Peterson's

Graduate Schools in the U.S. 2009

PETERSON'S

A nelnet COMPANY

PETERSON'S

A nelnet COMPANY

About Peterson's, a Nelnet company

Peterson's (www.petersons.com) is a leading provider of education information and advice, with books and online resources focusing on education search, test preparation, and financial aid. Its Web site offers searchable databases and interactive tools for contacting educational institutions, online practice tests and instruction, and planning tools for securing financial aid. Peterson's serves 110 million education consumers annually.

For more information, contact Peterson's, 2000 Lenox Drive, Lawrenceville, NJ 08648; 800-338-3282; or find us on the World Wide Web at www.petersons.com/about.

Editor: Fern A. Oram; Production Editor: Jill C. Schwartz; Research Project Manager: Ken Britschge; Research Associate: Amy Weber; Programmer: Phyllis Johnson; Manufacturing Manager: Ray Golaszewski; Composition Manager: Linda M. Williams

ISSN 1528-5901
ISBN 13: 978-0-7689-2599-9
ISBN 10: 0-7689-2599-1

Printed in the United States of America

10 9 8 7 6 5 4 3 2 1 10 09 08

Ninth Edition

Contents

A Note
from the Peterson's Editors

If you are a student seeking to continue your education beyond college, *Peterson's Graduate Schools in the U.S.* is just what you need to discover an array of possibilities in a wide variety of academic disciplines available at nearly 1,000 graduate schools across the United States.

Inside you'll find advice on graduate education, including topics such as admission tests, financial aid, and accreditation. **The Graduate Adviser** includes two essays and information about accreditation. The first essay, "The Admissions Process," discusses general admission requirements, admission tests, factors to consider when selecting a graduate school or program, when and how to apply, and how admission decisions are made. Special information for international students and tips for minority students are also included. The second essay, "Financial Support," is an overview of the broad range of support available at the graduate level. Fellowships, scholarships, and grants; assistantships and internships; federal and private loan programs, as well as Federal Work-Study; and the GI bill are detailed. This essay concludes with advice on applying for need-based financial aid. "Accreditation and Accrediting Agencies" gives information on accreditation and its purpose and lists first institutional accrediting agencies and then specialized accrediting agencies relevant to specific fields of study.

If you know the field of study that interests you, turn to the **Directory of Graduate and Professional Programs by Field.** You will find, at a glance, all institutions that offer that field of study.

For geographical or financial reasons, you may already have a specific institution in mind. Turn to the **Profiles of Institutions Offering Graduate and Professional Work,** which contain information on nearly 1,000 graduate schools. **Profiles** detail information from student enrollment and the number of full-time faculty members to tuition and application contacts and are followed by a list of graduate units and the specific programs of study they offer.

Peterson's publishes a full line of resources to help guide you through the graduate admissions process. Peterson's publications can be found at your local bookstore or library—or you can access us online at www.petersons.com.

We welcome any comments or suggestions you may have about this publication and invite you to complete our online survey at www.petersons.com/booksurvey.

Your feedback will help us make your educational dreams possible.

Colleges and universities will be pleased to know that Peterson's helped you in your selection. Admissions staff members are more than happy to answer questions, address specific problems, and help in any way they can. The editors at Peterson's wish you great success in your graduate school search!

The Graduate Adviser

The Admissions Process

Generalizations about graduate admissions practices are not always helpful because each institution has its own set of guidelines and procedures. Nevertheless, some broad statements can be made about the admissions process that may help you plan your strategy.

Factors Involved in Selecting a Graduate School or Program

Selecting a graduate school and a specific program of study is a complex matter. Quality of the faculty; program and course offerings; the nature, size, and location of the institution; admission requirements; cost; and the availability of financial assistance are among the many factors that affect one's choice of institution. Other considerations are job placement and achievements of the program's graduates and the institution's resources, such as libraries, laboratories, and computer facilities. If you are to make the best possible choice, you need to learn as much as you can about the schools and programs you are considering before you apply.

The following steps may help you narrow your choices.

- Talk to alumni of the programs or institutions you are considering to get their impressions of how well they were prepared for work in their fields of study.
- Remember that graduate school requirements change, so be sure to get the most up-to-date information possible.
- Talk to department faculty members and the graduate adviser at your undergraduate institution. They often have information about programs of study at other institutions.
- Visit the Web sites of the graduate schools in which you are interested to request a graduate catalog. Contact the department chair in your chosen field of study for additional information about the department and the field.
- Visit as many campuses as possible. Call ahead for an appointment with the graduate adviser in your field of interest and be sure to check out the facilities and talk to students.

General Requirements

Graduate schools and departments have requirements that applicants for admission must meet. Typically, these requirements include undergraduate transcripts (which provide information about undergraduate grade point average and course work applied toward a major), admission test scores, and letters of recommendation. Most graduate programs also ask for an essay or personal statement that describes your personal reasons for seeking graduate study. In some fields, such as art and music, portfolios or auditions may be required in addition to other evidence of talent. Some institutions require that the applicant have an undergraduate degree in the same subject as the intended graduate major.

Most institutions evaluate each applicant on the basis of the applicant's total record, and the weight accorded any given factor varies widely from institution to institution and from program to program.

The Application Process

You should begin the application process at least one year before you expect to begin your graduate study. Find out the application deadline for each institution (many are provided in the **Profile** section of this guide). Go to the institution's Web site and find out if you can apply online. If not, request a paper application form. Fill out this form thoroughly and neatly. Assume that the school needs all the information it is requesting and that the admissions officer will be sensitive to the neatness and overall quality of what you submit. Do not supply more information than the school requires.

The institution may ask at least one question that will require a three- or four-paragraph answer. Compose your response on the assumption that the admissions officer is interested in both what you think and how you express yourself. Keep your statement brief and to the point, but, at the same time, include all pertinent information about your past experiences and your educational goals. Individual statements vary greatly in style and content, which helps admissions officers differentiate among applicants. Many graduate departments give considerable weight to the statement in making their admissions decisions, so be sure to take the time to prepare a thoughtful and concise statement.

If recommendations are a part of the admissions requirements, carefully choose the individuals you ask to write them. It is generally best to ask current or former professors to write the recommendations, provided they are able to attest to your intellectual ability and motivation for doing the work required of a graduate student. It is advisable to provide stamped, preaddressed envelopes to people being asked to submit recommendations on your behalf.

Completed applications, including references, transcripts, and admission test scores, should be received at the institution by the specified date.

Be advised that institutions do not usually make admissions decisions until all materials have been received. Enclose a self-addressed postcard with your application, requesting confirmation of receipt. Allow at least 10 days for the return of the postcard before making further inquiries.

If you plan to apply for financial support, it is imperative that you file your application early.

Admission Tests

The major testing program used in graduate admissions is the Graduate Record Examinations (GRE) testing program, sponsored by the GRE Board and administered by Educational Testing Service, Princeton, New Jersey.

The Graduate Record Examinations testing program consists of a General Test and eight Subject Tests. The General Test measures critical thinking, verbal reasoning, quantitative reasoning, and analytical writing skills. It is offered as an Internet-based test (iBT) in the United States, Canada, and many other countries.

The typical computer-based General Test consists of one 30-minute verbal reasoning section, one 45-minute quantitative reasoning sections, one 45-minute issue analysis (writing) section, and one 30-minute argument analysis (writing) section. In addition, an unidentified verbal or quantitative section that doesn't count toward a score may be included and an identified research section that is not scored may also be included.

The Subject Tests measure achievement and assume undergraduate majors or extensive background in the following eight disciplines:

- Biochemistry, Cell and Molecular Biology
- Biology
- Chemistry
- Computer Science
- Literature in English
- Mathematics
- Physics
- Psychology

The Subject Tests are available three times per year as paper-based administrations around the world. Testing time is approximately 2 hours and 50 minutes. You can obtain more information about the GRE by visiting the ETS Web site at www.ets.org or consulting the *GRE Information and Registration Bulletin*. The *Bulletin* can be obtained at many undergraduate colleges. You can also download it from the ETS Web site or obtain it by contacting Graduate Record Examinations,

Educational Testing Service, PO Box 6000, Princeton, NJ 08541-6000, telephone 1-609-771-7670.

If you expect to apply for admission to a program that requires any of the GRE tests, you should select a test date well in advance of the application deadline. Scores on the computer-based General Test are reported within ten to fifteen days; scores on the paper-based Subject Tests are reported within six weeks.

Another testing program, the Miller Analogies Test (MAT), is administered at more than 500 Controlled Testing Centers, licensed by Harcourt Assessment, Inc., in the United States, Canada, and other countries. The MAT computer-based test is now available. Testing time is 60 minutes. The test consists of 120 partial analogies. You can obtain the *Candidate Information Booklet*, which contains a list of test centers and instructions for taking the test, from http://www.milleranalogies.com or by calling 1-800-622-3231.

Check the specific requirements of the programs to which you are applying.

How Admission Decisions Are Made

The program you apply to is directly involved in the admissions process. Although the final decision is usually made by the graduate dean (or an associate) or the faculty admissions committee, recommendations from faculty members in your intended field are important. At some institutions, an interview is incorporated into the decision process.

A Special Note for International Students

In addition to the steps already described, there are some special considerations for international students who intend to apply for graduate study in the United States. All graduate schools require an indication of competence in English. The purpose of the Test of English as a Foreign Language (TOEFL) is to evaluate the English proficiency of people who are nonnative speakers of English and want to study at colleges and universities where English is the language of instruction. The TOEFL is administered by Educational Testing Service (ETS) under the general direction of a policy board established by the College Board and the Graduate Record Examinations Board.

The TOEFL iBT assesses the four basic language skills: listening, reading, writing, and speaking. It was administered for the first time in September 2005, and ETS continues to introduce the TOEFL iBT in selected cities. The Internet-based test is administered at secure, official test centers. The testing time is approximately 4 hours. Because the TOEFL iBT includes a speaking section, the Test of Spoken English (TSE) is no longer needed.

The TOEFL is also offered in the paper-based format in areas of the world where Internet-based testing is not available. The paper-based TOEFL consists of three sections—listening comprehension, structure and written expression, and reading comprehension. The testing time is approximately 3 hours. The Test of Written English (TWE) is also given. The TWE is a 30-minute essay that measures the examinee's ability to compose in English. Examinees receive a TWE score separate from their TOEFL score. The *Information Bulletin* contains information on local fees and registration procedures.

Additional information and registration materials are available from TOEFL Services, Educational Testing Service, P.O. Box 6151, Princeton, New Jersey 08541-6151. Telephone: 1-609-771-7100. Web site: www.toefl.org.

International students should apply especially early because of the number of steps required to complete the admissions process. Furthermore, many United States graduate schools have a limited number of spaces for international students, and many more students apply than the schools can accommodate.

International students may find financial assistance from institutions very limited. The U.S. government requires international applicants to submit a certification of support, which is a statement attesting to the applicant's financial resources. In addition, international students *must* have health insurance coverage.

Tips for Minority Students

Indicators of a university's values in terms of diversity are found both in its recruitment programs and its resources directed to student success. Important questions: Does the institution vigorously recruit minorities for its graduate programs? Is there funding available to help with the costs associated with visiting the school? Are minorities represented in the institution's brochures or Web site or on their faculty rolls? What campus-based resources or services (including assistance in locating housing or career counseling and placement) are available? Is funding available to members of underrepresented groups?

At the program level, it is particularly important for minority students to investigate the "climate" of a program under consideration. How many minority students are enrolled and how many have graduated? What opportunities are there to work with diverse faculty and mentors whose research interests match yours? How are conflicts resolved or concerns addressed? How interested are faculty in building strong and supportive relations with students? "Climate" concerns should be addressed by posing questions to various individuals, including faculty members, current students, and alumni.

Information is also available through various organizations, such as the Hispanic Association of Colleges & Universities (HACU), and publications such as *Diverse Issues in Higher Education* and *Hispanic Outlook* magazine. There are also books devoted to this topic, such as *The Multicultural Student's Guide to Colleges* by Robert Mitchell.

Financial Support

The range of financial support at the graduate level is very broad. The following descriptions will give you a general idea of what you might expect and what will be expected of you as a financial support recipient.

Fellowships, Scholarships, and Grants

These are usually outright awards of a few hundred to many thousands of dollars with no service to the institution required in return. Fellowships and scholarships are usually awarded on the basis of merit and are highly competitive. Grants are made on the basis of financial need or special talent in a field of study. Many fellowships, scholarships, and grants not only cover tuition, fees, and supplies but also include stipends for living expenses with allowances for dependents. However, the terms of each should be examined because some do not permit recipients to supplement their income with outside work. Fellowships, scholarships, and grants may vary in the number of years for which they are awarded.

In addition to the availability of these funds at the university or program level, many excellent fellowship programs are available at the national level and may be applied for before and during enrollment in a graduate program. A listing of many of these programs can be found at the Council of Graduate Schools' Web site: http://www.cgsnet.org. There is a wealth of information in the "Programs and Awards" section.

Assistantships and Internships

Many graduate students receive financial support through assistantships, particularly involving teaching or research duties. It is important to recognize that such appointments should not be viewed simply as employment relationships but rather should constitute an integral and important part of a student's graduate education. As such, the appointments should be accompanied by strong faculty mentoring and increasingly responsible apprenticeship experiences. The specific nature of these appointments in a given program should be considered in selecting that graduate program.

Teaching Assistantships

These usually provide a salary and full or partial tuition remission and may also provide health benefits. Unlike fellowships, scholarships, and grants, which require no service to the institution, teaching assistantships require recipients to provide the institution with a specific amount of undergraduate teaching, ideally related to the student's field of study. Some teaching assistants are limited to grading papers, compiling bibliographies, taking notes, or monitoring laboratories. At some graduate schools, teaching assistants must carry lighter course loads than regular full-time students.

Research Assistantships

These are very similar to teaching assistantships in the manner in which financial assistance is provided. The difference is that recipients are given basic research assignments in their disciplines rather than teaching responsibilities. The work required is normally related to the student's field of study; in most instances, the assistantship supports the student's thesis or dissertation research.

Administrative Internships

These are similar to assistantships in application of financial assistance funds, but the student is given an assignment on a part-time basis, usually as a special assistant with one of the university's administrative offices. The assignment may not necessarily be directly related to the recipient's discipline.

Residence Hall and Counseling Assistantships

These assistantships are frequently assigned to graduate students in psychology, counseling, and social work, but may be offered to students in other disciplines, especially if they have worked in this capacity during their undergraduate years. Duties can vary from being available in a dean's office for a specific number of hours for consultation with undergraduates to living in campus residences and being responsible for both counseling and administrative tasks or advising student activity groups. Residence hall assistantships often include a room and board allowance and, in some cases, tuition assistance and stipends. Contact the Housing and Student Life Office for more information.

Health Insurance

The availability and affordability of health insurance is an important issue and one that should be considered in an applicant's choice of institution and program. While often included with assistantships and fellowships, this is not always the case and, even if provided, the benefits may be limited. It is important to note that the U.S. government requires international students to have health insurance.

The GI Bill

This provides financial assistance for students who are veterans of the United States armed forces. If you are a veteran, contact your local Veterans Administration office to determine your eligibility and to get full details about benefits. There are a number of programs that offer educational benefits to current military enlistees. Some states have tuition assistance programs for members of the National Guard. Contact the VA office at the college for more information.

Federal Work-Study Program (FWS)

Employment is another way some students finance their graduate studies. The federally funded Federal Work-Study Program provides eligible students with employment opportunities, usually in public and private nonprofit organizations. Federal funds pay up to 75 percent of the wages, with the remainder paid by the employing agency. FWS is available to graduate students who demonstrate financial need. Not all schools have these funds, and some only award them to undergraduates. Each school sets its application deadline and work-study earnings limits. Wages vary and are related to the type of work done. You must file the Free Application for Federal Student Aid (FAFSA) to be eligible for this program.

Loans

Many graduate students borrow to finance their graduate programs when other sources of assistance (which do not have to be repaid) prove insufficient. You should always read and understand the terms of any loan program before submitting your application.

Federal Loans

Federal Stafford Loans. The Federal Stafford Loan Program offers government-sponsored, low-interest loans to students through a private lender such as a bank, credit union, or savings and loan association.

There are two components of the Federal Stafford Loan program. Under the *subsidized* component of the program, the federal government pays the interest on the loan while you are enrolled in graduate school on at least a half-time basis, as well as during any period of deferment. Under the *unsubsidized* component of the program, you pay the interest on the loan from the day proceeds are issued. Eligibility for the federal subsidy is based on demonstrated financial need as determined by the financial aid office from the information you provide on the FAFSA. A cosigner is not required, since the loan is not based on creditworthiness.

Although *unsubsidized* Federal Stafford Loans may not be as desirable as *subsidized* Federal Stafford Loans from the student's perspective, they are a useful source of support for those who may not qualify for the subsidized loans or who need additional financial assistance.

Graduate students may borrow up to $20,500 per year through the Stafford Loan Program, up to a cumulative maximum of $138,500, including undergraduate borrowing. This may include up to $8500 in *subsidized* Stafford Loans annually, depending on eligibility, up to a cumulative maximum of $65,500, including undergraduate borrowing. The amount of the loan borrowed through the *unsubsidized* Stafford Program equals the total amount of the loan (as much as $20,500) minus your eligibility for a *subsidized* Stafford Loan (as much as $8500). You may borrow up to the cost of attendance at the school in which you are enrolled or will attend, minus estimated financial assistance from other federal, state, and private sources, up to a maximum of $20,500.

Stafford Loans made on or after July 1, 2006, carry a fixed interest rate of 6.8% both for in-school and in-repayment borrowers.

Two fees may be deducted from the loan proceeds upon disbursement: a Federal Default Fee of 1 percent, which is deposited in an insurance pool to ensure repayment to the lender if the borrower defaults, and a federally mandated 1.5 percent origination fee, for loans made after July 1, 2007, which is used to offset the administrative cost of the Federal Stafford Loan Program. Many lenders do offer reduced-fee or "zero fee" loans. The origination fees are scheduled to be eliminated by July 1, 2010.

Under the *subsidized* Federal Stafford Loan Program, repayment begins six months after your last date of enrollment on at least a half-time basis. Under the *unsubsidized* program, repayment of interest begins within thirty days from disbursement of the loan proceeds, and repayment of the principal begins six months after your last enrollment on at least a half-time basis. Some borrowers may choose to defer interest payments while they are in school. The accrued interest is added to the loan balance when the borrower begins repayment. There are several repayment options.

Federal Direct Loans. Some schools participate in the Department of Education's William D. Ford Direct Loan Program instead of the Federal Stafford Loan Program. The two programs are essentially the same except that with the Direct Loans, schools themselves provide the loans with funds from the federal government. Terms and interest rates are virtually the same except that there are a few additional repayment options with Federal Direct Loans.

Federal Perkins Loans. The Federal Perkins Loan is available to students demonstrating financial need and is administered directly by the school. Not all schools have these funds, and some may award them to undergraduates only. Eligibility is determined from the information you provide on the FAFSA. The school will notify you of your eligibility.

Eligible graduate students may borrow up to $6000 per year, up to a maximum of $40,000, including undergraduate borrowing (even if your previous Perkins Loans have been repaid). The interest rate for Federal Perkins Loans is 5 percent, and no interest accrues while you remain in school at least half-time. There are no guarantee, loan, or disbursement fees. Repayment begins nine months after your last date of enrollment on at least a half-time basis and may extend over a maximum of ten years with no prepayment penalty.

Federal Graduate PLUS Loans. Effective July 1, 2006, graduate and professional students are eligible for Graduate PLUS loans. Graduate PLUS loans are identical to Parent PLUS loans, except that students borrow on their own behalf. This program allows students to borrow up to their cost of attendance, less any other aid received through this federal program. These loans have a fixed interest rate of 8.5% (7.9% for the Federal Direct PLUS), and interest begins to accrue at the time of disbursement. For more information, contact your FFELP lender or your college financial aid office.

Deferring Your Federal Loan Repayments. If you borrowed under the Federal Stafford Loan Program, Federal Direct Loan Program, or the Federal Perkins Loan Program for previous undergraduate or graduate study, your repayments may be deferred when you return to graduate school, depending on when you borrowed and under which program.

There are other deferment options available if you are temporarily unable to repay your loan. Information about these deferments is provided at your entrance and exit interviews. If you believe you are eligible for a deferment of your loan repayments, you must contact your lender to request a deferment form. The deferment must be filed prior to the time your repayment is due, and it must be refiled when it expires if you remain eligible for deferment at that time.

Supplemental (Private) Loans

Many lending institutions offer supplemental loan programs and other financing plans, such as the ones described here, to students seeking additional assistance in meeting their educational expenses. Some loan programs target all types of graduate students; others are designed specifically for business, law, or medical students. In addition, you can use private loans not specifically designed for education to help finance your graduate degree.

If you are considering borrowing through a supplemental or private loan program, you should carefully consider the terms and be sure to "read the fine print." Check with the program sponsor for the most current terms that will be applicable to the amounts you intend to borrow for graduate study. Most supplemental loan programs for graduate study offer unsubsidized, credit-based loans. In general, a credit-ready borrower is one who has a satisfactory credit history or no credit history at all. A creditworthy borrower generally must pass a credit test to be eligible to borrow or act as a cosigner for the loan funds.

Many supplemental loan programs have minimum and maximum annual loan limits. Some offer amounts equal to the cost of attendance minus any other aid you will receive for graduate study. If you are planning to borrow for several years of graduate study, consider whether there is a cumulative or aggregate limit on the amount you may borrow. Often this cumulative or aggregate limit will include any amounts you borrowed and have not repaid for undergraduate or previous graduate study.

The combination of the annual interest rate, loan fees, and the repayment terms you choose will determine how much you will repay over time. Compare these features in combination before you decide which loan program to use. Some loans offer interest rates that are adjusted monthly, some quarterly, some annually. Some offer interest rates that are lower during the in-school, grace, and deferment periods and then increase when you begin repayment. Some programs include a loan "origination" fee, which is usually deducted from the principal amount you receive when the loan is disbursed and must be repaid along with the interest and other principal when you graduate, withdraw from school, or drop below half-time study. Sometimes the loan fees are reduced if you borrow with a qualified cosigner. Some programs allow you to defer interest and/or principal payments while you are enrolled in graduate school. Many programs allow you to capitalize your interest payments; the interest due on your loan is added to the outstanding balance of your loan, so you don't have to repay immediately, but this increases the amount you owe. Other programs allow you to pay the interest as you go, which reduces the amount you later have to repay.

Some examples of supplemental programs follow. The private loan market is very competitive, and your financial aid office can help you evaluate these and other programs.

CitiAssist Loans. Offered by Citibank, these no-fee loans help graduate students fill the gap between the financial aid they receive and the money they need for school. Visit www.studentloan.com for more loan information from Citibank.

EXCEL Loan. This program, sponsored by Nellie Mae, is designed for students who are not ready to borrow on their own and wish to borrow with a creditworthy cosigner. Visit www.nelliemae.com for more information.

Graduate Access Loan. Sponsored by the Access Group, this is for graduate students enrolled at least half-time. The Web site is www.accessgroup.com.

Signature Student Loan. A loan program for students who are enrolled at least half-time, this is sponsored by Sallie Mae. Visit www.salliemae.com for more information.

Nelnet Graduate and Professional Loans. These private loans are for graduate and professional students attending participating degree-granting institutions. For more information, go to www.nelnet.com.

Applying for Need-Based Financial Aid

Schools that award federal and institutional financial assistance based on need will require you to complete the FAFSA and, in some cases, an institutional financial aid application.

If you are applying for federal student assistance, you **must** complete the FAFSA. A service of the U.S. Department of Education, it is free to all applicants. Most applicants apply online at www.fafsa.ed.gov. Paper applications are available at the financial aid office of your local college.

After your FAFSA information has been processed, you will receive a Student Aid Report (SAR). If you provided an e-mail address on the FAFSA, this will be sent to you electronically; otherwise, it will be mailed to your home address.

Follow the instructions on the SAR if you need to correct information reported on your original application. If your situation changes after you file your FAFSA, contact your financial aid officer to discuss amending your information. You can also appeal your financial aid award if you have extenuating circumstances.

If you would like more information on federal student financial aid, visit the FAFSA Web site or download the most recent version of *Funding Education Beyond High School: The Guide to Federal Student Aid* at http://studentaid.ed.gov/students/publications/student_guide/index.html. This guide is also available in Spanish.

The U.S. Department of Education also has a toll-free number for questions concerning federal student aid programs. The number is 1-800-4-FED AID (1-800-433-3243). If you are hearing impaired, call toll-free, 1-800-730-8913.

Summary

Remember that these are generalized statements about financial assistance at the graduate level. Because each institution allots its aid differently, you should communicate directly with the school and the specific department of interest to you. It is not unusual, for example, to find that an endowment vested within a specific department supports one or more fellowships. You may fit its requirements and specifications precisely.

Accreditation and Accrediting Agencies

Colleges and universities in the United States, and their individual academic and professional programs, are accredited by nongovernmental agencies concerned with monitoring the quality of education in this country. Agencies with both regional and national jurisdictions grant accreditation to institutions as a whole, while specialized bodies acting on a nationwide basis—often national professional associations—grant accreditation to departments and programs in specific fields.

Institutional and specialized accrediting agencies share the same basic concerns: the purpose an academic unit—whether university or program—has set for itself and how well it fulfills that purpose, the adequacy of its financial and other resources, the quality of its academic offerings, and the level of services it provides. Agencies that grant institutional accreditation take a broader view, of course, and examine university-wide or college-wide services with which a specialized agency may not concern itself.

Both types of agencies follow the same general procedures when considering an application for accreditation. The academic unit prepares a self-evaluation, focusing on the concerns mentioned above and usually including an assessment of both its strengths and weaknesses; a team of representatives of the accrediting body reviews this evaluation, visits the campus, and makes its own report; and finally, the accrediting body makes a decision on the application. Often, even when accreditation is granted, the agency makes a recommendation regarding how the institution or program can improve. All institutions and programs are also reviewed every few years to determine whether they continue to meet established standards; if they do not, they may lose their accreditation.

Accrediting agencies themselves are reviewed and evaluated periodically by the U.S. Department of Education and the Council for Higher Education Accreditation (CHEA). Recognized agencies adhere to certain standards and practices, and their authority in matters of accreditation is widely accepted in the educational community.

This does not mean, however, that accreditation is a simple matter, either for schools wishing to become accredited or for students deciding where to apply. Indeed, in certain fields the very meaning and methods of accreditation are the subject of a good deal of debate. For their part, those applying to graduate school should be aware of the safeguards provided by regional accreditation, especially in terms of degree acceptance and institutional longevity. Beyond this, applicants should understand the role that specialized accreditation plays in their field, as this varies considerably from one discipline to another. In certain professional fields, it is necessary to have graduated from a program that is accredited in order to be eligible for a license to practice, and in some fields the federal government also makes this a hiring requirement. In other disciplines, however, accreditation is not as essential, and there can be excellent programs that are not accredited. In fact, some programs choose not to seek accreditation, although most do.

Institutions and programs that present themselves for accreditation are sometimes granted the status of candidate for accreditation, or what is known as "preaccreditation." This may happen, for example, when an academic unit is too new to have met all the requirements for accreditation. Such status signifies initial recognition and indicates that the school or program in question is working to fulfill all requirements; it does not, however, guarantee that accreditation will be granted.

Institutional Accrediting Agencies—Regional

MIDDLE STATES ASSOCIATION OF COLLEGES AND SCHOOLS

Accredits institutions in Delaware, District of Columbia, Maryland, New Jersey, New York, Pennsylvania, Puerto Rico, and the Virgin Islands.
Jean Avnet Morse, President
Middle States Commission on Higher Education
3624 Market Street
Philadelphia, Pennsylvania 19104
Telephone: 267-284-5025
Fax: 215-662-5501
E-mail: info@msche.org
World Wide Web: www.msche.org

NEW ENGLAND ASSOCIATION OF SCHOOLS AND COLLEGES

Accredits institutions in Connecticut, Maine, Massachusetts, New Hampshire, Rhode Island, and Vermont.
Barbara E. Brittingham, Director
Commission on Institutions of Higher Education
209 Burlington Road
Bedford, Massachusetts 01730-1433
Telephone: 781-541-5447
Fax: 781-271-0950
E-mail: bbrittingham@neasc.org
World Wide Web: www.neasc.org

NORTH CENTRAL ASSOCIATION OF COLLEGES AND SCHOOLS

Accredits institutions in Arizona, Arkansas, Colorado, Illinois, Indiana, Iowa, Kansas, Michigan, Minnesota, Missouri, Nebraska, New Mexico, North Dakota, Ohio, Oklahoma, South Dakota, West Virginia, Wisconsin, and Wyoming.
Steven D. Crow, President
The Higher Learning Commission
30 North LaSalle Street, Suite 2400
Chicago, Illinois 60602
Telephone: 312-263-0456
Fax: 312-263-7462
E-mail: scrow@hlcommission.org
World Wide Web:
www.ncahigherlearningcommission.org

NORTHWEST COMMISSION ON COLLEGES AND UNIVERSITIES

Accredits institutions in Alaska, Idaho, Montana, Nevada, Oregon, Utah, and Washington.
Sandra E. Elman, President
8060 165th Avenue, NE, Suite 100
Redmond, Washington 98052
Telephone: 425-558-4224
Fax: 425-376-0596
E-mail: selman@nwccu.org
World Wide Web: www.nwccu.org

SOUTHERN ASSOCIATION OF COLLEGES AND SCHOOLS

Accredits institutions in Alabama, Florida, Georgia, Kentucky, Louisiana, Mississippi, North Carolina, South Carolina, Tennessee, Texas, and Virginia.
Belle S. Wheelan, President
Commission on Colleges
1866 Southern Lane
Decatur, Georgia 30033
Telephone: 404-679-4512
Fax: 404-679-4558
E-mail: bwheelan@sacscoc.org
World Wide Web: www.sacscoc.org

WESTERN ASSOCIATION OF SCHOOLS AND COLLEGES

Accredits institutions in California, Guam, and Hawaii.
Ralph A. Wolff, President and Executive Director
The Senior College Commission
985 Atlantic Avenue, Suite 100
Alameda, California 94501
Telephone: 510-748-9001
Fax: 510-748-9797
E-mail: wascsr@wascsenior.org
World Wide Web: www.wascsenior.org/wasc/

Institutional Accrediting Agencies—Other

ACCREDITING COUNCIL FOR INDEPENDENT COLLEGES AND SCHOOLS

Sheryl L. Moody, Executive Director
750 First Street, NE, Suite 980
Washington, DC 20002-4242
Telephone: 202-336-6780
Fax: 202-842-2593
E-mail: smoody@acics.org
World Wide Web: www.acics.org

DISTANCE EDUCATION AND TRAINING COUNCIL

Accrediting Commission
Michael P. Lambert, Executive Director
1601 18th Street, NW
Washington, DC 20009
Telephone: 202-234-5100 Ext. 101
Fax: 202-332-1386
E-mail: detc@detc.org
World Wide Web: www.detc.org

Specialized Accrediting Agencies

[Only Book 1 of *Peterson's Graduate and Professional Programs* Series includes the complete list of specialized accrediting groups recognized by the U.S. Department of Education and the Council on Higher Education Accreditation (CHEA). The lists in Books 2, 3, 4, 5, and 6 are abridged.]

ACUPUNCTURE AND ORIENTAL MEDICINE

Dort S. Bigg, Executive Director
Accreditation Commission for Acupuncture and Oriental Medicine
Maryland Trade Center #3
7501 Greenway Center Drive, Suite 820
Greenbelt, Maryland 20770
Telephone: 301-313-0855
Fax: 301-313-0912
E-mail: acaom1@compuserve.com
World Wide Web: www.acaom.org

ART AND DESIGN

Samuel Hope, Executive Director
National Association of Schools of Art and Design
11250 Roger Bacon Drive, Suite 21
Reston, Virginia 20190
Telephone: 703-437-0700
Fax: 703-437-6312
E-mail: shope@arts-accredit.org
World Wide Web: nasad.arts-accredit.org

BUSINESS

Jerry E. Trapnell, Executive Vice President/Chief Accreditation Officer
AACSB International--The Association to Advance Collegiate Schools of Business
777 South Harbour Island Boulevard, Suite 750
Tampa, Florida 33602
Telephone: 813-769-6500
Fax: 813-769-6559
E-mail: jerryt@aacsb.edu
World Wide Web: www.aacsb.edu

CHIROPRACTIC

Martha S. O'Connor, Executive Director
Council on Chiropractic Education
8049 North 85th Way
Scottsdale, Arizona 85258-4321
Telephone: 480-443-8877
Fax: 480-483-7333
E-mail: cce@cce-usa.org
World Wide Web: www.cce-usa.org

CLINICAL LABORATORY SCIENCES

Dianne M. Cearlock, Chief Executive Officer
National Accrediting Agency for Clinical Laboratory Sciences
8410 West Bryn Mawr Avenue, Suite 670
Chicago, Illinois 60631
Telephone: 773-714-8880
Fax: 773-714-8886
E-mail: dcearlocknaacls.org
World Wide Web: www.naacls.org

CLINICAL PASTORAL EDUCATION

Teresa E. Snorton, Executive Director
Accreditation Commission
Association for Clinical Pastoral Education, Inc.
1549 Clairmont Road, Suite 103
Decatur, Georgia 30033-4611
Telephone: 404-320-1472
Fax: 404-320-0849
E-mail: acpe@acpe.edu
World Wide Web: www.acpe.edu

DANCE

Samuel Hope, Executive Director
National Association of Schools of Dance
11250 Roger Bacon Drive, Suite 21
Reston, Virginia 20190
Telephone: 703-437-0700
Fax: 703-437-6312
E-mail: shope@arts-accredit.org
World Wide Web: nasd.arts-accredit.org

DENTISTRY

Laura M. Neumann, Interim Director
Commission on Dental Accreditation
American Dental Association
211 East Chicago Avenue, 18th Floor
Chicago, Illinois 60611
Telephone: 312-440-2712
Fax: 312-440-2915
E-mail: neumannl@ada.org
World Wide Web: www.ada.org

DIETETICS

Beverly E. Mitchell, Director
American Dietetic Association
Commission on Accreditation for Dietetics Education (CADE-ADA)
120 South Riverside Plaza, Suite 2000
Chicago, Illinois 60606-6995
Phone: 312-899-4872
Fax: 312-899-4817
E-mail: bmitchell@eatright.org
Web: www.eatright.org/cade

ENGINEERING

George D. Peterson, Executive Director
Accreditation Board for Engineering and Technology, Inc.
111 Market Place, Suite 1050
Baltimore, Maryland 21202

Telephone: 410-347-7700
Fax: 410-625-2238
E-mail: info@abet.org
World Wide Web: www.abet.org

FORESTRY

Michael T. Goergen Jr.
Executive Vice President and CEO
Society of American Foresters
5400 Grosvenor Lane
Bethesda, Maryland 20814
Telephone: 301-897-8720
Fax: 301-897-3690
E-mail: goergenm@safnet.org
World Wide Web: www.safnet.org

HEALTH SERVICES ADMINISTRATION

Commission on Accreditation of Healthcare Management Education
Pamela S. Jenness
Director of Accreditation Operations
2000 14th Street North, Suite 780
Arlington, Virginia 22201
Telephone: 703-894-0960
Fax: 703-894-0941
E-mail: pjenness@cahme.org
World Wide Web: cahmeweb.org

INTERIOR DESIGN

Holly Mattson, Executive Director
Council for Interior Design Accreditation
146 Monroe Center, NW, Suite 1318
Grand Rapids, Michigan 49503
Telephone: 616-458-0400
Fax: 616-458-0460
E-mail: holly@accredit-id.org
World Wide Web: www.accredit-id.org

JOURNALISM AND MASS COMMUNICATIONS

Susanne Shaw, Executive Director
Accrediting Council on Education in Journalism and Mass Communications
School of Journalism
Stauffer-Flint Hall
University of Kansas
1435 Jayhawk Boulevard
Lawrence, Kansas 66045-7575
Telephone: 785-864-3973
Fax: 785-864-5225
E-mail: sshaw@ku.edu
World Wide Web: www.ku.edu/~acejmc

LANDSCAPE ARCHITECTURE

Ronald C. Leighton, Executive Director
Landscape Architectural Accreditation Board
American Society of Landscape Architects
636 Eye Street, NW
Washington, DC 20001
Telephone: 202-898-2444
Fax: 202-898-1185
E-mail: rleighton@asla.org
World Wide Web: www.asla.org

LAW

Hulett H. Askew, Consultant on Legal Education
American Bar Association
321 North Clark Street, 21st Floor
Chicago, Illinois 60610
Telephone: 312-988-6746
Fax: 312-988-5681
E-mail: askewh@staff.abanet.org
World Wide Web: www.abanet.org/legaled/

LIBRARY

Karen O'Brien, Executive Director
Office for Accreditation
American Library Association
50 East Huron Street
Chicago, Illinois 60611
Telephone: 312-280-2434
Fax: 312-280-2433
E-mail: kobrien@ala.org
World Wide Web: www.ala.org/ala/accreditation/accreditation.htm

MARRIAGE AND FAMILY THERAPY

Jeff S. Harmon, Director of Accreditation Services
Commission on Accreditation for Marriage and Family Therapy Education
American Association for Marriage and Family Therapy
112 South Alfred Street
Alexandria, Virginia 22314-3061
Telephone: 703-838-9808
Fax: 703-253-0508
E-mail: jharmon@aamft.org
World Wide Web: www.aamft.org

MEDICAL ILLUSTRATION

Commission on Accreditation of Allied Health Education
Programs (CAAHEP)
Kathleen Megivern, Executive Director
1361 Park Street
Clearwater, Florida 33756
Telephone: 727-210-2350
Fax: 727-210-2354
E-mail: megivern@caahep.org
World Wide Web: www.caahep.org

MEDICINE

Liaison Committee on Medical Education (LCME)
In even-numbered years beginning each July 1, contact:

Robert H. Eaglen
Interim AAMC Secretary to the LCME
Association of American Medical Colleges
2450 N Street, NW
Washington, DC 20037
Telephone: 202-828-0596
Fax: 202-828-1125
E-mail: reaglen@aamc.org
World Wide Web: www.lcme.org

In odd-numbered years beginning each July 1, contact:
Barbara Barzansky
Interim AMA Secretary to the LCME
American Medical Association
Council on Medical Education
515 North State Street
Chicago, Illinois 60610
Telephone: 312-464-1690
Fax: 312-464-5830
E-mail: barbara_barzansky@ama-assn.org
World Wide Web: www.ama-assn.org

MUSIC

Samuel Hope, Executive Director
National Association of Schools of Music
11250 Roger Bacon Drive, Suite 21
Reston, Virginia 20190
Telephone: 703-437-0700
Fax: 703-437-6312
E-mail: shope@arts-accredit.org
World Wide Web: nasm.arts-accredit.org

NATUROPATHIC MEDICINE

Daniel Seitz, Executive Director
Council on Naturopathic Medical Education
P.O. Box 178
Great Barrington, Massachusetts 01230
Telephone: 413-528-8877
Fax: 413-528-8880
E-mail: council@cnme.org
World Wide Web: www.cnme.org

NURSE ANESTHESIA

Francis Gerbasi, Director of Accreditation and Education
Council on Accreditation of Nurse Anesthesia Educational Programs
222 South Prospect Avenue
Park Ridge, Illinois 60068
Telephone: 847-692-7050
Fax: 847-692-7137
E-mail: fgerbasi@aana.com
World Wide Web: www.aana.com

NURSE EDUCATION

Jennifer Butlin, Director
Commission on Collegiate Nursing Education (CCNE)
One Dupont Circle, NW, Suite 530
Washington, DC 20036-1120
Telephone: 202-887-6791
Fax: 202-887-8476
E-mail: jbutlin@aacn.nche.edu
World Wide Web: www.aacn.nche.edu/accreditation

NURSE MIDWIFERY

Diane Boyer, Chair
ACNM Division of Accreditation
American College of Nurse-Midwives
8403 Colesville Road, Suite 1550
Silver Spring, Maryland 20910
Telephone: 240-485-1800
Fax: 240-485-1818
E-mail: dboyer@luc.edu
World Wide Web: www.midwife.org

Mary Ann Baul, Executive Director
Midwifery Education Accreditation Council
20 East Cherry Avenue
Flagstaff, Arizona 86001-4607
Telephone: 928-214-0997
Fax: 928-773-9694
E-mail: info@meacschools.org
World Wide Web: www.meacschools.org

NURSE PRACTITIONER

Susan Wysocki, President
National Association of Nurse Practitioners in Women's Health
Council on Accreditation
505 C Street, NE
Washington, DC 20002
Telephone: 202-543-9693
Fax: 202-543-9858
E-mail: info@npwh.org
World Wide Web: www.npwh.org

NURSING

Sharon J. Tanner, Executive Director
National League for Nursing Accrediting Commission
61 Broadway, 33rd Floor
New York, New York 10006
Telephone: 800-669-1656 Ext. 451
Fax: 212-812-0364
E-mail: stanner@nlnac.org
World Wide Web: www.nlnac.org

OCCUPATIONAL THERAPY

Neil Harvison, Director of Accreditation
American Occupational Therapy Association
4720 Montgomery Lane
P.O. Box 31220
Bethesda, Maryland 20824-1220

Telephone: 301-652-2682 Ext. 2912
Fax: 301-652-7711
E-mail: nharvison@aota.org
World Wide Web: www.aota.org

OPTOMETRY

Joyce L. Urbeck, Administrative Director
Accreditation Council on Optometric Education
American Optometric Association
243 North Lindbergh Boulevard
St. Louis, Missouri 63141
Telephone: 314-991-4100 Ext. 246
Fax: 314-991-4101
E-mail: jlurbeck@aoa.org
World Wide Web: www.aoanet.org

OSTEOPATHIC MEDICINE

Konrad C. Miskowicz-Retz, Director
Commission on Osteopathic College Accreditation
American Osteopathic Association
142 East Ontario Street
Chicago, Illinois 60611
Telephone: 312-202-8048
Fax: 312-202-8202
E-mail: kretz@osteopathic.org
World Wide Web: www.osteopathic.org

PHARMACY

Peter H. Vlasses, Executive Director
Accreditation Council for Pharmacy Education
20 North Clark Street, Suite 2500
Chicago, Illinois 60602-5109
Telephone: 312-664-3575
Fax: 312-664-4652
E-mail: pvlasses@acpe-accredit.org
World Wide Web: www.acpe-accredit.org

PHYSICAL THERAPY

Mary Jane Harris, Director
Commission on Accreditation
American Physical Therapy Association
1111 North Fairfax Street
Alexandria, Virginia 22314
Telephone: 703-684-2782
Fax: 703-684-7343
E-mail: maryjaneharris@apta.org
World Wide Web: www.apta.org

PHYSICIAN ASSISTANT STUDIES

John McCarty, Executive Director
Accreditation Review Commission on Education for the Physician
Assistant
12000 Findley Road, Suite 240
Duluth, Georgia 30097
Telephone: 770-476-1224
Fax: 770-476-1738
E-mail: johnmccarty@arc-pa.org
World Wide Web: www.arc-pa.org

PLANNING

Shonagh Merits, Executive Director
American Institute of Certified Planners/Association of Collegiate Schools of Planning/American Planning Association
Planning Accreditation Board (PAB)
122 South Michigan Avenue, Suite 1600
Chicago, Illinois 60603
Telephone: 312-334-1271
Fax: 312-334-1273
E-mail: pab@planning.org
World Wide Web: showcase.netins.net/web/pab_fi66/

PODIATRIC MEDICINE

Alan R. Tinkleman, Director
Council on Podiatric Medical Education
American Podiatric Medical Association
9312 Old Georgetown Road
Bethesda, Maryland 20814-1621
Telephone: 301-581-9200
Fax: 301-571-4903
E-mail: artinkleman@apma.org
World Wide Web: www.cpme.org

PSYCHOLOGY AND COUNSELING

Susan F. Zlotlow, Director
Office of Program Consultation and Accreditation
American Psychological Association
750 First Street, NE
Washington, DC 20002-4242
Telephone: 202-336-5979
Fax: 202-336-5978
E-mail: szlotlow@apa.org
World Wide Web: www.apa.org/ed/accreditation/
Carol L. Bobby, Executive Director
Council for Accreditation of Counseling and Related Educational Programs
1001 North Fairfax Street, Suite 510
Alexandria, Virginia 22314
Telephone: 703-535-5990
Fax: 703-739-6209
E-mail: cacrep@cacrep.org
World Wide Web: www.cacrep.org

PUBLIC AFFAIRS AND ADMINISTRATION

Crystal Calarusse, Academic Director
Commission on Peer Review and Accreditation
National Association of Schools of Public Affairs and Administration
1120 G Street, NW, Suite 730
Washington, DC 20005
Telephone: 202-628-8965 Ext. 103
Fax: 202-626-4978
E-mail: calarusse@naspaa.org

World Wide Web: www.naspaa.org

PUBLIC HEALTH

Laura Rasar King, Executive Director
Council on Education for Public Health
800 Eye Street, NW, Suite 202
Washington, DC 20001-3710
Telephone: 202-789-1050
Fax: 202-789-1895
E-mail: lking@ceph.org
World Wide Web: www.ceph.org

REHABILITATION EDUCATION

Marv Kuehn, Executive Director
Council on Rehabilitation Education
Commission on Standards and Accreditation
300 North Martingale Road, Suite 460
Schaumburg, Illinois 60173
Telephone: 847-944-1345
Fax: 847-944-1324
E-mail: mkuehn@emporia.edu
World Wide Web: www.core-rehab.org

SOCIAL WORK

Dean Pierce, Director
Office of Social Work Accreditation and Educational Excellence
Council on Social Work Education
1725 Duke Street, Suite 500
Alexandria, Virginia 22314
Telephone: 703-519-2044
Fax: 703-739-9048
E-mail: dpierce@cswe.org
World Wide Web: www.cswe.org

SPEECH-LANGUAGE PATHOLOGY AND AUDIOLOGY

Patrima Tice, Director of Credentialing
American Speech-Language-Hearing Association
10801 Rockville Pike
Rockville, Maryland 20852
Telephone: 301-897-5700
Fax: 301-571-0457
E-mail: ptice@asha.org
World Wide Web: www.asha.org

TEACHER EDUCATION

Arthur E. Wise, President
National Council for Accreditation of Teacher Education
2010 Massachusetts Avenue, NW, Suite 500
Washington, DC 20036
Telephone: 202-466-7496
Fax: 202-296-6620
E-mail: art@ncate.org
World Wide Web: www.ncate.org
Frank B. Murray, President
Teacher Education Accreditation Council (TEAC)
One Dupont Circle, Suite 320
Washington, DC 20036-0110
Telephone: 202-466-7236
Fax: 202-466-7238
E-mail: frank@teac.org
World Wide Web: www.teac.org

TECHNOLOGY

Elise Scanlon, Executive Director
Accrediting Commission of Career Schools and Colleges of Technology
2101 Wilson Boulevard, Suite 302
Arlington, Virginia 22201
Telephone: 703-247-4212
Fax: 703-247-4533
E-mail: escanlon@accsct.org
World Wide Web: www.accsct.org

THEATER

Samuel Hope, Executive Director
National Association of Schools of Theatre
11250 Roger Bacon Drive, Suite 21
Reston, Virginia 20190
Telephone: 703-437-0700
Fax: 703-437-6312
E-mail: shope@arts-accredit.org
World Wide Web: nast.arts-accredit.org

THEOLOGY

Bernard Fryshman, Executive Vice President
Association of Advanced Rabbinical and Talmudic Schools
11 Broadway, Suite 405
New York, New York 10004
Telephone: 212-363-1991
Fax: 212-533-5335

Daniel O. Aleshire, Executive Director
Association of Theological Schools in the United States and Canada
10 Summit Park Drive
Pittsburgh, Pennsylvania 15275
Telephone: 412-788-6505 Ext. 237
Fax: 412-788-6510
E-mail: ats@ats.edu
World Wide Web: www.ats.edu

Russell Guy Fitzgerald, Executive Director
Transnational Association of Christian Colleges and Schools
Accreditation Commission
15935 Forest Road
P.O. Box 328
Forest, Virginia 24551
Telephone: 434-525-9539
Fax: 434-525-9538
E-mail: rfitzgerald@tracs.org
World Wide Web: www.tracs.org

VETERINARY MEDICINE

Donald G. Simmons, Director of Education and Research Division
American Veterinary Medical Association
1931 North Meacham Road, Suite 100
Schaumburg, Illinois 60173
Telephone: 847-925-8070 Ext. 6674
Fax: 847-925-9329
E-mail: dsimmons@avma.org
World Wide Web: www.avma.org

How to Use This Guide

The graduate and professional programs in *Peterson's Graduate Schools in the U.S.* are offered by colleges and universities in the United States and U.S. territories. They are accredited by U.S. accrediting bodies recognized by the Department of Education or the Council for Higher Education Accreditation. Each institution qualifies as a doctorate/research- or master's-level institution according to the *Carnegie Classification of Institutions of Higher Education*, and most are regionally accredited.

Profiles of Institutions Offering Graduate and Professional Work

Information in this guide is presented in **Profile** form. Each **Profile** provides basic information about an institution. The format of the **Profiles** is consistent throughout the guide, making it easier to compare institutions. Any item that does not apply to or was not provided by a graduate unit is omitted. Information about the overall institution comes first. Information about autonomous graduate units follows with lists of the specific graduate degree programs offered. For complex institutions that combine their graduate studies under a unified administrative structure, degrees may be listed under divisional subheadings.

Institution Information

The institution's name, city, and Web address make up the heading. The following paragraph begins with information about the institution's control, gender makeup of the student body, and category of institutional structure. The total figure for graduate, professional, and undergraduate student enrollment precedes specific figures for full-time and part-time graduate students, including number of women. Next comes the number of full-time and part-time graduate faculty members. Information about the institution's computer and library facilities follows. Graduate tuition and fee information for full-time and part-time students follows. (Please be aware that tuition can be different, and frequently higher, in specific graduate programs. You should always check with the particular program if a tuition difference will be a factor in your selection.) A general graduate program application contact and telephone number ends this first paragraph.

Graduate Units

The name of the unit is followed by the name and title of the head of the unit. Institutions have varying levels of discreteness in defining administrative units, and these are presented according to the information that the institution has provided to Peterson's. Each degree-program field of study offered by the unit is listed with abbreviations for all postbaccalaureate degrees awarded.

For Further Information

For many programs there is more in-depth narrative style information that can be located at www.petersons.com/gradchannel. There is a notation of the availability of this information at the end of the relevant profiles.

Data Collection Procedures

The information published in this book was collected through *Peterson's Annual Survey of Graduate and Professional Institutions.* Each spring and summer, this survey is sent to accredited institutions in the United States and U.S. territories that offer postbaccalaureate degree programs. Deans and other administrators provide information on specific programs as well as overall institutional information.

While every effort is made to ensure the accuracy and completeness of the data, information is sometimes unavailable or changes occur after publication deadlines. The omission of any particular item from a **Profile** signifies either that the item is not applicable to the institution or program or that information was not available.

Directory of Graduate and Professional Programs by Field

Graduate and Professional Programs by Field

■ ACCOUNTING

Abilene Christian University	M
Adelphi University	M
Alabama State University	M
American InterContinental University (FL)	M
American InterContinental University Buckhead Campus	M
American University	M
Anderson University	M,D
Andrews University	M
Angelo State University	M
Appalachian State University	M
Argosy University, Orange County Campus	M,D,O
Argosy University, Sarasota Campus	M,D,O
Argosy University, Tampa Campus	M,D,O
Argosy University, Twin Cities Campus	M,D
Arizona State University	M,D
Arizona State University at the West campus	M,O
Arkansas State University	M
Auburn University	M
Avila University	M
Baldwin-Wallace College	M
Ball State University	M
Barry University	M
Bayamón Central University	M
Baylor University	M
Benedictine University	M
Bentley College	M,D
Bernard M. Baruch College of the City University of New York	M,D
Bob Jones University	P,M,D,O
Boise State University	M
Boston College	M
Boston University	M,D,O
Bowling Green State University	M
Bradley University	M
Brenau University	M
Bridgewater State College	M
Brigham Young University	M
Brooklyn College of the City University of New York	M
Bryant University	M,O
Caldwell College	M
California State University, East Bay	M
California State University, Fresno	M
California State University, Fullerton	M
California State University, Los Angeles	M
California State University, Sacramento	M
Canisius College	M
Capella University	M,D,O
Carnegie Mellon University	D
Case Western Reserve University	M,D
Centenary College	M
Central Michigan University	M
Central Washington University	M
Charleston Southern University	M
City University of Seattle	M,O
Clark University	M
Clemson University	M
Cleveland State University	M
College of Charleston	M
The College of Saint Rose	M
The College of William and Mary	M
Colorado State University	M
Colorado Technical University—Colorado Springs	M,D
Colorado Technical University—Denver	M
Columbia University	M,D
Cornell University	D
Dallas Baptist University	M
Delta State University	M
DePaul University	M
Dominican University	M
Drexel University	M,D,O
Duquesne University	M
East Carolina University	M
Eastern Illinois University	M,O
Eastern Michigan University	M
Eastern University	M
East Tennessee State University	M
Elmhurst College	M
Fairfield University	M,O
Fairleigh Dickinson University, College at Florham	M
Fairleigh Dickinson University, Metropolitan Campus	M,O
Fitchburg State College	M
Florida Agricultural and Mechanical University	M
Florida Atlantic University	M
Florida Gulf Coast University	M
Florida International University	M
Florida State University	M,D
Fontbonne University	M
Fordham University	M
Fort Hays State University	M
Gannon University	O
The George Washington University	M,D
Georgia College & State University	M
Georgia Institute of Technology	M,D,O
Georgia Southern University	M
Georgia State University	M,D,O
Golden Gate University	M,D,O
Gonzaga University	M
Governors State University	M
Graduate School and University Center of the City University of New York	D
Grand Valley State University	M
Hawai'i Pacific University	M
Hofstra University	M
Houston Baptist University	M
Howard University	M
Hunter College of the City University of New York	M
Illinois State University	M
Indiana University Northwest	M,O
Indiana University South Bend	M
Indiana University Southeast	M,O
Indiana Wesleyan University	M
Inter American University of Puerto Rico, Metropolitan Campus	M,D
Inter American University of Puerto Rico, San Germán Campus	M,D
Iowa State University of Science and Technology	M
Ithaca College	M
Jackson State University	M
James Madison University	M
John Carroll University	M
Johnson & Wales University	M
Kansas State University	M
Kean University	M
Kennesaw State University	M
Kent State University	M,D
Lamar University	M
Lehigh University	M
Lehman College of the City University of New York	M
Lincoln University (MO)	M
Lindenwood University	M
Lipscomb University	M
Long Island University, Brooklyn Campus	M
Long Island University, C.W. Post Campus	M,O
Louisiana State University and Agricultural and Mechanical College	M,D
Louisiana Tech University	M,D
Loyola University Chicago	M
Marquette University	M
Maryville University of Saint Louis	M,O
Mercer University	M
Miami University	M
Michigan State University	M,D
Middle Tennessee State University	M
Minnesota State University Mankato	M
Mississippi College	M,O
Mississippi State University	M,D
Missouri State University	M
Monmouth University	M,O
Montana State University	M
Montclair State University	M
Murray State University	M
National University	M
New Jersey City University	M
New Mexico State University	M
New York Institute of Technology	M,O
New York University	M,D
North Carolina State University	M
Northeastern Illinois University	M
Northeastern State University	M
Northeastern University	M,O
Northern Illinois University	M
Northern Kentucky University	M
Northwestern University	D
Northwest Missouri State University	M
Nova Southeastern University	M
Nyack College	M
Oakland University	M,O
The Ohio State University	M,D
Oklahoma City University	M
Oklahoma State University	M,D
Old Dominion University	M
Oral Roberts University	M

Pace University M
Penn State University Park M,D
Pittsburg State University M
Pontifical Catholic University of Puerto Rico M,D
Prairie View A&M University M
Purdue University M,D
Purdue University Calumet M
Queens College of the City University of New York M
Quinnipiac University M
Regis University M,O
Rhode Island College M
Rider University M
Robert Morris University M
Rochester Institute of Technology M
Roosevelt University M
Rutgers, The State University of New Jersey, Newark M,D,O
St. Ambrose University M
St. Bonaventure University M,O
St. Edward's University M,O
St. John's University (NY) M,O
St. Joseph's College, Suffolk Campus M
Saint Joseph's University M
Saint Leo University M
Saint Louis University M
St. Mary's University of San Antonio M
Saint Peter's College M,O
St. Thomas University M,O
San Diego State University M
San Jose State University M
Seattle University M
Seton Hall University M
Southeastern University M
Southeast Missouri State University M
Southern Illinois University Carbondale M,D
Southern Illinois University Edwardsville M
Southern Methodist University M
Southern New Hampshire University M,D,O
Southern University and Agricultural and Mechanical College M
Southern Utah University M
State University of New York at Binghamton M,D
State University of New York at Fredonia M
State University of New York at New Paltz M
State University of New York Institute of Technology M
Stephen F. Austin State University M
Stetson University M
Strayer University M
Suffolk University M,O
Syracuse University M,D
Tarleton State University M
Temple University M,D
Texas A&M International University M
Texas A&M University M,D
Texas A&M University–Corpus Christi M
Texas A&M University–Texarkana M
Texas Christian University M
Texas State University-San Marcos M
Texas Tech University M,D
Towson University M
Trinity University M
Truman State University M
Universidad del Turabo M
Universidad Metropolitana M,O
University at Albany, State University of New York M
University at Buffalo, the State University of New York M,D,O
The University of Akron M
The University of Alabama M,D
The University of Alabama in Huntsville M,O
The University of Arizona M
University of Arkansas M
University of Baltimore M
University of California, Berkeley D
University of Central Arkansas M
University of Central Florida M
University of Central Missouri M
University of Cincinnati M,D
University of Colorado at Boulder D
University of Colorado at Colorado Springs M
University of Colorado Denver M
University of Connecticut M,D
University of Dallas M
University of Delaware M
University of Denver M
University of Florida M,D
University of Georgia M
University of Hartford M,O
University of Hawaii at Manoa M,D
University of Houston M,D
University of Houston–Clear Lake M
University of Houston–Victoria M
University of Idaho M
University of Illinois at Chicago M
University of Illinois at Springfield M
University of Illinois at Urbana–Champaign M,D
The University of Iowa M,D
University of Kansas M
University of Kentucky M
University of La Verne M
University of Louisville M
University of Maine M
University of Mary Hardin-Baylor M
University of Maryland University College M,O
University of Massachusetts Amherst M
University of Massachusetts Dartmouth M,O
University of Memphis M,D
University of Miami M
University of Michigan–Dearborn M
University of Minnesota, Twin Cities Campus M,D
University of Mississippi M,D
University of Missouri–Columbia M,D
University of Missouri–Kansas City M,D
University of Missouri–St. Louis M,O
The University of Montana M
University of Nebraska at Omaha M
University of Nebraska–Lincoln M,D
University of Nevada, Las Vegas M
University of Nevada, Reno M
University of New Hampshire M
University of New Haven M
University of New Mexico M
University of New Orleans M
The University of North Carolina at Chapel Hill M,D
The University of North Carolina at Charlotte M
The University of North Carolina at Greensboro M,O
The University of North Carolina Wilmington M
University of Northern Iowa M
University of North Florida M
University of North Texas M,D
University of Notre Dame M
University of Oklahoma M
University of Oregon M,D
University of Pennsylvania M,D
University of Phoenix–Central Florida Campus M
University of Phoenix–Denver Campus M
University of Phoenix–Fort Lauderdale Campus M
University of Phoenix–Hawaii Campus M
University of Phoenix–North Florida Campus M
University of Phoenix M
University of Phoenix–Oregon Campus M
University of Phoenix–Sacramento Valley Campus M
University of Phoenix–Southern Arizona Campus M
University of Phoenix–Southern California Campus M
University of Phoenix–West Michigan Campus M
University of Rhode Island M
University of St. Thomas (MN) M
University of San Diego M,O
The University of Scranton M
University of South Alabama M
University of South Carolina M
The University of South Dakota M
University of Southern California M
University of Southern Indiana M
University of Southern Maine M
University of Southern Mississippi M
University of South Florida M
The University of Tampa M
The University of Tennessee M,D
The University of Tennessee at Chattanooga M
The University of Tennessee at Martin M
The University of Texas at Arlington M,D
The University of Texas at Austin M,D
The University of Texas at Dallas M
The University of Texas at El Paso M
The University of Texas at San Antonio M,D
The University of Texas of the Permian Basin M
The University of Toledo M
University of Utah M,D
University of Virginia M
University of Washington M,D
University of Washington, Tacoma M
University of West Florida M
University of West Georgia M
University of Wisconsin–Madison D
University of Wisconsin–Whitewater M
University of Wyoming M
Upper Iowa University M
Utah State University M
Utica College M
Villanova University M
Virginia Commonwealth University M,D
Virginia Polytechnic Institute and State University M,D
Wagner College M
Wake Forest University M
Washington State University M,D
Washington University in St. Louis M
Wayne State University M,D
Weber State University M
Western Carolina University M
Western Connecticut State University M
Western Illinois University M
Western Michigan University M

Western New England College M
West Texas A&M University M
West Virginia University M
Wheeling Jesuit University M
Wichita State University M
Widener University M
Wilkes University M
Worcester State College M
Wright State University M
Yale University D
Youngstown State University M

■ ACOUSTICS

The Catholic University of America M,D
Penn State University Park M,D
University of Massachusetts Dartmouth M,D,O

■ ACTUARIAL SCIENCE

Ball State University M
Boston University M
Central Connecticut State University M,O
Columbia University M
Georgia State University M
Maryville University of Saint Louis M
Roosevelt University M
St. John's University (NY) M
Temple University M
University of Central Florida M,O
University of Connecticut M,D
The University of Iowa M,D
University of Nebraska–Lincoln M
University of Wisconsin–Madison M

■ ACUPUNCTURE AND ORIENTAL MEDICINE

University of Bridgeport M

■ ACUTE CARE/CRITICAL CARE NURSING

Barry University M,O
Case Western Reserve University M,D
The College of New Rochelle M,O
Columbia University M,O
Duke University M,D,O
Duquesne University M,O
Indiana University–Purdue University Indianapolis M
The Johns Hopkins University M,O
Loyola University Chicago M
New York University M,O
Northeastern University M,O
Seton Hall University M
University at Buffalo, the State University of New York M,D,O
University of Cincinnati M,D
University of Connecticut M,D,O
University of Miami M,D
University of Michigan M
University of Pennsylvania M
University of Pittsburgh M,D
University of South Carolina M,O
Vanderbilt University M,D
Wayne State University M
Wright State University M

■ ADDICTIONS/SUBSTANCE ABUSE COUNSELING

Capella University M,D,O
The College of New Jersey M,O
College of St. Joseph M
The College of William and Mary M,D
Coppin State University M
East Carolina University M
Eastern Kentucky University M
Georgian Court University M,O
Governors State University M
Hofstra University M,O
The Johns Hopkins University M,D,O
Kean University M,O
Lewis & Clark College M
Loyola College in Maryland M,O
Marywood University M
Mercy College M,O
Minnesota State University Mankato M
Monmouth University M,O
Montclair State University M,O
National-Louis University M,O
Notre Dame de Namur University M,O
Pace University M
Palm Beach Atlantic University M
St. Mary's University of San Antonio M,D,O
Southern New Hampshire University M,O
Springfield College M,O
Stony Brook University, State University of New York M
University of Central Florida M,O
University of Central Oklahoma M
University of Detroit Mercy M,O
University of Great Falls O
University of Illinois at Springfield M
University of Louisiana at Monroe M
University of New England M,O
Wayne State University O

■ ADULT EDUCATION

Alverno College M
Armstrong Atlantic State University M
Auburn University M,D,O
Ball State University M,D
Buffalo State College, State University of New York M,O
Capella University M,D,O
Cheyney University of Pennsylvania M
Cleveland State University M,O
Colorado State University M,D
Coppin State University M
Cornell University M,D
DePaul University M
Drake University M
East Carolina University M,O
Eastern Washington University M
Florida Agricultural and Mechanical University M,D
Florida Atlantic University M,D,O
Florida International University M,D
Florida State University M,D,O
Fordham University M,D,O
Grand Valley State University M
Indiana University of Pennsylvania M
Kansas State University M,D
Kean University M
Marshall University M
Marygrove College M
Michigan State University M,D,O
Morehead State University M,O
National-Louis University M,D,O
North Carolina Agricultural and Technical State University M
North Carolina State University M,D
Northern Illinois University M,D
Northwestern State University of Louisiana M
Nova Southeastern University D
Oregon State University M
Penn State Harrisburg M,D
Penn State University Park M,D
Portland State University M,D
Regis University M,O
Robert Morris University M
Rutgers, The State University of New Jersey, New Brunswick M
San Francisco State University M,O
Seattle University M,O
Suffolk University M,O
Texas A&M University–Kingsville M
Texas A&M University–Texarkana M
Troy University M
Tusculum College M
University of Alaska Anchorage M
University of Arkansas M,D,O
University of Arkansas at Little Rock M
University of Central Oklahoma M
University of Cincinnati M,D,O
University of Connecticut M,D
University of Denver M,D,O
University of Georgia M,D,O
University of Idaho M,D,O
University of Memphis M,D
University of Minnesota, Twin Cities Campus M,D,O
University of Missouri–Columbia M,D,O
University of Missouri–St. Louis M,D,O
The University of North Carolina at Greensboro M,D,O
University of Oklahoma M,D
University of Phoenix M
University of Phoenix–Sacramento Valley Campus M,O
University of Rhode Island M
University of St. Francis (IL) M
University of Southern Maine M,O
University of Southern Mississippi M,D,O
University of South Florida M,D,O
The University of Tennessee M,D
The University of Texas at San Antonio M,D
University of the Incarnate Word M,D,O
The University of West Alabama M
University of Wisconsin–Platteville M
University of Wyoming M,D,O
Valdosta State University M,D
Virginia Commonwealth University M
Virginia Polytechnic Institute and State University M,D
Walden University M,D
Wayne State University M,D,O
Western Washington University M
Widener University M,D
Wright State University O

■ ADULT NURSING

Angelo State University M
Bloomsburg University of Pennsylvania M
Boston College M,D
Case Western Reserve University M,D
The Catholic University of America M,D
College of Mount Saint Vincent M,O
College of Staten Island of the City University of New York M,O
Columbia University M,O
Daemen College M,O
DeSales University M
Duke University M,D,O
Eastern Michigan University M,O
Emory University M
Fairfield University M,O
The George Washington University M,D,O
Georgia State University M,D,O
Gwynedd-Mercy College M
Hunter College of the City University of New York M
The Johns Hopkins University M,O
Kent State University M,D
La Salle University M,O

Lehman College of the City University of New York	M
Long Island University, Brooklyn Campus	M,O
Loyola University Chicago	M
Madonna University	M
Marian College of Fond du Lac	M
Marquette University	M,D,O
Mercy College	M,O
Molloy College	M,O
Mount Saint Mary College	M
New Mexico State University	M
New York University	M,O
Oakland University	M
Otterbein College	M,O
Quinnipiac University	M,O
Rutgers, The State University of New Jersey, Newark	M
Saint Xavier University	M,O
Seton Hall University	M
Spalding University	M
State University of New York at New Paltz	M,O
State University of New York Institute of Technology	M,O
Stony Brook University, State University of New York	M,O
Texas Christian University	M
Texas Woman's University	M,D
University at Buffalo, the State University of New York	M,D,O
University of Central Florida	M,D,O
University of Cincinnati	M,D
University of Colorado at Colorado Springs	M,D
University of Connecticut	M,D,O
University of Delaware	M,O
University of Hawaii at Manoa	M,D,O
University of Massachusetts Lowell	M
University of Miami	M,D
University of Michigan	M
University of Minnesota, Twin Cities Campus	M
University of Missouri–Kansas City	M,D
The University of North Carolina at Charlotte	M
The University of North Carolina at Greensboro	M,D,O
University of Pennsylvania	M
University of Pittsburgh	M,D
University of San Diego	M,D,O
The University of Scranton	M,O
University of South Alabama	M,D
University of South Carolina	M
University of Southern Maine	M,O
University of Southern Mississippi	M,D
The University of Tampa	M
The University of Tennessee at Chattanooga	M
The University of Texas–Pan American	M
University of Wisconsin–Oshkosh	M
Vanderbilt University	M,D
Villanova University	M,D,O
Virginia Commonwealth University	M,D,O
Wayne State University	M
Western Connecticut State University	M
Wilmington University (DE)	M
Winona State University	M,O
Wright State University	M

■ ADVERTISING AND PUBLIC RELATIONS

Ball State University	M
Boston University	M
California State University, Fullerton	M
Colorado State University	M
Emerson College	M
Golden Gate University	M,D,O
Iona College	M
Marquette University	M
Michigan State University	M,D
Mississippi College	M
Monmouth University	M,O
Montana State University–Billings	M
Montclair State University	M
New York Institute of Technology	M,O
New York University	M
Northwestern University	M
Rowan University	M
San Diego State University	M
Syracuse University	M
Texas Christian University	M
Towson University	O
The University of Alabama	M
University of Colorado Denver	M,O
University of Denver	M
University of Florida	M
University of Houston	M
University of Illinois at Urbana–Champaign	M
University of Maryland, College Park	M,D
University of Miami	M,D
University of New Haven	M
University of Oklahoma	M
University of Southern California	M
University of Southern Mississippi	M,D
The University of Tennessee	M,D
The University of Texas at Austin	M,D
University of Wisconsin–Stevens Point	M
Virginia Commonwealth University	M
Wayne State University	M,D
Webster University	M

■ AEROSPACE/AERONAUTICAL ENGINEERING

Arizona State University	M,D
Arizona State University at the Polytechnic Campus	M
Auburn University	M,D
Boston University	M,D
Brown University	M,D
California Institute of Technology	M,D,O
California Polytechnic State University, San Luis Obispo	M
California State University, Long Beach	M
Case Western Reserve University	M,D
Cornell University	M,D
Embry-Riddle Aeronautical University (FL)	M
Embry-Riddle Aeronautical University Worldwide	M
Florida Institute of Technology	M,D
The George Washington University	M,D,O
Georgia Institute of Technology	M,D
Illinois Institute of Technology	M,D
Iowa State University of Science and Technology	M,D
Massachusetts Institute of Technology	M,D,O
Middle Tennessee State University	M
Mississippi State University	M
Missouri University of Science and Technology	M,D
North Carolina State University	M,D
The Ohio State University	M,D
Oklahoma State University	M
Old Dominion University	M
Penn State University Park	M,D
Princeton University	M,D
Purdue University	M,D
Rensselaer Polytechnic Institute	M,D
Rutgers, The State University of New Jersey, New Brunswick	M,D
San Diego State University	M,D
San Jose State University	M
Stanford University	M,D,O
Syracuse University	M,D
Texas A&M University	M,D
University at Buffalo, the State University of New York	M,D
The University of Alabama	M,D
The University of Alabama in Huntsville	M,D
The University of Arizona	M,D
University of California, Davis	M,D,O
University of California, Irvine	M,D
University of California, Los Angeles	M,D
University of California, San Diego	M,D
University of Central Florida	M
University of Cincinnati	M,D
University of Colorado at Boulder	M,D
University of Colorado at Colorado Springs	M
University of Dayton	M,D
University of Florida	M,D,O
University of Houston	M,D
University of Illinois at Urbana–Champaign	M,D
University of Kansas	M,D
University of Maryland, College Park	M,D,O
University of Miami	M,D
University of Michigan	M,D
University of Minnesota, Twin Cities Campus	M,D
University of Missouri–Columbia	M,D
University of Notre Dame	M,D
University of Oklahoma	M,D
University of Southern California	M,D,O
The University of Tennessee	M,D
The University of Texas at Arlington	M,D
The University of Texas at Austin	M,D
University of Virginia	M,D
University of Washington	M,D
Utah State University	M,D
Virginia Polytechnic Institute and State University	M,D
Webster University	M,D
West Virginia University	M,D
Wichita State University	M,D

■ AFRICAN-AMERICAN STUDIES

Boston University	M
Clark Atlanta University	M,D
Columbia University	M
Cornell University	M,D
Florida Agricultural and Mechanical University	M
Harvard University	D
Indiana University Bloomington	M
Michigan State University	M,D
Morgan State University	M,D
North Carolina Agricultural and Technical State University	M
The Ohio State University	M
Rutgers, The State University of New Jersey, New Brunswick	D
Syracuse University	M
Temple University	M,D
University at Albany, State University of New York	M
University of California, Berkeley	D
University of California, Los Angeles	M
The University of Iowa	M

University of Massachusetts Amherst M,D
University of Wisconsin–Madison M
West Virginia University M,D
Yale University M,D

■ AFRICAN STUDIES

Boston University M,O
Claremont Graduate University M,D,O
Columbia University O
Cornell University M,D
Florida International University M
Harvard University D
Howard University M,D
The Johns Hopkins University M,D,O
Michigan State University M,D
New York University M,D,O
Northwestern University O
The Ohio State University M
Ohio University M
Rutgers, The State University of New Jersey, New Brunswick D
St. John's University (NY) M,O
Syracuse University M
University at Albany, State University of New York M
University of California, Los Angeles M
University of Connecticut M
University of Florida O
University of Illinois at Urbana–Champaign M
University of Louisville M
University of Pittsburgh O
University of South Florida M
University of Wisconsin–Madison M,D
West Virginia University M,D
Yale University M

■ AGRICULTURAL ECONOMICS AND AGRIBUSINESS

Alabama Agricultural and Mechanical University M
Alcorn State University M
Arizona State University at the Polytechnic Campus M
Auburn University M,D
California Polytechnic State University, San Luis Obispo M
Colorado State University M,D
Cornell University M,D
Florida Agricultural and Mechanical University M
Illinois State University M
Iowa State University of Science and Technology M,D
Kansas State University M,D
Louisiana State University and Agricultural and Mechanical College M,D
Michigan State University M,D
Mississippi State University M,D
Montana State University M
New Mexico State University M
North Carolina Agricultural and Technical State University M
North Carolina State University M
North Dakota State University M,D
Northwest Missouri State University M
The Ohio State University M,D
Oklahoma State University M,D
Oregon State University M,D
Penn State University Park M,D
Prairie View A&M University M
Purdue University M,D
Rutgers, The State University of New Jersey, New Brunswick M
South Carolina State University M
Southern Illinois University Carbondale M
Texas A&M University M,D
Texas A&M University–Kingsville M
Texas Tech University M,D
The University of Arizona M
University of Arkansas M
University of California, Berkeley D
University of California, Davis M,D
University of California, Santa Barbara M,D
University of Connecticut M,D
University of Delaware M
University of Florida M,D
University of Georgia M,D
University of Idaho M
University of Illinois at Urbana–Champaign M,D
University of Kentucky M,D
University of Maine M
University of Maryland, College Park M,D
University of Massachusetts Amherst M,D
University of Missouri–Columbia M,D
University of Nebraska–Lincoln M,D
University of Nevada, Reno M,D
University of Puerto Rico, Mayagüez Campus M
University of Vermont M
University of Wisconsin–Madison M,D
University of Wyoming M
Virginia Polytechnic Institute and State University M,D
Washington State University M,D,O
West Texas A&M University M
West Virginia University M
William Woods University M,O

■ AGRICULTURAL EDUCATION

Alcorn State University M,O
Arkansas State University M,O
Clemson University M
Cornell University M,D
Eastern Kentucky University M
Iowa State University of Science and Technology M,D
Louisiana State University and Agricultural and Mechanical College M,D
Mississippi State University M
Missouri State University M
Murray State University M
New Mexico State University M
North Carolina Agricultural and Technical State University M
North Carolina State University M
North Dakota State University M
Northwest Missouri State University M
The Ohio State University M,D
Oklahoma State University M,D
Oregon State University M
Penn State University Park M,D
Purdue University M,D,O
State University of New York at Oswego M
Stephen F. Austin State University M
Tarleton State University M
Texas A&M University M,D
Texas A&M University–Commerce M
Texas A&M University–Kingsville M
Texas State University-San Marcos M
Texas Tech University M,D
The University of Arizona M
University of Arkansas M
University of Connecticut M,D
University of Florida M,D
University of Georgia M
University of Idaho M,D
University of Illinois at Urbana–Champaign M,D
University of Minnesota, Twin Cities Campus M,D
University of Missouri–Columbia M,D,O
University of Nebraska–Lincoln M
University of Puerto Rico, Mayagüez Campus M
The University of Tennessee M
University of Wisconsin–River Falls M
Utah State University M
West Virginia University M

■ AGRICULTURAL ENGINEERING

Cornell University M,D
Illinois Institute of Technology M,D
Iowa State University of Science and Technology M,D
Kansas State University M,D
Louisiana State University and Agricultural and Mechanical College M,D
Michigan State University M,D
New York University M,D
North Carolina Agricultural and Technical State University M
North Carolina State University M,D
North Dakota State University M,D
The Ohio State University M,D
Oklahoma State University M,D
Penn State Great Valley M
Penn State University Park M,D
Purdue University M,D
South Dakota State University M,D
Texas A&M University M,D
The University of Arizona M,D
University of Arkansas M,D
University of Dayton M
University of Florida M,D,O
University of Georgia M,D
University of Idaho M,D
University of Illinois at Urbana–Champaign M,D
University of Kentucky M,D
University of Minnesota, Twin Cities Campus M,D
University of Missouri–Columbia M,D
University of Nebraska–Lincoln M,D
The University of Tennessee M
University of Wisconsin–Madison M,D
Utah State University M,D
Virginia Polytechnic Institute and State University M,D
Washington State University M,D

■ AGRICULTURAL SCIENCES—GENERAL

Alabama Agricultural and Mechanical University M,D
Alcorn State University M
Angelo State University M
Arkansas State University M,O
Auburn University M,D
Brigham Young University M,D
California Polytechnic State University, San Luis Obispo M
California State Polytechnic University, Pomona M
California State University, Fresno M
Clemson University M,D
Colorado State University M,D
Florida Agricultural and Mechanical University M

Illinois State University	M
Iowa State University of Science and Technology	M,D
Kansas State University	M,D
Louisiana State University and Agricultural and Mechanical College	M,D
McNeese State University	M
Michigan State University	M,D
Mississippi State University	M,D
Missouri State University	M
Montana State University	M,D
Murray State University	M
New Mexico State University	M
North Carolina Agricultural and Technical State University	M
North Carolina State University	M,D
North Dakota State University	M,D
Northwest Missouri State University	M
The Ohio State University	M,D
Oklahoma State University	M,D
Oregon State University	M,D
Penn State University Park	M,D
Prairie View A&M University	M
Purdue University	M,D
Sam Houston State University	M
South Dakota State University	M,D
Southern Illinois University Carbondale	M
Southern University and Agricultural and Mechanical College	M
Tarleton State University	M
Tennessee State University	M
Texas A&M University	M,D
Texas A&M University–Commerce	M
Texas A&M University–Kingsville	M,D
Texas Tech University	M,D
The University of Arizona	M,D
University of Arkansas	M,D
University of California, Davis	M
University of Connecticut	M,D
University of Delaware	M,D
University of Florida	M,D
University of Georgia	M,D
University of Hawaii at Manoa	M,D
University of Illinois at Urbana–Champaign	M,D
University of Kentucky	M,D
University of Maine	M,D
University of Maryland, College Park	P,M,D
University of Maryland Eastern Shore	M,D
University of Minnesota, Twin Cities Campus	M,D
University of Missouri–Columbia	M,D
University of Nebraska–Lincoln	M,D
University of Nevada, Reno	M,D
University of Puerto Rico, Mayagüez Campus	M
The University of Tennessee	M,D
The University of Tennessee at Martin	M
University of Vermont	M,D
University of Wisconsin–Madison	M,D
University of Wisconsin–River Falls	M
University of Wyoming	M,D
Utah State University	M,D
Virginia Polytechnic Institute and State University	M,D
Washington State University	M
Western Kentucky University	M
West Texas A&M University	M,D
West Virginia University	M,D

■ AGRONOMY AND SOIL SCIENCES

Alabama Agricultural and Mechanical University	M,D
Alcorn State University	M
Auburn University	M,D
Brigham Young University	M,D
Colorado State University	M,D
Cornell University	M,D
Iowa State University of Science and Technology	M,D
Kansas State University	M,D
Louisiana State University and Agricultural and Mechanical College	M,D
Michigan State University	M,D
Mississippi State University	M,D
New Mexico State University	M,D
North Carolina State University	M,D
North Dakota State University	M,D
The Ohio State University	M,D
Oklahoma State University	M,D
Oregon State University	M,D
Penn State University Park	M,D
Prairie View A&M University	M
Purdue University	M,D
South Dakota State University	M,D
Southern Illinois University Carbondale	M
Texas A&M University	M,D
Texas A&M University–Kingsville	M,D
Texas Tech University	M,D
The University of Arizona	M,D
University of Arkansas	M,D
University of California, Davis	M,D
University of California, Riverside	M,D
University of Connecticut	M,D
University of Delaware	M,D
University of Florida	M,D
University of Georgia	M,D
University of Idaho	M,D
University of Illinois at Urbana–Champaign	M,D
University of Kentucky	M,D
University of Maine	M,D
University of Maryland, College Park	M,D
University of Massachusetts Amherst	M,D
University of Minnesota, Twin Cities Campus	M,D
University of Missouri–Columbia	M,D
University of Nebraska–Lincoln	M,D
University of New Hampshire	M
University of Puerto Rico, Mayagüez Campus	M
University of Vermont	M,D
University of Wisconsin–Madison	M,D
University of Wyoming	M,D
Utah State University	M,D
Virginia Polytechnic Institute and State University	M,D
Washington State University	M,D
West Virginia University	M,D

■ ALLIED HEALTH—GENERAL

Alabama State University	D
Andrews University	M
Arkansas State University	M,O
Baylor University	M,D
Belmont University	M,D
Bennington College	O
Boston University	M,D
Cleveland State University	M
Creighton University	P,M,D
Dominican College	M,D
Drexel University	M,D,O
Duquesne University	M,D
East Carolina University	M,D
Eastern Kentucky University	M
East Tennessee State University	M,D,O
Emory University	M,D
Ferris State University	M
Florida Agricultural and Mechanical University	M
Florida Gulf Coast University	M
Georgia Southern University	M,O
Georgia State University	M,D,O
Grand Valley State University	M,D
Idaho State University	M,D,O
Ithaca College	M,D
Long Island University, C.W. Post Campus	M,O
Marymount University	M,D,O
Maryville University of Saint Louis	M,D
Mercy College	M,O
Misericordia University	M,D
Mountain State University	M
New Jersey City University	M
Northeastern University	P,M,D,O
Northern Arizona University	M,D,O
Nova Southeastern University	M,D
Oakland University	M,D,O
The Ohio State University	M
Old Dominion University	M,D
Quinnipiac University	M,D,O
Regis University	M,D
Saint Louis University	M,D,O
Seton Hall University	M,D
Shenandoah University	M,D,O
South Carolina State University	M
Southwestern Oklahoma State University	M
Temple University	M,D
Tennessee State University	M,D
Texas Christian University	M
Texas State University-San Marcos	M
Texas Woman's University	M,D
Towson University	M
University at Buffalo, the State University of New York	M,D,O
The University of Alabama at Birmingham	M,D,O
University of Connecticut	M
University of Detroit Mercy	M,O
University of Florida	M,D
University of Illinois at Chicago	M,D
University of Kansas	M,D,O
University of Kentucky	M,D
University of Massachusetts Lowell	M,D
The University of North Carolina at Chapel Hill	M,D
University of North Florida	M,O
University of Phoenix–Las Vegas Campus	M
University of St. Francis (IL)	M
University of Saint Francis (IN)	M
University of South Alabama	M,D
The University of South Dakota	M,D
The University of Texas at El Paso	M
University of Vermont	M,D
University of Wisconsin–Milwaukee	M,D
Virginia Commonwealth University	D
Washington University in St. Louis	M,D,O
Wichita State University	M

■ ALLOPATHIC MEDICINE

Boston University	P
Brown University	P
Case Western Reserve University	P
Columbia University	P

Creighton University	P
Drexel University	P
Duke University	P
East Carolina University	P
East Tennessee State University	P
Emory University	P
Florida State University	P,D
Georgetown University	P
The George Washington University	P
Harvard University	P,D
Howard University	P,D
The Johns Hopkins University	P
Loyola University Chicago	P
Marshall University	P
Mercer University	P,M
Michigan State University	P
New York University	P
Northwestern University	
The Ohio State University	P
Saint Louis University	P
Stanford University	P
Stony Brook University, State University of New York	P
Temple University	P
Tufts University	P
Tulane University	P
University at Buffalo, the State University of New York	P
The University of Alabama at Birmingham	P,M,D
The University of Arizona	P
University of California, Berkeley	
University of California, Davis	P
University of California, Irvine	P
University of California, Los Angeles	P
University of California, San Diego	P
University of Chicago	P
University of Cincinnati	P,M
University of Colorado Denver	P
University of Florida	P
University of Hawaii at Manoa	P
University of Illinois at Chicago	P
University of Illinois at Urbana–Champaign	
The University of Iowa	P
University of Kansas	P
University of Kentucky	P
University of Louisville	P
University of Miami	P
University of Michigan	P
University of Minnesota, Duluth	P
University of Minnesota, Twin Cities Campus	P
University of Missouri–Columbia	P
University of Missouri–Kansas City	P
University of New Mexico	P
The University of North Carolina at Chapel Hill	P
University of North Dakota	P
University of Pennsylvania	P
University of Pittsburgh	P
University of Rochester	P
University of South Alabama	P
University of South Carolina	P
The University of South Dakota	P
University of Southern California	P
The University of Toledo	M
University of Utah	P
University of Vermont	P
University of Virginia	P,M,D
University of Washington	P
University of Wisconsin–Madison	P
Vanderbilt University	M,D
Virginia Commonwealth University	P
Wake Forest University	P
Washington University in St. Louis	P
Wayne State University	P
West Virginia University	P
Wright State University	P
Yale University	P

■ AMERICAN INDIAN/NATIVE AMERICAN STUDIES

Montana State University	M
The University of Arizona	M,D
University of California, Davis	M,D
University of California, Los Angeles	M
University of Kansas	M
University of Oklahoma	M

■ AMERICAN STUDIES

American University	M,D,O
Appalachian State University	M
Baylor University	M
Boston University	D
Bowling Green State University	M,D
Brandeis University	M,D
Brown University	M,D
California State University, Fullerton	M
Claremont Graduate University	M,D,O
The College of William and Mary	M,D
Columbia University	M
Cornell University	M,D
Drake University	M
East Carolina University	M
Eastern Michigan University	M
Fairfield University	M
Florida State University	M,O
The George Washington University	M,D
Harvard University	D
Lehigh University	M
Michigan State University	M,D
New Mexico Highlands University	M
New York University	M,D
Northeastern State University	M
Penn State Harrisburg	M
Pepperdine University	M
Purdue University	M,D
Saint Louis University	M,D
State University of New York College at Cortland	O
Stony Brook University, State University of New York	M,O
University at Buffalo, the State University of New York	M,D
The University of Alabama	M
University of Central Oklahoma	M
University of Dallas	M
University of Delaware	M
University of Hawaii at Manoa	M,D,O
The University of Iowa	M,D
University of Kansas	M,D
University of Louisiana at Lafayette	D
University of Maryland, College Park	M,D
University of Massachusetts Boston	M
University of Michigan	M,D
University of Michigan–Flint	M
University of Minnesota, Twin Cities Campus	D
University of Mississippi	M
University of New Mexico	M,D
University of Pennsylvania	M,D
University of Southern California	D
University of Southern Maine	M
University of South Florida	M
The University of Texas at Austin	M,D
University of Utah	M,D
University of Wyoming	M
Utah State University	M
Washington State University	M,D
Western Carolina University	M
West Virginia University	M,D
Wheaton College	M
Yale University	M,D

■ ANALYTICAL CHEMISTRY

Auburn University	M,D
Brigham Young University	M,D
California State University, Fullerton	M
California State University, Los Angeles	M
Case Western Reserve University	M,D
Clarkson University	M,D
Cleveland State University	M,D
Cornell University	D
Florida State University	M,D
Georgetown University	M,D
The George Washington University	M,D
Governors State University	M
Howard University	M,D
Illinois Institute of Technology	M,D
Indiana University Bloomington	M,D
Kansas State University	M,D
Kent State University	M,D
Marquette University	M,D
Miami University	M,D
Northeastern University	M,D
Old Dominion University	M,D
Oregon State University	M,D
Purdue University	M,D
Rensselaer Polytechnic Institute	M,D
Rutgers, The State University of New Jersey, Newark	M,D
Seton Hall University	M,D
Southern University and Agricultural and Mechanical College	M
State University of New York at Binghamton	M,D
Stevens Institute of Technology	M,D,O
Tufts University	M,D
University of Cincinnati	M,D
University of Georgia	M,D
University of Louisville	M,D
University of Maryland, College Park	M,D
University of Michigan	D
University of Missouri–Columbia	M,D
University of Missouri–Kansas City	M,D
The University of Montana	M,D
University of Nebraska–Lincoln	M,D
University of Southern Mississippi	M,D
University of South Florida	M,D
The University of Tennessee	M,D
The University of Texas at Austin	M,D
The University of Toledo	M,D
Vanderbilt University	M,D
Virginia Commonwealth University	M,D
Wake Forest University	M,D
West Virginia University	M,D

■ ANATOMY

Auburn University	M,D
Barry University	M
Boston University	M,D
Case Western Reserve University	M,D
Columbia University	M,D
Cornell University	M,D
Creighton University	M
Duke University	D
East Carolina University	D
East Tennessee State University	M,D
Howard University	M,D
Indiana University–Purdue University Indianapolis	M,D

The Johns Hopkins University	D
Kansas State University	M,D
Loyola University Chicago	M,D
The Ohio State University	M,D
Purdue University	M,D
Saint Louis University	M,D
Stony Brook University, State University of New York	D
Temple University	M,D
Texas A&M University	M,D
University at Buffalo, the State University of New York	M,D
The University of Arizona	D
University of California, Irvine	M,D
University of California, Los Angeles	D
University of Chicago	D
University of Georgia	M
University of Illinois at Chicago	M,D
The University of Iowa	D
University of Kansas	M,D
University of Kentucky	D
University of Louisville	M,D
University of North Dakota	M,D
University of Rochester	M,D
University of South Florida	M,D
The University of Tennessee	M,D
University of Utah	D
University of Vermont	D
University of Wisconsin–Madison	M,D
Virginia Commonwealth University	M,D,O
Wake Forest University	D
Wayne State University	M,D
Wright State University	M

■ ANESTHESIOLOGIST ASSISTANT STUDIES

Case Western Reserve University	M
Emory University	M

■ ANIMAL BEHAVIOR

Arizona State University	M,D
Bucknell University	M
Cornell University	D
Emory University	D
Illinois State University	M,D
University of California, Davis	D
University of Colorado at Boulder	M,D
University of Minnesota, Twin Cities Campus	M,D
University of Missouri–St. Louis	M,D,O
The University of Montana	M,D,O
The University of Tennessee	M,D
The University of Texas at Austin	D

■ ANIMAL SCIENCES

Alabama Agricultural and Mechanical University	M,D
Alcorn State University	M
Angelo State University	M
Auburn University	M,D
Boise State University	M
Brigham Young University	M,D
California State Polytechnic University, Pomona	M
California State University, Fresno	M
Clemson University	M,D
Colorado State University	M,D
Cornell University	M,D
Florida Agricultural and Mechanical University	M
Fort Valley State University	M
Iowa State University of Science and Technology	M,D
Kansas State University	M,D
Louisiana State University and Agricultural and Mechanical College	M,D
Michigan State University	M,D
Mississippi State University	M
Montana State University	M,D
New Mexico State University	M,D
North Carolina State University	M,D
North Dakota State University	M,D
The Ohio State University	M,D
Oklahoma State University	M,D
Oregon State University	M,D
Penn State University Park	M,D
Prairie View A&M University	M
Purdue University	M,D
Rutgers, The State University of New Jersey, New Brunswick	M,D
South Dakota State University	M,D
Southern Illinois University Carbondale	M
Sul Ross State University	M
Texas A&M University	M,D
Texas A&M University–Kingsville	M
Texas Tech University	M,D
The University of Arizona	M,D
University of Arkansas	M,D
University of California, Davis	M,D
University of Connecticut	M,D
University of Delaware	M,D
University of Florida	M,D
University of Georgia	M,D
University of Hawaii at Manoa	M
University of Idaho	M,D
University of Illinois at Urbana–Champaign	M,D
University of Kentucky	M,D
University of Maine	M
University of Maryland, College Park	M,D
University of Massachusetts Amherst	M,D
University of Minnesota, Twin Cities Campus	M,D
University of Missouri–Columbia	M,D
University of Nebraska–Lincoln	M,D
University of Nevada, Reno	M
University of New Hampshire	M,D
University of Puerto Rico, Mayagüez Campus	M
University of Rhode Island	M,D
The University of Tennessee	M,D
University of Vermont	M,D
University of Wisconsin–Madison	M,D
University of Wyoming	M,D
Utah State University	M,D
Virginia Polytechnic Institute and State University	M,D
Washington State University	M,D
West Texas A&M University	M
West Virginia University	M,D

■ ANTHROPOLOGY

American University	M,D,O
Arizona State University	M,D
Ball State University	M
Boston University	M,D
Brandeis University	M,D
Brigham Young University	M
Brown University	M,D
California Institute of Integral Studies	M,D
California State University, Bakersfield	M
California State University, Chico	M
California State University, East Bay	M
California State University, Fullerton	M
California State University, Long Beach	M
California State University, Los Angeles	M
California State University, Northridge	M
California State University, Sacramento	M
Case Western Reserve University	M,D
The Catholic University of America	M,D
The College of William and Mary	M,D
Colorado State University	M
Columbia University	M,D
Cornell University	D
Duke University	D
East Carolina University	M
Eastern New Mexico University	M
Emory University	D
Florida Atlantic University	M
Florida State University	M,D
The George Washington University	M,D
Georgia State University	M
Graduate School and University Center of the City University of New York	D
Harvard University	M,D
Hunter College of the City University of New York	M
Idaho State University	M
Indiana University Bloomington	M,D
Iowa State University of Science and Technology	M
The Johns Hopkins University	D
Kent State University	M
Louisiana State University and Agricultural and Mechanical College	M,D
Michigan State University	M,D
Minnesota State University Mankato	M
Mississippi State University	M,D
New Mexico Highlands University	M
New Mexico State University	M
The New School: A University	M,D
New York University	M,D
North Carolina State University	M
Northern Arizona University	M
Northern Illinois University	M
Northwestern University	D
The Ohio State University	M,D
Oregon State University	M
Penn State University Park	M,D
Portland State University	M,D,O
Princeton University	D
Purdue University	M,D
Rice University	M,D
Roosevelt University	M
Rutgers, The State University of New Jersey, New Brunswick	M,D
San Diego State University	M
San Francisco State University	M
Southern Illinois University Carbondale	M,D
Southern Methodist University	M,D
Stanford University	M,D
State University of New York at Binghamton	M,D
Stony Brook University, State University of New York	M,D
Syracuse University	M,D
Temple University	D
Texas A&M University	M,D
Texas State University-San Marcos	M
Texas Tech University	M
Tulane University	M,D
University at Albany, State University of New York	M,D
University at Buffalo, the State University of New York	M,D

The University of Alabama M,D
The University of Alabama at Birmingham M
University of Alaska Anchorage M
University of Alaska Fairbanks M,D
The University of Arizona M,D
University of Arkansas M,D
University of California, Berkeley D
University of California, Davis M,D
University of California, Irvine M,D
University of California, Los Angeles M,D
University of California, Riverside M,D
University of California, San Diego D
University of California, Santa Barbara M,D
University of California, Santa Cruz D
University of Central Florida M,O
University of Chicago M,D
University of Cincinnati M
University of Colorado at Boulder M,D
University of Colorado Denver M
University of Connecticut M,D
University of Denver M
University of Florida M,D
University of Georgia M,D
University of Hawaii at Manoa M,D
University of Houston M
University of Idaho M
University of Illinois at Chicago M,D
University of Illinois at Urbana–Champaign M,D
The University of Iowa M,D
University of Kansas M,D
University of Kentucky M,D
University of Maryland, College Park M
University of Massachusetts Amherst M,D
University of Memphis M
University of Michigan D
University of Minnesota, Duluth M
University of Minnesota, Twin Cities Campus M,D
University of Mississippi M
University of Missouri–Columbia M,D
The University of Montana M,D
University of Nebraska–Lincoln M
University of Nevada, Las Vegas M,D
University of Nevada, Reno M,D
University of New Mexico M,D
The University of North Carolina at Chapel Hill M,D
University of North Texas M
University of Oklahoma M,D
University of Oregon M,D
University of Pennsylvania M,D
University of Pittsburgh M,D
University of South Carolina M,D
University of Southern California M,D,O
University of Southern Mississippi M
University of South Florida M,D
The University of Tennessee M,D
The University of Texas at Arlington M
The University of Texas at Austin M,D
The University of Texas at San Antonio M,D
University of Tulsa M
University of Utah M,D
University of Virginia M,D
University of Washington M,D
University of West Florida M
University of Wisconsin–Madison M,D
University of Wisconsin–Milwaukee M,D,O
University of Wyoming M,D
Vanderbilt University M,D
Washington State University M,D
Washington University in St. Louis M,D
Wayne State University M,D
West Chester University of Pennsylvania M,O
Western Kentucky University M
Western Michigan University M
Western Washington University M
Wichita State University M
Yale University M,D

■ APPLIED ARTS AND DESIGN—GENERAL

Alfred University M
Arizona State University M
Bowling Green State University M
Bradley University M
California State University, Fresno M
California State University, Fullerton M,O
California State University, Los Angeles M
Cardinal Stritch University M
Carnegie Mellon University D
Drexel University M
Ferris State University M
Florida Atlantic University M
Florida State University M,D
The George Washington University M,D
Howard University M
Illinois Institute of Technology M,D
Indiana University–Purdue University Indianapolis M
Iowa State University of Science and Technology M
Lamar University M
Louisiana State University and Agricultural and Mechanical College M
Louisiana Tech University M
New Mexico State University M
The New School: A University M
New York University M
North Carolina State University M,D
Oklahoma State University M,D
Purdue University M
Rutgers, The State University of New Jersey, New Brunswick M
San Diego State University M
San Jose State University M
Southern Illinois University Carbondale M
Stephen F. Austin State University M
Suffolk University M
Sul Ross State University M
Syracuse University M
University of California, Berkeley M
University of California, Los Angeles M
University of Central Oklahoma M
University of Cincinnati M
University of Delaware M
University of Idaho M
University of Illinois at Urbana–Champaign M,D
University of Kansas M
University of Kentucky M
University of Massachusetts Dartmouth M
University of Michigan M
University of Minnesota, Twin Cities Campus M,D,O
University of Notre Dame M
University of Oklahoma M
The University of Texas at Austin M
University of Wisconsin–Madison M,D
Virginia Commonwealth University M
Virginia Polytechnic Institute and State University M
Wayne State University M
Western Michigan University M
Yale University M

■ APPLIED ECONOMICS

American University M,D,O
Auburn University M,D
Buffalo State College, State University of New York M
Clemson University M,D
Cornell University D
Eastern Michigan University M
The Johns Hopkins University M
Mississippi State University M,D
Montana State University M
New York University M,D,O
North Carolina Agricultural and Technical State University M
Northeastern University M,D
Ohio University M
Portland State University M,D
Roosevelt University M
St. Cloud State University M
San Jose State University M
Southern Methodist University M,D
Texas Tech University M,D
University of California, Santa Cruz M
University of Georgia M,D
University of Michigan M
University of Minnesota, Twin Cities Campus M,D
University of Nevada, Reno M,D
The University of North Carolina at Greensboro M
University of North Dakota M
University of North Texas M
The University of Texas at Dallas M,D
University of Vermont M
University of Wisconsin–Madison M,D
University of Wyoming M
Utah State University M
Virginia Polytechnic Institute and State University M,D
Washington State University M,D,O
Western Michigan University M,D
Wright State University M

■ APPLIED MATHEMATICS

Arizona State University M,D
Auburn University M,D
Bowie State University M
Brown University M,D
California Institute of Technology M,D
California State Polytechnic University, Pomona M
California State University, Fullerton M
California State University, Long Beach M,D
California State University, Los Angeles M
California State University, Northridge M
Case Western Reserve University M,D
Claremont Graduate University M,D
Clark Atlanta University M
Clemson University M,D
Columbia University M,D,O
Cornell University M,D
DePaul University M,O
East Carolina University M
Florida Atlantic University M,D
Florida Institute of Technology M,D
Florida State University M,D
The George Washington University M,D
Georgia Institute of Technology M,D
Hampton University M

Institution	Degrees
Harvard University	M,D
Hofstra University	M
Howard University	M,D
Hunter College of the City University of New York	M
Illinois Institute of Technology	M,D
Indiana University Bloomington	M,D
Indiana University of Pennsylvania	M
Indiana University–Purdue University Fort Wayne	M,O
Indiana University–Purdue University Indianapolis	M,D
Indiana University South Bend	M
Inter American University of Puerto Rico, San Germán Campus	M
Iowa State University of Science and Technology	M,D
The Johns Hopkins University	M,D
Kent State University	M,D
Lehigh University	M,D
Long Island University, C.W. Post Campus	M
Michigan State University	M,D
Missouri University of Science and Technology	M
Montclair State University	M,O
New Jersey Institute of Technology	M
New Mexico Institute of Mining and Technology	M,D
North Carolina State University	M,D
North Dakota State University	M,D
Northeastern University	M,D
Northwestern University	M,D
Oakland University	M,D
Oklahoma State University	M,D
Penn State University Park	M,D
Princeton University	M,D
Rensselaer Polytechnic Institute	M
Rice University	M,D
Rochester Institute of Technology	M
Rutgers, The State University of New Jersey, New Brunswick	M,D
St. John's University (NY)	M
San Diego State University	M
Santa Clara University	M
Southern Methodist University	M,D
Stevens Institute of Technology	M,D
Stony Brook University, State University of New York	M,D
Temple University	M,D
Texas A&M University–Corpus Christi	M
Texas State University-San Marcos	M
Towson University	M
Tulane University	M,D
The University of Akron	M,D
The University of Alabama	M,D
The University of Alabama at Birmingham	M,D
The University of Alabama in Huntsville	M,D
The University of Arizona	M,D
University of Arkansas at Little Rock	M
University of California, Berkeley	D
University of California, Davis	M,D
University of California, San Diego	M,D
University of California, Santa Barbara	M,D
University of Central Florida	M,D,O
University of Central Missouri	M
University of Central Oklahoma	M
University of Chicago	M,D
University of Cincinnati	M,D
University of Colorado at Boulder	M,D
University of Colorado at Colorado Springs	M
University of Colorado Denver	M,D
University of Connecticut	M
University of Dayton	M
University of Delaware	M,D
University of Denver	M,D
University of Georgia	M,D
University of Illinois at Chicago	M,D
University of Illinois at Urbana–Champaign	M,D
The University of Iowa	D
University of Kansas	M,D
University of Kentucky	M,D
University of Louisville	M,D
University of Maryland, Baltimore County	M,D
University of Maryland, College Park	M,D
University of Massachusetts Amherst	M
University of Massachusetts Lowell	M,D
University of Memphis	M,D
University of Michigan–Dearborn	M
University of Minnesota, Duluth	M
University of Missouri–Columbia	M
University of Missouri–St. Louis	M,D
University of Nevada, Las Vegas	M,D
University of New Hampshire	M,D
University of Notre Dame	M,D
University of Pittsburgh	M,D
University of Puerto Rico, Mayagüez Campus	M
University of Rhode Island	M,D,O
University of Southern California	M,D
The University of Tennessee	M,D
The University of Texas at Austin	M,D
The University of Texas at Dallas	M,D
The University of Toledo	M,D
University of Washington	M,D
Utah State University	M,D
Virginia Commonwealth University	M,O
Virginia Polytechnic Institute and State University	M,D
Washington State University	M,D
Wayne State University	M,D
Western Illinois University	M,O
Western Michigan University	M
West Virginia University	M,D
Wichita State University	M,D
Worcester Polytechnic Institute	M,D,O
Wright State University	M
Yale University	M,D

■ APPLIED PHYSICS

Institution	Degrees
Alabama Agricultural and Mechanical University	M,D
Appalachian State University	M
Brooklyn College of the City University of New York	M,D
California Institute of Technology	M,D
Colorado School of Mines	M,D
Columbia University	M,D,O
Cornell University	M,D
DePaul University	M
George Mason University	M
Harvard University	M,D
Iowa State University of Science and Technology	M,D
The Johns Hopkins University	M
New Jersey Institute of Technology	M,D
Northern Arizona University	M
Pittsburg State University	M
Princeton University	M,D
Rensselaer Polytechnic Institute	M,D
Rice University	M,D
Rutgers, The State University of New Jersey, Newark	M,D
Southern Illinois University Carbondale	M,D
Stanford University	M,D
State University of New York at Binghamton	M
Texas A&M University	M,D
Texas Tech University	M,D
The University of Arizona	M
University of Arkansas	M
University of California, San Diego	M,D
University of Maryland, Baltimore County	M,D
University of Massachusetts Boston	M
University of Massachusetts Lowell	M,D
University of Michigan	D
University of Missouri–St. Louis	M,D
The University of North Carolina at Charlotte	M,D
University of South Florida	M,D
University of Washington	M,D
Virginia Commonwealth University	M,D
Virginia Polytechnic Institute and State University	M,D
West Virginia University	M,D
Yale University	M,D

■ APPLIED SCIENCE AND TECHNOLOGY

Institution	Degrees
American University	M,O
The College of William and Mary	M,D
Harvard University	M,O
James Madison University	M
Louisiana State University and Agricultural and Mechanical College	M
Oklahoma State University	M
Rensselaer Polytechnic Institute	M
Southeastern Louisiana University	M
Southern Methodist University	M,D
University of Arkansas at Little Rock	M,D
University of California, Berkeley	D
University of California, Davis	M,D
University of Colorado Denver	M
University of Mississippi	M,D
University of Northern Colorado	M

■ APPLIED SOCIAL RESEARCH

Institution	Degrees
American University	M,O
California State University, Dominguez Hills	M,O
Hunter College of the City University of New York	M
The New School: A University	M,D
Portland State University	M,D
University of California, Los Angeles	M,D
Virginia Commonwealth University	M,O
West Virginia University	M

■ APPLIED STATISTICS

Institution	Degrees
American University	M,O
Bowling Green State University	M,D
Brigham Young University	M
California State University, East Bay	M
Cornell University	M,D
DePaul University	M,O
Florida State University	M,D
Indiana University–Purdue University Fort Wayne	M,O
Indiana University–Purdue University Indianapolis	M
Kennesaw State University	M
Louisiana State University and Agricultural and Mechanical College	M
Michigan State University	M,D

Montclair State University	M,O
New Jersey Institute of Technology	M
North Dakota State University	M,D,O
Oakland University	M
Oregon State University	M,D
Penn State University Park	M,D
Rochester Institute of Technology	M,O
Rutgers, The State University of New Jersey, New Brunswick	M,D
St. Cloud State University	M
Stevens Institute of Technology	O
Syracuse University	M
The University of Alabama	M,D
University of California, Riverside	M,D
University of California, Santa Barbara	M,D
University of Memphis	M,D
University of Michigan	M,D
University of Nevada, Las Vegas	M,D
University of Northern Colorado	M,D
University of Pittsburgh	M,D
University of South Carolina	M,D,O
The University of Texas at San Antonio	M,D
Villanova University	M
Worcester Polytechnic Institute	M,D,O
Wright State University	M

■ AQUACULTURE

Auburn University	M,D
Clemson University	M,D
Purdue University	M,D
Texas A&M University–Corpus Christi	M
University of Florida	M,D
University of Rhode Island	M,D

■ ARCHAEOLOGY

Boston University	M,D
Brown University	M,D
Columbia University	M,D
Cornell University	M,D
Florida State University	M,D
George Mason University	M
Graduate School and University Center of the City University of New York	D
Harvard University	M,D
Illinois State University	M
Michigan Technological University	M,D
New York University	M,D
Northern Arizona University	M
Northwestern State University of Louisiana	M
Princeton University	D
Trinity International University	P,M,D,O
Tufts University	M
University of California, Berkeley	M,D
University of California, Los Angeles	M,D
University of California, Santa Barbara	M,D
University of Chicago	M,D
University of Massachusetts Boston	M
University of Memphis	M
University of Michigan	D
University of Minnesota, Twin Cities Campus	M,D
University of Missouri–Columbia	M,D
The University of North Carolina at Chapel Hill	M,D
University of Pennsylvania	M,D
The University of Tennessee	M,D
The University of Texas at Austin	M,D
University of Virginia	M,D
University of West Florida	M
Washington State University	M,D
Washington University in St. Louis	M,D
Wheaton College	M
Yale University	M

■ ARCHITECTURAL ENGINEERING

Illinois Institute of Technology	M,D
Kansas State University	M
North Carolina Agricultural and Technical State University	M
Oklahoma State University	M
Penn State University Park	M,D
University of Colorado at Boulder	M,D
University of Detroit Mercy	M
University of Kansas	M
University of Louisiana at Lafayette	M
University of Miami	M,D
University of Nebraska–Lincoln	M
The University of Texas at Austin	M

■ ARCHITECTURAL HISTORY

Arizona State University	D
Cornell University	M,D
Graduate School and University Center of the City University of New York	D
Harvard University	D
Massachusetts Institute of Technology	M,D
University of California, Berkeley	M,D
University of Pittsburgh	M,D
University of Virginia	M,D
Virginia Commonwealth University	M,D

■ ARCHITECTURE

Andrews University	M
Arizona State University	M
Auburn University	M
Ball State University	M
California Polytechnic State University, San Luis Obispo	M
California State Polytechnic University, Pomona	M
Carnegie Mellon University	M,D
The Catholic University of America	M
City College of the City University of New York	M
Clemson University	M
Columbia College Chicago	M
Columbia University	M,D
Cornell University	M,D
Drexel University	M
Florida Agricultural and Mechanical University	M
Florida International University	M
Georgia Institute of Technology	M,D
Harvard University	M,D
Idaho State University	M
Illinois Institute of Technology	M,D
Iowa State University of Science and Technology	M
Kansas State University	M
Kent State University	M,O
Lawrence Technological University	M
Louisiana State University and Agricultural and Mechanical College	M
Massachusetts Institute of Technology	M,D
Miami University	M
Mississippi State University	M
Montana State University	M
Morgan State University	M
New Jersey Institute of Technology	M
The New School: A University	M
New York Institute of Technology	M
North Carolina State University	M
Northeastern University	M
The Ohio State University	M
Oklahoma State University	M
Penn State University Park	M
Prairie View A&M University	M
Princeton University	M,D
Rensselaer Polytechnic Institute	M,D
Rice University	M,D
Roger Williams University	M
Syracuse University	M
Texas A&M University	M,D
Texas Tech University	M
Tulane University	M
University at Buffalo, the State University of New York	M
The University of Arizona	M
University of California, Berkeley	M,D
University of California, Los Angeles	M,D
University of Cincinnati	M
University of Colorado Denver	M
University of Florida	M,D
University of Hartford	M
University of Hawaii at Manoa	D
University of Houston	M
University of Idaho	M
University of Illinois at Chicago	M
University of Illinois at Urbana–Champaign	M,D
University of Kansas	M
University of Kentucky	M
University of Maryland, College Park	M
University of Massachusetts Amherst	M
University of Miami	M
University of Michigan	M,D
University of Minnesota, Twin Cities Campus	M
University of Missouri–Columbia	M
University of Nebraska–Lincoln	M
University of Nevada, Las Vegas	M
University of New Mexico	M
The University of North Carolina at Charlotte	M
The University of North Carolina at Greensboro	M,O
University of Notre Dame	M
University of Oklahoma	M
University of Oregon	M
University of Pennsylvania	M,D,O
University of Puerto Rico, Río Piedras	M
University of Southern California	M,O
University of South Florida	M
The University of Tennessee	M
The University of Texas at Arlington	M
The University of Texas at Austin	M,D
The University of Texas at San Antonio	M
University of Utah	M
University of Virginia	M
University of Washington	M,D,O
University of Wisconsin–Milwaukee	M,D,O
Virginia Polytechnic Institute and State University	M
Washington State University	M
Washington University in St. Louis	M
Woodbury University	M
Yale University	M

■ ART/FINE ARTS

Adams State College	M
Adelphi University	M
Alfred University	M,D
American University	M
Anna Maria College	M
Antioch University McGregor	M
Arizona State University	M
Arkansas State University	M
Arkansas Tech University	M
Azusa Pacific University	M

Ball State University M
Barry University M
Bob Jones University P,M,D,O
Boise State University M
Boston University M
Bowling Green State University M
Bradley University M
Brandeis University O
Brigham Young University M
Brooklyn College of the City University of New York M,D
California State University, Chico M
California State University, Fresno M
California State University, Fullerton M,O
California State University, Long Beach M
California State University, Los Angeles M
California State University, Northridge M
California State University, Sacramento M
California State University, San Bernardino M
Carnegie Mellon University M
Central Michigan University M
Central Washington University M
City College of the City University of New York M
Claremont Graduate University M
Clemson University M
Cleveland State University M
The College of New Rochelle M
Colorado State University M
Columbia University M
Cornell University M
Drake University M
East Carolina University M
Eastern Illinois University M
Eastern Michigan University M
East Tennessee State University M
Edinboro University of Pennsylvania M
Fairleigh Dickinson University, Metropolitan Campus M
Ferris State University M
Florida Atlantic University M
Florida International University M
Florida State University M
Fontbonne University M
Fort Hays State University M
Framingham State College M
The George Washington University M,D
Georgia Southern University M
Georgia State University M
Governors State University M
Hofstra University M,O
Hollins University M,O
Hood College M,O
Howard University M
Hunter College of the City University of New York M
Idaho State University M
Illinois State University M
Indiana State University M
Indiana University Bloomington M,D
Indiana University of Pennsylvania M
Indiana University–Purdue University Indianapolis M
Inter American University of Puerto Rico, San Germán Campus M
James Madison University M
John F. Kennedy University M
Johnson State College M
Kansas State University M
Kean University M
Kent State University M
Lamar University M
Lehman College of the City University of New York M
Lesley University M
Lindenwood University M
Long Island University, C.W. Post Campus M
Louisiana State University and Agricultural and Mechanical College M
Louisiana Tech University M
Marshall University M
Marywood University M
Massachusetts Institute of Technology M,D,O
Miami University M
Michigan State University M
Mills College M
Minnesota State University Mankato M
Mississippi College M
Mississippi State University M
Missouri State University M
Montana State University M
Montclair State University M
Morehead State University M
National University M
New Jersey City University M
New Mexico State University M
The New School: A University M
New York University M,D
Norfolk State University M
Northern Illinois University M
Northwestern State University of Louisiana M
Northwestern University M
The Ohio State University M
Ohio University M
Oklahoma City University M
Old Dominion University M
Penn State University Park M,D
Pittsburg State University M
Portland State University M
Purchase College, State University of New York M
Purdue University M
Queens College of the City University of New York M
Radford University M
Regent University M,D
Regis University M,O
Rensselaer Polytechnic Institute M,D
Rhode Island College M
Rochester Institute of Technology M
Rutgers, The State University of New Jersey, New Brunswick M
Sam Houston State University M
San Diego State University M
San Francisco State University M
San Jose State University M
Seattle Pacific University M
Seton Hall University M
Southern Illinois University Carbondale M
Southern Illinois University Edwardsville M
Southern Methodist University M
Stanford University M,D
State University of New York at New Paltz M
State University of New York at Oswego M
State University of New York College at Brockport M
Stephen F. Austin State University M
Stony Brook University, State University of New York M
Sul Ross State University M
Syracuse University M
Temple University M
Texas A&M International University
Texas A&M University–Commerce M
Texas A&M University–Corpus Christi M
Texas A&M University–Kingsville M
Texas Christian University M
Texas Tech University M
Texas Woman's University M
Towson University M
Troy University M
Tufts University M
Tulane University M
Union Institute & University M
University at Albany, State University of New York M
University at Buffalo, the State University of New York M,O
The University of Alabama M
University of Alaska Fairbanks M
The University of Arizona M
University of Arkansas M
University of Arkansas at Little Rock M
University of California, Berkeley M
University of California, Davis M
University of California, Irvine M
University of California, Los Angeles M
University of California, Riverside M
University of California, San Diego M,D
University of California, Santa Barbara M,D
University of California, Santa Cruz M
University of Central Florida M
University of Chicago M,D
University of Cincinnati M
University of Colorado at Boulder M
University of Connecticut M
University of Dallas M
University of Delaware M
University of Denver M
University of Florida M,D
University of Georgia M,D
University of Guam M
University of Hartford M
University of Hawaii at Manoa M
University of Houston M
University of Idaho M
University of Illinois at Chicago M
University of Illinois at Urbana–Champaign M
University of Indianapolis M
The University of Iowa M
University of Kansas M
University of Kentucky M
University of Louisville M
University of Maryland, Baltimore County M
University of Maryland, College Park M
University of Massachusetts Amherst M
University of Massachusetts Dartmouth M,O
University of Memphis M
University of Miami M
University of Michigan M
University of Minnesota, Duluth M
University of Minnesota, Twin Cities Campus M
University of Mississippi M
University of Missouri–Columbia M
University of Missouri–Kansas City M,D
The University of Montana M
University of Nebraska–Lincoln M
University of Nevada, Las Vegas M

University of Nevada, Reno M
University of New Hampshire M
University of New Mexico M
University of New Orleans M
The University of North Carolina at Chapel Hill M
The University of North Carolina at Greensboro M
University of North Dakota M
University of Northern Colorado M
University of Northern Iowa M
University of North Texas M,D
University of Notre Dame M
University of Oklahoma M
University of Oregon M
University of Pennsylvania M
University of Rochester M,D
University of Saint Francis (IN) M
University of South Carolina M
The University of South Dakota M
University of Southern California M
University of South Florida M
The University of Tennessee M
The University of Texas at Austin M
The University of Texas at El Paso M
The University of Texas at San Antonio M
The University of Texas at Tyler M
The University of Texas–Pan American M
University of Tulsa M
University of Utah M
University of Washington M
University of Wisconsin–Madison M
University of Wisconsin–Milwaukee M
University of Wisconsin–Superior M
Utah State University M
Virginia Commonwealth University M,D
Washington State University M
Washington University in St. Louis M
Wayne State University M
Webster University M
Western Carolina University M
Western Connecticut State University M
West Texas A&M University M
West Virginia University M
Wichita State University M
William Paterson University of New Jersey M
Winthrop University M
Yale University M

■ ART EDUCATION

Arcadia University M,D,O
Ball State University M
Bennington College M
Boise State University M
Boston University M
Bowling Green State University M
Bridgewater State College M
Brigham Young University M
Brooklyn College of the City University of New York M,O
Buffalo State College, State University of New York M
California State University, Los Angeles M
California State University, Northridge M
Carlow University M
Case Western Reserve University M
Central Connecticut State University M,O
Chatham University M
City University of Seattle M,O
Cleveland State University M
College of Mount St. Joseph M
The College of New Rochelle M
The College of Saint Rose M,O
Columbus State University M
Concordia University Wisconsin M
Converse College M,O
Eastern Illinois University M
Eastern Kentucky University M
Eastern Michigan University M
East Tennessee State University M
Endicott College M
Fitchburg State College M,O
Florida Atlantic University M,D,O
Florida International University M,D
Florida State University M,D,O
Georgia Southern University M
Georgia State University M,D,O
Harding University M,O
Harvard University M
Hofstra University M
Indiana University Bloomington M,D,O
Indiana University–Purdue University Indianapolis M
Iowa State University of Science and Technology M
James Madison University M
Kean University M
Kent State University M
Kutztown University of Pennsylvania M,O
Lesley University M,D,O
Long Island University, C.W. Post Campus M
Manhattanville College M
Mansfield University of Pennsylvania M
Maryville University of Saint Louis M,D
Marywood University M
Miami University M
Millersville University of Pennsylvania M
Mills College M,D
Minnesota State University Mankato M
Mississippi College M,O
Missouri State University M
Montclair State University M,O
Morehead State University M
Nazareth College of Rochester M
New Jersey City University M
New York University M,D
North Carolina Agricultural and Technical State University M
North Georgia College & State University M,O
Nova Southeastern University M,O
The Ohio State University M,D
Ohio University M
Penn State University Park M,D
Pittsburg State University M
Purdue University M,D,O
Queens College of the City University of New York M,O
Rhode Island College M
Rochester Institute of Technology M
Rockford College M
Saint Michael's College M,O
Salem State College M
Salisbury University M
Southern Connecticut State University M
Southern Illinois University Edwardsville M
Southwestern Oklahoma State University M
Stanford University M,D
State University of New York at New Paltz M
State University of New York at Oswego M
Sul Ross State University M
Syracuse University M,O
Temple University M
Texas Tech University M
Towson University M,O
The University of Alabama at Birmingham M
The University of Arizona M
University of Arkansas at Little Rock M
University of Central Florida M
University of Cincinnati M
University of Dayton M
University of Florida M,D
University of Georgia M,D,O
University of Houston M,D
University of Idaho M
University of Illinois at Urbana–Champaign M,D
University of Indianapolis M
The University of Iowa M,D
University of Kansas M
University of Kentucky M
University of Louisville M
University of Massachusetts Dartmouth M
University of Minnesota, Twin Cities Campus M,D,O
University of Mississippi M
University of Missouri–Columbia M,D,O
University of Nebraska at Kearney M
University of New Mexico M
The University of North Carolina at Charlotte M
The University of North Carolina at Pembroke M
University of Northern Iowa M
University of North Texas M,D
University of Rio Grande M
University of South Carolina M,D
University of Southern Mississippi M
The University of Tennessee M,D,O
The University of Texas at Austin M
The University of Texas at Tyler M
The University of Toledo M
University of Utah M
University of West Georgia M
University of Wisconsin–Madison M,D
University of Wisconsin–Milwaukee M
University of Wisconsin–Superior M
Virginia Commonwealth University M
Wayne State University M,D,O
Western Carolina University M
Western Kentucky University M
West Virginia University M
Wichita State University M
William Carey University M,O
Winthrop University M

■ ART HISTORY

American University M
Boston University M,D,O
Bowling Green State University M
Brigham Young University M
Brooklyn College of the City University of New York M,D
Brown University M,D
California State University, Chico M
California State University, Fullerton M,O
California State University, Los Angeles M
California State University, Northridge M
Case Western Reserve University M,D
City College of the City University of New York M
Cleveland State University M
Columbia University M,D
Cornell University D

Duke University D
East Tennessee State University M
Emory University D
Florida State University M,D,O
The George Washington University M,D
Georgia State University M
Graduate School and University Center of the City University of New York D
Harvard University D
Howard University M
Hunter College of the City University of New York M
Illinois State University M
Indiana University Bloomington M,D
James Madison University M
The Johns Hopkins University M,D
Kent State University M
Lamar University M
Louisiana State University and Agricultural and Mechanical College M
Massachusetts Institute of Technology M,D
Montclair State University M
New Mexico State University M
New York University M,D
Northwestern University D
The Ohio State University M,D
Ohio University M
Penn State University Park M,D
Purchase College, State University of New York M
Queens College of the City University of New York M
Rutgers, The State University of New Jersey, New Brunswick M,D,O
San Diego State University M
San Francisco State University M
San Jose State University M
Southern Methodist University M
State University of New York at Binghamton M,D
Stony Brook University, State University of New York M,D
Sul Ross State University M
Syracuse University M
Temple University M,D
Texas A&M University–Commerce M
Texas Christian University M
Tufts University M
Tulane University M
University at Buffalo, the State University of New York M,O
The University of Alabama M
The University of Alabama at Birmingham M
The University of Arizona M,D
University of Arkansas at Little Rock M
University of California, Berkeley D
University of California, Davis M
University of California, Irvine M,D
University of California, Los Angeles M,D
University of California, Riverside M
University of California, Santa Barbara D
University of Chicago M,D
University of Cincinnati M
University of Colorado at Boulder M
University of Connecticut M
University of Delaware M,D
University of Denver M
University of Florida M,D
University of Georgia M
University of Hawaii at Manoa M
University of Illinois at Chicago M,D
University of Illinois at Urbana–Champaign M,D
The University of Iowa M,D
University of Kansas M,D
University of Kentucky M
University of Louisville M,D
University of Maryland, College Park M,D
University of Massachusetts Amherst M
University of Memphis M
University of Miami M
University of Michigan D
University of Minnesota, Twin Cities Campus M,D
University of Mississippi M
University of Missouri–Columbia M,D
University of Missouri–Kansas City M,D
University of Nebraska–Lincoln M
University of New Mexico M,D
The University of North Carolina at Chapel Hill M,D
University of North Texas M,D
University of Notre Dame M
University of Oklahoma M
University of Oregon M,D
University of Pennsylvania M,D
University of Pittsburgh M,D
University of Rochester M,D
University of St. Thomas (MN) M
University of South Carolina M
University of Southern California M,D,O
University of South Florida M
The University of Texas at Austin M,D
The University of Texas at San Antonio M
University of Utah M
University of Virginia M,D
University of Washington M,D
University of Wisconsin–Madison M,D
University of Wisconsin–Milwaukee M,O
University of Wisconsin–Superior M
Virginia Commonwealth University M,D
Washington University in St. Louis M,D
Wayne State University M
West Virginia University M
Yale University D

■ ARTIFICIAL INTELLIGENCE/ROBOTICS

Carnegie Mellon University M,D
The Catholic University of America M,D
Cornell University M,D
Indiana University–Purdue University Indianapolis M,D
Portland State University M,D,O
University of California, Irvine M
University of California, Riverside M,D
University of California, San Diego M,D
University of Georgia M
University of Southern California M
The University of Tennessee M,D
Villanova University M,O

■ ARTS ADMINISTRATION

American University M,O
Boston University M,O
Carnegie Mellon University M
Claremont Graduate University M
Columbia College Chicago M
Drexel University M
Eastern Michigan University M
Florida State University M,D
Montclair State University M
New York University M
The Ohio State University M
Regis University M,O
Rhode Island College M
Saint Mary's University of Minnesota M
Seton Hall University M
Shenandoah University M,D,O
Southern Methodist University
Southern Utah University M
Temple University M,D
The University of Akron M
University of Cincinnati M
University of Florida M
University of New Orleans M
University of Oregon M
University of Southern California M
University of Wisconsin–Madison M
Virginia Polytechnic Institute and State University M
Webster University M
Winthrop University M

■ ART THERAPY

Avila University M
Caldwell College M
California Institute of Integral Studies M,D
California State University, Los Angeles M
The College of New Rochelle M
Drexel University M
Emporia State University M
The George Washington University M,O
Hofstra University M
Lesley University M,D,O
Long Island University, C.W. Post Campus M
Marylhurst University M,O
Marywood University M,O
Mount Mary College M
Naropa University M
Nazareth College of Rochester M
New York University M
Notre Dame de Namur University M
Salve Regina University M,O
Seton Hill University M,O
Southern Illinois University Edwardsville M,O
Springfield College M,O
University of Louisville M
University of Wisconsin–Superior M
Ursuline College M

■ ASIAN-AMERICAN STUDIES

California State University, Long Beach M,O
San Francisco State University M
University of California, Los Angeles M

■ ASIAN LANGUAGES

Columbia University M,D
Cornell University M,D
Harvard University M,D
Indiana University Bloomington M,D
Naropa University M
The Ohio State University M,D
St. John's College (NM) M
University of California, Berkeley M,D
University of California, Irvine M,D
University of California, Los Angeles M,D
University of California, Santa Barbara D
University of Chicago M,D
University of Hawaii at Manoa M,D
University of Illinois at Urbana–Champaign M,D
University of Kansas M
University of Michigan M,D

Institution	Degrees
University of Minnesota, Twin Cities Campus	D
University of Oregon	M,D
University of Southern California	M,D
The University of Texas at Austin	M,D
University of Washington	M,D
University of Wisconsin–Madison	M,D
Washington University in St. Louis	M,D
Yale University	D

■ ASIAN STUDIES

Institution	Degrees
California Institute of Integral Studies	M,D
California State University, Long Beach	M,O
Columbia University	M,D,O
Cornell University	M,D
Duke University	M,O
Florida State University	M
The George Washington University	M
Harvard University	M,D
Indiana University Bloomington	M,D
The Johns Hopkins University	M,D,O
Maharishi University of Management	M,D
Ohio University	M
Princeton University	D
Rutgers, The State University of New Jersey, New Brunswick	D
St. John's College (NM)	M
St. John's University (NY)	M,O
San Diego State University	M
Seton Hall University	M
Stanford University	M
The University of Arizona	M,D
University of California, Berkeley	M,D
University of California, Los Angeles	M,D
University of California, Santa Barbara	M,D
University of Chicago	M,D
University of Colorado at Boulder	M,D
University of Hawaii at Manoa	M,O
University of Illinois at Urbana–Champaign	M,D
The University of Iowa	M
University of Kansas	M
University of Michigan	M,D,O
University of Minnesota, Twin Cities Campus	D
University of Oregon	M
University of Pennsylvania	M,D
University of Pittsburgh	M,O
University of San Francisco	M
University of Southern California	M,D
The University of Texas at Austin	M,D
University of Virginia	M
University of Washington	M
University of Wisconsin–Madison	M,D
Valparaiso University	M
Washington State University	M,D
Washington University in St. Louis	M,D
West Virginia University	M,D
Yale University	M

■ ASTRONOMY

Institution	Degrees
Arizona State University	M,D
Boston University	M,D
Brigham Young University	M,D
California Institute of Technology	D
Case Western Reserve University	M,D
Clemson University	M,D
Columbia University	M,D
Cornell University	D
Dartmouth College	M,D
Georgia State University	D
Harvard University	D
Indiana University Bloomington	M,D
Iowa State University of Science and Technology	M,D
The Johns Hopkins University	D
Louisiana State University and Agricultural and Mechanical College	M,D
Michigan State University	M,D
Minnesota State University Mankato	M
New Mexico State University	M,D
Northwestern University	M,D
The Ohio State University	M,D
Ohio University	M,D
Penn State University Park	M,D
Rice University	M,D
San Diego State University	M
Stony Brook University, State University of New York	M,D
Texas Christian University	M,D
The University of Arizona	M,D
University of California, Los Angeles	M,D
University of California, Riverside	M,D
University of California, Santa Cruz	D
University of Chicago	M,D
University of Delaware	M,D
University of Florida	M,D
University of Georgia	M,D
University of Hawaii at Manoa	M,D
University of Illinois at Urbana–Champaign	M,D
The University of Iowa	M
University of Kansas	M,D
University of Kentucky	M,D
University of Maryland, College Park	M,D
University of Massachusetts Amherst	M,D
University of Michigan	M,D
University of Minnesota, Twin Cities Campus	M,D
University of Missouri–Columbia	M,D
University of Nebraska–Lincoln	M,D
The University of North Carolina at Chapel Hill	M,D
University of Rochester	M,D
University of South Carolina	M,D
The University of Texas at Austin	M,D
University of Virginia	M,D
University of Washington	M,D
University of Wisconsin–Madison	D
Vanderbilt University	M,D
West Chester University of Pennsylvania	M
Yale University	M,D

■ ASTROPHYSICS

Institution	Degrees
Clemson University	M,D
Cornell University	D
Harvard University	D
Indiana University Bloomington	M,D
Iowa State University of Science and Technology	M,D
Louisiana State University and Agricultural and Mechanical College	M,D
Michigan State University	M,D
New Mexico Institute of Mining and Technology	M,D
Northwestern University	M,D
Penn State University Park	M,D
Princeton University	D
Rensselaer Polytechnic Institute	M,D
Texas Christian University	M,D
University of Alaska Fairbanks	M,D
University of California, Berkeley	D
University of California, Los Angeles	M,D
University of California, Santa Cruz	D
University of Chicago	M,D
University of Colorado at Boulder	M,D
University of Maryland, Baltimore County	M,D
University of Minnesota, Twin Cities Campus	M,D
University of Missouri–St. Louis	M,D
The University of North Carolina at Chapel Hill	M,D
University of Oklahoma	M,D
University of Pennsylvania	M,D

■ ATHLETIC TRAINING AND SPORTS MEDICINE

Institution	Degrees
Armstrong Atlantic State University	M
Barry University	M
Boston University	D
Brigham Young University	M,D
California University of Pennsylvania	M
Eastern Michigan University	M
Florida International University	M
Georgia State University	M
Humboldt State University	M
Indiana State University	M,D
Indiana University Bloomington	M,D,O
Kent State University	M
Long Island University, Brooklyn Campus	M
Montana State University–Billings	M
Ohio University	M
Old Dominion University	M
Plymouth State University	M
Seton Hall University	M
Shenandoah University	M
Stephen F. Austin State University	M
The University of Findlay	M
University of Florida	M,D
University of Miami	M
The University of North Carolina at Chapel Hill	M
University of Pittsburgh	M
The University of Tennessee	M,D
The University of West Alabama	M
University of Wisconsin–La Crosse	M
Virginia Commonwealth University	M,D
West Chester University of Pennsylvania	M
Western Michigan University	M
West Virginia University	M,D

■ ATMOSPHERIC SCIENCES

Institution	Degrees
City College of the City University of New York	M,D
Clemson University	M,D
Colorado State University	M,D
Columbia University	M,D
Cornell University	M,D
Creighton University	M
George Mason University	D
Georgia Institute of Technology	M,D
Howard University	M,D
Massachusetts Institute of Technology	M,D
New Mexico Institute of Mining and Technology	M,D
North Carolina State University	M,D
The Ohio State University	M,D
Oregon State University	M,D
Princeton University	D
Purdue University	M,D
Rutgers, The State University of New Jersey, New Brunswick	M,D
Stony Brook University, State University of New York	M,D
Texas Tech University	M,D
University at Albany, State University of New York	M,D

The University of Alabama in Huntsville M,D
University of Alaska Fairbanks M,D
The University of Arizona M,D
University of California, Davis M,D
University of California, Los Angeles M,D
University of Chicago M,D
University of Colorado at Boulder M,D
University of Delaware D
University of Illinois at Urbana–Champaign M,D
University of Maryland, Baltimore County M,D
University of Michigan M,D
University of Missouri–Columbia M,D
University of Nevada, Reno M,D
The University of North Carolina at Chapel Hill M,D
University of North Dakota M
University of Washington M,D
University of Wisconsin–Madison M,D
University of Wyoming M,D

■ AUTOMOTIVE ENGINEERING

Central Michigan University M,O
Clemson University M,D
Lawrence Technological University M,D
Minnesota State University Mankato M
Old Dominion University M
University of Detroit Mercy M,D
University of Michigan M
University of Michigan–Dearborn M

■ AVIATION

Middle Tennessee State University M
Southeastern Oklahoma State University M
University of Central Missouri M
University of Illinois at Urbana–Champaign M
University of North Dakota M
The University of Tennessee M

■ AVIATION MANAGEMENT

Delta State University M
Dowling College M,O
Embry-Riddle Aeronautical University (FL) M
Embry-Riddle Aeronautical University Worldwide M
Lynn University M,D
Southeastern Oklahoma State University M

■ BACTERIOLOGY

Illinois State University M,D
The University of Iowa M,D
University of Washington M,D
University of Wisconsin–Madison M

■ BIOCHEMICAL ENGINEERING

Cornell University M,D
Dartmouth College M,D
Drexel University M
Hofstra University M,O
Rutgers, The State University of New Jersey, New Brunswick M,D
University of California, Irvine M,D
The University of Iowa M,D
University of Maryland, Baltimore County M,D,O
University of Massachusetts Dartmouth D

■ BIOCHEMISTRY

Arizona State University M,D
Auburn University M,D
Boston College M,D
Boston University M,D
Brandeis University M,D
Brigham Young University M,D
Brown University M,D
California Institute of Technology M,D
California Polytechnic State University, San Luis Obispo M
California State University, East Bay M
California State University, Fullerton M
California State University, Long Beach M
California State University, Los Angeles M
California State University, Northridge M
Carnegie Mellon University M,D
Case Western Reserve University M,D
City College of the City University of New York M,D
Clemson University M,D
Colorado State University M,D
Columbia University M,D
Cornell University D
Dartmouth College D
DePaul University M
Drexel University M,D
Duke University D,O
Duquesne University M,D
East Carolina University D
East Tennessee State University M,D
Emory University D
Florida Atlantic University M,D
Florida State University M,D
Georgetown University M,D
The George Washington University M,D
Georgia Institute of Technology M,D
Georgia State University M,D
Graduate School and University Center of the City University of New York D
Harvard University D
Howard University M,D
Hunter College of the City University of New York M
Illinois State University M,D
Indiana University Bloomington M,D
Indiana University–Purdue University Indianapolis D
Iowa State University of Science and Technology M,D
The Johns Hopkins University M,D
Kansas State University M,D
Kent State University M,D
Lehigh University M,D
Louisiana State University and Agricultural and Mechanical College M,D
Loyola University Chicago M,D
Massachusetts Institute of Technology D
Mayo Graduate School D
Miami University M,D
Michigan State University M,D
Mississippi State University M,D
Montana State University M,D
Montclair State University M
New Mexico Institute of Mining and Technology M,D
New Mexico State University M,D
North Carolina State University M,D
North Dakota State University M,D
Northeastern University M,D
Northern Arizona University M
Northern Michigan University M
Northwestern University D
The Ohio State University M
Ohio University M,D
Oklahoma State University M,D
Old Dominion University M,D
Oregon State University M,D
Penn State University Park M,D
Purdue University M,D
Queens College of the City University of New York M
Rensselaer Polytechnic Institute M,D
Rice University M,D
Rutgers, The State University of New Jersey, Newark M,D
Rutgers, The State University of New Jersey, New Brunswick M,D
Saint Louis University D
San Francisco State University M
Seton Hall University M,D
Southern Illinois University Carbondale M,D
Southern University and Agricultural and Mechanical College M
Stanford University D
State University of New York College of Environmental Science and Forestry M,D
Stevens Institute of Technology M,D,O
Stony Brook University, State University of New York D
Syracuse University D
Temple University M,D
Texas A&M University M,D
Texas State University-San Marcos M
Tufts University D
Tulane University M,D
University at Albany, State University of New York M,D
University at Buffalo, the State University of New York M,D
The University of Alabama at Birmingham D
University of Alaska Fairbanks M,D
The University of Arizona M,D
University of California, Berkeley D
University of California, Davis M,D
University of California, Irvine M,D
University of California, Los Angeles M,D
University of California, Riverside M,D
University of California, San Diego M,D
University of California, Santa Barbara M,D
University of California, Santa Cruz M,D
University of Chicago D
University of Cincinnati M,D
University of Colorado at Boulder M,D
University of Colorado Denver D
University of Connecticut M,D
University of Delaware M,D
University of Detroit Mercy M
University of Florida M,D
University of Georgia M,D
University of Houston M,D
University of Idaho M,D
University of Illinois at Chicago M,D
University of Illinois at Urbana–Champaign M,D
The University of Iowa M,D
University of Kansas M,D
University of Kentucky D
University of Louisville M,D
University of Maine M,D
University of Maryland, Baltimore County M,D
University of Maryland, College Park M,D

University of Massachusetts Amherst M,D
University of Massachusetts Lowell M,D
University of Miami D
University of Michigan D
University of Minnesota, Duluth M,D
University of Minnesota, Twin Cities Campus D
University of Missouri–Columbia M,D
University of Missouri–Kansas City D
University of Missouri–St. Louis M,D,O
The University of Montana M,D
University of Nebraska–Lincoln M,D
University of Nevada, Las Vegas M,D
University of Nevada, Reno M,D
University of New Hampshire M,D
University of New Mexico M,D
The University of North Carolina at Chapel Hill M,D
The University of North Carolina at Greensboro M
University of North Dakota M,D
University of North Texas M,D
University of Notre Dame M,D
University of Oklahoma M,D
University of Oregon M,D
University of Pennsylvania D
University of Pittsburgh M,D
University of Rhode Island M,D
University of Rochester M,D
The University of Scranton M
University of South Alabama D
University of South Carolina M,D
University of Southern California M,D
University of Southern Mississippi M,D
University of South Florida M,D
The University of Tennessee M,D
The University of Texas at Austin M,D
The University of Toledo M,D
University of Utah M,D
University of Vermont M,D
University of Virginia D
University of Washington D
University of West Florida M
University of Wisconsin–Madison M,D
Utah State University M,D
Vanderbilt University M,D
Virginia Commonwealth University M,D,O
Virginia Polytechnic Institute and State University M,D
Wake Forest University D
Washington State University M,D
Washington University in St. Louis D
Wayne State University M,D
West Virginia University M,D
Worcester Polytechnic Institute M,D
Wright State University M
Yale University M,D

■ BIOENGINEERING

Alfred University M,D
Arizona State University M,D
California Institute of Technology M,D
Carnegie Mellon University M,D
Clemson University M,D
Cornell University M,D
Georgia Institute of Technology M,D,O
Illinois Institute of Technology M,D
Iowa State University of Science and Technology M,D
The Johns Hopkins University M,D
Kansas State University M,D
Louisiana State University and Agricultural and Mechanical College M,D
Massachusetts Institute of Technology M,D
Mississippi State University M,D
North Carolina State University M,D
The Ohio State University M,D
Oklahoma State University M,D
Oregon State University M,D
Penn State University Park M,D
Rensselaer Polytechnic Institute M,D
Rice University M,D
Stanford University M,D
Syracuse University M,D
Texas A&M University M,D
Tufts University O
University at Buffalo, the State University of New York M,D
University of Arkansas M
University of California, Berkeley D
University of California, Davis M,D
University of California, Riverside M,D
University of California, San Diego M,D
University of California, Santa Barbara M,D
University of Florida M,D,O
University of Georgia M,D
University of Hawaii at Manoa M,D
University of Illinois at Chicago M,D
University of Illinois at Urbana–Champaign M,D
University of Maine M
University of Maryland, College Park M,D
University of Missouri–Columbia M,D
University of Nebraska–Lincoln M,D
University of Notre Dame M,D
University of Oklahoma M,D
University of Pennsylvania M,D
University of Pittsburgh M,D
The University of Toledo M,D
University of Utah M,D
University of Washington M,D
University of Wisconsin–Madison M,D
Virginia Commonwealth University M,D
Virginia Polytechnic Institute and State University M,D
Washington State University M,D

■ BIOETHICS

Boston University M
Case Western Reserve University M,D
Cleveland State University M,O
Drew University M,D,O
Duquesne University M,D,O
Indiana University–Purdue University Indianapolis M,D,O
Loyola Marymount University M
Michigan State University M
Saint Louis University D,O
Trinity International University M
University of Pennsylvania M
University of Pittsburgh M
The University of Tennessee M,D
University of Virginia M

■ BIOINFORMATICS

Boston University M,D
California State University, Dominguez Hills M
Duke University D
Eastern Michigan University M
George Mason University M,D,O
The George Washington University M
Georgia Institute of Technology M,D
Grand Valley State University M
Indiana University Bloomington M,D
Iowa State University of Science and Technology D
The Johns Hopkins University M,D,O
Marquette University M
Mississippi Valley State University M
Morgan State University M
North Carolina State University M,D
North Dakota State University M,D
Northeastern University M
Northwestern University M
Polytechnic University, Brooklyn Campus M
Rochester Institute of Technology M
Stevens Institute of Technology M,D,O
Texas Tech University M,D
University of Arkansas at Little Rock M,D
University of California, Riverside D
University of California, San Diego D
University of California, Santa Cruz M,D
University of Cincinnati D
University of Colorado Denver D
University of Idaho M,D
University of Illinois at Urbana–Champaign M,D,O
University of Michigan M,D
University of Pittsburgh M,D,O
University of South Florida M,D
The University of Texas at El Paso M
The University of Toledo M,O
University of Utah M,D
University of Washington M,D
Vanderbilt University M,D
Virginia Commonwealth University M
Virginia Polytechnic Institute and State University D
Yale University D

■ BIOLOGICAL AND BIOMEDICAL SCIENCES—GENERAL

Adelphi University M
Alabama Agricultural and Mechanical University M
Alabama State University M
Alcorn State University M
American University M
Andrews University M
Angelo State University M
Appalachian State University M
Arizona State University M,D
Arizona State University at the Polytechnic Campus M
Arkansas State University M,D,O
Auburn University M,D
Austin Peay State University M
Ball State University M,D
Barry University M
Baylor University M,D
Bemidji State University M
Bloomsburg University of Pennsylvania M
Boise State University M
Boston College M,D
Boston University M,D
Bowling Green State University M,D
Bradley University M
Brandeis University M,D,O
Brigham Young University M,D
Brooklyn College of the City University of New York M,D
Brown University M,D
Bucknell University M
Buffalo State College, State University of New York M
California Institute of Technology M,D
California Polytechnic State University, San Luis Obispo M
California State Polytechnic University, Pomona M
California State University, Bakersfield M

California State University, Chico	M
California State University, Dominguez Hills	M
California State University, East Bay	M
California State University, Fresno	M
California State University, Fullerton	M
California State University, Long Beach	M
California State University, Los Angeles	M
California State University, Northridge	M
California State University, Sacramento	M
California State University, San Bernardino	M
California State University, San Marcos	M
Carnegie Mellon University	M,D
Case Western Reserve University	M,D
The Catholic University of America	M,D
Central Connecticut State University	M,O
Central Michigan University	M
Central Washington University	M
Chatham University	M
Chicago State University	M
The Citadel, The Military College of South Carolina	M
City College of the City University of New York	M,D
Clarion University of Pennsylvania	M
Clark Atlanta University	M,D
Clark University	M,D
Clemson University	M,D
Cleveland State University	M,D
College of Staten Island of the City University of New York	M
The College of William and Mary	M
Colorado State University	M,D
Columbia University	M,D
Cornell University	P,M,D
Creighton University	M,D
Dartmouth College	D
Delaware State University	M
Delta State University	M
DePaul University	M
Drexel University	M,D,O
Duke University	D,O
Duquesne University	M,D
East Carolina University	M,D
Eastern Illinois University	M
Eastern Kentucky University	M
Eastern Michigan University	M
Eastern New Mexico University	M
Eastern Washington University	M
East Stroudsburg University of Pennsylvania	M
East Tennessee State University	M,D
Edinboro University of Pennsylvania	M
Emory University	D
Emporia State University	M
Fairleigh Dickinson University, College at Florham	M
Fairleigh Dickinson University, Metropolitan Campus	M
Fayetteville State University	M
Fitchburg State College	M
Florida Agricultural and Mechanical University	M
Florida Atlantic University	M,D
Florida Institute of Technology	M,D
Florida International University	M,D
Florida State University	P,M,D
Fordham University	M,D
Fort Hays State University	M
Framingham State College	M
Frostburg State University	M
George Mason University	M,D,O
Georgetown University	M,D
The George Washington University	M,D
Georgia College & State University	M
Georgia Institute of Technology	M,D
Georgian Court University	M,O
Georgia Southern University	M
Georgia State University	M,D
Graduate School and University Center of the City University of New York	D
Grand Valley State University	M
Hampton University	M
Harvard University	M,D,O
Heritage University	M
Hofstra University	M
Hood College	M
Howard University	M,D
Humboldt State University	M
Hunter College of the City University of New York	M,D
Idaho State University	M,D
Illinois Institute of Technology	M,D
Illinois State University	M,D
Indiana State University	M,D
Indiana University Bloomington	M,D
Indiana University of Pennsylvania	M
Indiana University–Purdue University Fort Wayne	M
Indiana University–Purdue University Indianapolis	M,D
Iowa State University of Science and Technology	M,D
Jackson State University	M,D
Jacksonville State University	M
James Madison University	M
John Carroll University	M
The Johns Hopkins University	M,D
Kansas State University	M,D
Kent State University	M,D
Lamar University	M
Lehigh University	M,D
Lehman College of the City University of New York	M
Long Island University, Brooklyn Campus	M
Long Island University, C.W. Post Campus	M
Louisiana State University and Agricultural and Mechanical College	M,D
Louisiana Tech University	M
Loyola University Chicago	M
Marquette University	M,D
Marshall University	M,D
Massachusetts Institute of Technology	P,M,D
Mayo Graduate School	D
McNeese State University	M
Michigan State University	M,D
Michigan Technological University	M,D
Middle Tennessee State University	M
Midwestern State University	M
Millersville University of Pennsylvania	M
Mills College	O
Minnesota State University Mankato	M
Mississippi College	M
Mississippi State University	M,D
Missouri State University	M
Missouri University of Science and Technology	M
Montana State University	M,D
Montclair State University	M,O
Morehead State University	M
Morgan State University	M,D
Murray State University	M,D
New Jersey Institute of Technology	M,D
New Mexico Highlands University	M
New Mexico Institute of Mining and Technology	M
New Mexico State University	M,D
New York University	M,D
North Carolina Agricultural and Technical State University	M
North Carolina Central University	M
North Carolina State University	M,D
North Dakota State University	M,D
Northeastern Illinois University	M
Northeastern University	M,D
Northern Arizona University	M,D
Northern Illinois University	M,D
Northern Michigan University	M
Northwestern University	D
Northwest Missouri State University	M
Notre Dame de Namur University	O
Nova Southeastern University	M
Oakland University	M
The Ohio State University	M,D
Ohio University	M,D
Old Dominion University	M,D
Penn State University Park	M,D
Pittsburg State University	M
Point Loma Nazarene University	M
Pontifical Catholic University of Puerto Rico	M
Portland State University	M,D
Prairie View A&M University	M
Princeton University	D
Purdue University	M,D
Purdue University Calumet	M
Queens College of the City University of New York	M
Quinnipiac University	M
Rensselaer Polytechnic Institute	M,D
Rhode Island College	M
Rochester Institute of Technology	M
Rutgers, The State University of New Jersey, Camden	M
Rutgers, The State University of New Jersey, Newark	M,D
Rutgers, The State University of New Jersey, New Brunswick	D
St. Cloud State University	M
Saint Francis University	M
St. John's University (NY)	M,D
Saint Joseph College	M
Saint Joseph's University	M
Saint Louis University	M,D
Sam Houston State University	M
San Diego State University	M,D
San Francisco State University	M
San Jose State University	M
Seton Hall University	M,D
Shippensburg University of Pennsylvania	M
Sonoma State University	M
South Dakota State University	M,D
Southeastern Louisiana University	M
Southeast Missouri State University	M
Southern Connecticut State University	M
Southern Illinois University Carbondale	M,D
Southern Illinois University Edwardsville	M
Southern Methodist University	M,D
Southern University and Agricultural and Mechanical College	M
Stanford University	M,D

State University of New York at Binghamton	M,D
State University of New York at Fredonia	M
State University of New York at New Paltz	M
State University of New York College at Brockport	M
State University of New York College at Oneonta	M
Stephen F. Austin State University	M
Stony Brook University, State University of New York	D
Sul Ross State University	M
Syracuse University	M,D
Tarleton State University	M
Temple University	M,D
Tennessee State University	M,D
Tennessee Technological University	M
Texas A&M International University	M
Texas A&M University	M,D
Texas A&M University–Commerce	M
Texas A&M University–Corpus Christi	M
Texas A&M University–Kingsville	M
Texas Christian University	M
Texas Southern University	M
Texas State University-San Marcos	M
Texas Tech University	M,D
Texas Woman's University	M,D
Touro College	M
Towson University	M
Truman State University	M
Tufts University	M,D
Tulane University	M,D
University at Albany, State University of New York	M,D
University at Buffalo, the State University of New York	M,D
The University of Akron	M,D
The University of Alabama	M,D
The University of Alabama at Birmingham	M,D
The University of Alabama in Huntsville	M
University of Alaska Anchorage	M
University of Alaska Fairbanks	M,D
The University of Arizona	M,D
University of Arkansas	M,D
University of Arkansas at Little Rock	M
University of California, Berkeley	D
University of California, Irvine	M,D
University of California, Los Angeles	M,D
University of California, Riverside	M,D
University of California, San Diego	M,D
University of Central Arkansas	M
University of Central Florida	M,D,O
University of Central Missouri	M
University of Central Oklahoma	M
University of Chicago	D
University of Cincinnati	M,D
University of Colorado Denver	M,D
University of Connecticut	M,D
University of Dayton	M,D
University of Delaware	M,D
University of Denver	M,D
University of Florida	D
University of Georgia	D
University of Guam	M
University of Hartford	M
University of Hawaii at Manoa	M,D
University of Houston	M,D
University of Houston–Clear Lake	M
University of Idaho	M
University of Illinois at Chicago	M,D
University of Illinois at Springfield	M
University of Illinois at Urbana–Champaign	M,D
University of Indianapolis	M
The University of Iowa	M,D
University of Kansas	M,D
University of Kentucky	M,D
University of Louisiana at Lafayette	M,D
University of Louisiana at Monroe	M
University of Louisville	M
University of Maine	D
University of Maryland, Baltimore County	M,D
University of Maryland, College Park	M,D
University of Massachusetts Amherst	M,D
University of Massachusetts Boston	M
University of Massachusetts Dartmouth	M
University of Massachusetts Lowell	M,D
University of Memphis	M,D
University of Miami	M,D
University of Michigan	M,D
University of Michigan–Flint	M
University of Minnesota, Duluth	M
University of Minnesota, Twin Cities Campus	M,D
University of Mississippi	M,D
University of Missouri–Columbia	M,D
University of Missouri–Kansas City	M,D
University of Missouri–St. Louis	M,D,O
The University of Montana	M,D
University of Nebraska at Kearney	M
University of Nebraska at Omaha	M
University of Nebraska–Lincoln	M,D
University of Nevada, Las Vegas	M,D
University of Nevada, Reno	M,D
University of New England	M
University of New Mexico	M,D
University of New Orleans	M,D
The University of North Carolina at Chapel Hill	M,D
The University of North Carolina at Charlotte	M,D
The University of North Carolina at Greensboro	M
The University of North Carolina Wilmington	M,D
University of North Dakota	M,D
University of Northern Colorado	M,D
University of Northern Iowa	M
University of North Florida	M
University of North Texas	M,D
University of Notre Dame	M,D
University of Oregon	M,D
University of Pennsylvania	M,D
University of Pittsburgh	D
University of Puerto Rico, Mayagüez Campus	M
University of Puerto Rico, Río Piedras	M,D
University of Rhode Island	M,D
University of Richmond	M
University of Rochester	M,D
University of San Francisco	M
University of South Alabama	M,D
University of South Carolina	M,D,O
The University of South Dakota	M,D
University of Southern California	M,D
University of Southern Maine	M
University of Southern Mississippi	M,D
University of South Florida	M,D
The University of Tennessee	M,D
The University of Texas at Arlington	M,D
The University of Texas at Austin	M,D
The University of Texas at Brownsville	M
The University of Texas at Dallas	M,D
The University of Texas at El Paso	M,D
The University of Texas at San Antonio	M,D
The University of Texas at Tyler	M
The University of Texas of the Permian Basin	M
The University of Texas–Pan American	M
University of the Incarnate Word	M
University of the Pacific	M
The University of Toledo	M,D
University of Tulsa	M,D
University of Utah	M,D
University of Vermont	M,D
University of Virginia	M,D
University of Washington	M,D
University of West Florida	M
University of West Georgia	M
University of Wisconsin–Eau Claire	M
University of Wisconsin–La Crosse	M
University of Wisconsin–Madison	M,D
University of Wisconsin–Milwaukee	M,D
University of Wisconsin–Oshkosh	M
Utah State University	M,D
Vanderbilt University	M,D
Villanova University	M
Virginia Commonwealth University	M,D,O
Virginia Polytechnic Institute and State University	M,D
Virginia State University	M
Wagner College	M
Wake Forest University	M,D
Walla Walla University	M
Washington State University	M
Washington University in St. Louis	D
Wayne State University	M,D
West Chester University of Pennsylvania	M
Western Carolina University	M
Western Connecticut State University	M
Western Illinois University	M,O
Western Kentucky University	M
Western Michigan University	M,D
Western Washington University	M
West Texas A&M University	M
West Virginia University	M,D
Wichita State University	M
William Paterson University of New Jersey	M
Winthrop University	M
Worcester Polytechnic Institute	M,D
Wright State University	M,D
Yale University	D
Youngstown State University	M

■ BIOLOGICAL ANTHROPOLOGY

Duke University	D
Kent State University	D
Mercyhurst College	M

■ BIOMEDICAL ENGINEERING

Baylor University	M
Boston University	M,D
Brown University	M,D
Carnegie Mellon University	M,D
Case Western Reserve University	M,D
The Catholic University of America	M,D
City College of the City University of New York	M,D
Cleveland State University	D
Columbia University	M,D
Cornell University	M,D
Dartmouth College	M,D
Drexel University	M,D
Duke University	M,D

Florida Agricultural and Mechanical University	M,D
Florida International University	M,D
Florida State University	M,D
Georgia Institute of Technology	M,D,O
Graduate School and University Center of the City University of New York	D
Harvard University	M,D
Illinois Institute of Technology	D
Indiana University–Purdue University Indianapolis	M,D,O
The Johns Hopkins University	M,D
Louisiana Tech University	M,D
Marquette University	M,D
Massachusetts Institute of Technology	M,D,O
Mayo Graduate School	D
Michigan Technological University	D
Mississippi State University	M,D
New Jersey Institute of Technology	M,D
North Carolina State University	M,D
Northwestern University	M,D
The Ohio State University	M,D
Ohio University	M,D
Penn State University Park	M,D
Polytechnic University, Brooklyn Campus	M,D
Purdue University	M,D
Rensselaer Polytechnic Institute	M,D
Rice University	M,D
Rutgers, The State University of New Jersey, New Brunswick	M,D
St. Cloud State University	M
Saint Louis University	M,D
Stanford University	M
Stevens Institute of Technology	M,O
Stony Brook University, State University of New York	M,D,O
Syracuse University	M,D
Texas A&M University	M,D
Tufts University	M,D
Tulane University	M,D
The University of Akron	M,D
The University of Alabama at Birmingham	M,D
University of Arkansas	M
University of California, Davis	M,D
University of California, Irvine	M,D
University of California, Los Angeles	M,D
University of Cincinnati	D
University of Connecticut	M,D
University of Florida	M,D,O
University of Houston	M,D
The University of Iowa	M,D
University of Kentucky	M,D
University of Memphis	M,D
University of Miami	M,D
University of Michigan	M,D
University of Minnesota, Twin Cities Campus	M,D
University of Nevada, Reno	M,D
The University of North Carolina at Chapel Hill	M,D
University of Rochester	M,D
University of Southern California	M,D
University of South Florida	M,D
The University of Tennessee	M,D
The University of Texas at Arlington	M,D
The University of Texas at Austin	M,D
The University of Texas at San Antonio	M,D
University of Vermont	M
University of Virginia	M,D
University of Wisconsin–Madison	M,D
Vanderbilt University	M,D
Virginia Commonwealth University	M,D
Virginia Polytechnic Institute and State University	M,D
Wake Forest University	M,D
Washington University in St. Louis	M,D
Wayne State University	M,D
Worcester Polytechnic Institute	M,D,O
Wright State University	M

■ BIOMETRICS

Cornell University	M,D
North Carolina State University	M,D
Oregon State University	M,D
San Diego State University	D
University of California, Los Angeles	M,D
University of Nebraska–Lincoln	M
University of Southern California	M
University of Wisconsin–Madison	M

■ BIOPHYSICS

Boston University	M,D
Brandeis University	M,D
California Institute of Technology	D
Carnegie Mellon University	M,D
Case Western Reserve University	M,D
Clemson University	M,D
Columbia University	M,D
Cornell University	D
East Carolina University	M,D
East Tennessee State University	M,D
Emory University	D
Georgetown University	M,D
Harvard University	D
Howard University	D
Illinois State University	M,D
Iowa State University of Science and Technology	M,D
The Johns Hopkins University	M,D
Northwestern University	D
The Ohio State University	M,D
Oregon State University	M,D
Princeton University	D
Purdue University	M,D
Rensselaer Polytechnic Institute	M,D
Stanford University	D
Stony Brook University, State University of New York	D
Syracuse University	D
Texas A&M University	M,D
University at Buffalo, the State University of New York	M,D
The University of Alabama at Birmingham	M,D
University of California, Berkeley	D
University of California, Davis	M,D
University of California, Irvine	D
University of California, San Diego	M,D
University of California, Santa Barbara	M,D
University of Chicago	D
University of Cincinnati	D
University of Colorado Denver	D
University of Connecticut	M,D
University of Illinois at Chicago	M,D
University of Illinois at Urbana–Champaign	D
The University of Iowa	M,D
University of Kansas	M,D
University of Louisville	M,D
University of Miami	D
University of Michigan	D
University of Minnesota, Duluth	M,D
University of Minnesota, Twin Cities Campus	M,D
University of Missouri–Kansas City	D
University of New Mexico	M,D
The University of North Carolina at Chapel Hill	M,D
University of Rochester	M,D
University of Southern California	M,D
University of South Florida	M,D
University of Vermont	M,D
University of Virginia	M,D
University of Washington	D
University of Wisconsin–Madison	D
Vanderbilt University	M,D
Washington State University	M,D
Wright State University	M
Yale University	M,D

■ BIOPSYCHOLOGY

American University	M
Argosy University, Twin Cities Campus	M,D,O
Boston University	M
Carnegie Mellon University	D
Columbia University	M,D
Cornell University	D
Drexel University	M,D
Duke University	D
Graduate School and University Center of the City University of New York	D
Harvard University	D
Howard University	M,D
Hunter College of the City University of New York	M
Indiana University–Purdue University Indianapolis	M,D
Louisiana State University and Agricultural and Mechanical College	M,D
Northwestern University	D
Penn State University Park	M,D
Rutgers, The State University of New Jersey, Newark	D
Rutgers, The State University of New Jersey, New Brunswick	D
State University of New York at Binghamton	M,D
Stony Brook University, State University of New York	D
Texas A&M University	M,D
University at Albany, State University of New York	M,D,O
University of Connecticut	M,D
University of Michigan	D
University of Minnesota, Twin Cities Campus	D
University of Nebraska at Omaha	M,D,O
University of Oregon	M,D
The University of Texas at Austin	M,D
The University of Toledo	M,D
University of Wisconsin–Madison	D
Wayne State University	M

■ BIOSTATISTICS

Arizona State University	M,D
Boston University	M,D
Brown University	M,D
California State University, East Bay	M
Case Western Reserve University	M,D
Columbia University	M,D
Drexel University	M,D
Emory University	M,D
Florida State University	M,D
Georgetown University	M
The George Washington University	M,D
Grand Valley State University	M
Harvard University	M,D

Iowa State University of Science and Technology D
The Johns Hopkins University M,D
The Ohio State University D
Rice University M,D
Rutgers, The State University of New Jersey, New Brunswick M,D
San Diego State University M,D
Tufts University M,D
Tulane University M,D
University at Albany, State University of New York M,D
University at Buffalo, the State University of New York M,D
The University of Alabama at Birmingham M,D
The University of Arizona M,D
University of California, Berkeley M,D
University of California, Davis M,D
University of California, Los Angeles M,D
University of Cincinnati M,D
University of Colorado Denver M,D
University of Florida M
University of Illinois at Chicago M,D
The University of Iowa M,D
University of Louisville M,D
University of Michigan M,D
University of Minnesota, Twin Cities Campus M,D
The University of North Carolina at Chapel Hill M,D
University of Pennsylvania M,D
University of Pittsburgh M,D
University of Rochester M,D
University of South Carolina M,D
University of Southern California M,D
University of Southern Mississippi M
University of South Florida M,D
University of Utah M,D
University of Vermont M
University of Washington M,D
Virginia Commonwealth University M,D
Western Michigan University M
Yale University M,D

■ BIOSYSTEMS ENGINEERING

Clemson University M,D
Iowa State University of Science and Technology M,D
Michigan State University M,D
North Dakota State University M,D
South Dakota State University M,D
The University of Arizona M,D
The University of Tennessee M,D

■ BIOTECHNOLOGY

American University M
Brigham Young University M,D
Brown University M,D
Cabrini College M,O
Dartmouth College M,D
Duquesne University M
East Carolina University M
Florida Institute of Technology M,D
The George Washington University M
Harvard University M,O
Howard University M,D
Illinois State University M
The Johns Hopkins University M
Kean University M
Marywood University M
North Carolina State University M
Northeastern University M,D
Northwestern University D
Oklahoma State University M,D
Penn State University Park M,D
Polytechnic University, Brooklyn Campus M,D
Purdue University Calumet M
Regis College (MA) M
Roosevelt University M
Southern Illinois University Edwardsville M
Stephen F. Austin State University M
Texas Tech University M
Tufts University O
University at Buffalo, the State University of New York M
The University of Alabama in Huntsville M,D
University of California, Irvine M
University of Connecticut M
University of Delaware M,D
University of Houston–Clear Lake M
University of Illinois at Chicago M,D
University of Maryland University College M,O
University of Massachusetts Amherst M,D
University of Massachusetts Boston M
University of Massachusetts Dartmouth D
University of Massachusetts Lowell M,D
University of Minnesota, Twin Cities Campus M
University of Missouri–St. Louis M,D,O
University of Nevada, Reno M
University of Pennsylvania M
The University of Texas at Dallas M,D
The University of Texas at San Antonio M,D
University of Utah M
University of Washington D
William Paterson University of New Jersey M
Worcester Polytechnic Institute M,D
Worcester State College M

■ BOTANY

Auburn University M,D
California State University, Chico M
California State University, Fullerton M
Claremont Graduate University M,D
Colorado State University M,D
Emporia State University M
Illinois State University M,D
Miami University M,D
North Carolina State University M,D
North Dakota State University M,D
Oklahoma State University M,D
Oregon State University M,D
Purdue University M,D
Texas A&M University M,D
University of Alaska Fairbanks M,D
University of California, Riverside M,D
University of Connecticut M,D
University of Florida M,D
University of Hawaii at Manoa M,D
University of Kansas M,D
University of Maine M
University of Missouri–St. Louis M,D,O
The University of North Carolina at Chapel Hill M,D
University of North Dakota M,D
University of Oklahoma M,D
University of South Florida M,D
University of Vermont M,D
University of Washington M,D
University of Wisconsin–Madison M,D
University of Wisconsin–Oshkosh M
University of Wyoming M,D
Virginia Polytechnic Institute and State University M,D
Washington State University M,D

■ BUILDING SCIENCE

Arizona State University M
Auburn University M
Carnegie Mellon University M,D
Cornell University M,D
Georgia Institute of Technology M,D
University of California, Berkeley M,D
University of Florida M,D
University of Southern California M,O

■ BUSINESS ADMINISTRATION AND MANAGEMENT—GENERAL

Adelphi University M,O
Alabama Agricultural and Mechanical University M
Alabama State University M
Alaska Pacific University M
Albany State University M
Alcorn State University M
Alfred University M
Alvernia College M
Alverno College M
Amberton University M
American InterContinental University (CA) M
American InterContinental University (FL) M
American InterContinental University Buckhead Campus M
American International College M
American University M,O
Anderson University M,D
Andrews University M
Angelo State University M
Anna Maria College M,O
Antioch University Los Angeles M
Antioch University McGregor M
Antioch University New England M
Antioch University Seattle M
Appalachian State University M
Aquinas College M
Arcadia University M
Argosy University, Orange County Campus M,D,O
Argosy University, Sarasota Campus M,D,O
Argosy University, Tampa Campus M,D,O
Argosy University, Twin Cities Campus M,D
Arizona State University M,D
Arizona State University at the West campus M
Arkansas State University M,O
Ashland University M
Assumption College M,O
Auburn University M,D
Auburn University Montgomery M
Augsburg College M
Augusta State University M
Aurora University M
Austin Peay State University M
Avila University M
Azusa Pacific University M
Baldwin-Wallace College M
Ball State University M
Barry University M,O
Bayamón Central University M
Baylor University M
Belhaven College (MS) M
Bellarmine University M
Bellevue University M
Belmont University M

Institution	Degrees
Benedictine College	M
Benedictine University	M
Bentley College	M,D,O
Bernard M. Baruch College of the City University of New York	M,D,O
Bethel University	M
Biola University	M
Bloomsburg University of Pennsylvania	M
Bob Jones University	P,M,D,O
Boise State University	M
Boston College	M
Boston University	M,D,O
Bowie State University	M
Bowling Green State University	M
Bradley University	M
Brandeis University	M
Brenau University	M
Bridgewater State College	M
Brigham Young University	M
Bryant University	M,O
Butler University	M
Caldwell College	M
California Baptist University	M
California Lutheran University	M,O
California Polytechnic State University, San Luis Obispo	M
California State Polytechnic University, Pomona	M
California State University, Bakersfield	M
California State University, Chico	M
California State University, Dominguez Hills	M
California State University, East Bay	M
California State University, Fresno	M
California State University, Fullerton	M
California State University, Long Beach	M
California State University, Los Angeles	M
California State University, Northridge	M
California State University, Sacramento	M
California State University, San Bernardino	M
California State University, San Marcos	M
California State University, Stanislaus	M
California University of Pennsylvania	M
Cambridge College	M
Cameron University	M
Campbell University	M
Canisius College	M
Capella University	M,D,O
Capital University	M
Cardinal Stritch University	M
Carnegie Mellon University	M,D
Case Western Reserve University	M,D
The Catholic University of America	M
Centenary College	M
Central Connecticut State University	M,O
Central Michigan University	M
Chaminade University of Honolulu	M
Chapman University	M,O
Charleston Southern University	M
Chatham University	M
Christian Brothers University	M,O
The Citadel, The Military College of South Carolina	M
City University of Seattle	M,O
Claremont Graduate University	M,D,O
Clarion University of Pennsylvania	M
Clark Atlanta University	M
Clarkson University	M
Clark University	M
Clemson University	M,D
Cleveland State University	M,D
College of Charleston	M
College of Notre Dame of Maryland	M
College of Saint Elizabeth	M
College of St. Joseph	M
The College of Saint Rose	M
The College of St. Scholastica	M
College of Santa Fe	M
College of Staten Island of the City University of New York	M
The College of William and Mary	M
Colorado Christian University	M
Colorado State University	M
Colorado Technical University—Colorado Springs	M,D
Colorado Technical University—Denver	M
Colorado Technical University—Sioux Falls	M
Columbia College (MO)	M
Columbia University	M,D
Columbus State University	M
Concordia University (CA)	M
Concordia University (OR)	M
Concordia University, St. Paul	M
Concordia University Wisconsin	M
Cornell University	M,D
Cornerstone University	M,O
Creighton University	M
Cumberland University	M
Daemen College	M
Dallas Baptist University	M
Dartmouth College	M
Davenport University	M
Delaware State University	M
Delta State University	M
DePaul University	M
DeSales University	M
DeVry University	M
Doane College	M
Dominican University	M
Dominican University of California	M
Dowling College	M,O
Drake University	M
Drexel University	M,D,O
Drury University	M
Duke University	M,D
Duquesne University	M
East Carolina University	M,D,O
Eastern Illinois University	M,O
Eastern Kentucky University	M
Eastern Mennonite University	M
Eastern Michigan University	M
Eastern New Mexico University	M
Eastern University	M
Eastern Washington University	M
East Tennessee State University	M,O
Edgewood College	M
Elmhurst College	M
Elon University	M
Embry-Riddle Aeronautical University (FL)	M
Emmanuel College	M
Emory University	M,D
Emporia State University	M
Endicott College	M
Everest University	M
Fairfield University	M,O
Fairleigh Dickinson University, College at Florham	M,O
Fairleigh Dickinson University, Metropolitan Campus	M,O
Ferris State University	M
Fitchburg State College	M
Florida Agricultural and Mechanical University	M
Florida Atlantic University	M
Florida Gulf Coast University	M
Florida Institute of Technology	M
Florida International University	M,D
Florida State University	M,D
Fontbonne University	M
Fordham University	M
Fort Hays State University	M
Framingham State College	M
Franciscan University of Steubenville	M
Francis Marion University	M
Freed-Hardeman University	M
Fresno Pacific University	M
Friends University	M
Frostburg State University	M
Gannon University	M,O
Gardner-Webb University	M
Geneva College	M
George Fox University	M,D
George Mason University	M
Georgetown University	M
The George Washington University	M,D
Georgia College & State University	M
Georgia Institute of Technology	M,D,O
Georgian Court University	M
Georgia Southern University	M
Georgia Southwestern State University	M
Georgia State University	M,D
Goddard College	M
Golden Gate University	M,D,O
Gonzaga University	M
Governors State University	M
Graduate School and University Center of the City University of New York	D
Grand Canyon University	M
Grand Valley State University	M
Gwynedd-Mercy College	M
Hamline University	M
Hampton University	M
Harding University	M
Hardin-Simmons University	M
Harvard University	M,D,O
Hawai'i Pacific University	M
Heidelberg College	M
Henderson State University	M
High Point University	M
Hodges University	M
Hofstra University	M,O
Holy Family University	M
Holy Names University	M
Hood College	M
Houston Baptist University	M
Howard University	M
Humboldt State University	M
Husson College	M
Idaho State University	M,O
Illinois Institute of Technology	M,D
Illinois State University	M
Indiana State University	M
Indiana University Bloomington	M,D
Indiana University Northwest	M,O
Indiana University of Pennsylvania	M
Indiana University–Purdue University Fort Wayne	M
Indiana University–Purdue University Indianapolis	M
Indiana University South Bend	M
Indiana University Southeast	M,O
Indiana Wesleyan University	M
Inter American University of Puerto Rico, San Germán Campus	M,D

Iona College	M,O
Iowa State University of Science and Technology	M
Ithaca College	M
Jackson State University	M,D
Jacksonville State University	M
Jacksonville University	M
James Madison University	M
John Brown University	M
John Carroll University	M
John F. Kennedy University	M,O
The Johns Hopkins University	M,O
Kansas State University	M
Kean University	M
Kennesaw State University	M
Kent State University	M
King's College	M
Kutztown University of Pennsylvania	M
Lakeland College	M
Lamar University	M
La Salle University	M,O
La Sierra University	M,O
Lawrence Technological University	M,D
Lehigh University	M,D,O
Le Moyne College	M
LeTourneau University	M
Lewis University	M
Liberty University	M
Lincoln Memorial University	M
Lincoln University (MO)	M
Lindenwood University	M
Lipscomb University	M
Long Island University, Brooklyn Campus	M
Long Island University, C.W. Post Campus	M,O
Longwood University	M
Louisiana State University and Agricultural and Mechanical College	M,D
Louisiana State University in Shreveport	M
Louisiana Tech University	M,D
Loyola College in Maryland	M
Loyola Marymount University	M
Loyola University Chicago	M
Loyola University New Orleans	M
Lynchburg College	M
Lynn University	M,D
Madonna University	M
Maharishi University of Management	M,D
Malone College	M
Marian College of Fond du Lac	M
Marist College	M,O
Marquette University	M
Marshall University	M
Marylhurst University	M
Marymount University	M,O
Maryville University of Saint Louis	M,O
Marywood University	M
Massachusetts Institute of Technology	M,D
McNeese State University	M
Medaille College	M
Mercer University	M
Mercy College	M
Metropolitan College of New York	M
Metropolitan State University	M
Miami University	M
Michigan State University	M,D
Michigan Technological University	M
MidAmerica Nazarene University	M
Middle Tennessee State University	M
Midwestern State University	M
Millersville University of Pennsylvania	M
Mills College	M
Minnesota State University Mankato	M
Minot State University	M
Mississippi College	M,O
Mississippi State University	M,D
Missouri Baptist University	M,O
Missouri State University	M
Monmouth University	M,O
Montclair State University	M
Monterey Institute of International Studies	M
Morehead State University	M
Morgan State University	D
Mount Marty College	M
Mount Mary College	M
Mount Saint Mary College	M
Mount St. Mary's University	M
Murray State University	M
National-Louis University	M
National University	M
Nazareth College of Rochester	M
New Jersey City University	M
New Jersey Institute of Technology	M
Newman University	M
New Mexico Highlands University	M
New Mexico State University	M,D
New York Institute of Technology	M,O
New York University	P,M,D,O
Niagara University	M
Nicholls State University	M
North Carolina Central University	M
North Carolina State University	M
North Central College	M
North Dakota State University	M
Northeastern Illinois University	M
Northeastern State University	M
Northeastern University	M,O
Northern Arizona University	M
Northern Illinois University	M
Northern Kentucky University	M
North Park University	M
Northwestern University	M
Northwest Missouri State University	M
Northwest Nazarene University	M
Norwich University	M
Notre Dame de Namur University	M
Nova Southeastern University	M,D
Nyack College	M
Oakland City University	M
Oakland University	M,O
Ohio Dominican University	M
The Ohio State University	M,D
Ohio University	M
Oklahoma City University	M
Oklahoma State University	M,D
Old Dominion University	M,D
Olivet Nazarene University	M
Oral Roberts University	M
Oregon State University	M,O
Otterbein College	M
Our Lady of the Lake University of San Antonio	M
Pace University	M,D,O
Pacific Lutheran University	M
Palm Beach Atlantic University	M
Park University	M
Penn State Great Valley	M
Penn State Harrisburg	M
Pepperdine University	M
Pfeiffer University	M
Philadelphia University	M
Piedmont College	M
Pittsburg State University	M
Plymouth State University	M
Point Loma Nazarene University	M
Point Park University	M
Polytechnic University, Brooklyn Campus	M,D
Polytechnic University, Westchester Graduate Center	M
Pontifical Catholic University of Puerto Rico	M,D
Portland State University	M,D,O
Prairie View A&M University	M
Providence College	M
Purdue University	M,D
Purdue University Calumet	M
Queens University of Charlotte	M
Quinnipiac University	M
Radford University	M
Regent University	M,D,O
Regis College (MA)	M
Regis University	M,O
Rensselaer Polytechnic Institute	M,D
Rice University	M
The Richard Stockton College of New Jersey	M
Rider University	M
Rivier College	M
Robert Morris University	M
Roberts Wesleyan College	M,O
Rochester Institute of Technology	M
Rockford College	M
Rockhurst University	M
Rollins College	M
Roosevelt University	M
Rosemont College	M
Rowan University	M
Rutgers, The State University of New Jersey, Camden	M
Rutgers, The State University of New Jersey, Newark	M,D,O
Sacred Heart University	M
Saginaw Valley State University	M
St. Ambrose University	M,D
St. Bonaventure University	M,O
St. Cloud State University	M
St. Edward's University	M,O
Saint Francis University	M
St. John Fisher College	M
St. John's University (NY)	M,O
Saint Joseph College	M
Saint Joseph's College of Maine	M
St. Joseph's College, Suffolk Campus	M,O
Saint Joseph's University	M,O
Saint Leo University	M
Saint Louis University	M
Saint Martin's University	M
Saint Mary's College of California	M
Saint Mary's University of Minnesota	M,O
St. Mary's University of San Antonio	M
Saint Michael's College	M,O
Saint Peter's College	M
St. Thomas Aquinas College	M
St. Thomas University	M,O
Saint Xavier University	M,O
Salem State College	M
Salisbury University	M
Salve Regina University	M,O
Samford University	M
Sam Houston State University	M
San Diego State University	M
San Francisco State University	M
San Jose State University	M
Santa Clara University	M
Schiller International University (United States)	M
School for International Training	M

Institution	Degrees
Seattle Pacific University	M
Seattle University	M,O
Seton Hall University	M,O
Seton Hill University	M
Shenandoah University	M,O
Shippensburg University of Pennsylvania	M
Silver Lake College	M
Simmons College	M,O
Slippery Rock University of Pennsylvania	M
Sonoma State University	M
Southeastern Louisiana University	M
Southeastern Oklahoma State University	M
Southeastern University	M
Southeast Missouri State University	M
Southern Connecticut State University	M
Southern Illinois University Carbondale	M,D
Southern Illinois University Edwardsville	M
Southern Methodist University	M
Southern Nazarene University	M
Southern New Hampshire University	M,D,O
Southern Oregon University	M
Southern Polytechnic State University	M
Southern University and Agricultural and Mechanical College	M
Southern Utah University	M
Southern Wesleyan University	M
Southwest Baptist University	M
Southwestern Oklahoma State University	M
Southwest Minnesota State University	M
Spalding University	M
Spring Arbor University	M
Spring Hill College	M
Stanford University	M,D
State University of New York at Binghamton	M,D
State University of New York at Fredonia	M
State University of New York at New Paltz	M
State University of New York at Oswego	M
State University of New York Empire State College	M
State University of New York Institute of Technology	M
Stephen F. Austin State University	M
Stetson University	M
Stevens Institute of Technology	M
Stony Brook University, State University of New York	M,O
Strayer University	M
Suffolk University	M,O
Sullivan University	M
Sul Ross State University	M
Syracuse University	M,D
Tarleton State University	M
Temple University	M,D
Tennessee State University	M
Tennessee Technological University	M
Texas A&M International University	M
Texas A&M University	M,D
Texas A&M University–Commerce	M
Texas A&M University–Corpus Christi	M
Texas A&M University–Kingsville	M
Texas A&M University–Texarkana	M
Texas Christian University	M,D
Texas Southern University	M
Texas State University-San Marcos	M
Texas Tech University	M,D
Texas Wesleyan University	M
Texas Woman's University	M
Thomas More College	M
Tiffin University	M
Towson University	M
Trevecca Nazarene University	M
Trinity International University	P,M,D,O
Trinity University	M
Trinity (Washington) University	M
Troy University	M
Tulane University	M,D
Union University	M
Universidad del Turabo	M,D
Universidad Metropolitana	M,O
University at Albany, State University of New York	M
University at Buffalo, the State University of New York	M,D,O
The University of Akron	M
The University of Alabama	M,D
The University of Alabama at Birmingham	M,D
The University of Alabama in Huntsville	M,O
University of Alaska Anchorage	M
University of Alaska Fairbanks	M
University of Alaska Southeast	M
The University of Arizona	M,D
University of Arkansas	M,D
University of Arkansas at Little Rock	M
University of Baltimore	M
University of Bridgeport	M
University of California, Berkeley	M,D
University of California, Davis	M
University of California, Irvine	M,D
University of California, Los Angeles	M,D
University of California, Riverside	M
University of California, San Diego	M
University of Central Arkansas	M
University of Central Florida	M,D,O
University of Central Missouri	M
University of Central Oklahoma	M
University of Chicago	M,D
University of Cincinnati	M,D
University of Colorado at Boulder	M,D
University of Colorado at Colorado Springs	M
University of Colorado Denver	M
University of Connecticut	M,D
University of Dallas	M
University of Dayton	M
University of Delaware	M,D
University of Denver	M,O
University of Detroit Mercy	M,O
University of Dubuque	M
University of Evansville	M
The University of Findlay	M
University of Florida	M,D,O
University of Georgia	M,D,O
University of Guam	M
University of Hartford	M
University of Hawaii at Manoa	M
University of Houston	M,D
University of Houston–Clear Lake	M
University of Houston–Victoria	M
University of Idaho	M
University of Illinois at Chicago	M,D
University of Illinois at Springfield	M
University of Illinois at Urbana–Champaign	M,D
University of Indianapolis	M,O
The University of Iowa	M,D
University of Kansas	M,D
University of Kentucky	M,D
University of La Verne	M,O
University of Louisiana at Lafayette	M
University of Louisiana at Monroe	M
University of Louisville	M
University of Maine	M
University of Mary	M
University of Mary Hardin-Baylor	M
University of Maryland, College Park	M,D
University of Maryland University College	M,D,O
University of Mary Washington	M
University of Massachusetts Amherst	M,D
University of Massachusetts Boston	M
University of Massachusetts Dartmouth	M,O
University of Massachusetts Lowell	M
University of Memphis	M,D
University of Miami	M
University of Michigan	D
University of Michigan–Dearborn	M
University of Michigan–Flint	M
University of Minnesota, Duluth	M
University of Minnesota, Twin Cities Campus	M,D
University of Mississippi	M,D
University of Missouri–Columbia	M,D
University of Missouri–Kansas City	M,D
University of Missouri–St. Louis	M,O
University of Mobile	M
The University of Montana	M
University of Nebraska at Kearney	M
University of Nebraska at Omaha	M
University of Nebraska–Lincoln	M,D
University of Nevada, Las Vegas	M
University of Nevada, Reno	M
University of New Hampshire	M
University of New Haven	M
University of New Mexico	M
University of New Orleans	M
University of North Alabama	M
The University of North Carolina at Chapel Hill	M,D
The University of North Carolina at Charlotte	M,D
The University of North Carolina at Greensboro	M,O
The University of North Carolina at Pembroke	M
The University of North Carolina Wilmington	M
University of North Dakota	M
University of Northern Iowa	M
University of North Florida	M
University of North Texas	M,D
University of Notre Dame	M
University of Oklahoma	M,D
University of Oregon	M,D
University of Pennsylvania	M,D
University of Phoenix–Central Florida Campus	M
University of Phoenix–Denver Campus	M
University of Phoenix–Fort Lauderdale Campus	M
University of Phoenix–Hawaii Campus	M
University of Phoenix–Las Vegas Campus	M
University of Phoenix–Louisiana Campus	M
University of Phoenix–New Mexico Campus	M
University of Phoenix–North Florida Campus	M
University of Phoenix	M,D
University of Phoenix–Oregon Campus	M

University of Phoenix–Philadelphia Campus M
University of Phoenix–Phoenix Campus M
University of Phoenix–Sacramento Valley Campus M
University of Phoenix–San Diego Campus M
University of Phoenix–Southern Arizona Campus M
University of Phoenix–Southern California Campus M
University of Phoenix–Southern Colorado Campus M
University of Phoenix–Utah Campus M
University of Phoenix–West Florida Campus M
University of Phoenix–West Michigan Campus M
University of Pittsburgh M,D
University of Portland M
University of Puerto Rico, Mayagüez Campus M
University of Puerto Rico, Río Piedras M,D
University of Redlands M
University of Rhode Island M,D
University of Richmond M
University of Rochester M,D
University of St. Francis (IL) M
University of Saint Francis (IN) M
University of Saint Mary M
University of St. Thomas (MN) M
University of St. Thomas (TX) M
University of San Diego M,O
University of San Francisco M
The University of Scranton M
University of Sioux Falls M
University of South Alabama M
University of South Carolina M,D
The University of South Dakota M
University of Southern California M,D
University of Southern Indiana M
University of Southern Maine M
University of Southern Mississippi M
University of South Florida M,D
The University of Tampa M
The University of Tennessee M,D
The University of Tennessee at Chattanooga M
The University of Tennessee at Martin M
The University of Texas at Arlington M,D
The University of Texas at Austin M,D
The University of Texas at Brownsville M
The University of Texas at Dallas M,D
The University of Texas at El Paso M
The University of Texas at San Antonio M,D
The University of Texas at Tyler M
The University of Texas of the Permian Basin M
The University of Texas–Pan American M,D
University of the District of Columbia M
University of the Incarnate Word M,O
University of the Pacific M
The University of Toledo M,D
University of Tulsa M
University of Utah M,D
University of Vermont M
University of Virginia M,D
University of Washington M,D
University of Washington, Bothell M
University of West Florida M
University of West Georgia M
University of Wisconsin–Eau Claire M
University of Wisconsin–La Crosse M
University of Wisconsin–Madison M
University of Wisconsin–Milwaukee M,D,O
University of Wisconsin–Oshkosh M
University of Wisconsin–River Falls M
University of Wisconsin–Stevens Point M
University of Wisconsin–Whitewater M
University of Wyoming M
Upper Iowa University M
Ursuline College M
Utah State University M
Valdosta State University M
Valparaiso University M,O
Vanderbilt University M,D
Vanguard University of Southern California M
Villanova University M
Virginia Commonwealth University M,D
Virginia Polytechnic Institute and State University M,D
Wagner College M
Wake Forest University M
Walden University M,D,O
Walsh University M
Washburn University M
Washington State University M,D
Washington University in St. Louis M,D
Wayland Baptist University M
Waynesburg University M
Wayne State College M
Wayne State University M,D
Weber State University M
Webster University M,D
Wesley College M
West Chester University of Pennsylvania M
Western Carolina University M
Western Connecticut State University M
Western Illinois University M
Western International University M
Western Kentucky University M
Western Michigan University M
Western New England College M
Western New Mexico University M
Western Washington University M
Westminster College (UT) M,O
West Texas A&M University M
West Virginia University M
Wheeling Jesuit University M
Whitworth University M
Wichita State University M
Widener University M
Wilkes University M
Willamette University M
William Carey University M
William Paterson University of New Jersey M
Wilmington University (DE) M
Winthrop University M
Woodbury University M
Worcester Polytechnic Institute M,O
Worcester State College M
Wright State University M
Xavier University M
Yale University M,D
Youngstown State University M

■ BUSINESS EDUCATION

Albany State University M
Arkansas State University M,O
Armstrong Atlantic State University M
Auburn University M,D,O
Ball State University M
Bloomsburg University of Pennsylvania M
Bowling Green State University M
Buffalo State College, State University of New York M
Canisius College M
Central Connecticut State University M,O
Central Michigan University M
The College of Saint Rose M,O
Drake University M
Eastern Kentucky University M
Emporia State University M
Florida Agricultural and Mechanical University M
Georgia Southern University M
Hofstra University M
Inter American University of Puerto Rico, Metropolitan Campus M,D
Inter American University of Puerto Rico, San Germán Campus M
Lehman College of the City University of New York M
Louisiana State University and Agricultural and Mechanical College M,D
Louisiana Tech University M,D
Maryville University of Saint Louis M,O
Middle Tennessee State University M
Mississippi College M,O
Nazareth College of Rochester M
New York University M,O
Northwestern State University of Louisiana M
Old Dominion University M,D
Penn State Harrisburg M,D
Rider University M,O
Salisbury University M
South Carolina State University M
Southern New Hampshire University M,O
State University of New York at Oswego M
University of Delaware M,D
University of Minnesota, Twin Cities Campus M,D
University of Missouri–Columbia M,D,O
University of South Carolina M,D
The University of Toledo M
University of Washington M,D
University of West Georgia M,O
University of Wisconsin–Whitewater M
Utah State University M,D
Valdosta State University M,D
Wayne State College M
Wayne State University M,D,O
Western Kentucky University M,O
Wright State University M

■ CANADIAN STUDIES

The Johns Hopkins University M,D,O

■ CANCER BIOLOGY/ONCOLOGY

Brown University M,D
Dartmouth College D
Drexel University M,D
Duke University D
Mayo Graduate School D
New York University M,D
Northwestern University D
Stanford University D
University at Buffalo, the State University of New York D
The University of Arizona D
University of California, San Diego D
University of Chicago D
University of Cincinnati D
University of Colorado Denver D
University of Delaware M,D
University of Miami D

Institution	Degrees
Illinois State University	M
Indiana University Bloomington	M,D
Indiana University of Pennsylvania	M
Indiana University–Purdue University Indianapolis	M,D
Iowa State University of Science and Technology	M,D
Jackson State University	M,D
The Johns Hopkins University	D
Kansas State University	M,D
Kent State University	M,D
Lamar University	M
Lehigh University	M,D
Long Island University, Brooklyn Campus	M
Louisiana State University and Agricultural and Mechanical College	M,D
Louisiana Tech University	M
Loyola University Chicago	M,D
Marquette University	M,D
Marshall University	M
Massachusetts Institute of Technology	D
McNeese State University	M
Miami University	M,D
Michigan State University	M,D
Michigan Technological University	M,D
Middle Tennessee State University	M,D
Mississippi College	M
Mississippi State University	M,D
Missouri State University	M
Missouri University of Science and Technology	M,D
Montana State University	M,D
Montclair State University	M
Morgan State University	M
Murray State University	M
New Jersey Institute of Technology	M,D
New Mexico Highlands University	M
New Mexico Institute of Mining and Technology	M,D
New Mexico State University	M,D
New York University	M,D
North Carolina Agricultural and Technical State University	M
North Carolina Central University	M
North Carolina State University	M,D
North Dakota State University	M,D
Northeastern Illinois University	M
Northeastern University	M,D
Northern Arizona University	M
Northern Illinois University	M,D
Northern Michigan University	M
Northwestern University	D
Oakland University	M,D
The Ohio State University	M,D
Oklahoma State University	M,D
Old Dominion University	M,D
Oregon State University	M,D
Penn State University Park	M,D
Pittsburg State University	M
Polytechnic University, Brooklyn Campus	M,D
Polytechnic University, Westchester Graduate Center	M
Pontifical Catholic University of Puerto Rico	M
Portland State University	M,D
Prairie View A&M University	M
Princeton University	M,D
Purdue University	M,D
Queens College of the City University of New York	M
Rensselaer Polytechnic Institute	M,D
Rice University	M,D
Rochester Institute of Technology	M
Roosevelt University	M
Rutgers, The State University of New Jersey, Camden	M
Rutgers, The State University of New Jersey, Newark	M,D
Rutgers, The State University of New Jersey, New Brunswick	M,D
Sacred Heart University	M
St. John's University (NY)	M
Saint Joseph College	M
Saint Louis University	M
Sam Houston State University	M
San Diego State University	M,D
San Francisco State University	M
San Jose State University	M
Seton Hall University	M,D
South Dakota State University	M,D
Southeast Missouri State University	M
Southern Connecticut State University	M
Southern Illinois University Carbondale	M,D
Southern Illinois University Edwardsville	M
Southern Methodist University	M,D
Southern University and Agricultural and Mechanical College	M
Stanford University	D
State University of New York at Binghamton	M,D
State University of New York at Fredonia	M
State University of New York at New Paltz	M
State University of New York at Oswego	M
State University of New York College of Environmental Science and Forestry	M,D
Stephen F. Austin State University	M
Stevens Institute of Technology	M,D,O
Stony Brook University, State University of New York	M,D
Sul Ross State University	M
Syracuse University	M,D
Temple University	M,D
Tennessee State University	M
Tennessee Technological University	M
Texas A&M University	M,D
Texas A&M University–Commerce	M
Texas A&M University–Kingsville	M
Texas Christian University	M,D
Texas Southern University	M
Texas State University-San Marcos	M
Texas Tech University	M,D
Texas Woman's University	M
Tufts University	M,D
Tulane University	M,D
University at Albany, State University of New York	M,D
University at Buffalo, the State University of New York	M,D
The University of Akron	M,D
The University of Alabama	M,D
The University of Alabama at Birmingham	M,D
The University of Alabama in Huntsville	M
University of Alaska Fairbanks	M,D
The University of Arizona	M,D
University of Arkansas	M,D
University of Arkansas at Little Rock	M
University of California, Berkeley	D
University of California, Davis	M,D
University of California, Irvine	M,D
University of California, Los Angeles	M,D
University of California, Riverside	M,D
University of California, San Diego	M,D
University of California, Santa Barbara	M,D
University of California, Santa Cruz	M,D
University of Central Florida	M,D,O
University of Central Oklahoma	M
University of Chicago	D
University of Cincinnati	M,D
University of Colorado at Boulder	M,D
University of Colorado Denver	M
University of Connecticut	M,D
University of Dayton	M
University of Delaware	M,D
University of Denver	M,D
University of Detroit Mercy	M
University of Florida	M,D
University of Georgia	M,D
University of Hawaii at Manoa	M,D
University of Houston	M,D
University of Houston–Clear Lake	M
University of Idaho	M,D
University of Illinois at Chicago	M,D
University of Illinois at Urbana–Champaign	M,D
The University of Iowa	M,D
University of Kansas	M,D
University of Kentucky	M,D
University of Louisville	M,D
University of Maine	M,D
University of Maryland, Baltimore County	M,D
University of Maryland, College Park	M,D
University of Massachusetts Amherst	M,D
University of Massachusetts Boston	M
University of Massachusetts Dartmouth	M
University of Massachusetts Lowell	M,D
University of Memphis	M,D
University of Miami	M,D
University of Michigan	D
University of Minnesota, Duluth	M
University of Minnesota, Twin Cities Campus	M,D
University of Mississippi	M,D
University of Missouri–Columbia	M,D
University of Missouri–Kansas City	M,D
University of Missouri–St. Louis	M,D
The University of Montana	M,D
University of Nebraska–Lincoln	M,D
University of Nevada, Las Vegas	M,D
University of Nevada, Reno	M,D
University of New Hampshire	M,D
University of New Mexico	M,D
University of New Orleans	M,D
The University of North Carolina at Chapel Hill	M,D
The University of North Carolina at Charlotte	M
The University of North Carolina at Greensboro	M
The University of North Carolina Wilmington	M
University of North Dakota	M,D
University of Northern Colorado	M,D
University of Northern Iowa	M
University of North Texas	M,D
University of Notre Dame	M,D
University of Oklahoma	M,D
University of Oregon	M,D
University of Pennsylvania	M,D
University of Pittsburgh	M,D

University of Puerto Rico, Mayagüez Campus M,D
University of Puerto Rico, Río Piedras M,D
University of Rhode Island M,D
University of Rochester M,D
University of San Francisco M
The University of Scranton M
University of South Carolina M,D
The University of South Dakota M
University of Southern California M,D
University of Southern Mississippi M,D
University of South Florida M,D
The University of Tennessee M,D
The University of Texas at Arlington M,D
The University of Texas at Austin M,D
The University of Texas at Dallas M,D
The University of Texas at El Paso M
The University of Texas at San Antonio M,D
The University of Toledo M,D
University of Tulsa M
University of Utah M,D
University of Vermont M,D
University of Virginia M,D
University of Washington M,D
University of Wisconsin–Madison M,D
University of Wisconsin–Milwaukee M,D
University of Wyoming M,D
Utah State University M,D
Vanderbilt University M,D
Villanova University M
Virginia Commonwealth University M,D
Virginia Polytechnic Institute and State University M,D
Wake Forest University M,D
Washington State University M,D
Washington University in St. Louis M,D
Wayne State University M,D
West Chester University of Pennsylvania M
Western Carolina University M
Western Illinois University M
Western Kentucky University M
Western Michigan University M,D
Western Washington University M
West Texas A&M University M
West Virginia University M,D
Wichita State University M,D
Worcester Polytechnic Institute M,D
Wright State University M
Yale University D
Youngstown State University M

■ CHILD AND FAMILY STUDIES

Arizona State University M,D
Auburn University M,D
Bowling Green State University M
Brandeis University M
Brigham Young University M,D
Capella University M,D,O
Central Michigan University M
Central Washington University M
Clemson University D
Colorado State University M
Concordia University, St. Paul M,O
Concordia University Wisconsin M
Cornell University D
East Carolina University M
Florida State University M,D
Indiana State University M
Indiana University Bloomington M,D
Iowa State University of Science and Technology M,D
Kansas State University M,D
Miami University M
Michigan State University M,D
Middle Tennessee State University M
Missouri State University M
North Dakota State University M,D
Northern Illinois University M
Nova Southeastern University M,D
The Ohio State University M,D
Ohio University M
Oklahoma State University M,D
Oregon State University M,D
Penn State University Park M,D
Purdue University M,D
Roberts Wesleyan College M
St. Cloud State University M
Saint Joseph College M,O
San Diego State University M
San Jose State University M
South Carolina State University M
Spring Arbor University M
Springfield College M,O
Stanford University D
State University of New York at Oswego M
Syracuse University M,D
Texas State University-San Marcos M
Texas Tech University M,D
Texas Woman's University M,D
Towson University O
Tufts University M,D,O
The University of Akron M
The University of Alabama M
The University of Arizona M,D
University of California, Santa Barbara M,D
University of Central Florida M,O
University of Connecticut M,D
University of Delaware M,D
University of Denver M,D,O
University of Georgia M,D
University of Illinois at Springfield M
University of Kentucky M,D
University of La Verne M
University of Maryland, College Park M,D
University of Minnesota, Twin Cities Campus M,D
University of Missouri–Columbia M,D
University of Nebraska–Lincoln M,D
University of Nevada, Reno M
University of New Hampshire M
University of New Mexico M,D
The University of North Carolina at Greensboro M,D
University of North Texas M,D
University of Rhode Island M
University of Southern Mississippi M
The University of Tennessee M,D
The University of Tennessee at Martin M
The University of Texas at Austin M,D
The University of Texas at Dallas M,D
University of Utah M
University of Wisconsin–Madison M,D
University of Wisconsin–Stout M
Utah State University M,D
Vanderbilt University M
Virginia Polytechnic Institute and State University M,D
Wayne State University O
West Virginia University M
Wheelock College M

■ CHILD DEVELOPMENT

American International College M,D,O
Appalachian State University M
Arcadia University M,D,O
California State University, Los Angeles M
California State University, San Bernardino M
East Carolina University M
Florida State University M,D
Indiana State University M
Michigan State University M,D
Middle Tennessee State University M
North Dakota State University M,D
Ohio University M
Purdue University M,D
Rutgers, The State University of New Jersey, Camden M,D
San Diego State University M
Sarah Lawrence College M
Southern New Hampshire University M,O
Texas Woman's University M,D
Tufts University M,D,O
The University of Akron M
University of California, Davis M
University of La Verne M
University of Minnesota, Twin Cities Campus M,D
The University of North Carolina at Charlotte M,D
The University of Tennessee at Martin M
The University of Texas at Austin M,D
Virginia Polytechnic Institute and State University M,D

■ CHINESE

Cornell University M,D
Harvard University D
Indiana University Bloomington M,D
San Francisco State University M
Stanford University M,D
University of California, Berkeley D
University of California, Irvine M,D
University of Colorado at Boulder M,D
University of Hawaii at Manoa M,D
University of Kansas M
University of Massachusetts Amherst M
University of Oregon M,D
University of Washington M,D
University of Wisconsin–Madison M,D
Washington University in St. Louis M,D

■ CHIROPRACTIC

D'Youville College P
University of Bridgeport P

■ CIVIL ENGINEERING

Arizona State University M,D
Auburn University M,D
Boise State University M
Bradley University M
Brigham Young University M,D
Bucknell University M
California Institute of Technology M,D,O
California Polytechnic State University, San Luis Obispo M
California State Polytechnic University, Pomona M
California State University, Fresno M
California State University, Fullerton M
California State University, Long Beach M
California State University, Los Angeles M
California State University, Northridge M
California State University, Sacramento M
Carnegie Mellon University M,D
Case Western Reserve University M,D
The Catholic University of America M,D
City College of the City University of New York M,D

Clarkson University	M,D
Clemson University	M,D
Cleveland State University	M,D
Colorado State University	M,D
Columbia University	M,D,O
Cornell University	M,D
Drexel University	M,D
Duke University	M,D
Florida Agricultural and Mechanical University	M,D
Florida Atlantic University	M
Florida Institute of Technology	M,D
Florida International University	M,D
Florida State University	M,D
George Mason University	M
The George Washington University	M,D,O
Georgia Institute of Technology	M,D
Graduate School and University Center of the City University of New York	D
Howard University	M
Idaho State University	M,D,O
Illinois Institute of Technology	M,D
Iowa State University of Science and Technology	M,D
The Johns Hopkins University	M,D
Kansas State University	M,D
Lamar University	M,D
Lawrence Technological University	M,D
Lehigh University	M,D
Louisiana State University and Agricultural and Mechanical College	M,D
Louisiana Tech University	M,D
Loyola Marymount University	M
Manhattan College	M
Marquette University	M,D
Massachusetts Institute of Technology	M,D,O
McNeese State University	M
Michigan State University	M,D
Michigan Technological University	M,D
Mississippi State University	M,D
Missouri University of Science and Technology	M,D
Montana State University	M,D
Morgan State University	M,D
New Jersey Institute of Technology	M,D
New Mexico State University	M,D
North Carolina Agricultural and Technical State University	M
North Carolina State University	M,D
North Dakota State University	M,D
Northeastern University	M,D
Northwestern University	M,D
Norwich University	M
The Ohio State University	M,D
Ohio University	M,D
Oklahoma State University	M,D
Old Dominion University	M,D
Oregon State University	M,D
Penn State University Park	M,D
Polytechnic University, Brooklyn Campus	M,D
Portland State University	M,D,O
Princeton University	M,D
Purdue University	M,D
Rensselaer Polytechnic Institute	M,D
Rice University	M,D
Rutgers, The State University of New Jersey, New Brunswick	M,D
Saint Martin's University	M
San Diego State University	M
San Jose State University	M
Santa Clara University	M
South Carolina State University	M
South Dakota State University	M
Southern Illinois University Carbondale	M
Southern Illinois University Edwardsville	M
Southern Methodist University	M,D
Stanford University	M,D,O
Stevens Institute of Technology	M,D,O
Syracuse University	M,D
Temple University	M
Tennessee Technological University	M,D
Texas A&M University	M,D
Texas A&M University–Kingsville	M
Texas Tech University	M,D
Tufts University	M,D
Tulane University	M,D
University at Buffalo, the State University of New York	M,D
The University of Akron	M,D
The University of Alabama	M,D
The University of Alabama at Birmingham	M,D
The University of Alabama in Huntsville	M,D
University of Alaska Anchorage	M,O
University of Alaska Fairbanks	M,D
The University of Arizona	M,D
University of Arkansas	M,D
University of California, Berkeley	M,D
University of California, Davis	M,D,O
University of California, Irvine	M,D
University of California, Los Angeles	M,D
University of Central Florida	M,D,O
University of Cincinnati	M,D
University of Colorado at Boulder	M,D
University of Colorado Denver	M,D
University of Connecticut	M,D
University of Dayton	M
University of Delaware	M,D
University of Detroit Mercy	M
University of Florida	M,D,O
University of Hawaii at Manoa	M,D
University of Houston	M,D
University of Idaho	M,D
University of Illinois at Chicago	M,D
University of Illinois at Urbana–Champaign	M,D
The University of Iowa	M,D
University of Kansas	M,D
University of Kentucky	M,D
University of Louisiana at Lafayette	M
University of Louisville	M,D
University of Maine	M,D
University of Maryland, Baltimore County	M,D
University of Maryland, College Park	M,D,O
University of Massachusetts Amherst	M,D
University of Massachusetts Dartmouth	M
University of Massachusetts Lowell	M
University of Memphis	M,D
University of Miami	M,D
University of Michigan	M,D,O
University of Minnesota, Twin Cities Campus	M,D
University of Missouri–Columbia	M,D
University of Missouri–Kansas City	M,D
University of Nebraska–Lincoln	M,D
University of Nevada, Las Vegas	M,D
University of Nevada, Reno	M,D
University of New Hampshire	M,D
University of New Mexico	M,D
The University of North Carolina at Charlotte	M,D
University of North Dakota	M
University of Notre Dame	M,D
University of Oklahoma	M,D
University of Pittsburgh	M,D
University of Puerto Rico, Mayagüez Campus	M,D
University of Rhode Island	M,D
University of South Carolina	M,D
University of Southern California	M,D,O
University of South Florida	M,D
The University of Tennessee	M,D
The University of Texas at Arlington	M,D
The University of Texas at Austin	M,D
The University of Texas at El Paso	M,D
The University of Texas at San Antonio	M
The University of Toledo	M,D
University of Utah	M,D
University of Vermont	M,D
University of Virginia	M,D
University of Washington	M,D
University of Wisconsin–Madison	M,D
University of Wyoming	M,D
Utah State University	M,D,O
Vanderbilt University	M,D
Villanova University	M
Virginia Polytechnic Institute and State University	M,D
Washington State University	M,D
Washington University in St. Louis	M,D
Wayne State University	M,D
West Virginia University	M,D
Widener University	M
Worcester Polytechnic Institute	M,D,O
Youngstown State University	M

■ CLASSICS

Boston College	M
Boston University	M,D
Brown University	M,D
The Catholic University of America	M,D
Columbia University	M,D
Cornell University	D
Duke University	D
Florida State University	M,D
Fordham University	M,D
Graduate School and University Center of the City University of New York	M,D
Harvard University	D
Hunter College of the City University of New York	M
Indiana University Bloomington	M,D
The Johns Hopkins University	D
Kent State University	M,D
New York University	M,D,O
The Ohio State University	M,D
Princeton University	D
Rutgers, The State University of New Jersey, New Brunswick	M,D
San Francisco State University	M
Stanford University	M,D
Texas Tech University	M
Tufts University	M
Tulane University	M
University at Buffalo, the State University of New York	M,D
The University of Arizona	M
University of California, Berkeley	M,D
University of California, Irvine	M,D
University of California, Los Angeles	M,D
University of California, Riverside	D
University of California, Santa Barbara	M,D
University of Chicago	M,D
University of Cincinnati	M,D

University of Colorado at Boulder M,D
University of Florida M,D
University of Georgia M
University of Hawaii at Manoa M
University of Illinois at Urbana–Champaign M,D
The University of Iowa M,D
University of Kansas M
University of Kentucky M
University of Maryland, College Park M
University of Massachusetts Amherst M
University of Michigan M,D,O
University of Minnesota, Twin Cities Campus M,D
University of Mississippi M
University of Missouri–Columbia M,D
University of Nebraska–Lincoln M
The University of North Carolina at Chapel Hill M,D
The University of North Carolina at Greensboro M
University of Oregon M
University of Pennsylvania M,D
University of Pittsburgh M,D
University of Southern California M,D
The University of Texas at Austin M,D
University of Vermont M
University of Virginia M,D
University of Washington M,D
University of Wisconsin–Madison M,D
University of Wisconsin–Milwaukee M
Vanderbilt University M
Villanova University M
Washington University in St. Louis M
Wayne State University M
West Chester University of Pennsylvania M
Yale University D

■ CLINICAL LABORATORY SCIENCES/MEDICAL TECHNOLOGY

The Catholic University of America M,D
Duke University M
Emory University M,D
Fairleigh Dickinson University, Metropolitan Campus M
Inter American University of Puerto Rico, Metropolitan Campus M
Long Island University, C.W. Post Campus M
Michigan State University M
Pontifical Catholic University of Puerto Rico O
Quinnipiac University M
Rochester Institute of Technology M
San Francisco State University M
University at Buffalo, the State University of New York M
The University of Alabama at Birmingham M
University of Colorado Denver M,D
University of Kentucky M,D
University of Massachusetts Lowell M
University of North Dakota M
University of Rhode Island M
University of Southern Mississippi M
University of Utah M
University of Washington M
University of Wisconsin–Milwaukee M
Virginia Commonwealth University M,D
Wayne State University M,O

■ CLINICAL PSYCHOLOGY

Abilene Christian University M
Adelphi University D,O
Alabama Agricultural and Mechanical University M,O
American International College M
American University D
Antioch University Los Angeles M
Antioch University New England M,D
Antioch University Santa Barbara D
Appalachian State University M
Argosy University, Orange County Campus M,D,O
Argosy University, Sarasota Campus M,D,O
Argosy University, Tampa Campus M,D
Argosy University, Twin Cities Campus M,D,O
Arizona State University D
Azusa Pacific University M,D
Ball State University M
Barry University M,O
Baylor University M,D
Benedictine University M
Bowling Green State University M,D
Brigham Young University M,D
California Institute of Integral Studies M,D
California Lutheran University M
California State University, Dominguez Hills M
California State University, Fullerton M
California State University, San Bernardino M
Capella University M,D,O
Cardinal Stritch University M
Carlos Albizu University M,D
Case Western Reserve University D
The Catholic University of America D
Central Michigan University D
Chestnut Hill College D
City College of the City University of New York M,D
Clark University D
Cleveland State University M,O
College of St. Joseph M
The College of William and Mary D
DePaul University M,D
Drexel University M,D
Duke University D
Duquesne University D
East Carolina University M
Eastern Illinois University M,O
Eastern Kentucky University M,O
Eastern Michigan University M,D
East Tennessee State University M
Edinboro University of Pennsylvania M
Emory University D
Emporia State University M
Fairleigh Dickinson University, College at Florham M
Fairleigh Dickinson University, Metropolitan Campus M,D
Florida Institute of Technology M,D
Florida State University D
Fordham University D
Francis Marion University M
Gallaudet University D
George Fox University M,D
George Mason University M,D
The George Washington University D
Graduate School and University Center of the City University of New York D
Hofstra University M,D
Howard University M,D
Idaho State University D
Illinois Institute of Technology M,D
Illinois State University M,D,O
Immaculata University M,D,O
Indiana State University M,D
Indiana University of Pennsylvania D
Indiana University–Purdue University Indianapolis M,D
Jackson State University D
James Madison University D
The Johns Hopkins University M,D
Kent State University M,D
Lamar University M
La Salle University M,D
Lesley University M,D,O
Long Island University, Brooklyn Campus D
Long Island University, C.W. Post Campus D
Louisiana State University and Agricultural and Mechanical College M,D
Loyola College in Maryland M,D,O
Loyola University Chicago D
Madonna University M
Marquette University M,D
Marshall University M,D
Marywood University M,D
Miami University D
Millersville University of Pennsylvania M
Minnesota State University Mankato M
Mississippi State University M,D
Montclair State University M,O
Morehead State University M
Murray State University M
Naropa University M
New College of California M
The New School: A University M,D
Norfolk State University M
North Dakota State University M,D
Northwestern State University of Louisiana M
Northwestern University D
Nova Southeastern University D,O
The Ohio State University M,D
Ohio University D
Oklahoma State University M,D
Old Dominion University D
Pace University D
Penn State Harrisburg M,D
Penn State University Park M,D
Pepperdine University M
Pontifical Catholic University of Puerto Rico M,D
Prairie View A&M University M,D
Queens College of the City University of New York M
Radford University M,D,O
Regent University M,D,O
Roosevelt University M,D
Rutgers, The State University of New Jersey, New Brunswick M,D
St. John's University (NY) D
Saint Louis University M,D
St. Mary's University of San Antonio M
Saint Michael's College M
Sam Houston State University M,D
San Diego State University M,D
San Jose State University M
Seattle Pacific University D
Southern Illinois University Carbondale M,D
Southern Illinois University Edwardsville M
Southern Methodist University M,D
Southern New Hampshire University M,O
Spalding University M,D

State University of New York at Binghamton M,D
Stony Brook University, State University of New York D
Suffolk University D
Syracuse University D
Temple University D
Texas A&M University M,D
Texas Tech University M,D
Towson University M
Troy University M
Union Institute & University D
University at Albany, State University of New York M,D,O
University at Buffalo, the State University of New York M,D
The University of Alabama D
The University of Alabama at Birmingham M,D
University of Alaska Anchorage M,D
University of Alaska Fairbanks D
University of California, San Diego D
University of California, Santa Barbara M,D
University of Central Florida M,D
University of Cincinnati D
University of Connecticut M,D
University of Dayton M
University of Delaware D
University of Denver M,D
University of Detroit Mercy M,D
University of Florida D
University of Hartford M,D
University of Hawaii at Manoa M,D,O
University of Houston M,D
University of Houston–Clear Lake M
University of Indianapolis M,D
University of Kansas M,D
University of Kentucky M,D
University of La Verne D
University of Louisville D
University of Maine M,D
University of Maryland, College Park M,D
University of Massachusetts Amherst M,D
University of Massachusetts Boston D
University of Massachusetts Dartmouth M
University of Memphis M,D
University of Miami M,D
University of Michigan D
University of Michigan–Dearborn M
University of Minnesota, Twin Cities Campus D
University of Mississippi M,D
University of Missouri–Kansas City M,D
University of Missouri–St. Louis M,D,O
The University of Montana M,D,O
University of Nevada, Las Vegas M,D
University of New Mexico M,D
The University of North Carolina at Chapel Hill D
The University of North Carolina at Charlotte M
The University of North Carolina at Greensboro M,D
University of North Dakota M,D
University of North Texas M,D
University of Oregon D
University of Pennsylvania D
University of Rhode Island D
University of Rochester M,D
University of South Carolina M,D
The University of South Dakota M,D
University of Southern California M,D
University of Southern Mississippi M,D
University of South Florida M,D
The University of Tennessee M,D
The University of Texas at El Paso M,D
The University of Texas at Tyler M
The University of Texas of the Permian Basin M
The University of Texas–Pan American M
University of the District of Columbia M
The University of Toledo M,D
University of Tulsa M,D
University of Vermont D
University of Virginia M,D,O
University of Washington D
University of Wisconsin–Madison D
University of Wisconsin–Milwaukee M,D
Utah State University M,D
Valdosta State University M,O
Valparaiso University M,O
Vanguard University of Southern California M
Virginia Commonwealth University D
Virginia Polytechnic Institute and State University M,D
Washburn University M
Washington State University M,D
Washington University in St. Louis M,D
Wayne State University M,D,O
West Chester University of Pennsylvania M
Western Carolina University M
Western Illinois University M,O
Western Michigan University M,D,O
West Virginia University M,D
Wheaton College M,D
Wichita State University M,D
Widener University D
William Paterson University of New Jersey M
Wright State University D
Xavier University M,D
Yeshiva University D

■ CLINICAL RESEARCH

Case Western Reserve University M
Duke University M
Eastern Michigan University M
Emory University M
The Johns Hopkins University M,D
New York University P,M,D
Northwestern University M,O
Tufts University M,D
University of California, Davis M
University of California, Los Angeles M
University of California, San Diego M
University of Florida M
The University of Iowa M,D
University of Louisville M,D,O
University of Michigan M
University of Minnesota, Twin Cities Campus M
University of Pittsburgh M,O
University of Virginia M
Vanderbilt University M
Washington University in St. Louis M

■ CLOTHING AND TEXTILES

Auburn University M
Cornell University M,D
Eastern Michigan University M
Florida State University M,D
Indiana State University M
Iowa State University of Science and Technology M,D
Kansas State University M,D
North Carolina State University D
The Ohio State University M,D
Oklahoma State University M,D
Oregon State University M,D
Philadelphia University M
Purdue University M,D
South Dakota State University M
The University of Akron M
The University of Alabama M
University of California, Davis M
University of Georgia M,D
University of Kentucky M
University of Minnesota, Twin Cities Campus M,D,O
University of Missouri–Columbia M
University of Nebraska–Lincoln M
University of North Texas M
University of Rhode Island M
The University of Tennessee M,D
Virginia Polytechnic Institute and State University M,D
Washington State University M,D

■ COGNITIVE SCIENCES

Arizona State University D
Ball State University M
Boston University M,D
Brandeis University M,D
Brown University M,D
Carnegie Mellon University D
Claremont Graduate University M,D,O
Cornell University D
Dartmouth College D
Duke University D
Emory University D
Florida State University D
The George Washington University D
Graduate School and University Center of the City University of New York D
Harvard University M,D
Hunter College of the City University of New York M
Indiana University Bloomington M,D
Iowa State University of Science and Technology M,D
The Johns Hopkins University D
Louisiana State University and Agricultural and Mechanical College M,D
Loyola University Chicago M
Massachusetts Institute of Technology D
Mississippi State University M,D
New Mexico Highlands University M
New York University M,D,O
North Dakota State University M,D
Northwestern University D
The Ohio State University M,D
Penn State University Park M,D
Rensselaer Polytechnic Institute D
Rice University M,D
Rutgers, The State University of New Jersey, Newark D
Rutgers, The State University of New Jersey, New Brunswick D
State University of New York at Binghamton M,D
Stevens Institute of Technology O
Temple University D
Texas A&M University M,D
University at Buffalo, the State University of New York M,D
The University of Akron M,D
University of California, San Diego D
University of Colorado at Colorado Springs M,D
University of Connecticut M,D

University of Delaware D
University of Florida M,D
University of Louisiana at Lafayette D
University of Maryland, Baltimore County D
University of Maryland, College Park D
University of Minnesota, Twin Cities Campus D
The University of North Carolina at Chapel Hill D
The University of North Carolina at Greensboro M,D
University of Notre Dame D
University of Oregon M,D
University of Pittsburgh D
University of Rochester M,D
The University of Texas at Austin M,D
The University of Texas at Dallas M,D
The University of Toledo M,D
University of Wisconsin–Madison D
Wayne State University M,D

■ COMMUNICATION—GENERAL

Abilene Christian University M
American University M
Andrews University M
Angelo State University M
Arizona State University M,D
Arizona State University at the West campus M,O
Arkansas State University M,O
Arkansas Tech University M
Auburn University M
Austin Peay State University M
Ball State University M
Barry University M,O
Baylor University M
Bellevue University M
Bethel University M,O
Boise State University M
Boston University M
Bowling Green State University M,D
Brigham Young University M
California State University, Chico M
California State University, East Bay M
California State University, Fresno M
California State University, Fullerton M
California State University, Long Beach M
California State University, Los Angeles M
California State University, Northridge M
California State University, Sacramento M
California State University, San Bernardino M
Carnegie Mellon University M,D
Central Connecticut State University M
Central Michigan University M
Clarion University of Pennsylvania M
Clark University M
Clemson University M,D
Cleveland State University M,O
The College of New Rochelle M,O
College of Notre Dame of Maryland M
Columbia University M,D
Cornell University M,D
DePaul University M
Drake University M
Drexel University M
Drury University M
Duquesne University M,D
Eastern Michigan University M
Eastern New Mexico University M
Eastern Washington University M
East Tennessee State University M
Edinboro University of Pennsylvania M
Emerson College M
Fairleigh Dickinson University, Metropolitan Campus M
Fitchburg State College M,O
Florida Atlantic University M
Florida Institute of Technology M
Florida State University M,D
Fordham University M
Fort Hays State University M
George Mason University M
Georgetown University M
Georgia State University M,D
Gonzaga University M
Governors State University M
Grand Valley State University M
Harvard University M,O
Hawai'i Pacific University M
Hofstra University M
Howard University M,D
Illinois Institute of Technology M,D
Illinois State University M
Indiana State University M
Indiana University Bloomington M,D
Indiana University–Purdue University Fort Wayne M
Ithaca College M
The Johns Hopkins University M
Kean University M
Kent State University M,D
Liberty University M
Lindenwood University M
Louisiana State University and Agricultural and Mechanical College M,D
Loyola University New Orleans M
Marquette University M
Marshall University M
Marywood University M,O
Miami University M
Michigan State University M,D
Mississippi College M
Missouri State University M
Monmouth University M,O
Montana State University–Billings M
Montclair State University M
Morehead State University M
National University M
New Mexico State University M
The New School: A University M
New York Institute of Technology M,O
New York University M,D
Norfolk State University M
North Carolina State University M
North Dakota State University M,D
Northeastern State University M
Northern Arizona University M
Northern Illinois University M
Northern Kentucky University M
Northwestern University M,D
The Ohio State University M,D
Ohio University M,D
Penn State University Park M,D
Pepperdine University M
Pittsburg State University M
Point Park University M
Polytechnic University, Brooklyn Campus O
Purdue University M,D
Purdue University Calumet M
Quinnipiac University M
Regent University M,D
Regis University M,O
Rensselaer Polytechnic Institute M,D
Rochester Institute of Technology M
Roosevelt University M
Rutgers, The State University of New Jersey, New Brunswick D
Saginaw Valley State University M
St. John's University (NY) M,O
Saint Louis University M
St. Mary's University of San Antonio M
St. Thomas University M,O
San Diego State University M
San Jose State University M
Seton Hall University M
Shippensburg University of Pennsylvania M
South Dakota State University M
Southeastern Louisiana University M
Southern Illinois University Carbondale M,D
Southern Utah University M
Spalding University M
Spring Arbor University M
Stanford University M,D
State University of New York College at Brockport M
State University of New York College of Environmental Science and Forestry M,D
Stephen F. Austin State University M
Suffolk University M
Syracuse University M,D
Temple University M,D
Texas A&M University M,D
Texas Southern University M
Texas State University-San Marcos M
Texas Tech University M
Towson University M,O
Trinity International University M
Trinity (Washington) University M
Troy University M
University at Albany, State University of New York M,D
University at Buffalo, the State University of New York M,D
The University of Akron M
The University of Alabama M,D
The University of Alabama at Birmingham M
University of Alaska Fairbanks M
The University of Arizona M,D
University of Arkansas M
University of Baltimore M,D
University of California, Davis M
University of California, San Diego M,D
University of California, Santa Barbara D
University of California, Santa Cruz O
University of Central Florida M
University of Central Missouri M
University of Cincinnati M
University of Colorado at Boulder M,D
University of Colorado at Colorado Springs M
University of Colorado Denver M
University of Connecticut M,D
University of Dayton M
University of Delaware M
University of Denver M,D,O
University of Dubuque M
University of Florida M,D
University of Georgia M,D
University of Hartford M
University of Hawaii at Manoa M,O
University of Houston M
University of Illinois at Chicago M
University of Illinois at Springfield M

Institution	Degrees
University of Illinois at Urbana–Champaign	D
The University of Iowa	M,D
University of Kansas	M,D
University of Kentucky	M,D
University of Louisiana at Lafayette	M
University of Louisiana at Monroe	M
University of Maine	M
University of Maryland, Baltimore County	M
University of Maryland, College Park	M,D
University of Massachusetts Amherst	M,D
University of Memphis	M,D
University of Miami	M,D
University of Michigan	D
University of Minnesota, Twin Cities Campus	M,D,O
University of Missouri–Columbia	M,D
University of Missouri–St. Louis	M
The University of Montana	M
University of Nebraska at Omaha	M
University of Nebraska–Lincoln	M,D
University of Nevada, Las Vegas	M
University of New Mexico	M,D
The University of North Carolina at Chapel Hill	M,D
The University of North Carolina at Charlotte	M
The University of North Carolina at Greensboro	M
University of North Dakota	M,D
University of Northern Colorado	M
University of Northern Iowa	M
University of North Texas	M
University of Oklahoma	M,D
University of Oregon	M,D
University of Pennsylvania	D
University of Pittsburgh	M,D
University of Portland	M
University of Rhode Island	M
University of South Alabama	M
The University of South Dakota	M
University of Southern California	M,D
University of South Florida	M,D
The University of Tennessee	M,D
The University of Texas at Arlington	M
The University of Texas at Austin	M,D
The University of Texas at Dallas	D
The University of Texas at El Paso	M
The University of Texas at San Antonio	M
The University of Texas at Tyler	M
The University of Texas–Pan American	M
University of the Incarnate Word	M,O
University of the Pacific	M
The University of Toledo	O
University of Utah	M,D
University of Vermont	M
University of Washington	M,D
University of West Florida	M
University of Wisconsin–Madison	M,D
University of Wisconsin–Milwaukee	M,O
University of Wisconsin–Stevens Point	M
University of Wisconsin–Superior	M
University of Wisconsin–Whitewater	M
University of Wyoming	M
Utah State University	M
Villanova University	M
Virginia Commonwealth University	D
Virginia Polytechnic Institute and State University	M
Wake Forest University	M
Washington State University	M,D
Wayne State College	M
Wayne State University	M,D
Webster University	M
West Chester University of Pennsylvania	M
Western Illinois University	M
Western Kentucky University	M
Western Michigan University	M
Westminster College (UT)	M
West Texas A&M University	M
West Virginia University	M
Wichita State University	M

■ COMMUNICATION DISORDERS

Institution	Degrees
Abilene Christian University	M
Adelphi University	M,D
Alabama Agricultural and Mechanical University	M
Appalachian State University	M
Arizona State University	M,D
Arkansas State University	M
Armstrong Atlantic State University	M
Auburn University	M,D
Ball State University	M,D
Barry University	M
Baylor University	M
Bloomsburg University of Pennsylvania	M,D
Boston University	M,D,O
Bowling Green State University	M,D
Brigham Young University	M
Brooklyn College of the City University of New York	M,D
Buffalo State College, State University of New York	M
California State University, Chico	M
California State University, East Bay	M
California State University, Fresno	M
California State University, Fullerton	M
California State University, Long Beach	M
California State University, Los Angeles	M
California State University, Northridge	M
California State University, Sacramento	M
California University of Pennsylvania	M
Canisius College	M
Carlos Albizu University	M,D
Case Western Reserve University	M,D,O
Central Michigan University	M,D
Clarion University of Pennsylvania	M
Cleveland State University	M
The College of New Jersey	M
The College of New Rochelle	M
The College of Saint Rose	M
Duquesne University	M,D
East Carolina University	M,D
Eastern Illinois University	M
Eastern Kentucky University	M
Eastern Michigan University	M
Eastern New Mexico University	M
Eastern Washington University	M
East Stroudsburg University of Pennsylvania	M
East Tennessee State University	M,D
Edinboro University of Pennsylvania	M
Emerson College	M
Florida Atlantic University	M
Florida International University	M
Florida State University	M,D
Fontbonne University	M
Fort Hays State University	M
Gallaudet University	M,D
The George Washington University	M
Georgia State University	M
Governors State University	M
Graduate School and University Center of the City University of New York	D
Hampton University	M
Harvard University	D
Hofstra University	M,D
Howard University	M,D
Hunter College of the City University of New York	M
Idaho State University	M,D
Illinois State University	M
Indiana State University	M
Indiana University Bloomington	M,D
Indiana University of Pennsylvania	M
Ithaca College	M
Jackson State University	M
James Madison University	M,D
Kean University	M
Kent State University	M,D
Lamar University	M,D
La Salle University	M
Lehman College of the City University of New York	M
Lewis & Clark College	M
Long Island University, Brooklyn Campus	M
Long Island University, C.W. Post Campus	M
Longwood University	M
Louisiana State University and Agricultural and Mechanical College	M,D
Louisiana Tech University	M
Loyola College in Maryland	M,O
Marquette University	M
Marshall University	M
Marywood University	M
Massachusetts Institute of Technology	D
Mercy College	M
Miami University	M
Michigan State University	M,D
Minnesota State University Mankato	M
Minnesota State University Moorhead	M
Minot State University	M
Misericordia University	M
Mississippi University for Women	M
Missouri State University	M,D
Montclair State University	M,D
Murray State University	M
National University	M
Nazareth College of Rochester	M
New Mexico State University	M,D
New York University	M,D
North Carolina Central University	M
Northeastern State University	M
Northeastern University	M,D
Northern Arizona University	M
Northern Illinois University	M,D
Northern Michigan University	M
Northwestern University	M,D
Nova Southeastern University	M,D
The Ohio State University	M,D
Ohio University	M,D
Oklahoma State University	M
Old Dominion University	M
Our Lady of the Lake University of San Antonio	M
Penn State University Park	M,D
Portland State University	M
Purdue University	M,D
Queens College of the City University of New York	M
Radford University	M
Rockhurst University	M

St. Cloud State University M
Saint Louis University M
Saint Xavier University M
San Diego State University M,D
San Francisco State University M
San Jose State University M
Seton Hall University M
South Carolina State University M
Southeastern Louisiana University M
Southeast Missouri State University M
Southern Connecticut State University M
Southern Illinois University Carbondale M
Southern Illinois University Edwardsville M
State University of New York at Fredonia M
State University of New York at New Paltz M
State University of New York at Plattsburgh M
State University of New York College at Geneseo M
Stephen F. Austin State University M
Syracuse University M,D
Temple University M
Tennessee State University M
Texas A&M University–Kingsville M
Texas Christian University M
Texas State University-San Marcos M
Texas Woman's University M
Towson University M,D
Truman State University M
University at Buffalo, the State University of New York M,D
The University of Akron M,D
The University of Alabama M
The University of Arizona M,D
University of Arkansas M
University of California, San Diego D
University of Central Arkansas M
University of Central Florida M,D,O
University of Central Missouri M
University of Central Oklahoma M
University of Cincinnati M,D,O
University of Colorado at Boulder M,D
University of Connecticut M,D
University of Florida M,D
University of Georgia M,D,O
University of Hawaii at Manoa M
University of Houston M
University of Illinois at Urbana–Champaign M,D
The University of Iowa M,D
University of Kansas M,D
University of Kentucky M
University of Louisiana at Lafayette M,D
University of Louisiana at Monroe M
University of Louisville M,D
University of Maine M
University of Maryland, College Park M,D
University of Massachusetts Amherst M,D
University of Memphis M,D
University of Minnesota, Duluth M
University of Minnesota, Twin Cities Campus M,D
University of Mississippi M
University of Missouri–Columbia M
University of Montevallo M
University of Nebraska at Kearney M
University of Nebraska at Omaha M
University of Nebraska–Lincoln M
University of Nevada, Reno M,D
University of New Hampshire M
University of New Mexico M
The University of North Carolina at Chapel Hill M,D
The University of North Carolina at Greensboro M,D
University of North Dakota M,D
University of Northern Colorado M,D
University of Northern Iowa M
University of North Texas M,D
University of Pittsburgh M,D
University of Redlands M
University of Rhode Island M,D
University of South Alabama M,D
University of South Carolina M,D
The University of South Dakota M,D
University of Southern Mississippi M,D
University of South Florida D
The University of Tennessee M,D,O
The University of Texas at Austin M,D
The University of Texas at Dallas M,D
The University of Texas at El Paso M
The University of Texas–Pan American M
University of the District of Columbia M
University of the Pacific M
The University of Toledo M,D,O
University of Tulsa M
University of Utah M,D
University of Virginia M
University of Washington M,D
University of West Georgia M
University of Wisconsin–Eau Claire M
University of Wisconsin–Madison M,D
University of Wisconsin–Milwaukee M
University of Wisconsin–River Falls M
University of Wisconsin–Stevens Point M,D
University of Wisconsin–Whitewater M
University of Wyoming M,D
Utah State University M,D,O
Valdosta State University M,O
Vanderbilt University M,D
Washington University in St. Louis M,D
Wayne State University M,D
West Chester University of Pennsylvania M
Western Carolina University M
Western Illinois University M
Western Kentucky University M
Western Michigan University M
Western Washington University M
West Texas A&M University M
West Virginia University M,D
Wichita State University M,D
William Paterson University of New Jersey M
Worcester State College M

■ COMMUNITY COLLEGE EDUCATION

Argosy University, Orange County Campus M,D
Argosy University, Tampa Campus M,D,O
Arkansas State University M,D,O
Colorado State University M,D
Eastern Washington University M
George Mason University D,O
Morgan State University D
North Carolina State University M,D
Northern Arizona University M,D
Old Dominion University M,D
Pittsburg State University O
Princeton University D
University of Central Florida M,D,O
University of South Florida M,D,O
Walden University M,D
Western Carolina University M

■ COMMUNITY HEALTH

Adelphi University M,O
Arcadia University M
Bloomsburg University of Pennsylvania M
Brooklyn College of the City University of New York M
Brown University M,D
Columbia University M,D
Eastern Kentucky University M
East Stroudsburg University of Pennsylvania M
East Tennessee State University M,O
The George Washington University M,O
Idaho State University O
Indiana State University M
The Johns Hopkins University M,D
Long Island University, Brooklyn Campus M
Minnesota State University Mankato M
New Jersey City University M
Old Dominion University M
Saint Louis University M
Southern Illinois University Carbondale M
Southern New Hampshire University M,O
Stony Brook University, State University of New York M,D,O
Temple University M
University at Buffalo, the State University of New York M,D
University of California, Los Angeles M,D
University of Illinois at Chicago M,D
University of Illinois at Urbana–Champaign M,D
The University of Iowa M,D
University of Miami M,D
University of Minnesota, Twin Cities Campus M
The University of North Carolina at Greensboro M,D
University of Northern Colorado M
University of Northern Iowa M,D
University of North Florida M,O
University of North Texas M
University of Pittsburgh M,D,O
University of South Florida M,D
The University of Tennessee M,D
University of Wisconsin–La Crosse M
University of Wisconsin–Madison M,D
Virginia Commonwealth University D
Wayne State University M,O
West Virginia University M

■ COMMUNITY HEALTH NURSING

Augsburg College M
Boston College M,D
Case Western Reserve University M
Cleveland State University M
D'Youville College M,O
Georgia Southern University M,O
Hawai'i Pacific University M
Holy Names University M
Hunter College of the City University of New York M
Indiana University–Purdue University Indianapolis M,D
Indiana Wesleyan University M,O
The Johns Hopkins University M
Kean University M
La Salle University M,O
New Mexico State University M
Northeastern University M,O

Rutgers, The State University of New Jersey, Newark M
Saint Xavier University M,O
Seattle University M
Southern Illinois University Edwardsville M,O
University of Cincinnati M,D
University of Colorado at Colorado Springs M,D
University of Connecticut M,D,O
University of Hartford M
University of Hawaii at Manoa M,D,O
University of Illinois at Chicago M
University of Massachusetts Dartmouth M,D,O
University of Massachusetts Lowell M
University of Michigan M
University of Minnesota, Twin Cities Campus M
The University of North Carolina at Chapel Hill M
The University of North Carolina at Charlotte M
University of South Alabama M,D
University of South Carolina M
University of Southern Mississippi M,D
The University of Texas at Brownsville M
The University of Texas at El Paso M
Wayne State University M
Worcester State College M
Wright State University M

■ COMPARATIVE AND INTERDISCIPLINARY ARTS

Bradley University M
Brigham Young University M
Columbia College Chicago M
Florida Atlantic University D
Goddard College M
John F. Kennedy University M
Ohio University D

■ COMPARATIVE LITERATURE

American University M
Antioch University McGregor M
Arizona State University M,D
Brigham Young University M
Brown University M,D
California State University, Fullerton M
California State University, Northridge M
Carnegie Mellon University M,D
Case Western Reserve University M,D
The Catholic University of America M,D
Claremont Graduate University M,D
Columbia University M,D
Cornell University D
Dartmouth College M
Duke University D
Emory University D,O
Fairleigh Dickinson University, Metropolitan Campus M
Florida Atlantic University M
Graduate School and University Center of the City University of New York M,D
Harvard University D
Hofstra University M
Indiana University Bloomington M,D
The Johns Hopkins University D
Kent State University M,D
Long Island University, Brooklyn Campus M
Louisiana State University and Agricultural and Mechanical College M,D
New York University M,D
Northwestern University M,D,O
Oklahoma City University M
Penn State University Park M,D
Princeton University D
Purdue University M,D
Rutgers, The State University of New Jersey, New Brunswick M,D
San Francisco State University M
San Jose State University M,O
Stanford University D
State University of New York at Binghamton M,D
Stony Brook University, State University of New York M,D
University at Buffalo, the State University of New York M,D
The University of Arizona M,D
University of Arkansas M,D
University of California, Berkeley D
University of California, Davis D
University of California, Irvine M,D
University of California, Los Angeles M,D
University of California, Riverside M,D
University of California, San Diego M,D
University of California, Santa Barbara D
University of California, Santa Cruz M,D
University of Chicago M,D
University of Colorado at Boulder M,D
University of Connecticut M,D
University of Dallas D
University of Georgia M,D
University of Illinois at Urbana–Champaign M,D
The University of Iowa M,D
University of Maryland, College Park M,D
University of Massachusetts Amherst M,D
University of Michigan D
University of Minnesota, Twin Cities Campus D
University of Missouri–Columbia M,D
University of New Hampshire M,D
University of New Mexico M,D
The University of North Carolina at Chapel Hill M,D
University of Notre Dame D
University of Oregon M,D
University of Pennsylvania M,D
University of Puerto Rico, Río Piedras M
University of South Carolina M,D
University of Southern California M,D
The University of Texas at Austin M,D
The University of Texas at Dallas M,D
University of Utah M,D
University of Washington M,D
University of Wisconsin–Madison M,D
University of Wisconsin–Milwaukee M,D,O
Washington University in St. Louis M,D
Wayne State University M
Western Kentucky University M
West Virginia University M
Yale University D

■ COMPUTATIONAL BIOLOGY

Arizona State University M
Carnegie Mellon University M,D
Claremont Graduate University M,D
Florida State University D
George Mason University M,D,O
Iowa State University of Science and Technology D
Massachusetts Institute of Technology D
New Jersey Institute of Technology M
New York University D
Northwestern University M
Princeton University D
Rutgers, The State University of New Jersey, Newark M
Rutgers, The State University of New Jersey, New Brunswick D
University of Idaho M,D
University of Illinois at Urbana–Champaign D
The University of Iowa M,D,O
University of Pennsylvania D
University of Pittsburgh D
University of Rochester M,D
University of Southern California D
Virginia Polytechnic Institute and State University D
Washington University in St. Louis D
Yale University D

■ COMPUTATIONAL SCIENCES

Arizona State University M,D
California Institute of Technology M,D
Carnegie Mellon University M,D
Claremont Graduate University M,D
Clemson University M,D
The College of William and Mary M
Cornell University M,D
George Mason University M,D,O
Kean University M
Lehigh University M,D
Louisiana Tech University M,D
Massachusetts Institute of Technology M
Michigan Technological University D
Northwestern University M
Princeton University D
Rice University M,D
Sam Houston State University M
San Diego State University M,D
South Dakota State University M,D
Southern Methodist University M,D
Stanford University M,D
State University of New York College at Brockport M
Temple University M,D
University of Alaska Fairbanks M,D
University of Central Florida M,D
The University of Iowa D
University of Massachusetts Lowell M,D
University of Michigan–Dearborn M
University of Minnesota, Duluth M
University of Minnesota, Twin Cities Campus M,D
University of Mississippi M,D
University of Nevada, Las Vegas M,D
University of Puerto Rico, Mayagüez Campus M
The University of South Dakota D
University of Southern Mississippi M,D
University of South Florida M,D
The University of Tennessee at Chattanooga D
The University of Texas at Austin M,D
University of Utah M
Western Michigan University M

■ COMPUTER AND INFORMATION SYSTEMS SECURITY

American InterContinental University (FL) M
Benedictine University M
Capella University M,D,O
Carnegie Mellon University M
Colorado Technical University—Colorado Springs M,D
Colorado Technical University—Denver M

Colorado Technical University—Sioux Falls	M
DePaul University	M,D
Eastern Illinois University	M,O
Eastern Michigan University	M
The Johns Hopkins University	M,O
Marymount University	M,O
New Jersey City University	M
Northern Kentucky University	M,O
Nova Southeastern University	M
Polytechnic University, Brooklyn Campus	O
Purdue University	M
Rochester Institute of Technology	M
Sacred Heart University	M,O
Saint Leo University	M
Stevens Institute of Technology	M,D,O
Syracuse University	O
Towson University	O
University of St. Thomas (MN)	M,O
University of Wisconsin–Madison	M
Worcester Polytechnic Institute	M,O

■ COMPUTER ART AND DESIGN

Alfred University	M
Bowling Green State University	M
Carnegie Mellon University	M
Chatham University	M
Claremont Graduate University	M
Clemson University	M
Columbia University	M
Cornell University	M,D
DePaul University	M,D
East Tennessee State University	M
Indiana University Bloomington	M,D
Long Island University, Brooklyn Campus	M
Long Island University, C.W. Post Campus	M
Mississippi State University	M
National University	M
New Mexico Highlands University	M
The New School: A University	M
New York University	M
Philadelphia University	M
Rensselaer Polytechnic Institute	M,D
Rochester Institute of Technology	M
St. Edward's University	M
San Jose State University	M
Syracuse University	M
University of Baltimore	M,D
University of California, Santa Cruz	M
University of Central Florida	M
University of Denver	M
University of Florida	M,D
University of Missouri–Columbia	M
University of Pennsylvania	M
Washington State University	M

■ COMPUTER EDUCATION

Arcadia University	M,D,O
California State University, Dominguez Hills	M,O
California State University, Los Angeles	M
Cardinal Stritch University	M
DeSales University	M,O
Eastern Washington University	M
Florida Institute of Technology	M,D,O
Fontbonne University	M
Jacksonville University	M
Kean University	M
Lesley University	M,D,O
Long Island University, C.W. Post Campus	M
Mississippi College	M,O
Morningside College	M
Nova Southeastern University	M,D,O
Ohio University	M,D
Providence College	M
Southern New Hampshire University	M,O
Stanford University	M,D
Stony Brook University, State University of New York	M
University of Bridgeport	M,O
University of Central Oklahoma	M
University of Maryland, Baltimore County	M,O
University of Michigan	M,D
University of North Texas	M,D
University of Phoenix–Fort Lauderdale Campus	M
University of Phoenix–North Florida Campus	M
The University of Texas at Tyler	M
Wilkes University	M,D
Wright State University	M

■ COMPUTER ENGINEERING

Arizona State University at the Polytechnic Campus	M
Auburn University	M,D
Baylor University	M
Boise State University	M,D
Boston University	M,D
California State University, Chico	M
California State University, East Bay	M
California State University, Long Beach	M
Carnegie Mellon University	M,D
Case Western Reserve University	M,D
Clarkson University	M,D
Clemson University	M,D
Colorado Technical University—Colorado Springs	M
Colorado Technical University—Denver	M
Columbia University	M,D,O
Cornell University	M,D
Dartmouth College	M,D
Drexel University	M
Duke University	M,D
Fairfield University	M
Fairleigh Dickinson University, Metropolitan Campus	M
Florida Atlantic University	M,D
Florida Institute of Technology	M,D
Florida International University	M
George Mason University	M,D
The George Washington University	M,D
Georgia Institute of Technology	M,D
Grand Valley State University	M
Illinois Institute of Technology	M,D
Indiana State University	M
Indiana University–Purdue University Indianapolis	M,D
Iowa State University of Science and Technology	M,D
The Johns Hopkins University	M,D
Kansas State University	M,D
Lawrence Technological University	M,D
Lehigh University	M,D
Louisiana State University and Agricultural and Mechanical College	M,D
Manhattan College	M
Marquette University	M,D
Massachusetts Institute of Technology	M,D,O
Mercer University	M
Michigan Technological University	D
Mississippi State University	M,D
Missouri University of Science and Technology	M,D
New Jersey Institute of Technology	M,D
New Mexico State University	M,D
New York Institute of Technology	M
Norfolk State University	M
North Carolina State University	M,D
Northeastern University	M,D
Northwestern University	M,D,O
Oakland University	M
Oklahoma State University	M,D
Old Dominion University	M,D
Oregon State University	M,D
Penn State University Park	M,D
Polytechnic University, Brooklyn Campus	M,O
Polytechnic University, Westchester Graduate Center	M
Portland State University	M,D
Purdue University	M,D
Rensselaer Polytechnic Institute	M,D
Rice University	M,D
Rochester Institute of Technology	M
Rutgers, The State University of New Jersey, New Brunswick	M,D
St. Mary's University of San Antonio	M
San Jose State University	M
Santa Clara University	M,D,O
Southern Illinois University Carbondale	M,D
Southern Methodist University	M,D
Southern Polytechnic State University	M
State University of New York at New Paltz	M
Stevens Institute of Technology	M,D,O
Stony Brook University, State University of New York	M,D
Syracuse University	M,D,O
Temple University	M
Texas A&M University	M,D
The University of Akron	M,D
The University of Alabama	M,D
The University of Alabama at Birmingham	D
The University of Alabama in Huntsville	M,D
University of Alaska Fairbanks	M,D
The University of Arizona	M,D
University of Arkansas	M,D
University of Bridgeport	M,D
University of California, Davis	M,D
University of California, Riverside	M,D
University of California, San Diego	M,D
University of California, Santa Barbara	M,D
University of California, Santa Cruz	M,D
University of Central Florida	M,D
University of Cincinnati	M,D
University of Colorado at Boulder	M,D
University of Colorado Denver	M,D
University of Dayton	M,D
University of Delaware	M,D
University of Denver	M,D
University of Florida	M,D,O
University of Houston	M,D
University of Houston–Clear Lake	M
University of Idaho	M
University of Illinois at Chicago	M,D
University of Illinois at Urbana–Champaign	M,D
The University of Iowa	M,D
University of Kansas	M
University of Louisiana at Lafayette	M,D
University of Louisville	M,D

University of Maine M,D
University of Maryland, Baltimore County M,D
University of Maryland, College Park M,D
University of Massachusetts Amherst M,D
University of Massachusetts Dartmouth M,D,O
University of Massachusetts Lowell M
University of Memphis M,D
University of Miami M,D
University of Michigan M,D
University of Michigan–Dearborn M
University of Minnesota, Duluth M
University of Minnesota, Twin Cities Campus M,D
University of Missouri–Kansas City M,D
University of Nebraska–Lincoln M,D
University of Nevada, Las Vegas M,D
University of Nevada, Reno M,D
University of New Mexico M,D
The University of North Carolina at Charlotte M,D
University of Notre Dame M,D
University of Oklahoma M,D
University of Puerto Rico, Mayagüez Campus M
University of Rochester M,D
University of South Carolina M,D
University of Southern California M,D
University of South Florida M,D
The University of Tennessee M,D
The University of Texas at Arlington M,D
The University of Texas at Austin M,D
The University of Texas at Dallas M,D
The University of Texas at El Paso M,D
University of Virginia M,D
University of Washington, Tacoma M
Villanova University M,O
Virginia Polytechnic Institute and State University M,D
Walden University M,O
Washington State University M,D
Washington University in St. Louis M,D
Wayne State University M,D
Western Michigan University M,D
Western New England College M
West Virginia University D
Widener University M
Worcester Polytechnic Institute M,D,O
Wright State University M,D

■ COMPUTER SCIENCE

Alabama Agricultural and Mechanical University M
Alcorn State University M
American University M,O
Appalachian State University M
Arizona State University M,D
Arizona State University at the Polytechnic Campus M
Arkansas State University M
Armstrong Atlantic State University M
Auburn University M,D
Ball State University M
Baylor University M
Boise State University M
Boston University M,D
Bowie State University M,D
Bowling Green State University M
Bradley University M
Brandeis University M,D,O
Bridgewater State College M
Brigham Young University M,D
Brooklyn College of the City University of New York M,D
Brown University M,D
California Institute of Technology M,D
California Polytechnic State University, San Luis Obispo M
California State Polytechnic University, Pomona M
California State University, Chico M
California State University, East Bay M
California State University, Fresno M
California State University, Fullerton M
California State University, Long Beach M
California State University, Los Angeles M
California State University, Northridge M
California State University, Sacramento M
California State University, San Bernardino M
California State University, San Marcos M
Carnegie Mellon University M,D
Case Western Reserve University M,D
The Catholic University of America M,D
Central Connecticut State University M
Central Michigan University M
Chicago State University M
The Citadel, The Military College of South Carolina M
City College of the City University of New York M,D
City University of Seattle M,O
Clark Atlanta University M
Clarkson University M,D
Clemson University M,D
College of Charleston M
The College of Saint Rose M
College of Staten Island of the City University of New York M
The College of William and Mary M,D
Colorado School of Mines M,D
Colorado State University M,D
Colorado Technical University—Colorado Springs M,D
Colorado Technical University—Denver M
Colorado Technical University—Sioux Falls M
Columbia University M,D,O
Columbus State University M
Cornell University M,D
Dartmouth College M,D
DePaul University M,D
Drexel University M,D
Duke University M,D
East Carolina University M,D,O
Eastern Illinois University M,O
Eastern Michigan University M
Eastern Washington University M
East Stroudsburg University of Pennsylvania M
East Tennessee State University M
Elmhurst College M
Emory University M,D
Fairleigh Dickinson University, Metropolitan Campus M
Ferris State University M
Fitchburg State College M
Florida Atlantic University M,D
Florida Gulf Coast University M
Florida Institute of Technology M,D
Florida International University M,D
Florida State University M,D
Fordham University M
Frostburg State University M
Gannon University M
George Mason University M,D
Georgetown University M
The George Washington University M,D,O
Georgia Institute of Technology M,D
Georgia Southwestern State University M
Georgia State University M,D
Governors State University M
Graduate School and University Center of the City University of New York D
Grand Valley State University M
Hampton University M
Harvard University M,D
Hofstra University M
Hood College M
Howard University M
Illinois Institute of Technology M,D
Indiana State University M
Indiana University Bloomington M,D
Indiana University–Purdue University Fort Wayne M
Indiana University–Purdue University Indianapolis M,D
Indiana University South Bend M
Inter American University of Puerto Rico, Metropolitan Campus M
Iona College M
Iowa State University of Science and Technology M,D
Jackson State University M
Jacksonville State University M
James Madison University M
The Johns Hopkins University M,D
Kansas State University M,D
Kennesaw State University M
Kent State University M,D
Kutztown University of Pennsylvania M
Lamar University M
La Salle University M
Lawrence Technological University M
Lehigh University M,D
Lehman College of the City University of New York M
Long Island University, Brooklyn Campus M
Long Island University, C.W. Post Campus M
Louisiana State University and Agricultural and Mechanical College M,D
Louisiana Tech University M
Loyola College in Maryland M
Loyola Marymount University M
Loyola University Chicago M
Maharishi University of Management M
Marist College M,O
Marquette University M,D
Marymount University M,O
Massachusetts Institute of Technology M,D,O
McNeese State University M
Michigan State University M,D
Michigan Technological University M,D
Middle Tennessee State University M
Midwestern State University M
Mills College M,O
Minnesota State University Mankato M,O
Mississippi College M
Mississippi State University M,D
Missouri State University M
Missouri University of Science and Technology M,D
Monmouth University M
Montana State University M,D
Montclair State University M,O
National University M

New Jersey Institute of Technology M,D
New Mexico Highlands University M
New Mexico Institute of Mining and Technology M,D
New Mexico State University M,D
New York Institute of Technology M
New York University M,D
Nicholls State University M
Norfolk State University M
North Carolina Agricultural and Technical State University M
North Carolina State University M,D
North Central College M
North Dakota State University M,D,O
Northeastern Illinois University M
Northeastern University M,D
Northern Illinois University M
Northern Kentucky University M
Northwestern University M,D,O
Northwest Missouri State University M
Nova Southeastern University M,D
Oakland University M
The Ohio State University M,D
Ohio University M,D
Oklahoma City University M
Oklahoma State University M,D
Old Dominion University M,D
Pace University M,D,O
Penn State Harrisburg M
Penn State University Park M,D
Polytechnic University, Brooklyn Campus M,D
Polytechnic University, Westchester Graduate Center M,D
Portland State University M,D
Prairie View A&M University M,D
Princeton University M,D
Purdue University M,D
Queens College of the City University of New York M
Regis University M,O
Rensselaer Polytechnic Institute M,D
Rice University M,D
Rivier College M
Rochester Institute of Technology M,O
Roosevelt University M
Rutgers, The State University of New Jersey, Camden M
Rutgers, The State University of New Jersey, New Brunswick M,D
Sacred Heart University M,O
St. Cloud State University M
St. John's University (NY) M
Saint Joseph's University M,O
St. Mary's University of San Antonio M
Saint Xavier University M
Sam Houston State University M
San Diego State University M
San Francisco State University M
San Jose State University M,O
Santa Clara University M,D,O
Shippensburg University of Pennsylvania M
Southeastern University M
Southern Connecticut State University M
Southern Illinois University Carbondale M,D
Southern Illinois University Edwardsville M
Southern Methodist University M,D
Southern Oregon University M
Southern Polytechnic State University M
Southern University and Agricultural and Mechanical College M
Stanford University M,D
State University of New York at Binghamton M,D
State University of New York at New Paltz M
State University of New York Institute of Technology M
Stephen F. Austin State University M
Stevens Institute of Technology M,D,O
Stony Brook University, State University of New York M,D,O
Suffolk University M
Syracuse University M,D,O
Temple University M,D
Tennessee Technological University M
Texas A&M University M,D
Texas A&M University–Commerce M
Texas A&M University–Corpus Christi M
Texas A&M University–Kingsville M
Texas Southern University M
Texas State University-San Marcos M
Texas Tech University M,D
Towson University M
Troy University M
Tufts University M,D,O
Tulane University M,D
University at Albany, State University of New York M,D
University at Buffalo, the State University of New York M,D
The University of Akron M
The University of Alabama M,D
The University of Alabama at Birmingham M,D
The University of Alabama in Huntsville M,D,O
University of Alaska Fairbanks M
The University of Arizona M,D
University of Arkansas M,D
University of Arkansas at Little Rock M
University of Bridgeport M,D
University of California, Berkeley M,D
University of California, Davis M,D
University of California, Irvine M,D
University of California, Los Angeles M,D
University of California, Riverside M,D
University of California, San Diego M,D
University of California, Santa Cruz M,D
University of Central Arkansas M
University of Central Florida M,D
University of Central Oklahoma M
University of Chicago M
University of Cincinnati M,D
University of Colorado at Boulder M,D
University of Colorado at Colorado Springs M,D
University of Colorado Denver M,D
University of Connecticut M,D
University of Dayton M
University of Delaware M,D
University of Denver M,D,O
University of Detroit Mercy M
University of Evansville M
University of Florida M,D
University of Georgia M,D
University of Hawaii at Manoa M,D
University of Houston M,D
University of Houston–Clear Lake M
University of Houston–Victoria M
University of Idaho M,D
University of Illinois at Chicago M,D
University of Illinois at Springfield M
University of Illinois at Urbana–Champaign M,D
The University of Iowa M,D
University of Kansas M,D
University of Kentucky M,D
University of Louisiana at Lafayette M,D
University of Louisville M,D
University of Maine M,D
University of Maryland, Baltimore County M,D
University of Maryland, College Park M,D
University of Maryland Eastern Shore M
University of Massachusetts Amherst M,D
University of Massachusetts Boston M,D
University of Massachusetts Dartmouth M,O
University of Massachusetts Lowell M,D
University of Memphis M,D
University of Miami M
University of Michigan M,D
University of Michigan–Dearborn M
University of Michigan–Flint M
University of Minnesota, Duluth M
University of Minnesota, Twin Cities Campus M,D
University of Missouri–Columbia M,D
University of Missouri–Kansas City M,D
University of Missouri–St. Louis M,D
The University of Montana M
University of Nebraska at Omaha M
University of Nebraska–Lincoln M,D
University of Nevada, Las Vegas M,D
University of Nevada, Reno M,D
University of New Hampshire M,D
University of New Haven M
University of New Mexico M,D
University of New Orleans M
The University of North Carolina at Chapel Hill M,D
The University of North Carolina at Charlotte M
The University of North Carolina at Greensboro M
The University of North Carolina Wilmington M
University of North Dakota M
University of Northern Iowa M
University of North Florida M
University of North Texas M,D
University of Notre Dame M,D
University of Oklahoma M,D
University of Oregon M,D
University of Pennsylvania M,D
University of Pittsburgh M,D
University of Rhode Island M,D,O
University of Rochester M,D
University of San Francisco M
University of South Alabama M
University of South Carolina M,D
The University of South Dakota M,D
University of Southern California M,D
University of Southern Maine M
University of Southern Mississippi M,D
University of South Florida M,D
The University of Tennessee M,D
The University of Tennessee at Chattanooga M,O
The University of Texas at Arlington M,D
The University of Texas at Austin M,D
The University of Texas at Dallas M,D
The University of Texas at El Paso M
The University of Texas at San Antonio M,D
The University of Texas at Tyler M
The University of Texas–Pan American M
The University of Toledo M,D
University of Tulsa M,D

University of Utah M,D
University of Vermont M,D
University of Virginia M,D
University of Washington M,D
University of West Florida M
University of West Georgia M
University of Wisconsin–Madison M,D
University of Wisconsin–Milwaukee M,D
University of Wisconsin–Platteville M
University of Wyoming M,D
Utah State University M,D
Vanderbilt University M,D
Villanova University M,O
Virginia Commonwealth University M,D,O
Virginia Polytechnic Institute and State University M,D
Wake Forest University M
Walden University M,O
Washington State University M,D
Washington University in St. Louis M,D
Wayne State University M,D,O
Webster University M,O
West Chester University of Pennsylvania M,O
Western Carolina University M
Western Illinois University M
Western Kentucky University M
Western Michigan University M,D
Western Washington University M
West Virginia University M,D
Wichita State University M
Worcester Polytechnic Institute M,D,O
Wright State University M,D
Yale University D

■ CONDENSED MATTER PHYSICS

Cleveland State University M
Emory University D
Iowa State University of Science and Technology M,D
Rutgers, The State University of New Jersey, New Brunswick M,D
West Virginia University M,D

■ CONFLICT RESOLUTION AND MEDIATION/PEACE STUDIES

Abilene Christian University M,O
American University M,D,O
Antioch University McGregor M
Arcadia University M
Brandeis University M
California State University, Dominguez Hills M
Chaminade University of Honolulu M
Columbia College (SC) M,O
Cornell University M,D
Creighton University M
Dallas Baptist University M
Duquesne University M,O
Eastern Mennonite University M,O
Florida International University O
Fresno Pacific University M
George Mason University M,D
Georgetown University M,D
The Johns Hopkins University M,D,O
Kennesaw State University M
Lipscomb University M,O
Montclair State University M,O
Nova Southeastern University M,D
Pepperdine University M
Portland State University M
Regis University M,O
St. Edward's University M,O
School for International Training M
Sullivan University M
Tufts University M,D
University of Baltimore M
University of Denver M
University of Hawaii at Manoa O
University of Massachusetts Boston M,O
University of Missouri–Columbia M
University of Missouri–St. Louis M
The University of North Carolina at Greensboro M,O
University of Notre Dame M
University of Pittsburgh M
University of San Diego M
Wayne State University M,O
Woodbury University M,O

■ CONSERVATION BIOLOGY

Arizona State University M,D
Central Michigan University M
Columbia University M,D,O
Frostburg State University M
Illinois State University M,D
North Dakota State University M,D
Oklahoma State University M,D
San Francisco State University M
State University of New York College of Environmental Science and Forestry M,D
Texas State University-San Marcos M
University at Albany, State University of New York M
University of Central Florida M,D,O
University of Hawaii at Manoa M,D
University of Maryland, College Park M
University of Michigan M,D
University of Minnesota, Twin Cities Campus M,D
University of Missouri–St. Louis M,D,O
University of Nevada, Reno D
University of Wisconsin–Madison M

■ CONSTRUCTION ENGINEERING

Arizona State University M
Auburn University M,D
Bradley University M
Carnegie Mellon University M,D
Columbia University M,D,O
Illinois Institute of Technology M,D
Iowa State University of Science and Technology M,D
Lawrence Technological University M,D
Massachusetts Institute of Technology M,D,O
Missouri University of Science and Technology M,D
Ohio University M,D
Oregon State University M,D
Southern Polytechnic State University M
Stevens Institute of Technology M,O
Texas A&M University M,D
The University of Alabama M,D
University of Colorado at Boulder M,D
University of Florida M,D
University of Michigan M,D,O
University of Nevada, Las Vegas M,D
University of Southern California M
University of Southern Mississippi M
University of Washington M,D
Virginia Polytechnic Institute and State University M
Western Michigan University M

■ CONSTRUCTION MANAGEMENT

Auburn University M
Bowling Green State University M
Brigham Young University M
The Catholic University of America M,D
Central Connecticut State University M
Clemson University M
Colorado State University M
Columbia University M,D,O
Eastern Michigan University M
Florida International University M
Marquette University M,D
Michigan State University M,D
New York University M,O
Polytechnic University, Brooklyn Campus M
State University of New York College of Environmental Science and Forestry M,D
Stevens Institute of Technology M,O
Texas A&M University M,D
University of Cincinnati M,D
University of Denver M
University of Kansas M
University of Nevada, Las Vegas M,D
University of New Mexico M,D
University of Southern California M
University of Washington M
Washington University in St. Louis M
Western Carolina University M
Western Michigan University M
Worcester Polytechnic Institute M,D,O

■ CONSUMER ECONOMICS

California State University, Long Beach M
Colorado State University M
Cornell University M,D
Eastern Illinois University M
Florida State University M,D
Indiana State University M
Iowa State University of Science and Technology M,D
North Dakota State University M,D
The Ohio State University M,D
Purdue University M,D
State University of New York at Oswego M
Texas Tech University D
The University of Alabama M
The University of Arizona M,D
University of Georgia M,D
University of Idaho M
University of Illinois at Urbana–Champaign M,D
University of Missouri–Columbia M
University of Nebraska–Lincoln M,D
University of South Carolina M
The University of Tennessee M,D
University of Utah M
University of Wisconsin–Madison M,D
University of Wyoming M
Utah State University M
Virginia Polytechnic Institute and State University M,D

■ CORPORATE AND ORGANIZATIONAL COMMUNICATION

Antioch University Seattle M
Barry University M,O
Bernard M. Baruch College of the City University of New York M
Bowie State University M,O
Canisius College M
Central Connecticut State University M
Central Michigan University M
College of Charleston O

Columbia University M
Concordia University Wisconsin M
Dallas Baptist University M
DePaul University M
Emerson College M
Fairleigh Dickinson University, College at Florham M
Florida State University M,D
Fordham University M
Hawai'i Pacific University M
Howard University M,D
Illinois Institute of Technology M
Iowa State University of Science and Technology M,D
John Carroll University M
La Salle University M
Loyola University Chicago M
Manhattanville College M
Marist College M
Marywood University M,O
Metropolitan College of New York M
Mississippi College M
Monmouth University M,O
Montclair State University M
Murray State University M
New Mexico State University M,D
New York University M
North Carolina State University M
Northwestern University M
Oklahoma City University M
Queens University of Charlotte M
Radford University M
Regis College (MA) M
Roosevelt University M
Seton Hall University M
Simmons College M
Southern Illinois University Edwardsville O
Spalding University M
Stevens Institute of Technology O
Syracuse University M
Temple University M,D
Towson University M
University of Alaska Fairbanks M
University of Arkansas at Little Rock M
University of Connecticut M,D
University of Portland M
University of St. Thomas (MN) M
University of Southern California M,D
University of Wisconsin–Stevens Point M
University of Wisconsin–Whitewater M
Washington State University M,D
Wayne State University M,D
Webster University M
Western Michigan University M
West Virginia University M

■ COUNSELING PSYCHOLOGY

Abilene Christian University M
Adelphi University M
Alabama Agricultural and Mechanical University M,O
Alaska Pacific University M
Amberton University M
Andrews University D
Angelo State University M
Anna Maria College M
Antioch University McGregor M
Antioch University New England M
Antioch University Santa Barbara M
Argosy University, Orange County Campus M,D
Argosy University, Sarasota Campus M,D,O
Argosy University, Tampa Campus M,D
Arizona State University D
Assumption College M,O
Auburn University M,D,O
Avila University M
Ball State University M,D
Bemidji State University M
Bethel University M,O
Boston College M,D
Boston University M,D
Bowie State University M
Bowling Green State University M
Brigham Young University M,D,O
Brooklyn College of the City University of New York M,D,O
Caldwell College M
California Baptist University M
California Institute of Integral Studies M,D
California State University, Bakersfield M
California State University, Sacramento M
California State University, San Bernardino M
Cambridge College M,O
Capella University M,D,O
Carlow University M
Centenary College M
Central Washington University M
Chaminade University of Honolulu M
Chatham University M
Chestnut Hill College M,O
City University of Seattle M
Cleveland State University D
The College of New Rochelle M,O
College of Saint Elizabeth M,O
College of St. Joseph M
Colorado Christian University M
Columbus State University M,O
Concordia University Chicago (IL) M
Concordia University Wisconsin M
Dallas Baptist University M
Dominican University of California M
Eastern Nazarene College M
Eastern University M
Eastern Washington University M
Emporia State University M
Fitchburg State College M,O
Florida Atlantic University M,O
Florida International University M
Florida State University M,D,O
Fordham University M,D,O
Fort Valley State University M
Franciscan University of Steubenville M
Frostburg State University M
Gallaudet University M
Gannon University D
Gardner-Webb University M
Geneva College M
George Fox University M,O
Georgian Court University M,O
Georgia State University M,D,O
Goddard College M
Gonzaga University M
Governors State University M
Harding University M
Heidelberg College M
Hofstra University M,O
Holy Family University M
Holy Names University M,O
Hope International University M
Houston Baptist University M
Howard University M,D,O
Idaho State University M,D,O
Illinois State University M,D,O
Immaculata University M,D,O
Indiana State University M,D
Indiana University Bloomington M,D,O
Indiana Wesleyan University M
Inter American University of Puerto Rico, San Germán Campus M,D
Iona College M
Iowa State University of Science and Technology M,D
James Madison University M,O
John Carroll University M,O
John F. Kennedy University M
Kean University M
Kent State University M
Kutztown University of Pennsylvania M
La Salle University M
Lee University M
Lehigh University M,D,O
Lesley University M
Lewis & Clark College M,O
Lewis University M
Liberty University M,D
Lindenwood University M,D,O
Lipscomb University M,O
Louisiana State University in Shreveport M,O
Louisiana Tech University M,D
Loyola College in Maryland M,O
Loyola University Chicago D
Marist College M,O
Marylhurst University M,O
Marymount University M,O
Marywood University M
McNeese State University M
Medaille College M
Mercy College M,O
MidAmerica Nazarene University M
Mississippi College M,O
Monmouth University M,O
Morehead State University M
Mount St. Mary's College M
Naropa University M
National University M
New Jersey City University M,O
New Mexico State University M,D,O
New York Institute of Technology M
New York University M,D,O
Nicholls State University M,O
Northeastern State University M
Northeastern University M,D,O
Northern Arizona University D
Northwestern University M
Notre Dame de Namur University M,O
Nova Southeastern University M
Oakland University M,D,O
Our Lady of the Lake University of San Antonio M,D
Palm Beach Atlantic University M
Penn State University Park M,D
Prescott College M
Radford University M,D,O
Regent University M,D,O
Regis University M,O
Rivier College M,O
Rosemont College M
Rowan University M,O
Rutgers, The State University of New Jersey, New Brunswick M
St. Edward's University M
St. John Fisher College M
Saint Joseph College M,O
Saint Martin's University M
Saint Mary's University of Minnesota M
St. Mary's University of San Antonio M,D,O
St. Thomas University M
Saint Xavier University M,O
Salem State College M

Salve Regina University M,O
San Francisco State University M
Santa Clara University M,O
Seton Hall University M,D
Sonoma State University M
Southern Illinois University Carbondale M,D
Southern Methodist University M
Southern Nazarene University M
Spring Arbor University M
Springfield College M,O
Stanford University D
State University of New York at New Paltz M
State University of New York at Oswego M,O
State University of New York College at Brockport M,O
Tarleton State University M
Temple University M,D
Tennessee State University M,D
Texas A&M International University M
Texas A&M University M,D
Texas A&M University–Commerce M,D
Texas A&M University–Texarkana M
Texas Tech University M,D
Texas Wesleyan University M
Texas Woman's University M,D,O
Towson University M,O
Trevecca Nazarene University M
Trinity International University P,M,D,O
University at Albany, State University of New York M,D,O
University at Buffalo, the State University of New York M,D,O
The University of Akron M,D
University of Baltimore M
University of California, Santa Barbara M,D
University of Central Arkansas M
University of Central Oklahoma M
University of Colorado Denver M,O
University of Connecticut M,D
University of Denver M,D,O
University of Florida M,D
University of Great Falls M
University of Houston M,D
University of Indianapolis M,D
The University of Iowa M,D,O
University of Kansas M,D
University of Kentucky M,D,O
University of La Verne M
University of Louisville M,D
University of Mary Hardin-Baylor M
University of Maryland, College Park M,D,O
University of Massachusetts Boston M,O
University of Memphis M,D
University of Miami D
University of Minnesota, Twin Cities Campus D
University of Missouri–Columbia M,D,O
University of Missouri–Kansas City M,D,O
The University of Montana M,D,O
The University of North Carolina at Greensboro M,D,O
University of North Dakota M
University of Northern Colorado D
University of North Florida M
University of North Texas M,D
University of Notre Dame D
University of Oklahoma D
University of Pennsylvania M
University of Phoenix–Las Vegas Campus M
University of Phoenix–Utah Campus M
University of Rhode Island M
University of Saint Francis (IN) M
University of St. Thomas (MN) M,D,O
University of San Francisco M,D
The University of Scranton M,O
University of Southern California M
University of Southern Mississippi M,D
The University of Tennessee M,D
The University of Texas at Austin M,D
The University of Texas at Tyler M
University of the District of Columbia M
University of Utah M,D
University of Vermont M
University of Wisconsin–Madison D
University of Wisconsin–Stout M
Utah State University M,D
Valdosta State University M,O
Valparaiso University M,O
Virginia Commonwealth University M,D,O
Walden University M,D
Walla Walla University M
Walsh University M
Washington State University M,D
Wayland Baptist University M
Webster University M
Western Michigan University M,D
Western Washington University M
Westfield State College M
Westminster College (UT) M
West Virginia University D
William Carey University M
Yeshiva University M

■ COUNSELOR EDUCATION

Adams State College M
Alabama Agricultural and Mechanical University M,O
Alabama State University M,O
Albany State University M
Alcorn State University M,O
Alfred University M,O
Angelo State University M
Appalachian State University M
Argosy University, Sarasota Campus M,D,O
Argosy University, Tampa Campus M,D
Arizona State University M
Arkansas State University M,O
Auburn University M,D,O
Auburn University Montgomery M,O
Augusta State University M
Austin Peay State University M
Azusa Pacific University M
Barry University M,D,O
Bayamón Central University M
Bloomsburg University of Pennsylvania M
Bob Jones University P,M,D,O
Boise State University M
Boston University M,O
Bowie State University M
Bowling Green State University M
Bradley University M
Bridgewater State College M,O
Brooklyn College of the City University of New York M,O
Bucknell University M
Butler University M
Caldwell College M
California Lutheran University M
California State University, Bakersfield M
California State University, Dominguez Hills M
California State University, East Bay M
California State University, Fresno M
California State University, Fullerton M
California State University, Long Beach M
California State University, Los Angeles M
California State University, Northridge M
California State University, Sacramento M
California State University, San Bernardino M
California University of Pennsylvania M
Campbell University M
Canisius College M
Carson-Newman College M
The Catholic University of America M,D
Central Connecticut State University M,O
Central Michigan University M
Central Washington University M
Chapman University M
Chicago State University M
The Citadel, The Military College of South Carolina M
Clark Atlanta University M,D
Clemson University M
Cleveland State University M,D,O
The College of New Jersey M
College of St. Joseph M
The College of Saint Rose M
College of Santa Fe M
College of the Southwest M
The College of William and Mary M,D
Colorado State University M,D
Columbus State University M,O
Concordia University Chicago (IL) M,O
Concordia University Wisconsin M
Creighton University M
Dallas Baptist University M
Delta State University M
DePaul University M,D
Doane College M
Drake University M
Duquesne University M,D
East Carolina University M,O
East Central University M
Eastern Illinois University M
Eastern Kentucky University M
Eastern Michigan University M,O
Eastern New Mexico University M
Eastern University M
Eastern Washington University M
East Tennessee State University M
Edinboro University of Pennsylvania M,O
Emporia State University M
Fairfield University M,O
Fitchburg State College M,O
Florida Agricultural and Mechanical University M,D
Florida Atlantic University M,O
Florida Gulf Coast University M
Florida International University M
Florida State University M,D,O
Fordham University M,D,O
Fort Hays State University M
Fort Valley State University M,O
Freed-Hardeman University M,O
Fresno Pacific University M
Frostburg State University M
Gallaudet University M
Gannon University M,O
Geneva College M
George Fox University M,O
George Mason University M
The George Washington University M,D,O
Georgia Southern University M,O
Georgia State University M,D,O
Gwynedd-Mercy College M

Hampton University M
Harding University M,O
Hardin-Simmons University M
Henderson State University M
Heritage University M
Hofstra University M,O
Houston Baptist University M
Howard University M,O
Hunter College of the City University of New York M
Idaho State University M,D,O
Illinois State University M,D
Immaculata University M,D,O
Indiana State University M,D
Indiana University Bloomington M,D,O
Indiana University of Pennsylvania M
Indiana University–Purdue University Fort Wayne M
Indiana University South Bend M
Indiana University Southeast M
Indiana Wesleyan University M
Inter American University of Puerto Rico, Metropolitan Campus M
Inter American University of Puerto Rico, San Germán Campus M,D
Iowa State University of Science and Technology M,D
Jackson State University M,O
Jacksonville State University M
John Brown University M
John Carroll University M,O
The Johns Hopkins University M,O
Johnson State College M
Kansas State University M,D
Kean University M,O
Keene State College M,O
Kent State University M,D,O
Kutztown University of Pennsylvania M
Lamar University M,D,O
La Sierra University M,O
Lee University M
Lehigh University M,D,O
Lehman College of the City University of New York M
Lewis University M
Liberty University M,D,O
Lincoln Memorial University M,O
Lincoln University (MO) M,O
Long Island University, Brentwood Campus M
Long Island University, Brooklyn Campus M,O
Long Island University, C.W. Post Campus M
Longwood University M
Louisiana State University and Agricultural and Mechanical College M,D,O
Louisiana Tech University M,D
Loyola College in Maryland M,O
Loyola Marymount University M
Loyola University Chicago M,O
Loyola University New Orleans M
Lynchburg College M
Malone College M
Manhattan College M,O
Marshall University M,O
Marymount University M
Marywood University M,O
McDaniel College M
McNeese State University M
Mercy College M
Michigan State University M,D,O
Middle Tennessee State University M,O
Midwestern State University M
Minnesota State University Mankato M,D,O
Minnesota State University Moorhead M
Mississippi College M,O
Mississippi State University M,D,O
Missouri Baptist University M,O
Missouri State University M
Montana State University–Billings M
Montclair State University M,O
Morehead State University M,O
Mount Mary College M
Murray State University M,O
National-Louis University M,O
National University M
New Mexico Highlands University M
New Mexico State University M,D,O
New York Institute of Technology M
New York University M,D,O
Niagara University M,O
Nicholls State University M
North Carolina Agricultural and Technical State University M
North Carolina Central University M
North Carolina State University M,D
North Dakota State University M,D
Northeastern Illinois University M
Northeastern State University M
Northeastern University M
Northern Arizona University M
Northern Illinois University M,D
Northern Kentucky University M
Northwestern State University of Louisiana M,O
Northwest Missouri State University M
Northwest Nazarene University M
Nova Southeastern University M
Ohio University M,D
Oklahoma State University M,D,O
Old Dominion University M,D,O
Oregon State University M,D
Our Lady of the Lake University of San Antonio M
Palm Beach Atlantic University M
Penn State University Park M,D
Pittsburg State University M
Plymouth State University M
Portland State University M,D
Prairie View A&M University M,D
Providence College M
Purdue University M,D,O
Purdue University Calumet M
Queens College of the City University of New York M
Radford University M
Regent University M,D,O
Rhode Island College M,O
Rider University M,O
Rivier College M,O
Roberts Wesleyan College M
Rollins College M
Roosevelt University M
Rosemont College M
Rowan University M
St. Bonaventure University M,O
St. Cloud State University M
St. John's University (NY) M
Saint Joseph College M,O
Saint Louis University M,D,O
Saint Martin's University M
Saint Mary's College of California M
St. Mary's University of San Antonio D
St. Thomas University M,O
Saint Xavier University M
Salem State College M
Sam Houston State University M,D
San Diego State University M
San Jose State University M
Santa Clara University M
Seattle Pacific University M
Seattle University M,O
Seton Hall University M
Shippensburg University of Pennsylvania M,O
Siena Heights University M,O
Simmons College M,D,O
Slippery Rock University of Pennsylvania M
Sonoma State University M
South Carolina State University M
South Dakota State University M
Southeastern Louisiana University M
Southeastern Oklahoma State University M
Southeast Missouri State University M,O
Southern Connecticut State University M,O
Southern Illinois University Carbondale M,D
Southern Oregon University M
Southern University and Agricultural and Mechanical College M
Southwestern Oklahoma State University M
Springfield College M,O
State University of New York at Plattsburgh M,O
State University of New York College at Brockport M,O
State University of New York College at Oneonta M,O
Stephen F. Austin State University M
Stetson University M
Suffolk University M,O
Sul Ross State University M
Syracuse University D
Tarleton State University M
Tennessee State University M,D
Texas A&M International University M
Texas A&M University M,D
Texas A&M University–Commerce M,D
Texas A&M University–Corpus Christi M,D
Texas A&M University–Kingsville M
Texas Christian University M,O
Texas Southern University M,D
Texas State University-San Marcos M
Texas Tech University M,D,O
Texas Wesleyan University M
Texas Woman's University M,D
Trevecca Nazarene University M
Trinity (Washington) University M
Troy University M,O
University at Albany, State University of New York M,D,O
University at Buffalo, the State University of New York M,D,O
The University of Akron M,D
The University of Alabama M,D,O
The University of Alabama at Birmingham M
University of Alaska Anchorage M
University of Alaska Fairbanks M
University of Arkansas M,D,O
University of Arkansas at Little Rock M
University of Central Arkansas M
University of Central Florida M,D
University of Central Missouri M,O
University of Central Oklahoma M
University of Cincinnati M,D,O

University of Colorado at Colorado Springs M,D
University of Colorado Denver M,O
University of Connecticut M,D
University of Dayton M,O
University of Delaware M,D
University of Detroit Mercy M
University of Florida M,D,O
University of Georgia M,D,O
University of Guam M
University of Hartford M,O
University of Hawaii at Manoa M
University of Houston–Clear Lake M
University of Idaho M,D,O
University of Illinois at Urbana–Champaign M,D,O
The University of Iowa M,D
University of La Verne M,O
University of Louisiana at Lafayette M
University of Louisiana at Monroe M
University of Louisville M,D
University of Maine M,D,O
University of Mary Hardin-Baylor M
University of Maryland, College Park M,D,O
University of Maryland Eastern Shore M
University of Massachusetts Amherst M,D,O
University of Massachusetts Boston M,O
University of Memphis M,D
University of Miami M,O
University of Minnesota, Twin Cities Campus M,D,O
University of Mississippi M,D,O
University of Missouri–St. Louis M
The University of Montana M,D,O
University of Montevallo M
University of Nebraska at Kearney M,O
University of Nebraska at Omaha M
University of Nevada, Las Vegas M,D,O
University of Nevada, Reno M,D,O
University of New Hampshire M
University of New Mexico M,D
University of New Orleans M,D,O
University of North Alabama M
The University of North Carolina at Chapel Hill M
The University of North Carolina at Charlotte M,D
The University of North Carolina at Greensboro M,D,O
The University of North Carolina at Pembroke M
University of Northern Colorado D
University of Northern Iowa M,D
University of North Florida M
University of North Texas M,D
University of Oklahoma M
University of Phoenix–Southern Arizona Campus M,O
University of Puerto Rico, Río Piedras M,D
University of Puget Sound M
University of Saint Francis (IN) M
University of San Diego M
University of San Francisco M,D
The University of Scranton M
University of South Alabama M,D
University of South Carolina D,O
The University of South Dakota M,D,O
University of Southern California M
University of Southern Maine M,O
University of South Florida M,D
The University of Tennessee M,D,O
The University of Tennessee at Chattanooga M,D,O
The University of Tennessee at Martin M
The University of Texas at Austin M,D
The University of Texas at Brownsville M
The University of Texas at San Antonio M,D
The University of Texas of the Permian Basin M
The University of Texas–Pan American M
University of the District of Columbia M
The University of Toledo M,D,O
University of Utah M,D
University of Vermont M
University of Virginia M,D,O
University of Washington M,D
The University of West Alabama M
University of West Florida M
University of West Georgia M,O
University of Wisconsin–Madison M
University of Wisconsin–Oshkosh M
University of Wisconsin–Platteville M
University of Wisconsin–River Falls M,O
University of Wisconsin–Stevens Point M
University of Wisconsin–Superior M
University of Wisconsin–Whitewater M
University of Wyoming M,D
Utah State University M,D
Valdosta State University M,O
Vanderbilt University M
Villanova University M
Virginia Commonwealth University M
Virginia Polytechnic Institute and State University M,D,O
Virginia State University M
Wake Forest University M
Walsh University M
Wayne State College M
Wayne State University M,D,O
West Chester University of Pennsylvania M
Western Carolina University M
Western Connecticut State University M
Western Illinois University M
Western Kentucky University M,O
Western Michigan University M,D
Western New Mexico University M
Western Washington University M
Westfield State College M
West Texas A&M University M
West Virginia University M
Whitworth University M
Wichita State University M,D,O
Widener University M,D
William Paterson University of New Jersey M
Wilmington University (DE) M
Winona State University M
Winthrop University M
Wright State University M
Xavier University M
Xavier University of Louisiana M
Youngstown State University M

■ CRIMINAL JUSTICE AND CRIMINOLOGY

Albany State University M
American International College M
American University M,D
Anna Maria College M
Appalachian State University M
Arizona State University at the West campus M
Arkansas State University M,O
Armstrong Atlantic State University M
Auburn University Montgomery M
Bayamón Central University M
Bellevue University M
Boise State University M
Boston University M
Bowling Green State University M
Bridgewater State College M
Buffalo State College, State University of New York M
California State University, Fresno M
California State University, Long Beach M
California State University, Los Angeles M
California State University, Sacramento M
California State University, San Bernardino M
California State University, Stanislaus M
California University of Pennsylvania M
Capella University M,D,O
Carnegie Mellon University M
Central Connecticut State University M
Central Michigan University M
Chaminade University of Honolulu M
Charleston Southern University M
Chicago State University M
Clark Atlanta University M
Colorado Technical University—Colorado Springs M
Colorado Technical University—Denver M
Colorado Technical University—Sioux Falls M
Columbia College (MO) M
Concordia University, St. Paul M
Coppin State University M
Dallas Baptist University M
Delta State University M
DeSales University M
Drury University M
East Carolina University M
East Central University M
Eastern Kentucky University M
Eastern Michigan University M
East Tennessee State University M
Fayetteville State University M
Ferris State University M
Fitchburg State College M
Florida Agricultural and Mechanical University M
Florida Atlantic University M
Florida Gulf Coast University M
Florida International University M
Florida State University M,D
The George Washington University M
Georgia College & State University M
Georgia State University M
Graduate School and University Center of the City University of New York D
Grambling State University M
Grand Valley State University M
Hodges University M
Illinois State University M
Indiana State University M
Indiana University Bloomington M,D
Indiana University Northwest M,O
Indiana University of Pennsylvania M,D
Indiana University–Purdue University Indianapolis M
Inter American University of Puerto Rico, Metropolitan Campus M
Iona College M
Jackson State University M
Jacksonville State University M

John Jay College of Criminal Justice of the City University of New York M,D
The Johns Hopkins University M
Kean University M
Kent State University M
Lamar University M
Lewis University M
Lincoln University (MO) M
Lindenwood University M
Long Island University, Brentwood Campus M
Long Island University, C.W. Post Campus M
Longwood University M
Loyola University Chicago M
Loyola University New Orleans M
Lynn University M,O
Madonna University M
Marshall University M
Marywood University M
Mercyhurst College M,O
Metropolitan State University M
Michigan State University M,D
Middle Tennessee State University M
Midwestern State University M
Minnesota State University Mankato M
Minot State University M
Mississippi College M,O
Mississippi Valley State University M
Missouri State University M
Monmouth University M,O
Morehead State University M
Mountain State University M
New Jersey City University M
New Mexico State University M
Niagara University M
Norfolk State University M
North Carolina Central University M
North Dakota State University M,D
Northeastern State University M
Northeastern University M,D
Northern Arizona University M,O
Northern Michigan University M
Norwich University M
Nova Southeastern University M
Oklahoma City University M
Oklahoma State University M,D
Old Dominion University D
Penn State Harrisburg M,D
Penn State University Park M,D
Point Park University M
Polytechnic University, Brooklyn Campus M,D,O
Pontifical Catholic University of Puerto Rico M,D
Portland State University M,D
Radford University M
The Richard Stockton College of New Jersey M
Roger Williams University M
Rosemont College M
Rutgers, The State University of New Jersey, Camden M
Rutgers, The State University of New Jersey, Newark M,D
Sacred Heart University M
St. Ambrose University M
St. Cloud State University M
St. John's University (NY) M
Saint Joseph's University M,O
Saint Leo University M
Saint Louis University M
St. Thomas University M,O
Salem State College M
Salve Regina University M
Sam Houston State University M,D
San Diego State University M
San Jose State University M
Seattle University M
Shippensburg University of Pennsylvania M
Southeast Missouri State University M
Southern Illinois University Carbondale M
Southern University and Agricultural and Mechanical College M
Suffolk University M
Sul Ross State University M
Tarleton State University M
Temple University M,D
Tennessee State University M
Texas A&M International University M
Texas State University-San Marcos M
Tiffin University M
Troy University M
Universidad del Turabo M
University at Albany, State University of New York M,D
The University of Alabama M
The University of Alabama at Birmingham M
University of Alaska Fairbanks M
University of Arkansas at Little Rock M
University of Baltimore M
University of California, Irvine M,D
University of Central Florida M,O
University of Central Missouri M,O
University of Central Oklahoma M
University of Cincinnati M,D
University of Colorado at Colorado Springs M
University of Colorado Denver M
University of Delaware M,D
University of Denver M,O
University of Detroit Mercy M
University of Florida M,D
University of Great Falls M
University of Houston–Clear Lake M
University of Illinois at Chicago M
University of Louisiana at Monroe M
University of Louisville M
University of Maryland, College Park M,D
University of Maryland Eastern Shore M
University of Massachusetts Lowell M
University of Memphis M
University of Minnesota, Duluth M
University of Missouri–Kansas City M,D
University of Missouri–St. Louis M,D
The University of Montana M
University of Nebraska at Omaha M,D
University of Nevada, Las Vegas M
University of Nevada, Reno M
University of New Haven M
University of North Alabama M
The University of North Carolina at Charlotte M
The University of North Carolina at Greensboro M
The University of North Carolina Wilmington M
University of North Dakota D
University of Northern Iowa M
University of North Florida M
University of North Texas M
University of Pennsylvania M,D
University of Phoenix–Hawaii Campus M
University of Phoenix–Louisiana Campus M
University of Phoenix M
University of Phoenix–Oregon Campus M
University of Phoenix–Sacramento Valley Campus M
University of Phoenix–San Diego Campus M
University of Phoenix–Southern Arizona Campus M,O
University of Pittsburgh D
University of South Carolina M
University of Southern Mississippi M,D
University of South Florida M,D
The University of Tennessee M,D
The University of Tennessee at Chattanooga M
The University of Texas at Arlington M
The University of Texas at San Antonio M
The University of Texas at Tyler M
The University of Texas of the Permian Basin M
The University of Texas–Pan American M
The University of Toledo M,O
University of West Florida M
University of Wisconsin–Milwaukee M
University of Wisconsin–Platteville M
Upper Iowa University M
Utica College M
Valdosta State University M
Villanova University M
Virginia Commonwealth University M,O
Washburn University M
Washington State University M,D
Wayland Baptist University M
Wayne State University M
Webster University M,D
West Chester University of Pennsylvania M
Western Connecticut State University M
Western Illinois University M,O
Western Oregon University M
Westfield State College M
West Texas A&M University M
Wichita State University M
Widener University M
Wilmington University (DE) M
Wright State University M
Xavier University M
Youngstown State University M

■ CULTURAL STUDIES

Biola University M,D,O
Chapman University D
Claremont Graduate University M,D,O
Cornell University M,D
Eastern Michigan University M
George Mason University D
Lewis & Clark College M,O
New York University M,D,O
San Francisco State University M
Simmons College M
Southern Illinois University Carbondale M
Stony Brook University, State University of New York M,O
Union University M
University of Alaska Fairbanks M
University of California, Davis M,D
University of Hawaii at Manoa M,O
University of Houston–Clear Lake M
University of Minnesota, Twin Cities Campus D
University of Pittsburgh M,D
The University of Texas at San Antonio M,D

Washington State University	M,D
Wheaton College	M,O

■ CURRICULUM AND INSTRUCTION

Andrews University	M,D,O
Angelo State University	M
Appalachian State University	M
Arizona State University	M,D
Arizona State University at the Polytechnic Campus	M,D
Arkansas State University	M,D,O
Arkansas Tech University	M,O
Armstrong Atlantic State University	M
Ashland University	M
Auburn University	M,D,O
Aurora University	M,D
Austin Peay State University	M,O
Azusa Pacific University	M
Ball State University	M,O
Barry University	D,O
Baylor University	M,D,O
Benedictine University	M
Bloomsburg University of Pennsylvania	M
Bob Jones University	P,M,D,O
Boise State University	D
Boston College	M,D,O
Boston University	M,D,O
Bowling Green State University	M
Bradley University	M
Bucknell University	M
Caldwell College	M
California Baptist University	M
California State University, Bakersfield	M
California State University, Chico	M
California State University, Dominguez Hills	M
California State University, East Bay	M
California State University, Fresno	M
California State University, Sacramento	M
California State University, San Bernardino	M
California State University, Stanislaus	M
Capella University	M,D,O
Carson-Newman College	M
Castleton State College	M
The Catholic University of America	M,D
Chapman University	M,D
Christian Brothers University	M
City University of Seattle	M,O
Clarion University of Pennsylvania	M
Clark Atlanta University	M,O
Clemson University	D
The College of St. Scholastica	M
College of Santa Fe	M
College of the Southwest	M
The College of William and Mary	M,D
Colorado Christian University	M
Concordia University (CA)	M
Concordia University Chicago (IL)	M
Concordia University (NE)	M
Concordia University (OR)	M
Concordia University Wisconsin	M
Converse College	O
Coppin State University	M
Cornell University	M,D
Dallas Baptist University	M
Delaware State University	M
DePaul University	D
Doane College	M
Dominican University	M
Dominican University of California	M
Drexel University	M
Duquesne University	M,D
East Carolina University	M
Eastern Kentucky University	M
Eastern Michigan University	M
Eastern Washington University	M
East Tennessee State University	M
Emporia State University	M
Fairleigh Dickinson University, Metropolitan Campus	M
Ferris State University	M
Florida Atlantic University	M,D,O
Florida Gulf Coast University	M
Florida International University	M,D,O
Fordham University	M,D,O
Framingham State College	M
Franciscan University of Steubenville	M
Freed-Hardeman University	M,O
Fresno Pacific University	M
Frostburg State University	M
Gannon University	M
Gardner-Webb University	D
The George Washington University	M,D,O
Georgia Southern University	D
Grambling State University	M,D
Harvard University	M
Henderson State University	M,O
Holy Names University	M,O
Hood College	M,O
Houston Baptist University	M
Idaho State University	M,O
Illinois State University	M,D
Indiana State University	M,D
Indiana University Bloomington	M,D,O
Indiana University of Pennsylvania	M,D
Indiana Wesleyan University	M
Iowa State University of Science and Technology	M,D
The Johns Hopkins University	M
Johnson State College	M
Kansas State University	M,D
Kean University	M
Keene State College	M
Kent State University	M,D,O
Kutztown University of Pennsylvania	M,O
La Sierra University	M,D,O
Lesley University	M,D,O
Lewis University	M
Liberty University	M,D,O
Lincoln Memorial University	M,O
Lipscomb University	M
Louisiana Tech University	M,D
Loyola College in Maryland	M,O
Loyola University Chicago	M,D
Malone College	M
McDaniel College	M
McNeese State University	M
Medaille College	M
Miami University	M
Michigan State University	M,D,O
MidAmerica Nazarene University	M
Middle Tennessee State University	M,O
Midwestern State University	M
Mills College	M,D
Minnesota State University Mankato	M,O
Minnesota State University Moorhead	M
Misericordia University	M
Mississippi College	M,O
Mississippi State University	M,D,O
Missouri State University	M
Montana State University–Billings	M
Montclair State University	M,D,O
Morehead State University	O
National-Louis University	M,D,O
Newman University	M
New Mexico Highlands University	M
New Mexico State University	M,D,O
Nicholls State University	M
North Carolina State University	M,D
Northern Arizona University	D
Northern Illinois University	M,D
Northwestern State University of Louisiana	M
Northwest Nazarene University	M
Nova Southeastern University	M,O
Ohio University	M,D
Oklahoma State University	M,D
Old Dominion University	M,D
Olivet Nazarene University	M
Oral Roberts University	M,D
Our Lady of the Lake University of San Antonio	M,D
Pace University	M,O
Pacific Lutheran University	M
Penn State Great Valley	M
Penn State Harrisburg	M,D
Penn State University Park	M,D
Philadelphia Biblical University	M
Piedmont College	M,O
Point Park University	M
Pontifical Catholic University of Puerto Rico	M,D
Portland State University	M,D
Prairie View A&M University	M
Purdue University	M,D,O
Purdue University Calumet	M
Regis University	M,O
Rider University	M,O
Rivier College	M,O
Rosemont College	M
Rowan University	M
St. Cloud State University	M
Saint Leo University	M
Saint Louis University	M,D
Saint Mary's College of California	M
Saint Michael's College	M,O
Saint Peter's College	M,O
Saint Xavier University	M,O
San Diego State University	M
Seattle University	M,O
Shippensburg University of Pennsylvania	M
Siena Heights University	M
Sonoma State University	M
South Dakota State University	M
Southeastern Louisiana University	M
Southern Illinois University Carbondale	M,D
Southern Nazarene University	M
Southern New Hampshire University	M,O
Stanford University	M,D
State University of New York at Plattsburgh	M
State University of New York College at Brockport	M
State University of New York College at Potsdam	M
Stetson University	O
Suffolk University	M,O
Syracuse University	M,D,O
Tarleton State University	M
Tennessee State University	M,D
Tennessee Technological University	M,O
Texas A&M International University	M,D
Texas A&M University	M,D
Texas A&M University–Commerce	M,D
Texas A&M University–Corpus Christi	M,D
Texas A&M University–Texarkana	M
Texas Southern University	M,D
Texas Tech University	M,D
Trevecca Nazarene University	M
Universidad Metropolitana	M

University at Albany, State University of New York M,D,O
University of Alaska Fairbanks M
University of Arkansas D
University of California, Davis M,D
University of Central Florida M,D,O
University of Central Missouri M,O
University of Cincinnati M,D
University of Colorado at Boulder M,D
University of Colorado at Colorado Springs M,D
University of Connecticut M,D
University of Delaware M,D
University of Denver M,D,O
University of Detroit Mercy M
University of Florida M,D,O
University of Hawaii at Manoa M,D
University of Houston M,D
University of Houston–Clear Lake M
University of Idaho M,D
University of Illinois at Chicago M,D
University of Illinois at Urbana–Champaign M,D,O
University of Indianapolis M
The University of Iowa M,D
University of Kansas M,D
University of Kentucky M,D
University of Louisiana at Lafayette M
University of Louisiana at Monroe M,D
University of Louisville D
University of Maine M
University of Mary M
University of Maryland, Baltimore County M,O
University of Maryland, College Park M,D,O
University of Massachusetts Amherst M,D,O
University of Massachusetts Boston M
University of Massachusetts Lowell M,D,O
University of Memphis M,D
University of Michigan M,D
University of Minnesota, Twin Cities Campus M,D,O
University of Mississippi M,D,O
University of Missouri–Columbia M,D,O
University of Missouri–Kansas City M,D,O
University of Missouri–St. Louis M,D
The University of Montana M,D
University of Nebraska at Kearney M
University of Nebraska–Lincoln M,D,O
University of Nevada, Las Vegas M,D,O
University of Nevada, Reno M,D,O
University of New Orleans M,D,O
The University of North Carolina at Chapel Hill M,D
The University of North Carolina at Charlotte M,D,O
The University of North Carolina at Greensboro M,D,O
The University of North Carolina Wilmington M
University of Northern Iowa M,D
University of North Texas D
University of Oklahoma M,D,O
University of Phoenix–Central Florida Campus M
University of Phoenix–Denver Campus M
University of Phoenix–Fort Lauderdale Campus M
University of Phoenix–Hawaii Campus M
University of Phoenix–Las Vegas Campus M
University of Phoenix–New Mexico Campus M
University of Phoenix–North Florida Campus M
University of Phoenix M
University of Phoenix–Phoenix Campus M
University of Phoenix–Sacramento Valley Campus M,O
University of Phoenix–San Diego Campus M
University of Phoenix–Southern Arizona Campus M,O
University of Phoenix–Southern California Campus M
University of Phoenix–Southern Colorado Campus M,O
University of Phoenix–Utah Campus M
University of Phoenix–West Florida Campus M
University of Phoenix–West Michigan Campus M
University of Puerto Rico, Río Piedras M,D
University of St. Francis (IL) M
University of Saint Mary M
University of St. Thomas (MN) M,D,O
University of San Diego M,D
University of San Francisco M,D
The University of Scranton M
University of South Carolina M,D,O
The University of South Dakota M,D,O
University of Southern California M
University of Southern Mississippi M,D,O
The University of Tennessee M,D,O
The University of Texas at Arlington M
The University of Texas at Austin M,D
The University of Texas at Brownsville M
The University of Texas at El Paso M
The University of Texas at San Antonio M
The University of Texas at Tyler M
University of the Pacific M,D
The University of Toledo M,D,O
University of Vermont M
University of Virginia M,D,O
University of Washington M,D
University of West Florida M,D,O
University of Wisconsin–Madison M,D
University of Wisconsin–Milwaukee M
University of Wisconsin–Oshkosh M
University of Wisconsin–Superior M
University of Wisconsin–Whitewater M
University of Wyoming M,D
Utah State University D
Valdosta State University M,D,O
Vanderbilt University M,D
Virginia Commonwealth University M,O
Virginia Polytechnic Institute and State University M,D,O
Walden University M,D
Walla Walla University M
Washburn University M
Washington State University M,D
Wayne State University M,D,O
Weber State University M
Western Connecticut State University M
West Texas A&M University M
West Virginia University M,D
Wichita State University M
William Woods University M,O
Wright State University M,O
Xavier University of Louisiana M

■ DANCE

American University M,O
Arizona State University M
Bennington College M
California State University, Fullerton M
California State University, Long Beach M
California State University, Sacramento M
Case Western Reserve University M
Florida State University M
George Mason University M
Hollins University M
Mills College M
New York University M,D
Northern Illinois University M
The Ohio State University M,D
Purchase College, State University of New York M
Sam Houston State University M
Sarah Lawrence College M
Shenandoah University M,D,O
Southern Methodist University M
State University of New York College at Brockport M
Temple University M,D
Texas Tech University M,D
Texas Woman's University M,D
Tufts University M,D
Tulane University M
University of California, Irvine M
University of California, Los Angeles M,D
University of California, Riverside M,D
University of Colorado at Boulder M,D
University of Hawaii at Manoa M,D
University of Illinois at Urbana–Champaign M
The University of Iowa M
University of Maryland, College Park M
University of Michigan M
University of Minnesota, Twin Cities Campus M,D
University of New Mexico M
The University of North Carolina at Charlotte M
The University of North Carolina at Greensboro M
University of Oklahoma M
University of Oregon M
The University of Texas at Austin M,D
University of Utah M
University of Washington M
University of Wisconsin–Milwaukee M

■ DECORATIVE ARTS

The New School: A University M

■ DEMOGRAPHY AND POPULATION STUDIES

Arizona State University M,D
Bowling Green State University M,D
Brown University D
Cornell University M,D
Duke University D
Florida State University M,O
Georgetown University M
Harvard University M,D
The Johns Hopkins University M,D
Princeton University D,O
University at Albany, State University of New York M,D,O
University of California, Berkeley M,D
University of California, Irvine M
University of Hawaii at Manoa O
University of Illinois at Urbana–Champaign M,D
University of Pennsylvania M,D
The University of Texas at San Antonio D

Washington State University M,D

■ DENTAL HYGIENE

Boston University P,M,D,O
Idaho State University M,O
Old Dominion University M
University of Missouri–Kansas City P,M,D,O
University of New Mexico M

■ DENTISTRY

Boston University P,M,D,O
Case Western Reserve University P
Columbia University P
Creighton University P
Harvard University P,M,D,O
Howard University P,O
Idaho State University M,O
Indiana University–Purdue University Indianapolis P,M,D,O
Marquette University P
New York University P
Nova Southeastern University P,M
The Ohio State University P,M
Southern Illinois University Edwardsville P
Stony Brook University, State University of New York P,O
Temple University P
Tufts University P
University at Buffalo, the State University of New York P,M,D,O
The University of Alabama at Birmingham P
University of California, Los Angeles P,O
University of Colorado Denver P
University of Detroit Mercy P
University of Florida P,O
University of Illinois at Chicago P
The University of Iowa P,M,D,O
University of Kentucky P,M
University of Louisville P
University of Michigan P
University of Minnesota, Twin Cities Campus P
University of Missouri–Kansas City P,M,D,O
The University of North Carolina at Chapel Hill P
University of Pennsylvania P
University of Pittsburgh P,M,O
University of Southern California P,O
University of the Pacific P,M,O
University of Washington P
Virginia Commonwealth University P,M
West Virginia University P

■ DEVELOPMENTAL BIOLOGY

Arizona State University M,D
Brigham Young University M,D
Brown University M,D
California Institute of Technology D
Carnegie Mellon University M,D
Case Western Reserve University M,D
Columbia University M,D
Cornell University M,D
Duke University D,O
Emory University D
Florida State University M,D
Illinois State University M,D
Iowa State University of Science and Technology M,D
The Johns Hopkins University D
Marquette University M,D
Massachusetts Institute of Technology D
New York University M,D
Northwestern University D
The Ohio State University M,D
Penn State University Park M,D
Purdue University M,D
Rensselaer Polytechnic Institute M,D
Rutgers, The State University of New Jersey, New Brunswick M,D
Stanford University D
Stony Brook University, State University of New York M,D
Tufts University D
University at Albany, State University of New York M,D
University of California, Davis M,D
University of California, Irvine M,D
University of California, Los Angeles M,D
University of California, Riverside M,D
University of California, San Diego D
University of California, Santa Barbara M,D
University of Chicago D
University of Cincinnati D
University of Colorado at Boulder M,D
University of Colorado Denver D
University of Connecticut M,D
University of Delaware M,D
University of Illinois at Chicago M,D
University of Illinois at Urbana–Champaign D
University of Kansas M,D
University of Massachusetts Amherst D
University of Miami D
University of Michigan M,D
University of Minnesota, Twin Cities Campus M,D
University of Missouri–St. Louis M,D,O
The University of North Carolina at Chapel Hill M,D
University of Pennsylvania D
University of Pittsburgh D
University of South Carolina M,D
The University of Texas at Austin D
Virginia Polytechnic Institute and State University M,D
Washington University in St. Louis D
West Virginia University M,D
Yale University D

■ DEVELOPMENTAL EDUCATION

Edinboro University of Pennsylvania O
Ferris State University M
Grambling State University M,D
National-Louis University M,O
North Carolina State University M
Rutgers, The State University of New Jersey, New Brunswick M
Texas State University-San Marcos M,D
University of California, Berkeley
The University of Iowa M,D

■ DEVELOPMENTAL PSYCHOLOGY

Andrews University M,D
Arizona State University D
Boston College M,D
Bowling Green State University M,D
Brandeis University M,D
Carnegie Mellon University D
Claremont Graduate University M,D,O
Clark University D
Cornell University D
Duke University D
Emory University D
Florida International University M,D
Florida State University D
Fordham University D
Gallaudet University M,O
George Mason University M,D
Graduate School and University Center of the City University of New York D
Harvard University D
Howard University M,D
Illinois State University M,D,O
Indiana University Bloomington M,D
Louisiana State University and Agricultural and Mechanical College M,D
Loyola University Chicago D
New York University M,D,O
North Carolina State University D
The Ohio State University M,D
Penn State University Park M,D
Stanford University D
Suffolk University D
Temple University D
Texas A&M University M,D
Tufts University M,D,O
The University of Alabama at Birmingham M,D
University of California, Santa Barbara M,D
University of Connecticut M,D
University of Florida M,D
University of Kansas M,D
University of Maine M,D
University of Maryland, Baltimore County D
University of Maryland, College Park M,D
University of Miami M,D
University of Michigan D
The University of Montana M,D,O
University of Nebraska at Omaha M,D,O
The University of North Carolina at Chapel Hill D
The University of North Carolina at Greensboro M,D
University of Notre Dame D
University of Oregon M,D
University of Pittsburgh M,D
University of Rochester M,D
University of Wisconsin–Madison D
Virginia Polytechnic Institute and State University M,D
Wayne State University M,D
West Virginia University M,D

■ DISABILITY STUDIES

Chapman University D
Suffolk University M,O
Syracuse University O
University of Hawaii at Manoa O
University of Illinois at Chicago M,D
University of Pittsburgh O
Utah State University M,D,O

■ DISTANCE EDUCATION DEVELOPMENT

Barry University O
Endicott College M
Florida State University M,D,O
New York Institute of Technology M,O
Nova Southeastern University M,D
University of Maryland, Baltimore County M,O
University of Maryland University College M,O
University of Wyoming M,D,O
Western Illinois University M,O

■ EARLY CHILDHOOD EDUCATION

Adelphi University M,O
Alabama Agricultural and Mechanical University M,O

Institution	Degrees
Alabama State University	M,O
Albany State University	M
Anna Maria College	M,O
Arcadia University	M,D,O
Arkansas State University	M,O
Armstrong Atlantic State University	M
Ashland University	M
Auburn University	M,D,O
Auburn University Montgomery	M,O
Barry University	M,D,O
Bayamón Central University	M
Bellarmine University	M
Belmont University	M
Bennington College	M
Bloomsburg University of Pennsylvania	M
Boise State University	M
Boston College	M
Boston University	M,D,O
Bowling Green State University	M
Brenau University	M,O
Bridgewater State College	M
Brooklyn College of the City University of New York	M
Buffalo State College, State University of New York	M
California State University, Bakersfield	M
California State University, Fresno	M
California State University, Northridge	M
California State University, Sacramento	M
Canisius College	M
Carlow University	M
Central Connecticut State University	M
Central Michigan University	M
Chatham University	M
Chestnut Hill College	M
Cheyney University of Pennsylvania	O
Chicago State University	M
City College of the City University of New York	M
Clarion University of Pennsylvania	M
Cleveland State University	M
College of Charleston	M
College of Mount St. Joseph	M
The College of New Jersey	M
The College of New Rochelle	M
The College of Saint Rose	M,O
Columbus State University	M,O
Concordia University Chicago (IL)	M,D
Concordia University (NE)	M
Concordia University, St. Paul	M,O
Concordia University Wisconsin	M
Converse College	M,O
Daemen College	M
Dallas Baptist University	M
Dominican University	M
Duquesne University	M
Eastern Connecticut State University	M
Eastern Illinois University	M
Eastern Michigan University	M
Eastern Nazarene College	M,O
Eastern Washington University	M
East Tennessee State University	M
Edinboro University of Pennsylvania	M
Emporia State University	M
Fitchburg State College	M
Florida Agricultural and Mechanical University	M
Florida International University	M,D
Florida State University	M,D,O
Fordham University	M,D,O
Fort Valley State University	M
Framingham State College	M
Francis Marion University	M
Furman University	M
Gallaudet University	M,D,O
Gannon University	M,O
George Mason University	M
The George Washington University	M
Georgia College & State University	M,O
Georgia Southern University	M
Georgia Southwestern State University	M,O
Georgia State University	M,D,O
Governors State University	M
Grambling State University	M
Grand Valley State University	M
Harding University	M,O
Henderson State University	M,O
Hofstra University	M,O
Hood College	M,O
Howard University	M,O
Hunter College of the City University of New York	M,O
Indiana State University	M
Indiana University of Pennsylvania	M
Jackson State University	M,D,O
Jacksonville State University	M
Jacksonville University	M,O
James Madison University	M
John Carroll University	M
Kean University	M
Kennesaw State University	M
Kent State University	M
Kutztown University of Pennsylvania	M,O
Lehman College of the City University of New York	M
Lesley University	M,D,O
Liberty University	M,D,O
Long Island University, C.W. Post Campus	M
Long Island University, Southampton Graduate Campus	M
Loyola College in Maryland	M,O
Manhattan College	M
Manhattanville College	M
Marshall University	M
Maryville University of Saint Louis	M,D
Marywood University	M
McNeese State University	M
Mercer University	M,D,O
Mercy College	M
Miami University	M
Middle Tennessee State University	M,O
Millersville University of Pennsylvania	M
Mills College	M,D
Minnesota State University Mankato	M
Minot State University	M
Missouri State University	M
Montana State University–Billings	M
Montclair State University	M,O
Mount Saint Mary College	M
Murray State University	M
National-Louis University	M,O
Nazareth College of Rochester	M
New Jersey City University	M
New York University	M,D,O
Norfolk State University	M
North Carolina Agricultural and Technical State University	M
Northeastern State University	M
Northern Arizona University	M
Northern Illinois University	M,D
North Georgia College & State University	M,O
Northwestern State University of Louisiana	M
Northwest Missouri State University	M
Nova Southeastern University	M,D,O
Oakland University	M,D,O
Ohio University	M
Oklahoma City University	M
Old Dominion University	M,D
Pacific University	M
Penn State University Park	M,D
Piedmont College	M,O
Pittsburg State University	M
Portland State University	M,D
Queens College of the City University of New York	M,O
Regis University	M,O
Rhode Island College	M
Rivier College	M,O
Roberts Wesleyan College	M,O
Roosevelt University	M
Rutgers, The State University of New Jersey, New Brunswick	M,D
Saginaw Valley State University	M
St. John's University (NY)	M
Saint Joseph College	M
St. Joseph's College, Suffolk Campus	M
Saint Mary's College of California	M
Saint Xavier University	M,O
Salem State College	M
Salisbury University	M
Samford University	M,D,O
Sam Houston State University	M
San Francisco State University	M
Siena Heights University	M
Slippery Rock University of Pennsylvania	M
South Carolina State University	M
Southern Oregon University	M
Southwestern Oklahoma State University	M
Spring Hill College	M
State University of New York at Binghamton	M
State University of New York at New Paltz	M
State University of New York College at Cortland	M
State University of New York College at Geneseo	M
Stephen F. Austin State University	M
Syracuse University	M
Temple University	M,D
Tennessee Technological University	M,O
Texas A&M International University	M,D
Texas A&M University–Commerce	M,D
Texas A&M University–Corpus Christi	M,D
Texas A&M University–Kingsville	M
Texas Southern University	M,D
Texas State University-San Marcos	M
Texas Woman's University	M,D
Towson University	M,O
Trinity (Washington) University	M
Troy University	M,O
Tufts University	M,D,O
Universidad Metropolitana	M
University at Buffalo, the State University of New York	M,D,O
The University of Alabama at Birmingham	M,D
University of Alaska Anchorage	M,O
University of Alaska Southeast	M
University of Arkansas	M
University of Arkansas at Little Rock	M
University of Bridgeport	M,O
University of Central Arkansas	M
University of Central Florida	M
University of Central Oklahoma	M
University of Cincinnati	M
University of Colorado Denver	M

University of Dayton M
University of Detroit Mercy M
The University of Findlay M
University of Florida M,D,O
University of Georgia M,D,O
University of Hartford M
University of Hawaii at Manoa M
University of Houston M,D
University of Houston–Clear Lake M
The University of Iowa M,D
University of Kentucky M,D
University of Louisville M
University of Mary M
University of Maryland, Baltimore County M
University of Maryland, College Park M,D
University of Massachusetts Amherst M,D,O
University of Memphis M,D
University of Miami M,O
University of Michigan M,D
University of Michigan–Flint M
University of Minnesota, Twin Cities Campus M,D,O
University of Missouri–Columbia M,D,O
University of Montevallo M
University of New Hampshire M
The University of North Carolina at Chapel Hill M,D
The University of North Carolina at Greensboro M,D,O
University of North Dakota M
University of Northern Colorado M,D
University of Northern Iowa M
University of North Texas M,D
University of Oklahoma M,D,O
University of Pennsylvania M
University of Phoenix–Louisiana Campus M
University of Phoenix M
University of Phoenix–Oregon Campus M
University of Pittsburgh M
University of Portland M
University of Puerto Rico, Río Piedras M
The University of Scranton M
University of South Alabama M,O
University of South Carolina M,D
University of Southern Mississippi M,D,O
University of South Florida M,D,O
The University of Tennessee M,D,O
The University of Texas at Brownsville M
The University of Texas at San Antonio M
The University of Texas at Tyler M
The University of Texas of the Permian Basin M
The University of Texas–Pan American M
University of the District of Columbia M
University of the Incarnate Word M,D
The University of Toledo M,O
The University of West Alabama M
University of West Florida M
University of West Georgia M,O
University of Wisconsin–Milwaukee M
University of Wisconsin–Oshkosh M
Valdosta State University M,O
Vanderbilt University M,D
Virginia Commonwealth University M,O
Wagner College M
Walden University M,D
Wayne State College M
Wayne State University M,D,O
Webster University M
Western Kentucky University M
Western Michigan University M
Western Oregon University M
Westfield State College M
West Virginia University M,D
Wheelock College M
Widener University M,D
Worcester State College M
Wright State University M
Xavier University M
Youngstown State University M

■ EAST EUROPEAN AND RUSSIAN STUDIES

Boston College M
Columbia University M,O
Cornell University M,D
Florida State University M
Georgetown University M
The George Washington University M
Harvard University M
Indiana University Bloomington M,O
The Johns Hopkins University M,D,O
La Salle University M
The Ohio State University M
Stanford University M
University of Illinois at Chicago M,D
University of Illinois at Urbana–Champaign M
University of Kansas M
University of Michigan M,O
The University of North Carolina at Chapel Hill M
University of Pittsburgh O
The University of Texas at Austin M
University of Washington M
Yale University M

■ ECOLOGY

Arizona State University M,D
Brown University D
Clemson University M,D
Colorado State University M,D
Columbia University D,O
Cornell University M,D
Dartmouth College D
Duke University M,D,O
Eastern Kentucky University M
Emory University D
Florida Institute of Technology M
Florida State University M,D
Frostburg State University M
Illinois State University M,D
Indiana State University M,D
Indiana University Bloomington M,D
Iowa State University of Science and Technology M,D
Kent State University M,D
Lesley University M,D,O
Marquette University M,D
Michigan State University D
Michigan Technological University M
Montana State University M,D
North Carolina State University M,D
North Dakota State University M,D
Northern Arizona University M,O
The Ohio State University M,D
Ohio University M,D
Old Dominion University D
Penn State University Park M,D
Prescott College M
Princeton University D
Purdue University M,D
Rice University M,D
Rutgers, The State University of New Jersey, New Brunswick M,D
San Diego State University M,D
San Francisco State University M
San Jose State University M
State University of New York College of Environmental Science and Forestry M,D
Stony Brook University, State University of New York D
Texas Christian University M
Tulane University M,D
University at Albany, State University of New York M,D
University at Buffalo, the State University of New York M,D,O
The University of Arizona M,D
University of California, Davis M,D
University of California, Irvine M,D
University of California, Los Angeles M,D
University of California, San Diego D
University of California, Santa Barbara M,D
University of California, Santa Cruz M,D
University of Chicago D
University of Colorado at Boulder M,D
University of Connecticut M,D
University of Delaware M,D
University of Florida M,D
University of Georgia M,D
University of Hawaii at Manoa M,D
University of Illinois at Chicago M,D
University of Illinois at Urbana–Champaign M,D
University of Kansas M,D
University of Maine M,D
University of Maryland, College Park M,D
University of Michigan M,D
University of Minnesota, Twin Cities Campus M,D
University of Missouri–Columbia M,D
University of Missouri–St. Louis M,D,O
The University of Montana M,D
University of Nevada, Reno D
The University of North Carolina at Chapel Hill M,D
University of North Dakota M,D
University of Notre Dame M,D
University of Oregon M,D
University of Pittsburgh D
University of South Carolina M,D
University of South Florida M,D
The University of Tennessee M,D
The University of Texas at Austin D
The University of Toledo M,D
University of Utah M,D
University of Wisconsin–Madison M,D
Utah State University M,D
Virginia Polytechnic Institute and State University M,D
Washington University in St. Louis D
William Paterson University of New Jersey M
Yale University D

■ ECONOMICS

Alabama Agricultural and Mechanical University M
Albany State University M
American University M,D,O
Andrews University M
Arizona State University M,D
Auburn University M
Baylor University M
Bernard M. Baruch College of the City University of New York M
Boston College D
Boston University M,D

Economics

Institution	Degrees
Bowling Green State University	M
Brandeis University	M,D
Brooklyn College of the City University of New York	M
Brown University	M,D
Buffalo State College, State University of New York	M
California State Polytechnic University, Pomona	M
California State University, East Bay	M
California State University, Fullerton	M
California State University, Long Beach	M
California State University, Los Angeles	M
Carnegie Mellon University	M,D
Case Western Reserve University	M
The Catholic University of America	M
Central Michigan University	M
City College of the City University of New York	M
Claremont Graduate University	M,D,O
Clark Atlanta University	M
Clark University	D
Clemson University	M,D
Cleveland State University	M,O
Colorado State University	M,D
Columbia University	M,D
Cornell University	M,D
DePaul University	M
Drexel University	M,D,O
Duke University	M,D
East Carolina University	M
Eastern Illinois University	M
Eastern Michigan University	M
Eastern University	M
East Tennessee State University	M
Emory University	D
Florida Agricultural and Mechanical University	M
Florida Atlantic University	M
Florida International University	M,D
Florida State University	M,D
Fordham University	M,D,O
George Mason University	M,D
Georgetown University	D
The George Washington University	M,D
Georgia Institute of Technology	M
Georgia State University	M,D
Graduate School and University Center of the City University of New York	D
Harvard University	D
Hawai'i Pacific University	M
Howard University	M,D
Hunter College of the City University of New York	M
Illinois State University	M
Indiana University Bloomington	M,D
Indiana University–Purdue University Indianapolis	M
Indiana University Southeast	M,O
Iowa State University of Science and Technology	M,D
The Johns Hopkins University	D
Kansas State University	M,D
Kent State University	M
Lehigh University	M,D
Long Island University, Brooklyn Campus	M
Louisiana State University and Agricultural and Mechanical College	M,D
Louisiana Tech University	M,D
Loyola College in Maryland	M
Marquette University	M
Massachusetts Institute of Technology	M,D
Miami University	M
Michigan State University	M,D
Middle Tennessee State University	M,D
Mississippi State University	M,D
Montclair State University	M
Morgan State University	M
Murray State University	M
National University	M
New Mexico State University	M
The New School: A University	M,D
New York Institute of Technology	M,O
New York University	M,D,O
North Carolina State University	M,D
Northeastern University	M,D
Northern Illinois University	M,D
Northwestern University	M,D
Oakland University	O
The Ohio State University	M,D
Ohio University	M
Oklahoma State University	M,D
Old Dominion University	M
Oregon State University	M,D
Pace University	M
Penn State University Park	M,D
Pepperdine University	M
Portland State University	M,D,O
Princeton University	D,O
Purdue University	D
Quinnipiac University	M
Regent University	M
Rensselaer Polytechnic Institute	M
Rice University	M,D
Roosevelt University	M
Rutgers, The State University of New Jersey, Newark	M
Rutgers, The State University of New Jersey, New Brunswick	M,D
St. Cloud State University	M
San Diego State University	M
San Francisco State University	M
San Jose State University	M
Seattle Pacific University	M
South Dakota State University	M
Southern Illinois University Carbondale	M,D
Southern Illinois University Edwardsville	M
Southern Methodist University	M,D
Southern New Hampshire University	M,D
Stanford University	D
State University of New York at Binghamton	M,D
Stony Brook University, State University of New York	M,D
Suffolk University	M,D
Syracuse University	M,D
Tarleton State University	M
Temple University	M,D
Texas A&M University	M,D
Texas A&M University–Commerce	M
Texas Tech University	M,D
Tufts University	M
Tulane University	M,D
University at Albany, State University of New York	M,D,O
University at Buffalo, the State University of New York	M,D,O
The University of Akron	M
The University of Alabama	M,D
University of Alaska Fairbanks	M
The University of Arizona	M,D
University of Arkansas	M,D
University of California, Berkeley	D
University of California, Davis	M,D
University of California, Irvine	M,D
University of California, Los Angeles	M,D
University of California, Riverside	M,D
University of California, San Diego	M,D
University of California, Santa Barbara	M,D
University of California, Santa Cruz	D
University of Central Arkansas	M
University of Central Florida	M,D
University of Chicago	D
University of Cincinnati	M
University of Colorado at Boulder	M,D
University of Colorado Denver	M
University of Connecticut	M,D
University of Delaware	M,D
University of Denver	M
University of Florida	M,D
University of Georgia	M,D
University of Hawaii at Manoa	M,D
University of Houston	M,D
University of Houston–Victoria	M
University of Illinois at Chicago	M,D
University of Illinois at Urbana–Champaign	M,D
The University of Iowa	D
University of Kansas	M,D
University of Kentucky	M,D
University of Maine	M
University of Maryland, Baltimore County	M
University of Maryland, College Park	M,D
University of Massachusetts Amherst	M,D
University of Massachusetts Lowell	M
University of Memphis	M,D
University of Miami	M,D
University of Michigan	M,D
University of Minnesota, Twin Cities Campus	D
University of Mississippi	M,D
University of Missouri–Columbia	M,D
University of Missouri–Kansas City	M,D
University of Missouri–St. Louis	M,O
The University of Montana	M
University of Nebraska at Omaha	M
University of Nebraska–Lincoln	M,D
University of Nevada, Las Vegas	M
University of Nevada, Reno	M
University of New Hampshire	M,D
University of New Mexico	M,D
University of New Orleans	D
The University of North Carolina at Chapel Hill	M,D
The University of North Carolina at Charlotte	M
The University of North Carolina at Greensboro	D
University of North Texas	M
University of Notre Dame	M,D
University of Oklahoma	M,D
University of Oregon	M,D
University of Pennsylvania	M,D
University of Pittsburgh	M,D,O
University of Puerto Rico, Río Piedras	M
University of Rhode Island	M,D
University of Rochester	M,D
University of San Francisco	M
University of South Carolina	M,D
University of Southern California	M,D
University of Southern Mississippi	M,D
University of South Florida	M,D
The University of Tampa	M
The University of Tennessee	M,D

The University of Texas at Arlington	M
The University of Texas at Austin	M,D
The University of Texas at Dallas	M,D
The University of Texas at El Paso	M
The University of Texas at San Antonio	M
The University of Toledo	M
University of Utah	M,D
University of Virginia	M,D
University of Washington	M,D
University of Wisconsin–Madison	D
University of Wisconsin–Milwaukee	M,D
University of Wyoming	M,D
Utah State University	M,D
Vanderbilt University	P,M,D
Virginia Commonwealth University	M
Virginia Polytechnic Institute and State University	M,D
Virginia State University	M
Washington State University	M,D,O
Washington University in St. Louis	M,D
Wayne State University	M,D,O
West Chester University of Pennsylvania	M
Western Illinois University	M
Western Michigan University	M,D
West Texas A&M University	M
West Virginia University	M,D
Wichita State University	M
Wright State University	M
Yale University	M,D
Youngstown State University	M

■ EDUCATION—GENERAL

Abilene Christian University	M,O
Adams State College	M
Adelphi University	M,D,O
Alabama Agricultural and Mechanical University	M,O
Alabama State University	M,D,O
Alaska Pacific University	M
Albany State University	M,O
Alcorn State University	M,O
Alfred University	M,O
Alvernia College	M
Alverno College	M
American InterContinental University (CA)	M
American International College	M,D,O
American University	M,D,O
Anderson University	M
Andrews University	M,D,O
Angelo State University	M
Anna Maria College	M,O
Antioch University Los Angeles	M
Antioch University McGregor	M
Antioch University New England	M
Antioch University Santa Barbara	M
Antioch University Seattle	M
Appalachian State University	M,D,O
Aquinas College	M
Arcadia University	M,D,O
Argosy University, Orange County Campus	M,D
Argosy University, Sarasota Campus	M,D,O
Argosy University, Tampa Campus	M,D,O
Argosy University, Twin Cities Campus	M,D,O
Arizona State University	M,D
Arizona State University at the Polytechnic Campus	M,D
Arizona State University at the West campus	M,D,O
Arkansas State University	M,D,O
Arkansas Tech University	M,O
Armstrong Atlantic State University	M
Ashland University	M,D
Auburn University	M,D,O
Auburn University Montgomery	M,O
Augsburg College	M
Augusta State University	M,O
Aurora University	M,D
Austin Peay State University	M,O
Avila University	M,O
Azusa Pacific University	M,D
Baldwin-Wallace College	M
Ball State University	M,D,O
Barry University	M,D,O
Bayamón Central University	M
Baylor University	M,D,O
Belhaven College (MS)	M
Bellarmine University	M
Belmont University	M
Bemidji State University	M
Benedictine University	M
Bennington College	M
Bethel College (TN)	M
Bethel University	M,D,O
Biola University	M
Bloomsburg University of Pennsylvania	M
Boise State University	M,D
Boston College	M,D,O
Boston University	M,D,O
Bowie State University	M
Bradley University	M,D
Brenau University	M,O
Bridgewater State College	M,O
Brigham Young University	M,D,O
Brooklyn College of the City University of New York	M,O
Brown University	M
Bucknell University	M
Butler University	M
Cabrini College	M,O
California Baptist University	M
California Lutheran University	M,O
California Polytechnic State University, San Luis Obispo	M
California State Polytechnic University, Pomona	M
California State University, Bakersfield	M,O
California State University, Chico	M
California State University, Dominguez Hills	M,O
California State University, East Bay	M
California State University, Fresno	M,D
California State University, Fullerton	M
California State University, Long Beach	M,D
California State University, Los Angeles	M
California State University, Northridge	M
California State University, Sacramento	M
California State University, San Bernardino	M
California State University, San Marcos	M
California State University, Stanislaus	M
California University of Pennsylvania	M
Cambridge College	M,D,O
Cameron University	M
Campbell University	M
Canisius College	M
Capella University	M,D,O
Cardinal Stritch University	M,D
Carlow University	M
Carnegie Mellon University	M,D
Carroll College	M
Carson-Newman College	M
Castleton State College	M,O
The Catholic University of America	M,D
Centenary College	M
Central Connecticut State University	M,D,O
Central Michigan University	M,D,O
Central Washington University	M
Chaminade University of Honolulu	M
Chapman University	M,D,O
Charleston Southern University	M
Chatham University	M
Chestnut Hill College	M
Cheyney University of Pennsylvania	M,O
Chicago State University	M,D
Christian Brothers University	M
The Citadel, The Military College of South Carolina	M,O
City College of the City University of New York	M,O
City University of Seattle	M,O
Claremont Graduate University	M,D,O
Clarion University of Pennsylvania	M,O
Clark Atlanta University	M,D,O
Clark University	M
Clemson University	M,D,O
Cleveland State University	M,D,O
College of Charleston	M,O
College of Mount St. Joseph	M
College of Mount Saint Vincent	M,O
The College of New Jersey	M,O
The College of New Rochelle	M,O
College of Notre Dame of Maryland	M
College of St. Catherine	M
College of Saint Elizabeth	M,O
College of St. Joseph	M
The College of Saint Rose	M,O
The College of St. Scholastica	M,O
College of Santa Fe	M
College of Staten Island of the City University of New York	M,O
College of the Southwest	M
The College of William and Mary	M,D,O
Colorado Christian University	M
Colorado State University	M,D
Columbia College (MO)	M
Columbia College (SC)	M
Columbia College Chicago	M
Columbus State University	M,O
Concordia University (CA)	M
Concordia University Chicago (IL)	M
Concordia University (NE)	M
Concordia University (OR)	M
Concordia University, St. Paul	M,O
Concordia University Wisconsin	M
Converse College	M,O
Coppin State University	M
Cornell University	M,D
Cornerstone University	M,O
Creighton University	M
Cumberland University	M
Daemen College	M
Dallas Baptist University	M
Delaware State University	M
Delta State University	M,D,O
DePaul University	M
DeSales University	M,O
Doane College	M
Dominican College	M
Dominican University	M
Dominican University of California	M,O
Dowling College	M,D,O
Drake University	M,D,O
Drexel University	M,D,O
Drury University	M
Duke University	M
Duquesne University	M,D,O
D'Youville College	M,O

Institution	Degrees
East Carolina University	M,D,O
East Central University	M
Eastern Connecticut State University	M
Eastern Illinois University	M,O
Eastern Kentucky University	M
Eastern Mennonite University	M
Eastern Michigan University	M,D,O
Eastern Nazarene College	M,O
Eastern New Mexico University	M
Eastern Oregon University	M
Eastern University	M,O
Eastern Washington University	M
East Stroudsburg University of Pennsylvania	M
East Tennessee State University	M,D,O
Edgewood College	M,D,O
Edinboro University of Pennsylvania	M,O
Elon University	M
Emmanuel College	M,O
Emory University	M,D,O
Emporia State University	M,O
The Evergreen State College	M
Fairfield University	M,O
Fairleigh Dickinson University, College at Florham	M,O
Fairleigh Dickinson University, Metropolitan Campus	M,O
Ferris State University	M
Florida Agricultural and Mechanical University	M,D
Florida Atlantic University	M,D,O
Florida Gulf Coast University	M
Florida International University	M,D,O
Florida State University	M,D,O
Fontbonne University	M
Fordham University	M,D,O
Fort Hays State University	M,O
Franciscan University of Steubenville	M
Francis Marion University	M
Freed-Hardeman University	M,O
Fresno Pacific University	M
Friends University	M
Frostburg State University	M
Furman University	M
Gallaudet University	M,D,O
Gannon University	M,O
Gardner-Webb University	M,D
Geneva College	M
George Fox University	M,D,O
George Mason University	M,D
Georgetown College	M
The George Washington University	M,D,O
Georgia College & State University	M,O
Georgian Court University	M,O
Georgia Southern University	M,D,O
Georgia Southwestern State University	M,O
Georgia State University	M,D,O
Goddard College	M
Gonzaga University	M
Governors State University	M
Graceland University	M
Grambling State University	M,D
Grand Canyon University	M
Grand Valley State University	M
Gratz College	M
Gwynedd-Mercy College	M
Hamline University	M,D
Hampton University	M
Harding University	M,O
Hardin-Simmons University	M
Harvard University	M,D
Heidelberg College	M
Henderson State University	M,O
Heritage University	M
Hodges University	M
Hofstra University	M,D,O
Hollins University	M
Holy Family University	M
Holy Names University	M,O
Hood College	M,O
Hope International University	M
Houston Baptist University	M
Howard University	M,D,O
Humboldt State University	M
Hunter College of the City University of New York	M,O
Idaho State University	M,D,O
Illinois State University	M,D
Indiana State University	M,D,O
Indiana University Bloomington	M,D,O
Indiana University Northwest	M
Indiana University of Pennsylvania	M,D,O
Indiana University–Purdue University Fort Wayne	M
Indiana University–Purdue University Indianapolis	M,O
Indiana University South Bend	M
Indiana University Southeast	M
Indiana Wesleyan University	M
Inter American University of Puerto Rico, Metropolitan Campus	M,D
Jackson State University	M,D,O
Jacksonville State University	M,O
Jacksonville University	M,O
John Carroll University	M
John F. Kennedy University	M
The Johns Hopkins University	M,D,O
Johnson & Wales University	M
Johnson State College	M,O
Kansas State University	M,D
Kean University	M,O
Keene State College	M,O
Kennesaw State University	M,D,O
Kent State University	M,D,O
Kutztown University of Pennsylvania	M,O
Lakeland College	M
Lamar University	M,D,O
La Salle University	M
La Sierra University	M,D,O
Lee University	M
Lehigh University	M,D,O
Lehman College of the City University of New York	M
Le Moyne College	M
Lesley University	M,D,O
Lewis & Clark College	M,D,O
Lewis University	M,O
Liberty University	M,D,O
Lincoln Memorial University	M,O
Lincoln University (MO)	M,O
Lindenwood University	M,D,O
Lipscomb University	M
Lock Haven University of Pennsylvania	M
Long Island University, Brentwood Campus	M
Long Island University, Brooklyn Campus	M,O
Long Island University, C.W. Post Campus	M,O
Long Island University, Southampton Graduate Campus	M
Longwood University	M
Louisiana State University and Agricultural and Mechanical College	M,D,O
Louisiana State University in Shreveport	M
Louisiana Tech University	M,D
Loyola College in Maryland	M,O
Loyola Marymount University	M,D
Loyola University Chicago	M,D,O
Loyola University New Orleans	M
Lynchburg College	M
Madonna University	M
Maharishi University of Management	M
Malone College	M
Manhattan College	M,O
Manhattanville College	M
Mansfield University of Pennsylvania	M
Marian College of Fond du Lac	M,D
Marist College	M,O
Marquette University	M,D,O
Marshall University	M,D,O
Mary Baldwin College	M
Marygrove College	M
Marymount University	M,O
Maryville University of Saint Louis	M,D
Marywood University	M
McNeese State University	M
Medaille College	M
Mercer University	M,D,O
Mercy College	M
Miami University	M,D,O
Michigan State University	M,D,O
MidAmerica Nazarene University	M
Middle Tennessee State University	M,D,O
Midwestern State University	M
Millersville University of Pennsylvania	M
Mills College	M,D
Minnesota State University Mankato	M,D,O
Minnesota State University Moorhead	M,O
Misericordia University	M
Mississippi College	M,O
Mississippi State University	M,D,O
Mississippi University for Women	M
Mississippi Valley State University	M
Missouri Baptist University	M,O
Missouri State University	M
Monmouth University	M,O
Montana State University	M,D,O
Montana State University–Billings	M,O
Montclair State University	M,O
Morehead State University	M,O
Morgan State University	M,D
Morningside College	M
Mount Mary College	M
Mount Saint Mary College	M
Mount St. Mary's College	M
Mount St. Mary's University	M
Murray State University	M,D,O
Muskingum College	M
Naropa University	M
National-Louis University	M,D,O
National University	M
Nazareth College of Rochester	M
Neumann College	M
New College of California	M
Newman University	M
New Mexico Highlands University	M
New Mexico State University	M,D,O
New York Institute of Technology	M,O
New York University	M,D,O
Niagara University	M,O
Nicholls State University	M
Norfolk State University	M
North Carolina Agricultural and Technical State University	M
North Carolina Central University	M
North Carolina State University	M,D,O
North Central College	M
North Dakota State University	M,D,O
Northeastern Illinois University	M

Northeastern State University	M
Northern Arizona University	M,D,O
Northern Illinois University	M,D,O
Northern Kentucky University	M,O
Northern Michigan University	M,O
North Georgia College & State University	M,O
North Park University	M
Northwestern State University of Louisiana	M,O
Northwestern University	M,D
Northwest Missouri State University	M,O
Northwest Nazarene University	M
Norwich University	M
Notre Dame de Namur University	M
Nova Southeastern University	M,D,O
Nyack College	M
Oakland City University	M,D
Oakland University	M,D,O
Ohio Dominican University	M
The Ohio State University	M,D
Ohio University	M,D
Oklahoma City University	M
Oklahoma State University	M,D,O
Old Dominion University	M,D,O
Olivet Nazarene University	M
Oral Roberts University	M,D
Oregon State University	M,D
Otterbein College	M
Our Lady of the Lake University of San Antonio	M,D
Pace University	M,O
Pacific Lutheran University	M
Pacific University	M
Palm Beach Atlantic University	M
Park University	M
Penn State Great Valley	M
Penn State Harrisburg	M,D
Penn State University Park	M,D
Pfeiffer University	M
Philadelphia Biblical University	M
Piedmont College	M,O
Pittsburg State University	M,O
Plymouth State University	O
Point Loma Nazarene University	M,O
Point Park University	M
Pontifical Catholic University of Puerto Rico	M,D
Portland State University	M,D
Prairie View A&M University	M,D
Prescott College	M,D
Providence College	M
Purdue University	M,D,O
Purdue University Calumet	M
Queens College of the City University of New York	M,O
Queens University of Charlotte	M
Quinnipiac University	M
Radford University	M
Regent University	M,D,O
Regis College (MA)	M
Regis University	M,O
Rhode Island College	D
Rice University	M
The Richard Stockton College of New Jersey	M
Rider University	M,O
Rivier College	M,O
Roberts Wesleyan College	M,O
Rockford College	M
Rockhurst University	M
Roger Williams University	M
Rollins College	M
Roosevelt University	M,D
Rowan University	M,D,O
Rutgers, The State University of New Jersey, New Brunswick	M,D
Sacred Heart University	M,O
Saginaw Valley State University	M,O
St. Ambrose University	M
St. Bonaventure University	M,O
St. Cloud State University	M,O
St. Edward's University	M
Saint Francis University	M
St. John Fisher College	M,D,O
St. John's University (NY)	M,D,O
Saint Joseph College	M
Saint Joseph's College of Maine	M
Saint Joseph's University	M,D,O
Saint Leo University	M
Saint Louis University	M,D
Saint Martin's University	M
Saint Mary's College of California	M,D
Saint Mary's University of Minnesota	M
St. Mary's University of San Antonio	M,O
Saint Michael's College	M,O
Saint Peter's College	M,O
St. Thomas Aquinas College	M,O
St. Thomas University	M,D,O
Saint Xavier University	M,O
Salem State College	M
Salisbury University	M
Samford University	M,D,O
San Diego State University	M,D
San Francisco State University	M,D,O
San Jose State University	M,O
Santa Clara University	M,O
Sarah Lawrence College	M
School for International Training	M
Seattle Pacific University	M,D
Seattle University	M,D,O
Seton Hall University	M,D,O
Seton Hill University	M
Shenandoah University	M,D,O
Shippensburg University of Pennsylvania	M,O
Siena Heights University	M
Silver Lake College	M
Simmons College	M,D,O
Slippery Rock University of Pennsylvania	M
Sonoma State University	M
South Dakota State University	M
Southeastern Louisiana University	M,D
Southeastern Oklahoma State University	M
Southern Connecticut State University	M,D,O
Southern Illinois University Carbondale	M,D
Southern Illinois University Edwardsville	M,O
Southern Methodist University	M
Southern Nazarene University	M
Southern New Hampshire University	M,O
Southern Oregon University	M
Southern University and Agricultural and Mechanical College	M,D
Southern Utah University	M
Southern Wesleyan University	M
Southwest Baptist University	M,O
Southwestern College (KS)	M
Southwestern Oklahoma State University	M
Southwest Minnesota State University	M
Spalding University	M,D
Spring Arbor University	M
Springfield College	M
Spring Hill College	M
Stanford University	M,D
State University of New York at Binghamton	M,D
State University of New York at Fredonia	M,O
State University of New York at New Paltz	M,O
State University of New York at Oswego	M,O
State University of New York College at Brockport	M
State University of New York College at Cortland	M,O
State University of New York College at Geneseo	M
State University of New York College at Oneonta	M,O
State University of New York Empire State College	M
Stephen F. Austin State University	M,D
Stetson University	M,O
Suffolk University	M,O
Sul Ross State University	M
Syracuse University	M,D,O
Tarleton State University	M,D,O
Temple University	M,D
Tennessee State University	M,D,O
Tennessee Technological University	M,D,O
Texas A&M International University	M,D
Texas A&M University	M,D
Texas A&M University–Commerce	M,D
Texas A&M University–Corpus Christi	M,D
Texas A&M University–Kingsville	M,D
Texas A&M University–Texarkana	M
Texas Christian University	M,D,O
Texas Southern University	M,D
Texas State University-San Marcos	M,D
Texas Tech University	M,D,O
Texas Wesleyan University	M
Texas Woman's University	M,D
Towson University	M
Trevecca Nazarene University	M,D
Trinity International University	M
Trinity University	M
Trinity (Washington) University	M
Troy University	M,O
Truman State University	M
Tufts University	M,D,O
Tusculum College	M
Union College (KY)	M
Union Institute & University	M,O
Union University	M,D,O
Universidad del Turabo	M
Universidad Metropolitana	M
University at Albany, State University of New York	M,D,O
University at Buffalo, the State University of New York	M,D,O
The University of Akron	M,D
The University of Alabama at Birmingham	M,D,O
University of Alaska Anchorage	M,O
University of Alaska Fairbanks	M
University of Alaska Southeast	M
The University of Arizona	M,D,O
University of Arkansas	M,D,O
University of Arkansas at Little Rock	M,D,O
University of Arkansas at Monticello	M
University of Bridgeport	M,D,O
University of California, Berkeley	M,D
University of California, Davis	M,D
University of California, Irvine	M,D
University of California, Los Angeles	M,D
University of California, Riverside	M,D

Institution	Degrees
University of California, San Diego	M,D
University of California, Santa Barbara	M,D
University of California, Santa Cruz	M,D
University of Central Arkansas	M
University of Central Florida	M,D,O
University of Central Missouri	M,D,O
University of Central Oklahoma	M
University of Cincinnati	M,D,O
University of Colorado at Boulder	M,D
University of Colorado at Colorado Springs	M,D
University of Colorado Denver	M,D,O
University of Connecticut	M,D
University of Dayton	M,D,O
University of Delaware	M,D
University of Denver	M,D,O
University of Detroit Mercy	M
University of Evansville	M
The University of Findlay	M
University of Florida	M,D,O
University of Georgia	M,D,O
University of Great Falls	M
University of Guam	M
University of Hartford	M,D,O
University of Hawaii at Manoa	M,D,O
University of Houston	M,D
University of Houston–Clear Lake	M,D
University of Houston–Victoria	M
University of Idaho	M,D,O
University of Illinois at Chicago	M,D
University of Illinois at Urbana–Champaign	M,D,O
University of Indianapolis	M
The University of Iowa	M,D,O
University of Kansas	M,D,O
University of Kentucky	M,D,O
University of La Verne	M,O
University of Louisiana at Lafayette	M,D
University of Louisiana at Monroe	M,D,O
University of Louisville	M,D,O
University of Maine	M,D,O
University of Mary	M
University of Mary Hardin-Baylor	M,D
University of Maryland, Baltimore County	M,O
University of Maryland, College Park	M,D,O
University of Maryland Eastern Shore	M
University of Maryland University College	M
University of Mary Washington	M
University of Massachusetts Amherst	M,D,O
University of Massachusetts Boston	M,D,O
University of Massachusetts Dartmouth	M,O
University of Massachusetts Lowell	M,D,O
University of Memphis	M,D
University of Miami	M,D,O
University of Michigan	M,D
University of Michigan–Dearborn	M
University of Michigan–Flint	M
University of Minnesota, Duluth	D
University of Minnesota, Twin Cities Campus	M,D,O
University of Mississippi	M,D,O
University of Missouri–Columbia	M,D,O
University of Missouri–Kansas City	M,D,O
University of Missouri–St. Louis	M,D,O
University of Mobile	M
The University of Montana	M,D,O
University of Montevallo	M,O
University of Nebraska at Kearney	M,O
University of Nebraska at Omaha	M,D,O
University of Nebraska–Lincoln	M,D,O
University of Nevada, Las Vegas	M,D,O
University of Nevada, Reno	M,D,O
University of New England	M
University of New Hampshire	M,D,O
University of New Haven	M
University of New Mexico	M,O
University of New Orleans	M,D,O
University of North Alabama	M,O
The University of North Carolina at Chapel Hill	M,D
The University of North Carolina at Charlotte	M
The University of North Carolina at Greensboro	M,D,O
The University of North Carolina at Pembroke	M
The University of North Carolina Wilmington	M
University of North Dakota	M,D,O
University of Northern Colorado	M,D,O
University of Northern Iowa	M,D,O
University of North Florida	M,D
University of North Texas	M,D,O
University of Notre Dame	M
University of Oklahoma	M,D
University of Oregon	M,D
University of Pennsylvania	M,D
University of Phoenix–Central Florida Campus	M
University of Phoenix–Denver Campus	M
University of Phoenix–Fort Lauderdale Campus	M
University of Phoenix–Hawaii Campus	M
University of Phoenix–Las Vegas Campus	M
University of Phoenix–Louisiana Campus	M
University of Phoenix–New Mexico Campus	M
University of Phoenix–North Florida Campus	M
University of Phoenix	M,D
University of Phoenix–Oregon Campus	M
University of Phoenix–Phoenix Campus	M
University of Phoenix–Sacramento Valley Campus	M,O
University of Phoenix–San Diego Campus	M
University of Phoenix–Southern Arizona Campus	M,O
University of Phoenix–Southern California Campus	M
University of Phoenix–Southern Colorado Campus	M,O
University of Phoenix–Utah Campus	M
University of Phoenix–West Florida Campus	M
University of Phoenix–West Michigan Campus	M
University of Pittsburgh	M,D
University of Portland	M
University of Puerto Rico, Río Piedras	M,D
University of Puget Sound	M
University of Redlands	M,D,O
University of Rhode Island	M
University of Rio Grande	M
University of Rochester	M,D
University of St. Francis (IL)	M
University of Saint Francis (IN)	M
University of Saint Mary	M
University of St. Thomas (MN)	M
University of St. Thomas (TX)	M
University of San Diego	M,D,O
University of San Francisco	M,D
The University of Scranton	M
University of Sioux Falls	M,O
University of South Alabama	M,D,O
University of South Carolina	M,D,O
The University of South Dakota	M,D,O
University of Southern Indiana	M
University of Southern Maine	M,D,O
University of Southern Mississippi	M,D,O
University of South Florida	M,D,O
The University of Tampa	M
The University of Tennessee	M,D,O
The University of Tennessee at Chattanooga	M,D,O
The University of Tennessee at Martin	M
The University of Texas at Arlington	M
The University of Texas at Austin	M,D
The University of Texas at Brownsville	M
The University of Texas at El Paso	M,D
The University of Texas at San Antonio	M,D
The University of Texas at Tyler	M
The University of Texas of the Permian Basin	M
The University of Texas–Pan American	M,D
University of the District of Columbia	M
University of the Incarnate Word	M,D
University of the Pacific	M,D,O
The University of Toledo	M,D,O
University of Tulsa	M
University of Utah	M,D
University of Vermont	M,D
University of Virginia	M,D,O
University of Washington	M,D,O
University of Washington, Bothell	M
University of Washington, Tacoma	M
The University of West Alabama	M
University of West Georgia	M,D,O
University of Wisconsin–Eau Claire	M
University of Wisconsin–La Crosse	M
University of Wisconsin–Madison	M,D,O
University of Wisconsin–Milwaukee	M,D,O
University of Wisconsin–Oshkosh	M
University of Wisconsin–Platteville	M
University of Wisconsin–River Falls	M
University of Wisconsin–Stevens Point	M
University of Wisconsin–Stout	M,O
University of Wisconsin–Superior	M
University of Wisconsin–Whitewater	M
Ursuline College	M
Utah State University	M,D,O
Utica College	M,O
Valdosta State University	M,D,O
Valparaiso University	M
Vanderbilt University	M,D
Vanguard University of Southern California	M
Villanova University	M
Virginia Commonwealth University	M,D,O
Virginia State University	M,O
Viterbo University	M
Wagner College	M,O
Wake Forest University	M
Walla Walla University	M
Walsh University	M
Washburn University	M
Washington State University	M,D
Washington University in St. Louis	M,D
Wayland Baptist University	M
Wayne State College	M,O
Wayne State University	M,D,O
Weber State University	M
Webster University	M,O
Wesley College	M
West Chester University of Pennsylvania	M,O

Western Carolina University M,D,O
Western Connecticut State University M
Western Illinois University M,D,O
Western Michigan University M,D,O
Western New Mexico University M
Western Oregon University M
Western Washington University M
Westfield State College M,O
Westminster College (UT) M
West Texas A&M University M
West Virginia University M,D
Wheaton College M
Wheelock College M
Whitworth University M
Wichita State University M,D,O
Widener University M,D
Wilkes University M,D
Willamette University M
William Carey University M,O
William Paterson University of New Jersey M
Wilmington University (DE) M
Winona State University M
Winthrop University M
Worcester State College M
Wright State University M,O
Xavier University M
Xavier University of Louisiana M
Youngstown State University M,D

■ EDUCATIONAL ADMINISTRATION

Abilene Christian University M,O
Adelphi University M,O
Alabama Agricultural and Mechanical University M,O
Alabama State University M,D,O
Albany State University M,O
Alverno College M
American International College M,D,O
American University M,D
Andrews University M,D,O
Angelo State University M
Antioch University McGregor M
Antioch University New England M
Appalachian State University M,D,O
Arcadia University M,D,O
Argosy University, Orange County Campus M,D
Argosy University, Sarasota Campus M,D,O
Argosy University, Tampa Campus M,D,O
Argosy University, Twin Cities Campus M,D,O
Arizona State University M,D
Arizona State University at the Polytechnic Campus M,D
Arizona State University at the West campus M,D,O
Arkansas State University M,D,O
Arkansas Tech University M,O
Ashland University M,D
Auburn University M,D,O
Auburn University Montgomery M,O
Augusta State University M,O
Aurora University M,D
Austin Peay State University M,O
Azusa Pacific University M,D
Baldwin-Wallace College M
Ball State University M,D,O
Barry University M,D,O
Bayamón Central University M
Baylor University M,O
Bellarmine University M
Benedictine College M
Benedictine University M,D
Bernard M. Baruch College of the City University of New York M
Bethel College (TN) M
Bethel University M,D,O
Bob Jones University P,M,D,O
Boise State University M,D
Boston College M,D,O
Boston University M,O
Bowie State University M,D
Bowling Green State University M,D,O
Bradley University M
Bridgewater State College M,O
Brigham Young University M,D
Brooklyn College of the City University of New York O
Bucknell University M
Buffalo State College, State University of New York O
Butler University M
Cabrini College M,O
Caldwell College M
California Baptist University M
California Lutheran University M
California State University, Bakersfield M
California State University, Chico M
California State University, Dominguez Hills M
California State University, East Bay M
California State University, Fresno M,D
California State University, Fullerton M
California State University, Northridge M
California State University, Sacramento M
California State University, San Bernardino M
California University of Pennsylvania M
Cambridge College M,D,O
Cameron University M
Campbell University M
Canisius College M
Capella University M,D,O
Cardinal Stritch University M,D
Carlow University M
Castleton State College M,O
The Catholic University of America M,D
Centenary College M
Central Connecticut State University M,D,O
Central Michigan University M,D,O
Central Washington University M
Chapman University M
Charleston Southern University M
Chestnut Hill College M
Cheyney University of Pennsylvania M,O
Chicago State University M,D
Christian Brothers University M
The Citadel, The Military College of South Carolina M,O
City College of the City University of New York M,O
City University of Seattle M,O
Claremont Graduate University M,D,O
Clark Atlanta University M,D,O
Clemson University M,D,O
Cleveland State University M,D,O
College of Mount St. Joseph M
The College of New Jersey M,O
The College of New Rochelle M,O
College of Notre Dame of Maryland M,D
College of Saint Elizabeth M,O
The College of Saint Rose M,O
College of Santa Fe M
College of Staten Island of the City University of New York O
College of the Southwest M
The College of William and Mary M,D
Colorado State University M,D
Columbus State University M,O
Concordia University (CA) M
Concordia University Chicago (IL) M,D,O
Concordia University (NE) M
Concordia University (OR) M
Concordia University Wisconsin M
Converse College M,O
Creighton University M
Dallas Baptist University M
Delta State University M,D,O
DePaul University D
Doane College M
Dominican University M
Dowling College M,D,O
Drake University M,D,O
Drexel University M,D
Duquesne University M,D
East Carolina University M,D,O
Eastern Illinois University M,O
Eastern Kentucky University M
Eastern Michigan University M,D,O
Eastern Nazarene College M,O
Eastern Washington University M
East Tennessee State University M,D,O
Edgewood College M,D,O
Edinboro University of Pennsylvania M,O
Elmhurst College M
Emmanuel College M,O
Emporia State University M
Fairleigh Dickinson University, College at Florham M
Fairleigh Dickinson University, Metropolitan Campus M
Fayetteville State University M,D
Ferris State University M
Fitchburg State College M,O
Florida Agricultural and Mechanical University M,D
Florida Atlantic University M,D,O
Florida Gulf Coast University M
Florida International University M,D,O
Florida State University M,D,O
Fordham University M,D,O
Fort Hays State University M,O
Framingham State College M
Franciscan University of Steubenville M
Freed-Hardeman University M,O
Fresno Pacific University M
Friends University M
Frostburg State University M
Furman University M
Gallaudet University M,D,O
Gannon University M,O
Gardner-Webb University M,D
Geneva College M
George Fox University M,D,O
George Mason University M
The George Washington University M,D,O
Georgia College & State University M,O
Georgian Court University M,O
Georgia Southern University M,D,O
Georgia State University M,D,O
Gonzaga University M,D
Governors State University M
Grambling State University M,D
Grand Valley State University M
Gwynedd-Mercy College M
Harding University M,O
Harvard University M,D
Henderson State University M,O
Heritage University M
High Point University M
Hofstra University M,D,O
Hood College M,O
Houston Baptist University M

Institution	Degrees
Howard University	M,D,O
Hunter College of the City University of New York	O
Idaho State University	M,D,O
Illinois State University	M,D
Immaculata University	M,D,O
Indiana State University	M,D,O
Indiana University Bloomington	M,D,O
Indiana University of Pennsylvania	M,D,O
Indiana University–Purdue University Fort Wayne	M
Inter American University of Puerto Rico, Metropolitan Campus	M
Inter American University of Puerto Rico, San Germán Campus	M,D
Iona College	M
Iowa State University of Science and Technology	M,D
Jackson State University	M,D,O
Jacksonville State University	M,O
James Madison University	M
John Carroll University	M
The Johns Hopkins University	M,D,O
Johnson & Wales University	D
Kansas State University	M,D
Kean University	M
Keene State College	M,O
Kennesaw State University	M,D,O
Kent State University	M,D,O
Kutztown University of Pennsylvania	M
Lamar University	M,D,O
La Sierra University	M,D,O
Lee University	M
Lehigh University	M,D,O
LeTourneau University	M
Lewis & Clark College	M,D
Lewis University	M
Liberty University	M,D,O
Lincoln Memorial University	M,O
Lincoln University (MO)	M,O
Lindenwood University	M,D,O
Lipscomb University	M
Long Island University, Brentwood Campus	M
Long Island University, Brooklyn Campus	M
Long Island University, C.W. Post Campus	M,O
Longwood University	M
Louisiana State University and Agricultural and Mechanical College	M,D,O
Louisiana Tech University	M,D
Loyola College in Maryland	M,O
Loyola Marymount University	M,D
Loyola University Chicago	M,D,O
Lynchburg College	M
Lynn University	M,D
Madonna University	M
Manhattan College	M,O
Manhattanville College	M
Marian College of Fond du Lac	M,D
Marshall University	M,D,O
Marygrove College	M
Marymount University	M,O
Maryville University of Saint Louis	M,D
Marywood University	M,D
McDaniel College	M
McNeese State University	M,O
Mercer University	M,D,O
Mercy College	M
Mercyhurst College	M,O
Miami University	M,D
Michigan State University	M,D,O
Middle Tennessee State University	M,O
Midwestern State University	M
Mills College	M,D
Minnesota State University Mankato	M,O
Minnesota State University Moorhead	M,O
Mississippi College	M,O
Mississippi State University	M,D,O
Missouri Baptist University	M,O
Missouri State University	M,O
Monmouth University	M,O
Montclair State University	M,O
Morehead State University	M,O
Morgan State University	M,D
Mount St. Mary's College	M
Murray State University	M,O
National-Louis University	M,D,O
National University	M
New Jersey City University	M
Newman University	M
New Mexico Highlands University	M
New Mexico State University	M,D
New York Institute of Technology	O
New York University	M,D,O
Niagara University	M,O
Nicholls State University	M
Norfolk State University	M
North Carolina Agricultural and Technical State University	M
North Carolina Central University	M
North Carolina State University	M,D
North Central College	M
North Dakota State University	M,O
Northeastern Illinois University	M
Northeastern State University	M
Northern Arizona University	M,D
Northern Illinois University	M,D,O
Northern Kentucky University	M
Northern Michigan University	M,O
North Georgia College & State University	M,O
Northwestern State University of Louisiana	M,O
Northwest Missouri State University	M,O
Northwest Nazarene University	M
Notre Dame de Namur University	M,O
Nova Southeastern University	M,D,O
Oakland City University	M,D
Oakland University	M,D,O
The Ohio State University	M,D
Ohio University	M,D
Oklahoma State University	M,D
Old Dominion University	M,D,O
Oral Roberts University	M,D
Oregon State University	M
Our Lady of the Lake University of San Antonio	M,D
Pace University	M,O
Pacific Lutheran University	M
Park University	M
Penn State University Park	M,D
Philadelphia Biblical University	M
Pittsburg State University	M
Plymouth State University	M
Point Park University	M
Portland State University	M,D
Prairie View A&M University	M,D
Providence College	M
Purdue University	M,D,O
Purdue University Calumet	M
Queens College of the City University of New York	O
Radford University	M
Regent University	M,D,O
Regis University	M,O
Rhode Island College	M,O
Rider University	M,O
Rivier College	M,O
Roosevelt University	M,D
Rowan University	M,D,O
Rutgers, The State University of New Jersey, Camden	M
Rutgers, The State University of New Jersey, New Brunswick	M,D
Sacred Heart University	M,O
Saginaw Valley State University	M,O
St. Ambrose University	M
St. Bonaventure University	M,O
St. Cloud State University	M
Saint Francis University	M
St. John Fisher College	M,D
St. John's University (NY)	M,D,O
Saint Joseph's University	M,D,O
Saint Leo University	M
Saint Louis University	M,D,O
Saint Martin's University	M
Saint Mary's College of California	M,D
Saint Mary's University of Minnesota	M,D,O
St. Mary's University of San Antonio	M,O
Saint Michael's College	M,O
Saint Peter's College	M,O
St. Thomas University	M,D,O
Saint Xavier University	M,O
Salem State College	M
Salisbury University	M
Samford University	M,D,O
Sam Houston State University	M,D
San Diego State University	M
San Francisco State University	M,O
San Jose State University	M,O
Santa Clara University	M
Seattle Pacific University	M,D
Seattle University	M,D,O
Seton Hall University	M,D,O
Shenandoah University	M,D,O
Shippensburg University of Pennsylvania	M
Silver Lake College	M
Simmons College	M,O
Slippery Rock University of Pennsylvania	M
Sonoma State University	M
South Carolina State University	D,O
South Dakota State University	M
Southeastern Louisiana University	M,D
Southeastern Oklahoma State University	M
Southeast Missouri State University	M,O
Southern Connecticut State University	D,O
Southern Illinois University Carbondale	M,D
Southern Illinois University Edwardsville	M,O
Southern Nazarene University	M
Southern New Hampshire University	M,O
Southern Oregon University	M
Southern University and Agricultural and Mechanical College	M
Southwest Baptist University	M,O
Southwestern Oklahoma State University	M
Southwest Minnesota State University	M
Spalding University	M,D
Stanford University	M,D
State University of New York at Fredonia	O
State University of New York at New Paltz	M,O

State University of New York at Oswego O
State University of New York at Plattsburgh O
State University of New York College at Brockport M,O
State University of New York College at Cortland O
Stephen F. Austin State University M,D
Stetson University M,O
Stony Brook University, State University of New York M,O
Suffolk University M,O
Sul Ross State University M
Syracuse University M,D,O
Tarleton State University M,D,O
Temple University M,D
Tennessee State University M,D,O
Tennessee Technological University M,O
Texas A&M International University M
Texas A&M University M,D
Texas A&M University–Commerce M,D
Texas A&M University–Corpus Christi M,D
Texas A&M University–Kingsville M,D
Texas A&M University–Texarkana M
Texas Christian University M
Texas Southern University M,D
Texas State University-San Marcos M
Texas Tech University M,D,O
Texas Woman's University M,D
Towson University M
Trevecca Nazarene University M,D
Trinity International University M
Trinity University M
Trinity (Washington) University M
Troy University M,O
Union College (KY) M,O
Union University M,D,O
Universidad del Turabo M
Universidad Metropolitana M
University at Albany, State University of New York M,D,O
University at Buffalo, the State University of New York M,D,O
The University of Akron M,D
The University of Alabama M,D,O
The University of Alabama at Birmingham M,D,O
University of Alaska Anchorage M,O
The University of Arizona M,D,O
University of Arkansas M,D,O
University of Arkansas at Little Rock M,D,O
University of Arkansas at Monticello M
University of Bridgeport D,O
University of California, Berkeley M,D
University of California, Irvine M,D
University of California, Santa Barbara M,D
University of Central Arkansas O
University of Central Florida M,D,O
University of Central Missouri M,O
University of Central Oklahoma M
University of Cincinnati M,D,O
University of Colorado at Colorado Springs M,D
University of Colorado Denver M,D,O
University of Connecticut D
University of Dayton M,D,O
University of Delaware M,D
University of Denver M,D,O
University of Detroit Mercy M
The University of Findlay M
University of Florida M,D,O
University of Georgia M,D,O
University of Guam M
University of Hartford D,O
University of Hawaii at Manoa M,D
University of Houston M,D
University of Houston–Clear Lake M,D
University of Idaho M,D,O
University of Illinois at Chicago M,D
University of Illinois at Springfield M
University of Illinois at Urbana–Champaign M,D,O
University of Indianapolis M
The University of Iowa M,D,O
University of Kansas M,D,O
University of Kentucky M,D,O
University of La Verne M,D,O
University of Louisiana at Lafayette M,D
University of Louisiana at Monroe M,D
University of Louisville M,D,O
University of Maine M,D,O
University of Mary M
University of Mary Hardin-Baylor M,D
University of Maryland, College Park M,D,O
University of Maryland Eastern Shore D
University of Massachusetts Amherst M,D,O
University of Massachusetts Boston M,D,O
University of Massachusetts Lowell M,D,O
University of Memphis M,D
University of Miami M,O
University of Michigan M,D
University of Michigan–Dearborn M,O
University of Minnesota, Twin Cities Campus M,D,O
University of Mississippi M,D,O
University of Missouri–Columbia M,D,O
University of Missouri–Kansas City M,D,O
University of Missouri–St. Louis M,D,O
The University of Montana M,D,O
University of Montevallo M,O
University of Nebraska at Kearney M,O
University of Nebraska at Omaha M,D,O
University of Nebraska–Lincoln M,D,O
University of Nevada, Las Vegas M,D,O
University of Nevada, Reno M,D,O
University of New England O
University of New Hampshire M,O
University of New Mexico M,D,O
University of New Orleans M,D,O
University of North Alabama M,O
The University of North Carolina at Chapel Hill M,D
The University of North Carolina at Charlotte M,D,O
The University of North Carolina at Greensboro M,D,O
The University of North Carolina at Pembroke M
The University of North Carolina Wilmington M
University of North Dakota M,D,O
University of Northern Colorado M,D,O
University of Northern Iowa M,D
University of North Florida M,D
University of North Texas M,D
University of Oklahoma M,D
University of Pennsylvania M,D
University of Phoenix–Central Florida Campus M
University of Phoenix–Denver Campus M
University of Phoenix–Fort Lauderdale Campus M
University of Phoenix–Hawaii Campus M
University of Phoenix–Las Vegas Campus M
University of Phoenix–New Mexico Campus M
University of Phoenix–North Florida Campus M
University of Phoenix M
University of Phoenix–Phoenix Campus M
University of Phoenix–Southern Colorado Campus M,O
University of Phoenix–Utah Campus M
University of Phoenix–West Florida Campus M
University of Phoenix–West Michigan Campus M
University of Pittsburgh M,D
University of Puerto Rico, Río Piedras M,D
University of St. Francis (IL) M
University of St. Thomas (MN) M,D,O
University of San Diego M,D,O
University of San Francisco M,D
The University of Scranton M
University of Sioux Falls M,O
University of South Alabama M,O
University of South Carolina M,D,O
The University of South Dakota M,D,O
University of Southern California D
University of Southern Maine M,O
University of Southern Mississippi M,D,O
University of South Florida M,D,O
The University of Tennessee M,D,O
The University of Tennessee at Chattanooga M,D,O
The University of Tennessee at Martin M
The University of Texas at Arlington M
The University of Texas at Austin M,D
The University of Texas at Brownsville M
The University of Texas at El Paso M,D
The University of Texas at San Antonio M,D
The University of Texas at Tyler M
The University of Texas of the Permian Basin M
The University of Texas–Pan American M,D
University of the Pacific M,D
The University of Toledo M,D,O
University of Utah M,D
University of Vermont M,D
University of Virginia M,D,O
University of Washington M,D,O
University of Washington, Tacoma M
The University of West Alabama M
University of West Florida M,O
University of West Georgia M,O
University of Wisconsin–Madison M,D,O
University of Wisconsin–Milwaukee M,O
University of Wisconsin–Oshkosh M
University of Wisconsin–Stevens Point M
University of Wisconsin–Superior M,O
University of Wisconsin–Whitewater M
University of Wyoming M,D,O
Ursuline College M
Valdosta State University M,D,O
Vanderbilt University M,D
Villanova University M
Virginia Commonwealth University D
Virginia Polytechnic Institute and State University D,O
Virginia State University M
Wagner College O
Walden University M,D
Walla Walla University M
Washburn University M
Washington State University M,D
Wayne State College M,O
Wayne State University M,D,O
Webster University M,O

Western Carolina University M,D,O
Western Connecticut State University D
Western Illinois University M,D,O
Western Kentucky University M,O
Western Michigan University M,D,O
Western New Mexico University M
Western Washington University M
Westfield State College M,O
West Texas A&M University M
West Virginia University M,D
Wheelock College M
Whitworth University M
Wichita State University M,D,O
Widener University M,D
Wilkes University M,D
William Paterson University of New Jersey M
William Woods University M,O
Wilmington University (DE) M,D
Winona State University M,O
Winthrop University M
Worcester State College M
Wright State University M,O
Xavier University M
Xavier University of Louisiana M
Yeshiva University M,D,O
Youngstown State University M,D

■ EDUCATIONAL MEASUREMENT AND EVALUATION

Abilene Christian University M
Angelo State University M
Arkansas State University M,O
Boston College M,D
Bucknell University M
Claremont Graduate University M,D,O
College of the Southwest M
Florida State University M,D
Gallaudet University O
George Mason University M
Georgia State University M,D
Harvard University D
Hofstra University M
Houston Baptist University M
Iowa State University of Science and Technology M,D
Kent State University M,D
Louisiana State University and Agricultural and Mechanical College M,D,O
Loyola University Chicago M,D
Michigan State University M,D,O
New York University M,D,O
North Carolina State University D
Ohio University M,D
Rutgers, The State University of New Jersey, New Brunswick M
Southern Connecticut State University M
Southern Illinois University Carbondale M,D
Southwestern Oklahoma State University M
Stanford University M,D
Sul Ross State University M
Syracuse University M,D,O
Texas A&M University M,D
Texas Christian University M
Texas Southern University M,D
University at Albany, State University of New York M,D,O
University of California, Berkeley M,D
University of California, Santa Barbara M,D
University of Colorado at Boulder D
University of Connecticut M,D
University of Denver M,D,O
University of Florida M,D,O
The University of Iowa M,D,O
University of Kansas M,D
University of Kentucky M,D
University of Maryland, College Park M,D
University of Massachusetts Amherst M,D,O
University of Memphis M,D
University of Miami M,D
University of Michigan M,D
University of Michigan–Dearborn M,O
University of Minnesota, Twin Cities Campus M,D
University of Missouri–St. Louis M,D,O
University of New England M
The University of North Carolina at Chapel Hill M,D
The University of North Carolina at Greensboro D
University of North Dakota D
University of Northern Colorado M,D
University of North Texas D
University of Pennsylvania M,D
University of Pittsburgh M,D
University of Puerto Rico, Río Piedras M
University of South Carolina M,D
University of South Florida M,D,O
The University of Tennessee M,D,O
The University of Texas–Pan American M
The University of Toledo M,D
University of Virginia M,D
University of Washington M,D
University of West Georgia D
Utah State University M,D
Vanderbilt University M,D
Virginia Commonwealth University D
Virginia Polytechnic Institute and State University D
Washington University in St. Louis D
Wayne State University M,D,O
West Chester University of Pennsylvania M
Western Michigan University M,D
West Texas A&M University M
Wilkes University M,D

■ EDUCATIONAL MEDIA/ INSTRUCTIONAL TECHNOLOGY

Adelphi University M,O
Alabama State University M,O
Alverno College M
American InterContinental University (CA) M
American InterContinental University (FL) M
American University M,D
Appalachian State University M
Arcadia University M,D,O
Argosy University, Orange County Campus M,D
Argosy University, Sarasota Campus M,D,O
Argosy University, Twin Cities Campus M,D,O
Arizona State University M,D
Ashland University M
Auburn University M,D,O
Azusa Pacific University M
Baldwin-Wallace College M
Barry University M,D,O
Belmont University M
Bloomsburg University of Pennsylvania M
Boise State University M
Boston University M,D,O
Bowling Green State University M
Bridgewater State College M
Brigham Young University M,D
Buffalo State College, State University of New York M
Cabrini College M,O
California Baptist University M
California State University, Bakersfield M
California State University, Chico M
California State University, East Bay M
California State University, Fullerton M
California State University, Los Angeles M
California State University, San Bernardino M
Capella University M,D,O
Cardinal Stritch University M
Carlow University M
Central Connecticut State University M
Central Michigan University M
Chestnut Hill College M,O
Chicago State University M
City University of Seattle M,O
College of Mount Saint Vincent M,O
The College of New Jersey M
College of Saint Elizabeth M,O
The College of Saint Rose M,O
The College of St. Scholastica M
The College of William and Mary M,D
DeSales University M,O
Dowling College M,D,O
Drexel University D
Duquesne University M,D
East Carolina University M,O
Eastern Connecticut State University M
Eastern Michigan University M
Eastern Washington University M
East Stroudsburg University of Pennsylvania M
East Tennessee State University M
Emporia State University M
Fairfield University M,O
Fairleigh Dickinson University, College at Florham M,O
Fairleigh Dickinson University, Metropolitan Campus M,O
Ferris State University M
Fitchburg State College M,O
Florida Atlantic University M
Florida Gulf Coast University M
Florida International University M,D,O
Florida State University M,D,O
Fort Hays State University M
Framingham State College M
Fresno Pacific University M
Frostburg State University M
Gallaudet University O
Gannon University M,O
George Mason University M
The George Washington University M
Georgia College & State University M,O
Georgian Court University M,O
Georgia Southern University M
Georgia State University M,D,O
Governors State University M
Grand Valley State University M
Harvard University M,O
Hofstra University M
Idaho State University M,D,O
Indiana State University M,D
Indiana University Bloomington M,D,O
Indiana University of Pennsylvania M
Inter American University of Puerto Rico, Metropolitan Campus M
Iona College M,O

Iowa State University of Science and Technology M,D
Jackson State University M,D,O
Jacksonville State University M
Jacksonville University M
The Johns Hopkins University M,D,O
Kean University M
Kennesaw State University M
Kent State University M
Kutztown University of Pennsylvania M,O
Lamar University M,D,O
Lawrence Technological University M
Lehigh University M,D,O
Lindenwood University M,D,O
Long Island University, Brooklyn Campus M
Long Island University, C.W. Post Campus M
Longwood University M
Louisiana State University and Agricultural and Mechanical College M,D,O
Loyola College in Maryland M
Loyola University Chicago M
Malone College M
McDaniel College M
McNeese State University M
Mercy College M
Michigan State University M,D,O
MidAmerica Nazarene University M
Midwestern State University M
Minnesota State University Mankato M,O
Mississippi State University M,D,O
Mississippi University for Women M
Missouri State University M
Montana State University–Billings M
Montclair State University M,O
National-Louis University M,O
National University M
Nazareth College of Rochester M
New Jersey City University M
New York Institute of Technology M,O
New York University M,D,O
North Carolina Agricultural and Technical State University M
North Carolina Central University M
North Carolina State University M,D
Northeastern State University M
Northern Arizona University M,O
Northern Illinois University M,D
Northwestern State University of Louisiana M,O
Northwestern University M,D
Northwest Missouri State University M
Notre Dame de Namur University M,O
Nova Southeastern University M,D,O
Oakland University O
Ohio University M,D
Old Dominion University M,D
Our Lady of the Lake University of San Antonio M
Penn State Great Valley M
Penn State University Park M,D
Philadelphia University M
Pittsburg State University M
Pontifical Catholic University of Puerto Rico M,D
Portland State University M,D
Purdue University M,D,O
Purdue University Calumet M
Regis University M,O
The Richard Stockton College of New Jersey M
Rochester Institute of Technology M
Rosemont College M
Rowan University M
Sacred Heart University M,O
Saginaw Valley State University M
St. Cloud State University M
Saint Joseph's University M,D,O
Saint Michael's College M,O
Salem State College M
Salisbury University M
San Diego State University M,D
San Francisco State University M,O
San Jose State University M,O
Seton Hall University M
Seton Hill University M
Simmons College M,D,O
Southeastern Oklahoma State University M
Southern Connecticut State University M,O
Southern Illinois University Edwardsville M
Southern University and Agricultural and Mechanical College M
State University of New York College at Potsdam M
Stony Brook University, State University of New York M,O
Syracuse University M,O
Texas A&M University M,D
Texas A&M University–Commerce M,D
Texas A&M University–Corpus Christi M,D
Texas A&M University–Texarkana M
Texas Tech University M,D,O
Towson University M,D
University at Albany, State University of New York M,D,O
The University of Akron M
University of Alaska Southeast M
University of Arkansas M
University of Arkansas at Little Rock M
University of Central Arkansas M
University of Central Florida M,D,O
University of Central Missouri M
University of Central Oklahoma M
University of Colorado Denver M
University of Connecticut M,D
University of Dayton M
The University of Findlay M
University of Georgia M,D,O
University of Hartford M
University of Hawaii at Manoa M
University of Houston–Clear Lake M
University of Kentucky M,D
University of Louisville M
University of Maine M
University of Maryland, Baltimore County M,O
University of Maryland, College Park M,D,O
University of Massachusetts Amherst M,D,O
University of Memphis M,D
University of Michigan M,D
University of Michigan–Flint M
University of Minnesota, Twin Cities Campus M,D,O
University of Missouri–Columbia M,D,O
University of Nebraska at Kearney M
University of Nebraska at Omaha M,O
University of Nevada, Las Vegas M,D,O
University of New Mexico M,D,O
The University of North Carolina at Charlotte M,D,O
The University of North Carolina at Greensboro M,D,O
The University of North Carolina Wilmington M
University of North Dakota M
University of Northern Colorado M,D
University of Northern Iowa M
University of Phoenix M
University of Phoenix–West Florida Campus M
University of St. Thomas (MN) M,D,O
University of San Francisco M
University of Sioux Falls M,O
University of South Alabama M,D
University of South Carolina M
The University of South Dakota M,O
University of Southern California M
University of South Florida M,D,O
The University of Tennessee M,D,O
The University of Tennessee at Chattanooga O
The University of Texas at Brownsville M
The University of Texas at San Antonio M
University of the Incarnate Word M,D,O
The University of Toledo M,D,O
University of Washington M,D
The University of West Alabama M
University of West Florida M
University of West Georgia M,O
University of Wyoming M,D,O
Utah State University M,D,O
Valdosta State University M,D,O
Virginia Polytechnic Institute and State University M,D,O
Walden University M,D
Wayne State University M,D,O
Webster University M,O
West Chester University of Pennsylvania M,O
Western Connecticut State University M
Western Illinois University M,O
Western Kentucky University M
Western Oregon University M
Westfield State College M
West Texas A&M University M
Widener University M,D
Wilkes University M,D
Wilmington University (DE) M

■ EDUCATIONAL POLICY

Alabama State University M,D,O
The College of William and Mary M,D
DeSales University M,O
The George Washington University M,D
Georgia State University M,D,O
Harvard University M,D
Illinois State University M,D
Indiana University Bloomington M,D,O
Loyola University Chicago M,D
Michigan State University D
New York University M,D
The Ohio State University M,D
Portland State University M,D
Rutgers, The State University of New Jersey, Camden M
Rutgers, The State University of New Jersey, New Brunswick D
University of Georgia M,D,O
University of Hawaii at Manoa D
University of Illinois at Chicago M,D
University of Illinois at Urbana–Champaign M,D
The University of Iowa M,D,O
University of Kansas D
University of Kentucky M,D
University of Minnesota, Twin Cities Campus M,D,O
University of Pennsylvania M,D

University of St. Thomas (MN) M,D,O
University of Virginia M,D
University of Washington M,D
University of Wisconsin–Madison M,D,O
University of Wisconsin–Milwaukee M
Vanderbilt University M,D
Wayne State University M,D,O

■ EDUCATIONAL PSYCHOLOGY

American International College M,D,O
Andrews University M,D
Arcadia University M,D,O
Arizona State University M,D
Auburn University M,D,O
Ball State University M,D,O
Baylor University M,D,O
Boston College M,D
Brigham Young University M,D
California State University, Northridge M
California State University, San Bernardino M
Capella University M,D,O
The Catholic University of America M,D
Chapman University M,O
Clark Atlanta University M,D
The College of Saint Rose M,O
Eastern Michigan University M
Eastern University M
Edinboro University of Pennsylvania M
Florida Atlantic University M,D,O
Florida State University M,D
Fordham University M,D,O
Georgian Court University M,O
Georgia State University M,D
Graduate School and University Center of the City University of New York D
Harvard University M
Holy Names University M,O
Howard University M,D,O
Illinois State University M,D,O
Indiana State University M,D,O
Indiana University Bloomington M,D,O
Indiana University of Pennsylvania M,O
John Carroll University M
Johnson State College M
Kansas State University M,D
Kean University M
Kent State University M,D
La Sierra University M,O
Loyola Marymount University M
Loyola University Chicago M
Marist College M,O
Miami University M,O
Michigan State University M,D,O
Mississippi State University M,D,O
Montclair State University M,O
National-Louis University M,D,O
New Jersey City University M,O
New York University M,D,O
Northeastern University M
Northern Arizona University D
Northern Illinois University M,D,O
Oklahoma City University M
Oklahoma State University M,D,O
Penn State University Park M,D
Purdue University M,D,O
Rutgers, The State University of New Jersey, New Brunswick M,D
Southern Illinois University Carbondale M,D
Stanford University D
State University of New York College at Oneonta M,O
Temple University M,D
Tennessee Technological University M,O
Texas A&M University M,D
Texas A&M University–Commerce M,D
Texas Christian University M,O
Texas Tech University M,D,O
University at Albany, State University of New York M,D,O
University at Buffalo, the State University of New York M,D,O
The University of Arizona M,D
University of California, Davis M,D
University of Colorado at Boulder M,D
University of Colorado Denver M
University of Connecticut M,D
University of Denver M,D,O
University of Florida M,D,O
University of Georgia M,D,O
University of Hawaii at Manoa M,D
University of Houston M,D
University of Illinois at Chicago M,D
University of Illinois at Urbana–Champaign M,D,O
The University of Iowa M,D,O
University of Kansas M,D
University of Kentucky M,D,O
University of Louisville M,D
University of Mary Hardin-Baylor M,D
University of Maryland, College Park M,D
University of Memphis M,D
University of Minnesota, Twin Cities Campus M,D,O
University of Missouri–Columbia M,D,O
University of Missouri–St. Louis D,O
University of Nebraska at Omaha M,D,O
University of Nebraska–Lincoln M,O
University of Nevada, Las Vegas M,D,O
University of Nevada, Reno M,D,O
University of New Mexico M,D
The University of North Carolina at Chapel Hill M,D
University of Northern Colorado M,D
University of Northern Iowa M,O
University of Oklahoma M,D
University of Pennsylvania M,D
University of Phoenix–Southern Arizona Campus M,O
University of South Carolina M,D
The University of South Dakota M,D,O
University of Southern California D
The University of Tennessee M,D,O
The University of Texas at Austin M,D
The University of Texas at San Antonio M
The University of Texas–Pan American M
University of the Pacific M,D,O
The University of Toledo M,D
University of Utah M,D
University of Virginia M,D,O
University of Washington M,D
University of Wisconsin–Madison M,D
University of Wisconsin–Milwaukee M,O
Virginia Polytechnic Institute and State University M,D,O
Washington State University M,D
Wayne State University M,D,O
Western Kentucky University M,O
West Virginia University M
Wichita State University M,D,O
Widener University M,D

■ EDUCATION OF THE GIFTED

Arkansas State University M,D,O
Arkansas Tech University M,O
Ashland University M
Barry University M,D,O
Belmont University M
Bowling Green State University M
Clark Atlanta University M,O
The College of New Rochelle M,O
The College of William and Mary M
Converse College M
Drury University M
Elon University M
Emporia State University M
Grand Valley State University M
Hardin-Simmons University M
Hofstra University M,O
The Johns Hopkins University M,D,O
Johnson State College M
Kent State University M
Liberty University M,D,O
Lynn University M,D
Maryville University of Saint Louis M,D
Minnesota State University Mankato M,O
Mississippi University for Women M
Northeastern Illinois University M
Nova Southeastern University M,O
Purdue University M,D,O
St. John's University (NY) M
Saint Leo University M
Samford University M,D,O
Southern Methodist University M,D
Tennessee Technological University D
Texas A&M University M,D
The University of Alabama M,D,O
University of Arkansas at Little Rock M
University of Central Florida M,D,O
University of Connecticut M,D
University of Houston M,D
University of Louisiana at Lafayette M
University of Minnesota, Twin Cities Campus M,D,O
University of Missouri–Columbia M,D
University of Nevada, Las Vegas M,D,O
The University of North Carolina at Charlotte M,D
University of St. Thomas (MN) M,D,O
University of Southern Mississippi M,D,O
University of South Florida M
The University of Texas–Pan American M
The University of Toledo O
Western Washington University M
West Virginia University M,D
Whitworth University M
William Carey University M,O
Wilmington University (DE) M
Wright State University M
Youngstown State University M

■ EDUCATION OF THE MULTIPLY HANDICAPPED

Cleveland State University M
Fresno Pacific University M
Gallaudet University M,D,O
Georgia State University M
Hunter College of the City University of New York M
Minot State University M
Montclair State University M,O
Norfolk State University M
University of Arkansas at Little Rock M
University of Illinois at Urbana–Champaign M,D,O
Western Oregon University M
West Virginia University M,D

■ ELECTRICAL ENGINEERING

Alfred University M
Arizona State University M,D

Arizona State University at the Polytechnic Campus M
Auburn University M,D
Baylor University M
Boise State University M,D
Boston University M,D
Bradley University M
Brigham Young University M,D
Brown University M,D
Bucknell University M
California Institute of Technology M,D,O
California Polytechnic State University, San Luis Obispo M
California State Polytechnic University, Pomona M
California State University, Chico M
California State University, Fresno M
California State University, Fullerton M
California State University, Long Beach M
California State University, Los Angeles M
California State University, Northridge M
California State University, Sacramento M
Carnegie Mellon University M,D
Case Western Reserve University M,D
The Catholic University of America M,D
City College of the City University of New York M,D
Clarkson University M,D
Clemson University M,D
Cleveland State University M,D
Colorado State University M,D
Colorado Technical University—Colorado Springs M
Colorado Technical University—Denver M
Columbia University M,D,O
Cornell University M,D
Dartmouth College M,D
Drexel University M,D
Duke University M,D
Fairfield University M
Fairleigh Dickinson University, Metropolitan Campus M
Florida Agricultural and Mechanical University M,D
Florida Atlantic University M,D
Florida Institute of Technology M,D
Florida International University M,D
Florida State University M,D
Gannon University M
George Mason University M,D
The George Washington University M,D
Georgia Institute of Technology M,D
Georgia Southern University M
Graduate School and University Center of the City University of New York D
Grand Valley State University M
Howard University M,D
Illinois Institute of Technology M,D
Indiana University–Purdue University Indianapolis M,D
Iowa State University of Science and Technology M,D
The Johns Hopkins University M,D
Kansas State University M,D
Lamar University M,D
Lawrence Technological University M,D
Lehigh University M,D
Louisiana State University and Agricultural and Mechanical College M,D
Louisiana Tech University M,D
Loyola Marymount University M
Manhattan College M
Marquette University M,D
Massachusetts Institute of Technology M,D,O
McNeese State University M
Mercer University M
Michigan State University M,D
Michigan Technological University M,D
Minnesota State University Mankato M
Mississippi State University M,D
Missouri University of Science and Technology M,D
Montana State University M,D
Morgan State University M,D
New Jersey Institute of Technology M,D
New Mexico Institute of Mining and Technology M
New Mexico State University M,D
New York Institute of Technology M
Norfolk State University M
North Carolina Agricultural and Technical State University M,D
North Carolina State University M,D
North Dakota State University
Northeastern University M,D
Northern Illinois University M
Northwestern University M,D,O
Oakland University M
The Ohio State University M,D
Ohio University M,D
Oklahoma State University M,D
Old Dominion University M,D
Penn State Harrisburg M
Penn State University Park M,D
Polytechnic University, Brooklyn Campus M,D
Polytechnic University, Westchester Graduate Center M,D
Portland State University M,D
Prairie View A&M University M,D
Princeton University M,D
Purdue University M,D
Rensselaer Polytechnic Institute M,D
Rice University M,D
Rochester Institute of Technology M
Rutgers, The State University of New Jersey, New Brunswick M,D
St. Cloud State University M
St. Mary's University of San Antonio M
San Diego State University M
San Jose State University M
Santa Clara University M,D,O
South Dakota State University M,D
Southern Illinois University Carbondale M,D
Southern Illinois University Edwardsville M
Southern Methodist University M,D
Southern Polytechnic State University M
Stanford University M,D,O
State University of New York at Binghamton M,D
State University of New York at New Paltz M
Stevens Institute of Technology M,D,O
Stony Brook University, State University of New York M,D
Syracuse University M,D,O
Temple University M
Tennessee Technological University M,D
Texas A&M University M,D
Texas A&M University–Kingsville M
Texas Tech University M,D
Tufts University M,D,O
Tulane University M,D
University at Buffalo, the State University of New York M,D
The University of Akron M,D
The University of Alabama M,D
The University of Alabama at Birmingham M
The University of Alabama in Huntsville M,D
University of Alaska Fairbanks M,D
The University of Arizona M,D
University of Arkansas M,D
University of Bridgeport M
University of California, Berkeley M,D
University of California, Davis M,D
University of California, Irvine M,D
University of California, Los Angeles M,D
University of California, Riverside M,D
University of California, San Diego M,D
University of California, Santa Barbara M,D
University of California, Santa Cruz M,D
University of Central Florida M,D,O
University of Cincinnati M,D
University of Colorado at Boulder M,D
University of Colorado at Colorado Springs M,D
University of Colorado Denver M
University of Connecticut M,D
University of Dayton M,D
University of Delaware M,D
University of Denver M,D
University of Detroit Mercy M,D
University of Evansville M
University of Florida M,D,O
University of Hawaii at Manoa M,D
University of Houston M,D
University of Idaho M,D
University of Illinois at Chicago M,D
University of Illinois at Urbana–Champaign M,D
The University of Iowa M,D
University of Kansas M,D
University of Kentucky M,D
University of Louisville M,D
University of Maine M,D
University of Maryland, Baltimore County M,D
University of Maryland, College Park M,D,O
University of Massachusetts Amherst M,D
University of Massachusetts Dartmouth M,D,O
University of Massachusetts Lowell M,D
University of Memphis M,D
University of Miami M,D
University of Michigan M,D
University of Michigan–Dearborn M
University of Minnesota, Duluth M
University of Minnesota, Twin Cities Campus M,D
University of Missouri–Columbia M,D
University of Missouri–Kansas City M,D
University of Nebraska–Lincoln M,D
University of Nevada, Las Vegas M,D
University of Nevada, Reno M,D
University of New Hampshire M,D
University of New Haven M
University of New Mexico M,D
The University of North Carolina at Charlotte M,D
University of North Dakota M
University of North Texas M
University of Notre Dame M,D
University of Oklahoma M,D

University of Pennsylvania M,D
University of Pittsburgh M,D
University of Puerto Rico, Mayagüez Campus M
University of Rhode Island M,D
University of Rochester M,D
University of South Alabama M
University of South Carolina M,D
University of Southern California M,D,O
University of South Florida M,D
The University of Tennessee M,D
The University of Texas at Arlington M,D
The University of Texas at Austin M,D
The University of Texas at Dallas M,D
The University of Texas at El Paso M,D
The University of Texas at San Antonio M,D
The University of Toledo M,D
University of Tulsa M
University of Utah M,D,O
University of Vermont M,D
University of Virginia M,D
University of Washington M,D
University of Wisconsin–Madison M,D
University of Wyoming M,D
Utah State University M,D
Vanderbilt University M,D
Villanova University M,O
Virginia Commonwealth University M,D
Virginia Polytechnic Institute and State University M,D
Walden University M,O
Washington State University M,D
Washington University in St. Louis M,D
Wayne State University M,D
Western Michigan University M,D
Western New England College M
West Virginia University M,D
Wichita State University M,D
Wilkes University M
Worcester Polytechnic Institute M,D,O
Wright State University M
Yale University M,D
Youngstown State University M

■ ELECTRONIC COMMERCE

Adelphi University M
American University M
Arkansas State University M,O
Boston University M
Bryant University M,O
California State University, East Bay M
Cambridge College M
Carnegie Mellon University M
City University of Seattle M,O
Claremont Graduate University M,D,O
Clemson University M,D
Cleveland State University M,D,O
Dallas Baptist University M
DePaul University M,D
Eastern Michigan University M
Fairleigh Dickinson University, Metropolitan Campus M
Ferris State University M
Florida Atlantic University M
Florida Institute of Technology M
Georgia Institute of Technology M,O
Hawai'i Pacific University M
Maryville University of Saint Louis M,O
Marywood University M,O
Mercy College M
National University M
New York Institute of Technology M,O
New York University M,O
Northwestern University M
Regis University M,O
Rensselaer Polytechnic Institute M,D
Saint Joseph's University M,O
Saint Xavier University M,O
Stevens Institute of Technology M,O
Temple University M
University at Buffalo, the State University of New York M,D,O
The University of Akron M
University of Cincinnati M
University of Denver M
University of Florida M
University of Massachusetts Dartmouth M,O
University of Phoenix–Denver Campus M
University of Phoenix–New Mexico Campus M
University of Phoenix M
University of Phoenix–West Michigan Campus M
University of San Francisco M
West Chester University of Pennsylvania M
Xavier University M

■ ELECTRONIC MATERIALS

Colorado School of Mines M,D
Massachusetts Institute of Technology M,D,O
Northwestern University M,D,O
Princeton University D
University of Arkansas M,D

■ ELEMENTARY EDUCATION

Adelphi University M
Alabama Agricultural and Mechanical University M,O
Alabama State University M,O
Alaska Pacific University M
Alcorn State University M,O
American International College M,D,O
American University M,O
Andrews University M,D,O
Anna Maria College M,O
Appalachian State University M
Arcadia University M,D,O
Argosy University, Orange County Campus M,D
Argosy University, Sarasota Campus M,D,O
Argosy University, Tampa Campus M,D,O
Argosy University, Twin Cities Campus M,D,O
Arizona State University at the West campus M,D,O
Arkansas State University M,O
Armstrong Atlantic State University M
Auburn University M,D,O
Auburn University Montgomery M,O
Augusta State University M,O
Ball State University M,D
Barry University M,D,O
Bayamón Central University M
Belhaven College (MS) M
Belmont University M
Benedictine University M
Bennington College M
Bethel College (TN) M
Bloomsburg University of Pennsylvania M
Bob Jones University P,M,D,O
Boston College M
Boston University M
Bowie State University M
Brandeis University M
Bridgewater State College M
Brooklyn College of the City University of New York M
Brown University M
Buffalo State College, State University of New York M
Butler University M
California State University, Fullerton M
California State University, Los Angeles M
California State University, Northridge M
California State University, San Bernardino M
California State University, Stanislaus M
California University of Pennsylvania M
Campbell University M
Capella University M,D,O
Carlow University M
Carson-Newman College M
Central Connecticut State University M,O
Central Michigan University M
Chapman University M
Charleston Southern University M
Chatham University M
Chestnut Hill College M
Cheyney University of Pennsylvania M
Chicago State University M
Clarion University of Pennsylvania M
Clemson University M
College of Charleston M
The College of New Jersey M
The College of New Rochelle M
College of St. Joseph M
The College of Saint Rose M,O
College of Staten Island of the City University of New York M
The College of William and Mary M
Columbia College (SC) M
Columbia College Chicago M
Concordia University (OR) M
Converse College M
Dallas Baptist University M
Delta State University M,O
DePaul University M,D
Drake University M
Drury University M
Duquesne University M
D'Youville College M,O
East Carolina University M
Eastern Connecticut State University M
Eastern Illinois University M
Eastern Kentucky University M
Eastern Michigan University M
Eastern Nazarene College M,O
Eastern Oregon University M
Eastern Washington University M
East Stroudsburg University of Pennsylvania M
East Tennessee State University M
Edinboro University of Pennsylvania M
Elon University M
Emmanuel College M,O
Emporia State University M
Endicott College M
Fairfield University M,O
Fayetteville State University M
Ferris State University M
Fitchburg State College M
Florida Agricultural and Mechanical University M
Florida Atlantic University M,D,O
Florida Gulf Coast University M
Florida Institute of Technology M,D,O
Florida International University M,D
Florida State University M,D,O
Fordham University M,D,O
Fort Hays State University M
Framingham State College M

Francis Marion University M
Friends University M
Frostburg State University M
Furman University M
Gallaudet University M,D,O
Gardner-Webb University M
The George Washington University M
Grambling State University M
Grand Canyon University M
Grand Valley State University M
Hampton University M
Harding University M,O
High Point University M
Hofstra University M,O
Holy Family University M
Hood College M,O
Howard University M
Hunter College of the City University of New York M
Idaho State University M,O
Immaculata University M,D,O
Indiana State University M
Indiana University Bloomington M,D,O
Indiana University Northwest M
Indiana University–Purdue University Fort Wayne M
Indiana University South Bend M
Indiana University Southeast M
Inter American University of Puerto Rico, Metropolitan Campus M
Inter American University of Puerto Rico, San Germán Campus M
Iona College M
Iowa State University of Science and Technology M,D
Jackson State University M,D,O
Jacksonville State University M
Jacksonville University M
The Johns Hopkins University M
Kansas State University M,D
Kennesaw State University M
Kent State University M,D,O
Kutztown University of Pennsylvania M,O
Lee University M
Lehigh University M,D
Lehman College of the City University of New York M
Lesley University M,D,O
Lewis & Clark College M
Liberty University M,D,O
Lincoln University (MO) M,O
Lock Haven University of Pennsylvania M
Long Island University, Brentwood Campus M
Long Island University, Brooklyn Campus M
Long Island University, C.W. Post Campus M
Long Island University, Southampton Graduate Campus M
Longwood University M
Louisiana State University and Agricultural and Mechanical College M,D,O
Loyola Marymount University M
Loyola University Chicago M
Loyola University New Orleans M
Lynchburg College M
Maharishi University of Management M
Manhattanville College M
Mansfield University of Pennsylvania M
Marshall University M
Mary Baldwin College M
Marygrove College M
Marymount University M,O
Maryville University of Saint Louis M,D
Marywood University M
McDaniel College M
McNeese State University M
Medaille College M
Mercy College M
Metropolitan College of New York M
Miami University M
Middle Tennessee State University M,O
Millersville University of Pennsylvania M
Mills College M,D
Minnesota State University Mankato M
Minot State University M
Mississippi College M,O
Mississippi State University M,D,O
Mississippi Valley State University M
Missouri State University M,O
Monmouth University M,O
Montclair State University M,O
Morehead State University M
Morgan State University M
Morningside College M
Mount Saint Mary College M
Mount St. Mary's College M
Murray State University M,O
National-Louis University M
Nazareth College of Rochester M
New Jersey City University M
New York Institute of Technology M,O
New York University M,D,O
Niagara University M
North Carolina Agricultural and Technical State University M
North Carolina Central University M
Northern Arizona University M
Northern Illinois University M,D
Northern Michigan University M
Northwestern State University of Louisiana M,O
Northwestern University M
Northwest Missouri State University M,O
Nova Southeastern University M,O
Oklahoma City University M
Old Dominion University M
Olivet Nazarene University M
Oregon State University M
Pacific University M
Palm Beach Atlantic University M
Penn State University Park M,D
Pfeiffer University M
Pittsburg State University M
Plymouth State University M
Portland State University M,D
Purdue University M,D,O
Purdue University Calumet M
Queens College of the City University of New York M,O
Queens University of Charlotte M
Quinnipiac University M
Regent University M,D,O
Regis University M,O
Rhode Island College M
Rider University M,O
Rivier College M,O
Rockford College M
Roger Williams University M
Rollins College M
Roosevelt University M
Rosemont College M
Rutgers, The State University of New Jersey, New Brunswick M,D
Sacred Heart University M,O
Saginaw Valley State University M
St. John Fisher College M
St. John's University (NY) M
Saint Joseph's University M,D,O
Saint Mary's University of Minnesota M,O
Saint Peter's College M,O
St. Thomas Aquinas College M,O
St. Thomas University M,D,O
Saint Xavier University M,O
Salem State College M
Salisbury University M
Samford University M,D,O
Sam Houston State University M
San Diego State University M
San Francisco State University M
San Jose State University M,O
Seton Hill University M,O
Shenandoah University M,D,O
Siena Heights University M
Simmons College M,O
Slippery Rock University of Pennsylvania M
Sonoma State University M
South Carolina State University M
Southeastern Louisiana University M
Southeastern Oklahoma State University M
Southeast Missouri State University M
Southern Connecticut State University M,O
Southern Illinois University Edwardsville M
Southern New Hampshire University M,O
Southern Oregon University M
Southern University and Agricultural and Mechanical College M
Southwestern Oklahoma State University M
Spalding University M
Spring Hill College M
State University of New York at Binghamton M
State University of New York at Fredonia M
State University of New York at New Paltz M
State University of New York at Oswego M
State University of New York at Plattsburgh M
State University of New York College at Geneseo M
State University of New York College at Oneonta M
State University of New York College at Potsdam M
Stephen F. Austin State University M
Sul Ross State University M
Temple University M,D
Tennessee State University M,D
Tennessee Technological University M,O
Texas A&M University–Commerce M,D
Texas A&M University–Corpus Christi M
Texas A&M University–Kingsville M
Texas Christian University M,O
Texas Southern University M,D
Texas State University-San Marcos M
Texas Tech University M,D
Texas Woman's University M,D
Towson University M
Trevecca Nazarene University M
Trinity (Washington) University M
Troy University M,O
Tufts University M,D
Union College (KY) M

University at Buffalo, the State University of New York M,D,O
The University of Akron M,D
The University of Alabama at Birmingham M
University of Alaska Southeast M
The University of Arizona M,D
University of Arkansas M,O
University of Bridgeport M,O
University of California, Irvine M,D
University of Central Florida M,D
University of Central Missouri M,O
University of Central Oklahoma M
University of Cincinnati M
University of Connecticut M,D
The University of Findlay M
University of Florida M,D,O
University of Georgia M,D,O
University of Hartford M
University of Houston M,D
University of Illinois at Chicago M,D
University of Indianapolis M
The University of Iowa M,D
University of Louisiana at Monroe M
University of Louisville M
University of Maine M,O
University of Maryland, Baltimore County M
University of Massachusetts Amherst M,D,O
University of Massachusetts Boston M,D,O
University of Memphis M,D
University of Miami M
University of Michigan M,D
University of Michigan–Flint M
University of Minnesota, Twin Cities Campus M,D,O
University of Missouri–Columbia M,D,O
University of Missouri–St. Louis M,D
University of Montevallo M
University of Nebraska at Omaha M
University of Nevada, Las Vegas M,D,O
University of Nevada, Reno M,D,O
University of New Hampshire M
University of New Mexico M,O
University of North Alabama M,O
The University of North Carolina at Charlotte M
The University of North Carolina at Greensboro D
The University of North Carolina at Pembroke M
The University of North Carolina Wilmington M
University of North Dakota M,D
University of Northern Colorado M,D
University of Northern Iowa M
University of North Florida M
University of Oklahoma M,D,O
University of Pennsylvania M
University of Phoenix–Central Florida Campus M
University of Phoenix–Denver Campus M
University of Phoenix–Fort Lauderdale Campus M
University of Phoenix–Hawaii Campus M
University of Phoenix–Las Vegas Campus M
University of Phoenix–New Mexico Campus M
University of Phoenix–North Florida Campus M
University of Phoenix M
University of Phoenix–Oregon Campus M
University of Phoenix–Phoenix Campus M
University of Phoenix–Sacramento Valley Campus M,O
University of Phoenix–San Diego Campus M
University of Phoenix–Southern Arizona Campus M,O
University of Phoenix–Southern California Campus M
University of Phoenix–Southern Colorado Campus M,O
University of Phoenix–Utah Campus M
University of Phoenix–West Florida Campus M
University of Pittsburgh M
University of Puget Sound M
University of Rhode Island M
University of St. Francis (IL) M
The University of Scranton M
University of South Alabama M,O
University of South Carolina M,D
The University of South Dakota M
University of Southern Indiana M
University of Southern Mississippi M,D,O
University of South Florida M,D,O
The University of Tennessee M,D,O
The University of Tennessee at Chattanooga M,D,O
The University of Tennessee at Martin M
The University of Texas at San Antonio M
The University of Texas–Pan American M
University of the Incarnate Word M
The University of Toledo D,O
University of Utah M,D
The University of West Alabama M
University of West Florida M
University of Wisconsin–Eau Claire M
University of Wisconsin–La Crosse M
University of Wisconsin–Milwaukee M
University of Wisconsin–Platteville M
University of Wisconsin–River Falls M
University of Wisconsin–Stevens Point M
Utah State University M
Vanderbilt University M,D
Villanova University M
Wagner College M
Walden University M,D
Washington State University M,D
Washington University in St. Louis M
Wayne State College M
Wayne State University M,D,O
West Chester University of Pennsylvania M
Western Carolina University M
Western Illinois University M
Western Kentucky University M,O
Western Michigan University M
Western New England College M
Western New Mexico University M
Western Washington University M
Westfield State College M
West Virginia University M
Wheaton College M
Wheelock College M
Whitworth University M
Widener University M,D
Wilkes University M,D
William Carey University M,O
William Paterson University of New Jersey M
Wilmington University (DE) M
Worcester State College M
Wright State University M
Xavier University M
Youngstown State University M

■ EMERGENCY MANAGEMENT

Adelphi University O
Anna Maria College M,O
Arkansas Tech University M
Benedictine University M
California State University, Long Beach M
Drexel University M
The George Washington University M,D,O
Jacksonville State University M
Lynn University M,O
North Dakota State University M,D
Oklahoma State University M
Park University M
San Diego State University M,D
University of Nevada, Las Vegas M,D,O
Virginia Commonwealth University M,O
West Chester University of Pennsylvania M,O

■ EMERGENCY MEDICAL SERVICES

Drexel University M
San Diego State University M,D

■ ENERGY AND POWER ENGINEERING

New York Institute of Technology M,O
Rensselaer Polytechnic Institute M,D
Southern Illinois University Carbondale D
University of Massachusetts Lowell M,D
University of Memphis M,D
University of Wisconsin–Madison M,D
Worcester Polytechnic Institute M,D

■ ENERGY MANAGEMENT AND POLICY

Boston University M
New York Institute of Technology M,O
University of California, Berkeley M,D

■ ENGINEERING AND APPLIED SCIENCES—GENERAL

Alabama Agricultural and Mechanical University M
Alfred University M,D
Andrews University M
Arizona State University M,D
Arizona State University at the Polytechnic Campus M
Auburn University M,D
Baylor University M
Boise State University M,D
Boston University M,D
Bradley University M
Brigham Young University M,D
Brown University M,D
Bucknell University M
California Institute of Technology M,D,O
California Polytechnic State University, San Luis Obispo M
California State Polytechnic University, Pomona M
California State University, Chico M
California State University, Fresno M
California State University, Fullerton M
California State University, Los Angeles M
California State University, Northridge M
California State University, Sacramento M
Carnegie Mellon University M,D

Case Western Reserve University M,D
The Catholic University of America M,D
Central Connecticut State University M
Central Washington University M
Christian Brothers University M
City College of the City University of New York M,D
Clarkson University M,D
Clemson University M,D
Cleveland State University M,D
Colorado School of Mines M,D,O
Colorado State University M,D
Columbia University M,D,O
Cornell University M,D
Dartmouth College M,D
Drexel University M,D
Duke University M,D
Eastern Illinois University M,O
Eastern Michigan University M
Fairfield University M
Fairleigh Dickinson University, Metropolitan Campus M
Florida Agricultural and Mechanical University M,D
Florida Atlantic University M,D
Florida Institute of Technology M,D
Florida International University M,D
Florida State University M,D
George Mason University M,D,O
The George Washington University M,D,O
Georgia Institute of Technology M,D,O
Graduate School and University Center of the City University of New York D
Grand Valley State University M
Harvard University M,D
Howard University M,D
Idaho State University M,D,O
Illinois Institute of Technology M,D
Indiana State University M,D
Indiana University–Purdue University Fort Wayne M
Iowa State University of Science and Technology M,D
The Johns Hopkins University M,D,O
Kansas State University M,D
Kent State University M
Lamar University M,D
Lawrence Technological University M,D
Lehigh University M,D
Louisiana State University and Agricultural and Mechanical College M,D
Louisiana Tech University M,D
Loyola College in Maryland M
Manhattan College M
Marquette University M,D
Marshall University M
Massachusetts Institute of Technology M,D,O
McNeese State University M
Mercer University M
Miami University M,O
Michigan State University M,D
Michigan Technological University M,D
Mississippi State University M,D
Missouri University of Science and Technology M,D
Montana State University M,D
Morgan State University M,D
National University M
New Jersey Institute of Technology M,D,O
New Mexico State University M,D
New York Institute of Technology M,O

North Carolina Agricultural and Technical State University M,D
North Carolina State University M,D
North Dakota State University M,D
Northeastern University M,D
Northern Arizona University M,D,O
Northern Illinois University M
Northwestern University M,D,O
Oakland University M,D
The Ohio State University M,D
Ohio University M,D
Oklahoma State University M,D
Old Dominion University M,D
Oregon State University M,D
Penn State Harrisburg M
Penn State University Park M,D
Pittsburg State University M
Portland State University M,D,O
Prairie View A&M University M,D
Purdue University M,D,O
Purdue University Calumet M
Rensselaer Polytechnic Institute M,D
Rice University M,D
Rochester Institute of Technology M,D,O
Rowan University M
Saginaw Valley State University M
St. Cloud State University M
St. Mary's University of San Antonio M
San Diego State University M,D
San Francisco State University M
San Jose State University M
Santa Clara University M,D,O
Seattle University M
Sonoma State University M
South Dakota State University M,D
Southern Illinois University Carbondale M,D
Southern Illinois University Edwardsville M
Southern Methodist University M,D
Southern Polytechnic State University M
Southern University and Agricultural and Mechanical College M
Stanford University M,D,O
State University of New York at Binghamton M,D
State University of New York Institute of Technology M
Stevens Institute of Technology M,D,O
Stony Brook University, State University of New York M,D,O
Syracuse University M,D,O
Temple University M,D
Tennessee State University M,D
Tennessee Technological University M,D
Texas A&M University M,D
Texas A&M University–Kingsville M,D
Texas Tech University M,D
Tufts University M,D
University at Buffalo, the State University of New York M,D
The University of Akron M,D
The University of Alabama M,D
The University of Alabama at Birmingham M,D
The University of Alabama in Huntsville M,D
University of Alaska Anchorage M,O
University of Alaska Fairbanks M,D
The University of Arizona M,D
University of Arkansas M,D
University of Bridgeport M,D
University of California, Berkeley M,D
University of California, Davis M,D,O

University of California, Irvine M,D
University of California, Los Angeles M,D
University of California, Santa Barbara M,D
University of California, Santa Cruz M,D
University of Central Florida M,D,O
University of Central Oklahoma M
University of Cincinnati M,D
University of Colorado at Boulder M,D
University of Colorado at Colorado Springs M,D
University of Connecticut M,D
University of Dayton M,D
University of Delaware M,D
University of Denver M,D
University of Detroit Mercy M,D
University of Evansville M
University of Florida M,D,O
University of Hartford M
University of Hawaii at Manoa M,D,O
University of Houston M,D
University of Idaho M,D
University of Illinois at Chicago M,D
University of Illinois at Urbana–Champaign M,D
The University of Iowa M,D
University of Kansas M,D
University of Kentucky M,D
University of Louisville M,D
University of Maine M,D
University of Maryland, Baltimore County M,D,O
University of Maryland, College Park M
University of Massachusetts Amherst M,D
University of Massachusetts Dartmouth M,D,O
University of Massachusetts Lowell M,D,O
University of Memphis M,D
University of Miami M,D
University of Michigan M,D,O
University of Michigan–Dearborn M,D
University of Minnesota, Twin Cities Campus M,D
University of Mississippi M,D
University of Missouri–Columbia M,D
University of Missouri–Kansas City M,D
University of Nebraska–Lincoln M,D
University of Nevada, Las Vegas M,D
University of Nevada, Reno M,D,O
University of New Haven M,O
University of New Mexico M,D
University of New Orleans M,D,O
The University of North Carolina at Charlotte M,D
University of North Dakota D
University of North Texas M
University of Notre Dame M,D
University of Oklahoma M,D
University of Pennsylvania M,D,O
University of Pittsburgh M,D
University of Portland M
University of Puerto Rico, Mayagüez Campus M,D
University of Rhode Island M,D
University of Rochester M,D
University of St. Thomas (MN) M,O
University of South Alabama M
University of South Carolina M,D
University of Southern California M,D,O
University of Southern Indiana M
University of Southern Mississippi M,D
University of South Florida M,D
The University of Tennessee M,D
The University of Tennessee at Chattanooga M,D,O
The University of Texas at Arlington M,D

The University of Texas at Austin M,D
The University of Texas at Dallas M,D
The University of Texas at El Paso M,D
The University of Texas at San Antonio M,D
The University of Texas at Tyler M
The University of Toledo M
University of Tulsa M,D
University of Utah M,D,O
University of Vermont M,D
University of Virginia M,D
University of Washington M,D
University of Wisconsin–Madison M,D,O
University of Wisconsin–Milwaukee M,D,O
University of Wisconsin–Platteville M
University of Wyoming M,D
Utah State University M,D,O
Vanderbilt University M,D
Villanova University M,D,O
Virginia Commonwealth University M,D,O
Virginia Polytechnic Institute and State University M,D
Walden University M,O
Washington State University M,D
Washington University in St. Louis M,D
Wayne State University M,D,O
Western Michigan University M,D
Western New England College M
West Texas A&M University M
West Virginia University M,D
Wichita State University M,D
Widener University M
Wilkes University M
Wright State University M,D
Yale University M,D
Youngstown State University M

■ ENGINEERING DESIGN

The Catholic University of America M,D
Rochester Institute of Technology M
San Diego State University M,D
Santa Clara University M,D,O
Stanford University M
Stevens Institute of Technology M
University of Central Florida M,D,O
University of Illinois at Urbana–Champaign M
University of New Haven M,O

■ ENGINEERING MANAGEMENT

California State Polytechnic University, Pomona M
California State University, East Bay M
California State University, Long Beach M,D
California State University, Northridge M
Carnegie Mellon University M,D
Case Western Reserve University M
The Catholic University of America M
Clarkson University M
Colorado School of Mines M,D
Columbia University M,D,O
Cornell University M,D
Dallas Baptist University M
Dartmouth College M
Drexel University M,D
Duke University M
Eastern Michigan University M
Florida Institute of Technology M
Gannon University M
The George Washington University M,D,O
Hofstra University M
Kansas State University M,D
Lamar University M,D
Lawrence Technological University M,D
Long Island University, C.W. Post Campus M
Loyola Marymount University M,O
Marquette University M,D
Marshall University M
Massachusetts Institute of Technology M,D
McNeese State University M
Mercer University M
Michigan State University M,D
Missouri University of Science and Technology M,D
National University M
New Jersey Institute of Technology M
New Mexico Institute of Mining and Technology M
Northeastern University M,D
Northwestern University M
Oakland University M
Oklahoma State University M
Old Dominion University M,D
Point Park University M
Portland State University M,D,O
Rensselaer Polytechnic Institute M,D
Rochester Institute of Technology M
St. Cloud State University M
Saint Martin's University M
St. Mary's University of San Antonio M
Santa Clara University M
Southern Methodist University M,D
Stanford University M,D
Stevens Institute of Technology M,D,O
Syracuse University M
Texas Tech University M,D
Tufts University M
The University of Akron M
University of Alaska Anchorage M
University of Alaska Fairbanks M
University of California, Berkeley M,D
University of Central Florida M,D,O
University of Colorado at Boulder M
University of Colorado at Colorado Springs M
University of Dayton M
University of Detroit Mercy M
University of Kansas M
University of Louisiana at Lafayette M
University of Louisville M
University of Maryland, Baltimore County M
University of Massachusetts Amherst M
University of Michigan–Dearborn M
University of Minnesota, Duluth M
University of New Haven M
University of New Orleans M,O
The University of North Carolina at Charlotte M
University of St. Thomas (MN) M,O
University of Southern California M
University of South Florida M,D
The University of Tennessee M,D
The University of Tennessee at Chattanooga M,O
University of Tulsa M
University of Wisconsin–Madison M
Valparaiso University M,O
Virginia Polytechnic Institute and State University M,D
Walden University M,D,O
Wayne State University M
Webster University M
Western Michigan University M
Widener University M

■ ENGINEERING PHYSICS

Cornell University M,D
Dartmouth College M,D
Embry-Riddle Aeronautical University (FL) M
George Mason University M
Michigan Technological University D
Mississippi State University M,D
Polytechnic University, Brooklyn Campus M
Rensselaer Polytechnic Institute M,D
Stevens Institute of Technology M,D,O
University of California, San Diego M,D
University of Maine M
University of Oklahoma M,D
University of Virginia M,D
University of Wisconsin–Madison M,D
Yale University M,D

■ ENGLISH

Abilene Christian University M
Andrews University M
Angelo State University M
Appalachian State University M
Arcadia University M
Arizona State University M,D
Arkansas State University M,O
Arkansas Tech University M
Auburn University M,D
Austin Peay State University M
Ball State University M,D
Baylor University M,D
Belmont University M
Bemidji State University M
Bennington College M
Bob Jones University P,M,D,O
Boise State University M
Boston College M,D
Boston University M,D
Bowie State University M
Bowling Green State University M,D
Bradley University M
Brandeis University M,D
Bridgewater State College M
Brigham Young University M
Brooklyn College of the City University of New York M,D
Brown University M,D
Bucknell University M
Buffalo State College, State University of New York M
Butler University M
California Baptist University M
California Polytechnic State University, San Luis Obispo M
California State Polytechnic University, Pomona M
California State University, Bakersfield M
California State University, Chico M
California State University, Dominguez Hills M,O
California State University, East Bay M
California State University, Fresno M
California State University, Fullerton M
California State University, Long Beach M
California State University, Los Angeles M
California State University, Northridge M
California State University, Sacramento M
California State University, San Bernardino M
California State University, San Marcos M
California State University, Stanislaus M
Carnegie Mellon University M,D
Case Western Reserve University M,D
The Catholic University of America M,D

Institution	Degrees
Central Connecticut State University	M,O
Central Michigan University	M
Central Washington University	M
Chapman University	M
Chicago State University	M
The Citadel, The Military College of South Carolina	M
City College of the City University of New York	M
Claremont Graduate University	M,D
Clarion University of Pennsylvania	M
Clark Atlanta University	M
Clark University	M
Clemson University	M
Cleveland State University	M
College of Charleston	M
The College of New Jersey	M
The College of Saint Rose	M
College of Staten Island of the City University of New York	M
Columbia University	M,D
Converse College	M
Cornell University	M,D
Creighton University	M
DePaul University	M
Drew University	M,D
Duke University	D
Duquesne University	M,D
East Carolina University	M
Eastern Illinois University	M
Eastern Kentucky University	M
Eastern Michigan University	M
Eastern New Mexico University	M
Eastern Washington University	M
East Tennessee State University	M
Elmhurst College	M
Emory University	D,O
Emporia State University	M
Fairleigh Dickinson University, Metropolitan Campus	M
Fayetteville State University	M
Fitchburg State College	M
Florida Atlantic University	M
Florida Gulf Coast University	M
Florida International University	M
Florida State University	M,D
Fordham University	M,D
Fort Hays State University	M
Gannon University	M
Gardner-Webb University	M
George Mason University	M
Georgetown University	M
The George Washington University	M,D
Georgia College & State University	M
Georgia Southern University	M
Georgia State University	M,D
Governors State University	M
Graduate School and University Center of the City University of New York	D
Grand Valley State University	M
Hardin-Simmons University	M
Harvard University	M,D,O
Heritage University	M
Hofstra University	M
Hollins University	M
Howard University	M,D
Humboldt State University	M
Hunter College of the City University of New York	M
Idaho State University	M,D,O
Illinois State University	M,D
Indiana State University	M
Indiana University Bloomington	M,D
Indiana University of Pennsylvania	M,D
Indiana University–Purdue University Fort Wayne	M,O
Indiana University–Purdue University Indianapolis	M
Indiana University South Bend	M
Iona College	M
Iowa State University of Science and Technology	M,D
Jackson State University	M
Jacksonville State University	M
James Madison University	M
John Carroll University	M
The Johns Hopkins University	D
Kansas State University	M
Kent State University	M,D
Kutztown University of Pennsylvania	M
Lamar University	M
La Sierra University	M
Lehigh University	M,D
Lehman College of the City University of New York	M
Long Island University, Brooklyn Campus	M
Long Island University, C.W. Post Campus	M
Longwood University	M
Louisiana State University and Agricultural and Mechanical College	M,D
Louisiana Tech University	M
Loyola Marymount University	M
Loyola University Chicago	M,D
Marquette University	M,D
Marshall University	M
Mary Baldwin College	M
Marymount University	M
McNeese State University	M
Mercy College	M
Miami University	M,D
Michigan State University	M,D
Middle Tennessee State University	M,D
Midwestern State University	M
Millersville University of Pennsylvania	M
Mills College	M
Minnesota State University Mankato	M,O
Mississippi College	M
Mississippi State University	M
Missouri State University	M
Monmouth University	M
Montana State University	M
Montclair State University	M
Morehead State University	M
Morgan State University	M,D
Mount Mary College	M
Murray State University	M
National University	M
New Mexico Highlands University	M
New Mexico State University	M,D
New York University	M,D
North Carolina Agricultural and Technical State University	M
North Carolina Central University	M
North Carolina State University	M
North Dakota State University	M
Northeastern Illinois University	M
Northeastern State University	M
Northeastern University	M,D,O
Northern Arizona University	M
Northern Illinois University	M,D
Northern Michigan University	M
Northwestern State University of Louisiana	M
Northwestern University	M,D
Northwest Missouri State University	M
Notre Dame de Namur University	M,O
Oakland University	M
The Ohio State University	M,D
Ohio University	M,D
Oklahoma State University	M,D
Old Dominion University	M,D
Oregon State University	M
Our Lady of the Lake University of San Antonio	M
Penn State University Park	M,D
Pittsburg State University	M
Portland State University	M
Prairie View A&M University	M
Princeton University	D
Purdue University	M,D
Purdue University Calumet	M
Queens College of the City University of New York	M
Radford University	M
Rhode Island College	M
Rice University	M,D
Rivier College	M
Roosevelt University	M
Rosemont College	M
Rutgers, The State University of New Jersey, Camden	M
Rutgers, The State University of New Jersey, Newark	M
Rutgers, The State University of New Jersey, New Brunswick	D
St. Bonaventure University	M
St. Cloud State University	M
St. John's University (NY)	M,D
Saint Louis University	M,D
St. Mary's University of San Antonio	M
Saint Xavier University	M,O
Salem State College	M
Salisbury University	M
Sam Houston State University	M
San Diego State University	M
San Francisco State University	M,O
San Jose State University	M,O
Seton Hall University	M
Simmons College	M
Slippery Rock University of Pennsylvania	M
Sonoma State University	M
South Dakota State University	M
Southeastern Louisiana University	M
Southeast Missouri State University	M
Southern Connecticut State University	M
Southern Illinois University Carbondale	M,D
Southern Illinois University Edwardsville	M,O
Southern Methodist University	M,D
Stanford University	M,D
State University of New York at Binghamton	M,D
State University of New York at Fredonia	M
State University of New York at New Paltz	M
State University of New York at Oswego	M
State University of New York College at Brockport	M
State University of New York College at Cortland	M
State University of New York College at Potsdam	M
Stephen F. Austin State University	M
Stetson University	M

Stony Brook University, State University of New York M,D,O
Sul Ross State University M
Syracuse University M,D
Tarleton State University M
Temple University M,D
Tennessee State University M
Tennessee Technological University M
Texas A&M International University M,D
Texas A&M University M,D
Texas A&M University–Commerce M,D
Texas A&M University–Corpus Christi M
Texas A&M University–Kingsville M
Texas A&M University–Texarkana M
Texas Christian University M,D
Texas Southern University M
Texas State University-San Marcos M
Texas Tech University M,D
Texas Woman's University M,D
Truman State University M
Tufts University M,D
Tulane University M,D
University at Albany, State University of New York M,D
University at Buffalo, the State University of New York M,D
The University of Akron M
The University of Alabama M,D
The University of Alabama at Birmingham M
The University of Alabama in Huntsville M,O
University of Alaska Anchorage M
University of Alaska Fairbanks M
The University of Arizona M,D
University of Arkansas M,D
University of California, Berkeley D
University of California, Davis M,D
University of California, Irvine M,D
University of California, Los Angeles M,D
University of California, Riverside M,D
University of California, San Diego M
University of California, Santa Barbara D
University of Central Arkansas M
University of Central Florida M
University of Central Missouri M
University of Central Oklahoma M
University of Chicago M,D
University of Cincinnati M,D
University of Colorado at Boulder M,D
University of Colorado Denver M,O
University of Connecticut M,D
University of Dallas M
University of Dayton M
University of Delaware M,D
University of Denver M,D
University of Florida M,D
University of Georgia M,D
University of Hawaii at Manoa M,D
University of Houston M,D
University of Houston–Clear Lake M
University of Idaho M
University of Illinois at Chicago M,D
University of Illinois at Springfield M
University of Illinois at Urbana–Champaign M,D
University of Indianapolis M
The University of Iowa M,D
University of Kansas M,D
University of Kentucky M,D
University of Louisiana at Lafayette M,D
University of Louisiana at Monroe M
University of Louisville M,D
University of Maine M
University of Maryland, College Park M,D
University of Massachusetts Amherst M,D
University of Massachusetts Boston M
University of Memphis M,D
University of Miami M,D
University of Michigan M,D,O
University of Michigan–Flint M
University of Minnesota, Duluth M
University of Minnesota, Twin Cities Campus M,D
University of Mississippi M,D
University of Missouri–Columbia M,D
University of Missouri–Kansas City M,D
University of Missouri–St. Louis M,O
The University of Montana M
University of Montevallo M
University of Nebraska at Kearney M
University of Nebraska at Omaha M,O
University of Nebraska–Lincoln M,D
University of Nevada, Las Vegas M,D
University of Nevada, Reno M,D
University of New Hampshire M,D
University of New Mexico M,D
University of New Orleans M
University of North Alabama M
The University of North Carolina at Chapel Hill M,D
The University of North Carolina at Charlotte M
The University of North Carolina at Greensboro M,D
The University of North Carolina Wilmington M
University of North Dakota M,D
University of Northern Colorado M
University of Northern Iowa M
University of North Florida M
University of North Texas M,D
University of Notre Dame M,D
University of Oklahoma M,D
University of Oregon M,D
University of Pennsylvania M,D
University of Pittsburgh M,D
University of Puerto Rico, Mayagüez Campus M
University of Puerto Rico, Río Piedras M,D
University of Rhode Island M,D
University of Richmond M
University of Rochester M,D
University of St. Thomas (MN) M
University of South Alabama M
University of South Carolina M,D
The University of South Dakota M,D
University of Southern Mississippi M,D
University of South Florida M,D
The University of Tennessee M,D
The University of Tennessee at Chattanooga M
The University of Texas at Arlington M,D
The University of Texas at Austin M,D
The University of Texas at Brownsville M
The University of Texas at El Paso M
The University of Texas at San Antonio M,D
The University of Texas at Tyler M
The University of Texas of the Permian Basin M
The University of Texas–Pan American M
University of the District of Columbia M
University of the Incarnate Word M,O
The University of Toledo M,O
University of Tulsa M,D
University of Utah M,D
University of Vermont M
University of Virginia M,D
University of Washington M,D
University of West Florida M
University of West Georgia M
University of Wisconsin–Eau Claire M
University of Wisconsin–Madison M,D
University of Wisconsin–Milwaukee M,D,O
University of Wisconsin–Oshkosh M
University of Wisconsin–Stevens Point M
University of Wyoming M
Utah State University M
Valdosta State University M
Valparaiso University M,O
Vanderbilt University M,D
Villanova University M
Virginia Commonwealth University M
Virginia Polytechnic Institute and State University M,D
Virginia State University M
Wake Forest University M
Washington State University M,D
Washington University in St. Louis M,D
Wayne State University M,D
Weber State University M
West Chester University of Pennsylvania M
Western Carolina University M
Western Connecticut State University M
Western Illinois University M
Western Kentucky University M
Western Michigan University M,D
Western Washington University M
Westfield State College M
West Texas A&M University M
West Virginia University M,D
Wichita State University M
William Paterson University of New Jersey M
Winona State University M
Winthrop University M
Wright State University M
Xavier University M
Yale University M,D
Youngstown State University M

■ ENGLISH AS A SECOND LANGUAGE

Adelphi University M,O
American University M,O
Andrews University M,D,O
Arizona State University M,D
Arkansas Tech University M
Avila University M,O
Azusa Pacific University M
Ball State University M,D
Barry University M,D,O
Biola University M,D,O
Boston University M,O
Brigham Young University M,O
California State University, Dominguez Hills M,O
California State University, Fresno M
California State University, Fullerton M
California State University, Los Angeles M
California State University, Sacramento M
California State University, San Bernardino M
Cardinal Stritch University M
Carson-Newman College M
The Catholic University of America M,D
Central Connecticut State University O
Central Michigan University M
Central Washington University M

City University of Seattle M,O
Cleveland State University M
College of Charleston O
The College of New Jersey M,O
The College of New Rochelle M,O
College of Notre Dame of Maryland M
Cornerstone University M,O
Dallas Baptist University M
DeSales University M,O
Drexel University M,D,O
Duquesne University M,D
Eastern Michigan University M
Eastern Nazarene College M,O
Eastern University O
Emporia State University M
Fairfield University M,O
Florida International University M,D,O
Fordham University M,D,O
Framingham State College M
Fresno Pacific University M
Furman University M
Gannon University O
George Mason University M
Georgetown University M,D,O
Georgia State University M,D,O
Gonzaga University M
Grand Canyon University M
Grand Valley State University M
Hawai'i Pacific University M
Henderson State University M,O
Heritage University M
Hofstra University M,O
Holy Names University M,O
Houston Baptist University M
Hunter College of the City University of New York M
Indiana State University M,O
Indiana University of Pennsylvania M,D
Indiana University–Purdue University Fort Wayne M,O
Inter American University of Puerto Rico, Metropolitan Campus M
Inter American University of Puerto Rico, San Germán Campus M
The Johns Hopkins University M
Kean University M
Kennesaw State University M
Kent State University M,D
Lehman College of the City University of New York M
Long Island University, Brooklyn Campus M
Long Island University, C.W. Post Campus M
Madonna University M
Manhattanville College M
Marymount University M,O
Mercy College M
Michigan State University M,D
Middle Tennessee State University M,O
Mississippi College M
Montclair State University M,O
Monterey Institute of International Studies M
Murray State University M
Nazareth College of Rochester M
New Jersey City University M
Newman University M
The New School: A University M
New York University M,D,O
Northern Arizona University M,D,O
Notre Dame de Namur University M,O
Nova Southeastern University M,O
Oakland University M,O
Ohio Dominican University M
Ohio University M
Oklahoma City University M
Oral Roberts University M,D
Pontifical Catholic University of Puerto Rico M,D
Portland State University M
Prescott College M,D
Queens College of the City University of New York M
Regent University M,D,O
Regis University M,O
Rhode Island College M,O
Rider University M,O
Rutgers, The State University of New Jersey, New Brunswick M,D
St. Cloud State University M
St. John's University (NY) M
Saint Martin's University M
Saint Michael's College M,O
Salem State College M
Salisbury University M
San Diego State University M,O
San Francisco State University M
San Jose State University M,O
School for International Training M
Seattle Pacific University M
Seattle University M,O
Shenandoah University M,D,O
Simmons College M
Southeast Missouri State University M
Southern Connecticut State University M
Southern Illinois University Carbondale M
Southern Illinois University Edwardsville M,O
Southern New Hampshire University M,O
State University of New York at Fredonia M
State University of New York at New Paltz M
State University of New York College at Cortland M
Stony Brook University, State University of New York M,D
Temple University M,D
Texas A&M University–Kingsville M
Trevecca Nazarene University M
Trinity (Washington) University M
Universidad del Turabo M
University at Buffalo, the State University of New York M,D,O
The University of Alabama M,D
The University of Alabama in Huntsville M,O
The University of Arizona M,D
University of California, Los Angeles M
University of Central Florida M,O
University of Central Missouri M
University of Central Oklahoma M
University of Cincinnati M,D,O
University of Colorado Denver M,O
University of Delaware M,D
The University of Findlay M
University of Florida M,D,O
University of Guam M
University of Hawaii at Manoa M,D,O
University of Houston M,D
University of Idaho M
University of Illinois at Chicago M
University of Illinois at Urbana–Champaign M
University of Maryland, College Park M,D,O
University of Massachusetts Boston M
University of Miami M,D
University of Michigan M,D
University of Minnesota, Twin Cities Campus M
University of Nebraska at Omaha M,O
University of Nevada, Las Vegas M,D,O
University of Nevada, Reno M,D,O
The University of North Carolina at Charlotte M
The University of North Carolina at Greensboro M,D,O
University of Northern Iowa M
University of Pennsylvania M,D
University of Phoenix M
University of Pittsburgh O
University of Puerto Rico, Río Piedras M
University of San Francisco M,D
The University of Scranton M
University of South Carolina M,D,O
University of Southern California M
University of Southern Maine M,O
The University of Tennessee M,D,O
The University of Texas at Arlington M
The University of Texas at Brownsville M
The University of Texas at San Antonio M,D
The University of Texas of the Permian Basin M
The University of Texas–Pan American M
The University of Toledo M,O
University of Washington M,D
Wayne State College M
Webster University M
West Chester University of Pennsylvania M
Western Kentucky University M
Western New Mexico University M
West Virginia University M
Wheaton College M,O
Wright State University M

■ ENGLISH EDUCATION

Alabama State University M,O
Albany State University M
Andrews University M,D,O
Appalachian State University M
Arcadia University M,D,O
Arkansas State University M,O
Arkansas Tech University M,O
Armstrong Atlantic State University M
Auburn University M,D,O
Belmont University M
Bennington College M
Bethel College (TN) M
Bob Jones University P,M,D,O
Boston College M
Boston University M,O
Brooklyn College of the City University of New York M,O
Brown University M
Buffalo State College, State University of New York M
California State University, San Bernardino M
Campbell University M
Charleston Southern University M
Chatham University M
City College of the City University of New York M,O
Clarion University of Pennsylvania M
Clemson University M
College of St. Joseph M
The College of William and Mary M
Columbia College Chicago M
Columbus State University M,O

Converse College	M
Delta State University	M
DeSales University	M,O
Drake University	M
East Carolina University	M
Eastern Kentucky University	M
Edinboro University of Pennsylvania	M
Fitchburg State College	M
Florida Agricultural and Mechanical University	M
Florida Gulf Coast University	M
Florida International University	M,D
Florida State University	M,D,O
Framingham State College	M
Gardner-Webb University	M
Georgia College & State University	M,O
Georgia Southern University	M
Georgia State University	M,D,O
Grand Valley State University	M
Harding University	M,O
Henderson State University	M,O
Hofstra University	M
Hunter College of the City University of New York	M
Indiana University of Pennsylvania	M,D
Indiana University–Purdue University Fort Wayne	M,O
Indiana University–Purdue University Indianapolis	M
Iona College	M
Ithaca College	M
Jackson State University	M
Kennesaw State University	M
Kent State University	M,D
Kutztown University of Pennsylvania	M,O
Lehman College of the City University of New York	M
Long Island University, Brooklyn Campus	M
Long Island University, C.W. Post Campus	M
Longwood University	M
Louisiana Tech University	M,D
Lynchburg College	M
Manhattanville College	M
Marymount University	M
Maryville University of Saint Louis	M,D
Miami University	M,D
Millersville University of Pennsylvania	M
Mills College	M,D
Minnesota State University Mankato	M,O
Mississippi College	M,O
Montclair State University	M,O
National-Louis University	M,O
New York University	M,D,O
North Carolina Agricultural and Technical State University	M
Northeastern Illinois University	M
Northern Arizona University	M
North Georgia College & State University	M,O
Northwestern State University of Louisiana	M
Northwest Missouri State University	M
Nova Southeastern University	M,O
Plymouth State University	M
Purdue University	M,D,O
Queens College of the City University of New York	M,O
Quinnipiac University	M
Rhode Island College	M,O
Rider University	M,O
Rockford College	M
Rollins College	M
Rutgers, The State University of New Jersey, New Brunswick	M
St. John Fisher College	M
Salem State College	M
Salisbury University	M
San Francisco State University	M,O
San Jose State University	M,O
South Carolina State University	M
Southern Illinois University Edwardsville	M,O
Southwestern Oklahoma State University	M
Stanford University	M,D
State University of New York at Binghamton	M
State University of New York at Plattsburgh	M
State University of New York College at Brockport	M
State University of New York College at Cortland	M
Stony Brook University, State University of New York	M,O
Syracuse University	M,D
Temple University	M,D
Texas A&M University	M,D
Texas A&M University–Commerce	M,D
Texas Tech University	M,D
Trinity (Washington) University	M
University at Buffalo, the State University of New York	M,D,O
University of Alaska Fairbanks	M
The University of Arizona	M,D
University of Central Florida	M
University of Colorado Denver	M,O
University of Connecticut	M,D
University of Florida	M,D,O
University of Illinois at Chicago	M,D
University of Indianapolis	M
The University of Iowa	M,D
University of Michigan	M,D
University of Minnesota, Twin Cities Campus	M
University of Missouri–Columbia	M,D,O
The University of Montana	M
University of Nevada, Las Vegas	M,D,O
University of New Hampshire	M,D
University of New Orleans	M
The University of North Carolina at Chapel Hill	M
The University of North Carolina at Charlotte	M
The University of North Carolina at Greensboro	M,D
The University of North Carolina at Pembroke	M
University of Oklahoma	M,D,O
University of Phoenix	M
University of Pittsburgh	M,D
University of Puerto Rico, Mayagüez Campus	M
University of Puerto Rico, Río Piedras	M,D
University of St. Francis (IL)	M
University of South Carolina	M,D
University of South Florida	M,D,O
The University of Tennessee	M,D,O
The University of Texas at El Paso	M
The University of Texas at Tyler	M
The University of Toledo	M
University of Washington	M,D
The University of West Alabama	M
University of West Georgia	M,O
University of Wisconsin–Eau Claire	M
Vanderbilt University	M,D
Virginia Polytechnic Institute and State University	M,D,O
Washington State University	M,D
Wayne State College	M
Wayne State University	M,D,O
Western Carolina University	M
Western Connecticut State University	M
Western Kentucky University	M
Western Michigan University	M,D
Western New England College	M
Widener University	M,D
Wilkes University	M,D
William Carey University	M,O
Worcester State College	M

■ ENTOMOLOGY

Auburn University	M,D
Clemson University	M,D
Colorado State University	M,D
Cornell University	M,D
Florida Agricultural and Mechanical University	M
Illinois State University	M,D
Iowa State University of Science and Technology	M,D
Kansas State University	M,D
Louisiana State University and Agricultural and Mechanical College	M,D
Michigan State University	M,D
Mississippi State University	M,D
New Mexico State University	M
North Carolina State University	M,D
North Dakota State University	M,D
The Ohio State University	M,D
Oklahoma State University	D
Penn State University Park	M,D
Purdue University	M,D
Rutgers, The State University of New Jersey, New Brunswick	M,D
State University of New York College of Environmental Science and Forestry	M,D
Texas A&M University	M,D
Texas Tech University	M,D
The University of Arizona	M,D
University of Arkansas	M,D
University of California, Davis	M,D
University of California, Riverside	M,D
University of Connecticut	M,D
University of Delaware	M,D
University of Florida	M,D
University of Georgia	M,D
University of Hawaii at Manoa	M,D
University of Idaho	M,D
University of Illinois at Urbana–Champaign	M,D
University of Kansas	M,D
University of Kentucky	M,D
University of Maine	M
University of Maryland, College Park	M,D
University of Massachusetts Amherst	M,D
University of Minnesota, Twin Cities Campus	M,D
University of Missouri–Columbia	M,D
University of Nebraska–Lincoln	M,D
University of North Dakota	M,D
University of Rhode Island	M,D
The University of Tennessee	M,D
University of Wisconsin–Madison	M,D
University of Wyoming	M,D
Virginia Polytechnic Institute and State University	M,D
Washington State University	M,D
West Virginia University	M,D

■ ENTREPRENEURSHIP

American University	M
Baldwin-Wallace College	M
Benedictine University	M
Bernard M. Baruch College of the City University of New York	M,D
California Lutheran University	M,O
California State University, East Bay	M
Cameron University	M
Columbia University	M
Concordia University (CA)	M
Dallas Baptist University	M
DePaul University	M
Eastern Michigan University	M
Fairleigh Dickinson University, College at Florham	M,O
Fairleigh Dickinson University, Metropolitan Campus	M,O
Florida Atlantic University	M
Georgia Institute of Technology	M,O
Georgia State University	M,D
Illinois Institute of Technology	M
Inter American University of Puerto Rico, San Germán Campus	D
Lamar University	M
Lincoln University (MO)	M
Lindenwood University	M
Northeastern University	M
Oakland University	M,O
Park University	M
Penn State Great Valley	M
Regent University	M,D,O
Rensselaer Polytechnic Institute	M,D
St. Edward's University	M,O
San Diego State University	M
Simmons College	M,O
South Carolina State University	M
Stevens Institute of Technology	M,O
Syracuse University	M
Texas Tech University	M
The University of Akron	M
University of Central Florida	M,O
University of Dallas	M
University of Delaware	M,D
University of Florida	M,D,O
University of Hawaii at Manoa	M
University of Houston	D
University of Houston–Victoria	M
The University of Iowa	M
University of Louisville	D
University of Minnesota, Twin Cities Campus	M
University of San Francisco	M
University of South Florida	M,O
The University of Tampa	M
University of the Incarnate Word	M,D
University of Wisconsin–Madison	M
Western Carolina University	M
Wilkes University	M

■ ENVIRONMENTAL AND OCCUPATIONAL HEALTH

Anna Maria College	M
Boston University	M,D
California State University, Fresno	M
California State University, Northridge	M
Colorado State University	M,D
Columbia University	M,D
Duke University	M,D,O
East Carolina University	M
Eastern Kentucky University	M
East Tennessee State University	M
Emory University	M
Fort Valley State University	M
Gannon University	M,O
The George Washington University	M,D
Harvard University	M,D
Hunter College of the City University of New York	M
Illinois Institute of Technology	M
Indiana State University	M
Indiana University of Pennsylvania	M
The Johns Hopkins University	M,D
Loyola University Chicago	M
Mississippi Valley State University	M
Montclair State University	M,D,O
Murray State University	M
New Jersey Institute of Technology	M
New York University	M,D
Oakland University	M
Old Dominion University	M
Oregon State University	M
Penn State University Park	M,D
Saint Joseph's University	M,O
Saint Mary's University of Minnesota	M
San Diego State University	M,D
Stony Brook University, State University of New York	M,O
Temple University	M
Towson University	D
Tufts University	M,D
Tulane University	M,D
University at Albany, State University of New York	M,D
The University of Alabama at Birmingham	D
University of California, Berkeley	M,D
University of California, Los Angeles	M,D
University of Central Missouri	M,O
University of Cincinnati	M,D
University of Connecticut	M
University of Florida	M
University of Georgia	M,D
University of Illinois at Chicago	M,D
The University of Iowa	M,D,O
University of Miami	M
University of Michigan	M,D
University of Minnesota, Twin Cities Campus	M,D,O
University of Nevada, Reno	M,D
University of New Haven	M
The University of North Carolina at Chapel Hill	M,D
University of Oklahoma	M,D
University of Pittsburgh	M
University of South Alabama	M
University of South Carolina	M,D
University of Southern Mississippi	M
University of South Florida	M,D
The University of Toledo	M
University of Washington	M,D
University of Wisconsin–Eau Claire	M
University of Wisconsin–Whitewater	M
Virginia Commonwealth University	M
Wayne State University	M,O
West Chester University of Pennsylvania	M,O
West Virginia University	D
Yale University	M,D

■ ENVIRONMENTAL BIOLOGY

Antioch University New England	M
Baylor University	M,D
Emporia State University	M
Georgia State University	M,D
Governors State University	M
Hood College	M
Massachusetts Institute of Technology	M,D,O
Missouri University of Science and Technology	M
Montana State University	M,D
Morgan State University	D
Nicholls State University	M
Ohio University	M,D
Rutgers, The State University of New Jersey, New Brunswick	M,D
Sonoma State University	M
State University of New York College of Environmental Science and Forestry	M,D
Tennessee Technological University	M
University of California, Santa Cruz	M,D
University of Louisiana at Lafayette	M,D
University of Louisville	D
University of Massachusetts Amherst	M,D
University of Massachusetts Boston	D
University of North Dakota	M,D
University of Southern Mississippi	M,D
University of West Florida	M
University of Wisconsin–Madison	M,D
Washington University in St. Louis	D
West Virginia University	M,D

■ ENVIRONMENTAL DESIGN

Arizona State University	D
Clemson University	D
Columbia University	M
Cornell University	M
Michigan State University	M,D
Minnesota State University Mankato	M,O
San Diego State University	M
Texas Tech University	M,D
University of California, Berkeley	M
University of Missouri–Columbia	M
Virginia Polytechnic Institute and State University	D
Yale University	M

■ ENVIRONMENTAL EDUCATION

Alaska Pacific University	M
Antioch University New England	M
Arcadia University	M,D,O
Brooklyn College of the City University of New York	M
California State University, Fullerton	M
California State University, San Bernardino	M
Chatham University	M
Concordia University Wisconsin	M
Florida Institute of Technology	M,D,O
Gannon University	M
Lesley University	M,D,O
Maryville University of Saint Louis	M,D
New York University	M
Prescott College	M
Slippery Rock University of Pennsylvania	M
Southern Connecticut State University	M,O
Southern Oregon University	M
Universidad Metropolitana	M
University of Minnesota, Twin Cities Campus	M,D,O
University of New Hampshire	M
Western Washington University	M
West Virginia University	M

■ ENVIRONMENTAL ENGINEERING

Auburn University	M,D
California Institute of Technology	M,D
California Polytechnic State University, San Luis Obispo	M
Carnegie Mellon University	M,D
The Catholic University of America	M,D

Clarkson University	M,D
Clemson University	M,D
Cleveland State University	M,D
Colorado School of Mines	M,D
Columbia University	M,D,O
Cornell University	M,D
Drexel University	M,D
Duke University	M,D
Florida Agricultural and Mechanical University	M,D
Florida International University	M
Florida State University	M,D
Gannon University	M
The George Washington University	M,D,O
Georgia Institute of Technology	M,D
Idaho State University	M,D,O
Illinois Institute of Technology	M,D
Iowa State University of Science and Technology	M,D
The Johns Hopkins University	M,D,O
Lamar University	M,D
Lehigh University	M,D
Louisiana State University and Agricultural and Mechanical College	M,D
Manhattan College	M
Marquette University	M,D
Marshall University	M
Massachusetts Institute of Technology	M,D,O
Michigan State University	M,D
Michigan Technological University	M,D
Missouri University of Science and Technology	M
Montana State University	M,D
National University	M
New Jersey Institute of Technology	M,D
New Mexico Institute of Mining and Technology	M
New Mexico State University	M,D
New York Institute of Technology	M
North Carolina Agricultural and Technical State University	M
North Dakota State University	M,D
Northeastern University	M,D
Northwestern University	M,D
Ohio University	M,D
Oklahoma State University	M,D
Old Dominion University	M,D
Oregon State University	M,D
Penn State Harrisburg	M
Penn State University Park	M,D
Polytechnic University, Brooklyn Campus	M
Portland State University	M,D
Princeton University	M,D
Rensselaer Polytechnic Institute	M,D
Rice University	M,D
Rutgers, The State University of New Jersey, New Brunswick	M,D
Southern Methodist University	M,D
Stanford University	M,D,O
State University of New York College of Environmental Science and Forestry	M,D
Stevens Institute of Technology	M,D,O
Syracuse University	M,D
Texas A&M University	M,D
Texas A&M University–Kingsville	M,D
Texas Tech University	M,D
Tufts University	M,D
Tulane University	M,D
University at Buffalo, the State University of New York	M,D
The University of Alabama	M,D
The University of Alabama at Birmingham	M
The University of Alabama in Huntsville	M,D
University of Alaska Anchorage	M
University of Alaska Fairbanks	M,D
The University of Arizona	M,D
University of Arkansas	M
University of California, Berkeley	M,D
University of California, Davis	M,D,O
University of California, Irvine	M,D
University of California, Los Angeles	M,D
University of California, Riverside	M,D
University of Central Florida	M,D,O
University of Cincinnati	M,D
University of Colorado at Boulder	M,D
University of Connecticut	M,D
University of Dayton	M
University of Delaware	M,D
University of Detroit Mercy	M
University of Florida	M,D,O
University of Hawaii at Manoa	M,D
University of Houston	M,D
University of Idaho	M
University of Illinois at Urbana–Champaign	M,D
The University of Iowa	M,D
University of Kansas	M,D
University of Louisville	M,D
University of Maine	M,D
University of Maryland, Baltimore County	M,D
University of Maryland, College Park	M,D
University of Massachusetts Amherst	M
University of Massachusetts Lowell	M
University of Memphis	M,D
University of Michigan	M,D,O
University of Missouri–Columbia	M,D
University of Nebraska–Lincoln	M,D
University of New Haven	M,O
The University of North Carolina at Chapel Hill	M,D
The University of North Carolina at Charlotte	D
University of North Dakota	M
University of Notre Dame	M,D
University of Oklahoma	M,D
University of Pittsburgh	M,D
University of Rhode Island	M
University of Southern California	M,D
University of South Florida	M,D
The University of Tennessee	M
The University of Texas at Arlington	M,D
The University of Texas at Austin	M
The University of Texas at El Paso	M,D
The University of Texas at San Antonio	M,D
University of Utah	M,D
University of Vermont	M,D
University of Washington	M,D
University of Wisconsin–Madison	M,D
University of Wyoming	M
Utah State University	M,D,O
Vanderbilt University	M,D
Villanova University	M
Virginia Polytechnic Institute and State University	M,D
Washington State University	M
Washington University in St. Louis	M,D
West Virginia University	M,D
Worcester Polytechnic Institute	M,D,O
Youngstown State University	M

■ ENVIRONMENTAL MANAGEMENT AND POLICY

Adelphi University	M
American University	M,D,O
Antioch University New England	M,D
Antioch University Seattle	M
Arizona State University at the Polytechnic Campus	M
Baylor University	M
Bemidji State University	M
Boise State University	M
Boston University	M,D,O
Brown University	M
California Polytechnic State University, San Luis Obispo	M
California State University, Fullerton	M
Central Washington University	M
Clark University	M
Clemson University	M,D
Cleveland State University	M
Colorado State University	M,D
Columbia University	M
Cornell University	M,D
Drexel University	M
Duke University	M,D
Duquesne University	M,O
East Carolina University	D
The Evergreen State College	M
Florida Gulf Coast University	M
Florida Institute of Technology	M,D
Florida International University	M
Friends University	M
Gannon University	M
The George Washington University	M,D
Georgia Institute of Technology	M,D
Goddard College	M
Hardin-Simmons University	M
Harvard University	M,O
Illinois Institute of Technology	M
Indiana University–Purdue University Indianapolis	M
Iowa State University of Science and Technology	M,D
The Johns Hopkins University	M
Kansas State University	M
Kean University	M
Lamar University	M,D
Long Island University, C.W. Post Campus	M
Louisiana State University and Agricultural and Mechanical College	M
Michigan State University	M,D
Michigan Technological University	M
Missouri State University	M
Montana State University	M,D
Montclair State University	M,D
Monterey Institute of International Studies	M
Morehead State University	M
Naropa University	M
New Jersey Institute of Technology	M,D
New Mexico Highlands University	M
New York Institute of Technology	M,O
North Dakota State University	M,D
Northeastern Illinois University	M
Northern Arizona University	M,O
The Ohio State University	M,D
Ohio University	M
Oregon State University	M,D
Penn State University Park	M
Plymouth State University	M
Portland State University	M,D
Prescott College	M

Princeton University	M,D
Purdue University	M,D
Rensselaer Polytechnic Institute	M,D
Rice University	M
Rochester Institute of Technology	M
St. Cloud State University	M
Saint Joseph's University	M,O
Samford University	M
San Francisco State University	M
San Jose State University	M
Shippensburg University of Pennsylvania	M
Slippery Rock University of Pennsylvania	M
Southeast Missouri State University	M
Southern Illinois University Edwardsville	M
Stanford University	M
State University of New York College of Environmental Science and Forestry	M,D
Stony Brook University, State University of New York	M,O
Texas State University-San Marcos	M
Texas Tech University	M,D
Towson University	M
Troy University	M
Tufts University	M,D,O
Universidad del Turabo	M
Universidad Metropolitana	M
University at Albany, State University of New York	M
University of Alaska Fairbanks	M
University of California, Berkeley	M,D
University of California, Santa Barbara	M,D
University of California, Santa Cruz	D
University of Chicago	M,D
University of Colorado at Boulder	M,D
University of Connecticut	M,D
University of Delaware	M,D
University of Denver	M,O
The University of Findlay	M
University of Hawaii at Manoa	M,D,O
University of Houston–Clear Lake	M
University of Idaho	M
University of Illinois at Springfield	M
University of Maine	M,D
University of Maryland University College	M,O
University of Massachusetts Lowell	M,D,O
University of Miami	M,D
University of Michigan	M,D
University of Minnesota, Twin Cities Campus	M,D
University of Missouri–St. Louis	M,D,O
The University of Montana	M,D
University of Nevada, Reno	M
University of New Hampshire	M
The University of North Carolina at Chapel Hill	M,D
University of Oregon	M,D
University of Pennsylvania	M
University of Pittsburgh	M
University of Rhode Island	M,D
University of San Francisco	M
University of South Carolina	M
University of South Florida	M
The University of Tennessee	M,D
The University of Texas at Austin	M
University of Vermont	M,D
University of Washington	M,D
University of Wisconsin–Madison	M,D
Utah State University	M,D
Vanderbilt University	M,D
Virginia Commonwealth University	M
Webster University	M,D
Wesley College	M
West Virginia University	M,D
Yale University	M,D
Youngstown State University	M,O

■ ENVIRONMENTAL SCIENCES

Alabama Agricultural and Mechanical University	M,D
Alaska Pacific University	M
American University	M
Antioch University New England	M,D
Arkansas State University	M,D,O
California State Polytechnic University, Pomona	M
California State University, Chico	M
California State University, Fullerton	M
California State University, Northridge	M
California State University, San Bernardino	M
City College of the City University of New York	M,D
Clarkson University	M,D
Clemson University	M,D
Cleveland State University	M,D
College of Charleston	M
College of Staten Island of the City University of New York	M
Columbia University	M
Columbus State University	M
Cornell University	M,D
Drexel University	M,D
Duke University	M,D
Duquesne University	M,O
Florida Agricultural and Mechanical University	M,D
Florida Atlantic University	M
Florida Gulf Coast University	M
Florida Institute of Technology	M,D
Florida International University	M
Gannon University	O
Georgia Institute of Technology	M,D
Graduate School and University Center of the City University of New York	D
Hawai'i Pacific University	M
Howard University	M,D
Humboldt State University	M
Hunter College of the City University of New York	M,O
Idaho State University	M
Indiana University Bloomington	M,D
Indiana University Northwest	M,O
Inter American University of Puerto Rico, San Germán Campus	M
Iowa State University of Science and Technology	M,D
Jackson State University	M,D
The Johns Hopkins University	M
Lehigh University	M,D
Long Island University, C.W. Post Campus	M
Louisiana State University and Agricultural and Mechanical College	M,D
Loyola Marymount University	M
Marshall University	M
Massachusetts Institute of Technology	M,D,O
McNeese State University	M
Miami University	M
Michigan State University	M,D
Minnesota State University Mankato	M
Montana State University	M,D
Montclair State University	M,D,O
Murray State University	M
New Jersey Institute of Technology	M,D
New Mexico Institute of Mining and Technology	M,D
North Carolina Agricultural and Technical State University	M
North Dakota State University	M,D
Northern Arizona University	M,O
Nova Southeastern University	M
Oakland University	M,D
The Ohio State University	M,D
Oklahoma State University	M,D
Oregon State University	M,D
Pace University	M
Penn State Harrisburg	M
Penn State University Park	M
Polytechnic University, Brooklyn Campus	M
Pontifical Catholic University of Puerto Rico	M
Portland State University	M,D
Queens College of the City University of New York	M
Rensselaer Polytechnic Institute	M,D
Rice University	M,D
Rochester Institute of Technology	M
Rutgers, The State University of New Jersey, Newark	M,D
Rutgers, The State University of New Jersey, New Brunswick	M,D
Southern Illinois University Carbondale	D
Southern Illinois University Edwardsville	M
Southern Methodist University	M,D
Southern University and Agricultural and Mechanical College	M
Stanford University	M,D,O
State University of New York College at Brockport	M
State University of New York College of Environmental Science and Forestry	M,D
Stephen F. Austin State University	M
Tarleton State University	M
Tennessee Technological University	D
Texas A&M University–Corpus Christi	M
Texas Christian University	M
Texas Tech University	M,D
Towson University	M,O
Tufts University	M,D
University at Albany, State University of New York	M
The University of Alabama in Huntsville	M,D
University of Alaska Anchorage	M
University of Alaska Fairbanks	M,D
The University of Arizona	M,D
University of California, Berkeley	M,D
University of California, Davis	M,D
University of California, Los Angeles	D
University of California, Riverside	M,D
University of California, Santa Barbara	M,D
University of Chicago	M,D
University of Cincinnati	M,D
University of Colorado at Colorado Springs	M
University of Colorado Denver	M,O
University of Guam	M
University of Houston–Clear Lake	M
University of Idaho	M,D
University of Illinois at Springfield	M
University of Illinois at Urbana–Champaign	M,D

University of Kansas	M,D
University of Maine	M,D
University of Maryland, Baltimore County	M,D
University of Maryland, College Park	M,D
University of Maryland Eastern Shore	M,D
University of Massachusetts Boston	D
University of Massachusetts Lowell	M,D,O
University of Michigan	M,D
University of Michigan–Dearborn	M
The University of Montana	M
University of Nevada, Las Vegas	M,D
University of Nevada, Reno	M,D
University of New Haven	M
University of New Orleans	M
The University of North Carolina at Chapel Hill	M,D
University of Northern Iowa	M
University of North Texas	M,D
University of Oklahoma	M,D
University of Rhode Island	M,D
University of South Carolina	M,D
University of South Florida	M
The University of Tennessee at Chattanooga	M
The University of Texas at Arlington	M,D
The University of Texas at El Paso	M,D
The University of Texas at San Antonio	M,D
The University of Toledo	M,D
University of Utah	M
University of Virginia	M,D
University of West Florida	M
University of Wisconsin–Madison	M,D
Vanderbilt University	M
Virginia Commonwealth University	M
Virginia Polytechnic Institute and State University	M,D
Washington State University	M,D
Western Connecticut State University	M
Western Washington University	M
West Texas A&M University	M
Wichita State University	M
Wright State University	M,D
Yale University	M,D

■ EPIDEMIOLOGY

Boston University	M,D
Brown University	M,D
Case Western Reserve University	M,D
Columbia University	M,D
Cornell University	M,D
East Tennessee State University	M,O
Emory University	M,D
Georgetown University	M
The George Washington University	M,D
Harvard University	M,D
The Johns Hopkins University	M,D
Michigan State University	M,D
New York University	M,D
North Carolina State University	M,D
Purdue University	M,D
San Diego State University	M,D
Stanford University	M,D
Temple University	M
Texas A&M University	M,D
Tufts University	M,D,O
Tulane University	M,D
University at Albany, State University of New York	M,D
University at Buffalo, the State University of New York	M,D
The University of Alabama at Birmingham	D
The University of Arizona	M,D
University of California, Berkeley	M,D
University of California, Davis	M,D
University of California, Irvine	M,D
University of California, Los Angeles	M,D
University of California, San Diego	D
University of Cincinnati	M,D
University of Colorado Denver	D
University of Florida	M
University of Hawaii at Manoa	D
University of Illinois at Chicago	M,D
The University of Iowa	M,D
University of Maryland, Baltimore County	M
University of Massachusetts Lowell	M,D,O
University of Miami	D
University of Michigan	M,D
University of Minnesota, Twin Cities Campus	M,D
The University of North Carolina at Chapel Hill	M,D
University of Pennsylvania	M,D
University of Pittsburgh	M,D
University of Rochester	M,D
University of South Carolina	M,D
University of Southern California	M,D
University of Southern Mississippi	M
University of South Florida	M,D
University of Washington	M,D
Virginia Commonwealth University	D
Yale University	M,D

■ ERGONOMICS AND HUMAN FACTORS

Bentley College	M
The Catholic University of America	M
Clemson University	D
Cornell University	M
Embry-Riddle Aeronautical University (FL)	M
Florida Institute of Technology	M
Indiana University Bloomington	M,D,O
New York University	M,D
North Carolina State University	D
Old Dominion University	D
San Jose State University	M
Tufts University	M,D
University of Central Florida	M,D,O
University of Cincinnati	M,D
The University of Iowa	M,D
University of Massachusetts Lowell	M,D,O
University of Miami	M,D
The University of Tennessee	M,D
University of Washington	M,D
Wright State University	M,D

■ ETHICS

American University	M,D,O
Azusa Pacific University	M
Biola University	P,M,D
Claremont Graduate University	M,D
Drew University	M,D
Duquesne University	M
Eastern Michigan University	M
Fordham University	O
Marquette University	M,D
St. Edward's University	M
University of Baltimore	M
University of Nevada, Las Vegas	M
University of North Florida	M,O
University of North Texas	M,D
Valparaiso University	M,O

■ ETHNIC STUDIES

Cornell University	M,D
Minnesota State University Mankato	M
San Francisco State University	M
University of California, Berkeley	D
University of California, San Diego	M,D
Washington State University	M,D

■ EVOLUTIONARY BIOLOGY

Arizona State University	M,D
Brown University	D
Clemson University	M,D
Columbia University	D,O
Cornell University	D
Dartmouth College	D
Emory University	D
Florida State University	M,D
George Mason University	M,D,O
Harvard University	D
Illinois State University	M,D
Indiana University Bloomington	M,D
Iowa State University of Science and Technology	M,D
The Johns Hopkins University	D
Marquette University	M,D
Michigan State University	D
Northwestern University	D
The Ohio State University	M,D
Ohio University	M,D
Penn State University Park	M,D
Princeton University	D
Purdue University	M,D
Rice University	M,D
Rutgers, The State University of New Jersey, New Brunswick	M,D
Stony Brook University, State University of New York	D
Tulane University	M,D
University at Albany, State University of New York	M,D
University at Buffalo, the State University of New York	M,D,O
The University of Arizona	M,D
University of California, Davis	D
University of California, Irvine	M,D
University of California, Los Angeles	M,D
University of California, Riverside	M,D
University of California, San Diego	D
University of California, Santa Barbara	M,D
University of California, Santa Cruz	M,D
University of Chicago	D
University of Colorado at Boulder	M,D
University of Delaware	M,D
University of Hawaii at Manoa	M,D
University of Illinois at Chicago	M,D
University of Illinois at Urbana–Champaign	M,D
The University of Iowa	M,D
University of Kansas	M,D
University of Louisiana at Lafayette	M,D
University of Maryland, College Park	M,D
University of Massachusetts Amherst	M,D
University of Miami	M,D
University of Michigan	M,D
University of Minnesota, Twin Cities Campus	M,D
University of Missouri–Columbia	M,D
University of Missouri–St. Louis	M,D,O
University of Nevada, Reno	D
The University of North Carolina at Chapel Hill	M,D
University of Notre Dame	M,D
University of Oregon	M,D
University of Pittsburgh	D
University of South Carolina	M,D
The University of Tennessee	M,D
The University of Texas at Austin	D
University of Utah	M,D

Virginia Polytechnic Institute and State University M,D
Washington University in St. Louis D
West Virginia University M,D
Yale University D

■ EXERCISE AND SPORTS SCIENCE

American University M
Appalachian State University M
Arizona State University D
Arizona State University at the Polytechnic Campus M,D
Arkansas State University M,O
Armstrong Atlantic State University M
Ashland University M
Auburn University M,D,O
Austin Peay State University M
Ball State University D
Barry University M
Baylor University M,D
Bemidji State University M
Benedictine University M
Bloomsburg University of Pennsylvania M
Boise State University M
Brigham Young University M,D
Brooklyn College of the City University of New York M
California State University, Fresno M
California University of Pennsylvania M
Central Connecticut State University M,O
Central Michigan University M
Cleveland State University M
The College of St. Scholastica M
Colorado State University M,D
Concordia University Chicago (IL) M
East Carolina University M,D
Eastern Michigan University M
East Stroudsburg University of Pennsylvania M
East Tennessee State University M
Florida Atlantic University M
Florida International University M
Florida State University M,D
Gardner-Webb University M
George Mason University M
The George Washington University M
Georgia State University M,D
High Point University M
Howard University M
Humboldt State University M
Indiana State University M
Indiana University Bloomington M,D,O
Indiana University of Pennsylvania M
Iowa State University of Science and Technology M,D
Ithaca College M
Kean University M
Kent State University M,D
Long Island University, Brooklyn Campus M
Louisiana Tech University M
Manhattanville College M
Marshall University M
Marywood University M
McNeese State University M
Miami University M
Middle Tennessee State University M,D
Mississippi State University M
Montclair State University M,O
Morehead State University M
Murray State University M
New Mexico Highlands University M
North Dakota State University M
Northeastern University M
Northern Arizona University M
Northern Michigan University M
Oakland University M,O
Ohio University M,D
Old Dominion University M
Oregon State University M,D
Purdue University M,D
Queens College of the City University of New York M
St. Cloud State University M
San Diego State University M
Southeast Missouri State University M
Southern Connecticut State University M
Springfield College M,D,O
State University of New York College at Cortland M
Syracuse University M
Tennessee State University M
Texas Tech University M
Texas Woman's University M
University at Buffalo, the State University of New York M,D
The University of Akron M
The University of Alabama M,D
University of California, Davis M
University of Central Florida M
University of Central Missouri M
University of Connecticut M,D
University of Dayton M,D
University of Delaware M
University of Florida M,D
University of Houston M,D
University of Houston–Clear Lake M
The University of Iowa M,D
University of Kentucky M,D
University of Louisiana at Monroe M
University of Louisville M
University of Mary Hardin-Baylor M,D
University of Memphis M
University of Miami M,D
University of Minnesota, Twin Cities Campus M,D,O
University of Mississippi M,D
University of Missouri–Columbia M,D
The University of Montana M
University of Nebraska at Kearney M
University of Nevada, Las Vegas M
The University of North Carolina at Chapel Hill M
The University of North Carolina at Charlotte M
The University of North Carolina at Greensboro M,D
University of Northern Colorado M,D
University of Oklahoma M,D
University of Pittsburgh M,D
University of Puerto Rico, Río Piedras M
University of Rhode Island M,D
University of South Alabama M
University of South Carolina M,D
University of Southern Mississippi M,D
The University of Tennessee M,D,O
The University of Texas at Arlington M
The University of Texas at El Paso M
The University of Texas at Tyler M
University of the Pacific M
The University of Toledo M,D
University of Utah M,D
University of West Florida M
University of Wisconsin–La Crosse M
Virginia Commonwealth University M,D
Wake Forest University M
Washington State University M,D
Wayne State College M
West Chester University of Pennsylvania M,O
Western Michigan University M
Western Washington University M
West Texas A&M University M
West Virginia University M,D
Wichita State University M

■ EXPERIMENTAL PSYCHOLOGY

American University M
Appalachian State University M
Auburn University M,D
Bowling Green State University M,D
Brooklyn College of the City University of New York M,D
California State University, San Bernardino M
Case Western Reserve University D
The Catholic University of America M,D
Central Michigan University M,D
Central Washington University M
City College of the City University of New York M,D
Cleveland State University M,O
The College of William and Mary M
Columbia University M,D
Cornell University D
Dallas Baptist University M
DePaul University M,D
Duke University D
Eastern Michigan University M,D
Fairleigh Dickinson University, Metropolitan Campus M,O
George Mason University M,D
Graduate School and University Center of the City University of New York D
Harvard University D
Howard University M,D
Illinois State University M,D,O
Iona College M
Kent State University M,D
Long Island University, C.W. Post Campus M,O
Miami University D
Mississippi State University M,D
Morehead State University M
North Carolina State University D
Northeastern University M,D
Ohio University D
Oklahoma State University M,D
Old Dominion University D
Radford University M,D,O
St. John's University (NY) M
Saint Louis University M,D
San Jose State University M
Seton Hall University M
Southern Illinois University Carbondale M,D
Stony Brook University, State University of New York D
Syracuse University D
Texas Tech University M,D
Towson University M
University at Albany, State University of New York M,D,O
The University of Alabama D
University of Central Florida D
University of Cincinnati D
University of Connecticut M,D
University of Hartford M
University of Kentucky M,D
University of Louisville D
University of Maine M,D

University of Maryland, College Park	M,D
University of Memphis	M,D
University of Michigan	D
University of Mississippi	M,D
The University of Montana	M,D,O
University of Nevada, Las Vegas	M,D
The University of North Carolina at Chapel Hill	D
University of North Dakota	M,D
University of North Texas	M,D
University of South Carolina	M,D
University of Southern Mississippi	M,D
University of South Florida	M,D
The University of Tennessee	M,D
The University of Tennessee at Chattanooga	M
The University of Texas at Arlington	M,D
The University of Texas at El Paso	M,D
The University of Texas–Pan American	M
The University of Toledo	M,D
University of Wisconsin–Oshkosh	M
Washington State University	M,D
Washington University in St. Louis	M,D
Western Michigan University	M,D,O
Western Washington University	M

■ FACILITIES MANAGEMENT

Cornell University	M
Indiana University of Pennsylvania	M
Southern Methodist University	M,D

■ FAMILY AND CONSUMER SCIENCES-GENERAL

Alabama Agricultural and Mechanical University	M,D
Appalachian State University	M
Ball State University	M
Bowling Green State University	M
California State University, Fresno	M
California State University, Long Beach	M
California State University, Northridge	M
Central Michigan University	M
Central Washington University	M
Clemson University	D
Cornell University	M,D
Eastern Illinois University	M
Florida State University	M,D
Fontbonne University	M
Illinois State University	M
Indiana State University	M
Iowa State University of Science and Technology	M
Kansas State University	M,D
Kent State University	M
Lamar University	M,O
Louisiana State University and Agricultural and Mechanical College	M,D
Louisiana Tech University	M
Marshall University	M
Missouri State University	M
New Mexico State University	M
North Carolina Central University	M
North Dakota State University	M
The Ohio State University	M
Ohio University	M
Oklahoma State University	M,D
Oregon State University	M
Prairie View A&M University	M
Purdue University	M,D
Queens College of the City University of New York	M
Sam Houston State University	M
San Francisco State University	M
South Carolina State University	M
South Dakota State University	M
Southeast Missouri State University	M
State University of New York College at Oneonta	M
Stephen F. Austin State University	M
Tennessee State University	M
Texas A&M University–Kingsville	M
Texas Southern University	M
Texas Tech University	M,D,O
Tufts University	M,D,O
The University of Akron	M
The University of Alabama	M,D
The University of Arizona	M,D
University of Arkansas	M
University of Central Arkansas	M
University of Central Oklahoma	M
University of Florida	M
University of Georgia	M,D
University of Houston	M
University of Louisiana at Lafayette	M
University of Maryland, College Park	M,D
University of Memphis	M
University of Missouri–Columbia	M,D
University of Nebraska–Lincoln	M,D
The University of North Carolina at Greensboro	M,D,O
University of Puerto Rico, Río Piedras	M
The University of Tennessee	D
The University of Tennessee at Martin	M
The University of Texas at Austin	M,D
University of Wisconsin–Madison	M,D
University of Wisconsin–Stevens Point	M
Utah State University	M,D
Western Michigan University	M

■ FAMILY NURSE PRACTITIONER STUDIES

Barry University	M,O
Baylor University	M
Bloomsburg University of Pennsylvania	M
Bowie State University	M
Brenau University	M
Brigham Young University	M
California State University, Fresno	M
Carson-Newman College	M
Case Western Reserve University	D
The Catholic University of America	M,D
College of Mount Saint Vincent	M,O
The College of New Rochelle	M,O
Columbia University	M,O
Concordia University Wisconsin	M
Coppin State University	M,O
DeSales University	M
Dominican College	M
Duke University	M,D,O
Duquesne University	M,O
D'Youville College	M,O
Eastern Kentucky University	M
Edinboro University of Pennsylvania	M
Emory University	M
Fairfield University	M,O
Florida State University	M,O
George Mason University	M,D,O
The George Washington University	M,D,O
Georgia Southern University	M,O
Georgia State University	M,D,O
Graceland University	M,O
Grambling State University	M,O
Gwynedd-Mercy College	M
Hardin-Simmons University	M
Hawai'i Pacific University	M
Holy Names University	M
Howard University	M,O
Hunter College of the City University of New York	M,O
Husson College	M
Illinois State University	M,O
Indiana University–Purdue University Indianapolis	M,D
The Johns Hopkins University	M,O
Kent State University	M,D
La Roche College	M
La Salle University	M,O
Long Island University, C.W. Post Campus	M,O
Loyola University Chicago	M
Loyola University New Orleans	M
Malone College	M
Marymount University	M,O
Midwestern State University	M
Minnesota State University Mankato	M,D
Molloy College	M,O
Montana State University	M,O
Mountain State University	M,O
Murray State University	M
Northern Kentucky University	M,O
North Georgia College & State University	M
Oakland University	M,O
Otterbein College	M,O
Pacific Lutheran University	M
Prairie View A&M University	M
Quinnipiac University	M,O
Regis College (MA)	M,O
Rivier College	M
Rutgers, The State University of New Jersey, Newark	M
Sacred Heart University	M
Saginaw Valley State University	M
St. John Fisher College	M,O
Saint Joseph College	M,O
Saint Xavier University	M,O
San Francisco State University	M
Seattle Pacific University	O
Shenandoah University	M,O
Sonoma State University	M
Southern Illinois University Edwardsville	M,O
Southern University and Agricultural and Mechanical College	M,D,O
Spalding University	M
State University of New York Institute of Technology	M,O
Stony Brook University, State University of New York	M,O
Texas A&M University–Corpus Christi	M
University at Buffalo, the State University of New York	M,D,O
The University of Alabama in Huntsville	M,O
University of Alaska Anchorage	M,O
University of Central Arkansas	M
University of Colorado at Colorado Springs	M,D
University of Delaware	M,O
University of Detroit Mercy	M,O
University of Hawaii at Manoa	M,D,O
University of Mary	M
University of Miami	M,D
University of Michigan	M
University of Minnesota, Twin Cities Campus	M
University of Missouri–Kansas City	M,D
University of Nevada, Las Vegas	M,D,O
The University of North Carolina at Charlotte	M

University of Northern Colorado M,D
University of Pennsylvania M,O
University of Phoenix–Hawaii Campus M
University of Phoenix–Phoenix Campus M,O
University of Phoenix–Sacramento Valley Campus M
University of Phoenix–Southern Arizona Campus M,O
University of Phoenix–Southern California Campus M,O
University of Pittsburgh M,D
University of Rhode Island M,D
University of San Diego M,D,O
University of San Francisco M,D
The University of Scranton M,O
University of South Carolina M
University of Southern Maine M,O
University of Southern Mississippi M,D
The University of Tampa M
The University of Tennessee at Chattanooga M
The University of Texas at Arlington M,D
The University of Texas at El Paso M
The University of Texas at Tyler M
The University of Texas–Pan American M
The University of Toledo M,O
University of Wisconsin–Oshkosh M
Vanderbilt University M,D
Virginia Commonwealth University M,O
Wagner College O
Westminster College (UT) M
Wichita State University M
Wilmington University (DE) M
Winona State University M,O
Wright State University M

■ FILM, TELEVISION, AND VIDEO PRODUCTION

American University M
Antioch University McGregor M
Bob Jones University P,M,D,O
Boston University M
Bowling Green State University M,D
Brigham Young University M
Brooklyn College of the City University of New York M
California State University, Fullerton M
California State University, Northridge M
Carnegie Mellon University M
Central Michigan University M
Chapman University M
Chatham University M
Chestnut Hill College M,O
Columbia College Chicago M
Columbia University M
Emerson College M
Florida State University M
George Mason University M
Georgia State University M,D
Hofstra University M
Hollins University M
Howard University M
Loyola Marymount University M
Marywood University M,O
Montana State University M
New Mexico Highlands University M
New York University M
Northwestern University M,D
Ohio University M
Polytechnic University, Brooklyn Campus O
Regent University M,D
Rochester Institute of Technology M
San Diego State University M
San Francisco State University M
San Jose State University M
Southern Methodist University M
Syracuse University M
Temple University M
The University of Alabama M
University of California, Los Angeles M,D
University of California, Santa Barbara
University of Central Arkansas M
University of Central Florida M
University of Denver M
The University of Iowa M
University of Memphis M,D
University of Miami M,D
University of Michigan O
The University of Montana M
University of Nevada, Las Vegas M
University of New Orleans M
University of North Texas M
University of Oklahoma M
University of Southern California M
The University of Texas at Austin M,D
University of Utah M
University of Wisconsin–Milwaukee M

■ FILM, TELEVISION, AND VIDEO THEORY AND CRITICISM

Boston University M
Claremont Graduate University M,D
College of Staten Island of the City University of New York M
Emory University M,D,O
Hollins University M
New York University M,D
Ohio University M
San Francisco State University M
Syracuse University M
University of Chicago M,D
University of Georgia M,D
The University of Iowa M,D
University of Kansas M,D
University of Miami M,D
University of Michigan D,O
University of Southern California M,D

■ FINANCE AND BANKING

Adelphi University M
Alabama Agricultural and Mechanical University M
Alaska Pacific University M
American InterContinental University (FL) M
American InterContinental University Buckhead Campus M
American University M,D,O
Andrews University M
Argosy University, Orange County Campus M,D,O
Argosy University, Sarasota Campus M,D,O
Argosy University, Tampa Campus M,D,O
Argosy University, Twin Cities Campus M,D
Arizona State University M,D
Auburn University M
Avila University M
Barry University O
Bayamón Central University M
Benedictine University M
Bentley College M
Bernard M. Baruch College of the City University of New York M,D
Boston College M,D
Boston University P,M,D
Brandeis University M,D
Bridgewater State College M
Bryant University M,O
California Lutheran University M,O
California State University, East Bay M
California State University, Fullerton M
California State University, Los Angeles M
California State University, Stanislaus M
Capella University M,D,O
Carnegie Mellon University D
Case Western Reserve University M,D
Central Michigan University M
Charleston Southern University M
Christian Brothers University M,O
City University of Seattle M,O
Clark Atlanta University M
Clark University M
Cleveland State University M,D,O
College of Santa Fe M
Columbia University M,D
Concordia University Wisconsin M
Cornell University D
Dallas Baptist University M
DePaul University M,O
Dowling College M,O
Drexel University M,D,O
Eastern Michigan University M
Eastern University M
East Tennessee State University M
Fairfield University M,O
Fairleigh Dickinson University, College at Florham M,O
Fairleigh Dickinson University, Metropolitan Campus M,O
Florida Agricultural and Mechanical University M
Florida Atlantic University M
Florida International University M
Florida State University M,D
Fordham University M
Gannon University O
The George Washington University M,D
Georgia Institute of Technology M,D,O
Georgia State University M,D,O
Golden Gate University M,D,O
Graduate School and University Center of the City University of New York D
Hawai'i Pacific University M
Hofstra University M
Howard University M
Illinois Institute of Technology P,M
Indiana University Southeast M,O
Inter American University of Puerto Rico, Metropolitan Campus M,D
Inter American University of Puerto Rico, San Germán Campus M,D
Iona College M,O
The Johns Hopkins University M,O
Johnson & Wales University M,O
Kent State University D
Lamar University M
Lehigh University M
Lindenwood University M
Lipscomb University M
Long Island University, C.W. Post Campus M,O
Louisiana State University and Agricultural and Mechanical College M,D
Louisiana Tech University M,D
Loyola College in Maryland M
Marywood University M
Mercy College M

Metropolitan State University	M
Miami University	M
Michigan State University	M,D
Middle Tennessee State University	M,D
Minnesota State University Mankato	M
Mississippi State University	M,D
Montclair State University	M
Mount Saint Mary College	M
National University	M
New Jersey City University	M
New Mexico Highlands University	M
The New School: A University	M
New York Institute of Technology	M,O
New York University	M,D,O
Northeastern Illinois University	M
Northeastern State University	M
Northeastern University	M
Northwestern University	D
Oakland University	M,O
The Ohio State University	M,D
Ohio University	M
Oklahoma City University	M
Oklahoma State University	M,D
Old Dominion University	D
Oral Roberts University	M
Our Lady of the Lake University of San Antonio	M
Pace University	M
Penn State University Park	M,D
Philadelphia University	M
Polytechnic University, Brooklyn Campus	M,O
Polytechnic University, Westchester Graduate Center	M,O
Pontifical Catholic University of Puerto Rico	M,D
Portland State University	M
Princeton University	M
Purdue University	M,D
Quinnipiac University	M
Regis University	M,O
Rensselaer Polytechnic Institute	M,D
Rhode Island College	M
Robert Morris University	M
Rochester Institute of Technology	M
Rutgers, The State University of New Jersey, Newark	M,D,O
Rutgers, The State University of New Jersey, New Brunswick	M,D
St. Bonaventure University	M,O
St. Cloud State University	M
St. Edward's University	M,O
St. John's University (NY)	M,O
Saint Joseph's University	M,O
Saint Louis University	M
Saint Mary's University of Minnesota	M,O
St. Mary's University of San Antonio	M
Saint Peter's College	M
St. Thomas Aquinas College	M
Saint Xavier University	M,O
Sam Houston State University	M
San Diego State University	M
Schiller International University (United States)	M
Seattle University	M,O
Seton Hall University	M
Southeastern University	M
Southeast Missouri State University	M
Southern Illinois University Edwardsville	M
Southern New Hampshire University	M,D,O
State University of New York at Binghamton	M,D
Stevens Institute of Technology	M
Stony Brook University, State University of New York	M,O
Suffolk University	M,O
Syracuse University	M,D
Tarleton State University	M
Temple University	M,D
Texas A&M International University	M
Texas A&M University	M,D
Texas Tech University	M,D
Universidad Metropolitana	M
University at Albany, State University of New York	M
University at Buffalo, the State University of New York	M,D,O
The University of Akron	M
The University of Alabama	M,D
University of Alaska Fairbanks	M
The University of Arizona	M,D
University of Baltimore	M
University of California, Berkeley	D
University of Cincinnati	M,D
University of Colorado at Boulder	D
University of Colorado at Colorado Springs	M
University of Colorado Denver	M
University of Connecticut	M,D,O
University of Dallas	M
University of Denver	M
The University of Findlay	M
University of Florida	M,D,O
University of Hawaii at Manoa	M,D
University of Houston	M
University of Houston–Clear Lake	M
University of Houston–Victoria	M
University of Illinois at Urbana–Champaign	M,D
University of Indianapolis	M,O
The University of Iowa	M,D
University of La Verne	M
University of Maryland University College	M,O
University of Massachusetts Dartmouth	M,O
University of Memphis	M,D
University of Miami	M
University of Michigan–Dearborn	M
University of Minnesota, Twin Cities Campus	M,D
University of Missouri–St. Louis	M,O
University of Nebraska–Lincoln	M,D
University of Nevada, Reno	M
University of New Haven	M
University of New Mexico	M
University of New Orleans	M,D
The University of North Carolina at Chapel Hill	D
The University of North Carolina at Greensboro	M,O
University of North Texas	M,D
University of Oregon	D
University of Pennsylvania	M,D
University of Puerto Rico, Mayagüez Campus	M
University of Rhode Island	D
University of San Diego	M,O
University of San Francisco	M
The University of Scranton	M
University of Southern California	M
University of South Florida	M
The University of Tampa	M
The University of Tennessee	M,D
The University of Texas at Arlington	M,D
The University of Texas at Austin	D
The University of Texas at San Antonio	M,D
The University of Toledo	M
University of Tulsa	M
University of Utah	M,D
University of Washington, Tacoma	M
University of Wisconsin–Madison	M,D
University of Wisconsin–Whitewater	M
University of Wyoming	M
Upper Iowa University	M
Vanderbilt University	M,D
Villanova University	M
Virginia Commonwealth University	M
Virginia Polytechnic Institute and State University	M,D
Wagner College	M
Walden University	M,D
Washington State University	M,D
Washington University in St. Louis	M
Webster University	M
West Chester University of Pennsylvania	M
Western International University	M
West Texas A&M University	M
Wilkes University	M
Wilmington University (DE)	M
Wright State University	M
Xavier University	M
Yale University	D
Youngstown State University	M

■ FINANCIAL ENGINEERING

Claremont Graduate University	M,D
Columbia University	M,D,O
Kent State University	M
North Carolina State University	M
Polytechnic University, Brooklyn Campus	M,O
Polytechnic University, Westchester Graduate Center	M,O
Princeton University	M,D
University of California, Berkeley	M
University of Michigan	M
University of Tulsa	M

■ FIRE PROTECTION ENGINEERING

Anna Maria College	M
Oklahoma State University	M
University of Central Missouri	M,O
University of Maryland, College Park	M,O
University of New Haven	M
Worcester Polytechnic Institute	M,D,O

■ FISH, GAME, AND WILDLIFE MANAGEMENT

Arkansas Tech University	M
Auburn University	M,D
Brigham Young University	M,D
Clemson University	M,D
Colorado State University	M,D
Cornell University	M,D
Frostburg State University	M
Iowa State University of Science and Technology	M,D
Louisiana State University and Agricultural and Mechanical College	M,D
Michigan State University	M,D
Mississippi State University	M
Montana State University	M,D
New Mexico Highlands University	M
New Mexico State University	M
North Carolina State University	M
Oregon State University	M,D
Penn State University Park	M,D
Purdue University	M,D
South Dakota State University	M,D

State University of New York College of Environmental Science and Forestry M,D
Sul Ross State University M
Tennessee Technological University M
Texas A&M University M,D
Texas A&M University–Kingsville M,D
Texas State University-San Marcos M
Texas Tech University M,D
University of Alaska Fairbanks M,D
The University of Arizona M,D
University of Delaware M,D
University of Florida M,D
University of Idaho M,D
University of Maine M,D
University of Massachusetts Amherst M,D
University of Miami M,D
University of Minnesota, Twin Cities Campus M,D
University of Missouri–Columbia M,D
The University of Montana M,D
University of New Hampshire M
University of North Dakota M,D
University of Rhode Island M,D
The University of Tennessee M
University of Washington M,D
Utah State University M,D
Virginia Polytechnic Institute and State University M,D
West Virginia University M

■ FOLKLORE

The George Washington University M
Indiana University Bloomington M,D
University of California, Berkeley M
University of Louisiana at Lafayette M,D
The University of North Carolina at Chapel Hill M
University of Oregon M
University of Pennsylvania M,D
The University of Texas at Austin M,D
Utah State University M

■ FOOD SCIENCE AND TECHNOLOGY

Alabama Agricultural and Mechanical University M,D
Auburn University M,D
Brigham Young University M
California State Polytechnic University, Pomona M
California State University, Fresno M
Chapman University M
Clemson University M,D
Colorado State University M,D
Cornell University M,D
Drexel University M,D
Florida Agricultural and Mechanical University M
Florida State University M,D
Framingham State College M
Illinois Institute of Technology M
Iowa State University of Science and Technology M,D
Kansas State University M,D
Louisiana State University and Agricultural and Mechanical College M,D
Michigan State University M,D
Mississippi State University M,D
Montclair State University M,O
New York University M,D
North Carolina State University M,D
North Dakota State University M,D
The Ohio State University M,D
Oklahoma State University M,D
Oregon State University M,D
Penn State University Park M,D
Purdue University M,D
Rutgers, The State University of New Jersey, New Brunswick M,D
South Dakota State University M
Texas A&M University M,D
Texas Tech University M,D
Texas Woman's University M,D
University of Arkansas M,D
University of California, Davis M,D
University of Delaware M,D
University of Florida M,D
University of Georgia M,D
University of Hawaii at Manoa M
University of Idaho M,D
University of Illinois at Urbana–Champaign M,D
University of Maine M,D
University of Maryland, College Park M,D
University of Maryland Eastern Shore M,D
University of Massachusetts Amherst M,D
University of Minnesota, Twin Cities Campus M,D
University of Missouri–Columbia M,D
University of Nebraska–Lincoln M,D
University of Puerto Rico, Mayagüez Campus M
University of Rhode Island M,D
University of Southern Mississippi M,D
The University of Tennessee M,D
The University of Tennessee at Martin M
University of Vermont D
University of Wisconsin–Madison M,D
University of Wisconsin–Stout M
University of Wyoming M
Utah State University M,D
Virginia Polytechnic Institute and State University M,D
Washington State University M,D
Wayne State University M,D
West Virginia University M,D

■ FOREIGN LANGUAGES EDUCATION

Andrews University M,D,O
Auburn University M,D,O
Bennington College M
Boston College M
Boston University M
Bowling Green State University M
Brigham Young University M
Brooklyn College of the City University of New York M,O
California State University, Chico M
California State University, Sacramento M
Central Connecticut State University M,O
Cleveland State University M
College of Charleston M
The College of New Jersey M
The College of William and Mary M
Colorado State University M
Cornell University M,D
Eastern Washington University M
Fairfield University M,O
Florida Atlantic University M
Florida International University M,D,O
Framingham State College M
George Mason University M
Georgia Southern University M
Harding University M,O
Hofstra University M
Hood College O
Hunter College of the City University of New York M
Indiana University Bloomington M,D
Iona College M
Ithaca College M
Kent State University M,D
Long Island University, C.W. Post Campus M
Louisiana Tech University M,D
Manhattanville College M
Marquette University M
Michigan State University D
Middle Tennessee State University M
Mississippi State University M
Missouri State University M
Monterey Institute of International Studies M
New College of California M
New York University M,D,O
Northern Arizona University M
Portland State University M
Purdue University M,D,O
Queens College of the City University of New York M,O
Quinnipiac University M
Rhode Island College M,O
Rider University M,O
Rivier College M
Rutgers, The State University of New Jersey, New Brunswick M,D
St. John Fisher College M
Salisbury University M
School for International Training M
Southern Illinois University Edwardsville M
Stanford University M
State University of New York at Binghamton M
State University of New York at Plattsburgh M
State University of New York College at Cortland M
Stony Brook University, State University of New York M,O
Temple University M,D
Texas A&M International University M,D
Texas A&M University–Kingsville M
University at Buffalo, the State University of New York M,D,O
The University of Arizona M,D
University of California, Irvine M,D
University of Central Arkansas M
University of Central Florida M,O
University of Connecticut M,D
University of Delaware M
University of Hawaii at Manoa M,D,O
University of Illinois at Urbana–Champaign M,D,O
University of Indianapolis M
The University of Iowa M,D
University of Kentucky M
University of Louisville M,D
University of Maine M
University of Maryland, College Park M,D
University of Massachusetts Amherst M,D
University of Massachusetts Boston M
University of Michigan M,D
University of Minnesota, Twin Cities Campus M
University of Missouri–Columbia M,D,O
University of Nebraska at Kearney M
University of Nebraska at Omaha M
University of Nevada, Reno M

The University of North Carolina at Chapel Hill M
The University of North Carolina at Charlotte M
The University of North Carolina at Greensboro M,D,O
University of Northern Colorado M
University of Pittsburgh M,D
University of Puerto Rico, Río Piedras M,D
University of South Carolina M,D
University of Southern Mississippi M
University of South Florida M,D,O
The University of Tennessee M,D,O
The University of Texas at Austin M,D
The University of Toledo M
University of Utah M,D
University of Vermont M
University of West Georgia M
University of Wisconsin–Madison M,D
Vanderbilt University M,D
Wayne State University M,D,O
West Chester University of Pennsylvania M
Worcester State College M

■ FORENSIC NURSING

Cleveland State University M
Duquesne University M,O
Fitchburg State College M,O
Quinnipiac University M,O
University of Colorado at Colorado Springs M,D
Vanderbilt University M,D

■ FORENSIC PSYCHOLOGY

American International College M
Argosy University, Orange County Campus M
Argosy University, Sarasota Campus M,D,O
Argosy University, Twin Cities Campus M,D,O
Castleton State College M
Drexel University M,D
Holy Names University M,O
John Jay College of Criminal Justice of the City University of New York M,D
Marymount University
Prairie View A&M University M,D
Roger Williams University M
Tiffin University M
University of Massachusetts Boston M,O
University of North Dakota M,D

■ FORENSIC SCIENCES

Arcadia University M
Boston University M
Chaminade University of Honolulu M
Duquesne University M
Florida International University M,D
The George Washington University M
John Jay College of Criminal Justice of the City University of New York M,D
Marshall University M
Mercyhurst College M
Michigan State University M,D
National University M
Pace University M
Sam Houston State University M,D
Southern Utah University M
University at Albany, State University of New York M,D
The University of Alabama at Birmingham M
University of California, Davis M
University of Central Florida M,D,O
University of Florida M,O
University of Illinois at Chicago M
University of New Haven M
University of Rhode Island M,D,O
Virginia Commonwealth University M

■ FORESTRY

California Polytechnic State University, San Luis Obispo M
Clemson University M,D
Colorado State University M,D
Cornell University M,D
Duke University M
Harvard University M
Iowa State University of Science and Technology M,D
Louisiana State University and Agricultural and Mechanical College M,D
Michigan State University M,D
Michigan Technological University M,D
Mississippi State University M,D
North Carolina State University M,D
Northern Arizona University M,D
Oklahoma State University M
Oregon State University M,D
Penn State University Park M,D
Purdue University M,D
Southern Illinois University Carbondale M
Southern University and Agricultural and Mechanical College M
State University of New York College of Environmental Science and Forestry M,D
Stephen F. Austin State University M,D
Texas A&M University M,D
The University of Arizona M,D
University of Arkansas at Monticello M
University of California, Berkeley M,D
University of Florida M,D
University of Georgia M,D
University of Idaho M
University of Kentucky M
University of Maine M,D
University of Massachusetts Amherst M,D
University of Michigan M,D,O
University of Minnesota, Twin Cities Campus M,D
University of Missouri–Columbia M,D
The University of Montana M,D
University of New Hampshire M
The University of Tennessee M
University of Vermont M,D
University of Washington M,D
University of Wisconsin–Madison M,D
Utah State University M,D
Virginia Polytechnic Institute and State University M,D
West Virginia University M,D
Yale University M,D

■ FOUNDATIONS AND PHILOSOPHY OF EDUCATION

Antioch University New England M
Arizona State University M
Arkansas State University M,D,O
Ashland University M
Ball State University D
Brigham Young University M,D
California State University, Los Angeles M
Central Connecticut State University M
Chicago State University M
Duquesne University M
Eastern Michigan University M
Eastern Washington University M
Fairfield University M,O
Fairleigh Dickinson University, Metropolitan Campus M
Florida Atlantic University M,D,O
Florida State University M,D,O
George Fox University M,D,O
Georgia State University M,D
Harvard University M,O
Hofstra University M,O
Indiana University Bloomington M,D,O
Iowa State University of Science and Technology M,D
Kent State University M,D
Millersville University of Pennsylvania M
Montclair State University M,D,O
New York University M,D
Niagara University M
Northeastern State University M
Northern Illinois University M,D,O
Oakland University M
Penn State University Park M,D
Purdue University M,D,O
Regis University M,O
Rutgers, The State University of New Jersey, New Brunswick M,D
Saint Louis University M,D
Southeast Missouri State University M
Southern Connecticut State University O
Southern Illinois University Edwardsville M
Stanford University M,D
State University of New York at Binghamton D
Suffolk University M,O
Syracuse University M,D
Texas A&M University M,D
University of Arkansas M,D
University of California, Berkeley M,D
University of Cincinnati M,D
University of Colorado at Boulder M,D
University of Connecticut D
University of Florida M,D,O
University of Georgia M,D,O
University of Hawaii at Manoa M,D
University of Houston M,D
University of Houston–Clear Lake M
The University of Iowa M,D,O
University of Kansas D
University of Maryland, College Park M,D,O
University of Michigan M,D
University of Minnesota, Twin Cities Campus M,D,O
University of New Mexico M,D
University of New Orleans M,D,O
University of Oklahoma M,D
University of Pittsburgh M,D
University of South Carolina D
The University of Tennessee M,D,O
The University of Texas of the Permian Basin M
The University of Toledo M,D
University of Utah M,D
University of Washington M,D
The University of West Alabama M
University of Wisconsin–Milwaukee M
Wayne State University M,D,O
Western Illinois University M
Widener University M,D
Youngstown State University M,D

■ FRENCH

American University O
Appalachian State University M

Arizona State University M
Bennington College M
Boston College M,D
Boston University M,D
Bowling Green State University M
Brigham Young University M
Brooklyn College of the City University of New York M,D
Brown University M,D
California State University, Fullerton M
California State University, Long Beach M
California State University, Los Angeles M
California State University, Sacramento M
Case Western Reserve University M,D
The Catholic University of America M,D
Central Connecticut State University M,O
Columbia University M,D
Cornell University D
Duke University D
Eastern Michigan University M
Emory University D,O
Florida Atlantic University M
Florida State University M,D
Georgia State University M
Graduate School and University Center of the City University of New York D
Harvard University M,D
Hofstra University M
Howard University M
Hunter College of the City University of New York M
Illinois State University M
Indiana State University M,O
Indiana University Bloomington M,D
The Johns Hopkins University D
Kansas State University M
Kent State University M,D
Louisiana State University and Agricultural and Mechanical College M,D
Miami University M
Michigan State University M,D
Millersville University of Pennsylvania M
Minnesota State University Mankato M
Mississippi State University M
Missouri State University M
Montclair State University M,O
New York University M,D,O
North Carolina State University M
Northern Illinois University M
Northwestern University D,O
The Ohio State University M,D
Ohio University M
Penn State University Park M,D
Portland State University M
Princeton University D
Purdue University M,D
Queens College of the City University of New York M
Rice University M,D
Rutgers, The State University of New Jersey, New Brunswick M,D
Saint Louis University M
San Francisco State University M
San Jose State University M
Southern Connecticut State University M
Stanford University M,D
State University of New York at Binghamton M
Stony Brook University, State University of New York M,D
Syracuse University M
Texas Tech University M
Tufts University M
Tulane University M,D
University at Albany, State University of New York M,D
University at Buffalo, the State University of New York M,D
The University of Alabama M,D
The University of Arizona M,D
University of Arkansas M
University of California, Berkeley D
University of California, Davis D
University of California, Irvine M,D
University of California, Los Angeles M,D
University of California, San Diego M
University of California, Santa Barbara M,D
University of Chicago M,D
University of Cincinnati M,D
University of Colorado at Boulder M,D
University of Connecticut M,D
University of Delaware M
University of Florida M,D
University of Georgia M
University of Hawaii at Manoa M
University of Houston M,D
University of Illinois at Chicago M
University of Illinois at Urbana–Champaign M,D
The University of Iowa M,D
University of Kansas M,D
University of Kentucky M
University of Louisiana at Lafayette M,D
University of Louisville M
University of Maine M
University of Maryland, College Park M,D
University of Massachusetts Amherst M,D
University of Memphis M
University of Miami D
University of Michigan D
University of Minnesota, Twin Cities Campus M,D
University of Mississippi M
University of Missouri–Columbia M,D
The University of Montana M
University of Nebraska–Lincoln M,D
University of Nevada, Reno M
University of New Mexico M,D
The University of North Carolina at Chapel Hill M,D
The University of North Carolina at Greensboro M
University of Northern Iowa M
University of North Texas M
University of Notre Dame M
University of Oklahoma M,D
University of Oregon M
University of Pennsylvania M,D
University of Pittsburgh M,D
University of South Carolina M,D
University of Southern California M,D
University of South Florida M
The University of Tennessee M,D
The University of Texas at Arlington M
The University of Texas at Austin M,D
The University of Toledo M
University of Utah M,D
University of Vermont M
University of Virginia M,D
University of Washington M,D
University of Wisconsin–Madison M,D,O
University of Wisconsin–Milwaukee M
University of Wyoming M
Vanderbilt University M,D
Washington University in St. Louis M,D
Wayne State University M
West Chester University of Pennsylvania M
West Virginia University M
Yale University M,D

■ GENDER STUDIES

Cornell University M,D
Eastern Michigan University M
Northwestern University
Roosevelt University M,O
Rutgers, The State University of New Jersey, New Brunswick M,D
Simmons College M
University of Florida M,O
The University of North Carolina at Greensboro M,O
University of Northern Iowa M
Virginia Commonwealth University M,O

■ GENETIC COUNSELING

Arcadia University M
Brandeis University M
California State University, Northridge M
Case Western Reserve University M
The Johns Hopkins University M,D
Northwestern University M
Sarah Lawrence College M
University of California, Irvine M
University of Cincinnati M
University of Colorado Denver M
University of Minnesota, Twin Cities Campus M,D
The University of North Carolina at Greensboro M
University of Pittsburgh M
University of South Carolina M
Virginia Commonwealth University M,D

■ GENETICS

Arizona State University M,D
Brandeis University M,D
California Institute of Technology D
Carnegie Mellon University M,D
Case Western Reserve University D
Clemson University M,D
Columbia University M,D
Cornell University D
Dartmouth College D
Drexel University M,D
Duke University D
Emory University D
Florida State University M,D
The George Washington University M,D
Harvard University D
Illinois State University M,D
Indiana University Bloomington M,D
Iowa State University of Science and Technology M,D
The Johns Hopkins University M,D
Kansas State University M,D
Marquette University M,D
Mayo Graduate School D
Michigan State University M,D
New York University M,D
North Carolina State University M,D
Northwestern University D
The Ohio State University M,D
Oregon State University M,D
Penn State University Park M,D
Purdue University M,D
Rutgers, The State University of New Jersey, New Brunswick M,D
Stanford University D

Stony Brook University, State University of New York	D
Temple University	D
Texas A&M University	M,D
Tufts University	D
University at Albany, State University of New York	M,D
The University of Alabama at Birmingham	D
The University of Arizona	M,D
University of California, Davis	M,D
University of California, Irvine	D
University of California, Riverside	D
University of California, San Diego	D
University of Chicago	D
University of Colorado at Boulder	M,D
University of Colorado Denver	D
University of Connecticut	M,D
University of Delaware	M,D
University of Florida	D
University of Georgia	M,D
University of Hawaii at Manoa	M,D
University of Illinois at Chicago	M,D
The University of Iowa	M,D
University of Miami	M,D
University of Minnesota, Twin Cities Campus	M,D
University of Missouri–Columbia	M,D
University of Missouri–St. Louis	M,D,O
University of New Hampshire	M,D
University of New Mexico	M,D
The University of North Carolina at Chapel Hill	M,D
University of North Dakota	M,D
University of Notre Dame	M,D
University of Oregon	M,D
University of Pennsylvania	D
University of Rochester	M,D
University of Southern California	M,D
The University of Tennessee	M,D
The University of Texas at Austin	D
The University of Toledo	M
University of Utah	M,D
University of Washington	M,D
University of Wisconsin–Madison	M,D
Virginia Commonwealth University	M,D
Virginia Polytechnic Institute and State University	M,D
Washington State University	M,D
Washington University in St. Louis	M,D,O
Wayne State University	M,D
West Virginia University	M,D
Yale University	D

■ GENOMIC SCIENCES

Case Western Reserve University	D
The George Washington University	M
Harvard University	D
North Carolina State University	M,D
North Dakota State University	M,D
University of California, Riverside	D
University of Cincinnati	M,D
University of Connecticut	M
University of Florida	D
University of Pennsylvania	D
The University of Tennessee	M,D
The University of Toledo	M,O
University of Washington	D
Wake Forest University	D
Yale University	D

■ GEOCHEMISTRY

California Institute of Technology	M,D
California State University, Fullerton	M
Colorado School of Mines	M,D,O
Columbia University	M,D
Cornell University	M,D
Georgia Institute of Technology	M,D
Indiana University Bloomington	M,D
Massachusetts Institute of Technology	M,D
Missouri University of Science and Technology	M,D
New Mexico Institute of Mining and Technology	M,D
Ohio University	M
Rensselaer Polytechnic Institute	M,D
University of California, Los Angeles	M,D
University of Hawaii at Manoa	M,D
University of Illinois at Chicago	M,D
University of Illinois at Urbana–Champaign	M,D
University of Michigan	M,D
University of Nevada, Reno	M,D,O
University of New Hampshire	M
Washington University in St. Louis	M,D
Yale University	D

■ GEODETIC SCIENCES

Columbia University	M,D
George Mason University	M,D,O
The Ohio State University	M,D

■ GEOGRAPHIC INFORMATION SYSTEMS

Boston University	M
Clark University	M
Cleveland State University	M,O
Florida State University	M,D
George Mason University	M,D,O
Georgia Institute of Technology	M,D
Georgia State University	O
Hunter College of the City University of New York	M,O
Idaho State University	M,O
North Carolina State University	M,D
Northern Arizona University	M,O
Northwest Missouri State University	M
Saint Louis University	M,D,O
Saint Mary's University of Minnesota	M,O
Texas State University-San Marcos	M,D
University at Albany, State University of New York	M,O
University at Buffalo, the State University of New York	M,D,O
The University of Akron	M
University of Central Arkansas	O
University of Colorado Denver	M,D,O
University of Connecticut	M,D,O
University of Denver	M,O
University of Minnesota, Twin Cities Campus	M
The University of Montana	M
The University of North Carolina at Greensboro	M,D,O
University of Pittsburgh	M,D
University of Redlands	M
The University of Texas at Dallas	M,D
The University of Toledo	D
University of Wisconsin–Madison	M,D,O
Virginia Commonwealth University	M,O
West Virginia University	M,D

■ GEOGRAPHY

Appalachian State University	M
Arizona State University	M,D
Boston University	M,D
California State University, Chico	M
California State University, East Bay	M
California State University, Fullerton	M
California State University, Long Beach	M
California State University, Los Angeles	M
California State University, Northridge	M
Central Connecticut State University	M
Chicago State University	M
Clark University	M,D
East Carolina University	M
Eastern Michigan University	M
Florida Atlantic University	M
Florida State University	M,D
George Mason University	M
The George Washington University	M
Georgia State University	M
Hunter College of the City University of New York	M,O
Indiana State University	M,D
Indiana University Bloomington	M,D
Indiana University of Pennsylvania	M
The Johns Hopkins University	M,D
Kansas State University	M,D
Kent State University	M,D
Louisiana State University and Agricultural and Mechanical College	M,D
Marshall University	M
Miami University	M
Michigan State University	M,D
Minnesota State University Mankato	M
Missouri State University	M
New Mexico State University	M
Northeastern Illinois University	M
Northern Arizona University	M,O
Northern Illinois University	M
Northwest Missouri State University	M
The Ohio State University	M,D
Ohio University	M
Oklahoma State University	M,D
Oregon State University	M,D
Penn State University Park	M,D
Portland State University	M,D
Rutgers, The State University of New Jersey, New Brunswick	M,D
St. Cloud State University	M
Salem State College	M
San Diego State University	M,D
San Francisco State University	M
San Jose State University	M,O
South Dakota State University	M
Southern Illinois University Carbondale	M,D
Southern Illinois University Edwardsville	M
State University of New York at Binghamton	M
Syracuse University	M,D
Temple University	M
Texas A&M University	M,D
Texas State University-San Marcos	M,D
Towson University	M
University at Albany, State University of New York	M,O
University at Buffalo, the State University of New York	M,D,O
The University of Akron	M
The University of Alabama	M
The University of Arizona	M,D
University of Arkansas	M
University of California, Berkeley	D
University of California, Davis	M,D
University of California, Los Angeles	M,D
University of California, Santa Barbara	M,D
University of Central Arkansas	O

University of Cincinnati M,D
University of Colorado at Boulder M,D
University of Colorado at Colorado Springs M
University of Connecticut M,D
University of Delaware M,D
University of Denver M,D
University of Florida M,D
University of Georgia M,D
University of Hawaii at Manoa M,D
University of Idaho M,D
University of Illinois at Chicago M
University of Illinois at Urbana–Champaign M,D
The University of Iowa M,D
University of Kansas M,D
University of Kentucky M,D
University of Maryland, College Park M,D
University of Massachusetts Amherst M
University of Miami M
University of Minnesota, Twin Cities Campus M,D
University of Missouri–Columbia M
The University of Montana M
University of Nebraska at Omaha M,O
University of Nebraska–Lincoln M,D
University of Nevada, Reno M,D
University of New Mexico M
University of New Orleans M
The University of North Carolina at Chapel Hill M,D
The University of North Carolina at Charlotte M,D
The University of North Carolina at Greensboro M,D,O
University of North Dakota M
University of Northern Iowa M
University of North Texas M
University of Oklahoma M,D
University of Oregon M,D
University of South Carolina M,D
University of Southern California M,D
University of Southern Mississippi M,D
University of South Florida M
The University of Tennessee M,D
The University of Texas at Austin M,D
The University of Toledo M,D,O
University of Utah M,D
University of Washington M,D
University of Wisconsin–Madison M,D,O
University of Wisconsin–Milwaukee M,D
University of Wyoming M
Utah State University M,D
Virginia Polytechnic Institute and State University M,D
Wayne State University M
West Chester University of Pennsylvania M
Western Illinois University M,O
Western Kentucky University M
Western Michigan University M
Western Washington University M
West Virginia University M,D

■ GEOLOGICAL ENGINEERING

Arizona State University M,D
Colorado School of Mines M,D,O
Drexel University M
Michigan Technological University M,D
Missouri University of Science and Technology M,D
University of Alaska Anchorage M
University of Alaska Fairbanks M,O
University of Connecticut M,D
University of Hawaii at Manoa M,D
University of Idaho M
University of Minnesota, Twin Cities Campus M,D
University of Nevada, Reno M,D,O
University of North Dakota M
University of Oklahoma M,D
University of Utah M,D
University of Wisconsin–Madison M,D

■ GEOLOGY

Auburn University M
Ball State University M
Baylor University M,D
Boise State University M,D
Boston College M
Bowling Green State University M
Brigham Young University M
Brooklyn College of the City University of New York M,D
California Institute of Technology M,D
California State University, Bakersfield M
California State University, Chico M
California State University, East Bay M
California State University, Fresno M
California State University, Fullerton M
California State University, Long Beach M
California State University, Los Angeles M
California State University, Northridge M
Case Western Reserve University M,D
Central Washington University M
Cornell University M,D
Duke University M,D
East Carolina University M
Eastern Kentucky University M,D
Eastern Michigan University M
Florida Atlantic University M
Florida State University M,D
Fort Hays State University M
The George Washington University M,D
Georgia State University M
Idaho State University M,O
Indiana University Bloomington M,D
Indiana University–Purdue University Indianapolis M
Iowa State University of Science and Technology M,D
Kansas State University M
Kent State University M,D
Lehigh University M,D
Louisiana State University and Agricultural and Mechanical College M,D
Massachusetts Institute of Technology M,D
Miami University M,D
Michigan Technological University M,D
Missouri State University M
Missouri University of Science and Technology M,D
New Mexico Institute of Mining and Technology M,D
New Mexico State University M
Northern Arizona University M
Northern Illinois University M,D
Northwestern University M,D
The Ohio State University M,D
Ohio University M
Oklahoma State University M
Oregon State University M,D
Portland State University M,D
Princeton University D
Queens College of the City University of New York M
Rensselaer Polytechnic Institute M,D
Rutgers, The State University of New Jersey, Newark M
Rutgers, The State University of New Jersey, New Brunswick M,D
San Diego State University M
San Jose State University M
Southern Illinois University Carbondale M,D
Southern Methodist University M,D
State University of New York at Binghamton M,D
State University of New York at New Paltz M
Stephen F. Austin State University M
Sul Ross State University M
Syracuse University M,D
Temple University M
Texas A&M University M,D
Texas A&M University–Kingsville M
Texas Christian University M
Tulane University M,D
University at Albany, State University of New York M,D
University at Buffalo, the State University of New York M,D
The University of Akron M
The University of Alabama M,D
University of Alaska Fairbanks M,D
University of Arkansas M
University of California, Berkeley M,D
University of California, Davis M,D
University of California, Los Angeles M,D
University of California, Riverside M,D
University of California, Santa Barbara M,D
University of Cincinnati M,D
University of Colorado at Boulder M,D
University of Connecticut M,D
University of Delaware M,D
University of Florida M,D
University of Georgia M,D
University of Hawaii at Manoa M,D
University of Houston M,D
University of Idaho M,D
University of Illinois at Chicago M,D
University of Illinois at Urbana–Champaign M,D
University of Kansas M,D
University of Kentucky M,D
University of Louisiana at Lafayette M
University of Maine M,D
University of Maryland, College Park M,D
University of Memphis M,D
University of Michigan M,D
University of Minnesota, Duluth M,D
University of Minnesota, Twin Cities Campus M,D
University of Missouri–Columbia M,D
University of Missouri–Kansas City M,D
The University of Montana M,D
University of Nevada, Reno M,D,O
University of New Hampshire M
The University of North Carolina at Chapel Hill M,D
The University of North Carolina Wilmington M
University of North Dakota M,D
University of Oklahoma M,D
University of Oregon M,D
University of Pennsylvania M,D
University of Pittsburgh M,D
University of Puerto Rico, Mayagüez Campus M
University of Rochester M,D
University of South Carolina M,D

University of Southern Mississippi	M,D
University of South Florida	M,D
The University of Tennessee	M,D
The University of Texas at Arlington	M,D
The University of Texas at Austin	M,D
The University of Texas at El Paso	M,D
The University of Texas at San Antonio	M,D
The University of Texas of the Permian Basin	M
The University of Toledo	M,D
University of Tulsa	M
University of Utah	M,D
University of Vermont	M
University of Washington	M,D
University of Wisconsin–Madison	M,D
University of Wisconsin–Milwaukee	M,D
University of Wyoming	M,D
Utah State University	M
Virginia Polytechnic Institute and State University	M,D
Washington State University	M,D
Washington University in St. Louis	M,D
Wayne State University	M
West Chester University of Pennsylvania	M
Western Kentucky University	M
Western Michigan University	M,D
Western Washington University	M
West Virginia University	M,D
Wichita State University	M
Wright State University	M
Yale University	D

■ GEOPHYSICS

Boise State University	M,D
Boston College	M
Bowling Green State University	M
California Institute of Technology	M,D
Columbia University	M,D
Cornell University	M,D
Florida State University	D
Georgia Institute of Technology	M,D
Idaho State University	M,O
Indiana University Bloomington	M,D
Louisiana State University and Agricultural and Mechanical College	M,D
Massachusetts Institute of Technology	M,D
Michigan Technological University	M
Missouri University of Science and Technology	M,D
New Mexico Institute of Mining and Technology	M,D
Ohio University	M
Oregon State University	M,D
Princeton University	D
Rensselaer Polytechnic Institute	M,D
Rice University	M
Saint Louis University	M,D
Southern Methodist University	M,D
Stanford University	M,D
Texas A&M University	M,D
The University of Akron	M
University of Alaska Fairbanks	M,D
University of California, Berkeley	M,D
University of California, Los Angeles	M,D
University of California, Santa Barbara	M,D
University of Chicago	M,D
University of Colorado at Boulder	M,D
University of Hawaii at Manoa	M,D
University of Houston	M,D
University of Illinois at Chicago	M,D
University of Illinois at Urbana–Champaign	M,D
University of Miami	M,D
University of Minnesota, Twin Cities Campus	M,D
University of Nevada, Reno	M,D,O
University of Oklahoma	M
The University of Texas at El Paso	M
University of Utah	M,D
University of Washington	M,D
University of Wisconsin–Madison	M,D
University of Wyoming	M,D
Virginia Polytechnic Institute and State University	M,D
Washington University in St. Louis	M,D
West Virginia University	M,D
Wright State University	M
Yale University	D

■ GEOSCIENCES

Arizona State University	M,D
Ball State University	M
Baylor University	M,D
Boise State University	M
Boston University	M,D
Brown University	M,D
California State University, Chico	M
California State University, Long Beach	M
Case Western Reserve University	M,D
Central Connecticut State University	M
City College of the City University of New York	M,D
Colorado School of Mines	M,D,O
Colorado State University	M,D
Columbia University	M,D
Cornell University	M,D
Dartmouth College	M,D
Emporia State University	M,O
Florida International University	M,D
The George Washington University	M,D
Georgia Institute of Technology	M,D
Georgia State University	M,O
Graduate School and University Center of the City University of New York	D
Harvard University	M,D
Hunter College of the City University of New York	M,O
Idaho State University	M,O
Indiana State University	M,D
Indiana University Bloomington	M,D
Iowa State University of Science and Technology	M,D
The Johns Hopkins University	M,D
Lehigh University	M,D
Massachusetts Institute of Technology	M,D
Michigan State University	M,D
Middle Tennessee State University	O
Mississippi State University	M
Missouri State University	M
Montana State University	M,D
Montclair State University	M,D,O
Murray State University	M
New Mexico Institute of Mining and Technology	M,D
North Carolina Central University	M
North Carolina State University	M,D
Northeastern Illinois University	M
Northern Arizona University	M
Northwestern University	M,D
Oregon State University	M,D
Penn State University Park	M,D
Princeton University	D
Purdue University	M,D
Rensselaer Polytechnic Institute	M,D
Rice University	M,D
Saint Louis University	M,D
San Francisco State University	M
South Dakota State University	D
Stanford University	M,D,O
State University of New York College at Oneonta	M
Stony Brook University, State University of New York	M,D
Texas A&M University–Commerce	M
Texas Christian University	M
Texas Tech University	M,D
University at Albany, State University of New York	M,D
The University of Akron	M
The University of Arizona	M,D
University of California, Irvine	M,D
University of California, Los Angeles	M,D
University of California, San Diego	M,D
University of California, Santa Barbara	M,D
University of California, Santa Cruz	M,D
University of Chicago	M,D
University of Florida	M,D
University of Illinois at Chicago	M,D
University of Illinois at Urbana–Champaign	M,D
The University of Iowa	M,D
University of Maine	M,D
University of Massachusetts Amherst	M,D
University of Missouri–Kansas City	M,D
The University of Montana	M,D
University of Nebraska–Lincoln	M,D
University of Nevada, Las Vegas	M,D
University of New Hampshire	M
University of New Mexico	M,D
University of New Orleans	M
The University of North Carolina at Charlotte	M
The University of North Carolina Wilmington	M
University of North Dakota	M,D
University of Northern Colorado	M
University of Notre Dame	M,D
University of Rhode Island	M
University of Rochester	M,D
University of South Carolina	M,D
University of Southern California	M,D
The University of Texas at Arlington	M,D
The University of Texas at Austin	M,D
The University of Texas at Dallas	M,D
The University of Toledo	M,D
University of Tulsa	M,D
Virginia Polytechnic Institute and State University	M,D
Washington State University	M,D
Washington University in St. Louis	M,D
Western Connecticut State University	M
Western Michigan University	M
Yale University	D

■ GEOTECHNICAL ENGINEERING

Auburn University	M,D
The Catholic University of America	M,D
Cornell University	M,D
Illinois Institute of Technology	M,D
Iowa State University of Science and Technology	M,D
Louisiana State University and Agricultural and Mechanical College	M,D
Marquette University	M,D
Massachusetts Institute of Technology	M,D,O
Missouri University of Science and Technology	M,D
Northwestern University	M,D
Ohio University	M,D

Rensselaer Polytechnic Institute	M,D
Texas A&M University	M,D
Tufts University	M,D
University of California, Berkeley	M,D
University of California, Los Angeles	M,D
University of Colorado at Boulder	M,D
University of Delaware	M,D
University of Illinois at Chicago	D
University of Maine	M,D
University of Missouri–Columbia	M,D
University of Oklahoma	M,D
University of Southern California	M
The University of Texas at Austin	M,D
University of Washington	M,D
Worcester Polytechnic Institute	M,D,O

■ GERMAN

Arizona State University	M
Bowling Green State University	M
Brigham Young University	M
Brown University	M,D
California State University, Fullerton	M
California State University, Long Beach	M
California State University, Sacramento	M
Columbia University	M,D
Cornell University	M,D
Duke University	D
Eastern Michigan University	M
Florida Atlantic University	M
Florida State University	M
Georgetown University	M,D
Georgia State University	M
Graduate School and University Center of the City University of New York	M,D
Harvard University	D
Hofstra University	M
Illinois State University	M
Indiana University Bloomington	M,D
The Johns Hopkins University	D
Kansas State University	M
Kent State University	M,D
Michigan State University	M,D
Millersville University of Pennsylvania	M
Mississippi State University	M
Missouri State University	M
New York University	M,D
Northwestern University	D
The Ohio State University	M,D
Penn State University Park	M,D
Portland State University	M
Princeton University	D
Purdue University	M,D
Rutgers, The State University of New Jersey, New Brunswick	M,D
San Francisco State University	M
Stanford University	M,D
Stony Brook University, State University of New York	M,D
Texas Tech University	M
Tufts University	M
The University of Alabama	M,D
The University of Arizona	M,D
University of Arkansas	M
University of California, Berkeley	D
University of California, Davis	M,D
University of California, Irvine	M,D
University of California, Los Angeles	M,D
University of California, San Diego	M
University of California, Santa Barbara	M,D
University of Chicago	M,D
University of Cincinnati	M,D
University of Colorado at Boulder	M
University of Connecticut	M,D
University of Delaware	M
University of Florida	M,D
University of Georgia	M
University of Illinois at Chicago	M,D
University of Illinois at Urbana–Champaign	M,D
The University of Iowa	M,D
University of Kansas	M,D
University of Kentucky	M
University of Maryland, College Park	M,D
University of Massachusetts Amherst	M,D
University of Michigan	M,D
University of Minnesota, Twin Cities Campus	M,D
University of Mississippi	M
University of Missouri–Columbia	M
The University of Montana	M
University of Nebraska–Lincoln	M,D
University of Nevada, Reno	M
University of New Mexico	M,D
The University of North Carolina at Chapel Hill	M,D
University of Northern Iowa	M
University of Oklahoma	M
University of Oregon	M,D
University of Pennsylvania	M,D
University of Pittsburgh	M,D
University of South Carolina	M,D
The University of Tennessee	M,D
The University of Texas at Austin	M,D
The University of Toledo	M
University of Utah	M,D
University of Vermont	M
University of Virginia	M,D
University of Washington	M,D
University of Wisconsin–Madison	M,D
University of Wisconsin–Milwaukee	M
University of Wyoming	M
Vanderbilt University	M,D
Washington University in St. Louis	M,D
Wayne State University	M,D
West Chester University of Pennsylvania	M
West Virginia University	M
Yale University	M,D

■ GERONTOLOGICAL NURSING

Abilene Christian University	O
Arkansas State University	M,O
Boston College	M,D
Case Western Reserve University	M,D
The Catholic University of America	M,D
College of Mount Saint Vincent	M,O
College of Staten Island of the City University of New York	M,O
Columbia University	M,O
Concordia University Wisconsin	M
Duke University	M,D,O
Emory University	M
Gwynedd-Mercy College	M
Hunter College of the City University of New York	M
Kent State University	M,D
Lehman College of the City University of New York	M
Marquette University	M,D,O
Nazareth College of Rochester	M
New York University	M,O
Oakland University	M,O
Rutgers, The State University of New Jersey, Newark	M
San Jose State University	M,O
Seton Hall University	M
Southern University and Agricultural and Mechanical College	M,D,O
State University of New York at New Paltz	M,O
State University of New York Institute of Technology	M,O
Stony Brook University, State University of New York	M
Texas Wesleyan University	M
University at Buffalo, the State University of New York	M,D,O
University of Colorado at Colorado Springs	M,D
University of Delaware	M,O
University of Massachusetts Lowell	M
University of Michigan	M
University of Minnesota, Twin Cities Campus	M
The University of North Carolina at Greensboro	M,D,O
University of Utah	M,O
Vanderbilt University	M,D
Villanova University	M,D,O

■ GERONTOLOGY

Abilene Christian University	M,O
Adelphi University	M,O
Appalachian State University	M
Arizona State University at the West campus	O
Arkansas State University	M,O
Ball State University	M
Bethel University	M
California State University, Dominguez Hills	M
California State University, Fullerton	M
California State University, Long Beach	M
Case Western Reserve University	M,D,O
Chestnut Hill College	M,O
The College of New Rochelle	M,O
Concordia University Chicago (IL)	M
Dominican University of California	M
Eastern Illinois University	M
Eastern Michigan University	M,O
East Tennessee State University	M,O
Emory University	M
Florida Gulf Coast University	M
Gannon University	O
George Mason University	M
Georgia State University	M
Hofstra University	M,O
Kent State University	M
La Salle University	M,O
Lindenwood University	M
Long Island University, C.W. Post Campus	M,O
Marywood University	M,O
Miami University	M
Middle Tennessee State University	O
Minnesota State University Mankato	M,O
Morehead State University	M
National-Louis University	M,O
North Dakota State University	M,D
Northeastern Illinois University	M
Notre Dame de Namur University	M,O
Oklahoma State University	M
Oregon State University	M
Portland State University	O
Rochester Institute of Technology	O
Sacred Heart University	M
St. Cloud State University	M
Saint Joseph College	O
Saint Joseph's University	M,O
San Diego State University	M
San Francisco State University	M
San Jose State University	M,O

Texas A&M University–Kingsville M
Texas Tech University M,D
Towson University M,O
University of Arkansas at Little Rock M,O
University of Central Florida M,O
University of Central Missouri M
University of Central Oklahoma M
University of Georgia O
University of Hawaii at Manoa O
University of Illinois at Springfield M
University of Indianapolis M,O
University of Kansas M,D
University of Kentucky D
University of La Verne M,O
University of Louisiana at Monroe M,O
University of Maryland, Baltimore County M,D,O
University of Massachusetts Boston M,D,O
University of Missouri–St. Louis M,O
University of Nebraska at Omaha M,O
University of New England M,O
The University of North Carolina at Charlotte M
The University of North Carolina at Greensboro M,O
University of Northern Colorado M
University of North Florida M,O
University of North Texas M,D,O
University of Pittsburgh M,D,O
University of Rhode Island M,D
University of South Alabama O
University of South Carolina O
University of Southern California M,D,O
University of South Florida M,D
The University of Tennessee M
The University of Toledo O
University of Utah M,O
University of West Georgia M
Valparaiso University M,O
Virginia Commonwealth University M,D,O
Virginia Polytechnic Institute and State University M,D
Wayne State University O
Webster University M
West Chester University of Pennsylvania M,O
Wichita State University M
Wilmington University (DE) M

■ GRAPHIC DESIGN

Bob Jones University P,M,D,O
Boston University M
Bowling Green State University M
California State University, Los Angeles M
Cardinal Stritch University M
City College of the City University of New York M
The College of New Rochelle M
George Mason University M
Illinois State University M
Indiana State University M
Iowa State University of Science and Technology M
Kean University M
Kent State University M
Louisiana State University and Agricultural and Mechanical College M
Louisiana Tech University M
Marywood University M
New York University M
North Carolina State University M
Pittsburg State University M,O
Rochester Institute of Technology M
San Diego State University M
Suffolk University M
Syracuse University M
Temple University M
University of Baltimore M
University of Cincinnati M
University of Florida M,D
University of Guam M
University of Illinois at Chicago M
University of Illinois at Urbana–Champaign M
University of Memphis M
University of Miami M
University of Minnesota, Duluth M
University of North Texas M,D
University of Notre Dame M
The University of Tennessee M
University of Utah M
Western Illinois University M,O
Western Michigan University M
West Virginia University M
Yale University M

■ HAZARDOUS MATERIALS MANAGEMENT

Idaho State University M
New Mexico Institute of Mining and Technology M
Rutgers, The State University of New Jersey, New Brunswick M,D
Southern Methodist University M,D
Stony Brook University, State University of New York M,O
Tufts University M,D
University of Oklahoma M,D
University of South Carolina M,D
Wayne State University M,O

■ HEALTH COMMUNICATION

Cleveland State University M,O
East Carolina University M
Emerson College M
Marquette University M
Marywood University M,O
Michigan State University M
Tufts University M
Tulane University M
University of Florida M,D,O
University of Southern California M
University of West Florida M
Washington State University M,D

■ HEALTH EDUCATION

Adams State College M
Adelphi University M,O
Alabama State University M
Albany State University M
Alcorn State University M,O
Arcadia University M
Arkansas State University M,O
Auburn University M,D,O
Augusta State University M
Austin Peay State University M
Ball State University M
Baylor University M,D
Benedictine University M
Boston University M,O
Brigham Young University M
Brooklyn College of the City University of New York M,O
California State University, Dominguez Hills M
California State University, Long Beach M
California State University, Los Angeles M
California State University, Northridge M
California State University, San Bernardino M
Central Washington University M
The Citadel, The Military College of South Carolina M
Cleveland State University M
The College of New Jersey M
East Carolina University M
Eastern Kentucky University M
Eastern Michigan University M
Eastern University M
East Stroudsburg University of Pennsylvania M
Emory University M,D
Florida Agricultural and Mechanical University M
Florida State University M,D
Fort Hays State University M
Framingham State College M
Georgia College & State University M,O
Georgia Southern University M
Georgia Southwestern State University M,O
Georgia State University M
Harding University M,O
Hofstra University M
Howard University M
Idaho State University M
Illinois State University M
Indiana State University M
Indiana University Bloomington M,D
Indiana University of Pennsylvania M
Indiana University–Purdue University Indianapolis M,D
Inter American University of Puerto Rico, Metropolitan Campus M
Iowa State University of Science and Technology M,D
Ithaca College M
Jackson State University M
Jacksonville State University M
James Madison University M
John F. Kennedy University M
The Johns Hopkins University M,D
Kent State University M,D
Lehman College of the City University of New York M
Long Island University, Brooklyn Campus M
Louisiana Tech University M,D
Marshall University M
Marywood University D
Middle Tennessee State University M,D
Mills College M,D
Minnesota State University Mankato M
Mississippi State University M
Mississippi University for Women M
Montana State University M
Montclair State University M,O
Morehead State University M
Mount Mary College M
New Jersey City University M
New Mexico Highlands University M
New York University M,D
North Carolina Agricultural and Technical State University M
Northeastern State University M
Northern Arizona University M
Northwestern State University of Louisiana M
Northwest Missouri State University M
Nova Southeastern University D

Oklahoma State University M,D,O
Penn State Harrisburg M,D
Plymouth State University M
Portland State University M,O
Prairie View A&M University M
Rhode Island College M
Saint Francis University M
Saint Joseph's University M
San Francisco State University M
San Jose State University M,O
Simmons College M,D,O
South Dakota State University M
Southeastern Louisiana University M
Southern Connecticut State University M
Southern Illinois University Carbondale M,D
Southern Illinois University Edwardsville M,O
Springfield College M,D,O
State University of New York College at Brockport M
State University of New York College at Cortland M
Temple University M
Tennessee Technological University M
Texas A&M University M,D
Texas A&M University–Commerce M,D
Texas A&M University–Kingsville M
Texas Southern University M
Texas State University-San Marcos M
Texas Woman's University M,D
Tulane University M
Union College (KY) M
The University of Alabama M,D
The University of Alabama at Birmingham M,D
University of Arkansas M,D
University of California, Berkeley M
University of Central Arkansas M
University of Central Oklahoma M
University of Cincinnati M,D
University of Colorado Denver D
University of Florida M,D,O
University of Georgia M,D,O
University of Houston M,D
University of Illinois at Chicago M
University of Louisville M
University of Maryland, Baltimore County M
University of Maryland, College Park M,D
University of Michigan–Flint M
University of Missouri–Columbia M,D,O
The University of Montana M
University of Nebraska at Omaha M
University of Nebraska–Lincoln M
University of New Mexico M
The University of North Carolina at Chapel Hill M,D
University of Northern Iowa M,D
University of Pennsylvania M,D
University of Pittsburgh M,O
University of Rhode Island M,D
University of South Alabama M
University of South Carolina M,D,O
The University of South Dakota M
University of Southern Mississippi M
The University of Tennessee M
The University of Texas at Austin M,D
The University of Texas at El Paso M
The University of Texas at Tyler M
The University of Toledo M,D
University of Utah M,D
University of Virginia M,D
University of West Florida M
University of Wisconsin–La Crosse M
University of Wyoming M
Utah State University M
Valdosta State University M
Virginia Commonwealth University M,D
Virginia Polytechnic Institute and State University M,D,O
Wayne State University M,D,O
West Chester University of Pennsylvania M,O
Western Illinois University M,O
Western Oregon University M
West Virginia University M,D
Widener University M,D
Worcester State College M
Wright State University M

■ HEALTH INFORMATICS

Barry University O
Benedictine University M
The College of St. Scholastica M,O
Emory University M,D
The George Washington University M
Indiana University Bloomington M,D
The Johns Hopkins University M
Northeastern University M,D
Northern Kentucky University M
Touro College M,O
The University of Alabama at Birmingham M
University of Illinois at Urbana–Champaign M,D,O
The University of Iowa M,D,O
University of La Verne M
University of Maryland University College M,O
University of Minnesota, Twin Cities Campus M,D
University of Missouri–Columbia M
University of Pittsburgh M
University of Virginia M
University of Washington M,D
University of Wisconsin–Milwaukee M

■ HEALTH PHYSICS/ RADIOLOGICAL HEALTH

Bloomsburg University of Pennsylvania M
Drexel University M,D
Emory University D
Georgetown University M
Georgia Institute of Technology M,D
Illinois Institute of Technology M,D
Midwestern State University M
Oregon State University M,D
Quinnipiac University M
San Diego State University M
Texas A&M University M,D
University of Cincinnati M
University of Illinois at Urbana–Champaign M,D
University of Kentucky M
University of Massachusetts Lowell M,D
University of Michigan M,D,O
University of Missouri–Columbia M,D
University of Nevada, Las Vegas M
The University of Toledo M
Virginia Commonwealth University D
Wayne State University M,D

■ HEALTH PROMOTION

Auburn University M,D,O
Ball State University M
Benedictine University M
Boston University M,D
Bridgewater State College M
Brigham Young University M,D
California State University, Fresno M
Canisius College M
Central Michigan University M
Eastern Michigan University M
Emory University M
Florida Atlantic University M
Georgetown University M,D
The George Washington University M,O
Georgia State University M,D,O
Goddard College M
Harvard University M,D
Indiana State University M
Indiana University Bloomington M,D
Lehman College of the City University of New York M
Marymount University M
McNeese State University M
Missouri State University M
New York University M,D,O
Northern Arizona University M
Oakland University O
Old Dominion University M
Oregon State University M
Portland State University M,O
Purdue University M,D
San Diego State University M,D
Simmons College M,O
The University of Alabama M,D
The University of Alabama at Birmingham D
University of Central Florida M,O
University of Chicago M
University of Delaware M
University of Georgia M,D,O
University of Kentucky M,D
University of Massachusetts Lowell D
University of Memphis M
University of Michigan M,D
The University of Montana M
University of Nevada, Las Vegas M
The University of North Carolina at Chapel Hill M
University of North Texas M
University of South Carolina M,D,O
University of Southern California M
The University of Tennessee M
University of Utah M,D
University of Wisconsin–Madison M,D
University of Wisconsin–Stevens Point M
Virginia Polytechnic Institute and State University M,D,O
West Virginia University M,D
Wright State University M

■ HEALTH PSYCHOLOGY

Appalachian State University M
Argosy University, Twin Cities Campus M,D,O
California Institute of Integral Studies M,D
Central Connecticut State University M
Drexel University M,D
Duke University D
East Carolina University D
The George Washington University D
Lesley University M
National-Louis University M,O
Northern Arizona University M
Rutgers, The State University of New Jersey, New Brunswick D
San Diego State University M,D
Stony Brook University, State University of New York D
Texas State University-San Marcos M
University of Florida D
University of Michigan–Dearborn M

The University of North Carolina at Charlotte D
University of North Texas M,D
West Chester University of Pennsylvania M,O
Yeshiva University D

■ HEALTH SERVICES MANAGEMENT AND HOSPITAL ADMINISTRATION

Alaska Pacific University M
Albany State University M
Argosy University, Orange County Campus M,D,O
Argosy University, Sarasota Campus M,D,O
Argosy University, Tampa Campus M,D,O
Argosy University, Twin Cities Campus M,D
Arizona State University M
Armstrong Atlantic State University M
Avila University M
Baldwin-Wallace College M
Barry University M,O
Baylor University M
Bellevue University M
Benedictine University M
Bernard M. Baruch College of the City University of New York M
Boston University M,D,O
Brandeis University M
Brenau University M
Brooklyn College of the City University of New York M
California State University, Bakersfield M
California State University, Chico M
California State University, East Bay M
California State University, Fresno M
California State University, Long Beach M,O
California State University, Los Angeles M
California State University, Northridge M
California State University, San Bernardino M
Capella University M,D,O
Carnegie Mellon University M
Case Western Reserve University M,D
Central Michigan University M,D,O
Charleston Southern University M
Clark University M
Cleveland State University M
College of Saint Elizabeth M
Colorado Technical University—Sioux Falls M
Columbia University M
Concordia University Wisconsin M
Cornell University M,D
Dallas Baptist University M
DePaul University M,O
Duke University O
Duquesne University M,D
D'Youville College M,O
Eastern Kentucky University M
East Tennessee State University M,D,O
Emory University M,D
Fairfield University M,O
Fairleigh Dickinson University, Metropolitan Campus M
Florida Atlantic University M
Florida International University M
Framingham State College M
Francis Marion University M
Friends University M
The George Washington University M,D,O
Georgia Institute of Technology M
Georgia Southern University M
Georgia State University M
Governors State University M
Grand Valley State University M
Harvard University M,D
Hofstra University M,O
Houston Baptist University M
Illinois Institute of Technology M
Indiana University Northwest M,O
Indiana University–Purdue University Indianapolis M
Indiana University South Bend M,O
Indiana Wesleyan University M
Iona College M,O
The Johns Hopkins University M,D,O
Kean University M
Kennesaw State University M
King's College M
Lamar University M
Lindenwood University M
Lipscomb University M
Long Island University, Brooklyn Campus M
Long Island University, C.W. Post Campus M,O
Louisiana State University in Shreveport M
Loyola University Chicago M
Loyola University New Orleans M
Madonna University M
Marshall University M
Marymount University M
Marywood University M
Mercy College M,O
Middle Tennessee State University O
Midwestern State University M
Mississippi College M
Missouri State University M
Monmouth University M,O
Montana State University–Billings M
National University M
New Jersey City University M
The New School: A University M,O
New York Institute of Technology M,O
New York University M,O
Northeastern University M
Northwest Missouri State University M
The Ohio State University M
Ohio University M
Oklahoma City University M
Oklahoma State University M
Old Dominion University M
Oregon State University M
Our Lady of the Lake University of San Antonio M
Pace University M
Park University M
Penn State Great Valley M
Penn State Harrisburg M,D
Penn State University Park M,D
Pfeiffer University M
Philadelphia University M
Portland State University M,O
Quinnipiac University M
Regent University M
Regis University M,D
Roberts Wesleyan College M
Rochester Institute of Technology M,O
Rutgers, The State University of New Jersey, Newark M,D
St. Ambrose University M,D
Saint Joseph's College of Maine M
St. Joseph's College, Suffolk Campus M,O
Saint Joseph's University M
Saint Louis University M,D
Saint Mary's University of Minnesota M
St. Thomas University M,O
Saint Xavier University M,O
Salve Regina University M,O
San Diego State University M,D
Seton Hall University M
Shenandoah University M,O
Simmons College M,O
Southeastern University M
Southeast Missouri State University M
Southwest Baptist University M
Springfield College M
State University of New York at Binghamton M,D
State University of New York Institute of Technology M
Stony Brook University, State University of New York M,D,O
Suffolk University M,O
Syracuse University O
Temple University M,D
Texas A&M University–Corpus Christi M
Texas State University-San Marcos M
Texas Tech University M,D
Texas Wesleyan University M
Texas Woman's University M,D
Touro College O
Towson University O
Trinity University M
Tulane University M,D
University at Albany, State University of New York M
The University of Akron M
The University of Alabama at Birmingham M,D
University of Arkansas at Little Rock M
University of Baltimore M
University of California, Berkeley M,D
University of California, Los Angeles M,D
University of California, San Diego M
University of Central Florida M,O
University of Colorado at Colorado Springs M
University of Colorado Denver M
University of Connecticut M,D
University of Dallas M
University of Detroit Mercy M
University of Evansville M
University of Florida M,D
University of Houston–Clear Lake M
University of Illinois at Chicago M,D
The University of Iowa M,D
University of Kansas M
University of Kentucky M
University of La Verne M,O
University of Louisiana at Lafayette M
University of Maryland, Baltimore County M
University of Maryland University College M,O
University of Massachusetts Boston M,D,O
University of Massachusetts Lowell M
University of Memphis M
University of Michigan M,D
University of Minnesota, Twin Cities Campus M,D
University of Missouri–Columbia M
University of Missouri–St. Louis M,O
University of New Hampshire M
University of New Haven M
University of New Orleans M
The University of North Carolina at Chapel Hill M,D

The University of North Carolina at Charlotte	M
University of North Florida	M,O
University of Oklahoma	M
University of Pennsylvania	M,D
University of Phoenix–Central Florida Campus	M
University of Phoenix–Denver Campus	M
University of Phoenix–Fort Lauderdale Campus	M
University of Phoenix–Hawaii Campus	M
University of Phoenix–Louisiana Campus	M
University of Phoenix–New Mexico Campus	M
University of Phoenix–North Florida Campus	M
University of Phoenix	M,D
University of Phoenix–Oregon Campus	M
University of Phoenix–Philadelphia Campus	M
University of Phoenix–Phoenix Campus	M,O
University of Phoenix–Sacramento Valley Campus	M
University of Phoenix–Southern Arizona Campus	M,O
University of Phoenix–Southern California Campus	M,O
University of Phoenix–Southern Colorado Campus	M
University of Phoenix–West Florida Campus	M
University of Phoenix–West Michigan Campus	M
University of Pittsburgh	M,D,O
University of St. Francis (IL)	M
University of St. Thomas (MN)	M
University of San Francisco	M
The University of Scranton	M
University of South Carolina	M,D
University of Southern California	M
University of Southern Indiana	M
University of Southern Maine	M,O
University of Southern Mississippi	M
University of South Florida	M,D
The University of Tennessee	M
The University of Texas at Arlington	M
The University of Texas at Dallas	M
The University of Texas at Tyler	M
The University of Toledo	M
University of Virginia	M
University of Washington	M
University of Wisconsin–Oshkosh	M
Villanova University	M,D,O
Virginia Commonwealth University	M,D
Wagner College	M
Walden University	M,D
Washington State University	M
Washington University in St. Louis	M
Wayland Baptist University	M
Weber State University	M
Webster University	M,D
West Chester University of Pennsylvania	M,O
Western Carolina University	M
Western Connecticut State University	M
Western Illinois University	M,O
Western Kentucky University	M
Widener University	M
William Woods University	M,O
Wilmington University (DE)	M
Worcester State College	M
Wright State University	M
Xavier University	M
Yale University	M,D
Youngstown State University	M

■ HEALTH SERVICES RESEARCH

Arizona State University	M,D
Brown University	M,D
Clarkson University	M
Dartmouth College	M,D
Emory University	M,D
Florida State University	M
The George Washington University	M,D,O
The Johns Hopkins University	M,D
Old Dominion University	D
Stanford University	M
Texas State University-San Marcos	M
University of Florida	M,D
University of La Verne	M
University of Minnesota, Twin Cities Campus	M,D
The University of North Carolina at Charlotte	D
University of North Florida	M,O
University of Rochester	D
University of Southern California	D
University of Virginia	M
University of Washington	M,D
Virginia Commonwealth University	D
Wake Forest University	M

■ HIGHER EDUCATION

Abilene Christian University	M
Angelo State University	M
Appalachian State University	M,O
Argosy University, Orange County Campus	M,D
Argosy University, Sarasota Campus	M,D,O
Argosy University, Tampa Campus	M,D,O
Argosy University, Twin Cities Campus	M,D,O
Arizona State University	M,D
Auburn University	M,D,O
Azusa Pacific University	M,D
Ball State University	M,D
Barry University	M,D
Benedictine University	D
Bernard M. Baruch College of the City University of New York	M
Bethel University	M,O
Boston College	M,D
Bowling Green State University	D
Capella University	M,D,O
Chicago State University	M,D
Claremont Graduate University	M,D,O
College of Saint Elizabeth	M,O
Dallas Baptist University	M
Drexel University	M
Eastern Kentucky University	M
Eastern Washington University	M
Fitchburg State College	M,O
Florida Atlantic University	M,D,O
Florida International University	D
Florida State University	M,D,O
Geneva College	M
The George Washington University	M,D,O
Georgia Southern University	M
Grand Valley State University	M
Harvard University	D
Illinois State University	M,D
Indiana University Bloomington	M,D,O
Indiana University of Pennsylvania	M
Inter American University of Puerto Rico, Metropolitan Campus	M
Iowa State University of Science and Technology	M,D
Kent State University	M
Louisiana State University and Agricultural and Mechanical College	M,D,O
Loyola University Chicago	M,D
Marywood University	M,D
Michigan State University	M,D,O
Minnesota State University Mankato	M,O
Mississippi College	M,O
Morehead State University	M,O
Morgan State University	D
New York University	M,D
North Carolina State University	M,D
Northeastern State University	M
Northern Illinois University	M,D
Northwestern University	M
Nova Southeastern University	D
Oakland University	M,D,O
The Ohio State University	M
Ohio University	M,D
Oklahoma State University	M,D
Old Dominion University	M,D,O
Oral Roberts University	M,D
Penn State University Park	M,D
Pittsburg State University	M,O
Portland State University	M,D
Purdue University	M,D,O
Rowan University	M
St. Cloud State University	M
Saint Louis University	M,D,O
Salem State College	M
San Diego State University	M
San Jose State University	M,O
Seton Hall University	D
Southeast Missouri State University	M,O
Southern Illinois University Carbondale	M
Stanford University	M,D
Syracuse University	M,D
Texas A&M University–Commerce	M,D
Texas A&M University–Kingsville	D
Texas Southern University	M,D
Texas Tech University	M,D,O
Union University	M,D,O
University at Buffalo, the State University of New York	M,D,O
The University of Akron	M
The University of Alabama	M,D
The University of Arizona	M,D
University of Arkansas	M,D,O
University of Arkansas at Little Rock	D
University of Central Florida	D
University of Central Oklahoma	M
University of Connecticut	M
University of Delaware	M
University of Denver	M,D,O
University of Florida	M,D,O
University of Georgia	D
University of Houston	M,D
University of Illinois at Urbana–Champaign	M,D,O
The University of Iowa	M,D,O
University of Kansas	M,D
University of Kentucky	M,D
University of Louisville	M,O
University of Maine	M,D,O
University of Mary	M
University of Massachusetts Amherst	M,D,O
University of Massachusetts Boston	M,D,O
University of Memphis	M,D
University of Miami	M,O
University of Michigan	M,D
University of Minnesota, Twin Cities Campus	M,D
University of Mississippi	M,D,O

Institution	Degrees
University of Missouri–Columbia	M,D,O
University of Missouri–St. Louis	M,D,O
University of New Hampshire	M
The University of North Carolina at Greensboro	D
University of Northern Iowa	M
University of North Texas	M,D
University of Oklahoma	M,D
University of Pittsburgh	M,D
University of South Carolina	M
University of Southern Mississippi	M,D,O
University of South Florida	M,D,O
The University of Texas at San Antonio	M,D
The University of Toledo	M,D
University of Virginia	D,O
University of Washington	M,D
University of Wisconsin–Whitewater	M
Vanderbilt University	M,D
Virginia Polytechnic Institute and State University	M,D,O
Walden University	M,D
Washington State University	M,D
Wayne State University	M,D,O
Western Washington University	M
West Virginia University	M,D
Wilkes University	M,D
Wright State University	M,O

■ HISPANIC STUDIES

Institution	Degrees
Brown University	M,D
California State University, Los Angeles	M
California State University, Northridge	M
Eastern Michigan University	M,O
La Salle University	M
Michigan State University	M,D
New Mexico Highlands University	M
Pontifical Catholic University of Puerto Rico	M,O
St. Thomas University	M,O
San Jose State University	M
Stony Brook University, State University of New York	M,D
Texas A&M International University	M,D
University of California, Berkeley	M,D
University of California, Los Angeles	D
University of California, Riverside	M,D
University of California, Santa Barbara	M,D
University of Illinois at Chicago	M,D
University of Kentucky	M,D
The University of North Carolina at Greensboro	M,O
The University of North Carolina Wilmington	O
University of Pittsburgh	M,D
University of Puerto Rico, Mayagüez Campus	M
University of Puerto Rico, Río Piedras	M,D
The University of Texas at San Antonio	M
University of Washington	M
Villanova University	M

■ HISTORIC PRESERVATION

Institution	Degrees
Ball State University	M
Boston University	M
Buffalo State College, State University of New York	M,O
Clemson University	M
Columbia University	M
Cornell University	M,D
Eastern Michigan University	M
The George Washington University	M
Georgia State University	M
Kent State University	M,O
Michigan Technological University	D
Middle Tennessee State University	M,D
New York University	
Rensselaer Polytechnic Institute	M
Rutgers, The State University of New Jersey, New Brunswick	M,D,O
Texas Tech University	M
University of California, Riverside	M,D
University of Delaware	M,D
University of Georgia	M
University of Hawaii at Manoa	O
University of Kentucky	M
University of Maryland, College Park	M,O
The University of North Carolina at Greensboro	M,O
University of Oregon	M
University of Pennsylvania	M,O
University of South Carolina	M,O
University of Southern California	O
University of Vermont	M
University of Washington	O
Ursuline College	M
Virginia Commonwealth University	M,O

■ HISTORY

Institution	Degrees
American University	M,D
Andrews University	M
Angelo State University	M
Appalachian State University	M
Arizona State University	M,D
Arkansas State University	M,D,O
Arkansas Tech University	M
Armstrong Atlantic State University	M
Ashland University	M
Auburn University	M,D
Ball State University	M
Baylor University	M
Bob Jones University	P,M,D,O
Boise State University	M
Boston College	M,D
Boston University	M,D
Bowling Green State University	M,D
Brandeis University	M,D
Brigham Young University	M
Brooklyn College of the City University of New York	M,D
Brown University	M,D
Buffalo State College, State University of New York	M
Butler University	M
California Polytechnic State University, San Luis Obispo	M
California State Polytechnic University, Pomona	M
California State University, Bakersfield	M
California State University, Chico	M
California State University, East Bay	M
California State University, Fresno	M
California State University, Fullerton	M
California State University, Long Beach	M
California State University, Los Angeles	M
California State University, Northridge	M
California State University, Stanislaus	M
Cardinal Stritch University	M
Carnegie Mellon University	M,D
Case Western Reserve University	M,D
The Catholic University of America	M,D
Central Connecticut State University	M,O
Central Michigan University	M,D
Central Washington University	M
Chicago State University	M
The Citadel, The Military College of South Carolina	M
City College of the City University of New York	M
Claremont Graduate University	M,D,O
Clark Atlanta University	M
Clark University	M,D,O
Clemson University	M
Cleveland State University	M
College of Charleston	M
The College of Saint Rose	M
College of Staten Island of the City University of New York	M
The College of William and Mary	M,D
Colorado State University	M
Columbia University	M,D
Converse College	M
Cornell University	M,D
DePaul University	M
Drake University	M
Drew University	M,D
Duke University	M,D
Duquesne University	M
East Carolina University	M
Eastern Illinois University	M
Eastern Kentucky University	M
Eastern Michigan University	M
Eastern Washington University	M
East Stroudsburg University of Pennsylvania	M
East Tennessee State University	M
Emory University	D
Emporia State University	M
Fairleigh Dickinson University, Metropolitan Campus	M
Fayetteville State University	M
Fitchburg State College	M
Florida Agricultural and Mechanical University	M
Florida Atlantic University	M
Florida International University	M,D
Florida State University	M,D
Fordham University	M,D
Fort Hays State University	M
George Mason University	M,D
Georgetown University	M,D
The George Washington University	M,D
Georgia College & State University	M
Georgia Southern University	M
Georgia State University	M,D
Graduate School and University Center of the City University of New York	D
Hardin-Simmons University	M
Harvard University	D
High Point University	M
Howard University	M,D
Hunter College of the City University of New York	M
Idaho State University	M
Illinois State University	M
Indiana State University	M
Indiana University Bloomington	M,D
Indiana University of Pennsylvania	M
Indiana University–Purdue University Indianapolis	M
Iona College	M
Iowa State University of Science and Technology	M,D
Jackson State University	M
Jacksonville State University	M
James Madison University	M
John Carroll University	M
The Johns Hopkins University	D

Institution	Degrees
Kansas State University	M,D
Kent State University	M,D
Lamar University	M
La Salle University	M
Lehigh University	M,D
Lehman College of the City University of New York	M
Lincoln University (MO)	M
Long Island University, Brooklyn Campus	M,O
Long Island University, C.W. Post Campus	M
Louisiana State University and Agricultural and Mechanical College	M,D
Louisiana Tech University	M
Loyola University Chicago	M,D
Marquette University	M,D
Marshall University	M
Miami University	M,D
Michigan State University	M,D
Middle Tennessee State University	M,D
Midwestern State University	M
Millersville University of Pennsylvania	M
Minnesota State University Mankato	M
Mississippi College	M,O
Mississippi State University	M,D
Missouri State University	M
Monmouth University	M
Montana State University	M,D
Montclair State University	M
Morgan State University	M,D
Murray State University	M
New Jersey Institute of Technology	M
New Mexico Highlands University	M
New Mexico State University	M
The New School: A University	M,D
New York University	M,D,O
North Carolina Central University	M
North Carolina State University	M
North Dakota State University	M,D
Northeastern Illinois University	M
Northeastern University	M,D
Northern Arizona University	M,D
Northern Illinois University	M,D
Northwestern University	D
Northwest Missouri State University	M
Oakland University	M
The Ohio State University	M,D
Ohio University	M,D
Oklahoma State University	M,D
Old Dominion University	M
Oregon State University	M,D
Penn State University Park	M,D
Pepperdine University	M
Pittsburg State University	M
Pontifical Catholic University of Puerto Rico	M
Portland State University	M
Prescott College	M
Princeton University	D
Providence College	M
Purdue University	M,D
Purdue University Calumet	M
Queens College of the City University of New York	M
Rhode Island College	M
Rice University	M,D
Roosevelt University	M
Rutgers, The State University of New Jersey, Camden	M
Rutgers, The State University of New Jersey, Newark	M
Rutgers, The State University of New Jersey, New Brunswick	D
St. Cloud State University	M
St. John's University (NY)	M,D
Saint Louis University	M,D
Salem State College	M
Salisbury University	M
Sam Houston State University	M
San Diego State University	M
San Francisco State University	M
San Jose State University	M
Sarah Lawrence College	M
Seton Hall University	M
Shippensburg University of Pennsylvania	M,O
Slippery Rock University of Pennsylvania	M
Sonoma State University	M
Southeastern Louisiana University	M
Southeast Missouri State University	M
Southern Connecticut State University	M
Southern Illinois University Carbondale	M,D
Southern Illinois University Edwardsville	M
Southern Methodist University	M,D
Southern University and Agricultural and Mechanical College	M
Stanford University	M,D
State University of New York at Binghamton	M,D
State University of New York at Oswego	M
State University of New York College at Brockport	M
State University of New York College at Cortland	M
Stephen F. Austin State University	M
Stony Brook University, State University of New York	M,D
Sul Ross State University	M
Syracuse University	M,D
Tarleton State University	M
Temple University	M,D
Texas A&M International University	M
Texas A&M University	M,D
Texas A&M University–Commerce	M
Texas A&M University–Corpus Christi	M
Texas A&M University–Kingsville	M
Texas A&M University–Texarkana	M
Texas Christian University	M,D
Texas Southern University	M
Texas State University-San Marcos	M
Texas Tech University	M,D
Texas Woman's University	M
Tufts University	M,D
Tulane University	M,D
University at Albany, State University of New York	M,D,O
University at Buffalo, the State University of New York	M,D
The University of Akron	M,D
The University of Alabama	M,D
The University of Alabama at Birmingham	M
The University of Alabama in Huntsville	M
The University of Arizona	M,D
University of Arkansas	M,D
University of California, Berkeley	M,D
University of California, Davis	M,D
University of California, Irvine	M,D
University of California, Los Angeles	M,D
University of California, Riverside	M,D
University of California, San Diego	M,D
University of California, Santa Barbara	D
University of California, Santa Cruz	M,D
University of Central Arkansas	M
University of Central Florida	M
University of Central Missouri	M
University of Central Oklahoma	M
University of Chicago	D
University of Cincinnati	M,D
University of Colorado at Boulder	M,D
University of Colorado at Colorado Springs	M
University of Colorado Denver	M
University of Connecticut	M,D
University of Delaware	M,D
University of Florida	M,D
University of Georgia	M,D
University of Hawaii at Manoa	M,D
University of Houston	M,D
University of Houston–Clear Lake	M
University of Idaho	M,D
University of Illinois at Chicago	M,D
University of Illinois at Urbana–Champaign	M,D
University of Indianapolis	M
The University of Iowa	M,D
University of Kansas	M,D
University of Kentucky	M,D
University of Louisiana at Lafayette	M
University of Louisiana at Monroe	M
University of Louisville	M
University of Maine	M,D
University of Maryland, Baltimore County	M
University of Maryland, College Park	M,D
University of Massachusetts Amherst	M,D
University of Massachusetts Boston	M
University of Memphis	M,D
University of Miami	M,D
University of Michigan	D,O
University of Minnesota, Twin Cities Campus	M,D
University of Mississippi	M,D
University of Missouri–Columbia	M,D
University of Missouri–Kansas City	M,D
The University of Montana	M,D
University of Nebraska at Kearney	M
University of Nebraska at Omaha	M
University of Nebraska–Lincoln	M,D
University of Nevada, Las Vegas	M,D
University of Nevada, Reno	M,D
University of New Hampshire	M,D
University of New Mexico	M,D
University of New Orleans	M
The University of North Carolina at Chapel Hill	M,D
The University of North Carolina at Charlotte	M
The University of North Carolina at Greensboro	M,D,O
The University of North Carolina Wilmington	M
University of North Dakota	M,D
University of Northern Colorado	M
University of Northern Iowa	M
University of North Florida	M
University of North Texas	M,D
University of Notre Dame	M,D
University of Oklahoma	M,D
University of Oregon	M,D
University of Pennsylvania	M,D
University of Pittsburgh	M,D
University of Puerto Rico, Río Piedras	M,D
University of Rhode Island	M

University of Richmond M
University of Rochester M,D
University of San Diego M
The University of Scranton M
University of South Alabama M
University of South Carolina M,D,O
The University of South Dakota M
University of Southern California M,D
University of Southern Mississippi M,D
University of South Florida M
The University of Tennessee M,D
The University of Texas at Arlington M,D
The University of Texas at Austin M,D
The University of Texas at Brownsville M
The University of Texas at El Paso M,D
The University of Texas at San Antonio M
The University of Texas at Tyler M
The University of Texas of the Permian Basin M
The University of Texas–Pan American M
The University of Toledo M,D
University of Tulsa M
University of Utah M,D
University of Vermont M
University of Virginia M,D
University of Washington M,D
University of West Florida M
University of West Georgia M
University of Wisconsin–Eau Claire M
University of Wisconsin–Madison M,D
University of Wisconsin–Milwaukee M,D
University of Wisconsin–Stevens Point M
University of Wyoming M
Utah State University M
Valdosta State University M
Valparaiso University M,O
Vanderbilt University M,D
Villanova University M
Virginia Commonwealth University M,D
Virginia Polytechnic Institute and State University M
Virginia State University M
Washington State University M,D
Washington University in St. Louis M,D
Wayne State University M,D
West Chester University of Pennsylvania M
Western Carolina University M
Western Connecticut State University M
Western Illinois University M
Western Kentucky University M
Western Michigan University M,D
Western Washington University M
Westfield State College M
West Texas A&M University M
West Virginia University M,D
Wichita State University M
William Paterson University of New Jersey M
Winthrop University M
Wright State University M
Yale University M,D
Youngstown State University M

■ HISTORY OF MEDICINE

Duke University
Rutgers, The State University of New Jersey, New Brunswick D
University of Minnesota, Twin Cities Campus M,D
Yale University M,D

■ HISTORY OF SCIENCE AND TECHNOLOGY

Arizona State University M,D
Brown University M,D
Cornell University M,D
Drexel University M
Georgia Institute of Technology M,D
Harvard University M,D
Indiana University Bloomington M,D
Iowa State University of Science and Technology M,D
The Johns Hopkins University M,D
Massachusetts Institute of Technology D
Polytechnic University, Brooklyn Campus M
Princeton University D
Rensselaer Polytechnic Institute M,D
Rutgers, The State University of New Jersey, New Brunswick D
University of California, Berkeley D
University of California, San Diego M,D
University of Delaware M,D
University of Massachusetts Amherst M,D
University of Minnesota, Twin Cities Campus M,D
University of Notre Dame M,D
University of Oklahoma M,D
University of Pennsylvania M,D
University of Pittsburgh M,D
University of Wisconsin–Madison M,D
Virginia Polytechnic Institute and State University M,D
West Virginia University M,D
Yale University M,D

■ HIV/AIDS NURSING

Duke University M,D,O
University of Delaware M,O

■ HOLOCAUST STUDIES

Clark University D
Drew University M,D,O
Kean University M
The Richard Stockton College of New Jersey M

■ HOME ECONOMICS EDUCATION

Appalachian State University M
Central Washington University M
Eastern Kentucky University M
Harding University M,O
Indiana State University M
Iowa State University of Science and Technology M,D
Louisiana State University and Agricultural and Mechanical College M,D
Montclair State University M,O
Northwestern State University of Louisiana M
The Ohio State University M
Purdue University M,D,O
Queens College of the City University of New York M
South Carolina State University M
State University of New York College at Oneonta M
Texas Tech University M,D,O
University of Central Oklahoma M
University of Indianapolis M,O
Utah State University M
Wayne State College M
Western Carolina University M

■ HOMELAND SECURITY

Arkansas Tech University M
The Johns Hopkins University M,O
Long Island University, Southampton Graduate Campus M,O
National University M
Regent University M
Salve Regina University M,O
Texas A&M University M,O
Tiffin University M
Towson University M,O
University of Connecticut M
Upper Iowa University M
Virginia Commonwealth University M,O

■ HORTICULTURE

Auburn University M,D
Colorado State University M,D
Cornell University M,D
Iowa State University of Science and Technology M,D
Kansas State University M,D
Louisiana State University and Agricultural and Mechanical College M,D
Michigan State University M,D
New Mexico State University M,D
North Carolina State University M,D
The Ohio State University M,D
Oklahoma State University M,D
Oregon State University M,D
Penn State University Park M,D
Purdue University M,D
Rutgers, The State University of New Jersey, New Brunswick M,D
Southern Illinois University Carbondale M
Texas A&M University M,D
Texas Tech University M,D
University of Arkansas M
University of California, Davis M
University of Delaware M
University of Florida M,D
University of Georgia M,D
University of Hawaii at Manoa M,D
University of Maine M
University of Maryland, College Park D
University of Missouri–Columbia M,D
University of Nebraska–Lincoln M,D
University of Puerto Rico, Mayagüez Campus M
University of Vermont M,D
University of Washington M,D
University of Wisconsin–Madison M,D
Virginia Polytechnic Institute and State University M,D
Washington State University M,D
West Virginia University M,D

■ HOSPICE NURSING

Madonna University M

■ HOSPITALITY MANAGEMENT

Central Michigan University M
Cornell University M,D
Eastern Michigan University M
East Stroudsburg University of Pennsylvania M
Endicott College M
Fairleigh Dickinson University, College at Florham M
Fairleigh Dickinson University, Metropolitan Campus M
Florida International University M

The George Washington University	M,O
Iowa State University of Science and Technology	M,D
Johnson & Wales University	M,O
Kansas State University	M,D
Lynn University	M,D
Michigan State University	M
New York University	M,D,O
The Ohio State University	M,D
Oklahoma State University	M,D
Penn State University Park	M,D
Purdue University	M,D
Rochester Institute of Technology	M
Roosevelt University	M
Schiller International University (United States)	M
South Dakota State University	M
Southern New Hampshire University	M,D,O
Temple University	M
Texas Tech University	M,D
Texas Woman's University	M,D
The University of Alabama	M
University of Central Florida	M
University of Delaware	M
University of Houston	M
University of Kentucky	M
University of Massachusetts Amherst	M
University of Missouri–Columbia	M,D
University of Nevada, Las Vegas	M,D
University of New Haven	M
University of New Orleans	M
University of North Texas	M
University of South Carolina	M
The University of Tennessee	M
Virginia Polytechnic Institute and State University	M,D

■ HUMAN-COMPUTER INTERACTION

Carnegie Mellon University	M,D
Cornell University	D
DePaul University	M,D
Georgia Institute of Technology	M
Indiana University Bloomington	M,D
Iowa State University of Science and Technology	M,D
Rensselaer Polytechnic Institute	M
State University of New York at Oswego	M
Tufts University	O
University of Baltimore	M,D
University of Illinois at Urbana–Champaign	M,D,O
University of Michigan	M,D

■ HUMAN DEVELOPMENT

Arizona State University	M,D
Auburn University	M,D
Boston University	M,D,O
Bowling Green State University	M
Bradley University	M
Brigham Young University	M,D
California State University, San Bernardino	M
The Catholic University of America	D
Central Michigan University	M
Claremont Graduate University	M,D,O
Clemson University	M
Colorado State University	M
Cornell University	D
DePaul University	M,D
Dowling College	M,D,O
Duke University	D
East Tennessee State University	M
The George Washington University	M,D
Harvard University	M,D
Hood College	M,O
Howard University	M
Indiana University Bloomington	M,D
Iowa State University of Science and Technology	M,D
Kansas State University	D
Kent State University	M,D
Lehigh University	M,D
Marywood University	D
Montana State University	M
National-Louis University	M,D,O
New York Institute of Technology	M
New York University	M,D,O
North Dakota State University	D
Northwestern University	D
The Ohio State University	M,D
Oregon State University	M,D
Our Lady of the Lake University of San Antonio	M
Penn State University Park	M,D
Purdue University	M,D
Saint Joseph College	O
Saint Louis University	M,D,O
Saint Mary's University of Minnesota	M
South Dakota State University	M
Southern Illinois University Carbondale	M,D
Texas A&M University	M,D
Texas Southern University	M
Texas Tech University	M,D
The University of Alabama	M
The University of Arizona	M,D
University of California, Berkeley	M,D
University of California, Davis	D
University of Central Arkansas	M
University of Central Oklahoma	M
University of Chicago	D
University of Connecticut	M,D
University of Dayton	M,O
University of Delaware	M,D
University of Houston	M
University of Illinois at Chicago	M,D
University of Illinois at Springfield	M
University of Illinois at Urbana–Champaign	M,D
University of Kansas	M,D
University of Maine	M
University of Maryland, College Park	M,D
University of Missouri–Columbia	M,D
University of Nevada, Reno	M
The University of North Carolina at Greensboro	M,D
University of North Texas	M,D
University of Pennsylvania	M,D
University of St. Thomas (MN)	M,D,O
The University of Texas at Austin	M,D
University of Washington	M,D
University of Wisconsin–Madison	M,D
University of Wisconsin–Stevens Point	M
University of Wisconsin–Stout	M
Utah State University	M,D
Vanderbilt University	M
Virginia Polytechnic Institute and State University	M,D
Washington State University	M
Wayne State University	M
Wheelock College	M

■ HUMAN GENETICS

Case Western Reserve University	D
Drexel University	M,D
The Johns Hopkins University	D
Sarah Lawrence College	M
Tulane University	M,D
University of California, Los Angeles	M,D
University of Chicago	D
University of Michigan	M,D
University of Pittsburgh	M,D,O
University of Utah	M,D
Virginia Commonwealth University	M,D,O
Wake Forest University	D
West Virginia University	M,D

■ HUMANITIES

Arcadia University	M
Arizona State University	M
Brigham Young University	M
California Institute of Integral Studies	M,D
California State University, Dominguez Hills	M
Carlow University	M
Central Michigan University	M
Claremont Graduate University	M,D,O
Clark Atlanta University	D
Dominican University of California	M
Drew University	M,D,O
Duke University	M
Florida State University	M,D
Hofstra University	M
Hollins University	M,O
Hood College	M
John Carroll University	M
Marshall University	M
Marymount University	M
Massachusetts Institute of Technology	M
Michigan State University	M
Mount St. Mary's College	M
National University	M
New College of California	M
New York University	M,O
Nova Southeastern University	M
Old Dominion University	M
Penn State Harrisburg	M
Pepperdine University	M
Polytechnic University, Brooklyn Campus	M,O
Prescott College	M
Salve Regina University	M,D
Sam Houston State University	M,D
San Francisco State University	M
Stanford University	M
Texas Tech University	M,D
Tiffin University	M
Towson University	M
University of California, Santa Cruz	D
University of Chicago	M
University of Colorado Denver	M
University of Dallas	M
University of Houston–Clear Lake	M
University of Louisville	M,D
The University of Texas at Arlington	M
The University of Texas at Dallas	M,D
University of West Florida	M
Wright State University	M

■ HUMAN RESOURCES DEVELOPMENT

Abilene Christian University	M
Amberton University	M
American International College	M
Antioch University Los Angeles	M
Azusa Pacific University	M
Barry University	M,D
Bowie State University	M
California State University, Sacramento	M
Clemson University	M
The College of New Rochelle	M,O

Florida International University M,D
Florida State University M,D,O
Friends University M
The George Washington University M,D,O
Illinois Institute of Technology M,D
Indiana State University M
Indiana University of Pennsylvania M
Inter American University of Puerto Rico, Metropolitan Campus M,D
Inter American University of Puerto Rico, San Germán Campus M,D
Iowa State University of Science and Technology M,D
John F. Kennedy University M,O
The Johns Hopkins University M,O
Johnson & Wales University O
Manhattanville College M
Marquette University M
McDaniel College M
Midwestern State University M
Mississippi State University M,D,O
National-Louis University M
New York University M,O
North Carolina Agricultural and Technical State University M
Northeastern Illinois University M
Oakland University M
Palm Beach Atlantic University M
Penn State University Park M
Pittsburg State University M
Rochester Institute of Technology M,O
Rollins College M
Roosevelt University M
St. John Fisher College M
Salve Regina University M,O
Siena Heights University M
Southern New Hampshire University M,O
Suffolk University M,O
Syracuse University D
Texas A&M University M,D
Towson University M
University of Bridgeport M
University of Connecticut M
University of Illinois at Urbana–Champaign M,D,O
University of Louisville M
University of Minnesota, Twin Cities Campus M,D,O
University of Missouri–St. Louis M,O
The University of Scranton M
The University of Tennessee M
The University of Texas at Austin M
The University of Texas at Tyler M
University of Wisconsin–Milwaukee M,O
University of Wisconsin–Stout M
Vanderbilt University M,D
Villanova University M
Virginia Commonwealth University M
Virginia Polytechnic Institute and State University M,D
Webster University M,D
Western Carolina University M
Western Michigan University M,D,O
William Woods University M,O
Xavier University M

■ HUMAN RESOURCES MANAGEMENT

Adelphi University M,O
Alabama Agricultural and Mechanical University M,O
Albany State University M
Amberton University M
American InterContinental University (FL) M
Auburn University M,D
Baldwin-Wallace College M
Barry University O
Benedictine University M
Bernard M. Baruch College of the City University of New York M,D
Boston University M,O
Buffalo State College, State University of New York M,O
California State University, East Bay M
California State University, Sacramento M
Capella University M,D,O
Case Western Reserve University M
Central Michigan University M,O
Chapman University M,O
City University of Seattle M,O
Claremont Graduate University M
Clarkson University M
Cleveland State University M
College of Santa Fe M
Colorado Technical University—Colorado Springs M,D
Colorado Technical University—Denver M
Colorado Technical University—Sioux Falls M
Columbia University M
Concordia University, St. Paul M
Concordia University Wisconsin M
Cornell University M,D
Cumberland University M
Dallas Baptist University M
DePaul University M
East Central University M
Eastern Michigan University M
Emmanuel College M,O
Fairfield University M,O
Fairleigh Dickinson University, College at Florham M
Fairleigh Dickinson University, Metropolitan Campus M,O
Fitchburg State College M
Florida Institute of Technology M
Fordham University M,D,O
Framingham State College M
Gannon University O
George Mason University M
The George Washington University M,D,O
Georgia State University M,D
Golden Gate University M,D,O
Hawai'i Pacific University M
Hofstra University M,O
Holy Family University M
Houston Baptist University M
Inter American University of Puerto Rico, Metropolitan Campus M,D
Inter American University of Puerto Rico, San Germán Campus M,D
Iona College M,O
La Roche College M,O
Lindenwood University M
Long Island University, Brooklyn Campus M
Loyola University Chicago M
Manhattanville College M
Marquette University M
Marshall University M
Marygrove College M
Marymount University M,O
Mercy College M
Metropolitan State University M
Michigan State University M,D
National-Louis University M
Nazareth College of Rochester M
New Mexico Highlands University M
New York Institute of Technology M,O
New York University M,D,O
North Carolina Agricultural and Technical State University M
Nova Southeastern University M
Oakland University M,O
The Ohio State University M,D
Pontifical Catholic University of Puerto Rico M,D
Purdue University M,D
Regis University M,O
Rivier College M
Robert Morris University M
Rollins College M
Roosevelt University M
Rutgers, The State University of New Jersey, Newark M,D
Rutgers, The State University of New Jersey, New Brunswick M,D
St. Ambrose University M,D
St. Edward's University M,O
Saint Francis University M
St. Joseph's College, Suffolk Campus M,O
Saint Joseph's University M
Saint Leo University M
Saint Mary's University of Minnesota M
St. Thomas University M,O
Salve Regina University M,O
San Diego State University M
Southern New Hampshire University M,D,O
Stevens Institute of Technology M,O
Stony Brook University, State University of New York M,O
Suffolk University M,O
Tarleton State University M
Temple University M,D
Texas A&M University M,D
Trinity (Washington) University M
Troy University M
Universidad Metropolitana M
University at Albany, State University of New York M
University at Buffalo, the State University of New York M,D,O
The University of Akron M
The University of Alabama in Huntsville M,O
University of Central Florida M,O
University of Connecticut M
University of Dallas M
University of Denver M,O
The University of Findlay M
University of Florida M
University of Hawaii at Manoa M
University of Houston–Clear Lake M
University of Illinois at Urbana–Champaign M,D
University of Minnesota, Twin Cities Campus M,D
University of Missouri–St. Louis M,O
University of New Haven M
University of New Mexico M
University of Phoenix–Denver Campus M
University of Phoenix–Fort Lauderdale Campus M
University of Phoenix–Hawaii Campus M
University of Phoenix–Louisiana Campus M
University of Phoenix–New Mexico Campus M

University of Phoenix–North Florida Campus	M
University of Phoenix	M
University of Phoenix–Oregon Campus	M
University of Phoenix–Sacramento Valley Campus	M
University of Phoenix–Southern California Campus	M
University of Phoenix–West Florida Campus	M
University of Phoenix–West Michigan Campus	M
University of Puerto Rico, Mayagüez Campus	M
University of Rhode Island	M
The University of Scranton	M
University of South Carolina	M
The University of Texas at Arlington	M
The University of Toledo	M
University of Wisconsin–Madison	M,D
University of Wisconsin–Whitewater	M
Upper Iowa University	M
Utah State University	M
Walden University	M,D
Wayland Baptist University	M
Webster University	M,D
Widener University	M
Wilkes University	M
Wilmington University (DE)	M

■ HUMAN SERVICES

Abilene Christian University	M,O
Andrews University	M
Anna Maria College	M
Bellevue University	M
Brandeis University	M
California State University, Sacramento	M
Canisius College	M
Capella University	M,D,O
Chestnut Hill College	M,O
Concordia University Chicago (IL)	M
Concordia University Wisconsin	M,D
Coppin State University	M
DePaul University	M,D
Drury University	M
Eastern New Mexico University	M
Ferris State University	M
Georgia State University	M
Indiana University Northwest	M,O
Kansas State University	M
Kent State University	M,D,O
Lehigh University	M,D,O
Lincoln University (PA)	M
Louisiana State University in Shreveport	M
McDaniel College	M
Minnesota State University Mankato	M
Minnesota State University Moorhead	M,O
Montana State University–Billings	M
Murray State University	M
National-Louis University	M,O
National University	M
Nova Southeastern University	D
Pontifical Catholic University of Puerto Rico	M,D
Roberts Wesleyan College	M
Rosemont College	M
St. Edward's University	M,O
St. John Fisher College	M
Saint Joseph's University	M,O
St. Mary's University of San Antonio	M,D,O
South Carolina State University	M
Southern Oregon University	M
Springfield College	M
State University of New York at Oswego	M
Texas Southern University	M
Universidad del Turabo	M
University of Baltimore	M
University of Bridgeport	M
University of Central Missouri	M,O
University of Colorado at Colorado Springs	M,D
University of Great Falls	M
University of Illinois at Springfield	M
University of Maryland, Baltimore County	M,D
University of Massachusetts Boston	M
University of Oklahoma	M
Upper Iowa University	M
Walden University	M,D
Wayne State University	O
West Virginia University	M
Wichita State University	M
Wilmington University (DE)	M
Youngstown State University	M

■ HYDRAULICS

Auburn University	M,D
Massachusetts Institute of Technology	M,D,O
Missouri University of Science and Technology	M,D

■ HYDROGEOLOGY

California State University, Chico	M
Clemson University	M
Colorado School of Mines	M,D,O
Georgia State University	M,O
Indiana University Bloomington	M,D
Ohio University	M
Rensselaer Polytechnic Institute	M,D
University of Hawaii at Manoa	M,D
University of Illinois at Chicago	M,D
University of Nevada, Reno	M,D
West Virginia University	M,D

■ HYDROLOGY

Auburn University	M,D
California State University, Bakersfield	M
California State University, Chico	M
Colorado State University	M,D
Cornell University	M,D
Georgia Institute of Technology	M,D
Idaho State University	M,O
Illinois State University	M
Massachusetts Institute of Technology	M,D,O
Missouri University of Science and Technology	M,D
Murray State University	M
New Mexico Institute of Mining and Technology	M,D
State University of New York College of Environmental Science and Forestry	M,D
The University of Arizona	M,D
University of California, Davis	M,D
University of California, Los Angeles	M,D
University of Idaho	M
University of Nevada, Reno	M,D
University of New Hampshire	M
University of Southern Mississippi	M,D
University of Washington	M,D
West Virginia University	M,D

■ ILLUSTRATION

Bob Jones University	P,M,D,O
Bradley University	M
Kent State University	M
Marywood University	M
University of Utah	M
Western Connecticut State University	M

■ IMMUNOLOGY

Boston University	D
Brown University	M,D
California Institute of Technology	D
Case Western Reserve University	M,D
Colorado State University	M,D
Cornell University	P,M,D
Creighton University	M,D
Dartmouth College	D
Drexel University	M,D
Duke University	D
East Carolina University	D
Emory University	D
Florida State University	M,D
Georgetown University	M,D
The George Washington University	D
Harvard University	D
Illinois State University	M,D
Indiana University–Purdue University Indianapolis	M,D
Iowa State University of Science and Technology	M,D
The Johns Hopkins University	M,D
Long Island University, C.W. Post Campus	M
Loyola University Chicago	M,D
Massachusetts Institute of Technology	D
Mayo Graduate School	D
New York University	M,D
North Carolina State University	M,D
Northwestern University	D
The Ohio State University	M,D
Purdue University	M,D
Rutgers, The State University of New Jersey, New Brunswick	M,D
Saint Louis University	D
Stanford University	D
Stony Brook University, State University of New York	M,D
Temple University	M,D
Tufts University	D
Tulane University	M,D
University at Albany, State University of New York	M,D
University at Buffalo, the State University of New York	M,D
The University of Arizona	M,D
University of California, Berkeley	D
University of California, Davis	M,D
University of California, Los Angeles	M,D
University of California, San Diego	D
University of Chicago	D
University of Cincinnati	M,D
University of Colorado Denver	D
University of Florida	D
University of Illinois at Chicago	D
The University of Iowa	M,D
University of Kansas	D
University of Louisville	M,D
University of Miami	D
University of Michigan	D
University of Minnesota, Duluth	M,D
University of Missouri–Columbia	M,D
The University of North Carolina at Chapel Hill	M,D
University of North Dakota	M,D
University of Pennsylvania	D
University of Pittsburgh	M,D
University of Rochester	M,D
University of South Alabama	D
The University of South Dakota	M,D
University of Southern California	M,D

University of Southern Maine	M
University of South Florida	M,D
The University of Texas at Austin	D
The University of Toledo	M,D
University of Virginia	D
University of Washington	D
Vanderbilt University	M,D
Virginia Commonwealth University	M,D
Wake Forest University	D
Washington University in St. Louis	D
Wayne State University	M,D
West Virginia University	M,D
Wright State University	M
Yale University	D

■ INDUSTRIAL/MANAGEMENT ENGINEERING

Arizona State University	M,D
Auburn University	M,D
Bradley University	M
Buffalo State College, State University of New York	M
California Polytechnic State University, San Luis Obispo	M
California State University, Fresno	M
California State University, Northridge	M
Central Washington University	M
Clemson University	M,D
Cleveland State University	M,D
Columbia University	M,D,O
Cornell University	M,D
East Carolina University	M,D,O
Eastern Kentucky University	M
Florida Agricultural and Mechanical University	M,D
Florida International University	M,D
Florida State University	M,D
Georgia Institute of Technology	M,D
Illinois State University	M
Indiana State University	M
Iowa State University of Science and Technology	M,D
Kansas State University	M,D
Lamar University	M,D
Lehigh University	M,D
Louisiana State University and Agricultural and Mechanical College	M,D
Louisiana Tech University	M,D
Mississippi State University	M,D
Montana State University	M,D
Morehead State University	M
Morgan State University	M,D
New Jersey Institute of Technology	M,D
New Mexico State University	M,D
North Carolina Agricultural and Technical State University	M,D
North Carolina State University	M,D
North Dakota State University	M,D
Northeastern University	M,D
Northern Illinois University	M
Northwestern University	M,D
The Ohio State University	M,D
Ohio University	M,D
Oklahoma State University	M,D
Oregon State University	M,D
Penn State University Park	M,D
Polytechnic University, Brooklyn Campus	M
Purdue University	M,D
Rensselaer Polytechnic Institute	M,D
Rochester Institute of Technology	M
Rutgers, The State University of New Jersey, New Brunswick	M,D
St. Mary's University of San Antonio	M
Sam Houston State University	M
San Jose State University	M
South Dakota State University	M
Southern Polytechnic State University	M
Stanford University	M,D
State University of New York at Binghamton	M,D
Texas A&M University	M,D
Texas A&M University–Commerce	M
Texas A&M University–Kingsville	M
Texas Southern University	M
Texas State University-San Marcos	M
Texas Tech University	M,D
University at Buffalo, the State University of New York	M,D
The University of Alabama	M
The University of Alabama in Huntsville	M,D
The University of Arizona	M,D
University of Arkansas	M,D
University of California, Berkeley	M,D
University of Central Florida	M,D,O
University of Central Missouri	M
University of Cincinnati	M,D
University of Dayton	M
University of Florida	M,D,O
University of Houston	M,D
University of Illinois at Chicago	M,D
University of Illinois at Urbana–Champaign	M,D
The University of Iowa	M,D
University of Louisville	M,D
University of Massachusetts Amherst	M,D
University of Massachusetts Lowell	M,D,O
University of Memphis	M,D
University of Miami	M,D
University of Michigan	M,D
University of Michigan–Dearborn	M
University of Minnesota, Twin Cities Campus	M,D
University of Missouri–Columbia	M,D
University of Nebraska–Lincoln	M,D
University of New Haven	M,O
University of Oklahoma	M,D
University of Pittsburgh	M,D
University of Puerto Rico, Mayagüez Campus	M
University of Rhode Island	D
University of Southern California	M,D,O
University of South Florida	M,D
The University of Tennessee	M,D
The University of Texas at Arlington	M
The University of Texas at Austin	M,D
The University of Texas at El Paso	M
The University of Toledo	M,D
University of Washington	M,D
University of Wisconsin–Madison	M,D
University of Wisconsin–Stout	M
Virginia Polytechnic Institute and State University	M,D
Wayne State University	M,D
Western Carolina University	M
Western Michigan University	M
Western New England College	M
West Virginia University	M,D
Wichita State University	M,D
Youngstown State University	M

■ INDUSTRIAL AND LABOR RELATIONS

Bernard M. Baruch College of the City University of New York	M
Case Western Reserve University	M
Cleveland State University	M
Cornell University	M,D
Georgia State University	M,D
Indiana University of Pennsylvania	M
Inter American University of Puerto Rico, Metropolitan Campus	M,D
Inter American University of Puerto Rico, San Germán Campus	M,D
Loyola University Chicago	M
Michigan State University	M,D
New York Institute of Technology	M,O
The Ohio State University	M,D
Penn State University Park	M
Rutgers, The State University of New Jersey, New Brunswick	M,D
State University of New York Empire State College	M
Stony Brook University, State University of New York	M,O
University of California, Berkeley	D
University of Cincinnati	M
University of Illinois at Urbana–Champaign	M,D
University of Louisville	M
University of Massachusetts Amherst	M
University of Minnesota, Twin Cities Campus	M,D
University of New Haven	M
University of North Texas	M,D
University of Rhode Island	M
University of Wisconsin–Madison	M,D
University of Wisconsin–Milwaukee	M,O
Wayne State University	M
West Virginia University	M

■ INDUSTRIAL AND MANUFACTURING MANAGEMENT

Boston University	D
Bryant University	M,O
California Polytechnic State University, San Luis Obispo	M
California State University, East Bay	M
Carnegie Mellon University	M,D
Case Western Reserve University	M,D
Central Michigan University	M
Clarkson University	M
Clemson University	M,D
Cleveland State University	D
DePaul University	M
Eastern Michigan University	M
Florida Institute of Technology	M
Friends University	M
The George Washington University	M
Illinois Institute of Technology	M
Indiana University Southeast	M,O
Inter American University of Puerto Rico, Metropolitan Campus	M,D
Lawrence Technological University	M,D
Marist College	M,O
Northeastern State University	M
Northern Illinois University	M
Oakland University	M,O
Oklahoma State University	M,D
Penn State University Park	M,D
Portland State University	M,D
Purdue University	M,D
Regis University	M,O
Rensselaer Polytechnic Institute	M,D
Rochester Institute of Technology	M
San Diego State University	M
San Jose State University	M
Southeastern Oklahoma State University	M
Southeast Missouri State University	M

Stevens Institute of Technology M
Stony Brook University, State University of New York M,O
Syracuse University D
Texas A&M University M,D
Texas Tech University M,D
University of Arkansas M
University of Central Missouri M
University of Cincinnati M,D
The University of Iowa M
University of Massachusetts Lowell M
University of Minnesota, Twin Cities Campus M,D
University of Missouri–St. Louis M,O
University of North Dakota M
University of North Texas M,D
University of Puerto Rico, Mayagüez Campus M
University of Rhode Island M,D
University of St. Thomas (MN) M,O
University of Southern Indiana M
The University of Tennessee M,D
The University of Texas at Tyler M
The University of Toledo M,D
University of Wisconsin–Madison D
Washington State University M,D

■ INDUSTRIAL AND ORGANIZATIONAL PSYCHOLOGY

Angelo State University M
Antioch University Seattle M
Appalachian State University M
Auburn University M,D
Avila University M
Bernard M. Baruch College of the City University of New York M,D,O
Bowling Green State University M,D
Brooklyn College of the City University of New York M,D
California State University, San Bernardino M
Capella University M,D,O
Carlos Albizu University M,D
Central Michigan University M,D
Claremont Graduate University M,D,O
Clemson University D
Cleveland State University M,O
DePaul University M,D
Eastern Kentucky University M,O
Elmhurst College M
Emporia State University M
Fairleigh Dickinson University, College at Florham M
Florida Institute of Technology M,D
George Mason University M,D
The George Washington University D
Goddard College M
Graduate School and University Center of the City University of New York D
Hofstra University M,D
Illinois Institute of Technology M,D
Illinois State University M,D,O
Indiana University–Purdue University Indianapolis M,D
Iona College M
John F. Kennedy University M,O
Kean University M
Lamar University M
Louisiana State University and Agricultural and Mechanical College M,D
Louisiana Tech University M,D
Marshall University M,D
Middle Tennessee State University M,O
Minnesota State University Mankato M
Montclair State University M,O
National-Louis University M,O
National University M
New York University M,D,O
North Carolina State University D
Northern Kentucky University M
Ohio University D
Old Dominion University D
Penn State University Park M,D
Pontifical Catholic University of Puerto Rico M,D
Radford University M,D,O
Rice University M,D
Roosevelt University M
Rutgers, The State University of New Jersey, New Brunswick M,D
St. Cloud State University M
Saint Louis University M,D
St. Mary's University of San Antonio M
San Diego State University M,D
San Jose State University M
Seattle Pacific University M,D
Southern Illinois University Edwardsville M
Springfield College M,O
Temple University M
Texas A&M University M,D
University at Albany, State University of New York M,D,O
The University of Akron M,D
University of Baltimore M
University of Central Florida M,D
University of Connecticut M,D
University of Detroit Mercy M
University of Houston M,D
University of Maryland, College Park M,D
University of Michigan D
University of Minnesota, Twin Cities Campus D
University of Missouri–St. Louis M,D,O
University of Nebraska at Omaha M,D,O
University of New Haven M,O
The University of North Carolina at Charlotte M,D
University of North Texas M,D
University of South Florida M,D
The University of Tennessee D
The University of Tennessee at Chattanooga M
University of Tulsa M,D
University of Wisconsin–Oshkosh M
Valdosta State University M,O
Virginia Polytechnic Institute and State University M,D
Wayne State University M,D
West Chester University of Pennsylvania M
Western Michigan University M,D,O
Wright State University M,D

■ INDUSTRIAL DESIGN

Auburn University M
Brigham Young University M
North Carolina State University M
The Ohio State University M
Rochester Institute of Technology M
San Francisco State University M
University of Cincinnati M
University of Illinois at Chicago M
University of Illinois at Urbana–Champaign M
University of Notre Dame M

■ INDUSTRIAL HYGIENE

California State University, Northridge M
Murray State University M
New Jersey Institute of Technology M
The University of Alabama at Birmingham D
University of Central Missouri M,O
University of Cincinnati M,D
University of Massachusetts Lowell M,D,O
University of Michigan M,D
University of Minnesota, Twin Cities Campus M,D
University of New Haven M
The University of North Carolina at Chapel Hill M,D
University of South Carolina M,D
University of Washington M,D
University of Wisconsin–Stout M
West Virginia University M

■ INFECTIOUS DISEASES

Cornell University M,D
Georgetown University M,D
The George Washington University M
Harvard University D
The Johns Hopkins University M,D
Loyola University Chicago M
Purdue University M,D
Tulane University M,D,O
University of California, Berkeley M,D
University of Georgia M,D
University of Minnesota, Twin Cities Campus M,D
The University of Montana D
University of Pittsburgh M,D
Yale University D

■ INFORMATION SCIENCE

Alcorn State University M
American InterContinental University (FL) M
American InterContinental University Dunwoody Campus M
Arizona State University at the Polytechnic Campus M
Arkansas Tech University M
Ball State University M
Barry University M
Bellevue University M
Bentley College M
Bradley University M
Brigham Young University M
Brooklyn College of the City University of New York M,D
Bryant University M
California State University, Fullerton M
Carnegie Mellon University M,D
Case Western Reserve University M,D
The Citadel, The Military College of South Carolina M
Claremont Graduate University M,D,O
Clark Atlanta University M
Clarkson University M
Clark University M
The College of Saint Rose M
Colorado Technical University—Colorado Springs M,D
Cornell University D
DePaul University M,D
DeSales University M
Drexel University D
East Carolina University M
East Tennessee State University M
Florida Gulf Coast University M

Florida International University	M,D
Gannon University	M
George Mason University	M,D,O
Georgia Southwestern State University	M
Georgia State University	M
Grand Valley State University	M
Harvard University	M,D,O
Hood College	M
Indiana University Bloomington	M,D,O
Indiana University–Purdue University Indianapolis	M,D
Iowa State University of Science and Technology	M
Kansas State University	M,D
Kennesaw State University	M
Kent State University	M
Lamar University	M
Lehigh University	M
Long Island University, C.W. Post Campus	M
Loyola University Chicago	M
Marshall University	M
Marywood University	M
Massachusetts Institute of Technology	M,D,O
Missouri University of Science and Technology	M
Montclair State University	M,O
National University	M
New Jersey Institute of Technology	M,D
Northeastern University	M,D
Northern Kentucky University	M
Northwestern University	M
Nova Southeastern University	M,D
The Ohio State University	M,D
Pace University	M,D,O
Penn State Great Valley	M
Polytechnic University, Westchester Graduate Center	M
Regis University	M,O
Rensselaer Polytechnic Institute	M
Robert Morris University	M,D
Rochester Institute of Technology	M
Sacred Heart University	M,O
St. Mary's University of San Antonio	M
Saint Xavier University	M
Sam Houston State University	M
Shippensburg University of Pennsylvania	M
Southern Methodist University	M,D
Southern Polytechnic State University	M
State University of New York Institute of Technology	M
Stevens Institute of Technology	M,O
Strayer University	M
Syracuse University	D
Temple University	M,D
Towson University	O
Trevecca Nazarene University	M
University at Albany, State University of New York	M,D,O
The University of Alabama at Birmingham	M,D
University of Baltimore	M,D
University of California, Irvine	M,D
University of Colorado at Colorado Springs	M
University of Colorado Denver	D
University of Delaware	M,D
University of Detroit Mercy	M
University of Florida	M,D
University of Great Falls	M
University of Hawaii at Manoa	M,D,O
University of Houston	M,D
University of Houston–Clear Lake	M
University of Illinois at Urbana–Champaign	M,D,O
The University of Iowa	M,D,O
University of Maryland, Baltimore County	M,D
University of Maryland University College	M,O
University of Michigan	M,D
University of Michigan–Dearborn	M
University of Michigan–Flint	M
University of Minnesota, Twin Cities Campus	M,D
University of Nebraska at Omaha	M,D
University of Nevada, Las Vegas	M,D
University of New Haven	M
The University of North Carolina at Charlotte	M,D
University of North Florida	M
University of Oregon	M,D
University of Pennsylvania	M,D
University of Phoenix–Phoenix Campus	M
University of Pittsburgh	M,D,O
University of Puerto Rico, Mayagüez Campus	D
University of South Alabama	M
The University of Tennessee	M,D
The University of Texas at El Paso	M
The University of Texas at San Antonio	M,D
The University of Texas at Tyler	M
University of Washington	M,D
University of Wisconsin–Stout	M
Virginia Polytechnic Institute and State University	M

■ INFORMATION STUDIES

The Catholic University of America	M
Central Connecticut State University	M
Claremont Graduate University	M,D,O
College of St. Catherine	M
Cornell University	D
Dominican University	M,O
Drexel University	M,D,O
Emporia State University	M,D,O
Florida State University	M,D,O
Indiana University Bloomington	M,D,O
Long Island University, C.W. Post Campus	M,D,O
Louisiana State University and Agricultural and Mechanical College	M,O
Mansfield University of Pennsylvania	M
Metropolitan State University	M
North Carolina Central University	M
Queens College of the City University of New York	M,O
Rutgers, The State University of New Jersey, New Brunswick	M,D
St. John's University (NY)	M,O
San Jose State University	M
Simmons College	M,D,O
Southern Connecticut State University	M,O
Syracuse University	M
University at Buffalo, the State University of New York	M,O
The University of Alabama	M,D
The University of Arizona	M,D
University of California, Berkeley	M,D
University of California, Los Angeles	M,D,O
University of Central Missouri	M,O
University of Denver	M,O
University of Hawaii at Manoa	M,D,O
University of Illinois at Urbana–Champaign	M,D,O
The University of Iowa	M
University of Maryland, College Park	M,D
University of Michigan	M,D
University of Missouri–Columbia	M,D,O
The University of North Carolina at Chapel Hill	M,D,O
The University of North Carolina at Greensboro	M
University of North Texas	M,D
University of Oklahoma	M,O
University of Pittsburgh	M,D,O
University of Puerto Rico, Río Piedras	M,O
University of Rhode Island	M
University of South Carolina	M,O
University of South Florida	M
The University of Texas at Austin	M,D
University of Wisconsin–Madison	M,D,O
University of Wisconsin–Milwaukee	M,O
Valdosta State University	M
Wayne State University	M,O

■ INORGANIC CHEMISTRY

Auburn University	M,D
Boston College	M,D
Brandeis University	M,D
Brigham Young University	M,D
California State University, Fullerton	M
California State University, Los Angeles	M
Case Western Reserve University	M,D
Clark Atlanta University	M,D
Clarkson University	M,D
Cleveland State University	M,D
Columbia University	M,D
Cornell University	D
Florida State University	M,D
Georgetown University	M,D
The George Washington University	M,D
Harvard University	D
Howard University	M,D
Indiana University Bloomington	M,D
Kansas State University	M,D
Kent State University	M,D
Marquette University	M,D
Massachusetts Institute of Technology	D
Miami University	M,D
Northeastern University	M,D
Oregon State University	M,D
Purdue University	M,D
Rensselaer Polytechnic Institute	M,D
Rice University	M,D
Rutgers, The State University of New Jersey, Newark	M,D
Rutgers, The State University of New Jersey, New Brunswick	M,D
Seton Hall University	M,D
Southern University and Agricultural and Mechanical College	M
State University of New York at Binghamton	M,D
Tufts University	M,D
University of Cincinnati	M,D
University of Georgia	M,D
University of Louisville	M,D
University of Maryland, College Park	M,D
University of Miami	M,D
University of Michigan	D
University of Missouri–Columbia	M,D
University of Missouri–Kansas City	M,D
University of Missouri–St. Louis	M,D
The University of Montana	M,D
University of Nebraska–Lincoln	M,D
University of Notre Dame	M,D
University of Southern Mississippi	M,D
University of South Florida	M,D

The University of Tennessee M,D
The University of Texas at Austin M,D
The University of Toledo M,D
Vanderbilt University M,D
Virginia Commonwealth University M,D
Wake Forest University M,D
West Virginia University M,D
Yale University D

■ INSURANCE

Florida State University M,D
Georgia State University M,D
St. John's University (NY) M
Temple University M,D
University of Florida M,D,O
University of North Texas M,D
University of Pennsylvania M,D
University of Wisconsin–Madison M,D
Virginia Commonwealth University M
Washington State University D

■ INTERDISCIPLINARY STUDIES

Alaska Pacific University M
Amberton University M
American University M
Angelo State University M
Arizona State University at the West campus M
Baylor University M,D
Boise State University M
Boston University M,D
Bowling Green State University M,D
Buffalo State College, State University of New York M
California State University, Bakersfield M
California State University, Chico M
California State University, East Bay M,O
California State University, Long Beach M
California State University, Northridge M
California State University, Sacramento M
California State University, San Bernardino M
California State University, Stanislaus M
Campbell University M
Central Washington University M
Clemson University D,O
Columbia University M
Dallas Baptist University M
DePaul University M
Drew University M,D,O
Eastern Michigan University M
Eastern Washington University M
Emory University D
Fitchburg State College O
Fresno Pacific University M
Frostburg State University M
George Mason University M
Goddard College M
Graduate School and University Center of the City University of New York M,D
Hodges University M
Hofstra University M
Hollins University M,O
Idaho State University M
Iowa State University of Science and Technology M
John F. Kennedy University M
Lesley University M
Long Island University, C.W. Post Campus M
Marquette University D
Marylhurst University M
Marywood University M,O
Minnesota State University Mankato M
Montana State University–Billings M
Mountain State University M
New Mexico State University M,D
New York University M
Nova Southeastern University M
The Ohio State University M,D
Ohio University D
Oregon State University M
Regis University M,O
Rensselaer Polytechnic Institute M,D
Rochester Institute of Technology M
Rutgers, The State University of New Jersey, New Brunswick D
San Diego State University M
San Jose State University M
Sarah Lawrence College M
Sonoma State University M
Southern Methodist University M
Stanford University M,D
State University of New York at Fredonia M
State University of New York at New Paltz M
Stephen F. Austin State University M
Texas A&M University M,D
Texas A&M University–Texarkana M
Texas State University-San Marcos M
Texas Tech University M
Union Institute & University M,D
University of Alaska Anchorage M
University of Alaska Fairbanks M,D
The University of Arizona M,D
University of Arkansas D
University of Central Florida M
University of Chicago D
University of Cincinnati D
University of Houston–Victoria M
University of Idaho M
University of Illinois at Springfield M
University of Kansas M,D
University of Louisville M
University of Maine D
University of Maryland, College Park D
University of Minnesota, Twin Cities Campus D
University of Missouri–Kansas City D
The University of Montana M,D
University of Northern Colorado M
University of North Texas M
University of Oklahoma M,D
University of Oregon M
University of Pittsburgh D
The University of South Dakota M
The University of Texas at Arlington M
The University of Texas at Brownsville M
The University of Texas at Dallas M
The University of Texas at El Paso M
The University of Texas at San Antonio M
The University of Texas at Tyler M
The University of Texas–Pan American M
University of the Incarnate Word M
University of Washington, Tacoma M
University of Wisconsin–Milwaukee D
Villanova University D
Virginia Commonwealth University M
Virginia Polytechnic Institute and State University M,D
Virginia State University M
Washington State University D
Wayland Baptist University M
Wayne State University M,D
Western Kentucky University M
Western New Mexico University M
West Texas A&M University M
Worcester Polytechnic Institute M,D
Wright State University M

■ INTERIOR DESIGN

Chatham University M
Columbia College Chicago M
Cornell University M
Drexel University M
Eastern Michigan University M
Florida State University M
The George Washington University M,D
Iowa State University of Science and Technology M
Lawrence Technological University M
Louisiana Tech University M
Marymount University M
Marywood University M
Michigan State University M,D
The New School: A University M
The Ohio State University M
San Diego State University M
South Dakota State University M
Suffolk University M
The University of Alabama M
University of Central Oklahoma M
University of Cincinnati M
University of Florida M,D
University of Georgia M,D
University of Houston M
University of Kentucky M
University of Massachusetts Amherst M
University of Memphis M
University of Minnesota, Twin Cities Campus M,D,O
The University of North Carolina at Greensboro M,O
University of North Texas M,D
University of Oregon M
Utah State University M
Virginia Commonwealth University M
Virginia Polytechnic Institute and State University M,D
Washington State University M,D

■ INTERNATIONAL AFFAIRS

American University M,D,O
Arcadia University M
Baylor University M,D
Boston University M,O
Brandeis University M,D
California State University, Fresno M
California State University, Sacramento M
The Catholic University of America M,D
Central Connecticut State University M
Central Michigan University M,O
City College of the City University of New York M
Claremont Graduate University M,D
Clark Atlanta University M,D
Colorado School of Mines M,O
Columbia University M
Concordia University (CA) M
Cornell University D
Creighton University M
East Carolina University M
Fairleigh Dickinson University, Metropolitan Campus M
Florida Agricultural and Mechanical University M
Florida International University M,D
Florida State University M
Fordham University M,O
George Mason University M

Georgetown University	M,D
The George Washington University	M
Georgia Institute of Technology	M
Harvard University	D
Indiana State University	M
The Johns Hopkins University	M,D,O
Kansas State University	M
Lesley University	M,O
Long Island University, Brooklyn Campus	M,O
Long Island University, C.W. Post Campus	M
Loyola University Chicago	M,D
Marquette University	M
Michigan State University	M
Missouri State University	M
Monterey Institute of International Studies	M
Morgan State University	M
The New School: A University	M
New York University	M,D,O
North Carolina State University	M
Northeastern University	M,D
Northwestern University	O
Norwich University	M
Ohio University	M
Oklahoma State University	M
Old Dominion University	M,D
Pepperdine University	M
Princeton University	M,D
Rutgers, The State University of New Jersey, Camden	M
Rutgers, The State University of New Jersey, Newark	M,D
Rutgers, The State University of New Jersey, New Brunswick	D
St. John Fisher College	M
St. Mary's University of San Antonio	M
Salve Regina University	M,O
San Francisco State University	M
School for International Training	M
Seton Hall University	M
Stanford University	M
Syracuse University	M
Texas A&M University	M,O
Texas State University-San Marcos	M
Troy University	M
Tufts University	M,D
University of California, Berkeley	M
University of California, San Diego	M,D
University of California, Santa Barbara	M
University of California, Santa Cruz	D
University of Central Florida	M
University of Central Oklahoma	M
University of Chicago	M
University of Colorado at Boulder	M,D
University of Connecticut	M
University of Delaware	M,D
University of Denver	M,D
University of Florida	M
University of Hawaii at Manoa	O
University of Indianapolis	M
University of Kansas	M
University of Kentucky	M
University of Miami	M,D
University of Oklahoma	M
University of Oregon	M
University of Pennsylvania	M
University of Pittsburgh	M,D,O
University of Rhode Island	M,O
University of San Diego	M
University of South Carolina	M,D
University of Southern California	M,D
University of Southern Mississippi	M,D
University of South Florida	M
University of the Pacific	P,M,D
University of Virginia	M,D
University of Washington	M
University of Wyoming	M
Virginia Polytechnic Institute and State University	M
Washington State University	M,D
Webster University	M
West Virginia University	M,D
Yale University	M

▪ INTERNATIONAL AND COMPARATIVE EDUCATION

American University	M
Boston University	M
California State University, Dominguez Hills	M
The College of New Jersey	M,O
Drexel University	M
Endicott College	M
Florida International University	M,D
Florida State University	M,D,O
The George Washington University	M
Harvard University	M
Indiana University Bloomington	M,D,O
Louisiana State University and Agricultural and Mechanical College	M,D
Lynn University	M,D
Morehead State University	M
New York University	M,D,O
School for International Training	M
Stanford University	M,D
Tufts University	M,D
University of Bridgeport	M,O
University of California, Santa Barbara	M,D
University of Central Florida	M,D,O
University of Massachusetts Amherst	M,D,O
University of Minnesota, Twin Cities Campus	M,D
University of Pennsylvania	M,D
University of Pittsburgh	M,D
University of San Francisco	M,D
Vanderbilt University	M,D
Wright State University	M

▪ INTERNATIONAL BUSINESS

American InterContinental University (FL)	M
American InterContinental University Dunwoody Campus	M
American University	M
Argosy University, Orange County Campus	M,D,O
Argosy University, Sarasota Campus	M,D,O
Argosy University, Tampa Campus	M,D,O
Argosy University, Twin Cities Campus	M,D
Avila University	M
Azusa Pacific University	M
Baldwin-Wallace College	M
Barry University	O
Baylor University	M
Benedictine University	M
Bernard M. Baruch College of the City University of New York	M
Boston University	M
Brandeis University	M,D
California Lutheran University	M,O
California State University, East Bay	M
California State University, Fullerton	M
California State University, Los Angeles	M
Central Connecticut State University	M
Central Michigan University	M
City University of Seattle	M,O
Clark Atlanta University	M,D
Clark University	M
Cleveland State University	M,D,O
Columbia University	M
Concordia University Wisconsin	M
Daemen College	M
Dallas Baptist University	M
DePaul University	M
Dominican University of California	M
Drury University	M
D'Youville College	M
Eastern Michigan University	M
Emerson College	M
Fairfield University	M,O
Fairleigh Dickinson University, College at Florham	M,O
Fairleigh Dickinson University, Metropolitan Campus	M
Florida Atlantic University	M
Florida International University	M
The George Washington University	M,D
Georgia Institute of Technology	M,O
Georgia State University	M
Golden Gate University	M,D,O
Hawai'i Pacific University	M
Hofstra University	M,O
Hope International University	M
Howard University	M
Illinois Institute of Technology	M
Inter American University of Puerto Rico, Metropolitan Campus	M,D
Inter American University of Puerto Rico, San Germán Campus	M,D
Iona College	M,O
Johnson & Wales University	M
Kean University	M
Lindenwood University	M
Long Island University, C.W. Post Campus	M,O
Lynn University	M,D
Madonna University	M
Manhattanville College	M
Metropolitan State University	M
Minnesota State University Mankato	M
Montclair State University	M
Monterey Institute of International Studies	M
Newman University	M
New Mexico Highlands University	M
The New School: A University	M
New York Institute of Technology	M,O
New York University	M,D
Nova Southeastern University	M,D
Oakland University	M,O
Oklahoma City University	M
Oral Roberts University	M
Our Lady of the Lake University of San Antonio	M
Pace University	M
Park University	M
Pepperdine University	M
Philadelphia University	M
Pontifical Catholic University of Puerto Rico	M,D
Portland State University	M
Purdue University	M
Quinnipiac University	M
Regis University	M,O
Rochester Institute of Technology	M
Roosevelt University	M
Rutgers, The State University of New Jersey, Newark	M,D

St. Edward's University	M,O
St. John's University (NY)	M,O
Saint Joseph's University	M
Saint Louis University	M,D
Saint Mary's University of Minnesota	M
St. Mary's University of San Antonio	M
Saint Peter's College	M
St. Thomas University	M,O
San Diego State University	M
Schiller International University (United States)	M
School for International Training	M
Seton Hall University	M,O
Southeastern University	M
Southeast Missouri State University	M
Southern New Hampshire University	M,D,O
Stevens Institute of Technology	M
Suffolk University	M,D
Sul Ross State University	M
Temple University	M,D
Texas A&M International University	M
Texas A&M University–Corpus Christi	M
Texas Christian University	M
Texas Tech University	M
Tufts University	M,D
Universidad Metropolitana	M
The University of Akron	M
University of Chicago	M
University of Colorado at Colorado Springs	M
University of Colorado Denver	M
University of Dallas	M
University of Denver	M
The University of Findlay	M
University of Florida	P,M,D
University of Hawaii at Manoa	M,D
University of Houston–Victoria	M
University of Kentucky	M
University of La Verne	M
University of Maryland University College	M,O
University of Memphis	M
University of Miami	M
University of Minnesota, Twin Cities Campus	M
University of New Haven	M
University of New Mexico	M
University of Oklahoma	M
University of Pennsylvania	M
University of Phoenix–Central Florida Campus	M
University of Phoenix–Denver Campus	M
University of Phoenix–Fort Lauderdale Campus	M
University of Phoenix–Hawaii Campus	M
University of Phoenix–New Mexico Campus	M
University of Phoenix–North Florida Campus	M
University of Phoenix–Oregon Campus	M
University of Phoenix–Philadelphia Campus	M
University of Phoenix–Sacramento Valley Campus	M
University of Phoenix–San Diego Campus	M
University of Phoenix–Southern Arizona Campus	M
University of Phoenix–West Florida Campus	M
University of Phoenix–West Michigan Campus	M
University of Pittsburgh	M
University of Rhode Island	M,D
University of San Francisco	M
The University of Scranton	M
University of South Carolina	M
University of Southern California	M
The University of Tampa	M
The University of Texas at Dallas	M,D
The University of Texas at San Antonio	M,D
University of the Incarnate Word	M,O
The University of Toledo	M
University of Washington	M,D,O
University of Wisconsin–Whitewater	M
Upper Iowa University	M
Valparaiso University	M
Wagner College	M
Washington State University	M,D,O
Wayland Baptist University	M
Webster University	M
Western International University	M
Whitworth University	M
Wilkes University	M
Wright State University	M
Xavier University	M

■ INTERNATIONAL DEVELOPMENT

American University	M,D,O
Andrews University	M
Brandeis University	M
Clark Atlanta University	M,D
Clark University	M
Cornell University	M
Duke University	M,O
Fordham University	M,O
The George Washington University	M
Harvard University	M
Hope International University	M
The Johns Hopkins University	M,D,O
The New School: A University	M
Ohio University	M
Rutgers, The State University of New Jersey, Camden	M
Texas A&M University	M,O
Tufts University	M,D
Tulane University	M,D
University of Florida	M,D,O
University of Pittsburgh	M,O
University of Southern Mississippi	M,D

■ INTERNATIONAL HEALTH

Boston University	M,D,O
Brandeis University	M
Emory University	M,D
The George Washington University	M
Harvard University	M,D
The Johns Hopkins University	M,D
New York University	M,D
Tufts University	M,D
Tulane University	M,D
University of Michigan	M,D
University of South Florida	M,D
University of Washington	M,D
Yale University	M

■ INTERNET AND INTERACTIVE MULTIMEDIA

Alfred University	M
Brooklyn College of the City University of New York	M,O
California State University, East Bay	M
Chestnut Hill College	M,O
City University of Seattle	M,O
Duquesne University	M,O
Georgetown University	M
Georgia Institute of Technology	M
Indiana University–Purdue University Indianapolis	M,D
Long Island University, C.W. Post Campus	M
National University	M
New Jersey Institute of Technology	M
New Mexico Highlands University	M
New York Institute of Technology	M,O
New York University	M
Polytechnic University, Brooklyn Campus	M,O
Quinnipiac University	M
Robert Morris University	M
Rochester Institute of Technology	M,O
Sacred Heart University	M,O
San Diego State University	M
Southern Polytechnic State University	M
Syracuse University	M
Towson University	M,D,O
University of Central Florida	M
University of Florida	M,D
University of Georgia	M
University of Miami	M
University of San Francisco	M
University of Southern California	M,D
Virginia Commonwealth University	M,D,O
Western Illinois University	M,O
Wilmington University (DE)	M

■ INVESTMENT MANAGEMENT

Boston University	M
Gannon University	O
The George Washington University	M,D
The Johns Hopkins University	M,O
Lindenwood University	M
Lynn University	M,D
Marywood University	M
Pace University	M
Quinnipiac University	M
The University of Iowa	M
University of Tulsa	M
University of Wisconsin–Madison	D

■ ITALIAN

Boston College	M,D
Brown University	M,D
The Catholic University of America	M,D
Central Connecticut State University	M,O
Columbia University	M,D
Cornell University	D
Florida State University	M
Graduate School and University Center of the City University of New York	M,D
Harvard University	M,D
Hunter College of the City University of New York	M
Indiana University Bloomington	M,D
The Johns Hopkins University	D
New York University	M,D
Northwestern University	D,O
The Ohio State University	M,D
Princeton University	D
Queens College of the City University of New York	M
Rutgers, The State University of New Jersey, New Brunswick	M,D
San Francisco State University	M
Stanford University	M,D
State University of New York at Binghamton	M
Stony Brook University, State University of New York	M,D
University at Albany, State University of New York	M

University of California, Berkeley	D
University of California, Los Angeles	M,D
University of Chicago	M,D
University of Connecticut	M,D
University of Massachusetts Amherst	M,D
The University of North Carolina at Chapel Hill	M,D
University of Notre Dame	M
University of Oregon	M
University of Pennsylvania	M,D
University of Pittsburgh	M
The University of Tennessee	D
University of Virginia	M
University of Washington	M,D
University of Wisconsin–Madison	M,D
University of Wisconsin–Milwaukee	M
Wayne State University	M
Yale University	D

■ JAPANESE

Cornell University	M,D
Harvard University	D
Indiana University Bloomington	M,D
Kent State University	M,D
The Ohio State University	M,D
Portland State University	M
San Francisco State University	M
Stanford University	M,D
University at Buffalo, the State University of New York	M,D,O
University of California, Berkeley	D
University of California, Irvine	M,D
University of Colorado at Boulder	M,D
University of Hawaii at Manoa	M,D
University of Kansas	M
University of Maryland, College Park	M,D
University of Massachusetts Amherst	M
University of Oregon	M,D
University of Washington	M,D
University of Wisconsin–Madison	M,D
Washington University in St. Louis	M,D

■ JEWISH STUDIES

Brandeis University	M,D
Brooklyn College of the City University of New York	M
Brown University	M,D
Columbia University	M,D
Cornell University	M,D
Emory University	M
Gratz College	M
Harvard University	M,D
New York University	M,D,O
Seton Hall University	M
Touro College	M
University of California, Berkeley	D
University of California, San Diego	M,D
University of Connecticut	M
University of Maryland, College Park	M
The University of Montana	M
University of Wisconsin–Madison	M,D
University of Wisconsin–Milwaukee	M
Washington University in St. Louis	M
Yeshiva University	M,D

■ JOURNALISM

American University	M
Angelo State University	M
Arizona State University	M
Arkansas State University	M
Arkansas Tech University	M
Ball State University	M
Baylor University	M
Bob Jones University	P,M,D,O
Boston University	M
California State University, Fresno	M
California State University, Fullerton	M
California State University, Northridge	M
Columbia College Chicago	M
Columbia University	M,D
Drake University	M
Drexel University	M
Emerson College	M
Florida Agricultural and Mechanical University	M
Harvard University	M,O
Hofstra University	M
Indiana University Bloomington	M,D
Iona College	M
Iowa State University of Science and Technology	M
Kent State University	M
Marquette University	M
Marshall University	M
Michigan State University	M
Middle Tennessee State University	M
New York Institute of Technology	M,O
New York University	M,D,O
Northeastern University	M
Northwestern University	M
Ohio University	M,D
Point Park University	M
Polytechnic University, Brooklyn Campus	M
Quinnipiac University	M
Regent University	M,D
Roosevelt University	M
South Dakota State University	M
Southern Illinois University Carbondale	D
Stanford University	M,D
Syracuse University	M
Temple University	M
Texas A&M University	M
Texas Christian University	M
Texas Southern University	M
The University of Alabama	M
University of Arkansas	M
University of California, Berkeley	M
University of Colorado at Boulder	M,D
University of Florida	M
University of Georgia	M,D
University of Illinois at Springfield	M
University of Illinois at Urbana–Champaign	M
The University of Iowa	M
University of Kansas	M
University of Maryland, College Park	M,D
University of Memphis	M
University of Miami	M,D
University of Mississippi	M
University of Missouri–Columbia	M,D
The University of Montana	M
University of Nebraska–Lincoln	M
University of Nevada, Las Vegas	M
University of Nevada, Reno	M
University of North Texas	M
University of Oklahoma	M
University of Oregon	M,D
University of South Carolina	M,D
University of Southern California	M
The University of Tennessee	M,D
The University of Texas at Austin	M,D
The University of Texas at Tyler	M
University of Wisconsin–Madison	M,D
University of Wisconsin–Milwaukee	M
Virginia Commonwealth University	M
West Virginia University	M

■ KINESIOLOGY AND MOVEMENT STUDIES

Angelo State University	M
Arizona State University	M,D
Barry University	M
Bowling Green State University	M
California Baptist University	M
California Polytechnic State University, San Luis Obispo	M
California State Polytechnic University, Pomona	M
California State University, Chico	M
California State University, Fresno	M
California State University, Long Beach	M
California State University, Los Angeles	M
California State University, Northridge	M
California State University, San Bernardino	M
Columbia University	M,D
Florida State University	M,D
Fresno Pacific University	M
Georgia Southern University	M
Humboldt State University	M
Indiana University Bloomington	M,D,O
Inter American University of Puerto Rico, San Germán Campus	M
James Madison University	M
Kansas State University	M
Lamar University	M
Louisiana State University and Agricultural and Mechanical College	M,D
Michigan State University	M,D
Midwestern State University	M
Mississippi State University	M
New York University	M,D
Old Dominion University	D
Oregon State University	M
Penn State University Park	M,D
Saint Mary's College of California	M
Sam Houston State University	M
San Francisco State University	M
San Jose State University	M
Sonoma State University	M
Southeastern Louisiana University	M
Southern Illinois University Edwardsville	M,O
Southwestern Oklahoma State University	M
Springfield College	M,D
Stephen F. Austin State University	M
Temple University	M,D
Tennessee Technological University	M
Texas A&M University	M,D
Texas A&M University–Commerce	M,D
Texas A&M University–Corpus Christi	M,D
Texas A&M University–Kingsville	M
Texas Christian University	M
Texas Woman's University	M,D
The University of Alabama	M,D
University of Arkansas	M,D
University of Central Arkansas	M
University of Colorado at Boulder	M,D
University of Connecticut	M,D
University of Delaware	M,D
University of Florida	M,D
University of Georgia	M,D,O
University of Hawaii at Manoa	M
University of Houston	M,D
University of Illinois at Chicago	M
University of Illinois at Urbana–Champaign	M,D

University of Kentucky M,D
University of Maine M
University of Maryland, College Park M,D
University of Massachusetts Amherst M,D
University of Michigan M,D
University of Minnesota, Twin Cities Campus M,D
University of Nevada, Las Vegas M
University of New Hampshire M
The University of North Carolina at Chapel Hill M,D
The University of North Carolina at Charlotte M
University of North Dakota M
University of North Texas M
University of Southern California M,D
The University of Tennessee M,D
The University of Texas at Austin M,D
The University of Texas at El Paso M
The University of Texas at Tyler M
The University of Texas of the Permian Basin M
The University of Texas–Pan American M
University of the Incarnate Word M,D
University of Virginia M,D
University of Wisconsin–Madison M,D
University of Wisconsin–Milwaukee M
Washington University in St. Louis D
Wayne State University M
West Chester University of Pennsylvania M,O
Western Illinois University M

■ LANDSCAPE ARCHITECTURE

Arizona State University M
Auburn University M
Ball State University M
California State Polytechnic University, Pomona M
Chatham University M
City College of the City University of New York M,O
Clemson University M
Columbia University M
Cornell University M
Florida Agricultural and Mechanical University M
Florida International University M
Harvard University M,D
Iowa State University of Science and Technology M
Kansas State University M
Louisiana State University and Agricultural and Mechanical College M
Mississippi State University M
Morgan State University M
North Carolina State University M
The Ohio State University M
Oklahoma State University M,D
Penn State University Park M
State University of New York College of Environmental Science and Forestry M
Texas A&M University M,D
Texas Tech University M
The University of Arizona M
University of California, Berkeley M
University of Colorado Denver M
University of Florida M,D
University of Georgia M
University of Idaho M
University of Illinois at Urbana–Champaign M,D
University of Massachusetts Amherst M
University of Michigan M,D
University of Minnesota, Twin Cities Campus M
University of New Mexico M
University of Oklahoma M
University of Oregon M
University of Pennsylvania M,O
University of Southern California M,O
The University of Tennessee M
The University of Texas at Arlington M
University of Virginia M
University of Washington M
University of Wisconsin–Madison M
Utah State University M
Virginia Polytechnic Institute and State University M
Washington State University M,D

■ LATIN AMERICAN STUDIES

American University M,O
Arizona State University M,D
Brown University M,D
California State University, Los Angeles M
Columbia University O
Cornell University M,D
Duke University M,D,O
Florida International University M
Fordham University O
Georgetown University M
The George Washington University M
Indiana University Bloomington M
The Johns Hopkins University M,D,O
La Salle University M
Michigan State University D
New York University M,O
Ohio University M
San Diego State University M
Tulane University M,D
University at Albany, State University of New York M,O
The University of Arizona M
University of California, Berkeley M,D
University of California, Los Angeles M
University of California, San Diego M
University of California, Santa Barbara M,D
University of Central Florida M,O
University of Chicago M
University of Connecticut M
University of Florida M,O
University of Illinois at Urbana–Champaign M
University of Kansas M,O
University of Massachusetts Dartmouth M,D
University of New Mexico M,D
The University of North Carolina at Chapel Hill M,D,O
University of Notre Dame M
University of Pittsburgh O
University of South Florida M,O
The University of Texas at Austin M,D
University of Wisconsin–Madison M
Vanderbilt University M
West Virginia University M,D

■ LAW

American University P,M,O
Arizona State University P
Barry University P
Baylor University P
Boston College P
Boston University P,M
Brigham Young University P,M
Campbell University P
Capital University P,M
Case Western Reserve University P,M
The Catholic University of America P
Chapman University P,M
Cleveland State University P,M
The College of William and Mary P,M
Columbia University P,M,D
Cornell University P,M,D
Creighton University P,M
DePaul University P,M
Drake University P
Duke University P,M,D
Duquesne University P,M
Elon University P
Emory University P,M,O
Florida Agricultural and Mechanical University P
Florida International University P
Florida State University P
Fordham University P,M
Friends University M
George Mason University P,M
Georgetown University P,M,D
The George Washington University P,M,D
Georgia State University P
Golden Gate University P,M,D
Gonzaga University P
Hamline University P,M
Harvard University P,M,D
Hodges University M
Hofstra University P,M
Howard University P,M
Illinois Institute of Technology P,M
Indiana University Bloomington P,M,D,O
Indiana University–Purdue University Indianapolis P,M,D
John F. Kennedy University P
The Johns Hopkins University M,D,O
Lewis & Clark College P,M
Liberty University P
Louisiana State University and Agricultural and Mechanical College P,M
Loyola Marymount University P,M
Loyola University Chicago P,M,D
Loyola University New Orleans P
Marquette University P
Mercer University P
Mississippi College P,O
New College of California P
New York University P,M,D,O
North Carolina Central University P
Northeastern University P
Northern Illinois University P
Northern Kentucky University P
Northwestern University P,M,O
Nova Southeastern University P,M
The Ohio State University P,M
Oklahoma City University P
Pace University P,M,D
Park University M
Pepperdine University P
Pontifical Catholic University of Puerto Rico P
Quinnipiac University P,M
Regent University P,M
Roger Williams University P
Rutgers, The State University of New Jersey, Camden P
Rutgers, The State University of New Jersey, Newark P
St. John's University (NY) P
Saint Joseph's University M,O
Saint Louis University P,M
St. Mary's University of San Antonio P

St. Thomas University	P,M
Samford University	P,M
Santa Clara University	P,M,O
Seattle University	P
Seton Hall University	P,M
Southern Illinois University Carbondale	P,M
Southern Methodist University	P,M,D
Southern University and Agricultural and Mechanical College	P
Stanford University	P,M,D
Stetson University	P,M
Suffolk University	P,M
Syracuse University	P
Temple University	P,M
Texas Southern University	P
Texas Tech University	P
Texas Wesleyan University	P
Touro College	P,M
Trinity International University	P
Tulane University	P,M,D
University at Buffalo, the State University of New York	P,M
The University of Akron	P
The University of Alabama	P,M
The University of Arizona	P,M
University of Arkansas	P,M
University of Arkansas at Little Rock	P
University of Baltimore	P,M
University of California, Berkeley	P,M,D
University of California, Davis	P,M
University of California, Los Angeles	P,M
University of Chicago	P,M,D
University of Cincinnati	P
University of Colorado at Boulder	P
University of Connecticut	P
University of Dayton	P,M
University of Denver	P,M
University of Detroit Mercy	P
University of Florida	P,M,D
University of Georgia	P,M
University of Hawaii at Manoa	P,O
University of Houston	P,M
University of Idaho	P
University of Illinois at Urbana–Champaign	P,M,D
The University of Iowa	P,M
University of Kansas	P
University of Kentucky	P
University of La Verne	P
University of Louisville	P
University of Maryland, College Park	
University of Memphis	P
University of Miami	P,M
University of Michigan	P,M,D
University of Minnesota, Twin Cities Campus	P,M
University of Mississippi	P
University of Missouri–Columbia	P,M
University of Missouri–Kansas City	P,M
The University of Montana	P
University of Nebraska–Lincoln	P,M
University of Nevada, Las Vegas	P
University of New Mexico	P
The University of North Carolina at Chapel Hill	P
University of North Dakota	P
University of Notre Dame	P,M,D
University of Oklahoma	P
University of Oregon	P,M
University of Pennsylvania	P,M,D
University of Pittsburgh	P,M,O
University of Puerto Rico, Río Piedras	P,M
University of Richmond	P
University of St. Thomas (MN)	P
University of San Diego	P,M,O
University of San Francisco	P,M
University of South Carolina	P
The University of South Dakota	P
University of Southern California	P,M
University of Southern Maine	P
The University of Tennessee	P
The University of Texas at Austin	P,M
University of the District of Columbia	P
University of the Pacific	P,M,D
The University of Toledo	P,M
University of Tulsa	P,M,O
University of Utah	P,M
University of Virginia	P,M,D
University of Washington	P,M,D
University of Wisconsin–Madison	M,D
University of Wyoming	P
Valparaiso University	P,M
Vanderbilt University	P,M,D
Villanova University	P
Wake Forest University	P,M
Washburn University	P
Washington University in St. Louis	P,M,D
Wayne State University	P,M,D
Western New England College	P,M
West Virginia University	P
Widener University	P,M,D
Willamette University	P,M
Yale University	P,M,D
Yeshiva University	P,M

■ LEGAL AND JUSTICE STUDIES

American University	M,D,O
Arizona State University	M,D
Boston University	M
California University of Pennsylvania	M
Capital University	M
Case Western Reserve University	P,M
The Catholic University of America	D,O
College of Charleston	M,O
DePaul University	M,O
The George Washington University	M,O
Golden Gate University	P,M,D
Governors State University	M
Hofstra University	P,M
John Jay College of Criminal Justice of the City University of New York	M,D
Marygrove College	M
Marymount University	M,O
Mississippi College	M,O
Montclair State University	M,O
New York University	M,D
Northeastern University	M,D
Nova Southeastern University	M
Pace University	P,M,D
Prairie View A&M University	M,D
Quinnipiac University	M
Regis University	M,O
The Richard Stockton College of New Jersey	O
Rutgers, The State University of New Jersey, New Brunswick	D
St. John's University (NY)	M
Salve Regina University	M
San Francisco State University	M,O
Southern Illinois University Carbondale	P,M
State University of New York at Binghamton	M,D
Texas State University-San Marcos	M
University of Baltimore	M
University of California, Berkeley	D
University of Denver	M,O
University of Illinois at Springfield	M
University of Nebraska–Lincoln	M
University of Nevada, Reno	M
University of New Hampshire	M
University of Pittsburgh	M,O
University of San Diego	P,M,O
University of the Pacific	P,M,D
University of Washington	P,M,D
University of Wisconsin–Madison	M
Weber State University	M
Webster University	M
West Virginia University	M

■ LEISURE STUDIES

Aurora University	M
Bowling Green State University	M
California State University, Long Beach	M
Central Michigan University	M
East Carolina University	M
Florida International University	M
Gallaudet University	M
Howard University	M
Indiana University Bloomington	M,D,O
Murray State University	M
Oklahoma State University	M,D,O
Penn State University Park	M,D
Prescott College	M
San Francisco State University	M
Southeast Missouri State University	M
Southern Connecticut State University	M
State University of New York College at Brockport	M
Temple University	M
Texas State University-San Marcos	M
Universidad Metropolitana	M
University of Connecticut	M,D
University of Illinois at Urbana–Champaign	M,D
The University of Iowa	M
University of Memphis	M
University of Minnesota, Twin Cities Campus	M,D
University of Mississippi	M,D
University of Nevada, Las Vegas	M
The University of North Carolina at Chapel Hill	M
University of Northern Iowa	M,D
University of North Texas	M,O
University of South Alabama	M
University of Southern Mississippi	M,D
The University of Tennessee	M,D
The University of Toledo	M
University of Utah	M,D
University of West Florida	M

■ LIBERAL STUDIES

Abilene Christian University	M
Alaska Pacific University	M
Alvernia College	M
Antioch University McGregor	M
Armstrong Atlantic State University	M
Auburn University Montgomery	M
Barry University	M
Boston University	M
Bradley University	M
Brooklyn College of the City University of New York	M
California State University, Sacramento	M
Cardinal Stritch University	M
Clark University	M
College of Notre Dame of Maryland	M
College of Staten Island of the City University of New York	M
Columbia University	M
Concordia University Chicago (IL)	M

Converse College M
Creighton University M
Dallas Baptist University M
Dartmouth College M
DePaul University M
Dowling College M
Duke University M
Duquesne University M
East Tennessee State University M
Fitchburg State College M
Florida Atlantic University M
Florida International University M
Fordham University M
Fort Hays State University M
Friends University M
George Mason University M
Georgetown University M
Graduate School and University Center of the City University of New York M
Hamline University M,O
Harvard University M,O
Henderson State University M
Hollins University M,O
Houston Baptist University M
Indiana University–Purdue University Fort Wayne M
Indiana University–Purdue University Indianapolis M,D,O
Indiana University South Bend M
Indiana University Southeast M
Jacksonville State University M
The Johns Hopkins University M,O
Kean University M
Kent State University M
Lock Haven University of Pennsylvania M
Louisiana State University and Agricultural and Mechanical College M
Louisiana State University in Shreveport M
Loyola College in Maryland M
Madonna University M
Manhattanville College M
McDaniel College M
Minnesota State University Moorhead M
Mississippi College M
Monmouth University M
Nazareth College of Rochester M
The New School: A University M
North Carolina State University M
North Central College M
Northern Arizona University M
Northern Kentucky University M
Northwestern University M
Oakland University M
Ohio Dominican University M
Oklahoma City University M
Queens College of the City University of New York M
Ramapo College of New Jersey M
Rollins College M
Rutgers, The State University of New Jersey, Camden M
Rutgers, The State University of New Jersey, Newark M
St. Edward's University M,O
St. John's College (MD) M
St. John's College (NM) M
St. John's University (NY) M
Saint Mary's College of California M
San Diego State University M
Spring Hill College M
State University of New York at Plattsburgh M
State University of New York College at Brockport M
State University of New York Empire State College M
Stony Brook University, State University of New York M,O
Tarleton State University M
Temple University M
Texas Christian University M
Towson University M
Tulane University M
University at Albany, State University of New York M
University of Arkansas at Little Rock M
University of Delaware M
University of Denver M,O
University of Detroit Mercy M
The University of Findlay M
University of Maine M
University of Memphis M
University of Miami M
University of Michigan–Dearborn M
University of Minnesota, Duluth M
University of New Hampshire M
The University of North Carolina at Charlotte M
The University of North Carolina at Greensboro M
The University of North Carolina Wilmington M
University of Oklahoma M
University of Pennsylvania M
University of Richmond M
University of St. Thomas (TX) M
University of Southern Indiana M
University of South Florida M
The University of Toledo M
University of Wisconsin–Milwaukee M
Ursuline College M
Utica College M
Valparaiso University M,O
Vanderbilt University M
Villanova University M
Wake Forest University M
Washburn University M
West Virginia University M
Wichita State University M
Widener University M
Winthrop University M

■ LIBRARY SCIENCE

Appalachian State University M
Azusa Pacific University M
The Catholic University of America M
Chicago State University M
Clarion University of Pennsylvania M,O
College of St. Catherine M
Columbia University M
Dominican University M,O
Drexel University M,D,O
East Carolina University M,O
Emporia State University M,D,O
Florida State University M,D,O
Gratz College O
Indiana University Bloomington M,D,O
Indiana University–Purdue University Indianapolis M
Inter American University of Puerto Rico, San Germán Campus M
Kent State University M
Kutztown University of Pennsylvania M,O
Long Island University, C.W. Post Campus M,D,O
Louisiana State University and Agricultural and Mechanical College M,O
Mansfield University of Pennsylvania M
Marywood University M,O
McDaniel College M
North Carolina Central University M
Old Dominion University M
Queens College of the City University of New York M,O
Rowan University M
Rutgers, The State University of New Jersey, New Brunswick M
St. John's University (NY) M,O
Sam Houston State University M
San Jose State University M
Simmons College M,D,O
Southern Connecticut State University M,O
Syracuse University M,O
Tennessee Technological University M,O
Texas Woman's University M,D
Trevecca Nazarene University M
University at Albany, State University of New York M,D,O
University at Buffalo, the State University of New York M,O
The University of Alabama M,D
The University of Arizona M,D
University of California, Los Angeles M,D,O
University of Central Arkansas M
University of Central Missouri M,O
University of Denver M,D,O
University of Hawaii at Manoa M,D,O
University of Houston–Clear Lake M
University of Illinois at Urbana–Champaign M,D,O
The University of Iowa M
University of Kentucky M
University of Maryland, College Park
University of Michigan M,D
University of Missouri–Columbia M,D,O
University of Nevada, Las Vegas M,D,O
The University of North Carolina at Chapel Hill M,D,O
The University of North Carolina at Greensboro M
University of North Texas M,D
University of Oklahoma M,O
University of Pittsburgh M,D,O
University of Puerto Rico, Río Piedras M,O
University of Rhode Island M
University of South Carolina M,O
University of Southern Mississippi M,O
University of South Florida M
The University of Texas at Austin M,D
University of Washington M,D
University of Wisconsin–Madison M,D,O
University of Wisconsin–Milwaukee M,O
Valdosta State University M
Wayne State University M,O
Wright State University M

■ LIMNOLOGY

Baylor University M,D
Cornell University D
University of Florida M,D
University of Wisconsin–Madison M,D
William Paterson University of New Jersey M

■ LINGUISTICS

Arizona State University M,D
Ball State University D
Biola University M,D,O
Boston College M

Boston University	M,D
Brigham Young University	M,O
Brown University	M,D
California State University, Fresno	M
California State University, Fullerton	M
California State University, Long Beach	M
California State University, Northridge	M
Carnegie Mellon University	M,D
Cornell University	M,D
Eastern Michigan University	M
Florida International University	M
Gallaudet University	M
George Mason University	M
Georgetown University	M,D,O
Georgia State University	M,D
Graduate School and University Center of the City University of New York	M,D
Harvard University	D
Hofstra University	M
Indiana State University	M,O
Indiana University Bloomington	M,D
Indiana University of Pennsylvania	M,D
Louisiana State University and Agricultural and Mechanical College	M,D
Massachusetts Institute of Technology	D
Michigan State University	M,D
Montclair State University	M
New York University	M,D
Northeastern Illinois University	M
Northern Arizona University	M,D,O
Northwestern University	M,D
Oakland University	M,O
The Ohio State University	M,D
Ohio University	M
Old Dominion University	M
Purdue University	M,D
Queens College of the City University of New York	M
Rice University	M,D
Rutgers, The State University of New Jersey, New Brunswick	D
San Diego State University	M,O
San Francisco State University	M
San Jose State University	M,O
Southern Illinois University Carbondale	M
Stanford University	M,D
Stony Brook University, State University of New York	M,D
Syracuse University	M
Temple University	M
Texas Tech University	M
University at Buffalo, the State University of New York	M,D
University of Alaska Fairbanks	M
The University of Arizona	M,D
University of California, Berkeley	D
University of California, Davis	M,D
University of California, Los Angeles	M,D
University of California, San Diego	D
University of California, Santa Barbara	M,D
University of California, Santa Cruz	M,D
University of Chicago	M,D
University of Colorado at Boulder	M,D
University of Colorado Denver	M,O
University of Connecticut	D
University of Delaware	M,D
University of Florida	M,D,O
University of Georgia	M,D
University of Hawaii at Manoa	M,D
University of Houston	M,D
University of Illinois at Chicago	M
University of Illinois at Urbana–Champaign	M,D
The University of Iowa	M,D
University of Kansas	M,D
University of Maryland, Baltimore County	M
University of Maryland, College Park	M,D
University of Massachusetts Amherst	M,D
University of Massachusetts Boston	M
University of Michigan	D
University of Minnesota, Twin Cities Campus	M,D
University of Missouri–St. Louis	M,O
The University of Montana	M,D
University of New Hampshire	M,D
University of New Mexico	M,D
The University of North Carolina at Chapel Hill	M,D
University of North Dakota	M
University of Oregon	M,D
University of Pennsylvania	M,D
University of Pittsburgh	M,D
University of Puerto Rico, Río Piedras	M
University of South Carolina	M,D,O
University of Southern California	M,D
University of South Florida	M
The University of Tennessee	D
The University of Texas at Arlington	M,D
The University of Texas at Austin	M,D
The University of Texas at El Paso	M
University of Utah	M,D
University of Virginia	M
University of Washington	M,D
University of Wisconsin–Madison	M,D
Wayne State University	M
West Virginia University	M
Yale University	D

■ LOGISTICS

Benedictine University	M
Case Western Reserve University	M,D
Colorado Technical University—Colorado Springs	M,D
East Carolina University	M,D,O
Florida Institute of Technology	M
George Mason University	M
The George Washington University	M
Georgia College & State University	M
Massachusetts Institute of Technology	M,D
North Dakota State University	M,D
The Ohio State University	M
Penn State University Park	M,D
Stevens Institute of Technology	M,D,O
Universidad del Turabo	M
University at Buffalo, the State University of New York	M,D,O
University of Alaska Anchorage	M,O
University of Arkansas	M
University of Dallas	M
University of Houston	M
University of Minnesota, Twin Cities Campus	M,D
University of Missouri–St. Louis	M,D,O
University of New Hampshire	M,D
University of New Haven	M,O
The University of Tennessee	M,D
The University of Texas at Arlington	M
University of Washington	O
Virginia Polytechnic Institute and State University	M,D
Wilmington University (DE)	M
Wright State University	M

■ MANAGEMENT INFORMATION SYSTEMS

Adelphi University	M
American InterContinental University (CA)	M
American InterContinental University Dunwoody Campus	M
American University	M,O
Argosy University, Orange County Campus	M,D,O
Argosy University, Sarasota Campus	M,D,O
Argosy University, Tampa Campus	M,D,O
Argosy University, Twin Cities Campus	M,D
Arizona State University	M,D
Arizona State University at the Polytechnic Campus	M
Arkansas State University	M,O
Auburn University	M,D
Avila University	M
Barry University	O
Baylor University	M
Bellarmine University	M
Bellevue University	M
Benedictine University	M
Bernard M. Baruch College of the City University of New York	M,D
Boise State University	M
Boston University	D
Bowie State University	M,O
Brigham Young University	M
Bryant University	M,O
California Lutheran University	M,O
California State University, East Bay	M
California State University, Fullerton	M
California State University, Los Angeles	M
California State University, Sacramento	M
Capella University	M,D,O
Carnegie Mellon University	M,D
Case Western Reserve University	M,D
Central Michigan University	M,O
Charleston Southern University	M
City University of Seattle	M,O
Claremont Graduate University	M,D,O
Clarkson University	M
Clark University	M
Cleveland State University	M,D
The College of St. Scholastica	M
Colorado State University	M
Colorado Technical University—Colorado Springs	M,D
Colorado Technical University—Denver	M
Colorado Technical University—Sioux Falls	M
Concordia University Wisconsin	M
Creighton University	M
Dallas Baptist University	M
DePaul University	M,D
Dominican University	M
Duquesne University	M
East Carolina University	M,D,O
Eastern Michigan University	M
Edinboro University of Pennsylvania	M,O
Fairfield University	M,O
Fairleigh Dickinson University, Metropolitan Campus	M,O
Ferris State University	M
Florida Agricultural and Mechanical University	M
Florida Institute of Technology	M
Florida International University	D
Florida State University	M,D
Fordham University	M

Friends University M
The George Washington University M
Georgia College & State University M
Georgia Institute of Technology M,D,O
Georgia State University M,D
Golden Gate University M,D,O
Governors State University M
Graduate School and University Center of the City University of New York D
Grand Valley State University M
Harvard University D
Hawai'i Pacific University M
Hodges University M
Hofstra University M
Holy Family University M
Howard University M
Idaho State University M,O
Illinois Institute of Technology M,D
Illinois State University M
Indiana University South Bend M
Indiana University Southeast M,O
Inter American University of Puerto Rico, San Germán Campus M,D
Iowa State University of Science and Technology M
The Johns Hopkins University M
Kean University M
Kent State University D
Lawrence Technological University M,D
Lindenwood University M
Long Island University, C.W. Post Campus M,O
Louisiana State University and Agricultural and Mechanical College M,D
Loyola University Chicago M
Marist College M,O
Marymount University M,O
Marywood University M
Metropolitan State University M
Miami University M
Michigan State University M,D
Middle Tennessee State University M
Minnesota State University Mankato M,O
Minot State University M
Mississippi State University M
Missouri State University M
Montclair State University M
Morehead State University M
National University M
Newman University M
New York Institute of Technology M,O
New York University M,D,O
North Central College M
Northeastern University M,D
Northern Arizona University M
Northern Illinois University M
Northwestern University M
Northwest Missouri State University M
Norwich University M
Nova Southeastern University M,D
Oakland University M,O
The Ohio State University M,D
Oklahoma City University M
Oklahoma State University M,D
Pace University M
Park University M
Penn State Harrisburg M
Penn State University Park M,D
Polytechnic University, Westchester Graduate Center M,O
Pontifical Catholic University of Puerto Rico M,D
Prairie View A&M University M,D
Purdue University M,D
Quinnipiac University M
Regis University M,O
Rensselaer Polytechnic Institute M,D
Rivier College M
Robert Morris University M,D
Rochester Institute of Technology M,O
Roosevelt University M
Rutgers, The State University of New Jersey, Newark M,D
Sacred Heart University M,O
St. Edward's University M,O
St. John's University (NY) M,O
Saint Joseph's University M
Saint Peter's College M
San Diego State University M
San Jose State University M
Santa Clara University M
Schiller International University (United States) M
Seattle Pacific University M
Seton Hall University M
Shenandoah University M,O
Southeastern University M
Southern Illinois University Edwardsville M
Southern New Hampshire University M,D,O
Stevens Institute of Technology M,D,O
Stony Brook University, State University of New York M,D,O
Strayer University M
Syracuse University M,D,O
Tarleton State University M
Temple University M,D
Texas A&M International University M
Texas A&M University M,D
Texas Tech University M,D
Towson University M,D,O
Universidad del Turabo D
University at Buffalo, the State University of New York M,D,O
The University of Akron M
The University of Alabama in Huntsville M,O
The University of Arizona M,D
University of Arkansas M
University of Arkansas at Little Rock M
University of Baltimore M
University of Central Florida M
University of Central Missouri M
University of Cincinnati M
University of Colorado at Colorado Springs M
University of Colorado Denver M,D
University of Dallas M
University of Delaware M
University of Denver M
University of Detroit Mercy M
University of Florida M,D
University of Hawaii at Manoa M,D,O
University of Houston–Clear Lake M
University of Illinois at Chicago M,D
University of Illinois at Springfield M
The University of Iowa M
University of Kansas M,D
University of La Verne M
University of Maine M
University of Mary Hardin-Baylor M
University of Maryland University College M,O
University of Mary Washington M
University of Memphis M,D
University of Miami M
University of Michigan–Dearborn M
University of Minnesota, Twin Cities Campus M,D
University of Mississippi M,D
University of Missouri–St. Louis M,D
University of Nebraska at Omaha M,D
University of Nebraska–Lincoln M
University of Nevada, Las Vegas M
University of New Haven M
University of New Mexico M
The University of North Carolina at Chapel Hill D
The University of North Carolina at Greensboro M,D,O
University of North Texas M,D
University of Oklahoma M
University of Oregon M
University of Pennsylvania M,D
University of Phoenix–Central Florida Campus M
University of Phoenix–Denver Campus M
University of Phoenix–Fort Lauderdale Campus M
University of Phoenix–Hawaii Campus M
University of Phoenix–Las Vegas Campus M
University of Phoenix–Louisiana Campus M
University of Phoenix–New Mexico Campus M
University of Phoenix–North Florida Campus M
University of Phoenix M
University of Phoenix–Oregon Campus M
University of Phoenix–Philadelphia Campus M
University of Phoenix–Sacramento Valley Campus M
University of Phoenix–San Diego Campus M
University of Phoenix–Southern Arizona Campus M
University of Phoenix–Southern California Campus M
University of Phoenix–Southern Colorado Campus M
University of Phoenix–Utah Campus M
University of Phoenix–West Florida Campus M
University of Phoenix–West Michigan Campus M
University of Pittsburgh M
University of Redlands M
University of Rhode Island D
University of St. Thomas (MN) M,O
University of San Francisco M
The University of Scranton M
University of South Alabama M
University of Southern California M
University of Southern Mississippi M
University of South Florida M
The University of Tampa M
The University of Texas at Arlington M,D
The University of Texas at Austin D
The University of Texas at Dallas M
The University of Texas at San Antonio M,D
The University of Texas–Pan American M,D
The University of Toledo M
University of Virginia M
University of Wisconsin–Madison M,D
University of Wisconsin–Oshkosh M
Utah State University M,D
Virginia Commonwealth University M,D

Virginia Polytechnic Institute and State University M,D
Walden University M,D
Washington State University M,D
Wayland Baptist University M
Webster University M,D,O
Western International University M
Western New England College M
Wilmington University (DE) M
Worcester Polytechnic Institute M,D
Wright State University M
Xavier University M

■ MANAGEMENT OF TECHNOLOGY

Boston University M
Capella University M,D,O
Carlow University M
Carnegie Mellon University M,D
Central Connecticut State University M
City University of Seattle M,O
Colorado School of Mines M,D
Colorado Technical University—Colorado Springs M,D
Colorado Technical University—Denver M
Colorado Technical University—Sioux Falls M
Columbia University M
Dallas Baptist University M
East Carolina University M,D,O
Eastern Michigan University D
Embry-Riddle Aeronautical University Worldwide M
Fairfield University M
Fairleigh Dickinson University, College at Florham M,O
George Mason University M,D
The George Washington University M,D
Georgia Institute of Technology M,O
Golden Gate University M,D,O
Harvard University D
Hodges University M
Idaho State University M
Illinois Institute of Technology M
Illinois State University M
Indiana State University D
Iona College M,O
The Johns Hopkins University M,O
La Salle University M
Lawrence Technological University M,D
Marist College M,O
Marquette University M,D
Marshall University M
Mercer University M
Murray State University M
National University M
New Jersey Institute of Technology M,D
New York Institute of Technology M,O
New York University M
North Carolina Agricultural and Technical State University M
North Carolina State University D
Oklahoma State University M
Pacific Lutheran University M
Polytechnic University, Brooklyn Campus M,D
Polytechnic University, Westchester Graduate Center M
Portland State University M,D
Regis University M,O
Rensselaer Polytechnic Institute M,D
Saginaw Valley State University M
St. Ambrose University M
State University of New York Institute of Technology M
Stevens Institute of Technology M,D,O
Stony Brook University, State University of New York M,O
Sullivan University M
Texas A&M University–Commerce M
Texas State University-San Marcos M
University at Albany, State University of New York M
The University of Akron M
University of Bridgeport M
University of Cincinnati M,D
University of Colorado at Colorado Springs M
University of Dallas M
University of Delaware M
University of Denver M,O
University of Illinois at Urbana–Champaign M
University of Indianapolis M,O
University of Maryland University College M,O
University of Miami M,D
University of Minnesota, Twin Cities Campus M
University of New Hampshire M
University of New Haven M
University of New Mexico M
University of Pennsylvania M
University of Phoenix–Central Florida Campus M
University of Phoenix–Denver Campus M
University of Phoenix–Hawaii Campus M
University of Phoenix–Las Vegas Campus M
University of Phoenix–Louisiana Campus M
University of Phoenix–New Mexico Campus M
University of Phoenix M
University of Phoenix–Oregon Campus M
University of Phoenix–Philadelphia Campus M
University of Phoenix–Sacramento Valley Campus M
University of Phoenix–San Diego Campus M
University of Phoenix–Southern Arizona Campus M
University of Phoenix–Southern California Campus M
University of Phoenix–Southern Colorado Campus M
University of Phoenix–West Florida Campus M
University of Phoenix–West Michigan Campus M
University of St. Thomas (MN) M,O
The University of Scranton M
The University of Tampa M
University of Tulsa M
University of Washington M,D
University of Wisconsin–Madison M
University of Wisconsin–Stout M
University of Wisconsin–Whitewater M
Villanova University M
Walden University M,D
Westminster College (UT) M,O

■ MANAGEMENT STRATEGY AND POLICY

Azusa Pacific University M
Bernard M. Baruch College of the City University of New York M,D
Brenau University M
California State University, East Bay M
Case Western Reserve University M
Claremont Graduate University M,D,O
Clemson University M,D
DePaul University M
Dominican University of California M
Drexel University M,D,O
Duquesne University M
The George Washington University M,D
Georgia Institute of Technology M,D,O
Illinois Institute of Technology M
Lamar University M
Manhattanville College M
Mountain State University M
Neumann College M
New York Institute of Technology M,O
New York University M,D
Northwestern University D
Pace University M
Purdue University M,D
Regent University M,D,O
Roberts Wesleyan College M,O
Rutgers, The State University of New Jersey, Newark M
Stevens Institute of Technology M
Syracuse University D
Temple University M,D
Tennessee Technological University M
Towson University O
Tufts University O
The University of Arizona M,D
University of Dallas M
University of Denver M,O
University of Florida M
The University of Iowa M
University of Minnesota, Twin Cities Campus M,D
University of New Haven M
University of New Mexico M
The University of North Carolina at Chapel Hill D
University of North Texas M,D
University of Oklahoma M
University of Wisconsin–Madison M
Western International University M

■ MANUFACTURING ENGINEERING

Arizona State University at the Polytechnic Campus M
Boston University M,D
Bowling Green State University M
Bradley University M
California State University, Northridge M
Clemson University M
Cornell University M,D
Dartmouth College M,D
Drexel University M,D
East Carolina University M,D,O
Eastern Kentucky University M
East Tennessee State University M
Florida State University M,D
Grand Valley State University M
Illinois Institute of Technology M,D
Kansas State University M,D
Lawrence Technological University M,D
Lehigh University M
Louisiana Tech University M,D
Marquette University M,D
Massachusetts Institute of Technology M,D,O
Michigan State University M,D
Minnesota State University Mankato M
Missouri University of Science and Technology M
New Jersey Institute of Technology M
North Carolina State University M

North Dakota State University M,D
Northeastern University M,D
Northwestern University M
Ohio University M,D
Oklahoma State University M
Old Dominion University M,D
Oregon State University M,D
Penn State University Park M,D
Polytechnic University, Brooklyn Campus M
Portland State University M
Rensselaer Polytechnic Institute M,D
Rochester Institute of Technology M
Southern Illinois University Carbondale M
Southern Methodist University M,D
Stevens Institute of Technology M
Texas A&M University M
Texas Tech University M,D
Tufts University O
University of California, Los Angeles M
University of Central Florida M,D,O
University of Colorado at Colorado Springs M
University of Detroit Mercy M,D
The University of Iowa M,D
University of Kentucky M
University of Maryland, College Park M,D
University of Massachusetts Amherst M
University of Massachusetts Lowell M,D,O
University of Memphis M
University of Michigan M,D
University of Michigan–Dearborn M,D
University of Missouri–Columbia M,D
University of Nebraska–Lincoln M,D
University of New Mexico M
University of Rhode Island M
University of St. Thomas (MN) M,O
University of Southern California M
University of Southern Maine M
The University of Tennessee M,D
The University of Texas at Austin M,D
University of Wisconsin–Madison M
University of Wisconsin–Stout M
Villanova University M,O
Wayne State University M
Western Illinois University M
Western Michigan University M
Western New England College M
Wichita State University M,D
Worcester Polytechnic Institute M,D,O

■ MARINE AFFAIRS

Duke University M
East Carolina University D
Florida Institute of Technology M,D
Louisiana State University and Agricultural and Mechanical College M,D
Nova Southeastern University M
Oregon State University M
Stevens Institute of Technology M
University of Delaware M,D
University of Maine M
University of Miami M
University of Rhode Island M,D
University of San Diego M
University of Washington M
University of West Florida M

■ MARINE BIOLOGY

California State University, Stanislaus M
College of Charleston M
Florida Institute of Technology M
Florida State University M,D
Nicholls State University M
Northeastern University M,D
Nova Southeastern University M,D
Rutgers, The State University of New Jersey, New Brunswick M,D
San Francisco State University M
Texas State University-San Marcos M
University of Alaska Fairbanks M,D
University of California, San Diego M,D
University of California, Santa Barbara M,D
University of Colorado at Boulder M,D
University of Guam M
University of Hawaii at Manoa M,D
University of Maine M,D
University of Massachusetts Dartmouth M
University of Miami M,D
The University of North Carolina Wilmington M,D
University of Oregon M,D
University of Southern California D
University of Southern Mississippi M,D
Western Illinois University M,O

■ MARINE GEOLOGY

Cornell University M,D
Massachusetts Institute of Technology M,D
University of Delaware M,D
University of Hawaii at Manoa M,D
University of Miami M,D
University of Michigan M,D
University of Washington M,D

■ MARINE SCIENCES

American University M
California State University, East Bay M
California State University, Fresno M
California State University, Sacramento M
The College of William and Mary M,D
Cornell University M,D
Duke University M
Florida Institute of Technology M,D
Hawai'i Pacific University M
North Carolina State University M,D
Nova Southeastern University M
Oregon State University M
San Francisco State University M
San Jose State University M
Savannah State University M
Stony Brook University, State University of New York M,D
Texas A&M University–Corpus Christi D
University of California, San Diego M
University of California, Santa Barbara M,D
University of California, Santa Cruz M,D
University of Connecticut M,D
University of Delaware M,D
University of Florida M,D
University of Georgia M,D
University of Maine M,D
University of Maryland, Baltimore County M,D
University of Maryland, College Park M,D
University of Maryland Eastern Shore M,D
University of Massachusetts Amherst M
University of Massachusetts Boston D
University of Massachusetts Dartmouth M,D
University of Miami M,D
University of Michigan M,D
University of New England M
The University of North Carolina at Chapel Hill M,D
The University of North Carolina Wilmington M,D
University of Puerto Rico, Mayagüez Campus M,D
University of Rhode Island M,D
University of San Diego M
University of South Alabama M,D
University of South Carolina M,D
University of Southern California D
University of Southern Mississippi M,D
University of South Florida M,D
The University of Texas at Austin M,D
University of Wisconsin–La Crosse M
University of Wisconsin–Madison M,D
Western Washington University M

■ MARKETING

Adelphi University M
Alabama Agricultural and Mechanical University M
American InterContinental University (FL) M
American InterContinental University Buckhead Campus M
American University M
Andrews University M
Argosy University, Orange County Campus M,D,O
Argosy University, Sarasota Campus M,D,O
Argosy University, Tampa Campus M,D,O
Argosy University, Twin Cities Campus M,D
Arizona State University M,D
Avila University M
Barry University O
Bayamón Central University M
Benedictine University M
Bentley College M
Bernard M. Baruch College of the City University of New York M,D
Boston University D
Bryant University M,O
California Lutheran University M,O
California State University, East Bay M
California State University, Fullerton M
California State University, Los Angeles M
Canisius College M
Capella University M,D,O
Carnegie Mellon University D
Case Western Reserve University M,D
Central Michigan University M
City University of Seattle M,O
Clark Atlanta University M
Clark University M
Clemson University M
Cleveland State University M,D,O
Columbia University M,D
Concordia University Wisconsin M
Cornell University D
Dallas Baptist University M
Delta State University M
DePaul University M
Drexel University M,D,O
Eastern Michigan University M
Eastern University M
Emerson College M
Fairfield University M,O
Fairleigh Dickinson University, College at Florham M,O
Fairleigh Dickinson University, Metropolitan Campus M,O
Florida Agricultural and Mechanical University M
Florida Atlantic University M
Florida State University M,D
Fordham University M
Gannon University O
The George Washington University M,D
Georgia Institute of Technology M,D,O

Georgia State University M,D
Golden Gate University M,D,O
Hawai'i Pacific University M
Hofstra University M,O
Howard University M
Illinois Institute of Technology M
Indiana University Southeast M,O
Inter American University of Puerto Rico, Metropolitan Campus M,D
Inter American University of Puerto Rico, San Germán Campus M,D
Iona College M,O
The Johns Hopkins University M
Johnson & Wales University M
Kent State University D
Lindenwood University M
Long Island University, C.W. Post Campus M,O
Louisiana State University and Agricultural and Mechanical College D
Louisiana Tech University M,D
Loyola College in Maryland M
Loyola University Chicago M
Lynn University M,D
Manhattanville College M
Maryville University of Saint Louis M,O
Mercy College M
Metropolitan State University M
Miami University M
Michigan State University M,D
Middle Tennessee State University M
Minnesota State University Mankato M
Mississippi State University M,D
Montclair State University M
New Mexico State University D
New York Institute of Technology M,O
New York University M,D,O
Northeastern Illinois University M
Northwestern University M,D
Oakland University M,O
Oklahoma City University M
Oklahoma State University M,D
Old Dominion University D
Oral Roberts University M
Pace University M
Penn State University Park M,D
Philadelphia University M
Pontifical Catholic University of Puerto Rico M,D
Purdue University M,D
Quinnipiac University M
Regis University M,O
Rensselaer Polytechnic Institute M,D
Roberts Wesleyan College M,O
Rutgers, The State University of New Jersey, Newark M,D
St. Bonaventure University M,O
St. Cloud State University M
St. Edward's University M,O
St. John's University (NY) M,O
Saint Joseph's University M,O
Saint Peter's College M
St. Thomas Aquinas College M
Saint Xavier University M,O
San Diego State University M
Seton Hall University M
Southeastern University M
Southern New Hampshire University M,D,O
Stephen F. Austin State University M
Syracuse University M,D
Temple University M,D
Texas A&M University M,D
Texas Tech University M,D
Universidad del Turabo M
Universidad Metropolitana M
University at Albany, State University of New York M
The University of Akron M
The University of Alabama M,D
The University of Arizona D
University of Baltimore M
University of California, Berkeley D
University of Cincinnati M,D
University of Colorado at Boulder D
University of Colorado at Colorado Springs M
University of Colorado Denver M
University of Connecticut M,D
University of Dallas M
University of Denver M
The University of Findlay M
University of Florida M,D
University of Georgia M
University of Hawaii at Manoa M,D
University of Houston D
University of Houston–Victoria M
University of Indianapolis M,O
The University of Iowa M,D
University of La Verne M
University of Massachusetts Dartmouth M,O
University of Memphis M,D
University of Miami M
University of Minnesota, Twin Cities Campus M,D
University of Missouri–St. Louis M,O
University of Nebraska–Lincoln M,D
University of New Haven M
University of New Mexico M
The University of North Carolina at Chapel Hill D
The University of North Carolina at Charlotte M
The University of North Carolina at Greensboro M,D
University of North Texas M,D
University of Oregon D
University of Pennsylvania M,D
University of Phoenix–Central Florida Campus M
University of Phoenix–Denver Campus M
University of Phoenix–Fort Lauderdale Campus M
University of Phoenix–Hawaii Campus M
University of Phoenix–North Florida Campus M
University of Phoenix M
University of Phoenix–Sacramento Valley Campus M
University of Phoenix–Southern California Campus M
University of Phoenix–West Florida Campus M
University of Rhode Island D
University of San Francisco M
The University of Scranton M
The University of Tampa M
The University of Tennessee M,D
The University of Texas at Arlington M,D
The University of Texas at Austin D
The University of Texas at San Antonio M
The University of Toledo M
University of Wisconsin–Whitewater M
Vanderbilt University D
Virginia Commonwealth University O
Virginia Polytechnic Institute and State University M,D
Wagner College M
Walden University M,D
Washington State University M,D
Webster University M,D
Western International University M
West Virginia University M
Wilkes University M
Worcester Polytechnic Institute M,O
Wright State University M
Xavier University M
Yale University D
Youngstown State University M

■ MARKETING RESEARCH

Hofstra University M,O
Pace University M
Southern Illinois University Edwardsville M
University of Georgia M
The University of Texas at Arlington M
University of Wisconsin–Madison M

■ MARRIAGE AND FAMILY THERAPY

Abilene Christian University M,O
Antioch University New England M
Appalachian State University M
Argosy University, Orange County Campus M,D,O
Argosy University, Sarasota Campus M,D,O
Argosy University, Tampa Campus M,D
Argosy University, Twin Cities Campus M,D,O
Azusa Pacific University M,D
Barry University M,O
Brigham Young University M,D
California Baptist University M
California Lutheran University M
California State University, Chico M
California State University, Dominguez Hills M
California State University, Fresno M
California State University, Northridge M
Capella University M,D,O
Central Connecticut State University M,O
Chapman University M
The College of New Jersey O
The College of William and Mary M,D
Converse College O
Drexel University M,D
East Carolina University M
Eastern Nazarene College M
Eastern University D
East Tennessee State University M
Edgewood College M
Fairfield University M
Fitchburg State College M,O
Florida Atlantic University M,O
Florida State University M,D
Friends University M
Geneva College M
George Fox University M,O
Harding University M
Hardin-Simmons University M
Hofstra University M,O
Hope International University M
Idaho State University M,D,O
Indiana State University M,D
Indiana Wesleyan University M
Iona College M,O
Iowa State University of Science and Technology M,D
John Brown University M
Kansas State University D
Kean University O

Kutztown University of Pennsylvania M
La Salle University D
Lewis & Clark College M
Loyola Marymount University M
Mercy College M,O
Michigan State University M,D
Minnesota State University Mankato M,D,O
Mississippi College M,O
Montclair State University M,O
North Dakota State University M,D
Northwestern University M
Northwest Nazarene University M
Notre Dame de Namur University M
Nova Southeastern University M,D,O
Our Lady of the Lake University of San Antonio M,D
Pacific Lutheran University M
Palm Beach Atlantic University M
Purdue University M,D
Purdue University Calumet M
Regis University M,O
St. Cloud State University M
Saint Joseph College M,O
Saint Louis University M,D,O
Saint Mary's College of California M
Saint Mary's University of Minnesota M,O
St. Mary's University of San Antonio M,D
St. Thomas University M,O
San Francisco State University M
Seattle Pacific University M
Seton Hall University M,O
Seton Hill University M
Shippensburg University of Pennsylvania M,O
Sonoma State University M
Southern Connecticut State University M
Southern Nazarene University M
Springfield College M,O
Stetson University M
Syracuse University M,D
Texas Tech University M,D,O
Texas Woman's University M,D
Trevecca Nazarene University M
The University of Akron M
The University of Alabama at Birmingham M
University of Central Florida M,O
University of Florida M,D,O
University of Great Falls M
University of Houston–Clear Lake M
University of La Verne M
University of Louisiana at Monroe M,D
University of Louisville M,D,O
University of Mary Hardin-Baylor M
University of Maryland, College Park M,D
University of Massachusetts Boston M,O
University of Miami M,O
University of Minnesota, Twin Cities Campus M,D
University of Mobile M
University of Montevallo M
University of Nevada, Las Vegas M,O
University of New Hampshire M
The University of North Carolina at Greensboro M,D,O
University of Phoenix–Denver Campus M
University of Phoenix–Hawaii Campus M
University of Phoenix–Las Vegas Campus M
University of Phoenix–New Mexico Campus M
University of Phoenix–Sacramento Valley Campus M
University of Phoenix–San Diego Campus M
University of Phoenix–Southern Arizona Campus M,O
University of Phoenix–Southern California Campus M,O
University of Phoenix–Southern Colorado Campus M
University of Rochester M
University of St. Thomas (MN) M,D,O
University of San Diego M
University of San Francisco M,D
University of Southern California M
University of Southern Mississippi M
The University of Texas at Tyler M
University of Wisconsin–Stout M
Utah State University M,D
Valdosta State University M
Virginia Polytechnic Institute and State University M,D
Western Michigan University M,D

■ MASS COMMUNICATION

American University M
Auburn University M
Boston University M
Brigham Young University M
California State University, Fresno M
California State University, Northridge M
Central Michigan University M
The College of Saint Rose M
Florida International University M
Florida State University M,D
Fordham University M
The George Washington University M
Georgia State University M,D
Grambling State University M
Howard University M,D
Indiana University Bloomington M,D
Iona College M
Iowa State University of Science and Technology M
Jackson State University M
Kansas State University M
Kent State University M
Louisiana State University and Agricultural and Mechanical College M,D
Loyola University New Orleans M
Lynn University M,D
Marquette University M
Marshall University M
Miami University M
Middle Tennessee State University M
Murray State University M
The New School: A University M
North Dakota State University M,D
Oklahoma City University M
Oklahoma State University M
Penn State University Park M,D
Point Park University M
St. Cloud State University M
San Jose State University M
Seton Hall University M
Southern Illinois University Carbondale M
Southern Illinois University Edwardsville M
Southern University and Agricultural and Mechanical College M
Stephen F. Austin State University M
Syracuse University M,D
Temple University D
Texas State University-San Marcos M
Texas Tech University M,D
University of Arkansas at Little Rock M
University of Central Missouri M
University of Colorado at Boulder M,D
University of Denver M
University of Florida M,D
University of Georgia M,D
University of Houston M
University of Illinois at Chicago M
The University of Iowa M,D
University of Louisiana at Lafayette M
University of Michigan D
University of Minnesota, Twin Cities Campus M,D
University of Nebraska–Lincoln M
The University of North Carolina at Chapel Hill M,D
University of Oklahoma M
University of Puerto Rico, Río Piedras M
University of Southern California M,D
University of Southern Mississippi M,D
University of South Florida M
University of Wisconsin–Madison M,D
University of Wisconsin–Milwaukee M
University of Wisconsin–Stevens Point M
University of Wisconsin–Superior M
University of Wisconsin–Whitewater M
Virginia Commonwealth University M

■ MATERIALS ENGINEERING

Arizona State University M,D
Auburn University M,D
Boise State University M
California State University, Northridge M
Carnegie Mellon University M,D
Case Western Reserve University M,D
Clemson University M,D
Colorado School of Mines M,D
Columbia University M,D,O
Cornell University M,D
Dartmouth College M,D
Drexel University M,D
Florida International University M,D
Georgia Institute of Technology M,D
Illinois Institute of Technology M,D
Iowa State University of Science and Technology M,D
The Johns Hopkins University M,D
Lehigh University M,D
Massachusetts Institute of Technology M,D,O
Michigan State University M,D
Michigan Technological University M,D
New Jersey Institute of Technology M,D
New Mexico Institute of Mining and Technology M,D
North Carolina State University M,D
Northwestern University M,D,O
The Ohio State University M,D
Penn State University Park M,D
Purdue University M,D
Rensselaer Polytechnic Institute M,D
Rochester Institute of Technology M
Rutgers, The State University of New Jersey, New Brunswick M,D
San Jose State University M
Santa Clara University M,D,O
Stanford University M,D,O
State University of New York at Binghamton M,D
Stevens Institute of Technology M,D
Stony Brook University, State University of New York M,D
Texas A&M University M,D
The University of Alabama M,D
The University of Alabama at Birmingham M,D

The University of Arizona M,D
University of California, Berkeley M,D
University of California, Davis M,D
University of California, Irvine M,D
University of California, Los Angeles M,D
University of California, Santa Barbara M,D
University of Central Florida M,D
University of Cincinnati M,D
University of Connecticut M,D
University of Dayton M,D
University of Delaware M,D
University of Florida M,D,O
University of Houston M,D
University of Idaho M,D
University of Illinois at Chicago M,D
University of Illinois at Urbana–Champaign M,D
University of Maryland, College Park M,D,O
University of Massachusetts Lowell M,D
University of Michigan M,D
University of Minnesota, Twin Cities Campus M,D
University of Nebraska–Lincoln M,D
University of Pennsylvania M,D
University of Southern California M,D,O
The University of Tennessee M,D
The University of Texas at Arlington M,D
The University of Texas at Austin M,D
The University of Texas at Dallas M,D
The University of Texas at El Paso D
University of Utah M,D
University of Washington M,D
University of Wisconsin–Madison M,D
Virginia Polytechnic Institute and State University M,D
Washington State University M
Wayne State University M,D,O
Worcester Polytechnic Institute M,D,O
Wright State University M

■ MATERIALS SCIENCES

Alabama Agricultural and Mechanical University M,D
Alfred University M,D
Arizona State University M,D
Brown University M,D
California Institute of Technology M,D
Carnegie Mellon University M,D
Case Western Reserve University M,D
Clemson University M,D
Colorado School of Mines M,D
Columbia University M,D,O
Cornell University M,D
Dartmouth College M,D
Duke University M,D
The George Washington University M,D
Illinois Institute of Technology M,D
Iowa State University of Science and Technology M,D
Jackson State University M
The Johns Hopkins University M,D
Lehigh University M,D
Massachusetts Institute of Technology M,D,O
Michigan State University M,D
Missouri State University M
New Jersey Institute of Technology M,D
Norfolk State University M
North Carolina State University M,D
Northwestern University M,D,O
The Ohio State University M,D
Oregon State University M,D
Penn State University Park M,D
Polytechnic University, Brooklyn Campus M
Polytechnic University, Westchester Graduate Center D
Rensselaer Polytechnic Institute M,D
Rice University M,D
Rochester Institute of Technology M
Rutgers, The State University of New Jersey, New Brunswick M,D
Stanford University M,D,O
State University of New York at Binghamton M,D
Stony Brook University, State University of New York M,D
University at Buffalo, the State University of New York M
The University of Alabama D
The University of Alabama at Birmingham D
The University of Alabama in Huntsville M,D
The University of Arizona M,D
University of California, Berkeley M,D
University of California, Davis M,D
University of California, Irvine M,D
University of California, Los Angeles M,D
University of California, San Diego M,D
University of California, Santa Barbara M,D
University of Central Florida M,D
University of Cincinnati M,D
University of Connecticut M,D
University of Delaware M,D
University of Denver M,D
University of Florida M,D,O
University of Idaho M,D
University of Illinois at Urbana–Champaign M,D
University of Kentucky M,D
University of Maryland, College Park M,D,O
University of Michigan M,D
University of Minnesota, Twin Cities Campus M,D
University of New Hampshire M,D
The University of North Carolina at Chapel Hill M,D
University of North Texas M,D
University of Pennsylvania M,D
University of Pittsburgh M,D
University of Rochester M,D
University of Southern California M,D,O
The University of Tennessee M,D
The University of Texas at Arlington M,D
The University of Texas at Austin M,D
The University of Texas at El Paso D
University of Utah M,D
University of Vermont M,D
University of Virginia M,D
University of Washington M,D
University of Wisconsin–Madison M,D
Vanderbilt University M,D
Virginia Polytechnic Institute and State University M,D
Washington State University M,D
Wayne State University M,D,O
Worcester Polytechnic Institute M,D,O
Wright State University M

■ MATERNAL AND CHILD/ NEONATAL NURSING

Baylor University M
Boston College M,D
Case Western Reserve University M,D
Columbia University M,O
Duke University M,D,O
Hardin-Simmons University M
Hunter College of the City University of New York M
Indiana University–Purdue University Indianapolis M,D
Lehman College of the City University of New York M
Marquette University M,D,O
Northeastern University M,O
Rutgers, The State University of New Jersey, Newark M
Saint Joseph College M,O
Stony Brook University, State University of New York M,O
University at Buffalo, the State University of New York M,D,O
University of Cincinnati M,D
University of Colorado at Colorado Springs M,D
University of Connecticut M,D,O
University of Delaware M,O
University of Illinois at Chicago M
University of Missouri–Kansas City M,D
University of Pennsylvania M,O
University of South Alabama M,D
University of Southern Mississippi M,D
Vanderbilt University M,D
Wayne State University M,O

■ MATERNAL AND CHILD HEALTH

Boston University M,O
Columbia University M
The George Washington University M,O
Oakland University M,D,O
Tulane University M,D
The University of Alabama at Birmingham M
University of California, Berkeley M
University of California, Davis M
University of Minnesota, Twin Cities Campus M
The University of North Carolina at Chapel Hill M,D
University of Washington M,D

■ MATHEMATICAL AND COMPUTATIONAL FINANCE

Bernard M. Baruch College of the City University of New York M
Boston University M,D
Carnegie Mellon University M,D
DePaul University M,D
Florida State University M,D
Georgia Institute of Technology M,D
Illinois Institute of Technology M
New York University M,D
North Carolina State University M
Polytechnic University, Brooklyn Campus M,O
Polytechnic University, Westchester Graduate Center M,O
Rice University M,D
Stanford University M,D
University of California, Santa Barbara M,D
University of Chicago M
University of Connecticut M
University of Dayton M
The University of North Carolina at Charlotte M
University of Pittsburgh M,D

■ MATHEMATICAL PHYSICS

New Mexico Institute of Mining and Technology M,D
Princeton University D
University of Colorado at Boulder M,D

Virginia Polytechnic Institute and State University M,D

▪ MATHEMATICS

Alabama State University M,O
American University M
Andrews University M
Appalachian State University M
Arizona State University M,D
Arkansas State University M
Auburn University M,D
Aurora University M
Ball State University M
Baylor University M,D
Boston College M
Boston University M,D
Bowling Green State University M,D
Brandeis University M,D
Brigham Young University M,D
Brooklyn College of the City University of New York M,D
Brown University M,D
Bucknell University M
California Institute of Technology D
California Polytechnic State University, San Luis Obispo M
California State Polytechnic University, Pomona M
California State University, East Bay M
California State University, Fresno M
California State University, Fullerton M
California State University, Long Beach M
California State University, Los Angeles M
California State University, Northridge M
California State University, Sacramento M
California State University, San Bernardino M
California State University, San Marcos M
Carnegie Mellon University M,D
Case Western Reserve University M,D
Central Connecticut State University M,O
Central Michigan University M,D
Central Washington University M
Chicago State University M
City College of the City University of New York M
Claremont Graduate University M,D
Clarkson University M,D
Clemson University M,D
Cleveland State University M
College of Charleston M,O
Colorado State University M,D
Columbia University M,D
Cornell University D
Dartmouth College D
Delaware State University M
DePaul University M,O
Dowling College M
Drexel University M,D
Duke University D
Duquesne University M
East Carolina University M
Eastern Illinois University M
Eastern Kentucky University M
Eastern Michigan University M
Eastern New Mexico University M
Eastern Washington University M
East Tennessee State University M
Emory University M,D
Emporia State University M
Fairfield University M
Fairleigh Dickinson University, Metropolitan Campus M
Fayetteville State University M
Florida Atlantic University M,D
Florida International University M
Florida State University M,D
The George Washington University M,D
Georgia Institute of Technology M,D
Georgian Court University M,O
Georgia Southern University M
Georgia State University M
Graduate School and University Center of the City University of New York D
Hardin-Simmons University M,D
Harvard University D
Hofstra University M
Howard University M,D
Hunter College of the City University of New York M
Idaho State University M,D
Illinois State University M
Indiana State University M
Indiana University Bloomington M,D
Indiana University of Pennsylvania M
Indiana University–Purdue University Fort Wayne M,O
Iowa State University of Science and Technology M,D
Jackson State University M
Jacksonville State University M
James Madison University M
John Carroll University M
The Johns Hopkins University D
Kansas State University M,D
Kean University M
Kent State University M,D
Lamar University M
Lehigh University M,D
Lehman College of the City University of New York M
Long Island University, C.W. Post Campus M
Louisiana State University and Agricultural and Mechanical College M,D
Louisiana Tech University M
Loyola University Chicago M
Marquette University M,D
Marshall University M
Massachusetts Institute of Technology D
McNeese State University M
Miami University M
Michigan State University M,D
Michigan Technological University M,D
Middle Tennessee State University M
Minnesota State University Mankato M
Mississippi College M
Mississippi State University M,D
Missouri State University M
Missouri University of Science and Technology M,D
Montana State University M,D
Montclair State University M,O
Morgan State University M
Murray State University M
New Jersey Institute of Technology D
New Mexico Institute of Mining and Technology M,D
New Mexico State University M,D
New York University M,D
Nicholls State University M
North Carolina Central University M
North Carolina State University M,D
North Dakota State University M,D
Northeastern Illinois University M
Northeastern University M,D
Northern Arizona University M
Northern Illinois University M,D
Northwestern University D
Oakland University M
The Ohio State University M,D
Ohio University M,D
Oklahoma State University M,D
Old Dominion University M,D
Oregon State University M,D
Penn State University Park M,D
Pittsburg State University M
Polytechnic University, Brooklyn Campus M,D
Portland State University M,D,O
Prairie View A&M University M
Princeton University D
Purdue University M,D
Purdue University Calumet M
Queens College of the City University of New York M
Rensselaer Polytechnic Institute M,D
Rhode Island College M
Rice University M,D
Rivier College M
Roosevelt University M
Rowan University M
Rutgers, The State University of New Jersey, Camden M
Rutgers, The State University of New Jersey, Newark D
Rutgers, The State University of New Jersey, New Brunswick M,D
St. Cloud State University M
St. John's University (NY) M
Saint Joseph's University M,O
Saint Louis University M,D
Saint Xavier University M
Salem State College M
Sam Houston State University M
San Diego State University M,D
San Francisco State University M
San Jose State University M
South Dakota State University M,D
Southeast Missouri State University M
Southern Connecticut State University M
Southern Illinois University Carbondale M,D
Southern Illinois University Edwardsville M
Southern Methodist University M,D
Southern Oregon University M
Southern University and Agricultural and Mechanical College M
Stanford University M,D
State University of New York at Binghamton M,D
State University of New York at Fredonia M
State University of New York at New Paltz M
State University of New York College at Brockport M
State University of New York College at Cortland M
State University of New York College at Potsdam M
Stephen F. Austin State University M
Stevens Institute of Technology M,D
Stony Brook University, State University of New York M,D
Syracuse University M,D
Tarleton State University M
Temple University M,D

Tennessee State University	M
Tennessee Technological University	M
Texas A&M International University	M
Texas A&M University	M,D
Texas A&M University–Commerce	M
Texas A&M University–Corpus Christi	M
Texas A&M University–Kingsville	M
Texas Christian University	M
Texas Southern University	M
Texas State University-San Marcos	M
Texas Tech University	M,D
Texas Woman's University	M
Tufts University	M,D
Tulane University	M,D
University at Albany, State University of New York	M,D
University at Buffalo, the State University of New York	M,D
The University of Akron	M
The University of Alabama	M,D
The University of Alabama at Birmingham	M,D
The University of Alabama in Huntsville	M,D
University of Alaska Fairbanks	M,D
The University of Arizona	M,D
University of Arkansas	M,D
University of Arkansas at Little Rock	M
University of California, Berkeley	M,D
University of California, Davis	M,D
University of California, Irvine	M,D
University of California, Los Angeles	M,D
University of California, Riverside	M,D
University of California, San Diego	M,D
University of California, Santa Barbara	M,D
University of California, Santa Cruz	M,D
University of Central Arkansas	M
University of Central Florida	M,D,O
University of Central Missouri	M
University of Central Oklahoma	M
University of Chicago	M,D
University of Cincinnati	M,D
University of Colorado at Boulder	M,D
University of Colorado Denver	M
University of Connecticut	M,D
University of Delaware	M,D
University of Denver	M,D
University of Detroit Mercy	M
University of Florida	M,D
University of Georgia	M,D
University of Hawaii at Manoa	M,D
University of Houston	M,D
University of Houston–Clear Lake	M
University of Idaho	M,D
University of Illinois at Chicago	M,D
University of Illinois at Urbana–Champaign	M,D
The University of Iowa	M,D
University of Kansas	M,D
University of Kentucky	M,D
University of Louisiana at Lafayette	M,D
University of Louisville	M,D
University of Maine	M
University of Maryland, College Park	M,D
University of Massachusetts Amherst	M,D
University of Massachusetts Lowell	M,D
University of Memphis	M,D
University of Miami	M,D
University of Michigan	M,D
University of Minnesota, Twin Cities Campus	M,D
University of Mississippi	M,D
University of Missouri–Columbia	M,D
University of Missouri–Kansas City	M,D
University of Missouri–St. Louis	M,D
The University of Montana	M,D
University of Nebraska at Omaha	M
University of Nebraska–Lincoln	M,D
University of Nevada, Las Vegas	M,D
University of Nevada, Reno	M
University of New Hampshire	M,D
University of New Mexico	M,D
University of New Orleans	M
The University of North Carolina at Chapel Hill	M,D
The University of North Carolina at Charlotte	M,D
The University of North Carolina at Greensboro	M
The University of North Carolina Wilmington	M
University of North Dakota	M
University of Northern Colorado	M,D
University of Northern Iowa	M
University of North Florida	M
University of North Texas	M,D
University of Notre Dame	M,D
University of Oklahoma	M,D
University of Oregon	M,D
University of Pennsylvania	M,D
University of Pittsburgh	M,D
University of Puerto Rico, Mayagüez Campus	M
University of Puerto Rico, Río Piedras	M,D
University of Rhode Island	M,D
University of Rochester	M,D
University of South Alabama	M
University of South Carolina	M,D
The University of South Dakota	M
University of Southern California	M,D
University of Southern Mississippi	M,D
University of South Florida	M,D,O
The University of Tennessee	M,D
The University of Texas at Arlington	M,D
The University of Texas at Austin	M,D
The University of Texas at Brownsville	M
The University of Texas at Dallas	M,D
The University of Texas at El Paso	M
The University of Texas at Tyler	M
The University of Texas–Pan American	M
University of the Incarnate Word	M
The University of Toledo	M,D
University of Tulsa	M
University of Utah	M,D
University of Vermont	M,D
University of Virginia	M,D
University of Washington	M,D
University of West Florida	M
University of Wisconsin–Madison	M,D
University of Wisconsin–Milwaukee	M,D
University of Wyoming	M,D
Utah State University	M,D
Vanderbilt University	M,D
Villanova University	M
Virginia Commonwealth University	M,O
Virginia Polytechnic Institute and State University	M,D
Virginia State University	M
Wake Forest University	M
Washington State University	M,D
Washington University in St. Louis	M,D
Wayne State University	M,D
West Chester University of Pennsylvania	M
Western Carolina University	M
Western Connecticut State University	M
Western Illinois University	M,O
Western Kentucky University	M
Western Michigan University	M,D
Western Washington University	M
West Texas A&M University	M
West Virginia University	M,D
Wichita State University	M,D
Wilkes University	M
Worcester Polytechnic Institute	M,D,O
Wright State University	M
Yale University	M,D
Youngstown State University	M

■ MATHEMATICS EDUCATION

Alabama State University	M,O
Albany State University	M
Appalachian State University	M
Arcadia University	M,D,O
Arkansas Tech University	M
Armstrong Atlantic State University	M
Auburn University	M,D,O
Ball State University	M
Belmont University	M
Bemidji State University	M
Bennington College	M
Bob Jones University	P,M,D,O
Boston College	M
Boston University	M,D,O
Bowling Green State University	M,D
Bridgewater State College	M
Brigham Young University	M
Brooklyn College of the City University of New York	M,D,O
Buffalo State College, State University of New York	M
California State University, Bakersfield	M
California State University, Chico	M
California State University, Dominguez Hills	M
California State University, Fresno	M
California State University, Fullerton	M
California State University, Long Beach	M
California State University, Northridge	M
Campbell University	M
Chatham University	M
Cheyney University of Pennsylvania	O
City College of the City University of New York	M,O
Clemson University	M
Cleveland State University	M
College of Charleston	M
College of St. Joseph	M
The College of William and Mary	M
Columbus State University	M,O
Converse College	M
Cornell University	M,D
Delta State University	M
DePaul University	M,O
DeSales University	M,O
Drake University	M
East Carolina University	M
Eastern Illinois University	M
Eastern Kentucky University	M
Eastern Michigan University	M
Eastern Washington University	M
Edinboro University of Pennsylvania	M
Florida Agricultural and Mechanical University	M
Florida Gulf Coast University	M
Florida Institute of Technology	M,D,O
Florida International University	M,D
Florida State University	M,D,O
Framingham State College	M
Fresno Pacific University	M
Georgia College & State University	M,O
Georgia Southern University	M

Georgia State University M,D,O
Harding University M,O
Harvard University M,O
Henderson State University M,O
Hofstra University M
Hood College M,O
Hunter College of the City University of New York M
Idaho State University M,D
Illinois Institute of Technology M,D
Illinois State University D
Indiana University Bloomington M,D,O
Indiana University of Pennsylvania M
Indiana University–Purdue University Indianapolis M
Iona College M
Iowa State University of Science and Technology M,D
Ithaca College M
Jackson State University M
Jacksonville University M
Kean University M
Kennesaw State University M
Kutztown University of Pennsylvania M,O
Lehman College of the City University of New York M
Long Island University, Brooklyn Campus M
Long Island University, C.W. Post Campus M
Louisiana Tech University M,D
Loyola Marymount University M
Manhattanville College M
Marquette University M,D
Miami University M
Michigan State University M,D
Middle Tennessee State University M
Millersville University of Pennsylvania M
Mills College M,D
Minnesota State University Mankato M
Minot State University M
Mississippi College M,O
Missouri University of Science and Technology M,D
Montclair State University M,D,O
Morgan State University D
National-Louis University M,O
New Jersey City University M
New York University M
Nicholls State University M
North Carolina Agricultural and Technical State University M
North Carolina State University M,D
North Dakota State University M,D,O
Northeastern Illinois University M
Northeastern State University M
Northern Arizona University M
North Georgia College & State University M,O
Northwestern State University of Louisiana M
Northwest Missouri State University M
Nova Southeastern University M,O
Oakland University M,D,O
Ohio University M,D
Oklahoma State University M,D
Oregon State University M,D
Plymouth State University M
Portland State University M,D
Providence College M
Purdue University M,D,O
Purdue University Calumet M
Queens College of the City University of New York M,O
Quinnipiac University M
Rhode Island College M,O
Rider University M,O
Rollins College M
Rutgers, The State University of New Jersey, New Brunswick M,D
St. John Fisher College M
Salisbury University M
San Diego State University M,D
San Francisco State University M
San Jose State University M
Slippery Rock University of Pennsylvania M
South Carolina State University M
Southern Illinois University Edwardsville M
Southern University and Agricultural and Mechanical College D
Southwestern Oklahoma State University M
Stanford University M,D
State University of New York at Binghamton M
State University of New York at Plattsburgh M
State University of New York College at Brockport M
State University of New York College at Cortland M
Stephen F. Austin State University M
Stony Brook University, State University of New York M,O
Syracuse University M,D
Temple University M,D
Texas A&M University M,D
Texas A&M University–Corpus Christi M
Texas State University-San Marcos M
Texas Woman's University M
Towson University M
Trinity (Washington) University M
University at Albany, State University of New York M,D
University at Buffalo, the State University of New York M,D,O
University of Arkansas M
University of California, Berkeley M,D
University of California, San Diego D
University of Central Florida M,D,O
University of Central Oklahoma M
University of Cincinnati M,D
University of Connecticut M,D
University of Dayton M
University of Detroit Mercy M
University of Florida M,D,O
University of Georgia M,D,O
University of Houston M,D
University of Illinois at Chicago M
University of Illinois at Urbana–Champaign M,D
University of Indianapolis M
The University of Iowa M,D
University of Massachusetts Lowell M,D,O
University of Miami M,D,O
University of Michigan M,D
University of Minnesota, Twin Cities Campus M
University of Missouri–Columbia M,D,O
The University of Montana M,D
University of Nevada, Las Vegas M,D,O
University of Nevada, Reno M
University of New Hampshire M,D
The University of North Carolina at Chapel Hill M
The University of North Carolina at Charlotte M
The University of North Carolina at Greensboro M,D,O
The University of North Carolina at Pembroke M
University of Northern Colorado M,D
University of Northern Iowa M
University of Oklahoma M,D,O
University of Phoenix M
University of Pittsburgh M,D
University of Puerto Rico, Río Piedras M,D
University of Rio Grande M
University of St. Francis (IL) M
University of South Carolina M,D
University of Southern Mississippi M,D
University of South Florida M,D,O
The University of Tampa M
The University of Tennessee M,D,O
The University of Texas at Austin M,D
The University of Texas at Dallas M
The University of Texas at San Antonio M
The University of Texas at Tyler M
University of the District of Columbia M
University of the Incarnate Word M,D
The University of Toledo M
University of Tulsa M
University of Vermont M,D
University of Washington M,D
The University of West Alabama M
University of West Georgia M,O
University of Wisconsin–Eau Claire M
University of Wisconsin–Madison M,D
University of Wisconsin–Oshkosh M
University of Wisconsin–River Falls M
University of Wyoming M,D
Vanderbilt University M,D
Virginia Polytechnic Institute and State University M,D,O
Virginia State University M
Walden University M,D
Washington State University M,D
Washington University in St. Louis M,D
Wayne State College M
Wayne State University M,D,O
Webster University M,O
Western Carolina University M
Western Connecticut State University M
Western Michigan University M,D
Western New England College M
Western Oregon University M
West Virginia University M,D
Widener University M,D
Wilkes University M
Wright State University M

■ MECHANICAL ENGINEERING

Alfred University M
Arizona State University M,D
Arizona State University at the Polytechnic Campus M
Auburn University M,D
Baylor University M
Boise State University M
Boston University M,D
Bradley University M
Brigham Young University M,D
Brown University M,D
Bucknell University M
California Institute of Technology M,D,O
California Polytechnic State University, San Luis Obispo M
California State Polytechnic University, Pomona M

California State University, Fresno M
California State University, Fullerton M
California State University, Long Beach M,D
California State University, Los Angeles M
California State University, Northridge M
California State University, Sacramento M
Carnegie Mellon University M,D
Case Western Reserve University M,D
The Catholic University of America M,D
City College of the City University of New York M,D
Clarkson University M,D
Clemson University M,D
Cleveland State University M,D
Colorado State University M,D
Columbia University M,D,O
Cornell University M,D
Dartmouth College M,D
Drexel University M,D
Duke University M,D
Fairfield University M
Florida Agricultural and Mechanical University M,D
Florida Atlantic University M,D
Florida Institute of Technology M,D
Florida International University M,D
Florida State University M,D
Gannon University M
The George Washington University M,D,O
Georgia Institute of Technology M,D
Georgia Southern University M
Graduate School and University Center of the City University of New York D
Grand Valley State University M
Howard University M,D
Idaho State University M,D,O
Illinois Institute of Technology M,D
Indiana University–Purdue University Indianapolis M,D,O
Iowa State University of Science and Technology M,D
The Johns Hopkins University M,D
Kansas State University M,D
Lamar University M,D
Lawrence Technological University M,D
Lehigh University M,D
Louisiana State University and Agricultural and Mechanical College M,D
Louisiana Tech University M,D
Loyola Marymount University M
Manhattan College M
Marquette University M,D
Massachusetts Institute of Technology M,D,O
McNeese State University M
Mercer University M
Michigan State University M,D
Michigan Technological University M,D
Mississippi State University M,D
Missouri University of Science and Technology M,D
Montana State University M,D
New Jersey Institute of Technology M,D,O
New Mexico State University M,D
North Carolina Agricultural and Technical State University M,D
North Carolina State University M,D
North Dakota State University M,D
Northeastern University M,D
Northern Illinois University M
Northwestern University M,D
Oakland University M,D
The Ohio State University M,D
Ohio University M,D
Oklahoma State University M,D
Old Dominion University M,D
Oregon State University M,D
Penn State University Park M,D
Polytechnic University, Brooklyn Campus M,D
Portland State University M,D,O
Princeton University M,D
Purdue University M,D,O
Rensselaer Polytechnic Institute M,D
Rice University M,D
Rochester Institute of Technology M
Rutgers, The State University of New Jersey, New Brunswick M,D
St. Cloud State University M
San Diego State University M,D
San Jose State University M
Santa Clara University M,D,O
South Carolina State University M
South Dakota State University M
Southern Illinois University Carbondale M
Southern Illinois University Edwardsville M
Southern Methodist University M,D
Stanford University M,D,O
State University of New York at Binghamton M,D
Stevens Institute of Technology M,D,O
Stony Brook University, State University of New York M,D,O
Syracuse University M,D
Temple University M
Tennessee Technological University M,D
Texas A&M University M,D
Texas A&M University–Kingsville M
Texas Tech University M,D
Tufts University M,D
Tulane University M,D
University at Buffalo, the State University of New York M,D
The University of Akron M,D
The University of Alabama M,D
The University of Alabama at Birmingham M,D
The University of Alabama in Huntsville M,D
University of Alaska Fairbanks M,D
The University of Arizona M,D
University of Arkansas M,D
University of Bridgeport M
University of California, Berkeley M,D
University of California, Davis M,D,O
University of California, Irvine M,D
University of California, Los Angeles M,D
University of California, Riverside M,D
University of California, San Diego M,D
University of California, Santa Barbara M,D
University of Central Florida M,D,O
University of Cincinnati M,D
University of Colorado at Boulder M,D
University of Colorado at Colorado Springs M
University of Colorado Denver M
University of Connecticut M,D
University of Dayton M,D
University of Delaware M,D
University of Denver M,D
University of Detroit Mercy M,D
University of Florida M,D,O
University of Hawaii at Manoa M,D
University of Houston M,D
University of Idaho M,D
University of Illinois at Chicago M,D
University of Illinois at Urbana–Champaign M,D
The University of Iowa M,D
University of Kansas M,D
University of Kentucky M,D
University of Louisiana at Lafayette M
University of Louisville M
University of Maine M,D
University of Maryland, Baltimore County M,D,O
University of Maryland, College Park M,D,O
University of Massachusetts Amherst M,D
University of Massachusetts Dartmouth M
University of Massachusetts Lowell M,D,O
University of Memphis M,D
University of Miami M,D
University of Michigan M,D
University of Michigan–Dearborn M
University of Minnesota, Twin Cities Campus M,D
University of Missouri–Columbia M,D
University of Missouri–Kansas City M,D
University of Nebraska–Lincoln M,D
University of Nevada, Las Vegas M,D
University of Nevada, Reno M,D
University of New Hampshire M,D
University of New Haven M
University of New Mexico M,D
University of New Orleans M
The University of North Carolina at Charlotte M,D
University of North Dakota M
University of Notre Dame M,D
University of Oklahoma M,D
University of Pennsylvania M,D
University of Pittsburgh M,D
University of Puerto Rico, Mayagüez Campus M
University of Rhode Island M,D
University of Rochester M,D
University of South Alabama M
University of South Carolina M,D
University of Southern California M,D,O
University of South Florida M,D
The University of Tennessee M,D
The University of Texas at Arlington M,D
The University of Texas at Austin M,D
The University of Texas at El Paso M
The University of Texas at San Antonio M
The University of Toledo M,D
University of Tulsa M,D
University of Utah M,D
University of Vermont M,D
University of Virginia M,D
University of Washington M,D
University of Wisconsin–Madison M,D
University of Wyoming M,D
Utah State University M,D
Vanderbilt University M,D
Villanova University M,O
Virginia Commonwealth University M,D
Virginia Polytechnic Institute and State University M,D
Washington State University M,D
Washington University in St. Louis M,D
Wayne State University M,D
Western Michigan University M,D
Western New England College M
West Virginia University M,D
Wichita State University M,D

Widener University M
Worcester Polytechnic Institute M,D,O
Wright State University M
Yale University M,D
Youngstown State University M

■ MECHANICS

Brown University M,D
California Institute of Technology M,D
California State University, Fullerton M
Case Western Reserve University M,D
The Catholic University of America M,D
Columbia University M,D,O
Cornell University M,D
Drexel University M,D
Georgia Institute of Technology M,D
Idaho State University M,D,O
Iowa State University of Science and Technology M,D
Lehigh University M,D
Louisiana State University and Agricultural and Mechanical College M,D
Massachusetts Institute of Technology M,D,O
Michigan State University M,D
Michigan Technological University M
Mississippi State University M
Missouri University of Science and Technology M,D
New Mexico Institute of Mining and Technology M
North Dakota State University M,D
Northwestern University M,D
The Ohio State University M,D
Penn State University Park M,D
Rutgers, The State University of New Jersey, New Brunswick M,D
San Diego State University M,D
Southern Illinois University Carbondale M,D
The University of Alabama M,D
The University of Arizona M,D
University of California, Berkeley M,D
University of California, San Diego M,D
University of Cincinnati M,D
University of Dayton M
University of Illinois at Urbana–Champaign M,D
University of Maryland, College Park M,D
University of Massachusetts Lowell M,D
University of Minnesota, Twin Cities Campus M,D
University of Nebraska–Lincoln M,D
University of Pennsylvania M,D
University of Rhode Island M,D
University of Southern California M
The University of Tennessee M,D
The University of Texas at Austin M,D
University of Virginia M
University of Wisconsin–Madison M,D
Virginia Polytechnic Institute and State University M,D
Yale University M,D

■ MEDIA STUDIES

American University M
Arkansas State University M
Bob Jones University P,M,D,O
Boston University M
California State University, Fullerton M
Carnegie Mellon University M
Central Michigan University M
City College of the City University of New York M
College of Staten Island of the City University of New York M
Columbia College Chicago M
Edinboro University of Pennsylvania M
Emerson College M
Fairleigh Dickinson University, Metropolitan Campus M
Florida State University M,D
Fordham University M
Governors State University M
Howard University M,D
Hunter College of the City University of New York M
Indiana State University M
Kutztown University of Pennsylvania M
Louisiana State University and Agricultural and Mechanical College M,D
Lynn University M,D
Marquette University M
Marywood University M,O
Massachusetts Institute of Technology M,D
Metropolitan College of New York M
Michigan State University M,D
Monmouth University M,O
National University M
New College of California M
The New School: A University M
New York University M,D
Norfolk State University M
Northwestern University M,D
Ohio University M,D
Rochester Institute of Technology M
Saginaw Valley State University M
San Diego State University M
San Francisco State University M
Southern Illinois University Carbondale M
Southern Illinois University Edwardsville O
Syracuse University M
Temple University M,D
Texas Southern University M
University at Buffalo, the State University of New York M,O
The University of Alabama M
The University of Arizona M
University of California, Santa Barbara M,D
University of Chicago M,D
University of Colorado at Boulder D
University of Denver M
University of Florida M
The University of Iowa M,D
University of Maryland, College Park M,D
University of Michigan M
University of Nevada, Las Vegas M
University of South Carolina M
University of Southern California M
The University of Tennessee M,D
The University of Texas at Austin M,D
Virginia Commonwealth University D
Washington State University M,D
Wayne State University M,D
Webster University M
William Paterson University of New Jersey M

■ MEDICAL/SURGICAL NURSING

Angelo State University M
Case Western Reserve University M,D
Columbia University M,O
Daemen College M,O
Emory University M
Gannon University M,O
George Mason University M,D,O
Hunter College of the City University of New York M
La Salle University M,O
New Mexico State University M
Pontifical Catholic University of Puerto Rico M
University of Illinois at Chicago M
University of Michigan M
University of South Carolina M
University of Southern Maine M,O
Vanderbilt University M,D

■ MEDICAL ILLUSTRATION

The Johns Hopkins University M
Rochester Institute of Technology M
University of Illinois at Chicago M

■ MEDICAL IMAGING

Illinois Institute of Technology M,D
University of Cincinnati D
University of Florida M,D
University of Southern California M

■ MEDICAL INFORMATICS

Columbia University M,D,O
Grand Valley State University M
Harvard University M
Marymount University M,O
Massachusetts Institute of Technology M
Stanford University M,D
University of California, Davis M
University of Illinois at Urbana–Champaign M,D,O
University of Washington M,D
University of Wisconsin–Milwaukee D

■ MEDICAL MICROBIOLOGY

Creighton University M,D
Idaho State University M,D
Rutgers, The State University of New Jersey, New Brunswick M,D
University of Hawaii at Manoa M,D
University of Minnesota, Duluth M,D
University of South Florida M,D
University of Wisconsin–La Crosse M
University of Wisconsin–Madison D

■ MEDICAL PHYSICS

Cleveland State University M
Columbia University M,D,O
Drexel University M,D
East Carolina University M,D
Georgia Institute of Technology M,D
Harvard University D
Massachusetts Institute of Technology D
Oakland University M,D
Stony Brook University, State University of New York D
University of California, Los Angeles M,D
University of Central Arkansas M
University of Cincinnati M
University of Colorado at Boulder M,D
University of Kentucky M
University of Minnesota, Twin Cities Campus M,D
University of Missouri–Columbia M,D
University of Pennsylvania M,D
The University of Toledo M
University of Wisconsin–Madison M,D
Vanderbilt University M
Virginia Commonwealth University M,D
Wayne State University M,D
Wright State University M

■ MEDICINAL AND PHARMACEUTICAL CHEMISTRY

Duquesne University M,D
Florida Agricultural and Mechanical University M,D
Idaho State University M,D
Lehigh University M,D
Long Island University, C.W. Post Campus M
The Ohio State University M,D
Purdue University M,D
Rutgers, The State University of New Jersey, New Brunswick M,D
Temple University M,D
University at Buffalo, the State University of New York M,D
University of Connecticut M,D
University of Florida P,M,D
University of Georgia M,D
University of Kansas M,D
University of Michigan D
University of Minnesota, Twin Cities Campus M,D
University of Mississippi M,D
University of Rhode Island M,D
The University of Toledo M,D
University of Utah M,D
University of Washington D
Wayne State University P,M,D
West Virginia University M,D

■ MEDIEVAL AND RENAISSANCE STUDIES

The Catholic University of America M,D,O
Columbia University M
Cornell University M,D
Duke University O
Fordham University M,O
Graduate School and University Center of the City University of New York M,D
Harvard University D
Indiana University Bloomington M,D
Marquette University M,D
Rutgers, The State University of New Jersey, New Brunswick D
Southern Methodist University M
Tufts University M,D
University of Colorado at Boulder M,D
University of Connecticut M,D
University of Minnesota, Twin Cities Campus M,D
University of Notre Dame M,D
Western Michigan University M
Yale University M,D

■ METALLURGICAL ENGINEERING AND METALLURGY

Colorado School of Mines M,D
Columbia University M,D,O
Massachusetts Institute of Technology M,D,O
Michigan Technological University M,D
Missouri University of Science and Technology M,D
The Ohio State University M,D
Penn State University Park M,D
Rensselaer Polytechnic Institute M,D
The University of Alabama M,D
University of California, Los Angeles M,D
University of Cincinnati M,D
University of Connecticut M,D
University of Idaho M
University of Nevada, Reno M,D,O
The University of Texas at El Paso M
University of Utah M,D
Wayne State University M,D,O

■ METEOROLOGY

Columbia University M
Florida Institute of Technology M,D
Florida State University M,D
Iowa State University of Science and Technology M,D
North Carolina State University M,D
Penn State University Park M,D
Plymouth State University M
Saint Louis University M,D
San Jose State University M
Texas A&M University M,D
University of Hawaii at Manoa M,D
University of Maryland, College Park M,D
University of Miami M,D
University of Oklahoma M,D
University of Utah M,D
Utah State University M,D
Yale University D

■ MICROBIOLOGY

Arizona State University M,D
Auburn University M,D
Boston University M,D
Brandeis University M,D
Brigham Young University M,D
Brown University M,D
California State University, Fullerton M
California State University, Long Beach M
Case Western Reserve University D
The Catholic University of America M,D
Clemson University M,D
Colorado State University M,D
Columbia University M,D
Cornell University D
Dartmouth College D
Drexel University M,D
Duke University D
East Carolina University D
East Tennessee State University M,D
Emory University D
Emporia State University M
Florida State University M,D
George Mason University M,D,O
Georgetown University M,D
The George Washington University M,D,O
Georgia State University M,D
Harvard University D
Howard University D
Idaho State University M,D
Illinois State University M,D
Indiana State University M,D
Indiana University Bloomington M,D
Indiana University–Purdue University Indianapolis M,D
Iowa State University of Science and Technology M,D
The Johns Hopkins University M,D
Kansas State University D
Long Island University, C.W. Post Campus M
Loyola University Chicago M,D
Marquette University M,D
Miami University M,D
Michigan State University M,D
Montana State University M,D
New York University M,D
North Carolina State University M,D
North Dakota State University M,D
Northwestern University D
The Ohio State University M,D
Ohio University M,D
Oklahoma State University M,D
Oregon State University M,D
Penn State University Park M,D
Purdue University M,D
Quinnipiac University M
Rensselaer Polytechnic Institute M,D
Rutgers, The State University of New Jersey, New Brunswick M,D
Saint Louis University D
San Diego State University M
San Francisco State University M
San Jose State University M
Seton Hall University M,D
South Dakota State University M,D
Southern Illinois University Carbondale M,D
Southwestern Oklahoma State University M
Stanford University D
Stony Brook University, State University of New York D
Temple University M,D
Texas A&M University M,D
Texas Tech University M,D
Tufts University D
Tulane University M,D
University at Buffalo, the State University of New York M,D
The University of Alabama at Birmingham D
The University of Arizona M,D
University of California, Berkeley D
University of California, Davis M,D
University of California, Irvine M,D
University of California, Los Angeles M,D
University of California, Riverside M,D
University of California, San Diego D
University of Central Florida M
University of Chicago D
University of Cincinnati M,D
University of Colorado at Boulder M,D
University of Colorado Denver D
University of Connecticut M,D
University of Delaware M,D
University of Florida M,D
University of Georgia M,D
University of Hawaii at Manoa M,D
University of Idaho M,D
University of Illinois at Chicago D
University of Illinois at Urbana–Champaign D
The University of Iowa M,D
University of Kansas M,D
University of Kentucky D
University of Louisville M,D
University of Maine M,D
University of Massachusetts Amherst M,D
University of Miami D
University of Michigan D
University of Minnesota, Twin Cities Campus D
University of Missouri–Columbia M,D
The University of Montana M,D
University of New Hampshire M,D
University of New Mexico M,D
The University of North Carolina at Chapel Hill M,D
University of North Dakota M,D
University of Oklahoma M,D
University of Pennsylvania D
University of Pittsburgh M,D
University of Rhode Island M,D
University of Rochester M,D

University of South Alabama	D
The University of South Dakota	M,D
University of Southern California	M,D
University of Southern Mississippi	M,D
University of South Florida	M,D
The University of Tennessee	M,D
The University of Texas at Austin	M,D
The University of Toledo	M
University of Utah	M,D
University of Vermont	M,D
University of Virginia	D
University of Washington	D
University of Wisconsin–La Crosse	M
University of Wisconsin–Madison	D
University of Wisconsin–Oshkosh	M
Utah State University	M,D
Vanderbilt University	M,D
Virginia Commonwealth University	M,D,O
Virginia Polytechnic Institute and State University	M,D
Wagner College	M
Wake Forest University	D
Washington State University	M,D
Washington University in St. Louis	D
Wayne State University	M,D
West Virginia University	M,D
Wright State University	M
Yale University	D

■ MIDDLE SCHOOL EDUCATION

Alaska Pacific University	M
Albany State University	M
Armstrong Atlantic State University	M
Ashland University	M
Augusta State University	M,O
Bellarmine University	M
Belmont University	M
Brenau University	M,O
Brooklyn College of the City University of New York	M
California State University, Bakersfield	M
California State University, Fullerton	M
Campbell University	M
Capella University	M,D,O
Central Michigan University	M
Chicago State University	M
City College of the City University of New York	M,O
Clemson University	M
Cleveland State University	M
College of Mount St. Joseph	M
College of Mount Saint Vincent	M,O
Columbus State University	M,O
Daemen College	M
Drury University	M
East Carolina University	M
Eastern Illinois University	M
Eastern Michigan University	M
Eastern Nazarene College	M,O
Emory University	M,D,O
Fayetteville State University	M
Fitchburg State College	M
Fort Valley State University	M
Furman University	M
Gardner-Webb University	M
George Mason University	M
Georgia College & State University	M,O
Georgia Southern University	M
Georgia Southwestern State University	M,O
Georgia State University	M,O
Grand Valley State University	M
Henderson State University	M,O
Hofstra University	O
James Madison University	M
John Carroll University	M
Kennesaw State University	M
Kent State University	M
Lesley University	M,D,O
Long Island University, C.W. Post Campus	M
Manhattanville College	M
Mary Baldwin College	M
Maryville University of Saint Louis	M,D
Mercer University	M,D,O
Mercy College	M
Middle Tennessee State University	M,O
Montclair State University	M,O
Morehead State University	M
Morgan State University	M,D
Mount Saint Mary College	M
Murray State University	M,O
Nazareth College of Rochester	M
North Carolina Agricultural and Technical State University	M
North Carolina State University	M
North Georgia College & State University	M,O
Northwestern State University of Louisiana	M
Northwest Missouri State University	M
Ohio University	M,D
Old Dominion University	M,D
Pacific University	M
Park University	M
Plymouth State University	M
Quinnipiac University	M
Roberts Wesleyan College	M,O
Rosemont College	M
Saginaw Valley State University	M
St. John Fisher College	M
St. Thomas Aquinas College	M,O
Salem State College	M
Shenandoah University	M,D,O
Siena Heights University	M
Simmons College	M,O
Southeast Missouri State University	M
Spalding University	M
State University of New York College at Brockport	M
State University of New York College at Oneonta	M
Tufts University	M,D
Union College (KY)	M
University at Buffalo, the State University of New York	M,D,O
University of Arkansas	M,D,O
University of Arkansas at Little Rock	M
University of Dayton	M
University of Georgia	M,D,O
University of Kentucky	M,D
University of Louisville	M
University of Memphis	M,D
University of Missouri–St. Louis	M,D
University of Montevallo	M
The University of North Carolina at Charlotte	M
The University of North Carolina at Greensboro	M,D,O
The University of North Carolina at Pembroke	M
The University of North Carolina Wilmington	M
University of Northern Iowa	M
University of Puget Sound	M
University of Southern Maine	M,O
University of South Florida	M,D,O
The University of Toledo	M
University of West Florida	M
University of West Georgia	M,O
University of Wisconsin–Milwaukee	M
University of Wisconsin–Platteville	M
Valdosta State University	M,O
Virginia Commonwealth University	M,O
Wagner College	M
Walden University	M,D
Western Carolina University	M
Western Kentucky University	M,O
Western Michigan University	M
Widener University	M,D
Winthrop University	M
Worcester State College	M
Wright State University	M
Youngstown State University	M

■ MILITARY AND DEFENSE STUDIES

Austin Peay State University	M
The George Washington University	M
Hawai'i Pacific University	M
Missouri State University	M
Norwich University	M
University of Pittsburgh	M

■ MINERAL/MINING ENGINEERING

Colorado School of Mines	M,D
Columbia University	M,D,O
Michigan Technological University	M,D
Missouri University of Science and Technology	M,D
New Mexico Institute of Mining and Technology	M
Penn State University Park	M,D
Southern Illinois University Carbondale	M
University of Alaska Fairbanks	M
The University of Arizona	M,O
University of Kentucky	M,D
University of Nevada, Reno	M,O
University of North Dakota	M
The University of Texas at Austin	M
University of Utah	M,D
Virginia Polytechnic Institute and State University	M,D
West Virginia University	M,D

■ MINERAL ECONOMICS

Colorado School of Mines	M,D
Michigan Technological University	M
The University of Texas at Austin	M

■ MINERALOGY

Cornell University	M,D
Indiana University Bloomington	M,D
University of Illinois at Chicago	M,D
University of Michigan	M,D
Yale University	D

■ MISSIONS AND MISSIOLOGY

Abilene Christian University	M
Anderson University	P,M,D
Biola University	M,D,O
Dallas Baptist University	M
Eastern University	D
Gardner-Webb University	P,D
Oral Roberts University	P,M,D
Regent University	P,M,D
Trinity International University	P,M,D,O
Wheaton College	M,O

■ MOLECULAR BIOLOGY

Arkansas State University	M,D,O
Auburn University	M,D
Boston University	M,D
Brandeis University	M,D

Brigham Young University	M,D
Brown University	M,D
California Institute of Technology	D
Carnegie Mellon University	M,D
Case Western Reserve University	M,D
Central Connecticut State University	M
Clemson University	M,D
Colorado State University	M,D
Columbia University	M,D
Cornell University	D
Dartmouth College	D
Drexel University	M,D
Duke University	D,O
East Carolina University	M,D
Emory University	D
Florida Institute of Technology	M,D
Florida State University	M,D
George Mason University	M,D,O
Georgetown University	D
The George Washington University	M,D
Georgia State University	M,D
Grand Valley State University	M
Harvard University	D
Howard University	M,D
Illinois Institute of Technology	M,D
Illinois State University	M,D
Indiana University Bloomington	M,D
Indiana University–Purdue University Indianapolis	D
Iowa State University of Science and Technology	M,D
The Johns Hopkins University	M,D
Kent State University	M,D
Lehigh University	M,D
Loyola University Chicago	D
Marquette University	M,D
Mayo Graduate School	D
Michigan State University	M,D
Mississippi State University	M,D
Missouri State University	M
Montana State University	M,D
Montclair State University	M,O
New Mexico State University	M,D
New York University	M,D
North Dakota State University	M,D
Northwestern University	D
The Ohio State University	M,D
Ohio University	M,D
Oklahoma State University	M,D
Oregon State University	M,D
Penn State University Park	M,D
Princeton University	D
Purdue University	M,D
Quinnipiac University	M
Rensselaer Polytechnic Institute	M,D
Rutgers, The State University of New Jersey, New Brunswick	M,D
Saint Joseph College	M
Saint Louis University	D
San Diego State University	M,D
San Francisco State University	M
San Jose State University	M
Seton Hall University	M,D
Southern Illinois University Carbondale	M,D
Stony Brook University, State University of New York	M,D
Temple University	D
Texas Woman's University	M,D
Tufts University	D
Tulane University	M,D
University at Albany, State University of New York	M,D
University at Buffalo, the State University of New York	D
The University of Alabama at Birmingham	M,D
The University of Arizona	M,D
University of Arkansas	M,D
University of California, Berkeley	D
University of California, Davis	M,D
University of California, Irvine	M,D
University of California, Los Angeles	M,D
University of California, Riverside	M,D
University of California, San Diego	D
University of California, Santa Barbara	M,D
University of California, Santa Cruz	M,D
University of Central Florida	M
University of Chicago	D
University of Cincinnati	M,D
University of Colorado at Boulder	M,D
University of Colorado Denver	D
University of Connecticut	M
University of Delaware	M,D
University of Florida	M,D
University of Georgia	M,D
University of Hawaii at Manoa	M,D
University of Idaho	M,D
University of Illinois at Chicago	M,D
The University of Iowa	D
University of Kansas	M,D
University of Louisville	M,D
University of Maine	M,D
University of Maryland, Baltimore County	M,D
University of Maryland, College Park	D
University of Massachusetts Amherst	D
University of Massachusetts Boston	D
University of Miami	D
University of Michigan	M,D
University of Minnesota, Duluth	M,D
University of Minnesota, Twin Cities Campus	M,D
University of Missouri–Kansas City	D
University of Missouri–St. Louis	M,D,O
University of Nevada, Reno	M,D
University of New Haven	M
University of New Mexico	M,D
The University of North Carolina at Chapel Hill	M,D
University of North Texas	M,D
University of Notre Dame	M,D
University of Oregon	M,D
University of Pennsylvania	D
University of Pittsburgh	D
University of Rhode Island	M,D
University of South Alabama	D
University of South Carolina	M,D
The University of South Dakota	M,D
University of Southern California	M,D
University of Southern Maine	M
University of Southern Mississippi	M,D
University of South Florida	M,D
The University of Texas at Austin	D
The University of Texas at Dallas	M,D
The University of Texas at San Antonio	M,D
The University of Toledo	M,D
University of Vermont	M,D
University of Washington	D
University of Wisconsin–La Crosse	M
University of Wisconsin–Madison	M,D
University of Wyoming	M,D
Utah State University	M,D
Vanderbilt University	M,D
Virginia Commonwealth University	M,D
Wake Forest University	D
Washington State University	M,D
Washington University in St. Louis	D
Wayne State University	M,D
West Virginia University	M,D
William Paterson University of New Jersey	M
Wright State University	M
Yale University	D

■ MOLECULAR BIOPHYSICS

California Institute of Technology	M,D
Duke University	O
Florida State University	D
Illinois Institute of Technology	M,D
Rutgers, The State University of New Jersey, New Brunswick	D
University of Pennsylvania	D
University of Pittsburgh	D
Virginia Commonwealth University	M,D
Washington University in St. Louis	D
Yale University	D

■ MOLECULAR GENETICS

Duke University	D
Emory University	D
Georgia State University	M,D
Harvard University	D
Illinois State University	M,D
Indiana University–Purdue University Indianapolis	M,D
Michigan State University	M,D
New York University	M,D
The Ohio State University	M,D
Oklahoma State University	M,D
Rutgers, The State University of New Jersey, New Brunswick	M,D
Stony Brook University, State University of New York	D
The University of Alabama at Birmingham	D
University of California, Irvine	M,D
University of California, Los Angeles	M,D
University of California, Riverside	D
University of Chicago	D
University of Cincinnati	M,D
University of Florida	M,D
University of Illinois at Chicago	D
University of Kansas	D
University of Maryland, College Park	M,D
University of Pittsburgh	M,D
University of Rhode Island	M,D
University of Vermont	M,D
University of Virginia	D
Wake Forest University	D
Washington University in St. Louis	D

■ MOLECULAR MEDICINE

Boston University	D
Cleveland State University	M,D
Cornell University	M,D
Dartmouth College	D
The George Washington University	D
The Johns Hopkins University	D
Penn State University Park	M,D
University of Cincinnati	D
University of Washington	M,D
Wake Forest University	M,D
Yale University	D

■ MOLECULAR PATHOGENESIS

Dartmouth College	D
Emory University	D
Massachusetts Institute of Technology	M,D
North Dakota State University	M,D

University at Albany, State University of New York M,D
Washington University in St. Louis D

■ MOLECULAR PATHOLOGY

University of California, San Diego D
University of Pittsburgh M,D
Yale University D

■ MOLECULAR PHARMACOLOGY

Brown University M,D
Dartmouth College D
Harvard University D
Massachusetts Institute of Technology M,D
Mayo Graduate School D
New York University D
Purdue University M,D
Rutgers, The State University of New Jersey, New Brunswick D
Stanford University D
University at Buffalo, the State University of New York D
University of Nevada, Reno M,D
University of Pittsburgh D
University of Southern California M,D

■ MOLECULAR PHYSIOLOGY

Loyola University Chicago M,D
Stony Brook University, State University of New York D
Tufts University D
The University of Alabama at Birmingham M,D
University of Chicago D
The University of North Carolina at Chapel Hill D
University of Pittsburgh M,D
University of Vermont M,D
University of Virginia M,D
Vanderbilt University M,D
Yale University D

■ MOLECULAR TOXICOLOGY

Massachusetts Institute of Technology M,D
New York University M,D
North Carolina State University M,D
Oregon State University M,D
University of California, Berkeley D
University of California, Los Angeles D
University of Cincinnati M,D
University of Pittsburgh M,D,O

■ MULTILINGUAL AND MULTICULTURAL EDUCATION

Azusa Pacific University M
Belhaven College (MS) M
Bennington College M
Boston University M,O
Brooklyn College of the City University of New York M
Brown University M,D
Buffalo State College, State University of New York M
California Baptist University M
California State University, Bakersfield M
California State University, Chico M
California State University, Dominguez Hills M
California State University, Fullerton M
California State University, Sacramento M
California State University, San Bernardino M
California State University, Stanislaus M
Capella University M,D,O
Chicago State University M
City College of the City University of New York M
College of Mount St. Joseph M
College of Mount Saint Vincent M,O
The College of New Rochelle M,O
The College of Saint Rose M,O
College of Santa Fe M
Columbia College Chicago M
DePaul University M,D
DeSales University M,O
Eastern Michigan University M
Eastern University M
Fairfield University M,O
Fairleigh Dickinson University, Metropolitan Campus M
Florida Atlantic University M,D,O
Florida State University M,D,O
Fordham University M,D,O
Fresno Pacific University M
George Mason University M
Georgetown University M,D,O
Harvard University D
Heritage University M
Hofstra University M,O
Howard University M,D
Hunter College of the City University of New York M
Immaculata University M
Indiana State University M,O
Iona College M
Kean University M
Lehman College of the City University of New York M
Long Island University, Brooklyn Campus M
Long Island University, C.W. Post Campus M
Loyola Marymount University M
McNeese State University M
Mercy College M,O
Mercyhurst College M,O
Minnesota State University Mankato M
National University M
New Jersey City University M
New York University M,D,O
Northeastern Illinois University M
Northern Arizona University M,O
Nova Southeastern University M,O
Park University M
Penn State University Park M,D
Prescott College M,D
Queens College of the City University of New York M,O
Rhode Island College M,O
Rutgers, The State University of New Jersey, New Brunswick M,D
St. John's University (NY) M
Salem State College M
San Diego State University M,D
Seton Hall University O
Southern Connecticut State University M
Southern Methodist University M,D
State University of New York at New Paltz M
State University of New York College at Brockport M
Sul Ross State University M
Texas A&M International University M,D
Texas A&M University M,D
Texas A&M University–Kingsville M,D
Texas Southern University M,D
Texas State University-San Marcos M
Texas Tech University M,D
Universidad del Turabo M
University at Buffalo, the State University of New York M,D,O
University of Alaska Fairbanks M
The University of Arizona M,D,O
University of California, Berkeley M,D
University of Colorado at Boulder M,D
University of Connecticut M,D
University of Delaware M,D
The University of Findlay M
University of Florida M,D,O
University of Houston M,D
University of Houston–Clear Lake M
University of La Verne O
University of Maryland, Baltimore County M,D,O
University of Massachusetts Amherst M,D,O
University of Massachusetts Boston M
University of Michigan M,D
University of Michigan–Flint M
University of Minnesota, Twin Cities Campus M
University of Nevada, Las Vegas M,D,O
University of New Mexico D,O
The University of North Carolina at Greensboro M,D,O
University of Oklahoma M,D,O
University of Pennsylvania M,D
University of San Francisco M,D
The University of Tennessee M,D,O
The University of Texas at Brownsville M
The University of Texas at San Antonio M,D
The University of Texas–Pan American M
University of Washington M,D
Utah State University M
Vanderbilt University M,D
Washington State University M,D
Wayne State University M,D,O
Western New Mexico University M
Western Oregon University M
Xavier University M

■ MUSEUM EDUCATION

The College of New Rochelle O
The George Washington University M

■ MUSEUM STUDIES

Baylor University M
Boston University M,D,O
California State University, Chico M
California State University, Fullerton M,O
Case Western Reserve University M,D
City College of the City University of New York M
Cleveland State University M
Duquesne University M
Florida State University M,D,O
The George Washington University M,D,O
Hampton University M
Harvard University M,O
John F. Kennedy University M,O
New York University M,D,O
San Francisco State University M
Seton Hall University M
Southern Illinois University Edwardsville O
State University of New York College at Oneonta M
Syracuse University M
Texas Tech University M
Tufts University O
University at Buffalo, the State University of New York M,O
University of California, Riverside M,D
University of Central Oklahoma M

University of Colorado at Boulder M
University of Delaware O
University of Denver M
University of Florida M,D
University of Hawaii at Manoa O
University of Kansas M
University of Missouri–St. Louis M,O
University of Nebraska–Lincoln M
University of New Hampshire M,D
The University of North Carolina at Greensboro M,D,O
University of Oklahoma M
University of South Carolina M,O
University of Washington M
University of Wisconsin–Milwaukee M,O
Virginia Commonwealth University M,D

■ MUSIC

Alabama Agricultural and Mechanical University M
Alabama State University M
Andrews University M
Appalachian State University M
Arizona State University M,D
Arkansas State University M,O
Austin Peay State University M
Azusa Pacific University M
Baylor University M
Belmont University M
Bennington College M
Bob Jones University P,M,D,O
Boise State University M
Boston University M,D,O
Bowling Green State University M,D
Brandeis University M,D
Brigham Young University M
Brooklyn College of the City University of New York M,D,O
Brown University M,D
Butler University M
California Baptist University M
California State University, Chico M
California State University, East Bay M
California State University, Fresno M
California State University, Fullerton M
California State University, Long Beach M
California State University, Los Angeles M
California State University, Northridge M
California State University, Sacramento M
Capital University M
Cardinal Stritch University M
Carnegie Mellon University M
Case Western Reserve University M,D
The Catholic University of America M,D
Central Michigan University M
Central Washington University M
City College of the City University of New York M
Claremont Graduate University M,D
Cleveland State University M
The College of Saint Rose M
Colorado State University M
Columbia University M,D
Concordia University Chicago (IL) M
Concordia University Wisconsin M
Converse College M
Cornell University M,D
Dartmouth College M
DePaul University M,O
Duke University M,D
Duquesne University M,O
East Carolina University M
Eastern Illinois University M
Eastern Kentucky University M
Eastern Michigan University M
Eastern Washington University M
Emory University M
Emporia State University M
Florida Atlantic University M
Florida International University M
Florida State University M,D
George Mason University M
Georgia Southern University M
Georgia State University M
Graduate School and University Center of the City University of New York D
Gratz College M,O
Hardin-Simmons University M
Harvard University M,D
Hofstra University M
Hollins University M,O
Holy Names University M,O
Hope International University M
Howard University M
Hunter College of the City University of New York M
Illinois State University M
Indiana State University M
Indiana University Bloomington M,D
Indiana University of Pennsylvania M
Indiana University–Purdue University Indianapolis M
Indiana University South Bend M
Ithaca College M
Jacksonville State University M
James Madison University M
The Johns Hopkins University M,D,O
Kansas State University M
Kent State University M,D
Lamar University M
Lee University M
Long Island University, C.W. Post Campus M
Louisiana State University and Agricultural and Mechanical College M,D
Loyola University New Orleans M
Lynn University M,O
Mansfield University of Pennsylvania M
Marshall University M
Mercer University M
Miami University M
Michigan State University M,D
Middle Tennessee State University M
Mills College M
Minnesota State University Mankato M
Mississippi College M
Missouri State University M
Montclair State University M,O
Morehead State University M
Morgan State University M
Murray State University M
New Jersey City University M
New Mexico State University M
The New School: A University M,O
New York University M,D,O
Norfolk State University M
North Dakota State University M,D
Northeastern Illinois University M
Northern Arizona University M
Northern Illinois University M,O
Northwestern State University of Louisiana M
Northwestern University M,D,O
Notre Dame de Namur University M
Oakland University M,D
The Ohio State University M,D
Ohio University M,O
Oklahoma City University M
Oklahoma State University M
Penn State University Park M,D
Pittsburg State University M
Point Park University M
Portland State University M
Princeton University D
Purchase College, State University of New York M
Queens College of the City University of New York M
Radford University M
Regis University M,O
Rice University M,D
Roosevelt University M,O
Rowan University M
Rutgers, The State University of New Jersey, Newark M
Rutgers, The State University of New Jersey, New Brunswick M,D,O
St. Cloud State University M
Samford University M
Sam Houston State University M
San Diego State University M
San Francisco State University M
San Jose State University M
Santa Clara University M
Seton Hall University M
Shenandoah University M,D,O
Southeastern Louisiana University M
Southern Illinois University Carbondale M
Southern Illinois University Edwardsville M
Southern Methodist University M,O
Southern Oregon University M
Southwestern Oklahoma State University M
Stanford University M,D
State University of New York at Binghamton M
State University of New York at Fredonia M
State University of New York College at Potsdam M
Stephen F. Austin State University M
Stony Brook University, State University of New York M,D
Syracuse University M
Temple University M,D
Texas A&M International University
Texas A&M University–Commerce M
Texas Christian University M,O
Texas Southern University M
Texas State University-San Marcos M
Texas Tech University M,D
Texas Woman's University M
Towson University M
Truman State University M
Tufts University M
Tulane University M
University at Buffalo, the State University of New York M,D
The University of Akron M
The University of Alabama M,D
University of Alaska Fairbanks M
The University of Arizona M,D
University of Arkansas M
University of California, Berkeley D
University of California, Davis M,D
University of California, Irvine M
University of California, Los Angeles M,D

Institution	Degrees
University of California, Riverside	M
University of California, San Diego	M,D
University of California, Santa Barbara	M,D
University of California, Santa Cruz	M,D
University of Central Arkansas	M
University of Central Florida	M
University of Central Missouri	M
University of Central Oklahoma	M
University of Chicago	M,D
University of Cincinnati	M,D,O
University of Colorado at Boulder	M,D
University of Colorado Denver	M
University of Connecticut	M,D,O
University of Delaware	M
University of Denver	M,O
University of Florida	M,D
University of Georgia	M,D
University of Hartford	M,D,O
University of Hawaii at Manoa	M,D
University of Houston	M,D
University of Idaho	M
University of Illinois at Urbana–Champaign	M,D
The University of Iowa	M,D
University of Kansas	M,D
University of Kentucky	M,D
University of Louisiana at Lafayette	M
University of Louisiana at Monroe	M
University of Louisville	M,D
University of Maine	M
University of Maryland, Baltimore County	O
University of Maryland, College Park	M,D
University of Massachusetts Amherst	M,D
University of Massachusetts Lowell	M
University of Memphis	M,D
University of Miami	M,D,O
University of Michigan	M,D,O
University of Minnesota, Duluth	M
University of Minnesota, Twin Cities Campus	M,D
University of Mississippi	M,D
University of Missouri–Columbia	M
University of Missouri–Kansas City	M,D
The University of Montana	M
University of Montevallo	M
University of Nebraska at Omaha	M
University of Nebraska–Lincoln	M,D
University of Nevada, Las Vegas	M,D
University of Nevada, Reno	M
University of New Hampshire	M
University of New Mexico	M
University of New Orleans	M
The University of North Carolina at Chapel Hill	M,D
The University of North Carolina at Greensboro	M,D
University of North Dakota	M,D
University of Northern Colorado	M,D
University of Northern Iowa	M
University of North Texas	M,D
University of Oklahoma	M,D
University of Oregon	M,D
University of Pennsylvania	M,D
University of Pittsburgh	M,D
University of Portland	M
University of Redlands	M
University of Rhode Island	M
University of Rochester	M,D
University of South Carolina	M,D,O
The University of South Dakota	M
University of Southern California	M,D,O
University of Southern Maine	M
University of Southern Mississippi	M,D
University of South Florida	M
The University of Tennessee	M
The University of Tennessee at Chattanooga	M
The University of Texas at Arlington	M
The University of Texas at Austin	M,D
The University of Texas at El Paso	M
The University of Texas at San Antonio	M
The University of Texas at Tyler	M
The University of Texas–Pan American	M
University of the Pacific	M
The University of Toledo	M
University of Utah	M,D
University of Virginia	M,D
University of Washington	M,D
University of West Georgia	M
University of Wisconsin–Madison	M,D
University of Wisconsin–Milwaukee	M,O
University of Wyoming	M
Valdosta State University	M
Virginia Commonwealth University	M
Washington State University	M
Washington University in St. Louis	M,D
Wayne State University	M,O
Webster University	M
West Chester University of Pennsylvania	M
Western Carolina University	M
Western Illinois University	M
Western Michigan University	M
Western Oregon University	M
Western Washington University	M
West Texas A&M University	M
West Virginia University	M,D
Wichita State University	M
William Paterson University of New Jersey	M
Winthrop University	M
Wright State University	M
Yale University	M,D,O
Youngstown State University	M

■ MUSIC EDUCATION

Institution	Degrees
Alabama Agricultural and Mechanical University	M
Albany State University	M
Appalachian State University	M
Arcadia University	M,D,O
Arkansas State University	M,O
Auburn University	M,D,O
Austin Peay State University	M
Azusa Pacific University	M
Ball State University	M,D
Baylor University	M
Belmont University	M
Bennington College	M
Bob Jones University	P,M,D,O
Boise State University	M
Boston University	M,D
Bowling Green State University	M,D
Brigham Young University	M
Brooklyn College of the City University of New York	M,D,O
Butler University	M
California State University, Fresno	M
California State University, Fullerton	M
California State University, Los Angeles	M
California State University, Northridge	M
Capital University	M
Carnegie Mellon University	M
Case Western Reserve University	M,D
The Catholic University of America	M,D
Central Connecticut State University	M,O
Central Michigan University	M
Cleveland State University	M
College of Mount St. Joseph	M
The College of Saint Rose	M,O
Columbus State University	M
Converse College	M
DePaul University	M,O
Duquesne University	M,O
East Carolina University	M
Eastern Kentucky University	M
Eastern Michigan University	M
Eastern Washington University	M
Emporia State University	M
Florida International University	M
Florida State University	M,D
George Mason University	M
Georgia State University	M,D,O
Hardin-Simmons University	M
Hofstra University	M
Holy Names University	M,O
Howard University	M
Hunter College of the City University of New York	M
Indiana University of Pennsylvania	M
Inter American University of Puerto Rico, San Germán Campus	M
Ithaca College	M
Jackson State University	M
Jacksonville University	M
James Madison University	M
Kansas State University	M
Kent State University	M,D
Kutztown University of Pennsylvania	O
Lamar University	M
Lee University	M
Lehman College of the City University of New York	M
Long Island University, C.W. Post Campus	M
Louisiana State University and Agricultural and Mechanical College	M,D
Manhattanville College	M
Marywood University	M
McNeese State University	M
Miami University	M
Michigan State University	M,D
Minot State University	M
Mississippi College	M
Montclair State University	M,O
Morehead State University	M
Murray State University	M
Nazareth College of Rochester	M
New Jersey City University	M
New York University	M,D,O
Norfolk State University	M
North Dakota State University	M,D,O
Northern Arizona University	M
Northwestern University	M,D
Northwest Missouri State University	M
Notre Dame de Namur University	M
Oakland University	M,D
Ohio University	M,O
Oklahoma State University	M
Old Dominion University	M
Oregon State University	M
Penn State University Park	M,D
Pittsburg State University	M
Portland State University	M
Queens College of the City University of New York	M,O
Rhode Island College	M
Rollins College	M
Roosevelt University	M,O

Rowan University M,O
Rutgers, The State University of New Jersey, New Brunswick M,D,O
St. Cloud State University M
Salisbury University M
Samford University M
Sam Houston State University M
San Diego State University M
San Francisco State University M
Shenandoah University M,D,O
Silver Lake College M
Southeast Missouri State University M
Southern Illinois University Carbondale M
Southern Illinois University Edwardsville M
Southern Methodist University M,O
Southwestern Oklahoma State University M
State University of New York at Fredonia M
State University of New York College at Potsdam M
Syracuse University M
Temple University M,D
Tennessee State University M
Texas A&M University–Commerce M
Texas A&M University–Kingsville M
Texas Christian University M,O
Texas State University-San Marcos M
Texas Tech University M,D
Towson University M,O
Union College (KY) M
University at Buffalo, the State University of New York M,D,O
The University of Akron M
The University of Alabama M,D,O
University of Alaska Fairbanks M
The University of Arizona M,D
University of Central Arkansas M
University of Central Oklahoma M
University of Cincinnati M
University of Colorado at Boulder M,D
University of Connecticut M,D,O
University of Dayton M
University of Delaware M
University of Denver M,O
University of Florida M,D
University of Georgia M,D,O
University of Hartford M,D,O
University of Houston M,D
The University of Iowa M,D
University of Kansas M,D
University of Kentucky M,D
University of Louisiana at Lafayette M
University of Louisville M
University of Maryland, College Park M,D
University of Massachusetts Lowell M
University of Memphis M,D
University of Miami M,D,O
University of Michigan M,D,O
University of Minnesota, Duluth M
University of Missouri–Columbia M,D,O
University of Missouri–Kansas City M,D
University of Missouri–St. Louis M
The University of Montana M
University of Montevallo M
University of Nebraska at Kearney M
University of Nevada, Las Vegas M,D
University of New Hampshire M
The University of North Carolina at Chapel Hill M
The University of North Carolina at Charlotte M
The University of North Carolina at Greensboro M,D
The University of North Carolina at Pembroke M
University of North Dakota M,D
University of Northern Colorado M,D
University of Northern Iowa M
University of North Texas M,D
University of Oklahoma M,D
University of Oregon M,D
University of Rhode Island M
University of Rochester M,D
University of St. Thomas (MN) M
University of South Carolina M,D,O
University of Southern California M,D
University of Southern Mississippi M,D
University of South Florida M
The University of Tennessee M
The University of Texas at El Paso M
The University of Texas at Tyler M
The University of Texas–Pan American M
University of the Pacific M
The University of Toledo M
University of Washington M,D
University of West Georgia M
University of Wisconsin–Madison M,D
University of Wisconsin–Stevens Point M
University of Wyoming M
Valdosta State University M
Virginia Commonwealth University M
Washington State University M
Wayne State College M
Wayne State University M,O
Webster University M
West Chester University of Pennsylvania M
Western Carolina University M
Western Connecticut State University M
Western Kentucky University M
West Virginia University M,D
Wichita State University M
Winthrop University M
Wright State University M
Youngstown State University M

■ NANOTECHNOLOGY

George Mason University M,D,O
Rice University M
University at Albany, State University of New York M,D
University of Washington M,D

■ NATIONAL SECURITY

California State University, San Bernardino M
Georgetown University M
New Jersey City University M
Texas A&M University M,O
University of Pittsburgh M

■ NATURAL RESOURCES

Auburn University M,D
Ball State University M
Cornell University M,D
Duke University M,D
Georgia Institute of Technology M,D
Humboldt State University M
Iowa State University of Science and Technology M,D
Louisiana State University and Agricultural and Mechanical College M,D
Montana State University M,D
North Carolina State University M
The Ohio State University M,D
Oklahoma State University M,D
Purdue University M,D
State University of New York College of Environmental Science and Forestry M,D
Texas A&M University M,D
The University of Arizona M,D
University of Arkansas at Monticello M
University of Connecticut M,D
University of Florida M,D
University of Georgia M,D
University of Hawaii at Manoa M,D
University of Idaho M,D
University of Illinois at Urbana–Champaign M,D
University of Maine M,D
University of Maryland, College Park M,D
University of Michigan M,D,O
The University of Montana M,D
University of Nebraska–Lincoln M,D
University of New Hampshire D
University of Oklahoma M,D
University of Rhode Island M,D
University of Vermont M,D
University of Wisconsin–Stevens Point M
University of Wyoming M,D
Utah State University M
Virginia Polytechnic Institute and State University M
Washington State University M,D

■ NATUROPATHIC MEDICINE

University of Bridgeport D

■ NEAR AND MIDDLE EASTERN LANGUAGES

Brandeis University M,D
The Catholic University of America M,D
Columbia University M,D
Georgetown University M,D
Harvard University M,D
Indiana University Bloomington M,D
The Ohio State University M,D
University of California, Los Angeles M,D
University of Chicago M,D
University of Michigan M,D
The University of Texas at Austin M,D
University of Utah M,D
University of Wisconsin–Madison M,D
Yale University M,D

■ NEAR AND MIDDLE EASTERN STUDIES

Brandeis University M,D
Columbia University M,D,O
Cornell University M,D
Drew University M,D
Emory University D,O
Georgetown University M,O
Gratz College O
Harvard University M,D
The Johns Hopkins University M,D,O
New York University M,D,O
Princeton University M,D
The University of Arizona M,D
University of California, Berkeley M,D
University of California, Los Angeles M,D
University of Chicago M,D
University of Kansas M
University of Michigan M,D
University of Pennsylvania M,D
The University of Texas at Austin M,D
University of Utah M,D
University of Washington M,D

Washington University in St. Louis M
Wayne State University M

▪ NEUROBIOLOGY

Brandeis University M,D
California Institute of Technology D
Carnegie Mellon University M,D
Case Western Reserve University D
Columbia University M,D
Cornell University D
Duke University D
Georgia State University M,D
Harvard University D
Illinois State University M,D
Loyola University Chicago M,D
Marquette University M,D
Massachusetts Institute of Technology D
New York University M,D
Northwestern University M,D
Purdue University M,D
University at Albany, State University of New York M,D
The University of Alabama at Birmingham D
University of California, Irvine M,D
University of California, Los Angeles D
University of California, San Diego D
University of Chicago D
University of Colorado at Boulder M,D
University of Connecticut M,D
University of Illinois at Chicago M,D
The University of Iowa M,D
University of Kentucky D
University of Louisville M,D
University of Missouri–Columbia M,D
The University of North Carolina at Chapel Hill D
University of Pittsburgh M,D
University of Rochester M,D
University of Southern California M,D
The University of Texas at Austin M,D
The University of Texas at San Antonio M,D
University of Utah D
University of Vermont D
University of Washington D
University of Wisconsin–Madison D
Virginia Commonwealth University D
Wake Forest University D
Wayne State University D
Yale University D

▪ NEUROSCIENCE

American University D
Argosy University, Tampa Campus M,D
Arizona State University M,D
Baylor University M,D
Boston University M,D
Brandeis University M,D
Brigham Young University M,D
Brown University D
California Institute of Technology M,D
Carnegie Mellon University D
Case Western Reserve University D
College of Staten Island of the City University of New York M
Colorado State University M,D
Dartmouth College D
Drexel University D
Duke University D,O
Emory University D
Florida Atlantic University D
Florida State University D
George Mason University M,D,O
Georgetown University D
The George Washington University D
Graduate School and University Center of the City University of New York D
Harvard University D
Illinois State University M,D
Iowa State University of Science and Technology M,D
The Johns Hopkins University D
Kent State University M,D
Loyola University Chicago M,D
Massachusetts Institute of Technology D
Mayo Graduate School D
Michigan State University M,D
Montana State University M,D
New York University D
Northwestern University D
The Ohio State University M,D
Ohio University M,D
Penn State University Park M,D
Princeton University D
Rutgers, The State University of New Jersey, Newark D
Rutgers, The State University of New Jersey, New Brunswick D
Seton Hall University M
Stanford University D
Stony Brook University, State University of New York D
Syracuse University M,D
Temple University M,D
Texas A&M University M,D
Tufts University D
Tulane University M,D
University at Albany, State University of New York M,D
University at Buffalo, the State University of New York M,D
The University of Alabama at Birmingham M,D
The University of Arizona D
University of California, Berkeley D
University of California, Davis D
University of California, Los Angeles D
University of California, Riverside D
University of California, San Diego D
University of Chicago D
University of Cincinnati D
University of Colorado Denver D
University of Connecticut M,D
University of Delaware D
University of Florida M,D
University of Georgia D
University of Hartford M
University of Idaho M,D
University of Illinois at Chicago D
University of Illinois at Urbana–Champaign D
The University of Iowa D
University of Kansas M,D
University of Maryland, Baltimore County D
University of Maryland, College Park M,D
University of Massachusetts Amherst M,D
University of Miami M,D
University of Michigan D
University of Minnesota, Twin Cities Campus M,D
University of Missouri–St. Louis M,D,O
The University of Montana M,D
University of New Mexico M,D
University of Oregon M,D
University of Pennsylvania D
University of Pittsburgh D
University of Rochester M,D
University of South Alabama D
The University of South Dakota M,D
University of Southern California D
The University of Texas at Austin M,D
The University of Texas at Dallas M,D
The University of Toledo M,D
University of Utah D
University of Vermont D
University of Virginia D
University of Washington D
University of Wisconsin–Madison M,D
University of Wyoming D
Vanderbilt University D
Virginia Commonwealth University M,D
Wake Forest University D
Washington State University M,D
Washington University in St. Louis D
Wayne State University M,D
West Virginia University D
Yale University D

▪ NONPROFIT MANAGEMENT

Azusa Pacific University M
Boston University M,O
Capella University M,D,O
Carlow University M
Case Western Reserve University M,O
Cleveland State University M,O
College of Notre Dame of Maryland M
The College of Saint Rose O
Columbia University M
DePaul University M,O
Eastern Michigan University M
Eastern University M
Fairleigh Dickinson University, Metropolitan Campus M,O
Florida Atlantic University M
The George Washington University M
Hamline University M
High Point University M
Hope International University M
Illinois Institute of Technology M
Indiana University Bloomington M,D,O
Indiana University Northwest M,O
Indiana University–Purdue University Indianapolis M
Indiana University South Bend M,O
John Carroll University M
Kean University M
Lindenwood University M
Lipscomb University M
Long Island University, C.W. Post Campus M,O
Metropolitan State University M
New Mexico Highlands University M
The New School: A University M
New York University M,D,O
North Central College M
Northern Kentucky University M,O
Oral Roberts University M
Pace University M
Park University M
Regis College (MA) M,O
Regis University M,O
Robert Morris University M
Roberts Wesleyan College M,O
Rosemont College M
St. Cloud State University M
Saint Xavier University M,O
San Francisco State University M
Seattle University M
Seton Hall University M
Southern New Hampshire University M,D,O
Suffolk University M,O
Texas A&M University M,O

Trinity (Washington) University	M
Tufts University	O
University of Central Florida	M,O
University of Connecticut	M,O
University of Dallas	M
University of Delaware	M,D
University of Georgia	M,D,O
The University of Iowa	M
University of La Verne	M,O
University of Maryland, Baltimore County	M,O
University of Memphis	M
University of Michigan–Dearborn	M,O
University of Missouri–St. Louis	M,O
The University of North Carolina at Greensboro	M,O
University of Northern Iowa	M
University of Notre Dame	M
University of Pittsburgh	M
University of San Diego	M,D,O
University of San Francisco	M
University of Southern Maine	M,O
Virginia Commonwealth University	O
Western Illinois University	M,O
Willamette University	M
Worcester State College	M

■ NORTHERN STUDIES

University of Alaska Fairbanks	M

■ NUCLEAR ENGINEERING

Cornell University	M,D
Georgia Institute of Technology	M,D
Idaho State University	M,D,O
Kansas State University	M,D
Massachusetts Institute of Technology	M,D,O
Missouri University of Science and Technology	M,D
North Carolina State University	M,D
The Ohio State University	M,D
Oregon State University	M,D
Penn State University Park	M,D
Purdue University	M,D
Rensselaer Polytechnic Institute	M,D
Texas A&M University	M,D
University of California, Berkeley	M,D
University of Cincinnati	M,D
University of Florida	M,D,O
University of Idaho	M,D
University of Illinois at Urbana–Champaign	M,D
University of Maryland, College Park	M,D
University of Massachusetts Lowell	M
University of Michigan	M,D,O
University of Missouri–Columbia	M,D
University of New Mexico	M,D
The University of Tennessee	M,D
University of Utah	M,D
University of Wisconsin–Madison	M,D
Virginia Commonwealth University	M

■ NURSE ANESTHESIA

Arkansas State University	M,O
Barry University	M
Boston College	M,D
Bradley University	M
Case Western Reserve University	M
Central Connecticut State University	M,O
Columbia University	M,O
DePaul University	M
Drexel University	M
Duke University	M,D,O
Emory University	M,D
Fairfield University	M,O
Gannon University	M,O
Gonzaga University	M
La Roche College	M
Missouri State University	M
Mountain State University	M,O
Mount Marty College	M
Murray State University	M
Newman University	M
Northeastern University	M
Oakland University	M,O
Saint Joseph's University	M
Saint Mary's University of Minnesota	M
Southern Illinois University Edwardsville	M,O
Texas Christian University	M
Texas Wesleyan University	M
Union University	M,O
University at Buffalo, the State University of New York	M,D,O
The University of Alabama at Birmingham	M
University of Cincinnati	M,D
University of Detroit Mercy	M
University of Kansas	M
University of Miami	M,D
University of Michigan–Flint	M
University of Minnesota, Twin Cities Campus	M
University of New England	M
The University of North Carolina at Charlotte	M
The University of North Carolina at Greensboro	M,D,O
University of Pennsylvania	M
University of Pittsburgh	M
The University of Scranton	M,O
University of South Carolina	M
The University of Tennessee at Chattanooga	M
University of Wisconsin–La Crosse	M
Villanova University	M,D,O
Virginia Commonwealth University	M,D
Wayne State University	M,O
Webster University	M
Westminster College (UT)	M

■ NURSE MIDWIFERY

Boston University	M,O
Case Western Reserve University	M,D
Columbia University	M
Emory University	M
Marquette University	M,D,O
New York University	M,O
Philadelphia University	M,O
Shenandoah University	M,O
Stony Brook University, State University of New York	M,O
University of Cincinnati	M,D
University of Illinois at Chicago	M
University of Indianapolis	M
University of Kansas	M,D,O
University of Miami	M,D
University of Michigan	M
University of Minnesota, Twin Cities Campus	M
University of Pennsylvania	M
University of Rhode Island	M,D
The University of Texas at El Paso	M
Vanderbilt University	M,D
Wichita State University	M

■ NURSING—GENERAL

Abilene Christian University	M
Adelphi University	M,D,O
Albany State University	M
Alcorn State University	M
Alverno College	M
American International College	M
Andrews University	M
Arizona State University	M
Arkansas State University	M,O
Armstrong Atlantic State University	M
Augsburg College	M
Austin Peay State University	M
Azusa Pacific University	M,D
Ball State University	M
Barry University	M,D,O
Baylor University	M
Bellarmine University	M,D
Belmont University	M
Bethel University	M,O
Bloomsburg University of Pennsylvania	M
Boston College	M,D
Bowie State University	M
Bradley University	M
Brigham Young University	M
California State University, Bakersfield	M
California State University, Chico	M
California State University, Dominguez Hills	M
California State University, Fresno	M
California State University, Fullerton	M
California State University, Long Beach	M
California State University, Los Angeles	M
California State University, Sacramento	M
California State University, San Bernardino	M
Capital University	M
Cardinal Stritch University	M
Carlow University	M,O
Carson-Newman College	M
Case Western Reserve University	M,D
The Catholic University of America	M,D
Chatham University	M,D
Clarion University of Pennsylvania	M
Clemson University	M
Cleveland State University	M
College of Mount St. Joseph	M
College of Mount Saint Vincent	M,O
The College of New Jersey	M,O
The College of New Rochelle	M,O
College of St. Catherine	M
The College of St. Scholastica	M,O
College of Staten Island of the City University of New York	M,O
Columbia University	M,D,O
Concordia University Wisconsin	M
Coppin State University	M,O
Creighton University	M
Daemen College	M,O
Delta State University	M
DePaul University	M
DeSales University	M
Dominican College	M
Dominican University of California	M
Drexel University	M
Duke University	D
Duquesne University	M,D,O
D'Youville College	M,O
East Carolina University	M,D
Eastern Kentucky University	M
Eastern Washington University	M
East Tennessee State University	M,D,O
Edgewood College	M
Edinboro University of Pennsylvania	M
Elmhurst College	M
Emory University	M,D
Fairfield University	M,O

Fairleigh Dickinson University, Metropolitan Campus	M,O
Ferris State University	M
Florida Agricultural and Mechanical University	M
Florida Atlantic University	M,D,O
Florida Gulf Coast University	M
Florida International University	M,D
Florida State University	M,O
Fort Hays State University	M
Franciscan University of Steubenville	M
Gannon University	M,O
Gardner-Webb University	M,O
George Mason University	M,D,O
Georgetown University	M
Georgia College & State University	M
Georgia Southern University	M,O
Georgia State University	M,D,O
Gonzaga University	M
Governors State University	M
Graceland University	M,O
Graduate School and University Center of the City University of New York	D
Grambling State University	M,O
Grand Valley State University	M
Gwynedd-Mercy College	M
Hampton University	M
Hardin-Simmons University	M
Hawai'i Pacific University	M
Holy Family University	M
Holy Names University	M
Howard University	M,O
Hunter College of the City University of New York	M,O
Husson College	M
Idaho State University	M,O
Illinois State University	M,O
Immaculata University	M
Indiana State University	M
Indiana University of Pennsylvania	M
Indiana University–Purdue University Fort Wayne	M,O
Indiana University–Purdue University Indianapolis	M,D
Indiana Wesleyan University	M,O
Jacksonville State University	M
Jacksonville University	M
James Madison University	M
The Johns Hopkins University	M,D,O
Kean University	M
Kennesaw State University	M
Kent State University	M,D
Lamar University	M
La Roche College	M
La Salle University	M,O
Lehman College of the City University of New York	M
Le Moyne College	M
Lewis University	M
Liberty University	M,D
Lincoln Memorial University	M
Long Island University, Brooklyn Campus	M,O
Long Island University, C.W. Post Campus	M,O
Loyola University Chicago	M
Loyola University New Orleans	M
Madonna University	M
Malone College	M
Mansfield University of Pennsylvania	M
Marian College of Fond du Lac	M
Marquette University	M,D,O
Marshall University	M
Marymount University	M,O
Maryville University of Saint Louis	M
McNeese State University	M
Mercer University	M,O
Mercy College	M
Metropolitan State University	M
Michigan State University	M,D
Middle Tennessee State University	M
Midwestern State University	M
Millersville University of Pennsylvania	M
Minnesota State University Mankato	M,D
Minnesota State University Moorhead	M,O
Misericordia University	M
Mississippi University for Women	M,O
Missouri State University	M
Molloy College	M,O
Monmouth University	M,O
Montana State University	M,O
Mountain State University	M,O
Mount Saint Mary College	M
Mount St. Mary's College	M
Murray State University	M
Nazareth College of Rochester	M
Neumann College	M
New Jersey City University	M
New Mexico State University	M
New York University	M,O
North Dakota State University	M,D
Northeastern University	M,O
Northern Arizona University	M,O
Northern Illinois University	M
Northern Kentucky University	M,O
Northern Michigan University	M
North Park University	M
Northwestern State University of Louisiana	M
Nova Southeastern University	M
Oakland University	M,D,O
The Ohio State University	M,D
Oklahoma City University	M
Old Dominion University	M
Otterbein College	M,O
Pace University	M,O
Pacific Lutheran University	M
Penn State University Park	M,D
Pittsburg State University	M
Point Loma Nazarene University	M
Pontifical Catholic University of Puerto Rico	M
Prairie View A&M University	M
Purdue University Calumet	M
Queens University of Charlotte	M
Radford University	M
Regis College (MA)	M,O
Regis University	M
Rhode Island College	M
The Richard Stockton College of New Jersey	M
Rivier College	M
Robert Morris University	M
Roberts Wesleyan College	M
Rutgers, The State University of New Jersey, Newark	M
Sacred Heart University	M
Saginaw Valley State University	M
St. Ambrose University	M
St. John Fisher College	M,O
Saint Joseph College	M,O
Saint Joseph's College of Maine	M,O
St. Joseph's College, Suffolk Campus	M
Saint Louis University	M,D,O
Saint Peter's College	M
Saint Xavier University	M,O
Salem State College	M
Salisbury University	M
Samford University	M
San Diego State University	M
San Francisco State University	M
San Jose State University	M,O
Seattle Pacific University	M,O
Seattle University	M
Seton Hall University	M,D
Shenandoah University	M,O
Simmons College	M,D,O
Slippery Rock University of Pennsylvania	M
South Dakota State University	M,D
Southeastern Louisiana University	M
Southeast Missouri State University	M
Southern Connecticut State University	M
Southern Illinois University Edwardsville	M,O
Southern Nazarene University	M
Southern University and Agricultural and Mechanical College	M,D,O
Spalding University	M
Spring Hill College	M
State University of New York at Binghamton	M,D,O
State University of New York at New Paltz	M,O
State University of New York Institute of Technology	M,O
Stony Brook University, State University of New York	M,O
Temple University	M
Tennessee State University	M
Tennessee Technological University	M
Texas A&M International University	M
Texas A&M University–Corpus Christi	M
Texas Christian University	M
Texas Woman's University	M,D
Towson University	M,O
Troy University	M
Union University	M,O
University at Buffalo, the State University of New York	M,D,O
The University of Akron	M,D
The University of Alabama	M
The University of Alabama at Birmingham	M,D
The University of Alabama in Huntsville	M,O
University of Alaska Anchorage	M,O
The University of Arizona	M,D
University of Arkansas	M
University of California, Los Angeles	M,D
University of Central Arkansas	M
University of Central Florida	M,D,O
University of Central Missouri	M
University of Cincinnati	M,D
University of Colorado at Colorado Springs	M,D
University of Colorado Denver	M,D,O
University of Connecticut	M,D,O
University of Delaware	M,O
University of Evansville	M
University of Florida	M,D
University of Hartford	M
University of Hawaii at Manoa	M,D,O
University of Illinois at Chicago	M,D
University of Indianapolis	M
The University of Iowa	M,D
University of Kansas	M,D,O
University of Kentucky	M,D
University of Louisiana at Lafayette	M
University of Louisville	M,D
University of Maine	M,O

University of Mary	M
University of Massachusetts Amherst	M,D
University of Massachusetts Boston	M,D
University of Massachusetts Lowell	M,D
University of Miami	M,D
University of Michigan	M,D,O
University of Michigan–Flint	M
University of Minnesota, Twin Cities Campus	M,D
University of Missouri–Columbia	M,D
University of Missouri–Kansas City	M,D
University of Missouri–St. Louis	M,D,O
University of Mobile	M
University of Nevada, Las Vegas	M,D,O
University of Nevada, Reno	M
University of New Hampshire	M
University of New Mexico	M,D
University of North Alabama	M
The University of North Carolina at Chapel Hill	M,D
The University of North Carolina at Charlotte	M
The University of North Carolina at Greensboro	M,D,O
The University of North Carolina Wilmington	M
University of North Dakota	M,D
University of Northern Colorado	M,D
University of North Florida	M,O
University of Pennsylvania	M,D,O
University of Phoenix–Central Florida Campus	M
University of Phoenix–Denver Campus	M
University of Phoenix–Fort Lauderdale Campus	M
University of Phoenix–Hawaii Campus	M
University of Phoenix–Louisiana Campus	M
University of Phoenix–New Mexico Campus	M
University of Phoenix–North Florida Campus	M
University of Phoenix	M
University of Phoenix–Phoenix Campus	M,O
University of Phoenix–Sacramento Valley Campus	M
University of Phoenix–San Diego Campus	M
University of Phoenix–Southern California Campus	M,O
University of Phoenix–Southern Colorado Campus	M
University of Phoenix–Utah Campus	M
University of Phoenix–West Florida Campus	M
University of Phoenix–West Michigan Campus	M
University of Pittsburgh	M
University of Portland	M
University of Rhode Island	M,D
University of Rochester	M,D,O
University of St. Francis (IL)	M
University of Saint Francis (IN)	M
University of San Diego	M,D,O
University of San Francisco	M,D
The University of Scranton	M,O
University of South Alabama	M,D
University of South Carolina	M,O
University of Southern Indiana	M
University of Southern Maine	M,O
University of Southern Mississippi	M,D
University of South Florida	M,D
The University of Tampa	M
The University of Tennessee	M,D
The University of Tennessee at Chattanooga	M
The University of Texas at Arlington	M,D
The University of Texas at Austin	M,D
The University of Texas at El Paso	M
The University of Texas at Tyler	M
The University of Texas–Pan American	M
University of the Incarnate Word	M
The University of Toledo	M,O
University of Utah	M,D
University of Vermont	M
University of Virginia	M,D
University of Washington	M,D
University of Washington, Bothell	M
University of Washington, Tacoma	M
University of West Georgia	M
University of Wisconsin–Eau Claire	M
University of Wisconsin–Madison	M,D
University of Wisconsin–Milwaukee	M,D,O
University of Wisconsin–Oshkosh	M
University of Wyoming	M
Ursuline College	M
Valdosta State University	M
Valparaiso University	M,O
Vanderbilt University	M,D
Villanova University	M,D,O
Virginia Commonwealth University	M,D,O
Viterbo University	M
Wagner College	M
Walden University	M,D
Wayne State University	D
Webster University	M
Wesley College	M
West Chester University of Pennsylvania	M
Western Carolina University	M
Western Connecticut State University	M
Western Kentucky University	M
Westminster College (UT)	M
West Texas A&M University	M
West Virginia University	M,D,O
Wheeling Jesuit University	M
Wichita State University	M
Widener University	M,D,O
Wilkes University	M
William Carey University	M
William Paterson University of New Jersey	M
Wilmington University (DE)	M
Winona State University	M,O
Wright State University	M
Xavier University	M
Yale University	M,D,O
Youngstown State University	M

■ NURSING AND HEALTHCARE ADMINISTRATION

Barry University	M,D,O
Baylor University	M
Bellarmine University	M,D
Bloomsburg University of Pennsylvania	M
Bowie State University	M
Bradley University	M
Capital University	M
Carlow University	M,O
The Catholic University of America	M,D
College of Mount Saint Vincent	M,O
The College of New Rochelle	M,O
Daemen College	M,O
Duke University	M,D,O
Duquesne University	M,O
D'Youville College	M,O
Eastern Michigan University	M
Emory University	M
Ferris State University	M
Florida Agricultural and Mechanical University	M
Florida Atlantic University	M
Gannon University	M,O
George Mason University	M,D,O
The George Washington University	M,D,O
Graceland University	M,O
Grand Valley State University	M
Indiana University–Purdue University Fort Wayne	M,O
Indiana Wesleyan University	M,O
The Johns Hopkins University	M
Kean University	M
Kent State University	M,D
Lamar University	M
La Roche College	M
La Salle University	M,O
Lewis University	M
Long Island University, Brooklyn Campus	M
Loyola University Chicago	M
Madonna University	M
Marymount University	M,O
Marywood University	M
Mercy College	M
Minnesota State University Mankato	M,D
Molloy College	M,O
Mountain State University	M,O
Mount Saint Mary College	M
Northeastern University	M
Norwich University	M
Otterbein College	M,O
Pacific Lutheran University	M
Prairie View A&M University	M
Queens University of Charlotte	M
Rivier College	M
Roberts Wesleyan College	M
Sacred Heart University	M
Saginaw Valley State University	M
Saint Joseph's College of Maine	M,O
Saint Xavier University	M,O
San Francisco State University	M
San Jose State University	M,O
Seattle Pacific University	M
Seattle University	M
Seton Hall University	M
Southern Connecticut State University	M
Southern Illinois University Edwardsville	M,O
Southern Nazarene University	M
Southern University and Agricultural and Mechanical College	M,D,O
Spalding University	M
State University of New York Institute of Technology	M,O
Texas A&M University–Corpus Christi	M
University of Cincinnati	M,D
University of Colorado at Colorado Springs	M,D
University of Connecticut	M,D,O
University of Delaware	M,O
University of Hawaii at Manoa	M,D,O
University of Illinois at Chicago	M
University of Indianapolis	M
University of Mary	M
University of Massachusetts Lowell	D
University of Michigan	M
University of Minnesota, Twin Cities Campus	M
University of Missouri–Kansas City	M,D
The University of North Carolina at Greensboro	M,D,O

University of Pennsylvania	M,D
University of Pittsburgh	M
University of Rhode Island	M,D
University of San Diego	M,D,O
University of San Francisco	M,D
University of South Carolina	M
University of Southern Mississippi	M,D
The University of Tampa	M
The University of Tennessee at Chattanooga	M
The University of Texas at Arlington	M,D
The University of Texas at El Paso	M
The University of Texas at Tyler	M
Vanderbilt University	M,D
Villanova University	M,D,O
Virginia Commonwealth University	M,D,O
Wichita State University	M
Winona State University	M,O
Wright State University	M
Xavier University	M

■ NURSING EDUCATION

Angelo State University	M
Azusa Pacific University	M,D
Barry University	M,O
Bellarmine University	M,D
Bethel University	M,O
Bowie State University	M
Brenau University	M
The Catholic University of America	M,D
College of Mount Saint Vincent	M,O
The College of New Rochelle	M,O
Concordia University Wisconsin	M
DeSales University	M
Dominican University of California	M
Duke University	M,D,O
Duquesne University	M,O
D'Youville College	M,O
Eastern Michigan University	M,O
Eastern Washington University	M
Ferris State University	M
Florida State University	M,O
George Mason University	M,D,O
Graceland University	M,O
Grambling State University	M,O
Grand Valley State University	M
Indiana Wesleyan University	M,O
Lamar University	M
La Salle University	M,O
Lewis University	M
Marian College of Fond du Lac	M
Marymount University	M,O
Mercy College	M
Midwestern State University	M
Minnesota State University Mankato	M,D
Minnesota State University Moorhead	M
Molloy College	M,O
Montana State University	M,O
Mountain State University	M,O
Mount Saint Mary College	M
New York University	M,O
North Georgia College & State University	M
Oakland University	M,O
Prairie View A&M University	M
Regis College (MA)	M,O
Rivier College	M
Roberts Wesleyan College	M
St. John Fisher College	M,O
Saint Joseph's College of Maine	M,O
San Francisco State University	M
San Jose State University	M,O
Seton Hall University	M
Southern Connecticut State University	M
Southern Illinois University Edwardsville	M,O
Southern Nazarene University	M
Southern University and Agricultural and Mechanical College	M,D,O
State University of New York Institute of Technology	M,O
Texas Woman's University	M,D
Towson University	M,O
Union University	M,O
University of Alaska Anchorage	M,O
University of Central Florida	M,D,O
University of Hartford	M
University of Indianapolis	M
University of Kansas	M,D,O
University of Mary	M
University of Missouri–Kansas City	M,D
University of Nevada, Las Vegas	M,D,O
The University of North Carolina at Greensboro	M,D,O
University of Northern Colorado	M,D
University of Phoenix–Fort Lauderdale Campus	M
University of Phoenix–North Florida Campus	M
University of Phoenix	M
University of Phoenix–Sacramento Valley Campus	M
University of Phoenix–Southern California Campus	M,O
University of Phoenix–West Florida Campus	M
University of Pittsburgh	M
University of Rhode Island	M,D
The University of Tampa	M
The University of Tennessee at Chattanooga	M
The University of Texas at Arlington	M,D
The University of Texas at Tyler	M
Villanova University	M,D,O
Wayne State University	M,O
West Chester University of Pennsylvania	M
Westminster College (UT)	M
Winona State University	M,O

■ NURSING INFORMATICS

Case Western Reserve University	M
Duke University	M,D,O
Ferris State University	M
La Salle University	M,O
Molloy College	M,O
New York University	M,O
Tennessee State University	M
Vanderbilt University	M,D

■ NUTRITION

Andrews University	M
Arizona State University at the Polytechnic Campus	M
Auburn University	M,D
Baylor University	M,D
Benedictine University	M
Boston University	M,D
Bowling Green State University	M
Brigham Young University	M
Brooklyn College of the City University of New York	M
California State Polytechnic University, Pomona	M
California State University, Chico	M
California State University, Long Beach	M
California State University, Los Angeles	M
Case Western Reserve University	M,D
Central Michigan University	M
Central Washington University	M
Chapman University	M
Clemson University	M
College of Saint Elizabeth	M,O
Colorado State University	M,D
Columbia University	M,D
Cornell University	M,D
Drexel University	M,D
D'Youville College	M
East Carolina University	M
Eastern Illinois University	M
Eastern Kentucky University	M
Eastern Michigan University	M
East Tennessee State University	M
Emory University	M,D
Florida International University	M,D
Florida State University	M,D
Framingham State College	M
Georgia State University	M,O
Harvard University	D
Howard University	M,D
Idaho State University	M,O
Immaculata University	M
Indiana State University	M
Indiana University Bloomington	M,D
Indiana University of Pennsylvania	M
Indiana University–Purdue University Indianapolis	M,D
Iowa State University of Science and Technology	M,D
The Johns Hopkins University	M,D
Kansas State University	M,D
Kent State University	M
Lehman College of the City University of New York	M
Long Island University, C.W. Post Campus	M,O
Louisiana Tech University	M
Marshall University	M
Marywood University	M
Michigan State University	M,D
Middle Tennessee State University	M
Mississippi State University	M,D
Montclair State University	M,O
Mount Mary College	M
New York Institute of Technology	M
New York University	M,D
North Carolina Agricultural and Technical State University	M
North Carolina State University	M,D
North Dakota State University	M
Northern Illinois University	M
The Ohio State University	M,D
Ohio University	M
Oklahoma State University	M,D
Oregon State University	M,D
Penn State University Park	M,D
Purdue University	M,D
Rutgers, The State University of New Jersey, New Brunswick	M,D
Saint Louis University	M
San Diego State University	M
San Jose State University	M
Simmons College	M,O
South Carolina State University	M
South Dakota State University	M
Southeast Missouri State University	M
Southern Illinois University Carbondale	M
Syracuse University	M
Texas Southern University	M
Texas Tech University	M,D

Texas Woman's University	M,D
Tufts University	M,D
Tulane University	M
University at Buffalo, the State University of New York	M,D
The University of Akron	M
The University of Alabama	M
The University of Alabama at Birmingham	M,D,O
University of Alaska Fairbanks	M,D
University of Bridgeport	M
University of California, Berkeley	M,D
University of California, Davis	M,D
University of Central Oklahoma	M
University of Chicago	D
University of Cincinnati	M
University of Connecticut	M,D
University of Delaware	M
University of Florida	M,D
University of Georgia	M,D
University of Hawaii at Manoa	M
University of Illinois at Chicago	M,D
University of Illinois at Urbana–Champaign	M,D
University of Kansas	M,O
University of Kentucky	M,D
University of Maine	M,D
University of Maryland, College Park	M,D
University of Massachusetts Amherst	M,D
University of Memphis	M
University of Michigan	M
University of Minnesota, Twin Cities Campus	M,D
University of Missouri–Columbia	M,D
University of Nebraska–Lincoln	M,D
University of Nevada, Reno	M
University of New Hampshire	M,D
University of New Haven	M
University of New Mexico	M
The University of North Carolina at Chapel Hill	M,D
The University of North Carolina at Greensboro	M,D
University of North Florida	M,O
University of Pittsburgh	M
University of Puerto Rico, Río Piedras	M
University of Rhode Island	M,D
University of Southern California	M
University of Southern Mississippi	M,D
The University of Tennessee	M
The University of Tennessee at Martin	M
The University of Texas at Austin	M,D
University of the Incarnate Word	M,O
University of Utah	M
University of Vermont	M,D
University of Washington	M,D
University of Wisconsin–Madison	M,D
University of Wisconsin–Stevens Point	M
University of Wisconsin–Stout	M
University of Wyoming	M
Utah State University	M,D
Virginia Polytechnic Institute and State University	M,D
Washington State University	M,D
Wayne State University	M,D
West Virginia University	M
Winthrop University	M

■ OCCUPATIONAL HEALTH NURSING

University of Cincinnati	M,D
University of Massachusetts Lowell	M
University of Michigan	M
University of Minnesota, Twin Cities Campus	M,D
The University of North Carolina at Chapel Hill	M
University of Pennsylvania	M

■ OCCUPATIONAL THERAPY

Alvernia College	M
American International College	M
Barry University	M
Belmont University	M,D
Boston University	M,D
Brenau University	M
California State University, Dominguez Hills	M
Chatham University	M,D
Cleveland State University	M
College of St. Catherine	M
The College of St. Scholastica	M
Colorado State University	M
Columbia University	M,D
Concordia University Wisconsin	M
Creighton University	D
Dominican College	M
Dominican University of California	M
Duquesne University	M,D
D'Youville College	M
East Carolina University	M
Eastern Kentucky University	M
Eastern Michigan University	M
Eastern Washington University	M
Florida Gulf Coast University	M
Florida International University	M
Gannon University	M,O
Governors State University	M
Grand Valley State University	M
Idaho State University	M
Indiana University–Purdue University Indianapolis	M,D
Ithaca College	M
James Madison University	M
Kean University	M
Maryville University of Saint Louis	M
Mercy College	M
Misericordia University	M
Mount Mary College	M
New York Institute of Technology	M
New York University	M,D
Nova Southeastern University	M,D
The Ohio State University	M
Pacific University	M
Philadelphia University	M
Quinnipiac University	M
The Richard Stockton College of New Jersey	M
Rockhurst University	M
Sacred Heart University	M
Saginaw Valley State University	M
St. Ambrose University	M
Saint Francis University	M
Saint Louis University	M
Salem State College	M
San Jose State University	M
Seton Hall University	M
Shenandoah University	M
Spalding University	M
Springfield College	M,O
Stony Brook University, State University of New York	M,D,O
Temple University	M
Texas Woman's University	M,D
Touro College	M
Towson University	M
Tufts University	M,D,O
University at Buffalo, the State University of New York	M
The University of Alabama at Birmingham	M
University of Central Arkansas	M
The University of Findlay	M
University of Florida	M
University of Illinois at Chicago	M
University of Indianapolis	M,D
University of Kansas	M,D
University of Mary	M
University of Missouri–Columbia	M
University of New England	M
University of New Hampshire	M
University of New Mexico	M
The University of North Carolina at Chapel Hill	M,D
University of North Dakota	M
University of Pittsburgh	M
University of Puget Sound	M
The University of Scranton	M
University of South Alabama	M
The University of South Dakota	M
University of Southern California	M,D
University of Southern Indiana	M
University of Southern Maine	M
The University of Texas–Pan American	M
The University of Toledo	M,D
University of Utah	M
University of Washington	M,D
University of Wisconsin–La Crosse	M
University of Wisconsin–Madison	M,D
University of Wisconsin–Milwaukee	M
Utica College	M
Virginia Commonwealth University	M,D
Washington University in St. Louis	M,D
Wayne State University	M
Western Michigan University	M
West Virginia University	M
Worcester State College	M
Xavier University	M

■ OCEAN ENGINEERING

Florida Atlantic University	M,D
Florida Institute of Technology	M,D
Georgia Institute of Technology	M,D
Massachusetts Institute of Technology	M,D,O
Oregon State University	M
Stevens Institute of Technology	M,D
Texas A&M University	M,D
University of Alaska Anchorage	M,O
University of California, San Diego	M,D
University of Delaware	M,D
University of Florida	M,D,O
University of Hawaii at Manoa	M,D
University of Michigan	M,D,O
University of New Hampshire	M,D
University of Rhode Island	M,D
University of Southern California	M
Virginia Polytechnic Institute and State University	M,D

■ OCEANOGRAPHY

Columbia University	M,D
Cornell University	D
Florida Institute of Technology	M,D
Florida State University	M,D
Louisiana State University and Agricultural and Mechanical College	M,D
Massachusetts Institute of Technology	M,D,O
North Carolina State University	M,D
Nova Southeastern University	M,D
Old Dominion University	M,D
Oregon State University	M,D

Institution	Degrees
Princeton University	D
Rutgers, The State University of New Jersey, New Brunswick	M,D
Texas A&M University	M,D
University of Alaska Fairbanks	M,D
University of California, San Diego	M,D
University of Colorado at Boulder	M,D
University of Connecticut	M,D
University of Delaware	M,D
University of Georgia	M,D
University of Hawaii at Manoa	M,D
University of Maine	M,D
University of Maryland, College Park	M,D
University of Miami	M,D
University of Michigan	M,D
University of New Hampshire	M,D
University of Rhode Island	M,D
University of Southern California	D
University of South Florida	M,D
University of Washington	M,D
University of Wisconsin–Madison	M,D
Yale University	D

■ ONCOLOGY NURSING

Institution	Degrees
Columbia University	M,O
Duke University	M,D,O
Emory University	M
Gwynedd-Mercy College	M
Loyola University Chicago	M
University of Delaware	M,O
University of Pennsylvania	M

■ OPERATIONS RESEARCH

Institution	Degrees
Bowling Green State University	M
California State University, East Bay	M
California State University, Fullerton	M
Carnegie Mellon University	D
Case Western Reserve University	M
Claremont Graduate University	M,D
Clemson University	M,D
The College of William and Mary	M
Columbia University	M,D,O
Cornell University	M,D
Florida Institute of Technology	M,D
George Mason University	M
Georgia Institute of Technology	M
Georgia State University	M,D
Idaho State University	M,D,O
Indiana University–Purdue University Fort Wayne	M,O
Iowa State University of Science and Technology	M,D
The Johns Hopkins University	M,D
Kansas State University	M,D
Louisiana Tech University	M,D
Massachusetts Institute of Technology	M,D
Miami University	M
New Mexico Institute of Mining and Technology	M,D
North Carolina State University	M,D
North Dakota State University	M,D,O
Northeastern University	M,D
Northwestern University	M,D
Oklahoma State University	M,D
Oregon State University	M,D
Princeton University	M,D
Rensselaer Polytechnic Institute	M,D
Rutgers, The State University of New Jersey, New Brunswick	D
St. Mary's University of San Antonio	M
Southern Methodist University	M,D
Temple University	D
The University of Alabama in Huntsville	M
University of Arkansas	M
University of California, Berkeley	M,D
University of California, Los Angeles	M,D
University of Central Florida	M,D,O
University of Colorado at Boulder	M
University of Delaware	M,D
University of Illinois at Chicago	D
The University of Iowa	M,D
University of Massachusetts Amherst	M,D
University of Miami	M
University of Michigan	M,D
University of New Haven	M
The University of North Carolina at Chapel Hill	M,D
University of Southern California	M
The University of Texas at Austin	M,D
Virginia Commonwealth University	M,O
Virginia Polytechnic Institute and State University	M,D
Western Michigan University	M

■ OPTICAL SCIENCES

Institution	Degrees
Alabama Agricultural and Mechanical University	M,D
Cleveland State University	M
Norfolk State University	M
The Ohio State University	M,D
Rochester Institute of Technology	M,D
The University of Alabama in Huntsville	D
The University of Arizona	M,D
University of Central Florida	M,D
University of Colorado at Boulder	M,D
University of Dayton	M,D
University of Maryland, Baltimore County	M,D
University of Massachusetts Lowell	M,D
University of New Mexico	M,D
The University of North Carolina at Charlotte	M,D
University of Rochester	M,D

■ OPTOMETRY

Institution	Degrees
Ferris State University	P
Indiana University Bloomington	P,M,D
Northeastern State University	P
Nova Southeastern University	P,M
The Ohio State University	P
The University of Alabama at Birmingham	P
University of California, Berkeley	P,O
University of Houston	P
University of Missouri–St. Louis	P

■ ORAL AND DENTAL SCIENCES

Institution	Degrees
Boston University	P,M,D,O
Case Western Reserve University	M,O
Columbia University	M,D,O
The George Washington University	M
Harvard University	M,D,O
Howard University	P,O
Idaho State University	M,O
Jacksonville University	O
Marquette University	M
New York University	M,D,O
The Ohio State University	D
Saint Louis University	M
Stony Brook University, State University of New York	P,D,O
Temple University	M,O
Tufts University	M,O
University at Buffalo, the State University of New York	M,D,O
The University of Alabama at Birmingham	M
University of California, Los Angeles	M,D
University of Connecticut	M
University of Detroit Mercy	M,O
University of Florida	M,D,O
University of Illinois at Chicago	M
The University of Iowa	M,D,O
University of Kentucky	M
University of Louisville	M
University of Michigan	M,D,O
University of Minnesota, Twin Cities Campus	M,D,O
University of Missouri–Kansas City	P,M,D,O
The University of North Carolina at Chapel Hill	M,D
University of Pittsburgh	M,O
University of Rochester	M
University of Southern California	M,D
University of the Pacific	M,O
The University of Toledo	M
University of Washington	M,D
West Virginia University	M

■ ORGANIC CHEMISTRY

Institution	Degrees
Auburn University	M,D
Boston College	M,D
Brandeis University	M,D
Brigham Young University	M,D
California State University, Fullerton	M
California State University, Los Angeles	M
Case Western Reserve University	M,D
Clark Atlanta University	M,D
Clarkson University	M,D
Cleveland State University	M,D
Columbia University	M,D
Cornell University	D
Florida State University	M,D
Georgetown University	M,D
The George Washington University	M,D
Harvard University	D
Howard University	M,D
Kansas State University	M,D
Kent State University	M,D
Marquette University	M,D
Massachusetts Institute of Technology	M,D,O
Miami University	M,D
Northeastern University	M,D
Old Dominion University	M,D
Oregon State University	M,D
Purdue University	M,D
Rensselaer Polytechnic Institute	M,D
Rice University	M,D
Rutgers, The State University of New Jersey, Newark	M,D
Rutgers, The State University of New Jersey, New Brunswick	M,D
Seton Hall University	M,D
Southern University and Agricultural and Mechanical College	M
State University of New York at Binghamton	M,D
State University of New York College of Environmental Science and Forestry	M,D
Stevens Institute of Technology	M,D,O
Tufts University	M,D
University of Cincinnati	M,D
University of Georgia	M,D
University of Louisville	M,D
University of Maryland, College Park	M,D
University of Miami	M,D
University of Michigan	D
University of Missouri–Columbia	M,D
University of Missouri–Kansas City	M,D
University of Missouri–St. Louis	M,D
The University of Montana	M,D

University of Nebraska–Lincoln M,D
University of Notre Dame M,D
University of Southern Mississippi M,D
University of South Florida M,D
The University of Tennessee M,D
The University of Texas at Austin M,D
The University of Toledo M,D
Vanderbilt University M,D
Virginia Commonwealth University M,D
Wake Forest University M,D
West Virginia University M,D
Yale University D

■ ORGANIZATIONAL BEHAVIOR

Benedictine University M
Bernard M. Baruch College of the City University of New York M,D
Boston College D
Boston University D
California Lutheran University M,O
Carnegie Mellon University D
Case Western Reserve University M
Columbia College (SC) M,O
Cornell University M,D
Drexel University M,D,O
Fairleigh Dickinson University, College at Florham M,O
The George Washington University M,D
Georgia Institute of Technology M,D,O
Graduate School and University Center of the City University of New York D
Harvard University D
John Jay College of Criminal Justice of the City University of New York M,D
Lindenwood University M
New York University M,D
Northwestern University M,D
Oral Roberts University M
Polytechnic University, Brooklyn Campus M
Purdue University M,D
Silver Lake College M
Syracuse University D
Towson University O
University of California, Berkeley D
University of Hartford M
University of Hawaii at Manoa M
The University of North Carolina at Chapel Hill D
University of Oklahoma M
University of Pennsylvania M

■ ORGANIZATIONAL MANAGEMENT

American International College M
American University M
Antioch University Los Angeles M
Antioch University New England O
Antioch University Santa Barbara M
Antioch University Seattle M
Argosy University, Orange County Campus M,D,O
Argosy University, Sarasota Campus M,D,O
Argosy University, Tampa Campus M,D
Augsburg College M
Avila University M,O
Azusa Pacific University M
Benedictine University M,D
Bernard M. Baruch College of the City University of New York M,D
Bethel University M
Biola University M
Boston College D
Bowling Green State University M
Brenau University M
Cabrini College M,O
Capella University M,D,O
Carlow University M
Carnegie Mellon University D
Charleston Southern University M
Chatham University M
College of Mount St. Joseph M
College of St. Catherine M
Colorado Technical University—Colorado Springs M,D
Colorado Technical University—Sioux Falls M
Concordia University, St. Paul M
Cumberland University M
Dominican University M
Duquesne University M
Eastern Connecticut State University M
Eastern Michigan University M
Eastern University D
Endicott College M
Fairleigh Dickinson University, College at Florham M,O
Gannon University O
Geneva College M
George Fox University M
George Mason University M
The George Washington University M,O
Georgia State University M,D
Gonzaga University M
Hawai'i Pacific University M
Immaculata University M
Indiana University–Purdue University Fort Wayne M
Indiana Wesleyan University D
John F. Kennedy University M,O
Johnson & Wales University M
Lehigh University M,D,O
Lewis University M
Lindenwood University M
Manhattanville College M
Marian College of Fond du Lac M
Medaille College M
Mercy College M
Mercyhurst College M,O
Metropolitan State University M
Misericordia University M
National University M
Newman University M
The New School: A University M
New York University M,D
Northern Kentucky University M
Northwestern University M,D
Norwich University M
Nova Southeastern University D
Olivet Nazarene University M
Palm Beach Atlantic University M
Pfeiffer University M
Philadelphia Biblical University M
Point Park University M
Regent University M,D,O
Regis College (MA) M
Regis University M,O
Rider University M
Rivier College M
Roosevelt University M,D
Rutgers, The State University of New Jersey, Newark D
St. Ambrose University M
St. Edward's University M
St. Joseph's College, Suffolk Campus M,O
Saint Joseph's University M,D,O
Saint Louis University M,D,O
Saint Mary's University of Minnesota M
School for International Training M
Seattle University M,O
Shippensburg University of Pennsylvania M
Southern New Hampshire University M,D,O
Spring Arbor University M
Trevecca Nazarene University M
Trinity (Washington) University M
Tusculum College M
University of Cincinnati M
University of Dallas M
University of Denver M,O
University of Hawaii at Manoa M,D
University of La Verne M,D,O
University of Maryland Eastern Shore D
University of Massachusetts Dartmouth M,O
University of New Mexico M
University of North Texas M,D
University of Pennsylvania M
University of Phoenix D
University of St. Thomas (MN) M,D,O
University of San Francisco M
The University of Scranton M
University of the Incarnate Word M,D,O
Upper Iowa University M
Vanderbilt University M,D
Walden University M,D
Wayland Baptist University M
Wayne State College M
Webster University M
Wilmington University (DE) M
Woodbury University M
Worcester Polytechnic Institute M
Worcester State College M

■ OSTEOPATHIC MEDICINE

Michigan State University P
New York Institute of Technology P
Nova Southeastern University P,M
Ohio University P
University of New England P

■ PALEONTOLOGY

Cornell University M,D
Duke University D
Tulane University M,D
University of Chicago M,D
University of Illinois at Chicago M,D
West Virginia University M,D
Yale University D

■ PAPER AND PULP ENGINEERING

Miami University M
North Carolina State University M,D
Oregon State University M,D
State University of New York College of Environmental Science and Forestry M,D
University of Washington M,D
Western Michigan University M,D

■ PARASITOLOGY

Illinois State University M,D
New York University D
Purdue University M,D
Texas A&M University M,D
Tulane University M,D,O
University of Notre Dame M,D
University of Pennsylvania D
University of Washington M,D
Yale University D

■ PASTORAL MINISTRY AND COUNSELING

Abilene Christian University M,D
Andrews University P,M,D,O

Anna Maria College	M
Argosy University, Sarasota Campus	M,D,O
Azusa Pacific University	P,M
Barry University	M,D
Bayamón Central University	P,M
Bob Jones University	P,M,D,O
Boston College	P,M,D,O
Caldwell College	M
California Baptist University	M
Cardinal Stritch University	M
Chaminade University of Honolulu	M
Chestnut Hill College	M,O
College of Mount St. Joseph	M
Concordia University (NE)	M
Concordia University, St. Paul	M,O
Dallas Baptist University	M
Eastern Mennonite University	P,M,O
Eastern University	D
Fordham University	M,D,O
Freed-Hardeman University	M
Gannon University	M,O
Gardner-Webb University	P,D
George Fox University	P,M,D,O
Gonzaga University	M
Graceland University	M
Hardin-Simmons University	P,M
Holy Names University	M,O
Hope International University	M
Houston Baptist University	M
Iona College	M,O
John Brown University	M
The Johns Hopkins University	M,O
La Salle University	M
Liberty University	M,D
Loyola College in Maryland	M,D,O
Loyola Marymount University	M
Loyola University Chicago	M
Madonna University	M
Malone College	M
Marygrove College	M
Marymount University	M,O
Missouri Baptist University	M,O
Mount Marty College	M
Neumann College	M,O
Northwest Nazarene University	P,M
Oklahoma Christian University	P,M
Olivet Nazarene University	M
Oral Roberts University	P,M,D
Philadelphia Biblical University	M
Providence College	M
Regent University	P,M,D
Roberts Wesleyan College	M
St. Ambrose University	M
St. John's University (NY)	P,M,O
Saint Joseph College	M,O
Saint Leo University	M
Saint Mary's University of Minnesota	M
St. Mary's University of San Antonio	M
St. Thomas University	M,D,O
Santa Clara University	M
Seattle University	M
Seton Hall University	P,M,O
Southern Wesleyan University	M
Spring Arbor University	M
Texas Christian University	P,M,D,O
Trinity International University	P,M,D,O
University of Dallas	M
University of Dayton	M,D
University of Portland	M
University of Puget Sound	M
University of Saint Francis (IN)	M
University of St. Thomas (MN)	M
University of San Diego	M,O
University of San Francisco	M
Wake Forest University	M
Wayland Baptist University	M
Wheaton College	M,D
Xavier University of Louisiana	M

■ PATHOBIOLOGY

Auburn University	M,D
Brown University	M,D
Columbia University	M,D
Drexel University	D
The Johns Hopkins University	D
Kansas State University	M,D
Michigan State University	M,D
New York University	D
The Ohio State University	M,D
Penn State University Park	D
Purdue University	M,D
Texas A&M University	M,D
The University of Arizona	M,D
University of Cincinnati	D
University of Connecticut	M,D
University of Illinois at Urbana–Champaign	M,D
University of Missouri–Columbia	M,D
University of Southern California	M,D
University of Washington	M,D
University of Wyoming	M
Wake Forest University	M,D
Yale University	D

■ PATHOLOGY

Boston University	D
Brown University	M,D
Case Western Reserve University	M,D
Colorado State University	M,D
Columbia University	M,D
Duke University	M,D
East Carolina University	D
Georgetown University	M,D
Harvard University	D
Indiana University–Purdue University Indianapolis	M,D
Iowa State University of Science and Technology	M,D
The Johns Hopkins University	D
Michigan State University	M,D
North Carolina State University	M,D
North Dakota State University	M,D
The Ohio State University	M
Oregon State University	M
Purdue University	M,D
Quinnipiac University	M
Saint Louis University	D
Stony Brook University, State University of New York	M,D
Temple University	D
Texas A&M University	M,D
University at Buffalo, the State University of New York	M,D
The University of Alabama at Birmingham	D
University of California, Davis	M,D
University of California, Los Angeles	M,D
University of Chicago	D
University of Cincinnati	D
University of Florida	D
University of Georgia	M,D
The University of Iowa	M
University of Kansas	M,D
University of Michigan	D
University of New Mexico	M,D
The University of North Carolina at Chapel Hill	D
University of Pittsburgh	M,D
University of Rochester	M,D
University of Southern California	M,D
University of South Florida	M,D
The University of Toledo	O
University of Utah	M,D
University of Vermont	M
University of Washington	M,D
University of Wisconsin–Madison	D
Vanderbilt University	D
Virginia Commonwealth University	M,D
Washington State University	M,D
Wayne State University	M,D
Yale University	D

■ PEDIATRIC NURSING

Baylor University	M
Case Western Reserve University	M,D
The Catholic University of America	M,D
Columbia University	M,O
Duke University	M,D,O
Emory University	M
Florida State University	M,O
Georgia State University	M,D,O
Gwynedd-Mercy College	M
Hunter College of the City University of New York	M,O
Indiana University–Purdue University Indianapolis	M,D
The Johns Hopkins University	M,O
Kent State University	M,D
Lehman College of the City University of New York	M
Marquette University	M,D,O
Molloy College	M,O
New York University	M,O
Seton Hall University	M
Spalding University	M
Stony Brook University, State University of New York	M,O
University at Buffalo, the State University of New York	M,D,O
University of Central Florida	M,D,O
University of Cincinnati	M,D
University of Delaware	M,O
University of Illinois at Chicago	M
University of Michigan	M
University of Minnesota, Twin Cities Campus	M
University of Missouri–Kansas City	M,D
University of Nevada, Las Vegas	M,D,O
University of Pennsylvania	M
University of Pittsburgh	M,D
University of San Diego	M,D,O
University of South Carolina	M
The University of Texas–Pan American	M
Vanderbilt University	M,D
Villanova University	M,D,O
Virginia Commonwealth University	M,D,O
Wayne State University	M,O
Wright State University	M

■ PETROLEUM ENGINEERING

Colorado School of Mines	M,D
Louisiana State University and Agricultural and Mechanical College	M,D
Missouri University of Science and Technology	M,D
New Mexico Institute of Mining and Technology	M,D
Penn State University Park	M,D
Stanford University	M,D,O
Texas A&M University	M,D
Texas A&M University–Kingsville	M
Texas Tech University	M,D
University of Alaska Fairbanks	M

University of Houston M,D
University of Kansas M,D
University of Louisiana at Lafayette M
University of Oklahoma M,D
University of Pittsburgh M,D
University of Southern California M,D,O
The University of Texas at Austin M,D
University of Tulsa M,D
University of Wyoming M,D
West Virginia University M,D

▪ PHARMACEUTICAL ADMINISTRATION

Duquesne University M
Fairleigh Dickinson University, Metropolitan Campus M,O
Florida Agricultural and Mechanical University M,D
Idaho State University P,M,D
Long Island University, Brooklyn Campus M
The Ohio State University M,D
Purdue University M,D,O
St. John's University (NY) M
San Diego State University M
Seton Hall University M
University of Colorado Denver M
University of Florida M,D
University of Georgia M,D
University of Houston P,M,D
University of Illinois at Chicago M,D
University of Michigan D
University of Minnesota, Twin Cities Campus M,D
University of Mississippi M,D
The University of Toledo M
University of Wisconsin–Madison M,D
Wayne State University P,M,D,O
West Virginia University M,D

▪ PHARMACEUTICAL ENGINEERING

New Jersey Institute of Technology M
University of Michigan M

▪ PHARMACEUTICAL SCIENCES

Auburn University M,D
Boston University M,D
Butler University P,M
Campbell University P,M
Creighton University M,D
Dartmouth College D
Duquesne University M,D
Florida Agricultural and Mechanical University M,D
Idaho State University M,D
Long Island University, Brooklyn Campus M,D
Mercer University P,M,D
North Dakota State University M,D
Northeastern University P,M,D
The Ohio State University M,D
Oregon State University P,M,D
Purdue University M,D
Rutgers, The State University of New Jersey, New Brunswick M,D
St. John's University (NY) M,D
South Dakota State University M,D
Stevens Institute of Technology M,O
Temple University M,D
University at Buffalo, the State University of New York M,D
The University of Arizona M,D
University of Cincinnati M,D
University of Colorado Denver D
University of Connecticut M,D
University of Florida D
University of Georgia M,D
University of Houston P,M,D
University of Illinois at Chicago M,D
University of Kansas M
University of Kentucky M,D
University of Louisiana at Monroe M
University of Michigan D
University of Minnesota, Twin Cities Campus M,D
University of Mississippi M,D
University of Missouri–Kansas City P,M,D
The University of Montana M,D
University of New Mexico M,D
The University of North Carolina at Chapel Hill M,D
University of Rhode Island M,D
University of South Carolina M,D
University of Southern California M,D
The University of Texas at Austin M,D
University of the Pacific M,D
The University of Toledo M
University of Washington M,D
University of Wisconsin–Madison M,D
Virginia Commonwealth University P,M,D
Wayne State University P,M,D,O
West Virginia University M,D

▪ PHARMACOLOGY

Auburn University M,D
Boston University M,D
Case Western Reserve University M,D
Columbia University M,D
Cornell University P,M,D
Creighton University M,D
Dartmouth College D
Drexel University M,D
Duke University D
Duquesne University M,D
East Carolina University D
East Tennessee State University M,D
Emory University D
Fairleigh Dickinson University, College at Florham M,O
Florida Agricultural and Mechanical University M,D
Georgetown University D
The George Washington University D
Howard University M,D
Idaho State University M,D
Indiana University–Purdue University Indianapolis M,D
The Johns Hopkins University D
Kent State University M,D
Long Island University, Brooklyn Campus M,D
Loyola University Chicago M,D
Michigan State University M,D
New York University D
North Carolina State University M,D
Northeastern University M,D
Northwestern University D
Nova Southeastern University M
The Ohio State University M,D
Purdue University M,D
Saint Louis University D
Southern Illinois University Carbondale M,D
Stony Brook University, State University of New York D
Temple University M,D
Tufts University D
Tulane University M,D
University at Buffalo, the State University of New York M,D
The University of Alabama at Birmingham D
The University of Arizona M,D
University of California, Davis M,D
University of California, Irvine M,D
University of California, Los Angeles D
University of California, San Diego D
University of Chicago D
University of Cincinnati D
University of Colorado Denver D
University of Connecticut M,D
University of Florida M,D
University of Georgia M,D
University of Houston P,M,D
University of Illinois at Chicago D
The University of Iowa M,D
University of Kansas M,D
University of Kentucky D
University of Louisville M,D
University of Miami D
University of Michigan D
University of Minnesota, Duluth M,D
University of Minnesota, Twin Cities Campus M,D
University of Mississippi M,D
University of Missouri–Columbia M,D
The University of North Carolina at Chapel Hill D
University of North Dakota M,D
University of Pennsylvania D
University of Rhode Island M,D
University of Rochester M,D
University of South Alabama D
The University of South Dakota M,D
University of South Florida M,D
The University of Toledo M
University of Utah M,D
University of Vermont M,D
University of Virginia D
University of Washington M,D
University of Wisconsin–Madison M,D
Vanderbilt University D
Virginia Commonwealth University M,D,O
Wake Forest University D
Washington State University M,D
Wayne State University P,M,D
West Virginia University M,D
Wright State University M
Yale University D

▪ PHARMACY

Auburn University P
Butler University P,M
Campbell University P,M
Creighton University P
Drake University P
Duquesne University P
Ferris State University P
Florida Agricultural and Mechanical University P,D
Harding University P
Howard University P
Idaho State University P,M,D
Mercer University P,M,D
Nova Southeastern University P
The Ohio State University P
Oregon State University P,M,D
Pacific University P
Palm Beach Atlantic University P
Purdue University P
Rutgers, The State University of New Jersey, New Brunswick P,M,D
St. John Fisher College P

St. John's University (NY) P
Samford University P
Shenandoah University P
South Dakota State University P
Southern Illinois University Edwardsville P
Southwestern Oklahoma State University P
Temple University P
Texas Southern University P,M
University at Buffalo, the State University of New York P
The University of Arizona P
University of California, San Diego P
University of Cincinnati P
University of Colorado Denver P,D
University of Connecticut P
University of Florida P
University of Georgia P
University of Houston P,M,D
University of Illinois at Chicago P,M,D
The University of Iowa M,D
University of Kentucky P
University of Louisiana at Monroe P,D
University of Michigan P
University of Minnesota, Twin Cities Campus P
University of Mississippi P
University of Missouri–Kansas City P,M,D
The University of Montana P,M,D
University of New Mexico P
University of Pittsburgh P
University of Rhode Island M,D
University of South Alabama P
University of South Carolina P
University of Southern California P
The University of Texas at Austin P
University of the Incarnate Word P
University of the Pacific P
University of Utah P,M
University of Washington P
University of Wisconsin–Madison P
University of Wyoming P
Virginia Commonwealth University P
Washington State University P
Wayne State University P,M,D,O
West Virginia University P,M,D
Wilkes University P
Xavier University of Louisiana P

■ PHILANTHROPIC STUDIES

Saint Mary's University of Minnesota M

■ PHILOSOPHY

American University M
Arizona State University M,D
Baylor University M,D
Boston College M,D
Boston University M,D
Bowling Green State University M,D
Brown University M,D
California Institute of Integral Studies M,D
California State University, Long Beach M
California State University, Los Angeles M
Carnegie Mellon University M,D
The Catholic University of America M,D,O
Claremont Graduate University M,D
Cleveland State University M,O
Colorado State University M
Columbia University M,D
Cornell University D
DePaul University M,D
Duke University M,D
Duquesne University M,D
Emory University D,O
Florida State University M,D
Fordham University M,D
Franciscan University of Steubenville M
Georgetown University M,D
The George Washington University M,D
Georgia State University M
Gonzaga University M
Graduate School and University Center of the City University of New York M,D
Harvard University M,D
Howard University M
Indiana University Bloomington M,D
Indiana University–Purdue University Indianapolis M,D,O
The Johns Hopkins University M,D
Kent State University M
Louisiana State University and Agricultural and Mechanical College M
Loyola Marymount University M
Loyola University Chicago M,D
Marquette University M,D
Massachusetts Institute of Technology D
Miami University M
Michigan State University M,D
Montclair State University M,D,O
The New School: A University M,D
New York University M,D
Northern Illinois University M
Northwestern University D
The Ohio State University M,D
Ohio University M
Oklahoma City University M
Oklahoma State University M
Penn State University Park M,D
Princeton University D
Purdue University M,D
Purdue University Calumet M
Rice University M,D
Rutgers, The State University of New Jersey, New Brunswick D
St. John's University (NY) M
Saint Louis University M,D
San Diego State University M
San Francisco State University M,O
San Jose State University M,O
Southern Illinois University Carbondale M,D
Stanford University M,D
State University of New York at Binghamton M,D
Stony Brook University, State University of New York M,D
Syracuse University M,D
Temple University M,D
Texas A&M University M,D
Texas Tech University M
Tufts University M
Tulane University M,D
University at Albany, State University of New York M,D
University at Buffalo, the State University of New York M,D
The University of Arizona M,D
University of Arkansas M,D
University of California, Berkeley D
University of California, Davis M,D
University of California, Irvine M,D
University of California, Los Angeles M,D
University of California, Riverside M,D
University of California, San Diego D
University of California, Santa Barbara D
University of California, Santa Cruz M,D
University of Chicago M,D
University of Cincinnati M,D
University of Colorado at Boulder M,D
University of Connecticut M,D
University of Dallas M,D
University of Florida M,D
University of Georgia M,D
University of Hawaii at Manoa M,D
University of Houston M
University of Illinois at Chicago M,D
University of Illinois at Urbana–Champaign M,D
The University of Iowa M,D
University of Kansas M,D
University of Kentucky M,D
University of Louisville M
University of Maryland, College Park M,D
University of Massachusetts Amherst M,D
University of Memphis M,D
University of Miami M,D
University of Michigan M,D
University of Minnesota, Twin Cities Campus M,D
University of Mississippi M
University of Missouri–Columbia M,D
University of Missouri–St. Louis M
The University of Montana M
University of Nebraska–Lincoln M,D
University of Nevada, Reno M
University of New Mexico M,D
The University of North Carolina at Chapel Hill M,D
University of North Florida M,O
University of North Texas M,D
University of Notre Dame D
University of Oklahoma M,D
University of Oregon M,D
University of Pennsylvania M,D
University of Pittsburgh M,D
University of Puerto Rico, Río Piedras M
University of Rochester M,D
University of St. Thomas (TX) M,D
University of South Carolina M,D
University of Southern California M,D
University of Southern Mississippi M
University of South Florida M,D
The University of Tennessee M,D
The University of Texas at Austin M,D
The University of Toledo M
University of Utah M,D
University of Virginia M,D
University of Washington M,D
University of Wisconsin–Madison M,D
University of Wisconsin–Milwaukee M
University of Wyoming M
Vanderbilt University M,D
Villanova University D
Virginia Polytechnic Institute and State University M
Washington State University M
Washington University in St. Louis M,D
Wayne State University M,D
West Chester University of Pennsylvania M
Western Michigan University M
Yale University D

■ PHOTOGRAPHY

Barry University M
Bradley University M
Brooklyn College of the City University of New York M,D
California State University, Fullerton M,O

California State University, Los Angeles M
Claremont Graduate University M
Columbia College Chicago M
Columbia University M
Cornell University M
The George Washington University M,D
Georgia State University M,D
Howard University M
Illinois State University M
Indiana State University M
Inter American University of Puerto Rico, San Germán Campus M
James Madison University M
Lamar University M
Louisiana State University and Agricultural and Mechanical College M
Louisiana Tech University M
Marywood University M
Mills College M
New Mexico State University M
The New School: A University M
Ohio University M
Penn State University Park M,D
Rochester Institute of Technology M
San Jose State University M
Southern Methodist University M
Syracuse University M
Temple University M
The University of Alabama M
University of Colorado at Boulder M
University of Florida M,D
University of Houston M
University of Illinois at Chicago M
University of Illinois at Urbana–Champaign M
University of Memphis M
University of Miami M
The University of Montana M
University of North Texas M,D
University of Notre Dame M
University of Oklahoma M
The University of Tennessee M
University of Utah M
Virginia Commonwealth University M
Washington State University M
Yale University M

■ PHOTONICS

Boston University M,D
Lehigh University M,D
Oklahoma State University M,D
Princeton University D
Stevens Institute of Technology O
University of Arkansas M,D
University of California, San Diego M,D
University of Central Florida M,D

■ PHYSICAL CHEMISTRY

Auburn University M,D
Boston College M,D
Brandeis University M,D
Brigham Young University M,D
California State University, Fullerton M
California State University, Los Angeles M
Case Western Reserve University M,D
Clark Atlanta University M,D
Clarkson University M,D
Cleveland State University M,D
Cornell University D
Florida State University M,D
Georgetown University M,D
The George Washington University M,D
Harvard University D
Howard University M,D
Indiana University Bloomington M,D
Kansas State University M,D
Kent State University M,D
Marquette University M,D
Massachusetts Institute of Technology D
Miami University M,D
Northeastern University M,D
Old Dominion University M,D
Oregon State University M,D
Purdue University M,D
Rensselaer Polytechnic Institute M,D
Rice University M,D
Rutgers, The State University of New Jersey, Newark M,D
Rutgers, The State University of New Jersey, New Brunswick M,D
Seton Hall University M,D
Southern University and Agricultural and Mechanical College M
State University of New York at Binghamton M,D
Stevens Institute of Technology M,D,O
Tufts University M,D
University of Cincinnati M,D
University of Georgia M,D
University of Louisville M,D
University of Maryland, College Park M,D
University of Miami M,D
University of Michigan D
University of Missouri–Columbia M,D
University of Missouri–Kansas City M,D
University of Missouri–St. Louis M,D
The University of Montana M,D
University of Nebraska–Lincoln M,D
University of Notre Dame M,D
University of Southern Mississippi M,D
University of South Florida M,D
The University of Tennessee M,D
The University of Texas at Austin M,D
The University of Toledo M,D
Vanderbilt University M,D
Virginia Commonwealth University M,D
Wake Forest University M,D
West Virginia University M,D
Yale University D

■ PHYSICAL EDUCATION

Adams State College M
Adelphi University M,O
Alabama Agricultural and Mechanical University M
Alabama State University M
Albany State University M
Alcorn State University M,O
Arizona State University at the Polytechnic Campus M,D
Arkansas State University M,O
Ashland University M
Auburn University M,D,O
Auburn University Montgomery M,O
Augusta State University M
Austin Peay State University M
Azusa Pacific University M
Ball State University M,D
Bayamón Central University M
Baylor University M,D
Bethel College (TN) M
Boston University M,D,O
Bridgewater State College M
Brigham Young University M,D
Brooklyn College of the City University of New York M,O
California State University, Dominguez Hills M
California State University, East Bay M
California State University, Fullerton M
California State University, Long Beach M
California State University, Los Angeles M
California State University, Sacramento M
Campbell University M
Canisius College M
Central Connecticut State University M,O
Central Michigan University M
Central Washington University M
Chicago State University M
The Citadel, The Military College of South Carolina M
Cleveland State University M
The College of New Jersey M
Columbus State University M,O
Concordia University (CA) M
Delta State University M
DePaul University M,D
Drury University M
Eastern Illinois University M
Eastern Kentucky University M
Eastern Michigan University M
Eastern New Mexico University M
Eastern Washington University M
East Stroudsburg University of Pennsylvania M
East Tennessee State University M
Emporia State University M
Florida Agricultural and Mechanical University M
Florida International University M,D,O
Florida State University M,D,O
Fort Hays State University M
Frostburg State University M
Gardner-Webb University M
Georgia College & State University M,O
Georgia Southern University M
Georgia Southwestern State University M,O
Georgia State University M
Hardin-Simmons University M
Henderson State University M
Hofstra University M
Howard University M
Humboldt State University M
Idaho State University M
Illinois State University M
Indiana State University M
Indiana University Bloomington M,D,O
Indiana University of Pennsylvania M
Indiana University–Purdue University Indianapolis M
Inter American University of Puerto Rico, Metropolitan Campus M
Inter American University of Puerto Rico, San Germán Campus M
Iowa State University of Science and Technology M,D
Ithaca College M
Jackson State University M
Jacksonville State University M
Kent State University M,D
Long Island University, Brooklyn Campus M
Louisiana Tech University M,D
McDaniel College M
Middle Tennessee State University M,D
Minnesota State University Mankato M,O
Mississippi State University M
Missouri State University M

Montana State University–Billings M
Montclair State University M,O
Morehead State University M
Murray State University M,O
North Carolina Agricultural and Technical State University M
North Carolina Central University M
North Dakota State University M
Northern Arizona University M
Northern Illinois University M
North Georgia College & State University M,O
Northwest Missouri State University M
The Ohio State University M,D
Ohio University M
Oklahoma State University M,D,O
Old Dominion University M
Oregon State University M
Pittsburg State University M
Prairie View A&M University M
Purdue University M,D
Saginaw Valley State University M
St. Cloud State University M
Salem State College M
San Diego State University M
Slippery Rock University of Pennsylvania M
South Dakota State University M
Southern Connecticut State University M
Southern Illinois University Carbondale M
Springfield College M,D,O
State University of New York College at Brockport M
State University of New York College at Cortland M
Stony Brook University, State University of New York M,O
Sul Ross State University M
Tarleton State University M
Temple University M,D
Tennessee State University M
Tennessee Technological University M
Texas A&M University M,D
Texas A&M University–Commerce M,D
Texas Southern University M
Texas State University-San Marcos M
Union College (KY) M
Universidad Metropolitana M
The University of Akron M
The University of Alabama M,D
The University of Alabama at Birmingham M
University of Arkansas M
University of California, Berkeley M,D
University of Central Florida M
University of Central Missouri M
University of Dayton M,D
University of Florida M,D
University of Houston M,D
University of Idaho M,D
University of Indianapolis M
The University of Iowa M,D
University of Kansas M,D
University of Louisville M
University of Maine M
University of Massachusetts Amherst M,D,O
University of Memphis M
University of Minnesota, Twin Cities Campus M,D,O
The University of Montana M
University of Nebraska at Kearney M
University of Nebraska at Omaha M
University of Nebraska–Lincoln M
University of Nevada, Las Vegas M,D
University of New Mexico M,D,O
The University of North Carolina at Chapel Hill M
The University of North Carolina at Pembroke M
University of Northern Colorado M,D
University of Northern Iowa M
University of Rhode Island M,D
University of South Alabama M
University of South Carolina M,D
The University of South Dakota M
University of Southern Mississippi M,D
University of South Florida M
The University of Tennessee at Chattanooga M
The University of Texas at Arlington M
The University of Texas at El Paso M
University of the Incarnate Word M
The University of Toledo M
University of Virginia M,D
The University of West Alabama M
University of West Florida M
University of West Georgia M,O
University of Wisconsin–La Crosse M
University of Wyoming M
Utah State University M
Valdosta State University M
Virginia Commonwealth University M,D
Virginia Polytechnic Institute and State University M,D,O
Wayne State College M
Wayne State University M
West Chester University of Pennsylvania M,O
Western Carolina University M
Western Kentucky University M
Western Michigan University M
Western Washington University M
Westfield State College M
West Virginia University M,D
Wichita State University M
Winthrop University M
Wright State University M

■ PHYSICAL THERAPY

Alabama State University D
American International College M,D
Andrews University D
Angelo State University M
Arcadia University D
Arkansas State University M
Armstrong Atlantic State University M
Azusa Pacific University D
Baylor University M,D
Bellarmine University M,D
Belmont University D
Boston University D
Bradley University D
California State University, Fresno M
California State University, Long Beach M
California State University, Northridge M
Carroll College M,D
Central Michigan University M,D
Chapman University D
Chatham University D
Clarkson University M,D
Cleveland State University D
College of Mount St. Joseph M,D
College of St. Catherine M,D
The College of St. Scholastica D
Columbia University D
Concordia University Wisconsin M,D
Creighton University D
Daemen College D
Dominican College M,D
Drexel University M,D,O
Duke University D
Duquesne University M,D
D'Youville College M,D,O
East Carolina University M,D
Eastern Washington University D
East Tennessee State University D
Elon University D
Emory University D
Florida Agricultural and Mechanical University M
Florida Gulf Coast University M
Florida International University M
Gannon University D
The George Washington University D
Georgia State University D
Governors State University M,D
Graduate School and University Center of the City University of New York D
Grand Valley State University M,D
Hampton University D
Hardin-Simmons University D
Humboldt State University M
Hunter College of the City University of New York M
Husson College M
Idaho State University D
Indiana University–Purdue University Indianapolis M,D
Ithaca College D
Long Island University, Brooklyn Campus D
Marquette University D
Marymount University D
Maryville University of Saint Louis D
Mercy College M
Misericordia University M,D
Missouri State University M
Mount St. Mary's College D
Nazareth College of Rochester M,D
Neumann College M,D
New York Institute of Technology M,D
New York University M,D
Northern Arizona University D
Northern Illinois University M
North Georgia College & State University D
Northwestern University D
Nova Southeastern University D
Oakland University M,D,O
The Ohio State University M
Ohio University D
Old Dominion University D
Pacific University D
Quinnipiac University D
Regis University D
The Richard Stockton College of New Jersey M,D
Rockhurst University D
Rutgers, The State University of New Jersey, Camden M
Sacred Heart University D
St. Ambrose University D
Saint Francis University D
Saint Louis University M,D
San Francisco State University M,D
Seton Hall University D
Shenandoah University D
Simmons College D
Slippery Rock University of Pennsylvania D

Southwest Baptist University D
Springfield College M
Stony Brook University, State University of New York M,D,O
Temple University D
Tennessee State University M,D
Texas State University-San Marcos M
Texas Woman's University M,D
Touro College M
University at Buffalo, the State University of New York D
The University of Alabama at Birmingham D
University of Central Arkansas D
University of Central Florida M
University of Colorado Denver M,D
University of Connecticut M
University of Delaware D
The University of Findlay M
University of Florida D
University of Hartford M,D
University of Illinois at Chicago M
University of Indianapolis M,D
The University of Iowa D
University of Kansas M,D
University of Kentucky M
University of Mary D
University of Maryland Eastern Shore D
University of Massachusetts Lowell M
University of Miami D
University of Michigan–Flint D
University of Minnesota, Twin Cities Campus D
University of Missouri–Columbia M
The University of Montana D
University of Nevada, Las Vegas M,D
University of New England D
University of New Mexico M
The University of North Carolina at Chapel Hill M,D
University of North Dakota M,D
University of North Florida M
University of Pittsburgh M,D
University of Puget Sound D
University of Rhode Island D
The University of Scranton M,D
University of South Alabama D
The University of South Dakota M,D
University of Southern California M,D
University of South Florida M
The University of Tennessee at Chattanooga D
The University of Texas at El Paso M
University of the Pacific M,D
The University of Toledo M,D
University of Utah D,O
University of Vermont D
University of Washington M,D
University of Wisconsin–La Crosse M,D
Utica College D
Virginia Commonwealth University M,D
Walsh University M
Washington University in St. Louis D,O
Wayne State University M
Western Carolina University M
West Virginia University D
Wheeling Jesuit University D
Wichita State University M
Widener University M,D
Youngstown State University M

■ PHYSICIAN ASSISTANT STUDIES

Augsburg College M
Barry University M
Butler University P,M
California State University, Dominguez Hills M
Central Michigan University M,D
Chatham University M
Daemen College M
DeSales University M
Drexel University M
Duke University M
Duquesne University M,D
D'Youville College M
East Carolina University M
Emory University M
Gannon University M
The George Washington University M
Grand Valley State University M
Harding University M
Idaho State University M
James Madison University M
King's College M
Le Moyne College M
Lock Haven University of Pennsylvania M
Marquette University M
Marywood University M
Mercy College M
Missouri State University M
Mountain State University M
New York Institute of Technology M
Northeastern University M
Nova Southeastern University M
Pacific University M
Philadelphia University M
Quinnipiac University M
Regis University M,D
Saint Francis University M
Saint Louis University M
Seton Hall University M
Seton Hill University M
Shenandoah University M
Springfield College M
Towson University M
Trevecca Nazarene University M
The University of Alabama at Birmingham M
University of Colorado Denver M
University of Detroit Mercy M
University of Florida M
The University of Iowa M
University of Kentucky M
University of New England M
University of North Dakota M
University of St. Francis (IL) M
University of Saint Francis (IN) M
University of South Alabama M
The University of South Dakota M
University of Southern California M
The University of Toledo M
University of Utah M
University of Wisconsin–La Crosse M
Wagner College M
Wayne State University M
Western Michigan University M
Yale University M

■ PHYSICS

Adelphi University M
Alabama Agricultural and Mechanical University M,D
American University M
Arizona State University M,D
Auburn University M,D
Ball State University M
Baylor University M,D
Boston College M,D
Boston University M,D
Bowling Green State University M
Brandeis University M,D
Brigham Young University M,D
Brooklyn College of the City University of New York M,D
Brown University M,D
California Institute of Technology D
California State University, Fresno M
California State University, Fullerton M
California State University, Long Beach M
California State University, Los Angeles M
California State University, Northridge M
Carnegie Mellon University D
Case Western Reserve University M,D
The Catholic University of America M,D
Central Connecticut State University M
Central Michigan University M
City College of the City University of New York M,D
Clark Atlanta University M
Clarkson University M,D
Clark University M,D
Clemson University M,D
Cleveland State University M
The College of William and Mary M,D
Colorado State University M,D
Columbia University M,D
Cornell University M,D
Creighton University M
Dartmouth College M,D
Delaware State University M
DePaul University M
Drexel University M,D
Duke University M,D
East Carolina University M,D
Eastern Michigan University M
Emory University D
Florida Agricultural and Mechanical University M,D
Florida Atlantic University M,D
Florida Institute of Technology M,D
Florida International University M,D
Florida State University M,D
The George Washington University M,D
Georgia Institute of Technology M,D
Georgia State University M,D
Graduate School and University Center of the City University of New York D
Hampton University M,D
Harvard University D
Howard University M,D
Hunter College of the City University of New York M,D
Idaho State University M,D
Illinois Institute of Technology M,D
Indiana University Bloomington M,D
Indiana University of Pennsylvania M
Indiana University–Purdue University Indianapolis M,D
Iowa State University of Science and Technology M,D
The Johns Hopkins University D
Kansas State University M,D
Kent State University M,D
Lehigh University M,D
Louisiana State University and Agricultural and Mechanical College M,D
Louisiana Tech University M,D
Marshall University M
Massachusetts Institute of Technology D
Miami University M

Institution	Degrees
Michigan State University	M,D
Michigan Technological University	M,D
Minnesota State University Mankato	M
Mississippi State University	M,D
Missouri University of Science and Technology	M,D
Montana State University	M,D
New Mexico Institute of Mining and Technology	M,D
New Mexico State University	M,D
New York University	M,D
North Carolina State University	M,D
North Dakota State University	M,D
Northeastern University	M,D
Northern Illinois University	M,D
Northwestern University	M,D
Oakland University	M,D
The Ohio State University	M,D
Ohio University	M,D
Oklahoma State University	M,D
Old Dominion University	M,D
Oregon State University	M,D
Penn State University Park	M,D
Pittsburg State University	M
Polytechnic University, Brooklyn Campus	M,D
Portland State University	M,D
Princeton University	D
Purdue University	M,D
Queens College of the City University of New York	M,D
Rensselaer Polytechnic Institute	M,D
Rice University	M,D
Rutgers, The State University of New Jersey, New Brunswick	M,D
San Diego State University	M
San Francisco State University	M
San Jose State University	M
South Dakota State University	M
Southern Illinois University Carbondale	M,D
Southern Illinois University Edwardsville	M
Southern Methodist University	M,D
Southern University and Agricultural and Mechanical College	M
Stanford University	D
State University of New York at Binghamton	M
Stephen F. Austin State University	M
Stevens Institute of Technology	M,D,O
Stony Brook University, State University of New York	M,D
Syracuse University	M,D
Temple University	M,D
Texas A&M International University	M
Texas A&M University	M,D
Texas A&M University–Commerce	M
Texas Christian University	M,D
Texas State University-San Marcos	M
Texas Tech University	M,D
Tufts University	M,D
Tulane University	M,D
University at Albany, State University of New York	M,D
University at Buffalo, the State University of New York	M,D
The University of Akron	M
The University of Alabama	M,D
The University of Alabama at Birmingham	M,D
The University of Alabama in Huntsville	M,D
University of Alaska Fairbanks	M,D
The University of Arizona	M,D
University of Arkansas	M,D
University of California, Berkeley	D
University of California, Davis	M,D
University of California, Irvine	M,D
University of California, Los Angeles	M,D
University of California, Riverside	M,D
University of California, San Diego	M,D
University of California, Santa Barbara	D
University of California, Santa Cruz	M,D
University of Central Florida	M,D
University of Central Oklahoma	M
University of Chicago	M,D
University of Cincinnati	M,D
University of Colorado at Boulder	M,D
University of Connecticut	M,D
University of Delaware	M,D
University of Denver	M,D
University of Florida	M,D
University of Georgia	M,D
University of Hawaii at Manoa	M,D
University of Houston	M,D
University of Houston–Clear Lake	M
University of Idaho	M,D
University of Illinois at Chicago	M,D
University of Illinois at Urbana–Champaign	M,D
The University of Iowa	M,D
University of Kansas	M,D
University of Kentucky	M,D
University of Louisiana at Lafayette	M
University of Louisville	M
University of Maine	M,D
University of Maryland, Baltimore County	M,D
University of Maryland, College Park	M,D
University of Massachusetts Amherst	M,D
University of Massachusetts Dartmouth	M
University of Massachusetts Lowell	M,D
University of Memphis	M
University of Miami	M,D
University of Michigan	M,D
University of Minnesota, Duluth	M
University of Minnesota, Twin Cities Campus	M,D
University of Mississippi	M,D
University of Missouri–Columbia	M,D
University of Missouri–Kansas City	M,D
University of Missouri–St. Louis	M,D
University of Nebraska–Lincoln	M,D
University of Nevada, Las Vegas	M,D
University of Nevada, Reno	M,D
University of New Hampshire	M,D
University of New Mexico	M,D
University of New Orleans	M,D
The University of North Carolina at Chapel Hill	M,D
University of North Dakota	M,D
University of Northern Iowa	M
University of North Texas	M,D
University of Notre Dame	D
University of Oklahoma	M,D
University of Oregon	M,D
University of Pennsylvania	M,D
University of Pittsburgh	M,D
University of Puerto Rico, Mayagüez Campus	M
University of Puerto Rico, Río Piedras	M,D
University of Rhode Island	M,D
University of Rochester	M,D
University of South Carolina	M,D
University of Southern California	M,D
University of Southern Mississippi	M,D
University of South Florida	M,D
The University of Tennessee	M,D
The University of Texas at Arlington	M,D
The University of Texas at Austin	M,D
The University of Texas at Brownsville	M
The University of Texas at Dallas	M,D
The University of Texas at El Paso	M
The University of Texas at San Antonio	M,D
The University of Toledo	M,D
University of Utah	M,D
University of Vermont	M
University of Virginia	M,D
University of Washington	M,D
University of Wisconsin–Madison	M,D
University of Wisconsin–Milwaukee	M,D
Utah State University	M,D
Vanderbilt University	M,D
Virginia Commonwealth University	M,D
Virginia Polytechnic Institute and State University	M,D
Virginia State University	M
Wake Forest University	M,D
Washington State University	M,D
Washington University in St. Louis	M,D
Wayne State University	M,D
Western Illinois University	M
Western Michigan University	M,D
West Virginia University	M,D
Wichita State University	M
Worcester Polytechnic Institute	M,D
Wright State University	M
Yale University	D

■ PHYSIOLOGY

Institution	Degrees
Arizona State University	M,D
Ball State University	M
Boston University	M,D
Brigham Young University	M,D
Brown University	M,D
Case Western Reserve University	M,D
Columbia University	M,D
Cornell University	P,M,D
Dartmouth College	D
East Carolina University	D
East Tennessee State University	M,D
Florida State University	M,D
Georgetown University	M,D
Georgia Institute of Technology	M
Georgia State University	M,D
Harvard University	M,D
Howard University	D
Illinois State University	M,D
Indiana State University	M,D
The Johns Hopkins University	M,D
Kansas State University	M,D
Kent State University	M,D
Maharishi University of Management	M,D
Marquette University	M,D
Michigan State University	M,D
New York University	D
North Carolina State University	M,D
Northwestern University	M
The Ohio State University	M,D
Ohio University	M,D
Penn State University Park	M,D
Purdue University	M,D
Saint Louis University	D
Salisbury University	M
San Francisco State University	M
San Jose State University	M
Southern Illinois University Carbondale	M,D
Stanford University	D
Stony Brook University, State University of New York	D

Temple University	D
Texas A&M University	M,D
Tufts University	D
Tulane University	M,D
University at Buffalo, the State University of New York	M,D
The University of Alabama at Birmingham	M,D
The University of Arizona	D
University of California, Berkeley	M,D
University of California, Davis	M,D
University of California, Irvine	D
University of California, Los Angeles	M,D
University of California, San Diego	D
University of Chicago	D
University of Cincinnati	D
University of Colorado at Boulder	M,D
University of Colorado Denver	D
University of Connecticut	M,D
University of Delaware	M,D
University of Florida	M,D
University of Georgia	M,D
University of Hawaii at Manoa	M,D
University of Illinois at Chicago	M,D
University of Illinois at Urbana–Champaign	M,D
The University of Iowa	M,D
University of Kansas	M,D
University of Kentucky	M,D
University of Louisville	M,D
University of Miami	D
University of Michigan	D
University of Minnesota, Duluth	M,D
University of Minnesota, Twin Cities Campus	M,D
University of Missouri–Columbia	M,D
University of Missouri–St. Louis	M,D,O
University of Nevada, Reno	M,D
University of New Mexico	M,D
University of North Dakota	M,D
University of Notre Dame	M,D
University of Oregon	M,D
University of Pennsylvania	D
University of Rochester	M,D
University of South Alabama	D
The University of South Dakota	M,D
University of Southern California	M,D
University of South Florida	M,D
The University of Tennessee	M,D
University of Utah	D
University of Virginia	D
University of Washington	D
University of Wisconsin–La Crosse	M
University of Wisconsin–Madison	M,D
University of Wyoming	M,D
Virginia Commonwealth University	M,D,O
Wake Forest University	D
Wayne State University	M,D
West Virginia University	M,D
William Paterson University of New Jersey	M
Wright State University	M
Yale University	D

■ PLANETARY AND SPACE SCIENCES

California Institute of Technology	M,D
Columbia University	M,D
Cornell University	D
Embry-Riddle Aeronautical University (FL)	M
Florida Institute of Technology	M,D
Harvard University	M,D
Massachusetts Institute of Technology	M,D
Stony Brook University, State University of New York	M,D
The University of Arizona	M,D
University of Arkansas	M,D
University of California, Los Angeles	M,D
University of Chicago	M,D
University of Hawaii at Manoa	M,D
University of Michigan	M,D
University of New Mexico	M,D
University of North Dakota	M
University of Pittsburgh	M,D
Washington University in St. Louis	M,D
Western Connecticut State University	M

■ PLANT BIOLOGY

Clemson University	M,D
Cornell University	M,D
Florida State University	M,D
Illinois State University	M,D
Indiana University Bloomington	M,D
Miami University	M,D
Michigan State University	M,D
New York University	M,D
The Ohio State University	M,D
Ohio University	M,D
Rutgers, The State University of New Jersey, New Brunswick	M,D
Southern Illinois University Carbondale	M,D
Texas A&M University	M,D
University of California, Berkeley	D
University of California, Davis	M,D
University of California, Riverside	M,D
University of California, San Diego	D
University of Connecticut	M,D
University of Florida	M,D
University of Georgia	M,D
University of Illinois at Chicago	M,D
University of Illinois at Urbana–Champaign	M,D
The University of Iowa	M,D
University of Maine	M,D
University of Maryland, College Park	M,D
University of Massachusetts Amherst	M,D
University of Minnesota, Twin Cities Campus	M,D
University of Missouri–Columbia	M,D
University of New Hampshire	M,D
The University of Texas at Austin	M,D
University of Utah	M,D
University of Vermont	M,D
Washington University in St. Louis	D
Yale University	D

■ PLANT MOLECULAR BIOLOGY

Cornell University	M,D
Illinois State University	M,D
Michigan Technological University	M,D
Rutgers, The State University of New Jersey, New Brunswick	M,D
University of California, San Diego	D
University of Connecticut	M,D
University of Florida	M,D
University of Massachusetts Amherst	M,D
Washington State University	M,D

■ PLANT PATHOLOGY

Auburn University	M,D
Colorado State University	M,D
Cornell University	M,D
Iowa State University of Science and Technology	M,D
Kansas State University	M,D
Louisiana State University and Agricultural and Mechanical College	M,D
Michigan State University	M,D
Mississippi State University	M,D
Montana State University	M,D
New Mexico State University	M
North Carolina State University	M,D
North Dakota State University	M,D
The Ohio State University	M,D
Oklahoma State University	D
Oregon State University	M,D
Penn State University Park	M,D
Purdue University	M,D
Rutgers, The State University of New Jersey, New Brunswick	M,D
State University of New York College of Environmental Science and Forestry	M,D
Texas A&M University	M,D
The University of Arizona	M,D
University of Arkansas	M
University of California, Davis	M,D
University of California, Riverside	M,D
University of Florida	M,D
University of Georgia	M,D
University of Hawaii at Manoa	M,D
University of Kentucky	M,D
University of Maine	M
University of Minnesota, Twin Cities Campus	M,D
University of Missouri–Columbia	M,D
The University of Tennessee	M,D
University of Wisconsin–Madison	M,D
Virginia Polytechnic Institute and State University	M,D
Washington State University	M,D
West Virginia University	M,D

■ PLANT PHYSIOLOGY

Cornell University	M,D
Iowa State University of Science and Technology	M,D
Oregon State University	M,D
Penn State University Park	M,D
Purdue University	M,D
University of Kentucky	D
University of Massachusetts Amherst	M,D
The University of Tennessee	M,D
Virginia Polytechnic Institute and State University	M,D

■ PLANT SCIENCES

Alabama Agricultural and Mechanical University	M,D
Brigham Young University	M,D
California State University, Fresno	M
Clemson University	M,D
Colorado State University	M,D
Cornell University	M,D
Florida Agricultural and Mechanical University	M
Illinois State University	M,D
Lehman College of the City University of New York	D
Miami University	M,D
Michigan State University	M,D
Mississippi State University	M,D
Missouri State University	M
Montana State University	M,D
New Mexico State University	M
North Carolina Agricultural and Technical State University	M
North Dakota State University	M,D
Oklahoma State University	M,D

South Dakota State University M,D
Southern Illinois University Carbondale M
State University of New York College of Environmental Science and Forestry M,D
Texas A&M University M,D
Texas A&M University–Kingsville M,D
Texas Tech University M,D
The University of Arizona M,D
University of Arkansas D
University of California, Riverside M,D
University of Connecticut M,D
University of Delaware M,D
University of Florida D
University of Hawaii at Manoa M,D
University of Idaho M,D
University of Kentucky M
University of Maine M,D
University of Massachusetts Amherst M,D
University of Minnesota, Twin Cities Campus M,D
University of Missouri–Columbia M,D
University of Rhode Island M,D
The University of Tennessee M
University of Vermont M,D
University of Wisconsin–Madison M,D
Utah State University M,D
West Texas A&M University M
West Virginia University M,D

■ PLASMA PHYSICS

Massachusetts Institute of Technology M,D,O
Princeton University D
University of Colorado at Boulder M,D
West Virginia University M,D

■ PODIATRIC MEDICINE

Barry University P
Temple University P

■ POLITICAL SCIENCE

American University M,D,O
Appalachian State University M
Arizona State University M,D
Arkansas State University M,O
Ashland University M
Auburn University M,D
Auburn University Montgomery M,D
Augusta State University M
Ball State University M
Baylor University M,D
Boston College M,D
Boston University M,D
Bowling Green State University
Brandeis University M,D
Brooklyn College of the City University of New York M,D
Brown University M,D
California Polytechnic State University, San Luis Obispo M
California State University, Chico M
California State University, Fullerton M
California State University, Long Beach M
California State University, Los Angeles M
California State University, Northridge M
California State University, Sacramento M
California State University, Stanislaus M
Case Western Reserve University M,D
The Catholic University of America M,D
Central Michigan University M
Claremont Graduate University M,D
Clark Atlanta University M,D
The College of Saint Rose M
Colorado State University M,D
Columbia University M,D
Converse College M
Cornell University D
Duke University M,D
East Carolina University M
Eastern Illinois University M
Eastern Kentucky University M
East Stroudsburg University of Pennsylvania M
Emory University D
Fairleigh Dickinson University, Metropolitan Campus M
Fayetteville State University M
Florida Agricultural and Mechanical University M
Florida Atlantic University M
Florida International University M,D
Florida State University M,D
Fordham University M
Georgetown University M,D
The George Washington University M,D
Georgia State University M,D
Governors State University M
Graduate School and University Center of the City University of New York M,D
Harvard University M,D
Hawai'i Pacific University M
Howard University M,D
Idaho State University M,D
Illinois State University M
Indiana State University M
Indiana University Bloomington M,D
Indiana University of Pennsylvania M
Indiana University–Purdue University Indianapolis M,O
Iowa State University of Science and Technology M
Jackson State University M
Jacksonville State University M
The Johns Hopkins University M,D,O
Kansas State University M
Kean University M
Kent State University M,D
Lamar University M
Lehigh University M
Lincoln University (MO) M
Long Island University, Brooklyn Campus M
Long Island University, C.W. Post Campus M
Louisiana State University and Agricultural and Mechanical College M,D
Loyola University Chicago M,D
Marquette University M
Marshall University M
Massachusetts Institute of Technology M,D
Miami University M,D
Michigan State University M,D
Midwestern State University M
Minnesota State University Mankato M
Mississippi College M,O
Mississippi State University M,D
Missouri State University M
New Mexico Highlands University M
New Mexico State University M
The New School: A University M,D
New York University M,D
North Dakota State University M,D
Northeastern Illinois University M
Northeastern University M,D
Northern Arizona University M,D,O
Northern Illinois University M,D
Northwestern University M,D
The Ohio State University M,D
Ohio University M
Oklahoma State University M
Penn State University Park M,D
Pepperdine University M
Portland State University M,D
Princeton University D
Purdue University M,D
Purdue University Calumet M
Regent University M
Rice University M,D
Roosevelt University M
Rutgers, The State University of New Jersey, Newark M
Rutgers, The State University of New Jersey, New Brunswick D
St. John's University (NY) M,O
St. Mary's University of San Antonio M
Sam Houston State University M
San Diego State University M
San Francisco State University M
Sonoma State University M
Southern Connecticut State University M
Southern Illinois University Carbondale M,D
Southern University and Agricultural and Mechanical College M
Stanford University M,D
State University of New York at Binghamton M,D
Stony Brook University, State University of New York M,D
Suffolk University M
Sul Ross State University M
Syracuse University M,D
Tarleton State University M
Temple University M,D
Texas A&M International University M
Texas A&M University M,D
Texas A&M University–Kingsville M
Texas State University-San Marcos M
Texas Tech University M,D
Texas Woman's University M
Tulane University M,D
University at Albany, State University of New York M,D
University at Buffalo, the State University of New York M,D
The University of Akron M
The University of Alabama M,D
The University of Arizona M,D
University of Arkansas M
University of California, Berkeley D
University of California, Davis M,D
University of California, Irvine D
University of California, Los Angeles M,D
University of California, Riverside M,D
University of California, San Diego M,D
University of California, Santa Barbara M,D
University of California, Santa Cruz D
University of Central Florida M
University of Central Oklahoma M
University of Chicago D
University of Cincinnati M,D
University of Colorado at Boulder M,D
University of Colorado Denver M
University of Connecticut M,D
University of Dallas M,D
University of Delaware M,D
University of Florida M,D,O
University of Georgia M,D

University of Hawaii at Manoa M,D
University of Houston M,D
University of Idaho M,D
University of Illinois at Chicago M,D
University of Illinois at Springfield M
University of Illinois at Urbana–Champaign M,D
The University of Iowa M,D
University of Kansas M,D
University of Kentucky M,D
University of Louisville M
University of Maryland, College Park D
University of Massachusetts Amherst M,D
University of Massachusetts Boston M,D,O
University of Memphis M
University of Miami M
University of Michigan M,D
University of Minnesota, Twin Cities Campus D
University of Mississippi M,D
University of Missouri–Columbia M,D
University of Missouri–Kansas City M,D
University of Missouri–St. Louis M,D
The University of Montana M
University of Nebraska at Omaha M
University of Nebraska–Lincoln M,D
University of Nevada, Las Vegas M
University of Nevada, Reno M,D
University of New Hampshire M
University of New Mexico M,D
University of New Orleans M,D
The University of North Carolina at Chapel Hill M,D
The University of North Carolina at Greensboro M,O
University of North Texas M,D
University of Notre Dame D
University of Oklahoma M,D
University of Oregon M,D
University of Pennsylvania M,D
University of Pittsburgh M,D
University of Rhode Island M,O
University of Rochester M,D
University of South Carolina M,D
The University of South Dakota M
University of Southern California M,D
University of Southern Mississippi M,D
University of South Florida M
The University of Tennessee M,D
The University of Texas at Arlington M
The University of Texas at Austin M,D
The University of Texas at Brownsville M
The University of Texas at Dallas M,D
The University of Texas at El Paso M
The University of Texas at San Antonio M
The University of Texas at Tyler M
The University of Toledo M
University of Utah M,D
University of Virginia M,D
University of Washington M,D
University of West Florida M
University of Wisconsin–Madison M,D
University of Wisconsin–Milwaukee M,D
University of Wisconsin–Oshkosh M
University of Wyoming M
Utah State University M
Vanderbilt University M,D
Villanova University M
Virginia Polytechnic Institute and State University M
Washington State University M,D
Washington University in St. Louis M,D
Wayne State University M,D
Western Illinois University M,O
Western Kentucky University M
Western Michigan University M,D
Western Washington University M
West Texas A&M University M
West Virginia University M,D
Wichita State University M
Yale University D

■ POLYMER SCIENCE AND ENGINEERING

California Polytechnic State University, San Luis Obispo M
Carnegie Mellon University M,D
Case Western Reserve University M,D
Clemson University M,D
Cornell University M,D
DePaul University M
Eastern Michigan University M
Georgia Institute of Technology M,D
Lehigh University M,D
Massachusetts Institute of Technology M,D,O
North Carolina State University D
North Dakota State University M,D
Penn State University Park M,D
Polytechnic University, Brooklyn Campus M
Princeton University M,D
Rensselaer Polytechnic Institute M,D
Stevens Institute of Technology M,D,O
The University of Akron M,D
University of Cincinnati M,D
University of Connecticut M,D
University of Detroit Mercy M,D
University of Massachusetts Amherst M,D
University of Massachusetts Lowell M,D
University of Missouri–Kansas City M,D
University of Southern Mississippi M,D
The University of Tennessee M,D
University of Wisconsin–Madison M,D
Wayne State University M,D,O

■ PORTUGUESE

Brigham Young University M
Emory University D,O
Harvard University M,D
Indiana University Bloomington M,D
Michigan State University M,D
New York University M,D
The Ohio State University M,D
Princeton University D
Tulane University M,D
University of California, Los Angeles M
University of California, Santa Barbara M,D
University of Maryland, College Park M,D
University of Massachusetts Dartmouth M,D
University of Minnesota, Twin Cities Campus M,D
University of New Mexico M,D
The University of North Carolina at Chapel Hill M,D
The University of Tennessee D
The University of Texas at Austin M,D
University of Washington M
University of Wisconsin–Madison M,D
Vanderbilt University M,D
Yale University M,D

■ PROJECT MANAGEMENT

Avila University M,O
Boston University M
Cabrini College M,O
Capella University M,D,O
Christian Brothers University M,O
City University of Seattle M,O
Colorado Technical University—Colorado Springs M,D
Colorado Technical University—Denver M
Colorado Technical University—Sioux Falls M
Dallas Baptist University M
The George Washington University M,D
Lehigh University M,D,O
Marymount University M,O
Mississippi State University M,D
Missouri State University M
New York Institute of Technology M,O
Northwestern University M
Regis University M,O
Rosemont College M
St. Edward's University M
Saint Mary's University of Minnesota M
Southern New Hampshire University M,D,O
Stevens Institute of Technology M,O
University of Alaska Anchorage M
University of Dallas M
University of Denver M,O
University of San Francisco M
University of the Incarnate Word M,O
University of Wisconsin–Platteville M
Western Carolina University M
Winthrop University M,O
Worcester Polytechnic Institute M
Wright State University M

■ PSYCHIATRIC NURSING

Boston College M,D
Case Western Reserve University M,D
The Catholic University of America M,D
Columbia University M,O
Duquesne University M,O
Fairfield University M,O
Georgia State University M,D,O
Hunter College of the City University of New York M
Husson College M
Indiana University–Purdue University Indianapolis M,D
Kent State University M,D
Molloy College M,O
New Mexico State University M
New York University M,O
Northeastern University M,O
Pontifical Catholic University of Puerto Rico M
Rutgers, The State University of New Jersey, Newark M
Saint Joseph College M,O
Saint Xavier University M,O
Seattle University M
Shenandoah University M,O
Stony Brook University, State University of New York M,O
University at Buffalo, the State University of New York M,D,O
University of Alaska Anchorage M,O
University of Cincinnati M,D
University of Connecticut M,D,O
University of Delaware M,O
University of Illinois at Chicago M
University of Kansas M,D,O
University of Massachusetts Lowell M
University of Miami M,D
University of Michigan M
University of Minnesota, Twin Cities Campus M
University of Pennsylvania M
University of Pittsburgh M,D
University of Rhode Island M,D

University of South Carolina M,O
University of Southern Maine M,O
University of Southern Mississippi M,D
Vanderbilt University M,D
Virginia Commonwealth University M,D,O
Wayne State University M,O

■ PSYCHOANALYSIS AND PSYCHOTHERAPY

Naropa University M
New York University M,D,O

■ PSYCHOLOGY—GENERAL

Abilene Christian University M
Adelphi University M,D,O
Alabama Agricultural and Mechanical University M,O
American International College M,D
American University M,D
Andrews University M,D,O
Angelo State University M
Anna Maria College M
Antioch University Los Angeles M
Antioch University McGregor M
Antioch University New England M,O
Antioch University Santa Barbara M
Antioch University Seattle M,D
Appalachian State University M,O
Arcadia University M,D,O
Argosy University, Orange County Campus M,D,O
Argosy University, Sarasota Campus M,D,O
Argosy University, Tampa Campus M,D
Argosy University, Twin Cities Campus M,D,O
Arizona State University D
Arizona State University at the Polytechnic Campus M
Auburn University M,D
Auburn University Montgomery M
Augusta State University M
Austin Peay State University M
Avila University M
Azusa Pacific University M,D
Ball State University M
Barry University M,O
Bayamón Central University M
Baylor University M,D
Biola University M,D
Boston College M,D
Boston University M,D
Bowling Green State University M,D
Brandeis University M
Brenau University M
Bridgewater State College M
Brigham Young University M,D
Brooklyn College of the City University of New York M,D
Brown University M,D
Bucknell University M
Caldwell College M
California Institute of Integral Studies M,D
California Lutheran University M
California Polytechnic State University, San Luis Obispo M
California State Polytechnic University, Pomona M
California State University, Bakersfield M
California State University, Chico M
California State University, Dominguez Hills M
California State University, Fresno M
California State University, Fullerton M
California State University, Long Beach M
California State University, Los Angeles M
California State University, Northridge M
California State University, Sacramento M
California State University, San Bernardino M
California State University, San Marcos M
California State University, Stanislaus M
Cameron University M
Capella University M,D,O
Cardinal Stritch University M
Carlos Albizu University M,D
Carnegie Mellon University D
Case Western Reserve University D
Castleton State College M
The Catholic University of America M,D
Central Connecticut State University M
Central Michigan University M,D,O
Central Washington University M
Chestnut Hill College M,D,O
The Citadel, The Military College of South Carolina M
City College of the City University of New York M,D
Claremont Graduate University M,D,O
Clark University D
Clemson University M,D
Cleveland State University M,O
College of Saint Elizabeth M,O
College of St. Joseph M
The College of William and Mary M,D
Colorado State University M,D
Columbia University M,D
Concordia University Chicago (IL) M
Concordia University Wisconsin M
Cornell University D
Dartmouth College D
DePaul University M,D
Drexel University M,D
Duke University D
Duquesne University D
East Carolina University M
East Central University M
Eastern Illinois University M,O
Eastern Kentucky University M,O
Eastern Michigan University M,D
Eastern Washington University M
East Tennessee State University M
Edinboro University of Pennsylvania M
Emory University D
Emporia State University M
Fairfield University M,O
Fairleigh Dickinson University, College at Florham M,O
Fairleigh Dickinson University, Metropolitan Campus M,D,O
Fayetteville State University M
Florida Agricultural and Mechanical University M
Florida Atlantic University M,D
Florida Institute of Technology M,D
Florida International University M,D
Florida State University M,D
Fordham University D
Fort Hays State University M,O
Framingham State College M
Francis Marion University M
Frostburg State University M
Gallaudet University M,D,O
Gardner-Webb University M
Geneva College M
George Fox University M,D
George Mason University M,D
Georgetown University D
The George Washington University D
Georgia Institute of Technology M,D
Georgia Southern University M
Georgia State University M,D
Golden Gate University M,D,O
Governors State University M
Graduate School and University Center of the City University of New York D
Hardin-Simmons University M
Harvard University D
Hodges University M
Hofstra University M,D,O
Hood College M,O
Hope International University M
Houston Baptist University M
Howard University M,D
Humboldt State University M
Hunter College of the City University of New York M
Idaho State University M,D
Illinois Institute of Technology M,D
Illinois State University M,D,O
Immaculata University M,D,O
Indiana State University M,D
Indiana University Bloomington M,D
Indiana University of Pennsylvania M,D
Indiana University–Purdue University Indianapolis M,D
Inter American University of Puerto Rico, Metropolitan Campus M
Inter American University of Puerto Rico, San Germán Campus M,D
Iona College M
Iowa State University of Science and Technology M,D
Jackson State University D
Jacksonville State University M
James Madison University M,D,O
John F. Kennedy University M,D,O
The Johns Hopkins University D
Kansas State University M,D
Kent State University M,D
Lamar University M
La Salle University D
Lehigh University M,D
Lesley University M,D,O
Lipscomb University M,O
Long Island University, Brooklyn Campus M,D
Long Island University, C.W. Post Campus M,D,O
Louisiana State University and Agricultural and Mechanical College M,D
Louisiana Tech University M,D
Loyola College in Maryland M,D,O
Loyola University Chicago M,D
Lynn University M,O
Madonna University M
Marist College M,O
Marquette University M,D
Marshall University M,D
Marywood University M
McNeese State University M
Medaille College M
Mercy College M
Miami University D
Michigan State University M,D
Middle Tennessee State University M
Midwestern State University M
Millersville University of Pennsylvania M
Minnesota State University Mankato M
Mississippi State University M,D

Missouri State University	M
Monmouth University	M,O
Montana State University	M
Montana State University–Billings	M
Montclair State University	M,O
Morehead State University	M
Morgan State University	M,D
Murray State University	M
National-Louis University	M,O
National University	M
New College of California	M
New Jersey City University	M,O
New Mexico Highlands University	M
New Mexico State University	M,D
The New School: A University	M,D
New York University	M,D,O
Norfolk State University	M,D
North Carolina Central University	M
North Carolina State University	D
North Dakota State University	M,D
Northeastern State University	M
Northeastern University	M,D,O
Northern Arizona University	M
Northern Illinois University	M,D
Northern Michigan University	M
Northwestern State University of Louisiana	M
Northwestern University	D
Northwest Missouri State University	M
Notre Dame de Namur University	M,O
Nova Southeastern University	M,D,O
The Ohio State University	M,D
Ohio University	D
Oklahoma State University	M,D
Old Dominion University	M,D
Our Lady of the Lake University of San Antonio	M,D
Pace University	M,D
Pacific University	M,D
Penn State Harrisburg	M,D
Penn State University Park	M,D
Pepperdine University	M
Pittsburg State University	M
Polytechnic University, Brooklyn Campus	M
Pontifical Catholic University of Puerto Rico	M,D
Portland State University	M,D,O
Princeton University	D
Purdue University	D
Queens College of the City University of New York	M
Radford University	M,D,O
Regis University	M,O
Rhode Island College	M
Rice University	M,D
Rochester Institute of Technology	M
Roosevelt University	D
Rowan University	M,O
Rutgers, The State University of New Jersey, Camden	M
Rutgers, The State University of New Jersey, Newark	D
Rutgers, The State University of New Jersey, New Brunswick	M,D
St. Cloud State University	M
St. John's University (NY)	M,D
Saint Joseph's University	M,O
Saint Louis University	M,D
St. Mary's University of San Antonio	M
Saint Xavier University	M,O
Salem State College	M
Sam Houston State University	M,D
San Diego State University	M,D
San Francisco State University	M
San Jose State University	M
Seattle University	M
Seton Hall University	M,D,O
Shippensburg University of Pennsylvania	M
Southeastern Louisiana University	M
Southern Connecticut State University	M
Southern Illinois University Carbondale	M,D
Southern Illinois University Edwardsville	M,O
Southern Methodist University	M,D
Southern Nazarene University	M
Southern New Hampshire University	M,O
Southern Oregon University	M
Southern University and Agricultural and Mechanical College	M
Spalding University	M,D
Stanford University	D
State University of New York at Binghamton	M,D
State University of New York at New Paltz	M
State University of New York at Plattsburgh	M,O
State University of New York College at Brockport	M
Stephen F. Austin State University	M
Stony Brook University, State University of New York	D
Suffolk University	D
Sul Ross State University	M
Syracuse University	D
Temple University	D
Tennessee State University	M,D
Texas A&M International University	M
Texas A&M University	M,D
Texas A&M University–Commerce	M,D
Texas A&M University–Corpus Christi	M
Texas A&M University–Kingsville	M
Texas A&M University–Texarkana	M
Texas Christian University	M,D
Texas Southern University	M
Texas State University-San Marcos	M
Texas Tech University	M,D
Texas Woman's University	M,D,O
Tufts University	M,D
Tulane University	M,D
Union Institute & University	M,D
University at Albany, State University of New York	M,D,O
University at Buffalo, the State University of New York	M,D
The University of Akron	M,D
The University of Alabama	D
The University of Alabama at Birmingham	M,D
The University of Alabama in Huntsville	M
University of Alaska Anchorage	M,D
University of Alaska Fairbanks	D
The University of Arizona	D
University of Arkansas	M,D
University of Arkansas at Little Rock	M
University of Baltimore	M
University of California, Berkeley	D
University of California, Davis	D
University of California, Irvine	D
University of California, Los Angeles	M,D
University of California, Riverside	M,D
University of California, San Diego	D
University of California, Santa Barbara	D
University of California, Santa Cruz	D
University of Central Arkansas	M,D
University of Central Florida	M,D
University of Central Missouri	M
University of Central Oklahoma	M
University of Chicago	D
University of Cincinnati	D
University of Colorado at Boulder	M,D
University of Colorado at Colorado Springs	M,D
University of Colorado Denver	M
University of Connecticut	M,D
University of Dallas	M
University of Dayton	M
University of Delaware	D
University of Denver	M,D
University of Detroit Mercy	M,D,O
University of Florida	M,D
University of Georgia	M,D
University of Hartford	M,D
University of Hawaii at Manoa	M,D,O
University of Houston	M,D
University of Houston–Clear Lake	M
University of Houston–Victoria	M
University of Idaho	M
University of Illinois at Chicago	D
University of Illinois at Urbana–Champaign	M,D
University of Indianapolis	M,D
The University of Iowa	M,D,O
University of Kansas	M,D
University of Kentucky	M,D
University of La Verne	M,D
University of Louisiana at Lafayette	M
University of Louisiana at Monroe	M,O
University of Louisville	M,D
University of Maine	M,D
University of Mary Hardin-Baylor	M
University of Maryland, Baltimore County	M,D
University of Maryland, College Park	M,D
University of Massachusetts Amherst	M,D
University of Massachusetts Dartmouth	M
University of Massachusetts Lowell	M
University of Memphis	M,D
University of Miami	M,D
University of Michigan	D,O
University of Minnesota, Twin Cities Campus	D
University of Mississippi	M,D
University of Missouri–Columbia	M,D
University of Missouri–Kansas City	M,D
University of Missouri–St. Louis	M,D,O
The University of Montana	M,D,O
University of Nebraska at Omaha	M,D,O
University of Nebraska–Lincoln	M,D
University of Nevada, Las Vegas	M,D
University of Nevada, Reno	M,D
University of New Hampshire	D
University of New Mexico	M,D
University of New Orleans	M,D
The University of North Carolina at Chapel Hill	D
The University of North Carolina at Charlotte	M,D
The University of North Carolina at Greensboro	M,D
The University of North Carolina Wilmington	M
University of North Dakota	M,D
University of Northern Colorado	M,D
University of Northern Iowa	M
University of North Florida	M
University of North Texas	M,D
University of Notre Dame	D

University of Oklahoma	M,D
University of Oregon	M,D
University of Pennsylvania	D
University of Phoenix–Hawaii Campus	M
University of Phoenix–Louisiana Campus	M
University of Phoenix	M
University of Phoenix–Oregon Campus	M
University of Pittsburgh	M,D
University of Puerto Rico, Río Piedras	M,D
University of Rhode Island	D
University of Richmond	M
University of Rochester	M,D
University of Saint Francis (IN)	M
University of Saint Mary	M
University of St. Thomas (MN)	M,D,O
University of South Alabama	M
University of South Carolina	M,D
The University of South Dakota	M,D
University of Southern California	M,D
University of Southern Mississippi	M,D
University of South Florida	M,D
The University of Tennessee	M,D
The University of Tennessee at Chattanooga	M
The University of Texas at Arlington	M,D
The University of Texas at Austin	D
The University of Texas at Brownsville	M
The University of Texas at Dallas	M,D
The University of Texas at El Paso	M,D
The University of Texas at San Antonio	M
The University of Texas at Tyler	M
The University of Texas of the Permian Basin	M
The University of Texas–Pan American	M
University of the Pacific	M
The University of Toledo	M,D
University of Tulsa	M,D
University of Utah	M,D
University of Vermont	D
University of Virginia	M,D
University of Washington	D
University of West Florida	M
University of West Georgia	M,D
University of Wisconsin–Eau Claire	M,O
University of Wisconsin–La Crosse	M,O
University of Wisconsin–Madison	D
University of Wisconsin–Milwaukee	M,D
University of Wisconsin–Oshkosh	M
University of Wisconsin–Stout	M
University of Wisconsin–Whitewater	M,O
University of Wyoming	M,D
Utah State University	M,D
Valdosta State University	M,O
Valparaiso University	M,O
Vanderbilt University	M,D
Villanova University	M
Virginia Commonwealth University	D
Virginia Polytechnic Institute and State University	M,D
Virginia State University	M
Wake Forest University	M
Washburn University	M
Washington State University	M,D
Washington University in St. Louis	M,D
Wayne State University	M,D
West Chester University of Pennsylvania	M
Western Carolina University	M
Western Illinois University	M,O
Western Kentucky University	M,O
Western Michigan University	M,D,O
Western Washington University	M
Westfield State College	M
West Texas A&M University	M
West Virginia University	M,D
Wheaton College	M,D
Wichita State University	M,D
Widener University	
William Carey University	M
Winthrop University	M,O
Wright State University	M,D
Xavier University	M,D
Yale University	D
Yeshiva University	M,D

■ PUBLIC ADMINISTRATION

Adelphi University	O
Albany State University	M
American International College	M
American University	M,D
Angelo State University	M
Appalachian State University	M
Argosy University, Orange County Campus	M,D,O
Argosy University, Tampa Campus	M,D,O
Arkansas State University	M,O
Auburn University	M,D
Auburn University Montgomery	M,D
Ball State University	M
Barry University	M
Baylor University	M,D
Bernard M. Baruch College of the City University of New York	M
Boise State University	M
Boston University	M,O
Bowie State University	M
Bowling Green State University	M
Brandeis University	M,D
Bridgewater State College	M
Brigham Young University	M
California Baptist University	M
California Lutheran University	M
California State Polytechnic University, Pomona	M
California State University, Bakersfield	M
California State University, Chico	M
California State University, Dominguez Hills	M
California State University, East Bay	M
California State University, Fresno	M
California State University, Fullerton	M
California State University, Long Beach	M
California State University, Los Angeles	M
California State University, Northridge	M
California State University, Sacramento	M
California State University, San Bernardino	M
California State University, Stanislaus	M
Carnegie Mellon University	M
Central Michigan University	M,O
Clark Atlanta University	M
Clark University	M,O
Clemson University	M
Cleveland State University	M,O
College of Charleston	M
Columbia University	M
Columbus State University	M
Concordia University Wisconsin	M
Cumberland University	M
DePaul University	M,O
Drake University	M
Duquesne University	M,O
East Carolina University	M
Eastern Kentucky University	M
Eastern Michigan University	M
Eastern Washington University	M
The Evergreen State College	M
Fairleigh Dickinson University, College at Florham	M
Fairleigh Dickinson University, Metropolitan Campus	M,O
Florida Agricultural and Mechanical University	M
Florida Atlantic University	M,D
Florida Gulf Coast University	M
Florida Institute of Technology	M
Florida International University	M,D
Florida State University	M,D,O
Framingham State College	M
Gannon University	M,O
The George Washington University	M,D
Georgia College & State University	M
Georgia Southern University	M
Georgia State University	M
Governors State University	M
Grambling State University	M
Grand Valley State University	M
Hamline University	M
Harvard University	M
Hodges University	M
Howard University	M
Idaho State University	M
Illinois Institute of Technology	M
Indiana State University	M
Indiana University Bloomington	M,D,O
Indiana University Northwest	M,O
Indiana University–Purdue University Indianapolis	M
Indiana University South Bend	M,O
Iowa State University of Science and Technology	M
Jackson State University	M,D
James Madison University	M
John Jay College of Criminal Justice of the City University of New York	M
Kansas State University	M
Kean University	M
Kennesaw State University	M
Kent State University	M
Kutztown University of Pennsylvania	M
Lamar University	M
Lewis University	M
Lincoln University (MO)	M
Lindenwood University	M
Long Island University, Brooklyn Campus	M
Long Island University, C.W. Post Campus	M,O
Louisiana State University and Agricultural and Mechanical College	M,D
Marist College	M
Marquette University	M
Marywood University	M
Metropolitan College of New York	M
Metropolitan State University	M
Midwestern State University	M
Minnesota State University Mankato	M
Minnesota State University Moorhead	M
Mississippi State University	M,D
Missouri State University	M
Montana State University	M
Montana State University–Billings	M
Monterey Institute of International Studies	M
Morehead State University	M
New York University	M,D,O
North Carolina Central University	M
North Carolina State University	M,D

Northeastern University M
Northern Arizona University M,D,O
Northern Illinois University M
Northern Kentucky University M
Northern Michigan University M
North Georgia College & State University M
Norwich University M
Notre Dame de Namur University M
Nova Southeastern University M,D
Oakland University M
Ohio University M
Old Dominion University M,D
Pace University M
Park University M
Penn State Harrisburg M,D
Pepperdine University M
Pontifical Catholic University of Puerto Rico M,D
Portland State University M,D
Regent University M
Regis College (MA) M,O
Rhode Island College M
Roger Williams University M
Roosevelt University M
Rutgers, The State University of New Jersey, Camden M
Rutgers, The State University of New Jersey, Newark M,D
Saginaw Valley State University M
St. Edward's University M,O
Saint Louis University M,D,O
Saint Mary's University of Minnesota M,O
St. Mary's University of San Antonio M
St. Thomas University M,O
Sam Houston State University M
San Diego State University M
San Francisco State University M
San Jose State University M
Savannah State University M
Seattle University M
Seton Hall University M
Shenandoah University M,D,O
Shippensburg University of Pennsylvania M
Sonoma State University M
Southeastern University M
Southeast Missouri State University M
Southern Illinois University Carbondale M
Southern Illinois University Edwardsville M
Southern University and Agricultural and Mechanical College M,D
State University of New York at Binghamton M
State University of New York College at Brockport M
Stephen F. Austin State University M
Suffolk University M,O
Sul Ross State University M
Syracuse University M,D,O
Tennessee State University M,D
Texas A&M International University M
Texas A&M University M,O
Texas A&M University–Corpus Christi M
Texas Southern University M
Texas State University-San Marcos M
Texas Tech University M,D
Troy University M
Tufts University O
University at Albany, State University of New York M,D,O
The University of Akron M
The University of Alabama M,D
The University of Alabama at Birmingham M
University of Alaska Anchorage M
University of Alaska Southeast M
The University of Arizona M,D
University of Arkansas M
University of Arkansas at Little Rock M
University of Baltimore D
University of Central Florida M,O
University of Colorado at Colorado Springs M
University of Colorado Denver M
University of Connecticut M
University of Dayton M
University of Delaware M
University of Evansville M
The University of Findlay M
University of Georgia M,D
University of Guam M
University of Hawaii at Manoa M,O
University of Idaho M
University of Illinois at Chicago M,D
University of Illinois at Springfield M,D
University of Kansas M,D
University of Kentucky M,D
University of La Verne M,D,O
University of Louisville M
University of Maine M,D
University of Maryland, College Park M
University of Massachusetts Amherst M
University of Memphis M
University of Michigan–Dearborn M,O
University of Michigan–Flint M
University of Missouri–Kansas City M,D
University of Missouri–St. Louis M,D,O
The University of Montana M
University of Nebraska at Omaha M,D
University of Nevada, Las Vegas M,D,O
University of Nevada, Reno M
University of New Hampshire M
University of New Haven M
University of New Mexico M
University of New Orleans M
The University of North Carolina at Chapel Hill M
The University of North Carolina at Charlotte M
The University of North Carolina at Pembroke M
The University of North Carolina Wilmington M
University of North Dakota M
University of North Florida M
University of North Texas M
University of Oklahoma M
University of Pennsylvania M
University of Phoenix–Denver Campus M
University of Phoenix–Fort Lauderdale Campus M
University of Phoenix–Hawaii Campus M
University of Phoenix–Louisiana Campus M
University of Phoenix–North Florida Campus M
University of Phoenix M
University of Phoenix–Sacramento Valley Campus M
University of Phoenix–West Florida Campus M
University of Pittsburgh M,D
University of Puerto Rico, Río Piedras M
University of Rhode Island M,O
University of San Francisco M
University of South Alabama M
University of South Carolina M
The University of South Dakota M
University of Southern California M,D,O
University of Southern Indiana M
University of South Florida M
The University of Tennessee M
The University of Tennessee at Chattanooga M
The University of Texas at Arlington M
The University of Texas at Brownsville M
The University of Texas at San Antonio M
The University of Texas at Tyler M
The University of Texas–Pan American M
University of the District of Columbia M
The University of Toledo M
University of Utah M,O
University of Vermont M
University of West Georgia M
University of Wisconsin–Milwaukee M
University of Wyoming M
Upper Iowa University M
Valdosta State University M
Villanova University M
Virginia Commonwealth University M,O
Virginia Polytechnic Institute and State University M,D,O
Walden University M,D
Wayland Baptist University M
Wayne State University M
Webster University M,D
West Chester University of Pennsylvania M
Western Illinois University M,O
Western International University M
Western Michigan University M,D
West Virginia University M
Wichita State University M
Widener University M
Willamette University M
Wilmington University (DE) M
Wright State University M

■ PUBLIC AFFAIRS

American University M
Arizona State University M,D
Cornell University M
DePaul University M,O
George Mason University M
Georgia College & State University M
Howard University M
Indiana University Bloomington M,D,O
Indiana University Northwest M,O
Indiana University of Pennsylvania M
Indiana University–Purdue University Fort Wayne M,O
Indiana University–Purdue University Indianapolis M
Indiana University South Bend M,O
Jackson State University M
Murray State University M
New Mexico Highlands University M
Northeastern University M,D
The Ohio State University M,D
Park University M
Princeton University M,D
Stony Brook University, State University of New York M,O
Texas A&M University M,O
The University of Alabama in Huntsville M
University of Arkansas at Little Rock M
University of Baltimore M,D
University of Central Florida D

University of Colorado at Colorado Springs M
University of Colorado Denver D
University of Florida M,D,O
University of Idaho M,D
University of Louisville D
University of Massachusetts Boston M
University of Minnesota, Twin Cities Campus M
University of Missouri–Columbia M
University of Missouri–Kansas City M,D
University of Nevada, Las Vegas M,D,O
The University of North Carolina at Greensboro M,O
The University of Texas at Arlington D
The University of Texas at Austin M,D
The University of Texas at Dallas M,D
University of Washington M,D
University of Wisconsin–Madison M
Western Carolina University M
Western Michigan University M,D

■ PUBLIC HEALTH—GENERAL

Adelphi University O
Armstrong Atlantic State University M
Barry University M
Benedictine University M
Boise State University M
Boston University P,M,D,O
Bowling Green State University M
Brooklyn College of the City University of New York M
Brown University M
California State University, Fresno M
California State University, Fullerton M
Case Western Reserve University M
College of St. Catherine M
Columbia University M,D
Dartmouth College M
Dominican University of California M
Drexel University M
East Carolina University M
East Stroudsburg University of Pennsylvania M
East Tennessee State University M,O
Emory University M,D
Florida Agricultural and Mechanical University M
Florida International University M
Fort Valley State University M
Georgetown University M,D
The George Washington University M,D,O
Georgia Southern University M
Georgia State University M,O
Graduate School and University Center of the City University of New York D
Harvard University M,D
Hunter College of the City University of New York M
Idaho State University M,O
Indiana University Bloomington M,D
Indiana University–Purdue University Indianapolis M
The Johns Hopkins University M,D
Kansas State University M
Kent State University M
Missouri State University M
Morgan State University M,D
New Jersey Institute of Technology M
New Mexico State University M
Northern Arizona University M
Northern Illinois University M
Northwestern University M
Nova Southeastern University M
The Ohio State University M,D
Old Dominion University M
Oregon State University M,D
Portland State University M,O
Purdue University M,D
Rutgers, The State University of New Jersey, New Brunswick M,D
Saint Louis University M,D
Saint Xavier University M,O
San Diego State University M,D
San Francisco State University M
San Jose State University M,O
Sarah Lawrence College M
Southern Connecticut State University M
Stony Brook University, State University of New York M
Temple University M,D
Texas A&M University M,D
Texas Wesleyan University M
Trinity (Washington) University M
Tufts University M
Tulane University M,D,O
University at Albany, State University of New York M,D
University at Buffalo, the State University of New York M,D
The University of Akron M,D
The University of Alabama at Birmingham M,D
University of Alaska Anchorage M
The University of Arizona M,D
University of California, Berkeley M,D
University of California, Los Angeles M,D
University of California, San Diego D
University of Colorado Denver M
University of Connecticut M
University of Florida M
University of Hawaii at Manoa M
University of Illinois at Chicago M,D
University of Illinois at Springfield M
The University of Iowa M,D,O
University of Kansas M
University of Kentucky M
University of Louisville M,O
University of Maryland, College Park M,D
University of Massachusetts Amherst M,D
University of Miami M
University of Michigan M,D
University of Minnesota, Twin Cities Campus M,D,O
University of Missouri–Columbia M
The University of Montana M,O
University of Nebraska at Omaha M
University of Nevada, Las Vegas M
University of Nevada, Reno M
University of New England M,O
University of New Hampshire M
University of New Mexico M
The University of North Carolina at Chapel Hill M,D
The University of North Carolina at Charlotte M
University of Northern Colorado M
University of North Florida M,O
University of Pittsburgh M,D,O
University of Rochester M
University of South Carolina M
University of Southern California M
University of Southern Mississippi M
University of South Florida M,D
The University of Tennessee M
The University of Toledo M,D,O
University of Utah M,D
University of Virginia M
University of Washington M,D
University of West Florida M
University of Wisconsin–Eau Claire M
University of Wisconsin–La Crosse M
Vanderbilt University M
Virginia Commonwealth University M,D
Walden University M,D
Wayne State University M,O
West Chester University of Pennsylvania M,O
Western Kentucky University M
West Virginia University M
Wichita State University M
Wright State University M
Yale University M,D

■ PUBLIC HISTORY

Appalachian State University M
Arizona State University M,D
California State University, Sacramento M
Eastern Illinois University M
Florida State University M,D
Indiana University–Purdue University Indianapolis M
Loyola University Chicago M,D
New York University M,D,O
North Carolina State University M
Northeastern University M,D
Rutgers, The State University of New Jersey, Camden M
Shippensburg University of Pennsylvania M,O
Simmons College
Sonoma State University M
University at Albany, State University of New York M,D,O
University of Arkansas at Little Rock M
University of California, Santa Barbara D
University of Houston M,D
University of Illinois at Springfield M
University of Massachusetts Amherst M,D
University of Massachusetts Boston M
University of South Carolina M,O
The University of Texas at Austin M,D
Washington State University M,D

■ PUBLIC POLICY

Albany State University M
American University M
Baylor University M,D
Boise State University M
Brandeis University M,D
Brooklyn College of the City University of New York M,D
Brown University M
California Lutheran University M
California State University, Long Beach M
California State University, Sacramento M
Carnegie Mellon University M
Claremont Graduate University M,D,O
Clemson University D,O
The College of William and Mary M
Columbia University M
Cornell University M,D
Duke University M,D,O
Duquesne University M,O
Florida State University M,D,O
George Mason University M,D
Georgetown University M
The George Washington University M,D
Georgia Institute of Technology M,D
Georgia State University D

Graduate School and University Center of the City University of New York M,D
Harvard University M,D
Indiana University Bloomington D
Indiana University–Purdue University Indianapolis M
Jackson State University M,D
John Jay College of Criminal Justice of the City University of New York M,D
The Johns Hopkins University M
Kent State University M,D
Lincoln University (MO) M
Mills College M
Mississippi State University M,D
Monmouth University M
The New School: A University D
Northeastern University M,D
Northern Arizona University M,D,O
Northwestern University D
Pepperdine University M
Regent University M
Regis College (MA) M,O
Rochester Institute of Technology M
Rutgers, The State University of New Jersey, Camden M
Rutgers, The State University of New Jersey, Newark M,D
Rutgers, The State University of New Jersey, New Brunswick M
Saint Louis University M,D,O
San Francisco State University M
Seton Hall University M
State University of New York at Binghamton M,D
State University of New York Empire State College M
Stony Brook University, State University of New York M,D
Texas A&M University M,O
Tufts University M
University at Albany, State University of New York M,D,O
The University of Arizona M,D
University of Arkansas D
University of California, Berkeley M,D
University of California, Los Angeles M
University of Chicago M,D
University of Colorado at Boulder M,D
University of Connecticut M,O
University of Delaware M,D
University of Denver M
University of Georgia M,D
University of Illinois at Chicago M,D
University of Louisville M
University of Maryland, Baltimore County M,D
University of Maryland, College Park M,D
University of Massachusetts Amherst M
University of Massachusetts Boston D
University of Massachusetts Dartmouth M
University of Memphis M
University of Michigan M,D
University of Michigan–Dearborn M
University of Minnesota, Twin Cities Campus M
University of Missouri–St. Louis M,D,O
University of Nevada, Las Vegas M
The University of North Carolina at Chapel Hill D
The University of North Carolina at Charlotte D
University of Northern Iowa M
University of Oregon M
University of Pennsylvania M,D
University of Pittsburgh M,D
University of Rhode Island M,O
University of Southern California M
University of Southern Maine M,D,O
The University of Texas at Austin M,D
The University of Texas at Brownsville M
The University of Texas at Dallas M
University of the Pacific P,M,D
University of Washington, Bothell M
Vanderbilt University M,D
Virginia Commonwealth University D
Virginia Polytechnic Institute and State University M,D,O
Washington State University M,D
Washington University in St. Louis M
West Virginia University M,D
William Paterson University of New Jersey M

■ PUBLISHING

Drexel University M
Emerson College M
The George Washington University M
New York University M
Northwestern University M
Pace University M
Rosemont College M
University of Baltimore M

■ QUALITY MANAGEMENT

California State University, Dominguez Hills M
Case Western Reserve University M,D
Dowling College M,O
Eastern Michigan University M
Ferris State University M
Hofstra University M,O
Illinois Institute of Technology M
Madonna University M
Marian College of Fond du Lac M
Penn State University Park M
Regis College (MA) M
Rutgers, The State University of New Jersey, New Brunswick M,D
Saint Joseph's College of Maine M
San Jose State University M
Southern Polytechnic State University M
Stevens Institute of Technology M,O
University of Miami M
Upper Iowa University M
Webster University M,D

■ QUANTITATIVE ANALYSIS

Bernard M. Baruch College of the City University of New York M
California State University, East Bay M
Clark Atlanta University M
Drexel University M,D,O
Hofstra University M
Lehigh University M
Loyola College in Maryland M
New York University M,D,O
Purdue University M,D
St. John's University (NY) M,O
Saint Joseph's University M
Syracuse University D
Texas Tech University M,D
University of California, Santa Barbara M,D
University of Cincinnati M,D
University of Florida M
University of Missouri–St. Louis M,O
University of North Texas M,D
University of Oregon M
The University of Texas at Arlington M,D
Virginia Commonwealth University M
Walden University M,D

■ RADIATION BIOLOGY

Auburn University M,D
Colorado State University M,D
Georgetown University M
The University of Iowa M,D

■ RANGE SCIENCE

Colorado State University M,D
Kansas State University M,D
Montana State University M,D
New Mexico State University M,D
North Dakota State University M,D
Oregon State University M,D
Sul Ross State University M
Texas A&M University M,D
Texas A&M University–Kingsville M
Texas Tech University M,D
The University of Arizona M,D
University of California, Berkeley M
University of Idaho M
University of Wyoming M,D
Utah State University M,D

■ READING EDUCATION

Abilene Christian University M
Adelphi University M
Albany State University M
Alfred University M,O
Alverno College M
American International College M,D,O
Andrews University M
Angelo State University M
Anna Maria College M,O
Appalachian State University M
Arcadia University M,D,O
Arkansas State University M,O
Auburn University M,D,O
Auburn University Montgomery M,O
Aurora University M,D
Austin Peay State University M,O
Avila University M,O
Baldwin-Wallace College M
Barry University M,D,O
Bellarmine University M
Benedictine University M
Bethel University M,D,O
Bloomsburg University of Pennsylvania M
Boise State University M
Boston College M,O
Boston University M,D,O
Bowie State University M
Bowling Green State University M,O
Bridgewater State College M,O
Brigham Young University M
Bucknell University M
Buffalo State College, State University of New York M
Butler University M
California Baptist University M
California Lutheran University M
California State University, Bakersfield M,O
California State University, Chico M
California State University, Fresno M
California State University, Fullerton M
California State University, Los Angeles M
California State University, Sacramento M
California State University, San Bernardino M
California State University, Stanislaus M
California University of Pennsylvania M
Canisius College M

Capella University M,D,O
Cardinal Stritch University M
Castleton State College M,O
Central Connecticut State University M,O
Central Michigan University M
Central Washington University M
Chapman University M
Chicago State University M
The Citadel, The Military College of South Carolina M
City College of the City University of New York M
City University of Seattle M,O
Clarion University of Pennsylvania M
Clemson University M
College of Mount St. Joseph M
The College of New Jersey M,O
The College of New Rochelle M
College of St. Joseph M
The College of Saint Rose M,O
The College of William and Mary M
Concordia University Chicago (IL) M
Concordia University (NE) M
Concordia University Wisconsin M
Coppin State University M
Dallas Baptist University M
DePaul University M,D
Dominican University M
Dowling College M,D,O
Duquesne University M
East Carolina University M
Eastern Connecticut State University M
Eastern Kentucky University M
Eastern Michigan University M
Eastern Nazarene College M,O
Eastern Washington University M
East Stroudsburg University of Pennsylvania M
East Tennessee State University M
Edinboro University of Pennsylvania M,O
Emporia State University M
Endicott College M
Fairleigh Dickinson University, College at Florham M,O
Fairleigh Dickinson University, Metropolitan Campus M,O
Fayetteville State University M
Ferris State University M
Florida Atlantic University M,D,O
Florida Gulf Coast University M
Florida International University M,D
Florida State University M,D,O
Fordham University M,D,O
Framingham State College M
Fresno Pacific University M
Frostburg State University M
Furman University M
Gannon University M,O
George Mason University M
Georgia Southern University M
Georgia Southwestern State University M,O
Georgia State University M,D,O
Governors State University M
Grand Canyon University M
Grand Valley State University M
Gwynedd-Mercy College M
Harding University M,O
Hardin-Simmons University M
Harvard University M
Henderson State University M,O
Heritage University M
Hofstra University M,D,O
Holy Family University M
Hood College M,O

Houston Baptist University M
Howard University M,O
Hunter College of the City University of New York M,O
Idaho State University M,O
Illinois State University M
Indiana State University M
Indiana University Bloomington M,D,O
Indiana University of Pennsylvania M
Jacksonville State University M
Jacksonville University M
James Madison University M
The Johns Hopkins University M,D,O
Johnson State College M
Kean University M
Kent State University M
King's College M
Kutztown University of Pennsylvania M
Lehman College of the City University of New York M
Lesley University M,D,O
Liberty University M,D,O
Long Island University, Brentwood Campus M
Long Island University, Brooklyn Campus M
Long Island University, C.W. Post Campus M
Long Island University, Southampton Graduate Campus M
Longwood University M
Loyola College in Maryland M,O
Loyola Marymount University M
Loyola University Chicago M
Loyola University New Orleans M
Madonna University M
Malone College M
Manhattanville College M
Marshall University M,O
Marygrove College M
Maryville University of Saint Louis M,D
Marywood University M
McDaniel College M
Medaille College M
Mercer University M,D,O
Mercy College M
Miami University M
Michigan State University M
Middle Tennessee State University M
Midwestern State University M
Millersville University of Pennsylvania M
Minnesota State University Moorhead M
Missouri State University M
Monmouth University M,O
Montana State University–Billings M
Montclair State University M,O
Morehead State University M
Morningside College M
Mount Saint Mary College M
Murray State University M,O
National-Louis University M,D,O
Nazareth College of Rochester M
New Jersey City University M
New Mexico State University M,D,O
New York University M
Niagara University M
North Carolina Agricultural and Technical State University M
Northeastern Illinois University M
Northeastern State University M
Northern Illinois University M,D
Northwestern State University of Louisiana M,O
Northwest Missouri State University M

Northwest Nazarene University M
Notre Dame de Namur University M,O
Nova Southeastern University M,O
Oakland University M,D,O
Ohio University M,D
Old Dominion University M,D
Oregon State University M
Penn State University Park M,D
Pittsburg State University M
Plymouth State University M
Portland State University M,D
Providence College M
Purdue University M,D,O
Queens College of the City University of New York M
Radford University M
Regis University M,O
Rhode Island College M
Rider University M,O
Rivier College M,O
Roberts Wesleyan College M,O
Rockford College M
Roger Williams University M
Roosevelt University M
Rowan University M
Rutgers, The State University of New Jersey, New Brunswick M,D
Sacred Heart University M,O
Saginaw Valley State University M
St. Bonaventure University M
Saint Francis University M
St. John Fisher College M
St. John's University (NY) M
St. Joseph's College, Suffolk Campus M
Saint Joseph's University M,D,O
Saint Leo University M
Saint Martin's University M
Saint Mary's College of California M
Saint Mary's University of Minnesota M,O
St. Mary's University of San Antonio M
Saint Michael's College M,O
Saint Peter's College M
St. Thomas Aquinas College M,O
St. Thomas University M,D,O
Saint Xavier University M,O
Salem State College M,O
Salisbury University M
Sam Houston State University M
San Diego State University M
San Francisco State University M,O
Seattle Pacific University M
Seattle University M,O
Shippensburg University of Pennsylvania M
Siena Heights University M
Slippery Rock University of Pennsylvania M
Southern Connecticut State University M,O
Southern Illinois University Edwardsville M
Southern Oregon University M
State University of New York at Binghamton M
State University of New York at Fredonia M
State University of New York at New Paltz M
State University of New York at Oswego M
State University of New York at Plattsburgh M
State University of New York College at Brockport M

State University of New York College at Cortland M
State University of New York College at Geneseo M
State University of New York College at Oneonta M
State University of New York College at Potsdam M
Stetson University M
Sul Ross State University M
Syracuse University M,D
Temple University M,D
Tennessee Technological University M,O
Texas A&M International University M,D
Texas A&M University M,D
Texas A&M University–Commerce M,D
Texas A&M University–Corpus Christi M,D
Texas A&M University–Kingsville M
Texas Southern University M,D
Texas State University-San Marcos M
Texas Tech University M,D
Texas Woman's University M,D
Towson University M,O
Trevecca Nazarene University M
Trinity (Washington) University M
Union College (KY) M
University at Albany, State University of New York M,D,O
University at Buffalo, the State University of New York M,D,O
University of Alaska Fairbanks M
The University of Arizona M,D,O
University of Arkansas at Little Rock M
University of Bridgeport M,O
University of California, Berkeley M,D
University of Central Arkansas M
University of Central Florida M,O
University of Central Missouri M,O
University of Central Oklahoma M
University of Cincinnati M,D
University of Connecticut M,D
University of Dayton M
University of Florida M,D,O
University of Georgia M,D,O
University of Guam M
University of Houston M,D
University of Houston–Clear Lake M
University of Illinois at Chicago M,D
University of La Verne M,O
University of Louisiana at Monroe M
University of Louisville M
University of Maine M,D,O
University of Mary M
University of Mary Hardin-Baylor M,D
University of Maryland, College Park M,D,O
University of Massachusetts Amherst M,D,O
University of Massachusetts Lowell M,D,O
University of Memphis M,D
University of Miami M,D,O
University of Michigan M,D
University of Michigan–Flint M
University of Minnesota, Twin Cities Campus M,D,O
University of Missouri–Columbia M,D,O
University of Missouri–Kansas City M,D,O
University of Missouri–St. Louis M,D
University of Nebraska at Kearney M
University of Nebraska at Omaha M
University of Nevada, Las Vegas M,D,O
University of Nevada, Reno M,D,O
University of New England M
University of New Hampshire M
The University of North Carolina at Chapel Hill M,D
The University of North Carolina at Charlotte M
The University of North Carolina at Greensboro M,D,O
The University of North Carolina at Pembroke M
The University of North Carolina Wilmington M
University of North Dakota M
University of Northern Colorado M
University of Northern Iowa M
University of North Texas M,D
University of Oklahoma M,D,O
University of Pennsylvania M,D
University of Pittsburgh M,D
University of Rhode Island M
University of Rio Grande M
University of St. Francis (IL) M
University of St. Thomas (MN) M,D,O
University of San Francisco M
The University of Scranton M
University of Sioux Falls M,O
University of South Alabama M,O
University of South Carolina M,D
University of Southern Maine M,O
University of Southern Mississippi M,D,O
University of South Florida M
The University of Tampa M
The University of Tennessee M,D,O
The University of Texas at Brownsville M
The University of Texas at San Antonio M
The University of Texas at Tyler M
The University of Texas of the Permian Basin M
The University of Texas–Pan American M
University of the Incarnate Word M,D
University of Vermont M
University of Washington M,D
University of West Florida M
University of West Georgia M
University of Wisconsin–Eau Claire M
University of Wisconsin–La Crosse M
University of Wisconsin–Milwaukee M
University of Wisconsin–Oshkosh M
University of Wisconsin–River Falls M
University of Wisconsin–Stevens Point M
University of Wisconsin–Superior M
University of Wisconsin–Whitewater M
Valdosta State University M,O
Vanderbilt University M,D
Virginia Commonwealth University M
Wagner College M
Walden University M,D
Walla Walla University M
Washburn University M
Washington State University M,D
Wayne State University M,D,O
West Chester University of Pennsylvania M
Western Carolina University M
Western Connecticut State University M
Western Illinois University M
Western Kentucky University M
Western Michigan University M
Western New Mexico University M
Westfield State College M
West Texas A&M University M
West Virginia University M
Wheelock College M
Widener University M,D
William Paterson University of New Jersey M
Wilmington University (DE) M
Winthrop University M
Worcester State College M
Xavier University M
Youngstown State University M

■ REAL ESTATE

American University M
Bentley College M
California State University, Sacramento M
Clemson University M
Cleveland State University M,O
Columbia University M
Cornell University M
DePaul University M
Florida Atlantic University M
The George Washington University M
Georgia State University M,D,O
The Johns Hopkins University M
Massachusetts Institute of Technology M
New York University M,O
Nova Southeastern University M
Penn State University Park M,D
Roosevelt University M,O
Texas A&M University M
University of California, Berkeley D
University of Denver M
University of Florida M,D,O
University of Hawaii at Manoa M
University of Memphis M,D
University of Michigan M,O
University of North Texas M,D
University of Pennsylvania M,D
University of St. Thomas (MN) M
University of Southern California M
The University of Texas at Arlington M,D
University of Wisconsin–Madison M,D
Virginia Commonwealth University M,O
Washington State University D
Woodbury University M

■ RECREATION AND PARK MANAGEMENT

Arizona State University M
Bowling Green State University M
Brigham Young University M
California State University, Chico M
California State University, Long Beach M
California State University, Northridge M
California State University, Sacramento M
Central Michigan University M
Clemson University M,D
Colorado State University M,D
Delta State University M
East Carolina University M
Eastern Kentucky University M
Florida Agricultural and Mechanical University M
Florida Gulf Coast University M
Florida International University M
Florida State University M,D,O
Frostburg State University M
Georgia Southern University M
Hardin-Simmons University M
Indiana University Bloomington M,D,O
Kent State University M
Lehman College of the City University of New York M
Michigan State University M,D
Middle Tennessee State University M,D
Naropa University M
North Carolina Central University M
North Carolina State University M,D
Northwest Missouri State University M

Ohio University M
Old Dominion University M
Penn State University Park M,D
San Francisco State University M
San Jose State University M
South Dakota State University M
Southern Connecticut State University M
Southern Illinois University Carbondale M
Southern University and Agricultural and Mechanical College M
Southwestern Oklahoma State University M
Springfield College M
State University of New York College at Brockport M
State University of New York College at Cortland M
State University of New York College of Environmental Science and Forestry M,D
Temple University M
Texas A&M University M,D
Texas State University-San Marcos M
Universidad Metropolitana M
University of Arkansas M,D
University of Florida M,D
University of Idaho M
The University of Iowa M
University of Minnesota, Twin Cities Campus M,D
University of Mississippi M,D
University of Missouri–Columbia M
The University of Montana M,D
University of Nebraska at Omaha M
University of Nebraska–Lincoln M
University of New Hampshire M
The University of North Carolina at Chapel Hill M
The University of North Carolina at Greensboro M
University of North Texas M,O
University of Rhode Island M,D
University of South Alabama M
University of Southern Mississippi M,D
The University of Tennessee M,D
University of Utah M,D
University of Wisconsin–La Crosse M
University of Wisconsin–Madison M
Utah State University M,D
Virginia Commonwealth University M
Virginia Polytechnic Institute and State University M,D
Wayne State University M
Western Illinois University M
Western Kentucky University M
West Virginia University M
Wright State University M

■ REHABILITATION COUNSELING

Arkansas State University M,O
Assumption College M,O
Auburn University M,D,O
Barry University M,O
Bowling Green State University M
California State University, Fresno M
California State University, Los Angeles M
California State University, San Bernardino M
Central Connecticut State University M,O
Coppin State University M
Drake University M
East Carolina University M
East Central University M
Edinboro University of Pennsylvania M
Emporia State University M
Florida Atlantic University M,O
Florida International University M
Florida State University M,D,O
Fort Valley State University M
The George Washington University M
Georgia State University M
Hofstra University M,O
Hunter College of the City University of New York M
Illinois Institute of Technology M,D
Indiana University–Purdue University Indianapolis M,D
Jackson State University M,O
Kent State University M,O
La Salle University D
Maryville University of Saint Louis M
Michigan State University M,D,O
Minnesota State University Mankato M
Montana State University–Billings M
Northeastern University M
Ohio University M,D
Pontifical Catholic University of Puerto Rico M
St. Cloud State University M
Salve Regina University M,O
San Diego State University M
San Francisco State University M
South Carolina State University M
Southern Illinois University Carbondale M,D
Southern University and Agricultural and Mechanical College M
Springfield College M,O
Syracuse University M
Troy University M,O
University at Albany, State University of New York M
University at Buffalo, the State University of New York M,D,O
The University of Alabama at Birmingham M
The University of Arizona M,D,O
University of Arkansas M,D
University of Florida M
The University of Iowa M,D
University of Kentucky M,D
University of Louisiana at Lafayette M
University of Maryland, College Park M,D,O
University of Maryland Eastern Shore M
University of Massachusetts Boston M,O
University of Memphis M,D
University of Nevada, Las Vegas M,O
The University of North Carolina at Chapel Hill M,D
University of Northern Colorado M,D
University of North Florida M,O
University of North Texas M
University of Pittsburgh M
University of Puerto Rico, Río Piedras M
The University of Scranton M
University of South Alabama M,D
University of South Carolina M,O
University of South Florida M
The University of Tennessee M,D
The University of Texas–Pan American M
University of Wisconsin–Madison M,D
University of Wisconsin–Stout M
Utah State University M
Virginia Commonwealth University M,O
Wayne State University M,D,O
Western Michigan University M
Western Oregon University M
Western Washington University M
West Virginia University M
Wright State University M

■ REHABILITATION SCIENCES

Boston University D
California University of Pennsylvania M
Canisius College M
Central Michigan University M,D
Clarion University of Pennsylvania M
Concordia University Wisconsin M
Drake University M
East Carolina University M
East Stroudsburg University of Pennsylvania M
Indiana University–Purdue University Indianapolis M,D
University at Buffalo, the State University of New York M,D,O
The University of Alabama at Birmingham O
University of Cincinnati D
University of Florida D
The University of Iowa D
University of Kansas M,D
University of Kentucky D
University of Maryland Eastern Shore M
University of Northern Iowa M,D
University of North Texas M
University of Pittsburgh M,D,O
University of South Carolina M,O
University of Washington M,D
University of Wisconsin–La Crosse M
University of Wisconsin–Madison M
Virginia Commonwealth University M,D
Wayne State University M,O

■ RELIABILITY ENGINEERING

The University of Arizona M
University of Maryland, College Park M,D,O

■ RELIGION

Arizona State University M,D
Azusa Pacific University M
Baylor University M,D
Bellarmine University M
Biola University P,M,D
Bob Jones University P,M,D,O
Boston University M,D
Brown University M,D
California Institute of Integral Studies M,D
California State University, Long Beach M
Cardinal Stritch University M
The Catholic University of America P,M,D,O
Chestnut Hill College M,O
Christian Brothers University M
Claremont Graduate University M,D
Columbia University M,D
Concordia University Chicago (IL) M
Cornell University D
Drew University M,D
Duke University M,D
Eastern Mennonite University P,M,O
Edgewood College M
Emory University D,O
Florida International University M
Florida State University M,D
Fordham University M,D,O
George Fox University P,M,D,O
The George Washington University M
Georgia State University M
Gonzaga University M
Graceland University M
Hardin-Simmons University M

Harvard University	D
Holy Names University	M,O
Indiana University Bloomington	M,D
John Carroll University	M
La Salle University	M
La Sierra University	M
Lee University	M
Liberty University	P,M,D
Lipscomb University	P,M
Loyola University Chicago	P,M,O
Loyola University New Orleans	M
Miami University	M
Missouri State University	M
Mount St. Mary's College	M
Naropa University	M
New York University	M,O
Northwest Nazarene University	P,M
Oklahoma City University	M
Olivet Nazarene University	M
Pepperdine University	P,M
Point Loma Nazarene University	M
Princeton University	D
Providence College	M
Rice University	D
Sacred Heart University	M
Santa Clara University	M
Seton Hall University	M
Southern Methodist University	M,D
Southern Nazarene University	M
Stanford University	M,D
Syracuse University	M,D
Temple University	M,D
Trevecca Nazarene University	M
Trinity International University	P,M,D,O
Union University	M
University of California, Berkeley	D
University of California, Santa Barbara	M,D
University of Chicago	P,M,D
University of Colorado at Boulder	M
University of Denver	M,D
University of Detroit Mercy	M
University of Florida	M,D
University of Georgia	M
University of Hawaii at Manoa	M
The University of Iowa	M,D
University of Kansas	M
University of Minnesota, Twin Cities Campus	M,D
University of Missouri–Columbia	M
University of Mobile	M
The University of North Carolina at Chapel Hill	M,D
The University of North Carolina at Charlotte	M
University of North Texas	M,D
University of Notre Dame	M
University of Pennsylvania	D
University of Pittsburgh	M,D
University of St. Thomas (MN)	M
University of South Carolina	M
University of Southern California	M,D
University of South Florida	M
The University of Tennessee	M,D
University of the Incarnate Word	M
University of Virginia	M,D
University of Washington	M
Vanderbilt University	M,D
Vanguard University of Southern California	M
Wake Forest University	M
Washington University in St. Louis	M
Wayland Baptist University	M
Western Michigan University	M,D
Wheaton College	M
Yale University	D

■ RELIGIOUS EDUCATION

Andrews University	M,D,O
Azusa Pacific University	M
Biola University	P,M,D
Boston College	P,M,D,O
Brandeis University	M
Brigham Young University	M
Campbell University	P,M,D
Concordia University Chicago (IL)	M
Concordia University (NE)	M
Concordia University, St. Paul	M,O
Dallas Baptist University	M
Fordham University	M,D,O
Gardner-Webb University	P,D
Gratz College	M,O
Harding University	M,O
Indiana Wesleyan University	M
La Sierra University	M
Loyola Marymount University	M
Loyola University Chicago	P,M,O
Nova Southeastern University	M,O
Oral Roberts University	P,M,D
Pfeiffer University	M
Pontifical Catholic University of Puerto Rico	M,D
Regent University	M,D,O
Trinity International University	P,M,D,O
University of St. Thomas (MN)	M
University of San Francisco	M,D
Wheaton College	M
Yeshiva University	M,D,O

■ REPRODUCTIVE BIOLOGY

Cornell University	M,D
New York University	D
Northwestern University	D
University of Wyoming	M,D
West Virginia University	M,D

■ RHETORIC

Abilene Christian University	M
Ball State University	M
Bob Jones University	P,M,D,O
Bowling Green State University	M,D
California State University, Dominguez Hills	M,O
California State University, Northridge	M
Carnegie Mellon University	M
The Catholic University of America	M,D
Clemson University	D
Duquesne University	M,D
Florida State University	M,D
Georgia State University	M,D
Indiana University of Pennsylvania	M,D
Iowa State University of Science and Technology	M,D
Kansas State University	M
Kent State University	M,D
Miami University	M,D
Michigan State University	M,D
Michigan Technological University	M,D
New Mexico Highlands University	M
New Mexico State University	M,D
Northern Arizona University	M
Rensselaer Polytechnic Institute	M,D
San Diego State University	M
Southern Illinois University Carbondale	M,D
Syracuse University	M,D
Texas State University-San Marcos	M
Texas Tech University	M,D
Texas Woman's University	M,D
The University of Alabama	M,D
The University of Arizona	M,D
University of Arkansas at Little Rock	M
University of California, Berkeley	D
University of Illinois at Chicago	M,D
The University of Iowa	M,D
University of Louisiana at Lafayette	M,D
University of Louisville	D
The University of North Carolina at Greensboro	M,D
The University of Texas at Arlington	M,D
The University of Texas at El Paso	M
University of Utah	M,D
Virginia Commonwealth University	M
Wright State University	M

■ ROMANCE LANGUAGES

Appalachian State University	M
Boston University	M,D
The Catholic University of America	M,D
Clark Atlanta University	M
Columbia University	M,D
Cornell University	M,D
Hunter College of the City University of New York	M
The Johns Hopkins University	D
Michigan State University	M,D
New York University	M,D
Northern Illinois University	M
Queens College of the City University of New York	M
San Diego State University	M
Southern Connecticut State University	M
Stony Brook University, State University of New York	M,D
Texas Tech University	M,D
University at Buffalo, the State University of New York	M,D
The University of Alabama	M,D
University of California, Berkeley	D
University of California, Los Angeles	M,D
University of Chicago	M,D
University of Cincinnati	M,D
University of Georgia	M,D
University of Michigan	D
University of Missouri–Columbia	M,D
University of Missouri–Kansas City	M
University of New Orleans	M
The University of North Carolina at Chapel Hill	M,D
University of Notre Dame	M
University of Oregon	M,D
University of Pennsylvania	M,D
The University of Texas at Austin	M,D
University of Virginia	M,D
University of Washington	M,D
Washington University in St. Louis	M,D
Wayne State University	M,D

■ RURAL PLANNING AND STUDIES

California State University, Chico	M
Cornell University	M
Iowa State University of Science and Technology	M,D
University of Alaska Fairbanks	M
The University of Montana	M
University of West Georgia	M
University of Wyoming	M

■ RURAL SOCIOLOGY

Auburn University	M
Cornell University	M,D
Iowa State University of Science and Technology	M,D
North Carolina State University	M,D
The Ohio State University	M,D

Penn State University Park M,D
South Dakota State University M,D
University of Missouri–Columbia M,D
The University of Montana M
University of Wisconsin–Madison M,D

■ RUSSIAN

American University O
Boston College M
Brown University M,D
Columbia University M,D
Harvard University D
Hofstra University M
Kent State University M,D
New York University M
Penn State University Park M,D
Stanford University M,D
University at Albany, State University of New York M,O
The University of Arizona M
University of California, Berkeley D
University of Illinois at Urbana–Champaign M,D
University of Michigan M,D
The University of North Carolina at Chapel Hill M,D
University of Oregon M
The University of Tennessee D
University of Washington M,D
Wayne State University M,D

■ SAFETY ENGINEERING

Indiana University Bloomington M,D
Murray State University M
National University M
New Jersey Institute of Technology M
University of Minnesota, Duluth M
West Virginia University M

■ SCANDINAVIAN LANGUAGES

Cornell University M,D
Harvard University D
University of California, Berkeley D
University of California, Los Angeles M,D
University of Minnesota, Twin Cities Campus M,D
University of Washington M,D
University of Wisconsin–Madison M,D

■ SCHOOL NURSING

Kutztown University of Pennsylvania O
La Salle University M,O
Monmouth University M,O
Seton Hall University M
Wright State University M

■ SCHOOL PSYCHOLOGY

Abilene Christian University M
Adelphi University M
Alabama Agricultural and Mechanical University M,O
Alfred University M,D,O
Andrews University M,O
Appalachian State University M,O
Arcadia University M
Argosy University, Sarasota Campus M,D,O
Arkansas State University M,O
Assumption College M,O
Auburn University M,D,O
Azusa Pacific University M
Ball State University M,D,O
Barry University M,O
Bowling Green State University M,O
Brigham Young University M,D,O
Brooklyn College of the City University of New York M,O
Bucknell University M
California State University, Los Angeles M
California State University, Northridge M
California State University, Sacramento M
California University of Pennsylvania M
Canisius College M
Capella University M,D,O
Central Connecticut State University M,O
Central Michigan University D,O
Central Washington University M
Chapman University M,D,O
The Citadel, The Military College of South Carolina M,O
City University of Seattle M,O
Cleveland State University M,O
The College of New Rochelle M
College of St. Joseph M
The College of Saint Rose M,O
The College of William and Mary M,O
Duquesne University M,D,O
East Carolina University
Eastern Illinois University M,O
Eastern Kentucky University M,O
Eastern Washington University M
Emporia State University M,O
Fairfield University M,O
Fairleigh Dickinson University, Metropolitan Campus M,D
Florida Agricultural and Mechanical University M
Florida International University M,O
Florida State University M,O
Fordham University M,D,O
Fort Hays State University O
Francis Marion University M
Fresno Pacific University M
Gallaudet University M,O
Gardner-Webb University M
George Fox University M,O
George Mason University M
Georgia Southern University M,O
Georgia State University M,D,O
Grand Valley State University M
Hofstra University M,D,O
Howard University M,D,O
Idaho State University M,D,O
Illinois State University D,O
Immaculata University M,D,O
Indiana State University M,D,O
Indiana University Bloomington M,D,O
Indiana University of Pennsylvania D,O
Inter American University of Puerto Rico, San Germán Campus M,D
Iona College M
James Madison University M,D,O
Kean University O
Kent State University M,D,O
La Sierra University M,O
Lehigh University D,O
Lesley University M
Lewis & Clark College M,O
Lindenwood University M,D,O
Long Island University, Brooklyn Campus M
Louisiana State University and Agricultural and Mechanical College M,D
Louisiana State University in Shreveport M,O
Loyola Marymount University M
Loyola University Chicago M,D,O
Marist College M,O
Marshall University O
Marywood University M,O
McNeese State University M
Mercy College M
Miami University M,O
Michigan State University M,D,O
Middle Tennessee State University M,O
Millersville University of Pennsylvania M
Minnesota State University Moorhead M,O
Minot State University O
Montclair State University M,O
National-Louis University M,D,O
National University M
New Jersey City University M,O
New Mexico State University M,D,O
New York University M,D,O
Niagara University M
Nicholls State University M,O
North Carolina State University D
Northeastern University M,D,O
Northern Arizona University M,D
Northwest Nazarene University M
Nova Southeastern University O
Our Lady of the Lake University of San Antonio M,D
Pace University M
Penn State University Park M,D
Pittsburg State University O
Pontifical Catholic University of Puerto Rico M,D
Queens College of the City University of New York M,O
Radford University O
Regent University M,D,O
Rider University M,O
Roberts Wesleyan College M
Rochester Institute of Technology M,O
Rowan University M,O
Rutgers, The State University of New Jersey, New Brunswick M,D
St. John's University (NY) M,D
St. Mary's University of San Antonio M
Sam Houston State University M,D
San Diego State University M
Seattle University M,O
Seton Hall University O
Southeast Missouri State University M,O
Southern Connecticut State University M,O
Southern Illinois University Edwardsville O
Southern New Hampshire University M,O
Southwestern Oklahoma State University M
State University of New York at Oswego M,O
State University of New York at Plattsburgh M,O
Stephen F. Austin State University M
Syracuse University M,D
Tarleton State University M
Temple University M,D
Tennessee State University M,D
Texas A&M University M,D
Texas State University-San Marcos M
Texas Woman's University M,D,O
Towson University M,O
Trinity University M
Troy University M
Tufts University M,O
University at Albany, State University of New York M,D,O
University at Buffalo, the State University of New York M,D,O

The University of Akron	M
The University of Alabama at Birmingham	M
University of California, Berkeley	
University of Central Arkansas	M,D
University of Central Florida	O
University of Cincinnati	D,O
University of Colorado Denver	M,O
University of Connecticut	M,D
University of Dayton	M,O
University of Delaware	M,D
University of Denver	M,D,O
University of Detroit Mercy	O
University of Florida	M,D,O
University of Great Falls	M
University of Hartford	M
University of Houston–Clear Lake	M
University of Idaho	O
The University of Iowa	M,D,O
University of Kansas	D,O
University of Kentucky	M,D,O
University of Louisiana at Monroe	O
University of Mary Hardin-Baylor	M
University of Maryland, College Park	M,D,O
University of Massachusetts Amherst	D
University of Massachusetts Boston	M,O
University of Memphis	M,D
University of Minnesota, Twin Cities Campus	M,D,O
University of Missouri–Columbia	M,D,O
University of Missouri–St. Louis	D,O
The University of Montana	M,D,O
University of Nebraska at Kearney	M,O
University of Nebraska at Omaha	M,D,O
University of Nevada, Las Vegas	M,D,O
The University of North Carolina at Chapel Hill	M,D
The University of North Carolina at Greensboro	M,D,O
University of Northern Colorado	D,O
University of Northern Iowa	M,O
University of North Texas	M,D
University of Oklahoma	M,D
University of Pennsylvania	D
University of Phoenix–Denver Campus	M
University of Phoenix–Las Vegas Campus	M
University of Phoenix–Southern Colorado Campus	M,O
University of Phoenix–Utah Campus	M
University of Rhode Island	M,D
University of South Alabama	M,D
University of South Carolina	D
University of Southern Maine	M,D,O
University of Southern Mississippi	M,D
University of South Florida	M,D,O
The University of Tennessee	M,D,O
The University of Tennessee at Chattanooga	O
The University of Texas at Austin	M,D
The University of Texas at Tyler	M
The University of Texas–Pan American	M
University of the Pacific	M,D,O
The University of Toledo	M,D,O
University of Virginia	M,D,O
University of Washington	M,D
University of Wisconsin–Eau Claire	M,O
University of Wisconsin–La Crosse	M,O
University of Wisconsin–Milwaukee	O
University of Wisconsin–River Falls	M,O
University of Wisconsin–Stout	M,O
University of Wisconsin–Whitewater	M,O
Utah State University	M,D
Valdosta State University	M,O
Valparaiso University	
Wayne State University	M,D,O
Western Carolina University	M
Western Illinois University	M,O
Western Kentucky University	M,O
Western Michigan University	M,D,O
Western New Mexico University	M
Wichita State University	M,D,O
Yeshiva University	D

■ SCIENCE EDUCATION

Alabama State University	M,O
Albany State University	M
Alverno College	M
Andrews University	M,D,O
Antioch University New England	M
Arcadia University	M,D,O
Arizona State University	M,D
Arkansas State University	M,D,O
Armstrong Atlantic State University	M
Auburn University	M,D,O
Ball State University	M,D
Belmont University	M
Bemidji State University	M
Benedictine University	M
Bennington College	M
Bethel College (TN)	M
Bloomsburg University of Pennsylvania	M
Boise State University	M,D
Boston College	M,D
Boston University	M,D,O
Bowling Green State University	M
Bridgewater State College	M
Brigham Young University	M,D
Brooklyn College of the City University of New York	M,O
Brown University	M
Buffalo State College, State University of New York	M
California State University, Chico	M
California State University, Fullerton	M
California State University, Long Beach	M
California State University, San Bernardino	M
Central Michigan University	M
Charleston Southern University	M
Chatham University	M
City College of the City University of New York	M
Clarion University of Pennsylvania	M
Clark Atlanta University	M,D
Clemson University	M
Cleveland State University	M
College of Charleston	M
The College of William and Mary	M
Columbia University	M,D,O
Columbus State University	M,O
Converse College	M
Cornell University	M,D
Delaware State University	M
DeSales University	M,O
Drake University	M
East Carolina University	M
Eastern Connecticut State University	M
Eastern Kentucky University	M
Eastern Michigan University	M
Eastern Washington University	M
East Stroudsburg University of Pennsylvania	M
Edinboro University of Pennsylvania	M
Fairleigh Dickinson University, Metropolitan Campus	M
Fitchburg State College	M
Florida Agricultural and Mechanical University	M
Florida Gulf Coast University	M
Florida Institute of Technology	M,D,O
Florida International University	M,D
Florida State University	M,D,O
Framingham State College	M
Fresno Pacific University	M
Gannon University	M
Georgia College & State University	M,O
Georgia Southern University	M
Georgia State University	M,D,O
Grambling State University	M,O
Harding University	M,O
Hardin-Simmons University	M,D
Harvard University	M
Heritage University	M
Hofstra University	M,O
Hood College	M,O
Hunter College of the City University of New York	M,O
Illinois Institute of Technology	M,D
Indiana State University	M,D
Indiana University Bloomington	M,D,O
Inter American University of Puerto Rico, Metropolitan Campus	M
Inter American University of Puerto Rico, San Germán Campus	M
Iona College	M
Ithaca College	M
Jackson State University	M,D
John Carroll University	M
The Johns Hopkins University	M,D,O
Johnson State College	M
Kean University	M
Kutztown University of Pennsylvania	M,O
Lawrence Technological University	M
Lehman College of the City University of New York	M
Lesley University	M,D,O
Long Island University, C.W. Post Campus	M
Louisiana Tech University	M,D
Loyola University Chicago	M
Lynchburg College	M
Manhattanville College	M
McNeese State University	M
Michigan State University	M
Michigan Technological University	M
Middle Tennessee State University	M
Mills College	M,D
Minnesota State University Mankato	M
Minot State University	M
Mississippi College	M,O
Missouri State University	M
Montclair State University	M,D,O
Morgan State University	D
National-Louis University	M,O
New Mexico Institute of Mining and Technology	M
New York University	M
North Carolina Agricultural and Technical State University	M
North Carolina State University	M,D
North Dakota State University	M,D,O
Northeastern State University	M
Northern Arizona University	M,D
North Georgia College & State University	M,O
Northwestern State University of Louisiana	M
Northwest Missouri State University	M
Nova Southeastern University	M,O
Ohio University	M

Old Dominion University	M
Oregon State University	M,D
Penn State University Park	M,D
Plymouth State University	M
Portland State University	M,D
Purdue University	M,D,O
Purdue University Calumet	M
Queens College of the City University of New York	M,O
Quinnipiac University	M
Regis University	M,O
Rensselaer Polytechnic Institute	M
Rider University	M,O
Rutgers, The State University of New Jersey, New Brunswick	M,D
Saginaw Valley State University	M
St. John Fisher College	M
Salem State College	M
Salisbury University	M
San Diego State University	M,D
Slippery Rock University of Pennsylvania	M
South Carolina State University	M
Southeast Missouri State University	M
Southern Connecticut State University	M,O
Southern Illinois University Edwardsville	M
Southern University and Agricultural and Mechanical College	D
Southwestern Oklahoma State University	M
Stanford University	M,D
State University of New York at Binghamton	M
State University of New York at Fredonia	M
State University of New York at Plattsburgh	M
State University of New York College at Brockport	M
State University of New York College at Cortland	M
Stony Brook University, State University of New York	M,O
Syracuse University	M,D
Temple University	M,D
Texas A&M University	M,D
Texas Christian University	M,D
Texas State University-San Marcos	M
Texas Woman's University	M,D
Towson University	M
Trinity (Washington) University	M
University at Albany, State University of New York	M,D
University at Buffalo, the State University of New York	M,D,O
The University of Arizona	M,D
University of California, Berkeley	M,D
University of California, Los Angeles	M,D
University of California, San Diego	D
University of Central Florida	M,D,O
University of Chicago	D
University of Cincinnati	M,D,O
University of Connecticut	M,D
University of Florida	M,D,O
University of Georgia	M,D,O
University of Houston	M,D
University of Idaho	M,D
University of Indianapolis	M
The University of Iowa	M,D
University of Maine	M,O
University of Massachusetts Lowell	M,D,O
University of Miami	M,D,O
University of Michigan	M,D
University of Michigan–Dearborn	M
University of Minnesota, Twin Cities Campus	M
University of Missouri–Columbia	M,D,O
University of Nebraska at Kearney	M
University of New Hampshire	M,D
University of New Orleans	M
The University of North Carolina at Chapel Hill	M
The University of North Carolina at Greensboro	M,D,O
The University of North Carolina at Pembroke	M
University of Northern Colorado	M,D
University of Northern Iowa	M,O
University of Oklahoma	M,D,O
University of Pittsburgh	M,D
University of Puerto Rico, Río Piedras	M,D
University of St. Francis (IL)	M
University of South Alabama	M,O
University of South Carolina	M,D
University of Southern Mississippi	M,D
University of South Florida	M,D
The University of Tampa	M
The University of Tennessee	M,D,O
The University of Texas at Austin	M,D
The University of Texas at Dallas	M
The University of Texas at Tyler	M
University of the Incarnate Word	M
The University of Toledo	M
University of Tulsa	M
University of Utah	M,D
University of Vermont	M,D
University of Virginia	M,D
University of Washington	M,D
University of Washington, Tacoma	M
The University of West Alabama	M
University of West Florida	M
University of West Georgia	M,O
University of Wisconsin–Eau Claire	M
University of Wisconsin–Madison	M,D
University of Wisconsin–River Falls	M
University of Wisconsin–Stevens Point	M
University of Wyoming	M
Vanderbilt University	M,D
Walden University	M,D
Wayne State College	M
Wayne State University	M,D,O
West Chester University of Pennsylvania	M
Western Carolina University	M
Western Kentucky University	M
Western Michigan University	D
Western Oregon University	M
Western Washington University	M
Widener University	M,D
Wilkes University	M,D
Wright State University	M

■ SECONDARY EDUCATION

Adelphi University	M
Alabama Agricultural and Mechanical University	M,O
Alabama State University	M,O
Alcorn State University	M,O
American International College	M,D,O
American University	M,O
Andrews University	M,D,O
Appalachian State University	M
Arcadia University	M,D,O
Argosy University, Orange County Campus	M,D
Argosy University, Sarasota Campus	M,D,O
Argosy University, Tampa Campus	M,D,O
Argosy University, Twin Cities Campus	M,D,O
Arizona State University at the West campus	M,D,O
Arkansas Tech University	M,O
Armstrong Atlantic State University	M
Auburn University	M,D,O
Auburn University Montgomery	M,O
Augusta State University	M,O
Ball State University	M
Belhaven College (MS)	M
Bellarmine University	M
Belmont University	M
Benedictine University	M
Bennington College	M
Bethel University	M,D,O
Bob Jones University	P,M,D,O
Boston College	M
Bowie State University	M
Brandeis University	M
Bridgewater State College	M
Brooklyn College of the City University of New York	M,O
Brown University	M
Butler University	M
California State University, Bakersfield	M
California State University, Fullerton	M
California State University, Los Angeles	M
California State University, Northridge	M
California State University, San Bernardino	M
California State University, Stanislaus	M
California University of Pennsylvania	M
Campbell University	M
Canisius College	M
Carlow University	M
Carson-Newman College	M
Central Connecticut State University	M
Central Michigan University	M
Chapman University	M
Charleston Southern University	M
Chatham University	M
Chestnut Hill College	M
Chicago State University	M
The Citadel, The Military College of South Carolina	M
City College of the City University of New York	M,O
Clemson University	M
College of Mount St. Joseph	M
The College of New Jersey	M
College of St. Joseph	M
The College of Saint Rose	M,O
College of Staten Island of the City University of New York	M
The College of William and Mary	M
Columbus State University	M,O
Concordia University (OR)	M
Converse College	M
Delta State University	M,O
DePaul University	M,D
Dowling College	M,D,O
Drake University	M
Drury University	M
Duquesne University	M
D'Youville College	M,O
Eastern Connecticut State University	M
Eastern Kentucky University	M
Eastern Michigan University	M
Eastern Nazarene College	M,O
Eastern Oregon University	M
East Stroudsburg University of Pennsylvania	M

East Tennessee State University M
Edinboro University of Pennsylvania M
Emmanuel College M,O
Emory University M,D,O
Emporia State University M
Fairfield University M,O
Fayetteville State University M
Fitchburg State College M
Florida Agricultural and Mechanical University M
Florida Gulf Coast University M
Fordham University M,D,O
Fort Hays State University M
Francis Marion University M
Friends University M
Frostburg State University M
Gallaudet University M,D,O
George Mason University M
The George Washington University M
Georgia College & State University M,O
Georgia Southwestern State University M,O
Grand Canyon University M
Harding University M,O
Hawai'i Pacific University M
Hofstra University M,O
Holy Family University M
Hood College M,O
Howard University M,O
Hunter College of the City University of New York M
Idaho State University M,O
Immaculata University M,D,O
Indiana University Bloomington M,D,O
Indiana University Northwest M
Indiana University–Purdue University Fort Wayne M
Indiana University South Bend M
Indiana University Southeast M
Iona College M
Ithaca College M
Jackson State University M,D,O
Jacksonville State University M
James Madison University M
John Carroll University M
The Johns Hopkins University M
Johnson State College M,O
Kansas State University M,D
Kennesaw State University M
Kent State University M
Kutztown University of Pennsylvania M,O
Lee University M
Lehigh University M,D
Lewis & Clark College M
Liberty University M,D,O
Lincoln University (MO) M,O
Long Island University, C.W. Post Campus M
Longwood University M
Louisiana State University and Agricultural and Mechanical College M,D,O
Louisiana Tech University M,D
Loyola Marymount University M
Loyola University Chicago M
Loyola University New Orleans M
Maharishi University of Management M
Manhattanville College M
Mansfield University of Pennsylvania M
Marshall University M
Marygrove College M
Marymount University M,O
Maryville University of Saint Louis M,D
Marywood University M
McDaniel College M
McNeese State University M
Mercer University M,D,O
Mercy College M
Miami University M
Mills College M,D
Minnesota State University Mankato M,O
Mississippi College M,O
Mississippi State University M,D,O
Missouri State University M,O
Montana State University–Billings M
Morehead State University M
Morgan State University M
Mount Saint Mary College M
Mount St. Mary's College M
Murray State University M,O
National-Louis University M
New Jersey City University M
Niagara University M
Norfolk State University M
Northern Arizona University M
Northern Illinois University M,D
Northern Michigan University M
North Georgia College & State University M,O
Northwestern State University of Louisiana M,O
Northwestern University M
Northwest Missouri State University M,O
Nova Southeastern University M,O
Oakland University M
Ohio University M,D
Old Dominion University M,D
Olivet Nazarene University M
Pacific University M
Park University M
Piedmont College M,O
Pittsburg State University M
Plymouth State University M
Portland State University M,D
Purdue University Calumet M
Queens College of the City University of New York M,O
Quinnipiac University M
Regis University M,O
Rhode Island College M,O
Roberts Wesleyan College M,O
Rochester Institute of Technology M
Rockford College M
Rollins College M
Roosevelt University M
Rowan University M
Sacred Heart University M,O
Saginaw Valley State University M
St. John's University (NY) M
Saint Joseph's University M,D,O
Saint Mary's University of Minnesota M,O
St. Thomas Aquinas College M,O
Saint Xavier University M,O
Salem State College M
Salisbury University M
Sam Houston State University M
San Diego State University M
San Francisco State University M
San Jose State University M,O
Seattle Pacific University M
Shenandoah University M,D,O
Siena Heights University M
Simmons College M,O
Slippery Rock University of Pennsylvania M
South Carolina State University M
Southeastern Louisiana University M
Southeastern Oklahoma State University M
Southeast Missouri State University M
Southern Illinois University Edwardsville M
Southern New Hampshire University M,O
Southern Oregon University M
Southern University and Agricultural and Mechanical College M
Southwestern Oklahoma State University M
Spalding University M
Springfield College M
Spring Hill College M
State University of New York at Binghamton M
State University of New York at Fredonia M
State University of New York at New Paltz M
State University of New York at Oswego M
State University of New York at Plattsburgh M
State University of New York College at Cortland M
State University of New York College at Geneseo M
State University of New York College at Oneonta M
State University of New York College at Potsdam M
Stephen F. Austin State University M,D
Suffolk University M
Sul Ross State University M
Tarleton State University M,D,O
Tennessee Technological University M,O
Texas A&M University–Commerce M,D
Texas A&M University–Corpus Christi M
Texas A&M University–Kingsville M
Texas Southern University M,D
Texas State University-San Marcos M
Texas Tech University M,D
Towson University M
Trevecca Nazarene University M
Trinity (Washington) University M
Troy University M,O
Tufts University M,D
Union College (KY) M
The University of Akron M,D
The University of Alabama at Birmingham M
University of Alaska Southeast M
The University of Arizona M,D
University of Arkansas M,O
University of Arkansas at Little Rock M
University of Bridgeport M,O
University of California, Irvine M,D
University of Central Missouri M,O
University of Central Oklahoma M
University of Cincinnati M
University of Connecticut M,D
University of Dayton M
University of Great Falls M
University of Guam M
University of Houston M,D
University of Illinois at Chicago M,D
University of Indianapolis M
The University of Iowa M,D
University of Louisiana at Monroe M
University of Louisville M
University of Maine M,O
University of Maryland, Baltimore County M
University of Maryland, College Park M,D,O
University of Massachusetts Amherst M,D,O

University of Massachusetts Boston	M,D,O
University of Memphis	M,D
University of Michigan	M,D
University of Mississippi	M,D,O
University of Missouri–St. Louis	M,D
University of Montevallo	M
University of Nebraska at Omaha	M
University of Nevada, Las Vegas	M,D,O
University of Nevada, Reno	M,D,O
University of New Hampshire	M
University of New Mexico	M,O
University of North Alabama	M
The University of North Carolina at Chapel Hill	M
The University of North Carolina at Charlotte	M
The University of North Carolina Wilmington	M
University of North Dakota	D
University of North Florida	M
University of North Texas	M
University of Oklahoma	M,D,O
University of Pennsylvania	M
University of Phoenix–Central Florida Campus	M
University of Phoenix–Denver Campus	M
University of Phoenix–Fort Lauderdale Campus	M
University of Phoenix–Hawaii Campus	M
University of Phoenix–New Mexico Campus	M
University of Phoenix–North Florida Campus	M
University of Phoenix	M
University of Phoenix–Oregon Campus	M
University of Phoenix–Phoenix Campus	M
University of Phoenix–Sacramento Valley Campus	M,O
University of Phoenix–San Diego Campus	M
University of Phoenix–Southern Arizona Campus	M,O
University of Phoenix–Southern California Campus	M
University of Phoenix–Southern Colorado Campus	M,O
University of Phoenix–Utah Campus	M
University of Phoenix–West Florida Campus	M
University of Pittsburgh	M,D
University of Portland	M
University of Puerto Rico, Río Piedras	M,D
University of Puget Sound	M
University of Rhode Island	M
University of St. Francis (IL)	M
The University of Scranton	M
University of South Alabama	M,O
University of South Carolina	M,D
The University of South Dakota	M
University of Southern Indiana	M
University of Southern Mississippi	M,D,O
University of South Florida	M,D,O
The University of Tennessee	M,D,O
The University of Tennessee at Chattanooga	M,D,O
The University of Tennessee at Martin	M
The University of Texas at Tyler	M
The University of Texas–Pan American	M
University of the Incarnate Word	M
The University of Toledo	M,D,O
University of Utah	M,D
University of Washington, Tacoma	M
The University of West Alabama	M
University of West Florida	M
University of West Georgia	M,O
University of Wisconsin–Eau Claire	M
University of Wisconsin–La Crosse	M
University of Wisconsin–Milwaukee	M
University of Wisconsin–Platteville	M
University of Wisconsin–Whitewater	M
Utah State University	M
Valdosta State University	M,O
Vanderbilt University	M,D
Villanova University	M
Virginia Commonwealth University	M,O
Wagner College	M
Wake Forest University	M
Washington State University	M,D
Washington University in St. Louis	M
Wayne State University	M,D,O
West Chester University of Pennsylvania	M
Western Carolina University	M
Western Illinois University	M
Western Kentucky University	M,O
Western New Mexico University	M
Western Oregon University	M
Western Washington University	M
Westfield State College	M
West Virginia University	M,D
Wheaton College	M
Whitworth University	M
Wilkes University	M,D
William Carey University	M,O
Wilmington University (DE)	M
Winthrop University	M
Worcester State College	M
Wright State University	M
Xavier University	M
Youngstown State University	M

■ SLAVIC LANGUAGES

Boston College	M
Brown University	M,D
Columbia University	M,D
Cornell University	M,D
Duke University	M
Florida State University	M
Harvard University	D
Indiana University Bloomington	M,D
New York University	M
Northwestern University	D
The Ohio State University	M,D
Princeton University	D
Stanford University	M,D
Stony Brook University, State University of New York	M
University of California, Berkeley	D
University of California, Los Angeles	M,D
University of Chicago	M,D
University of Illinois at Chicago	M,D
University of Illinois at Urbana–Champaign	M,D
University of Kansas	M,D
University of Michigan	M,D
The University of North Carolina at Chapel Hill	M,D
University of Pittsburgh	M,D
University of Southern California	M,D
The University of Texas at Austin	M,D
University of Virginia	M,D
University of Washington	M,D
University of Wisconsin–Madison	M,D
University of Wisconsin–Milwaukee	M
Yale University	D

■ SOCIAL PSYCHOLOGY

Alvernia College	M
American University	M
Andrews University	M
Appalachian State University	M
Arcadia University	M
Argosy University, Sarasota Campus	M,D,O
Arizona State University	D
Auburn University	M,D,O
Ball State University	M
Bowling Green State University	M,D
Brandeis University	M,D
Brigham Young University	M,D
Brooklyn College of the City University of New York	M,D
California State University, Fullerton	M
Canisius College	M
Carnegie Mellon University	D
Central Connecticut State University	M
Claremont Graduate University	M,D,O
Clark University	D
The College of New Rochelle	M
College of St. Joseph	M
Columbia University	M,D
Cornell University	M,D
DePaul University	M,D
Eastern Illinois University	M
Eastern Michigan University	M,O
Florida Agricultural and Mechanical University	M
Florida State University	D
Francis Marion University	M
The George Washington University	D
Graduate School and University Center of the City University of New York	D
Harvard University	D
Henderson State University	M
Hofstra University	M,D,O
Howard University	M,D
Hunter College of the City University of New York	M
Indiana University Bloomington	M,D
Indiana Wesleyan University	M
Iowa State University of Science and Technology	M,D
Lamar University	M
Lesley University	M,D,O
Loyola University Chicago	M,D
Marymount University	
Miami University	D
Minnesota State University Mankato	M,D,O
Montclair State University	M,O
Naropa University	M
National-Louis University	M,O
New College of California	M
New York University	M,D,O
Norfolk State University	M
North Carolina State University	M
North Dakota State University	M,D
Northern Kentucky University	M
North Georgia College & State University	M
Northwestern University	D
Northwest Nazarene University	M
The Ohio State University	M,D
Penn State Harrisburg	M,D
Penn State University Park	M,D
Pittsburg State University	M
Prescott College	M
Regent University	M,D,O
Regis University	M,O
Rutgers, The State University of New Jersey, Newark	D
Rutgers, The State University of New Jersey, New Brunswick	D

St. Cloud State University M
Saint Joseph College M,O
Saint Martin's University M
St. Mary's University of San Antonio M
Southeast Missouri State University M,O
Stony Brook University, State University of New York D
Syracuse University M,D
Temple University D
Texas A&M University M,D
University at Albany, State University of New York M,D,O
University at Buffalo, the State University of New York M,D
University of Alaska Anchorage M,D
University of Alaska Fairbanks D
University of Central Arkansas M
University of Connecticut M,D
University of Dayton M,O
University of Delaware D
University of Florida M,D
University of Hawaii at Manoa M,D,O
University of Houston M,D
University of La Verne D
University of Maine M,D
University of Mary Hardin-Baylor M
University of Maryland, College Park M,D
University of Massachusetts Lowell M
University of Michigan D
University of Minnesota, Twin Cities Campus D
University of Missouri–Kansas City M,D
University of Missouri–St. Louis M,D,O
University of Montevallo M
University of Nevada, Reno D
University of New Haven M,O
The University of North Carolina at Chapel Hill D
The University of North Carolina at Charlotte M
The University of North Carolina at Greensboro M,D
University of Oklahoma M
University of Oregon M,D
University of Pennsylvania D
University of Phoenix–Denver Campus M
University of Phoenix–Hawaii Campus M
University of Phoenix–Phoenix Campus M,O
University of Phoenix–Southern Colorado Campus M
University of Puget Sound M
University of Rochester M,D
The University of Scranton M
University of South Carolina M,D
The University of Toledo M,D,O
University of Wisconsin–Madison D
University of Wisconsin–Superior M
University of Wisconsin–Whitewater M
Washington State University M,D
Washington University in St. Louis M,D
Western Carolina University M
Western Connecticut State University M
Western Illinois University M,O
Wichita State University M,D
Wilmington University (DE) M

■ SOCIAL SCIENCES

Arizona State University M,D
Arkansas Tech University M
Ball State University M
California Institute of Technology M,D
California State University, Chico M
California State University, San Bernardino M
California University of Pennsylvania M
Carnegie Mellon University D
The Citadel, The Military College of South Carolina M
Cleveland State University M
Columbia University M
Eastern Michigan University M
Edinboro University of Pennsylvania M
Florida Agricultural and Mechanical University M
Florida State University M
George Mason University M,D,O
Hollins University M,O
Humboldt State University M
Indiana University Bloomington P,M,D,O
The Johns Hopkins University M,D
Lincoln University (MO) M
Long Island University, Brooklyn Campus M,O
Long Island University, C.W. Post Campus M
Massachusetts Institute of Technology D
Michigan State University M
Mississippi College M,O
Montclair State University M,O
The New School: A University M,D
North Dakota State University M,D
Northwestern University M,O
Nova Southeastern University M
Ohio University M
Queens College of the City University of New York M
Regis University M,O
San Francisco State University M
Southern Oregon University M
Southern University and Agricultural and Mechanical College M
State University of New York at Binghamton M
Stony Brook University, State University of New York M,O
Syracuse University M,D
Texas A&M International University M
Texas A&M University–Commerce M
Towson University M
University of California, Irvine M,D
University of California, Santa Cruz D
University of Chicago M,D
University of Colorado Denver M
University of Florida M
University of Idaho M
University of Illinois at Springfield M
University of Kansas M,D
University of Maryland, Baltimore County D
University of Michigan D
University of Michigan–Flint M
The University of Texas at Tyler M
The University of Toledo D
University of Wisconsin–Madison D
Worcester Polytechnic Institute M,D
Yale University M,D

■ SOCIAL SCIENCES EDUCATION

Alabama State University M,O
Albany State University M
Andrews University M,D,O
Appalachian State University M
Arcadia University M,D,O
Arkansas State University M,D,O
Arkansas Tech University M
Armstrong Atlantic State University M
Auburn University M,D,O
Belmont University M
Bennington College M
Bethel College (TN) M
Bob Jones University P,M,D,O
Boston College M
Boston University M,D,O
Bridgewater State College M
Brooklyn College of the City University of New York M,O
Brown University M
Buffalo State College, State University of New York M
California State University, Chico M
California State University, San Bernardino M
Campbell University M
Chaminade University of Honolulu M
Charleston Southern University M
Chatham University M
City College of the City University of New York M,O
Clarion University of Pennsylvania M
College of St. Joseph M
The College of William and Mary M
Columbus State University M,O
Converse College M
Delta State University M
Drake University M
East Carolina University M
Eastern Kentucky University M
Eastern Washington University M
East Stroudsburg University of Pennsylvania M
Emporia State University M
Fayetteville State University M
Fitchburg State College M
Florida Agricultural and Mechanical University M
Florida Gulf Coast University M
Florida International University M,D
Florida State University M,D,O
Framingham State College M
Georgia College & State University M,O
Georgia Southern University M
Georgia State University M,D,O
Grambling State University M
Harding University M,O
Henderson State University M,O
Hofstra University M
Hunter College of the City University of New York M
Indiana University Bloomington M,D,O
Iona College M
Ithaca College M
Kutztown University of Pennsylvania M,O
Lehman College of the City University of New York M
Louisiana Tech University M,D
Manhattanville College M
McNeese State University M
Miami University M
Michigan State University M,D
Mills College M,D
Minnesota State University Mankato M
Mississippi College M,O
Missouri State University M
Montclair State University M
New York University M,D
North Carolina Agricultural and Technical State University M
North Dakota State University M,D,O
North Georgia College & State University M,O
Northwestern State University of Louisiana M
Northwest Missouri State University M

Nova Southeastern University M,O
Ohio University M,D
Penn State University Park M,D
Portland State University M
Princeton University D
Purdue University M,D,O
Queens College of the City University of New York M,O
Quinnipiac University M
Rhode Island College M,O
Rider University M,O
Rivier College M
Rockford College M
Rutgers, The State University of New Jersey, New Brunswick M,D
St. John Fisher College M
Salisbury University M
South Carolina State University M
Southern Illinois University Edwardsville M
Southwestern Oklahoma State University M
Stanford University M,D
State University of New York at Binghamton M
State University of New York at Plattsburgh M
State University of New York College at Brockport M
State University of New York College at Cortland M
Stony Brook University, State University of New York M,O
Syracuse University M,O
Texas A&M University–Commerce M
Texas State University-San Marcos D
Trinity (Washington) University M
University at Buffalo, the State University of New York M,D,O
University of California, Santa Cruz M
University of Central Florida M
University of Cincinnati M,D,O
University of Colorado Denver M
University of Connecticut M,D
University of Florida M,D,O
University of Georgia M,D,O
University of Houston M,D
University of Indianapolis M
The University of Iowa M,D
University of Maine M,O
University of Michigan M,D
University of Minnesota, Twin Cities Campus M
University of Missouri–Columbia M,D,O
University of New Orleans M
The University of North Carolina at Chapel Hill M
The University of North Carolina at Greensboro M,D,O
The University of North Carolina at Pembroke M
University of Oklahoma M,D,O
University of Pittsburgh M,D
University of Puerto Rico, Río Piedras M,D
University of St. Francis (IL) M
University of South Carolina M,D,O
University of Southern Mississippi M,D,O
University of South Florida M,D,O
The University of Tennessee M,D,O
The University of Texas at Tyler M
The University of Toledo M,D
University of Washington M,D
The University of West Alabama M
University of West Georgia M,O
University of Wisconsin–Eau Claire M
University of Wisconsin–River Falls M
Virginia Commonwealth University M,O
Wayne State College M
Wayne State University M,D,O
Webster University M,O
Western Carolina University M
Western Oregon University M
Widener University M,D
Wilkes University M,D
William Carey University M,O
Worcester State College M

■ SOCIAL WORK

Abilene Christian University M
Adelphi University M,D
Alabama Agricultural and Mechanical University M
Andrews University M
Appalachian State University M
Arizona State University M,D
Arizona State University at the West campus M
Arkansas State University M
Augsburg College M
Aurora University M
Barry University M,D
Baylor University M
Boise State University M
Boston College M,D
Boston University M,D
Bridgewater State College M
Brigham Young University M
California State University, Bakersfield M
California State University, Chico M
California State University, Dominguez Hills M
California State University, East Bay M
California State University, Fresno M
California State University, Long Beach M
California State University, Los Angeles M
California State University, Northridge M
California State University, Sacramento M
California State University, San Bernardino M
California State University, Stanislaus M
California University of Pennsylvania M
Case Western Reserve University M,D
The Catholic University of America M,D
Chicago State University M
Clark Atlanta University M,D
Cleveland State University M
College of St. Catherine M
Colorado State University M
Columbia University M,D
Cornell University M,D
Delaware State University M
Dominican University M
East Carolina University M
Eastern Michigan University M,O
Eastern Washington University M
East Tennessee State University M
Edinboro University of Pennsylvania M
Fayetteville State University M
Florida Agricultural and Mechanical University M
Florida Atlantic University M
Florida Gulf Coast University M
Florida International University M,D
Florida State University M,D
Fordham University M,D
Gallaudet University M
George Mason University M,D,O
Georgia State University M
Governors State University M
Graduate School and University Center of the City University of New York D
Grambling State University M
Grand Valley State University M
Gratz College M,O
Hawai'i Pacific University M
Howard University M,D
Humboldt State University M
Hunter College of the City University of New York M,D
Illinois State University M
Indiana University Northwest M
Indiana University–Purdue University Indianapolis M,D,O
Indiana University South Bend M
Inter American University of Puerto Rico, Metropolitan Campus M
Jackson State University M,D
Kean University M
Kennesaw State University M
Kutztown University of Pennsylvania M
Louisiana State University and Agricultural and Mechanical College M,D
Loyola University Chicago M,D
Marywood University M,D
Michigan State University M,D
Millersville University of Pennsylvania M
Missouri State University M
Monmouth University M
Morgan State University M,D
Nazareth College of Rochester M
Newman University M
New Mexico Highlands University M
New Mexico State University M
New York University M,D
Norfolk State University M,D
North Carolina Agricultural and Technical State University M
Northwest Nazarene University M
The Ohio State University M,D
Ohio University M
Our Lady of the Lake University of San Antonio M
Pontifical Catholic University of Puerto Rico M,D
Portland State University M,D
Radford University M
Rhode Island College M
Roberts Wesleyan College M
Rutgers, The State University of New Jersey, New Brunswick M,D
St. Ambrose University M
Saint Louis University M
Salem State College M
Salisbury University M
San Diego State University M
San Francisco State University M
San Jose State University M,O
Savannah State University M
Shippensburg University of Pennsylvania M
Simmons College M,D
Southern Connecticut State University M
Southern Illinois University Carbondale M
Southern Illinois University Edwardsville M
Southern University at New Orleans M
Spalding University M
Springfield College M,O

Institution	Degrees
State University of New York College at Brockport	M
Stephen F. Austin State University	M
Stony Brook University, State University of New York	M,D
Syracuse University	M
Temple University	M
Texas A&M University–Commerce	M
Texas State University-San Marcos	M
Tulane University	M
University at Albany, State University of New York	M,D
University at Buffalo, the State University of New York	M,D
The University of Akron	M
The University of Alabama	M,D
University of Alaska Anchorage	M,O
University of Arkansas	M
University of Arkansas at Little Rock	M
University of California, Berkeley	M,D
University of California, Los Angeles	M,D
University of Central Florida	M,O
University of Chicago	M,D
University of Cincinnati	M
University of Connecticut	M,D
University of Denver	M,D,O
University of Georgia	M,D,O
University of Hawaii at Manoa	M,D
University of Houston	M,D
University of Illinois at Chicago	M,D
University of Illinois at Urbana–Champaign	M,D
The University of Iowa	M,D
University of Kentucky	M,D
University of Louisville	M,D,O
University of Maine	M
University of Maryland, College Park	
University of Michigan	M,D
University of Minnesota, Duluth	M
University of Minnesota, Twin Cities Campus	M,D
University of Missouri–Columbia	M
University of Missouri–Kansas City	M
University of Missouri–St. Louis	M
The University of Montana	M
University of Nebraska at Omaha	M
University of Nevada, Las Vegas	M
University of Nevada, Reno	M
University of New England	M,O
University of New Hampshire	M
The University of North Carolina at Chapel Hill	M,D
The University of North Carolina at Charlotte	M
The University of North Carolina at Greensboro	M
The University of North Carolina Wilmington	M
University of North Dakota	M
University of Northern Iowa	M
University of Oklahoma	M
University of Pennsylvania	M,D
University of Pittsburgh	M,D,O
University of Puerto Rico, Río Piedras	M,D
University of St. Francis (IL)	M
University of St. Thomas (MN)	M
University of South Carolina	M,D
University of Southern California	M,D
University of Southern Indiana	M
University of Southern Maine	M
University of Southern Mississippi	M
University of South Florida	M
The University of Tennessee	M,D
The University of Texas at Arlington	M,D
The University of Texas at Austin	M,D
The University of Texas at San Antonio	M
The University of Texas–Pan American	M
The University of Toledo	M
University of Utah	M,D
University of Vermont	M
University of Washington	M,D
University of Washington, Tacoma	M
University of Wisconsin–Madison	M,D
University of Wisconsin–Milwaukee	M,O
University of Wisconsin–Oshkosh	M
University of Wyoming	M
Valdosta State University	M
Virginia Commonwealth University	M,D
Walla Walla University	M
Washburn University	M
Washington University in St. Louis	M,D
Wayne State University	M,D,O
West Chester University of Pennsylvania	M
Western Kentucky University	M
Western Michigan University	M
West Virginia University	M
Wheelock College	M
Wichita State University	M
Widener University	M
Winthrop University	M
Yeshiva University	M,D

■ SOCIOLOGY

Institution	Degrees
American University	M,O
Arizona State University	M,D
Arkansas State University	M,O
Auburn University	M
Ball State University	M
Baylor University	M,D
Boston College	M,D
Boston University	M,D
Bowling Green State University	M,D
Brandeis University	M,D
Brigham Young University	M,D
Brooklyn College of the City University of New York	M,D
Brown University	M,D
California State University, Bakersfield	M
California State University, Dominguez Hills	M,O
California State University, East Bay	M
California State University, Fullerton	M
California State University, Los Angeles	M
California State University, Northridge	M
California State University, Sacramento	M
California State University, San Marcos	M
Case Western Reserve University	D
The Catholic University of America	M,D
Central Michigan University	M
City College of the City University of New York	M
Clark Atlanta University	M
Clemson University	M
Cleveland State University	M
Colorado State University	M,D
Columbia University	M,D
Cornell University	M,D
DePaul University	M
Drake University	M
Duke University	M,D
East Carolina University	M
Eastern Michigan University	M
East Tennessee State University	M
Emory University	M,D
Fayetteville State University	M
Florida Agricultural and Mechanical University	M
Florida Atlantic University	M
Florida International University	M,D
Florida State University	M,D
Fordham University	M,D
George Mason University	M
The George Washington University	M
Georgia Southern University	M
Georgia State University	M,D
Graduate School and University Center of the City University of New York	D
Harvard University	D
Howard University	M,D
Humboldt State University	M
Idaho State University	M
Illinois State University	M
Indiana University Bloomington	M,D
Indiana University of Pennsylvania	M
Indiana University–Purdue University Fort Wayne	M
Indiana University–Purdue University Indianapolis	M
Iowa State University of Science and Technology	M,D
Jackson State University	M
The Johns Hopkins University	D
Kansas State University	M,D
Kent State University	M,D
Lehigh University	M
Lincoln University (MO)	M
Louisiana State University and Agricultural and Mechanical College	M,D
Loyola University Chicago	M,D
Marshall University	M
Michigan State University	M,D
Middle Tennessee State University	M,O
Minnesota State University Mankato	M
Mississippi College	M
Mississippi State University	M,D
Montclair State University	M
Morehead State University	M
Morgan State University	M
New Mexico Highlands University	M
New Mexico State University	M
The New School: A University	M,D
New York University	M,D
Norfolk State University	M
North Carolina Central University	M
North Carolina State University	M,D
North Dakota State University	M,D
Northeastern University	M,D
Northern Arizona University	M
Northern Illinois University	M
Northwestern University	D
The Ohio State University	M,D
Ohio University	M
Oklahoma State University	M,D
Old Dominion University	M
Our Lady of the Lake University of San Antonio	M
Penn State University Park	M,D
Portland State University	M,D,O
Prairie View A&M University	M
Princeton University	D,O
Purdue University	M,D
Queens College of the City University of New York	M
Roosevelt University	M
Rutgers, The State University of New Jersey, New Brunswick	M,D
St. John's University (NY)	M

Sam Houston State University	M
San Diego State University	M
San Jose State University	M
Shippensburg University of Pennsylvania	M
Southeastern Louisiana University	M
Southern Connecticut State University	M
Southern Illinois University Carbondale	M,D
Southern Illinois University Edwardsville	M
Stanford University	D
State University of New York at Binghamton	M,D
State University of New York Institute of Technology	M
Stony Brook University, State University of New York	M,D
Syracuse University	M,D
Temple University	M,D
Texas A&M International University	M
Texas A&M University	M,D
Texas A&M University–Commerce	M
Texas A&M University–Kingsville	M
Texas Southern University	M
Texas State University-San Marcos	M
Texas Tech University	M
Texas Woman's University	M,D
Tulane University	M,D
University at Albany, State University of New York	M,D,O
University at Buffalo, the State University of New York	M,D
The University of Akron	M,D
The University of Alabama at Birmingham	M,D
The University of Arizona	M,D
University of Arkansas	M
University of California, Berkeley	D
University of California, Davis	M,D
University of California, Irvine	M,D
University of California, Los Angeles	M,D
University of California, Riverside	M,D
University of California, San Diego	D
University of California, Santa Barbara	D
University of California, Santa Cruz	D
University of Central Florida	M,D,O
University of Central Missouri	M
University of Chicago	D
University of Cincinnati	M,D
University of Colorado at Boulder	D
University of Colorado at Colorado Springs	M
University of Colorado Denver	M
University of Connecticut	M,D
University of Delaware	M,D
University of Florida	M,D
University of Georgia	M,D
University of Hawaii at Manoa	M,D,O
University of Houston	M
University of Houston–Clear Lake	M
University of Illinois at Chicago	M,D
University of Illinois at Urbana–Champaign	M,D
University of Indianapolis	M
The University of Iowa	M,D
University of Kansas	M,D
University of Kentucky	M,D
University of Louisville	M
University of Maryland, Baltimore County	M,O
University of Maryland, College Park	M,D
University of Massachusetts Amherst	M,D
University of Massachusetts Boston	M
University of Massachusetts Lowell	M
University of Memphis	M
University of Miami	M,D
University of Michigan	D
University of Minnesota, Duluth	M
University of Minnesota, Twin Cities Campus	M,D
University of Mississippi	M
University of Missouri–Columbia	M,D
University of Missouri–Kansas City	M,D
University of Missouri–St. Louis	M
The University of Montana	M
University of Nebraska–Lincoln	M,D
University of Nevada, Las Vegas	M,D
University of Nevada, Reno	M
University of New Hampshire	M,D
University of New Mexico	M,D
University of New Orleans	M
The University of North Carolina at Chapel Hill	M,D
The University of North Carolina at Charlotte	M
The University of North Carolina at Greensboro	M
The University of North Carolina Wilmington	M
University of North Dakota	M
University of Northern Colorado	M
University of Northern Iowa	M
University of North Florida	M
University of North Texas	M,D
University of Notre Dame	D
University of Oklahoma	M,D
University of Oregon	M,D
University of Pennsylvania	M,D
University of Pittsburgh	M,D
University of Puerto Rico, Río Piedras	M
University of South Alabama	M
University of South Carolina	M,D
University of Southern California	M,D
University of South Florida	M
The University of Tennessee	M,D
The University of Texas at Arlington	M
The University of Texas at Austin	M,D
The University of Texas at Dallas	M
The University of Texas at El Paso	M
The University of Texas at San Antonio	M
The University of Texas at Tyler	M
The University of Texas–Pan American	M
The University of Toledo	M
University of Utah	M,D
University of Virginia	M,D
University of Washington	M,D
University of West Georgia	M
University of Wisconsin–Madison	M,D
University of Wisconsin–Milwaukee	M
University of Wyoming	M
Utah State University	M,D
Valdosta State University	M
Vanderbilt University	M,D
Virginia Commonwealth University	M,O
Virginia Polytechnic Institute and State University	M,D
Washington State University	M,D
Wayne State University	M,D
West Chester University of Pennsylvania	M,O
Western Illinois University	M
Western Kentucky University	M
Western Michigan University	M,D
West Virginia University	M
Wichita State University	M
William Paterson University of New Jersey	M
Yale University	D

■ SOFTWARE ENGINEERING

Andrews University	M
Auburn University	M,D
Bowling Green State University	M
California State University, East Bay	M
California State University, Fullerton	M
California State University, Sacramento	M
Carnegie Mellon University	M,D
Carroll College	M
Central Michigan University	M,O
Cleveland State University	M,D
Colorado Technical University—Colorado Springs	M,D
Colorado Technical University—Denver	M
Colorado Technical University—Sioux Falls	M
DePaul University	M,D
Drexel University	M
East Tennessee State University	M
Embry-Riddle Aeronautical University (FL)	M
Fairfield University	M
Florida Agricultural and Mechanical University	M
Florida Institute of Technology	M,D
Florida State University	M,D
Gannon University	M
George Mason University	M
Grand Valley State University	M
Illinois Institute of Technology	M,D
Jacksonville State University	M
Kansas State University	M,D
Loyola College in Maryland	M
Loyola University Chicago	M
Marist College	M,O
Mercer University	M
Miami University	M,O
Monmouth University	M,O
National University	M
North Dakota State University	M,D,O
Northern Kentucky University	M,O
Oakland University	M
Penn State Great Valley	M
Polytechnic University, Brooklyn Campus	O
Portland State University	M,D
Regis University	M,O
Rochester Institute of Technology	M
St. Mary's University of San Antonio	M
San Jose State University	M
Santa Clara University	M,D,O
Seattle University	M
Southern Methodist University	M,D
Southern Polytechnic State University	M
Stevens Institute of Technology	M,O
Stony Brook University, State University of New York	M,D,O
Texas State University-San Marcos	M
Texas Tech University	M,D
Towson University	M,D,O
The University of Alabama in Huntsville	M,D,O
University of Alaska Fairbanks	M
University of Colorado at Colorado Springs	M
University of Connecticut	M,D
University of Houston–Clear Lake	M
University of Michigan–Dearborn	M
University of Missouri–Kansas City	M,D
University of New Haven	M

University of St. Thomas (MN)	M,O
The University of Scranton	M
University of South Carolina	M,D
University of Southern California	M
The University of Texas at Arlington	M,D
The University of Texas at Dallas	M,D
University of Washington, Tacoma	M
University of West Florida	M
University of Wisconsin–La Crosse	M
Walden University	M,O
West Virginia University	M
Widener University	M
Winthrop University	M,O

■ SPANISH

American University	M,O
Appalachian State University	M
Arizona State University	M,D
Arkansas Tech University	M
Auburn University	M
Baylor University	M
Bennington College	M
Boston College	M,D
Boston University	M,D
Bowling Green State University	M
Brigham Young University	M
Brooklyn College of the City University of New York	M,D
California State University, Bakersfield	M
California State University, Fresno	M
California State University, Fullerton	M
California State University, Long Beach	M
California State University, Los Angeles	M
California State University, Northridge	M
California State University, Sacramento	M
California State University, San Bernardino	M
California State University, San Marcos	M
The Catholic University of America	M,D
Central Connecticut State University	M,O
Central Michigan University	M
City College of the City University of New York	M
Cleveland State University	M
The College of New Jersey	M
Columbia University	M,D
Cornell University	D
Duke University	D
Eastern Michigan University	M
Emory University	D,O
Florida Atlantic University	M
Florida International University	M,D
Florida State University	M,D
Framingham State College	M
Georgetown University	M,D
Georgia State University	M
Graduate School and University Center of the City University of New York	D
Harvard University	M,D
Hofstra University	M
Howard University	M
Hunter College of the City University of New York	M
Illinois State University	M
Indiana State University	M,O
Indiana University Bloomington	M,D
Inter American University of Puerto Rico, Metropolitan Campus	M
Iona College	M
The Johns Hopkins University	D
Kansas State University	M
Kent State University	M,D
Lehman College of the City University of New York	M
Long Island University, C.W. Post Campus	M
Louisiana State University and Agricultural and Mechanical College	M
Loyola University Chicago	M
Marquette University	M
Miami University	M
Michigan State University	M,D
Millersville University of Pennsylvania	M
Minnesota State University Mankato	M
Mississippi State University	M
Missouri State University	M
Montclair State University	M,O
New Mexico Highlands University	M
New Mexico State University	M
New York University	M,D
North Carolina State University	M
Northern Illinois University	M
Nova Southeastern University	M,O
The Ohio State University	M,D
Ohio University	M
Penn State University Park	M,D
Portland State University	M
Princeton University	D
Purdue University	M,D
Queens College of the City University of New York	M
Rice University	M
Roosevelt University	M
Rutgers, The State University of New Jersey, New Brunswick	M,D
St. John's University (NY)	M,O
Saint Louis University	M
Salem State College	M
San Diego State University	M
San Francisco State University	M
San Jose State University	M
Simmons College	M
Southern Connecticut State University	M
Stanford University	M,D
State University of New York at Binghamton	M,O
Syracuse University	M
Temple University	M,D
Texas A&M International University	M,D
Texas A&M University	M,D
Texas A&M University–Commerce	M,D
Texas A&M University–Kingsville	M
Texas State University-San Marcos	M
Texas Tech University	M,D
Tulane University	M,D
University at Albany, State University of New York	M,D
University at Buffalo, the State University of New York	M,D
The University of Akron	M
The University of Alabama	M,D
The University of Arizona	M,D
University of Arkansas	M
University of California, Berkeley	M,D
University of California, Davis	M,D
University of California, Irvine	M,D
University of California, Los Angeles	M
University of California, Riverside	M,D
University of California, San Diego	M
University of California, Santa Barbara	M,D
University of Central Florida	M
University of Chicago	M,D
University of Cincinnati	M,D
University of Colorado at Boulder	M,D
University of Colorado Denver	M
University of Connecticut	M,D
University of Delaware	M
University of Florida	M,D
University of Georgia	M
University of Hawaii at Manoa	M
University of Houston	M,D
The University of Iowa	M,D
University of Kansas	M,D
University of Louisville	M
University of Maryland, College Park	M,D
University of Massachusetts Amherst	M,D
University of Memphis	M
University of Miami	M,D
University of Michigan	D
University of Minnesota, Twin Cities Campus	M,D
University of Mississippi	M
University of Missouri–Columbia	M,D
The University of Montana	M
University of Nebraska–Lincoln	M,D
University of Nevada, Las Vegas	M
University of Nevada, Reno	M
University of New Hampshire	M
University of New Mexico	M,D
The University of North Carolina at Chapel Hill	M,D
The University of North Carolina at Charlotte	M
The University of North Carolina at Greensboro	M,O
University of Northern Colorado	M
University of Northern Iowa	M
University of North Texas	M
University of Notre Dame	M
University of Oklahoma	M,D
University of Oregon	M
University of Pennsylvania	M,D
University of Pittsburgh	M,D
University of Rhode Island	M
University of South Carolina	M,D
University of South Florida	M
The University of Tennessee	M,D
The University of Texas at Arlington	M
The University of Texas at Austin	M,D
The University of Texas at Brownsville	M
The University of Texas at El Paso	M
The University of Texas at San Antonio	M
The University of Texas–Pan American	M
The University of Toledo	M
University of Utah	M,D
University of Virginia	M,D
University of Washington	M
University of Wisconsin–Madison	M,D
University of Wisconsin–Milwaukee	M
University of Wyoming	M
Vanderbilt University	M,D
Washington State University	M
Washington University in St. Louis	M,D
Wayne State University	M
West Chester University of Pennsylvania	M
Western Michigan University	M
West Virginia University	M
Wichita State University	M
Winthrop University	M
Yale University	M,D

■ SPECIAL EDUCATION

Adams State College	M
Adelphi University	M,O
Alabama Agricultural and Mechanical University	M,O
Alabama State University	M
Albany State University	M

Alcorn State University	M,O
American International College	M,D,O
American University	M
Andrews University	M,D,O
Appalachian State University	M
Arcadia University	M,D,O
Arizona State University	M
Arizona State University at the West campus	M,D,O
Arkansas State University	M,D,O
Armstrong Atlantic State University	M
Ashland University	M
Assumption College	M
Auburn University	M,D,O
Auburn University Montgomery	M,O
Augusta State University	M,O
Azusa Pacific University	M
Baldwin-Wallace College	M
Ball State University	M,D,O
Barry University	M,D,O
Bayamón Central University	M
Bellarmine University	M
Bemidji State University	M
Benedictine University	M
Bethel College (TN)	M
Bethel University	M,D,O
Bloomsburg University of Pennsylvania	M
Bob Jones University	P,M,D,O
Boise State University	M
Boston College	M,O
Boston University	M,D,O
Bowie State University	M
Bowling Green State University	M
Brenau University	M,O
Bridgewater State College	M
Brigham Young University	M,D,O
Brooklyn College of the City University of New York	M
Buffalo State College, State University of New York	M
Butler University	M
Caldwell College	M
California Baptist University	M
California Lutheran University	M
California State University, Bakersfield	M
California State University, Chico	M
California State University, Dominguez Hills	M
California State University, East Bay	M
California State University, Fresno	M
California State University, Fullerton	M
California State University, Long Beach	M
California State University, Los Angeles	M
California State University, Northridge	M
California State University, Sacramento	M
California State University, San Bernardino	M
California University of Pennsylvania	M
Canisius College	M
Cardinal Stritch University	M
Carlow University	M
Castleton State College	M,O
Centenary College	M
Central Connecticut State University	M
Central Michigan University	M
Central Washington University	M
Chapman University	M
Chatham University	M
Cheyney University of Pennsylvania	M
Chicago State University	M
City College of the City University of New York	M
Clarion University of Pennsylvania	M
Clemson University	M
Cleveland State University	M
College of Charleston	M
The College of New Jersey	M,O
The College of New Rochelle	M
College of St. Joseph	M
The College of Saint Rose	M,O
College of Santa Fe	M
College of Staten Island of the City University of New York	M
The College of William and Mary	M
Columbus State University	M,O
Concordia University, St. Paul	M,O
Concordia University Wisconsin	M
Converse College	M
Coppin State University	M
Creighton University	M
Daemen College	M
Delaware State University	M
Delta State University	M
DePaul University	M,D
DeSales University	M,O
Dominican College	M
Dominican University	M
Dominican University of California	O
Dowling College	M,D,O
Drake University	M
Duquesne University	M
D'Youville College	M,O
East Carolina University	M
Eastern Illinois University	M
Eastern Kentucky University	M
Eastern Michigan University	M,O
Eastern Nazarene College	M,O
Eastern New Mexico University	M
Eastern Washington University	M
East Stroudsburg University of Pennsylvania	M
East Tennessee State University	M,D
Edgewood College	M,D,O
Edinboro University of Pennsylvania	M
Elmhurst College	M
Elon University	M
Emporia State University	M
Endicott College	M
Fairfield University	M,O
Fairleigh Dickinson University, Metropolitan Campus	M
Ferris State University	M
Fitchburg State College	M
Florida Atlantic University	M,D
Florida Gulf Coast University	M
Florida International University	M,D,O
Florida State University	M,D,O
Fontbonne University	M
Fordham University	M,D,O
Fort Hays State University	M
Framingham State College	M
Francis Marion University	M
Fresno Pacific University	M
Frostburg State University	M
Furman University	M
Gallaudet University	M,D,O
Geneva College	M
George Mason University	M
The George Washington University	M,D,O
Georgia College & State University	M
Georgian Court University	M,O
Georgia Southern University	M
Georgia Southwestern State University	M,O
Georgia State University	M,D
Gonzaga University	M
Governors State University	M
Grambling State University	M,D
Grand Valley State University	M
Gwynedd-Mercy College	M
Hampton University	M
Harding University	M,O
Henderson State University	M,O
Heritage University	M
High Point University	M
Hofstra University	M,O
Holy Names University	M,O
Hood College	M,O
Howard University	M,O
Hunter College of the City University of New York	M
Idaho State University	M,D,O
Illinois State University	M,D
Immaculata University	M,D,O
Indiana University Bloomington	M,D,O
Indiana University of Pennsylvania	M
Indiana University South Bend	M
Inter American University of Puerto Rico, Metropolitan Campus	M
Inter American University of Puerto Rico, San Germán Campus	M
Iowa State University of Science and Technology	M,D
Jackson State University	M,O
Jacksonville State University	M
James Madison University	M
The Johns Hopkins University	M,D,O
Johnson State College	M
Kansas State University	M,D
Kean University	M
Keene State College	M,O
Kennesaw State University	M
Kent State University	M,D,O
Kutztown University of Pennsylvania	M,O
Lamar University	M,D
La Sierra University	M,D,O
Lee University	M
Lehigh University	M,D,O
Lehman College of the City University of New York	M
Lesley University	M,D,O
Lewis & Clark College	M
Lewis University	M
Liberty University	M,D,O
Lincoln University (MO)	M,O
Lipscomb University	M
Long Island University, Brentwood Campus	M
Long Island University, Brooklyn Campus	M
Long Island University, C.W. Post Campus	M
Long Island University, Southampton Graduate Campus	M
Longwood University	M
Louisiana Tech University	M,D
Loyola College in Maryland	M,O
Loyola Marymount University	M
Loyola University Chicago	M
Lynchburg College	M
Lynn University	M,D
Madonna University	M
Malone College	M
Manhattan College	M
Manhattanville College	M
Marshall University	M
Marymount University	M,O
Marywood University	M
McDaniel College	M
Medaille College	M
Mercy College	M

Institution	Degrees
Mercyhurst College	M,O
Miami University	M
Michigan State University	M,D,O
MidAmerica Nazarene University	M
Middle Tennessee State University	M,O
Midwestern State University	M
Millersville University of Pennsylvania	M
Minnesota State University Mankato	M,O
Minnesota State University Moorhead	M
Minot State University	M
Mississippi College	M,O
Mississippi State University	M,D,O
Missouri State University	M,O
Monmouth University	M,O
Montana State University–Billings	M
Montclair State University	M,O
Morehead State University	M
Morningside College	M
Mount Saint Mary College	M
Mount St. Mary's College	M
Murray State University	M
National-Louis University	M,O
National University	M
New Jersey City University	M
New Mexico Highlands University	M
New Mexico State University	M,D
New York University	M
Niagara University	M
Norfolk State University	M
North Carolina Central University	M
North Carolina State University	M
Northeastern Illinois University	M
Northeastern University	M,D,O
Northern Arizona University	M
Northern Illinois University	M,D
Northern Kentucky University	O
Northern Michigan University	M
North Georgia College & State University	M,O
Northwestern State University of Louisiana	M,O
Northwestern University	M,D
Northwest Missouri State University	M
Northwest Nazarene University	M
Notre Dame de Namur University	M,O
Nova Southeastern University	M,D,O
Oakland University	M,O
Ohio University	M,D
Old Dominion University	M,D
Our Lady of the Lake University of San Antonio	M
Pacific University	M
Park University	M
Penn State Great Valley	M
Penn State University Park	M,D
Pittsburg State University	M
Plymouth State University	M,O
Portland State University	M,D
Prairie View A&M University	M
Providence College	M
Purdue University	M,D,O
Queens College of the City University of New York	M
Radford University	M
Regent University	M,D,O
Regis University	M,O
Rhode Island College	M,O
Rider University	M,O
Rivier College	M,O
Roberts Wesleyan College	M,O
Rochester Institute of Technology	M
Rockford College	M
Roosevelt University	M
Rowan University	M
Rutgers, The State University of New Jersey, New Brunswick	M,D
Saginaw Valley State University	M
St. Ambrose University	M
St. Cloud State University	M
St. John Fisher College	M,O
St. John's University (NY)	M
Saint Joseph College	M
St. Joseph's College, Suffolk Campus	M
Saint Joseph's University	M,D,O
Saint Louis University	M,D
Saint Martin's University	M
Saint Mary's College of California	M
Saint Michael's College	M,O
St. Thomas Aquinas College	M,O
St. Thomas University	M,D,O
Saint Xavier University	M,O
Salem State College	M
Sam Houston State University	M
San Diego State University	M
San Francisco State University	M,D,O
San Jose State University	M,O
Santa Clara University	M,O
Seattle University	M,O
Seton Hill University	M,O
Shippensburg University of Pennsylvania	M
Silver Lake College	M
Simmons College	M,D,O
Slippery Rock University of Pennsylvania	M
Sonoma State University	M
South Carolina State University	M
Southeastern Louisiana University	M
Southeast Missouri State University	M
Southern Connecticut State University	M,O
Southern Illinois University Carbondale	M
Southern Illinois University Edwardsville	M
Southern New Hampshire University	M,O
Southern Oregon University	M
Southern University and Agricultural and Mechanical College	M,D
Southwestern College (KS)	M
Southwestern Oklahoma State University	M
Southwest Minnesota State University	M
Spalding University	M
State University of New York at Binghamton	M
State University of New York at New Paltz	M
State University of New York at Oswego	M
State University of New York at Plattsburgh	M
State University of New York College at Cortland	M
State University of New York College at Potsdam	M
Stephen F. Austin State University	M
Stetson University	M
Syracuse University	M,D
Tarleton State University	M,D,O
Temple University	M,D
Tennessee State University	M,D
Tennessee Technological University	M,O
Texas A&M International University	M
Texas A&M University	M,D
Texas A&M University–Commerce	M,D
Texas A&M University–Corpus Christi	M
Texas A&M University–Kingsville	M
Texas A&M University–Texarkana	M
Texas Christian University	M
Texas Southern University	M,D
Texas State University-San Marcos	M
Texas Tech University	M,D,O
Texas Woman's University	M,D
Towson University	M
Trinity (Washington) University	M
Union College (KY)	M
Universidad del Turabo	M
Universidad Metropolitana	M
University at Albany, State University of New York	M
University at Buffalo, the State University of New York	M,D,O
The University of Akron	M
The University of Alabama	M,D,O
The University of Alabama at Birmingham	M
University of Alaska Anchorage	M,O
The University of Arizona	M,D,O
University of Arkansas	M
University of Arkansas at Little Rock	M
University of California, Berkeley	D
University of California, Los Angeles	D
University of California, Santa Barbara	M,D
University of Central Arkansas	M
University of Central Florida	M,D
University of Central Missouri	M,O
University of Central Oklahoma	M
University of Cincinnati	M,D
University of Colorado at Colorado Springs	M,D
University of Connecticut	M,D
University of Dayton	M
University of Delaware	M,D
University of Detroit Mercy	M
The University of Findlay	M
University of Florida	M,D,O
University of Georgia	M,D,O
University of Guam	M
University of Hawaii at Manoa	M,D
University of Houston	M,D
University of Idaho	M,O
University of Illinois at Chicago	M,D
University of Illinois at Urbana–Champaign	M,D,O
The University of Iowa	M,D
University of Kansas	M,D
University of Kentucky	M,D
University of La Verne	M
University of Louisiana at Monroe	M
University of Louisville	M,D
University of Maine	M,O
University of Mary	M
University of Maryland, College Park	M,D,O
University of Maryland Eastern Shore	M
University of Massachusetts Amherst	M,D,O
University of Massachusetts Boston	M
University of Memphis	M,D
University of Miami	M,D,O
University of Michigan	M,D
University of Michigan–Dearborn	M
University of Michigan–Flint	M
University of Minnesota, Twin Cities Campus	M,D,O
University of Missouri–Columbia	M,D
University of Missouri–Kansas City	M,D,O
University of Missouri–St. Louis	M,D
University of Nebraska at Kearney	M
University of Nebraska at Omaha	M
University of Nebraska–Lincoln	M
University of Nevada, Las Vegas	M,D,O
University of Nevada, Reno	M,D,O
University of New Hampshire	M

University of New Mexico M,D,O
University of New Orleans M,D,O
University of North Alabama M
The University of North Carolina at Charlotte M,D
The University of North Carolina at Greensboro M,D,O
The University of North Carolina Wilmington M
University of North Dakota M,D
University of Northern Colorado M,D
University of Northern Iowa M,D
University of North Florida M
University of North Texas M,D
University of Oklahoma M,D
University of Phoenix–Southern Arizona Campus M,O
University of Pittsburgh M,D
University of Portland M
University of Puerto Rico, Río Piedras M
University of Rio Grande M
University of St. Francis (IL) M
University of Saint Francis (IN) M
University of Saint Mary M
University of St. Thomas (MN) M,O
The University of Scranton M
University of South Alabama M,O
University of South Carolina M,D
The University of South Dakota M
University of Southern Maine M
University of Southern Mississippi M,D,O
University of South Florida M
The University of Tennessee M,D,O
The University of Tennessee at Chattanooga M,D,O
The University of Texas at Austin M,D
The University of Texas at Brownsville M
The University of Texas at San Antonio M
The University of Texas at Tyler M
The University of Texas of the Permian Basin M
The University of Texas–Pan American M
University of the District of Columbia M
University of the Incarnate Word M,D
University of the Pacific M,D
The University of Toledo M,D,O
University of Utah M,D
University of Vermont M
University of Virginia M,D,O
University of Washington M,D
University of Washington, Tacoma M
The University of West Alabama M
University of West Florida M
University of West Georgia M,O
University of Wisconsin–Eau Claire M
University of Wisconsin–La Crosse M
University of Wisconsin–Madison M,D
University of Wisconsin–Milwaukee M
University of Wisconsin–Oshkosh M
University of Wisconsin–Stevens Point M
University of Wisconsin–Superior M
University of Wisconsin–Whitewater M
University of Wyoming M,O
Utah State University M,D,O
Valdosta State University M,O
Vanderbilt University M,D
Virginia Commonwealth University M
Virginia Polytechnic Institute and State University D,O
Walden University M,D
Walla Walla University M
Washburn University M
Washington University in St. Louis M,D
Wayne State College M
Wayne State University M,D,O
Webster University M,O
West Chester University of Pennsylvania M
Western Carolina University M
Western Connecticut State University M
Western Illinois University M
Western Kentucky University M
Western Michigan University M,D
Western New Mexico University M
Western Oregon University M
Westfield State College M
West Texas A&M University M
West Virginia University M,D
Wheelock College M
Whitworth University M
Wichita State University M
Widener University M,D
Wilkes University M,D
William Carey University M,O
William Paterson University of New Jersey M
Wilmington University (DE) M
Winona State University M
Winthrop University M
Worcester State College M
Wright State University M
Xavier University M
Youngstown State University M

■ SPEECH AND INTERPERSONAL COMMUNICATION

Abilene Christian University M
Arizona State University M,D
Arkansas State University M,O
Ball State University M
Bob Jones University P,M,D,O
Bowling Green State University M,D
Brooklyn College of the City University of New York M,D
California State University, Fullerton M
California State University, Los Angeles M
California State University, Northridge M
Central Michigan University M
Colorado State University M
Drake University M
Eastern Illinois University M
Eastern Michigan University M
Florida State University M,D
Georgia State University M,D
Hofstra University M
Idaho State University M
Indiana University Bloomington M,D
Kansas State University M
Louisiana Tech University M
Marquette University M
Miami University M
Minnesota State University Mankato M
Montclair State University M
New York University M,D
North Dakota State University M,D
Northeastern Illinois University M
Northeastern University D
Northwestern University M,D
Ohio University D
Portland State University M,O
Rensselaer Polytechnic Institute M,D
San Francisco State University M
San Jose State University M
Seton Hall University M
Southern Illinois University Carbondale M,D
Southern Illinois University Edwardsville M
Texas A&M University–Commerce M
Texas Christian University M
Texas Southern University M
The University of Alabama M
University of Arkansas at Little Rock M
University of Central Missouri M
University of Denver M,D
University of Georgia M,D
University of Hawaii at Manoa M
University of Houston M
University of Illinois at Urbana–Champaign M,D
University of Maryland, College Park M,D
University of Nevada, Reno M
University of South Carolina M,D
University of Southern California M,D
University of Southern Mississippi M,D
The University of Tennessee M,D
The University of Texas at Tyler M
University of Wisconsin–Stevens Point M
University of Wisconsin–Superior M
Wake Forest University M
Washington University in St. Louis M,D
Wayne State University M,D

■ SPORT PSYCHOLOGY

Barry University M
California State University, Fresno M
California University of Pennsylvania M
Capella University M,D,O
Cleveland State University M
Florida State University M,D
John F. Kennedy University M
Purdue University M,D
Southern Connecticut State University M
Springfield College M,D,O
University of Florida M,D
The University of Iowa M,D
University of Rhode Island M,D
West Virginia University M,D

■ SPORTS MANAGEMENT

Ashland University M
Barry University M
Belmont University M
Boise State University M
Bowling Green State University M
Brooklyn College of the City University of New York M
California University of Pennsylvania M
Canisius College M
Central Michigan University M
Cleveland State University M
Concordia University (CA) M
Duquesne University M
Eastern Kentucky University M
Eastern Michigan University M
East Stroudsburg University of Pennsylvania M
East Tennessee State University M
Endicott College M
Florida Atlantic University M
Florida International University M
Florida State University M,D,O
The George Washington University M,O
Georgia Southern University M
Georgia State University M
Gonzaga University M
Grambling State University M
Hardin-Simmons University M
Henderson State University M
Howard University M
Indiana State University M

Indiana University Bloomington	M,D,O
Indiana University of Pennsylvania	M
Ithaca College	M
Kent State University	M
Lindenwood University	M
Lynn University	M,D
Manhattanville College	M
Marshall University	M
Millersville University of Pennsylvania	M
Mississippi State University	M
Missouri State University	M
Montana State University–Billings	M
Montclair State University	M,O
Morehead State University	M
Neumann College	M
New Mexico Highlands University	M
New York University	M,O
North Carolina State University	M,D
North Dakota State University	M
Northern Illinois University	M
Nova Southeastern University	M,O
Ohio University	M
Old Dominion University	M
Robert Morris University	M
St. Cloud State University	M
St. Edward's University	M,O
Saint Leo University	M
Seattle University	M
Seton Hall University	M
Slippery Rock University of Pennsylvania	M
Southern New Hampshire University	M,D,O
Springfield College	M,D,O
State University of New York College at Cortland	M
Temple University	M
Tiffin University	M
Troy University	M
The University of Alabama	M,D
University of Central Florida	M,O
University of Dallas	M
University of Florida	M
The University of Iowa	M
University of Louisville	M
University of Mary Hardin-Baylor	M
University of Massachusetts Amherst	M,D
University of Miami	M
University of Michigan	M,D
University of Minnesota, Twin Cities Campus	M,D,O
University of Nevada, Las Vegas	M,D
University of New Haven	M
The University of North Carolina at Chapel Hill	M
The University of North Carolina at Charlotte	M
University of Northern Colorado	M,D
University of Northern Iowa	M,D
University of Rhode Island	M,D
University of San Francisco	M
University of South Carolina	M
University of Southern Maine	M,O
University of Southern Mississippi	M,D
The University of Tennessee	M,D
University of the Incarnate Word	M,O
University of Wisconsin–La Crosse	M
Valparaiso University	M
Washington State University	M,D
Wayne State College	M
Wayne State University	M
West Chester University of Pennsylvania	M,O
Western Illinois University	M
Western Michigan University	M
West Virginia University	M,D
Wichita State University	M
Xavier University	M

■ STATISTICS

American University	M,O
Arizona State University	M,D
Auburn University	M,D
Ball State University	M
Baylor University	M,D
Bernard M. Baruch College of the City University of New York	M
Bowling Green State University	M,D
Brigham Young University	M
California State University, East Bay	M
California State University, Fullerton	M
California State University, Sacramento	M
Carnegie Mellon University	M,D
Case Western Reserve University	M,D
Central Connecticut State University	M,O
Claremont Graduate University	M,D
Clemson University	M,D
Colorado State University	M,D
Columbia University	M,D
Cornell University	M,D
Duke University	D
Eastern Michigan University	M
Florida Atlantic University	M,D
Florida International University	M
Florida State University	M,D
George Mason University	M,D,O
The George Washington University	M,D,O
Georgia Institute of Technology	M,D
Harvard University	M,D
Indiana University Bloomington	M,D
Iowa State University of Science and Technology	M,D
James Madison University	M
The Johns Hopkins University	M,D
Kansas State University	M,D
Kean University	M
Lehigh University	M,D
Louisiana State University and Agricultural and Mechanical College	M
Louisiana Tech University	M
Loyola University Chicago	M
Marquette University	M,D
McNeese State University	M
Miami University	M
Michigan State University	M,D
Minnesota State University Mankato	M
Mississippi State University	M,D
Missouri University of Science and Technology	M,D
Montana State University	M,D
Montclair State University	M,O
Murray State University	M
New Mexico State University	M
New York University	M,D
North Carolina State University	M,D
North Dakota State University	M,D,O
Northern Arizona University	M
Northern Illinois University	M
Northwestern University	M,D
Oakland University	O
The Ohio State University	M,D
Oklahoma State University	M,D
Oregon State University	M,D
Penn State University Park	M,D
Portland State University	M,D
Princeton University	M,D
Purdue University	M,D,O
Rensselaer Polytechnic Institute	M,D
Rice University	M,D
Rochester Institute of Technology	M,O
Rutgers, The State University of New Jersey, New Brunswick	M,D
St. John's University (NY)	M
Sam Houston State University	M
San Diego State University	M
South Dakota State University	M,D
Southern Illinois University Carbondale	M,D
Southern Methodist University	M,D
Stanford University	M,D
State University of New York at Binghamton	M,D
Stephen F. Austin State University	M
Stevens Institute of Technology	M,O
Stony Brook University, State University of New York	M,D
Temple University	M,D
Texas A&M University	M,D
Texas Tech University	M
Tulane University	M,D
University at Albany, State University of New York	M,D,O
The University of Akron	M
The University of Alabama	M,D
University of Alaska Fairbanks	M,D
The University of Arizona	M,D
University of Arkansas	M
University of Arkansas at Little Rock	M
University of California, Berkeley	M,D
University of California, Davis	M,D
University of California, Los Angeles	M,D
University of California, Riverside	M,D
University of California, San Diego	M,D
University of California, Santa Barbara	M,D
University of California, Santa Cruz	M
University of Central Florida	M,O
University of Central Oklahoma	M
University of Chicago	M,D
University of Cincinnati	M,D
University of Connecticut	M,D
University of Delaware	M
University of Denver	M
University of Florida	M,D
University of Georgia	M,D
University of Houston–Clear Lake	M
University of Idaho	M
University of Illinois at Chicago	M,D
University of Illinois at Urbana–Champaign	M,D
The University of Iowa	M,D,O
University of Kentucky	M,D
University of Maryland, Baltimore County	M,D
University of Maryland, College Park	M,D
University of Massachusetts Amherst	M,D
University of Memphis	M,D
University of Miami	M
University of Michigan	M,D
University of Minnesota, Twin Cities Campus	M,D
University of Missouri–Columbia	M,D
University of Missouri–Kansas City	M,D
University of Nebraska–Lincoln	M,D
University of Nevada, Las Vegas	M,D
University of New Hampshire	M,D
University of New Mexico	M,D
The University of North Carolina at Chapel Hill	M,D
University of North Florida	M
University of Pennsylvania	M,D
University of Pittsburgh	M,D
University of Puerto Rico, Mayagüez Campus	M

University of Rhode Island M,D,O
University of Rochester M,D
University of South Carolina M,D,O
The University of South Dakota D
University of Southern California M
University of Southern Maine M
The University of Tennessee M,D
The University of Texas at Austin M
The University of Texas at Dallas M,D
The University of Texas at El Paso M
The University of Texas at San Antonio M,D
The University of Toledo M,D
University of Utah M,D
University of Vermont M
University of Virginia M,D
University of Washington M,D
University of Wisconsin–Madison M,D
University of Wyoming M,D
Utah State University M,D
Virginia Commonwealth University M,O
Virginia Polytechnic Institute and State University M,D
Washington State University M
Washington University in St. Louis M,D
Wayne State University M,D
Western Michigan University M,D
West Virginia University M,D
Wichita State University M,D
Yale University M,D

■ STRUCTURAL BIOLOGY

Brandeis University M,D
Cornell University M,D
Duke University O
Florida State University D
Harvard University D
Illinois State University M,D
Iowa State University of Science and Technology D
Massachusetts Institute of Technology D
Mayo Graduate School D
New York University D
Northwestern University D
Stanford University D
Stony Brook University, State University of New York D
Syracuse University D
Tulane University M,D
University at Albany, State University of New York M,D
University at Buffalo, the State University of New York M,D
University of California, San Diego D
University of Connecticut M,D
University of Pittsburgh D
University of Washington D
Yale University D

■ STRUCTURAL ENGINEERING

Auburn University M,D
California State University, Northridge M
The Catholic University of America M,D
Cornell University M,D
Illinois Institute of Technology M,D
Iowa State University of Science and Technology M,D
Louisiana State University and Agricultural and Mechanical College M,D
Marquette University M,D
Massachusetts Institute of Technology M,D,O
Northwestern University M,D
Ohio University M,D
Penn State University Park M,D
Princeton University M,D
Rensselaer Polytechnic Institute M,D
Stevens Institute of Technology M,D,O
Texas A&M University M,D
Tufts University M,D
University at Buffalo, the State University of New York M,D
University of California, Berkeley M,D
University of California, Los Angeles M,D
University of California, San Diego M,D
University of Central Florida M,D,O
University of Colorado at Boulder M,D
University of Dayton M
University of Delaware M,D
University of Maine M,D
University of Memphis M,D
University of Michigan M,D,O
University of Missouri–Columbia M,D
University of North Dakota M
University of Oklahoma M,D
University of Rhode Island M,D
University of Southern California M
University of Washington M,D
Washington University in St. Louis M,D
Western Michigan University M
Worcester Polytechnic Institute M,D,O

■ STUDENT AFFAIRS

Arkansas State University M,O
Arkansas Tech University M,O
Ashland University M
Azusa Pacific University M
Bloomsburg University of Pennsylvania M
Bob Jones University P,M,D,O
Bowling Green State University M
Buffalo State College, State University of New York M
California State University, Bakersfield M
Canisius College M
Cleveland State University M,O
College of Saint Elizabeth M,O
The College of Saint Rose M,O
Colorado State University M,D
Concordia University Wisconsin M
Eastern Illinois University M
Fresno Pacific University M
Hampton University M
Kansas State University M,D
Kent State University M
Lewis University M
Miami University M
Minnesota State University Mankato M,D,O
New York University M,D
Northeastern University M
Northwestern State University of Louisiana M,O
Nova Southeastern University M
The Ohio State University M
Ohio University M,D
Oklahoma State University M,D,O
Oregon State University M
Penn State University Park M,D
St. Cloud State University M
Saint Louis University M,D,O
San Jose State University M
Seton Hall University M
Slippery Rock University of Pennsylvania M
Springfield College M,O
Tennessee Technological University M,O
University of Bridgeport M
University of Central Arkansas M
University of Central Missouri M
University of Dayton M,O
University of Florida M,D,O
The University of Iowa M,D
University of Louisville M,D
University of Maryland, College Park M,D,O
University of Memphis M,D
University of Miami M,O
University of Minnesota, Twin Cities Campus M,D,O
University of Mississippi M,D,O
University of Northern Iowa M
University of Rhode Island M
University of St. Thomas (MN) M,D,O
University of South Carolina M
University of Southern California M
University of South Florida M,D,O
The University of Tennessee M
University of Wisconsin–La Crosse M
Washington State University M,D
Western Illinois University M
Western Kentucky University M,O

■ SUPPLY CHAIN MANAGEMENT

Arizona State University M,D
California State University, East Bay M
Case Western Reserve University M
Eastern Michigan University M
Elmhurst College M
Howard University M
Lehigh University M,D,O
Michigan State University M,D
North Carolina State University M
Rutgers, The State University of New Jersey, Newark D
Syracuse University M,D
The University of Akron M
University of Dallas M
University of Florida M,D
University of Indianapolis M,O
University of La Verne M
University of Massachusetts Dartmouth M,O
University of Memphis M,D
University of Minnesota, Twin Cities Campus M
University of Missouri–St. Louis M,D,O
The University of North Carolina at Greensboro M,D,O
University of San Diego M,O
University of Wisconsin–Madison M
University of Wisconsin–Whitewater M
Worcester Polytechnic Institute M
Wright State University M

■ SURVEYING SCIENCE AND ENGINEERING

The Ohio State University M,D

■ SURVEY METHODOLOGY

University of Maryland, College Park M,D
University of Michigan M,D,O
University of Nebraska–Lincoln M

■ SUSTAINABLE DEVELOPMENT

Brandeis University M
Carnegie Mellon University M
Clark University M
Columbia University M,D
Goddard College M
Hawai'i Pacific University M
Illinois Institute of Technology M
Iowa State University of Science and Technology M,D
Michigan Technological University O
New College of California M
Prescott College M
School for International Training M

Slippery Rock University of Pennsylvania M
University of Connecticut M
University of Georgia M,D
University of Maryland, College Park M
University of Michigan M,D
University of Washington P,M,D
University of Wisconsin–Madison M
Western Illinois University M,O
West Virginia University D

■ SYSTEMS BIOLOGY

Dartmouth College D
Harvard University D
Massachusetts Institute of Technology D
Rutgers, The State University of New Jersey, New Brunswick D
University of California, San Diego D

■ SYSTEMS ENGINEERING

Auburn University M,D
Boston University M,D
California Institute of Technology M,D
California State University, Fullerton M
California State University, Northridge M
Carnegie Mellon University M
Case Western Reserve University M,D
Colorado School of Mines M,D
Colorado Technical University—Colorado Springs M
Colorado Technical University—Denver M
Cornell University M
Embry-Riddle Aeronautical University (FL) M
Florida Institute of Technology M
George Mason University M
The George Washington University M,D,O
Georgia Institute of Technology M,D
Iowa State University of Science and Technology M
The Johns Hopkins University M,O
Lehigh University M,D
Louisiana State University in Shreveport M
Loyola Marymount University M,O
Massachusetts Institute of Technology M,D
Mississippi State University M,D
Missouri University of Science and Technology M,D
National University M
North Carolina Agricultural and Technical State University M,D
Northeastern University M
Oakland University M,D
The Ohio State University M,D
Ohio University M
Oklahoma State University M
Old Dominion University M
Penn State Great Valley M
Polytechnic University, Brooklyn Campus M
Portland State University M,O
Regis University M,O
Rensselaer Polytechnic Institute M,D
Rochester Institute of Technology M,D
Rutgers, The State University of New Jersey, New Brunswick M,D
San Jose State University M
Southern Methodist University M,D
Southern Polytechnic State University M
Stevens Institute of Technology M,D,O
Stony Brook University, State University of New York M,D,O
Texas Tech University M,D
The University of Arizona M,D
University of Central Florida M,D,O
University of Florida M,D,O
University of Houston M,D
University of Houston–Clear Lake M
University of Idaho M
University of Illinois at Urbana–Champaign M
University of Maryland, Baltimore County O
University of Maryland, College Park M,O
University of Michigan M,D
University of Michigan–Dearborn M
University of Minnesota, Twin Cities Campus M
The University of North Carolina at Charlotte D
University of Pennsylvania M,D
University of Rhode Island M,D
University of St. Thomas (MN) M,O
University of Southern California M,D,O
The University of Texas at Arlington M
University of Virginia M,D
University of Wisconsin–Madison M,D
Virginia Polytechnic Institute and State University M
Walden University M,O
Western International University M
Worcester Polytechnic Institute M,D

■ SYSTEMS SCIENCE

Arkansas Tech University M
Claremont Graduate University M,D,O
Eastern Illinois University M,O
Fairleigh Dickinson University, Metropolitan Campus M
Florida Institute of Technology M
Hood College M
Louisiana State University and Agricultural and Mechanical College M,D
Louisiana State University in Shreveport M
Miami University M
Oakland University M
Portland State University M,D,O
Southern Methodist University M,D
State University of New York at Binghamton M,D
Stevens Institute of Technology M
University of Michigan–Dearborn M
The University of North Carolina at Charlotte M,D
The University of North Carolina Wilmington M
Washington University in St. Louis M,D
Worcester Polytechnic Institute M,O

■ TAXATION

American University M
Bentley College M
Bernard M. Baruch College of the City University of New York M
Boise State University M
Boston University P,M
Bryant University M,O
California Polytechnic State University, San Luis Obispo M
California State University, East Bay M
California State University, Fullerton M
California State University, Los Angeles M
Capital University M
Chapman University P,M
Cleveland State University M
DePaul University M
Drexel University M
Duquesne University M
Fairfield University M,O
Fairleigh Dickinson University, College at Florham M,O
Fairleigh Dickinson University, Metropolitan Campus M
Florida Atlantic University M
Florida Gulf Coast University M
Florida International University M
Florida State University M,D
Fontbonne University M
Fordham University M
Georgetown University P,M,D
Georgia State University M
Golden Gate University P,M,D,O
Grand Valley State University M
Hofstra University M
Illinois Institute of Technology P,M
Long Island University, Brooklyn Campus M
Long Island University, C.W. Post Campus M,O
Loyola Marymount University P,M
Mississippi State University M
National University M
New York University P,M,D,O
Northeastern University M,O
Northern Illinois University M
Nova Southeastern University M
Pace University M
Philadelphia University M
Robert Morris University M
Rutgers, The State University of New Jersey, Newark M
St. John's University (NY) M,O
St. Mary's University of San Antonio M
St. Thomas University P,M
San Jose State University M
Seton Hall University M
Southeastern University M
Southern Methodist University P,M,D
Southern New Hampshire University M,D,O
Suffolk University M,O
Temple University P,M
University at Albany, State University of New York M
The University of Akron M
The University of Alabama M,D
University of Baltimore P,M
University of Central Florida M
University of Cincinnati M
University of Denver M
University of Florida P,M,D
University of Hartford M,O
University of Hawaii at Manoa M
University of Memphis M
University of Miami M
University of Minnesota, Twin Cities Campus M
University of Mississippi M,D
University of Missouri–Kansas City P,M
University of New Haven M
University of New Mexico M
University of New Orleans M
The University of North Carolina at Greensboro M,O
University of San Diego P,M,O
University of Southern California M
The University of Texas at Arlington M
The University of Texas at San Antonio M,D
University of Tulsa M

University of Washington P,M,D
Villanova University M
Virginia Commonwealth University M,D
Washington State University M
Wayne State University M,D
Widener University M

■ TECHNICAL COMMUNICATION

Boise State University M
Bowling Green State University M,D
Colorado State University M
Harvard University M
Lawrence Technological University M
Michigan Technological University M,D
Minnesota State University Mankato M,O
New Jersey Institute of Technology M
North Carolina State University M
Polytechnic University, Brooklyn Campus O
Rensselaer Polytechnic Institute M
Rochester Institute of Technology O
Southern Polytechnic State University M
Texas State University-San Marcos M
University of Colorado Denver M
University of Nebraska at Omaha M,O
University of Washington M,D

■ TECHNICAL WRITING

Carnegie Mellon University M
Colorado State University M
Drexel University M
Fitchburg State College M,O
Illinois Institute of Technology M,D
James Madison University M
The Johns Hopkins University M
Massachusetts Institute of Technology M
Metropolitan State University M
Miami University M
Oklahoma State University M,D
Polytechnic University, Brooklyn Campus M
Regis University M,O
Texas Tech University M,D
The University of Alabama in Huntsville M,O
University of Arkansas at Little Rock M
University of Central Florida M,D,O
The University of North Carolina at Greensboro M,D,O

■ TECHNOLOGY AND PUBLIC POLICY

Carnegie Mellon University M,D
Eastern Michigan University M
The George Washington University M
Massachusetts Institute of Technology M,D
Rensselaer Polytechnic Institute M,D
Rochester Institute of Technology M
St. Cloud State University M
University of Minnesota, Twin Cities Campus M
The University of Texas at Austin M
Western Illinois University M

■ TELECOMMUNICATIONS

Ball State University M
Boston University M
California State University, East Bay M
Claremont Graduate University M,D,O
DePaul University M,D
Drexel University M
Florida International University M
George Mason University M,D,O
The George Washington University M,D
Illinois Institute of Technology M,D
Indiana University Bloomington M
Iona College M,O
The Johns Hopkins University M
Michigan State University M
National University M
Ohio University M
Pace University M,D,O
Polytechnic University, Brooklyn Campus M
Polytechnic University, Westchester Graduate Center M
Rochester Institute of Technology M
Roosevelt University M
Saint Mary's University of Minnesota M
Southern Illinois University Carbondale M
Southern Methodist University M,D
State University of New York Institute of Technology M
Stevens Institute of Technology M,D,O
Syracuse University M
University of Arkansas M
University of California, San Diego M,D
University of California, Santa Cruz M,D
University of Colorado at Boulder M
University of Denver M,O
University of Hawaii at Manoa O
University of Louisiana at Lafayette M
University of Maryland, College Park M
University of Massachusetts Dartmouth M,D,O
University of Missouri–Kansas City M,D
University of Oklahoma M,D
University of Pennsylvania M
University of Pittsburgh M,O
The University of Texas at Dallas M,D
Widener University M

■ TELECOMMUNICATIONS MANAGEMENT

Alaska Pacific University M
Carnegie Mellon University M
Morgan State University M
Murray State University M
Northeastern University M,D
Oklahoma State University M,D
Polytechnic University, Brooklyn Campus M
San Diego State University M
Santa Clara University M,D,O
Stevens Institute of Technology M,D,O
Syracuse University M,O
University of Colorado at Boulder M
University of Denver M,O
University of Missouri–St. Louis M,O
University of Pennsylvania M
University of San Francisco M
University of Wisconsin–Stout M
Webster University M,D

■ TEXTILE DESIGN

California State University, Los Angeles M
Cornell University M,D
Drexel University M
Florida State University M,D
Illinois State University M
James Madison University M
Kent State University M
Marywood University M
Philadelphia University M
Sul Ross State University M
Temple University M
University of California, Davis M
University of Cincinnati M
University of Minnesota, Twin Cities Campus M,D,O
The University of North Carolina at Greensboro M,D
University of North Texas M,D
Western Michigan University M

■ TEXTILE SCIENCES AND ENGINEERING

Auburn University M,D
Clemson University M,D
Cornell University M,D
Georgia Institute of Technology M,D
North Carolina State University M,D
Philadelphia University M,D
University of Massachusetts Dartmouth M

■ THANATOLOGY

Brooklyn College of the City University of New York M
Hood College M,O

■ THEATER

Antioch University McGregor M
Arcadia University M,D,O
Arizona State University M,D
Arkansas State University M,O
Baylor University M
Bennington College M
Bob Jones University P,M,D,O
Boston University M,O
Bowling Green State University M,D
Brandeis University M
Brigham Young University M
Brooklyn College of the City University of New York M,D
Brown University M
California State University, Fullerton M
California State University, Long Beach M
California State University, Los Angeles M
California State University, Northridge M
California State University, Sacramento M
California State University, San Bernardino M
Carnegie Mellon University M
Case Western Reserve University M
The Catholic University of America M
Central Michigan University M
Central Washington University M
Columbia University M,D
Cornell University D
DePaul University M,O
Drake University M
Eastern Kentucky University M
Eastern Michigan University M
Emerson College M
Florida Atlantic University M
Florida State University M,D
Fontbonne University M
The George Washington University M
Graduate School and University Center of the City University of New York D
Hollins University M
Humboldt State University M
Hunter College of the City University of New York M
Idaho State University M
Illinois State University M
Indiana State University M
Indiana University Bloomington M,D
Kansas State University M

Kent State University	M
Lamar University	M
Lindenwood University	M
Long Island University, C.W. Post Campus	M
Louisiana State University and Agricultural and Mechanical College	M,D
Mary Baldwin College	M
Miami University	M
Michigan State University	M
Minnesota State University Mankato	M
Missouri State University	M
Montclair State University	M
Naropa University	M
The New School: A University	M
New York University	M,D,O
Northern Illinois University	M
Northwestern University	M,D
The Ohio State University	M,D
Ohio University	M
Oklahoma City University	M
Oklahoma State University	M
Pace University	M
Penn State University Park	M
Pittsburg State University	M
Point Park University	M
Portland State University	M
Purchase College, State University of New York	M
Purdue University	M
Regent University	M,D
Rhode Island College	M
Roosevelt University	M
Rowan University	M
Rutgers, The State University of New Jersey, New Brunswick	M
St. John's University (NY)	M,O
San Diego State University	M
San Francisco State University	M
San Jose State University	M
Sarah Lawrence College	M
Southern Illinois University Carbondale	M,D
Southern Methodist University	M
Stanford University	D
State University of New York at Binghamton	M
Stony Brook University, State University of New York	M
Temple University	M
Texas A&M University–Commerce	M
Texas State University-San Marcos	M
Texas Tech University	M,D
Texas Woman's University	M
Towson University	M
Tufts University	M,D
Tulane University	M
University at Albany, State University of New York	M
The University of Akron	M
The University of Alabama	M
The University of Arizona	M
University of Arkansas	M
University of California, Berkeley	D
University of California, Davis	M,D
University of California, Irvine	M,D
University of California, Los Angeles	M,D
University of California, San Diego	M,D
University of California, Santa Barbara	M,D
University of California, Santa Cruz	O
University of Central Florida	M
University of Central Missouri	M
University of Cincinnati	M
University of Colorado at Boulder	M,D
University of Connecticut	M
University of Delaware	M
University of Florida	M
University of Georgia	M,D
University of Hawaii at Manoa	M,D
University of Houston	M
University of Idaho	M
University of Illinois at Urbana–Champaign	M,D
The University of Iowa	M
University of Kansas	M,D
University of Kentucky	M
University of Louisville	M
University of Maryland, College Park	M,D
University of Massachusetts Amherst	M
University of Memphis	M
University of Michigan	M,D
University of Minnesota, Twin Cities Campus	M,D
University of Mississippi	M
University of Missouri–Columbia	M,D
University of Missouri–Kansas City	M
The University of Montana	M
University of Nebraska at Omaha	M
University of Nebraska–Lincoln	M,D
University of Nevada, Las Vegas	M
University of New Mexico	M
University of New Orleans	M
The University of North Carolina at Chapel Hill	M
The University of North Carolina at Charlotte	M
The University of North Carolina at Greensboro	M
University of North Dakota	M
University of North Texas	M
University of Oklahoma	M
University of Oregon	M,D
University of Pittsburgh	M,D
University of Portland	M
University of San Diego	M
University of South Carolina	M,D
The University of South Dakota	M
University of Southern California	M
University of Southern Mississippi	M
The University of Tennessee	M
The University of Texas at Austin	M,D
The University of Texas at El Paso	M
The University of Texas at Tyler	M
The University of Texas–Pan American	M
University of Virginia	M
University of Washington	M,D
University of Wisconsin–Madison	M,D
University of Wisconsin–Milwaukee	M
University of Wisconsin–Superior	M
Utah State University	M
Villanova University	M
Virginia Commonwealth University	M
Virginia Polytechnic Institute and State University	M
Washington University in St. Louis	M
Wayne State University	M,D
Western Illinois University	M
Western Washington University	M
West Virginia University	M
Yale University	M,D,O

■ THEOLOGY

Abilene Christian University	P,M
Anderson University	P,M,D
Andrews University	P,M,D,O
Azusa Pacific University	M,D
Barry University	M,D
Bayamón Central University	P,M
Baylor University	P,M,D
Biola University	P,M,D
Bob Jones University	P,M,D,O
Boston College	P,M,D,O
Boston University	P,M,D
California Institute of Integral Studies	M,D
Campbell University	P,M,D
The Catholic University of America	P,M,D,O
Chaminade University of Honolulu	M
Claremont Graduate University	M,D
College of Mount St. Joseph	M
College of St. Catherine	M
College of Saint Elizabeth	M
Concordia University (CA)	M
Concordia University, St. Paul	M,O
Creighton University	M
Drew University	P,M,D,O
Duke University	P,M
Duquesne University	M,D
Eastern Mennonite University	P,M,O
Eastern University	P,M,D
Emory University	P,M,D
Fordham University	M,D
Franciscan University of Steubenville	M
Freed-Hardeman University	P,M
Friends University	M
Gardner-Webb University	P,D
George Fox University	P,M,D,O
Georgian Court University	M,O
Harding University	M
Hardin-Simmons University	P,M
Harvard University	P,M,D
Houston Baptist University	M
Howard University	P,M,D
Indiana Wesleyan University	M
Inter American University of Puerto Rico, Metropolitan Campus	D
Lakeland College	M
La Salle University	M
Lee University	M
Liberty University	P,M,D
Lipscomb University	P,M
Loyola Marymount University	M
Loyola University Chicago	P,M,D
Loyola University New Orleans	M,O
Lubbock Christian University	M
Madonna University	M
Malone College	M
Marquette University	M,D
Marylhurst University	P,M
Mercer University	P,D
Mount St. Mary's University	P,M
Naropa University	P
Oakland City University	P,D
Ohio Dominican University	M
Oklahoma Christian University	P,M
Olivet Nazarene University	M
Oral Roberts University	P,M,D
Philadelphia Biblical University	P,M
Pontifical Catholic University of Puerto Rico	P
Providence College	M
Regent University	P,M,D
St. Bonaventure University	M,O
St. John's University (NY)	P,M,O
Saint Louis University	M,D
St. Mary's University of San Antonio	M
Saint Michael's College	M,O
St. Thomas University	M,D,O
Samford University	P,M,D
Seattle University	P,M,O
Seton Hall University	P,M,O
Southern Methodist University	P,M,D
Southern Nazarene University	M

Spring Arbor University M
Spring Hill College M
Texas Christian University P,M,D,O
Trevecca Nazarene University M
Trinity International University P,M,D,O
University of Chicago P,M,D
University of Dallas M
University of Dayton M,D
University of Denver D
University of Dubuque P,M,D
University of Mobile M
University of Notre Dame P,M,D
University of St. Thomas (MN) P,M
University of St. Thomas (TX) P,M
University of San Francisco M
The University of Scranton M
Ursuline College M
Valparaiso University M,O
Vanderbilt University P,M
Vanguard University of Southern California M
Villanova University M
Walsh University M
Wheaton College M,D
Xavier University M
Xavier University of Louisiana M
Yale University P,M

■ THEORETICAL CHEMISTRY

Cornell University D
Georgetown University M,D
The University of Tennessee M,D
Vanderbilt University M,D
West Virginia University M,D

■ THEORETICAL PHYSICS

Cornell University M,D
Harvard University D
Rutgers, The State University of New Jersey, New Brunswick M,D
West Virginia University M,D

■ THERAPIES—DANCE, DRAMA, AND MUSIC

Antioch University New England M
Appalachian State University M
California Institute of Integral Studies M,D
Columbia College Chicago M,O
Drexel University M
East Carolina University M
Florida State University M,D
Georgia College & State University M,O
Immaculata University M
Lesley University M,D,O
Maryville University of Saint Louis M
Marywood University M,O
Michigan State University M,D
Montclair State University M,O
Naropa University M
Nazareth College of Rochester M
New York University M,D
Ohio University M,O
Radford University M
Shenandoah University M,D,O
Temple University M,D
University of Kansas M
University of Miami M,D,O
University of the Pacific M

■ TOXICOLOGY

American University M,O
Brown University M,D
Columbia University M,D
Cornell University M,D
Dartmouth College D
Duke University D,O
Florida Agricultural and Mechanical University M,D
The George Washington University M
Indiana University–Purdue University Indianapolis M,D
Iowa State University of Science and Technology M,D
The Johns Hopkins University M,D
Long Island University, Brooklyn Campus M,D
Louisiana State University and Agricultural and Mechanical College M
Massachusetts Institute of Technology M,D
Michigan State University M,D
New York University M,D
North Carolina State University M,D
Northeastern University M
Northwestern University D
The Ohio State University M,D
Oregon State University M,D
Purdue University M,D
Rutgers, The State University of New Jersey, New Brunswick M,D
St. John's University (NY) M
San Diego State University M,D
Texas A&M University M,D
Texas Southern University M,D
Texas Tech University M,D
University at Albany, State University of New York M,D
University at Buffalo, the State University of New York M,D
The University of Alabama at Birmingham M,D
University of California, Davis M,D
University of California, Irvine M,D
University of California, Riverside M,D
University of California, Santa Cruz M,D
University of Colorado Denver P,D
University of Connecticut M,D
University of Florida M,D,O
University of Georgia M,D
The University of Iowa M,D
University of Kansas M,D
University of Kentucky M,D
University of Louisville M,D
University of Maryland Eastern Shore M,D
University of Michigan M,D
University of Minnesota, Duluth M,D
University of Minnesota, Twin Cities Campus M,D
The University of Montana M,D
University of Nebraska–Lincoln M,D
University of New Mexico M,D
The University of North Carolina at Chapel Hill M,D
University of Rhode Island M,D
University of Rochester M,D
University of South Alabama M
University of Southern California M,D
University of Utah M,D
University of Washington M,D
University of Wisconsin–Madison M,D
Utah State University M,D
Virginia Commonwealth University M,D
Washington State University M,D
Wayne State University M,D
West Virginia University M,D
Wright State University M

■ TRANSCULTURAL NURSING

Augsburg College M
New Jersey City University M

■ TRANSLATIONAL BIOLOGY

The University of Iowa M,D

■ TRANSLATION AND INTERPRETATION

American University M,O
Gallaudet University M
Georgia State University O
Kent State University M,D
Marygrove College M
Montclair State University M,O
Monterey Institute of International Studies M
Rutgers, The State University of New Jersey, New Brunswick M,D
State University of New York at Binghamton M,O
University at Albany, State University of New York M,O
University of Arkansas M
University of Denver M,O
The University of Iowa M
University of Puerto Rico, Río Piedras M,O

■ TRANSPERSONAL AND HUMANISTIC PSYCHOLOGY

Naropa University M
Seattle University M

■ TRANSPORTATION AND HIGHWAY ENGINEERING

Auburn University M,D
Cornell University M,D
Illinois Institute of Technology M,D
Iowa State University of Science and Technology M,D
Louisiana State University and Agricultural and Mechanical College M,D
Marquette University M,D
Massachusetts Institute of Technology M,D,O
Morgan State University M,D
New Jersey Institute of Technology M,D
Northwestern University M,D
Ohio University M,D
Penn State University Park M,D
Polytechnic University, Brooklyn Campus M,D
Princeton University M,D
Rensselaer Polytechnic Institute M,D
Texas A&M University M,D
Texas Southern University M
University of Arkansas M
University of California, Berkeley M,D
University of California, Davis M,D
University of California, Irvine M,D
University of Central Florida M,D,O
University of Dayton M
University of Delaware M,D
University of Memphis M,D
University of Missouri–Columbia M,D
University of Nevada, Las Vegas M,D
University of Rhode Island M,D
University of Southern California M
University of Washington M,D
Villanova University M
Western Michigan University M
Worcester Polytechnic Institute M,D,O

■ TRANSPORTATION MANAGEMENT

Arizona State University O
Arizona State University at the Polytechnic Campus M

Florida Institute of Technology	M
George Mason University	M
Iowa State University of Science and Technology	M
Morgan State University	M
New Jersey Institute of Technology	M,D
North Dakota State University	M,D
Polytechnic University, Brooklyn Campus	M
San Jose State University	M
State University of New York Maritime College	M
University at Buffalo, the State University of New York	M,D,O
University of Arkansas	M
University of California, Davis	M,D
University of Central Missouri	M,O
University of Denver	M
The University of Tennessee	M,D
University of Washington	O
Wilmington University (DE)	M

■ TRAVEL AND TOURISM

Boston University	M
Clemson University	M,D
East Stroudsburg University of Pennsylvania	M
The George Washington University	M,O
Indiana University–Purdue University Indianapolis	M
New York University	M,O
North Carolina State University	M,D
Old Dominion University	M
Purdue University	M,D
Rochester Institute of Technology	M
Saint Xavier University	M,O
Schiller International University (United States)	M
Temple University	M,D
University of Central Florida	M
University of Hawaii at Manoa	M
University of Massachusetts Amherst	M
University of New Haven	M
University of New Orleans	M
University of South Carolina	M
The University of Tennessee	M
Virginia Polytechnic Institute and State University	M,D
Western Illinois University	M

■ URBAN AND REGIONAL PLANNING

Alabama Agricultural and Mechanical University	M
Arizona State University	M
Auburn University	M
Ball State University	M
Boston University	M
California Polytechnic State University, San Luis Obispo	M
California State Polytechnic University, Pomona	M
California State University, Chico	M
The Catholic University of America	M
Clark University	M
Clemson University	M
Cleveland State University	M,O
Columbia University	M,D
Cornell University	M,D
Delta State University	M
DePaul University	M,O
Eastern Kentucky University	M
Eastern Washington University	M
East Tennessee State University	M
Florida Atlantic University	M
Florida State University	M,D
Georgia Institute of Technology	M,D
Harvard University	M,D
Hunter College of the City University of New York	M
Iowa State University of Science and Technology	M
Jackson State University	M
Kansas State University	M
Massachusetts Institute of Technology	M,D
Michigan State University	M,D
Minnesota State University Mankato	M,O
Missouri State University	M
Morgan State University	M
New York University	M,O
North Park University	M
The Ohio State University	M,D
Old Dominion University	M
Portland State University	M
Rutgers, The State University of New Jersey, New Brunswick	M,D
San Diego State University	M
San Jose State University	M,O
State University of New York College of Environmental Science and Forestry	M,D
Temple University	M
Texas A&M University	M,D
Texas Southern University	M
Texas Tech University	M
Tufts University	M
University at Albany, State University of New York	M
University at Buffalo, the State University of New York	M
The University of Akron	M
University of California, Berkeley	M,D
University of California, Davis	M
University of California, Irvine	M,D
University of California, Los Angeles	M,D
University of Central Florida	M,O
University of Cincinnati	M
University of Colorado Denver	M,D
University of Florida	M,D
University of Hawaii at Manoa	M,D,O
University of Illinois at Chicago	M,D
University of Illinois at Urbana–Champaign	M,D
The University of Iowa	M
University of Kansas	M
University of Louisville	M
University of Maryland, College Park	M,D
University of Massachusetts Amherst	M,D
University of Memphis	M
University of Michigan	M,D,O
University of Minnesota, Twin Cities Campus	M
University of Nebraska–Lincoln	M
University of New Mexico	M
University of New Orleans	M
The University of North Carolina at Chapel Hill	M,D
University of Oklahoma	M
University of Oregon	M
University of Pennsylvania	M,D,O
University of Pittsburgh	M
University of Puerto Rico, Río Piedras	M
University of Southern California	M,D
University of Southern Maine	M,O
The University of Texas at Arlington	M
The University of Texas at Austin	M,D
The University of Toledo	M,D,O
University of Utah	M
University of Virginia	M
University of Washington	M,D
University of Wisconsin–Madison	M,D
University of Wisconsin–Milwaukee	M,O
Utah State University	M,D
Vanderbilt University	M
Virginia Commonwealth University	M,O
Virginia Polytechnic Institute and State University	M
Wayne State University	M
West Chester University of Pennsylvania	M
West Virginia University	M,D

■ URBAN DESIGN

City College of the City University of New York	M
Cleveland State University	M,O
Columbia University	M
Cornell University	M,D
Georgia Institute of Technology	M,D
Harvard University	M
Kent State University	M,O
New York Institute of Technology	M
Prairie View A&M University	M
Rice University	M,D
State University of New York College of Environmental Science and Forestry	M
University at Buffalo, the State University of New York	M
University of California, Berkeley	M,D
University of California, Los Angeles	M,D
University of Colorado Denver	M
University of Miami	M
University of Michigan	M
University of Pennsylvania	D
University of Washington	M,D,O
Washington University in St. Louis	M

■ URBAN EDUCATION

Cardinal Stritch University	M,D
Claremont Graduate University	M,D,O
Cleveland State University	D
College of Mount Saint Vincent	M,O
Columbia College Chicago	M
Concordia University Chicago (IL)	M
DePaul University	M,D
Florida International University	M
Graduate School and University Center of the City University of New York	D
Harvard University	D
Holy Names University	M,O
The Johns Hopkins University	M,D,O
Marygrove College	M
Mercy College	M
New Jersey City University	M
Norfolk State University	M
Northeastern Illinois University	M
Nova Southeastern University	M,O
Roberts Wesleyan College	M,O
Saint Peter's College	M
Simmons College	M,O
Temple University	M,D
Texas A&M University	M,D
Texas Southern University	M,D
University of Central Florida	M,D,O
University of Illinois at Chicago	M,D
University of Massachusetts Boston	M,D,O
University of Michigan–Flint	M
University of Nebraska at Omaha	M,O
University of Wisconsin–Milwaukee	M,D
Virginia Commonwealth University	D

■ URBAN STUDIES

Boston University	M
Brooklyn College of the City University of New York	M,D
Cleveland State University	M,D
East Tennessee State University	M
Georgia State University	M
Graduate School and University Center of the City University of New York	M,D
Hunter College of the City University of New York	M
Long Island University, Brooklyn Campus	M
Massachusetts Institute of Technology	M,D
Minnesota State University Mankato	M,O
New Jersey City University	M
New Jersey Institute of Technology	D
The New School: A University	M
Norfolk State University	M
Old Dominion University	M,D
Portland State University	M,D
Queens College of the City University of New York	M
Rutgers, The State University of New Jersey, Newark	M,D
Saint Louis University	M,D,O
Savannah State University	M
Southern Connecticut State University	M
Temple University	M
Tufts University	M
University at Albany, State University of New York	M,D,O
The University of Akron	M,D
University of California, Irvine	M,D
University of Central Oklahoma	M
University of Delaware	M,D
University of Louisville	D
University of New Orleans	M,D
University of the Incarnate Word	M,O
University of Wisconsin–Milwaukee	M,D
Wright State University	M

■ VETERINARY MEDICINE

Auburn University	P
Colorado State University	P
Cornell University	P,D
Iowa State University of Science and Technology	P,M
Kansas State University	P
Louisiana State University and Agricultural and Mechanical College	P
Michigan State University	P
Mississippi State University	P
North Carolina State University	P,M
The Ohio State University	P
Oklahoma State University	P
Oregon State University	P
Purdue University	P
Texas A&M University	P,M
Tufts University	P
University of California, Davis	P
University of Florida	P
University of Georgia	P
University of Illinois at Urbana–Champaign	P
University of Maryland, College Park	P
University of Minnesota, Twin Cities Campus	P
University of Missouri–Columbia	P
University of Pennsylvania	P
The University of Tennessee	P
University of Wisconsin–Madison	P
Virginia Polytechnic Institute and State University	P
Washington State University	P

■ VETERINARY SCIENCES

Auburn University	M,D
Clemson University	M,D
Colorado State University	M,D
Drexel University	M
Iowa State University of Science and Technology	M,D
Kansas State University	M
Louisiana State University and Agricultural and Mechanical College	M,D
Michigan State University	M,D
Mississippi State University	M,D
Montana State University	M,D
North Carolina State University	M,D
North Dakota State University	M,D
The Ohio State University	M,D
Oklahoma State University	M,D
Oregon State University	M,D
Penn State University Park	D
Purdue University	M,D
South Dakota State University	M,D
Texas A&M University	M
Tufts University	M,D
University of California, Davis	M,O
University of Florida	M,D,O
University of Georgia	M,D
University of Idaho	M,D
University of Illinois at Urbana–Champaign	M,D
University of Kentucky	M,D
University of Maryland, College Park	M,D
University of Minnesota, Twin Cities Campus	M,D
University of Missouri–Columbia	M,D
University of Nebraska–Lincoln	M,D
University of Washington	M
University of Wisconsin–Madison	M,D
Utah State University	M,D
Virginia Polytechnic Institute and State University	M,D
Washington State University	M,D

■ VIROLOGY

Loyola University Chicago	M,D
Mayo Graduate School	D
The Ohio State University	M,D
Purdue University	M,D
Rutgers, The State University of New Jersey, New Brunswick	M,D
University of California, San Diego	D
The University of Iowa	M,D
University of Pennsylvania	D
University of Pittsburgh	M,D
Yale University	D

■ VISION SCIENCES

Emory University	M
Nova Southeastern University	P,M
The University of Alabama at Birmingham	M,D
The University of Alabama in Huntsville	M,D
University of California, Berkeley	M,D
University of Chicago	D
University of Houston	M,D
University of Louisville	D
University of Missouri–St. Louis	M,D

■ VOCATIONAL AND TECHNICAL EDUCATION

Alabama Agricultural and Mechanical University	M
Alcorn State University	M,O
Appalachian State University	M
Ball State University	M
Bemidji State University	M
Bowling Green State University	M
Buffalo State College, State University of New York	M
California Baptist University	M
California State University, Long Beach	M
California State University, Sacramento	M
California State University, San Bernardino	M
California University of Pennsylvania	M
Central Connecticut State University	M,O
Central Michigan University	M
Chicago State University	M
Clarion University of Pennsylvania	M
Colorado State University	M,D
East Carolina University	M
Eastern Kentucky University	M
Eastern Michigan University	M
East Tennessee State University	M
Fitchburg State College	M
Florida Agricultural and Mechanical University	M
Georgia Southern University	M
Idaho State University	M
Indiana State University	M
Inter American University of Puerto Rico, Metropolitan Campus	M
Iowa State University of Science and Technology	M,D
Jackson State University	M
James Madison University	M
Kent State University	M,O
Louisiana State University and Agricultural and Mechanical College	M,D
Marshall University	M
Middle Tennessee State University	M
Millersville University of Pennsylvania	M
Mississippi State University	M,D,O
Morehead State University	M
Murray State University	M
North Carolina Agricultural and Technical State University	M
Northern Arizona University	M
Nova Southeastern University	D
The Ohio State University	D
Oklahoma State University	M,D
Old Dominion University	M,D
Penn State University Park	M,D
Pittsburg State University	M,O
Purdue University	M,D,O
Rhode Island College	M,O
Saint Martin's University	M
Sam Houston State University	M
South Carolina State University	M
Southern Illinois University Carbondale	M,D
Southern New Hampshire University	M,O
State University of New York at Oswego	M
Sul Ross State University	M
Temple University	M,D
Texas A&M University–Corpus Christi	M
Texas State University-San Marcos	M
Trevecca Nazarene University	M
The University of Akron	M

University of Arkansas M,D,O
University of Central Florida M
University of Central Missouri M,O
University of Georgia M,D,O
University of Idaho M,D,O
University of Illinois at Urbana–Champaign M,D,O
University of Kentucky M
University of Louisville M
University of Maryland Eastern Shore M
University of Minnesota, Twin Cities Campus M,D,O
University of Missouri–Columbia M,D,O
University of North Dakota M
University of Northern Iowa M,D
University of North Texas M,D
University of South Carolina M,D,O
University of Southern Maine M
University of Southern Mississippi M
University of South Florida M,D,O
The University of Texas at Tyler M
The University of Toledo M,O
University of West Florida M
University of Wisconsin–Platteville M
University of Wisconsin–Stout M,O
Utah State University M
Valdosta State University M,D
Virginia Polytechnic Institute and State University M,D,O
Virginia State University M,O
Wayne State College M
Wayne State University M,D,O
Western Michigan University M
Westfield State College M,O
West Virginia University M
Wilmington University (DE) M
Wright State University M

■ WATER RESOURCES

Albany State University M
Colorado State University M,D
Duke University M
Iowa State University of Science and Technology M,D
Missouri University of Science and Technology M,D
Montclair State University M,D,O
Rutgers, The State University of New Jersey, New Brunswick M,D
State University of New York College of Environmental Science and Forestry M,D
The University of Arizona M,D
University of California, Riverside M,D
University of Florida M,D
University of Illinois at Chicago M,D
University of Kansas M
University of Minnesota, Twin Cities Campus M,D
University of Nevada, Las Vegas M
University of New Hampshire M
University of New Mexico M
University of Oklahoma M,D
University of Wisconsin–Madison M
University of Wyoming M,D
Utah State University M,D

■ WATER RESOURCES ENGINEERING

Cornell University M,D
Louisiana State University and Agricultural and Mechanical College M,D
Marquette University M,D
New Mexico Institute of Mining and Technology M
Ohio University M,D
Oregon State University M,D
Penn State University Park M,D
Princeton University M,D
Stevens Institute of Technology M,D,O
Texas A&M University M,D
Tufts University M,D
The University of Arizona M,D
University of California, Berkeley M,D
University of California, Los Angeles M,D
University of Central Florida M,D,O
University of Colorado at Boulder M,D
University of Delaware M,D
University of Memphis M,D
University of Missouri–Columbia M,D
University of Southern California M
The University of Texas at Austin M
University of Washington M,D
Utah State University M,D
Villanova University M

■ WESTERN EUROPEAN STUDIES

Boston College M,D
Brown University M,D
The Catholic University of America M
Claremont Graduate University M,D,O
Columbia University M,O
Cornell University M,D
East Carolina University M
Georgetown University M
The George Washington University M
Indiana University Bloomington M
The Johns Hopkins University M,D,O
New York University M
San Diego State University M
University of California, Santa Barbara M
University of Connecticut M
University of Nevada, Reno D
University of Pittsburgh O
Washington State University M,D

■ WOMEN'S HEALTH NURSING

Case Western Reserve University M,D
Columbia University O
Emory University M
Georgia Southern University M,O
Georgia State University M,D,O
Indiana University–Purdue University Indianapolis M,D
Kent State University M,D
Loyola University Chicago M
Seton Hall University M
Stony Brook University, State University of New York M,O
University at Buffalo, the State University of New York M,D,O
University of Cincinnati M,D
University of Colorado at Colorado Springs M,D
University of Delaware M,O
University of Michigan M,O
University of Minnesota, Twin Cities Campus M
University of Missouri–Kansas City M,D
University of Pennsylvania M
University of South Carolina M
The University of Texas at El Paso M
Vanderbilt University M,D
Virginia Commonwealth University M,D,O
Wilmington University (DE) M

■ WOMEN'S STUDIES

Brandeis University M
California Institute of Integral Studies M,D
Claremont Graduate University M,D
Clark Atlanta University M,D
Cornell University M,D
Drew University M
Duke University O
Eastern Michigan University M
Emory University D,O
Florida Atlantic University M,O
The George Washington University M,D,O
Georgia State University M
Graduate School and University Center of the City University of New York M,D
Lesley University M
Minnesota State University Mankato M,O
New College of California M
The Ohio State University M,D
Roosevelt University M,O
Rutgers, The State University of New Jersey, New Brunswick M,D
San Diego State University M
San Francisco State University M
Sarah Lawrence College M
Shenandoah University M,D,O
Southern Connecticut State University M
Stony Brook University, State University of New York M,O
Texas Woman's University M
Towson University M,O
University at Albany, State University of New York M,D
The University of Alabama M
The University of Arizona M
University of California, Los Angeles M,D
University of California, Santa Barbara M,D
University of Cincinnati M,O
University of Florida M,O
University of Georgia O
University of Hawaii at Manoa O
The University of Iowa D
University of Louisville M,O
University of Maryland, Baltimore County O
University of Maryland, College Park M,D
University of Massachusetts Boston M,D,O
University of Michigan D,O
University of Minnesota, Twin Cities Campus D
University of Nevada, Las Vegas O
The University of North Carolina at Greensboro M,D,O
University of Northern Iowa M
University of Pittsburgh O
University of South Carolina O
University of South Florida M
University of Washington M,D
Washington State University M,D

■ WRITING

Abilene Christian University M
Adelphi University M
American University M
Antioch University Los Angeles M,O
Antioch University McGregor M
Arizona State University M
Ball State University M,D
Belmont University M
Bennington College M
Boise State University M
Boston University M,D
Bowling Green State University M,D
Brooklyn College of the City University of New York M
Brown University M

California State University, Fresno M
California State University, Long Beach M
California State University, Northridge M
California State University, Sacramento M
California State University, San Marcos M
Carlow University M
Carnegie Mellon University M
Central Michigan University M
Chapman University M
Chatham University M
Chicago State University M
City College of the City University of New York M
Claremont Graduate University M,D
Clemson University M
Cleveland State University M
Colorado State University M
Columbia College Chicago M
Columbia University M
Cornell University M,D
DePaul University M
Eastern Kentucky University M
Eastern Michigan University M
Eastern Washington University M
Emerson College M
Fairleigh Dickinson University, College at Florham M
Florida Atlantic University M
Florida International University M
Florida State University M,D
George Mason University M
Georgia College & State University M
Georgia State University M,D
Goddard College M
Hofstra University M
Hollins University M
Hunter College of the City University of New York M
Illinois State University M
Indiana University Bloomington M,D
Indiana University of Pennsylvania M,D
The Johns Hopkins University M
Kennesaw State University M
Kent State University M,D
Lesley University M
Lindenwood University M
Long Island University, Brooklyn Campus M
Longwood University M
Louisiana State University and Agricultural and Mechanical College M,D
Loyola Marymount University M
Manhattanville College M
Massachusetts Institute of Technology M
McNeese State University M
Miami University M,D
Michigan State University M,D
Mills College M
Minnesota State University Mankato M,O
Minnesota State University Moorhead M
Murray State University M
Naropa University M
National-Louis University M
National University M
New College of California M
New Mexico Highlands University M
New Mexico State University M,D
The New School: A University M
New York University M
North Carolina State University M
Northeastern Illinois University M
Northern Arizona University M
Northern Michigan University M
Northwestern University M
Oklahoma City University M
Oklahoma State University M,D
Old Dominion University M
Pacific Lutheran University M
Penn State University Park M,D
Purdue University M,D
Queens College of the City University of New York M
Queens University of Charlotte M
Rhode Island College M
Rivier College M
Roosevelt University M
Rowan University M
Rutgers, The State University of New Jersey, New Brunswick M
Saint Joseph's University M
Saint Mary's College of California M
Saint Xavier University M,O
Salisbury University M
San Diego State University M
San Francisco State University M
San Jose State University M,O
Sarah Lawrence College M
Seton Hill University M
Sonoma State University M
Southern Illinois University Carbondale M
Southern Illinois University Edwardsville M
Southern New Hampshire University M,O
Spalding University M
Syracuse University M,D
Temple University M
Texas State University-San Marcos M
Towson University M
Union Institute & University M
The University of Akron M
The University of Alabama M,D
University of Alaska Anchorage M
University of Alaska Fairbanks M
The University of Arizona M
University of Arkansas M
University of Arkansas at Little Rock M
University of Baltimore M
University of California, Davis M,D
University of California, Irvine M
University of California, Riverside M
University of California, Santa Cruz M
University of Central Florida M
University of Central Oklahoma M
University of Colorado at Boulder M,D
University of Florida M,D
University of Houston M,D
University of Idaho M
University of Illinois at Chicago M,D
The University of Iowa M,D
University of Kansas M,D
University of Louisiana at Lafayette M,D
University of Maryland, College Park M,D
University of Massachusetts Amherst M,D
University of Massachusetts Dartmouth M,O
University of Memphis M,D
University of Miami M,D
University of Michigan M
University of Missouri–St. Louis M,O
The University of Montana M
University of Nebraska at Kearney M
University of Nebraska at Omaha M,O
University of Nevada, Las Vegas M,D
University of New Hampshire M,D
University of New Mexico M
The University of North Carolina at Greensboro M
The University of North Carolina Wilmington M
University of North Florida M
University of Notre Dame M
University of Oklahoma M
University of Oregon M
University of Pennsylvania M,D
University of Pittsburgh M,D
University of San Francisco M
University of South Carolina M,D
University of Southern California M
University of Southern Maine M
The University of Texas at Austin M
The University of Texas at El Paso M
The University of Toledo M,O
University of Utah M
University of Virginia M
University of West Florida M
University of Wyoming M
Utah State University M
Vanderbilt University M
Virginia Commonwealth University M
Washington University in St. Louis M
Wayne State University M,D
Western Illinois University M
Western Kentucky University M
Western Michigan University M,D
Westminster College (UT) M
West Virginia University M
Wichita State University M
Wilkes University M
Wright State University M

■ ZOOLOGY

Auburn University M,D
Clemson University M,D
Colorado State University M,D
Cornell University P,M,D
Emporia State University M
Illinois State University M,D
Indiana University Bloomington M,D
Miami University M,D
Michigan State University M,D
Montana State University M,D
North Carolina State University M,D
North Dakota State University M,D
Oklahoma State University M,D
Oregon State University M,D
Southern Illinois University Carbondale M,D
Texas A&M University M,D
Texas Tech University M,D
University of Alaska Fairbanks M,D
University of California, Davis M
University of Chicago D
University of Connecticut M,D
University of Florida M,D
University of Hawaii at Manoa M,D
University of Illinois at Urbana–Champaign M,D
University of Maine M,D
The University of Montana M,D
University of New Hampshire M,D
University of North Dakota M,D
University of Oklahoma M,D
University of South Florida M,D
University of Washington D
University of Wisconsin–Madison M,D
University of Wisconsin–Oshkosh M
University of Wyoming M,D
Virginia Polytechnic Institute and State University M,D
Washington State University M,D
Western Illinois University M,O

Profiles of Institutions Offering Graduate and Professional Work

Alabama

■ ALABAMA AGRICULTURAL AND MECHANICAL UNIVERSITY

Huntsville, AL 35811

http://www.aamu.edu/

State-supported, coed, university. CGS member. *Enrollment:* 6,076 graduate, professional, and undergraduate students; 390 full-time matriculated graduate/professional students (295 women), 708 part-time matriculated graduate/professional students (496 women). *Graduate faculty:* 183. *Computer facilities:* 1,000 computers available on campus for general student use. A campuswide network can be accessed from student residence rooms and from off campus. Internet access is available. *Library facilities:* J. F. Drake Learning Resources Center. *General application contact:* Dr. Caula Beyl, Dean, School of Graduate Studies, 256-372-5266.

School of Graduate Studies
Dr. Caula Beyl, Dean, School of Graduate Studies

School of Agricultural and Environmental Sciences
Dr. James W. Shuford, Dean
Programs in:
- agribusiness (MS)
- agricultural and environmental sciences (MS, MURP, PhD)
- animal sciences (MS)
- environmental science (MS)
- family and consumer sciences (MS)
- food science (MS, PhD)
- plant and soil science (PhD)
- urban and regional planning (MURP)

School of Arts and Sciences
Dr. Jerry Shipman, Dean
Programs in:
- arts and sciences (MS, MSW, PhD)
- biology (MS)
- physics (MS, PhD)
- social work (MSW)

School of Business
Dr. Barbara A. P. Jones, Dean
Programs in:
- business (MBA, MS)
- economics and finance (MS)
- management and marketing (MBA)

School of Education
Dr. John Vickers, Interim Dean
Programs in:
- communicative disorders (M Ed, MS)
- early childhood education (MS Ed, Ed S)
- education (M Ed, Ed S)
- elementary and early childhood education (MS Ed, Ed S)
- elementary education (MS Ed, Ed S)
- health and physical education (M Ed, MS)
- higher administration (MS)
- music (MS)
- music education (M Ed, MS)
- physical education (M Ed, MS)
- psychology and counseling (MS, Ed S)
- secondary education (M Ed, MS, Ed S)
- special education (M Ed, MS)

School of Engineering and Technology
Dr. Arthur Bond, Dean
Programs in:
- computer science (MS)
- engineering and technology (M Ed, MS)
- industrial technology (M Ed, MS)

■ ALABAMA STATE UNIVERSITY

Montgomery, AL 36101-0271

http://www.alasu.edu/

State-supported, coed, comprehensive institution. *Enrollment:* 5,565 graduate, professional, and undergraduate students; 291 full-time matriculated graduate/professional students (184 women), 682 part-time matriculated graduate/professional students (512 women). *Graduate faculty:* 73 full-time (36 women), 56 part-time/adjunct (34 women). *Computer facilities:* Computer purchase and lease plans are available. 380 computers available on campus for general student use. A campuswide network can be accessed from off campus. Internet access and online class registration, e-mail are available. *Library facilities:* Levi Watkins Learning Center. *Graduate expenses:* Tuition, state resident: full-time $1,728; part-time $192 per hour. Tuition, nonresident: full-time $3,456; part-time $334 per hour. *General application contact:* Dr. Nathaniel Alan Sheppard, Dean of Graduate Studies, 334-229-4274.

School of Graduate Studies
Dr. Nathaniel Alan Sheppard, Dean of Graduate Studies
Programs in:
- instrumental music (M Ed)
- vocal/choral music (M Ed)

College of Arts and Sciences
Dr. Thelma Ivery, Dean
Programs in:
- arts and sciences (M Ed, MS, Ed S)
- biological sciences (MS)
- mathematics (M Ed, MS, Ed S)

College of Business Administration
Dr. Percy Vaughn, Dean
Programs in:
- accountancy (M Acc)
- business administration (M Acc)

College of Education
Dr. Katie Bell, Acting Dean
Programs in:
- biology education (M Ed, Ed S)
- early childhood education (M Ed, Ed S)
- education (M Ed, MS, Ed D, Ed S)
- educational administration (M Ed, Ed D, Ed S)
- educational leadership, policy and law (Ed D)
- elementary education (M Ed, Ed S)
- English/language arts (M Ed)
- general counseling (MS, Ed S)
- guidance and counseling (M Ed, MS, Ed S)
- health education (M Ed)
- history education (M Ed, Ed S)
- library education media (M Ed, Ed S)
- mathematics education (M Ed)
- physical education (M Ed)
- school counseling (M Ed, Ed S)
- secondary education (M Ed, Ed S)
- social studies (Ed S)
- special education (M Ed)

College of Health Sciences
Dr. Denise Chapman, Dean
Programs in:
- health sciences (DPT)
- physical therapy (DPT)

■ AUBURN UNIVERSITY

Auburn University, AL 36849

http://www.auburn.edu/

State-supported, coed, university. CGS member. *Enrollment:* 23,547 graduate, professional, and undergraduate students; 2,303 full-time matriculated graduate/professional students (1,219 women), 1,823 part-time matriculated graduate/professional students (911 women). *Graduate faculty:* 1,054 full-time (270 women), 3 part-time/adjunct (0 women). *Computer facilities:* 1,722 computers available on campus for general student use. A campuswide network can be accessed from student residence rooms and from off campus. Internet access and online class registration, online grades, pay Bursar online, course materials are available. *Library facilities:* R. B. Draughon Library plus 2 others. *Graduate expenses:* Tuition, state resident: full-time $5,000. Tuition, nonresident: full-time $15,000. Required fees: $416. Tuition and fees vary according to program. *General application contact:* Dr. Joe Pittman, Interim Dean of the Graduate School, 334-844-4700.

Find University Details at www.petersons.com/gradchannel.

College of Veterinary Medicine
Dr. Timothy R. Boosinger, Dean
Program in:
- veterinary medicine (DVM, MS, PhD)

Graduate Programs in Veterinary Medicine
Program in:
- biomedical sciences (MS, PhD)

Graduate School
Dr. Joe Pittman, Interim Dean of the Graduate School
Programs in:
- cell and molecular biology (PhD)
- integrated textile and apparel sciences (MS, PhD)
- rural sociology (MS)
- sociology (MA, MS)
- sociology, anthropology, criminology, and social work (MA, MS)
- textile science (MS)

College of Agriculture
Dr. Richard Guthrie, Dean
Programs in:
- agricultural economics (M Ag, MS)
- agriculture (M Ag, M Aq, MS, PhD)
- agronomy and soils (M Ag, MS, PhD)
- animal sciences (M Ag, MS, PhD)
- applied economics (PhD)
- entomology (M Ag, MS, PhD)
- fisheries and allied aquacultures (M Aq, MS, PhD)
- horticulture (M Ag, MS, PhD)
- plant pathology (M Ag, MS, PhD)
- poultry science (M Ag, MS, PhD)

College of Architecture, Design, and Construction
Dan D. Bennett, Dean
Programs in:
- architecture, design, and construction (MBS, MCP, MID, MLA)
- building science (MBS)
- community planning (MCP)
- construction management (MBS)
- industrial design (MID)
- landscape architecture (MLA)

College of Business
Dr. Paul M Bobrowski, Dean
Programs in:
- accountancy (M Acc)
- business (M Acc, MBA, MMIS, MS, PhD)
- business administration (MBA)
- economics (MS)
- finance (MS)
- human resource management (PhD)
- management (MS, PhD)
- management information systems (MMIS, PhD)

College of Education
Dr. Frances Kochan, Dean
Programs in:
- adult education (M Ed, MS, Ed D)
- business education (M Ed, MS, PhD)
- collaborative teacher special education (M Ed, MS)
- community agency counseling (M Ed, MS, Ed D, PhD, Ed S)
- counseling psychology (PhD)
- counselor education (Ed D, PhD)
- curriculum and instruction (M Ed, MS, Ed D, Ed S)
- curriculum supervision (M Ed, MS, Ed D, Ed S)
- early childhood education (M Ed, MS, PhD, Ed S)
- early childhood special education (M Ed, MS)
- education (M Ed, MS, Ed D, PhD, Ed S)
- educational psychology (PhD)
- elementary education (M Ed, MS, PhD, Ed S)
- exercise science (M Ed, MS, PhD)
- foreign languages (M Ed, MS)
- health promotion (M Ed, MS)
- higher education administration (M Ed, MS, Ed D, Ed S)
- media instructional design (MS)
- media specialist (M Ed)
- music education (M Ed, MS, PhD, Ed S)
- physical education/teacher education (M Ed, MS, Ed D, Ed S)
- postsecondary education (PhD)
- reading education (PhD, Ed S)
- rehabilitation counseling (M Ed, MS, PhD)
- school administration (M Ed, MS, Ed D, Ed S)
- school counseling (M Ed, MS, Ed D, PhD, Ed S)
- school psychometry (M Ed, MS, Ed D, PhD, Ed S)
- secondary education (M Ed, MS, PhD, Ed S)

College of Engineering
Dr. Larry Benefield, Dean
Programs in:
- aerospace engineering (MAE, MS, PhD)
- chemical engineering (M Ch E, MS, PhD)
- computer science and software engineering (MS, MSWE, PhD)
- construction engineering and management (MCE, MS, PhD)
- electrical and computer engineering (MEE, MS, PhD)
- engineering (M Ch E, M Mtl E, MAE, MCE, MEE, MISE, MME, MS, MSWE, PhD)
- environmental engineering (MCE, MS, PhD)
- geotechnical/materials engineering (MCE, MS, PhD)
- hydraulics/hydrology (MCE, MS, PhD)
- industrial and systems engineering (MISE, MS, PhD)
- materials engineering (M Mtl E, MS, PhD)
- mechanical engineering (MME, MS, PhD)
- structural engineering (MCE, MS, PhD)
- transportation engineering (MCE, MS, PhD)

College of Human Sciences
Dr. June Henton, Dean
Programs in:
- apparel and textiles (MS)
- human development and family studies (MS, PhD)
- human sciences (MS, PhD)
- nutrition and food science (MS, PhD)

College of Liberal Arts
Dr. Anne-Katrin Gramberg, Dean
Programs in:
- applied behavior analysis in developmental disabilities (MS)
- audiology (MCD, MS, Au D)
- clinical psychology (PhD)
- communication (MA)
- English (MA, MTPC, PhD)
- experimental psychology (PhD)
- history (MA, PhD)
- industrial/organizational psychology (PhD)
- liberal arts (MA, MCD, MFA, MHS, MPA, MS, MTPC, Au D, PhD)
- mass communications (MA)
- public administration (MPA, PhD)
- Spanish (MA, MHS)
- speech pathology (MCD, MS)

College of Sciences and Mathematics
Dr. Stewart W. Schneller, Dean
Programs in:
- analytical chemistry (MS, PhD)
- applied mathematics (MAM, MS)
- biochemistry (MS, PhD)
- botany (MS, PhD)
- geology (MS)
- inorganic chemistry (MS, PhD)
- mathematics (MS, PhD)
- microbiology (MS, PhD)
- organic chemistry (MS, PhD)
- physical chemistry (MS, PhD)
- physics (MS, PhD)
- probability and statistics (M Prob S)
- sciences and mathematics (M Prob S, MAM, MS, PhD)
- statistics (MS)
- zoology (MS, PhD)

School of Forestry and Wildlife Sciences
Richard W. Brinker, Dean
Programs in:
- forest economics (PhD)
- forestry (MS, PhD)
- natural resource conservation (MNR)
- wildlife sciences (MS, PhD)

School of Pharmacy
Dr. R. Lee Evans, Dean
Programs in:
- pharmacal sciences (MS, PhD)
- pharmaceutical sciences (PhD)
- pharmacy (Pharm D, MS, PhD)
- pharmacy care systems (MS, PhD)

■ AUBURN UNIVERSITY MONTGOMERY
Montgomery, AL 36124-4023
http://www.aum.edu/

State-supported, coed, comprehensive institution. *Enrollment:* 5,079 graduate, professional, and undergraduate students; 213 full-time matriculated graduate/professional students (156 women), 562 part-time matriculated graduate/professional students (404 women). *Graduate faculty:* 97 full-time (35 women), 7 part-time/adjunct (1

Auburn University Montgomery (continued)
woman). *Computer facilities:* 285 computers available on campus for general student use. A campuswide network can be accessed from student residence rooms and from off campus. Internet access and online class registration are available. *Library facilities:* Auburn University Montgomery Library. *General application contact:* Valerie Crawford, Associate Director of Enrollment Services, 334-244-3614.

School of Business
Dr. Jane Goodson, Dean
Program in:
business (MBA)

School of Education
Dr. Jennifer A. Brown, Dean
Programs in:
counseling (M Ed, Ed S)
early childhood education (M Ed, Ed S)
education (M Ed, Ed S)
education administration (M Ed, Ed S)
elementary education (M Ed, Ed S)
physical education (M Ed)
reading education (M Ed, Ed S)
secondary education (M Ed, Ed S)
special education (M Ed, Ed S)

School of Liberal Arts
Dr. Larry C. Mullins, Dean
Program in:
liberal arts (MLA)

School of Sciences
Dr. Bayo Lawal, Dean
Programs in:
justice and public safety (MSJPS)
psychology (MSPG)
public administration and political science (MPA, MPS, PhD)
sciences (MPA, MPS, MSJPS, MSPG, PhD)

■ JACKSONVILLE STATE UNIVERSITY
Jacksonville, AL 36265-1602
http://www.jsu.edu/

State-supported, coed, comprehensive institution. *Enrollment:* 8,957 graduate, professional, and undergraduate students; 365 full-time matriculated graduate/professional students (257 women), 1,281 part-time matriculated graduate/professional students (828 women). *Graduate faculty:* 109 full-time (69 women), 22 part-time/adjunct (15 women). *Computer facilities:* 330 computers available on campus for general student use. A campuswide network can be accessed from student residence rooms and from off campus. *Library facilities:* Houston Cole Library. *Graduate expenses:* Tuition, state resident: full-time $5,400; part-time $225 per credit hour. Tuition, nonresident: full-time $10,800; part-time $450 per credit hour. One-time fee: $20 full-time. *General application contact:* Dr. William D. Carr, Dean of the College of Graduate Studies and Continuing Education, 256-782-5329.

College of Graduate Studies and Continuing Education
Dr. William D. Carr, Dean
Program in:
liberal studies (MA)

College of Arts and Sciences
Dr. Earl Wade, Dean
Programs in:
arts and sciences (MA, MPA, MS)
biology (MS)
computer systems and software design (MS)
criminal justice (MS)
emergency management (MS)
English (MA)
history (MA)
mathematics (MS)
music (MA)
political science (MPA)
psychology (MS)

College of Commerce and Business Administration
Dr. William Fielding, Dean
Program in:
commerce and business administration (MBA)

College of Education and Professional Studies
Dr. Cynthia Harper, Dean
Programs in:
early childhood education (MS Ed)
education (Ed S)
education and professional studies (MS, MS Ed, Ed S)
educational administration (MS Ed, Ed S)
elementary education (MS Ed)
guidance and counseling (MS)
health and physical education (MS Ed)
instructional media (MS Ed)
reading specialist (MS Ed)
secondary education (MS Ed)
special education (MS Ed)

College of Nursing
Dr. Sarah Latham, Dean
Program in:
nursing (MSN)

■ SAMFORD UNIVERSITY
Birmingham, AL 35229-0002
http://www.samford.edu/

Independent-religious, coed, university. *Enrollment:* 4,478 graduate, professional, and undergraduate students; 1,295 full-time matriculated graduate/professional students (661 women), 301 part-time matriculated graduate/professional students (192 women). *Graduate faculty:* 128 full-time (45 women), 27 part-time/adjunct (10 women). *Computer facilities:* Computer purchase and lease plans are available. 350 computers available on campus for general student use. A campuswide network can be accessed from student residence rooms. Internet access is available. *Library facilities:* Samford University Library plus 3 others. *Graduate expenses:* Tuition: part-time $500 per credit. One-time fee: $25 part-time. Full-time tuition and fees vary according to program and student level. *General application contact:* Dr. Phil Kimrey, Dean of Admissions and Financial Aid, 205-726-2871.

Beeson School of Divinity
Dr. Timothy George, Dean
Program in:
divinity (M Div, MTS, D Min)

Cumberland School of Law
John L. Carroll, Dean
Program in:
law (JD, MCL)

Howard College of Arts and Sciences
Dr. David W. Chapman, Dean
Program in:
arts and sciences (MSEM)

Ida V. Moffett School of Nursing
Dr. Nena F. Sanders, Dean
Program in:
nursing (MSN, MSNA)

McWhorter School of Pharmacy
Dr. Bobby G. Bryant, Dean
Program in:
pharmacy (Pharm D)

School of Business
Dr. Beck Taylor, Dean
Program in:
business (M Acc, MBA)

School of Education
Dr. Jean Ann Box, Dean
Programs in:
early childhood education (Ed S)
early childhood/elementary education (MS Ed)
educational administration (Ed S)
educational leadership (Ed D)
elementary education (Ed S)
gifted education (MS Ed)

School of Performing Arts
Dr. Joseph H. Hopkins, Dean
Programs in:
church music (MM)
music education (MME)

■ SPRING HILL COLLEGE
Mobile, AL 36608-1791
http://www.shc.edu/

Independent-religious, coed, comprehensive institution. *Enrollment:* 1,446 graduate, professional, and undergraduate students; 23 full-time matriculated graduate/professional students (19 women), 169 part-time matriculated graduate/professional students (107 women). *Graduate faculty:* 16 full-time (7 women), 17 part-time/adjunct (10 women). *Computer facilities:* 194 computers available on campus for general student use. A campuswide network can be accessed from student residence rooms and from off campus. Internet access is available. *Library facilities:* Marnie and John Burke Memorial Library plus 1 other. *Graduate expenses:* Tuition: part-time $242 per credit hour. *General application contact:* Joyce Genz, Dean of Life Long Learning and Director of Graduate Programs, 251-380-3094.

Graduate Programs

Joyce Genz, Dean of Life Long Learning and Director of Graduate Programs
Programs in:
- business administration (MBA)
- clinical nurse leader (MSN)
- early childhood education (MAT, MS Ed)
- elementary education (MAT, MS Ed)
- liberal arts (MLA)
- secondary education (MAT, MS Ed)
- theology (MA, MPS, MTS)

■ TROY UNIVERSITY
Troy, AL 36082
http://www.troy.edu/

State-supported, coed, comprehensive institution. *Enrollment:* 27,938 graduate, professional, and undergraduate students; 2,748 full-time matriculated graduate/professional students (1,955 women), 5,121 part-time matriculated graduate/professional students (3,294 women). *Computer facilities:* 557 computers available on campus for general student use. A campuswide network can be accessed from student residence rooms and from off campus. Internet access is available. *Library facilities:* Wallace Library plus 3 others. *Graduate expenses:* Tuition, state resident: full-time $4,368; part-time $182 per hour. Tuition, nonresident: full-time $8,736; part-time $364 per hour. Required fees: $50 per term. *General application contact:* Brenda K. Campbell, Director of Graduate Admissions, 334-670-3178.

Graduate School

Dr. Dianne Barron, Associate Provost/ Dean of Graduate School
Programs in:
- business administration (EMBA, MBA)
- human resources management (MS)
- management (MS, MSM)

College of Arts and Sciences
Dr. Don Jeffrey, Interim Dean
Programs in:
- administration of criminal justice (MS)
- arts and sciences (MPA, MS)
- computer and information science (MS)
- environmental analysis and management (MS)
- international relations (MS)
- public administration (MPA)

College of Business
Dr. Don Hines, Dean
Programs in:
- business administration (EMBA, MBA)
- human resource management (MS)
- management (MS, MSM)

College of Communication and Fine Arts
Dr. Maryjo Cochran, Dean
Program in:
- communication and fine arts (MS)

College of Education
Dr. Lance Tatum, Interim Dean
Programs in:
- adult education (MS)
- clinical mental health (MS)
- community counseling (MS, Ed S)
- counselor education (MS)
- early childhood education (MS, MSE, Ed S)
- education (M Ed, ME, MS, MSE, Ed S)
- educational administration/leadership (MS, Ed S)
- guidance services (MS)
- K–6 elementary and collaborative education (MS, MSE, Ed S)
- postsecondary education (M Ed)
- rehabilitation counseling (Ed S)
- school counseling (Ed S)
- school psychology (MS)
- secondary education (MS, Ed S)
- student affairs counseling (MS)
- teacher education-multiple levels (MS, Ed S)

College of Health and Human Services
Dr. Edith Smith, Interim Dean
Programs in:
- health and human services (MS, MSN)
- nursing (MSN)
- sport and fitness management (MS)

■ THE UNIVERSITY OF ALABAMA
Tuscaloosa, AL 35487
http://www.ua.edu/

State-supported, coed, university. CGS member. *Enrollment:* 23,838 graduate, professional, and undergraduate students; 2,436 full-time matriculated graduate/professional students (1,250 women), 1,686 part-time matriculated graduate/professional students (1,053 women). *Graduate faculty:* 649 full-time (193 women), 4 part-time/adjunct (2 women). *Computer facilities:* 2,000 computers available on campus for general student use. A campuswide network can be accessed from student residence rooms and from off campus. Internet access and online class registration are available. *Library facilities:* Amelia Gayle Gorgas Library plus 8 others. *General application contact:* Louise F. Labosier, Admissions Officer, 205-348-5921.

Graduate School

Dr. Ronald W. Rogers, Dean

Capstone College of Nursing
Dr. Sara E. Barger, Dean
Program in:
- nursing (MSN)

College of Arts and Sciences
Dr. Robert F. Olin, Dean
Programs in:
- acting (MFA)
- American studies (MA)
- anthropology (MA, PhD)
- applied mathematics (PhD)
- art history (MA)
- arts and sciences (MA, MATESOL, MFA, MM, MPA, MS, DMA, PhD)
- biological sciences (MS, PhD)
- chemistry (MS, PhD)
- clinical psychology (PhD)
- communicative disorders (MS)
- composition (DMA)
- composition and rhetoric (PhD)
- costume design (MFA)
- creative writing (MFA)
- criminal justice (MS)
- directing (MFA)
- experimental psychology (PhD)
- French (MA, PhD)
- French and Spanish (PhD)
- geography (MS)
- geological sciences (MS, PhD)
- German (MA)
- history (MA, PhD)
- literature (MA, PhD)
- mathematics (MA, PhD)
- musicology (MM)
- performance (MM, DMA)
- physics (MS, PhD)
- political science (MA, PhD)
- public administration (MPA)
- pure mathematics (PhD)
- rhetoric and composition (MA)
- Romance languages (MA, PhD)
- scene design/technical production (MFA)
- Spanish (MA, PhD)
- stage management (MFA)
- studio art (MA, MFA)
- teaching English as a second language (MATESOL)
- theatre (MFA)
- theatre management/administration (MFA)
- theory (DMA)
- theory and composition (MM)
- women's studies (MA)

College of Communication and Information Sciences
Dr. Jennings Bryant, Associate Dean for Graduate Studies
Programs in:
- advertising and public relations (MA)
- book arts (MFA)
- communication and information sciences (MA, MFA, MLIS, PhD)
- communication studies (MA)
- journalism (MA)
- library and information studies (MLIS, PhD)
- telecommunication and film (MA)

The University of Alabama (continued)

College of Education
Dr. James E. McLean, Dean
Programs in:
- alternative sport pedagogy (MA)
- choral music education (MA)
- collaborative teacher program (M Ed, Ed S)
- curriculum and instruction (MA, Ed D, PhD, Ed S)
- early intervention (M Ed, Ed S)
- education (M Ed, MA, Ed D, PhD, Ed S)
- educational administration (Ed D, PhD)
- educational leadership (MA, Ed S)
- educational studies in psychology, research methodology and counseling (MA, Ed D, PhD, Ed S)
- exercise science (MA, PhD)
- gifted education (M Ed, Ed S)
- higher education administration (MA, Ed D, PhD)
- human performance (MA)
- instructional leadership (Ed D, PhD)
- instrumental music education (MA)
- multiple abilities program (M Ed)
- music education (Ed D, PhD, Ed S)
- special education (Ed D, PhD)
- sport management (MA)
- sport pedagogy (MA, PhD)

College of Engineering
Dr. Charles Karr, Dean
Programs in:
- aerospace engineering (MAE)
- chemical and biological engineering (MS Ch E, PhD)
- civil engineering (MSCE, PhD)
- computer science (MS, PhD)
- electrical engineering (MS, PhD)
- engineering (MAE, MES, MS, MS Ch E, MS Met E, MSCE, MSE, MSIE, PhD)
- engineering science and mechanics (MES, PhD)
- environmental engineering (MS)
- industrial engineering (MSE, MSIE)
- materials science (PhD)
- mechanical engineering (MS, PhD)
- metallurgical and materials engineering (MS Met E, PhD)

College of Human Environmental Sciences
Dr. Milla D. Boschung, Dean
Programs in:
- clothing, textiles, and interior design (MSHES)
- consumer sciences (MS)
- health education and promotion (PhD)
- health studies (MA)
- human development and family studies (MSHES)
- human environmental sciences (MA, MS, MSHES, PhD)
- human nutrition and hospitality management (MSHES)

Manderson Graduate School of Business
Dr. J. Barry Mason, Dean
Programs in:
- accounting (M Acc, MA, PhD)
- applied statistics (MS, PhD)
- business (Exec MBA, M Acc, MA, MBA, MS, MSC, MTA, PhD)
- economics (MA, PhD)
- finance (MS, PhD)
- general commerce and business (MBA)
- information systems, statistics, and management science—applied statistics (MS, PhD)
- information systems, statistics, and management science—operations management (MS, PhD)
- management (MA, MS, PhD)
- marketing (MS, PhD)
- operations management (MS, PhD)
- statistics (MS)
- tax accounting (MA, MTA)

School of Social Work
Dr. James P. Adams, Dean
Program in:
- social work (MSW, PhD)

School of Law
Kenneth C. Randall, Dean
Program in:
- law (JD, LL M, LL M in Tax)

■ THE UNIVERSITY OF ALABAMA AT BIRMINGHAM
Birmingham, AL 35294
http://main.uab.edu/

State-supported, coed, university. CGS member. *Enrollment:* 16,561 graduate, professional, and undergraduate students; 3,243 full-time matriculated graduate/professional students (1,762 women), 1,504 part-time matriculated graduate/professional students (1,003 women). *Computer facilities:* 400 computers available on campus for general student use. A campuswide network can be accessed from student residence rooms and from off campus. Internet access and online class registration are available. *Library facilities:* Mervyn Sterne Library plus 1 other. *Graduate expenses:* Tuition, state resident: part-time $170 per credit hour. Tuition, nonresident: part-time $425 per credit hour. Required fees: $15 per credit hour. $122 per term. Tuition and fees vary according to program. *General application contact:* Julie Bryant, Director of Graduate Admissions, 205-934-8227.

Find University Details at www.petersons.com/gradchannel.

Graduate Programs in Joint Health Sciences
Dr. Robert R. Rich, Vice President/Dean, School of Medicine
Programs in:
- basic medical sciences (MSBMS)
- biochemistry (PhD)
- biochemistry and molecular genetics (PhD)
- biophysical sciences (PhD)
- cell biology (PhD)
- cellular and molecular biology (PhD)
- cellular and molecular physiology (PhD)
- genetics (PhD)
- integrative biomedical sciences (PhD)
- microbiology (PhD)
- neurobiology (PhD)
- neuroscience (PhD)
- pathology (PhD)
- pharmacology (PhD)
- pharmacology and toxicology (PhD)
- physiology and biophysics (MSBMS, PhD)
- toxicology (PhD)

School of Arts and Humanities
Bert Brouwer, Dean
Programs in:
- art history (MA)
- arts and humanities (MA)
- communication studies (MA)
- English (MA)

School of Business
Dr. Robert E. Holmes, Dean
Program in:
- business (M Acct, MBA, PhD)

School of Dentistry
Dr. Huw F. Thomas, Dean
Programs in:
- dentistry (DMD, MS, MSBMS, PhD)
- dentistry and oral biology (MS)

School of Education
Dr. Michael J. Froning, Dean
Programs in:
- agency counseling (MA)
- arts education (MA Ed)
- counseling and school psychology (MA, MA Ed)
- early childhood education (MA Ed, PhD)
- education (Ed S)
- educational leadership (MA Ed, Ed D, PhD, Ed S)
- elementary education (MA Ed)
- health education (MA Ed)
- health education/health promotion (PhD)
- high school education (MA Ed)
- marriage and family counseling (MA)
- physical education (MA Ed)
- rehabilitation counseling (MA)
- school counseling (MA)
- school psychology (MA Ed)
- special education (MA Ed)

School of Engineering
Dr. Linda C. Lucas, Dean
Programs in:
- biomedical engineering (MSBME, PhD)
- civil engineering (MSCE, PhD)
- computer engineering (PhD)
- electrical engineering (MSEE)

engineering (MS Mt E, MSBME, MSCE, MSEE, MSME, PhD)
environmental health engineering (MSCE)
materials engineering (MS Mt E, PhD)
materials science (PhD)
mechanical engineering (MSME, PhD)

School of Health Professions
Dr. Harold P. Jones, Dean
Programs in:
administration-health services (PhD)
clinical laboratory science (MS)
clinical nutrition (MS)
clinical nutrition and dietetics (MS, Certificate)
dietetic internship (Certificate)
health administration (MSHA)
health informatics (MS)
health professions (MNA, MS, MSHA, DPT, Dr Sc PT, PhD, Certificate)
low vision rehabilitation (Certificate)
nurse anesthesia (MNA)
nutrition sciences (PhD)
occupational therapy (MS)
physical therapy (DPT, Dr Sc PT)
physician assistant (MS)

School of Medicine
Dr. Robert R. Rich, Vice President/Dean, School of Medicine
Program in:
medicine (MD, MSBMS, PhD)

School of Natural Sciences and Mathematics
Dr. Lowell E. Wenger, Dean
Programs in:
applied mathematics (PhD)
biology (MS, PhD)
chemistry (MS, PhD)
computer and information sciences (MS, PhD)
mathematics (MS)
natural sciences and mathematics (MS, PhD)
physics (MS, PhD)

School of Nursing
Dr. Doreen C. Harper, Dean
Program in:
nursing (MSN, PhD)

School of Optometry
Dr. John F. Amos, Dean
Programs in:
optometry (OD, MS, PhD)
vision science (MS, PhD)

School of Public Health
Dr. Max Michael, Dean
Programs in:
biomathematics (MS, PhD)
biostatistics (MS, PhD)
environmental health (PhD)
environmental toxicology (PhD)
epidemiology (PhD)
health care organization and policy (MPH, MSPH)
health education promotion (PhD)
industrial hygiene (PhD)
maternal and child health (MSPH)
public health (MPH, MS, MSPH, DPH, PhD)

School of Social and Behavioral Sciences
Dr. Tennant S. McWilliams, Dean
Programs in:
anthropology (MA)
behavioral neuroscience (PhD)
clinical psychology (PhD)
criminal justice (MSCJ)
developmental psychology (PhD)
forensic science (MSFS)
history (MA)
medical psychology (PhD)
medical sociology (PhD)
psychology (MA, PhD)
public administration (MPA)
social and behavioral sciences (MA, MPA, MSCJ, MSFS, PhD)
sociology (MA)

■ THE UNIVERSITY OF ALABAMA IN HUNTSVILLE
Huntsville, AL 35899
http://www.uah.edu/

State-supported, coed, university. CGS member. *Enrollment:* 7,091 graduate, professional, and undergraduate students; 470 full-time matriculated graduate/professional students (209 women), 777 part-time matriculated graduate/professional students (288 women). *Graduate faculty:* 185 full-time (42 women), 41 part-time/adjunct (12 women). *Computer facilities:* 1,091 computers available on campus for general student use. A campuswide network can be accessed from student residence rooms and from off campus. Internet access and online class registration are available. *Library facilities:* University of Alabama in Huntsville Library. *Graduate expenses:* Tuition, state resident: full-time $6,072; part-time $253 per credit hour. Tuition, nonresident: full-time $12,476; part-time $519 per credit hour. *General application contact:* Dr. Debra Moriarity, Dean of Graduate Studies, 256-824-6002.

School of Graduate Studies
Dr. Debra Moriarity, Dean of Graduate Studies
Programs in:
information assurance (Certificate)
optical science and engineering (PhD)

College of Administrative Science
Dr. C. David Billings, Dean
Programs in:
accounting (M Acc, Certificate)
administrative science (M Acc, MS, MSM, MSMIS, Certificate)
human resource management (Certificate)
management (MS, MSM)
management information systems (MSMIS, Certificate)

College of Engineering
Dr. Jorge Aunon, Dean
Programs in:
aerospace engineering (MSE)
biotechnology science and engineering (PhD)
chemical engineering (MSE)
civil and environmental engineering (MSE, PhD)
computer engineering (PhD)
electrical and computer engineering (MSE)
electrical engineering (PhD)
engineering (MSE, MSOR, MSSE, PhD)
industrial engineering (MSE, PhD)
mechanical engineering (MSE, PhD)
operations research (MSOR)
optical science and engineering (PhD)
software engineering (MSE, MSSE)

College of Liberal Arts
Dr. Sue Kirkpatrick, Dean
Programs in:
English (MA)
history (MA)
liberal arts (MA, Certificate)
psychology (MA)
public affairs (MA)
teaching of English to speakers of other languages (Certificate)
technical communications (Certificate)

College of Nursing
Dr. Fay Raines, Dean
Programs in:
family nurse practitioner (Certificate)
nursing (MSN)

College of Science
Dr. Jack Fix, Dean
Programs in:
applied mathematics (PhD)
atmospheric and environmental science (MS, PhD)
biological sciences (MS)
biotechnology science and engineering (PhD)
chemistry (MS)
computer science (MS, PhD)
materials science (MS, PhD)
mathematics (MA, MS)
physics (MS, PhD)
science (MA, MS, MSSE, PhD, Certificate)
software engineering (MSSE, Certificate)

■ UNIVERSITY OF MOBILE
Mobile, AL 36613
http://www.umobile.edu/

Independent-religious, coed, comprehensive institution. *Enrollment:* 1,639 graduate, professional, and undergraduate students; 62 full-time matriculated graduate/professional students (54 women), 132 part-time

University of Mobile (continued)
matriculated graduate/professional students (105 women). *Graduate faculty:* 28 full-time (15 women), 36 part-time/adjunct (17 women). *Computer facilities:* 110 computers available on campus for general student use. A campuswide network can be accessed from off campus. Internet access is available. *Library facilities:* J. L. Bedsole Library. *Graduate expenses:* Tuition: part-time $340 per hour. Required fees: $121 per term. Tuition and fees vary according to course load. *General application contact:* Dr. Kaye F. Brown, Associate Vice President for Academic Affairs, 251-442-2289.

Graduate Programs
Dr. Kaye F. Brown, Dean
Programs in:
- biblical/theological studies (MA)
- business administration (MBA)
- education (MA)
- marriage and family counseling (MA)
- nursing (MSN)
- religious studies (MA)

■ UNIVERSITY OF MONTEVALLO
Montevallo, AL 35115
http://www.montevallo.edu/

State-supported, coed, comprehensive institution. *Computer facilities:* 250 computers available on campus for general student use. A campuswide network can be accessed from student residence rooms and from off campus. Internet access and online class registration are available. *Library facilities:* Carmichael Library. *General application contact:* Coordinator for Graduate Studies, 205-665-6350.

College of Arts and Sciences
Programs in:
- arts and sciences (MA, MS)
- English (MA)
- speech pathology and audiology (MS)

College of Education
Programs in:
- early childhood education (M Ed)
- education (M Ed, Ed S)
- educational administration (M Ed, Ed S)
- elementary education (M Ed)
- guidance and counseling (M Ed)
- secondary education (M Ed)
- teacher leader (Ed S)

College of Fine Arts
Programs in:
- fine arts (MM)
- music (MM)

■ UNIVERSITY OF NORTH ALABAMA
Florence, AL 35632-0001
http://www.una.edu/

State-supported, coed, comprehensive institution. *Enrollment:* 6,810 graduate, professional, and undergraduate students; 349 full-time matriculated graduate/professional students (182 women), 721 part-time matriculated graduate/professional students (440 women). *Graduate faculty:* 7 full-time (3 women), 69 part-time/adjunct (26 women). *Computer facilities:* 750 computers available on campus for general student use. A campuswide network can be accessed from student residence rooms and from off campus. Internet access and online class registration are available. *Library facilities:* Collier Library. *Graduate expenses:* Tuition, state resident: full-time $4,080. Tuition, nonresident: full-time $8,160. Required fees: $764. *General application contact:* Kim Mauldin, Director of Admissions, 256-765-4608.

College of Arts and Sciences
Dr. Vagn Hansen, Dean
Programs in:
- arts and sciences (MAEN, MSCJ)
- criminal justice (MSCJ)
- English (MAEN)

College of Business
Dr. Kerry Gatlin, Dean
Program in:
- business (MBA)

College of Education
Dr. Donna Jacobs, Dean
Programs in:
- counseling (MA, MA Ed)
- education (MA, MA Ed, Ed S)
- education leadership (Ed S)
- elementary education (MA Ed, Ed S)
- learning disabilities (MA Ed)
- mentally retarded (MA Ed)
- mild learning handicapped (MA Ed)
- non-school-based counseling (MA)
- non-school-based teaching (MA)
- principalship (MA Ed)
- principalship, superintendency, and supervision of instruction (MA Ed)
- secondary education (MA Ed)
- special education (MA Ed)
- superintendency (MA Ed)
- supervision of instruction (MA Ed)

College of Nursing
Dr. Birdie Bailey, Dean
Program in:
- nursing (MSN)

■ UNIVERSITY OF SOUTH ALABAMA
Mobile, AL 36688-0002
http://www.usouthal.edu/

State-supported, coed, university. CGS member. *Enrollment:* 13,090 graduate, professional, and undergraduate students; 2,270 full-time matriculated graduate/professional students (1,583 women), 742 part-time matriculated graduate/professional students (560 women). *Graduate faculty:* 492 full-time (150 women), 41 part-time/adjunct (20 women). *Computer facilities:* 500 computers available on campus for general student use. A campuswide network can be accessed from student residence rooms and from off campus. Internet access and online class registration are available. *Library facilities:* University Library plus 1 other. *General application contact:* Dr. B. Keith Harrison, Interim Dean of the Graduate School, 251-460-6310.

Find University Details at www.petersons.com/gradchannel.

College of Medicine
Dr. Samuel J Strada, Interim Dean
Programs in:
- biochemistry and molecular biology (PhD)
- cell biology and neuroscience (PhD)
- medicine (MD, PhD)
- microbiology and immunology (PhD)
- pharmacology (PhD)
- physiology (PhD)

Graduate School
Dr. B. Keith Harrison, Interim Dean of the Graduate School
Programs in:
- environmental toxicology (MS)
- pharmacy (Pharm D)

College of Allied Health Professions
Dr. Richard Talbot, Dean
Programs in:
- allied health professions (MHS, MS, Au D, DPT, PhD)
- audiology (Au D)
- communication sciences and disorders (PhD)
- occupational therapy (MS)
- physical therapy (DPT, PhD)
- physician assistant studies (MHS)
- speech and hearing sciences (MS)

College of Arts and Sciences
Dr. G. David Johnson, Dean
Programs in:
- arts and sciences (MA, MPA, MS, PhD, Certificate)
- biological sciences (MS)
- communication (MA)
- English (MA)
- gerontology (Certificate)
- history (MA)
- marine sciences (MS, PhD)
- mathematics (MS)
- psychology (MS)
- public administration (MPA)
- sociology (MA)

College of Education
Dr. Richard L Hayes, Dean
Programs in:
- community counseling (MS)
- early childhood education (M Ed)
- education (M Ed, MS, PhD, Ed S)
- educational administration (Ed S)
- educational leadership (M Ed)
- educational media (M Ed, MS)
- elementary education (M Ed)

exercise science (MS)
health education (M Ed)
instructional design and development (MS, PhD)
physical education (M Ed)
reading education (M Ed)
rehabilitation counseling (MS)
school counseling (M Ed)
school psychometry (M Ed)
science education (M Ed)
secondary education (M Ed)
special education (M Ed, Ed S)
therapeutic recreation (MS)

College of Engineering
Dr. John W. Steadman, Dean
Programs in:
chemical engineering (MS Ch E)
electrical engineering (MSEE)
engineering (MS Ch E, MSEE, MSME)
mechanical engineering (MSME)

College of Nursing
Dr. Debra C. Davis, Dean
Programs in:
adult health nursing (MSN)
community/mental health nursing (MSN)
maternal/child nursing (MSN)
nursing (DSN)

Mitchell College of Business
Dr. Carl Moore, Dean
Programs in:
accounting (M Acct)
business (M Acct, MBA)
general management (MBA)

School of Computer and Information Sciences
Dr. David Feinstein, Dean
Programs in:
computer science (MS)
information systems (MS)

■ THE UNIVERSITY OF WEST ALABAMA
Livingston, AL 35470
http://www.uwa.edu/

State-supported, coed, comprehensive institution. *Enrollment:* 3,633 graduate, professional, and undergraduate students; 758 full-time matriculated graduate/professional students (636 women), 1,002 part-time matriculated graduate/professional students (855 women). *Graduate faculty:* 24 full-time (6 women), 7 part-time/adjunct (2 women). *Computer facilities:* 400 computers available on campus for general student use. A campuswide network can be accessed from student residence rooms and from off campus. Internet access is available. *Library facilities:* Julia Tutwiler Library. *General application contact:* Dr. Tom DeVaney, Dean of Graduate Studies, 205-652-3647 Ext. 421.

School of Graduate Studies
Dr. Tom DeVaney, Dean of Graduate Studies

College of Education
Dr. Martha Hocutt, Dean, College of Education
Programs in:
continuing education (MSCE)
early childhood education (M Ed)
education (M Ed, MAT, MSCE)
elementary education (M Ed)
guidance and counseling (M Ed, MSCE)
library media (M Ed)
physical education (M Ed, MAT)
school administration (M Ed)
secondary education (MAT)
special education (M Ed)

College of Liberal Arts
Dr. Michael Cook, Dean, College of Liberal Arts
Programs in:
history (MAT)
language arts (MAT)
liberal arts (MAT)
social science (MAT)

College of Natural Sciences and Mathematics
Dr. Judy Massey, Dean
Programs in:
biological sciences (MAT)
mathematics (MAT)
natural sciences and mathematics (MAT)

Alaska

■ ALASKA PACIFIC UNIVERSITY
Anchorage, AK 99508-4672
http://www.alaskapacific.edu/

Independent, coed, comprehensive institution. *Enrollment:* 733 graduate, professional, and undergraduate students; 74 full-time matriculated graduate/professional students (55 women), 99 part-time matriculated graduate/professional students (56 women). *Graduate faculty:* 21 full-time (11 women), 9 part-time/adjunct (3 women). *Computer facilities:* 40 computers available on campus for general student use. A campuswide network can be accessed from student residence rooms. Internet access is available. *Library facilities:* Consortium Library. *Graduate expenses:* Tuition: part-time $550 per credit hour. Required fees: $100 per semester. Tuition and fees vary according to program. *General application contact:* Michael Warner, Director of Admissions, 907-564-8248.

Graduate Programs
Dr. Marilyn Barry, Academic Dean
Programs in:
business administration (MBA)
counseling psychology (MSCP)
environmental science (MSES)
global finance (MBA)
health services administration (MBA)
information and communication technology (MBAICT, MBATM)
outdoor and environmental education (MSOEE)
self-designed study (MA)
teaching (MAT)
teaching (K-8) (MAT)

■ UNIVERSITY OF ALASKA ANCHORAGE
Anchorage, AK 99508-8060
http://www.uaa.alaska.edu/

State-supported, coed, comprehensive institution. CGS member. *Enrollment:* 17,023 graduate, professional, and undergraduate students; 242 full-time matriculated graduate/professional students (170 women), 490 part-time matriculated graduate/professional students (327 women). *Computer facilities:* 500 computers available on campus for general student use. A campuswide network can be accessed from student residence rooms and from off campus. Internet access is available. *Library facilities:* Consortium Library. *Graduate expenses:* Tuition, state resident: part-time $268 per credit. Tuition, nonresident: part-time $547 per credit. Required fees: $124 per semester. Tuition and fees vary according to reciprocity agreements and student level. *General application contact:* Elisa S. Mattison, Coordinator for Graduate Studies, 907-786-1096.

College of Arts and Sciences
Dr. James Liszka, Dean
Programs in:
anthropology (MA)
arts and sciences (MA, MFA, MS, PhD)
biological sciences (MS)
clinical psychology (MS)
clinical-community psychology with rural-indigenous emphasis (PhD)
creative writing and literary arts (MFA)
English (MA)
interdisciplinary studies (MA, MS)

College of Business and Public Policy
Gen. Tom Case, Dean
Programs in:
business administration (MBA)
business and public policy (MBA, MPA, MS, Certificate)
global supply chain management (MS)
public administration (MPA)
supply chain management (Certificate)

College of Education
Dr. Mary Snyder, Dean
Programs in:
adult education (M Ed)
counseling and guidance (M Ed)

University of Alaska Anchorage (continued)
early childhood special education (M Ed)
education (M Ed, MAT, Certificate)
educational leadership (M Ed)
master teacher (M Ed)
principal licensure (Certificate)
special education (M Ed, Certificate)
superintendent (Certificate)
teaching (MAT)

College of Health and Social Welfare
Dr. Cheryl Easley, Dean
Program in:
health and social welfare (MPH, MS, MSW, Certificate)

Division of Health Sciences
Dr. Rhonda Johnson, Chair
Program in:
public health practice (MPH)

School of Nursing
Dr. Jean Ballantyne, Director
Programs in:
family nurse practitioner (Certificate)
nursing (MS)
nursing education (Certificate)
psychiatric nurse practitioner (Certificate)

School of Social Work
Dr. Elizabeth Sirles, Director
Programs in:
clinical social work practice (Certificate)
social work (MSW)
social work management (Certificate)

School of Engineering
Dr. Robert Lang, Director
Programs in:
applied environmental science and technology (M AEST, MS)
arctic engineering (MS)
civil engineering (MCE, MS)
engineering (M AEST, MCE, MS, Certificate)
engineering management (MS)
port and coastal engineering (Certificate)
project management (MS)
science management (MS)

■ UNIVERSITY OF ALASKA FAIRBANKS

Fairbanks, AK 99775-7520

http://www.uaf.edu/

State-supported, coed, university. CGS member. *Enrollment:* 8,341 graduate, professional, and undergraduate students; 600 full-time matriculated graduate/professional students (295 women), 426 part-time matriculated graduate/professional students (251 women). *Graduate faculty:* 491 full-time (167 women), 13 part-time/adjunct (7 women). *Computer facilities:* Computer purchase and lease plans are available. 56 computers available on campus for general student use. A campuswide network can be accessed from student residence rooms and from off campus. Internet access and online class registration, university portal are available. *Library facilities:* Rasmuson Library plus 1 other. *General application contact:* Nancy D. Dix, Director of Admissions, 907-474-7500.

College of Engineering and Mines
Dr. Douglas J. Goering, Acting Dean
Programs in:
arctic engineering (MS)
civil engineering (MCE, MS)
electrical engineering (MEE, MS)
engineering (PhD)
engineering and mines (MCE, MEE, MS, PhD, EM)
engineering and science management (MS)
environmental engineering (MS)
environmental quality science (MS)
geological engineering (MS, EM)
mechanical engineering (MS)
mineral preparation engineering (MS)
mining engineering (MS, EM)
petroleum engineering (MS)

College of Liberal Arts
Phyliss Morrow, Dean
Programs in:
Alaskan ethnomusicology (MA)
anthropology (MA, PhD)
applied linguistics (MA)
art (MFA)
clinical-community psychology (PhD)
creative writing (MFA)
criminal justice management and administration (MA)
cross cultural studies (MA)
English (MA)
liberal arts (MA, MFA, PhD)
music education (MA)
music history (MA)
music theory (MA)
northern studies (MA)
performance (MA)
professional communications (MA)

College of Natural Sciences and Mathematics
Dr. Joan Braddock, Dean
Programs in:
atmospheric science (MS, PhD)
biochemistry and molecular biology (MS, PhD)
biological sciences (MS, PhD)
biology (MAT)
chemistry (MA, MS)
computational physics (MS, PhD)
computer science (MS)
environmental chemistry (MS, PhD)
general physics (MS)
geology (MS, PhD)
geophysics (MS, PhD)
mathematics (MAT, MS, PhD)
natural sciences and mathematics (MA, MAT, MS, MSE, PhD)
physics (MAT, PhD)
software engineering (MSE)
space physics (MS, PhD)
statistics (MS)
wildlife biology (MS, PhD)

College of Rural and Community Development
Dr. Bernice M. Joseph, Vice Chancellor
Programs in:
Alaska native and rural development (MA)
rural and community development (MA)

Graduate School for Interdisciplinary Studies
Dr. Susan M. Henrichs, Vice Provost
Program in:
interdisciplinary studies (MA, MS, PhD)

School of Education
Dr. Eric C. Madsen, Dean
Programs in:
cross cultural education (M Ed)
curriculum instruction (M Ed)
education (M Ed)
guidance and counseling (M Ed)
k-12 reading (M Ed)
language and literacy (M Ed)

School of Fisheries and Ocean Sciences
Dr. Denis Wiesenberg, Dean
Programs in:
fisheries (MS, PhD)
fisheries and ocean sciences (MS, PhD)
marine biology (MS, PhD)
oceanography (MS, PhD)

School of Management
Dr. Maurice Marr, Dean
Programs in:
capital markets (MBA)
general management (MBA)
management (MBA, MS)
resource economics and applied economics (MS)

School of Natural Resources and Agricultural Sciences
Dr. Carol E. Lewis, Dean
Programs in:
natural resources and agricultural sciences (MS)
nature resource management (MS)

■ UNIVERSITY OF ALASKA SOUTHEAST

Juneau, AK 99801

http://www.uas.alaska.edu/

State-supported, coed, comprehensive institution. *Enrollment:* 2,965 graduate, professional, and undergraduate students; 93 full-time matriculated graduate/professional students (58 women), 174 part-time matriculated graduate/professional students (128 women). *Graduate faculty:* 17 full-time

(9 women), 6 part-time/adjunct (5 women). *Computer facilities:* 75 computers available on campus for general student use. A campuswide network can be accessed from student residence rooms and from off campus. Internet access and online class registration are available. *Library facilities:* Egan Memorial Library plus 1 other. *General application contact:* Susan A. Stuck, Administrative Assistant, 866-465-6424.

Graduate Programs
Dr. Roberta Stell, Provost
Programs in:
- business administration (MBA)
- early childhood education (M Ed, MAT)
- educational technology (M Ed)
- elementary education (MAT)
- public administration (MPA)
- reading (M Ed)
- secondary education (MAT)

Arizona

■ ARIZONA STATE UNIVERSITY
Tempe, AZ 85287
http://www.asu.edu/

State-supported, coed, university. CGS member. *Computer facilities:* Computer purchase and lease plans are available. 5,000 computers available on campus for general student use. A campuswide network can be accessed from student residence rooms and from off campus. Internet access and online class registration are available. *Library facilities:* Hayden Library plus 5 others. *General application contact:* Graduate Admissions, 480-965-6113.

College of Law
Program in:
- law (JD)

Division of Graduate Studies
Programs in:
- science and engineering of materials (MS, PhD)
- statistics (MS)
- transportation systems (Certificate)

College of Architecture and Environmental Design
Programs in:
- architecture (M Arch)
- architecture and environmental design (M Arch, MEP, MS, MSD, PhD)
- building design (MS)
- design (MSD, PhD)
- history, theory, and criticism (PhD)
- planning (MEP, PhD)

College of Education
Programs in:
- counseling (M Ed, MC)
- counseling psychology (PhD)
- curriculum and instruction (M Ed, MA, Ed D, PhD)
- education (M Ed, MA, MC, Ed D, PhD)
- educational administration and supervision (M Ed, Ed D)
- educational leadership and policy studies (M Ed, MA, Ed D, PhD)
- educational psychology (M Ed, MA, PhD)
- higher and post-secondary education (M Ed, Ed D)
- learning and instructional technology (M Ed, MA, PhD)
- psychology in education (M Ed, MA, MC, PhD)
- social and philosophical foundations of education (MA)
- special education (M Ed, MA)

College of Fine Arts
Programs in:
- art (MA, MFA)
- dance (MFA)
- fine arts (MA, MFA, MM, DMA, PhD)
- music (MA, MM, DMA)
- theater (MA, MFA, PhD)

College of Liberal Arts and Sciences
Programs in:
- anthropology (MA, PhD)
- applied mathematics (MA, PhD)
- Asian history (MA, PhD)
- audiology (Au D)
- behavior (MS, PhD)
- behavioral neuroscience (PhD)
- biology (MNS)
- biology education (MS, PhD)
- British history (MA, PhD)
- cell and developmental biology (MS, PhD)
- chemistry and biochemistry (MNS, MS, PhD)
- clinical psychology (PhD)
- cognitive/behavioral systems (PhD)
- communication (PhD)
- communication disorders (MS)
- computational biosciences (MS, PSM)
- computational, statistical, and mathematical biology (MS, PhD)
- conservation (MS, PhD)
- creative writing (MFA)
- demography and population studies (MA, PhD)
- developmental psychology (PhD)
- ecology (MS, PhD)
- English (MA, PhD)
- environmental psychology (PhD)
- European history (MA, PhD)
- evolution (MS, PhD)
- exercise science (PhD)
- family and human development (MS)
- family science (PhD)
- French (MA)
- genetics (MS, PhD)
- geography (MA, MAS, PhD)
- geological engineering (MS, PhD)
- German (MA)
- history and philosophy of biology (MS, PhD)
- humanities (MA, MFA, MTESL, PhD)
- justice and social inquiry (MS, PhD)
- kinesiology (MS, PhD)
- Latin American studies (MA, PhD)
- liberal arts and sciences (MA, MAS, MFA, MNS, MPE, MS, MTESL, PSM, Au D, PhD)
- mathematics (MA, MNS, PhD)
- microbiology (MNS, MS, PhD)
- molecular and cellular biology (MS, PhD)
- natural science (MNS)
- natural sciences and mathematics (MA, MNS, MS, PSM, Au D, PhD)
- neuroscience (MS, PhD)
- philosophy (MA, PhD)
- physics and astronomy (MNS, MS, PhD)
- physiology (MS, PhD)
- political science (MA, PhD)
- public history (MA)
- quantitative research methods (PhD)
- religious studies (MA, PhD)
- social psychology (PhD)
- social sciences (MA, MAS, MS, PhD)
- sociology (MA, PhD)
- Spanish (MA, PhD)
- speech and hearing science (MS, Au D, PhD)
- speech and interpersonal communication (MA)
- statistics (MA, PhD)
- teaching English as a second language (MTESL)
- U.S. history (PhD)
- U.S. western history (MA)

College of Nursing
Program in:
- nursing (MS)

College of Public Programs
Programs in:
- journalism and mass communication (MMC)
- public affairs (MPA, PhD)
- public programs (MA, MMC, MPA, MS, MSW, PhD)
- recreation (MS)
- social work (MSW, PhD)

The Ira A. Fulton School of Engineering
Programs in:
- aerospace engineering (MS, MSE, PhD)
- bioengineering (MS, PhD)
- chemical engineering (MS, MSE, PhD)
- civil engineering (MS, MSE, PhD)
- computer science (MCS, MS, PhD)
- construction (MS)
- electrical engineering (MS, MSE, PhD)
- engineering (M Eng, MCS, MS, MSE, PhD)
- engineering science (MS, MSE, PhD)
- industrial engineering (MS, MSE, PhD)

Arizona State University (continued)
materials science and engineering (MS, MSE, PhD)
mechanical engineering (MS, MSE, PhD)

Walter Cronkite School of Journalism and Mass Communication
Program in:
journalism and mass communication (MMC)

W.P. Carey School of Business
Programs in:
accountancy (PhD)
accountancy and information management (M Tax, MAIS)
business (M Tax, MAIS, MBA, MHSM, MPH, MS, PhD)
business administration (MBA)
economics (MS, PhD)
finance (PhD)
health management and policy (MHSM, MPH)
health services research (PhD)
information management (PhD)
information systems (MS)
management (PhD)
marketing (PhD)
supply chain management (PhD)

■ ARIZONA STATE UNIVERSITY AT THE POLYTECHNIC CAMPUS

Mesa, AZ 85212

http://www.poly.asu.edu/

State-supported, coed, comprehensive institution. *Enrollment:* 6,545 graduate, professional, and undergraduate students; 268 full-time matriculated graduate/professional students (178 women), 446 part-time matriculated graduate/professional students (234 women). *Graduate faculty:* 97 full-time (23 women). *Computer facilities:* Computer purchase and lease plans are available. 456 computers available on campus for general student use. A campuswide network can be accessed from off campus. Internet access and online class registration, specialized software applications are available. *Library facilities:* ASU East Library Services at the Polytechnic campus plus 1 other. *Graduate expenses:* Tuition, state resident: part-time $310 per credit hour. Tuition, nonresident: part-time $688 per credit hour. *General application contact:* Dr. Glenn Irvin, Vice Provost Academic Programs, 480-727-1435.

College of Science and Technology
Dr. Timothy Lindquist, Interim Dean
Programs in:
aeronautical management technology (MS)
electronic systems (MS)
mechanical and manufacturing engineering technology (MS)
science and technology (MCST, MS)
technology management (MS)

Division of Computing Studies
Dr. Ben Huey, Division Chair
Programs in:
computing studies (MCST)
technology (MS)

East College
Dr. David Schwalm, Dean
Programs in:
applied biological sciences (MS)
applied psychology (MS)
exercise and wellness (MS)
human nutrition (MS)
physical activity, nutrition and wellness (PhD)

Morrison School of Management and Agribusiness
Dr. Paul Patterson, Dean
Program in:
agribusiness (MS)

■ ARIZONA STATE UNIVERSITY AT THE WEST CAMPUS

Phoenix, AZ 85069-7100

http://www.west.asu.edu/

State-supported, coed, comprehensive institution. *Enrollment:* 8,211 graduate, professional, and undergraduate students; 372 full-time matriculated graduate/professional students (285 women), 623 part-time matriculated graduate/professional students (385 women). *Graduate faculty:* 81 full-time (40 women), 41 part-time/adjunct (30 women). *Computer facilities:* 400 computers available on campus for general student use. A campuswide network can be accessed from off campus. Internet access and online class registration are available. *Library facilities:* Fletcher Library at the West campus. *Graduate expenses:* Tuition, state resident: full-time $5,930. Tuition, nonresident: full-time $16,516. Tuition and fees vary according to course load. *General application contact:* Marge A. Williams, Student Support Coordinator, 602-543-4567.

College of Human Services
Dr. John Hepburn, Dean
Programs in:
communication (MA)
communication/human relations (Certificate)
criminal justice (MA)
gerontology (Certificate)
human services (MA, MSW, Certificate)
social work (MSW)

College of Teacher Education and Leadership
Dr. Mari Koerner, Dean
Programs in:
educational administration and supervision (M Ed)
elementary education (M Ed, Certificate)
leadership/innovation (administration) (Ed D)
leadership/innovation (teaching) (Ed D)
secondary education (M Ed, Certificate)
special education (M Ed)

New College of Interdisciplinary Arts and Sciences
Dr. Barry G. Ritchie, Interim Dean
Program in:
interdisciplinary studies (MA)

School of Global Management and Leadership
Dr. Gary Waissi, Dean
Programs in:
business administration (MBA)
global management and leadership (MBA, Certificate)
professional accountancy (Certificate)

■ DEVRY UNIVERSITY

Phoenix, AZ 85021-2995

http://www.devry.edu/

Proprietary, coed, comprehensive institution. *Computer facilities:* Computer purchase and lease plans are available. 436 computers available on campus for general student use. A campuswide network can be accessed from off campus. Internet access and online class registration are available. *Library facilities:* Learning Resource Center. *General application contact:* Student Application Contact, 602-870-9222.

Keller Graduate School of Management
Program in:
management (MAFM, MBA, MHRM, MISM, MNCM, MPA, MPM)

■ GRAND CANYON UNIVERSITY

Phoenix, AZ 85017-1097

http://www.gcu.edu/

Independent-religious, coed, comprehensive institution. *Computer facilities:* 119 computers available on campus for general student use. Internet access is available. *Library facilities:* Grand Canyon University Library. *General application contact:* Director of Admissions, 602-589-2855 Ext. 2811.

College of Business
Program in:
business (MBA)

College of Education
Programs in:
elementary education (M Ed, MA)
reading education (MA)

secondary education (M Ed)
teaching (MAT)
teaching English as a second language (MA)

■ NORTHERN ARIZONA UNIVERSITY
Flagstaff, AZ 86011
http://www.nau.edu/

State-supported, coed, university. CGS member. *Computer facilities:* Computer purchase and lease plans are available. 903 computers available on campus for general student use. A campuswide network can be accessed from student residence rooms and from off campus. Internet access and online class registration, e-mail are available. *Library facilities:* Cline Library plus 1 other. *General application contact:* Director of Graduate Admissions, 928-523-4348.

Consortium of Professional Schools and Colleges

College of Health Professions
Programs in:
case management (Certificate)
communications sciences and disorders (MS)
exercise science (MS)
health education and health promotion (MPH)
health professions (MPH, MS, MSN, DPT, Certificate)
nursing (MSN)
physical education (MS)
physical therapy (DPT)

School of Forestry
Program in:
forestry (MF, MSF, PhD)

Graduate College

College of Arts and Letters
Programs in:
applied linguistics (PhD)
arts and letters (MA, MAT, MLS, MM, PhD, Certificate)
choral conducting (MM)
creative writing (MA)
English (MA)
English education (MA)
general English (MA)
history (MA, PhD)
instrumental conducting (MM)
instrumental performance (MM)
liberal studies (MLS)
literature (MA)
modern languages (MAT)
music education (MM)
music history (MM)
rhetoric (MA)
teaching English as a second language (MA)
teaching English as a second language/ applied linguistics (MA, PhD, Certificate)
teaching English as a second language/ English as a second language (Certificate)
theory and composition (MM)
vocal performance (MM)

College of Business Administration
Programs in:
general management (MBA)
management information systems (MBA)

College of Education
Programs in:
administration (M Ed)
bilingual multicultural education (M Ed)
community college (M Ed)
counseling (M Ed, MA)
counseling psychology (Ed D)
curriculum and instruction (Ed D)
early childhood education (M Ed)
education (M Ed, MA, Ed D, Certificate)
educational leadership (Ed D)
educational technology (M Ed)
elementary education (M Ed)
English as a Second Language/Teaching English as a second language (Certificate)
learning and instruction (Ed D)
school leadership (M Ed)
school psychology (Ed D)
secondary education (M Ed)
special education (M Ed)
teaching (M Ed)

College of Engineering and Natural Science
Programs in:
applied physics (MS)
biology (MS, PhD)
biology education (MAT)
chemistry (MS)
conservation ecology (Certificate)
earth science (MAT, MS)
engineering (M Eng, MAT, MS, PhD, Certificate)
environmental sciences and policy (MS)
geology (MS)
mathematics (MAT, MS)
physical science (MAT)
quaternary sciences (MS)
statistics (MS)

College of Social and Behavioral Sciences
Programs in:
anthropology (MA)
applied communication (MA)
applied geographic information science (MS)
applied health psychology (MA)
applied sociology (MA)
archaeology (MA)
criminal justice (MS)
criminal justice policy and planning (Certificate)
general (MA)
geographic information systems (Certificate)
political science (MA, PhD, Certificate)
public administration (MPA)
public management (Certificate)
public policy (PhD)
rural geography (MA)
social and behavioral sciences (MA, MPA, MS, PhD, Certificate)

■ PRESCOTT COLLEGE
Prescott, AZ 86301
http://www.prescott.edu/

Independent, coed, comprehensive institution. *Enrollment:* 1,053 graduate, professional, and undergraduate students; 195 full-time matriculated graduate/professional students (138 women), 100 part-time matriculated graduate/professional students (60 women). *Graduate faculty:* 5 full-time (2 women), 172 part-time/adjunct (92 women). *Computer facilities:* 30 computers available on campus for general student use. A campuswide network can be accessed. Internet access is available. *Library facilities:* Prescott College Library. *Graduate expenses:* Tuition: full-time $12,408; part-time $517 per credit. One-time fee: $130. *General application contact:* Kerstin Alicki, Admissions Counselor, 877-350-2100 Ext. 2102.

Graduate Programs
Paul Burkhart, Interim Dean
Programs in:
adventure education/wilderness leadership (MA)
agroecology (MA)
bilingual education (MA)
counseling and psychology (MA)
ecopsychology (MA)
education (MA, PhD)
environmental education (MA)
environmental studies (MA)
humanities (MA)
multicultural education (MA)
Southwestern regional history (MA)
sustainability (MA)

■ THE UNIVERSITY OF ARIZONA
Tucson, AZ 85721
http://www.arizona.edu/

State-supported, coed, university. CGS member. *Enrollment:* 36,805 graduate, professional, and undergraduate students; 4,551 full-time matriculated graduate/ professional students (2,244 women), 1,759 part-time matriculated graduate/professional students (1,040 women). *Graduate faculty:* 1,392 full-time (362 women), 103 part-time/ adjunct (32 women). *Computer facilities:* 1,950 computers available on campus for general student use. A campuswide network can be accessed from student residence rooms and from off campus. Internet access is available. *Library facilities:* University of Arizona Main Library plus 5 others. *General application contact:* Information Contact, 520-621-3132.

The University of Arizona (continued)

College of Medicine
Programs in:
- biochemistry (MS, PhD)
- cell biology and anatomy (PhD)
- immunobiology (MS, PhD)
- medicine (MD, MPH, MS, PhD)
- public health (MPH)

College of Optical Sciences
Dr. James Wyant, Dean
Program in:
- optical sciences (MS, PhD)

Graduate College
Dr. Andrew Comrie, Dean
Programs in:
- American Indian studies (MA, PhD)
- anthropology (MA, PhD)
- applied mathematics (MS, PMS, PhD)
- arid lands resource sciences (PhD)
- cancer biology (PhD)
- communication (MA, PhD)
- genetics (MS, PhD)
- geography (MA, PhD)
- history (MA, PhD)
- human language technology (MS)
- insect science (PhD)
- Latin American studies (MA)
- library science (MA, PhD)
- linguistics and anthropology (PhD)
- mathematical sciences (PMS)
- Native American linguistics (MA)
- Near Eastern studies (MA, PhD)
- neuroscience (PhD)
- philosophy (MA, PhD)
- physiological sciences (PhD)
- political science (MA, PhD)
- psychology (PhD)
- second language acquisition and teaching (PhD)
- social and behavioral sciences (MA, MS, PhD)
- sociology (MA, PhD)
- statistics (MS, PhD)
- theoretical linguistics (PhD)
- women's studies (MA)

Arizona Graduate Program in Public Health
Program in:
- public health (MPH)

College of Agriculture and Life Sciences
Dr. Eugene G. Sander, Dean
Programs in:
- agricultural and biosystems engineering (MS, PhD)
- agricultural and resource economics (MS)
- agricultural education (M Ag Ed, MS)
- agriculture and life sciences (M Ag Ed, MHE Ed, MS, PhD)
- animal sciences (MS, PhD)
- entomology (MS, PhD)
- family and consumer sciences (MS)
- family studies and human development (PhD)
- natural resources (MS, PhD)
- pathobiology (MS, PhD)
- plant pathology (MS, PhD)
- plant sciences (MS, PhD)
- rangeland ecology and management (MS, PhD)
- retailing and consumer sciences (MS, PhD)
- soil, water and environmental science (MS, PhD)
- watershed resources (MS, PhD)
- wildlife, fisheries conservation, and management (MS, PhD)

College of Architecture and Landscape Architecture
Charles Albanese, Dean
Programs in:
- architecture (M Arch)
- landscape architecture (ML Arch)

College of Education
Dr. Ronald Marx, Dean
Programs in:
- bilingual education (M Ed)
- bilingual/multicultural education (MA)
- education (M Ed, MA, MS, Ed D, PhD, Ed S)
- educational leadership (M Ed, Ed D, Ed S)
- educational psychology (MA, PhD)
- elementary education (M Ed, Ed D)
- higher education (MA, PhD)
- language, reading and culture (MA, Ed D, PhD, Ed S)
- school counseling and guidance (M Ed)
- secondary education (M Ed, Ed D)
- special education, rehabilitation and school psychology (M Ed, MA, MS, Ed D, PhD, Ed S)
- teaching and teacher education (MA, PhD)

College of Engineering
Dr. Thomas W. Peterson, Dean
Programs in:
- aerospace engineering (MS, PhD)
- chemical engineering (MS, PhD)
- civil engineering (MS, PhD)
- electrical and computer engineering (M Eng, MS, PhD)
- engineering (M Eng, ME, MS, PhD)
- engineering mechanics (MS, PhD)
- environmental engineering (MS, PhD)
- geological engineering (MS, PhD)
- hydrology (MS, PhD)
- industrial engineering (MS)
- materials science and engineering (ME, MS, PhD)
- mechanical engineering (MS, PhD)
- mine health and safety (Certificate)
- mine information and production technology (Certificate)
- mining engineering (M Eng, Certificate)
- nuclear engineering (MS, PhD)
- reliability and quality engineering (MS)
- rock mechanics (Certificate)
- systems and industrial engineering (PhD)
- systems engineering (MS)
- water resources engineering (M Eng)

College of Fine Arts
Dr. Maurice Sevigny, Dean
Programs in:
- art (studio) (MFA)
- art education (MA)
- art history (MA, PhD)
- composition (MM, A Mus D)
- conducting (MM, A Mus D)
- fine arts (MA, MFA, MM, A Mus D, PhD)
- history and theory of art (PhD)
- media arts (MA)
- music education (MM, PhD)
- music theory (MM, PhD)
- musicology (MM)
- performance (MM, A Mus D)
- theatre arts (MA, MFA)

College of Humanities
Programs in:
- classics (MA)
- creative writing (MFA)
- East Asian studies (MA, PhD)
- English (MA, PhD)
- English language/linguistics (MA)
- ESL (MA)
- French (MA, PhD)
- German (MA, PhD)
- humanities (M Ed, MA, MFA, PhD)
- literature (MA, PhD)
- rhetoric, composition and teaching of English (PhD)
- rhetoric, composition, and the teaching of English (MA)
- Russian (M Ed, MA)
- Spanish (M Ed, MA, PhD)

College of Nursing
Dr. Marjorie A. Isenberg, Dean
Program in:
- nursing (MS, DNP, PhD)

College of Pharmacy
Dr. J. Lyle Bootman, Dean
Programs in:
- medical pharmacology (MS, PhD)
- medicinal and natural products chemistry (MS, PhD)
- perfusion science (MS)
- pharmaceutical economics (MS, PhD)
- pharmaceutics and pharmacokinetics (MS, PhD)
- pharmacy (Pharm D, MS, PhD)

College of Science
Dr. Joaquin Ruiz, Dean
Programs in:
- applied and industrial physics (MS)
- applied biosciences (MS)
- astronomy (MS, PhD)
- atmospheric sciences (MS, PhD)
- chemistry (MA, MS, PhD)
- computer science (MS, PhD)
- ecology and evolutionary biology (MS, PhD)
- geosciences (MS, PhD)
- mathematical sciences (PMS)
- mathematics (M Ed, MA, MS, PMS, PhD)

molecular and cellular biology (MS, PhD)
physics (M Ed, MS, PhD)
planetary sciences/lunar and planetary laboratory (MS, PhD)
science (M Ed, MA, MS, PMS, Au D, PhD)
speech and hearing sciences (MS, Au D, PhD)

Eller Graduate School of Management
Dr. E. LaBrent Chrite, Associate Dean and MBA Director
Programs in:
accounting (M Ac)
business administration (MBA)
economics (MA, PhD)
finance (MS, PhD)
management (MS, PhD)
management and organizations (MS, PhD)
management information systems (MS)
marketing (MS, PhD)

James E. Rogers College of Law
Programs in:
international indigenous peoples' rights and policy (LL M)
international trade law (LL M)
law (JD)

■ UNIVERSITY OF PHOENIX
Phoenix, AZ 85034-7209
http://www.uopxonline.com/

Proprietary, coed, comprehensive institution. *Enrollment:* 160,150 graduate, professional, and undergraduate students; 46,920 full-time matriculated graduate/professional students (31,156 women). *Graduate faculty:* 61 full-time (37 women), 10,799 part-time/adjunct (4,201 women). *Computer facilities:* A campuswide network can be accessed from off campus. *Library facilities:* University Library. *Graduate expenses:* Tuition: full-time $12,664. Required fees: $760.

The Artemis School
Dr. Adam Honea, Provost

College of Education
Dr. Marla LaRue, Dean/Executive Director
Programs in:
administration and supervision (MAEd)
adult education and training (MAEd)
curriculum and instruction-adult education (MAEd)
curriculum and instruction-English and language arts education (MAEd)
curriculum and instruction-mathematics education (MAEd)
curriculum education (MAEd)
curriculum instruction (MAEd)
early childhood (MAEd)
English as a second language (MAEd)
teacher education elementary (MAEd)
teacher education secondary (MAEd)

College of Health and Human Services
Dr. Gil Linne, Dean/Executive Director
Programs in:
administration of justice and security (MS)
health care administration (MHA)
health care management (MBA, MSN)
nurse practitioner (MSN)
nursing (MSN)
nursing education (MSN)
psychology (MS)

John Sperling School of Business
Dr. Adam Honea, Provost
Program in:
business (MBA, MIS, MM)

College of Graduate Business and Management
Brian Lindquist, Dean/Executive Director and Associate Vice President
Programs in:
accounting (MBA)
administration (MBA)
global management (MBA)
human resources management (MBA)
management (MM)
marketing (MBA)
public administration (MBA, MM)

College of Information Systems and Technology
Dr. Adam Honea, Dean/Executive Director
Programs in:
e-business (MBA)
management (MIS)
technology management (MBA)

School of Advanced Studies
Dr. Dawn Iwamoto, Dean/Executive Director
Programs in:
business administration (DBA)
education (Ed D)
health administration (DHA)
organizational management (DM)

■ UNIVERSITY OF PHOENIX–PHOENIX CAMPUS
Phoenix, AZ 85040-1958
http://www.phoenix.edu/

Proprietary, coed, comprehensive institution. CGS member. *Enrollment:* 8,497 graduate, professional, and undergraduate students; 2,734 full-time matriculated graduate/professional students (1,710 women). *Graduate faculty:* 178 full-time (61 women), 2,189 part-time/adjunct (868 women). *Computer facilities:* Computer purchase and lease plans are available. A campuswide network can be accessed from off campus. Internet access is available. *Library facilities:* University Library. *General application contact:* Campus Information Center, 480-804-7600.

The Artemis School
Dr. Adam Honea, Provost

College of Education
Dr. Marla LaRue, Dean/Executive Director
Programs in:
administration and supervision (MA Ed)
curriculum and instruction (MA Ed)
elementary licensure (MA Ed)
secondary licensure (MA Ed)

College of Health and Human Services
Dr. Gil Linne, Dean/Executive Director
Programs in:
community counseling (MSC)
family nurse practitioner (MSN)
health care management (MBA)
nurse practitioner (Certificate)
nursing (MSN)
nursing health care education (Certificate)

The John Sperling School of Business
Dr. Adam Honea, Provost
Program in:
business (MBA, MIS, MM)

College of Graduate Business and Management
Dr. Brian Lindquist, Dean/Executive Director
Programs in:
business administration (MBA)
management (MM)

College of Information Systems and Technology
Dr. Adam Honea, Provost
Program in:
management (MIS)

■ UNIVERSITY OF PHOENIX–SOUTHERN ARIZONA CAMPUS
Tucson, AZ 85712-2732
http://www.phoenix.edu/

Proprietary, coed, comprehensive institution. *Enrollment:* 2,839 graduate, professional, and undergraduate students; 742 full-time matriculated graduate/professional students (434 women). *Graduate faculty:* 91 full-time (51 women), 644 part-time/adjunct (243 women). *Computer facilities:* A campuswide network can be accessed from off campus. Internet access is available. *Library facilities:* University Library. *Graduate expenses:* Tuition: full-time $8,669. Required fees: $760. *General application contact:* Campus Information Center, 520-881-6512.

The Artemis School
Dr. Adam Honea, Provost

College of Education
Dr. Marla LaRue, Dean/Executive Director

University of Phoenix–Southern Arizona Campus (continued)
Programs in:
- curriculum instruction (MA Ed)
- educational counseling (MA Ed)
- elementary licensure (MA Ed)
- school counseling (MSC)
- secondary licensure (MA Ed)
- special education (Certificate)

College of Health and Human Services
Dr. Gil Linne, Dean/Executive Director
Programs in:
- administration of justice and security (MS)
- family nurse practitioner (Certificate)
- health administration (MHA)
- marriage, family and child therapy (MSC)
- nursing (MSN)

John Sperling School of Business
Dr. Adam Honea, Provost
Program in:
- business (MBA, MIS, MM)

College of Graduate Business and Management
Dr. Brian Lindquist, Associate Vice President and Dean/Executive Director
Programs in:
- accounting (MBA)
- business administration (MBA)
- global management (MBA)
- management (MM)

College of Information Systems and Technology
Dr. Adam Honea, Provost/Dean, Vice President Academic Research and Development
Programs in:
- information systems (MIS)
- technology management (MBA)

■ WESTERN INTERNATIONAL UNIVERSITY
Phoenix, AZ 85021-2718
http://www.wintu.edu/

Proprietary, coed, comprehensive institution. *Enrollment:* 2,229 graduate, professional, and undergraduate students; 576 full-time matriculated graduate/professional students (281 women). *Graduate faculty:* 149 part-time/adjunct (49 women). *Computer facilities:* 30 computers available on campus for general student use. A campuswide network can be accessed. Internet access is available. *Library facilities:* Learning Resource Center. *Graduate expenses:* Tuition: full-time $9,600; part-time $400 per credit. One-time fee: $85 full-time. *General application contact:* Karen Janitell, Director of Enrollment, 602-943-2311 Ext. 1063.

Graduate Programs in Business
Dr. Deborah DeSimone, Chief Academic Officer
Programs in:
- business (MA, MBA, MPA, MS)
- finance (MBA)
- information systems engineering (MS)
- information technology (MBA, MS)
- innovative leadership (MA)
- international business (MBA)
- management (MBA)
- marketing (MBA)
- public administration (MPA)

Arkansas

■ ARKANSAS STATE UNIVERSITY
Jonesboro, State University, AR 72467
http://www.astate.edu/

State-supported, coed, comprehensive institution. CGS member. *Enrollment:* 10,727 graduate, professional, and undergraduate students; 425 full-time matriculated graduate/professional students (254 women), 962 part-time matriculated graduate/professional students (640 women). *Graduate faculty:* 212 full-time (76 women), 32 part-time/adjunct (13 women). *Computer facilities:* 510 computers available on campus for general student use. A campuswide network can be accessed from student residence rooms and from off campus. Internet access and online class registration are available. *Library facilities:* Dean B. Ellis Library. *Graduate expenses:* Tuition, state resident: full-time $3,393; part-time $189 per hour. Tuition, nonresident: full-time $8,577; part-time $477 per hour. Required fees: $752; $39 per hour. $25 per semester. *General application contact:* Dr. Andrew Sustich, Dean of the Graduate School, 870-972-3029.

Graduate School
Dr. Andrew Sustich, Dean of the Graduate School

College of Agriculture
Dr. Gregory Phillips, Dean
Programs in:
- agricultural education (MSA, SCCT)
- agriculture (MSA)
- vocational-technical administration (MS, SCCT)

College of Business
Dr. Len Frey, Dean
Programs in:
- accountancy (M Acc)
- business (EMBA, M Acc, MBA, MS, MSE, SCCT)
- business administration (EMBA, MBA, SCCT)
- business education (SCCT)
- business technology education (MSE)
- information systems and e-commerce (MS)

College of Communications
Dr. Russell Shain, Dean
Programs in:
- communications (MA, MSMC, SCCT)
- journalism (MSMC)
- radio-television (MSMC)
- speech communications and theater (MA, SCCT)

College of Education
Dr. John Beineke, Dean
Programs in:
- college student personnel services (MS)
- community college administration education (SCCT)
- counselor education (Ed S)
- early childhood education (MSE)
- early childhood services (MS)
- education (MRC, MS, MSE, Ed D, Certificate, Ed S, SCCT)
- education theory and practice (MSE)
- educational leadership (MSE, Ed D, Ed S)
- elementary education (MSE)
- exercise science (MS)
- physical education (MS, MSE, SCCT)
- reading (MSE, SCCT)
- rehabilitation counseling (MRC)
- school counseling (MSE)
- special education (MSE)
- special education program administration (Ed S)
- student affairs (Certificate)

College of Fine Arts
Dr. Daniel Reeves, Dean
Programs in:
- art (MA)
- fine arts (MA, MM, MME, SCCT)
- music education (MME, SCCT)
- performance (MM)
- speech communication and theater (MA, SCCT)

College of Humanities and Social Sciences
Dr. Gloria Gibson, Dean
Programs in:
- criminal justice (Certificate)
- English (MA)
- English education (MSE, SCCT)
- heritage studies (PhD)
- history (MA, SCCT)
- humanities and social sciences (MA, MPA, MSE, PhD, Certificate, SCCT)
- political science (MA, SCCT)
- public administration (MPA)
- social science (MSE)
- sociology (MA, SCCT)

College of Nursing and Health Professions
Dr. Susan Hanrahan, Dean
Programs in:
- aging studies (Certificate)
- communication disorders (MCD)

health sciences (MS, Certificate)
health sciences education (Certificate)
nurse anesthesia (MSN)
nursing (MSN, Certificate)
physical therapy (MPT)
social work (MSW)

College of Sciences and Mathematics
Dr. Gregory Phillips, Dean
Programs in:
biological sciences (MA)
biology (MS)
biology education (MSE, SCCT)
chemistry (MS)
chemistry education (MSE, SCCT)
computer science (MS)
environmental sciences (MS, PhD)
mathematics (MS, MSE)
molecular biosciences (PhD)
sciences and mathematics (MA, MS, MSE, PhD, SCCT)

■ ARKANSAS TECH UNIVERSITY

Russellville, AR 72801

http://www.atu.edu/

State-supported, coed, comprehensive institution. *Enrollment:* 7,038 graduate, professional, and undergraduate students; 147 full-time matriculated graduate/professional students (83 women), 456 part-time matriculated graduate/professional students (326 women). *Graduate faculty:* 62 full-time (26 women), 5 part-time/adjunct (4 women). *Computer facilities:* 700 computers available on campus for general student use. A campuswide network can be accessed from student residence rooms and from off campus. Internet access and online class registration are available. *Library facilities:* Ross Pendergraft Library and Technology Center. *Graduate expenses:* Tuition, state resident: full-time $3,060; part-time $170 per hour. Tuition, nonresident: full-time $6,120; part-time $340 per hour. Required fees: $312; $4 per hour. $84 per term. Part-time tuition and fees vary according to course load. *General application contact:* Dr. Eldon G. Clary, Dean of Graduate School, 479-968-0398.

Graduate School
Dr. Eldon G. Clary, Dean of Graduate School

School of Community Education
Dr. Mary Ann Rollans, Dean
Program in:
emergency management and homeland security (MS)

School of Education
Dr. C. Glenn Sheets, Dean
Programs in:
college student personnel (MSE)
educational leadership (M Ed, Ed S)
English education (M Ed)
gifted education (MSE)
instructional improvement (M Ed)
secondary education (M Ed)
teaching, learning and leadership (M Ed)

School of Liberal and Fine Arts
Dr. Georgena Duncan, Dean
Programs in:
communication (MLA)
English (M Ed, MA)
fine arts (MLA)
history (MA)
multi-media journalism (MA)
social science (MLA)
social studies (M Ed)
Spanish (MA, MLA)
teaching English as a second language (MA, MLA)

School of Physical and Life Sciences
Dr. Richard Cohoon, Dean
Program in:
fisheries and wildlife biology (MS)

School of System Science
Dr. John Watson, Dean
Programs in:
information technology (MS)
mathematics (M Ed)

■ HARDING UNIVERSITY

Searcy, AR 72149-0001

http://www.harding.edu/

Independent-religious, coed, comprehensive institution. *Enrollment:* 6,085 graduate, professional, and undergraduate students; 305 full-time matriculated graduate/professional students (217 women), 564 part-time matriculated graduate/professional students (370 women). *Graduate faculty:* 16 full-time (3 women), 87 part-time/adjunct (36 women). *Computer facilities:* 327 computers available on campus for general student use. A campuswide network can be accessed from student residence rooms and from off campus. Internet access and online class registration are available. *Library facilities:* Brackett Library plus 1 other. *Graduate expenses:* Tuition: part-time $455 per semester hour. Required fees: $20 per semester hour. Tuition and fees vary according to course load. *General application contact:* Dr. Larry Long, Vice President, Academic Affairs, 501-279-4335.

College of Bible and Religion
Bruce McLarty, Dean
Programs in:
Bible and religion (M Min, MS)
marriage and family therapy (MS)
mental health counseling (MS)
ministry (M Min)

College of Business Administration
Allen Figley, Director of Graduate Studies
Program in:
business administration (MBA)

College of Education
Pat Bashaw, Chair
Programs in:
advanced studies in teaching and learning (M Ed)
art (MSE)
behavioral science (MSE)
Bible and religion (MSE)
counseling (MS, Ed S)
early childhood education (M Ed)
early childhood special education (M Ed, MSE)
education (MSE)
educational leadership (M Ed, Ed S)
elementary education (M Ed)
English (MSE)
family and consumer science (MSE)
French (MSE)
history/social science (MSE)
kinesiology (MSE)
math (MSE)
physical science (MSE)
reading (M Ed)
secondary education (M Ed)
Spanish (MSE)
special education licensure (M Ed)
teaching (MAT)

■ HENDERSON STATE UNIVERSITY

Arkadelphia, AR 71999-0001

http://www.hsu.edu

State-supported, coed, comprehensive institution. *Enrollment:* 3,664 graduate, professional, and undergraduate students; 132 full-time matriculated graduate/professional students (80 women), 314 part-time matriculated graduate/professional students (236 women). *Graduate faculty:* 57 full-time (17 women), 9 part-time/adjunct (4 women). *Computer facilities:* 125 computers available on campus for general student use. A campuswide network can be accessed from student residence rooms and from off campus. *Library facilities:* Huie Library. *Graduate expenses:* Tuition, state resident: full-time $3,294; part-time $183 per credit hour. Tuition, nonresident: full-time $6,588; part-time $366 per credit hour. Required fees: $176 per term. *General application contact:* Dr. Marck L. Beggs, Graduate Dean, 870-230-5126.

Graduate Studies
Dr. Marck L. Beggs, Graduate Dean

Ellis College of Arts and Sciences
Dr. Maralyn Sommer, Dean
Program in:
arts and sciences (MLA)

School of Business Administration
Dr. Paul Huo, Dean
Program in:
business administration (MBA)

School of Education
Dr. Judy Harrison, Dean

Henderson State University (continued)
Programs in:
- community counseling (MS)
- early childhood (P-4) (MSE)
- early childhood special education (MSE)
- education (MAT)
- educational leadership (Ed S)
- elementary school counseling (MSE)
- English (MSE)
- English as a second language (MSE, CP)
- instructional specialist (MSE)
- math (MSE)
- middle school (MSE)
- reading (MSE)
- recreation (MS)
- school administration (MSE)
- secondary school counseling (MSE)
- social science (MSE)
- sports administration (MS)

■ JOHN BROWN UNIVERSITY
Siloam Springs, AR 72761-2121
http://www.jbu.edu/

Independent-religious, coed, comprehensive institution. *Computer facilities:* 100 computers available on campus for general student use. A campuswide network can be accessed from student residence rooms and from off campus. Internet access is available. *Library facilities:* Arutunoff Learning Resource Center plus 6 others. *General application contact:* Director of Graduate and Professional Studies, 479-524-7343.

Department of Business Administration
Programs in:
- business administration (MBA)
- leadership and ethics (MS)

Program in Counseling
Programs in:
- community counseling (MS)
- marriage and family therapy (MS)
- school counseling (MS)

Program in Ministry
Program in:
- ministry (MA)

■ UNIVERSITY OF ARKANSAS
Fayetteville, AR 72701-1201
http://www.uark.edu/

State-supported, coed, university. CGS member. *Enrollment:* 17,926 graduate, professional, and undergraduate students; 3,399 full-time matriculated graduate/professional students (1,684 women). *Graduate faculty:* 655 full-time (169 women), 13 part-time/adjunct (2 women). *Computer facilities:* Computer purchase and lease plans are available. 1,252 computers available on campus for general student use. A campuswide network can be accessed from student residence rooms and from off campus. Internet access and online class registration are available. *Library facilities:* David W. Mullins Library plus 5 others. *General application contact:* Lynn Mosesso, Director of Graduate and International Recruitment and Admissions, 479-575-6246.

Find University Details at www.petersons.com/gradchannel.

Graduate School
Dr. Patricia R. Koski, Associate Dean
Programs in:
- cell and molecular biology (MS, PhD)
- environmental dynamics (PhD)
- microelectronics and photonics (MS, PhD)
- public policy (PhD)
- space and planetary science (MS, PhD)

College of Education and Health Professions
M. Reed Greenwood, Dean
Programs in:
- adult education (M Ed, Ed D, Ed S)
- childhood education (MAT)
- communication disorders (MS)
- counseling education (MS, PhD, Ed S)
- curriculum and instruction (PhD)
- education and health professions (M Ed, MAT, MS, MSN, Ed D, PhD, Ed S)
- educational administration (M Ed, Ed D, Ed S)
- educational foundations (MS, PhD)
- educational technology (M Ed)
- elementary education (M Ed, Ed S)
- health science (MS, PhD)
- higher education (M Ed, Ed D, Ed S)
- kinesiology (MS, PhD)
- middle-level education (MAT)
- nursing (MSN)
- physical education (M Ed, MAT)
- recreation (M Ed, Ed D)
- rehabilitation (MS, PhD)
- secondary education (M Ed, MAT, Ed S)
- special education (M Ed, MAT)
- vocational education (M Ed, MAT, Ed D, Ed S)
- workforce development education (M Ed)

College of Engineering
Ashok Saxena, Dean
Programs in:
- biological and agricultural engineering (MSE, PhD)
- biological engineering (MSBE)
- biomedical engineering (MSBME)
- chemical engineering (MS Ch E, MSE, PhD)
- civil engineering (MSCE, MSE, PhD)
- computer engineering (MSCSE, MSE, PhD)
- computer science (MS, PhD)
- electrical engineering (MSEE, PhD)
- engineering (MS, MS Ch E, MS En E, MS Tc E, MSBE, MSBME, MSCE, MSCSE, MSE, MSEE, MSIE, MSME, MSOR, MSTE, PhD)
- environmental engineering (MS En E, MSE)
- industrial engineering (MSE, MSIE, PhD)
- mechanical engineering (MSE, MSME, PhD)
- operations management (MS)
- operations research (MSE, MSOR)
- telecommunications engineering (MS Tc E)
- transportation engineering (MSE, MSTE)

Dale Bumpers College of Agricultural, Food and Life Sciences
Dr. Greg Weidemann, Dean
Programs in:
- agricultural and extension education (MS)
- agricultural economics (MS)
- agricultural, food and life sciences (MS, PhD)
- agronomy (MS, PhD)
- animal science (MS, PhD)
- entomology (MS, PhD)
- food science (MS, PhD)
- horticulture (MS)
- human environmental sciences (MS)
- plant pathology (MS)
- plant science (PhD)
- poultry science (MS, PhD)

J. William Fulbright College of Arts and Sciences
Don Bobbitt, Dean
Programs in:
- anthropology (MA)
- applied physics (MS)
- art (MFA)
- arts and sciences (MA, MFA, MM, MPA, MS, MSW, PhD)
- biology (MA, MS, PhD)
- chemistry (MS, PhD)
- communication (MA)
- comparative literature (MA, PhD)
- comparative literature and cultural studies (MA, PhD)
- creative writing (MFA)
- drama (MA, MFA)
- English (MA, PhD)
- French (MA)
- geography (MA)
- geology (MS)
- German (MA)
- history (MA, PhD)
- journalism (MA)
- mathematics (MS, PhD)
- music (MM)
- philosophy (MA, PhD)
- physics (MS, PhD)
- physics education (MA)
- political science (MA)
- psychology (MA, PhD)
- public administration (MPA)
- secondary mathematics (MA)
- social work (MSW)

sociology (MA)
Spanish (MA)
statistics (MS)
translation (MFA)

Sam M. Walton College of Business Administration
Dr. Dan Worrell, Dean
Programs in:
accounting (M Acc)
business administration (M Acc, MA, MBA, MIS, MTLM, PhD)
economics (MA, PhD)
information systems (MIS)
transportation and logistics management (MTLM)

School of Law
Cynthia Nance, Dean
Programs in:
agricultural law (LL M)
law (JD)

■ UNIVERSITY OF ARKANSAS AT LITTLE ROCK
Little Rock, AR 72204-1099
http://www.ualr.edu/

State-supported, coed, university. CGS member. *Computer facilities:* 500 computers available on campus for general student use. A campuswide network can be accessed from off campus. Internet access is available. *Library facilities:* Ottenheimer Library plus 1 other. *General application contact:* Dean of the Graduate School, 501-569-3206.

Graduate School

Clinton School of Public Service
Program in:
public service (MPS)

College of Arts, Humanities, and Social Science
Programs in:
applied gerontology (CG)
applied psychology (MAP)
art education (MA)
art history (MA)
arts, humanities, and social science (MA, MALS, MAP, CG)
gerontology (MA)
philosophy and liberal studies (MALS)
professional writing (MA)
public history (MA)
studio art (MA)
technical writing (MA)

College of Business Administration
Programs in:
business administration (MBA)
management information system (MIS)

College of Education
Programs in:
adult education (M Ed)
college student affairs (MA)
counseling rehabilitation (MA)
counselor education (M Ed)
early childhood education (M Ed)
early childhood special education (M Ed)
education (M Ed, MA, Ed D, Ed S)
educational administration (M Ed, Ed D, Ed S)
educational administration and supervision (M Ed, Ed D, Ed S)
higher education (MA)
higher education administration (Ed D)
learning systems technology (M Ed)
middle childhood education (M Ed)
reading (M Ed)
rehabilitation of the blind (MA)
school counseling (M Ed)
secondary education (M Ed)
special education (M Ed)
teaching deaf and hard of hearing (M Ed)
teaching of the mildly disabled student (M Ed)
teaching persons with severe disabilities (M Ed)
teaching the gifted and talented (M Ed)
teaching the visually impaired (M Ed)

College of Information Science and Systems Engineering
Programs in:
applied science (MS, PhD)
bioinformatics (MS, PhD)
computer science (MS)
information science and systems engineering (MS, PhD)

College of Professional Studies
Programs in:
clinical social work (MSW)
criminal justice (MA)
health services administration (MHSA)
interpersonal communications (MA)
mass communication (MA)
organizational communications (MA)
professional studies (MA, MHSA, MPA, MSW, CG)
public administration (MPA)
social program administration (MSW)
social work (MSW, CG)

College of Science and Mathematics
Programs in:
applied mathematics (MS)
biology (MS)
chemistry (MA, MS)
integrated science and mathematics (MS)
science and mathematics (MA, MS)

William H. Bowen School of Law
Program in:
law (JD)

■ UNIVERSITY OF ARKANSAS AT MONTICELLO
Monticello, AR 71656
http://www.uamont.edu/

State-supported, coed, comprehensive institution. *Enrollment:* 3,179 graduate, professional, and undergraduate students; 25 full-time matriculated graduate/professional students (16 women), 81 part-time matriculated graduate/professional students (57 women). *Graduate faculty:* 48 full-time (14 women), 2 part-time/adjunct (1 woman). *Computer facilities:* 140 computers available on campus for general student use. *Library facilities:* Fred J. Taylor Library and Technology Center. *Graduate expenses:* Tuition, state resident: full-time $2,646; part-time $135 per hour. Tuition, nonresident: full-time $5,940; part-time $315 per hour. Required fees: $594; $30 per hour. Tuition and fees vary according to campus/location. *General application contact:* Mary Whiting, Director, Office of Admissions, 870-460-1026.

School of Education
Dr. Peggy Doss, Dean
Programs in:
education (M Ed, MAT)
educational leadership (M Ed)

School of Forest Resources
Dr. Richard Kluender, Dean
Program in:
forest resources (MS)

■ UNIVERSITY OF CENTRAL ARKANSAS
Conway, AR 72035-0001
http://www.uca.edu/

State-supported, coed, comprehensive institution. CGS member. *Enrollment:* 12,330 graduate, professional, and undergraduate students; 585 full-time matriculated graduate/professional students (415 women), 980 part-time matriculated graduate/professional students (782 women). *Graduate faculty:* 228 full-time (83 women), 11 part-time/adjunct (5 women). *Computer facilities:* Computer purchase and lease plans are available. 1,500 computers available on campus for general student use. A campuswide network can be accessed from student residence rooms and from off campus. Internet access and online class registration are available. *Library facilities:* Torreyson Library. *Graduate expenses:* Tuition, state resident: full-time $4,194; part-time $233 per semester. Tuition, nonresident: full-time $5,963; part-time $429 per semester. International tuition: $6,162 full-time. Required fees: $65; $23 per semester. One-time fee: $65 part-time. *General application contact:* Brenda Herring, Admissions Assistant, 501-450-5065.

University of Central Arkansas (continued)

Graduate School
Dr. Elaine M. McNiece, Dean

College of Business Administration
Dr. Pat Cantrell, Dean
Programs in:
- accounting (M Acc)
- business administration (M Acc, MBA)

College of Education
Dr. Larry Robinson, Dean
Programs in:
- collaborative instructional specialist (ages 0–8) (MSE)
- collaborative instructional specialist (grades 4–12) (MSE)
- early childhood education (MSE)
- education (MAT, MS, MSE)
- education media and library science (MS)
- reading education (MSE)
- special education (MSE)
- teaching (MAT)
- teaching and learning (MSE)
- training systems (MSE)

College of Fine Arts and Communication
Dr. Rollin Potter, Dean
Programs in:
- choral conducting (MM)
- filmmaking (MFA)
- fine arts and communication (MFA, MM)
- instrumental conducting (MM)
- music education (MM)
- music theory (MM)
- performance (MM)

College of Health and Behavioral Sciences
Dr. Neil Hattlestad, Dean
Programs in:
- clinical nurse specialist (MSN)
- community service counseling (MS)
- counseling psychology (MS)
- elementary school counseling (MS)
- family and consumer sciences (MS)
- health and behavioral sciences (MS, MSN, DPT, PhD)
- health education (MS)
- health systems (MS)
- kinesiology (MS)
- nurse practitioner (MSN)
- occupational therapy (MS)
- physical therapy (DPT, PhD)
- school counseling (MS)
- school psychology (MS, PhD)
- secondary school counseling (MS)
- speech-language pathology (MS)

College of Liberal Arts
Maurice Lee, Dean
Programs in:
- English (MA)
- foreign languages (MA)
- geographic information systems (Certificate)
- history (MA)
- liberal arts (MA, Certificate)

College of Natural Sciences and Math
Dr. Stephen Seidman, Dean
Programs in:
- applied computing (MS)
- biological science (MS)
- mathematics (MA)
- natural sciences and math (MA, MS)

Graduate School of Management, Leadership, and Administration
Dr. Elaine M. McNiece, Dean
Programs in:
- college student personnel (MS)
- community and economic development (MS)
- educational leadership—district level (Ed S)
- management, leadership, and administration (MS, Ed S)

California

■ AMERICAN INTERCONTINENTAL UNIVERSITY

Los Angeles, CA 90066

http://www.aiuniv.edu/

Proprietary, coed, comprehensive institution. *Enrollment:* 56 full-time matriculated graduate/professional students (25 women), 6 part-time matriculated graduate/professional students (4 women). *Graduate faculty:* 11 full-time (2 women). *Computer facilities:* Computer purchase and lease plans are available. 40 computers available on campus for general student use. A campuswide network can be accessed from off campus. Internet access is available. *Library facilities:* Library plus 1 other. *Graduate expenses:* Tuition: full-time $26,400. *General application contact:* Admissions Advisor, 888-594-9888.

Program in Business Administration
Dr. James Carroll, Dean of School of Business
Programs in:
- business administration (MBA)
- global technology management (MBA)

Program in Education
Dr. Eleanore Miller, Associate Dean of Education
Program in:
- instructional technology (M Ed)

Program in Information Technology
Dr. Shantaram Vasikarla, Dean of Information Technology
Program in:
- information technology (MIT)

■ ANTIOCH UNIVERSITY LOS ANGELES

Culver City, CA 90230

http://www.antiochla.edu/

Independent, coed, upper-level institution. *Computer facilities:* 12 computers available on campus for general student use. A campuswide network can be accessed from off campus. Internet access is available. *Library facilities:* Ohiolink plus 1 other. *General application contact:* Information Contact, 310-578-1090.

Find University Details at www.petersons.com/gradchannel.

Graduate Programs
Programs in:
- clinical psychology (MA)
- creative writing (MFA)
- education (MA)
- human resource development (MA)
- leadership (MA)
- organizational development (MA)
- pedagogy of creative writing (Certificate)
- psychology (MA)

■ ANTIOCH UNIVERSITY SANTA BARBARA

Santa Barbara, CA 93101-1581

http://www.antiochsb.edu/

Independent, coed, upper-level institution. *Enrollment:* 284 graduate, professional, and undergraduate students; 155 full-time matriculated graduate/professional students (130 women), 63 part-time matriculated graduate/professional students (53 women). *Graduate faculty:* 16 full-time (11 women), 55 part-time/adjunct (21 women). *Computer facilities:* 14 computers available on campus for general student use. A campuswide network can be accessed from off campus. *Graduate expenses:* Tuition: part-time $515 per unit. Part-time tuition and fees vary according to course load and program. *General application contact:* Director of Admissions, 805-962-8179.

Master's Program in Psychology
Dr. Catherine Radecki-Bush, Chair
Program in:
- psychology (MA)

Program in Education/Teacher Credentialing
Dr. Michele Britton Bass, Chair
Program in:
- education/teacher credentialing (MA)

Program in Organizational Management
Dr. Esther Lopez-Mulnix, Chair
Program in:
- organizational management (MA)

Psychology Program
Dr. Catherine Radecki-Bush, Chair

Program in:
- professional development and career counseling (MA)

■ ARGOSY UNIVERSITY, ORANGE COUNTY CAMPUS
Santa Ana, CA 92704
http://www.argosyu.edu/

Proprietary, coed, university. CGS member. *Enrollment:* 646 graduate, professional, and undergraduate students; 507 full-time matriculated graduate/professional students (293 women), 132 part-time matriculated graduate/professional students (75 women). *Graduate faculty:* 15 full-time (8 women), 72 part-time/adjunct (28 women). *Computer facilities:* 12 computers available on campus for general student use. Internet access and online class registration are available. *Library facilities:* Carrie Lixey. *General application contact:* Mark Betz, Director of Admissions, 800-716-9598.

College of Business
Dr. Ray London, Dean
Programs in:
- accounting (DBA, Adv C)
- customized professional concentration (MBA, DBA)
- finance (MBA, Certificate)
- healthcare administration (MBA, Certificate)
- information systems (DBA, Adv C)
- information systems management (MBA)
- international business (MBA, DBA, Adv C, Certificate)
- management (MBA, MSM, DBA, EDBA)
- mangement (Adv C)
- marketing (MBA, DBA, Adv C, Certificate)
- organizational leadership (Ed D)
- public administration (MBA, Certificate)

College of Education
Dr. Christine Zeppos, Dean
Programs in:
- community college executive leadership (Ed D)
- educational leadership (MA Ed, Ed D)
- instructional leadership (MA Ed, Ed D)

College of Psychology and Behavioral Sciences
Dr. Gary Bruss, Dean
Programs in:
- child and adolescent psychology (Psy D)
- clinical psychology (Postdoctoral Respecialization Certificate)
- counseling psychology (Ed D)
- forensic psychology (Psy D)
- marriage and family therapy (MA)
- psychology and behavioral sciences (MA, Ed D, Psy D, Postdoctoral Respecialization Certificate)

■ AZUSA PACIFIC UNIVERSITY
Azusa, CA 91702-7000
http://www.apu.edu/

Independent-religious, coed, comprehensive institution. CGS member. *Enrollment:* 8,128 graduate, professional, and undergraduate students; 504 full-time matriculated graduate/professional students (320 women), 2,902 part-time matriculated graduate/professional students (1,907 women). *Graduate faculty:* 129 full-time (74 women). *Computer facilities:* Computer purchase and lease plans are available. 300 computers available on campus for general student use. A campuswide network can be accessed from off campus. Internet access and online class registration are available. *Library facilities:* Marshburn Memorial Library plus 2 others. *Graduate expenses:* Tuition: part-time $475 per credit. *General application contact:* Linda Witte, Graduate Admissions Office, 626-969-3434.

College of Liberal Arts and Sciences
Dr. David Weeks, Dean
Programs in:
- fine arts in visual art (MFA)
- liberal arts and sciences (MA, MFA)
- teaching English to speakers of other languages (MA)

Haggard School of Theology
Dr. Enrique Zone, Associate Dean
Programs in:
- Christian education (MA)
- Christian non-profit leadership (MA)
- divinity (M Div)
- ministry (D Min)
- ministry management (MAMM)
- pastoral studies (MAPS)
- religion: Biblical studies (MAR)
- religion: theology and ethics (MAR)
- theology (M Div, MA, MAMM, MAPS, MAR, MAWL, D Min)
- worship leadership (MAWL)

School of Business and Management
Dr. Ilene Bezjian, Dean
Programs in:
- business administration (MBA)
- human and organizational development (MA)
- international business (MBA)
- strategic management (MBA)

School of Education
Dr. Paul Gray, Dean
Programs in:
- curriculum and instruction in a multicultural setting (MA)
- education (M Ed, MA, Ed D)
- educational counseling (MA)
- educational leadership (Ed D)
- educational psychology (MA)
- educational technology (M Ed)
- language development (MA)
- physical education (M Ed)
- pupil personnel services (MA)
- school administration (MA)
- school librarianship (MA)
- special education (MA)
- teaching (MA)

School of Music
Dr. Duane Funderburk, Dean
Programs in:
- education (M Mus)
- performance (M Mus)

School of Nursing
Dr. Aja Lesh, Interim Dean/Professor
Programs in:
- nursing (MSN)
- nursing education (PhD)

■ BIOLA UNIVERSITY
La Mirada, CA 90639-0001
http://www.biola.edu/

Independent-religious, coed, university. *Computer facilities:* Computer purchase and lease plans are available. 165 computers available on campus for general student use. A campuswide network can be accessed from student residence rooms and from off campus. Internet access and online class registration are available. *Library facilities:* The Biola University Library. *General application contact:* Director of Graduate Admissions, 562-903-4752.

Crowell School of Business
Program in:
- business (MBA)

Rosemead School of Psychology
Program in:
- psychology (MA, PhD, Psy D)

School of Arts and Sciences
Program in:
- arts and sciences (MA Ed)

School of Intercultural Studies
Programs in:
- applied linguistics (MA)
- intercultural education (PhD)
- intercultural studies (MAICS)
- missiology (D Miss)
- missions (MA)
- teaching English to speakers of other languages (MA, Certificate)

School of Professional Studies
Programs in:
- Christian apologetics (MA)
- organizational leadership (MA)

Talbot School of Theology
Programs in:
- Bible exposition (MA)
- biblical and theological studies (MA)
- Christian education (MACE)

Biola University (continued)
- Christian ministry and leadership (MA)
- divinity (M Div)
- education (PhD)
- ministry (MA Min)
- New Testament (MA)
- Old Testament (MA)
- philosophy of religion and ethics (MA)
- spiritual formation (MA)
- spiritual formation and soul care (MA)
- theology (MA, Th M, D Min)

■ CALIFORNIA BAPTIST UNIVERSITY
Riverside, CA 92504-3206
http://www.calbaptist.edu/

Independent-religious, coed, comprehensive institution. *Enrollment:* 3,409 graduate, professional, and undergraduate students; 268 full-time matriculated graduate/professional students (186 women), 518 part-time matriculated graduate/professional students (414 women). *Graduate faculty:* 44 full-time (22 women), 29 part-time/adjunct (19 women). *Computer facilities:* 154 computers available on campus for general student use. A campuswide network can be accessed from student residence rooms and from off campus. Internet access and online class registration, intranet are available. *Library facilities:* Annie Gabriel Library. *Graduate expenses:* Tuition: full-time $7,812; part-time $434 per unit. Required fees: $120 per semester. Tuition and fees vary according to program. *General application contact:* Gail Ronveaux, Dean of Graduate Enrollment, 951-343-5045.

Program in Business Administration
Dr. Andrew Herrity, Dean, School of Business
Program in:
- business administration (MBA)

Program in Education
Dr. Mary Crist, Dean, School of Education
Programs in:
- cross-cultural language and academic development (MA Ed)
- educational leadership (MS Ed)
- educational technology (MS Ed)
- instructional computer applications (MS Ed)
- reading (MS Ed)
- special education (MS Ed)
- teaching (MS Ed)

Program in English
Dr. Jennifer Newton, Director
Program in:
- English (MA)

Program in Kinesiology
Dr. Sean Sullivan, Chair, Department of Kinesiology
Program in:
- kinesiology (MS)

Program in Marriage and Family Therapy: Counseling Psychology
Dr. Gary Collins, Director and Associate Dean, School of Business
Program in:
- counseling psychology (MS)

Program in Music
Dr. Gary Bonner, Dean, School of Music
Program in:
- music (MM)

■ CALIFORNIA INSTITUTE OF INTEGRAL STUDIES
San Francisco, CA 94103
http://www.ciis.edu/

Independent, coed, upper-level institution. CGS member. *Enrollment:* 1,034 matriculated graduate/professional students. *Graduate faculty:* 55 full-time (28 women), 154 part-time/adjunct. *Computer facilities:* A campuswide network can be accessed from off campus. Internet access is available. *Library facilities:* The Laurance S. Rockefeller. *Graduate expenses:* Tuition: part-time $750 per unit. Tuition and fees vary according to course load, degree level and program. *General application contact:* Gwyneth Merner, Admissions Inquiries Coordinator, 415-575-6151.

Graduate Programs
Dr. Judie Wexler, Academic Vice President

School of Consciousness and Transformation
Dr. Judie Wexler, Academic Vice President
Programs in:
- cultural anthropology and social transformation (MA)
- East-West psychology (MA, PhD)
- integrative health studies (MA)
- philosophy and religion (MA, PhD)
- social and cultural anthropology (PhD)
- transformative leadership (MA)
- transformative studies (PhD)

School of Professional Psychology
Dr. Judie Wexler, Academic Vice President
Programs in:
- drama therapy (MA)
- expressive arts therapy (MA)
- integral counseling psychology (MA)
- psychology (Psy D)
- somatic psychology (MA)

■ CALIFORNIA INSTITUTE OF TECHNOLOGY
Pasadena, CA 91125-0001
http://www.caltech.edu/

Independent, coed, university. CGS member. *Computer facilities:* Computer purchase and lease plans are available. 600 computers available on campus for general student use. A campuswide network can be accessed from student residence rooms and from off campus. Internet access is available. *Library facilities:* Millikan Library plus 10 others. *General application contact:* Graduate Office, 626-395-3812.

Division of Biology
Elliot Meyerowitz, Chairman
Programs in:
- biochemistry and molecular biophysics (MS, PhD)
- cell biology and biophysics (PhD)
- developmental biology (PhD)
- genetics (PhD)
- immunology (PhD)
- molecular biology (PhD)
- neurobiology (PhD)

Division of Chemistry and Chemical Engineering
Dr. David A. Tirrell, Chairman
Programs in:
- biochemistry and molecular biophysics (MS, PhD)
- chemical engineering (MS, PhD)
- chemistry (MS, PhD)

Division of Engineering and Applied Science
Dr. David Rutledge, Chair to Division of Engineering and Applied Science
Programs in:
- aeronautics (MS, PhD, Engr)
- applied and computational mathematics (MS, PhD)
- applied mechanics (MS, PhD)
- applied physics (MS, PhD)
- bioengineering (MS, PhD)
- civil engineering (MS, PhD, Engr)
- computation and neural systems (MS, PhD)
- computer science (MS, PhD)
- control and dynamical systems (MS, PhD)
- electrical engineering (MS, PhD, Engr)
- environmental science and engineering (MS, PhD)
- materials science (MS, PhD)
- mechanical engineering (MS, PhD, Engr)

Division of Geological and Planetary Sciences
Dr. Kenneth A. Farley, Chairman
Programs in:
- geobiology (PhD)
- geochemistry (MS, PhD)
- geology (MS, PhD)
- geophysics (MS, PhD)
- planetary science (MS, PhD)

Division of Physics, Mathematics and Astronomy
Programs in:
- astronomy (PhD)
- mathematics (PhD)
- physics (PhD)

Division of the Humanities and Social Sciences
Peter L. Bossaerts, Chair
Programs in:
economics (PhD)
humanities and social sciences (MS, PhD)
political science (PhD)
social science (MS)

■ CALIFORNIA LUTHERAN UNIVERSITY
Thousand Oaks, CA 91360-2787
http://www.callutheran.edu/

Independent-religious, coed, comprehensive institution. *Computer facilities:* 267 computers available on campus for general student use. A campuswide network can be accessed from student residence rooms and from off campus. Internet access is available. *Library facilities:* Pearson Library. *General application contact:* Information Contact, 805-493-3127.

Find University Details at www.petersons.com/gradchannel.

Graduate Studies
Programs in:
clinical psychology (MS)
marital and family therapy (MS)
public policy and administration (MPPA)

School of Business
Programs in:
business (IMBA)
finance (MBA)
financial planning (MBA, MS, Certificate)
general business (MBA)
information technology management (MBA)
international business (MBA)
management and organization behavior (MBA)
marketing (MBA)
small business/entrepreneurship (MBA)

School of Education
Programs in:
counseling and guidance (MS)
curriculum and instruction (MA)
education (M Ed)
educational administration (MA)
reading education (MA)
special education (MS)
teacher preparation (Certificate)

■ CALIFORNIA POLYTECHNIC STATE UNIVERSITY, SAN LUIS OBISPO
San Luis Obispo, CA 93407
http://www.calpoly.edu/

State-supported, coed, comprehensive institution. *Enrollment:* 18,722 graduate, professional, and undergraduate students; 508 full-time matriculated graduate/professional students (229 women), 292 part-time matriculated graduate/professional students (130 women). *Graduate faculty:* 131 full-time (34 women), 54 part-time/adjunct (15 women). *Computer facilities:* 1,880 computers available on campus for general student use. A campuswide network can be accessed from student residence rooms and from off campus. *Library facilities:* Kennedy Library plus 1 other. *General application contact:* Dr. Jim Maraviglia, Assistant Vice President of Admissions, Recruitment and Financial Aid, 805-756-2311.

College of Agriculture, Food and Environmental Sciences
Dr. David J. Wehner, Dean
Programs in:
agribusiness (MS)
agriculture (MS)
agriculture, food and environmental sciences (MS)
forestry science (MS)

College of Architecture and Environmental Design
R. Thomas Jones, Dean
Programs in:
architecture (MS)
architecture and environmental design (MCRP, MS)
city and regional planning (MCRP)

College of Education
Dr. Bonnie Konopak, Dean
Program in:
education (MA)

College of Engineering
Dr. Mohammad Noori, Dean
Programs in:
aerospace engineering (MS)
civil and environmental engineering (MS)
computer science (MS)
electrical engineering (MS)
engineering (MS)
general engineering (MS)
industrial engineering (MS)
mechanical engineering (MS)

College of Liberal Arts
Dr. Linda Halisky, Dean
Programs in:
English (MA)
history (MA)
liberal arts (MA, MPP, MS)
political science (MPP)
psychology (MS)

College of Science and Mathematics
Dr. Philip S. Bailey, Dean
Programs in:
biological sciences (MS)
kinesiology (MS)
mathematics (MS)
polymers and coating science (MS)
science and mathematics (MS)

Orfalea College of Business
Dr. David P. Christy, Dean
Programs in:
business (MBA)
industrial and technical studies (MS)
taxation (MS Acct)

■ CALIFORNIA STATE POLYTECHNIC UNIVERSITY, POMONA
Pomona, CA 91768-2557
http://www.csupomona.edu/

State-supported, coed, comprehensive institution. CGS member. *Enrollment:* 20,510 graduate, professional, and undergraduate students; 654 full-time matriculated graduate/professional students (335 women), 475 part-time matriculated graduate/professional students (210 women). *Graduate faculty:* 533 full-time (192 women), 602 part-time/adjunct (238 women). *Computer facilities:* 1,864 computers available on campus for general student use. A campuswide network can be accessed from student residence rooms and from off campus. Internet access is available. *Library facilities:* University Library. *Graduate expenses:* Tuition, state resident: part-time $226 per unit. Tuition, nonresident: part-time $226 per unit. Required fees: $2,486 per year. *General application contact:* Scott Duncan, Associate Director, Admissions and Outreach, 909-869-3258.

Academic Affairs
Dr. Tomas D. Morales, Provost/Vice President for Academic Affairs

College of Agriculture
Dr. Wayne R. Bidlack, Dean
Programs in:
agricultural science (MS)
animal science (MS)
foods and nutrition (MS)

College of Business Administration
Dr. David Klock, Dean
Program in:
business administration (MBA, MSBA)

College of Education and Integrative Studies
Dr. Barbara J. Way, Interim Dean
Program in:
education and integrative studies (MA)

College of Engineering
Dr. Edward Hohmann, Dean
Programs in:
civil engineering (MS)
electrical engineering (MSEE)
engineering (MSE)
engineering management (MS)
mechanical engineering (MS)

College of Environmental Design
Karen C. Hanna, Dean

California State Polytechnic University, Pomona (continued)
Programs in:
architecture (M Arch)
environmental design (M Arch, M Land Arch, MS, MURP)
landscape architecture (M Land Arch)
regenerative studies (MS)
urban and regional planning (MURP)

College of Letters, Arts, and Social Sciences
Dr. Barbara J. Way, Dean
Programs in:
economics (MS)
English (MA)
history (MA)
kinesiology (MS)
letters, arts, and social sciences (MA, MPA, MS)
psychology (MS)
public administration (MPA)

College of Science
Dr. Donald O. Straney, Dean
Programs in:
applied mathematics (MS)
biological sciences (MS)
chemistry (MS)
computer science (MS)
pure mathematics (MS)
science (MS)

■ CALIFORNIA STATE UNIVERSITY, BAKERSFIELD
Bakersfield, CA 93311-1022
http://www.csubak.edu/

State-supported, coed, comprehensive institution. CGS member. *Enrollment:* 948 full-time matriculated graduate/professional students (673 women), 658 part-time matriculated graduate/professional students (466 women). *Graduate faculty:* 165 full-time (96 women), 103 part-time/adjunct (63 women). *Computer facilities:* 600 computers available on campus for general student use. A campuswide network can be accessed from student residence rooms and from off campus. Internet access and online class registration are available. *Library facilities:* Walter W. Stiern Library. *General application contact:* Dr. Kendyl Magnoson, Associate Dean, 661-664-2161.

Division of Graduate Studies
Programs in:
administration (MS)
interdisciplinary studies (MA)

School of Business and Public Administration
Dr. Mark O. Evans, Interim Dean
Programs in:
business administration (MBA)
business and public administration (MBA, MPA, MSA)
health care management (MSA)
public administration (MPA)

School of Education
Programs in:
bilingual/multicultural education (MA Ed)
curriculum and instruction (MA Ed)
early childhood education (MA)
education (MA, MA Ed, MS, Certificate)
educational administration (MA)
educational technology (MA Ed)
reading/literacy (MA Ed, Certificate)
school counseling (MS)
special education (MA)
student affairs (MS)

School of Humanities and Social Sciences
Programs in:
anthropology (MA)
counseling psychology (MS)
English (MA)
history (MA)
humanities and social sciences (MA, MS, MSW)
psychology (MA)
social work (MSW)
sociology (MA)
Spanish (MA)

School of Natural Sciences and Mathematics
Dr. Julio R. Blanco, Dean
Programs in:
biology (MS)
geology (MS)
hydrogeology (MS)
natural sciences and mathematics (MA, MS)
nursing (MS)
petroleum geology (MS)
teaching mathematics (MA)

■ CALIFORNIA STATE UNIVERSITY, CHICO
Chico, CA 95929-0722
http://www.csuchico.edu/

State-supported, coed, comprehensive institution. CGS member. *Enrollment:* 16,250 graduate, professional, and undergraduate students; 470 full-time matriculated graduate/professional students (289 women), 365 part-time matriculated graduate/professional students (219 women). *Graduate faculty:* 533 full-time (203 women), 432 part-time/adjunct (212 women). *Computer facilities:* 840 computers available on campus for general student use. A campuswide network can be accessed from student residence rooms and from off campus. Internet access and online class registration, student account information, e-mail, calendar, transcripts are available. *Library facilities:* Meriam Library. *General application contact:* Dr. Susan E. Place, School of Graduate, International, and Interdisciplinary Studies, 530-898-6880.

Graduate School
Dr. Susan E. Place, School of Graduate, International, and Interdisciplinary Studies
Programs in:
interdisciplinary studies (MA, MS)
science teaching (MS)
simulation science (MS)
teaching international languages (MA)

College of Behavioral and Social Sciences
Gayle Hutchinson, Dean
Programs in:
applied psychology (MA)
behavioral and social sciences (MA, MPA, MS, MSW)
geography (MA)
health administration (MPA)
local government management (MPA)
marriage and family therapy (MS)
museum studies (MA)
political science (MA)
psychological science (MA)
psychology (MA)
public administration (MPA)
rural and town planning (MA)
social science (MA)
social science education (MA)
social work (MSW)

College of Business
Dr. Willie Hopkins, Dean
Programs in:
business (MBA)
business administration (MBA)

College of Communication and Education
Dr. Phyllis Fernlund, Dean
Programs in:
communication and education (MA, MS)
communication science and disorders (MA)
communication studies (MA)
curriculum and instruction (MA)
education (MA)
educational administration (MA)
instructional technology (MS)
kinesiology (MA)
linguistically and culturally diverse learners (MA)
reading/language arts (MA)
recreation administration (MA)
special education (MA)

College of Engineering, Computer Science, and Technology
Dr. Kenneth Derucher, Dean
Programs in:
computer engineering (MS)
computer science (MS)
electronics engineering (MS)
engineering, computer science, and technology (MS)

College of Humanities and Fine Arts
Dr. Sarah Blackstone, Dean

Programs in:
- art history (MA)
- English (MA)
- fine arts (MFA)
- history (MA)
- humanities and fine arts (MA, MFA)
- music (MA)

College of Natural Sciences
Dr. James Houpis, Dean
Programs in:
- biological sciences (MS)
- botany (MS)
- environmental science (MS)
- geosciences (MS)
- hydrology/hydrogeology (MS)
- math education (MS)
- natural sciences (MS)
- nursing (MS)
- nutrition education (MS)
- nutritional and food science (MS)

■ CALIFORNIA STATE UNIVERSITY, DOMINGUEZ HILLS

Carson, CA 90747-0001

http://www.csudh.edu/

State-supported, coed, comprehensive institution. CGS member. *Enrollment:* 12,068 graduate, professional, and undergraduate students; 1,372 full-time matriculated graduate/professional students (990 women), 1,634 part-time matriculated graduate/professional students (1,216 women). *Graduate faculty:* 101 full-time (57 women), 132 part-time/adjunct (100 women). *Computer facilities:* 200 computers available on campus for general student use. *Library facilities:* Leo F. Cain Educational Resource Center. *Graduate expenses:* Tuition, nonresident: part-time $339 per unit. Required fees: $1,148 per term. Tuition and fees vary according to program. *General application contact:* Linda Wise, Associate Director, 310-243-3613.

Find University Details at www.petersons.com/gradchannel.

College of Business Administration and Public Policy
Dr. James Strong, Dean
Programs in:
- business administration (MBA)
- business administration and public policy (MBA, MPA)
- public administration (MPA)

College of Education
Dr. Lynne Cook, Dean
Program in:
- education (MA, Certificate)

Division of Graduate Education
Dr. Farah Fisher, Chairperson
Programs in:
- counseling (MA)
- curriculum and instruction (MA)
- early childhood (MA)
- educational administration (MA)
- individualized education (MA)
- mild/moderate (MA)
- moderate/severe (MA)
- multicultural education (MA)
- special education (MA)
- technology-based education (MA, Certificate)

College of Extended and International Education
Programs in:
- extended and international education (MA, MS)
- humanities (MA)

College of Health and Human Services
Dr. Mitchell T. Maki, Dean
Programs in:
- health and human services (MA, MS, MSN, MSW)
- marital and family therapy (MS)
- nursing (MSN)
- occupational therapy (MS)
- physical education administration (MA)
- social work (MSW)

Division of Health Sciences
Dr. Mitchell T. Maki, Dean, College of Health and Human Services
Programs in:
- gerontology (MA)
- health sciences (MS)

College of Liberal Arts
Dr. Garry Hart, Acting Dean
Programs in:
- English (MA)
- humanities (MA)
- liberal arts (MA, MS, Certificate)
- negotiation, conflict resolution and peacebuilding (MA)
- rhetoric and composition (Certificate)
- teaching English as a second language (Certificate)

College of Natural and Behavioral Science
Dr. Charles Hohm, Dean
Programs in:
- biology (MS)
- clinical psychology (MA)
- general psychology (MA)
- natural and behavioral science (MA, MS, Certificate)
- quality assurance (MS)
- social research (Certificate)
- sociology (MA)
- teaching of mathematics (MA)

■ CALIFORNIA STATE UNIVERSITY, EAST BAY

Hayward, CA 94542-3000

http://www.csueastbay.edu/

State-supported, coed, comprehensive institution. CGS member. *Enrollment:* 983 full-time matriculated graduate/professional students (679 women), 1,410 part-time matriculated graduate/professional students (870 women). *Graduate faculty:* 368. *Computer facilities:* 700 computers available on campus for general student use. A campuswide network can be accessed from student residence rooms and from off campus. Internet access and online class registration are available. *Library facilities:* California State University, East Bay Library plus 1 other. *General application contact:* My Huynh, Graduate Prospect Specialist, 510-885-2989.

Academic Programs and Graduate Studies
Dr. Carl Bellone, Associate Vice President
Programs in:
- interdisciplinary studies (MA, MS, Certificate)
- multimedia (MA)

College of Business and Economics
John Kohl, Dean
Programs in:
- accounting (MBA)
- business administration (MBA)
- business and economics (MA, MBA, MS)
- business economics (MBA)
- computer information systems (MBA, MS)
- e-business (MBA)
- economics (MA, MBA)
- economics for teachers (MBA)
- entrepreneurship (MBA)
- finance (MBA)
- human resources management (MBA)
- international business (MBA)
- management sciences (MBA)
- marketing management (MBA)
- new ventures/small business management (MBA)
- operations and material management (MBA)
- operations research (MBA)
- quantitative business methods (MS)
- strategic management (MBA)
- supply chain management (MBA)
- taxation (MBA, MS)
- telecommunications (MS)

College of Education and Allied Studies
Dr. Emily Brizendine, Interim Dean
Programs in:
- counseling (MS)
- education (MS)
- education and allied studies (MS)
- educational leadership (MS)
- physical education (MS)
- special education (MS)
- specializing in urban teaching leadership (MS)

College of Letters, Arts, and Social Sciences
Dr. Benjamin Bowser, Interim Dean

California State University, East Bay (continued)
Programs in:
- anthropology (MA)
- communication (MA)
- English (MA)
- geography (MA)
- health care administration (MS)
- history (MA)
- letters, arts, and social sciences (MA, MPA, MS, MSW)
- music (MA)
- public administration (MPA)
- social work (MSW)
- sociology (MA)
- speech pathology and audiology (MS)

College of Science
Dr. Michael Leung, Dean
Programs in:
- actuarial statistics (MS)
- biochemistry (MS)
- biological sciences (MS)
- biostatistics (MS)
- chemistry (MS)
- computational statistics (MS)
- computer science (MS)
- engineering management (MS)
- geology (MS)
- marine sciences (MS)
- mathematical statistics (MS)
- mathematics (MS)
- multimedia (MA)
- science (MA, MS)
- statistics (MS)
- telecommunication (MS)
- theoretical and applied statistics (MS)

■ CALIFORNIA STATE UNIVERSITY, FRESNO
Fresno, CA 93740-8027
http://www.csufresno.edu/

State-supported, coed, comprehensive institution. CGS member. *Computer facilities:* 853 computers available on campus for general student use. A campuswide network can be accessed from off campus. Internet access, common applications are available. *Library facilities:* Henry Madden Library. *General application contact:* Administrative Analyst/Specialist, 559-278-2448.

Division of Graduate Studies

College of Agricultural Sciences and Technology
Programs in:
- agricultural sciences and technology (MA, MS)
- animal science (MA)
- family and consumer sciences (MS)
- food science and nutritional sciences (MS)
- industrial technology (MS)
- plant science (MS)
- viticulture and enology (MS)

College of Arts and Humanities
Programs in:
- art (MA)
- arts and humanities (MA, MFA)
- communication (MA)
- composition theory (MA)
- creative writing (MFA)
- linguistics (MA)
- literature (MA)
- mass communication and journalism (MA)
- music (MA)
- music education (MA)
- performance (MA)
- Spanish (MA)

College of Engineering and Computer Science
Programs in:
- civil engineering (MS)
- computer science (MS)
- electrical engineering (MS)
- engineering and computer science (MS)
- mechanical engineering (MS)

College of Health and Human Services
Programs in:
- communicative disorders (MA)
- environmental/occupational health (MPH)
- exercise science (MA)
- health administration (MPH)
- health and human services (MA, MPH, MPT, MS, MSW)
- health promotion (MPH)
- nursing (MS)
- physical therapy (MPT)
- social work education (MSW)
- sport psychology (MA)

College of Science and Mathematics
Programs in:
- biology (MA)
- chemistry (MS)
- geology (MS)
- marine sciences (MS)
- mathematics (MA)
- physics (MS)
- psychology (MA, MS)
- science and mathematics (MA, MS)
- teaching (MA)

College of Social Sciences
Programs in:
- criminology (MS)
- history (MA)
- international relations (MA)
- public administration (MPA)
- social sciences (MA, MPA, MS)

Craig School of Business
Programs in:
- accountancy (MS)
- business (MBA, MS)
- business administration (MBA)

School of Education and Human Development
Programs in:
- counseling and student services (MS)
- education (MA)
- education and human development (MA, MS, Ed D)
- educational leadership (Ed D)
- marriage and family therapy (MS)
- rehabilitation counseling (MS)
- special education (MA)

■ CALIFORNIA STATE UNIVERSITY, FULLERTON
Fullerton, CA 92834-9480
http://www.fullerton.edu/

State-supported, coed, comprehensive institution. CGS member. *Enrollment:* 35,921 graduate, professional, and undergraduate students; 1,309 full-time matriculated graduate/professional students (856 women), 2,802 part-time matriculated graduate/professional students (1,727 women). *Computer facilities:* 1,993 computers available on campus for general student use. A campuswide network can be accessed from student residence rooms and from off campus. Internet access is available. *Library facilities:* California State University, Fullerton Pollak Library. *Graduate expenses:* Tuition, nonresident: part-time $339 per unit. Required fees: $1,155 per semester. *General application contact:* Admissions/Applications, 714-278-2300.

Graduate Studies
Dr. Ray Young, Associate Vice President, Academic Programs

College of Business and Economics
Dr. Anil Puri, Dean
Programs in:
- accounting (MBA, MS)
- business administration (MBA)
- business and economics (MA, MBA, MS)
- business economics (MBA)
- economics (MA)
- finance (MBA)
- international business (MBA)
- management (MBA)
- management information systems (MS)
- management science (MBA, MS)
- marketing (MBA)
- operations research (MS)
- statistics (MS)
- taxation (MS)

College of Communications
Dr. Rick Pullen, Dean
Programs in:
- advertising (MA)
- communications (MA)
- communicative disorders (MA)
- journalism education (MA)
- news editorial (MA)
- photo communication (MA)
- public relations (MA)
- radio, television and film (MA)
- speech communication (MA)
- technical communication (MA)
- theory and process (MA)

College of Education
Dr. Claire Cavallaro, Dean
Programs in:
- bilingual/bicultural education (MS)
- education (MS)
- educational leadership (MS)
- elementary curriculum and instruction (MS)
- instructional design and technology (MS)
- middle school mathematics (MS)
- reading (MS)
- secondary education (MS)
- special education (MS)
- teacher induction (MS)

College of Engineering and Computer Science
Dr. Raman Unnikrishnan, Dean
Programs in:
- applications administrative information systems (MS)
- applications mathematical methods (MS)
- civil engineering and engineering mechanics (MS)
- computer science (MS)
- electrical engineering (MS)
- engineering and computer science (MS)
- engineering science (MS)
- information processing systems (MS)
- mechanical engineering (MS)
- software engineering (MS)
- systems engineering (MS)

College of Health and Human Development
Dr. Roberta Rikli, Dean
Programs in:
- counseling (MS)
- health and human development (MPH, MS)
- nursing (MS)
- physical education (MS)
- public health (MPH)

College of Humanities and Social Sciences
Dr. Thomas Klammer, Dean
Programs in:
- American studies (MA)
- analysis of specific language structures (MA)
- anthropological linguistics (MA)
- anthropology (MA)
- applied linguistics (MA)
- clinical/community psychology (MS)
- communication and semantics (MA)
- comparative literature (MA)
- disorders of communication (MA)
- English (MA)
- environmental education and communication (MS)
- environmental policy and planning (MS)
- environmental sciences (MS)
- experimental phonetics (MA)
- French (MA)
- geography (MA)
- German (MA)
- gerontology (MS)
- history (MA)
- humanities and social sciences (MA, MPA, MS)
- political science (MA)
- psychology (MA)
- public administration (MPA)
- sociology (MA)
- Spanish (MA)
- teaching English to speakers of other languages (MS)
- technological studies (MS)

College of Natural Science and Mathematics
Dr. Steven Murray, Dean
Programs in:
- analytical chemistry (MS)
- applied mathematics (MA)
- biochemistry (MS)
- biological science (MS)
- botany (MS)
- geochemistry (MS)
- geological sciences (MS)
- inorganic chemistry (MS)
- mathematics (MA)
- mathematics for secondary school teachers (MA)
- microbiology (MS)
- natural science and mathematics (MA, MAT, MS)
- organic chemistry (MS)
- physical chemistry (MS)
- physics (MA)
- teaching science (MAT)

College of the Arts
Jerry Samuelson, Dean
Programs in:
- acting (MFA)
- acting and directing (MA)
- art (MA, MFA)
- art history (MA)
- arts (MA, MFA, MM, Certificate)
- dance (MA)
- design (MA)
- directing (MFA)
- dramatic literature/criticism (MA)
- museum studies (Certificate)
- music education (MA)
- music history and literature (MA)
- oral interpretation (MA)
- performance (MM)
- playwriting (MA)
- technical theater (MA)
- technical theater and design (MFA)
- television (MA)
- theatre for children (MA)
- theatre history (MA)
- theory-composition (MM)

■ CALIFORNIA STATE UNIVERSITY, LONG BEACH
Long Beach, CA 90840
http://www.csulb.edu/

State-supported, coed, comprehensive institution. CGS member. *Enrollment:* 35,574 graduate, professional, and undergraduate students; 1,975 full-time matriculated graduate/professional students (1,297 women), 2,884 part-time matriculated graduate/professional students (1,634 women). *Graduate faculty:* 852 full-time (345 women), 1,179 part-time/adjunct (614 women). *Computer facilities:* 2,000 computers available on campus for general student use. A campuswide network can be accessed from off campus. Internet access is available. *Library facilities:* University Library. *General application contact:* Rachel Brophy, Students Programs Coordinator, 562-985-4546.

Graduate Studies
Dr. Cecile Lindsay, Director
Program in:
- interdisciplinary studies (MA, MS)

College of Business Administration
Dr. Mohammed B. Khan, Interim Dean
Program in:
- business administration (MBA)

College of Education
Dr. Jean Houck, Dean
Programs in:
- counseling (MS)
- counseling-guidance (MS)
- education (MA)
- special education (MS)

College of Engineering
Dr. Forouzan Golshani, Dean
Programs in:
- aerospace engineering (MSAE)
- civil engineering (MSCE)
- computer engineering and computer science (MS)
- electrical engineering (MSEE)
- engineering (MS, MSAE, MSCE, MSE, MSEE, MSME, PhD)
- engineering and industrial applied mathematics (PhD)
- interdisciplinary engineering (MSE)
- management engineering (MSE)
- mechanical engineering (MSME)

College of Health and Human Services
Dr. Ronald Vogel, Dean
Programs in:
- communicative disorders (MA)
- criminal justice (MS)
- emergency services administration (MS)
- family and consumer sciences (MA)
- gerontology (MS)
- health and human services (MA, MPA, MPH, MPT, MS, MSW, Certificate)
- health care administration (MS, Certificate)
- health science (MPH)
- kinesiology (MA, MS)
- nursing (MS)
- nursing-health care administration (MS)
- nutritional sciences (MS)
- nutritional sciences/dietetics and food administration (MS)
- occupational studies (MA)
- physical therapy (MPT)
- public policy and administration (MPA)
- recreation administration (MS)
- social work (MSW)

California State University, Long Beach (continued)

College of Liberal Arts
Dr. Gerry Riposa, Dean
Programs in:
anthropology (MA)
Asian American studies (Certificate)
Asian studies (MA)
communication studies (MA)
creative writing (MFA)
economics (MA)
English (MA)
French (MA)
geography (MA)
German (MA)
history (MA)
liberal arts (MA, MFA, MS, Certificate)
linguistics (MA)
philosophy (MA)
political science (MA)
psychology (MA, MS)
religious studies (MA)
Spanish (MA)

College of Natural Sciences and Mathematics
Dr. Laura Kingsford, Dean
Programs in:
biochemistry (MS)
biology (MS)
chemistry (MS)
geology/geosciences (MS)
mathematics (MS)
mathematics and science education (MS)
microbiology (MS)
natural sciences and mathematics (MS)
physics (MS)

College of the Arts
Dr. Donald Para, Dean
Programs in:
art (MA, MFA)
arts (MA, MFA, MM)
dance (performance) (MFA)
music (MA)
music (performing) (MM)
theatre arts (professional performance/design) (MFA)
theatre arts/drama (MA)

■ CALIFORNIA STATE UNIVERSITY, LOS ANGELES
Los Angeles, CA 90032-8530
http://www.calstatela.edu/

State-supported, coed, comprehensive institution. CGS member. *Enrollment:* 20,565 graduate, professional, and undergraduate students; 1,476 full-time matriculated graduate/professional students (1,017 women), 3,365 part-time matriculated graduate/professional students (2,228 women). *Graduate faculty:* 291 full-time (138 women), 147 part-time/adjunct (67 women). *Computer facilities:* 1,500 computers available on campus for general student use. A campuswide network can be accessed from off campus. Internet access is available. *Library facilities:* John F. Kennedy Memorial Library. *Graduate expenses:* Tuition, nonresident: part-time $226 per unit. *General application contact:* Dr. Jose L. Galvan, Dean of Graduate Studies, 323-343-3820.

Graduate Studies
Dr. Jose L. Galvan, Dean of Graduate Studies

Charter College of Education
Dr. Mary Falvey, Dean
Programs in:
applied and advanced studies in education (MA)
applied behavior analysis (MS)
community college counseling (MS)
computer education (MA)
counseling (MS)
education (MA, MS)
elementary teaching (MA)
instructional technology (MA)
psychological foundations (MA)
reading (MA)
rehabilitation counseling (MS)
school counseling and school psychology (MS)
secondary teaching (MA)
social foundations (MA)
special education (MA)
teaching English to speakers of other languages (MA)

College of Arts and Letters
Dr. Terry Allison, Dean
Programs in:
art (MA)
arts and letters (MA, MFA, MM)
English (MA)
fine arts (MFA)
French (MA)
music composition (MM)
music education (MA)
musicology (MA)
performance (MM)
philosophy (MA)
Spanish (MA)
speech communication (MA)
theater arts (MA)

College of Business and Economics
Dr. Dong-Woo Lee, Acting Dean
Programs in:
accountancy (MS)
accounting (MBA)
analytical quantitative economics (MA)
business and economics (MA, MBA, MS)
business economics (MA, MBA, MS)
business information systems (MBA)
economics (MA)
finance and banking (MBA, MS)
finance and law (MBA, MS)
health care management (MS)
information systems (MBA, MS)
international business (MBA, MS)
management (MBA, MS)
management information systems (MS)
marketing (MBA, MS)
office management (MBA)

College of Engineering, Computer Science, and Technology
Dr. Keith Moo-Young, Dean
Programs in:
civil engineering (MS)
computer science (MS)
electrical engineering (MS)
engineering, computer science, and technology (MS)
mechanical engineering (MS)

College of Health and Human Services
Dr. Beatrice Yorker, Dean
Programs in:
child development (MA)
criminal justice (MS)
criminalistics (MS)
health and human services (MA, MS, MSW)
health science (MA)
kinesiology (MA)
nursing (MS)
nutritional science (MS)
physical education (MA)
physical education and kinesiology (MA)
social work (MSW)
speech and hearing (MA)
speech-language pathology (MA)

College of Natural and Social Sciences
Dr. Desdemona Cardoza, Dean
Programs in:
analytical chemistry (MS)
anthropology (MA)
biochemistry (MS)
biology (MS)
chemistry (MS)
geography (MA)
geological sciences (MS)
history (MA)
inorganic chemistry (MS)
Latin American studies (MA)
mathematics (MS)
Mexican-American studies (MA)
natural and social sciences (MA, MS)
organic chemistry (MS)
physical chemistry (MS)
physics (MS)
political science (MA)
psychology (MA, MS)
public administration (MS)
sociology (MA)

■ CALIFORNIA STATE UNIVERSITY, NORTHRIDGE
Northridge, CA 91330
http://www.csun.edu/

State-supported, coed, comprehensive institution. CGS member. *Enrollment:* 34,560 graduate, professional, and undergraduate students; 1,693 full-time matriculated graduate/professional students (1,179 women), 2,855 part-time matriculated graduate/professional students (1,778 women). *Graduate faculty:* 732 full-time (318 women), 1,028 part-time/adjunct (553 women). *Computer facilities:* A campuswide network can be accessed from off campus. Internet access and online class registration are available. *Library facilities:* Oviatt Library. *Graduate expenses:* Tuition, nonresident: full-time $8,136; part-time $4,068 per year. Required fees: $3,624; $1,161 per term. *General application contact:* Dr. Mack Johnson, Associate Vice President, 818-677-2138.

Graduate Studies
Dr. Mack Johnson, Associate Vice President
Program in:
interdisciplinary studies (MA, MS)

College of Arts, Media, and Communication
Prof. David Moon, Interim Dean
Programs in:
art education (MA)
art history (MA)
arts, media, and communication (MA, MFA, MM)
communication studies (MA)
composition (MM)
conducting (MM)
mass communication (MA)
music education (MA)
performance (MM)
screenwriting (MA)
studio art (MA, MFA)
theater (MA)
visual communication (MA, MFA)

College of Business and Economics
Dr. William Jennings, Interim Dean
Program in:
business and economics (MBA)

College of Education
Dr. Philip J. Rusche, Dean
Programs in:
counseling (MS)
early childhood special education (MA)
education (MA)
education of the deaf and hard of hearing (MA)
educational administration (MA)
educational psychology (MA Ed)
educational therapy (MA)
elementary education (MA)
genetic counseling (MS)
mild/moderate disabilities (MA)
moderate/severe disabilities (MA)
secondary education (MA)

College of Engineering and Computer Science
Dr. S.K. Ramesh, Dean
Programs in:
computer science (MS)
electrical engineering (MS)
engineering (MS)
engineering and computer science (MS)
engineering management (MS)
manufacturing systems engineering (MS)
materials engineering (MS)
mechanical engineering (MS)

College of Health and Human Development
Dr. Helen M. Castillo, Dean
Programs in:
communication disorders and sciences (MS)
family and consumer sciences (MS)
health administration (MS)
health and human development (MPH, MPT, MS)
health education (MPH)
industrial hygiene (MS)
kinesiology (MS)
physical therapy (MPT)
recreation administration (MS)

College of Humanities
Dr. Elizabeth Say, Dean
Programs in:
Chicana and Chicano studies (MA)
creative writing (MA)
humanities (MA)
linguistics (MA)
literature (MA)
rhetoric and composition theory (MA)
Spanish (MA)

College of Science and Mathematics
Dr. Jerry Stinner, Dean
Programs in:
applied mathematics (MS)
biochemistry (MS)
biology (MS)
chemistry (MS)
genetic counseling (MS)
geology (MS)
mathematics (MS)
mathematics for educational careers (MS)
physics (MS)
science and mathematics (MS)

College of Social and Behavioral Sciences
Dr. Stella Z. Theodoulou, Dean
Programs in:
anthropology (MA)
geography (MA)
history (MA)
political science (MA)
psychology (MA)
public administration (MPA)
social and behavioral sciences (MA, MPA, MSW)
social work (MSW)
sociology (MA)

■ CALIFORNIA STATE UNIVERSITY, SACRAMENTO
Sacramento, CA 95819-6048
http://www.csus.edu/

State-supported, coed, comprehensive institution. CGS member. *Enrollment:* 28,529 graduate, professional, and undergraduate students; 1,694 full-time matriculated graduate/professional students (1,186 women), 1,784 part-time matriculated graduate/professional students (1,132 women). *Computer facilities:* 700 computers available on campus for general student use. A campuswide network can be accessed from student residence rooms and from off campus. Internet access and online class registration are available. *Library facilities:* California State University, Sacramento Library. *General application contact:* Dr. Chevelle Newsome, Associate Dean of Graduate Admissions, 916-278-6470.

Graduate Studies
Dr. Chevelle Newsome, Associate Dean
Program in:
special majors (MA, MS)

College of Arts and Letters
Jeffrey Mason, Dean
Programs in:
arts and letters (MA, MM)
communication studies (MA)
creative writing (MA)
foreign languages (MA)
French (MA)
German (MA)
music (MM)
public history (MA)
Spanish (MA)
studio art (MA)
teaching English to speakers of other languages (MA)
theater arts (MA)
theatre and dance (MA)

College of Business Administration
Dr. Sanjay Varshney, Dean
Programs in:
accountancy (MS)
business administration (MBA)
human resources (MBA)
management information science (MS)
urban land development (MBA)

College of Education
Dr. Vanessa Sheared, Dean
Programs in:
bilingual/cross-cultural education (MA)
career counseling (MS)
curriculum and instruction (MA)
early childhood education (MA)
education (MA, MS)
educational administration (MA)
generic counseling (MS)
guidance (MA)
reading education (MA)
school counseling (MS)
school psychology (MS)
special education (MA)
vocational rehabilitation (MS)

College of Engineering and Computer Science
Dr. Emir Jose Macari, Dean
Programs in:
civil engineering (MS)
computer systems (MS)
electrical engineering (MS)
engineering and computer science (MS)
mechanical engineering (MS)
software engineering (MS)

College of Health and Human Services
Dr. Marilyn Hopkins, Dean

California State University, Sacramento (continued)

Programs in:
- audiology (MS)
- criminal justice (MS)
- family and children's services (MSW)
- health and human services (MS, MSW)
- health care (MSW)
- mental health (MSW)
- nursing (MS)
- physical education (MS)
- recreation administration (MS)
- social justice and corrections (MSW)
- speech pathology (MS)

College of Natural Sciences and Mathematics
Laurel Hefferman, Dean
Programs in:
- biological sciences (MA, MS)
- chemistry (MS)
- immunohematology (MS)
- marine science (MS)
- mathematics and statistics (MA)
- natural sciences and mathematics (MA, MS)

College of Social Sciences and Interdisciplinary Studies
Otis Scott, Dean
Programs in:
- anthropology (MA)
- counseling psychology (MA)
- government (MA)
- international affairs (MA)
- public policy and administration (MPPA)
- social sciences and interdisciplinary studies (MA, MPPA)
- sociology (MA)

■ CALIFORNIA STATE UNIVERSITY, SAN BERNARDINO

San Bernardino, CA 92407-2397
http://www.csusb.edu/

State-supported, coed, comprehensive institution. CGS member. *Enrollment:* 16,479 graduate, professional, and undergraduate students; 1,527 full-time matriculated graduate/professional students (1,028 women), 738 part-time matriculated graduate/professional students (477 women). *Graduate faculty:* 431 full-time, 516 part-time/adjunct. *Computer facilities:* 1,300 computers available on campus for general student use. A campuswide network can be accessed from student residence rooms and from off campus. Internet access and online class registration are available. *Library facilities:* Pfau Library. *General application contact:* Olivia Rosas, Director of Admissions, 909-537-5188.

Graduate Studies
Dr. Sandra Kamusikiri, Dean of Graduate Studies
Program in:
- interdisciplinary studies (MA)

College of Arts and Letters
Dr. Eri F. Yasuhara, Dean
Programs in:
- art (MA)
- arts and letters (MA)
- communication studies (MA)
- English composition (MA)
- Spanish (MA)
- theatre arts (MA)

College of Business and Public Administration
Dr. Karen Dill-Bowerman, Dean
Programs in:
- business administration (MBA)
- business and public administration (MBA, MPA)
- public administration (MPA)

College of Education
Dr. Patricia Arlin, Dean
Programs in:
- bilingual/cross-cultural education (MA)
- counseling and guidance (MS)
- curriculum and instruction (MA)
- educational administration (MA)
- educational psychology and counseling (MA, MS)
- elementary education (MA)
- English as a second language (MA)
- environmental education (MA)
- history and English for secondary teachers (MA)
- instructional technology (MA)
- reading (MA)
- rehabilitation counseling (MA)
- secondary education (MA)
- special education (MA)
- special education and rehabilitation counseling (MA)
- teaching of science (MA)
- vocational and career education (MA)

College of Natural Sciences
Dr. B. Robert Carlson, Dean
Programs in:
- biology (MS)
- computer science (MS)
- environmental sciences and chemistry (MS)
- health science (MS)
- health services administration (MS)
- kinesiology (MA Ed)
- mathematics (MA, MAT)
- natural sciences (MA, MA Ed, MAT, MS)
- nursing (MS)

College of Social and Behavioral Sciences
Dr. John Conley, Chair
Programs in:
- clinical/counseling psychology (MS)
- criminal justice (MA)
- general experimental psychology (MA)
- human development (MA)
- industrial organizational psychology (MS)
- national security studies (MA)
- social and behavioral sciences (MA, MS, MSW)
- social sciences (MA)
- social work (MSW)

■ CALIFORNIA STATE UNIVERSITY, SAN MARCOS

San Marcos, CA 92096-0001
http://www.csusm.edu/

State-supported, coed, comprehensive institution. CGS member. *Enrollment:* 6,956 graduate, professional, and undergraduate students; 172 full-time matriculated graduate/professional students (106 women), 468 part-time matriculated graduate/professional students (346 women). *Graduate faculty:* 104 full-time (60 women), 143 part-time/adjunct (85 women). *Computer facilities:* 1,300 computers available on campus for general student use. A campuswide network can be accessed from student residence rooms and from off campus. Internet access and online class registration are available. *Library facilities:* Kellogg Library. *Graduate expenses:* Tuition, nonresident: part-time $339 per unit. Required fees: $1,186 per term. *General application contact:* Admissions, 760-750-4848.

College of Arts and Sciences
Dr. Vicki Golich, Dean
Programs in:
- arts and sciences (MA, MS)
- biological sciences (MS)
- computer science (MS)
- literature and writing studies (MA)
- mathematics (MS)
- psychology (MA)
- sociological practice (MA)
- Spanish (MA)

College of Business Administration
Dennis Guseman, Dean
Programs in:
- business management (MBA)
- government management (MBA)

College of Education
Dr. Mark Baldwin, Dean
Program in:
- education (MA)

■ CALIFORNIA STATE UNIVERSITY, STANISLAUS

Turlock, CA 95382
http://www.csustan.edu/

State-supported, coed, comprehensive institution. CGS member. *Computer facilities:* 150 computers available on campus for general student use. A campuswide network can be accessed from student residence rooms and from off campus. Internet access and online class registration are available.

Library facilities: University Library. *General application contact:* Coordinator, Graduate School, 209-667-3129.

College of Arts, Letters, and Sciences
Programs in:
- arts, letters, and sciences (MA, MPA, MS, MSW)
- behavior analysis psychology (MS)
- criminal justice (MA)
- English (MA)
- general psychology (MA)
- history (MA)
- marine sciences (MS)
- public administration (MPA)
- social work (MSW)

College of Business Administration
Programs in:
- business administration (MBA)
- international finance (MSBA)

College of Education
Programs in:
- curriculum and instruction (MA Ed)
- education (MA Ed)

Programs in Interdisciplinary Studies
Program in:
- interdisciplinary studies (MA, MS)

■ CHAPMAN UNIVERSITY
Orange, CA 92866
http://www.chapman.edu/

Independent-religious, coed, comprehensive institution. *Enrollment:* 5,908 graduate, professional, and undergraduate students; 1,142 full-time matriculated graduate/professional students (640 women), 565 part-time matriculated graduate/professional students (345 women). *Graduate faculty:* 132 full-time (53 women), 116 part-time/adjunct (44 women). *Computer facilities:* Computer purchase and lease plans are available. 453 computers available on campus for general student use. A campuswide network can be accessed from student residence rooms and from off campus. Internet access and online class registration are available. *Library facilities:* Leatherby Libraries plus 1 other. *General application contact:* Saundra Hoover, Director of Graduate Admissions, 714-997-6786.

Find University Details at www.petersons.com/gradchannel.

Graduate Studies
Dr. Raymond Sfeir, Associate Provost

Dodge College of Film and Media Arts
Robert Bassett, Dean
Programs in:
- film and media arts (MA, MFA)
- film and television producing (MFA)
- film production (MFA)
- film studies (MA)
- screenwriting (MFA)

The George L. Argyros School of Business and Economics
Dr. Arthur Kraft, Dean
Programs in:
- business and economics (Exec MBA, MBA, MSHRM, Certificate)
- human resources and management (MSHRM)
- human resources management (Certificate)

School of Education
Dr. Donald Cardinal, Dean
Programs in:
- cultural and curricular studies (PhD)
- curriculum and instruction (MA)
- disability studies (PhD)
- education (MA, PhD, Ed S)
- educational leadership and administration (MA)
- educational psychology (MA)
- reading education (MA)
- school counseling (MA)
- school psychology (Ed S)
- special education (MA)
- teaching: elementary education (MA)
- teaching: secondary education (MA)

School of Law
Dr. Parham Williams, Dean
Programs in:
- law (JD)
- taxation (LL M)

Wilkinson College of Letters and Sciences
Dr. Roberta Lessor, Dean
Programs in:
- creative writing (MFA)
- food science and nutrition (MS)
- letters and sciences (MA, MFA, MS, DPT)
- literature (MA)
- marriage and family therapy (MA)
- physical therapy (DPT)

■ CLAREMONT GRADUATE UNIVERSITY
Claremont, CA 91711-6160
http://www.cgu.edu/

Independent, coed, graduate-only institution. CGS member. *Graduate faculty:* 91 full-time (35 women), 81 part-time/adjunct (30 women). *Computer facilities:* 90 computers available on campus for general student use. Internet access and online class registration are available. *Library facilities:* Honnold Library plus 3 others. *General application contact:* Brenda Wright, Assistant Director of Admissions, 909-627-0434.

Graduate Programs
Yi Feng, Provost and Vice President for Academic Affairs
Programs in:
- applied women's studies (MA)
- botany (MS, PhD)
- financial engineering (MS, MSFE, PhD)

Peter F. Drucker and Masatoshi Ito Graduate School of Management
Ira A. Jackson, Henry Y. Hwang Dean and Professor of Management
Programs in:
- advanced management (MS)
- executive management (EMBA, MA, MS, PhD, Certificate)
- leadership (Certificate)
- management (MA, MBA, PhD, Certificate)
- strategy (Certificate)

School of Arts and Humanities
Patricia Easton, Dean
Programs in:
- Africana history (Certificate)
- Africana studies (Certificate)
- American studies (MA, PhD)
- archival studies (MA)
- arts and cultural management (MA)
- arts and humanities (M Phil, MA, MFA, DCM, DMA, PhD, Certificate)
- church music (MA, DCM)
- composition (MA, DMA)
- critical theory (MA, PhD)
- cultural studies (MA, PhD)
- digital media (MA, MFA)
- drawing (MA, MFA)
- early modern studies (MA, PhD)
- English (M Phil, MA, PhD)
- European studies (MA, PhD)
- installation (MA, MFA)
- literary theory (PhD)
- literature (MA, PhD)
- literature and creative writing (MA)
- literature and film (MA)
- musicology (MA, PhD)
- new genre (MA, MFA)
- oral history (MA, PhD)
- painting (MA, MFA)
- performance (MA, MFA, DMA)
- philosophy (MA, PhD)
- photography (MA, MFA)
- sculpture (MA, MFA)

School of Behavioral and Organizational Sciences
Stewart Donaldson, Dean
Programs in:
- advanced study in evaluation (Certificate)
- behavioral and organizational sciences (MA, MS, PhD, Certificate)
- cognitive psychology (MA, PhD)
- developmental psychology (MA, PhD)
- evaluation and applied methods (MA, PhD)
- human resources design (MS)
- organizational behavior (MA, PhD)
- social psychology (MA, PhD)

School of Educational Studies
Philip H. Dreyer, Dean

Claremont Graduate University (continued)
Programs in:
Africana education (Certificate)
education policy issues (MA, PhD)
higher education (PhD)
higher education administration (MA)
human development (MA, PhD)
public school administration (MA, PhD)
teacher education (MA, PhD)
teaching and learning (MA, PhD)
urban education administration (MA, PhD)

School of Information Systems and Technology
Lorne Olfman, Dean
Programs in:
electronic commerce (MS, PhD)
information systems (Certificate)
knowledge management (MS, PhD)
systems development (MS, PhD)
telecommunications and networking (MS, PhD)

School of Mathematical Sciences
John Angus, Dean
Programs in:
computational and systems biology (PhD)
computational science (PhD)
engineering mathematics (PhD)
operations research and statistics (MA, MS)
physical applied mathematics (MA, MS)
pure mathematics (MA, MS)
scientific computing (MA, MS)
systems and control theory (MA, MS)

School of Politics and Economics
Thomas Willett, Dean
Programs in:
American politics (MA, PhD)
business and financial economics (MA, PhD)
comparative politics (PhD)
economic development (Certificate)
economics (PhD)
international economic policy and management (MA, PhD)
international political economy (MA)
international studies (MA)
political economy and public policy (MA, PhD)
political philosophy (PhD)
political science (PhD)
politics and economics (MA, PhD, Certificate)
politics, economics and business (MA)
public policy (MA, PhD)
world politics (PhD)

School of Religion
Karen Torjesen, Dean
Programs in:
Hebrew Bible (MA, PhD)
history of Christianity and religion in North America (MA, PhD)
New Testament (MA, PhD)
philosophy of religion and theology (MA, PhD)
theology, ethics and culture (MA, PhD)
women's studies in religion (MA, PhD)

■ CONCORDIA UNIVERSITY
Irvine, CA 92612-3299
http://www.cui.edu/

Independent-religious, coed, comprehensive institution. *Enrollment:* 2,317 graduate, professional, and undergraduate students; 328 full-time matriculated graduate/professional students (220 women), 556 part-time matriculated graduate/professional students (417 women). *Graduate faculty:* 31 full-time, 22 part-time/adjunct. *Computer facilities:* 42 computers available on campus for general student use. A campuswide network can be accessed from student residence rooms and from off campus. Internet access is available. *Library facilities:* Concordia University Library. *General application contact:* Information Contact, 800-229-1200.

School of Arts and Sciences
Dr. Kenneth Mangels, Dean
Program in:
coaching and athletic administration (MA)

School of Business and Professional Studies
Dr. Timothy Peters, Dean
Programs in:
entrepreneurial business administration (MBA)
international studies (MA)

School of Education
Dr. Joseph Bordeaux, Dean
Programs in:
curriculum and instruction (MA)
education (M Ed)
educational administration and administrative services credential (MA)

School of Theology
Rev. Dr. James V. Bachman, Dean
Program in:
theology (MA)

■ DEVRY UNIVERSITY
Pomona, CA 91768-2642
http://www.devry.edu/

Proprietary, coed, comprehensive institution. *Computer facilities:* Computer purchase and lease plans are available. 513 computers available on campus for general student use. A campuswide network can be accessed from off campus. Internet access and online class registration are available. *Library facilities:* Learning Resource Center.

Keller Graduate School of Management
Program in:
management (MAFM, MBA, MHRM, MISM, MNCM, MPA, MPM)

■ DOMINICAN UNIVERSITY OF CALIFORNIA
San Rafael, CA 94901-2298
http://www.dominican.edu/

Independent-religious, coed, comprehensive institution. *Computer facilities:* 45 computers available on campus for general student use. A campuswide network can be accessed from student residence rooms and from off campus. Internet access, Microsoft Office Application (Word, Excel, Powerpoint) are available. *Library facilities:* Archbishop Alemany Library plus 1 other. *General application contact:* Graduate Admissions Counselor, 415-485-3246.

Graduate Programs

School of Arts and Sciences
Programs in:
arts and sciences (MA, MS)
counseling psychology (MS)
geriatric and nurse educator (MS)
humanities (MA)
integrated health practices (MS)
occupational therapy (MS)

School of Business, Education and Leadership
Programs in:
business and international studies (MAM, MBA)
business, education and leadership (MAM, MBA, MS, Credential)
curriculum and instruction (MS)
education (MS, Credential)
global strategic management (MBA)
management (MAM)
multiple subject teaching (Credential)
single subject teaching (Credential)
special education (Credential)
strategic leadership (MBA)

■ FRESNO PACIFIC UNIVERSITY
Fresno, CA 93702-4709
http://www.fresno.edu/

Independent-religious, coed, comprehensive institution. *Enrollment:* 2,324 graduate, professional, and undergraduate students; 161 full-time matriculated graduate/professional students (117 women), 577 part-time matriculated graduate/professional students (416 women). *Graduate faculty:* 16 full-time (6 women), 22 part-time/adjunct (9 women). *Computer facilities:* 72 computers available on campus for general student use. A campuswide network can be accessed from student residence rooms and from off campus. Internet access is available. *Library facilities:* Hiebert Library. *Graduate expenses:*

Tuition: full-time $7,470; part-time $415 per credit. *General application contact:* Vivian Galba, Admissions Coordinator, 559-453-3667.

Graduate Programs

Programs in:
- individualized study (MA)
- kinesiology (MA)
- leadership and organizational studies (MA)
- peacemaking and conflict studies (MA)
- teaching English to speakers of other languages (MA)

Programs in Education

Programs in:
- administration (MA Ed)
- administrative services (MA Ed)
- bilingual/cross-cultural education (MA Ed)
- curriculum and teaching (MA Ed)
- educational technology (MA Ed)
- foundations, curriculum and teaching (MA Ed)
- integrated mathematics/science education (MA Ed)
- language development (MA Ed)
- language, literacy, and culture (MA Ed)
- mathematics education (MA Ed)
- mathematics/science/computer education (MA Ed)
- middle school mathematics (MA Ed)
- mild/moderate (MA Ed)
- moderate/severe (MA Ed)
- multilingual contexts (MA Ed)
- physical and health impairments (MA Ed)
- pupil personnel services (MA Ed)
- reading (MA Ed)
- reading/English as a second language (MA Ed)
- reading/language arts (MA Ed)
- school counseling (MA Ed)
- school library and information technology (MA Ed)
- school psychology (MA Ed)
- secondary school mathematics (MA Ed)
- special education (MA Ed)

■ GOLDEN GATE UNIVERSITY
San Francisco, CA 94105-2968
http://www.ggu.edu/

Independent, coed, university. *Enrollment:* 1,166 full-time matriculated graduate/professional students (658 women), 1,963 part-time matriculated graduate/professional students (1,019 women). *Graduate faculty:* 97 full-time, 398 part-time/adjunct. *Computer facilities:* Computer purchase and lease plans are available. 52 computers available on campus for general student use. A campuswide network can be accessed. Internet access and online class registration are available. *Library facilities:* Golden Gate University Library plus 1 other. *General application contact:* Angela Williams, Enrollment Services, 415-442-7800.

Ageno School of Business

Terry Connelly, Dean
Programs in:
- accounting (M Ac, MBA)
- business administration (EMBA, MBA, DBA)
- finance (MBA, MS, Certificate)
- financial planning (MS, Certificate)
- human resource management (MBA, MS)
- human resources management (Certificate)
- information technology (MBA)
- information technology management (MS, Certificate)
- integrated marketing and communications (MS, Certificate)
- international business (MBA)
- management (MBA)
- marketing (MBA, MS, Certificate)
- operations management (Certificate)
- psychology (MA, Certificate)
- public relations (MS, Certificate)

School of Law

Frederic White, Dean
Programs in:
- environmental law (LL M)
- intellectual property law (LL M)
- international legal studies (LL M, SJD)
- law (JD)
- taxation (LL M)
- U.S. legal studies (LL M)

School of Taxation

Mary Canning, Dean
Program in:
- taxation (MS, Certificate)

■ HOLY NAMES UNIVERSITY
Oakland, CA 94619-1699
http://www.hnu.edu/

Independent-religious, coed, primarily women, comprehensive institution. *Enrollment:* 1,048 graduate, professional, and undergraduate students; 176 full-time matriculated graduate/professional students (152 women), 249 part-time matriculated graduate/professional students (188 women). *Graduate faculty:* 12 full-time (10 women), 50 part-time/adjunct (35 women). *Computer facilities:* 86 computers available on campus for general student use. A campuswide network can be accessed from student residence rooms and from off campus. Internet access is available. *Library facilities:* Cushing Library. *Graduate expenses:* Tuition: full-time $10,800; part-time $600 per unit. Required fees: $240; $120 per term. *General application contact:* Gary Murdough, Graduate Admissions Office, 510-436-1351.

Graduate Division

Dr. Lizbeth Martin, Vice President for Academic Affairs
Programs in:
- advanced curriculum studies (M Ed)
- community health nursing/case manager (MS)
- counseling psychology (MA)
- educational therapy (M Ed)
- family nurse practitioner (MS)
- Kodály music education (Certificate)
- management (MBA)
- mild/moderate disabilities (Ed S)
- multiple subject credential (M Ed)
- music education with a Kodály emphasis (MM)
- pastoral counseling (MA, Certificate)
- pastoral ministries (MA)
- performance (MM)
- piano pedagogy (MM)
- piano pedagogy with Suzuki emphasis (Certificate)
- single subject credential (M Ed)
- special education (M Ed)
- teaching English as a second language (M Ed, Certificate)
- urban education (M Ed)

Sophia Center: Spirituality for the New Millennium

Dr. James Conlon, Program Director
Programs in:
- creation spirituality (Certificate)
- culture and creation spirituality (MA)

■ HOPE INTERNATIONAL UNIVERSITY
Fullerton, CA 92831-3138
http://www.hiu.edu/

Independent-religious, coed, comprehensive institution. *Enrollment:* 903 graduate, professional, and undergraduate students; 126 full-time matriculated graduate/professional students (92 women), 146 part-time matriculated graduate/professional students (80 women). *Graduate faculty:* 6 full-time (1 woman), 37 part-time/adjunct (15 women). *Computer facilities:* 44 computers available on campus for general student use. A campuswide network can be accessed from off campus. Internet access is available. *Library facilities:* Darling Library. *General application contact:* Teresa Smith, Director of Graduate and Adult Admissions, 714-879-3901.

School of Graduate Studies

Dr. Alan Rabe, Dean
Programs in:
- church music (MA, MCM)
- congregational leadership (MA)
- counseling (MA)
- education (ME)
- intercultural studies/urban ministries (MA)
- international development (MBA, MSM)
- marriage and family therapy (MFT)
- marriage, family, and child counseling (MA)
- nonprofit management (MBA)
- psychology (MA)

■ HUMBOLDT STATE UNIVERSITY

Arcata, CA 95521-8299

http://www.humboldt.edu/

State-supported, coed, comprehensive institution. CGS member. *Enrollment:* 7,435 graduate, professional, and undergraduate students; 322 full-time matriculated graduate/professional students (201 women), 125 part-time matriculated graduate/professional students (74 women). *Graduate faculty:* 288 full-time (109 women), 263 part-time/adjunct (153 women). *Computer facilities:* 778 computers available on campus for general student use. A campuswide network can be accessed from student residence rooms and from off campus. Internet access and online class registration are available. *Library facilities:* Humbolot State University Library. *General application contact:* Carla Douglas, Research and Graduate Studies, 707-826-3949.

Graduate Studies

Dr. Chris Hopper, Interim Dean

College of Arts, Humanities, and Social Sciences
Dr. Robert Snyder, Dean
Programs in:
- arts, humanities, and social sciences (MA, MFA, MSW)
- English (MA)
- environment and community (MA)
- sociology (MA)
- theatre, film and dance (MA)

College of Natural Resources and Sciences
Dr. Jim Howard, Dean
Programs in:
- biological sciences (MA)
- environmental systems (MS)
- natural resources (MS)
- natural resources and sciences (MA, MS)
- psychology (MA)

College of Professional Studies
Dr. Susan Higgins, Dean
Programs in:
- athletic training education (MS)
- business (MBA)
- education (MA)
- exercise science/wellness management (MS)
- pre-physical therapy (MS)
- social work (MSW)
- teaching/coaching (MS)

■ JOHN F. KENNEDY UNIVERSITY

Pleasant Hill, CA 94523-4817

http://www.jfku.edu/

Independent, coed, comprehensive institution. *Computer facilities:* 50 computers available on campus for general student use. Internet access is available. *Library facilities:* Robert M. Fisher Library plus 1 other. *General application contact:* Vice President, Enrollment Services, 925-969-3509.

Graduate School of Holistic Studies

Programs in:
- consciousness studies (MA)
- counseling psychology (MA)
- dream studies (Certificate)
- holistic health education (MA)
- holistic studies (MA, MFA, Certificate)
- integral psychology (MA, Certificate)
- life coaching (Certificate)
- studio arts (MFA)
- transformative arts (MA)

Graduate School of Professional Psychology

Programs in:
- counseling psychology (MA)
- organizational psychology (MA, Certificate)
- professional psychology (MA, Psy D, Certificate)
- psychology (Psy D)
- sport psychology (MA)

School of Education and Liberal Arts

Programs in:
- education (MAT)
- education and liberal arts (MA, MAT, Certificate)
- museum studies (MA, Certificate)

School of Law

Program in:
- law (JD)

School of Management

Programs in:
- business administration (MBA)
- career coaching (Certificate)
- career development (MA, Certificate)
- management (MA, MBA, Certificate)
- organizational leadership (Certificate)

■ LA SIERRA UNIVERSITY

Riverside, CA 92515

http://www.lasierra.edu/

Independent-religious, coed, comprehensive institution. CGS member. *Computer facilities:* 125 computers available on campus for general student use. A campuswide network can be accessed from student residence rooms and from off campus. Internet access and online class registration are available. *Library facilities:* University Library. *General application contact:* Director of Admissions, 909-785-2176.

College of Arts and Sciences

Programs in:
- arts and sciences (MA)
- English (MA)

School of Business and Management

Programs in:
- business administration and management (MBA)
- executive business administration (EMBA)
- leadership, values, and ethics for business and management (Certificate)

School of Education

Programs in:
- administration and leadership (MA, Ed D, Ed S)
- counseling (MA)
- curriculum and instruction (MA, Ed D, Ed S)
- education (MA, Ed D, Ed S)
- educational psychology (Ed S)
- school psychology (Ed S)
- special education (MA)

School of Religion

Programs in:
- religion (MA)
- religious education (MA)
- religious studies (MA)

■ LOYOLA MARYMOUNT UNIVERSITY

Los Angeles, CA 90045-2659

http://www.lmu.edu/

Independent-religious, coed, comprehensive institution. CGS member. *Enrollment:* 8,903 graduate, professional, and undergraduate students; 2,385 full-time matriculated graduate/professional students (1,353 women), 841 part-time matriculated graduate/professional students (479 women). *Graduate faculty:* 461 full-time (169 women), 436 part-time/adjunct (251 women). *Computer facilities:* Computer purchase and lease plans are available. 300 computers available on campus for general student use. A campuswide network can be accessed from student residence rooms and from off campus. Internet access is available. *Library facilities:* Charles von der Ahe Library plus 1 other. *General application contact:* Chake H. Kouyoumjian, Director, Graduate Admissions, 310-338-2721.

Find University Details at www.petersons.com/gradchannel.

Graduate Division

Dr. Ernest Rose, Academic Vice President and Chair of Graduate Council
Program in:
- marital and family therapy (MA)

College of Business Administration
Dr. John T. Wholihan, Dean
Program in:
- business administration (MBA)

College of Liberal Arts
Dr. Michael Engh, Dean

Programs in:
- bioethics (MA)
- creative writing (MA)
- liberal arts (MA)
- literature (MA)
- pastoral theology (MA)
- philosophy (MA)
- theology (MA)

College of Science and Engineering
Dr. Richard S. Plumb, Dean
Programs in:
- civil engineering (MS, MSE)
- computer science (MS)
- electrical engineering (MSE)
- engineering and production management (MS)
- environmental science (MS)
- mathematics (MAT)
- mechanical engineering (MSE)
- science and engineering (MAT, MS, MSE, Certificate)
- systems engineering (MS, Certificate)

School of Education
Dr. Shane Martin, Dean
Programs in:
- bilingual and bicultural education (MA)
- Catholic inclusive education (MA)
- Catholic school administration (MA)
- child/adolescent literacy (MA)
- counseling (MA)
- education (M Ed, MA, Ed D)
- educational leadership in social justice (Ed D)
- elementary education (MA)
- general education (M Ed)
- literacy/language arts (M Ed)
- school administration (M Ed)
- school psychology (MA)
- secondary education (MA)
- special education (MA)
- special education specialist in mild and moderate disabilities (MA)

School of Film and Television
Teri Schwartz, Dean
Programs in:
- film and television (MFA)
- film production (MFA)
- screen writing (MFA)
- television production (MFA)

Loyola Law School
David W. Burcham, Dean
Programs in:
- American law and international practice (LL M)
- law (JD)
- taxation (LL M)

■ MILLS COLLEGE
Oakland, CA 94613-1000
http://www.mills.edu/

Independent, Undergraduate: women only; graduate: coed, comprehensive institution. *Enrollment:* 1,410 graduate, professional, and undergraduate students; 430 full-time matriculated graduate/professional students (343 women), 51 part-time matriculated graduate/professional students (45 women). *Graduate faculty:* 89 full-time (53 women), 94 part-time/adjunct (70 women). *Computer facilities:* Computer purchase and lease plans are available. 267 computers available on campus for general student use. A campuswide network can be accessed from student residence rooms and from off campus. Internet access is available. *Library facilities:* F. W. Olin Library plus 1 other. *General application contact:* Marianne B. Sheldon, Director of Graduate Studies, 510-430-2355.

Find University Details at www.petersons.com/gradchannel.

Graduate Studies
Marianne B. Sheldon, Director
Programs in:
- administration (Ed D)
- ceramics (MFA)
- child life in health care settings (MA)
- computer science (Certificate)
- creative writing (MFA)
- dance (MA, MFA)
- early childhood education (MA)
- education (MA)
- English (MA, MFA)
- interdisciplinary computer science (MA)
- management (MBA)
- multimedia/art (MFA)
- multimedia/music (MFA)
- music (MA, MFA)
- painting (MFA)
- photography (MFA)
- pre-med (Certificate)
- sculpture (MFA)

Program in Management
Nancy Thornborrow, Director
Program in:
- management (MBA)

■ MONTEREY INSTITUTE OF INTERNATIONAL STUDIES
Monterey, CA 93940-2691
http://www.miis.edu/

Independent, coed, graduate-only institution. *Enrollment:* 632 full-time matriculated graduate/professional students (426 women), 83 part-time matriculated graduate/professional students (56 women). *Graduate faculty:* 59 full-time (24 women), 77 part-time/adjunct (45 women). *Computer facilities:* 140 computers available on campus for general student use. A campuswide network can be accessed from off campus. Internet access is available. *Library facilities:* William Tell Coleman Library. *Graduate expenses:* Tuition: full-time $26,500; part-time $1,200 per credit. Required fees: $200. *General application contact:* Admissions Office, 831-647-4123.

Fisher Graduate School of International Business
Dr. Ernest J. Scalberg, Dean
Program in:
- international business (MBA)

Graduate School of International Policy Studies
Dr. Edward J. Lawrence, Dean
Programs in:
- international environmental policy (MA)
- international management (MPA)
- international policy studies (MA, MPA)
- international trade policy (MA)

Graduate School of Language and Educational Linguistics
Dr. Ruth Larimer, Dean
Programs in:
- language and educational linguistics (MATESOL, MATFL)
- teaching English to speakers of other languages (MATESOL)
- teaching foreign language (MATFL)

Graduate School of Translation and Interpretation
Dr. Chuanyun Bao, Dean
Programs in:
- conference interpretation (MA)
- translation (MA)
- translation and interpretation (MA)
- translation and localization management (MA)

■ MOUNT ST. MARY'S COLLEGE
Los Angeles, CA 90049-1599
http://www.msmc.la.edu/

Independent-religious, coed, primarily women, comprehensive institution. *Enrollment:* 2,384 graduate, professional, and undergraduate students; 245 full-time matriculated graduate/professional students (191 women), 218 part-time matriculated graduate/professional students (173 women). *Graduate faculty:* 16 full-time (all women), 23 part-time/adjunct (19 women). *Computer facilities:* 85 computers available on campus for general student use. A campuswide network can be accessed from student residence rooms and from off campus. *Library facilities:* Charles Williard Coe Memorial Library. *Graduate expenses:* Tuition: part-time $630 per unit. *General application contact:* Tom Hoener, Director, Graduate Recruitment, 213-477-2800.

Graduate Division
Programs in:
- administrative studies (MS)
- counseling psychology (MS)
- elementary education (MS)
- humanities (MA)
- nursing (MS)
- physical therapy (DPT)
- religious studies (MA)
- secondary education (MS)
- special education (MS)

■ NATIONAL UNIVERSITY
La Jolla, CA 92037-1011
http://www.nu.edu/

Independent, coed, comprehensive institution. CGS member. *Enrollment:* 25,992 graduate, professional, and undergraduate students; 6,652 full-time matriculated graduate/professional students (4,423 women), 12,152 part-time matriculated graduate/professional students (7,594 women). *Graduate faculty:* 201 full-time (88 women), 2,974 part-time/adjunct (1,455 women). *Computer facilities:* 2,253 computers available on campus for general student use. A campuswide network can be accessed from off campus. Internet access and online class registration are available. *Library facilities:* Central Library. *Graduate expenses:* Tuition: full-time $7,722; part-time $286 per unit. One-time fee: $60. *General application contact:* Dominick Giovanniello, Associate Regional Dean—San Diego, 800-NAT-UNIV.

Academic Affairs
Dr. Thomas M. Green, Senior Vice President of Academic Affairs

College of Letters and Sciences
Dr. Michael Mcanear, Dean
Programs in:
- counseling psychology (MA)
- creative writing (MFA)
- English (MA)
- human behavior (MA)
- industrial organizational psychology (MS)
- letters and sciences (MA, MFA, MS)

School of Business and Management
Dr. Wali Mondal, Dean
Programs in:
- business and management (EMBA, MA, MBA, MFS, MS)
- e-business (MS)
- finance (MS)
- finance, accounting, and economics (EMBA, MBA)
- forensic science (MFS)
- human resource management and organizational development (MA)
- management (MA)
- organizational leadership (MS)
- taxation (MS)

School of Education
Dr. Gloria Johnston, Dean
Programs in:
- best practices (MA)
- cross-cultural teaching (M Ed)
- deaf and hard of hearing education (MS)
- education (M Ed, MA, MS)
- educational administration (MS)
- educational counseling (MS)
- educational technology (MS)
- exceptional student education (MS)
- school psychology (MS)
- special education (MS)
- teaching (MA)

School of Engineering and Technology
Dr. Howard Evans, Dean
Programs in:
- computer science (MS)
- database administration (MS)
- engineering and technology (MS)
- engineering management (MS)
- environmental engineering (MS)
- homeland security and safety engineering (MS)
- information systems (MS)
- software engineering (MS)
- system engineering (MS)
- technology management (MS)
- wireless communications (MS)

School of Health and Human Services
Dr. Thomas M. Green, Interim Dean
Programs in:
- health and human services (MHCA, MS)
- health care administration (MS)

School of Media and Communication
Debra B. Schneiger, Dean
Programs in:
- digital cinema (MFA)
- educational and instructional technology (MS)
- media (MFA, MS)
- video game production and design (MFA)

■ NEW COLLEGE OF CALIFORNIA
San Francisco, CA 94102-5206
http://www.newcollege.edu/

Independent, coed, comprehensive institution. *Computer facilities:* 10 computers available on campus for general student use. A campuswide network can be accessed from off campus. Internet access is available. *Library facilities:* New College Library plus 2 others. *General application contact:* Information Contact, 415-437-3460.

Find University Details at www.petersons.com/gradchannel.

School of Graduate Psychology
Programs in:
- feminist clinical psychology (MA)
- social-clinical psychology (MA)
- spiritual/transformatives clinical psychology (MA)

School of Humanities
Programs in:
- humanities and leadership (MA)
- Irish studies (MA)
- media studies (MA)
- poetics (MA, MFA)
- poetics and writing (MFA)
- teaching (MAT)
- women's spirituality (MA)
- writing and consciousness (MA)

School of Law
Debrenia Madison, Dean
Program in:
- law (JD)

■ NOTRE DAME DE NAMUR UNIVERSITY
Belmont, CA 94002-1908
http://www.ndnu.edu

Independent-religious, coed, comprehensive institution. *Enrollment:* 1,583 graduate, professional, and undergraduate students; 193 full-time matriculated graduate/professional students (154 women), 533 part-time matriculated graduate/professional students (420 women). *Graduate faculty:* 28 full-time (13 women), 63 part-time/adjunct (44 women). *Computer facilities:* 50 computers available on campus for general student use. A campuswide network can be accessed from off campus. Internet access is available. *Library facilities:* Carl Gellert and Celia Berta Gellert Library. *Graduate expenses:* Tuition: part-time $655 per credit. *General application contact:* Helen Valine, Director of Graduate Admissions, 650-508-3534.

Division of Academic Affairs
Dr. Judith Maxwell Greig, Executive Vice President and Provost

School of Arts and Humanities
Dr. Gregory B. White, Interim Dean
Programs in:
- arts and humanities (MA, MM, Certificate)
- English (MA)
- music (MM)
- pedagogy (MM)
- performance (MM)
- teaching English to speakers of other languages (Certificate)

School of Business and Management
Dr. George Klemic, Dean
Programs in:
- business administration (MBA)
- business and management (MBA, MPA, MSM)
- management (MSM)
- public administration (MPA)

School of Education and Leadership
Dr. Joanne Rossi, Dean
Programs in:
- education (MA)
- education and leadership (MA, MAT, Certificate)
- education in technology leadership (MA, Certificate)
- reading (MA, Certificate)
- special education (MA, Certificate)
- teaching (MAT)

School of Sciences
Dr. Gregory B. White, Dean
Programs in:
- art therapy psychology (MAAT, MAMFT)

chemical dependency (MACP)
counseling psychology (MACP)
gerontology (MA, Certificate)
marital and family therapy (MACP, MAMFT)
premedical studies (Certificate)
sciences (MA, MAAT, MACP, MAMFT, Certificate)

■ PEPPERDINE UNIVERSITY
Malibu, CA 90263
http://www.pepperdine.edu/

Independent-religious, coed, university. CGS member. *Enrollment:* 7,593 graduate, professional, and undergraduate students; 1,080 full-time matriculated graduate/professional students (577 women), 157 part-time matriculated graduate/professional students (80 women). *Graduate faculty:* 96 full-time (25 women), 41 part-time/adjunct (12 women). *Computer facilities:* Computer purchase and lease plans are available. 292 computers available on campus for general student use. A campuswide network can be accessed from student residence rooms. Internet access and online class registration are available. *Library facilities:* Payson Library plus 2 others. *Graduate expenses:* Tuition: full-time $32,744; part-time $1,026 per unit. Full-time tuition and fees vary according to program. *General application contact:* Paul A. Long, Dean of Admission and Enrollment Management, 310-506-6165.

Find University Details at www.petersons.com/gradchannel.

Graduate School of Education and Psychology
Dr. Margaret J. Weber, Dean of Graduate School of Education and Psychology
Program in:
clinical psychology (MA)

Malibu Graduate Business Programs
Dr. Mark Mallinger, Director, Full-Time Programs
Programs in:
business administration (MBA)
international business (MIB)

School of Law
Kenneth W. Starr, Dean
Programs in:
dispute resolution (LL M, MDR)
law (JD, LL M, MDR)

School of Public Policy
Dr. James R. Wilburn, Dean
Programs in:
American politics (MPP)
economics (MPP)
international relations (MPP)
public policy (MPP)
state and local policy (MPP)

Seaver College
Dr. David W. Baird, Dean
Programs in:
American studies (MA)
communication (MA)
history (MA)
ministry (MS)
religion (M Div, MA)

■ POINT LOMA NAZARENE UNIVERSITY
San Diego, CA 92106-2899
http://www.pointloma.edu/

Independent-religious, coed, comprehensive institution. *Enrollment:* 3,437 graduate, professional, and undergraduate students; 528 full-time matriculated graduate/professional students (366 women), 621 part-time matriculated graduate/professional students (424 women). *Graduate faculty:* 31 full-time (18 women), 83 part-time/adjunct (50 women). *Computer facilities:* 196 computers available on campus for general student use. A campuswide network can be accessed from student residence rooms and from off campus. Internet access and online class registration are available. *Library facilities:* Ryan Library. *General application contact:* Steve Guthrie, Director of Graduate Admissions, 866-692-4723.

Graduate Studies
Dr. Maggie Bailey, Vice Provost for Graduate Studies
Programs in:
biology (MA, MS)
business administration (MBA)
education (MA, Ed S)
nursing (MSN)
religion (M Min, MA)

■ SAINT MARY'S COLLEGE OF CALIFORNIA
Moraga, CA 94575
http://www.stmarys-ca.edu/

Independent-religious, coed, comprehensive institution. *Enrollment:* 3,962 graduate, professional, and undergraduate students; 540 full-time matriculated graduate/professional students (310 women), 587 part-time matriculated graduate/professional students (488 women). *Graduate faculty:* 111 full-time (61 women), 277 part-time/adjunct (154 women). *Computer facilities:* 250 computers available on campus for general student use. A campuswide network can be accessed from student residence rooms and from off campus. Internet access and online class registration are available. *Library facilities:* St. Albert Hall. *General application contact:* Michael Beseda, Vice Provost for Enrollment, 925-631-4277.

Graduate Business Programs
Guido Krickx, Associate Dean, Director
Programs in:
business (MBA)
business administration (MBA)
executive business administration (MBA)

School of Education
Dr. Nancy L. Sorenson, Dean
Programs in:
early childhood education and Montessori teacher training (M Ed, MA)
education (M Ed, MA, MAT, PhD)
educational leadership (MA, PhD)
general counseling (MA)
instruction (M Ed)
marital and family therapy (MA)
reading leadership (MA)
school counseling (MA)
special education (M Ed, MA)
teachers for tomorrow (MAT)
teaching leadership (MA)

School of Liberal Arts
Stephen Woolpert, Dean
Programs in:
creative writing (MFA)
kinesiology (MA)
leadership (MA)
liberal arts (MA, MFA)
liberal studies (MA)

■ SAN DIEGO STATE UNIVERSITY
San Diego, CA 92182
http://www.sdsu.edu/

State-supported, coed, university. CGS member. *Enrollment:* 34,305 graduate, professional, and undergraduate students; 3,038 full-time matriculated graduate/professional students (1,983 women), 2,520 part-time matriculated graduate/professional students (1,437 women). *Graduate faculty:* 741 full-time (299 women). *Computer facilities:* 400 computers available on campus for general student use. A campuswide network can be accessed from student residence rooms and from off campus. Internet access and online class registration are available. *Library facilities:* Malcolm A. Love Library. *General application contact:* Information Contact, 619-594-5213.

Graduate and Research Affairs
Dr. Patrick Papin, Associate Dean
Program in:
interdisciplinary studies (MA, MS)

College of Arts and Letters
Paul Wong, Dean
Programs in:
anthropology (MA)
applied linguistics and English as a second language (CAL)
arts and letters (MA, MFA, PhD, CAL)
Asian studies (MA)
computational linguistics (MA)
creative writing (MFA)

San Diego State University (continued)
economics (MA)
English (MA)
English as a second language/applied linguistics (MA)
European studies (MA)
general linguistics (MA)
geography (MA, PhD)
history (MA)
Latin American studies (MA)
liberal arts and sciences (MA)
philosophy (MA)
political science (MA)
rhetoric and writing (MA)
sociology (MA)
Spanish (MA)
women's studies (MA)

College of Business Administration
Dr. Gail K. Naughton, Dean
Programs in:
accountancy (MS)
business administration (MBA, MS)
entrepreneurship (MS)
finance (MS)
human resources management (MS)
information and decision systems (MS)
international business (MS)
management science (MS)
marketing (MS)
production and operations management (MS)

College of Education
Lionel R. Meno, Dean
Programs in:
counseling and school psychology (MS)
education (MA, MS, Ed D, PhD)
educational leadership (MA)
educational leadership in post-secondary education (MA)
educational technology (MA)
educational technology and teaching and learning (Ed D)
elementary curriculum and instruction (MA)
multi-cultural emphasis (PhD)
policy studies in language and cross cultural education (MA)
reading education (MA)
rehabilitation counseling (MS)
secondary curriculum and instruction (MA)
special education (MA)

College of Engineering
David A. Hayhurst, Dean
Programs in:
aerospace engineering (MS)
civil engineering (MS)
electrical engineering (MS)
engineering (MS, PhD)
engineering mechanics (MS)
engineering sciences and applied mechanics (PhD)
flight dynamics (MS)
fluid dynamics (MS)
manufacture and design (MS)
mechanical engineering (MS)

College of Health and Human Services
Marilyn Newhoff, Dean
Programs in:
audiology (Au D)
communicative disorders (MA)
environmental health (MPH)
epidemiology (MPH, PhD)
gerontology (MS)
global emergency preparedness and response (MS)
health and human services (MA, MPH, MS, MSW, Au D, PhD)
health behavior (PhD)
health promotion (MPH)
health services administration (MPH)
language and communicative disorders (PhD)
nursing (MS)
social work (MSW)
toxicology (MS)

College of Professional Studies and Fine Arts
Joyce M. Gattas, Dean
Programs in:
advertising and public relations (MA)
art history (MA)
child development (MS)
city planning (MCP)
composition (acoustic and electronic) (MM)
conducting (MM)
criminal justice administration (MPA)
criminal justice and criminology (MS)
critical-cultural studies (MA)
ethnomusicology (MA)
exercise physiology (MA)
interaction studies (MA)
intercultural and international studies (MA)
jazz studies (MM)
musicology (MA)
new media studies (MA)
news and information studies (MA)
nutritional science (MS)
nutritional sciences (MS)
performance (MM)
physical education (MS)
piano pedagogy (MA)
professional studies and fine arts (MA, MCP, MFA, MM, MPA, MS)
public administration (MPA)
studio arts (MA, MFA)
telecommunications and media management (MA)
television, film, and new media production (MA)
theatre arts (MA, MFA)
theory (MA)

College of Sciences
Programs in:
applied mathematics (MS)
astronomy (MS)
biology (MA, MS)
biostatistics and biometry (PhD)
cell and molecular biology (PhD)
chemistry (MA, MS, PhD)
clinical psychology (MS, PhD)
computational science (MS, PhD)
computer science (MS)
ecology (MS, PhD)
geological sciences (MS)
industrial and organizational psychology (MS)
mathematics (MA)
mathematics and science education (PhD)
microbiology (MS)
molecular biology (MA, MS)
physics (MA, MS)
program evaluation (MS)
psychology (MA)
radiological physics (MS)
regulatory affairs (MS)
sciences (MA, MS, PhD)
statistics (MS)

■ SAN FRANCISCO STATE UNIVERSITY
San Francisco, CA 94132-1722
http://www.sfsu.edu/

State-supported, coed, comprehensive institution. CGS member. *Enrollment:* 29,628 graduate, professional, and undergraduate students; 4,642 matriculated graduate/professional students. *Graduate faculty:* 795 full-time (285 women). *Computer facilities:* 1,474 computers available on campus for general student use. A campuswide network can be accessed from student residence rooms and from off campus. *Library facilities:* J. Paul Leonard Library. *General application contact:* Brian Gallagher, Director of Admissions, Division of Graduate Studies, 415-338-2234.

Division of Graduate Studies
Dr. Ann Hallum, Dean

College of Behavioral and Social Sciences
Joel Kassiola, Dean
Programs in:
anthropology (MA)
behavioral and social sciences (MA, MPA, MS)
economics (MA)
geography (MA)
history (MA)
human sexuality studies (MA)
integrated and collaborative services (MPA)
international relations (MA)
nonprofit administration (MPA)
policy analysis (MPA)
political science (MA)
psychology (MA, MS)
public management (MPA)
social science (MA)
urban administration (MPA)

College of Business
Nancy Mayes, Dean

Programs in:
business (MBA)
business administration (MBA)

College of Creative Arts
Ron Compesi, Interim Dean
Programs in:
art (MFA)
art history (MA)
chamber music (MM)
cinema (MFA)
cinema studies (MA)
classical performance (MM)
composition (MA)
conducting (MM)
creative arts (MA, MFA, MM)
drama (MA)
industrial arts (MA)
music education (MA)
music history (MA)
radio and television (MA)
theatre arts (MFA)

College of Education
Dr. Jacob Perea, Dean
Programs in:
adult education (MA Ed, AC)
communicative disorders (MS)
early childhood education (MA)
education (MA, MA Ed, MS, Ed D, PhD, AC)
educational administration (MA, AC)
educational technology (MA)
elementary education (MA)
equity and social justice (AC)
equity and social justice in education (MA Ed)
language and literacy education (MA)
mathematics education (MA)
secondary education (MA Ed)
special education (MA, Ed D, PhD, AC)
special interest (MA Ed)
training systems development (AC)

College of Ethnic Studies
Dr. Kenneth P. Montiero, Dean
Programs in:
Asian American studies (MA)
ethnic studies (MA)

College of Health and Human Services
Dr. Don Taylor, Dean
Programs in:
case management (MS)
counseling (MS)
family and consumer sciences (MA)
geriatric care management (MA)
health and human services (MA, MPH, MS, MSC, MSW, DPT, Dr Sc PT)
health education (MPH)
health, wellness and aging (MA)
kinesiology (MS)
long-term care administration (MA)
marriage, family, and child counseling (MSC)
nursing administration (MS)
nursing education (MS)
physical therapy (MS, DPT, Dr Sc PT)
recreation (MS)
rehabilitation counseling (MS)
social work (MSW)

College of Humanities
Dr. Paul Sherwin, Dean
Programs in:
Chinese (MA)
classics (MA)
communication studies (MA)
comparative literature (MA)
composition (MA, Certificate)
creative writing (MA, MFA)
French (MA)
German (MA)
humanities (MA, MFA, Certificate)
Italian (MA)
Japanese (MA)
linguistics (MA)
literature (MA)
museum studies (MA)
philosophy (MA)
Spanish (MA)
teaching composition (Certificate)
teaching critical thinking (Certificate)
teaching English to speakers of other languages (MA)
teaching post-secondary reading (Certificate)
women studies (MA)

College of Science and Engineering
Dr. Sheldon Axler, Dean
Programs in:
applied geosciences (MS)
biomedical laboratory science (MS)
cell and molecular biology (MS)
chemistry (MS)
computer science (MS)
conservation biology (MS)
ecology and systematic biology (MS)
engineering (MS)
marine biology (MS)
marine science (MS)
mathematics (MA)
microbiology (MS)
physics (MS)
physiology and behavioral biology (MS)
science and engineering (MA, MS)

■ SAN JOSE STATE UNIVERSITY
San Jose, CA 95192-0001
http://www.sjsu.edu/

State-supported, coed, comprehensive institution. CGS member. *Enrollment:* 29,604 graduate, professional, and undergraduate students; 3,555 full-time matriculated graduate/professional students (2,312 women), 3,567 part-time matriculated graduate/professional students (2,229 women). *Computer facilities:* A campuswide network can be accessed from student residence rooms and from off campus. Internet access and online class registration are available. *Library facilities:* Dr. Martin Luther King Jr. Library plus 1 other. *General application contact:* Andy Hernandez, Associate Director, Undergraduate and Graduate Admissions, 408-924-2359.

Graduate Studies and Research
Dr. Pam Stacks, Associate Vice President
Programs in:
human factors and ergonomics (MS)
interdisciplinary studies (MA, MS)

College of Applied Sciences and Arts
Barbara Conry, Interim Dean
Programs in:
applied sciences and arts (MA, MLIS, MPH, MS, MSW, Certificate)
applied social gerontology (Certificate)
community health education (MPH)
gerontology nurse practitioner (MS)
justice studies (MS)
kinesiology (MA)
library and information science (MLIS)
mass communication (MS)
nursing (Certificate)
nursing administration (MS)
nursing education (MS)
nutritional science (MS)
occupational therapy (MS)
recreation (MS)
social work (MSW, Certificate)

College of Education
Dr. Susan Meyers, Dean
Programs in:
child and adolescent development (MA)
education (MA, Certificate)
education (counseling and student personnel) (MA)
educational administration (MA)
elementary education (MA, Certificate)
higher education administration (MA)
instructional technology (MA, Certificate)
school business management (Certificate)
secondary education (Certificate)
special education (MA, Certificate)
speech pathology (MA)

College of Engineering
Dr. Belle Wei, Dean
Programs in:
aerospace engineering (MS)
chemical engineering (MS)
civil engineering (MS)
computer engineering (MS)
electrical engineering (MS)
engineering (MS)
general engineering (MS)
industrial and systems engineering (MS)
materials engineering (MS)
mechanical engineering (MS)
quality assurance (MS)
software engineering (MS)

College of Humanities and the Arts
Karl Toepfer, Dean
Programs in:
art history (MA)
computational linguistics (Certificate)
creative writing (MFA)
digital media arts (MFA)
English (MA)
French (MA)
humanities and the arts (MA, MFA, Certificate)
linguistics (MA, Certificate)

San Jose State University (continued)
- music (MA)
- philosophy (MA, Certificate)
- photography (MFA)
- pictorial arts (MFA)
- secondary English education (Certificate)
- Spanish (MA)
- spatial arts (MFA)
- teaching English to speakers of other languages (MA, Certificate)
- theatre arts (MA)

College of Science
J. Michael Parrish, Dean
Programs in:
- biological sciences (MA, MS)
- chemistry (MA, MS)
- computational physics (MS)
- computer science (MS, Certificate)
- geology (MS)
- marine science (MS)
- mathematics (MA, MS)
- mathematics education (MA)
- meteorology (MS)
- molecular biology and microbiology (MS)
- organismal biology, conservation and ecology (MS)
- physics (MS)
- physiology (MS)
- science (MA, MS, Certificate)

College of Social Sciences
Tim Hegstrom, Dean
Programs in:
- applied economics (MA)
- clinical psychology (MS)
- communication (MA)
- criminology (MA)
- economics (MA)
- environmental studies (MS)
- experimental psychology (MA)
- geography (MA, Certificate)
- history (MA)
- history education (MA)
- industrial/organizational psychology (MS)
- Mexican-American studies (MA)
- psychology (MA)
- public administration (MPA)
- social sciences (MA, MPA, MS, MUP, Certificate)
- sociology (MA)
- urban and regional planning (MUP, Certificate)

Lucas Graduate School of Business
Dr. Nancie Fimbel, Interim Dean
Programs in:
- accounting (MS)
- business (MBA, MS)
- business administration (MBA)
- taxation (MS)
- transportation management (MS)

■ SANTA CLARA UNIVERSITY
Santa Clara, CA 95053
http://www.scu.edu/

Independent-religious, coed, university. CGS member. *Enrollment:* 7,952 graduate, professional, and undergraduate students; 1,407 full-time matriculated graduate/professional students (703 women), 1,736 part-time matriculated graduate/professional students (681 women). *Graduate faculty:* 212 full-time (68 women), 124 part-time/adjunct (38 women). *Computer facilities:* Computer purchase and lease plans are available. 800 computers available on campus for general student use. A campuswide network can be accessed from student residence rooms and from off campus. Internet access and online class registration are available. *Library facilities:* University Library plus 1 other. *Graduate expenses:* Tuition: part-time $627 per unit. Tuition and fees vary according to program. *General application contact:* Ricahrd Toomey, Associate Vice Provost, Enrollment Mangement, 408-554-4966.

Leavey School of Business
Dr. Barry Posner, Dean
Programs in:
- business (EMBA, MBA, MSIS)
- business administration (EMBA, MBA)
- information systems (MSIS)

School of Education, Counseling Psychology, and Pastoral Ministries
Dr. Terry Shoup, Interim Dean
Programs in:
- catechetics (MA)
- counseling (MA)
- counseling psychology (MA)
- education (MA)
- education, counseling psychology, and pastoral ministries (MA, Certificate)
- educational administration (MA)
- liturgical music (MA)
- multiple subject teaching (Certificate)
- pastoral liturgy (MA)
- single subject teaching (Certificate)
- special education (MA, Certificate)
- spirituality (MA)
- teacher education (Certificate)

School of Engineering
Daniel Pitt, Dean
Programs in:
- analog circuit design (Certificate)
- applied mathematics (MSAM)
- ASIC design and test (Certificate)
- civil engineering (MSCE)
- computer science and engineering (MSCSE, PhD, Engineer)
- controls (Certificate)
- data storage technologies (Certificate)
- digital signal processing (Certificate)
- dynamics (Certificate)
- electrical engineering (MSEE, PhD, Engineer)
- engineering (MS, MSAM, MSCE, MSCSE, MSE, MSE Mgt, MSEE, MSME, PhD, Certificate, Engineer)
- engineering management (MSE Mgt)
- fundamentals of electrical engineering (Certificate)
- grid computing (Certificate)
- information assurance (Certificate)
- materials engineering (Certificate)
- mechanical design analysis (Certificate)
- mechanical engineering (MSME, PhD, Engineer)
- mechatronics systems engineering (Certificate)
- networking (Certificate)
- software engineering (MS, Certificate)
- technology jump-start (Certificate)
- telecommunications management (Certificate)
- thermofluids (Certificate)

School of Law
Donald Polden, Dean
Programs in:
- high technology law (Certificate)
- intellectual property law (LL M)
- international and comparative law (LL M)
- international law (Certificate)
- law (JD)
- public interest and social justice law (Certificate)
- U.S. law for foreign lawyers (LL M)

■ SONOMA STATE UNIVERSITY
Rohnert Park, CA 94928-3609
http://www.sonoma.edu/

State-supported, coed, comprehensive institution. *Enrollment:* 7,749 graduate, professional, and undergraduate students; 746 full-time matriculated graduate/professional students (539 women), 416 part-time matriculated graduate/professional students (297 women). *Graduate faculty:* 71 full-time (34 women), 16 part-time/adjunct (12 women). *Computer facilities:* 400 computers available on campus for general student use. A campuswide network can be accessed from student residence rooms and from off campus. Internet access is available. *Library facilities:* Jean and Charles Schultz Information Center. *Graduate expenses:* Tuition, nonresident: part-time $339 per unit. Required fees: $1,464 per term. *General application contact:* Elaine Sundberg, Associate Vice Provost, Academic Programs/Graduate Studies, 707-664-2215.

Institute of Interdisciplinary Studies/Special Major
Dr. Ellen Carlton, Coordinator
Program in:
- special major (MA, MS)

School of Arts and Humanities
Dr. William Babula, Dean

Programs in:
- American literature (MA)
- arts and humanities (MA)
- creative writing (MA)
- English literature (MA)
- world literature (MA)

School of Business and Economics
Jim Robertson, Dean
Programs in:
- business administration (MBA)
- business and economics (MBA)

School of Education
Dr. Mary Gendernalik-Cooper, Dean
Programs in:
- curriculum and secondary education (MA)
- education (MA)
- educational leadership (MA)
- literacy studies and elementary education (MA)
- special education (MA)

School of Science and Technology
Dr. Saeid Rahimi, Dean
Programs in:
- computer and engineering sciences (MSCES)
- environmental biology (MA)
- family nurse practitioner (MS)
- general biology (MA)
- kinesiology (MA)
- science and technology (MA, MS, MSCES)

School of Social Sciences
Dr. Elaine Leeder, Dean
Programs in:
- counseling (MA)
- cultural resources management (MA)
- history (MA)
- marriage, family, and child counseling (MA)
- public administration (MPA)
- pupil personnel services (MA)
- social sciences (MA, MPA)

■ STANFORD UNIVERSITY
Stanford, CA 94305-9991
http://www.stanford.edu/

Independent, coed, university. CGS member. *Computer facilities:* 1,000 computers available on campus for general student use. A campuswide network can be accessed from student residence rooms and from off campus. Internet access and online class registration are available. *Library facilities:* Green Library plus 18 others. *General application contact:* Graduate Admissions, 650-723-4291.

Graduate School of Business
Program in:
- business (MBA, PhD)

Law School
Program in:
- law (JD, JSM, MLS, JSD)

School of Earth Sciences
Programs in:
- earth sciences (MS, PhD, Eng)
- earth systems (MS)
- geological and environmental sciences (MS, PhD, Eng)
- geophysics (MS, PhD)
- petroleum engineering (MS, PhD, Eng)

School of Education
Programs in:
- administration and policy analysis (Ed D, PhD)
- anthropology of education (PhD)
- art education (MA, PhD)
- child and adolescent development (PhD)
- counseling psychology (PhD)
- dance education (MA)
- economics of education (PhD)
- education (MA, Ed D, PhD)
- educational linguistics (PhD)
- educational psychology (PhD)
- English education (MA, PhD)
- evaluation (MA)
- general curriculum studies (MA, PhD)
- higher education (PhD)
- history of education (PhD)
- interdisciplinary studies (PhD)
- international comparative education (MA, PhD)
- international education administration and policy analysis (MA)
- languages education (MA)
- learning, design, and technology (MA, PhD)
- mathematics education (MA, PhD)
- philosophy of education (PhD)
- policy analysis (MA)
- prospective principal's program (MA)
- science education (MA, PhD)
- social studies education (MA, PhD)
- sociology of education (PhD)
- symbolic systems in education (PhD)
- teacher education (MA, PhD)

School of Engineering
Programs in:
- aeronautics and astronautics (MS, PhD, Eng)
- biomechanical engineering (MS)
- chemical engineering (MS, PhD, Eng)
- civil and environmental engineering (MS, PhD, Eng)
- computer science (MS, PhD)
- electrical engineering (MS, PhD, Eng)
- engineering (MS, PhD, Eng)
- management science and engineering (MS, PhD)
- materials science and engineering (MS, PhD, Eng)
- mechanical engineering (MS, PhD, Eng)
- product design (MS)
- scientific computing and computational mathematics (MS, PhD)

School of Humanities and Sciences
Programs in:
- anthropological sciences (MA, MS, PhD)
- applied physics (MS, PhD)
- art history (PhD)
- art practice (MFA)
- biological sciences (MS, PhD)
- biophysics (PhD)
- chemistry (PhD)
- Chinese (MA, PhD)
- classics (MA, PhD)
- communication (journalism specialization) (MA)
- communication theory and research (PhD)
- comparative literature (PhD)
- computer-based music theory and acoustics (MA, PhD)
- cultural and social anthropology (MA, PhD)
- drama (PhD)
- economics (PhD)
- English (MA, PhD)
- financial mathematics (MS)
- French (MA, PhD)
- German studies (MA, PhD)
- history (MA, PhD)
- humanities (MA)
- humanities and sciences (MA, MFA, MS, DMA, PhD)
- international policy studies (MA)
- Italian (MA, PhD)
- Japanese (MA, PhD)
- linguistics (MA, PhD)
- mathematics (MS, PhD)
- modern thought and literature (PhD)
- music composition (MA, DMA)
- music history (MA)
- music, science, and technology (MA)
- musicology (PhD)
- philosophy (MA, PhD)
- physics (PhD)
- political science (MA, PhD)
- psychology (PhD)
- religious studies (MA, PhD)
- Russian (MA)
- Slavic languages and literatures (PhD)
- sociology (PhD)
- Spanish (MA, PhD)
- statistics (MS, PhD)

Center for East Asian Studies
Program in:
- East Asian studies (MA)

Center for Russian and East European Studies
Program in:
- Russian and East European studies (MA)

School of Medicine
Programs in:
- bioengineering (MS, PhD)
- medicine (MD, MS, PhD)

Stanford University (continued)

Graduate Programs in Medicine
Programs in:
biochemistry (PhD)
biomedical informatics (MS, PhD)
cancer biology (PhD)
developmental biology (PhD)
epidemiology (MS, PhD)
genetics (PhD)
health services research (MS)
immunology (PhD)
medicine (MS, PhD)
microbiology and immunology (PhD)
molecular and cellular physiology (PhD)
molecular pharmacology (PhD)
neurosciences (PhD)
structural biology (PhD)

■ UNIVERSITY OF CALIFORNIA, BERKELEY
Berkeley, CA 94720-1500
http://www.berkeley.edu/

State-supported, coed, university. CGS member. *Enrollment:* 33,933 graduate, professional, and undergraduate students; 9,887 matriculated graduate/professional students. *Graduate faculty:* 1,500. *Computer facilities:* Computer purchase and lease plans are available. 700 computers available on campus for general student use. A campuswide network can be accessed from student residence rooms and from off campus. Internet access and online class registration are available. *Library facilities:* Doe Library plus 30 others. *General application contact:* Information Contact, 510-642-7405.

Graduate Division
Dr. Mary Ann Mason, Dean, Graduate Division
Programs in:
ancient history and Mediterranean archaeology (MA, PhD)
Asian studies (PhD)
bioengineering (PhD)
biophysics (PhD)
Buddhist studies (PhD)
comparative biochemistry (PhD)
demography (MA, PhD)
East Asian studies (MA)
endocrinology (MA, PhD)
energy and resources (MA, MS, PhD)
ethnic studies (PhD)
folklore (MA)
French (PhD)
international and area studies (MA)
Italian (PhD)
Jewish studies (PhD)
Latin American studies (MA, PhD)
neuroscience (PhD)
Northeast Asian studies (MA)
performance studies (PhD)
range management (MS)
sociology and demography (PhD)
South Asian studies (MA)
Southeast Asian studies (MA)
Spanish (PhD)
vision science (MS, PhD)

College of Chemistry
Dr. Charles B. Harris, Dean, College of Chemistry
Programs in:
chemical engineering (MS, PhD)
chemistry (MS, PhD)

College of Engineering
Dr. Fiona Doyle, Dean, College of Engineering
Programs in:
applied science and technology (PhD)
computer science (MS, PhD)
electrical engineering (MS, PhD)
engineering (M Eng, MS, D Eng, PhD)
engineering and project management (M Eng, MS, D Eng, PhD)
engineering science (M Eng, MS, PhD)
environmental engineering (M Eng, MS, D Eng, PhD)
geoengineering (M Eng, MS, D Eng, PhD)
industrial engineering and operations research (M Eng, MS, D Eng, PhD)
mechanical engineering (M Eng, MS, D Eng, PhD)
nuclear engineering (M Eng, MS, D Eng, PhD)
structural engineering, mechanics and materials (M Eng, MS, D Eng, PhD)
transportation engineering (M Eng, MS, D Eng, PhD)

College of Environmental Design
Harrison Fraker, Dean
Programs in:
architecture (M Arch)
building science (MS, PhD)
building structures, construction and materials (MS, PhD)
city and regional planning (MCP, PhD)
design (MA)
design theories, methods, and practices (MS, PhD)
environmental design (M Arch, MA, MCP, MLA, MS, MUD, PhD)
environmental design in developing countries (MS, PhD)
environmental planning (MLA)
history of architecture and urbanism (MS, PhD)
landscape architecture (MLA)
landscape architecture and environmental planning (PhD)
landscape design and site planning (MLA)
social and cultural processes in architecture and urbanism (MS, PhD)
urban and community design (MLA)
urban design (MUD)

College of Letters and Science
Dr. Mark Richards, Chair of Deans
Programs in:
African American studies (PhD)
anthropology (PhD)
applied mathematics (PhD)
art practice (MFA)
astrophysics (PhD)
Chinese language (PhD)
classical archaeology (MA, PhD)
classics (MA, PhD)
comparative literature (PhD)
composition (PhD)
Czech (PhD)
economics (PhD)
English (PhD)
ethnomusicology (PhD)
French (PhD)
geography (PhD)
geology (MA, MS, PhD)
geophysics (MA, MS, PhD)
German (PhD)
Greek (MA)
Hindi (MA, PhD)
Hispanic languages and literature (MA, PhD)
history (PhD)
history of art (PhD)
Indonesian (MA, PhD)
integrative biology (PhD)
Italian studies (PhD)
Japanese language (PhD)
Latin (MA)
letters and science (MA, MFA, MS, PhD)
linguistics (PhD)
logic and the methodology of science (PhD)
mathematics (MA, PhD)
medical anthropology (PhD)
molecular and cell biology (PhD)
musicology (PhD)
Near Eastern religions (PhD)
Near Eastern studies (MA, PhD)
philosophy (PhD)
physics (PhD)
Polish (PhD)
political science (PhD)
psychology (PhD)
rhetoric (PhD)
Russian (PhD)
Sanskrit (MA, PhD)
Scandinavian languages and literatures (PhD)
Serbo-Croatian (PhD)
sociology (PhD)
statistics (MA, PhD)
Tamil (MA, PhD)

College of Natural Resources
Paul W. Ludden, Dean, College of Natural Resources
Programs in:
agricultural and environmental chemistry (PhD)
agricultural and resource economics (PhD)
environmental science, policy, and management (MS, PhD)
forestry (MF)
microbiology (PhD)
molecular and biochemical nutrition (PhD)

molecular toxicology (PhD)
natural resources (MF, MS, PhD)
plant biology (PhD)

Graduate School of Journalism
Orville Schell, Dean
Program in:
journalism (MJ)

Graduate School of Public Policy
Michael Nacht, Dean
Program in:
public policy (MPP, PhD)

Haas School of Business
Tom Campbell, Dean
Programs in:
accounting (PhD)
business (MBA, MFE, PhD)
business administration (MBA)
business and public policy (PhD)
finance (PhD)
financial engineering (MFE)
marketing (PhD)
organizational behavior and industrial relations (PhD)
real estate (PhD)

School of Education
Dr. P. David Pearson, Dean
Programs in:
development in mathematics and science (MA)
developmental teacher education)
education (MA, Ed D, PhD)
education and single subject credential: English (MA)
education in mathematics, science, and technology (MA, PhD)
educational leadership (Ed D)
human development and education (MA, PhD)
language, literacy, and culture (MA, Ed D, PhD)
policy and organizational research (MA, PhD)
principal leadership (MA)
program evaluation and assessment (Ed D)
quantitative methods and evaluation (MA, PhD)
school psychology)
science and mathematics education)
social and cultural studies in education (MA, PhD)
special education (PhD)

School of Information Management and Systems
AnnaLee Saxenian, Dean, School of Information Management and Systems
Program in:
information management and systems (MIMS, PhD)

School of Public Health
Ralph Catalano, Dean, School of Public Health
Programs in:
biostatistics (MA, PhD)
community health education (MPH)
environmental health sciences (MPH, MS, Dr PH, PhD)
epidemiology (MPH, MS, PhD)
health and medical sciences)
health and social behavior (MPH)
health policy and management (MPH)
health services and policy analysis (PhD)
infectious diseases (MPH, PhD)
infectious diseases and immunity (PhD)
interdisciplinary (MPH)
maternal and child health (MPH)
public health (MA, MPH, MS, Dr PH, PhD)
public health nutrition (MPH)

School of Social Welfare
Lorraine Midanik, Dean, School of Social Welfare
Program in:
social welfare (MSW, PhD)

School of Law
Programs in:
jurisprudence and social policy (PhD)
law (JD, LL M, JSD)

School of Optometry
Dr. Dennis M. Levi, Dean
Program in:
optometry (OD, Certificate)

■ UNIVERSITY OF CALIFORNIA, DAVIS
Davis, CA 95616
http://www.ucdavis.edu/

State-supported, coed, university. CGS member. *Computer facilities:* Computer purchase and lease plans are available. 600 computers available on campus for general student use. A campuswide network can be accessed from student residence rooms and from off campus. Internet access, software packages are available. *Library facilities:* Peter J. Shields Library plus 5 others. *General application contact:* Director of Outreach, Recruitment and Retention, 530-752-2119.

College of Engineering
Programs in:
aeronautical engineering (M Engr, MS, D Engr, PhD, Certificate)
applied science (MS, PhD)
biological systems engineering (M Engr, MS, D Engr, PhD)
biomedical engineering (MS, PhD)
chemical engineering (MS, PhD)
civil and environmental engineering (M Engr, MS, D Engr, PhD, Certificate)
computer science (MS, PhD)
electrical and computer engineering (MS, PhD)
engineering (M Engr, MS, D Engr, PhD, Certificate)
materials science and engineering (MS, PhD)
mechanical engineering (M Engr, MS, D Engr, PhD, Certificate)
transportation, technology and policy (MS, PhD)

Graduate School of Management
Nicole W. Biggart, Dean
Programs in:
business administration (MBA)
management (MBA)

Graduate Studies
Programs in:
acting (MFA)
agricultural and environmental chemistry (MS, PhD)
agricultural and resource economics (MS, PhD)
animal behavior (PhD)
animal biology (MAM, MS, PhD)
anthropology (MA, PhD)
applied linguistics (MA, PhD)
applied mathematics (MS, PhD)
art (MFA)
art history (MA)
atmospheric sciences (MS, PhD)
avian sciences (MS)
biochemistry and molecular biology (MS, PhD)
biophysics (MS, PhD)
biostatistics (MS, PhD)
cell and developmental biology (MS, PhD)
chemistry (MS, PhD)
child development (MS)
clinical research (MAS)
communication (MA)
community development (MS)
comparative literature (PhD)
comparative pathology (MS, PhD)
composition (MA, PhD)
conducting (MA, PhD)
creative writing (MA)
cultural studies (MA, PhD)
dramatic art (PhD)
ecology (MS, PhD)
economics (MA, PhD)
education (MA, Ed D)
English (MA, PhD)
entomology (MS, PhD)
epidemiology (MS, PhD)
exercise science (MS)
food science (MS, PhD)
forensic science (MS)
French (PhD)
genetics (MS, PhD)
geography (MA, PhD)
geology (MS, PhD)
German (MA, PhD)
health informatics (MS)
history (MA, PhD)
horticulture and agronomy (MS)
human development (PhD)
hydrologic sciences (MS, PhD)
immunology (MS, PhD)
instructional studies (PhD)
integrated pest management (MS)

University of California, Davis (continued)
- international agricultural development (MS)
- linguistics (MA)
- mathematics (MA, MAT, PhD)
- microbiology (MS, PhD)
- molecular, cellular and integrative physiology (MS, PhD)
- musicology (MA, PhD)
- Native American studies (MA, PhD)
- neuroscience (PhD)
- nutrition (MS, PhD)
- pharmacology/toxicology (MS, PhD)
- philosophy (MA, PhD)
- physics (MS, PhD)
- plant biology (MS, PhD)
- plant pathology (MS, PhD)
- political science (MA, PhD)
- population biology (PhD)
- psychological studies (PhD)
- psychology (PhD)
- sociocultural studies (PhD)
- sociology (MA, PhD)
- soils and biogeochemistry (MS, PhD)
- Spanish (MA, PhD)
- statistics (MS, PhD)
- textile arts and costume design (MFA)
- textiles (MS)
- viticulture and enology (MS, PhD)

School of Law
Rex R. Perschbacher, Dean
Program in:
- law (JD, LL M)

School of Medicine
Dr. Claire Pomeroy, Dean, School of Medicine; Vice Chancellor, Human Health Services
Program in:
- medicine (MD)

School of Veterinary Medicine
Programs in:
- preventive veterinary medicine (MPVM)
- veterinary medicine (DVM, MPVM, Certificate)

■ UNIVERSITY OF CALIFORNIA, IRVINE
Irvine, CA 92697
http://www.uci.edu/

State-supported, coed, university. CGS member. *Enrollment:* 25,229 graduate, professional, and undergraduate students; 4,140 matriculated graduate/professional students. *Graduate faculty:* 1,144. *Computer facilities:* 1,732 computers available on campus for general student use. A campuswide network can be accessed from student residence rooms and from off campus. Internet access and online class registration are available. *General application contact:* Ashley Brooks, Office of Graduate Studies, 949-824-4611.

College of Medicine
Dr. Thomas Cesario, Dean
Programs in:
- biological sciences (MS, PhD)
- genetic counseling (MS)
- medicine (MD, MS, PhD)
- pharmacology and toxicology (MS, PhD)
- research medical science training)

Office of Graduate Studies
Dr. William H. Parker, Vice Chancellor for Research and Dean of Graduate Studies
Programs in:
- educational administration (Ed D)
- educational administration and leadership (Ed D)
- elementary and secondary education (MAT)

Claire Trevor School of the Arts
Nohema Fernandez, Dean
Programs in:
- accompanying (MFA)
- acting (MFA)
- arts (MFA, PhD)
- choral conducting (MFA)
- composition and technology (MFA)
- dance (MFA)
- design and stage management (MFA)
- directing (MFA)
- drama (MFA)
- drama and theatre (PhD)
- guitar/lute performance (MFA)
- instrumental performance (MFA)
- jazz instrumental/composition (MFA)
- piano performance (MFA)
- studio art (MFA)
- vocal performance (MFA)

Donald Bren School of Information and Computer Sciences
Debra J. Richardson, Interim Dean
Programs in:
- information and computer science (MS, PhD)
- networked systems (MS, PhD)

The Paul Merage School of Business
Jone Pearce, Dean
Programs in:
- business administration (MBA)
- management (PhD)

School of Biological Sciences
Dr. Susan V. Bryant, Dean
Programs in:
- biological science (MS)
- biological sciences (MS, PhD)
- biotechnology (MS)

School of Engineering
Dr. Nicolaos G. Alexopoulos, Dean
Programs in:
- biomedical engineering (MS, PhD)
- chemical and biochemical engineering (MS, PhD)
- civil and environmental engineering (MS, PhD)
- electrical engineering and computer science (MS, PhD)
- engineering (MS, PhD)
- materials science and engineering (MS, PhD)
- mechanical and aerospace engineering (MS, PhD)
- networked systems (MS, PhD)

School of Humanities
Karen Lawrence, Dean
Programs in:
- Chinese (MA, PhD)
- classics (MA, PhD)
- comparative literature (MA, PhD)
- creative writing (MFA)
- East Asian languages and literatures (MA, PhD)
- English (MA, PhD)
- English (summer program) (MA)
- English and American literature (PhD)
- French (MA, PhD)
- German (MA, PhD)
- history (MA, PhD)
- humanities (MA, MAT, MFA, PhD)
- Japanese (MA, PhD)
- philosophy (MA, PhD)
- Spanish (MA, MAT, PhD)
- visual studies (MA, PhD)
- writing (MFA)

School of Physical Sciences
Ronald Stern, Dean
Programs in:
- chemical and material physics (PhD)
- chemical and materials physics (MS)
- chemistry (MS, PhD)
- earth system science (MS, PhD)
- mathematics (MS, PhD)
- physical sciences (MS, PhD)
- physics (MS, PhD)

School of Social Ecology
C. Ronald Huff, Dean
Programs in:
- criminology, law and society (MAS, PhD)
- planning, policy and design (PhD)
- psychology and social behavior (PhD)
- social ecology (MAS, MS, MURP, PhD)
- urban and regional planning (MURP)

School of Social Sciences
Barbara Anne Dosher, Dean
Programs in:
- anthropology (MA, PhD)
- demographic and social analysis (MA)
- economics (MA, PhD)
- philosophy (PhD)
- political psychology (PhD)
- political sciences (PhD)
- psychology (PhD)
- public choice (MA, PhD)
- social networks (PhD)
- social networks-social science (MA)
- social science (MA, PhD)
- social sciences (MA, PhD)
- sociology and social relations-social science (MA, PhD)
- transportation economics (MA, PhD)
- transportation science (MA, PhD)

■ UNIVERSITY OF CALIFORNIA, LOS ANGELES

Los Angeles, CA 90095
http://www.ucla.edu/

State-supported, coed, university. CGS member. *Computer facilities:* Computer purchase and lease plans are available. A campuswide network can be accessed from student residence rooms and from off campus. Internet access and online class registration are available. *Library facilities:* Charles E. Young Research Library plus 13 others. *General application contact:* Graduate Admissions, 310-825-1711.

Graduate Division
Program in:
- East Asian studies (MA)

College of Letters and Science
Programs in:
- African studies (MA)
- Afro-American studies (MA)
- American Indian studies (MA)
- anthropology (MA, PhD)
- applied linguistics (PhD)
- applied linguistics and teaching English as a second language (MA)
- archaeology (MA, PhD)
- art history (MA, PhD)
- Asian-American studies (MA)
- astronomy (MAT, MS, PhD)
- atmospheric sciences (MS, PhD)
- biochemistry and molecular biology (MS, PhD)
- biology (MA, PhD)
- chemistry (MS, PhD)
- classics (MA, PhD)
- comparative literature (MA, PhD)
- East Asian languages and cultures (MA, PhD)
- economics (MA, PhD)
- English (MA, PhD)
- French and Francophone studies (MA, PhD)
- geochemistry (MS, PhD)
- geography (MA, PhD)
- geology (MS, PhD)
- geophysics and space physics (MS, PhD)
- German (MA)
- Germanic languages (MA, PhD)
- Greek (MA)
- Hispanic languages and literature (PhD)
- history (MA, PhD)
- Indo-European studies (PhD)
- Islamic studies (MA, PhD)
- Italian (MA, PhD)
- Latin (MA)
- Latin American studies (MA)
- letters and science (MA, MAT, MS, PhD, Certificate)
- linguistics (MA, PhD)
- mathematics (MA, MAT, PhD)
- molecular and cellular life sciences (PhD)
- molecular biology (PhD)
- molecular, cellular and integrative physiology (PhD)
- musicology (MA, PhD)
- Near Eastern languages and cultures (MA, PhD)
- philosophy (MA, PhD)
- physics (MAT, MS, PhD)
- physics education (MAT)
- physiological science (MS, PhD)
- plant molecular biology (PhD)
- political science (MA, PhD)
- Portuguese (MA)
- psychology (MA, PhD)
- Romance linguistics and literature (MA, PhD)
- Scandinavian (MA, PhD)
- Slavic languages and literatures (MA, PhD)
- sociology (MA, PhD)
- Spanish (MA)
- statistics (MS, PhD)
- women's studies (MS, PhD)

Graduate School of Education and Information Studies
Programs in:
- archival studies (MLIS)
- education (M Ed, MA, Ed D, PhD)
- education and information studies (M Ed, MA, MLIS, Ed D, PhD, Certificate)
- informatics (MLIS)
- information studies (PhD)
- library and information science (Certificate)
- library studies (MLIS)
- special education (PhD)

Henry Samueli School of Engineering and Applied Science
Dr. Stephen E. Jacobsen, Associate Dean, Academic and Student Affairs
Programs in:
- aerospace engineering (MS, PhD)
- biomedical engineering (MS, PhD)
- ceramics engineering (MS, PhD)
- chemical and biomolecular engineering (MS, PhD)
- computer science (MS, PhD)
- electrical engineering (MS, PhD)
- engineering and applied science (MS, PhD)
- engineering optimization/operations research (MS, PhD)
- environmental engineering (MS, PhD)
- geotechnical engineering (MS, PhD)
- hydrology and water resources engineering (MS)
- manufacturing engineering (MS)
- mechanical engineering (MS, PhD)
- metallurgy (MS, PhD)
- structures (MS, PhD)
- water resource systems engineering (PhD)

School of Nursing
Program in:
- nursing (MSN, PhD)

School of Public Health
Programs in:
- biostatistics (MS, PhD)
- environmental health sciences (MS, PhD)
- environmental science and engineering (D Env)
- epidemiology (MS, PhD)
- health services (MS, PhD)
- molecular toxicology (PhD)
- public health (MS, PhD)
- public health for health professionals (MPH)

School of Public Policy and Social Research
Programs in:
- public policy (MPP)
- public policy and social research (MA, MPP, MSW, PhD)
- social welfare (MSW, PhD)
- urban planning (MA, PhD)

School of the Arts and Architecture
Programs in:
- architecture and urban design (M Arch, MA, PhD)
- art (MA, MFA)
- arts and architecture (M Arch, MA, MFA, MM, DMA, PhD)
- composition (MA, PhD)
- culture and performance (MA, PhD)
- dance (MA, MFA)
- design/media arts (MFA)
- ethnomusicology (MA, PhD)
- performance (MM, DMA)

School of Theater, Film and Television
Programs in:
- film and television (MA, MFA, PhD)
- film, television, and digital media (MA, MFA, PhD)
- theater (MFA, PhD)

UCLA Anderson School of Management
Judy D. Olian, Dean
Program in:
- management (MBA, MS, PhD)

School of Dentistry
Programs in:
- dentistry (DDS, MS, PhD, Certificate)
- oral biology (MS, PhD)

School of Law
Program in:
- law (JD, LL M)

School of Medicine
Program in:
- medicine (MD, MA, MS, PhD)

Graduate Programs in Medicine
Programs in:
- anatomy and cell biology (PhD)
- biological chemistry (MS, PhD)
- biomathematics (MS, PhD)
- biomedical physics (MS, PhD)
- clinical research (MS)

University of California, Los Angeles (continued)
- experimental pathology (MS, PhD)
- human genetics (MS, PhD)
- medicine (MA, MS, PhD)
- microbiology, immunology and molecular genetics (MS, PhD)
- molecular and medical pharmacology (PhD)
- molecular, cell and developmental biology (MA, PhD)
- neuroscience (PhD)
- physiology (MS, PhD)

■ UNIVERSITY OF CALIFORNIA, RIVERSIDE
Riverside, CA 92521-0102
http://www.ucr.edu/

State-supported, coed, university. CGS member. *Enrollment:* 16,875 graduate, professional, and undergraduate students; 1,944 full-time matriculated graduate/professional students (934 women), 21 part-time matriculated graduate/professional students (8 women). *Graduate faculty:* 635 full-time (184 women). *Computer facilities:* Computer purchase and lease plans are available. 793 computers available on campus for general student use. A campuswide network can be accessed from student residence rooms and from off campus. Internet access and online class registration, online viewing of grades, enrollment data and financial information are available. *Library facilities:* Tomas Rivera Library plus 6 others. *General application contact:* Graduate Admissions, 951-827-3313.

Graduate Division
Dr. Dallas Rabenstein, Dean
Programs in:
- anthropology (MA, MS, PhD)
- applied statistics (PhD)
- archival management (MA)
- art history (MA)
- biochemistry and molecular biology (MS, PhD)
- bioengineering (MS, PhD)
- biology (MS, PhD)
- biomedical sciences (PhD)
- cell, molecular, and developmental biology (MS, PhD)
- chemical and environmental engineering (MS, PhD)
- chemistry (MS, PhD)
- classics (PhD)
- comparative literature (MA, PhD)
- computer science (MS, PhD)
- creative writing (MFA)
- dance (MFA)
- dance history and theory (MA, PhD)
- economics (MA, PhD)
- electrical engineering (MS, PhD)
- English (MA, PhD)
- entomology (MS, PhD)
- environmental sciences (MS, PhD)
- environmental toxicology (MS, PhD)
- evolution, ecology and organismal biology (MS, PhD)
- genomics and bioinformatics (PhD)
- geological sciences (MS, PhD)
- historic preservation (MA)
- history (MA, PhD)
- mathematics (MA, MS, PhD)
- mechanical engineering (MS, PhD)
- microbiology (MS, PhD)
- molecular genetics (PhD)
- museum curatorship (MA)
- music (MA)
- neuroscience (PhD)
- philosophy (MA, PhD)
- physics and astronomy (MS, PhD)
- plant biology (MS, PhD)
- plant biology (plant genetics) (PhD)
- plant pathology (MS, PhD)
- political science (MA, PhD)
- population and evolutionary genetics (PhD)
- psychology (MA, PhD)
- sociology (MA, PhD)
- soil and water sciences (MS, PhD)
- Spanish (MA, PhD)
- statistics (MS)
- visual arts (MFA)
- writing for the performing arts (MFA)

A. Gary Anderson Graduate School of Management
Dr. Anil Deolalikar, Interim Dean
Program in:
- management (MBA)

Graduate School of Education
Dr. Steven T. Bossert, Dean
Program in:
- education (M Ed, MA, PhD)

■ UNIVERSITY OF CALIFORNIA, SAN DIEGO
La Jolla, CA 92093
http://www.ucsd.edu/

State-supported, coed, university. CGS member. *Computer facilities:* Computer purchase and lease plans are available. 1,500 computers available on campus for general student use. A campuswide network can be accessed from student residence rooms and from off campus. Internet access and online class registration, e-mail are available. *Library facilities:* Geisel Library plus 9 others. *General application contact:* Graduate Admissions Office, 858-534-1193.

Office of Graduate Studies
Richard Attiyeh, Dean
Programs in:
- acting (MFA)
- aerospace engineering (MS, PhD)
- anthropology (PhD)
- applied mathematics (MA)
- applied mechanics (MS, PhD)
- applied ocean science (MS, PhD)
- applied physics (MS, PhD)
- bilingual education (MA)
- bioengineering (M Eng, MS, PhD)
- bioinformatics (PhD)
- biophysics (MS, PhD)
- chemical engineering (MS, PhD)
- chemistry (MS, PhD)
- clinical psychology (PhD)
- cognitive science (PhD)
- cognitive science/anthropology (PhD)
- cognitive science/communication (PhD)
- cognitive science/computer science and engineering (PhD)
- cognitive science/linguistics (PhD)
- cognitive science/neuroscience (PhD)
- cognitive science/philosophy (PhD)
- cognitive science/psychology (PhD)
- cognitive science/sociology (PhD)
- communication (MA, PhD)
- communication theory and systems (MS, PhD)
- comparative literature (MA, PhD)
- computer engineering (MS, PhD)
- computer science (MS, PhD)
- curriculum design (MA)
- design (MFA)
- directing (MFA)
- drama and theatre (PhD)
- earth sciences (PhD)
- economics (PhD)
- economics and international affairs (PhD)
- electrical engineering (M Eng)
- electronic circuits and systems (MS, PhD)
- engineering physics (MS, PhD)
- ethnic studies (MA, PhD)
- French literature (MA)
- German literature (MA)
- history (MA, PhD)
- intelligent systems, robotics and control (MS, PhD)
- Judaic studies (MA)
- language and communicative disorders (PhD)
- Latin American studies (MA)
- linguistics (PhD)
- literature (PhD)
- literatures in English (MA)
- marine biodiversity and conservation (MAS)
- marine biology (PhD)
- materials science and engineering (MS, PhD)
- mathematics (MA, PhD)
- mathematics and science education (PhD)
- mechanical engineering (MS, PhD)
- music (MA, DMA, PhD)
- oceanography (PhD)
- philosophy (PhD)
- photonics (MS, PhD)
- physics (MS, PhD)
- physics/materials physics (MS)
- playwriting (MFA)
- political science (PhD)

political science and international affairs (PhD)
psychology (PhD)
public health and epidemiology (PhD)
science studies (PhD)
signal and image processing (MS, PhD)
sociology (PhD)
Spanish literature (MA)
stage management (MFA)
statistics (MS)
structural engineering (MS, PhD)
teacher education (M Ed)
teaching and learning (Ed D)
theatre (PhD)
visual arts (MFA, PhD)

Division of Biological Sciences
Programs in:
biochemistry (PhD)
biology (MS)
cell and developmental biology (PhD)
computational neurobiology (PhD)
ecology, behavior, and evolution (PhD)
genetics and molecular biology (PhD)
immunology, virology, and cancer biology (PhD)
molecular and cellular biology (PhD)
neurobiology (PhD)
plant molecular biology (PhD)
plant systems biology (PhD)
signal transduction (PhD)

Graduate School of International Relations and Pacific Studies
Programs in:
economics and international affairs (PhD)
Pacific international affairs (MPIA)
political science and international affairs (PhD)

Rady School of Management
Program in:
business administration and management (MBA)

School of Medicine
Programs in:
audiology (Au D)
bioinformatics (PhD)
cancer biology/oncology (PhD)
cardiovascular sciences and disease (PhD)
clinical research (MAS)
leadership in healthcare organizations (MAS)
medicine (MD, MAS, Au D, PhD)
microbiology (PhD)
molecular pathology (PhD)
neurological disease (PhD)
neurosciences (PhD)
stem cell and developmental biology (PhD)
structural biology/drug design (PhD)

Graduate Studies in Biomedical Sciences
Programs in:
molecular cell biology (PhD)
pharmacology (PhD)
physiology (PhD)
regulatory biology (PhD)

School of Pharmacy and Pharmaceutical Sciences
Program in:
pharmacy and pharmaceutical sciences (Pharm D)

■ UNIVERSITY OF CALIFORNIA, SANTA BARBARA
Santa Barbara, CA 93106
http://www.ucsb.edu/

State-supported, coed, university. CGS member. *Enrollment:* 21,062 graduate, professional, and undergraduate students; 2,870 full-time matriculated graduate/professional students (1,265 women). *Graduate faculty:* 684 full-time, 165 part-time/adjunct. *Computer facilities:* 3,000 computers available on campus for general student use. A campuswide network can be accessed from off campus. *Library facilities:* Davidson Library. *General application contact:* Rebecca Letts, Graduate Admissions Coordinator, 805-893-2278.

Graduate Division
Dr. Gale Morrison, Acting Dean

College of Engineering
Matthew Tirrell, Dean
Programs in:
chemical engineering (MS, PhD)
computer science (MS, PhD)
electrical and computer engineering (MS, PhD)
engineering (MS, PhD)
materials science and engineering (MS, PhD)
mechanical engineering (MS, PhD)

College of Letters and Sciences
David Marshall, Executive Dean
Programs in:
applied mathematics (MA)
applied statistics (MA)
archaeology (MA, PhD)
art studio (MFA)
biochemistry and molecular biology (MS, PhD)
biomolecular science and engineering (PhD)
biophysics and bioengineering (MS, PhD)
biosocial anthropology (PhD)
brass (MM)
chemistry (MA, MS, PhD)
Chicana and Chicano studies (PhD)
choral conducting (MM, DMA)
classics (MA, PhD)
communication (PhD)
comparative literature (PhD)
composition (MA, PhD)
East Asian languages (PhD)
East Asian literatures (PhD)
ecology, evolution, and marine biology (MA, PhD)
economics (MA, PhD)
electronic music and sound design (MA, PhD)
English literature (PhD)
ethnomusicology (MA, PhD)
film and media studies)
French (MA, PhD)
geography (MA, PhD)
geological sciences (MS, PhD)
geophysics (MS)
Germanic languages and literature (MA, PhD)
global and international studies (MA)
Hispanic languages and literature (PhD)
history (PhD)
history of art and architecture (PhD)
humanities and fine arts (MA, MFA, MM, MS, DMA, PhD)
keyboard (MM, DMA)
Latin American and Iberian studies (MA)
letters and sciences (MA, MFA, MM, MS, DMA, PhD)
linguistics (MA, PhD)
marine science (MS, PhD)
mathematical and empirical finance (PhD)
mathematical statistics (MA)
mathematics (MA, PhD)
mathematics, life, and physical sciences (MA, MS, PhD)
molecular, cellular, and developmental biology (MA, PhD)
multimedia engineering (MS, PhD)
musicology (MA, PhD)
philosophy (PhD)
physics (PhD)
political science (MA, PhD)
Portuguese (MA)
psychology (PhD)
public history (PhD)
quantitative methods in the social sciences (PhD)
religious studies (MA, PhD)
social sciences (MA, PhD)
sociocultural anthropology (PhD)
sociology (PhD)
Spanish (MA)
statistics and applied probability (PhD)
strings (MM, DMA)
theater (MA, PhD)
theory (MA, PhD)
visual and spatial arts (MA, PhD)
voice (MM, DMA)
women's studies (PhD)
woodwinds (MM)

Donald Bren School of Environmental Science and Management
Dr. Ernst Von Weizsacker, Dean
Programs in:
economics and environmental science (PhD)
environmental science and management (MESM, PhD)

Gevirtz Graduate School of Education
Dr. Jane Conoley, Chair

University of California, Santa Barbara (continued)
Programs in:
counseling, clinical and school psychology (PhD)
education (M Ed, MA, PhD)
educational leadership (Ed D)

■ UNIVERSITY OF CALIFORNIA, SANTA CRUZ
Santa Cruz, CA 95064
http://www.ucsc.edu/

State-supported, coed, university. CGS member. *Computer facilities:* 200 computers available on campus for general student use. A campuswide network can be accessed from student residence rooms and from off campus. Internet access and online class registration are available. *Library facilities:* McHenry Library plus 1 other. *General application contact:* Reporting Analyst for Graduate Admissions, 831-459-5906.

Division of Graduate Studies

Division of Arts
Programs in:
arts (MA, MFA, DMA, Certificate)
digital arts/new media (MFA)
music (MA, DMA)
theater arts (Certificate)

Division of Humanities
Programs in:
history (MA, PhD)
history of consciousness (PhD)
humanities (MA, PhD)
linguistics (MA, PhD)
literature (MA, PhD)
philosophy (MA, PhD)

Division of Physical and Biological Sciences
Programs in:
astronomy and astrophysics (PhD)
chemistry and biochemistry (MS, PhD)
earth sciences (MS, PhD)
ecology and evolutionary biology (MA, PhD)
environmental toxicology (MS, PhD)
mathematics (MA, PhD)
molecular, cellular, and developmental biology (MA, PhD)
ocean sciences (MS, PhD)
physical and biological sciences (MA, MS, PhD, Certificate)
physics (MS, PhD)
science communication (Certificate)

Division of Social Sciences
Programs in:
anthropology (PhD)
applied economics (MS)
education (MA, Ed D, PhD)
environmental studies (PhD)
international economics (PhD)
politics (PhD)
psychology (PhD)
social documentation (MA)
social sciences (MA, MS, Ed D, PhD)
sociology (PhD)

Jack Baskin School of Engineering
Programs in:
bioinformatics (MS, PhD)
computer engineering (MS, PhD)
computer science (MS, PhD)
electrical engineering (MS, PhD)
engineering (MS, PhD)
network engineering (MS)
statistics and stochastic modeling (MS)

■ UNIVERSITY OF LA VERNE
La Verne, CA 91750-4443
http://www.ulv.edu/

Independent, coed, university. *Enrollment:* 3,876 graduate, professional, and undergraduate students; 1,571 full-time matriculated graduate/professional students (987 women), 1,693 part-time matriculated graduate/professional students (1,162 women). *Graduate faculty:* 70 full-time (34 women), 162 part-time/adjunct (82 women). *Computer facilities:* 150 computers available on campus for general student use. A campuswide network can be accessed from student residence rooms and from off campus. Internet access and online class registration, online grade information are available. *Library facilities:* Wilson Library. *General application contact:* Jo Nell Baker, Director, Graduate Admissions and Academic Services, 909-593-3511 Ext. 4244.

College of Arts and Sciences
Dr. Fred Yaffe, Dean
Programs in:
arts and sciences (MS, Psy D)
clinical-community psychology (Psy D)
counseling (MS)
general counseling (MS)
higher education counseling (MS)
marriage and family therapy (MS)

College of Business and Public Management
Dr. Gordon Badovick, Dean
Programs in:
accounting (MBA)
business (MBIT)
business administration (MS)
business and public management (MBA, MBA-EP, MBIT, MHA, MPA, MS, DPA, Certificate)
counseling (MS)
executive management (MBA-EP)
finance (MBA, MBA-EP)
financial management (MHA)
gerontology (Certificate)
gerontology administration (MS)
health administration (MHA)
health services management (MBA, MS)
human resources (MHA)
information management (MHA)
information technology (MBA, MBA-EP)
international business (MBA, MBA-EP)
leadership (MBA-EP)
leadership and management (MHA, MS)
managed care (MBA, MHA)
management (MBA, MBA-EP)
marketing (MBA, MBA-EP)
marketing and business development (MHA)
nonprofit management (Certificate)
organizational leadership (Certificate)
public administration (MS)

College of Education and Organizational Leadership
Dr. Leonard Pellicer, Dean
Programs in:
advanced teaching skills (M Ed)
child development (MS)
child development/child life (MS)
child life (MS)
education (M Ed)
education (special emphasis) (M Ed)
education and organizational leadership (M Ed, MS, Ed D, Certificate, Credential)
educational management (M Ed, Credential)
multiple subject (Credential)
organizational leadership (Ed D)
preliminary administrative services (Credential)
professional administrative services (Credential)
pupil personnel services (Credential)
reading (M Ed, Certificate, Credential)
reading and language arts specialist (Credential)
school counseling (MS, Credential)
single subject (Credential)
teacher education (Credential)

College of Law
Donald J. Dunn, Dean
Program in:
law (JD)

Regional Campus Administration
Dr. Stephen E. Lesniak, Dean
Programs in:
advanced teaching (M Ed)
business (MBA-EP)
cross cultural language and academic development (Credential)
educational management (M Ed)
health administration (MHA)
leadership and management (MS)
multiple subject (Credential)
reading (M Ed)
school counseling (MS)
single subject (Credential)

■ UNIVERSITY OF PHOENIX–SACRAMENTO VALLEY CAMPUS
Sacramento, CA 95833-3632
http://www.phoenix.edu/

Proprietary, coed, comprehensive institution. *Enrollment:* 4,585 graduate, professional, and undergraduate students; 1,103 full-time matriculated graduate/professional students (728 women). *Graduate faculty:* 96 full-time (55 women), 801 part-time/adjunct (271 women). *Computer facilities:* A campuswide network can be accessed from off campus. Internet access is available. *Library facilities:* University Library. *Graduate expenses:* Tuition: full-time $12,024. Required fees: $760. *General application contact:* Campus Information Center, 916-923-2107.

The Artemis School
Dr. Adam Honea, Provost

College of Education
Dr. Marla LaRue, Dean
Programs in:
- adult education (MA Ed)
- curriculum instruction (MA Ed)
- elementary education (MA Ed)
- secondary education (MA Ed)
- teacher education (Certificate)

College of Health and Human Services
Dr. Gil Linne, Dean/Executive Director
Programs in:
- administration of justice and security (MS)
- family nurse practitioner (MSN)
- health care management (MBA)
- marriage, family and child counseling (MSC)
- nursing (MSN)
- nursing education (MSN)

John Sperling School of Business
Dr. Adam Honea, Provost
Program in:
- business (MBA, MIS)

College of Graduate Business and Management
Dr. Brian Lindquist, Associate Vice President and Dean/Executive Director
Programs in:
- accounting (MBA)
- business administration (MBA)
- global management (MBA)
- human resources management (MBA)
- marketing (MBA)
- public administration (MBA)

College of Information Systems and Technology
Dr. Adam Honea, Provost/Dean, Vice President Academic Research and Development
Programs in:
- management (MIS)
- technology management (MBA)

■ UNIVERSITY OF PHOENIX–SAN DIEGO CAMPUS
San Diego, CA 92123
http://www.phoenix.edu/

Proprietary, coed, comprehensive institution. *Enrollment:* 3,781 graduate, professional, and undergraduate students; 999 full-time matriculated graduate/professional students (625 women). *Graduate faculty:* 90 full-time (27 women), 585 part-time/adjunct (158 women). *Computer facilities:* A campuswide network can be accessed from off campus. Internet access is available. *Library facilities:* University Library. *Graduate expenses:* Tuition: full-time $11,419. Required fees: $760. *General application contact:* Campus Information Center, 888-UOP-INFO.

The Artemis School
Dr. Adam Honea, Provost

College of Education
Dr. Marla LaRue, Dean/Executive Director
Programs in:
- curriculum and instruction (MA Ed)
- elementary education (MA Ed)
- secondary education (MA Ed)

College of Health and Human Services
Dr. Gil Linne, Dean/Executive Director
Programs in:
- administration of justice and security (MS)
- marriage, family and child counseling (MSC)
- marriage, family and child therapy (MSC)
- nursing (MSN)

John Sperling School of Business
Dr. Adam Honea, Provost
Program in:
- business (MBA, MIS, MM)

College of Graduate Business and Management
Dr. Brian Lindquist, Associate Vice President and Dean/Executive Director
Programs in:
- business administration (MBA)
- global management (MBA)
- management (MM)

College of Information Systems and Technology
Dr. Adam Honea, Provost/Dean, Vice President Academic Research and Development
Programs in:
- management (MIS)
- technology management (MBA)

■ UNIVERSITY OF PHOENIX–SOUTHERN CALIFORNIA CAMPUS
Costa Mesa, CA 92626
http://www.phoenix.edu/

Proprietary, coed, comprehensive institution. *Enrollment:* 14,760 graduate, professional, and undergraduate students; 3,593 full-time matriculated graduate/professional students (2,460 women). *Graduate faculty:* 147 full-time (63 women), 1,450 part-time/adjunct (535 women). *Computer facilities:* A campuswide network can be accessed from off campus. Internet access is available. *Library facilities:* University Library. *Graduate expenses:* Tuition: full-time $13,512. Required fees: $760. *General application contact:* Campus Information Center, 714-378-1878.

The Artemis School
Dr. Adam Honea, Provost

College of Education
Dr. Marla LaRue, Dean/Executive Director
Programs in:
- curriculum and instruction (MA Ed)
- elementary education (MA Ed)
- secondary education (MA Ed)

College of Health and Human Services
Dr. Gil Linne, Dean/Executive Director
Programs in:
- family nurse practitioner (MSN, Certificate)
- health care education (MSN)
- health care management (MBA)
- marriage, family and child therapy (MSC)
- nursing (MSN)

John Sperling School of Business
Dr. Adam Honea, Provost
Program in:
- business (MBA, MM)

College of Graduate Business and Management
Dr. Brian Lindquist, Associate Vice President and Dean/Executive Director
Programs in:
- accounting (MBA)
- business administration (MBA)
- business and management (MM)
- human resource management (MBA)
- marketing (MBA)

College of Information Systems and Technology
Dr. Adam Honea, Provost/Dean, Vice President Research and Development
Program in:
- technology management (MBA)

■ UNIVERSITY OF REDLANDS

Redlands, CA 92373-0999

http://www.redlands.edu/

Independent, coed, comprehensive institution. *Enrollment:* 2,407 graduate, professional, and undergraduate students; 1,243 full-time matriculated graduate/professional students (727 women), 11 part-time matriculated graduate/professional students (6 women). *Graduate faculty:* 60 full-time, 217 part-time/adjunct. *Computer facilities:* 655 computers available on campus for general student use. A campuswide network can be accessed from student residence rooms and from off campus. Internet access is available. *Library facilities:* Armacost Library. *Graduate expenses:* Tuition: part-time $584 per credit. Required fees: $20 per course. Full-time tuition and fees vary according to program.

College of Arts and Sciences
Dr. Barbara Morris, Acting Dean
Programs in:
arts and sciences (MM, MS)
communicative disorders (MS)
geographic information systems (MS)

School of Music
Dr. Andrew Glendening, Director
Program in:
music (MM)

School of Business
Dr. Stuart Noble-Goodman, Interim Dean
Programs in:
business (MBA)
information technology (MS)
management (MA)

School of Education
Dr. Hank Robin, Dean
Program in:
education (MA, Ed D, Certificate)

■ UNIVERSITY OF SAN DIEGO

San Diego, CA 92110-2492

http://www.sandiego.edu/

Independent-religious, coed, university. CGS member. *Enrollment:* 7,483 graduate, professional, and undergraduate students; 1,358 full-time matriculated graduate/professional students (738 women), 1,112 part-time matriculated graduate/professional students (656 women). *Graduate faculty:* 149 full-time (68 women), 143 part-time/adjunct (79 women). *Computer facilities:* 260 computers available on campus for general student use. A campuswide network can be accessed from student residence rooms and from off campus. Internet access and online class registration are available. *Library facilities:* Helen K. and James S. Copley Library plus 1 other. *General application contact:* Stephen Pultz, Director of Admissions, 619-260-4524.

Find University Details at www.petersons.com/gradchannel.

College of Arts and Sciences
Dr. Nicholas Healy, Dean
Programs in:
arts and sciences (MA, MFA, MS, CAS)
dramatic arts (MFA)
history (MA)
international relations (MA)
marine science (MS)
pastoral care and counseling (MA, CAS)
peace and justice studies (MA)

Hahn School of Nursing and Health Sciences
Dr. Sally Hardin, Dean
Programs in:
accelerated nursing (for RNs only) (MSN)
adult clinical nurse specialist (MSN, Post Master's Certificate)
adult nurse practitioner (MSN, Post Master's Certificate)
clinical nursing (MSN)
entry-level nursing (for non-RNs) (MSN)
executive nurse leader (MSN)
family nurse practitioner (MSN, Post Master's Certificate)
nursing science (PhD)
pediatric nurse practitioner (MSN, Post Master's Certificate)

School of Business Administration
Dr. Andy Allen, Interim Dean
Programs in:
accounting and financial management (MS)
business administration (MBA)
executive leadership (MSEL)
global leadership (MSGL)
international business administration (IMBA)
real estate (MSRE)
supply chain management (MS, Certificate)
taxation (MS)

School of Law
Kevin Cole, Dean
Programs in:
business and corporate law (LL M)
comparative law (LL M)
general studies (LL M)
international law (LL M)
law (JD)
taxation (LL M, Diploma)

School of Leadership and Education Sciences
Dr. Paula A. Cordeiro, Dean
Programs in:
counseling (MA)
educational leadership (M Ed)
leadership and education sciences (M Ed, MA, MAT, Ed D, PhD, Certificate)
leadership studies (MA, PhD)
learning and teaching (M Ed)
marital and family therapy (MA)
nonprofit leadership and management (Certificate)
teaching (MAT)
teaching and learning (Ed D)

■ UNIVERSITY OF SAN FRANCISCO

San Francisco, CA 94117-1080

http://www.usfca.edu/

Independent-religious, coed, university. *Enrollment:* 8,549 graduate, professional, and undergraduate students; 2,510 full-time matriculated graduate/professional students (1,467 women), 613 part-time matriculated graduate/professional students (373 women). *Graduate faculty:* 139 full-time (50 women), 341 part-time/adjunct (154 women). *Computer facilities:* 350 computers available on campus for general student use. A campuswide network can be accessed from student residence rooms and from off campus. Internet access and online class registration are available. *Library facilities:* Gleeson Library plus 2 others. *Graduate expenses:* Tuition: full-time $17,370; part-time $965 per unit. Tuition and fees vary according to degree level, campus/location and program. *General application contact:* Information Contact, 415-422-4723.

College of Arts and Sciences
Dr. Jennifer Turpin, Dean
Programs in:
arts and sciences (MA, MFA, MS)
Asia Pacific studies (MA)
biology (MS)
chemistry (MS)
computer science (MS)
economics (MA)
environmental management (MS)
financial economics (MS)
international and development economics (MA)
Internet engineering (MS)
sport management (MA)
theology (MA)
writing (MA, MFA)

College of Professional Studies
Dr. Larry Brewster, Dean
Programs in:
health services administration (MPA)
information systems (MS)
nonprofit administration (MNA)
organization development (MS)
professional studies (MNA, MPA, MS)
project management (MS)
public administration (MPA)

Masagung Graduate School of Management
Dr. Michael Duffy, Dean
Programs in:
business economics (MBA)
e-business (MBA)
entrepreneurship (MBA)
finance and banking (MBA)
international business (MBA)
management (MBA)
marketing (MBA)
professional business administration (MBA)
telecommunications management and policy (MBA)

School of Education
Dr. Walter Gmelch, Dean
Programs in:
Catholic school leadership (MA, Ed D)
Catholic school teaching (MA)
counseling (MA)
counseling psychology (Ed D)
digital media and learning (MA)
education (MA, Ed D)
international and multicultural education (MA, Ed D)
learning and instruction (MA, Ed D)
multicultural literature for children and young adults (MA)
organization and leadership (MA, Ed D)
private school administration (Ed D)
teaching English as a second language (MA)

School of Law
Jeffrey Brand, Dean
Programs in:
intellectual property and technology law (LL M)
international transactions and comparative law (LL M)
law (JD, LL M)

School of Nursing
Dr. Judith Karshmer, Dean
Programs in:
advanced practice nursing-nurse practitioner and clinical nurse specialist (MSN)
nursing administration (MSN)

■ UNIVERSITY OF SOUTHERN CALIFORNIA
Los Angeles, CA 90089
http://www.usc.edu/

Independent, coed, university. CGS member. *Enrollment:* 33,389 graduate, professional, and undergraduate students; 13,205 full-time matriculated graduate/professional students (6,620 women), 3,454 part-time matriculated graduate/professional students (1,184 women). *Graduate faculty:* 1,917 full-time (568 women), 1,024 part-time/adjunct (383 women). *Computer facilities:* Computer purchase and lease plans are available. 2,500 computers available on campus for general student use. A campuswide network can be accessed from student residence rooms and from off campus. Internet access and online class registration, online degree progress, grades, financial aid summary are available. *Library facilities:* Doheny Memorial Library plus 19 others. *Graduate expenses:* Tuition: full-time $33,314; part-time $1,121 per credit. Required fees: $522. Full-time tuition and fees vary according to program. *General application contact:* Susan Ikerd, Director of Graduate Admission, 213-740-1111.

Graduate School
Dr. Jean Morrison, Viec Provost
Programs in:
biokinesiology (MS, PhD)
occupational science (PhD)
occupational therapy (MA, OTD)
physical therapy (MS, DPT)

Annenberg School for Communication
Ernest Wilson, Dean
Programs in:
broadcast journalism (MA)
communication (MA, PhD)
communication management (MCM)
global communication)
online journalism (MA)
print journalism (MA)
public diplomacy (MPD)
specialized journalism (MA)
strategic public relations (MA)

College of Letters, Arts and Sciences
Dr. Peter Starr, Dean
Programs in:
American studies and ethnicity (PhD)
anthropology (MA)
applied mathematics (MA, MS, PhD)
art history (MA, PhD, Certificate)
biological anthropology (PhD)
chemical physics (PhD)
chemistry (MA, MS, PhD)
classics (MA, PhD)
clinical psychology (PhD)
comparative literature (MA, PhD)
computational linguistics (MS)
earth sciences (MS, PhD)
East Asian area studies (MA)
East Asian languages and cultures (MA, PhD)
economic development programming (MA)
economics (MA, PhD)
English (MA, PhD)
French (MA, PhD)
geography (MA, MS, PhD)
Hispanic linguistics (PhD)
history (MA, PhD)
international relations (MA, PhD)
letters, arts and sciences (MA, MPW, MS, PhD, Certificate)
linguistics (MA, PhD)
marine environmental biology (PhD)
mathematics (MA, PhD)
molecular and computational biology (PhD)
neuroscience (PhD)
philosophy (MA, PhD)
physics (MA, MS, PhD)
political economy (MA)
political science (MA, PhD)
professional writing (MPW)
psychology (MA, PhD)
Slavic languages and literatures (MA, PhD)
social anthropology (PhD)
social ethics (MA, PhD)
sociology (MA, PhD)
statistics (MS)
visual anthropology (Certificate)

Davis School of Gerontology
Dr. Gerald Davison, Dean
Program in:
gerontology (MS, PhD, Certificate)

Gould School of Law
Edward McCaffy, Dean
Program in:
law (JD, LL M)

Marshall School of Business
James Ellis, Dean
Programs in:
accounting (M Acc)
business (M Acc, MBA, MBT, MS, PhD)
business administration (MBA, MS, PhD)
business taxation (MBT)
finance and business economics (MBA)
information and operations management (MS)
international business (MBA)

Roski School of Fine Arts
Ruth Weisberg, Dean
Programs in:
fine arts (MFA, MPAS)
public art studies (MPAS)

Rossier School of Education
Dr. Karen Symms Gallagher, Dean
Program in:
education (MS, Ed D, PhD)

School of Architecture
Qingyun Ma, Dean
Programs in:
architecture (M Arch, MBS, ML Arch, AC)
building science (MBS)
historic preservation (AC)
landscape architecture (ML Arch)

School of Cinematic Arts
Dr. Elizabeth Daley, Dean
Programs in:
cinematic arts (MA, MFA, PhD)
critical studies (MA, PhD)
film and video production (MFA)
film, video, and computer animation (MFA)
interactive media (MFA)
producing (MFA)
screen and television writing (MFA)

School of Dentistry
Dr. Harold Slavkin, Dean

University of Southern California (continued)
Programs in:
craniofacial biology (MS, PhD)
dentistry (DDS, MA, MS, DPT, OTD, PhD, Certificate)

School of Pharmacy
Dr. Pete Vanderveen, Dean
Programs in:
molecular pharmacology and toxicology (MS, PhD)
pharmaceutical economics and policy (MS, PhD)
pharmaceutical sciences (MS, PhD)
pharmacy (Pharm D, MS, PhD)
regulatory sciences (MS)

School of Policy, Planning and Development
Dr. Jack Knott, Dean
Programs in:
health administration (MHA)
planning (M Pl)
planning and development studies (MPDS, DPDS)
policy, planning and development (M Pl, MHA, MPA, MPDS, MPP, MRED, DPA, DPDS, PhD, Certificate)
public administration (MPA, DPA, PhD, Certificate)
public policy (MPP)
real estate development (MRED)
urban and regional planning (PhD)

School of Social Work
Dr. Marilyn L. Flynn, Dean
Program in:
social work (MSW, PhD)

School of Theatre
Madeline Puzo, Dean
Programs in:
acting (MFA)
design (MFA)
playwriting (MFA)

Thornton School of Music
Dr. Robert A. Cutietta, Dean
Programs in:
choral and church music (MM, DMA)
composition (MA, MM, DMA, PhD)
early music performance (MA)
jazz studies (MM, DMA)
keyboard collaborative arts (MM, DMA, Graduate Certificate)
music (MA, MM, MM Ed, DMA, PhD, Graduate Certificate)
music education (MM, MM Ed, DMA)
music history and literature (MA)
organ studies (MM, DMA, Graduate Certificate)
strings (MM, DMA, Graduate Certificate)
studio/jazz guitar (MM, DMA, Graduate Certificate)
vocal arts and opera (MM, DMA, Graduate Certificate)
winds and percussion (MM, DMA, Graduate Certificate)

Viterbi School of Engineering
Dr. Yannis Yortsos, Dean
Programs in:
aerospace engineering (MSAE, PhD, Engr)
applied mechanics (MS)
astronautical engineering (MS, PhD, Engr, Graduate Certificate)
astronautics (MSAE)
astronautics and space technology (MS, PhD, Engr, Graduate Certificate)
biomedical engineering (MS, PhD)
chemical engineering (MS, PhD, Engr)
civil engineering (MS, PhD, Engr)
coastal and ocean engineering (MS)
computer engineering (MS, PhD)
computer networks (MS)
computer science (MS, PhD)
computer-aided engineering (ME, Certificate)
construction engineering and management (MS)
construction management (MCM)
dynamics and control (MSME)
earthquake engineering (MS)
electrical engineering (MS, PhD, Engr)
engineering (MCM, ME, MS, MSAE, MSEE, MSME, PhD, Certificate, Engr, Graduate Certificate)
engineering management (MS)
environmental engineering (MS, MSEE, PhD)
environmental quality management (ME)
geotechnical engineering (MS)
industrial and systems engineering (MS, PhD, Engr)
manufacturing engineering (MS)
materials engineering (MS)
materials science (MS, PhD, Engr)
materials science and engineering (MS, PhD, Engr)
mechanical engineering (MSME, PhD, Engr)
medical device and diagnostic engineering (MS)
medical imaging and imaging informatics (MS)
multimedia and creative technologies (MS)
neuroengineering (MS)
operations research (MS)
petroleum engineering (MS, PhD, Engr)
robotics and automation (MS)
software engineering (MS)
structural design (ME)
structural engineering (MS)
structural mechanics (MS)
systems architecture and engineering (MS)
transportation engineering (MS)
VLSI design (MS)
water resources engineering (MS)

Keck School of Medicine
Dr. Brian E. Henderson, Dean
Program in:
medicine (MD, MPAP, MPH, MS, PhD)

Graduate Programs in Medicine
Dr. Francis S. Markland, Associate Dean for Research
Programs in:
applied biostatistics/epidemiology (MS)
biochemistry and molecular biology (MS, PhD)
biometry/epidemiology (MPH)
biostatistics (MS, PhD)
cell and neurobiology (MS, PhD)
epidemiology (PhD)
experimental and molecular pathology (MS)
genetic epidemiology and statistical genetics (PhD)
health behavior research (PhD)
health communication (MPH)
health promotion (MPH)
medicine (MPAP, MPH, MS, PhD)
molecular epidemiology (MS, PhD)
molecular microbiology and immunology (MS, PhD)
pathobiology (PhD)
physiology and biophysics (MS, PhD)
preventive nutrition (MPH)
primary care physician assistant (MPAP)
public health (MPH)

■ UNIVERSITY OF THE PACIFIC

Stockton, CA 95211-0197
http://www.pacific.edu/

Independent, coed, university. CGS member. *Enrollment:* 6,251 graduate, professional, and undergraduate students; 2,028 full-time matriculated graduate/professional students (1,045 women), 689 part-time matriculated graduate/professional students (376 women). *Graduate faculty:* 266 full-time (101 women), 255 part-time/adjunct (104 women). *Computer facilities:* Computer purchase and lease plans are available. 350 computers available on campus for general student use. A campuswide network can be accessed from student residence rooms and from off campus. Internet access and online class registration are available. *Library facilities:* Holt Memorial Library plus 1 other. *Graduate expenses:* Tuition: full-time $26,920. Required fees: $430. Tuition and fees vary according to course load. *General application contact:* Connie Henderson, Graduate Recruit/Admissions Director, 209-946-2261.

Arthur A. Dugoni School of Dentistry
Dr. Arthur A. Dugoni, Dean
Programs in:
advanced education in general dentistry (Certificate)
dentistry (MSD)
international dental studies (DDS)
oral and maxillofacial surgery (Certificate)

College of the Pacific
Dr. Robert Cox, Dean

Programs in:
biological sciences (MS)
communication (MA)
psychology (MA)
sport sciences (MA)

Conservatory of Music
Dr. Steven Anderson, Dean
Programs in:
music (MA, MM)
music education (MM)
music therapy (MA)

Eberhardt School of Business
Dr. Charles Williams, Dean
Program in:
business (MBA)

McGeorge School of Law
Elizabeth Rindskopf Parker, Dean
Programs in:
government and public policy (LL M)
international law (LL M)
international waters resources law (LL M)
law (JD)
transnational business practice (LL M)

School of Education
Dr. Lynn Beck, Dean
Programs in:
curriculum and instruction (M Ed, MA, Ed D)
education (M Ed)
educational administration (MA, Ed D)
educational psychology (MA, Ed D)
school psychology (Ed S)
special education (MA)

School of International Studies
Dr. Margee Ensign, Dean
Programs in:
intercultural relations (MA)
international studies (MA)

School of Pharmacy and Health Sciences
Dr. Philip Oppenheimer, Dean
Programs in:
pharmaceutical sciences (MS, PhD)
pharmacy (Pharm D, MS, DPT, PhD)
physical therapy (MS, DPT)
speech-language pathology (MS)

■ VANGUARD UNIVERSITY OF SOUTHERN CALIFORNIA
Costa Mesa, CA 92626-9601
http://www.vanguard.edu/

Independent-religious, coed, comprehensive institution. *Enrollment:* 2,146 graduate, professional, and undergraduate students; 120 full-time matriculated graduate/professional students (77 women), 172 part-time matriculated graduate/professional students (89 women). *Graduate faculty:* 16 full-time (7 women), 22 part-time/adjunct (13 women). *Computer facilities:* 150 computers available on campus for general student use. A campuswide network can be accessed from student residence rooms and from off campus. Internet access and online class registration, online registration for select programs are available. *Library facilities:* O. Cope Budge Library. *General application contact:* Drake Levasheff, Director of Graduate Admissions, 714-966-5499.

School of Business and Management
Dr. David Alford, Dean
Program in:
business and management (MBA)

School of Education
Dr. Jerry Ternes, Dean
Program in:
education (MA)

School of Psychology
Dr. Jerre White, Dean
Program in:
clinical psychology (MS)

School of Religion
April Westbrook, Dean
Programs in:
leadership studies (MA)
religion (MA)
theological studies (MTS)

■ WOODBURY UNIVERSITY
Burbank, CA 91504-1099
http://www.woodbury.edu/

Independent, coed, comprehensive institution. *Enrollment:* 1,485 graduate, professional, and undergraduate students; 149 full-time matriculated graduate/professional students (87 women), 26 part-time matriculated graduate/professional students (12 women). *Graduate faculty:* 27 part-time/adjunct (6 women). *Computer facilities:* 135 computers available on campus for general student use. A campuswide network can be accessed from off campus. Internet access and online class registration are available. *Library facilities:* Los Angeles Times Library. *Graduate expenses:* Tuition: full-time $8,052; part-time $671 per unit. Tuition and fees vary according to course load and campus/location. *General application contact:* Mauro Diaz, Director of Admissions, 800-784-9663.

Graduate Programs in Mediation and Applied Conflict Studies
Programs in:
conflict studies (Graduate Certificate)
mediation (MM)

School of Architecture
Norman Millar, Chair
Program in:
real estate development (M Arch)

School of Business and Management
Dr. Andre Van Niekerk, Dean
Programs in:
business administration (MBA)
organizational leadership (MA)

Colorado

■ ADAMS STATE COLLEGE
Alamosa, CO 81102
http://www.adams.edu/

State-supported, coed, comprehensive institution. *Computer facilities:* 353 computers available on campus for general student use. A campuswide network can be accessed from student residence rooms and from off campus. Internet access and online class registration are available. *Library facilities:* Nielsen Library. *General application contact:* Administrative Assistant, 719-587-8152.

The Graduate School
Programs in:
art (MA)
counseling (MA)
education (MA)
health and physical education (MA)
special education (MA)

■ COLORADO CHRISTIAN UNIVERSITY
Lakewood, CO 80226
http://www.ccu.edu/

Independent-religious, coed, comprehensive institution. *Computer facilities:* 141 computers available on campus for general student use. A campuswide network can be accessed from student residence rooms and from off campus. Internet access and online class registration are available. *Library facilities:* Clifton Fowler Library plus 1 other. *General application contact:* Executive Director of Graduate Programs, 303-963-3309.

Program in Business Administration
Program in:
business administration (MBA)

Program in Counseling
Program in:
counseling (MA)

Program in Curriculum and Instruction
Program in:
curriculum and instruction (MA)

■ COLORADO SCHOOL OF MINES

Golden, CO 80401-1887

http://www.mines.edu/

State-supported, coed, university. CGS member. *Enrollment:* 4,056 graduate, professional, and undergraduate students; 636 full-time matriculated graduate/professional students (164 women), 140 part-time matriculated graduate/professional students (34 women). *Graduate faculty:* 253 full-time (41 women), 155 part-time/adjunct (21 women). *Computer facilities:* 400 computers available on campus for general student use. A campuswide network can be accessed from student residence rooms and from off campus. Internet access and online class registration are available. *Library facilities:* Arthur Lakes Library. *Graduate expenses:* Tuition, state resident: full-time $8,064; part-time $523 per credit. Tuition, nonresident: full-time $20,340; part-time $1,338 per credit. Required fees: $983; $492 per semester. *General application contact:* Kay Leaman, Graduate Admissions Coordinator, 303-273-3249.

Find University Details at www.petersons.com/gradchannel.

Graduate School

Dr. Tom M. Boyd, Dean of Graduate Studies

Programs in:

- applied chemistry (PhD)
- applied physics (PhD)
- chemical engineering (MS, PhD)
- chemistry (MS, PhD)
- engineering geology (Diploma)
- exploration geosciences (Diploma)
- geochemistry (MS, PhD)
- geological engineering (ME, MS, PhD, Diploma)
- geology (MS, PhD)
- geophysical engineering (ME, MS, PhD)
- geophysics (MS, PhD, Diploma)
- hydrogeology (Diploma)
- international political economy (Graduate Certificate)
- liberal arts and international studies (MIPER)
- materials science (MS, PhD)
- mathematical and computer sciences (MS, PhD)
- metallurgical and materials engineering (ME, MS, PhD)
- mining engineering (ME, MS, PhD)
- petroleum engineering (ME, MS, PhD)
- physics (MS)
- science and technology policy (Graduate Certificate)

Division of Economics and Business

Dr. Roderick G. Eggert, Head

Programs in:

- engineering and technology management (MS)
- mineral economics (MS, PhD)

Division of Engineering

Dr. Terence Parker, Head

Program in:

- engineering systems (ME, MS, PhD)

Division of Environmental Science and Engineering

Dr. Robert Seigrist, Director

Program in:

- environmental science and engineering (MS, PhD)

■ COLORADO STATE UNIVERSITY

Fort Collins, CO 80523-0015

http://www.colostate.edu/

State-supported, coed, university. CGS member. *Enrollment:* 26,723 graduate, professional, and undergraduate students; 2,411 full-time matriculated graduate/professional students (1,462 women), 3,029 part-time matriculated graduate/professional students (1,374 women). *Graduate faculty:* 879 full-time (250 women), 37 part-time/adjunct (5 women). *Computer facilities:* 2,095 computers available on campus for general student use. A campuswide network can be accessed from student residence rooms and from off campus. Internet access is available. *Library facilities:* William E. Morgan Library plus 3 others. *Graduate expenses:* Tuition, state resident: full-time $4,248; part-time $236 per credit. Tuition, nonresident: full-time $15,642; part-time $869 per credit. Required fees: $66 per credit. Tuition and fees vary according to program. *General application contact:* Sandra Dailey, Graduate School, 970-491-6817.

College of Veterinary Medicine and Biomedical Sciences

Dr. Lance Perryman, Dean

Programs in:

- biomedical sciences (MS, PhD)
- clinical sciences (MS, PhD)
- environmental health (MS, PhD)
- microbiology (MS, PhD)
- pathology (PhD)
- radiological health sciences (MS, PhD)
- veterinary medicine (DVM)
- veterinary medicine and biomedical sciences (DVM, MS, PhD)

Graduate School

Peter K. Dorhout, Vice Provost for Graduate Studies

Programs in:

- cell and molecular biology (MS, PhD)
- ecology (MS, PhD)
- molecular, cellular and integrative neurosciences (PhD)

College of Agricultural Sciences

Marc Johnson, Dean

Programs in:

- agricultural and resource economics (MS, PhD)
- agricultural sciences (M Agr, MS, PhD)
- animal sciences (MS, PhD)
- entomology (MS, PhD)
- floriculture (MS, PhD)
- plant pathology and weed science (MS, PhD)
- soil and crop sciences (MS, PhD)

College of Applied Human Sciences

April C. Mason, Dean

Programs in:

- applied human sciences (M Ed, MS, MSW, PhD)
- construction management (MS)
- design and merchandising (MS)
- education and human resource studies (M Ed, PhD)
- food science and human nutrition (MS, PhD)
- health and exercise science (MS)
- human bioenergetics (PhD)
- human development and family studies (MS)
- occupational therapy (MS)
- social work (MSW)
- student affairs in higher education (MS)

College of Business

Dr. John Hoxmeier, Associate Dean

Programs in:

- accounting (M Acc)
- business (M Acc, MBA, MS, MSBA)
- business administration (MBA)
- computer information systems (MSBA)

College of Engineering

Dr. Sandra L. Woods, Interim Dean

Programs in:

- atmospheric science (MS, PhD)
- chemical engineering (MS, PhD)
- civil engineering (ME, MS, PhD)
- electrical engineering (MEE, MS, PhD)
- engineering (ME)
- mechanical engineering (ME, MS, PhD)

College of Liberal Arts

Ann Gill, Dean

Programs in:

- anthropology (MA)
- art (MFA)
- creative writing (MFA)
- economics (MA, PhD)
- English (MA)
- foreign languages and literatures (MA)
- history (MA)
- liberal arts (MA, MFA, MM, MS, PhD)
- music (MM)
- philosophy (MA)
- political science (MA, PhD)
- sociology (MA, PhD)
- speech communication (MA)
- technical communication (MS)

College of Natural Sciences

Rick Miranda, Dean

Programs in:

- biochemistry (MS, PhD)
- botany (MS, PhD)
- chemistry (MS, PhD)
- computer science (MCS, MS, PhD)

mathematics (MS, PhD)
natural sciences (MCS, MS, PhD)
physics (MS, PhD)
psychology (MS, PhD)
statistics (MS, PhD)
zoology (MS, PhD)

Warner College of Natural Resources
Dr. Joseph T. O'Leary, Dean
Programs in:
earth sciences (PhD)
fishery and wildlife biology (MFWB, MS, PhD)
forest sciences (MS, PhD)
geosciences (MS)
human dimensions of natural resources (MS, PhD)
natural resources (MFWB, MNRS, MS, PhD)
natural resources stewardship (MNRS)
rangeland ecology (MS, PhD)
watershed science (MS)

■ COLORADO TECHNICAL UNIVERSITY—COLORADO SPRINGS
Colorado Springs, CO 80907-3896
http://www.coloradotech.edu

Proprietary, coed, comprehensive institution. *Computer facilities:* 130 computers available on campus for general student use. A campuswide network can be accessed from off campus. Internet access is available. *Library facilities:* Colorado Technical University Library. *General application contact:* Graduate Admissions, 719-590-6720.

Graduate Studies
Programs in:
accounting (MBA)
business administration (MBA)
business management (MSM)
business technology (MSM)
communication systems (MSEE)
computer engineering (MSCE)
computer science (DCS)
computer systems security (MSCS)
criminal justice (MSM)
database management (MSM)
electronic systems (MSEE)
human resources management (MSM)
information systems security (MSM)
information technology (MSM)
logistics/supply chain management (MSM)
management (DM)
organizational leadership (MSM)
project management (MSM)
software engineering (MSCS)
software project management (MSCS)
systems engineering (MS)
technology management (MBA)

■ COLORADO TECHNICAL UNIVERSITY—DENVER
Greenwood Village, CO 80111
http://www.coloradotech.edu/

Proprietary, coed, comprehensive institution. *Computer facilities:* 112 computers available on campus for general student use. A campuswide network can be accessed. Internet access is available. *Library facilities:* Colorado Technical University Resource Center. *General application contact:* Director of Admissions, 303-694-6600.

Program in Computer Engineering
Program in:
computer engineering (MS)

Program in Computer Science
Programs in:
computer systems security (MSCS)
software engineering (MSCS)
software project management (MSCS)

Program in Electrical Engineering
Program in:
electrical engineering (MS)

Program in Information Science
Program in:
information systems security (MSM)

Program in Systems Engineering
Program in:
systems engineering (MS)

Programs in Business Administration and Management
Programs in:
accounting (MBA)
business administration (MBA)
business administration and management (EMBA)
business technology (MSM)
database management (MSM)
human resource management (MBA)
information technology (MSM)
project management (MSM)
technology management (MBA)

■ NAROPA UNIVERSITY
Boulder, CO 80302-6697
http://www.naropa.edu/

Independent, coed, comprehensive institution. *Enrollment:* 1,136 graduate, professional, and undergraduate students; 391 full-time matriculated graduate/professional students (274 women), 243 part-time matriculated graduate/professional students (175 women). *Graduate faculty:* 39 full-time (18 women), 80 part-time/adjunct (59 women). *Computer facilities:* 48 computers available on campus for general student use. A campuswide network can be accessed. Internet access and online class registration are available. *Library facilities:* Allen Ginsberg Library. *Graduate expenses:* Tuition: full-time $15,070; part-time $646 per credit. Tuition and fees vary according to course load. *General application contact:* Office of Admissions, 303-546-3572.

Graduate Programs
Thomas B. Coburn, President
Programs in:
art therapy (MA)
body psychotherapy (MA)
contemplative education (MA)
contemplative psychotherapy (MA)
creative writing (MFA)
dance/movement therapy (MA)
divinity (M Div)
ecopsychology (MA)
environmental leadership (MA)
Indo-Tibetan Buddhism (MA)
Indo-Tibetan Buddhism with language (MA)
religious studies (MA)
religious studies with language (MA)
theater: contemporary performance (MFA)
theater: Lecoq-based actor-created theater (MFA)
transpersonal counseling psychology (MA)
transpersonal psychology (MA)
wilderness therapy (MA)
writing and poetics (MFA)

■ REGIS UNIVERSITY
Denver, CO 80221-1099
http://www.regis.edu/

Independent-religious, coed, comprehensive institution. *Enrollment:* 16,004 graduate, professional, and undergraduate students; 5,328 matriculated graduate/professional students. *Graduate faculty:* 730. *Computer facilities:* 300 computers available on campus for general student use. A campuswide network can be accessed from student residence rooms and from off campus. Internet access and online class registration are available. *Library facilities:* Dayton Memorial Library. *General application contact:* Information Contact, 303-458-4300.

Regis College
Dr. Paul Ewald, Dean
Program in:
education (MA)

Rueckert-Hartman School for Health Professions
Dr. Patricia Ladewig, Academic Dean
Programs in:
clinical leadership for physician assistants (MS)
health services administration (MS)
nursing (MSN)
physical therapy (DPT, TDPT)

School for Professional Studies
Dr. Steven Berkshire, Dean

Regis University (continued)
Programs in:
accounting (MS)
adult learning, training, and development (M Ed)
business administration (MBA)
community counseling (MAC)
computer information technology (MSOL)
counseling children and adolescents (Post-Graduate Certificate)
curriculum, instruction, and assessment (M Ed)
database administration with IBM DB2 (Certificate)
database administration with Oracle (Certificate)
database development (Certificate)
database technologies (MSCIT)
early childhood (M Ed)
educational technology (Certificate)
elementary (M Ed)
enterprise Java software development (Certificate)
ESL (M Ed)
executive information technologies (Certificate)
executive information technology (MSCIT)
executive international management (Certificate)
executive leadership (Certificate)
finance (MBA)
finance and accounting (MBA)
fine arts (M Ed)
fine arts administration (Certificate)
human resource management (MSOL)
information assurance (Certificate)
instructional technology (M Ed)
international business (MBA)
language and communication (MA)
leadership (Certificate)
marketing (MBA)
marriage and family therapy (Post-Graduate Certificate)
mediation (Certificate)
nonprofit management (MNM)
operations management (MBA)
organization leadership (MS)
organizational leadership (MSOL)
professional leadership (M Ed)
program management (Certificate)
project leadership and management (MSOL, Certificate)
project management (Certificate)
psychology (MA)
reading (M Ed)
resource development (Certificate)
secondary (M Ed)
self-designed (M Ed)
social justice, peace, and reconciliation (Certificate)
social science (MA)
software and information systems (M Sc)
software engineering (MSCIT, Certificate)
space studies (M Ed)
special education (M Ed)
storage area networks (Certificate)
strategic business (Certificate)
strategic human resource (Certificate)
systems engineering (MSCIT, Certificate)
teacher licensure (M Ed)
technical communication (Certificate)
technical management (Certificate)

■ UNIVERSITY OF COLORADO AT BOULDER
Boulder, CO 80309
http://www.colorado.edu/

State-supported, coed, university. CGS member. *Enrollment:* 31,399 graduate, professional, and undergraduate students; 3,675 full-time matriculated graduate/professional students (1,636 women), 1,320 part-time matriculated graduate/professional students (568 women). *Graduate faculty:* 953 full-time (265 women). *Computer facilities:* 1,525 computers available on campus for general student use. A campuswide network can be accessed from student residence rooms and from off campus. Internet access and online class registration, standard and academic software, student government voting are available. *Library facilities:* Norlin Library plus 5 others. *General application contact:* Philip Distefano, Chancellor, 303-492-8908.

Graduate School
Susan Avery, Dean

College of Arts and Sciences
Todd T. Gleeson, Dean
Programs in:
animal behavior (MA)
anthropology (MA, PhD)
applied mathematics (MS, PhD)
art history (MA)
arts and sciences (MA, MFA, MS, Au D, PhD)
astrophysics (MS, PhD)
atmospheric and oceanic sciences (MS, PhD)
audiology (Au D, PhD)
biochemistry (PhD)
biology (MA, PhD)
cellular structure and function (MA, PhD)
ceramics (MFA)
chemical physics (PhD)
chemistry (MS)
Chinese (MA, PhD)
classics (MA, PhD)
clinical research and practice in audiology (PhD)
communication (MA, PhD)
comparative literature and humanities (MA, PhD)
dance (MFA)
developmental biology (MA, PhD)
drawing (MFA)
economics (MA, PhD)
environmental biology (MA, PhD)
environmental studies (MS, PhD)
evolutionary biology (MA, PhD)
French (MA, PhD)
geography (MA, PhD)
geology (MS, PhD)
geophysics (PhD)
German (MA)
Hispanic linguistics (MA)
history (MA, PhD)
integrative physiology (MS, PhD)
international affairs (MA)
Japanese (MA, PhD)
linguistics (MA, PhD)
liquid crystal science and technology (PhD)
literature (MA, PhD)
mathematical physics (PhD)
mathematics (MA, MS, PhD)
medical physics (PhD)
medieval/early modern Hispanic literatures (PhD)
molecular biology (MA, PhD)
museum and field studies (MS)
neurobiology (MA)
optical sciences and engineering (PhD)
painting (MFA)
philosophy (MA, PhD)
photography and media arts (MFA)
physics (MS, PhD)
planetary science (MS, PhD)
political science (MA, PhD)
population biology (MA)
population genetics (PhD)
printmaking (MFA)
psychology (MA, PhD)
public policy (MA)
religious studies (MA)
sculpture (MFA)
sociology (PhD)
Spanish literature (MA, PhD)
speech, language and hearing science (MA)
speech-language pathology (MA, PhD)
speech-language-hearing sciences (PhD)
theatre (MA, PhD)

College of Engineering and Applied Science
Robert Davis, Dean
Programs in:
aerospace engineering sciences (ME, MS, PhD)
building systems (MS, PhD)
chemical engineering (ME, MS, PhD)
computer science (ME, MS, PhD)
construction engineering and management (MS, PhD)
electrical and computer engineering (ME, MS)
electrical engineering (PhD)
engineering and applied science (ME, MS, PhD)
environmental engineering (MS, PhD)
geoenvironmental engineering (MS, PhD)
geotechnical engineering (MS, PhD)

mechanical engineering (ME, MS, PhD)
operations and logistics (ME)
quality and process (ME)
research and development (ME)
structural engineering (MS, PhD)
telecommunications (ME, MS)
water resources engineering (MS, PhD)

College of Music
Daniel P. Sher, Dean
Programs in:
church music (M Mus)
composition (M Mus, D Mus A)
conducting (M Mus, D Mus A)
music education (M Mus Ed, PhD)
music literature (M Mus)
musicology (PhD)
pedagogy (M Mus, D Mus A)
performance (M Mus, D Mus A)

School of Education
Lorrie Shepard, Dean
Programs in:
education (MA, PhD)
educational and psychological studies (MA, PhD)
educational foundations, policy, and practice (MA, PhD)
instruction and curriculum (MA, PhD)
research and evaluation methodology (PhD)
social multicultural and bilingual foundations (MA, PhD)

School of Journalism and Mass Communication
Paul Voakes, Dean
Programs in:
communication (PhD)
mass communication research (MA)
media studies (PhD)
newsgathering (MA)

Leeds School of Business
Dennis Ahlburg, Dean
Programs in:
accounting (MS, PhD)
business (PhD)
business administration (MBA, PhD)
finance (PhD)
management (PhD)
marketing (PhD)

School of Law
Harold H. Bruff, Dean
Program in:
law (JD)

■ UNIVERSITY OF COLORADO AT COLORADO SPRINGS
Colorado Springs, CO 80933-7150
http://www.uccs.edu/

State-supported, coed, comprehensive institution. *Enrollment:* 8,583 graduate, professional, and undergraduate students; 865 full-time matriculated graduate/professional students (528 women), 593 part-time matriculated graduate/professional students (330 women). *Graduate faculty:* 157 full-time (56 women), 85 part-time/adjunct (44 women). *Computer facilities:* 250 computers available on campus for general student use. A campuswide network can be accessed from student residence rooms and from off campus. *Library facilities:* University of Colorado at Colorado Springs Kraemer Family Library. *Graduate expenses:* Tuition, state resident: part-time $303 per credit hour. Tuition, nonresident: part-time $840 per credit hour. Tuition and fees vary according to course load, campus/location and program. *General application contact:* Jackie Francis, Graduate Recruitment Coordinator, 719-262-3072.

Graduate School
Dr. Tom Huber, Dean

Beth-El College of Nursing
Dr. Carole Schoffstall, Dean
Programs in:
adult health nurse practitioner and clinical specialist (MSN)
family practitioner (MSN)
gerontology (MSN)
neonatal nurse practitioner and clinical specialist (MSN)
nursing administration (MSN)
women nurse practitioner (MSN)

College of Education
Dr. LaVonne Neal, Dean
Programs in:
counseling and human services (MA)
curriculum and instruction (MA)
educational administration (MA)
educational leadership (MA, PhD)
special education (MA)

College of Engineering and Applied Science
Dr. Jeremy Haefner, Dean
Programs in:
computer science (MS)
electrical engineering (MS, PhD)
engineering (PhD)
engineering and applied science (ME, MS, PhD)
engineering management (ME)
information operations (ME)
manufacturing (ME)
mechanical engineering (MS)
software engineering (ME)
space operations (ME)
space systems (MS)

College of Letters, Arts and Sciences
Dr. Tom Christensen, Dean
Programs in:
applied mathematics (MS)
communications (MA)
geography and environmental studies (MA)
geropsychology (PhD)
history (MA)
letters, arts and sciences (M Sc, MA, MS, PhD)
psychology (MA)
sciences (M Sc)
sociology (MA)

Graduate School of Business Administration
Dr. Venkateshwar Reddy, Dean
Programs in:
accounting (MBA)
finance (MBA)
general health care administration (MBA)
information systems (MBA)
international business management (MBA)
marketing (MBA)
service management/technology management (MBA)

Graduate School of Public Affairs
Dr. Kathleen Beatty, Dean
Programs in:
criminal justice (MCJ)
public administration (MPA)

■ UNIVERSITY OF COLORADO DENVER
Denver, CO 80217-3364
http://www.ucdhsc.edu/

State-supported, coed, university. CGS member. *Enrollment:* 19,766 graduate, professional, and undergraduate students; 3,611 full-time matriculated graduate/professional students (2,176 women), 2,788 part-time matriculated graduate/professional students (1,651 women). *Graduate faculty:* 2,154 full-time (990 women), 75 part-time/adjunct (34 women). *Computer facilities:* 750 computers available on campus for general student use. A campuswide network can be accessed from student residence rooms and from off campus. Internet access and online class registration are available. *Library facilities:* Auraria Library. *General application contact:* Graduate School Admissions, 303-556-2400.

Business School
Cliff Young, Interim Associate Dean
Programs in:
accounting (MS)
business (Exec MBA, MBA, MS, MSIB, PhD)
business administration (Exec MBA, MBA)
computer science and information systems (PhD)
finance (MS)
health administration (MBA)
information systems (MS)
international business (MSIB)
management and organization (MS)
marketing (MS)
pharmaceutical management (MBA)

College of Architecture and Planning
Mark Gelernter, Dean

University of Colorado Denver (continued)
Programs in:
architecture (M Arch)
architecture and planning (M Arch, MLA, MUD, MURP, PhD)
design and planning (PhD)
landscape architecture (MLA)
urban and regional planning (MURP)
urban design (MUD)

College of Arts and Media
David Dynak, Dean
Programs in:
arts and media (MS)
recording arts (MS)

College of Engineering and Applied Science
Paul Rakowski, Assistant Dean of Student Services
Programs in:
civil engineering (MS, PhD)
computer science and engineering (MS)
computer science and information systems (PhD)
electrical engineering (M Eng, MS)
engineering and applied science (M Eng, MS, PhD)
geographic information systems (M Eng)
mechanical engineering (M Eng, MS)

College of Liberal Arts and Sciences
Dr. Jon Harbor, Dean
Programs in:
anthropology (MA)
applied linguistics (MA)
applied mathematics (MS, PhD)
applied science (MIS)
biology (MS)
chemistry (MS)
communication (MA)
computer science (MIS)
economics (MA)
English studies (MA)
environmental sciences (MS)
geographic information science (Certificate)
health and behavioral sciences (PhD)
history (MA)
humanities (MH)
interactive media (Certificate)
liberal arts and sciences (MA, MH, MIS, MS, MSS, PhD, Certificate)
literature (MA)
mathematics (MIS)
political science (MA)
psychology (MA)
public relations (Certificate)
social science (MSS)
sociology (MA)
Spanish (MA)
teaching English to speakers of other languages (Certificate)
teaching of writing (MA)
technical and professional communication (Certificate)
technical communication (MS)
usability testing and interface design (Certificate)

Graduate School
Dr. John Freed, Dean
Programs in:
analytic health sciences (PhD)
analytical health sciences (PhD)
bioinformatics (PhD)
biostatistics (MS, PhD)
clinical science (MS, PhD)
epidemiology (PhD)
genetic counseling (MS)
public health (MSPH)

Program in Biomedical Sciences
Dr. Steven Anderson, Director
Programs in:
biochemistry (PhD)
biomedical sciences (PhD)
cancer biology (PhD)
cell and developmental biology (PhD)
human medical genetics (PhD)
microbiology (PhD)
molecular biology (PhD)
neuroscience (PhD)
pharmacology (PhD)
physiology and biophysics (PhD)

Graduate School of Public Affairs
Kathleen Beatty, Dean
Programs in:
criminal justice (MCJ)
public administration (Exec MPA, MPA)
public affairs (Exec MPA, MCJ, MPA, PhD)

School of Dentistry
Dr. Denise K. Kassebaum, Interim ean
Program in:
dentistry (DDS)

School of Education and Human Development
Lynn K Rhodes, Dean
Programs in:
administration leadership and policy studies (MA, Ed S)
counseling psychology and counselor education (MA)
early childhood education (MA)
education and human development (MA, PhD, Ed S)
educational leadership and innovation (PhD)
educational psychology (MA)
professional learning and advancement networks (MA)
school psychology (Ed S)
special education (MA)

School of Medicine
Dr. Richard Krugman, Dean
Programs in:
medicine (MD, MPAS, DPT)
pediatrics (MPAS)
physical therapy (DPT)

School of Nursing
Patricia Moritz, Dean
Programs in:
nursing (MS, PhD, Post Master's Certificate)
nursing practice (DNP)

School of Pharmacy
Ralpha Altiere, Dean
Programs in:
pharmaceutical sciences (PhD)
pharmacy (Pharm D, PhD)
toxicology (PhD)

■ UNIVERSITY OF DENVER
Denver, CO 80208
http://www.du.edu/

Independent, coed, university. CGS member. *Enrollment:* 10,374 graduate, professional, and undergraduate students; 3,138 full-time matriculated graduate/professional students (1,827 women), 1,928 part-time matriculated graduate/professional students (1,043 women). *Graduate faculty:* 884. *Computer facilities:* 150 computers available on campus for general student use. A campuswide network can be accessed from student residence rooms and from off campus. Internet access and online class registration, online grade reports are available. *Library facilities:* Penrose Library. *Graduate expenses:* Tuition: full-time $29,628; part-time $823 per credit. *General application contact:* Information Contact, 360-871-2706.

Find University Details at www.petersons.com/gradchannel.

College of Education
Dr. Virginia Maloney, Dean
Programs in:
counseling psychology (MA, PhD)
curriculum and instruction (MA, PhD, Certificate)
educational administration and policy studies (Certificate)
educational psychology (MA, PhD, Ed S)
higher education and adult studies (MA, PhD)
library and information science (MLIS)
library and information sciences (Certificate)
school administration (PhD)

College of Law
Jose Roberto Juarez, Dean
Programs in:
American and comparative law (LL M)
international natural resources law (LL M, MRLS)
law (JD, LL M, MRLS, MSLA, MT, Certificate)
legal administration (MSLA, Certificate)
taxation (LL M, MT)

Daniels College of Business
Dr. Karen Newman, Dean

Programs in:
business (IMBA, M Acc, MBA, MS)
business administration (MBA)
data mining (MS)
finance (IMBA, MBA, MS)
general business administration (IMBA, MBA, MS)
information technology and electronic commerce (IMBA, MBA)
international business/management (IMBA, MBA)
management (MS)
marketing (IMBA, MBA, MS)

School of Accountancy
Dr. Ronald Kucic, Director
Programs in:
accountancy (M Acc)
accounting (IMBA, MBA)

School of Real Estate and Construction Management
Dr. Mark Levine, Director
Programs in:
construction management (IMBA, MS)
real estate (IMBA, MBA, MS)

Faculty of Arts and Humanities/ Social Sciences
Dr. George Potts, Interim Dean
Programs in:
anthropology (MA)
arts and humanities/social sciences (MA, MFA, MM, MPP, MS, PhD, Certificate)
economics (MA)
English (MA, PhD)
psychology (MA, PhD)
public policy (MPP)
religious studies (MA)

Lamont School of Music
Joseph Docksey, Director
Programs in:
composition (MA)
conducting (MA)
jazz and commercial music (Certificate)
music (MM)
music education (MA)
music history and literature (MA)
Orff-Schulwerk (MA)
performance (MA)
piano pedagogy (MA)
Suzuki pedagogy (MA)
Suzuki teaching (Certificate)
theory (MA)

School of Art and Art History
Dr. Annette Stott, Director
Programs in:
art history (MA)
art history/museum studies (MA)
electronic media arts and design (MFA)
studio art (MFA)

School of Communication
Programs in:
advertising management (MS)
communication (MA, MS, PhD)
digital media studies (MA)
human communication studies (MA, PhD)
international and intercultural communication (MA)
mass communications (MA)
public relations (MS)
video production (MA)

Faculty of Natural Sciences and Mathematics
Dr. James Fogleman, Dean
Programs in:
applied mathematics (MA, MS)
biological sciences (MS, PhD)
chemistry (MA, MS, PhD)
computer science (MS)
geography (MA, MS, PhD)
mathematics (PhD)
natural sciences and mathematics (MA, MS, PhD)
physics and astronomy (MS, PhD)

Graduate School of International Studies
Dr. Tom Farer, Dean
Programs in:
global studies (MGS)
international studies (MA, PhD)

Graduate School of Professional Psychology
Dr. Peter Buirski, Dean
Programs in:
clinical psychology (Psy D)
psychology (MA)

Graduate School of Social Work
Dr. Christian Molidor, Interim Dean
Program in:
social work (MSW, PhD, Certificate)

Graduate Studies
Dr. James Moran, Vice Provost
Program in:
joint (PhD)

Conflict Resolution Institute
Dr. Karen Feste, Director
Program in:
conflict resolution (MA)

Intermodal Transportation Institute
Dr. Bill Zaranka, Director
Program in:
intermodal transportation (MS)

School of Engineering and Computer Science
Dr. Rahmat Shoureshi, Dean
Programs in:
computer engineering (MS)
computer science (MS, PhD)
computer science and engineering (MS)
electrical engineering (MS)
engineering (PhD)
engineering and computer science (MS, PhD)
materials science (PhD)
mechanical engineering (MS)

University College
Dr. James Davis, Dean
Programs in:
applied communication (MAS, MPS, Certificate)
computer information systems (MAS, Certificate)
environmental policy and management (MAS, Certificate)
geographic information systems (MAS, Certificate)
human resource administration (MPS, Certificate)
knowledge and information technologies (MAS)
liberal studies (MLS, Certificate)
modern languages (MLS, Certificate)
organizational leadership (MPS, Certificate)
security management (Certificate)
technology management (MAS, Certificate)
telecommunications (MAS, Certificate)

■ UNIVERSITY OF NORTHERN COLORADO
Greeley, CO 80639
http://www.unco.edu/

State-supported, coed, university. CGS member. *Enrollment:* 12,981 graduate, professional, and undergraduate students; 977 full-time matriculated graduate/professional students (680 women), 521 part-time matriculated graduate/professional students (376 women). *Graduate faculty:* 240 full-time (112 women). *Computer facilities:* Computer purchase and lease plans are available. 1,100 computers available on campus for general student use. A campuswide network can be accessed from student residence rooms and from off campus. Internet access and online class registration are available. *Library facilities:* James A. Michener Library plus 2 others. *Graduate expenses:* Tuition, state resident: full-time $5,118; part-time $213 per credit hour. Tuition, nonresident: full-time $14,832; part-time $618 per credit hour. Required fees: $674; $34 per credit hour. *General application contact:* Linda Sisson, Graduate Student Admission Coordinator, 970-351-1807.

Find University Details at www.petersons.com/gradchannel.

Graduate School
Dr. Robbyn Wacker, Assistant Vice President, Research and Extended Studies/Dean of Graduate School
Program in:
interdisciplinary studies (MA)

College of Education and Behavioral Sciences
Dr. Eugene P. Sheehan, Dean
Programs in:
applied psychology and counselor education (PhD, Psy D, Ed S)

University of Northern Colorado (continued)

applied statistics and research methods (MS, PhD)
counseling psychology (Psy D)
counselor education and supervision (PhD)
early childhood education (MA)
education and behavioral sciences (MA, MAT, MS, Ed D, PhD, Psy D, Ed S)
educational leadership (MA, Ed D, Ed S)
educational media (MA)
educational psychology (MA, PhD)
educational research, leadership and technology (MA, MS, Ed D, PhD, Ed S)
educational studies (Ed D)
educational technology (MA, PhD)
elementary education (MAT)
interdisciplinary studies (MA)
psychological sciences (MA, PhD)
reading (MA)
school psychology (PhD, Ed S)
special education (MA, Ed D)
teacher education (MA, MAT, Ed D)

College of Humanities and Social Sciences
Dr. David Caldwell, Dean
Programs in:
clinical sociology (MA)
communication (MA)
English (MA)
history (MA)
humanities and social sciences (MA)
modern languages and cultural studies (MA)
social sciences (MA)
Spanish/teaching (MA)

College of Natural and Health Sciences
Dr. Denise A. Battles, Dean
Programs in:
audiology (Au D)
biological education (PhD)
biological sciences (MS)
chemistry education (PhD)
chemistry, earth sciences and physics (MA, MS, PhD)
chemistry: education (MS)
chemistry: research (MS)
clinical nurse specialist in chronic illness (MS)
earth sciences (MA)
exercise science (MS, PhD)
family nurse practitioner (MS)
gerontology (MA)
human rehabilitation (PhD)
human sciences (MA, MPH, Au D, PhD)
mathematical teaching (MA)
mathematics education (PhD)
mathematics: liberal arts (MA)
middle level mathematics (MA)
natural and health sciences (MA, MPH, MS, Au D, PhD)
natural sciences (MA)
nursing education (MS, PhD)
public health education (MPH)
rehabilitation counseling (MA)
speech language pathology (MA)
sport administration (MS, PhD)
sport pedagogy (MS, PhD)

College of Performing and Visual Arts
Dr. Andrew J. Svedlow, Dean
Programs in:
collaborative keyboard (MM)
conducting (MM)
instrumental performance (MM)
jazz studies (MM)
music conducting (DA)
music education (MM, DA)
music history and literature (MM, DA)
music performance (DA)
music theory and composition (MM, DA)
performing and visual arts (MA, MM, MME, DA)
visual arts (MA)
vocal performance (MM)

■ UNIVERSITY OF PHOENIX–DENVER CAMPUS
Lone Tree, CO 80124-5453
http://www.phoenix.edu/

Proprietary, coed, comprehensive institution. *Enrollment:* 2,948 graduate, professional, and undergraduate students; 564 full-time matriculated graduate/professional students (345 women). *Graduate faculty:* 125 full-time (52 women), 639 part-time/adjunct (227 women). *Computer facilities:* A campuswide network can be accessed from off campus. *Library facilities:* University Library. *Graduate expenses:* Tuition: full-time $10,032. Required fees: $760. *General application contact:* Campus Information Center, 303-694-9093.

The Artemis School
Dr. Adam Honea, Provost

College of Education
Dr. Marla LaRue, Dean/Executive Director
Programs in:
administration and supervision (MAEd)
curriculum instruction (MAEd)
elementary teacher education (MAEd)
school counseling (MSC)
secondary teacher education (MAEd)

College of Health and Human Services
Dr. Gil Linne, Dean/Executive Director
Programs in:
community counseling (MSC)
health care management (MBA)
marriage, family and child therapy (MSC)
nursing (MSN)

John Sperling School of Business
Dr. Adam Honea, Provost
Program in:
business (MBA, MIS, MM)

College of Graduate Business and Management
Dr. Brian Lindquist, Associate Vice President and Dean/Executive Director
Programs in:
accounting (MBA)
business administration (MBA)
e-business (MBA)
global management (MBA)
human resources management (MBA, MM)
management (MM)
marketing (MBA)
public administration (MBA, MM)

College of Information Systems and Technology
Dr. Adam Honea, Dean/Executive Director
Programs in:
e-business (MBA)
management (MIS)
technology management (MBA)

■ UNIVERSITY OF PHOENIX–SOUTHERN COLORADO CAMPUS
Colorado Springs, CO 80919-2335
http://www.phoenix.edu/

Proprietary, coed, comprehensive institution. *Enrollment:* 1,090 graduate, professional, and undergraduate students; 471 full-time matriculated graduate/professional students (306 women). *Graduate faculty:* 13 full-time (5 women), 489 part-time/adjunct (161 women). *Computer facilities:* A campuswide network can be accessed from off campus. Internet access is available. *Library facilities:* University Library. *Graduate expenses:* Tuition: full-time $10,291. Required fees: $760. *General application contact:* Campus Information Center, 719-599-5282.

The Artemis School
Dr. Adam Honea, Provost

College of Education
Dr. Marla LaRue, Dean/Executive Director
Programs in:
administration and supervision (MA Ed)
curriculum and instruction (MA Ed)
elementary licensure (MA Ed)
principal licensure certification (Certificate)
school counseling (MSC)
secondary licensure (MA Ed)

College of Health and Human Services
Dr. Gil Linne, Dean/Executive Director

Programs in:
- community counseling (MSC)
- health care management (MBA)
- marriage, family and child therapy (MSC)
- nursing (MSN)

John Sperling School of Business
Dr. William Pepicello, Provost and Senior Vice President of Academic Affairs
Program in:
- business (MBA)

College of Graduate Business and Management
Dr. Brian Lindquist, Associate Vice President and Dean/Executive Director
Program in:
- business administration (MBA)

College of Information Systems and Technology
Dr. Adam Honea, Provost/Dean, Vice President Academic Research and Development
Program in:
- technology management (MBA)

Connecticut

■ CENTRAL CONNECTICUT STATE UNIVERSITY
New Britain, CT 06050-4010
http://www.ccsu.edu/

State-supported, coed, comprehensive institution. CGS member. *Enrollment:* 12,144 graduate, professional, and undergraduate students; 536 full-time matriculated graduate/professional students (351 women), 1,595 part-time matriculated graduate/professional students (1,047 women). *Graduate faculty:* 332 full-time (140 women), 415 part-time/adjunct (197 women). *Computer facilities:* 880 computers available on campus for general student use. A campuswide network can be accessed from student residence rooms and from off campus. Internet access is available. *Library facilities:* Burritt Library plus 1 other. *Graduate expenses:* Full-time $3,970; part-time $380 per credit. Tuition, state resident: full-time $5,955; part-time $380 per credit. Tuition, nonresident: full-time $11,061; part-time $380 per credit. Required fees: $3,189. One-time fee: $62 part-time. Tuition and fees vary according to degree level and program. *General application contact:* Patricia Gardner, Graduate Admissions, 860-832-2350.

School of Graduate Studies
Patricia Gardner, Graduate Admissions

School of Arts and Sciences
Dr. Susan Pease, Dean
Programs in:
- anesthesia (MS)
- art education (MS, Certificate)
- arts and sciences (MA, MS, Certificate)
- biological sciences (MA, MS)
- biology (Certificate)
- community psychology (MA)
- computer information technology (MS)
- criminal justice (MS)
- earth science (MS)
- English (MA, Certificate)
- French (MA)
- general health (MS)
- general psychology (MA)
- geography (MS)
- graphic information design (MA)
- health psychology (MA)
- history (MA, Certificate)
- international studies (MS)
- Italian (Certificate)
- mathematics (MA, MS, Certificate)
- modern language (MA, Certificate)
- music education (MS, Certificate)
- natural sciences (MS)
- organizational communication (MS)
- physics (MS)
- public history (MA)
- Spanish (MA, MS, Certificate)
- Spanish language and Hispanic culture (MA)
- teaching English to speakers of other languages (Certificate)

School of Business
Dr. Christopher Galligan, Acting Dean
Programs in:
- business (MBA, MS, Certificate)
- business education (MS, Certificate)
- international business administration (MBA)

School of Education and Professional Studies
Dr. Mitchell Sakofs, Acting Dean
Programs in:
- early childhood education (MS)
- education and professional studies (MS, Ed D, Certificate, Sixth Year Certificate)
- educational foundations policy/secondary education (MS)
- educational leadership (MS, Ed D, Sixth Year Certificate)
- educational technology and media (MS)
- elementary education (MS, Certificate)
- marriage and family therapy (MS)
- physical education (MS, Certificate)
- professional counseling (MS, Certificate)
- reading (MS, Sixth Year Certificate)
- school counseling (MS)
- special education for special educators (MS)
- special education for teachers certified in areas other than education (MS)
- student development in higher education (MS)

School of Technology
Dr. Zdzislaw Kremens, Dean
Programs in:
- biomolecular sciences (MA)
- engineering technology (MS)
- technology (MA, MS, Certificate)
- technology education (MS, Certificate)
- technology management (MS)

■ EASTERN CONNECTICUT STATE UNIVERSITY
Willimantic, CT 06226-2295
http://www.easternct.edu

State-supported, coed, comprehensive institution. *Enrollment:* 5,239 graduate, professional, and undergraduate students; 84 full-time matriculated graduate/professional students (56 women), 352 part-time matriculated graduate/professional students (265 women). *Graduate faculty:* 19 full-time (10 women), 16 part-time/adjunct (7 women). *Computer facilities:* 637 computers available on campus for general student use. A campuswide network can be accessed from student residence rooms and from off campus. Internet access and online class registration are available. *Library facilities:* J. Eugene Smith Library. *Graduate expenses:* Tuition, state resident: full-time $3,970. Tuition, nonresident: full-time $11,061; part-time $336 per credit. Required fees: $35 per credit. *General application contact:* Dr. Tuesday L. Cooper, Associate Dean, 860-465-4543.

School of Education and Professional Studies/Graduate Division
Dr. Patricia A. Kleine, Dean
Programs in:
- early childhood education (MS)
- education and professional studies (MS)
- educational technology (MS)
- elementary education (MS)
- organizational management (MS)
- reading and language arts (MS)
- science education (MS)
- secondary education (MS)

■ FAIRFIELD UNIVERSITY
Fairfield, CT 06824-5195
http://www.fairfield.edu/

Independent-religious, coed, comprehensive institution. *Enrollment:* 5,091 graduate, professional, and undergraduate students; 270 full-time matriculated graduate/professional students (180 women), 813 part-time matriculated graduate/professional students (514 women). *Graduate faculty:* 78 full-time (43 women), 49 part-time/adjunct (18 women). *Computer facilities:* Computer purchase and lease plans are available. 150 computers available on campus for general student use. A campuswide network can be accessed from student residence rooms and from off campus. Internet access and online class registration are available. *Library facilities:* Dimenna-Nyselius Library. *General*

Fairfield University (continued)
application contact: Marianne Gumpper, Director of Graduate and Continuing Studies Admissions, 203-254-4184.

Charles F. Dolan School of Business

Dr. Norman A. Solomon, Dean
Programs in:
- accounting (MBA, MS, CAS)
- finance (MBA, MS, CAS)
- general management (MBA)
- human resource management (MBA, CAS)
- information systems and operations (MBA)
- information systems and operations management (CAS)
- international business (MBA, CAS)
- marketing (MBA, CAS)
- taxation (MBA, MS, CAS)

College of Arts and Sciences

Dr. Timothy L. Snyder, Dean
Programs in:
- American studies (MA)
- arts and sciences (MA, MS)
- mathematics and quantitative methods (MS)

Graduate School of Education and Allied Professions

Dr. Susan D. Franzosa, Dean
Programs in:
- applied psychology (MA)
- community counseling (MA)
- computers in education (MA, CAS)
- counselor education (CAS)
- education and allied professions (MA, CAS)
- educational media (MA, CAS)
- elementary education (MA)
- marriage and family therapy (MA)
- school counseling (MA)
- school media specialist (MA, CAS)
- school psychology (MA, CAS)
- secondary education (MA)
- special education (MA, CAS)
- teaching and foundations (MA, CAS)
- TESOL, foreign language and bilingual/multicultural education (MA, CAS)

School of Engineering

Dr. Evangelos Hadjimichael, Dean
Programs in:
- electrical and computer engineering (MS)
- management of technology (MS)
- mechanical engineering (MS)
- software engineering (MS)

School of Nursing

Dr. Jeanne M. Novotny, Dean
Programs in:
- adult nurse practitioner (MSN, PMC)
- family nurse practitioner (MSN, PMC)
- healthcare management (MSN)
- nurse anesthesia (MSN)
- psychiatric nurse practitioner (MSN, PMC)

■ QUINNIPIAC UNIVERSITY
Hamden, CT 06518-1940
http://www.quinnipiac.edu/

Independent, coed, comprehensive institution. *Enrollment:* 7,341 graduate, professional, and undergraduate students; 531 full-time matriculated graduate/professional students (377 women), 314 part-time matriculated graduate/professional students (189 women). *Computer facilities:* Computer purchase and lease plans are available. 600 computers available on campus for general student use. A campuswide network can be accessed from student residence rooms and from off campus. Internet access and online class registration are available. *Library facilities:* Arnold Bernhard Library plus 1 other. *Graduate expenses:* Tuition: part-time $675 per credit. Required fees: $30 per credit. *General application contact:* Information Contact, 800-462-1944.

Division of Education

Dr. Cynthia Dubea, Dean—Division of Education, College of Liberal Arts
Programs in:
- biology (MAT)
- chemistry (MAT)
- education (MAT)
- elementary education (MAT)
- English (MAT)
- French (MAT)
- history/social studies (MAT)
- mathematics (MAT)
- physics (MAT)
- Spanish (MAT)

School of Business

Dr. Mark Thompson, Dean
Programs in:
- accounting (MBA)
- business (MBA, MS)
- chartered financial analyst (MBA)
- economics (MBA)
- finance (MBA)
- health care management (MBA)
- healthcare management (MBA)
- information systems (MS)
- information systems management (MBA)
- international business (MBA)
- management (MBA)
- marketing (MBA)

School of Communications

Dr. David Donnelly, Dean
Programs in:
- communications (MS)
- interactive communications (MS)
- journalism (MS)

School of Health Sciences

Dr. Edward O'Connor, Dean
Programs in:
- adult nurse practitioner (MSN, Post Master's Certificate)
- biomedical sciences (MHS)
- family nurse practitioner (MSN, Post Master's Certificate)
- forensic nurse clinical specialist (MSN, Post Master's Certificate)
- health sciences (MHS, MOT, MS, MSN, DPT, Post Master's Certificate)
- laboratory management (MHS)
- microbiology (MHS)
- molecular and cell biology (MS)
- occupational therapy (MOT)
- pathologists' assistant (MHS)
- physical therapy (DPT)
- physician assistant (MHS)

School of Law

Brad Saxton, Dean
Programs in:
- health law (LL M)
- law (JD)

■ SACRED HEART UNIVERSITY
Fairfield, CT 06825-1000
http://www.sacredheart.edu/

Independent-religious, coed, comprehensive institution. *Enrollment:* 5,756 graduate, professional, and undergraduate students; 548 full-time matriculated graduate/professional students (407 women), 1,005 part-time matriculated graduate/professional students (698 women). *Graduate faculty:* 62 full-time (35 women), 81 part-time/adjunct (40 women). *Computer facilities:* Computer purchase and lease plans are available. 330 computers available on campus for general student use. A campuswide network can be accessed from student residence rooms and from off campus. Internet access and online class registration, intranet are available. *Library facilities:* Ryan-Matura Library. *Graduate expenses:* Tuition: part-time $510 per credit. Required fees: $118 per term. Full-time tuition and fees vary according to degree level and program. *General application contact:* Alexis Haakonsen, Dean of Graduate Admissions, 203-365-7619.

Find University Details at www.petersons.com/gradchannel.

Graduate Studies

College of Arts and Sciences
Dr. Claire Paolini, Dean
Programs in:
- arts and sciences (MA, MS, CPS)
- chemistry (MS)
- computer science (MS, CPS)
- criminal justice (MA)
- information technology (MS, CPS)
- information technology and network security (CPS)
- interactive multimedia (CPS)
- religious studies (MA)
- Web development (CPS)

College of Education and Health Professions
Dr. Patricia Walker, Dean

Programs in:
- administration (CAS)
- clinical nurse leader (MSN)
- education and health professions (MAT, MS, MSN, MSOT, DPT, CAS)
- educational technology (MAT)
- elementary education (MAT)
- family nurse practitioner (MSN)
- geriatric health and wellness (MS)
- occupational therapy (MSOT)
- patient care services administration (MSN)
- physical therapy (DPT)
- reading (CAS)
- secondary education (MAT)
- teaching (CAS)

The John F. Welch College of Business
Dr. Stephen Brown, Dean
Program in:
- business (MBA)

■ SAINT JOSEPH COLLEGE
West Hartford, CT 06117-2700
http://www.sjc.edu/

Independent-religious, Undergraduate: women only; graduate: coed, comprehensive institution. *Computer facilities:* 150 computers available on campus for general student use. A campuswide network can be accessed from student residence rooms and from off campus. Internet access and online class registration, Blackboard course management system, online grades are available. *Library facilities:* Pope Pius XII Library plus 1 other. *General application contact:* Assistant to the Coordinator of Academic Affairs, 860-231-5381.

Graduate Division
Programs in:
- biology (MS)
- biology/chemistry (MS)
- chemistry (MS)
- community counseling (MA)
- early childhood education (MA)
- education (MA)
- family health nurse practitioner (MS)
- family health nursing (MS)
- management science (MS)
- marriage and family therapy (MA, Certificate)
- nursing (Post Master's Certificate)
- psychiatric/mental health nursing (MS)
- special education (MA)
- spirituality (Certificate)

Institute in Gerontology
Program in:
- human development/gerontology (Certificate)

■ SOUTHERN CONNECTICUT STATE UNIVERSITY
New Haven, CT 06515-1355
http://www.southernct.edu/

State-supported, coed, comprehensive institution. CGS member. *Enrollment:* 12,326 graduate, professional, and undergraduate students; 569 full-time matriculated graduate/professional students, 1,490 part-time matriculated graduate/professional students. *Graduate faculty:* 402 full-time (175 women), 337 part-time/adjunct. *Computer facilities:* Computer purchase and lease plans are available. 750 computers available on campus for general student use. A campuswide network can be accessed from student residence rooms and from off campus. Internet access and online class registration are available. *Library facilities:* Hilton C. Buley Library. *General application contact:* Lisa Galvin, Assistant Dean, 203-392-5240.

Find University Details at www.petersons.com/gradchannel.

School of Graduate Studies
Dr. Sandra C. Holley, Dean
Programs in:
- audiology (MS)
- health and human services (MFT, MPH, MS, MSN, MSW)
- marriage and family therapy (MFT)
- nursing administration (MSN)
- nursing education (MSN)
- public health (MPH)
- recreation and leisure studies (MS)
- social work (MSW)
- speech pathology (MS)

School of Arts and Sciences
Dr. Donna Jean Fredeen, Dean
Programs in:
- art education (MS)
- arts and sciences (MA, MS, Diploma)
- biology (MS)
- biology for nurse anesthetists (MS)
- chemistry (MS)
- English (MA, MS)
- environmental education (MS)
- French (MA)
- history (MA, MS)
- mathematics (MS)
- multicultural-bilingual education/teaching English to speakers of other languages (MS)
- political science (MS)
- psychology (MA)
- Romance languages (MA)
- science education (MS, Diploma)
- sociology (MS)
- Spanish (MA)
- urban studies (MS)
- women's studies (MA)

School of Business
Dr. Henry Hein, Interim Dean
Programs in:
- business (MBA)
- business administration (MBA)

School of Communication, Information and Library Science
Dr. Edward Harris, Dean
Programs in:
- communication, information and library science (MLS, MS, Diploma)
- computer science (MS)
- instructional technology (MS)
- library science (MLS)
- library/information studies (Diploma)

School of Education
Dr. James Granfield, Interim Dean
Programs in:
- classroom teacher specialist (Diploma)
- community counseling (MS)
- counseling (Diploma)
- education (MS, MS Ed, Ed D, Diploma)
- educational leadership (Ed D, Diploma)
- elementary education (MS)
- foundational studies (Diploma)
- human performance (MS)
- physical education (MS)
- reading (MS, Diploma)
- research, measurement and quantitative analysis (MS)
- school counseling (MS)
- school health education (MS)
- school psychology (MS, Diploma)
- special education (MS Ed, Diploma)
- sport psychology (MS)

■ UNIVERSITY OF BRIDGEPORT
Bridgeport, CT 06604
http://www.bridgeport.edu/

Independent, coed, comprehensive institution. CGS member. *Enrollment:* 4,018 graduate, professional, and undergraduate students; 1,263 full-time matriculated graduate/professional students (564 women), 1,061 part-time matriculated graduate/professional students (617 women). *Graduate faculty:* 102 full-time (31 women), 260 part-time/adjunct (120 women). *Computer facilities:* 500 computers available on campus for general student use. A campuswide network can be accessed from student residence rooms and from off campus. Internet access is available. *Library facilities:* Wahlstrom Library. *General application contact:* Audrey Ashton-Savage, Vice President of Enrollment Management, 203-576-4552.

Acupuncture Institute
Dr. Jennifer Brett, Director
Program in:
- acupuncture (MS)

College of Chiropractic
Dr. Francis A. Zolli, Dean
Program in:
- chiropractic (DC)

University of Bridgeport (continued)

College of Naturopathic Medicine
Dr. Guru Sandesh Singh Khalsa, Dean
Program in:
naturopathic medicine (ND)

Nutrition Institute
Dr. David M. Brady, Director
Program in:
human nutrition (MS)

School of Business
Merrill Jay Forgotson, Dean
Programs in:
business (MBA)
business administration (MBA)

School of Education and Human Resources
Dr. James J. Ritchie, Dean
Program in:
education and human resources (MS, Ed D, Diploma)

Division of Education
Dr. Allen P. Cook, Associate Dean
Programs in:
computer specialist (Diploma)
early childhood education (MS, Diploma)
education (MS)
educational management (Ed D, Diploma)
elementary education (MS, Diploma)
intermediate administrator or supervisor (Diploma)
international education (Diploma)
leadership (Ed D)
reading specialist (MS, Diploma)
secondary education (MS, Diploma)

Division of Human Resources
Dr. Joseph T. Cullen, Head
Programs in:
college student personnel (MS)
community counseling (MS)
human resource development (MS)

School of Engineering
Dr. Tarek M. Sobh, Dean
Programs in:
computer engineering (MS)
computer science (MS)
computer science and engineering (PhD)
electrical engineering (MS)
engineering (MS, PhD)
mechanical engineering (MS)
technology management (MS)

■ UNIVERSITY OF CONNECTICUT
Storrs, CT 06269
http://www.uconn.edu/

State-supported, coed, university. CGS member. *Enrollment:* 23,557 graduate, professional, and undergraduate students; 3,344 full-time matriculated graduate/professional students (1,768 women), 2,244 part-time matriculated graduate/professional students (1,116 women). *Graduate faculty:* 1,242 full-time (387 women). *Computer facilities:* Computer purchase and lease plans are available. 1,318 computers available on campus for general student use. A campuswide network can be accessed from student residence rooms and from off campus. Internet access and online class registration, e-mail are available. *Library facilities:* Homer Babbidge Library plus 3 others. *General application contact:* Anne K. Lanzit, Associate Director of Graduate Admissions, 860-486-3617.

Find University Details at www.petersons.com/gradchannel.

Graduate School
Janet L. Greger, Dean and Vice Provost, Research and Graduate Education

Center for Continuing Studies
Programs in:
continuing studies (MPS)
homeland security leadership (MPS)
humanitarian services administration (MPS)
labor relations (MPS)
occupational safety and health management (MPS)
personnel (MPS)

College of Agriculture and Natural Resources
Kirklyn M. Kerr, Dean
Programs in:
agricultural and resource economics (MS, PhD)
agriculture and natural resources (MS, PhD)
animal science (MS, PhD)
natural resources (MS, PhD)
natural resources management and engineering (MS, PhD)
nutritional sciences (MS, PhD)
pathobiology (MS, PhD)
pathobiology and veterinary science (MS, PhD)
plant and soil sciences (MS, PhD)
plant science (MS, PhD)

College of Liberal Arts and Sciences
Ross D. MacKinnon, Dean
Programs in:
actuarial science (MS, PhD)
African studies (MA)
anthropology (MA, PhD)
applied financial mathematics (MS)
applied genomics (MS, PSM)
audiology (Au D, PhD)
behavioral neuroscience (PhD)
biobehavioral science (PhD)
biochemistry (MS, PhD)
biophysics and structural biology (MS, PhD)
biopsychology (PhD)
biotechnology (MS)
botany (MS, PhD)
cell and developmental biology (MS, PhD)
chemistry (MS, PhD)
clinical psychology (MA, PhD)
cognition and instruction (PhD)
communication processes (MA)
communication processes and marketing communication (PhD)
communication sciences (MA, Au D, PhD)
comparative literature and cultural studies (MA, PhD)
comparative physiology (MS, PhD)
developmental psychology (MA, PhD)
ecological psychology (PhD)
ecology (MS, PhD)
economics (MA, PhD)
English (MA, PhD)
entomology (MS, PhD)
European studies (MA)
experimental psychology (PhD)
French (MA, PhD)
general psychology (MA, PhD)
genetics (MS, PhD)
genetics, genomics, and bioinformatics (MS, PhD)
geographic information systems (Certificate)
geography (MS, PhD)
geological sciences (MS, PhD)
German (MA, PhD)
history (MA, PhD)
industrial/organizational psychology (PhD)
international studies (MA)
Italian (MA, PhD)
Italian history and culture (MA)
Judaic studies (MA)
language and cognition (PhD)
Latin American studies (MA)
liberal arts and sciences (MA, MPA, MS, PSM, Au D, PhD, Certificate, Graduate Certificate)
linguistics (PhD)
mathematics (MS, PhD)
medieval studies (MA, PhD)
microbial systems analysis (MS, PSM)
microbiology (MS, PhD)
neurobiology (MS, PhD)
neuroscience (PhD)
nonprofit management (Graduate Certificate)
oceanography (MS, PhD)
philosophy (MA, PhD)
physics (MS, PhD)
physiology and neurobiology (MS, PhD)
plant cell and molecular biology (MS, PhD)
political science (MA, PhD)
psychology (MA, PhD)
public administration (MPA)
public financial management (Graduate Certificate)
social psychology (MA, PhD)
sociology (MA, PhD)
Spanish (MA, PhD)
speech-language pathology (MA, PhD)
statistics (MS, PhD)
survey research (MA)
zoology (MS, PhD)

Neag School of Education
Richard L. Schwab, Dean
Programs in:
adult learning (MA, PhD)
agriculture education (MA, PhD)
bilingual and bicultural education (MA, PhD)
cognition and instruction (MA, PhD)
counseling psychology (MA, PhD)
curriculum and instruction (MA, PhD)
education (MA, Ed D, PhD)
education policy analysis (PhD)
educational administration (Ed D, PhD)
educational psychology (MA, PhD)
elementary education (MA, PhD)
English education (MA, PhD)
exercise science (MA, PhD)
gifted and talented education (MA, PhD)
higher education and student affairs (MA)
history and social sciences education (MA, PhD)
kinesiology (MA, PhD)
learning technology (MA, PhD)
mathematics education (MA, PhD)
measurement, evaluation, and assessment (MA, PhD)
reading education (MA, PhD)
school counseling (MA)
school psychology (MA, PhD)
science education (MA, PhD)
secondary education (MA, PhD)
special education (MA, PhD)
sport management and sociology (MA, PhD)
world languages education (MA, PhD)

School of Allied Health
Joseph W. Smey, Dean
Programs in:
allied health (MS)
physical therapy (MS)

School of Business
William Curt Hunter, Dean
Programs in:
accounting (MS, PhD)
business administration (Exec MBA, MBA, PhD)
finance (PhD)
health care management and insurance studies (MBA)
management (PhD)
management consulting (MBA)
marketing (PhD)
marketing intelligence (MBA)

School of Engineering
Amir Faghri, Dean
Programs in:
artificial intelligence (MS, PhD)
biomedical engineering (MS, PhD)
chemical engineering (MS, PhD)
civil engineering (MS, PhD)
computer architecture (MS, PhD)
computer science (MS, PhD)
electrical engineering (MS, PhD)
engineering (M Eng, MS, PhD)
environmental engineering (MS, PhD)
materials science and engineering (MS, PhD)
mechanical engineering (MS, PhD)
metallurgy and materials engineering (MS, PhD)
operating systems (MS, PhD)
polymer science and engineering (MS, PhD)
robotics (MS, PhD)
software engineering (MS, PhD)

School of Family Studies
Charles M. Super, Dean
Programs in:
family studies (MA, PhD)
human development and family studies (MA, PhD)

School of Fine Arts
David G. Woods, Dean
Programs in:
acting (MFA)
art history (MA)
conducting (M Mus, DMA)
costume design (MFA)
dramatic arts (MA, MFA)
fine arts (M Mus, MA, MFA, DMA, PhD, Performer's Certificate)
historical musicology (MA)
lighting design (MFA)
music (M Mus, MA, DMA, PhD, Performer's Certificate)
music education (M Mus, PhD)
music theory (MA)
music theory and history (PhD)
performance (M Mus, DMA)
puppetry (MA, MFA)
scenic design (MFA)
studio art (MFA)

School of Nursing
Laura Dzurec, Dean
Programs in:
adult acute care (Post-Master's Certificate)
adult primary care (Post-Master's Certificate)
community health (Post-Master's Certificate)
neonatal acute care (Post-Master's Certificate)
nursing (MS, PhD)
patient care services and systems administration (Post-Master's Certificate)
psychiatric mental health (Post-Master's Certificate)

School of Pharmacy
Robert L. McCarthy, Dean
Programs in:
medicinal chemistry (MS, PhD)
pharmaceutical sciences (MS, PhD)
pharmaceutics (MS, PhD)
pharmacology (MS, PhD)
pharmacology and toxicology (MS, PhD)
pharmacy (Pharm D, MS, PhD)
toxicology (MS, PhD)

School of Social Work
Kay Davidson, Dean
Program in:
social work (MSW, PhD)

University of Connecticut Health Center
Dr. Gerald Maxwell, Head
Programs in:
biomedical science (PhD)
dental science (M Dent Sc)
health (M Dent Sc, MPH, PhD)
public health (MPH)

School of Law
Ellen Keane Rutt, Associate Dean of Admissions, Career Services, and Student Finance
Program in:
law (JD)

■ UNIVERSITY OF HARTFORD
West Hartford, CT 06117-1599
http://www.hartford.edu/

Independent, coed, comprehensive institution. CGS member. *Enrollment:* 7,308 graduate, professional, and undergraduate students; 569 full-time matriculated graduate/professional students (347 women), 1,137 part-time matriculated graduate/professional students (703 women). *Graduate faculty:* 138 full-time (53 women), 97 part-time/adjunct (40 women). *Computer facilities:* Computer purchase and lease plans are available. 400 computers available on campus for general student use. A campuswide network can be accessed from student residence rooms and from off campus. Internet access and online class registration, student Web pages are available. *Library facilities:* Mortenson Library plus 1 other. *Graduate expenses:* Tuition: part-time $515 per credit. Required fees: $200 per term. *General application contact:* Reneé Murphy, Assistant Director of Graduate Admissions, 860-768-4373.

Barney School of Business
James W. Fairfield-Sonn, Interim Dean
Programs in:
business (EMBA, MBA, MSAT, Certificate)
business administration (EMBA, MBA)
professional accounting (Certificate)
taxation (MSAT)

College of Arts and Sciences
Dr. Joseph C. Voelker, Dean
Programs in:
arts and sciences (MA, MS, Psy D)
biology (MS)
clinical practices (MA, Psy D)
communication (MA)
general experimental psychology (MA)
neuroscience (MS)
organizational behavior (MS)
psychology (MA)
school psychology (MS)

University of Hartford (continued)

College of Education, Nursing, and Health Professions

Dr. Dorothy A. Zeiser, Dean
Programs in:
- administration and supervision (CAGS)
- community/public health nursing (MSN)
- counseling (M Ed, MS, Sixth Year Certificate)
- early childhood education (M Ed)
- education, nursing, and health professions (M Ed, MS, MSN, MSPT, DPT, Ed D, CAGS, Sixth Year Certificate)
- educational leadership (Ed D, CAGS)
- educational technology (M Ed)
- elementary education (M Ed)
- nursing education (MSN)
- nursing management (MSN)
- physical therapy (MSPT, DPT)

College of Engineering, Technology and Architecture

Louis Manzione, Dean
Programs in:
- architecture (M Arch)
- engineering (M Eng)
- engineering, technology and architecture (M Arch, M Eng)

Hartford Art School

Power Boothe, Dean
Program in:
- art (MFA)

The Hartt School

Dr. Malcolm Morrison, Dean
Programs in:
- choral conducting (MM Ed)
- composition (MM, DMA, Artist Diploma, Diploma)
- conducting (MM, DMA, Artist Diploma, Diploma)
- early childhood education (MM Ed)
- instrumental conducting (MM Ed)
- Kodály (MM Ed)
- music (CAGS)
- music education (DMA, PhD)
- music history (MM)
- music theory (MM)
- pedagogy (MM Ed)
- performance (MM, MM Ed, DMA, Artist Diploma, Diploma)
- research (MM Ed)
- technology (MM Ed)

■ UNIVERSITY OF NEW HAVEN

West Haven, CT 06516-1916
http://www.newhaven.edu/

Independent, coed, comprehensive institution. CGS member. *Computer facilities:* Computer purchase and lease plans are available. 300 computers available on campus for general student use. A campuswide network can be accessed from student residence rooms and from off campus. Internet access, e-mail are available. *Library facilities:* Marvin K. Peterson Library. *General application contact:* Director of Graduate Admissions, 203-932-7448.

Find University Details at www.petersons.com/gradchannel.

Graduate School

College of Arts and Sciences

Programs in:
- arts and sciences (MA, MS, Certificate)
- cellular and molecular biology (MS)
- community psychology (MA, Certificate)
- education (MS)
- environmental sciences (MS)
- executive tourism and hospitality (MS)
- hotel, restaurant, tourism and dietetics administration (MS)
- human nutrition (MS)
- industrial and organizational psychology (MA, Certificate)
- tourism and hospitality management (MS)

Henry C. Lee College of Criminal Justice and Forensic Sciences

Programs in:
- advanced investigation (MS)
- correctional counseling (MS)
- criminal justice and forensic sciences (MS)
- criminal justice management (MS)
- criminalistics (MS)
- fire science (MS)
- forensic science (MS)
- industrial hygiene (MS)
- occupational safety and health management (MS)
- security management (MS)

School of Business

Programs in:
- accounting (MBA)
- business (EMBA, MBA, MPA, MS)
- business administration (EMBA, MBA)
- business policy and strategy (MBA)
- corporate taxation (MS)
- finance (MBA)
- finance and financial services (MS)
- financial accounting (MS)
- health care administration (MS)
- health care management (MBA, MPA)
- human resources management (MBA)
- industrial relations (MS)
- international business (MBA)
- managerial accounting (MS)
- marketing (MBA)
- personnel and labor relations (MPA)
- public relations (MBA)
- public taxation (MS)
- sports management (MBA)
- taxation (MS)
- technology management (MBA)

Tagliatela College of Engineering

Programs in:
- applications software (MS)
- civil engineering design (Certificate)
- electrical engineering (MSEE)
- engineering (EMS, MS, MSEE, MSIE, MSME, Certificate)
- engineering management (EMS)
- environmental engineering (MS)
- industrial engineering (MSIE)
- logistics (Certificate)
- management information systems (MS)
- mechanical engineering (MSME)
- operations research (MS)
- systems software (MS)

■ WESTERN CONNECTICUT STATE UNIVERSITY

Danbury, CT 06810-6885
http://www.wcsu.edu/

State-supported, coed, comprehensive institution. *Enrollment:* 6,086 graduate, professional, and undergraduate students; 44 full-time matriculated graduate/professional students (32 women), 541 part-time matriculated graduate/professional students (345 women). *Graduate faculty:* 64 full-time (25 women), 9 part-time/adjunct (3 women). *Computer facilities:* 400 computers available on campus for general student use. A campuswide network can be accessed from student residence rooms and from off campus. Internet access and online class registration are available. *Library facilities:* Ruth Haas Library plus 1 other. *General application contact:* Chris Shankle, Associate Director of Graduate Admissions, 203-837-8244.

Division of Graduate Studies

Dr. Ellen D. Durnin, Dean Graduate Studies
Programs in:
- illustration (MFA)
- music education (MS)
- painting (MFA)
- visual and performing arts (MFA, MS)

Ancell School of Business

Dr. Allen Morton, Dean
Programs in:
- accounting (MBA)
- business (MBA, MHA, MS)
- business administration (MBA)
- health administration (MHA)
- justice administration (MS)

School of Arts and Sciences

Dr. Linda Vaden-Goad, Dean
Programs in:
- arts and sciences (MA)
- biological and environmental sciences (MA)
- earth and planetary sciences (MA)
- English (MA)
- history (MA)
- mathematics (MA)
- theoretical mathematics (MA)

School of Professional Studies

Dr. Lynne Clark, Dean

Programs in:
- adult nurse practitioner (MSN)
- clinical nurse specialist (MSN)
- community counseling (MS)
- curriculum (MS)
- English education (MS)
- instructional leadership (Ed D)
- instructional technology (MS)
- mathematics education (MS)
- professional studies (MS, MSN, Ed D)
- reading (MS)
- school counseling (MS)
- special education (MS)

■ YALE UNIVERSITY
New Haven, CT 06520
http://www.yale.edu/

Independent, coed, university. CGS member. *Computer facilities:* 350 computers available on campus for general student use. A campuswide network can be accessed from student residence rooms and from off campus. Internet access and online class registration are available. *Library facilities:* Sterling Memorial Library plus 20 others. *General application contact:* Admissions Information, 203-432-2772.

Divinity School
Dr. Harold W. Attridge, Dean
Program in:
- divinity (M Div, MAR, STM)

Graduate School of Arts and Sciences
Programs in:
- African studies (MA)
- African-American studies (MA, PhD)
- American studies (MA, PhD)
- anthropology (MA, PhD)
- applied mathematics (M Phil, MS, PhD)
- applied mechanics and mechanical engineering (M Phil, MS, PhD)
- applied physics (MS, PhD)
- archaeological studies (MA)
- arts and sciences (M Phil, MA, MS, PhD)
- astronomy (MS, PhD)
- biophysical chemistry (PhD)
- cell biology (PhD)
- cellular and molecular physiology (PhD)
- chemical engineering (MS, PhD)
- classics (PhD)
- comparative literature (PhD)
- computer science (PhD)
- developmental biology (PhD)
- East Asian languages and literatures (PhD)
- East Asian studies (MA)
- ecology and evolutionary biology (PhD)
- economics (PhD)
- electrical engineering (MS, PhD)
- English language and literature (MA, PhD)
- environmental sciences (PhD)
- experimental pathology (PhD)
- forestry (PhD)
- French (MA, PhD)
- genetics (PhD)
- geochemistry (PhD)
- geophysics (PhD)
- Germanic language and literature (MA, PhD)
- history (MA, PhD)
- history of art (PhD)
- history of medicine and the life sciences (MS, PhD)
- immunobiology (PhD)
- inorganic chemistry (PhD)
- international and development economics (MA)
- international relations (MA)
- Italian language and literature (PhD)
- linguistics (PhD)
- mathematics (MS, PhD)
- mechanical engineering (M Phil, MS, PhD)
- medieval studies (MA, PhD)
- meteorology (PhD)
- mineralogy and crystallography (PhD)
- molecular biology (PhD)
- molecular biophysics and biochemistry (MS, PhD)
- music (MA, PhD)
- Near Eastern languages and civilizations (MA, PhD)
- neurobiology (PhD)
- neuroscience (PhD)
- oceanography (PhD)
- organic chemistry (PhD)
- paleoecology (PhD)
- paleontology and stratigraphy (PhD)
- petrology (PhD)
- pharmacology (PhD)
- philosophy (PhD)
- physical chemistry (PhD)
- physics (PhD)
- plant sciences (PhD)
- political science (PhD)
- psychology (PhD)
- religious studies (PhD)
- Renaissance studies (PhD)
- Russian and East European studies (MA)
- Slavic languages and literatures (PhD)
- sociology (PhD)
- Spanish and Portuguese (MA, PhD)
- statistics (MS, PhD)
- structural geology (PhD)

School of Architecture
Robert A. M. Stern, Dean
Program in:
- architecture (M Arch, M Env Des, MEM)

School of Art
Robert Storr, Dean
Programs in:
- graphic design (MFA)
- painting/printmaking (MFA)
- photography (MFA)
- sculpture (MFA)

School of Drama
James Bundy, Dean/Artistic Director
Program in:
- drama (MFA, DFA, Certificate)

School of Forestry and Environmental Studies
James Gustave Speth, Dean
Program in:
- forestry and environmental studies (MEM, MES, MF, MFS, PhD)

School of Medicine
Programs in:
- biological and biomedical sciences (PhD)
- computational biology and bioinformatics (PhD)
- immunology (PhD)
- medicine (MD, MM Sc, MPH, MS, PhD)
- microbiology (PhD)
- molecular biophysics and biochemistry (PhD)
- molecular cell biology, genetics, and development (PhD)
- neuroscience (PhD)
- pharmacological sciences and molecular medicine (PhD)
- physician associate (MM Sc)
- physiology and integrative medical biology (PhD)

School of Public Health
Dr. Paul D. Cleary, Dean and Chairman
Programs in:
- biostatistics (MPH, MS, PhD)
- chronic disease epidemiology (MPH, PhD)
- environmental health sciences (MPH, PhD)
- epidemiology of microbial diseases (MPH, PhD)
- global health (MPH)
- health management (MPH)
- health policy and administration (MPH, PhD)
- parasitology (PhD)
- social and behavioral sciences (MPH)

School of Music
Robert Blocker, Dean
Program in:
- music (MM, MMA, DMA, AD, Certificate)

School of Nursing
Program in:
- nursing (MSN, DN Sc, Post Master's Certificate)

Yale Law School
Harold Hongju Koh, Dean
Program in:
- law (JD, LL M, MSL, JSD)

Yale School of Management
Joel M. Podolny, Dean
Programs in:
- accounting (PhD)
- business administration (MBA, PhD)
- financial economics (PhD)
- management (MBA, PhD)
- marketing (PhD)

Delaware

■ DELAWARE STATE UNIVERSITY

Dover, DE 19901-2277

http://www.desu.edu/

State-supported, coed, comprehensive institution. *Computer facilities:* 641 computers available on campus for general student use. A campuswide network can be accessed from student residence rooms and from off campus. Internet access and online class registration, online grade access, e-mail are available. *Library facilities:* William C. Jason Library. *General application contact:* Dean of Graduate Studies and Research, 302-857-6800.

Graduate Programs

Programs in:
- applied chemistry (MS)
- biology (MS)
- biology education (MS)
- business administration (MBA)
- chemistry (MS)
- curriculum and instruction (MA)
- education (MA)
- mathematics (MS)
- physics (MS)
- physics teaching (MS)
- science education (MA)
- social work (MSW)
- special education (MA)

■ UNIVERSITY OF DELAWARE

Newark, DE 19716

http://www.udel.edu/

State-related, coed, university. CGS member. *Computer facilities:* 908 computers available on campus for general student use. A campuswide network can be accessed from student residence rooms and from off campus. Internet access and online class registration, e-mail, personal Web page are available. *Library facilities:* Hugh Morris Library plus 5 others. *General application contact:* Assistant Provost for Graduate Studies, 302-831-8916.

Alfred Lerner College of Business and Economics

Programs in:
- accounting (MS)
- business administration (MBA)
- business and economics (MA, MBA, MS, PhD)
- economics (MA, MS, PhD)
- economics for entrepreneurship and educators (MA)
- information systems and technology management (MS)

College of Agriculture and Natural Resources

Programs in:
- agricultural economics (MS)
- agriculture and natural resources (MS, PhD)
- animal sciences (MS, PhD)
- entomology and applied ecology (MS, PhD)
- food sciences (MS)
- operations research (MS, PhD)
- plant and soil sciences (MS, PhD)
- public horticulture (MS)
- statistics (MS)

College of Arts and Sciences

Programs in:
- acting (MFA)
- applied mathematics (MS, PhD)
- art (MA, MFA)
- art history (MA, PhD)
- arts and sciences (MA, MALS, MFA, MM, MS, DPT, PhD, Certificate)
- behavioral neuroscience (PhD)
- biochemistry (MA, MS, PhD)
- biomechanics and movement science (MS, PhD)
- biotechnology (MS)
- cancer biology (MS, PhD)
- cell and extracellular matrix biology (MS, PhD)
- cell and systems physiology (MS, PhD)
- chemistry (MA, MS, PhD)
- climatology (PhD)
- clinical psychology (PhD)
- cognitive psychology (PhD)
- communication (MA)
- composition (MM)
- computer and information sciences (MS, PhD)
- criminology (MA, PhD)
- developmental biology (MS, PhD)
- early American culture (MA)
- ecology and evolution (MS, PhD)
- English and American literature (MA, PhD)
- foreign languages and literatures (MA)
- foreign languages pedagogy (MA)
- geography (MA, MS)
- geology (MS, PhD)
- history (MA, PhD)
- history of technology and industrialization (MA, PhD)
- liberal studies (MALS)
- linguistics (MA, PhD)
- mathematics (MS, PhD)
- microbiology (MS, PhD)
- molecular biology and genetics (MS, PhD)
- museum studies (Certificate)
- music education (MM)
- performance (MM)
- physical therapy (DPT)
- physics and astronomy (MS, PhD)
- political science and international relations (MA, PhD)
- practicing art conservation (MS)
- social psychology (PhD)
- sociology (MA, PhD)
- stage management (MFA)
- technical production (MFA)

College of Engineering

Programs in:
- chemical engineering (M Ch E, PhD)
- electrical and computer engineering (MS, MSECE, PhD)
- engineering (M Ch E, MAS, MCE, MEM, MMSE, MS, MSECE, MSME, PhD)
- environmental engineering (MAS, MCE, PhD)
- geotechnical engineering (MAS, MCE, PhD)
- materials science and engineering (MMSE, PhD)
- mechanical engineering (MEM, MSME, PhD)
- ocean engineering (MAS, MCE, PhD)
- structural engineering (MAS, MCE, PhD)
- transportation engineering (MAS, MCE, PhD)
- water resource engineering (MAS, MCE, PhD)

College of Health Sciences

Programs in:
- adult nurse practitioner (MSN, PMC)
- cardiopulmonary clinical nurse specialist (MSN, PMC)
- cardiopulmonary clinical nurse specialist/adult nurse practitioner (MSN, PMC)
- exercise science (MS)
- family nurse practitioner (MSN, PMC)
- gerontology clinical nurse specialist (MSN, PMC)
- gerontology clinical nurse specialist geriatric nurse practitioner (PMC)
- gerontology clinical nurse specialist/ geriatric nurse practitioner (MSN)
- health promotion (MS)
- health sciences (MS, MSN, PMC)
- health services administration (MSN, PMC)
- human nutrition (MS)
- nursing of children clinical nurse specialist (MSN, PMC)
- nursing of children clinical nurse specialist/pediatric nurse practitioner (MSN, PMC)
- oncology/immune deficiency clinical nurse specialist (MSN, PMC)
- oncology/immune deficiency clinical nurse specialist/adult nurse practitioner (MSN, PMC)
- perinatal/women's health clinical nurse specialist (MSN, PMC)
- perinatal/women's health clinical nurse specialist/women's health nurse practitioner (MSN, PMC)
- psychiatric nursing clinical nurse specialist (MSN, PMC)

College of Human Services, Education and Public Policy
Programs in:
counseling in higher education (M Ed, MA)
hospitality information management (MS)
human development and family studies (MS, PhD)
human services, education and public policy (M Ed, MA, MEEP, MI, MPA, MS, Ed D, PhD)

Center for Energy and Environmental Policy
Programs in:
environmental and energy policy (MEEP, PhD)
urban affairs and public policy (MA, PhD)

School of Education
Programs in:
curriculum and instruction (M Ed)
education (PhD)
educational leadership (M Ed, Ed D)
exceptional children and youth (M Ed)
instruction (MI)
school counseling (M Ed)
school psychology (MA)
teaching English as a second language (TESL) (MA)

School of Urban Affairs and Public Policy
Programs in:
community development and nonprofit leadership (MA)
energy and environmental policy (MA)
governance, planning and management (PhD)
historic preservation (MA)
public administration (MPA)
social and urban policy (PhD)
technology, environment and society (PhD)
urban affairs and public policy (MA, MPA, PhD)

College of Marine Studies
Programs in:
geology (MS, PhD)
marine management (MMM)
marine policy (MS)
marine studies (MMP, MS, PhD)
oceanography (MS, PhD)

■ WESLEY COLLEGE
Dover, DE 19901-3875
http://www.wesley.edu/

Independent-religious, coed, comprehensive institution. *Enrollment:* 2,306 graduate, professional, and undergraduate students; 68 full-time matriculated graduate/professional students (47 women), 110 part-time matriculated graduate/professional students (83 women). *Graduate faculty:* 12 full-time (8 women), 7 part-time/adjunct (4 women). *Computer facilities:* Computer purchase and lease plans are available. 225 computers available on campus for general student use. A campuswide network can be accessed from student residence rooms and from off campus. Internet access and online class registration are available. *Library facilities:* Robert H. Parker Library. *Graduate expenses:* Tuition: full-time $6,120; part-time $340 per credit. Required fees: $60; $60 per year. *General application contact:* G. R. Myers, Director of Graduate Admissions, 302-736-2343.

Business Program
G. R. Myers, Director of Graduate Admissions
Programs in:
environmental management (MBA)
executive leadership (MBA)
management (MBA)

Education Program
G. R. Myers, Director of Graduate Admissions
Program in:
education (M Ed, MA Ed, MAT)

Environmental Studies Program
G. R. Myers, Director of Graduate Admissions
Program in:
environmental studies (MS)

Nursing Program
G. R. Myers, Director of Graduate Admissions
Program in:
nursing (MSN)

■ WILMINGTON UNIVERSITY
New Castle, DE 19720-6491
http://www.wilmu.edu/

Independent, coed, comprehensive institution. *Enrollment:* 7,911 graduate, professional, and undergraduate students; 1,216 full-time matriculated graduate/professional students (832 women), 2,213 part-time matriculated graduate/professional students (1,615 women). *Graduate faculty:* 70 full-time (25 women), 507 part-time/adjunct (316 women). *Computer facilities:* Computer purchase and lease plans are available. 516 computers available on campus for general student use. A campuswide network can be accessed. Internet access, online available in 6 months are available. *Library facilities:* Robert C. and Dorothy M. Peoples Library plus 1 other. *General application contact:* Chris Ferguson, Director of Admissions and Financial Aid, 302-356-4636 Ext. 256.

Division of Behavioral Science
Dr. Thomas Cupples, Chair
Programs in:
administration of human services (MS)
administration of justice (MS)
community counseling (MS)

Division of Business
Dr. Robert Edelson, Chair
Programs in:
business administration (MBA)
finance (MBA)
health care administration (MBA, MS)
human resource management (MS)
management (MS)
management information systems (MBA)
organizational leadership (MS)
public administration (MS)
transportation and logistics (MBA, MS)

Division of Education
Dr. Richard Gochnauer, Chair
Programs in:
applied education technology (M Ed)
career and technical education (M Ed)
elementary and secondary school counseling (M Ed)
elementary special education (M Ed)
elementary studies (M Ed)
instruction: gifted and talented (M Ed)
instruction: teaching and learning (M Ed)
literacy (M Ed)
reading (M Ed)
school leadership (M Ed)
secondary teaching (MAT)

Division of Information Technology and Advanced Communications
Dr. Jack Nold, Head
Programs in:
corporate training (MS)
information systems technologies (MS)
Internet web design (MS)
management information systems (MS)

Division of Nursing
Dr. Mary Letitia Gallagher, Chair
Programs in:
adult nurse practitioner (MSN)
family nurse practitioner (MSN)
gerontology (MSN)
leadership (MSN)
nursing (MSN)
women's nurse practitioner (MSN)

Program in Innovation and Leadership
Dr. Joe Deardorff, Head
Programs in:
education innovation (Ed D)
organizational leadership (Ed D)

District of Columbia

■ AMERICAN UNIVERSITY
Washington, DC 20016-8001
http://www.american.edu/

Independent-religious, coed, university. CGS member. *Enrollment:* 11,279 graduate,

American University (continued)
professional, and undergraduate students; 2,732 full-time matriculated graduate/professional students (1,652 women), 2,468 part-time matriculated graduate/professional students (1,499 women). *Graduate faculty:* 554 full-time (250 women), 429 part-time/adjunct (190 women). *Computer facilities:* Computer purchase and lease plans are available. 760 computers available on campus for general student use. A campuswide network can be accessed from student residence rooms and from off campus. Internet access and online class registration, printers, scanners, online course support, wireless campus, USENET feed are available. *Library facilities:* American University Bender Library plus 1 other. *Graduate expenses:* Tuition: full-time $18,864; part-time $1,048 per credit. Required fees: $380. Tuition and fees vary according to program. *General application contact:* Information Contact, 202-885-6000.

College of Arts and Sciences
Dr. Kay Mussell, Dean
Programs in:
- anthropology (PhD)
- applied economics (Certificate)
- applied science (MS)
- applied statistics (Certificate)
- art history (MA)
- arts and sciences (MA, MAT, MFA, MS, PhD, Certificate)
- arts management (MA, Certificate)
- behavior, cognition, and neuroscience (PhD)
- biology (MA, MS)
- chemistry (MS)
- clinical psychology (PhD)
- computer science (MS, Certificate)
- creative writing (MFA)
- dance (MA, Certificate)
- economics (MA, PhD, Certificate)
- environmental science (MS)
- ethics, peace, and global affairs (MA)
- experimental/biological psychology (MA)
- French studies (Certificate)
- general psychology (MA)
- history (MA, PhD)
- interdisciplinary studies (MA)
- international economic relations (Certificate)
- literature (MA)
- marine science (MS)
- mathematics (MA)
- painting, sculpture and printmaking (MFA)
- personality/social psychology (MA)
- philosophy (MA)
- psychology (MA)
- public anthropology (MA, Certificate)
- Russian studies (Certificate)
- social research (Certificate)
- sociology (MA, Certificate)
- Spanish: Latin American studies (MA, Certificate)
- statistics (MS, Certificate)
- statistics for policy analysis (MS)
- teaching English to speakers of other languages (MA, Certificate)
- toxicology (Certificate)
- translation (Certificate)

School of Education, Teaching, and Health
Dr. Sarah Irvine-Belson, Dean
Programs in:
- education (PhD)
- educational leadership (MA)
- educational technology (MA)
- elementary education (MAT, Certificate)
- English for speakers of other languages (MAT, Certificate)
- health promotion management (MS)
- international education (MA)
- learning disabilities (MA)
- secondary teaching (MAT, Certificate)

Kogod School of Business
Dr. Richard Durand, Dean
Programs in:
- accounting (MBA)
- business (MBA, MS, Certificate)
- business administration (MBA)
- entrepreneurship and management (MBA)
- finance (MBA)
- information systems (MS, Certificate)
- interdisciplinary (MBA)
- international finance (MBA)
- international management (MBA)
- international marketing (MBA)
- law and business)
- management of global information technology (MBA)
- marketing (MBA)
- marketing information and technology (MBA)
- marketing management (MBA)
- real estate (MBA)
- taxation (MS)

School of Communication
Prof. Larry Kirkman, Dean
Programs in:
- broadcast journalism (MA)
- communication (MA, MFA)
- film and electronic media (MFA)
- film and video (MA)
- interactive journalism (MA)
- news media studies (MA)
- print journalism (MA)
- producing film and video (MA)
- producing for film and video (MA)
- public communication (MA)

School of International Service
Dr. Louis W. Goodman, Dean
Programs in:
- comparative and regional studies (MA)
- cross-cultural communication (Certificate)
- development management (MS)
- environmental policy (MA)
- ethics, peace, and global affairs (MA)
- global environmental policy (MA)
- international communication (MA)
- international development (MA)
- international development management (Certificate)
- international economic policy (MA)
- international economic relations (Certificate)
- international peace and conflict resolution (MA)
- international politics (MA)
- international relations (PhD)
- international service (MIS)
- the Americas (Certificate)
- U.S. foreign policy (MA)

School of Public Affairs
Dr. William Leo Grande, Dean
Programs in:
- advanced leadership studies (Certificate)
- justice, law and society (MS, PhD)
- organization development (MSOD)
- organizational change (Certificate)
- political science (MA, PhD)
- public administration (MPA, PhD)
- public affairs (MA, MPA, MPP, MS, MSOD, PhD, Certificate)
- public financial management (Certificate)
- public management (Certificate)
- public policy (MPP)

Washington College of Law
Dr. Claudio Grossman, Dean
Programs in:
- human rights and the law (Certificate)
- international legal studies (LL M, Certificate)
- judicial sciences (SJD)
- law (JD)
- law and government (LL M)

■ THE CATHOLIC UNIVERSITY OF AMERICA
Washington, DC 20064
http://www.cua.edu/

Independent-religious, coed, university. CGS member. *Enrollment:* 6,148 graduate, professional, and undergraduate students; 1,335 full-time matriculated graduate/professional students (658 women), 1,584 part-time matriculated graduate/professional students (830 women). *Graduate faculty:* 344 full-time (129 women), 347 part-time/adjunct (154 women). *Computer facilities:* Computer purchase and lease plans are available. 450 computers available on campus for general student use. A campuswide network can be accessed from student residence rooms and from off campus. Internet access and online class registration, internet 2, video streaming, online voting, pedagogical software are available. *Library facilities:* Mullen Library plus 7 others. *Graduate expenses:* Tuition: full-time $27,700; part-time $1,045 per credit hour. Required fees: $1,290. Part-time tuition and fees vary according to campus/

location and program. *General application contact:* Christine Mica, Director, University Admissions, 202-319-5305.

The Benjamin T. Rome School of Music

Murry Sidlin, Dean
Programs in:
accompanying and chamber music (MM)
chamber music (DMA)
composition (MM, DMA)
instrumental conducting (MM, DMA)
liturgical music (M Lit M, DMA)
music (M Lit M, MA, MM, MMSM, DMA, PhD)
music education (MM, DMA)
musicology (MA, PhD)
orchestral instruments (MM, DMA)
performance (MM, DMA)
piano pedagogy (MM, DMA)
vocal accompanying (DMA)
vocal pedagogy (MM)
vocal performance (MM)
voice pedagogy and performance (DMA)

Columbus School of Law

Program in:
law (JD)

National Catholic School of Social Service

Dr. James R. Zabora, Dean
Program in:
social service (MSW, PhD)

School of Architecture and Planning

Randall Ott, Dean
Program in:
architecture and planning (M Arch, M Arch Studies)

School of Arts and Sciences

Dr. Lawrence R. Poos, Dean
Programs in:
acting, directing, and playwriting (MFA)
administration, curriculum, and policy studies (MA)
American government (MA, PhD)
anthropology (MA, PhD)
applied experimental psychology (MA, PhD)
arts and sciences (MA, MFA, MS, MTS, PhD, Certificate)
Byzantine studies (MA, Certificate)
Catholic school leadership (MA)
cell and microbial biology (MS, PhD)
chemistry (MS)
classics (MA)
clinical laboratory science (MS, PhD)
clinical psychology (PhD)
comparative literature (MA, PhD)
congressional studies (MA)
counselor education (MA)
early Christian studies (MA, PhD, Certificate)
educational administration (PhD)
educational psychology (PhD)
English as a second language (MA)
English language and literature (MA, PhD)
French (MA, PhD)
general psychology (MA, PhD)
Greek and Latin (PhD)
history (MA, PhD)
human development (PhD)
human factors (MA)
international affairs (MA)
international political economics (MA)
Irish studies (MA)
Italian (MA)
Latin (MA)
learning and instruction (MA)
medieval studies (MA, PhD, Certificate)
physics (MS, PhD)
policy studies (PhD)
political theory (MA, PhD)
rhetoric (MA, PhD)
Romance languages and literatures (MA, PhD)
Semitic and Egyptian languages and literature (MA, PhD)
sociology (MA, PhD)
Spanish (MA, PhD)
teacher education (MA)
theatre history and criticism (MA)
world politics (MA, PhD)

School of Canon Law

Rev. Msgr. Brian Ferme, Dean
Program in:
canon law (JCD, JCL)

School of Engineering

Dr. Charles C. Nguyen, Dean
Programs in:
biomedical engineering (MBE, MS Engr, D Engr, PhD)
civil engineering (MCE, D Engr, PhD)
construction management (MCE, MS Engr, PhD)
design (D Engr, PhD)
design and robotics (MME, D Engr, PhD)
electrical engineering and computer science (MEE, MS Engr, MSCS, D Engr, PhD)
engineering (MBE, MCE, MEE, MME, MS Engr, MSCS, D Engr, PhD)
engineering management (MS Engr)
environmental engineering (MCE, MS Engr)
fluid mechanics and thermal science (MME, D Engr, PhD)
geotechnical engineering (MCE)
mechanical design (MME)
ocean and structural acoustics (MME, MS Engr, PhD)
structures and structural mechanics (MCE)

School of Library and Information Science

Dr. Martha L. Hale, Dean
Program in:
library and information science (MSLS)

School of Nursing

Dr. Nalini Jairath, Dean
Programs in:
advanced practice nursing (MSN)
clinical nursing (DN Sc)

School of Philosophy

Rev. Kurt Pritzl, OP, Dean
Program in:
philosophy (MA, PhD, Ph L)

School of Theology and Religious Studies

Msgr. Kevin W. Irwin, Dean
Program in:
religious studies (M Div, STB, MA, MRE, D Min, PhD, STD, STL)

■ GALLAUDET UNIVERSITY
Washington, DC 20002-3625
http://www.gallaudet.edu/

Independent, coed, university. CGS member. *Computer facilities:* 240 computers available on campus for general student use. A campuswide network can be accessed from student residence rooms and from off campus. Internet access and online class registration are available. *Library facilities:* Merrill Learning Center. *General application contact:* Coordinator of Prospective Graduate Student Services, 202-651-5647.

The Graduate School

College of Arts and Sciences
Programs in:
arts and sciences (MA, MSW, PhD, Psy S)
clinical psychology (PhD)
developmental psychology (MA)
school psychology (MA, Psy S)
social work (MSW)

School of Communication
Programs in:
audiology (Au D)
communication (MA, MS, Au D)
interpretation (MA)
linguistics (MA)
speech and language pathology (MS)

School of Education and Human Services
Programs in:
administration (MS)
administration and supervision (PhD, Ed S)
community counseling (MA)
early childhood education (MA, Ed S)
education and human services (MA, MS, PhD, Certificate, Ed S)
education of deaf and hard of hearing students and multihandicapped deaf and hard of hearing students (MA, Ed S)
elementary education (MA, Ed S)
individualized program of study (PhD)
instructional supervision (Ed S)
integrating technology in the classroom (Certificate)

Gallaudet University (continued)
leadership training (MS)
leisure services administration (MS)
mental health counseling (MA)
parent/infant specialty (MA, Ed S)
school counseling (MA)
secondary education (MA, Ed S)
special education administration (PhD)

■ GEORGETOWN UNIVERSITY
Washington, DC 20057
http://www.georgetown.edu/

Independent-religious, coed, university. CGS member. *Computer facilities:* Computer purchase and lease plans are available. 400 computers available on campus for general student use. A campuswide network can be accessed from student residence rooms and from off campus. Internet access and online class registration, online grade reports are available. *Library facilities:* Lauinger Library plus 6 others. *General application contact:* Dean of the Graduate School, 202-687-5974.

Graduate School of Arts and Sciences
Programs in:
American government (MA, PhD)
analytical chemistry (MS, PhD)
Arab studies (MA, Certificate)
Arabic language, literature, and linguistics (MS, PhD)
arts and sciences (MA, MALS, MAT, MBA, MPP, MS, PhD, Certificate)
bilingual education (Certificate)
biochemistry (MS, PhD)
biology (MS, PhD)
British and American literature (MA)
chemical physics (MS, PhD)
communication, culture, and technology (MA)
comparative government (PhD)
conflict resolution (MA)
demography (MA)
economics (PhD)
German (MS, PhD)
history (MA, PhD)
inorganic chemistry (MS, PhD)
international relations (PhD)
linguistics (MS, PhD)
national security studies (MA)
organic chemistry (MS, PhD)
philosophy (MA, PhD)
physical chemistry (MS, PhD)
political theory (PhD)
psychology (PhD)
Russian and East European studies (MA)
Spanish (MS, PhD)
teaching English as a second language (MAT, Certificate)
teaching English as a second language and bilingual education (MAT)
theoretical chemistry (MS, PhD)

BMW Center for German and European Studies
Program in:
German and European studies (MA)

Center for Latin American Studies
Program in:
Latin American studies (MA)

Edmund A. Walsh School of Foreign Service
Program in:
foreign service (MS)

The Georgetown Public Policy Institute
Program in:
public policy (MPP)

McDonough School of Business
Program in:
business administration (MBA)

Programs in Biomedical Sciences
Programs in:
biochemistry and molecular biology (PhD)
biohazardous threat agents and emerging infectious diseases (MS)
biomedical sciences (MS, PhD)
biostatistics and epidemiology (MS)
cell biology (PhD)
general microbiology and immunology (MS)
global infectious diseases (PhD)
health physics (MS)
microbiology and immunology research (PhD)
neuroscience (PhD)
pathology (MS, PhD)
pharmacology (PhD)
physiology and biophysics (MS, PhD)
radiobiology (MS)
science policy and advocacy (MS)

School for Summer and Continuing Education
Program in:
summer and continuing education (MALS)

School of Nursing and Health Studies
Program in:
nursing (MS)

Law Center
Programs in:
advocacy (LL M)
common law studies (LL M)
general (LL M)
international and comparative law (LL M)
labor and employment law (LL M)
law (JD, SJD)
securities regulation (LL M)
taxation (LL M)

National Institutes of Health Sponsored Programs
Program in:
biomedical sciences (MS, PhD)

School of Medicine
Program in:
medicine (MD)

■ THE GEORGE WASHINGTON UNIVERSITY
Washington, DC 20052
http://www.gwu.edu/

Independent, coed, university. CGS member. *Computer facilities:* 550 computers available on campus for general student use. A campuswide network can be accessed from student residence rooms and from off campus. *Library facilities:* Gelman Library plus 2 others. *General application contact:* Director, Graduate Student Enrollment Management, 202-994-0467.

College of Professional Studies
Programs in:
healthcare corporate compliance (Graduate Certificate)
molecular biotechnology (MPS)
paralegal studies (MPS, Graduate Certificate)
professional service firm management (MPS)
publishing (MPS)

Graduate School of Political Management
Programs in:
legislative affairs (MA)
PAC and political management (Certificate)
political management (MA)

Columbian College of Arts and Sciences
Programs in:
American studies (MA, PhD)
analytical chemistry (MS, PhD)
anthropology (MA)
applied mathematics (MA, MS)
applied social psychology (PhD)
art history (MA, PhD)
art therapy (MA, Certificate)
arts and sciences (MA, MFA, MFS, MPA, MPP, MS, MSFS, PhD, Psy D, Certificate, Graduate Certificate)
biochemistry (PhD)
biological sciences (MS, PhD)
biostatistics (MS, PhD)
ceramics (MFA)
classical acting (MFA)
clinical psychology (PhD)
cognitive neuropsychology (PhD)
crime scene investigation (MFS)
criminal justice (MA)
design (MFA)
economics (MA, PhD)
English (MA, PhD)
epidemiology (MS, PhD)
folklife (MA)
forensic chemistry (MFS, MSFS)

forensic molecular biology (MFS, MSFS)
forensic sciences (MFS, MSFS)
forensic toxicology (MFS, MSFS)
genomics, proteomics, and bioinformatics (MS)
geography (MA)
geology (MS, PhD)
geosciences (MS, PhD)
high-technology crime investigation (MFS)
Hinduism and Islam (MA)
historic preservation (MA)
history (MA, PhD)
hominid paleobiology (MS, PhD)
human resource management (MA)
human sciences (PhD)
industrial and engineering statistics (MS)
industrial-organizational psychology (PhD)
inorganic chemistry (MS, PhD)
interior design (MFA)
leadership and coaching (Certificate)
material culture (MA)
materials science (MS, PhD)
museum studies (MA, Certificate)
museum training (MA)
organic chemistry (MS, PhD)
organizational management (MA)
painting (MFA)
photography (MFA)
physical chemistry (MS, PhD)
physics (MA, PhD)
political science (MA, PhD)
printmaking (MFA)
professional psychology (Psy D)
pure mathematics (MA, PhD)
sculpture (MFA)
security management (MFS)
sociology (MA)
speech pathology (MA)
statistics (MS, PhD)
survey design and data analysis (Graduate Certificate)
theater design (MFA)
women's studies (MA, Certificate)

Institute for Biomedical Sciences
Programs in:
biochemistry and molecular biology (PhD)
genetics (MS, PhD)
microbiology and immunology (PhD)
molecular and cellular oncology (PhD)
molecular medicine (PhD)
neuroscience (PhD)
neurosciences (PhD)
pharmacology (PhD)
pharmacology and physiology (PhD)

School of Media and Public Affairs
Program in:
media and public affairs (MA)

School of Public Policy and Public Administration
Programs in:
budget and public finance (MPA)
environmental and resource policy (MA)
federal policy, politics, and management (MPA)
international development management (MPA)
managing public organizations (MPA)
managing state and local governments and urban policy (MPA)
nonprofit management (MPA)
philosophy and social policy (MA)
policy analysis and evaluation (MPA)
public administration (MPA)
public policy (MA, MPP)
public policy and administration (PhD)
public policy and public administration (MPA)
women's studies (MA)

Elliott School of International Affairs
Programs in:
Asian studies (MA)
European and Eurasian studies (MA)
international affairs (MA, MIPP, MIS)
international development studies (MA)
international policy and practice (MIPP, MIS)
international trade and investment policy (MA)
Latin American and hemispheric studies (MA)
science, technology, and public policy (MA)
security policy studies (MA)

Graduate School of Education and Human Development
Programs in:
counseling (PhD, Ed S)
counseling: school, community and rehabilitation (MA Ed)
curriculum and instruction (MA Ed, Ed D, Ed S)
early childhood special education (MA Ed)
education and human development (M Ed, MA Ed, MAT, Ed D, PhD, Certificate, Ed S)
education policy (Ed D)
education policy studies (MA Ed)
educational administration (Ed D)
educational administration and policy studies (Ed D)
educational human development (MA Ed)
educational leadership and administration (MA Ed, Ed S)
educational technology leadership (MA Ed)
elementary education (M Ed)
higher education administration (MA Ed, Ed D, Ed S)
human resource development (MA Ed, Ed D, Ed S)
infant special education (MA Ed)
international education (MA Ed)
museum education (MAT)
secondary education (M Ed)
special education (Ed D, Ed S)
special education of seriously emotionally disturbed students (MA Ed)
transitional special education (MA Ed, Certificate)

Law School
Program in:
law (JD, LL M, SJD)

National Institutes of Health Sponsored Programs
Program in:
biomedical sciences (PhD)

School of Business
Programs in:
accountancy (M Accy, MBA, PhD)
business (M Accy, MBA, MS, MSF, MSIST, MTA, PMBA, PhD, Professional Certificate)
business economics and public policy (MBA)
event and meeting management (MTA)
event management (Professional Certificate)
finance (MSF, PhD)
finance and investments (MBA)
human resources management (MBA)
information systems (MSIST)
information systems development (MSIST)
information systems management (MBA)
information systems project management (MSIST)
international business (MBA, PhD)
international hotel management (MTA)
logistics, operations, and materials management (MBA)
management and organization (PhD)
management decision making (MBA, PhD)
management information systems (MSIST)
management of science, technology, and innovation (MBA)
marketing (MBA, PhD)
organizational behavior and development (MBA)
project management (MS)
real estate development (MBA)
sports management (MTA)
strategic management and public policy (PhD)
sustainable destination management (MTA)
tourism administration (MTA)
tourism and hospitality management (MBA)
tourism destination management (Professional Certificate)

School of Engineering and Applied Science
Programs in:
civil and environmental engineering (MS, D Sc, App Sc, Engr)

The George Washington University (continued)

computer science (MS, D Sc, App Sc, Engr)
electrical and computer engineering (MS, D Sc)
engineering and applied science (MEM, MS, D Sc, App Sc, Engr)
engineering management and systems engineering (MEM, MS, D Sc, App Sc, Engr)
mechanical and aerospace engineering (MS, D Sc, App Sc, Engr)
telecommunication and computers (MS)

School of Medicine and Health Sciences

Programs in:
adult nurse practitioner (MSN, Post Master's Certificate)
advanced family nurse practitioner (Post Master's Certificate)
clinical practice management (MSHS)
clinical research administration (MSHS)
clinical research administration for nurses (MSN)
emergency services management (MSHS)
end-of-life care (MSHS, MSN)
family nurse practitioner (MSN)
immunohematology (MSHS)
medicine (MD)
medicine and health sciences (MD, MSHS, MSN, DPT, Post Master's Certificate)
nursing leadership and management (MSN)
oral biology (MSHS)
physical therapy (DPT)
physician assistant (MSHS)

School of Public Health and Health Services

Programs in:
biostatistics (MPH)
community-oriented primary care (MPH)
environmental and occupational health (Dr PH)
epidemiology (MPH)
exercise science (MS)
health behavior (Dr PH)
health information systems (MPH)
health management and leadership (MHSA)
health policy (MHSA, Dr PH)
health promotion (MPH)
health services administration (Specialist)
international health policy and programs (MPH)
international health promotion (MPH)
maternal and child health (MPH)
microbiology and emerging infectious diseases (MSPH)
public health and emergency management (Certificate)
public health and health services (MHSA, MPH, MS, MSPH, Dr PH, Certificate, Specialist)
public health management (MPH)

■ HOWARD UNIVERSITY

Washington, DC 20059-0002
http://www.howard.edu/

Independent, coed, university. CGS member. *Computer facilities:* Computer purchase and lease plans are available. 6,343 computers available on campus for general student use. A campuswide network can be accessed from student residence rooms and from off campus. Internet access and online class registration, student residential network are available. *Library facilities:* Founders Library plus 8 others. *General application contact:* Associate Dean for Student Relations, 202-806-4676.

College of Dentistry

Programs in:
advanced education program general dentistry (Certificate)
dentistry (DDS)
general dentistry (Certificate)
oral and maxillofacial surgery (Certificate)
orthodontics (Certificate)
pediatric dentistry (Certificate)

College of Engineering, Architecture, and Computer Sciences

Program in:
engineering, architecture, and computer sciences (M Eng, MCS, MS, PhD)

School of Engineering and Computer Science
Programs in:
chemical engineering (MS)
civil engineering (M Eng)
electrical engineering (M Eng, PhD)
engineering and computer science (M Eng, MCS, MS, PhD)
mechanical engineering (M Eng, PhD)
systems and computer science (MCS)

College of Medicine

Programs in:
biochemistry and molecular biology (PhD)
biotechnology (MS)
medicine (MD, MS, PhD)
microbiology (PhD)
pharmacology (MS, PhD)

College of Pharmacy, Nursing and Allied Health Sciences

Dr. Beatrice Adderley-Kelly, Interim Dean
Program in:
pharmacy, nursing and allied health sciences (Pharm D, MSN, Certificate)

Division of Nursing
Dr. Mamie C. Montague, Associate Dean (Interim)
Programs in:
nurse practitioner (Certificate)
primary family health nursing (MSN)

School of Pharmacy
Dr. Clarence E. Curry, Associate Dean (Interim)
Program in:
pharmacy (Pharm D)

Graduate School

Dr. Orlando L. Taylor, Dean
Programs in:
African diaspora (MA, PhD)
African history (MA, PhD)
African studies (MA, PhD)
analytical chemistry (MS, PhD)
anatomy (MS, PhD)
applied mathematics (MS, PhD)
atmospheric (MS, PhD)
atmospheric sciences (MS, PhD)
biochemistry (MS, PhD)
biology (MS, PhD)
biophysics (PhD)
clinical psychology (PhD)
developmental psychology (PhD)
economics (MA, PhD)
English (MA, PhD)
environmental (MS, PhD)
exercise physiology (MS)
experimental psychology (PhD)
French (MA)
health education (MS)
inorganic chemistry (MS, PhD)
Latin America and the Caribbean (MA, PhD)
mathematics (MS, PhD)
neuropsychology (PhD)
nutrition (MS, PhD)
organic chemistry (MS, PhD)
personality psychology (PhD)
philosophy (MA)
physical chemistry (MS, PhD)
physics (MS, PhD)
physiology (PhD)
political science (MA, PhD)
psychology (MS)
public administration (MAPA)
public affairs (MA)
public history (MA)
social psychology (PhD)
sociology (MA, PhD)
Spanish (MA)
sports studies (MS)
United States history (MA, PhD)
urban recreation (MS)

Division of Fine Arts
Programs in:
3D reality (sculpture and ceramics) (MFA)
applied music (MM)
art history (MA)
design (MFA)
electronic studio (MFA)
fine arts (MFA)
history of art and visual culture (MA)
instrument (MM Ed)
jazz studies (MM)
organ (MM Ed)
painting (MFA)
photography (MFA)
piano (MM Ed)
voice (MM Ed)

School of Business
Programs in:
- accounting (MBA)
- business (MBA)
- entrepreneurship (MBA)
- finance (MBA)
- information systems (MBA)
- international business (MBA)
- marketing (MBA)
- supply chain management (MBA)

School of Communications
Programs in:
- communication sciences (PhD)
- communications (MA, MFA, MS, PhD)
- film (MFA)
- intercultural communication (MA, PhD)
- organizational communication (MA, PhD)
- speech pathology (MS)

Division of Mass Communication and Media Studies
Programs in:
- mass communication (MA, PhD)
- media studies (MA, PhD)

School of Divinity
Program in:
- theology (M Div, MARS, D Min)

School of Education
Dr. Leslie T. Fenwick
Programs in:
- counseling and guidance (M Ed, MA, CAGS)
- counseling psychology (M Ed, MA, PhD, CAGS)
- early childhood education (M Ed, MA, MAT, CAGS)
- education (M Ed, MA, MAT, MS, Ed D, PhD, CAGS)
- educational administration (M Ed, MA, Ed D, CAGS)
- educational administration and policy (Ed D)
- educational psychology (M Ed, MA, Ed D, PhD, CAGS)
- elementary education (M Ed)
- human development (MS)
- reading (M Ed, MA, MAT, CAGS)
- school psychology (M Ed, MA, Ed D, PhD, CAGS)
- secondary education (M Ed, MA, MAT, CAGS)
- special education (M Ed, MA, CAGS)

School of Law
Program in:
- law (JD, LL M)

School of Social Work
Program in:
- social work (MSW, PhD)

■ SOUTHEASTERN UNIVERSITY
Washington, DC 20024-2788
http://www.seu.edu/

Independent, coed, comprehensive institution. *Computer facilities:* 137 computers available on campus for general student use. A campuswide network can be accessed from off campus. *Library facilities:* The Learning Resources Center plus 1 other. *General application contact:* Director of Admissions, 202-265-5343.

College of Graduate Studies
Programs in:
- accounting (MBA)
- business (MBA, MPA, MS, MSMOT)
- computer science (MBA, MS)
- financial management (MBA)
- government program management (MPA, MSMOT)
- health services administration (MPA)
- international management (MBA)
- management (MBA)
- management information systems (MBA)
- marketing (MBA)
- public administration (MPA)
- taxation (MS)

■ STRAYER UNIVERSITY
Washington, DC 20005-2603
http://www.strayer.edu/

Proprietary, coed, comprehensive institution. *Computer facilities:* 1,500 computers available on campus for general student use. A campuswide network can be accessed. Internet access and online class registration are available. *Library facilities:* Wilkes Library plus 20 others. *General application contact:* Campus Manager, 202-408-2400.

Graduate Studies
Programs in:
- accounting (MS)
- acquisition (MBA)
- business administration (MBA)
- communications technology (MS)
- educational management (M Ed)
- finance (MBA)
- health services administration (MHSA)
- hospitality and tourism management (MBA)
- human resource management (MBA)
- information systems (MS)
- management (MBA)
- management information systems (MS)
- marketing (MBA)
- professional accounting (MS)
- public administration (MPA)
- supply chain management (MBA)
- technology in education (M Ed)

■ TRINITY (WASHINGTON) UNIVERSITY
Washington, DC 20017-1094
http://www.trinitydc.edu/

Independent-religious, Undergraduate: women only; graduate: coed, comprehensive institution. *Computer facilities:* 80 computers available on campus for general student use. A campuswide network can be accessed from student residence rooms and from off campus. Internet access and online class registration are available. *Library facilities:* Sister Helen Sheehan Library plus 1 other. *General application contact:* Director of Admissions for School of Education and School of Professional Studies, 202-884-9400.

School of Education
Programs in:
- democracy, diversity, and social justice (M Ed)
- early childhood (MAT)
- educational administration (MSA)
- elementary education (MAT)
- English as a second language (M Ed, MAT)
- literacy and reading education (M Ed)
- school counseling (MA)
- secondary education (MAT)
- special education (MAT)

School of Professional Studies
Programs in:
- business administration (MBA)
- communication (MA)
- information security management (MS)
- organizational management (MSA)

■ UNIVERSITY OF THE DISTRICT OF COLUMBIA
Washington, DC 20008-1175
http://www.udc.edu/

District-supported, coed, comprehensive institution. CGS member. *Enrollment:* 5,534 graduate, professional, and undergraduate students; 70 full-time matriculated graduate/professional students (43 women), 92 part-time matriculated graduate/professional students (61 women). *Graduate faculty:* 30. *Computer facilities:* 1,500 computers available on campus for general student use. A campuswide network can be accessed. *Library facilities:* Learning Resources Division Library plus 1 other. *General application contact:* LaVerne Hill Flannigan, Processor, Graduate Applications, 202-274-5008.

College of Arts and Sciences
Dr. Rachel Petty, Dean
Programs in:
- arts and sciences (MA, MS, MST)
- clinical psychology (MS)
- counseling (MS)

University of the District of Columbia (continued)
- early childhood education (MA)
- English composition and rhetoric (MA)
- mathematics (MST)
- special education (MA)
- speech and language pathology (MS)

David A. Clarke School of Law
Program in:
- law (JD)

School of Business and Public Administration
Dr. Melanie Anderson, Dean
Programs in:
- business administration (MBA)
- business and public administration (MBA, MPA)
- public administration (MPA)

Florida

■ AMERICAN INTERCONTINENTAL UNIVERSITY
Weston, FL 33326
http://www.aiufl.edu/

Proprietary, coed, comprehensive institution. *Enrollment:* 1,844 graduate, professional, and undergraduate students; 99 full-time matriculated graduate/professional students (58 women), 8 part-time matriculated graduate/professional students (5 women). *Graduate faculty:* 8 full-time (1 woman), 4 part-time/adjunct (0 women). *Computer facilities:* Computer purchase and lease plans are available. 35 computers available on campus for general student use. A campuswide network can be accessed from off campus. Internet access is available. *Library facilities:* AIU Fort Lauderdale Library. *General application contact:* Dr. Tom Takach, Vice President, Academic Affairs, 954-446-6119.

Program in Information Technology
Andy Blitz, Associate Dean
Programs in:
- Internet security (MIT)
- wireless computer forensics (MIT)

Program in Instructional Technology
Dr. Fabian Cone, Director of Institutional Effectiveness
Program in:
- instructional technology (M Ed)

Program in International Business
Dr. David Kalichavan, Acting Dean, School of Business
Programs in:
- accounting and finance (MBA)
- human resource management (MBA)
- management (MBA)
- marketing (MBA)

■ ARGOSY UNIVERSITY, SARASOTA CAMPUS
Sarasota, FL 34235-8246
http://www.sarasota.edu/

Proprietary, coed, upper-level institution. CGS member. *Enrollment:* 1,400 full-time matriculated graduate/professional students (1,000 women), 600 part-time matriculated graduate/professional students (400 women). *Graduate faculty:* 37 full-time (19 women), 100 part-time/adjunct (44 women). *Computer facilities:* 80 computers available on campus for general student use. A campuswide network can be accessed. Internet access and online class registration are available. *Library facilities:* Doris Pickett Library. *General application contact:* Dr. Linda Volz, Director of Admissions, 800-331-5995 Ext. 222.

College of Business
Dr. Kathleen Cornett, Dean
Programs in:
- accounting (DBA, Adv C)
- customized professional concentration (MBA, DBA)
- finance (MBA, Certificate)
- healtcare administration (Certificate)
- healthcare administration (MBA)
- information systems (DBA, Adv C)
- information systems management (MBA, Certificate)
- international business (MBA, DBA, Adv C, Certificate)
- management (MBA, MSM, DBA)
- mangement (Adv C)
- marketing (MBA, DBA, Adv C, Certificate)

College of Education
Dr. Chuck Mlynarczyk, Dean
Programs in:
- community college educational leadership (Ed D)
- educational leadership (MA Ed, Ed D, Ed S)
- instructional leadership (MA Ed, Ed D, Ed S)

College of Psychology and Behavioral Sciences
Dr. Douglas Riedmiller, Dean
Programs in:
- clinical psychology (Psy D)
- community counseling (MA)
- counseling psychology (Ed D)
- counselor education and supervision (Ed D)
- forensic psychology (MA)
- marriage and family therapy (MA)
- mental health counseling (MA)
- organizational leadership (Ed D)
- pastoral community counseling (Ed D)
- school counseling (MA, Ed S)
- school psychology (MA)

■ ARGOSY UNIVERSITY, TAMPA CAMPUS
Tampa, FL 33614
http://www.argosyu.edu/

Proprietary, coed, upper-level institution. CGS member. *Enrollment:* 385 full-time matriculated graduate/professional students (304 women), 184 part-time matriculated graduate/professional students (146 women). *Graduate faculty:* 6. *Library facilities:* Main library plus 1 other. *General application contact:* Susan Beecroft, Campus Administration Coordinator, 800-850-6488.

College of Business
Dr. Andrew Ghillyer, Dean
Programs in:
- accounting (DBA)
- customized professional concentration (MBA, DBA)
- finance (MBA, Certificate)
- healthcare administration (MBA, Certificate)
- information systems (DBA)
- information systems management (MBA)
- international business (MBA, DBA, Certificate)
- management (MBA, MSM, DBA)
- marketing (MBA, DBA, Certificate)
- public administration (MBA)

College of Education
Dr. Patty O'Grady, Head
Programs in:
- community college executive leadership (Ed D)
- educational leadership (MA Ed, Ed D, Ed S)
- instructional leadership (MA Ed, Ed D, Ed S)

College of Psychology and Behavioral Sciences
Programs in:
- clinical psychology (MA, Psy D)
- counselor education and supervision (Ed D)
- marriage and family therapy (MA)
- mental health counseling (MA)
- organizational leadership (Ed D)
- school counseling (MA)

Program in Clinical Psychology
Dr. Melanie Storms, Department Head
Programs in:
- child and adolescent psychology (MA)
- clinical psychology (Psy D)
- geropsychology (MA)
- marriage/couples and family therapy (MA)
- neuropsychology (MA)

■ BARRY UNIVERSITY
Miami Shores, FL 33161-6695
http://www.barry.edu/

Independent-religious, coed, university. *Enrollment:* 8,885 graduate, professional, and undergraduate students; 1,935 full-time matriculated graduate/professional students (1,249 women), 1,497 part-time matriculated graduate/professional students (1,111 women). *Graduate faculty:* 142 full-time (80 women). *Computer facilities:* Computer purchase and lease plans are available. 368 computers available on campus for general student use. A campuswide network can be accessed from student residence rooms and from off campus. Internet access is available. *Library facilities:* Monsignor William Barry Memorial Library plus 1 other. *General application contact:* Dave Fletcher, Director of Graduate Admissions, 305-899-3113.

Find University Details at www.petersons.com/gradchannel.

Andreas School of Business
Dr. Jack Scarborough, Dean
Programs in:
accounting (MSA)
business (MBA, MSA, MSM, Certificate)
business administration (MBA)
finance (Certificate)
health services administration (Certificate)
international business (Certificate)
management (Certificate)
management information systems (Certificate)
marketing (Certificate)

School of Adult and Continuing Education
Dr. Carol Rae Sodano, Dean
Programs in:
administrative studies (MA)
adult and continuing education (MA, MPA, MS)
information technology (MS)
public administration (MPA)

School of Arts and Sciences
Dr. Christopher Starratt, Interim Dean
Programs in:
arts and sciences (MA, MFA, MS, D Min, Certificate, SSP)
broadcasting (Certificate)
clinical psychology (MS)
communication (MA)
liberal studies (MA)
ministry (D Min)
organizational communication (MS)
pastoral ministry for Hispanics (MA)
pastoral theology (MA)
photography (MA, MFA)
practical theology (MA)
school psychology (MS, SSP)

School of Education
Dr. Terry Piper, Dean
Programs in:
accomplished teacher (Ed S)
advanced teaching and learning with technology (Certificate)
counseling (MS, PhD, Ed S)
culture, language and literacy (TESOL) (PhD)
curriculum evaluation and research (PhD)
distance education (Certificate)
early childhood (Ed S)
early childhood education (PhD)
education (MS, Ed D, PhD, Certificate, Ed S)
education for teachers of students with hearing impairments (MS)
educational computing and technology (MS, Ed S)
educational leadership (MS, Ed D, Certificate, Ed S)
educational technology (PhD)
elementary (Ed S)
elementary education (MS, PhD)
elementary education/ESOL (MS)
ESOL (Ed S)
exceptional student education (MS, PhD, Ed S)
gifted (Ed S)
higher education administration (MS, PhD)
higher education technology integration (Certificate)
human resource development (PhD)
human resource development and administration (MS)
human resources: not for profit and religious organizations (Certificate)
K-12 technology integration (Certificate)
leadership (PhD)
marital, couple and family counseling/therapy (MS, Ed S)
mental health counseling (MS, Ed S)
Montessori (Ed S)
Montessori education (MS, Ed S)
PKP/elementary (Ed S)
pre-k/primary (MS)
pre-k/primary/ESOL (MS)
reading (Ed S)
reading, language and cognition (PhD)
rehabilitation counseling (MS, Ed S)
school counseling (MS, Ed S)
technology and TESOL (MS, Ed S)
TESOL (MS)
TESOL international (MS)

School of Graduate Medical Sciences
Dr. Chet Evans, Dean
Programs in:
anatomy (MS)
medical sciences (DPM, MCMS, MPH, MS)
physician assistant (MCMS)
podiatric medicine and surgery (DPM)
public health (MPH)

School of Human Performance and Leisure Sciences
Dr. G. Jean Cerra, Dean
Programs in:
athletic training (MS)
biomechanics (MS)
exercise science (MS)
human performance and leisure sciences (MS)
movement science (MS)
sport and exercise psychology (MS)
sport management (MS)

School of Law
Leticia Diaz, Dean
Program in:
law (JD)

School of Natural and Health Sciences
Sr. John Karen Frei, Dean
Programs in:
anesthesiology (MS)
biology (MS)
biomedical sciences (MS)
health care leadership (Certificate)
health care planning and informatics (Certificate)
health services administration (MS)
histotechnology (Certificate)
long term care management (Certificate)
medical group practice management (Certificate)
natural and health sciences (MS, Certificate)
occupational therapy (MS)
quality improvement and outcomes management (Certificate)

School of Nursing
Dr. Pegge L. Bell, Dean
Programs in:
acute care nurse practitioner (MSN)
family nurse practitioner (MSN)
nurse practitioner (Certificate)
nursing (MSN, PhD, Certificate)
nursing administration (MSN, PhD, Certificate)
nursing education (MSN, Certificate)

School of Social Work
Dr. Debra McPhee, Dean
Program in:
social work (MSW, PhD)

■ DEVRY UNIVERSITY
Orlando, FL 32839
http://www.devry.edu/

Proprietary, coed, comprehensive institution. *Computer facilities:* Computer purchase and lease plans are available. 310 computers available on campus for general student use. A campuswide network can be accessed from off campus. Internet access and online class registration are available. *Library facilities:* Learning Resource Center.

Keller Graduate School of Management
Program in:
management (MAFM, MBA, MHRM, MISM, MNCM, MPA, MPM)

■ EMBRY-RIDDLE AERONAUTICAL UNIVERSITY
Daytona Beach, FL 32114-3900
http://www.embryriddle.edu/

Independent, coed, comprehensive institution. *Enrollment:* 4,863 graduate, professional, and undergraduate students; 283 full-time matriculated graduate/professional students (71 women), 107 part-time matriculated graduate/professional students (27 women). *Graduate faculty:* 46 full-time (6 women), 4 part-time/adjunct (1 woman). *Computer facilities:* 884 computers available on campus for general student use. A campuswide network can be accessed from student residence rooms and from off campus. Internet access and online class registration are available. *Library facilities:* Jack R. Hunt Memorial Library. *Graduate expenses:* Tuition: full-time $12,240; part-time $1,020 per credit. *General application contact:* Tom Shea, Director, International and Graduate Admissions, 800-388-3728.

Daytona Beach Campus Graduate Program
Dr. Thomas Connolly, Chancellor
Programs in:
- aeronautics (MBAA, MS, MS Sp C, MSA, MSAE, MSE, MSHFS)
- aerospace engineering (MSAE)
- applied aviation sciences (MSA)
- business administration in aviation (MBAA)
- engineering physics (space science) (MS)
- human factors engineering (MSHFS)
- software engineering (MSE)
- space science (MS Sp C)
- systems engineering (MSHFS)

■ EMBRY-RIDDLE AERONAUTICAL UNIVERSITY WORLDWIDE
Daytona Beach, FL 32114-3900
http://www.embryriddle.edu/

Independent, coed, comprehensive institution. *Enrollment:* 16,826 graduate, professional, and undergraduate students; 1,857 full-time matriculated graduate/professional students (310 women), 2,118 part-time matriculated graduate/professional students (343 women). *Graduate faculty:* 69 full-time (15 women), 326 part-time/adjunct (38 women). *Library facilities:* Jack R. Hunt Memorial Library. *Graduate expenses:* Tuition: full-time $7,800; part-time $325 per credit. *General application contact:* Pam Thomas, Director of Enrollment Management, 386-226-6910.

Worldwide Headquarters
Dr. Martin A. Smith, Chancellor
Programs in:
- aeronautics (MAS)
- management (MSM)
- technical management (MSTM)

■ EVEREST UNIVERSITY
Clearwater, FL 33759
http://www.everest.edu/

Proprietary, coed, comprehensive institution. *Computer facilities:* 42 computers available on campus for general student use. A campuswide network can be accessed. Internet access is available. *Library facilities:* Laurel Raffel Memorial Library. *General application contact:* Information Contact, 727-725-2688.

Graduate School of Business
Program in:
- business (MBA)

■ FLORIDA AGRICULTURAL AND MECHANICAL UNIVERSITY
Tallahassee, FL 32307-3200
http://www.famu.edu/

State-supported, coed, university. CGS member. *Computer facilities:* A campuswide network can be accessed from student residence rooms and from off campus. Internet access is available. *Library facilities:* Coleman Memorial Library plus 5 others. *General application contact:* Dean of Graduate Studies, Research, and Continuing Education, 850-599-3315.

College of Law
Program in:
- law (JD)

Division of Graduate Studies, Research, and Continuing Education

College of Arts and Sciences
Programs in:
- African American history (MASS)
- arts and sciences (MASS, MS, MSW, PhD)
- biology (MS)
- chemistry (MS)
- community psychology (MS)
- criminal justice (MASS)
- economics (MASS)
- history (MASS)
- history and political sciences (MASS, MSW)
- physics (MS, PhD)
- political science (MASS)
- public administration (MASS)
- public management (MASS)
- school psychology (MS)
- social work (MASS)
- sociology (MASS)
- software engineering (MS)

College of Education
Programs in:
- administration and supervision (M Ed, MS Ed, PhD)
- adult education (M Ed, MS Ed)
- biology (M Ed)
- business education (MBE)
- chemistry (MS Ed)
- early childhood and elementary education (M Ed, MS Ed)
- education (M Ed, MBE, MS Ed, PhD)
- educational leadership (PhD)
- English (MS Ed)
- guidance and counseling (M Ed, MS Ed)
- health, physical education, and recreation (M Ed, MS Ed)
- history (MS Ed)
- industrial education (M Ed, MS Ed)
- math (MS Ed)
- physics (MS Ed)

College of Engineering Science, Technology, and Agriculture
Programs in:
- agribusiness (MS)
- animal science (MS)
- engineering science, technology, and agriculture (MS)
- engineering technology (MS)
- entomology (MS)
- food science (MS)
- international programs (MS)
- plant science (MS)

College of Pharmacy and Pharmaceutical Sciences
Programs in:
- environmental toxicology (PhD)
- medicinal chemistry (MS, PhD)
- pharmaceutics (MS, PhD)
- pharmacology/toxicology (MS, PhD)
- pharmacy administration (MS)
- pharmacy and pharmaceutical sciences (Pharm D, MPH, MS, Ex Doc, PhD)
- public health (MPH)

FAMU-FSU College of Engineering
Programs in:
- biomedical engineering (MS, PhD)
- chemical engineering (MS, PhD)
- civil engineering (MS, PhD)
- electrical engineering (MS, PhD)
- engineering (MS, PhD)
- environmental engineering (MS, PhD)
- industrial engineering (MS, PhD)
- mechanical engineering (MS, PhD)

School of Allied Health Sciences
Programs in:
- health administration (MS)
- physical therapy (MPT)

School of Architecture
Programs in:
- architectural studies (MS Arch)
- architecture (professional) (M Arch)
- landscape architecture (MLA)

School of Business and Industry
Programs in:
- accounting (MBA)

finance (MBA)
management information systems (MBA)
marketing (MBA)

School of Journalism Media and Graphic Arts
Program in:
journalism (MS)

School of Nursing
Program in:
nursing (MS)

Environmental Sciences Institute
Dr. Henry Neal Williams, Director
Program in:
environmental sciences (MS, PhD)

■ FLORIDA ATLANTIC UNIVERSITY
Boca Raton, FL 33431-0991
http://www.fau.edu/

State-supported, coed, university. CGS member. *Enrollment:* 25,385 graduate, professional, and undergraduate students; 1,500 full-time matriculated graduate/professional students (909 women), 1,976 part-time matriculated graduate/professional students (1,291 women). *Graduate faculty:* 1,023 full-time (452 women), 548 part-time/adjunct (257 women). *Computer facilities:* 822 computers available on campus for general student use. A campuswide network can be accessed from student residence rooms and from off campus. Internet access and online class registration are available. *Library facilities:* S. E. Wimberly Library plus 2 others. *Graduate expenses:* Full-time $4,394. Tuition, nonresident: full-time $16,441. *General application contact:* Joann Arlington, Graduate Studies-Admissions, 561-297-3624.

Charles E. Schmidt College of Science
Dr. Gary Perry, Dean
Programs in:
applied mathematics and statistics (MS)
biological sciences (MS, MST)
chemistry and biochemistry (MS, MST, PhD)
environmental sciences (MS)
geography (MA, MAT)
geology (MS)
mathematics (MS, MST, PhD)
physics (MS, MST, PhD)
psychology (MA, PhD)
science (MA, MAT, MS, MST, PhD)

Center for Complex Systems and Brain Sciences
Dr. J. A. Scott Kelso, Director
Program in:
complex systems and brain sciences (PhD)

College of Architecture, Urban and Public Affairs
Dr. Rosalyn Carter, Dean
Programs in:
architecture, urban and public affairs (MCJ, MNM, MPA, MSW, MURP, PhD)
criminology and criminal justice (MCJ)
urban and regional planning (MURP)

School of Public Administration
Dr. Hugh T. Miller, Director
Programs in:
nonprofit management (MNM)
public administration (MNM, MPA, PhD)

School of Social Work
Dr. Michele Hawkins, Director
Program in:
social work (MSW)

College of Biomedical Science
Dr. Michael Friedland, Dean
Program in:
biomedical science (MS, PhD)

College of Business
Dr. Dennis Coates, Dean
Programs in:
business (Exec MBA, M Ac, M Tax, MBA, MHA, MS, MST)
business administration (Exec MBA, MBA)
economics (MS, MST)
finance (MS)
health administration (MHA)

School of Accounting
Dr. Carl Borgia, Director
Programs in:
accounting (M Ac, M Tax)
taxation (M Tax)

College of Education
Dr. Gregory Aloia, Dean
Programs in:
adult/community education (M Ed, PhD, Ed S)
art teacher education (M Ed)
counselor education (M Ed)
curriculum and instruction (M Ed, Ed D, Ed S)
education (M Ed, MS, MSF, Ed D, PhD, Ed S)
educational leadership (M Ed, PhD, Ed S)
educational psychology (MSF)
educational research (MSF)
educational technology (MSF)
elementary education (M Ed)
emotional handicaps (M Ed)
exceptional student education (M Ed, Ed D)
exercise science and health promotion (M Ed, MS)
family counseling (Ed S)
foundations of education (M Ed)
foundations-educational research (M Ed)
foundations-educational technology (M Ed)
higher education management (M Ed, PhD)
learning disabilities (M Ed)
mental health counseling (M Ed, Ed S)
mental retardation (M Ed)
multicultural education (MSF)
reading teacher education (M Ed)
rehabilitation counseling (M Ed)
school counseling (Ed S)
special education (Ed D)
speech-language pathology (MS)
varying exceptionalities (M Ed)

College of Engineering
Dr. Karl Stevens, Dean
Programs in:
civil engineering (MS)
computer engineering (MS, PhD)
computer science (MS, PhD)
electrical engineering (MS, PhD)
engineering (MS, PhD)
mechanical engineering (MS, PhD)
ocean engineering (MS, PhD)

College of Nursing
Dr. Anne Boykin, Dean
Program in:
nursing (MS, DNS, Post Master's Certificate)

Dorothy F. Schmidt College of Arts and Letters
Dr. Sandra Norman, Interim Dean
Programs in:
American literature (MA)
anthropology (MA, MAT)
art education (MAT)
arts and letters (MA, MAT, MFA, MLBLST, PhD, Certificate)
ceramics (MFA)
communication (MA)
comparative literature (MA)
comparative studies (PhD)
creative writing (MFA)
English literature (MA)
fantasy and science fiction (MA)
French (MA)
German (MA)
history (MA)
liberal studies (MLBLST)
multicultural literature (MA)
music (MA)
painting (MFA)
political science (MA, MAT)
sociology (MA, MAT)
Spanish (MA)
teaching French (MAT)
teaching German (MAT)
teaching Spanish (MAT)
theatre (MFA)

Women's Studies Center
Dr. Marsha Rose, Director
Program in:
women's studies (MA, Certificate)

■ FLORIDA GULF COAST UNIVERSITY
Fort Myers, FL 33965-6565
http://www.fgcu.edu/

State-supported, coed, comprehensive institution. *Enrollment:* 8,292 graduate,

Florida Gulf Coast University (continued)
professional, and undergraduate students; 247 full-time matriculated graduate/professional students (184 women), 550 part-time matriculated graduate/professional students (378 women). *Graduate faculty:* 278 full-time (136 women), 194 part-time/adjunct (87 women). *Computer facilities:* 323 computers available on campus for general student use. A campuswide network can be accessed from student residence rooms and from off campus. Internet access and online class registration, online admissions and advising are available. *Library facilities:* Library Services. *Graduate expenses:* Tuition, state resident: full-time $4,326. Tuition, nonresident: full-time $18,523. Required fees: $1,211. One-time fee: $5 full-time. *General application contact:* Michael Sayarese, Director of Graduate Studies, 239-590-7988.

College of Arts and Sciences
Dr. Donna Price Henry, Dean
Programs in:
- arts and sciences (MA, MS)
- English (MA)
- environmental science (MS)

College of Business
Dr. Richard Pegnetter, Dean
Programs in:
- accounting and taxation (MS)
- business (MBA, MS)
- business administration (MBA)
- computer and information systems (MS)

College of Education
Dr. Marci Greene, Dean
Programs in:
- behavior disorders (MA)
- biology (MAT)
- counselor education (M Ed, MA)
- education (M Ed, MA, MAT)
- educational leadership (M Ed)
- educational technology (M Ed, MA)
- elementary education (M Ed, MA)
- English (MAT)
- mathematics (MAT)
- mental retardation (MA)
- reading education (M Ed)
- social sciences (MAT)
- specific learning disabilities (MA)
- varying exceptionalities (MA)

College of Health Professions
Dr. Denise Heinemann, Dean
Programs in:
- geriatric recreational therapy (MS)
- health professions (MS, MSN)
- health sciences (MS)
- occupational therapy (MS)
- physical therapy (MS)

School of Nursing
Dr. Peg Gray-Vickrey, Interim Director
Program in:
- nursing (MSN)

College of Public and Social Services
Dr. Barbara Stites, Assistant Director
Programs in:
- criminal justice (MPA)
- environmental policy (MPA)
- general public administration (MPA)
- management (MPA)
- public and social services (MPA, MSW)
- social work (MSW)

■ FLORIDA INSTITUTE OF TECHNOLOGY
Melbourne, FL 32901-6975
http://www.fit.edu/

Independent, coed, university. *Enrollment:* 4,741 graduate, professional, and undergraduate students; 627 full-time matriculated graduate/professional students (291 women), 1,687 part-time matriculated graduate/professional students (621 women). *Graduate faculty:* 155 full-time (24 women), 149 part-time/adjunct (19 women). *Computer facilities:* 400 computers available on campus for general student use. A campuswide network can be accessed from student residence rooms and from off campus. Internet access and online class registration are available. *Library facilities:* Evans Library. *Graduate expenses:* Tuition: part-time $900 per credit. *General application contact:* Carolyn P. Farrior, Director of Graduate Admissions, 321-674-7118.

Find University Details at www.petersons.com/gradchannel.

Graduate Programs
Antionet Mortara, Director Graduate Programs

College of Aeronautics
Dr. Ken Stackpoole, Dean
Programs in:
- airport development and management (MSA)
- applied aviation safety (MSA)
- aviation human factors (MS)

College of Business
Dr. Robert H. Fronk, Interim Dean
Program in:
- business (EMBA, MBA)

College of Engineering
Dr. Thomas Waite, Dean
Programs in:
- aerospace engineering (MS, PhD)
- biological oceanography (MS)
- chemical engineering (MS, PhD)
- chemical oceanography (MS)
- civil engineering (MS, PhD)
- coastal zone management (MS)
- computer engineering (MS, PhD)
- computer science (MS, PhD)
- electrical engineering (MS, PhD)
- engineering (MS, PhD)
- engineering management (MS)
- environmental resource management (MS)
- environmental science (MS, PhD)
- geological oceanography (MS)
- mechanical engineering (MS, PhD)
- meteorology (MS)
- ocean engineering (MS, PhD)
- oceanography (MS, PhD)
- physical oceanography (MS)
- software engineering (MS)
- systems engineering (MS)

College of Psychology and Liberal Arts
Dr. Mary Beth Kenkel, Dean
Programs in:
- applied behavior analysis (MS)
- clinical psychology (Psy D)
- communication (MS)
- humanities and communication (MS)
- industrial/organizational psychology (MS, PhD)
- psychology (MS, PhD, Psy D)

College of Science
Dr. Gordon L. Nelson, Dean
Programs in:
- applied mathematics (MS, PhD)
- biological sciences (PhD)
- biotechnology (MS)
- cell and molecular biology (MS, PhD)
- chemistry (MS, PhD)
- computer education (MS)
- ecology (MS)
- elementary science education (M Ed)
- environmental education (MS)
- marine biology (MS)
- mathematics education (MS, Ed D, PhD, Ed S)
- operations research (MS, PhD)
- physics (MS, PhD)
- science (M Ed, MAT, MS, Ed D, PhD, Ed S)
- science and mathematics education (MAT)
- science education (MS, Ed D, PhD, Ed S)
- space sciences (MS, PhD)

University College
Dr. Clifford Bragdon, Dean
Programs in:
- acquisition and contract management (MS, PMBA)
- aerospace engineering (MS)
- business administration (PMBA)
- computer information systems (MS)
- computer science (MS)
- e-business (PMBA)
- electrical engineering (MS)
- engineering management (MS)
- human resource management (PMBA)
- human resources management (MS)
- information systems (PMBA)
- logistics management (MS)
- management (MS)
- materiel acquisition management (MS)
- mechanical engineering (MS)
- operations research (MS)

project management (MS)
public administration (MPA)
software engineering (MS)
space systems (MS)
space systems management (MS)
systems management (MS)

■ FLORIDA INTERNATIONAL UNIVERSITY
Miami, FL 33199
http://www.fiu.edu/

State-supported, coed, university. CGS member. *Enrollment:* 37,997 graduate, professional, and undergraduate students; 3,330 full-time matriculated graduate/professional students (1,882 women), 2,415 part-time matriculated graduate/professional students (1,495 women). *Graduate faculty:* 759 full-time (259 women), 11 part-time/adjunct (5 women). *Computer facilities:* 600 computers available on campus for general student use. A campuswide network can be accessed from student residence rooms and from off campus. Internet access and online class registration are available. *Library facilities:* University Park Library plus 2 others. *Graduate expenses:* Tuition, state resident: part-time $249 per credit hour. Tuition, nonresident: part-time $753 per credit hour. Tuition and fees vary according to program. *General application contact:* Nanette Rojas, Coordinator of Graduate Admissions, 305-348-7442.

Find University Details at www.petersons.com/gradchannel.

Alvah H. Chapman, Jr. Graduate School of Business
Dr. Joyce J. Elam, Executive Dean
Programs in:
business administration (M Acc, MBA, MIB, MS, MSF, MST, PhD)
decision sciences and information systems (PhD)
finance (MSF)
international business (MIB)

School of Accounting
Dr. Christos Koulamas, Acting Director
Programs in:
accounting (M Acc)
taxation (MST)

College of Architecture and the Arts
Juan A. Bueno, Dean
Programs in:
architecture (MS)
art and art history (MFA)
landscape architecture (MS)
music (MM, MS)

School of Art and Art History
Dr. Juan Martinez, Director
Program in:
visual arts (MFA)

College of Arts and Sciences
Dr. Mark Szuchman, Interim Dean
Programs in:
African-new world studies (MA)
arts and sciences (MA, MFA, MM, MS, PhD)
biological management (MS)
biology (MS, PhD)
chemistry (MS, PhD)
comparative sociology (MA)
creative writing (MFA)
developmental psychology (PhD)
earth sciences (MS, PhD)
economics (MA, PhD)
energy (MS)
English (MA)
forensic science (MS)
general psychology (MS)
history (MA, PhD)
international relations (PhD)
international studies (MA)
Latin American and Caribbean studies (MA)
liberal studies (MA)
linguistics (MA)
mathematical sciences (MS)
physics (MS, PhD)
political science (MS, PhD)
pollution (MS)
psychology (MS)
religious studies (MA)
sociology (PhD)
Spanish (MA, PhD)
statistics (MS)

School of Music
Dr. Joseph Rohm, Director
Programs in:
music (MM)
music education (MS)

College of Education
Dr. Luis Miron, Unit Head
Programs in:
adult education (MS)
adult education in human resource development (Ed D)
advanced athletic injury training/sports medicine (MS)
advanced teacher preparation (MS)
art education (MAT, MS, Ed D)
conflict resolution and consensus building (Certificate)
counselor education (MS)
curriculum and instruction (Ed S)
curriculum development (MS)
curriculum studies (PhD)
early childhood education (MS, Ed D)
education (MA, MAT, MS, Ed D, PhD, Certificate, Ed S)
educational administration and supervision (Ed D)
educational leadership (MS, Certificate, Ed S)
elementary education (MS, Ed D)
English education (MAT, MS, Ed D)
exceptional student education (MS, Ed D)
exercise and sports science (MS)
foreign language education (Certificate)
foreign language education—teaching English to speakers of other languages (TESOL) (Certificate)
foreign language education- teaching English to speakers of other languages (TESOL) (MS)
French education—initial teacher preparation (MAT)
higher education (Ed D)
higher education administration (MS)
human resource development (MS)
international and intercultural development education (Ed D)
international and intercultural developmental education (MS)
language, literacy and culture (PhD)
learning technologies (MS, Ed D, PhD)
leisure services (MS)
mathematics education (MAT, MS, Ed D, PhD)
mental health counseling (MS)
modern language education/bilingual education (MS, Ed D)
parks and recreation management (MS)
physical education (MS)
reading education (MS, Ed D)
rehabilitation counseling (MS)
school counseling (MS)
school psychology (Ed S)
science education (MAT, MS, Ed D, PhD)
social studies education (MAT, MS, Ed D)
Spanish education—initial teacher preparation (MAT)
special education (MS)
sports management (MS)
strength and conditioning (MS)
teaching English (MS)
therapeutic recreation (MS)
urban education (MS)

College of Engineering and Computing
Dr. Vish Prasad, Executive Dean
Programs in:
biomedical engineering (MS, PhD)
civil engineering (MS, PhD)
computer engineering (MS)
construction management (MS)
electrical engineering (MS, PhD)
engineering and computing (MS, PhD)
environmental and urban systems (MS)
environmental engineering (MS)
industrial engineering (MS, PhD)
mechanical and materials engineering (MS, PhD)
telecommunications and networking (MS)

School of Computing and Information Sciences
Dr. Yi Deng, Director
Program in:
computing and information sciences (MS, PhD)

College of Law
Dr. Leonard Strickman, Dean

Florida International University (continued)
Program in:
law (JD)

College of Nursing and Health Sciences
Dr. Ray Thomlison, Acting Executive Dean
Programs in:
communication sciences and disorders (MS)
health sciences (MS)
health services administration (MHSA)
nursing and health sciences (MHSA, MS, MSN, PhD)
occupational therapy (MS)
physical therapy (MS)

School of Nursing
Dr. Divina Grossman, Dean
Program in:
nursing (MSN, PhD)

College of Social Work, Justice and Public Affairs
Dr. Ray Thomlison, Director
Program in:
social work, justice and public affairs (MPA, MS, MSW, PhD)

School of Criminal Justice
Dr. Lisa Stolzenberg, Head
Program in:
criminal justice (MS)

School of Public Administration
Dr. Meredith Newman, Director
Program in:
public administration (MPA, PhD)

School of Social Work
Dr. Gary Lowe, Acting Dean
Program in:
social work (MSW, PhD)

School of Hospitality Management
Dr. Joseph West, Dean
Program in:
hotel and food service management (MS)

School of Journalism and Mass Communication
Dr. Lillian Kopenhaver, Dean
Program in:
mass communication (MS)

School of Public Health
Dr. Michele Ciccazzo, Dean
Programs in:
dietetics and nutrition (MS, PhD)
public health (MHSA, MPH, MS, PhD)

■ FLORIDA STATE UNIVERSITY
Tallahassee, FL 32306
http://www.fsu.edu/

State-supported, coed, university. CGS member. *Enrollment:* 39,973 graduate, professional, and undergraduate students; 5,429 full-time matriculated graduate/professional students (2,854 women), 2,745 part-time matriculated graduate/professional students (1,722 women). *Graduate faculty:* 1,159 full-time (385 women), 119 part-time/adjunct (56 women). *Computer facilities:* Computer purchase and lease plans are available. 3,771 computers available on campus for general student use. A campuswide network can be accessed from student residence rooms and from off campus. Internet access and online class registration, course home pages, course search, online fee payment are available. *Library facilities:* Robert Manning Strozier Library plus 8 others. *Graduate expenses:* Tuition, state resident: full-time $5,822; part-time $243 per credit hour. Tuition, nonresident: full-time $20,976; part-time $874 per credit hour. Tuition and fees vary according to program. *General application contact:* Melanie Booker, Associate Director for Graduate Admissions, 850-644-3420.

Find University Details at www.petersons.com/gradchannel.

College of Law
Donald J. Weidner, Dean
Program in:
law (JD)

College of Medicine
Dr. J. Ocie Harris, Dean
Programs in:
biomedical sciences (PhD)
medicine (MD)

Graduate Studies
Dr. Nancy Marcus, Dean, Graduate Studies

College of Arts and Sciences
Dr. Joseph Travis, Dean
Programs in:
American and Florida studies (MA, Certificate)
analytical chemistry (MS, PhD)
anthropology (MA, MS, PhD)
applied behavior analysis (MS)
applied mathematics (MS, PhD)
applied statistics (MS)
arts and sciences (MA, MFA, MS, PhD, Certificate)
biochemistry (MS, PhD)
biochemistry, molecular and cell biology (PhD)
biomedical mathematics (MS, PhD)
biostatistics (MS, PhD)
cell biology (MS, PhD)
chemical physics (MS, PhD)
classical archaeology (MA)
classical civilization (MA, PhD)
classics (MA)
clinical psychology (PhD)
cognitive psychology (PhD)
computational structural biology (PhD)
computer science (MA, MS, PhD)
creative writing (MFA)
developmental biology (MS, PhD)
developmental psychology (PhD)
ecology (MS, PhD)
evolutionary biology (MS, PhD)
financial mathematics (MS, PhD)
French (MA, PhD)
genetics (MS, PhD)
geological sciences (MS, PhD)
geophysical fluid dynamics (PhD)
German (MA)
Greek (MA)
Greek and Latin (MA)
historical administration (MA)
history (MA, PhD)
history and philosophy of science (MA)
humanities (PhD)
immunology (MS, PhD)
information security (MS)
inorganic chemistry (MS, PhD)
interdisciplinary humanities (MA, PhD)
Italian (MA)
Italian studies (MA)
Latin (MA)
literature (MA, PhD)
marine biology (MS, PhD)
mathematical statistics (MS, PhD)
meteorology (MS, PhD)
microbiology (MS, PhD)
molecular biology (MS, PhD)
molecular biophysics (PhD)
neuroscience (PhD)
oceanography (MS, PhD)
organic chemistry (MS, PhD)
philosophy (MA, PhD)
physical chemistry (MS, PhD)
physics (MS, PhD)
plant sciences (MS, PhD)
pure mathematics (MS, PhD)
religion (MA, PhD)
rhetoric and composition (MA, PhD)
Slavic languages and literatures (MA)
Slavic languages/Russian (MA)
social psychology (PhD)
software engineering (MA, MS)
Spanish (MA, PhD)

College of Business
Dr. Caryn Beck-Duolley, Dean
Programs in:
accounting (M Acc)
business administration (MBA, PhD)
insurance (MSM)
management information systems (MS)

College of Communication
Dr. John K. Mayo, Dean
Programs in:
communication (Adv M, MA, MS, PhD)
communication sciences and disorders (Adv M, MS, PhD)
integrated marketing communication (MA, MS)
mass communication (MA, MS, PhD)
media and communication studies (MA, MS)
speech communication (PhD)

College of Criminology and Criminal Justice
Dr. Thomas Blomberg, Dean

Program in:
- criminology and criminal justice (MA, MSC, PhD)

College of Education
Dr. Marcy P Driscoll, Dean
Programs in:
- adult education and human resource development (MS, Ed D, PhD, Ed S)
- counseling/school psychology (PhD)
- early childhood education (MS, Ed D, PhD, Ed S)
- education (MS, Ed D, PhD, Ed S)
- educational administration/leadership (MS, Ed D, PhD, Ed S)
- educational leadership/administration (MS, Ed D, PhD, Ed S)
- educational psychology (MS, PhD)
- elementary education (MS, Ed D, PhD, Ed S)
- emotional disturbance/learning disabilities (MS)
- English education (MS, PhD, Ed S)
- health education (MS)
- higher education (MS, Ed D, PhD, Ed S)
- history and philosophy of education (MS, PhD, Ed S)
- institutional research (MS, Ed D, PhD, Ed S)
- instructional systems (MS, PhD, Ed S)
- international and intercultural education (MS, PhD, Ed S)
- learning and cognition (MS, PhD)
- mathematics education (MS, PhD, Ed S)
- measurement and statistics (MS, PhD)
- mental retardation (MS)
- multilingual-multicultural education (MS, PhD, Ed S)
- open and distance learning (MS)
- physical education (MS, Ed D, PhD, Ed S)
- policy planning and analysis (MS, Ed D, PhD, Ed S)
- program evaluation (MS, PhD)
- psychological services (MS, PhD, Ed S)
- reading education/language arts (MS, Ed D, PhD, Ed S)
- recreation management (MS)
- rehabilitation counseling (MS, PhD, Ed S)
- school psychology (MS, Ed S)
- science education (MS, PhD, Ed S)
- social science education (MS, Ed D, PhD, Ed S)
- social, history and philosophy of education (MS, PhD, Ed S)
- special education (MS, PhD, Ed S)
- sport management (MS, Ed D, PhD, Ed S)
- sports psychology (MS, PhD)
- visual disabilities (MS)

College of Human Sciences
Dr. Billie J. Collier, Dean
Programs in:
- apparel product development (MS)
- apparel/textile product development (PhD)
- child development (MS, PhD)
- creative design (MS)
- exercise science (PhD)
- family relations (MS, PhD)
- global product development (MS)
- human sciences (MS, PhD)
- marriage and family therapy (PhD)
- nutrition and food science (PhD)
- nutrition and food sciences (MS)
- professional merchandising (MS)
- retail merchandising (MS, PhD)
- textiles (MS)

College of Information
Dr. Lawrence Dennis, Dean
Program in:
- library and information studies (MS, PhD, Specialist)

College of Motion Picture, Television, and Recording Arts
Frank Patterson, Dean
Programs in:
- production (MFA)
- screen and play writing (MFA)

College of Music
Don Gibson, Dean
Programs in:
- accompanying (MM)
- arts administration (MA)
- choral conducting (MM)
- composition (MM, DM)
- ethnomusicology (MM)
- instrumental accompanying (MM)
- instrumental conducting (MM)
- jazz studies (MM)
- music education (MM Ed, Ed D, PhD)
- music theory (MM, PhD)
- music therapy (MM)
- musicology (MM, PhD)
- opera (MM)
- performance (MM, DM)
- piano pedagogy (MM)
- vocal accompanying (MM)

College of Nursing
Dr. Katherine P. Mason, Dean
Programs in:
- family nurse practitioner (MSN, Certificate)
- nurse educator (MSN, Certificate)
- pediatric nurse practitioner (MSN, Certificate)

College of Social Sciences
Dr. David W. Rasmussen, Dean
Programs in:
- Asian studies (MA)
- demography and population health (MS, Certificate)
- economics (MS, PhD)
- geographic information systems (MS)
- geography (MA, MS, PhD)
- international affairs (MA, MS)
- political science (MA, MS, PhD)
- public administration and policy (MPA, PhD, Certificate)
- Russian and East European studies (MA)
- social health sciences (MHPR, MPA, MPH, MS)
- social science (MA, MS)
- social sciences (MA, MHPR, MPA, MPH, MS, MSP, PhD, Certificate)
- sociology (MA, MS, PhD)
- urban and regional planning (MSP, PhD)

College of Social Work
Dr. C. Aaron McNeece, Dean
Programs in:
- clinical social work (MSW)
- social policy and administration (MSW)
- social work (PhD)

College of Visual Arts, Theatre and Dance
Dr. Sally E. McRorie, Dean
Programs in:
- American dance studies (MA)
- art education (MA, MS, Ed D, PhD, Ed S)
- art history (MA, PhD)
- dance (MFA)
- interior design (MA, MFA, MS)
- museum studies (Certificate)
- studio and related studies (MA)
- studio art (MFA)
- visual arts, theatre and dance (MA, MFA, MS, Ed D, PhD, Certificate, Ed S)

FAMU-FSU College of Engineering
Dr. Ching-Jen Chen, Dean and Professor
Programs in:
- biomedical engineering (MS, PhD)
- chemical engineering (MS, PhD)
- civil and environmental engineering (MS, PhD)
- electrical engineering (MS, PhD)
- engineering (MS, PhD)
- industrial engineering (MS, PhD)
- mechanical engineering (MS, PhD)

School of Theatre
Cameron Jackson, Director
Programs in:
- acting (MFA)
- directing (MFA)
- lighting, costume, and scenic design (MFA)
- technical production (MFA)
- theater management (MFA)
- theatre (MA, MS, PhD)

■ HODGES UNIVERSITY
Naples, FL 34119
http://www.internationalcollege.edu/

Independent, coed, comprehensive institution. *Enrollment:* 1,640 graduate, professional, and undergraduate students; 35 full-time matriculated graduate/professional students (22 women), 156 part-time matriculated graduate/professional students (100 women). *Graduate faculty:* 17 full-time (4 women). *Computer facilities:* 500 computers available on campus for general student use. A campuswide network can be

Hodges University (continued)
accessed. Internet access is available. *Library facilities:* Information Resource Center plus 1 other. *General application contact:* Terry McMahan, President, 239-513-1122.

■ JACKSONVILLE UNIVERSITY
Jacksonville, FL 32211-3394
http://www.ju.edu/

Independent, coed, comprehensive institution. *Computer facilities:* 450 computers available on campus for general student use. A campuswide network can be accessed from student residence rooms and from off campus. Internet access and online class registration are available. *Library facilities:* Carl S. Swisher Library. *General application contact:* Executive Director, Transfer and Graduate Enrollment, 904-256-7144.

College of Arts and Sciences
Program in:
arts and sciences (MAT, MSN, Certificate)

School of Education
Programs in:
computer sciences (MAT)
early childhood education (Certificate)
elementary education (MAT)
integrated learning with educational technology (MAT)
mathematics education (MAT)
music education (MAT)
reading education (MAT)
second career as a teacher (Certificate)
second careers as a teacher (Certificate)

School of Nursing
Program in:
nursing (MSN)

School of Orthodontics
Program in:
orthodontics (Certificate)

Davis College of Business
Programs in:
business (Exec MBA, MBA)
business administration (Exec MBA, MBA)

■ LYNN UNIVERSITY
Boca Raton, FL 33431-5598
http://www.lynn.edu/

Independent, coed, comprehensive institution. *Enrollment:* 2,715 graduate, professional, and undergraduate students; 143 full-time matriculated graduate/professional students (76 women), 272 part-time matriculated graduate/professional students (144 women). *Graduate faculty:* 36 full-time (16 women), 33 part-time/adjunct (10 women). *Computer facilities:* 150 computers available on campus for general student use. A campuswide network can be accessed from student residence rooms and from off campus. Internet access and online class registration are available. *Library facilities:* Eugene M. and Christine E. Lynn Library. *Graduate expenses:* Tuition: full-time $26,200. Required fees: $1,500. Tuition and fees vary according to class time, course load and degree level. *General application contact:* Dr. Larissa Baia, Assistant Director of Graduate Admissions, 561-237-7916 Ext. 7845.

College of Arts and Sciences
Dr. Pamela J. Monaco, Dean
Programs in:
applied psychology (MS)
criminal justice administration (MS)
emergency planning and administration (MS, Certificate)

College of Business and Management
Dr. Russell Boisjoly, Dean
Programs in:
aviation management (MBA)
financial valuation and investment management (MBA)
global leadership (PhD)
hospitality management (MBA)
international business (MBA)
marketing (MBA)
mass communication and media management (MBA)
sports and athletics administration (MBA)

Conservatory of Music
Dr. Jon Robertson, Dean
Programs in:
music performance (MM)
professional performance (Certificate)

Donald and Helen Ross College of Education
Dr. Patrick Hartwick, Dean
Programs in:
exceptional student education (M Ed)
global leadership (PhD)

Eugene M. and Christine E. Lynn College of International Communication
Dr. David L. Jaffe, Dean
Program in:
mass communication (MS)

■ NOVA SOUTHEASTERN UNIVERSITY
Fort Lauderdale, FL 33314-7796
http://www.nova.edu/

Independent, coed, university. CGS member. *Enrollment:* 25,960 graduate, professional, and undergraduate students; 10,055 full-time matriculated graduate/professional students (6,920 women), 10,492 part-time matriculated graduate/professional students (7,612 women). *Computer facilities:* 2,000 computers available on campus for general student use. A campuswide network can be accessed from student residence rooms and from off campus. Internet access and online class registration are available. *Library facilities:* Alvin Sherman Library, Research, and Information Technology Center plus 4 others. *General application contact:* Information Contact, 800-541-6682.

Center for Psychological Studies
Karen Grosby, Dean
Programs in:
clinical pharmacology (MS)
clinical psychology (PhD, Psy D, SPS)
mental health counseling (MS)
psychological studies (MS, PhD, Psy D, Psy S, SPS)
school guidance and counseling (MS)
school psychology (Psy S)

Fischler School of Education and Human Services
Dr. H. Wells Singleton, Provost/Dean
Programs in:
adult education (Ed D)
athletic administration (MS)
child and youth care administration (MS)
child and youth studies (Ed D)
cognitive and behavioral disabilities (MS)
computer science education (Ed S)
computer science education (K-12) (MS)
computing and information technology (Ed D)
curriculum and teaching (Ed S)
curriculum, instruction and technology (MS)
curriculum, instruction, management and administration (Ed S)
early childhood education administration (MS)
early childhood special education (MS)
early literacy and reading (Ed S)
early literacy education (MS)
education and human services (MA, MS, Ed D, SLPD, Ed S)
education technology (MS)
educational leaders (Ed D)
educational leadership (Ed D)
educational leadership (administration K–12) (MS, Ed S)
educational media (Ed S)
educational media (K-12) (MS)
elementary education (MS, Ed S)
English (MS, Ed S)
exceptional student education (MS)
family support studies (MS)
gifted education (MS, Ed S)
health care education (Ed D)
higher education (Ed D)
human serviced administration (Ed D)
instructional leadership (Ed D)
instructional technology and distance education (MS, Ed D)
instructional technology distance education (Ed D)
interdisciplinary arts education (MS)

management and administration of educational programs (MS)
mathematics (MS, Ed S)
multicultural early intervention (MS)
organizational leadership (Ed D)
pre-kindergarten/primary (MS)
preschool education (MS)
reading (MS, Ed S)
science (MS, Ed S)
secondary education (MS)
social studies (MS, Ed S)
Spanish language (MS)
special education (Ed D)
speech language pathology (Ed D)
speech-language pathology (MS, SLPD)
substance abuse counseling and education (MS)
teaching and learning (MA, MS)
teaching English to speakers of other languages (MS, Ed S)
technology management and administration (Ed S)
urban studies education (MS)
varying exceptionalities (Ed S)
vocational, occupational and technical education (Ed D)

Graduate School of Computer and Information Sciences
Dr. Edward Lieblein, Dean
Programs in:
computer information systems (MS, PhD)
computer science (MS, PhD)
computing technology in education (MS, PhD)
information security (MS)
information systems (PhD)
management information systems (MS)

Graduate School of Humanities and Social Sciences
Dr. Honggang Yang, Dean
Programs in:
college student affairs (MS)
college student personnel administration (Certificate)
community solutions and partnership (MS)
conflict analysis and resolution (MS, PhD)
conflict analysis and resolution studies (Certificate)
cross-disciplinary studies (MA)
family ministry (Certificate)
family studies (Certificate)
family systems healthcare (Certificate)
family therapy (MS, PhD, Certificate)
health care conflict resolution (Certificate)
humanities and social sciences (MA, MS, DMFT, PhD, Certificate)
marriage and family therapy (DMFT)
peace studies (Certificate)

Health Professions Division
Dr. Frederick Lippman, Chancellor
Program in:
health professions (DMD, DO, OD, Pharm D, MBS, MH Sc, MMS, MOT, MPH, MS, MSN, Au D, DHSc, DPT, OTD, PhD, TDPT)

College of Allied Health and Nursing
Dr. Richard Davis, Dean
Programs in:
allied health and nursing (MH Sc, MMS, MOT, MSN, Au D, DHSc, DPT, OTD, PhD, TDPT)
audiology (Au D)
health science (MH Sc, DHSc)
medical science/physician assistant (MMS)
nursing (MSN)
occupational therapy (MOT, OTD, PhD)
physical therapy (DPT, PhD, TDPT)

College of Dental Medicine
Dr. Robert A. Uchin, Dean
Programs in:
dental medicine (DMD)
dentistry (MS)

College of Medical Sciences
Dr. Harold E. Laubach, Dean
Program in:
biomedical sciences (MBS)

College of Optometry
Dr. David Loshin, Dean
Programs in:
clinical vision research (MS)
optometry (OD)

College of Osteopathic Medicine
Dr. Anthony J. Silavgni, Dean
Programs in:
osteopathic medicine (DO)
public health (MPH)

College of Pharmacy
Dr. Andrés Malavé, Dean
Program in:
pharmacy (Pharm D)

H. Wayne Huizenga School of Business and Entrepreneurship
Dr. Randolph A. Pohlman, Dean
Programs in:
accounting (M Acc)
business administration (MBA, DBA)
human resources management (MSHRM)
international business administration (MIBA, DIBA)
leadership (MS)
public administration (MPA, DPA)
real estate development (MBA)
taxation (MT)

Institute Studies
Dr. Tammy Kushner, Director
Programs in:
counseling (MS)
criminal justice (MS)

Oceanographic Center
Dr. Richard Dodge, Dean
Programs in:
coastal zone management (MS)
marine biology (MS, PhD)
marine biology and oceanography (PhD)
marine environmental science (MS)
oceanography (PhD)
physical oceanography (MS)

Shepard Broad Law Center
Joseph D. Harbaugh, Dean
Programs in:
education law (MS)
employment law (MS)
health law (MS)
law (JD)

■ PALM BEACH ATLANTIC UNIVERSITY
West Palm Beach, FL 33416-4708
http://www.pba.edu/

Independent-religious, coed, comprehensive institution. *Enrollment:* 3,264 graduate, professional, and undergraduate students; 548 full-time matriculated graduate/professional students (385 women), 192 part-time matriculated graduate/professional students (117 women). *Graduate faculty:* 26 full-time (15 women), 31 part-time/adjunct (12 women). *Computer facilities:* 147 computers available on campus for general student use. A campuswide network can be accessed from student residence rooms and from off campus. Internet access and online class registration are available. *Library facilities:* Warren Library. *Graduate expenses:* Tuition: full-time $10,665; part-time $395 per credit. Required fees: $90 per semester. *General application contact:* Laura A. Leinweber, Director of Graduate and Evening Admissions, 888-468-6722.

MacArthur School of Continuing Education
Dr. Jim Laub, Dean
Program in:
organizational leadership (MS)

Rinker School of Business
Dr. Edgar Langlois, Interim Dean
Program in:
business (MBA)

School of Education and Behavioral Studies
Dr. Melise Bunker, Dean
Programs in:
counseling psychology (MSCP)
elementary education (M Ed)

School of Pharmacy
Dr. Daniel Brown, Dean
Program in:
pharmacy (Pharm D)

■ ROLLINS COLLEGE
Winter Park, FL 32789-4499
http://www.rollins.edu/

Independent, coed, comprehensive institution. *Enrollment:* 2,454 graduate, professional, and undergraduate students; 343 full-time matriculated graduate/professional students (176 women), 391 part-time matriculated graduate/professional students (237 women). *Graduate faculty:* 23 full-time (3 women). *Computer facilities:* 195 computers available on campus for general student use. A campuswide network can be accessed from student residence rooms and from off campus. Internet access is available. *Library facilities:* Olin Library. *General application contact:* Information Contact, 407-646-2000.

Crummer Graduate School of Business
Dr. Craig M. McAllaster, Dean
Program in:
business (MBA)

Hamilton Holt School
Dr. Sharon M. Carrier, Dean
Programs in:
elementary education (M Ed, MAT)
human resources (MA)
liberal studies (MLS)
mental health counseling (MA)
school counseling (MA)
secondary education (MAT)

■ SAINT LEO UNIVERSITY
Saint Leo, FL 33574-6665
http://www.saintleo.edu/

Independent-religious, coed, comprehensive institution. *Enrollment:* 2,774 graduate, professional, and undergraduate students; 483 full-time matriculated graduate/professional students (317 women), 724 part-time matriculated graduate/professional students (453 women). *Graduate faculty:* 37 full-time (11 women), 44 part-time/adjunct (18 women). *Computer facilities:* 750 computers available on campus for general student use. A campuswide network can be accessed from student residence rooms and from off campus. Internet access and online class registration are available. *Library facilities:* Cannon Memorial Library. *General application contact:* Scott Cathcart, Vice President of Enrollment, 800-707-8846.

Graduate Business Studies
Dr. Robert Robertson, Director
Programs in:
accounting (MBA)
business (MBA)
criminal justice (MBA)
human resource administration (MBA)
information security management (MBA)
sport business (MBA)

Graduate Pastoral Studies
Dr. Michael Tkacik, Director
Program in:
pastoral studies (MA)

Graduate Studies in Criminal Justice
Dr. Robert Diemer, Director
Programs in:
criminal justice (MS)
critical incident management (MS)

Graduate Studies in Education
Dr. John Smith, Director
Programs in:
education (MAT)
educational leadership (M Ed)
exceptional student education (M Ed)
instructional leadership (M Ed)
reading (M Ed)

■ ST. THOMAS UNIVERSITY
Miami Gardens, FL 33054-6459
http://www.stu.edu/

Independent-religious, coed, comprehensive institution. *Computer facilities:* 60 computers available on campus for general student use. A campuswide network can be accessed. *Library facilities:* St. Thomas University Library plus 1 other. *General application contact:* Assistant Director of Admissions, 305-628-6546.

School of Graduate Studies
Programs in:
accounting (MBA)
business administration (M Acc, MBA, Certificate)
communication arts (MA)
educational administration (MS, Certificate)
educational leadership (Ed D)
elementary education (MS)
general management (MSM, Certificate)
guidance and counseling (MS, Post-Master's Certificate)
health management (MBA, MSM, Certificate)
Hispanic media (MA, Certificate)
human resource management (MBA, MSM, Certificate)
international business (MBA, MIB, MSM, Certificate)
justice administration (MSM, Certificate)
management accounting (MSM, Certificate)
marriage and family therapy (MS, Post-Master's Certificate)
mental health counseling (MS)
public management (MSM, Certificate)
reading (MS)
special education (MS)

Institute for Pastoral Ministries
Programs in:
pastoral ministries (MA, Certificate)
practical theology (PhD)

School of Law
Programs in:
international human rights (LL M)
international taxation (LL M)
law (JD)

■ SCHILLER INTERNATIONAL UNIVERSITY
Largo, FL 33770
http://www.schiller.edu/

Independent, coed, comprehensive institution. *Enrollment:* 246 graduate, professional, and undergraduate students; 146 matriculated graduate/professional students. *Graduate faculty:* 5 full-time (0 women), 10 part-time/adjunct (1 woman). *Computer facilities:* 17 computers available on campus for general student use. Internet access is available. *Library facilities:* SIU Library. *Graduate expenses:* Tuition: full-time $17,920; part-time $1,420 per course. *General application contact:* Susan Russeff, Associate Director of Admissions, 727-736-5082.

MBA Programs, Florida
Dr. Cathy Eberhart, Head
Programs in:
financial planning (MBA)
information technology (MBA)
international business (MBA)
international hotel and tourism management (MBA)

■ STETSON UNIVERSITY
DeLand, FL 32723
http://www.stetson.edu/

Independent, coed, comprehensive institution. *Enrollment:* 3,762 graduate, professional, and undergraduate students; 999 full-time matriculated graduate/professional students (518 women), 459 part-time matriculated graduate/professional students (270 women). *Graduate faculty:* 87 full-time (38 women), 43 part-time/adjunct (20 women). *Computer facilities:* 400 computers available on campus for general student use. A campuswide network can be accessed from student residence rooms and from off campus. Internet access and online class registration are available. *Library facilities:* DuPont-Ball Library plus 1 other. *General application contact:* Office of Graduate Studies, 386-822-7075.

College of Arts and Sciences
Dr. Grady Ballenger, Dean
Programs in:
arts and sciences (M Ed, MA, MS, Ed S)
curriculum and instruction (Ed S)
education (M Ed, MS, Ed S)
educational leadership (M Ed, Ed S)
exceptional student education (M Ed)

marriage and family therapy (MS)
mental health counseling (MS)
reading education (M Ed)
school guidance and family consultation (MS)

Division of Humanities
Programs in:
English (MA)
humanities (MA)

College of Law
Dr. Darby Dickerson, Dean
Program in:
law (JD, LL M)

School of Business Administration
Dr. James Scheiner, Dean
Programs in:
accounting (M Acc)
business administration (M Acc, MBA)

■ UNIVERSITY OF CENTRAL FLORIDA
Orlando, FL 32816
http://www.ucf.edu/

State-supported, coed, university. CGS member. *Enrollment:* 46,719 graduate, professional, and undergraduate students; 3,274 full-time matriculated graduate/professional students (1,822 women), 3,097 part-time matriculated graduate/professional students (1,905 women). *Graduate faculty:* 1,166 full-time (434 women), 464 part-time/adjunct (255 women). *Computer facilities:* Computer purchase and lease plans are available. 2,420 computers available on campus for general student use. A campuswide network can be accessed from student residence rooms and from off campus. Internet access and online class registration are available. *Library facilities:* University Library. *Graduate expenses:* Tuition, state resident: full-time $6,167; part-time $257 per credit hour. Tuition, nonresident: full-time $22,790; part-time $950 per credit hour. *General application contact:* Dr. Patricia Bishop, Vice Provost and Dean of Graduate Studies, 407-823-2766.

Burnett College of Biomedical Sciences
Dr. Pappachan E. Kolattukudy, Dean
Programs in:
biomedical sciences (MS, PhD)
molecular biology and microbiology (MS)

College of Arts and Humanities
Dr. José Fernandez, Dean, College of Arts an Humanities
Programs in:
arts and humanities (MA, MFA, MS, PhD, Certificate)
creative writing (MFA)
English (MA, MFA)
history (MA)
literature (MA)
professional writing (Certificate)
Spanish (MA)
studio art and the computer (MFA)
teaching English to speakers of other languages (MA, Certificate)
technical writing (MA)
texts and technology (PhD)
theatre (MA, MFA)

School of Film and Digital Media
Dr. Terry Frederick, Interim Director
Program in:
film and digital media (MA, MFA, MS)

College of Business Administration
Dr. Thomas Keon, Dean
Programs in:
business administration (MBA, MS, MSA, MSBM, MSM, MST, PhD)
economics (MS, PhD)
management (MSM)
management information systems (MS)
sport business management (MSBM)

Kenneth G. Dixon School of Accounting
Dr. Robin J. Roberts, Director
Programs in:
accounting (MSA, MST)
taxation (MST)

College of Education
Dr. Sandra Robinson, Dean
Programs in:
art education (M Ed, MA)
coaching (Certificate)
communication sciences and disorders (PhD)
community college education (Certificate)
counselor education (M Ed, MA, PhD)
curriculum and instruction (PhD)
e-learning (MA, Certificate)
e-learning professional development (Certificate)
early childhood education (M Ed, MA)
education (M Ed, MA, Ed D, PhD, Certificate, Ed S)
educational leadership (M Ed, MA, Ed D, Ed S)
educational media (M Ed)
educational studies (M Ed, MA, Ed D, Ed S)
educational technology (MA)
elementary education (M Ed, MA, PhD)
English language arts education (M Ed, MA)
exceptional education (M Ed, MA, PhD)
foreign language education (Certificate)
health and wellness (Certificate)
hospitality education (PhD)
instructional systems (MA)
instructional technology (PhD)
instructional technology/media and e-learning (MA)
K-8 mathematics and science education (M Ed, Certificate)
marriage and family therapy (MA)
mathematics education (M Ed, MA, PhD)
music education (M Ed, MA)
online educational media (Certificate)
physical education-exercise physiology (M Ed, MA)
pre-kindergarten handicapped endorsement (Certificate)
reading education (M Ed, MA, Certificate)
school psychology (Ed S)
science education (M Ed, MA)
social science education (M Ed, MA)
sports leadership (Certificate)
vocational education (M Ed, MA)
world studies education (Certificate)
writing education (Certificate)

College of Engineering and Computer Science
Dr. Neal Gallagher, Dean
Programs in:
aerospace engineering (MSAE)
applied operations research (Certificate)
CAD/CAM technology (Certificate)
civil engineering (MS, MSCE, PhD, Certificate)
computer-integrated manufacturing (MS)
construction engineering (Certificate)
design for usability (Certificate)
engineering (MS, MS Cp E, MS Env E, MSAE, MSCE, MSEE, MSIE, MSME, MSMSE, PhD, Certificate)
engineering management (MS)
environmental engineering (MS, MS Env E, PhD, Certificate)
HVAC engineering (Certificate)
industrial engineering (MSIE)
industrial engineering and management systems (PhD)
industrial ergonomics and safety (Certificate)
launch/spacecraft vehicle processing (Certificate)
materials failure analysis (Certificate)
materials science and engineering (MSMSE, PhD)
mechanical engineering (MSME, PhD, Certificate)
operations research (MS)
project engineering (Certificate)
quality assurance (Certificate)
simulation systems (MS)
structural engineering (Certificate)
surface water modeling (Certificate)
systems simulations for engineers (Certificate)
training simulation (Certificate)
transportation engineering (Certificate)
wastewater treatment (Certificate)

School of Electrical Engineering and Computer Science
Dr. Issa Batarseh, Interim Chair

University of Central Florida (continued)
Programs in:
communications systems (Certificate)
computer engineering (MS Cp E, PhD)
computer science (MS, PhD)
electrical engineering (MSEE, PhD, Certificate)
electronic circuits (Certificate)

College of Health and Public Affairs
Dr. Joyce Dorner, Interim Dean
Programs in:
child language disorders (Certificate)
communication sciences and disorders (MA)
corrections leadership (Certificate)
crime analysis (Certificate)
criminal justice (MS)
health and public affairs (MA, MNM, MPA, MS, MSW, DNP, PhD, Certificate, Post-Master's Certificate)
health services administration (MS, Certificate)
juvenile justice leadership (Certificate)
medical speech-language pathology (Certificate)
multicultural/multilingual speech-language pathology (Certificate)
non-profit management (MNM, Certificate)
physical therapy (MS)
police leadership (Certificate)
public administration (MPA, Certificate)
public affairs (PhD)
urban and regional planning (Certificate)
victim assistance (Certificate)

School of Social Work
Dr. John Ronnau, Director
Programs in:
addictions (Certificate)
aging studies (Certificate)
children's services (Certificate)
school social work (Certificate)
social work (MSW)
social work administration (Certificate)

College of Nursing
Dr. Jean D. Leuner, Dean, College of Nursing
Programs in:
adult practitioner (Post-Master's Certificate)
family practitioner (Post-Master's Certificate)
nursing (DNP, PhD)
nursing education (Post-Master's Certificate)
pediatric practitioner (Post-Master's Certificate)

College of Optics and Photonics
Dr. Eric W. Van Stryland, Dean and Director
Program in:
optics (MS, PhD)

College of Sciences
Dr. Peter Panousis, Dean
Programs in:
actuarial science (MS)
anthropology (MA)
applied environmental and human factors psychology (MA)
applied experimental and human factors psychology (PhD)
applied mathematics (Certificate)
applied sociology (MA)
biology (MS)
chemistry (MS, PhD)
clinical psychology (MA, MS, PhD)
conservation biology (PhD, Certificate)
data mining (MS, Certificate)
domestic violence (Certificate)
gender studies (Certificate)
industrial/organizational psychology (MS, PhD)
mathematical science (MS)
mathematics (PhD)
Mayan studies (Certificate)
physics (MS, PhD)
political science (MA)
sciences (MA, MS, PhD, Certificate)
sociology (PhD)
statistical computing (MS)

Nicholson School of Communication
Dr. Mary Alice Shaver, Director
Program in:
communication (MA)

Division of Graduate Studies
Dr. Patricia Bishop, Vice Provost and Dean
Programs in:
interdisciplinary studies (MA, MS)
modeling and simulation (MS, PhD)

Rosen College of Hospitality Management
Dr. Abraham C. Pizam, Dean
Program in:
hospitality and tourism management (MS)

■ UNIVERSITY OF FLORIDA
Gainesville, FL 32611
http://www.ufl.edu/

State-supported, coed, university. CGS member. *Enrollment:* 50,822 graduate, professional, and undergraduate students; 13,818 matriculated graduate/professional students. *Graduate faculty:* 3,271 full-time (949 women), 114 part-time/adjunct (44 women). *Computer facilities:* Computer purchase and lease plans are available. 472 computers available on campus for general student use. A campuswide network can be accessed from student residence rooms and from off campus. Internet access and online class registration are available. *Library facilities:* George A. Smathers Library plus 8 others. *Graduate expenses:* Tuition, state resident: full-time $6,827. Tuition, nonresident: full-time $21,951. Required fees: $999. *General application contact:* Graduate Admissions, 352-392-3261.

Find University Details at www.petersons.com/gradchannel.

College of Dentistry
Dr. Teresa A. Dolan, Dean
Programs in:
dentistry (DMD)
endodontics (MS, Certificate)
foreign trained dentistry (Certificate)
oral biology (PhD)
orthodontics (MS, Certificate)
periodontology (MS, Certificate)
prosthodontics (MS, Certificate)

College of Medicine
Dr. C. Craig Tisher, Dean
Programs in:
biochemistry and molecular biology (MS, PhD)
biomedical sciences (PhD)
clinical investigation (MS)
epidemiology (MS)
genetics (PhD)
imaging science and technology (MS, PhD)
immunology and microbiology (PhD)
immunology and molecular pathology (PhD)
medicine (MD, MPAS, MPH, MS, PhD)
molecular cell biology (PhD)
molecular genetics and microbiology (MS, PhD)
neuroscience (MS, PhD)
pharmacology and therapeutics (PhD)
physician assistant (MPAS)
physiology and functional genomics (PhD)
physiology and pharmacology (PhD)
public health (MPH)

College of Pharmacy
Dr. William H. Riffee, Dean
Programs in:
clinical pharmaceutical sciences (PhD)
forensic DNA and serology (MS, Certificate)
forensic drug chemistry (MS, Certificate)
forensic toxicology (MS, Certificate)
medicinal chemistry (Pharm D, MSP, PhD)
pharmaceutical sciences (MSP, PhD)
pharmaceutics (PhD)
pharmacodynamics (MSP, PhD)
pharmacology (PhD)
pharmacy (Pharm D, MSP, PhD)
pharmacy health care administration (MSP, PhD)
pharmacy practice (PhD)

College of Veterinary Medicine
Dr. James P. Thompson, Interim Dean
Programs in:
forensic toxicology (Certificate)

veterinary medical sciences (MS, PhD)
veterinary medicine (DVM, MS, PhD, Certificate)

Graduate School

Dr. Kenneth J. Gerhardt, Interim Dean

College of Agricultural and Life Sciences
R. Kirby Barrick, Dean
Programs in:
- agricultural and life sciences (M Ag, MAB, MFAS, MFRC, MFYCS, MS, DPM, PhD)
- agricultural education and communication (M Ag, MS, PhD)
- agronomy (MS, PhD)
- anatomy and development (MS, PhD)
- animal sciences (M Ag, MS, PhD)
- biochemistry and molecular biology (MS, PhD)
- breeding and genetics (MS, PhD)
- ecology (MS, PhD)
- entomology and nematology (MS, PhD)
- family, youth, and community sciences (MFYCS, MS)
- fisheries and aquatic sciences (MFAS, MS, PhD)
- food and resource economics (MAB, MS, PhD)
- food science (MS, PhD)
- forest resources and conservation (MFRC, MS, PhD)
- microbiology and cell science (MS, PhD)
- nutritional sciences (MS, PhD)
- plant biotechnology (MS, PhD)
- plant breeding and genetics (MS, PhD)
- plant medicine (DPM)
- plant molecular and cellular biology (MS, PhD)
- plant pathology (MS, PhD)
- plant production and nutrient management (MS, PhD)
- postharvest biology (MS, PhD)
- soil and water science (MS, PhD)
- stress physiology (MS, PhD)
- sustainable/organic practice (MS, PhD)
- taxonomy (MS, PhD)
- tissue culture (MS, PhD)
- weed science (MS, PhD)
- wildlife ecology and conservation (MS, PhD)

College of Design, Construction and Planning
Dr. Christopher Silver, Dean
Programs in:
- architecture (M Arch, MSAS, PhD)
- building construction (MBC, MICM, MSBC, PhD)
- design, construction and planning (M Arch, MAURP, MBC, MICM, MID, MLA, MSAS, MSBC, PhD)
- interior design (MID, PhD)
- landscape architecture (MLA, PhD)
- urban and regional planning (MAURP, PhD)

College of Education
Dr. Catherine Emihovich, Dean
Programs in:
- bilingual/ESOL education (M Ed, MAE, Ed D, PhD, Ed S)
- curriculum and instruction (M Ed, MAE, Ed D, PhD, Ed S)
- early childhood education (Ed D, PhD, Ed S)
- education (M Ed, MAE, Ed D, PhD, Ed S)
- educational leadership (M Ed, MAE, Ed D, PhD, Ed S)
- educational psychology (M Ed, MAE, Ed D, PhD, Ed S)
- elementary education (M Ed, MAE)
- English education (M Ed, MAE)
- higher education administration (Ed D, PhD, Ed S)
- marriage and family counseling (M Ed, MAE, Ed D, PhD, Ed S)
- mathematics education (M Ed, MAE)
- mental health counseling (M Ed, MAE, Ed D, PhD, Ed S)
- reading education (M Ed, MAE)
- research and evaluation methodology (M Ed, MAE, Ed D, PhD, Ed S)
- school counseling and guidance (M Ed, MAE, Ed D, PhD, Ed S)
- school psychology (M Ed, MAE, Ed D, PhD, Ed S)
- science education (M Ed, MAE)
- social foundations (M Ed, MAE, Ed D, PhD)
- social studies education (M Ed, MAE)
- special education (M Ed, MAE, Ed D, PhD, Ed S)
- student personnel in higher education (M Ed, MAE)

College of Engineering
Dr. Pramod P. Khargonekar, Dean
Programs in:
- aerospace engineering (ME, MS, PhD, Engr)
- agricultural and biological engineering (ME, MS, PhD, Engr)
- biomedical engineering (ME, MS, PhD, Certificate)
- chemical engineering (ME, MS, PhD)
- civil engineering (MCE, MS, PhD, Engr)
- coastal and oceanographic engineering (ME, MS, PhD, Engr)
- computer engineering (ME, MS, PhD)
- computer science (MS)
- digital arts and sciences (MS)
- electrical and computer engineering (ME, MS, PhD, Engr)
- engineering (MCE, ME, MS, PhD, Certificate, Engr)
- environmental engineering sciences (ME, MS, PhD, Engr)
- industrial and systems engineering (ME, MS, PhD, Engr)
- materials science and engineering (ME, MS, PhD, Engr)
- mechanical engineering (ME, MS, PhD, Engr)
- nuclear engineering sciences (ME, MS, PhD, Engr)

College of Fine Arts
Lucinda Lavelli, Interim Dean
Programs in:
- art (MFA)
- art education (MA)
- art history (MA, PhD)
- choral conducting (MM, PhD)
- composition/theory (MM, PhD)
- digital arts and sciences (MA)
- ethnomusicology (PhD)
- fine arts (MA, MFA, MM, PhD)
- instrumental conducting (MM, PhD)
- museology (museum studies) (MA)
- music (MM, PhD)
- music education (MM, PhD)
- music history and literature (MM)
- musicology (PhD)
- performance (MM)
- sacred music (MM)
- theatre (MFA)

College of Health and Human Performance
Dr. Steve Dorman, Dean
Programs in:
- athletic training/sport medicine (MS, PhD)
- biomechanics (MS, PhD)
- clinical exercise physiology (MS)
- exercise physiology (MS, PhD)
- health and human performance (PhD)
- health behavior (PhD)
- health communication (Graduate Certificate)
- health education and behavior (MS)
- human performance (MS)
- motor learning/control (MS, PhD)
- recreational studies (MS)
- sport and exercise psychology (MS)

College of Journalism and Communications
Dr. John W. Wright, Interim Dean
Programs in:
- advertising (M Adv)
- journalism (MAMC)
- mass communication (MAMC, PhD)
- public relations (MAMC)
- telecommunication (MAMC)

College of Liberal Arts and Sciences
Joe Glover, Interim Dean
Programs in:
- African studies (Certificate)
- anthropology (MA, PhD)
- astronomy (MS, PhD)
- behavior analysis (PhD)
- behavioral neuroscience (MS, PhD)
- botany (M Ag, MS, MST, PhD)
- chemistry (MS, MST, PhD)
- classical studies (MA, PhD)
- cognitive and sensory processes (PhD)
- communication sciences and disorders (MA, Au D, PhD)
- counseling psychology (PhD)
- creative writing (MFA)
- criminology and law (MA, PhD)
- developmental psychology (PhD)
- English (MA, PhD)

University of Florida (continued)
- French (MA, PhD)
- gender and development (Graduate Certificate)
- geography (MA, MS, PhD)
- geology (MS, MST, PhD)
- German (MA, PhD)
- history (MA, PhD)
- international development policy and administration (MA, Certificate)
- international relations (MA, MAT)
- Latin (MA, MAT, ML)
- Latin American studies (MA, Certificate)
- liberal arts and sciences (M Ag, M Stat, MA, MAT, MFA, ML, MS, MS Stat, MST, MWS, Au D, PhD, Certificate, Graduate Certificate)
- linguistics (MA, PhD)
- mathematics (MA, MAT, MS, MST, PhD)
- philosophy (MA, PhD)
- physics (MS, MST, PhD)
- political campaigning (MA, Certificate)
- political science (MA, MAT, PhD)
- public affairs (MA, Certificate)
- religion (MA, PhD)
- social psychology (MS, PhD)
- sociology (MA, PhD)
- Spanish (MA, PhD)
- statistics (M Stat, MS Stat, PhD)
- teaching English as a second language (Certificate)
- women's studies (MA, MWS, Graduate Certificate)
- zoology (MS, MST, PhD)

College of Nursing
Dr. Kathleen A. Long, Dean
Programs in:
- nursing (MSN)
- nursing sciences (PhD)

College of Public Health and Health Professions
Dr. Robert G. Frank, Dean
Programs in:
- audiology (Au D)
- biostatistics (MPH)
- clinical and health psychology (PhD)
- environmental health (MPH)
- epidemiology (MPH)
- health administration (MHA)
- health services research (PhD)
- occupational therapy (MHS, MOT)
- physical therapy (DPT)
- public health and health professions (MHA, MHS, MOT, MPH, Au D, DPT, PhD)
- public health management and policy (MPH)
- public health practice (MPH)
- rehabilitation counseling (MHS)
- rehabilitation science (PhD)
- social and behavioral sciences (MPH)

School of Natural Resources and Environment
James C. Cato, Senior Associate Dan
Program in:
- interdisciplinary ecology (MS, PhD)

Warrington College of Business Administration
Dr. John Kraft, Dean
Programs in:
- accounting (MBA)
- arts administration (MBA)
- business administration (MS)
- business strategy and public policy (MBA)
- competitive strategy (MBA)
- decision and information sciences (MBA, MS, PhD)
- economics (MA, PhD)
- electronic commerce (MBA)
- finance (MBA, PhD)
- financial services (Certificate)
- general business (MBA)
- global management (MBA)
- Graham-Buffett security analysis (MBA)
- health administration (MBA)
- human resources management (MBA)
- insurance (PhD)
- international business (MAIB)
- international studies (MBA)
- Latin American business (MBA)
- management (MBA, MS, PhD)
- marketing (MBA)
- real estate and urban analysis (PhD)
- sports administration (MBA)
- supply chain management (MS)

Interdisciplinary Concentration in Animal Molecular and Cell Biology
Program in:
- animal molecular and cell biology (MS, PhD)

Levin College of Law
Robert Jerry, Dean
Programs in:
- comparative law (LL M)
- international taxation (LL M)
- law (JD)
- taxation (LL M, SJD)

■ UNIVERSITY OF MIAMI
Coral Gables, FL 33124
http://www.miami.edu/

Independent, coed, university. CGS member. *Enrollment:* 15,670 graduate, professional, and undergraduate students; 4,485 full-time matriculated graduate/professional students (2,089 women), 550 part-time matriculated graduate/professional students (355 women). *Graduate faculty:* 1,192 full-time (314 women), 9 part-time/adjunct (4 women). *Computer facilities:* Computer purchase and lease plans are available. 1,800 computers available on campus for general student use. A campuswide network can be accessed from student residence rooms and from off campus. Internet access and online class registration, online student account and grade information are available. *Library facilities:* Otto G. Richter Library plus 7 others. *General application contact:* 305-284-4154.

Find University Details at www.petersons.com/gradchannel.

Graduate School
Dr. Terri A. Scandura, Dean

College of Arts and Sciences
Dr. Michael R. Halleran, Dean
Programs in:
- adult clinical (PhD)
- applied developmental psychology (PhD)
- art history (MA)
- arts and sciences (MA, MAIA, MALS, MFA, MS, DA, PhD)
- behavioral neuroscience (PhD)
- biology (MS, PhD)
- ceramics/glass (MFA)
- chemistry (MS)
- child clinical (PhD)
- computer science (MS)
- creative writing (MFA)
- English (MA, PhD)
- French (PhD)
- genetics and evolution (MS, PhD)
- geography (MA)
- graphic design/multimedia (MFA)
- health clinical (PhD)
- history (MA, PhD)
- inorganic chemistry (PhD)
- international administration (MAIA)
- international studies (MA, PhD)
- liberal studies (MALS)
- mathematics (MA, MS, DA, PhD)
- organic chemistry (PhD)
- painting (MFA)
- philosophy (MA, PhD)
- photography/digital imaging (MFA)
- physical chemistry (PhD)
- physics (MS, PhD)
- printmaking (MFA)
- psychology (MS)
- sculpture (MFA)
- sociology (MA, PhD)
- Spanish (PhD)

College of Engineering
Dr. M. Lewis Temares, Dean
Programs in:
- architectural engineering (MSAE)
- biomedical engineering (MSBE, PhD)
- civil engineering (MSCE, DA, PhD)
- electrical and computer engineering (MSECE, PhD)
- engineering (MS, MSAE, MSBE, MSCE, MSECE, MSEVH, MSIE, MSME, MSOES, DA, PhD)
- environmental health and safety (MS, MSEVH, MSOES)
- ergonomics (PhD)
- industrial engineering (MSIE, PhD)
- management of technology (MS)
- mechanical and aerospace engineering (MSME, PhD)
- occupational ergonomics and safety (MSOES)

Frost School of Music
Shelton Berg, Dean
Programs in:
accompanying and chamber music (MM, DMA)
choral conducting (MM, DMA)
composition (MM, DMA)
electronic music (MM)
instrumental conducting (MM, DMA)
instrumental performance (MM, DMA, AD)
jazz composition (DMA)
jazz pedagogy (MM)
jazz performance (MM, DMA)
keyboard performance and pedagogy (MM, DMA)
media writing and production (MM)
multiple woodwinds (MM, DMA)
music (MM, MS, DMA, PhD, AD, Spec M)
music business and entertainment industries (MM)
music education (MM, PhD, Spec M)
music engineering (MS)
music theory (MM)
music therapy (MM)
musicology (MM)
piano performance (MM, DMA, AD)
studio jazz writing (MM)
vocal pedagogy (DMA)
vocal performance (MM, DMA, AD)

Miller School of Medicine
Dr. Paschal Goldschmidt, Vice President for Medical Affairs/Dean
Programs in:
biochemistry and molecular biology (PhD)
cancer biology (PhD)
epidemiology (PhD)
medicine (MD, MPH, MSPH, DPT, PhD)
microbiology and immunology (PhD)
molecular and cellular pharmacology (PhD)
molecular cell and developmental biology (PhD)
neuroscience (PhD)
physical therapy (DPT, PhD)
physiology and biophysics (PhD)
public health (MPH, MSPH)

Rosenstiel School of Marine and Atmospheric Science
Dr. Otis Brown, Dean
Programs in:
applied marine physics (MS, PhD)
marine affairs and policy (MA, MS)
marine and atmospheric chemistry (MS, PhD)
marine and atmospheric science (MA, MS, PhD)
marine biology and fisheries (MA, MS, PhD)
marine geology and geophysics (MS, PhD)
meteorology (PhD)
physical oceanography (MS, PhD)

School of Architecture
Programs in:
architecture (M Arch)
suburb and town design (M Arch)

School of Business Administration
Dr. Harold W. Berkman, Vice Dean
Programs in:
accounting (MBA)
business administration (MA, MBA, MP Acc, MPA, MS, MS Tax, MSPM, PhD)
computer information systems (MBA)
economic development (MA, PhD)
environmental economics (PhD)
executive and professional (MBA)
finance (MBA)
human resource economics (MA, PhD)
international business (MBA)
international economics (MA, PhD)
macroeconomics (PhD)
management (MBA)
management science (MBA, MS)
marketing (MBA)
political science (MPA)
professional accounting (MP Acc)
professional management (MSPM)
taxation (MS Tax)

School of Communication
Dr. Sam L. Grogg, Dean
Programs in:
communication (PhD)
communication studies (MA)
film studies (MA, PhD)
motion pictures (MFA)
print journalism (MA)
public relations (MA)
Spanish language journalism (MA)
television broadcast journalism (MA)

School of Education
Dr. Isaac Prilleltensky, Dean
Programs in:
advanced professional studies (MS Ed, Ed S)
bilingual and bicultural counseling (Certificate)
counseling (MS Ed, Certificate)
counseling psychology (PhD)
education (MS Ed, PhD, Certificate, Ed S)
elementary education/TESOL (MS Ed)
exceptional student education (PhD)
exceptional student education, pre–K disabilities and ESOL (Ed S)
exceptional student education, pre-K disabilities and ESOL (MS Ed)
exceptional student education, reading and ESOL (MS Ed, Ed S)
exercise physiology (MS Ed, PhD)
higher education administration (MS Ed, Certificate)
higher education administration/ enrollment management (Certificate)
marriage and family therapy (MS Ed)
mathematics and science education (PhD)
mathematics and science resource teaching (MS Ed, Ed S)
mental health counseling (MS Ed)
reading (MS Ed, PhD, Ed S)
research, measurement, and evaluation (MS Ed, PhD)
sport administration (MS Ed)
sports medicine (MS Ed)
teaching and learning (PhD)
teaching English to speakers of other languages (PhD)

School of Law
Michael Goodnight, Assistant Dean of Admissions
Programs in:
comparative law (LL M)
estate planning (LL M)
inter-American law (LL M)
international law (LL M)
law (JD)
ocean and coastal law (LL M)
real property development (LL M)
taxation (LL M)

School of Nursing and Health Studies
Dr. Nilda Peragallo, Dean
Programs in:
acute care (MSN)
community health (MSN)
nursing (PhD)
primary care (MSN)

■ UNIVERSITY OF NORTH FLORIDA
Jacksonville, FL 32224-2645
http://www.unf.edu/

State-supported, coed, comprehensive institution. *Enrollment:* 15,954 graduate, professional, and undergraduate students; 603 full-time matriculated graduate/ professional students (422 women), 1,009 part-time matriculated graduate/professional students (615 women). *Graduate faculty:* 309 full-time (118 women). *Computer facilities:* 750 computers available on campus for general student use. A campuswide network can be accessed from student residence rooms and from off campus. Internet access and online class registration, applications software are available. *Library facilities:* Thomas G. Carpenter Library. *Graduate expenses:* Tuition, state resident: full-time $4,948; part-time $206 per semester hour. Tuition, nonresident: full-time $19,140; part-time $408 per semester hour. *General application contact:* Michelle Mouton, Graduate Coordinator, The Graduate School, 904-620-1360.

Coggin College of Business
Dr. John P McAllister, Dean
Programs in:
accounting (M Acct)
business (M Acct, MBA)
business administration (MBA)

College of Arts and Sciences
Dr. Dale L. Clifford, Acting Dean

University of North Florida (continued)
Programs in:
- applied ethics (Graduate Certificate)
- applied sociology (MS)
- arts and sciences (MA, MAC, MPA, MS, MSCJ, Graduate Certificate)
- biology (MA, MS)
- counseling psychology (MAC)
- criminal justice (MSCJ)
- English (MA)
- European history (MA)
- general psychology (MA)
- mathematical sciences (MS)
- practical philosophy and applied ethics (MA)
- public administration (MPA)
- statistics (MS)
- US history (MA)

College of Computing, Engineering, and Construction
Dr. Neal Coulter, Dean
Program in:
- computer and information sciences (MS)

College of Education and Human Services
Dr. Larry Daniel, Dean
Programs in:
- counselor education (M Ed)
- deaf education (M Ed)
- disability services (M Ed)
- education and human services (M Ed, Ed D)
- educational leadership (M Ed, Ed D)
- exceptional student education (M Ed)
- instructional leadership (M Ed)
- mental health counseling (M Ed)
- school counseling (M Ed)

Division of Curriculum and Instruction
Dr. Sandra Gupton, Chair
Programs in:
- elementary education (M Ed)
- secondary education (M Ed)

College of Health
Dr. Pamela Chally, Dean
Programs in:
- community health (MPH)
- geriatric management (MSH)
- health (MHA, MPH, MPT, MS, MSH, MSN, Certificate)
- health administration (MHA)
- health behavior research and evaluation (Certificate)
- nutrition (MSH)
- physical therapy (MPT)
- rehabilitation counseling (MS)

School of Nursing
Dr. Lilia Loriz, Director
Programs in:
- advanced practice nursing (MSN)
- primary care nurse practitioner (Certificate)

■ UNIVERSITY OF PHOENIX–CENTRAL FLORIDA CAMPUS
Maitland, FL 32751-7057
http://www.phoenix.edu/

Proprietary, coed, comprehensive institution. *Enrollment:* 2,072 graduate, professional, and undergraduate students; 510 full-time matriculated graduate/professional students (329 women). *Graduate faculty:* 110 full-time (38 women), 264 part-time/adjunct (74 women). *Computer facilities:* A campuswide network can be accessed from off campus. Internet access is available. *Library facilities:* University Library. *Graduate expenses:* Tuition: full-time $9,450. Required fees: $760. *General application contact:* Campus Information Center, 407-667-0555.

The Artemis School
Dr. Adam Honea, Provost/Dean/Vice President of Research and Development

College of Education
Dr. Marla LaRue, Dean/Executive Director
Programs in:
- administration and supervision (MA Ed)
- curriculum and instruction (MA Ed)
- elementary teacher education (MA Ed)
- secondary teacher education (MA Ed)

College of Health and Human Services
Dr. Gil Linne, Dean/Executive Director
Programs in:
- health administration (MHA)
- health and human services (MSN)
- health care management (MBA)

John Sperling School of Business
Dr. Adam Honea, Provost/Dean/Vice President of Research and Development
Program in:
- business (MBA, MIS, MM)

College of Graduate Business and Management
Dr. Brian Lindquist, Associate Vice President and Dean/Executive Director
Programs in:
- accounting (MBA)
- business administration (MBA)
- business and management (MM)
- global management (MBA)
- management (MM)
- marketing (MBA)

College of Information Systems and Technology
Programs in:
- management (MIS)
- technology management (MBA)

■ UNIVERSITY OF PHOENIX–FORT LAUDERDALE CAMPUS
Fort Lauderdale, FL 33309
http://www.phoenix.edu/

Proprietary, coed, comprehensive institution. *Enrollment:* 3,121 graduate, professional, and undergraduate students; 778 full-time matriculated graduate/professional students (568 women). *Graduate faculty:* 77 full-time (32 women), 256 part-time/adjunct (72 women). *Computer facilities:* A campuswide network can be accessed from off campus. Internet access is available. *Library facilities:* University Library. *Graduate expenses:* Tuition: full-time $9,450. Required fees: $760. *General application contact:* Campus Information Center, 954-832-5503.

The Artemis School
Dr. Adam Honea, Provost

College of Education
Dr. Marla LaRue, Dean/Executive Director
Programs in:
- administration and supervision (MA Ed)
- computer education (MA Ed)
- curriculum and instruction (MA Ed)
- elementary teacher education (MA Ed)
- secondary teacher education (MA Ed)

College of Health and Human Services
Dr. Gil Linne, Dean/Executive Director
Programs in:
- health administration (MHA)
- health care education (MSN)
- health care management (MBA)
- nursing (MSN)

John Sperling School of Business
Dr. Adam Honea, Provost
Program in:
- business (MBA, MIS, MM)

College of Graduate Business and Management
Dr. Brian Linquist, Associate Vice President and Dean/Executive Director
Programs in:
- accounting (MBA)
- business administration (MBA)
- global management (MBA)
- human resource management (MBA)
- human resources management (MM)
- management (MM)
- marketing (MBA)
- public administration (MBA)

College of Information Systems and Technology
Programs in:
- management (MIS)
- technology management (MBA)

■ UNIVERSITY OF PHOENIX–NORTH FLORIDA CAMPUS

Jacksonville, FL 32216-0959

http://www.phoenix.edu/

Proprietary, coed, comprehensive institution. *Enrollment:* 2,211 graduate, professional, and undergraduate students; 579 full-time matriculated graduate/professional students (370 women). *Graduate faculty:* 84 full-time (35 women), 228 part-time/adjunct (79 women). *Computer facilities:* A campuswide network can be accessed from off campus. Internet access is available. *Library facilities:* University Library. *General application contact:* Campus Information Center, 904-636-6645.

The Artemis School

Dr. Adam Honea, Provost

College of Education
Dr. Marla LaRue, Dean
Programs in:
- administration (MA Ed)
- curriculum and instruction (MA Ed)
- curriculum and instruction—computer education (MA Ed)
- elementary teacher education (MA Ed)
- secondary teacher education (MA Ed)

College of Health and Human Services
Dr. Gil Linne, Dean
Programs in:
- health administration (MHA)
- health care education (MSN)
- health care management (MBA)
- nursing (MSN)

John Sperling School of Business

Dr. Adam Honea, Provost
Program in:
- business (MBA, MIS, MM)

College of Graduate Business and Management
Dr. Brian Lindquist, Associate Vice President and Dean/Executive Director
Programs in:
- accounting (MBA)
- business administration (MBA)
- global management (MBA)
- human resources management (MBA, MM)
- management (MM)
- marketing (MBA)
- public administration (MBA)

College of Information Systems and Technology
Dr. Adam Honea, Dean
Programs in:
- information systems (MIS)
- management (MIS)

■ UNIVERSITY OF PHOENIX–WEST FLORIDA CAMPUS

Temple Terrace, FL 33637

http://www.phoenix.edu/

Proprietary, coed, comprehensive institution. *Enrollment:* 2,659 graduate, professional, and undergraduate students; 675 full-time matriculated graduate/professional students (422 women). *Graduate faculty:* 84 full-time (42 women), 316 part-time/adjunct (85 women). *Computer facilities:* A campuswide network can be accessed from off campus. Internet access is available. *Library facilities:* University Library. *Graduate expenses:* Tuition: full-time $9,450. Required fees: $760. *General application contact:* Campus Information Center, 813-626-7911.

The Artemis School

Dr. Adam Honea, Provost

College of Education
Dr. Marla LaRue, Dean
Programs in:
- administration and supervision (MA Ed)
- curriculum and instruction (MA Ed)
- curriculum and technology (MA Ed)
- elementary teacher education (MA Ed)
- secondary teacher education (MA Ed)

College of Health and Human Services
Dr. Gil Linne, Dean
Programs in:
- health administration (MHA)
- health care education (MSN)
- health care management (MBA)

The John Sperling School of Business

Dr. Adam Honea, Provost
Program in:
- business (MBA, MIS, MM)

College of Graduate Business and Management
Dr. Brian Lindquist, Associate Vice President and Dean/Executive Director
Programs in:
- business administration (MBA)
- global management (MBA)
- human resource management (MBA)
- human resources management (MM)
- management (MM)
- marketing (MBA)
- public administration (MBA)

College of Information Systems and Technology
Programs in:
- information systems and technology (MIS)
- technology management (MBA)

■ UNIVERSITY OF SOUTH FLORIDA

Tampa, FL 33620-9951

http://www.usf.edu

State-supported, coed, university. CGS member. *Computer facilities:* 593 computers available on campus for general student use. A campuswide network can be accessed from student residence rooms and from off campus. Internet access and online class registration are available. *Library facilities:* Tampa Campus Library plus 2 others. *General application contact:* Dr. Kelli MacCormack-Brown, Dean, Graduate School, 813-974-2846.

Find University Details at www.petersons.com/gradchannel.

Center for Entrepreneurship

Dr. Michael W. Fountain, Director
Program in:
- entrepreneurship (MS, Graduate Certificate)

College of Medicine

Dr. Robert S. Belsole, Interim Dean
Programs in:
- anatomy (PhD)
- biochemistry and molecular biology (MS, PhD)
- medical microbiology and immunology (PhD)
- medicine (MD, MS, PhD)
- pathology (PhD)
- pharmacology and therapeutics (PhD)
- physiology and biophysics (PhD)

School of Physical Therapy
Dr. William S. Quillen, Associate Dean/Director
Program in:
- physical therapy (MS)

Graduate School

Delcie Durham, Associate Provost for Research and Graduate Dean
Programs in:
- applied behavior analysis (MA)
- cancer biology (PhD)

College of Arts and Sciences
Dr. Kathleen Heide, Interim Dean
Programs in:
- Africana studies (MLA)
- aging studies (PhD)
- American studies (MA)
- analytical chemistry (MS, PhD)
- applied anthropology (MA, PhD)
- applied physics (PhD)
- arts and sciences (MA, MLA, MPA, MS, MSW, PhD, Graduate Certificate)
- biochemistry (MS, PhD)
- biology (PhD)
- botany (MS)
- clinical psychology (PhD)
- communication (MA, PhD)

University of South Florida (continued)
- communication sciences and disorders (PhD)
- criminal justice administration (MA)
- criminology (MA, PhD)
- Cuban studies (Graduate Certificate)
- ecology (PhD)
- English (MA, PhD)
- environmental science and policy (MS)
- experimental psychology (PhD)
- French (MA)
- geography (MA)
- geology (MS, PhD)
- gerontology (MA)
- history (MA)
- industrial/organizational psychology (PhD)
- inorganic chemistry (MS, PhD)
- Latin American and Caribbean studies (Graduate Certificate)
- Latin American, Caribbean and Latino studies (MA)
- liberal arts (MLA)
- library and information sciences (MA)
- linguistics (MA)
- mass communications (MA)
- mathematics (MA, PhD, Graduate Certificate)
- microbiology (MS)
- organic chemistry (MS, PhD)
- philosophy (MA, PhD)
- physical chemistry (MS, PhD)
- physics (MS)
- physiology (PhD)
- political science (MA)
- polymer chemistry (PhD)
- psychology (MA)
- public administration (MPA)
- rehabilitation and mental health counseling (MA)
- religious studies (MA)
- social work (MSW)
- sociology (MA)
- Spanish (MA)
- statistics (MA, Graduate Certificate)
- women's studies (MA)
- zoology (MS)

College of Business Administration
Dr. Steve Baumgarten, Director, MBA Programs
Programs in:
- accounting (M Acc)
- business administration (Exec MBA, M Acc, MA, MBA, MS, MSM, PhD)
- economics (MA, PhD)
- finance (MS)
- management information systems (MS)

College of Education
Colleen S. Kennedy, Dean
Programs in:
- adult education (MA, Ed D, PhD, Ed S)
- career and technical education (MA)
- college student affairs (M Ed)
- counselor education (MA, PhD)
- early childhood education (M Ed, MAT, PhD)
- education (M Ed, MA, MAT, Ed D, PhD, Ed S)
- education of the mentally handicapped (MA)
- educational leadership (M Ed, Ed D, Ed S)
- educational measurement and research (M Ed, PhD, Ed S)
- elementary education (MA, Ed D, PhD, Ed S)
- English education (M Ed, MA, PhD)
- foreign language education (M Ed, MA)
- gifted education (online) (MA)
- higher education/community college teaching (MA, PhD, Ed S)
- industrial-technical education (MA)
- instructional technology (M Ed)
- interdisciplinary education (PhD, Ed S)
- learning disabilities (MA)
- mathematics education (M Ed, MA, PhD, Ed S)
- middle school education (M Ed)
- physical education (MA)
- reading education (M Ed, MA, PhD, Ed S)
- school psychology (PhD, Ed S)
- science education (M Ed, MA, MAT, PhD)
- second language acquisition/instructional technology (PhD)
- secondary education (PhD)
- social science education (M Ed, MA)
- varying exceptionalities (MA, MAT)
- vocational education (Ed D, PhD, Ed S)

College of Engineering
Dr. Rafael Perez, Associate Dean for Academics and Student Affairs
Programs in:
- biomedical engineering (MSBE, PhD)
- chemical engineering (MCHE, ME, MSCH, PhD)
- civil and environmental engineering (MEVE, MSES, MSEV)
- civil engineering (MCE, MSCE, PhD)
- computer science (MSCP, MSCS)
- computer science and engineering (ME, MSES, PhD)
- electrical engineering (ME, MSEE, MSES, PhD)
- engineering (ME)
- engineering management (MIE, MSIE)
- engineering science (PhD)
- industrial engineering (MIE, MSES, MSIE, PhD)
- mechanical engineering (ME, MME, MSME, PhD)

College of Marine Science
Dr. Peter R. Betzer, Dean
Program in:
- marine science (MS, PhD)

College of Nursing
Dr. Patricia A. Burns, Dean
Program in:
- nursing (MS, PhD)

College of Public Health
Dr. Donna J. Petersen, Dean
Programs in:
- community and family health (MPH, MSPH, PhD)
- environmental and occupational health (MPH, MSPH, PhD)
- epidemiology and biostatistics (MPH, MSPH, PhD)
- global health (MPH, MSPH, PhD)
- health policy and management (MHA, MPH, MSPH, PhD)
- public health (MHA, MPH, MSPH, PhD)
- public health practice (MPH)

College of Visual and Performing Arts
Ron Jones, Dean
Programs in:
- art history (MA)
- chamber music (MM)
- composition (MM)
- conducting (MM)
- electro-acoustic music (MM)
- jazz studies (MM)
- performance (MM)
- piano pedagogy (MM)
- studio art (MFA)
- theory (MM)
- visual and performing arts (MA, MFA, MM)

School of Architecture and Community Design
Stephen Schreiber, Director
Program in:
- architecture and community design (M Arch)

■ THE UNIVERSITY OF TAMPA
Tampa, FL 33606-1490
http://www.utampa.edu/

Independent, coed, comprehensive institution. *Enrollment:* 5,381 graduate, professional, and undergraduate students; 151 full-time matriculated graduate/professional students (60 women), 485 part-time matriculated graduate/professional students (245 women). *Graduate faculty:* 57 full-time (23 women), 22 part-time/adjunct (11 women). *Computer facilities:* Computer purchase and lease plans are available. 493 computers available on campus for general student use. A campuswide network can be accessed from student residence rooms and from off campus. Internet access and online class registration are available. *Library facilities:* Macdonald Keloe Library. *Graduate expenses:* Tuition: part-time $426 per credit hour. Required fees: $35 per year. *General application contact:* Barbara P. Strickler, Vice President for Enrollment, 888-646-2738.

John H. Sykes College of Business
Dr. William L. Rhey, Dean Graduate Studies

Programs in:
- accounting (MBA, MS)
- economics (MBA)
- entrepreneurship (MBA)
- finance (MBA, MS)
- information systems management (MBA)
- innovation management (MS)
- international business (MBA)
- management (MBA)
- marketing (MBA, MS)

Nursing Program
Dr. Nancy Ross, Director
Programs in:
- adult nurse practitioner (MSN)
- family nurse practitioner (MSN)
- nursing administration (MSN)
- nursing education (MSN)

Program in Teaching
Dr. Martine Harrison, Associate Professor of Education
Programs in:
- education (MAT)
- math education (MAT)
- reading (M Ed)
- science education (MAT)

■ UNIVERSITY OF WEST FLORIDA
Pensacola, FL 32514-5750
http://uwf.edu/

State-supported, coed, comprehensive institution. CGS member. *Enrollment:* 9,819 graduate, professional, and undergraduate students; 365 full-time matriculated graduate/professional students (240 women), 907 part-time matriculated graduate/professional students (576 women). *Graduate faculty:* 165 full-time (60 women), 56 part-time/adjunct (29 women). *Computer facilities:* 900 computers available on campus for general student use. A campuswide network can be accessed from student residence rooms and from off campus. Internet access and online class registration are available. *Library facilities:* John C. Pace Library plus 2 others. *Graduate expenses:* Tuition, state resident: full-time $5,871; part-time $245 per credit hour. Tuition, nonresident: full-time $21,241; part-time $885 per credit hour. *General application contact:* Dr. Richard A. Barth, Director of Admissions, 850-474-2230.

College of Arts and Sciences: Arts
Dr. Jane Halonen, Dean
Programs in:
- anthropology (MA)
- applied politics (MA)
- arts and sciences: arts (MA)
- communication arts (MA)
- creative writing (MA)
- historical archaeology (MA)
- history (MA)
- interdisciplinary humanities (MA)
- literature (MA)
- political science (MA)
- psychology (MA)

College of Arts and Sciences: Sciences
Dr. Jane Halonen, Dean
Programs in:
- arts and sciences: sciences (MA, MPH, MS, MST)
- biological chemistry (MS)
- biology (MS, MST)
- biology education (MST)
- coastal zone studies (MS)
- computer science (MS)
- environmental biology (MS)
- environmental science (MS)
- general biology (MS)
- health communication (MA)
- mathematics and statistics (MS)
- public health (MPH)
- software engineering (MS)

College of Business
Dr. F. Edward Ranelli, Dean
Programs in:
- accounting (MA)
- business (MA, MBA)
- business administration (MBA)

College of Professional Studies
Dr. Donald Chu, Dean
Programs in:
- career and technical studies (M Ed)
- clinical teaching (MA)
- criminal justice (MSA)
- curriculum and instruction (M Ed)
- elementary education (M Ed)
- guidance and counseling (M Ed)
- habilitative science (MA)
- middle and secondary level education (M Ed)
- primary education (M Ed)
- professional studies (M Ed, MA, MS, MSA, Ed D, Ed S)
- reading education (M Ed)
- teacher education (M Ed, MA)

Division of Graduate Education
Dr. Thomas J. Kramer, Chairperson
Programs in:
- curriculum and instruction (Ed D, Ed S)
- educational leadership (M Ed, Ed S)
- instructional technology (M Ed)

Division of Health, Leisure, and Exercise Science
Dr. Stuart W. Ryan, Chairperson
Programs in:
- exercise science (MS)
- health education (MS)
- health, leisure, and exercise science (MS)
- physical education (MS)

Georgia

■ ALBANY STATE UNIVERSITY
Albany, GA 31705-2717
http://www.asurams.edu/

State-supported, coed, comprehensive institution. CGS member. *Computer facilities:* 1,000 computers available on campus for general student use. A campuswide network can be accessed from student residence rooms and from off campus. Internet access, e-mail are available. *Library facilities:* James Pendergrast Memorial Library. *General application contact:* Graduate Admissions Counselor, 229-430-5118.

College of Arts and Sciences
Programs in:
- arts and sciences (MPA, MS)
- community and economic development (MPA)
- criminal justice (MPA, MS)
- fiscal management (MPA)
- general management (MPA)
- health administration and policy (MPA)
- human resources management (MPA)
- public policy (MPA)
- water resource management and policy (MPA)

College of Education
Programs in:
- biology (M Ed)
- business education (M Ed)
- chemistry (M Ed)
- early childhood education (M Ed)
- education (M Ed, Certificate, Ed S)
- educational administration and supervision (M Ed, Certificate, Ed S)
- English education (M Ed)
- health and physical education (M Ed)
- mathematics education (M Ed)
- middle grades education (M Ed)
- music education (M Ed)
- reading education (M Ed)
- school counseling (M Ed)
- social science education (M Ed)
- special education (M Ed)

College of Health Professions
Program in:
- nursing (MS)

School of Business
Program in:
- water policy (MBA)

■ AMERICAN INTERCONTINENTAL UNIVERSITY BUCKHEAD CAMPUS
Atlanta, GA 30326-1016
http://buckhead.aiuniv.edu/

Proprietary, coed, comprehensive institution. *Enrollment:* 1,152 graduate, professional,

American InterContinental University Buckhead Campus (continued)
and undergraduate students; 19 full-time matriculated graduate/professional students (16 women). *Graduate faculty:* 2 full-time (1 woman), 1 part-time/adjunct (0 women). *Computer facilities:* 86 computers available on campus for general student use. A campuswide network can be accessed from off campus. Internet access is available. *Library facilities:* American Intercontinental University Library-Buckhead Campus. *General application contact:* Mike Betz, Vice President Admissions and Marketing, 404-965-5719.

Program in Business Administration

Dr. Sonia Heywood, Dean of Business
Programs in:
accounting and finance (MBA)
management (MBA)
marketing (MBA)

■ AMERICAN INTERCONTINENTAL UNIVERSITY DUNWOODY CAMPUS

Atlanta, GA 30328
http://www.aiudunwoody.com/

Proprietary, coed, comprehensive institution. *General application contact:* Information Contact, 888-754-4422 Ext. 8072.

Program in Global Technology Management

Program in:
global technology management (MBA)

Program in Information Technology

Program in:
information technology (MIT)

■ ARMSTRONG ATLANTIC STATE UNIVERSITY

Savannah, GA 31419-1997
http://www.armstrong.edu/

State-supported, coed, comprehensive institution. CGS member. *Enrollment:* 6,728 graduate, professional, and undergraduate students; 195 full-time matriculated graduate/professional students (153 women), 447 part-time matriculated graduate/professional students (338 women). *Graduate faculty:* 62 full-time (29 women). *Computer facilities:* 160 computers available on campus for general student use. A campuswide network can be accessed from student residence rooms and from off campus. Internet access and online class registration are available. *Library facilities:* Lane Library. *Graduate expenses:* Tuition, state resident: full-time $2,286; part-time $127 per credit. Tuition, nonresident: full-time $9,144; part-time $508 per credit. One-time fee: $257. *General application contact:* Dr. Michael Price, Assistant Vice President of Graduate Studies, 912-921-5711.

Find University Details at www.petersons.com/gradchannel.

School of Graduate Studies

Dr. Michael Price, Assistant Vice President of Graduate Studies
Programs in:
adult education (M Ed)
computer science (MS)
criminal justice (MS)
early childhood education (M Ed)
education (M Ed)
elementary education (M Ed)
health services administration (MHSA)
history (MA)
liberal and professional studies (MALPS)
middle grades education (M Ed)
nursing (MSN)
physical therapy (MSPT)
public health (MPH)
secondary education (M Ed)
special education (M Ed)
sports health sciences (MSSM)

■ AUGUSTA STATE UNIVERSITY

Augusta, GA 30904-2200
http://www.aug.edu/

State-supported, coed, comprehensive institution. *Enrollment:* 6,552 graduate, professional, and undergraduate students; 189 full-time matriculated graduate/professional students (133 women), 370 part-time matriculated graduate/professional students (276 women). *Graduate faculty:* 39 full-time (23 women), 13 part-time/adjunct (11 women). *Computer facilities:* 325 computers available on campus for general student use. A campuswide network can be accessed from off campus. Internet access and online class registration are available. *Library facilities:* Reese Library plus 1 other. *Graduate expenses:* Tuition, state resident: full-time $3,044; part-time $127 per credit hour. Tuition, nonresident: full-time $12,172; part-time $508 per credit hour. *General application contact:* Katherine Sweeney, Director of Admissions/Registrar, 706-737-1405.

Graduate Studies

Dr. Samuel Sullivan, Vice President for Academic Affairs

College of Arts and Sciences

Dr. Robert R. Parham, Dean
Programs in:
arts and sciences (MPA, MS)
political science (MPA)
psychology (MS)

College of Business Administration

Dr. Marc D Miller, Dean
Program in:
business administration (MBA)

College of Education

Dr. Thomas E. Deering, Dean
Programs in:
counseling/guidance (M Ed)
education (M Ed, Ed S)
educational leadership (M Ed, Ed S)
elementary education (M Ed, Ed S)
health and physical education (M Ed)
middle grades education (M Ed, Ed S)
secondary education (M Ed, Ed S)
special education (M Ed, Ed S)

■ BRENAU UNIVERSITY

Gainesville, GA 30501
http://www.brenau.edu/

Independent, Undergraduate: women only; graduate: coed, comprehensive institution. *Enrollment:* 846 graduate, professional, and undergraduate students; 209 full-time matriculated graduate/professional students (173 women), 344 part-time matriculated graduate/professional students (264 women). *Graduate faculty:* 45 full-time (33 women), 38 part-time/adjunct (16 women). *Computer facilities:* 200 computers available on campus for general student use. A campuswide network can be accessed from student residence rooms and from off campus. Internet access and online class registration are available. *Library facilities:* Trustee Library. *General application contact:* Nathan Goss, Admissions Coordinator, 770-534-6162.

Graduate Programs

Dr. Helen Ray, Dean

School of Business and Mass Communication

Dr. Bill Haney, Dean
Programs in:
accounting (MBA)
healthcare management (MBA)
leadership development (MBA)
management (MBA)
organizational development (MS)

School of Education

Dr. William B. Ware, Dean
Programs in:
early childhood education (M Ed, Ed S)
learning disabilities (M Ed)
middle grades education (M Ed, Ed S)

School of Health and Science

Dr. Gale Starich, Dean
Programs in:
family nurse practitioner (MS)
nurse educator (MS)
occupational therapy (MS)
psychology (MS)

■ CLARK ATLANTA UNIVERSITY
Atlanta, GA 30314
http://www.cau.edu/

Independent-religious, coed, university. CGS member. *Computer facilities:* 640 computers available on campus for general student use. A campuswide network can be accessed from off campus. Internet access and online class registration are available. *Library facilities:* Robert W. Woodruff Library. *General application contact:* Graduate Program Assistant, 404-880-8709.

School of Arts and Sciences
Programs in:
African-American studies (MA)
Africana women's studies (MA, DA)
applied mathematics (MS)
arts and sciences (MA, MPA, MS, DA, PhD)
biology (MS, PhD)
computer and information science (MS)
computer science (MS)
criminal justice (MA)
economics (MA)
English (MA)
history (MA)
humanities (DA)
inorganic chemistry (MS, PhD)
organic chemistry (MS, PhD)
physical chemistry (MS, PhD)
physics (MS)
political science (MA, PhD)
public administration (MPA)
Romance languages (MA)
science education (DA)
sociology (MA)

School of Business Administration
Programs in:
business administration (MBA)
decision science (MBA)
finance (MBA)
marketing (MBA)

School of Education
Programs in:
counseling (MA, PhD)
curriculum (MA, Ed S)
education (MA, Ed D, PhD, Ed S)
education psychology (MA)
educational leadership (MA, Ed D, Ed S)
exceptional student education (MA, Ed S)

School of International Affairs and Development
Programs in:
international affairs and development (PhD)
international business and development (MA)
international development administration (MA)
international development education and planning (MA)
international relations (MA)
regional studies (MA)

School of Social Work
Program in:
social work (MSW, PhD)

■ COLUMBUS STATE UNIVERSITY
Columbus, GA 31907-5645
http://www.colstate.edu/

State-supported, coed, comprehensive institution. *Enrollment:* 7,597 graduate, professional, and undergraduate students; 291 full-time matriculated graduate/professional students (172 women), 524 part-time matriculated graduate/professional students (264 women). *Graduate faculty:* 58 full-time (27 women), 19 part-time/adjunct (9 women). *Computer facilities:* 300 computers available on campus for general student use. A campuswide network can be accessed from student residence rooms and from off campus. Internet access and online class registration are available. *Library facilities:* Simon Schwob Memorial Library. *Graduate expenses:* Tuition, state resident: part-time $127 per semester hour. Tuition, nonresident: part-time $508 per semester hour. Required fees: $264 per semester. Tuition and fees vary according to course load. *General application contact:* Katie Thornton, Graduate Admissions Specialist, 706-568-2035.

Graduate Studies
Dr. George E. Stanton, Vice President for Academic Affairs

College of Arts and Letters
Dr. James Patrick McHenry, Acting Dean
Programs in:
art education (M Ed)
arts and letters (M Ed, MM, MPA)
music education (MM)
public administration (MPA)

College of Education
Dr. David Rock, Dean
Programs in:
community counseling (MS)
early childhood education (M Ed, Ed S)
education (M Ed, MS, Ed S)
educational leadership (M Ed, Ed S)
instructional technology (MS)
middle grades education (M Ed, Ed S)
physical education (M Ed)
school counseling (M Ed, Ed S)
secondary education (M Ed, Ed S)
special education (Ed S)

College of Science
Dr. Glenn Stokes, Acting Dean
Programs in:
applied computer science (MS)
environmental science (MS)
science (MS)

D. Abbott Turner College of Business
Dr. Linda U. Hadley, Dean
Program in:
business administration (MBA)

■ DEVRY UNIVERSITY
Decatur, GA 30030-2198
http://www.devry.edu/

Proprietary, coed, comprehensive institution. *Computer facilities:* Computer purchase and lease plans are available. A campuswide network can be accessed from off campus. Internet access and online class registration are available. *Library facilities:* Learning Resource Center.

Keller Graduate School of Management
Program in:
management (MAFM, MBA, MHRM, MISM, MNCM, MPA, MPM)

■ EMORY UNIVERSITY
Atlanta, GA 30322-1100
http://www.emory.edu/

Independent-religious, coed, university. CGS member. *Enrollment:* 12,338 graduate, professional, and undergraduate students; 4,877 full-time matriculated graduate/professional students (2,799 women), 815 part-time matriculated graduate/professional students (483 women). *Graduate faculty:* 2,760 full-time (966 women), 374 part-time/adjunct (214 women). *Computer facilities:* Computer purchase and lease plans are available. 600 computers available on campus for general student use. A campuswide network can be accessed from student residence rooms and from off campus. Internet access and online class registration are available. *Library facilities:* Robert W. Woodruff Library plus 7 others. *Graduate expenses:* Tuition: full-time $30,246. *General application contact:* Kharen Fulton, Director of Admissions, 404-727-0184.

Find University Details at www.petersons.com/gradchannel.

Candler School of Theology
Program in:
theology (M Div, MTS, Th M, Th D)

Graduate School of Arts and Sciences
Programs in:
anthropology (PhD)
art history (PhD)
arts and sciences (M Ed, MA, MAT, MM, MPH, MS, MSM, MSPH, PhD, Certificate, DAST)
biophysics (PhD)
biostatistics (MPH, MSPH, PhD)
chemistry (PhD)

Emory University (continued)
- choral conducting (MM, MSM)
- clinical psychology (PhD)
- clinical research (MS)
- cognition and development (PhD)
- comparative literature (PhD, Certificate)
- computer science (MS)
- condensed matter physics (PhD)
- economics (PhD)
- English (Certificate)
- film studies (Certificate)
- French (PhD, Certificate)
- French and educational studies (PhD)
- history (PhD)
- Jewish studies (MA)
- mathematics (PhD)
- Middle Eastern studies (PhD)
- neuroscience and animal behavior (PhD)
- non-linear physics (PhD)
- nursing (PhD)
- organ performance (MM, MSM)
- philosophy (Certificate)
- political science (PhD)
- psychoanalytic studies (PhD)
- public health informatics (MSPH)
- radiological physics (PhD)
- religion (PhD)
- sociology (MA, PhD)
- soft condensed matter physics (PhD)
- solid-state physics (PhD)
- Spanish (PhD, Certificate)
- statistical physics (PhD)
- women studies (Certificate)
- women's studies (Certificate)

Division of Biological and Biomedical Sciences
Dr. Keith Wilkinson, Acting Director
Programs in:
- biochemistry, cell and developmental biology (PhD)
- biological and biomedical sciences (PhD)
- genetics and molecular biology (PhD)
- immunology and molecular pathogenesis (PhD)
- microbiology and molecular genetics (PhD)
- molecular and systems pharmacology (PhD)
- neuroscience (PhD)
- nutrition and health sciences (PhD)
- population biology, ecology and evolution (PhD)

Division of Educational Studies
Programs in:
- educational studies (MA, PhD, DAST)
- middle grades teaching (M Ed, MAT)
- secondary teaching (M Ed, MAT)

Division of Religion
Program in:
- religion (PhD)

Graduate Institute of Liberal Arts
Program in:
- liberal arts (PhD)

Nell Hodgson Woodruff School of Nursing
Programs in:
- adult and elder health advanced practice nursing (MSN)
- emergency nurse practitioner (MSN)
- family nurse practitioner (MSN)
- family nurse-midwife (MSN)
- leadership in healthcare (MSN)
- nurse midwifery (MSN)
- nursing administration (MSN)
- pediatric advanced nursing practice (MSN)
- public health nursing (MSN)
- women's health nurse practitioner (MSN)

Roberto C. Goizueta Business School
Lawrence Benveniste, Dean
Program in:
- business (EMBA, MBA, WEMBA, PhD)

Rollins School of Public Health
Dr. Richard Levinson, Executive Associate Dean for Academic Affairs
Programs in:
- applied epidemiology (MPH)
- behavioral sciences and health education (MPH, PhD)
- biostatistics (MPH, MSPH, PhD)
- environmental and occupational health (MPH, MSPH)
- epidemiology (MPH, MSPH, PhD)
- global environmental health (MPH)
- health policy (MPH)
- health services management (MPH)
- health services research and health policy (PhD)
- healthcare outcomes (MPH)
- prevention option (MPH)
- public health (MPH, MSPH, PhD)
- public health informatics (MSPH)
- public nutrition (MSPH, PhD)

School of Law
David F. Partlett, Dean
Program in:
- law (JD, LL M, Certificate)

School of Medicine
Dr. John William Eley, Executive Associate Dean, Medical Education and Student Affairs
Programs in:
- anesthesiology (MM Sc)
- anesthesiology/patient monitoring systems (MM Sc)
- medicine (MD, MM Sc, DPT)
- ophthalmic technology (MM Sc)
- physical therapy (DPT)
- physician assistant (MM Sc)

■ FORT VALLEY STATE UNIVERSITY
Fort Valley, GA 31030-4313
http://www.fvsu.edu/

State-supported, coed, comprehensive institution. *Computer facilities:* 633 computers available on campus for general student use. A campuswide network can be accessed from off campus. Online grade reports available. *Library facilities:* Henry A. Hunt Memorial Library plus 2 others. *General application contact:* Dean of Admissions and Enrollment Management, 478-825-6307.

College of Graduate Studies and Extended Education
Programs in:
- animal science (MS)
- early childhood education (MS)
- environmental health (MPH)
- guidance and counseling (MS, Ed S)
- mental health counseling (MS)
- middle grades education (MS)
- vocational rehabilitation counseling (MS)

■ GEORGIA COLLEGE & STATE UNIVERSITY
Milledgeville, GA 31061
http://www.gcsu.edu/

State-supported, coed, comprehensive institution. *Enrollment:* 6,041 graduate, professional, and undergraduate students; 390 full-time matriculated graduate/professional students (254 women), 510 part-time matriculated graduate/professional students (327 women). *Graduate faculty:* 298 full-time (157 women). *Computer facilities:* 500 computers available on campus for general student use. A campuswide network can be accessed from student residence rooms and from off campus. Internet access and online class registration are available. *Library facilities:* Ina Dillard Russell Library. *Graduate expenses:* Tuition, state resident: full-time $3,222; part-time $179 per credit hour. Tuition, nonresident: full-time $12,870; part-time $715 per credit hour. Tuition and fees vary according to course load. *General application contact:* Leah Donna Douglas, Research and Graduate Services, Research Coordinator, 478-445-6278.

Graduate School
Dr. Mark Pelton, Associate Vice President of the Extended University, Research and Graduate Services

The J. Whitney Bunting School of Business
Dr. Faye Gilbert, Dean
Programs in:
- accountancy (MACCT)
- business (MBA)
- information systems (MIS)

School of Education
Dr. Linda Irwin-Devitis, Dean
Programs in:
- administration and supervision (M Ed, Ed S)
- behavior disorders (M Ed)
- early childhood education (M Ed, Ed S)
- education (M Ed, MAT, Ed S)
- English education (M Ed)
- instructional technology (M Ed)
- interrelated teaching (M Ed)
- learning disabilities (M Ed)
- mathematics education (M Ed)
- mental retardation (M Ed)
- middle grades education (M Ed, Ed S)
- natural science education (M Ed, Ed S)
- secondary education (MAT)
- social science education (M Ed, Ed S)
- special education (M Ed)

School of Health Sciences
Dr. Sandra Gangstead, Dean
Programs in:
- health and physical education (M Ed, Ed S)
- kinesiology (M Ed, Ed S)
- music therapy (MMT)
- nursing (MSN)

School of Liberal Arts and Sciences
Dr. Beth Rushing, Dean
Programs in:
- biology (MS)
- creative writing (MFA)
- criminal justice (MS)
- English (MA)
- history (MA)
- liberal arts and sciences (MA, MFA, MPA, MS, MSA, MSLS)
- logistics (MSA, MSLS)
- logistics management (MSA)
- logistics systems (MSLS)
- public administration and public affairs (MPA, MS)

■ GEORGIA INSTITUTE OF TECHNOLOGY
Atlanta, GA 30332-0001
http://www.gatech.edu/

State-supported, coed, university. CGS member. *Computer facilities:* 2,160 computers available on campus for general student use. A campuswide network can be accessed from student residence rooms and from off campus. Internet access and online class registration are available. *Library facilities:* Library and Information Center plus 1 other. *General application contact:* Manager, Graduate Academic and Enrollment Services, 404-894-4612.

Graduate Studies and Research
Programs in:
- algorithms, combinatorics, and optimization (PhD)
- statistics (MS Stat)

College of Architecture
Programs in:
- architecture (PhD)
- economic development (MCRP)
- environmental planning and management (MCRP)
- geographic information systems (MCRP)
- integrated facility management (MS)
- integrated project delivery systems (MS)
- land development (MCRP)
- land use planning (MCRP)
- transportation (MCRP)
- urban design (MCRP)

College of Computing
Programs in:
- algorithms, combinatorics, and optimization (PhD)
- computer science (MS, MSCS, PhD)
- human computer interaction (MSHCI)

College of Engineering
Programs in:
- aerospace engineering (MS, MSAE, PhD)
- algorithms, combinatorics, and optimization (PhD)
- bioengineering (MS Bio E, PhD)
- biomedical engineering (MS Bio E)
- chemical engineering (MS Ch E, PhD)
- civil engineering (MS, MSCE, PhD)
- electrical and computer engineering (MS, MSEE, PhD)
- engineering (MS, MS Bio E, MS Ch E, MS Env E, MS Poly, MS Stat, MSAE, MSCE, MSEE, MSESM, MSHS, MSIE, MSME, MSNE, MSOR, PhD, Certificate)
- engineering science and mechanics (MS, MSESM, PhD)
- environmental engineering (MS, MS Env E, PhD)
- health systems (MSHS)
- industrial and systems engineering (MS, MS Stat, MSIE, PhD)
- industrial engineering (MS, MSIE)
- materials science and engineering (MS, PhD)
- mechanical engineering (MS, MS Bio E, MSME, PhD)
- medical physics (MS)
- nuclear and radiological engineering (MSNE, PhD)
- nuclear and radiological engineering and medical physics (MS, MSNE, PhD)
- operations research (MSOR)
- paper science and engineering (MS, PhD)
- polymer, textile and fiber engineering (MS, PhD)
- polymers (MS Poly)
- statistics (MS Stat)

College of Management
Programs in:
- accounting (MBA, PhD)
- e-commerce (Certificate)
- engineering entrepreneurship (MBA)
- entrepreneurship (Certificate)
- finance (MBA, PhD)
- information technology management (MBA, PhD)
- international business (MBA, Certificate)
- management (MBA, MS, MSMOT, PhD, Certificate)
- management of technology (Certificate)
- marketing (MBA, PhD)
- operations management (MBA, PhD)
- organizational behavior (MBA, PhD)
- quantitative and computational finance (MS)
- strategic management (MBA, PhD)

College of Sciences
Programs in:
- algorithms, combinatorics, and optimization (PhD)
- applied biology (MS, PhD)
- applied mathematics (MS)
- atmospheric chemistry and air pollution (MS, PhD)
- atmospheric dynamics and climate (MS, PhD)
- bioinformatics (MS, PhD)
- biology (MS)
- chemistry and biochemistry (MS, MS Chem, PhD)
- geochemistry (MS, PhD)
- human computer interaction (MSHCI)
- hydrologic cycle (MS, PhD)
- mathematics (PhD)
- ocean sciences (MS, PhD)
- physics (MS, PhD)
- prosthetics and orthotics (MS)
- psychology (MS, MS Psy, PhD)
- quantitative and computational finance (MS)
- sciences (MS, MS Chem, MS Phys, MS Psy, MS Stat, MSA Phy, MSHCI, PhD)
- solid-earth and environmental geophysics (MS, PhD)
- statistics (MS Stat)

Ivan Allen College of Policy and International Affairs
Programs in:
- economics (MS)
- history of technology (MSHT, PhD)
- human computer interaction (MSHCI)
- information design and technology (MSIDT)
- international affairs (MS Int A)
- policy and international affairs (MS, MS Int A, MS Pub P, MSHCI, MSHT, MSIDT, PhD)
- public policy (MS Pub P, PhD)

■ GEORGIA SOUTHERN UNIVERSITY
Statesboro, GA 30460
http://www.georgiasouthern.edu/

State-supported, coed, comprehensive institution. CGS member. *Enrollment:* 16,425 graduate, professional, and undergraduate students; 583 full-time matriculated graduate/professional students (367

Georgia Southern University (continued)
women), 1,195 part-time matriculated graduate/professional students (898 women). *Graduate faculty:* 427 full-time (169 women), 27 part-time/adjunct (17 women). *Computer facilities:* 1,675 computers available on campus for general student use. A campuswide network can be accessed from student residence rooms and from off campus. Internet access and online class registration are available. *Library facilities:* Henderson Library. *General application contact:* Office of Graduate Admissions, 912-681-5384.

Jack N. Averitt College of Graduate Studies
Dr. Saundra Nettles, Interim Dean of Graduate Studies and Research

Allen E. Paulson College of Science and Technology
Dr. Bret Danilowicz, Dean
Programs in:
- biology (MS)
- mathematics (MS)
- mechanical and electrical engineering (M Tech)
- science and technology (M Tech, MS)

College of Business Administration
Dr. Ron Shiffler, Dean
Programs in:
- accounting (M Acc)
- business administration (M Acc, MBA)

College of Education
Dr. Lucindia Chance, Dean
Programs in:
- art education (M Ed, MAT)
- business education (M Ed, MAT)
- counselor education (M Ed, Ed S)
- curriculum studies (Ed D)
- early childhood education (M Ed)
- education (M Ed, MAT, Ed D, Ed S)
- educational administration (Ed D)
- educational leadership (M Ed, Ed S)
- English education (M Ed, MAT)
- French education (M Ed)
- health and physical education (M Ed)
- higher education (M Ed)
- instructional technology (M Ed)
- mathematics education (M Ed, MAT)
- middle grades education (M Ed, MAT)
- reading education (M Ed)
- school psychology (M Ed, Ed S)
- science education (M Ed, MAT)
- social science education (M Ed, MAT)
- Spanish education (MAT)
- special education (M Ed, MAT)
- teaching and learning (Ed S)
- technology education (M Ed)

College of Health and Human Sciences
Dr. Frederick Whitt, Dean
Programs in:
- health and human sciences (MS, MSN, Certificate)
- health and kinesiology (MS)
- recreation administration (MS)
- rural community health nurse practitioner (MSN)
- rural community health nurse specialist (Certificate)
- rural family nurse practitioner (MSN, Certificate)
- sport management (MS)
- women's health nurse practitioner (MSN, Certificate)

College of Liberal Arts and Social Sciences
Dr. Jane Rhoades Hudak, Dean
Programs in:
- English (MA)
- fine arts (MFA)
- foreign languages (MA)
- history (MA)
- liberal arts and social sciences (MA, MFA, MM, MPA, MS)
- music (MM)
- psychology (MS)
- public administration (MPA)
- sociology (MA)

Jiann-Ping Hsu College of Public Health
Dr. Charlie Hardy, Dean
Programs in:
- health services administration (MHSA)
- public health (MHSA, MPH)

■ GEORGIA SOUTHWESTERN STATE UNIVERSITY
Americus, GA 31709-4693
http://www.gsw.edu/

State-supported, coed, comprehensive institution. *Computer facilities:* 550 computers available on campus for general student use. A campuswide network can be accessed from student residence rooms and from off campus. Internet access and online class registration are available. *Library facilities:* James Earl Carter Library.

Graduate Studies

School of Business Administration
Program in:
- business administration (MBA)

School of Computer and Information Sciences
Programs in:
- computer information systems (MS)
- computer science (MS)

School of Education
Programs in:
- early childhood education (M Ed, Ed S)
- health and physical education (M Ed)
- middle grades education (M Ed, Ed S)
- reading (M Ed)
- secondary education (M Ed)
- special education (M Ed)

■ GEORGIA STATE UNIVERSITY
Atlanta, GA 30303-3083
http://www.gsu.edu/

State-supported, coed, university. CGS member. *Enrollment:* 26,134 graduate, professional, and undergraduate students; 4,045 full-time matriculated graduate/professional students (2,474 women), 2,967 part-time matriculated graduate/professional students (1,730 women). *Graduate faculty:* 762 full-time (313 women). *Computer facilities:* Computer purchase and lease plans are available. 775 computers available on campus for general student use. A campuswide network can be accessed from student residence rooms and from off campus. Internet access and online class registration are available. *Library facilities:* Pullen Library plus 1 other. *General application contact:* Daniel Niccum, Associate Director, 404-651-2365.

Andrew Young School of Policy Studies
Dr. Roy Bahl, Dean
Programs in:
- economics (MA, PhD)
- policy studies (MA, MPA, MS, PhD)
- public administration (MPA)
- public policy (PhD)
- urban policy studies (MS)

College of Arts and Sciences
Dr. Lauren B. Adamson, Dean
Programs in:
- anthropology (MA)
- applied and environmental microbiology (MS, PhD)
- applied linguistics (MA, PhD)
- arts and sciences (M Mu, MA, MA Ed, MAT, MFA, MHP, MS, PhD, Certificate)
- astronomy (PhD)
- cellular and molecular biology and physiology (MS, PhD)
- chemistry (MS, PhD)
- computer science (MS, PhD)
- creative writing (MA, MFA, PhD)
- English (MA, PhD)
- fiction (MFA)
- film/video/digital imaging (MA)
- French (MA, Certificate)
- geographic information systems (Certificate)
- geography (MA)
- geology (MS)
- German (MA, Certificate)
- gerontology (MA)
- heritage preservation (MHP)
- history (MA, PhD)
- human communication and social influence (MA)
- hydrogeology (Certificate)
- literary studies and composition (MA, PhD)

mass communication (MA)
mathematics (MAT, MS)
molecular genetics and biochemistry (MS, PhD)
moving image studies (PhD)
neurobiology and behavior (MS, PhD)
philosophy (MA)
physics (MS, PhD)
poetry (MFA)
political science (MA, PhD)
psychology (MA, PhD)
public communication (PhD)
religious studies (MA)
rhetoric (MA, PhD)
sociology (MA, PhD)
Spanish (MA, Certificate)
translation and interpretation (Certificate)

Ernest G. Welch School of Art and Design
Prof. Cheryl Goldsleger, Director
Programs in:
art and design (MA, MA Ed, MFA)
art education (MA Ed)
art history (MA)
studio art (MFA)

School of Music
Dr. John Haberlen, Director
Program in:
music (M Mu)

Women's Studies Institute
Dr. Susan Talburt, Director
Program in:
women's studies (MA)

College of Education
Dr. Ron P. Colarusso, Dean
Programs in:
art education (Ed S)
behavior and learning disabilities (M Ed)
communication disorders (M Ed)
counseling psychology (PhD)
counselor education and practice (PhD)
early childhood education (M Ed, PhD, Ed S)
education (M Ed, MLM, MS, PhD, Ed S)
education of students with exceptionalities (PhD)
educational leadership (M Ed, PhD, Ed S)
educational psychology (MS, PhD)
educational research (MS, PhD)
English education (M Ed, Ed S)
exercise science (MS)
health and physical education (M Ed)
instructional technology (MS, PhD, Ed S)
library media technology (MLM, PhD, Ed S)
library science/media (MLM, MS, PhD, Ed S)
mathematics education (M Ed, PhD, Ed S)
middle childhood education (M Ed, Ed S)
multiple and severe disabilities (M Ed)
music education (PhD)
professional counseling (MS, PhD, Ed S)
reading instruction (M Ed, PhD, Ed S)
reading, language and literacy (M Ed)
reading, language, and literacy (PhD, Ed S)
rehabilitation counseling (MS)
research, measurements and statistics (PhD)
school counseling (M Ed, Ed S)
school psychology (M Ed, PhD, Ed S)
science education (M Ed, PhD, Ed S)
secondary education (M Ed, PhD, Ed S)
social foundations of education (MS, PhD)
social studies education (M Ed, PhD, Ed S)
sport science (PhD)
sports administration (MS)
sports medicine (MS)
teaching English as a second language (M Ed)

College of Health and Human Sciences
Dr. Susan Kelley, Dean
Programs in:
criminal justice (MS)
health and human sciences (MPH, MS, MSW, DPT, PhD, Certificate)

Institute of Public Health
Michael P Eriksen, Director
Program in:
public health (MPH, Certificate)

School of Health Professions
Dr. Lynda Goodfellow, Director
Programs in:
health professions (MS, DPT, Certificate)
nutrition (MS, Certificate)
physical therapy (DPT)

School of Nursing
Dr. Barbara Woodring, Director
Programs in:
adult health (MS)
child health (MS)
family nurse practitioner (MS)
health promotion, protection and restoration (PhD)
nursing (Certificate)
perinatal/women's health (MS)
psychiatric/mental health (MS)

School of Social Work
Dr. Nancy Kropf, Director
Program in:
community partnerships (MSW)

College of Law
Dr. Steven J. Kaminshine, Dean
Program in:
law (JD)

J. Mack Robinson College of Business
Dr. H. Fenwick Huss, Dean
Programs in:
accounting/information systems (MBA)
actuarial science (MAS, MBA)
business (EMBA, MAS, MBA, MHA, MIB, MPA, MS, MSHA, MSIS, MSRE, MTX, PMBA, PhD, Certificate)
business analysis (MBA, MS)
computer information systems (MBA, MSIS, PhD)
enterprise risk management (MBA)
entrepreneurship (MBA)
finance (MBA, MS, PhD)
general business (MBA)
general business administration (EMBA, PMBA)
human resources management (MBA, MS)
information systems consulting (MBA)
information systems risk management (MBA)
international business and information technology (MBA)
international entrepreneurship (MBA)
management (MBA, PhD)
marketing (MBA, MS, PhD)
operations management (MBA, MS, PhD)
organization change (MS)
personal financial planning (MS, Certificate)
real estate (MBA, MSRE, PhD, Certificate)
risk management and insurance (MBA, MS, PhD)

Institute of Health Administration
Dr. Andrew T. Sumner, Director
Program in:
health administration (MBA, MHA, MSHA)

Institute of International Business
Dr. Joan Gabel, Director
Program in:
international business (MBA, MIB)

School of Accountancy
Dr. Galen R. Sevcik, Interim Director
Programs in:
accountancy (MBA, MPA, MTX, PhD, Certificate)
taxation (MTX)

W. T. Beebe Institute of Personnel and Employee Relations
Dr. Todd J. Maurer, Director
Program in:
personnel and employee relations (MBA, MS, PhD)

■ KENNESAW STATE UNIVERSITY
Kennesaw, GA 30144-5591
http://www.kennesaw.edu/

State-supported, coed, comprehensive institution. CGS member. *Enrollment:* 19,854 graduate, professional, and undergraduate students; 625 full-time matriculated graduate/professional students (420

Kennesaw State University (continued)
women), 1,283 part-time matriculated graduate/professional students (735 women). *Graduate faculty:* 221 full-time (88 women), 34 part-time/adjunct (12 women). *Computer facilities:* 1,087 computers available on campus for general student use. A campuswide network can be accessed from student residence rooms and from off campus. Internet access and online class registration are available. *Library facilities:* Horace W. Sturgis Library. *Graduate expenses:* Tuition, state resident: full-time $3,044; part-time $127 per semester hour. Tuition, nonresident: full-time $12,172; part-time $508 per semester hour. Required fees: $353 per semester. Full-time tuition and fees vary according to campus/location and program. *General application contact:* Vilma Marquez, Admissions Counselor, 770-420-4377.

College of Health and Human Services

Dr. Richard Sowell, Dean
Programs in:
- advanced care management and leadership (MSN)
- health and human services (MSN, MSW)
- primary care nurse practitioner (MSN)
- social work (MSW)

College of Humanities and Social Sciences

Dr. Richard Vengroff, Dean
Programs in:
- conflict management (MSCM)
- humanities and social sciences (MAPW, MPA, MSCM)
- professional writing (MAPW)
- public administration (MPA)

College of Science and Mathematics

Dr. Laurence I. Peterson, Dean
Programs in:
- applied computer science (MSaCS)
- applied statistics (MSAS)
- information systems (MSIS)
- science and mathematics (MSAS, MSIS, MSaCS)

Leland and Clarice C. Bagwell College of Education

Dr. Frank Butler, Interim Dean
Programs in:
- adolescent education (M Ed)
- early childhood education (M Ed)
- education (M Ed, MAT, Ed D, Ed S)
- educational leadership (M Ed)
- leadership for learning (Ed D, Ed S)
- special education (M Ed)
- teaching (MAT)

Michael J. Coles College of Business

Dr. Timothy Mescon, Dean
Programs in:
- accounting (M Acc)
- business (M Acc, MBA)
- business administration (MBA)

■ MERCER UNIVERSITY
Macon, GA 31207-0003
http://www.mercer.edu/

Independent-religious, coed, comprehensive institution. *Enrollment:* 5,090 graduate, professional, and undergraduate students; 1,802 full-time matriculated graduate/professional students (1,000 women), 712 part-time matriculated graduate/professional students (454 women). *Graduate faculty:* 125 full-time (52 women), 27 part-time/adjunct (10 women). *Computer facilities:* 350 computers available on campus for general student use. A campuswide network can be accessed from student residence rooms and from off campus. Internet access and online class registration are available. *Library facilities:* Jack Tarver Library plus 3 others. *General application contact:* Information Contact, 478-301-2700.

Graduate Studies, Cecil B. Day Campus

College of Pharmacy and Health Sciences

Dr. Hewitt W. Matthews, Dean
Programs in:
- medical sciences (MS)
- pharmacy (Pharm D, PhD)

Eugene W. Stetson School of Business and Economics

Karen G. Herlitz, Assistant Vice President of Admissions
Program in:
- business administration (MBA, XMBA)

Georgia Baptist College of Nursing

Dr. Susan S. Gunby, Dean/Professor
Programs in:
- nurse education (Certificate)
- nursing (MSN)

James and Carolyn McAfee School of Theology

Dr. R. Alan Culpepper, Dean
Program in:
- theology (M Div, D Min)

Tift College of Education

Dr. Carl R. Martray, Dean
Programs in:
- early childhood education (M Ed, MAT)
- educational leadership (M Ed, PhD)
- middle grades education (M Ed, MAT)
- reading education (M Ed)
- secondary education (M Ed, MAT)
- teacher leadership (Ed S)

Graduate Studies, Macon Campus

Eugene W. Stetson School of Business and Economics

Dr. William S. Mounts, Dean
Program in:
- business and economics (MBA)

School of Engineering

Dr. M. Dayne Aldridge, Dean
Programs in:
- computer engineering (MSE)
- electrical engineering (MSE)
- engineering management (MSE)
- mechanical engineering (MSE)
- software engineering (MSE)
- software systems (MS)
- technical communications management (MS)
- technical management (MS)

School of Music

John E. Simons, Director of Graduate Studies
Programs in:
- choral conducting (MM)
- church music (MM)
- performance (MM)

Tift College of Education

Dr. Carl R. Martray, Dean
Programs in:
- collaborative education (M Ed)
- educational leadership (M Ed, PhD)

School of Medicine

Dr. Martin Dalton, Dean
Program in:
- medicine (MD, MFT, MPH, MSA)

Walter F. George School of Law

Daisy H. Floyd, Dean
Program in:
- law (JD)

■ NORTH GEORGIA COLLEGE & STATE UNIVERSITY
Dahlonega, GA 30597
http://www.ngcsu.edu/

State-supported, coed, comprehensive institution. *Enrollment:* 4,922 graduate, professional, and undergraduate students; 127 full-time matriculated graduate/professional students (92 women), 439 part-time matriculated graduate/professional students (331 women). *Graduate faculty:* 125 full-time (56 women), 28 part-time/adjunct (17 women). *Computer facilities:* 470 computers available on campus for general student use. A campuswide network can be accessed from student residence rooms and from off campus. Internet access and online class registration are available. *Library facilities:* Stewart Library. *Graduate expenses:* Tuition, state resident: full-time $3,044; part-time $127 per credit hour. Tuition, nonresident: full-time $12,172; part-time $508 per credit hour. Required fees: $892; $458 per semester. *General application contact:* Dr. Donna A. Gessell, Director of Graduate Studies and External Programs, 706-864-1528.

Graduate Studies
Dr. Donna A. Gessell, Director of Graduate Studies and External Programs
Programs in:
- community counseling (MS)
- early childhood education (M Ed)
- educational leadership (Ed S)
- family nurse practitioner (MSN)
- middle grades education (M Ed)
- nursing education (MSN)
- physical therapy (DPT)
- public administration (MPA)
- secondary education (M Ed)
- special education (M Ed)

■ PIEDMONT COLLEGE
Demorest, GA 30535-0010
http://www.piedmont.edu/

Independent-religious, coed, comprehensive institution. *Enrollment:* 2,118 graduate, professional, and undergraduate students; 311 full-time matriculated graduate/professional students (213 women), 858 part-time matriculated graduate/professional students (730 women). *Graduate faculty:* 40 full-time (29 women), 50 part-time/adjunct (23 women). *Computer facilities:* 150 computers available on campus for general student use. A campuswide network can be accessed from student residence rooms and from off campus. Internet access, e-mail are available. *Library facilities:* Arrendale Library. *Graduate expenses:* Tuition: part-time $310 per credit hour. *General application contact:* Carol E. Kokesh, Director of Graduate Studies, 706-778-8500 Ext. 1181.

School of Business
Dr. William Piper, Dean
Program in:
- business (MBA)

School of Education
Dr. Jane McFerrin, Dean
Programs in:
- early childhood education (MA, MAT)
- instruction (Ed S)
- secondary education (MA, MAT)

■ SAVANNAH STATE UNIVERSITY
Savannah, GA 31404
http://www.savstate.edu/

State-supported, coed, comprehensive institution. *Computer facilities:* 440 computers available on campus for general student use. A campuswide network can be accessed. Internet access is available. *Library facilities:* Asa H. Gordon Library. *General application contact:* Associate Director of Admissions, 912-356-2345.

Program in Marine Science
Program in:
- marine science (MS)

Program in Public Administration
Program in:
- public administration (MPA)

Program in Social Work
Program in:
- social work (MSW)

Program in Urban Studies
Program in:
- urban studies (MS)

■ SOUTHERN POLYTECHNIC STATE UNIVERSITY
Marietta, GA 30060-2896
http://www.spsu.edu/

State-supported, coed, comprehensive institution. *Enrollment:* 4,206 graduate, professional, and undergraduate students; 163 full-time matriculated graduate/professional students (61 women), 339 part-time matriculated graduate/professional students (115 women). *Graduate faculty:* 46 full-time (15 women), 8 part-time/adjunct (1 woman). *Computer facilities:* 1,500 computers available on campus for general student use. A campuswide network can be accessed from student residence rooms and from off campus. Internet access and online class registration are available. *Library facilities:* Lawrence V. Johnson Library. *Graduate expenses:* Tuition, state resident: part-time $422 per credit hour. Tuition, nonresident: part-time $835 per credit hour. *General application contact:* Virginia A. Head, Director of Admissions, 678-915-4188.

School of Architecture, Civil Engineering Technology and Construction
Dr. Wilson Barnes, Dean
Programs in:
- architecture, civil engineering technology and construction (MS)
- construction (MS)

School of Arts and Sciences
Dr. Alan Gabrielli, Dean
Programs in:
- arts and sciences (MS)
- information design and communication (MS)

School of Computing and Software Engineering
Dr. Michael G. Murphy, Dean
Programs in:
- computer science (MS)
- computing and software engineering (MS, MS SwE, MSIT)
- information technology (MSIT)
- software engineering (MS SwE)

School of Engineering Technology and Management
Dr. David Caudill, Interim Dean
Programs in:
- business administration (MBA)
- engineering technology (MS)
- engineering technology and management (MBA, MS, MS SEng)
- quality assurance (MS)
- systems engineering (MS SEng)

■ UNIVERSITY OF GEORGIA
Athens, GA 30602
http://www.uga.edu/

State-supported, coed, university. CGS member. *Enrollment:* 33,959 graduate, professional, and undergraduate students; 5,982 full-time matriculated graduate/professional students (3,407 women), 2,018 part-time matriculated graduate/professional students (1,260 women). *Graduate faculty:* 1,423 full-time (427 women), 13 part-time/adjunct (6 women). *Computer facilities:* Computer purchase and lease plans are available. 2,500 computers available on campus for general student use. A campuswide network can be accessed from student residence rooms and from off campus. Internet access and online class registration, e-mail, Web pages are available. *Library facilities:* Ilah Dunlap Little Memorial Library plus 2 others. *General application contact:* Krista Haynes, Director of Graduate Admissions, 706-425-1789.

College of Pharmacy
Dr. Svein Oie, Dean
Programs in:
- experimental therapeutics (MS, PhD)
- medicinal chemistry (MS, PhD)
- pharmaceutical and biomedical regulatory affairs (Certificate)
- pharmaceutics (MS, PhD)
- pharmacology (MS, PhD)
- pharmacy (Pharm D, MS, PhD, Certificate)
- pharmacy care administration (MS, PhD)
- toxicology (MS, PhD)

College of Public Health
Dr. Phillip L. Williams, Dean
Programs in:
- environmental health science (MS, PhD)
- health promotion and behavior (M Ed, MA, MPH, PhD, Ed S)
- public health (M Ed, MA, MPH, MS, PhD, Certificate, Ed S)

Institute of Gerontology
Leonard W. Pooh, Director
Program in:
- gerontology (Certificate)

College of Veterinary Medicine
Dr. Sheila W. Allen, Dean
Programs in:
- infectious diseases (MS, PhD)
- pathology (MS, PhD)

University of Georgia (continued)
pharmacology (MS, PhD)
physiology (MS, PhD)
physiology and pharmacology (MS, PhD)
population health (MAM, MFAM)
toxicology (MS, PhD)
veterinary anatomy (MS)
veterinary anatomy and radiology (MS)
veterinary medicine (DVM, MAM, MFAM, MS, PhD)

Graduate School
Dr. Maureen Grasso, Dean

Biomedical and Health Sciences Institute
Dr. Harry A. Dailey, Director
Program in:
neuroscience (PhD)

College of Agricultural and Environmental Sciences
Dr. J. Scott Angle, Dean
Programs in:
agricultural and environmental sciences (MA Ext, MADS, MAE, MAL, MCCS, MFT, MPPPM, MS, PhD)
agricultural economics (MAE, MS, PhD)
agricultural engineering (MS)
agricultural leadership, education, and communication (MA Ext, MAL)
agronomy (MS, PhD)
animal and dairy science (PhD)
animal and dairy sciences (MADS)
animal nutrition (PhD)
animal science (MS)
biological and agricultural engineering (PhD)
biological engineering (MS)
crop and soil sciences (MCCS)
dairy science (MS)
entomology (MS, PhD)
environmental economics (MS)
food science (MS, PhD)
food technology (MFT)
horticulture (MS, PhD)
plant pathology (MS, PhD)
plant protection and pest management (MPPPM)
poultry science (MS, PhD)

College of Arts and Sciences
Dr. Garnett Stokes, Head
Programs in:
analytical chemistry (MS, PhD)
anthropology (MA, PhD)
applied mathematical science (MAMS)
art (MFA, PhD)
art education (MA Ed, Ed D, Ed S)
art history (MA)
artificial intelligence (MS)
arts and sciences (MA, MA Ed, MAMS, MAT, MFA, MM, MS, DMA, Ed D, PhD, Certificate, Ed S)
biochemistry and molecular biology (MS, PhD)
cellular biology (MS, PhD)
classical languages (MA)
comparative literature (MA, PhD)
computer science (MS, PhD)
drama (MFA, PhD)
English (MA, MAT, PhD)
French (MA, MAT)
genetics (MS, PhD)
geography (MA, MS, PhD)
geology (MS, PhD)
German (MA)
Greek (MA)
history (MA, PhD)
inorganic chemistry (MS, PhD)
Latin (MA)
linguistics (MA, PhD)
marine sciences (MS, PhD)
mathematics (MA, PhD)
microbiology (MS, PhD)
music (MA, MM, DMA, PhD)
organic chemistry (MS, PhD)
philosophy (MA, PhD)
physical chemistry (MS, PhD)
physics (MS, PhD)
plant biology (MS, PhD)
psychology (MS, PhD)
religion (MA)
Romance languages (MA, MAT, PhD)
sociology (MA, PhD)
Spanish (MA, MAT)
speech communication (MA, PhD)
statistics (MS, PhD)
women's studies (Certificate)

College of Education
Dr. Louis A. Castenell, Dean
Programs in:
communication sciences and special education (M Ed, MA, Ed D, PhD, Ed S)
counseling and human development services (M Ed, MA, Ed D, PhD, Ed S)
early childhood education (M Ed, PhD, Ed S)
education (M Ed, MA, MAT, MM Ed, Ed D, PhD, Ed S)
educational psychology and instructional technology (M Ed, MA, Ed D, PhD, Ed S)
elementary and middle school education (M Ed, PhD, Ed S)
higher education (Ed D, PhD)
kinesiology (M Ed, MA, Ed D, PhD, Ed S)
language and literacy education (M Ed, MA, Ed D, PhD, Ed S)
lifelong education, administration and policy (M Ed, MA, Ed D, PhD, Ed S)
mathematics and science education (M Ed, MA, Ed D, PhD, Ed S)
music education (MM Ed, Ed D, Ed S)
social foundations of education (PhD)
workforce education, leadership and social foundations (M Ed, MA, MAT, Ed D, PhD, Ed S)

College of Environment and Design
Prof. Scott S. Weinberg, Acting Dean
Programs in:
conservation ecology and sustainable development (MS)
ecology (MS, PhD)
environment and design (MHP, MLA, MS, PhD)
environmental design (MHP, MLA)
historic preservation (MHP)
landscape architecture (MLA)

College of Family and Consumer Sciences
Dr. Jan M. Hathcote, Interim Dean
Programs in:
child and family development (MFCS, MS, PhD)
family and consumer sciences (MFCS, MS, PhD)
foods and nutrition (MFCS, MS, PhD)
housing and consumer economics (MS, PhD)
textiles, merchandising, and interiors (MS, PhD)

Grady School of Journalism and Mass Communication
Dr. E. Culpepper Clark, Dean
Programs in:
journalism and mass communication (MA)
mass communication (PhD)

School of Forestry and Natural Resources
Dr. Robert J. Warren, Acting Dean
Program in:
forestry and natural resources (MFR, MS, PhD)

School of Social Work
Dr. Maurice Daniels, Dean
Programs in:
non-profit organizations (MA, Certificate)
social work (MA, MSW, PhD, Certificate)

Terry College of Business
Dr. Robert E. Hoyt, Dean
Programs in:
accounting (M Acc)
business (M Acc, MA, MBA, MIT, MMR, PhD)
business administration (MA, MBA, PhD)
economics (MA, PhD)
Internet technology (MIT)
marketing (MMR)

School of Law
Rebecca H. White, Dean
Program in:
law (JD, LL M)

School of Public and International Affairs
Dr. Thomas P. Lauth, Dean
Programs in:
non profit organization (MA)
political science (MA, PhD)
public administration (MPA, PhD)
public and international affairs (MA, MPA, DPA, PhD)

■ UNIVERSITY OF WEST GEORGIA
Carrollton, GA 30118
http://www.westga.edu/

State-supported, coed, comprehensive institution. CGS member. *Enrollment:* 10,163 graduate, professional, and undergraduate students; 360 full-time matriculated graduate/professional students (261 women), 1,328 part-time matriculated graduate/professional students (1,049 women). *Graduate faculty:* 230 full-time (104 women), 20 part-time/adjunct (11 women). *Computer facilities:* 745 computers available on campus for general student use. A campuswide network can be accessed from student residence rooms and from off campus. Internet access and online class registration are available. *Library facilities:* Irvine Sullivan Ingram Library. *Graduate expenses:* Tuition, state resident: full-time $2,286; part-time $127 per credit. Tuition, nonresident: full-time $9,144; part-time $508 per credit. Required fees: $494; $27 per credit. $121 per semester. *General application contact:* Dr. Charles W. Clark, Chair, 678-839-6508.

Graduate School
Dr. Charles W. Clark, Chair

College of Arts and Sciences
Dr. David White, Dean
Programs in:
- applied computer science (MS)
- arts and sciences (M Mus, MA, MPA, MS, MSN, Psy D)
- biology (MS)
- consciousness and society (Psy D)
- English (MA)
- gerontology (MA)
- history (MA)
- music education (M Mus)
- nursing (MSN)
- performance (M Mus)
- psychology (MA)
- public administration (MPA)
- rural and small town planning (MS)
- sociology (MA)

College of Education
Dr. Kent Layton, Dean
Programs in:
- administration and supervision (M Ed, Ed S)
- art education (M Ed)
- business education (M Ed, Ed S)
- counseling and guidance (M Ed, Ed S)
- curriculum and instruction (Ed S)
- early childhood education (M Ed, Ed S)
- education (M Ed, Ed D, Ed S)
- education-French (M Ed)
- education-Spanish (M Ed)
- leadership (Ed S)
- learning disabled (Ed S)
- media (M Ed, Ed S)
- middle grades education (M Ed, Ed S)
- physical education (M Ed, Ed S)
- reading education (M Ed)
- school improvement (Ed D)
- secondary education—English (M Ed, Ed S)
- secondary education—mathematics (M Ed, Ed S)
- secondary education—science (M Ed, Ed S)
- secondary education—social studies (M Ed, Ed S)
- special education-behavior disorders (M Ed)
- special education-emotionally handicapped (M Ed)
- special education-general (Ed S)
- special education-interrelated (M Ed)
- speech-language pathology (M Ed)

Richards College of Business
Dr. Faye S. McIntyre, Dean
Programs in:
- accounting and finance (MP Acc)
- business (MBA, MP Acc)
- business administration (MBA)

■ VALDOSTA STATE UNIVERSITY
Valdosta, GA 31698
http://www.valdosta.edu/

State-supported, coed, university. CGS member. *Computer facilities:* 1,400 computers available on campus for general student use. A campuswide network can be accessed from student residence rooms and from off campus. Internet access and online class registration are available. *Library facilities:* Odum Library. *General application contact:* Acting Dean, 229-333-5694.

Graduate School
Program in:
- library and information science (MLIS)

College of Arts and Sciences
Programs in:
- arts and sciences (MA, MPA, MS)
- criminal justice (MS)
- English (MA)
- history (MA)
- marriage and family therapy (MS)
- public administration (MPA)
- sociology (MS)

College of Education
Programs in:
- adult and career education (M Ed, Ed D)
- business education (M Ed)
- clinical/counseling psychology (MS)
- communication disorders (M Ed)
- curriculum and instruction (Ed D)
- early childhood education (M Ed, Ed S)
- education (M Ed, MS, Ed D, Ed S)
- educational leadership (M Ed, Ed D, Ed S)
- health and physical education (M Ed)
- industrial/organizational psychology (MS)
- instructional technology (M Ed, Ed S)
- middle grades education (M Ed, Ed S)
- reading education (M Ed)
- school counseling (M Ed, Ed S)
- school psychology (Ed S)
- secondary education (M Ed, Ed S)
- special education (M Ed, Ed S)

College of Nursing
Program in:
- nursing (MSN)

College of the Fine Arts
Programs in:
- arts (MME, MMP)
- music education (MME)
- performance (MMP)

Division of Social Work
Program in:
- social work (MSW)

Langdale College of Business Administration
Program in:
- business administration (MBA)

Guam

■ UNIVERSITY OF GUAM
Mangilao, GU 96923
http://www.uog.edu/

Territory-supported, coed, comprehensive institution. *Computer facilities:* 150 computers available on campus for general student use. *Library facilities:* Robert F. Kennedy Memorial Library. *General application contact:* Dean, Graduate School and Research, 671-735-2173.

Graduate School and Research

College of Arts and Sciences
Programs in:
- arts and sciences (MA, MS)
- ceramics (MA)
- environmental science (MS)
- graphics (MA)
- Micronesian studies (MA)
- painting (MA)
- tropical marine biology (MS)

College of Business and Public Administration
Programs in:
- business administration (MBA)
- business and public administration (MBA, MPA)
- public administration (MPA)

College of Education
Programs in:
- administration and supervision (M Ed)
- counseling (MA)
- education (M Ed, MA)

University of Guam (continued)
instructional leadership (MA)
language and literacy (M Ed)
secondary education (M Ed)
special education (M Ed)
teaching English to speakers of other languages (M Ed)

Hawaii

■ CHAMINADE UNIVERSITY OF HONOLULU

Honolulu, HI 96816-1578
http://www.chaminade.edu/

Independent-religious, coed, comprehensive institution. *Enrollment:* 465 full-time matriculated graduate/professional students (337 women), 239 part-time matriculated graduate/professional students (174 women). *Graduate faculty:* 30. *Computer facilities:* 90 computers available on campus for general student use. A campuswide network can be accessed from student residence rooms and from off campus. Internet access is available. *Library facilities:* Sullivan Library. *Graduate expenses:* Tuition: part-time $465 per credit. *General application contact:* Dr. Michael Fassiotto, Assistant to the Provost, 808-739-4674.

Graduate Services

Dr. Michael Fassiotto, Assistant to the Provost
Programs in:
business administration (MBA)
counseling psychology (MSCP)
criminal justice administration (MSCJA)
forensic science (MSFS)
pastoral leadership (MPL)
pastoral theology (MPT)
social science via peace education (M Ed)

■ HAWAI'I PACIFIC UNIVERSITY

Honolulu, HI 96813
http://www.hpu.edu/

Independent, coed, comprehensive institution. *Enrollment:* 8,080 graduate, professional, and undergraduate students; 708 full-time matriculated graduate/professional students (384 women), 516 part-time matriculated graduate/professional students (249 women). *Graduate faculty:* 77 full-time, 38 part-time/adjunct. *Computer facilities:* Computer purchase and lease plans are available. 590 computers available on campus for general student use. A campuswide network can be accessed from student residence rooms and from off campus. Internet access and online class registration are available. *Library facilities:* Meader Library plus 2 others. *Graduate expenses:* Tuition: full-time $10,080; part-time $560 per credit. *General application contact:* Danny Lam, Assistant Director of Graduate Admissions, 808-544-1135.

Find University Details at www.petersons.com/gradchannel.

College of Business Administration

Dr. Charles Steilen, Dean
Programs in:
accounting/CPA (MBA)
communication (MBA)
e-business (MBA)
economics (MBA)
finance (MBA)
human resource management (MBA)
information systems (MBA)
international business (MBA)
management (MBA)
marketing (MBA)
organizational change (MBA)
travel industry management (MBA)

College of Communication

Dr. James Whitfield, Dean
Program in:
communication (MA)

College of International Studies

Dr. Carlos Juarez, Dean
Program in:
teaching English as a second language (MA)

College of Liberal Arts

Dr. Leslie Correa, Associate Vice President and Dean
Programs in:
diplomacy and military studies (MA)
social work (MA)

College of Natural Sciences

Dr. Alissa Arp, Vice President, Research/Dean
Program in:
marine science (MS)

College of Professional Studies

Dr. Gordon Jones, Dean
Programs in:
global leadership and sustainable development (MA)
human resource management (MA)
information systems (MSIS)
organizational change (MA)

Program in Secondary Education

Dr. Valentina Abordonado, Director, Teacher Education Program
Program in:
secondary education (M Ed)

School of Nursing

Dr. Patricia Langotsuka, Interim Dean
Programs in:
community clinical nurse specialist (MSN)
community clinical nurse specialist educator option (MSN)
family nurse practitioner (MSN)

■ UNIVERSITY OF HAWAII AT MANOA

Honolulu, HI 96822
http://www.uhm.hawaii.edu/

State-supported, coed, university. CGS member. *Computer facilities:* Computer purchase and lease plans are available. 1,400 computers available on campus for general student use. A campuswide network can be accessed from student residence rooms and from off campus. Internet access and online class registration are available. *Library facilities:* Hamilton Library plus 6 others. *General application contact:* Joseph Q. Salas, Director of Graduate Admissions, 808-956-8544.

Graduate Division

Programs in:
ecology, evolution and conservation biology (MS, PhD)
marine biology (MS, PhD)

College of Education
Programs in:
counseling and guidance (M Ed)
curriculum and instruction (PhD)
curriculum studies (M Ed)
disability studies (Graduate Certificate)
early childhood education (M Ed)
education (M Ed, M Ed T, MS, PhD, Graduate Certificate)
education in teaching (M Ed T)
educational administration (PhD)
educational foundations (PhD)
educational policy studies (PhD)
educational psychology (M Ed, PhD)
educational technology (M Ed)
exceptionalities (PhD)
kinesiology (MS)
special education (M Ed)

College of Engineering
Programs in:
civil and environmental engineering (MS, PhD)
electrical engineering (MS, PhD)
engineering (MS, PhD, Graduate Certificate)
mechanical engineering (MS, PhD)
telecommunications and entrepreneurship (Graduate Certificate)

College of Health Sciences and Social Welfare
Programs in:
clinical nurse specialist (MS)
health sciences and social welfare (MS, MSW, PhD, Graduate Certificate)
nurse practitioner (MS)
nursing (PhD, Graduate Certificate)
nursing administration (MS)
social welfare (PhD)
social work (MSW)

College of Tropical Agriculture and Human Resources
Programs in:
animal sciences (MS)
bioengineering (MS)
biosystems engineering (MS)
entomology (MS, PhD)
food science (MS)
human nutrition (MS)
molecular biosystems and bioengineering (MS, PhD)
natural resources and environmental management (MS, PhD)
tropical agriculture and human resources (MS, PhD)
tropical plant and soil sciences (MS, PhD)
tropical plant pathology (MS, PhD)

Colleges of Arts and Sciences
Programs in:
advanced library and information science (Graduate Certificate)
advanced women's studies (Graduate Certificate)
American studies (MA, PhD)
anthropology (MA, PhD)
art (MA)
art history (MA)
arts and humanities (M Mus, MA, MFA, PhD, Graduate Certificate)
arts and sciences (M Mus, MA, MFA, MLI Sc, MPA, MS, MURP, PhD, Graduate Certificate)
astronomy (MS, PhD)
botany (MS, PhD)
chemistry (MS, PhD)
Chinese (MA, PhD)
classics (MA)
clinical psychology (PhD)
communication (MA)
communication and information science (PhD)
community and cultural psychology (PhD)
community and culture (MA)
community planning and social policy (MURP)
computer science (MS, PhD)
dance (MA, MFA)
economics (MA, PhD)
English (MA, PhD)
English as a second language (MA, Graduate Certificate)
environmental planning and management (MURP)
French (MA)
geography (MA, PhD)
Hawaiian (MA)
historic preservation (Graduate Certificate)
history (MA, PhD)
Japanese (MA, PhD)
Korean (MA, PhD)
land use and infrastructure planning (MURP)
language, linguistics and literature (MA, PhD, Graduate Certificate)
library and information science (MLI Sc, PhD, Graduate Certificate)
linguistics (MA, PhD)
mathematics (MA, PhD)
microbiology (MS, PhD)
museum studies (Graduate Certificate)
music (M Mus, MA, PhD)
natural sciences (MA, MLI Sc, MS, PhD, Graduate Certificate)
peace (Graduate Certificate)
philosophy (MA, PhD)
physics (MS, PhD)
political science (MA, PhD)
population studies (Graduate Certificate)
psychology (MA, PhD, Graduate Certificate)
public administration (MPA, Graduate Certificate)
religion (MA)
second language acquisition (PhD)
social sciences (MA, MPA, MURP, PhD, Graduate Certificate)
sociology (MA, PhD)
Spanish (MA)
speech (MA)
telecommunication and information resource management (Graduate Certificate)
theatre (MA, MFA, PhD)
urban and regional planning (PhD, Graduate Certificate)
urban and regional planning in Asia and Pacific (MURP)
visual arts (MFA)
zoology (MS, PhD)

School of Architecture
Program in:
architecture (D Arch)

School of Hawaiian, Asian and Pacific Studies
Programs in:
Asian studies (MA, Graduate Certificate)
Hawaiian studies (MA)
Hawaiian, Asian and Pacific studies (MA, Graduate Certificate)
Pacific Island studies (MA, Graduate Certificate)

School of Ocean and Earth Science and Technology
Programs in:
high-pressure geophysics and geochemistry (MS, PhD)
hydrogeology and engineering geology (MS, PhD)
marine geology and geophysics (MS, PhD)
meteorology (MS, PhD)
ocean and earth science and technology (MS, PhD)
ocean and resources engineering (MS, PhD)
oceanography (MS, PhD)
planetary geosciences and remote sensing (MS, PhD)
seismology and solid-earth geophysics (MS, PhD)
volcanology, petrology, and geochemistry (MS, PhD)

School of Travel Industry Management
Program in:
travel industry management (MS)

Shidler College of Business
Programs in:
accounting (M Acc)
accounting law (M Acc)
Asian business studies (MBA)
Asian finance (PhD)
business administration (MBA)
Chinese business studies (MBA)
decision sciences (MBA)
entrepreneurship (MBA)
executive business administration (EMBA)
executive education (EMBA)
finance (MBA)
finance and banking (MBA)
global information technology management (PhD)
human resources management (MBA, MHRM)
information management (MBA)
information systems (M Acc)
information technology (MBA)
international accounting (PhD)
international business (MBA)
international management (PhD)
international marketing (PhD)
international organization and strategy (PhD)
Japanese business studies (MBA)
marketing (MBA)
organizational behavior (MBA)
organizational management (MBA)
real estate (MBA)
student-designed track (MBA)
taxation (M Acc)
Vietnam focused business administration (EMBA)

John A. Burns School of Medicine

Programs in:
epidemiology (PhD)
medicine (MD, MPH, MS, PhD, Graduate Certificate)
public health (MPH, MS)

Center on Aging
Program in:
gerontology (Graduate Certificate)

Graduate Programs in Biomedical Sciences
Programs in:
biomedical sciences (MS, PhD)
cell and molecular biology (MS, PhD)
physiology (MS, PhD)
speech pathology and audiology (MS)
tropical medicine (MS, PhD)

William S. Richardson School of Law

Program in:
law (JD, Graduate Certificate)

University of Hawaii at Manoa (continued)

East-West Center
Program in:
international cultural studies (Graduate Certificate)

■ UNIVERSITY OF PHOENIX–HAWAII CAMPUS

Honolulu, HI 96813-4317
http://www.phoenix.edu/

Proprietary, coed, comprehensive institution. *Enrollment:* 1,730 graduate, professional, and undergraduate students; 396 full-time matriculated graduate/professional students (254 women). *Graduate faculty:* 54 full-time (24 women), 295 part-time/adjunct (111 women). *Computer facilities:* A campuswide network can be accessed from off campus. Internet access is available. *Library facilities:* University Library. *Graduate expenses:* Tuition: full-time $11,520. Required fees: $760. *General application contact:* Campus Information Center, 808-536-2686.

The Artemis School

Dr. Adam Honea, Provost

College of Education
Dr. Marla LaRue, Dean/Executive Director
Programs in:
administration and supervision (MA Ed)
curriculum and instruction (MA Ed)
elementary education (MA Ed)
secondary education (MA Ed)
teacher education for elementary licensure (MA Ed)

College of Health and Human Services
Dr. Gil Linne, Dean/Executive Director
Programs in:
administration of justice and security (MS)
community counseling (MSC)
family nurse practitioner (MSN)
health administration (MHA)
health care management (MBA)
marriage, family and child therapy (MSC)
nursing (MSN)
psychology (MS)

John Sperling School of Business

Dr. Adam Honea, Provost
Program in:
business (MBA, MIS, MM)

College of Graduate Business and Management
Dr. Brian Lindquist, Associate Vice President and Dean/Executive Director
Programs in:
accounting (MBA)
business administration (MBA)
global management (MBA)
human resources management (MBA, MM)
management (MM)
marketing (MBA)
public administration (MBA, MM)

College of Information Systems and Technology
Dr. Adam Honea, Dean/Executive Director
Programs in:
management (MIS)
technology management (MBA)

Idaho

■ BOISE STATE UNIVERSITY

Boise, ID 83725-0399
http://www.boisestate.edu/

State-supported, coed, comprehensive institution. CGS member. *Enrollment:* 18,826 graduate, professional, and undergraduate students; 372 full-time matriculated graduate/professional students (206 women), 1,184 part-time matriculated graduate/professional students (676 women). *Graduate faculty:* 658. *Computer facilities:* 900 computers available on campus for general student use. A campuswide network can be accessed from student residence rooms and from off campus. Internet access and online class registration are available. *Library facilities:* Albertsons Library. *General application contact:* Dr. John R. Pelton, Dean, 208-426-3647.

Graduate College

Dr. John R. Pelton, Dean

College of Arts and Sciences
Martin E. Schimpf, Dean
Programs in:
art education (MA)
arts and sciences (MA, MFA, MM, MS, PhD)
biology (MA, MS)
creative writing (MFA)
earth science (MS)
English (MA)
geology (MS, PhD)
geophysics (MS, PhD)
interdisciplinary studies (MA, MS)
music (MM)
music education (MM)
pedagogy (MM)
performance (MM)
raptor biology (MS)
technical communication (MA)
visual arts (MFA)

College of Business and Economics
Howard Smith, Dean
Programs in:
accountancy (MSA)
business administration (MBA)
business and economics (MBA, MSA)
information technology management (MBA)
taxation (MSA)

College of Education
Diane Boothe, Dean
Programs in:
athletic administration (MPE)
counseling (MA)
counselor education (MA)
curriculum and instruction (Ed D)
curriculum instruction (MA)
early childhood education (M Ed, MA)
education (M Ed, MA, MET, MPE, MS, MS Ed, Ed D)
educational leadership (M Ed)
educational technology (MET, MS, MS Ed)
exercise and sports studies (MS)
physical education (MPE)
reading (MA)
special education (M Ed, MA)

College of Engineering
Dr. Cheryl B. Schrader, Dean
Programs in:
civil engineering (M Engr, MS)
computer engineering (M Engr, MS)
computer science (MS)
electrical and computer engineering (PhD)
electrical engineering (M Engr, MS)
engineering (M Engr, MS, PhD)
instructional and performance technology (MS)
materials science and engineering (M Engr, MS)
mechanical engineering (M Engr, MS)

College of Health Science
Dr. James T. Girvan, Dean
Program in:
health science (MHS)

College of Social Sciences and Public Affairs
Joanne Klein, Interim Associate Dean
Programs in:
communication (MA)
criminal justice administration (MA)
environmental and natural resources policy and administration (MPA)
general public administration (MPA)
history (MA)
social sciences and public affairs (MA, MPA, MSW)
social work (MSW)
state and local government policy and administration (MPA)

■ IDAHO STATE UNIVERSITY

Pocatello, ID 83209
http://www.isu.edu/

State-supported, coed, university. CGS member. *Enrollment:* 12,679 graduate, professional, and undergraduate students; 1,081 full-time matriculated graduate/professional students (545 women), 958 part-time matriculated graduate/professional students (523 women). *Graduate faculty:* 232 full-time (65 women), 10 part-time/adjunct (6 women). *Computer facilities:* 562 computers available on campus for general student use. A campuswide network can be accessed from student residence rooms and from off campus. Internet access and online class registration are available. *Library facilities:* Eli M. Oboler Library. *Graduate expenses:* Tuition, state resident: part-time $251 per credit. Tuition, nonresident: part-time $366 per credit. Tuition and fees vary according to degree level, program and reciprocity agreements. *General application contact:* Dr. Thomas Jackson, Dean, 208-282-2390.

Office of Graduate Studies

Dr. Thomas Jackson, Dean
Programs in:
- general interdisciplinary (M Ed, MA, MNS)
- waste management and environmental science (MS)

College of Arts and Sciences
Dr. John Kijinski, Dean
Programs in:
- anthropology (MA, MS)
- art and pre-architecture (MFA)
- arts and sciences (MA, MFA, MNS, MPA, MS, DA, PhD, Post-Master's Certificate, Postbaccalaureate Certificate)
- biology (MNS, MS, DA, PhD)
- chemistry (MNS, MS)
- clinical laboratory science (MS)
- clinical psychology (PhD)
- English (MA, DA, Post-Master's Certificate)
- geographic information science (MS)
- geology (MNS, MS)
- geophysics/hydrology (MS)
- geotechnology (Postbaccalaureate Certificate)
- historical resources management (MA)
- mathematics (MS, DA)
- mathematics for secondary teachers (MA)
- microbiology (MS)
- physics (MNS, MS, PhD)
- political science (MA, DA)
- psychology (MS)
- public administration (MPA)
- sociology (MA)
- speech communication (MA)
- theatre (MA)

College of Business
Dr. William Stratton, Dean
Programs in:
- business administration (MBA, Postbaccalaureate Certificate)
- computer information systems (MS, Postbaccalaureate Certificate)

College of Education
Dr. Deborah Hedeen, Dean
Programs in:
- child and family studies (M Ed)
- curriculum leadership (M Ed)
- education (M Ed)
- educational administration (M Ed, 6th Year Certificate, Ed S)
- educational foundations (5th Year Certificate)
- educational leadership (Ed D)
- elementary education (M Ed)
- human exceptionality (M Ed)
- instructional design (PhD)
- instructional technology (M Ed)
- physical education (MPE)
- school psychology (Ed S)
- special education (Ed S)

College of Engineering
Dr. Richard Jacobsen, Dean
Programs in:
- civil engineering (MS)
- engineering and applied science (PhD)
- engineering structures and mechanics (MS)
- environmental engineering (MS)
- measurement and control engineering (MS)
- mechanical engineering (MS)
- nuclear science and engineering (MS, PhD, Postbaccalaureate Certificate)

College of Pharmacy
Dr. Joseph Steiner, Dean
Programs in:
- biopharmaceutical analysis (PhD)
- biopharmaceutics (PhD)
- pharmaceutical chemistry (MS)
- pharmaceutical science (PhD)
- pharmaceutics (MS)
- pharmacognosy (MS)
- pharmacokinetics (PhD)
- pharmacology (MS, PhD)
- pharmacy (Pharm D)
- pharmacy administration (MS, PhD)

College of Technology
Dr. Marilyn Davis, Interim Dean
Programs in:
- technology (MTD)
- training and development (MTD)

Kasiska College of Health Professions
Dr. Linda Hatzenbuehler, Dean
Programs in:
- advanced general dentistry (Post-Doctoral Certificate)
- audiology (MS, Au D)
- counseling (M Coun, Ed S, Postbaccalaureate Certificate)
- counselor education and counseling (PhD)
- deaf education (MS)
- dental hygiene (MS)
- dietetics (Certificate)
- family medicine (Post-Master's Certificate)
- health education (MHE)
- health professions (M Coun, MHE, MOT, MPAS, MPH, MS, Au D, DPT, PhD, Certificate, Ed S, Post-Doctoral Certificate, Post-Master's Certificate, Postbaccalaureate Certificate)
- nursing (MS, Post-Master's Certificate)
- occupational therapy (MOT)
- physical therapy (DPT)
- physician assistant studies (MPAS)
- public health (MPH)
- speech language pathology (MS)

■ NORTHWEST NAZARENE UNIVERSITY

Nampa, ID 83686-5897
http://www.nnu.edu/

Independent-religious, coed, comprehensive institution. *Enrollment:* 1,749 graduate, professional, and undergraduate students; 453 full-time matriculated graduate/professional students (242 women), 56 part-time matriculated graduate/professional students (35 women). *Graduate faculty:* 42 full-time (15 women), 47 part-time/adjunct (19 women). *Computer facilities:* Computer purchase and lease plans are available. 400 computers available on campus for general student use. A campuswide network can be accessed from student residence rooms and from off campus. Internet access, various software packages are available. *Library facilities:* John E. Riley Library. *General application contact:* Dr. Mark Maddix, Director, Graduate Studies, 208-467-8817.

Graduate Studies

Dr. Mark Maddix, Director, Graduate Studies
Programs in:
- business administration (MBA)
- Christian education (MA)
- community counseling (MS)
- counselor education (MS)
- curriculum and instruction (M Ed)
- educational leadership (M Ed)
- exceptional child (M Ed)
- marriage and family counseling (MS)
- pastoral ministry (MA)
- reading education (M Ed)
- religion (M Div, MA)
- school counseling (M Ed, MS)
- social work (MSW)
- spiritual formation (MA)
- teacher education (M Ed)

■ UNIVERSITY OF IDAHO

Moscow, ID 83844-2282
http://www.uidaho.edu/

State-supported, coed, university. CGS member. *Enrollment:* 11,739 graduate, professional, and undergraduate students; 1,246 full-time matriculated graduate/professional students (536 women), 1,099 part-time matriculated graduate/professional students (513 women). *Graduate faculty:* 407 full-time (96 women), 130 part-time/adjunct (23 women). *Computer facilities:* Computer purchase and lease plans are available. 670 computers available on

University of Idaho (continued)
campus for general student use. A campuswide network can be accessed from student residence rooms and from off campus. Internet access and online class registration, student evaluations of teaching are available. *Library facilities:* University of Idaho Library plus 1 other. *Graduate expenses:* Tuition, nonresident: full-time $9,600; part-time $140 per credit. Required fees: $4,740; $227 per credit. *General application contact:* Dr. Margrit von Braun, Associate Dean of the College of Graduate Studies, 208-885-6243.

College of Graduate Studies
Dr. Margrit von Braun, Associate Dean
Programs in:
- architecture and interior design (M Arch, MS)
- art (MFA)
- art and architecture (M Arch, MAT, MFA, MS)
- art education (MAT)
- bioinformatics and computational biology (MS, PhD)
- landscape architecture (MS)
- neuroscience (MS, PhD)

College of Agricultural and Life Sciences
Dr. John Hammel, Dean
Programs in:
- agricultural and life sciences (M Engr, MS, PhD)
- agricultural economics (MS)
- agricultural education (MS)
- animal physiology (PhD)
- animal science (MS)
- biological and agricultural engineering (M Engr, MS, PhD)
- education (PhD)
- entomology (MS, PhD)
- family and consumer sciences (MS)
- food science (MS, PhD)
- microbiology, molecular biology and biochemistry (MS, PhD)
- plant science (MS, PhD)
- soil and land resources (MS, PhD)
- veterinary science (MS)

College of Business and Economics
Dr. John Morris, Dean
Programs in:
- accounting (M Acct)
- business and economics (M Acct)

College of Education
Dr. Paul Rowland, Dean
Programs in:
- adult and organizational learning (MS, Ed D, PhD, Ed S)
- counseliing and human services (PhD)
- counseling and human services (M Ed, MS, Ed D, Ed S)
- curriculm and intstruction (Ed D)
- curriculum and instruction (PhD)
- education (M Ed, MS, Ed D, PhD, Ed S, Ed Sp PTE)
- educational leadership (M Ed, MS, Ed D, PhD, Ed S)
- physical education (M Ed, MS, PhD)
- professional-technical and technology education (M Ed, MS, PhD, Ed Sp PTE)
- professional-technical and tecnology education (Ed D)
- recreation (MS)
- school psychology (Ed S)
- special education (M Ed, MS, Ed S)

College of Engineering
Dr. Aicha Elshabini, Dean
Programs in:
- chemical engineering (M Engr, MS, PhD)
- civil engineering (M Engr, MS, PhD)
- computer engineering (M Engr, MS)
- computer science (MS, PhD)
- electrical engineering (M Engr, MS, PhD)
- engineering (M Engr, MS, PhD)
- environmental engineering (M Engr, MS)
- geological engineering (MS)
- materials science and engineering (MS, PhD)
- mechanical engineering (M Engr, MS, PhD)
- metallurgical engineering (MS)
- nuclear engineering (M Engr, MS, PhD)
- systems engineering (M Engr)

College of Letters, Arts and Social Sciences
Dr. Katherine Aiken, Dean
Programs in:
- anthropology (MA)
- creative writing (MFA)
- English (MA, MAT)
- environmental science (MS, PhD)
- history (MA, MAT, PhD)
- interdisciplinary studies (MA, MS)
- letters, arts and social sciences (M Mus, MA, MAT, MFA, MPA, MS, PhD)
- music (M Mus, MA)
- political science (MA, PhD)
- psychology (MS)
- public administration (MPA)
- teaching English as a second language (MA)
- theatre arts (MFA)

College of Natural Resources
Steven B. Daley-Laursen, Dean
Programs in:
- conservation social sciences (MS)
- fish and wildlife resources (MS)
- fishery resources (MS)
- forest products (MS)
- forest resources (MS)
- natural resources (MNR, PhD)
- natural resources management and administration (MNR)
- rangeland ecology and management (MS)
- wildlife resources (MS)

College of Science
Judith Totman Parrish, Dean
Programs in:
- biological sciences (M Nat Sci)
- chemistry (MAT, MS, PhD)
- earth science (MAT)
- geography (MAT, MS, PhD)
- geology (MS, PhD)
- hydrology (MS)
- mathematics (MAT, MS, PhD)
- physics (MS, PhD)
- physics education (MAT)
- science (M Nat Sci, MAT, MS, PhD)
- statistics (MS)

College of Law
Donald L. Burnett, Dean
Program in:
- law (JD)

Illinois

■ AURORA UNIVERSITY
Aurora, IL 60506-4892
http://www.aurora.edu/

Independent, coed, comprehensive institution. *Enrollment:* 3,791 graduate, professional, and undergraduate students; 378 full-time matriculated graduate/professional students (297 women), 1,384 part-time matriculated graduate/professional students (987 women). *Graduate faculty:* 38 full-time (19 women), 126 part-time/adjunct (72 women). *Computer facilities:* 90 computers available on campus for general student use. A campuswide network can be accessed from student residence rooms and from off campus. Internet access is available. *Library facilities:* Charles B. Phillips Library plus 1 other. *Graduate expenses:* Tuition: part-time $330 per credit hour. Tuition and fees vary according to campus/location and program. *General application contact:* Donna DeSpain, Dean of Adult and Graduate Studies, 800-742-5281.

College of Education
Dr. Donald C. Wold, Dean
Programs in:
- curriculum and instruction (Ed D)
- education (MAT)
- education and administration (Ed D)
- educational leadership (MEL)
- reading instruction (MA)

College of Professional Studies
Dr. Michael Carroll, Dean

Dunham School of Business
Dr. Shawn Green, Director
Program in:
- business (MBA)

School of Social Work
Dr. Fred Mckenzie, Dean
Program in:
- social work (MSW)

■ BENEDICTINE UNIVERSITY
Lisle, IL 60532-0900
http://www.ben.edu/

Independent-religious, coed, comprehensive institution. *Enrollment:* 3,900 graduate, professional, and undergraduate students; 275 full-time matriculated graduate/professional students (165 women), 968 part-time matriculated graduate/professional students (596 women). *Graduate faculty:* 20 full-time (7 women), 92 part-time/adjunct (50 women). *Computer facilities:* A campuswide network can be accessed from student residence rooms and from off campus. Internet access is available. *Library facilities:* Benedictine Library. *Graduate expenses:* Tuition: full-time $12,150; part-time $450 per credit hour. *General application contact:* Kari Gibbons, Director, Admissions, 630-829-6200.

Graduate Programs
Dr. Daniel Julius, Provost and Vice President for Academic Affairs
Programs in:
- accounting (MBA)
- administration of health care institutions (MPH)
- clinical exercise physiology (MS)
- clinical psychology (MS)
- curriculum and instruction and collaborative teaching (M Ed)
- dietetics (MPH)
- disaster management (MPH)
- elementary education (MA Ed)
- entrepreneurship and managing innovation (MBA)
- financial management (MBA)
- health administration (MBA)
- health education (MPH)
- health information systems (MPH)
- higher education and organizational change (Ed D)
- human resource management (MBA)
- information systems security (MBA)
- international business (MBA)
- leadership and administration (M Ed)
- management and organizational behavior (MS)
- management consulting (MBA)
- management information systems (MBA)
- marketing management (MBA)
- nutrition and wellness (MS)
- operations management and logistics (MBA)
- organizational development (PhD)
- organizational leadership (MBA)
- reading and literacy (M Ed)
- science content and process (MS)
- secondary education (MA Ed)
- special education (MA Ed)

■ BRADLEY UNIVERSITY
Peoria, IL 61625-0002
http://www.bradley.edu/

Independent, coed, comprehensive institution. CGS member. *Enrollment:* 6,126 graduate, professional, and undergraduate students; 226 full-time matriculated graduate/professional students (105 women), 481 part-time matriculated graduate/professional students (213 women). *Graduate faculty:* 245. *Computer facilities:* 2,000 computers available on campus for general student use. A campuswide network can be accessed from student residence rooms and from off campus. Internet access and online class registration are available. *Library facilities:* Cullom-Davis Library. *General application contact:* Leslie M. Betz, Director, Graduate Admissions, 309-677-2375.

Graduate School
Dr. Robert I. Bolla, Dean of the Graduate School

College of Education and Health Sciences
Dr. Joan Sattler, Dean
Programs in:
- curriculum and instruction (MA)
- education and health sciences (MA, MSN, DPT)
- human development counseling (MA)
- leadership in educational administration (MA)
- leadership in human service administration (MA)
- nurse administered anesthesia (MSN)
- nursing administration (MSN)
- physical therapy (DPT)

College of Engineering and Technology
Dr. Richard Johnson, Dean
Programs in:
- civil engineering and construction (MSCE)
- electrical engineering (MSEE)
- engineering and technology (MSCE, MSEE, MSIE, MSME, MSMFE)
- industrial engineering (MSIE)
- manufacturing engineering (MSIE)
- mechanical engineering (MSME)

College of Liberal Arts and Sciences
Dr. Claire Etaugh, Dean
Programs in:
- biology (MS)
- chemistry (MS)
- computer information systems (MS)
- computer science (MS)
- English (MA)
- liberal arts and sciences (MA, MLS, MS)
- liberal studies (MLS)

Foster College of Business Administration
Dr. Rob Baer, Dean
Programs in:
- accounting (MSA)
- business administration (MBA, MSA)

Slane College of Communications and Fine Arts
Dr. Jeffrey Huberman, Dean
Programs in:
- ceramics (MA, MFA)
- communications and fine arts (MA, MFA)
- drawing/illustration (MA, MFA)
- interdisciplinary art (MA, MFA)
- painting (MA, MFA)
- photography (MA, MFA)
- printmaking (MA, MFA)
- sculpture (MA, MFA)
- visual communication and design (MA, MFA)

■ CHICAGO STATE UNIVERSITY
Chicago, IL 60628
http://www.csu.edu/

State-supported, coed, comprehensive institution. *Computer facilities:* 75 computers available on campus for general student use. A campuswide network can be accessed from student residence rooms and from off campus. Internet access and online class registration are available. *Library facilities:* Paul and Emily Douglas Library. *General application contact:* Admissions and Records Officer II, 773-995-2404.

School of Graduate and Professional Studies

College of Arts and Sciences
Programs in:
- arts and sciences (MA, MFA, MS, MSW)
- biological sciences (MS)
- computer science (MS)
- counseling (MA)
- creative writing (MFA)
- criminal justice (MS)
- English (MA)
- geography and economic development (MA)
- history, philosophy, and political science (MA)
- mathematics (MS)
- social work (MSW)

College of Education
Programs in:
- bilingual education (M Ed)
- curriculum and instruction (MS Ed)
- early childhood education (MAT, MS Ed)
- education (M Ed, MA, MAT, MS Ed, Ed D)
- educational leadership (MA, Ed D)
- elementary education (MAT)
- general administration (MA)
- higher education administration (MA)
- instructional foundations (MS Ed)
- library information and media studies (MS Ed)
- middle school education (MAT)

Chicago State University (continued)
- physical education (MS Ed)
- reading (MS Ed)
- secondary education (MAT)
- special education (M Ed)
- teaching of reading (MS Ed)
- technology and education (MS Ed)

■ COLUMBIA COLLEGE CHICAGO
Chicago, IL 60605-1996
http://www.colum.edu/

Independent, coed, comprehensive institution. *Computer facilities:* 730 computers available on campus for general student use. A campuswide network can be accessed. Internet access is available. *Library facilities:* Columbia College Library plus 2 others. *General application contact:* Acting Dean of the Graduate School, 312-344-7261.

Graduate School
Programs in:
- architectural studies (MFA)
- arts, entertainment, and media management (MA)
- creative writing (MFA)
- dance/movement therapy (MA, Certificate)
- elementary (MAT)
- English (MAT)
- film and video (MFA)
- interdisciplinary arts (MA, MAT)
- interdisciplinary book and paper arts (MFA)
- interior design (MFA)
- multicultural education (MA)
- photography (MA, MFA)
- poetry (MFA)
- public affairs journalism (MA)
- teaching of writing (MA)
- urban teaching (MA)

■ CONCORDIA UNIVERSITY CHICAGO
River Forest, IL 60305-1499
http://www.cuchicago.edu/

Independent-religious, coed, comprehensive institution. CGS member. *Computer facilities:* 70 computers available on campus for general student use. A campuswide network can be accessed from student residence rooms and from off campus. Internet access is available. *Library facilities:* Klinck Memorial Library. *General application contact:* Director of Graduate Admissions, 708-209-3454.

College of Arts and Sciences
Programs in:
- church music (MCM)
- community counseling (MA)
- gerontology (MA)
- human services (MA)
- liberal studies (MA)
- music (MA)
- psychology (MA)
- religion (MA)

College of Education
Programs in:
- Christian education (MA)
- curriculum and instruction (MA)
- early childhood education (MA, Ed D)
- educational leadership (Ed D)
- reading education (MA)
- school administration (MA, CAS)
- school counseling (MA, CAS)
- teaching (MAT)
- urban teaching (MA)

■ DEPAUL UNIVERSITY
Chicago, IL 60604-2287
http://www.depaul.edu/

Independent-religious, coed, university. *Enrollment:* 23,149 graduate, professional, and undergraduate students; 15,971 full-time matriculated graduate/professional students (8,766 women), 7,177 part-time matriculated graduate/professional students (3,886 women). *Graduate faculty:* 390 full-time (156 women), 251 part-time/adjunct (98 women). *Computer facilities:* 1,361 computers available on campus for general student use. A campuswide network can be accessed from student residence rooms and from off campus. Internet access and online class registration are available. *Library facilities:* John T. Richardson Library plus 2 others. *General application contact:* Information Contact, 312-362-6709.

Charles H. Kellstadt Graduate School of Business
Robert T. Ryan, Assistant Dean and Director
Programs in:
- applied economics (MBA)
- behavioral finance (MBA)
- brand management (MBA)
- business (M Acc, MA, MBA, MS, MSA, MSF, MSHR, MSMA, MST)
- computational finance (MS)
- customer relationship management (MBA)
- economics (MA)
- entrepreneurship (MBA)
- finance (MBA, MSF)
- financial analysis (MBA)
- financial management and control (MBA)
- health sector management (MBA)
- human resource management (MBA, MSHR)
- integrated marketing communication (MBA)
- international business (MBA)
- international marketing and finance (MBA)
- leadership/change management (MBA)
- management planning and strategy (MBA)
- managerial finance (MBA)
- marketing analysis (MSMA)
- marketing and management (MBA)
- marketing strategy and analysis (MBA)
- marketing strategy and planning (MBA)
- new product management (MBA)
- operations management (MBA)
- real estate (MS)
- real estate finance and investment (MBA)
- sales leadership (MBA)
- strategy, execution and valuation (MBA)

School of Accountancy and Management Information Systems
Programs in:
- accountancy (M Acc, MSA)
- business information technology (MS)
- e-business (MBA, MS)
- financial management and control (MBA)
- management accounting (MBA)
- management information systems (MBA)
- taxation (MST)

College of Law
Glen Weissenberger, Dean
Program in:
- law (JD, LL M)

College of Liberal Arts and Sciences
Michael Mezey, Dean
Programs in:
- advanced practice nursing (MS)
- applied mathematics (MS)
- applied physics (MS)
- applied statistics (MS, Certificate)
- biochemistry (MS)
- biological sciences (MA, MS)
- chemistry (MS)
- clinical psychology (MA, PhD)
- English (MA)
- experimental psychology (MA, PhD)
- general psychology (MS)
- history (MA)
- industrial/organizational psychology (MA, PhD)
- interdisciplinary studies (MA, MS)
- liberal arts and sciences (MA, MBA, MS, PhD, Certificate)
- liberal studies (MA)
- masters entry into nursing practice (MS)
- mathematics education (MA)
- multicultural communication (MA)
- nurse anesthesia (MS)
- organizational communication (MA)
- philosophy (MA, PhD)
- polymer chemistry and coatings technology (MS)
- sociology (MA)
- writing (MA)

School for New Learning
Dr. Barbara Radner, Program Director

Programs in:
- applied technology (MS)
- educating adults (MA)
- integrated professional studies (MA)

School of Computer Science, Telecommunications, and Information Systems
Dr. David Miller, Dean
Programs in:
- business information technology (MS)
- computational finance (MS)
- computer graphics and animation (MS)
- computer science (MS, PhD)
- computer, information and network security (MS)
- digital cinema (MFA, MS)
- e-commerce technology (MS)
- human-computer interaction (MS)
- information systems (MS)
- information technology (MA)
- instructional technology systems (MS)
- software engineering (MS)
- telecommunication systems (MS)

School of Education
Dr. Clara Jennings, Dean
Programs in:
- bilingual and bicultural education (M Ed, MA)
- curriculum studies (M Ed, MA, Ed D)
- education (Ed D)
- educational leadership (M Ed, MA, Ed D)
- human development and learning (MA)
- human services and counseling (M Ed, MA)
- reading and learning disabilities (M Ed, MA)
- social culture studies in education and development (M Ed, MA)
- teaching and learning (early childhood, elementary and secondary) (M Ed)
- teaching and learning (early childhood, elementary, and secondary) (MA)

School of Music
Dr. Donald E. Casey, Dean
Programs in:
- applied music (performance) (MM, Certificate)
- jazz studies (MM)
- music composition (MM)
- music education (MM)

School of Public Service
Dr. J. Patrick Murphy, Director
Programs in:
- financial administration management (Certificate)
- health administration (Certificate)
- health law and policy (MS)
- international public services (MS)
- metropolitan planning (Certificate)
- public administration (MS)
- public service management (MS)
- public services (Certificate)

The Theatre School
John Culbert, Chair
Programs in:
- acting (MFA, Certificate)
- directing (MFA)

■ DOMINICAN UNIVERSITY
River Forest, IL 60305-1099
http://www.dom.edu/

Independent-religious, coed, comprehensive institution. *Enrollment:* 3,292 graduate, professional, and undergraduate students; 449 full-time matriculated graduate/professional students (261 women), 1,381 part-time matriculated graduate/professional students (1,065 women). *Graduate faculty:* 49 full-time (30 women), 114 part-time/adjunct (61 women). *Computer facilities:* 212 computers available on campus for general student use. A campuswide network can be accessed from student residence rooms and from off campus. Internet access and online class registration, e-mail are available. *Library facilities:* Rebecca Crown Library. *Graduate expenses:* Tuition: full-time $12,420; part-time $690 per credit hour. Required fees: $10 per course. Tuition and fees vary according to campus/location and program. *General application contact:* Pam Johnson, Vice President of Enrollment Management, 708-524-6544.

Edward A. and Lois L. Brennan School of Business
Dr. Molly Burke, Dean
Programs in:
- accounting (MSA)
- business administration (MBA)
- computer information systems (MSCIS)
- management information systems (MSMIS)
- organization management (MSOM)

Graduate School of Library and Information Science
Susan Roman, Dean
Program in:
- library and information science (MLIS, CSS)

Graduate School of Social Work
Dr. Mark Rodgers, Dean
Program in:
- social work (MSW)

Institute for Adult Learning
Bryan J. Watkins, Executive Director
Program in:
- adult learning (MSOL)

School of Education
Sr. Colleen McNicholas, Dean
Programs in:
- curriculum and instruction (MA Ed)
- early childhood education (MS)
- education (MAT)
- educational administration (MA)
- literacy (MS)
- special education (MS)

■ EASTERN ILLINOIS UNIVERSITY
Charleston, IL 61920-3099
http://www.eiu.edu/

State-supported, coed, comprehensive institution. CGS member. *Enrollment:* 12,349 graduate, professional, and undergraduate students; 611 full-time matriculated graduate/professional students, 1,143 part-time matriculated graduate/professional students. *Graduate faculty:* 448. *Computer facilities:* Computer purchase and lease plans are available. 798 computers available on campus for general student use. A campuswide network can be accessed from student residence rooms and from off campus. Internet access and online class registration are available. *Library facilities:* Booth Library. *Graduate expenses:* Tuition, state resident: part-time $169 per semester hour. Tuition, nonresident: part-time $508 per semester hour. Required fees: $60 per semester hour. *General application contact:* Rodney Ranes, Director of Graduate Admissions, 217-581-7489.

Find University Details at www.petersons.com/gradchannel.

Graduate School
Dr. Robert M. Augustine, Dean

College of Arts and Humanities
James Johnson, Dean
Programs in:
- art (MA)
- art education (MA)
- arts and humanities (MA)
- communication studies (MA)
- English (MA)
- historical administration (MA)
- history (MA)
- music (MA)

College of Education and Professional Studies
Dr. Diane Jackman, Dean
Programs in:
- college student affairs (MS)
- community counseling (MS)
- education and professional studies (MS, MS Ed, Ed S)
- educational administration (MS Ed, Ed S)
- elementary education (MS Ed)
- physical education (MS)
- school counseling (MS)
- special education (MS Ed)

College of Sciences
Dr. Mary Ann Hanner, Dean
Programs in:
- biological sciences (MS)
- chemistry (MS)
- clinical psychology (MA)
- communication disorders and sciences (MS)
- economics (MA)

Eastern Illinois University (continued)
- mathematics (MA)
- mathematics and computer science (MA)
- mathematics education (MA)
- natural sciences (MS)
- political science (MA)
- psychology (MA, SSP)
- school psychology (SSP)

Lumpkin College of Business and Applied Sciences
Dr. Diane Hoadley, Dean
Programs in:
- accountancy (Certificate)
- business and applied sciences (MA, MBA, MS, Certificate)
- computer technology (Certificate)
- dietetics (MS)
- family and consumer sciences (MS)
- general management (MBA)
- gerontology (MA)
- quality systems (Certificate)
- technology (MS)
- technology security (Certificate)
- work performance improvement (Certificate)

■ ELMHURST COLLEGE
Elmhurst, IL 60126-3296
http://www.elmhurst.edu/

Independent-religious, coed, comprehensive institution. *Enrollment:* 3,107 graduate, professional, and undergraduate students; 266 part-time matriculated graduate/professional students (153 women). *Graduate faculty:* 21 full-time (9 women), 19 part-time/adjunct (6 women). *Computer facilities:* 345 computers available on campus for general student use. A campuswide network can be accessed from student residence rooms and from off campus. Internet access and online class registration are available. *Library facilities:* Buehler Library. *Graduate expenses:* Tuition: part-time $781 per hour. Required fees: $75 per hour. Part-time tuition and fees vary according to course load and student level. *General application contact:* Elizabeth D. Kuebler, Director of Adult and Graduate Admission, 630-617-3069.

Graduate Programs
Dr. John E. Bohnert, Dean of Graduate Studies
Programs in:
- business administration (MBA)
- computer network systems (MS)
- early childhood special education (M Ed)
- English studies (MA)
- industrial/organizational psychology (MA)
- nursing (MSN)
- professional accountancy (MPA)
- supply chain management (MS)
- teacher leadership (M Ed)

■ GOVERNORS STATE UNIVERSITY
University Park, IL 60466-0975
http://www.govst.edu/

State-supported, coed, upper-level institution. *Enrollment:* 203 full-time matriculated graduate/professional students (143 women), 2,558 part-time matriculated graduate/professional students (1,930 women). *Graduate faculty:* 185 full-time (78 women), 27 part-time/adjunct (13 women). *Computer facilities:* 165 computers available on campus for general student use. A campuswide network can be accessed from off campus. *Library facilities:* University Library. *Graduate expenses:* Tuition, state resident: full-time $4,104; part-time $171 per hour. Tuition, nonresident: part-time $513 per hour. *General application contact:* Dr. William T. Craig, Associate Director of Admission, 708-534-4492.

College of Arts and Sciences
Dr. Eric V. Martin, Interim Dean
Programs in:
- analytical chemistry (MS)
- art (MA)
- arts and sciences (MA, MS)
- communication studies (MA)
- computer science (MS)
- English (MA)
- environmental biology (MS)
- instructional and training technology (MA)
- media communication (MA)
- political and justice studies (MA)

College of Business and Public Administration
Dr. William Nowlin, Dean
Programs in:
- accounting (MS)
- business administration (MBA)
- business and public administration (MBA, MPA, MS)
- management information systems (MS)
- public administration (MPA)

College of Education
Dr. Steven C. Russell, Dean
Programs in:
- counseling (MA)
- early childhood education (MA)
- education (MA)
- educational administration and supervision (MA)
- multi-categorical special education (MA)
- psychology (MA)
- reading (MA)

College of Health Professions
Dr. Linda Samson, Dean
Programs in:
- addictions studies (MHS)
- communication disorders (MHS)
- health administration (MHA)
- health professions (MHA, MHS, MOT, MPT, MSN, MSW, DPT)
- nursing (MSN)
- occupational therapy (MOT)
- physical therapy (MPT, DPT)
- social work (MSW)

■ ILLINOIS INSTITUTE OF TECHNOLOGY
Chicago, IL 60616-3793
http://www.iit.edu/

Independent, coed, university. CGS member. *Enrollment:* 6,795 graduate, professional, and undergraduate students; 2,725 full-time matriculated graduate/professional students (1,035 women), 1,525 part-time matriculated graduate/professional students (521 women). *Graduate faculty:* 353 full-time (77 women), 286 part-time/adjunct (67 women). *Computer facilities:* Computer purchase and lease plans are available. 650 computers available on campus for general student use. A campuswide network can be accessed from student residence rooms and from off campus. Internet access and online class registration are available. *Library facilities:* Paul V. Galvin Library plus 5 others. *Graduate expenses:* Tuition: full-time $13,086; part-time $727 per credit. Required fees: $7 per credit. $235 per term. Tuition and fees vary according to class time, course level, course load, program and student level. *General application contact:* Morgan Frederick, Office of Graduate Admissions, 866-472-3448.

Chicago-Kent College of Law
Harold J. Krent, Dean
Programs in:
- family law (LL M)
- financial services (LL M)
- international intellectual property (LL M)
- international law (LL M)
- law (JD)
- taxation (LL M)

Graduate College
Dr. Ali Cinar, Dean/Vice Provost

Armour College of Engineering
Dr. Hamid Arastoopour, Dean
Programs in:
- architectural engineering (M Arch E)
- biological engineering (MBE)
- biomedical engineering (PhD)
- biomedical imaging and signals (MS)
- chemical engineering (M Ch E, MS, PhD)
- civil engineering (MS, PhD)
- computer engineering (MS, PhD)
- computer/electrical engineering (MS)
- construction engineering and management (MCEM)
- electrical and computer engineering (MECE)
- electrical engineering (MS, PhD)

electricity markets (MEM)
engineering (M Arch E, M Ch E, M Env E, M Geoenv E, M Trans E, MBE, MCEM, MECE, MEM, MFPE, MGE, MGE, MMAE, MME, MMME, MNE, MPW, MS, MSE, MTSE, PhD)
environmental engineering (M Env E, MS, PhD)
food process engineering (MFPE)
food processing engineering (MS)
gas engineering (MGE)
geoenvironmental engineering (M Geoenv E)
geotechnical engineering (MGE)
manufacturing engineering (MME, MS)
materials science and engineering (MMME, MS, PhD)
mechanical and aerospace engineering (MMAE, MS, PhD)
network engineering (MNE)
power engineering (MS)
public works (MPW)
structural engineering (MSE)
telecommunications and software engineering (MTSE)
transportation engineering (M Trans E)
VLSI and microelectronics (MS)

Center for Professional Development
C. Robert Carlson, Director
Programs in:
industrial technology and operations (MITO)
information technology and management (MITM)

College of Architecture
Donna V. Robertson, Dean
Program in:
architecture (M Ar, PhD)

College of Science and Letters
Dr. Fred R. McMorris, Dean
Programs in:
analytical chemistry (M Ch, MS, PhD)
applied mathematics (MS, PhD)
biology (MBS, MS, PhD)
chemistry (M Ch, M Chem, MS, PhD)
computer science (MCS, MS, PhD)
food safety and technology (MS)
health physics (MHP)
information architecture (MS)
materials and chemical synthesis (M Ch)
mathematical finance (MMF)
mathematics education (MME, MS, PhD)
molecular biochemistry and biophysics (MS, PhD)
nonprofit management (MPA)
physics (MHP, MS, PhD)
public administration (MPA)
public safety and crisis management (MPA)
science and letters (M Ch, M Chem, MBS, MCS, MHP, MME, MMF, MPA, MS, MSE, MST, MTSE, PhD)
science education (MS, MSE, PhD)
teaching (MST)
technical communication (PhD)
technical communication and information design (MS)
telecommunications and software engineering (MTSE)

Institute of Design
Rachel Smothers, Director of Admissions and Retention
Program in:
design (M Des, MSDM, PhD)

Institute of Psychology
Dr. M. Ellen Mitchell, Director
Programs in:
clinical psychology (PhD)
industrial/organizational psychology (PhD)
personnel/human resource development (MS)
psychology (MS)
rehabilitation counseling (MS)
rehabilitation counseling education (PhD)

Stuart School of Business
Dr. Harvey Kahalas, Dean
Programs in:
business (MBA, MMF, MS, PhD)
entrepreneurship (MBA)
environmental management (MS)
finance (MS)
financial management (MBA)
financial markets (MBA)
healthcare management (MBA)
information technology management (MBA)
international business (MBA)
management science (MBA)
marketing (MBA)
marketing communication (MS)
mathematical finance (MMF)
operations, quality, and technology management (MBA)
strategic management of organizations (MBA)
sustainable enterprise (MBA)

■ ILLINOIS STATE UNIVERSITY
Normal, IL 61790-2200
http://www.ilstu.edu/

State-supported, coed, university. CGS member. *Enrollment:* 20,521 graduate, professional, and undergraduate students; 1,083 full-time matriculated graduate/professional students (656 women), 1,210 part-time matriculated graduate/professional students (805 women). *Graduate faculty:* 616 full-time (238 women), 15 part-time/adjunct (5 women). *Computer facilities:* 1,869 computers available on campus for general student use. A campuswide network can be accessed from student residence rooms and from off campus. Internet access is available. *Library facilities:* Milner Library. *Graduate expenses:* Tuition, state resident: full-time $3,330; part-time $185 per credit hour. Tuition, nonresident: full-time $6,948; part-time $438 per credit hour. Required fees: $1,259; $52 per credit hour. *General application contact:* Dr. Gary McGinnis, Associate Vice President of Research, Graduate Studies and International Education, 309-438-2583.

Find University Details at www.petersons.com/gradchannel.

Graduate School
Dr. Gary McGinnis, Associate Vice President of Research, Graduate Studies and International Education

College of Applied Science and Technology
Dr. J. Robert Rossman, Dean
Programs in:
agribusiness (MS)
applied science and technology (MA, MS)
criminal justice sciences (MA, MS)
family and consumer sciences (MA, MS)
health education (MS)
information technology (MS)
physical education (MS)
technology (MS)

College of Arts and Sciences
Dr. Gary Olson, Dean
Programs in:
animal behavior (MS)
arts and sciences (MA, MS, MSW, PhD, SSP)
bacteriology (MS)
biochemistry (MS)
biological sciences (MS)
biology (PhD)
biophysics (MS)
biotechnology (MS)
botany (MS, PhD)
cell biology (MS)
chemistry (MS)
communication (MA, MS)
conservation biology (MS)
developmental biology (MS)
ecology (MS, PhD)
economics (MA, MS)
English (MA, MS, PhD)
English studies (PhD)
entomology (MS)
evolutionary biology (MS)
French (MA)
French and German (MA)
French and Spanish (MA)
genetics (MS, PhD)
geohydrology (MS)
German (MA)
German and Spanish (MA)
historical archaeology (MA, MS)
history (MA, MS)
immunology (MS)
mathematics (MA, MS)
mathematics education (PhD)
microbiology (MS, PhD)
molecular biology (MS)
molecular genetics (MS)
neurobiology (MS)

Illinois State University (continued)
- neuroscience (MS)
- parasitology (MS)
- physiology (MS, PhD)
- plant biology (MS)
- plant molecular biology (MS)
- plant sciences (MS)
- politics and government (MA, MS)
- psychology (MA, MS)
- school psychology (PhD, SSP)
- social work (MSW)
- sociology (MA, MS)
- Spanish (MA)
- speech pathology and audiology (MA, MS)
- structural biology (MS)
- writing (MA, MS)
- zoology (MS, PhD)

College of Business
Dr. Dixie Mills, Dean
Programs in:
- accounting (MPA, MS)
- business (MBA, MPA, MS)
- business administration (MBA)

College of Education
Dr. Deborah Curtis, Dean
Programs in:
- curriculum and instruction (MS, MS Ed, Ed D)
- education (MS, MS Ed, Ed D, PhD)
- educational administration and foundations (MS, MS Ed, Ed D, PhD)
- educational policies (Ed D)
- guidance and counseling (MS, MS Ed)
- postsecondary education (Ed D)
- reading (MS Ed)
- special education (MS, MS Ed, Ed D)
- supervision (Ed D)

College of Fine Arts
Dr. Lonny Gordon, Dean
Programs in:
- art history (MA, MS)
- arts technology (MS)
- ceramics (MFA, MS)
- drawing (MFA, MS)
- fibers (MFA, MS)
- fine arts (MA, MFA, MM, MM Ed, MS)
- glass (MFA, MS)
- graphic design (MFA, MS)
- metals (MFA, MS)
- music (MM, MM Ed)
- painting (MFA, MS)
- photography (MFA, MS)
- printmaking (MFA, MS)
- sculpture (MFA, MS)
- theatre (MA, MFA, MS)

Mennonite College of Nursing
Nancy Ridenour, Dean
Programs in:
- family nurse practitioner (PMC)
- nursing (MSN)

■ LEWIS UNIVERSITY
Romeoville, IL 60446
http://www.lewisu.edu/

Independent-religious, coed, comprehensive institution. *Computer facilities:* 310 computers available on campus for general student use. A campuswide network can be accessed from student residence rooms and from off campus. Internet access and online class registration, e-mail are available. *Library facilities:* Lewis University Library. *General application contact:* Coordinator, 800-897-9000.

College of Arts and Sciences
Programs in:
- administration/education (MA)
- arts and sciences (M Ed, MA, MA Ed, MAE, MPSA, MS, CAS)
- child and adolescent counseling (MA)
- criminal/social justice (MS)
- curriculum and instruction (MA Ed)
- education (M Ed, MAE)
- educational leadership (MA Ed)
- general administrative program (CAS)
- higher education/student services (MA)
- instructional leadership (MA Ed)
- mental health counseling (MA)
- organizational management (MA)
- public administration (MA)
- school counseling and guidance (MA)
- special education (MA)
- superintendent endorsement program (CAS)
- training and development (MA)

College of Business
Program in:
- business (MBA)

Graduate School of Management
Programs in:
- accounting (MBA)
- e-business (MBA)
- finance (MBA)
- healthcare management (MBA)
- human resources management (MBA)
- international business (MBA)
- management information systems (MBA)
- marketing (MBA)
- technology and operations management (MBA)

College of Nursing and Health Professions
Programs in:
- case management (MSN)
- nursing administration (MSN)
- nursing and health professions (MSN)
- nursing education (MSN)

■ LOYOLA UNIVERSITY CHICAGO
Chicago, IL 60611-2196
http://www.luc.edu/

Independent-religious, coed, university. CGS member. *Enrollment:* 15,194 graduate, professional, and undergraduate students; 2,886 full-time matriculated graduate/professional students (1,684 women), 1,981 part-time matriculated graduate/professional students (1,181 women). *Graduate faculty:* 1,274 full-time (501 women), 913 part-time/adjunct (300 women). *Computer facilities:* 318 computers available on campus for general student use. A campuswide network can be accessed from student residence rooms and from off campus. Internet access is available. *Library facilities:* Cudahy Library plus 2 others. *General application contact:* Janice K. Atkinson, Director, Graduate and Professional Enrollment Management, 312-915-8902.

Find University Details at www.petersons.com/gradchannel.

Graduate School
Dr. Samuel Attoh, Dean
Programs in:
- American politics and policy (MA, PhD)
- applied human perception and performance (MS)
- applied social psychology (MA, PhD)
- applied sociology (MA)
- biochemistry (MS, PhD)
- biology (MA, MS)
- cell and molecular physiology (MS, PhD)
- cell biology, neurobiology and anatomy (MS, PhD)
- chemistry (MS, PhD)
- clinical psychology (PhD)
- criminal justice (MA)
- developmental psychology (PhD)
- English (MA, PhD)
- history (MA, PhD)
- immunology (MS, PhD)
- information technology (MS)
- international studies (MA, PhD)
- mathematics (MS)
- microbiology (MS, PhD)
- molecular biology (PhD)
- neuroscience (MS, PhD)
- pharmacology and experimental therapeutics (MS, PhD)
- philosophy (MA, PhD)
- political theory and philosophy (MA, PhD)
- public library (MA)
- scientific technical computing (MS)
- sociology (MA, PhD)
- software technology (MS)
- Spanish (MA)
- theology (MA, PhD)
- virology (MS, PhD)

Marcella Niehoff School of Nursing
Dr. Ida Androwich, Dean
Programs in:
- acute care clinical nurse specialist (MSN)
- acute care nurse practitioner (MSN)
- adult clinical nurse specialist (MSN)
- adult nurse practitioner (MSN)

cardiovascular health and disease management clinical nurse specialist (MSN)
emergency nurse practitioner (MSN)
family nurse practitioner (MSN)
health systems management (MSN)
nursing (PhD)
oncology clinical nurse specialist (MSN)
population-based infection control and environmental safety (MSN)
women's health nurse practitioner (MSN)

Graduate School of Business
Dr. Mary Ann McGrath, Associate Dean
Programs in:
accountancy (MS, MSA)
business administration (MBA)
healthcare management (MBA)
human resources and employee relations (MS, MSHR)
information systems and operations management (MS)
information systems management (MS)
integrated marketing communications (MS)
marketing (MS, MSIMC)
strategic financial services (MBA)

Institute of Human Resources and Employee Relations
Dr. Arup Varma, Chair
Programs in:
human resources (MS)
human resources and employee relations (MS, MSHR)

Institute of Pastoral Studies
Dr. Robert A. Ludwig, Director
Programs in:
divinity (M Div)
pastoral counseling (MA, Certificate)
pastoral studies (MA)
religious education (Certificate)
social justice (MA)
spiritual direction (Certificate)
spirituality (MA)

School of Education
Dr. David Prasse, Dean
Programs in:
administration and supervision (M Ed, Ed D, Certificate)
community counseling (M Ed, MA)
counseling psychology (PhD)
cultural and educational policy studies (M Ed, MA, Ed D, PhD)
curriculum and instruction (M Ed, Ed D)
education (M Ed, MA, Ed D, PhD, Certificate, Ed S)
educational psychology (M Ed)
elementary education (M Ed)
higher education (M Ed, PhD)
instructional leadership (M Ed)
reading specialist (M Ed)
research methods (M Ed, MA, PhD)
school counseling (M Ed, Certificate)
school psychology (M Ed, PhD, Ed S)
school technology (M Ed)
science education (M Ed)
secondary education (M Ed)
special education (M Ed)

School of Law
David N. Yellen, Dean
Programs in:
business law (LL M, MJ)
child and family law (LL M, MJ)
health law (LL M, MJ, D Law, SJD)
law (JD)

School of Social Work
Program in:
social work (MSW, PhD)

Stritch School of Medicine
Dr. John M. Lee, Dean
Program in:
medicine (MD)

■ NATIONAL-LOUIS UNIVERSITY
Chicago, IL 60603
http://www.nl.edu/

Independent, coed, university. *Enrollment:* 1,391 full-time matriculated graduate/professional students (1,042 women), 3,830 part-time matriculated graduate/professional students (3,020 women). *Graduate faculty:* 246 full-time (163 women), 856 part-time/adjunct (574 women). *Computer facilities:* A campuswide network can be accessed from off campus. Internet access is available. *Library facilities:* NLU Library plus 5 others. *Graduate expenses:* Tuition: full-time $17,685. One-time fee: $40 full-time. *General application contact:* Dr. Larry Poselli, Vice President of Enrollment Management, 312-261-3021.

College of Arts and Sciences
Dr. Martha Casazza, Coordinator
Programs in:
addictions counseling (Certificate)
addictions treatment (Certificate)
arts and sciences (M Ed, MA, MS, Ed D, Certificate)
career counseling and development studies (Certificate)
community counseling (MS)
community wellness and prevention (Certificate)
counseling (Certificate)
cultural psychology (MA)
eating disorders counseling (Certificate)
employee assistance programs (MS, Certificate)
gerontology administration (Certificate)
gerontology counseling (MS, Certificate)
health psychology (MA)
human development (MA)
human services administration (MS, Certificate)
long-term care administration (Certificate)
organizational psychology (MA)
psychology (Certificate)
school counseling (MS)
written communication (MS)

Division of Language and Academic Development
Judith Kent, Dean
Programs in:
adult education (Ed D)
adult literacy and developmental studies (M Ed, Certificate)
adult, continuing, and literacy education (M Ed, Certificate)

College of Management and Business
Dr. Richard Magner, Dean
Programs in:
business administration (MBA)
human resource management and development (MS)
management (MS)
management and business (MBA, MS)

National College of Education
Dr. Alison Hilsobeck, Dean
Programs in:
administration and supervision (M Ed, CAS, Ed S)
adult education (Ed D)
curriculum and instruction (M Ed, MS Ed, CAS)
curriculum and social inquiry (Ed D)
early childhood administration (M Ed, CAS)
early childhood curriculum and instruction specialist (M Ed, MS Ed, CAS)
early childhood education (M Ed, MAT, CAS)
education (M Ed, MAT, MS Ed, Ed D, CAS, Ed S)
educational leadership (Ed D)
educational leadership/superintendent endorsement (Ed D)
educational psychology (CAS, Ed S)
educational psychology/human learning and development (M Ed, MS Ed)
educational psychology/school psychology (Ed D)
elementary education (MAT)
general special education (M Ed, MAT, CAS)
human learning and development (Ed D)
interdisciplinary studies in curriculum and instruction (M Ed)
language and literacy (M Ed, MS Ed, CAS)
learning disabilities (M Ed, CAS)
learning disabilities/behavior disorders (M Ed, MAT, CAS)
mathematics education (M Ed, MS Ed, CAS)
reading and language (Ed D)

National-Louis University (continued)
- reading recovery (CAS)
- reading specialist (M Ed, MS Ed, CAS)
- school psychology (M Ed, Ed S)
- science education (M Ed, MS Ed, CAS)
- secondary education (MAT)
- technology in education (M Ed, MS Ed, CAS)

■ NORTH CENTRAL COLLEGE

Naperville, IL 60566-7063

http://www.noctrl.edu/

Independent-religious, coed, comprehensive institution. *Computer facilities:* Computer purchase and lease plans are available. 200 computers available on campus for general student use. A campuswide network can be accessed from student residence rooms and from off campus. Internet access and online class registration, software packages are available. *Library facilities:* Oesterle Library. *General application contact:* Director and Graduate and Continuing Education Admissions, 630-637-5840.

Graduate Programs

Programs in:
- business administration (MBA)
- computer science (MS)
- education (MA Ed)
- leadership studies (MLD)
- liberal studies (MALS)
- management information systems (MS)

■ NORTHEASTERN ILLINOIS UNIVERSITY

Chicago, IL 60625-4699

http://www.neiu.edu/

State-supported, coed, comprehensive institution. CGS member. *Enrollment:* 12,056 graduate, professional, and undergraduate students; 340 full-time matriculated graduate/professional students (179 women), 1,454 part-time matriculated graduate/professional students (1,011 women). *Graduate faculty:* 259 full-time (110 women), 170 part-time/adjunct (85 women). *Computer facilities:* 360 computers available on campus for general student use. A campuswide network can be accessed from off campus. Internet access and online class registration, productivity software are available. *Library facilities:* Ronald Williams Library. *General application contact:* Dr. Janet P. Fredericks, Dean of the Graduate College, 773-442-6010.

Graduate College

Dr. Janet P. Fredericks, Dean of the Graduate College

College of Arts and Sciences

Programs in:
- arts and sciences (MA, MS)
- biology (MS)
- chemistry (MS)
- communication, media and theatre (MA)
- composition/writing (MA)
- computer science (MS)
- earth science (MS)
- English (MA)
- geography and environmental studies (MA)
- gerontology (MA)
- history (MA)
- linguistics (MA)
- literature (MA)
- mathematics (MA, MS)
- mathematics for elementary school teachers (MA)
- music (MA)
- political science (MA)

College of Business and Management

Programs in:
- accounting (MBA)
- finance (MBA)
- management (MBA)
- marketing (MBA)

College of Education

Programs in:
- bilingual/bicultural education (MAT, MSI)
- early childhood special education (MA)
- educating children with behavior disorders (MA)
- educating individuals with mental retardation (MA)
- education (MA, MAT, MSI)
- educational administration and supervision (MA)
- educational leadership (MA)
- gifted education (MA)
- guidance and counseling (MA)
- human resource development (MA)
- inner city studies (MA)
- instruction (MSI)
- language arts (MAT, MSI)
- reading (MA)
- special education (MA)
- teaching (MAT)
- teaching children with learning disabilities (MA)

■ NORTHERN ILLINOIS UNIVERSITY

De Kalb, IL 60115-2854

http://www.niu.edu/

State-supported, coed, university. CGS member. *Enrollment:* 25,313 graduate, professional, and undergraduate students; 2,211 full-time matriculated graduate/professional students (1,150 women), 3,159 part-time matriculated graduate/professional students (1,947 women). *Graduate faculty:* 672 full-time (248 women), 66 part-time/adjunct (17 women). *Computer facilities:* 1,200 computers available on campus for general student use. A campuswide network can be accessed from student residence rooms and from off campus. Internet access and online class registration are available. *Library facilities:* Founders Memorial Library plus 8 others. *General application contact:* Dr. Bradley G. Bond, Associate Dean, Graduate School, 815-753-0395.

College of Law

LeRoy Pernell, Dean

Program in:
- law (JD)

Graduate School

Dr. Rathindra N. Bose, Dean of the Graduate School and Vice President for Research

College of Business

Dr. Denise Schownbachler, Dean

Programs in:
- accountancy (MAS, MST)
- business (MAS, MBA, MS, MST)
- business administration (MBA)
- management information systems (MS)

College of Education

Dr. Christine Sorensen, Dean

Programs in:
- adult and higher education (MS Ed, Ed D)
- counseling (MS Ed, Ed D)
- curriculum and instruction (MS Ed, Ed D)
- early childhood education (MS Ed)
- education (MS, MS Ed, Ed D, Ed S)
- educational administration (MS Ed, Ed D, Ed S)
- educational psychology (MS Ed, Ed D)
- educational research and evaluation (MS)
- elementary education (MS Ed)
- foundations of education (MS Ed)
- instructional technology (MS Ed, Ed D)
- literacy education (MS Ed)
- physical education (MS Ed)
- school business management (MS Ed)
- special education (MS Ed)
- sport management (MS)

College of Engineering and Engineering Technology

Dr. Promod Vohra, Acting Dean

Programs in:
- electrical engineering (MS)
- engineering and engineering technology (MS)
- industrial engineering (MS)
- industrial management (MS)
- mechanical engineering (MS)

College of Health and Human Sciences

Dr. Shirley Richmond, Dean

Programs in:
- applied family and child studies (MS)
- communicative disorders (MA, Au D)
- health and human sciences (MA, MPH, MPT, MS, Au D)
- nursing (MS)

nutrition and dietetics (MS)
physical therapy (MPT)
public health (MPH)

College of Liberal Arts and Sciences
Dr. Joeseph Grush, Acting Dean
Programs in:
anthropology (MA)
biological sciences (MS, PhD)
chemistry (MS, PhD)
communication studies (MA)
computer science (MS)
economics (MA, PhD)
English (MA, PhD)
French (MA)
geography (MS)
geology (MS, PhD)
history (MA, PhD)
liberal arts and sciences (MA, MPA, MS, PhD)
mathematical sciences (PhD)
mathematics (MS)
philosophy (MA)
physics (MS, PhD)
political science (MA, PhD)
psychology (MA, PhD)
public administration (MPA)
sociology (MA)
Spanish (MA)
statistics (MS)

College of Visual and Performing Arts
Dr. Harold Kafer, Dean
Programs in:
art (MA, MFA, MS)
music (MM, Performer's Certificate)
theatre and dance (MFA)
visual and performing arts (MA, MFA, MM, MS, Performer's Certificate)

■ NORTH PARK UNIVERSITY
Chicago, IL 60625-4895
http://www.northpark.edu/

Independent-religious, coed, comprehensive institution. *Computer facilities:* 105 computers available on campus for general student use. A campuswide network can be accessed from student residence rooms and from off campus. *Library facilities:* Consolidated Library plus 4 others. *General application contact:* Vice President for Admissions and Financial Aid, 773-244-5500.

Center for Management Education
Program in:
management education (MBA, MM)

School of Community Development
Program in:
community development (MA)

School of Education
Program in:
education (MA)

School of Nursing
Program in:
nursing (MS)

■ NORTHWESTERN UNIVERSITY
Evanston, IL 60208
http://www.northwestern.edu/

Independent, coed, university. CGS member. *Computer facilities:* Computer purchase and lease plans are available. 678 computers available on campus for general student use. A campuswide network can be accessed from student residence rooms and from off campus. Internet access and online class registration are available. *Library facilities:* University Library plus 6 others. *General application contact:* Graduate Admissions, 847-491-8532.

The Graduate School
Programs in:
African studies (Certificate)
biochemistry, molecular biology, and cell biology (PhD)
biotechnology (PhD)
cell and molecular biology (PhD)
clinical investigation (MSCI, Certificate)
clinical psychology (PhD)
counseling psychology (MA)
developmental biology and genetics (PhD)
genetic counseling (MS)
hormone action and signal transduction (PhD)
law and social science (Certificate)
liberal studies (MA)
literature (MA)
management and organizations and sociology (PhD)
marital and family therapy (MS)
mathematical methods in social science (MS)
neuroscience (PhD)
public health (MPH)
structural biology, biochemistry, and biophysics (PhD)

Center for International and Comparative Studies
Program in:
international and comparative studies (Certificate)

Institute for Neuroscience
Program in:
neuroscience (PhD)

Judd A. and Marjorie Weinberg College of Arts and Sciences
Programs in:
anthropology (PhD)
art history (PhD)
arts and sciences (MA, MFA, MS, PhD, Certificate)
astrophysics (PhD)
brain, behavior and cognition (PhD)
chemistry (PhD)
clinical psychology (PhD)
cognitive psychology (PhD)
comparative literary studies (PhD)
economics (MA, PhD)
eighteenth-century studies (Certificate)
English (MA, PhD)
French (PhD)
French and comparative literature (PhD)
geological sciences (MS, PhD)
German literature and critical thought (PhD)
history (PhD)
Italian studies (Certificate)
linguistics (MA, PhD)
mathematics (PhD)
neurobiology and physiology (MS)
personality (PhD)
philosophy (PhD)
physics (MS, PhD)
political science (MA, PhD)
Slavic languages and literature (PhD)
social psychology (PhD)
sociology (PhD)
statistics (MS, PhD)
visual arts (MFA)

Kellogg School of Management
Programs in:
accounting (PhD)
business administration (MBA)
finance (PhD)
management (MBA, PhD)
management and organizations (PhD)
managerial economics and strategy (PhD)
marketing (PhD)

School of Communication
Programs in:
audiology and hearing sciences (MA, PhD)
clinical audiology (Au D)
communication (MA, MFA, MSC, Au D, PhD)
communication studies (MA, PhD)
communication systems strategy and management (MSC)
directing (MFA)
learning disabilities (MA, PhD)
managerial communication (MSC)
performance studies (MA, PhD)
radio/television/film (MA, MFA, PhD)
speech and language pathology (MA, PhD)
speech and language pathology and learning disabilities (MA)
stage design (MFA)
theatre (MA)
theatre and drama (PhD)

School of Education and Social Policy
Mark P. Hoffman, Graduate Student Advisor
Programs in:
advanced teaching (MS)
education (MS)
elementary education and policy (MS)
higher education administration (MS)

Northwestern University (continued)
human development and social policy (PhD)
learning and organizational change (MS)
learning sciences (MA, PhD)
secondary teaching (MS)

Law School
David Van Zandt, Chair
Programs in:
executive law (LL M)
international law (JD)
law (JD, LL M)

McCormick School of Engineering and Applied Science
Programs in:
applied mathematics (MS, PhD)
biomedical engineering (MS, PhD)
chemical engineering (MS, PhD)
computational biology and bioinformatics (MS)
computer science (MS, PhD)
electrical and computer engineering (MS, PhD)
electronic materials (MS, PhD, Certificate)
engineering and applied science (MEM, MIT, MME, MMM, MPD, MPM, MS, PhD, Certificate)
engineering management (MEM)
environmental engineering and science (MS, PhD)
fluid mechanics (MS, PhD)
geotechnical engineering (MS, PhD)
industrial engineering and management science (MS, PhD)
information technology (MIT)
manufacturing engineering (MME)
materials science and engineering (MS, PhD)
mechanical engineering (MS, PhD)
mechanics of materials and solids (MS, PhD)
operations research (MS, PhD)
project management (MPM, PhD)
solid mechanics (MS, PhD)
structural engineering and materials (MS, PhD)
theoretical and applied mechanics (MS, PhD)
transportation systems analysis and planning (MS, PhD)

Medill School of Journalism
Programs in:
advertising/sales promotion (MSIMC)
broadcast journalism (MSJ)
direct database and e-commerce marketing (MSIMC)
general studies (MSIMC)
integrated marketing communications (MSIMC)
magazine publishing (MSJ)
new media (MSJ)
public relations (MSIMC)
reporting and writing (MSJ)

Northwestern University Feinberg School of Medicine
Lewis Landsberg, Dean
Programs in:
cancer biology (PhD)
cell biology (PhD)
clinical investigation (MSCI)
developmental biology (PhD)
evolutionary biology (PhD)
immunology and microbial pathogenesis (PhD)
medicine (MD, MS, MSCI, DPT, PhD)
molecular biology and genetics (PhD)
neurobiology (PhD)
pharmacology and toxicology (PhD)
physical therapy and human movement sciences (DPT)
structural biology and biochemistry (PhD)

School of Music
Programs in:
collaborative arts (DM)
conducting (MM, DM)
jazz pedagogy (MM)
keyboard (MM, DM, CP)
music (MM, DM, PhD, CP)
music cognition (PhD)
music composition (MM, DM)
music education (MM, PhD)
music technology (MM, PhD)
music theory (MM, PhD)
musicology (MM, PhD)
opera production (MM)
performance (MM)
piano performance and pedagogy (MM)
string performance and pedagogy (MM)
strings (MM, DM)
strings, winds and percussion (CP)
voice (MM, DM, CP)
winds and percussion (MM, DM)

■ OLIVET NAZARENE UNIVERSITY
Bourbonnais, IL 60914-2271
http://www.olivet.edu/

Independent-religious, coed, comprehensive institution. *Computer facilities:* Computer purchase and lease plans are available. 339 computers available on campus for general student use. A campuswide network can be accessed from student residence rooms and from off campus. Internet access and online class registration are available. *Library facilities:* Benner Library. *General application contact:* Dean of the Graduate School, 815-939-5291.

Graduate School
Programs in:
business administration (MBA)
practical ministries (MPM)

Division of Education
Programs in:
curriculum and instruction (MAE)
elementary education (MAT)
secondary education (MAT)

Division of Religion and Philosophy
Programs in:
biblical literature (MA)
religion (MA)
theology (MA)

Institute for Church Management
Programs in:
church management (MCM)
pastoral counseling (MPC)

Program in Organizational Leadership
Program in:
organizational leadership (MOL)

■ ROCKFORD COLLEGE
Rockford, IL 61108-2393
http://www.rockford.edu/

Independent, coed, comprehensive institution. *Computer facilities:* 65 computers available on campus for general student use. A campuswide network can be accessed from student residence rooms. Internet access is available. *Library facilities:* Howard Colman Library. *General application contact:* Administrative Assistant, 815-226-4041.

Graduate Studies
Programs in:
art education (MAT)
business administration (MBA)
elementary education (MAT)
English (MAT)
history (MAT)
learning disabilities (MAT)
political science (MAT)
reading (MAT)
secondary education (MAT)
social sciences (MAT)

■ ROOSEVELT UNIVERSITY
Chicago, IL 60605-1394
http://www.roosevelt.edu/

Independent, coed, comprehensive institution. *Enrollment:* 7,186 graduate, professional, and undergraduate students; 853 full-time matriculated graduate/professional students (572 women), 2,277 part-time matriculated graduate/professional students (1,597 women). *Graduate faculty:* 210 full-time (85 women), 424 part-time/adjunct (181 women). *Computer facilities:* 250 computers available on campus for general student use. A campuswide network can be accessed from student residence rooms and from off campus. Internet access and online class registration are available. *Library facilities:* Murray-Green Library plus 4 others. *General application contact:* Joanne Canyon-Heller, Coordinator of Graduate Admission, 877-APPLY RU.

Find University Details at www.petersons.com/gradchannel.

Graduate Division
Dr. Janett Trubatch, Dean of Graduate Studies

Chicago College of Performing Arts
James Gandre, Dean
Programs in:
- directing and dramaturgy (MFA)
- music (MM)
- musical theatre (MFA)
- performing arts (MA, MFA, MM, Diploma)
- piano pedagogy (Diploma)
- theatre (MA, MFA)
- theatre-directing (MA)
- theatre-performance (MFA)

College of Arts and Sciences
Lynn Weiner, Dean
Programs in:
- anthropology (MA)
- applied economics (MA)
- arts and sciences (MA, MFA, MPA, MS, MSC, MSIMC, MSJ, MST, Psy D, Certificate)
- biotechnology and chemical science (MS)
- clinical professional psychology (MA, Psy D)
- computer science (MSC)
- creative writing (MFA)
- economics (MA)
- English (MA)
- history (MA)
- industrial/organizational psychology (MA)
- integrated marketing communications (MSIMC)
- journalism (MSJ)
- mathematical sciences (MS)
- mathematics (MS)
- political science (MA)
- psychology (Psy D)
- public administration (MPA)
- sociology (MA)
- Spanish (MA)
- telecommunications (MST)
- women's and gender studies (MA, Certificate)

College of Education
James Gandre, Interim Dean
Programs in:
- counseling and human services (MA)
- early childhood education/early childhood professions (MA)
- education (MA, Ed D)
- educational leadership and organizational change (MA, Ed D)
- elementary education (MA)
- reading teacher education (MA)
- secondary education (MA)
- special education (MA)
- teacher leadership (MA)

Evelyn T. Stone University College
Douglas G. Knerr, Interim Dean
Programs in:
- hospitality management (MS)
- training and development (MA)

Walter E. Heller College of Business Administration
Joe Chan, Interim Dean
Programs in:
- accounting (MSA)
- business administration (MBA, MS, MSA, MSHRM, MSIB, MSIS, Certificate)
- commercial real estate development (Certificate)
- human resource management (MSHRM)
- information systems (MSIS)
- international business (MSIB)
- real estate (MBA, MS)

■ SAINT XAVIER UNIVERSITY
Chicago, IL 60655-3105
http://www.sxu.edu/

Independent-religious, coed, comprehensive institution. *Enrollment:* 5,657 graduate, professional, and undergraduate students; 221 full-time matriculated graduate/professional students (147 women), 2,120 part-time matriculated graduate/professional students (1,717 women). *Graduate faculty:* 152. *Computer facilities:* 306 computers available on campus for general student use. A campuswide network can be accessed from student residence rooms and from off campus. Internet access is available. *Library facilities:* Byrne Memorial Library. *General application contact:* Beth Gierach, Vice President of Enrollment Services, 773-298-3050.

Graduate Studies
Vice President of Academic Affairs

Graham School of Management
Dr. John Eber, Dean
Programs in:
- e-commerce (MBA)
- employee health benefits (Certificate)
- finance (MBA, MS)
- financial analysis and investments (MBA)
- financial planning (MBA, Certificate)
- financial trading and practice (MBA, Certificate)
- generalist/administration (MBA)
- health administration (MBA, MS)
- managed care (Certificate)
- management (MBA, MS)
- marketing (MBA)
- public and non-profit management (MBA)
- public health (MPH)
- service management (MBA)
- training and performance management (MBA)

School of Arts and Sciences
Dr. Lawrence Frank, Dean
Programs in:
- adult counseling (Certificate)
- applied computer science in Internet information systems (MS)
- arts and sciences (MA, MS, CAS, Certificate)
- child/adolescent counseling (Certificate)
- core counseling (Certificate)
- counseling psychology (MA)
- English (CAS)
- literary studies (MA)
- mathematics and computer science (MA)
- speech-language pathology (MS)
- teaching of writing (MA)
- writing pedagogy (CAS)

School of Education
Dr. Beverly Gulley, Dean
Programs in:
- counseling (MA)
- counselor education (MA)
- curriculum and instruction (MA)
- early childhood education (MA)
- education (CAS)
- educational administration (MA)
- elementary education (MA)
- field-based education (MA)
- general educational studies (MA)
- individualized program (MA)
- learning disabilities (MA)
- reading (MA)
- secondary education (MA)

School of Nursing
Beth Gierach, Managing Director of Admission
Programs in:
- adult health clinical nurse specialist (MS)
- family nurse practitioner (MS, PMC)
- leadership in community health nursing (MS)
- psychiatric-mental health clinical nurse specialist (MS)
- psychiatric-mental health clinical specialist (PMC)

■ SOUTHERN ILLINOIS UNIVERSITY CARBONDALE
Carbondale, IL 62901-4701
http://www.siu.edu/siuc/

State-supported, coed, university. CGS member. *Enrollment:* 21,003 graduate, professional, and undergraduate students; 1,648 full-time matriculated graduate/professional students (851 women), 2,632 part-time matriculated graduate/professional students (1,387 women). *Graduate faculty:* 1,074 full-time (262 women), 112 part-time/adjunct. *Computer facilities:* Computer purchase and lease plans are available. 1,827 computers available on campus for general student use. A campuswide network can be accessed from student residence rooms and from off campus. Internet access and online class registration are available. *Library facilities:* Morris Library plus 1 other. *General application contact:* Associate Dean of the Graduate School, 618-536-7791.

Graduate School
Dr. John Koropchak, Dean
Programs in:
- general law (MLS)

Southern Illinois University Carbondale (continued)
- health law and policy (MLS)
- molecular, cellular and systemic physiology (MS)
- pharmacology (MS, PhD)
- physiology (MS, PhD)

College of Agriculture
Gary L. Minish, Dean
Programs in:
- agribusiness economics (MS)
- agriculture (MS)
- animal science (MS)
- food and nutrition (MS)
- forestry (MS)
- horticultural science (MS)
- plant and soil science (MS)

College of Business and Administration
Dr. Dennis Cradit, Dean
Programs in:
- accountancy (M Acc, PhD)
- business administration (MBA, PhD)
- business and administration (M Acc, MBA, PhD)

College of Education
Patricia Elmore, Interim Dean
Programs in:
- behavior analysis and therapy (MS)
- behavioral analysis and therapy (MS)
- communication disorders and sciences (MS)
- community health education (MPH)
- counselor education (MS Ed, PhD)
- curriculum and instruction (MS Ed, PhD)
- education (MPH, MS, MS Ed, MSW, PhD, Rh D)
- educational administration (MS Ed, PhD)
- educational psychology (MS Ed, PhD)
- health education (MS Ed, PhD)
- higher education (MS Ed)
- human learning and development (MS Ed)
- measurement and statistics (PhD)
- physical education (MS Ed)
- recreation (MS Ed)
- rehabilitation (Rh D)
- rehabilitation administration and services (MS)
- rehabilitation counseling (MS)
- social work (MSW)
- special education (MS Ed)
- workforce education and development (MS Ed, PhD)

College of Engineering
Dr. William Osborne, Dean
Programs in:
- civil engineering (MS)
- electrical and computer engineering (MS, PhD)
- electrical systems (PhD)
- engineering (MS, PhD)
- fossil energy (PhD)
- manufacturing systems (MS)
- mechanical engineering and energy processes (MS)
- mechanics (PhD)
- mining engineering (MS)

College of Liberal Arts
Dr. Alan Vaux, Interim Dean
Programs in:
- administration of justice (MA)
- anthropology (MA, PhD)
- applied linguistics (MA)
- ceramics (MFA)
- clinical psychology (MA, MS, PhD)
- composition (MA, PhD)
- composition and theory (MM)
- counseling psychology (MA, MS, PhD)
- creative writing (MFA)
- drawing (MFA)
- economics (MA, MS, PhD)
- experimental psychology (MA, MS, PhD)
- fiber/weaving (MFA)
- foreign languages and literatures (MA)
- geography (MS, PhD)
- glass (MFA)
- history (MA, PhD)
- history and literature (MM)
- jewelry (MFA)
- liberal arts (MA, MFA, MM, MPA, MS, PhD)
- metalsmithing/blacksmithing (MFA)
- music education (MM)
- opera/music theater (MM)
- painting (MFA)
- performance (MM)
- philosophy (MA, PhD)
- piano pedagogy (MM)
- political science (MA, PhD)
- printmaking (MFA)
- public administration (MPA)
- sculpture (MFA)
- sociology (MA, PhD)
- speech communication (MA, MS, PhD)
- speech/theater (PhD)
- teaching English to speakers of other languages (MA)
- theater (MFA)

College of Mass Communication and Media Arts
Dr. Manjumath Pendakur, Dean
Programs in:
- journalism (PhD)
- mass communication and media arts (MA, MFA, PhD)
- professional media and media management studies (MA)
- telecommunications (MA)

College of Science
Dr. Jack Parker, Dean
Programs in:
- biological sciences (MS)
- chemistry and biochemistry (MS, PhD)
- computer science (MS, PhD)
- environmental resources and policy (PhD)
- geology (MS, PhD)
- mathematics (MA, MS, PhD)
- molecular biology, microbiology, and biochemistry (MS, PhD)
- physics (MS, PhD)
- plant biology (MS, PhD)
- science (MA, MS, PhD)
- statistics (MS)
- zoology (MS, PhD)

School of Law
Peter C. Alexander, Dean
Programs in:
- general law (LL M)
- health law and policy (LL M)
- law (JD)
- legal studies (MLS)

■ SOUTHERN ILLINOIS UNIVERSITY EDWARDSVILLE

Edwardsville, IL 62026-0001
http://www.siue.edu/

State-supported, coed, comprehensive institution. CGS member. *Enrollment:* 13,449 graduate, professional, and undergraduate students; 1,033 full-time matriculated graduate/professional students (584 women), 1,257 part-time matriculated graduate/professional students (818 women). *Graduate faculty:* 465 full-time (176 women). *Computer facilities:* Computer purchase and lease plans are available. 600 computers available on campus for general student use. A campuswide network can be accessed from student residence rooms and from off campus. Internet access, online job finder are available. *Library facilities:* Lovejoy Library. *General application contact:* Dr. Stephen L. Hansen, Dean of Graduate School, 618-650-3010.

Find University Details at www.petersons.com/gradchannel.

Graduate Studies and Research
Dr. Stephen L. Hansen, Dean of Graduate School

College of Arts and Sciences
Dr. M. Kent Neely, Dean
Programs in:
- American and English literature (MA, Postbaccalaureate Certificate)
- art therapy counseling (MA, Postbaccalaureate Certificate)
- arts and sciences (MA, MFA, MM, MPA, MS, MSW, Postbaccalaureate Certificate)
- biology (MA, MS)
- biotechnology management (MS)
- chemistry (MS)
- corporate and organizational communication (Postbaccalaureate Certificate)
- creative writing (MA)
- environmental science management (MS)
- environmental sciences (MS)

geography (MS)
history (MA)
mass communications (MS)
mathematics (MS)
media literacy (Postbaccalaureate Certificate)
museum studies (Postbaccalaureate Certificate)
music education (MM)
music performance (MM)
physics (MS)
public administration and policy analysis (MPA)
social work (MSW)
sociology (MA)
speech communication (MA)
studio art (MFA)
teaching English as a second language (MA, Postbaccalaureate Certificate)
teaching of writing (MA, Postbaccalaureate Certificate)

School of Business
Dr. Timothy Schoenecker, Acting Dean
Programs in:
accounting (MSA)
business (MA, MBA, MMR, MS, MSA)
business administration (MBA)
computer management and information systems (MS)
economics and finance (MA, MS)
management information systems (MBA)
marketing research (MMR)

School of Education
Dr. Bill Searcy, Interim Dean
Programs in:
art (MS Ed)
biology (MS Ed)
chemistry (MS Ed)
clinical child and school psychology (MS)
clinical-adult psychology (MA)
education (MA, MAT, MS, MS Ed, Ed S, Postbaccalaureate Certificate, SD)
educational administration (MS Ed, Ed S)
elementary education (MS Ed)
English (MS Ed)
exercise physiology (Postbaccalaureate Certificate)
foreign languages (MS Ed)
history (MS Ed)
industrial-organizational psychology (MA)
instructional design and learning technologies (MS Ed)
kinesiology (MS Ed)
learning, culture and society (MS Ed)
literacy education (MS Ed)
mathematics (MS Ed)
pedagogy administration (Postbaccalaureate Certificate)
physics (MS Ed)
psychology (MA, MS)
reading (MS Ed)
school psychology (SD)
science (MS Ed)
secondary education (MS Ed)
special education (MS Ed)
speech language pathology (MS)
sport and exercise behavior (Postbaccalaureate Certificate)
teaching (MAT)

School of Engineering
Dr. Hasan Sevim, Dean
Programs in:
civil engineering (MS)
computer science (MS)
electrical engineering (MS)
engineering (MS)
mechanical engineering (MS)

School of Nursing
Dr. Marcia Maurer, Dean
Programs in:
family nurse practitioner (MS, Post-Master's Certificate)
health care and nursing administration (MS, Post-Master's Certificate)
nurse anesthesia (MS, Post-Master's Certificate)
nurse educator (MS, Post-Master's Certificate)
nursing (MS, Post-Master's Certificate)
public health nursing (MS, Post-Master's Certificate)

School of Dental Medicine
Dr. Ann Boyle, Dean
Program in:
dental medicine (DMD)

School of Pharmacy
Dr. Philip J. Medon, Head
Program in:
pharmacy (Pharm D)

■ TRINITY INTERNATIONAL UNIVERSITY
Deerfield, IL 60015-1284
http://www.tiu.edu/

Independent-religious, coed, university. *Enrollment:* 2,855 graduate, professional, and undergraduate students; 696 full-time matriculated graduate/professional students (215 women), 912 part-time matriculated graduate/professional students (293 women). *Graduate faculty:* 47 full-time (7 women), 128 part-time/adjunct (28 women). *Computer facilities:* 130 computers available on campus for general student use. A campuswide network can be accessed from student residence rooms and from off campus. Internet access and online class registration are available. *Library facilities:* Rolfing Memorial Library. *Graduate expenses:* Tuition: full-time $13,200; part-time $630 per hour. Required fees: $43 per semester. *General application contact:* Ron Campbell, Director of Admissions, 800-345-8337.

Trinity Evangelical Divinity School
Dr. Tite Tiénou, Academic Dean
Programs in:
Biblical and Near Eastern archaeology and languages (MA)
Christian studies (MA, Certificate)
Christian thought (MA)
church history (MA, Th M)
congregational ministry: pastor-teacher (M Div)
congregational ministry: team ministry (M Div)
counseling ministries (MA)
counseling psychology (MA)
cross-cultural ministry (M Div)
educational studies (PhD)
evangelism (MA)
general studies (MAR)
history of Christianity in America (MA)
intercultural studies (MA, PhD)
leadership and ministry management (D Min)
military chaplaincy (D Min)
ministry (MA)
mission and evangelism (Th M)
missions and evangelism (D Min)
New Testament (MA, Th M)
Old Testament (Th M)
Old Testament and Semitic languages (MA)
pastoral care (M Div)
pastoral care and counseling (D Min)
pastoral counseling and psychology (Th M)
pastoral theology (Th M)
philosophy of religion (MA)
preaching (D Min)
research ministry (M Div)
systematic theology (Th M)
theological studies (PhD)
urban ministry (MA, MAR)

Trinity Graduate School
Dr. James Stamoolis, Academic Dean
Programs in:
bioethics (MA)
communication and culture (MA)
counseling psychology (MA)
instructional leadership (M Ed)
teaching (MA)

Trinity Law School
Kevin P. Holsclaw, Academic Dean
Program in:
law (JD)

■ UNIVERSITY OF CHICAGO
Chicago, IL 60637-1513
http://www.uchicago.edu/

Independent, coed, university. CGS member. *Enrollment:* 11,730 graduate, professional, and undergraduate students; 6,844 full-time matriculated graduate/professional students (3,072 women), 2,219 part-time matriculated graduate/professional students (628 women). *Graduate faculty:* 2,261 full-time (656 women), 573 part-time/adjunct (212 women). *Computer facilities:* 1,000 computers available on campus for general student

University of Chicago (continued)
use. A campuswide network can be accessed from student residence rooms and from off campus. Internet access and online class registration are available. *Library facilities:* Joseph Regenstein Library plus 6 others. *Graduate expenses:* Tuition: full-time $34,920. Required fees: $612. One-time fee: $35 full-time. Full-time tuition and fees vary according to course load, degree level and program. *General application contact:* Martha Jackson, Manager, Office of Graduate Affairs, 773-702-7813.

Divinity School
Program in:
- divinity (M Div, AM, AMRS, PhD)

Division of Social Sciences
Prof. John Mark Hansen, Dean
Programs in:
- anthropology (PhD)
- comparative human development (PhD)
- conceptual and historical studies of science (PhD)
- economics (PhD)
- history (PhD)
- international relations (AM)
- Latin American and Caribbean studies (AM)
- Middle Eastern studies (AM)
- political science (PhD)
- psychology (PhD)
- social sciences (AM, PhD)
- social thought (PhD)
- sociology (PhD)

Division of the Biological Sciences
Dr. James Madara, Dean
Programs in:
- biochemistry and molecular biology (PhD)
- biological sciences (MD, MS, PhD)
- biophysics and synthetic biology (PhD)
- cancer biology (PhD)
- cell physiology (PhD)
- cellular and molecular physiology (PhD)
- cellular differentiation (PhD)
- computational neuroscience (PhD)
- developmental biology (PhD)
- developmental endocrinology (PhD)
- developmental genetics (PhD)
- developmental neurobiology (PhD)
- ecology and evolution (PhD)
- evolutionary biology (PhD)
- functional and evolutionary biology (PhD)
- gene expression (PhD)
- genetics (PhD)
- health studies (MS)
- human genetics (PhD)
- immunology (PhD)
- integrative neuroscience (PhD)
- interdisciplinary scientist training (PhD)
- microbiology (PhD)
- molecular genetics and cell biology (PhD)
- molecular metabolism and nutrition (PhD)
- neurobiology (PhD)
- ophthalmology and visual science (PhD)
- organismal biology and anatomy (PhD)
- pathology (PhD)
- pharmacological and physiological sciences (PhD)

Pritzker School of Medicine
Dr. James Madara, Dean
Program in:
- medicine (MD)

Division of the Humanities
Thomas B. Thuerer, Dean of Students
Programs in:
- ancient philosophy (AM, PhD)
- anthropology and linguistics (PhD)
- art history (AM, PhD)
- cinema and media studies (AM, PhD)
- classical archaeology (AM, PhD)
- classical languages and literatures (AM, PhD)
- comparative literature (AM, PhD)
- East Asian languages and civilizations (AM, PhD)
- English language and literature (AM, PhD)
- French (AM, PhD)
- Germanic languages and literatures (AM, PhD)
- humanities (AM, MA, MFA, PhD)
- Italian (AM, PhD)
- linguistics (AM, PhD)
- music (AM, PhD)
- Near Eastern languages and civilizations (AM, PhD)
- New Testament and early Christian culture (AM, PhD)
- philosophy (AM, PhD)
- Slavic languages and literatures (AM, PhD)
- South Asian languages and civilizations (AM, PhD)
- Spanish (AM, PhD)
- visual arts (MFA)

Division of the Physical Sciences
Robert Fefferman, Dean
Programs in:
- applied mathematics (SM, PhD)
- astronomy and astrophysics (MS, PhD)
- atmospheric sciences (SM, PhD)
- chemistry (PhD)
- computer science (SM, PhD)
- earth sciences (SM, PhD)
- financial mathematics (MS)
- mathematics (SM, PhD)
- paleobiology (PhD)
- physical sciences (MS, SM, PhD)
- physics (PhD)
- planetary and space sciences (SM, PhD)
- statistics (SM, PhD)

Graduate School of Business
Edward A. Snyder, Dean
Programs in:
- business (IMBA, MBA, PhD)
- business administration (MBA)
- executive business administration (MBA)
- international business administration (IMBA)

The Irving B. Harris Graduate School of Public Policy Studies
Programs in:
- environmental science and policy (MS)
- public policy studies (AM, MPP, PhD)

The Law School
Saul Levmore, Dean
Program in:
- law (JD, LL M, MCL, DCL, JSD)

School of Social Service Administration
Dr. Jeanne Marsh, Dean
Programs in:
- social service administration (PhD)
- social work (AM)

■ UNIVERSITY OF ILLINOIS AT CHICAGO
Chicago, IL 60607-7128
http://www.uic.edu/

State-supported, coed, university. CGS member. *Computer facilities:* 1,100 computers available on campus for general student use. A campuswide network can be accessed from student residence rooms and from off campus. Internet access and online class registration are available. *Library facilities:* Richard J. Daley Library plus 3 others. *General application contact:* Graduate College Receptionist, 312-413-2550.

College of Dentistry
Programs in:
- dentistry (DDS, MS)
- oral sciences (MS)

College of Medicine
Programs in:
- anatomy and cell biology (MS, PhD)
- biochemistry and molecular biology (MS, PhD)
- cellular and systems neuroscience and cell biology (PhD)
- genetics (PhD)
- health professions education (MHPE)
- medicine (MD, MHPE, MS, PhD)
- microbiology and immunology (PhD)
- molecular genetics (PhD)
- neuroscience (PhD)
- pharmacology (PhD)
- physiology and biophysics (MS, PhD)
- surgery (MS)

College of Pharmacy
Programs in:
- forensic science (MS)
- medicinal chemistry (MS, PhD)
- pharmaceutics (MS, PhD)
- pharmacodynamics (MS, PhD)
- pharmacognosy (MS, PhD)
- pharmacy (Pharm D, MS, PhD)
- pharmacy administration (MS, PhD)

Center for Pharmaceutical Biotechnology
Program in:
- pharmaceutical biotechnology (MS, PhD)

Graduate College
Program in:
- neuroscience (PhD)

College of Applied Health Sciences
Programs in:
- applied health sciences (MAMS, MS, PhD)
- biomedical visualization (MAMS)
- disability and human development (MS)
- disability studies (PhD)
- human nutrition and dietetics (MS, PhD)
- movement sciences (MS)
- occupational therapy (MS)
- physical therapy (MS)

College of Architecture and Art
Programs in:
- architecture (M Arch)
- architecture and art (M Arch, MA, MFA, PhD)
- art history (MA, PhD)
- electronic visualization (MFA)
- film animation (MFA)
- graphic design (MFA)
- industrial design (MFA)
- photography (MFA)
- studio arts (MFA)

College of Education
Programs in:
- curriculum and instruction (PhD)
- education (M Ed, PhD)
- educational psychology (PhD)
- instructional leadership (M Ed)
- leadership and administration (M Ed)
- policy and administration (PhD)
- policy studies in urban education (PhD)
- special education (M Ed, PhD)

College of Engineering
Programs in:
- bioengineering (MS, PhD)
- chemical engineering (MS, PhD)
- civil and materials engineering (MS, PhD)
- computer science (MS, PhD)
- electrical and computer engineering (MS, PhD)
- engineering (MS, PhD)
- industrial engineering (MS)
- industrial engineering and operations research (PhD)
- mechanical engineering (MS, PhD)

College of Liberal Arts and Sciences
Programs in:
- anthropology (MA, PhD)
- applied linguistics (teaching English as a second language) (MA)
- applied mathematics (MS, DA, PhD)
- cell and developmental biology (PhD)
- chemistry (MS, PhD)
- communication (MA)
- computer science (MS, DA, PhD)
- criminal justice (MA)
- crystallography (MS, PhD)
- ecology and evolution (MS, DA, PhD)
- English (MA, PhD)
- environmental and urban geography (MA)
- environmental geology (MS, PhD)
- environmental studies (MA)
- French (MA)
- genetics and development (PhD)
- geochemistry (MS, PhD)
- geology (MS, PhD)
- geomorphology (MS, PhD)
- geophysics (MS, PhD)
- geotechnical engineering and geosciences (PhD)
- Germanic studies (MA, PhD)
- Hispanic studies (MA, PhD)
- history (MA, MAT, PhD)
- hydrogeology (MS, PhD)
- language, literacy, and rhetoric (PhD)
- liberal arts and sciences (MA, MAT, MS, MST, DA, PhD)
- linguistics (MA)
- low-temperature and organic geochemistry (MS, PhD)
- mass communication (MA)
- math and information science for the industry (MS)
- mineralogy (MS, PhD)
- molecular biology (MS, PhD)
- neurobiology (MS, PhD)
- paleoclimatology (MS, PhD)
- paleontology (MS, PhD)
- petrology (MS, PhD)
- philosophy (MA, PhD)
- physics (MS, PhD)
- plant biology (MS, DA, PhD)
- political science (MA, PhD)
- probability and statistics (MS, DA, PhD)
- psychology (PhD)
- pure mathematics (MS, DA, PhD)
- quaternary geology (MS, PhD)
- sedimentology (MS, PhD)
- Slavic languages and literatures (PhD)
- Slavic studies (MA)
- sociology (MA, PhD)
- teaching of mathematics (MST)
- urban geography (MA)
- water resources (MS, PhD)

College of Nursing
Programs in:
- maternity nursing/nurse midwifery (MS)
- nursing (MS, PhD)
- nursing research (PhD)
- nursing science (PhD)
- nursing sciences (medical surgical) (MS)
- nursing sciences (nursing administration) (MS)
- nursing sciences (psychiatric nursing) (MS)
- nursing sciences (public health nursing) (MS)
- pediatric nursing (MS)
- perinatal nursing (MS)

College of Urban Planning and Public Affairs
Programs in:
- public administration (MPA, PhD)
- public policy analysis (PhD)
- urban planning and policy (MUPP)
- urban planning and public affairs (MPA, MUPP, PhD)

Jane Addams College of Social Work
Program in:
- social work (MSW, PhD)

Liautaud Graduate School of Business
Programs in:
- accounting (MS)
- business administration (MA, MBA, MS, PhD)
- economics (MA, PhD)
- management information systems (MS, PhD)
- public policy analysis (PhD)

School of Public Health
Programs in:
- biostatistics (MS, PhD)
- community health sciences (MPH, MS, Dr PH, PhD)
- environmental and occupational health sciences (MPH, MS, Dr PH, PhD)
- epidemiology (MPH, MS, Dr PH, PhD)
- health policy administration (MPH, MS, Dr PH, PhD)

■ UNIVERSITY OF ILLINOIS AT SPRINGFIELD
Springfield, IL 62703-5407
http://www.uis.edu/

State-supported, coed, comprehensive institution. CGS member. *Enrollment:* 4,761 graduate, professional, and undergraduate students; 508 full-time matriculated graduate/professional students (245 women), 1,246 part-time matriculated graduate/professional students (736 women). *Graduate faculty:* 180 full-time (71 women), 50 part-time/adjunct (19 women). *Computer facilities:* Computer purchase and lease plans are available. 132 computers available on campus for general student use. A campuswide network can be accessed from student residence rooms and from off campus. Internet access and online class registration are available. *Library facilities:* Norris L. Brookens Library. *Graduate expenses:* Tuition, state resident: full-time $4,722; part-time $197 per credit hour. Tuition, nonresident: full-time $12,558; part-time $523 per credit hour. Required fees: $1,614; $8 per credit hour. $597 per term. *General application contact:* Dr. Lynn Pardie, Office of Graduate Studies, 800-252-8533.

Graduate Programs
Dr. Lynn Pardie, Office of Graduate Studies

College of Business and Management
Dr. Ronald McNeil, Dean

University of Illinois at Springfield (continued)
Programs in:
- accountancy (MA)
- business administration (MBA)
- business and management (MA, MBA, MS)
- management information systems (MS)

College of Education and Human Services
Dr. Larry Stonecipher, Dean
Programs in:
- alcoholism and substance abuse (MA)
- child and family services (MA)
- education and human services (MA)
- educational leadership (MA)
- gerontology (MA)
- human development counseling (MA)
- social services administration (MA)
- teacher leadership (MA)

College of Liberal Arts and Sciences
Dr. Margot Duley, Dean
Programs in:
- biology (MS)
- communication (MA)
- computer science (MS)
- English (MA)
- history (MA)
- interdisciplinary studies (MA)
- liberal arts and sciences (MA, MS)

College of Public Affairs and Administration
Dr. Pinky Sue Wassenberg, Dean
Programs in:
- environmental science (MS)
- environmental studies (MA)
- legal studies (MA)
- political studies (MA)
- public administration (MPA, DPA)
- public affairs and administration (MA, MPA, MPH, MS, DPA)
- public affairs reporting (MA)
- public health (MPH)

■ UNIVERSITY OF ILLINOIS AT URBANA–CHAMPAIGN
Champaign, IL 61820
http://www.uiuc.edu/

State-supported, coed, university. CGS member. *Enrollment:* 42,728 graduate, professional, and undergraduate students; 8,911 full-time matriculated graduate/professional students (3,988 women), 1,896 part-time matriculated graduate/professional students (1,095 women). *Graduate faculty:* 2,083 full-time (599 women), 167 part-time/adjunct (67 women). *Computer facilities:* Computer purchase and lease plans are available. 3,500 computers available on campus for general student use. A campuswide network can be accessed from student residence rooms and from off campus. Internet access and online class registration, wireless available in many buildings are available. *Library facilities:* University Library plus 36 others. *General application contact:* William Welburn, Associate Dean, 217-333-6715.

College of Law
Heidi M. Hurd, Dean
Program in:
- law (JD, LL M, MCL, JSD)

College of Veterinary Medicine
Herbert Whiteley, Dean
Programs in:
- pathobiology (MS, PhD)
- veterinary biosciences (MS, PhD)
- veterinary clinical medicine (MS, PhD)
- veterinary medicine (DVM, MS, PhD)

Graduate College
Richard P. Wheeler, Dean
Program in:
- medical scholars)

College of Agricultural, Consumer and Environmental Sciences
Robert A. Easter, Dean
Programs in:
- agricultural and biological engineering (MS, PhD)
- agricultural and consumer economics (MS, PhD)
- agricultural, consumer and environmental sciences (MS, PhD)
- animal sciences (MS, PhD)
- crop sciences (MS, PhD)
- extension education (MS)
- food science and human nutrition (MS, PhD)
- human and community development (MS, PhD)
- natural resources and environmental science (MS, PhD)
- nutritional sciences (MS, PhD)

College of Applied Health Studies
Tanya Gallagher, Dean
Programs in:
- applied health studies (MA, MS, MSPH, Au D, PhD)
- community health (MS, MSPH, PhD)
- kinesiology (MS, PhD)
- recreation, sport and tourism (MS, PhD)
- speech and hearing science (MA, Au D, PhD)

College of Business
Avijit Ghosh, Dean
Programs in:
- accountancy (MAS, MS, PhD)
- business (MAS, MBA, MS, MSTM, PhD)
- business administration (PhD)
- finance (MS, PhD)
- technology management (MSTM)

College of Communications
Ronald E. Yates, Dean
Programs in:
- advertising (MS)
- communications (PhD)
- journalism (MS)

College of Education
Mary A. Kalantzis, Dean
Programs in:
- curriculum and instruction (Ed M, MA, MS, Ed D, PhD, CAS)
- education (Ed M, MA, MS, Ed D, PhD, CAS)
- education, organization and leadership (Ed M, MA, MS, Ed D, PhD, CAS)
- educational policy studies (Ed M, MA, Ed D, PhD)
- educational psychology (Ed M, MA, MS, PhD, CAS)
- human resource education (Ed M, MA, MS, Ed D, PhD, CAS)
- special education (Ed M, MA, MS, PhD, CAS)

College of Engineering
Dr. Ilesanmi Adesida, Dean
Programs in:
- aerospace engineering (MS, PhD)
- bioengineering (MS, PhD)
- civil and environmental engineering (MS, PhD)
- civil engineering (MS, PhD)
- computer engineering (MS, PhD)
- computer science (MCS, MS, PhD)
- electrical engineering (MS, PhD)
- engineering (MCS, MS, PhD)
- health physics (MS, PhD)
- materials science and engineering (MS, PhD)
- mechanical engineering (MS, PhD)
- nuclear engineering (MS, PhD)
- physics (MS, PhD)
- systems engineering and engineering design (MS)
- theoretical and applied mechanics (MS, PhD)

College of Fine and Applied Arts
Robert F. Graves, Dean
Programs in:
- architecture (M Arch, PhD)
- art and design (MA, MFA, Ed D, PhD)
- art education (MA, Ed D)
- art history (MA, PhD)
- dance (MFA)
- fine and applied arts (M Arch, M Mus, MA, MFA, MLA, MME, MS, MUP, DMA, Ed D, PhD)
- graphics (MFA)
- industrial design (MFA)
- landscape architecture (MLA, PhD)
- music (M Mus, MME, MS, DMA, Ed D, PhD)
- painting (MFA)
- photography (MFA)
- regional planning (PhD)
- sculpture (MFA)
- theatre (MA, MFA, PhD)
- urban and regional planning (MUP)

College of Liberal Arts and Sciences
Dr. Sarah C. Mangelsdorf, Dean
Programs in:
- African studies (MA)
- animal biology (MS, PhD)
- anthropology (MA, PhD)
- applied mathematics (MS)

astronomy (MS, PhD)
atmospheric science (MS, PhD)
biochemistry (MS, PhD)
biophysics and computational biology (PhD)
cell and developmental biology (PhD)
chemical and biomolecular engineering (MS, PhD)
chemical sciences (MS, PhD)
chemistry (MS, PhD)
classics (MA, PhD)
comparative and world literature (MA, PhD)
demography (MA, PhD)
earth sciences (MS, PhD)
East Asian languages and cultures (MA, PhD)
ecology and evolutionary biology (MS, PhD)
economics (MS, PhD)
English (MA, MFA, PhD)
English as an international language (MA)
entomology (PhD)
French (MA, MAT, PhD)
geochemistry (MS, PhD)
geography (MA, MS, PhD)
geology (MS, PhD)
geophysics (MS, PhD)
Germanic languages and literatures (MA, MAT, PhD)
history (MA, PhD)
insect pest management (MS)
integrative biology (MS, PhD)
Italian (PhD)
Latin American and Caribbean studies (MA)
liberal arts and sciences (MA, MAT, MFA, MS, PhD, CAS)
linguistics (MA, PhD)
mathematics (MA, MS, PhD)
microbiology (PhD)
molecular and cellular biology (MS, PhD)
molecular and integrative physiology (MS, PhD)
neuroscience (PhD)
philosophy (MA, PhD)
physiological and molecular plant biology (PhD)
plant biology (MS, PhD)
political science (MA, PhD)
psychology (MA, MS, PhD)
Russian (MA, PhD)
Russian, East European and Eurasian (MA)
second language aquisition and teacher education (CAS)
Slavic languages and literatures (MA, PhD)
sociology (MA, PhD)
Spanish, Italian and Portuguese (MA)
speech communication (MA, PhD)
statistics (MS, PhD)
teaching of mathematics (MS)

Graduate School of Library and Information Science
John Unsworth, Dean
Programs in:
biological informatics (MS)
digital libraries (CAS)
library and information science (MS, PhD, CAS)

Institute of Labor and Industrial Relations
Dr. Joe Cutcher Gershenfeld, Director
Programs in:
human resources (MHRIR, PhD)
labor and industrial relations (MHRIR, PhD)

School of Social Work
Wynne S. Korr, Dean
Program in:
social work (MSW, PhD)

■ UNIVERSITY OF ST. FRANCIS
Joliet, IL 60435-6169
http://www.stfrancis.edu/

Independent-religious, coed, comprehensive institution. *Enrollment:* 2,060 graduate, professional, and undergraduate students; 249 full-time matriculated graduate/professional students (186 women), 1,182 part-time matriculated graduate/professional students (969 women). *Graduate faculty:* 33 full-time (22 women), 74 part-time/adjunct (36 women). *Computer facilities:* 250 computers available on campus for general student use. A campuswide network can be accessed from student residence rooms and from off campus. Internet access and online class registration are available. *Library facilities:* University of St. Francis Library. *Graduate expenses:* Tuition: part-time $445 per credit hour. Part-time tuition and fees vary according to campus/location and program. *General application contact:* Sandra Sloka, Director of Admissions for Graduate and Degree Completion Programs, 800-735-7500.

College of Business
Dr. Michael LaRocco, Dean
Programs in:
business (MBA)
management (MS)

College of Education
Dr. John Gambro, Dean
Programs in:
curriculum and instruction (MS)
educational leadership (MS)
elementary education certification (M Ed)
secondary education certification (M Ed)
special education (M Ed)
teaching and learning (MS)

College of Nursing and Allied Health
Dr. Maria Connolly, Dean
Programs in:
nursing (MSN)
physician assistant studies (MS)

College of Professional Studies
Dr. Michael LaRocco, Dean
Programs in:
health services administration (MS)
training and development (MS)

■ WESTERN ILLINOIS UNIVERSITY
Macomb, IL 61455-1390
http://www.wiu.edu/

State-supported, coed, comprehensive institution. CGS member. *Enrollment:* 13,602 graduate, professional, and undergraduate students; 798 full-time matriculated graduate/professional students (387 women), 1,140 part-time matriculated graduate/professional students (750 women). *Computer facilities:* 1,000 computers available on campus for general student use. A campuswide network can be accessed from student residence rooms and from off campus. Internet access and online class registration, course registration are available. *Library facilities:* Leslie Malpass Library plus 4 others. *Graduate expenses:* Tuition, state resident: part-time $200 per credit hour. Tuition, nonresident: part-time $400 per credit hour. *General application contact:* Dr. Barbara Baily, Director of Graduate Studies/Associate Provost, 309-298-1806.

School of Graduate Studies
Dr. Barbara Baily, Director of Graduate Studies/Associate Provost

College of Arts and Sciences
Dr. Inessa Levi, Dean
Programs in:
applied math (Certificate)
arts and sciences (MA, MS, Certificate, SSP)
biological sciences (MS)
chemistry (MS)
clinical/community mental health (MS)
community development (Certificate)
general psychology (MS)
geography (MA)
history (MA)
literature and language (MA)
mathematics (MS)
physics (MS)
political science (MA)
psychology (MS, SSP)
public and non-profit management (Certificate)
school psychology (SSP)
sociology (MA)
writing (MA)
zoo and aquarium studies (Certificate)

College of Business and Technology
Dr. Tom Erekson, Dean
Programs in:
accountancy (M Acct)
business administration (MBA)

Western Illinois University (continued)
business and technology (M Acct, MA, MBA, MS)
computer science (MS)
economics (MA)
manufacturing engineering systems (MS)

College of Education and Human Services
Dr. Bonnie Smith, Dean
Programs in:
college student personnel (MS)
counseling (MS Ed)
distance learning (Certificate)
education and human services (MA, MAT, MS, MS Ed, Ed D, Certificate, Ed S)
educational and interdisciplinary studies (MS Ed)
educational leadership (MS Ed, Ed D, Ed S)
elementary education (MS Ed)
graphic applications (Certificate)
health education (MS)
health services administration (Certificate)
instructional technology and telecommunications (MS)
kinesiology (MS)
law enforcement and justice administration (MA)
multimedia (Certificate)
police executive administration (Certificate)
reading (MS Ed)
recreation, park, and tourism administration (MS)
secondary education (MAT)
special education (MS Ed)
sport management (MS)
technology integration in education (Certificate)
training development (Certificate)

College of Fine Arts and Communication
Dr. Paul K. Kreider, Dean
Programs in:
acting (MFA)
communication (MA)
communication sciences and disorders (MS)
costume design (MFA)
directing (MFA)
fine arts and communication (MA, MFA, MM, MS)
lighting design/theatre technology (MFA)
music (MM)
scenic design (MFA)

■ WHEATON COLLEGE
Wheaton, IL 60187-5593
http://www.wheaton.edu/

Independent-religious, coed, comprehensive institution. *Enrollment:* 2,924 graduate, professional, and undergraduate students; 284 full-time matriculated graduate/professional students (161 women), 275 part-time matriculated graduate/professional students (148 women). *Graduate faculty:* 26 full-time (5 women), 4 part-time/adjunct (1 woman). *Computer facilities:* 238 computers available on campus for general student use. A campuswide network can be accessed from student residence rooms and from off campus. Internet access and online class registration, financial information, degree requirements evaluation are available. *Library facilities:* Buswell Memorial Library. *General application contact:* Julie A. Huebner, Director of Graduate Admissions, 630-752-5195.

Find University Details at www.petersons.com/gradchannel.

Graduate School
Programs in:
biblical and theological studies (MA, PhD)
biblical archaeology (MA)
biblical exegesis (MA)
biblical studies (MA)
Christian formation and ministry (MA)
clinical psychology (MA, Psy D)
counseling ministries (MA)
elementary level (MAT)
evangelism (MA)
general history of Christianity (MA)
historical and systematic theology (MA)
intercultural studies (MA)
intercultural studies/teaching English as a second language (MA)
missions (MA)
religion in American life (MA)
secondary level (MAT)
teaching English as a second language (Certificate)

Indiana

■ ANDERSON UNIVERSITY
Anderson, IN 46012-3495
http://www.anderson.edu/

Independent-religious, coed, comprehensive institution. *Computer facilities:* 200 computers available on campus for general student use. A campuswide network can be accessed from student residence rooms and from off campus. Microcomputer software available. *Library facilities:* Robert A. Nicholson Library. *General application contact:* Director of Seminary Advancement, 765-641-4526.

Falls School of Business
Programs in:
accountancy (MA)
business administration (MBA, DBA)

School of Education
Program in:
education (M Ed)

School of Theology
Programs in:
missions (MA)
theology (M Div, MTS, D Min)

■ BALL STATE UNIVERSITY
Muncie, IN 47306-1099
http://www.bsu.edu/

State-supported, coed, university. CGS member. *Enrollment:* 17,082 graduate, professional, and undergraduate students; 1,044 full-time matriculated graduate/professional students (613 women), 1,729 part-time matriculated graduate/professional students (1,095 women). *Graduate faculty:* 712. *Computer facilities:* 1,500 computers available on campus for general student use. A campuswide network can be accessed from student residence rooms and from off campus. *Library facilities:* Bracken Library plus 3 others. *General application contact:* Dr. Mary E. Kite, Acting Dean, 765-285-1300.

Graduate School
Dr. Mary E. Kite, Acting Dean

College of Applied Science and Technology
Dr. Nancy Kingsbury, Dean
Programs in:
applied gerontology (MA)
applied science and technology (MA, MAE, MS, PhD)
family and consumer sciences (MA, MS)
human bioenergetics (PhD)
industry and technology (MA, MAE)
nursing (MS)
physical education (MA, MAE, MS, PhD)
wellness management (MA, MS)

College of Architecture and Planning
Dr. Joseph Bilello, Dean
Programs in:
architecture (M Arch)
architecture and planning (M Arch, MLA, MS, MURP)
historic preservation (M Arch, MS)
landscape architecture (MLA)
urban planning (MURP)

College of Communication, Information, and Media
Roger Lavery, Dean
Programs in:
communication, information, and media (MA, MS)
digital storytelling (MA)
information and communication sciences (MS)
journalism (MA)
public relations (MA)
speech, public address, forensics, and rhetoric (MA)

College of Fine Arts
Dr. Robert Kvam, Dean

Programs in:
- art (MA)
- art education (MA, MAE)
- fine arts (MA, MAE, MM, DA)
- music education (MA, MM, DA)

College of Sciences and Humanities
Dr. Michael Maggioto, Dean
Programs in:
- actuarial science (MA)
- anthropology (MA)
- applied linguistics (PhD)
- biology (MA, MAE, MS)
- biology education (Ed D)
- chemistry (MA, MS)
- clinical psychology (MA)
- cognitive and social processes (MA)
- computer science (MA, MS)
- earth sciences (MA)
- English (MA, PhD)
- geology (MA, MS)
- health education (MA, MAE)
- history (MA)
- linguistics (MA, PhD)
- linguistics and teaching English to speakers of other languages (MA)
- mathematical statistics (MA)
- mathematics (MA, MAE, MS)
- mathematics education (MAE)
- natural resources (MA, MS)
- physics (MA, MS)
- physiology (MA, MS)
- political science (MA)
- public administration (MPA)
- sciences and humanities (MA, MAE, MPA, MS, Au D, Ed D, PhD)
- social sciences (MA)
- sociology (MA)
- speech pathology and audiology (MA, Au D)
- teaching English to speakers of other languages (MA)

Miller College of Business
Dr. Lynne D. Richardson, Dean
Programs in:
- accounting (MS)
- business (MAE, MBA, MS)
- business administration (MBA)
- information systems and operations management (MAE)

Teachers College
Dr. Roy Weaver, Dean
Programs in:
- adult and community education (MA)
- adult education (MA, Ed D)
- adult, community, and higher education (Ed D)
- counseling psychology (MA, PhD)
- curriculum (MAE, Ed S)
- curriculum and instruction (MAE, Ed S)
- education (MA, MAE, Ed D, PhD, Ed S)
- educational administration (MAE, Ed D)
- educational psychology (MA, PhD, Ed S)
- educational studies (MAE, PhD)
- elementary education (MAE, Ed D, PhD)
- executive development (MA)
- school psychology (MA, PhD, Ed S)
- school superintendency (Ed S)
- secondary education (MA)
- social psychology (MA)
- special education (MA, MAE, Ed D, Ed S)
- student affairs administration in higher education (MA)

■ BUTLER UNIVERSITY
Indianapolis, IN 46208-3485
http://www.butler.edu/

Independent, coed, comprehensive institution. *Enrollment:* 4,437 graduate, professional, and undergraduate students; 429 full-time matriculated graduate/professional students (304 women), 355 part-time matriculated graduate/professional students (211 women). *Graduate faculty:* 84 full-time (33 women), 33 part-time/adjunct (18 women). *Computer facilities:* 430 computers available on campus for general student use. A campuswide network can be accessed from student residence rooms and from off campus. Internet access, e-mail are available. *Library facilities:* Irwin Library System plus 1 other. *Graduate expenses:* Tuition: full-time $6,030; part-time $335 per credit. Tuition and fees vary according to program. *General application contact:* Pamela Bender, Student Services Specialist, 317-940-8100.

College of Business Administration
Dr. Richard Fetter, Dean
Program in:
- business administration (MBA, MP Acc)

College of Education
Dr. Ena Shelley, Dean
Programs in:
- administration (MS)
- elementary education (MS)
- reading (MS)
- school counseling (MS)
- secondary education (MS)
- special education (MS)

College of Liberal Arts and Sciences
Dr. Michael Zimmerman, Dean
Programs in:
- English (MA)
- history (MA)
- liberal arts and sciences (MA)

College of Pharmacy
Dr. Mary Andritz, Dean
Programs in:
- pharmaceutical science (Pharm D, MS)
- physician assistance studies (MS)

Jordan College of Fine Arts
Dr. Peter Alexander, Dean
Programs in:
- composition (MM)
- conducting (MM)
- fine arts (MM)
- music (MM)
- music education (MM)
- music history (MM)
- organ (MM)
- performance (MM)

■ CALUMET COLLEGE OF SAINT JOSEPH
Whiting, IN 46394-2195
http://www.ccsj.edu/

Independent-religious, coed, comprehensive institution. *Computer facilities:* Computer purchase and lease plans are available. 98 computers available on campus for general student use. A campuswide network can be accessed from off campus. Internet access is available. *Library facilities:* Mary Gorman Specker Memorial Library.

Program in Public Safety Administration
Dr. David J. Plebanski, Program Director

■ INDIANA STATE UNIVERSITY
Terre Haute, IN 47809-1401
http://web.indstate.edu/

State-supported, coed, university. CGS member. *Enrollment:* 10,568 graduate, professional, and undergraduate students; 767 full-time matriculated graduate/professional students (424 women), 1,264 part-time matriculated graduate/professional students (751 women). *Graduate faculty:* 269 full-time (85 women), 101 part-time/adjunct (46 women). *Computer facilities:* 450 computers available on campus for general student use. A campuswide network can be accessed from student residence rooms and from off campus. Internet access is available. *Library facilities:* Cunningham Memorial Library plus 1 other. *Graduate expenses:* Tuition, state resident: part-time $278 per credit. Tuition, nonresident: part-time $552 per credit. *General application contact:* Dr. Jolynn Kuhlman, Interim Dean, School of Graduate Studies, 800-444-GRAD.

Find University Details at www.petersons.com/gradchannel.

School of Graduate Studies
Dr. Jolynn Kuhlman, Interim Dean
Program in:
- technology management (PhD)

College of Arts and Sciences
Dr. Thomas Sauer, Interim Dean
Programs in:
- arts and sciences (MA, MFA, MM, MPA, MS, PhD, Psy D, CAS)

Indiana State University (continued)

ceramics (MA, MFA)
child development and family life (MS)
clinical psychology (Psy D)
clothing and textiles (MS)
communication studies (MA, MS)
computer science (MS)
criminology (MA, MS)
dietetics (MS)
drawing (MA, MFA)
earth sciences (MA, MS)
ecology (PhD)
economic geography (PhD)
English (MA, MS)
European history (MA, MS)
family and consumer sciences education (MS)
French (MA, MS)
general psychology (MA, MS)
geography (MA)
geology (MS)
graphic design (MA, MFA)
history of labor and reform movements in the U.S. (MA)
life sciences (MS)
linguistics/teaching English as a second language (MA, MS)
mathematics (MS)
mathematics and computer science (MA)
microbiology (PhD)
music performance (MM)
non-west history (MA, MS)
nutrition and foods (MS)
painting (MA, MFA)
photography (MA, MFA)
physical geography (PhD)
physiology (PhD)
political science (MA, MS)
printmaking (MA, MFA)
public administration (MPA)
radio, television and film (MA, MS)
science education (MS)
sculpture (MA, MFA)
Spanish (MA, MS)
sports medicine (PhD)
TESL/TEFL (CAS)
theatre (MA, MS)
U.S. history (MA, MS)

College of Business
Dr. Ronald Green, Dean
Program in:
business (MBA)

College of Education
Dr. Bradley Balch, Dean
Programs in:
counseling psychology (MS, PhD)
counselor education (PhD)
curriculum and instruction (M Ed, PhD)
early childhood education (M Ed)
education (M Ed, MA, MS, PhD, Ed S)
educational administration (PhD, Ed S)
educational technology (MS)
elementary education (M Ed)
literacy (M Ed)
marriage and family counseling (MS)
school administration and supervision (M Ed)
school counseling (M Ed)
school psychology (M Ed, PhD, Ed S)
speech-language pathology (MA, MS)
student affairs administration (PhD)
student affairs and higher education (MS)

College of Health and Human Performance
Dr. Douglas Timmons, Interim Dean
Programs in:
adult fitness (MA, MS)
athletic training (MS)
coaching (MA, MS)
community health promotion (MA, MS)
exercise science (MA, MS)
health and human performance (MA, MS)
master teacher (MA, MS)
occupational safety management (MA, MS)
recreation and sport management (MA, MS)
school health and safety (MA, MS)

College of Nursing
Dr. Esther Acree, Interim Dean
Program in:
nursing (MS)

College of Technology
Dr. W. Tad Foster, Dean
Programs in:
career and technical education (MS)
electronics and computer technology (MS)
human resource development (MS)
industrial technology (MS)
technology (MS, PhD)
technology education (MS)

■ INDIANA UNIVERSITY BLOOMINGTON
Bloomington, IN 47405-7000
http://www.iub.edu/

State-supported, coed, university. CGS member. *Enrollment:* 38,247 graduate, professional, and undergraduate students; 5,381 full-time matriculated graduate/professional students (2,683 women), 2,567 part-time matriculated graduate/professional students (1,378 women). *Graduate faculty:* 1,080 full-time (328 women), 4 part-time/adjunct (2 women). *Computer facilities:* 2,262 computers available on campus for general student use. A campuswide network can be accessed from student residence rooms and from off campus. Internet access and online class registration, various software packages are available. *Library facilities:* Indiana University Library plus 32 others. *Graduate expenses:* Tuition, state resident: full-time $5,791; part-time $241 per credit hour. Tuition, nonresident: full-time $16,866; part-time $703 per credit hour. *General application contact:* Information Contact, 812-855-0661.

Graduate School

College of Arts and Sciences
Bennett Bertenthal, Dean
Programs in:
acting (MFA)
African American and African diaspora studies (MA)
African languages and linguistics (PhD)
analytical chemistry (PhD)
anthropology (MA, PhD)
applied mathematics–numerical analysis (MA, PhD)
arts and sciences (MA, MAT, MFA, MS, Au D, PhD, Certificate)
astronomy (MA, PhD)
astrophysics (PhD)
audiology (Au D)
auditory sciences (PhD)
biogeochemistry (MS, PhD)
biological chemistry (PhD)
biology and behavior (PhD)
biology teaching (MAT)
Central Eurasian studies (MA, PhD)
chemistry (MAT)
Chinese (MA, PhD)
classical studies (MA, MAT, PhD)
clinical science (PhD)
cognitive psychology (PhD)
communication and culture (MA, PhD)
comparative literature (MA, MAT, PhD)
composition, literacy, and culture (PhD)
computational linguistics (MA)
computer science (MS, PhD)
creative writing (MA, MFA)
crime (MA, PhD)
criminal justice (MA, PhD)
cross-cultural perspectives of crime and justice (MA, PhD)
design and technology (MFA)
developmental psychology (PhD)
directing (MFA)
East Asian languages and cultures (PhD)
East Asian studies (MA)
economic geology (MS, PhD)
economics (MA, PhD)
evolution, ecology, and behavior (MA, PhD)
fine arts (MA, MFA, PhD)
folklore (MA, PhD)
French (MA, PhD)
genetics (PhD)
geobiology (MS, PhD)
geography (MA, MAT, MS, PhD)
geophysics, structural geology and tectonics (MS, PhD)
German literature and studies (PhD)
German studies (MA, PhD)
Hispanic linguistics (MA, PhD)
Hispanic literature (MA)
history (MA, MAT, PhD)
history and philosophy of science (MA, PhD)
history of art (MA, PhD)
hydrogeology (MS, PhD)
inorganic chemistry (PhD)
Italian (MA, PhD)
Japanese (MA, PhD)

journalism (MA, MAT)
language (MA)
language pedagogy (MA)
language sciences (PhD)
Latin American and Caribbean studies (MA)
law and society (MA, PhD)
linguistics (PhD)
literature (MA, PhD)
Luso-Brazilian literature (MA)
Luso-Brazilian studies (PhD)
mass communication (PhD)
mass communications (PhD)
mathematics education (MAT)
medieval German studies (PhD)
microbiology (MA, PhD)
mineralogy (MS, PhD)
molecular, cellular, and developmental biology (PhD)
Near Eastern languages and cultures (MA, PhD)
philosophy (MA, PhD)
physical chemistry (PhD)
physics (MAT, MS, PhD)
plant sciences (MA, PhD)
playwriting (MFA)
political science (MA, PhD)
probability-statistics (MA, PhD)
psychological and brain sciences (MA)
religious studies (MA, PhD)
Russian and East European studies (MA, Certificate)
Slavic languages and literatures (MA, MAT, PhD)
social psychology (PhD)
sociology (MA, PhD)
Spanish literatures (PhD)
speech and voice sciences (PhD)
speech-language pathology (MA)
stratigraphy and sedimentology (MS, PhD)
teaching German (MAT)
teaching Spanish (MAT)
telecommunications (MA, MS)
theatre and drama (MAT)
theatre history (MA, PhD)
theory (MA, PhD)
West European studies (MA)
writing (MA)
zoology (MA, PhD)

Jacobs School of Music
Gwyn Richards, Dean
Programs in:
church music (DM)
music (MA, MM, MME, MS, DM, DME, PhD, AD, Performance Diploma, Spec)
music literature and performance (DM)
performance (MM)
performance and church music (MM)

Kelley School of Business
Daniel Smith, Dean
Programs in:
business (MBA, MPA, MS, DBA, PhD)
business economics and public policy (PhD)

School of Education
Dr. Gerardo Gonzalez, Dean
Programs in:
art education (MS, Ed D, PhD)
counseling (MS, PhD, Ed S)
counseling psychology (PhD)
counselor education (MS, Ed S)
curriculum studies (Ed D, PhD)
education (MS, Ed D, PhD, Ed S)
education policy studies (PhD)
educational leadership (MS, Ed D, PhD, Ed S)
educational psychology (MS, PhD)
elementary education (MS, Ed D, PhD, Ed S)
higher education (MS, Ed D, PhD)
history and philosophy of education (MS)
history of education (PhD)
instructional systems technology (MS, PhD, Ed S)
international and comparative education (MS, PhD)
language education (MS, Ed D, PhD, Ed S)
learning and developmental sciences (MS, PhD)
mathematics education (MS, Ed D, PhD)
philosophy of education (PhD)
school psychology (PhD, Ed S)
science education (MS, Ed D, PhD)
secondary education (MS, Ed D, PhD)
social studies education (MS, PhD)
special education (MS, Ed D, PhD, Ed S)
student affairs administration (MS)

School of Health, Physical Education and Recreation
David Gallahue, Dean
Programs in:
adapted physical education (MS)
applied sport science (MS)
athletic training (MS)
biomechanics (MS)
clinical exercise physiology (MS)
ergonomics (MS)
exercise physiology (MS)
health behavior (PhD)
health promotion (MS)
health, physical education and recreation (MPH, MS, PhD, PE Dir, Re Dir)
human development/family studies (MS)
human performance (MS, PhD, PE Dir)
leisure behavior (PhD)
motor control (MS)
nutrition science (MS)
outdoor recreation management (MS)
park and recreation administration (MS)
public health (MPH)
recreation (Re Dir)
recreational sports administration (MS)
safety management (MS)
school and college health education (MS)
sport management (MS)
therapeutic recreation (MS)

School of Informatics
J. Michael Dunn, Dean
Programs in:
bioinformatics (MS)
chemical informatics (MS)
health informatics (MS)
human computer interaction (MS)
informatics (PhD)
laboratory informatics (MS)
media arts and science (MS)
music informatics (MS)

School of Law
Lauren K. Robel, Dean
Programs in:
comparative law (MCL)
juridical science (SJD)
law (JD, LL M)
law and social sciences (PhD)
legal studies (Certificate)

School of Library and Information Science
Debora Shaw, Dean
Program in:
library and information science (MIS, MLS, PhD, Sp LIS)

School of Optometry
Dr. Gerald E. Lowther, Dean
Program in:
optometry (OD, MS, PhD)

School of Public and Environmental Affairs
Charles Kurt Zorn, Interim Dean
Programs in:
environmental science (MSES, PhD)
nonprofit management (Certificate)
public affairs (MPA, PhD)
public and environmental affairs (MA, MPA, MSES, PhD, Certificate)
public management (Certificate)
public policy (PhD)

■ INDIANA UNIVERSITY NORTHWEST
Gary, IN 46408-1197
http://www.iun.edu/

State-supported, coed, comprehensive institution. *Enrollment:* 4,819 graduate, professional, and undergraduate students; 59 full-time matriculated graduate/professional students (49 women), 342 part-time matriculated graduate/professional students (252 women). *Graduate faculty:* 44 full-time (15 women). *Computer facilities:* 250 computers available on campus for general student use. A campuswide network can be accessed from off campus. Internet access and online class registration are available. *Library facilities:* IUN Library. *Graduate expenses:* Tuition, state resident: full-time $4,332; part-time $181 per credit hour. Tuition, nonresident: full-time $10,081; part-time $420 per credit hour. Tuition and fees vary according to course load, campus/location and program. *General application contact:* Admissions Counselor, 219-980-6760.

Indiana University Northwest (continued)

Division of Social Work
Dr. Denise Travis, Director
Program in:
social work (MSW)

School of Business and Economics
Anna Rominger, Dean
Programs in:
accountancy (M Acc)
accounting (Certificate)
business administration (MBA)

School of Education
Dr. Stanley E. Wigle, Dean
Programs in:
elementary education (MS Ed)
secondary education (MS Ed)

School of Public and Environmental Affairs
Karen Evans, Interim Assistant Dean/Division Director
Programs in:
criminal justice (MPA)
environmental affairs (Certificate)
health services administration (MPA)
human services administration (MPA)
nonprofit management (Certificate)
public administration (MPA)
public management (MPA, Certificate)

■ INDIANA UNIVERSITY–PURDUE UNIVERSITY FORT WAYNE

Fort Wayne, IN 46805-1499

http://www.ipfw.edu/

State-supported, coed, comprehensive institution. CGS member. *Enrollment:* 11,672 graduate, professional, and undergraduate students; 93 full-time matriculated graduate/professional students (49 women), 539 part-time matriculated graduate/professional students (323 women). *Graduate faculty:* 178 full-time (63 women), 3 part-time/adjunct (1 woman). *Computer facilities:* 285 computers available on campus for general student use. A campuswide network can be accessed from off campus. Internet access and online class registration, students academic records are available. *Library facilities:* Helmke Library. *Graduate expenses:* Tuition, state resident: full-time $4,039; part-time $224 per credit. Tuition, nonresident: full-time $9,220; part-time $512 per credit. Required fees: $429; $24 per credit. Tuition and fees vary according to course load. *General application contact:* Susan Humphreys, Graduate Applications Coordinator, 260-481-6145.

College of Arts and Sciences
Dr. Marc Lipman, Dean
Programs in:
applied mathematics (MS)
applied statistics (Certificate)
arts and sciences (MA, MAT, MLS, MS, Certificate)
biology (MS)
English (MA, MAT)
liberal studies (MLS)
mathematics (MS)
operations research (MS)
professional communication (MA, MS)
sociological practice (MA)
TENL (teaching English as a new language) (Certificate)

College of Engineering, Technology, and Computer Science
Dr. Gerard Voland, Dean
Programs in:
applied computer science (MS)
engineering, technology, and computer science (MS)

Division of Public and Environmental Affairs
Dr. Geralyn Miller, Interim Assistant Dean and Director
Programs in:
public affairs (MPA)
public management (MPM, Certificate)

School of Business and Management Sciences
Dr. John L. Wellington, Dean
Program in:
business administration (MBA)

School of Education
Dr. Barry Kanpol, Dean
Programs in:
counselor education (MS Ed)
education (MS Ed)
educational administration (MS Ed)
elementary education (MS Ed)
secondary education (MS Ed)

School of Health Sciences
Dr. Linda Finke, Dean
Programs in:
health sciences (MS, Certificate)
nursing administration (MS, Certificate)

■ INDIANA UNIVERSITY–PURDUE UNIVERSITY INDIANAPOLIS

Indianapolis, IN 46202-2896

http://www.iupui.edu/

State-supported, coed, university. *Enrollment:* 29,764 graduate, professional, and undergraduate students; 3,735 full-time matriculated graduate/professional students (2,024 women), 3,989 part-time matriculated graduate/professional students (2,224 women). *Graduate faculty:* 599 full-time (195 women), 2 part-time/adjunct (1 woman). *Computer facilities:* 500 computers available on campus for general student use. A campuswide network can be accessed from student residence rooms and from off campus. Internet access and online class registration are available. *Library facilities:* University Library plus 5 others. *Graduate expenses:* Tuition, state resident: full-time $5,437; part-time $227 per credit hour. Tuition, nonresident: full-time $15,694; part-time $654 per credit hour. Required fees: $620. Tuition and fees vary according to course load, campus/location and program. *General application contact:* Dr. Sherry Queener, Director, Graduate Studies and Associate Dean, 317-274-1577.

Department of Economics
Paul Carlin, Chair
Program in:
economics (MA)

Department of English
Susanmarie Harrington, Chair
Programs in:
English (MA)
teaching English (MA)

Department of History
Robert Barrows, Chair
Programs in:
history (MA)
public history (MA)

Herron School of Art and Design
Valerie Eickmeier, Dean
Programs in:
art education (MAE)
furniture design (MFA)
printmaking (MFA)
sculpture (MFA)
visual communication (MFA)

Indiana University School of Medicine
Dr. D. Craig Brater, Dean
Programs in:
anatomy and cell biology (MS, PhD)
biochemistry and molecular biology (PhD)
genetic counseling (MS)
medical and molecular genetics (MS, PhD)
medicine (MD, MPH, MS, DPT, PhD)
microbiology and immunology (MS, PhD)
pathology and laboratory medicine (MS, PhD)
pharmacology (MS, PhD)
public health (MPH)
toxicology (MS, PhD)

School of Health and Rehabilitation Sciences
Dr. Mark S. Sothmann, Dean of the School of Allied Health Sciences
Programs in:
health sciences education (MS)
nutrition and dietetics (MS)
occupational therapy (MS)
physical therapy (DPT)

Kelley School of Business
Roger W. Schmenner, Associate Dean, Indianapolis Programs
Program in:
business (MBA, MPA)

School of Dentistry
Lawrence I. Goldblatt, Dean
Program in:
dentistry (DDS, MS, MSD, PhD, Certificate)

School of Education
Dr. Khaula Murtadha, Executive Associate Dean
Program in:
education (MS, Certificate)

School of Engineering and Technology
Dr. H. Oner Yurtseven, Dean
Programs in:
biomedical engineering (MS, MS Bm E, PhD)
computer-aided mechanical engineering (Certificate)
electrical and computer engineering (MS, MSECE, PhD)
engineering (interdisciplinary) (MSE)
engineering and technology (MS, MS Bm E, MSE, MSECE, MSME, PhD, Certificate)
mechanical engineering (MSME, PhD)

School of Informatics
Darrell L. Bailey, Executive Associate Dean
Programs in:
informatics (PhD)
media arts and science (MS)

School of Law
Susanah M. Mead, Interim Dean
Program in:
law (JD, LL M, SJD)

School of Liberal Arts
Robert W. White, Dean, School of Liberal Arts
Programs in:
American philosophy (Certificate)
bioethics (Certificate)
liberal arts (MA, PhD, Certificate)
philosophy (MA, PhD)
political science (MA, Certificate)
sociology (MA)

School of Library and Information Science
Dr. Daniel Collison, Executive Associate Dean
Program in:
library and information science (MLS)

School of Music
G. David Peters, Director
Program in:
music technology (MS)

School of Nursing
Associate Dean for Graduate Programs
Programs in:
acute care nurse practitioner (MSN)
adult clinical nurse specialist (MSN)
adult health clinical nurse specialist (MSN)
adult health nursing (MSN)
adult nurse practitioner (MSN)
adult psychiatric/mental health nursing (MSN)
child psychiatric/mental health nursing (MSN)
community health nursing (MSN)
family nurse practitioner (MSN)
neonatal nurse practitioner (MSN)
nursing science (PhD)
pediatric clinical nurse specialist (MSN)
women's health nurse practitioner (MSN)

School of Physical Education and Tourism Management
P. Nicholas Kellum, Dean
Program in:
physical education and tourism management (MS)

School of Public and Environmental Affairs
Dr. Greg Lindsey, Associate Dean
Programs in:
criminal justice (MPA)
environmental management (MPA)
health administration (MHA)
nonprofit management (MPA)
policy analysis (MPA)
public affairs (MPA)
public management (MPA)

School of Science
William Bosran, Dean, School of Science
Programs in:
applied mathematics (MS, PhD)
applied statistics (MS)
biology (MS, PhD)
chemistry (MS, PhD)
clinical rehabilitation psychology (MS, PhD)
computer science (MS, PhD)
geology (MS)
industrial/organizational psychology (MS)
math education (MS)
mathematics (MS, PhD)
physics (MS, PhD)
psychobiology of addictions (PhD)
science (MS, PhD)

School of Social Work
Michael Patchner, Dean
Program in:
social work (MSW, PhD, Certificate)

■ INDIANA UNIVERSITY SOUTH BEND
South Bend, IN 46634-7111
http://www.iusb.edu/

State-supported, coed, comprehensive institution. *Enrollment:* 7,420 graduate, professional, and undergraduate students; 196 full-time matriculated graduate/professional students (130 women), 538 part-time matriculated graduate/professional students (364 women). *Graduate faculty:* 60 full-time (26 women). *Computer facilities:* 200 computers available on campus for general student use. Internet access is available. *Library facilities:* Franklin D. Schurz Library plus 1 other. *Graduate expenses:* Tuition, state resident: full-time $4,450; part-time $185 per credit hour. Tuition, nonresident: full-time $10,954; part-time $456 per credit hour. Tuition and fees vary according to course load, campus/location and program. *General application contact:* Admissions Counselor, 574-520-4839.

College of Liberal Arts and Sciences
Dr. Lynn R. Williams, Dean
Programs in:
applied mathematics and computer science (MS)
English (MA)
liberal studies (MLS)

School of Business and Economics
Dr. P. N. Saksena, Assistant Dean, Director of Graduate Studies
Programs in:
accounting (MSA)
business administration (MBA)
management of information technologies (MS)

School of Education
Dr. Michael Horvath, Professor and Dean, School of Education
Programs in:
counseling and human services (MS Ed)
elementary education (MS Ed)
secondary education (MS Ed)
special education (MS Ed)

School of Public and Environmental Affairs
Leda M. Hall, Dean
Programs in:
health systems administration and policy (MPA)
health systems management (Certificate)
nonprofit management (Certificate)
public and community services administration and policy (MPA)
public management (Certificate)
urban affairs (Certificate)

School of Social Work
Dr. Paul R. Newcomb, Program Director
Program in:
social work (MSW)

School of the Arts
Dr. Thomas Miller, Dean
Program in:
music (MM)

■ INDIANA UNIVERSITY SOUTHEAST

New Albany, IN 47150-6405

http://www.ius.edu/

State-supported, coed, comprehensive institution. *Enrollment:* 6,183 graduate, professional, and undergraduate students; 18 full-time matriculated graduate/professional students (10 women), 568 part-time matriculated graduate/professional students (358 women). *Graduate faculty:* 63 full-time (22 women). *Computer facilities:* 200 computers available on campus for general student use. A campuswide network can be accessed from off campus. Internet access is available. *Library facilities:* Main library plus 1 other. *Graduate expenses:* Tuition, state resident: full-time $4,458; part-time $186 per credit hour. Tuition, nonresident: full-time $10,196; part-time $425 per credit hour. Tuition and fees vary according to course load, campus/location and program. *General application contact:* Admissions Counselor, 812-941-2212.

Program in Liberal Studies
Dr. Sandra S. French, Director
Program in:
liberal studies (MLS)

School of Business
Chris Bjornson, Dean
Programs in:
accounting (Certificate)
business administration (MBA)
economics (Certificate)
finance (Certificate)
general business (Certificate)
information and operations management (Certificate)
management and marketing (Certificate)
strategic finance (MS)

School of Education
Dr. Gloria Murray, Dean
Programs in:
counselor education (MS Ed)
elementary education (MS Ed)
secondary education (MS Ed)

■ INDIANA WESLEYAN UNIVERSITY

Marion, IN 46953-4974

http://www.indwes.edu/

Independent-religious, coed, comprehensive institution. *Enrollment:* 4,461 full-time matriculated graduate/professional students (2,836 women), 156 part-time matriculated graduate/professional students (92 women). *Graduate faculty:* 30 full-time (14 women). *Computer facilities:* A campuswide network can be accessed from student residence rooms. Internet access is available. *Library facilities:* Jackson Library. *Graduate expenses:* Tuition: full-time $16,000; part-time $400 per credit. Required fees: $3,000. Tuition and fees vary according to degree level, campus/location and program. *General application contact:* Dr. Jim Freemyer, Director of Graduate Education, 765-677-2278.

College of Adult and Professional Studies
Dr. Tom Griffin, Dean
Programs in:
accounting (MBA)
adult and professional studies (M Ed, MBA, MS)
applied management (MBA)
curriculum and instruction (M Ed)
health care management (MBA)
management (MS)

College of Graduate Studies
Dr. Jim Fuller, Dean
Programs in:
community counseling (MS)
marriage and family counseling (MS)
ministerial education (MA)
ministry (MA)
organizational leadership (Ed D)
school counseling (MS)

Division of Nursing
Pam Giles, Director
Programs in:
community health nursing (MS)
nursing (Post Master's Certificate)
nursing administration (MS)
nursing education (MS)
primary care nursing (MS)

■ OAKLAND CITY UNIVERSITY

Oakland City, IN 47660-1099

http://www.oak.edu/

Independent-religious, coed, comprehensive institution. *Computer facilities:* 92 computers available on campus for general student use. A campuswide network can be accessed from student residence rooms. Internet access is available. *Library facilities:* Barger-Richardson Library. *General application contact:* Counselor for Graduate Admissions, 812-749-1241.

Chapman Seminary
Program in:
religious studies (M Div, D Min)

School of Adult and Extended Learning
Program in:
management (MS Mgt)

School of Education and Technology
Programs in:
educational leadership (Ed D)
teaching (MA)

■ PURDUE UNIVERSITY

West Lafayette, IN 47907

http://www.purdue.edu/

State-supported, coed, university. CGS member. *Enrollment:* 39,228 graduate, professional, and undergraduate students; 5,762 full-time matriculated graduate/professional students (2,499 women), 1,939 part-time matriculated graduate/professional students (725 women). *Graduate faculty:* 1,721 full-time (405 women), 305 part-time/adjunct (74 women). *Computer facilities:* 2,925 computers available on campus for general student use. A campuswide network can be accessed from student residence rooms and from off campus. Internet access is available. *Library facilities:* Hicks Undergraduate Library plus 13 others. *General application contact:* Graduate School Admissions, 765-494-2600.

College of Engineering
Dr. Leah H. Jamieson, Dean
Programs in:
agricultural and biological engineering (MS, MSABE, MSE, PhD)
engineering (MS, MSAAE, MSABE, MSBME, MSCE, MSChE, MSE, MSECE, MSIE, MSME, MSMSE, MSNE, PhD, Certificate)
engineering education (PhD)
engineering professional education (MS, MSE)

School of Aeronautics and Astronautics Engineering
Prof. Anastansias Lyrintzis, Graduate Chair
Program in:
aeronautics and astronautics engineering (MS, MSAAE, MSE, PhD)

School of Chemical Engineering
Osman Basaran, Graduate Chair
Program in:
chemical engineering (MSChE, PhD)

School of Civil Engineering
Darcy Bullock, Associate Head
Program in:
civil engineering (MS, MSCE, MSE, PhD)

School of Electrical and Computer Engineering
Chee-Mun Ong, Graduate Coordinator
Program in:
electrical and computer engineering (MS, MSE, MSECE, PhD)

School of Industrial Engineering
Srinivasan Chandrasekar, Associate Head
Program in:
industrial engineering (MS, MSIE, PhD)

School of Materials Engineering
David Johnson, Graduate Coordinator
Program in:
materials engineering (MSMSE, PhD)

School of Mechanical Engineering
Arill K. Bajaj, Associate Head

Program in:
- mechanical engineering (MS, MSE, MSME, PhD, Certificate)

School of Nuclear Engineering
Chan Choi, Graduate Chair
Program in:
- nuclear engineering (MS, MSNE, PhD)

College of Pharmacy and Pharmacal Sciences
Dr. Craig Svensson, Dean
Program in:
- pharmacy and pharmacal sciences (Pharm D, MS, PhD, Certificate)

Graduate Programs in Pharmacy and Pharmacal Sciences
Dr. G. Marc Loudon, Associate Dean
Programs in:
- analytical medicinal chemistry (PhD)
- clinical pharmacy (MS, PhD)
- computational and biophysical medicinal chemistry (PhD)
- industrial and physical pharmacy (MS, PhD, Certificate)
- medicinal and bioorganic chemistry (PhD)
- medicinal biochemistry and molecular biology (PhD)
- medicinal chemistry and molecular pharmacology (MS, PhD)
- molecular pharmacology and toxicology (PhD)
- natural products and pharmacognosy (PhD)
- nuclear pharmacy (MS)
- pharmaceutics (PhD)
- pharmacy administration (MS, PhD)
- pharmacy practice (MS, PhD)
- radiopharmaceutical chemistry and nuclear pharmacy (PhD)
- regulatory quality compliance (MS, Certificate)

Graduate School
Dr. Cindy H. Nakatsu, Interim Dean
Program in:
- life sciences (PhD)

Center for Education and Research in Information Assurance and Security (CERIAS)
Program in:
- information security (MS)

College of Agriculture
Dr. Victor L. Lechtenberg, Dean
Programs in:
- agricultural economics (MS, PhD)
- agriculture (EMBA, M Agr, MA, MS, MSF, PhD)
- agronomy (MS, PhD)
- animal sciences (MS, PhD)
- aquaculture, fisheries, aquatic science (MSF)
- aquaculture, fisheries, aquatic sciences (MS, PhD)
- biochemistry (MS, PhD)
- botany and plant pathology (MS, PhD)
- entomology (MS, PhD)
- food and agricultural business (EMBA)
- food science (MS, PhD)
- forest biology (MS, MSF, PhD)
- horticulture (M Agr, MS, PhD)
- natural resources and environmental policy (MS, MSF)
- natural resources environmental policy (PhD)
- quantitative resource analysis (MS, MSF, PhD)
- wildlife science (MS, MSF, PhD)
- wood science and technology (MS, MSF, PhD)
- youth development and agricultural education (MA, PhD)

College of Consumer and Family Sciences
Dr. Dennis A. Savaiano, Dean
Programs in:
- consumer and family sciences (MS, PhD)
- consumer behavior (MS, PhD)
- developmental studies (MS, PhD)
- family and consumer economics (MS, PhD)
- family studies (MS, PhD)
- hospitality and tourism management (MS, PhD)
- marriage and family therapy (MS, PhD)
- nutrition (MS, PhD)
- retail management (MS, PhD)
- textile science (MS, PhD)

College of Liberal Arts
Dr. John J. Contreni, Dean
Programs in:
- American studies (MA, PhD)
- anthropology (MS, PhD)
- art and design (MA)
- audiology (MS, Au D, PhD)
- communication (MA, MS, PhD)
- comparative literature (MA, PhD)
- creative writing (MFA)
- exercise, human physiology of movement and sport (PhD)
- French (MA, MAT, PhD)
- German (MA, MAT, PhD)
- health and fitness (MS)
- health promotion (MS)
- health promotion and disease prevention (PhD)
- history (MA, PhD)
- liberal arts (MA, MAT, MFA, MS, Au D, PhD)
- linguistics (MS, PhD)
- literature (MA, PhD)
- movement and sport science (MS)
- pedagogy and administration (MS)
- pedagogy of physical activity and health (PhD)
- philosophy (MA, PhD)
- political science (MA, PhD)
- psychological sciences (PhD)
- psychology of sport and exercise, and motor behavior (PhD)
- sociology (MS, PhD)
- Spanish (MA, MAT, PhD)
- speech and hearing science (MS, PhD)
- speech-language pathology (MS, PhD)
- theatre (MA, MFA)

College of Science
Dr. Jeffrey S Vitter, Dean
Programs in:
- analytical chemistry (MS, PhD)
- biochemistry (MS, PhD)
- biophysics (PhD)
- cell and developmental biology (PhD)
- chemical education (MS, PhD)
- computer sciences (MS, PhD)
- earth and atmospheric sciences (MS, PhD)
- ecology, evolutionary and population biology (MS, PhD)
- genetics (MS, PhD)
- inorganic chemistry (MS, PhD)
- mathematics (MS, PhD)
- microbiology (MS, PhD)
- molecular biology (PhD)
- neurobiology (MS, PhD)
- organic chemistry (MS, PhD)
- physical chemistry (MS, PhD)
- physics (MS, PhD)
- plant physiology (PhD)
- science (MS, PhD, Certificate)
- statistics (MS, PhD, Certificate)

College of Technology
Dr. Dennis R Depew, Dean
Programs in:
- industrial technology (MS)
- technology (MS)

Krannert School of Management
Dr. R. A. Cosier, Dean
Programs in:
- accounting (PhD)
- business (EMBA, MBA)
- business administration (MBA)
- economics (PhD)
- executive business administration (EMBA)
- finance (PhD)
- human resource management (MS)
- industrial administration (MSIA)
- management (EMBA, MBA, MS, MSIA, PhD)
- management information systems (PhD)
- marketing (PhD)
- operations management (PhD)
- organizational behavior and human resource management (MS, PhD)
- quantitative methods (PhD)
- strategic management (PhD)

School of Education
Dr. George W Hynd, Head
Programs in:
- administration (MS Ed, PhD, Ed S)
- agricultural and extension education (PhD, Ed S)
- agriculture and extension education (MS, MS Ed)
- art education (PhD)
- consumer and family sciences and extension education (MS Ed, PhD, Ed S)

Purdue University (continued)
counseling and development (MS Ed, PhD)
curriculum studies (MS Ed, PhD, Ed S)
education (MS, MS Ed, PhD, Ed S)
education of the gifted (MS Ed)
educational psychology (MS Ed, PhD)
educational technology (MS Ed, PhD, Ed S)
elementary education (MS Ed)
foreign language education (MS Ed, PhD, Ed S)
foundations of education (MS Ed, PhD)
higher education administration (MS Ed, PhD)
industrial technology (PhD, Ed S)
language arts (MS Ed, PhD, Ed S)
literacy (MS Ed, PhD, Ed S)
mathematics/science education (MS, MS Ed, PhD, Ed S)
social studies (MS Ed, PhD)
social studies education (Ed S)
special education (MS Ed, PhD)
vocational/industrial education (MS Ed, PhD, Ed S)
vocational/technical education (MS Ed, PhD, Ed S)

School of Health Sciences
Dr. George A. Sandison, Head
Program in:
health sciences (MS, PhD)

School of Veterinary Medicine
Dr. Willie Reed, Dean
Programs in:
anatomy (MS, PhD)
basic medical sciences (MS, PhD)
biochemistry and molecular biology (MS, PhD)
comparative epidemiology (MS, PhD)
comparative pathobiology (MS, PhD)
epidemiology (MS, PhD)
immunology (MS, PhD)
infectious diseases (MS, PhD)
interdisciplinary genetics (PhD)
laboratory animal medicine (MS, PhD)
microbiology (MS, PhD)
molecular virology (MS, PhD)
parasitology (MS, PhD)
pathobiology (MS, PhD)
pharmacology (MS, PhD)
physiology (MS, PhD)
public health epidemiology (MS, PhD)
toxicology (MS, PhD)
veterinary anatomic pathology (MS, PhD)
veterinary clinical pathology (MS, PhD)
veterinary clinical sciences (MS, PhD)
veterinary medicine (DVM, MS, PhD)
virology (MS, PhD)

■ PURDUE UNIVERSITY CALUMET
Hammond, IN 46323-2094
http://www.calumet.purdue.edu/

State-supported, coed, comprehensive institution. *Computer facilities:* 1,500 computers available on campus for general student use. A campuswide network can be accessed from off campus. Internet access and online class registration are available. *Library facilities:* Purdue University Calumet Library. *General application contact:* Assistant to the Graduate School, 219-989-2257.

Graduate School

School of Education
Programs in:
counseling and personnel services (MS Ed)
educational administration (MS Ed)
elementary education (MS Ed)
instructional development (MS Ed)
media sciences (MS Ed)
secondary education (MS Ed)

School of Engineering, Mathematics, and Science
Programs in:
biology (MS)
biology teaching (MS)
biotechnology (MS)
engineering (MSE)
engineering, mathematics, and science (MAT, MS, MSE)
mathematics (MAT, MS)

School of Liberal Arts and Sciences
Programs in:
communication (MA)
English and philosophy (MA)
history and political science (MA)
liberal arts and sciences (MA, MS)
marriage and family therapy (MS)

School of Management
Programs in:
accountancy (M Acc)
business administration (MBA)

School of Nursing
Program in:
nursing (MS)

■ UNIVERSITY OF EVANSVILLE
Evansville, IN 47722
http://www.evansville.edu/

Independent-religious, coed, comprehensive institution. *Enrollment:* 2,879 graduate, professional, and undergraduate students; 57 full-time matriculated graduate/professional students (39 women), 9 part-time matriculated graduate/professional students (7 women). *Graduate faculty:* 7 full-time (1 woman), 11 part-time/adjunct (4 women). *Computer facilities:* Computer purchase and lease plans are available. 312 computers available on campus for general student use. A campuswide network can be accessed from student residence rooms and from off campus. Internet access and online class registration are available. *Library facilities:* Bower Suhrheinrich Library plus 1 other. *Graduate expenses:* Tuition: full-time $6,534; part-time $580 per credit hour. Tuition and fees vary according to course load and program. *General application contact:* Carla Doty, Interim Director of Continuing Education, 812-488-2981.

Center for Continuing Education
Carla Doty, Interim Director of Continuing Education
Program in:
public service administration (MS)

College of Education and Health Sciences
Dr. Lynn Penland, Director
Programs in:
education and health sciences (MS)
health services administration (MS)

College of Engineering and Computer Science
Dr. Philip Gerhart, Dean
Programs in:
electrical engineering and computer science (MS)
engineering and computer science (MS)

■ UNIVERSITY OF INDIANAPOLIS
Indianapolis, IN 46227-3697
http://www.uindy.edu/

Independent-religious, coed, comprehensive institution. *Enrollment:* 4,389 graduate, professional, and undergraduate students; 396 full-time matriculated graduate/professional students (300 women), 630 part-time matriculated graduate/professional students (459 women). *Graduate faculty:* 68 full-time (34 women), 35 part-time/adjunct (20 women). *Computer facilities:* 218 computers available on campus for general student use. A campuswide network can be accessed from student residence rooms and from off campus. Internet access is available. *Library facilities:* Krannert Memorial Library. *General application contact:* Dr. E. John McIlvried, Associate Provost for Graduate Programs and International Programs, 317-788-3274.

Graduate Programs
Dr. E. John McIlvried, Associate Provost for Graduate Programs and International Programs

Center for Aging and Community
Dr. Ellen Miller, Executive Director
Program in:
gerontology (MS, Certificate)

College of Arts and Sciences
Dr. Daniel Briere, Dean
Programs in:
applied sociology (MA)
art (MA)
arts and sciences (MA, MS)
English (MA)
history (MA)
human biology (MS)
international relations (MA)

Krannert School of Physical Therapy
Dr. Mary Huer, Dean of Health Sciences
Program in:
physical therapy (MHS, DHS, DPT, TDPT)

School of Business
Dr. Mitch B. Shapiro, Dean
Programs in:
business (EMBA)
business administration (MBA)
finance (Graduate Certificate)
global supply chains management (Graduate Certificate)
marketing (Graduate Certificate)
organizational leadership (Graduate Certificate)
technology management (Graduate Certificate)

School of Education
Dr. E. Lynne Weisenbach, Dean
Programs in:
art education (MAT)
biology (MAT)
chemistry (MAT)
curriculum and instruction (MA)
earth sciences (MAT)
education (MA, MAT)
educational leadership (MA)
elementary education (MA)
English (MAT)
French (MAT)
math (MAT)
physical education (MAT)
physics (MAT)
secondary education (MA)
social studies (MAT)
Spanish (MAT)

School of Nursing
Dr. Sharon Isaac, Dean
Programs in:
family practice (post-RN) (MSN)
gerontological nurse practitioner (MSN)
nurse-midwifery (MSN)
nursing (MSN)
nursing administration (MSN)
nursing education (MSN)

School of Occupational Therapy
Dr. Mary Huer, Dean of Health Sciences
Program in:
occupational therapy (MHS, MOT, DHS)

School of Psychological Sciences
Dr. E. John McIlvried, Dean
Programs in:
clinical psychology (Psy D)
clinical psychology/mental health counseling (MA)

■ UNIVERSITY OF NOTRE DAME

Notre Dame, IN 46556
http://www.nd.edu/

Independent-religious, coed, university. CGS member. *Computer facilities:* Computer purchase and lease plans are available. 400 computers available on campus for general student use. A campuswide network can be accessed from student residence rooms and from off campus. Internet access and online class registration are available. *Library facilities:* University Libraries of Notre Dame plus 9 others. *General application contact:* Dr. Cecilia Lucero, Director of Graduate Admissions, 574-631-7706.

Graduate School
Dr. Donald Pope-Davis, Vice President for Graduate Studies and Research and Dean of the Graduate School

College of Arts and Letters
Dr. Mark W. Roche, Dean
Programs in:
art history (MA)
arts and letters (M Div, M Ed, MA, MFA, MMS, MSM, MTS, PhD)
cognitive psychology (PhD)
counseling psychology (PhD)
creative writing (MFA)
design (MFA)
developmental psychology (PhD)
early Christian studies (MA)
economics and econometrics (MA, PhD)
educational initiatives (M Ed)
English (MA, PhD)
French and Francophone studies (MA)
history (MA, PhD)
history and philosophy of science (MA, PhD)
humanities (M Div, MA, MFA, MMS, MSM, MTS, PhD)
Iberian and Latin American studies (MA)
international peace studies (MA)
Italian studies (MA)
literature (PhD)
medieval studies (MMS, PhD)
philosophy (PhD)
political science (PhD)
quantitative psychology (PhD)
Romance literatures (MA)
social science (M Ed, MA, PhD)
sociology (PhD)
studio art (MFA)
theology (M Div, MA, MSM, MTS, PhD)

College of Engineering
Dr. James Merz, Dean
Programs in:
aerospace and mechanical engineering (M Eng, PhD)
aerospace engineering (MS Aero E)
bioengineering (MS Bio E)
chemical and biomolecular engineering (MS Ch E, PhD)
civil engineering (MSCE)
civil engineering and geological sciences (PhD)
computer science and engineering (MSCSE, PhD)
electrical engineering (MSEE, PhD)
engineering (M Eng, MEME, MS, MS Aero E, MS Bio E, MS Ch E, MS Env E, MSCE, MSCSE, MSEE, MSME, PhD)
environmental engineering (MS Env E)
geological sciences (MS)
mechanical engineering (MEME, MSME)

College of Science
Dr. Joseph P. Marino, Dean
Programs in:
algebra (PhD)
algebraic geometry (PhD)
applied mathematics (MSAM)
aquatic ecology, evolution and environmental biology (MS, PhD)
biochemistry (MS, PhD)
cellular and molecular biology (MS, PhD)
complex analysis (PhD)
differential geometry (PhD)
genetics (MS, PhD)
inorganic chemistry (MS, PhD)
logic (PhD)
organic chemistry (MS, PhD)
partial differential equations (PhD)
physical chemistry (MS, PhD)
physics (PhD)
physiology (MS, PhD)
science (MS, MSAM, PhD)
topology (PhD)
vector biology and parasitology (MS, PhD)

School of Architecture
Prof. Philip Bess, Director of Graduate Studies
Programs in:
architectural design and urbanism (M ADU, M Arch)
architecture (M Arch)

Law School
Patricia A. O'Hara, Dean
Programs in:
human rights (LL M, JSD)
international and comparative law (LL M)
law (JD)

Mendoza College of Business
Dr. Carolyn Y. Woo, Dean
Programs in:
accountancy (MS)
administration (MNA)
business (MBA, MNA, MS)
business administration (MBA)
executive business administration (MBA)

■ UNIVERSITY OF SAINT FRANCIS

Fort Wayne, IN 46808-3994
http://www.sf.edu/

Independent-religious, coed, comprehensive institution. *Enrollment:* 2,039 graduate, professional, and undergraduate students; 94 full-time matriculated graduate/professional students (75 women), 161 part-time matriculated graduate/professional students (120 women). *Graduate faculty:* 36 full-time

University of Saint Francis (continued)
(24 women), 17 part-time/adjunct (10 women). *Computer facilities:* Computer purchase and lease plans are available. 217 computers available on campus for general student use. A campuswide network can be accessed from student residence rooms. Internet access and online class registration are available. *Library facilities:* Lee and Jim Vann Library. *General application contact:* James Lashdollar, Admissions Counselor, 260-434-3279.

Graduate School
Dr. Rolf Daniel, Chair
Programs in:
business administration (MBA, MS)
fine art (MA)
general psychology (MS)
mental health counseling (MS)
nursing (MSN)
pastoral counseling (MS)
physician assistant studies (MS)
school counseling (MS Ed)
special education (MS Ed)

■ UNIVERSITY OF SOUTHERN INDIANA
Evansville, IN 47712-3590
http://www.usi.edu/

State-supported, coed, comprehensive institution. CGS member. *Enrollment:* 10,021 graduate, professional, and undergraduate students; 103 full-time matriculated graduate/professional students (83 women), 521 part-time matriculated graduate/professional students (380 women). *Graduate faculty:* 73 full-time (36 women), 7 part-time/adjunct (4 women). *Computer facilities:* 778 computers available on campus for general student use. A campuswide network can be accessed from student residence rooms and from off campus. Internet access and online class registration are available. *Library facilities:* David L. Rice Library plus 1 other. *Graduate expenses:* Tuition, state resident: full-time $3,888; part-time $216 per credit hour. Tuition, nonresident: full-time $7,688; part-time $426 per credit hour. Required fees: $220; $23 per term. Tuition and fees vary according to course load and reciprocity agreements. *General application contact:* Dr. Peggy F. Harrel, Director, Graduate Studies, 812-465-7015.

Graduate Studies
Dr. Peggy F. Harrel, Director

College of Business
Dr. Mohammed F. Khayum, Dean
Programs in:
accountancy (MSA)
business (MBA, MSA)
business administration (MBA)

College of Education and Human Services
Dr. Jane Davis-Brezette, Acting Dean
Programs in:
education and human services (MS, MSW)
elementary education (MS)
secondary education (MS)
social work (MSW)

College of Liberal Arts
Dr. David L. Glassman, Dean
Programs in:
liberal arts (MA, MPA)
liberal studies (MA)
public administration (MPA)

College of Nursing and Health Professions
Dr. Nadine Coudret, Dean
Programs in:
health administration (MHA)
nursing (MSN)
nursing and health professions (MHA, MSN, MSOT)
occupational therapy (MSOT)

College of Science and Engineering
Dr. Scott A. Gordon, Dean
Programs in:
industrial management (MS)
science and engineering (MS)

■ VALPARAISO UNIVERSITY
Valparaiso, IN 46383
http://www.valpo.edu/

Independent-religious, coed, comprehensive institution. *Enrollment:* 3,868 graduate, professional, and undergraduate students; 684 full-time matriculated graduate/professional students (331 women), 197 part-time matriculated graduate/professional students (126 women). *Graduate faculty:* 31 full-time (13 women), 124 part-time/adjunct (55 women). *Computer facilities:* 634 computers available on campus for general student use. A campuswide network can be accessed from student residence rooms and from off campus. Internet access and online class registration, Web academic information (grades, program evaluation) are available. *Library facilities:* Christopher Center for Library and Information Resources plus 1 other. *Graduate expenses:* Tuition: part-time $390 per credit hour. Required fees: $60 per term. Tuition and fees vary according to program. *General application contact:* Dr. David L. Rowland, Dean, Graduate Studies and Continuing Education, 219-464-5313.

Graduate Division
Dr. David L. Rowland, Dean, Graduate Studies and Continuing Education
Programs in:
Chinese studies (MA)
clinical mental health counseling (MA)
community counseling (MA)
counseling (Certificate)
English (MALS, Post-Master's Certificate)
ethics and values (MALS, Post-Master's Certificate)
gerontology (MALS, Post-Master's Certificate)
history (MALS, Post-Master's Certificate)
human behavior and society (MALS, Post-Master's Certificate)
initial licensure (M Ed)
international commerce and policy (MS)
liberal studies (MALS, Post-Master's Certificate)
sports administration (MS)
teaching and learning (M Ed)
theology (MALS, Post-Master's Certificate)
theology and ministry (MALS, Post-Master's Certificate)

College of Business Administration
Dr. Dean Schroeder, Director
Programs in:
business administration (MBA)
engineering management (MEM)
management (Certificate)

College of Nursing
Dr. Janet Brown, Dean
Programs in:
management (Certificate)
nursing (MSN, Post-Master's Certificate)

School of Law
Jay Conison, Dean
Program in:
law (JD, LL M)

Iowa

■ DRAKE UNIVERSITY
Des Moines, IA 50311-4516
http://www.drake.edu/

Independent, coed, university. *Enrollment:* 5,366 graduate, professional, and undergraduate students; 977 full-time matriculated graduate/professional students (579 women), 1,143 part-time matriculated graduate/professional students (755 women). *Graduate faculty:* 32 full-time (14 women), 58 part-time/adjunct (25 women). *Computer facilities:* Computer purchase and lease plans are available. 1,000 computers available on campus for general student use. A campuswide network can be accessed from student residence rooms and from off campus. Internet access is available. *Library facilities:* Cowles Library plus 1 other. *General application contact:* Ann J. Martin, Graduate Coordinator, 515-271-2034.

Find University Details at www.petersons.com/gradchannel.

College of Business and Public Administration
Dr. Charles Edwards, Dean
Program in:
business and public administration (M Acc, MBA, MFM, MPA)

College of Pharmacy and Health Sciences
Dr. Raylene Rospond, Dean
Programs in:
pharmacy (Pharm D)
pharmacy and health sciences (Pharm D)

Law School
David Walker, Dean
Program in:
law (JD)

School of Education
Dr. Janet McMahill, Dean
Programs in:
adult development (MS)
adult learning and performance development (MS)
art (MAT)
biology (MAT)
business (MAT)
chemistry (MAT)
community agency counseling (MSE)
counseling (MSE)
education (MAT, MS, MSE, MST, Ed D, Ed S)
education leadership (MSE, Ed D, Ed S)
effective teaching, learning and leadership (MSE)
elementary education (MST)
English (MAT)
general science (MAT)
guidance counseling (MSE)
history-American (MAT)
history-world (MAT)
journalism (MAT)
mathematics (MAT)
physical science (MAT)
physics (MAT)
rehabilitation (MS)
rehabilitation administration (MS)
rehabilitation counseling (MS)
rehabilitation placement (MS)
secondary education (MAT)
sociology (MAT)
special education (MSE)
speech (MAT)
speech communication (MAT)
teacher education (MSE)
theatre (MAT)

■ GRACELAND UNIVERSITY
Lamoni, IA 50140
http://www.graceland.edu/

Independent-religious, coed, comprehensive institution. *Enrollment:* 2,116 graduate, professional, and undergraduate students; 696 full-time matriculated graduate/professional students (543 women), 157 part-time matriculated graduate/professional students (122 women). *Graduate faculty:* 18 full-time (16 women), 39 part-time/adjunct (23 women). *Computer facilities:* 106 computers available on campus for general student use. A campuswide network can be accessed from student residence rooms and from off campus. Internet access and online class registration are available. *Library facilities:* Frederick Madison Smith Library. *General application contact:* John D. Koehler, Manager of Recruiting, 816-833-0524 Ext. 4804.

Community of Christ Seminary
Dr. Don H. Compier, Dean
Programs in:
Christian ministry (MACM)
religion (MAR)

School of Education
Dr. William L. Armstrong, Dean
Program in:
education (M Ed)

School of Nursing
Dr. Kathryn A Ballou, Dean
Programs in:
family nurse practitioner (MSN, PMC)
health care administration (MSN, PMC)
nurse educator (MSN, PMC)

■ IOWA STATE UNIVERSITY OF SCIENCE AND TECHNOLOGY
Ames, IA 50011
http://www.iastate.edu/

State-supported, coed, university. CGS member. *Enrollment:* 25,462 graduate, professional, and undergraduate students; 2,761 full-time matriculated graduate/professional students (1,155 women), 1,207 part-time matriculated graduate/professional students (561 women). *Graduate faculty:* 1,384 full-time, 163 part-time/adjunct. *Computer facilities:* Computer purchase and lease plans are available. 2,400 computers available on campus for general student use. A campuswide network can be accessed from student residence rooms and from off campus. Internet access and online class registration, e-mail, network services are available. *Library facilities:* University Library plus 1 other. *Graduate expenses:* Tuition, state resident: full-time $5,936; part-time $330 per credit. Tuition, nonresident: full-time $16,350; part-time $330 per credit. *General application contact:* Information Contact, 515-294-5836.

Find University Details at www.petersons.com/gradchannel.

College of Veterinary Medicine
Dr. John Thomson, Dean
Programs in:
biomedical sciences (MS, PhD)
veterinary clinical sciences (MS)
veterinary diagnostic and production animal medicine (MS)
veterinary medicine (DVM, MS, PhD)
veterinary microbiology (MS, PhD)
veterinary microbiology and preventive medicine (MS, PhD)
veterinary pathology (MS, PhD)
veterinary preventative medicine (MS)

Graduate College
Dr. David K. Holger, Associate Provost for Academic Progress and Dean of the Graduate College
Programs in:
bioinformatics and computational biology (PhD)
biorenewable resources and technology (MS, PhD)
ecology and evolutionary biology (MS, PhD)
environmental sciences (MS, PhD)
genetics (MS, PhD)
human-computer interaction (MS, PhD)
immunobiology (MS, PhD)
information assurance (MS)
interdisciplinary graduate studies (MA, MS)
interdisciplinary studies (MA, MBA, MS, PhD)
microbiology (MS, PhD)
molecular, cellular, and developmental biology (MS, PhD)
neuroscience (MS, PhD)
nutritional sciences (MS, PhD)
plant physiology (MS, PhD)
sustainable agriculture (MS, PhD)
toxicology (MS, PhD)
transportation (MS)

College of Agriculture
Dr. Wendy Wintersteen, Dean
Programs in:
agricultural education and studies (MS, PhD)
agricultural meteorology (MS, PhD)
agriculture (M Ag, MS, PhD)
agronomy (MS)
animal breeding and genetics (MS, PhD)
animal ecology (MS, PhD)
animal physiology (MS)
animal psychology (PhD)
animal science (MS, PhD)
biochemistry (MS, PhD)
biophysics (MS, PhD)
crop production and physiology (MS, PhD)
entomology (MS, PhD)
forestry (MS, PhD)
genetics (MS, PhD)
horticulture (MS, PhD)
industrial education and technology (MS, PhD)
meat science (MS, PhD)
molecular, cellular, and developmental biology (MS, PhD)
plant breeding (MS, PhD)
plant pathology (MS, PhD)
soil science (MS, PhD)
toxicology (MS, PhD)

Iowa State University of Science and Technology (continued)

College of Business
Dr. Labh S Hira, Dean
Programs in:
- accounting (M Acc)
- business (M Acc, MBA, MS)
- business administration (MBA, MS)
- information systems (MS)

College of Design
Mark Engelbrecht, Dean
Programs in:
- architectural studies (MSAS)
- architecture (M Arch)
- art and design (MA)
- art education (MA)
- community and regional planning (MCRP)
- design (M Arch, MA, MCRP, MFA, MLA, MS, MSAS)
- graphic design (MFA)
- integrated visual arts (MFA)
- interior design (MFA)
- landscape architecture (MLA)
- transportation (MS)

College of Engineering
Dr. Mark J Kushner, Dean
Programs in:
- aerospace engineering (M Eng, MS, PhD)
- agricultural and biosystems engineering (M Eng, MS, PhD)
- chemical and biological engineering (M Eng, MS, PhD)
- civil engineering (MS, PhD)
- computer engineering (MS, PhD)
- electrical engineering (MS, PhD)
- engineering (M Eng, MS, PhD)
- engineering mechanics (M Eng, MS, PhD)
- industrial engineering (MS, PhD)
- materials science and engineering (MS, PhD)
- mechanical engineering (MS, PhD)
- operations research (MS)
- systems engineering (M Eng)

College of Human Sciences
Dr. Cheryl Acterberg, Dean
Programs in:
- counselor education (M Ed, MS)
- curriculum and instructional technology (M Ed, MS, PhD)
- education (M Ed)
- educational administration (M Ed, MS)
- educational leadership (PhD)
- elementary education (M Ed, MS)
- exercise and sport science (MS)
- family and consumer sciences (MFCS)
- family and consumer sciences education and studies (M Ed, MS, PhD)
- food science and technology (MS, PhD)
- foodservice and lodging management (MFCS, MS, PhD)
- health and human performance (PhD)
- higher education (M Ed, MS)
- historical, philosophical, and comparative studies in education (M Ed, MS)
- human development and family studies (MFCS, MS, PhD)
- human sciences (M Ed, MFCS, MS, PhD)
- marriage and family therapy (PhD)
- nutrition (MS, PhD)
- organizational learning and human resource development (M Ed, MS)
- research and evaluation (MS)
- special education (M Ed, MS)
- textiles and clothing (MFCS, MS, PhD)

College of Liberal Arts and Sciences
Dr. Michael Whiteford, Dean
Programs in:
- agricultural economics (MS, PhD)
- agricultural history and rural studies (PhD)
- anthropology (MA)
- applied mathematics (MS, PhD)
- applied physics (MS, PhD)
- astrophysics (MS, PhD)
- chemistry (MS, PhD)
- cognitive psychology (PhD)
- computer science (MS, PhD)
- condensed matter physics (MS, PhD)
- counseling psychology (PhD)
- earth science (MS, PhD)
- ecology, evolution, and organismal biology (MS, PhD)
- economics (MS, PhD)
- English (MA)
- general psychology (MS)
- genetics, developmental and cell biology (MS, PhD)
- geology (MS, PhD)
- high energy physics (MS, PhD)
- history (MA)
- history of technology and science (MA, PhD)
- journalism and mass communication (MS)
- liberal arts and sciences (MA, MPA, MS, MSM, PhD)
- mathematics (MS, PhD)
- meteorology (MS, PhD)
- nuclear physics (MS, PhD)
- physics (MS, PhD)
- political science (MA)
- public administration (MPA)
- rhetoric and professional communication (PhD)
- rural sociology (MS, PhD)
- school mathematics (MSM)
- social psychology (PhD)
- sociology (MS, PhD)
- statistics (MS, PhD)
- water resources (MS, PhD)

■ MAHARISHI UNIVERSITY OF MANAGEMENT
Fairfield, IA 52557
http://www.mum.edu/

Independent, coed, university. *Computer facilities:* 120 computers available on campus for general student use. A campuswide network can be accessed from student residence rooms and from off campus. Internet access is available. *Library facilities:* Maharishi University of Management Library. *General application contact:* Director of Admissions, 641-472-1140.

Graduate Studies
Programs in:
- business administration (MBA, PhD)
- computer science (MS)
- Maharishi consciousness-based health care (MS, PhD)
- Maharishi Vedic science (MA, PhD)
- teaching elementary education (MA)
- teaching secondary education (MA)

■ MORNINGSIDE COLLEGE
Sioux City, IA 51106
http://www.morningside.edu/

Independent-religious, coed, comprehensive institution. *Computer facilities:* Computer purchase and lease plans are available. 800 computers available on campus for general student use. A campuswide network can be accessed from student residence rooms and from off campus. Internet access, online access for students to academic and financial records are available. *Library facilities:* Hickman-Johnson-Furrow Learning Center. *General application contact:* Director, Graduate Division, 712-274-5375.

Graduate Division
Programs in:
- elementary education (MAT)
- reading specialist (MAT)
- special education (MAT)
- technology based learning (MAT)

■ ST. AMBROSE UNIVERSITY
Davenport, IA 52803-2898
http://www.sau.edu/

Independent-religious, coed, comprehensive institution. CGS member. *Enrollment:* 3,780 graduate, professional, and undergraduate students; 310 full-time matriculated graduate/professional students (214 women), 641 part-time matriculated graduate/professional students (379 women). *Graduate faculty:* 75 full-time (22 women), 50 part-time/adjunct (22 women). *Computer facilities:* Computer purchase and lease plans are available. 190 computers available on campus for general student use. A campuswide network can be accessed from student residence rooms and from off campus. Internet access and online class registration, online course syllabi, class listings, grades are available. *Library facilities:* O'Keefe Library plus 1 other. *General application contact:* Elizabeth Berridge, Director of Graduate Student Recruitment, 563-333-6271.

College of Arts and Sciences
Dr. Aron R. Aji, Dean
Programs in:
- arts and sciences (MCJ, MOL, MPS, MSW)
- criminal justice (MCJ)
- juvenile justice education (MCJ)
- leadership studies (MOL)
- pastoral studies (MPS)
- social work (MSW)

College of Business
Dr. Richard M. Dienesch, Dean
Programs in:
- accounting (M Ac)
- business (M Ac, MBA, MSITM, DBA)
- business administration (DBA)
- health care (MBA)
- human resources (MBA)
- information technology management (MSITM)

College of Education and Health Sciences
Dr. Robert Ristow, Dean
Programs in:
- education and health sciences (M Ed, MEA, MOT, MSN, DPT)
- educational leadership (MEA)
- occupational therapy (MOT)
- physical therapy (DPT)
- special education (M Ed)
- teaching (M Ed)

■ UNIVERSITY OF DUBUQUE
Dubuque, IA 52001-5099
http://www.dbq.edu/

Independent-religious, coed, comprehensive institution. *Enrollment:* 20 full-time matriculated graduate/professional students (11 women), 67 part-time matriculated graduate/professional students (33 women). *Graduate faculty:* 9 full-time (1 woman), 5 part-time/adjunct (4 women). *Computer facilities:* 220 computers available on campus for general student use. A campuswide network can be accessed from student residence rooms and from off campus. Internet access, intranet are available. *Library facilities:* Charles C. Myer's Library. *General application contact:* Carol A. Knockle, Graduate Program Coordinator, 563-589-3300.

Program in Business Administration
Richard Birkenbeuel, Director of Domestic and International MBA Programs
Program in:
- business administration (MBA)

Program in Communication
Dr. Robert Reid, Program Director
Program in:
- communication (MAC)

Theological Seminary
Dr. Bradley Longfield, Dean
Program in:
- theology (M Div, MAR, D Min)

■ THE UNIVERSITY OF IOWA
Iowa City, IA 52242-1316
http://www.uiowa.edu/

State-supported, coed, university. CGS member. *Enrollment:* 28,816 graduate, professional, and undergraduate students; 4,684 full-time matriculated graduate/professional students (2,496 women), 3,892 part-time matriculated graduate/professional students (1,791 women). *Graduate faculty:* 1,584 full-time (455 women), 89 part-time/adjunct (23 women). *Computer facilities:* Computer purchase and lease plans are available. 1,200 computers available on campus for general student use. A campuswide network can be accessed from student residence rooms and from off campus. Internet access and online class registration, online degree process, grades, financial aid summary, bills are available. *Library facilities:* Main Library plus 12 others. *General application contact:* Betty Wood, Associate Director of Admissions, 319-335-1525.

College of Dentistry
Programs in:
- dental public health (MS)
- dentistry (DDS, MS, PhD, Certificate)
- endodontics (MS, Certificate)
- operative dentistry (MS, Certificate)
- oral and maxillofacial pathology (Certificate)
- oral and maxillofacial radiology (Certificate)
- oral and maxillofacial surgery (MS, Certificate)
- oral pathology, radiology and medicine (MS, Certificate)
- oral science (MS, PhD)
- orthodontics (MS, Certificate)
- pediatric dentistry (Certificate)
- periodontics (MS, Certificate)
- preventive and community dentistry (MS)
- prosthodontics (MS, Certificate)
- stomatology (MS)

College of Law
Carolyn Jones, Dean
Program in:
- law (JD, LL M)

College of Pharmacy
Jordan Cohen, Dean
Program in:
- pharmacy (MS, PhD)

Graduate College
Dr. John C. Keller, Dean
Programs in:
- applied mathematical and computational sciences (PhD)
- bioinformatics and computational biology (Certificate)
- genetics (PhD)
- health informatics (MS, PhD, Certificate)
- human toxicology (MS, PhD)
- immunology (PhD)
- information science (MS, PhD, Certificate)
- molecular and cellular biology (PhD)
- neuroscience (PhD)
- second language acquisition (PhD)
- urban and regional planning (MA, MS)

College of Education
Sandra Bowman Damico, Dean
Programs in:
- administration and research (PhD)
- art education (MA, PhD)
- counseling psychology (PhD)
- counselor education and supervision (PhD)
- curriculum and supervision (MA, PhD)
- curriculum supervision (MA)
- developmental reading (MA)
- early childhood and elementary education (MA, PhD)
- early childhood education and care (MA)
- education (MA, MAT, PhD, Ed S)
- educational administration (MA, PhD, Ed S)
- educational measurement and statistics (MA, PhD)
- educational psychology (MA, PhD)
- elementary education (MA, PhD)
- English education (MA, MAT, PhD)
- foreign language education (MA, MAT)
- foreign language/ESL education (PhD)
- higher education (MA, PhD, Ed S)
- language, literature and culture (PhD)
- math education (PhD)
- mathematics education (MA)
- music education (MA, PhD)
- rehabilitation counseling (MA)
- rehabilitation counselor education (PhD)
- school counseling (MA)
- school psychology (PhD, Ed S)
- secondary education (MA, MAT, PhD)
- social foundations (MA, PhD)
- social studies (MA, PhD)
- special education (MA, PhD)
- student development (MA, PhD)

College of Engineering
Dr. P. Barry Butler, Dean
Programs in:
- biomedical engineering (MS, PhD)
- chemical and biochemical engineering (MS, PhD)
- civil and environmental engineering (MS, PhD)
- electrical and computer engineering (MS, PhD)
- engineering (MS, PhD)
- engineering design and manufacturing (MS, PhD)

The University of Iowa (continued)
- ergonomics (MS, PhD)
- information and engineering management (MS, PhD)
- mechanical engineering (MS, PhD)
- operations research (MS, PhD)
- quality engineering (MS, PhD)

College of Liberal Arts and Sciences
Linda Maxson, Dean
Programs in:
- African American world studies (MA)
- American studies (MA, PhD)
- anthropology (MA, PhD)
- art (MA, MFA)
- art history (MA, PhD)
- Asian languages and literature (MA)
- astronomy (MS)
- biology (MS, PhD)
- cell and developmental biology (MS, PhD)
- chemistry (MS, PhD)
- classics (MA, PhD)
- communication research (MA, PhD)
- comparative literature (MA, PhD)
- comparative literature translation (MFA)
- computer science (MCS, MS, PhD)
- dance (MFA)
- English (PhD)
- evolution (MS, PhD)
- exercise science (MS)
- film and video production (MA, MFA)
- film studies (MA, PhD)
- French (MA, PhD)
- genetics (MS, PhD)
- geography (MA, PhD)
- geoscience (MS, PhD)
- German (MA, PhD)
- history (MA, PhD)
- integrative physiology (PhD)
- leisure and recreational sport management (MA)
- liberal arts and sciences (MA, MCS, MFA, MS, MSW, Au D, DMA, PhD)
- linguistics (MA, PhD)
- linguistics with TESL (MA)
- literary criticism (PhD)
- literary history (PhD)
- literary studies (MA)
- mass communication (PhD)
- mathematics (MS, PhD)
- media communication (MA)
- music (MA, MFA, DMA, PhD)
- neural and behavioral sciences (PhD)
- neurobiology (MS, PhD)
- nonfiction writing (MFA)
- philosophy (MA, PhD)
- physics (MS, PhD)
- plant biology (MS, PhD)
- political science (MA, PhD)
- professional journalism (MA)
- professional speech pathology and audiology (MA, Au D)
- psychology (MA, PhD)
- psychology of sport and physical activity (MA, PhD)
- religious studies (MA, PhD)
- rhetorical studies (MA, PhD)
- rhetorical theory and stylistics (PhD)
- science education (MS, PhD)
- social work (MSW, PhD)
- sociology (MA, PhD)
- Spanish (MA, PhD)
- speech and hearing science (PhD)
- sports studies (MA, PhD)
- statistics and actuarial science (MS, PhD)
- theatre arts (MFA)
- therapeutic recreation (MA)
- women's studies (PhD)
- writer's workshop (MFA)

College of Nursing
Martha Craft-Rosenberg, Interim Dean
Program in:
- nursing (MSN, PhD)

College of Public Health
Dr. James A. Merchant, Dean
Programs in:
- biostatistics (MS, PhD)
- clinical investigation (MS)
- community and behavioral health (MS, PhD)
- epidemiology (MS, PhD)
- health management and policy (MHA, PhD)
- occupational and environmental health (MS, PhD, Certificate)
- public health (MHA, MPH, MS, PhD, Certificate)

School of Library and Information Science
James Elmborg, Director
Program in:
- library and information science (MA)

Henry B. Tippie College of Business
Prof. William C. (Curt) Hunter, Dean
Programs in:
- accountancy (M Ac)
- business (M Ac, MBA, PhD)
- business administration (PhD)
- economics (PhD)

Henry B. Tippie School of Management
Prof. Gary J. Gaeth, Associate Dean, MBA Programs
Programs in:
- accounting (MBA)
- corporate finance (MBA)
- entrepreneurship (MBA)
- finance (MBA)
- individually designed concentration (MBA)
- investment management (MBA)
- management information systems (MBA)
- marketing (MBA)
- nonprofit management (MBA)
- operations management (MBA)
- strategic management and consulting (MBA)

Roy J. and Lucille A. Carver College of Medicine
Dr. Jean E. Robillard, Dean
Programs in:
- anatomy and biology (PhD)
- biochemistry (PhD)
- biology (PhD)
- chemistry (PhD)
- free radical and radiation biology (PhD)
- genetics (PhD)
- human toxicology (PhD)
- immunology (PhD)
- medicine (MD, MA, MPAS, MS, DPT, PhD)
- microbiology (PhD)
- molecular and cellular biology (PhD)
- molecular physiology and biophysics (PhD)
- neuroscience (PhD)
- pharmacology (PhD)
- speech and hearing (PhD)

Graduate Programs in Medicine
Programs in:
- anatomy and cell biology (PhD)
- biochemistry (MS, PhD)
- free radical and radiation biology (MS, PhD)
- general microbiology and microbial physiology (MS, PhD)
- immunology (MS, PhD)
- medicine (MA, MPAS, MS, DPT, PhD)
- microbial genetics (MS, PhD)
- pathogenic bacteriology (MS, PhD)
- pathology (MS)
- pharmacology (MS, PhD)
- physical therapy (DPT)
- physician assistant (MPAS)
- physiology and biophysics (PhD)
- physiology and biophysiology (MS)
- rehabilitation science (PhD)
- translational biomedicine (MS, PhD)
- virology (MS, PhD)

■ UNIVERSITY OF NORTHERN IOWA
Cedar Falls, IA 50614
http://www.uni.edu/

State-supported, coed, comprehensive institution. CGS member. *Enrollment:* 12,327 graduate, professional, and undergraduate students; 624 full-time matriculated graduate/professional students (396 women), 615 part-time matriculated graduate/professional students (426 women). *Computer facilities:* Computer purchase and lease plans are available. 1,900 computers available on campus for general student use. A campuswide network can be accessed from student residence rooms and from off campus. Internet access and online class registration, course registration, student account and grade information, degree audit, program of study are available. *Library facilities:* Rod Library. *Graduate expenses:* Tuition, state resident: full-time $5,936. Tuition, nonresident: full-time $14,074. *General application contact:* Laurie S. Russell, Record Analyst, 319-273-2623.

Graduate College
Dr. Susan Koch, Dean
Programs in:
- philanthropy/nonprofit development (MA)
- public policy (MPP)
- women's and gender studies (MA)

College of Business Administration
Dr. Farzad Moussavi, Dean
Programs in:
- accounting (M Acc)
- business administration (M Acc, MBA)

College of Education
Dr. Jeffrey Cornett, Dean
Programs in:
- communication and training technology (MA)
- community health education (Ed D)
- counseling (MA, MAE, Ed D)
- curriculum and instruction (MAE, Ed D)
- early childhood education (MAE)
- education (MA, MAE, Ed D, Ed S)
- educational administration (Ed D)
- educational leadership (MAE, Ed D)
- educational media (MA)
- educational psychology (MAE)
- educational technology (MA)
- elementary education (MAE)
- elementary principal (MAE)
- elementary reading and language arts (MAE)
- health education (MA, Ed D)
- leisure services (MA, Ed D)
- middle school/junior high education (MAE)
- physical education (MA)
- postsecondary education (MAE)
- program administration (MA)
- reading (MAE)
- reading education (MAE)
- rehabilitation studies (Ed D)
- school counseling (MAE)
- school library media studies (MA)
- school psychology (Ed S)
- scientific basis of physical education (MA)
- secondary principal (MAE)
- secondary reading (MAE)
- special education (MAE, Ed D)
- student affairs (MAE)
- teaching/coaching (MA)
- youth/human services administration (MA)

College of Humanities and Fine Arts
Dr. Reinhold Bubser, Interim Dean
Programs in:
- art (MA)
- art education (MA)
- audiology (MA)
- communication studies (MA)
- composition (MM)
- conducting (MM)
- English (MA)
- French (MA)
- German (MA)
- humanities and fine arts (MA, MM)
- jazz pedagogy (MM)
- music (MA, MM)
- music education (MA, MM)
- music history (MM)
- performance (MM)
- piano performance and pedagogy (MM)
- Spanish (MA)
- speech pathology (MA)
- teaching English to speakers of other languages (MA)
- teaching English to speakers of other languages/French (MA)
- teaching English to speakers of other languages/German (MA)
- teaching English to speakers of other languages/Spanish (MA)
- two languages (MA)

College of Natural Sciences
Dr. Joel Haack, Interim Dean
Programs in:
- biology (MA, MS, PSM)
- chemistry (MA, MS, PSM)
- computer science (MA, MS)
- environmental health (MS)
- environmental science (MS)
- environmental technology (MS)
- industrial technology (MA, PSM, DIT)
- mathematics (MA)
- mathematics for middle grades (MA)
- natural sciences (MA, MS, PSM, DIT, SP)
- physics (MA, PSM)
- science education (MA, SP)

College of Social and Behavioral Sciences
Dr. Julia E. Wallace, Dean
Programs in:
- criminology (MA)
- geography (MA)
- history (MA)
- psychology (MA)
- social and behavioral sciences (MA, MSW)
- social work (MSW)
- sociology (MA)

■ UPPER IOWA UNIVERSITY
Fayette, IA 52142-1857
http://www.uiu.edu/

Independent, coed, comprehensive institution. *Computer facilities:* 75 computers available on campus for general student use. A campuswide network can be accessed. Internet access is available. *Library facilities:* Henderson Wilder Library. *General application contact:* Online Program Office Manager, 515-369-7777.

Online Master's Programs
Programs in:
- accounting (MBA)
- corporate financial management (MBA)
- global business (MBA)
- health and human services (MPA)
- homeland security (MPA)
- human resources management (MBA)
- justice administration (MPA)
- organizational development (MBA)
- public personnel management (MPA)
- quality management (MBA)

Kansas

■ BENEDICTINE COLLEGE
Atchison, KS 66002-1499
http://www.benedictine.edu/

Independent-religious, coed, comprehensive institution. *Computer facilities:* 80 computers available on campus for general student use. A campuswide network can be accessed from student residence rooms and from off campus. Internet access is available. *Library facilities:* Benedictine College Library. *General application contact:* Administrative Assistant of Graduation Programs, 913-367-5340 Ext. 2524.

Executive Master of Business Administration Program
Program in:
- business administration (EMBA)

Program in Business Administration
Program in:
- business administration (MBA)

Program in Educational Administration
Program in:
- educational administration (MA)

■ EMPORIA STATE UNIVERSITY
Emporia, KS 66801-5087
http://www.emporia.edu/

State-supported, coed, comprehensive institution. CGS member. *Enrollment:* 6,473 graduate, professional, and undergraduate students; 252 full-time matriculated graduate/professional students (146 women), 1,382 part-time matriculated graduate/professional students (1,008 women). *Graduate faculty:* 215 full-time (79 women), 22 part-time/adjunct (18 women). *Computer facilities:* 410 computers available on campus for general student use. A campuswide network can be accessed from student residence rooms and from off campus. Internet access and online class registration, various software packages are available. *Library facilities:* William Allen White Library. *Graduate expenses:* Tuition, state resident: full-time $3,438; part-time $143 per credit hour. Tuition, nonresident: full-time $10,398; part-time $433 per credit

Emporia State University (continued)
hour. Required fees: $724; $44 per credit hour. *General application contact:* Mary Sewell, Admissions Coordinator, 800-950-GRAD.

Find University Details at www.petersons.com/gradchannel.

School of Graduate Studies
Dr. Gerrit Bleeker, Interim Dean

College of Liberal Arts and Sciences
Dr. Rodney Sobieski, Dean
Programs in:
- American history (MAT)
- anthropology (MAT)
- botany (MS)
- earth science (MS)
- economics (MAT)
- English (MA)
- environmental biology (MS)
- general biology (MS)
- geography (MAT)
- geospatial analysis (Postbaccalaureate Certificate)
- history (MA)
- liberal arts and sciences (MA, MAT, MM, MS, Postbaccalaureate Certificate)
- mathematics (MS)
- microbial and cellular biology (MS)
- music education (MM)
- performance (MM)
- physical science (MS)
- political science (MAT)
- social sciences (MAT)
- social studies education (MAT)
- sociology (MAT)
- teaching English to speakers of other languages (MA)
- world history (MAT)
- zoology (MS)

School of Business
Dr. Robert Hite, Dean
Programs in:
- business (MBA, MSBE)
- business administration (MBA)
- business education (MSBE)

School of Library and Information Management
Dr. Robert Grover, Interim Dean
Programs in:
- archives studies (Certificate)
- legal information management (MLM, Certificate)
- library and information management (MLS, PhD, Certificate)

The Teachers College
Dr. Teresa Mehring, Dean
Programs in:
- art therapy (MS)
- behavior disorders (MS)
- clinical psychology (MS)
- counselor education (MS)
- curriculum and instruction (MS)
- early childhood education (MS)
- education (MS, Ed S)
- educational administration (MS)
- general psychology (MS)
- gifted, talented, and creative (MS)
- industrial/organizational psychology (MS)
- instructional design and technology (MS)
- interrelated special education (MS)
- learning disabilities (MS)
- master teacher (MS)
- mental health counseling (MS)
- mental retardation (MS)
- physical education (MS)
- psychology (MS)
- rehabilitation counseling (MS)
- school counseling (MS)
- school psychology (MS, Ed S)
- special education (MS)

■ FORT HAYS STATE UNIVERSITY
Hays, KS 67601-4099
http://www.fhsu.edu/

State-supported, coed, comprehensive institution. CGS member. *Enrollment:* 7,403 graduate, professional, and undergraduate students; 186 full-time matriculated graduate/professional students (114 women), 651 part-time matriculated graduate/professional students (397 women). *Graduate faculty:* 127 full-time (31 women). *Computer facilities:* Computer purchase and lease plans are available. 813 computers available on campus for general student use. A campuswide network can be accessed from student residence rooms and from off campus. Internet access is available. *Library facilities:* Forsyth Library. *General application contact:* Dr. Steven Trout, Interim Dean, 785-628-4236.

Graduate School
Dr. Steven Trout, Interim Dean

College of Arts and Sciences
Dr. Paul Faber, Dean
Programs in:
- arts and sciences (MA, MFA, MLS, MS, Ed S)
- communication (MS)
- English (MA)
- geology (MS)
- history (MA)
- liberal studies (MLS)
- psychology (MS)
- school psychology (Ed S)
- studio art (MFA)

College of Business and Leadership
Dr. Steve Williams, Dean
Programs in:
- accounting (MBA)
- business and leadership (MBA)
- management (MBA)

College of Education and Technology
Dr. Deb Mercer, Dean
Programs in:
- counseling (MS)
- education (MSE)
- education and technology (MS, MSE, Ed S)
- educational administration (MS, Ed S)
- elementary education (MS)
- instructional technology (MS)
- secondary education (MS)
- special education (MS)

College of Health and Life Sciences
Dr. Jeff Briggs, Dean
Programs in:
- biology (MS)
- health and human performance (MS)
- health and life sciences (MS, MSN)
- nursing (MSN)
- speech-language pathology (MS)

■ FRIENDS UNIVERSITY
Wichita, KS 67213
http://www.friends.edu/

Independent, coed, comprehensive institution. *Enrollment:* 650 full-time matriculated graduate/professional students. *Graduate faculty:* 19 full-time (7 women). *Computer facilities:* 190 computers available on campus for general student use. A campuswide network can be accessed from student residence rooms and from off campus. *Library facilities:* Edmund Stanley Library plus 3 others. *General application contact:* Craig Davis, Director of Graduate Admissions, 800-794-6945 Ext. 5573.

Graduate School
Dr. Al Saber, Dean

Division of Business, Technology, and Leadership
Dr. William Wunder, Division Chair
Programs in:
- business administration (MBA)
- business law (MBL)
- business, technology, and leadership (EMBA, MBA, MBL, MHCL, MMIS, MSM, MSOD, MSPM)
- executive business administration (EMBA)
- health care leadership (MHCL)
- management (MSM)
- management information systems (MMIS)
- organization development (MSOD)
- service/production management (MSPM)

Division of Science, Arts, and Education
Dr. Dan Lord, Division Chair
Programs in:
- Christian ministry (MACM)
- elementary education (MAT)
- environmental studies (MSES)
- family therapy (MSFT)
- liberal studies (MALS)
- school leadership (MSL)

science, arts, and education (MACM, MALS, MAT, MSES, MSFT, MSL)
secondary education (MAT)

■ KANSAS STATE UNIVERSITY
Manhattan, KS 66506
http://www.ksu.edu/

State-supported, coed, university. CGS member. *Enrollment:* 23,141 graduate, professional, and undergraduate students; 2,120 full-time matriculated graduate/professional students (991 women), 1,672 part-time matriculated graduate/professional students (1,171 women). *Graduate faculty:* 906 full-time (231 women), 207 part-time/adjunct (48 women). *Computer facilities:* 326 computers available on campus for general student use. A campuswide network can be accessed from student residence rooms and from off campus. Internet access and online class registration are available. *Library facilities:* Hale Library plus 3 others. *Graduate expenses:* Tuition, state resident: full-time $6,352; part-time $240 per credit hour. Tuition, nonresident: full-time $14,296; part-time $571 per credit hour. Required fees: $585. *General application contact:* Dr. James Guikema, Associate Dean, 785-532-7927.

Find University Details at www.petersons.com/gradchannel.

College of Veterinary Medicine
Ralph Richardson, Dean
Programs in:
anatomy and physiology (MS, PhD)
biomedical science (MS)
clinical sciences (MS)
diagnostic medicine/pathobiology (MS, PhD)
physiology (PhD)
veterinary medicine (DVM, MS, PhD)

Graduate School
Ron Trewyn, Dean
Programs in:
food science (MS, PhD)
genetics (MS, PhD)

College of Agriculture
Fred Cholick, Dean
Programs in:
agricultural economics (MAB, MS, PhD)
agriculture (MAB, MS, PhD)
animal breeding and genetics (MS, PhD)
crop science (MS, PhD)
entomology (MS, PhD)
grain science and industry (MS, PhD)
horticulture (MS, PhD)
meat science (MS, PhD)
monogastric nutrition (MS, PhD)
physiology (MS, PhD)
plant pathology (MS, PhD)
range management (MS, PhD)
ruminant nutrition (MS, PhD)
soil science (MS, PhD)
weed science (MS, PhD)

College of Architecture, Planning and Design
Dennis Law, Dean
Programs in:
architecture (M Arch)
architecture, planning and design (M Arch, MLA, MRCP)
landscape architecture (MLA)
regional and community planning (MRCP)

College of Arts and Sciences
Stephen White, Dean
Programs in:
analytical chemistry (MS)
art (MFA)
arts and sciences (MA, MFA, MM, MPA, MS, PhD)
biochemistry (MS, PhD)
biological chemistry (MS)
biology (MS, PhD)
chemistry (PhD)
economics (MA, PhD)
English (MA)
French (MA)
geography (MA, PhD)
geology (MS)
German (MA)
history (MA, PhD)
inorganic chemistry (MS)
international service (MA)
kinesiology (MS)
mass communications (MS)
materials chemistry (MS)
mathematics (MS, PhD)
microbiology (PhD)
music education (MM)
music education/band conducting (MM)
music history and literature (MM)
organic chemistry (MS)
performance (MM)
performance with pedagogy emphasis (MM)
physical chemistry (MS)
physics (MS, PhD)
political science (MA)
psychology (MS, PhD)
public administration (MPA)
rhetoric/communication (MA)
sociology (MA, PhD)
Spanish (MA)
statistics (MS, PhD)
theatre (MA)
theory and composition (MM)

College of Business Administration
Yar M. Ebadi, Interim Dean
Programs in:
accounting (M Acc)
business administration (M Acc, MBA)

College of Education
Michael Holen, Dean
Programs in:
adult and continuing education (MS, Ed D)
counseling and student development-college student personnel work (MS)
counseling and student development-school counseling (MS)
counselor education and supervisors (PhD)
curriculum and instruction (MS, Ed D, PhD)
education (MS, Ed D, PhD)
educational administration (MS, Ed D)
school counseling (Ed D)
special education (MS, Ed D)
student affairs in higher education (PhD)

College of Engineering
Richard Gallagher, Dean
Programs in:
architectural engineering (MS)
bioengineering (MS, PhD)
biological and agricultural engineering (MS)
chemical engineering (MS)
civil engineering (MS)
communications systems (MS, PhD)
computer engineering (MS, PhD)
computer science (MS, PhD)
control systems (MS, PhD)
electromagnetics (MS, PhD)
engineering (PhD)
engineering management (MEM)
industrial engineering (MS, PhD)
instrumentation (MS, PhD)
mechanical engineering (MS)
nuclear engineering (MS)
operations research (MS)
power systems (MS, PhD)
signal processing (MS, PhD)
software engineering (MSE)
solid-state electronics (MS, PhD)

College of Human Ecology
Dr. Virginia Moxley, Interim Dean
Programs in:
apparel and textiles (MS, PhD)
dietetics and administration (MS)
family life education and consultation (PhD)
family studies and human services (MS)
food science (MS, PhD)
food service and hospitality management (MS)
food service, hospitality management, and administrative dietetics (PhD)
human ecology (MS, PhD)
human nutrition (MS, PhD)
institutional management (PhD)
lifespan and human development (PhD)
marriage and family therapy (PhD)
public health (MS)

■ MIDAMERICA NAZARENE UNIVERSITY
Olathe, KS 66062-1899
http://www.mnu.edu/

Independent-religious, coed, comprehensive institution. *Computer facilities:* 85 computers available on campus for general student use. A campuswide network can be accessed from student residence rooms and from off campus. Internet access is available. *Library*

MidAmerica Nazarene University (continued)
facilities: Mabee Library. *General application contact:* Director of Admissions for Graduate and Adult Studies, 913-791-3277.

Graduate Studies in Counseling
Program in:
counseling (MAC)

Graduate Studies in Education
Programs in:
curriculum and instruction (M Ed)
educational technology (MET)
special education (MA)

Graduate Studies in Management
Program in:
management (MAOA, MBA)

■ NEWMAN UNIVERSITY
Wichita, KS 67213-2097
http://www.newmanu.edu/

Independent-religious, coed, comprehensive institution. *Enrollment:* 2,104 graduate, professional, and undergraduate students; 114 full-time matriculated graduate/professional students (78 women), 199 part-time matriculated graduate/professional students (124 women). *Graduate faculty:* 18 full-time (4 women), 13 part-time/adjunct (11 women). *Computer facilities:* Computer purchase and lease plans are available. 90 computers available on campus for general student use. A campuswide network can be accessed from student residence rooms and from off campus. Internet access and online class registration are available. *Library facilities:* Dungan Library and Campus Center plus 1 other. *General application contact:* Linda Kay Sabala, Director of Graduate Admissions, 316-942-4291 Ext. 2230.

School of Business
Dr. Joe Goetz, Dean
Programs in:
international business (MBA)
leadership (MBA)
management (MBA)
technology (MBA)

School of Education
Dr. Guy Glidden, Director
Programs in:
building leadership (MS Ed)
curriculum and instruction (MS Ed)

School of Nursing and Allied Health
Sharon Niemann, Director
Program in:
nurse anesthesia (MS)

School of Social Work
Dr. Kevin Brown, Dean
Program in:
social work (MSW)

■ PITTSBURG STATE UNIVERSITY
Pittsburg, KS 66762
http://www.pittstate.edu/

State-supported, coed, comprehensive institution. CGS member. *Enrollment:* 6,859 graduate, professional, and undergraduate students; 374 full-time matriculated graduate/professional students (213 women), 738 part-time matriculated graduate/professional students (497 women). *Graduate faculty:* 223 full-time (74 women), 129 part-time/adjunct (68 women). *Computer facilities:* A campuswide network can be accessed from student residence rooms and from off campus. Internet access and online class registration are available. *Library facilities:* Leonard H. Axe Library plus 1 other. *Graduate expenses:* Tuition, state resident: full-time $2,144; part-time $181 per credit hour. Tuition, nonresident: full-time $5,273; part-time $442 per credit hour. Tuition and fees vary according to course load and campus/location. *General application contact:* Jamie Vanderbeck, Assistant Director, 620-235-4223.

Graduate School
Dr. Peggy Snyder, Dean of Continuing and Graduate Studies

College of Arts and Sciences
Dr. Lynette Olson, Dean
Programs in:
applied communication (MA)
applied physics (MS)
art education (MA)
arts and sciences (MA, MM, MS, MSN)
biology (MS)
chemistry (MS)
communication education (MA)
English (MA)
history (MA)
instrumental music education (MM)
mathematics (MS)
music history/music literature (MM)
nursing (MSN)
performance (MM)
physics (MS)
professional physics (MS)
studio art (MA)
theatre (MA)
theory and composition (MM)
vocal music education (MM)

College of Education
Programs in:
behavioral disorders (MS)
classroom reading teacher (MS)
community college and higher education (Ed S)
counseling (MS)
counselor education (MS)
early childhood education (MS)
education (MAT, MS, Ed S)
educational leadership (MS)
educational technology (MS)
elementary education (MS)
learning disabilities (MS)
mentally retarded (MS)
physical education (MS)
psychology (MS)
reading (MS)
reading specialist (MS)
school psychology (Ed S)
secondary education (MS)
special education teaching (MS)
teaching (MAT)

College of Technology
Dr. Bruce Dallman, Dean
Programs in:
engineering technology (MET)
human resource development (MS, Ed S)
industrial education (Ed S)
technical teacher education (MS)
technology (MS)
technology education (MS)

Kelce College of Business
Programs in:
accounting (MBA)
business (MBA)
general administration (MBA)

■ SOUTHWESTERN COLLEGE
Winfield, KS 67156-2499
http://www.sckans.edu/

Independent-religious, coed, comprehensive institution. *Computer facilities:* 55 computers available on campus for general student use. A campuswide network can be accessed from student residence rooms and from off campus. Internet access, laptops, wireless campus are available. *Library facilities:* Memorial Library plus 1 other. *General application contact:* Director of Graduate Studies, 800-846-1543 Ext. 6115.

Center for Teaching Excellence
Program in:
special education (M Ed)

MBA Program

■ UNIVERSITY OF KANSAS
Lawrence, KS 66045
http://www.ku.edu

State-supported, coed, university. CGS member. *Enrollment:* 28,924 graduate, professional, and undergraduate students; 4,655 full-time matriculated graduate/professional students (2,549 women), 2,489 part-time matriculated graduate/professional students (1,436 women). *Graduate faculty:* 1,953. *Computer facilities:* Computer purchase and lease plans are available. 1,500 computers available on campus for general student use. A campuswide network can be accessed from student residence rooms and from off campus. Internet access and online class registration are available. *Library facilities:* Watson Library plus 11 others. *Graduate expenses:* Part-time $227 per credit. Tuition, state resident: part-time $543 per credit. Tuition and fees vary according to course load, campus/location, program and reciprocity agreements. *General application contact:* Information Contact, 785-864-6161.

Graduate Studies

College of Liberal Arts and Sciences
Joseph Steinmetz, Dean
Programs in:
- American studies (MA, PhD)
- anthropology (MA, PhD)
- applied behavioral science (MA)
- applied mathematics (MA, PhD)
- audiology (PhD)
- behavioral psychology (PhD)
- biochemistry and biophysics (MA, PhD)
- biological sciences (MA, PhD)
- botany (MA, PhD)
- Brazilian studies (Certificate)
- Central American and Mexican studies (Certificate)
- chemistry (MA, MS, PhD)
- child language (MA, PhD)
- Chinese language and literature (MA)
- classical languages (MA)
- clinical child psychology (MA, PhD)
- communication studies (MA, PhD)
- computational physics and astronomy (MS)
- creative writing (MFA)
- developmental and child psychology (PhD)
- East Asian cultures (MA)
- ecology and evolutionary biology (MA, PhD)
- economics (MA, PhD)
- English (MA, PhD)
- entomology (MA, PhD)
- French (MA, PhD)
- geography (MA, PhD)
- geology (MS, PhD)
- German (MA, PhD)
- gerontology (MA, PhD)
- history (MA, PhD)
- history of art (MA, PhD)
- human development (MA)
- indigenous nations studies (MA)
- international studies (MA)
- Japanese language and literature (MA)
- Latin American studies (MA)
- liberal arts and sciences (MA, MFA, MPA, MS, PhD, Certificate)
- linguistics (MA, PhD)
- mathematics (MA, PhD)
- microbiology (MA, PhD)
- molecular, cellular, and developmental biology (MA, PhD)
- museum studies (MA)
- philosophy (MA, PhD)
- physics (MS, PhD)
- political science (MA, PhD)
- psychology (MA, PhD)
- public administration (MPA, PhD)
- religious studies (MA)
- Russian, East European and Eurasian studies (MA)
- Slavic languages and literatures (MA, PhD)
- sociology (MA, PhD)
- Spanish (MA, PhD)
- speech-language pathology (MA, PhD)
- systematics and ecology (MA)
- theatre and film (MA, PhD)

School of Architecture and Urban Planning
John C. Gaunt, Dean
Programs in:
- academic track (M Arch)
- architecture and urban planning (M Arch, MUP)
- management track (M Arch)
- professional track (M Arch)
- urban planning (MUP)

School of Business
William L. Fuerst, Head
Programs in:
- accounting and information systems (MAIS)
- business (MAIS, MBA, MS, PhD)
- business administration (MBA)

School of Education
Dr. Rick Ginsberg, Dean
Programs in:
- counseling psychology (MS, PhD)
- curriculum and instruction (MA, MS Ed, Ed D, PhD)
- education (MA, MS, MS Ed, Ed D, PhD, Ed S)
- education administration (MS Ed, Ed S)
- educational psychology and research (MS Ed, PhD)
- foundations (Ed D, PhD)
- foundations of education (MS Ed)
- health, sports, and exercise sciences (Ed D)
- higher education (Ed D, PhD)
- higher education administration (MS Ed)
- physical education (MS Ed, PhD)
- policy studies (Ed D, PhD)
- school administration (Ed D, PhD)
- school psychology (PhD, Ed S)
- special education (MS Ed, Ed D, PhD)

School of Engineering
Stuart R. Bell, Dean
Programs in:
- aerospace engineering (ME, MS, DE, PhD)
- architectural engineering (MS)
- chemical engineering (MS)
- chemical/petroleum engineering (PhD)
- civil engineering (MCE, MS, DE, PhD)
- computer engineering (MS)
- computer science (MS, PhD)
- construction management (MCM)
- electrical engineering (MS, DE, PhD)
- engineering (MCE, MCM, ME, MS, DE, PhD)
- engineering management (MS)
- environmental engineering (MS, PhD)
- environmental science (MS, PhD)
- information technology (MS)
- mechanical engineering (MS, DE, PhD)
- petroleum engineering (MS)
- water resources science (MS)

School of Fine Arts
Dr. Steven K. Hedden, Dean
Programs in:
- art (MFA)
- church music (MM, DMA)
- composition (MM, DMA)
- conducting (MM, DMA)
- design (MA, MFA)
- fine arts (MA, MFA, MM, MME, DMA, PhD)
- music and dance (MM, MME, DMA, PhD)
- music education (MME, PhD)
- music theory (MM, PhD)
- music therapy (MME)
- musicology (MM, PhD)
- opera (MM)
- performance (MM, DMA)
- special studies (MA)
- visual arts education (MA)

School of Journalism and Mass Communications
Ann Brill, Dean
Program in:
- journalism (MS)

School of Pharmacy
Kenneth L. Audus, Dean
Programs in:
- hospital pharmacy (MS)
- medicinal chemistry (MS, PhD)
- neurosciences (MS, PhD)
- pharmaceutical chemistry (MS, PhD)
- pharmacology and toxicology (MS, PhD)
- pharmacy (MS, PhD)

School of Social Welfare
Mary Ellen Kondrat, Dean
Programs in:
- social welfare (MSW)
- social work (PhD)

Graduate Studies Medical Center

Dr. Allen Rawitch, Vice Chancellor for Academic Affairs and Dean of Graduate Studies
Programs in:
- anatomy and cell biology (MA, PhD)
- audiology (MA, Au D, PhD)
- biochemistry and molecular biology (MS, PhD)
- biomedical sciences (MA, MPH, MS, PhD)
- health policy and management (MHSA)
- medicine (MA, MHSA, MOT, MPH, MS, Au D, DPT, PhD, Certificate, PMC)
- microbiology, molecular genetics and immunology (PhD)
- molecular and integrative physiology (MS, PhD)

University of Kansas (continued)
- pathology and laboratory medicine (MA, PhD)
- pharmacology (MS, PhD)
- preventive medicine (MPH, MS)
- speech-language pathology (MA, PhD)
- toxicology (MS, PhD)

School of Allied Health
Dr. Karen L. Miller, Dean
Programs in:
- allied health (MA, MOT, MS, Au D, DPT, PhD, Certificate)
- dietetic internship (Certificate)
- dietetics and nutrition (MS)
- nurse anesthesia (MS)
- occupational therapy (MOT, MS)
- physical therapy and rehabilitation science (MS, DPT, PhD)
- therapeutic science (PhD)

School of Nursing
Dr. Karen L. Miller, Dean
Programs in:
- nurse educator (PMC)
- nurse midwife (PMC)
- nursing (MS, PhD)
- psychiatric/mental health nurse practitioner (PMC)

School of Law
Gail B Agrawal, Dean
Program in:
- law (JD)

School of Medicine
Dr. Barbara Atkinson, Executive Dean
Program in:
- medicine (MD)

■ UNIVERSITY OF SAINT MARY
Leavenworth, KS 66048-5082
http://www.stmary.edu/

Independent-religious, coed, comprehensive institution. *Computer facilities:* 95 computers available on campus for general student use. A campuswide network can be accessed from student residence rooms. Internet access and online class registration are available. *Library facilities:* De Paul Library. *General application contact:* Graduate Dean, 913-345-8288.

Graduate Programs
Programs in:
- business administration (MBA)
- curriculum and instruction (MAT)
- education (MA, MAT)
- management (MS)
- psychology (MA)
- special education (MA)
- teaching (MA)

■ WASHBURN UNIVERSITY
Topeka, KS 66621
http://www.washburn.edu/

City supported, coed, comprehensive institution. *Enrollment:* 7,153 graduate, professional, and undergraduate students; 599 full-time matriculated graduate/professional students (298 women), 257 part-time matriculated graduate/professional students (178 women). *Computer facilities:* 400 computers available on campus for general student use. A campuswide network can be accessed from off campus. Internet access and online class registration are available. *Library facilities:* Mabee Library plus 1 other. *Graduate expenses:* Tuition, state resident: full-time $4,338; part-time $241 per credit hour. Tuition, nonresident: full-time $8,820; part-time $490 per credit hour. Required fees: $62; $31 per semester. *General application contact:* Gordon McQuere, Dean, 785-670-1561.

College of Arts and Sciences
Gordon McQuere, Dean
Programs in:
- arts and sciences (M Ed, MA, MLS)
- clinical psychology (MA)
- curriculum and instruction (M Ed)
- educational leadership (M Ed)
- liberal studies (MLS)
- reading (M Ed)
- special education (M Ed)

School of Applied Studies
Programs in:
- applied studies (MCJ, MSW)
- clinical social work (MSW)
- criminal justice (MCJ)

School of Business
Dr. David L. Sollars, Dean
Program in:
- business (MBA)

School of Law
Program in:
- law (JD)

■ WICHITA STATE UNIVERSITY
Wichita, KS 67260
http://www.wichita.edu/

State-supported, coed, university. CGS member. *Computer facilities:* 1,500 computers available on campus for general student use. A campuswide network can be accessed from student residence rooms and from off campus. Internet access and online class registration, online grades, e-mail are available. *Library facilities:* Ablah Library plus 2 others. *General application contact:* Dean of the Graduate School, 316-978-3095.

Graduate School

College of Education
Programs in:
- communications sciences (MA, PhD)
- counseling (M Ed)
- curriculum and instruction (M Ed)
- education (M Ed, MA, Ed D, PhD, Ed S)
- education administration (M Ed, Ed D)
- educational psychology (M Ed)
- physical education (M Ed)
- school psychology (Ed S)
- special education (M Ed)
- sports administration (M Ed)

College of Engineering
Programs in:
- aerospace engineering (MS, PhD)
- electrical engineering (MS, PhD)
- engineering (MEM, MS, PhD)
- industrial and manufacturing engineering (MEM, MS, PhD)
- mechanical engineering (MS, PhD)

College of Fine Arts
Programs in:
- art education (MA)
- fine arts (MA, MFA, MM, MME)
- music (MM)
- music education (MME)
- studio arts (MFA)

College of Health Professions
Programs in:
- clinical nurse specialist (MSN)
- health professions (MPH, MPT, MSN)
- nurse midwifery (MSN)
- nurse practitioner (MSN)
- nursing and health care systems administration (MSN)
- physical therapy (MPT)
- public health (MPH)

Fairmount College of Liberal Arts and Sciences
Programs in:
- anthropology (MA)
- applied mathematics (PhD)
- biological sciences (MS)
- chemistry (MS, PhD)
- communication (MA)
- community/clinical psychology (PhD)
- computer science (MS)
- creative writing (MA, MFA)
- criminal justice (MA)
- English (MA, MFA)
- environmental science (MS)
- geology (MS)
- gerontology (MA)
- history (MA)
- human factors (PhD)
- liberal arts and sciences (MA, MFA, MPA, MS, MSW, PhD)
- mathematics (MS)
- physics (MS)
- political science (MA)
- psychology (MA)
- public administration (MPA)
- social work (MSW)

sociology (MA)
Spanish (MA)
statistics (MS)

W. Frank Barton School of Business
Programs in:
accountancy (MPA)
business (EMBA, MBA, MS)
business economics (MA)
economic analysis (MA)
economics (MA)
professional accountancy (MPA)

Kentucky

■ BELLARMINE UNIVERSITY
Louisville, KY 40205-0671
http://www.bellarmine.edu/

Independent-religious, coed, comprehensive institution. *Enrollment:* 2,627 graduate, professional, and undergraduate students; 290 full-time matriculated graduate/professional students (198 women), 341 part-time matriculated graduate/professional students (226 women). *Graduate faculty:* 44 full-time (24 women), 32 part-time/adjunct (17 women). *Computer facilities:* 160 computers available on campus for general student use. A campuswide network can be accessed from student residence rooms. Internet access is available. *Library facilities:* W.L. Lyons Brown Library. *Graduate expenses:* Tuition: part-time $490 per credit hour. Tuition and fees vary according to program. *General application contact:* Dr. Julie F. Toner, Graduate School Dean, 502-452-8494.

Annsley Frazier Thornton School of Education
Dr. Milton Brown, Dean (Interim)
Programs in:
early elementary education (MA, MAT)
education (MA, MAT)
instructional leadership and school administration/school principal (MA)
learning and behavior disorders (MA)
middle school education (MA, MAT)
reading and writing endorsement (MA)
secondary school education (MAT)
Waldorf inspired curriculum (MA)

Bellarmine Center for Interdisciplinary Technology and Entrepreneurship
Dr. Michael D. Mattei, Executive Director
Program in:
technology and entrepreneurship (MAIT)

Bellarmine College of Arts and Sciences
Dr. Robert Kingsolver, Dean

Donna and Allan Lansing School of Nursing and Health Sciences
Dr. Susan H. Davis, Dean
Programs in:
nursing administration (MSN)
nursing education (MSN)
physical therapy (DPT)

W. Fielding Rubel School of Business
Daniel L. Bauer, Dean
Program in:
business (EMBA, MBA)

■ EASTERN KENTUCKY UNIVERSITY
Richmond, KY 40475-3102
http://www.eku.edu/

State-supported, coed, comprehensive institution. CGS member. *Enrollment:* 15,763 graduate, professional, and undergraduate students; 618 full-time matriculated graduate/professional students (413 women), 1,522 part-time matriculated graduate/professional students (1,051 women). *Graduate faculty:* 218 full-time (109 women), 40 part-time/adjunct (24 women). *Computer facilities:* Computer purchase and lease plans are available. 1,200 computers available on campus for general student use. A campuswide network can be accessed from student residence rooms and from off campus. Internet access and online class registration are available. *Library facilities:* John Grant Crabbe Library plus 2 others. *Graduate expenses:* Tuition, state resident: full-time $5,610. Tuition, nonresident: full-time $15,910. *General application contact:* Dr. Gerald Pogatshnik, Dean, 859-622-1742.

The Graduate School
Dr. Gerald Pogatshnik, Dean

College of Arts and Sciences
Dr. Andrew Schoomaster, Dean
Programs in:
arts and sciences (MA, MFA, MM, MPA, MS, PhD, Psy S)
biological sciences (MS)
chemistry (MS)
choral conducting (MM)
clinical psychology (MS)
community development (MPA)
community health administration (MPA)
creative writing (MFA)
ecology (MS)
English (MA)
general public administration (MPA)
geology (MS, PhD)
history (MA)
industrial/organizational psychology (MS)
mathematical sciences (MS)
performance (MM)
political science (MA)
school psychology (Psy S)
theory/composition (MM)

College of Business and Technology
Dr. Robert Rogow, Dean
Programs in:
business administration (MBA)
business and technology (MBA, MS)
industrial education (MS)
industrial technology (MS)
occupational training and development (MS)
technical administration (MS)
technology education (MS)

College of Education
Dr. William Phillips, Dean
Programs in:
agricultural education (MA Ed)
allied health sciences education (MA Ed)
art education (MA Ed)
biological sciences education (MA Ed)
business education (MA Ed)
chemistry education (MA Ed)
communication disorders (MA Ed)
earth science education (MA Ed)
education (MA, MA Ed)
elementary education general (MA Ed)
English education (MA Ed)
general science education (MA Ed)
geography education (MA Ed)
history education (MA Ed)
home economics education (MA Ed)
human services (MA)
industrial education (MA Ed)
instructional leadership (MA Ed)
mathematical sciences education (MA Ed)
mental health counseling (MA)
music education (MA Ed)
physical education (MA Ed)
physics education (MA Ed)
political science education (MA Ed)
psychology education (MA Ed)
reading (MA Ed)
school counseling (MA Ed)
school health education (MA Ed)
secondary and higher education (MA Ed)
sociology education (MA Ed)
special education (MA Ed)

College of Health Sciences
Dr. David D. Gale, Dean
Programs in:
chemical abuse and dependency (MPH)
community health (MPH)
community nutrition (MS)
environmental health science (MPH)
health sciences (MPH, MS, MSN)
occupational therapy (MS)
physical education (MS)
recreation and park administration (MS)
rural community health care (MSN)
rural health family nurse practitioner (MSN)
sports administration (MS)

College of Justice and Safety
Dr. Allen Ault, Dean

Eastern Kentucky University (continued)
Programs in:
correctional and juvenile justice studies (MS)
criminal justice (MS)
criminal justice education (MS)
justice and safety (MS)
loss prevention and safety (MS)
police studies (MS)

■ GEORGETOWN COLLEGE
Georgetown, KY 40324-1696
http://www.georgetowncollege.edu/

Independent-religious, coed, comprehensive institution. *Computer facilities:* 175 computers available on campus for general student use. A campuswide network can be accessed from student residence rooms and from off campus. Internet access is available. *Library facilities:* Anna Ashcraft Ensor Learning Resource Center plus 1 other. *General application contact:* Director of Graduate Education, 502-863-8176.

Department of Education
Program in:
education (MA Ed)

■ MOREHEAD STATE UNIVERSITY
Morehead, KY 40351
http://www.moreheadstate.edu/

State-supported, coed, comprehensive institution. *Enrollment:* 9,025 graduate, professional, and undergraduate students; 344 full-time matriculated graduate/professional students (209 women), 777 part-time matriculated graduate/professional students (534 women). *Graduate faculty:* 218 full-time (84 women), 78 part-time/adjunct (38 women). *Computer facilities:* 1,000 computers available on campus for general student use. A campuswide network can be accessed from student residence rooms and from off campus. Internet access and online class registration are available. *Library facilities:* Camden Carroll Library. *General application contact:* Michelle Barber, Graduate Admissions Counselor, 606-783-2039.

Graduate Programs
Dr. Deborah Abell, Associate Vice President for Graduate and Undergraduate Programs

Caudill College of Humanities
Dr. Michael Seelig, Dean
Programs in:
art education (MA)
communication (MA)
criminology (MA)
English (MA)
general sociology (MA)
gerontology (MA)
humanities (MA, MM)
music education (MM)
music performance (MM)
studio art (MA)

College of Business
Dr. Robert L. Albert, Dean
Programs in:
business (MBA, MSIS)
information systems (MSIS)

College of Education
Dr. Cathy Gunn, Dean
Programs in:
adult and higher education (MA, Ed S)
counseling (MA Ed, Ed S)
curriculum and instruction (Ed S)
education (MA, MA Ed, MAT, Ed S)
elementary education (MA Ed, MAT)
exercise physiology (MA)
health and physical education (MA)
instructional leadership (Ed S)
international education (MA Ed)
middle school education (MA Ed, MAT)
reading (MA Ed)
school administration (MA, Ed S)
secondary education (MA Ed, MAT)
special education (MA Ed, MAT)
sports management (MA)

College of Science and Technology
Dr. Gerald DeMoss, Dean
Programs in:
biology (MS)
career and technical education (MS)
clinical psychology (MA)
counseling psychology (MA)
experimental/general psychology (MA)
industrial technology (MS)
regional analysis and public policy (MS)
science and technology (MA, MS)

Institute for Regional Analysis and Public Policy
Dr. David Rudy, Dean
Program in:
public administration (MPA)

■ MURRAY STATE UNIVERSITY
Murray, KY 42071
http://www.murraystate.edu/

State-supported, coed, comprehensive institution. CGS member. *Enrollment:* 10,298 graduate, professional, and undergraduate students; 538 full-time matriculated graduate/professional students (314 women), 1,151 part-time matriculated graduate/professional students (844 women). *Graduate faculty:* 354. *Computer facilities:* Computer purchase and lease plans are available. 1,800 computers available on campus for general student use. A campuswide network can be accessed from student residence rooms and from off campus. Internet access and online class registration are available. *Library facilities:* Waterfield Library plus 1 other. *General application contact:* Dr. Sandra J. Jordan, University Coordinator of Graduate Studies, 270-809-3027.

College of Business and Public Affairs
Dr. Dannie Harrison, Dean
Programs in:
business administration (MBA)
business and public affairs (MA, MBA, MPAC, MS)
economics (MS)
mass communications (MA, MS)
organizational communication (MA, MS)
professional accountancy (MPAC)
telecommunications systems management (MS)

College of Education
Dr. Russ Wall, Dean
Programs in:
advanced learning behavior disorders (MA Ed)
community and agency counseling (Ed S)
early childhood education (MA Ed)
education (MA Ed, MS, Ed D, PhD, Ed S)
elementary education and reading and writing (MA Ed, Ed S)
health, physical education, and recreation (MA)
human development and leadership (MS)
industrial and technical education (MS)
learning disabilities (MA Ed)
middle school education (MA Ed, Ed S)
moderate/severe disorders (MA Ed)
reading and writing (MA Ed)
school administration (MA Ed, Ed S)
school guidance and counseling (MA Ed, Ed S)
secondary education (MA Ed, Ed S)
special education (MA Ed)

College of Health Sciences and Human Services
Dr. Elizabeth Blodgett, Dean
Programs in:
clinical nurse specialist (MSN)
environmental science (MS)
exercise and leisure studies (MS)
family nurse practitioner (MSN)
health sciences and human services (MS, MSN)
industrial hygiene (MS)
nurse anesthesia (MSN)
safety management (MS)
speech-language pathology (MS)

College of Humanities and Fine Arts
Dr. Ted Brown, Graduate Coordinator
Programs in:
clinical psychology (MA, MS)
creative writing (MFA)
English (MA)

history (MA)
humanities and fine arts (MA, MFA, MME, MPA, MS)
music education (MME)
psychology (MA, MS)
public administration (MPA)
public affairs (MPA)
teaching English to speakers of other languages (MA)

College of Science, Engineering and Technology
Dr. Neil V. Weber, Interim ean
Programs in:
biological sciences (MAT, MS, PhD)
chemistry (MS)
geosciences (MS)
management of technology (MS)
mathematics (MA, MAT, MS)
science, engineering and technology (MA, MAT, MS, PhD)
water science (MS)

School of Agriculture
Dr. Tony L. Brannon, Dean
Programs in:
agriculture (MS)
agriculture education (MS)

■ NORTHERN KENTUCKY UNIVERSITY
Highland Heights, KY 41099
http://www.nku.edu/

State-supported, coed, comprehensive institution. CGS member. *Enrollment:* 14,617 graduate, professional, and undergraduate students; 461 full-time matriculated graduate/professional students (242 women), 1,306 part-time matriculated graduate/professional students (820 women). *Computer facilities:* 600 computers available on campus for general student use. A campuswide network can be accessed from student residence rooms and from off campus. Internet access and online class registration are available. *Library facilities:* Steely Library plus 1 other. *Graduate expenses:* Tuition, state resident: full-time $5,274; part-time $293 per hour. Tuition, nonresident: full-time $10,314; part-time $573 per hour. Tuition and fees vary according to course load, program and reciprocity agreements. *General application contact:* Dr. Peg Griffin, Director of Graduate Programs, 859-572-1555.

Office of Graduate Programs
Dr. Carole A. Beere, Associate Provost for Outreach/Dean of Graduate Studies

College of Arts and Sciences
Dr. Kevin Corcoran, Dean
Programs in:
industrial psychology (Certificate)
industrial-organizational psychology (MSIO)
liberal studies (MALS)
non-profit management (Certificate)
occupational health psychology (Certificate)
organizational psychology (Certificate)
public administration (MPA)

College of Business
Michael Carrell, Dean
Programs in:
accountancy (M Acc)
business (M Acc, MA, MBA)
business administration (MBA)
executive leadership and organizational change (MA)

College of Education and Human Services
Dr. Elaine McNally Jarchow, Dean
Programs in:
community counseling (MSCC)
education (M Ed)
instructional leadership (MA)
school counseling (MASC)
special education (Certificate)
teaching (MAT)

College of Informatics
Dr. Douglas Perry, Dean
Programs in:
business informatics (MS)
communication (MA Comm)
computer science (MSCS)
corporate information security (Certificate)
health informatics (MHI)
secure software engineering (Certificate)

School of Nursing and Health Professions
Dr. Margaret M. Anderson, Chair, Nursing and Health Professions
Programs in:
nurse practitioner advancement (Certificate)
nursing (MSN, Post-Master's Certificate)

Salmon P. Chase College of Law
Dennis R. Honabach, Dean
Program in:
law (JD)

■ SPALDING UNIVERSITY
Louisville, KY 40203-2188
http://www.spalding.edu/

Independent-religious, coed, comprehensive institution. CGS member. *Computer facilities:* 80 computers available on campus for general student use. A campuswide network can be accessed. Internet access is available. *Library facilities:* Spalding Library. *General application contact:* Admissions Office, 502-585-7111.

Find University Details at www.petersons.com/gradchannel.

Graduate Studies

College of Business and Communication
Program in:
business communication (MS)

College of Education
Programs in:
education (MA, MAT, Ed D)
elementary school education (MAT)
general education (MA)
high school education (MAT)
leadership education (Ed D)
middle school education (MAT)
school administration (MA)
special education (learning and behavioral disorders) (MAT)

College of Health and Natural Sciences
Programs in:
adult nurse practitioner (MSN)
family nurse practitioner (MSN)
health and natural sciences (MS, MSN)
leadership in nursing and healthcare (MSN)
occupational therapy (advanced-level) (MS)
occupational therapy (entry-level) (MS)
pediatric nurse practitioner (MSN)

College of Social Sciences and Humanities
Programs in:
clinical psychology (MA, Psy D)
social sciences and humanities (MA, MFA, MSW, Psy D)
social work (MSW)
writing (MFA)

■ SULLIVAN UNIVERSITY
Louisville, KY 40205
http://www.sullivan.edu/

Proprietary, coed, comprehensive institution. *Computer facilities:* 125 computers available on campus for general student use. A campuswide network can be accessed from student residence rooms and from off campus. Internet access is available. *Library facilities:* McWhorter Library. *General application contact:* Admissions Officer, 502-456-6505.

School of Business
Programs in:
business (EMBA, MBA)
dispute resolution (MSDR)
management of information technology (MSMIT)

■ THOMAS MORE COLLEGE
Crestview Hills, KY 41017-3495
http://www.thomasmore.edu/

Independent-religious, coed, comprehensive institution. *Enrollment:* 1,400 graduate, professional, and undergraduate students; 75

Thomas More College (continued)
full-time matriculated graduate/professional students (36 women). *Graduate faculty:* 11 full-time (3 women). *Computer facilities:* 100 computers available on campus for general student use. A campuswide network can be accessed from student residence rooms and from off campus. Internet access is available. *Library facilities:* Thomas More Library. *Graduate expenses:* Tuition: full-time $10,330. One-time fee: $125 full-time. *General application contact:* Nathan Hartman, Director of Lifelong Learning, 859-344-3602.

Program in Business Administration
Nathan Hartman, Director of Lifelong Learning
Program in:
business administration (MBA)

■ UNION COLLEGE
Barbourville, KY 40906-1499
http://www.unionky.edu/

Independent-religious, coed, comprehensive institution. *Computer facilities:* 70 computers available on campus for general student use. A campuswide network can be accessed from student residence rooms and from off campus. Internet access and online class registration are available. *Library facilities:* Weeks-Townsend Memorial Library. *General application contact:* Dean of Graduate Academic Affairs, 606-546-1210.

Graduate Programs
Programs in:
elementary education (MA)
elementary principalship (Certificate)
health (MA Ed)
health and physical education (MA)
middle grades (MA)
middle grades principalship (Certificate)
music education (MA)
principalship (MA)
reading specialist (MA)
secondary education (MA)
secondary school principalship (Certificate)
special education (MA)
supervisor of instruction (Certificate)

■ UNIVERSITY OF KENTUCKY
Lexington, KY 40506-0032
http://www.uky.edu/

State-supported, coed, university. CGS member. *Enrollment:* 26,382 graduate, professional, and undergraduate students; 3,827 full-time matriculated graduate/professional students (2,089 women), 1,444 part-time matriculated graduate/professional students (938 women). *Graduate faculty:* 1,881 full-time (510 women), 128 part-time/adjunct (22 women). *Computer facilities:* 1,400 computers available on campus for general student use. A campuswide network can be accessed from student residence rooms and from off campus. Internet access and online class registration, various software packages are available. *Library facilities:* William T. Young Library plus 15 others. *Graduate expenses:* Tuition, state resident: full-time $7,670; part-time $401 per credit hour. Tuition, nonresident: full-time $16,158; part-time $873 per credit hour. *General application contact:* Dr. Brian Jackson, Senior Associate Dean, 859-257-8176.

College of Dentistry
Program in:
dentistry (DMD, MS)

College of Law
Program in:
law (JD)

College of Medicine
Dr. Carol L. Elam, Assistant Dean for Admissions
Program in:
medicine (MD)

College of Pharmacy
Dr. Kenneth B. Roberts, Dean
Programs in:
pharmaceutical sciences (MS, PhD)
pharmacy (Pharm D, MS, PhD)

Graduate School
Dr. Jeannine Blackwell, Dean
Programs in:
biomedical engineering (MSBE, PBME, PhD)
health administration (MHA)
nutritional sciences (MSNS, PhD)
public administration (MPA, MPP, PhD)

College of Agriculture
Dr. M. Scott Smith, Dean
Programs in:
agricultural economics (MS, PhD)
agriculture (MS, MSFAM, MSFOR, PhD)
animal sciences (MS, PhD)
biosystems and agricultural engineering (MS, PhD)
career, technology and leadership education (MS)
crop science (MS, PhD)
entomology (MS, PhD)
family studies, human development, and resource management (MSFAM, PhD)
forestry (MSFOR)
hospitality and dietetic administration (MS)
plant and soil science (MS)
plant pathology (MS, PhD)
plant physiology (PhD)
soil science (PhD)
veterinary science (MS, PhD)

College of Arts and Sciences
Dr. Steven Hoch, Dean
Programs in:
anthropology (MA, PhD)
applied mathematics (MS)
arts and sciences (MA, MS, PhD)
biology (MS, PhD)
chemistry (MS, PhD)
classics (MA)
clinical psychology (MA)
English (MA, PhD)
experimental psychology (MA)
French (MA)
geography (MA, PhD)
geology (MS, PhD)
German (MA)
Hispanic studies (MA, PhD)
history (MA, PhD)
mathematics (MA, MS, PhD)
philosophy (MA, PhD)
physics (MS, PhD)
political science (MA, PhD)
sociology (MA, PhD)
statistics (MS, PhD)
teaching world languages (MA)

College of Communications and Information Studies
Dr. David Johnson, Dean
Programs in:
communication (MA, PhD)
communications and information studies (MA, MSLS, PhD)
library science (MA, MSLS)

College of Design
Dr. David Mohney, Dean
Programs in:
architecture (M Arch)
design (M Arch, MAIDM, MHP, MSIDM)
historic preservation (MHP)
interior design, merchandising, and textiles (MAIDM, MSIDM)

College of Education
Dr. James Cibulka, Dean
Programs in:
administration and supervision (Ed S)
counseling psychology (MS Ed, PhD, Ed S)
curriculum and instruction (MA Ed, Ed D)
early childhood special education (MS Ed)
education (M Ed, MA Ed, MRC, MS, MS Ed, Ed D, PhD, Ed S)
educational and counseling psychology (MS Ed)
educational policy studies and evaluation (Ed D)
educational psychology (Ed D, PhD, Ed S)
exercise science (PhD)
higher education (MS Ed, PhD)
instruction and administration (Ed D)
instruction system design (MS Ed)
kinesiology (MS, Ed D)
middle school education (MS Ed)
rehabilitation counseling (MRC)
school administration (M Ed)

school psychometrist and school psychology (MA Ed)
special education (MS Ed)
special education leadership personnel preparation (Ed D)

College of Engineering
Dr. Thomas W. Lester, Dean
Programs in:
chemical engineering (MS, PhD)
civil engineering (MCE, MSCE, PhD)
computer science (MS, PhD)
electrical engineering (MSEE, PhD)
engineering (M Eng, MCE, MME, MS, MS Ch E, MS Min, MSCE, MSEE, MSEM, MSMAE, MSME, MSMSE, PhD)
manufacturing systems engineering (MSMSE)
materials science and engineering (MSMAE, PhD)
mechanical engineering (MSME, PhD)
mining engineering (MME, MS Min, PhD)

College of Fine Arts
Dr. Robert Shay, Dean
Programs in:
art education (MA)
art history (MA)
art studio (MFA)
fine arts (MA, MFA, MM, DMA, PhD)
music (PhD)
music composition (MM)
music education (MM)
music performance (MM)
music theory (MA)
musical arts (DMA)
musicology (MA)
theatre (MA)

College of Health Sciences
Dr. Lori Gonzalez, Dean
Programs in:
clinical sciences (MS, DS)
communication disorders (MSCD)
health physics (MSHP)
health sciences (MS, MSCD, MSHP, MSPAS, MSPT, MSRMP, DS, PhD)
physical therapy (MSPT)
physician assistant studies (MSPAS)
radiological medical physics (MSRMP)
rehabilitation sciences (PhD)

College of Public Health
Dr. Stephen Wyatt, Dean
Programs in:
gerontology (PhD)
public health (MPH, PhD)

College of Social Work
Dr. Kay Hoffman, Dean
Program in:
social work (MSW, PhD)

Gatton College of Business and Economics
Dr. Devanathan Sudharshan, Dean
Programs in:
accounting (MSACC)
business administration (MBA, PhD)
business and economics (MBA, MS, MSACC, PhD)
economics (MS, PhD)

Graduate School Programs from the College of Medicine
Dr. Jay Perman, Dean of College of Medicine
Programs in:
anatomy (PhD)
biochemistry (PhD)
medical science (MS)
medicine (MS, PhD)
microbiology (PhD)
pharmacology (PhD)
physiology (MS, PhD)
toxicology (MS, PhD)

Graduate School Programs in the College of Nursing
Dr. Jane Marie Kirschling, Dean
Program in:
nursing (MSN, PhD)

Patterson School of Diplomacy and International Commerce
Dr. Evan Hillebrand, Director of Graduate Studies
Program in:
diplomacy and international commerce (MA)

■ UNIVERSITY OF LOUISVILLE
Louisville, KY 40292-0001
http://www.louisville.edu/

State-supported, coed, university. CGS member. *Enrollment:* 20,804 graduate, professional, and undergraduate students; 3,161 full-time matriculated graduate/professional students (1,668 women), 1,973 part-time matriculated graduate/professional students (1,149 women). *Graduate faculty:* 1,462 full-time (512 women), 572 part-time/adjunct (252 women). *Computer facilities:* Computer purchase and lease plans are available. 265 computers available on campus for general student use. A campuswide network can be accessed from student residence rooms and from off campus. Internet access and online class registration are available. *Library facilities:* William F. Ekstrom Library plus 5 others. *General application contact:* Libby Leggett, Information Contact, 502-852-3108.

Find University Details at www.petersons.com/gradchannel.

Graduate School
Dr. Ronald M. Atlas, Dean

College of Arts and Sciences
Dr. J. Blaine Hudson, Dean
Programs in:
analytical chemistry (MS, PhD)
applied and industrial mathematics (PhD)
art history (MA, PhD)
arts and sciences (MA, MFA, MPA, MS, MUP, PhD, Certificate)
biochemistry (MS, PhD)
biology (MS)
chemical physics (PhD)
clinical psychology (PhD)
creative art (MA)
English (MA)
English literature (MA)
English rhetoric and composition (PhD)
environmental biology (PhD)
experimental psychology (PhD)
French (MA)
history (MA)
humanities (MA, PhD)
inorganic chemistry (MS, PhD)
justice administration (MS)
labor and public management (MPA)
mathematics (MA)
organic chemistry (MS, PhD)
Pan-African studies (MA)
performance (MFA)
philosophy (MA)
physical chemistry (MS, PhD)
physics (MS)
political science (MA)
production (MFA)
psychology (MA)
public administration (MPA)
public policy and administration (MPA)
sociology (MA)
Spanish (MA)
systems science (MA)
theatre arts (MA)
urban and public affairs (PhD)
urban and regional development (MPA)
urban planning (MUP)
women's and gender studies (MA, Certificate)

College of Business
Dr. Charles Moyer, Dean
Programs in:
accountancy (MAC)
business (MA, MAC, MBA, PhD)
business administration (MBA)
entrepreneurship (PhD)

College of Education and Human Development
Dr. Robert Felner, Dean
Programs in:
art education (MAT)
college student personnel services (M Ed)
counseling and personnel services (M Ed, PhD)
counseling psychology (M Ed, PhD)
curriculum and instruction (Ed D)
early elementary education (M Ed, MAT)
education and human development (M Ed, MA, MAT, MS, Ed D, PhD, Ed S)
educational leadership and organizational development (PhD)
exercise physiology (MS)
expressive therapies (M Ed)

University of Louisville (continued)
- foreign language education (MAT)
- health education (M Ed)
- higher education (MA, Ed S)
- human resource education (M Ed)
- instructional technology (M Ed)
- interdisciplinary early childhood education (M Ed)
- mental health counseling (PhD)
- middle school education (M Ed, MAT)
- music education (MAT)
- occupational training and development (M Ed)
- p-12 educational administration (M Ed, PhD, Ed S)
- physical education (teacher preparation) (M Ed, MAT)
- reading education (M Ed)
- school counseling and guidance (M Ed, PhD)
- secondary education (M Ed, MAT)
- special education (M Ed, PhD)
- sport administration (MS)

Interdisciplinary Studies
Program in:
- interdisciplinary studies (MA, MS)

J.B. Speed School of Engineering
Dr. Mickey R. Wilhelm, Dean
Programs in:
- chemical engineering (M Eng, MS, PhD)
- civil and environmental engineering (M Eng, MS, PhD)
- computer engineering and computer science (M Eng, MS)
- computer science (MS)
- computer science and engineering (PhD)
- electrical and computer engineering (M Eng, MS, PhD)
- engineering (M Eng, MS, PhD)
- engineering management (M Eng)
- industrial engineering (M Eng, MS, PhD)
- mechanical engineering (M Eng, MS)

Raymond A. Kent School of Social Work
Dr. Terry Singer, Dean
Programs in:
- marriage and family therapy (PMC)
- social work (MSSW, PhD)

School of Music
Dr. Christopher Doane, Dean
Programs in:
- music education (MAT, MME)
- music history (MM, PhD)
- music history and literature (MM)
- music literature (PhD)
- music performance (MM)
- music theory and composition (MM)
- musicology (PhD)
- performance (MM)
- theory and composition (MM)

School of Nursing
Dr. Cynthia A. McCurren, Interim Dean
Program in:
- nursing (MSN, PhD)

School of Public Health
Dr. Richard D. Clover, Dean
Programs in:
- bioinformatics and biostatistics (MS, PhD)
- clinical investigation (Certificate)
- clinical investigation sciences (MS, PhD)
- public health (MPH)

Louis D. Brandeis School of Law
James Chen, Dean
Program in:
- law (JD)

School of Dentistry
Dr. Wood E. Currens, Acting Dean
Programs in:
- dentistry (DMD, MS)
- oral biology (MS)

School of Medicine
Dr. Edward C. Halperin, Dean
Programs in:
- anatomical sciences and neurobiology (MS, PhD)
- audiology (Au D)
- biochemistry and molecular biology (MS, PhD)
- communicative disorders (MS, Au D)
- medicine (MD, MS, Au D, PhD)
- microbiology and immunology (MS, PhD)
- ophthalmology and visual sciences (PhD)
- pharmacology and toxicology (MS, PhD)
- physiology and biophysics (MS, PhD)

■ WESTERN KENTUCKY UNIVERSITY
Bowling Green, KY 42101
http://www.wku.edu/

State-supported, coed, comprehensive institution. CGS member. *Enrollment:* 18,660 graduate, professional, and undergraduate students; 766 full-time matriculated graduate/professional students (467 women), 1,299 part-time matriculated graduate/professional students (941 women). *Graduate faculty:* 230 full-time (100 women), 35 part-time/adjunct (15 women). *Computer facilities:* 1,300 computers available on campus for general student use. A campuswide network can be accessed from student residence rooms and from off campus. Internet access and online class registration, online grade reports are available. *Library facilities:* Helm-Cravens Library plus 3 others. *Graduate expenses:* Tuition, state resident: full-time $6,520; part-time $226 per hour. Tuition, nonresident: full-time $7,140; part-time $357 per hour. International tuition: $15,820 full-time. *General application contact:* Dean, Graduate Studies, 270-745-2446.

Graduate Studies
Dr. Richard G. Bowker, Interim Dean, Graduate Studies

College of Education and Behavioral Sciences
Dr. Sam Evans, Dean
Programs in:
- business and marketing education (MA Ed, MAE)
- counseling (MA Ed)
- counselor education (Ed S)
- education and behavioral science (MA Ed)
- education and behavioral sciences (MA, MAE, MS, Ed S)
- educational administration (MAE)
- elementary education (MA Ed, MAE, Ed S)
- exceptional child education (MAE)
- interdisciplinary early child education (MAE)
- library media education (MS)
- literacy (MAE)
- middle grades education (MAE)
- middle years education (MA Ed)
- psychology (MA)
- school administration (Ed S)
- school psychology (Ed S)
- secondary education (MA Ed, MAE, Ed S)
- student affairs (MA Ed)

College of Health and Human Services
Dr. John A Bonaguro, Dean
Programs in:
- communication disorders (MS)
- health and human services (MHA, MPH, MS, MSN, MSW)
- healthcare administration (MHA)
- nursing (MSN)
- physical education (MS)
- public health (MPH)
- recreation (MS)
- social work (MSW)

Gordon Ford College of Business
Dr. William Tallon, Dean
Programs in:
- business (MBA)
- business administration (MBA)

Ogden College of Science and Engineering
Dr. Blaine R. Ferrell, Dean
Programs in:
- agriculture (MA Ed, MS)
- biology (MA Ed, MS)
- chemistry (MA Ed, MS)
- computer science (MS)
- geography and geology (MAE, MS)
- mathematics (MA Ed, MS)
- science and engineering (MA Ed, MAE, MS)

Potter College of Arts and Letters
Dr. David D Lee, Dean
Programs in:
- art education (MA Ed)
- arts and letter (MA, MA Ed, MPA)
- communication (MA)
- education (MA)

English (MA Ed)
folk studies (MA)
history (MA, MA Ed)
literature (MA)
music (MA Ed)
political science (MPA)
sociology (MA)
teaching English as a second language (MA)
writing (MA)

Louisiana

■ GRAMBLING STATE UNIVERSITY
Grambling, LA 71245
http://www.gram.edu/

State-supported, coed, university. CGS member. *Enrollment:* 5,065 graduate, professional, and undergraduate students; 314 full-time matriculated graduate/professional students (228 women), 148 part-time matriculated graduate/professional students (111 women). *Graduate faculty:* 45 full-time (24 women), 14 part-time/adjunct (5 women). *Computer facilities:* Computer purchase and lease plans are available. 250 computers available on campus for general student use. A campuswide network can be accessed from student residence rooms and from off campus. Internet access is available. *Library facilities:* A. C. Lewis Memorial Library. *Graduate expenses:* Tuition, state resident: full-time $2,232; part-time $124 per credit hour. Tuition, nonresident: full-time $7,582; part-time $124 per credit hour. Required fees: $1,127. *General application contact:* Jacklen Greer-Hill, Administrative Assistant, School of Graduate Studies and Research, 318-274-2158.

School of Graduate Studies and Research
Dr. Janet Guyden, Dean

College of Arts and Sciences
Dr. Connie Walton, Dean
Programs in:
arts and sciences (MAT, MPA)
public administration (MPA)
social sciences (MAT)

College of Education
Dr. Sean Warner, Dean
Programs in:
curriculum and instruction (Ed D)
developmental education (Ed D)
education (M Ed, MS, Ed D)
educational leadership (M Ed, Ed D)
elementary/early childhood education (MS)
special education (M Ed)
sports administration (MS)

College of Professional Studies
Dr. Marianne Fisher-Giorlando, Acting Dean
Programs in:
criminal justice (MS)
family nurse practitioner (MSN, PMC)
mass communication (MA)
nurse educator (MSN)
social work (MSW)

■ LOUISIANA STATE UNIVERSITY AND AGRICULTURAL AND MECHANICAL COLLEGE
Baton Rouge, LA 70803
http://www.lsu.edu/

State-supported, coed, university. CGS member. *Enrollment:* 29,925 graduate, professional, and undergraduate students; 3,326 full-time matriculated graduate/professional students (1,738 women), 1,129 part-time matriculated graduate/professional students (650 women). *Graduate faculty:* 1,214 full-time (284 women), 22 part-time/adjunct (8 women). *Computer facilities:* 7,000 computers available on campus for general student use. A campuswide network can be accessed from student residence rooms and from off campus. Internet access and online class registration, e-mail, wireless, grades, payroll, storage, e-portfolio are available. *Library facilities:* Troy H. Middleton Library plus 7 others. *General application contact:* Reneé Renegar, Office of Graduate Admissions, 225-578-1641.

Graduate School
Dr. Stacia Haynie, Associate Dean

College of Agriculture
Dr. Kenneth Koonce, Dean
Programs in:
agricultural economics and agribusiness (MS, PhD)
agriculture (M App St, MS, MSBAE, PhD)
agronomy (MS, PhD)
animal sciences (MS, PhD)
applied statistics (M App St)
biological and agricultural engineering (MSBAE)
comprehensive vocational education (MS, PhD)
engineering science (MS, PhD)
entomology (MS, PhD)
extension and international education (MS, PhD)
fisheries (MS)
food science (MS, PhD)
forestry (MS, PhD)
horticulture (MS, PhD)
human ecology (MS, PhD)
industrial education (MS)
plant health (MS, PhD)
vocational agriculture education (MS, PhD)
vocational business education (MS)
vocational home economics education (MS)
wildlife (MS)
wildlife and fisheries science (PhD)

College of Art and Design
David Cronrath, Dean
Programs in:
architecture (M Arch)
art and design (M Arch, MA, MFA, MLA)
art history (MA)
ceramics (MFA)
graphic design (MFA)
landscape architecture (MLA)
painting and drawing (MFA)
photography (MFA)
printmaking (MFA)
sculpture (MFA)
studio art (MFA)

College of Arts and Sciences
Dr. Guillermo Ferreya, Dean
Programs in:
anthropology (MA)
arts and sciences (MA, MALA, MFA, MS, PhD)
biological psychology (MA, PhD)
clinical psychology (MA, PhD)
cognitive psychology (MA, PhD)
communication sciences and disorders (MA, PhD)
communication studies (MA, PhD)
comparative literature (MA, PhD)
creative writing (MFA)
developmental psychology (MA, PhD)
English (MA, PhD)
French literature and linguistics (MA, PhD)
geography (MA, MS, PhD)
history (MA, PhD)
industrial/organizational psychology (MA, PhD)
liberal arts (MALA)
linguistics (MA, PhD)
mathematics (MS, PhD)
philosophy (MA)
political science (MA, PhD)
school psychology (MA, PhD)
sociology (MA, PhD)
Spanish (MA)

College of Basic Sciences
Dr. Kevin Carman, Dean
Programs in:
astronomy (PhD)
astrophysics (PhD)
basic sciences (MNS, MS, MSSS, PhD)
biochemistry (MS, PhD)
biological science (MS, PhD)
chemistry (MS, PhD)
computer science (MSSS, PhD)
geology and geophysics (MS, PhD)
natural sciences (MNS)
physics (MS, PhD)
systems science (MSSS)

College of Education
Dr. Jayne Fleener, Dean
Programs in:
counseling (M Ed, MA, Ed S)
education (M Ed, MA, MS, PhD, Ed S)
educational administration (M Ed, MA, PhD, Ed S)

Louisiana State University and Agricultural and Mechanical College (continued)

educational technology (MA)
elementary education (M Ed)
higher education (PhD)
kinesiology (MS, PhD)
research methodology (PhD)
secondary education (M Ed)

College of Engineering
Dr. Zaki Bassiouni, Dean
Programs in:
chemical engineering (MS Ch E, PhD)
electrical and computer engineering (MSEE, PhD)
engineering (MS Ch E, MS Pet E, MSCE, MSEE, MSES, MSIE, MSME, PhD)
engineering science (MSES, PhD)
environmental engineering (MSCE, PhD)
geotechnical engineering (MSCE, PhD)
industrial engineering (MSIE)
mechanical engineering (MSME, PhD)
petroleum engineering (MS Pet E, PhD)
structural engineering and mechanics (MSCE, PhD)
transportation engineering (MSCE, PhD)
water resources (MSCE, PhD)

College of Music and Dramatic Arts
Dr. Sara Lyn Baird, Interim Dean
Programs in:
acting (MFA)
directing (MFA)
music (MM, DMA, PhD)
music and dramatic arts (MFA, MM, DMA, PhD)
music education (PhD)
theatre (PhD)
theatre design/technology (MFA)

E. J. Ourso College of Business
Dr. William R. Lane, Interim Dean
Programs in:
accounting (MS, PhD)
business (EMBA, MBA, MPA, MS, PMBA, PhD)
business administration (PhD)
economics (MS, PhD)
finance (MS)
information systems and decision sciences (MS, PhD)
public administration (MPA)

Manship School of Mass Communication
Dr. John Maxwell Hamilton, Dean
Program in:
mass communication (MMC, PhD)

School of Library and Information Science
Dr. Beth M. Paskoff, Dean
Program in:
library and information science (MLIS, CAS)

School of Social Work
Dr. Pamela Ann Monroe, Dean
Program in:
social work (MSW, PhD)

School of the Coast and Environment
Dr. Ed Laws, Dean
Programs in:
environmental planning and management (MS)
environmental toxicology (MS)
oceanography and coastal sciences (MS, PhD)
the coast and environment (MS, PhD)

Paul M. Hebert Law Center
John J. Costonis, Chancellor
Program in:
law (JD, LL M, MCL)

School of Veterinary Medicine
Dr. Peter Haynes, Dean
Programs in:
comparative biomedical sciences (MS, PhD)
pathobiological sciences (MS, PhD)
veterinary clinical sciences (MS, PhD)
veterinary medicine (DVM, MS, PhD)

■ LOUISIANA STATE UNIVERSITY IN SHREVEPORT
Shreveport, LA 71115-2399
http://www.lsus.edu/

State-supported, coed, comprehensive institution. *Enrollment:* 4,023 graduate, professional, and undergraduate students; 102 full-time matriculated graduate/professional students (75 women), 301 part-time matriculated graduate/professional students (220 women). *Graduate faculty:* 91 full-time (31 women), 9 part-time/adjunct (7 women). *Computer facilities:* Computer purchase and lease plans are available. A campuswide network can be accessed from off campus. Internet access is available. *Library facilities:* Noel Memorial Library. *General application contact:* Dr. Patricia Doerr, Dean of Graduate Studies, 318-797-5247.

College of Business Administration
Program in:
healthcare (MBA)

College of Education and Human Development
Dr. David B. Gustavson, Chair
Programs in:
counseling psychology (MS)
education (M Ed)
education and human development (M Ed, MS, SSP)
school psychology (SSP)

College of Liberal Arts
Dr. Larry Anderson, Dean
Programs in:
health administration (MHA)
human services administration (MS)
liberal arts (MA, MHA, MS)

College of Sciences
Dr. John Sigle, Chair, Computer Science Department
Program in:
systems technology (MSST)

■ LOUISIANA TECH UNIVERSITY
Ruston, LA 71272
http://www.latech.edu/

State-supported, coed, university. *Computer facilities:* 1,800 computers available on campus for general student use. A campuswide network can be accessed from student residence rooms and from off campus. *Library facilities:* Prescott Memorial Library. *General application contact:* Dean of the Graduate School, 318-257-2924.

Graduate School

College of Administration and Business
Programs in:
administration and business (MBA, MPA, DBA)
business administration (MBA, DBA)
business economics (MBA, DBA)
finance (MBA, DBA)
management (MBA, DBA)
marketing (MBA, DBA)
professional accountancy (MBA, MPA, DBA)

College of Applied and Natural Sciences
Programs in:
applied and natural sciences (MS)
biological sciences (MS)
dietetics (MS)
human ecology (MS)

College of Education
Programs in:
counseling (MA)
counseling psychology (PhD)
curriculum and instruction (MS, Ed D)
education (M Ed, MA, MS, Ed D, PhD)
educational leadership (Ed D)
health and exercise science (MS)
industrial/organizational psychology (MA)
secondary education (M Ed)
special education (MA)

College of Engineering and Science
Programs in:
applied computational analysis and modeling (PhD)
biomedical engineering (MS, PhD)
chemical engineering (MS, PhD)
chemistry (MS)
civil engineering (MS, PhD)

computer science (MS)
electrical engineering (MS, PhD)
engineering (PhD)
engineering and science (MS, PhD)
industrial engineering (MS, PhD)
manufacturing systems engineering (MS)
mathematics and statistics (MS)
mechanical engineering (MS, PhD)
operations research (MS)
physics (MS)

College of Liberal Arts
Programs in:
art and graphic design (MFA)
English (MA)
history (MA)
interior design (MFA)
liberal arts (MA, MFA)
photography (MFA)
speech (MA)
speech pathology and audiology (MA)
studio art (MFA)

■ LOYOLA UNIVERSITY NEW ORLEANS
New Orleans, LA 70118-6195
http://www.loyno.edu/

Independent-religious, coed, comprehensive institution. *Computer facilities:* Computer purchase and lease plans are available. 458 computers available on campus for general student use. A campuswide network can be accessed from student residence rooms and from off campus. Internet access and online class registration are available. *Library facilities:* University Library plus 1 other. *General application contact:* Dean of Admissions and Enrollment Management, 504-865-3240.

City College
Programs in:
criminal justice (MCJ)
family nurse practitioner (MSN)
health care systems management (MSN)

Loyola Institute for Ministry
Programs in:
pastoral studies (MPS)
religious education (MRE)
theology and ministry (Certificate)

College of Arts and Sciences
Programs in:
arts and sciences (MA, MS)
counseling (MS)
elementary education (MS)
mass communication (MA)
reading education (MS)
religious studies (MA)
secondary education (MS)

College of Music
Program in:
music (MM, MME, MMT)

Joseph A. Butt, S.J., College of Business Administration
Program in:
business administration (MBA)

School of Law
Program in:
law (JD)

■ MCNEESE STATE UNIVERSITY
Lake Charles, LA 70609
http://www.mcneese.edu/

State-supported, coed, comprehensive institution. *Enrollment:* 8,343 graduate, professional, and undergraduate students; 323 full-time matriculated graduate/professional students (160 women), 463 part-time matriculated graduate/professional students (355 women). *Graduate faculty:* 97 full-time (32 women), 5 part-time/adjunct (4 women). *Computer facilities:* 700 computers available on campus for general student use. A campuswide network can be accessed from student residence rooms and from off campus. Internet access and online class registration are available. *Library facilities:* Frazer Memorial Library plus 2 others. *Graduate expenses:* Full-time $2,226; part-time $193 per hour. Required fees: $919; $106 per hour. *General application contact:* Tammie Pettis, Director of Admissions, 337-475-5282.

Graduate School
Dr. George F. Mead, Interim Dean

College of Business
Dr. Mitchell Adrian, Dean
Programs in:
business (MBA)
business administration (MBA)

College of Education
Dr. Wayne R Fetter, Dean
Programs in:
counseling psychology (MA)
curriculum and instruction (M Ed)
early childhood education (M Ed)
education (M Ed, MA, MAT, MS, Ed S)
educational leadership (M Ed, Ed S)
educational technology leadership (M Ed)
elementary education (M Ed, MAT)
exercise physiology (MS)
general psychology (MA)
health promotion (MS)
instructional technology (MS)
school counseling (M Ed)
secondary education (M Ed, MAT)
special education (mild/moderate) (MAT)
teaching (MAT)

College of Engineering and Technology
Dr. Nikos Kiritsis, Dean
Programs in:
chemical engineering (M Eng)
civil engineering (M Eng)
electrical engineering (M Eng)
engineering management (M Eng)
mechanical engineering (M Eng)

College of Liberal Arts
Dr. Ray Miles, Dean
Programs in:
creative writing (MFA)
English (MA)
liberal arts (MA, MFA, MM Ed)
music education (MM Ed)

College of Nursing
Dr. Peggy L. Wolfe, Dean
Program in:
nursing (MSN)

College of Science
Dr. George F. Mead, Dean
Programs in:
agricultural sciences (MS)
chemistry (MS)
chemistry environmental science education (MS)
environmental and chemical sciences (MS)
environmental sciences (MS)
mathematical science (MS)
science (MS)

■ NICHOLLS STATE UNIVERSITY
Thibodaux, LA 70310
http://www.nicholls.edu

State-supported, coed, comprehensive institution. *Enrollment:* 6,805 graduate, professional, and undergraduate students; 109 full-time matriculated graduate/professional students (67 women), 275 part-time matriculated graduate/professional students (211 women). *Graduate faculty:* 66 full-time (24 women), 25 part-time/adjunct (10 women). *Computer facilities:* 250 computers available on campus for general student use. A campuswide network can be accessed from student residence rooms and from off campus. Internet access and online class registration are available. *Library facilities:* Allen J. Ellender Memorial Library plus 3 others. *Graduate expenses:* Tuition, state resident: part-time $450 per hour. Tuition, nonresident: part-time $450 per hour. *General application contact:* Dr. Betty A. Kleen, Director, University Graduate Studies, 985-448-4191.

Graduate Studies
Dr. Betty A. Kleen, Director, University Graduate Studies

College of Arts and Sciences
Dr. Badiollah R. Asrabadi, Dean
Programs in:
arts and sciences (MS)
community/technical college mathematics (MS)
marine and environmental biology (MS)

College of Business Administration
Dr. Shawn Mauldin, Dean
Program in:
business administration (MBA)

College of Education
Dr. Deborah Bordelon, Dean

Nicholls State University (continued)
Programs in:
- administration and supervision (M Ed)
- counselor education (M Ed)
- curriculum and instruction (M Ed)
- education (M Ed, MA, SSP)
- psychological counseling (MA)
- school psychology (SSP)

■ NORTHWESTERN STATE UNIVERSITY OF LOUISIANA
Natchitoches, LA 71497
http://www.nsula.edu/

State-supported, coed, comprehensive institution. CGS member. *Enrollment:* 9,431 graduate, professional, and undergraduate students; 280 full-time matriculated graduate/professional students (214 women), 698 part-time matriculated graduate/professional students (568 women). *Graduate faculty:* 74 full-time (41 women), 29 part-time/adjunct (22 women). *Computer facilities:* Computer purchase and lease plans are available. 1,132 computers available on campus for general student use. A campuswide network can be accessed from student residence rooms and from off campus. Internet access and online class registration are available. *Library facilities:* Eugene P. Watson Memorial Library. *General application contact:* Dr. Steven G. Horton, Associate Provost/Dean, Graduate Studies, Research, and Information Systems, 318-357-5851.

Graduate Studies and Research
Dr. Steven G. Horton, Associate Provost/Dean, Graduate Studies, Research, and Information Systems
Programs in:
- clinical psychology (MS)
- English (MA)
- health and human performance (MS)
- heritage resources (MA)

College of Education
Dr. Vickie Gentry, Chair
Programs in:
- adult and continuing education (M Ed)
- business and distributive education (M Ed)
- counseling (M Ed, Ed S)
- counseling and guidance (M Ed, Ed S)
- curriculum and instruction (M Ed)
- early childhood education (M Ed)
- early childhood education and teaching (M Ed)
- education (M Ed)
- education leadership (M Ed)
- educational leadership (Ed S)
- educational technology (M Ed, Ed S)
- educational technology leadership (M Ed)
- elementary education (MAT)
- elementary teaching (M Ed, Ed S)
- English education (M Ed)
- home economics education (M Ed)
- mathematics education (M Ed)
- middle school education (MAT)
- reading (M Ed, Ed S)
- science education (M Ed)
- secondary education (MAT)
- secondary teaching (M Ed, Ed S)
- social sciences education (M Ed)
- special education (M Ed, Ed S)
- student personnel services (MA)
- teacher education and professional development, specific levels and methods (M Ed)

College of Nursing
Dr. Norann Planchock, Director
Program in:
- nursing (MSN)

School of Creative and Performing Arts
William E. Brent, Chairman
Programs in:
- art (MA)
- fine and graphic arts (MA)
- music (MM)

■ SOUTHEASTERN LOUISIANA UNIVERSITY
Hammond, LA 70402
http://www.selu.edu/

State-supported, coed, comprehensive institution. *Enrollment:* 15,118 graduate, professional, and undergraduate students; 369 full-time matriculated graduate/professional students (241 women), 742 part-time matriculated graduate/professional students (587 women). *Graduate faculty:* 182 full-time (80 women), 3 part-time/adjunct (1 woman). *Computer facilities:* 837 computers available on campus for general student use. A campuswide network can be accessed from student residence rooms and from off campus. Internet access and online class registration, campus Webmail, student newspaper, transcripts, bookstore are available. *Library facilities:* Sims Memorial Library. *Graduate expenses:* Tuition, state resident: full-time $2,216; part-time $123 per credit. Tuition, nonresident: full-time $6,212; part-time $345 per credit. Required fees: $986; $55 per credit. Part-time tuition and fees vary according to course load. *General application contact:* Sandra Meyers, Graduate Admissions Analyst, 985-549-2066.

College of Arts, Humanities and Social Sciences
Dr. Tammy Bourg, Dean
Programs in:
- applied sociology (MS)
- arts, humanities and social sciences (M Mus, MA, MS)
- English (MA)
- history (MA)
- music (M Mus)
- organizational communication (MA)
- psychology (MA)

College of Business
Dr. Randy Settoon, Dean
Program in:
- business administration (MBA)

College of Education and Human Development
Dr. Diane Allen, Dean
Programs in:
- counselor education (M Ed)
- curriculum and instruction (M Ed)
- education and human development (M Ed, MAT, Ed D)
- educational leadership (M Ed, Ed D)
- elementary education (MAT)
- secondary education (MAT)
- special education (M Ed, MAT)

College of Nursing and Health Sciences
Dr. Donnie Booth, Dean
Programs in:
- communication sciences and disorders (MS)
- health and kinesiology (MA)
- nursing and health sciences (MA, MS, MSN)

School of Nursing
Dr. Barbara Moffett, Director
Program in:
- nursing (MSN)

College of Science and Technology
Dr. Daniel McCarthy, Dean
Programs in:
- biology (MS)
- integrated science and technology (MS)
- science and technology (MS)

■ SOUTHERN UNIVERSITY AND AGRICULTURAL AND MECHANICAL COLLEGE
Baton Rouge, LA 70813
http://www.subr.edu/

State-supported, coed, comprehensive institution. CGS member. *Computer facilities:* 1,500 computers available on campus for general student use. A campuswide network can be accessed from student residence rooms and from off campus. Internet access and online class registration are available. *Library facilities:* John B. Cade Library plus 2 others. *General application contact:* Director of Graduate Admissions and Recruitment, 225-771-5390.

Graduate School
Programs in:
- criminal justice (MS)
- public policy analysis (PhD)
- science/mathematics education (PhD)
- special education (M Ed, PhD)

College of Agricultural, Family and Consumer Sciences
Program in:
- urban forestry (MS)

College of Arts and Humanities
Programs in:
- arts and humanities (MA)
- mass communications (MA)
- social sciences (MA)

College of Business
Programs in:
- accountancy (MPA)
- business (MPA)

College of Education
Programs in:
- administration and supervision (M Ed)
- counselor education (MA)
- education (M Ed, MA, MS, PhD)
- elementary education (M Ed)
- media (M Ed)
- mental health counseling (MA)
- secondary education (M Ed)
- therapeutic recreation (MS)

College of Engineering
Program in:
- engineering (ME)

College of Sciences
Programs in:
- analytical chemistry (MS)
- biochemistry (MS)
- biology (MS)
- environmental sciences (MS)
- information systems (MS)
- inorganic chemistry (MS)
- mathematics (MS)
- micro/minicomputer architecture (MS)
- operating systems (MS)
- organic chemistry (MS)
- physical chemistry (MS)
- physics (MS)
- rehabilitation counseling (MS)
- sciences (MA, MS)

School of Public Policy and Urban Affairs
Programs in:
- public administration (MPA)
- public policy (PhD)
- public policy and urban affairs (MA, MPA, MS, PhD)
- social sciences (MA)

School of Nursing
Programs in:
- educator/administrator (PhD)
- family health nursing (MSN)
- family nurse practitioner (Post Master's Certificate)
- geriatric nurse practitioner/gerontology (PhD)

Southern University Law Center
Program in:
- law (JD)

■ SOUTHERN UNIVERSITY AT NEW ORLEANS
New Orleans, LA 70126-1009
http://www.suno.edu/

State-supported, coed, comprehensive institution. *Computer facilities:* 100 computers available on campus for general student use. *Library facilities:* Leonard Washington Library. *General application contact:* Director of Student Affairs, 504-286-5376.

School of Social Work
Program in:
- social work (MSW)

■ TULANE UNIVERSITY
New Orleans, LA 70118-5669
http://www.tulane.edu/

Independent, coed, university. CGS member. *Enrollment:* 10,606 graduate, professional, and undergraduate students; 7,110 full-time matriculated graduate/professional students (3,543 women), 1,172 part-time matriculated graduate/professional students (510 women). *Graduate faculty:* 1,428. *Computer facilities:* Computer purchase and lease plans are available. 592 computers available on campus for general student use. A campuswide network can be accessed from student residence rooms and from off campus. Internet access and online class registration, wireless access to the internet are available. *Library facilities:* Howard Tilton Memorial Library plus 8 others. *General application contact:* Dr. Michael Herman, Dean, 504-865-5100.

A. B. Freeman School of Business
Angelo S. DeNisi, Dean
Program in:
- business (EMBA, M Acct, M Fin, MBA, PMBA, PhD)

Program in Liberal Arts
Dr. Ronna Burger, Director
Program in:
- liberal arts (MLA)

School of Architecture
Reed Kroloff, Dean
Program in:
- architecture (M Arch, MPS)

School of Law
Lawrence Ponoroff, Dean
Programs in:
- admiralty (LL M)
- American business law (LL M)
- energy and environment (LL M)
- international and comparative law (LL M)
- law (JD, LL M, SJD)

School of Liberal Arts
George L. Bernstein, Dean
Programs in:
- anthropology (MA, PhD)
- applied mathematics (MS)
- art (MFA)
- art history (MA)
- cell and molecular biology (MS, PhD)
- chemistry (MS, PhD)
- classical studies (MA)
- design and technical production (MFA)
- ecology and evolutionary biology (MS, PhD)
- economics (MA, PhD)
- English (MA, PhD)
- French (MA, PhD)
- geology (MS, PhD)
- history (MA, PhD)
- liberal arts (MA, MFA, MS, PhD)
- mathematics (MS, PhD)
- music (MA, MFA)
- paleontology (PhD)
- philosophy (MA, PhD)
- physics (MS, PhD)
- political science (MA, PhD)
- Portuguese (MA)
- sociology (MA, PhD)
- Spanish (MA)
- Spanish and Portuguese (PhD)
- statistics (MS)

The Payson Center for International Development and Technology Transfer
Dr. Eamon M. Kelly, Academic Director
Program in:
- international development (MS, PhD)

Roger Thayer Stone Center for Latin American Studies
Dr. Thomas Reese, Executive Director
Program in:
- Latin American studies (MA, PhD)

School of Medicine
Dr. L. Lee Hamm, Interim Dean
Program in:
- medicine (MD, MBS, MS, PhD)

Graduate Programs in Biomedical Sciences
Dr. Michael Herman, Dean, Graduate School
Programs in:
- biochemistry (MS, PhD)
- biomedical sciences (MBS, MS, PhD)
- human genetics (MBS, PhD)
- microbiology and immunology (MS, PhD)
- molecular and cellular biology (PhD)
- neuroscience (MS, PhD)
- pharmacology (MS, PhD)
- physiology (MS, PhD)
- structural and cellular biology (MS, PhD)

School of Public Health and Tropical Medicine
Dr. Pierre Beukens, Dean
Programs in:
- biostatistics (MS, MSPH, PhD, Sc D)
- clinical tropical medicine and travelers health (Diploma)
- environmental health sciences (MPH, MSPH, Dr PH, PhD)
- epidemiology (MPH, MS, Dr PH, PhD)
- health education and communication (MPH)

Tulane University (continued)
- health systems management (MHA, MMM, MPH, PhD, Sc D)
- international health and development (MPH, Dr PH, PhD)
- maternal and child health (MPH, Dr PH)
- nutrition (MPH)
- parasitology (MSPH, PhD)
- public health and tropical medicine (MPHTM)
- vector borne infectious diseases (MS, PhD)

School of Science and Engineering
Dr. Nicholas J. Altiero, Dean
Programs in:
- biomedical engineering (M Eng, MS, PhD)
- chemical and biomolecular engineering (M Eng, MS, PhD)
- civil engineering (M Eng, MS, PhD, Sc D)
- computer science (MS, PhD)
- electrical engineering (MS, PhD)
- engineering science (Sc D)
- environmental engineering (M Eng, Sc D)
- mechanical engineering (M Eng, MS, PhD, Sc D)
- psychology (MS, PhD)
- science and engineering (M Eng, MS, PhD, Sc D)

School of Social Work
Dr. Ronald Marks, Dean
Program in:
- social work (MSW)

■ UNIVERSITY OF LOUISIANA AT LAFAYETTE
Lafayette, LA 70504
http://www.louisiana.edu/

State-supported, coed, university. CGS member. *Enrollment:* 16,302 graduate, professional, and undergraduate students; 725 full-time matriculated graduate/professional students (342 women), 480 part-time matriculated graduate/professional students (296 women). *Graduate faculty:* 322 full-time (100 women), 5 part-time/adjunct (1 woman). *Computer facilities:* 1,000 computers available on campus for general student use. A campuswide network can be accessed from off campus. Internet access and online class registration are available. *Library facilities:* Edith Garland Dupre Library. *Graduate expenses:* Tuition, state resident: full-time $3,247; part-time $93 per credit hour. Tuition, nonresident: full-time $9,427; part-time $350 per credit hour. *General application contact:* Dr. C. E. Palmer, Dean, 337-482-6965.

Graduate School
Dr. C. E. Palmer, Dean
Program in:
- counselor education (MS)

College of Business Administration
Ellen Cook, Acting Dean
Programs in:
- business administration (MBA)
- health care administration (MBA)
- health care certification (MBA)

College of Education
Dr. Gerald B. Carlson, Dean
Programs in:
- administration and supervision (M Ed)
- curriculum and instruction (M Ed)
- education (M Ed, Ed D)
- education of the gifted (M Ed)
- educational leadership (M Ed, Ed D)

College of Engineering
Dr. Mark Zappi, Dean
Programs in:
- chemical engineering (MSE)
- civil engineering (MSE)
- computer engineering (MS, PhD)
- computer science (MS, PhD)
- engineering (MS, MSE, MSET, MSTC, PhD)
- engineering and technology management (MSET)
- mechanical engineering (MSE)
- petroleum engineering (MSE)
- telecommunications (MSTC)

College of Liberal Arts
Dr. A. David Barry, Dean
Programs in:
- British and American literature (MA)
- communicative disorders (MS, PhD)
- creative writing (PhD)
- Francophone studies (PhD)
- French (MA)
- history (MA)
- liberal arts (MA, MS, PhD)
- literature (PhD)
- mass communications (MS)
- psychology (MS)
- rehabilitation counseling (MS)
- rhetoric (PhD)

College of Nursing
Dr. Gail Poirrier, Dean
Program in:
- nursing (MSN)

College of Sciences
Dr. Bradd D. Clark, Dean
Programs in:
- biology (MS)
- cognitive science (PhD)
- computer science (MS, PhD)
- environmental and evolutionary biology (PhD)
- geology (MS)
- mathematics (MS, PhD)
- physics (MS)
- sciences (MS, PhD)

College of the Arts
H. Gordon Brooks, Dean
Programs in:
- architecture (M Arch)
- arts (M Arch, MM)
- conducting (MM)
- pedagogy (MM)
- vocal and instrumental performance (MM)

School of Human Resources
Dr. Rachel Fournet, Director
Program in:
- human resources (MS)

■ UNIVERSITY OF LOUISIANA AT MONROE
Monroe, LA 71209-0001
http://www.ulm.edu/

State-supported, coed, university. *Enrollment:* 8,571 graduate, professional, and undergraduate students; 759 full-time matriculated graduate/professional students (517 women), 351 part-time matriculated graduate/professional students (275 women). *Graduate faculty:* 98 full-time (37 women), 9 part-time/adjunct (5 women). *Computer facilities:* 1,400 computers available on campus for general student use. A campuswide network can be accessed from student residence rooms and from off campus. Internet access and online class registration are available. *Library facilities:* University Library. *Graduate expenses:* Tuition, state resident: part-time $124 per credit hour. Tuition, nonresident: part-time $124 per credit hour. *General application contact:* Dr. Virginia Eaton, Executive Director, 318-342-1043.

Graduate Studies and Research
Dr. Virginia Eaton, Graduate Studies and Research Director
Programs in:
- pharmaceutical sciences (MS)
- pharmacy (Pharm D, MS, PhD)

College of Arts and Sciences
Dr. Mark Arant, Dean-Interim
Programs in:
- arts and sciences (MA, MM, MS, CGS)
- biology (MS)
- communication (MA)
- criminal justice (MA)
- English (MA)
- gerontological studies (CGS)
- gerontology (MA, CGS)
- history (MA)
- music (MM)
- visual and performing arts (MM)

College of Business Administration
Dr. Ron Berry, Dean
Program in:
- business administration (MBA)

College of Education and Human Development
Dr. Luke Thomas, Dean

Programs in:
- administration and supervision (M Ed)
- counseling (M Ed)
- curriculum and instruction (M Ed, Ed D)
- education (M Ed, MA, MAT, MS, Ed D, PhD, SSP)
- educational leadership (Ed D)
- elementary education (M Ed, MAT)
- exercise science (MS)
- marriage and family therapy (MA, PhD)
- psychology (MS)
- reading (M Ed)
- school psychology (SSP)
- secondary education (M Ed, MAT)
- special education (M Ed, MAT)
- substance abuse counseling (MA)

College of Health Sciences
Dr. Jan Corder, Dean-Interim
Programs in:
- communicative disorders (MS)
- health sciences (MS)

■ UNIVERSITY OF NEW ORLEANS
New Orleans, LA 70148
http://www.uno.edu/

State-supported, coed, university. CGS member. *Enrollment:* 11,747 graduate, professional, and undergraduate students; 2,591 matriculated graduate/professional students (1,566 women). *Graduate faculty:* 679. *Computer facilities:* 1,084 computers available on campus for general student use. A campuswide network can be accessed from student residence rooms and from off campus. Internet access is available. *Library facilities:* Earl K. Long Library. *Graduate expenses:* Tuition, state resident: full-time $3,292. Tuition, nonresident: full-time $10,336. Required fees: $158. *General application contact:* Amanda M. Athey, Coordinator of Program Reviews and Electronic Theses and Dissertations, 504-280-1155.

Graduate School
Dr. Robert Cashner, Dean

College of Business Administration
Programs in:
- accounting (MS)
- business administration (MBA, MS, PhD)
- economics and finance (MS)
- financial economics (PhD)
- health care management (MS)
- hospitality and tourism management (MS)
- taxation (MS)

College of Education and Human Development
Dr. James Meza, Dean
Programs in:
- counselor education (M Ed, PhD, GCE)
- curriculum and instruction (M Ed, PhD, GCE)
- education and human development (M Ed, PhD, GCE)
- educational leadership (M Ed, PhD, GCE)
- special education (M Ed, PhD, GCE)

College of Engineering
Dr. Russell Trahan, Dean
Programs in:
- engineering (MS, PhD, Certificate)
- engineering and applied sciences (PhD)
- engineering management (MS, Certificate)
- mechanical engineering (MS)

College of Liberal Arts
Dr. Susan Krantz, Dean
Programs in:
- arts administration (MA)
- English (MA)
- English teaching (MAET)
- film production (MFA)
- fine arts (MFA)
- foreign languages (MA)
- geography (MA)
- history (MA)
- history teaching (MAHT)
- liberal arts (MA, MAET, MAHT, MFA, MM, MPA, MS, MURP, PhD)
- music (MM)
- political science (MA, PhD)
- public administration (MPA)
- sociology (MA)
- theatre directing (MFA)
- theatre performance (MFA)
- urban and regional planning (MURP)
- urban planning and regional studies (MS, MURP, PhD)
- urban studies (MS, PhD)

College of Sciences
Dr. Joe King, Dean
Programs in:
- biological sciences (MS, PhD)
- chemistry (MS, PhD)
- computer science (MS)
- earth and environmental sciences (MS)
- mathematics (MS)
- physics (MS, PhD)
- psychology (MS, PhD)
- science teaching (MAST)
- sciences (MAST, MS, PhD)

■ UNIVERSITY OF PHOENIX–LOUISIANA CAMPUS
Metairie, LA 70001-2082
http://www.phoenix.edu/

Proprietary, coed, comprehensive institution. *Enrollment:* 481 full-time matriculated graduate/professional students (367 women). *Graduate faculty:* 25 full-time (12 women), 240 part-time/adjunct (99 women). *Computer facilities:* A campuswide network can be accessed from off campus. Internet access is available. *Library facilities:* University Library. *Graduate expenses:* Tuition: full-time $11,832. Required fees: $760. *General application contact:* Campus Information Center, 504-461-8852.

The Artemis School
Dr. Adam Honea, Provost
Program in:
- early childhood education (MA Ed)

College of Health and Human Services
Dr. Gil Linne, Dean/Executive Director
Programs in:
- administration of justice and security (MS)
- health care management (MBA)
- nursing (MSN)
- psychology (MS)

John Sperling School of Business
Dr. Adam Honea, Provost
Program in:
- business (MBA, MIS, MM)

College of Graduate Business and Management
Dr. Brian Lindquist, Associate Vice President and Dean/Executive Director
Programs in:
- business administration (MBA)
- human resource management (MBA, MM)
- public administration (MBA)

College of Information Systems and Technology
Dr. Adam Honea, Dean
Programs in:
- information systems/management (MIS)
- technology management (MBA)

■ XAVIER UNIVERSITY OF LOUISIANA
New Orleans, LA 70125-1098
http://www.xula.edu/

Independent-religious, coed, comprehensive institution. CGS member. *Computer facilities:* 250 computers available on campus for general student use. A campuswide network can be accessed from student residence rooms and from off campus. *Library facilities:* Xavier Library plus 1 other. *General application contact:* Director of Graduate Admissions, 504-520-7487.

College of Pharmacy
Dr. Wayne T. Harris, Dean
Program in:
- pharmacy (Pharm D)

Graduate School
Programs in:
- curriculum and instruction (MA)
- education administration and supervision (MA)
- guidance and counseling (MA)

Institute for Black Catholic Studies
Program in:
- pastoral theology (Th M)

Maine

■ HUSSON COLLEGE
Bangor, ME 04401-2999
http://www.husson.edu/

Independent, coed, comprehensive institution. *Computer facilities:* 57 computers available on campus for general student use. A campuswide network can be accessed from student residence rooms. Internet access is available. *Library facilities:* Sawyer Library. *General application contact:* Dean of Graduate Studies, 207-941-7062.

Graduate Studies Division
Programs in:
- business (MSB)
- family nurse practitioner (MSN)
- nursing (MSN)
- physical therapy (MSPT)
- psychiatric nursing (MSN)

■ SAINT JOSEPH'S COLLEGE OF MAINE
Standish, ME 04084-5263
http://www.sjcme.edu/

Independent-religious, coed, comprehensive institution. *Enrollment:* 1,050 graduate, professional, and undergraduate students; 884 matriculated graduate/professional students (678 women). *Graduate faculty:* 5 full-time (4 women), 67 part-time/adjunct (46 women). *Computer facilities:* Computer purchase and lease plans are available. 102 computers available on campus for general student use. A campuswide network can be accessed from student residence rooms. Internet access is available. *Library facilities:* Wellehan Library. *Graduate expenses:* Tuition: part-time $350 per credit. *General application contact:* Admissions Department/ Graduate and Professional Studies, 800-752-4723.

Department of Nursing
Dr. Margaret Hourigan, Chair
Programs in:
- nursing (MS)
- nursing administration and leadership (Certificate)
- nursing and health care education (Certificate)

Program in Business Administration
Dr. Gregory Gull, Director
Program in:
- quality leadership (MBA)

Program in Health Services Administration
John Pratt, Interim Director
Program in:
- health services administration (MHSA)

Program in Teacher Education
Dr. Richard Willis, Director
Program in:
- teacher education (MS)

■ UNIVERSITY OF MAINE
Orono, ME 04469
http://www.umaine.edu/

State-supported, coed, university. CGS member. *Enrollment:* 11,435 graduate, professional, and undergraduate students; 1,110 full-time matriculated graduate/ professional students (631 women), 1,160 part-time matriculated graduate/professional students (844 women). *Graduate faculty:* 527 full-time (176 women), 284 part-time/ adjunct (158 women). *Computer facilities:* Computer purchase and lease plans are available. 500 computers available on campus for general student use. A campuswide network can be accessed from student residence rooms and from off campus. Internet access and online class registration, online grade and financial aid information, e-mail are available. *Library facilities:* Fogler Library plus 2 others. *General application contact:* Scott G. Delcourt, Associate Dean of the Graduate School, 207-581-3219.

Graduate School
Scott G. Delcourt, Associate Dean of the Graduate School
Programs in:
- biomedical sciences (PhD)
- information systems (MS)
- interdisciplinary studies (PhD)
- liberal studies (MA)
- teaching (MST)

Climate Change Institute
Dr. Paul Mayewski, Director
Program in:
- climate change (MS)

College of Business, Public Policy and Health
Dr. Daniel E. Innis, Dean
Programs in:
- accounting (MS)
- business administration (MBA)
- business, public policy and health (MA, MBA, MPA, MS, MSW, PhD, CAS)
- economics (MA)
- financial economics (MA)
- nursing (MS, CAS)
- public administration (MPA, PhD)
- social work (MSW)

College of Education and Human Development
Dr. Robert A. Cobb, Dean
Programs in:
- counselor education (M Ed, MA, MS, Ed D, CAS)
- curriculum, assessment, and instruction (M Ed)
- educational leadership (M Ed, Ed D, CAS)
- elementary and secondary education (M Ed)
- elementary education (M Ed, MAT, MS, CAS)
- higher education (M Ed, MA, MS, Ed D, CAS)
- human development (MS)
- human development and family relations (MS)
- instructional technology (M Ed)
- kinesiology and physical education (M Ed, MS)
- literacy education (M Ed, MA, MS, Ed D, CAS)
- science education (M Ed, MS, CAS)
- secondary education (M Ed, MA, MAT, MS, CAS)
- social studies education (M Ed, MA, MS, CAS)
- special education (M Ed, CAS)

College of Engineering
Dr. Dana Humphrey, Interim Dean
Programs in:
- biological engineering (MS)
- chemical engineering (MS, PhD)
- civil engineering (MS, PhD)
- computer engineering (MS)
- electrical engineering (MS, PhD)
- engineering (MS, PhD)
- mechanical engineering (MS, PhD)
- spatial information science and engineering (MS, PhD)

College of Liberal Arts and Sciences
Dr. Ann Leffler, Dean
Programs in:
- chemistry (MS, PhD)
- clinical psychology (PhD)
- communication (MA)
- communication sciences and disorders (MA)
- computer science (MS, PhD)
- developmental psychology (MA)
- engineering physics (M Eng)
- English (MA)
- experimental psychology (MA, PhD)
- French (MA, MAT)
- history (MA, PhD)
- liberal arts and sciences (M Eng, MA, MAT, MM, MS, PhD)
- mathematics (MA)
- music (MM)
- physics (MS, PhD)
- social psychology (MA)

College of Natural Sciences, Forestry, and Agriculture
Dr. G. Bruce Wiersma, Dean
Programs in:
- animal sciences (MPS, MS)
- biochemistry (MPS, MS)
- biochemistry and molecular biology (PhD)
- biological sciences (PhD)
- botany and plant pathology (MS)
- earth sciences (MS, PhD)

ecology and environmental science (MS, PhD)
ecology and environmental sciences (MS, PhD)
entomology (MS)
food and nutritional sciences (PhD)
food science and human nutrition (MS)
forest resources (PhD)
forestry (MF, MS)
horticulture (MS)
marine biology (MS, PhD)
marine policy (MS)
microbiology (MPS, MS, PhD)
natural sciences, forestry, and agriculture (MF, MPS, MS, MWC, PhD)
oceanography (MS, PhD)
plant science (PhD)
plant, soil, and environmental sciences (MS)
resource economics and policy (MS)
resource utilization (MS)
wildlife conservation (MWC)
wildlife ecology (MS, PhD)
zoology (MS, PhD)

■ UNIVERSITY OF NEW ENGLAND
Biddeford, ME 04005-9526
http://www.une.edu/

Independent, coed, comprehensive institution. *Enrollment:* 3,379 graduate, professional, and undergraduate students; 870 full-time matriculated graduate/professional students (543 women), 558 part-time matriculated graduate/professional students (422 women). *Graduate faculty:* 125 full-time (66 women), 119 part-time/adjunct (59 women). *Computer facilities:* 150 computers available on campus for general student use. A campuswide network can be accessed from student residence rooms and from off campus. Internet access and online class registration are available. *Library facilities:* Ketchum Library plus 1 other. *General application contact:* Peggy Warden, Assistant Dean of Graduate Admissions, 207-221-4225.

College of Arts and Sciences
Paul Burlin, Interim Dean
Programs in:
applied biosciences (MS)
arts and sciences (MS, MS Ed, CAGS)
educational leadership (CAGS)
general studies (MS Ed)
literacy (MS Ed)
marine science (MS)
teaching methodologies (MS Ed)

College of Health Professions
Dr. David Ward, Dean
Programs in:
health professions (MS, MSW, DPT, Certificate)
nurse anesthesia (MS)
occupational therapy (MS)
physical therapy (DPT)
physician assistant (MS)
post professional occupational therapy (MS)
post professional physical therapy (DPT)

School of Social Work
Martha Wilson, Director
Programs in:
addictions counseling (Certificate)
gerontology (Certificate)
social work (MSW)

College of Osteopathic Medicine
Dr. Boyd Buser, Dean
Programs in:
osteopathic medicine (DO, MPH, Certificate)
public health (MPH, Certificate)

■ UNIVERSITY OF SOUTHERN MAINE
Portland, ME 04104-9300
http://www.usm.maine.edu/

State-supported, coed, comprehensive institution. CGS member. *Enrollment:* 10,478 graduate, professional, and undergraduate students; 511 full-time matriculated graduate/professional students (388 women), 1,798 part-time matriculated graduate/professional students (1,195 women). *Graduate faculty:* 166. *Computer facilities:* Computer purchase and lease plans are available. 485 computers available on campus for general student use. A campuswide network can be accessed from student residence rooms and from off campus. Internet access and online class registration are available. *Library facilities:* University of Southern Maine Library plus 4 others. *Graduate expenses:* Tuition, state resident: full-time $4,860; part-time $270 per credit hour. Tuition, nonresident: full-time $13,572; part-time $754 per credit hour. Required fees: $222 per semester. Tuition and fees vary according to course load. *General application contact:* Mary Sloan, Director of Graduate Admissions, 207-780-4386.

College of Arts and Sciences
Devinder Malhotra, Dean
Programs in:
American and New England studies (MA)
arts and sciences (MA, MFA, MM, MS, MSW)
biology (MS)
creative writing (MFA)
music (MM)
social work (MSW)
statistics (MS)

College of Education and Human Development
Betty Lou Whitford, Dean
Programs in:
adult education (MS)
adult learning (CAS)
applied behavior analysis (Certificate)
applied literacy (MS Ed)
assistant principal (Certificate)
athletic administration (Certificate)
counseling (MS, CAS)
education and human development (MS, MS Ed, Psy D, CAS, Certificate)
educational leadership (MS Ed, CAS)
English as a second language (MS Ed, CAS)
industrial/technology education (MS Ed)
literacy education (MS Ed, CAS, Certificate)
mental health rehabilitation technician/community (Certificate)
middle-level education (Certificate)
school psychology (MS, Psy D)
special education (MS)
teaching and learning (MS Ed)

College of Nursing and Health Professions
Susan Sepples, Director of Nursing Program
Programs in:
adult health nursing (PMC)
clinical nurse leader (MS)
clinical nurse specialist psychiatric-mental health nursing (MS)
family nursing (PMC)
medical/surgical nursing (MS)
nurse practitioner adult health nursing (MS)
nurse practitioner family nursing (MS)
nurse practitioner psychiatric/mental health nursing (MS)
psychiatric-mental health nursing (PMC)

Edmund S. Muskie School of Public Service
Programs in:
child and family policy (Certificate)
community planning and development (MCPD, Certificate)
health policy and management (MS, Certificate)
non-profit management (Certificate)
public policy (PhD)
public policy and management (MPPM)
public service (MCPD, MPPM, MS, PhD, Certificate)

Program in Occupational Therapy
Program in:
occupational therapy (MOT)

School of Applied Science, Engineering, and Technology
Dr. John R. Wright, Dean
Programs in:
applied medical sciences (MS)
applied science, engineering, and technology (MS)
computer science (MS)
manufacturing systems (MS)

University of Southern Maine (continued)

School of Business
James B. Shaffer, Dean
Programs in:
accounting (MSA)
business administration (MBA)

University of Maine School of Law
Peter R. Pitegoff, Dean
Program in:
law (JD)

Maryland

■ BOWIE STATE UNIVERSITY
Bowie, MD 20715-9465
http://www.bowiestate.edu/

State-supported, coed, comprehensive institution. CGS member. *Enrollment:* 5,291 graduate, professional, and undergraduate students; 304 full-time matriculated graduate/professional students (236 women), 835 part-time matriculated graduate/professional students (628 women). *Graduate faculty:* 61 full-time (32 women), 57 part-time/adjunct (20 women). *Computer facilities:* 3,144 computers available on campus for general student use. A campuswide network can be accessed from student residence rooms and from off campus. Internet access and online class registration are available. *Library facilities:* Thurgood Marshall Library. *Graduate expenses:* Tuition, state resident: full-time $7,344; part-time $306 per credit. Tuition, nonresident: full-time $14,304; part-time $396 per credit. Required fees: $1,078; $77 per credit. $539 per term. One-time fee: $40. *General application contact:* Dr. Beverly O'Bryant, Dean, 301-860-3406.

Graduate Programs
Dr. Beverly O'Bryant, Dean
Programs in:
administration of nursing services (MS)
applied and computational mathematics (MS)
business administration (MBA)
computer science (MS, App Sc D)
counseling psychology (MA)
educational leadership (Ed D)
elementary and secondary school administration (M Ed)
elementary education (M Ed)
English (MA)
family nurse practitioner (MS)
guidance and counseling (M Ed)
human resource development (MA)
information systems analyst (Certificate)
management information systems (MS)
mental halth counseling (MA)
nursing education (MS)
organizational communication (MA, Certificate)
public administration (MPA)
reading education (M Ed)
school administration and supervision (M Ed)
secondary education (M Ed)
special education (M Ed)
teaching (MAT)

■ COLLEGE OF NOTRE DAME OF MARYLAND
Baltimore, MD 21210-2476
http://www.ndm.edu/

Independent-religious, Undergraduate: women only; graduate: coed, comprehensive institution. *Enrollment:* 111 full-time matriculated graduate/professional students (96 women), 1,502 part-time matriculated graduate/professional students (1,217 women). *Graduate faculty:* 40 full-time (25 women), 125 part-time/adjunct (100 women). *Computer facilities:* Computer purchase and lease plans are available. 80 computers available on campus for general student use. A campuswide network can be accessed from student residence rooms and from off campus. Internet access, online classroom assignments and information are available. *Library facilities:* Loyola/Notre Dame Library. *General application contact:* Erica D. Jones, Graduate Admissions Coordinator, 410-532-5317.

Graduate Studies
Dr. Carolyn Boulger Karlson, Dean of Graduate Studies
Programs in:
contemporary communication (MA)
instructional leadership for changing populations (PhD)
leadership in teaching (MA)
liberal studies (MA)
management (MA)
nonprofit management (MA)
teaching (MA)
teaching English to speakers of other languages (MA)

■ COPPIN STATE UNIVERSITY
Baltimore, MD 21216-3698
http://www.coppin.edu/

State-supported, coed, comprehensive institution. CGS member. *Enrollment:* 177 full-time matriculated graduate/professional students (142 women), 207 part-time matriculated graduate/professional students (152 women). *Graduate faculty:* 35 full-time (22 women), 28 part-time/adjunct (15 women). *Computer facilities:* 130 computers available on campus for general student use. A campuswide network can be accessed from off campus. Internet access is available. *Library facilities:* Parlett L. Moore Library. *General application contact:* Dr. Mary Owens, Dean, Graduate Studies and Research Evaluation, 410-951-3090.

Division of Graduate Studies
Dr. Mary Owens, Dean, Graduate Studies and Research Evaluation

Division of Arts and Sciences
Dr. Clyde Mathura, Dean
Programs in:
alcohol and substance abuse counseling (MS)
arts and sciences (M Ed, MS)
criminal justice (MS)
human services administration (MS)
rehabilitation counseling (M Ed)

Division of Education
Dr. Julius Chapman, Chair
Programs in:
adult and general education (MS)
curriculum and instruction (M Ed, MA, MS)
reading education (MS)
special education (M Ed)
teacher education (MA)
teaching (MA)

Helene Fuld School of Nursing
Dr. Marcella Copes, Dean
Programs in:
family nurse practitioner (PMC)
nursing (MSN)

■ FROSTBURG STATE UNIVERSITY
Frostburg, MD 21532-1099
http://www.frostburg.edu/

State-supported, coed, comprehensive institution. *Computer facilities:* 577 computers available on campus for general student use. A campuswide network can be accessed from student residence rooms and from off campus. Internet access and online class registration are available. *Library facilities:* Lewis J. Ort Library. *General application contact:* Director, Graduate Services, 301-687-7053.

Graduate School

College of Business
Programs in:
business (MBA)
business administration (MBA)

College of Education
Programs in:
curriculum and instruction (M Ed)
education (M Ed, MAT, MS)
educational administration and supervision (M Ed)
educational technology (M Ed)
elementary (M Ed)
elementary education (M Ed)
elementary teaching (MAT)

human performance (MS)
interdisciplinary education (M Ed)
parks and recreational management (MS)
reading (M Ed)
school counseling (M Ed)
secondary (M Ed)
secondary education (M Ed)
secondary teaching (MAT)
special education (M Ed)

College of Liberal Arts and Sciences
Programs in:
applied computer science (MS)
applied ecology and conservation biology (MS)
counseling psychology (MS)
fisheries and wildlife management (MS)
liberal arts and sciences (MS)

■ HOOD COLLEGE
Frederick, MD 21701-8575
http://www.hood.edu/

Independent, coed, comprehensive institution. CGS member. *Enrollment:* 2,248 graduate, professional, and undergraduate students; 63 full-time matriculated graduate/professional students (38 women), 891 part-time matriculated graduate/professional students (657 women). *Graduate faculty:* 31 full-time (11 women), 67 part-time/adjunct (27 women). *Computer facilities:* 277 computers available on campus for general student use. A campuswide network can be accessed from student residence rooms and from off campus. Internet access and online class registration are available. *Library facilities:* Beneficial-Hodson Library and Information Technology Center. *Graduate expenses:* Tuition: part-time $350 per credit. Required fees: $20 per semester. *General application contact:* Dr. Kathleen C. Bands, Associate Dean of Graduate School, 301-696-3811.

Graduate School
Dr. Frank Sweeney, Dean of the Graduate School
Programs in:
administration and management (MBA)
biomedical science (MS)
ceramic arts (MFA, Certificate)
computer and information sciences (MS)
computer science (MS)
curriculum and instruction (MS)
educational leadership (MS)
environmental biology (MS)
foreign language proficiency (Certificate)
human sciences (MA)
humanities (MA)
management of information technology (MS)
reading specialization (MS)
secondary mathematics education (Certificate)
teaching the struggling reader (Certificate)
thanatology (MA, Certificate)

■ THE JOHNS HOPKINS UNIVERSITY
Baltimore, MD 21218-2699
http://www.jhu.edu/

Independent, coed, university. CGS member. *Enrollment:* 6,140 full-time matriculated graduate/professional students (3,269 women), 8,060 part-time matriculated graduate/professional students (4,091 women). *Graduate faculty:* 3,430 full-time (1,243 women), 217 part-time/adjunct (96 women). *Computer facilities:* 140 computers available on campus for general student use. A campuswide network can be accessed from student residence rooms and from off campus. Internet access and online class registration are available. *Library facilities:* Milton S. Eisenhower Library plus 6 others. *Graduate expenses:* Tuition: full-time $32,976. Tuition and fees vary according to degree level and program. *General application contact:* Graduate Admissions Office, 410-516-8174.

Find University Details at www.petersons.com/gradchannel.

Bloomberg School of Public Health
Dr. Michael J. Klag, Dean
Programs in:
behavioral sciences and health education (MHS)
biochemistry and molecular biology (MHS, Sc M, PhD)
bioinformatics (MHS)
biostatistics (MHS, Sc M, PhD)
cancer epidemiology (MHS, Sc M, PhD, Sc D)
cardiovascular disease epidemiology (MHS, Sc M, PhD, Sc D)
child and adolescent health and development (Dr PH, PhD)
children's mental health services (PhD)
clinical epidemiology (MHS, Sc M, PhD, Sc D)
clinical investigation (MHS, Sc M, PhD)
clinical trials (PhD, Sc D)
demography (MHS)
disease prevention and control (MHS, PhD)
drug dependence epidemiology (PhD)
environmental health engineering (PhD)
environmental health sciences (MHS, Dr PH)
epidemiology (Dr PH)
epidemiology (general) (MHS, Sc M, PhD, Sc D)
epidemiology of aging (MHS, Sc M, PhD, Sc D)
genetic counseling (Sc M)
health and public policy (PhD)
health care management and leadership (Dr PH)
health finance and management (MHS)
health policy (MHS)
health services research (PhD)
health systems (MHS, PhD)
human genetics/genetic epidemiology (MHS, Sc M, PhD, Sc D)
human nutrition (MHS, PhD)
infectious disease epidemiology (MHS, Sc M, PhD, Sc D)
international health (Dr PH)
mental health (MHS)
molecular imaging (PhD)
molecular microbiology and immunology (MHS, Sc M, PhD)
occupational and environmental health (PhD)
occupational and environmental hygiene (MHS)
occupational/environmental epidemiology (MHS, Sc M, PhD, Sc D)
physiology (PhD)
population and health (Dr PH, PhD)
population, family and reproductive health (MHS)
psychiatric epidemiology (PhD)
public health (MHS, MPH, Sc M, Dr PH, PhD, Sc D)
reproductive, perinatal women's health (Dr PH, PhD)
social and behavioral interventions (MHS, PhD)
social and behavioral sciences (PhD, Sc D)
toxicology (PhD)

Carey Business School
Dr. Pamela Cranston, Interim Dean
Programs in:
business administration (MBA)
business of health (MBA, Certificate)
business of medicine (Certificate)
business of nursing (Certificate)
competitive intelligence (Certificate)
finance (MS, Certificate)
financial management (Certificate)
information and telecommunication systems (Certificate)
information security management (Certificate)
information technology (MS, Certificate)
information technology and telecommunication systems for business (MS)
investments (Certificate)
leadership and management in the life sciences (MBA, Certificate)
leadership development (Certificate)
management (MS, Certificate)
marketing (MS)
medical services management (MBA)
organization development and strategic human resources (MS)
real estate (MS)
senior living and health care real estate (Certificate)
skilled facilitator (Certificate)

Engineering and Applied Science Programs for Professionals
Dr. Allan Bjerkaas, Associate Dean

The Johns Hopkins University (continued)
Programs in:
- applied and computational mathematics (MS)
- applied biomedical engineering (MS)
- applied physics (MS)
- bioinformatics (MS)
- chemical and biomolecular engineering (M Ch E)
- civil engineering (MCE)
- computer science (MS)
- electrical and computer engineering (MS)
- engineering and applied science (M Ch E, M Mat SE, MCE, MEE, MME, MS, MSE, Certificate, Post-Master's Certificate)
- environmental engineering (MS)
- environmental engineering and science (MEE, MS, Certificate)
- environmental planning and management (MS)
- information systems and technology (MS)
- materials science and engineering (M Mat SE, MSE)
- mechanical engineering (MME)
- systems engineering (MS, Certificate, Post-Master's Certificate)
- technical innovation and new ventures (Graduate Certificate)
- technical management (MS, Post-Master's Certificate)
- telecommunications and networking (MS)

G. W. C. Whiting School of Engineering
Dr. Nicholas P. Jones, Interim Dean
Programs in:
- biomedical engineering (MSE, PhD)
- chemical and biomolecular engineering (MSE, PhD)
- civil engineering (MCE, MSE, PhD)
- computer science (MSE, PhD)
- discrete mathematics (MA, MSE, PhD)
- electrical and computer engineering (MSE, PhD)
- engineering (M Ch E, M Mat SE, MA, MCE, MEE, MME, MS, MSE, PhD, Certificate, Post-Master's Certificate)
- geography and environmental engineering (MA, MS, MSE, PhD)
- materials science and engineering (M Mat SE, MSE, PhD)
- mechanical engineering (MSE, PhD)
- operations research/optimization/decision science (MA, MSE, PhD)
- statistics/probability/stochastic processes (MA, MSE, PhD)

Information Security Institute
Dr. Gerald M. Masson, Director
Program in:
- security informatics (MS)

National Institutes of Health Sponsored Programs
Programs in:
- biology (PhD)
- cell, molecular, and developmental biology and biophysics)

Paul H. Nitze School of Advanced International Studies
Programs in:
- emerging markets (Certificate)
- interdisciplinary studies (MA, PhD)
- international public policy (MIPP)
- international studies (Certificate)

Peabody Conservatory of Music
Jeffrey Sharkey, Director
Program in:
- music (MA, MM, DMA, AD, GPD)

School of Education
Dr. Ralph Fessler, Dean
Programs in:
- addictions counseling (Certificate)
- adult learning (Certificate)
- advanced methods for differential instruction and inclusive education (Certificate)
- assistive technology for communication and social interaction (Certificate)
- business leadership for independent schools (Certificate)
- clinical community counseling (Certificate)
- counseling (MS, CAGS)
- counseling at-risk youth (Certificate)
- early intervention/preschool special education specialist (Certificate)
- earth/space science (Certificate)
- education (MAT, MS, Ed D, CAGS, Certificate)
- education of students with autism and other pervasive developmental disorders (Certificate)
- educational leadership for independent schools (Certificate)
- educational studies (MS)
- effective teaching of reading (Certificate)
- elementary education (MAT)
- English for speakers of other languages (MAT)
- ESL instruction (Certificate)
- gifted education (Certificate)
- leadership for school, family and community collaboration (Certificate)
- management (MS)
- organizational counseling (Certificate)
- reading (MS)
- school administration and supervision (MS, Certificate)
- secondary education (MAT)
- special education (MS, Ed D, CAGS)
- spiritual and existential counseling and therapy (Certificate)
- teacher development and leadership (Ed D)
- teacher leadership (Certificate)
- technology for educators (MS)
- urban education (Certificate)

Division of Public Safety Leadership
Dr. Sheldon Greenberg, Associate Dean
Program in:
- management (MS)

School of Medicine
Dr. Edward D. Miller, Dean of Medical Faculty and Chief Executive Officer
Program in:
- medicine (MD, MA, MS, PhD)

Division of Health Sciences Informatics
Dr. Harold P. Lehmann, Director, Training Program
Program in:
- health sciences informatics (MS)

Graduate Programs in Medicine
Dr. Peter Maloney, Associate Dean for Graduate Programs
Programs in:
- biochemistry, cellular and molecular biology (PhD)
- biological chemistry (PhD)
- biophysics and biophysical chemistry (MS, PhD)
- cellular and molecular medicine (PhD)
- cellular and molecular physiology (PhD)
- functional anatomy and evolution (PhD)
- human genetics and molecular biology (PhD)
- immunology (PhD)
- medical and biological illustration (MA)
- medicine (MA, MS, PhD)
- neuroscience (PhD)
- pathobiology (PhD)
- pharmacology and molecular sciences (PhD)
- physiology (PhD)

School of Nursing
Dr. Martha N. Hill, Dean
Programs in:
- adult acute/critical care (MSN, Certificate)
- adult and pediatric primary care (MSN)
- adult or pediatric primary care (Certificate)
- clinical nurse specialist (MSN)
- clinical nurse specialist and health systems management (MSN)
- family primary care (MSN, Certificate)
- health systems management (MSN)
- nursing (MSN, PhD, Certificate)
- public health nursing (MSN)

Zanvyl Krieger School of Arts and Sciences
Dr. Adam Falk, Dean
Programs in:
- anthropology (PhD)
- applied economics (MA)
- arts and sciences (MA, MFA, MS, PhD)
- astronomy (PhD)
- bioinformatics (MS)
- biology (PhD)
- biophysics (MA, PhD)
- bioscience regulatory affairs (MS)

biotechnology (MS)
chemistry (PhD)
chemistry-biology (PhD)
classics (PhD)
cognitive science (PhD)
communication in contemporary society (MA)
earth and planetary sciences (MA, PhD)
economics (PhD)
English and American literature (PhD)
environmental sciences and policy (MS)
fiction writing (MFA)
French (PhD)
German (PhD)
government (MA, Certificate)
history (PhD)
history of art (MA, PhD)
history of science and technology (MA, PhD)
homeland security (Certificate)
Italian (PhD)
liberal arts (MA, Certificate)
mathematics (PhD)
Near Eastern studies (PhD)
philosophy (MA, PhD)
physics (PhD)
poetry (MFA)
political science (MA, PhD)
psychological and brain sciences (PhD)
science writing (MA)
sociology (PhD)
Spanish (PhD)
writing (MA)

Humanities Center
Ruth Leys, Chair
Program in:
humanities (PhD)

Institute for Public Policy
Dr. Sandra J. Newman, Director
Program in:
public policy (MA)

■ LOYOLA COLLEGE IN MARYLAND
Baltimore, MD 21210-2699
http://www.loyola.edu/

Independent-religious, coed, comprehensive institution. *Enrollment:* 6,035 graduate, professional, and undergraduate students; 704 full-time matriculated graduate/professional students (474 women), 1,732 part-time matriculated graduate/professional students (1,039 women). *Graduate faculty:* 94 full-time (45 women), 105 part-time/adjunct (42 women). *Computer facilities:* 292 computers available on campus for general student use. A campuswide network can be accessed from student residence rooms and from off campus. Internet access is available. *Library facilities:* Loyola/Notre Dame Library. *General application contact:* Scott Greatorex, Director, Graduate Admissions, 410-617-5020.

Graduate Programs
Rev. Brian Linnane, President

College of Arts and Sciences
Dr. James Buckley, Dean
Programs in:
administration and supervision (M Ed, MA, CAS)
arts and sciences (M Ed, MA, MES, MMS, MS, PhD, Psy D, CAS)
clinical psychology (MS, Psy D, CAS)
computer science (MS)
counseling psychology (MS, CAS)
curriculum and instruction (M Ed, MA, CAS)
educational technology (M Ed)
employee assistance and substance abuse (CAS)
engineering science (MES, MS)
guidance and counseling (M Ed, MA, CAS)
liberal studies (MMS)
Montessori education (M Ed, CAS)
pastoral counseling (MS, PhD, CAS)
reading (M Ed, CAS)
software engineering (MS)
special education (M Ed, CAS)
speech-language pathology and audiology (MS, CAS)
spiritual and pastoral care (MA)

Sellinger School of Business and Management
John Moran, Associate Dean
Programs in:
business and management (MBA, MSF, XMBA)
decision sciences (MBA)
economics (MBA)
executive business administration (MBA, XMBA)
finance (MBA)
marketing/management (MBA)

■ MCDANIEL COLLEGE
Westminster, MD 21157-4390
http://www.mcdaniel.edu/

Independent, coed, comprehensive institution. *Computer facilities:* 171 computers available on campus for general student use. A campuswide network can be accessed from student residence rooms and from off campus. Internet access and online class registration are available. *Library facilities:* Hoover Library. *General application contact:* Dean of Graduate and Professional Studies, 410-857-2500.

Graduate and Professional Studies
Programs in:
curriculum and instruction (MS)
education of the deaf (MS)
educational administration (MS)
elementary education (MS)
guidance and counseling (MS)
human resources development (MS)
human services management in special education (MS)
liberal studies (MLA)
media/library science (MS)
physical education (MS)
reading education (MS)
secondary education (MS)
special education (MS)

■ MORGAN STATE UNIVERSITY
Baltimore, MD 21251
http://www.morgan.edu/

State-supported, coed, university. CGS member. *Enrollment:* 450 full-time matriculated graduate/professional students, 362 part-time matriculated graduate/professional students. *Graduate faculty:* 222. *Computer facilities:* 285 computers available on campus for general student use. A campuswide network can be accessed from student residence rooms and from off campus. Internet access and online class registration, engineering lab supercomputer are available. *Library facilities:* Morris Soper Library. *Graduate expenses:* Tuition, state resident: part-time $272 per credit. Tuition, nonresident: part-time $478 per credit. Required fees: $38 per credit. *General application contact:* Dr. Maurice C. Taylor, Dean, 443-885-3185.

School of Graduate Studies
Dr. Maurice C. Taylor, Dean
Program in:
public health and policy (MPH, Dr PH)

Clarence M. Mitchell, Jr. School of Engineering
Dr. Eugene DeLoatch, Dean
Programs in:
civil engineering (M Eng, D Eng)
electrical engineering (M Eng, D Eng)
industrial engineering (M Eng, D Eng)
transportation (MS)

College of Liberal Arts
Dr. Burney J. Hollis, Dean
Programs in:
African-American studies (MA)
economics (MA)
English (MA, PhD)
history (MA, PhD)
international studies (MA)
liberal arts (MA, MS, PhD)
music (MA)
psychometrics (MS, PhD)
sociology (MA, MS)
telecommunications management (MS)

Earl G. Graves School of Business and Management
Dr. Otis A. Thomas, Dean
Programs in:
business administration (MBA, PhD)
business and management (MBA, PhD)

Institute of Architecture and Planning
Dr. Richard E. Lloyd, Director
Programs in:
architecture (M Arch)
city and regional planning (MCRP)
landscape architecture (MLA, MSLA)

Morgan State University (continued)

School of Computer, Mathematical, and Natural Sciences
Dr. Joseph Whittaker, Dean
Programs in:
bio-environmental science (PhD)
bioinformatics (MS)
biology (MS)
chemistry (MS)
computer, mathematical, and natural sciences (MA, MS, PhD)
mathematics (MA)
physics (MS)

School of Education and Urban Studies
Dr. Patricia L. Welch, Dean
Programs in:
education and urban studies (MAT, MS, MSW, Ed D, PhD)
educational administration and supervision (MS)
elementary and middle school education (MS)
elementary education (MAT, MS)
high school education (MAT)
higher education administration (PhD)
higher education-community college leadership (Ed D)
mathematics education (MS, Ed D)
middle school education (MAT)
science education (MS, Ed D)
social work (MSW, PhD)

School of Public Health and Policy
Dr. Allan Noonan, Dean
Program in:
public health and policy (MPH, Dr PH)

■ MOUNT ST. MARY'S UNIVERSITY
Emmitsburg, MD 21727-7799
http://www.msmary.edu/

Independent-religious, coed, comprehensive institution. *Enrollment:* 2,186 graduate, professional, and undergraduate students; 221 full-time matriculated graduate/professional students (52 women), 270 part-time matriculated graduate/professional students (155 women). *Graduate faculty:* 24 full-time (4 women), 24 part-time/adjunct (6 women). *Computer facilities:* Computer purchase and lease plans are available. 150 computers available on campus for general student use. A campuswide network can be accessed from student residence rooms and from off campus. Internet access and online class registration are available. *Library facilities:* Phillips Library. *Graduate expenses:* Tuition: part-time $395 per credit hour. Required fees: $12 per credit hour. Tuition and fees vary according to program. *General application contact:* David Rehm, Vice President for Academic Affairs, 301-447-5218.

Graduate Seminary
Rev. Steven P. Rohlfs, Vice President/ Rector
Program in:
theology (M Div, MA)

Program in Business Administration
Program in:
business administration (MBA)

Program in Education
Laura Frazier, Director
Program in:
education (M Ed, MAT)

■ ST. JOHN'S COLLEGE
Annapolis, MD 21404
http://www.stjohnscollege.edu/

Independent, coed, comprehensive institution. *Enrollment:* 600 graduate, professional, and undergraduate students; 90 matriculated graduate/professional students (34 women). *Graduate faculty:* 13 full-time (2 women), 5 part-time/adjunct (1 woman). *Computer facilities:* 16 computers available on campus for general student use. A campuswide network can be accessed from student residence rooms and from off campus. Internet access is available. *Library facilities:* Greenfield Library plus 1 other. *Graduate expenses:* Tuition: full-time $12,762. Required fees: $582. *General application contact:* Miriam L. Callahan-Hean, Graduate Admissions Administrator, 410-626-2541.

Graduate Institute in Liberal Education
Dr. Joan E. Silver, Director
Program in:
liberal arts (MA)

■ SALISBURY UNIVERSITY
Salisbury, MD 21801-6837
http://www.ssu.edu/

State-supported, coed, comprehensive institution. *Enrollment:* 7,383 graduate, professional, and undergraduate students; 147 full-time matriculated graduate/professional students (100 women), 287 part-time matriculated graduate/professional students (221 women). *Graduate faculty:* 71 full-time (30 women), 14 part-time/adjunct (12 women). *Computer facilities:* Computer purchase and lease plans are available. 275 computers available on campus for general student use. A campuswide network can be accessed from student residence rooms and from off campus. Internet access and online class registration, e-mail services/accounts for all students are available. *Library facilities:* Blackwell Library plus 1 other. *Graduate expenses:* Tuition, state resident: part-time $260 per credit hour. Tuition, nonresident: part-time $546 per credit hour. Required fees: $52 per credit hour. *General application contact:* Gary E. Grodzicki, Associate Dean of Admissions, 410-543-6161.

Graduate Division
Programs in:
applied health physiology (MS)
art (MAT)
biology (MAT)
business administration (MBA)
business education (MAT)
chemistry (MAT)
composition, language and rhetoric (MA)
early childhood education (M Ed)
educational administration (M Ed)
elementary education (M Ed)
English (M Ed, MAT)
French (MAT)
geography (MAT)
history (MAT)
literature (MA)
mathematics (MAT)
mathematics education (MS)
media and technology (MAT)
music (MAT)
nursing (MS)
psychology (MAT)
public school administration (MS Ed)
reading (M Ed)
reading education (MAT)
science (MAT)
secondary education (MAT)
social studies (MAT)
social work (MSW)
Spanish (MAT)
teaching English to speakers of other languages (MA)

■ TOWSON UNIVERSITY
Towson, MD 21252-0001
http://www.towson.edu/

State-supported, coed, university. CGS member. *Enrollment:* 18,921 graduate, professional, and undergraduate students; 886 full-time matriculated graduate/professional students (663 women), 2,661 part-time matriculated graduate/professional students (1,976 women). *Graduate faculty:* 484. *Computer facilities:* A campuswide network can be accessed from student residence rooms and from off campus. Internet access and online class registration are available. *Library facilities:* Cook Library. *Graduate expenses:* Tuition, state resident: part-time $275 per unit. Tuition, nonresident: part-time $577 per unit. Required fees: $72 per unit. *General application contact:* Fran Musotto, Information Contact, 410-704-2501.

Graduate School
Dr. Jin Gong, Dean
Programs in:
applied and industrial mathematics (MS)
applied gerontology (MS, Certificate)
applied information technology (MS, D Sc)
art education (M Ed)
audiology (Au D)

biology (MS)
clinical psychology (MA)
clinician-administrator transition (Certificate)
communications management (MS)
computer science (MS)
counseling psychology (MA, CAS)
Dalcroze (Certificate)
early childhood education (M Ed, CAS)
educational leadership (Certificate)
educational leadership (administrator I certification) (CAS)
educational technology (MS)
elementary education (M Ed)
environmental science (MS, Certificate)
experimental psychology (MA)
family-professional collaboration (Certificate)
geography and environmental planning (MA)
health science (MS)
human resource development (MS)
humanities (MA)
information security and assurance (Certificate)
information systems management (Certificate)
instructional design and training (MS)
instructional technology (Ed D)
integrated homeland security management (MS)
Internet application development (Certificate)
Kodaly (Certificate)
management and leadership development (Certificate)
mathematics education (MS)
music education (MS)
music performance and composition (MM)
networking technologies (Certificate)
nursing (MS, Certificate)
occupational science (Sc D)
occupational therapy (MS)
Orff (Certificate)
organizational change (CAS)
physician assistant studies (MS)
professional studies (MA)
professional writing (MS)
reading (M Ed)
reading education (CAS)
school library media (MS)
school psychology (MA, CAS)
science education (MS)
secondary education (M Ed)
security assessment and management (Certificate)
social science (MS)
software engineering (Certificate)
special education certification (M Ed)
special education leadership (M Ed)
speech-language pathology (MS)
strategic public relations and integrated communications (Certificate)
studio arts (MFA)
teaching (MAT)
theatre (MFA)
women's studies (MS)

Joint University of Baltimore/ Towson University (UB/Towson) MBA Program
Ron Desi, Graduate Program Director
Programs in:
accounting and business advisory services (MS)
business administration (MBA)

■ UNIVERSITY OF BALTIMORE
Baltimore, MD 21201-5779
http://www.ubalt.edu/

State-supported, coed, upper-level institution. *Enrollment:* 4,948 graduate, professional, and undergraduate students; 1,452 full-time matriculated graduate/professional students (824 women), 1,380 part-time matriculated graduate/professional students (865 women). *Graduate faculty:* 152 full-time (60 women), 172 part-time/adjunct (49 women). *Computer facilities:* 135 computers available on campus for general student use. A campuswide network can be accessed from off campus. Internet access and online class registration are available. *Library facilities:* Langsdale Library plus 1 other. *Graduate expenses:* Tuition, state resident: full-time $5,322; part-time $591 per credit. Tuition, nonresident: full-time $7,527; part-time $830 per credit. *General application contact:* Dean Dreibelbis, Assistant Director, Office of Graduate Admissions, 410-837-6565.

Graduate School
Dr. Wim Wiewel, Provost

Merrick School of Business
Dr. Susan Zacur, Dean
Programs in:
accounting and business advisory services (MS)
business (MBA, MS)
business/finance (MS)
business/management information systems (MS)
business/marketing and venturing (MS)
taxation (MS)

The Yale Gordon College of Liberal Arts
Dr. Larry Thomas, Dean
Programs in:
applied psychology (MS)
communications design (DCD)
creative writing and publishing arts (MFA)
criminal justice (MS)
health systems management (MS)
human services administration (MS)
human-computer interaction (MS)
integrated design (MFA)
interaction design and information technology (MS)
legal and ethical studies (MA)
liberal arts (MA, MFA, MPA, MS, DCD, DPA)
negotiations and conflict management (MS)
public administration (MPA, DPA)
publications design (MA)

Joint University of Baltimore/ Towson University (UB/Towson) MBA Program
Ray Frederick, Graduate Advisor
Program in:
business administration (MBA)

School of Law
Phillip J. Closius, Dean
Programs in:
law (JD)
taxation (LL M)

■ UNIVERSITY OF MARYLAND, BALTIMORE COUNTY
Baltimore, MD 21250
http://www.umbc.edu/

State-supported, coed, university. CGS member. *Enrollment:* 11,798 graduate, professional, and undergraduate students; 881 full-time matriculated graduate/ professional students (469 women), 1,363 part-time matriculated graduate/professional students (709 women). *Graduate faculty:* 325 full-time, 15 part-time/adjunct. *Computer facilities:* Computer purchase and lease plans are available. 762 computers available on campus for general student use. A campuswide network can be accessed from student residence rooms and from off campus. Internet access and online class registration, student account and grade information are available. *Library facilities:* Albin O. Kuhn Library and Gallery plus 1 other. *Graduate expenses:* Tuition, state resident: part-time $412 per credit hour. Tuition, nonresident: part-time $681 per credit hour. Required fees: $91 per credit hour. One-time fee: $75 part-time. *General application contact:* Kathryn Nee, Coordinator of Domestic Admissions, 410-455-2944.

Find University Details at www.petersons.com/gradchannel.

Graduate School
Dr. Scott A. Bass, Dean and Vice President for Research
Programs in:
aging policy for the elderly (PhD)
epidemiology of aging (PhD)
marine-estuarine-environmental sciences (MS, PhD)
social, cultural, and behavioral sciences (PhD)

College of Arts, Humanities and Social Sciences
Dr. John Jeffries, Dean

University of Maryland, Baltimore County (continued)
Programs in:
administration, planning, and policy (MS)
American contemporary music (Postbaccalaureate Certificate)
applied behavioral analysis (MA)
applied developmental psychology (PhD)
applied sociology (MA, Postbaccalaureate Certificate)
arts, humanities and social science (MA, MAT, MFA, MPP, MS, PhD, Postbaccalaureate Certificate)
computer/web-based instruction (Postbaccalaureate Certificate)
distance education (Postbaccalaureate Certificate)
early childhood education (MAT)
economic policy analysis (MA)
education (MA, MS)
elementary education (MAT)
emergency health services (MS)
ESOL/bilingual education (Postbaccalaureate Certificate)
ESOL/bilingual training systems (MA)
French (MA)
gender and women's studies (Postbaccalaureate Certificate)
German (MA)
historical studies (MA)
human services psychology (MA, PhD)
human services psychology/clinical (PhD)
imaging and digital arts (MFA)
instructional systems development (MA, Postbaccalaureate Certificate)
intercultural communication (MA)
language, literacy, and culture (PhD)
non-profit sector (Postbaccalaureate Certificate)
preventive medicine and epidemiology (MS)
psychology (MS)
public policy (MPP, PhD)
Russian (MA)
secondary education (MA, MAT)
Spanish (MA)
teaching (MA)

College of Engineering and Information Technology
Dr. Warren DeVries, Dean
Programs in:
biochemical and regulatory engineering (Postbaccalaureate Certificate)
biochemical regulatory engineering (Postbaccalaureate Certificate)
chemical and biochemical engineering (MS, PhD)
chemical engineering (MS, PhD)
civil and environmental engineering (MS, PhD)
computer engineering (MS, PhD)
computer science (MS, PhD)
electrical engineering (MS, PhD)
engineering and information technology (MS, PhD, Postbaccalaureate Certificate)
engineering management (MS)
human-centered computing (MS, PhD)
information systems (MS, PhD)
mechanical engineering (MS, PhD)
mechatronics (Postbaccalaureate Certificate)
systems engineering (Postbaccalaureate Certificate)

College of Natural and Mathematical Sciences
Dr. Geoffrey P. Summers, Dean of Natural and Mathematical Sciences
Programs in:
applied mathematics (MS, PhD)
applied molecular biology (MS)
applied physics (MS, PhD)
astrophysics (PhD)
atmospheric physics (MS, PhD)
biochemistry (MS, PhD)
biological sciences (MS, PhD)
chemistry (MS, PhD)
molecular and cell biology (PhD)
natural and mathematical sciences (MS, PhD)
neurosciences and cognitive sciences (PhD)
optics (MS, PhD)
quantum optics (PhD)
solid state physics (MS, PhD)
statistics (MS, PhD)

■ UNIVERSITY OF MARYLAND, COLLEGE PARK

College Park, MD 20742
http://www.maryland.edu/

State-supported, coed, university. CGS member. *Enrollment:* 35,300 graduate, professional, and undergraduate students; 6,695 full-time matriculated graduate/professional students (3,247 women), 3,195 part-time matriculated graduate/professional students (1,589 women). *Graduate faculty:* 2,896 full-time (1,012 women), 856 part-time/adjunct (395 women). *Computer facilities:* Computer purchase and lease plans are available. 773 computers available on campus for general student use. A campuswide network can be accessed from student residence rooms and from off campus. Internet access and online class registration, student account information, financial aid summary are available. *Library facilities:* McKeldin Library plus 6 others. *General application contact:* Dean of Graduate School, 301-405-4190.

Graduate Studies
Dr. Charles Caramello, Dean of the Graduate School
Program in:
neurosciences and cognitive sciences (PhD)

A. James Clark School of Engineering
Dr. Nariman Farvardin, Dean
Programs in:
aerospace engineering (M Eng)
bioengineering (MS, PhD)
chemical engineering (M Eng, MS, PhD)
civil and environmental engineering (M Eng, MS, PhD)
civil engineering (M Eng)
electrical and computer engineering (M Eng, MS, PhD)
electrical engineering (M Eng, MS, PhD)
electronic packaging and reliability (MS, PhD)
engineering (Certificate)
engineering and public policy (MS)
fire protection engineering (M Eng)
manufacturing and design (MS, PhD)
materials science and engineering (M Eng, MS, PhD)
mechanical engineering (M Eng)
mechanics and materials (MS, PhD)
nuclear engineering (ME, MS, PhD)
reliability engineering (M Eng, MS, PhD)
systems engineering (M Eng)
telecommunications (MS)
thermal and fluid sciences (MS, PhD)

College of Agriculture and Natural Resources
Dr. Cheng-i Wei, Dean
Programs in:
agriculture and natural resources (DVM, MS, PhD)
agriculture economics (MS, PhD)
agronomy (MS, PhD)
animal sciences (MS, PhD)
food science (MS, PhD)
horticulture (PhD)
natural resource sciences (MS, PhD)
nutrition (MS, PhD)
resource economics (MS, PhD)
veterinary medical sciences (MS, PhD)
veterinary medicine (DVM, MS, PhD)

College of Arts and Humanities
Dr. James F. Harris, Dean
Programs in:
American studies (MA, PhD)
art (MFA)
art history (MA, PhD)
arts and humanities (M Ed, MA, MFA, MM, DMA, Ed D, PhD)
classics (MA)
communication (MA, PhD)
comparative literature (MA, PhD)
creative writing (MA, MFA, PhD)
dance (MFA)
English language and literature (MA, PhD)
ethnomusicology (MA)
French (MA)
French language and literature (MA)
German (MA)

Germanic language and literature (MA, PhD)
history (MA, PhD)
Japanese (MA)
Jewish studies (MA)
languages, literature, and cultures (MA, PhD)
linguistics (MA, PhD)
modern French studies (PhD)
music (M Ed, MA, MM, DMA, Ed D, PhD)
philosophy (MA, PhD)
Russian (MA)
second language instruction (PhD)
second language learning (PhD)
second language measurement and assessment (PhD)
second language use (PhD)
Spanish (MA)
Spanish and Portuguese (MA, PhD)
theatre (MA, MFA, PhD)
women's studies (MA, PhD)

College of Behavioral and Social Sciences
Dr. Edward Montgomery, Dean
Programs in:
American politics (PhD)
applied anthropology (MAA)
audiology (MA, PhD)
behavioral and social sciences (MA, MAA, MS, Au D, PhD)
clinical psychology (PhD)
comparative politics (PhD)
criminology and criminal justice (MA, PhD)
developmental psychology (PhD)
economics (MA, PhD)
experimental psychology (PhD)
geography (MA, PhD)
hearing and speech sciences (Au D)
industrial psychology (MA, MS, PhD)
international relations (PhD)
language pathology (MA, PhD)
neuroscience (PhD)
political economy (PhD)
political theory (PhD)
social psychology (PhD)
sociology (MA, PhD)
speech (MA, PhD)
survey methodology (MS, PhD)

College of Chemical and Life Sciences
Dr. Norma M. Allewell, Dean
Programs in:
analytical chemistry (MS, PhD)
behavior, ecology, and systematics (PhD)
behavior, ecology, evolution, and systematics (MS)
biochemistry (MS, PhD)
biology (MS, PhD)
cell biology and molecular genetics (MS, PhD)
chemical and life sciences (MLS, MS, PhD)
chemistry (MS, PhD)
entomology (MS, PhD)
inorganic chemistry (MS, PhD)
life sciences (MLS)
marine-estuarine-environmental sciences (MS, PhD)
molecular and cellular biology (PhD)
organic chemistry (MS, PhD)
physical chemistry (MS, PhD)
plant biology (MS, PhD)
sustainable development and conservation biology (MS)

College of Computer, Mathematical and Physical Sciences
Dr. Stephen Halperin, Dean
Programs in:
applied mathematics (MS, PhD)
astronomy (MS, PhD)
atmospheric and oceanic science (MS, PhD)
chemical physics (MS, PhD)
computer science (MS, PhD)
computer, mathematical and physical sciences (MA, MS, PhD)
geology (MS, PhD)
mathematical statistics (MA, PhD)
mathematics (MA, PhD)
physics (MS, PhD)

College of Education
Dr. Dennis M. Kivlighan, Dean
Programs in:
college student personnel (M Ed, MA)
college student personnel administration (PhD)
community counseling (CAGS)
community/career counseling (M Ed, MA)
counseling and personnel services (M Ed, MA, PhD)
counseling psychology (PhD)
counselor education (PhD)
curriculum and educational communications (M Ed, MA, Ed D, PhD)
early childhood/elementary education (M Ed, MA, Ed D, PhD)
education (M Ed, MA, Ed D, PhD, CAGS)
human development (M Ed, MA, Ed D, PhD)
measurement (MA, PhD)
program evaluation (MA, PhD)
reading (M Ed, MA, PhD, CAGS)
rehabilitation counseling (M Ed, MA)
school counseling (M Ed, MA)
school psychology (M Ed, MA, PhD)
secondary education (M Ed, MA, Ed D, PhD, CAGS)
social foundations of education (M Ed, MA, Ed D, PhD, CAGS)
special education (M Ed, MA, PhD, CAGS)
statistics (MA, PhD)
teaching English to speakers of other languages (M Ed)

College of Health and Human Performance
Dr. Robert Gold, Dean
Programs in:
community health education (MPH)
family studies (PhD)
health and human performance (MA, MPH, MS, PhD)
kinesiology (MA, PhD)
marriage and family therapy (MS)
public/community health (PhD)

College of Information Studies
Dr. Jennifer Preece, Dean
Program in:
information studies (MIM, MLS, PhD)

Phillip Merrill College of Journalism
Thomas Kunkel, Dean
Programs in:
broadcast journalism (MA)
journalism (MA)
journalism and media studies (PhD)
online news (MA)
public affairs reporting (MA)

Robert H. Smith School of Business
Dr. Howard Frank, Dean
Programs in:
business (EMBA, MBA, MS, PhD)
business administration (EMBA, MBA)
business and management (MS, PhD)

School of Architecture, Planning and Preservation
Garth Rockcastle, Dean
Programs in:
architecture (M Arch)
architecture, planning and preservation (M Arch, MCP, MHP, PhD, Certificate)
historic preservation (MHP, Certificate)
urban and regional planning/design (PhD)
urban studies and planning (MCP)

School of Public Policy
Dr. Steve Fetter, Dean
Programs in:
policy studies (PhD)
public management (MPM)
public policy (MPM, MPP, PhD)
public policy/law)

■ UNIVERSITY OF MARYLAND EASTERN SHORE

Princess Anne, MD 21853-1299

http://www.umes.edu/

State-supported, coed, university. CGS member. *Enrollment:* 190 full-time matriculated graduate/professional students (105 women), 217 part-time matriculated graduate/professional students (131 women). *Graduate faculty:* 65 full-time (24 women), 51 part-time/adjunct (15 women). *Computer facilities:* Computer purchase and lease plans are available. 120 computers available on campus for general student use. A campuswide network can be accessed. *Library facilities:* Frederick Douglass Library.

University of Maryland Eastern Shore (continued)

General application contact: Dr. C. Dennis Ignasias, Associate Vice President for Academic Affairs, 410-651-6507.

Find University Details at www.petersons.com/gradchannel.

Graduate Programs

Dr. C. Dennis Ignasias, Associate Vice President for Academic Affairs

Programs in:

- applied computer science (MS)
- career and technology education (M Ed)
- criminology and criminal justice (MS)
- education leadership (Ed D)
- food and agricultural sciences (MS)
- food science and technology (PhD)
- guidance and counseling (M Ed)
- marine-estuarine-environmental sciences (MS, PhD)
- organizational leadership (PhD)
- physical therapy (DPT)
- rehabilitation counseling (MS)
- special education (M Ed)
- teaching (MAT)
- toxicology (MS, PhD)

■ UNIVERSITY OF MARYLAND UNIVERSITY COLLEGE

Adelphi, MD 20783

http://www.umuc.edu/

State-supported, coed, comprehensive institution. CGS member. *Enrollment:* 33,096 graduate, professional, and undergraduate students; 267 full-time matriculated graduate/professional students (150 women), 9,253 part-time matriculated graduate/professional students (4,960 women). *Graduate faculty:* 103 full-time (41 women), 312 part-time/adjunct (88 women). *Computer facilities:* 375 computers available on campus for general student use. A campuswide network can be accessed from off campus. *Library facilities:* Information and Library Services plus 1 other. *General application contact:* Coordinator, Graduate Admissions, 301-985-7155.

Graduate School of Management and Technology

Dr. Christina A. Hannah, Acting Associate Vice President and Dean of Graduate Studies

Programs in:

- accounting and financial management (MS, Certificate)
- accounting and information technology (MS, Certificate)
- biotechnology studies (MS, Certificate)
- business administration (Exec MBA, MBA)
- distance education (MDE, Certificate)
- education (M Ed)
- environmental management (MS, Certificate)
- financial management and information systems (MS, Certificate)
- health administration informatics (MS, Certificate)
- health care administration (MS, Certificate)
- information technology (Exec MS, MS, Certificate)
- international management (MIM, Certificate)
- management (MS, DM, Certificate)
- management and technology (Exec MBA, Exec MS, M Ed, MBA, MDE, MIM, MS, DM, Certificate)
- technology management (Exec MS, MS, Certificate)

Massachusetts

■ AMERICAN INTERNATIONAL COLLEGE

Springfield, MA 01109-3189

http://www.aic.edu/

Independent, coed, comprehensive institution. *Enrollment:* 173 full-time matriculated graduate/professional students (116 women), 398 part-time matriculated graduate/professional students (310 women). *Graduate faculty:* 55 full-time (28 women), 60 part-time/adjunct (27 women). *Computer facilities:* 125 computers available on campus for general student use. A campuswide network can be accessed. Internet access is available. *Library facilities:* James J. Shea Jr. Library. *Graduate expenses:* Tuition: part-time $585 per semester hour. Required fees: $100 per year. Full-time tuition and fees vary according to program. *General application contact:* Keshawn Dodds, Associate Director of Graduate Admissions, 413-205-3549.

School of Business Administration

Dr. John Rogers, Dean

Program in:

- business administration (MBA, MSAT)

School of Continuing Education and Graduate Studies

Dr. Roland E. Holstead, Dean

Programs in:

- organization development (MSOD)
- public administration (MPA)

School of Health Sciences

Dr. Carol Jobe, Dean

Programs in:

- health sciences (MPT, MSN, MSOT, DPT)
- nursing (MSN)
- occupational therapy (MSOT)
- physical therapy (MPT, DPT)

School of Psychology and Education

Dr. Gregory Schmutte, Dean

Programs in:

- administration (M Ed, CAGS)
- child development (MA, Ed D)
- clinical psychology (MA)
- criminal justice studies (MS)
- elementary education (M Ed, CAGS)
- forensic psychology (MS)
- psychology and education (M Ed, MA, MAT, MS, Ed D, CAGS)
- reading (M Ed, CAGS)
- secondary education (M Ed, CAGS)
- special education (M Ed, CAGS)
- teaching (MAT)

Center for Human Resource Development

Dr. Debra D. Anderson, Director

Program in:

- human resource development (MA)

■ ANNA MARIA COLLEGE

Paxton, MA 01612

http://www.annamaria.edu/

Independent-religious, coed, comprehensive institution. *Enrollment:* 1,200 graduate, professional, and undergraduate students; 52 full-time matriculated graduate/professional students (32 women), 313 part-time matriculated graduate/professional students (210 women). *Graduate faculty:* 16 full-time (8 women), 60 part-time/adjunct (31 women). *Computer facilities:* 59 computers available on campus for general student use. A campuswide network can be accessed from student residence rooms and from off campus. Internet access, online class schedules, student account information are available. *Library facilities:* Mondor-Eagen Library. *General application contact:* Janet LaPointe, Admissions Coordinator, Graduate and Continuing Education, 508-849-3234.

Graduate Division

Dr. Paul Erickson, Academic Dean

Programs in:

- business administration (MBA, AC)
- counseling psychology (MA)
- criminal justice (MS)
- early childhood development (M Ed)
- education (CAGS)
- elementary education (M Ed)
- emergency management (MS, Graduate Certificate)
- fire science (MA)
- human services administration (MS)
- justice administration (MS)
- occupational and environmental health and safety (MS)
- pastoral ministry (MA)
- psychology (MA)
- reading (M Ed)
- visual art (MA)

■ ASSUMPTION COLLEGE
Worcester, MA 01609-1296
http://www.assumption.edu/

Independent-religious, coed, comprehensive institution. *Enrollment:* 2,498 graduate, professional, and undergraduate students; 133 full-time matriculated graduate/professional students (103 women), 264 part-time matriculated graduate/professional students (174 women). *Graduate faculty:* 16 full-time (4 women), 34 part-time/adjunct (12 women). *Computer facilities:* Computer purchase and lease plans are available. 190 computers available on campus for general student use. A campuswide network can be accessed from student residence rooms and from off campus. Internet access is available. *Library facilities:* Emmanuel d'Alzon Library. *General application contact:* Adrian O. Dumas, Director of Graduate Enrollment Management and Services, 508-767-7365.

Find University Details at www.petersons.com/gradchannel.

Graduate School
Dr. MaryLou Anderson, Dean
Programs in:
- business administration (MBA, CAGS)
- counseling psychology (MA, CAGS)
- rehabilitation counseling (MA, CAGS)
- school counseling (MA, CAGS)
- special education (MA)

■ BENTLEY COLLEGE
Waltham, MA 02452-4705
http://www.bentley.edu

Independent, coed, comprehensive institution. *Enrollment:* 5,497 graduate, professional, and undergraduate students; 236 full-time matriculated graduate/professional students (114 women), 1,020 part-time matriculated graduate/professional students (474 women). *Graduate faculty:* 271 full-time (105 women), 202 part-time/adjunct (72 women). *Computer facilities:* Computer purchase and lease plans are available. 4,441 computers available on campus for general student use. A campuswide network can be accessed from student residence rooms and from off campus. Internet access and online class registration, grade checking, online admission, Blackboard, resume review, student employment, interlibrary loan are available. *Library facilities:* Baker Library. *Graduate expenses:* Tuition: full-time $28,440; part-time $2,844 per course. Required fees: $404; $105 per year. *General application contact:* Sharon Hill, Director of Graduate Admissions, 781-891-2108.

The Elkin B. McCallum Graduate School of Business
Dr. Margrethe H. Olson, Dean
Programs in:
- accountancy (PhD)
- accounting (GBC)
- accounting information systems (GBC)
- business (GSS)
- business administration (MBA)
- business ethics (GBC)
- data analysis (GBC)
- finance (MSF)
- financial planning (GBC)
- human factors in information design (MSHFID)
- information technology (MSIT)
- marketing analytics (GBC)
- real estate management (MSREM)
- taxation (GBC)

■ BOSTON COLLEGE
Chestnut Hill, MA 02467-3800
http://www.bc.edu/

Independent-religious, coed, university. CGS member. *Enrollment:* 13,652 graduate, professional, and undergraduate students; 2,383 full-time matriculated graduate/professional students (1,462 women), 2,249 part-time matriculated graduate/professional students (1,241 women). *Graduate faculty:* 679. *Computer facilities:* Computer purchase and lease plans are available. 1,000 computers available on campus for general student use. A campuswide network can be accessed from student residence rooms and from off campus. Internet access and online class registration are available. *Library facilities:* Thomas P. O'Neill Library plus 6 others. *General application contact:* Robert V. Howe, Associate Dean, 617-552-3265.

The Carroll School of Management
Dr. Jeffrey L. Ringuest, Associate Dean for Graduate Programs
Programs in:
- accounting (MSA)
- business administration (MBA)
- finance (MSF, PhD)
- management (MBA, MSA, MSF, PhD)
- organization studies (PhD)

Graduate School of Arts and Sciences
Dr. Michael A. Smyer, Dean
Programs in:
- arts and sciences (MA, MS, MST, PhD)
- biochemistry (MS, PhD)
- biology (PhD)
- classics (MA)
- economics (PhD)
- English (MA, PhD)
- European national studies (MA)
- French (MA, PhD)
- geology and geophysics (MS)
- Greek (MA)
- history (MA, PhD)
- inorganic chemistry (PhD)
- Italian (MA)
- Latin (MA)
- linguistics (MA)
- mathematics (MA)
- medieval language (PhD)
- medieval studies (MA)
- organic chemistry (PhD)
- philosophy (MA, PhD)
- physical chemistry (PhD)
- physics (MS, PhD)
- political science (MA, PhD)
- psychology (MA, PhD)
- Russian and Slavic languages and literature (MA)
- science education (MST)
- Slavic studies (MA)
- sociology (MA, PhD)
- Spanish (MA, PhD)
- theology (MA, PhD)

Institute of Religious Education and Pastoral Ministry
Dr. Thomas Groome, Chairperson
Programs in:
- church leadership (MA)
- pastoral ministry (MA)
- religious education (MA, PhD)
- social justice/social ministry (MA)
- youth ministry (MA)

Graduate School of Social Work
Dr. Alberto Godenzi, Dean
Program in:
- social work (MSW, PhD)

Law School
John H. Garvey, Dean
Program in:
- law (JD)

Lynch Graduate School of Education
Rev. Joseph O'Keefe, SJ, Dean
Programs in:
- biology (MST)
- chemistry (MST)
- counseling psychology (MA, PhD)
- curriculum and instruction (M Ed, PhD, CAES)
- developmental and educational psychology (MA, PhD)
- early childhood education/teacher option (M Ed)
- early childhood/specialist option (MA)
- education (M Ed, MA, MAT, MST, Ed D, PhD, CAES)
- educational administration (M Ed, Ed D, PhD, CAES)
- educational research, measurement, and evaluation (M Ed, PhD)
- elementary education (M Ed)
- English (MAT)
- French (MAT)
- geology (MST)
- higher education (MA, PhD)
- history (MAT)
- Latin and classical humanities (MAT)
- mathematics (MST)
- physics (MST)
- professional school administrator (Ed D)
- reading specialist (M Ed, CAES)
- religious education (M Ed, CAES)

Boston College (continued)
- secondary education (M Ed, MAT, MST)
- secondary teaching (M Ed)
- Spanish (MAT)
- special needs: moderate disabilities (M Ed, CAES)
- special needs: severe disabilities (M Ed)

William F. Connell School of Nursing
Dr. Barbara Hazard, Dean
Programs in:
- adult health nursing (MS)
- community health nursing (MS)
- family health (MS)
- gerontology (MS)
- maternal/child health nursing (MS)
- nurse anesthesia (MS)
- nursing (PhD)
- psychiatric-mental health nursing (MS)

■ BOSTON UNIVERSITY
Boston, MA 02215
http://www.bu.edu/

Independent, coed, university. CGS member. *Enrollment:* 31,574 graduate, professional, and undergraduate students; 8,508 full-time matriculated graduate/professional students (4,624 women), 4,330 part-time matriculated graduate/professional students (2,271 women). *Graduate faculty:* 3,856. *Computer facilities:* Computer purchase and lease plans are available. 750 computers available on campus for general student use. A campuswide network can be accessed from student residence rooms and from off campus. Internet access and online class registration, research and educational networks are available. *Library facilities:* Mugar Memorial Library plus 18 others. *Graduate expenses:* Tuition: full-time $33,330; part-time $1,042 per credit. Required fees: $462; $40. *General application contact:* Information Contact, 617-353-2000.

Find University Details at www.petersons.com/gradchannel.

College of Communication
Dr. John J. Schulz, Dean
Programs in:
- advertising (MS)
- broadcast journalism (MS)
- business and economics journalism (MS)
- communication (MFA, MS)
- communication research (MS)
- communication studies (MS)
- film production (MFA)
- film studies (MFA)
- photo journalism (MS)
- print journalism (MS)
- public relations (MS)
- science journalism (MS)
- screenwriting (MFA)
- television (MS)
- television management (MS)

College of Engineering
Dr. Kenneth R. Lutchen, Dean
Programs in:
- aerospace engineering (MS, PhD)
- biomedical engineering (MS, PhD)
- computer engineering (PhD)
- computer systems engineering (MS)
- electrical engineering (MS, PhD)
- engineering (MS, PhD)
- general engineering (MS)
- global manufacturing (MS)
- manufacturing (MS)
- manufacturing engineering (PhD)
- mechanical engineering (MS, PhD)
- photonics (MS)
- systems engineering (PhD)

College of Fine Arts
Walt Meissner, Interim Dean
Programs in:
- art education (MFA)
- collaborative piano (MM, DMA)
- composition (MM, DMA)
- conducting (MM, Artist Diploma, Performance Diploma)
- costume design (MFA)
- costume production (MFA)
- directing (MFA)
- fine arts (MFA, MM, DMA, Artist Diploma, Certificate, Performance Diploma)
- graphic design (MFA)
- historical performance (MM, DMA, Artist Diploma, Performance Diploma)
- lighting design (MFA)
- music education (MM, DMA)
- music theory (MM)
- musicology (MM)
- opera performance (Certificate)
- painting (MFA)
- performance (MM, DMA, Artist Diploma, Performance Diploma)
- scene design (MFA)
- sculpture (MFA)
- studio teaching (MFA)
- technical production (MFA, Certificate)
- theatre crafts (Certificate)
- theatre education (MFA)

College of Health and Rehabilitation Sciences—Sargent College
Dr. Gloria S. Waters, Dean
Programs in:
- applied anatomy and physiology (MS, PhD)
- audiology (PhD)
- health and rehabilitation sciences (MS, MSOT, D Sc, DPT, PhD, CAGS)
- nutrition (MS)
- occupational therapy (MS, MSOT)
- physical therapy (DPT)
- rehabilitation sciences (D Sc)
- speech-language pathology (MS, PhD, CAGS)

Goldman School of Dental Medicine
Dr. Spencer Frankl, Dean
Programs in:
- advanced general dentistry (CAGS)
- dental medicine (DMD, MS, MSD, D Sc, D Sc D, PhD, CAGS)
- dental public health (MS, MSD, D Sc D, CAGS)
- dentistry (DMD)
- endodontics (MSD, D Sc D, CAGS)
- implantology (CAGS)
- operative dentistry (MSD, D Sc D, CAGS)
- oral and maxillofacial surgery (MSD, D Sc D, CAGS)
- oral biology (MSD, D Sc, D Sc D, PhD)
- orthodontics (MSD, D Sc D, CAGS)
- pediatric dentistry (MSD, D Sc D, CAGS)
- periodontology (MSD, D Sc D, CAGS)
- prosthodontics (MSD, D Sc D, CAGS)

Graduate School of Arts and Sciences
J. Scott Whittaker, Associate Dean
Programs in:
- African American studies (MA)
- African studies (Certificate)
- American and New England studies (PhD)
- anthropology (PhD)
- applied anthropology (MA)
- applied linguistics (MA, PhD)
- archaeological heritage management (MA)
- archaeology (MA, PhD)
- art history (MA, PhD)
- arts and sciences (MA, MAEP, MAPE, MS, PhD, Certificate)
- astronomy (MA, PhD)
- bioinformatics (MS, PhD)
- biology (MA, PhD)
- biostatistics (MA, PhD)
- cellular biophysics (PhD)
- chemistry (MA, PhD)
- classical studies (MA, PhD)
- cognitive and neural systems (MA, PhD)
- composition (MA)
- computer science (MA, PhD)
- creative writing (MA)
- earth sciences (MA, PhD)
- economic policy (MAEP)
- economics (MA, PhD)
- energy and environmental analysis (MA)
- English (MA, PhD)
- environmental remote sensing and geographic information systems (MA)
- French language and literature (MA, PhD)
- geoarchaeology (MA)
- geography and environment (MA, PhD)
- Hispanic language and literatures (MA, PhD)
- history (MA, PhD)
- international relations (MA)
- international relations and environmental policy (MA)
- international relations and environmental policy management (MA)

international relations and international communication (MA)
mathematical finance (MA)
mathematics (MA, PhD)
molecular biology, cell biology, and biochemistry (MA, PhD)
museum studies (Certificate)
music education (MA)
music history/theory (PhD)
musicology (MA, PhD)
neuroscience (MA, PhD)
philosophy (MA, PhD)
physics (MA, PhD)
political economy (MAPE)
political science (MA, PhD)
preservation studies (MA)
psychology (MA, PhD)
religious and theological studies (MA, PhD)
sociology (MA, PhD)
sociology and social work (PhD)

Editorial Institute
Archie Burnett, Co-Director
Program in:
editorial studies (MA, PhD)

Metropolitan College (Continuing Education)
Dr. Jay Halfond, Dean
Programs in:
actuarial science (MS)
advertising (MS)
arts administration (MS, Graduate Certificate)
banking and financial management (MSM)
business continuity in emergency management (MSM)
city planning (MCP)
computer information systems (MS)
computer science (MS)
continuing education (MCJ, MCP, MLA, MS, MSAS, MSM, MUA, Graduate Certificate)
criminal justice (MCJ)
economics development and tourism management (MSAS)
electronic commerce, systems, and technology (MSAS)
financial economics (MSAS)
fundraising management (Graduate Certificate)
human resource management (MSM)
innovation and technology (MSAS)
insurance management (MSM)
international market management (MSM)
liberal studies (MLA)
multinational commerce (MSAS)
project management (MSM)
telecommunications (MS)
urban affairs (MUA)

School of Education
Dr. Charles L. Glenn, Dean ad interim
Programs in:
administration, training, and policy studies (Ed D)
bilingual education (Ed M, CAGS)
counseling (Ed M, CAGS)
counseling psychology (Ed D)
curriculum and teaching (Ed M, MAT, Ed D, CAGS)
developmental studies (Ed M, Ed D, CAGS)
early childhood education (Ed M, Ed D, CAGS)
education (Ed M, MAT, Ed D, CAGS)
education of the deaf (Ed M, CAGS)
educational administration (Ed M)
educational media and technology (Ed M, Ed D, CAGS)
elementary education (Ed M)
English and language arts education (Ed M, CAGS)
health education (Ed M, CAGS)
human resource education (Ed M, CAGS)
international educational development (Ed M)
Latin and classical studies (MAT)
literacy and language (Ed D)
mathematics education (Ed M, MAT, Ed D, CAGS)
modern foreign language education (Ed M, MAT)
physical education and coaching (Ed M, Ed D, CAGS)
policy, planning, and administration (Ed M, CAGS)
reading education (Ed M, Ed D, CAGS)
science education (Ed M, MAT, Ed D, CAGS)
social studies education (Ed M, MAT, Ed D, CAGS)
special education (Ed M, Ed D, CAGS)
teaching of English to speakers of other languages (Ed M, CAGS)

School of Law
Maureen O'Rourke, Interim Dean
Programs in:
American law (LL M)
banking law (LL M)
intellectual property law (LL M)
law (JD)
taxation (LL M)

School of Management
Louis Lataif, Dean
Programs in:
accounting (DBA)
advanced accounting (Certificate)
business administration (Exec MBA, MBA, DBA, Certificate)
general management (MBA)
healthcare management (MBA)
information systems (DBA)
investment management (MSIM)
management policy (DBA)
marketing (DBA)
operations management (DBA)
organizational behavior (DBA)
public and nonprofit management (MBA)

School of Medicine
Dr. Karen H. Antman, Dean
Programs in:
biomedical forensics (MS)
medicine (MD, MA, MS, PhD)

Division of Graduate Medical Sciences
Dr. Carl Franzblau, Associate Dean
Programs in:
biochemistry (MA, PhD)
cell and molecular biology (PhD)
experimental pathology (PhD)
immunology (PhD)
medical nutrition sciences (MA, PhD)
medical sciences (MA, MS, PhD)
mental health and behavioral medicine (MA)
microbiology (MA, PhD)
molecular medicine (PhD)
pharmacology and experimental therapeutics (MA, PhD)
physiology and biophysics (MA, PhD)

School of Public Health
Dr. Robert F. Meenan, Dean
Programs in:
biostatistics (MA, MPH, PhD)
environmental health (MPH, D Sc)
epidemiology (M Sc, MPH, D Sc)
health behavior, health promotion, and disease prevention (MPH)
health law, bioethics and human rights (MPH)
health policy and management (M Sc, MPH, D Sc)
international health (MPH, Dr PH, Certificate)
maternal and child health (MPH)
nurse midwifery education (Certificate)
public health (M Sc, MA, MPH, D Sc, Dr PH, PhD, Certificate)
social behavioral sciences (Dr PH)

School of Social Work
Wilma Peebles-Wilkins, Dean
Programs in:
clinical practice with groups (MSW)
clinical practice with individuals and families (MSW)
macro social work practice (MSW)
social work and sociology (PhD)

School of Theology
Dr. Ray Hart, Interim Dean
Program in:
theology (M Div, MSM, MTS, STM, D Min, Th D)

University Professors Program
Bruce Redford, Director
Program in:
interdisciplinary studies (MA, PhD)

■ BRANDEIS UNIVERSITY
Waltham, MA 02454-9110
http://www.brandeis.edu/

Independent, coed, university. CGS member. *Enrollment:* 5,313 graduate, professional, and undergraduate students; 1,323 full-time matriculated graduate/professional students (731 women), 255 part-time matriculated

Brandeis University (continued)
graduate/professional students (94 women). *Graduate faculty:* 348 full-time (130 women), 153 part-time/adjunct (75 women). *Computer facilities:* Computer purchase and lease plans are available. 104 computers available on campus for general student use. A campuswide network can be accessed from student residence rooms and from off campus. Internet access and online class registration, educational software are available. *Library facilities:* Goldfarb Library plus 2 others. *General application contact:* Margaret Haley, Assistant Dean, Graduate Admissions, 781-736-3406.

Find University Details at www.petersons.com/gradchannel.

Graduate School of Arts and Sciences

Dr. Gregory L. Freeze, Dean
Programs in:
- acting (MFA)
- American history (MA, PhD)
- anthropology (MA, PhD)
- anthropology and women's and gender studies (MA)
- arts and sciences (MA, MAT, MFA, MS, PhD, Certificate)
- biochemistry (MS, PhD)
- biophysics and structural biology (MS, PhD)
- coexistence and conflict (MA)
- cognitive neuroscience (PhD)
- comparative history (MA, PhD)
- composition and theory (MA, MFA, PhD)
- design (MFA)
- English and American literature (MA, PhD)
- English and women's and gender studies (MA)
- English and women's studies (MA)
- general psychology (MA)
- genetic counseling (MS)
- genetics (PhD)
- inorganic chemistry (MS, PhD)
- Jewish day school (MAT)
- Jewish professional leadership)
- mathematics (MA, PhD)
- microbiology (PhD)
- molecular and cell biology (MS, PhD)
- molecular biology (PhD)
- music and women's and gender studies (MA)
- music and women's studies (MA)
- musicology (MA, MFA, PhD)
- Near Eastern and Judaic studies (MA, PhD)
- Near Eastern and Judaic studies and sociology (PhD)
- Near Eastern and Judaic studies and women's and gender studies (MA)
- Near Eastern and Judaic studies and women's studies (MA)
- neurobiology (PhD)
- neuroscience (MS, PhD)
- organic chemistry (MS, PhD)
- physical chemistry (MS, PhD)
- physics (MS, PhD)
- politics (MA, PhD)
- premedical studies (Certificate)
- public education elementary (MAT)
- secondary education (English, history, biology, Bible) (MAT)
- social policy and sociology (PhD)
- social/developmental psychology (PhD)
- sociology (MA, PhD)
- sociology and women's and gender studies (MA)
- studio art (Certificate)
- teaching of Hebrew (MAT)

Michtom School of Computer Science
Dr. James Pustejovsky, Director of Graduate Studies
Program in:
- computer science (MA, PhD, Certificate)

The Heller School for Social Policy and Management

Programs in:
- child, youth, and family policy and management (MBA)
- health care policy and management (MBA)
- international development (MA)
- international health policy and management (MS)
- social policy (MPP, PhD)
- social policy and management (MBA)
- sustainable development (MA, MBA)

International Business School

Programs in:
- finance (MSF)
- international business (MBAi)
- international economics and finance (MA, PhD)
- international finance/international economics (MBAi)

■ BRIDGEWATER STATE COLLEGE

Bridgewater, MA 02325-0001
http://www.bridgew.edu/

State-supported, coed, comprehensive institution. *Enrollment:* 9,655 graduate, professional, and undergraduate students; 2,150 matriculated graduate/professional students. *Graduate faculty:* 140 full-time. *Computer facilities:* Computer purchase and lease plans are available. 780 computers available on campus for general student use. A campuswide network can be accessed from student residence rooms and from off campus. Internet access and online class registration, student account information, application software are available. *Library facilities:* Clement Maxwell Library. *General application contact:* Dr. Raymond Charles Guillette, Assistant Dean School of Graduate Studies, 508-531-2919.

School of Graduate Studies

Dr. William Smith, Dean

School of Arts and Sciences
Dr. Howard London, Dean
Programs in:
- art (MAT)
- arts and sciences (MA, MAT, MPA, MS, MSW)
- biological sciences (MAT)
- computer science (MS)
- criminal justice (MS)
- English (MA, MAT)
- history (MAT)
- mathematics (MAT)
- physical sciences (MAT)
- physics (MAT)
- psychology (MA)
- public administration (MPA)
- social work (MSW)

School of Business
Dr. Catherine Morgan, Dean
Programs in:
- accounting and finance (MSM)
- business (MSM)
- management (MSM)

School of Education and Allied Science
Dr. Anna Bradfield, Dean
Programs in:
- counseling (M Ed, CAGS)
- early childhood education (M Ed)
- education and allied science (M Ed, MAT, MS, CAGS)
- educational leadership (M Ed, CAGS)
- elementary education (M Ed)
- health promotion (M Ed)
- instructional technology (M Ed)
- physical education (MS)
- reading (M Ed, CAGS)
- secondary education (MAT)
- special education (M Ed)

■ CAMBRIDGE COLLEGE

Cambridge, MA 02138-5304
http://www.cambridgecollege.edu/

Independent, coed, comprehensive institution. *Enrollment:* 4,670 graduate, professional, and undergraduate students; 1,857 full-time matriculated graduate/professional students (1,368 women), 1,945 part-time matriculated graduate/professional students (1,501 women). *Graduate faculty:* 24 full-time (10 women), 759 part-time/adjunct (468 women). *Computer facilities:* Computer purchase and lease plans are available. A campuswide network can be accessed. Internet access and online class registration are available. *Library facilities:* Cambridge College Online Library. *Graduate expenses:* Tuition: full-time $10,935; part-time $405 per credit hour. One-time fee: $130 full-time. Tuition and fees vary according to degree level and program. *General application contact:* Farah Favanbaksh, Senior Director of Admissions, 617-868-1000 Ext. 1124.

Program in Counseling Psychology
Dr. Niti Seth, Director
Program in:
counseling psychology (M Ed, CAGS)

Program in Education
Dr. Anthony DeMatteo, Dean
Programs in:
education (CAGS)
education leadership (Ed D)
education/integrated studies (M Ed)

Program in Management
Dr. Bill Hancock, Associate Dean
Programs in:
e-commerce (M Mgt)
management (M Mgt)

■ CLARK UNIVERSITY
Worcester, MA 01610-1477
http://www.clarku.edu/

Independent, coed, university. CGS member. *Enrollment:* 3,071 graduate, professional, and undergraduate students; 568 full-time matriculated graduate/professional students (344 women), 203 part-time matriculated graduate/professional students (96 women). *Graduate faculty:* 179 full-time (70 women), 131 part-time/adjunct (60 women). *Computer facilities:* 200 computers available on campus for general student use. A campuswide network can be accessed from student residence rooms and from off campus. Internet access, online course support are available. *Library facilities:* Robert Hutchings Goddard Library plus 4 others. *General application contact:* Denise Robertson, Graduate School Coordinator, 508-793-7676.

Find University Details at www.petersons.com/gradchannel.

Graduate School
Dr. Nancy Budwig, Director
Programs in:
biology (MA, PhD)
chemistry (MA, PhD)
clinical psychology (PhD)
community development and planning (MA)
developmental psychology (PhD)
economics (PhD)
education (MA Ed)
English (MA)
environmental science and policy (MA)
geographic information science (MA)
geographic information science for development and environment (MA)
geography (PhD)
history (MA, CAGS)
holocaust history (PhD)
international development and social change (MA)
physics (MA, PhD)
social-personality psychology (PhD)

College of Professional and Continuing Education
Dr. Thomas Massey, Director
Programs in:
information technology (MIT)
liberal studies (MALA)
professional and continuing education (MALA, MIT, MPA, MSPC, CAGS, Certificate)
professional communication (MSPC)
public administration (MPA, Certificate)

Graduate School of Management
Dr. Edward Ottensmeyer, Dean
Programs in:
accounting (MBA)
finance (MBA)
global business (MBA)
health care management (MBA)
management (MBA)
management of information technology (MBA)
marketing (MBA)

■ EASTERN NAZARENE COLLEGE
Quincy, MA 02170-2999
http://www.enc.edu/

Independent-religious, coed, comprehensive institution. *Enrollment:* 1,212 graduate, professional, and undergraduate students; 50 full-time matriculated graduate/professional students (30 women), 120 part-time matriculated graduate/professional students (80 women). *Graduate faculty:* 8 full-time (3 women), 8 part-time/adjunct (5 women). *Computer facilities:* 98 computers available on campus for general student use. A campuswide network can be accessed from student residence rooms and from off campus. Internet access is available. *Library facilities:* Nease Library. *General application contact:* Christine Galbraith, Graduate Studies Recruiter, 617-774-6703.

Adult and Graduate Studies
John G. Moran, Director of Adult and Graduate Studies
Program in:
marriage and family therapy (MS)

Division of Education
Dr. Lorne Ranstrom, Chair
Programs in:
early childhood education (M Ed, Certificate)
elementary education (M Ed, Certificate)
English as a second language (M Ed, Certificate)
instructional enrichment and development (M Ed, Certificate)
middle school education (M Ed, Certificate)
moderate special needs education (M Ed, Certificate)
principal (Certificate)
program development and supervision (M Ed, Certificate)
secondary education (M Ed, Certificate)
special education administrator (Certificate)
supervisor (Certificate)
teacher of reading (M Ed, Certificate)

■ EMERSON COLLEGE
Boston, MA 02116-4624
http://www.emerson.edu/

Independent, coed, comprehensive institution. CGS member. *Computer facilities:* 385 computers available on campus for general student use. A campuswide network can be accessed from student residence rooms and from off campus. Internet access and online class registration are available. *Library facilities:* Emerson Library plus 1 other. *General application contact:* Director of Graduate Admission, 617-824-8608.

Graduate Studies

School of Communication
Programs in:
broadcast journalism (MA)
communication (MA, MS)
communication management (MA)
communication sciences and disorders (MS)
global marketing communication and advertising (MA)
health communication (MA)
integrated journalism (MA)
integrated marketing communication (MA)
print/multimedia journalism (MA)
print/multimedia journalism, broadcast journalism, integrated journalism (MA)
speech-language pathology (MS)

School of the Arts
Programs in:
arts (MA, MFA)
audio production (MA)
audio, television/video, and new media production (MA)
creative writing (MFA)
new media production (MA)
publishing and writing (MA)
television/video production (MA)
theatre education (MA)

■ EMMANUEL COLLEGE
Boston, MA 02115
http://www.emmanuel.edu/

Independent-religious, coed, comprehensive institution. *Enrollment:* 2,340 graduate, professional, and undergraduate students; 5 full-time matriculated graduate/professional students (all women), 179 part-time matriculated graduate/professional students (142 women). *Graduate faculty:* 5 full-time (4 women), 30 part-time/adjunct (9 women). *Computer facilities:* 115 computers available on campus for general student use. A campuswide network can be accessed from

Emmanuel College (continued)
student residence rooms and from off campus. Internet access, software applications are available. *Library facilities:* Cardinal Cushing Library. *Graduate expenses:* Tuition: full-time $5,256. *General application contact:* Brian Minchello, Associate Director, Graduate and Professional Programs, 617-735-9928.

Graduate Programs
Ellen Sweeney, Director of Operations-Graduate and Professional Programs
Programs in:
- educational leadership (CAGS)
- elementary education (MAT)
- human resource management (MS, Certificate)
- management (MSM)
- school administration (M Ed)
- secondary education (MAT)

■ ENDICOTT COLLEGE
Beverly, MA 01915-2096
http://www.endicott.edu/

Independent, coed, comprehensive institution. *Graduate faculty:* 3 full-time (2 women), 128 part-time/adjunct (56 women). *Computer facilities:* 150 computers available on campus for general student use. A campuswide network can be accessed from student residence rooms and from off campus. Internet access and online class registration, e-mail are available. *Library facilities:* Endicott College Library. *Graduate expenses:* Tuition: part-time $279 per credit. Tuition and fees vary according to program. *General application contact:* Dr. Paul A. Squarcia, Vice President and Dean of Graduate and Professional Studies, 978-232-2084.

Van Loan School of Graduate and Professional Studies
Dr. Paul A. Squarcia, Vice President and Dean of Graduate and Professional Studies
Programs in:
- arts and learning (M Ed)
- business administration (MBA)
- hospitality organizational training and management (M Ed)
- initial and professional licensure (M Ed)
- integrative learning (M Ed)
- international education (M Ed)
- organizational management (M Ed)
- sport management (M Ed)

■ FITCHBURG STATE COLLEGE
Fitchburg, MA 01420-2697
http://www.fsc.edu/

State-supported, coed, comprehensive institution. CGS member. *Enrollment:* 5,508 graduate, professional, and undergraduate students; 200 full-time matriculated graduate/professional students (144 women), 721 part-time matriculated graduate/professional students (544 women). *Computer facilities:* 135 computers available on campus for general student use. A campuswide network can be accessed from student residence rooms and from off campus. Internet access and online class registration are available. *Library facilities:* Hammond Library. *Graduate expenses:* Tuition, state resident: part-time $150 per credit. Tuition, nonresident: part-time $150 per credit. Required fees: $90 per credit. *General application contact:* Director of Admissions, 978-665-3144.

Division of Graduate and Continuing Education
Catherine Canney, Dean, Graduate and Continuing Education
Programs in:
- accounting (MBA)
- applied communications (MS, Certificate)
- arts education (M Ed)
- biology and teaching biology (MA, MAT)
- computer science (MS)
- criminal justice (MS)
- early childhood education (M Ed)
- educational technology (Certificate)
- elementary education (M Ed)
- elementary school guidance counseling (MS)
- English and teaching English (secondary level) (MA, MAT)
- fine arts director (Certificate)
- forensic nursing (MS, Certificate)
- general studies education (M Ed)
- guided studies (M Ed)
- higher education administration (CAGS)
- history and teaching history (secondary level) (MA, MAT)
- human resource management (MBA)
- interdisciplinary studies (CAGS)
- library media (MS)
- management (MBA)
- marriage and family therapy (Certificate)
- media technology (MS)
- mental health counseling (MS)
- middle school education (M Ed)
- non-licensure (M Ed, CAGS)
- occupational education (M Ed)
- professional mentoring for teachers (Certificate)
- reading specialist (M Ed)
- school principal (M Ed, CAGS)
- science education (M Ed)
- secondary education (M Ed)
- secondary school guidance counseling (MS)
- supervisor director (M Ed, CAGS)
- teaching students with moderate disabilities (M Ed)
- teaching students with severe disabilities (M Ed)
- technical and professional writing (MS)
- technology education (M Ed)
- technology leader (M Ed, CAGS)

■ FRAMINGHAM STATE COLLEGE
Framingham, MA 01701-9101
http://www.framingham.edu/

State-supported, coed, comprehensive institution. *Enrollment:* 5,861 graduate, professional, and undergraduate students; 1,404 matriculated graduate/professional students. *Graduate faculty:* 25 full-time, 50 part-time/adjunct. *Computer facilities:* Computer purchase and lease plans are available. 575 computers available on campus for general student use. A campuswide network can be accessed from student residence rooms and from off campus. Internet access and online class registration, TELNET are available. *Library facilities:* Whittemore Library. *General application contact:* Dr. Janet Castleman, Dean of Graduate and Continuing Education.

Division of Graduate and Continuing Education
Dr. Janet Castleman, Dean of Graduate and Continuing Education
Programs in:
- art (M Ed)
- biology (M Ed)
- business administration (MA)
- counseling psychology (MA)
- curriculum and instructional technology (M Ed)
- dietetics (MS)
- early childhood education (M Ed)
- educational leadership (MA)
- elementary education (M Ed)
- English (M Ed)
- food science and nutrition science (MS)
- health care administration (MA)
- history (M Ed)
- human nutrition: education and media technologies (MS)
- human resource management (MA)
- literacy and language (M Ed)
- mathematics (M Ed)
- public administration (MA)
- Spanish (M Ed)
- special education (M Ed)
- teaching of English as a second language (M Ed)

■ HARVARD UNIVERSITY
Cambridge, MA 02138
http://www.harvard.edu/

Independent, coed, university. CGS member. *Enrollment:* 19,538 graduate, professional, and undergraduate students; 12,034 full-time matriculated graduate/professional students (5,674 women), 980 part-time matriculated graduate/professional students (506 women). *Graduate faculty:* 2,497. *Computer facilities:* A campuswide network can be accessed from student residence rooms and from off campus. Internet access is available. *Library facilities:* Widener Library. *Graduate expenses:* Tuition: full-time $30,275. Full-time tuition and fees vary according to program and student level. *General application contact:* Admissions Office, 617-495-1814.

Find University Details at www.petersons.com/gradchannel.

Business School

Programs in:
- business (MBA, DBA, PhD)
- business administration (DBA)
- business economics (PhD)
- health policy management (PhD)
- information and technology management (PhD)
- organizational behavior (PhD)

Divinity School

William A. Graham, Dean

Program in:
- divinity (M Div, MTS, Th M, PhD, Th D)

Extension School

Michael Shinagel, Dean

Programs in:
- applied sciences (CAS)
- biotechnology (ALM)
- educational technologies (ALM)
- educational technology (CET)
- English for graduate and professional studies (DGP)
- environmental management (ALM, CEM)
- information technology (ALM)
- journalism (ALM)
- liberal arts (ALM)
- management (ALM, CM)
- mathematics for teaching (ALM)
- museum studies (ALM)
- premedical studies (Diploma)
- publication and communication (CPC)

Graduate School of Arts and Sciences

Dr. Theda Skocpol, Dean

Programs in:
- African and African American studies (PhD)
- African history (PhD)
- Akkadian and Sumerian (AM, PhD)
- American history (PhD)
- ancient art (PhD)
- ancient Near Eastern art (PhD)
- ancient, medieval, early modern, and modern Europe (PhD)
- anthropology and Middle Eastern studies (PhD)
- Arabic (AM, PhD)
- archaeology (PhD)
- architecture (PhD)
- Armenian (AM, PhD)
- arts and sciences (AM, ME, MFS, SM, PhD)
- astronomy (PhD)
- astrophysics (PhD)
- baroque art (PhD)
- biblical history (AM, PhD)
- biochemical chemistry (PhD)
- biological anthropology (PhD)
- biological sciences in dental medicine (PhD)
- biological sciences in public health (PhD)
- biology (PhD)
- biophysics (PhD)
- business economics (PhD)
- Byzantine art (PhD)
- Byzantine Greek (PhD)
- chemical biology (PhD)
- chemical physics (PhD)
- Chinese (PhD)
- Chinese studies (AM)
- classical archaeology (PhD)
- classical art (PhD)
- classical philology (PhD)
- classical philosophy (PhD)
- comparative literature (PhD)
- composition (AM, PhD)
- critical theory (PhD)
- descriptive linguistics (PhD)
- diplomatic history (PhD)
- earth and planetary sciences (AM, PhD)
- East Asian history (PhD)
- economic and social history (PhD)
- economics (PhD)
- economics and Middle Eastern studies (PhD)
- eighteenth-century literature (PhD)
- experimental physics (PhD)
- fine arts and Middle Eastern studies (PhD)
- forest science (MFS)
- French (AM, PhD)
- German (PhD)
- health policy (PhD)
- Hebrew (AM, PhD)
- historical linguistics (PhD)
- history and Middle Eastern studies (PhD)
- history of American civilization (PhD)
- history of science (AM, PhD)
- Indian art (PhD)
- Indian philosophy (AM, PhD)
- Indo-Muslim culture (AM, PhD)
- information, technology and management (PhD)
- Inner Asian and Altaic studies (PhD)
- inorganic chemistry (PhD)
- intellectual history (PhD)
- Iranian (AM, PhD)
- Irish (PhD)
- Islamic art (PhD)
- Italian (AM, PhD)
- Japanese (PhD)
- Japanese and Chinese art (PhD)
- Japanese studies (AM)
- Jewish history and literature (AM, PhD)
- Korean (PhD)
- Korean studies (AM)
- landscape architecture (PhD)
- Latin American history (PhD)
- legal anthropology (AM)
- literature: nineteenth-century to the present (PhD)
- mathematics (PhD)
- medical anthropology (AM)
- medical engineering/medical physics (PhD)
- medieval art (PhD)
- medieval Latin (PhD)
- medieval literature and language (PhD)
- modern art (PhD)
- modern British and American literature (PhD)
- molecular and cellular biology (PhD)
- Mongolian (PhD)
- Mongolian studies (AM)
- musicology (AM)
- musicology and ethnomusicology (PhD)
- Near Eastern history (PhD)
- neurobiology (PhD)
- oceanic history (PhD)
- oral literature (PhD)
- organic chemistry (PhD)
- organizational behavior (PhD)
- Pali (AM, PhD)
- Persian (AM, PhD)
- philosophy (PhD)
- physical chemistry (PhD)
- Polish (PhD)
- political economy and government (PhD)
- political science (PhD)
- Portuguese (AM, PhD)
- psychology (PhD)
- public policy (PhD)
- regional studies–Middle East (AM)
- regional studies-Russia, Eastern Europe, and Central Asia (AM)
- Renaissance and modern architecture (PhD)
- Renaissance art (PhD)
- Renaissance literature (PhD)
- Russian (PhD)
- Sanskrit (AM, PhD)
- Scandinavian (PhD)
- Semitic philology (AM, PhD)
- Serbo-Croatian (PhD)
- Slavic philology (PhD)
- social anthropology (AM, PhD)
- social change and development (AM)
- social policy (PhD)
- social psychology (PhD)
- sociology (PhD)
- Spanish (AM, PhD)
- statistics (AM, PhD)
- study of religion (PhD)
- Syro-Palestinian archaeology (AM, PhD)
- systems biology (PhD)
- theoretical linguistics (PhD)
- theoretical physics (PhD)
- theory (AM, PhD)
- Tibetan (AM, PhD)
- Turkish (AM, PhD)
- Ukrainian (PhD)
- urban planning (PhD)
- Urdu (AM, PhD)
- Vietnamese (PhD)
- Vietnamese studies (AM)
- Welsh (PhD)

Division of Medical Sciences

Leah Wade Simons, Administrator

Harvard University (continued)
Programs in:
biological chemistry and molecular pharmacology (PhD)
cell biology (PhD)
genetics (PhD)
microbiology and molecular genetics (PhD)
pathology (PhD)

School of Engineering and Applied Sciences
Ventatesh Narayanamurti, Dean
Programs in:
applied mathematics (ME, SM, PhD)
applied physics (ME, SM, PhD)
computer science (ME, SM, PhD)
engineering science (ME)
engineering sciences (SM, PhD)

Graduate School of Design
Alan Altshuler, Dean
Programs in:
architecture (M Arch)
design (M Arch, M Des S, MAUD, MLA, MLAUD, MUP, Dr DES)
design studies (M Des S)
landscape architecture (MLA)
urban planning (MUP)
urban planning and design (MAUD, MLAUD)

Graduate School of Education
Dr. Kathleen McCartney, Dean
Programs in:
arts in education (Ed M)
culture, communities and education (Ed D)
education (Ed M, Ed D)
education policy (Ed D)
education policy and management (Ed M)
education policy, leadership and instructional practice (Ed D)
higher education (Ed M, Ed D)
human development and education (Ed D)
human development and psychology (Ed M)
international education policy (Ed M)
language and literacy (Ed M)
learning and teaching (Ed M)
mid-career mathematics and science (teaching certificate) (Ed M)
mind brain and education (Ed M)
quantitative policy analysis in education (Ed D)
risk and prevention (Ed M)
school leadership (Ed M)
special studies (Ed M)
teaching and curriculum (teaching certificate) (Ed M)
technology innovation and education (Ed M)
urban superintendency (Ed D)

Harvard Medical School
Dr. Joseph B. Martin, Dean of the Faculty of Medicine
Program in:
medicine (MD, M Eng, SM, PhD, Sc D)

Division of Health Sciences and Technology
Programs in:
biomedical engineering (M Eng)
biomedical enterprise (SM)
biomedical informatics (SM)
health sciences and technology (MD, M Eng, SM, PhD, Sc D)
medical engineering (PhD)
medical engineering/medical physics (Sc D)
medical physics (PhD)
medical sciences (MD)
speech and hearing bioscience and technology (PhD, Sc D)

John F. Kennedy School of Government
Dr. David Ellwood, Dean
Programs in:
government (MPA, MPAID, MPP, MPPUP, PhD)
political economy and government (PhD)
public administration (MPA)
public administration and international development (MPAID)
public policy (MPP, PhD)
public policy and urban planning (MPPUP)

Law School
Program in:
law (JD, LL M, SJD)

School of Dental Medicine
Programs in:
advanced general dentistry (Certificate)
dental medicine (DMD, M Med Sc, D Med Sc, Certificate)
dental public health (Certificate)
endodontics (Certificate)
general practice residency (Certificate)
oral biology (M Med Sc, D Med Sc)
oral pathology (Certificate)
oral surgery (Certificate)
orthodontics (Certificate)
pediatric dentistry (Certificate)
periodontics (Certificate)
prosthodontics (Certificate)

School of Public Health
Programs in:
biostatistics (SM, PhD)
clinical effectiveness (MPH)
environmental health (MOH, SM, DPH, PhD, SD)
epidemiology (SM, DPH, SD)
exposure, epidemiology and risk (SM, SD)
family and community health (MPH)
genetics and complex diseases (PhD)
health care management and policy (MPH)
health policy (PhD)
health policy and management (SM, SD)
immunology and infectious diseases (PhD, SD)
international health (MPH)
nutrition (DPH, PhD, SD)
nutritional epidemiology (DPH, SD)
occupational and environmental health (MPH)
occupational health (MOH, SM, DPH, SD)
physiology (PhD, SD)
population and international health (SM, DPH, SD)
public health (MOH, MPH, SM, DPH, PhD, SD)
public health nutrition (DPH, SD)
quantitative methods (MPH)
society, human development and health (SM, DPH, SD)

■ LESLEY UNIVERSITY
Cambridge, MA 02138-2790
http://www.lesley.edu/

Independent, coed, comprehensive institution. CGS member. *Enrollment:* 6,539 graduate, professional, and undergraduate students; 1,028 full-time matriculated graduate/professional students (909 women), 4,996 part-time matriculated graduate/professional students (4,405 women). *Graduate faculty:* 103 full-time (83 women), 403 part-time/adjunct (276 women). *Computer facilities:* Computer purchase and lease plans are available. 175 computers available on campus for general student use. A campuswide network can be accessed from student residence rooms and from off campus. Internet access and online class registration are available. *Library facilities:* Eleanor DeWolfe Ludcke Library plus 2 others. *General application contact:* Kristen Card, Associate Director of On-Campus Admissions, 617-349-8734.

Graduate School of Arts and Social Sciences
Dr. Julia Halevy, Dean
Programs in:
clinical mental health counseling (MA)
counseling psychology (MA, CAGS)
creative arts in learning (CAGS)
creative writing (MFA)
ecological teaching and learning (MS)
environmental education (MS)
expressive therapies (MA, PhD, CAGS)
independent studies (CAGS)
independent study (MA)
individualized studies (MA)
integrative holistic health (MA)
intercultural relations (MA, CAGS)
interdisciplinary studies (MA)
professional counseling (MA)
school counseling (MA)
visual arts (MFA)
women's studies (MA)

Division of Expressive Therapies
Julia Byers, Director
Programs in:
art (MA)

dance (MA)
expressive therapies (MA, PhD, CAGS)
music (MA)

School of Education
Dr. Mario Borunda, Dean
Programs in:
curriculum and instruction (M Ed, CAGS)
early childhood education (M Ed)
educational studies (PhD)
elementary education (M Ed)
individually designed (M Ed)
middle school education (M Ed)
moderate special needs (M Ed)
reading (M Ed, CAGS)
science in education (M Ed)
severe special needs (M Ed)
special needs (CAGS)
technology in education (M Ed, CAGS)

■ MASSACHUSETTS INSTITUTE OF TECHNOLOGY
Cambridge, MA 02139-4307
http://web.mit.edu/

Independent, coed, university. CGS member. *Enrollment:* 10,253 graduate, professional, and undergraduate students; 5,911 full-time matriculated graduate/professional students (1,760 women), 62 part-time matriculated graduate/professional students (19 women). *Graduate faculty:* 986 full-time (186 women), 12 part-time/adjunct (2 women). *Computer facilities:* Computer purchase and lease plans are available. 1,100 computers available on campus for general student use. A campuswide network can be accessed from student residence rooms and from off campus. Internet access is available. *Library facilities:* MIT Libraries plus 11 others. *Graduate expenses:* Tuition: full-time $33,400; part-time $525 per unit. Required fees: $200. Part-time tuition and fees vary according to course load. *General application contact:* Stuart Schmill, Interim Director of Admissions, 617-253-2917.

Operations Research Center
Dr. Dimitris J. Bertsimas, Co-Director
Program in:
operations research (SM, PhD)

School of Architecture and Planning
Prof. Adèle Naudé Santos, Dean
Programs in:
architecture (M Arch, SM Arch S, SM Vis S, SMBT, PhD)
architecture and planning (M Arch, MCP, MSRED, SM, SM Arch S, SM Vis S, SMBT, PhD)
city planning (MCP)
media arts and sciences (SM, PhD)
media technology (SM)
urban and regional planning (PhD)
urban and regional studies (PhD)
urban studies and planning (SM)

Center for Real Estate
David Geltner, Director
Program in:
real estate (MSRED)

School of Engineering
Prof. Thomas L. Magnanti, Dean
Programs in:
aeroacoustics (PhD, Sc D)
aerodynamics (PhD, Sc D)
aeroelasticity (PhD, Sc D)
aeronautics and astronautics (SM, PhD, Sc D, EAA)
aerospace systems (PhD, Sc D)
aircraft propulsion (PhD, Sc D)
applied biosciences (PhD, Sc D)
astrodynamics (PhD, Sc D)
bio- and polymeric materials (PhD, Sc D)
bioengineering (PhD, Sc D)
biological oceanography (PhD, Sc D)
biomaterials (PhD, Sc D)
biomedical engineering (M Eng, PhD, Sc D)
ceramics (PhD, Sc D)
chemical engineering (SM, PhD, Sc D)
chemical engineering practice (SM, PhD)
chemical oceanography (PhD, Sc D)
civil and environmental engineering (M Eng, SM, PhD, Sc D, CE)
civil and environmental systems (PhD, Sc D)
civil engineering (PhD, Sc D)
coastal engineering (PhD, Sc D)
computation for design and optimization (SM)
computational and systems biology (PhD)
computational fluid dynamics (PhD, Sc D)
computer science (PhD, Sc D, ECS)
computer systems (PhD, Sc D)
construction engineering and management (PhD, Sc D)
dynamics energy conversion (PhD, Sc D)
electrical engineering (PhD, Sc D, EE)
electrical engineering and computer science (M Eng, SM, PhD, Sc D)
electronic materials (PhD, Sc D)
electronic, photonic and magnetic materials (PhD, Sc D)
emerging, fundamental and computational studies in materials science (Sc D)
emerging, fundamental, and computational studies in materials science (PhD)
engineering (M Eng, SM, PhD, Sc D, CE, EAA, ECS, EE, Mat E, Mech E, Met E, NE, Naval E)
environmental biology (PhD, Sc D)
environmental chemistry (PhD, Sc D)
environmental engineering (PhD, Sc D)
environmental fluid mechanics (PhD, Sc D)
estimation and control (PhD, Sc D)
flight transportation (PhD, Sc D)
fluid mechanics (PhD, Sc D)
gas turbine structures (PhD, Sc D)
gas turbines (PhD, Sc D)
genetic toxicology (PhD, Sc D)
geotechnical and geoenvironmental engineering (PhD, Sc D)
humans and automation (PhD, Sc D)
hydrology (PhD, Sc D)
information technology (PhD, Sc D)
instrumentation (PhD, Sc D)
manufacturing engineering (M Eng)
materials engineering (PhD, Sc D, Mat E)
materials science (PhD, Sc D)
materials science and engineering (M Eng, SM, PhD, Sc D)
mechanical engineering (SM, PhD, Sc D, Mech E)
metallurgical engineering (Met E)
molecular and systems bacterial pathogenesis (PhD, Sc D)
molecular and systems toxicology and pharmacology (PhD, Sc D)
molecular systems toxicology (PhD, Sc D)
naval architecture and marine engineering (SM, PhD, Sc D)
navigation and control systems (PhD, Sc D)
nuclear science and engineering (SM, PhD, Sc D, NE)
ocean engineering (SM, PhD, Sc D, Naval E)
oceanographic engineering (SM, PhD, Sc D)
physics of fluids (PhD, Sc D)
plasma physics (PhD, Sc D)
polymers (PhD, Sc D)
space propulsion (PhD, Sc D)
structural and environmental materials (PhD, Sc D)
structural dynamics (PhD, Sc D)
structures and materials (PhD, Sc D)
structures technology (PhD, Sc D)
toxicology (SM, PhD, Sc D)
transportation (PhD, Sc D)
vehicle design (PhD, Sc D)

Engineering Systems Division
Prof. Joel Moses, Acting Director
Programs in:
engineering and management (SM)
engineering systems (SM, PhD)
logistics (M Eng)
technology and policy (SM)
technology, management and policy (PhD)

School of Humanities, Arts, and Social Sciences
Prof. Deborah Fitzgerald, Dean
Programs in:
comparative media studies (SM)
economics (SM, PhD)
history, anthropology, and science, technology and society (PhD)

Massachusetts Institute of Technology (continued)

- humanities, arts, and social sciences (SM, PhD)
- linguistics (PhD)
- philosophy (PhD)
- political science (SM, PhD)
- science writing (SM)

School of Science

Prof. Marc A. Kastner, Dean
Programs in:

- atmospheric chemistry (PhD, Sc D)
- atmospheric science (SM, PhD, Sc D)
- biochemistry (PhD)
- biological chemistry (PhD, Sc D)
- biological oceanography (PhD)
- biophysical chemistry and molecular structure (PhD)
- cell biology (PhD)
- climate physics and chemistry (PhD, Sc D)
- cognitive science (PhD)
- developmental biology (PhD)
- earth and planetary sciences (SM)
- genetics/microbiology (PhD)
- geochemistry (PhD, Sc D)
- geology (PhD, Sc D)
- geophysics (PhD, Sc D)
- immunology (PhD)
- inorganic chemistry (PhD, Sc D)
- marine geology and geophysics (SM)
- mathematics (PhD)
- neurobiology (PhD)
- neuroscience (PhD)
- oceanography (SM)
- organic chemistry (PhD, Sc D)
- physical chemistry (PhD, Sc D)
- physical oceanography (PhD, Sc D)
- physics (PhD)
- planetary sciences (PhD, Sc D)
- science (SM, PhD, Sc D)

Sloan School of Management

Richard L. Schmalensee, Dean
Program in:

- management (MBA, MS, SM, PhD)

Whitaker College of Health Sciences and Technology

Dr. Martha L. Gray, Director
Programs in:

- biomedical engineering (M Eng)
- biomedical enterprise (SM)
- biomedical informatics (SM)
- health sciences and technology (MD, M Eng, SM, PhD, Sc D)
- medical engineering (PhD)
- medical engineering and medical physics (Sc D)
- medical physics (PhD)
- medical sciences (MD)
- speech and hearing bioscience and technology (PhD, Sc D)

■ NORTHEASTERN UNIVERSITY
Boston, MA 02115-5096
http://www.northeastern.edu

Independent, coed, university. CGS member. *Enrollment:* 20,605 graduate, professional, and undergraduate students; 3,298 full-time matriculated graduate/professional students (1,773 women), 2,112 part-time matriculated graduate/professional students (1,098 women). *Graduate faculty:* 884 full-time (314 women), 424 part-time/adjunct (246 women). *Computer facilities:* 1,993 computers available on campus for general student use. A campuswide network can be accessed from student residence rooms and from off campus. Internet access and online class registration are available. *Library facilities:* Snell Library plus 4 others. *General application contact:* Information Contact, 617-373-2000.

Find University Details at www.petersons.com/gradchannel.

Bouvé College of Health Sciences Graduate School

Suzanne B. Greenberg, Director
Programs in:

- applied behavior analysis (MS)
- applied educational psychology (MS)
- audiology (Au D)
- biotechnology (PSM)
- clinical exercise physiology (MS)
- college student development and counseling (MS)
- counseling psychology (MS, PhD, CAGS)
- health sciences (Pharm D, MS, MS Ed, PSM, Au D, PhD, CAGS, CAS)
- pharmaceutical sciences (PhD)
- pharmacology (MS)
- pharmacy (Pharm D)
- school counseling (MS)
- school psychology (MS, PhD, CAGS)
- special needs and intensive special needs (MS Ed)
- speech-language pathology (MS)
- toxicology (MS)

School of Health Professions

Program in:

- physician assistant (MS)

School of Nursing

Dr. Nancy Hoffart, Dean
Programs in:

- community health nursing (MS, CAS)
- critical care-acute care nurse practitioner (MS, CAS)
- critical care-neonatal nurse practitioner (MS, CAS)
- nurse anesthesia (MS)
- nursing (MS, PhD, CAS)
- nursing administration (MS)
- primary care nursing (MS, CAS)
- psychiatric-mental health nursing (MS, CAS)

College of Arts and Sciences

Dr. Mary Loeffelholz, Associate Dean and Director of the Graduate School
Programs in:

- analytical chemistry (PhD)
- applied mathematics (MS)
- arts and sciences (M Arch, MA, MAW, MPA, MS, MSOR, PMS, PSM, PhD, Certificate)
- bioinformatics (PMS)
- biology (MS, PhD)
- biotechnology (MS)
- chemistry (MS, PhD)
- cinema studies (Certificate)
- development administration (MPA)
- economics (MA, PhD)
- English (MA, PhD)
- experimental psychology (MA, PhD)
- health administration and policy (MPA)
- history (MA)
- inorganic chemistry (PhD)
- law, policy, and society (MS, PhD)
- marine biology (MS)
- mathematics (MS, PhD)
- operations research (MSOR)
- organic chemistry (PhD)
- physical chemistry (PhD)
- physics (MS, PhD)
- political science (MA)
- public administration (MPA)
- public and international affairs (PhD)
- public history (MA)
- sociology (MA, PhD)
- state and local government (MPA)
- women's studies (Certificate)
- world history (PhD)

School of Journalism

Prof. Stephen Burgard, Graduate Coordinator
Program in:

- journalism (MA)

College of Computer and Information Science

Dr. Larry A. Finkelstein, Dean
Programs in:

- computer and information science (PhD)
- computer science (MS)
- health informatics (MS)
- information assurance (MS)
- telecommunication systems management (MS)

College of Criminal Justice

Jack McDevitt, Dean
Program in:

- criminal justice (MS, PhD)

College of Engineering

Dr. Yaman Yener, Associate Dean of Engineering for Research and Graduate Studies
Programs in:

- chemical engineering (MS, PhD)
- civil and environmental engineering (MS, PhD)
- computer engineering (PhD)

computer systems engineering (MS)
electrical engineering (MS, PhD)
engineering (MS, PSM, PhD)
engineering management (MS)
industrial engineering (MS, PhD)
information systems (MS)
mechanical engineering (MS, PhD)
operations research (MS)
telecommunication systems management (MS)

Graduate School of Business Administration
Kate Klepper, Director of Graduate Programs
Programs in:
business administration (EMBA, MBA, MSF, MST, CAGS)
finance (MSF)

Graduate School of Professional Accounting
Annarita Meeker, Director
Programs in:
professional accounting (MST, CAGS)
taxation (MST, CAGS)

School of Architecture
George Thrush, Chair
Program in:
architecture (M Arch)

School of Law
Emily A. Spieler, Dean
Program in:
law (JD)

School of Technological Entrepreneurship
Paul M. Zavracky, Dean
Program in:
technological entrepreneurship (MS)

■ REGIS COLLEGE
Weston, MA 02493
http://www.regiscollege.edu/

Independent-religious, coed, comprehensive institution. *Enrollment:* 1,314 graduate, professional, and undergraduate students; 166 full-time matriculated graduate/professional students (150 women), 289 part-time matriculated graduate/professional students (267 women). *Graduate faculty:* 24 full-time (22 women), 39 part-time/adjunct (33 women). *Computer facilities:* 159 computers available on campus for general student use. A campuswide network can be accessed from student residence rooms and from off campus. Internet access and online class registration are available. *Library facilities:* Regis College Library. *Graduate expenses:* Tuition: full-time $23,680; part-time $665 per credit hour. *General application contact:* Christine Petherick, Administrative Coordinator—Graduate Admission, 866-438-7344.

Department of Education
Dr. Leona McCaughey-Oreszak, Program Director
Program in:
education (MAT)

Department of Health Product Regulation and Health Policy
Charles Burr, Director
Program in:
health product regulation and health policy (MS)

Department of Management and Leadership
Dr. Phillip Jutras, Director
Program in:
leadership and organizational change (MS)

Department of Nursing
Dr. Antoinette Hays, Dean, School of Nursing and Health Professions
Programs in:
nurse educator (Certificate)
nurse practitioner (Certificate)
nursing (MS)

Department of Organizational and Professional Communication
Dr. Joan Murray, Director
Program in:
organizational and professional communication (MS)

■ SALEM STATE COLLEGE
Salem, MA 01970-5353
http://www.salemstate.edu/

State-supported, coed, comprehensive institution. CGS member. *Enrollment:* 10,230 graduate, professional, and undergraduate students; 271 full-time matriculated graduate/professional students (223 women), 1,108 part-time matriculated graduate/professional students (869 women). *Graduate faculty:* 320 full-time (160 women), 397 part-time/adjunct (169 women). *Computer facilities:* Computer purchase and lease plans are available. 426 computers available on campus for general student use. A campuswide network can be accessed from student residence rooms and from off campus. Internet access is available. *Library facilities:* Salem State College Library. *General application contact:* Dr. Marc Glasser, Dean of the Graduate School, 978-542-6323.

Graduate School
Dr. Marc Glasser, Dean of the Graduate School
Programs in:
advanced practice in rehabilitation (MSN)
art (MAT)
bilingual education (M Ed)
biology (MAT)
business administration (MBA)
chemistry (MAT)
counseling and psychological services (MS)
criminal justice (MS)
direct entry nursing (MSN)
early childhood education (M Ed)
educational leadership (CAGS)
elementary education (M Ed)
English (MA, MAT)
English as a second language (MAT)
field-based education (M Ed)
geo-information science (MS)
higher education in student affairs (M Ed)
history (MA, MAT)
innovative practices (CAGS)
library media studies (M Ed)
mathematics (MS)
middle school education (M Ed, MAT)
nursing (MSN)
physical education 5-12 (M Ed)
physical education K-9 (M Ed)
reading (M Ed, CAGS)
reading, literacy and language (CAGS)
school business officer (M Ed)
school counseling (M Ed)
secondary education (M Ed)
social work (MSW)
Spanish (MAT)
special education (M Ed, MAT)
teaching English as a second language (MAT)
technology in education (M Ed)

■ SIMMONS COLLEGE
Boston, MA 02115
http://www.simmons.edu/

Independent, Undergraduate: women only; graduate: coed, university. *Enrollment:* 4,849 graduate, professional, and undergraduate students; 568 full-time matriculated graduate/professional students (498 women), 1,765 part-time matriculated graduate/professional students (1,509 women). *Graduate faculty:* 143 full-time (107 women), 220 part-time/adjunct (155 women). *Computer facilities:* 420 computers available on campus for general student use. A campuswide network can be accessed from student residence rooms and from off campus. Internet access and online class registration are available. *Library facilities:* Beatley Library plus 2 others. *General application contact:* Donna M. Dolan, Registrar, 617-521-2111.

Graduate School
Dr. Diane Raymond, Dean

College of Arts and Sciences Graduate Studies
Programs in:
applied behavior analysis (PhD)
arts and sciences (MA, MAT, MFA, MS, MS Ed, PhD, CAGS, Ed S)
assistive technology (MS Ed, Ed S)
behavioral education (MS Ed, Ed S)
children's literature (MA)

Simmons College (continued)
- communications management (MS)
- educational leadership (MS Ed, CAGS)
- elementary education (MAT, CAGS)
- English (MA)
- gender/cultural studies (MA)
- general education (CAGS)
- general purposes (MS)
- health professions education (PhD)
- language and literacy (MS Ed, Ed S)
- middle school education (MAT, CAGS)
- moderate disabilities (Ed S)
- moderate special needs (MS Ed)
- professional license (CAGS)
- professional license: elementary (MS Ed)
- professional license: middle/high (MS Ed)
- secondary education (MAT, CAGS)
- severe disabilities (Ed S)
- severe special needs (MS Ed)
- Spanish (MA)
- special education (MS Ed, PhD, Ed S)
- special education administration (MS Ed, PhD, Ed S)
- teacher preparation (MAT, MS, MS Ed, CAGS)
- teaching English as a second language (MAT)
- urban education (MS Ed, CAGS)
- writing for children (MFA)

Graduate School of Library and Information Science
Dr. Michele V. Cloonan, Dean
Programs in:
- history and archives management)
- library and information science (PhD)
- school library teacher (MS, Certificate)

School for Health Studies
Dr. Gerald P. Koocher, Dean
Programs in:
- didactic program in dietetics (Certificate)
- health care administration (MHA, CAGS)
- health professions education (PhD)
- health studies (MHA, MS, DPT, PhD, CAGS, Certificate)
- nutrition (dietetic internship) (Certificate)
- nutrition and health promotion (MS)
- physical therapy (DPT)
- primary health care nursing (MS, CAGS)
- sports nutrition (Certificate)

School of Social Work
Dr. Stefan Krug, Dean
Program in:
- clinical social work (MSW, PhD)

Simmons School of Management
Dr. Deborah Merrill-Sands, Dean
Programs in:
- entrepreneurship (Certificate)
- management (MBA)

■ SPRINGFIELD COLLEGE
Springfield, MA 01109-3797
http://www.spfldcol.edu/

Independent, coed, comprehensive institution. *Enrollment:* 1,170 full-time matriculated graduate/professional students, 323 part-time matriculated graduate/professional students. *Graduate faculty:* 156 full-time (78 women), 98 part-time/adjunct (46 women). *Computer facilities:* Computer purchase and lease plans are available. 95 computers available on campus for general student use. A campuswide network can be accessed from student residence rooms and from off campus. Internet access is available. *Library facilities:* Babson Library. *Graduate expenses:* Tuition: full-time $12,222; part-time $679 per credit. Required fees: $25; $25 per year. One-time fee: $25 full-time. *General application contact:* Donald James Shaw, Director of Graduate Admissions, 413-748-3060.

Find University Details at www.petersons.com/gradchannel.

Graduate Programs
Dr. Betty L. Mann, Dean
Programs in:
- adapted physical education (M Ed, MPE, MS)
- advanced level coaching (M Ed, MPE, MS)
- alcohol rehabilitation/substance abuse counseling (M Ed, MS, CAS)
- art therapy (M Ed, MS, CAS)
- athletic administration (M Ed, MPE, MS)
- athletic counseling (M Ed, MS, CAS)
- biomechanics (MS)
- counseling and secondary education (M Ed, MS)
- deaf counseling (M Ed, MS, CAS)
- developmental disabilities (M Ed, MS, CAS)
- education (M Ed, MS)
- exercise physiology (MS, DPE)
- general counseling (M Ed)
- general counseling and casework (M Ed, MS, CAS)
- general physical education (DPE, CAS)
- health care management (MS)
- health education licensure (MPE, MS)
- health education licensure program (M Ed)
- human services (MS)
- industrial/organizational psychology (MS, CAS)
- interdisciplinary movement sciences (MS)
- marriage and family therapy (M Ed, MS, CAS)
- mental health counseling (M Ed, MS, CAS)
- occupational therapy (M Ed, MS, CAS)
- outdoor recreational management (M Ed, MS)
- physical education licensure (MPE, MS)
- physical education licensure program (M Ed)
- physical therapy (MS)
- physician assistant studies (MS)
- psychiatric rehabilitation/mental health counseling (M Ed, MS, CAS)
- recreational management (M Ed, MS)
- school guidance and counseling (M Ed, MS, CAS)
- special services (M Ed, MS, CAS)
- sport management (M Ed, MS)
- sport performance (M Ed, MPE, MS)
- sport psychology (MS, DPE)
- student personnel in higher education (M Ed, MS, CAS)
- teaching and administration (MS)
- therapeutic recreational management (M Ed, MS)
- vocational evaluation and work adjustment (M Ed, MS, CAS)

School of Social Work
Dr. Francine Vecchiolla, Dean
Programs in:
- advanced generalist (MSW)
- advanced standing (MSW)
- practice with children and adolescents (PMC)

■ SUFFOLK UNIVERSITY
Boston, MA 02108-2770
http://www.suffolk.edu/

Independent, coed, comprehensive institution. *Enrollment:* 8,863 graduate, professional, and undergraduate students; 1,518 full-time matriculated graduate/professional students (804 women), 1,777 part-time matriculated graduate/professional students (1,020 women). *Graduate faculty:* 210 full-time (81 women), 96 part-time/adjunct (30 women). *Computer facilities:* 400 computers available on campus for general student use. A campuswide network can be accessed from student residence rooms and from off campus. Internet access and online class registration are available. *Library facilities:* Mildred Sawyer Library plus 3 others. *General application contact:* Judith Reynolds, Director of Graduate Admissions, 617-573-8302.

College of Arts and Sciences
Dr. Kenneth S. Greenberg, Dean
Programs in:
- administration of higher education (M Ed)
- adult and organizational learning (MS, CAGS)
- arts and sciences (M Ed, MA, MS, MSCJ, MSEP, MSIE, PhD, CAGS)
- clinical-developmental psychology (PhD)
- communication (MA)
- computer science (MS)
- counseling and human relations (M Ed, MS, CAGS)
- criminal justice (MSCJ)

economic policy (MSEP)
economics (PhD)
educational administration (M Ed)
foundations of education (M Ed, CAGS)
higher education administration (M Ed, CAGS)
human resources (MS, CAGS)
instructional design (CAGS)
international economics (MSIE)
leadership (CAGS)
mental health counseling (MS)
organizational development (CAGS)
organizational learning (CAGS)
political science (MS)
professional development in teaching programs (CAGS)
school counseling (M Ed)
secondary school teaching (MS)

New England School of Art and Design
Dr. William Davis, Director
Programs in:
graphic design (MA)
interior design (MA)

Law School
Gail N. Ellis, Dean of Admissions
Programs in:
civil litigation (JD)
financial services (JD)
global law and technology (LL M)
health care/biotechnology law (JD)
intellectual property law (JD)
international law (JD)
U.S. law for international business lawyers (LL M)

Sawyer Business School
Dr. William J. O'Neill, Dean
Programs in:
accounting (MSA, GDPA)
banking and financial services (MS)
business (EMBA, GMBA, MBA, MBAH, MHA, MPA, MS, MSA, MSF, MST, APC, CASPA, CPASF, GDPA)
business administration (MBA, APC)
disability studies (MPA)
executive business administration (EMBA)
finance (MSF, CPASF)
global business administration (GMBA)
health administration (MPA)
nonprofit management (MPA)
public administration (CASPA)
public finance and human resources (MPA)
state and local government (MPA)
taxation (MST)

■ TUFTS UNIVERSITY
Medford, MA 02155
http://www.tufts.edu/

Independent, coed, university. CGS member. *Enrollment:* 9,638 graduate, professional, and undergraduate students; 3,823 full-time matriculated graduate/professional students (2,250 women), 468 part-time matriculated graduate/professional students (242 women). *Graduate faculty:* 789 full-time, 419 part-time/adjunct. *Computer facilities:* 254 computers available on campus for general student use. A campuswide network can be accessed from student residence rooms and from off campus. Internet access and online class registration are available. *Library facilities:* Tisch Library plus 1 other. *Graduate expenses:* Tuition: full-time $33,672. Tuition and fees vary according to degree level and program. *General application contact:* Information Contact, 617-628-5000.

Find University Details at www.petersons.com/gradchannel.

Cummings School of Veterinary Medicine
Dr. Deborah T. Kochevar, Dean
Programs in:
animals and public policy (MS)
comparative biomedical sciences (PhD)
veterinary medicine (DVM, MS, PhD)

Fletcher School of Law and Diplomacy
Stephen W. Bosworth, Dean
Program in:
law and diplomacy (MA, MAHA, MALD, PhD)

The Gerald J. and Dorothy R. Friedman School of Nutrition Science and Policy
Stacey M. Herman, Director of Student Affairs
Programs in:
humanitarian assistance (MAHA)
nutrition (MS, PhD)

Graduate School of Arts and Sciences
Lynne Pepall, Deam
Programs in:
analytical chemistry (MS, PhD)
applied developmental psychology (PhD)
art history (MA)
arts and sciences (MA, MAT, MFA, MPP, MS, OTD, PhD, CAGS, Certificate)
bioengineering (Certificate)
biology (MS, PhD)
bioorganic chemistry (MS, PhD)
biotechnology (Certificate)
biotechnology engineering (Certificate)
child development (MA, CAGS)
classical archaeology (MA)
classics (MA)
community development (MA)
community environmental studies (Certificate)
computer science (Certificate)
computer science minor (Certificate)
dance (MA, PhD)
drama (MA)
dramatic literature and criticism (PhD)
early childhood education (MAT)
economics (MA)
education (MA, MAT, MS, PhD)
elementary education (MAT)
English (MA, PhD)
environmental chemistry (MS, PhD)
environmental management (Certificate)
environmental policy (MA)
epidemiology (Certificate)
ethnomusicology (MA)
French (MA)
German (MA)
health and human welfare (MA)
history (MA, PhD)
housing policy (MA)
human-computer interaction (Certificate)
inorganic chemistry (MS, PhD)
international environment/development policy (MA)
management of community organizations (Certificate)
manufacturing engineering (Certificate)
mathematics (MA, MS, PhD)
microwave and wireless engineering (Certificate)
middle and secondary education (MA, MAT)
museum studies (Certificate)
music history and literature (MA)
music theory and composition (MA)
occupational therapy (Certificate)
organic chemistry (MS, PhD)
philosophy (MA)
physical chemistry (MS, PhD)
physics (MS, PhD)
program evaluation (Certificate)
psychology (MS, PhD)
public policy (MPP)
public policy and citizen participation (MA)
school psychology (MA, CAGS)
secondary education (MA)
studio art (MFA)
theater history (PhD)

Sackler School of Graduate Biomedical Sciences
Naomi Rosenberg, Dean
Programs in:
biochemistry (PhD)
biomedical sciences (MS, PhD)
cell, molecular and developmental biology (PhD)
cellular and molecular physiology (PhD)
genetics (PhD)
immunology (PhD)
integrated studies (PhD)
molecular microbiology (PhD)
neuroscience (PhD)
pharmacology and experimental therapeutics (PhD)

Division of Clinical Care Research
Dr. Harry P. Selker, Program Director
Program in:
clinical care research (MS, PhD)

School of Dental Medicine
Programs in:
dental medicine (DMD, MS, Certificate)
dentistry (Certificate)

Tufts University (continued)

School of Engineering
Linda Abriola, Dean
Programs in:
- biomedical engineering (ME, MS, PhD)
- chemical and biological engineering (ME, MS, PhD)
- civil engineering (ME, MS, PhD)
- computer science (MS, PhD)
- electrical engineering (MS, PhD)
- engineering (ME, MS, MSEM, PhD)
- environmental engineering (ME, MS, PhD)
- human factors (MS)
- mechanical engineering (ME, MS, PhD)

The Gordon Institute
Arthur Winston, Director
Program in:
- engineering management (MSEM)

School of Medicine
Dr. Michael Rosenblatt, Dean
Programs in:
- biomedical sciences (MS)
- health communication (MS)
- medicine (MD, MPH, MS)
- pain research, education and policy (MS)
- public health (MPH)

■ UNIVERSITY OF MASSACHUSETTS AMHERST
Amherst, MA 01003
http://www.umass.edu/

State-supported, coed, university. CGS member. *Enrollment:* 25,593 graduate, professional, and undergraduate students; 2,946 full-time matriculated graduate/professional students (1,500 women), 2,125 part-time matriculated graduate/professional students (1,073 women). *Graduate faculty:* 1,200 full-time (379 women). *Computer facilities:* 450 computers available on campus for general student use. A campuswide network can be accessed from student residence rooms and from off campus. Internet access and online class registration, online course and grade information are available. *Library facilities:* W. E. B. Du Bois Library plus 1 other. *Graduate expenses:* Tuition, state resident: full-time $2,640; part-time $110 per credit. Tuition, nonresident: full-time $9,936; part-time $414 per credit. Required fees: $8,969; $3,129 per term. One-time fee: $257 full-time. Tuition and fees vary according to class time, course load, campus/location and reciprocity agreements. *General application contact:* Jean Ames, Supervisor of Admissions, 413-545-0721.

Graduate School
Dr. John Mullin, Dean
Programs in:
- interdisciplinary studies (MS, PhD)
- marine science and technology (MS)
- neuroscience and behavior (MS, PhD)
- organismic and evolutionary biology (MS, PhD)
- plant biology (MS, PhD)

College of Engineering
Dr. Michael Malone, Dean
Programs in:
- chemical engineering (MS, PhD)
- civil engineering (MS, PhD)
- electrical and computer engineering (MS, PhD)
- engineering (MS, PhD)
- engineering management (MS)
- environmental engineering (MS)
- industrial engineering and operations research (MS, PhD)
- manufacturing engineering (MS)
- mechanical engineering (MS, PhD)

College of Humanities and Fine Arts
Dr. Joel Martin, Dean
Programs in:
- Afro-American studies (MA, PhD)
- ancient history (MA)
- architecture (M Arch, MS)
- architecture and design (M Arch)
- art (MA, MFA)
- art history (MA)
- British Empire history (MA)
- Chinese (MA)
- comparative literature (MA, PhD)
- creative writing (MFA)
- English and American literature (MA, PhD)
- European (medieval and modern) history (MA, PhD)
- French and Francophone studies (MA, MAT, PhD)
- Germanic languages and literatures (MA, PhD)
- Hispanic literatures and linguistics (MA, PhD)
- humanities and fine arts (M Arch, MA, MAT, MFA, MM, MS, PhD)
- interior design (MS)
- Islamic history (MA)
- Italian studies (MAT)
- Japanese (MA)
- Latin American history (MA, PhD)
- Latin and classical humanities (MAT)
- linguistics (MA, PhD)
- modern global history (MA)
- music (MM, PhD)
- philosophy (MA, PhD)
- public history (MA)
- science and technology history (MA)
- teaching Spanish (MAT)
- theater (MFA)
- U.S. history (MA, PhD)

College of Natural Resources and the Environment
Dr. Cleve Willis, Director
Programs in:
- entomology (MS, PhD)
- food science (MS, PhD)
- forest resources (MS, PhD)
- landscape architecture (MLA)
- mammalian and avian biology (MS, PhD)
- microbiology (MS, PhD)
- natural resources and the environment (MLA, MRP, MS, PhD)
- plant science (PhD)
- regional planning (MRP, PhD)
- resource economics (MS, PhD)
- soil science (MS, PhD)
- wildlife and fisheries conservation (MS, PhD)

College of Natural Sciences and Mathematics
Dr. George M. Langford, Dean
Programs in:
- applied mathematics (MS)
- astronomy (MS, PhD)
- biochemistry (MS, PhD)
- biological chemistry (PhD)
- cell and developmental biology (PhD)
- chemistry (MS, PhD)
- computer science (MS, PhD)
- geography (MS)
- geosciences (MS, PhD)
- mathematics and statistics (MS, PhD)
- natural sciences and mathematics (MS, PhD)
- physics (MS, PhD)
- polymer science and engineering (MS, PhD)

College of Social and Behavioral Sciences
Dr. Janet Rifkin, Dean
Programs in:
- anthropology (MA, PhD)
- clinical psychology (MS, PhD)
- communication (MA, PhD)
- economics (MA, PhD)
- labor studies (MS)
- political science (MA, PhD)
- public policy and administration (MPA)
- social and behavioral sciences (MA, MPA, MS, PhD)
- sociology (MA, PhD)

Isenberg School of Management
Dr. Soren Bisgaard, Dean
Programs in:
- accounting (MS)
- business administration (PMBA)
- hospitality and tourism management (MS)
- management (MBA, MS, PMBA, PhD)
- sport management (MS, PhD)

School of Education
Dr. Christine McCormick, Dean
Programs in:
- cultural diversity and curriculum reform (M Ed, Ed D, CAGS)
- early childhood education and development (M Ed, Ed D, CAGS)
- education (M Ed, Ed D, PhD, CAGS)
- educational administration (M Ed, Ed D, CAGS)
- elementary teacher education (M Ed, Ed D, CAGS)

higher education (M Ed, Ed D, CAGS)
international education (M Ed, Ed D, CAGS)
mathematics, science, and instructional technology (M Ed, Ed D, CAGS)
physical education teacher education (M Ed, Ed D, CAGS)
reading and writing (M Ed, Ed D, CAGS)
research and evaluation methods (M Ed, Ed D, CAGS)
school psychology (PhD)
school psychology and school counseling (M Ed, Ed D, CAGS)
secondary teacher education (M Ed, Ed D, CAGS)
social justice education (M Ed, Ed D, CAGS)
special education (M Ed, Ed D, CAGS)

School of Nursing
Dr. Eileen T. Breslin, Dean
Program in:
nursing (MS, PhD)

School of Public Health and Health Sciences
Dr. John Cunningham, Dean
Programs in:
communication disorders (MA, PhD)
kinesiology (MS, PhD)
nutrition (MPH, MS)
public health (PhD)
public health and health sciences (MA, MPH, MS, PhD)

■ UNIVERSITY OF MASSACHUSETTS BOSTON

Boston, MA 02125-3393

http://www.umb.edu/

State-supported, coed, university. CGS member. *Enrollment:* 12,362 graduate, professional, and undergraduate students; 913 full-time matriculated graduate/professional students (634 women), 2,203 part-time matriculated graduate/professional students (1,511 women). *Graduate faculty:* 448 full-time (172 women). *Computer facilities:* Computer purchase and lease plans are available. 260 computers available on campus for general student use. A campuswide network can be accessed from off campus. Internet access and online class registration are available. *Library facilities:* Joseph P. Healey Library. *Graduate expenses:* Tuition, state resident: full-time $2,590; part-time $301 per credit. Tuition, nonresident: full-time $9,758; part-time $427 per credit. One-time fee: $495 full-time. *General application contact:* Peggy Roldan, Graduate Admissions Coordinator, 617-287-6400.

Find University Details at www.petersons.com/gradchannel.

Office of Graduate Studies
Dr. Kristy Alster, Associate Provost

College of Liberal Arts
Dr. Donna Kuizenga, Dean, College of Liberal Arts
Programs in:
American studies (MA)
applied sociology (MA)
archival methods (MA)
bilingual education (MA)
clinical psychology (PhD)
English (MA)
English as a second language (MA)
foreign language pedagogy (MA)
historical archaeology (MA)
history (MA)
liberal arts (MA, PhD)

College of Management
Dr. Philip Quaglieri, Dean
Programs in:
business administration (MBA)
management (MBA)

College of Nursing and Health Sciences
Dr. Greer Glazer, Dean
Program in:
nursing (MS, PhD)

College of Public and Community Service
Adenrele Awotona, Dean
Programs in:
dispute resolution (MA, Certificate)
human services (MS)
public and community service (MA, MS, Certificate)

College of Science and Mathematics
Dr. William Hagar, Interim Dean
Programs in:
applied physics (MS)
biology (MS)
biotechnology and biomedical science (MS)
chemistry (MS)
computer science (MS, PhD)
environmental biology (PhD)
environmental sciences (MS)
environmental, earth and ocean sciences (PhD)
molecular, cellular and organismal biology (PhD)
science and mathematics (MS, PhD)

Division of Continuing Education
Dr. Dirk Messelaar, Head
Programs in:
continuing education (Certificate)
women in politics and government (Certificate)

Graduate College of Education
Dr. Peter Langer, Interim Dean
Programs in:
critical and creative thinking (MA, Certificate)
education (M Ed, Ed D)
educational administration (M Ed, CAGS)
elementary and secondary education/certification (M Ed)
family therapy (M Ed, CAGS)
forensic counseling (M Ed, CAGS)
higher education administration (Ed D)
instructional design (M Ed)
mental health counseling (M Ed, CAGS)
rehabilitation counseling (M Ed, CAGS)
school guidance counseling (M Ed, CAGS)
school psychology (M Ed, CAGS)
special education (M Ed)
teacher certification (M Ed)
urban school leadership (Ed D)

John W. McCormack Graduate School of Policy Studies
Dr. Stephen Crosby, Dean
Programs in:
gerontology (MA, MS, PhD, Certificate)
gerontology research (MA)
management in aging services (MA)
public affairs (MS)
public policy (PhD)
women in politics and government (Certificate)

■ UNIVERSITY OF MASSACHUSETTS DARTMOUTH

North Dartmouth, MA 02747-2300

http://www.umassd.edu/

State-supported, coed, university. *Enrollment:* 8,756 graduate, professional, and undergraduate students; 342 full-time matriculated graduate/professional students (147 women), 572 part-time matriculated graduate/professional students (330 women). *Graduate faculty:* 271 full-time (98 women), 134 part-time/adjunct (76 women). *Computer facilities:* Computer purchase and lease plans are available. 368 computers available on campus for general student use. A campuswide network can be accessed from student residence rooms and from off campus. Internet access and online class registration are available. *Library facilities:* University of Massachusetts Dartmouth Library. *Graduate expenses:* Tuition, state resident: full-time $2,071; part-time $86 per credit. Tuition, nonresident: full-time $8,099; part-time $337 per credit. *General application contact:* Carol Novo, Graduate Admissions Officer, 508-999-8604.

Graduate School
Dr. Richard J. Panofsky, Associate Vice Chancellor for Academic Affairs/Graduate Studies
Program in:
biomedical engineering/biotechnology (PhD)

Charlton College of Business
Dr. Eileen Peacock, Dean

University of Massachusetts Dartmouth (continued)
Programs in:
- accounting (Postbaccalaureate Certificate)
- business (MBA, PMC, Postbaccalaureate Certificate)
- business administration (MBA)
- e-commerce (PMC)
- finance (PMC)
- general management (PMC)
- leadership (PMC)
- management (Postbaccalaureate Certificate)
- marketing (PMC)
- supply chain management (PMC)

College of Arts and Sciences
Dr. William Hogan, Dean
Programs in:
- arts and sciences (MA, MAT, MPP, MS, PhD, Certificate, Postbaccalaureate Certificate)
- biology (MS)
- chemistry (MS)
- clinical psychology (MA)
- general psychology (MA)
- marine biology (MS)
- policy studies (MPP)
- Portuguese (MA)
- professional writing (MA, Postbaccalaureate Certificate)
- teaching (MAT, Certificate)
- WSO-Afro-Brazilian studies (PhD)

College of Engineering
Antonio Costa, Interim Dean
Programs in:
- acoustics (Certificate)
- civil engineering (MS)
- communications (Certificate)
- computer engineering (MS)
- computer science (MS, Certificate)
- computer systems engineering (Certificate)
- digital signal processing (Certificate)
- electrical engineering (MS, PhD)
- electrical engineering systems (Certificate)
- engineering (MS, PhD, Certificate)
- mechanical engineering (MS)
- physics (MS)
- textile chemistry (MS)
- textile technology (MS)

College of Nursing
Dr. James Fain, Dean
Programs in:
- community nursing (MS, PhD, Certificate, PMC)
- nursing (MS, PhD, Certificate, PMC)

College of Visual and Performing Arts
Michael Taylor, Interim Dean
Programs in:
- art education (MAE)
- artisanry (MFA, Certificate)
- fine arts (MFA)
- visual and performing arts (MAE, MFA, Certificate)
- visual design (MFA)

School of Marine Science and Technology
Dr. Avijit Gangopadhyay, Director
Program in:
- marine science and technology (MS, PhD)

■ UNIVERSITY OF MASSACHUSETTS LOWELL
Lowell, MA 01854-2881
http://www.uml.edu/

State-supported, coed, university. CGS member. *Computer facilities:* 4,000 computers available on campus for general student use. A campuswide network can be accessed from student residence rooms and from off campus. *Library facilities:* O'Leary Library plus 2 others. *General application contact:* Information Contact, 978-934-2380.

Find University Details at www.petersons.com/gradchannel.

Graduate School

College of Arts and Sciences
Programs in:
- applied mathematics (MS)
- applied mechanics (PhD)
- applied physics (MS, PhD)
- arts and sciences (MA, MM, MMS, MS, MS Eng, PhD, Sc D)
- biochemistry (PhD)
- biological sciences (MS)
- biotechnology (MS)
- chemistry (MS, PhD)
- community and social psychology (MA)
- computational mathematics (PhD)
- computer science (MS, PhD, Sc D)
- criminal justice (MA)
- energy engineering (PhD)
- environmental studies (PhD)
- mathematics (MS)
- music education (MM)
- music theory (MM)
- performance (MM)
- physics (MS, PhD)
- polymer sciences (MS, PhD)
- radiological sciences and protection (MS, PhD)
- regional economic and social development (MS)
- sound recording technology (MMS)

College of Health Professions
Programs in:
- administration of nursing services (PhD)
- adult psychiatric nursing (MS)
- advanced practice (MS)
- clinical laboratory studies (MS)
- family and community health nursing (MS)
- gerontological nursing (MS)
- health professions (MS, PhD)
- health promotion (PhD)
- health services administration (MS)
- occupational health nursing (MS)
- physical therapy (MS)

College of Management
Programs in:
- business administration (MBA)
- management (MBA, MMS)
- manufacturing management (MMS)

Graduate School of Education
Programs in:
- administration, planning, and policy (CAGS)
- curriculum and instruction (M Ed, CAGS)
- educational administration (M Ed)
- language arts and literacy (Ed D)
- leadership in schooling (Ed D)
- math and science education (Ed D)
- reading and language (M Ed, CAGS)

James B. Francis College of Engineering
Programs in:
- chemical engineering (MS Eng)
- chemistry (PhD)
- civil engineering (MS Eng)
- cleaner production and pollution prevention (MS, Sc D)
- computer engineering (MS Eng)
- electrical engineering (MS Eng, D Eng)
- energy engineering (MS Eng)
- engineering (MS, MS Eng, D Eng, PhD, Sc D, Certificate)
- environmental risk assessment (Certificate)
- environmental studies (MS Eng)
- identification and control of ergonomic hazards (Certificate)
- industrial hygiene (MS, Sc D)
- job stress and healthy job redesign (Certificate)
- manufacturing (Certificate)
- mechanical engineering (MS Eng, D Eng)
- occupational epidemiology (MS, Sc D)
- occupational ergonomics (MS, Sc D)
- plastics engineering (MS Eng, D Eng)
- radiological health physics and general work environment protection (Certificate)
- work environmental policy (MS, Sc D)

■ WESTERN NEW ENGLAND COLLEGE
Springfield, MA 01119
http://www.wnec.edu/

Independent, coed, comprehensive institution. *Computer facilities:* 460 computers available on campus for general student use. A campuswide network can be accessed from student residence rooms and from off campus. Internet access and online class registration are available. *Library facilities:* D'Amour Library plus 1 other. *General application contact:* Assistant Vice President, Graduate Studies and Continuing Education, 413-782-1249.

School of Arts and Sciences
Programs in:
- arts and sciences (M Ed, MAET, MAMT)
- elementary education (M Ed)
- English for teachers (MAET)
- mathematics for teachers (MAMT)

School of Business
Programs in:
- accounting (MSA)
- business (MBA, MSA)
- business administration (general) (MBA)

School of Engineering
Programs in:
- computer and engineering information systems (MSEE)
- computer engineering (MSEE)
- engineering (MSEE, MSEM, MSME)
- mechanical engineering (MSME)
- production management (MSEM)

School of Law
Programs in:
- estate planning/elder law (LL M)
- law (JD)

■ WESTFIELD STATE COLLEGE
Westfield, MA 01086
http://www.wsc.ma.edu/

State-supported, coed, comprehensive institution. *Computer facilities:* 238 computers available on campus for general student use. A campuswide network can be accessed from student residence rooms and from off campus. Internet access and online class registration, online transcripts, grade reports, billing information are available. *Library facilities:* Ely Library. *General application contact:* Admissions Clerk, 413-572-8022.

Division of Graduate and Continuing Education
Programs in:
- criminal justice (MS)
- early childhood education (M Ed)
- elementary education (M Ed)
- English (MA)
- history (M Ed)
- mental health counseling (MA)
- occupational education (M Ed, CAGS)
- physical education (M Ed)
- reading (M Ed)
- school administration (M Ed, CAGS)
- school guidance (MA)
- secondary education (M Ed)
- special education (M Ed)
- technology for educators (M Ed)

■ WHEELOCK COLLEGE
Boston, MA 02215-4176
http://www.wheelock.edu/

Independent, coed, primarily women, comprehensive institution. *Computer facilities:* 120 computers available on campus for general student use. A campuswide network can be accessed from student residence rooms and from off campus. Internet access is available. *Library facilities:* Wheelock College Library. *General application contact:* Associate Director of Graduate Admissions, 617-879-2206.

Graduate Programs
Program in:
- education (MS, MSW)

Division of Arts and Sciences
Program in:
- human development (MS)

Division of Child and Family Studies
Programs in:
- family studies (MS)
- family support and parent education (MS)
- family, culture, and society (MS)

Division of Education
Programs in:
- early childhood education (MS)
- education leadership (MS)
- elementary education (MS)
- language, literacy, and reading (MS)
- teaching students with moderate disabilities (MS)

Division of Social Work
Program in:
- social work (MSW)

■ WORCESTER POLYTECHNIC INSTITUTE
Worcester, MA 01609-2280
http://www.wpi.edu/

Independent, coed, university. CGS member. *Enrollment:* 3,918 graduate, professional, and undergraduate students; 496 full-time matriculated graduate/professional students (133 women), 399 part-time matriculated graduate/professional students (75 women). *Graduate faculty:* 203 full-time (38 women), 25 part-time/adjunct (4 women). *Computer facilities:* 700 computers available on campus for general student use. A campuswide network can be accessed from student residence rooms and from off campus. Internet access and online class registration, online course content, wireless network are available. *Library facilities:* George C. Gordon Library. *Graduate expenses:* Tuition: part-time $1,042 per credit hour. Required fees: $1,009 per year. *General application contact:* Lynne Dougherty, Administrative Assistant, 508-831-5301.

Find University Details at www.petersons.com/gradchannel.

Graduate Studies and Enrollment
Arlene R. Lowenstein, Dean of Special Academic Programs

Programs in:
- applied mathematics (MS)
- applied statistics (MS)
- biochemistry (MS)
- biology (MS)
- biomedical engineering (M Eng, MS, PhD, Certificate)
- bioscience administration (MS)
- biotechnology (MS, PhD)
- building regulatory integration in construction management (Advanced Certificate)
- chemical engineering (MS, PhD)
- chemistry (MS, PhD)
- civil engineering (MS, PhD)
- clinical engineering (M Eng)
- computer based support systems for construction management (Advanced Certificate)
- computer science (MS, PhD, Advanced Certificate, Certificate)
- construction project management (MS, Certificate)
- customized management (Certificate)
- electrical and computer engineering (Advanced Certificate, Certificate)
- electrical engineering (MS, PhD)
- engineering (M Eng, MBA, MME, MS, PhD, Advanced Certificate, Certificate, Graduate Certificate)
- environmental engineering (MS, Certificate)
- financial mathematics (MS)
- fire protection engineering (MS, PhD, Advanced Certificate, Certificate)
- geotechnical engineering (Certificate)
- impact engineering (MS)
- industrial mathematics (MS)
- information security management (MS, Certificate)
- information technology (MS, Certificate)
- information technology and entrepreneurship (MS)
- information technology applications development (MS)
- information technology project management (MS)
- management of technology (Certificate)
- manufacturing and service information technology applications (MS)
- manufacturing engineering (MS, PhD, Certificate)
- manufacturing engineering management (MS)
- marketing and technological innovation (MS)
- marketing information technology applications (MS)
- master builder (Certificate)
- master builder environmental engineering (M Eng)
- materials process engineering (MS)
- materials science and engineering (MS, PhD, Certificate)
- materials/transportation (Certificate)
- mathematical sciences (PhD, Certificate)

Worcester Polytechnic Institute (continued)
mathematics (MME)
mechanical engineering (MS, PhD, Advanced Certificate)
operations design and leadership (MS)
physics (MS, PhD)
power systems management (MS)
process design (MS)
social science (PhD)
structural engineering (Certificate)
supply chain management (MS)
system dynamics (MS, Graduate Certificate)
systems engineering (MS)
systems modeling (MS)
technology (MBA)
technology marketing (Certificate)
waste minimization and management (Advanced Certificate)

■ WORCESTER STATE COLLEGE
Worcester, MA 01602-2597
http://www.worcester.edu/

State-supported, coed, comprehensive institution. *Enrollment:* 5,440 graduate, professional, and undergraduate students; 90 full-time matriculated graduate/professional students (83 women), 724 part-time matriculated graduate/professional students (528 women). *Graduate faculty:* 42 full-time (27 women), 20 part-time/adjunct (9 women). *Computer facilities:* Computer purchase and lease plans are available. 102 computers available on campus for general student use. A campuswide network can be accessed from student residence rooms. Internet access is available. *Library facilities:* Learning Resources Center. *Graduate expenses:* Tuition, state resident: full-time $4,518; part-time $251 per credit hour. Tuition, nonresident: full-time $4,518; part-time $251 per credit hour. *General application contact:* Nicole Brown, Assistant Dean of Graduate and Continuing Education, 508-929-8787.

Graduate Studies
Dr. William H. White, Associate Vice President for Continuing Education and Outreach, Dean of the Graduate School
Programs in:
accounting (MS)
biotechnology (MS)
community health nursing (MS)
early childhood education (M Ed)
elementary education (M Ed)
English (M Ed)
health care administration (MS)
health education (M Ed)
history (M Ed)
leadership and administration (M Ed)
middle school education (M Ed)
moderate special needs (M Ed)
non-profit management (MS)
occupational therapy (MOT)
organizational leadership (MS)
reading (M Ed)
secondary education (M Ed)
Spanish (M Ed)
speech-language pathology (MS)

Michigan

■ ANDREWS UNIVERSITY
Berrien Springs, MI 49104
http://www.andrews.edu/

Independent-religious, coed, university. CGS member. *Computer facilities:* Computer purchase and lease plans are available. 130 computers available on campus for general student use. A campuswide network can be accessed from student residence rooms and from off campus. Internet access is available. *Library facilities:* James White Library plus 2 others. *General application contact:* Supervisor of Graduate Admission, 800-253-2874.

School of Graduate Studies

College of Arts and Sciences
Programs in:
allied health (MSMT)
arts and sciences (M Mus, MA, MAT, MS, MSA, MSMT, MSW, Dr Sc PT, TDPT)
biology (MAT, MS)
communication (MA)
community services management (MSA)
English (MA, MAT)
history (MA, MAT)
international development (MSA)
international language studies (MAT)
mathematics and physical science (MS)
music (M Mus, MA)
nursing (MS)
nutrition (MS)
physical therapy (DPT, Dr Sc PT, TDPT)
social work (MSW)

College of Technology
Programs in:
software engineering (MS)
technology (MS)

Division of Architecture
Program in:
architecture (M Arch)

School of Business
Programs in:
accounting, economics and finance (MBA, MSA)
business (MBA, MSA)
management and marketing (MBA, MSA)

School of Education
Programs in:
community counseling (MA)
counseling psychology (PhD)
curriculum and instruction (MA, Ed D, PhD, Ed S)
education (MA, MAT, MS, Ed D, PhD, Ed S)
educational administration and leadership (MA, Ed D, PhD, Ed S)
educational and developmental psychology (MA, Ed D, PhD)
educational psychology (Ed D, PhD)
elementary education (MAT)
leadership (MA, Ed D, PhD)
reading (MA)
school counseling (MA)
school psychology (Ed S)
secondary education (MAT)
special education (MS)
special education/learning disabilities (MS)
teacher education (MAT)

Seventh-day Adventist Theological Seminary
Programs in:
ministry (M Div, D Min)
pastoral ministry (MA)
religious education (MA, Ed D, PhD, Ed S)
theology (M Th, Th D)

■ AQUINAS COLLEGE
Grand Rapids, MI 49506-1799
http://www.aquinas.edu/

Independent-religious, coed, comprehensive institution. *Enrollment:* 2,098 graduate, professional, and undergraduate students; 76 full-time matriculated graduate/professional students (53 women), 242 part-time matriculated graduate/professional students (182 women). *Graduate faculty:* 36 full-time (21 women), 39 part-time/adjunct (29 women). *Computer facilities:* 176 computers available on campus for general student use. A campuswide network can be accessed from student residence rooms and from off campus. Internet access is available. *Library facilities:* Grace Hauenstein Library. *Graduate expenses:* Tuition: part-time $450 per credit. *General application contact:* Lynn Atkins-Rykert, Executive Assistant, School of Management, 616-632-2924.

School of Education
Nanette Clatterbuck, Dean
Program in:
education (MAT, ME, MS)

School of Management
Cynthia VanGelderen, Dean
Program in:
management (M Mgt)

■ CENTRAL MICHIGAN UNIVERSITY
Mount Pleasant, MI 48859
http://www.cmich.edu/

State-supported, coed, university. CGS member. *Computer facilities:* Computer purchase and lease plans are available. 1,585 computers available on campus for general student use. A campuswide network can be accessed from student residence rooms and from off campus. Internet access and online class registration, online bill payment are available. *Library facilities:* Charles V. Park Library plus 1 other. *General application contact:* Director of Graduate Student Services, 989-774-1059.

Central Michigan University Off-Campus Programs

Dr. Merodie Hancock, Vice President and Executive Director

Programs in:

- acquisitions administration (MSA, Certificate)
- counseling (MA)
- education (MA)
- educational administration (Ed S)
- educational administration and community leadership (Ed D)
- educational technology (MA)
- general administration (MSA, Certificate)
- health administration (DHA)
- health services administration (MSA, Certificate)
- human resources administration (MSA, Certificate)
- humanities (MA)
- information resource management (MSA, Certificate)
- international administration (MSA, Certificate)
- leadership (MSA, Certificate)
- public administration (MSA, Certificate)
- reading and literacy (MA)
- school principalship (MA)
- software engineering administration (MSA, Certificate)
- sport administration (MA)
- vehicle design and manufacturing administration (MSA, Certificate)

College of Graduate Studies

Programs in:

- acquisitions administration (MSA)
- general administration (MSA)
- health services administration (MSA)
- hospitality and tourism administration (MSA)
- human resources administration (MSA)
- information resource management (MSA)
- international administration (MSA)
- leadership (MSA)
- long-term care administration (MSA)
- organizational communication (MSA)
- public administration (MSA)
- recreation and park administration (MSA)
- sport administration (MSA)

College of Business Administration

Programs in:

- accounting (MBA)
- business administration (MA, MBA, MBE, MS)
- business education (MBE)
- economics (MA)
- finance and law (MBA)
- information systems (MS)
- management (MBA)
- marketing and hospitality services administration (MBA)

College of Communication and Fine Arts

Programs in:

- art (MA, MFA)
- broadcast and cinematic arts (MA)
- communication and fine arts (MA, MFA, MM)
- interpersonal and public communication (MA)
- music education and supervision (MM)
- music performance (MM)
- oral interpretation (MA)
- theatre (MA)

College of Education and Human Services

Programs in:

- community leadership (MA)
- counseling (MA)
- education and human services (MA, MS, Ed D, Ed S)
- educational administration (MA, Ed S)
- educational leadership (Ed D)
- educational technology (MA)
- elementary education (MA)
- human development and family studies (MA)
- library, media, and technology (MA)
- middle level education (MA)
- nutrition and dietetics (MS)
- professional counseling (MA)
- reading improvement (MA)
- recreation and park administration (MA)
- school counseling (MA)
- school principalship (MA)
- secondary education (MA)
- special education (MA)
- teaching senior high (MA)
- therapeutic recreation (MA)

College of Humanities and Social and Behavioral Sciences

Programs in:

- applied experimental psychology (PhD)
- clinical psychology (PhD)
- composition and communication (MA)
- creative writing (MA)
- English language and literature (MA)
- general, applied, and experimental psychology (MS, PhD)
- general/experimental psychology (MS)
- history (MA, PhD)
- humanities and social and behavioral sciences (MA, MPA, MS, PhD, S Psy S)
- industrial/organizational psychology (MA, PhD)
- political science (MA)
- public administration (MPA)
- public management (MPA)
- school psychology (PhD, S Psy S)
- social and criminal justice (MA)
- sociology (MA)
- Spanish (MA)
- state and local government (MPA)
- teaching English to speakers of other languages (MA)

College of Science and Technology

Programs in:

- biology (MS)
- chemistry (MS)
- computer science (MS)
- conservation biology (MS)
- industrial education (MA)
- industrial management and technology (MA)
- mathematics (MA, MAT, PhD)
- physics (MS)
- science and technology (MA, MAT, MS, PhD)
- teaching chemistry (MA)

The Herbert H. and Grace A. Dow College of Health Professions

Programs in:

- athletic administration (MA)
- audiology (Au D)
- coaching (MA)
- exercise science (MA)
- health professions (MA, MS, Au D, DPT)
- health promotion and program management (MA)
- physical therapy (DPT)
- physician assistant (MS)
- speech and language pathology (MA)
- sport administration (MA)
- teaching (MA)

Interdisciplinary Programs

Programs in:

- humanities (MA)
- interdisciplinary studies (MA, MSA)

■ CORNERSTONE UNIVERSITY

Grand Rapids, MI 49525-5897

http://www.cornerstone.edu/

Independent-religious, coed, comprehensive institution. *Computer facilities:* 531 computers available on campus for general student use. A campuswide network can be accessed from student residence rooms and from off campus. Internet access is available. *Library facilities:* Miller Library. *General application contact:* Graduate Admissions Director, 616-222-1559.

Graduate Programs

Programs in:

- business administration (MBA)
- education (MA Ed)
- management (MSM)
- teaching English to speakers of other languages (MA, Graduate Certificate)

■ DAVENPORT UNIVERSITY
Grand Rapids, MI 49503
http://www.davenport.edu/

Independent, coed, comprehensive institution. *General application contact:* Program Coordinator, 616-233-2597.

Sneden Graduate School
Program in:
business (MBA)

■ EASTERN MICHIGAN UNIVERSITY
Ypsilanti, MI 48197
http://www.emich.edu/

State-supported, coed, comprehensive institution. CGS member. *Enrollment:* 22,821 graduate, professional, and undergraduate students; 836 full-time matriculated graduate/professional students (543 women), 2,989 part-time matriculated graduate/professional students (1,913 women). *Graduate faculty:* 636 full-time (301 women). *Computer facilities:* Computer purchase and lease plans are available. 1,500 computers available on campus for general student use. A campuswide network can be accessed from student residence rooms and from off campus. Internet access is available. *Library facilities:* Bruce T. Halle Library. *Graduate expenses:* Tuition, state resident: part-time $341 per credit hour. Tuition, nonresident: full-time $16,104; part-time $671 per credit hour. Required fees: $816; $34 per credit hour. $40 per term. One-time fee: $82 full-time. Tuition and fees vary according to course level, course load, degree level and reciprocity agreements. *General application contact:* Graduate Admissions, 734-487-3400.

Find University Details at www.petersons.com/gradchannel.

Graduate School
Dr. Deborah deLaski-Smith, Interim Dean

College of Arts and Sciences
Dr. Hartmut Hoft, Interim Dean
Programs in:
applied economics (MA)
art (MA)
art education (MA)
arts administration (MA)
arts and sciences (MA, MFA, MLS, MPA, MS, PhD, Graduate Certificate)
bioinformatics (MS)
biology (MS)
chemistry (MS)
children's literature (MA)
clinical psychology (MS, PhD)
clinical/behavioral psychology (MS)
communication (MA)
computer science (MA)
creative writing (MA)
criminology and criminal justice (MA)
development, trade and planning (MA)
drama/theatre for the young (MA, MFA)
economics (MA)
English linguistics (MA)
foreign languages (MA)
French (MA)
general science (MS)
geography and geology (MS)
German (MA)
German for business practices (Graduate Certificate)
health economics (MA)
Hispanic language and cultures (Graduate Certificate)
historic preservation (MS)
history (MA)
individualized studies program (MLS)
international economics and development (MA)
interpretation/performance studies (MA)
language and international trade (MA)
literature (MA)
mathematics (MA)
mathematics education (MA)
music (MA)
music education (MA)
music performance (MA)
music theory-literature (MA)
physics (MS)
physics education (MS)
piano pedagogy (MA)
public administration (MPA)
social science (MA, MLS)
social science and American culture (MLS)
sociology (MA)
Spanish (MA)
Spanish (bilingual-bicultural education) (MA)
statistics (MA)
studio art (MA, MFA)
teaching English to speakers of other languages (MA, Graduate Certificate)
theatre (MA)
women's and gender studies (MA, MLS)
written communication (MA)

College of Business
Dr. David Mielke, Dean
Programs in:
accounting (MSA)
accounting and taxation (MBA)
accounting, financial, and operational control (MBA)
business (MBA, MSA, MSHROD, MSIS)
business administration (MBA)
computer information systems (MBA)
computer-based information systems (MSIS)
e-business (MBA)
enterprise business intelligence (MBA)
entrepreneurship (MBA)
finance (MBA)
human resources (MBA)
human resources management and organizational development (MSHROD)
information systems (MBA)
internal auditing (MBA)
international business (MBA)
management of human resources (MBA)
management organizational development (MBA)
nonprofit management (MBA)
production and operations management (MBA)
strategic quality management (MBA)
supply chain management (MBA)

College of Education
Dr. Vernon C. Polite, Dean
Programs in:
college counseling (MA)
community counseling (MA)
counseling (MA, Post Master's Certificate)
early childhood education (MA)
education (MA, Ed D, Post Master's Certificate, SPA)
educational leadership (Ed D)
educational media and technology (MA)
educational psychology (MA)
elementary education (MA)
higher education general administration (MA)
higher education student affairs (MA)
interdisciplinary cultural studies (MA)
K–12 curriculum (MA)
K-12 administration (MA)
leadership (MA, Ed D, SPA)
middle school education (MA)
reading (MA)
school counseling (MA)
school counselor (MA)
school counselor licensure (Post Master's Certificate)
secondary school teaching (MA)
social foundations (MA)
special education (MA, SPA)
speech and language pathology (MA)
teaching for diversity (MA)

College of Health and Human Services
Dr. Jeanne Thomas, Dean
Programs in:
Alzheimer's education (Graduate Certificate)
clinical research administration (MS)
dietetics/nutrition (MS)
gerontology (Graduate Certificate)
health and human services (MOT, MS, MSN, MSW, Advanced Certificate, Graduate Certificate)
health and physical education (MS)
nursing (MSN)
nursing education (Advanced Certificate)
occupational therapy (MOT, MS)
orthotics and prosthetics (MS)
social work (MSW)
sports management (MS)
sports medicine (MS)

College of Technology
Dr. Morell Boone, Interim Dean

Programs in:
- apparel, textile merchandising (MS)
- career, technical and workforce education (MS)
- computer aided engineering (MS)
- construction management (MS)
- engineering management (MS)
- hotel and restaurant management (MS)
- information security (MLS, Graduate Certificate)
- interior design (MS)
- liberal studies in technology (MLS)
- polymers and coatings technology (MS)
- quality and quality management (MS)
- technology (MLS, MS, PhD, Graduate Certificate)

■ FERRIS STATE UNIVERSITY
Big Rapids, MI 49307
http://www.ferris.edu/

State-supported, coed, comprehensive institution. *Enrollment:* 12,575 graduate, professional, and undergraduate students; 739 full-time matriculated graduate/professional students (424 women), 427 part-time matriculated graduate/professional students (266 women). *Graduate faculty:* 84 full-time (40 women), 127 part-time/adjunct (59 women). *Computer facilities:* Computer purchase and lease plans are available. 2,373 computers available on campus for general student use. A campuswide network can be accessed from student residence rooms and from off campus. Internet access and online class registration are available. *Library facilities:* FLITE: Ferris Library for Information, Technology and Education. *Graduate expenses:* Tuition, state resident: part-time $355 per credit hour. Tuition, nonresident: part-time $687 per credit hour. *General application contact:* Craig Westman, Interim Dean Enrollment Services/Director Admissions and Records, 231-591-2100.

College of Allied Health Sciences
Program in:
- allied health sciences (MS)

School of Nursing
Dr. Julie A. Coon, Director
Programs in:
- nursing (MS)
- nursing administration (MS)
- nursing education (MS)
- nursing informatics (MS)

College of Business
Dr. Bill Boras, Department Chair
Programs in:
- application development (MSISM)
- database administration (MSISM)
- e-business (MSISM)
- information systems (MBA)
- networking (MSISM)
- quality management (MBA)
- security (MSISM)

College of Education and Human Services
Michelle Johnston, Dean
Program in:
- education and human services (M Ed, MS, MSCTE)

School of Criminal Justice
Dr. Frank Crowe, Director
Program in:
- criminal justice administration (MS)

School of Education
Interim Director
Programs in:
- administration (MSCTE)
- curriculum and instruction (M Ed)
- education technology (MSCTE)
- instructor (MSCTE)
- post-secondary administration (MSCTE)
- training and development (MSCTE)

College of Pharmacy
Dr. Ian Mathison, Dean
Program in:
- pharmacy (Pharm D)

Kendall College of Art and Design
Dr. Oliver H. Evans, President
Program in:
- art and design (MFA)

Michigan College of Optometry
Dr. Kevin L. Alexander, Dean
Program in:
- optometry (OD)

■ GRAND VALLEY STATE UNIVERSITY
Allendale, MI 49401-9403
http://www.gvsu.edu/

State-supported, coed, comprehensive institution. CGS member. *Enrollment:* 23,295 graduate, professional, and undergraduate students; 792 full-time matriculated graduate/professional students (558 women), 2,381 part-time matriculated graduate/professional students (1,620 women). *Graduate faculty:* 261 full-time (115 women), 89 part-time/adjunct (39 women). *Computer facilities:* 2,600 computers available on campus for general student use. A campuswide network can be accessed from student residence rooms and from off campus. Internet access and online class registration, transcript, degree audit, credit card payments, grades are available. *Library facilities:* James H. Zumberge Library plus 2 others. *Graduate expenses:* Tuition, state resident: full-time $5,850; part-time $325 per credit. Tuition, nonresident: full-time $10,800; part-time $600 per credit. Tuition and fees vary according to course load. *General application contact:* Tracey James-Heer, Associate Director for Graduate Recruitment, 616-331-2025.

Find University Details at www.petersons.com/gradchannel.

College of Community and Public Service
Dr. Rodney Mulder, Dean
Program in:
- community and public service (MHA, MPA, MS, MSW)

School of Criminal Justice
Dr. Jonathan White, Director
Program in:
- criminal justice (MS)

School of Public and Nonprofit Administration
Dr. Mark Hoffman, Director
Programs in:
- health administration (MHA)
- public and nonprofit administration (MHA, MPA)

School of Social Work
Dr. Elaine Schott, Director
Program in:
- social work (MSW)

College of Education
Dr. Elaine C. Collins, Dean
Programs in:
- adult and higher education (M Ed)
- early childhood developmental delay (M Ed)
- early childhood education (M Ed)
- education (M Ed)
- education of the gifted and talented (M Ed)
- educational leadership (M Ed)
- educational technology (M Ed)
- elementary education (M Ed)
- emotional impairment (M Ed)
- learning disabilities (M Ed)
- middle and high school education (M Ed)
- reading and language arts (M Ed)
- school counseling (M Ed)
- special education endorsements (M Ed)
- student affairs leadership (M Ed)
- teaching English to speakers of other languages (M Ed)

College of Health Professions
Dr. Jane Toot, Dean
Programs in:
- health professions (MPAS, MS, DPT)
- occupational therapy (MS)
- physical therapy (MS, DPT)
- physician assistant studies (MPAS)

College of Liberal Arts and Sciences
Dr. Frederick Antczak, Dean
Programs in:
- biology (MS)
- biomedical sciences (MHS)
- biostatistics (MS)
- cell and molecular biology (MS)
- English (MA)
- liberal arts and sciences (MA, MHS, MS)

School of Communications
Dr. Alex Nesterenko, Director
Program in:
- communications (MS)

Grand Valley State University (continued)

Kirkhof College of Nursing
Dr. Phyllis Gendler, Dean
Programs in:
advanced practice (MSN)
case management (MSN)
nursing administration (MSN)
nursing education (MSN)

Padnos College of Engineering and Computing
Dr. Paul Plotkowski, Dean
Programs in:
engineering and computing (MS, MSE)
medical and bioinformatics (MS)

School of Computing and Information Systems
Paul Leidig, Director
Program in:
computer information systems (MS)

School of Engineering
Dr. Jeff Ray, Director
Programs in:
electrical and computer engineering (MSE)
manufacturing engineering (MSE)
manufacturing operations (MSE)
mechanical engineering (MSE)
product design and manufacturing engineering (MSE)

Seidman College of Business
Dr. H. James Williams, Dean
Programs in:
accounting (MSA)
business (MBA, MSA, MST)
business administration (MBA)
taxation (MST)

■ LAWRENCE TECHNOLOGICAL UNIVERSITY

Southfield, MI 48075-1058

http://www.ltu.edu/

Independent, coed, university. *Enrollment:* 4,049 graduate, professional, and undergraduate students; 79 full-time matriculated graduate/professional students (28 women), 1,223 part-time matriculated graduate/professional students (397 women). *Graduate faculty:* 43 full-time (13 women), 97 part-time/adjunct (15 women). *Computer facilities:* Computer purchase and lease plans are available. 60 computers available on campus for general student use. A campuswide network can be accessed from student residence rooms and from off campus. Internet access and online class registration, degree audit, black board, SCT Banner (student information) are available. *Library facilities:* Lawrence Technological University Library plus 1 other. *General application contact:* Jane Rohrback, Director of Admissions, 248-204-3160.

College of Architecture and Design
Glen LeRoy, Dean of the College of Architecture and Design
Programs in:
architecture (M Arch)
interior design (MID)

College of Arts and Sciences
Dr. Hsiao-Ping Moore, Interim Dean
Programs in:
computer science (MS)
educational technology (MET)
science education (MSE)
technical communication (MS)

College of Engineering
Dr. Laird Johnston, Dean
Programs in:
automotive engineering (MAE)
civil engineering (MCE)
construction engineering management (MS)
electrical and computer engineering (MS)
engineering management (ME)
manufacturing systems (MEMS, DE)
mechanical engineering (MS)
mechatronic systems engineering (MS)

College of Management
Dr. Lou DeGennaro, Dean
Programs in:
business administration (MBA, DBA)
information systems (MS)
information technology (DM)
operations management (MS)

■ MADONNA UNIVERSITY

Livonia, MI 48150-1173

http://www.madonna.edu

Independent-religious, coed, comprehensive institution. *Enrollment:* 4,156 graduate, professional, and undergraduate students; 104 full-time matriculated graduate/professional students (76 women), 790 part-time matriculated graduate/professional students (600 women). *Graduate faculty:* 40 full-time (20 women), 39 part-time/adjunct (12 women). *Computer facilities:* Computer purchase and lease plans are available. 175 computers available on campus for general student use. A campuswide network can be accessed from student residence rooms and from off campus. Internet access and online class registration, wireless network are available. *Library facilities:* Madonna University Library. *General application contact:* Sandra Kellums, Coordinator of Graduate Admissions and Records, 734-432-5667.

Department of English
Dr. Andrew Domzalski, Director
Program in:
teaching English to speakers of other languages (MATESOL)

Department of Psychology
Dr. Robert Cohen, Chairperson
Program in:
clinical psychology (MSCP)

Program in Health Services
Dr. Ted Biermann, Dean
Program in:
health services (MSHS)

Program in Hospice
Program in:
hospice (MSH)

Program in Liberal Studies
Dr. Dwight Lang, Director
Program in:
liberal studies (MALS)

Program in Nursing
Dr. Nancy O'Connor, Chairperson
Programs in:
adult health: chronic health conditions (MSN)
adult nurse practitioner (MSN)
nursing administration (MSN)

Program in Religious Studies
Program in:
pastoral ministry (MA)

Programs in Education
Dr. Robert Kimball, Dean
Programs in:
Catholic school leadership (MSA)
educational leadership (MSA)
learning disabilities (MAT)
literacy education (MAT)
teaching and learning (MAT)

School of Business
Dr. Stuart Arends, Dean
Programs in:
business administration (MBA)
international business (MSBA)
leadership studies (MSBA)
leadership studies in criminal justice (MSBA)
quality and operations management (MSBA)

■ MARYGROVE COLLEGE

Detroit, MI 48221-2599

http://www.marygrove.edu/

Independent-religious, coed, primarily women, comprehensive institution. *Computer facilities:* Computer purchase and lease plans are available. 115 computers available on campus for general student use. A campuswide network can be accessed from student residence rooms. Internet access is available. *Library facilities:* Marygrove College Library plus 1 other. *General application contact:* Director, Graduate Admissions, 313-927-1390.

Graduate Division
Programs in:
educational leadership (MA)
modern language translation (MA)
pastoral ministry (MA)
social justice (MA)

Education Unit
Programs in:
- adult learning (MA)
- art of teaching (MAT)
- griot (M Ed)
- reading education (M Ed)
- sage (M Ed)

Human Resource Management Unit
Program in:
- human resource management (MA)

■ MICHIGAN STATE UNIVERSITY
East Lansing, MI 48824
http://www.msu.edu/

State-supported, coed, university. CGS member. *Enrollment:* 45,520 graduate, professional, and undergraduate students; 6,734 full-time matriculated graduate/professional students (3,492 women), 1,695 part-time matriculated graduate/professional students (1,164 women). *Graduate faculty:* 1,944 full-time (611 women), 17 part-time/adjunct (5 women). *Computer facilities:* Computer purchase and lease plans are available. 2,000 computers available on campus for general student use. A campuswide network can be accessed from student residence rooms and from off campus. Internet access and online class registration are available. *Library facilities:* Main Library plus 14 others. *Graduate expenses:* Tuition, state resident: part-time $346 per credit hour. Tuition, nonresident: part-time $730 per credit hour. Tuition and fees vary according to program. *General application contact:* Dr. Karen Klomparens, Dean of the Graduate School and Associate Provost for Graduate Education, 517-432-1236.

Find University Details at www.petersons.com/gradchannel.

College of Human Medicine
Dr. Marsha D. Rappley, Dean
Programs in:
- biochemistry and molecular biology (MS, PhD)
- bioethics, humanities, and society (MA)
- epidemiology (MS, PhD)
- human medicine (MD)
- human medicine/medical scientist training program (MD)
- microbiology (MS)
- microbiology and molecular genetics (PhD)
- pharmacology and toxicology (MS, PhD)
- physiology (MS, PhD)

College of Osteopathic Medicine
Dr. William D. Strampel, Dean
Programs in:
- biochemistry and molecular biology (MS, PhD)
- microbiology (MS)
- microbiology and molecular genetics (PhD)
- osteopathic medicine (DO, MS, PhD)
- pharmacology and toxicology (MS, PhD)
- pharmacology and toxicology-environmental toxicology (PhD)
- physiology (MS, PhD)

College of Veterinary Medicine
Dr. Christopher Brown, Dean
Programs in:
- animal science–environmental toxicology (PhD)
- biochemistry and molecular biology–environmental toxicology (PhD)
- chemistry–environmental toxicology (PhD)
- comparative medicine and integrative biology (MS, PhD)
- crop and soil sciences–environmental toxicology (PhD)
- environmental engineering–environmental toxicology (PhD)
- environmental geosciences–environmental toxicology (PhD)
- fisheries and wildlife–environmental toxicology (PhD)
- food safety (MS)
- food safety and toxicology (MS)
- food science–environmental toxicology (PhD)
- forestry–environmental toxicology (PhD)
- industrial microbiology (MS)
- integrative toxicology (PhD)
- large animal clinical sciences (MS, PhD)
- microbiology (MS, PhD)
- microbiology and molecular genetics (MS, PhD)
- microbiology–environmental toxicology (PhD)
- pathobiology and diagnostic investigation (MS, PhD)
- pathology (MS, PhD)
- pathology–environmental toxicology (PhD)
- pharmacology and toxicology–environmental toxicology (PhD)
- small animal clinical sciences (MS)
- veterinary medicine (DVM)
- veterinary medicine/medical scientist training program (DVM)
- zoology–environmental toxicology (PhD)

The Graduate School
Dr. Karen Klomparens, Dean of the Graduate School and Associate Provost for Graduate Education

College of Agriculture and Natural Resources
Dr. Jeffrey D. Armstrong, Dean
Programs in:
- agricultural economics (MS, PhD)
- agricultural technology and systems management (MS, PhD)
- agriculture and natural resources (MA, MIPS, MS, MURP, PhD)
- animal science (MS, PhD)
- animal science-environmental toxicology (PhD)
- biosystems engineering (MS, PhD)
- community, agriculture, recreation, and resource studies (MS, PhD)
- construction management (MS, PhD)
- crop and soil sciences (MS, PhD)
- crop and soil sciences-environmental toxicology (PhD)
- entomology (MS, PhD)
- environmental design (MA)
- fisherics and wildlife (MS, PhD)
- fisheries and wildlife—environmental toxicology (PhD)
- food science (MS, PhD)
- food science—environmental toxicology (PhD)
- forestry (MS, PhD)
- forestry-environmental toxicology (PhD)
- horticulture (MS, PhD)
- human nutrition (MS, PhD)
- human nutrition-environmental toxicology (PhD)
- integrated pest management (MS)
- interior design and facilities management (MA)
- international planning studies (MIPS)
- packaging (MS, PhD)
- plant breeding and genetics (MS, PhD)
- plant breeding and genetics-crop and soil sciences (MS, PhD)
- plant breeding and genetics-forestry (MS, PhD)
- plant breeding and genetics-horticulture (MS, PhD)
- plant pathology (MS, PhD)
- urban and regional planning (MURP)

College of Arts and Letters
Dr. Karin A. Warst, Dean
Programs in:
- African-American and African studies (MA, PhD)
- American studies (MA, PhD)
- applied Spanish linguistics (MA)
- arts and letters (MA, MFA, PhD)
- critical studies in literacy and pedagogy (MA)
- digital rhetoric and professional writing (MA)
- English (PhD)
- French (MA)
- French language and literature (PhD)
- German studies (MA, PhD)
- Hispanic cultural studies (PhD)
- Hispanic literatures (MA)
- history (MA, PhD)
- history-secondary school teaching (MA)
- linguistics (MA, PhD)
- literature in English (MA)
- philosophy (MA, PhD)
- rhetoric and writing (PhD)
- second language studies (PhD)
- studio art (MFA)
- teaching English to speakers of other languages (MA)
- theatre (MA, MFA)

Michigan State University (continued)

College of Communication Arts and Sciences
Dr. Charles T. Salmon, Dean
Programs in:
- advertising (MA)
- communication (MA, PhD)
- communication arts and sciences (MA, MS, PhD)
- communicative sciences and disorders (MA, PhD)
- health communication (MA)
- journalism (MA)
- media and information studies (PhD)
- public relations (MA)
- retailing (MS, PhD)
- telecommunication, information studies, and media (MA)

College of Education
Dr. Carole Ames, Dean
Programs in:
- counseling (MA)
- curriculum and teaching (MA)
- curriculum, teaching and education policy (PhD, Ed S)
- education (MA, MS, PhD, Ed S)
- education for professional teachers (MA)
- educational policy (PhD)
- educational psychology and educational technology (PhD)
- educational technology (MA)
- higher, adult and lifelong education (MA, PhD)
- K–12 educational administration (MA, PhD, Ed S)
- kinesiology (MS, PhD)
- literacy instruction (MA)
- measurement and quantitative methods (PhD)
- rehabilitation counseling (MA)
- rehabilitation counselor education (PhD)
- school psychology (MA, PhD, Ed S)
- special education (MA, PhD)
- student affairs administration (MA)

College of Engineering
Dr. Satish Udpa, Dean
Programs in:
- chemical engineering (MS, PhD)
- civil engineering (MS, PhD)
- computer science (MS, PhD)
- electrical engineering (MS, PhD)
- engineering (MS, PhD)
- engineering mechanics (MS, PhD)
- environmental engineering (MS, PhD)
- environmental engineering-environmental toxicology (PhD)
- materials science and engineering (MS, PhD)
- mechanical engineering (MS, PhD)

College of Music
Prof. James B. Forger, Dean
Programs in:
- music (PhD)
- music composition (M Mus, DMA)
- music conducting (M Mus, DMA)
- music education (M Mus)
- music performance (M Mus, DMA)
- music theory (M Mus)
- music therapy (M Mus)
- musicology (MA)
- piano pedagogy (M Mus)

College of Natural Science
Dr. Estelle E. McGroarty, Acting Dean
Programs in:
- applied mathematics (MS, PhD)
- applied statistics (MS)
- astrophysics and astronomy (MS, PhD)
- biochemistry and molecular biology (MS, PhD)
- biochemistry and molecular biology/environmental toxicology (PhD)
- biological science (MS)
- biological, physical and general science for teachers (MAT, MS)
- biomedical laboratory operations (MS)
- cell and molecular biology (MS, PhD)
- cell and molecular biology/environmental toxicology (PhD)
- chemical physics (PhD)
- chemistry (MS, PhD)
- chemistry-environmental toxicology (PhD)
- clinical laboratory sciences (MS)
- computational chemistry (MS)
- ecology, evolutionary biology and behavior (PhD)
- environmental geosciences (MS, PhD)
- environmental geosciences-environmental toxicology (PhD)
- general science (MAT)
- genetics (MS, PhD)
- geological sciences (MS, PhD)
- industrial mathematics (MS)
- mathematics (MAT, MS, PhD)
- mathematics education (MS, PhD)
- natural science (MAT, MS, PhD)
- neuroscience (MS, PhD)
- physical science (MS)
- physics (MS, PhD)
- plant biology (MS, PhD)
- plant breeding and genetics—plant biology (MS, PhD)
- statistics (MS, PhD)
- zoo and aquarium management (MS)
- zoology (MS, PhD)
- zoology-environmental toxicology (PhD)

College of Nursing
Dr. Mary Mundt, Dean
Program in:
- nursing (MSN, PhD)

College of Social Science
Dr. Marietta Baba, Dean
Programs in:
- anthropology (MA, PhD)
- Chicano/Latino studies (PhD)
- child development (MA)
- clinical social work (MSW)
- community services (MS)
- criminal justice (MS, PhD)
- economics (MA, PhD)
- family and child ecology (PhD)
- family studies (MA)
- forensic science (MS)
- geographic information science (MS)
- geography (MA, PhD)
- human resources and labor relations (MLRHR)
- industrial relations and human resources (PhD)
- marriage and family therapy (MA)
- organizational and community practice (MSW)
- political science (MA, PhD)
- professional applications in anthropology (MA)
- psychology (MA, PhD)
- public policy (MPP)
- social science (MA, MIPS, MLRHR, MPP, MS, MSW, MURP, PhD)
- social science—global applications (MA)
- social work (PhD)
- sociology (MA, PhD)
- youth development (MA)

Eli Broad Graduate School of Management
Dr. Robert B. Duncan, Dean
Programs in:
- accounting (MS)
- business administration (MBA, PhD)
- corporate business administration (MBA)
- finance (MS)
- food service management (MS)
- hospitality business (MS)
- integrative management (MBA)
- management (MBA, MS, PhD)
- manufacturing and engineering management (MS)
- supply chain management (MS)

■ MICHIGAN TECHNOLOGICAL UNIVERSITY
Houghton, MI 49931-1295
http://www.mtu.edu/

State-supported, coed, university. CGS member. *Computer facilities:* 1,555 computers available on campus for general student use. A campuswide network can be accessed from student residence rooms and from off campus. Internet access and online class registration are available. *Library facilities:* J. R. Van Pelt Library. *General application contact:* Senior Staff Assistant, 906-487-2327.

Find University Details at www.petersons.com/gradchannel.

Graduate School

College of Engineering
Programs in:
- biomedical engineering (PhD)
- chemical engineering (MS, PhD)
- civil engineering (ME, MS, PhD)
- electrical engineering (MS, PhD)
- engineering (ME, MS, PhD)
- engineering mechanics (MS)

environmental engineering (ME, MS, PhD)
environmental engineering science (MS)
geological engineering (MS, PhD)
geology (MS, PhD)
geophysics (MS)
materials science and engineering (MS, PhD)
mechanical engineering (MS, PhD)
mechanical engineering-engineering mechanics (PhD)
mining engineering (MS, PhD)

College of Sciences and Arts
Programs in:
applied science education (MS)
biological sciences (MS, PhD)
chemistry (MS, PhD)
computational science and engineering (PhD)
computer science (MS, PhD)
engineering physics (PhD)
environmental policy (MS)
industrial archaeology (MS)
industrial heritage and archeology (PhD)
mathematical sciences (MS, PhD)
physics (MS, PhD)
rhetoric and technical communication (MS, PhD)
sciences and arts (MS, PhD)

School of Business and Economics
Programs in:
business administration (MS)
business and economics (MS)
mineral economics (MS)

School of Forest Resources and Environmental Science
Programs in:
applied ecology (MS)
forest ecology and management (MS)
forest molecular genetics and biotechnology (MS, PhD)
forest science (PhD)
forestry (MF, MS)

Sustainable Futures Institute
Program in:
sustainability (Certificate)

■ NORTHERN MICHIGAN UNIVERSITY
Marquette, MI 49855-5301
http://www.nmu.edu/

State-supported, coed, comprehensive institution. CGS member. *Computer facilities:* Computer purchase and lease plans are available. 9,000 computers available on campus for general student use. A campuswide network can be accessed from student residence rooms and from off campus. Internet access and online class registration are available. *Library facilities:* Lydia Olson Library plus 1 other. *General application contact:* Dean of Graduate Studies and Research, 906-227-2300.

College of Graduate Studies

College of Arts and Sciences
Programs in:
administrative services (MA)
arts and sciences (MA, MFA, MPA, MS)
biochemistry (MS)
biology (MS)
chemistry (MS)
creative writing (MFA)
literature (MA)
pedagogy (MA)
public administration (MPA)
writing (MA)

College of Professional Studies
Programs in:
administration and supervision (MA Ed, Ed S)
behavioral sciences and human services (MA, MA Ed, MS, MSN, Ed S)
communication disorders (MA)
criminal justice (MS)
elementary education (MA Ed)
exercise science (MS)
nursing (MSN)
psychology (MS)
secondary education (MA Ed)
special education (MA Ed)

■ OAKLAND UNIVERSITY
Rochester, MI 48309-4401
http://www.oakland.edu/

State-supported, coed, university. CGS member. *Enrollment:* 17,737 graduate, professional, and undergraduate students; 1,319 full-time matriculated graduate/professional students (892 women), 2,479 part-time matriculated graduate/professional students (1,579 women). *Graduate faculty:* 298 full-time (119 women), 83 part-time/adjunct (42 women). *Computer facilities:* A campuswide network can be accessed from student residence rooms and from off campus. Internet access and online class registration are available. *Library facilities:* Kresge Library plus 1 other. *Graduate expenses:* Tuition, state resident: full-time $9,936; part-time $414 per credit. Tuition, nonresident: full-time $17,202; part-time $716 per credit. *General application contact:* Christina J. Grabowski, Associate Director of Graduate Study and Lifelong Learning, 248-370-3167.

Find University Details at www.petersons.com/gradchannel.

Graduate Study and Lifelong Learning
Graduate Admissions

College of Arts and Sciences
Graduate Admissions
Programs in:
applied mathematical sciences (PhD)
applied statistics (MS)
arts and sciences (MA, MM, MPA, MS, PhD, Certificate)
biological sciences (MA, MS)
cellular biology of aging (MS)
chemistry (MS)
English (MA)
health and environmental chemistry (PhD)
history (MA)
industrial applied mathematics (MS)
liberal studies (MA)
linguistics (MA)
mathematics (MA)
medical physics (PhD)
music (MM)
music education (PhD)
physics (MS)
public administration (MPA)
statistical methods (Certificate)
teaching English as a second language (Certificate)

School of Business Administration
Dr. Jonathan Silberman, Dean
Programs in:
accounting (M Acc, Certificate)
business administration (MBA)
economics (Certificate)
entrepreneurship (Certificate)
finance (Certificate)
general management (Certificate)
human resource management (Certificate)
information technology management (MS)
international business (Certificate)
management information systems (Certificate)
marketing (Certificate)
production and operations management (Certificate)

School of Education and Human Services
Dr. Mary L. Otto, Dean
Programs in:
advanced microcomputer applications (Certificate)
counseling (MA, PhD, Certificate)
early childhood education (M Ed, PhD, Certificate)
early mathematics education (Certificate)
education and human services (M Ed, MA, MAT, MTD, PhD, Certificate, Ed S)
education studies (M Ed)
educational leadership (M Ed, PhD)
higher education (Certificate)
higher education administration (Certificate)
human resource development (MTD)
microcomputer applications (Certificate)
reading (Certificate)
reading and language arts (MAT)
reading education (PhD)
reading, language arts and literature (Certificate)
school administration (Ed S)
secondary education (MAT)
special education (M Ed, Certificate)

Oakland University (continued)

School of Engineering and Computer Science
Dr. Pieter A. Frick, Dean
Programs in:
- computer science (MS)
- electrical and computer engineering (MS)
- embedded systems (MS)
- engineering and computer science (MS, PhD)
- engineering management (MS)
- information systems engineering (MS)
- mechanical engineering (MS, PhD)
- software engineering (MS)
- systems engineering (MS, PhD)

School of Health Sciences
Dr. Kenneth R. Hightower, Dean
Programs in:
- complimentary medicine and wellness (Certificate)
- exercise science (MS, Certificate)
- health sciences (MS, MSPT, DPT, Dr Sc PT, Certificate)
- neurological rehabilitation (Certificate)
- orthopedic manual physical therapy (Certificate)
- orthopedic physical therapy (Certificate)
- pediatric rehabilitation (Certificate)
- physical therapy (MSPT, DPT, Dr Sc PT)
- safety management (MS)
- teaching and learning for rehabilitation professionals (Certificate)

School of Nursing
Dr. Linda Thompson, Dean
Programs in:
- adult gerontological nurse practitioner (MSN, Certificate)
- adult health (MSN)
- family nurse practitioner (MSN, Certificate)
- nurse anesthetist (MSN, Certificate)
- nursing (MSN, DNP, Certificate)
- nursing education (MSN, Certificate)
- nursing practice (DNP)

■ SAGINAW VALLEY STATE UNIVERSITY
University Center, MI 48710
http://www.svsu.edu/

State-supported, coed, comprehensive institution. *Enrollment:* 9,543 graduate, professional, and undergraduate students; 154 full-time matriculated graduate/professional students (107 women), 1,456 part-time matriculated graduate/professional students (1,097 women). *Graduate faculty:* 81 full-time (47 women), 55 part-time/adjunct (37 women). *Computer facilities:* Computer purchase and lease plans are available. 1,033 computers available on campus for general student use. A campuswide network can be accessed from student residence rooms and from off campus. Internet access and online class registration are available. *Library facilities:* Zahnow Library. *Graduate expenses:* Tuition, state resident: full-time $7,225; part-time $301 per credit hour. Tuition, nonresident: full-time $13,888; part-time $579 per credit hour. Required fees: $330; $14 per credit hour. Tuition and fees vary according to course load. *General application contact:* Information Contact, 989-964-4200.

College of Arts and Behavioral Sciences
Dr. Mary Hedberg, Dean
Programs in:
- administrative science (MA)
- arts and behavioral sciences (MA)
- communication and multimedia (MA)

College of Business and Management
Dr. Marwan A. Wafa, Dean
Programs in:
- business administration (MBA)
- business and management (MBA)

College of Education
Dr. Steve P. Barbus, Dean
Programs in:
- adapted physical activity (MAT)
- chief business officers (M Ed)
- early childhood education (MAT)
- education (M Ed, MAT, Ed S)
- education leadership (Ed S)
- educational administration and supervision (M Ed)
- elementary (MAT)
- elementary classroom teaching (MAT)
- instructional technology (MAT)
- learning and behavioral disorders (MAT)
- middle school (MAT)
- middle school classroom teaching (MAT)
- principalship (M Ed)
- reading education (MAT)
- secondary classroom teaching (MAT)
- secondary school (MAT)
- special education (MAT)
- superintendency (M Ed)

College of Science, Engineering, and Technology
Dr. Ron Williams, Dean
Programs in:
- science, engineering, and technology (MS)
- technological processes (MS)

Crystal M. Lange College of Nursing and Health Sciences
Dr. Janalou Blecke, Dean
Programs in:
- clinical nurse specialist (MSN)
- health system nurse specialist (MSN)
- nurse practitioner (MSN)
- nursing (MSN)
- nursing and health sciences (MSN, MSOT)
- occupational therapy (MSOT)

■ SIENA HEIGHTS UNIVERSITY
Adrian, MI 49221-1796
http://www.sienaheights.edu/

Independent-religious, coed, comprehensive institution. *Computer facilities:* 75 computers available on campus for general student use. A campuswide network can be accessed from student residence rooms and from off campus. Internet access is available. *General application contact:* Dean, Graduate College, 517-264-7663.

Graduate College
Programs in:
- agency counseling (MA)
- community counseling (Spt)
- curriculum and instruction (MA)
- early childhood education (MA)
- elementary education (MA)
- elementary education/reading (MA)
- human resource development (MA)
- middle school education (MA)
- Montessori education (MA)
- school counseling (MA)
- secondary education (MA)
- secondary education/reading (MA)

■ SPRING ARBOR UNIVERSITY
Spring Arbor, MI 49283-9799
http://www.arbor.edu/

Independent-religious, coed, comprehensive institution. *Enrollment:* 3,714 graduate, professional, and undergraduate students; 759 full-time matriculated graduate/professional students (580 women), 425 part-time matriculated graduate/professional students (310 women). *Graduate faculty:* 21 full-time (5 women), 173 part-time/adjunct (76 women). *Computer facilities:* 168 computers available on campus for general student use. A campuswide network can be accessed from student residence rooms and from off campus. Internet access and online class registration are available. *Library facilities:* Hugh A. White Library. *Graduate expenses:* Tuition: full-time $4,200; part-time $350 per credit. Required fees: $140; $48 per term. Tuition and fees vary according to course load and program. *General application contact:* Dale N. Glinz, Graduate Recruiter, Admissions Office.

School of Adult Studies
Natalie Gianetti, Dean of Adult Studies
Programs in:
- counseling (MAC)
- family studies (MAFS)
- organizational management (MAOM)

School of Arts and Sciences
Dr. Wally Metts, Chair of the Department of Communication
Programs in:
- communication (MA)
- spiritual formation and leadership (MA)

School of Business and Management
Dr. Caleb K. Chan, Director, MBA Program
Program in:
business and management (MBA)

School of Education
Carla Koontz, Interim Dean of Education
Program in:
education (MAE)

■ UNIVERSITY OF DETROIT MERCY
Detroit, MI 48221
http://www.udmercy.edu/

Independent-religious, coed, university. *Enrollment:* 1,424 full-time matriculated graduate/professional students (659 women), 964 part-time matriculated graduate/professional students (611 women). *Graduate faculty:* 175. *Computer facilities:* 250 computers available on campus for general student use. A campuswide network can be accessed from student residence rooms and from off campus. Internet access is available. *Library facilities:* McNichols Campus Library plus 3 others. *Graduate expenses:* Tuition: full-time $15,750; part-time $875 per credit hour. Required fees: $570. *General application contact:* Michael Joseph, Vice President, Enrollment Management, 313-993-1245.

College of Business Administration
Dr. Hossein Nivi, Dean
Programs in:
business administration (EMBA, MBA, MS, MSCIS, Certificate)
business turnaround management (MS, Certificate)
computer information systems (MSCIS)
information assurance (MS)

College of Engineering and Science
Programs in:
automotive engineering (DE)
chemical engineering (ME, DE)
civil and environmental engineering (ME)
computer science (MSCS)
electrical engineering (ME, DE)
elementary mathematics education (MATM)
engineering and science (M Eng Mgt, MATM, ME, MS, MSCS, DE)
engineering management (M Eng Mgt)
junior high mathematics education (MATM)
macromolecular chemistry (MS)
manufacturing engineering (DE)
mechanical engineering (ME, DE)
polymer engineering (ME)
secondary mathematics education (MATM)
teaching of mathematics (MATM)

College of Health Professions
Programs in:
family nurse practitioner (MSN, Certificate)
health professions (MS, MSN, Certificate)
health services administration (MS)
health systems management (MSN)
nurse anesthesiology (MS)
physician assistant (MS)

College of Liberal Arts and Education
Programs in:
addiction counseling (MA)
addiction studies (Certificate)
clinical psychology (MA, PhD)
community counseling (MA)
counseling (MA)
criminal justice (MA)
curriculum and instruction (MA)
early childhood education (MA)
educational administration (MA)
emotionally impaired (MA)
industrial/organizational psychology (MA)
learning disabilities (MA)
liberal arts and education (MA, MALS, MS, PhD, Certificate, Spec)
liberal studies (MALS)
religious studies (MA)
school counseling (MA)
school psychology (Spec)
security administration (MS)
special education (MA)
teaching and learning (MA)

School of Architecture
Program in:
architecture (M Arch)

School of Dentistry
Programs in:
dentistry (DDS, MS, Certificate)
endodontics (MS, Certificate)
orthodontics (MS, Certificate)

School of Law
Program in:
law (JD)

■ UNIVERSITY OF MICHIGAN
Ann Arbor, MI 48109
http://www.umich.edu/

State-supported, coed, university. CGS member. *Computer facilities:* Computer purchase and lease plans are available. 2,600 computers available on campus for general student use. A campuswide network can be accessed from student residence rooms and from off campus. Internet access and online class registration are available. *Library facilities:* University Library plus 20 others. *General application contact:* Admissions Office, 734-764-8129.

A. Alfred Taubman College of Architecture and Urban Planning
Programs in:
architecture (M Arch, M Sc, PhD)
architecture and urban planning (M Arch, M Sc, MUD, MUP, PhD, Certificate)
real estate development (Certificate)
urban and regional planning (MUP, PhD, Certificate)
urban design (MUD)
urban planning (MUP)

College of Pharmacy
Programs in:
medicinal chemistry (PhD)
pharmaceutical sciences (PhD)
pharmacy (Pharm D, PhD)
social and administrative sciences (PhD)

Horace H. Rackham School of Graduate Studies
Programs in:
biophysics (PhD)
chemical biology (PhD)
education and psychology (PhD)
English and education (PhD)
modern Middle Eastern and North African studies (AM)
neuroscience (PhD)
survey methodology (MS, PhD, Certificate)

College of Engineering
Programs in:
aerospace engineering (M Eng, MS, MSE, PhD)
applied physics (PhD)
atmospheric (MS)
atmospheric and space sciences (PhD)
automotive engineering (M Eng)
biomedical engineering (MS, MSE, PhD)
chemical engineering (MSE, PhD, Ch E)
civil engineering (MSE, PhD, CE)
computer science and engineering (MS, MSE, PhD)
concurrent marine design (M Eng)
construction engineering and management (M Eng, MSE)
electrical engineering (MS, MSE, PhD)
electrical engineering systems (MS, MSE, PhD)
engineering (M Eng, MS, MSE, D Eng, PhD, CE, Certificate, Ch E, Mar Eng, Nav Arch, Nuc E)
environmental engineering (MSE, PhD)
financial engineering (MS)
geoscience and remote sensing (PhD)
global automotive and manufacturing engineering (M Eng)
industrial and operations engineering (MS, MSE, PhD)
integrated microsystems (M Eng)
macromolecular science and engineering (MS, MSE, PhD)
manufacturing (M Eng, D Eng)

University of Michigan (continued)
- materials science and engineering (MS, PhD)
- mechanical engineering (MSE, PhD)
- naval architecture and marine engineering (MS, MSE, PhD, Mar Eng, Nav Arch)
- nuclear engineering (Nuc E)
- nuclear engineering and radiological sciences (MSE, PhD)
- nuclear science (MS, PhD)
- pharmaceutical engineering (M Eng)
- space and planetary sciences (PhD)
- space engineering (M Eng)
- space sciences (MS)
- structural engineering (M Eng)

College of Literature, Science, and the Arts
Programs in:
- American culture (AM, PhD)
- analytical chemistry (PhD)
- ancient Israel/Hebrew Bible (AM, PhD)
- anthropology (PhD)
- anthropology and history (PhD)
- applied and interdisciplinary mathematics (AM, MS, PhD)
- applied economics (AM)
- applied statistics (AM)
- Arabic (AM, PhD)
- Armenian (AM, PhD)
- Asian languages and cultures (MA, PhD)
- astronomy (MS, PhD)
- biopsychology (PhD)
- Chinese studies (AM)
- classical art and archaeology (PhD)
- classical studies (PhD)
- clinical psychology (PhD)
- cognition and perception (PhD)
- communication studies (PhD)
- comparative literature (PhD)
- creative writing (MFA)
- developmental psychology (PhD)
- early Christian studies (AM, PhD)
- ecology and evolutionary biology (MS, PhD)
- economics (AM, PhD)
- Egyptology (AM, PhD)
- English and education (PhD)
- English and women's studies (PhD)
- English language and literature (PhD)
- film and video studies (Certificate)
- French (PhD)
- general linguistics (PhD)
- geology (MS, PhD)
- German (AM, PhD)
- Greek (AM)
- Greek and Roman history (PhD, Certificate)
- Hebrew (AM, PhD)
- history (PhD)
- history and women's studies (PhD)
- history of art (PhD)
- inorganic chemistry (PhD)
- Islamic studies (AM, PhD)
- Japanese studies (AM)
- Latin (AM)
- linguistics and Germanic languages and literatures (PhD)
- literature, science, and the arts (AM, MA, MAT, MFA, MS, PhD, Certificate)
- material chemistry (PhD)
- mathematics (AM, MS, PhD)
- Mesopotamian and ancient Near Eastern studies (AM, PhD)
- mineralogy (MS, PhD)
- molecular, cellular, and developmental biology (MS, PhD)
- oceanography: marine geology and geochemistry (MS, PhD)
- organic chemistry (PhD)
- organizational psychology (PhD)
- Persian (AM, PhD)
- personality psychology (PhD)
- philosophy (AM, PhD)
- physical chemistry (PhD)
- physics (MS, PhD)
- political science (AM, PhD)
- psychology and women's studies (PhD)
- public policy and economics (PhD)
- public policy and sociology (PhD)
- Romance linguistics (PhD)
- Russian (AM, PhD)
- Russian and East European studies (AM, Certificate)
- screen arts and cultures (PhD, Certificate)
- social psychology (PhD)
- social work and economics (PhD)
- social work and political science (PhD)
- social work and sociology (PhD)
- sociology (PhD)
- South Asian studies (AM, Certificate)
- Southeast Asian studies (AM)
- Spanish (PhD)
- statistics (AM, PhD)
- teaching Latin (MAT)
- teaching of Arabic as a foreign Language (AM)
- Turkish (AM, PhD)
- women's studies (Certificate)
- women's studies and sociology (PhD)

Division of Kinesiology
Programs in:
- kinesiology (MS, PhD)
- sport management (AM)

Gerald R. Ford School of Public Policy
Program in:
- public policy (MPA, MPP, PhD)

School of Art and Design
Program in:
- art and design (MFA)

School of Education
Deborah Loewenberg Ball, Dean
Programs in:
- academic affairs and student development (PhD)
- curriculum development (MA)
- early childhood education (MA, PhD)
- education (AM)
- educational administration and policy (MA, PhD)
- educational foundation, administration, policy, and research methods (MA)
- educational foundations and policy (MA, PhD)
- elementary education (MA, PhD)
- English education (MA)
- English language learning in school settings (MA)
- higher education (AM)
- individually designed concentration (PhD)
- learning technologies (MA, PhD)
- literacy, language, and culture (MA, PhD)
- mathematics education (MA, PhD)
- organizational behavior and management (PhD)
- public policy (PhD)
- research methods (MA)
- research, evaluation, and assessment (PhD)
- science education (MA, PhD)
- secondary education (MA, PhD)
- social studies education (MA)
- special education (PhD)
- teaching and teacher education (PhD)

School of Information
Programs in:
- archives and records management (MS)
- human-computer interaction (MS)
- information (MS, PhD)
- information economics, management and policy (MS)
- library and information services (MS)

The School of Music, Theatre, and Dance
Programs in:
- composition (MA, MM, A Mus D)
- composition and theory (PhD)
- conducting (MM, A Mus D)
- design (MFA)
- media arts (MA)
- modern dance performance and choreography (MFA)
- music education (MM, PhD, Spec M)
- music, theatre, and dance (MA, MFA, MM, A Mus D, PhD, Spec M)
- musicology (MA, PhD)
- performance (MM, A Mus D, Spec M)
- theatre (PhD)
- theory (MA, PhD)

School of Nursing
Programs in:
- adult acute care nurse practitioner (MS)
- adult primary care/adult nurse practitioner (MS)
- community care/home care (MS)
- community health nursing (MS)
- family nurse practitioner (MS)
- gerontology nurse practitioner (MS)
- gerontology nursing (MS)
- infant, child, adolescent health nurse practitioner (MS)

medical-surgical clinical nurse specialist (MS)
nurse midwifery (MS)
nursing (MS, PhD, Post Master's Certificate)
nursing business and health systems (MS)
occupational health nursing (MS)
parent-child nursing (MS)
psychiatric mental health nurse practitioner (MS)
psychiatric mental health nursing (MS)
women's health (Post Master's Certificate)

Law School
Programs in:
comparative law (MCL)
law (JD, LL M, SJD)

Medical School
Programs in:
bioinformatics (MS, PhD)
biological chemistry (PhD)
biomedical sciences (MS, PhD)
cell and developmental biology (MS, PhD)
cellular and molecular biology (PhD)
human genetics (MS, PhD)
immunology (PhD)
medicine (MD, MS, PhD)
microbiology and immunology (PhD)
pathology (PhD)
pharmacology (PhD)
physiology (PhD)

Ross School of Business at the University of Michigan
Programs in:
business (M Acc, MBA)
business administration (PhD)

School of Dentistry
Program in:
dentistry (DDS, MS, PhD, Certificate)

School of Natural Resources and Environment
Dr. Rosina Bierbaum, Dean
Programs in:
aquatic sciences: research and management (MS)
behavior, education and communication (MS)
conservation biology (MS)
environmental informatics (MS)
environmental justice (MS)
environmental policy and planning (MS)
industrial ecology (Certificate)
landscape architecture (MLA, PhD)
natural resources and environment (MS, PhD)
spatial analysis (Certificate)
sustainable systems (MS)
terrestrial ecosystems (MS)

School of Public Health
Programs in:
biostatistics (MPH, MS, PhD)
clinical research design and statistical analysis (MS)
dental public health (MPH)
environmental health (MPH, MS, Dr PH, PhD)
epidemiological science (PhD)
epidemiology (MPH, Dr PH)
health behavior and health education (MPH, PhD)
health management and policy (MHSA, MPH)
health services organization and policy (PhD)
hospital and molecular epidemiology (MPH)
human nutrition (MPH, MS)
industrial hygiene (MS, PhD)
international health (MPH)
occupational and environmental epidemiology (MPH)
occupational health (MPH, MS, PhD)
public health (MHSA, MPH, MS, Dr PH, PhD)
toxicology (MPH, MS, PhD)

School of Social Work
Programs in:
social work (MSW, PhD)
social work and social science (PhD)

■ UNIVERSITY OF MICHIGAN–DEARBORN
Dearborn, MI 48128-1491
http://www.umd.umich.edu/

State-supported, coed, comprehensive institution. *Graduate faculty:* 277 full-time (93 women), 234 part-time/adjunct (88 women). *Computer facilities:* 350 computers available on campus for general student use. A campuswide network can be accessed from off campus. Internet access is available. *Library facilities:* Mardigian Library. *General application contact:* Julie Tigani, Graduate Coordinator, 313-593-1494.

Find University Details at www.petersons.com/gradchannel.

College of Arts, Sciences, and Letters
Dr. Kathryn Anderson-Levitt, Dean
Programs in:
applied and computational mathematics (MS)
arts, sciences, and letters (MA, MPP, MS)
environmental science (MS)
health psychology (MS)
liberal studies (MA)
public policy (MPP)

College of Engineering and Computer Science
Programs in:
automotive systems engineering (MSE)
computer and information science (MS)
computer engineering (MSE)
electrical engineering (MSE)
engineering (MS, MSE)
engineering management (MS)
industrial and systems engineering (MSE)
information systems and technology (MS)
manufacturing systems engineering (MSE, D Eng)
mechanical engineering (MSE)
software engineering (MS)

School of Education
Programs in:
education (M Ed, MA, MPA, Certificate)
educational administration (Certificate)
emotional impairments endorsement (M Ed)
inclusion specialist (M Ed)
learning disabilities endorsement (M Ed)
nonprofit leadership (Certificate)
public administration (MPA)
teaching (MA)

School of Management
Programs in:
accounting (MS)
finance (MS)
management (MBA)

■ UNIVERSITY OF MICHIGAN–FLINT
Flint, MI 48502-1950
http://www.umflint.edu/

State-supported, coed, comprehensive institution. *Enrollment:* 6,527 graduate, professional, and undergraduate students; 207 full-time matriculated graduate/professional students (150 women), 720 part-time matriculated graduate/professional students (467 women). *Graduate faculty:* 69 full-time (35 women), 27 part-time/adjunct (14 women). *Computer facilities:* 213 computers available on campus for general student use. A campuswide network can be accessed from off campus. Internet access and online class registration are available. *Library facilities:* Frances Willson Thompson Library. *Graduate expenses:* Tuition, state resident: full-time $6,790; part-time $377 per credit. Tuition, nonresident: full-time $10,186; part-time $566 per credit. Required fees: $258 per term. Full-time tuition and fees vary according to degree level and program. Part-time tuition and fees vary according to course load and degree level. *General application contact:* Bradley T. Maki, Director of Graduate Admissions, 810-762-3171.

College of Arts and Sciences
Dr. D. J. Trela, Dean
Programs in:
arts and sciences (MA, MS)
biology (MS)
computer science (MS)

University of Michigan–Flint (continued)
English (MA)
information systems (MS)
social sciences (MA)

Graduate Programs
Dr. Vahid Lotfi, Associate Provost
Programs in:
American culture (MLS)
public administration (MPA)

School of Education and Human Services
Dr. Susanne Chandler, Dean
Programs in:
early childhood education (MA, MA Ed)
education (MA Ed)
elementary education with teacher certification (MA)
elementary education with teaching certificate (MA Ed)
literacy (K-12) (MA, MA Ed)
special education (MA, MA Ed)
technology in education (MA)
urban and multicultural education (MA, MA Ed)

School of Health Professions and Studies
Dr. Augustine O. Agho, Dean
Programs in:
anesthesia (MSA)
health education (MS)
health professions and studies (MS, MSA, MSN, DPT)
nursing (MSN)
physical therapy (DPT)

School of Management
Dr. Douglas Moon, Dean
Program in:
management (MBA)

■ UNIVERSITY OF PHOENIX–WEST MICHIGAN CAMPUS
Walker, MI 49544
http://www.phoenix.edu/

Proprietary, coed, comprehensive institution. *Enrollment:* 1,004 graduate, professional, and undergraduate students; 170 full-time matriculated graduate/professional students (97 women). *Graduate faculty:* 48 full-time (4 women), 187 part-time/adjunct (88 women). *Computer facilities:* A campuswide network can be accessed from off campus. Internet access is available. *Library facilities:* University Library. *Graduate expenses:* Tuition: full-time $12,043. Required fees: $760. *General application contact:* Campus Information Center, 888-345-9699.

The Artemis School
Dr. Adam Honea, Provost

College of Education
Dr. Marla LaRue, Dean/Executive Director
Programs in:
administration and supervision (MA Ed)
curriculum and instruction (MA Ed)

College of Health and Human Services
Dr. Gil Linne, Dean/Executive Director
Programs in:
health care management (MBA)
nursing (MSN)

The John Sperling School of Business
Dr. Adam Honea, Provost
Program in:
business (MBA)

College of Graduate Business and Management
Dr. Brian Lindquist, Associate Vice President and Dean/Executive Director
Programs in:
accounting (MBA)
business administration (MBA)
global management (MBA)
human resource management (MBA)

College of Information Systems and Technology
Dr. Adam Honea, Dean/Executive Director
Programs in:
e-business (MBA)
technology management (MBA)

■ WAYNE STATE UNIVERSITY
Detroit, MI 48202
http://www.wayne.edu/

State-supported, coed, university. CGS member. *Enrollment:* 6,629 full-time matriculated graduate/professional students (3,575 women), 5,461 part-time matriculated graduate/professional students (3,448 women). *Graduate faculty:* 1,236 full-time (460 women), 155 part-time/adjunct (56 women). *Computer facilities:* 1,800 computers available on campus for general student use. A campuswide network can be accessed from student residence rooms and from off campus. Internet access and online class registration are available. *Library facilities:* David Adamany Undergraduate Library plus 6 others. *General application contact:* Susan Zwieg, Director, 313-577-9753.

College of Education
Dr. Paula Wood, Dean
Program in:
education (M Ed, MA, MAT, Ed D, PhD, Certificate, Ed S)

Division of Administrative and Organizational Studies
Dr. JoAnne Holbert, Assistant Dean
Programs in:
administration and supervision-secondary (Ed S)
college and university teaching (Certificate)
curriculum and instruction (PhD)
educational leadership (M Ed, Ed S)
educational leadership and policy studies (Ed D, PhD)
elementary education curriculum and instruction (MA, Ed S)
general administration and supervision (Ed D, PhD, Ed S)
higher education (Ed D, PhD)
instructional technology (M Ed, Ed D, PhD, Ed S)
secondary curriculum and instruction (M Ed, Ed S)

Division of Kinesiology, Health and Sports Studies
Dr. Sally Erbaugh, Assistant Dean
Programs in:
health education (M Ed)
kinesiology (M Ed)
physical education (M Ed)
recreation and park services (MA)
sports administration (MA)

Division of Teacher Education
Dr. Joann Snyder, Academic Director
Programs in:
adult and continuing education (M Ed)
art education (M Ed)
bilingual/bicultural education (M Ed, MAT)
business education (M Ed, MAT)
career and technical education (M Ed, Ed D, PhD, Ed S)
curriculum and instruction (Ed D, PhD, Ed S)
distributive education (M Ed, MAT)
early childhood education (M Ed)
elementary education (M Ed, MAT, Ed D, PhD, Ed S)
elementary education curriculum and instruction (M Ed)
English education (M Ed)
English education-secondary (M Ed, Ed S)
foreign language education (M Ed)
general education (Ed D, Ed S)
health occupations education (M Ed)
industrial education (M Ed)
mathematics education (M Ed, Ed S)
pre-school and parent education (M Ed)
reading (M Ed, Ed D, Ed S)
reading, languages and literature (Ed D)
school music-vocal (M Ed)
science education (M Ed, MAT, Ed S)
secondary education (MAT)
secondary school reading (M Ed)
social studies education (M Ed, Ed S)
special education (M Ed, Ed D, PhD, Ed S)
teacher education (MAT, Ed D, PhD)

Division of Theoretical and Behavioral Foundations
Dr. JoAnne Holbert, Assistant Dean

Programs in:
- counseling (M Ed, MA, Ed D, PhD, Ed S)
- education evaluation and research (M Ed, Ed D, PhD)
- educational psychology (M Ed, Ed D, PhD, Ed S)
- educational sociology (M Ed, Ed D, PhD, Ed S)
- history and philosophy of education (M Ed, Ed D, PhD)
- rehabilitation counseling and community inclusion (MA, Ed S)
- school and community psychology (MA, Ed S)
- school clinical psychology (Ed S)

College of Engineering
Dr. Ralph Kummler, Dean
Programs in:
- biomedical engineering (MS, PhD)
- chemical engineering (MS, PhD)
- civil engineering (MS, PhD)
- computer engineering (MS, PhD)
- electrical engineering (MS, PhD)
- electronics and computer control systems (MS)
- engineering (MS, PhD, Certificate)
- engineering management (MS)
- environmental auditing (Certificate)
- hazardous materials management on public lands (Certificate)
- hazardous waste (MS, Certificate)
- hazardous waste control (Certificate)
- hazardous waste management (MS)
- industrial engineering (MS, PhD)
- manufacturing engineering (MS)
- materials science and engineering (MS, PhD, Certificate)
- mechanical engineering (MS, PhD)
- metallurgical engineering (MS, PhD)
- polymer engineering (Certificate)

Division of Engineering Technology
Dr. Chih-Ping Yeh, Department Chair
Program in:
- engineering technology (MS)

College of Fine, Performing and Communication Arts
Sharon Vasquez, Dean
Programs in:
- art (MA, MFA)
- art history (MA)
- choral conducting (MM)
- communication studies (MA, PhD)
- composition (MM)
- design and merchandising (MA)
- fine, performing and communication arts (MA, MFA, MM, PhD, Certificate)
- music (MA, MM)
- music education (MM)
- orchestral studies (Certificate)
- performance (MM)
- public relations and organizational communication (MA)
- radio-TV-film (MA, PhD)
- speech communication (MA, PhD)
- theatre (MA, MFA, PhD)
- theory (MM)

College of Liberal Arts and Sciences
Robert Thomas, Dean
Programs in:
- anthropology (MA, PhD)
- applied mathematics (MA, PhD)
- audiology (MA, MS, Au D, PhD)
- behavioral and cognitive neuroscience (PhD)
- biological sciences (MA, MS, PhD)
- chemistry (MA, MS, PhD)
- classics (MA)
- clinical psychology (PhD)
- cognitive and social psychology (PhD)
- communication disorders and science (MA, PhD)
- comparative literature (MA)
- computer science (MA, MS, PhD)
- criminal justice (MPA)
- dispute resolution (MADR, Certificate)
- economic development (Certificate)
- economics (MA, PhD)
- English (MA, PhD)
- French (MA)
- geography (MA)
- geology (MA, MS)
- German (MA)
- history (MA, PhD)
- human development (MA)
- industrial relations (MAIR)
- industrial/organizational psychology (PhD)
- interdisciplinary studies (MIS, PhD)
- Italian (MA)
- language learning (MA)
- Latin (MA)
- liberal arts and sciences (MA, MADR, MAIR, MIS, MPA, MS, MUP, Au D, PhD, Certificate)
- linguistics (MA)
- mathematical statistics (MA, PhD)
- mathematics (MA, MS, PhD)
- modern languages (PhD)
- molecular biotechnology (MS)
- Near Eastern studies (MA)
- nutrition and food science (MA, MS, PhD)
- philosophy (MA, PhD)
- physics (MA, MS, PhD)
- political science (MA, PhD)
- psychology (MA, MS, PhD)
- public administration (MPA)
- Romance languages (MA)
- Russian (MA)
- scientific computing (Certificate)
- sociology (MA, PhD)
- Spanish (MA)
- speech-language pathology (MA, PhD)
- urban planning (MUP)

College of Nursing
Dr. Barbara Redman, Dean
Programs in:
- adult acute care nursing (MSN)
- adult primary care nursing (MSN)
- advanced practice nursing with women, neonates and children (MSN, Certificate)
- community health nursing (MSN)
- neonatal nurse practitioner (Certificate)
- nursing (MSN, PhD, Certificate)
- nursing education (Certificate)
- psychiatric mental health nurse practitioner (MSN, Certificate)
- transcultural nursing (MSN, Certificate)

Eugene Applebaum College of Pharmacy and Health Sciences
Beverly J. Schmoll, Dean
Programs in:
- clinical laboratory science (MS)
- clinical laboratory sciences (MS, Certificate)
- experimental technology in pharmaceutical sciences (Certificate)
- health systems pharmacy management (MS)
- hospital pharmacy (MS)
- medical technology (Certificate)
- medicinal chemistry (MS, PhD)
- nurse anesthesia (MS)
- nursing anesthesia (MS, Certificate)
- occupational and environmental health sciences (MPH, MS, Certificate, Post-Master's Certificate)
- occupational therapy (MOT, MS)
- pediatric nurse anesthesia (Certificate)
- pharmaceutical administration (MS, PhD)
- pharmaceutical sciences (MS, PhD)
- pharmaceutics (MS, PhD)
- pharmacology (MS, PhD)
- pharmacy (Pharm D)
- pharmacy and health sciences (Pharm D, MOT, MPH, MPT, MS, PhD, Certificate, Post-Master's Certificate)
- physical therapy (MPT)
- physician assistant studies (MS)

Law School
Frank Wu, Dean
Program in:
- law (JD, LL M, PhD)

School of Business Administration
Dr. Richard Gabrys, Dean
Programs in:
- accounting (MS)
- business administration (MBA, PhD)
- interdisciplinary studies (PhD)
- taxation (MS)

School of Medicine
Dr. Bernard Frank, Dean
Program in:
- medicine (MD, MPH, MS, PhD, Certificate)

Graduate Programs in Medicine
Dr. Kenneth C. Palmer, Assistant Dean
Programs in:
- anatomy (MS, PhD)
- basic medical science (MS)
- biochemistry and molecular biology (MS, PhD)
- cancer biology (MS, PhD)

Wayne State University (continued)
- cellular and clinical neurobiology (PhD)
- community health (MS)
- community health services (Certificate)
- immunology and microbiology (MS, PhD)
- medical physics (PhD)
- medical research (MS)
- medicine (MPH, MS, PhD, Certificate)
- pathology (MS, PhD)
- pharmacology (MS, PhD)
- physiology (MS, PhD)
- psychiatry and behavioral neurosciences (MS)
- public health (MPH)
- public health practice (Certificate)
- radiological physics (MS)
- rehabilitation science administration (Certificate)
- rehabilitation sciences (MS)

School of Social Work
Phyllis Vroom, Dean
Programs in:
- interdisciplinary studies (PhD)
- social work (MSW)
- social work practice with families and couples (Certificate)

■ WESTERN MICHIGAN UNIVERSITY
Kalamazoo, MI 49008-5202
http://www.wmich.edu/

State-supported, coed, university. CGS member. *Computer facilities:* 2,000 computers available on campus for general student use. A campuswide network can be accessed from student residence rooms and from off campus. *Library facilities:* Waldo Library plus 4 others. *General application contact:* Admissions and Orientation, 616-387-2000.

Graduate College

College of Arts and Sciences
Programs in:
- anthropology (MA)
- applied behavior analysis (MA, PhD)
- applied economics (PhD)
- applied mathematics (MS)
- arts and sciences (MA, MDA, MFA, MPA, MS, DPA, PhD, Ed S)
- biological sciences (MS, PhD)
- biostatistics (MS)
- chemistry (MA, PhD)
- clinical psychology (MA, PhD)
- comparative religion (MA, PhD)
- computational mathematics (MS)
- creative writing (MFA)
- development administration (MDA)
- earth science (MS)
- economics (MA)
- English (MA, PhD)
- English education (MA, PhD)
- experimental analysis of behavior (PhD)
- experimental psychology (MA)
- geography (MA)
- geology (MS, PhD)
- graph theory and computer science (PhD)
- history (MA, PhD)
- industrial/organizational psychology (MA)
- mathematics (MA, PhD)
- mathematics education (MA, PhD)
- medieval studies (MA)
- molecular biotechnology (MS)
- organizational communication (MA)
- philosophy (MA)
- physics (MA, PhD)
- political science (MA, PhD)
- professional writing (MA)
- public affairs and administration (MPA, DPA)
- school psychology (PhD, Ed S)
- science education (PhD)
- sociology (MA, PhD)
- Spanish (MA)
- statistics (MS, PhD)

College of Education
Programs in:
- administration (MA)
- athletic training (MA)
- career and technical education (MA)
- coaching and sports studies (MA)
- counseling psychology (PhD)
- counselor education (MA, Ed D, PhD)
- counselor education and counseling psychology (MA, PhD)
- counselor psychology (MA)
- early childhood education (MA)
- education (MA, Ed D, PhD, Ed S)
- education and professional development (MA)
- educational leadership (MA, Ed D, PhD, Ed S)
- educational studies (MA, Ed D)
- educational technology (MA)
- elementary education (MA)
- evaluation, measurement, and research (MA, PhD)
- exercise science (MA)
- family and consumer sciences (MA)
- human resources development (MA)
- marriage and family therapy (MA)
- middle school education (MA)
- motor development (MA)
- physical education (MA)
- reading (MA)
- socio-cultural foundations and educational thought (MA)
- special education for handicapped children (MA)

College of Engineering and Applied Sciences
Programs in:
- computer engineering (MSE, PhD)
- computer science (MS, PhD)
- construction engineering and management (MS)
- electrical engineering (MSE, PhD)
- engineering and applied sciences (MS, MSE, PhD)
- engineering management (MS)
- industrial engineering (MSE)
- manufacturing engineering (MS)
- mechanical engineering (MSE, PhD)
- operations research (MS)
- paper and printing science and engineering (MS, PhD)
- structural engineering (MS)
- transportation engineering (MS)

College of Fine Arts
Programs in:
- fine arts (MA, MFA, MM)
- graphic design (MFA)
- music (MA, MM)
- performing arts administration (MFA)
- textile design (MA, MFA)

College of Health and Human Services
Programs in:
- audiology (MA)
- blind rehabilitation (MA)
- health and human services (MA, MS, MSW)
- occupational therapy (MS)
- physician assistant (MS)
- social work (MSW)
- speech pathology (MA)

Haworth College of Business
Programs in:
- accountancy (MSA)
- business (MBA, MSA)
- business administration (MBA)

Minnesota

■ ARGOSY UNIVERSITY, TWIN CITIES CAMPUS
Eagan, MN 55121
http://www.argosyu.edu/

Proprietary, coed, university. *Enrollment:* 1,700 graduate, professional, and undergraduate students; 406 full-time matriculated graduate/professional students (309 women), 219 part-time matriculated graduate/professional students (178 women). *Graduate faculty:* 19 full-time (10 women), 73 part-time/adjunct (33 women). *Computer facilities:* 50 computers available on campus for general student use. Internet access and online class registration are available. *Library facilities:* Argosy University/Twin Cities Library. *General application contact:* Jennifer Radke, 2nd Director of Graduate Admissions, 651-846-3300.

College of Business
Dr. Paula King, Department Head
Programs in:
- accounting (DBA)
- corporate compliance (MBA)
- customized professional certification (DBA)

customized professional concentration (MBA)
finance (MBA)
healthcare administration (MBA)
information systems (DBA)
information systems management (MBA)
international business (MBA, DBA)
management (MBA, MSM, DBA, EDBA)
marketing (MBA, DBA)

College of Education
Dr. David Lange, Program Chair
Programs in:
educational leadership (MA Ed, Ed D, Ed S)
instructional leadership (MA Ed, Ed D, Ed S)

College of Psychology and Behavioral Sciences
Dr. Kenneth Solberg, Dean
Programs in:
clinical psychology (MA, Psy D, Postdoctoral Respecialization Certificate)
forensic counseling (Post-Graduate Certificate)
marriage and family therapy (MA, Post-Graduate Certificate)

■ AUGSBURG COLLEGE
Minneapolis, MN 55454-1351
http://www.augsburg.edu/

Independent-religious, coed, comprehensive institution. *Enrollment:* 3,732 graduate, professional, and undergraduate students; 573 full-time matriculated graduate/professional students (342 women), 238 part-time matriculated graduate/professional students (175 women). *Graduate faculty:* 30 full-time (19 women), 18 part-time/adjunct (8 women). *Computer facilities:* 260 computers available on campus for general student use. A campuswide network can be accessed from student residence rooms and from off campus. Internet access and online class registration are available. *Library facilities:* James G. Lindell Library. *Graduate expenses:* Tuition: full-time $10,584; part-time $1,764 per course. Required fees: $300; $35 per course. Tuition and fees vary according to program. *General application contact:* Mike Bilden, Director, Weekend College and Graduate Admissions, 612-330-1101 Ext. 1792.

Program in Business Administration
Dr. Robert Kramarczuk, Director
Program in:
business administration (MBA)

Program in Education
Vicki Olson, Professor
Program in:
education (MAE)

Program in Leadership
Dr. Norma Noonan, Director
Program in:
leadership (MA)

Program in Physicians Assistant Studies
Dawn B. Ludwig, Director
Program in:
physicians assistant studies (MS)

Program in Social Work
Dr. Tony Bibus, Director
Program in:
social work (MSW)

Program in Transcultural Community Health Nursing
Dr. Cheryl J. Leuning, Director
Program in:
transcultural community health nursing (MA)

■ BEMIDJI STATE UNIVERSITY
Bemidji, MN 56601-2699
http://www.bemidjistate.edu/

State-supported, coed, comprehensive institution. *Enrollment:* 4,918 graduate, professional, and undergraduate students; 43 full-time matriculated graduate/professional students (27 women), 196 part-time matriculated graduate/professional students (125 women). *Graduate faculty:* 156 part-time/adjunct (59 women). *Computer facilities:* 1,200 computers available on campus for general student use. A campuswide network can be accessed from student residence rooms and from off campus. Internet access and online class registration are available. *Library facilities:* A. C. Clark Library. *Graduate expenses:* Tuition, nonresident: part-time $284 per credit. Required fees: $86 per credit. *General application contact:* Carol Nielsen, Interim Dean, School of Graduate/Professional Studies, 218-755-3732.

School of Graduate Studies
Carol Nielsen, Interim Dean, School of Graduate/Professional Studies

College of Arts and Letters
Dr. Nancy Erickson, Dean
Programs in:
arts and letters (MA, MS)
English (MA, MS)

College of Professional Studies
Programs in:
education (M Ed, MS)
professional studies (M Ed, M Sp Ed, MS)
special education (M Sp Ed, MS)
sport studies (MS)
technical education (MS)
technology/career technical education (MS)

College of Social and Natural Sciences
Dr. Ranae Womack, Dean
Programs in:
biology (MS)
environmental studies (MS)
mathematics (MS)
psychology (MS)
science (MS)
social and natural sciences (MS)

■ BETHEL UNIVERSITY
St. Paul, MN 55112-6999
http://www.bethel.edu/

Independent-religious, coed, comprehensive institution. *Enrollment:* 5,185 graduate, professional, and undergraduate students; 634 full-time matriculated graduate/professional students (428 women), 155 part-time matriculated graduate/professional students (103 women). *Graduate faculty:* 59 full-time (26 women), 79 part-time/adjunct (30 women). *Computer facilities:* Computer purchase and lease plans are available. 124 computers available on campus for general student use. A campuswide network can be accessed from student residence rooms and from off campus. Internet access and online class registration are available. *Library facilities:* Bethel College Library plus 1 other. *Graduate expenses:* Tuition: part-time $395 per credit. Tuition and fees vary according to program. *General application contact:* Michael Price, Director of Admissions, 651-635-8000 Ext. 8017.

Graduate School
Dr. Carl Polding, Dean
Programs in:
business administration (MBA)
child and adolescent mental health (Certificate)
Christian health ministry (MA)
communication (MA)
counseling psychology (MA)
education K-12 (MA)
educational administration (Ed D)
gerontology (MA)
healthcare leadership (MA)
literacy (Certificate)
literacy education (MA)
nursing education (MA, Certificate)
organizational leadership (MA)
postsecondary teaching (Certificate)
secondary education (MA)
special education (M Ed)

■ CAPELLA UNIVERSITY
Minneapolis, MN 55402
http://www.capella.edu/

Proprietary, coed, upper-level institution. CGS member. *Computer facilities:* Online

Capella University (continued)
class registration is available. *Library facilities:* Capella University Library. *General application contact:* Enrollment Services Office, 888-CAPELLA.

Harold Abel School of Psychology

Programs in:
- clinical psychology (MS)
- counseling psychology (MS)
- educational psychology (MS, PhD)
- general psychology (MS, PhD)
- industrial/organizational psychology (MS, PhD)
- school psychology (MS, Certificate)
- sport psychology (MS)

School of Business and Technology

Programs in:
- accounting (MBA)
- business (Certificate)
- finance (MBA)
- general business (MBA)
- health care management (MBA)
- information technology (MS, Certificate)
- information technology management (MBA)
- marketing (MBA)
- organization and management (MBA, MS, PhD)
- project management (MBA)

■ COLLEGE OF ST. CATHERINE

St. Paul, MN 55105-1789
http://www.stkate.edu/

Independent-religious, Undergraduate: women only; graduate: coed, comprehensive institution. *Computer facilities:* Computer purchase and lease plans are available. 350 computers available on campus for general student use. A campuswide network can be accessed from student residence rooms and from off campus. Internet access, transcript are available. *Library facilities:* St. Catherine Library plus 2 others. *General application contact:* Information Contact, 651-690-6933.

Graduate Programs

Programs in:
- education (MA)
- holistic health studies (MA)
- library and information science (MA)
- nursing (MA)
- occupational therapy (MA)
- organizational leadership (MA)
- physical therapy (MPT, DPT)
- social work (MSW)
- theology (MA)

■ COLLEGE OF ST. CATHERINE–MINNEAPOLIS

Minneapolis, MN 55454-1494
http://www.stkate.edu/

Independent-religious, coed, primarily women, comprehensive institution. *Computer facilities:* Computer purchase and lease plans are available. 40 computers available on campus for general student use. A campuswide network can be accessed from student residence rooms and from off campus. Internet access is available. *Library facilities:* Minneapolis Campus Library.

■ THE COLLEGE OF ST. SCHOLASTICA

Duluth, MN 55811-4199
http://www.css.edu/

Independent-religious, coed, comprehensive institution. *Enrollment:* 3,304 graduate, professional, and undergraduate students; 291 full-time matriculated graduate/professional students (233 women), 281 part-time matriculated graduate/professional students (203 women). *Graduate faculty:* 44 full-time (29 women), 56 part-time/adjunct (33 women). *Computer facilities:* 129 computers available on campus for general student use. A campuswide network can be accessed from student residence rooms and from off campus. Internet access and online class registration, student account information and transcripts online are available. *Library facilities:* College of St. Scholastica Library. *General application contact:* Tonya J. Roth, Graduate Recruitment Counselor, 218-723-6285.

Graduate Studies

Dr. Collette Garrity, Vice President of Graduate and Extended Studies
Programs in:
- computer information systems (MA)
- curriculum and instruction (M Ed)
- educational media and technology (M Ed)
- exercise physiology (MA)
- health information management (MA, Certificate)
- management (MA)
- nursing (MA, PMC)
- occupational therapy (MA)
- physical therapy (DPT)
- teaching (M Ed, Certificate)

■ CONCORDIA UNIVERSITY, ST. PAUL

St. Paul, MN 55104-5494
http://www.csp.edu/

Independent-religious, coed, comprehensive institution. *Enrollment:* 2,046 graduate, professional, and undergraduate students; 287 full-time matriculated graduate/professional students (209 women), 51 part-time matriculated graduate/professional students (34 women). *Graduate faculty:* 23 full-time (9 women), 37 part-time/adjunct (16 women). *Computer facilities:* Computer purchase and lease plans are available. 1,000 computers available on campus for general student use. A campuswide network can be accessed from student residence rooms and from off campus. Internet access is available. *Library facilities:* Library Technology Center. *General application contact:* Kimberly Craig, Director of Graduate and Cohort Admission, 651-603-6223.

College of Business and Organizational Leadership

Dr. Robert DeGregorio, Dean
Programs in:
- business and organizational leadership (MBA)
- criminal justice (MAHS)
- human resources (MAOM)
- organizational management (MAOM)

College of Education

Prof. Lonn Maly, Dean
Programs in:
- differentiated instruction (MA Ed)
- early childhood (MA Ed)
- family life education (MAHS)
- special education (Certificate)

College of Vocation and Ministry

Dr. Steven Arnold, Dean
Programs in:
- Christian education (Certificate)
- Christian outreach (MA)

■ HAMLINE UNIVERSITY

St. Paul, MN 55104-1284
http://www.hamline.edu/

Independent-religious, coed, comprehensive institution. *Enrollment:* 4,575 graduate, professional, and undergraduate students; 1,158 full-time matriculated graduate/professional students (655 women), 1,144 part-time matriculated graduate/professional students (873 women). *Graduate faculty:* 78 full-time (44 women), 185 part-time/adjunct (119 women). *Computer facilities:* 130 computers available on campus for general student use. A campuswide network can be accessed from student residence rooms and from off campus. Internet access and online class registration are available. *Library facilities:* Bush Library plus 1 other. *Graduate expenses:* Tuition: full-time $5,104; part-time $319 per credit. One-time fee: $175. Tuition and fees vary according to course load, degree level and program. *General application contact:* Rae A. Lenway, Director Graduate Recruitment and Admission, 651-523-2592.

Graduate School of Education

Mary K. Boyd, Interim Dean

Program in:
- education (MA Ed, MAESL, MAT, Ed D)

Graduate School of Liberal Studies
Mary Francóis Rockcastle, Dean
Program in:
- liberal studies (MALS, MFA, CALS)

Graduate School of Management
Julian Schuster, Dean
Programs in:
- management (MAM)
- nonprofit management (MANM)
- public administration (MAPA)

School of Law
Jon M. Garon, Dean
Program in:
- law (JD, LL M)

■ MAYO GRADUATE SCHOOL
Rochester, MN 55905
http://www.mayo.edu/mgs/index.html

Independent, coed, graduate-only institution. *Computer facilities:* A campuswide network can be accessed from off campus. Internet access is available. *Library facilities:* Plummer Library plus 7 others. *General application contact:* Admissions Coordinator, 507-538-1160.

Graduate Programs in Biomedical Sciences
Programs in:
- biochemistry and structural biology (PhD)
- biomedical engineering (PhD)
- biomedical sciences (PhD)
- cell biology and genetics (PhD)
- immunology (PhD)
- molecular biology (PhD)
- molecular neuroscience (PhD)
- molecular pharmacology and experimental therapeutics (PhD)
- tumor biology (PhD)
- virology and gene therapy (PhD)

■ METROPOLITAN STATE UNIVERSITY
St. Paul, MN 55106-5000
http://www.metrostate.edu

State-supported, coed, comprehensive institution. *Computer facilities:* 525 computers available on campus for general student use. A campuswide network can be accessed from off campus. Internet access and online class registration are available. *Library facilities:* Library and Learning Center. *General application contact:* Recruiter/Admissions Adviser, 612-659-7258.

College of Arts and Sciences
Program in:
- technical communication (MS)

College of Management
Programs in:
- finance (MBA)
- human resource management (MBA)
- information management (MMIS)
- international business (MBA)
- law enforcement (MPNA)
- management information systems (MBA)
- marketing (MBA)
- nonprofit management (MPNA)
- organizational studies (MBA)
- public administration (MPNA)
- purchasing management (MBA)
- systems management (MMIS)

School of Nursing
Program in:
- nursing (MSN)

■ MINNESOTA STATE UNIVERSITY MANKATO
Mankato, MN 56001
http://www.mnsu.edu/

State-supported, coed, comprehensive institution. CGS member. *Enrollment:* 14,148 graduate, professional, and undergraduate students; 544 full-time matriculated graduate/professional students (319 women), 1,047 part-time matriculated graduate/professional students (644 women). *Computer facilities:* 900 computers available on campus for general student use. A campuswide network can be accessed from student residence rooms and from off campus. Internet access and online class registration are available. *Library facilities:* Memorial Library. *General application contact:* Information Contact, 507-389-2321.

College of Graduate Studies
Dr. Anne Blackhurst, Interim Dean
Program in:
- multidisciplinary studies (MS)

College of Allied Health and Nursing
Dr. Kaye Herth, Dean
Programs in:
- allied health and nursing (MA, MS, MSN, MT, SP)
- chemical dependency studies (MS)
- communication disorders (MS)
- community health (MS)
- family nursing (MSN)
- health science (MS, MT)
- human performance (MA, MS, MT, SP)
- managed care (MSN)
- rehabilitation counseling (MS)
- school health (MS)

College of Arts and Humanities
Dr. Jane F. Earley, Dean
Programs in:
- art education (MS)
- arts and humanities (MA, MAT, MFA, MM, MS, MT, Certificate)
- creative writing (MFA)
- English (MA, MS)
- English literature (MA)
- forensics (MFA)
- French (MAT, MS)
- music (MM, MT)
- Spanish (MAT, MS)
- speech communication (MA, MS, MT)
- studio art (MA)
- teaching art (MAT, MT)
- teaching English (MS, MT)
- teaching English as a second language (MA)
- technical communication (Certificate)
- theatre and dance (MA, MFA)

College of Business
Scott Johnson, Dean
Programs in:
- accounting and business law (MBA)
- finance (MBA)
- management (MBA)
- marketing and international business (MBA)

College of Education
Dr. Michael Miller, Dean
Programs in:
- college student affairs (MS)
- computer services administration (MS)
- curriculum and instruction (SP)
- early education for exceptional children (MS)
- education (MA, MAT, MS, MT, Certificate, SP)
- educational administration (Certificate)
- educational leadership (MS)
- educational studies: elementary and early childhood (MS)
- elementary school administration (MS, SP)
- emotional/behavioral disorders (MS, Certificate)
- experiential education (MS, Certificate, SP)
- general school administration (MS)
- higher education administration (MS)
- learning disabilities (MS, Certificate)
- library media education (MS, Certificate, SP)
- marriage and family (Certificate)
- professional community counseling (MS)
- professional school counseling (MS)
- secondary administration (MS, SP)
- talent development and gifted education (MS, Certificate, SP)
- teaching and learning (MS, Certificate)
- vocational-technical administration (MS)

College of Science, Engineering and Technology
Dr. John Frey, Dean
Programs in:
- biology (MS)
- biology education (MS)

Minnesota State University Mankato (continued)

computer and information sciences (MS, Certificate)
computer science (MS, Graduate Certificate)
electrical and computer engineering technology (MSE)
electrical engineering (MS)
environmental science (MS)
manufacturing engineering technology (MS)
mathematics (MA, MS)
mathematics education (MAT, MS)
physics (MS)
physics and astronomy (MT)
science, engineering and technology (MA, MAT, MS, MSE, MT, Certificate, Graduate Certificate)
statistics (MS)

College of Social and Behavioral Sciences
Dr. William Wagner, Interim Dean
Programs in:
anthropology (MS)
clinical psychology (MA)
ethnic and multicultural studies (MS)
geography (MS)
geography education (MT)
gerontology (MS, Certificate)
history (MA, MS)
human services planning and administration (MS)
industrial/organizational psychology (MA)
local government (Certificate)
political science (MA, MS, MT)
psychology (MT)
public administration (MAPA)
social and behavioral sciences (MA, MAPA, MS, MT, Certificate)
social studies (MS)
sociology (MA)
sociology: corrections (MS)
teaching history (MS, MT)
urban and regional studies (MA)
urban planning (Certificate)
women's studies (MS, Certificate)

■ MINNESOTA STATE UNIVERSITY MOORHEAD
Moorhead, MN 56563-0002
http://www.mnstate.edu/

State-supported, coed, comprehensive institution. *Enrollment:* 81 full-time matriculated graduate/professional students (59 women), 228 part-time matriculated graduate/professional students (168 women). *Graduate faculty:* 129. *Computer facilities:* 450 computers available on campus for general student use. A campuswide network can be accessed from student residence rooms and from off campus. Internet access and online class registration are available. *Library facilities:* Livingston Lord Library. *General application contact:* Karla Wenger, Graduate Studies Office, 218-477-2344.

Graduate Studies
Dr. Richard K. Adler, Director of Graduate Studies

College of Arts and Humanities
Dr. Kathleen Enz Finken, Dean of Arts and Humanities
Programs in:
arts and humanities (MFA, MLA)
creative writing (MFA)
liberal studies (MLA)

College of Education and Human Services
Dr. Michael Parsons, Dean of Education and Human Services
Programs in:
counseling and student affairs (MS)
curriculum and instruction (MS)
educational leadership (MS, Ed S)
nursing (MS)
reading (MS)
special education (MS)
speech-language pathology (MS)

College of Social and Natural Sciences
Dr. Ron Jeppson, Dean
Programs in:
public, human services, and health administration (MS)
school psychology (MS, Psy S)
social and natural sciences (MS, Psy S)

■ ST. CLOUD STATE UNIVERSITY
St. Cloud, MN 56301-4498
http://www.stcloudstate.edu/

State-supported, coed, comprehensive institution. CGS member. *Enrollment:* 15,964 graduate, professional, and undergraduate students; 641 full-time matriculated graduate/professional students (375 women), 951 part-time matriculated graduate/professional students (604 women). *Graduate faculty:* 540 full-time (194 women), 34 part-time/adjunct (16 women). *Computer facilities:* Computer purchase and lease plans are available. 1,335 computers available on campus for general student use. A campuswide network can be accessed from student residence rooms and from off campus. Internet access and online class registration are available. *Library facilities:* James W. Miller Learning Resources Center. *General application contact:* Dr. Dennis Nunes, Dean of Graduate Studies, 320-308-2113.

School of Graduate Studies
Dr. Dennis Nunes, Dean

College of Education
Dr. Kate Steffens, Interim Dean
Programs in:
applied behavior analysis (MS)
child and family studies (MS)
college counseling and student development (MS)
community counseling (MS)
curriculum and instruction (MS)
educable mentally handicapped (MS)
education (MS, Spt)
educational administration and leadership (MS)
educational leadership and community psychology (Spt)
emotionally disturbed (MS)
exercise science (MS)
gifted and talented (MS)
higher education administration (MS)
information media (MS)
learning disabled (MS)
marriage and family therapy (MS)
physical education (MS)
rehabilitation counseling (MS)
school counseling (MS)
social responsibility (MS)
special education (MS)
sports management (MS)
trainable mentally retarded (MS)

College of Fine Arts and Humanities
Dr. Roland Specht-Jarvis, Dean
Programs in:
communication sciences and disorders (MS)
conducting and literature (MM)
English (MA, MS)
fine arts and humanities (MA, MM, MS)
mass communication (MS)
music education (MM)
piano pedagogy (MM)
teaching English as a second language (MA)

College of Science and Engineering
Dr. David DeGroote, Chairperson
Programs in:
applied statistics (MS)
biological sciences (MA, MS)
computer science (MS)
electrical engineering and computer engineering (MS)
engineering management (MEM)
environmental and technological studies (MS)
mathematics (MS)
mechanical engineering (MS)
science and engineering (MA, MEM, MS)

College of Social Sciences
Dr. Sharon Cogdill, Interim Dean
Programs in:
applied economics (MS)
criminal justice administration (MS)
criminal justice counseling (MS)
geography (MS)
gerontology (MS)
history (MA, MS)
industrial-organizational psychology (MS)

public and nonprofit institutions (MS)
public safety executive leadership (MS)
social sciences (MA, MS)

G.R. Herberger College of Business
Dr. P.N. Subba, Graduate Director
Programs in:
management and finance (MBA)
marketing and general business (MBA)

■ SAINT MARY'S UNIVERSITY OF MINNESOTA
Winona, MN 55987-1399
http://www.smumn.edu/

Independent-religious, coed, comprehensive institution. *Enrollment:* 5,566 graduate, professional, and undergraduate students; 592 full-time matriculated graduate/professional students (379 women), 3,012 part-time matriculated graduate/professional students (2,001 women). *Graduate faculty:* 8 full-time (2 women), 368 part-time/adjunct (169 women). *Computer facilities:* 374 computers available on campus for general student use. A campuswide network can be accessed from student residence rooms and from off campus. Internet access and online class registration are available. *Library facilities:* Fitzgerald Library plus 1 other. *General application contact:* Becky Copper, Director of Admissions for Graduate and Professional Programs, 612-728-5207.

School of Graduate and Professional Programs
James M. Bedtke, Vice President, Graduate and Professional Programs
Programs in:
arts and cultural management (MA)
business administration (MBA)
counseling and psychological services (MA)
education (MA)
educational administration (MA, Certificate, Ed S)
educational leadership (Ed D)
executive business leadership (Certificate)
finance manager (Certificate)
geographic information science (MS, Certificate)
health and human services administration (MA)
human development (MA)
human resource management (MA)
instruction (MA, Certificate)
international business (MA)
K-12 reading teacher (Certificate)
literacy education (MA)
management (MA)
marriage and family therapy (MA, Certificate)
nurse anesthesia (MS)
organizational leadership (MA)
philanthropy and development (MA)
project management (MS)
public safety administration (MA)
teaching and learning (M Ed)
telecommunications (MS)

Institute in Pastoral Ministries
Dr. Gregory Sobolewski, Director
Programs in:
pastoral administration (MA)
pastoral ministries (MA)

■ SOUTHWEST MINNESOTA STATE UNIVERSITY
Marshall, MN 56258
http://www.southwest.msus.edu/

State-supported, coed, comprehensive institution. *Enrollment:* 6,126 graduate, professional, and undergraduate students; 131 full-time matriculated graduate/professional students (93 women), 305 part-time matriculated graduate/professional students (223 women). *Graduate faculty:* 21 full-time (7 women), 3 part-time/adjunct (2 women). *Computer facilities:* 350 computers available on campus for general student use. A campuswide network can be accessed from student residence rooms and from off campus. Internet access and online class registration are available. *Library facilities:* Southwest State University. *Graduate expenses:* Full-time $4,835. Tuition, state resident: full-time $4,835; part-time $269 per credit. Tuition, nonresident: part-time $269 per credit. Required fees: $589; $33 per credit. Tuition and fees vary according to course load and reciprocity agreements. *General application contact:* Rich Shearer, Director of Enrollment Management, 507-537-6286.

Department of Business Administration
Dr. Mark Goodenow, Department Chair
Programs in:
business administration (MBA)
management (MS)

Department of Education
Donna Burgraff, Dean
Programs in:
education (MS)
education development and leadership (MS)
special education (MS)

■ UNIVERSITY OF MINNESOTA, DULUTH
Duluth, MN 55812-2496
http://www.d.umn.edu/

State-supported, coed, comprehensive institution. *Enrollment:* 11,090 graduate, professional, and undergraduate students; 443 full-time matriculated graduate/professional students (257 women), 153 part-time matriculated graduate/professional students (76 women). *Graduate faculty:* 284 full-time (71 women), 68 part-time/adjunct (23 women). *Computer facilities:* 680 computers available on campus for general student use. A campuswide network can be accessed from student residence rooms and from off campus. Internet access and online class registration are available. *Library facilities:* University of Minnesota Duluth Library. *General application contact:* M.J. Leone, Executive Administrative Specialist, 218-726-7523.

Graduate School
Larry Knopp, Associate Dean
Program in:
toxicology (MS, PhD)

College of Education and Human Service Professions
Dr. Paul N. Deputy, Dean
Programs in:
communication sciences and disorders (MA)
education (Ed D)
education and human service professions (MA, MSW, Ed D)
social work (MSW)

College of Liberal Arts
Dr. Linda Krug, Dean
Programs in:
criminology (MA)
English (MA)
liberal arts (MA, MLS)
liberal studies (MLS)

College of Science and Engineering
Dr. James Riehl, Dean
Programs in:
applied and computational mathematics (MS)
chemistry and biochemistry (MS)
computer science (MS)
electrical and computer engineering (MSECE)
engineering management (MSEM)
environmental health and safety (MEHS)
geological sciences (MS, PhD)
integrated biosciences (MS)
physics (MS)
science and engineering (MEHS, MS, MSECE, MSEM, PhD)

Labovitz School of Business and Economics
Kjell Knudsen, Dean
Programs in:
business administration (MBA)
business and economics (MBA)

School of Fine Arts
Dr. Jack Bowman, Dean
Programs in:
fine arts (MFA, MM)
graphic design (MFA)
music education (MM)
performance (MM)

Medical School
Dr. Richard J. Ziegler, Dean

University of Minnesota, Duluth (continued)
Programs in:
- biochemistry, molecular biology and biophysics (MS, PhD)
- medicine (MD, MS, PhD)
- microbiology, immunology and molecular pathobiology (MS, PhD)
- pharmacology (MS, PhD)
- physiology (MS, PhD)

■ UNIVERSITY OF MINNESOTA, TWIN CITIES CAMPUS

Minneapolis, MN 55455-0213
http://www.umn.edu/tc/

State-supported, coed, university. CGS member. *Enrollment:* 50,402 graduate, professional, and undergraduate students; 10,904 matriculated graduate/professional students (5,675 women). *Graduate faculty:* 2,405. *Computer facilities:* Computer purchase and lease plans are available. A campuswide network can be accessed from student residence rooms and from off campus. Internet access and online class registration, e-mail are available. *Library facilities:* Wilson Library plus 17 others. *Graduate expenses:* Tuition, state resident: full-time $9,302; part-time $775 per credit. Tuition, nonresident: full-time $16,400; part-time $1,367 per credit. Full-time tuition and fees vary according to class time, course load, program, reciprocity agreements and student level. *General application contact:* Information Contact, 612-625-3014.

Carlson School of Management
Dr. Allison Davis-Blake, Dean
Programs in:
- accountancy (M Acc)
- accounting (MBA, PhD)
- business administration (MBA, PhD)
- business taxation (MBT)
- entrepreneurship (MBA)
- finance (MBA, PhD)
- healthcare management (MBA)
- human resources and industrial relations (MA, PhD)
- information and decision sciences (MBA, PhD)
- international business (MBA)
- management (EMBA, M Acc, MA, MBA, MBT, MS, MSMOT, PhD)
- marketing and logistics management (MBA, PhD)
- operations and management science (MBA, PhD)
- strategic management and organization (MBA, PhD)
- supply chain management (MBA)

College of Pharmacy
Programs in:
- medicinal chemistry (MS, PhD)
- pharmaceutics (MS, PhD)
- pharmacy (Pharm D, MS, PhD)
- social and administrative pharmacy (MS, PhD)

College of Veterinary Medicine
Dr. Jeffrey Klausner, Dean
Programs in:
- comparative and molecular bioscience (MS, PhD)
- veterinary medicine (MS, PhD)

Graduate School
Dr. Gail Dubrow, Vice Provost and Dean
Programs in:
- biophysical sciences and medical physics (MS, PhD)
- cellular and integrative physiology (MS, PhD)
- genetic counseling (MS)
- health informatics (MHI, MS, PhD)
- history of science, technology and medicine (MA, PhD)
- microbial engineering (MS)
- microbiology, immunology and cancer biology (PhD)
- molecular, cellular, developmental biology and genetics (PhD)
- natural resource sciences and management (MS, PhD)
- neuroscience (MS, PhD)
- scientific computation (MS, PhD)

College of Biological Sciences
Dr. Robert Elde, Dean
Programs in:
- biochemistry, molecular biology and biophysics (PhD)
- biological science (MBS)
- biological sciences (MBS, MS, PhD)
- ecology, evolution, and behavior (MS, PhD)
- plant biological sciences (MS, PhD)

College of Design
Thomas Fisher, Dean
Programs in:
- apparel (MA, MS, PhD)
- architecture (M Arch)
- design (M Arch, MA, MFA, MLA, MS, PhD, Postbaccalaureate Certificate)
- design communication (MA, MS, PhD)
- housing studies (MA, MS, PhD, Postbaccalaureate Certificate)
- interactive design (MFA)
- interior design (MA, MS, PhD)
- landscape architecture (MLA, MS)
- sustainable design (MS)

College of Education and Human Development
Dr. Darlyne Bailey, Dean
Programs in:
- adapted physical education (MA, PhD)
- adult education (M Ed, MA, Ed D, PhD, Certificate)
- agricultural, food and environmental education (M Ed, MA, Ed D, PhD)
- art education (M Ed, MA, PhD)
- biomechanics (MA)
- biomechanics and neural control (PhD)
- business and industry education (M Ed, MA, Ed D, PhD)
- business education (M Ed)
- child psychology (MA, PhD)
- children's literature (M Ed, MA, PhD)
- Chinese (M Ed)
- coaching (Certificate)
- comparative and international development education (MA, PhD)
- counseling and student personnel psychology (MA, PhD, Ed S)
- curriculum and instruction (MA, PhD)
- developmental adapted physical education (M Ed)
- disability policy and services (Certificate)
- early childhood education (M Ed, MA, PhD)
- earth science (M Ed)
- education and human development (M Ed, MA, MSW, Ed D, PhD, Certificate, Ed S)
- educational administration (MA, Ed D, PhD)
- educational psychology (PhD)
- elementary education (M Ed, MA, PhD)
- elementary special education (M Ed)
- English (M Ed)
- English as a second language (M Ed)
- English education (MA, PhD)
- environmental education (M Ed)
- evaluation studies (MA, PhD)
- exercise physiology (MA, PhD)
- family education (M Ed, MA, Ed D, PhD)
- French (M Ed)
- German (M Ed)
- Hebrew (M Ed)
- higher education (MA, PhD)
- human factors/ergonomics (MA, PhD)
- human resource development (M Ed, MA, Ed D, PhD, Certificate)
- instructional systems and technology (M Ed, MA, PhD)
- international/comparative sport (MA, PhD)
- Japanese (M Ed)
- kinesiology (M Ed, MA, PhD)
- language arts (MA, PhD)
- language immersion education (Certificate)
- leisure services/management (MA, PhD)
- life sciences (M Ed)
- literacy education (MA)
- marketing education (M Ed)
- marriage and family therapy (MA, PhD)
- mathematics (M Ed)
- mathematics education (MA, PhD)
- middle school science (M Ed)
- motor development (MA, PhD)
- motor learning/control (MA, PhD)
- outdoor education/recreation (MA, PhD)
- physical education (M Ed)
- postsecondary administration (Ed D)
- program evaluation (Certificate)
- psychological foundations of education (MA, PhD, Ed S)

reading education (MA, PhD)
recreation, park, and leisure studies (M Ed, MA, PhD)
school psychology (MA, PhD, Ed S)
school-to-work (Certificate)
science (M Ed)
science education (MA, PhD)
second languages and cultures (M Ed)
second languages and cultures education (MA, PhD)
social studies (M Ed)
social studies education (MA, PhD)
social work (MSW, PhD)
Spanish (M Ed)
special education (M Ed, MA, PhD, Ed S)
sport and exercise science (M Ed)
sport management (M Ed, MA, PhD)
sport psychology (MA, PhD)
sport sociology (MA, PhD)
staff development (Certificate)
talent development and gifted education (Certificate)
teacher leadership (M Ed)
teaching (M Ed)
technical education (Certificate)
technology education (M Ed, MA)
technology enhanced learning (Certificate)
therapeutic recreation (MA, PhD)
work and human resource education (M Ed, MA, Ed D, PhD)
writing education (M Ed, MA, PhD)
youth development leadership (M Ed)

College of Food, Agricultural and Natural Resource Sciences
Dr. Allen S. Levine, Dean
Programs in:
animal science (MS, PhD)
applied economics (MS, PhD)
applied plant sciences (MS, PhD)
biosystems and agricultural engineering (MBAE, MSBAE, PhD)
conservation biology (MS, PhD)
entomology (MS, PhD)
food science (MS, PhD)
food, agricultural and natural resource sciences (MBAE, MS, MSBAE, PhD)
natural resources science and management (MS, PhD)
natural resources, science and management (MS, PhD)
nutrition (MS, PhD)
plant pathology (MS, PhD)
soil science (MS, PhD)
water resources science (MS, PhD)

College of Liberal Arts
Steven J. Rosenstone, Dean
Programs in:
American studies (MA, PhD)
ancient and medieval art and archaeology (MA, PhD)
anthropology (MA, PhD)
art (MFA)
art history (MA, PhD)
Asian literatures, cultures, and media (PhD)
audiology (Au D)
biological psychopathology (PhD)
classics (MA, PhD)
clinical psychology (PhD)
cognitive and biological psychology (PhD)
communication studies (MA, PhD)
comparative literature (PhD)
comparative studies in discourse and society (PhD)
counseling psychology (PhD)
design technology (MFA)
economics (PhD)
English (MA, MFA, PhD)
English as a second language (MA)
feminist studies (PhD)
French (MA, PhD)
geographic information science (MGIS)
geography (MA, PhD)
Germanic studies: German and Scandinavian studies track (PhD)
Germanic studies: German track (MA, PhD)
Germanic studies: Germanic medieval studies track (MA, PhD)
Germanic studies: Scandinavian studies track (MA)
Germanic studies: teaching track (MA)
Greek (MA, PhD)
health journalism (professional program) (MA)
Hispanic and Luso-Brazilian literatures and linguistics (PhD)
Hispanic linguistics (MA)
Hispanic literature (MA)
history (MA, PhD)
industrial/organizational psychology (PhD)
Latin (MA, PhD)
liberal arts (MA, MFA, MGIS, MM, MS, Au D, DMA, PhD)
linguistics (MA, PhD)
Lusophone literature (MA)
mass communication (MA, PhD)
music (MA, MM, DMA, PhD)
personality, individual differences, and behavior genetics (PhD)
philosophy (MA, PhD)
political science (MA, PhD)
quantitative/psychometric methods (PhD)
religions in antiquity (MA)
school psychology (PhD)
social psychology (PhD)
sociology (MA, PhD)
speech-language pathology (MA)
speech-language-hearing sciences (PhD)
statistics (MS, PhD)
strategic communication (professional program) (MA)
theater arts and dance (MA)
theatre arts and dance (PhD)

Hubert H. Humphrey Institute of Public Affairs
Programs in:
advanced policy analysis methods (MPP)
economic and community development (MPP)
environmental planning (MURP)
foreign policy (MPP)
housing and community development (MURP)
land use and urban design (MURP)
public affairs (MPA, MPP, MS, MURP)
public and nonprofit leadership and management (MPP)
regional, economic and workforce development (MURP)
science technology and environmental policy (MPP)
science, technology, and environmental policy (MS)
social policy (MPP)
transportation planning (MURP)
women and public policy (MPP)

School of Nursing
Dr. Connie Delaney, Dean
Programs in:
adolescent nursing (MS)
adult health clinical nurse specialist (MS)
advanced clinical specialist in gerontology (MS)
children with special health care needs (MS)
family nurse practitioner (MS)
gerontological nurse practitioner (MS)
nurse anesthetist (MS)
nurse midwifery (MS)
nursing (MN, MS, DNP, PhD)
nursing and health care systems administration (MS)
pediatric clinical nurse specialist (MS)
pediatric nurse practitioner (MS)
psychiatric mental health clinical nurse specialist (MS)
public health nursing (MS)
women's health nurse practitioner (MS)

Institute of Technology
H. Ted Davis, Dean
Programs in:
aerospace engineering (M Aero E)
aerospace engineering and mechanics (MS, PhD)
biomedical engineering (MS, PhD)
chemical engineering (M Ch E, MS Ch E, PhD)
chemistry (MS, PhD)
civil engineering (MCE, MS, PhD)
computer and information sciences (MCIS, MS, PhD)
computer engineering (M Comp E, MS)
electrical engineering (MEE, MSEE, PhD)
geological engineering (M Geo E, MS, PhD)
geology (MS, PhD)
geophysics (MS, PhD)
history of science and technology (MA, PhD)
industrial engineering (MSIE, PhD)
materials science and engineering (M Mat SE, MS Mat SE, PhD)

University of Minnesota, Twin Cities Campus (continued)

mechanical engineering (MSME, PhD)
technology (M Aero E, M Ch E, M Comp E, M Geo E, M Mat SE, MA, MCE, MCIS, MCS, MEE, MS, MS Ch E, MS Mat SE, MSEE, MSIE, MSME, MSMOT, PhD)

Center for the Development of Technological Leadership
Dr. Massond Amin, Director
Programs in:
infrastructure systems engineering (MS)
management of technology (MSMOT)

School of Mathematics
Naresh Jain, Head
Program in:
mathematics (MS, PhD)

School of Physics and Astronomy
Allen M. Goldman, Head
Programs in:
astronomy (MS, PhD)
astrophysics (MS, PhD)
physics (MS, PhD)

Law School
Program in:
law (JD, LL M)

Medical School
Programs in:
medicine (MD, MA, MS, DPT, PhD)
pharmacology (MS, PhD)

Graduate Programs in Medicine
Programs in:
biochemistry, molecular biology and biophysics (PhD)
experimental surgery (MS)
medicine (MA, MS, DPT, PhD)
physical therapy (DPT)
surgery (MS, PhD)

School of Dentistry
Programs in:
dentistry (DDS, MS, PhD, Certificate)
endodontics (MS, Certificate)
oral biology (MS, PhD)
oral health services for older adults (geriatrics) (MS, Certificate)
orthodontics (MS)
pediatric dentistry (MS)
periodontology (MS)
prosthodontics (MS)
temporomandibular joint disorders (MS)

School of Public Health
Programs in:
biostatistics (MPH, MS, PhD)
clinical research (MS)
community health education (MPH)
core concepts (Certificate)
environmental and occupational epidemiology (MPH, MS, PhD)
environmental chemistry (MS, PhD)
environmental health policy (MPH, MS, PhD)
environmental infectious diseases (MPH, MS, PhD)
environmental toxicology (MPH, MS, PhD)
epidemiology (MPH, PhD)
food safety and biosecurity (Certificate)
general environmental health (MPH, MS)
health services research, policy, and administration (MS, PhD)
healthcare management (MHA)
industrial hygiene (MPH, MS, PhD)
maternal and child health (MPH)
occupational health and safety (Certificate)
occupational health nursing (MPH, MS, PhD)
occupational medicine (MPH)
preparedness, response and recovery (Certificate)
public health (MHA, MPH, MS, PhD, Certificate)
public health administration and policy (MPH)
public health nutrition (MPH)
public health practice (MPH)

■ UNIVERSITY OF ST. THOMAS
St. Paul, MN 55105-1096
http://www.stthomas.edu/

Independent-religious, coed, university. *Enrollment:* 10,712 graduate, professional, and undergraduate students; 1,016 full-time matriculated graduate/professional students (563 women), 3,675 part-time matriculated graduate/professional students (1,887 women). *Graduate faculty:* 178 full-time (74 women), 307 part-time/adjunct (103 women). *Computer facilities:* 1,549 computers available on campus for general student use. A campuswide network can be accessed from student residence rooms and from off campus. Internet access and online class registration are available. *Library facilities:* O'Shaughnessy-Frey Library plus 3 others. *General application contact:* Dr. Angeline Barretta-Herman, Associate Vice President for Academic Affairs, 651-962-6033.

Graduate Studies
Dr. Thomas R. Rochon, Executive Vice President for Academic Affairs
Programs in:
computer security (Certificate)
information systems (MSDD, Certificate)
software design and development (Certificate)
software engineering (MS)
software systems (MSS)

College of Arts and Sciences
Dr. Marisa Kelly, Dean
Programs in:
art history (MA)
arts and sciences (MA)
Catholic studies (MA)
English (MA)
music education (MA)

Graduate School of Professional Psychology
Dr. David Welch, Dean
Programs in:
counseling psychology (MA, Psy D)
family psychology (Certificate)

Opus College of Business
Dr. Chistopher P. Puto, Dean
Programs in:
accountancy (MS)
business (MBA, MBC, MS)
business administration (MBA)
business communication (MBC)
health care business administration (MBA)
real estate (MS)

Saint Paul Seminary School of Divinity
Rev. Msgr. Aloysius R. Callaghan, Rector
Programs in:
divinity (M Div, MA, MARE)
religious education (MARE)
theology (MA)

School of Education
Dr. Miriam Q. Williams, Dean
Programs in:
athletics and activities administration (MA)
autism spectrum disorders (Certificate)
community education administration (MA)
critical pedagogy (Ed D)
curriculum and instruction (MA, Ed S)
director of special education (Ed S)
education (MA, MAT, Ed D, Certificate, Ed S)
educational leadership (Ed S)
educational leadership and administration (MA)
gifted, creative, and talented education (MA, Certificate)
leadership (Ed D)
leadership in student affairs (MA, Certificate)
learning technology (MA, Certificate)
organization learning and development (MA, Ed D, Certificate)
Orton-Gillingham reading (Certificate)
police leadership (MA)
public policy and leadership (MA, Certificate)
reading (MA)
special education (MA)
teacher education (MAT)

School of Engineering
Ron Bennett, Dean
Programs in:
engineering and technology management (Certificate)
manufacturing systems (MS)

manufacturing systems engineering (MMSE)
systems engineering (MS)
technology management (MS)

School of Law
Thomas M. Mengler, Dean
Program in:
law (JD)

School of Social Work
Dr. Barbara W. Shank, Dean and Professor
Program in:
social work (MSW)

■ WALDEN UNIVERSITY
Minneapolis, MN 55401
http://www.waldenu.edu/

Proprietary, coed, upper-level institution. CGS member. *Enrollment:* 27,633 graduate, professional, and undergraduate students; 19,263 full-time matriculated graduate/professional students (15,151 women), 6,787 part-time matriculated graduate/professional students (4,920 women). *Graduate faculty:* 1,079. *General application contact:* Seth Saunders, Director of Student Enrollment, 866-4-WALDEN.

Find University Details at www.petersons.com/gradchannel.

Graduate Programs
Dr. Paula Peinovich, President

NTU College of Engineering and Applied Science
Dr. Ahmed Naumaan, Chair
Programs in:
computer engineering (MS)
computer science (MS)
electrical engineering (MS)
engineering (MS)
engineering management (MBA, Certificate)
high-tech business administration (MBA)
software engineering (MS)
systems engineering (MS)

College of Education
Dr. Manual Barrera, Dean
Programs in:
administrator leadership for teaching and learning (Ed D)
adult education leadership (PhD)
community college leadership (PhD)
curriculum, instruction, and assessment (MS)
early childhood education (PhD)
education (MS)
educational leadership (MS)
educational technology (PhD)
elementary reading and literacy (MS)
elementary reading and mathematics (MS)
higher education (PhD)
integrating technology in the classroom (MS)
K–12 educational leadership (PhD)
literacy and learning in the content areas (MS)
mathematics (grades 6–8) (MS)
mathematics (grades K–5) (MS)
middle level education (MS)
science (grades K–8) (MS)
special education (PhD)
teacher leadership (Ed D)

School of Health Sciences
Dr. Gary J. Burkholder, Dean
Programs in:
health services (PhD)
human services (PhD)
nursing (MS)
public health (MPH, PhD)

School of Management
Dr. Kathleen Simmons, Chair
Programs in:
applied management and decision sciences (PhD)
business administration (MBA)
human resource management (MBA)
marketing (MBA)
technology (MBA)

School of Psychology
Dr. Nina Nabors, Interim Dean
Programs in:
mental health counseling (MS)
psychology (MS, PhD)

School of Public Policy and Administration
Dr. Marion Angelica, Dean
Program in:
public policy and administration (MPA, PhD)

■ WINONA STATE UNIVERSITY
Winona, MN 55987-5838

State-supported, coed, comprehensive institution. *Enrollment:* 8,220 graduate, professional, and undergraduate students; 2 full-time matriculated graduate/professional students (both women), 390 part-time matriculated graduate/professional students (299 women). *Graduate faculty:* 57 full-time (38 women). *Computer facilities:* Computer purchase and lease plans are available. 1,400 computers available on campus for general student use. A campuswide network can be accessed from student residence rooms and from off campus. Internet access and online class registration are available. *Library facilities:* Darrel W. Krueger. *General application contact:* Dr. Lee Gray, Director of Graduate Studies, 507-457-5346.

Graduate Studies
Dr. Lee Gray, Director of Graduate Studies

College of Education
Lorene Olsen, Acting Dean
Programs in:
community counseling (MS)
education (MS, Ed S)
educational leadership (Ed S)
general school leadership (MS)
K-12 principalship (MS)
professional development (MS)
school counseling (MS)
special education (MS)
teacher leadership (MS)

College of Liberal Arts
Dr. Troy Paino, Dean
Programs in:
English (MA, MS)
liberal arts (MA, MS)

College of Nursing and Health Sciences
Dr. Timothy Gaspar, Graduate Director
Programs in:
adult nurse practitioner (MS)
clinical nurse specialist (MS)
family nurse practitioner (MS)
nurse administrator (MS)
nurse educator (MS)

Mississippi

■ ALCORN STATE UNIVERSITY
Alcorn State, MS 39096-7500
http://www.alcorn.edu/

State-supported, coed, comprehensive institution. CGS member. *Enrollment:* 3,584 graduate, professional, and undergraduate students; 165 full-time matriculated graduate/professional students (100 women), 404 part-time matriculated graduate/professional students (323 women). *Graduate faculty:* 55 full-time (16 women), 23 part-time/adjunct (15 women). *Computer facilities:* 500 computers available on campus for general student use. A campuswide network can be accessed from student residence rooms and from off campus. Internet access and online class registration are available. *Library facilities:* John Dewey Boyd Library. *General application contact:* Lula Russell, Administrative Assistant to the Dean, School of Graduate Studies, 601-877-6122.

School of Graduate Studies
Dr. Donzell Lee, Dean
Program in:
workforce education leadership (MS)

School of Agriculture and Applied Science
Dalton McAfee, Interim Dean
Programs in:
agricultural economics (MS Ag)
agronomy (MS Ag)
animal science (MS Ag)

Alcorn State University (continued)

School of Arts and Sciences
Reginald Lindsey, Dean
Programs in:
arts and sciences (MS)
biology (MS)
computer and information sciences (MS)

School of Business
Dr. Steve Wells, Dean
Program in:
business (MBA)

School of Nursing
Dr. Mary Hill, Dean
Program in:
rural nursing (MSN)

School of Psychology and Education
Dr. Josephine M. Posey, Dean
Programs in:
agricultural education (MS Ed)
elementary education (MS Ed, Ed S)
guidance and counseling (MS Ed)
industrial education (MS Ed)
secondary education (MS Ed)
special education (MS Ed)

■ BELHAVEN COLLEGE
Jackson, MS 39202-1789
http://www.belhaven.edu/

Independent-religious, coed, comprehensive institution. *Computer facilities:* 40 computers available on campus for general student use. A campuswide network can be accessed from student residence rooms and from off campus. Internet access, e-mail are available. *Library facilities:* Hood Library. *General application contact:* Director of Marketing, 601-968-5988.

School of Business
Programs in:
business administration (MBA)
business management (MSM)

School of Education
Programs in:
elementary education (M Ed, MAT)
secondary education (M Ed, MAT)

■ DELTA STATE UNIVERSITY
Cleveland, MS 38733-0001
http://www.deltastate.edu/

State-supported, coed, comprehensive institution. *Enrollment:* 4,217 graduate, professional, and undergraduate students; 211 full-time matriculated graduate/professional students (156 women), 519 part-time matriculated graduate/professional students (405 women). *Graduate faculty:* 59 full-time (18 women), 74 part-time/adjunct (35 women). *Computer facilities:* 293 computers available on campus for general student use. A campuswide network can be accessed from student residence rooms and from off campus. Internet access and online class registration, e-mail are available. *Library facilities:* Roberts-LaForge Library plus 1 other. *General application contact:* Dr. Tyrone Jackson, Assistant Dean of Graduate and Continuing Studies, 662-846-4875.

Graduate Programs
Dr. John Thornell, Provost and Vice President for Academic Affairs

College of Arts and Sciences
Collier Parker, Dean
Programs in:
arts and sciences (M Ed, MSCD, MSCJ, MSNS)
biological and physical sciences (MSNS)
community development (MSCD)
criminal justice (MSCJ)
English education (M Ed)
history education (M Ed)
mathematics education (M Ed)
social science secondary education (M Ed)

College of Business
Dr. Billy Moore, Dean
Programs in:
accountancy (MPA)
business (MBA, MCA, MPA)
commercial aviation (MCA)
management (MBA)
marketing (MBA)

College of Education
Dr. Matthew Buckley, Dean
Programs in:
administration and supervision (M Ed)
administrative and supervision (Ed S)
counseling (M Ed)
education (M Ed, MAT, Ed D, Ed S)
educational administration and supervision (Ed S)
educational leadership (M Ed)
elementary education (M Ed, MAT, Ed S)
physical education and recreation (M Ed)
secondary education (Ed S)
special education (M Ed)
teaching (Ed D)

School of Nursing
Dr. Lizabeth Carlson, Dean
Program in:
nursing (MSN)

■ JACKSON STATE UNIVERSITY
Jackson, MS 39217
http://www.jsums.edu/

State-supported, coed, university. CGS member. *Enrollment:* 8,256 graduate, professional, and undergraduate students; 525 full-time matriculated graduate/professional students (349 women), 579 part-time matriculated graduate/professional students (374 women). *Graduate faculty:* 213 full-time (83 women), 15 part-time/adjunct (6 women). *Computer facilities:* A campuswide network can be accessed from off campus. Internet access is available. *Library facilities:* H. T. Sampson Library plus 1 other. *General application contact:* Dr. Dorris R. Robinson-Gardner, Dean of the Graduate School, 601-979-2455.

Graduate School
Dr. Dorris R. Robinson-Gardner, Dean

College of Public Service
Dr. Gwednolyn Prater, Dean
Programs in:
communicative disorders (MS)
public service (MS)

School of Business
Dr. Glenda B. Glover, Dean
Programs in:
accounting (MPA)
business (MBA, MPA, PhD)
business administration (MBA)

School of Education
Dr. Daniel Watkins, Interim Dean
Programs in:
community and agency counseling (MS)
early childhood education (MS Ed, Ed D)
education (MS, MS Ed, Ed D, PhD, Ed S)
education administration (Ed S)
educational administration (MS Ed, PhD)
elementary education (MS Ed, Ed S)
guidance and counseling (MS, MS Ed, Ed S)
health, physical education and recreation (MS Ed)
rehabilitative counseling (MS Ed)
rehabilitative counseling service (MS Ed)
secondary education (MS Ed, Ed S)
special education (MS Ed, Ed S)

School of Liberal Arts
Dr. Dollye M. E. Robinson, Dean
Programs in:
clinical psychology (PhD)
criminology and justice service (MA)
English (MA)
history (MA)
liberal arts (MA, MAT, MM Ed, MPPA, MS, PhD)
mass communications (MS)
music education (MM Ed)
political science (MA)
public policy and administration (MPPA, PhD)
sociology (MA)
teaching English (MAT)
urban and regional planning (MS)

School of Science and Technology
Dr. Mark G. Hardy, Interim Dean
Programs in:
biology education (MST)
chemistry (MS, PhD)
computer science (MS)
environmental science (MS, PhD)
hazardous materials management (MS)
industrial arts education (MS Ed)
mathematics (MS)

mathematics education (MST)
science and technology (MS, MS Ed, MST, PhD)
science education (MST)

School of Social Work
Dr. Gwednolyn Prater, Dean
Program in:
social work (MSW, PhD)

■ MISSISSIPPI COLLEGE
Clinton, MS 39058
http://www.mc.edu/

Independent-religious, coed, comprehensive institution. *Enrollment:* 4,039 graduate, professional, and undergraduate students; 764 full-time matriculated graduate/professional students (351 women), 620 part-time matriculated graduate/professional students (479 women). *Graduate faculty:* 97 full-time (31 women), 72 part-time/adjunct (32 women). *Computer facilities:* 250 computers available on campus for general student use. A campuswide network can be accessed from student residence rooms and from off campus. Internet access is available. *Library facilities:* Leland Speed Library plus 1 other. *Graduate expenses:* Tuition: full-time $7,290; part-time $405 per hour. Required fees: $150 per term. Tuition and fees vary according to campus/location and program. *General application contact:* Dr. Debbie C. Norris, Graduate Dean, 601-925-3260.

Graduate School
Dr. Debbie C. Norris, Graduate Dean
Programs in:
health services administration (MHSA)
liberal studies (MLS)

College of Arts and Sciences
Dr. Ron Howard, Dean
Programs in:
administration of justice (MSS)
applied communication (MSC)
applied music performance (MM)
art (M Ed, MA, MFA)
arts and sciences (M Ed, MA, MCS, MFA, MM, MS, MSC, MSS, Certificate)
biological science (M Ed)
biology (MCS)
biology-biological sciences (MS)
biology-medical sciences (MS)
chemistry (MCS, MS)
Christian studies and the arts (M Ed, MA, MFA, MM, MSC)
computer science (M Ed, MS)
conducting (MM)
English (M Ed, MA)
history (M Ed, MA, MSS)
humanities and social sciences (M Ed, MA, MS, MSS, Certificate)
mathematics (M Ed, MCS, MS)
music education (MM)
music performance: organ (MM)
paralegal studies (Certificate)
political science (MSS)
public relations and corporate communication (MSC)
science and mathematics (M Ed, MCS, MS)
social sciences (M Ed, MSS)
sociology (MSS)
teaching English to speakers of other languages (MA, MS)
vocal pedagogy (MM)

School of Business
Dr. Marcelo Eduardo, Dean
Programs in:
accounting (Certificate)
business administration (MBA)
business education (M Ed)

School of Education
Dr. Don Locke, Dean
Programs in:
art (M Ed)
biological science (M Ed)
business education (M Ed)
computer science (M Ed)
counseling (Ed S)
dyslexia therapy (M Ed)
education (M Ed, MS, Ed S)
educational leadership (M Ed, Ed S)
elementary education (M Ed, Ed S)
English (M Ed)
higher education administration (MS)
marriage and family counseling (MS)
mathematics (M Ed)
mental health counseling (MS)
school counseling (M Ed)
secondary education (M Ed)
social studies (history) (M Ed)
teaching arts (M Ed)

School of Law
James H. Rosenblatt, Dean
Programs in:
civil law studies (Certificate)
law (JD)

■ MISSISSIPPI STATE UNIVERSITY
Mississippi State, MS 39762
http://www.msstate.edu/

State-supported, coed, university. CGS member. *Enrollment:* 16,206 graduate, professional, and undergraduate students; 1,793 full-time matriculated graduate/professional students (824 women), 1,783 part-time matriculated graduate/professional students (966 women). *Graduate faculty:* 1,071 full-time (352 women), 197 part-time/adjunct (102 women). *Computer facilities:* 2,000 computers available on campus for general student use. A campuswide network can be accessed from student residence rooms and from off campus. Internet access and online class registration, wireless network with partial campus coverage are available. *Library facilities:* Mitchell Memorial Library plus 2 others. *Graduate expenses:* Tuition, state resident: full-time $4,550; part-time $253 per hour. Tuition, nonresident: full-time $10,552; part-time $584 per hour. International tuition: $10,882 full-time. Tuition and fees vary according to course load. *General application contact:* Dr. Phil Bonfanti, Director of Admissions, 662-325-4104.

Bagley College of Engineering
Dr. Kirk H. Schulz, Dean
Programs in:
aerospace engineering (MS)
civil engineering (MS)
computer engineering (MS, PhD)
computer science (MS, PhD)
electrical engineering (MS, PhD)
engineering (PhD)
engineering mechanics (MS)
industrial and systems engineering (MS, PhD)
mechanical engineering (MS, PhD)

David C. Swalm School of Chemical Engineering
Dr. Mark White, Director
Programs in:
chemical engineering (MS)
engineering (PhD)

College of Agriculture and Life Sciences
Dr. Vance Watson, Dean and Vice President
Programs in:
agribusiness management (MABM)
agricultural economics (PhD)
agricultural pest management (MS)
agriculture and extension education (MS)
agriculture and life sciences (MABM, MLA, MS, PhD)
agronomy (MS, PhD)
biochemistry (MS)
biological engineering (MS)
biomedical engineering (MS, PhD)
engineering (PhD)
entomology (MS, PhD)
food science (PhD)
food science, nutrition and health promotion (MS)
horticulture (MS, PhD)
landscape architecture (MLA)
molecular biology (PhD)
nutrition (MS, PhD)
plant pathology (MS, PhD)
poultry science (MS)
weed science (MS, PhD)

College of Architecture, Art and Design
James L. West, Dean
Programs in:
architecture, art and design (MFA, MS)
electronic visualization (MFA)

School of Architecture
Dr. Larry Barrow, Director
Program in:
architecture (MS)

Mississippi State University (continued)

College of Arts and Sciences

Dr. Philip B. Oldham, Dean
Programs in:
- applied anthropology (MA)
- arts and sciences (MA, MPPA, MS, PhD)
- biological sciences (MS, PhD)
- chemistry (MS, PhD)
- clinical psychology (MS)
- cognitive science (PhD)
- engineering physics (PhD)
- English (MA)
- experimental psychology (MS)
- French (MA)
- French/German (MA)
- geosciences (MS)
- German (MA)
- history (MA, PhD)
- mathematical sciences (PhD)
- mathematics (MS)
- physics (MS)
- political science (MA)
- public policy and administration (MPPA, PhD)
- sociology (MS, PhD)
- Spanish (MA)
- Spanish/French (MA)
- Spanish/German (MA)
- statistics (MS)

College of Business and Industry

Dr. Dan P. Hollingsworth, Interim Dean
Programs in:
- applied economics (PhD)
- business administration (MBA, PhD)
- business and industry (MA, MBA, MPA, MSBA, MSIS, MTX, PhD)
- economics (MA)
- finance (MSBA)
- information systems (MSIS)
- project management (MBA)

School of Accountancy
Dr. Clyde Herring, Interim Director
Program in:
- accountancy (MPA, MTX)

College of Education

Dr. Richard Blackbourn, Dean
Programs in:
- counselor education (MS, PhD, Ed S)
- curriculum and instruction (PhD)
- education (MS, MSIT, Ed D, PhD, Ed S)
- educational psychology (MS, PhD, Ed S)
- elementary education (MS, Ed D, PhD, Ed S)
- exercise science (MS)
- health education/health promotion (MS)
- instructional technology (MSIT)
- secondary education (MS, Ed D, PhD, Ed S)
- special education (MS, Ed S)
- sports administration (MS)
- teaching/coaching (MS)
- technology (MS, Ed D, PhD, Ed S)
- workforce education leadership (MS)

College of Forest Resources

Dr. George M. Hopper, Dean
Programs in:
- forest products (MS, PhD)
- forest resources (MS, PhD)
- forestry (MS)
- wildlife and fisheries science (MS)

College of Veterinary Medicine

Programs in:
- environmental toxicology (PhD)
- veterinary medical science (MS, PhD)
- veterinary medicine (DVM, MS, PhD)

■ MISSISSIPPI UNIVERSITY FOR WOMEN

Columbus, MS 39701-9998
http://www.muw.edu/

State-supported, coed, primarily women, comprehensive institution. *Computer facilities:* 250 computers available on campus for general student use. A campuswide network can be accessed from student residence rooms and from off campus. Internet access, various software packages are available. *Library facilities:* John Clayton Fant Memorial Library. *General application contact:* Director, Graduate School, 601-329-7150.

Graduate School

Division of Education and Human Sciences
Programs in:
- gifted studies (M Ed)
- instructional management (M Ed)
- speech/language pathology (MS)

Division of Health and Kinesiology
Program in:
- health education (MS)

Division of Nursing
Program in:
- nursing (MSN, Certificate)

■ MISSISSIPPI VALLEY STATE UNIVERSITY

Itta Bena, MS 38941-1400
http://www.mvsu.edu/

State-supported, coed, comprehensive institution. *Computer facilities:* 250 computers available on campus for general student use. A campuswide network can be accessed from student residence rooms and from off campus. Internet access and online class registration are available. *Library facilities:* James H. White Library. *General application contact:* Office of Admissions, 601-254-3344.

Department of Criminal Justice and Social Work

Program in:
- criminal justice (MS)

Department of Education

Programs in:
- education (MAT)
- elementary education (MA)

Department of Natural Science and Environmental Health

Programs in:
- bioinformatics (MS)
- environmental health (MS)

■ UNIVERSITY OF MISSISSIPPI

Oxford, University, MS 38677
http://www.olemiss.edu/

State-supported, coed, university. CGS member. *Enrollment:* 15,220 graduate, professional, and undergraduate students; 1,766 full-time matriculated graduate/professional students (900 women), 646 part-time matriculated graduate/professional students (433 women). *Graduate faculty:* 565 full-time (205 women), 116 part-time/adjunct (61 women). *Computer facilities:* Computer purchase and lease plans are available. 3,500 computers available on campus for general student use. A campuswide network can be accessed from student residence rooms and from off campus. Internet access and online class registration, application for admission, registration for orientation are available. *Library facilities:* J. D. Williams Library plus 3 others. *Graduate expenses:* Tuition, state resident: full-time $4,602; part-time $256 per credit hour. Tuition, nonresident: full-time $10,566; part-time $587 per credit hour. *General application contact:* Dr. Christy M. Wyandt, Associate Dean of Graduate School, 662-915-7474.

Graduate School

Dr. Maurice Eftink, Dean

College of Liberal Arts
Dr. Glenn Hopkins, Dean
Programs in:
- anthropology (MA)
- art education (MA)
- art history (MA)
- biology (MS, PhD)
- chemistry (MS, DA, PhD)
- classics (MA)
- clinical psychology (PhD)
- economics (MA, PhD)
- English (MA, PhD)
- experimental psychology (PhD)
- fine arts (MFA)
- French (MA)
- German (MA)
- history (MA, PhD)
- journalism (MA)
- liberal arts (MA, MFA, MM, MS, MSS, DA, PhD)
- mathematics (MA, MS, PhD)
- music (MM, DA)
- philosophy (MA)

physics (MA, MS, PhD)
political science (MA, PhD)
psychology (MA)
sociology (MA, MSS)
Southern studies (MA)
Spanish (MA)
theatre arts (MFA)

School of Accountancy
Dr. Mark Wilder, Interim Dean
Programs in:
accountancy (M Acc, PhD)
taxation accounting (M Tax)

School of Applied Sciences
Dr. Linda Chitwood, Dean
Programs in:
applied sciences (MA, MS, PhD)
communicative disorders (MS)
exercise science (MA, MS)
exercise science and leisure management (PhD)
leisure management (MA)
park and recreation management (MA)
wellness (MS)

School of Business Administration
Dr. Brian Reithel, Dean
Programs in:
business administration (MBA, PhD)
systems management (MS)

School of Education
Dr. Tom Burnham, Dean
Programs in:
counselor education (M Ed, PhD, Specialist)
curriculum and instruction (M Ed, Ed D, Ed S)
education (PhD)
educational leadership (PhD)
educational leadership and counselor education (M Ed, MA, Ed D, Ed S)
higher education/student personnel (MA)
secondary education (MA)

School of Engineering
Dr. Kai-Fong Lee, Dean
Programs in:
computational engineering science (MS, PhD)
engineering science (MS, PhD)

School of Pharmacy
Dr. Barbara G. Wells, Dean
Programs in:
medicinal chemistry (MS, PhD)
pharmaceutics (MS, PhD)
pharmacognosy (MS, PhD)
pharmacology (MS, PhD)
pharmacy (Pharm D, MS, PhD)
pharmacy administration (MS, PhD)

School of Law
Dr. Samuel Davis, Dean
Program in:
law (JD)

■ UNIVERSITY OF SOUTHERN MISSISSIPPI
Hattiesburg, MS 39406-0001
http://www.usm.edu/

State-supported, coed, university. CGS member. *Enrollment:* 14,777 graduate, professional, and undergraduate students; 1,358 full-time matriculated graduate/professional students (801 women), 1,297 part-time matriculated graduate/professional students (872 women). *Graduate faculty:* 465 full-time (154 women), 1 part-time/adjunct (0 women). *Computer facilities:* 600 computers available on campus for general student use. Internet access is available. *Library facilities:* Cook Memorial Library plus 4 others. *General application contact:* Dr. Susan Siltanen, University Director, 601-266-4369.

Graduate School
Dr. Susan Siltanen, University Director

College of Arts and Letters
Dr. Denise Von Hermann, Interim Dean
Programs in:
anthropology (MA)
art education (MAE)
arts and letters (MA, MAE, MATL, MFA, MM, MME, MS, DMA, PhD)
conducting (MM)
English (MA, PhD)
French (MATL)
history (MA, MS, PhD)
history and literature (MM)
international development (PhD)
mass communication (MA, MS, PhD)
music education (MME, PhD)
performance (MM)
performance and pedagogy (DMA)
philosophy (MA)
political science (MA, MS)
public relations (MS)
Spanish (MATL)
speech communication (MA, MS, PhD)
teaching English to speakers of other languages (TESOL) (MATL)
theatre (MFA)
theory and composition (MM)
woodwind performance (MM)

College of Business
Dr. Harold Doty, Dean
Programs in:
accountancy (MPA)
business (MBA, MPA)
business administration (MBA)

College of Education and Psychology
Dr. Wanda Maulding, Interim Chair
Programs in:
adult education (M Ed, Ed D, PhD, Ed S)
alternative secondary teacher education (MAT)
business technology education (MS)
child and family studies (MS)
clinical psychology (MA, PhD)
counseling psychology (PhD)
early childhood education (M Ed, Ed S)
early intervention (MS)
education and psychology (M Ed, MA, MAT, MLIS, MS, Ed D, PhD, Ed S, SLS)
education of the gifted (M Ed, Ed D, PhD, Ed S)
educational administration (M Ed, Ed D, PhD, Ed S)
elementary education (M Ed, Ed D, PhD, Ed S)
experimental psychology (MA, PhD)
higher education (PhD)
instructional technology (MS)
library and information science (MLIS, SLS)
marriage and family therapy (MS)
psychology (MS)
reading (M Ed, MS, Ed S)
school psychology (MA, PhD)
secondary education (M Ed, MS, Ed D, PhD, Ed S)
special education (M Ed, Ed D, PhD, Ed S)
technical occupational education (MS)

College of Health
Dr. Peter Fos, Dean
Programs in:
adult health nursing (MSN)
community health nursing (MSN)
epidemiology and biostatistics (MPH)
ethics (PhD)
family nurse practitioner (MSN)
health (MA, MPH, MS, MSN, MSW, Au D, Ed D, PhD)
health education (MPH)
health policy/administration (MPH)
human performance (MS, Ed D, PhD)
interscholastic athletic administration (MS)
leadership (PhD)
medical technology (MS)
nursing service administration (MSN)
nutrition and food systems (MS, PhD)
occupational/environmental health (MPH)
policy analysis (PhD)
psychiatric nursing (MSN)
public health nutrition (MPH)
recreation and leisure management (MS)
social work (MSW)
speech and hearing sciences (MA, MS, Au D)
sport administration (MS)
sport and coaching education (MS)
sport management (MS)
sports and high performance materials (MS)

College of Science and Technology
Dr. Rex Gandy, Dean
Programs in:
administration of justice (PhD)
analytical chemistry (MS, PhD)
architecture and construction visualization (MS)
biochemistry (MS, PhD)

University of Southern Mississippi (continued)

coastal sciences (MS, PhD)
computational science (MS, PhD)
computational science: mathematics (PhD)
computer science (MS, PhD)
construction management and technology (MS)
corrections (MA, MS)
economic development (MS)
engineering technology (MS)
environmental biology (MS, PhD)
geography (MS, PhD)
geology (MS)
human capital development (PhD)
hydrographic science (MS)
inorganic chemistry (MS, PhD)
juvenile justice (MA, MS)
law enforcement (MA, MS)
logistics management and technology (MS)
marine biology (MS, PhD)
marine science (MS, PhD)
mathematics (MS)
microbiology (MS, PhD)
molecular biology (MS, PhD)
organic chemistry (MS, PhD)
physical chemistry (MS, PhD)
physics (MS)
polymer science (MS)
polymer science and engineering (PhD)
science and mathematics education (MS, PhD)
science and technology (MA, MS, PhD)
workforce training and development (MS)

■ WILLIAM CAREY UNIVERSITY
Hattiesburg, MS 39401-5499
http://www.wmcarey.edu/

Independent-religious, coed, comprehensive institution. *Enrollment:* 2,493 graduate, professional, and undergraduate students; 319 full-time matriculated graduate/professional students (231 women), 534 part-time matriculated graduate/professional students (456 women). *Graduate faculty:* 38 full-time (24 women), 35 part-time/adjunct (24 women). *Computer facilities:* 50 computers available on campus for general student use. A campuswide network can be accessed from student residence rooms and from off campus. Internet access is available. *Library facilities:* Smith-Rouse Library. *Graduate expenses:* Tuition: full-time $5,040; part-time $240 per credit hour. Tuition and fees vary according to course load. *General application contact:* Jason Douglas, Clerical Assistant, Graduate Admissions, 601-318-6774.

School of Business
Dr. Cheryl D. Dale, Dean
Program in:
business (MBA)

School of Education
Dr. Patty Ward, Dean
Programs in:
art education (M Ed)
art of teaching (M Ed)
elementary education (M Ed, Ed S)
English education (M Ed)
gifted education (M Ed)
history and social science (M Ed)
mild/moderate disabilities (M Ed)
secondary education (M Ed)

School of Nursing
Dr. Mary Stewart, Dean
Program in:
nursing (MSN)

School of Psychology and Counseling
Dr. Frank G. Baugh, Dean, School of Psychology
Program in:
counseling psychology (MS)

Missouri

■ AVILA UNIVERSITY
Kansas City, MO 64145-1698
http://www.avila.edu/

Independent-religious, coed, comprehensive institution. *Enrollment:* 1,683 graduate, professional, and undergraduate students; 370 full-time matriculated graduate/professional students (273 women), 183 part-time matriculated graduate/professional students (112 women). *Graduate faculty:* 22 full-time (15 women), 42 part-time/adjunct (22 women). *Computer facilities:* 68 computers available on campus for general student use. A campuswide network can be accessed from student residence rooms. Internet access is available. *Library facilities:* Hooley Bundshu Library. *Graduate expenses:* Tuition: full-time $7,470; part-time $415 per credit. *General application contact:* Office of Admissions, 816-501-2400.

Department of Psychology
Regina Staves, PhD, Director of Graduate Psychology
Programs in:
counseling and art therapy (MS)
counseling psychology (MS)
general psychology (MS)
organizational development (MS)

Program in Organizational Development
Lacey Smith, Assistant Dean
Programs in:
organizational development (MS)
project management (Graduate Certificate)

School of Business
Dr. Richard Woodall, Dean
Programs in:
accounting (MBA)
finance (MBA)
general management (MBA)
health care administration (MBA)
international business (MBA)
management information systems (MBA)
marketing (MBA)

School of Education
Dr. Laura Sloan, Dean
Programs in:
education (MA)
English for speakers of other languages (Advanced Certificate)
special reading (Advanced Certificate)

■ COLUMBIA COLLEGE
Columbia, MO 65216-0002
http://www.ccis.edu/

Independent-religious, coed, comprehensive institution. *Enrollment:* 1,186 graduate, professional, and undergraduate students; 300 full-time matriculated graduate/professional students (173 women). *Graduate faculty:* 14 full-time (6 women), 40 part-time/adjunct (9 women). *Computer facilities:* Computer purchase and lease plans are available. 137 computers available on campus for general student use. A campuswide network can be accessed from student residence rooms and from off campus. Internet access is available. *Library facilities:* Stafford Library. *Graduate expenses:* Tuition: part-time $270 per credit hour. *General application contact:* Regina Morin, Director of Admissions, 573-875-7354.

Program in Business Administration
Dr. Ken Middleton, Chair
Program in:
business administration (MBA)

Program in Criminal Justice
Barry Longford, Chair
Program in:
criminal justice (MSCJ)

Program in Teaching
Dr. Judy Brown, Chair
Program in:
teaching (MAT)

■ DRURY UNIVERSITY
Springfield, MO 65802
http://www.drury.edu/

Independent, coed, comprehensive institution. *Computer facilities:* 323 computers available on campus for general student use. A campuswide network can be accessed from student residence rooms and from off campus. Internet access and online class registration, digital imaging lab, online bill payment/student information are available.

Library facilities: F. W. Olin Library plus 1 other. *General application contact:* Director of Teacher Education, 417-873-7271.

Breech School of Business Administration
Programs in:
business administration (MBA)
business and international management (MBA)

Graduate Programs in Education
Programs in:
elementary education (M Ed)
gifted education (M Ed)
human services (M Ed)
middle school teaching (M Ed)
physical education (M Ed)
secondary education (M Ed)

Program in Communication
Program in:
communication (MA)

Program in Criminology/ Criminal Justice
Programs in:
criminal justice (MS)
criminology (MA)

■ FONTBONNE UNIVERSITY
St. Louis, MO 63105-3098
http://www.fontbonne.edu/

Independent-religious, coed, comprehensive institution. *Enrollment:* 2,924 graduate, professional, and undergraduate students; 446 full-time matriculated graduate/ professional students (310 women), 360 part-time matriculated graduate/professional students (273 women). *Graduate faculty:* 27 full-time (15 women), 120 part-time/adjunct (55 women). *Computer facilities:* 120 computers available on campus for general student use. A campuswide network can be accessed from student residence rooms and from off campus. Internet access and online class registration are available. *Library facilities:* Fontbonne Library. *Graduate expenses:* Tuition: full-time $4,890; part-time $489 per credit. Required fees: $160; $76 per credit. Full-time tuition and fees vary according to course load and program. *General application contact:* Peggy Musen, Associate Dean of Enrollment Management and Director of Admissions, 314-889-1400.

Graduate Programs
Dr. Nancy Blattner, Vice President and Dean for Academic and Student Affairs
Programs in:
accounting (MS)
art (MA)
business administration (MBA)
computer education (MS)
early intervention in deaf education (MA)
education (MA)
family and consumer sciences (MA)
fine arts (MFA)
options in business administration (MBA)
options in management (MM)
speech-language pathology (MS)
taxation (MST)
theater education (MA)

■ LINCOLN UNIVERSITY
Jefferson City, MO 65102
http://www.lincolnu.edu/

State-supported, coed, comprehensive institution. *Enrollment:* 3,224 graduate, professional, and undergraduate students; 68 full-time matriculated graduate/professional students (50 women), 102 part-time matriculated graduate/professional students (75 women). *Graduate faculty:* 1 (woman) full-time, 28 part-time/adjunct (10 women). *Computer facilities:* Computer purchase and lease plans are available. 141 computers available on campus for general student use. A campuswide network can be accessed. Internet access and online class registration are available. *Library facilities:* Inman Page Library. *Graduate expenses:* Tuition, state resident: part-time $189 per credit hour. Tuition, nonresident: part-time $351 per credit hour. Required fees: $15 per credit hour. $20 per semester. *General application contact:* Dr. Linda S. Bickel, Dean of the School of Graduate Studies and Continuing Education, 573-681-5247.

School of Graduate Studies and Continuing Education
Dr. Linda S. Bickel, Dean of the School of Graduate Studies and Continuing Education

College of Business and Professional Studies
Dr. Felix M. Edoho, Dean
Programs in:
business administration (MBA)
business and professional studies (MBA)

College of Liberal Arts, Education and Journalism
Dr. Patrick Henry, Dean
Programs in:
educational leadership (Ed S)
guidance and counseling (M Ed)
history (MA)
liberal arts, education and journalism (M Ed, MA, Ed S)
school administration and supervision (M Ed)
school teaching (M Ed)
social science (MA)
sociology (MA)
sociology/criminal justice (MA)

■ LINDENWOOD UNIVERSITY
St. Charles, MO 63301-1695
http://www.lindenwood.edu/

Independent-religious, coed, comprehensive institution. *Enrollment:* 9,525 graduate, professional, and undergraduate students; 1,374 full-time matriculated graduate/ professional students (895 women), 2,083 part-time matriculated graduate/professional students (1,572 women). *Graduate faculty:* 67 full-time (23 women), 48 part-time/ adjunct (22 women). *Computer facilities:* Computer purchase and lease plans are available. 160 computers available on campus for general student use. A campuswide network can be accessed from student residence rooms and from off campus. Internet access, WEBCT are available. *Library facilities:* Butler Library. *Graduate expenses:* Tuition: part-time $340 per credit hour. Tuition and fees vary according to course level, course load, degree level and program. *General application contact:* Brett Barger, Dean, Adult, Corporate and Graduate Admissions, 636-949-4934.

Graduate Programs
Dr. John Weitzel, Vice President of Academic Affairs
Programs in:
administration (MSA)
business administration (MBA)
communications (MA)
criminal justice and administration (MS)
gerontology (MA)
health management (MS)
human resource management (MS)
management (MSA)
marketing (MSA)
writing (MFA)

Division of Education
Dr. John Dougherty, Dean of Education
Programs in:
education (MA)
educational administration (MA, Ed D, Ed S)
instructional leadership (Ed D, Ed S)
library media (MA)
professional and school counseling (MA)
professional counseling (MA)
school counseling (MA)
teaching (MA)

Division of Fine and Performing Arts
Marsha Parker, Dean of Fine Arts
Programs in:
arts management (MA)
communication arts (MA)
studio art (MFA)
theatre arts (MA, MFA)
theatre arts management (MFA)

Division of Management
Ed Morris, Dean
Programs in:
accounting (MBA, MS)

Lindenwood University (continued)

business administration (MBA)
entrepreneurial studies (MBA)
finance (MBA, MS)
human resource management (MBA)
human resources (MS)
international business (MBA, MS)
management (MBA, MS)
management information systems (MBA, MS)
managing business to business (MA)
managing human resources (MA)
managing international business (MA)
managing investment management (MA)
managing leadership (MA)
managing marketing (MA)
managing organizational behavior (MA)
managing sales (MA)
managing, training and development (MA)
marketing (MBA, MS)
nonprofit administration (MA)
public management (MBA, MS)
sport management (MA)

■ MARYVILLE UNIVERSITY OF SAINT LOUIS

St. Louis, MO 63141-7299

http://www.maryville.edu/

Independent, coed, comprehensive institution. *Enrollment:* 3,333 graduate, professional, and undergraduate students; 140 full-time matriculated graduate/professional students (108 women), 445 part-time matriculated graduate/professional students (329 women). *Graduate faculty:* 84 full-time (55 women), 36 part-time/adjunct (23 women). *Computer facilities:* 401 computers available on campus for general student use. A campuswide network can be accessed from student residence rooms and from off campus. Internet access, e-mail, specialized software, university catalog, schedules, wireless internet in some areas are available. *Library facilities:* Maryville University Library. *Graduate expenses:* Tuition: full-time $17,800; part-time $555 per credit. Required fees: $55 per semester. Tuition and fees vary according to degree level and program. *General application contact:* Kelli Anderson, Research Analyst, 314-529-9324.

The John E. Simon School of Business

Dr. Pamela Horwitz, Dean
Programs in:
accounting (MBA, PGC)
business studies (PGC)
e-business (MBA, PGC)
management (MBA, PGC)
marketing (MBA, PGC)

School of Education

Dr. Sam Hausfather, Dean
Programs in:
art education (MA Ed)
early childhood education (MA Ed)
education (Ed D)
elementary education (MA Ed)
elementary education/English (MA Ed)
environmental education (MA Ed)
gifted education (MA Ed)
middle grades education (MA Ed)
reading specialist (MA Ed)
secondary education (MA Ed)

School of Health Professions

Charles Gulas, Dean
Programs in:
health professions (MARC, MMT, MOT, MSN, DPT)
music therapy (MMT)
nursing (MSN)
occupational therapy (MOT)
physical therapy (DPT)
rehabilitation counseling (MARC)

■ MISSOURI BAPTIST UNIVERSITY

St. Louis, MO 63141-8660

http://www.mobap.edu/

Independent-religious, coed, comprehensive institution. *Computer facilities:* 122 computers available on campus for general student use. A campuswide network can be accessed from student residence rooms and from off campus. Internet access is available. *Library facilities:* Jung-Kellogg Library.

■ MISSOURI STATE UNIVERSITY

Springfield, MO 65804-0094

http://www.missouristate.edu/

State-supported, coed, comprehensive institution. CGS member. *Enrollment:* 19,218 graduate, professional, and undergraduate students; 1,136 full-time matriculated graduate/professional students (683 women), 1,159 part-time matriculated graduate/professional students (708 women). *Graduate faculty:* 404 full-time (139 women), 98 part-time/adjunct (23 women). *Computer facilities:* Computer purchase and lease plans are available. 1,800 computers available on campus for general student use. A campuswide network can be accessed from student residence rooms and from off campus. Internet access and online class registration are available. *Library facilities:* Meyer Library plus 3 others. *Graduate expenses:* Tuition, state resident: full-time $3,582; part-time $199 per credit hour. Tuition, nonresident: full-time $6,984; part-time $199 per credit hour. Required fees: $548. Full-time tuition and fees vary according to course level, course load, program and reciprocity agreements. *General application contact:* Tobin Bushman, Coordinator of Admissions and Recruitment, 417-836-5331.

Find University Details at www.petersons.com/gradchannel.

Graduate College

Frank A. Einhellig, Associate Provost
Programs in:
applied communication (MSAS)
criminal justice (MSAS)
environmental management (MSAS)
project management (MSAS)
sports management (MSAS)

College of Arts and Letters

Dean
Programs in:
arts and letters (MA, MM, MS Ed)
communication and mass media (MA)
English and writing (MA)
music (MM)
secondary education (MS Ed)
theatre (MA)

College of Business Administration

Dr. Ronald Bottin, Dean
Programs in:
accountancy (M Acc)
business administration (M Acc, MBA, MHA, MS, MS Ed)
computer information systems (MS)
health administration (MHA)
secondary education (MS Ed)

College of Education

Dr. David L. Hough, Dean
Programs in:
counseling (MS)
director of special education (Ed S)
early childhood and family development (MS)
education (MAT, MS, MS Ed, Ed S)
educational administration (MS Ed, Ed S)
elementary education (MS Ed)
elementary principal (Ed S)
instructional media technology (MS Ed)
reading education (MS Ed)
secondary education (MS Ed)
secondary principal (Ed S)
special education (MS Ed)
superintendent (Ed S)
teacher education (MAT, MS Ed)
teaching (MAT)

College of Health and Human Services

Dr. Helen Reid, Acting Dean
Programs in:
audiology (Au D)
cell and molecular biology (MS)
communication sciences and disorders (MS)
health and human services (MPH, MPT, MS, MS Ed, MSN, MSW, Au D)
health promotion and wellness management (MS)
nurse anesthesia (MS)
nursing (MSN)
physical therapy (MPT)
physician assistant studies (MS)
psychology (MS)
public health (MPH)
secondary education (MS Ed)
social work (MSW)

College of Humanities and Public Affairs
Dr. Lorene H. Stone, Dean
Programs in:
- defense and strategic studies (MS)
- history (MA)
- humanities and public affairs (MA, MIAA, MPA, MS, MS Ed)
- international affairs and administration (MIAA)
- public administration (MPA)
- religious studies (MA)
- secondary education (MS Ed)

College of Natural and Applied Sciences
Dr. Tamera Jahnke, Dean
Programs in:
- agriculture (MNAS)
- biology (MNAS, MS)
- chemistry (MNAS, MS)
- computer science (MNAS)
- consumer sciences (MNAS)
- fruit science (MNAS)
- geography, geology and planning (MNAS)
- geospatial sciences (MS)
- materials science (MS)
- mathematics (MS)
- natural and applied sciences (MNAS, MS, MS Ed)
- physics, astronomy, and materials science (MNAS)
- plant science (MS)
- secondary education (MS Ed)

■ MISSOURI UNIVERSITY OF SCIENCE AND TECHNOLOGY
Rolla, MO 65409-0910
http://www.mst.edu/

State-supported, coed, university. *Enrollment:* 5,858 graduate, professional, and undergraduate students; 847 full-time matriculated graduate/professional students (186 women), 373 part-time matriculated graduate/professional students (74 women). *Graduate faculty:* 238 full-time (13 women), 4 part-time/adjunct (0 women). *Computer facilities:* 800 computers available on campus for general student use. A campuswide network can be accessed from student residence rooms and from off campus. Internet access and online class registration are available. *Library facilities:* Curtis Laws Wilson Library. *General application contact:* Debbie Schwertz, Admissions Coordinator, 573-341-6013.

Graduate School
Dr. Warren K., Wray, Provost and Executive Vice Chancellor
Programs in:
- applied and environmental biology (MS)
- applied mathematics (MS)
- chemistry (MS, PhD)
- computer science (MS, PhD)
- information science and technology (MS)
- mathematics (MST, PhD)
- mathematics education (MST)
- physics (MS, PhD)
- statistics (PhD)

School of Engineering
Dr. O. Robert Mitchell, Dean
Programs in:
- aerospace engineering (MS, PhD)
- ceramic engineering (MS, DE, PhD)
- chemical engineering (MS, DE, PhD)
- civil engineering (MS, DE, PhD)
- computer engineering (MS, DE, PhD)
- construction engineering (MS, DE, PhD)
- electrical engineering (MS, DE, PhD)
- engineering (M Eng, MS, DE, PhD)
- engineering management (MS, DE, PhD)
- environmental engineering (MS)
- fluid mechanics (MS, DE, PhD)
- geochemistry (MS, PhD)
- geological engineering (MS, DE, PhD)
- geology (MS, PhD)
- geology and geophysics (MS, PhD)
- geophysics (MS, PhD)
- geotechnical engineering (MS, DE, PhD)
- groundwater and environmental geology (MS, PhD)
- hydrology and hydraulic engineering (MS, DE, PhD)
- manufacturing engineering (M Eng, MS)
- mechanical engineering (MS, DE, PhD)
- metallurgical engineering (MS, PhD)
- mining engineering (MS, DE, PhD)
- nuclear engineering (MS, DE, PhD)
- petroleum engineering (MS, DE, PhD)
- systems engineering (MS, PhD)

■ NORTHWEST MISSOURI STATE UNIVERSITY
Maryville, MO 64468-6001
http://www.nwmissouri.edu/

State-supported, coed, comprehensive institution. *Enrollment:* 6,220 graduate, professional, and undergraduate students; 255 full-time matriculated graduate/professional students (110 women), 431 part-time matriculated graduate/professional students (270 women). *Graduate faculty:* 134 full-time (47 women). *Computer facilities:* 2,450 computers available on campus for general student use. A campuswide network can be accessed from student residence rooms and from off campus. Internet access is available. *Library facilities:* B. D. Owens Library plus 1 other. *General application contact:* Dr. Frances Shipley, Dean of Graduate School, 660-562-1145.

Graduate School
Dr. Frances Shipley, Dean of Graduate School

College of Arts and Sciences
Dr. Charles McAdams, Dean
Programs in:
- arts and sciences (MA, MS, MS Ed)
- biology (MS)
- English (MA)
- English with speech emphasis (MA)
- geographic information sciences (MS)
- history (MA)
- teaching English with speech emphasis (MS Ed)
- teaching history (MS Ed)
- teaching mathematics (MS Ed)
- teaching music (MS Ed)

College of Education and Human Services
Dr. Max Ruhl, Dean
Programs in:
- education and human services (MS, MS Ed, Ed S)
- educational leadership (MS Ed, Ed S)
- educational leadership: elementary (MS Ed)
- educational leadership: secondary (MS Ed)
- elementary principalship (Ed S)
- guidance and counseling (MS Ed)
- health and physical education (MS Ed)
- reading (MS Ed)
- recreation (MS)
- secondary individualized prescribed programs (MS Ed)
- secondary principalship (Ed S)
- special education (MS Ed)
- superintendency (Ed S)
- teaching secondary (MS Ed)
- teaching: early childhood (MS Ed)
- teaching: elementary self contained (MS Ed)
- teaching: middle school (MS Ed)
- teaching: science (MS Ed)
- teaching: secondary (MS Ed)

Melvin and Valorie Booth College of Business and Professional Studies
Dr. Thomas Billesbach, Dean
Programs in:
- accounting (MBA)
- agricultural economics (MBA)
- agriculture (MS)
- applied computer science (MS)
- business administration (MBA)
- business and professional studies (MBA, MS, MS Ed)
- health management (MBA)
- management information systems (MBA)
- school computer studies (MS)
- teaching agriculture (MS Ed)
- teaching instructional technology (MS Ed)

■ PARK UNIVERSITY
Parkville, MO 64152-3795
http://www.park.edu/

Independent, coed, comprehensive institution. *Computer facilities:* 143 computers available on campus for general student use.

Park University (continued)
A campuswide network can be accessed from student residence rooms. Internet access and online class registration are available. *Library facilities:* McAfee Memorial Library. *General application contact:* Recruiter, 816-842-6182 Ext. 5530.

College of Graduate and Professional Studies

Programs in:
- adult education (M Ed)
- at-risk students (M Ed)
- disaster and emergency management (MPA)
- educational administration (M Ed)
- entrepreneurship (MBA)
- general business (MBA)
- general education (M Ed)
- government/business relations (MPA)
- healthcare/services management (MBA, MPA)
- international business (MBA)
- K-12 certification (MAT)
- management information systems (MBA)
- management of information systems (MPA)
- middle school certification (MAT)
- multi-cultural education (M Ed)
- nonprofit management (MPA)
- public management (MPA)
- school law (M Ed)
- secondary school certification (MAT)
- special education (M Ed)

■ ROCKHURST UNIVERSITY

Kansas City, MO 64110-2561
http://www.rockhurst.edu/

Independent-religious, coed, comprehensive institution. CGS member. *Enrollment:* 3,066 graduate, professional, and undergraduate students; 347 full-time matriculated graduate/professional students (221 women), 497 part-time matriculated graduate/professional students (259 women). *Graduate faculty:* 59 full-time (31 women), 23 part-time/adjunct (9 women). *Computer facilities:* 500 computers available on campus for general student use. A campuswide network can be accessed from student residence rooms and from off campus. Internet access is available. *Library facilities:* Greenlease Library. *Graduate expenses:* Tuition: full-time $9,810; part-time $6,540 per year. Required fees: $400 per term. *General application contact:* Director of Graduate Recruitment, 816-501-4100.

Helzberg School of Management

Dr. James Daley, Dean
Program in:
- management (MBA)

School of Graduate and Professional Studies

Dr. Robin Bowen, Dean
Programs in:
- arts and sciences (M Ed, MOT, MS, DPT)
- communication sciences and disorders (MS)
- education (M Ed)
- occupational therapy (MOT)
- physical therapy (DPT)

■ SAINT LOUIS UNIVERSITY

St. Louis, MO 63103-2097
http://www.slu.edu

Independent-religious, coed, university. CGS member. *Enrollment:* 12,034 graduate, professional, and undergraduate students; 2,937 full-time matriculated graduate/professional students (1,615 women). *Graduate faculty:* 1,051 full-time (382 women), 477 part-time/adjunct (223 women). *Computer facilities:* Computer purchase and lease plans are available. 1,350 computers available on campus for general student use. A campuswide network can be accessed from student residence rooms and from off campus. Internet access and online class registration are available. *Library facilities:* Pius XII Memorial Library plus 2 others. *Graduate expenses:* Tuition: part-time $800 per credit hour. Required fees: $105 per semester. *General application contact:* Gary Behrman, Associate Dean of the Graduate School, 314-977-3827.

Find University Details at www.petersons.com/gradchannel.

Graduate School

Dr. Donald G. Brennan, Interim Dean
Programs in:
- biochemistry and molecular biology (PhD)
- biomedical sciences (PhD)
- molecular microbiology and immunology (PhD)
- pathology (PhD)
- pharmacological and physiological science (PhD)

Center for Advanced Dental Education

Dr. Rolf Behrents, Executive Director
Program in:
- dentistry (MS)

Center for Health Care Ethics

Rev. Gerard Magill, PhD, Executive Director
Programs in:
- clinical health care ethics (Certificate)
- health care ethics (PhD)

College of Arts and Sciences

Dr. Donald G. Brennan, Interim Dean
Programs in:
- administration of justice (MA)
- American studies (MA, PhD)
- arts and sciences (M Pr Met, MA, MA-R, MS, MS-R, PhD)
- biology (MS, MS-R, PhD)
- chemistry (MS, MS-R)
- clinical psychology (MS-R, PhD)
- communication (MA, MA-R)
- English (MA, MA-R, PhD)
- experimental psychology (MS-R, PhD)
- French (MA)
- geophysics (PhD)
- geoscience (MS)
- historical theology (MA, PhD)
- history (MA, PhD)
- industrial-organizational psychology (PhD)
- mathematics (MA, MA-R, PhD)
- meteorology (M Pr Met, MS-R, PhD)
- philosophy (MA, PhD)
- psychology (PhD)
- Spanish (MA)
- theology (MA)

College of Public Service

Marla Berg-Weger, Interim Dean
Programs in:
- Catholic school leadership (MA)
- communication sciences and disorders (MA, MA-R)
- counseling and family therapy (PhD)
- curriculum and instruction (MA, Ed D, PhD)
- educational administration (MA, Ed D, PhD, Ed S)
- educational foundations (MA, Ed D, PhD)
- geographic information systems (Certificate)
- higher education (MA, Ed D, PhD)
- human development counseling (MA)
- marriage and family therapy (Certificate)
- organizational development (Certificate)
- public administration (MAPA)
- public policy analysis (PhD)
- public service (MA, MA-R, MAPA, MAT, MAUA, MSW, MUPRED, Ed D, PhD, Certificate, Ed S)
- school counseling (MA, MA-R)
- social work (MSW)
- special education (MA)
- student personnel administration (MA)
- teaching (MAT)
- urban affairs (MAUA)
- urban planning and real estate development (MUPRED)

Doisy College of Health Sciences

Dr. Charlotte Royeen, Dean
Programs in:
- health sciences (MMS, MOT, MS, MSN, MSN-R, MSPT, DPT, PhD, Certificate)
- nursing (MSN, MSN-R, PhD, Certificate)
- nutrition and dietetics (MS)
- occupational science and occupational therapy (MOT)
- physical therapy (MSPT, DPT)
- physician assistant (MMS)

John Cook School of Business

Dr. Ellen Harshman, Dean

Programs in:
accounting (M Acct, MBA)
business (EMIB, M Acct, MBA, MSF, PhD)
business administration (PhD)
executive international business (EMIB)
finance (MBA, MSF)
international business (MBA)

Parks College of Engineering, Aviation, and Technology
Dr. Neil E Seitz, Interim Dean
Programs in:
biomedical engineering (MS, MS-R, PhD)
engineering, aviation, and technology (MS, MS-R, PhD)

School of Medicine
Dr. Patricia L. Monteleone, Dean
Programs in:
anatomy (MS-R, PhD)
medicine (MD, MS-R, PhD)

School of Public Health
Dr. Connie J. Evashwick, Dean
Programs in:
biosecurity (Certificate)
community health (MPH)
health administration (MHA)
health management and policy (MHA, PhD)
public health (PhD)
public health studies (PhD)

School of Law
Dr. Jeffrey E. Lewis, Dean
Program in:
law (JD, LL M)

■ SOUTHEAST MISSOURI STATE UNIVERSITY
Cape Girardeau, MO 63701-4799
http://www.semo.edu/

State-supported, coed, comprehensive institution. CGS member. *Enrollment:* 10,477 graduate, professional, and undergraduate students; 231 full-time matriculated graduate/professional students (163 women), 1,269 part-time matriculated graduate/professional students (1,033 women). *Graduate faculty:* 215 full-time (85 women). *Computer facilities:* 1,022 computers available on campus for general student use. A campuswide network can be accessed from student residence rooms and from off campus. Internet access and online class registration are available. *Library facilities:* Kent Library. *General application contact:* Dr. Fred Janzow, Dean of the School of Graduate Studies, 573-651-2192.

School of Graduate Studies
Dr. Fred Janzow, Dean
Programs in:
biology (MNS)
chemistry (MNS)
communication disorders (MA)
community counseling (MA)
community wellness and leisure services (MPA)
counseling education (Ed S)
criminal justice (MS)
educational administration (MA, Ed S)
educational studies (MA)
elementary education (MA)
English (MA)
exceptional child education (MA)
guidance and counseling (MA, Ed S)
higher education (MA)
history (MA)
home economics (MA)
human environmental studies (MA)
mathematics (MNS)
middle level education (MA)
music education (MME)
nursing (MSN)
nutrition and exercise science (MS)
political science, philosophy and religion (MPA)
school counseling (MA)
teaching English to speakers of other languages (MA)

Godwin Center for Science and Mathematics Education
Dr. Sharon Coleman, Director
Program in:
science education (MNS)

Harrison College of Business
Dr. Kenneth Heischmidt, Director MBA Program
Programs in:
accounting (MBA)
environmental management (MBA)
finance (MBA)
general management (MBA)
health administration (MBA)
industrial management (MBA)
international business (MBA)

School of Polytechnic Studies
Dr. Randall Shaw, Dean
Program in:
industrial management (MS)

■ SOUTHWEST BAPTIST UNIVERSITY
Bolivar, MO 65613-2597
http://www.sbuniv.edu/

Independent-religious, coed, comprehensive institution. *Computer facilities:* 261 computers available on campus for general student use. A campuswide network can be accessed from student residence rooms and from off campus. Internet access is available. *Library facilities:* Harriett K. Hutchens Library plus 3 others. *General application contact:* Provost, 417-328-1601.

Graduate Studies
Programs in:
business administration (MBA)
education (MS)
educational administration (MS, Ed S)
health administration (MBA)
physical therapy (DPT)

■ TRUMAN STATE UNIVERSITY
Kirksville, MO 63501-4221
http://www.truman.edu/

State-supported, coed, comprehensive institution. CGS member. *Computer facilities:* Computer purchase and lease plans are available. 900 computers available on campus for general student use. A campuswide network can be accessed from student residence rooms and from off campus. Internet access and online class registration are available. *Library facilities:* Pickler Memorial Library. *General application contact:* Graduate Office Secretary, 660-785-4109.

Find University Details at www.petersons.com/gradchannel.

Graduate School

Division of Business and Accountancy
Programs in:
accountancy (M Ac)
accounting (M Ac)

Division of Education
Program in:
education (MAE)

Division of Fine Arts
Program in:
music (MA)

Division of Human Potential and Performance
Program in:
communication disorders (MA)

Division of Language and Literature
Program in:
English (MA)

Division of Science
Program in:
biology (MS)

■ UNIVERSITY OF CENTRAL MISSOURI
Warrensburg, MO 64093
http://www.ucmo.edu/

State-supported, coed, comprehensive institution. CGS member. *Enrollment:* 10,711 graduate, professional, and undergraduate students; 425 full-time matriculated graduate/professional students (237 women), 1,329 part-time matriculated graduate/professional students (888 women). *Graduate faculty:* 404 full-time (169 women). *Computer facilities:* 1,220 computers available on campus for general student

University of Central Missouri (continued)

use. A campuswide network can be accessed from student residence rooms and from off campus. Internet access and online class registration are available. *Library facilities:* James C. Kirkpatrick Library. *Graduate expenses:* Tuition, state resident: full-time $5,448; part-time $227 per credit hour. Tuition, nonresident: full-time $10,896; part-time $454 per credit hour. Required fees: $336; $14 per credit hour. *General application contact:* Dr. Novella Perrin, Associate Provost for Research/Dean of the Graduate School, 660-543-4092.

Find University Details at www.petersons.com/gradchannel.

The Graduate School

Dr. Novella Perrin, Assistant Provost for Research/Dean of the Graduate School
Programs in:
- college student personnel administration (MS)
- counseling (MS)
- counselor education (MS)
- curriculum and instruction (Ed S)
- education (MS, MSE, Ed D, Ed S)
- educational leadership (Ed D)
- educational technology (MSE)
- elementary education (MSE)
- human service/guidance counseling (Ed S)
- human services/ technology and occupational education (Ed S)
- human services/learning resources (Ed S)
- K–12 education (MSE)
- library science and information services (MS, Ed S)
- literacy education (MSE)
- school administration (MSE, Ed S)
- secondary education (MSE)
- secondary education/business and office education (MSE)
- special education (MSE, Ed S)
- special education/human services (Ed S)
- technology and occupational education (MS)

College of Arts, Humanities and Social Sciences
Dr. Steven Boone, Interim Dean
Programs in:
- applied mathematics (MS)
- arts, humanities and social sciences (MA, MS)
- biology (MS)
- communication (MA)
- English (MA)
- history (MA)
- mathematics (MS)
- music (MA)
- speech communication (MA)
- teaching English as a second language (MA)
- theatre (MA)

College of Health and Human Services
Dr. Rick Sluder, Interim Dean
Programs in:
- criminal justice (MS)
- fire science (MS)
- health and human services (MA, MS, Ed S)
- human services/public services (Ed S)
- industrial hygiene (MS)
- industrial safety management (MS)
- loss control (MS)
- occupational safety management (MS)
- physical education/exercise and sports science (MS)
- psychology (MS)
- public safety (MS)
- rural family nursing (MS)
- security (MS)
- social gerontology (MS)
- sociology (MA)
- speech pathology and audiology (MS)
- transportation safety (MS)

College of Science and Technology
Dr. Alice Greife, Dean
Programs in:
- aviation safety (MS)
- industrial management (MS)
- science and technology (MS)

Harmon College of Business Administration
Dr. George Wilson, Dean
Programs in:
- accounting (MA)
- business administration (MBA)
- information technology (MS)

■ UNIVERSITY OF MISSOURI–COLUMBIA
Columbia, MO 65211
http://www.missouri.edu/

State-supported, coed, university. CGS member. *Enrollment:* 28,253 graduate, professional, and undergraduate students; 3,885 full-time matriculated graduate/professional students (2,134 women), 2,817 part-time matriculated graduate/professional students (1,749 women). *Graduate faculty:* 1,678 full-time (520 women), 70 part-time/adjunct (32 women). *Computer facilities:* Computer purchase and lease plans are available. 1,615 computers available on campus for general student use. A campuswide network can be accessed from student residence rooms and from off campus. Internet access and online class registration, telephone registration are available. *Library facilities:* Ellis Library plus 11 others. *General application contact:* Norma J. Jackson, Coordinator of Graduate Student Affairs, 573-882-3292.

College of Veterinary Medicine

Dr. Joe Kornegay, Dean
Programs in:
- laboratory animal medicine (MS)
- pathobiology (MS, PhD)
- veterinary biomedical sciences (MS)
- veterinary clinical sciences (MS)
- veterinary medicine (DVM)
- veterinary medicine and surgery (MS)
- veterinary pathobiology (MS, PhD)

Graduate School

Dr. Pamela Benoit, Vice-Provost for Advanced Studies and Dean of the Graduate School
Programs in:
- dispute resolution (LL M)
- genetics (PhD)
- health administration (MHA)
- health informatics (MHA)
- health services management (MHA)

College of Agriculture, Food and Natural Resources
Dr. Thomas T. Payne, Dean
Programs in:
- agricultural economics (MS, PhD)
- agricultural education (MS, PhD)
- agriculture, food and natural resources (MS, PhD)
- animal sciences (MS, PhD)
- entomology (MS, PhD)
- food science (MS, PhD)
- foods and food systems management (MS)
- horticulture (MS, PhD)
- human nutrition (MS)
- nutrition (MS, PhD)
- plant pathology and microbiology (MS, PhD)
- plant sciences (MS, PhD)
- rural sociology (MS, PhD)

College of Arts and Sciences
Dr. Richard Schwartz, Dean
Programs in:
- analytical chemistry (MS, PhD)
- anthropology (MA, PhD)
- applied mathematics (MS)
- art (MFA)
- art history and archaeology (MA, PhD)
- arts and sciences (MA, MFA, MM, MS, MST, PhD)
- classical studies (MA, PhD)
- communication (MA, PhD)
- economics (MA, PhD)
- English (MA, PhD)
- evolutionary biology and ecology (MA, PhD)
- French (MA, PhD)
- genetic, cellular and developmental biology (MA, PhD)
- geography (MA)
- geological sciences (MS, PhD)
- German (MA)
- history (MA, PhD)
- inorganic chemistry (MS, PhD)
- literature (MA)
- mathematics (MA, MST, PhD)
- music (MA, MM)
- neurobiology and behavior (MA, PhD)
- organic chemistry (MS, PhD)
- philosophy (MA, PhD)
- physical chemistry (MS, PhD)
- physics and astronomy (MS, PhD)

political science (MA, PhD)
psychological sciences (MA, MS, PhD)
religious studies (MA)
sociology (MA, PhD)
Spanish (MA, PhD)
statistics (MA, PhD)
teaching (MA)
theatre (MA, PhD)

College of Business
Dr. Bruce Walker, Dean
Programs in:
accountancy (M Acc, PhD)
business (M Acc, MBA, PhD)

College of Education
Dr. Carolyn D. Herrington, Dean
Programs in:
administration and supervision of special education (PhD)
agricultural education (M Ed, PhD, Ed S)
art education (M Ed, PhD, Ed S)
behavior disorders (M Ed, PhD)
business and office education (M Ed, PhD, Ed S)
counseling psychology (M Ed, MA, PhD, Ed S)
curriculum development of exceptional students (M Ed, PhD)
early childhood education (M Ed, PhD, Ed S)
early childhood special education (M Ed, PhD)
education (M Ed, MA, Ed D, PhD, Ed S)
education administration (M Ed, MA, Ed D, PhD, Ed S)
educational psychology (M Ed, MA, PhD, Ed S)
educational technology (M Ed, Ed S)
elementary education (M Ed, PhD, Ed S)
English education (M Ed, PhD, Ed S)
foreign language education (M Ed, PhD, Ed S)
general special education (M Ed, MA, PhD)
health education and promotion (M Ed, PhD)
higher and adult education (M Ed, MA, Ed D, PhD, Ed S)
information science and learning technology (PhD)
learning and instruction (M Ed)
learning disabilities (M Ed, PhD)
library science (MA)
marketing education (M Ed, PhD, Ed S)
mathematics education (M Ed, PhD, Ed S)
mental retardation (M Ed, PhD)
music education (M Ed, PhD, Ed S)
reading education (M Ed, PhD, Ed S)
school psychology (M Ed, MA, PhD, Ed S)
science education (M Ed, PhD, Ed S)
social studies education (M Ed, PhD, Ed S)
vocational education (M Ed, PhD, Ed S)

College of Engineering
Dr. James Thompson, Dean
Programs in:
agricultural engineering (MS)
biological engineering (MS, PhD)
chemical engineering (MS, PhD)
civil engineering (MS, PhD)
computer science (MS, PhD)
electrical and computer engineering (MS, PhD)
engineering (MS, PhD)
environmental engineering (MS, PhD)
geotechnical engineering (MS, PhD)
industrial and manufacturing systems engineering (MS, PhD)
mechanical and aerospace engineering (MS, PhD)
nuclear power engineering (MS, PhD)
structural engineering (MS, PhD)
transportation and highway engineering (MS)
water resources (MS, PhD)

College of Human Environmental Science
Dr. Stephen R. Jorgensen, Dean
Programs in:
design with digital media (MA, MS)
environmental design (MS)
exercise physiology (MA, PhD)
human development and family studies (MA, MS, PhD)
human environmental science (MA, MS, PhD)
nutritional sciences (MS, PhD)
personal financial planning (MS)
textile and apparel management (MA, MS)

Harry S Truman School of Public Affairs
Guy B. Adams, Director of Graduate Studies
Program in:
public affairs (MPA)

School of Journalism
Dr. Esther Thorson, Associate Dean
Program in:
journalism (MA, PhD)

School of Natural Resources
Dr. Harold Gene Garrett, Director
Programs in:
atmospheric science (MS, PhD)
fisheries and wildlife (MS, PhD)
forestry (MS, PhD)
natural resources (MS, PhD)
parks, recreation and tourism (MS)
soil science (MS, PhD)

School of Social Work
Dr. Colleen Galambos, Director of Graduate Studies
Program in:
social work (MSW)

Sinclair School of Nursing
Dr. Roxanne W. McDaniel, Director of Graduate Studies
Program in:
nursing (MS, PhD)

School of Health Professions
Dr. Richard E. Oliver, Dean
Programs in:
communication science and disorders (MHS)
diagnostic medical ultrasound (MHS)
health professions (MHS, MOT, MPT)
occupational therapy (MOT)
physical therapy (MPT)

School of Law
Dr. R. Lawrence Dessem, Dean
Program in:
law (JD, LL M)

School of Medicine
Dr. William M. Crist, Dean
Program in:
medicine (MD, MPH, MS, PhD)

Graduate Programs in Medicine
Programs in:
biochemistry (MS, PhD)
medicine (MPH, MS, PhD)
molecular microbiology and immunology (MS, PhD)
pharmacology (MS, PhD)
physiology (MS, PhD)
public health (MPH)

■ UNIVERSITY OF MISSOURI–KANSAS CITY
Kansas City, MO 64110-2499
http://www.umkc.edu/

State-supported, coed, university. CGS member. *Enrollment:* 14,213 graduate, professional, and undergraduate students; 2,616 full-time matriculated graduate/professional students (1,395 women), 1,979 part-time matriculated graduate/professional students (1,185 women). *Graduate faculty:* 662 full-time (276 women), 439 part-time/adjunct (227 women). *Computer facilities:* Computer purchase and lease plans are available. 671 computers available on campus for general student use. A campuswide network can be accessed from student residence rooms and from off campus. Internet access and online class registration are available. *Library facilities:* Miller-Nichols Library plus 3 others. *Graduate expenses:* Tuition, state resident: full-time $4,975; part-time $276 per credit. Tuition, nonresident: full-time $12,847; part-time $713 per credit. Required fees: $595; $595 per year. *General application contact:* Jennifer DeHaemeas, Director of Admissions, 816-235-1111.

College of Arts and Sciences
Dr. Karen Vorst, Dean
Programs in:
acting (MFA)
analytical chemistry (MS, PhD)
art history (MA, PhD)
arts and sciences (MA, MFA, MS, MSW, PhD)
criminal justice and criminology (MS)
design technology (MFA)

University of Missouri–Kansas City (continued)

economics (MA, PhD)
English (MA, PhD)
environmental and urban geosciences (MS)
geosciences (PhD)
history (MA, PhD)
inorganic chemistry (MS, PhD)
mathematics and statistics (MA, MS, PhD)
organic chemistry (MS, PhD)
physical chemistry (MS, PhD)
physics (MS, PhD)
political science (MA, PhD)
polymer chemistry (MS, PhD)
psychology (MA, PhD)
Romance languages and literatures (MA)
sociology (MA, PhD)
studio art (MA)
theatre (MA)

School of Social Work
Dr. Walter Boulden, Chair
Program in:
social work (MSW)

Conservatory of Music
Dr. Randall G. Pembrook, Dean
Programs in:
composition (MM, DMA)
conducting (MM, DMA)
music (MA)
music education (MME, PhD)
music history and literature (MM)
music theory (MM)
performance (MM, DMA)

Henry W. Bloch School of Business and Public Administration
Dr. O. Homer Erekson, Dean
Programs in:
accounting (MS)
business administration (MBA)
public affairs (MPA, PhD)

School of Biological Sciences
Dr. Lawrence A. Dreyfus, Dean
Programs in:
biology (MA)
cell biology and biophysics (PhD)
cellular and molecular biology (MS)
molecular biology and biochemistry (PhD)

School of Computing and Engineering
Dr. Khosrow Sohraby, Dean
Programs in:
civil engineering (MS)
computer and electrical engineering (PhD)
computer science (MS)
computer science and informatics (PhD)
computing (PhD)
electrical engineering (MS)
engineering (PhD)
mechanical engineering (MS)
telecommunications (PhD)

School of Dentistry
Dr. Michael Reed, Dean
Programs in:
advanced education in dentistry (Graduate Dental Certificate)
dental hygiene education (MS)
dental specialties (Graduate Dental Certificate)
dentistry (DDS)
diagnostic sciences (Graduate Dental Certificate)
oral and maxillofacial surgery (Graduate Dental Certificate)
oral biology (MS, PhD)
orthodontics and dentofacial orthopedics (Graduate Dental Certificate)
pediatric dentistry (Graduate Dental Certificate)
periodontics (Graduate Dental Certificate)
prosthodontics (Graduate Dental Certificate)

School of Education
Dr. Linda Edwards, Dean
Programs in:
administration (Ed D)
counseling and guidance (MA, Ed S)
counseling psychology (PhD)
curriculum and instruction (MA, Ed S)
education (PhD)
educational administration (Ed S)
reading education (MA, Ed S)
special education (MA)

School of Graduate Studies
Dr. Ronald MacQuarrie, Dean
Program in:
interdisciplinary studies (PhD)

School of Law
Ellen Y. Suni, Dean
Program in:
law (JD, LL M)

School of Medicine
Dr. Betty Drees, Dean
Program in:
medicine (MD)

School of Nursing
Dr. Lora Lacey-Haun, Dean
Programs in:
adult clinical nurse specialist (MSN)
family nurse practitioner (MSN)
neonatal nurse practitioner (MSN)
nurse educator (MSN)
nurse executive (MSN)
nursing (PhD)
pediatric nurse practitioner (MSN)

School of Pharmacy
Dr. Robert W. Piepho, Dean
Programs in:
pharmaceutical sciences (MS, PhD)
pharmacy (Pharm D)

■ UNIVERSITY OF MISSOURI–ST. LOUIS

St. Louis, MO 63121
http://www.umsl.edu/

State-supported, coed, university. CGS member. *Enrollment:* 15,540 graduate, professional, and undergraduate students; 694 full-time matriculated graduate/professional students (407 women), 2,093 part-time matriculated graduate/professional students (1,366 women). *Graduate faculty:* 347 full-time (139 women), 50 part-time/adjunct (15 women). *Computer facilities:* Computer purchase and lease plans are available. 1,000 computers available on campus for general student use. A campuswide network can be accessed from student residence rooms and from off campus. Internet access and online class registration are available. *Library facilities:* Thomas Jefferson Library plus 2 others. *Graduate expenses:* Tuition, state resident: part-time $332 per credit hour. Tuition, nonresident: part-time $770 per credit hour. *General application contact:* Graduate Admissions, 314-516-5458.

Find University Details at www.petersons.com/gradchannel.

College of Arts and Sciences
Dr. Mark Burkholder, Dean
Programs in:
advanced social perspective (MA)
American literature (MA)
American politics (MA)
applied mathematics (MA, PhD)
applied physics (MS)
arts and sciences (MA, MFA, MS, MSW, PhD, Certificate, Graduate Certificate)
astrophysics (MS)
behavioral neuroscience (PhD)
biology (MS, PhD)
biotechnology (Certificate)
chemistry (MS, PhD)
clinical psychology respecialization (Certificate)
community conflict intervention (MA)
community psychology (PhD)
comparative politics (MA)
computer science (MS, PhD)
creative writing (MFA)
criminology and criminal justice (MA, PhD)
English (MA)
English literature (MA)
general economics (MA)
general psychology (MA)
industrial/organizational psychology (PhD)
international politics (MA)
linguistics (MA)
managerial economics (Certificate)
mathematics (PhD)
museum studies (MA, Certificate)
philosophy (MA)

physics (PhD)
political process and behavior (MA)
political science (PhD)
program design and evaluation research (MA)
public administration and public policy (MA)
social policy planning and administration (MA)
teaching of writing (Graduate Certificate)
tropical biology and conservation (Certificate)
urban and regional politics (MA)

School of Social Work
Dr. Lois Pierce, Director
Program in:
social work (MSW)

College of Business Administration
Karl Kottemann, Assistant Director
Programs in:
accounting (MBA)
business administration (Certificate)
finance (MBA)
human resource management (Certificate)
information systems (MSMIS, PhD)
logistics and supply chain management (MBA, PhD, Certificate)
management (MBA)
marketing (MBA)
marketing management (Certificate)
operations (MBA)
quantitative management science (MBA)
telecommunications management (Certificate)

College of Education
Dr. Kathleen Haywood, Director of Graduate Studies
Program in:
education (M Ed, Ed D, PhD, Certificate, Ed S)

Division of Counseling
Dr. Mark Pope, Chair
Programs in:
community counseling (M Ed)
elementary school counseling (M Ed)
secondary school counseling (M Ed)

Division of Educational Leadership and Policy Studies
Dr. E. Paulette Savage, Chair
Programs in:
adult and higher education (M Ed, Ed D)
educational administration (M Ed, Ed D, Ed S)
educational leadership and policy studies (PhD)
institutional research (Certificate)

Division of Educational Psychology, Research, and Evaluation
Dr. Matthew Keefer, Chairperson
Programs in:
education (Ed D)
educational psychology (PhD)
school psychology (Certificate, Ed S)

Division of Teaching and Learning
Dr. Gayle Wilkinson, Chair
Programs in:
elementary education (M Ed)
secondary education (M Ed)
special education (M Ed)
teaching-learning processes (Ed D, PhD)

College of Fine Arts and Communication
Dr. John Hylton, Dean
Programs in:
communication (MA)
fine arts and communication (MA, MME)
music education (MME)

College of Nursing
Dean Juliann Sebastian, Dean
Programs in:
nurse practitioner (Certificate)
nursing (MSN, PhD)

College of Optometry
Dr. Larry J. Davis, Dean
Programs in:
optometry (OD, MS, PhD)
vision science (MS, PhD)

Graduate School
Dr. Judith Walker de Félix, Dean
Programs in:
gerontology (MS, Certificate)
health policy (MPPA)
local government management (MPPA)
long term care administration (Certificate)
managing human resources and organization (MPPA)
nonprofit organization management (MPPA)
nonprofit organization management and leadership (Certificate)
policy research and analysis (MPPA)
public sector human resources management (MPPA)

■ WASHINGTON UNIVERSITY IN ST. LOUIS
St. Louis, MO 63130-4899
http://www.wustl.edu/

Independent, coed, university. CGS member. *Computer facilities:* Computer purchase and lease plans are available. 2,500 computers available on campus for general student use. A campuswide network can be accessed from student residence rooms and from off campus. Internet access and online class registration, e-mail are available. *Library facilities:* John M. Olin Library plus 13 others. *General application contact:* Information Contact, 314-935-6880.

Find University Details at www.petersons.com/gradchannel.

George Warren Brown School of Social Work
Dr. Edward F Lawlor, Dean and William E. Gordon Professor
Program in:
social work (MSW, PhD)

Graduate School of Arts and Sciences
Programs in:
American history (MA, PhD)
anthropology (MA, PhD)
art history (MA, PhD)
arts and sciences (MA, MA Ed, MAT, MFAW, MM, PhD)
Asian history (MA, PhD)
Asian language (MA)
Asian studies (MA)
British history (MA, PhD)
chemistry (MA, PhD)
Chinese (MA, PhD)
Chinese and comparative literature (PhD)
classical archaeology (MA, PhD)
classics (MA, MAT)
clinical psychology (PhD)
comparative literature (MA, PhD)
earth and planetary sciences (MA)
East Asian studies (MA)
economics (MA, PhD)
educational research (PhD)
elementary education (MA Ed)
English and American literature (MA, PhD)
European history (MA, PhD)
French (MA, PhD)
general experimental psychology (MA, PhD)
geochemistry (PhD)
geology (MA, PhD)
geophysics (PhD)
Germanic languages and literature (MA, PhD)
history (PhD)
Islamic and Near Eastern studies (MA)
Japanese (MA, PhD)
Japanese and comparative literature (PhD)
Jewish studies (MA)
Jewish, Islamic, and Near Eastern studies (MA)
Latin American history (MA, PhD)
mathematics (MA, PhD)
mathematics education (MAT)
Middle Eastern history (MA, PhD)
movement science (PhD)
music (MA, MM, PhD)
performing arts (MA)
philosophy (MA, PhD)
philosophy/neuroscience/psychology (PhD)
physics (MA, PhD)
planetary sciences (PhD)
political economy and public policy (MA)
political science (MA, PhD)
Romance languages (MA, PhD)
secondary education (MA Ed, MAT)

Washington University in St. Louis (continued)
social psychology (MA, PhD)
social work (PhD)
Spanish (MA, PhD)
statistics (MA, PhD)
writing (MFAW)

Division of Biology and Biomedical Sciences
Programs in:
biochemistry (PhD)
chemical biology (PhD)
computational biology (PhD)
developmental biology (PhD)
ecology (PhD)
environmental biology (PhD)
evolution, ecology and population biology (PhD)
evolutionary biology (PhD)
genetics (PhD)
immunology (PhD)
molecular biophysics (PhD)
molecular cell biology (PhD)
molecular genetics (PhD)
molecular microbiology and microbial pathogenesis (PhD)
neurosciences (PhD)
plant biology (PhD)

Henry Edwin Sever Graduate School of Engineering and Applied Science
Programs in:
biomedical engineering (MS, D Sc)
chemical engineering (MS, D Sc)
civil engineering (MSCE)
computer engineering (MS, D Sc)
computer science (MS, D Sc)
construction management (MCM)
electrical engineering (MS, D Sc, PhD)
engineering and applied science (MCE, MCM, MEM, MIM, MS, MSCE, MSE, MSEE, MSEE, MTM, D Sc, PhD)
environmental engineering (MS, D Sc)
mechanical and aerospace engineering (MS, D Sc)
structural engineering (MSCE, MSE, D Sc, PhD)
systems science and mathematics (MS, D Sc, PhD)

John M. Olin School of Business
Programs in:
accounting (MS)
business (EMBA, M Acc, MBA, MS, PhD)
business administration (EMBA, MBA)
finance (MS)

Sam Fox School of Design and Visual Arts
Program in:
design and visual arts (M Arch, MFA, MUD)

Graduate School of Architecture and Urban Design
Bruce Lindsey, Dean
Programs in:
architecture (M Arch)
architecture and urban design (M Arch, MUD)
urban design (MUD)

Graduate School of Art
Jeff Pike, Dean
Program in:
art (MFA)

School of Law
Kent D Syvervd, Dean
Program in:
law (JD, LL M, MJS, JSD)

School of Medicine
Dr. William A. Peck, Dean
Programs in:
audiology (Au D)
clinical (MS)
clinical investigation (MS)
computational (MS)
deaf education (MS)
genetic epidemiology (Certificate)
health administration (MHA)
medicine (MD, MHA, MS, MSOT, Au D, DPT, OTD, PhD, Certificate, PPDPT)
movement science (PhD)
occupational therapy (MSOT, OTD)
physical therapy (DPT, PhD, PPDPT)
speech and hearing sciences (PhD)

■ WEBSTER UNIVERSITY
St. Louis, MO 63119-3194
http://www.webster.edu/

Independent, coed, comprehensive institution. *Enrollment:* 3,894 full-time matriculated graduate/professional students (2,291 women), 11,651 part-time matriculated graduate/professional students (6,775 women). *Graduate faculty:* 81 full-time (23 women), 1,689 part-time/adjunct (426 women). *Computer facilities:* 330 computers available on campus for general student use. A campuswide network can be accessed. Internet access and online class registration are available. *Library facilities:* Emerson Library. *Graduate expenses:* Tuition: full-time $8,820; part-time $490 per credit. Tuition and fees vary according to degree level, campus/location and program. *General application contact:* Matt Nolan, Director of Graduate and Evening Student Admissions, 314-968-7089.

College of Arts and Sciences
Dr. David Carl Wilson, Dean
Programs in:
arts and sciences (MA, MS, MSN)
counseling (MA)
gerontology (MA)
international nongovernmental organizations (MA)
international relations (MA)
legal analysis (MA)
legal studies (MA)
nurse anesthesia (MS)
nursing (MSN)
patent agency (MA)
professional science management and leadership (MA)

Leigh Gerdine College of Fine Arts
Peter Sargent, Dean
Programs in:
art (MA)
arts management and leadership (MFA)
church music (MM)
composition (MM)
conducting (MM)
fine arts (MA, MFA, MM)
jazz studies (MM)
music (MA)
music education (MM)
performance (MM)
piano (MM)

School of Business and Technology
Dr. Benjamin Ola Akande, Dean
Programs in:
business (MA)
business and organizational security management (MA, MBA)
business and technology (MA, MBA, MS, DM, Certificate)
computer resources and information management (MA, MBA)
computer science/distributed systems (MS, Certificate)
environmental management (MBA, MS)
finance (MA, MBA)
health care management (MA)
health services management (MA, MBA)
human resources development (MA, MBA)
human resources management (MA, MBA)
international business (MA, MBA)
management (DM)
management and leadership (MA, MBA)
marketing (MA, MBA)
procurement and acquisitions management (MA, MBA)
public administration (MA)
quality management (MA)
space systems operations management (MS)
telecommunications management (MA, MBA)

School of Communications
Debra Carpenter, Dean
Programs in:
advertising and marketing communications (MA)
communications (MA)
communications management (MA)
media communications (MA)
media literacy (MA)
public relations (MA)

School of Education
Dr. Brenda Fyfe, Dean

Programs in:
- administrative leadership (Ed S)
- communications (MAT)
- early childhood education (MAT)
- education (MAT, Ed S)
- education leadership (Ed S)
- educational technology (MAT)
- mathematics (MAT)
- multidisciplinary studies (MAT)
- school systems, superintendency and leadership (Ed S)
- social science (MAT)
- special education (MAT)

■ WILLIAM WOODS UNIVERSITY
Fulton, MO 65251-1098
http://www.williamwoods.edu/

Independent-religious, coed, comprehensive institution. *Enrollment:* 2,893 graduate, professional, and undergraduate students; 1,944 full-time matriculated graduate/professional students (1,230 women). *Graduate faculty:* 38 full-time (14 women), 174 part-time/adjunct (50 women). *Computer facilities:* Computer purchase and lease plans are available. 105 computers available on campus for general student use. A campuswide network can be accessed from student residence rooms. Internet access and online class registration are available. *Library facilities:* Dulany Library. *Graduate expenses:* Tuition: part-time $255 per credit hour. Tuition and fees vary according to program. *General application contact:* Linda Rembish, Administrative Assistant, 800-995-3199.

Graduate and Adult Studies
Sean Siebert, Dean of Graduate and Adult Studies Enrollment Services
Programs in:
- administration (M Ed, Ed S)
- agribusiness (MBA)
- curriculum/instruction (M Ed)
- health management (MBA)
- human services (MBA)
- instructional leadership (Ed S)

Montana

■ MONTANA STATE UNIVERSITY
Bozeman, MT 59717
http://www.montana.edu/

State-supported, coed, university. CGS member. *Enrollment:* 12,338 graduate, professional, and undergraduate students; 421 full-time matriculated graduate/professional students (179 women), 806 part-time matriculated graduate/professional students (403 women). *Graduate faculty:* 526 full-time (183 women), 212 part-time/adjunct (117 women). *Computer facilities:* 850 computers available on campus for general student use. A campuswide network can be accessed from student residence rooms and from off campus. Internet access and online class registration, e-mail are available. *Library facilities:* Renne Library plus 2 others. *Graduate expenses:* Tuition, state resident: full-time $5,113. Tuition, nonresident: full-time $12,501. *General application contact:* Dr. Carl A. Fox, Vice Provost for Graduate Education, 406-994-4145.

College of Graduate Studies
Dr. Carl A. Fox, Vice Provost for Graduate Education

College of Agriculture
Dr. Jeffrey S. Jacobsen, Dean
Programs in:
- agriculture (MS, PhD)
- animal and range sciences (MS, PhD)
- applied economics (MS)
- land rehabilitation (interdisciplinary) (MS)
- land resources and environmental sciences (MS, PhD)
- plant pathology (MS)
- plant sciences (MS, PhD)
- veterinary molecular biology (MS, PhD)

College of Arts and Architecture
Susan Agre-Kippenhan, Dean, College of Arts and Architecture
Programs in:
- architecture (M Arch)
- art (MFA)
- arts and architecture (M Arch, MFA)
- science and natural history filmmaking (MFA)

College of Business
Dr. Richard J. Semenik, Dean, College of Business
Program in:
- professional accountancy (MP Ac)

College of Education, Health, and Human Development
Larry Baker, Dean, College of Education, Health and Human Development
Programs in:
- education (M Ed, Ed D, Ed S)
- education, health, and human development (M Ed, MS, Ed D, Ed S)
- health and human development (MS)

College of Engineering
Dr. Robert Marley, Dean, College of Engineering
Programs in:
- chemical engineering (MS)
- civil engineering (MS)
- computer science (MS, PhD)
- electrical engineering (MS)
- engineering (PhD)
- environmental engineering (MS)
- industrial and management engineering (MS)
- land rehabilitation (intercollege) (MS)
- mechanical engineering (MS)

College of Letters and Science
Dr. George Tuthill, Interim Dean
Programs in:
- applied psychology (MS)
- biochemistry (MS, PhD)
- biological sciences (MS, PhD)
- chemistry (MS, PhD)
- earth sciences (MS, PhD)
- English (MA)
- fish and wildlife biology (PhD)
- fish and wildlife management (MS)
- history (MA, PhD)
- land rehabilitation (intercollege) (MS)
- letters and science (MA, MPA, MS, PhD)
- mathematics (MS, PhD)
- microbiology (MS, PhD)
- Native American studies (MA)
- neuroscience (MS, PhD)
- physics (MS, PhD)
- public administration (MPA)
- statistics (MS, PhD)

College of Nursing
Dr. Elizabeth Kinion, Dean, College of Nursing
Programs in:
- clinical nurse specialist (CNS) (MN, Post-Master's Certificate)
- family nurse practitioner (MN, Post-Master's Certificate)
- nursing education (Certificate)

■ MONTANA STATE UNIVERSITY–BILLINGS
Billings, MT 59101-0298
http://www.msubillings.edu/

State-supported, coed, comprehensive institution. *Enrollment:* 4,799 graduate, professional, and undergraduate students; 345 full-time matriculated graduate/professional students (252 women). *Graduate faculty:* 60 full-time (24 women). *Computer facilities:* 863 computers available on campus for general student use. A campuswide network can be accessed from student residence rooms and from off campus. Internet access and online class registration, online degree programs are available. *Library facilities:* Montana State University-Billings Library plus 2 others. *Graduate expenses:* Tuition, state resident: full-time $4,599. Tuition, nonresident: full-time $10,786. *General application contact:* David M. Sullivan, Graduate Studies Counselor, 406-657-2053.

College of Allied Health Professions
Dr. David Garloff, Dean
Programs in:
- allied health professions (MHA, MS, MSRC)
- athletic training (MS)
- health administration (MHA)
- rehabilitation and human services (MSRC)
- sport management (MS)

Montana State University–Billings (continued)

College of Arts and Sciences

Dr. Tasneem Khaleel, Dean
Programs in:
- arts and sciences (MPA, MS)
- psychology (MS)
- public administration (MPA)
- public relations (MS)

College of Education and Human Services

Dr. Mary Susan Fishbaugh, Interim Dean
Programs in:
- advanced studies (MS Sp Ed)
- early childhood education (M Ed)
- education and human services (M Ed, MS Sp Ed, Certificate)
- educational technology (M Ed)
- general curriculum (M Ed)
- interdisciplinary studies (M Ed)
- reading (M Ed)
- school counseling (M Ed)
- secondary education (M Ed)
- special education (MS Sp Ed)
- special education generalist (MS Sp Ed)
- teaching (Certificate)

■ UNIVERSITY OF GREAT FALLS

Great Falls, MT 59405
http://www.ugf.edu/

Independent-religious, coed, comprehensive institution. *Enrollment:* 716 graduate, professional, and undergraduate students; 27 full-time matriculated graduate/professional students (22 women), 39 part-time matriculated graduate/professional students (33 women). *Graduate faculty:* 21 full-time (9 women), 19 part-time/adjunct (11 women). *Computer facilities:* 110 computers available on campus for general student use. A campuswide network can be accessed from student residence rooms. Internet access and online class registration are available. *Library facilities:* University of Great Falls Library. *General application contact:* Dr. Richard Fisher, Dean of Graduate Studies, 406-791-5332.

Graduate Studies

Dr. Richard Fisher, Dean of Graduate Studies
Programs in:
- addictions counseling (MAC, Certificate)
- counseling psychology (MSC)
- education (M Ed)
- effectiveness (MCJ)
- information systems (MIS)
- management (MCJ)
- marriage and family counseling (MSC)
- organizational management (MS)
- school psychology (MSC)
- secondary teaching (MAT)

■ THE UNIVERSITY OF MONTANA

Missoula, MT 59812-0002
http://www.umt.edu/

State-supported, coed, university. CGS member. *Computer facilities:* 545 computers available on campus for general student use. A campuswide network can be accessed from student residence rooms and from off campus. Internet access and online class registration are available. *Library facilities:* Maureen and Mike Mansfield Library plus 2 others. *General application contact:* Dean of the Graduate School, 406-243-2572.

Graduate School

Programs in:
- individual interdisciplinary programs (IIP) (PhD)
- interdisciplinary studies (MIS)

College of Arts and Sciences

Programs in:
- anthropology (MA)
- applied geoscience (PhD)
- arts and sciences (MA, MFA, MPA, MS, PhD, Ed S)
- biochemistry (MS)
- biochemistry and microbiology (MS, PhD)
- chemistry (MS, PhD)
- clinical psychology (PhD)
- communication studies (MA)
- computer science (MS)
- creative writing (MFA)
- criminology (MA)
- cultural heritage (MA)
- cultural heritage studies (PhD)
- ecology of infectious disease (PhD)
- economics (MA)
- environmental studies (MS)
- experimental psychology (PhD)
- fiction (MFA)
- forensic anthropology (MA)
- French (MA)
- geography (MA)
- geology (MS, PhD)
- German (MA)
- historical anthropology (PhD)
- history (MA, PhD)
- integrative microbiology and biochemistry (PhD)
- linguistics (MA)
- literature (MA)
- mathematics (MA, PhD)
- mathematics education (MA)
- microbial ecology (MS, PhD)
- microbiology (MS)
- non-fiction (MFA)
- organismal biology and ecology (MS, PhD)
- philosophy (MA)
- poetry (MFA)
- political science (MA)
- public administration (MPA)
- rural and environmental change (MA)
- school psychology (MA, PhD, Ed S)
- sociology (MA)
- Spanish (MA)
- teaching (MA)

College of Forestry and Conservation

Programs in:
- ecosystem management (MEM, MS)
- fish and wildlife biology (PhD)
- forestry (MS, PhD)
- recreation management (MS)
- resource conservation (MS)
- wildlife biology (MS)

School of Business Administration

Programs in:
- accounting (M Acct)
- business administration (M Acct, MBA)

School of Education

Programs in:
- counselor education (MA, Ed D, Ed S)
- counselor education and supervision (Ed D)
- curriculum and instruction (M Ed, Ed D)
- education (M Ed, MA, MS, Ed D, Ed S)
- educational leadership (M Ed, Ed D, Ed S)
- exercise science (MS)
- health and human performance (MS)
- health promotion (MS)
- mental health counseling (MA)
- school counseling (MA)

School of Fine Arts

Programs in:
- fine arts (MA, MFA)
- music (MM)

School of Journalism

Program in:
- journalism (MA)

School of Law

Program in:
- law (JD)

Nebraska

■ BELLEVUE UNIVERSITY

Bellevue, NE 68005-3098
http://www.bellevue.edu/

Independent, coed, comprehensive institution. *Computer facilities:* 1,000 computers available on campus for general student use. A campuswide network can be accessed from off campus. Internet access and online class registration are available. *Library facilities:* Freeman/Lozier Library plus 1 other. *General application contact:* Director of Graduate Enrollment, 402-682-4045.

Find University Details at www.petersons.com/gradchannel.

Graduate School
Programs in:
- business (MBA)
- communications studies (MA, MS)
- computer information systems (MS)
- health care administration (MS)
- human services (MS)
- leadership (MA)
- management (MA)
- security management (MS)

■ CONCORDIA UNIVERSITY
Seward, NE 68434-1599
http://www.cune.edu/

Independent-religious, coed, comprehensive institution. *Computer facilities:* 75 computers available on campus for general student use. A campuswide network can be accessed from student residence rooms and from off campus. Internet access and online class registration, academic plans, human resource data are available. *Library facilities:* Link Library. *General application contact:* Dean of Graduate Studies, 402-643-7464.

Graduate Programs in Education
Programs in:
- curriculum and instruction (M Ed)
- early childhood education (M Ed)
- education (M Ed, MPE, MS)
- educational administration (M Ed)
- family life ministry (MS)
- literacy education (M Ed)
- parish education (MPE)

■ CREIGHTON UNIVERSITY
Omaha, NE 68178-0001
http://www.creighton.edu/

Independent-religious, coed, university. CGS member. *Enrollment:* 6,981 graduate, professional, and undergraduate students; 2,417 full-time matriculated graduate/professional students (1,296 women), 489 part-time matriculated graduate/professional students (268 women). *Computer facilities:* Computer purchase and lease plans are available. 505 computers available on campus for general student use. A campuswide network can be accessed from student residence rooms and from off campus. Internet access and online class registration, online grade information, financial aid information are available. *Library facilities:* Reinert Alumni Memorial Library plus 2 others. *Graduate expenses:* Tuition: part-time $595 per credit hour. Required fees: $38 per semester. *General application contact:* LuAnn M. Schwery, Coordinator of Graduate Programs, 402-280-2870.

Graduate School
Dr. Gail M. Jenson, Dean

College of Arts and Sciences
Dr. Robert E, Kennedy, Interim Dean
Programs in:
- arts and sciences (M Ed, MA, MLS, MS)
- atmospheric sciences (MS)
- Christian spirituality (MA)
- education (M Ed)
- educational leadership (MS)
- English (MA)
- guidance and counseling (MS)
- international relations (MA)
- liberal studies (MLS)
- ministry (MA)
- physics (MS)
- special populations in education (MS)
- theology (MA)

Eugene C. Eppley College of Business Administration
Dr. Ravi Nath, Director
Programs in:
- business administration (MBA)
- information technology (MS)
- securities and portfolio management (MSAPM)

School of Dentistry
Program in:
- dentistry (DDS)

School of Law
Patrick J. Borchers, Dean
Programs in:
- law (JD, MS)
- negotiation and dispute resolution (MS)

School of Medicine
Dr. Cam E. Enarson, Dean
Programs in:
- biomedical sciences (MS, PhD)
- clinical anatomy (MS)
- medical microbiology and immunology (MS, PhD)
- medicine (MD, MS, PhD)
- pharmaceutical sciences (MS)
- pharmacology (MS, PhD)

School of Nursing
Dr. Eleanor V. Howell, Dean
Program in:
- nursing (MS)

School of Pharmacy and Health Professions
Programs in:
- occupational therapy (OTD)
- pharmaceutical sciences (MS)
- pharmacy (Pharm D)
- pharmacy and health professions (Pharm D, MS, DPT, OTD)
- physical therapy (DPT)

■ DOANE COLLEGE
Crete, NE 68333-2430
http://www.doane.edu/

Independent-religious, coed, comprehensive institution. *Computer facilities:* 240 computers available on campus for general student use. A campuswide network can be accessed from student residence rooms and from off campus. Internet access and online class registration are available. *Library facilities:* Perkins Library plus 1 other. *General application contact:* Assistant Dean, 402-464-1223.

Program in Counseling
Program in:
- counseling (MAC)

Program in Education
Programs in:
- curriculum and instruction (M Ed)
- educational leadership (M Ed)

Program in Management
Program in:
- management (MA)

■ UNIVERSITY OF NEBRASKA AT KEARNEY
Kearney, NE 68849-0001
http://www.unk.edu/

State-supported, coed, comprehensive institution. CGS member. *Enrollment:* 6,468 graduate, professional, and undergraduate students; 141 full-time matriculated graduate/professional students (99 women), 657 part-time matriculated graduate/professional students (422 women). *Graduate faculty:* 109 full-time (52 women). *Computer facilities:* 277 computers available on campus for general student use. A campuswide network can be accessed from student residence rooms and from off campus. Internet access and online class registration, online grade reports are available. *Library facilities:* Calvin T. Ryan Library. *Graduate expenses:* Tuition, state resident: part-time $161 per hour. Tuition, nonresident: part-time $332 per hour. Required fees: $57 per hour. *General application contact:* Dr. Kenya Taylor, Graduate Dean, 308-856-8843.

College of Graduate Study
Dr. Kenya Taylor, Graduate Dean

College of Business and Technology
Dr. Bruce A. Forster, Dean
Programs in:
- business administration (MBA)
- business and technology (MBA)

College of Education
Dr. Ed Scantling, Dean
Programs in:
- adapted physical education (MA Ed)
- counseling (MS Ed, Ed S)
- curriculum and instruction (MS Ed)
- education (MA Ed, MS Ed, Ed S)
- educational administration (MA Ed, Ed S)
- exercise science (MA Ed)
- instructional technology (MS Ed)
- master teacher (MA Ed)
- reading education (MA Ed)
- school psychology (Ed S)
- special education (MA Ed)
- speech pathology (MS Ed)
- supervisor (MA Ed)

University of Nebraska at Kearney (continued)

College of Fine Arts and Humanities
Dr. William Jurma, Dean
Programs in:
art education (MA Ed)
creative writing (MA)
fine arts and humanities (MA, MA Ed)
French (MA Ed)
German (MA Ed)
literature (MA)
music education (MA Ed)
Spanish (MA Ed)

College of Natural and Social Sciences
Dr. Francis Harrold, Dean
Programs in:
biology (MS)
history (MA)
natural and social sciences (MA, MS, MS Ed)
science education (MS Ed)

■ UNIVERSITY OF NEBRASKA AT OMAHA
Omaha, NE 68182
http://www.unomaha.edu/

State-supported, coed, university. CGS member. *Enrollment:* 13,906 graduate, professional, and undergraduate students; 565 full-time matriculated graduate/professional students (344 women), 1,716 part-time matriculated graduate/professional students (1,047 women). *Graduate faculty:* 338 full-time (114 women). *Computer facilities:* 2,000 computers available on campus for general student use. A campuswide network can be accessed from student residence rooms and from off campus. Internet access and online class registration are available. *Library facilities:* Criss Library. *General application contact:* Penny Harmoney, Director, Graduate Studies, 402-554-2341.

Graduate Studies and Research
Dr. Thomas Bragg, Dean for Graduate Studies
Programs in:
public health (MPH)
writing (MFA)

College of Arts and Sciences
Dr. Shelton Hendricks, Dean
Programs in:
advanced writing (Certificate)
arts and sciences (MA, MAT, MS, PhD, Certificate, Ed S)
biology (MS)
developmental psychology (PhD)
English (MA)
geographic information science (Certificate)
geography (MA)
history (MA)
industrial/organizational psychology (MS, PhD)
language teaching (MA)
mathematics (MA, MAT, MS)
political science (MS)
psychobiology (PhD)
psychology (MA)
school psychology (MS, Ed S)
teaching English to speakers of other languages (Certificate)
technical communication (Certificate)

College of Business Administration
Dr. Louis Pol, Associate
Programs in:
accounting (M Acc)
business administration (EMBA, M Acc, MA, MBA, MS)
economics (MA, MS)

College of Communication, Fine Arts and Media
Dr. Gail Baker, Dean
Programs in:
communication (MA)
communication, fine arts and media (MA, MM)
music (MM)
theatre (MA)

College of Education
Dr. John Langan, Chairperson
Programs in:
community counseling (MA, MS)
counseling gerontology (MA, MS)
education (MA, MS, Ed D, Certificate, Ed S)
educational administration and supervision (MS, Ed D, Ed S)
elementary education (MA, MS)
health, physical education, and recreation (MA, MS)
instruction in urban schools (Certificate)
instructional technology (Certificate)
reading education (MS)
school counseling-elementary (MA, MS)
school counseling-secondary (MA, MS)
secondary education (MA, MS)
special education (MS)
speech-language pathology (MA, MS)
student affairs practice in higher education (MA, MS)

College of Information Science and Technology
Dr. Hesham Ali, Dean
Programs in:
computer science (MA, MS)
information science and technology (MA, MS, PhD)
information technology (PhD)
management information systems (MS)

College of Public Affairs and Community Service
Dr. Burton J. Reed, Chairperson
Programs in:
criminal justice (MA, MS, PhD)
gerontology (Certificate)
public administration (MPA, PhD)
public affairs and community service (MA, MPA, MS, MSW, PhD, Certificate)
social gerontology (MA)
social work (MSW)
urban studies (MS)

■ UNIVERSITY OF NEBRASKA–LINCOLN
Lincoln, NE 68588
http://www.unl.edu/

State-supported, coed, university. CGS member. *Computer facilities:* Computer purchase and lease plans are available. 600 computers available on campus for general student use. A campuswide network can be accessed from student residence rooms and from off campus. Internet access and online class registration are available. *Library facilities:* Love Memorial Library plus 10 others. *General application contact:* Executive Associate Dean of Graduate Studies, 402-472-2875.

College of Law
Programs in:
law (JD, MLS)
legal studies (MLS)

Graduate College
Programs in:
museum studies (MA, MS)
survey research and methodology (MS)
toxicology (MS, PhD)

College of Agricultural Sciences and Natural Resources
Programs in:
agricultural economics (MS, PhD)
agricultural leadership, education and communication (MS)
agricultural sciences and natural resources (M Ag, MA, MS, PhD)
agriculture (M Ag)
agronomy (MS, PhD)
animal science (MS, PhD)
biochemistry (MS, PhD)
biometry (MS)
entomology (MS, PhD)
food science and technology (MS, PhD)
horticulture (MS, PhD)
mechanized systems management (MS)
natural resources (MS)
nutrition (MS, PhD)
veterinary and biomedical sciences (MS, PhD)

College of Architecture
Programs in:
architecture (M Arch, MS)
community and regional planning (MCRP)

College of Arts and Sciences
Programs in:
analytical chemistry (PhD)
anthropology (MA)

arts and sciences (M Sc T, MA, MAT, MS, PhD)
astronomy (MS, PhD)
biological sciences (MA, MS, PhD)
chemistry (MS)
classics and religious studies (MA)
communication studies and theatre arts (PhD)
communications studies (MA)
computer engineering (PhD)
computer science (MS, PhD)
English (MA, PhD)
French (MA, PhD)
geography (MA, PhD)
geosciences (MS, PhD)
German (MA, PhD)
history (MA, PhD)
inorganic chemistry (PhD)
mathematics and statistics (M Sc T, MA, MAT, MS, PhD)
organic chemistry (PhD)
philosophy (MA, PhD)
physical chemistry (PhD)
physics (MS, PhD)
political science (MA, PhD)
psychology (MA, PhD)
sociology (MA, PhD)
Spanish (MA, PhD)

College of Business Administration
Programs in:
accountancy (PhD)
actuarial science (MS)
business (MA, MBA, PhD)
business administration (MA, MBA, MPA, MS, PhD)
economics (MA, PhD)
finance (MA, PhD)
management (MA, PhD)
marketing (MA, PhD)

College of Education and Human Sciences
Programs in:
family and consumer sciences (MS)
human resources and family sciences (PhD)
nutritional science and dietetics (MS)
textiles, clothing and design (MA, MS)

College of Education and Human Services
Programs in:
administration, curriculum and instruction (Ed D, PhD)
community and human resources (Ed D, PhD)
curriculum and instruction (M Ed, MA, MST, Ed S)
education (M Ed, MA, MPE, MS, MST, Ed D, PhD, Certificate, Ed S)
educational administration (M Ed, MA, Ed D, Certificate)
educational psychology (MA, Ed S)
health, physical education, and recreation (M Ed, MPE)
psychological and cultural studies (Ed D, PhD)
special education (M Ed, MA)
special education and communication disorders (Ed S)
speech-language pathology and audiology (MS)

College of Engineering and Technology
Programs in:
agricultural and biological systems engineering (MS, PhD)
architectural engineering (MAE)
chemical engineering (MS)
civil engineering (MS)
electrical engineering (MS)
engineering (M Eng, PhD)
engineering and technology (M Eng, MAE, MEE, MS, PhD)
engineering mechanics (MS)
environmental engineering (MS)
industrial and management systems engineering (MS)
manufacturing systems engineering (MS)
mechanical engineering (MS)
mechanized systems management (MS)

College of Fine and Performing Arts
Programs in:
art and art history (MFA)
fine and performing arts (MFA, MM, DMA)
music (MM, DMA)
theatre arts (MFA)

College of Journalism and Mass Communications
Program in:
journalism and mass communications (MA)

■ WAYNE STATE COLLEGE
Wayne, NE 68787
http://www.wsc.edu/

State-supported, coed, comprehensive institution. CGS member. *Enrollment:* 3,407 graduate, professional, and undergraduate students; 49 full-time matriculated graduate/professional students (24 women), 492 part-time matriculated graduate/professional students (344 women). *Graduate faculty:* 74 part-time/adjunct (39 women). *Computer facilities:* 365 computers available on campus for general student use. A campuswide network can be accessed from student residence rooms and from off campus. Internet access and online class registration are available. *Library facilities:* U. S. Conn Library. *Graduate expenses:* Tuition, state resident: full-time $3,114; part-time $130 per credit hour. Tuition, nonresident: full-time $6,228; part-time $260 per credit hour. Required fees: $894; $37 per credit hour. Tuition and fees vary according to course load. *General application contact:* Dr. Carolyn Linster, Director of Graduate Studies, 402-375-7121.

Department of Health, Human Performance and Sport
Dr. Kevin Hill, Dean
Programs in:
exercise science (MSE)
organization management (MSE)

School of Business and Technology
Dr. Vaughn Benson, Dean
Program in:
business and technology (MBA)

School of Education and Counseling
Dr. Anthony Koyzis, Dean
Programs in:
counseling (MSE)
counselor education (MSE)
curriculum and instruction (MSE)
education and counseling (MSE, Ed S)
educational administration (MSE, Ed S)
elementary administration (MSE)
elementary and secondary administration (MSE)
guidance and counseling (MSE)
school counseling (MSE)
secondary administration (MSE)
special education (MSE)

Nevada

■ UNIVERSITY OF NEVADA, LAS VEGAS
Las Vegas, NV 89154-9900
http://www.unlv.edu/

State-supported, coed, university. CGS member. *Enrollment:* 27,933 graduate, professional, and undergraduate students; 1,836 full-time matriculated graduate/professional students (1,084 women), 1,972 part-time matriculated graduate/professional students (1,226 women). *Graduate faculty:* 776 full-time (238 women), 296 part-time/adjunct (115 women). *Computer facilities:* 1,900 computers available on campus for general student use. A campuswide network can be accessed from student residence rooms and from off campus. Internet access and online class registration are available. *Library facilities:* Lied Library. *General application contact:* Karen Maldonado, Administrative Assistant I, 702-895-3320.

Find University Details at www.petersons.com/gradchannel.

Graduate College
Dr. Ronald Smith, Interim Vice President of Research and Graduate Dean

College of Business
Dr. Richard Flaherty, Dean
Programs in:
accounting (MS)
business (MA, MBA, MS)
business administration (MBA)
economics (MA)
management information systems (MS)

University of Nevada, Las Vegas (continued)

College of Education
Dr. Jane McCarthy, Interim Dean
Programs in:
- assistive technology (Ed S)
- curriculum and instruction (Ed D, PhD, Ed S)
- education (M Ed, MS, Ed D, PhD, Ed S)
- education psychology (MS)
- educational administration (M Ed, Ed D, PhD, Ed S)
- educational leadership (MS)
- educational psychology (PhD)
- elementary education (M Ed, MS)
- emotional disturbance (Ed D)
- English education (M Ed, MS)
- general special education (Ed D)
- gifted and talented education (Ed D)
- learning and technology (PhD)
- learning disabilities (Ed D)
- library science (M Ed, MS)
- literacy education (M Ed, MS)
- mathematics education (M Ed, MS)
- mental retardation (Ed D)
- multicultural education (M Ed, MS)
- reading specialist (M Ed, MS)
- school counseling (M Ed)
- school counselor education (PhD)
- school psychology (PhD, Ed S)
- secondary education (M Ed, MS)
- special education (M Ed, MS, PhD, Ed S)
- sports education leadership (M Ed, MS, PhD)
- teacher leadership (M Ed, MS)
- teaching English as a second language (M Ed, MS)
- technology integration and leadership (M Ed, MS)

College of Fine Arts
Dr. Jeffrey Koep, Dean
Programs in:
- applied music (performance) (MM)
- architecture (M Arch)
- art (MFA)
- composition/theory (MM)
- design/technology (MFA)
- directing (MFA)
- fine arts (M Arch, MA, MFA, MM, DMA)
- music education (MM)
- performance (MFA)
- performance studies (DMA)
- playwriting (MFA)
- screenwriting (MFA)
- stage management (MFA)
- theatre (MA)
- theatre arts (MFA)

College of Liberal Arts
Dr. Edward Shoben, Dean
Programs in:
- anthropology (MA, PhD)
- clinical psychology (PhD)
- creative writing (MFA)
- English (PhD)
- ethics and policy studies (MA)
- experimental psychology (PhD)
- general psychology (MA)
- history (MA, PhD)
- language/composition theory study (MA)
- liberal arts (MA, MFA, PhD, Certificate)
- literature study (MA)
- political science (MA)
- sociology (MA, PhD)
- Spanish language, culture and technology (MA)
- women's studies (Certificate)

College of Science
Dr. Ronald Yasbin, Dean
Programs in:
- applied mathematics (MS, PhD)
- applied statistics (MS)
- biochemistry (MS)
- chemistry (MS)
- computational mathematics (PhD)
- environmental science/chemistry (PhD)
- geoscience (MS, PhD)
- life sciences (MS, PhD)
- physics (MS, PhD)
- pure mathematics (MS, PhD)
- radiochemistry (PhD)
- science (MAS, MS, PhD)
- statistics (PhD)
- teaching mathematics (MS)
- water resources management (MS)

Division of Health Sciences
Dr. Harvey Wallmann, Interim Director
Programs in:
- exercise physiology (MS)
- family nurse practitioner (MS, Post-Master's Certificate)
- health physics (MS)
- health promotion (M Ed)
- health sciences (M Ed, MPH, MS, DPT, PhD, Post-Master's Certificate)
- kinesiology (MS)
- nursing (PhD)
- nursing education (MS, Post-Master's Certificate)
- pediatric nurse practitioner (MS)
- physical therapy (MS, DPT)
- public health (MPH)

Greenspun College of Urban Affairs
Dr. Martha Watson, Dean
Programs in:
- communication studies (MA)
- community agency counseling (MS)
- criminal justice (MA)
- crisis and emergency management (MS)
- environmental science (MS, PhD)
- journalism and media studies (MA)
- marriage and family counseling (MS)
- marriage and family therapy (Certificate)
- public administration (MPA)
- public affairs (PhD)
- public management (Certificate)
- rehabilitation counseling (MS)
- social work (MSW)
- urban affairs (MA, MPA, MS, MSW, PhD, Certificate)

Howard R. Hughes College of Engineering
Dr. Eric Sandgren, Dean
Programs in:
- civil engineering (MSE, PhD)
- computer science (MS, PhD)
- construction (MSE)
- construction management (MS)
- electrical and computer engineering (MSE, PhD)
- engineering (MS, MSE, PhD)
- informatics (MS, PhD)
- mechanical engineering (MSE, PhD)
- transportation (MS, MSE)

William F. Harrah College of Hotel Administration
Dr. Stuart Mann, Dean
Programs in:
- hospitality administration (MHA, PhD)
- hotel administration (MS)
- leisure studies (MS)

William S. Boyd School of Law
Richard J. Morgan, Dean
Program in:
- law (JD)

■ UNIVERSITY OF NEVADA, RENO
Reno, NV 89557
http://www.unr.edu/

State-supported, coed, university. CGS member. *Enrollment:* 16,663 graduate, professional, and undergraduate students; 980 full-time matriculated graduate/professional students (575 women), 1,475 part-time matriculated graduate/professional students (815 women). *Graduate faculty:* 999. *Computer facilities:* Computer purchase and lease plans are available. 298 computers available on campus for general student use. A campuswide network can be accessed from student residence rooms and from off campus. Internet access and online class registration are available. *Library facilities:* Getchell Library plus 6 others. *General application contact:* John C. Green, Application Contact, 775-784-6869.

Graduate School
Dr. Marsha Read, Associate Dean of the Graduate School
Programs in:
- biomedical engineering (MS, PhD)
- environmental sciences and health (MS, PhD)
- judicial studies (MJS)

College of Agriculture, Biotechnology and Natural Resources
Dr. David Thawley, Dean
Programs in:
- agriculture, biotechnology and natural resources (MS, PhD)
- animal science (MS)
- biochemistry (MS, PhD)

natural resources and environmental sciences (MS)
nutrition (MS)
resource economics (MS, PhD)

College of Business Administration
Dr. Dana Edberg, Interim Dean
Programs in:
accounting and information systems (M Acc)
business administration (M Acc, MA, MBA, MS)
economics (MA, MS)
finance (MS)

College of Education
Dr. William E. Sparkman, Dean
Programs in:
counseling and educational psychology (M Ed, MA, MS, Ed D, PhD, Ed S)
curriculum, teaching and learning (Ed D, PhD)
education (M Ed, MA, MS, Ed D, PhD, Ed S)
educational leadership (M Ed, MA, MS, Ed D, PhD, Ed S)
educational specialties (MA, MS, PhD, Ed S)
elementary education (M Ed, MA, Ed S)
literacy studies (M Ed, MA, Ed D, PhD)
secondary education (M Ed, MA, MS, Ed S)
special education (M Ed)
special education and disability studies (PhD)
teaching English as a second language (MA)

College of Engineering
Dr. Theodore Batchman, Dean
Programs in:
chemical engineering (MS, PhD)
civil engineering (MS, PhD)
computer engineering (MS)
computer science (MS)
computer science and engineering (PhD)
electrical engineering (MS, PhD)
engineering (MS, PhD, Met E)
mechanical engineering (MS, PhD)
metallurgical engineering (MS, PhD, Met E)

College of Health and Human Sciences
Dr. Charles Bullock, Acting Dean
Programs in:
criminal justice (MA)
health and human sciences (MA, MPH, MS, MSN, MSW)
human development and family studies (MS)
nursing (MSN)
public health (MPH)
social work (MSW)

College of Liberal Arts
Dr. Heather Hardy, Dean
Programs in:
anthropology (MA, PhD)
Basque studies (PhD)
English (MA, MATE, PhD)
fine arts (MFA)
French (MA)
German (MA)
history (MA, PhD)
liberal arts (MA, MATE, MFA, MM, MPA, MS, PhD)
music (MA, MM)
philosophy (MA)
political science (MA, PhD)
psychology (MA, PhD)
public administration (MPA)
public administration and policy (MPA)
social psychology (PhD)
sociology (MA)
Spanish (MA)
speech communications (MA)

College of Science
Dr. Jeff Thompson, Acting Dean
Programs in:
atmospheric sciences (MS, PhD)
biology (MS)
biotechnology (MS)
chemical physics (PhD)
chemistry (MS, PhD)
earth sciences and engineering (MS, PhD, EM, Geol E)
ecology, evolution, and conservation biology (PhD)
geochemistry (MS, PhD)
geography (MS, PhD)
geological engineering (MS, Geol E)
geology (MS, PhD)
geophysics (MS, PhD)
hydrogeology (MS, PhD)
hydrology (MS, PhD)
land use planning (MS)
mathematics (MS)
mining engineering (MS, EM)
physics (MS, PhD)
science (MATM, MS, PhD, EM, Geol E)
teaching mathematics (MATM)

Donald W. Reynolds School of Journalism
Dr. Donica Mensing, Graduate Program Director
Program in:
journalism (MA)

School of Medicine
Dr. David Lupan, Dean
Program in:
medicine (MD, MS, PhD)

Graduate Programs in Medicine
Programs in:
cell and molecular biology (MS, PhD)
cellular and molecular pharmacology and physiology (MS, PhD)
medicine (MS, PhD)
speech pathology (PhD)
speech pathology and audiology (MS)

■ UNIVERSITY OF PHOENIX–LAS VEGAS CAMPUS
Las Vegas, NV 89128
http://www.phoenix.edu/

Proprietary, coed, comprehensive institution. *Enrollment:* 3,484 graduate, professional, and undergraduate students; 1,106 full-time matriculated graduate/professional students (757 women). *Graduate faculty:* 56 full-time (17 women), 335 part-time/adjunct (114 women). *Computer facilities:* A campuswide network can be accessed from off campus. Internet access is available. *Library facilities:* University Library. *Graduate expenses:* Tuition: full-time $9,576. Required fees: $760. *General application contact:* Campus Information Center, 702-638-7249.

The Artemis School
Dr. Adam Honea, Provost

College of Education
Dr. Marla LaRue, Dean/Executive Director
Programs in:
administration and supervision (MA Ed)
curriculum and instruction (MA Ed)
school counseling (MSC)
teacher education-elementary licensure (MA Ed)

College of Health and Human Services
Dr. Gil Linne, Dean/Executive Director
Programs in:
marriage, family, and child therapy (MSC)
mental health counseling (MSC)

John Sperling School of Business
Dr. Adam Honea, Provost
Program in:
business (MBA, MIS, MM)

College of Graduate Business and Management
Dr. Brian Lindquist, Associate Vice President and Dean/Executive Director
Programs in:
business administration (MBA)
management (MM)

College of Information Systems and Technology
Dr. Adam Honea, Dean/Executive Director
Programs in:
information systems (MIS)
technology management (MBA)

New Hampshire

■ ANTIOCH UNIVERSITY NEW ENGLAND
Keene, NH 03431-3552
http://www.antiochne.edu/

Independent, coed, graduate-only institution. *Graduate faculty:* 54 full-time (33 women), 34 part-time/adjunct (18 women). *Computer facilities:* 12 computers available on campus for general student use. A campuswide network can be accessed from off campus. Internet access, e-mail, intranet services are available. *Library facilities:* Antioch New England Graduate School Library. *Graduate expenses:* Tuition: full-time $22,000. Tuition and fees vary according to program and student level. *General application contact:* Leatrice A. Oram, Co-Director of Admissions, 800-490-3310.

Graduate School
Dr. David A. Caruso, President
Programs in:
- autism spectrum disorders (Certificate)
- clinical mental health counseling (MA)
- clinical psychology (Psy D)
- conservation biology (MS)
- dance/movement therapy and counseling (M Ed, MA)
- educational administration and supervision (M Ed)
- environmental advocacy (MS)
- environmental education (MS)
- environmental studies (MS, PhD)
- experienced educators (M Ed)
- integrated learning (M Ed)
- leadership and management (MS)
- marriage and family therapy (MA)
- organization development (Certificate)
- organizational and environmental sustainability (MBA)
- resource management and conservation (MS)
- teacher certification in biology (7th-12th grade) (MS)
- teacher certification in general science (5th-9th grade) (MS)
- Waldorf teacher training (M Ed)

■ DARTMOUTH COLLEGE
Hanover, NH 03755
http://www.dartmouth.edu/

Independent, coed, university. CGS member. *Enrollment:* 5,753 graduate, professional, and undergraduate students; 1,573 full-time matriculated graduate/professional students (619 women), 95 part-time matriculated graduate/professional students (51 women). *Graduate faculty:* 320 full-time (84 women), 39 part-time/adjunct (19 women). *Computer facilities:* 200 computers available on campus for general student use. A campuswide network can be accessed from student residence rooms and from off campus. Internet access and online class registration are available. *Library facilities:* Baker-Berry Library plus 10 others. *Graduate expenses:* Tuition: full-time $33,297. *General application contact:* Gary Hutchins, Assistant Dean/School of Arts and Sciences, 603-646-2107.

Find University Details at www.petersons.com/gradchannel.

Graduate Program in Molecular and Cellular Biology
Program in:
- molecular and cellular biology (PhD)

Program in Experimental and Molecular Medicine
Programs in:
- cancer biology and molecular therapeutics (PhD)
- molecular pharmacology, toxicology and experimental therapeutics (PhD)
- neuroscience (PhD)
- systems biology (PhD)
- vascular biology (PhD)

School of Arts and Sciences
Dr. Charles Barlowe, Dean of Graduate Studies
Programs in:
- arts and sciences (AM, MALS, MPH, MS, PhD)
- biology of integrated systems (PhD)
- cancer biology and molecular therapeutics (PhD)
- chemistry (PhD)
- cognitive neuroscience (PhD)
- comparative literature (AM)
- computer science (MS, PhD)
- earth sciences (MS, PhD)
- ecology and evolutionary biology (PhD)
- electro-acoustic music (AM)
- genetics (PhD)
- liberal studies (MALS)
- mathematics (PhD)
- microbiology and immunology (PhD)
- molecular and cellular biology (PhD)
- molecular pharmacology, toxicology and experimental therapeutics (PhD)
- neuroscience (PhD)
- pharmacology and toxicology (PhD)
- physics and astronomy (MS, PhD)
- physiology (PhD)
- psychology (PhD)
- vascular biology (PhD)

Center for the Evaluative Clinical Sciences
Dr. Gerald T. O'Connor, Director
Programs in:
- evaluative clinical sciences (MS, PhD)
- public health (MPH)

The Neuroscience Center
Program in:
- neuroscience (PhD)

Thayer School of Engineering
Dr. Joseph J. Helbie, Dean
Programs in:
- biomedical engineering (MS, PhD)
- biotechnology and biochemical engineering (MS, PhD)
- computer engineering (MS, PhD)
- electrical engineering (MS, PhD)
- engineering (MEM, MS, PhD)
- engineering management (MEM)
- engineering physics (MS, PhD)
- manufacturing systems (MS, PhD)
- materials sciences and engineering (MS, PhD)
- mechanical engineering (MS, PhD)

Tuck School of Business at Dartmouth
Paul Danos, Dean
Program in:
- business (MBA)

■ KEENE STATE COLLEGE
Keene, NH 03435
http://www.keene.edu/

State-supported, coed, comprehensive institution. *Enrollment:* 4,940 graduate, professional, and undergraduate students; 47 full-time matriculated graduate/professional students (35 women), 84 part-time matriculated graduate/professional students (61 women). *Graduate faculty:* 10 full-time (6 women), 7 part-time/adjunct (5 women). *Computer facilities:* Computer purchase and lease plans are available. 500 computers available on campus for general student use. A campuswide network can be accessed from student residence rooms and from off campus. Internet access, e-mail, personal Web pages are available. *Library facilities:* Mason Library. *Graduate expenses:* Part-time $265 per credit. Tuition, state resident: full-time $5,780; part-time $290 per credit. Tuition, nonresident: full-time $13,050. Required fees: $80 per credit. Part-time tuition and fees vary according to course load. *General application contact:* Peggy Richmond, Director of Admissions, 603-358-2276.

Division of Graduate and Professional Studies
Dr. John Couture, Dean
Programs in:
- curriculum and instruction (M Ed)
- educational administration (M Ed)
- educational leadership (PMC)
- school counselor (M Ed, PMC)
- special education (M Ed, PMC)

■ PLYMOUTH STATE UNIVERSITY
Plymouth, NH 03264-1595
http://www.plymouth.edu/

State-supported, coed, comprehensive institution. *Enrollment:* 5,872 graduate, professional, and undergraduate students; 28 full-time matriculated graduate/professional students (21 women), 1,692 part-time matriculated graduate/professional students (1,225 women). *Graduate faculty:* 73 full-time (33 women), 95 part-time/adjunct (54 women). *Computer facilities:* Computer purchase and lease plans are available. 500 computers available on campus for general student use. A campuswide network can be accessed from student residence rooms and from off campus. Internet access and online class registration, degree audit, academic history, account status are available. *Library facilities:* Lamson Library. *Graduate expenses:* Tuition, state resident: part-time $369 per credit. Tuition, nonresident: part-time $407 per credit. Tuition and fees vary according to course level. *General application contact:* Cheryl B. Baker, Director of Recruitment and Outreach, 603-535-2737.

College of Graduate Studies
Dr. Dennise M. Maslakowski, Associate Vice President
Program in:
business (MBA)

Graduate Studies in Education
Programs in:
applied meteorology (MS)
athletic training (M Ed, MS)
counselor education (M Ed)
education (CAGS)
educational leadership (M Ed)
elementary education (M Ed)
English education (M Ed)
environmental science and policy (MS)
health education (M Ed)
k-12 education (M Ed)
mathematics education (M Ed)
reading and writing specialist (M Ed)
science (MS)
science education (MS)
secondary education (M Ed)
special education administration (M Ed)
special education k-12 (M Ed)
teaching (MAT)

■ RIVIER COLLEGE
Nashua, NH 03060
http://www.rivier.edu/

Independent-religious, coed, comprehensive institution. *Enrollment:* 2,320 graduate, professional, and undergraduate students; 73 full-time matriculated graduate/professional students (40 women), 674 part-time matriculated graduate/professional students (530 women). *Graduate faculty:* 35 full-time (17 women), 71 part-time/adjunct (39 women). *Computer facilities:* 93 computers available on campus for general student use. A campuswide network can be accessed from student residence rooms and from off campus. *Library facilities:* Regina Library plus 1 other. *General application contact:* Diane Monahan, Director of Graduate Admissions, 603-897-8129.

School of Graduate Studies
Dr. Albert DeCiccio, Dean
Programs in:
arts and sciences (EMBA, M Ed, MA, MAT, MBA, MS, CAGS)
business administration (MBA)
computer information systems (MS)
computer science (MS)
curriculum and instruction (M Ed)
early childhood education (M Ed)
educational administration (M Ed)
educational studies (M Ed)
elementary education (M Ed)
elementary education and general special education (M Ed)
emotional and behavioral disorders (M Ed)
English (MA, MAT)
family nurse practitioner (MS)
general social education (M Ed)
health care administration (MBA)
human resources management (MS)
leadership and learning (CAGS)
learning disabilities (M Ed)
learning disabilities and reading (M Ed)
mathematics (MAT)
mental health counseling (MA)
nursing education (MS)
organizational leadership (EMBA)
reading (M Ed)
school counseling (M Ed)
social studies education (MAT)
Spanish (MAT)
writing and literature (MA)

■ SOUTHERN NEW HAMPSHIRE UNIVERSITY
Manchester, NH 03106-1045
http://www.snhu.edu/

Independent, coed, comprehensive institution. *Enrollment:* 3,490 graduate, professional, and undergraduate students; 467 full-time matriculated graduate/professional students (184 women), 1,104 part-time matriculated graduate/professional students (592 women). *Computer facilities:* Computer purchase and lease plans are available. 557 computers available on campus for general student use. A campuswide network can be accessed from student residence rooms and from off campus. Internet access and online class registration are available. *Library facilities:* Harry A. B. and Gertrude C. Shapiro Library. *General application contact:* Scott Durand, Director of Graduate Enrollment Services, 603-644-3102 Ext. 3338.

School of Business
Dr. Martin Bradley, Dean
Programs in:
accounting (MS)
business administration (MBA, Certificate)
finance (MS)
hospitality and tourism leadership (Certificate)
information technology (MS, Certificate)
information technology/international business (Certificate)
integrated marketing communications (Certificate)
international business (MS, DBA)
marketing (MS)
operations and project management (MS)
organizational leadership (MS)
project management (Certificate)
sport management (MS)

School of Community Economic Development
Dr. Michael Swack, Dean
Program in:
community economic development (MA, MS, PhD)

School of Education
Dr. Patrick J. Hartwick, Dean
Programs in:
business education (MS)
child development (M Ed)
computer technology education (Certificate)
curriculum and instruction (M Ed)
education (M Ed, CAS)
elementary education (M Ed)
general special education (Certificate)
school business administrator (Certificate)
school counseling (M Ed)
school psychology (M Ed)
secondary education (M Ed)
training and development (Certificate)

School of Liberal Arts
Dr. Karen Erickson, Dean
Programs in:
clinical services for adults psychiatric disabilities (Certificate)
clinical services for children and adolescents with psychiatric disabilities (Certificate)
clinical services for persons with co-occurring substance abuse and psychiatric disabilities (Certificate)
community mental health (MS)
fiction writing (MFA)
non-fiction writing (MFA)
teaching English as a foreign language (MS)

■ UNIVERSITY OF NEW HAMPSHIRE
Durham, NH 03824
http://www.unh.edu/

State-supported, coed, university. CGS member. *Enrollment:* 14,848 graduate, professional, and undergraduate students; 1,254 full-time matriculated graduate/professional students (773 women), 1,180 part-time matriculated graduate/professional students (682 women). *Graduate faculty:* 605 full-time. *Computer facilities:* 389 computers available on campus for general student use. A campuswide network can be accessed from student residence rooms and

University of New Hampshire (continued)
from off campus. Internet access and online class registration are available. *Library facilities:* Dimond Library plus 4 others. *Graduate expenses:* Tuition, state resident: full-time $8,540; part-time $474 per credit hour. Tuition, nonresident: full-time $20,990; part-time $862 per credit hour. Required fees: $1,343; $356 per term. Tuition and fees vary according to course load, program and reciprocity agreements. *General application contact:* Graduate Admissions Office, 603-862-3000.

Find University Details at www.petersons.com/gradchannel.

Graduate School
Dr. Harry J. Richards, Dean
Programs in:
college teaching (MST)
earth and environmental science (PhD)
environmental education (MA)
natural resources and environmental studies (PhD)

College of Engineering and Physical Sciences
Dr. Arthur Greenberg, Dean
Programs in:
applied mathematics (MS)
chemical engineering (MS, PhD)
chemistry (MS, MST, PhD)
chemistry education (PhD)
civil engineering (MS, PhD)
computer science (MS, PhD)
earth sciences (MS)
electrical engineering (MS, PhD)
engineering and physical sciences (MS, MST, PhD)
hydrology (MS)
materials science (MS, PhD)
mathematics (MS, MST, PhD)
mathematics education (PhD)
mechanical engineering (MS, PhD)
ocean engineering (MS, PhD)
ocean mapping (MS)
physics (MS, PhD)
statistics (MS)
systems design (PhD)

College of Liberal Arts
Dr. Marilyn Hoskin, Dean
Programs in:
counseling (M Ed, MA)
early childhood education (M Ed)
education (PhD)
educational administration (M Ed, CAGS)
elementary education (M Ed, MAT)
English (PhD)
English education (MST)
history (MA, PhD)
justice studies (MA)
language and linguistics (MA)
liberal arts (M Ed, MA, MALS, MAT, MFA, MPA, MST, PhD, CAGS)
liberal studies (MALS)
literature (MA)
museum studies (MA)
music education (MA)
music history (MA)
painting (MFA)
political science (MA)
psychology (PhD)
public administration (MPA)
reading (M Ed)
secondary education (M Ed, MAT)
sociology (MA, PhD)
Spanish (MA)
special education (M Ed)
special needs (M Ed)
teacher leadership (M Ed)
writing (MA)

College of Life Sciences and Agriculture
Dean
Programs in:
animal and nutritional sciences (PhD)
animal science (MS)
biochemistry (MS, PhD)
environmental conservation (MS)
forestry (MS)
genetics (MS, PhD)
life sciences and agriculture (MS, PhD)
microbiology (MS, PhD)
nutritional sciences (MS)
plant biology (MS, PhD)
resource administration (MS)
resource economics (MS)
soil science (MS)
water resources management (MS)
wildlife (MS)
zoology (MS, PhD)

School of Health and Human Services
Dr. James McCarthy, Dean
Programs in:
early childhood intervention (MS)
family studies (MS)
health and human services (MPH, MS, MSW)
kinesiology (MS)
language and literature disabilities (MS)
marriage and family therapy (MS)
nursing (MS)
occupational therapy (MS)
public health: ecology (MPH)
public health: nursing (MPH)
public health: policy and management (MPH)
recreation administration (MS)
social work (MSW)
therapeutic recreation (MS)

Whittemore School of Business and Economics
Dr. Steve Bolander, Dean
Programs in:
accounting (MS)
business administration (MBA)
business and economics (MA, MBA, MS, PhD)
economics (MA, PhD)
executive business administration (MBA)
health management (MBA)
management of technology (MS)

New Jersey

■ CALDWELL COLLEGE
Caldwell, NJ 07006-6195
http://www.caldwell.edu/

Independent-religious, coed, comprehensive institution. CGS member. *Computer facilities:* 197 computers available on campus for general student use. A campuswide network can be accessed from student residence rooms and from off campus. Internet access and online class registration are available. *Library facilities:* Jennings Library. *General application contact:* Graduate Admissions Counselor, 973-618-3408.

Find University Details at www.petersons.com/gradchannel.

Graduate Studies
Programs in:
accounting (MBA)
applied behavior analysis (MA)
art therapy (MA)
business administration (MBA)
counseling psychology (MA)
curriculum and instruction (MA)
educational administration (MA)
pastoral ministry (MA)
school counseling (MA)
special education (MA)

■ CENTENARY COLLEGE
Hackettstown, NJ 07840-2100
http://www.centenarycollege.edu/

Independent-religious, coed, comprehensive institution. *Computer facilities:* 30 computers available on campus for general student use. A campuswide network can be accessed from student residence rooms and from off campus. Internet access, laptop computer are available. *Library facilities:* Taylor Memorial Learning Resource Center. *General application contact:* Dean, 908-852-1400 Ext. 2322.

Program in Business Administration
Program in:
business administration (MBA)

Program in Counseling Psychology
Programs in:
counseling (MA)
counseling psychology (MA)

Program in Education
Programs in:
instructional leadership (MA)
special education (MA)

Program in Professional Accounting
Program in:
professional accounting (MS)

■ THE COLLEGE OF NEW JERSEY

Ewing, NJ 08628

http://www.tcnj.edu/

State-supported, coed, comprehensive institution. CGS member. *Enrollment:* 6,934 graduate, professional, and undergraduate students; 111 full-time matriculated graduate/professional students (86 women), 729 part-time matriculated graduate/professional students (585 women). *Computer facilities:* 800 computers available on campus for general student use. A campuswide network can be accessed from student residence rooms and from off campus. Internet access and online class registration are available. *Library facilities:* New Library. *General application contact:* Susan L. Hydro, Office of Graduate Studies, Assistant Dean, 609-771-2300.

Find University Details at www.petersons.com/gradchannel.

Graduate Division

Program in:
- overseas education (M Ed, Certificate)

School of Culture and Society

Dr. Susan Albertine, Dean

Programs in:
- applied Spanish studies (MA)
- culture and society (MA)
- English (MA)

School of Education

Dr. William Behre, Dean

Programs in:
- community counseling: human services (MA)
- community counseling: substance abuse and addiction (MA, Certificate)
- developmental reading (M Ed)
- education (M Ed, MA, MAT, MS, Certificate, Ed S)
- educational leadership (M Ed, Certificate)
- educational technology (MS)
- elementary education (M Ed, MAT)
- elementary teaching (MAT)
- English as a second language (M Ed)
- marriage and family therapy (Ed S)
- reading certification (Certificate)
- school counseling (MA)
- school personnel licensure: preschool-grade 3 (M Ed, MAT)
- secondary education (MAT)
- special education (M Ed, MAT)
- special education with learning disabilities (Certificate)
- speech pathology (MA)
- teaching English as a second language (M Ed, Certificate)

School of Nursing, Health and Exercise Science

Dr. Susan Bakewell-Sachs, Dean

Programs in:
- health (MAT)
- health education (M Ed, MAT)
- nursing (MSN, Certificate)
- nursing, health and exercise science (M Ed, MAT, MSN, Certificate)
- physical education (M Ed, MAT)

■ COLLEGE OF SAINT ELIZABETH

Morristown, NJ 07960-6989

http://www.cse.edu/

Independent-religious, Undergraduate: women only; graduate: coed, comprehensive institution. *Enrollment:* 1,982 graduate, professional, and undergraduate students; 119 full-time matriculated graduate/professional students (97 women), 580 part-time matriculated graduate/professional students (506 women). *Graduate faculty:* 23 full-time (11 women), 37 part-time/adjunct (23 women). *Computer facilities:* 152 computers available on campus for general student use. A campuswide network can be accessed from student residence rooms and from off campus. Internet access is available. *Library facilities:* Mahoney Library. *General application contact:* Michael Szarek, Director of Enrollment Management, 973-290-4112.

Department of Business Administration and Economics

Dr. Kathleen Reddick, Director of the Graduate Program in Management

Program in:
- management (MS)

Department of Education

Dr. Alan H. Markowitz, Director of Graduate Education Programs

Programs in:
- accelerated certification for teachers (Certificate)
- assistive technology (Certificate)
- education: human services leadership (MA)
- educational technology (MA)

Department of Foods and Nutrition

Dr. Anne Boresma, Director of the Graduate Program in Nutrition

Programs in:
- dietetic internship (Certificate)
- nutrition (MS)

Department of Health Professions and Related Sciences

Linda Hunter, Director of the Graduate Program in Health Care Management

Program in:
- health care management (MS)

Department of Psychology

Dr. Valerie Scott, Director of the Graduate Program in Counseling Psychology

Programs in:
- counseling psychology (MA)
- student affairs in higher education (Certificate)

Department of Theology

Sr. Kathleen Flanagan, Director of the Graduate Program in Theology

Program in:
- theology (MA)

■ DREW UNIVERSITY

Madison, NJ 07940-1493

http://www.drew.edu/

Independent-religious, coed, university. CGS member. *Computer facilities:* Computer purchase and lease plans are available. 200 computers available on campus for general student use. A campuswide network can be accessed from student residence rooms and from off campus. Internet access and online class registration are available. *Library facilities:* Drew University Library. *General application contact:* Director of Graduate Admissions, 973-408-3110.

Find University Details at www.petersons.com/gradchannel.

Caspersen School of Graduate Studies

Programs in:
- anthropology of religion (MA, PhD)
- Christian social ethics (MA, PhD)
- English literature (MA, PhD)
- historical studies (MA, PhD)
- holocaust and genocide studies (Certificate)
- interdisciplinary studies (M Litt, D Litt)
- liturgical studies (MA, PhD)
- medical humanities (MMH, DMH, CMH)
- Methodist studies (PhD)
- modern history and literature (MA, PhD)
- philosophy of religion (MA, PhD)
- psychology and religion (MA, PhD)
- religion in ancient Israel (MA, PhD)
- sociology of religion (MA, PhD)
- systematic theology (MA, PhD)
- the New Testament and early Christianity (MA, PhD)
- theological ethics (MA, PhD)
- Wesleyan and Methodist studies (MA, PhD)
- women's studies (MA)

The Theological School

Program in:
- theology (M Div, MTS, STM, D Min, Certificate)

■ FAIRLEIGH DICKINSON UNIVERSITY, COLLEGE AT FLORHAM
Madison, NJ 07940-1099
http://www.fdu.edu/

Independent, coed, comprehensive institution. *Enrollment:* 3,562 graduate, professional, and undergraduate students; 349 full-time matriculated graduate/professional students (200 women), 556 part-time matriculated graduate/professional students (297 women). *Graduate faculty:* 116 full-time, 189 part-time/adjunct. *Computer facilities:* 300 computers available on campus for general student use. A campuswide network can be accessed from student residence rooms and from off campus. *Library facilities:* College of Florham Library. *General application contact:* Thomas M. Shea, University Director of International and Graduate Admissions, 973-443-8905.

Find University Details at www.petersons.com/gradchannel.

Anthony J. Petrocelli College of Continuing Studies
Program in:
- continuing studies (MAS, MPA, MS)

International School of Hospitality and Tourism Management
Program in:
- hospitality management studies (MS)

Public Administration Institute
Program in:
- public administration (MPA)

School of Administrative Science
Program in:
- administrative science (MAS)

Maxwell Becton College of Arts and Sciences
Programs in:
- arts and sciences (MA, MFA, MS, Certificate)
- biology (MS)
- chemistry (MS)
- clinical/counseling psychology (MA)
- corporate and organizational communication (MA)
- creative writing (MFA)
- industrial/organizational psychology (MA)
- organizational behavior (MA, Certificate)
- organizational leadership (Certificate)

Silberman College of Business
Dr. David Steele, Dean
Programs in:
- accounting (MS)
- business (MBA, MS, Certificate)
- business administration (MBA)
- entrepreneurial studies (MBA, Certificate)
- evolving technology (Certificate)
- finance (MBA, Certificate)
- international business (MBA, Certificate)
- international taxation (Certificate)
- management (MBA, Certificate)
- marketing (MBA, Certificate)
- taxation (MS, Certificate)

Center for Healthcare Management Studies
Programs in:
- healthcare management studies (MBA, Certificate)
- pharmaceutical studies (MBA, Certificate)

Center for Human Resource Management Studies
Programs in:
- human resource management (MBA)
- human resource management studies (MBA)

University College: Arts, Sciences, and Professional Studies
Program in:
- arts, sciences, and professional studies (MA, MAT, Certificate)

Peter Sammartino School of Education
Programs in:
- education for certified teachers (MA, Certificate)
- educational leadership (MA)
- instructional technology (Certificate)
- literacy/reading (Certificate)
- teaching (MAT)

■ FAIRLEIGH DICKINSON UNIVERSITY, METROPOLITAN CAMPUS
Teaneck, NJ 07666-1914
http://www.fdu.edu/

Independent, coed, comprehensive institution. *Enrollment:* 8,491 graduate, professional, and undergraduate students; 937 full-time matriculated graduate/professional students (456 women), 1,622 part-time matriculated graduate/professional students (965 women). *Graduate faculty:* 185 full-time, 440 part-time/adjunct. *Computer facilities:* 210 computers available on campus for general student use. A campuswide network can be accessed from student residence rooms and from off campus. *Library facilities:* Weiner Library plus 3 others. *General application contact:* Thomas Shea, University Director of International and Graduate Admissions, 201-692-2554.

Find University Details at www.petersons.com/gradchannel.

Anthony J. Petrocelli College of Continuing Studies
Kenneth T. Vehrkens, Dean
Program in:
- continuing studies (MAS, MPA, MS, Certificate)

International School of Hospitality and Tourism Management
Dr. Richard Wisch, Director
Program in:
- hospitality management studies (MS)

Public Administration Institute
Dr. William Roberts, Director
Programs in:
- public administration (MPA, Certificate)
- public non-profit management (Certificate)

School of Administrative Science
Ronald Calissi, Director/Executive Associate Dean
Program in:
- administrative science (MAS, Certificate)

Maxwell Becton College of Arts and Sciences
Programs in:
- arts and sciences (MA)
- corporate communications (MA)

Silberman College of Business
Dr. Robert Greenfield, Dean
Programs in:
- accounting (MS, Certificate)
- business (MBA, MS, Certificate)
- business administration (MBA)
- entrepreneurial studies (MBA, Certificate)
- finance (MBA, Certificate)
- international business (MBA)
- management (MBA, Certificate)
- management information systems (Certificate)
- marketing (MBA, Certificate)
- taxation (MS)

Center for Healthcare Management Studies
Dr. Peter Caliguari, Director
Programs in:
- chemical studies (Certificate)
- management for health system executives (MBA)
- pharmaceutical studies (MBA, Certificate)

Center for Human Resources Management Studies
Programs in:
- executive education (MBA)
- human resource management (Certificate)

University College: Arts, Sciences, and Professional Studies
Dr. John Snyder, Dean
Programs in:
- art and media studies (MA)
- arts, sciences, and professional studies (MA, MAT, MS, MSEE, MSN, PhD, Psy D, Certificate)

English and literature (MA)
media and communications (MA)
systems science (MS)

Henry P. Becton School of Nursing and Allied Health
Dr. Minerva Guttman, Director
Programs in:
medical technology (MS)
nursing (MSN, Certificate)

Peter Sammartino School of Education
Dr. Vicki Cohen, Director
Programs in:
dyslexia specialist (Certificate)
education for certified teachers (MA)
educational leadership (MA)
instructional technology (Certificate)
learning disabilities (MA)
literacy/reading (Certificate)
multilingual education (MA)
teacher of the handicapped (Certificate)
teaching (MAT)

School of Computer Sciences and Engineering
Dr. Alfredo Tan, Director
Programs in:
computer engineering (MS)
computer science (MS)
e-commerce (MS)
electrical engineering (MSEE)
management information systems (MS)
mathematical foundation (MS)

School of History, Political and International Studies
Dr. Faramarz S. Fatemi, Director
Programs in:
history (MA)
international studies (MA)
political science (MA)

School of Natural Sciences
Dr. Irwin Isquith, Director
Programs in:
biology (MS)
chemistry (MS)
science (MA)

School of Psychology
Dr. Christopher Capuano, Director
Programs in:
clinical psychology (PhD)
clinical psychopharmacology (MA)
general-theoretical psychology (MA, Certificate)
school psychology (MA, Psy D)

■ GEORGIAN COURT UNIVERSITY
Lakewood, NJ 08701-2697
http://www.georgian.edu/

Independent-religious, Undergraduate: women only; graduate: coed, comprehensive institution. *Enrollment:* 3,047 graduate, professional, and undergraduate students; 199 full-time matriculated graduate/professional students (170 women), 880 part-time matriculated graduate/professional students (722 women). *Graduate faculty:* 54 full-time (29 women), 54 part-time/adjunct (28 women). *Computer facilities:* 180 computers available on campus for general student use. A campuswide network can be accessed from student residence rooms. Internet access is available. *Library facilities:* The Sister Mary Joseph Cunningham Library. *General application contact:* Eugene Soltys, Director of Graduate Admissions, 732-987-2760 Ext. 2760.

School of Arts and Humanities
Dr. Linda James, Dean
Program in:
theology (MA, Certificate)

School of Business
Dr. Siamack Shoisi, Dean
Program in:
business (MBA)

School of Education
Sr. Mary Gurley, OSF, Dean
Programs in:
administration, supervision, and curriculum planning (MA)
early intervention studies (Certificate)
education (MA)
instructional technology (MA, Certificate)
special education (MA)
substance awareness coordinator (Certificate)

School of Sciences and Mathematics
Dr. Linda James, Dean
Programs in:
biology (MS)
counseling psychology (MA)
holistic health (Certificate)
holistic health studies (MA)
mathematics (MA)
professional counselor (Certificate)
school psychology (Certificate)

■ KEAN UNIVERSITY
Union, NJ 07083
http://www.kean.edu/

State-supported, coed, comprehensive institution. CGS member. *Enrollment:* 13,050 graduate, professional, and undergraduate students; 626 full-time matriculated graduate/professional students (483 women), 1,592 part-time matriculated graduate/professional students (1,229 women). *Graduate faculty:* 215 full-time (110 women). *Computer facilities:* Computer purchase and lease plans are available. 2,000 computers available on campus for general student use. A campuswide network can be accessed from student residence rooms and from off campus. Internet access and online class registration are available. *Library facilities:* Nancy Thompson Library. *Graduate expenses:* Tuition, state resident: full-time $8,856; part-time $369 per credit. Tuition, nonresident: full-time $11,256; part-time $469 per credit. *General application contact:* Joanne Morris, Director of Graduate Admissions, 908-737-3355.

Find University Details at www.petersons.com/gradchannel.

College of Business and Public Administration
Dr. Alfred Ntoko, Dean
Programs in:
accounting (MS)
business and public administration (MPA, MS)
criminal justice (MPA)
environmental management (MPA)
health services administration (MPA)
non-profit management (MPA)
public administration (MPA)

College of Education
Dr. Frank Esposito, Dean
Programs in:
administration in early childhood and family studies (MA)
adult literacy (MA)
advanced curriculum and teaching (MA)
alcohol and drug abuse counseling (MA)
basic skills (MA)
bilingual/bicultural education (MA)
business and industry counseling (MA, PMC)
classroom instruction (MA)
community/agency counseling (MA)
developmental disabilities (MA)
early childhood education (MA)
earth science (MA)
education (MA, MS, PMC)
education for family living (MA)
educational media specialist (MA)
educational technology (MA)
elementary education (MA)
emotionally disturbed and socially maladjusted (MA)
exercise science (MS)
learning disabilities (MA)
mathematics/science/computer education (MA)
pre-school handicapped (MA)
principals and supervisors (MA)
reading specialization (MA)
school business administration (MA)
school counseling (MA)
speech language pathology (MA)
supervisors (MA)
teaching (MA)
teaching English as a second language (MA)

College of Humanities and Social Sciences
Dr. Kenneth Dollarhide, Dean
Programs in:
advanced standing (MSW)
behavioral sciences (MA)
business and industry counseling (MA)
communication studies (MA)
educational psychology (MA)

Kean University (continued)
human behavior and organizational psychology (MA)
humanities and social sciences (MA, MSW, Diploma)
marriage and family therapy (Diploma)
political science (MA)
psychological services (MA)
school psychology (Diploma)
social work (MSW)

College of Natural, Applied and Health Sciences

Dr. Xiaobo Yu, Dean
Programs in:
clinical management (MSN)
community health (MSN)
computer applications (MA)
computing, statistics and mathematics (MS)
natural, applied and health sciences (MA, MS, MSN)
nursing and public administration)
occupational therapy (MS)
supervision of math education (MA)
teaching of math (MA)

Nathan Weiss Graduate College

Dr. Kristie Reilly, Dean
Programs in:
biotechnology (MS)
global management (MBA)
holocaust and genocide studies (MA)
management information systems (MSMIS)

School of Visual and Performing Arts

Dr. Carole Shaffer-Koros, Dean
Programs in:
certification (MA)
graphic communication technology management (MS)
liberal studies (MA)
studio/research (MA)
supervision (MA)
visual and performing arts (MA, MS)

■ MONMOUTH UNIVERSITY
West Long Branch, NJ 07764-1898
http://www.monmouth.edu/

Independent, coed, comprehensive institution. *Enrollment:* 6,399 graduate, professional, and undergraduate students; 468 full-time matriculated graduate/professional students (342 women), 1,284 part-time matriculated graduate/professional students (956 women). *Graduate faculty:* 143 full-time (70 women), 53 part-time/adjunct (34 women). *Computer facilities:* 673 computers available on campus for general student use. A campuswide network can be accessed from student residence rooms and from off campus. Internet access is available. *Library facilities:* Monmouth University Library. *Graduate expenses:* Tuition: full-time $12,780; part-time $710 per credit. Required fees: $628; $314 per term. *General application contact:* Kevin Roane, Director, Office of Graduate Admission, 732-571-3452.

Find University Details at www.petersons.com/gradchannel.

Graduate School

Dr. Datta V. Naik, Dean
Programs in:
community and international development (MSW)
computer science (MS)
corporate and public communication (MA)
criminal justice administration (MA, Certificate)
English (MA)
history (MA)
human resources communication (Certificate)
liberal arts (MA)
media studies (Certificate)
practice with families and children (MSW)
professional counseling (PMC)
psychological counseling (MA)
public policy (MA)
public relations (Certificate)
software development (Certificate)
software engineering (MS, Certificate)

The Marjorie K. Unterberg School of Nursing and Health Studies

Dr. Janet Mahoney, Director
Programs in:
advanced practice nursing (Post-Master's Certificate)
nursing (MSN)
school nursing (Certificate)
substance awareness coordinator (Certificate)

School of Business Administration

Donald Smith, Program Director
Programs in:
accounting (MBA)
business administration (MBA)
health care management (MBA, Certificate)

School of Education

Dr. Lynn Romeo, Program Director
Programs in:
educational counseling (MS Ed)
elementary education (MAT)
learning disabilities-teacher consultant (Certificate)
principal studies (MS Ed)
reading specialist (MS Ed, Certificate)
special education (MS Ed)
supervisor (Certificate)
teacher of the handicapped (Certificate)

■ MONTCLAIR STATE UNIVERSITY
Montclair, NJ 07043-1624
http://www.montclair.edu/

State-supported, coed, comprehensive institution. CGS member. *Enrollment:* 16,076 graduate, professional, and undergraduate students; 803 full-time matriculated graduate/professional students (597 women), 2,571 part-time matriculated graduate/professional students (1,877 women). *Graduate faculty:* 491 full-time (218 women), 706 part-time/adjunct (404 women). *Computer facilities:* Computer purchase and lease plans are available. 218 computers available on campus for general student use. A campuswide network can be accessed from student residence rooms and from off campus. Internet access and online class registration are available. *Library facilities:* Sprague Library. *Graduate expenses:* Tuition, state resident: part-time $450 per credit. Tuition, nonresident: part-time $682 per credit. Tuition and fees vary according to degree level and program. *General application contact:* Dr. Kim C. O'Halloran, Associate Dean of the Graduate School, 973-655-5147.

Find University Details at www.petersons.com/gradchannel.

The Graduate School

Dr. Kim C. O'Halloran, Associate Dean of the Graduate School

College of Education and Human Services

Dr. Ada Beth Cutler, Dean
Programs in:
administration and supervision (MA)
advanced counseling (Certificate)
counseling and guidance (MA)
critical thinking (M Ed)
early childhood /elementary education (M Ed)
early childhood education and teaching students in disabilities (MAT)
early childhood special education (M Ed, Certificate)
education (M Ed)
education and human services (M Ed, MA, MAT, MS, Ed D, Certificate)
educational technology (M Ed)
elementary education with disabilities (MAT)
elementary school teacher (Certificate)
food safety instructor (Certificate)
health and physical education (Certificate)
health education (MA)
learning disabilities (Certificate)
mathematics education (Ed D)
nutrition and exercise science (MS, Certificate)
nutrition and food science (MS)
philosophy for children (M Ed, Ed D, Certificate)
physical education (MA, Certificate)
reading (MA, Certificate)
reading specialist (Certificate)
school administrator (Certificate)
school business administrator (Certificate)
school counselor (Certificate)

school library media specialist (Certificate)
substance awareness coordinator (Certificate)
teaching (MAT, Certificate)

College of Humanities and Social Sciences
Dr. Mary Papazian, Dean
Programs in:
- applied linguistics (MA)
- applied sociology (MA)
- audiology (Sc D)
- child advocacy (MA, Certificate)
- dispute resolution (MA)
- educational psychology (MA)
- English (MA)
- French (MA, Certificate)
- governance, compliance and regulation (MA)
- humanities and social sciences (MA, Sc D, Certificate)
- law office management and technology (MA)
- paralegal (Certificate)
- psychology (MA)
- public child welfare (MA)
- school psychologist (Certificate)
- social sciences (MA)
- Spanish (MA)
- speech/language pathology (MA)
- teaching English to speakers of other languages (MA)
- translating and interpreting Spanish (Certificate)

College of Science and Mathematics
Dr. Robert Prezant, Dean
Programs in:
- applied mathematics (MS)
- applied statistics (MS)
- biology (MS)
- chemistry (MS)
- CISCO (Certificate)
- environmental management (MA, D Env M)
- environmental studies (MS)
- geoscience (MS, Certificate)
- informatics (MS)
- mathematics (MS)
- molecular biology (Certificate)
- object oriented computing (Certificate)
- science and mathematics (MA, MS, D Env M, Certificate)
- teaching middle grades math (Certificate)

School of Business
Dr. Alan Oppenheim, Dean
Programs in:
- accounting (MBA)
- business (MA, MBA)
- business economics (MBA)
- finance (MBA)
- international business (MBA)
- management (MBA)
- management information systems (MBA)
- marketing (MBA)

School of the Arts
Dr. Geoffrey Newman, Dean
Programs in:
- art education (MA)
- art history (MA)
- arts (MA, MFA, AD, Certificate)
- music (AD)
- music education (MA)
- music therapy (MA)
- organizational communication (MA)
- performance (MA, Certificate)
- public relations (MA)
- speech communication (MA)
- studio arts (MA, MFA)
- theatre (MA)
- theory/composition (MA)

■ NEW JERSEY CITY UNIVERSITY
Jersey City, NJ 07305-1597
http://www.njcu.edu/

State-supported, coed, comprehensive institution. *Enrollment:* 8,523 graduate, professional, and undergraduate students; 47 full-time matriculated graduate/professional students (37 women), 965 part-time matriculated graduate/professional students (668 women). *Graduate faculty:* 177. *Computer facilities:* 1,400 computers available on campus for general student use. A campuswide network can be accessed from student residence rooms and from off campus. Internet access and online class registration are available. *Library facilities:* Congressman Frank J. Guarini Library. *Graduate expenses:* Tuition, state resident: full-time $7,038; part-time $391 per credit. Tuition, nonresident: full-time $12,510; part-time $695 per credit. Required fees: $65 per credit. *General application contact:* Dr. Richard Hendrix, Dean of Graduate Studies, 201-200-3409.

Graduate and Continuing Education
Dr. Richard Hendrix, Dean of Graduate Studies

College of Arts and Sciences
Dr. Liza Fiol-Mata, Dean
Programs in:
- art (MFA)
- art education (MA)
- arts and sciences (MA, MFA, MM, PD)
- counseling (MA)
- educational psychology (MA, PD)
- mathematics education (MA)
- music education (MA)
- performance (MM)
- school psychology (PD)
- studio art (MFA)

College of Education
Dr. Ivan Banks, Acting Dean
Programs in:
- basics and urban studies (MA)
- bilingual/bicultural education and English as a second language (MA)
- early childhood education (MA)
- education (MA, MAT)
- educational administration and supervision (MA)
- educational technology (MA)
- elementary education (MAT)
- elementary school reading (MA)
- reading specialist (MA)
- secondary education (MAT)
- secondary school reading (MA)
- special education (MA)

College of Professional Studies
Dr. Sandra Bloomberg, Dean
Programs in:
- accounting (MS)
- community health education (MS)
- criminal justice (MS)
- finance (MS)
- health administration (MS)
- holistic nursing (MSN)
- law enforcement (MS)
- professional security studies (MS)
- school health education (MS)
- urban health (MSN)

■ NEW JERSEY INSTITUTE OF TECHNOLOGY
Newark, NJ 07102
http://www.njit.edu/

State-supported, coed, university. CGS member. *Enrollment:* 8,209 graduate, professional, and undergraduate students; 1,569 full-time matriculated graduate/professional students (488 women), 1,260 part-time matriculated graduate/professional students (378 women). *Graduate faculty:* 399 full-time (59 women), 247 part-time/adjunct (42 women). *Computer facilities:* Computer purchase and lease plans are available. 1,938 computers available on campus for general student use. A campuswide network can be accessed from student residence rooms and from off campus. Internet access and online class registration are available. *Library facilities:* Van Houten Library plus 1 other. *Graduate expenses:* Tuition, state resident: full-time $11,896; part-time $648 per credit. Tuition, nonresident: full-time $16,900; part-time $892 per credit. Required fees: $336; $66 per credit. $168 per term. Tuition and fees vary according to course load. *General application contact:* Kathryn Kelly, Director of Admissions, 973-596-3300.

Office of Graduate Studies
Dr. Ronald Kane, Dean of Graduate Studies

College of Computing Science
Dr. Narain Gehani, Chairperson
Programs in:
- computational biology (MS)
- computer science (MS, PhD)
- information systems (MS, PhD)
- telecommunication (MS)

College of Science and Liberal Arts
Dr. Fadi P. Deek, Acting Dean

New Jersey Institute of Technology (continued)

Programs in:
- applied mathematics (MS)
- applied physics (MS, PhD)
- applied statistics (MS)
- biology (MS, PhD)
- chemistry (MS, PhD)
- computing biology (MS)
- environmental policy studies (MS, PhD)
- environmental science (MS, PhD)
- history (MA, MAT)
- materials science and engineering (MS, PhD)
- mathematics science (PhD)
- occupational safety and industrial hygiene (MS)
- professional and technical communication (MS)
- public health (MS)
- science and liberal arts (MA, MAT, MS, PhD)

Newark College of Engineering
Dr. John Schuring, Dean
Programs in:
- biomedical engineering (MS, PhD)
- chemical engineering (MS, PhD)
- civil engineering (MS, PhD)
- computer engineering (MS, PhD)
- electrical engineering (MS, PhD)
- engineering (MS, PhD, Engineer)
- engineering management (MS)
- engineering science (MS)
- environmental engineering (MS, PhD)
- industrial engineering (MS, PhD)
- Internet engineering (MS)
- manufacturing engineering (MS)
- mechanical engineering (MS, PhD, Engineer)
- occupational safety and health engineering (MS)
- pharmaceutical engineering (MS)
- transportation (MS, PhD)

School of Architecture
Urs P. Gauchat, Dean
Programs in:
- architecture (M Arch, MS)
- infrastructure planning (MIP)
- urban systems (PhD)

School of Management
Dr. David L Hawk, Dean
Programs in:
- management of business administration (MBA)
- management of technology (MS, PhD)

■ PRINCETON UNIVERSITY
Princeton, NJ 08544-1019
http://www.princeton.edu/

Independent, coed, university. CGS member. *Computer facilities:* Computer purchase and lease plans are available. 500 computers available on campus for general student use. A campuswide network can be accessed from student residence rooms and from off campus. Internet access and online class registration, academic applications and courseware are available. *Library facilities:* Harvey S. Firestone Memorial Library plus 14 others. *General application contact:* Director of Graduate Admission, 609-258-3034.

Center for Photonic and Optoelectronic Materials (POEM)
Program in:
- photonic and optoelectronic materials (PhD)

Graduate School
Programs in:
- ancient history (PhD)
- ancient Near Eastern studies (PhD)
- anthropology (PhD)
- applied and computational mathematics (PhD)
- applied physics (M Eng, MSE, PhD)
- astrophysical sciences (PhD)
- atmospheric and oceanic sciences (PhD)
- biology (PhD)
- chemical engineering (M Eng, MSE, PhD)
- chemistry (PhD)
- Chinese and Japanese art and archaeology (PhD)
- classical archaeology (PhD)
- classical art and archaeology (PhD)
- classical philosophy (PhD)
- community college history teaching (PhD)
- comparative literature (PhD)
- composition (PhD)
- computational methods (M Eng, MSE)
- computer science (M Eng, MSE, PhD)
- demography (PhD, Certificate)
- demography and public affairs (PhD)
- dynamics and control systems (M Eng, MSE, PhD)
- East Asian civilizations (PhD)
- East Asian studies (PhD)
- economics (PhD)
- economics and demography (PhD)
- electrical engineering (M Eng, MSE, PhD)
- energy and environmental policy (M Eng, MSE, PhD)
- energy conversion, propulsion, and combustion (M Eng, MSE, PhD)
- English (PhD)
- environmental engineering and water resources (PhD)
- financial engineering (M Eng)
- flight science and technology (M Eng, MSE, PhD)
- fluid mechanics (M Eng, MSE, PhD)
- French and Italian (PhD)
- geological and geophysical sciences (PhD)
- Germanic languages and literatures (PhD)
- history (PhD)
- history of science (PhD)
- history, archaeology and religions of the ancient world (PhD)
- industrial chemistry (MS)
- Islamic studies (PhD)
- mathematical physics (PhD)
- mathematics (PhD)
- mechanics, materials, and structures (M Eng, MSE, PhD)
- molecular biology (PhD)
- molecular biophysics (PhD)
- musicology (PhD)
- Near Eastern studies (MA)
- neuroscience (PhD)
- operations research and financial engineering (MSE, PhD)
- philosophy (PhD)
- physics (PhD)
- physics and chemical physics (PhD)
- plasma physics (PhD)
- plasma science and technology (MSE, PhD)
- political philosophy (PhD)
- politics (PhD)
- polymer sciences and materials (MSE, PhD)
- psychology (PhD)
- religion (PhD)
- Slavic languages and literatures (PhD)
- sociology (PhD)
- sociology and demography (PhD)
- Spanish and Portuguese languages and cultures (PhD)
- statistics and operations research (MSE, PhD)
- transportation systems (MSE, PhD)

Bendheim Center for Finance
Program in:
- finance (M Fin)

School of Architecture
Program in:
- architecture (M Arch, PhD)

Woodrow Wilson School of Public and International Affairs
Program in:
- public and international affairs (MPA, MPA-URP, MPP, PhD)

■ RAMAPO COLLEGE OF NEW JERSEY
Mahwah, NJ 07430-1680
http://www.ramapo.edu/

State-supported, coed, comprehensive institution. *Enrollment:* 5,499 graduate, professional, and undergraduate students; 47 matriculated graduate/professional students (31 women). *Graduate faculty:* 16. *Computer facilities:* 580 computers available on campus for general student use. A campuswide network can be accessed from student residence rooms and from off campus. Internet access and online class registration, part of the campus is WI FI accessible are available. *Library facilities:* George T. Potter Library. *Graduate expenses:* Tuition, state resident: part-time $450 per credit. Tuition, nonresident: part-time $578 per credit. *General application contact:* Dr. Anthony T. Padovano, Director, 201-684-7430.

Program in Liberal Studies
Dr. Anthony T. Padovano, Director
Program in:
liberal studies (MALS)

■ THE RICHARD STOCKTON COLLEGE OF NEW JERSEY
Pomona, NJ 08240-0195
http://www.stockton.edu/

State-supported, coed, comprehensive institution. *Enrollment:* 7,212 graduate, professional, and undergraduate students; 127 full-time matriculated graduate/professional students (101 women), 361 part-time matriculated graduate/professional students (257 women). *Graduate faculty:* 85 full-time (53 women), 22 part-time/adjunct (12 women). *Computer facilities:* 1,375 computers available on campus for general student use. A campuswide network can be accessed from student residence rooms and from off campus. Internet access and online class registration are available. *Library facilities:* The Richard Stockton College of New Jersey Library. *Graduate expenses:* Tuition, state resident: full-time $9,746. Tuition, nonresident: full-time $14,462. Required fees: $2,340. *General application contact:* John Iacovelli, Dean of Enrollment Management, 866-RSC-2885.

Graduate Programs
Dr. Deborah M. Figart, Dean of Graduate Studies
Programs in:
business studies (MBA)
criminal justice (MA)
education (MA)
Holocaust and genocide studies (MA)
instructional technology (MA)
nursing (MSN)
occupational therapy (MSOT)
paralegal (Certificate)
physical therapy (MPT, DPT)

■ RIDER UNIVERSITY
Lawrenceville, NJ 08648-3001
http://www.rider.edu/

Independent, coed, comprehensive institution. *Enrollment:* 5,790 graduate, professional, and undergraduate students; 255 full-time matriculated graduate/professional students (165 women), 749 part-time matriculated graduate/professional students (513 women). *Graduate faculty:* 78 full-time (27 women), 78 part-time/adjunct (35 women). *Computer facilities:* Computer purchase and lease plans are available. 403 computers available on campus for general student use. A campuswide network can be accessed from student residence rooms and from off campus. Internet access and online class registration are available. *Library facilities:* Franklin F. Moore Library plus 1 other. *Graduate expenses:* Tuition: part-time $525 per credit. Required fees: $35 per course. $30 per semester. *General application contact:* Jamie L Mitchell, Director of Graduate Admissions, 609-896-5036.

College of Business Administration
Dr. John Farrell, MBA Program Director
Programs in:
accountancy (M Acc)
business administration (M Acc, MBA)

Department of Graduate Education, Leadership and Counseling
Dr. Dennis C. Buss, Chair
Programs in:
business education (Certificate)
counseling services (MA, Ed S)
curriculum, instruction and supervision (MA)
director of school counseling services (Certificate)
educational administration (MA)
elementary education (Certificate)
English as a second language (Certificate)
English education (Certificate)
mathematics education (Certificate)
organizational leadership (MA)
preschool to grade 3 (Certificate)
principal (Certificate)
reading specialist (Certificate)
reading/language arts (MA, Certificate)
school business administrator (Certificate)
school counseling services (Certificate)
school psychology (Ed S)
science education (Certificate)
social studies education (Certificate)
special education (MA)
supervisor (Certificate)
teacher certification (Certificate)
teaching (MA)
world languages (Certificate)

■ ROWAN UNIVERSITY
Glassboro, NJ 08028-1701
http://www.rowan.edu/

State-supported, coed, comprehensive institution. CGS member. *Enrollment:* 9,578 graduate, professional, and undergraduate students; 199 full-time matriculated graduate/professional students (143 women), 582 part-time matriculated graduate/professional students (438 women). *Graduate faculty:* 90 full-time (39 women), 24 part-time/adjunct (7 women). *Computer facilities:* 350 computers available on campus for general student use. A campuswide network can be accessed from student residence rooms and from off campus. Internet access and online class registration are available. *Library facilities:* Keith and Shirley Campbell Library plus 2 others. *Graduate expenses:* Tuition, state resident: full-time $9,882; part-time $549 per credit. Tuition, nonresident: full-time $9,882; part-time $549 per credit. Tuition and fees vary according to degree level. *General application contact:* Dr. Jay Kuder, Dean, Graduate School, 856-256-4050.

Graduate School
Dr. Jay Kuder, Dean, Graduate School

College of Communication
Dr. Craig Monroe, Dean
Programs in:
public relations (MA)
writing (MA)

College of Education
Dr. Carol Sharp, Dean
Programs in:
business administration (MA)
collaborative teaching (MST)
counseling in educational settings (MA)
education (M Ed, MA, MST, Ed D, CAGS, Ed S)
educational leadership (Ed D)
higher education administration (MA)
learning disabilities (MA)
music education (MA)
principal preparation (MA)
reading education (MA)
school administration (MA, CAGS)
school and public librarianship (MA)
school psychology (MA, Ed S)
special education (MA)
standards-based practice (M Ed)
supervision and curriculum development (MA)
teaching-secondary (MST)

College of Engineering
Dr. Dianne Dorland, Dean
Program in:
engineering (MS)

College of Fine and Performing Arts
Dr. Donald Gephardt, Dean
Programs in:
fine and performing arts (MA, MM)
music (MM)
theatre (MA)

College of Liberal Arts and Sciences
Dr. Jay Harper, Dean
Programs in:
liberal arts and sciences (MA, CAGS)
mathematics (MA)
mental health counseling and applied psychology (MA, CAGS)

William G. Rohrer College of Business
Dr. Edward Schoen, Dean
Programs in:
business (MBA)
business administration (MBA)

■ RUTGERS, THE STATE UNIVERSITY OF NEW JERSEY, CAMDEN
Camden, NJ 08102-1401
http://camden-www.rutgers.edu/

State-supported, coed, university. *Enrollment:* 5,165 graduate, professional, and undergraduate students; 744 full-time

Rutgers, The State University of New Jersey, Camden (continued)
matriculated graduate/professional students (349 women), 727 part-time matriculated graduate/professional students (318 women). *Graduate faculty:* 228 full-time (88 women), 173 part-time/adjunct (65 women). *Computer facilities:* 184 computers available on campus for general student use. A campuswide network can be accessed from student residence rooms and from off campus. Internet access, online grade reports are available. *Library facilities:* Paul Robeson Library plus 2 others. *General application contact:* Information Contact, 856-225-6149.

Graduate School of Arts and Sciences

Dr. Michael Palis, Interim Dean
Programs in:
- American and public history (MA)
- biology (MS)
- chemistry (MS)
- childhood studies (MA, PhD)
- computer science (MS)
- criminal justice (MA)
- education policy and leadeship (MPA)
- English (MA)
- international public service and development (MPA)
- liberal studies (MA)
- mathematics (MS)
- physical therapy (MPT)
- psychology (MA)
- public management (MPA)

School of Business

Mitchell P. Koza, Dean
Program in:
- business (MBA)

School of Law

Rayman L. Solomon, Dean
Program in:
- law (JD)

■ RUTGERS, THE STATE UNIVERSITY OF NEW JERSEY, NEWARK

Newark, NJ 07102
http://www.newark.rutgers.edu/

State-supported, coed, university. CGS member. *Enrollment:* 10,203 graduate, professional, and undergraduate students; 1,406 full-time matriculated graduate/professional students (632 women), 2,294 part-time matriculated graduate/professional students (1,044 women). *Graduate faculty:* 403 full-time (151 women), 203 part-time/adjunct (85 women). *Computer facilities:* 708 computers available on campus for general student use. A campuswide network can be accessed from student residence rooms and from off campus. Internet access, online grade reports are available. *Library facilities:* John Cotton Dana Library plus 4 others. *General application contact:* Information Contact, 973-353-5205.

Find University Details at www.petersons.com/gradchannel.

Graduate School

Dr. Barry R. Komisarwk, Associate Dean
Programs in:
- accounting (PhD)
- accounting information systems (PhD)
- American political system (MA)
- analytical chemistry (MS, PhD)
- applied physics (MS, PhD)
- biochemistry (MS, PhD)
- biology (MS, PhD)
- cognitive neuroscience (PhD)
- cognitive science (PhD)
- computational biology (MS)
- computer information systems (PhD)
- criminal justice (PhD)
- economics (MA)
- English (MA)
- environmental geology (MS)
- environmental science (MS, PhD)
- finance (PhD)
- health care administration (MPA)
- history (MA, MAT)
- human resources administration (MPA)
- information technology (PhD)
- inorganic chemistry (MS, PhD)
- integrative neuroscience (PhD)
- international business (PhD)
- international relations (MA)
- jazz history and research (MA)
- liberal studies (MALS)
- management science (PhD)
- marketing (PhD)
- mathematical sciences (PhD)
- nursing (MS)
- organic chemistry (MS, PhD)
- organization management (PhD)
- perception (PhD)
- physical chemistry (MS, PhD)
- psychobiology (PhD)
- public administration (PhD)
- public management (MPA)
- public policy analysis (MPA)
- social cognition (PhD)
- urban systems (PhD)
- urban systems and issues (MPA)

Division of Global Affairs

Program in:
- global affairs (MS, PhD)

Program in Criminal Justice

Dr. Bonnie Veysey, Program Director
Program in:
- criminal justice (PhD)

Rutgers Business School: Graduate Programs-Newark/New Brunswick

Programs in:
- accounting (PhD)
- accounting information systems (PhD)
- business (M Accy, MBA, MQF, PhD, Certificate)
- business environment (MBA)
- customized concentration (MBA)
- finance (PhD)
- finance and economics (MBA, MQF)
- global business (MBA)
- government financial management (Certificate)
- governmental accounting (M Accy)
- individualized study (PhD)
- information technology (PhD)
- international business (PhD)
- management and business strategy (MBA)
- management science (PhD)
- management science and information systems (MBA)
- marketing (MBA)
- organizational management (PhD)
- professional accounting (MBA)
- supply chain management (PhD)
- taxation (M Accy)

School of Law

Stuart L. Deutsch, Dean
Program in:
- law (JD)

■ RUTGERS, THE STATE UNIVERSITY OF NEW JERSEY, NEW BRUNSWICK

New Brunswick, NJ 08901-1281
http://www.rutgers.edu/

State-supported, coed, university. CGS member. *Enrollment:* 34,392 graduate, professional, and undergraduate students; 3,894 full-time matriculated graduate/professional students (2,349 women), 3,807 part-time matriculated graduate/professional students (2,540 women). *Graduate faculty:* 1,527 full-time (488 women), 685 part-time/adjunct (335 women). *Computer facilities:* 1,450 computers available on campus for general student use. A campuswide network can be accessed from student residence rooms and from off campus. Internet access, online grade reports are available. *Library facilities:* Archibald S. Alexander Library plus 14 others. *General application contact:* Information Contact, 732-932-7711.

Edward J. Bloustein School of Planning and Public Policy

James W. Hughes, Dean
Programs in:
- planning and public policy (MCRP, MCRS, MPAP, MPH, MPP, Dr PH, PhD)
- public health (MPH, Dr PH, PhD)
- public policy (MPAP, MPP)
- urban planning and policy development (MCRP, MCRS, PhD)

Ernest Mario School of Pharmacy

John L. Colaizzi, Dean
Program in:
- pharmacy (Pharm D)

Graduate School

Programs in:

- African diaspora (PhD)
- air resources (MS, PhD)
- American political institutions (PhD)
- analytical chemistry (MS, PhD)
- anthropology (MA, PhD)
- applied mathematics (MS, PhD)
- applied microbiology (MS, PhD)
- aquatic biology (MS, PhD)
- aquatic chemistry (MS, PhD)
- art history (MA, PhD)
- astronomy (MS, PhD)
- atmospheric science (MS, PhD)
- biochemistry (MS, PhD)
- biological chemistry (PhD)
- biomedical engineering (MS, PhD)
- biophysics (PhD)
- biopsychology and behavioral neuroscience (PhD)
- bioresource engineering (MS)
- cell biology (MS, PhD)
- cellular and molecular pharmacology (PhD)
- ceramic and materials science and engineering (MS, PhD)
- chemical and biochemical engineering (MS, PhD)
- chemistry and physics of aerosol and hydrosol systems (MS, PhD)
- chemistry education (MST)
- civil and environmental engineering (MS, PhD)
- classics (MA, MAT, PhD)
- clinical microbiology (MS, PhD)
- clinical psychology (PhD)
- cognitive psychology (PhD)
- communication, information and library studies (PhD)
- communications and solid-state electronics (MS, PhD)
- comparative literature (MA, PhD)
- comparative politics (PhD)
- composition (MA, PhD)
- computational biology and molecular biophysics (PhD)
- computational fluid dynamics (MS, PhD)
- computational molecular biology (PhD)
- computer engineering (MS, PhD)
- computer science (MS, PhD)
- condensed matter physics (MS, PhD)
- control systems (MS, PhD)
- design and dynamics (MS, PhD)
- developmental biology (MS, PhD)
- digital signal processing (MS, PhD)
- diplomatic history (PhD)
- direct intervention in interpersonal situations (PhD)
- early American history (PhD)
- early modern European history (PhD)
- ecology and evolution (MS, PhD)
- economics (MA, PhD)
- elementary particle physics (MS, PhD)
- endocrine control of growth and metabolism (MS, PhD)
- entomology (MS, PhD)
- environmental chemistry (MS, PhD)
- environmental microbiology (MS, PhD)
- environmental toxicology (MS, PhD)
- exposure assessment (PhD)
- fate and effects of pollutants (MS, PhD)
- fluid mechanics (MS, PhD)
- food and business economics (MS)
- food science (M Phil, MS, PhD)
- French (MA, PhD)
- French studies (MAT)
- geography (MA, MS, PhD)
- geological sciences (MS, PhD)
- German (PhD)
- global/comparative history (PhD)
- heat transfer (MS, PhD)
- historic preservation (PhD)
- history (PhD)
- history of technology, environment and health (PhD)
- horticulture (MS, PhD)
- immunology (MS, PhD)
- industrial and systems engineering (MS, PhD)
- industrial relations and human resources (PhD)
- industrial-occupational toxicology (MS, PhD)
- information technology (MS)
- inorganic chemistry (MS, PhD)
- interdisciplinary developmental psychology (PhD)
- interdisciplinary health psychology (PhD)
- intermediate energy nuclear physics (MS)
- international relations (PhD)
- Italian (MA)
- Italian history (PhD)
- Italian literature and literary criticism (MA, PhD)
- language, literature and civilization (MAT)
- Latin American history (PhD)
- linguistics (PhD)
- literature (MA, PhD)
- literatures in English (PhD)
- manufacturing systems (MS)
- math finance (MS)
- mathematics (MS, PhD)
- mechanics (MS, PhD)
- medicinal chemistry (MS, PhD)
- medieval history (PhD)
- microbial biochemistry (MS, PhD)
- modern American history (PhD)
- modern British history (PhD)
- modern European history (PhD)
- molecular and cell biology (PhD)
- molecular biology (MS, PhD)
- molecular biology and biochemistry (MS, PhD)
- molecular biosciences (PhD)
- molecular genetics (MS, PhD)
- museum studies (MA)
- music history (MA, PhD)
- neuroscience (PhD)
- nuclear physics (MS, PhD)
- nutrition of ruminant and nonruminant animals (MS, PhD)
- nutritional sciences (MS, PhD)
- nutritional toxicology (MS, PhD)
- oceanography (MS, PhD)
- operations research (PhD)
- organic chemistry (MS, PhD)
- pathology (MS, PhD)
- pharmaceutical science (MS, PhD)
- pharmaceutical toxicology (MS, PhD)
- philosophy (PhD)
- physical chemistry (MS, PhD)
- physics (MST)
- physiology and neurobiology (PhD)
- plant ecology (MS, PhD)
- plant genetics (PhD)
- plant physiology (MS, PhD)
- political and cultural history (PhD)
- political economy (PhD)
- political theory (PhD)
- pollution prevention and control (MS, PhD)
- production and management (MS)
- public law (PhD)
- quality and productivity management (MS)
- quality and reliability engineering (MS)
- reproductive endocrinology and neuroendocrinology (MS, PhD)
- social policy analysis and administration (PhD)
- social psychology (PhD)
- social work (PhD)
- sociology (MA, PhD)
- solid mechanics (MS, PhD)
- Spanish (MA, MAT, PhD)
- Spanish-American literature (MA, PhD)
- statistics (MS, PhD)
- structure and plant groups (MS, PhD)
- surface science (PhD)
- theoretical physics (MS, PhD)
- translation (MA)
- virology (MS, PhD)
- water and wastewater treatment (MS, PhD)
- water resources (MS, PhD)
- women and politics (PhD)
- women's and gender studies (MA, PhD)
- women's history (PhD)

Graduate School of Applied and Professional Psychology

Dr. Stanley B. Messer, Dean

Programs in:

- applied and professional psychology (Psy M, Psy D)
- clinical psychology (Psy M, Psy D)
- organizational psychology (Psy M, Psy D)
- school psychology (Psy M, Psy D)

Graduate School of Education

Dr. Richard DeLisi, Dean

Programs in:

- adult and continuing education (Ed M)
- counseling psychology (Ed M)
- early childhood/elementary education (Ed M, Ed D)

Rutgers, The State University of New Jersey, New Brunswick (continued)
- education (Ed M, Ed D, PhD)
- educational administration and supervision (Ed M, Ed D)
- educational policy (PhD)
- educational psychology (PhD)
- educational statistics, measurement and evaluation (Ed M)
- English as a second language education (Ed M)
- English education (Ed M)
- language education (Ed M, Ed D)
- learning, cognition and development (Ed M)
- literacy education (Ed M, Ed D, PhD)
- mathematics education (Ed M, Ed D, PhD)
- reading education (Ed M)
- science education (Ed M, Ed D)
- social and philosophical foundations of education (Ed M, Ed D)
- social studies education (Ed M, Ed D)
- special education (Ed M, Ed D)

Mason Gross School of the Arts
George B. Stauffer, Dean
Programs in:
- acting (MFA)
- arts (MFA, MM, DMA, AD)
- collaborative piano (MM, DMA)
- conducting: choral (MM, DMA)
- conducting: instrumental (MM, DMA)
- conducting: orchestral (MM, DMA)
- design (MFA)
- directing (MFA)
- drawing (MFA)
- jazz studies (MM)
- music (DMA, AD)
- music education (MM, DMA)
- music performance (MM)
- painting (MFA)
- playwriting (MFA)
- sculpture (MFA)
- stage management (MFA)

School of Communication, Information and Library Studies
Dr. Gustav W. Friedrich, Dean
Programs in:
- communication and information studies (MCIS)
- library and information science (MLS)

School of Management and Labor Relations
Dr. Barbara A. Lee, Dean
Programs in:
- human resource management (MHRM)
- labor and employment relations (MLER)
- management and labor relations (MHRM, MLER)

School of Social Work
Dr. Richard L. Edwards, Dean
Program in:
- social work (MSW, PhD)

■ SAINT PETER'S COLLEGE
Jersey City, NJ 07306-5997
http://www.spc.edu/

Independent-religious, coed, comprehensive institution. *Computer facilities:* 150 computers available on campus for general student use. A campuswide network can be accessed from student residence rooms and from off campus. Internet access is available. *Library facilities:* Theresa and Edward O'Toole Library plus 1 other. *General application contact:* Graduate Admissions Coordinator, 201-915-9220.

Find University Details at www.petersons.com/gradchannel.

Graduate Programs in Education
Programs in:
- administration and supervision (MA)
- elementary teacher (Certificate)
- reading specialist (MA)
- supervisor of instruction (Certificate)
- teaching (MA, Certificate)
- urban education (MA)

MBA Programs
Programs in:
- finance (MBA)
- international business (MBA)
- management (MBA)
- management information systems (MBA)
- marketing (MBA)

Nursing Program
Program in:
- nursing (MSN)

Program in Accountancy
Program in:
- accountancy (MS, Certificate)

■ SETON HALL UNIVERSITY
South Orange, NJ 07079-2697
http://www.shu.edu/

Independent-religious, coed, university. CGS member. *Computer facilities:* Computer purchase and lease plans are available. 300 computers available on campus for general student use. A campuswide network can be accessed from student residence rooms and from off campus. Internet access and online class registration are available. *Library facilities:* Walsh Library plus 1 other. *General application contact:* Information Contact, 973-761-9000.

College of Arts and Sciences
Programs in:
- analytical chemistry (MS, PhD)
- arts administration (MPA)
- arts and sciences (MA, MHA, MPA, MS, PhD)
- Asian studies (MA)
- biochemistry (MS, PhD)
- biology (MS)
- Catholic history (MA)
- chemistry (MS)
- corporate and public communication (MA)
- English (MA)
- European history (MA)
- experimental psychology (MS)
- global history (MA)
- health policy and management (MPA)
- healthcare administration (MHA)
- inorganic chemistry (MS, PhD)
- Jewish-Christian studies (MA)
- microbiology (MS)
- molecular bioscience (PhD)
- museum professions (MA)
- nonprofit organization management (MPA)
- organic chemistry (MS, PhD)
- physical chemistry (MS, PhD)
- public service: leadership, governance, and policy (MPA)
- strategic communication and leadership (MA)
- US history (MA)

College of Education and Human Services
Dr. Joseph V. De Pierro, Dean
Programs in:
- bilingual education (Ed S)
- Catholic school leadership (MA)
- Catholic school teaching EPICS (MA)
- college student personnel administration (MA)
- counseling psychology (MA, PhD)
- counselor preparation (MA)
- education and human services (MA, MS, Ed D, Exec Ed D, PhD, Ed S)
- education media specialist (MA)
- higher education administration (PhD)
- human resource training and development (MA)
- instructional design (MA)
- K–12 administration and supervision (Ed D, Exec Ed D, Ed S)
- K–12 leadership, management and policy (Ed D, Exec Ed D, Ed S)
- marriage and family therapy (MS, Ed S)
- professional development (MA)
- psychological studies (MA)
- school psychology (Ed S)

College of Nursing
Programs in:
- acute care nurse practitioner (MSN)
- adult nurse practitioner (MSN)
- advanced practice in acute care nursing (MSN)
- advanced practice in primary health care (MSN)
- gerontological nurse practitioner (MSN)
- health systems administration (MSN)
- nursing (PhD)
- nursing case management (MSN)
- nursing education (MA)

pediatric nurse practitioner (MSN)
school nurse (MSN)
women's health nurse practitioner (MSN)

Immaculate Conception Seminary School of Theology
Programs in:
pastoral ministry (M Div, MA)
theology (MA, Certificate)

School of Graduate Medical Education
Dr. Brian B. Shulman, Dean
Programs in:
athletic training (MS)
health sciences (MS, PhD)
medical education (MS, DPT, PhD)
occupational therapy (MS)
physician assistant (MS)
professional physical therapy (DPT)
speech-language pathology (MS)

School of Law
Patrick E. Hobbs, Dean and Professor of Law
Program in:
law (JD, LL M, MSJ)

Stillman School of Business
Dr. Karen E. Boroff, Dean
Programs in:
accounting (MBA, MS)
business (MBA, MS, Certificate)
finance (MBA)
financial markets, institutions and instruments (MBA)
healthcare management (MBA)
information systems (MBA)
international business (MBA)
management (MBA)
marketing (MBA)
pharmaceutical management (MBA)
professional accounting (MS)
sport management (MBA)
taxation (MS)

Whitehead School of Diplomacy and International Relations
Ursula Sanjamino, Assistant Dean of Graduate Studies
Program in:
diplomacy and international relations (MA)

■ STEVENS INSTITUTE OF TECHNOLOGY
Hoboken, NJ 07030
http://www.stevens.edu/

Independent, coed, university. *Computer facilities:* Computer purchase and lease plans are available. 175 computers available on campus for general student use. A campuswide network can be accessed from student residence rooms and from off campus. Internet access and online class registration, online grade and account information are available. *Library facilities:* S. C. Williams Library. *General application contact:* Graduate Admissions, 800-496-4935.

Graduate School
Program in:
interdisciplinary sciences and engineering (M Eng, MS, PhD)

Arthur E. Imperatore School of Sciences and Arts
Programs in:
applied mathematics (MS, PhD)
applied optics (Certificate)
applied statistics (Certificate)
chemical biology (MS, PhD)
chemistry (MS, PhD)
chemistry and chemical biology (Certificate)
cognitive science (Certificate)
computer science (MS, PhD)
database systems (Certificate)
elements of computer science (Certificate)
engineering physics (M Eng)
information systems (MS)
mathematics (MS, PhD)
physics (MS, PhD)
professional communications (Certificate)
quantitative software engineering (MS, Certificate)
sciences and arts (M Eng, MS, PhD, Certificate)
stochastic systems analysis and optimization (MS, Certificate)
surface physics (Certificate)
theoretical computer science (Certificate)

Charles V. Schaefer Jr. School of Engineering
Programs in:
advanced manufacturing (Certificate)
agile systems engineering and design (Certificate)
air pollution technology (Certificate)
armament engineering (M Eng)
biomedical engineering (M Eng, Certificate)
chemical engineering (M Eng, PhD, Engr)
civil engineering (M Eng, PhD, Certificate, Engr)
computational fluid mechanics and heat transfer (Certificate)
computer and communications security (Certificate)
computer and electrical engineering (M Eng)
computer architecture and digital system design (M Eng, PhD, Engr)
computer engineering (M Eng, PhD, Certificate, Engr)
computer systems (M Eng, PhD, Engr)
concurrent design management (M Eng)
construction accounting/estimating (Certificate)
construction engineering (Certificate)
construction law/disputes (Certificate)
construction management (MS, Certificate)
construction/quality management (Certificate)
design and production management (Certificate)
digital systems and VLSI design (Certificate)
electrical engineering (M Eng, MS, PhD, Certificate, Engr)
engineering (M Eng, MS, PhD, Certificate, Engr)
engineering management (M Eng, PhD, Certificate)
environmental compatibility in engineering (Certificate)
environmental engineering (M Eng, PhD, Certificate)
environmental process (M Eng, PhD, Certificate)
geotechnical engineering (Certificate)
geotechnical/geoenvironmental engineering (M Eng, PhD, Engr)
groundwater and soil pollution control (M Eng, PhD, Certificate)
image processing and multimedia (M Eng, PhD, Engr)
information networks (Certificate)
inland and coastal environmental hydrodynamics (M Eng, PhD, Certificate)
integrated product development (M Eng)
manufacturing technologies (M Eng)
maritime systems (M Eng, MS)
materials engineering (M Eng, PhD)
mechanical engineering (M Eng, PhD, Engr)
microelectronics and photonics (Certificate)
ocean engineering (M Eng, PhD)
pharmaceutical manufacturing (M Eng, MS, Certificate)
polymer engineering (M Eng, PhD, Engr)
power generation (Certificate)
product architecture and engineering (M Eng)
robotics and control (Certificate)
signal processing for communications (M Eng, PhD, Engr)
software engineering (M Eng, PhD, Engr)
structural analysis and design (Certificate)
structural engineering (M Eng, PhD, Engr)
systems and supportability engineering (Certificate)
systems design and operational effectiveness (M Eng)
systems engineering (M Eng, PhD, Certificate)
systems engineering and architecting (Certificate)

Stevens Institute of Technology (continued)
systems reliability and design (M Eng)
telecommunications engineering (M Eng, PhD, Engr)
telecommunications management (MS, PhD, Certificate)
vibration and noise control (Certificate)
water quality control (Certificate)
water resources engineering (M Eng)

Wesley J. Howe School of Technology Management
Programs in:
business (MS)
computer science (MS)
e-commerce (MS, Certificate)
engineering management (MBA)
entrepreneurial information technology (MS)
financial management (MBA)
general management (MS)
global innovation management (MS)
global technology management (MBA)
human resource management (MS)
information management (MBA, MS, PhD, Certificate)
information security (MS)
information technology in financial services (MBA)
information technology in financial services industry (MS)
information technology in the pharmaceutical industry (MBA, MS)
information technology outsourcing (MBA)
information technology outsourcing management (MS)
integrated information architecture (MS)
management of wireless networks (MS)
online security, technology and business (MS)
pharmaceutical technology management (MBA)
project management (MBA, MS, Certificate)
quantitative software engineering (MS)
systems engineering (MS)
technical management (MS)
technology commercialization (MS)
technology management (EMBA, MS, PhD)
technology management for experienced professionals (EMTM, MS, MTM, Certificate)
telecommunications management (MBA, MS, PhD, Certificate)

■ WILLIAM PATERSON UNIVERSITY OF NEW JERSEY

Wayne, NJ 07470-8420
http://ww2.wpunj.edu/

State-supported, coed, comprehensive institution. CGS member. *Enrollment:* 10,600 graduate, professional, and undergraduate students; 326 full-time matriculated graduate/professional students, 1,411 part-time matriculated graduate/professional students. *Computer facilities:* 700 computers available on campus for general student use. A campuswide network can be accessed from student residence rooms and from off campus. Internet access and online class registration are available. *Library facilities:* David and Lorraine Cheng Library. *General application contact:* Danielle Liautaud Watkins, Assistant Director, 973-720-3579.

Find University Details at www.petersons.com/gradchannel.

College of Business
Sam Basu, Dean
Program in:
business (MBA)

College of Education
Leslie Agard-Jones, Dean
Programs in:
counseling (M Ed)
counseling services (M Ed)
education (M Ed, MAT)
educational leadership (M Ed)
elementary education (M Ed, MAT)
reading (M Ed)
special education (M Ed)

College of Science and Health
Programs in:
biotechnology (MS)
general biology (MA)
limnology and terrestrial ecology (MA)
molecular biology (MA)
nursing (MSN)
physiology (MA)
science and health (MA, MS, MSN)
speech pathology (MS)

College of the Arts and Communication
Dr. Steve Marcone, Interim Dean
Programs in:
art (MFA)
arts and communication (MA, MFA, MM)
media studies (MA)
music (MM)
visual arts (MA)

College of the Humanities and Social Sciences
Dr. Isabel Tirado, Dean
Programs in:
applied clinical psychology (MA)
English (MA)
history (MA)
humanities and social sciences (MA)
public policy and international affairs (MA)
sociology (MA)

New Mexico

■ COLLEGE OF SANTA FE

Santa Fe, NM 87505-7634
http://www.csf.edu

Independent, coed, comprehensive institution. *Computer facilities:* 180 computers available on campus for general student use. A campuswide network can be accessed from student residence rooms and from off campus. Internet access is available. *Library facilities:* Fogelson Library Center plus 2 others. *General application contact:* Director, Evening and Weekend Degree Program, 505-473-6177.

Department of Business Administration
Programs in:
finance (MBA)
human resources (MBA)

Department of Education
Programs in:
at-risk youth (MA)
curriculum and instruction (MA)
multicultural special education (MA)

■ COLLEGE OF THE SOUTHWEST

Hobbs, NM 88240-9129
http://www.csw.edu/

Independent, coed, comprehensive institution. *Enrollment:* 741 graduate, professional, and undergraduate students; 41 full-time matriculated graduate/professional students (28 women), 43 part-time matriculated graduate/professional students (35 women). *Graduate faculty:* 2 full-time (both women), 6 part-time/adjunct (1 woman). *Computer facilities:* 35 computers available on campus for general student use. A campuswide network can be accessed from student residence rooms. Internet access is available. *Library facilities:* Scarborough Memorial Library plus 1 other. *Graduate expenses:* Tuition: part-time $375 per credit hour. *General application contact:* Steve Hill, Dean/Recruiting, 505-392-6561 Ext. 1010.

School of Education
Dr. Dennis Atherton, Dean
Programs in:
curriculum and instruction (MS)
educational administration (MS)
educational counseling (MS)
educational diagnostician (MS)

■ EASTERN NEW MEXICO UNIVERSITY

Portales, NM 88130
http://www.enmu.edu/

State-supported, coed, comprehensive institution. CGS member. *Enrollment:* 4,033 graduate, professional, and undergraduate students; 35 full-time matriculated graduate/professional students (18 women), 477 part-time matriculated graduate/professional students (332 women). *Graduate faculty:* 76 full-time (29 women), 8 part-time/adjunct (7 women). *Computer facilities:* 493 computers available on campus for general student use. A campuswide network can be accessed from student residence rooms and from off campus. Internet access and online class registration are available. *Library facilities:* Golden Library. *Graduate expenses:* Tuition, state resident: full-time $2,478; part-time $103 per credit hour. Tuition, nonresident: full-time $8,034; part-time $335 per credit hour. Required fees: $35 per credit hour. *General application contact:* Dr. Phillip Shelley, Dean, Graduate School, 505-562-2147.

Graduate School
Dr. Phillip Shelley, Dean

College of Business
Dr. John Groesbeck, Dean
Program in:
business (MBA)

College of Education and Technology
Dr. Jerry Harmon, Dean
Programs in:
counseling (MA)
curriculum and instruction (M Ed)
education (M Ed)
education and technology (M Ed, M Sp Ed, MA, MS)
physical education (MS)
school counseling (M Ed)
special education (M Ed, M Sp Ed)

College of Liberal Arts and Sciences
Dr. Mary Ayala, Dean
Programs in:
anthropology (MA)
biology (MS)
chemistry (MS)
communicative arts and sciences (MA)
English (MA)
liberal arts and sciences (MA, MS)
mathematical sciences (MA)
speech pathology and audiology (MS)

■ NEW MEXICO HIGHLANDS UNIVERSITY
Las Vegas, NM 87701
http://www.nmhu.edu/

State-supported, coed, comprehensive institution. CGS member. *Enrollment:* 3,750 graduate, professional, and undergraduate students; 542 full-time matriculated graduate/professional students (377 women), 637 part-time matriculated graduate/professional students (439 women). *Graduate faculty:* 79 full-time (33 women), 33 part-time/adjunct (18 women). *Computer facilities:* 500 computers available on campus for general student use. A campuswide network can be accessed from student residence rooms and from off campus. Internet access and online class registration are available. *Library facilities:* Donnelly Library. *Graduate expenses:* Tuition, state resident: part-time $101 per credit hour. Tuition, nonresident: part-time $101 per credit hour. *General application contact:* Diane Trujillo, Administrative Assistant Graduate Studies, 505-454-3266.

Graduate Studies
Dr. Gilbert Rivera, Interim Vice President for Academic Affairs

College of Arts and Sciences
Dr. C.G. (Tino) Mendez, Dean
Programs in:
administration (MA)
anthropology (MA)
applied chemistry (MS)
applied sociology (MA)
arts and sciences (MA, MS)
biology (MS)
cognitive science (MA, MS)
computer graphics (MA, MS)
design studies (MA)
digital audio and video production (MA)
English (MA)
Hispanic language and literature (MA)
historical and cross-cultural perspective (MA)
history and political science (MA)
life science (MS)
multimedia systems (MA, MS)
natural resource management (MS)
networking technology (MA, MS)
political and governmental processes (MA)
psychology (MS)

School of Business
Dr. William Taylor, Dean
Program in:
business administration (MBA)

School of Education
Dr. Francisco Hidalgo, Dean
Programs in:
education (MA)
educational leadership (MA)
exercise and sport sciences (MA)
guidance and counseling (MA)
human performance and sport (MA)
special education (MA)
sports administration (MA)
teacher education (MA)

School of Social Work
Dr. Alfredo Garcia, Dean
Programs in:
bilingual/bicultural social work practice (MSW)
clinical practice (MSW)
community organization (MSW)

■ NEW MEXICO INSTITUTE OF MINING AND TECHNOLOGY
Socorro, NM 87801
http://www.nmt.edu/

State-supported, coed, university. *Enrollment:* 1,846 graduate, professional, and undergraduate students; 229 full-time matriculated graduate/professional students (68 women), 127 part-time matriculated graduate/professional students (55 women). *Graduate faculty:* 96 full-time (14 women), 36 part-time/adjunct (7 women). *Computer facilities:* 225 computers available on campus for general student use. A campuswide network can be accessed from student residence rooms and from off campus. Internet access and online class registration are available. *Library facilities:* New Mexico Tech Library plus 1 other. *Graduate expenses:* Tuition, state resident: full-time $3,593; part-time $200 per credit. Tuition, nonresident: full-time $11,554; part-time $642 per credit. Required fees: $419; $16 per credit. $34 per term. Tuition and fees vary according to course load. *General application contact:* Dr. David B. Johnson, Dean of Graduate Studies, 505-835-5513.

Find University Details at www.petersons.com/gradchannel.

Graduate Studies
Dr. David B. Johnson, Dean
Programs in:
advanced mechanics (MS)
applied math (PhD)
astrophysics (MS, PhD)
atmospheric physics (MS, PhD)
biochemistry (MS)
biology (MS)
chemistry (MS)
computer science (MS, PhD)
electrical engineering (MS)
engineering management (MEM)
environmental chemistry (PhD)
environmental engineering (MS)
explosives engineering (MS)
explosives technology and atmospheric chemistry (PhD)
geochemistry (MS, PhD)
geology (MS, PhD)
geology and geochemistry (MS, PhD)
geophysics (MS, PhD)
hydrology (MS, PhD)
instrumentation (MS)
materials engineering (MS, PhD)
mathematical physics (PhD)
mathematics (MS)
mining and mineral engineering (MS)
operations research (MS)
petroleum engineering (MS, PhD)
science teaching (MST)

■ NEW MEXICO STATE UNIVERSITY

Las Cruces, NM 88003-8001

http://www.nmsu.edu/

State-supported, coed, university. CGS member. *Enrollment:* 16,415 graduate, professional, and undergraduate students; 1,712 full-time matriculated graduate/professional students (901 women), 1,493 part-time matriculated graduate/professional students (911 women). *Graduate faculty:* 495 full-time (168 women), 57 part-time/adjunct (26 women). *Computer facilities:* 500 computers available on campus for general student use. A campuswide network can be accessed from student residence rooms and from off campus. Internet access and online class registration are available. *Library facilities:* New Mexico State University Library plus 2 others. *General application contact:* Elena Luna, Coordinator, 505-646-3498.

Graduate School
Dr. Linda Lacey, Dean
Programs in:
interdisciplinary studies (MA, MS, PhD)
molecular biology (MS, PhD)

College of Agriculture and Home Economics
Dr. Lowell Catlett, Interim Dean
Programs in:
agribusiness (M Ag, MBA)
agricultural biology (MS)
agricultural economics (MS)
agriculture and extension education (MA)
agriculture and home economics (M Ag, MA, MBA, MS, PhD)
animal science (M Ag, MS, PhD)
economics (MA)
family and consumer sciences (MS)
general agronomy (MS, PhD)
horticulture (MS)
range science (M Ag, MS, PhD)
wildlife science (MS)

College of Arts and Sciences
Dr. Waded Cruzado-Salas, Dean
Programs in:
anthropology (MA)
art history (MA)
arts and sciences (MA, MAG, MCJ, MFA, MM, MPA, MS, PhD)
astronomy (MS, PhD)
biology (MS, PhD)
ceramics (MA, MFA)
chemistry and biochemistry (MS, PhD)
communication studies (MA)
computer science (MS, PhD)
creative writing (MFA)
criminal justice (MCJ)
design (MA, MFA)
drawing (MA, MFA)
English (MA)
geography (MAG)
geological sciences (MS)
government (MA, MPA)
history (MA)
mathematical sciences (MS, PhD)
metals (MA, MFA)
music (MM)
painting (MA, MFA)
photography (MA, MFA)
physics (MS, PhD)
printmaking (MA, MFA)
psychology (MA, PhD)
rhetoric and professional communication (PhD)
sculpture (MA, MFA)
sociology (MA)
Spanish (MA)

College of Business
Dr. Garrey Carruthers, Dean
Programs in:
accounting and information systems (M Acct)
business (M Acct, MA, MBA, MS, PhD)
business administration (PhD)
economics (MA)
experimental statistics (MS)

College of Education
Dr. Robert Moulton, Dean
Programs in:
counseling and guidance (MA)
counseling psychology (PhD)
curriculum and instruction (MAT, Ed D, PhD, Ed S)
education (MA, MAT, Ed D, PhD, Ed S)
educational administration (MA, PhD)
educational management and development (Ed D)
general education (MA)
reading (Ed S)
school psychology (Ed S)
special education (MA, Ed D, PhD)

College of Engineering
Dr. Steven Castillo, Dean
Programs in:
chemical engineering (MS Ch E, PhD)
civil engineering (MSCE, PhD)
electrical and computer engineering (MSEE, PhD)
engineering (MS Ch E, MS Env E, MSCE, MSEE, MSIE, MSME, PhD)
environmental engineering (MS Env E)
industrial engineering (MSIE, PhD)
mechanical engineering (MSME, PhD)

College of Health and Social Services
Dr. Jeffrey Brandon, Dean
Programs in:
community/public health (MSN)
health and social services (MPH, MSN, MSW)
health science (MPH)
medical-surgical (adult health) (MSN)
psychiatric/mental health (MSN)
social work (MSW)

■ ST. JOHN'S COLLEGE

Santa Fe, NM 87505-4599

http://www.stjohnscollege.edu/

Independent, coed, comprehensive institution. *Computer facilities:* 30 computers available on campus for general student use. A campuswide network can be accessed from student residence rooms and from off campus. Internet access is available. *Library facilities:* Meem Library. *General application contact:* Associate Director of Graduate Admissions, 505-984-6083.

Graduate Institute in Liberal Education
Programs in:
Eastern classics (MA)
liberal arts (MA)
liberal education (MA)

■ UNIVERSITY OF NEW MEXICO

Albuquerque, NM 87131-2039

http://www.unm.edu/

State-supported, coed, university. CGS member. *Enrollment:* 26,172 graduate, professional, and undergraduate students; 3,085 full-time matriculated graduate/professional students (1,699 women), 2,757 part-time matriculated graduate/professional students (1,603 women). *Graduate faculty:* 1,509 full-time (666 women), 682 part-time/adjunct (359 women). *Computer facilities:* Computer purchase and lease plans are available. 446 computers available on campus for general student use. A campuswide network can be accessed from student residence rooms and from off campus. Internet access and online class registration are available. *Library facilities:* The University of New Mexico General Library plus 7 others. *General application contact:* Edwina Chavez-Salazar, Enrollment Management Specialist, 505-277-2711.

Find University Details at www.petersons.com/gradchannel.

Graduate School
Dr. Teresita E. Aguilar, Dean
Program in:
water resources (MWR)

College of Arts and Sciences
Dr. Vera Norwood, Dean
Programs in:
American studies (MA, PhD)
anthropology (MA, MS, PhD)
arts and sciences (MA, MFA, MS, PhD)
biology (MS, PhD)
biomedical physics (MS, PhD)
chemistry (MS, PhD)
clinical psychology (MS, PhD)
communication (MA, PhD)
comparative literature and cultural studies (MA)

earth and planetary sciences (MS, PhD)
economics (MA, PhD)
English (MA, MFA, MS, PhD)
French (MA)
French studies (PhD)
geography (MS)
German studies (MA)
history (MA, PhD)
Latin American studies (MA, PhD)
linguistics (MA, PhD)
mathematics (MS, PhD)
optical science and engineering (MS)
optical sciences and engineering (PhD)
philosophy (MA, PhD)
physics (MS, PhD)
political science (MA, PhD)
Portuguese (MA)
psychology (MS, PhD)
sociology (MA, PhD)
Spanish (MA)
Spanish and Portuguese (PhD)
speech and hearing sciences (MS)
statistics (MS, PhD)

College of Education
Dr. Viola E. Florez, Dean
Programs in:
art education (MA)
counselor education (MA, PhD)
education (MA, MS, Ed D, PhD, EDSPC)
educational leadership (MA, Ed D, EDSPC)
educational linguistics (Ed D, PhD)
educational psychology (MA, PhD)
elementary education (MA, EDSPC)
family studies (MA, PhD)
health education (MS)
language, literacy and sociocultural studies (MA, Ed D, PhD)
multicultural teacher and childhood education (Ed D, PhD, EDSPC)
nutrition (MS)
organizational learning and instructional technologies (MA, PhD, EDSPC)
physical education (MS, Ed D, PhD, EDSPC)
secondary education (MA, EDSPC)
special education (MA, Ed D, PhD, EDSPC)
teacher education (MA, EDSPC)

College of Fine Arts
Dr. James S. Moy, Dean
Programs in:
art history (MA, PhD)
dramatic writing (MFA)
fine arts (M Mu, MA, MFA, PhD)
music (M Mu)
studio arts (MFA)
theater and dance (MA)

College of Nursing
Dr. Robin Meize-Grochowski, Senior Associate Dean of Academic Affairs
Program in:
nursing (MSN, PhD)

College of Pharmacy
Dr. John Pieper, Dean
Programs in:
pharmaceutical sciences (MS, PhD)
pharmacy (Pharm D, MS, PhD)

School of Architecture and Planning
Dr. Roger L. Schluntz, Dean
Programs in:
architecture (M Arch)
architecture and planning (M Arch, MCRP, MLA)
community and regional planning (MCRP)
landscape architecture (MLA)

School of Engineering
Dr. Joseph L. Cecchi, Dean
Programs in:
chemical engineering (MS, PhD)
civil engineering (MS)
computer science (MS, PhD)
construction management (MCM)
electrical engineering (MS)
engineering (PhD)
manufacturing engineering (MEME)
mechanical engineering (MS)
nuclear engineering (MS, PhD)
optical sciences (PhD)

School of Public Administration
Dr. F. Lee Brown, Interim Director
Program in:
public administration (MPA)

Robert O. Anderson Graduate School of Management
Programs in:
accounting (M Acc, MBA)
financial management (MBA)
financial, international and technology management (MBA)
human resources management (MBA)
international management (MBA)
international management in Latin America (MBA)
management information systems (MBA)
management of technology (MBA)
marketing management (MBA)
marketing, information and decision sciences (MBA)
operations management (MBA)
organizational studies (MBA)
policy and planning (MBA)
tax accounting (MBA)

School of Law
Suellyn Scarnecchia, Dean
Program in:
law (JD)

School of Medicine
Programs in:
biochemistry and molecular biology (MS, PhD)
cell biology and physiology (MS, PhD)
dental hygiene (MS)
medicine (MD, MOT, MPH, MPT, MS, PhD)
molecular genetics and microbiology (MS, PhD)
neuroscience (MS, PhD)
occupational therapy (MOT)
pathology (MS, PhD)
physical therapy (MPT)
public health (MPH)
toxicology (MS, PhD)

■ UNIVERSITY OF PHOENIX–NEW MEXICO CAMPUS
Albuquerque, NM 87109-4645
http://www.phoenix.edu/

Proprietary, coed, comprehensive institution. *Enrollment:* 4,586 graduate, professional, and undergraduate students; 1,047 full-time matriculated graduate/professional students (669 women). *Graduate faculty:* 60 full-time (28 women), 621 part-time/adjunct (208 women). *Computer facilities:* A campuswide network can be accessed from off campus. Internet access is available. *Library facilities:* University Library. *Graduate expenses:* Tuition: full-time $9,005. Required fees: $760. *General application contact:* Campus Information Center, 505-821-4800.

The Artemis School
Dr. Adam Honea, Provost

College of Education
Dr. Marla LaRue, Dean/Executive Director
Programs in:
administration (MAEd)
curriculum and instruction (MAEd)
teacher education (MAEd)

College of Health and Human Services
Dr. Gil Linne, Dean/Executive Director
Programs in:
health care management (MBA)
marriage and family therapy (MSC)

John Sperling School of Business
Dr. Adam Honea, Provost
Program in:
business (MBA)

College of Graduate Business and Management
Dr. Brian Lindquist, Associate Vice President and Dean/Executive Director
Programs in:
business administration (MBA)
global management (MBA)
human resource management (MBA)

College of Information Systems and Technology
Dr. Adam Honea, Dean/Executive Director
Programs in:
e-business (MBA)
technology management (MBA)

■ WESTERN NEW MEXICO UNIVERSITY
Silver City, NM 88062-0680
http://www.wnmu.edu/

State-supported, coed, comprehensive institution. *Enrollment:* 80 full-time matriculated graduate/professional students (49 women), 374 part-time matriculated graduate/professional students (265 women). *Graduate faculty:* 35 full-time (18 women), 32 part-time/adjunct (19 women). *Computer facilities:* 85 computers available on campus for general student use. Internet access and online class registration, online classes in Spanish are available. *Library facilities:* Miller Library plus 2 others. *Graduate expenses:* Tuition, state resident: full-time $1,329. Tuition, nonresident: full-time $4,779. *General application contact:* Dan Tressler, Director of Admissions, 505-538-6106.

Graduate Division
Programs in:
- business management (MBA)
- interdisciplinary studies (MA)

School of Education
Programs in:
- counselor education (MA)
- elementary education (MAT)
- reading education (MAT)
- school administration (MA)
- secondary education (MAT)
- special education (MAT)

New York

■ ADELPHI UNIVERSITY
Garden City, NY 11530-0701
http://www.adelphi.edu/

Independent, coed, university. *Enrollment:* 8,053 graduate, professional, and undergraduate students; 900 full-time matriculated graduate/professional students (762 women), 2,195 part-time matriculated graduate/professional students (1,738 women). *Graduate faculty:* 280 full-time (136 women), 623 part-time/adjunct (407 women). *Computer facilities:* Computer purchase and lease plans are available. 540 computers available on campus for general student use. A campuswide network can be accessed from student residence rooms and from off campus. Internet access and online class registration, payment, grades, drop/add classes, check application status are available. *Library facilities:* Swirbul Library plus 1 other. *General application contact:* Christine Murphy, Director of Admissions, 516-877-3050.

Derner Institute of Advanced Psychological Studies
Dr. Jeau Lau Chir, Dean
Programs in:
- clinical psychology (PhD, Post-Doctoral Certificate)
- general psychology (MA)
- mental health counseling (MA)
- school psychology (MA)

Graduate School of Arts and Sciences
Dr. Gayle Insler, Dean
Programs in:
- art and art history (MA)
- arts and sciences (MA, MFA, MS, Certificate)
- biology (MS)
- creative writing (MFA)
- emergency management (Certificate)
- environmental studies (MS)
- physics (MS)

School of Business
Dr. Anthony F. Libertella, Dean
Programs in:
- accounting (MBA)
- business (MBA, MS, Certificate)
- finance (MBA, MS)
- human resource management (Certificate)
- management information systems (MBA)
- management/human resource management (MBA)
- marketing/e-commerce (MBA)

School of Education
Dr. Ronald Feingold, Dean
Programs in:
- adolescent education (MA)
- aging (Certificate)
- audiology (MS, DA)
- birth through grade 2 (Certificate)
- birth-grade 12 (MS)
- birth-grade 6 (MS)
- childhood special education (Certificate)
- childhood special education studies (MS)
- community health education (MA, Certificate)
- early childhood education (Certificate)
- education (MA, MS, DA, Certificate)
- educational leadership and technology (MA, Certificate)
- elementary teachers pre K-6 (MA)
- grades 1-6 (MA, MS)
- grades 5-12 (MS)
- in-service (MA, MS)
- inclusive setting, grades 1-6 preservice or in-service track (MS)
- physical/educational human performance science (MA)
- pre-certification (MA)
- preservice (MS)
- school health education (MA)
- speech-language pathology (MS, DA)
- teaching English to speakers of other languages (MA, Certificate)

School of Nursing
Dr. Patrick Coonan, Dean
Program in:
- nursing (MS, PhD, Certificate)

School of Social Work
Dr. Andrew Safyer, Dean
Programs in:
- social welfare (DSW)
- social work (MSW)

■ ALFRED UNIVERSITY
Alfred, NY 14802-1205
http://www.alfred.edu/

Independent, coed, university. CGS member. *Enrollment:* 2,310 graduate, professional, and undergraduate students; 182 full-time matriculated graduate/professional students (111 women), 105 part-time matriculated graduate/professional students (63 women). *Graduate faculty:* 87 full-time (24 women), 7 part-time/adjunct (2 women). *Computer facilities:* Computer purchase and lease plans are available. 450 computers available on campus for general student use. A campuswide network can be accessed from student residence rooms and from off campus. Internet access is available. *Library facilities:* Herrick Memorial Library plus 1 other. *Graduate expenses:* Tuition: full-time $29,600; part-time $630 per credit hour. Required fees: $850; $70 per semester. Tuition and fees vary according to program. *General application contact:* Valerie Stephens, Coordinator of Graduate Admissions, 607-871-2141.

Graduate School
Dr. William Hall, Associate Provost for Graduate and Professional Programs
Program in:
- school psychology (MA, Psy D, CAS)

College of Business
Lori Hollenbeck, Director of MBA Program
Program in:
- business administration (MBA)

Division of Education
Dr. James Curl, Chair
Programs in:
- counseling (MS Ed, CAS)
- literacy teacher (MS Ed)

New York State College of Ceramics
Dr. Alastair Cormack, Dean of School of Engineering
Programs in:
- biomedical materials engineering science (MS)
- ceramic art (MFA)
- ceramic engineering (MS)
- ceramics (PhD)
- electrical engineering (MS)
- electronic integrated arts (MFA)
- glass art (MFA)
- glass science (MS, PhD)
- materials science and engineering (MS, PhD)
- mechanical engineering (MS)
- sculpture (MFA)

■ BERNARD M. BARUCH COLLEGE OF THE CITY UNIVERSITY OF NEW YORK
New York, NY 10010-5585
http://www.baruch.cuny.edu/

State and locally supported, coed, comprehensive institution. *Enrollment:* 15,730 graduate, professional, and undergraduate students; 829 full-time matriculated graduate/professional students (417 women), 2,083 part-time matriculated graduate/professional students (1,039 women). *Graduate faculty:* 271 full-time (66 women), 259 part-time/adjunct (59 women). *Computer facilities:* 1,294 computers available on campus for general student use. A campuswide network can be accessed. Internet access and online class registration are available. *Library facilities:* The William and Anita Newman Library plus 1 other. *General application contact:* Frances Murphy, Office of Graduate Admissions, 646-312-1300.

Find University Details at www.petersons.com/gradchannel.

School of Public Affairs
David Birdsell, Dean
Programs in:
- educational administration and supervision (MS Ed)
- higher education administration (MS Ed)
- public administration (MPA)
- public affairs (MPA, MS Ed)

Weissman School of Arts and Sciences
Gary Hentzi, Director
Programs in:
- arts and sciences (MA, MS)
- corporate communication (MA)
- financial engineering (MS)
- industrial organizational psychology (MS)

Zicklin School of Business
John Elliott, Vice President and Dean
Programs in:
- accounting (MBA, MS, PhD)
- business (MBA, MS, PhD, Certificate)
- business administration (MBA)
- computer information systems (MBA, MS, PhD)
- decision sciences (MBA, MS)
- economics (MBA)
- entrepreneurship (MBA)
- finance (MBA, MS, PhD)
- general business (MBA)
- general management and policy (MBA)
- health care administration (MBA)
- human resources management (MBA)
- industrial and labor relations (MS)
- industrial and organizational psychology (MBA, MS, PhD, Certificate)
- international executive education (MBA)
- management planning systems (PhD)
- management science (MBA)
- marketing (MBA, MS, PhD)
- organization and policy studies (PhD)
- organizational behavior (MBA)
- statistics (MBA, MS)
- taxation (MBA, MS)

■ BROOKLYN COLLEGE OF THE CITY UNIVERSITY OF NEW YORK
Brooklyn, NY 11210-2889
http://www.brooklyn.cuny.edu/

State and locally supported, coed, comprehensive institution. CGS member. *Enrollment:* 15,947 graduate, professional, and undergraduate students; 356 full-time matriculated graduate/professional students (268 women), 2,883 part-time matriculated graduate/professional students (1,959 women). *Computer facilities:* 800 computers available on campus for general student use. A campuswide network can be accessed from off campus. Internet access and online class registration are available. *Library facilities:* Brooklyn College Library plus 1 other. *Graduate expenses:* Tuition, state resident: full-time $6,400; part-time $270 per credit. Tuition, nonresident: full-time $12,000; part-time $500 per credit. Required fees: $118 per semester. *General application contact:* Karen Alleyne-Pierre, Director of Admissions Services and Enrollment Communications, 718-951-5902.

Find University Details at www.petersons.com/gradchannel.

Division of Graduate Studies
Dr. Louise Hainline, Dean
Programs in:
- accounting (MA, MS)
- acting (MFA)
- applied biology (MA)
- applied chemistry (MA)
- applied geology (MA)
- applied physics (MA)
- art history (MA, PhD)
- audiology (Au D)
- biology (MA, PhD)
- chemistry (MA, PhD)
- community health (MA, MPH, MS)
- community health education (MA)
- computer and information science (MA, PhD)
- computer science and health science (MS)
- creative writing (MFA)
- criticism and history (MA)
- design and technical production (MFA)
- digital art (MFA)
- directing (MFA)
- dramaturgy (MFA)
- drawing and painting (MFA)
- economics (MA)
- economics and computer and information science (MPS)
- economics/accounting (MA)
- English (MA, PhD)
- exercise science and rehabilitation (MS)
- experimental psychology (MA)
- fiction (MFA)
- French (MA)
- geology (MA, PhD)
- grief counseling (CAS)
- health care management (MPH)
- health care policy and administration (MPH)
- history (MA, PhD)
- industrial and organizational psychology (MA)
- information systems (MS)
- Judaic studies (MA)
- liberal studies (MA)
- mathematics (MA, PhD)
- mental health counseling (MA)
- modern languages and literature (PhD)
- nutrition (MS)
- nutrition sciences (MS)
- performance and interactive media arts (MFA, CAS)
- performing arts management (MFA)
- photography (MFA)
- physical education (MS, MS Ed)
- physics (MA, PhD)
- playwriting (MFA)
- poetry (MFA)
- political science (MA, PhD)
- political science, urban policy and administration (MA)
- printmaking (MFA)
- psychology (PhD)
- public health (MPH)
- sculpture (MFA)
- secondary mathematics education (MA)
- sociology (MA, PhD)
- Spanish (MA)
- speech (MA, MS Ed)
- speech and hearing sciences (PhD)
- speech pathology (MS)
- television and radio (MS)
- television production (MFA)
- thanatology (MA)
- theater (PhD)

Conservatory of Music
Dr. Bruce MacIntyre, Chairperson
Programs in:
- composition (MM)
- music (DMA, PhD)
- music education (MA)
- musicology (MA)
- performance practice (MM)

School of Education
Dr. Deborah Shanley, Dean
Programs in:
- art teacher (MA)
- bilingual education (MS Ed)
- bilingual special education (MS Ed)
- biology teacher (MA)
- birth-grade 2 (MS Ed)
- chemistry teacher (MA)

Brooklyn College of the City University of New York (continued)

children with emotional handicaps (MS Ed)
children with neuropsychological learning disabilities (MS Ed)
children with retarded mental development (MS Ed)
education (MA, MS Ed, CAS)
educational leadership (CAS)
English teacher (MA)
French teacher (MA)
guidance and counseling (CAS)
health and nutrition sciences: health teacher (MS Ed)
liberal arts (MS Ed)
mathematics (MS Ed)
mathematics teacher (MA)
middle childhood education (math) (MS Ed)
middle childhood education (science) (MS Ed)
music education (CAS)
music teacher (MA)
physical education teacher (MS Ed)
physics teacher (MA)
school psychologist (MS Ed, CAS)
school psychologist-bilingual (CAS)
science/environmental education (MS Ed)
social studies teacher (MA)
Spanish teacher (MA)
teacher of students with disabilities (MS Ed)

■ BUFFALO STATE COLLEGE, STATE UNIVERSITY OF NEW YORK

Buffalo, NY 14222-1095

http://www.buffalostate.edu/

State-supported, coed, comprehensive institution. CGS member. *Computer facilities:* 836 computers available on campus for general student use. A campuswide network can be accessed from student residence rooms and from off campus. Internet access and online class registration are available. *Library facilities:* E. H. Butler Library. *General application contact:* Graduate Studies and Research, 716-878-5601.

Graduate Studies and Research
Program in:
multidisciplinary studies (MA, MS)

Faculty of Applied Science and Education
Programs in:
adult education (MS, Certificate)
applied science and education (MPS, MS, MS Ed, CAS, Certificate)
business and marketing education (MS Ed)
career and technical education (MS Ed)
childhood education (grades 1-6) (MS Ed)
creative studies (MS)
criminal justice (MS)
early childhood and childhood curriculum and instruction (MS Ed)
early childhood education (birth-grade 2) (MS Ed)
educational computing (MS Ed)
educational leadership and facilitation (CAS)
elementary education (MS Ed)
human resources development (Certificate)
industrial technology (MS)
literacy specialist (MPS, MS Ed)
literacy specialist (birth-grade 6) (MS Ed)
literacy specialist (grades 5-12) (MPS)
special education (MS Ed)
special education: adolescents (MS Ed)
special education: childhood (MS Ed)
special education: early childhood (MS Ed)
speech language pathology (MS Ed)
student personnel administration (MS)
teaching bilingual exceptional individuals (MS Ed)
technology education (MS Ed)

Faculty of Arts and Humanities
Programs in:
art conservation (CAS)
art education (MS Ed)
arts and humanities (MA, MS Ed, CAS)
conservation of historic works and art works (MA)
English (MA)
secondary education (MS Ed)

Faculty of Natural and Social Sciences
Programs in:
applied economics (MA)
biology (MA)
chemistry (MA)
history (MA)
mathematics education (MS Ed)
natural and social sciences (MA, MS Ed)
secondary education (MS Ed)
secondary education physics (MS Ed)

■ CANISIUS COLLEGE

Buffalo, NY 14208-1098

http://www.canisius.edu/

Independent-religious, coed, comprehensive institution. *Enrollment:* 4,850 graduate, professional, and undergraduate students; 684 full-time matriculated graduate/professional students (417 women), 705 part-time matriculated graduate/professional students (431 women). *Graduate faculty:* 77 full-time (25 women), 127 part-time/adjunct (68 women). *Computer facilities:* Computer purchase and lease plans are available. 348 computers available on campus for general student use. A campuswide network can be accessed from student residence rooms and from off campus. Internet access and online class registration, online accounts are available. *Library facilities:* Andrew L. Bouwhuis Library plus 1 other. *Graduate expenses:* Tuition: part-time $645 per credit hour. Required fees: $19 per credit hour. Tuition and fees vary according to program. *General application contact:* Ann Marie Muscovic, Director of Admissions, 716-888-2200.

Graduate Division
Dr. Herbert J. Nelson, Vice President for Academic Affairs

College of Arts and Sciences
Dr. Paula McNutt, Dean
Programs in:
arts and sciences (MS)
communication and leadership (MS)

Richard J. Wehle School of Business
Dr. Antone Alber, Dean
Programs in:
accounting (MBA)
business (MBA, MBAPA)
business administration (MBA)
professional accounting (MBAPA)

School of Education and Human Services
Dr. Margaret C. McCarthy, Dean
Programs in:
business education (MS)
childhood education (MS)
college student personnel (MS)
community mental health counseling (MS)
counseling and human services (MS)
differentiated instruction (MS Ed)
early childhood education (MS)
education administration (MS)
education and human services (MS, MS Ed)
education of the deaf and hard of hearing (MS)
general education (MS Ed)
health and human performance (MS)
literacy education (MS Ed)
physical education (MS)
physical education—birth to 12 (MS)
reading education (MS Ed)
school and agency counseling (MS)
secondary education (MS)
special education (MS)
sport administration (MS)

■ CITY COLLEGE OF THE CITY UNIVERSITY OF NEW YORK

New York, NY 10031-9198

http://www.ccny.cuny.edu/

State and locally supported, coed, university. *Enrollment:* 13,244 graduate, professional, and undergraduate students; 246 full-time matriculated graduate/professional students (115 women), 2,684 part-time matriculated graduate/professional students (1,550 women). *Graduate faculty:* 491 full-time (145 women), 475 part-time/adjunct (240 women). *Computer facilities:* 3,000 computers available on campus for general student use. A campuswide network can be accessed from off campus. Internet access is available. *Library facilities:* Morris Raphael Cohen Library plus 3 others. *General application contact:* Information Contact, 212-650-6977.

Find University Details at www.petersons.com/gradchannel.

Graduate School

College of Liberal Arts and Science
Programs in:
- advertising design (MFA)
- art history (MA)
- art history and museum studies (MA)
- biochemistry (MA, PhD)
- biology (MA, PhD)
- ceramic design (MFA)
- chemistry (MA, PhD)
- clinical psychology (PhD)
- creative writing (MFA)
- earth and environmental science (PhD)
- earth systems science (MA)
- economics (MA)
- English and American literature (MA)
- experimental cognition (PhD)
- fine arts (MFA)
- general psychology (MA)
- history (MA)
- humanities and arts (MA, MFA)
- international relations (MA)
- language and literacy (MA)
- liberal arts and science (MA, MFA, PhD)
- mathematics (MA)
- media arts production (MFA)
- mental health counseling (MA)
- museum studies (MA)
- music (MA)
- painting (MFA)
- physics (MA, PhD)
- printmaking (MFA)
- science (MA, PhD)
- sculpture (MFA)
- social science (MA, PhD)
- sociology (MA)
- Spanish (MA)
- wood and metal design (MFA)

School of Architecture and Environmental Studies
George Ranalli, Dean
Programs in:
- architecture (M Arch, PD)
- landscape architecture (PD)
- urban design (MUP)

School of Education
Dr. Alfred Posamentier, Dean
Programs in:
- administration and supervision (MS, AC)
- adolescent mathematics education (MA, AC)
- bilingual education (MS)
- childhood education (MS)
- education (MA, MS, AC)
- English education (MA)
- middle school mathematics education (MS)
- science education (MA)
- social studies education (AC)
- teaching students with disabilities (MA)

School of Engineering
Dr. Muntaz G. Kassir, Associate Dean for Graduate Studies
Programs in:
- biomedical engineering (ME, PhD)
- chemical engineering (ME, MS, PhD)
- civil engineering (ME, MS, PhD)
- computer sciences (MS, PhD)
- electrical engineering (ME, MS, PhD)
- engineering (ME, MS, PhD)
- mechanical engineering (ME, MS, PhD)

■ CLARKSON UNIVERSITY
Potsdam, NY 13699
http://www.clarkson.edu/

Independent, coed, university. *Enrollment:* 2,964 graduate, professional, and undergraduate students; 377 full-time matriculated graduate/professional students (89 women), 37 part-time matriculated graduate/professional students (16 women). *Graduate faculty:* 117 full-time (20 women), 10 part-time/adjunct (5 women). *Computer facilities:* Computer purchase and lease plans are available. 400 computers available on campus for general student use. A campuswide network can be accessed from student residence rooms and from off campus. Internet access and online class registration are available. *Library facilities:* Andrew S. Schuler Educational Resources Center plus 1 other. *Graduate expenses:* Tuition: full-time $22,776; part-time $949 per credit. Required fees: $215. *General application contact:* Donna Brockway, Graduate Admissions International Advisor/ Assistant to the Provost, 315-268-6447.

Graduate School

Center for Health Science
Dr. Scott Minor, Associate Dean of Health Sciences
Programs in:
- basic science (MS)
- health science (MPT, MS, DPT)
- physical therapy (MPT, DPT)

School of Arts and Sciences
Dr. Dick Pratt, Dean
Programs in:
- analytical chemistry (MS, PhD)
- arts and sciences (MS, PhD)
- computer science (MS)
- information technology (MS)
- inorganic chemistry (MS, PhD)
- mathematics (MS, PhD)
- organic chemistry (MS, PhD)
- physical chemistry (MS, PhD)
- physics (MS, PhD)

School of Business
Dr. Farzad Mahmoodi, Director
Programs in:
- business (MBA, MS)
- business administration (MBA)
- engineering and global operations management (MS)
- human resource management (MS)
- management information systems (MS)
- manufacturing management (MS)

School of Engineering
Dr. Goodarz Ahmadi, Dean
Programs in:
- chemical and biomolecular engineering (ME, MS, PhD)
- civil and environmental engineering (PhD)
- civil engineering (ME, MS)
- computer engineering (ME, MS)
- electrical and computer engineering (PhD)
- electrical engineering (ME, MS)
- engineering (ME, MS, PhD)
- environmental science and engineering (MS, PhD)
- interdisciplinary engineering science (MS, PhD)
- mechanical engineering (ME, MS, PhD)

■ COLLEGE OF MOUNT SAINT VINCENT
Riverdale, NY 10471-1093
http://www.mountsaintvincent.edu/

Independent, coed, comprehensive institution. *Enrollment:* 1,812 graduate, professional, and undergraduate students; 37 full-time matriculated graduate/professional students (27 women), 328 part-time matriculated graduate/professional students (273 women). *Graduate faculty:* 20 full-time (17 women), 25 part-time/adjunct (19 women). *Computer facilities:* 184 computers available on campus for general student use. A campuswide network can be accessed from student residence rooms and from off campus. Internet access and online class registration, e-mail are available. *Library facilities:* Elizabeth Seton Library. *General application contact:* Dr. Edward H. Meyer, Dean, School of Professional and Continuing Studies, 718-405-3373.

School of Professional and Continuing Studies

Dr. Edward H. Meyer, Dean, School of Professional and Continuing Studies
Programs in:
- adult nurse practitioner (MSN, PMC)
- family nurse practitioner (MSN, PMC)
- instructional technology and global perspectives (Certificate)
- middle level education (Certificate)
- multicultural studies (Certificate)
- nurse educator (PMC)
- nursing administration (MSN)
- nursing for the adult and aged (MSN)
- urban and multicultural education (MS Ed)

■ THE COLLEGE OF NEW ROCHELLE

New Rochelle, NY 10805-2308

http://cnr.edu/

Independent, coed, primarily women, comprehensive institution. CGS member. *Enrollment:* 2,341 graduate, professional, and undergraduate students; 206 full-time matriculated graduate/professional students (182 women), 1,168 part-time matriculated graduate/professional students (1,012 women). *Graduate faculty:* 25 full-time (16 women), 74 part-time/adjunct (52 women). *Computer facilities:* Computer purchase and lease plans are available. 120 computers available on campus for general student use. A campuswide network can be accessed from off campus. Internet access and online class registration are available. *Library facilities:* Gill Library. *Graduate expenses:* Tuition: part-time $575 per credit. Required fees: $90 per term. *General application contact:* Dr. Guy Lometti, Dean of the Graduate School, 914-654-5320.

Find University Details at www.petersons.com/gradchannel.

Graduate School

Dr. Guy Lometti, Dean of the Graduate School
Programs in:
- acute care nurse practitioner (MS, Certificate)
- clinical specialist in holistic nursing (MS, Certificate)
- family nurse practitioner (MS, Certificate)
- nursing and health care management (MS)
- nursing education (Certificate)

Division of Art and Communication Studies
Dr. John Patton, Head
Programs in:
- art education (MA)
- art museum education (Certificate)
- art therapy (MS)
- communication studies (MS, Certificate)
- fine art (MS)
- graphic art (MS)
- studio art (MS)

Division of Education
Dr. Marie Ribarich, Acting Division Head
Programs in:
- bilingual education (Certificate)
- creative teaching and learning (MS Ed, Certificate)
- elementary education/early childhood education (MS Ed)
- literacy education (MS Ed)
- school administration and supervision (MS Ed, Certificate, PD)
- special education (MS Ed)
- speech-language pathology (MS)
- teaching English as a second language (MS Ed)
- teaching English as a second language and multilingual/multicultural education (MS Ed, Certificate)

Division of Human Services
Dr. Marie Ribarich, Head
Programs in:
- career development (MS, Certificate)
- community-school psychology (MS)
- gerontology (MS, Certificate)
- guidance and counseling (MS)
- mental health counseling (Certificate)

■ THE COLLEGE OF SAINT ROSE

Albany, NY 12203-1419

http://www.strose.edu/

Independent, coed, comprehensive institution. CGS member. *Computer facilities:* 322 computers available on campus for general student use. A campuswide network can be accessed from student residence rooms and from off campus. Internet access and online class registration are available. *Library facilities:* Neil Hellman Library plus 1 other. *General application contact:* Dean of Graduate and Adult and Continuing Education Admissions, 518-454-5136.

Find University Details at www.petersons.com/gradchannel.

Graduate Studies

School of Arts and Humanities
Programs in:
- art education (MS Ed, Certificate)
- arts and humanities (MA, MS Ed, Adv C, Certificate)
- English (MA)
- history/political science (MA)
- music (MA)
- music education (MS Ed, Adv C, Certificate)
- public communications (MA)

School of Business
Programs in:
- accounting (MS)
- business (MBA, MS, Certificate)
- business administration (MBA)
- not-for-profit management (Certificate)

School of Education
Programs in:
- applied technology education (MS Ed)
- bilingual pupil personnel services (Certificate)
- business and marketing (MS Ed)
- childhood education (MS Ed)
- college student personnel (MS Ed)
- college student services administration (MS Ed)
- communication disorders (MS Ed)
- community counseling (MS Ed)
- counseling (MS Ed)
- early childhood education (MS Ed)
- education (MS, MS Ed, Adv C, Certificate)
- educational administration and supervision (MS Ed, Certificate)
- educational leadership and administration (MS Ed)
- educational psychology (MS Ed)
- ELA—school building leader (Certificate)
- ELA—school district leader (Certificate)
- elementary education (K-6) (MS Ed)
- literacy: birth-grade 6 (MS Ed)
- literacy: grades 5-12 (MS Ed)
- reading (Certificate)
- school administrator and supervisor (Certificate)
- school counseling (MS Ed)
- school psychology (MS, Adv C)
- secondary education (MS Ed, Certificate)
- special education (MS Ed)
- teacher education (MS Ed, Certificate)

School of Mathematics and Sciences
Programs in:
- computer information systems (MS)
- mathematics and sciences (MS)

■ COLLEGE OF STATEN ISLAND OF THE CITY UNIVERSITY OF NEW YORK

Staten Island, NY 10314-6600

http://www.csi.cuny.edu/

State and locally supported, coed, comprehensive institution. *Enrollment:* 12,313 graduate, professional, and undergraduate students; 96 full-time matriculated graduate/professional students (66 women), 875 part-time matriculated graduate/professional students (659 women). *Graduate faculty:* 59 full-time (32 women), 21 part-time/adjunct (11 women). *Computer facilities:* 1,100 computers available on campus for general student use. A campuswide network can be accessed from off campus. Internet access and online class registration are available. *Library facilities:* College of Staten Island Library. *Graduate expenses:* Tuition, state resident: full-time $6,400; part-time $270 per credit. Tuition, nonresident: part-time $500 per credit. Required fees: $53 per semester. *General application contact:* Emmanuel Esperance, Deputy Director of Office of Recruitment and Admissions, 718-982-2190.

Find University Details at www.petersons.com/gradchannel.

Graduate Programs

Dr. David Podell, Senior Vice President for Academic Affairs and Provost
Programs in:
- adolescence education (MS Ed)
- adult health nursing (MS, 6th Year Certificate)

biology (MS)
business management (MS)
childhood education (MS Ed)
cinema and media studies (MA)
computer science (MS)
English (MA)
gerontological nursing (MS, 6th Year Certificate)
history (MA)
leadership in education (6th Year Certificate)
liberal studies (MA)
special education (MS Ed)

Center for Developmental Neuroscience and Developmental Disabilities
Dr. Probal Banerjee, Coordinator
Program in:
neuroscience, mental retardation and developmental disabilities (MS)

Center for Environmental Science
Dr. Alfred Levine, Director
Program in:
environmental science (MS)

■ COLUMBIA UNIVERSITY
New York, NY 10027
http://www.columbia.edu/

Independent, coed, university. CGS member. *Graduate faculty:* 3,462 full-time (1,317 women), 1,027 part-time/adjunct (395 women). *General application contact:* Information Contact, 212-854-1754.

College of Physicians and Surgeons
Programs in:
medicine (MD, M Phil, MA, MS, DN Sc, DPT, Ed D, PhD, Adv C)
movement science (Ed D)
occupational therapy (professional) (MS)
occupational therapy administration or education (post-professional) (MS)
physical therapy (DPT)

Institute of Human Nutrition
Dr. Richard J. Deckelbaum, Director
Program in:
nutrition (MS, PhD)

Fu Foundation School of Engineering and Applied Science
Zvi Galil, Dean
Programs in:
applied mathematics (MS, PhD)
applied physics (MS, Eng Sc D, PhD)
applied physics and applied mathematics (Engr)
biomedical engineering (MS, Eng Sc D, PhD)
chemical engineering (MS, Eng Sc D, PhD)
civil engineering (MS, Eng Sc D, PhD, Engr)
computer engineering (MS)
computer science (MS, Eng Sc D, PhD, Engr)
construction engineering and management (MS)
earth and environmental engineering (MS, Eng Sc D, PhD)
electrical engineering (MS, Eng Sc D, PhD, Engr)
engineering and applied science (MS, Eng Sc D, PhD, Engr)
engineering management systems (MS)
engineering mechanics (MS, Eng Sc D, PhD, Engr)
financial engineering (MS)
industrial engineering (MS, Eng Sc D, PhD, Engr)
materials science and engineering (MS, Eng Sc D, PhD)
mechanical engineering (MS, Eng Sc D, PhD, Engr)
medical physics (MS)
metallurgical engineering (Engr)
mining engineering (Engr)
operations research (MS, Eng Sc D, PhD)
solid state science and engineering (MS, Eng Sc D, PhD)

Graduate School of Architecture, Planning, and Preservation
Programs in:
advanced architectural design (MS)
architecture (M Arch, PhD)
architecture and urban design (MS)
architecture, planning, and preservation (M Arch, MS, PhD)
historic preservation (MS)
real estate development (MS)
urban planning (MS, PhD)

Graduate School of Arts and Sciences
Dr. Henry C. Pinkham, Dean
Programs in:
African-American studies (MA)
American studies (MA)
arts and sciences (M Phil, MA, DMA, PhD, Certificate)
climate and society (MA)
conservation biology (MA)
East Asian regional studies (MA)
East Asian studies (MA)
French cultural studies (MA)
human rights studies (MA)
Islamic culture studies (MA)
Jewish studies (MA)
medieval studies (MA)
modern European studies (MA)
quantitative methods in the social sciences (MA)
Russian, Eurasian and East European regional studies (MA)
South Asian studies (MA)
sustainable development (PhD)
theatre (M Phil, MA, PhD)
Yiddish studies (MA)

Division of Humanities
Programs in:
archaeology (M Phil, MA, PhD)
art history and archaeology (M Phil, MA, PhD)
classics (M Phil, MA, PhD)
comparative literature (M Phil, MA, PhD)
East Asian languages and cultures (M Phil, MA, PhD)
English literature (M Phil, MA, PhD)
French and Romance philology (M Phil, PhD)
Germanic languages (M Phil, MA, PhD)
Hebrew language and literature (M Phil, MA, PhD)
humanities (M Phil, MA, DMA, PhD)
Italian (M Phil, MA, PhD)
Jewish studies (M Phil, MA, PhD)
literature-writing (M Phil, MA, PhD)
Middle Eastern languages and cultures (M Phil, MA, PhD)
modern art (MA)
music (M Phil, MA, DMA, PhD)
Oriental studies (M Phil, MA, PhD)
philosophy (M Phil, MA, PhD)
religion (M Phil, MA, PhD)
Romance languages (MA)
Russian literature (M Phil, MA, PhD)
Slavic languages (M Phil, MA, PhD)
South Asian languages and cultures (M Phil, MA, PhD)
Spanish and Portuguese (M Phil, MA, PhD)

Division of Natural Sciences
Programs in:
astronomy (M Phil, MA, PhD)
atmospheric and planetary science (M Phil, PhD)
biological sciences (M Phil, MA, PhD)
chemical physics (M Phil, PhD)
conservation biology (Certificate)
ecology and evolutionary biology (PhD)
environmental policy (Certificate)
experimental psychology (M Phil, MA, PhD)
geochemistry (M Phil, MA, PhD)
geodetic sciences (M Phil, MA, PhD)
geophysics (M Phil, MA, PhD)
inorganic chemistry (M Phil, MA, PhD)
mathematics (M Phil, MA, PhD)
natural sciences (M Phil, MA, PhD, Certificate)
oceanography (M Phil, MA, PhD)
organic chemistry (M Phil, MA, PhD)
philosophical foundations of physics (MA)
physics (M Phil, PhD)
psychobiology (M Phil, MA, PhD)
social psychology (M Phil, MA, PhD)
statistics (M Phil, MA, PhD)

Division of Social Sciences
Programs in:
American history (M Phil, MA, PhD)
anthropology (M Phil, MA, PhD)
economics (M Phil, MA, PhD)
history (M Phil, MA, PhD)

Columbia University (continued)
political science (M Phil, MA, PhD)
social sciences (M Phil, MA, PhD)
sociology (M Phil, MA, PhD)

Graduate School of Business
Prof. Robert Glenn Hubbard, Dean
Programs in:
accounting (MBA)
business (PhD)
business administration (EMBA, MBA)
decision, risk, and operations (MBA)
entrepreneurship (MBA)
finance and economics (MBA)
global business administration (EMBA)
human resource management (MBA)
international business (MBA)
management (MBA)
marketing (MBA)
media (MBA)
real estate (MBA)
social enterprise (MBA)

Graduate School of Journalism
Program in:
journalism (MS, PhD)

Mailman School of Public Health
Dr. Allan Rosenfield, Dean
Programs in:
biostatistics (MPH, MS, Dr PH, PhD)
environmental health sciences (MPH, Dr PH, PhD)
epidemiology (MPH, MS, Dr PH, PhD)
health policy and management (Exec MPH, MPH)
population and family health (MPH)
public health (MPH, Dr PH)
sociomedical sciences (MPH, Dr PH, PhD)

School of Continuing Education
Programs in:
actuarial science (MS)
construction administration (MS)
fundraising management (MS)
information and archive management (MS)
landscape design (MS)
strategic communications (MS)
technology management (Exec MS)

College of Dental Medicine
Programs in:
advanced education in general dentistry (Certificate)
biomedical informatics (MA, PhD)
dental and oral surgery (DDS)
dental medicine (DDS, MA, MS, PhD, Certificate)
endodontics (Certificate)
orthodontics (MS, Certificate)
periodontics (MS, Certificate)
prosthodontics (MS, Certificate)
science education (MA)

School of International and Public Affairs
Dr. John Coatsworth, Dean
Programs in:
environmental science and policy (MPA)
international affairs (MIA)
international and public affairs (MIA, MPA, Certificate)
public policy and administration (MPA)

The East Central Europe Center
Dr. John Micgiel, Director
Program in:
East Central European studies (Certificate)

The Harriman Institute
Dr. Catherine Theimer Nepomnyashchy, Director
Program in:
Russian, Eurasian, and Eastern European studies (Certificate)

Institute for the Study of Europe
Dr. Volker Berghahn, Director
Program in:
European studies (Certificate)

Institute of African Studies
Mamadou Diouf, Director
Program in:
African studies (Certificate)

Institute of Latin American Studies
Program in:
Latin American studies (Certificate)

Middle East Institute
Dr. Rashidi Khalidi, Director
Program in:
Middle East studies (Certificate)

Southern Asian Institute
Dr. Vidya Dehejia, Director
Program in:
Southern Asian studies (Certificate)

Weatherhead East Asian Institute
Myron Cohen, Director
Program in:
Asian studies (Certificate)

School of Law
Program in:
law (JD, LL M, JSD)

School of Nursing
Dr. Mary O'Neil Mundinger, Dean
Programs in:
acute care nurse practitioner (MS, Adv C)
adult nurse practitioner (MS, Adv C)
family nurse practitioner (MS, Adv C)
geriatric nurse practitioner (MS, Adv C)
neonatal nurse practitioner (MS, Adv C)
nurse anesthesia (MS, Adv C)
nurse midwifery (MS)
nursing (MS, DN Sc, DrNP, Adv C)
nursing practice (DrNP)
nursing science (DN Sc)
oncology nursing (MS, Adv C)
pediatric nurse practitioner (MS, Adv C)
psychiatric mental health nursing (MS, Adv C)
women's health nurse practitioner (Adv C)

School of Social Work
Dr. Jeanette Takamura, Dean
Program in:
social work (MSSW, PhD)

School of the Arts
Dan Kleinman, Acting Dean
Programs in:
arts (MFA)
digital media (MFA)
directing (MFA)
fiction (MFA)
new genres (MFA)
nonfiction (MFA)
painting (MFA)
photography (MFA)
poetry (MFA)
printmaking (MFA)
producing (MFA)
screen writing (MFA)
sculpture (MFA)

Theatre Arts Division
Steven Chaikelson, Chair
Programs in:
acting (MFA)
directing (MFA)
dramaturgy (MFA)
playwriting (MFA)
stage management (MFA)
theater management (MFA)

■ CORNELL UNIVERSITY
Ithaca, NY 14853-0001
http://www.cornell.edu/

Independent, coed, university. CGS member. *Enrollment:* 19,639 graduate, professional, and undergraduate students; 6,077 full-time matriculated graduate/professional students (2,533 women). *Graduate faculty:* 1,548 full-time (391 women), 85 part-time/adjunct (17 women). *Computer facilities:* Computer purchase and lease plans are available. 3,000 computers available on campus for general student use. A campuswide network can be accessed from student residence rooms and from off campus. Internet access and online class registration are available. *Library facilities:* Olin Library plus 17 others. *Graduate expenses:* Tuition: full-time $32,800. Full-time tuition and fees vary according to program. *General application contact:* Graduate School Application Requests, Caldwell Hall, 607-255-4884.

College of Veterinary Medicine
Dr. Donald F. Smith, Dean
Programs in:
comparative biomedical science (PhD)
immunology (PhD)
pharmacology (PhD)
physiology (PhD)
veterinary medicine (DVM)
zoology (PhD)

Cornell Law School
Stewart J. Schawb, Dean
Program in:
law (JD, LL M)

Graduate School
Dr. Alison G. Power, Dean
Programs in:
acarology (MS, PhD)
advanced composites and structures (M Eng)
advanced materials processing (M Eng, MS, PhD)
aerospace engineering (M Eng, MS, PhD)
African history (MA, PhD)
African studies (MPS)
African-American literature (PhD)
African-American studies (MPS)
agricultural economics (MPS, MS, PhD)
agricultural education (MAT)
agriculture and life sciences (M Eng, MAT, MFS, MLA, MPS, MS, PhD)
agronomy (MS, PhD)
algorithms (M Eng, PhD)
American art (PhD)
American history (MA, PhD)
American literature after 1865 (PhD)
American literature to 1865 (PhD)
American politics (PhD)
American studies (PhD)
analytical chemistry (PhD)
ancient art and archaeology (PhD)
ancient history (MA, PhD)
ancient Near Eastern studies (MA, PhD)
ancient philosophy (PhD)
animal breeding (MS, PhD)
animal cytology (MS, PhD)
animal genetics (MS, PhD)
animal nutrition (MPS, MS, PhD)
animal science (MPS, MS, PhD)
apiculture (MS, PhD)
apparel design (MA, MPS)
applied economics (PhD)
applied entomology (MS, PhD)
applied linguistics (MA, PhD)
applied logic and automated reasoning (M Eng, PhD)
applied mathematics (PhD)
applied mathematics and computational methods (M Eng, MS, PhD)
applied physics (PhD)
applied probability and statistics (PhD)
applied research in human-environment relations (MS)
applied statistics (MPS)
aquatic entomology (MS, PhD)
aquatic science (MPS, MS, PhD)
Arabic and Islamic studies (MA, PhD)
archaeological anthropology (PhD)
artificial intelligence (M Eng, PhD)
arts and sciences (MA, MFA, MPA, MPS, MS, DMA, PhD)
Asian art (PhD)
Asian religions (MA, PhD)
astronomy (PhD)
astrophysics (PhD)
atmospheric science (MS, PhD)
baroque art (PhD)
basic analytical economics (PhD)
behavioral biology (PhD)
behavioral physiology (MS, PhD)
biblical studies (MA, PhD)
bio-organic chemistry (PhD)
biochemical engineering (M Eng, MS, PhD)
biochemistry (PhD)
biological anthropology (PhD)
biological control (MS, PhD)
biological engineering (M Eng, MPS, MS, PhD)
biology (7-12) (MAT)
biomechanical engineering (M Eng, MS, PhD)
biomedical engineering (M Eng, MS, PhD)
biometry (MS, PhD)
biophysical chemistry (PhD)
biophysics (PhD)
biopsychology (PhD)
cardiovascular and respiratory physiology (MS, PhD)
cell biology (PhD)
cellular and molecular medicine (MS, PhD)
cellular and molecular toxicology (MS, PhD)
cellular immunology (MS, PhD)
chemical biology (PhD)
chemical physics (PhD)
chemical reaction engineering (M Eng, MS, PhD)
chemistry (7-12) (MAT)
Chinese linguistics (MA, PhD)
Chinese philology (MA, PhD)
classical and statistical thermodynamics (M Eng, MS, PhD)
classical archaeology (PhD)
classical Chinese literature (MA, PhD)
classical Japanese literature (MA, PhD)
classical myth (PhD)
classical rhetoric (PhD)
cognition (PhD)
collective bargaining, labor law and labor history (MILR, MPS, MS, PhD)
colonial and postcolonial literature (PhD)
combustion (M Eng, MS, PhD)
communication (MPS, MS, PhD)
communication research methods (MS, PhD)
community and regional society (MS)
community and regional sociology (MPS, PhD)
community development process (MPS)
community nutrition (MPS, MS, PhD)
comparative and functional anatomy (MS, PhD)
comparative biomedical sciences (MS, PhD)
comparative literature (PhD)
comparative politics (PhD)
composition (DMA)
computer engineering (M Eng, PhD)
computer graphics (M Eng, PhD)
computer science (M Eng, PhD)
computer vision (M Eng, PhD)
concurrency and distributed computing (M Eng, PhD)
consumer policy (PhD)
controlled environment agriculture (MPS, PhD)
controlled environment horticulture (MS)
creative writing (MFA)
cultural studies (PhD)
curriculum and instruction (MPS, MS, PhD)
cytology (MS, PhD)
dairy science (MPS, MS, PhD)
decision theory (MS, PhD)
development policy (MPS)
developmental and reproductive biology (MS, PhD)
developmental biology (MS, PhD)
developmental psychology (PhD)
drama and the theatre (PhD)
dramatic literature (PhD)
dynamics and space mechanics (MS, PhD)
early modern European history (MA, PhD)
earth science (7-12) (MAT)
East Asian linguistics (MA, PhD)
East Asian studies (MA)
ecological and environmental plant pathology (MPS, MS, PhD)
ecology (MS, PhD)
econometrics and economic statistics (PhD)
economic and social statistics (MILR, MS, PhD)
economic development (MPS)
economic development and planning (PhD)
economic geology (M Eng, MS, PhD)
economic theory (PhD)
economy and society (MA, PhD)
ecotoxicology and environmental chemistry (MS, PhD)
electrical engineering (M Eng, PhD)
electrical systems (M Eng, PhD)
electrophysics (M Eng, PhD)
endocrinology (MS, PhD)
energy (M Eng, MPS, MS, PhD)
energy and power systems (M Eng, MS, PhD)
engineering (M Eng, MS, PhD)
engineering geology (M Eng, MS, PhD)
engineering management (M Eng, MS, PhD)
engineering physics (M Eng)
engineering statistics (MS, PhD)
English history (MA, PhD)
English linguistics (MA, PhD)
English poetry (PhD)
English Renaissance to 1660 (PhD)
environmental and comparative physiology (MS, PhD)
environmental archaeology (MA)
environmental engineering (M Eng, MPS, MS, PhD)
environmental fluid mechanics and hydrology (M Eng, MS, PhD)
environmental geophysics (M Eng, MS, PhD)

Cornell University (continued)
environmental information science (MS, PhD)
environmental management (MPS)
environmental systems engineering (M Eng, MS, PhD)
epidemiological plant pathology (MPS, MS, PhD)
evaluation (PhD)
evolutionary biology (PhD)
experimental design (MS, PhD)
experimental physics (MS, PhD)
extension, and adult education (MPS, MS, PhD)
facilities planning and management (MS)
family and social welfare policy (PhD)
fiber science (MS, PhD)
field crop science (MS, PhD)
fishery science (MPS, MS, PhD)
fluid dynamics, rheology and biorheology (M Eng, MS, PhD)
fluid mechanics (M Eng, MS, PhD)
food chemistry (MPS, MS, PhD)
food engineering (MPS, MS, PhD)
food microbiology (MPS, MS, PhD)
food processing engineering (M Eng, MPS, MS, PhD)
food processing waste technology (MPS, MS, PhD)
food science (MFS, MPS, MS, PhD)
forest science (MPS, MS, PhD)
French history (MA, PhD)
French linguistics (PhD)
French literature (PhD)
gastrointestinal and metabolic physiology (MS, PhD)
gender and life course (MA, PhD)
general geology (M Eng, MS, PhD)
general linguistics (MA, PhD)
general space sciences (PhD)
genetics (PhD)
geobiology (M Eng, MS, PhD)
geochemistry and isotope geology (M Eng, MS, PhD)
geohydrology (M Eng, MS, PhD)
geomorphology (M Eng, MS, PhD)
geophysics (M Eng, MS, PhD)
geotechnical engineering (M Eng, MS, PhD)
geotectonics (M Eng, MS, PhD)
German area studies (MA, PhD)
German history (MA, PhD)
German intellectual history (MA, PhD)
Germanic linguistics (MA, PhD)
Germanic literature (MA, PhD)
Greek and Latin language and linguistics (PhD)
Greek language and literature (PhD)
greenhouse crops (MPS, MS, PhD)
health administration (MHA)
health management and policy (PhD)
heat and mass transfer (M Eng, MS, PhD)
heat transfer (M Eng, MS, PhD)
Hebrew and Judaic studies (MA, PhD)
Hispanic literature (PhD)
histology (MS, PhD)
historical archaeology (MA)
history and philosophy of science and technology (MA, PhD)
history of science (MA, PhD)
horticultural business management (MPS, MS, PhD)
horticultural physiology (MPS, MS, PhD)
hospitality management (MMH)
hotel administration (MS, PhD)
housing and design (MS)
human computer interaction (PhD)
human development and family studies (PhD)
human ecology (MA, MHA, MPS, MS, PhD)
human experimental psychology (PhD)
human factors and ergonomics (MS)
human nutrition (MPS, MS, PhD)
human resource studies (MILR, MPS, MS, PhD)
human-environment relations (MS)
immunochemistry (MS, PhD)
immunogenetics (MS, PhD)
immunopathology (MS, PhD)
Indo-European linguistics (MA, PhD)
industrial and labor relations problems (MILR, MPS, MS, PhD)
industrial organization and control (PhD)
infection and immunity (MS, PhD)
infectious diseases (MS, PhD)
information organization and retrieval (M Eng, PhD)
information systems (PhD)
infrared astronomy (PhD)
inorganic chemistry (PhD)
insect behavior (MS, PhD)
insect biochemistry (MS, PhD)
insect ecology (MS, PhD)
insect genetics (MS, PhD)
insect morphology (MS, PhD)
insect pathology (MS, PhD)
insect physiology (MS, PhD)
insect systematics (MS, PhD)
insect toxicology and insecticide chemistry (MS, PhD)
integrated pest management (MS, PhD)
interior design (MA, MPS)
international agriculture (M Eng, MPS, MS, PhD)
international agriculture and development (MPS)
international and comparative labor (MILR, MPS, MS, PhD)
international communication (MS, PhD)
international economics (PhD)
international food science (MPS, MS, PhD)
international nutrition (MPS, MS, PhD)
international planning (MPS)
international population (MPS)
international relations (PhD)
Italian linguistics (PhD)
Italian literature (PhD)
Japanese linguistics (MA, PhD)
kinetics and catalysis (M Eng, MS, PhD)
Korean literature (MA, PhD)
labor economics (MILR, MPS, MS, PhD)
landscape architecture (MLA)
landscape horticulture (MPS, MS, PhD)
Latin American archaeology (MA)
Latin American history (MA, PhD)
Latin language and literature (PhD)
lesbian, bisexual, and gay literature studies (PhD)
literary criticism and theory (PhD)
local government organizations and operations (MPS)
local roads (M Eng, MPS, MS, PhD)
machine systems (M Eng, MPS, MS, PhD)
manufacturing systems engineering (PhD)
marine geology (MS, PhD)
materials and manufacturing engineering (M Eng, MS, PhD)
materials chemistry (PhD)
materials engineering (M Eng, PhD)
materials science (M Eng, PhD)
mathematical programming (PhD)
mathematical statistics (MS, PhD)
mathematics (PhD)
mathematics (7-12) (MAT)
mechanical systems and design (M Eng, MS, PhD)
mechanics of materials (MS, PhD)
medical and veterinary entomology (MS, PhD)
medieval and Renaissance Latin literature (PhD)
medieval archaeology (MA, PhD)
medieval art (PhD)
medieval Chinese history (MA, PhD)
medieval history (MA, PhD)
medieval literature (PhD)
medieval music (PhD)
medieval philology and linguistics (PhD)
medieval philosophy (PhD)
Mediterranean and Near Eastern archaeology (MA)
membrane and epithelial physiology (MS, PhD)
methodology (MA, PhD)
methods of social research (MPS, MS, PhD)
microbiology (PhD)
mineralogy (M Eng, MS, PhD)
modern art (PhD)
modern Chinese history (MA, PhD)
modern Chinese literature (MA, PhD)
modern European history (MA, PhD)
modern Japanese history (MA, PhD)
modern Japanese literature (MA, PhD)
molecular and cell biology (PhD)
molecular and cellular physiology (MS, PhD)
molecular biology (PhD)
molecular plant pathology (MPS, MS, PhD)
monetary and macroeconomics (PhD)
multiphase flows (M Eng, MS, PhD)

musicology (PhD)
mycology (MPS, MS, PhD)
neural and sensory physiology (MS, PhD)
neurobiology (PhD)
nineteenth century (PhD)
nuclear engineering (M Eng, MS, PhD)
nuclear science (MS, PhD)
nursery crops (MPS, MS, PhD)
nutrition of horticultural crops (MPS, MS, PhD)
nutritional and food toxicology (MS, PhD)
nutritional biochemistry (MPS, MS, PhD)
Old and Middle English (PhD)
old Norse (MA, PhD)
operating systems (M Eng, PhD)
operations research and industrial engineering (M Eng)
organic chemistry (PhD)
organizational behavior (MILR, MPS, MS, PhD)
organizations (MA, PhD)
organometallic chemistry (PhD)
paleobotany (MS, PhD)
paleontology (M Eng, MS, PhD)
parallel computing (M Eng, PhD)
performance practice (DMA)
personality and social psychology (PhD)
petroleum geology (M Eng, MS, PhD)
petrology (M Eng, MS, PhD)
pharmacology (MS, PhD)
philosophy (PhD)
phonetics (MA, PhD)
phonological theory (MA, PhD)
physical chemistry (PhD)
physics (MS, PhD)
physics (7-12) (MAT)
physiological genomics (MS, PhD)
physiology of reproduction (MPS, MS, PhD)
planetary geology (M Eng, MS, PhD)
planetary studies (PhD)
plant breeding (MPS, MS, PhD)
plant cell biology (MS, PhD)
plant disease epidemiology (MPS, MS, PhD)
plant ecology (MS, PhD)
plant genetics (MPS, MS, PhD)
plant molecular biology (MS, PhD)
plant morphology, anatomy and biomechanics (MS, PhD)
plant pathology (MPS, MS, PhD)
plant physiology (MS, PhD)
plant propagation (MPS, MS, PhD)
plant protection (MPS)
policy analysis (MA, PhD)
political methodology (PhD)
political sociology/social movements (MA, PhD)
political thought (PhD)
polymer chemistry (PhD)
polymer science (MS, PhD)
polymers (M Eng, MS, PhD)
pomology (MPS, MS, PhD)
population and development (MPS, MS, PhD)
population medicine and epidemiology (MS)
population medicine and epidemiology sciences (PhD)
Precambrian geology (M Eng, MS, PhD)
premodern Islamic history (MA, PhD)
premodern Japanese history (MA, PhD)
probability (MS, PhD)
program development and planning (MPS)
programming environments (M Eng, PhD)
programming languages and methodology (M Eng, PhD)
prose fiction (PhD)
public affairs (MPA)
public finance (PhD)
public garden management (MPS, MS, PhD)
public policy (MPA, PhD)
Quaternary geology (M Eng, MS, PhD)
racial and ethnic relations (MA, PhD)
radio astronomy (PhD)
radiophysics (PhD)
remote sensing (M Eng, MS, PhD)
Renaissance art (PhD)
Renaissance history (MA, PhD)
reproductive physiology (MS, PhD)
resource economics (MPS, MS, PhD)
resource policy and management (MPS, MS, PhD)
Restoration and eighteenth century (PhD)
restoration ecology (MPS, MS, PhD)
risk assessment, management and public policy (MS, PhD)
robotics (M Eng, PhD)
rock mechanics (M Eng, MS, PhD)
Romance linguistics (MA, PhD)
rural and environmental sociology (MPS, MS, PhD)
Russian history (MA, PhD)
sampling (MS, PhD)
science and environmental communication (MS, PhD)
science and technology policy (MPS)
scientific computing (M Eng, PhD)
second language acquisition (MA, PhD)
sedimentology (M Eng, MS, PhD)
seismology (M Eng, MS, PhD)
semantics (MA, PhD)
sensory evaluation (MPS, MS, PhD)
Slavic linguistics (MA, PhD)
social aspects of information (PhD)
social networks (MA, PhD)
social psychology (MA, PhD)
social psychology of communication (MS, PhD)
social stratification (MA, PhD)
social studies of science and technology (MA, PhD)
sociocultural anthropology (PhD)
sociolinguistics (MA, PhD)
soil and water engineering (M Eng, MPS, MS, PhD)
soil science (MS, PhD)
solid mechanics (MS, PhD)
South Asian linguistics (MA, PhD)
South Asian studies (MA)
Southeast Asian art (PhD)
Southeast Asian history (MA, PhD)
Southeast Asian linguistics (MA, PhD)
Southeast Asian studies (MA)
Spanish linguistics (PhD)
state, economy and society (MS)
state, economy, and society (MPS, PhD)
statistical computing (MS, PhD)
statistics (MPS, MS, PhD)
stochastic processes (MS, PhD)
Stone Age archaeology (MA)
stratigraphy (M Eng, MS, PhD)
structural and functional biology (MS, PhD)
structural engineering (M Eng, MS, PhD)
structural geology (M Eng, MS, PhD)
structural mechanics (M Eng, MS)
structures and environment (M Eng, MPS, MS, PhD)
surface science (M Eng, MS, PhD)
syntactic theory (MA, PhD)
systematic botany (MS, PhD)
systems engineering (M Eng)
taxonomy of ornamental plants (MPS, MS, PhD)
textile science (MS, PhD)
theatre history (PhD)
theatre theory and aesthetics (PhD)
theoretical astrophysics (PhD)
theoretical chemistry (PhD)
theoretical physics (MS, PhD)
theory and criticism (PhD)
theory of computation (M Eng, PhD)
theory of music (MA)
transportation engineering (MS, PhD)
transportation systems engineering (M Eng)
turfgrass science (MPS, MS, PhD)
twentieth century (PhD)
urban horticulture (MPS, MS, PhD)
uses and effects of communication (MS, PhD)
vegetable crops (MPS, MS, PhD)
water resource systems (M Eng, MS, PhD)
weed science (MPS, MS, PhD)
wildlife science (MPS, MS, PhD)
women's literature (PhD)

Field of Environmental Management
Program in:
environmental management (MPS)

Graduate Field in the Law School
Director of Graduate Studies
Program in:
law (LL M, JSD)

Graduate Field of Management
Director of Graduate Studies
Programs in:
accounting (PhD)

Cornell University (continued)
behavioral decision theory (PhD)
finance (PhD)
marketing (PhD)
organizational behavior (PhD)
production and operations management (PhD)

Graduate Fields of Architecture, Art and Planning
Programs in:
architectural design (M Arch)
architectural science (MS)
architecture, art and planning (M Arch, MA, MFA, MPSRE, MRP, MS, PhD)
building technology and environmental science (MS)
city and regional planning (MRP, PhD)
computer graphics (MS)
creative visual arts (MFA)
environmental planning and design (MRP, PhD)
environmental studies (MA, MS, PhD)
historic preservation planning (MA)
history of architecture (MA, PhD)
history of urban development (MA, PhD)
international development planning (MRP, PhD)
international spatial problems (MA, MS, PhD)
location theory (MA, MS, PhD)
multiregional economic analysis (MA, MS, PhD)
peace science (MA, MS, PhD)
planning methods (MA, MS, PhD)
planning theory and systems analysis (MRP, PhD)
real estate (MPSRE)
regional economics and development planning (MRP, PhD)
regional science (MRP, PhD)
social and health systems planning (MRP, PhD)
theory and criticism of architecture (M Arch)
urban and regional economics (MA, MS, PhD)
urban and regional theory (MRP, PhD)
urban design (M Arch)
urban planning history (MRP, PhD)

Johnson Graduate School of Management
Robert J. Swieringa, Dean
Program in:
management (MBA)

■ DAEMEN COLLEGE
Amherst, NY 14226-3592
http://www.daemen.edu/

Independent, coed, comprehensive institution. *Enrollment:* 2,414 graduate, professional, and undergraduate students; 418 full-time matriculated graduate/professional students (330 women), 348 part-time matriculated graduate/professional students (292 women). *Graduate faculty:* 20 full-time (11 women), 64 part-time/adjunct (50 women). *Computer facilities:* 99 computers available on campus for general student use. A campuswide network can be accessed from student residence rooms and from off campus. Internet access is available. *Library facilities:* Marian Library plus 1 other. *Graduate expenses:* Tuition: full-time $11,700; part-time $650 per credit hour. Required fees: $15 per credit hour. Tuition and fees vary according to course load. *General application contact:* Karl Shallowhorn, Associate Director of Graduate Admissions, 716-839-8225.

Department of Accounting and Information Systems
Dr. Linda J. Kuechler, Chair
Program in:
global business (MS)

Department of Nursing
Dr. Mary Lou Rusin, Chair
Programs in:
adult nurse practitioner (MS, Certificate)
nursing executive leadership (MS)
palliative care nursing (MS, Certificate)

Department of Physical Therapy
Dr. Sharon L. Held, Chair
Program in:
physical therapy (DPT, TDPT)

Education Department
Dr. Mary H. Fox, Chair
Programs in:
adolescence education (MS)
childhood education (MS)
childhood special education (MS)

Physician Assistant Department
Gregg L. Shutts, Director
Program in:
physician assistant (MS)

Program in Executive Leadership and Change
Dr. John S. Frederick, Executive Director
Program in:
executive leadership and change (MS)

■ DOMINICAN COLLEGE
Orangeburg, NY 10962-1210
http://www.dc.edu/

Independent, coed, comprehensive institution. *Enrollment:* 1,856 graduate, professional, and undergraduate students; 48 full-time matriculated graduate/professional students (31 women), 105 part-time matriculated graduate/professional students (85 women). *Graduate faculty:* 12 full-time (11 women), 27 part-time/adjunct (21 women). *Computer facilities:* 38 computers available on campus for general student use. A campuswide network can be accessed from student residence rooms. Internet access is available. *Library facilities:* Pius X Hall plus 1 other. *General application contact:* Joyce Elbe, Director of Admissions, 845-848-7896 Ext. 15.

Find University Details at www.petersons.com/gradchannel.

Division of Allied Health
Sr. Beryl Herdt, Division Director
Programs in:
allied health (MS, DPT)
occupational therapy (MS)
physical therapy (MS, DPT)

Division of Nursing
Dr. Maureen Creegan, Division Director, Nursing
Programs in:
family nurse practitioner (MSN)
nursing (MSN)

Division of Teacher Education
Dr. Roger Tesi, Division Director, Teacher Education
Programs in:
teacher education (MS Ed)
teacher of students with disabilities (MS Ed)
teacher of visually impaired (MS Ed)

■ DOWLING COLLEGE
Oakdale, NY 11769-1999
http://www.dowling.edu/

Independent, coed, comprehensive institution. *Enrollment:* 5,546 graduate, professional, and undergraduate students; 831 full-time matriculated graduate/professional students (527 women), 1,663 part-time matriculated graduate/professional students (1,112 women). *Graduate faculty:* 117 full-time (43 women), 290 part-time/adjunct (146 women). *Computer facilities:* 118 computers available on campus for general student use. A campuswide network can be accessed. Internet access and online class registration are available. *Library facilities:* Dowling College Library. *Graduate expenses:* Tuition: full-time $16,008; part-time $667 per credit. Tuition and fees vary according to course load. *General application contact:* Franks S. Pizzardi, Director of Admissions Operations, 631-244-3227.

Graduate Programs in Education
Dr. Clyde Payne, Associate Provost
Programs in:
educational administration (Ed D, PD)
human development and learning (MS Ed)
literacy (MS Ed)
literacy/special education (MS Ed)
secondary education (MS Ed)
special education (MS Ed)

Programs in Arts and Sciences
Dr. Linda Ardito, Provost
Programs in:
integrated math and science (MS)
liberal studies (MA)

School of Business
Dr. Elana Zolfo, Dean of the School of Business
Programs in:
- aviation management (MBA, Certificate)
- banking and finance (MBA, Certificate)
- general management (MBA)
- public management (MBA, Certificate)
- total quality management (MBA, Certificate)

■ D'YOUVILLE COLLEGE
Buffalo, NY 14201-1084
http://www.dyc.edu/

Independent, coed, comprehensive institution. *Enrollment:* 3,024 graduate, professional, and undergraduate students; 1,048 full-time matriculated graduate/professional students (760 women), 610 part-time matriculated graduate/professional students (464 women). *Graduate faculty:* 100 full-time (66 women), 78 part-time/adjunct (47 women). *Computer facilities:* Computer purchase and lease plans are available. 72 computers available on campus for general student use. A campuswide network can be accessed from student residence rooms and from off campus. Internet access and online class registration are available. *Library facilities:* D'Youville College Library. *General application contact:* Linda Fisher, Graduate Admissions Director, 716-829-8400.

Find University Details at www.petersons.com/gradchannel.

Department of Business
Dr. Kushnood Haq, Chair
Program in:
- international business (MS)

Department of Dietetics
Dr. Edward Weiss, Chair
Program in:
- dietetics (MS)

Department of Education
Dr. David Gorlewski, Chair
Programs in:
- elementary education (MS Ed, Teaching Certificate)
- secondary education (MS Ed, Teaching Certificate)
- special education (MS Ed)

Department of Health Services Administration
Dr. Walter Iwanenko, Chair
Programs in:
- clinical research associate (Certificate)
- health services administration (MS, Certificate)
- long term care administration (Certificate)

Department of Holistic Health Studies
Dr. Paul Hageman, Chair of Holistic Health Studies
Program in:
- chiropractic (DC)

Department of Nursing
Dr. Verna Kieffer, Chair
Programs in:
- community health nursing/education (MSN)
- community health nursing/high risk parents and children (MSN)
- community health nursing/management (MSN)
- family nurse practitioner (MS)
- nursing and health-related professions (Certificate)
- nursing with clinical focus choice (MSN)

Department of Physical Therapy
Dr. Lynn Rivers, Chair
Programs in:
- advanced orthopedic physical therapy (Certificate)
- manual physical therapy (Certificate)
- physical therapy (MPT, MS, DPT)

Occupational Therapy Department
Dr. Merlene Gingher, Chair
Program in:
- occupational therapy (MS)

■ FORDHAM UNIVERSITY
New York, NY 10458
http://www.fordham.edu/

Independent-religious, coed, university. CGS member. *Enrollment:* 14,732 graduate, professional, and undergraduate students; 3,298 full-time matriculated graduate/professional students (2,020 women), 3,838 part-time matriculated graduate/professional students (2,407 women). *Graduate faculty:* 502 full-time, 416 part-time/adjunct. *Computer facilities:* Computer purchase and lease plans are available. 1,400 computers available on campus for general student use. A campuswide network can be accessed from student residence rooms and from off campus. Internet access and online class registration are available. *Library facilities:* Walsh Library plus 3 others. *General application contact:* Charlene Dundie, Director of Graduate Admissions, 718-817-4420.

Find University Details at www.petersons.com/gradchannel.

Graduate School of Arts and Sciences
Dr. Nancy A. Busch, Dean
Programs in:
- applied developmental psychology (PhD)
- arts and sciences (MA, MS, PhD, Certificate)
- biological sciences (MS, PhD)
- classical Greek and Latin literature (MA)
- classics (PhD)
- clinical psychology (PhD)
- computer science (MS)
- economics (MA, PhD)
- elections and campaign management (MA)
- English language and literature (MA, PhD)
- health care ethics (Certificate)
- history (MA, PhD)
- humanities and sciences (MA)
- international political economy and development (MA, Certificate)
- Latin American and Latino studies (Certificate)
- philosophical resources (MA)
- philosophy (MA, PhD)
- psychometrics (PhD)
- public communications (MA)
- sociology (MA, PhD)
- theology (MA, PhD)

Graduate School of Business
Dr. Howard Tuckman, Dean
Programs in:
- accounting (MBA)
- communications and media management (MBA)
- finance (MBA, MS)
- information systems (MBA, MS)
- management systems (MBA)
- marketing (MBA)
- media management (MS)
- taxation (MS)

Graduate School of Education
Dr. James Hennessy, Dean
Program in:
- education (MAT, MS, MSE, MST, Ed D, PhD, Adv C)

Division of Curriculum and Teaching
Dr. Terry Osborn, Chairperson
Programs in:
- adult education (MS, MSE)
- bilingual teacher education (MSE)
- curriculum and teaching (MSE)
- early childhood education (MSE)
- elementary education (MST)
- language, literacy, and learning (PhD)
- reading education (MSE, Adv C)
- secondary education (MAT, MSE)
- special education (MSE, Adv C)
- teaching English as a second language (MSE)

Division of Educational Leadership, Administration and Policy
Dr. Gerald Cattaro, Chairperson
Programs in:
- administration and supervision (MSE, Adv C)
- administration and supervision for church leaders (PhD)
- educational administration and supervision (Ed D, PhD)
- human resource program administration (MS)

Division of Psychological and Educational Services
Dr. Mitch Rabinowitz, Chairman

Fordham University (continued)
Programs in:
- counseling and personnel services (MSE, Adv C)
- counseling psychology (PhD)
- educational psychology (MSE, PhD)
- school psychology (PhD)
- urban and urban bilingual school psychology (Adv C)

Graduate School of Religion and Religious Education
Rev. Anthony J. Ciorra, Dean
Programs in:
- pastoral counseling and spiritual care (MA)
- pastoral ministry/spirituality/pastoral counseling (D Min)
- religion and religious education (MA)
- religious education (MS, PhD, PD)
- spiritual direction (Certificate)

Graduate School of Social Service
Dr. Peter B. Vaughan, Dean
Program in:
- social work (MSW, PhD)

School of Law
William Michael Treanor, Dean
Programs in:
- banking, corporate and finance law (LL M)
- intellectual property and information law (LL M)
- international business and trade law (LL M)
- law (JD)

■ GRADUATE SCHOOL AND UNIVERSITY CENTER OF THE CITY UNIVERSITY OF NEW YORK
New York, NY 10016-4039
http://www.gc.cuny.edu/

State and locally supported, coed, graduate-only institution. CGS member. *Graduate faculty:* 1,471 full-time (318 women). *Library facilities:* Mina Rees Library. *General application contact:* Les Gribben, Director of Admissions, 212-817-7470.

Graduate Studies
Dr. Linda Edwards, Acting Provost and Senior Vice President for Academic Affairs
Programs in:
- accounting (PhD)
- anthropological linguistics (PhD)
- archaeology (PhD)
- architecture (PhD)
- basic applied neurocognition (PhD)
- behavioral science (PhD)
- biochemistry (PhD)
- biology (PhD)
- biomedical engineering (PhD)
- biopsychology (PhD)
- chemical engineering (PhD)
- chemistry (PhD)
- civil engineering (PhD)
- classical studies (MA, PhD)
- clinical psychology (PhD)
- comparative literature (MA, PhD)
- computer science (PhD)
- criminal justice (PhD)
- cultural anthropology (PhD)
- developmental psychology (PhD)
- earth and environmental sciences (PhD)
- economics (PhD)
- educational psychology (PhD)
- electrical engineering (PhD)
- English (PhD)
- environmental psychology (PhD)
- experimental psychology (PhD)
- finance (PhD)
- French (PhD)
- Germanic languages and literatures (MA, PhD)
- graphic arts (PhD)
- Hispanic and Luso-Brazilian literatures (PhD)
- history (PhD)
- industrial psychology (PhD)
- learning processes (PhD)
- liberal studies (MA)
- linguistics (MA, PhD)
- management planning systems (PhD)
- mathematics (PhD)
- mechanical engineering (PhD)
- music (DMA, PhD)
- neuropsychology (PhD)
- painting (PhD)
- philosophy (MA, PhD)
- photography (PhD)
- physical anthropology (PhD)
- physics (PhD)
- political science (MA, PhD)
- psychology (PhD)
- sculpture (PhD)
- social personality (PhD)
- social welfare (DSW, PhD)
- sociology (PhD)
- speech and hearing sciences (PhD)
- theatre (PhD)
- urban education (PhD)

Interdisciplinary Studies
Programs in:
- language in social context (PhD)
- medieval studies (PhD)
- public policy (MA, PhD)
- urban studies (MA, PhD)
- women's studies (MA, PhD)

■ HOFSTRA UNIVERSITY
Hempstead, NY 11549
http://www.hofstra.edu/

Independent, coed, university. CGS member. *Enrollment:* 12,550 graduate, professional, and undergraduate students; 2,094 full-time matriculated graduate/professional students (1,273 women), 1,766 part-time matriculated graduate/professional students (1,118 women). *Graduate faculty:* 246 full-time (103 women), 183 part-time/adjunct (84 women). *Computer facilities:* Computer purchase and lease plans are available. 1,175 computers available on campus for general student use. A campuswide network can be accessed from student residence rooms and from off campus. Internet access and online class registration are available. *Library facilities:* Axinn Library plus 1 other. *Graduate expenses:* Tuition: full-time $13,320; part-time $740 per credit. Required fees: $930; $155 per term. *General application contact:* Carol Drummer, Dean of Graduate Admissions, 516-463-4876.

Find University Details at www.petersons.com/gradchannel.

College of Liberal Arts and Sciences
Dr. Bernard J. Firestone, Dean
Programs in:
- applied linguistics (MA)
- applied mathematics (MS)
- applied organizational psychology (PhD)
- audiology (MA, Au D)
- biology (MA, MS)
- clinical and school psychology (MA, PhD)
- comparative arts and culture (MA)
- computer science (MA, MS)
- engineering management (MS)
- English (literature) (MA)
- English and creative writing (MA)
- industrial/organizational psychology (MA)
- liberal arts and sciences (MA, MS, Au D, PhD, Psy D, CAS)
- mathematics (MA)
- school and community psychology (MS)
- school-community psychology (Psy D, CAS)
- Spanish (MA)
- speech-language pathology (MA)

Frank G. Zarb School of Business
Salvatore F. Sodano, Dean
Programs in:
- accounting (MBA, MS)
- business (EMBA, MBA, MS, Advanced Certificate)
- business administration (EMBA)
- business computer information systems (MBA)
- computer information systems (MS)
- finance (MBA, MS)
- health services management (MBA)
- human resource management (MS, Advanced Certificate)
- international business (MBA, MS, Advanced Certificate)
- management (EMBA, MBA)
- marketing (MBA, MS, Advanced Certificate)
- marketing research (MS)
- quality management (MBA)
- quantitative finance (MS)
- taxation (MBA, MS)

New College
Dr. Barry Nass, Vice Dean

Program in:
- interdisciplinary studies (MA)

School of Communication
Dr. Sybil A. DelGaudio, Dean
Programs in:
- audio, video, and film (MFA)
- communication (MA, MFA)
- journalism (MA)
- speech communication, rhetoric, and performance studies (MA)

School of Education and Allied Human Services
Dr. Maureen O. Murphy, Interim Dean
Programs in:
- addiction studies (CAS)
- advanced literacy studies (birth-6) (PD)
- advanced literacy studies (grades 5–12) (PD)
- bilingual education (MA)
- bilingual extension education (CAS)
- business education (MS Ed)
- counseling (MA, MS Ed, Advanced Certificate, PD)
- creative arts therapy (MA, MS Ed)
- creative arts therapy and special education (birth-grade 2) (MS Ed)
- creative arts therapy and special education (grades 1-12) (MS Ed)
- divorce mediation (CAS)
- early childhood and childhood education (MS Ed)
- early childhood education (MA, MS Ed)
- early childhood special education (MS Ed, Advanced Certificate)
- education and allied human services (MA, MHA, MS, MS Ed, Ed D, PhD, Advanced Certificate, CAS, PD)
- educational administration (MS Ed, CAS)
- educational administration and policy studies (MS Ed)
- educational and policy leadership (Ed D)
- educational leadership (CAS)
- elementary education (MA, MS Ed)
- elementary education-math/science/technology (MA)
- English education (MA, MS Ed)
- family therapy (CAS)
- fine arts education (MA, MS Ed)
- foreign language education (MA, MS Ed)
- foundations of education (MA, CAS)
- French (MA, MS Ed)
- German (MA, MS Ed)
- gerontology (MS, Advanced Certificate)
- gifted education (Advanced Certificate)
- health administration (MHA)
- health education (MS)
- inclusive early childhood special education (MS Ed)
- inclusive elementary special education (MS Ed)
- inclusive secondary special education (MS Ed)
- intensive program in fine arts or music (Advanced Certificate)
- intensive program in secondary education (CAS)
- literacy studies (MA, MS Ed, Ed D, PhD, CAS, PD)
- literacy studies (birth–grade 6) (MS Ed, CAS)
- literacy studies (birth-grade 6) and special education (birth-grade 2) (MS Ed)
- literacy studies (birth-grade 6) and special education (grades 1-6) (MS Ed)
- literacy studies (grades 5–12) (MS Ed, CAS)
- literacy studies and special education (MS Ed)
- marriage and family therapy (MA, CAS, PD)
- mathematics education (MA, MS Ed)
- mental health counseling (MA)
- middle level education (CAS)
- middle school extension (grades 5-6) (CAS)
- middle school extension (grades 7-9) (CAS)
- music education (MA, MS Ed)
- physical education (MS)
- program evaluation (MS Ed)
- rehabilitation administration (PD)
- rehabilitation counseling (MS Ed, PD)
- rehabilitation counseling in mental health (MS Ed)
- Russian (MA, MS Ed)
- school counselor (MS Ed)
- school counselor-bilingual extension (Advanced Certificate)
- school district business leader (CAS)
- science education (MA, MS Ed, CAS)
- science education (biology, chemistry, geology, physics, earth science) (MA)
- science education (biology, chemistry, physics, earth science, geology) (MS Ed)
- secondary education (intensive program) (CAS)
- social studies education (MA, MS Ed)
- Spanish (MA, MS Ed)
- special education (MA, MS Ed, Advanced Certificate, PD)
- special education assessment and diagnosis (Advanced Certificate)
- teaching of writing (birth–grade 6) (MA)
- teaching of writing (grades 5–12) (MA)
- teaching students with severe/multiple disabilities (Advanced Certificate)
- TESL/bilingual education (MA, MS Ed, CAS)
- TESOL (MS Ed, CAS)
- wind conducting (MA)

School of Law
Nora V. Demleitner, Interim Dean
Programs in:
- American legal studies (LL M)
- family law (LL M)
- international law (LL M)
- law (JD)

■ HUNTER COLLEGE OF THE CITY UNIVERSITY OF NEW YORK
New York, NY 10021-5085
http://www.hunter.cuny.edu/

State and locally supported, coed, comprehensive institution. *Enrollment:* 20,899 graduate, professional, and undergraduate students; 946 full-time matriculated graduate/professional students (769 women), 3,249 part-time matriculated graduate/professional students (2,522 women). *Graduate faculty:* 313 full-time (166 women), 198 part-time/adjunct (122 women). *Computer facilities:* 750 computers available on campus for general student use. A campuswide network can be accessed. Internet access is available. *Library facilities:* Hunter College Library. *Graduate expenses:* Tuition, state resident: part-time $270 per credit. Tuition, nonresident: part-time $500 per credit. Required fees: $45 per semester. *General application contact:* William Zlata, Director for Graduate Admissions, 212-772-4482.

Graduate School
William Zlata, Director of Admissions

School of Arts and Sciences
Dr. Judith Friedlander, Acting Dean
Programs in:
- accounting (MS)
- analytical geography (MA)
- anthropology (MA)
- applied and evaluative psychology (MA)
- applied mathematics (MA)
- applied social research (MS)
- art history (MA)
- arts and sciences (MA, MFA, MS, MUP, PhD, Certificate)
- biochemistry (MA)
- biological sciences (MA, PhD)
- biopsychology and comparative psychology (MA)
- British and American literature (MA)
- creative writing (MFA)
- earth system science (MA)
- economics (MA)
- English education (MA)
- environmental and social issues (MA)
- fine arts (MFA)
- French (MA)
- French education (MA)
- geographic information science (Certificate)
- geographic information systems (MA)
- history (MA)
- integrated media arts (MA, MFA)
- Italian (MA)
- Italian education (MA)
- mathematics for secondary education (MA)
- music (MA)
- music education (MA)
- physics (MA, PhD)

Hunter College of the City University of New York (continued)
- pure mathematics (MA)
- social research (MS)
- social, cognitive, and developmental psychology (MA)
- Spanish (MA)
- Spanish education (MA)
- studio art (MFA)
- teaching earth science (MA)
- teaching Latin (MA)
- theatre (MA)
- urban affairs (MS)
- urban planning (MUP)

School of Education
Dr. David Steiner, Dean
Programs in:
- bilingual education (MS)
- biology education (MA)
- blind or visually impaired (MS Ed)
- chemistry education (MA)
- corrective reading (K–12) (MS Ed)
- deaf or hard of hearing (MS Ed)
- early childhood education (MS)
- earth science (MA)
- education (MA, MS, MS Ed, AC)
- educational supervision and administration (AC)
- elementary education (MS)
- English education (MA)
- French education (MA)
- Italian education (MA)
- literacy education (MS)
- mathematics education (MA)
- music education (MA)
- physics education (MA)
- rehabilitation counseling (MS Ed)
- school counseling (MS Ed)
- school counseling with bilingual extension (MS Ed)
- school counselor (MS Ed)
- severe/multiple disabilities (MS Ed)
- social studies education (MA)
- Spanish education (MA)
- special education (MS Ed)
- teaching English as a second language (MA)

School of Social Work
Dr. Jacqueline B. Mondros, Dean
Program in:
- social work (MSW, DSW)

Schools of the Health Professions
Lauren N. Sherwen, Dean
Programs in:
- adult nurse practitioner (MS)
- audiology (MS)
- community health nursing (MS)
- community health nursing/community health education)
- environmental and occupational health sciences (MS)
- gerontological nurse practitioner (MS)
- health professions (MPH, MPT, MS, AC)
- maternal child-health nursing (MS)
- medical/surgical nursing (MS)
- nursing (MS, AC)
- pediatric nurse practitioner (MS, AC)
- physical therapy (MPT)
- psychiatric nursing (MS)
- public health (MPH)
- speech language pathology (MS)
- teacher of speech and hearing handicapped (MS)

■ IONA COLLEGE
New Rochelle, NY 10801-1890
http://www.iona.edu/

Independent-religious, coed, comprehensive institution. *Enrollment:* 4,242 graduate, professional, and undergraduate students; 172 full-time matriculated graduate/professional students (129 women), 603 part-time matriculated graduate/professional students (382 women). *Graduate faculty:* 114 full-time (33 women), 68 part-time/adjunct (33 women). *Computer facilities:* Computer purchase and lease plans are available. 500 computers available on campus for general student use. A campuswide network can be accessed from student residence rooms and from off campus. Internet access and online class registration are available. *Library facilities:* Ryan Library plus 2 others. *Graduate expenses:* Tuition: part-time $665 per credit. Required fees: $150 per term. *General application contact:* Thomas Weede, Director of Admissions, 914-633-2120.

Find University Details at www.petersons.com/gradchannel.

Hagan School of Business
Dr. Vincent Calluzo, Dean
Programs in:
- business (MBA, PMC)
- financial management (MBA, PMC)
- human resource management (MBA, PMC)
- information and decision technology management (MBA, PMC)
- international business (PMC)
- management (MBA, PMC)
- marketing (MBA)

School of Arts and Science
Dr. Alexander R. Eodice, Dean
Programs in:
- arts and science (MA, MS, MS Ed, MST, Certificate)
- biology education (MS Ed, MST)
- computer science (MS)
- criminal justice (MS)
- educational leadership (MS Ed)
- educational technology (MS, Certificate)
- English (MA)
- English education (MS Ed, MST)
- experimental psychology (MA)
- family counseling (MS, Certificate)
- health service administration (MS, Certificate)
- history (MA)
- industrial-organizational psychology (MA)
- journalism (MS)
- mathematics education (MS Ed, MST)
- mental health counseling (MA)
- multicultural education (MS Ed)
- pastoral counseling (MS)
- psychology (MA)
- public relations (MA)
- school psychology (MA)
- social studies education (MS Ed, MST)
- Spanish (MA)
- Spanish education (MS Ed, MST)
- teaching education (MST)
- telecommunications (MS, Certificate)

■ ITHACA COLLEGE
Ithaca, NY 14850-7020
http://www.ithaca.edu/

Independent, coed, comprehensive institution. CGS member. *Enrollment:* 6,409 graduate, professional, and undergraduate students; 339 full-time matriculated graduate/professional students (251 women), 33 part-time matriculated graduate/professional students (19 women). *Graduate faculty:* 153 full-time (62 women), 10 part-time/adjunct (9 women). *Computer facilities:* Computer purchase and lease plans are available. 640 computers available on campus for general student use. A campuswide network can be accessed from student residence rooms and from off campus. Internet access and online class registration are available. *Library facilities:* Ithaca College Library. *Graduate expenses:* Tuition: full-time $16,650; part-time $555 per credit hour. *General application contact:* Dr. Gregory Woodward, Dean of Graduate Studies, 607-274-3527.

Find University Details at www.petersons.com/gradchannel.

Graduate Studies
Dr. Gregory Woodward, Dean of Graduate Studies
Programs in:
- biology 7-12 (MAT)
- chemistry 7-12 (MAT)
- English 7-12 (MAT)
- French 7-12 (MAT)
- humanities and sciences (MAT)
- math 7-12 (MAT)
- physics 7-12 (MAT)
- social studies 7-12 (MAT)
- Spanish (MAT)

Roy H. Park School of Communications
Dianne Lynch, Dean
Program in:
- communications (MS)

School of Business
Dr. Susan West Engelkemeyer, Dean
Programs in:
- accountancy (MBA)
- business (MBA)
- business administration (MBA)

School of Health Sciences and Human Performance
Dr. Steven Siconolfi, Dean
Programs in:
exercise and sport sciences (MS)
health education (MS)
health sciences and human performance (MS, DPT)
occupational therapy (MS)
physical education (MS)
physical therapy (DPT)
speech pathology (MS)
sport management (MS)
teacher of the speech and hearing handicapped (MS)

School of Music
Dr. Arthur Ostrander, Dean
Programs in:
composition (MM)
conducting (MM)
music (MM, MS)
music education (MM, MS)
performance (MM)
Suzuki pedagogy (MM)

■ JOHN JAY COLLEGE OF CRIMINAL JUSTICE OF THE CITY UNIVERSITY OF NEW YORK

New York, NY 10019-1093
http://www.jjay.cuny.edu/

State and locally supported, coed, comprehensive institution. *Computer facilities:* 250 computers available on campus for general student use. A campuswide network can be accessed from off campus. Internet access is available. *Library facilities:* Lloyd George Sealy Library. *General application contact:* Director of Graduate Admissions, 212-237-8864.

Graduate Studies
Programs in:
criminal justice (MA, PhD)
criminology and deviance (PhD)
forensic computing (MS)
forensic psychology (PhD)
forensic science (PhD)
law and philosophy (PhD)
organizational behavior (PhD)
protection management (MS)
public administration (MPA)
public policy (PhD)

■ LEHMAN COLLEGE OF THE CITY UNIVERSITY OF NEW YORK

Bronx, NY 10468-1589
http://www.lehman.cuny.edu/

State and locally supported, coed, comprehensive institution. *Computer facilities:* 600 computers available on campus for general student use. Internet access is available. *Library facilities:* Leonard Lief Library plus 1 other. *General application contact:* Director of Graduate Admissions, 718-960-8856.

Division of Arts and Humanities
Programs in:
art (MA, MFA)
arts and humanities (MA, MAT, MFA)
English (MA)
history (MA)
music (MAT)
Spanish (MA)
speech-language pathology and audiology (MA)

Division of Education
Programs in:
bilingual special education (MS Ed)
business education (MS Ed)
early childhood education (MS Ed)
early special education (MS Ed)
education (MA, MS Ed)
elementary education (MS Ed)
emotional handicaps (MS Ed)
English education (MS Ed)
guidance and counseling (MS Ed)
learning disabilities (MS Ed)
mathematics 7–12 (MS Ed)
mental retardation (MS Ed)
music education (MS Ed)
reading teacher (MS Ed)
science education (MS Ed)
social studies 7–12 (MA)
teachers of special education (MS Ed)
teaching English to speakers of other languages (MS Ed)

Division of Natural and Social Sciences
Programs in:
accounting (MS)
adult health nursing (MS)
biology (MA)
clinical nutrition (MS)
community nutrition (MS)
computer science (MS)
dietetic internship (MS)
health education and promotion (MA)
health N–12 teacher (MS Ed)
mathematics (MA)
natural and social sciences (MA, MS, MS Ed, PhD)
nursing of older adults (MS)
nutrition (MS)
parent-child nursing (MS)
pediatric nurse practitioner (MS)
plant sciences (PhD)
recreation (MA, MS Ed)
recreation education (MA, MS Ed)

■ LE MOYNE COLLEGE

Syracuse, NY 13214
http://www.lemoyne.edu/

Independent-religious, coed, comprehensive institution. *Enrollment:* 3,536 graduate, professional, and undergraduate students; 153 full-time matriculated graduate/professional students (121 women), 423 part-time matriculated graduate/professional students (304 women). *Graduate faculty:* 38 full-time (15 women), 42 part-time/adjunct (23 women). *Computer facilities:* 325 computers available on campus for general student use. A campuswide network can be accessed from student residence rooms and from off campus. Internet access and online class registration, ECHO (campus-wide portal) are available. *Library facilities:* Noreen Reale Falcone Library. *Graduate expenses:* Tuition: full-time $9,846; part-time $547 per credit hour. Tuition and fees vary according to program. *General application contact:* Kristen P. Trapasso, Director of Graduate Admission, 315-445-4265.

Department of Education
Dr. Cathy Leogrande, Chair, Education Department and Director of Graduate Education
Program in:
education (MS Ed, MST)

Department of Physician Assistant Studies
Dr. Linda G. Allison, Professor and Chair of Department of Physician Assistant Studies
Program in:
physician assistant studies (MS)

Division of Management
Dr. George Kulick, Director of MBA Program
Program in:
management (MBA)

■ LONG ISLAND UNIVERSITY, BRENTWOOD CAMPUS

Brentwood, NY 11717
http://www.liu.edu/

Independent, coed, upper-level institution. *Computer facilities:* Computer purchase and lease plans are available. 42 computers available on campus for general student use. A campuswide network can be accessed. Internet access is available. *Library facilities:* Brentwood Campus Library. *General application contact:* Director of Admissions, 631-273-5112 Ext. 26.

School of Education
Programs in:
elementary education (MS)
reading (MS)
school counseling (MS)
school district administration and supervision (MS)
special education (MS)

School of Public Service
Program in:
criminal justice (MS)

■ LONG ISLAND UNIVERSITY, BROOKLYN CAMPUS

Brooklyn, NY 11201-8423

http://www.liu.edu/

Independent, coed, university. *Computer facilities:* 345 computers available on campus for general student use. A campuswide network can be accessed from student residence rooms and from off campus. Internet access is available. *Library facilities:* Salena Library. *General application contact:* Director of Graduate Admissions, 718-488-1011.

Arnold and Marie Schwartz College of Pharmacy and Health Sciences

Dr. Stephen M. Gross, Dean

Programs in:
- cosmetic science (MS)
- drug regulatory affairs (MS)
- industrial pharmacy (MS)
- pharmaceutical sciences (MS, PhD)
- pharmaceutics (PhD)
- pharmacology/toxicology (MS)
- pharmacy administration (MS)
- pharmacy and health sciences (MS, PhD)
- social and administrative sciences (MS)

Richard L. Conolly College of Liberal Arts and Sciences

Programs in:
- biology (MS)
- chemistry (MS)
- clinical psychology (PhD)
- economics (MA)
- English literature (MA)
- history (MS)
- liberal arts and sciences (MA, MS, PhD, Certificate)
- media arts (MA)
- political science (MA)
- professional and creative writing (MA)
- psychology (MA)
- speech-language pathology (MS)
- teaching of writing (MA)
- United Nations studies (Certificate)
- urban studies (MA)

School of Business, Public Administration and Information Sciences

Programs in:
- accounting (MS)
- business administration (MBA)
- business, public administration and information sciences (MBA, MPA, MS)
- computer science (MS)
- human resources management (MS)
- public administration (MPA)
- taxation (MS)

School of Education

Programs in:
- bilingual education (MS Ed)
- computers in education (MS)
- counseling and development (MS, MS Ed, Certificate)
- education (MS, MS Ed, Certificate)
- elementary education (MS Ed)
- leadership and policy (MS)
- mathematics education (MS Ed)
- reading (MS Ed)
- school psychology (MS Ed)
- secondary education (MS Ed)
- special education (MS Ed)
- teaching English to speakers of other languages (MS Ed)

School of Health Professions

Programs in:
- adapted physical education (MS)
- athletic training and sports sciences (MS)
- community mental health (MS)
- exercise physiology (MS)
- family health (MS)
- health management (MS)
- health professions (MS, DPT, TDPT)
- health sciences (MS)
- physical therapy (DPT, TDPT)

School of Nursing

Programs in:
- adult nurse practitioner (MS, Certificate)
- nurse executive (MS)
- nursing (MS, Certificate)

■ LONG ISLAND UNIVERSITY, C.W. POST CAMPUS

Brookville, NY 11548-1300

http://www.liu.edu/

Independent, coed, comprehensive institution. *Computer facilities:* 357 computers available on campus for general student use. A campuswide network can be accessed from student residence rooms and from off campus. Internet access is available. *Library facilities:* B. Davis Schwartz Memorial Library. *General application contact:* Director of Graduate and International Admissions, 516-299-2900.

Find University Details at www.petersons.com/gradchannel.

College of Information and Computer Science

Programs in:
- information and computer science (MS, PhD, Certificate)
- information systems (MS)
- information technology education (MS)
- management engineering (MS)

Palmer School of Library and Information Science

Programs in:
- archives and records management (Certificate)
- information studies (PhD)
- library and information science (MS)
- library media specialist (MS)
- public library management (Certificate)

College of Liberal Arts and Sciences

Programs in:
- applied behavior analysis (Advanced Certificate)
- applied mathematics (MS)
- biology (MS)
- biology education (MS)
- clinical psychology (Psy D)
- English (MA)
- English for adolescence education (MS)
- environmental management (MS)
- environmental science (MS)
- experimental psychology (MA, Advanced Certificate)
- history (MA)
- interdisciplinary studies (MA, MS)
- liberal arts and sciences (MA, MS, Psy D, Advanced Certificate)
- mathematics education (MS)
- mathematics for secondary school teachers (MS)
- political science/international studies (MA)
- Spanish (MA)
- Spanish education (MS)

College of Management

Program in:
- management (MBA, MPA, MS, Certificate)

School of Business

Programs in:
- accounting and taxation (Certificate)
- business administration (Certificate)
- finance (MBA, Certificate)
- general business administration (MBA)
- international business (MBA, Certificate)
- management (MBA, Certificate)
- management information systems (MBA, Certificate)
- marketing (MBA, Certificate)

School of Professional Accountancy

Programs in:
- accounting (MS)
- taxation (MS)

School of Public Service

Programs in:
- criminal justice (MS)
- fraud examination (MS)
- gerontology (Certificate)
- health care administration (MPA)
- health care administration/gerontology (MPA)
- nonprofit management (MPA, Certificate)
- public administration (MPA)
- public service (MPA, MS, Certificate)
- security administration (MS)

School of Education

Programs in:
- adolescence education (MS)
- adolescence education: biology (MS)
- adolescence education: earth science (MS)
- adolescence education: English (MS)
- adolescence education: mathematics (MS)
- adolescence education: social studies (MS)
- adolescence education: Spanish (MS)
- art education (MS)
- bilingual education (MS)
- childhood education (MS)
- childhood education/literacy (MS)
- childhood education/special education (MS)
- computers in education (MS)
- early childhood education (MS)
- education (MA, MS, MS Ed, PD)
- literacy (MS Ed)
- mental health counseling (MS)
- middle childhood education (MS)
- music education (MS)
- school administration and supervision (MS Ed)
- school business administration (PD)
- school counseling (MS)
- school district administration (PD)
- special education (MS Ed)
- speech language pathology (MA)
- teaching English to speakers of other languages (MS)

School of Health Professions and Nursing

Programs in:
- cardiovascular perfusion (MS, Certificate)
- clinical laboratory management (MS)
- clinical nurse specialist (MS)
- dietetic internship (Certificate)
- family nurse practitioner (MS, Certificate)
- health professions and nursing (MS, Certificate)
- hematology (MS)
- immunology (MS)
- medical biology (MS)
- medical chemistry (MS)
- medical microbiology (MS)
- nutrition (MS)

School of Visual and Performing Arts

Programs in:
- art (MA)
- art education (MS)
- clinical art therapy (MA)
- fine art and design (MFA)
- interactive multimedia arts (MA)
- music (MA)
- music education (MS)
- theatre (MA)
- visual and performing arts (MA, MFA, MS)

■ LONG ISLAND UNIVERSITY, SOUTHAMPTON GRADUATE CAMPUS

Southampton, NY 11968-4198

http://www.southampton.liu.edu/

Independent, coed, primarily women, graduate-only institution. *Enrollment:* 40 full-time matriculated graduate/professional students, 111 part-time matriculated graduate/professional students. *Graduate faculty:* 6 full-time (2 women), 11 part-time/adjunct (5 women). *Computer facilities:* 48 computers available on campus for general student use. A campuswide network can be accessed from off campus. Internet access is available. *Library facilities:* Southampton Graduate Campus Library. *Graduate expenses:* Tuition: part-time $790 per credit. Required fees: $220 per semester. *General application contact:* Joyce Tuttle, Director of Graduate Admissions and Program Administration, 631-287-8010.

Education Division

Dr. R. Lawrence McCann, Director

Programs in:
- childhood education (MS Ed)
- education (MS Ed)
- elementary education (MS Ed)
- literacy education (MS Ed)
- teaching students with disabilities (MS Ed)

Homeland Security Management Institute

Dr. Vincent E. Henry, Unit Head

Program in:
- homeland security management (MS, Advanced Certificate)

■ MANHATTAN COLLEGE

Riverdale, NY 10471

http://www.manhattan.edu/

Independent-religious, coed, comprehensive institution. *Enrollment:* 3,357 graduate, professional, and undergraduate students; 97 full-time matriculated graduate/professional students (52 women), 341 part-time matriculated graduate/professional students (207 women). *Graduate faculty:* 53 full-time (12 women), 49 part-time/adjunct (18 women). *Computer facilities:* 375 computers available on campus for general student use. A campuswide network can be accessed from student residence rooms and from off campus. Internet access and online class registration are available. *Library facilities:* O'Malley Library plus 1 other. *General application contact:* Dr. Weldon Jackson, Provost, 718-862-7303.

Graduate Division

Dr. Weldon Jackson, Provost

School of Education

Dr. William Merriman, Dean

Programs in:
- 5 year dual childhood/special education (MS Ed)
- counseling (MA, Diploma)
- dual childhood/special education (MS Ed)
- school building leadership (MS Ed, Diploma)
- special education (MS Ed)

School of Engineering

Dr. Richard H. Heist, Dean

Programs in:
- chemical engineering (MS)
- civil engineering (MS)
- computer engineering (MS)
- electrical engineering (MS)
- environmental engineering (ME, MS)
- mechanical engineering (MS)

■ MANHATTANVILLE COLLEGE

Purchase, NY 10577-2132

http://www.manhattanville.edu/

Independent, coed, comprehensive institution. *Enrollment:* 2,974 graduate, professional, and undergraduate students; 309 full-time matriculated graduate/professional students (225 women), 689 part-time matriculated graduate/professional students (483 women). *Computer facilities:* Computer purchase and lease plans are available. 200 computers available on campus for general student use. A campuswide network can be accessed from student residence rooms and from off campus. Internet access and online class registration are available. *Library facilities:* Manhattanville College Library. *General application contact:* Graduate Admissions, 914-694-3425.

Find University Details at www.petersons.com/gradchannel.

Graduate Programs

Dr. Scott F. Stoddert, Interim Provost

Programs in:
- integrated marketing communications (MS)
- international management (MS)
- leadership and strategic management (MS)
- liberal studies (MA)
- management communications (MS)
- organization development and human resources management (MS)
- sports business management (MS)
- writing (MA)

School of Education

Dr. Shelley Wepner, Dean

Programs in:
- biology (MAT)
- biology and special education (MPS)
- chemistry (MAT)
- chemistry and special education (MPS)

Manhattanville College (continued)
- child and early childhood education (MAT)
- childhood and early childhood education (MAT)
- childhood and special education (MPS)
- childhood education (MAT)
- early childhood education (birth-grade 2) (MAT)
- education (MAT, MPS)
- educational leadership (MPS)
- English (MAT)
- English and special education (MPS)
- literacy (MPS)
- literacy (birth-grade 6) (MPS)
- literacy (birth-grade 6)
- and special education (grades 1-6) (MPS)
- literacy and special education (MPS)
- math (MAT)
- math and special education (MPS)
- music education (MAT)
- physical education and sport pedagogy (MAT)
- second language (MAT)
- social studies (MAT)
- social studies and special education (MPS)
- special education (MPS)
- special education (birth-grade 2) (MPS)
- special education (birth-grade 6) (MPS)
- special education childhood (MPS)
- teaching English as a second language (MPS)

■ MARIST COLLEGE
Poughkeepsie, NY 12601-1387
http://www.marist.edu/

Independent, coed, comprehensive institution. *Enrollment:* 5,877 graduate, professional, and undergraduate students; 168 full-time matriculated graduate/professional students (102 women), 686 part-time matriculated graduate/professional students (352 women). *Graduate faculty:* 57 full-time (24 women), 36 part-time/adjunct (20 women). *Computer facilities:* Computer purchase and lease plans are available. 585 computers available on campus for general student use. A campuswide network can be accessed from student residence rooms and from off campus. Internet access and online class registration are available. *Library facilities:* James A. Cannavino Library. *Graduate expenses:* Tuition: full-time $11,340; part-time $630 per credit. Required fees: $60; $30 per semester. *General application contact:* Anu R. Ailawadhi, Director of Graduate Admissions, 845-575-3800.

Graduate Programs
Dr. Artin Arslanian, Academic Vice President

School of Communication and the Arts
Dr. Subir Sengupta, Assistant Dean
Program in:
- organizational communication and leadership (MA)

School of Computer Science and Mathematics
Dr. Roger Norton, Dean
Programs in:
- information systems (MS, Adv C)
- software development (MS)
- technology management (MS)

School of Management
Dr. Elmore R. Alexander, Interim Dean
Programs in:
- business administration (MBA, Adv C)
- executive leadership (Adv C)
- public administration (MPA)
- technology management (MS)

School of Social and Behavioral Sciences
Margaret Calista, Dean
Programs in:
- counseling psychology (MA)
- education (M Ed)
- education psychology (MA)
- school psychology (MA, Adv C)

■ MEDAILLE COLLEGE
Buffalo, NY 14214-2695
http://www.medaille.edu/

Independent, coed, comprehensive institution. *Enrollment:* 2,971 graduate, professional, and undergraduate students; 1,133 full-time matriculated graduate/professional students (864 women), 131 part-time matriculated graduate/professional students (99 women). *Graduate faculty:* 43 full-time (26 women), 117 part-time/adjunct (65 women). *Computer facilities:* 105 computers available on campus for general student use. A campuswide network can be accessed from student residence rooms and from off campus. Internet access is available. *Library facilities:* Medaille College Library. *Graduate expenses:* Tuition: part-time $580 per credit hour. Full-time tuition and fees vary according to program. *General application contact:* Susan Greenwald, Executive Director of Admissions, 716-635-5033 Ext. 2011.

Program in Business Administration—Amherst
Jennifer Bavifard, Associate Dean for Special Programs
Programs in:
- business administration (MBA)
- organizational leadership (MA)

Program in Business Administration—Rochester
Lorraine Beach-Horner, Branch Campus Director
Programs in:
- business administration (MBA)
- organizational leadership (MA)

Program in Education
Dr. Robert DiSibio, Director of Graduate Programs
Programs in:
- curriculum and instruction (MS Ed)
- education preparation (MS Ed)
- literacy (MS Ed)
- special education (MS)

Programs in Psychology
Dr. Judith Horowitz, Interim Dean of Adult and Graduate Studies
Programs in:
- mental health counseling (MA)
- psychology (MA)

■ MERCY COLLEGE
Dobbs Ferry, NY 10522-1189
http://www.mercy.edu/

Independent, coed, comprehensive institution. CGS member. *Enrollment:* 9,120 graduate, professional, and undergraduate students; 1,117 full-time matriculated graduate/professional students (885 women), 2,692 part-time matriculated graduate/professional students (2,039 women). *Computer facilities:* 138 computers available on campus for general student use. A campuswide network can be accessed from off campus. Internet access is available. *Library facilities:* Mercy College Library. *Graduate expenses:* Tuition: part-time $595 per credit. Required fees: $9 per credit. Tuition and fees vary according to program. *General application contact:* Kathleen Jackson, Director of Admissions, 800-Mercy-NY.

Division of Business and Accounting
Wayne L. Cioffari, Director
Programs in:
- banking (MS)
- business administration (MBA)
- direct marketing (MS)
- human resource management (MS)
- organizational leadership (MS)
- securities (MS)

Division of Education
Dr. William Prattella, Chairperson
Programs in:
- adolescence education: grades 7-12 (MS)
- applied behavior analysis (MS)
- bilingual education (MS)
- childhood education: grades 1-6 (MS)
- early childhood education: birth—grade 2 (MS)
- education (MS)
- elementary education (MS)
- learning technology (MS)
- middle childhood education: grades 5-9 (MS)
- reading (MS)
- school administration and supervision (MS)
- school building leadership (MS)

school business administration (MS)
secondary education (MS)
special education (MS)
students with disabilities: grades 5-9 (MS)
students with disabilities: grades 7-12 (MS)
teaching English to speakers of other languages (MS)
teaching literacy: birth—grade 6 (MS)
teaching literacy: grades 5-12 (MS)
urban education (MS)

Division of Health Professions
Dr. Pat Chute
Programs in:
adult nurse practitioner (MS, AC)
communication disorders (MS)
nursing (MS)
nursing administration (MS)
nursing education (MS)
occupational therapy (MS)
physical therapy (MS)
physician assistant (MPS, MS)

Division of Literature, Language, and Communication
Dr. Sean Dugan, Program Director
Program in:
English literature (MA)

Division of Mathematics and Computer Information Science
Nagaraj Rao, Division Chair
Program in:
Internet business systems (MS, Certificate)

Division of Social and Behavioral Sciences
Diana Juettner, Chair
Programs in:
alcohol and substance abuse counseling (AC)
counseling (MS, AC)
family counseling (AC)
health services management (MPA, MS, AC, Certificate)
marriage and family therapy (MS)
mental health counseling (MS)
psychology (MS)
retirement counseling (AC)
school psychology (MS)

■ METROPOLITAN COLLEGE OF NEW YORK

New York, NY 10013-1919

http://www.metropolitan.edu/

Independent, coed, primarily women, comprehensive institution. *Enrollment:* 1,238 graduate, professional, and undergraduate students; 389 full-time matriculated graduate/professional students (354 women). *Graduate faculty:* 13 full-time (6 women), 46 part-time/adjunct (17 women). *Computer facilities:* 130 computers available on campus for general student use. A campuswide network can be accessed from off campus. Internet access is available. *Library facilities:* Main Library. *Graduate expenses:* Tuition: full-time $9,800; part-time $840 per unit. Required fees: $100 per term. *General application contact:* Robert Hernandez, Graduate Admissions Coordinator, 212-343-1234 Ext. 2709.

Program in Childhood Education
Dr. Patrick Ianniello, Director
Program in:
childhood education (MS)

Program in General Management
Dr. Robert Gilmore, Dean, Graduate School for Business
Program in:
general management (MBA)

Program in Media Management
Dr. Fay Ran, Dean, Graduate School for Business
Program in:
media management (MBA)

Program in Public Administration
Prof. Humphrey Crookendale, Dean, Graduate School for Public Affairs Administration
Program in:
public administration (MPA)

■ MOLLOY COLLEGE

Rockville Centre, NY 11571-5002

http://www.molloy.edu/

Independent, coed, comprehensive institution. *Computer facilities:* 246 computers available on campus for general student use. A campuswide network can be accessed. Internet access is available. *Library facilities:* James Edward Tobin Library. *General application contact:* Director, Graduate Program, 516-678-5000 Ext. 6820.

Department of Nursing
Programs in:
adult nurse practitioner (Advanced Certificate)
clinical nurse specialist: adult health (Advanced Certificate)
family nurse practitioner (Advanced Certificate)
nurse practitioner psychiatry (Advanced Certificate)
nursing (MS)
nursing administration (Advanced Certificate)
nursing administration with informatics (Advanced Certificate)
nursing education (Advanced Certificate)
nursing informatics (Advanced Certificate)
pediatric nurse practitioner (Advanced Certificate)

■ MOUNT SAINT MARY COLLEGE

Newburgh, NY 12550-3494

http://www.msmc.edu/

Independent, coed, comprehensive institution. *Enrollment:* 2,601 graduate, professional, and undergraduate students; 108 full-time matriculated graduate/professional students (88 women), 439 part-time matriculated graduate/professional students (353 women). *Graduate faculty:* 20 full-time (12 women), 26 part-time/adjunct (20 women). *Computer facilities:* 336 computers available on campus for general student use. A campuswide network can be accessed from student residence rooms and from off campus. Internet access and online class registration, intranet are available. *Library facilities:* Curtin Memorial Library plus 1 other. *Graduate expenses:* Tuition: full-time $11,880; part-time $660 per credit. *General application contact:* Graduate Coordinator, 845-561-0800.

Division of Business
David R. Rant, Coordinator
Programs in:
business (MBA)
financial planning (MBA)

Division of Education
Theresa Lewis, Coordinator
Programs in:
adolescence and special education (MS Ed)
adolescence education (MS Ed)
childhood and special education (MS Ed)
childhood education (MS Ed)
literacy and special education (MS Ed)
literacy/childhood (MS Ed)
middle school (5-6) (MS Ed)
middle school (7-9) (MS Ed)
special education (1-6) (MS Ed)
special education (7-12) (MS Ed)

Division of Nursing
Dr. Karen Baldwin, Coordinator
Programs in:
adult nurse practitioner (MS)
clinical nurse specialist-adult health (MS)

■ NAZARETH COLLEGE OF ROCHESTER

Rochester, NY 14618-3790

http://www.naz.edu/

Independent, coed, comprehensive institution. *Enrollment:* 3,179 graduate, professional, and undergraduate students; 423 full-time matriculated graduate/professional students (360 women), 675 part-time matriculated graduate/professional students (549 women). *Graduate faculty:* 93. *Computer facilities:* 150 computers available on campus for general student use. A campuswide network can be accessed from

Nazareth College of Rochester (continued)
student residence rooms and from off campus. Internet access is available. *Library facilities:* Lorette Wilmot Library. *General application contact:* Judith G. Baker, Director, Graduate Admissions, 585-389-2050.

Graduate Studies
Dr. Kay F. Marshman, Associate Vice President for Graduate Studies
Programs in:
art education (MS Ed)
art therapy (MS)
business education (MS Ed)
communication sciences and disorders (MS)
creative arts therapy (MS)
educational technology/computer education (MS Ed)
gerontological nurse practitioner (MS)
human resource management (MS)
inclusive education-adolescence level (MS Ed)
inclusive education-childhood level (MS Ed)
inclusive education-early childhood level (MS Ed)
liberal studies (MA)
literacy education (MS Ed)
management (MS)
music education (MS Ed)
music therapy (MS)
physical therapy (MS, DPT)
social work (MSW)
teaching English to speakers of other languages (MS Ed)

■ THE NEW SCHOOL: A UNIVERSITY
New York, NY 10011
http://www.newschool.edu/

Independent, coed, university. *General application contact:* Christy Kalan, Director of Enrollment Management, 212-229-5154.

Find University Details at www.petersons.com/gradchannel.

Mannes College The New School for Music
Joel Lester, Dean
Program in:
music performance (MM, PD)

Milano The New School for Management and Urban Policy
Dr. Fred Hochberg, Dean
Programs in:
health services management and policy (MS)
human resources management (MS, Adv C)
management and urban policy (MS, PhD, Adv C)
medical group practice management (Adv C)
nonprofit management (MS)
organizational change management (MS)
public and urban policy (PhD)
urban policy analysis and management (MS)

The New School for Drama
Robert LuPone, Director
Programs in:
acting (MFA)
directing (MFA)
playwriting (MFA)

The New School for General Studies
Dr. Linda Dunne, Dean
Programs in:
communication theory (MA)
creative writing (MFA)
global management, trade, and finance (MA, MS)
international development (MA, MS)
international media and communication (MA, MS)
international politics and diplomacy (MA, MS)
media studies (MA)
service, civic, and non-profit management (MS)
teaching English to speakers of other languages (MA)

The New School for Social Research
Dr. Michael Schober, Dean
Programs in:
anthropology (MA, DS Sc, PhD)
clinical psychology (PhD)
economics (MA, DS Sc, PhD)
general psychology (MA, PhD)
global finance (MS)
historical studies (MA, PhD)
liberal studies (MA)
philosophy (MA, DS Sc, PhD)
political science (MA, DS Sc, PhD)
social research (MA, MS, DS Sc, PhD)
sociology (MA, DS Sc, PhD)

Parsons The New School for Design
Tim Marshall, Dean
Programs in:
architecture (M Arch)
design (M Arch, MA, MFA)
design and technology (MFA)
fine arts (MFA)
history of decorative arts (MA)
lighting design (MFA)
photography and related technologies (MFA)

■ NEW YORK INSTITUTE OF TECHNOLOGY
Old Westbury, NY 11568-8000
http://www.nyit.edu/

Independent, coed, university. CGS member. *Enrollment:* 11,404 graduate, professional, and undergraduate students; 2,460 full-time matriculated graduate/professional students (1,163 women), 2,158 part-time matriculated graduate/professional students (986 women). *Graduate faculty:* 256 full-time (81 women), 419 part-time/adjunct (146 women). *Computer facilities:* 815 computers available on campus for general student use. A campuswide network can be accessed from student residence rooms and from off campus. Internet access, e-mail are available. *Library facilities:* George and Gertrude Wisser Memorial Library plus 4 others. *Graduate expenses:* Tuition: full-time $16,800; part-time $700 per credit. *General application contact:* Jacquelyn Nealon, Dean of Admissions and Financial Aid, 516-686-7925.

Ellis College
Programs in:
accounting and information systems (MBA)
communication arts—advertising and public relations (MA)
e-commerce (MBA)
finance (MBA)
general business studies (MBA)
global management (MBA)
health care administration (MBA)
human resources management (MBA)
human resources management and labor relations (MS)
instructional technology for educators (MS)
instructional technology for professional trainers (MS)
leadership (MBA)
management of information systems (MBA)
management of technology (MBA)
marketing (MBA)
multimedia (Advanced Certificate)
professional accounting (MBA)
project management (MBA)
risk management (MBA)
strategy and economics (MBA)

Graduate Division
Dr. Spencer Turkel, Director of Academic Affairs

School of Allied Health and Life Sciences
Dr. Barbara Ross-Lee, Dean
Programs in:
allied health and life sciences (MPS, MS, DPT)
clinical nutrition (MS)
human relations (MPS)
occupational therapy (MS)
physical therapy (MS, DPT)
physician assistant (MS)

School of Architecture
Judith DiMaio, Dean
Program in:
urban and regional design (M Arch)

School of Arts, Sciences, and Communication
Dr. Roger Yu, Dean
Programs in:
arts, sciences, and communication (MA)
communication arts (MA)

School of Education and Professional Services
Dr. Jacqueline Kress, Dean
Programs in:
- distance learning (Advanced Certificate)
- district leadership and technology (Professional Diploma)
- education and professional services (MS, Advanced Certificate, Professional Diploma)
- elementary education (MS)
- instructional technology (MS)
- mental health counseling and school counseling (MS)
- multimedia (Advanced Certificate)
- school counseling (MS)
- school leadership and technology (Professional Diploma)

School of Engineering and Technology
Dr. Heskia Heskiaoff, Dean
Programs in:
- computer science (MS)
- electrical engineering and computer engineering (MS)
- energy management (MS)
- energy technology (Advanced Certificate)
- engineering and technology (MS, Advanced Certificate)
- environmental management (Advanced Certificate)
- environmental technology (MS)
- facilities management (Advanced Certificate)

School of Management
Dr. David R. Decker, Dean
Programs in:
- accounting (Advanced Certificate)
- business administration (MBA)
- finance (Advanced Certificate)
- human resources administration (Advanced Certificate)
- human resources management and labor relations (MS)
- international business (Advanced Certificate)
- labor relations (Advanced Certificate)
- management (MBA, MS, Advanced Certificate)
- management of information systems (Advanced Certificate)
- marketing (Advanced Certificate)

New York College of Osteopathic Medicine
Dr. Barbara Ross-Lee, Dean
Program in:
- osteopathic medicine (DO)

■ NEW YORK UNIVERSITY
New York, NY 10012-1019
http://www.nyu.edu/

Independent, coed, university. CGS member. *Enrollment:* 40,870 graduate, professional, and undergraduate students; 11,599 full-time matriculated graduate/professional students (6,593 women), 8,306 part-time matriculated graduate/professional students (4,713 women). *Graduate faculty:* 3,363 full-time (1,267 women), 3,392 part-time/adjunct. *Computer facilities:* Computer purchase and lease plans are available. 4,500 computers available on campus for general student use. A campuswide network can be accessed from student residence rooms and from off campus. Internet access and online class registration are available. *Library facilities:* Elmer H. Bobst Library plus 11 others. *Graduate expenses:* Tuition: part-time $1,080 per unit. Required fees: $56 per unit. $329 per term. Tuition and fees vary according to program. *General application contact:* New York University Information, 212-998-1212.

Find University Details at www.petersons.com/gradchannel.

College of Dentistry
Dr. Richard Vogel, Interim Dean
Programs in:
- clinical research (MS)
- dentistry (DDS, MS, PhD, Advanced Certificate)
- endodontics (Advanced Certificate)
- oral and maxillofacial surgery (Advanced Certificate)
- orthodontics (Advanced Certificate)
- pediatric dentistry (Advanced Certificate)
- periodontics (Advanced Certificate)
- prosthodontics (Advanced Certificate)
- prosthodontics (implantology) (Advanced Certificate)

College of Nursing
Dr. Terry Fulmer, Dean, College of Nursing
Programs in:
- advanced practice nursing: adult acute care (MS, Advanced Certificate)
- advanced practice nursing: adult primary care (MS, Advanced Certificate)
- advanced practice nursing: adult primary care/geriatrics (MS)
- advanced practice nursing: children with special needs (Advanced Certificate)
- advanced practice nursing: geriatrics (MS, Advanced Certificate)
- advanced practice nursing: holistic nursing (MS, Advanced Certificate)
- advanced practice nursing: home health nursing (Advanced Certificate)
- advanced practice nursing: mental health (MS)
- advanced practice nursing: mental health nursing (Advanced Certificate)
- advanced practice nursing: pediatrics (MS, Advanced Certificate)
- advanced practice nursing: pediatrics/children with special needs (MS)
- midwifery (MS, Advanced Certificate)
- nursing (MS, PhD, Advanced Certificate)
- nursing administration (MS, Advanced Certificate)
- nursing education (MS, Advanced Certificate)
- nursing informatics (MS, Advanced Certificate)
- palliative care (MS, Advanced Certificate)
- research and theory development in nursing science (PhD)

Gallatin School of Individualized Study
Dr. Ali Mirsepassi, Interim Dean
Program in:
- individualized study (MA)

Graduate School of Arts and Science
Catharine R. Stimpson, Dean
Programs in:
- African diaspora (PhD)
- African history (PhD)
- Africana studies (MA)
- American studies (MA, PhD)
- anthropology (MA, PhD)
- anthropology and French studies (PhD)
- applied economic analysis (Advanced Certificate)
- archival management and historical editing (Advanced Certificate)
- arts and science (MA, MFA, MS, PhD, Advanced Certificate)
- Atlantic history (PhD)
- biology (PhD)
- biomaterials science (MS)
- biomedical journalism (MS)
- cancer and molecular biology (PhD)
- chemistry (MS, PhD)
- classics (MA, PhD)
- cognition and perception (PhD)
- community psychology (PhD)
- comparative literature (MA, PhD)
- composition and theory (MA, PhD)
- computational biology (PhD)
- computers in biological research (MS)
- creative writing (MA, MFA)
- cultural reporting and criticism (MA)
- developmental genetics (PhD)
- early music performance (Advanced Certificate)
- economics (MA, PhD)
- English and American literature (MA, PhD)
- environmental health sciences (MS, PhD)
- ethnomusicology (MA, PhD)
- French studies and sociology (PhD)
- French studies/history (PhD)
- French studies/journalism (MA)
- general biology (MS)
- general psychology (MA)
- German studies and critical thought (MA, PhD)
- Hebrew and Judaic studies (MA, PhD)
- Hebrew and Judaic studies/history (PhD)
- Hebrew and Judaic studies/museum studies (MA)
- history (MA, PhD)

New York University (continued)
humanities and social thought (MA)
immunology and microbiology (PhD)
industrial/organizational psychology (MA)
Italian (MA, PhD)
Italian studies (MA)
journalism (MA)
Latin American and Caribbean studies/journalism (MA)
linguistics (MA, PhD)
Middle Eastern history (MA)
Middle Eastern studies/history (PhD)
molecular genetics (PhD)
museum studies (MA, Advanced Certificate)
Near Eastern studies/journalism (MA)
neurobiology (PhD)
oral biology (MS)
philosophy (MA, PhD)
physics (MS, PhD)
plant biology (PhD)
poetics and theory (Advanced Certificate)
political campaign management (MA)
politics (MA, PhD)
Portuguese (MA, PhD)
psychotherapy and psychoanalysis (Advanced Certificate)
public history (Advanced Certificate)
recombinant DNA technology (MS)
religion (Advanced Certificate)
religious studies (MA)
Russian literature (MA)
science and environmental reporting (Advanced Certificate)
Slavic literature (MA)
social theory (Advanced Certificate)
social/personality psychology (PhD)
sociology (MA, PhD)
Spanish (PhD)
Spanish and Latin American literatures and cultures (MA)
Spanish language and translation (MA)
world history (MA)

Center for European Studies
Katherine Fleming, Director
Program in:
European studies (MA)

Center for French Civilization and Culture
Judith Miller, Chair
Programs in:
French (PhD)
French civilization (PhD)
French civilization and culture (MA, PhD, Advanced Certificate)
French language and civilization (MA)
French literature (MA)
French studies (MA, PhD, Advanced Certificate)
French studies and anthropology (PhD)
French studies and history (PhD)
French studies and journalism (MA)
French studies and sociology (PhD)
Romance languages and literatures (MA)

Center for Latin American and Caribbean Studies
Tom Abercrombie, Director
Program in:
Latin American and Caribbean studies (MA)

Center for Neural Science
J. Anthony Movshon, Chair
Program in:
neural science (PhD)

Courant Institute of Mathematical Sciences
Fedor Bogomolov, Director of Graduate Studies
Programs in:
atmosphere ocean science and mathematics (PhD)
computer science (MS, PhD)
information systems (MS)
mathematics (MS, PhD)
mathematics and statistics/operations research (MS)
mathematics in finance (MS)
scientific computing (MS)

Hagop Kevorkian Center for Near Eastern Studies
Timothy Mitchell, Chair
Programs in:
Middle Eastern and Islamic studies (MA, PhD)
Middle Eastern and Islamic studies/history (PhD)
Near Eastern studies (MA)
Near Eastern studies (museum studies) (MA)
Near Eastern studies/journalism (MA)

Institute for Law and Society
Lewis Kornhauser, Director
Program in:
law and society (MA, PhD)

Institute of Fine Arts
Mariet Westermann, Chair
Programs in:
architectural studies (PhD)
art history and archaeology (MA, PhD)
classical art and archaeology (PhD)
curatorial studies (PhD)
East and South Asian art (PhD)
Near Eastern art and archaeology (PhD)

Leonard N. Stern School of Business
Programs in:
accounting (MBA, PhD)
economics (MBA, PhD)
entertainment, media and technology (MBA)
finance (MBA, PhD)
general marketing (MBA)
information systems (MBA, PhD)
information, operations and management sciences (MBA, PhD)
management and organizations (MBA, PhD, APC)
management organizations (MBA)
marketing (MBA, PhD)
operations management (MBA, PhD)
organization theory (PhD)
organizational behavior (PhD)
product management (MBA)
statistics (MBA, PhD)
strategy (PhD)

National Institutes of Health Sponsored Programs
Program in:
structural biology (PhD)

Robert F. Wagner Graduate School of Public Service
Prof. Ellen Schall, Dean
Programs in:
health finance (MPA)
health policy analysis (MPA)
health policy and management (Advanced Certificate)
health services management (MPA)
housing (Advanced Certificate)
international health (MPA)
international public service organizations management (MS)
management (MS)
public administration (PhD)
public and nonprofit management and policy (MPA, Advanced Certificate)
public economics (Advanced Certificate)
public service (MPA, MS, MUP, PhD, Advanced Certificate)
quantitative analysis and computer applications for policy and planning (Advanced Certificate)
urban planning (MUP)

School of Continuing and Professional Studies
Robert Lapiner, Dean
Programs in:
fundraising (MS)
graphic communications management and technology (MA)

Center for Advanced Digital Applications
Dr. Michael Hosenfeld, Director
Program in:
digital imaging and design (MS)

Center for Global Affairs
Dr. Vera Jelinek, Assistant Dean and Director
Program in:
global studies (MS)

Center for Management
Dr. Anthony Davidson, Assistant Dean
Programs in:
applied database technologies (MS)
benefits and compensation (Advanced Certificate)
enterprise and risk management (Advanced Certificate)
executive coaching and organizational development (Advanced Certificate)
human resource development (MS)

- human resource management (MS, Advanced Certificate)
- human resources management and development (MS)
- information technologies (Advanced Certificate)
- leadership and knowledge management (MS)
- management and systems (MS, Advanced Certificate)
- management in the Internet E-conomy (MS)
- organizational effectiveness (MS)
- strategy and leadership (Advanced Certificate)
- systems management (MS)

Center for Marketing
Dr. Marjorie Kalter, Director
Programs in:
- direct and interactive marketing (MS)
- public relations and corporate communications (MS, Advanced Certificate)

Center for Publishing
Andrea L. Chambers, Director
Program in:
- publishing (MS)

Real Estate Institute
D. Kenneth Patton, Associate Dean
Programs in:
- construction management (MS, Advanced Certificate)
- real estate (MS, Advanced Certificate)

Tisch Center for Hospitality, Tourism and Sports Management
Dr. Lalia Rach, Associate Dean
Programs in:
- hospitality industry studies (MS, Advanced Certificate)
- sports business (MS, Advanced Certificate)
- tourism and travel management (MS, Advanced Certificate)

School of Law
Richard L. Revesz, Dean
Programs in:
- law (JD, LL M, JSD)
- law and business (Advanced Certificate)
- tax (Advanced Certificate)

School of Medicine
Dr. Robert M. Glickman, Dean
Programs in:
- clinical investigation (MS)
- medicine (MD)

Sackler Institute of Graduate Biomedical Sciences
Dr. Joel D. Oppenheim, Senior Associate Dean for Graduate Studies
Programs in:
- cellular and molecular biology (PhD)
- computational biology (PhD)
- developmental genetics (PhD)
- immunology (PhD)
- medical and molecular parasitology (PhD)
- microbiology (PhD)
- molecular oncology (PhD)
- molecular oncology and immunology (PhD)
- molecular pharmacology and signal transduction (PhD)
- neuroscience (PhD)
- neuroscience and physiology (PhD)
- pathobiology (PhD)
- pharmacology (PhD)
- physiology (PhD)
- structural biology (PhD)

School of Social Work
Dr. Suzanne England, Dean
Program in:
- social work (MSW, PhD)

Steinhardt School of Culture, Education and Human Development
Dr. Mary Brabeck, Dean
Programs in:
- advanced occupational therapy (MA)
- art education (MA, PhD)
- art therapy (MA)
- arts and humanities education (MA, PhD)
- bilingual education (MA, PhD, Advanced Certificate)
- biology grades 7-12 (MA)
- business education (MA, Advanced Certificate)
- business education in higher education (MA)
- chemistry grades 7-12 (MA)
- childhood education (MA, PhD, Advanced Certificate)
- childhood special education (MA)
- clinical nutrition (MS)
- community health (MPH)
- community public health (MPH, PhD)
- counseling and guidance (MA, Advanced Certificate)
- counseling for mental health and wellness (MA)
- counseling psychology (PhD)
- counselor education (MA, PhD, Advanced Certificate)
- culture, education and human development (MA, MFA, MM, MPH, MS, DA, DPS, DPT, Ed D, PhD, Advanced Certificate)
- dance education (MA, Ed D, PhD)
- drama therapy (MA)
- early childhood and childhood education (MA, PhD, Advanced Certificate)
- early childhood education (MA, PhD, Advanced Certificate)
- early childhood special education (MA)
- education and Jewish studies (PhD)
- education policy (MA)
- educational and developmental psychology (MA, PhD)
- educational communication and technology (MA, PhD, Advanced Certificate)
- educational leadership (MA, Ed D, PhD, Advanced Certificate)
- educational psychology (MA)
- educational theatre (MA, Ed D, PhD, Advanced Certificate)
- educational theatre for colleges and communities (MA, PhD)
- educational theatre with English 7-12 (MA)
- English education (MA, PhD, Advanced Certificate)
- environmental conservation education (MA)
- food management (MA)
- food studies (MA)
- food studies and food management (MA, PhD)
- foods and nutrition (MS)
- for-profit sector (MA)
- foreign language education (MA, Advanced Certificate)
- foreign language education/TESOL (MA)
- higher education (MA, PhD)
- higher education administration (PhD)
- history of education (MA, PhD)
- international community health (MPH)
- international education (MA, PhD, Advanced Certificate)
- literacy education (MA)
- mathematics education (MA)
- media ecology/culture and communication (PhD)
- media, culture, and communication (MA)
- multilingual/multicultural studies (MA, PhD, Advanced Certificate)
- music business (MA)
- music education (MA, Ed D, PhD, Advanced Certificate)
- music performance and composition (MA, PhD)
- music technology (MM)
- music therapy (MA, DA)
- not-for-profit sector (MA)
- nutrition and dietetics (MS, PhD)
- occupational therapy (MA, MS, DPS, PhD)
- performing arts administration (MA)
- philosophy of education (MA, PhD)
- physical therapists pathokinesiology (MA)
- physical therapy (DPT)
- physics grades 7-12 (MA)
- practicing physical therapist (DPT)
- psychological development (PhD)
- public health (PhD)
- public health nutrition (MPH)
- research in physical therapy (PhD)
- school psychology (PhD)
- science education (MA)
- social and cultural studies of education (MA)
- social studies education (MA)

New York University (continued)
sociology of education (MA, PhD)
special education (MA)
speech-language pathology and audiology (MA, PhD)
student personnel administration higher education (MA)
studio art (MA, MFA)
teaching and learning (Ed D, PhD)
teaching educational theatre, all grades (MA)
teaching English to speakers of other languages (MA, PhD, Advanced Certificate)
visual arts administration (MA)
visual culture (MA, PhD)
visual culture: costume studies (MA)
visual culture: theory (MA, PhD)
workplace learning (Advanced Certificate)

Tisch School of the Arts
Mary Schmidt Campbell, Dean
Programs in:
acting (MFA)
arts (MA, MFA, MPS, PhD)
cinema studies (MA, PhD)
dance (MFA)
design for stage and film (MFA)
dramatic writing (MFA)
interactive telecommunications (MPS)
moving image archiving and preservation (MA)
musical theatre writing (MFA)
performance studies (MA, PhD)

Kanbar Institute of Film and Television
John Tintori, Chair
Program in:
film and television (MFA)

■ NIAGARA UNIVERSITY
Niagara Falls, Niagara University, NY 14109
http://www.niagara.edu/

Independent-religious, coed, comprehensive institution. *Enrollment:* 3,881 graduate, professional, and undergraduate students; 582 full-time matriculated graduate/professional students (396 women), 332 part-time matriculated graduate/professional students (233 women). *Graduate faculty:* 40 full-time (20 women), 30 part-time/adjunct (14 women). *Computer facilities:* 150 computers available on campus for general student use. A campuswide network can be accessed from student residence rooms. Internet access and online class registration are available. *Library facilities:* Our Lady of Angels Library. *General application contact:* Carlos Tejada, Associate Dean for Graduate Recruitment, 716-286-8769.

Graduate Division of Arts and Sciences
Dr. Nancy McGlen, Dean
Programs in:
criminal justice (MS)
criminal justice administration (MS)

Graduate Division of Business Administration
Wick Hannan, Director
Programs in:
business (MBA)
commerce (MBA)

Graduate Division of Education
Dr. Debra A. Colley, Dean
Programs in:
administration and supervision (MS Ed, Certificate)
elementary education (MS Ed)
foundations of teaching (MA, MS Ed)
inclusive education (MS Ed)
literacy instruction (MS Ed)
mental health counseling (MS Ed, Certificate)
school business administration (MS Ed, Certificate)
school counseling (MS Ed, Certificate)
school psychology (MS)
secondary education (MS Ed)
teacher education (MS Ed)

■ NYACK COLLEGE
Nyack, NY 10960-3698
http://www.nyack.edu

Independent-religious, coed, comprehensive institution. *Computer facilities:* 180 computers available on campus for general student use. A campuswide network can be accessed from student residence rooms and from off campus. Internet access is available. *Library facilities:* The Bailey Library plus 2 others. *General application contact:* Director of Admissions, 800-33-NYACK.

Graduate and Professional Programs

School of Business
Programs in:
accounting (MBA)
business administration (MBA)

School of Education
Program in:
inclusive education (MS)

■ PACE UNIVERSITY
New York, NY 10038
http://www.pace.edu/

Independent, coed, university. CGS member. *Enrollment:* 13,463 graduate, professional, and undergraduate students; 677 full-time matriculated graduate/professional students (452 women), 3,832 part-time matriculated graduate/professional students (2,314 women). *Graduate faculty:* 189 full-time, 139 part-time/adjunct. *Computer facilities:* 246 computers available on campus for general student use. A campuswide network can be accessed from student residence rooms and from off campus. Internet access and online class registration are available. *Library facilities:* Henry Birnbaum Library plus 3 others. *Graduate expenses:* Tuition: part-time $890 per credit. *General application contact:* Joanna Broda, Director of Admissions, 212-346-1652.

Dyson College of Arts and Sciences
Dr. Nira Hermann, Dean
Programs in:
acting (MFA)
arts and sciences (MA, MFA, MPA, MS, MS Ed, Psy D)
bilingual school psychology (MS Ed)
counseling-substance abuse (MS)
environmental science (MS)
forensic science (MS)
government management (MPA)
health care administration (MPA)
nonprofit management (MPA)
psychology (MA)
publishing (MS)
school psychology (MS Ed)
school-clinical child psychology (Psy D)

Lienhard School of Nursing
Dr. Harriet Feldman, Dean
Program in:
nursing (MS, Advanced Certificate)

Lubin School of Business
Dr. Arthur Centonze, Dean
Programs in:
banking and finance (MBA)
business (MBA, MS, DPS, APC)
corporate economic planning (MBA)
corporate financial management (MBA)
financial economics (MBA)
financial management (MBA)
information systems (MBA)
international business (MBA)
international economics (MBA)
investment management (MBA, MS)
management (MBA)
management science (MBA)
managerial accounting (MBA)
marketing management (MBA)
marketing research (MBA)
operations management (MBA)
professional studies (DPS)
public accounting (MBA, MS)
taxation (MBA, MS)

School of Computer Science and Information Systems
Dr. Susan Merritt, Dean
Programs in:
computer communications and networks (Certificate)
computer science (MS)
computing studies (DPS)
information systems (MS)
object-oriented programming (Certificate)
telecommunications (MS, Certificate)

School of Education
Dr. Harriet Feldman, Interim Dean

Programs in:
- administration and supervision (MS Ed)
- curriculum and instruction (MS)
- education (MST)
- school business management (Certificate)

School of Law
Stephen J. Friedman, Dean
Programs in:
- comparative legal studies (LL M)
- environmental law (LL M, SJD)
- law (JD)

■ POLYTECHNIC UNIVERSITY, BROOKLYN CAMPUS
Brooklyn, NY 11201-2990
http://www.poly.edu/

Independent, coed, university. CGS member. *Enrollment:* 2,919 graduate, professional, and undergraduate students; 806 full-time matriculated graduate/professional students (202 women), 457 part-time matriculated graduate/professional students (111 women). *Graduate faculty:* 138 full-time (24 women), 135 part-time/adjunct (29 women). *Computer facilities:* Computer purchase and lease plans are available. 1,334 computers available on campus for general student use. A campuswide network can be accessed from student residence rooms and from off campus. Internet access is available. *Library facilities:* Bern Dibner Library plus 1 other. *Graduate expenses:* Tuition: full-time $17,784; part-time $988 per credit. *General application contact:* Prof. Sunil Kumar, Associate Provost for Graduate School, 718-260-3482.

Department of Chemical and Biological Sciences
Programs in:
- biomedical engineering (MS, PhD)
- biotechnology and entrepreneurship (MS)
- chemistry (MS)
- materials chemistry (PhD)
- polymer science and engineering (MS)

Department of Civil Engineering
Dr. Roger Roess, Head
Programs in:
- civil engineering (MS, PhD)
- construction management (MS)
- environmental engineering (MS)
- environmental science (MS)
- transportation management (MS)
- transportation planning and engineering (MS, PhD)

Department of Computer and Information Science
Dr. Stuart Steele, Head
Programs in:
- computer science (MS, PhD)
- cyber security (Graduate Certificate)
- software engineering (Graduate Certificate)

Department of Electrical and Computer Engineering
Dr. Jonathan Chao, Head
Programs in:
- computer engineering (MS, Certificate)
- electrical engineering (MS, PhD)
- electrophysics (MS)
- image processing (Certificate)
- systems engineering (MS)
- telecommunication networks (MS)
- wireless communications (Certificate)

Department of Finance and Risk Engineering
Frederick Novomestky, Academic Director
Programs in:
- financial engineering (MS, Advanced Certificate)
- financial technology management (Advanced Certificate)
- risk management (Advanced Certificate)

Department of Humanities and Social Sciences
Dr. Harold Sjursen, Head
Programs in:
- environment-behavior studies (MS)
- history of science (MS)
- integrated digital media (MS, Graduate Certificate)
- technical communication (Graduate Certificate)
- technical writing and specialized journalism (MS)

Department of Management
Dr. Barry Blecherman, Associate Dean
Programs in:
- management (MS)
- management of technology (MS)
- organizational behavior (MS)
- technology management (PhD)
- telecommunications and information management (MS)

Department of Mathematics
Dr. Erwin Lutwak, Head
Program in:
- mathematics (MS, PhD)

Department of Mechanical and Aerospace Engineering
Dr. Said Nourbaksh, Head
Programs in:
- industrial engineering (MS)
- manufacturing engineering (MS)
- materials science (MS)
- mechanical engineering (MS, PhD)

Department of Physics
Dr. Edward Wolf, Head
Program in:
- physics (MS, PhD)

Othmer-Jacobs Department of Chemical and Biological Engineering
Dr. Jovan Mijovic, Head
Programs in:
- bioinformatics (MS)
- chemical engineering (MS, PhD)

■ POLYTECHNIC UNIVERSITY, WESTCHESTER GRADUATE CENTER
Hawthorne, NY 10532-1507
http://west.poly.edu/~www/

Independent, coed, graduate-only institution. *Graduate faculty:* 66 full-time (6 women), 66 part-time/adjunct (5 women). *Computer facilities:* 30 computers available on campus for general student use. A campuswide network can be accessed from off campus. Internet access is available. *Library facilities:* Dibner Library. *Graduate expenses:* Tuition: full-time $17,184; part-time $988 per credit. *General application contact:* Prof. Sunil Kumar, Graduate Admissions, 718-260-3482.

Graduate Programs
LaVerne Clark, Director of Campus Operations
Programs in:
- chemical engineering (MS)
- chemistry (MS)
- computer engineering (MS)
- computer science (MS, PhD)
- electrical engineering (MS, PhD)
- information systems engineering (MS)
- materials chemistry (PhD)
- telecommunication networks (MS)

Department of Management
Dr. Barry Blecherman, Associate Dean
Programs in:
- capital markets (MS)
- computational finance (MS)
- financial engineering (MS, AC)
- financial technology (MS)
- financial technology management (AC)
- information management (AC)
- management (MS)
- management of technology (MS)

■ PURCHASE COLLEGE, STATE UNIVERSITY OF NEW YORK
Purchase, NY 10577-1400
http://www.purchase.edu/

State-supported, coed, comprehensive institution. *Enrollment:* 3,901 graduate, professional, and undergraduate students; 134 full-time matriculated graduate/professional students (74 women), 13 part-time matriculated graduate/professional students (9 women). *Graduate faculty:* 266. *Computer facilities:* 350 computers available on campus for general student use. A

Purchase College, State University of New York (continued)
campuswide network can be accessed from student residence rooms and from off campus. Internet access, e-mail are available. *Library facilities:* Purchase College Library. *Graduate expenses:* Tuition, state resident: full-time $6,900; part-time $288 per credit. Tuition, nonresident: full-time $10,920; part-time $455 per credit. *General application contact:* Sabrina Johnston, Counselor, 914-251-6479.

Conservatory of Dance
Programs in:
choreography (MFA)
performance and pedagogy (MFA)

Conservatory of Music
Programs in:
composition (MFA)
instrumental (MFA)
voice (MFA)

Conservatory of Theatre Arts and Film
Programs in:
theatre design (MFA)
theatre technology (MFA)

Division of Humanities
Jonathan Levin, Dean, Division of Humanities
Program in:
art history (MA)

School of Art and Design
Program in:
art and design (MFA)

■ QUEENS COLLEGE OF THE CITY UNIVERSITY OF NEW YORK
Flushing, NY 11367-1597
http://www.qc.cuny.edu/

State and locally supported, coed, comprehensive institution. CGS member. *Enrollment:* 18,107 graduate, professional, and undergraduate students; 379 full-time matriculated graduate/professional students (282 women), 4,066 part-time matriculated graduate/professional students (2,883 women). *Graduate faculty:* 582 full-time (244 women). *Computer facilities:* 1,000 computers available on campus for general student use. A campuswide network can be accessed from off campus. Internet access is available. *Library facilities:* Main library plus 1 other. *General application contact:* Mario Caruso, Director of Graduate Admissions, 718-997-5200.

Find University Details at www.petersons.com/gradchannel.

Division of Graduate Studies
Dr. Steven Schwarz, Acting Dean of Research and Graduate Services

Arts and Humanities Division
Dr. Tamara Evans, Dean
Programs in:
applied linguistics (MA)
art history (MA)
arts and humanities (MA, MFA, MS Ed)
creative writing (MA)
English language and literature (MA)
fine arts (MFA)
French (MA)
Italian (MA)
music (MA)
Spanish (MA)
speech pathology (MA)
teaching English to speakers of other languages (MS Ed)

Division of Education
Dr. Penny Hammrich, Dean
Programs in:
art (MS Ed)
bilingual education (MS Ed)
biology (MS Ed, AC)
chemistry (MS Ed, AC)
childhood education (MA)
counselor education (MS Ed)
early childhood education (MA)
earth sciences (MS Ed, AC)
education (MA, MS Ed, AC)
educational leadership (AC)
elementary education (MS Ed, AC)
English (MS Ed, AC)
French (MS Ed, AC)
Italian (MS Ed, AC)
literacy (MS Ed)
mathematics (MS Ed, AC)
music (MS Ed, AC)
physics (MS Ed, AC)
school psychology (MS Ed, AC)
social studies (MS Ed, AC)
Spanish (MS Ed, AC)
special education (MS Ed)

Mathematics and Natural Sciences Division
Dr. Thomas Strekas, Dean
Programs in:
biochemistry (MA)
biology (MA)
chemistry (MA)
clinical behavioral applications in mental health settings (MA)
computer science (MA)
earth and environmental sciences (MA)
home economics (MS Ed)
mathematics (MA)
mathematics and natural sciences (MA, MS Ed, PhD)
physical education and exercise sciences (MS Ed)
physics (MA, PhD)
psychology (MA)

Social Science Division
Dr. Elizabeth Hendrey, Dean
Programs in:
accounting (MS)
history (MA)
liberal studies (MALS)
library and information studies (MLS, AC)
social science (MA, MALS, MASS, MLS, MS, AC)
social sciences (MASS)
sociology (MA)
urban studies (MA)

■ RENSSELAER POLYTECHNIC INSTITUTE
Troy, NY 12180-3590
http://www.rpi.edu/

Independent, coed, university. CGS member. *Enrollment:* 7,433 graduate, professional, and undergraduate students; 1,131 full-time matriculated graduate/professional students (344 women), 1,109 part-time matriculated graduate/professional students (326 women). *Graduate faculty:* 393 full-time (82 women), 78 part-time/adjunct (21 women). *Computer facilities:* Computer purchase and lease plans are available. 5,588 computers available on campus for general student use. A campuswide network can be accessed from student residence rooms and from off campus. Internet access and online class registration are available. *Library facilities:* Folsom Library plus 1 other. *Graduate expenses:* Tuition: full-time $32,600; part-time $1,358 per credit. Required fees: $1,629. *General application contact:* James G. Nondorf, Vice President for Enrollment, 518-276-6216.

Find University Details at www.petersons.com/gradchannel.

Graduate School
Dr. Lester A. Gerhardt, Vice Provost and Dean of Graduate Education, Acting

Lally School of Management and Technology
Dr. David A. Gautschi, Dean
Programs in:
finance (MBA, MS)
financial technology (MS)
management (PhD)
management and technology (MBA, MS, PhD)
management information systems (MBA, MS)
new product development and marketing (MBA)
new production and operations management (MS)
product development and marketing (MS)
production and operations management (MBA)
technical commercialization (MS)
technological entrepreneurship (MBA, MS)

School of Architecture
Prof. Ted Krueger, Chair

Programs in:
- architectural science (MS, PhD)
- architecture (M Arch)
- building conservation (MS)
- lighting (MS)

School of Engineering
Dr. Alan W. Cramb, Dean
Programs in:
- aerospace engineering (M Eng, MS, PhD)
- biomedical engineering (MS, PhD)
- ceramics and glass science (M Eng, MS, PhD)
- chemical and biological engineering (M Eng, MS, D Eng, PhD)
- civil engineering (M Eng, MS, D Eng, PhD)
- composites (M Eng, MS, PhD)
- computer and systems engineering (M Eng, MS, D Eng, PhD)
- decision sciences and engineering systems (PhD)
- electric power engineering (M Eng, MS, D Eng, PhD)
- electrical engineering (M Eng, MS, D Eng, PhD)
- electronic materials (M Eng, MS, PhD)
- engineering (M Eng, MS, D Eng, PhD)
- engineering physics (MS, PhD)
- engineering science (M Eng, MS, PhD)
- environmental engineering (M Eng, MS, D Eng, PhD)
- geotechnical engineering (M Eng, MS, D Eng, PhD)
- industrial and management engineering (M Eng, MS, PhD)
- manufacturing systems engineering (M Eng, MS, PhD)
- mechanical engineering (M Eng, MS, PhD)
- mechanics of composite materials and structures (M Eng, MS, D Eng, PhD)
- metallurgy (M Eng, MS, PhD)
- nuclear engineering (M Eng, MS, PhD)
- nuclear engineering and science (PhD)
- operations research and statistics (M Eng, MS, PhD)
- polymers (M Eng, MS, PhD)
- structural engineering (M Eng, MS, D Eng, PhD)
- transportation engineering (M Eng, MS, D Eng, PhD)

School of Humanities and Social Sciences
Dr. John P. Harrington, Dean
Programs in:
- cognitive science (PhD)
- communication and rhetoric (MS, PhD)
- ecological economics (PhD)
- ecological economics, values, and policy (MS)
- economics (MS)
- electronic arts (MFA)
- human-computer interaction (MS)
- humanities and social sciences (MFA, MS, PhD)
- science and technology studies (MS, PhD)
- technical communication (MS)

School of Science
Dr. Wei Zhao, Dean
Programs in:
- analytical chemistry (MS, PhD)
- applied mathematics (MS)
- applied science (MS)
- biochemistry (MS, PhD)
- biophysics (MS, PhD)
- cell biology (MS, PhD)
- computer science (MS, PhD)
- developmental biology (MS, PhD)
- environmental chemistry (MS, PhD)
- geochemistry (MS, PhD)
- geology (MS, PhD)
- geophysics (MS, PhD)
- information technology (MS)
- inorganic chemistry (MS, PhD)
- mathematics (MS, PhD)
- microbiology (MS, PhD)
- molecular biology (MS, PhD)
- multidisciplinary science (MS, PhD)
- natural sciences (MS)
- organic chemistry (MS, PhD)
- petrology (MS, PhD)
- physical chemistry (MS, PhD)
- physics (MS, PhD)
- polymer chemistry (MS, PhD)
- science (MS, PhD)

■ ROBERTS WESLEYAN COLLEGE

Rochester, NY 14624-1997

http://www.roberts.edu/

Independent-religious, coed, comprehensive institution. *Enrollment:* 1,903 graduate, professional, and undergraduate students; 168 full-time matriculated graduate/professional students (116 women), 121 part-time matriculated graduate/professional students (81 women). *Graduate faculty:* 11 full-time (2 women), 31 part-time/adjunct (10 women). *Computer facilities:* 170 computers available on campus for general student use. A campuswide network can be accessed from student residence rooms and from off campus. Internet access and online class registration are available. *Library facilities:* Ora A. Sprague Library. *General application contact:* Office of Admissions, 800-777-4RWC.

Division of Adult Professional Studies
Dr. William Walence, Chair
Program in:
- health administration (MS)

Division of Business
Dr. Steven Bovee, Chair
Programs in:
- nonprofit leadership (Certificate)
- strategic leadership (MS)
- strategic marketing (MS)

Division of Social Work
Dr. Harmon Meldrim, Chair
Programs in:
- child and family practice (MSW)
- congregational and community practice (MSW)
- mental health practice (MSW)

Division of Teacher Education
Dr. Richard Mace, Chair
Programs in:
- adolescence education (M Ed)
- childhood and special education (M Ed)
- literacy education (M Ed)
- urban education (M Ed)

■ ROCHESTER INSTITUTE OF TECHNOLOGY

Rochester, NY 14623-5603

http://www.rit.edu/

Independent, coed, comprehensive institution. CGS member. *Enrollment:* 15,557 graduate, professional, and undergraduate students; 1,279 full-time matriculated graduate/professional students (498 women), 976 part-time matriculated graduate/professional students (347 women). *Computer facilities:* 2,500 computers available on campus for general student use. A campuswide network can be accessed from student residence rooms and from off campus. Internet access and online class registration, student account information are available. *Library facilities:* Wallace Memorial Library. *Graduate expenses:* Tuition: full-time $28,491; part-time $800 per credit. Required fees: $201. *General application contact:* Diane Ellison, Director, Graduate Enrollment Services, 585-475-7284.

Find University Details at www.petersons.com/gradchannel.

Graduate Enrollment Services
Diane Ellison, Director, Graduate Enrollment Services

College of Applied Science and Technology
Dr. Carol Richardson, Interim Dean
Programs in:
- applied science and technology (MS, AC)
- cross-disciplinary professional studies (MS)
- environmental management (MS)
- health systems administration (MS, AC)
- health systems-finance (AC)
- hospitality-tourism management (MS)
- human resources development (MS, AC)
- integrated health systems (AC)
- manufacturing and mechanical systems integration (MS)
- multidisciplinary studies (MS, AC)
- packaging science (MS)
- senior living management (AC)
- service management (MS)
- technical information design (AC)
- telecommunications engineering technology (MS)

Rochester Institute of Technology (continued)

College of Engineering
Dr. Harvey Palmer, Dean
Programs in:
- applied statistics (MS)
- computer engineering (MS)
- electrical engineering (MSEE)
- engineering (ME, MS, MSEE, PhD, AC)
- engineering management (ME)
- industrial engineering (ME, MS)
- manufacturing engineering (ME, MS)
- manufacturing leadership (MS)
- mechanical engineering (ME, MS)
- microelectronic engineering (MS)
- microelectronic manufacturing engineering (ME)
- microsystems engineering (PhD)
- product development (MS)
- statistical quality (AC)
- systems engineering (ME)

College of Imaging Arts and Sciences
Dr. Joan Stone, Dean
Programs in:
- art education (MST)
- ceramics (MFA)
- computer graphics design (MFA)
- fine arts (MFA, MST)
- fine arts studio (MST)
- glass (MFA)
- graphic design (MFA)
- imaging arts (MFA)
- imaging arts and sciences (MFA, MS, MST)
- industrial design (MFA)
- medical illustration (MFA)
- metal crafts and jewelry (MFA)
- painting (MFA)
- print media (MS)
- printmaking (MFA)
- woodworking and furniture design (MFA)

College of Liberal Arts
Dr. Glenn Kist, Interim Dean
Programs in:
- communication and media technologies (MS)
- liberal arts (MS, AC)
- psychology (MS)
- public policy (MS)
- school psychology (MS, AC)

College of Science
Dr. Ian Gatley, Dean
Programs in:
- bioinformatics (MS)
- chemistry (MS)
- clinical chemistry (MS)
- color science (MS, PhD)
- environmental science (MS)
- imaging science (MS, PhD)
- industrial and applied mathematics (MS)
- materials science and engineering (MS)
- science (MS, PhD)

E. Philip Saunders College of Business
Ashok Rao, Dean
Programs in:
- accounting (MBA, MS)
- business (Exec MBA, MBA, MS)
- business administration (MBA)
- executive business administration (Exec MBA)
- finance (MS)
- management (MS)

Golisano College of Computing and Information Sciences
Jorge Diaz-Herrara, Dean
Programs in:
- computer science (MS)
- computing and information sciences (MS, AC)
- game design and development (MS)
- information technology (MS)
- interactive multimedia development (AC)
- learning and knowledge management systems (MS)
- networking and systems administration (AC)
- security and information assurance (MS)
- software development and management (MS)

National Technical Institute for the Deaf
Dr. Alan Hurwitz, Dean
Programs in:
- deaf studies (MS)
- secondary education (MS)

■ ST. BONAVENTURE UNIVERSITY
St. Bonaventure, NY 14778-2284
http://www.sbu.edu/

Independent-religious, coed, comprehensive institution. CGS member. *Computer facilities:* 200 computers available on campus for general student use. A campuswide network can be accessed from student residence rooms and from off campus. Internet access and online class registration are available. *Library facilities:* Friedsam Library. *General application contact:* Information Contact, 716-375-2021.

School of Graduate Studies

School of Arts and Sciences
Programs in:
- arts and sciences (MA)
- English (MA)

School of Business
Programs in:
- accounting (Adv C)
- accounting and finance (MBA)
- finance (Adv C)
- management (Adv C)
- management and marketing (MBA)
- marketing (Adv C)
- professional leadership (Adv C)

School of Education
Programs in:
- counseling education (Adv C)
- counseling education-agency (MS, MS Ed)
- counseling education-school (MS, MS Ed)
- education (MS, MS Ed, Adv C)
- educational leadership (MS Ed, Adv C)
- literacy (MS Ed)

School of Franciscan Studies
Program in:
- Franciscan studies (MA, Adv C)

■ ST. JOHN FISHER COLLEGE
Rochester, NY 14618-3597
http://www.sjfc.edu/

Independent-religious, coed, comprehensive institution. *Enrollment:* 3,704 graduate, professional, and undergraduate students; 274 full-time matriculated graduate/professional students (182 women), 637 part-time matriculated graduate/professional students (468 women). *Graduate faculty:* 60 full-time (27 women), 40 part-time/adjunct (25 women). *Computer facilities:* 260 computers available on campus for general student use. A campuswide network can be accessed from student residence rooms and from off campus. Internet access and online class registration are available. *Library facilities:* Charles J. Lavery Library. *Graduate expenses:* Tuition: part-time $615 per credit. Tuition and fees vary according to program. *General application contact:* Shannon Cleverley, Director of Graduate Admissions, 585-385-8161.

Office of the Provost

Dr. Ronald J. Ambrosetti, Provost and Dean of the College
Programs in:
- advanced practice nursing (MS)
- arts and sciences (MS)
- clinical nurse specialist (Certificate)
- family nurse practitioner (Certificate)
- human resources development (MS)
- human service administration (MS)
- international studies (MS)
- mathematics/science/technology education (MS)
- mental health counseling (MS)
- nurse educator (Certificate)
- nursing (MS, Certificate)
- pharmacy (Pharm D)

Ralph C. Wilson Jr. School of Education
Dr. Arthur Walton, Dean
Programs in:
- adolescence English (MS Ed)
- adolescence French (MS Ed)
- adolescence social studies (MS Ed)
- adolescence Spanish (MS Ed)
- childhood education (MS Ed)

education (MS, MS Ed, Ed D, Certificate)
educational leadership (MS Ed)
executive leadership (Ed D)
literacy birth to grade 6 (MS)
literacy grades 5 to 12 (MS)
special education (MS, Certificate)

Ronald L. Bittner School of Business
Dr. Selim Ilter, Interim Dean
Programs in:
business (MBA)
business administration and management (MBA)

■ ST. JOHN'S UNIVERSITY
Queens, NY 11439
http://www.stjohns.edu/

Independent-religious, coed, university. CGS member. *Enrollment:* 20,069 graduate, professional, and undergraduate students; 1,962 full-time matriculated graduate/professional students (1,231 women), 3,124 part-time matriculated graduate/professional students (2,077 women). *Graduate faculty:* 648 full-time (250 women), 865 part-time/adjunct (346 women). *Computer facilities:* Computer purchase and lease plans are available. 1,025 computers available on campus for general student use. A campuswide network can be accessed from student residence rooms and from off campus. Internet access and online class registration, various software packages are available. *Library facilities:* St. John's University Library plus 1 other. *Graduate expenses:* Tuition: full-time $18,480; part-time $770 per credit. Required fees: $125 per semester. Tuition and fees vary according to program. *General application contact:* Br. Shamus McGrenra, Senior Associate Director, Office of Admission, 718-990-1601.

College of Pharmacy and Allied Health Professions
Dr. Robert Mangione, Dean
Programs in:
pharmaceutical sciences (MS, PhD)
pharmacy (Pharm D, MS, PhD)
pharmacy administration (MS)
pharmacy and allied health professions (Pharm D, MS, PhD)
toxicology (MS)

College of Professional Studies
Dr. Kathleen Voute MacDonald, Dean
Program in:
criminal justice and legal studies (MPS)

The Peter J. Tobin College of Business
Dr. Steven Papamarcos, Dean
Programs in:
accounting (MBA, MS, Adv C)
business (MBA, MS, Adv C)
computer information systems and decision sciences (MBA, Adv C)
finance (MBA, Adv C)
international business (MBA, Adv C)
management (MBA, Adv C)
marketing (MBA, Adv C)
taxation (MBA, MS, Adv C)

School of Risk Management and Actuarial Science
Dr. Nicos Scordis, Chair
Program in:
risk management and actuarial science (MBA, MS)

St. John's College of Liberal Arts and Sciences
Dr. Jeffrey Fagen, Dean
Programs in:
algebra (MA)
analysis (MA)
applied mathematics (MA)
biological sciences (MS, PhD)
chemistry (MS)
clinical psychology (PhD)
clinical psychology-child (PhD)
clinical psychology-general (PhD)
computer science (MA)
criminology and justice (MA)
English (MA, DA)
general experimental psychology (MA)
geometry-topology (MA)
government and politics (MA, Adv C)
history (MA)
international law and diplomacy (Adv C)
languages and literatures (Adv C)
liberal arts and sciences (M Div, MA, MLS, MS, Au D, DA, PhD, Psy D, Adv C, Advanced Diploma, Certificate)
liberal studies (MA)
library and information science (MLS, Adv C)
logic and foundations (MA)
modern world history (DA)
pastoral ministry (Certificate)
philosophy (MA)
priestly studies (M Div)
probability and statistics (MA)
school psychology (MS, Psy D)
sociology (MA)
Spanish (MA)
speech, communication sciences and theatre (MA, Advanced Diploma)
theology (MA, Certificate)

Institute of Asian Studies
Dr. Bernadette Li, Chair
Programs in:
Asian and African cultural studies (Adv C)
Asian studies (Adv C)
Chinese studies (MA, Adv C)
East Asian culture studies (Adv C)
East Asian studies (MA)

The School of Education
Dr. Jerrold Ross, Dean
Programs in:
bilingual school counseling (MS Ed)
bilingual/multicultural education/teaching English to speakers of other languages (MS Ed)
education (MS Ed, Ed D, PD)
instructional leadership (Ed D, PD)
literacy (MS Ed, PD)
rehabilitation counseling (MS Ed, PD)
school building leadership (MS Ed, PD)
school counseling (MS Ed, PD)
school district leader (PD)
student development practice in higher education (PD)
teaching children with disabilities (MS Ed)

School of Law
Mary C. Daly, Dean
Programs in:
bankruptcy (LL M)
law (JD, LL M)

■ ST. JOSEPH'S COLLEGE, SUFFOLK CAMPUS
Patchogue, NY 11772-2399
http://www.sjcny.edu/

Independent, coed, comprehensive institution. *Computer facilities:* 223 computers available on campus for general student use. A campuswide network can be accessed from off campus. Internet access and online class registration are available. *Library facilities:* Callahan Library. *General application contact:* Coordinator of Graduate Admissions, 631-447-3383.

Executive MBA Program
Program in:
business administration (EMBA)

Program in Accounting
Program in:
accounting (MBA)

Program in Infant/Toddler Early Childhood Special Education
Program in:
infant/toddler early childhood special education (MA)

Program in Literacy and Cognition
Program in:
literacy and cognition (MA)

Program in Management
Programs in:
health care (AC)
health care management (MS)
human resource management (AC)
human resources management (MS)
organizational management (MS)

Program in Nursing
Program in:
nursing (MS)

■ ST. THOMAS AQUINAS COLLEGE

Sparkill, NY 10976
http://www.stac.edu/

Independent, coed, comprehensive institution. *Computer facilities:* 200 computers available on campus for general student use. A campuswide network can be accessed from student residence rooms and from off campus. Internet access is available. *Library facilities:* Lougheed Library. *General application contact:* Director of Admissions, 845-398-4102.

Division of Business Administration

Programs in:
- business administration (MBA)
- finance (MBA)
- management (MBA)
- marketing (MBA)

Division of Teacher Education

Programs in:
- adolescence education (MST)
- childhood and special education (MST)
- childhood education (MST)
- reading (MS Ed, PMC)
- special education (MS Ed, PMC)
- teaching (MS Ed)

■ SARAH LAWRENCE COLLEGE

Bronxville, NY 10708-5999
http://www.sarahlawrence.edu/

Independent, coed, comprehensive institution. CGS member. *Enrollment:* 1,709 graduate, professional, and undergraduate students; 219 full-time matriculated graduate/professional students (180 women), 99 part-time matriculated graduate/professional students (92 women). *Graduate faculty:* 134 part-time/adjunct (78 women). *Computer facilities:* 110 computers available on campus for general student use. A campuswide network can be accessed from student residence rooms and from off campus. Internet access is available. *Library facilities:* Esther Rauschenbush Library plus 2 others. *Graduate expenses:* Tuition: full-time $23,520. Required fees: $404. Tuition and fees vary according to program and student level. *General application contact:* Susan Guma, Dean of Graduate Studies, 914-395-2373.

Find University Details at www.petersons.com/gradchannel.

Graduate Studies

Susan Guma, Dean of Graduate Studies
Programs in:
- art of teaching (MS Ed)
- child development (MA)
- creative non-fiction (MFA)
- dance (MFA)
- fiction (MFA)
- health advocacy (MA)
- human genetics (MS)
- individualized study (MA)
- poetry (MFA)
- theater (MFA)
- women's history (MA)

■ STATE UNIVERSITY OF NEW YORK AT BINGHAMTON

Binghamton, NY 13902-6000
http://www.binghamton.edu/

State-supported, coed, university. CGS member. *Enrollment:* 14,373 graduate, professional, and undergraduate students; 1,589 full-time matriculated graduate/professional students (749 women), 1,157 part-time matriculated graduate/professional students (631 women). *Graduate faculty:* 461 full-time (162 women), 211 part-time/adjunct (92 women). *Computer facilities:* Computer purchase and lease plans are available. 7,200 computers available on campus for general student use. A campuswide network can be accessed from student residence rooms and from off campus. Internet access and online class registration are available. *Library facilities:* Glenn G. Bartle Library plus 1 other. *General application contact:* Dr. Nancy E. Stamp, Vice Provost and Dean of the Graduate School, 607-777-2070.

Graduate School

Dr. Nancy E. Stamp, Vice Provost and Dean of the Graduate School

College of Community and Public Affairs
Dr. Patricia Ingraham, Dean
Programs in:
- community and public affairs (MASS, MPA, MSW)
- social science (MASS)

Decker School of Nursing
Dr. Joyce Ferrario, Dean
Program in:
- nursing (MS, PhD, Certificate)

School of Arts and Sciences
Dr. Jean-Pierre Mileur, Dean
Programs in:
- analytical chemistry (PhD)
- anthropology (MA, PhD)
- applied physics (MS)
- art history (MA, PhD)
- arts and sciences (MA, MM, MS, PhD, Certificate)
- behavioral neuroscience (MA, PhD)
- biological sciences (MA, PhD)
- chemistry (MA, MS)
- clinical psychology (MA, PhD)
- cognitive and behavioral science (MA, PhD)
- comparative literature (MA, PhD)
- computer science (MA, PhD)
- economics (MA, PhD)
- economics and finance (MA, PhD)
- English (MA, PhD)
- French (MA)
- geography (MA)
- geological sciences (MA, PhD)
- history (MA, PhD)
- inorganic chemistry (PhD)
- Italian (MA)
- music (MA, MM)
- organic chemistry (PhD)
- philosophy (MA, PhD)
- physical chemistry (PhD)
- physics (MA, MS)
- political science (MA, PhD)
- probability and statistics (MA, PhD)
- public policy (MA, PhD)
- social, legal and legal philosophy (MA, PhD)
- sociology (MA, PhD)
- Spanish (MA, Certificate)
- theater (MA)
- translation (Certificate)
- translation research and instruction (Certificate)

School of Education
Dr. Susan Strahle, Interim Dean
Programs in:
- biology education (MAT, MS Ed, MST)
- early childhood and elementary education (MS Ed)
- earth science education (MAT, MS Ed, MST)
- education (MAT, MS Ed, MST, Ed D)
- educational theory and practice (Ed D)
- English education (MAT, MS Ed, MST)
- French education (MAT, MST)
- mathematical sciences education (MAT, MS Ed, MST)
- physics (MAT, MS Ed, MST)
- reading education (MS Ed)
- social studies (MAT, MS Ed, MST)
- Spanish education (MAT, MST)
- special education (MS Ed)

School of Management
Dr. Upinder S. Dhillon, Dean
Programs in:
- accounting (MS, PhD)
- business administration (MBA, PhD)
- health care professional executive (MBA)
- management (MBA, MS, PhD)

Thomas J. Watson School of Engineering and Applied Science
Dr. Seshu Desu, Dean
Programs in:
- computer science (M Eng, MS, PhD)
- electrical and computer engineering (M Eng, MS, PhD)
- engineering and applied science (M Eng, MS, MSAT, PhD)
- materials science and engineering (MS, PhD)
- mechanical engineering (M Eng, MS, PhD)

systems science and industrial engineering (M Eng, MS, MSAT, PhD)

■ STATE UNIVERSITY OF NEW YORK AT FREDONIA

Fredonia, NY 14063-1136

http://www.fredonia.edu/

State-supported, coed, comprehensive institution. *Enrollment:* 5,540 graduate, professional, and undergraduate students; 169 full-time matriculated graduate/professional students (106 women), 171 part-time matriculated graduate/professional students (73 women). *Graduate faculty:* 65 full-time (31 women), 9 part-time/adjunct (4 women). *Computer facilities:* 500 computers available on campus for general student use. A campuswide network can be accessed from student residence rooms and from off campus. *Library facilities:* Reed Library. *Graduate expenses:* Tuition, state resident: full-time $6,900; part-time $288 per credit hour. Tuition, nonresident: full-time $10,920; part-time $455 per credit hour. Required fees: $1,132; $47 per credit hour. *General application contact:* Dr. Jacqueline Swansinger, Interim Dean of Graduate Studies, 716-673-3808.

Graduate Studies

Dr. Jacqueline Swansinger, Dean of Graduate Studies (Interim)

Programs in:
- accounting (MS)
- biology (MS, MS Ed)
- chemistry (MS)
- curriculum and instruction science education (MS Ed)
- English (MA, MS Ed)
- interdisciplinary studies (MA, MS)
- mathematical sciences (MS Ed)
- speech pathology and audiology (MS, MS Ed)

College of Education

Dr. Christine Givner, Dean

Programs in:
- educational administration (CAS)
- elementary education (MS Ed)
- literacy (MS Ed)
- secondary education (MS Ed)
- teaching English to speakers of other languages (MS Ed)

School of Music

Dr. Karl Boelter, Director

Programs in:
- music (MM)
- music education (MM)

■ STATE UNIVERSITY OF NEW YORK AT NEW PALTZ

New Paltz, NY 12561

http://www.newpaltz.edu/

State-supported, coed, comprehensive institution. *Enrollment:* 7,699 graduate, professional, and undergraduate students; 525 full-time matriculated graduate/professional students (321 women), 725 part-time matriculated graduate/professional students (503 women). *Graduate faculty:* 185 full-time (96 women), 218 part-time/adjunct (135 women). *Computer facilities:* 600 computers available on campus for general student use. A campuswide network can be accessed from student residence rooms and from off campus. Internet access and online class registration, e-mail are available. *Library facilities:* Sojourner Truth Library. *Graduate expenses:* Tuition, state resident: full-time $6,900; part-time $288 per credit hour. Tuition, nonresident: full-time $10,920; part-time $455 per credit hour. *General application contact:* Caroline Murphy, Graduate Admissions Advisor, 845-257-3285.

Graduate School

Dr. Laurel M. Garrick-Duhaney, Associate Provost for Academic Affairs/Dean of the Graduate School

Faculty of Education

Dr. Robert Michael, Dean

Programs in:
- adolescence (7-12) (MS Ed)
- childhood (1-6) (MS Ed)
- childhood education (MS Ed)
- childhood education (1-6) (MST)
- early childhood education (B-2) (MST)
- education (MAT, MPS, MS Ed, MST, CAS)
- educational administration (MS Ed, CAS)
- English as a second language (MS Ed)
- humanistic/multicultural education (MPS)
- literacy education (5-12) (MS Ed)
- literacy education (B-6) (MS Ed)
- secondary education (MAT, MS Ed)
- special education (MS Ed)

Faculty of Fine and Performing Arts

Dr. Kurt Daw, Dean

Programs in:
- art studio (MFA)
- ceramics (MA)
- fine and performing arts (MA, MFA, MS Ed)
- interdisciplinary (MA)
- metal (MA)
- painting (MA)
- printmaking (MA)
- sculpture (MA)
- visual arts education (MS Ed)

Faculty of Liberal Arts and Sciences

Dr. Gerald Benjamin, Dean

Programs in:
- biology (MA)
- clinical nurse specialist adult health (CAS)
- communication disorders (MS)
- English (MA)
- gerontological nursing (MS)
- liberal arts and sciences (MA, MS, CAS)
- mental health counseling (MS)
- psychology (MA)

School of Business

Dr. Hadi Salavitabar, Dean

Programs in:
- business administration (MBA)
- public accountancy (MBA)

School of Science and Engineering

Dr. John Harrington, Dean

Programs in:
- chemistry (MA)
- computer science (MS)
- electrical and computer engineering (MS)
- geological sciences (MA)
- mathematics (MA)
- science and engineering (MA, MS)

■ STATE UNIVERSITY OF NEW YORK AT OSWEGO

Oswego, NY 13126

http://www.oswego.edu/

State-supported, coed, comprehensive institution. *Enrollment:* 8,183 graduate, professional, and undergraduate students; 378 full-time matriculated graduate/professional students (246 women), 481 part-time matriculated graduate/professional students (321 women). *Graduate faculty:* 76 full-time, 97 part-time/adjunct. *Computer facilities:* Computer purchase and lease plans are available. 600 computers available on campus for general student use. A campuswide network can be accessed from student residence rooms and from off campus. Internet access and online class registration are available. *Library facilities:* Penfield Library plus 1 other. *Graduate expenses:* Tuition, state resident: part-time $288 per credit. Tuition, nonresident: part-time $455 per credit. Tuition and fees vary according to program. *General application contact:* Dr. David W. King, Dean of Graduate Studies, 315-312-3152.

Graduate Studies

Dr. David W. King, Dean of Graduate Studies

College of Arts and Sciences

Dr. Rhonda Mandel, Interim Dean

Programs in:
- art (MA)
- arts and sciences (MA, MS)
- chemistry (MS)
- English (MA)
- history (MA)
- human computer interaction (MA)

School of Business

Dr. Lanny A. Karns, Dean

Programs in:
- business (MBA)
- business administration (MBA)

School of Education

Dr. Linda Markert, Dean

Programs in:
- agriculture (MS Ed)

State University of New York at Oswego (continued)

art education (MAT)
business and marketing (MS Ed)
counseling services (MS, CAS)
education (MAT, MS, MS Ed, CAS)
educational administration and supervision (CAS)
elementary education (MS Ed)
family and consumer sciences (MS Ed)
health careers (MS Ed)
human services/community counseling (MS)
literacy education (MS Ed)
school building leadership (CAS)
school psychology (MS, CAS)
secondary education (MS Ed)
special education (MS Ed)
technical education (MS Ed)
technology (MS Ed)
trade education (MS Ed)

■ STATE UNIVERSITY OF NEW YORK AT PLATTSBURGH

Plattsburgh, NY 12901-2681
http://www.plattsburgh.edu/

State-supported, coed, comprehensive institution. *Enrollment:* 6,217 graduate, professional, and undergraduate students; 277 full-time matriculated graduate/professional students (204 women), 259 part-time matriculated graduate/professional students (176 women). *Graduate faculty:* 54 full-time (31 women), 48 part-time/adjunct (26 women). *Computer facilities:* Computer purchase and lease plans are available. 475 computers available on campus for general student use. A campuswide network can be accessed from student residence rooms and from off campus. Internet access and online class registration are available. *Library facilities:* Feinberg Library. *Graduate expenses:* Tuition, state resident: full-time $6,900; part-time $288 per credit hour. Tuition, nonresident: full-time $10,920; part-time $455 per credit hour. *General application contact:* Richard Higgins, Director of Graduate Admissions, 518-564-2040.

Division of Education, Health, and Human Services

Dr. David Hill, Dean
Programs in:
adolescence education (MST)
biology 7-12 (MST)
birth to grade 2 (MS Ed)
birth-grade 6 (MS Ed)
chemistry 7-12 (MST)
childhood education (grades 1-6) (MST)
college/agency counseling (MS)
curriculum and instruction (MS Ed)
earth science 7-12 (MST)
education, health, and human services (MA, MS, MS Ed, MST, CAS)
educational leadership (CAS)
English 7-12 (MST)
French 7-12 (MST)
grades 1 to 6 (MS Ed)
grades 5-12 (MS Ed)
grades 7 to 12 (MS Ed)
mathematics 7-12 (MST)
physics 7-12 (MST)
school counselor (MS Ed, CAS)
social studies 7-12 (MST)
Spanish 7-12 (MST)
speech-language pathology (MA)

Faculty of Arts and Science

Dr. Kathleen Lavoie, Dean
Programs in:
arts and science (MA, CAS)
school psychology (MA, CAS)

■ STATE UNIVERSITY OF NEW YORK COLLEGE AT BROCKPORT

Brockport, NY 14420-2997
http://www.brockport.edu/

State-supported, coed, comprehensive institution. CGS member. *Enrollment:* 8,312 graduate, professional, and undergraduate students; 345 full-time matriculated graduate/professional students (243 women), 870 part-time matriculated graduate/professional students (554 women). *Graduate faculty:* 141 full-time (66 women), 53 part-time/adjunct (23 women). *Computer facilities:* 750 computers available on campus for general student use. A campuswide network can be accessed from student residence rooms and from off campus. Internet access and online class registration are available. *Library facilities:* Drake Memorial Library. *Graduate expenses:* Tuition, state resident: full-time $6,900; part-time $288 per credit. Tuition, nonresident: full-time $10,920; part-time $455 per credit. *General application contact:* Graduate Admissions Secretary, 585-395-5465.

Find University Details at www.petersons.com/gradchannel.

School of Arts and Performance

Dr. Francis X. Short, Dean
Programs in:
arts and performance (MA, MFA, MS Ed)
communication (MA)
dance (MA, MFA)
physical education and sport (MS Ed)
visual studies (MFA)

School of Letters and Sciences

Dr. Stuart Appelle, Graduate Admission Secretary
Programs in:
biological sciences (MS)
computational science (MS)
English (MA)
environmental science and biology (MS)
history (MA)
letters and sciences (MA, MS)
liberal studies (MA)
mathematics (MA)
psychology (MA)

School of Professions

Dr. Christine Murray, Dean
Programs in:
adolescence education (MS Ed)
bilingual education (MS Ed)
biology education (MS Ed)
chemistry education (MS Ed)
childhood curriculum specialist (MS Ed)
childhood literacy (MS Ed)
college counseling (MS Ed)
earth science education (MS Ed)
English education (MS Ed)
health science (MS Ed)
mathematics education (MS Ed)
mental health counseling (MS)
physics education (MS Ed)
public administration (MPA)
recreation and leisure studies (MS)
school administration and supervision (MS Ed, CAS)
school business administration (CAS)
school counseling (MS Ed, CAS)
school district administration (CAS)
social studies education (MS Ed)
social work (MSW)

■ STATE UNIVERSITY OF NEW YORK COLLEGE AT CORTLAND

Cortland, NY 13045
http://www.cortland.edu/

State-supported, coed, comprehensive institution. *Computer facilities:* 832 computers available on campus for general student use. A campuswide network can be accessed from student residence rooms and from off campus. *Library facilities:* Memorial Library. *General application contact:* Assistant Director of Graduate Studies, 607-753-4800.

Graduate Studies

School of Arts and Sciences
Programs in:
American civilization and culture (CAS)
arts and sciences (MA, MAT, MS Ed, CAS)
biology (MAT, MS Ed)
chemistry (MAT, MS Ed)
earth science (MAT, MS Ed)
English (MS Ed)
French (MS Ed)
history (MA, MS Ed)
mathematics (MAT, MS Ed)
physics (MAT, MS Ed)
second language education (MS Ed)
social studies (MS Ed)
Spanish (MS Ed)

School of Education
Programs in:
childhood/early child education (MS Ed, MST)
educational leadership (CAS)
literacy (MS Ed)
teaching students with disabilities (MS Ed)

School of Professional Studies
Programs in:
exercise science and sport studies (MS)
health education (MS Ed, MST)
international sport management (MS)
physical education (MS Ed)
professional studies (MS, MS Ed, MST)
recreation and leisure studies (MS, MS Ed)
sport management (MS)

■ STATE UNIVERSITY OF NEW YORK COLLEGE AT GENESEO

Geneseo, NY 14454-1401
http://www.geneseo.edu/

State-supported, coed, comprehensive institution. *Enrollment:* 5,530 graduate, professional, and undergraduate students; 78 full-time matriculated graduate/professional students (67 women), 94 part-time matriculated graduate/professional students (70 women). *Graduate faculty:* 25 full-time (11 women), 7 part-time/adjunct (5 women). *Computer facilities:* Computer purchase and lease plans are available. 900 computers available on campus for general student use. A campuswide network can be accessed from student residence rooms and from off campus. Internet access and online class registration are available. *Library facilities:* Milne Library. *General application contact:* Dr. Paul Schacht, Interim Dean of the College, 585-245-5546.

Graduate Studies
Dr. Susan Bailey, Dean of the College
Program in:
communicative disorders and sciences (MA)

School of Education
Dr. Osman Alawiye, Chairperson
Programs in:
early childhood education (MS Ed)
elementary education (MS Ed)
reading (MS Ed)
secondary education (MS Ed)

■ STATE UNIVERSITY OF NEW YORK COLLEGE AT ONEONTA

Oneonta, NY 13820-4015
http://www.oneonta.edu/

State-supported, coed, comprehensive institution. *Computer facilities:* Computer purchase and lease plans are available. 700 computers available on campus for general student use. A campuswide network can be accessed from student residence rooms and from off campus. Internet access and online class registration are available. *Library facilities:* Milne Library. *General application contact:* Dean, 607-436-2523.

Graduate Studies
Programs in:
biology (MA)
earth science (MA)
history museum studies (MA)

Division of Education
Programs in:
adolescence education (MS Ed)
childhood education (MS Ed)
educational psychology and counseling (MS Ed, CAS)
elementary and reading education (MS Ed)
family and consumer science education (MS Ed)
literacy education (MS Ed)
school counselor K-12 (MS Ed, CAS)

■ STATE UNIVERSITY OF NEW YORK COLLEGE AT POTSDAM

Potsdam, NY 13676
http://www.potsdam.edu/

State-supported, coed, comprehensive institution. *Enrollment:* 4,332 graduate, professional, and undergraduate students; 469 full-time matriculated graduate/professional students (351 women), 166 part-time matriculated graduate/professional students (126 women). *Graduate faculty:* 47 full-time (20 women), 21 part-time/adjunct (11 women). *Computer facilities:* Computer purchase and lease plans are available. 400 computers available on campus for general student use. A campuswide network can be accessed from student residence rooms and from off campus. Internet access and online class registration, online access to grades, financial aid status, and unofficial transcripts are available. *Library facilities:* F. W. Crumb Memorial Library plus 1 other. *General application contact:* Peter Cutler, Graduate Admissions Counselor, 315-267-3154.

Crane School of Music
Dr. Alan Solomon, Dean
Programs in:
composition (MM)
history and literature (MM)
music education (MM)
music theory (MM)
performance (MM)

School of Arts and Sciences
Dr. Galen K. Pletcher, Dean
Programs in:
arts and sciences (MA)
English (MA)
mathematics (MA)

School of Education
Dr. William Amoriell, Dean of Education and Graduate Studies
Programs in:
curriculum and instruction (MS Ed)
education (MS Ed, MST)
educational technology (MS Ed)
elementary education (MS Ed, MST)
literacy education (MS Ed)
secondary education (MS Ed, MST)
special education (MS Ed)

■ STATE UNIVERSITY OF NEW YORK COLLEGE OF ENVIRONMENTAL SCIENCE AND FORESTRY

Syracuse, NY 13210-2779
http://www.esf.edu/

State-supported, coed, university. *Enrollment:* 2,069 graduate, professional, and undergraduate students; 281 full-time matriculated graduate/professional students (151 women), 176 part-time matriculated graduate/professional students (77 women). *Graduate faculty:* 113 full-time (23 women), 23 part-time/adjunct (6 women). *Computer facilities:* 150 computers available on campus for general student use. A campuswide network can be accessed from student residence rooms and from off campus. Internet access and online class registration are available. *Library facilities:* F. Franklin Moon Library plus 1 other. *General application contact:* Dr. Dudley J. Raynal, Dean, Instruction and Graduate Studies, 315-470-6599.

Department of Construction Management and Wood Products Engineering
Dr. Susan E. Anagnost, Interim Chair
Program in:
environmental and resources engineering (MPS, MS, PhD)

Department of Paper and Bioprocess Engineering
Dr. Gary M. Scott, Chair
Program in:
environmental and resources engineering (MPS, MS, PhD)

Faculty of Chemistry
Dr. Arthur J. Stipanovic, Chair
Programs in:
biochemistry (MS, PhD)
environmental and forest chemistry (MS, PhD)
organic chemistry of natural products (MS, PhD)
polymer chemistry (MS, PhD)

Faculty of Environmental and Forest Biology
Dr. Donald J. Leopold, Chair

State University of New York College of Environmental Science and Forestry (continued)

Programs in:
- chemical ecology (MPS, MS, PhD)
- conservation biology (MPS, MS, PhD)
- ecology (MPS, MS, PhD)
- entomology (MPS, MS, PhD)
- environmental interpretation (MPS, MS, PhD)
- environmental physiology (MPS, MS, PhD)
- fish and wildlife biology (MPS, MS, PhD)
- forest pathology and mycology (MPS, MS, PhD)
- plant science and biotechnology (MPS, MS, PhD)

Faculty of Environmental Resources and Forest Engineering

Dr. James M. Hassett, Chair

Program in:
- environmental and resources engineering (MPS, MS, PhD)

Faculty of Environmental Studies

Chair

Programs in:
- environmental and community land planning (MPS, MS, PhD)
- environmental and natural resources policy (PhD)
- environmental communication and participatory processes (MPS, MS, PhD)
- environmental policy and democratic processes (MPS, MS, PhD)
- environmental systems and risk management (MPS, MS, PhD)
- water and wetland resource studies (MPS, MS, PhD)

Faculty of Forest and Natural Resources Management

Dr. David Newman, Chair

Programs in:
- environmental and natural resource policy (MS, PhD)
- environmental and natural resources policy (MPS)
- forest management and operations (MF)
- forestry ecosystems science and applications (MPS, MS, PhD)
- natural resources management (MPS, MS, PhD)
- quantitative methods and management in forest science (MPS, MS, PhD)
- recreation and resource management (MPS, MS, PhD)
- watershed management and forest hydrology (MPS, MS, PhD)

Faculty of Landscape Architecture

Richard S. Hawks, Chair

Programs in:
- community design and planning (MLA, MS)
- cultural landscape studies and conservation (MLA, MS)
- landscape and urban ecology (MLA, MS)

■ STATE UNIVERSITY OF NEW YORK EMPIRE STATE COLLEGE

Saratoga Springs, NY 12866-4391

http://www.esc.edu/

State-supported, coed, comprehensive institution. *Computer facilities:* 100 computers available on campus for general student use. A campuswide network can be accessed from off campus. Internet access and online class registration are available. *General application contact:* Assistant Director, 518-587-2100 Ext. 393.

Graduate Studies

Programs in:
- business administration (MBA)
- business and policy studies (MA)
- labor and policy studies (MA)
- liberal studies (MA)
- social policy (MA)
- teaching (MA)

■ STATE UNIVERSITY OF NEW YORK INSTITUTE OF TECHNOLOGY

Utica, NY 13504-3050

http://www.sunyit.edu/

State-supported, coed, comprehensive institution. *Enrollment:* 2,587 graduate, professional, and undergraduate students; 123 full-time matriculated graduate/professional students (59 women), 309 part-time matriculated graduate/professional students (145 women). *Graduate faculty:* 54 full-time (18 women), 16 part-time/adjunct (8 women). *Computer facilities:* 250 computers available on campus for general student use. A campuswide network can be accessed from student residence rooms and from off campus. Internet access and online class registration, various other software applications are available. *Library facilities:* Peter J. Cayan Library. *Graduate expenses:* Tuition, state resident: full-time $3,452; part-time $288 per credit hour. Tuition, nonresident: full-time $10,920; part-time $455 per credit hour. Required fees: $927; $38 per credit hour. *General application contact:* Marybeth Lyons, Director of Admissions, 315-792-7500.

Find University Details at www.petersons.com/gradchannel.

School of Arts and Sciences

Dr. Thomas McMillan, Dean

Programs in:
- applied sociology (MS)
- information design and technology (MS)

School of Business

Dr. Stephen Havlovic, Dean

Programs in:
- accountancy (MS)
- business administration in technology management (MBA)
- health services administration (MS)
- technology management (MBA)

School of Information Systems and Engineering Technology

Ray Jesaltis, Interim Dean

Programs in:
- advanced technology (MS)
- computer and information science (MS)
- telecommunications (MS)

School of Nursing and Health Systems

Dr. Esther Bankert, Dean

Programs in:
- adult nurse practitioner (MS, CAS)
- family nurse practitioner (MS, CAS)
- gerontological nurse practitioner (MS, CAS)
- nursing administration (MS, CAS)
- nursing education (MS, CAS)

■ STATE UNIVERSITY OF NEW YORK MARITIME COLLEGE

Throggs Neck, NY 10465-4198

http://www.sunymaritime.edu/

State-supported, coed, primarily men, comprehensive institution. *Computer facilities:* 110 computers available on campus for general student use. A campuswide network can be accessed from student residence rooms and from off campus. Internet access is available. *Library facilities:* Stephen Luce Library plus 1 other. *General application contact:* Director, 718-409-7285.

Program in International Transportation Management

Program in:
- international transportation management (MS)

■ STONY BROOK UNIVERSITY, STATE UNIVERSITY OF NEW YORK

Stony Brook, NY 11794

http://www.sunysb.edu/

State-supported, coed, university. CGS member. *Enrollment:* 22,522 graduate, professional, and undergraduate students; 4,413 full-time matriculated graduate/professional students (2,296 women), 2,216 part-time matriculated graduate/professional students (1,433 women). *Graduate faculty:* 1,254 full-time (394 women), 445 part-time/

adjunct (173 women). *Computer facilities:* 2,600 computers available on campus for general student use. A campuswide network can be accessed from student residence rooms and from off campus. Internet access and online class registration are available. *Library facilities:* Frank Melville, Jr. Building Library plus 6 others. *Graduate expenses:* Tuition, state resident: full-time $6,900; part-time $288 per credit. Tuition, nonresident: full-time $10,920; part-time $455 per credit. *General application contact:* Dr. Kent Marks, Director, Admissions and Records, 631-632-4723.

Find University Details at www.petersons.com/gradchannel.

Graduate School
Dr. Lawrence B. Martin, Dean

College of Arts and Sciences
Dr. James V. Staros, Dean
Programs in:
- anthropology (MA, PhD)
- art history and criticism (MA, PhD)
- arts and sciences (MA, MAPP, MAT, MFA, MM, MS, DA, DMA, PhD, Certificate)
- astronomy (MS, PhD)
- biochemistry and molecular biology (PhD)
- biochemistry and structural biology (PhD)
- biological and biomedical sciences (PhD)
- biological sciences (MA)
- biopsychology (PhD)
- cellular and developmental biology (PhD)
- chemistry (MAT, MS, PhD)
- clinical psychology (PhD)
- comparative literature (MA, PhD)
- composition studies (Certificate)
- dramaturgy (MFA)
- earth and space science (MS, PhD)
- earth and space sciences (MS, PhD)
- earth science (MAT)
- ecology and evolution (PhD)
- economics (MA, PhD)
- English (MA, MAT, PhD)
- ethnomusicology (MA, PhD)
- experimental psychology (PhD)
- foreign languages (DA)
- French (MA, MAT, DA)
- genetics (PhD)
- German (MA, MAT, DA)
- Germanic languages and literatures (MA)
- Hispanic languages and literature (MA, DA, PhD)
- history (MA, MAT, PhD)
- immunology and pathology (PhD)
- Italian (MA, MAT, DA)
- linguistics (MA, PhD)
- mathematics (MA, PhD)
- molecular and cellular biology (MA, PhD)
- music (MA, PhD)
- music history, theory and composition (MA, PhD)
- music performance (MM, DMA)
- neuroscience (PhD)
- philosophy (MA, PhD)
- physics (MA, MAT, MS, PhD)
- political science (MA, PhD)
- psychology (MA)
- public policy (MAPP)
- Romance languages and literatures (MA)
- Slavic languages and literatures (MA)
- social/health psychology (PhD)
- sociology (MA, PhD)
- studio art (MFA)
- teaching English to speakers of other languages (MA, DA)
- theatre (MA)

College of Business
William H. Turner, Interim Dean
Programs in:
- business (MBA, MS, Certificate)
- business administration (MBA)
- finance (Certificate)
- industrial management (Certificate)
- management policy (MS)
- technology management (MS)

College of Engineering and Applied Sciences
Dr. Yacov Shamash, Dean
Programs in:
- applied mathematics and statistics (MS, PhD)
- biomedical engineering (MS, PhD, Certificate)
- computer science (MS, PhD)
- educational technology (MS)
- electrical and computer engineering (MS, PhD)
- engineering and applied sciences (MS, PhD, Certificate)
- global operations management (MS)
- information systems (Certificate)
- information systems engineering (MS)
- materials science and engineering (MS, PhD)
- mechanical engineering (MS, PhD)
- medical physics (PhD)
- optoelectromechanical system engineering (MS)
- software engineering (Certificate)

Institute for Terrestrial and Planetary Atmospheres
Minghua Zhang, Director
Program in:
- terrestrial and planetary atmospheres (PhD)

Marine Sciences Research Center
Dr. David O. Conover, Dean and Director
Program in:
- marine and atmospheric sciences (MS, PhD)

School of Professional Development
Dr. Paul J. Edelson, Dean
Programs in:
- adolescence education: mathematics (Certificate)
- biology 7-12 (MAT)
- chemistry-grade 7-12 (MAT)
- coaching (Certificate)
- computer integrated engineering (Certificate)
- cultural studies (Certificate)
- earth science-grade 7-12 (MAT)
- educational computing (Advanced Certificate, Certificate)
- English-grade 7-12 (MAT)
- environmental and waste management (MS, Advanced Certificate)
- environmental systems management (Certificate)
- environmental/occupational health and safety (Certificate)
- French-grade 7-12 (MAT)
- German-grade 7-12 (MAT)
- human resource management (Certificate)
- industrial management (Certificate)
- information systems management (Certificate)
- Italian-grade 7-12 (MAT)
- liberal studies (MA)
- liberal studies online (MA)
- Long Island regional studies (Certificate)
- operation research (Certificate)
- physics-grade 7-12 (MAT)
- Russian-grade 7-12 (MAT)
- school administration and supervision (Certificate)
- school district administration (Certificate)
- social science and the professions (MPS)
- social studies 7-12 (MAT)
- waste management (Certificate)
- women's studies (Certificate)

■ SYRACUSE UNIVERSITY
Syracuse, NY 13244
http://www.syracuse.edu/

Independent, coed, university. CGS member. *Enrollment:* 17,492 graduate, professional, and undergraduate students; 3,229 full-time matriculated graduate/professional students (1,632 women), 1,564 part-time matriculated graduate/professional students (898 women). *Computer facilities:* Computer purchase and lease plans are available. 1,200 computers available on campus for general student use. A campuswide network can be accessed from student residence rooms and from off campus. Internet access and online class registration, online services, networked client and server computing are available. *Library facilities:* E. S. Bird Library plus 7 others. *Graduate expenses:* Tuition: full-time $16,920; part-time $940 per credit hour. Required fees: $930; $930 per year. *General application contact:* The Graduate Enrollment Management Center, 315-443-4492.

Syracuse University (continued)

College of Law

Program in:
law (JD)

Graduate School

Dr. Ben Ware, Dean
Program in:
disability studies (CAS)

College of Arts and Sciences

Dr. Cathryn Newton, Dean
Programs in:
applied statistics (MS)
art history (MA)
arts and sciences (MA, MFA, MS, Au D, PhD)
audiology (Au D, PhD)
biology (MS, PhD)
chemistry (MS, PhD)
clinical psychology (PhD)
college science teaching (PhD)
composition and cultural rhetoric (PhD)
creative writing (MFA)
English (MA, PhD)
experimental psychology (PhD)
French language, literature and culture (MA)
geology (MA, MS, PhD)
linguistic studies (MA)
mathematics (MS, PhD)
Pan-African studies (MA)
philosophy (MA, PhD)
physics (MS, PhD)
religion (MA, PhD)
school psychology (PhD)
social psychology (PhD)
Spanish language, literature and culture (MA)
speech language pathology (MS, PhD)
structural biology, biochemistry and biophysics (PhD)

College of Human Services and Health Professions

Dr. Diane Lyden Murphy, Dean
Programs in:
child and family studies (MA, MS, PhD)
human services and health professions (MA, MS, MSW, PhD)
marriage and family therapy (MA, PhD)
nutrition science and food management (MA, MS)
social work (MSW)

College of Visual and Performing Arts

Carole Brzozowski, Dean
Programs in:
art (MFA)
art photography (MFA)
art video (MFA)
arts education (MS)
ceramics (MFA)
communication and rhetorical studies (MA, MS)
computer art (MFA)
conducting (M Mu)
film (MFA)
metalsmithing (MFA)
museum studies (MA)
music composition (M Mus)
organ (M Mus)
painting (MFA)
percussion (M Mus)
piano (M Mus)
printmaking (MFA)
sculpture (MFA)
strings (M Mus)
transmedia (MFA)
visual and performing arts (M Mu, M Mus, MA, MFA, MS)
voice (M Mus)
wind instruments (M Mus)

L. C. Smith College of Engineering and Computer Science

Dr. Shiu-Kai Chen, Interim Dean
Programs in:
bioengineering (ME, MS, PhD)
chemical engineering (MS, PhD)
civil engineering (MS, PhD)
computer and information science and engineering (PhD)
computer engineering (MS, CE)
computer science (MS)
electrical and computer engineering (PhD)
electrical engineering (MS, EE)
engineering and computer science (ME, MS, PhD, CE, EE)
engineering management (MS)
environmental engineering (MS)
environmental engineering science (MS)
mechanical and aerospace engineering (MS, PhD)
neuroscience (MS)

Maxwell School of Citizenship and Public Affairs

Mitchel Wallerstein, Dean
Programs in:
anthropology (MA, PhD)
citizenship and public affairs (EMPA, MA, MPA, MS Sc, PhD, CAS)
economics (MA, PhD)
geography (MA, PhD)
health services management and policy (CAS)
history (MA, PhD)
international relations (MA)
political science (MA, PhD)
public administration (EMPA, MPA, PhD, CAS)
social sciences (MS Sc, PhD)
sociology (MA, PhD)

School of Architecture

Mark Robbins, Dean
Program in:
architecture (M Arch I, M Arch II)

School of Education

Dr. Douglas Biklen, Dean
Programs in:
art education (MS, CAS)
art education/professional certification (MS)
art education: preparation (MS)
childhood education: (1-6)
preparation (MS)
community counseling (MS)
counselor education (PhD)
cultural foundations of education (MS, PhD)
early childhood special education (MS)
education (M Mus, MS, Ed D, PhD, CAS)
educational leadership (MS, Ed D, CAS)
English education (PhD)
English education: preparation 7-12 (MS)
exercise science (MS)
higher education (MS, PhD)
inclusive special education (grades 1-6) (MS)
inclusive special education (grades 7-12) (MS)
instructional design, development, and evaluation (MS, PhD, CAS)
literacy education (MS)
literacy education: birth-grade 6 (MS)
literacy education: grades 5-12 (MS)
mathematics education (MS, PhD)
mathematics education: preparation 7-12 (MS)
music education (M Mus, MS)
music education/professional certification (M Mus, MS)
music education: teacher preparation (MS)
reading education (PhD)
rehabilitation and community counseling (MS)
rehabilitation counseling (MS)
school counseling (MS)
science education (MS, PhD)
science/biology education: preparation 7-12 (MS)
science/chemistry education: preparation 7-12 (MS)
science/earth science education: preparation 7-12 (MS)
science/physics education: preparation 7-12 (MS)
social studies education (MS, CAS)
social studies education: preparation 7-12 (MS)
special education (PhD)
teaching and curriculum (MS, PhD)

School of Information Studies

Dr. Raymond F. von Dran, Dean
Programs in:
digital libraries (CAS)
information management (MS)
information science and technology (PhD)
information security management (CAS)
information systems and telecommunications management (CAS)
library and information science (MS)
school library media (CAS)
school media (MS)
telecommunications and network management (MS)

S. I. Newhouse School of Public Communications
David M. Rubin, Dean
Programs in:
- advertising (MA)
- arts journalism (MA)
- broadcast journalism (MS)
- communications management (MS)
- documentary film and history (MA)
- magazine, newspaper and online journalism (MA)
- mass communications (PhD)
- media management (MS)
- media studies (MA)
- new media (MS)
- photography (MS)
- public communications (MA, MS, PhD)
- public relations (MS)

Martin J. Whitman School of Management
Dr. Melvin T. Stiten, Dean
Programs in:
- accounting (MBA, PhD)
- entrepreneurship (MBA)
- finance (MBA, PhD)
- management (MBA, MS Acct, MSF, PhD)
- management information systems (PhD)
- managerial statistics (PhD)
- marketing (MBA, PhD)
- operations management (PhD)
- organizational behavior (PhD)
- strategy and human resources (PhD)
- supply chain management (MBA, PhD)

■ TOURO COLLEGE
New York, NY 10010
http://www.touro.edu/

Independent, coed, comprehensive institution. *Computer facilities:* 350 computers available on campus for general student use. A campuswide network can be accessed from off campus. Internet access and online class registration are available. *Library facilities:* Touro College Library plus 14 others.

Barry Z. Levine School of Health Sciences
Programs in:
- biomedical sciences (MS)
- health information management (Certificate)
- occupational therapy (MS)
- physical therapy (MS)

Jacob D. Fuchsberg Law Center
Programs in:
- law (JD)
- U.S. law for foreign lawyers (LL M)

School of Jewish Studies
Program in:
- Jewish studies (MA)

■ UNIVERSITY AT ALBANY, STATE UNIVERSITY OF NEW YORK
Albany, NY 12222-0001
http://www.albany.edu/

State-supported, coed, university. CGS member. *Enrollment:* 17,434 graduate, professional, and undergraduate students; 2,336 full-time matriculated graduate/professional students (1,407 women), 2,129 part-time matriculated graduate/professional students (1,308 women). *Graduate faculty:* 635 full-time (222 women), 579 part-time/adjunct (275 women). *Computer facilities:* 500 computers available on campus for general student use. A campuswide network can be accessed from student residence rooms and from off campus. Internet access and online class registration are available. *Library facilities:* University Library plus 2 others. *Graduate expenses:* Tuition, state resident: full-time $6,900; part-time $288 per credit. Tuition, nonresident: full-time $10,920; part-time $455 per credit. Required fees: $1,139. *General application contact:* Michael DeRensis, Director, Graduate Admissions, 518-442-3980.

College of Arts and Sciences
Michael DeRensis, Director, Graduate Admissions
Programs in:
- African studies (MA)
- Afro-American studies (MA)
- anthropology (MA, PhD)
- art (MA, MFA)
- arts and sciences (MA, MFA, MRP, MS, DA, PhD, Certificate)
- atmospheric science (MS, PhD)
- autism (Certificate)
- biodiversity, conservation, and policy (MS)
- biopsychology (PhD)
- chemistry (MS, PhD)
- clinical psychology (PhD)
- communication (MA)
- demography (Certificate)
- ecology, evolution, and behavior (MS, PhD)
- economics (MA, PhD)
- English (MA, PhD)
- forensic molecular biology (MS)
- French (MA, PhD)
- general/experimental psychology (PhD)
- geographic information systems and spatial analysis (Certificate)
- geography (MA, Certificate)
- geology (MS, PhD)
- history (MA, PhD)
- industrial/organizational psychology (PhD)
- Italian (MA)
- Latin American, Caribbean, and US Latino studies (MA, Certificate)
- liberal studies (MA)
- mathematics (PhD)
- molecular, cellular, developmental, and neural biology (MS, PhD)
- philosophy (MA, PhD)
- physics (MS, PhD)
- psychology (MA)
- public history (Certificate)
- regional planning (MRP)
- regulatory economics (Certificate)
- Russian (MA, Certificate)
- Russian translation (Certificate)
- secondary teaching (MA)
- social/personality psychology (PhD)
- sociology (MA, PhD)
- sociology and communication (PhD)
- Spanish (MA, PhD)
- statistics (MA)
- theatre (MA)
- urban policy (Certificate)
- women's studies (MA, DA)

College of Computing and Information
Peter Bloniarz, Dean
Programs in:
- computer science (MS, PhD)
- information science (MS, PhD)
- information science and policy (CAS)
- library science (MLS)

College of Nanoscale Science and Engineering
Alain Kaloyeros, Dean
Program in:
- nanoscale science and engineering (MS, PhD)

Nelson A. Rockefeller College of Public Affairs and Policy
Dr. Jeffrey J. Straussman, Dean
Programs in:
- administrative behavior (PhD)
- comparative and development administration (MPA, PhD)
- human resources (MPA)
- legislative administration (MPA)
- nonprofit leadership and management (Certificate)
- planning and policy analysis (CAS)
- policy analysis (MPA)
- political science (MA, PhD)
- program analysis and evaluation (PhD)
- public affairs and policy (MA)
- public finance (MPA, PhD)
- public management (MPA, PhD)
- women and public policy (Certificate)

School of Business
Paul Leonard, Dean
Programs in:
- accounting (MS)
- business (MBA, MS)
- finance (MBA)
- human resource systems (MBA)
- information technology management (MBA)
- marketing (MBA)
- taxation (MS)

School of Criminal Justice
Julie Horney, Dean

University at Albany, State University of New York (continued)
Program in:
criminal justice (MA, PhD)

School of Education
Susanne K. Phillips, Dean
Programs in:
counseling psychology (MS, PhD, CAS)
curriculum and instruction (MS, Ed D, CAS)
curriculum planning and development (MA)
education (MA, MS, Ed D, PhD, Psy D, CAS)
educational administration (MS, PhD, CAS)
educational communications (MS, CAS)
educational psychology (Ed D)
educational psychology and statistics (MS)
measurements and evaluation (Ed D)
reading (MS, Ed D, CAS)
rehabilitation counseling (MS)
school counselor (CAS)
school psychology (Psy D, CAS)
special education (MS)
statistics and research design (Ed D)

School of Public Health
Dr. Mary Applegate, Dean
Programs in:
biochemistry, molecular biology, and genetics (MS, PhD)
cell and molecular structure (MS, PhD)
environmental and analytical chemistry (MS, PhD)
environmental and occupational health (MS, PhD)
epidemiology and biostatistics (MS, PhD)
health policy, management, and behavior (MS)
immunobiology and immunochemistry (MS, PhD)
molecular pathogenesis (MS, PhD)
neuroscience (MS, PhD)
public health (MPH, MS, Dr PH, PhD, Certificate)
toxicology (MS, PhD)

School of Social Welfare
Katharine Briar-Lawson, Dean
Program in:
social welfare (MSW, PhD)

■ UNIVERSITY AT BUFFALO, THE STATE UNIVERSITY OF NEW YORK
Buffalo, NY 14260
http://www.buffalo.edu/

State-supported, coed, university. CGS member. *Enrollment:* 27,220 graduate, professional, and undergraduate students; 6,969 full-time matriculated graduate/professional students (3,554 women), 2,036 part-time matriculated graduate/professional students (1,154 women). *Graduate faculty:* 1,277 full-time (418 women), 1,122 part-time/adjunct (417 women). *Computer facilities:* 2,391 computers available on campus for general student use. A campuswide network can be accessed from student residence rooms and from off campus. Internet access and online class registration are available. *Library facilities:* Lockwood Library plus 7 others. *General application contact:* Christopher S. Connor, Director of Graduate Student Recruitment Services, 716-645-6968.

Find University Details at www.petersons.com/gradchannel.

Graduate School
Dr. Myron A. Thompson, Associate Provost and Executive Director of the Graduate School
Programs in:
cancer pathology and prevention (PhD)
cancer research and biomedical sciences (MS, PhD)
cellular and molecular biology (PhD)
immunology (PhD)
molecular and cellular biophysics and biochemistry (PhD)
molecular pharmacology and cancer therapeutics (PhD)
natural and biomedical sciences (MS)

College of Arts and Sciences
Dr. Bruce D. Mc Combe, Dean
Programs in:
American studies (MA, PhD)
anthropology (MA, PhD)
art (MFA)
art history (MA, Certificate)
arts and sciences (MA, MFA, MM, MS, Au D, PhD, Certificate)
audiology (Au D)
behavioral neuroscience (PhD)
biological sciences (MA, MS, PhD)
chemistry (MA, PhD)
classics (MA, PhD)
clinical psychology (PhD)
cognitive psychology (PhD)
communication (MA, PhD)
communicative disorders and sciences (MA, PhD)
comparative literature (MA, PhD)
critical museum studies (Certificate)
economics (MA, MS, PhD)
English (MA, PhD)
evolution, ecology and behavior (MS, PhD, Certificate)
financial economics (Certificate)
fine arts (MFA)
French (MA, PhD)
general psychology (MA)
geographic information science (Certificate)
geography (MA, MS, PhD)
geology (MA, MS, PhD)
health services (Certificate)
historical musicology and music theory (PhD)
history (MA, PhD)
humanities (film studies concentration) (MA)
information and Internet economics (Certificate)
international economics (Certificate)
law and regulation (Certificate)
linguistics (MA, PhD)
mathematics (MA, PhD)
media arts production (MFA)
medicinal chemistry (MS, PhD)
music composition (MA, PhD)
music history (MA)
music performance (MM)
music theory (MA)
new media design (Certificate)
philosophy (MA, PhD)
physics (MS, PhD)
political science (MA, PhD)
social-personality psychology (PhD)
sociology (MA, PhD)
Spanish (MA, PhD)
transportation and business geographics (Certificate)
urban and regional economics (Certificate)

Graduate School of Education
Dr. Mary H. Gresham, Dean
Programs in:
adolescence education (Certificate)
biology (Ed M)
chemistry (Ed M)
childhood education (Ed M)
counseling/school psychology (PhD)
counselor education (PhD)
early childhood and childhood education with bilingual extension (Ed M)
early childhood education (Ed M)
earth science (Ed M)
education (Ed M, MA, MLS, MS, Ed D, PhD, Certificate)
educational administration (Ed M, Ed D, PhD)
educational psychology (MA, PhD)
elementary education (Ed D, PhD)
English (Ed M)
English education (PhD)
English for speakers of other languages (Ed M)
foreign and second language education (PhD)
French (Ed M)
general education (Ed M)
German (Ed M)
higher education (PhD)
higher education administration (Ed M)
Italian (Ed M)
Japanese (Ed M)
Latin (Ed M)
library and information studies (MLS, Certificate)
literary specialist (Ed M)
mathematics (Ed M)
mathematics education (PhD)
mental health counseling (MS)
mentoring teachers (Certificate)
music education (Ed M, Certificate)
physics (Ed M)

reading education (PhD)
rehabilitation counseling (MS)
Russian (Ed M)
school administrator and supervisor (Certificate)
school business and human resource administration (Certificate)
school counseling (Ed M, Certificate)
school psychology (MA)
science education (PhD)
social foundations (PhD)
social studies (Ed M)
Spanish (Ed M)
special education (PhD)
specialist in education administration (Certificate)
teaching and leading for diversity (Certificate)
teaching English to speakers of other languages (Ed M)

Law School
R. Nils Olsen, Dean
Programs in:
criminal law (LL M)
general law for international students (LL M)
law (JD)

School of Architecture and Planning
Brian Carter, Dean
Programs in:
architecture (M Arch)
architecture and planning (M Arch, MUP)
planning (MUP)

School of Dental Medicine
Dr. Richard N. Buchanan, Dean
Programs in:
advanced education in general dentistry (Certificate)
biomaterials (MS)
combined prosthodontics (Certificate)
dental medicine (DDS, MS, PhD, Certificate)
endodontics (Certificate)
general practice residency (Certificate)
oral and maxillofacial pathology (Certificate)
oral and maxillofacial surgery (Certificate)
oral biology (PhD)
oral diagnostic sciences (MS)
oral sciences (MS)
orthodontics (MS, Certificate)
pediatric dentistry (Certificate)
periodontics (Certificate)
temporomandibular disorders and oralfacial pain (Certificate)

School of Engineering and Applied Sciences
Dr. Harvey G. Stenger, Dean
Programs in:
aerospace engineering (MS, PhD)
chemical and biological engineering (M Eng, MS, PhD)
civil engineering (M Eng, MS, PhD)
computer science and engineering (MS, PhD)
electrical engineering (M Eng, MS, PhD)
engineering and applied sciences (M Eng, MS, PhD)
engineering science (MS)
industrial and systems engineering (M Eng, MS, PhD)
mechanical engineering (MS, PhD)

School of Management
John M. Thomas, Dean
Programs in:
accounting (MS)
business administration (MBA)
finance (MS)
information assurance (Certificate)
management (PhD)
management information systems (MS)
supply chains and operations management (MS)

School of Medicine and Biomedical Sciences
Dr. Michael E. Cain, Dean of Medicine
Programs in:
anatomical sciences (MA, PhD)
biochemical pharmacology (MS)
biochemistry (MA, PhD)
biomedical sciences (PhD)
biophysics (MS, PhD)
biotechnology (MS)
medicine (MD)
medicine and biomedical sciences (MD, MA, MS, PhD)
microbiology and immunology (MA, PhD)
neuroscience (MS, PhD)
pathology (MA, PhD)
pharmacology (MA, PhD)
physiology (MA, PhD)
structural biology (MS, PhD)

School of Nursing
Dr. Jean K. Brown, Dean, Interim
Programs in:
acute care nurse practitioner (MS, Certificate)
adult health nursing (MS, Certificate)
child health nursing (MS)
family nurse practitioner (Certificate)
family nursing (MS)
geriatric nurse practitioner (MS, Certificate)
maternal and women's health nurse practitioner (Certificate)
maternal and women's health nursing (MS)
nurse anesthetist (MS)
nursing (PhD)
nursing education (Certificate)
pediatric nurse practitioner (Certificate)
psychiatric/mental health nurse practitioner (Certificate)
psychiatric/mental health nursing (MS)

School of Pharmacy and Pharmaceutical Sciences
Dr. Wayne K. Anderson, Dean
Programs in:
pharmaceutical sciences (MS, PhD)
pharmacy (Pharm D)
pharmacy and pharmaceutical sciences (Pharm D, MS, PhD)

School of Public Health and Health Professions
Dr. Maurizio Trevisan, Dean
Programs in:
assistive and rehabilitation technology (Certificate)
biostatistics (MA, PhD)
community health (PhD)
epidemiology (MS, PhD)
exercise science (MS, PhD)
nutrition (MS)
occupational therapy (MS)
physical therapy (DPT)
public health (MPH)
public health and health professions (MA, MPH, MS, DPT, PhD, Certificate)

School of Social Work
Dr. Nancy J. Smyth, Dean
Program in:
social work (MSW, PhD)

■ UNIVERSITY OF ROCHESTER

Rochester, NY 14627-0250

http://www.rochester.edu/

Independent, coed, university. CGS member. *Computer facilities:* 260 computers available on campus for general student use. A campuswide network can be accessed from student residence rooms and from off campus. *Library facilities:* Rush Rhees Library plus 5 others. *General application contact:* Dean of Graduate Studies, 585-275-3540.

The College, Arts and Sciences
Programs in:
arts and sciences (MA, MS, PhD)
biology (MS, PhD)
brain and cognitive sciences (MS, PhD)
chemistry (MS, PhD)
clinical psychology (PhD)
computer science (MS, PhD)
developmental psychology (PhD)
economics (MA, PhD)
English (MA, PhD)
geological sciences (MS, PhD)
history (MA, PhD)
mathematics (MA, MS, PhD)
philosophy (MA, PhD)
physics (MA, MS, PhD)
physics and astronomy (PhD)
political science (MA, PhD)
psychology (MA)
social-personality psychology (PhD)
visual and cultural studies (MA, PhD)

University of Rochester (continued)

The College, School of Engineering and Applied Sciences

Programs in:
- biomedical engineering (MS, PhD)
- chemical engineering (MS, PhD)
- electrical and computer engineering (MS, PhD)
- engineering and applied sciences (MS, PhD)
- materials science (MS, PhD)
- mechanical engineering (MS, PhD)

Institute of Optics

Program in:
- optics (MS, PhD)

Eastman School of Music

Programs in:
- composition (MA, MM, DMA, PhD)
- conducting (MM, DMA)
- education (MA, PhD)
- jazz studies/contemporary media (MM)
- music education (MM, DMA)
- musicology (MA, PhD)
- pedagogy of music theory (MA)
- performance and literature (MM, DMA)
- piano accompanying and chamber music (MM, DMA)
- theory (MA, PhD)

Margaret Warner Graduate School of Education and Human Development

Program in:
- education and human development (MAT, MS, Ed D, PhD)

School of Medicine and Dentistry

Programs in:
- medicine (MD)
- medicine and dentistry (MD, MA, MPH, MS, PhD, Certificate)

Graduate Programs in Medicine and Dentistry

Programs in:
- biochemistry (MS, PhD)
- biomedical genetics (MS, PhD)
- biophysics (MS, PhD)
- epidemiology (MS, PhD)
- health services research and policy (PhD)
- marriage and family therapy (MS)
- medical statistics (MS)
- medicine and dentistry (MA, MPH, MS, PhD)
- microbiology (MS, PhD)
- neurobiology and anatomy (MS, PhD)
- neuroscience (MS, PhD)
- oral biology (MS)
- pathology (MS, PhD)
- pharmacology (MS, PhD)
- physiology (MS, PhD)
- public health (MPH)
- statistics (MA, PhD)
- toxicology (MS, PhD)

School of Nursing

Dr. Patricia Chiverton, Dean

Program in:
- nursing (MS, PhD, Certificate)

William E. Simon Graduate School of Business Administration

Program in:
- business administration (MBA, MS, PhD)

■ UTICA COLLEGE
Utica, NY 13502-4892
http://www.utica.edu/

Independent, coed, comprehensive institution. *Enrollment:* 2,952 graduate, professional, and undergraduate students; 117 full-time matriculated graduate/professional students (87 women), 376 part-time matriculated graduate/professional students (240 women). *Graduate faculty:* 65 full-time (28 women). *Computer facilities:* 140 computers available on campus for general student use. A campuswide network can be accessed from student residence rooms. Internet access is available. *Library facilities:* Frank E. Gannett Memorial Library. *Graduate expenses:* Tuition: full-time $20,480; part-time $550 per credit hour. Required fees: $310; $50 per term. Tuition and fees vary according to course load, degree level and program. *General application contact:* John D. Rowe, Director of Graduate Admissions, 315-792-3824.

Department of Physical Therapy

Dr. Dale Scalise-Smith, Director of Physical Therapy

Program in:
- physical therapy (DPT, TDPT)

Program in Economic Crime Management

Dr. R. Bruce McBride, Director of Economic Crime Graduate Programs

Program in:
- economic crime management (MS)

■ WAGNER COLLEGE
Staten Island, NY 10301-4495
http://www.wagner.edu/

Independent, coed, comprehensive institution. *Enrollment:* 2,280 graduate, professional, and undergraduate students; 210 full-time matriculated graduate/professional students (124 women), 129 part-time matriculated graduate/professional students (99 women). *Graduate faculty:* 24 full-time (13 women), 37 part-time/adjunct (23 women). *Computer facilities:* 150 computers available on campus for general student use. A campuswide network can be accessed from student residence rooms and from off campus. Internet access is available. *Library facilities:* August Horrmann Library. *Graduate expenses:* Tuition: full-time $15,120; part-time $840 per credit. *General application contact:* Susan Rosenberg, Office of Graduate Studies, 718-390-3106.

Division of Graduate Studies

Dr. Jeffrey Kraus, Coordinator of Graduate Studies

Programs in:
- accelerated MBA (MBA)
- accounting (MS)
- adolescent education (MS Ed)
- advanced physician assistant studies (MS)
- childhood education (MS Ed)
- early childhood education (birth-grade 2) (MS Ed)
- educational leadership (Certificate)
- family nurse practitioner (Certificate)
- finance (MBA)
- health care administration (MBA)
- international business (MBA)
- literacy (B-6) (MS Ed)
- management (Exec MBA, MBA)
- marketing (MBA)
- microbiology (MS)
- middle level education (5-9) (MS Ed)
- nursing (MS)
- school building leader (Certificate)
- school district leader (Certificate)

■ YESHIVA UNIVERSITY
New York, NY 10033-3201
http://www.yu.edu/

Independent, coed, university. CGS member. *Computer facilities:* 142 computers available on campus for general student use. Internet access is available. *Library facilities:* Mendel Gottesman Library plus 6 others. *General application contact:* Associate Director of Admissions, 212-960-5277.

Azrieli Graduate School of Jewish Education and Administration

Program in:
- Jewish education and administration (MS, Ed D, Specialist)

Benjamin N. Cardozo School of Law

David G. Martinidez, Dean of Admissions

Programs in:
- comparative legal thought (LL M)
- general studies (LL M)
- intellectual property law (LL M)
- law (JD)

Bernard Revel Graduate School of Jewish Studies

Program in:
- Jewish studies (MA, PhD)

Ferkauf Graduate School of Psychology

Dr. Lawrence J. Siegel, Dean

Programs in:
clinical psychology (Psy D)
health psychology (PhD)
mental health counseling psychology (MA)
psychology (MA, PhD, Psy D)
school/clinical-child psychology (Psy D)

Wurzweiler School of Social Work
Dr. Sheldon R. Gelman, Dean
Program in:
social work (MSW, PhD)

North Carolina

■ APPALACHIAN STATE UNIVERSITY

Boone, NC 28608
http://www.appstate.edu/

State-supported, coed, comprehensive institution. CGS member. *Enrollment:* 15,117 graduate, professional, and undergraduate students; 685 full-time matriculated graduate/professional students (440 women), 1,058 part-time matriculated graduate/professional students (740 women). *Graduate faculty:* 530 full-time (213 women), 30 part-time/adjunct (15 women). *Computer facilities:* Computer purchase and lease plans are available. 500 computers available on campus for general student use. A campuswide network can be accessed from student residence rooms and from off campus. Internet access is available. *Library facilities:* Carol Grotnes Belk Library plus 1 other. *Graduate expenses:* Tuition, state resident: full-time $2,600; part-time $127 per hour. Tuition, nonresident: full-time $13,200; part-time $597 per hour. Required fees: $2,000; $546 per term. *General application contact:* Dr. Holly Hirst, Associate Dean for Graduate Studies, 828-262-2130.

Cratis D. Williams Graduate School
Dr. E. D. Huntley, Dean of Graduate Studies and Research

College of Arts and Sciences
Dr. Robert Lyman, Dean
Programs in:
Appalachian studies (MA)
applied physics (MS)
arts and sciences (MA, MPA, MS, MSW, SSP)
biology (MS)
clinical health psychology (MA)
computer science (MS)
criminal justice (MS)
English (MA)
English education (MA)
general experimental psychology (MA)
geography (MA)
gerontology (MA)
history (MA)
history education (MA)
industrial and organizational psychology (MA)
mathematics (MA)
mathematics education (MA)
political science (MA)
political science and criminal justice (MA, MS)
public administration (MPA)
public history (MA)
romance languages-French (MA)
romance languages-Spanish (MA)
school psychology (MA, SSP)
social work (MSW)

College of Education
Dr. Charles Duke, Dean
Programs in:
communication disorders (MA)
community counseling (MA)
curriculum specialist (MA)
education (MA, MLS, MSA, Ed D, Ed S)
educational administration (Ed S)
educational leadership (Ed D)
educational media (MA)
elementary education (MA)
higher education (MA, Ed S)
library science (MLS)
marriage and family therapy (MA)
reading education (MA)
school administration (MSA, Ed S)
school counseling (MA)
secondary education (MA)
special education (MA)
student development (MA)

College of Fine and Applied Arts
Dr. Mark Estepp, Dean
Programs in:
child development (MA)
exercise science (MS)
family and consumer science (MA)
family and consumer science education (MA)
fine and applied arts (MA, MS)
industrial technology (MA)
technology education (MA)

John A. Walker College of Business
Dr. Randy Edwards, Dean
Programs in:
accounting (MS)
business (MBA, MS)
business administration (MBA)

School of Music
Dr. William Harbinson, Dean
Programs in:
music performance (MM)
music therapy (MMT)

■ CAMPBELL UNIVERSITY

Buies Creek, NC 27506
http://www.campbell.edu/

Independent-religious, coed, university. *Enrollment:* 6,033 graduate, professional, and undergraduate students; 1,002 full-time matriculated graduate/professional students (559 women), 606 part-time matriculated graduate/professional students (376 women). *Graduate faculty:* 99 full-time (32 women), 51 part-time/adjunct (14 women). *Computer facilities:* 256 computers available on campus for general student use. A campuswide network can be accessed from student residence rooms and from off campus. Internet access is available. *Library facilities:* Carrie Rich Memorial Library plus 2 others. *Graduate expenses:* Tuition: part-time $380 per semester hour. *General application contact:* James S. Farthing, Director of Graduate Admissions for Business and Education, 910-893-1200 Ext. 1318.

Graduate and Professional Programs
Dr. M. Dwaine Greene, Vice President for Academic Affairs and Provost

Divinity School
Dr. Michael Glenn Cogdill, Dean
Programs in:
Christian education (MA)
divinity (M Div)
ministry (D Min)

Lundy-Fetterman School of Business
Dr. Ben Hawkins, Dean
Program in:
business (MBA, MTIM)

Norman Adrian Wiggins School of Law
Melissa A. Essary, Dean
Program in:
law (JD)

School of Education
Dr. Karen P. Nery, Dean
Programs in:
administration (MSA)
community counseling (MA)
elementary education (M Ed)
English education (M Ed)
interdisciplinary studies (M Ed)
mathematics education (M Ed)
middle grades education (M Ed)
physical education (M Ed)
school counseling (M Ed)
secondary education (M Ed)
social science education (M Ed)

School of Pharmacy
Dr. Ronald W. Maddox, Dean
Programs in:
clinical research (MS)
pharmaceutical science (MS)
pharmacy (Pharm D)

■ DUKE UNIVERSITY

Durham, NC 27708-0586
http://www.duke.edu/

Independent-religious, coed, university. CGS member. *Enrollment:* 13,373 graduate, professional, and undergraduate students; 6,365 full-time matriculated graduate/

Duke University (continued)
professional students (2,900 women), 273 part-time matriculated graduate/professional students (208 women). *Graduate faculty:* 2,342. *Computer facilities:* Computer purchase and lease plans are available. 600 computers available on campus for general student use. A campuswide network can be accessed from student residence rooms and from off campus. Internet access and online class registration are available. *Library facilities:* Perkins Library plus 14 others. *General application contact:* Bertie S. Belvin, Associate Dean for Academic Services, 919-684-3913.

Divinity School
Program in:
theology (M Div, MCM, MTS, Th M)

Fuqua School of Business
Blair H. Sheppard, Dean
Programs in:
business (EMBA, GEMBA, MBA, MMS, WEMBA, PhD, Certificate)
cross continent executive business administration (EMBA)
EMBA held with Frankford University (EMBA)
global executive business administration (GEMBA)
health sector management (Certificate)
weekend executive business administration (WEMBA)

Graduate School
Jo Rae Wright, Dean
Programs in:
art and art history (PhD)
biological and biologically inspired materials (PhD, Certificate)
biological chemistry (PhD, Certificate)
biological psychology (PhD)
biology (PhD)
business administration (PhD)
cell biology (PhD)
cellular and molecular biology (PhD)
chemistry (PhD)
classical studies (PhD)
clinical psychology (PhD)
cognitive neuroscience (PhD, Certificate)
cognitive psychology (PhD)
computational biology and bioinformatics (PhD)
computer science (MS, PhD)
crystallography of macromolecules (PhD)
developmental biology (PhD, Certificate)
developmental psychology (PhD)
East Asian studies (AM, Certificate)
ecology (PhD, Certificate)
economics (AM, PhD)
English (PhD)
enzyme mechanisms (PhD)
experimental psychology (PhD)
French (PhD)
genetics and genomics (PhD)
German studies (PhD)
gross anatomy and physical anthropology (PhD)
health psychology (PhD)
history (AM, PhD)
human social development (PhD)
humanities (AM)
immunology (PhD)
integrated toxicology and environmental health (PhD, Certificate)
Latin American studies (PhD)
liberal studies (AM)
lipid biochemistry (PhD)
literature (PhD)
mathematics (PhD)
medical physics (MS, PhD)
medieval and Renaissance studies (Certificate)
membrane structure and function (PhD)
molecular cancer biology (PhD)
molecular genetics (PhD)
molecular genetics and microbiology (PhD)
music composition (AM, PhD)
musicology (AM, PhD)
natural resource economics/policy (AM, PhD)
natural resource science/ecology (AM, PhD)
natural resource systems science (AM, PhD)
neuroanatomy (PhD)
neurobiology (PhD)
neurochemistry (PhD)
nucleic acid structure and function (PhD)
pathology (PhD)
performance practice (AM, PhD)
pharmacology (PhD)
philosophy (AM, PhD)
physical anthropology (PhD)
physics (PhD)
political science (AM, PhD)
protein structure and function (PhD)
religion (MA, PhD)
Slavic languages and literatures (AM)
social/cultural anthropology (PhD)
sociology (AM, PhD)
Spanish (PhD)
structural biology and biophysics (Certificate)
teaching (MAT)
women's studies (Certificate)

Center for Demographic Studies
Dr. Kenneth C. Land, Director
Program in:
demographic studies (PhD)

Division of Earth and Ocean Sciences
Alan Boudreau, Director of Graduate Studies
Program in:
earth and ocean sciences (MS, PhD)

Institute of Statistics and Decision Sciences
Alan Gelfand, Director of Graduate Studies
Program in:
statistics and decision sciences (PhD)

Pratt School of Engineering
Dr. Kristina M. Johnson, Dean
Programs in:
biomedical engineering (MS, PhD)
civil and environmental engineering (MS, PhD)
electrical and computer engineering (MS, PhD)
engineering (MEM, MS, PhD)
engineering management (MEM)
environmental engineering (MS, PhD)
materials science (MS, PhD)
mechanical engineering (MS, PhD)

Terry Sanford Institute of Public Policy
Fritz Mayer, Director
Programs in:
international development policy (AM, Certificate)
public policy (AM, MPP, PhD, Certificate)

Nicholas School of the Environment and Earth Sciences
Dr. William Schlesinger, Dean
Programs in:
coastal environmental management (MEM)
DEL-environmental leadership (MEM)
energy and environment (MEM)
environmental economics and policy (MEM)
environmental health and security (MEM)
forest resource management (MF)
global environmental change (MEM)
resource ecology (MEM)
water and air resources (MEM)

School of Law
William J. Hoye, Associate Dean, Admissions and Financial Aid
Program in:
law (JD, LL M, MLS, SJD)

School of Medicine
Dr. Edward Buckley, Vice Dean of Medical Education
Programs in:
clinical leadership program (MHS)
clinical research (MHS)
medicine (MD, MHS, DPT)
pathologists' assistant (MHS)
physician assistant (MHS)

Physical Therapy Division
Dr. Jan K. Richardson, Professor of the Practice/Division Chief
Program in:
physical therapy (DPT)

School of Nursing
Dr. Catherine L. Gilliss, Dean/Vice Chancellor for Nursing Affairs
Programs in:
adult acute care (Certificate)

adult cardiovascular (Certificate)
adult oncology/HIV (Certificate)
adult primary care (Certificate)
clinical nurse specialist (MSN)
clinical research management (MSN, Certificate)
family (Certificate)
gerontology (Certificate)
health and nursing ministries (MSN, Certificate)
health systems leadership and outcomes (Certificate)
leadership in community based long term care (MSN, Certificate)
neonatal (Certificate)
neonatal/pediatric in rural health (MSN, Certificate)
nurse anesthetist (MSN, Certificate)
nurse practitioner (MSN)
nursing (PhD)
nursing and healthcare leadership (MSN)
nursing education (MSN)
nursing informatics (MSN, Certificate)
pediatric (Certificate)
pediatric acute care (Certificate)

■ EAST CAROLINA UNIVERSITY
Greenville, NC 27858-4353
http://www.ecu.edu/

State-supported, coed, university. CGS member. *Enrollment:* 24,351 graduate, professional, and undergraduate students; 2,058 full-time matriculated graduate/professional students (1,332 women), 2,347 part-time matriculated graduate/professional students (1,655 women). *Graduate faculty:* 586 full-time (201 women), 67 part-time/adjunct (34 women). *Computer facilities:* Computer purchase and lease plans are available. 1,692 computers available on campus for general student use. A campuswide network can be accessed from student residence rooms and from off campus. Internet access and online class registration are available. *Library facilities:* J. Y. Joyner Library plus 1 other. *General application contact:* Dr. Patrick Pellicane, Dean of Graduate School, 252-328-6012.

Find University Details at www.petersons.com/gradchannel.

Brody School of Medicine
Dr. Phyllis Horns, Interim Dean
Programs in:
anatomy and cell biology (PhD)
biochemistry and molecular biology (PhD)
medicine (MD, MPH, PhD)
microbiology and immunology (PhD)
Pathology (PhD)
pharmacology (PhD)
physiology (PhD)
public health (MPH)

Graduate School
Dr. Patrick Pellicane, Dean of Graduate School
Program in:
coastal resources management (PhD)

College of Business
Dr. Frederick D. Niswander, Dean
Programs in:
accounting (MS)
business (MBA, MS, MSA)
management (MBA)

College of Education
Dr. John Swope, Interim Dean
Programs in:
adult education (MA Ed)
behavior/emotional disabilities (MA Ed)
counselor education (MS, Ed S)
education (MA, MA Ed, MLS, MS, MSA, Ed D, CAS, Ed S)
educational administration and supervision (Ed S)
educational leadership (Ed D)
elementary education (MA Ed)
English education (MA Ed)
higher education administration (Ed D)
information technologies (MS)
instruction technology specialist (MA Ed)
learning disabilities (MA Ed)
library science (MLS, CAS)
low incidence disabilities (MA Ed)
mathematics (MA Ed)
mental retardation (MA Ed)
middle grade education (MA Ed)
reading education (MA Ed)
school administration (MSA)
science education (MA, MA Ed)
social studies education (MA Ed)
supervision (MA Ed)
vocation education (MA Ed)

College of Fine Arts and Communication
Jeffery Elwell, Dean
Programs in:
art and design (MA, MA Ed, MFA)
fine arts and communication (MA, MA Ed, MFA, MM)
health communication (MA)
music education (MM)
music therapy (MM)
performance (MM)
theory and composition (MM)

College of Health and Human Performance
Dr. Glen Gilbert, Dean
Programs in:
bioenergetics (PhD)
environmental health (MS)
exercise and sport science (MA, MA Ed)
health and human performance (MA, MA Ed, MS, PhD)
health education (MA, MA Ed)
recreation and leisure services administration (MS)
therapeutic recreation administration (MS)

College of Human Ecology
Dr. Karla Hughes, Dean
Programs in:
child development and family relations (MS)
criminal justice (MS)
human ecology (MS, MSW)
marriage and family therapy (MS)
nutrition (MS)
social work (MSW)

College of Technology and Computer Science
Dr. Ralph Rogers, Dean
Programs in:
computer network professional (Certificate)
computer science (MS)
industrial technology (MS)
information assurance (Certificate)
occupational safety (MS)
technology and computer science (MS, PhD, Certificate)
technology management (PhD)
Website developer (Certificate)

School of Allied Health Sciences
Dr. Stephen Thomas, Dean
Programs in:
allied health sciences (MPT, MS, MSOT, DPT, PhD)
communication sciences and disorders (PhD)
occupational therapy (MSOT)
physical therapy (MPT, DPT)
physician assistant studies (MS)
rehabilitation counseling (MS)
speech, language and auditory pathology (MS)
substance abuse and clinical counseling (MS)
vocational evaluation (MS)

School of Nursing
Dr. Sylvia Brown, Interim Dean
Program in:
nursing (MSN, PhD)

Thomas Harriot College of Arts and Sciences
Dr. Alan White, Dean
Programs in:
American history (MA)
anthropology (MA)
applied and biomedical physics (MS)
applied mathematics (MA)
applied resource economics (MS)
arts and sciences (MA, MA Ed, MPA, MS, PhD)
biology (MS)
chemistry (MS)
clinical psychology (MA)
English (MA)
European history (MA)
general psychology (MA)
geography (MA)
geology (MS)
health psychology (PhD)
international studies (MA)
maritime history (MA)
mathematics (MA)
medical physics (MS)

East Carolina University (continued)
- molecular biology/biotechnology (MS)
- physics (PhD)
- public administration (MPA)
- sociology (MA)

■ ELON UNIVERSITY
Elon, NC 27244-2010
http://www.elon.edu/

Independent-religious, coed, comprehensive institution. CGS member. *Enrollment:* 5,230 graduate, professional, and undergraduate students; 235 full-time matriculated graduate/professional students (135 women), 146 part-time matriculated graduate/professional students (72 women). *Graduate faculty:* 56 full-time (26 women), 17 part-time/adjunct (12 women). *Computer facilities:* Computer purchase and lease plans are available. 575 computers available on campus for general student use. A campuswide network can be accessed from student residence rooms and from off campus. Internet access and online class registration, e-mail are available. *Library facilities:* Carol Grotnes Belk. *General application contact:* Art Fadde, Director of Graduate Admissions, 800-334-8448 Ext. 3.

Program in Business Administration
Dr. Scott Buechler, Director
Program in:
- business administration (MBA)

Program in Education
Dr. Judith B. Howard, Director
Programs in:
- elementary education (M Ed)
- gifted education (M Ed)
- special education (M Ed)

Program in Physical Therapy
Dr. Elizabeth A. Rogers, Chair
Program in:
- physical therapy (DPT)

■ FAYETTEVILLE STATE UNIVERSITY
Fayetteville, NC 28301-4298
http://www.uncfsu.edu/

State-supported, coed, comprehensive institution. CGS member. *Enrollment:* 6,301 graduate, professional, and undergraduate students; 165 full-time matriculated graduate/professional students (133 women), 219 part-time matriculated graduate/professional students (173 women). *Graduate faculty:* 135 full-time (64 women), 6 part-time/adjunct (3 women). *Computer facilities:* 355 computers available on campus for general student use. A campuswide network can be accessed from student residence rooms and from off campus. Internet access and online class registration, access to student information are available. *Library facilities:* Charles W. Chestnut Library. *Graduate expenses:* Tuition, state resident: full-time $2,118. Tuition, nonresident: full-time $11,708. Required fees: $1,099. Tuition and fees vary according to course load. *General application contact:* Charles Darlington, Director of Admissions, 910-672-1371.

Graduate School
Programs in:
- biology (MA Ed, MS)
- criminal justice (MA)
- educational leadership (Ed D)
- elementary education (MA Ed)
- English (MA)
- history (MA, MA Ed)
- mathematics (MA Ed, MS)
- middle grades (MA Ed)
- political science (MA, MA Ed)
- psychology (MA)
- reading (MA Ed)
- school administration (MSA)
- social work (MSW)
- sociology (MA Ed)
- special education (MA Ed)

■ GARDNER-WEBB UNIVERSITY
Boiling Springs, NC 28017
http://www.gardner-webb.edu/

Independent-religious, coed, comprehensive institution. *Enrollment:* 3,840 graduate, professional, and undergraduate students; 203 full-time matriculated graduate/professional students (77 women), 1,008 part-time matriculated graduate/professional students (635 women). *Graduate faculty:* 46 full-time (20 women), 13 part-time/adjunct (5 women). *Computer facilities:* 150 computers available on campus for general student use. A campuswide network can be accessed from student residence rooms and from off campus. Internet access and online class registration are available. *Library facilities:* Dover Memorial Library. *Graduate expenses:* Tuition: full-time $3,144; part-time $262 per hour. *General application contact:* Dr. Gayle B. Price, Dean, Graduate School, 704-406-4723.

Graduate School
Dr. Gayle B. Price, Dean
Programs in:
- curriculum and instruction (Ed D)
- educational leadership (Ed D)
- elementary education (MA)
- English (MA)
- English education (MA)
- middle grades education (MA)
- nursing (MSN, PMC)
- school administration (MA, Ed D)
- sport science and pedagogy (MA)

Department of Education
Dr. Donna Simmons, Chair
Programs in:
- curriculum and instruction (Ed D)
- educational leadership (Ed D)
- elementary education (MA)
- middle grades education (MA)
- school administration (MA, Ed D)

Program in Nursing
Dr. Gayle B. Price, Dean, Graduate School
Program in:
- nursing (MSN, PMC)

School of Psychology
Dr. David Carscaddon, Chair
Programs in:
- mental health counseling (MA)
- school counseling (MA)

Graduate School of Business
Dr. Anthony Negbenebor, Director
Program in:
- business (IMBA, M Acc, MBA)

M. Christopher White School of Divinity
Dr. Robert W. Canoy, Dean
Programs in:
- business administration (MA)
- Christian education (M Div)
- English (MA)
- ministry (D Min)
- missiology (M Div)
- pastoral care and counseling (M Div)
- pastoral ministry (M Div)

■ HIGH POINT UNIVERSITY
High Point, NC 27262-3598
http://www.highpoint.edu/

Independent-religious, coed, comprehensive institution. CGS member. *Enrollment:* 2,811 graduate, professional, and undergraduate students; 49 full-time matriculated graduate/professional students (29 women), 202 part-time matriculated graduate/professional students (130 women). *Graduate faculty:* 31 full-time (11 women), 1 part-time/adjunct (0 women). *Computer facilities:* 176 computers available on campus for general student use. A campuswide network can be accessed from student residence rooms and from off campus. Internet access is available. *Library facilities:* Herman and Louise Smith Library. *Graduate expenses:* Tuition: full-time $9,270; part-time $1,545 per course. *General application contact:* Dr. Alberta Haynes Herron, Dean of Norcross Graduate School, 336-841-9198.

Norcross Graduate School
Programs in:
- business administration (MBA)
- educational leadership (M Ed)
- elementary education (M Ed)
- history (MA)
- nonprofit organizations (MPA)
- special education (M Ed)
- sport studies (MS)

■ NORTH CAROLINA AGRICULTURAL AND TECHNICAL STATE UNIVERSITY

Greensboro, NC 27411

http://www.ncat.edu/

State-supported, coed, university. CGS member. *Computer facilities:* 250 computers available on campus for general student use. A campuswide network can be accessed from off campus. Internet access and online class registration are available. *Library facilities:* F. D. Bluford Library plus 1 other. *General application contact:* Interim Dean of the Graduate School, 336-334-7920.

Find University Details at www.petersons.com/gradchannel.

Graduate School

College of Arts and Sciences
Programs in:
- art education (MS)
- arts and sciences (MA, MS, MSW)
- biology (MS)
- chemistry (MS)
- English (MA)
- English and Afro-American literature (MA)
- history education (MS)
- mathematics education (MS)
- social science education (MS)
- sociology and social work (MSW)

College of Engineering
Programs in:
- architectural, agricultural, civil and environmental engineering (MSAE, MSCE, MSE)
- chemical engineering (MSE)
- computer science (MSCS)
- electrical engineering (MSEE, PhD)
- engineering (MSAE, MSCE, MSCS, MSE, MSEE, MSISE, MSME, PhD)
- industrial and systems engineering (MSISE, PhD)
- mechanical engineering (MSME, PhD)

School of Agriculture and Environmental and Allied Sciences
Programs in:
- agricultural economics (MS)
- agricultural education (MS)
- agriculture and environmental and allied sciences (MS)
- food and nutrition (MS)
- plant science (MS)

School of Education
Programs in:
- adult education (MS)
- biology education (MS)
- chemistry education (MS)
- early childhood education (MS)
- education (MS)
- educational administration (MS)
- educational media (MS)
- elementary education (MS)
- English education (MS)
- guidance and counseling (MS)
- health and physical education (MS)
- history education (MS)
- human resources (MS)
- intermediate education (MS)
- reading (MS)
- social science education (MS)

School of Technology
Programs in:
- industrial arts education (MS)
- industrial technology (MS, MSIT)
- safety and driver education (MS)
- technology (MS, MSIT)
- technology education (MS)
- vocational-industrial education (MS)

■ NORTH CAROLINA CENTRAL UNIVERSITY

Durham, NC 27707-3129

http://www.nccu.edu/

State-supported, coed, comprehensive institution. CGS member. *Computer facilities:* Computer purchase and lease plans are available. 603 computers available on campus for general student use. A campuswide network can be accessed from student residence rooms and from off campus. Internet access and online class registration are available. *Library facilities:* Shepherd Library plus 4 others. *General application contact:* Interim Vice Chancellor for Academic Affairs and Provost, 919-560-6230.

Division of Academic Affairs

College of Arts and Sciences
Programs in:
- arts and sciences (MA, MPA, MS)
- biology (MS)
- chemistry (MS)
- criminal justice (MS)
- earth sciences (MS)
- English (MA)
- general physical education (MS)
- history (MA)
- human sciences (MS)
- mathematics (MS)
- psychology (MA)
- public administration (MPA)
- recreation administration (MS)
- sociology (MA)
- special physical education (MS)
- therapeutic recreation (MS)

School of Business
Program in:
- business (MBA)

School of Education
Programs in:
- agency counseling (MA)
- career counseling (MA)
- development leadership and professional studies (MA)
- education (M Ed, MA)
- education of the emotionally handicapped (M Ed)
- education of the mentally handicapped (M Ed)
- elementary education (M Ed, MA)
- instructional media (MA)
- school counseling (MA)
- speech pathology and audiology (M Ed)

School of Law
Program in:
- law (JD, LL B)

School of Library and Information Sciences
Program in:
- library and information sciences (MIS, MLS)

■ NORTH CAROLINA STATE UNIVERSITY

Raleigh, NC 27695

http://www.ncsu.edu/

State-supported, coed, university. CGS member. *Computer facilities:* Computer purchase and lease plans are available. 3,189 computers available on campus for general student use. A campuswide network can be accessed from student residence rooms and from off campus. Internet access and online class registration are available. *Library facilities:* D. H. Hill Library plus 6 others. *General application contact:* Office of Graduate Admissions, 919-515-2871.

College of Veterinary Medicine

Programs in:
- cell biology and morphology (MS, PhD)
- epidemiology and population medicine (MS, PhD)
- immunology (MS, PhD)
- microbiology and immunology (MS, PhD)
- pathology (MS, PhD)
- pharmacology (MS, PhD)
- specialized veterinary medicine (MS)
- veterinary medicine (DVM, MS, MSpVM, MVPH, PhD)
- veterinary public health (MVPH)

Graduate School

College of Agriculture and Life Sciences
Programs in:
- agricultural and resource economics (MS)
- agricultural education (MAEE, MS)
- agriculture and life sciences (M Tox, MAEE, MB, MBAE, MFG, MFM, MFS, MG, MMB, MN, MP, MS, MZS, PhD)
- animal science (MS)
- animal science and poultry science (PhD)
- biochemistry (MS, PhD)
- bioinformatics (MB, PhD)

North Carolina State University (continued)

biological and agricultural engineering (MBAE, MS, PhD)
botany (MS, PhD)
crop science (MS, PhD)
entomology (MS, PhD)
environmental and molecular toxicology (M Tox, MS, PhD)
extension education (MAEE, MS)
financial mathematics (MFM)
food science (MFS, MS, PhD)
functional genomics (MFG, MS, PhD)
genetics (MG, MS, PhD)
horticultural science (MS, PhD)
immunology (MS, PhD)
microbial biotechnology (MMB)
microbiology (MS, PhD)
nutrition (MN, MS, PhD)
physiology (MP, MS, PhD)
plant pathology (MS, PhD)
poultry science (MS)
soil science (MS, PhD)
zoology (MS, MZS, PhD)

College of Design
Programs in:
architecture (M Arch)
art and design (MAD)
design (M Arch, MAD, MID, MLA, UA Undergraduate Associate, PhD)
graphic design (UA Undergraduate Associate)
industrial design (MID)
landscape architecture (MLA)

College of Education
Programs in:
adult and community college education (M Ed, MS, Ed D)
agency counseling (M Ed, MS)
counselor education (M Ed, MS, PhD)
curriculum and instruction (M Ed, MS, PhD)
education (M Ed, MS, MSA, Ed D, PhD, Certificate)
educational administration and supervision (Ed D)
educational research and policy analysis (PhD)
higher education administration (M Ed, MS, Ed D)
mathematics education (M Ed, MS, PhD)
middle grades education (M Ed, MS)
school administration (MSA)
science education (M Ed, MS, PhD)
special education (M Ed, MS)
technology education (M Ed, MS, Ed D)
training and development (M Ed, MS)

College of Engineering
Programs in:
aerospace engineering (MS, PhD)
biomedical engineering (MS, PhD)
chemical engineering (M Ch E, MS, PhD)
civil engineering (MCE, MS, PhD)
computer engineering (MS, PhD)
computer networking (MS)
computer science (MC Sc, MS, PhD)
electrical engineering (MS, PhD)
engineering (M Ch E, M Eng, MC Sc, MCE, MIE, MIMS, MME, MMSE, MNE, MOR, MS, PhD)
industrial engineering (MIE, MS, PhD)
integrated manufacturing systems engineering (MIMS)
materials science and engineering (MMSE, MS, PhD)
mechanical engineering (MME, MS, PhD)
nuclear engineering (MNE, MS, PhD)
operations research (MOR, MS, PhD)

College of Humanities and Social Sciences
Programs in:
anthropology (MA)
bioarchaeology (MA)
creative writing (MFA)
cultural anthropology (MA)
developmental psychology (PhD)
English (MA)
environmental anthropology (MA)
ergonomics and experimental psychology (PhD)
French language and literature (MA)
history (MA)
humanities and social sciences (M Soc, MA, MAIS, MFA, MPA, MS, PhD)
industrial/organizational psychology (PhD)
international studies (MAIS)
liberal studies (MA)
organizational communication (MS)
psychology in the public interest (PhD)
public administration (MPA, PhD)
public history (MA)
rural sociology (MS)
school psychology (PhD)
sociology (M Soc, MS, PhD)
Spanish language and literature (MA)
technical communication (MS)

College of Management
Programs in:
accounting (MAC)
business administration (MBA)
economics (M Econ, MA, PhD)
financial management (MBA)
information technology management (MBA)
marketing management (MBA)
product innovation management (MBA)
supply chain management (MBA)
technology commercialization (MBA)

College of Natural Resources
Programs in:
fisheries and wildlife sciences (MFWS, MS)
forestry (MF, MS, PhD)
geographic information systems (MS)
maintenance management (MRRA, MS)
natural resources (MF, MFWS, MNR, MRRA, MS, MWPS, PhD)
parks, recreation and tourism management (PhD)
recreation planning (MRRA, MS)
recreation resources administration/public administration (MRRA)
recreation/park management (MRRA, MS)
sports management (MRRA, MS)
travel and tourism management (MS)
wood and paper science (MS, MWPS, PhD)

College of Physical and Mathematical Sciences
Programs in:
applied mathematics (MS, PhD)
biomathematics (M Biomath, MS, PhD)
chemistry (MCH, MS, PhD)
ecology (PhD)
marine, earth, and atmospheric sciences (MS, PhD)
mathematics (MS, PhD)
meteorology (MS, PhD)
oceanography (MS, PhD)
physical and mathematical sciences (M Biomath, M Stat, MCH, MS, PhD)
physics (MS, PhD)
statistics (M Stat, MS, PhD)

College of Textiles
Programs in:
fiber and polymer sciences (PhD)
textile and apparel technology and management (MS, MT)
textile chemistry (MS)
textile engineering (MS)
textile technology management (PhD)
textiles (MS, MT, PhD)

■ PFEIFFER UNIVERSITY
Misenheimer, NC 28109-0960
http://www.pfeiffer.edu/

Independent-religious, coed, comprehensive institution. *Enrollment:* 2,116 graduate, professional, and undergraduate students; 179 full-time matriculated graduate/professional students (100 women), 803 part-time matriculated graduate/professional students (563 women). *Graduate faculty:* 24 full-time (9 women), 29 part-time/adjunct (5 women). *Computer facilities:* 90 computers available on campus for general student use. A campuswide network can be accessed from student residence rooms and from off campus. Internet access, e-mail are available. *Library facilities:* Gustavus A. Pfeiffer Library. *Graduate expenses:* Tuition: part-time $380 per semester hour. Tuition and fees vary according to campus/location. *General application contact:* Michael Utsman, Assistant Dean, 704-521-9116 Ext. 253.

Program in Business Administration
Dr. Robert K. Spear, Director of the MBA Program
Programs in:
business administration (MBA)
organizational management (MS)

Program in Health Administration
Dr. Joel Vickers, Director
Program in:
health administration (MHA)

Program in Organizational Change and Leadership
Dr. Ron Hunady, Director
Program in:
organizational change and leadership (MS)

School of Education
Dr. Sandra Loehr, Director of Teacher Education
Programs in:
elementary education (MS)
teaching (MAT)

School of Religion and Christian Education
Kathleen Kilbourne, Coordinator
Program in:
religion and Christian education (MACE)

■ QUEENS UNIVERSITY OF CHARLOTTE

Charlotte, NC 28274-0002
http://www.queens.edu/

Independent-religious, coed, comprehensive institution. *Enrollment:* 2,118 graduate, professional, and undergraduate students; 150 full-time matriculated graduate/professional students (91 women), 255 part-time matriculated graduate/professional students (173 women). *Graduate faculty:* 24 full-time (9 women), 11 part-time/adjunct (8 women). *Computer facilities:* Computer purchase and lease plans are available. 125 computers available on campus for general student use. A campuswide network can be accessed from student residence rooms and from off campus. Internet access is available. *Library facilities:* Everett Library plus 1 other. *General application contact:* Robert Mobley, Director of MBA Admissions, 704-337-2224.

College of Arts and Sciences
Dr. Betty J. Powell, Dean
Program in:
creative writing (MFA)

Hayworth College
Dr. Darrel L. Miller, Dean
Programs in:
elementary education (MAT)
organizational communications (MA)

Division of Nursing
Dr. William K. Cody, Chair
Program in:
nursing management (MSN)

McColl Graduate School of Business
Terry Broderick, Chair
Program in:
business (EMBA, MBA)

■ THE UNIVERSITY OF NORTH CAROLINA AT CHAPEL HILL

Chapel Hill, NC 27599
http://www.unc.edu/

State-supported, coed, university. CGS member. *Computer facilities:* Computer purchase and lease plans are available. 600 computers available on campus for general student use. A campuswide network can be accessed from student residence rooms and from off campus. Internet access and online class registration, online grade reports are available. *Library facilities:* Davis Library plus 14 others. *General application contact:* Director of Admissions and Enrollment Services, 919-966-2611.

Graduate School
Programs in:
materials science (MS, PhD)
public policy (PhD)
Russian and east European studies (MA)

College of Arts and Sciences
Programs in:
acting (MFA)
anthropology (MA, PhD)
art history (MA, PhD)
arts and sciences (MA, MFA, MPA, MRP, MS, MSRA, PhD, Certificate)
athletic training (MA)
biological psychology (PhD)
botany (MA, MS, PhD)
cell biology, development, and physiology (MA, MS, PhD)
cell motility and cytoskeleton (PhD)
chemistry (MA, MS, PhD)
city and regional planning (MRP)
classical archaeology (MA, PhD)
classics (MA, PhD)
clinical psychology (PhD)
cognitive psychology (PhD)
communication studies (MA, PhD)
comparative literature (MA, PhD)
computer science (MS, PhD)
costume production (MFA)
developmental psychology (PhD)
ecology (MA, MS, PhD)
ecology and behavior (MA, MS, PhD)
economics (MS, PhD)
English (MA, PhD)
exercise physiology (MA)
folklore (MA)
French (MA, PhD)
genetics and molecular biology (MA, MS, PhD)
geography (MA, PhD)
geological sciences (MS, PhD)
history (MA, PhD)
Italian (MA, PhD)
Latin American studies (Certificate)
linguistics (MA, PhD)
literature and linguistics (MA, PhD)
marine sciences (MS, PhD)
mathematics (MA, MS, PhD)
morphology, systematics, and evolution (MA, MS, PhD)
music (MA, PhD)
operations research (MS, PhD)
philosophy (MA, PhD)
physics (MS, PhD)
planning (PhD)
Polish literature (PhD)
political science (MA, PhD)
Portuguese (MA, PhD)
public administration (MPA)
public policy analysis (PhD)
quantitative psychology (PhD)
recreation and leisure studies (MSRA)
religious studies (MA, PhD)
Romance languages (MA, PhD)
Romance philology (MA, PhD)
Russian literature (MA, PhD)
Serbo-Croatian literature (PhD)
Slavic linguistics (MA, PhD)
social psychology (PhD)
sociology (MA, PhD)
Spanish (MA, PhD)
sport administration (MA)
statistics (MS, PhD)
studio art (MFA)
technical production (MFA)
trans-Atlantic studies (MA)

School of Education
Dr. Jill Fitzgerald, Interim Dean
Programs in:
culture, curriculum and change (PhD)
culture, curriculum, and change (MA)
curriculum and instruction (Ed D)
early childhood, families, and literacy studies (MA, PhD)
education (M Ed, MA, MAT, MSA, Ed D, PhD)
education for experienced teachers (M Ed)
education for experienced teachers, early childhood intervention and family studies (birth-K) (M Ed)
educational leadership (Ed D)
educational psychology measurements, and evaluation (PhD)
educational psychology, measurement, and evaluation (MA)
English (Grades 9-12) (MAT)
French (Grades K-12) (MAT)
German (Grades K-12) (MAT)
Japanese (Grades K-12) (MAT)
Latin (Grades 9-12) (MAT)
mathematics (Grades 9-12) (MAT)
music (Grades K-12) (MAT)
school administration (MSA)
school counseling (M Ed)
school psychology (M Ed, MA, PhD)
science (Grades 9-12) (MAT)
social studies/social science (Grades 9-12) (MAT)
Spanish (Grades K-12) (MAT)

School of Information and Library Science
Dr. Jose-Marie Griffiths, Dean

The University of North Carolina at Chapel Hill (continued)
Program in:
information and library science (MSIS, MSLS, PhD, CAS)

School of Journalism and Mass Communication
Dr. Jean Folkerts, Dean
Program in:
mass communication (MA, PhD)

School of Public Health
Dr. Barbara K. Rimer, Dean
Programs in:
air, radiation and industrial hygiene (MPH, MS, MSEE, MSPH, PhD)
aquatic and atmospheric sciences (MPH, MS, MSPH, PhD)
biostatistics (MPH, MS, Dr PH, PhD)
environmental engineering (MPH, MS, MSEE, MSPH, PhD)
environmental health sciences (MPH, MS, MSPH, PhD)
environmental management and policy (MPH, MS, MSPH, PhD)
epidemiology (MPH, MSPH, PhD)
health behavior and health education (MPH, PhD)
health care and prevention (MPH)
health policy and administration (MHA, MPH, MSPH, Dr PH, PhD)
leadership (MPH)
maternal and child health (MPH, MSPH, Dr PH, PhD)
nutrition (MPH, Dr PH, PhD)
nutritional biochemistry (MS)
occupational health nursing (MPH)
professional practice program (MPH)
public health (MHA, MPH, MS, MSEE, MSPH, Dr PH, PhD)
public health nursing (MS)

School of Social Work
Program in:
social work (MSW, PhD)

Kenan-Flagler Business School
Programs in:
accounting (PhD)
business (MAC, MBA, PhD)
business administration (MBA, PhD)
finance (PhD)
marketing (PhD)
operations management (PhD)
organizational behavior (PhD)
strategy (PhD)

National Institutes of Health Sponsored Programs
Program in:
cell motility and cytoskeleton (PhD)

School of Dentistry
Dr. John N. Williams, Dean
Programs in:
dentistry (MS)
oral biology (PhD)

School of Law
Program in:
law (JD)

School of Medicine
Programs in:
allied health sciences (MPT, MS, Au D, DPT, PhD)
audiology (Au D)
biochemistry and biophysics (MS, PhD)
biomedical engineering (MS, PhD)
cell and developmental biology (PhD)
cell and molecular physiology (PhD)
experimental pathology (PhD)
genetics and molecular biology (PhD)
human movement science (MS, PhD)
immunology (MS, PhD)
medicine (MD, MPT, MS, Au D, DPT, PhD)
microbiology (MS, PhD)
microbiology and immunology (MS, PhD)
neurobiology (PhD)
occupational science (MS, PhD)
pathology and laboratory medicine (PhD)
pharmacology (PhD)
physical therapy (MPT, MS, DPT)
rehabilitation counseling and psychology (MS)
speech and hearing sciences (MS, Au D, PhD)
toxicology (MS, PhD)

School of Nursing
Program in:
nursing (MSN, PhD)

School of Pharmacy
Dr. Robert A. Blouin, Dean
Program in:
pharmacy (MS, PhD)

■ THE UNIVERSITY OF NORTH CAROLINA AT CHARLOTTE
Charlotte, NC 28223-0001
http://www.uncc.edu/

State-supported, coed, university. CGS member. *Enrollment:* 21,519 graduate, professional, and undergraduate students; 1,191 full-time matriculated graduate/professional students (667 women), 1,980 part-time matriculated graduate/professional students (1,213 women). *Graduate faculty:* 594 full-time (226 women), 63 part-time/adjunct (33 women). *Computer facilities:* Computer purchase and lease plans are available. 1,400 computers available on campus for general student use. A campuswide network can be accessed from student residence rooms and from off campus. Internet access and online class registration are available. *Library facilities:* J. Murrey Atkins Library. *Graduate expenses:* Tuition, state resident: full-time $2,719; part-time $170 per credit. Tuition, nonresident: full-time $12,926; part-time $808 per credit. Required fees: $1,555. *General application contact:* Dr. Thomas L. Reynolds, Dean and Associate Provost, 704-687-3372.

Graduate School
Dr. Thomas L. Reynolds, Dean and Associate Provost

Belk College of Business Administration
Dr. Claude C. Lilly, Dean
Programs in:
accounting (M Acc)
business administration (M Acc, MBA, MS, PhD)
economics (MS)
mathematical finance (MS)
sports marketing management (MS)

College of Architecture
Kenneth A. Lambla, Dean
Program in:
architecture (M Arch)

College of Arts and Sciences
Dr. Nancy A Gutierrez, Dean
Programs in:
applied mathematics (MS, PhD)
applied physics (MS)
arts and sciences (MA, MPA, MS, PhD)
biology (MA, MS, PhD)
chemistry (MS)
communication studies (MA)
community/clinical psychology (MA)
criminal justice (MS)
earth sciences (MS)
English (MA)
English education (MA)
geography (MA)
geography and urban and regional analysis (PhD)
gerontology (MA)
health psychology (PhD)
history (MA)
industrial/organizational psychology (MA)
liberal studies (MA)
mathematics (MS)
mathematics education (MA)
optical science and engineering (MS, PhD)
organizational science (PhD)
public administration (MPA)
public policy (PhD)
religious studies (MA)
sociology (MA)
Spanish (MA)

College of Computing and Informatics
Dr. Mirsad Hadzikadic, Dean
Programs in:
computer science (MS)
computing and informatics (MS, PhD)
information technology (MS, PhD)

College of Education
Dr. Mary Lynne Calhoun, Dean
Programs in:
art education (K-12) (MAT)
counseling (MA, PhD)
curriculum and supervision (M Ed)
dance education (K-12) (MAT)

education (M Ed, MA, MAT, MSA, Ed D, PhD, CAS)
educational administration (CAS)
educational leadership (Ed D)
elementary education (M Ed)
elementary education (K-6) (MAT)
English as a second language (K-12) (MAT)
foreign language education (K-12) (MAT)
general teacher education (MAT)
instructional systems technology (M Ed)
middle grades and secondary education (M Ed)
middle grades education (6-9) (MAT)
music education (K-12) (MAT)
reading education (M Ed)
school administration (MSA)
secondary education (9-12) (MAT)
special education (M Ed, PhD)
special education (K-12) (MAT)
teaching English as a second language (M Ed)
theatre education (K-12) (MAT)
urban education (PhD)
urban literacy (PhD)
urban math (PhD)

College of Health and Human Services
Dr. Karen Schmaling, Dean
Programs in:
clinical exercise physiology (MS)
family nurse practitioner (MSN)
health and human services (MHA, MS, MSN, MSPH, MSW, PhD)
health behavior and administration (MHA)
health services research (PhD)
nursing (MSN)
nursing adult health (MSN)
nursing-anesthesia (MSN)
nursing-community health (MSN)
public health (MSPH)
social work (MSW)

The William States Lee College of Engineering
Dr. Robert E. Johnson, Dean
Programs in:
civil engineering (MSCE)
electrical engineering (MSEE, PhD)
engineering (MS, MSCE, MSE, MSEE, MSME, PhD)
engineering management (MS)
infrastructure and environmental systems (PhD)
infrastructure and environmental systems design (PhD)
infrastructure and environmental systems management (PhD)
infrastructure and environmental systems science (PhD)
mechanical engineering (MSME, PhD)

■ THE UNIVERSITY OF NORTH CAROLINA AT GREENSBORO
Greensboro, NC 27412-5001
http://www.uncg.edu/

State-supported, coed, university. CGS member. *Enrollment:* 16,728 graduate, professional, and undergraduate students; 2,270 full-time matriculated graduate/professional students (1,565 women), 1,537 part-time matriculated graduate/professional students (1,107 women). *Graduate faculty:* 614 full-time (270 women), 163 part-time/adjunct (96 women). *Computer facilities:* Computer purchase and lease plans are available. 500 computers available on campus for general student use. A campuswide network can be accessed from student residence rooms and from off campus. Internet access and online class registration are available. *Library facilities:* Jackson Library plus 1 other. *Graduate expenses:* Tuition, state resident: full-time $2,692. Tuition, nonresident: full-time $13,742. *General application contact:* Michelle Harkleroad, Director of Graduate Admissions, 336-334-4884.

Find University Details at www.petersons.com/gradchannel.

Graduate School
Dr. James Peterson, Dean
Programs in:
conflict resolution (MA, Certificate)
genetic counseling (MS)
gerontology (MS, Certificate)
liberal studies (MALS)

Bryan School of Business and Economics
James K. Weeks, Dean
Programs in:
accounting (MS)
accounting systems (MS)
applied economics (MA)
business administration (MBA, PMC, Postbaccalaureate Certificate)
business and economics (MA, MBA, MS, PhD, Certificate, PMC, Postbaccalaureate Certificate)
economics (PhD)
financial accounting and reporting (MS)
financial analysis (PMC)
financial economics (MA)
information systems (PhD)
information technology (Certificate)
information technology and management (MS)
supply chain management (Certificate)
tax concentration (MS)

College of Arts and Sciences
Timothy Johnston, Dean
Programs in:
acting (MFA)
advanced Spanish language and Hispanic cultural studies (Certificate)
American literature (PhD)
applied geography (MA)
arts and sciences (M Ed, MA, MFA, MPA, MS, PhD, Certificate)
biochemistry (MS)
biology (MS)
chemistry (MS)
clinical psychology (MA, PhD)
cognitive psychology (MA, PhD)
communication studies (MA)
computer science (MS)
creative writing (MFA)
criminology (MA)
design (MFA)
developmental psychology (MA, PhD)
directing (MFA)
English (M Ed, MA, PhD, Certificate)
English literature (PhD)
French (MA)
geographic information science (Certificate)
geography (PhD)
historic preservation (Certificate)
history (MA)
Latin (M Ed)
mathematics (M Ed, MA)
museum studies (Certificate)
nonprofit management (Certificate)
public affairs (MPA)
rhetoric and composition (PhD)
social psychology (MA, PhD)
sociology (MA)
Spanish (MA, Certificate)
studio arts (MFA)
theater education (M Ed)
theater for youth (MFA)
U.S. history (PhD)
urban and economic development (Certificate)
women's and gender studies (MA, Certificate)

School of Education
Dr. Dale Schunk, Dean
Programs in:
advanced school counseling (PMC)
college teaching and adult learning (Certificate)
counseling and counselor education (PhD)
counseling and educational development (MS)
couple and family counseling (PMC)
cross-categorical special education (M Ed)
curriculum and instruction (M Ed)
curriculum and teaching (PhD)
education (M Ed, MLIS, MS, MSA, Ed D, PhD, Certificate, Ed S, PMC)
educational leadership (Ed D, Ed S)
educational research, measurement and evaluation (PhD)
English as a second language (Certificate)
higher education (M Ed, PhD)

The University of North Carolina at Greensboro (continued)
- interdisciplinary studies in special education (M Ed)
- leadership early care and education (Certificate)
- library and information studies (MLIS)
- school administration (MSA)
- school counseling (PMC)
- special education (M Ed, PhD)
- supervision (M Ed)
- teacher education and development (PhD)

School of Health and Human Performance
David Perrin, Dean
Programs in:
- community health education (MPH, Dr PH)
- dance (MA, MFA)
- exercise and sports science (M Ed, MS, Ed D, PhD)
- health and human performance (M Ed, MA, MFA, MPH, MS, Dr PH, Ed D, PhD)
- parks and recreation management (MS)
- speech language pathology (PhD)
- speech pathology and audiology (MA)

School of Human Environmental Sciences
Laura S. Sims, Dean
Programs in:
- consumer, apparel, and retail studies (MS, PhD)
- historic preservation (Certificate)
- human development and family studies (M Ed, MS, PhD)
- human environmental sciences (M Ed, MS, MSW, PhD, Certificate)
- interior architecture (MS)
- museum studies (Certificate)
- nutrition (MS, PhD)
- social work (MSW)

School of Music
Dr. John J. Deal, Dean
Programs in:
- composition (MM)
- education (MM)
- music education (PhD)
- performance (MM, DMA)

School of Nursing
Dr. Lynne Pearcey, Dean
Programs in:
- adult clinical nurse specialist (MSN, PMC)
- adult/gerontological nurse practitioner (MSN, PMC)
- nurse anesthesia (MSN, PMC)
- nursing (PhD)
- nursing administration (MSN)
- nursing education (MSN)

■ THE UNIVERSITY OF NORTH CAROLINA AT PEMBROKE

Pembroke, NC 28372-1510
http://www.uncp.edu/

State-supported, coed, comprehensive institution. CGS member. *Enrollment:* 5,827 graduate, professional, and undergraduate students; 82 full-time matriculated graduate/professional students (49 women), 587 part-time matriculated graduate/professional students (400 women). *Graduate faculty:* 27 full-time (9 women), 2 part-time/adjunct (1 woman). *Computer facilities:* 650 computers available on campus for general student use. A campuswide network can be accessed from student residence rooms and from off campus. Internet access and online class registration are available. *Library facilities:* Sampson-Livermore Library. *Graduate expenses:* Tuition, state resident: full-time $3,516; part-time $1,091 per semester. Tuition, nonresident: full-time $12,924; part-time $4,619 per semester. Tuition and fees vary according to class time, course load, degree level and campus/location. *General application contact:* Dr. Kathleen C. Hilton, Dean of Graduate Studies, 910-521-6271.

Graduate Studies
Dr. Kathleen C. Hilton, Dean of Graduate Studies
Programs in:
- art education (MA, MAT)
- English education (MA, MAT)
- mathematics education (MA, MAT)
- music education (MA, MAT)
- physical education (MA, MAT)
- public administration (MPA)
- school counseling (MA)
- science education (MA)
- service agency counseling (MA)
- social studies education (MA, MAT)

School of Business
Dr. Eric Dent, Dean
Programs in:
- business (MBA)
- business administration (MBA)

School of Education
Dr. Zoe Locklear, Dean
Programs in:
- elementary education (MA Ed)
- middle grades education (MA Ed, MAT)
- reading education (MA Ed)
- school administration (MSA)

■ THE UNIVERSITY OF NORTH CAROLINA WILMINGTON

Wilmington, NC 28403-3297
http://www.uncw.edu/

State-supported, coed, comprehensive institution. CGS member. *Enrollment:* 11,793 graduate, professional, and undergraduate students; 384 full-time matriculated graduate/professional students (238 women), 582 part-time matriculated graduate/professional students (371 women). *Graduate faculty:* 325 full-time (101 women), 35 part-time/adjunct (15 women). *Computer facilities:* Computer purchase and lease plans are available. 778 computers available on campus for general student use. A campuswide network can be accessed from student residence rooms and from off campus. Internet access and online class registration are available. *Library facilities:* William M. Randall Library. *General application contact:* Dr. Robert D. Roer, Dean, Graduate School, 910-962-4117.

College of Arts and Sciences
Dr. David Cordle, Dean
Programs in:
- arts and sciences (MA, MALS, MFA, MPA, MS, MSW, PhD, Graduate Certificate)
- biology (MS)
- chemistry (MS)
- computer science and information systems (MS)
- creative writing (MFA)
- criminology (MA)
- English (MA)
- geology (MS)
- Hispanic studies (Graduate Certificate)
- history (MA)
- liberal studies (MALS)
- marine biology (MS, PhD)
- marine science (MS)
- mathematical sciences (MA, MS)
- psychology (MA)
- public administration (MPA)
- public sociology (MA)
- social work (MSW)

School of Business
Dr. Lawrence Clark, Dean
Programs in:
- accountancy (MSA)
- business (MBA, MSA)
- business administration (MBA)

School of Education
Dr. Cathy L. Barlow, Dean
Programs in:
- curriculum, instruction and supervision (M Ed)
- education (M Ed, MAT, MS, MSA)
- educational leadership (MSA)
- elementary education (M Ed)
- instructional technology (MS)
- language and literacy education (M Ed)
- middle grades education (M Ed)
- secondary education (M Ed)
- special education (M Ed)
- teaching (MAT)

School of Nursing
Dr. Virginia W. Adams, Dean
Program in:
- nursing (MSN)

■ WAKE FOREST UNIVERSITY
Winston-Salem, NC 27109
http://www.wfu.edu/

Independent, coed, university. CGS member. *Enrollment:* 6,739 graduate, professional, and undergraduate students; 2,418 matriculated graduate/professional students. *Graduate faculty:* 1,900. *Computer facilities:* Computer purchase and lease plans are available. 150 computers available on campus for general student use. A campuswide network can be accessed from student residence rooms and from off campus. Internet access and online class registration, laptop computer for all students, financial information online, GPA, drop-add, transcript requests are available. *Library facilities:* Z. Smith Reynolds Library plus 3 others. *General application contact:* Carol DiGiantommaso, Admissions Coordinator, 336-758-5301.

Find University Details at www.petersons.com/gradchannel.

Babcock Graduate School of Management
Ajay Patel, Dean
Programs in:
- business administration (MA, MBA)
- management (MA, MBA)

Graduate School
Dr. Cecilia H. Solano, Interim Dean
Programs in:
- accountancy (MSA)
- analytical chemistry (MS, PhD)
- biology (MS, PhD)
- computer science (MS)
- counseling (MA)
- English (MA)
- health and exercise science (MS)
- inorganic chemistry (MS, PhD)
- liberal studies (MALS)
- mathematics (MA)
- organic chemistry (MS, PhD)
- pastoral counseling (MA)
- physical chemistry (MS, PhD)
- physics (MS, PhD)
- psychology (MA)
- religion (MA)
- secondary education (MA Ed)
- speech communication (MA)

School of Law
Robert K. Walsh, Dean
Program in:
- law (JD, LL M)

School of Medicine
Program in:
- medicine (MD, MS, PhD)

Graduate Programs in Medicine
Programs in:
- biochemistry (PhD)
- cancer biology (PhD)
- clinical epidemiology and health services research (MS)
- comparative medicine (MS)
- medicine (MS, PhD)
- microbiology and immunology (PhD)
- molecular and cellular pathobiology (MS, PhD)
- molecular genetics and genomics (PhD)
- molecular medicine (MS, PhD)
- neurobiology and anatomy (PhD)
- neuroscience (PhD)
- pharmacology (PhD)
- physiology (PhD)

Virginia Tech-Wake Forest University School of Biomedical Engineering and Sciences
Program in:
- biomedical engineering and sciences (MS, PhD)

■ WESTERN CAROLINA UNIVERSITY
Cullowhee, NC 28723
http://www.wcu.edu/

State-supported, coed, comprehensive institution. CGS member. *Computer facilities:* 823 computers available on campus for general student use. A campuswide network can be accessed from student residence rooms and from off campus. Internet access and online class registration, e-mail, student Web pages, online music services (Rhapsody pilot), WebCT are available. *Library facilities:* Hunter Library. *General application contact:* Assistant to the Dean, 828-227-7398.

Graduate School

College of Applied Science
Programs in:
- applied science (MCM, MHS, MPT, MS, MSN)
- construction management (MCM)
- health sciences (MHS)
- nursing (MSN)
- physical therapy (MPT)
- technology (MS)

College of Arts and Sciences
Programs in:
- American history (MA)
- applied mathematics (MS)
- art education (MA Ed, MAT)
- arts and sciences (MA, MA Ed, MAT, MFA, MPA, MS)
- biology (MAT, MS)
- chemistry (MAT, MS)
- comprehensive education (MA Ed)
- comprehensive education—art (MA Ed)
- comprehensive education-biology (MA Ed)
- comprehensive education-chemistry (MA Ed)
- comprehensive education-English (MA Ed)
- comprehensive education-mathematics (MA Ed)
- English (MA, MAT)
- history (MA)
- mathematics (MAT)
- music (MA)
- public affairs (MPA)
- science and entrepreneurship (PSM)
- social sciences (MAT)
- studio art (MFA)

College of Business
Programs in:
- accountancy (M Ac)
- business administration (MBA)
- entrepreneurship (ME)
- project management (MPM)

College of Education and Allied Professions
Programs in:
- art education (MAT)
- behavioral disorders (MA Ed)
- biology (MAT)
- chemistry (MAT)
- clinical psychology (MA)
- communication disorders (MS)
- community college education (MA Ed)
- community counseling (MS)
- comprehensive education (MA Ed)
- comprehensive education-elementary education (MA Ed)
- comprehensive education-reading (MA Ed)
- comprehensive education-special education (MA Ed, MS)
- counseling (M Ed, MA Ed, MS)
- education and allied professions (M Ed, MA, MA Ed, MAT, MS, MSA, Ed D, Ed S)
- educational leadership (Ed D, Ed S)
- educational supervision (MA Ed)
- elementary education (MA Ed)
- English (MAT)
- family and consumer sciences (MAT)
- general special education (MA Ed, MAT)
- human resource development (MS)
- learning disabilities (MA Ed)
- mathematics (MAT)
- mental retardation (MA Ed)
- middle grades education (MA Ed, MAT)
- physical education (MA Ed, MAT)
- reading (MAT)
- reading education (M Ed, MA Ed, MAT)
- school administration (MSA)
- school counseling (M Ed, MA Ed)
- school psychology (MA)
- secondary education (MA Ed, MAT)
- social sciences (MAT)
- special education-learning disabilities (MAT)

North Dakota

■ MINOT STATE UNIVERSITY
Minot, ND 58707-0002
http://www.minotstateu.edu/

State-supported, coed, comprehensive institution. *Enrollment:* 3,712 graduate, professional, and undergraduate students; 274 matriculated graduate/professional students (225 women). *Graduate faculty:* 76 full-time (24 women), 47 part-time/adjunct (26 women). *Computer facilities:* 460 computers available on campus for general student use. A campuswide network can be accessed from student residence rooms and from off campus. Internet access and online class registration are available. *Library facilities:* Gordon B. Olson Library. *General application contact:* Brenda Anderson, Administrative Assistant, 701-858-3250 Ext. 3150.

Graduate School
Dr. Linda Cresap, Dean
Programs in:
- audiology (MS)
- criminal justice (MS)
- education of the deaf (MS)
- elementary education (M Ed)
- information systems (MSIS)
- learning disabilities (MS)
- management (MS)
- mathematics (MAT)
- music education (MME)
- school psychology (Ed Sp)
- science (MAT)
- special education strategist (MS)
- speech-language pathology (MS)

■ NORTH DAKOTA STATE UNIVERSITY
Fargo, ND 58105
http://www.ndsu.edu/

State-supported, coed, university. CGS member. *Enrollment:* 12,258 graduate, professional, and undergraduate students; 550 full-time matriculated graduate/professional students (227 women), 1,112 part-time matriculated graduate/professional students (563 women). *Graduate faculty:* 432 full-time (65 women), 21 part-time/adjunct (6 women). *Computer facilities:* 500 computers available on campus for general student use. A campuswide network can be accessed from student residence rooms and from off campus. Internet access is available. *Library facilities:* North Dakota State University Library plus 3 others. *General application contact:* Dr. David A. Wittrock, Dean, 701-231-8909.

Find University Details at www.petersons.com/gradchannel.

The Graduate School
Dr. David A. Wittrock, Dean
Programs in:
- agricultural education (M Ed, MS)
- agricultural extension education (MS)
- applied mathematics (MS, PhD)
- applied statistics (MS, Certificate)
- biochemistry (MS, PhD)
- biological sciences (MS)
- botany (MS, PhD)
- cellular and molecular biology (PhD)
- chemistry (MS, PhD)
- child development and family science (MS)
- clinical psychology (MS)
- coatings and polymeric materials (MS, PhD)
- cognitive and visual neuroscience (PhD)
- computer science (MS, PhD)
- counseling (M Ed, MS, PhD)
- couple and family therapy (MS)
- curriculum and instruction (M Ed, MS)
- dietetics (MS)
- education (PhD)
- educational leadership (M Ed, MS, Ed S)
- entry level athletic training (MS)
- environmental and conservation sciences (MS, PhD)
- environmental science (MS)
- exercise science (MS)
- family and consumer sciences education (M Ed, MS)
- family financial planning (MS)
- genomics (MS, PhD)
- gerontology (MS, PhD)
- health/social psychology (PhD)
- history education (M Ed, MS)
- human development (PhD)
- human development and education (M Ed, MS, PhD, Ed S)
- mathematics (MS, PhD)
- mathematics education (M Ed, MS)
- music education (M Ed, MS)
- natural resource management (MS, PhD)
- natural resources (MS, PhD)
- nutrition science (MS)
- operations research (MS)
- pedagogy (M Ed, MS)
- physical education and athletic administration (M Ed, MS)
- physics (MS, PhD)
- psychology (MS)
- public health (MS)
- science and mathematics (MS, PhD, Certificate)
- science education (M Ed, MS)
- software engineering (MS, PhD, Certificate)
- sport pedagogy (MS)
- sports recreation management (MS)
- statistics (PhD)
- transportation and logistics (PhD)
- zoology (MS, PhD)

College of Agriculture, Food Systems, and Natural Resources
Dr. Kenneth F. Grafton, Dean
Programs in:
- agribusiness and applied economics (MS)
- agriculture, food systems, and natural resources (MS, PhD)
- animal science (MS, PhD)
- cellular and molecular biology (PhD)
- cereal science (MS, PhD)
- crop and weed sciences (MS)
- entomology (MS, PhD)
- environment and conservation science (MS, PhD)
- environmental and conservation science (PhD)
- environmental conservation science (MS)
- food safety (MS, PhD)
- genomics and bioinformatics (MS, PhD)
- horticulture (MS)
- international agribusiness (MS)
- microbiology (MS)
- molecular pathogenesis (PhD)
- natural resource management (MS, PhD)
- plant pathology (MS, PhD)
- plant sciences (PhD)
- range sciences (MS, PhD)
- soil sciences (MS, PhD)

College of Arts, Humanities and Social Sciences
Dr. Thomas J. Riley, Dean
Programs in:
- arts, humanities and social sciences (M Ed, MA, MM, MS, DMA, PhD)
- communication (PhD)
- criminal justice (MS, PhD)
- emergency management (MS, PhD)
- English (MA, MS)
- history (MA, MS, PhD)
- mass communication (MA, MS)
- music (M Ed, MM, DMA)
- social science (MA, MS)
- sociology (MS)
- speech communication (MA, MS)

College of Business Administration
Dr. Ron Johnson, Dean
Program in:
- business administration (MBA)

College of Engineering and Architecture
Dr. Gary R. Smith, Dean
Programs in:
- agricultural and biosystems engineering (MS, PhD)
- civil engineering (MS, PhD)
- electrical and computer engineering)
- engineering (PhD)
- engineering and architecture (MS, PhD)
- environmental engineering (MS, PhD)
- industrial and manufacturing engineering (PhD)
- industrial engineering and management (MS)
- manufacturing engineering (MS)
- mechanical engineering (MS, PhD)

natural resource management (MS, PhD)
natural resources management (PhD)
transportation and logistics (PhD)

College of Human Development and Education
Dr. Virginia Clark Johnson, Dean
Programs in:
agricultural education (M Ed, MS)
agricultural extension education (MS)
child development and family science (MS)
counselor education (M Ed, MS, PhD)
curriculum and instruction (M Ed, MS)
education (PhD)
education leadership (MS)
educational leadership (M Ed, Ed S)
entry level athletic training (MS)
exercise science (MS)
family and consumer sciences education (M Ed, MS)
gerontology (PhD)
history education (M Ed, MS)
human development (PhD)
human development and education (M Ed, MS, PhD, Ed S)
mathematics education (M Ed, MS)
music education (M Ed, MS)
nutrition science (MS)
pedagogy (M Ed, MS)
physical education and athletic administration (M Ed, MS)
public health (MS)
science education (M Ed, MS)
sport pedagogy (MS)
sports recreation management (MS)

College of Pharmacy, Nursing and Allied Sciences
Dr. Charles D. Peterson, Dean
Programs in:
nursing (MS, DNP)
pharmaceutical sciences (MS, PhD)
pharmacy, nursing and allied sciences (MS, DNP, PhD)

College of Science and Mathematics
Dr. Donald P. Schwert, Dean
Programs in:
applied mathematics (MS, PhD)
applied statistics (MS, Certificate)
biochemistry (MS, PhD)
biological sciences (MS)
botany (MS, PhD)
cellular and molecular biology (PhD)
chemistry (MS, PhD)
clinical psychology (MS)
coatings and polymeric materials (MS, PhD)
cognitive and visual neuroscience (PhD)
computer science (MS, PhD)
environmental and conservation sciences (MS, PhD)
genomics (MS, PhD)
health/social psychology (PhD)
mathematics (MS, PhD)
natural resource management (MS, PhD)
operations research (MS)
physics (MS, PhD)
psychology (MS)
science and mathematics (MS, PhD, Certificate)
software engineering (MS, PhD, Certificate)
statistics (PhD)
zoology (MS, PhD)

■ UNIVERSITY OF MARY
Bismarck, ND 58504-9652
http://www.umary.edu/

Independent-religious, coed, comprehensive institution. *Enrollment:* 2,765 graduate, professional, and undergraduate students; 498 full-time matriculated graduate/professional students (290 women), 161 part-time matriculated graduate/professional students (124 women). *Graduate faculty:* 41 full-time (21 women), 34 part-time/adjunct (13 women). *Computer facilities:* 233 computers available on campus for general student use. A campuswide network can be accessed from student residence rooms and from off campus. Internet access and online class registration are available. *Library facilities:* University of Mary Library. *General application contact:* Dr. Kathy Perrin, Director of Graduate Studies, 701-355-8119.

Department of Occupational Therapy
Janeene Sibla, Program Director
Program in:
occupational therapy (MS)

Department of Physical Therapy
Joellen Marie Roller, Program Director
Program in:
physical therapy (DPT)

Division of Nursing
Glenda Reemts, Director
Programs in:
family nurse practitioner (MSN)
nurse management (MSN)
nursing educator (MSN)

Program in Business Administration
Brenda Kaspari, Director of the School of Accelerated and Distance Education
Program in:
business administration (MBA)

Program in Education
Dr. Rebecca Yunker Salveson, Director
Programs in:
college teaching (MS Ed)
curriculum and instruction (MS Ed)
early childhood education (MS Ed)
early childhood special education (MS Ed)
elementary education administration (MS Ed)
reading (MS Ed)
secondary education administration (MS Ed)
special education (MS Ed)

Program in Management
Brenda Kaspari, Director of the School of Accelerated and Distance Education
Program in:
management (M Mgmt)

■ UNIVERSITY OF NORTH DAKOTA
Grand Forks, ND 58202
http://www.und.nodak.edu/

State-supported, coed, university. CGS member. *Enrollment:* 12,834 graduate, professional, and undergraduate students; 846 full-time matriculated graduate/professional students (512 women), 1,289 part-time matriculated graduate/professional students (777 women). *Graduate faculty:* 492 full-time (161 women), 69 part-time/adjunct (12 women). *Computer facilities:* Computer purchase and lease plans are available. 1,100 computers available on campus for general student use. A campuswide network can be accessed from student residence rooms and from off campus. Internet access and online class registration are available. *Library facilities:* Chester Fritz Library plus 2 others. *Graduate expenses:* Tuition, state resident: full-time $5,650; part-time $214 per credit. Tuition, nonresident: full-time $14,248; part-time $572 per credit. Required fees: $1,008; $42 per credit. Tuition and fees vary according to reciprocity agreements. *General application contact:* Linda M. Baeza, Admissions Officer, 701-777-2945.

Graduate School
Dr. Joseph N. Benoit, Dean
Program in:
earth system science and policy (MEM, MS, PhD)

College of Arts and Sciences
Dr. Martha Potvin, Dean
Programs in:
arts and sciences (M Ed, M Mus, MA, MFA, MS, DA, DMEd, PhD)
botany (MS, PhD)
chemistry (MS, PhD)
clinical psychology (PhD)
communication (MA, PhD)
communication sciences and disorders (PhD)
counseling psychology (PhD)
criminal justice (PhD)
ecology (MS, PhD)
English (MA, PhD)
entomology (MS, PhD)
environmental biology (MS, PhD)
experimental psychology (PhD)
fisheries/wildlife (MS, PhD)
forensic psychology (MA, MS)
genetics (MS, PhD)

University of North Dakota (continued)
geography (MA, MS)
history (MA, DA, PhD)
linguistics (MA)
mathematics (M Ed, MS)
music (M Mus)
music education (M Mus, DMEd)
physics (MS, PhD)
psychology (MA)
sociology (MA)
speech-language pathology (MS)
theatre arts (MA)
visual arts (MFA)
zoology (MS, PhD)

College of Business and Public Administration
Dr. Dennis J. Elbert, Dean
Programs in:
applied economics (MSAE)
business administration (MBA)
business and public administration (MBA, MPA, MS, MSAE)
career and technical education (MS)
public administration (MPA)
technology education (MS)

College of Education and Human Development
Dr. Dan R. Rice, Dean
Programs in:
counseling (MA)
early childhood education (MS)
education and human development (M Ed, MA, MS, MSW, Ed D, PhD, Specialist)
education/general studies (MS)
educational leadership (M Ed, MS, Ed D, PhD, Specialist)
elementary education (Ed D, PhD)
instructional design and technology (M Ed, MS)
kinesiology (MS)
measurement and statistics (Ed D, PhD)
reading education (M Ed, MS)
secondary education (Ed D, PhD)
social work (MSW)
special education (Ed D, PhD)

College of Nursing
Dr. Chandice Covington, Dean
Program in:
nursing (MS, PhD)

John D. Odegard School of Aerospace Sciences
Bruce A. Smith, Dean
Programs in:
aerospace sciences (MS)
atmospheric sciences (MS)
aviation (MS)
computer science (MS)
space studies (MS)

School of Engineering and Mines
Dr. John L. Watson, Dean
Programs in:
chemical engineering (M Engr, MS)
civil engineering (M Engr)
electrical engineering (M Engr, MS)
engineering (PhD)
engineering and mines (M Engr, MA, MS, PhD)
environmental engineering (M Engr, MS)
geological engineering (MS)
geology (MA, MS, PhD)
mechanical engineering (M Engr, MS)
sanitary engineering (M Engr)

School of Law
Paul LeBel, Dean
Program in:
law (JD)

School of Medicine
Dr. H. David Wilson, Dean
Programs in:
anatomy (MS, PhD)
biochemistry (MS, PhD)
clinical laboratory science (MS)
medicine (MD, MOT, MPAS, MPT, MS, DPT, PhD)
microbiology and immunology (MS, PhD)
occupational therapy (MOT)
pharmacology (MS, PhD)
physical therapy (MPT, DPT)
physician assistant (MPAS)
physiology (MS, PhD)

Ohio

■ ANTIOCH UNIVERSITY MCGREGOR
Yellow Springs, OH 45387-1609
http://www.mcgregor.edu/

Independent, coed, upper-level institution. *Enrollment:* 679 graduate, professional, and undergraduate students; 304 full-time matriculated graduate/professional students (222 women), 215 part-time matriculated graduate/professional students (160 women). *Graduate faculty:* 19 full-time (11 women), 40 part-time/adjunct (20 women). *Computer facilities:* 49 computers available on campus for general student use. A campuswide network can be accessed from off campus. Internet access is available. *Library facilities:* Olive Kettering Library. *General application contact:* Seth Gordon, Enrollment Services Officer, 937-769-1800 Ext. 1825.

Graduate Programs
Darlene Robertson, Director of Operations
Programs in:
community college management (MA)
conflict resolution (MA)
liberal and professional studies (MA)
management (MA)
teacher education (M Ed)

■ ASHLAND UNIVERSITY
Ashland, OH 44805-3702
http://www.exploreashland.com

Independent-religious, coed, comprehensive institution. CGS member. *Enrollment:* 6,648 graduate, professional, and undergraduate students; 738 full-time matriculated graduate/professional students (466 women), 1,191 part-time matriculated graduate/professional students (786 women). *Graduate faculty:* 67 full-time (29 women), 196 part-time/adjunct (111 women). *Computer facilities:* Computer purchase and lease plans are available. 600 computers available on campus for general student use. A campuswide network can be accessed from student residence rooms and from off campus. *Library facilities:* Ashland Library plus 2 others. *Graduate expenses:* Tuition: part-time $403 per credit. Tuition and fees vary according to degree level and program. *General application contact:* Dr. John P. Sikula, Associate Provost, 419-289-5751.

College of Arts and Sciences
Dr. John Bee, Head
Programs in:
American history and government (MAHG)
arts and sciences (MAHG)

College of Education
Dr. Frank E. Pettigrew, Dean
Programs in:
education (M Ed, Ed D)
educational leadership studies (Ed D)

Graduate Studies in Education
Dr. Ann C. Shelly, Associate Dean
Programs in:
adapted physical education (M Ed)
administration (M Ed)
applied exercise science (M Ed)
business manager (M Ed)
classroom instruction (M Ed)
curriculum specialist (M Ed)
early childhood education (M Ed)
early childhood intervention (M Ed)
educational administration (M Ed)
educational foundations (M Ed)
educational technology (M Ed)
intervention specialist-mild/moderate (M Ed)
intervention specialist-moderate/intensive (M Ed)
middle school education (M Ed)
principalship (M Ed)
pupil services (M Ed)
school treasurer (M Ed)
sport education (M Ed)
sport management (M Ed)
sport sciences (M Ed)
superintendency (M Ed)
talent development (M Ed)

Dauch College of Business and Economics
Dr. Beverly Heimann, Chair

Program in:
business and economics (MBA)

■ BALDWIN-WALLACE COLLEGE
Berea, OH 44017-2088
http://www.bw.edu/

Independent-religious, coed, comprehensive institution. *Enrollment:* 4,365 graduate, professional, and undergraduate students; 373 full-time matriculated graduate/professional students (208 women), 367 part-time matriculated graduate/professional students (259 women). *Graduate faculty:* 30 full-time (8 women), 24 part-time/adjunct (6 women). *Computer facilities:* Computer purchase and lease plans are available. 460 computers available on campus for general student use. A campuswide network can be accessed from student residence rooms. Internet access and online class registration are available. *Library facilities:* Ritter Library plus 2 others. *Graduate expenses:* Tuition: part-time $760 per credit hour. Tuition and fees vary according to program. *General application contact:* Winifred W. Gerhardt, Director of Admission for the Evening and Weekend College, 440-826-2222.

Graduate Programs
Mary Lou Higgerson, Dean of the College

Division of Business Administration
Programs in:
accounting (MBA)
business administration-systems management (MBA)
entrepreneurship (MBA)
executive management (MBA)
health care executive management (MBA)
human resources (MBA)
international management (MBA)

Division of Education
Karen Kaye, Chair
Programs in:
educational technology (MA Ed)
mild/moderate educational needs (MA Ed)
pre-administration (MA Ed)
reading (MA Ed)

■ BOWLING GREEN STATE UNIVERSITY
Bowling Green, OH 43403
http://www.bgsu.edu/

State-supported, coed, university. CGS member. *Enrollment:* 19,108 graduate, professional, and undergraduate students; 1,527 full-time matriculated graduate/professional students (881 women), 1,047 part-time matriculated graduate/professional students (734 women). *Computer facilities:* 6,240 computers available on campus for general student use. A campuswide network can be accessed from student residence rooms and from off campus. Internet access and online class registration are available. *Library facilities:* Jerome Library plus 2 others. *Graduate expenses:* Tuition, state resident: part-time $535 per hour. Tuition, nonresident: part-time $884 per hour. *General application contact:* Dr. Terry L. Lawrence, Assistant Dean for Graduate Admissions and Studies, 419-372-7713.

Find University Details at www.petersons.com/gradchannel.

Graduate College
Dr. Heinz Bulmahn, Vice Provost for Research and Dean

College of Arts and Sciences
Dr. Donald Nieman, Dean
Programs in:
2-D studio art (MA, MFA)
3-D studio art (MA, MFA)
American culture studies (MA, MAT, PhD)
applied philosophy (PhD)
applied statistics (MS)
art education (MA)
art history (MA)
arts and sciences (MA, MAT, MFA, MPA, MS, PhD)
biological sciences (MAT, MS, PhD)
chemistry (MAT, MS)
clinical psychology (MA, PhD)
communication studies (MA, PhD)
computer art (MA, MFA)
computer science (MS)
creative writing (MFA)
demography and population studies (MA)
design (MFA)
developmental psychology (MA, PhD)
English (MA, PhD)
experimental psychology (MA, PhD)
fiction (MFA)
French (MA, MAT)
French education (MAT)
geology (MS)
geophysics (MS)
German (MA, MAT)
graphics (MFA)
history (MA, MAT, PhD)
industrial/organizational psychology (MA, PhD)
institutional theory and history (PhD)
literature (MA)
mathematics (MA, MAT, PhD)
philosophy (MA)
photochemical sciences (PhD)
physics (MAT, MS)
poetry (MFA)
popular culture (MA)
probability and statistics (PhD)
public administration (MPA)
public history (MA)
quantitative psychology (MA, PhD)
rhetoric and writing (PhD)
scientific and technical communication (MA)
social psychology (MA)
sociology (PhD)
Spanish (MA, MAT)
Spanish education (MAT)
theatre and film (MA, MAT, PhD)

College of Business Administration
Dr. Rodney Rogers, Dean
Programs in:
accountancy (M Acc)
applied statistics (MS)
business (MBA)
business administration (M Acc, MA, MBA, MOD, MS)
economics (MA)
organization development (MOD)

College of Education and Human Development
Dr. Josué Cruz, Dean
Programs in:
assistive technology (M Ed)
business education (M Ed)
classroom technology (M Ed)
college student personnel (MA)
counseling (M Ed, MA)
curriculum (M Ed)
curriculum and teaching (M Ed)
developmental kinesiology (M Ed)
early childhood intervention (M Ed)
education and human development (M Ed, MA, MFCS, MRC, Ed D, PhD, Ed S, Sp Ed)
education and intervention services (M Ed, MA, MRC, Ed S, Sp Ed)
educational administration and supervision (M Ed, Ed S)
food and nutrition (MFCS)
gifted education (M Ed)
hearing impaired intervention (M Ed)
higher education administration (PhD)
human development and family studies (MFCS)
leadership and policy studies (M Ed, MA, Ed D, PhD, Ed S)
leadership studies (Ed D)
master teaching (M Ed)
mental health counseling (MA)
mild/moderate intervention (M Ed)
moderate/intensive intervention (M Ed)
reading (M Ed, Ed S)
recreation and leisure (M Ed)
rehabilitation counseling (MRC)
school counseling (M Ed)
school psychology (M Ed, Sp Ed)
special education (M Ed)
sport administration (M Ed)

College of Health and Human Services
Dr. Linda Petrosino, Dean
Programs in:
communication disorders (PhD)
criminal justice (MSCJ)
health and human services (MPH, MS, MSCJ, PhD)
public health (MPH)
speech-language pathology (MS)

College of Musical Arts
Dr. Richard Kennell, Dean

Bowling Green State University (continued)
Programs in:
- composition (MM)
- contemporary music (DMA)
- ethnomusicology (MM)
- music education (MM)
- music history (MM)
- music theory (MM)
- performance (MM)

College of Technology
Dr. C. Wayne Unsell, Dean
Programs in:
- career and technology education (M Ed)
- construction management (MIT)
- manufacturing technology (MIT)
- technology (M Ed, MIT)

Interdisciplinary Studies
Program in:
- interdisciplinary studies (M Ed, MA, MS, PhD)

■ CAPITAL UNIVERSITY
Columbus, OH 43209-2394
http://www.capital.edu/

Independent-religious, coed, comprehensive institution. *Enrollment:* 3,825 graduate, professional, and undergraduate students; 573 full-time matriculated graduate/professional students (268 women), 436 part-time matriculated graduate/professional students (216 women). *Graduate faculty:* 17 full-time (12 women), 16 part-time/adjunct (10 women). *Computer facilities:* 100 computers available on campus for general student use. A campuswide network can be accessed from student residence rooms and from off campus. Internet access is available. *Library facilities:* Blackmore Library. *Graduate expenses:* Tuition: part-time $920 per credit. Part-time tuition and fees vary according to program. *General application contact:* Dr. Jill D Steuer, Professor and Director of the MSN Program, 614-236-6393.

Conservatory of Music
Dr. William B. Dederer, Dean
Program in:
- music education (MM)

Law School
Programs in:
- business (LL M)
- business and taxation (LL M)
- law (JD, LL M, MT)
- taxation (LL M, MT)

School of Management
Dr. Keirsten Moore, Interim Dean
Program in:
- management (MBA)

School of Nursing
Dr. Elaine F. Haynes, Dean and Professor
Programs in:
- administration (MSN)
- legal studies (MSN)
- theological studies (MSN)

■ CASE WESTERN RESERVE UNIVERSITY
Cleveland, OH 44106
http://www.case.edu/

Independent, coed, university. CGS member. *Enrollment:* 9,592 graduate, professional, and undergraduate students; 3,756 full-time matriculated graduate/professional students (1,749 women), 1,486 part-time matriculated graduate/professional students (787 women). *Graduate faculty:* 1,992 full-time (640 women). *Computer facilities:* Computer purchase and lease plans are available. 280 computers available on campus for general student use. A campuswide network can be accessed from student residence rooms and from off campus. Internet access and online class registration, software library, online reference databases, electronic books and journals are available. *Library facilities:* University Library plus 6 others. *General application contact:* Susan M. Benedict, Assistant Dean of Graduate Studies, 216-368-4390.

Frances Payne Bolton School of Nursing
Dr. May L. Wykle, Dean
Programs in:
- acute care cardiovascular nursing (MSN)
- acute care nurse practitioner (MSN, DNP)
- acute care/flight nurse (MSN)
- adult nurse practitioner (MSN, DNP)
- community health nursing (MSN)
- family nurse practitioner (MSN, DNP)
- gerontological nurse practitioner (MSN, DNP)
- graduate entry/pre-licensure option (DNP)
- medical-surgical nursing (MSN, DNP)
- midwifery/family nursing (DNP)
- neonatal nurse practitioner (MSN, DNP)
- nurse anesthesia (MSN)
- nurse midwifery (MSN)
- nurse practitioner (MSN)
- nursing (MSN, DNP, PhD)
- nursing informatics (MSN)
- pediatric nurse practitioner (MSN, DNP)
- post-licensure option (DNP)
- psychiatric mental health nurse practitioner (DNP)
- psychiatric-mental health nurse practitioner (MSN)
- women's health nurse practitioner (MSN, DNP)

Mandel School of Applied Social Sciences
Programs in:
- social administration (MSSA)
- social welfare (PhD)

School of Dental Medicine
Dr. Jerold S. Goldberg, Dean
Programs in:
- advanced general dentistry (Certificate)
- dental medicine (DMD, MSD, Certificate)
- dentistry (DMD, MSD, Certificate)
- endodontics (MSD, Certificate)
- oral surgery (Certificate)
- orthodontics (MSD, Certificate)
- pedodontics (MSD, Certificate)
- periodontics (MSD, Certificate)

School of Graduate Studies
Dr. Charles E. Rozek, Dean
Programs in:
- acting (MFA)
- analytical chemistry (MS, PhD)
- anthropology (MA, PhD)
- applied mathematics (MS, PhD)
- art education (MA)
- art history (MA, PhD)
- art history and museum studies (MA, PhD)
- astronomy (MS, PhD)
- bioethics (MA, PhD)
- biology (MS, PhD)
- clinical psychology (PhD)
- comparative literature (MA)
- contemporary dance (MFA)
- early music (D Mus A)
- English and American literature (MA, PhD)
- experimental psychology (PhD)
- French (MA, PhD)
- geological sciences (MS, PhD)
- gerontology (Certificate)
- history (MA, PhD)
- inorganic chemistry (MS, PhD)
- mathematics (MS, PhD)
- mental retardation (PhD)
- music (MA, PhD)
- music education (MA, PhD)
- organic chemistry (MS, PhD)
- physical chemistry (MS, PhD)
- physics (MS, PhD)
- political science (MA, PhD)
- sociology (PhD)
- speech-language pathology (MA, PhD)
- statistics (MS, PhD)
- theater (MFA)
- world literature (MA)

The Case School of Engineering
John Blackwell, Associate Dean
Programs in:
- aerospace engineering (MS, PhD)
- biomedical engineering (MS, PhD)
- ceramics and materials science (MS)
- chemical engineering (MS, PhD)
- civil engineering (MS, PhD)
- computer engineering (MS, PhD)

computing and information science (MS, PhD)
electrical engineering (MS, PhD)
engineering (ME, MEM, MS, PhD)
engineering mechanics (MS)
fluid and thermal engineering sciences (MS, PhD)
integration of management and engineering (MEM)
macromolecular science (MS, PhD)
materials science and engineering (MS, PhD)
mechanical engineering (MS, PhD)
systems and control engineering (MS, PhD)

School of Law
Gary J. Simson, Dean
Programs in:
law (JD)
U.S. legal studies (LL M)

School of Medicine
Dr. Pamela Davis, Dean
Programs in:
clinical research (MS)
medicine (MD, MPH, MS, PhD)

Graduate Programs in Medicine
Dr. Charles E. Rozek, Dean
Programs in:
anesthesiology (MS)
applied anatomy (MS)
biochemical research (MS)
biochemistry (MS, PhD)
biological anthropology (MS, PhD)
biomedical sciences (PhD)
biostatistics (MS, PhD)
cell biology (MS, PhD)
cell physiology (PhD)
cellular biology (MS, PhD)
developmental biology (PhD)
dietetics (MS)
epidemiology (MS, PhD)
genetic and molecular epidemiology (MS, PhD)
genetic counseling (MS)
health policy (MS, PhD)
human, molecular, and developmental genetics and genomics (PhD)
immunology (MS, PhD)
medicine (MPH, MS, PhD)
microbiology (PhD)
molecular biology (PhD)
molecular/cellular biophysics (PhD)
neurobiology (PhD)
neuroscience (PhD)
nutrition (MS, PhD)
pathology (MS, PhD)
pharmacology (MS, PhD)
physiology and biophysics (PhD)
physiology and biotechnology (MS)
public health (MPH)
public health nutrition (MS)
systems physiology (PhD)

Weatherhead School of Management
Mohan Reddy, Dean
Programs in:
accountancy (M Acc, PhD)
banking and finance (MBA)
business administration (EMBA, MBA)
economics (MBA)
information systems (MBA)
labor and human resource policy (MBA)
management (MS, MSM, EDM)
management for liberal arts graduates (MSM)
management policy (MBA)
marketing (MBA)
operations research (MSM, PhD)
organizational behavior and analysis (MBA, MPOD, MS)
positive organization development and change (MPOD)
supply chain (MSM)

Mandel Center for Nonprofit Organizations
Susan Lajoie Eagan, Director
Program in:
nonprofit organizations (MNO, CNM)

■ CLEVELAND STATE UNIVERSITY
Cleveland, OH 44115
http://www.csuohio.edu/

State-supported, coed, university. CGS member. *Enrollment:* 15,483 graduate, professional, and undergraduate students; 1,728 full-time matriculated graduate/professional students (996 women), 4,216 part-time matriculated graduate/professional students (2,652 women). *Graduate faculty:* 637. *Computer facilities:* Computer purchase and lease plans are available. 600 computers available on campus for general student use. A campuswide network can be accessed. Internet access and online class registration are available. *Library facilities:* University Library plus 1 other. *General application contact:* Giannina Pianalto, Director of Graduate Admissions, 216-523-7572.

Cleveland-Marshall College of Law
Geoffrey S. Mearns, Dean
Program in:
law (JD, LL M)

College of Graduate Studies
Dr. Leo W. Jeffres, Interim Vice Provost for Research/Interim Dean

College of Education and Human Services
Dr. James A. McLoughlin, Dean
Programs in:
adult learning and development (M Ed)
art education (M Ed)
clinical nursing leader (MSN)
community agency counseling (M Ed)
community health education (M Ed)
counseling (PhD)
counseling and pupil personnel administration (Ed S)
counseling psychology (PhD)
early childhood education (M Ed)
education and human services (M Ed, MSN, PhD, Ed S)
educational administration (Ed S)
educational administration and supervision (M Ed)
exercise science (M Ed)
foreign language education (M Ed)
forensic nursing (MSN)
human performance (M Ed)
leadership and lifelong learning (PhD)
learning and development (PhD)
mathematics and science education (M Ed)
middle childhood education (M Ed)
physical education pedagogy (M Ed)
policy studies (PhD)
population health nursing (MSN)
school administration (PhD)
school counseling (M Ed)
school health education (M Ed)
special education (M Ed)
sport and exercise psychology (M Ed)
sports management (M Ed)
teaching English to speakers of other languages (M Ed)

College of Liberal Arts and Social Sciences
Dr. Gregory M. Sadlek, Dean
Programs in:
applied communication theory and methodology (MA)
art education (M Ed)
art history (MA)
bioethics (MA, Certificate)
composition (MM)
creative writing (MFA)
culture, communication and health care (Certificate)
economics (MA)
English (MA)
history (MA)
liberal arts and social sciences (M Ed, MA, MFA, MM, MSW, Certificate)
museum studies (MA)
music education (MM)
performance (MM)
philosophy (MA)
social studies (MA)
social work (MSW)
sociology (MA)
Spanish (MA)

College of Science
Dr. Bette R. Bonder, Dean
Programs in:
analytical chemistry (MS)
applied optics (MS)
biology (MS)
clinical chemistry (MS)
clinical psychology (MA)
clinical/bioanalytical chemistry (PhD)
condensed matter physics (MS)
consumer/industrial research (MA)
diversity management (MA)

Cleveland State University (continued)
- environmental chemistry (MS)
- environmental science (MS)
- experimental research psychology (MA)
- health sciences (MS)
- inorganic chemistry (MS)
- mathematics (MA, MS)
- medical physics (MS)
- occupational therapy (MOT)
- organic chemistry (MS)
- physical chemistry (MS)
- physical therapy (DPT)
- regulatory biology (PhD)
- school psychology (Psy S)
- science (MA, MOT, MS, DPT, PhD, Psy S)
- speech pathology and audiology (MA)

Fenn College of Engineering
Dr. Paul Bellini, Dean
Programs in:
- applied biomedical engineering (D Eng)
- chemical engineering (MS, D Eng)
- civil engineering (MS, D Eng)
- electrical engineering (MS, D Eng)
- engineering (MS, D Eng)
- engineering mechanics (MS)
- environmental engineering (MS)
- industrial engineering (MS, D Eng)
- mechanical engineering (MS, D Eng)
- software engineering (MS)

Maxine Goodman Levin College of Urban Affairs
Dr. Mark S. Rosentraub, Dean
Programs in:
- environmental studies (MAES)
- geographic information systems (Certificate)
- local and urban management (Certificate)
- non-profit management (Certificate)
- nonprofit administration and leadership (MNAL)
- public administration (MPA)
- urban affairs (MAES, MNAL, MPA, MS, MUPDD, PhD, Certificate)
- urban economic development (Certificate)
- urban planning, design, and development (MUPDD)
- urban real estate development and finance (Certificate)
- urban studies (MS)
- urban studies and public affairs (PhD)

Nance College of Business Administration
Dr. Robert F. Scherer, Dean
Programs in:
- business administration (DBA)
- business statistics (MBA)
- computer information science (MS)
- data-driven marketing planning (Graduate Certificate)
- e-commerce (MBA)
- finance (MBA, DBA)
- financial accounting/audit (MAC)
- global business (Graduate Certificate)
- health care administration (MBA)
- information systems (DBA)
- labor relations and human resources (MLRHR)
- marketing (MBA, DBA)
- operations management (MBA)
- production/operations management (DBA)
- taxation (MAC)

■ COLLEGE OF MOUNT ST. JOSEPH
Cincinnati, OH 45233-1670
http://www.msj.edu/

Independent-religious, coed, comprehensive institution. *Enrollment:* 2,259 graduate, professional, and undergraduate students; 146 full-time matriculated graduate/professional students (112 women), 197 part-time matriculated graduate/professional students (157 women). *Graduate faculty:* 46 full-time (31 women), 16 part-time/adjunct (9 women). *Computer facilities:* Computer purchase and lease plans are available. 278 computers available on campus for general student use. A campuswide network can be accessed from student residence rooms and from off campus. Internet access and online class registration, computer-aided instruction are available. *Library facilities:* Archbishop Alter Library. *Graduate expenses:* Tuition: part-time $440 per hour. Tuition and fees vary according to program. *General application contact:* Marilyn Hoskins, Assistant Director of Admissions for Graduate Recruitment, 513-244-4723.

Find University Details at www.petersons.com/gradchannel.

Graduate Education Program
Dr. Mifrando Obach, Chair
Programs in:
- adolescent young adult education (MA)
- art (MA)
- inclusive early childhood education (MA)
- instructional leadership (MA)
- middle childhood education (MA)
- multicultural special education (MA)
- music (MA)
- reading (MA)

Graduate Program in Religious Studies
Dr. John Trokan, Chair
Program in:
- spiritual and pastoral care (MA)

Master of Nursing Program
Dr. Darla Vale, Chair, Health Sciences Department
Program in:
- nursing (MN)

Multidisciplinary Program in Organizational Leadership
Dr. Jim Brodzinski, Chair
Program in:
- organizational leadership (MS)

Physical Therapy Program
Dr. Darla Vale, Chair, Health Sciences Department
Program in:
- physical therapy (MPT, DPT)

■ DEVRY UNIVERSITY
Columbus, OH 43209-2705
http://www.devry.edu/

Proprietary, coed, comprehensive institution. *Computer facilities:* Computer purchase and lease plans are available. 408 computers available on campus for general student use. A campuswide network can be accessed from off campus. Internet access and online class registration are available. *Library facilities:* Learning Resource Center.

Keller Graduate School of Management
Program in:
- management (MAFM, MBA, MHRM, MISM, MNCM, MPA, MPM)

■ FRANCISCAN UNIVERSITY OF STEUBENVILLE
Steubenville, OH 43952-1763
http://www.franciscan.edu/

Independent-religious, coed, comprehensive institution. *Computer facilities:* 126 computers available on campus for general student use. A campuswide network can be accessed. Internet access is available. *Library facilities:* John Paul II Library. *General application contact:* Director of Graduate Enrollment, 800-783-6220.

Graduate Programs
Programs in:
- administration (MS Ed)
- business (MBA)
- counseling (MA)
- nursing (MSN)
- philosophy (MA)
- teaching (MS Ed)
- theology and Christian ministry (MA)

■ HEIDELBERG COLLEGE
Tiffin, OH 44883-2462
http://www.heidelberg.edu/

Independent-religious, coed, comprehensive institution. *Enrollment:* 1,569 graduate, professional, and undergraduate students; 50 full-time matriculated graduate/professional students (28 women), 202 part-time matriculated graduate/professional students (148 women). *Graduate faculty:* 4 full-time (1 woman), 11 part-time/adjunct (6 women). *Computer facilities:* 125 computers available on campus for general student use. A campuswide network can be accessed from student residence rooms and from off campus. Internet access and online class registration are available. *Library facilities:* Beeghly Library. *Graduate expenses:* Tuition: part-time $345 per hour. Tuition and fees vary according to program. *General application contact:* Dr. G. Michael Pratt, Graduate Studies Office, 419-448-2288.

Program in Business
Dr. Henry G. Rennie, Director of Graduate Studies in Business
Program in:
business (MBA)

Program in Counseling
Dr. Jo-Ann Lipford Sanders, Director of Graduate Studies in Counseling
Program in:
counseling (MA)

Program in Education
Dr. Jim Getz, Director of Graduate Studies in Education
Program in:
education (MA)

■ JOHN CARROLL UNIVERSITY
University Heights, OH 44118-4581
http://www.jcu.edu/

Independent-religious, coed, comprehensive institution. CGS member. *Enrollment:* 188 full-time matriculated graduate/professional students (128 women), 515 part-time matriculated graduate/professional students (323 women). *Graduate faculty:* 140 full-time (41 women), 42 part-time/adjunct (23 women). *Computer facilities:* 210 computers available on campus for general student use. A campuswide network can be accessed from student residence rooms and from off campus. Internet access and online class registration are available. *Library facilities:* Grasselli Library. *Graduate expenses:* Tuition: full-time $9,675; part-time $645 per credit hour. Tuition and fees vary according to program. *General application contact:* Jennifer Tucker, Records Management Assistant, 216-397-1925.

Graduate School
Dr. Mary E. Beadle, Dean
Programs in:
administration (M Ed, MA)
biology (MA, MS)
clinical counseling (Certificate)
communications management (MA)
community counseling (MA)
educational and school psychology (M Ed, MA)
English (MA)
history (MA)
humanities (MA)
integrated science (MA)
mathematics (MA, MS)
nonprofit administration (MA)
professional teacher education (M Ed, MA)
religious studies (MA)
school based adolescent-young adult education (M Ed)
school based early childhood education (M Ed)
school based middle childhood education (M Ed)
school based multi-age education (M Ed)
school counseling (M Ed, MA)

John M. and Mary Jo Boler School of Business
Dr. Karen Schuele, Associate Dean
Programs in:
accountancy (MS)
business (MBA)

■ KENT STATE UNIVERSITY
Kent, OH 44242-0001
http://www.kent.edu/

State-supported, coed, university. CGS member. *Computer facilities:* 1,690 computers available on campus for general student use. A campuswide network can be accessed from student residence rooms and from off campus. Internet access is available. *Library facilities:* Kent State University Libraries and Media Services plus 7 others. *General application contact:* Division of Research and Graduate Studies, 330-672-2661.

College of Architecture and Environmental Design
Programs in:
architecture (M Arch)
architecture and environmental design (Certificate)

College of Arts and Sciences
Programs in:
analytical chemistry (MS, PhD)
anthropology (MA)
applied mathematics (MA, MS, PhD)
arts and sciences (MA, MFA, MLS, MPA, MS, PhD)
biochemistry (MS, PhD)
botany (MS)
chemical physics (MS, PhD)
chemistry (MA, MS, PhD)
clinical psychology (MA, PhD)
comparative literature (MA)
computer science (MA, MS, PhD)
creative writing (MFA)
ecology (MS, PhD)
English for teachers (MA)
experimental psychology (MA, PhD)
French (MA)
geography (MA, PhD)
geology (MS, PhD)
German (MA)
history (MA, PhD)
inorganic chemistry (MS, PhD)
Japanese (MA)
justice studies (MA)
Latin (MA)
liberal studies (MLS)
literature (PhD)
literature and writing (MA)
organic chemistry (MS, PhD)
philosophy (MA)
physical chemistry (MS, PhD)
physics (MA, MS, PhD)
physiology (MS, PhD)
political science (MA)
public administration (MPA)
public policy (PhD)
pure mathematics (MA, MS, PhD)
rhetoric and composition (PhD)
Russian (MA)
sociology (MA, PhD)
Spanish (MA)
teaching English as a second language (MA)
translation (MA)

College of Communication and Information
Program in:
communication and information (MA, MFA, MLS, MS, PhD)

School of Communication Studies
Program in:
communication studies (MA, PhD)

School of Journalism and Mass Communication
Program in:
journalism and mass communication (MA)

School of Library and Information Science
Programs in:
information architecture and knowledge management (MS)
library and information science (MLS, MS)

School of Visual Communication Design
Program in:
visual communication design (MA, MFA)

College of Fine and Professional Arts
Program in:
fine and professional arts (MA, MFA, MLS, MM, MPH, MS, Au D, PhD, Certificate)

Hugh A. Glauser School of Music
Programs in:
composition (MA)
conducting (MM)
ethnomusicology (MA)
music education (MM, PhD)
musicology (MA)
musicology-ethnomusicology (PhD)
performance (MM)
theory (MA)
theory and composition (PhD)

Kent State University (continued)
School of Art
Programs in:
art education (MA)
art history (MA)
crafts (MA, MFA)
fine arts (MA, MFA)

School of Theatre and Dance
Programs in:
acting (MFA)
design and technology (MFA)
theatre (MA, MFA)

College of Nursing
Programs in:
clinical nursing (MSN)
nursing (PhD)
nursing administration (MSN)
nursing education (MSN)
parent-child nursing (MSN)

Graduate School of Education, Health, and Human Services
Dr. David A. England, Dean
Programs in:
athletic training (MA)
career technical teacher education (M Ed, MA, Ed S)
community counseling (M Ed, MA)
computer technology (M Ed, MA)
counseling (Ed S)
counseling and human development services (PhD)
cultural foundations (M Ed, MA, PhD)
curriculum and instruction (M Ed, MA, PhD, Ed S)
deaf education (M Ed, MA)
early childhood education (M Ed, MA, MAT)
education, health, and human services (M Ed, MA, MAT, MPH, MS, Au D, PhD, Ed S)
educational administration (PhD, Ed S)
educational interpreter (M Ed, MA)
educational psychology (M Ed, MA, PhD)
evaluation and measurement (M Ed, MA, PhD)
exercise physiology (MA, PhD)
general special education (M Ed, MA)
gifted (M Ed, MA)
health education and promotion (M Ed, MA, PhD)
higher education administration and student personnel (M Ed, MA)
instructional technology (M Ed, MA)
instructional technology general (M Ed, MA)
intervention specialist (M Ed, MA)
junior high/middle school (M Ed, MA)
K-12 leadership (M Ed, MA, PhD, Ed S)
library media (M Ed, MA)
math specialization (M Ed, MA)
mild/moderate (M Ed, MA)
moderate/intensive (M Ed, MA)
physical teacher education (MA)
public health (MPH)
reading (M Ed, MA)
rehabilitation counseling (M Ed, MA, Ed S)
school counseling (M Ed, MA)
school psychology (M Ed, PhD, Ed S)
secondary education (MAT)
special education (PhD, Ed S)
sport and recreation management (MA)
sports studies (MA)
transition to work (M Ed, MA)

School of Exercise, Leisure and Sport
Wayne Munson, Interim Director
Program in:
exercise, leisure and sport (MA, PhD)

School of Family and Consumer Studies
Dr. Mary Dellmann-Jenkins, Director
Programs in:
dietetic internship (MS)
family and consumer studies (MA, MS)
gerontology (MA)
human development and family studies (MA)
nutrition (MS)

School of Speech Pathology and Audiology
Dr. Lynne B. Rowan, Director
Programs in:
audiology (Au D, PhD)
speech pathology and audiology (MA, Au D, PhD)

Graduate School of Management
Dr. Frederick W. Schroath, Associate Dean
Programs in:
accounting (MS, PhD)
business administration (MBA)
economics (MA)
finance (PhD)
financial engineering (MSFE)
management (MA, MBA, MS, MSFE, PhD)
management systems (PhD)
marketing (PhD)

School of Biomedical Sciences
Programs in:
biomedical sciences (MS, PhD)
cellular and molecular biology (MS, PhD)
neuroscience (MS, PhD)
pharmacology (MS, PhD)
physiology (MS, PhD)

School of Technology
Program in:
technology (M Tech, MA)

■ MALONE COLLEGE
Canton, OH 44709-3897
http://www.malone.edu/

Independent-religious, coed, comprehensive institution. *Enrollment:* 2,296 graduate, professional, and undergraduate students; 35 full-time matriculated graduate/professional students (28 women), 299 part-time matriculated graduate/professional students (212 women). *Graduate faculty:* 35 full-time (16 women), 36 part-time/adjunct (22 women). *Computer facilities:* 200 computers available on campus for general student use. A campuswide network can be accessed from student residence rooms and from off campus. Internet access is available. *Library facilities:* Everett L. Cattell Library. *Graduate expenses:* Tuition: part-time $399 per credit hour. *General application contact:* Dr. David Kleffman, Recruiter, 330-471-8447.

■ MIAMI UNIVERSITY
Oxford, OH 45056
http://www.muohio.edu/

State-related, coed, university. CGS member. *Computer facilities:* 1,000 computers available on campus for general student use. A campuswide network can be accessed from student residence rooms and from off campus. Internet access and online class registration are available. *Library facilities:* King Library plus 3 others. *General application contact:* Associate Provost for Research and Dean of the Graduate School, 513-529-3734.

Find University Details at www.petersons.com/gradchannel.

Graduate School

College of Arts and Sciences
Programs in:
analytical chemistry (MS, PhD)
arts and sciences (MA, MAT, MGS, MS, MS Stat, MTSC, PhD)
biochemistry (MS, PhD)
biological sciences (MAT)
botany (MA, MS, PhD)
chemical education (MS, PhD)
chemistry (MS, PhD)
clinical psychology (PhD)
comparative religion (MA)
composition and rhetoric (MA, PhD)
creative writing (MA)
criticism (PhD)
English and American literature and language (PhD)
English education (MAT)
experimental psychology (PhD)
French (MA)
geography (MA)
geology (MA, MS, PhD)
gerontology (MGS)
history (MA, PhD)
inorganic chemistry (MS, PhD)
library theory (PhD)
literature (MA, MAT, PhD)
mass communication (MA)
mathematics (MA, MAT, MS)
mathematics/operations research (MS)
microbiology (MS, PhD)
organic chemistry (MS, PhD)

philosophy (MA)
physical chemistry (MS, PhD)
physics (MAT, MS)
political science (MA, MAT, PhD)
social gerontology (PhD)
social psychology (PhD)
Spanish (MA)
speech communication (MA)
speech pathology and audiology (MA, MS)
statistics (MS Stat)
technical and scientific communication (MTSC)
zoology (MA, MS, PhD)

Institute of Environmental Sciences
Program in:
environmental sciences (M En S)

Richard T. Farmer School of Business Administration
Programs in:
accountancy (M Acc)
business administration (MBA)
economics (MA)
finance (MBA)
general management (MBA)
management information systems (MBA)
marketing (MBA)
quality and process improvement (MBA)

School of Education and Allied Professions
Programs in:
adolescent education (MAT)
child and family studies (MS)
college student personnel services (MS)
curriculum and teacher leadership (M Ed)
education and allied professions (M Ed, MAT, MS, Ed D, PhD, Ed S)
educational administration (Ed D, PhD)
educational leadership (M Ed, MS)
educational psychology (M Ed)
elementary education (M Ed, MAT)
elementary mathematics education (M Ed)
exercise and health studies (MS)
reading education (M Ed)
school psychology (MS, Ed S)
secondary education (M Ed, MAT)
special education (M Ed)
sport studies (MS)

School of Engineering and Applied Science
Programs in:
computer science (MCS)
computer science and systems analysis (MCS)
paper science and engineering (MS)
software development (Certificate)

School of Fine Arts
Programs in:
architecture (M Arch)
art education (MA)
fine arts (M Arch, MA, MFA, MM)
music education (MM)
music performance (MM)
studio art (MFA)
theatre (MA)

■ MUSKINGUM COLLEGE
New Concord, OH 43762
http://www.muskingum.edu/

Independent-religious, coed, comprehensive institution. *Computer facilities:* 76 computers available on campus for general student use. A campuswide network can be accessed from student residence rooms and from off campus. Internet access is available. *Library facilities:* College Library. *General application contact:* Director of Graduate Studies, 614-826-8037.

Graduate Program in Education
Program in:
education (MAE)

■ OHIO DOMINICAN UNIVERSITY
Columbus, OH 43219-2099
http://www.ohiodominican.edu/

Independent-religious, coed, comprehensive institution. *Enrollment:* 3,054 graduate, professional, and undergraduate students; 309 full-time matriculated graduate/professional students (156 women), 150 part-time matriculated graduate/professional students (102 women). *Computer facilities:* 198 computers available on campus for general student use. A campuswide network can be accessed from student residence rooms and from off campus. Internet access and online class registration are available. *Library facilities:* Spangler Library. *Graduate expenses:* Tuition: part-time $450 per credit. Required fees: $10 per semester. *General application contact:* Jill M. Westerfeld, Graduate Admissions Recruiter, 614-251-4725.

Graduate Programs
Dr. Mary Todd, Vice President for Academic Affairs
Programs in:
liberal studies (MA)
TESOL (MA)

Division of Business
Antonio Emanuel, Director of Graduate Business Programs
Program in:
business (MBA)

Division of Education
Dr. Mary Todd, Vice President for Academic Affairs
Program in:
education (M Ed)

Division of Theology, Arts and Ideas
Dr. Barbara Finan, Director, MA in Theology
Program in:
theology (MA)

■ THE OHIO STATE UNIVERSITY
Columbus, OH 43210
http://www.osu.edu/

State-supported, coed, university. CGS member. *Enrollment:* 51,818 graduate, professional, and undergraduate students; 10,205 full-time matriculated graduate/professional students (5,320 women), 3,134 part-time matriculated graduate/professional students (2,021 women). *Graduate faculty:* 2,876. *Computer facilities:* 800 computers available on campus for general student use. A campuswide network can be accessed from student residence rooms and from off campus. Internet access and online class registration are available. *Library facilities:* Main Library plus 12 others. *Graduate expenses:* Tuition, state resident: full-time $9,438. Tuition, nonresident: full-time $22,791. Tuition and fees vary according to course load, campus/location and program. *General application contact:* Information Contact, 614-292-9444.

College of Dentistry
Dr. Carole Anderson, Interim Dean
Programs in:
dentistry (DDS, MS, PhD)
oral biology (PhD)

College of Medicine
Dr. Wiley W. Souba, Dean
Programs in:
anatomy (MS, PhD)
biomedical science (MD, MS, PhD)
experimental pathobiology (MS)
immunology (PhD)
medical genetics (PhD)
medical science (PhD)
medicine (MD, MOT, MPT, MS, PhD)
molecular virology (PhD)
molecular virology, immunology and medical genetics (MS, PhD)
neuroscience (PhD)
pathology assistant (MS)
pharmacology (PhD)

School of Allied Medical Professions
Deborah S. Larsen, Director
Programs in:
allied medicine (MS)
circulation technology (MS)
occupational therapy (MOT)
physical therapy (MPT)

College of Optometry
Dr. Melvin D. Shipp, Dean
Programs in:
optometry (OD, MS, PhD)
vision science (MS, PhD)

College of Pharmacy
Dr. Robert W. Brueggemeier, Dean
Programs in:
health-system pharmacy administration (MS)

The Ohio State University (continued)

- medicinal chemistry and pharmacognosy (MS, PhD)
- pharmaceutical administration (MS, PhD)
- pharmaceutics (MS, PhD)
- pharmacology (MS, PhD)
- pharmacy (Pharm D, MS, PhD)
- pharmacy practice and administration (MS, PhD)

College of Veterinary Medicine

Thomas Rosol, Dean
Programs in:

- anatomy and cellular biology (MS, PhD)
- pathobiology (MS, PhD)
- pharmacology (MS, PhD)
- toxicology (MS, PhD)
- veterinary clinical sciences (MS, PhD)
- veterinary medicine (DVM, MS, PhD)
- veterinary physiology (MS, PhD)
- veterinary preventive medicine (MS, PhD)

Graduate School

Peter S. Osmer, Dean
Program in:

- textiles and clothing (MS, PhD)

College of Biological Sciences
Dr. Joan M. Herbers, Dean
Programs in:

- biochemistry (MS)
- biological sciences (MS, PhD)
- biophysics (MS, PhD)
- cell and developmental biology (MS, PhD)
- entomology (MS, PhD)
- environmental science (MS, PhD)
- evolution, ecology, and organismal biology (MS, PhD)
- genetics (MS, PhD)
- microbiology (MS, PhD)
- molecular biology (MS, PhD)
- molecular, cellular and developmental biology (MS, PhD)
- plant biology (MS, PhD)

College of Education and Human Ecology
Dr. David Andrews, Dean
Programs in:

- education and human ecology (M Ed, MA, MS, PhD)
- educational policy and leadership (M Ed, MA, PhD)
- family and consumer sciences education (M Ed, MS)
- family resource management (MS, PhD)
- food service management (MS, PhD)
- foods (MS, PhD)
- higher education and student affairs (MA)
- hospitality management (MS, PhD)
- human development and family science (M Ed, MS, PhD)
- nutrition (MS, PhD)
- physical activity and educational services (M Ed, MA, PhD)
- teaching and learning (M Ed, MA, PhD)

College of Engineering
Dr. William A. Baeslack, Dean
Programs in:

- aeronautical and astronautical engineering (MS, PhD)
- architecture (M Arch, M Land Arch, MCRP, PhD)
- biomedical engineering (MS, PhD)
- chemical engineering (MS, PhD)
- city and regional planning (MCRP, PhD)
- civil engineering (MS, PhD)
- computer and information science (MS, PhD)
- electrical engineering (MS, PhD)
- engineering (M Arch, M Land Arch, MCRP, MS, MWE, PhD)
- engineering mechanics (MS, PhD)
- geodetic science and surveying (MS, PhD)
- industrial and systems engineering (MS, PhD)
- landscape architecture (M Land Arch)
- materials science and engineering (MS, PhD)
- mechanical engineering (MS, PhD)
- nuclear engineering (MS, PhD)
- welding engineering (MS, MWE, PhD)

College of Food, Agricultural, and Environmental Sciences
Dr. Bobby D. Moser, Dean
Programs in:

- agricultural economics and rural sociology (MS, PhD)
- animal sciences (MS, PhD)
- environment and natural resources (MS, PhD)
- food science and nutrition (MS, PhD)
- food, agricultural, and biological engineering (MS, PhD)
- food, agricultural, and environmental sciences (M Ed, MS, PhD)
- horticulture and crop science (MS, PhD)
- human and community resource development (M Ed, MS, PhD)
- human dimensions in natural resources (MS, PhD)
- natural resources (MS, PhD)
- plant pathology (MS, PhD)
- rural sociology (MS, PhD)
- soil science (MS, PhD)
- vocational education (PhD)

College of Humanities
Dr. John W. Roberts, Dean
Programs in:

- African-American and African studies (MA)
- classics (MA)
- comparative studies (MA, PhD)
- East Asian languages and literatures (MA, PhD)
- English (MA, MFA, PhD)
- French (MA, PhD)
- Germanic languages and literatures (MA, PhD)
- Greek and Latin (MA, PhD)
- history (MA, PhD)
- humanities (MA, MFA, PhD)
- Italian (MA)
- Japanese (MA, PhD)
- linguistics (MA, PhD)
- Near Eastern languages and cultures (MA, PhD)
- philosophy (MA, PhD)
- Slavic and East European languages and literatures (MA, PhD)
- Slavic and East European studies (MA)
- Spanish and Portuguese (MA, PhD)
- women's studies (MA, PhD)

College of Mathematical and Physical Sciences
Dr. Richard R. Freeman, Dean
Programs in:

- astronomy (MS, PhD)
- biostatistics (PhD)
- chemical physics (MS, PhD)
- chemistry (MS, PhD)
- geological sciences (MS, PhD)
- mathematical and physical sciences (M Appl Stat, MA, MS, PhD)
- mathematics (MA, MS, PhD)
- physics (MS, PhD)
- statistics (M Appl Stat, MS, PhD)

College of Nursing
Dr. Elizabeth R. Lenz, Dean
Program in:

- nursing (MS, PhD)

College of Social and Behavioral Sciences
Dr. Paul A. Beck, Dean
Programs in:

- anthropology (MA, PhD)
- atmospheric sciences (MS, PhD)
- behavioral neuroscience (PhD)
- clinical psychology (PhD)
- cognitive psychology (PhD)
- communication (MA, PhD)
- developmental psychology (PhD)
- economics (MA, PhD)
- geography (MA, PhD)
- mental retardation and developmental disabilities (PhD)
- political science (MA, PhD)
- psychology (MA)
- quantitative psychology (PhD)
- social and behavioral science (MA, MS, Au D, PhD)
- social and behavioral sciences (MA, MS, Au D, PhD)
- social psychology (PhD)
- sociology (MA, PhD)
- speech and hearing science (MA, Au D, PhD)

College of Social Work
William Meezan, Dean
Program in:

- social work (MSW, PhD)

College of the Arts
Karen A. Bell, Dean
Programs in:

- art (MFA)

art education (MA, PhD)
arts (M Mus, MA, MFA, PhD)
arts policy and administration (MA)
dance (MA, MFA, PhD)
history of art (MA, PhD)
industrial, interior, and visual communication design (MA, MFA)
music (M Mus, MA, PhD)
theatre (MA, MFA, PhD)

Max M. Fisher College of Business
Dr. Steve Mangum, Acting Dean
Programs in:
accounting and management information systems (M Acc, MA, PhD)
business (M Acc, MA, MBA, MBLE, MLHR, PhD)
business administration (MA, MBA, PhD)
business logistics engineering (MBLE)
finance (MA, PhD)
labor and human resources (MLHR, PhD)

John Glenn School of Public Affairs
Mary K. Marvel, Graduate Studies Committee Chair
Program in:
public affairs (MA, MPA, PhD)

Moritz College of Law
Nancy H. Rogers, Dean
Program in:
law (JD, LL M, MSL)

■ OHIO UNIVERSITY
Athens, OH 45701-2979
http://www.ohio.edu/

State-supported, coed, university. CGS member. *Enrollment:* 20,593 graduate, professional, and undergraduate students; 2,422 full-time matriculated graduate/professional students (1,222 women), 729 part-time matriculated graduate/professional students (414 women). *Graduate faculty:* 938 full-time (331 women), 340 part-time/adjunct (152 women). *Computer facilities:* 1,500 computers available on campus for general student use. A campuswide network can be accessed from student residence rooms and from off campus. Internet access and online class registration are available. *Library facilities:* Alden Library plus 1 other. *General application contact:* Information Contact, 740-593-2800.

College of Osteopathic Medicine
Dr. John A. Brose, Dean
Program in:
osteopathic medicine (DO)

Graduate Studies
Dr. Michael J. Mumper, Associate Provost for Graduate Studies
Program in:
interdisciplinary studies (PhD)

Center for International Studies
Dr. Josep Rota, Director
Programs in:
African studies (MA)
communications and development studies (MA)
development studies (MA)
international studies (MA)
Latin American studies (MA)
Southeast Asian studies (MA)

College of Arts and Sciences
Dr. Ben M. Ogles, Interim Dean
Programs in:
applied economics (MA)
applied linguistics/TESOL (MA)
arts and sciences (MA, MPA, MS, MSS, MSW, PhD)
astronomy (MS, PhD)
biological sciences (MS, PhD)
cell biology and physiology (MS, PhD)
chemistry and biochemistry (MS, PhD)
clinical psychology (PhD)
ecology and evolutionary biology (MS, PhD)
English language and literature (MA, PhD)
environmental and plant biology (MS, PhD)
environmental geochemistry (MS)
environmental geology (MS)
environmental studies (MS)
environmental/hydrology (MS)
exercise physiology and muscle biology (MS, PhD)
experimental psychology (PhD)
financial economics (MA)
French (MA)
geography (MA)
geology (MS)
geology education (MS)
geomorphology/surficial processes (MS)
geophysics (MS)
history (MA, PhD)
hydrogeology (MS)
mathematics (MS, PhD)
microbiology (MS, PhD)
molecular and cellular biology (MS, PhD)
neuroscience (MS, PhD)
organizational psychology (PhD)
philosophy (MA)
physics (MS, PhD)
political science (MA)
public administration (MPA)
sedimentology (MS)
social sciences (MSS)
social work (MSW)
sociology (MA)
Spanish (MA)
structure/tectonics (MS)

College of Business
Dr. Edward B. Yost, Director, Executive Education
Programs in:
business (EMBA, MBA)
business administration (EMBA, MBA)

College of Education
Dr. Ren'ee A. Middleton, Dean
Programs in:
adolescent to young adult education (M Ed)
college student personnel (M Ed)
community/agency counseling (M Ed)
computer education and technology (M Ed)
counselor education (PhD)
curriculum and instruction (M Ed, PhD)
education (M Ed, Ed D, PhD)
educational administration (M Ed, Ed D)
educational research and evaluation (M Ed, PhD)
higher education (M Ed, PhD)
instructional technology (PhD)
mathematics education (PhD)
middle child education (M Ed)
reading and language arts (PhD)
reading education (M Ed)
rehabilitation counseling (M Ed)
school counseling (M Ed)
social studies education (PhD)
special education (M Ed, PhD)

College of Fine Arts
Charles A. McWeeney, Dean
Programs in:
accompanying (MM)
art education (MA)
art history (MA)
art history/studio (MFA)
ceramics (MFA)
composition (MM)
conducting (MM)
film (MFA)
film studies (MA)
fine arts (MA, MFA, MM, PhD, Certificate)
history/literature (MM)
interdisciplinary arts (PhD)
music education (MM)
music therapy (MM)
painting (MFA)
performance (MM, Certificate)
performance/pedagogy (MM)
photography (MFA)
printmaking (MFA)
sculpture (MFA)
theater (MA, MFA)
theory (MM)

College of Health and Human Services
Dr. Gary Neiman, Dean
Programs in:
athletic training education (MS RSS)
audiology (Au D)
child development and family life (MSHCS)
coaching education (MS)
early childhood education (MSHCS)
family studies (MSHCS)
food and nutrition (MSHCS)
health and human services (MA, MHA, MPH, MS, MS RSS, MSA, MSHCS, MSP Ex, Au D, DPT, PhD)
health sciences (MHA, MPH)
hearing science (PhD)

Ohio University (continued)
physical therapy (DPT)
physiology of exercise (MSP Ex)
recreation studies (MS)
speech language pathology (MA)
speech-language science (PhD)
sports administration and facility management (MSA)

Russ College of Engineering and Technology
Dr. Dennis Irwin, Dean
Programs in:
biomedical engineering (MS)
chemical engineering (MS, PhD)
civil (PhD)
computer science (MS)
construction (MS)
electrical engineering (MS, PhD)
engineering and technology (MS, PhD)
environmental (MS)
geotechnical and environmental engineering (MS)
industrial (PhD)
industrial and manufacturing systems engineering (MS)
integrated engineering (PhD)
manufacturing engineering (MS)
mechanical (PhD)
mechanical engineering (MS, PhD)
structures (MS)
transportation (MS)
water resources and structures (MS)

Scripps College of Communication
Dr. Gregory J. Shepherd, Dean
Programs in:
communication (MA, MCTP, MS, PhD)
communication studies (PhD)
information and telecommunication systems (MCTP)
journalism (MS, PhD)
telecommunications (MA, PhD)
visual communication (MA)

■ OTTERBEIN COLLEGE
Westerville, OH 43081
http://www.otterbein.edu/

Independent-religious, coed, comprehensive institution. *Enrollment:* 3,176 graduate, professional, and undergraduate students; 90 full-time matriculated graduate/professional students (51 women), 290 part-time matriculated graduate/professional students (240 women). *Graduate faculty:* 30 full-time (23 women), 10 part-time/adjunct (3 women). *Computer facilities:* 146 computers available on campus for general student use. A campuswide network can be accessed from student residence rooms and from off campus. Internet access is available. *Library facilities:* Courtright Memorial Library. *Graduate expenses:* Tuition: full-time $7,560; part-time $315 per credit. Tuition and fees vary according to program. *General application contact:* Deb Williams, Administrative Assistant, Office of Graduate Programs, 614-823-3210.

Department of Business, Accounting and Economics
Dr. Don Eskew, Chair
Program in:
business, accounting and economics (MBA)

Department of Education
Dr. Harriet Fayne, Chair
Program in:
education (MAE, MAT)

Department of Nursing
Dr. Barbara Schaffner, Chair
Programs in:
adult nurse practitioner (MSN, Certificate)
clinical nurse leader (MSN)
family nurse practitioner (MSN, Certificate)
nurse service administration (MSN)

■ TIFFIN UNIVERSITY
Tiffin, OH 44883-2161
http://www.tiffin.edu/

Independent, coed, comprehensive institution. *Enrollment:* 1,977 graduate, professional, and undergraduate students; 204 full-time matriculated graduate/professional students (143 women), 335 part-time matriculated graduate/professional students (156 women). *Graduate faculty:* 40 full-time (13 women), 40 part-time/adjunct (17 women). *Computer facilities:* 60 computers available on campus for general student use. A campuswide network can be accessed from student residence rooms and from off campus. Internet access and online class registration are available. *Library facilities:* Pfeiffer Library. *Graduate expenses:* Tuition: part-time $700 per credit hour. *General application contact:* Kristi Krintzline, Director of Graduate Admissions, 800-968-6446 Ext. 3445.

Program in Business Administration
Dr. Shawn P. Daly, Dean of the School of Business
Programs in:
general management (MBA)
leadership (MBA)
safety and security management (MBA)
sports management (MBA)

Program in Criminal Justice
Dr. Charles Christensen, Dean of Criminal Justice and Social Sciences
Programs in:
crime analysis (MSCJ)
criminal behavior (MSCJ)
forensic psychology (MSCJ)
homeland security administration (MSCJ)
justice administration (MSCJ)

■ UNION INSTITUTE & UNIVERSITY
Cincinnati, OH 45206-1925
http://www.tui.edu/

Independent, coed, university. *Computer facilities:* A campuswide network can be accessed from off campus. Internet access is available. *Library facilities:* Gary Library plus 1 other. *General application contact:* Admissions Director, 800-486-3116.

Program in Education (Florida Campus)
Program in:
education (M Ed, Ed S)

Program in Education (Vermont Campus)
Program in:
education (M Ed)

Program in Interdisciplinary Studies (Vermont Campus)
Programs in:
counseling (MA)
interdisciplinary studies (MA)
psychology (MA)

Program in Visual Art (Vermont Campus)
Program in:
visual art (MFA)

Program in Writing (Vermont Campus)
Programs in:
writing (MFA)
writing for children and young adults (MFA)

School of Interdisciplinary Arts and Sciences
Program in:
interdisciplinary studies (PhD)

School of Professional Psychology
Programs in:
clinical psychology (PhD)
interdisciplinary studies (PhD)

■ THE UNIVERSITY OF AKRON
Akron, OH 44325
http://www.uakron.edu/

State-supported, coed, university. CGS member. *Enrollment:* 21,882 graduate, professional, and undergraduate students; 2,039 full-time matriculated graduate/professional students (1,110 women), 1,828 part-time matriculated graduate/professional students (1,116 women). *Graduate faculty:* 524 full-time (176 women), 427 part-time/adjunct (216 women). *Computer facilities:* Computer purchase and lease plans are available. 2,450 computers available on campus for general student use. A campuswide network can be accessed from student residence rooms and from off campus. Internet access and online class registration, wireless campus, library laptops for student checkout are available. *Library facilities:* Bierce Library plus 2 others. *Graduate expenses:* Tuition, state resident: full-time $6,164; part-time $342 per credit. Tuition, nonresident: full-time $10,575; part-time $588 per credit. Required fees: $806; $43 per credit. $12 per term. Tuition and fees vary according to course load, degree level and program. *General application contact:* Dr. Mark Tausig, Associate Dean, 330-972-6266.

Graduate School

Dr. George R. Newkome, Vice President for Research and Dean of the Graduate School

Buchtel College of Arts and Sciences
Dr. Ronald Levant, Dean
Programs in:
- applied cognitive aging (MA, PhD)
- applied mathematics (MS)
- applied politics (MA)
- arts and sciences (MA, MFA, MPA, MS, PhD)
- biology (MS)
- chemistry (MS, PhD)
- composition (MA)
- computer science (MS)
- counseling psychology (MA, PhD)
- creative writing (MFA)
- earth science (MS)
- economics (MA)
- environmental (MS)
- geographic information science (MS)
- geology (MS)
- geophysics (MS)
- history (MA, PhD)
- industrial/gerontological (PhD)
- industrial/organizational psychology (MA, PhD)
- integrated bioscience (PhD)
- literature (MA)
- mathematics (MS)
- physics (MS)
- political science (MA)
- psychology (MA)
- public administration (MPA)
- sociology (MA, PhD)
- Spanish (MA)
- statistics (MS)
- urban planning (MA)
- urban studies (MA, PhD)
- urban studies and public affairs (PhD)

College of Business Administration
Dr. Raj Aggrawal, Dean
Programs in:
- accountancy (MS)
- accounting-information systems (MS)
- business administration (MBA, MS, MSM, MT)
- electronic business (MBA)
- entrepreneurship (MBA)
- finance (MBA)
- international business (MBA)
- international business for international executive (MBA)
- management (MBA)
- management of technology (MBA)
- management-health services administration (MSM)
- management-human resources (MSM)
- management-information systems (MSM)
- management-supply chain management (MSM)
- strategic marketing (MBA)
- taxation (MT)

College of Education
Dr. Patricia Nelson, Dean
Programs in:
- administrative specialist (MA, MS)
- classroom guidance for teachers (MA, MS)
- community counseling (MA, MS)
- counseling psychology (PhD)
- counselor education and supervision (PhD)
- education (MA, MS, Ed D, PhD)
- educational administration (MA, MS, Ed D)
- elementary education (MA, MS, PhD)
- elementary education—literacy (MA)
- elementary education with licensure (MS)
- exercise physiology/adult fitness (MA, MS)
- higher education administration (MA, MS)
- marriage and family therapy (MA, MS)
- physical education K–12 (MA, MS)
- principalship (MA, MS)
- school counseling (MA, MS)
- school psychology (MS)
- secondary education (MA, MS, PhD)
- secondary education with licensure (MS)
- special education (MA, MS)
- sports science/coaching (MA, MS)
- superintendent (MA, MS)
- technical education (MS)
- technical education guidance (MS)
- technical education instructional technology (MS)
- technical education teaching (MS)
- technical education training (MS)

College of Engineering
Dr. George Haritos, Dean
Programs in:
- biomedical engineering (MS, PhD)
- chemical and biomolecular engineering (MS, PhD)
- civil engineering (MS, PhD)
- electrical and computer engineering (MS, PhD)
- engineering (MS, PhD)
- engineering (biomedical engineering specialization) (MS)
- engineering (management specialization) (MS)
- engineering (polymer specialization) (MS)
- engineering-applied mathematics (PhD)
- mechanical engineering (MS, PhD)

College of Fine and Applied Arts
Dr. James Lynn, Interim Dean
Programs in:
- arts administration (MA)
- audiology (Au D)
- child and family development (MA)
- child development (MA)
- child life (MA)
- clothing, textiles and interiors (MA)
- communication (MA)
- composition (MM)
- family development (MA)
- fine and applied arts (MA, MM, MS, Au D)
- music education (MM)
- music history and literature (MM)
- music technology (MM)
- nutrition and dietetics (MS)
- performance (MM)
- social work (MS)
- speech-language pathology (MA)
- theatre arts (MA)
- theory (MM)

College of Nursing
Dr. Margaret Wineman, Interim Dean
Programs in:
- nursing (MSN, PhD)
- public health (MPH)

College of Polymer Science and Polymer Engineering
Dr. George R. Newkome, Interim Dean
Programs in:
- polymer engineering (MS, PhD)
- polymer science (MS, PhD)

School of Law

Richard L. Aynes, Dean
Program in:
- law (JD)

■ UNIVERSITY OF CINCINNATI

Cincinnati, OH 45221
http://www.uc.edu/

State-supported, coed, university. CGS member. *Computer facilities:* 325 computers available on campus for general student use. A campuswide network can be accessed from student residence rooms and from off campus. Internet access and online class registration are available. *Library facilities:* Langsam Library plus 7 others. *General application contact:* Associate Senior Vice President and University Dean, 513-556-2872.

College of Law

Louis D. Bilionois, Dean
Program in:
- law (JD)

Division of Research and Advanced Studies

Program in:
- neuroscience (PhD)

University of Cincinnati (continued)

College-Conservatory of Music
Programs in:
arts administration (MA)
choral conducting (MM, DMA)
composition (MM, DMA)
directing (MFA)
keyboard studies (MM, DMA, AD)
music (MA, MFA, MM, DMA, PhD, AD)
music education (MM)
music history (MM)
music theory (MM, PhD)
musicology (PhD)
orchestral conducting (MM, DMA)
performance (MM, DMA, AD)
theater design and production (MFA)
wind conducting (MM, DMA)

College of Allied Health Sciences
Programs in:
allied health sciences (MA, MS, Au D, DPT, PhD)
blood transfusion medicine (MS)
cellular therapies (MS)
communication sciences and disorders (MA, Au D, PhD)
medical genetics (MS)
nutritional science (MS)
rehabilitation science (DPT)

College of Business
Dr. Willard McIntosh, Dean
Programs in:
accounting (MBA)
accounting management/organizational behavior (PhD)
business (MBA, MS, PhD)
construction management (MBA)
e-business (MBA)
finance (MBA, MS, PhD)
general accounting (MS)
information systems (MBA, MS)
management (MBA, PhD)
management of advanced technology and innovation (MBA)
marketing (MBA, MS, PhD)
operations management (MBA, PhD)
quantitative analysis (MBA, MS, PhD)
taxation (MS)

College of Design, Architecture, Art, and Planning
Programs in:
architecture (M Arch)
art education (MA)
art history (MA)
community planning (MCP)
design, architecture, art, and planning (M Arch, M Des, MA, MCP, MFA, PhD)
fashion design (M Des)
fine arts (MFA)
graphic design (M Des)
industrial design (M Des)
interaction design (M Des)
planning (MCP)
product development (M Des)
regional development planning (PhD)

College of Education, Criminal Justice, and Human Services
Programs in:
community health (MS)
counseling (Ed D)
counselor education (CAGS)
criminal justice (MS, PhD)
curriculum and instruction (M Ed, Ed D)
deaf studies (Certificate)
early childhood education (M Ed)
education, criminal justice, and human services (M Ed, MA, MS, Ed D, PhD, CAGS, Certificate, Ed S)
educational leadership (M Ed, Ed S)
educational studies (M Ed, Ed D, PhD, Ed S)
health education (MS, PhD)
health promotion and education (M Ed)
human services (M Ed, MA, MS, Ed D, PhD, CAGS, Ed S)
mental health (MA)
middle childhood education (M Ed)
postsecondary literacy instruction (Certificate)
reading/literacy (M Ed, Ed D)
school counseling (M Ed)
school psychology (PhD, Ed S)
secondary education (M Ed)
special education (M Ed, Ed D)
teaching English as a second language (M Ed, Ed D, Certificate)
teaching science (MS)
urban educational leadership (Ed D)

College of Engineering
Programs in:
aerospace engineering and engineering mechanics (MS, PhD)
bioinformatics (PhD)
biomechanics (PhD)
ceramic science and engineering (MS, PhD)
chemical engineering (MS, PhD)
civil engineering (MS, PhD)
computer engineering (MS)
computer science (MS)
computer science and engineering (PhD)
electrical engineering (MS, PhD)
engineering (MS, PhD)
environmental engineering (MS, PhD)
environmental sciences (MS, PhD)
health physics (MS)
industrial engineering (MS, PhD)
materials science and engineering (MS, PhD)
materials science and metallurgical engineering (MS, PhD)
mechanical engineering (MS, PhD)
medical imaging (PhD)
metallurgical engineering (MS, PhD)
nuclear engineering (MS, PhD)
polymer science and engineering (MS, PhD)
tissue engineering (PhD)

College of Medicine
Dr. David Stern, Dean
Programs in:
biomedical sciences (MS, PhD)
cell and molecular biology (PhD)
cell biophysics (PhD)
environmental and industrial hygiene (MS, PhD)
environmental and occupational medicine (MS)
environmental genetics and molecular toxicology (MS, PhD)
epidemiology and biostatistics (MS, PhD)
immunobiology (MS, PhD)
medical physics (MS)
medicine (MD, MS, D Sc, PhD)
molecular and developmental biology (PhD)
molecular genetics, biochemistry and microbiology (MS, PhD)
occupational safety and ergonomics (MS, PhD)
pathology (PhD)
pharmacology (PhD)
physiology (PhD)
teratology (PhD)

College of Pharmacy
Programs in:
pharmaceutical sciences (MS, PhD)
pharmacy (Pharm D, MS, PhD)
pharmacy practice (Pharm D)

McMicken College of Arts and Sciences
Programs in:
analytical chemistry (MS, PhD)
anthropology (MA)
applied economics (MA)
applied mathematics (MS, PhD)
arts and sciences (MA, MALER, MAT, MS, PhD, Certificate)
biochemistry (MS, PhD)
biological sciences (MS, PhD)
classics (MA, PhD)
clinical psychology (PhD)
communication (MA)
English (MA, MAT, PhD)
experimental psychology (PhD)
French (MA)
geography (MA, PhD)
geology (MS, PhD)
German studies (MA, PhD)
history (MA, PhD)
inorganic chemistry (MS, PhD)
interdisciplinary studies (PhD)
labor and employment relations (MALER)
mathematics education (MAT)
organic chemistry (MS, PhD)
organizational leadership (MALER)
philosophy (MA, PhD)
physical chemistry (MS, PhD)
physics (MS, PhD)
political science (MA, PhD)
polymer chemistry (MS, PhD)
pure mathematics (MS, PhD)
Romance languages and literatures (PhD)
sensors (PhD)

sociology (MA, PhD)
Spanish (MA)
statistics (MS, PhD)
women's studies (MA, Certificate)

School of Social Work
Program in:
social work (MSW)

Graduate School

College of Nursing
Dr. Andrea R. Lindell, Dean
Programs in:
clinical nurse specialist (MSN)
nurse anesthesia (MSN)
nurse midwifery (MSN)
nurse practitioner (MSN)
nursing (PhD)

■ UNIVERSITY OF DAYTON
Dayton, OH 45469-1300
http://www.udayton.edu/

Independent-religious, coed, university. CGS member. *Enrollment:* 10,503 graduate, professional, and undergraduate students; 1,235 full-time matriculated graduate/professional students (693 women), 1,172 part-time matriculated graduate/professional students (770 women). *Graduate faculty:* 494. *Computer facilities:* Computer purchase and lease plans are available. 8,000 computers available on campus for general student use. A campuswide network can be accessed from student residence rooms and from off campus. Internet access and online class registration, apply online, check admission status, confirm enrollment, virtual orientation are available. *Library facilities:* Roesch Library plus 2 others. *Graduate expenses:* Tuition: part-time $601 per semester hour. Tuition and fees vary according to degree level and program. *General application contact:* Erika Eavers, Graduate Admission Processor, 937-229-3065.

Graduate School
Dr. F. Thomas Eggemeier, Dean of the Graduate School

College of Arts and Sciences
Dr. Mary Morton, Dean
Programs in:
applied mathematics (MS)
arts and sciences (MA, MCS, MPA, MS, PhD)
biology (MS, PhD)
chemistry (MS)
clinical psychology (MA)
communication (MA)
computer science (MCS)
English (MA)
financial mathematics (MS)
general psychology (MA)
mathematics education (MS)
pastoral ministry (MA)
public administration (MPA)
theological studies (MA)
theology (PhD)

School of Business Administration
Janice M. Glynn, Director
Program in:
business administration (MBA)

School of Education and Allied Professions
Dr. Thomas J. Lasley, Dean
Programs in:
adolescent/young adult (MS Ed)
art education (MS Ed)
college student personnel (MS Ed)
community counseling (MS Ed)
early childhood education (MS Ed)
education and allied professions (MS Ed, DPT, PhD, Ed S)
educational leadership (MS Ed, PhD, Ed S)
exercise sports science (MS Ed)
higher education administration (MS Ed)
human development services (MS Ed)
inclusive early childhood (MS Ed)
interdisciplinary education (MS Ed)
intervention specialist education, mild/moderate (MS Ed)
literacy (MS Ed)
middle childhood (MS Ed)
multi-age education (MS Ed)
music education (MS Ed)
physical education (MS Ed)
school counseling (MS Ed)
school psychology (MS Ed, Ed S)
teacher as child/youth development specialist (MS Ed)
teacher as leader (MS Ed)
technology in education (MS Ed)

School of Engineering
Dr. Joseph E. Saliba, Dean
Programs in:
aerospace engineering (MSAE, DE, PhD)
chemical engineering (MS Ch E)
electrical and computer engineering (MSEE, DE, PhD)
electro-optics (MSEO, PhD)
engineering (MS Ch E, MS Mat E, MSAE, MSCE, MSE, MSEE, MSEM, MSEM, MSEO, MSME, MSMS, DE, PhD)
engineering management and systems (MSEM)
engineering mechanics (MSEM)
environmental engineering (MSCE)
management science (MSMS)
materials engineering (MS Mat E, DE, PhD)
mechanical engineering (MSME, DE, PhD)
soil mechanics (MSCE)
structural engineering (MSCE)
transport engineering (MSCE)

School of Law
Lisa A. Kloppenberg, Dean
Program in:
law (JD, LL M, MSL)

■ THE UNIVERSITY OF FINDLAY
Findlay, OH 45840-3653
http://www.findlay.edu/

Independent-religious, coed, comprehensive institution. CGS member. *Enrollment:* 6,182 graduate, professional, and undergraduate students; 337 full-time matriculated graduate/professional students (208 women), 830 part-time matriculated graduate/professional students (409 women). *Graduate faculty:* 43 full-time, 8 part-time/adjunct. *Computer facilities:* Computer purchase and lease plans are available. 200 computers available on campus for general student use. A campuswide network can be accessed from student residence rooms and from off campus. Internet access and online class registration are available. *Library facilities:* Shafer Library. *General application contact:* Heather Riffle, Director, Graduate and Special Programs, 419-434-4640.

Graduate and Professional Studies
Dr. Thomas Dillion, Dean, Graduate and Professional Studies
Programs in:
administration (MA Ed)
early childhood (MA Ed)
elementary education (MA Ed)
human resource development (MA Ed)
leadership (MA Ed)
professional studies (MA, MA Ed, MALS, MAT, MBA, MOT, MPT, MSEM)
special education (MA Ed)
technology (MA Ed)
web instruction (MA Ed)

College of Health Professions
Dr. Lisa Dutton, Dean, College of Health Professions
Programs in:
athletic training (MAT)
health professions (MAT, MOT, MPT)
occupational therapy (MOT)
physical therapy (MPT)

College of Liberal Arts
Dr. Dennis Stevens, Dean
Programs in:
bilingual and multicultural education (MA)
liberal arts (MA, MALS)
liberal studies (MALS)
teaching English to speakers of other languages (MA)

College of Science
Programs in:
environmental management (MSEM)
science (MSEM)

MBA Program
Dr. Paul Sears, Dean

The University of Findlay (continued)
Programs in:
- financial management (MBA)
- human resource management (MBA)
- international management (MBA)
- management (MBA)
- marketing (MBA)
- public management (MBA)

■ UNIVERSITY OF RIO GRANDE

Rio Grande, OH 45674
http://www.rio.edu/

Independent, coed, comprehensive institution. *Computer facilities:* 300 computers available on campus for general student use. A campuswide network can be accessed from student residence rooms and from off campus. Internet access and online class registration are available. *Library facilities:* Jeanette Albiez Davis Library plus 2 others. *General application contact:* Graduate Secretary, 740-245-7167.

Graduate School

Program in:
- classroom teaching (M Ed)

■ THE UNIVERSITY OF TOLEDO

Toledo, OH 43606-3390
http://www.utoledo.edu/

State-supported, coed, university. CGS member. *Enrollment:* 19,374 graduate, professional, and undergraduate students; 1,705 full-time matriculated graduate/professional students (928 women), 1,370 part-time matriculated graduate/professional students (870 women). *Graduate faculty:* 358. *Computer facilities:* 2,800 computers available on campus for general student use. A campuswide network can be accessed from student residence rooms and from off campus. Internet access and online class registration, online transcripts, student account and grade information are available. *Library facilities:* Carlson Library plus 7 others. *General application contact:* Jamilah Jones, Recruitment Coordinator, 419-530-8582.

Find University Details at www.petersons.com/gradchannel.

College of Graduate Studies

Dr. Martin A. Abraham, Assistant Dean, Research and Graduate Studies

College of Arts and Sciences

Sue Rowlands, Interim Dean
Programs in:
- analytical chemistry (MS, PhD)
- applied mathematics (MS, PhD)
- arts and sciences (MA, MLS, MMP, MPA, MS, PhD, Certificate)
- behavioral (PhD)
- biological chemistry (MS, PhD)
- biology (MS, PhD)
- biology (ecology track) (MS, PhD)
- clinical psychology (PhD)
- communication studies (Certificate)
- economics (MA)
- English as a second language (MA)
- experimental psychology (MA)
- French (MA)
- geographic information systems and applied geographics (Certificate)
- geography (MA)
- geology (MS)
- German (MA)
- health care policy (MPA)
- health care policy and administration (Certificate)
- history (MA, PhD)
- inorganic chemistry (MS, PhD)
- liberal studies (MLS)
- literature (MA)
- mathematics (MA, PhD)
- municipal administration (MPA)
- organic chemistry (MS, PhD)
- performance (MMP)
- philosophy (MA)
- physical chemistry (MS, PhD)
- physics (MS, PhD)
- planning (MA)
- political science (MA)
- public administration (MPA)
- sociology (MA)
- Spanish (MA)
- spatially integrated social sciences (PhD)
- statistics (MS, PhD)
- teaching of writing (Certificate)

College of Business Administration

Dr. Thomas G. Gutteridge, Dean
Programs in:
- accounting (MBA, MS Acct, MSA)
- business administration (EMBA, MBA, MS Acct, MSA, DME)
- business administration-general (MBA)
- finance and business economics (MBA)
- human resource management (MBA)
- information systems (MBA)
- international business (MBA)
- management (MBA)
- manufacturing management (MBA, DME)
- marketing (MBA)
- operations management (MBA)

College of Education

Dr. Thomas J. Switzer, Dean
Programs in:
- art education (ME)
- career and technical education (Ed S)
- career and technical training (ME)
- curriculum and instruction (ME, DE, PhD, Ed S)
- early childhood education (ME, Ed S)
- education (MAE, ME, MES, MME, DE, PhD, Ed S)
- education and administration supervision (ME)
- education and biology (MES)
- education and chemistry (MES)
- education and economics (MAE)
- education and English (MAE)
- education and French (MAE)
- education and geology (MES)
- education and German (MAE)
- education and history (MAE)
- education and mathematics (MAE, MES)
- education and physics (MES)
- education and political science (MAE)
- education and sociology (MAE)
- education and Spanish (MAE)
- educational administration and supervision (DE, Ed S)
- educational media (DE, PhD, Ed S)
- educational psychology (ME, DE, PhD)
- educational research and measurement (ME, PhD)
- educational sociology (DE, PhD)
- educational technology (ME)
- educational theory and social foundations (ME)
- elementary (PhD, Ed S)
- English as a second language (MAE)
- foundations of education (DE, PhD)
- gifted and talented (Ed S)
- health education (ME)
- higher education (ME, PhD)
- history of education (DE, PhD)
- middle childhood education (ME)
- music education (MME)
- philosophy of education (DE, PhD)
- physical education (ME)
- secondary education (ME, DE, PhD, Ed S)
- special education (ME, DE, PhD, Ed S)

College of Engineering

Dr. Nagi Naganathan, Dean
Programs in:
- bioengineering (MS, PhD)
- chemical engineering (MS)
- civil engineering (MS)
- computer science (MS)
- electrical engineering (MS)
- engineering (MS, PhD)
- engineering sciences (PhD)
- general engineering (MS)
- industrial engineering (MS)
- mechanical engineering (MS)

College of Health Science and Human Service

Dr. Jerome M. Sulivan, Dean
Programs in:
- community counseling (MA)
- counselor education (MA, PhD, Ed S)
- counselor education and school psychology (MA, PhD, Ed S)
- counselor education and supervision (PhD)
- criminal justice (MA, Certificate)
- exercise science (MSX, PhD)
- gerontology (Certificate)
- guidance/counselor education (PhD)
- health education (PhD)

health science and human service (MA, MOT, MPH, MS, MSBS, MSX, OTD, PhD, Certificate, Ed S)
human donation science (MS)
juvenile justice (Certificate)
kinesiology (MSX, PhD)
occupational health (MS)
occupational therapy (MOT, OTD)
physical therapy (MS, DPT)
physician assistant studies (MSBS)
public health (MPH)
public health and rehabilitative services (MA, MPH)
recreation and leisure (MA)
school counseling (MA)
school psychology (MA, Ed S)
severe behavioral spectrum (Certificate)
social work (MS)
speech-language pathology (MA)

College of Medicine
Dr. Almira F. Gohara, Dean
Programs in:
bioinformatics (MS)
bioinformatics and proteomics/genomics (MSBS, Certificate)
cancer biology (MS, PhD)
cardiovascular and metabolic diseases (MS, PhD)
cellular and molecular neurobiology (MS, PhD)
infection, immunity and transplantation (MS)
infection, immunology and transplantation (PhD)
medical physics (MS)
medical sciences (MS)
medicine (MS, MSBS, PhD, Certificate)
molecular and cellular biology (MS, PhD)
molecular basis of disease (PhD)
neurosciences and neurological disorders (MS, PhD)
oral biology (MS)
orthopedic science (MS)
pathology (Certificate)
radiology (MS)
surgery (MS)
urology (MS)

College of Nursing
Dr. Jeri Millstead, Dean
Program in:
advanced practice nursing (MSN)

College of Pharmacy
Dr. Wayne P. Hoss, Vice Dean Graduate Studies and Research
Programs in:
administrative pharmacy (MSPS)
industrial pharmacy (MSPS)
medicinal and biological chemistry (MS, PhD)
pharmaceutical science (MSPS)
pharmacology (MSPS)
pharmacy (MS, MSPS, PhD)

College of Law
Douglas E. Ray, Dean
Program in:
law (JD, MLW)

■ URSULINE COLLEGE
Pepper Pike, OH 44124-4398
http://www.ursuline.edu/

Independent-religious, Undergraduate: women only; graduate: coed, comprehensive institution. *Enrollment:* 1,639 graduate, professional, and undergraduate students; 66 full-time matriculated graduate/professional students (59 women), 393 part-time matriculated graduate/professional students (346 women). *Graduate faculty:* 15 full-time (13 women), 27 part-time/adjunct (17 women). *Computer facilities:* 72 computers available on campus for general student use. A campuswide network can be accessed from student residence rooms. Internet access is available. *Library facilities:* Ralph M. Besse Library. *Graduate expenses:* Tuition: full-time $12,078; part-time $671 per credit hour. Required fees: $60 per semester. *General application contact:* Dean of Graduate Studies, 440-646-8119.

School of Graduate Studies
Dean of Graduate Studies
Programs in:
art therapy counseling (MA)
education (MA)
educational administration (MA)
historic preservation (MA)
liberal studies (MALS)
management (MM)
ministry (MA)
nursing (MSN)

■ WALSH UNIVERSITY
North Canton, OH 44720-3396
http://www.walsh.edu/

Independent-religious, coed, comprehensive institution. *Enrollment:* 2,396 graduate, professional, and undergraduate students; 103 full-time matriculated graduate/professional students (76 women), 207 part-time matriculated graduate/professional students (142 women). *Graduate faculty:* 28 full-time (18 women), 10 part-time/adjunct (4 women). *Computer facilities:* 262 computers available on campus for general student use. A campuswide network can be accessed from student residence rooms and from off campus. Internet access is available. *Library facilities:* Brother Edmond Drouin Library. *Graduate expenses:* Tuition: full-time $8,910; part-time $495 per credit. *General application contact:* Brett D. Freshour, Vice President of Enrollment Management, 330-490-7286.

Graduate Programs
Dr. Laurence Bove, Academic Dean
Programs in:
business administration (MBA)
education (MA)
mental health counseling (MA)
physical therapy (M Sc)
school counseling (MA)
theology (MA)

■ WRIGHT STATE UNIVERSITY
Dayton, OH 45435
http://www.wright.edu/

State-supported, coed, university. CGS member. *Enrollment:* 16,207 graduate, professional, and undergraduate students; 2,169 full-time matriculated graduate/professional students (1,162 women), 1,365 part-time matriculated graduate/professional students (896 women). *Graduate faculty:* 749 full-time (232 women), 354 part-time/adjunct (195 women). *Computer facilities:* 450 computers available on campus for general student use. A campuswide network can be accessed from student residence rooms and from off campus. *Library facilities:* Paul Laurence Dunbar Library plus 2 others. *General application contact:* John Kimble, Associate Director of Graduate Admissions and Records, 937-775-2957.

School of Graduate Studies
Dr. Jack A. Bantle, Vice President for Research and Graduate Studies
Program in:
interdisciplinary studies (MA, MS)

College of Education and Human Services
Dr. Gregory R. Bernhardt, Dean
Programs in:
adolescent young adult (M Ed, MA)
advanced curriculum and instruction (Ed S)
advanced educational leadership (Ed S)
career, technology and vocational education (M Ed, MA)
chemical dependency (MRC)
classroom teacher education (M Ed, MA)
computer/technology education (M Ed, MA)
counseling (M Ed, MA, MS)
curriculum and instruction: teacher leader (MA)
early childhood education (M Ed, MA)
education and human services (M Ed, MA, MRC, MS, MST, Ed S)
educational administrative specialist: teacher leader (M Ed)
educational administrative specialist: vocational education administration (M Ed, MA)
educational leadership (M Ed, MA)
gifted educational needs (M Ed, MA)
health, physical education, and recreation (M Ed, MA)
higher education-adult education (Ed S)
intervention specialist (M Ed, MA)
library/media (M Ed, MA)
middle childhood (M Ed)
middle childhood education (MA)
mild to moderate educational needs (M Ed, MA)

Wright State University (continued)
- moderate to intensive educational needs (M Ed, MA)
- multi age (M Ed, MA)
- pupil personnel services (M Ed, MA)
- rehabilitation counseling (MRC)
- severe disabilities (MRC)
- student affairs in higher education-administration (M Ed, MA)
- superintendent (Ed S)
- vocational education (M Ed, MA)
- workforce education (M Ed, MA)

College of Engineering and Computer Science
Dr. Bor Z. Jang, Dean
Programs in:
- biomedical and human factors engineering (MSE)
- biomedical engineering (MSE)
- computer engineering (MSCE)
- computer science (MS)
- computer science and engineering (PhD)
- electrical engineering (MSE)
- engineering (PhD)
- engineering and computer science (MS, MSCE, MSE, PhD)
- human factors engineering (MSE)
- materials science and engineering (MSE)
- mechanical and materials engineering (MSE)
- mechanical engineering (MSE)

College of Liberal Arts
Dr. Charles S. Taylor, Dean
Programs in:
- composition and rhetoric (MA)
- criminal justice and social problems (MA)
- English (MA)
- history (MA)
- humanities (M Hum)
- international and comparative politics (MA)
- liberal arts (M Hum, M Mus, MA, MPA)
- literature (MA)
- music education (M Mus)
- performance (M Mus)
- public administration (MPA)
- teaching English to speakers of other languages (MA)

College of Nursing and Health
Dr. Patricia A. Martin, Dean
Programs in:
- acute care nurse practitioner (MS)
- administration of nursing and health care systems (MS)
- adult health (MS)
- child and adolescent health (MS)
- community health (MS)
- family nurse practitioner (MS)
- nurse practitioner (MS)
- nursing and health (MS)
- school nurse (MS)

College of Science and Mathematics
Dr. Michele Wheatly, Dean
Programs in:
- anatomy (MS)
- applied mathematics (MS)
- applied statistics (MS)
- biochemistry and molecular biology (MS)
- biological sciences (MS)
- biomedical sciences (PhD)
- chemistry (MS)
- earth science education (MST)
- environmental sciences (MS)
- geological sciences (MS)
- geophysics (MS)
- human factors and industrial/organizational psychology (MS, PhD)
- mathematics (MS)
- medical physics (MS)
- microbiology and immunology (MS)
- physics (MS)
- physics education (MST)
- physiology and biophysics (MS)
- science and mathematics (MS, MST, PhD)

Raj Soin College of Business
Dr. Berkwood Farmer, Dean
Programs in:
- accountancy (M Acc)
- accounting (MBA)
- business (M Acc, MBA, MIS, MS)
- business administration (MBA)
- business economics (MBA)
- finance (MBA)
- flexible business (MBA)
- health care management (MBA)
- information systems (MIS)
- international business (MBA)
- logistics and supply chain management (MS)
- management information technology (MBA)
- management, innovation and change (MBA)
- marketing (MBA)
- project management (MBA)
- social and applied economics (MS)
- supply chain management (MBA)

School of Medicine
Dr. Howard Part, Dean
Programs in:
- aerospace medicine (MS)
- health promotion and education (MPH)
- medicine (MD, MPH, MS, PhD)
- pharmacology and toxicology (MS)
- public health management (MPH)
- public health nursing (MPH)

School of Professional Psychology
Dr. John R. Rudisill, Dean
Program in:
- clinical psychology (Psy D)

■ XAVIER UNIVERSITY
Cincinnati, OH 45207
http://www.xu.edu/

Independent-religious, coed, comprehensive institution. *Enrollment:* 6,666 graduate, professional, and undergraduate students; 804 full-time matriculated graduate/professional students (506 women), 1,652 part-time matriculated graduate/professional students (957 women). *Graduate faculty:* 162 full-time (79 women), 133 part-time/adjunct (62 women). *Computer facilities:* 210 computers available on campus for general student use. A campuswide network can be accessed from student residence rooms and from off campus. Internet access and online class registration are available. *Library facilities:* McDonald Library plus 1 other. *Graduate expenses:* Tuition: part-time $462 per credit hour. Part-time tuition and fees vary according to degree level, campus/location and program. *General application contact:* Roger Bosse, Interim Director of Graduate Studies, 513-745-3357.

College of Arts and Sciences
Dr. Janice B. Walker, Dean
Programs in:
- arts and sciences (MA)
- English (MA)
- theology (MA)

College of Social Sciences, Health and Education
Dr. Neil Heighberger, Dean
Programs in:
- clinical nurse leader (MSN)
- clinical psychology (Psy D)
- criminal justice (MS)
- forensic nursing (MSN)
- health services administration (MHSA)
- healthcare law (MSN)
- nursing administration (MSN)
- occupational therapy (MOT)
- psychology (MA)
- school nursing (MSN)
- social sciences, health and education (M Ed, MA, MHSA, MOT, MS, MSN, Psy D)
- sport administration (M Ed)

School of Education
Dr. James Boothe, Acting Dean
Programs in:
- community counseling (MA)
- education (M Ed, MA)
- educational administration (M Ed)
- elementary education (M Ed)
- human resource development (M Ed)
- Montessori (M Ed)
- multicultural literature for children (M Ed)
- reading specialist (M Ed)
- school counseling (MA)
- secondary education (M Ed)
- special education (M Ed)

Williams College of Business
Dr. Ali Malekzadeh, Dean
Programs in:
- business (Exec MBA, MBA)
- business administration (Exec MBA, MBA)
- e-commerce (MBA)

finance (MBA)
international business (MBA)
management information systems (MBA)
marketing (MBA)

■ YOUNGSTOWN STATE UNIVERSITY
Youngstown, OH 44555-0001
http://www.ysu.edu/

State-supported, coed, comprehensive institution. CGS member. *Computer facilities:* 1,619 computers available on campus for general student use. A campuswide network can be accessed from student residence rooms and from off campus. Internet access and online class registration are available. *Library facilities:* Maag Library. *General application contact:* Dean of Graduate Studies and Research, 330-941-3091.

Graduate School

College of Arts and Sciences
Programs in:
arts and sciences (MA, MS, Certificate)
biological sciences (MS)
chemistry (MS)
economics (MA)
English (MA)
environmental studies (MS)
history (MA)
industrial/institutional management (Certificate)
mathematics (MS)
risk management (Certificate)

College of Education
Programs in:
counseling (MS Ed)
early and middle childhood education (MS Ed)
education (MS Ed, Ed D)
educational administration (MS Ed)
educational leadership (Ed D)
gifted and talented education (MS Ed)
secondary education (MS Ed)
special education (MS Ed)
teaching—elementary education (MS Ed)
teaching—secondary reading (MS Ed)

College of Fine and Performing Arts
Programs in:
fine and performing arts (MM)
music education (MM)
music history and literature (MM)
music theory and composition (MM)
performance (MM)

College of Health and Human Services
Programs in:
criminal justice (MS)
health and human services (MHHS)
nursing (MSN)
physical therapy (MPT)
public health (MPH)

Warren P. Williamson Jr. College of Business Administration
Programs in:
accounting (MBA)
business administration (EMBA, MBA)
executive business administration (EMBA)
finance (MBA)
management (MBA)
marketing (MBA)

William Rayen College of Engineering
Programs in:
civil, chemical, and environmental engineering (MSE)
electrical engineering (MSE)
engineering (MSE)
mechanical and industrial engineering (MSE)

Oklahoma

■ CAMERON UNIVERSITY
Lawton, OK 73505-6377
http://www.cameron.edu/

State-supported, coed, comprehensive institution. CGS member. *Enrollment:* 5,734 graduate, professional, and undergraduate students; 139 full-time matriculated graduate/professional students (94 women), 254 part-time matriculated graduate/professional students (179 women). *Graduate faculty:* 47 full-time (20 women), 14 part-time/adjunct (6 women). *Computer facilities:* 350 computers available on campus for general student use. A campuswide network can be accessed from student residence rooms and from off campus. Internet access, online courses, e-mail accounts, student information system are available. *Library facilities:* Cameron University Library. *Graduate expenses:* Tuition, state resident: full-time $2,479; part-time $138 per credit hour. Tuition, nonresident: full-time $5,976; part-time $332 per credit hour. Tuition and fees vary according to campus/location. *General application contact:* Teresa Enriquez, Graduate Admissions/Enrollment Coordinator, 580-581-2987.

Office of Graduate Studies
Dr. Lance Janda, Assistant V.P. for Academic Affairs and Graduate Coordinator
Programs in:
behavioral sciences (MS)
business administration (MBA)
education (M Ed)
educational leadership (MS)
entrepreneurial studies (MS)
teaching (MAT)

■ EAST CENTRAL UNIVERSITY
Ada, OK 74820-6899
http://www.ecok.edu/

State-supported, coed, comprehensive institution. CGS member. *Enrollment:* 4,506 graduate, professional, and undergraduate students; 186 full-time matriculated graduate/professional students (142 women), 536 part-time matriculated graduate/professional students (418 women). *Graduate faculty:* 48. *Computer facilities:* 500 computers available on campus for general student use. A campuswide network can be accessed. Internet access is available. *Library facilities:* Linscheid Library. *General application contact:* Dr. B. Richard Wetherill, Interim Dean, 580-310-5709 Ext. 709.

School of Graduate Studies
Dr. B. Richard Wetherill, Interim Dean
Programs in:
administration (MSHR)
counseling (MSHR)
criminal justice (MSHR)
education (M Ed)
psychology (MSPS)
rehabilitation counseling (MSHR)

■ NORTHEASTERN STATE UNIVERSITY
Tahlequah, OK 74464-2399
http://www.nsuok.edu/

State-supported, coed, comprehensive institution. *Enrollment:* 9,540 graduate, professional, and undergraduate students; 338 full-time matriculated graduate/professional students (238 women), 651 part-time matriculated graduate/professional students (440 women). *Graduate faculty:* 121 full-time (35 women), 10 part-time/adjunct (5 women). *Computer facilities:* 534 computers available on campus for general student use. A campuswide network can be accessed from student residence rooms and from off campus. Internet access is available. *Library facilities:* John Vaughn Library. *General application contact:* Donna Trout, Graduate Program Coordinator, 918-449-6000 Ext. 6123.

College of Optometry
Dr. George E. Foster, Dean
Program in:
optometry (OD)

Graduate College
Dr. Thomas L. Jackson, Dean

College of Business and Technology
Dr. John Schleede, Dean
Programs in:
accounting and financial analysis (MS)
business administration (MBA)
business and technology (MBA, MS)
industrial management (MS)

Northeastern State University (continued)

College of Education
Dr. Kay Grant, Head
Programs in:
- collegiate scholarship and services (MS)
- counseling psychology (MS)
- early childhood education (M Ed)
- education (M Ed, MS, MS Ed)
- health and kinesiology (MS Ed)
- library media and information technology (MS Ed)
- mathematics education (M Ed)
- reading (M Ed)
- school administration (M Ed)
- school counseling (M Ed)
- teaching (M Ed)

College of Liberal Arts
Dr. Paul Westbrook, Interim Dean
Programs in:
- American studies (MA)
- communication (MA)
- criminal justice (MS)
- English (MA)
- liberal arts (MA, MS)

College of Science and Health Professions
Dr. Doug Penisten, Interim Dean
Programs in:
- science and health professions (M Ed, MS)
- science education (M Ed)
- speech-language pathology (MS)

■ OKLAHOMA CHRISTIAN UNIVERSITY
Oklahoma City, OK 73136-1100
http://www.oc.edu/

Independent-religious, coed, comprehensive institution. *Enrollment:* 2,120 graduate, professional, and undergraduate students; 11 full-time matriculated graduate/professional students (3 women), 44 part-time matriculated graduate/professional students (4 women). *Graduate faculty:* 12 full-time (0 women). *Computer facilities:* Computer purchase and lease plans are available. 101 computers available on campus for general student use. A campuswide network can be accessed from student residence rooms and from off campus. Internet access, each student has a laptop computer are available. *Library facilities:* Tom and Ada Beam Library. *General application contact:* Dr. Bob Young, Director, 405-425-5485.

Graduate School of Bible
Dr. John Harrison, Chair
Programs in:
- family life ministry (MA)
- ministry (M Div, MA)
- youth ministry (MA)

■ OKLAHOMA CITY UNIVERSITY
Oklahoma City, OK 73106-1402
http://www.okcu.edu/

Independent-religious, coed, comprehensive institution. *Enrollment:* 3,713 graduate, professional, and undergraduate students; 1,224 full-time matriculated graduate/professional students (530 women), 553 part-time matriculated graduate/professional students (246 women). *Graduate facuity:* 186 full-time (77 women), 160 part-time/adjunct (85 women). *Computer facilities:* 264 computers available on campus for general student use. A campuswide network can be accessed from student residence rooms and from off campus. Internet access and online class registration are available. *Library facilities:* Dulaney Browne Library plus 1 other. *Graduate expenses:* Tuition: full-time $12,780; part-time $710 per hour. Required fees: $89 per hour. *General application contact:* Leslie McKenzie, Director, Graduate Admissions, 800-633-7242.

Kramer School of Nursing
Dr. Marvel L. Williamson, Dean
Program in:
- nursing (MSN)

Margaret E. Petree College of Performing Arts
Programs in:
- costume design (MA)
- performing arts (MA, MM)
- technical theater (MA)
- theater (MA)
- theater for young audiences (MA)

Wanda L. Bass School of Music
Mark Parker, Dean
Programs in:
- composition (MM)
- conducting (MM)
- musical theatre (MM)
- opera performance (MM)
- performance (MM)

Meinders School of Business
Dr. Vince Orza, Dean
Programs in:
- accounting (MSA)
- business (MBA, MSA)
- finance (MBA)
- health administration (MBA)
- information technology (MBA)
- integrated marketing communications (MBA)
- international business (MBA)
- marketing (MBA)

Petree College of Arts and Sciences
Dr. David Evans, Dean
Programs in:
- art (MLA)
- arts and sciences (M Ed, MA, MCJ, MLA, MS)
- general studies (MLA)
- leadership/management (MLA)
- literature (MLA)
- mass communications (MLA)
- philosophy (MLA)
- writing (MLA)

Division of Computer Science
Dr. Art Kazmieczak, Program Director
Program in:
- computer science (MS)

Division of Education and Kinesiology Exercise Studies
Chair
Programs in:
- applied behavioral studies (M Ed)
- early childhood education (M Ed)
- education and kinesiology exercise studies (M Ed, MA)
- elementary education (M Ed)
- teaching English to speakers of other languages (MA)

Division of Social Sciences
Dr. Jody Horn, Director
Program in:
- criminal justice (MCJ)

School of Law
Dr. Larry Hellman, Dean
Program in:
- law (JD)

Wimberly School of Religion and Graduate Theological Center
Dr. Mark Davies, Dean
Program in:
- religion and theology (M Rel, MAR)

■ OKLAHOMA STATE UNIVERSITY
Stillwater, OK 74078
http://osu.okstate.edu/

State-supported, coed, university. CGS member. *Enrollment:* 23,307 graduate, professional, and undergraduate students; 1,501 full-time matriculated graduate/professional students (700 women), 2,238 part-time matriculated graduate/professional students (1,051 women). *Graduate faculty:* 996 full-time (277 women), 193 part-time/adjunct (85 women). *Computer facilities:* 2,456 computers available on campus for general student use. A campuswide network can be accessed from student residence rooms and from off campus. Internet access and online class registration are available. *Library facilities:* Edmon Low Library plus 3 others. *Graduate expenses:* Tuition, state resident: part-time $146 per credit hour. Tuition, nonresident: part-time $516 per credit hour. Required fees: $44 per credit hour. Tuition and fees vary according to program. *General application contact:* Dr. Gordon Emslie, Dean, 405-744-6368.

Center for Veterinary Health Sciences
Dr. Michael Lorenz, Dean
Programs in:
veterinary biomedical sciences (MS, PhD)
veterinary health sciences (DVM, MS, PhD)
veterinary medicine (DVM)

College of Agricultural Science and Natural Resources
Dr. Robert E. Whitson, Dean
Programs in:
agricultural economics (M Ag, MS, PhD)
agricultural education, communications and 4H youth development (M Ag, MS, PhD)
agricultural science and natural resources (M Ag, MS, PhD)
agronomy (M Ag, MS, PhD)
animal breeding and reproduction (PhD)
animal nutrition (PhD)
animal sciences (M Ag, MS)
biochemistry and molecular biology (MS, PhD)
biomechanical engineering (MS, PhD)
bioprocessing and biotechnology (MS, PhD)
crop science (PhD)
entomology (PhD)
environmental and natural resources (MS, PhD)
environmental science (PhD)
food processing (MS, PhD)
food science (MS, PhD)
forestry (M Ag, MS)
horticulture (M Ag, MS)
plant pathology (PhD)
plant science (PhD)
soil science (PhD)

College of Arts and Sciences
Peter M. A. Sherwood, Dean
Programs in:
applied history (MA)
applied mathematics (MS)
arts and sciences (MA, MM, MS, PhD)
botany (MS)
chemistry (MS, PhD)
clinical psychology (PhD)
communications sciences and disorders (MS)
computer science (MS, PhD)
conservation science (MS, PhD)
corrections (MS)
creative writing (MA, PhD)
environmental science (PhD)
experimental psychology (PhD)
fire and emergency management administration (MS)
general psychology (MS)
geography (MS, PhD)
history (MA, PhD)
literature (MA, PhD)
mathematics (pure and applied) (PhD)
mathematics (pure) (MS)
mathematics education (MS, PhD)
microbiology and molecular genetics (MS, PhD)
pedagogy and performance (MM)
philosophy (MA)
photonics (MS, PhD)
physics (MS, PhD)
plant science (PhD)
political science (MA)
sociology (MS, PhD)
statistics (MS, PhD)
technical writing (MA, PhD)
theatre (MA)
zoology (MS, PhD)

School of Geology
Dr. Jay Gregg, Head
Program in:
geology (MS)

School of Journalism and Broadcasting
Tom Weir, Director
Program in:
mass communication (MS)

College of Education
Dr. Pamela Fry, Dean
Program in:
education (MS, Ed D, PhD, Ed S)

School of Applied Health and Educational Psychology
Dr. John Romans, Head
Programs in:
applied behavioral studies (MS, Ed D, PhD)
counseling and student personnel (MS, PhD)
educational psychology (PhD)
health (MS, Ed D)
leisure sciences (MS, Ed D)
physical education (MS, Ed D)
physical education and leisure sciences (Ed D)
school psychology (Ed S)

School of Educational Studies
Dr. Bert Jacobson, Head
Programs in:
educational administration (MS)
higher education (MS, Ed D)
technical education (MS, Ed D)
trade and industrial education (MS, Ed D)

School of Teaching and Curriculum Leadership
Dr. Christine Ormsbee, Head
Program in:
teaching and curriculum leadership (MS, PhD)

College of Engineering, Architecture and Technology
Dr. Karl N. Reid, Dean
Program in:
engineering, architecture and technology (M Arch, M Arch E, M Bio E, MIEM, MS, PhD)

School of Architecture
Dr. Randy Seitsinger, Head
Programs in:
architectural engineering (M Arch E)
architecture (M Arch, M Arch E)

School of Chemical Engineering
Dr. Russell Rhinehart, Head
Program in:
chemical engineering (MS, PhD)

School of Civil and Environmental Engineering
Dr. John Veenstra, Interim Head
Programs in:
civil engineering (MS, PhD)
environmental engineering (MS, PhD)

School of Electrical and Computer Engineering
Dr. Keith Teague, Head
Programs in:
control systems engineering (MS)
electrical and computer engineering (MS, PhD)

School of Industrial Engineering and Management
Dr. William J. Kolarik, Head
Programs in:
engineering and technology management (MS)
industrial engineering and management (MIEM, MS, PhD)
manufacturing systems engineering (MS)

School of Mechanical and Aerospace Engineering
Dr. Lawrence L. Hoberock, Head
Program in:
mechanical engineering (MS, PhD)

College of Human Environmental Sciences
Dr. Patricia Knaub, Dean
Programs in:
design, housing and merchandising (MS, PhD)
human development and family science (MS, PhD)
human environmental sciences (MS, PhD)
nutritional sciences (MS, PhD)

School of Hotel and Restaurant Administration
Dr. Bill Ryan, Interim Head
Program in:
hotel and restaurant administration (MS, PhD)

Graduate College
Dr. Gordon Emslie, Dean
Programs in:
aviation and space science (MS)
biophotonics (MS, PhD)
environmental sciences (MS, PhD)
gerontology (MS)
health care administration (MS)
international studies (MS)
natural and applied sciences (MS)
plant science (PhD)

Oklahoma State University (continued)

William S. Spears School of Business

Dr. Sara M. Freedman, Dean
Programs in:
business (MBA, MS, MSQFE, PhD)
business administration (MBA)
economics and legal studies in business (MS, PhD)
finance (MBA, MSQFE, PhD)
management (MBA, PhD)
management information systems (PhD)
management information systems/ accounting information systems (MS)
management science (PhD)
marketing (MBA, PhD)
operations management (PhD)
telecommunications management (MS, PhD)

School of Accounting

Dr. Don Hansen, Head
Program in:
accounting (MS, PhD)

■ ORAL ROBERTS UNIVERSITY

Tulsa, OK 74171-0001

http://www.oru.edu/

Independent-religious, coed, comprehensive institution. *Enrollment:* 3,244 graduate, professional, and undergraduate students; 381 full-time matriculated graduate/ professional students (180 women), 393 part-time matriculated graduate/professional students (208 women). *Graduate faculty:* 35 full-time (5 women), 13 part-time/adjunct (6 women). *Computer facilities:* 253 computers available on campus for general student use. A campuswide network can be accessed from student residence rooms and from off campus. Internet access is available. *Library facilities:* John D. Messick Resources Center plus 1 other. *General application contact:* Graduate Admissions Coordinator, 918-495-6989.

School of Business

Dr. Mark Lewandowski, Dean
Programs in:
accounting (MBA)
finance (MBA)
international business (MBA)
management (MBA)
marketing (MBA)
non-profit management (M Man, MBA)
organizational dynamics (M Man)
sales marketing (M Man)

School of Education

Dr. David Hand, Dean
Programs in:
Christian school administration (MA Ed, Ed D)
Christian school administration (K-12) (MA Ed, Ed D)
Christian school curriculum development (MA Ed)
college and higher education administration (MA Ed, Ed D)
public school administration (K-12) (MA Ed, Ed D)
public school teaching (MA Ed)
teaching English as a second language (MA Ed)

School of Theology and Missions

Dr. Thomson K. Mathew, Dean
Programs in:
biblical literature (MA)
Christian counseling (MA)
Christian education (MA)
divinity (M Div)
missions (MA)
practical theology (MA)
theological/historical studies (MA)
theology (D Min)

■ SOUTHEASTERN OKLAHOMA STATE UNIVERSITY

Durant, OK 74701-0609

http://www.sosu.edu/

State-supported, coed, comprehensive institution. *Computer facilities:* 425 computers available on campus for general student use. A campuswide network can be accessed from student residence rooms. Internet access and online class registration, campus Blackboard classes are available. *Library facilities:* Henry G. Bennett Memorial Library. *General application contact:* Graduate Secretary, 580-745-2200.

Graduate School

Program in:
aerospace administration (MS)

School of Arts and Sciences

Program in:
technology (MT)

School of Behavioral Sciences

Program in:
guidance and counseling (MBS)

School of Business

Program in:
business (MBA, MS)

School of Education

Programs in:
educational administration (M Ed)
educational instruction and leadership (M Ed)
educational technology (M Ed)
elementary education (M Ed)
school counseling (M Ed)
secondary education (M Ed)

■ SOUTHERN NAZARENE UNIVERSITY

Bethany, OK 73008

http://www.snu.edu/

Independent-religious, coed, comprehensive institution. *Enrollment:* 382 full-time matriculated graduate/professional students (214 women), 11 part-time matriculated graduate/professional students (4 women). *Graduate faculty:* 18 full-time (6 women), 36 part-time/adjunct (16 women). *Computer facilities:* 120 computers available on campus for general student use. A campuswide network can be accessed from student residence rooms and from off campus. Internet access is available. *Library facilities:* R. T. Williams Learning Resources Center. *Graduate expenses:* Tuition: part-time $507 per credit. *General application contact:* Dr. W. Davis Berryman, Dean of Graduate College, 405-491-6316.

Graduate College

Dr. W. Davis Berryman, Dean of Graduate College
Program in:
theology (MA)

School of Business

Jeff Seyfert, Interim Chair
Program in:
business (MBA, MS Mgt)

School of Education

Dr. Rex Tullis, Director
Programs in:
curriculum and instruction (MA)
educational leadership (MA)

School of Nursing

Dr. Carol Dorough, Dean
Programs in:
nursing education (MS)
nursing leadership (MS)

School of Psychology

Dr. Phil Budd, Chair
Programs in:
counseling psychology (MSCP)
marriage and family therapy (MA)

■ SOUTHWESTERN OKLAHOMA STATE UNIVERSITY

Weatherford, OK 73096-3098

http://www.swosu.edu/

State-supported, coed, comprehensive institution. *Computer facilities:* 270 computers available on campus for general student use. A campuswide network can be accessed from student residence rooms and from off campus. Internet access is available. *Library facilities:* Al Harris Library. *General application contact:* Information Contact, 580-774-3790.

College of Arts and Sciences
Programs in:
- art education (M Ed)
- arts and sciences (M Ed, MM)
- English (M Ed)
- mathematics (M Ed)
- music education (MM)
- natural sciences (M Ed)
- performance (MM)
- social sciences (M Ed)

College of Pharmacy
Program in:
- pharmacy (Pharm D)

College of Professional and Graduate Studies

School of Behavioral Sciences and Education
Programs in:
- community counseling (M Ed)
- early childhood education (M Ed)
- educational administration (M Ed)
- elementary education (M Ed)
- health sciences and microbiology (M Ed)
- kinesiology (M Ed)
- parks and recreation management (M Ed)
- school counseling (M Ed)
- school psychology (MS)
- school psychometry (M Ed)
- secondary education (M Ed)
- special education (M Ed)

School of Business and Technology
Program in:
- business and technology (MBA)

■ UNIVERSITY OF CENTRAL OKLAHOMA
Edmond, OK 73034-5209
http://www.ucok.edu/

State-supported, coed, comprehensive institution. CGS member. *Computer facilities:* 400 computers available on campus for general student use. A campuswide network can be accessed from student residence rooms and from off campus. Internet access is available. *Library facilities:* Max Chambers Library. *General application contact:* Interim Dean, Graduate College, 405-974-3341.

College of Graduate Studies and Research

College of Arts, Media, and Design
Programs in:
- arts, media, and design (MFA, MM)
- design and interior design (MFA)
- music education (MM)
- performance (MM)

College of Business Administration
Program in:
- business administration (MBA)

College of Education
Programs in:
- adult education (M Ed)
- community services (M Ed)
- counseling psychology (MS)
- early childhood education (M Ed)
- education (M Ed, MA, MS)
- educational administration (M Ed)
- elementary education (M Ed)
- family and child studies (MS)
- family and consumer science education (MS)
- general education (M Ed)
- gerontology (M Ed)
- guidance and counseling (M Ed)
- instructional media (M Ed)
- interior design (MS)
- nutrition-food management (MS)
- professional health occupations (M Ed)
- psychology (MA)
- reading (M Ed)
- secondary education (M Ed)
- special education (M Ed)
- speech-language pathology (M Ed)

College of Liberal Arts
Programs in:
- composition skills (MA)
- contemporary literature (MA)
- creative writing (MA)
- criminal justice management and administration (MA)
- history (MA)
- international affairs (MA)
- liberal arts (MA)
- museum studies (MA)
- political science (MA)
- social studies teaching (MA)
- Southwestern studies (MA)
- teaching English as a second language (MA)
- traditional studies (MA)
- urban affairs (MA)

College of Mathematics and Science
Programs in:
- applied mathematical sciences (MS)
- biology (MS)
- chemistry (MS)
- mathematics and science (MS)
- physics and engineering (MS)

■ UNIVERSITY OF OKLAHOMA
Norman, OK 73019-0390
http://www.ou.edu/

State-supported, coed, university. CGS member. *Enrollment:* 26,002 graduate, professional, and undergraduate students; 3,219 full-time matriculated graduate/professional students (1,644 women), 3,142 part-time matriculated graduate/professional students (1,648 women). *Graduate faculty:* 1,130 full-time (341 women), 256 part-time/adjunct (115 women). *Computer facilities:* Computer purchase and lease plans are available. 2,356 computers available on campus for general student use. A campuswide network can be accessed from student residence rooms and from off campus. Internet access and online class registration are available. *Library facilities:* Bizzell Memorial Library plus 8 others. *Graduate expenses:* Tuition, state resident: full-time $3,180; part-time $133 per credit hour. Tuition, nonresident: full-time $11,347; part-time $473 per credit hour. Required fees: $1,729; $62 per credit hour. $117 per semester. Tuition and fees vary according to course load and program. *General application contact:* Patricia Lynch, Director of Admissions, 405-325-2251.

Find University Details at www.petersons.com/gradchannel.

College of Law
Dr. Andrew M. Coats, Dean
Program in:
- law (JD)

Graduate College
Lee Williams, Dean
Program in:
- interdisciplinary studies (MA, MS, PhD)

College of Architecture
Bob G. Fillpot, Dean
Programs in:
- architecture (M Arch, MLA, MRCP, MS)
- construction science (MS)
- landscape architecture (MLA)
- regional and city planning (MRCP)

College of Arts and Sciences
Programs in:
- anthropology (MA, PhD)
- arts and sciences (M Nat Sci, MA, MHR, MLIS, MPA, MS, MSW, PhD, Certificate)
- astrophysics (MS, PhD)
- botany (MS, PhD)
- chemistry and biochemistry (MS, PhD)
- communication (MA, PhD)
- economics (MA, PhD)
- English (MA, PhD)
- French (MA, PhD)
- German (MA)
- health and exercise science (MS, PhD)
- history (MA, PhD)
- history of science (MA, PhD)
- human relations (MHR)
- international studies (MA)
- knowledge management (MS)
- library and information studies (MLIS)
- mathematics (MA, MS, PhD)
- microbiology (MS, PhD)
- Native American studies (MA)
- organizational dynamics (MS)
- philosophy (MA, PhD)
- physics (MS, PhD)
- political science (MA, PhD)
- psychology (MS, PhD)
- public administration (MPA)
- school library media specialist (Certificate)
- social work (MSW)
- sociology (MA, PhD)
- Spanish (MA, PhD)
- zoology (M Nat Sci, MS, PhD)

University of Oklahoma (continued)

College of Atmospheric and Geographic Sciences
Dr. John T. Snow, Dean
Programs in:
- atmospheric and geographic sciences (M Pr Met, MA, MS, MS Metr, PhD)
- geography (MA, PhD)
- meteorology (M Pr Met, MS Metr, PhD)

College of Earth and Energy
Larry R Grillot, Dean
Programs in:
- earth and energy (MS, PhD)
- geological engineering (MS, PhD)
- geology (MS, PhD)
- geophysics (MS)
- natural gas engineering (MS)
- petroleum engineering (MS, PhD)

College of Education
Dr. Joan Karen Smith, Dean
Programs in:
- adult and higher education (M Ed, PhD)
- community counseling (M Ed)
- counseling psychology (PhD)
- education (Certificate)
- educational administration, curriculum and supervision (M Ed, Ed D, PhD)
- educational studies (M Ed, PhD)
- historical, philosophical, and social foundations of education (M Ed, PhD)
- instructional leadership and academic curriculum (M Ed, PhD)
- instructional psychology (M Ed, PhD)
- school counseling (M Ed)
- special education (M Ed, PhD)

College of Engineering
Dr. Thomas Landers, Dean
Programs in:
- aerospace engineering (MS, PhD)
- air (M Env Sc)
- bioengineering (MS, PhD)
- chemical engineering (MS, PhD)
- civil engineering (MS, PhD)
- computer science (MS, PhD)
- electrical and computer engineering (MS, PhD)
- engineering (M Env Sc, MS, D Engr, PhD)
- engineering physics (MS, PhD)
- environmental engineering (MS)
- environmental science (M Env Sc, PhD)
- geotechnical engineering (MS)
- groundwater management (M Env Sc)
- hazardous solid waste (M Env Sc)
- industrial engineering (MS, PhD)
- mechanical engineering (MS, PhD)
- occupational safety and health (M Env Sc)
- process design (M Env Sc)
- structures (MS)
- telecommunication systems (MS)
- water quality resources (M Env Sc)

College of Fine Arts
Eugene J. Enrico, Dean
Programs in:
- acting (MFA)
- art (MA, MFA)
- art history (MA, MFA)
- ceramics (MFA)
- choral conducting (M Mus)
- conducting (M Mus Ed, DMA)
- dance (MFA)
- design (MFA)
- directing (MFA)
- drama (MA)
- film and video (MFA)
- fine arts (M Mus, M Mus Ed, MA, MFA, DMA, PhD)
- general (M Mus Ed)
- instrumental (M Mus Ed)
- instrumental conducting (M Mus)
- music composition (M Mus, DMA)
- music education (M Mus Ed, PhD)
- music theory (M Mus)
- musicology (M Mus)
- organ (M Mus, DMA)
- painting (MFA)
- photography (MFA)
- piano (M Mus, DMA)
- printmaking (MFA)
- visual communications (MFA)
- voice (M Mus, DMA)
- wind/percussion/string (M Mus, DMA)

College of Liberal Studies
Dr. James Pappas, Dean
Programs in:
- administrative leadership (MLS)
- integrated studies (MLS)
- interprofessional human and health services (MLS)
- museum studies (MLS)

Gaylord College of Journalism and Mass Communication
Joe Foote, Dean
Programs in:
- advertising and public relations (MA)
- information gathering and distribution (MA)
- journalism and mass communication (MA)
- mass communication management and policy (MA)
- professional writing (MA, MPW)
- telecommunication and new technology (MA)

Michael F. Price College of Business
Dr. Kenneth Evans, Dean
Programs in:
- accounting (M Acc)
- business administration (MBA, PhD)
- management (MS)
- management information systems (MS)

■ UNIVERSITY OF TULSA
Tulsa, OK 74104-3189
http://www.utulsa.edu/

Independent-religious, coed, university. CGS member. *Enrollment:* 4,125 graduate, professional, and undergraduate students; 972 full-time matriculated graduate/professional students (362 women), 316 part-time matriculated graduate/professional students (158 women). *Graduate faculty:* 215 full-time (63 women), 7 part-time/adjunct (4 women). *Computer facilities:* Computer purchase and lease plans are available. 900 computers available on campus for general student use. A campuswide network can be accessed from student residence rooms and from off campus. Internet access and online class registration are available. *Library facilities:* McFarlin Library plus 1 other. *Graduate expenses:* Tuition: full-time $13,338; part-time $741 per credit hour. *General application contact:* Dr. Janet A. Haggerty, Associate Vice President of Research and Dean of the Graduate School, 918-631-2336.

Find University Details at www.petersons.com/gradchannel.

College of Law
Robert Butkin, Dean
Programs in:
- alternative methods of dispute resolution (Certificate)
- American Indian and indigenous law (LL M)
- American law for foreign lawyers (LL M)
- comparative and international law (Certificate)
- entrepreneurial law (Certificate)
- health law (Certificate)
- law (JD)
- lawyering skills (Certificate)
- Native American law (Certificate)
- public policy and regulation (Certificate)
- resources, energy, and environmental law (Certificate)

Graduate School
Dr. Janet A. Haggerty, Associate Vice President of Research and Dean of the Graduate School

College of Arts and Sciences
Dr. Dale Thomas Benediktson, Dean
Programs in:
- anthropology (MA)
- art (MA, MFA, MTA)
- arts and sciences (MA, MFA, MS, MSMSE, MTA, PhD)
- clinical psychology (MA, PhD)
- education (MA)
- English language and literature (MA, MTA, PhD)
- history (MA, MTA)
- industrial/organizational psychology (MA, PhD)
- mathematics and science education (MSMSE)
- speech-language pathology (MS)
- teaching arts (MTA)

College of Business Administration
Dr. W. Gale Sullenburger, Dean
Programs in:
- business administration (M Tax, MBA, METM, MS)
- chemical engineering (METM)

computer science (METM)
corporate finance (MS)
electrical engineering (METM)
geological science (METM)
investments and portfolio management (MS)
mathematics (METM)
mechanical engineering (METM)
petroleum engineering (METM)
risk management (MS)
taxation (M Tax)

College of Engineering and Natural Sciences
Dr. Steve J. Bellovich, Dean
Programs in:
biological sciences (MS, MTA, PhD)
chemical engineering (ME, MSE, PhD)
chemistry (MS)
computer science (MS, PhD)
electrical engineering (ME, MSE)
engineering and natural sciences (ME, METM, MS, MSE, MTA, PhD)
geosciences (MS, PhD)
mathematical sciences (MS, MTA)
mechanical engineering (ME, MSE, PhD)
petroleum engineering (ME, MSE, PhD)

Oregon

■ CONCORDIA UNIVERSITY
Portland, OR 97211-6099
http://www.cu-portland.edu/

Independent-religious, coed, comprehensive institution. *Computer facilities:* 60 computers available on campus for general student use. A campuswide network can be accessed from student residence rooms and from off campus. Internet access and online class registration are available. *Library facilities:* Concordia Library plus 3 others. *General application contact:* Graduate Admissions Counselor, 503-280-8501.

College of Education
Programs in:
curriculum and instruction (elementary) (M Ed)
educational administration (M Ed)
elementary education (MAT)
secondary education (MAT)

School of Management
Program in:
management (MBA)

■ EASTERN OREGON UNIVERSITY
La Grande, OR 97850-2899
http://www.eou.edu/

State-supported, coed, comprehensive institution. *Computer facilities:* Computer purchase and lease plans are available. 125 computers available on campus for general student use. A campuswide network can be accessed from student residence rooms and from off campus. Internet access and online class registration are available. *Library facilities:* Pierce Library plus 1 other. *General application contact:* Coordinator of Graduate Studies, 541-962-3399.

School of Education and Business
Programs in:
education (MS)
education and business (MS, MTE)
elementary education (MTE)
secondary education (MTE)

■ GEORGE FOX UNIVERSITY
Newberg, OR 97132-2697
http://www.georgefox.edu/

Independent-religious, coed, university. *Enrollment:* 3,252 graduate, professional, and undergraduate students; 444 full-time matriculated graduate/professional students (289 women), 944 part-time matriculated graduate/professional students (513 women). *Graduate faculty:* 80 full-time (38 women), 82 part-time/adjunct (40 women). *Computer facilities:* 1,300 computers available on campus for general student use. A campuswide network can be accessed from student residence rooms and from off campus. Internet access and online class registration are available. *Library facilities:* Murdock Learning Resource Center. *General application contact:* Brandon Connelly, Director of Admission for Graduate Programs, 503-554-6121.

Find University Details at www.petersons.com/gradchannel.

George Fox Evangelical Seminary
Dr. Jules Glanzer, Dean
Programs in:
divinity (M Div)
ministry (D Min)
ministry leadership (MA)
spiritual formation (MA)
spiritual formation and discipleship (Certificate)
theological studies (MA)

Graduate Department of Clinical Psychology
Dr. Wayne Adams, Director
Programs in:
clinical psychology (Psy D)
psychology (MA)

Program in Organizational Leadership
Dr. Mary Olson, Director
Program in:
organizational leadership (MAOL)

School of Education
Dr. James Worthington, Dean
Programs in:
counseling (MA, MS, Certificate)
educational foundations and leadership (M Ed, Ed D)
marriage and family therapy (MA, Certificate)
school counseling (MA)
school psychology (MS, Certificate)
teaching (MAT)
trauma (Certificate)

School of Management
Dr. Dirk Barran, Acting Dean
Program in:
management (MBA, DM)

■ LEWIS & CLARK COLLEGE
Portland, OR 97219-7899
http://www.lclark.edu/

Independent, coed, comprehensive institution. *Enrollment:* 3,641 graduate, professional, and undergraduate students; 234 full-time matriculated graduate/professional students (182 women), 257 part-time matriculated graduate/professional students (199 women). *Graduate faculty:* 39 full-time (27 women), 66 part-time/adjunct (40 women). *Computer facilities:* Computer purchase and lease plans are available. 158 computers available on campus for general student use. A campuswide network can be accessed from student residence rooms and from off campus. Internet access and online class registration are available. *Library facilities:* Aubrey Watzek Library plus 1 other. *Graduate expenses:* Tuition: part-time $610 per semester hour. *General application contact:* Helen L. Hayes, Administrative Specialist, Graduate Office of Admissions, 503-768-6200.

Graduate School of Education and Counseling
Dr. Peter W. Cookson, Dean
Programs in:
addictions treatment (MA)
counseling psychology (MA, MS)
early childhood/elementary education (MAT)
education (MAT)
education and counseling (M Ed, MA, MAT, MS, Ed D, Ed S)
educational leadership (M Ed, Ed D)
marriage and family therapy (MA)
middle level/high school education (MAT)
psychological and cultural studies (MA)
school counseling (M Ed)
school psychology (MS, Ed S)
special education (M Ed)

Lewis & Clark School of Law
Robert H. Klonoff, Dean, School of Law

Lewis & Clark College (continued)
Programs in:
environmental and natural resources law (LL M)
law (JD)

■ MARYLHURST UNIVERSITY
Marylhurst, OR 97036-0261
http://www.marylhurst.edu/

Independent-religious, coed, comprehensive institution. *Enrollment:* 1,249 graduate, professional, and undergraduate students; 86 full-time matriculated graduate/professional students (70 women), 306 part-time matriculated graduate/professional students (185 women). *Graduate faculty:* 6 full-time (2 women), 36 part-time/adjunct (14 women). *Computer facilities:* 40 computers available on campus for general student use. A campuswide network can be accessed. Internet access and online class registration are available. *Library facilities:* Shoen Library. *Graduate expenses:* Tuition: part-time $395 per credit. Required fees: $8 per credit. *General application contact:* Information Contact, 503-636-8141 Ext. 6268.

Department of Art Therapy Counseling
Christine Turner, Chairperson
Programs in:
art therapy (PGC)
art therapy counseling (MA)
counseling (PGC)

Department of Business Administration
Bob Hanks, Director of Business Programming
Program in:
business administration (MBA)

Department of Interdisciplinary Studies
Dr. Debrah B. Bokowski, Chair
Program in:
interdisciplinary studies (MA)

Department of Religious Studies–Applied Theology Program
Dr. Jerry Roussell, Chair
Program in:
applied theology (MAAT)

Department of Religious Studies–Divinity Program
Dr. Jerry Roussell, Chair
Program in:
divinity (M Div)

■ OREGON STATE UNIVERSITY
Corvallis, OR 97331
http://oregonstate.edu/

State-supported, coed, university. CGS member. *Enrollment:* 19,362 graduate, professional, and undergraduate students; 2,640 full-time matriculated graduate/professional students (1,341 women), 893 part-time matriculated graduate/professional students (479 women). *Graduate faculty:* 1,393 full-time (508 women), 207 part-time/adjunct (104 women). *Computer facilities:* 2,251 computers available on campus for general student use. A campuswide network can be accessed from student residence rooms and from off campus. Internet access and online class registration are available. *Library facilities:* Valley Library. *General application contact:* Dr. Sally K. Francis, Dean of the Graduate School, 541-737-4881.

College of Pharmacy
Dr. Wayne A. Kradjan, Dean
Program in:
pharmacy (Pharm D, MAIS, MS, PhD)

College of Veterinary Medicine
Dr. Cyril Clarke, Dean
Programs in:
comparative veterinary medicine (PhD)
microbiology (MS)
pathology (MS)
toxicology (MS)
veterinary medicine (DVM, MS, PhD)

Graduate School
Dr. Sally K. Francis, Dean
Programs in:
environmental sciences (MA, MS, PhD)
interdisciplinary studies (MAIS)
molecular and cellular biology (MS, PhD)
plant physiology (MS, PhD)
water resources engineering (MS, PhD)

College of Agricultural Sciences
Dr. Thayne R. Dutson, Dean
Programs in:
agricultural and resource economics (M Agr, MAIS, MS, PhD)
agricultural education (M Agr, MAIS, MAT, MS)
agricultural sciences (M Ag, M Agr, MA, MAIS, MAT, MS, PhD)
animal science (M Agr, MAIS, MS, PhD)
crop science (M Agr, MAIS, MS, PhD)
economics (MS, PhD)
fisheries science (M Agr, MAIS, MS, PhD)
food science and technology (M Agr, MAIS, MS, PhD)
genetics (MA, MAIS, MS, PhD)
horticulture (M Ag, MAIS, MS, PhD)
poultry science (M Agr, MAIS, MS, PhD)
rangeland ecology and management (M Agr, MAIS, MS, PhD)
soil science (M Agr, MAIS, MS, PhD)
toxicology (MS, PhD)
wildlife science (MAIS, MS, PhD)

College of Business
Dr. Ilene K. Kleinsorge, Dean
Program in:
business (MAIS, MBA, Certificate)

College of Education
Dr. Sam Stern, Dean
Programs in:
adult education and higher education leadership (Ed M, MAIS)
college student service administration (Ed M, MS)
counseling (MS, PhD)
education (Ed M, MAIS, MAT, MS, Ed D, PhD)
elementary education (MAT)
family and consumer sciences education (MAT, MS)
general education (Ed M, MAIS, MS, Ed D, PhD)
language arts education (MAT)
music education (MAT)

College of Engineering
Dr. Ronald L. Adams, Dean
Programs in:
bioscience engineering (MS, PhD)
chemical engineering (MS, PhD)
civil engineering (MS, PhD)
construction engineering management (MBE)
electrical engineering and computer science (MA, MAIS, MS, PhD)
engineering (M Engr, M Oc E, MA, MAIS, MBE, MS, PhD)
industrial engineering (MS, PhD)
manufacturing engineering (M Engr)
materials science (MAIS, MS, PhD)
mechanical engineering (MS, PhD)
nuclear engineering (MS, PhD)
ocean engineering (M Oc E)
radiation health physics (MS, PhD)

College of Forestry
Hal J. Salwasser, Dean
Programs in:
economics (MS, PhD)
forest engineering (MAIS, MF, MS, PhD)
forest products (MAIS, MF, MS, PhD)
forest resources (MAIS, MF, MS, PhD)
forest science (MAIS, MF, MS, PhD)
forestry (MAIS, MF, MS, PhD)
wood science and technology (MF, MS, PhD)

College of Health and Human Sciences
Dr. Tammy Bray, Dean
Programs in:
design and human environment (MA, MAIS, MS, PhD)
environmental health and occupational safety management (MAIS, MS)
exercise and sport science (MS, PhD)
gerontology (MAIS)
health and human sciences (MA, MAIS, MAT, MPH, MS, PhD)
health management and policy (MS)
health promotion and health behavior (MAIS, MAT, MS)
human development and family studies (MS, PhD)
human performance (MAIS, MS, PhD)

movement studies in disabilities (MAIS, MS)
nutrition and food management (MAIS, MS, PhD)
physical education teacher education (MAT)
public health (MPH, PhD)

College of Liberal Arts
Dr. Kay F. Schaffer, Dean
Programs in:
anthropology (MAIS)
applied anthropology (MA)
economics (MA, MS, PhD)
English (MA, MAIS, MFA)
history (MA, MS, PhD)
liberal arts (MA, MAIS, MAT, MFA, MS, PhD)
music education (MAT)

College of Oceanic and Atmospheric Sciences
Dr. Mark R. Abbott, Dean
Programs in:
atmospheric sciences (MA, MS, PhD)
geophysics (MA, MS, PhD)
marine resource management (MA, MS)
oceanography (MA, MS, PhD)

College of Science
Dr. Sherman H. Bloomer, Dean
Programs in:
advanced mathematics education (MAT)
analytical chemistry (MS, PhD)
applied statistics (MA, MS, PhD)
biochemistry and biophysics (MA, MAIS, MS, PhD)
biology education (MAT)
biometry (MA, MS, PhD)
chemistry (MA, MAIS)
chemistry education (MAT)
ecology (MA, MAIS, MS, PhD)
environmental statistics (MA, MS, PhD)
general science (MA, MS, PhD)
genetics (MA, MAIS, MS, PhD)
geography (MA, MAIS, MS, PhD)
geology (MA, MAIS, MS, PhD)
inorganic chemistry (MS, PhD)
integrated science education (MAT)
mathematical statistics (MA, MS, PhD)
mathematics (MA, MAIS, MS, PhD)
mathematics education (MA, MAT, MS, PhD)
microbiology (MA, MAIS, MS, PhD)
molecular and cellular biology (MA, MAIS, MS, PhD)
mycology (MA, MAIS, MS, PhD)
nuclear and radiation chemistry (MS, PhD)
operations research (MA, MAIS, MS)
organic chemistry (MS, PhD)
physical chemistry (MS, PhD)
physics (MA, MS, PhD)
physics education (MAT)
plant pathology (MA, MAIS, MS, PhD)
plant physiology (MA, MAIS, MS, PhD)
science (MA, MAIS, MAT, MS, PhD)
science education (MA, MAT, MS, PhD)
statistics (MA, MS, PhD)
structural botany (MA, MAIS, MS, PhD)
systematics (MA, MAIS, MS, PhD)
zoology (MA, MAIS, MS, PhD)

■ PACIFIC UNIVERSITY
Forest Grove, OR 97116-1797
http://www.pacificu.edu/

Independent, coed, comprehensive institution. *Enrollment:* 2,790 graduate, professional, and undergraduate students; 1,183 full-time matriculated graduate/professional students (753 women), 190 part-time matriculated graduate/professional students (158 women). *Graduate faculty:* 108 full-time (56 women), 86 part-time/adjunct (47 women). *Computer facilities:* Computer purchase and lease plans are available. 150 computers available on campus for general student use. A campuswide network can be accessed from student residence rooms and from off campus. Internet access, e-mail, Web space, printing, student and academic information, WebCT, wireless, computer peripherals are available. *Library facilities:* Pacific University Library. *General application contact:* Jon-Erik Larsen, Director of Graduate and Professional Admissions, 503-352-7221.

College of Education
Dr. Mark Ankeny, Acting Dean
Programs in:
early childhood education (MAT)
education (MAE)
elementary education (MAT)
high school education (MAT)
middle school education (MAT)
special education (MAT)
visual function in learning (M Ed)

College of Optometry
Dr. James E. Sheedy, Dean
Program in:
optometry (OD, MS)

School of Occupational Therapy
Dr. John A. White, Director
Program in:
occupational therapy (MOT)

School of Pharmacy
Dr. Robert Rosenow, Director
Program in:
pharmacy (Pharm D)

School of Physical Therapy
Dr. Richard Rutt, Director
Programs in:
entry level (DPT)
post-professional (DPT)

School of Physician Assistant Studies
Randy Randolph, Director
Program in:
physician assistant studies (MHS, MS)

School of Professional Psychology
Dr. Michel Hersen, Dean
Programs in:
clinical psychology (MS, Psy D)
counseling psychology (MA)

■ PORTLAND STATE UNIVERSITY
Portland, OR 97207-0751
http://www.pdx.edu/

State-supported, coed, university. CGS member. *Enrollment:* 24,254 graduate, professional, and undergraduate students; 2,244 full-time matriculated graduate/professional students (1,341 women), 2,319 part-time matriculated graduate/professional students (1,356 women). *Graduate faculty:* 643 full-time (261 women), 414 part-time/adjunct (194 women). *Computer facilities:* 800 computers available on campus for general student use. A campuswide network can be accessed from student residence rooms and from off campus. Internet access and online class registration are available. *Library facilities:* Branford P. Millar Library plus 1 other. *Graduate expenses:* Tuition, state resident: full-time $6,426; part-time $238 per credit. Tuition, nonresident: full-time $11,016; part-time $408 per credit. Tuition and fees vary according to course load. *General application contact:* Information Contact, 503-725-3511.

Graduate Studies
Dr. William H. Feyerherm, Vice Provost for Sponsored Research/Dean of Graduate Studies
Programs in:
computational intelligence (Certificate)
computer modeling and simulation (Certificate)
systems science (MS)
systems science/anthropology (PhD)
systems science/business administration (PhD)
systems science/civil engineering (PhD)
systems science/economics (PhD)
systems science/engineering management (PhD)
systems science/general (PhD)
systems science/mathematical sciences (PhD)
systems science/mechanical engineering (PhD)
systems science/psychology (PhD)
systems science/sociology (PhD)

College of Liberal Arts and Sciences
Dr. Marvin Kaiser, Dean
Programs in:
anthropology (MA)
applied economics (MA, MS)
biology (MA, MS, PhD)
chemistry (MA, MS, PhD)
conflict resolution (MA, MS)

Portland State University (continued)
economics (PhD)
English (MA)
environmental management (MEM)
environmental sciences and resources (PhD)
environmental sciences/biology (PhD)
environmental sciences/chemistry (PhD)
environmental sciences/civil engineering (PhD)
environmental sciences/geography (PhD)
environmental sciences/geology (PhD)
environmental sciences/physics (PhD)
environmental studies (MS)
foreign literature and language (MA)
French (MA)
general arts and letters education (MAT, MST)
general economics (MA, MS)
general science education (MAT, MST)
general social science education (MAT, MST)
general speech communication (MA, MS, Certificate)
geography (MA, MAT, MS, MST, PhD)
geology (MA, MS)
German (MA)
history (MA)
Japanese (MA)
liberal arts and sciences (MA, MAT, MEM, MS, MST, MST, PhD, Certificate)
mathematical sciences (PhD)
mathematics education (PhD)
physics (MA, MS, PhD)
psychology (MA, MS, PhD)
science/environmental science (MST)
science/geology (MAT, MST)
sociology (MA, MS, PhD)
Spanish (MA)
speech-language pathology (MA, MS)
statistics (MS)
teaching English to speakers of other languages (MA)

College of Urban and Public Affairs
Dr. Lawrence Wallack, Dean
Programs in:
criminology and criminal justice (MS, PhD)
gerontology (Certificate)
government (MA, MAT, MPA, MS, MST, PhD)
health administration (MPA)
health administration and policy (MPH)
health education (MA, MS)
health education and health promotion (MPH)
health studies (MPA, MPH)
political science (MA, MAT, MS, MST, PhD)
public administration (MPA)
public administration and policy (PhD)
urban and public affairs (MA, MAT, MPA, MPH, MS, MST, MURP, MUS, PhD, Certificate)
urban and regional planning (MURP)
urban studies (MUS, PhD)
urban studies and planning (MURP, MUS, PhD)

Graduate School of Social Work
Dr. Kristine E. Nelson, Dean
Programs in:
social work (MSW)
social work and social research (PhD)

Maseeh College of Engineering and Computer Science
Dr. Robert D. Dryden, Dean
Programs in:
civil and environmental engineering (M Eng, MS)
civil and environmental engineering management (M Eng)
civilian and environmental engineering (PhD)
computer science (MS, PhD)
electrical and computer engineering (M Eng, MS, PhD)
engineering and computer science (M Eng, ME, MS, MSE, PhD, Certificate)
engineering and technology management (M Eng)
engineering management (MS)
environmental sciences and resources (PhD)
manufacturing engineering (ME)
manufacturing management (M Eng)
mechanical engineering (M Eng, MS, PhD)
software engineering (MSE)
systems engineering (M Eng)
systems engineering fundamentals (Certificate)
systems science (PhD)
systems science/engineering management (PhD)

School of Business Administration
Dr. Scott Dawson, Dean
Programs in:
business administration (MBA, MIM, MSFA, PhD)
financial analysis (MSFA)
international management (MIM)

School of Education
Dr. Randy Hitz, Dean
Programs in:
counselor education (MA, MS)
early childhood education (MA, MS)
education (M Ed, MA, MS)
educational leadership (MA, MS, Ed D)
educational leadership: curriculum and instruction (Ed D)
educational media/school librarianship (MA, MS)
elementary education (M Ed, MAT, MST)
postsecondary, adult and continuing education (Ed D)
reading (MA, MS)
secondary education (M Ed, MAT, MST)
special and counselor education (Ed D)
special education (MA, MS)

School of Fine and Performing Arts
Barbara Sestak, Dean
Programs in:
conducting (MMC)
drawing (MFA)
fine and performing arts (MA, MAT, MFA, MMC, MMP, MS, MST)
mixed media (MFA)
music education (MAT, MST)
painting (MFA)
performance (MMP)
printmaking (MFA)
sculpture (MFA)
theater arts (MA, MS)

■ SOUTHERN OREGON UNIVERSITY
Ashland, OR 97520
http://www.sou.edu/

State-supported, coed, comprehensive institution. *Computer facilities:* 750 computers available on campus for general student use. A campuswide network can be accessed from student residence rooms and from off campus. Internet access and online class registration are available. *Library facilities:* Lenn and Dixie Hannon Library. *General application contact:* Director of Admissions, 541-552-6411.

Graduate Studies

School of Arts and Letters
Program in:
music (MA, MS)

School of Business
Program in:
business (MA Ed, MIM, MS Ed)

School of Sciences
Programs in:
environmental education (MA, MS)
mathematics/computer science (MA, MS)
science (MA, MS)

School of Social Sciences
Programs in:
applied psychology (MAP)
elementary education (MA Ed, MS Ed)
human service-organizational training and development (MA, MS)
secondary education (MA Ed, MS Ed)
social science (MA, MS)
social science, health and physical education (MA, MA Ed, MAP, MAT, MS, MS Ed)
teaching (MAT)

■ UNIVERSITY OF OREGON
Eugene, OR 97403
http://www.uoregon.edu/

State-supported, coed, university. CGS member. *Enrollment:* 20,348 graduate, professional, and undergraduate students; 3,349 full-time matriculated graduate/professional students (1,782 women), 536 part-time matriculated graduate/professional students (285 women). *Graduate faculty:* 715 full-time (273 women), 188 part-time/adjunct (106 women). *Computer facilities:* 1,600 computers available on campus for general student use. A campuswide network can be accessed from student residence rooms and from off campus. Internet access and online class registration are available. *Library facilities:* Knight Library plus 6 others. *General application contact:* Information Contact, 541-346-5129.

Graduate School
Marian Friestad, Associate Dean
Program in:
applied information management (MS)

Charles H. Lundquist College of Business
James C. Bean, Dean
Programs in:
accounting (M Actg, PhD)
business (M Actg, MA, MBA, MS, PhD)
decision sciences (MA, MS)
finance (PhD)
management (PhD)
management: general business (MBA)
marketing (PhD)

College of Arts and Sciences
Wendy Larson, Dean
Programs in:
anthropology (MA, MS, PhD)
arts and sciences (MA, MFA, MS, PhD)
Asian studies (MA)
biochemistry (MA, MS, PhD)
chemistry (MA, MS, PhD)
Chinese (MA, PhD)
classical civilization (MA)
classics (MA)
clinical psychology (PhD)
cognitive psychology (MA, MS, PhD)
comparative literature (MA, PhD)
computer and information science (MA, MS, PhD)
creative writing (MFA)
developmental psychology (MA, MS, PhD)
ecology and evolution (MA, MS, PhD)
economics (MA, MS, PhD)
English (MA, PhD)
environmental science, studies, and policy (PhD)
environmental studies (MA, MS)
French (MA)
geography (MA, MS, PhD)
geological sciences (MA, MS, PhD)
Germanic languages and literatures (MA, PhD)
Greek (MA)
history (MA, PhD)
human physiology (MS, PhD)
independent study: folklore (MA, MS)
international studies (MA)
Italian (MA)
Japanese (MA, PhD)
Latin (MA)
linguistics (MA, PhD)
marine biology (MA, MS, PhD)
mathematics (MA, MS, PhD)
molecular, cellular and genetic biology (PhD)
neuroscience and development (PhD)
philosophy (MA, PhD)
physics (MA, MS, PhD)
physiological psychology (MA, MS, PhD)
political science (MA, MS, PhD)
psychology (MA, MS, PhD)
Romance languages (MA, PhD)
Russian and East European Studies (MA)
social/personality psychology (MA, MS, PhD)
sociology (MA, MS, PhD)
Spanish (MA)
theater arts (MA, MFA, MS, PhD)

College of Education
Michael Bullis, Dean
Program in:
education (M Ed, MA, MS, D Ed, PhD)

School of Architecture and Allied Arts
Frances Bronet, Dean
Programs in:
architecture (M Arch)
architecture and allied arts (M Arch, MA, MCRP, MFA, MI Arch, MLA, MPA, MS, PhD)
art (MFA)
art history (MA, PhD)
arts management (MA, MS)
community and regional planning (MCRP)
historic preservation (MS)
interior architecture (MI Arch)
landscape architecture (MLA)
public policy and management (MA, MPA, MS)

School of Journalism and Communication
Timothy W. Gleason, Dean
Program in:
journalism and communication (MA, MS, PhD)

School of Music
C. Brad Foley, Dean
Programs in:
composition (M Mus, DMA, PhD)
conducting (M Mus)
dance (MA, MS)
jazz studies (M Mus)
music (MA)
music education (M Mus, DMA, PhD)
music history (PhD)
music theory (PhD)
performance (M Mus, DMA)
piano pedagogy (M Mus)

School of Law
Margaret Paris, Interim Dean
Program in:
law (JD, MA, MS)

■ UNIVERSITY OF PHOENIX–OREGON CAMPUS
Tigard, OR 97223
http://www.phoenix.edu/

Proprietary, coed, comprehensive institution. *Enrollment:* 1,836 graduate, professional, and undergraduate students; 355 full-time matriculated graduate/professional students (170 women). *Graduate faculty:* 50 full-time (10 women), 250 part-time/adjunct (75 women). *Computer facilities:* A campuswide network can be accessed from off campus. Internet access is available. *Library facilities:* University Library. *Graduate expenses:* Tuition: full-time $10,200. Required fees: $760. *General application contact:* Campus Information Center, 503-403-2900.

The Artemis School
Dr. Adam Honea, Provost

College of Education
Dr. Marla LaRue, Dean/Executive Director
Programs in:
early childhood and elementary education (MA Ed)
secondary education (MA Ed)

College of Health and Human Services
Dr. Gil Linne, Dean/Executive Director
Programs in:
administration of justice and security (MS)
health administration (MHA)
health care management (MBA)
nursing (MSN)
psychology (MS)

The John Sperling School of Business
Dr. Adam Honea, Provost
Program in:
business (MBA, MIS, MM)

College of Graduate Business and Management
Dr. Brian Lindquist, Associate Vice President and Dean/Executive Director
Programs in:
accounting (MBA)
business administration (MBA)
global management (MBA)
human resource management (MM)
human resources management (MBA)
management (MM)

College of Information Systems and Technology
Dr. Adam Honea, Provost/Dean
Programs in:
information systems (MIS)
technology management (MBA)

■ UNIVERSITY OF PORTLAND
Portland, OR 97203-5798
http://www.up.edu/

Independent-religious, coed, comprehensive institution. *Enrollment:* 3,478 graduate, professional, and undergraduate students; 158 full-time matriculated graduate/professional students (91 women), 315 part-time matriculated graduate/professional students (205 women). *Graduate faculty:* 84 full-time (26 women), 11 part-time/adjunct (5 women). *Computer facilities:* 575 computers available on campus for general student use. A campuswide network can be accessed from student residence rooms and from off campus. Internet access and online class registration are available. *Library facilities:* Wilson M. Clark Library plus 1 other. *Graduate expenses:* Tuition: part-time $728 per semester hour. Required fees: $5 per semester hour. Tuition and fees vary according to program. *General application contact:* Dr. Patricia L. Chadwick, Assistant to the Provost and Dean of the Graduate School, 503-943-7107.

Graduate School
Dr. Thomas G. Greene, Assistant to the Provost and Dean of the Graduate School

College of Arts and Sciences
Dr. Marlene Moore, Dean
Programs in:
arts and sciences (MA, MFA, MS)
communication (MA)
drama (MFA)
management communication (MS)
music (MA)
pastoral ministry (MA)

Dr. Robert B. Pamplin, Jr. School of Business
Dr. Robin Anderson, Dean
Program in:
business (MBA)

School of Education
Dr. Maria Ciriello, OP, Dean
Programs in:
early childhood education (M Ed, MA, MAT)
education (M Ed, MA, MAT)
secondary education (M Ed, MA, MAT)
special education (M Ed)

School of Engineering
Dr. Zia Yamayee, Dean
Program in:
engineering (ME)

School of Nursing
Dr. Terry Misener, Dean
Program in:
nursing (MS)

■ WESTERN OREGON UNIVERSITY
Monmouth, OR 97361-1394
http://www.wou.edu/

State-supported, coed, comprehensive institution. *Enrollment:* 4,885 graduate, professional, and undergraduate students; 173 full-time matriculated graduate/professional students (118 women), 529 part-time matriculated graduate/professional students (422 women). *Graduate faculty:* 33 full-time (20 women), 32 part-time/adjunct (19 women). *Computer facilities:* 411 computers available on campus for general student use. A campuswide network can be accessed from student residence rooms and from off campus. Internet access and online class registration are available. *Library facilities:* Wayne and Lynn Hamersly Library. *Graduate expenses:* Tuition, state resident: full-time $8,250; part-time $250 per credit. Tuition, nonresident: full-time $14,025; part-time $250 per credit. Required fees: $1,173. *General application contact:* Dr. David McDonald, Dean of Admissions, Retention and Enrollment Management, 503-838-8919.

Graduate Programs
Dr. Linda Stonecipher, Unit Head

College of Education
Dr. Hilda Rosselli, Dean
Programs in:
bilingual education (MS Ed)
deaf education (MS Ed)
early childhood education (MS Ed)
education (MAT, MS, MS Ed)
health (MS Ed)
humanities (MAT, MS Ed)
information technology (MS Ed)
initial licensure (MAT)
learning disabilities (MS Ed)
mathematics (MAT, MS Ed)
multihandicapped education (MS Ed)
rehabilitation counseling (MS)
science (MAT, MS Ed)
social science (MAT, MS Ed)
teacher education (MAT, MS, MS Ed)

College of Liberal Arts and Sciences
Dr. Stephen Scheck, Dean
Programs in:
contemporary music (MM)
criminal justice (MA, MS)
liberal arts and sciences (MA, MM, MS)

■ WILLAMETTE UNIVERSITY
Salem, OR 97301-3931
http://www.willamette.edu/

Independent-religious, coed, comprehensive institution. *Computer facilities:* 400 computers available on campus for general student use. A campuswide network can be accessed from student residence rooms and from off campus. Online class registration is available. *Library facilities:* Mark O. Hatfield Library plus 1 other. *General application contact:* Vice President for Enrollment, 503-370-6303.

College of Law
Symeon C. Symeonides, Dean
Program in:
law (JD, LL M)

George H. Atkinson Graduate School of Management
Debra J. Ringold, Interim Dean
Programs in:
business (MBA)
government (MBA)
not-for-profit management (MBA)

School of Education
Dr. Maureen Musser
Program in:
teaching (MAT)

Pennsylvania

■ ALVERNIA COLLEGE
Reading, PA 19607-1799
http://www.alvernia.edu/

Independent-religious, coed, comprehensive institution. *Computer facilities:* 60 computers available on campus for general student use. A campuswide network can be accessed from student residence rooms. Internet access is available. *Library facilities:* Franco Library. *General application contact:* Coordinator of Graduate Admissions and Student Services, 610-796-8296.

Graduate and Continuing Studies
Programs in:
business (MBA)
community counseling (MA)
education (M Ed)
liberal studies (MALS)
occupational therapy (MSOT)

■ ARCADIA UNIVERSITY
Glenside, PA 19038-3295
http://www.arcadia.edu/

Independent-religious, coed, comprehensive institution. CGS member. *Enrollment:* 3,595 graduate, professional, and undergraduate students; 464 full-time matriculated graduate/professional students (369 women), 1,017 part-time matriculated graduate/professional students (760 women). *Graduate faculty:* 71 full-time, 135 part-time/adjunct. *Computer facilities:* Computer purchase and lease plans are available. 110 computers available on campus for general student use. A campuswide network can be accessed from student residence rooms and from off campus. Internet access is available. *Library facilities:* Landman Library. *General application contact:* Information Contact, 215-572-2910.

Find University Details at www.petersons.com/gradchannel.

Graduate Studies

Mark Curchack, Dean of Graduate and Professional Studies
Programs in:
- allied health (MSHE, MSPH)
- art education (M Ed, MA Ed)
- biology education (MA Ed)
- business administration (MBA)
- chemistry education (MA Ed)
- child development (CAS)
- community counseling (MACP)
- computer education (M Ed, CAS)
- computer education 7–12 (MA Ed)
- early childhood education (M Ed, CAS)
- educational leadership (M Ed, CAS)
- educational psychology (CAS)
- elementary education (M Ed, CAS)
- English (MAE)
- English education (MA Ed)
- environmental education (MA Ed, CAS)
- fine arts, theater, and music (MAH)
- forensic science (MSFS)
- genetic counseling (MSGC)
- history education (MA Ed)
- history, philosophy, and religion (MAH)
- international peace and conflict management (MAIPCR)
- international relations and diplomacy (MA)
- language arts (M Ed, CAS)
- literature and language (MAH)
- mathematics education (M Ed, MA Ed, CAS)
- medical science and community health (MM Sc, MSHE, MSPH)
- music education (MA Ed)
- physical therapy (DPT)
- psychology (MA Ed)
- pupil personnel services (CAS)
- reading (M Ed, CAS)
- school counseling (MACP)
- school library science (M Ed)
- science education (M Ed, CAS)
- secondary education (M Ed, CAS)
- special education (M Ed, Ed D, CAS)
- theater arts (MA Ed)
- written communication (MA Ed)

■ BLOOMSBURG UNIVERSITY OF PENNSYLVANIA

Bloomsburg, PA 17815-1301
http://www.bloomu.edu/

State-supported, coed, comprehensive institution. CGS member. *Enrollment:* 8,723 graduate, professional, and undergraduate students; 344 full-time matriculated graduate/professional students (244 women), 394 part-time matriculated graduate/professional students (270 women). *Graduate faculty:* 186 full-time (65 women). *Computer facilities:* 1,250 computers available on campus for general student use. A campuswide network can be accessed from student residence rooms and from off campus. Internet access and online class registration are available. *Library facilities:* Andruss Library. *Graduate expenses:* Tuition, state resident: full-time $6,048; part-time $336 per credit. Tuition, nonresident: full-time $9,678; part-time $538 per credit. Required fees: $1,415. *General application contact:* Carol Arnold, Administrative Assistant, 570-389-4015.

School of Graduate Studies

Dr. James F. Matta, Dean of Graduate Studies

College of Business
Dr. David Martin, Dean
Programs in:
- business (M Ed, MBA)
- business administration (MBA)
- business education (M Ed)

College of Liberal Arts
Dr. George Agbango, Dean
Programs in:
- exercise science (MS)
- liberal arts (MS)

College of Professional Studies
Dr. Dianne Mark, Dean
Programs in:
- adult and family nurse practitioner (MSN)
- adult health and illness (MSN)
- audiology (Au D)
- community health (MSN)
- curriculum and instruction (M Ed)
- early childhood education (MS)
- education (M Ed, MS)
- education of the deaf/hard of hearing (MS)
- elementary education (M Ed)
- exceptionality programs (MS)
- guidance counseling and student affairs (M Ed)
- health sciences (MS, MSN, Au D)
- nursing (MSN)
- nursing administration (MSN)
- reading (M Ed)
- special education (MS)
- speech pathology (MS)

College of Science and Technology
Dr. Robert Marande, Dean
Programs in:
- biology (MS)
- biology education (M Ed)
- instructional technology (MS)
- radiologist assistant (MS)
- science and technology (M Ed, MS)

■ BUCKNELL UNIVERSITY

Lewisburg, PA 17837
http://www.bucknell.edu/

Independent, coed, comprehensive institution. *Computer facilities:* 620 computers available on campus for general student use. A campuswide network can be accessed from student residence rooms and from off campus. Internet access and online class registration are available. *Library facilities:* Ellen Clarke Bertrand Library plus 2 others. *General application contact:* Director of Graduate Studies, 570-577-1304.

Graduate Studies

College of Arts and Sciences
Programs in:
- animal behavior (MA, MS)
- arts and sciences (MA, MS, MS Ed)
- biology (MA, MS)
- chemistry (MA, MS)
- classroom teaching (MS Ed)
- educational research (MS Ed)
- elementary and secondary counseling (MA, MS Ed)
- elementary and secondary principalship (MA, MS Ed)
- English (MA)
- mathematics (MA, MS)
- psychology (MA, MS)
- reading (MA, MS Ed)
- school psychology (MS Ed)
- supervision of curriculum and instruction (MA, MS Ed)

College of Engineering
Programs in:
- chemical engineering (MS, MS Ch E)
- civil and environmental engineering (MS, MSCE, MSEV)
- electrical engineering (MS, MSEE)
- engineering (MS, MS Ch E, MSCE, MSEE, MSEV, MSME)
- mechanical engineering (MS, MSME)

■ CABRINI COLLEGE

Radnor, PA 19087-3698
http://www.cabrini.edu/

Independent-religious, coed, comprehensive institution. *Enrollment:* 2,389 graduate, professional, and undergraduate students; 91 full-time matriculated graduate/professional students (63 women), 484 part-time matriculated graduate/professional students (364 women). *Graduate faculty:* 11 full-time (7 women), 25 part-time/adjunct (11 women). *Computer facilities:* 195 computers available on campus for general student use. A campuswide network can be accessed from student residence rooms. Internet access and online class registration, student access to account balances, grades and other services are available. *Library facilities:* Holy Spirit Library. *Graduate expenses:* Tuition: part-time $310 per credit. Required fees: $45 per term. Tuition and fees vary according to course load. *General application contact:* Bruce D. Bryde, Director of Enrollment and Recruiting, 610-902-8291.

Graduate and Professional Studies

Dr. Michael W. Markowitz, Dean for Graduate and Professional Studies

Cabrini College (continued)
Programs in:
- biotechnology (Certificate)
- education (M Ed)
- educational leadership (Certificate)
- instructional systems technology (MS)
- organization leadership (MS)
- project management (Certificate)

■ CALIFORNIA UNIVERSITY OF PENNSYLVANIA
California, PA 15419-1394
http://www.cup.edu/

State-supported, coed, comprehensive institution. CGS member. *Enrollment:* 7,720 graduate, professional, and undergraduate students; 800 full-time matriculated graduate/professional students (461 women), 621 part-time matriculated graduate/professional students (387 women). *Graduate faculty:* 135 full-time (63 women), 29 part-time/adjunct (7 women). *Computer facilities:* 1,220 computers available on campus for general student use. A campuswide network can be accessed from student residence rooms. Internet access and online class registration are available. *Library facilities:* Manderino Library. *Graduate expenses:* Tuition, state resident: full-time $6,048; part-time $336 per credit. Tuition, nonresident: full-time $9,678; part-time $538 per credit. Required fees: $1,854; $263 per credit. Full-time tuition and fees vary according to course load, campus/location and program. *General application contact:* Suzanne C. Powers, Director of Graduate Admissions and Recruitment, 724-938-4029.

School of Graduate Studies and Research
Dr. Ronald W. Wagner, Dean
Program in:
- legal studies (MS)

College of Liberal Arts
Dr. Laura Ann Tuennerman, Interim Dean
Programs in:
- liberal arts (MA)
- social science—criminal justice (MA)

School of Education
Geraldine Jones, Dean
Programs in:
- athletic training (MS)
- communication disorders (MS)
- education (M Ed, MAT, MS, MSW)
- exercise science and health promotion (MS)
- fitness and wellness (MS)
- guidance and counseling (M Ed, MS)
- mentally and/or physically handicapped education (M Ed)
- performance enhancement and injury prevention (MS)
- reading specialist (M Ed)
- rehabilitation sciences (MS)
- school administration (M Ed)
- school psychology (MS)
- secondary education (MAT)
- social work (MSW)
- sport management (MS)
- sport psychology (MS)
- technology education (M Ed)

School of Science and Technology
Dr. Leonard Colelli, Dean
Programs in:
- business administration (MSBA)
- multimedia technology (MS)
- science and technology (MS, MSBA)

■ CARLOW UNIVERSITY
Pittsburgh, PA 15213-3165
http://www.carlow.edu/

Independent-religious, coed, primarily women, comprehensive institution. *Computer facilities:* 250 computers available on campus for general student use. A campuswide network can be accessed from student residence rooms and from off campus. Internet access and online class registration, applications software, e-mail, online access to registration and grades are available. *Library facilities:* Grace Library. *General application contact:* Administrative Assistant, Admissions, 412-578-6059.

Humanities Division
Program in:
- creative writing (MFA)

School for Social Change
Programs in:
- management of non-profit organization (MS)
- organizational influence (MS)
- professional counseling (MSPC)
- training and development (MS)

School of Education
Programs in:
- art education (M Ed)
- early childhood education (M Ed)
- early childhood supervision (M Ed)
- education with certificate options (M Ed)
- educational leadership (M Ed)
- educational praxis (MA)
- elementary education (M Ed)
- instructional technology specialist (M Ed)
- secondary education (M Ed)
- special education (M Ed)

School of Management
Program in:
- management and technology (MS)

School of Nursing
Programs in:
- home health advanced practice nursing (MSN, PMC)
- nursing case management/leadership (MSN)
- nursing leadership (MSN)

■ CARNEGIE MELLON UNIVERSITY
Pittsburgh, PA 15213-3891
http://www.cmu.edu/

Independent, coed, university. CGS member. *Computer facilities:* 402 computers available on campus for general student use. A campuswide network can be accessed from student residence rooms and from off campus. Internet access and online class registration are available. *Library facilities:* Hunt Library plus 2 others. *General application contact:* Information Contact, 412-268-2000.

Carnegie Institute of Technology
Programs in:
- advanced infrastructure systems (MS, PhD)
- architecture-engineering construction management (MS)
- bioengineering (MS, PhD)
- biomedical engineering (MS, PhD)
- chemical engineering (M Ch E, MS, PhD)
- civil and environmental engineering (MS, PhD)
- civil and environmental engineering/ engineering and public policy (PhD)
- civil engineering (MS, PhD)
- colloids, polymers and surfaces (MS)
- computational science and engineering (MS, PhD)
- computer-aided engineering (MS, PhD)
- computer-aided engineering and management (MS, PhD)
- electrical and computer engineering (MS, PhD)
- engineering (MS, PhD)
- engineering and public policy (PhD)
- environmental engineering (MS, PhD)
- environmental management and science (MS, PhD)
- materials science and engineering (MS, PhD)
- mechanical engineering (ME, MS, PhD)
- product development (MPD)
- technology (M Ch E, ME, MPD, MS, PhD)

Information Networking Institute
Programs in:
- information networking (MS)
- information security technology and management (MS)

Center for the Neural Basis of Cognition
Program in:
- neural basis of cognition (PhD)

College of Fine Arts
Programs in:
- art (MFA)
- fine arts (M Des, M Sc, MAM, MET, MFA, MM, MPD, MSA, PhD)

School of Architecture
Programs in:
- architecture (MSA)
- building performance and diagnostics (M Sc, PhD)
- computational design (M Sc, PhD)

School of Design
Programs in:
- communication planning and information design (M Des)
- design (PhD)
- design theory (PhD)
- interaction design (M Des)
- new product development (PhD)
- product development (MPD)
- typography and information design (PhD)

School of Drama
Programs in:
- design (MFA)
- directing (MFA)
- dramatic writing (MFA)
- performance technology and management (MFA)

School of Music
Programs in:
- composition (MM)
- conducting (MM)
- music education (MM)
- performance (MM)

College of Humanities and Social Sciences
Programs in:
- behavioral decision theory (PhD)
- cognitive neuroscience (PhD)
- cognitive psychology (PhD)
- communication planning and design (M Des)
- computer-assisted language learning (MCALL)
- design (MAPW)
- developmental psychology (PhD)
- English (MA)
- history (MA, MS)
- history and policy (MA, PhD)
- humanities and social sciences (M Des, MA, MAPW, MCALL, MS, PhD)
- literary and cultural studies (MA, PhD)
- logic and computation (MS)
- logic, computation and methodology (PhD)
- mathematical finance (PhD)
- organization science (PhD)
- philosophy (MA)
- professional writing (MAPW)
- research (MAPW)
- rhetoric (MA, PhD)
- rhetorical theory (MAPW)
- science writing (MAPW)
- second language acquisition (PhD)
- social and cultural history (PhD)
- social and decision science (PhD)
- social/personality/health psychology (PhD)
- statistics (MS, PhD)
- technical (MAPW)

Center for Innovation in Learning
Program in:
- instructional science (PhD)

H. John Heinz III School of Public Policy and Management
Programs in:
- arts management (MAM)
- entertainment industry management (MEIM)
- health care policy and management (MSHCPM)
- information security policy and management (MSISPM)
- information systems management (MISM)
- medical management (MMM)
- public management (MPM)
- public policy analysis (PhD)
- public policy and management (MAM, MEIM, MIS, MISM, MMM, MPM, MS, MSED, MSHCPM, MSISPM, PhD)
- sustainable economic development (MIS)

Joint CMU-Pitt PhD Program in Computational Biology
Program in:
- computational biology (PhD)

Mellon College of Science
Programs in:
- algorithms, combinatorics, and optimization (PhD)
- biochemistry (PhD)
- biophysics (PhD)
- cell biology (PhD)
- chemical instrumentation (MS)
- chemistry (MS, PhD)
- colloids, polymers and surfaces (MS)
- computational biology (MS, PhD)
- developmental biology (PhD)
- genetics (PhD)
- mathematical finance (PhD)
- mathematical sciences (MS, DA, PhD)
- molecular biology (PhD)
- neurobiology (PhD)
- physics (PhD)
- polymer science (MS)
- pure and applied logic (PhD)
- science (MS, DA, PhD)

School of Computer Science
Programs in:
- algorithms, combinatorics, and optimization (PhD)
- computer science (PhD)
- entertainment technology (MET)
- human-computer interaction (MHCI, PhD)
- knowledge discovery and data mining (MS)
- pure and applied logic (PhD)
- software engineering (MSE, PhD)

Language Technologies Institute
Program in:
- language technologies (MLT, PhD)

Robotics Institute
Program in:
- robotics (MS, PhD)

Tepper School of Business
Programs in:
- accounting (PhD)
- algorithms, combinatorics, and optimization (MS, PhD)
- business management and software engineering (MBMSE)
- civil engineering and industrial management (MS)
- computational finance (MSCF)
- economics (MS, PhD)
- electronic commerce (MS)
- environmental engineering and management (MEEM)
- finance (PhD)
- financial economics (PhD)
- industrial administration (MBA, PhD)
- information systems (PhD)
- management of manufacturing and automation (MOM, PhD)
- manufacturing (MOM)
- marketing (PhD)
- mathematical finance (PhD)
- operations research (PhD)
- organizational behavior and theory (PhD)
- political economy (PhD)
- production and operations management (PhD)
- public policy and management (MS, MSED)
- software engineering and business management (MS)

■ CHATHAM UNIVERSITY
Pittsburgh, PA 15232-2826
http://www.chatham.edu/

Independent, Undergraduate: women only; graduate: coed, comprehensive institution. *Enrollment:* 1,590 graduate, professional, and undergraduate students; 513 full-time matriculated graduate/professional students (421 women), 272 part-time matriculated graduate/professional students (213 women). *Graduate faculty:* 27 full-time, 54 part-time/adjunct. *Computer facilities:* Computer purchase and lease plans are available. 265 computers available on campus for general student use. A campuswide network can be accessed from student residence rooms and from off campus. Internet access and online class registration, computer-aided instruction are available. *Library facilities:* Jennie King Mellon Library. *General application contact:* Information Contact, 412-365-1825.

Program in Business Administration
Dr. Mary Reibe, Director
Programs in:
- business administration (MBA)
- healthcare professional (MBA)

Chatham University (continued)

Program in Counseling Psychology

Dr. Mary Beth Mannarino, Director
Program in:
counseling psychology (MSCP)

Program in Education

Dr. Wendy Weiner, Director
Programs in:
early childhood education (MAT)
elementary education (MAT)
English—secondary (MAT)
environmental education (K-12) (MAT)
secondary art (MAT)
secondary biology education (MAT)
secondary chemistry education (MAT)
secondary English education (MAT)
secondary math education (MAT)
secondary physics education (MAT)
secondary social studies education (MAT)
special education (MAT)

Program in Landscape Architecture

Lisa Kunst Vavaro, Director
Programs in:
landscape architecture (ML Arch)
landscape studies (MA)

Program in Physical Therapy

Dr. Patricia Downey, Director
Program in:
physical therapy (DPT, TDPT)

Program in Physician Assistant Studies

Luis Ramos, Director
Program in:
physician assistant studies (MPAS)

Program in Writing

Dr. Sheryl St. Germain, Director
Programs in:
creative writing (MFA)
fiction (MFA)
non-fiction (MFA)
poetry (MFA)
professional writing (MAPW)
writing for children/adolescent audience (MFA)

■ CHESTNUT HILL COLLEGE

Philadelphia, PA 19118-2693
http://www.chc.edu/

Independent-religious, coed, primarily women, comprehensive institution. *Enrollment:* 1,918 graduate, professional, and undergraduate students; 162 full-time matriculated graduate/professional students (131 women), 547 part-time matriculated graduate/professional students (455 women). *Graduate faculty:* 9 full-time (3 women), 75 part-time/adjunct (42 women). *Computer facilities:* Computer purchase and lease plans are available. 101 computers available on campus for general student use. A campuswide network can be accessed from student residence rooms. Internet access, e-mail are available. *Library facilities:* Logue Library. *Graduate expenses:* Tuition: part-time $470 per credit hour. Required fees: $30 per semester. Tuition and fees vary according to degree level. *General application contact:* Sr. Ann Harkin, SSJ, Administrative Assistant, 215-248-7170.

Find University Details at www.petersons.com/gradchannel.

School of Graduate Studies

Dr. Joyce Huth Munro, Dean of the School of Graduate Studies
Programs in:
administration of human services (MS)
adult and aging services (CAS)
applied spirituality (CAS)
clinical pastoral education (CAS)
clinical psychology (Psy D)
counseling psychology and human services (MA, MS, CAS)
e-communication (CAS)
early childhood education (M Ed)
education and technology (CAS)
educational leadership (M Ed)
elementary education (M Ed)
holistic spirituality (MA)
holistic spirituality and healthcare (MA)
holistic spirituality and spiritual direction (MA)
holistic spirituality/health care (CAS)
instructional design (CAS)
instructional technology specialist (CAS)
instructional technology/instruction design (MS)
instructional technology/leadership and technology (MS)
instructional technology/technology and education (MS)
leadership and technology (CAS)
leadership development (CAS)
multimedia design (CAS)
online learning (CAS)
restructured environments (CAS)
secondary education (M Ed)
spirituality (CAS)
supervision of spiritual directors (CAS)
video (CAS)

■ CHEYNEY UNIVERSITY OF PENNSYLVANIA

Cheyney, PA 19319-0200
http://www.cheyney.edu/

State-supported, coed, comprehensive institution. *Computer facilities:* 250 computers available on campus for general student use. A campuswide network can be accessed from student residence rooms and from off campus. Internet access and online class registration, online tutorials, various software packages, online payment/online praxis study guide are available. *Library facilities:* Leslie Pickney Hill Library. *General application contact:* Executive Dean of Graduate Studies, 215-560-7034.

School of Education

Programs in:
adult and continuing education (MS)
early childhood education (Certificate)
education (M Ed, MAT, MS, Certificate)
educational administration and supervision (M Ed, Certificate)
educational administration of adult and continuing education (M Ed, MS)
elementary and secondary principalship (Certificate)
elementary education (M Ed, MAT)
mathematics education (Certificate)
special education (M Ed, MS)

■ CLARION UNIVERSITY OF PENNSYLVANIA

Clarion, PA 16214
http://www.clarion.edu/

State-supported, coed, comprehensive institution. CGS member. *Enrollment:* 6,591 graduate, professional, and undergraduate students; 538 matriculated graduate/professional students. *Graduate faculty:* 71. *Computer facilities:* 400 computers available on campus for general student use. A campuswide network can be accessed from student residence rooms and from off campus. Internet access and online class registration are available. *Library facilities:* Carlson Library. *Graduate expenses:* Tuition, state resident: part-time $336 per credit. Tuition, nonresident: part-time $538 per credit. *General application contact:* Dr. Brenda Sanders Dédé, Assistant Vice President for Academic Affairs, 814-393-2337.

Find University Details at www.petersons.com/gradchannel.

Office of Research and Graduate Studies

Dr. Brenda Sanders Dédé, Assistant Vice President for Academic Affairs

College of Arts and Sciences

Dr. Stephen R. Johnson, Interim Dean
Programs in:
arts and sciences (MA, MS)
biology (MS)
English (MA)
mass media arts, journalism, and communication studies (MS)

College of Business Administration

Dr. James Pesek, Interim Dean
Program in:
business administration (MBA)

College of Education and Human Services

Dr. Nancy Sayre, Interim Dean
Programs in:
communication sciences and disorders (MS)
curriculum and instruction (M Ed)
early childhood (M Ed)

education (M Ed)
education and human services (M Ed, MS, MSLS, CAS)
English (M Ed)
history (M Ed)
library science (MSLS, CAS)
literacy (M Ed)
reading (M Ed)
rehabilitative sciences (MS)
science (M Ed)
science education (M Ed)
special education (MS)
technology (M Ed)

School of Nursing
Joyce Keenan, Acting Director
Program in:
nursing (MSN)

■ COLLEGE MISERICORDIA
Dallas, PA 18612-1098
http://www.misericordia.edu/

Independent-religious, coed, comprehensive institution. *Enrollment:* 2,358 graduate, professional, and undergraduate students; 62 full-time matriculated graduate/professional students (50 women), 261 part-time matriculated graduate/professional students (189 women). *Graduate faculty:* 17 full-time (9 women), 32 part-time/adjunct (19 women). *Computer facilities:* Computer purchase and lease plans are available. 75 computers available on campus for general student use. A campuswide network can be accessed from student residence rooms and from off campus. Internet access and online class registration are available. *Library facilities:* Mary Kintz Bevevino Library. *Graduate expenses:* Tuition: full-time $19,800; part-time $495 per credit. Required fees: $1,060. *General application contact:* Larree Brown, Coordinator of Part-Time Undergraduate and Graduate Programs, 570-674-6451.

College of Health Sciences
Dr. Ellen McLaughlin, Interim Dean of Health Sciences
Programs in:
health sciences (MSN, MSOT, MSPT, MSSLP, DPT)
nursing (MSN)
occupational therapy (MSOT)
physical therapy (MSPT, DPT)
speech-language pathology (MSSLP)

College of Professional Studies and Social Sciences
Tom O'Neill, Dean of Adult and Continuing Education
Programs in:
education/curriculum (MS)
organizational management (MS)

■ DESALES UNIVERSITY
Center Valley, PA 18034-9568
http://www.desales.edu

Independent-religious, coed, comprehensive institution. *Enrollment:* 2,936 graduate, professional, and undergraduate students; 58 full-time matriculated graduate/professional students, 752 part-time matriculated graduate/professional students. *Computer facilities:* Computer purchase and lease plans are available. 200 computers available on campus for general student use. A campuswide network can be accessed from student residence rooms and from off campus. Internet access is available. *Library facilities:* Trexler Library. *General application contact:* Rev. Peter J. Leonard, Dean of Graduate Education, 610-282-1100 Ext. 1289.

Graduate Division
Rev. Peter J. Leonard, Dean of Graduate Education
Programs in:
academic standards and information (Certificate)
adult advanced practice nurse specialist (MSN)
bilingual/ESL studies (Certificate)
biology (M Ed)
business administration (MBA)
chemistry (M Ed)
computers in education (K-12) (M Ed)
computers in education (K-8) (M Ed)
criminal justice (MACJ)
English (M Ed)
family nurse practitioner (MSN)
information systems (MSIS)
instructional technology specialist (Certificate)
mathematics (M Ed)
nurse educator (MSN)
physician assistant studies (MSPAS)
special education (M Ed, Certificate)
TESOL (M Ed)

■ DREXEL UNIVERSITY
Philadelphia, PA 19104-2875
http://www.drexel.edu/

Independent, coed, university. CGS member. *Computer facilities:* 6,500 computers available on campus for general student use. A campuswide network can be accessed from student residence rooms and from off campus. Internet access and online class registration, campuswide wireless network are available. *Library facilities:* W. W. Hagerty Library. *General application contact:* Director of Graduate Admissions, 215-895-6700.

Find University Details at www.petersons.com/gradchannel.

College of Arts and Sciences
Programs in:
arts and sciences (MA, MS, PhD)
biological science (MS, PhD)
chemistry (MS, PhD)
clinical psychology (MA, MS, PhD)
communication (MS)
environmental policy (MS)
environmental science (MS, PhD)
food science (MS)
forensic psychology (PhD)
health psychology (PhD)
law-psychology (PhD)
mathematics (MS, PhD)
neuropsychology (PhD)
nutrition and food sciences (MS, PhD)
nutrition science (PhD)
physics (MS, PhD)
publication management (MS)
science, technology and society (MS)

College of Engineering
Programs in:
biochemical engineering (MS)
chemical engineering (MS, PhD)
civil engineering (MS, PhD)
computer engineering (MS)
computer science (MS, PhD)
electrical and computer engineering (PhD)
electrical engineering (MSEE, PhD)
engineering (MS, MSEE, MSSE, PhD)
engineering geology (MS)
engineering management (MS, PhD)
environmental engineering (MS, PhD)
manufacturing engineering (MS, PhD)
materials engineering (MS, PhD)
mechanical engineering and mechanics (MS, PhD)
software engineering (MSSE)
telecommunications engineering (MSEE)

College of Information Science and Technology
Programs in:
information science and technology (PhD)
information studies (PhD, CAS)
information systems (MSIS)
library and information science (MS)

College of Media Arts and Design
Programs in:
architecture (M Arch)
arts administration (MS)
design (MS)
fashion design (MS)
interior design (MS)
media arts (MS)
performing arts (MS)

College of Medicine
Program in:
medicine (MD, MBS, MLAS, MMS, MS, PhD, Certificate)

Biomedical Graduate Programs
Programs in:
biochemistry (MS, PhD)
biomedical sciences (MBS, MLAS, MMS, MS, PhD, Certificate)
laboratory animal science (MLAS)
medical science (MBS, MMS, Certificate)
microbiology and immunology (MS, PhD)

Drexel University (continued)
molecular and cell biology (MS, PhD)
molecular and human genetics (MS, PhD)
molecular pathobiology (PhD)
neuroscience (PhD)
pharmacology and physiology (MS, PhD)
radiation (MS)
radiation biology (MS)
radiation physics (PhD)
radiation science (PhD)
radiopharmaceutical science (MS, PhD)

College of Nursing and Health Professions
Programs in:
advanced physician assistant studies (MHS)
art therapy (MA)
couples and family therapy (PhD)
dance/movement therapy (MA)
emergency and public safety services (MS)
family therapy (MFT)
hand/upper quarter rehabilitation (MHS, MS, PhD)
movement science (MHS, MS, PhD)
music therapy (MA)
nurse anesthesia (MSN)
nursing (MSN)
nursing and health professions (MA, MFT, MHS, MS, MSN, DPT, PhD, Certificate)
orthopedics (MHS, MS, PhD)
pediatrics (MHS, MS, PhD)
physical therapy (DPT, Certificate)

LeBow College of Business
Programs in:
accounting (MS)
business administration (MBA, PhD, APC)
business and administration (MBA, MS, PhD, APC)
decision sciences (MS)
finance (MS)
marketing (MS)
taxation (MS)

School of Biomedical Engineering, Science and Health Systems
Programs in:
biomedical engineering (MS, PhD)
biomedical science (MS, PhD)
biostatistics (MS)
clinical/rehabilitation engineering (MS)

School of Education
Programs in:
educational administration (MS)
educational administration and collaborative learning (MS)
educational leadership and learning technology (PhD)
global and international education (MS)
graduate intern teaching (Certificate)
higher education (MS)
instructional technology (Spt)
post-bachelor's teaching (Certificate)
school principal (Certificate)
school superintendent (Certificate)
science of instruction (MS)
teaching English as a second language (Certificate)
teaching, learning and curriculum (MS)

School of Journalism
Program in:
journalism (MA)

School of Public Health
Program in:
public health (MPH)

■ DUQUESNE UNIVERSITY
Pittsburgh, PA 15282-0001
http://www.duq.edu/

Independent-religious, coed, university. CGS member. *Enrollment:* 10,110 graduate, professional, and undergraduate students; 3,129 full-time matriculated graduate/professional students (1,808 women), 1,303 part-time matriculated graduate/professional students (776 women). *Graduate faculty:* 379. *Computer facilities:* 800 computers available on campus for general student use. A campuswide network can be accessed from student residence rooms and from off campus. Internet access and online class registration are available. *Library facilities:* Gumberg Library plus 1 other. *Graduate expenses:* Tuition: part-time $723 per credit. Required fees: $71 per credit. Tuition and fees vary according to degree level and program. *General application contact:* Dr. Ralph L. Pearson, Provost and Academic Vice President, 412-396-6054.

Find University Details at www.petersons.com/gradchannel.

Bayer School of Natural and Environmental Sciences
Dr. David W. Seybert, Dean
Programs in:
biochemistry (MS, PhD)
biological sciences (MS, PhD)
chemistry (MS, PhD)
environmental management (MEM, Certificate)
environmental science (Certificate)
environmental science and management (MS)
forensic science and the law (MS)
natural and environmental sciences (MEM, MS, PhD, Certificate)

Graduate School of Liberal Arts
Dr. Francesco C. Cesareo, Dean
Programs in:
archival, museum, and editing studies (MA)
clinical psychology (PhD)
communication (MA)
computational mathematics (MA, MS)
English (MA, PhD)
health care ethics (MA, DHCE, PhD, Certificate)
history (MA)
liberal arts (M Phil, MA, MS, DHCE, PhD, Certificate)
liberal studies (M Phil, MA)
multimedia technology (MS, Certificate)
pastoral ministry (MA)
philosophy (MA, PhD)
religious education (MA)
rhetoric (PhD)
systematic theology (PhD)
theology (MA)

Graduate Center for Social and Public Policy
Dr. Joseph Yenerall, Director
Programs in:
conflict resolution and peace studies (Certificate)
social and public policy (MA, Certificate)

John F. Donahue Graduate School of Business
Alan R. Miciak, Dean
Programs in:
business administration (MBA)
taxation (MS)

John G. Rangos, Sr. School of Health Sciences
Dr. Gregory H. Frazer, Dean
Programs in:
health management systems (MHMS)
occupational therapy (MS)
physical therapy (DPT)
physician assistant (MPA)
speech–language pathology (MS)

Mary Pappert School of Music
Dr. Edward W. Kocher, Dean
Programs in:
music composition (MM)
music education (MM)
music performance (MM, AD)
music technology (MM)
music theory (MM)
sacred music (MM)

School of Education
Dr. Olga Welch, Dean
Programs in:
child psychology (MS Ed)
community counseling (MS Ed)
counselor education (MS Ed, Ed D)
counselor education and supervision (Ed D)
early childhood education (MS Ed)
education (MS Ed, Ed D, PhD, CAGS)
educational leaders (Ed D)
educational studies (MS Ed)
elementary education (MS Ed)
English as a second language (MS Ed)
instructional leadership excellence (Ed D)

instructional technology (MS Ed, Ed D)
marriage and family therapy (MS Ed)
reading and language arts (MS Ed)
school administration (MS Ed)
school administration and supervision (MS Ed)
school counseling (MS Ed)
school psychology (MS Ed, PhD, CAGS)
school supervision (MS Ed)
secondary education (MS Ed)
special education (MS Ed)

School of Law
Donald J. Guter, Dean
Program in:
law (JD, LL M)

School of Leadership and Professional Advancement
Programs in:
community leadership (MS)
leadership and business ethics (MS)
leadership and information technology (MS)
leadership and liberal studies (MA)
sports leadership (MS)

School of Nursing
Dr. Eileen Zungolo, Dean/Professor
Programs in:
acute care nursing (Post-Master's Certificate)
acute care nursing specialist (MSN)
family nurse practitioner (MSN, Post-Master's Certificate)
forensic nursing (MSN, Post-Master's Certificate)
nursing (MSN, PhD, Post-Master's Certificate)
nursing administration (MSN, Post-Master's Certificate)
nursing education (MSN, Post-Master's Certificate)
psychiatric/mental health nursing (MSN, Post-Master's Certificate)

School of Pharmacy
Dr. J. Douglas Bricker, Dean
Program in:
pharmacy (Pharm D, MS, PhD)

Graduate School of Pharmaceutical Sciences
Dr. James K. Drennen, Head
Programs in:
medicinal chemistry (MS, PhD)
pharmaceutical administration (MS)
pharmaceutics (MS, PhD)
pharmacology/toxicology (MS, PhD)

■ EASTERN UNIVERSITY
St. Davids, PA 19087-3696
http://www.eastern.edu/

Independent-religious, coed, comprehensive institution. *Computer facilities:* 60 computers available on campus for general student use. A campuswide network can be accessed from student residence rooms and from off campus. Internet access is available. *Library facilities:* Warner Library plus 1 other. *General application contact:* Director of Graduate Admissions, 610-341-5972.

Graduate Business Programs
Programs in:
business administration (MBA)
economic development (MBA, MS)
nonprofit management (MBA, MS)

Graduate Education Programs
Programs in:
English as a second or foreign language (Certificate)
multicultural education (M Ed)
school health services (M Ed)

Office of Interdisciplinary Programs
Program in:
organizational leadership (PhD)

Palmer Theological Seminary
Programs in:
marriage and family (D Min)
renewal of the church for mission (D Min)
theology (M Div, MTS, D Min)

Programs in Counseling
Programs in:
community/clinical counseling (MA)
educational counseling (MA, MS)
marriage and family (MA)
school counseling (MA)
school psychology (MS)
student development (MA)

■ EAST STROUDSBURG UNIVERSITY OF PENNSYLVANIA
East Stroudsburg, PA 18301-2999
http://www3.esu.edu/

State-supported, coed, comprehensive institution. *Enrollment:* 7,013 graduate, professional, and undergraduate students; 287 full-time matriculated graduate/professional students (182 women), 546 part-time matriculated graduate/professional students (408 women). *Graduate faculty:* 87 full-time (35 women), 28 part-time/adjunct (17 women). *Computer facilities:* 500 computers available on campus for general student use. A campuswide network can be accessed from student residence rooms and from off campus. Internet access and online class registration are available. *Library facilities:* Kemp Library. *Graduate expenses:* Tuition, state resident: full-time $6,048; part-time $336 per credit. Tuition, nonresident: full-time $9,678; part-time $538 per credit. Required fees: $1,353; $67 per credit. One-time fee: $37 part-time. *General application contact:* Dr. Henry Gardner, Associate Provost for Enrollment Management, 570-422-2870.

Find University Details at www.petersons.com/gradchannel.

Graduate School
Dr. Alberto Cardelle, Interim Dean: Graduate Schools Faculty Research

School of Arts and Sciences
Dr. Peter Hawkes, Dean
Programs in:
arts and sciences (M Ed, MA, MS)
biology (M Ed, MS)
computer science (MS)
history (M Ed, MA)
political science (M Ed, MA)

School of Health Sciences and Human Performance
Dr. Mark Kilker, Dean
Programs in:
cardiac rehabilitation and exercise science (MS)
community health education (MPH)
health and physical education (M Ed)
health education (MS)
health sciences and human performance (M Ed, MPH, MS)
management and leadership (MS)
speech pathology and audiology (MS)
sports management (MS)

School of Professional Studies
Dr. Pamela Kramer, Interim Dean
Programs in:
elementary education (M Ed)
instructional technology (M Ed)
management and leadership (MS)
professional and secondary education (M Ed)
reading (M Ed)
special education (M Ed)

■ EDINBORO UNIVERSITY OF PENNSYLVANIA
Edinboro, PA 16444
http://www.edinboro.edu/

State-supported, coed, comprehensive institution. *Enrollment:* 7,579 graduate, professional, and undergraduate students; 483 full-time matriculated graduate/professional students (331 women), 653 part-time matriculated graduate/professional students (491 women). *Graduate faculty:* 89 full-time (43 women). *Computer facilities:* Computer purchase and lease plans are available. 818 computers available on campus for general student use. A campuswide network can be accessed from student residence rooms and from off campus. Internet access and online class registration, e-mail, software are available. *Library facilities:* Baron-Forness Library plus 1 other. *Graduate expenses:* Tuition, state resident: full-time $6,048; part-time $336

Edinboro University of Pennsylvania (continued)
per credit. Tuition, nonresident: full-time $9,678; part-time $538 per credit. Required fees: $1,849; $42 per credit. *General application contact:* Dr. R. Scott Baldwin, Dean of Graduate Studies and Research, 814-732-2856.

Graduate Studies and Research
Dr. R. Scott Baldwin, Dean

School of Education
Dr. Kenneth Adams, Interim Dean
Programs in:
- behavior management (Certificate)
- character education (M Ed, Certificate)
- community counseling (MA)
- counseling (MA)
- early childhood education (M Ed)
- education (M Ed, MA, Certificate)
- educational leadership (M Ed)
- educational psychology (M Ed)
- elementary education (M Ed)
- elementary guidance (MA)
- elementary school administration (M Ed)
- letter of eligibility (Certificate)
- reading (M Ed, Certificate)
- reading specialist (Certificate)
- rehabilitation counseling (MA)
- secondary education (M Ed)
- secondary guidance (MA)
- secondary school administration (M Ed)
- special education (M Ed)
- student personnel services (MA)

School of Liberal Arts
Dr. Terry L. Smith, Dean
Programs in:
- art (MA)
- ceramics (MFA)
- clinical psychology (MA)
- communications and media studies (MA)
- fine arts (MFA)
- jewelry/metalsmithing (MFA)
- liberal arts (MA, MFA, MSW)
- painting (MFA)
- printmaking (MFA)
- sculpture (MFA)
- social sciences (MA)
- social work (MSW)
- speech language pathology (MA)

School of Science, Management and Technology
Dr. Eric Randall, Dean
Programs in:
- biology (MS)
- family nurse practitioner (MSN)
- information technology (MS, Certificate)
- science, management and technology (MS, MSN, Certificate)

■ GANNON UNIVERSITY
Erie, PA 16541-0001
http://www.gannon.edu/

Independent-religious, coed, comprehensive institution. *Enrollment:* 3,815 graduate, professional, and undergraduate students; 410 full-time matriculated graduate/professional students (207 women), 680 part-time matriculated graduate/professional students (446 women). *Graduate faculty:* 67 full-time (32 women), 51 part-time/adjunct (17 women). *Computer facilities:* 175 computers available on campus for general student use. A campuswide network can be accessed from student residence rooms and from off campus. Internet access and online class registration are available. *Library facilities:* Nash Library plus 1 other. *Graduate expenses:* Tuition: full-time $12,240; part-time $680 per credit. Required fees: $496; $16 per credit. Tuition and fees vary according to course load, degree level, campus/location and program. *General application contact:* Debra Meszaros, Director of Graduate Recruitment, 814-871-5819.

School of Graduate Studies
Michael J. O'Neill, Dean

College of Humanities, Business, and Education
Dr. Timothy Downs, Dean
Programs in:
- accounting (Certificate)
- advanced counselor studies (Certificate)
- business (MBA, MPA, Certificate)
- business administration (MBA)
- community counseling (MS, Certificate)
- counseling psychology (PhD)
- curriculum and instruction (M Ed)
- early intervention (MS, Certificate)
- education (M Ed, MS, Certificate)
- educational computing technology (M Ed)
- educational leadership (M Ed)
- English (MA)
- English as a second language (Certificate)
- finance (Certificate)
- gerontology (Certificate)
- human resources management (Certificate)
- humanities (MA, MS, PhD, Certificate)
- humanities, business, and education (M Ed, MA, MBA, MPA, MS, PhD, Certificate)
- instructional technology specialist (Certificate)
- investments (Certificate)
- marketing (Certificate)
- organizational leadership (Certificate)
- pastoral studies (MA, Certificate)
- principal certification (Certificate)
- public administration (MPA, Certificate)
- reading (M Ed, Certificate)
- risk management (Certificate)
- school counselor preparation (Certificate)
- superintendent letter of eligibility certification (Certificate)

College of Sciences, Engineering, and Health Sciences
Dr. Carolynn Masters, Dean
Programs in:
- anesthesia (MSN)
- business administration (MSN)
- case management (MSN)
- computer and information science (MSCIS)
- electrical engineering (MSEE)
- embedded software engineering (MSES)
- engineering and computer science (MSCIS, MSE, MSEE, MSES, MSME)
- engineering management (MSE)
- environmental and occupational science and health (Certificate)
- environmental health and engineering (MS)
- environmental studies (MS)
- health sciences (MPAS, MS, MSN, DPT, Certificate)
- mechanical engineering (MSME)
- medical-surgical nursing (MSN)
- natural and environmental sciences (M Ed)
- nurse anesthesia (Certificate)
- nursing rural practitioner (MSN)
- occupational therapy (MS)
- physical therapy (DPT)
- physician assistant (MPAS)
- sciences (M Ed, MS, Certificate)
- sciences, engineering, and health sciences (M Ed, MPAS, MS, MSCIS, MSE, MSEE, MSES, MSME, MSN, DPT, Certificate)

■ GENEVA COLLEGE
Beaver Falls, PA 15010-3599
http://www.geneva.edu/

Independent-religious, coed, comprehensive institution. *Computer facilities:* 150 computers available on campus for general student use. A campuswide network can be accessed from student residence rooms and from off campus. Internet access and online class registration are available. *Library facilities:* McCartney Library plus 5 others. *General application contact:* Information Contact, 724-846-5100.

Program in Business Administration
Program in:
- business administration (MBA)

Program in Counseling
Programs in:
- marriage and family (MA)
- mental health (MA)
- school counseling (MA)

Program in Higher Education
Programs in:
- campus ministry (MA)
- college teaching (MA)
- educational leadership (MA)
- student affairs administration (MA)

Program in Organizational Leadership
Program in:
organizational leadership (MS)

Program in Special Education
Program in:
special education (M Ed)

■ GRATZ COLLEGE
Melrose Park, PA 19027
http://www.gratzcollege.edu/

Independent-religious, coed, comprehensive institution. *Computer facilities:* 2 computers available on campus for general student use. A campuswide network can be accessed from off campus. *Library facilities:* Tuttleman Library. *General application contact:* Director of Admissions, 215-635-7300 Ext. 140.

Graduate Programs
Programs in:
classical studies (MA)
education (MA)
Israel studies (Certificate)
Jewish communal studies (MA, Certificate)
Jewish education (MA, Certificate)
Jewish music (MA, Certificate)
Jewish studies (MA)
Judaica librarianship (Certificate)
modern studies (MA)

■ GWYNEDD-MERCY COLLEGE
Gwynedd Valley, PA 19437-0901
http://www.gmc.edu/

Independent-religious, coed, comprehensive institution. *Enrollment:* 2,727 graduate, professional, and undergraduate students; 100 full-time matriculated graduate/professional students (72 women), 492 part-time matriculated graduate/professional students (400 women). *Graduate faculty:* 13 full-time (9 women), 26 part-time/adjunct (13 women). *Computer facilities:* Computer purchase and lease plans are available. 97 computers available on campus for general student use. A campuswide network can be accessed from student residence rooms and from off campus. Internet access is available. *Library facilities:* Lourdes Library plus 1 other. *Graduate expenses:* Tuition: part-time $525 per credit hour. *General application contact:* Information Contact, 800-342-5462.

School of Business and Computer Information Sciences
Program in:
business and computer information sciences (MSM)

School of Education
Dr. Lorraine Cavaliere, EdD, Dean
Programs in:
educational administration (MS)
master teacher (MS)
reading (MS)
school counseling (MS)
special education (MS)

School of Nursing
Dr. Andrea D. Hollingsworth, Dean
Programs in:
clinical nurse specialist (MSN)
nurse practitioner (MSN)

■ HOLY FAMILY UNIVERSITY
Philadelphia, PA 19114-2094
http://www.holyfamily.edu/

Independent-religious, coed, comprehensive institution. *Computer facilities:* 148 computers available on campus for general student use. A campuswide network can be accessed. Internet access is available. *Library facilities:* Holy Family College Library plus 1 other. *General application contact:* Dean, Graduate Studies, 215-637-7700 Ext. 3230.

Graduate School

School of Arts and Sciences
Program in:
counseling psychology (MS)

School of Business
Programs in:
human resources management (MS)
information systems management (MS)

School of Education
Programs in:
education (M Ed)
elementary education (M Ed)
reading specialist (M Ed)
secondary education (M Ed)

School of Nursing
Program in:
nursing (MSN)

■ IMMACULATA UNIVERSITY
Immaculata, PA 19345
http://www.immaculata.edu/

Independent-religious, coed, primarily women, comprehensive institution. *Enrollment:* 4,067 graduate, professional, and undergraduate students; 102 full-time matriculated graduate/professional students (81 women), 875 part-time matriculated graduate/professional students (672 women). *Graduate faculty:* 44. *Computer facilities:* 254 computers available on campus for general student use. A campuswide network can be accessed from student residence rooms. Internet access is available. *Library facilities:* Gabriele Library. *General application contact:* Sandra A. Rollison, Director of Graduate Admission, 610-647-4400 Ext. 3215.

Find University Details at www.petersons.com/gradchannel.

College of Graduate Studies
Sr. Ann M. Heath, Dean
Programs in:
clinical psychology (Psy D)
counseling psychology (MA, Certificate)
cultural and linguistic diversity (MA)
educational leadership and administration (MA, Ed D)
elementary education (Certificate)
intermediate unit director (Certificate)
music therapy (MA)
nursing (MSN)
nutrition education (MA)
nutrition education/approved pre-professional practice program (MA)
organization studies (MA)
school principal (Certificate)
school psychology (Psy D)
school superintendent (Certificate)
secondary education (Certificate)
special education (Certificate)

■ INDIANA UNIVERSITY OF PENNSYLVANIA
Indiana, PA 15705-1087
http://www.iup.edu/

State-supported, coed, university. CGS member. *Enrollment:* 14,248 graduate, professional, and undergraduate students; 1,100 full-time matriculated graduate/professional students (677 women), 1,172 part-time matriculated graduate/professional students (761 women). *Graduate faculty:* 278 full-time (114 women), 14 part-time/adjunct (9 women). *Computer facilities:* Computer purchase and lease plans are available. 3,500 computers available on campus for general student use. A campuswide network can be accessed from student residence rooms and from off campus. Internet access and online class registration are available. *Library facilities:* Stapleton Library. *Graduate expenses:* Tuition, state resident: full-time $6,048; part-time $336 per credit. Tuition, nonresident: full-time $9,678; part-time $538 per credit. Required fees: $1,069; $148 per year. *General application contact:* Donna Griffith, Assistant Dean, 724-357-2222.

Find University Details at www.petersons.com/gradchannel.

School of Graduate Studies and Research
Dr. Alicia Linzey, Dean

College of Education and Educational Technology
Dr. Mary Ann Rafoth, Dean

Indiana University of Pennsylvania (continued)
Programs in:
administration and leadership studies (D Ed)
adult education and communication technology (MA)
communications technology (MA)
community counseling (MA)
counselor education (M Ed)
curriculum and instruction (M Ed, D Ed)
early childhood education (M Ed)
education (M Ed, Certificate)
education and educational technology (M Ed, MA, MS, D Ed, Certificate)
education of exceptional persons (M Ed)
educational psychology (M Ed, Certificate)
literacy (M Ed)
principal (Certificate)
reading (M Ed)
school psychology (D Ed, Certificate)
speech-language pathology (MS)
student affairs in higher education (MA)

College of Fine Arts
Michael Hood, Dean
Programs in:
art (MA, MFA)
fine arts (MA, MFA)
music (MA)
music education (MA)
music history and literature (MA)
music theory and composition (MA)
performance (MA)

College of Health and Human Services
Dr. Carleen Zoni, Dean
Programs in:
aquatics administration and facilities management (MS)
exercise science (MS)
food and nutrition (MS)
health and human services (MA, MS, Certificate)
industrial and labor relations (MA)
nursing (MS)
safety sciences (MS, Certificate)
sport management (MS)
sport science (MS)

College of Humanities and Social Sciences
Dr. Yaw Asamoah, Dean
Programs in:
administration and leadership studies (PhD)
composition and teaching English to speakers of other languages (MA, MAT, PhD)
criminology (MA, PhD)
generalist (MA)
geography (MA, MS)
history (MA)
humanities and social sciences (MA, MAT, MS, PhD)
literature (MA)
literature and criticism (MA, PhD)
public affairs (MA)
rhetoric and linguistics (PhD)
sociology (MA)
teaching English (MAT)
teaching English to speakers of other languages (MA)

College of Natural Sciences and Mathematics
Dr. Gerald Buriok, Interim Dean
Programs in:
applied mathematics (MS)
biology (MS)
chemistry (MA, MS)
clinical psychology (Psy D)
elementary and middle school mathematics education (M Ed)
mathematics education (M Ed)
natural sciences and mathematics (M Ed, MA, MS, Psy D)
physics (MA, MS)
psychology (MA)

Eberly College of Business and Information Technology
Dr. Robert Camp, Dean
Programs in:
business (M Ed, MBA)
business administration (MBA)
business/workforce development (M Ed)

■ KING'S COLLEGE
Wilkes-Barre, PA 18711-0801
http://www.kings.edu/

Independent-religious, coed, comprehensive institution. *Enrollment:* 2,386 graduate, professional, and undergraduate students; 64 full-time matriculated graduate/professional students (55 women), 219 part-time matriculated graduate/professional students (175 women). *Graduate faculty:* 14 full-time (8 women), 16 part-time/adjunct (10 women). *Computer facilities:* Computer purchase and lease plans are available. 318 computers available on campus for general student use. A campuswide network can be accessed from student residence rooms and from off campus. Internet access is available. *Library facilities:* D. Leonard Corgan Library. *Graduate expenses:* Tuition: full-time $26,598; part-time $625 per credit. Required fees: $900. *General application contact:* Dr. Elizabeth S. Lott, Director of Graduate Programs, 570-208-5991.

Program in Physician Assistant Studies
Dr. Elizabeth S. Lott, Director of Graduate Programs
Program in:
physician assistant studies (MSPAS)

Program in Reading
Dr. Elizabeth S. Lott, Director of Graduate Programs
Program in:
reading (M Ed)

William G. McGowan School of Business
Dr. John J. Ryan, Director
Program in:
health care administration (MS)

■ KUTZTOWN UNIVERSITY OF PENNSYLVANIA
Kutztown, PA 19530-0730
http://www.kutztown.edu/

State-supported, coed, comprehensive institution. CGS member. *Enrollment:* 10,193 graduate, professional, and undergraduate students; 291 full-time matriculated graduate/professional students (185 women), 590 part-time matriculated graduate/professional students (421 women). *Graduate faculty:* 71 full-time (30 women), 6 part-time/adjunct (4 women). *Computer facilities:* 650 computers available on campus for general student use. A campuswide network can be accessed from student residence rooms and from off campus. Internet access and online class registration are available. *Library facilities:* Rohrbach Library. *Graduate expenses:* Tuition, state resident: full-time $6,048; part-time $336 per credit. Tuition, nonresident: full-time $9,678; part-time $538 per credit. *General application contact:* Dr. Regis Bernhardt, Interim Dean of Graduate Studies, 610-683-4253.

Find University Details at www.petersons.com/gradchannel.

College of Graduate Studies and Extended Learning
Dr. Regis Bernhardt, Interim Dean of Graduate Studies
Programs in:
agency counseling (MA)
counselor education (M Ed)
marital and family therapy (MA)
student affairs in higher education (M Ed)

College of Business
Dr. Fidelis M. Ikem, Interim Dean
Programs in:
business (MBA)
business administration (MBA)

College of Education
Programs in:
biology (M Ed)
curriculum and instruction (M Ed)
early childhood education (Certificate)
education (M Ed, MLS, Certificate)
elementary education (M Ed, Certificate)
English (M Ed)
instructional technology (M Ed, Certificate)
library science (MLS, Certificate)
mathematics (M Ed)
reading (M Ed)
secondary education (Certificate)
social studies (M Ed)
special education (Certificate)

College of Liberal Arts and Sciences
Dr. Bashar Hanna, Dean
Programs in:
- computer science (MS)
- electronic media (MS)
- English (MA)
- liberal arts and sciences (MA, MPA, MS, MSW, Certificate)
- public administration (MPA)
- school nursing (Certificate)
- social work (MSW)

College of Visual and Performing Arts
Dr. William Mowder, Dean
Programs in:
- art education (M Ed, Certificate)
- music education (Certificate)
- visual and performing arts (M Ed, Certificate)

■ LA ROCHE COLLEGE
Pittsburgh, PA 15237-5898
http://www.laroche.edu/

Independent-religious, coed, comprehensive institution. *Enrollment:* 1,533 graduate, professional, and undergraduate students; 70 full-time matriculated graduate/professional students (41 women), 97 part-time matriculated graduate/professional students (77 women). *Graduate faculty:* 5 full-time (3 women), 11 part-time/adjunct (3 women). *Computer facilities:* 200 computers available on campus for general student use. A campuswide network can be accessed from student residence rooms and from off campus. Internet access and online class registration are available. *Library facilities:* John J. Wright Library. *Graduate expenses:* Tuition: full-time $9,900; part-time $550 per credit. Required fees: $14 per credit. *General application contact:* Hope Schiffgens, Director of Admissions for Graduate and Continuing Education, 412-536-1266.

School of Graduate Studies
Dr. Howard Ishiyama, Vice President for Academic Affairs and Graduate Dean
Programs in:
- family nurse practitioner (MSN)
- human resources management (MS, Certificate)
- nurse anesthesia (MS)
- nursing management (MSN)

■ LA SALLE UNIVERSITY
Philadelphia, PA 19141-1199
http://www.lasalle.edu/

Independent-religious, coed, comprehensive institution. *Computer facilities:* 1,000 computers available on campus for general student use. A campuswide network can be accessed from student residence rooms and from off campus. Internet access and online class registration, WEBCT are available. *Library facilities:* Connelly Library. *General application contact:* Director of Marketing/Graduate Enrollment, 215-951-1946.

School of Arts and Sciences
Programs in:
- arts and sciences (MA, MS, Psy D)
- bilingual/bicultural studies (Spanish) (MA)
- Central and Eastern European studies (MA)
- clinical psychology (Psy D)
- clinical-counseling psychology (MA)
- computer information science (MS)
- education (MA)
- family psychology (Psy D)
- history (MA)
- information technology leadership (MS)
- pastoral studies (MA)
- professional communication (MA)
- rehabilitation psychology (Psy D)
- religion (MA)
- theological studies (MA)

School of Business
Program in:
- business administration (MBA, MS, Certificate)

School of Nursing and Health Sciences
Programs in:
- adult health and illness, clinical nurse specialist (MSN)
- gerontology (Certificate)
- nursing administration (MSN)
- nursing education (Certificate)
- nursing informatics (Certificate)
- primary care of adults-nurse practitioner (MSN)
- public health nursing (MSN)
- school nursing (Certificate)
- speech-language-hearing science (MS)
- wound, ostomy and continence nursing (Certificate)
- wound, ostomy, and continence nursing (MSN)

■ LEHIGH UNIVERSITY
Bethlehem, PA 18015-3094
http://www.lehigh.edu/

Independent, coed, university. CGS member. *Enrollment:* 6,858 graduate, professional, and undergraduate students; 928 full-time matriculated graduate/professional students (402 women), 1,024 part-time matriculated graduate/professional students (495 women). *Graduate faculty:* 370 full-time (85 women), 100 part-time/adjunct (24 women). *Computer facilities:* 572 computers available on campus for general student use. A campuswide network can be accessed from student residence rooms and from off campus. Internet access and online class registration are available. *Library facilities:* E. W. Fairchild-Martindale Library plus 1 other. *General application contact:* Information Contact, 610-758-3000.

College of Arts and Sciences
Dr. Anne S. Meltzer, Dean
Programs in:
- American studies (MA)
- applied mathematics (MS, PhD)
- arts and sciences (MA, MS, PhD)
- biochemistry (PhD)
- chemistry (MS, PhD)
- clinical chemistry (MS)
- earth and environmental sciences (MS, PhD)
- English (MA, PhD)
- history (MA, PhD)
- human cognition and development (MS, PhD)
- integrative biology (PhD)
- mathematics (MS, PhD)
- molecular biology (MS, PhD)
- pharmaceutical chemistry (MS, PhD)
- photonics (MS)
- physics (MS, PhD)
- political science (MA)
- polymer science (MS, PhD)
- polymer science and engineering (MS, PhD)
- sociology (MA)
- statistics (MS)

College of Business and Economics
Michael G. Kolchin, Graduate Business Programs
Programs in:
- accounting (MS)
- accounting and information analysis (MS)
- analytical finance (MS)
- business administration (MBA)
- economics (MS, PhD)
- entrepreneurship (Certificate)
- finance (MS)
- health and bio-pharmaceutical economics (MS)
- organizational leadership (Certificate)
- project management (Certificate)
- supply chain management (Certificate)

College of Education
Dr. Sally A. White, Dean
Programs in:
- academic intervention (M Ed)
- counseling and human services (M Ed)
- counseling psychology (M Ed, PhD, Certificate)
- education (M Ed, MA, MS, Ed D, PhD, Certificate, Ed S)
- educational leadership (M Ed, Ed D, Certificate)
- educational technology (Ed D, PhD, Certificate)
- elementary education (M Ed)
- instructional technology (MS)
- international counseling (M Ed, Certificate)
- learning sciences and technology (PhD)
- project management (Certificate)
- school counseling (M Ed)
- school psychology (PhD, Ed S)

Lehigh University (continued)
secondary education (M Ed, MA)
special education (M Ed, PhD, Certificate)
technology use in schools (Certificate)
technology–based teacher education (M Ed, PhD)
technology-based teacher education (MA)

P.C. Rossin College of Engineering and Applied Science
Dr. John P. Coulter, Associate Dean of Graduate Studies and Research
Programs in:
analytical finance (MS)
chemical engineering (M Eng, MS, PhD)
civil and environmental engineering (M Eng, MS, PhD)
computational engineering and mechanics (MS, PhD)
computer engineering (MS, PhD)
computer science (MS, PhD)
electrical engineering (M Eng, MS, PhD)
engineering and applied science (M Eng, MS, PhD)
industrial engineering (M Eng, MS, PhD)
information and systems engineering (M Eng, MS)
management science (MS)
manufacturing systems engineering (MS)
materials science and engineering (M Eng, MS, PhD)
mechanical engineering (M Eng, MS, PhD)
photonics (MS)
polymer science/engineering (MS, PhD)
quality engineering (MS)
wireless network engineering (MS)

Center for Polymer Science and Engineering
Dr. Raymond A. Pearson, Director
Program in:
polymer science and engineering (M Eng, MS, PhD)

■ LINCOLN UNIVERSITY
Lincoln University, PA 19352
http://www.lincoln.edu/

State-related, coed, comprehensive institution. *Computer facilities:* Computer purchase and lease plans are available. 210 computers available on campus for general student use. A campuswide network can be accessed from student residence rooms and from off campus. Internet access is available. *Library facilities:* Langston Hughes Memorial Library. *General application contact:* Acting Director, Graduate Program in Human Services, 610-932-8300 Ext. 3360.

Graduate Program in Human Services
Program in:
human services (M Hum Svcs)

■ LOCK HAVEN UNIVERSITY OF PENNSYLVANIA
Lock Haven, PA 17745-2390
http://www.lhup.edu/

State-supported, coed, comprehensive institution. *Computer facilities:* 290 computers available on campus for general student use. A campuswide network can be accessed from student residence rooms and from off campus. Internet access and online class registration are available. *Library facilities:* Stevenson Library. *General application contact:* Assistant Director of Admissions, 800-332-8900.

Office of Graduate Studies
Programs in:
alternative education (M Ed)
liberal arts (MLA)
physician assistant in rural primary care (MHS)
teaching and learning (M Ed)

■ MANSFIELD UNIVERSITY OF PENNSYLVANIA
Mansfield, PA 16933
http://www.mansfield.edu/

State-supported, coed, comprehensive institution. *Enrollment:* 3,360 graduate, professional, and undergraduate students; 70 full-time matriculated graduate/professional students (60 women), 354 part-time matriculated graduate/professional students (305 women). *Graduate faculty:* 42 full-time (19 women), 13 part-time/adjunct (11 women). *Computer facilities:* Computer purchase and lease plans are available. 550 computers available on campus for general student use. A campuswide network can be accessed from student residence rooms and from off campus. Internet access and online class registration are available. *Library facilities:* North Hall Library. *Graduate expenses:* Tuition, state resident: part-time $336 per credit. Tuition, nonresident: part-time $538 per credit. Tuition and fees vary according to course load and reciprocity agreements. *General application contact:* Judi Brayer, Assistant Director of Enrollment Management/Graduate Admissions, 570-662-4818.

Graduate Studies
Dr. Denise Seigart, Interim Associate Provost
Programs in:
art education (M Ed)
band conducting (MA)
choral conducting (MA)
elementary education (M Ed)
library science (M Ed)
nursing (MSN)
performance (MA)
secondary education (MS)

■ MARYWOOD UNIVERSITY
Scranton, PA 18509-1598
http://www.marywood.edu/

Independent-religious, coed, comprehensive institution. *Enrollment:* 3,180 graduate, professional, and undergraduate students; 516 full-time matriculated graduate/professional students (410 women), 768 part-time matriculated graduate/professional students (596 women). *Graduate faculty:* 133 full-time (73 women), 177 part-time/adjunct (106 women). *Computer facilities:* 367 computers available on campus for general student use. A campuswide network can be accessed from student residence rooms and from off campus. Internet access and online class registration are available. *Library facilities:* Learning Resources Center plus 1 other. *Graduate expenses:* Tuition: part-time $672 per credit. Tuition and fees vary according to degree level, campus/location and program. *General application contact:* Dr. Deborah M. Flynn, Coordinator of Graduate Advising (Enrollment Management), 570-348-6211.

Academic Affairs
Dr. Barbara Rose Sadowski, Vice president for Academic Affairs (Interim)

College of Education and Human Development
Dr. Mary Anne Fedrick, Dean
Programs in:
addiction (MA)
child/clinical school psychology (MA)
clinical psychology (Psy D)
clinical services (MA)
counseling (Certificate)
early childhood intervention (MS)
education (M Ed)
education and human development (M Ed, MA, MAT, MS, PhD, Psy D, Certificate, Ed S)
educational administration (PhD)
elementary education (MAT)
elementary school counseling (MS)
general (MA)
general theoretical psychology (MA)
health promotion (PhD)
higher education administration (MS, PhD)
human development—general (PhD)
instructional leadership (M Ed, PhD)
mental health counseling (MA)
pastoral (MA)
psychology (MA)
reading education (MS)
school leadership (MS)
school psychology (Ed S)
secondary education (MAT)
secondary school counseling (MS)
social work (PhD)
special education (MS)
special education administration and supervision (MS)
speech-language pathology (MS)

College of Health and Human Services
Dr. Ronald Bulbulian, Dean
Programs in:
- clinical physician assistant (MS)
- criminal justice (MPA)
- dietetic internships (Certificate)
- dietetics/internships (Certificate)
- gerontology (MS, Certificate)
- health and human services (MHSA, MPA, MS, MSW, PhD, Certificate)
- health services administration (MHSA)
- human development (PhD)
- long-term care management (MHSA)
- managed care (MHSA)
- nursing administration (MS)
- nutrition (MS)
- physician assistant studies (MS)
- public administration (MPA)
- social work (MSW)
- sports nutrition and exercise science (MS)

College of Liberal Arts and Sciences
Dr. Kurt Torell, Dean
Programs in:
- biotechnology (MS)
- criminal justice (MS)
- liberal arts and sciences (MS)

Insalaco College of Creative Arts and Management
Dr. Devorah Namm, Dean
Programs in:
- advertising design (MA, MFA)
- art education (MA)
- art therapy (MA, Certificate)
- ceramics (MA)
- clay (MA, MFA)
- communication arts (MA, Certificate)
- corporate communication (MS, Certificate)
- creative arts and management (MA, MBA, MFA, MMT, MS, Certificate)
- e-business (MS, Certificate)
- fibers (MFA)
- finance and investments (MBA)
- general management (MBA)
- graphic design (MA, MFA)
- health communication (MS, Certificate)
- illustration (MA, MFA)
- information sciences (MS)
- instructional technology (MS, Certificate)
- interdisciplinary (MA)
- interior architecture (MA)
- library science/information science (MS)
- library science/information specialist (Certificate)
- management information systems (MBA, MS)
- media management (MA)
- metals (MFA)
- music education (MA)
- music therapy (MMT, Certificate)
- painting (MA, MFA)
- photography (MA, MFA)
- printmaking (MA, MFA)
- production (MA)
- sculpture (MA)
- studio art (MA)
- visual arts (MFA)
- vocal pedagogy (Certificate)
- weaving (MA)

■ MERCYHURST COLLEGE
Erie, PA 16546
http://www.mercyhurst.edu/

Independent-religious, coed, comprehensive institution. *Computer facilities:* Computer purchase and lease plans are available. 330 computers available on campus for general student use. A campuswide network can be accessed from student residence rooms and from off campus. Internet access and online class registration are available. *Library facilities:* Hammermill Library. *General application contact:* Academic Coordinator, 814-824-3363.

Graduate Program
Programs in:
- administration of justice (MS)
- applied intelligence (MS, Certificate)
- bilingual/bicultural special education (MS)
- educational leadership (Certificate)
- forensic and biological anthropology (MS)
- organizational leadership (MS, Certificate)
- special education (MS)

■ MILLERSVILLE UNIVERSITY OF PENNSYLVANIA
Millersville, PA 17551-0302
http://www.millersville.edu/

State-supported, coed, comprehensive institution. CGS member. *Enrollment:* 8,194 graduate, professional, and undergraduate students; 127 full-time matriculated graduate/professional students (96 women), 444 part-time matriculated graduate/professional students (304 women). *Graduate faculty:* 216 full-time (108 women), 95 part-time/adjunct (50 women). *Computer facilities:* Computer purchase and lease plans are available. 510 computers available on campus for general student use. A campuswide network can be accessed from student residence rooms and from off campus. Internet access and online class registration are available. *Library facilities:* Helen A. Ganser Library. *Graduate expenses:* Tuition, state resident: full-time $6,048; part-time $336 per credit. Tuition, nonresident: full-time $9,678; part-time $538 per credit. Required fees: $1,244. Tuition and fees vary according to course load. *General application contact:* Dr. Victor S. DeSantis, Dean of Graduate Studies and Research, 717-872-3099.

Graduate School
Dr. Victor S. DeSantis, Dean of Graduate Studies and Research

School of Education
Dr. Jane S. Bray, Dean
Programs in:
- athletic coaching (M Ed)
- athletic management (M Ed)
- clinical psychology (MS)
- early childhood education (M Ed)
- education (M Ed, MS)
- elementary education (M Ed)
- leadership for teaching and learning (M Ed)
- psychology (MS)
- reading/language arts education (M Ed)
- school counseling (M Ed)
- school psychology (MS)
- special education (M Ed)
- sport management (M Ed)
- technology education (M Ed)

School of Humanities and Social Sciences
Dr. John N. Short, Dean
Programs in:
- art education (M Ed)
- business administration (MBA)
- English (MA)
- English education (M Ed)
- French (M Ed, MA)
- German (M Ed, MA)
- history (MA)
- humanities and social sciences (M Ed, MA, MBA, MSW)
- social work (MSW)
- Spanish (M Ed, MA)

School of Science and Mathematics
Dr. Edward C. Shane, Dean
Programs in:
- biology (MS)
- mathematics (M Ed)
- nursing (MSN)

■ NEUMANN COLLEGE
Aston, PA 19014-1298
http://www.neumann.edu/

Independent-religious, coed, comprehensive institution. *Enrollment:* 2,969 graduate, professional, and undergraduate students; 105 full-time matriculated graduate/professional students (69 women), 446 part-time matriculated graduate/professional students (308 women). *Graduate faculty:* 26 full-time (15 women), 23 part-time/adjunct (18 women). *Computer facilities:* 200 computers available on campus for general student use. A campuswide network can be accessed from student residence rooms and from off campus. Internet access, e-mail are available. *Library facilities:* Neumann College Library. *General application contact:* Louise Bank, Assistant Director of Admissions, Graduate and Evening Programs, 610-558-5604.

Neumann College (continued)

Program in Education
Dr. Andrew DeSanto, Coordinator, Division of Education and Human Services
Program in:
education (MS)

Program in Nursing and Health Sciences
Dr. Kathleen Hoover, Dean, Division of Nursing and Health Services
Program in:
nursing (MS)

Program in Pastoral Counseling
Dr. Leonard DiPaul, Executive Director
Programs in:
pastoral counseling (MS, CAS)
spiritual direction (CSD)

Program in Physical Therapy
Dr. Robert Post, Director
Program in:
physical therapy (MS, DPT)

Program in Sports Management
Dr. Sandra L. Slabik, Coordinator
Program in:
sports management (MS)

Program in Strategic Leadership
Dr. Judith Stang, Coordinator, Division of Continuing Adult and Professional Studies
Program in:
strategic leadership (MS)

■ PENN STATE GREAT VALLEY
Malvern, PA 19355-1488
http://www.gv.psu.edu/

State-related, coed, graduate-only institution. *Computer facilities:* 331 computers available on campus for general student use. A campuswide network can be accessed from off campus. Internet access and online class registration are available. *Library facilities:* Great Valley Library. *Graduate expenses:* Tuition, state resident: full-time $13,224; part-time $551 per credit. Tuition, nonresident: full-time $26,064; part-time $1,003 per credit. Required fees: $69 per semester. *General application contact:* Dr. Kathy Mingioni, Assistant Director of Admissions, 610-648-3315.

Graduate Studies
Dr. Diane M. Disney, Chancellor

Education Division
Dr. Arlene Mitchell, Academic Division Head
Programs in:
curriculum and instruction (M Ed)
instructional systems (M Ed, MS)
special education (M Ed, MS)

Engineering Division
Unit Head
Programs in:
information science (MSIS)
software engineering (MSE)
systems engineering (M Eng)

Management Division
Programs in:
biotechnology and health industry management (MBA)
business administration (MBA)
finance (M Fin)
leadership development (MLD)
management (M Fin, MBA, MLD)
new venture and entrepreneurial studies (MBA)

■ PENN STATE HARRISBURG
Middletown, PA 17057-4898
http://www.hbg.psu.edu/

State-related, coed, comprehensive institution. *Computer facilities:* Computer purchase and lease plans are available. 132 computers available on campus for general student use. A campuswide network can be accessed from student residence rooms and from off campus. Internet access and online class registration are available. *Library facilities:* Penn State Harrisburg Library. *Graduate expenses:* Tuition, state resident: full-time $13,224; part-time $551 per credit. Tuition, nonresident: full-time $18,652; part-time $777 per credit. Required fees: $84 per semester. *General application contact:* Robert Coffman, Director of Admissions, 717-948-6250.

Find University Details at www.petersons.com/gradchannel.

Graduate School
Dr. Madlyn L. Hanes, Chancellor

School of Behavioral Sciences and Education
Dr. William D. Milheim, Director
Programs in:
adult education (D Ed)
applied behavior analysis (MA)
applied clinical psychology (MA)
applied psychological research (MA)
community psychology and social change (MA)
health education (M Ed)
teaching and curriculum (M Ed)
training and development (M Ed)

School of Business Administration
Dr. Mukund S. Kulkarni, Professor
Programs in:
business administration (MBA)
information systems (MS)

School of Humanities
Kathryn Robinson, Professor
Programs in:
American studies (MA)
humanities (MA)

School of Public Affairs
Dr. Steven A. Peterson, Professor of Politics
Programs in:
criminal justice (MA)
health administration (MHA)
public administration (MPA)
public affairs (PhD)

School of Science, Engineering and Technology
Dr. Omid Ansary, Director
Programs in:
computer science (MS)
electrical engineering (M Eng)
engineering science (M Eng)
environmental engineering (M Eng)
environmental pollution control (M Eng, MEPC, MS)

■ PENN STATE UNIVERSITY PARK
State College, University Park, PA 16802-1503
http://www.psu.edu/

State-related, coed, university. CGS member. *Computer facilities:* 3,589 computers available on campus for general student use. A campuswide network can be accessed from student residence rooms and from off campus. Internet access and online class registration are available. *Library facilities:* Pattee Library plus 14 others. *General application contact:* Cynthia E. Nicosia, Director, Graduate Enrollment Services, 814-865-1834.

Find University Details at www.petersons.com/gradchannel.

Graduate School
Dr. Eva J. Pell, Vice President, Research and Dean of the Graduate School
Programs in:
acoustics (M Eng, MS, PhD)
bioengineering (MS, PhD)
ecology (MS, PhD)
environmental pollution control (MEPC, MS)
genetics (MS, PhD)
integrative biosciences (MS, PhD)
mass communications (PhD)
nutrition (MS, PhD)
physiology (MS, PhD)
plant physiology (MS, PhD)
quality and manufacturing management (MMM)

College of Agricultural Sciences
Dr. Robert D. Steele, Dean
Programs in:
agricultural and biological engineering (MS, PhD)
agricultural and extension education (M Ed, MS, D Ed, PhD)
agricultural sciences (M Agr, M Ed, MFR, MS, D Ed, PhD)

agricultural, environmental and regional economics (M Agr, MS, PhD)
agronomy (M Agr, MS, PhD)
animal science (M Agr, MS, PhD)
entomology (M Agr, MS, PhD)
food science (MS, PhD)
forest resources (M Agr, MFR, MS, PhD)
horticulture (M Agr, MS, PhD)
pathobiology (PhD)
plant pathology (M Agr, MS, PhD)
rural sociology (M Agr, MS, PhD)
soil science (M Agr, PhD)
wildlife and fisheries sciences (M Agr, MFR, MS, PhD)
youth and family education (M Ed)

College of Arts and Architecture
Dr. Yvonne M. Gaudelius, Interim Dean
Programs in:
architecture (M Arch)
art (MFA)
art education (M Ed, MS, PhD)
art history (MA, PhD)
arts and architecture (M Arch, M Ed, M Mus, MA, MFA, MLA, MME, MS, PhD)
composition/theory (M Mus)
conducting (M Mus)
landscape architecture (MLA)
music education (MME, PhD)
music theory (MA)
music theory and history (MA)
musicology (MA)
performance (M Mus)
piano, pedagogy and performance (M Mus)
theatre (MFA)
voice performance and pedagogy (M Mus)

College of Communications
Dr. Douglas A. Anderson, Dean
Programs in:
communications (MA, PhD)
mass communications (PhD)
media studies (MA)
telecommunications studies (MA)

College of Earth and Mineral Sciences
Dr. Rob G. Crane, Dean
Programs in:
astrobiology (PhD)
ceramic science (MS, PhD)
earth and mineral sciences (M Ed, M Eng, MGIS, MS, PhD)
energy and geo-environmental engineering (MS, PhD)
fuel science (MS, PhD)
geography (MS, PhD)
geosciences (MS, PhD)
industrial health and safety (MS)
metals science and engineering (MS, PhD)
meteorology (MS, PhD)
mineral processing (MS, PhD)
mining engineering (MS, PhD)
petroleum and mining engineering (MS, PhD)
polymer science (MS, PhD)

College of Education
Dr. David H. Monk, Dean
Programs in:
adult education (M Ed, D Ed, PhD)
bilingual education (M Ed, MS, PhD)
college student affairs (M Ed)
counseling psychology (PhD)
counselor education (M Ed, MS)
counselor education, counseling psychology and rehabilitation services (D Ed)
early childhood education (M Ed, MS, PhD)
education (M Ed, MA, MS, D Ed, PhD)
educational leadership (M Ed, MS, D Ed, PhD)
educational psychology (MS, PhD)
educational theory and policy (MA, PhD)
elementary education (M Ed, MS, PhD)
higher education (M Ed, D Ed, PhD)
instructional systems (M Ed, MS, D Ed, PhD)
language arts and reading (M Ed, MS, PhD)
school psychology (M Ed, MS, PhD)
science education (M Ed, MS, PhD)
social studies education (MS, PhD)
special education (M Ed, MS, PhD)
supervisor and curriculum development (M Ed, MS, PhD)
workforce education and development (M Ed, MS, D Ed, PhD)

College of Engineering
Dr. David N. Wormley, Dean
Programs in:
aerospace engineering (M Eng, MS, PhD)
architectural engineering (M Eng, MAE, MS, PhD)
chemical engineering (MS, PhD)
civil engineering (M Eng, MS, PhD)
computer science and engineering (M Eng, MS, PhD)
electrical engineering (MS, PhD)
engineering (M Eng, MAE, MS, PhD)
engineering mechanics (M Eng, MS, PhD)
engineering science (M Eng, MS, PhD)
engineering science and mechanics (M Eng, MS, PhD)
environmental engineering (M Eng, MS, PhD)
industrial engineering (M Eng, MS, PhD)
manufacturing engineering (M Eng)
mechanical engineering (M Eng, MS, PhD)
nuclear engineering (M Eng, MS, PhD)
structural engineering (M Eng, MS, PhD)
transportation and highway engineering (M Eng, MS, PhD)
water resources engineering (M Eng, MS, PhD)

College of Health and Human Development
Dr. Ann Crouter, Dean
Programs in:
biobehavioral health (MS, PhD)
communication sciences and disorders (MS, PhD)
health and human development (M Ed, MHA, MHRIM, MS, PhD)
health policy and administration (MHA, MS, PhD)
hospitality management (MHRIM, MS, PhD)
hotel, restaurant, and institutional management (MHRIM, MS, PhD)
human development and family studies (MS, PhD)
human nutrition (M Ed)
kinesiology (MS, PhD)
leisure studies (MS, PhD)
nursing (MS, PhD)
nutrition (MS, PhD)
recreation, park and tourism management (M Ed)

College of Information Sciences and Technology
Dr. Henry Foley, Dean
Program in:
information sciences and technology (MS, PhD)

College of the Liberal Arts
Dr. Susan Welch, Dean
Programs in:
anthropology (MA, PhD)
applied linguistics (PhD)
classical American philosophy (MA, PhD)
clinical psychology (MS, PhD)
cognitive psychology (MS, PhD)
communication arts and sciences (MA, PhD)
comparative literature (MA, PhD)
contemporary European philosophy (MA, PhD)
crime, law, and justice (MA, PhD)
developmental psychology (MS, PhD)
economics (MA, PhD)
English (MA, MFA, PhD)
French (MA, PhD)
German (MA, PhD)
history (MA, PhD)
history of philosophy (MA, PhD)
industrial relations and human resources (MS)
industrial/organizational psychology (MS, PhD)
liberal arts (MA, MFA, MS, PhD)
political science (MA, PhD)
psychobiology (MS, PhD)
Russian and comparative literature (MA)
social psychology (MS, PhD)
sociology (MA, PhD)
Spanish (MA, PhD)
teaching English as a second language (MA)

Eberly College of Science
Dr. Daniel J. Larson, Dean
Programs in:
applied statistics (MAS)

Penn State University Park (continued)
astronomy and astrophysics (MS, PhD)
biochemistry, microbiology, and molecular biology (MS, PhD)
biology (MS, PhD)
biotechnology (MS)
cell and developmental biology (MS, PhD)
chemistry (MS, PhD)
mathematics (M Ed, MA, D Ed, PhD)
molecular evolutionary biology (MS, PhD)
physics (M Ed, MS, D Ed, PhD)
science (M Ed, MA, MAS, MS, D Ed, PhD)
statistics (MA, MAS, MS, PhD)

The Mary Jean and Frank P. Smeal College of Business Administration
Dr. Kenneth B. Thomas, Dean
Programs in:
accounting (PhD)
business administration (MBA)
finance (PhD)
management and organization (PhD)
management science/operations/logistics (PhD)
marketing (PhD)
real estate (PhD)
supply chain and information systems (PhD)

■ PHILADELPHIA BIBLICAL UNIVERSITY
Langhorne, PA 19047-2990
http://www.pbu.edu/

Independent-religious, coed, comprehensive institution. *Enrollment:* 1,389 graduate, professional, and undergraduate students; 29 full-time matriculated graduate/professional students (13 women), 302 part-time matriculated graduate/professional students (162 women). *Graduate faculty:* 18 full-time (7 women), 21 part-time/adjunct (9 women). *Computer facilities:* Computer purchase and lease plans are available. 85 computers available on campus for general student use. A campuswide network can be accessed from student residence rooms and from off campus. Internet access and online class registration are available. *Library facilities:* Masland Learning Resource Center. *Graduate expenses:* Tuition: full-time $8,820; part-time $490 per credit. *General application contact:* Binu Abraham, Assistant Director, Graduate Admissions, 800-572-2472.

School of Biblical Studies
Dr. O. Herbert Hirt, Dean
Program in:
biblical studies (M Div, MSB)

School of Business and Leadership
Ron Ferner, Dean
Program in:
organizational leadership (MSOL)

School of Church and Community Ministries
Donald Cheyney, Dean
Program in:
Christian counseling (MSCC)

School of Education
Dr. Martha MacCullough, Dean
Programs in:
educational leadership and administration (MS El)
teacher education (MS Ed)

■ PHILADELPHIA UNIVERSITY
Philadelphia, PA 19144-5497
http://www.philau.edu/

Independent, coed, comprehensive institution. *Enrollment:* 3,256 graduate, professional, and undergraduate students; 224 full-time matriculated graduate/professional students (164 women), 262 part-time matriculated graduate/professional students (152 women). *Graduate faculty:* 42 full-time (12 women), 40 part-time/adjunct (12 women). *Computer facilities:* 400 computers available on campus for general student use. A campuswide network can be accessed from student residence rooms and from off campus. Internet access and online class registration are available. *Library facilities:* Paul J. Gutman Library plus 1 other. *General application contact:* Jack A. Klett, Director of Graduate Admissions, 215-951-2943.

School of Business Administration
Dr. Elmore Alexander, Dean
Programs in:
business (MBA, MS, PhD)
business administration (MBA)
finance (MBA)
health care management (MBA)
international business (MBA)
marketing (MBA)
taxation (MS)

School of Design and Media
Programs in:
design and media (MS)
digital design (MS)
instructional design and technology (MS)

School of Engineering and Textiles
Dr. David Brookstein, Dean
Programs in:
engineering and textiles (MS, PhD)
fashion-apparel studies (MS)
textile design (MS)
textile engineering (MS, PhD)

School of Science and Health
Matt Dane Baker, Dean
Programs in:
midwifery (MS)
nurse midwifery (Postbaccalaureate Certificate)
occupational therapy (MS)
physician assistant studies (MS)
science and health (MS, Postbaccalaureate Certificate)

■ POINT PARK UNIVERSITY
Pittsburgh, PA 15222-1984
http://www.pointpark.edu/

Independent, coed, comprehensive institution. *Enrollment:* 3,546 graduate, professional, and undergraduate students; 219 full-time matriculated graduate/professional students (128 women), 255 part-time matriculated graduate/professional students (154 women). *Graduate faculty:* 31 full-time, 60 part-time/adjunct. *Computer facilities:* 170 computers available on campus for general student use. A campuswide network can be accessed from student residence rooms and from off campus. Internet access is available. *Library facilities:* Point Park University Library. *Graduate expenses:* Tuition: full-time $9,828; part-time $546 per credit. Required fees: $360; $20 per credit. *General application contact:* Marty Paonessa, Associate Director, Graduate and Adult Enrollment, 412-392-3915.

Conservatory of Performing Arts
Ronald Allan-Lindblom, Dean/Artistic Producing Director
Program in:
theatre arts-acting (MFA)

School of Adult and Professional Studies
Judy Bolsinger, Dean
Program in:
criminal justice administration (MS)

School of Arts and Sciences
Dr. Kathleen Rourke, Dean
Programs in:
arts and sciences (MA, MS)
curriculum and instruction (MA)
educational administration (MA)
engineering management (MS)
journalism and mass communication (MA)

School of Business
Margaret Gilfillan, Interim Dean
Programs in:
business (MBA)
organizational leadership (MA)

■ ROBERT MORRIS UNIVERSITY
Moon Township, PA 15108-1189
http://www.rmu.edu/

Independent, coed, university. *Enrollment:* 5,065 graduate, professional, and undergraduate students; 1,121 part-time matriculated graduate/professional students (537 women). *Graduate faculty:* 65 full-time

(23 women), 26 part-time/adjunct (9 women). *Computer facilities:* 300 computers available on campus for general student use. A campuswide network can be accessed from student residence rooms and from off campus. Internet access and online class registration are available. *Library facilities:* Robert Morris University Library plus 1 other. *Graduate expenses:* Tuition: part-time $580 per credit. Part-time tuition and fees vary according to degree level and program. *General application contact:* Kellie L. Laurenzi, Dean of Enrollment, 412-262-8235.

Find University Details at www.petersons.com/gradchannel.

Graduate Studies

Dr. William J. Katip, Senior Vice President for Academic and Student Affairs

School of Adult and Continuing Education

Dr. Kathleen V. Davis, Dean
Program in:
- adult and continuing education (MS)

School of Business

Dr. Derya A. Jacobs, Dean
Programs in:
- accounting (MS)
- business administration and management (MBA)
- finance (MS)
- human resource management (MS)
- nonprofit management (MS)
- sport management (MS)
- taxation (MS)

School of Communications and Information Systems

Dr. David L. Jamison, Dean
Programs in:
- communications and information systems (MS)
- competitive intelligence systems (MS)
- information security and assurance (MS)
- information systems and communications (D Sc)
- information systems management (MS)
- Internet information systems (MS)
- IT project management (MS)

School of Education and Social Sciences

Dr. John E. Graham, Dean
Program in:
- education and social sciences (MS, PhD, Postbaccalaureate Certificate)

School of Engineering, Mathematics and Science

Dr. Winston F. Erevelles, Dean
Program in:
- engineering, mathematics and science (MS, PhD)

School of Nursing

Dr. Lynda J. Davidson, Dean
Program in:
- nursing (MS)

■ ROSEMONT COLLEGE
Rosemont, PA 19010-1699
http://www.rosemont.edu/

Independent-religious, Undergraduate: women only; graduate: coed, comprehensive institution. *Computer facilities:* 77 computers available on campus for general student use. A campuswide network can be accessed from student residence rooms and from off campus. Internet access is available. *Library facilities:* Kistler Library plus 1 other. *General application contact:* Director, Enrollment and Student Services, 610-527-0200 Ext. 2187.

Find University Details at www.petersons.com/gradchannel.

Graduate School

Programs in:
- arts/culture/project management (MSM)
- business administration (MBA)
- criminal justice (MSM)
- elementary certification (MA)
- English (MA)
- English and publishing (MA)
- human services (MA)
- middle level education (M Ed)
- not for profit (MSM)
- school counseling (MA)
- technology in education (M Ed)
- training and leadership (MSM)

■ SAINT FRANCIS UNIVERSITY
Loretto, PA 15940-0600
http://www.francis.edu/

Independent-religious, coed, comprehensive institution. *Enrollment:* 2,014 graduate, professional, and undergraduate students; 188 full-time matriculated graduate/professional students (133 women), 291 part-time matriculated graduate/professional students (153 women). *Graduate faculty:* 22 full-time (14 women), 52 part-time/adjunct (12 women). *Computer facilities:* Computer purchase and lease plans are available. 60 computers available on campus for general student use. A campuswide network can be accessed from student residence rooms and from off campus. Internet access, billing, schedules and grades are available. *Library facilities:* Pasquerella Library. *Graduate expenses:* Tuition: part-time $661 per credit. Tuition and fees vary according to program. *General application contact:* Dr. Peter Raymond Skoner, Associate Vice President for Academic Affairs, 814-472-3085.

Department of Education and Educational Leadership

Dr. Janette D. Kelly, Director, Graduate Education
Programs in:
- education (M Ed)
- educational leadership (MEDL)
- reading (M Ed)

Department of Occupational Therapy

Dr. Donald Walkovich, Chair
Program in:
- occupational therapy (MOT)

Department of Physical Therapy

Dr. Patricia I. Fitzgerald, Interim Department Chair/Associate Professor
Program in:
- physical therapy (DPT)

Department of Physician Assistant Sciences

Donna L. Yeisley, Chair
Programs in:
- health science (MHS)
- medical science (MMS)
- physician assistant sciences (MPAS)

■ SAINT JOSEPH'S UNIVERSITY
Philadelphia, PA 19131-1395
http://www.sju.edu/

Independent-religious, coed, comprehensive institution. *Enrollment:* 7,535 graduate, professional, and undergraduate students; 440 full-time matriculated graduate/professional students (223 women), 1,653 part-time matriculated graduate/professional students (982 women). *Graduate faculty:* 95 full-time (40 women), 139 part-time/adjunct (53 women). *Computer facilities:* Computer purchase and lease plans are available. 400 computers available on campus for general student use. A campuswide network can be accessed from student residence rooms and from off campus. Internet access and online class registration are available. *Library facilities:* Francis A. Drexel Library plus 1 other. *General application contact:* Susan P. Kassab, Director of Admissions, 610-660-1306.

College of Arts and Sciences

Dr. Robert H. Palestini, Dean of Graduate and Continuing Studies
Programs in:
- administration/police executive (MS)
- arts and sciences (MA, MS, Ed D, Certificate, Post-Master's Certificate)
- behavior analysis (MS)
- behavior management and justice (MS)
- biology (MA, MS)
- computer science (MS)
- criminal justice (MS, Post-Master's Certificate)
- criminology (MS)
- educational leadership (Ed D)
- elementary education (MS)
- federal law (MS)
- gerontological counseling (MS)
- gerontological services (Post-Master's Certificate)
- health administration (MS)
- health education (MS)

Saint Joseph's University (continued)
- human services administration (MS)
- instructional technology (MS)
- intelligence and crime (MS)
- mathematics and computer science (Post-Master's Certificate)
- nurse anesthesia (MS)
- probation, parole, and corrections (MS)
- professional education (MS)
- psychology (MS)
- reading (MS)
- secondary education (MS)
- special education (MS)
- training and organizational development (MS, Certificate)
- writing studies (MA)

Public Safety and Environmental Protection Institute
Dr. Vincent P. McNally, Director
Programs in:
- environmental protection and safety management (MS, Post-Master's Certificate)
- public safety (MS, Post-Master's Certificate)

Erivan K. Haub School of Business
Dr. Joseph A. DiAngelo, Dean
Programs in:
- accounting (MBA)
- business (MBA, MS, Certificate, Post Master's Certificate)
- certified financial planner (Certificate)
- decision and system sciences (MBA)
- e-business (MBA)
- executive business administration (MBA)
- executive pharmaceutical marketing (MBA, Post Master's Certificate)
- finance (MBA, Certificate)
- financial services (MS)
- food marketing (MBA, MS)
- general business (MBA)
- health and medical services administration (MBA)
- human resource management (MBA)
- information systems (MBA)
- international business (MBA)
- international marketing (MBA)
- management (MBA)
- marketing (MBA)

■ SETON HILL UNIVERSITY
Greensburg, PA 15601
http://www.setonhill.edu/

Independent-religious, coed, comprehensive institution. *Enrollment:* 1,895 graduate, professional, and undergraduate students; 125 full-time matriculated graduate/professional students (100 women), 220 part-time matriculated graduate/professional students (168 women). *Graduate faculty:* 24 full-time (15 women), 36 part-time/adjunct (16 women). *Computer facilities:* 259 computers available on campus for general student use. A campuswide network can be accessed from student residence rooms and from off campus. Internet access and online class registration, e-mail are available. *Library facilities:* Reeves Memorial Library. *Graduate expenses:* Tuition: part-time $620 per credit. Required fees: $100 per semester. *General application contact:* Christine Schaeffer, Director of Graduate and Adult Studies, 724-838-4283.

Find University Details at www.petersons.com/gradchannel.

Program in Art Therapy
Nina Denninger, Director
Program in:
- art therapy (MA, Certificate)

Program in Business Administration
Paul Mahady, Interim Director
Program in:
- business administration (MBA)

Program in Elementary Education
Dr. Michele H. Conway, Director
Program in:
- elementary education (MA, Teaching Certificate)

Program in Instructional Design
Dr. Shirley Campbell, Director
Program in:
- instructional design (M Ed)

Program in Marriage and Family Therapy
Dr. Susan Cooley, Director
Program in:
- marriage and family therapy (MA)

Program in Physician Assistant
Cathy Shallenberger, Director
Program in:
- physician assistant (MS)

Program in Special Education
Dr. Sondra Lettrich, Director
Program in:
- special education (MA, Teaching Certificate)

Program in Writing Popular Fiction
Dr. Lee McClain, Director
Program in:
- writing popular fiction (MA)

■ SHIPPENSBURG UNIVERSITY OF PENNSYLVANIA
Shippensburg, PA 17257-2299
http://www.ship.edu/

State-supported, coed, comprehensive institution. CGS member. *Enrollment:* 7,516 graduate, professional, and undergraduate students; 239 full-time matriculated graduate/professional students (151 women), 712 part-time matriculated graduate/professional students (470 women). *Graduate faculty:* 146 full-time (51 women), 13 part-time/adjunct (6 women). *Computer facilities:* 800 computers available on campus for general student use. A campuswide network can be accessed from student residence rooms and from off campus. Internet access, personal Web pages are available. *Library facilities:* Ezra Lehman Memorial Library. *Graduate expenses:* Tuition, state resident: part-time $336 per credit. Tuition, nonresident: part-time $538 per credit. *General application contact:* Renee Payne, Associate Dean of Graduate Admissions, 717-477-1231.

Find University Details at www.petersons.com/gradchannel.

School of Graduate Studies
Dr. Tracy Schoolcraft, Interim Dean of Graduate Studies/Associate Provost

College of Arts and Sciences
Dr. James Mike, Dean
Programs in:
- applied history (MA, Certificate)
- arts and sciences (MA, MPA, MS, Certificate)
- biology (MS)
- communication studies (MS)
- computer science (MS)
- geoenvironmental studies (MS)
- information studies (MS)
- organizational development and leadership (MS)
- psychology (MS)
- public administration (MPA)

College of Education and Human Services
Dr. Robert B. Bartos, Dean
Programs in:
- Adlerian studies (Certificate)
- administration of justice (MS)
- advanced study in counseling (Certificate)
- counseling (MS)
- couple and family counseling (Certificate)
- curriculum and instruction (M Ed)
- education and human services (M Ed, MS, MSW, Certificate)
- guidance and counseling (M Ed)
- reading (M Ed)
- school administration (M Ed)
- social work (MSW)
- special education (M Ed)

John L. Grove College of Business
Dr. Robert Rollins, Director
Program in:
- business administration (MBA)

■ SLIPPERY ROCK UNIVERSITY OF PENNSYLVANIA
Slippery Rock, PA 16057-1383
http://www.sru.edu/

State-supported, coed, comprehensive institution. *Enrollment:* 8,230 graduate, professional, and undergraduate students;

311 full-time matriculated graduate/professional students (201 women), 374 part-time matriculated graduate/professional students (274 women). *Graduate faculty:* 62 full-time (34 women), 6 part-time/adjunct (4 women). *Computer facilities:* Computer purchase and lease plans are available. 940 computers available on campus for general student use. A campuswide network can be accessed from student residence rooms and from off campus. Internet access and online class registration are available. *Library facilities:* Bailey Library. *Graduate expenses:* Tuition, state resident: part-time $336 per credit. Tuition, nonresident: part-time $538 per credit. Required fees: $84 per credit. $37 per semester. *General application contact:* April Longwell, Interim Director of Graduate Studies, 724-738-2051 Ext. 2116.

Find University Details at www.petersons.com/gradchannel.

Graduate Studies (Recruitment)
April Longwell, Interim Director of Graduate Studies

College of Business, Information, and Social Sciences
Dr. Bruce Russell, Dean
Program in:
- business, information, and social sciences (MS)

College of Education
Dr. Jay Hertzog, Interim Director of Graduate Studies
Programs in:
- community counseling (MA)
- early childhood education (M Ed)
- education (M Ed, MA, MS)
- elementary guidance and counseling (M Ed)
- master teacher (M Ed)
- math/science (M Ed)
- physical education (M Ed)
- reading (M Ed)
- secondary education in math/science (M Ed)
- secondary guidance and counseling (M Ed)
- sport management (MS)
- student personnel (MA)
- supervision (M Ed)

College of Health, Environment, and Science
Dr. Susan Hannam, Dean
Programs in:
- environmental education (M Ed)
- health, environment, and science (M Ed, MS, MSN, DPT)
- nursing (MSN)
- physical therapy (DPT)
- resource management (MS)
- sustainable systems (MS)

College of Humanities, Fine and Performing Arts
Dr. William McKinney, Dean
Programs in:
- English (MA)
- history (MA)
- humanities, fine and performing arts (MA)

■ TEMPLE UNIVERSITY
Philadelphia, PA 19122-6096
http://www.temple.edu/

State-related, coed, university. CGS member. *Enrollment:* 33,865 graduate, professional, and undergraduate students; 4,632 full-time matriculated graduate/professional students (2,471 women), 3,373 part-time matriculated graduate/professional students (1,918 women). *Graduate faculty:* 1,421 full-time (482 women). *Computer facilities:* 2,000 computers available on campus for general student use. A campuswide network can be accessed from student residence rooms and from off campus. Internet access and online class registration, student account and grade information are available. *Library facilities:* Paley Library plus 11 others. *Graduate expenses:* Tuition, state resident: full-time $12,264; part-time $511 per credit. Tuition, nonresident: full-time $17,904; part-time $746 per credit. Required fees: $84 per course. Tuition and fees vary according to program. *General application contact:* Tara Schumacher, Coordinator of Outreach, 215-204-6575.

Find University Details at www.petersons.com/gradchannel.

Ambler College
Dr. James Hilty, Interim Dean
Program in:
- community and regional planning (MS)

Graduate School
Dr. Aquiles Iglesias, Dean

College of Education
Dr. C. Kent McGuire, Dean
Programs in:
- adult and organizational development (Ed M)
- applied behavioral analysis (MS Ed)
- career and technical education (MS Ed)
- counseling psychology (Ed M, PhD)
- early childhood education and elementary education (MS Ed)
- education (Ed M, MS Ed, Ed D, PhD)
- educational administration (Ed M, Ed D)
- educational psychology (Ed M, PhD)
- English education (MS Ed)
- language arts education (Ed D)
- math/science education (Ed D)
- mathematics education (MS Ed)
- school psychology (Ed M, PhD)
- science education (MS Ed)
- second and foreign language education (MS Ed)
- special education (MS Ed)
- teaching English as a second language (MS Ed)
- urban education (Ed M, Ed D)

College of Engineering
Dr. Keyanoush Sadeghipour, Dean
Programs in:
- civil engineering (MSE)
- electrical engineering (MSE)
- engineering (MS, MSE, PhD)
- mechanical engineering (MSE)

College of Liberal Arts
Dr. Carolyn Adams, Interim Dean
Programs in:
- African American studies (MA, PhD)
- anthropology (PhD)
- clinical psychology (PhD)
- cognitive psychology (PhD)
- creative writing (MA)
- criminal justice (MA, PhD)
- developmental psychology (PhD)
- English (MA, PhD)
- geography (MA)
- history (MA, PhD)
- liberal arts (MA, MLA, PhD)
- philosophy (MA, PhD)
- political science (MA, PhD)
- religion (MA, PhD)
- social psychology (PhD)
- sociology (MA, PhD)
- Spanish (MA, PhD)
- urban studies (MA)

College of Science and Technology
Dr. Hai-Lung Dai, Dean
Programs in:
- applied mathematics (MA)
- biology (MS, PhD)
- chemistry (MA, PhD)
- computer and information sciences (MS, PhD)
- geology (MS)
- mathematics (PhD)
- physics (MA, PhD)
- pure mathematics (MA)
- science and technology (MA, MS, PhD)

Esther Boyer College of Music and Dance
Dr. Robert T. Stroker, Dean
Programs in:
- choral activities (MM)
- composition (MM, DMA)
- dance (Ed M, MFA, PhD)
- instrumental studies (MM, DMA)
- keyboard instruction (MM, DMA)
- music and dance (Ed M, MFA, MM, MMT, DMA, PhD)
- music education (MM, PhD)
- music history (MM)
- music theory (MM)
- music therapy (MMT, PhD)
- voice and opera (MM, DMA)

Fox School of Business and Management
Programs in:
- accounting (MBA, PhD)
- accounting and financial management (MS)
- actuarial science (MS)
- business administration (EMBA, IMBA, MBA, MS)

Temple University (continued)
- business and management (EMBA, IMBA, MA, MBA, MS, PhD)
- e-business (MBA, MS)
- economics (MA, MBA, PhD)
- finance (MBA, MS, PhD)
- general and strategic management (MBA, PhD)
- healthcare financial management (MS)
- healthcare management (MBA, PhD)
- human resource administration (MBA, MS, PhD)
- international business (IMBA)
- international business administration (PhD)
- management information systems (MBA, MS, PhD)
- management science/operations management (MBA, MS)
- management science/operations research (PhD)
- marketing (MBA, MS, PhD)
- risk management and insurance (MBA)
- risk, insurance, and health-care management (PhD)
- statistics (MBA, MS, PhD)
- tourism (PhD)

School of Communications and Theater
Dr. Concetta M. Stewart, Dean
Programs in:
- acting (MFA)
- broadcasting, telecommunications and mass media (MA)
- communication management (MS)
- communications and theater (MA, MFA, MJ, MS, PhD)
- design (MFA)
- directing (MFA)
- film and media arts (MFA)
- journalism (MJ)
- mass media and communication (PhD)

School of Social Administration
Dr. Linda Mauro, Interim Dean
Programs in:
- social administration (MSW)
- social work (MSW)

School of Tourism and Hospitality Management
Dr. M. Moshe Porat, Dean
Programs in:
- sport and recreation administration (Ed M)
- tourism and hospitality management (Ed M, MTHM)

Tyler School of Art
Keith Morrison, Dean
Programs in:
- art (Ed M, MA, MFA, PhD)
- art and art education (Ed M)
- art history (MA, PhD)
- ceramics/glass (MFA)
- fibers and fabric design (MFA)
- graphic and interactive design (MFA)
- metals/jewelry/CAD-CAM (MFA)
- painting (MFA)
- photography (MFA)
- printmaking (MFA)
- sculpture (MFA)

Health Sciences Center
Program in:
- health sciences (DMD, DPM, MD, Pharm D, Ed M, MA, MOT, MPH, MS, MSN, DPT, PhD, Certificate)

College of Health Professions
Dr. Ronald T. Brown, Dean
Programs in:
- communication sciences (PhD)
- community health education (MPH)
- environmental health (MS)
- epidemiology (MS)
- health professions (Ed M, MA, MOT, MPH, MS, MSN, DPT, PhD)
- health studies (PhD)
- kinesiology (Ed M, PhD)
- linguistics (MA)
- nursing (MSN)
- occupational therapy (MOT, MS)
- physical therapy (DPT, PhD)
- public health (Ed M, MPH, MS, PhD)
- school health education (Ed M)
- speech-language-hearing (MA)
- therapeutic recreation (Ed M)

School of Dentistry
Dr. Martin F. Tansy, Dean
Programs in:
- advanced education in general dentistry (Certificate)
- dentistry (DMD, MS, Certificate)
- endodontology (Certificate)
- oral biology (MS)
- orthodontics (Certificate)
- periodontology (Certificate)

School of Medicine
Dr. John M. Daly, Dean
Programs in:
- anatomy and cell biology (MS, PhD)
- biochemistry (MS, PhD)
- medicine (MD, MS, PhD)
- microbiology and immunology (MS, PhD)
- molecular biology and genetics (PhD)
- neuroscience (MS, PhD)
- pathology and laboratory medicine (PhD)
- pharmacology (PhD)
- physiology (PhD)

School of Pharmacy
Dr. Peter H. Doukas, Dean
Programs in:
- medicinal chemistry (MS, PhD)
- pharmaceutics (MS, PhD)
- pharmacodynamics (MS, PhD)
- pharmacy (Pharm D, MS, PhD)
- quality assurance/regulatory affairs (MS)

School of Podiatric Medicine
Program in:
- podiatric medicine (DPM)

James E. Beasley School of Law
Programs in:
- law (JD)
- taxation (LL M)
- transnational law (LL M)
- trial advocacy (LL M)

■ UNIVERSITY OF PENNSYLVANIA
Philadelphia, PA 19104
http://www.upenn.edu/

Independent, coed, university. CGS member. *Enrollment:* 18,809 graduate, professional, and undergraduate students; 9,296 full-time matriculated graduate/professional students (4,603 women), 2,204 part-time matriculated graduate/professional students (1,302 women). *Graduate faculty:* 2,471 full-time (689 women), 1,871 part-time/adjunct (517 women). *Computer facilities:* 975 computers available on campus for general student use. A campuswide network can be accessed from student residence rooms and from off campus. Internet access and online class registration, billing information, financial aid application, status, academic records, student services are available. *Library facilities:* University of Pennsylvania Libraries plus 15 others. *General application contact:* Karen Lawrence, Assistant Vice Provost for Graduate Education, 215-898-1842.

Find University Details at www.petersons.com/gradchannel.

Annenberg School for Communication
Joseph Turow, Graduate Dean
Program in:
- communication (PhD)

Graduate School of Education
Dr. Andrew Porter, Graduate Dean
Programs in:
- applied psychology and human development (MS Ed, Ed D, PhD)
- counseling psychology (MS Ed)
- early childhood education (MS Ed)
- education (MS Ed, Ed D, PhD)
- education, culture and society (MS Ed, PhD)
- educational linguistics (PhD)
- educational policy and leadership (MS Ed, Ed D, PhD)
- elementary education (MS Ed)
- foundations and practices in education (MS Ed, Ed D, PhD)
- human development (MS Ed, PhD)
- human sexuality education (MS Ed, Ed D, PhD)
- intercultural communication (MS Ed, Ed D, PhD)
- policy, management and evaluation (MS Ed, Ed D, PhD)
- reading, writing, and literacy (MS Ed, Ed D, PhD)

school, community, and clinical child psychology (PhD)
secondary education (MS Ed)
teaching English to speakers of other languages (MS Ed)
teaching English to speakers of other languages and intercultural communication (MS Ed, PhD)

Law School
Michael A. Fitts, Dean
Program in:
law (JD, LL CM, LL M, SJD)

School of Arts and Sciences
Jack Nagel, Associate Dean
Programs in:
American civilization (AM, PhD)
ancient history (AM, PhD)
anthropology (AM, MS, PhD)
art and archaeology of the Mediterranean world (AM, PhD)
arts and sciences (AM, M Bioethics, MA, MBA, MES, MGA, MLA, MS, PhD)
bioethics (M Bioethics)
biology (PhD)
chemistry (MS, PhD)
classical studies (AM, PhD)
comparative literature (AM, PhD)
criminology (MA, MS, PhD)
demography (AM, PhD)
East Asian languages and civilization (AM, PhD)
economics (AM, PhD)
English (AM, PhD)
folklore and folklife (AM, PhD)
French (AM, PhD)
geology (MS, PhD)
Germanic languages (AM, PhD)
history (AM, PhD)
history and sociology of science (AM, PhD)
history of art (AM, PhD)
international studies (AM)
Italian (AM, PhD)
linguistics (AM, PhD)
literary theory (AM, PhD)
mathematics (AM, PhD)
medical physics (MS)
music (AM, PhD)
near eastern languages and civilization (AM, PhD)
organizational dynamics (MS)
philosophy (AM, PhD)
physics (PhD)
political science (AM, PhD)
psychology (PhD)
religious studies (PhD)
sociology (AM, PhD)
South Asian regional studies (AM, PhD)
Spanish (AM, PhD)

College of General Studies
Programs in:
environmental studies (MES)
individualized study (MLA)

Fels Institute of Government
Donald F. Kettl, Director
Program in:
government (MGA)

Joseph H. Lauder Institute of Management and International Studies
Dr. Richard J. Herring, Director
Programs in:
international studies (MA)
management and international studies (MBA)

School of Dental Medicine
Dr. Marjorie Jeffcoat, Dean
Program in:
dental medicine (DMD)

School of Design
David Leatherbarrow, Graduate Dean
Programs in:
architecture (M Arch, PhD)
city and regional planning (MCP, PhD, Certificate)
conservation and heritage management (Certificate)
design (M Arch, MCP, MFA, MLA, MS, PhD, Certificate)
fine arts (MFA)
historic conservation (Certificate)
historic preservation (MS)
landscape architecture and regional planning (MLA)
landscape studies (Certificate)
real estate design and development (PhD, Certificate)
urban design (PhD, Certificate)

School of Engineering and Applied Science
Eduardo D. Glandt, Dean
Programs in:
applied mechanics (MSE, PhD)
bioengineering (MSE, PhD)
biotechnology (MS)
chemical engineering (MSE, PhD)
computer and information science (MCIT, MSE, PhD)
computer graphics and game technology (MSE)
electrical and systems engineering (MSE, PhD)
engineering and applied science (EMBA, MCIT, MS, MSE, PhD, AC)
materials science and engineering (MSE, PhD)
mechanical engineering (MSE, PhD)
technology management (EMBA)
telecommunications and networking (MSE)

School of Medicine
Dr. Arthur M. Rubenstein, Dean
Program in:
medicine (MD, MS, MSCE, PhD)

Biomedical Graduate Studies
Dr. Susan R. Ross, Director
Programs in:
biochemistry and molecular biophysics (PhD)
biomedical studies (MS, PhD)
biostatistics (MS, PhD)
cell biology and physiology (PhD)
cell growth and cancer (PhD)
developmental biology (PhD)
gene therapy and vaccines (PhD)
genetics and gene regulation (PhD)
genomics and computational biology (PhD)
immunology (PhD)
microbiology, virology, and parasitology (PhD)
neuroscience (PhD)
pharmacology (PhD)

Center for Clinical Epidemiology and Biostatistics
Dr. Harold I. Feldman, Director
Programs in:
clinical epidemiology (MSCE)
epidemiology (PhD)

School of Nursing
Anne Keane, Graduate Dean
Programs in:
acute care nurse practitioner (MSN)
administration/consulting (MSN)
adult and special populations (MSN)
adult health nurse practitioner (MSN)
adult oncology nurse practitioner (MSN)
child and family (MSN)
family health nurse practitioner (MSN, Certificate)
geropsychiatrics (MSN)
health leadership (MSN)
neonatal nurse practitioner (MSN)
nurse anesthetist (MSN)
nurse midwifery (MSN)
nursing (MSN, PhD, Certificate)
nursing and health care administration (MSN, PhD)
pediatric acute/chronic care nurse practitioner (MSN)
pediatric critical care nurse practitioner (MSN)
pediatric nurse practitioner (MSN)
pediatric oncology nurse practitioner (MSN)
perinatal advanced practice nurse specialist (MSN)
primary care (MSN)
women's healthcare nurse practitioner (MSN)

School of Social Policy and Practice
Richard Gelles, Dean
Programs in:
social policy and practice (MSW, PhD)
social welfare (PhD)
social work (MSW)

School of Veterinary Medicine
Dr. Joan C. Hendricks, Dean
Program in:
veterinary medicine (VMD)

Wharton School
Programs in:
accounting (PhD)

University of Pennsylvania (continued)
business (MBA, PhD)
business and public policy (PhD)
finance (PhD)
health care systems (PhD)
insurance and risk management (PhD)
management (PhD)
marketing (PhD)
operations and information management (MBA, PhD)
operations and information management operations research (PhD)
real estate (PhD)
statistics (PhD)

Wharton Executive MBA Division
Program in:
executive business administration (MBA)

Wharton MBA Division
Program in:
business administration (MBA)

■ UNIVERSITY OF PHOENIX–PHILADELPHIA CAMPUS
Wayne, PA 19087-2121
http://www.phoenix.edu/

Proprietary, coed, comprehensive institution. *Enrollment:* 1,611 graduate, professional, and undergraduate students; 340 full-time matriculated graduate/professional students (199 women). *Graduate faculty:* 32 full-time (4 women), 133 part-time/adjunct (26 women). *Computer facilities:* A campuswide network can be accessed from off campus. Internet access is available. *Library facilities:* University Library. *Graduate expenses:* Tuition: full-time $13,560. Required fees: $760. *General application contact:* Campus Information Center, 610-989-0880.

The Artemis School
Dr. Adam Honea, Provost

College of Health and Human Services
Dr. Gil Linne, Dean/Executive Director
Program in:
health care management (MBA)

The John Sperling School of Business
Dr. Adam Honea, Provost
Program in:
business (MBA, MIS, MM)

College of Graduate Business and Management
Dr. Brian Lindquist, Associate Vice President and Dean/Executive Director
Programs in:
business administration (MBA)
global management (MBA)
management (MM)

College of Information Systems and Technology
Dr. Adam Honea, Provost/Dean, Vice President Academic Research and Development
Programs in:
information systems (MIS)
technology management (MBA)

■ UNIVERSITY OF PITTSBURGH
Pittsburgh, PA 15260
http://www.pitt.edu/

State-related, coed, university. CGS member. *Enrollment:* 26,860 graduate, professional, and undergraduate students; 6,701 full-time matriculated graduate/professional students (3,572 women), 2,913 part-time matriculated graduate/professional students (1,822 women). *Graduate faculty:* 3,655 full-time (1,345 women). *Computer facilities:* Computer purchase and lease plans are available. 600 computers available on campus for general student use. A campuswide network can be accessed from student residence rooms and from off campus. Internet access, online class listings are available. *Library facilities:* Hillman Library plus 25 others. *General application contact:* Information Contact, 412-624-4141.

Center for Neuroscience
Dr. Alan Sved, Co-Director, Graduate Program
Programs in:
neurobiology (PhD)
neuroscience (PhD)

Graduate School of Public and International Affairs
Dr. David Miller, Interim Dean
Programs in:
development planning (MPPM)
development policy (PhD)
foreign and security policy (PhD)
international development (MPPM)
international political economy (MPPM, PhD)
international security studies (MPPM)
management of non profit organizations (MPPM)
metropolitan management and regional development (MPPM)
policy analysis and evaluation (MPPM)
public administration (PhD)
public and international affairs (MID, MPA, MPIA, MPPM, PhD, Certificate)
public policy (PhD)

Division of International Development
Dr. Martin Staniland, Director, International Affairs and International Development Divisions
Programs in:
development planning and environmental sustainability (MID)
international development (MID)
nongovernmental organizations and civil society (MID)

Division of Public and Urban Affairs
Dr. Louise Comfort, Director, Public and Urban Affairs Division
Programs in:
policy research and analysis (MPA)
public and nonprofit management (MPA)
public and urban affairs (MPA)
urban and regional affairs (MPA)

International Affairs Division
Dr. Martin Staniland, Director, International Affairs and International Development Divisions
Programs in:
global political economy (MPIA)
human security (MPIA)
security and intelligence studies (MPIA)

Graduate School of Public Health
Dr. Donald S. Burke, Dean
Programs in:
behavioral and community health sciences (MPH, Dr PH)
biostatistics (MPH, MS, Dr PH, PhD)
environmental and occupational health (MPH)
epidemiology (MPH, MS, Dr PH, PhD)
genetic counseling (MS)
health policy and management (MHA, MPH)
human genetics (MS, PhD)
infectious diseases and microbiology (MPH, MS, Dr PH, PhD)
lesbian, gay, bisexual and transgender health and wellness (Certificate)
minority health and health disparities (Certificate)
molecular toxicology (MS, PhD)
occupational medicine (MPH)
program evaluation (Certificate)
public health (MHA, MPH, MS, Dr PH, PhD, Certificate)
public health and aging (Certificate)
public health genetics (MPH, Certificate)
public health preparedness (Certificate)
risk assessment (Certificate)

Joint CMU-Pitt PhD Program in Computational Biology
Dr. Ivet Bahar, Chair
Program in:
computational biology (PhD)

Joseph M. Katz Graduate School of Business
Dr. Lawrence F Feick, Dean
Programs in:
business (EMBA, MBA, MS, PhD)
business administration (EMBA, MBA, MS, PhD)
international business (MBA)
international business administration (MBA)
management of information systems (MS)

School of Arts and Sciences
Dr. Nicole Constable, Associate Dean, Graduate Studies and Research

Programs in:
- anthropology (MA, PhD)
- applied linguistics (PhD)
- applied mathematics (MA, MS)
- applied statistics (MA, MS)
- arts and sciences (MA, MFA, MS, PM Sc, PMS, PhD, Certificate, Doctoral Certificate, Master's Certificate)
- chemistry (MS, PhD)
- classics (MA, PhD)
- communication (MA, PhD)
- composition and theory (MA, PhD)
- computer science (MS, PhD)
- cultural and critical studies (PhD)
- East Asian studies (MA)
- ecology and evolution (PhD)
- English (MA)
- ethnomusicology (MA, PhD)
- financial mathematics (PMS)
- French (MA, PhD)
- geographical information systems (PM Sc)
- geology and planetary science (MS, PhD)
- Germanic languages and literatures (MA, PhD)
- Hispanic languages and literatures (MA, PhD)
- Hispanic linguistics (MA, PhD)
- historical musicology (MA, PhD)
- history (MA, PhD)
- history and philosophy of science (MA, PhD)
- history of art and architecture (MA, PhD)
- intelligent systems (MS, PhD)
- Italian (MA)
- linguistics (MA)
- mathematics (MA, MS, PhD)
- molecular, cellular, and developmental biology (PhD)
- performance pedagogy (MFA)
- philosophy (MA, PhD)
- physics (MS, PhD)
- political science (MA, PhD)
- psychology (MS, PhD)
- religion (PhD)
- religious studies (MA)
- Slavic languages and literatures (MA, PhD)
- sociolinguistics (PhD)
- sociology (MA, PhD)
- statistics (MA, MS, PhD)
- TESOL (Certificate)
- theatre and performance studies (MA, PhD)
- women's studies (Doctoral Certificate, Master's Certificate)
- writing (MFA)

Center for Bioethics and Health Law
Dr. Lisa S. Parker, Director of Graduate Education
Program in:
- bioethics (MA)

Department of Economics
Dr. David N. De Jong, Department Chair
Program in:
- economics (PhD)

School of Dental Medicine
Dr. Thomas W. Braun, Dean
Programs in:
- advanced education in general dentistry (Certificate)
- craniofacial and maxillofacial surgery (Certificate)
- dental medicine (DMD, MDS, Certificate)
- endodontics (MDS, Certificate)
- oral and maxillofacial surgery (Certificate)
- orthodontics (MDS, Certificate)
- pediatric dentistry (MDS, Certificate)
- periodontics (MDS, Certificate)
- prosthodontics (MDS, Certificate)

School of Education
Dr. Alan Lesgold, Dean
Programs in:
- applied developmental psychology (MS, PhD)
- cognitive studies (PhD)
- deaf and hard of hearing (M Ed)
- developmental movement (MS)
- early childhood education (M Ed)
- early education of disabled students (M Ed)
- education (M Ed, MA, MAT, MS, Ed D, PhD)
- education of students with mental and physical disabilities (M Ed)
- education of the visually impaired (M Ed)
- elementary education (M Ed, MAT)
- English/communications education (M Ed, MAT, Ed D, PhD)
- exercise physiology (MS, PhD)
- foreign languages education (M Ed, MAT, Ed D, PhD)
- general special education (M Ed)
- higher education (M Ed, Ed D)
- higher education management (M Ed, Ed D)
- international development education (MA, PhD)
- international developmental education (M Ed)
- mathematics education (M Ed, MAT, Ed D)
- reading education (M Ed, Ed D, PhD)
- research methodology (M Ed, MA, PhD)
- school leadership (M Ed, Ed D)
- science education (M Ed, MAT, MS, Ed D)
- secondary education (M Ed, MAT, MS, Ed D, PhD)
- social and comparative analysis in education (M Ed, MA, PhD)
- social studies education (M Ed, MAT, Ed D, PhD)
- social, philosophical, and historical foundations of education (M Ed, MA, PhD)
- special education (M Ed, Ed D, PhD)

School of Engineering
Dr. Gerald D. Holder, Dean
Programs in:
- bioengineering (MSBENG, PhD)
- chemical engineering (MS Ch E, PhD)
- civil and environmental engineering (MSCEE, PhD)
- electrical engineering (MSEE, PhD)
- engineering (MS Ch E, MSBENG, MSCEE, MSEE, MSIE, MSME, MSPE, PhD)
- industrial engineering (MSIE, PhD)
- mechanical engineering and materials science (MSME, PhD)
- petroleum engineering (MSPE)

School of Health and Rehabilitation Sciences
Dr. Clifford E. Brubaker, Dean
Programs in:
- assistive rehabilitation technology (Certificate)
- communication science and disorders (MA, MS, Au D, CScD, PhD)
- dietetics (MS)
- disability studies (Certificate)
- health and rehabilitation sciences (MS)
- occupational therapy (MOT)
- physical therapy (DPT)
- rehabilitation science (PhD)
- wellness and human performance (MS)

School of Information Sciences
Dr. Ronald L. Larsen, Dean
Programs in:
- information science (MSIS, Certificate)
- information science telecommunications (PhD)
- information sciences (MLIS, MSIS, MST, PhD, Certificate)
- library and information science (MLIS, PhD, Certificate)
- telecommunications and networking (MST, Certificate)

School of Law
Mary Crossley, Dean
Programs in:
- business law (MSL)
- civil litigation (Certificate)
- constitutional law (MSL)
- criminal justice (MSL)
- disabilities law (MSL)
- dispute resolution (MSL)
- education law (MSL)
- elder and estate planning law (MSL)
- employment and labor law (MSL)
- environment and real estate law (MSL)
- environmental law, science and policy (Certificate)
- family law (MSL)
- general law and jurisprudence (MSL)
- health law (MSL)
- intellectual property and technology (MSL)
- intellectual property and technology law (Certificate)

University of Pittsburgh (continued)
international and comparative law (LL M, MSL)
international law (Certificate)
law (JD, LL M, MA, MSL, Certificate)
personal injury and civil litigation (MSL)
regulatory law (MSL)
self-designed (MSL)

School of Medicine
Dr. Arthur S. Levine, Dean
Programs in:
biochemistry and molecular genetics (MS, PhD)
biomedical informatics (MS, PhD, Certificate)
cell biology and molecular physiology (MS, PhD)
cellular and molecular pathology (MS, PhD)
clinical research (MS, Certificate)
immunology (MS, PhD)
integrative molecular biology (PhD)
interdisciplinary biomedical sciences (PhD)
medical education (MS, Certificate)
medical research (Certificate)
medicine (MD, MS, PhD, Certificate)
molecular biophysics and structural biology (PhD)
molecular pharmacology (PhD)
molecular virology and microbiology (MS, PhD)
neurobiology (MS, PhD)

School of Nursing
Dr. Jacqueline Dunbar-Jacob, Dean
Programs in:
acute care nurse practitioner (MSN)
adult nurse practitioner (MSN)
anesthesia nursing (MSN)
family nurse practitioner (MSN)
medical/surgical clinical nurse specialist (MSN)
nursing (MSN, DNP, PhD)
nursing administration (MSN)
nursing education (MSN)
nursing informatics (MSN)
nursing practice (DNP)
nursing research (MSN)
pediatric nurse practitioner (MSN)
psychiatric and mental health clinical nurse specialist (MSN)
psychiatric primary care nurse practitioner (MSN)

School of Pharmacy
Dr. Patricia Dowley Kroboth, Dean
Programs in:
pharmaceutical sciences (MS, PhD)
pharmacy (Pharm D)

School of Social Work
Dr. Larry E. Davis, Dean
Programs in:
gerontology (Certificate)
social work (MSW, PhD, Certificate)

University Center for International Studies
Programs in:
African studies (Certificate)
Asian studies (Certificate)
European Union studies (Certificate)
global studies (Certificate)
Latin American studies (Certificate)
Russian and East European studies (Certificate)
West European studies (Certificate)

Center for Latin American Studies
Dr. Kathleen Musante DeWalt, Director
Program in:
Latin American studies (Certificate)

■ THE UNIVERSITY OF SCRANTON
Scranton, PA 18510
http://www.scranton.edu/

Independent-religious, coed, comprehensive institution. CGS member. *Enrollment:* 5,353 graduate, professional, and undergraduate students; 327 full-time matriculated graduate/professional students (219 women), 985 part-time matriculated graduate/professional students (664 women). *Graduate faculty:* 135 full-time (57 women), 68 part-time/adjunct (29 women). *Computer facilities:* 903 computers available on campus for general student use. A campuswide network can be accessed from student residence rooms and from off campus. Internet access and online class registration are available. *Library facilities:* Harry and Jeanette Weinberg Memorial Library plus 1 other. *Graduate expenses:* Tuition: part-time $684 per credit. Required fees: $25 per term. *General application contact:* James L. Goonan, Director of Admissions, 570-941-6304.

Graduate School
Dr. Duncan Perry, Dean
Programs in:
accounting (MBA)
adult health nursing (MSN)
biochemistry (MA, MS)
chemistry (MA, MS)
clinical chemistry (MA, MS)
community counseling (MS)
curriculum and instruction (MA, MS)
early childhood education (MA, MS)
educational administration (MS)
elementary education (MS)
English as a second language (MS)
enterprise management technology (MBA)
family nurse practitioner (MSN, PMC)
finance (MBA)
general business administration (MBA)
health administration (MHA)
history (MA)
human resources (MS)
human resources administration (MS)
human resources development (MS)
international business (MBA)
management information systems (MBA)
marketing (MBA)
nurse anesthesia (MSN, PMC)
occupational therapy (MS)
operations management (MBA)
organizational leadership (MS)
physical therapy (MPT, DPT)
professional counseling (CAGS)
reading education (MS)
rehabilitation counseling (MS)
school counseling (MS)
secondary education (MS)
software engineering (MS)
special education (MS)
theology (MA)

■ VILLANOVA UNIVERSITY
Villanova, PA 19085-1699
http://www.villanova.edu/

Independent-religious, coed, comprehensive institution. CGS member. *Enrollment:* 10,456 graduate, professional, and undergraduate students; 1,412 full-time matriculated graduate/professional students (687 women), 1,650 part-time matriculated graduate/professional students (756 women). *Graduate faculty:* 250. *Computer facilities:* Computer purchase and lease plans are available. 3,711 computers available on campus for general student use. A campuswide network can be accessed from student residence rooms and from off campus. Internet access and online class registration are available. *Library facilities:* Falvey Library plus 2 others. *Graduate expenses:* Tuition: part-time $565 per credit. *General application contact:* Dr. Gerald Long, Dean, Graduate School of Liberal Arts and Sciences, 610-519-7090.

Find University Details at www.petersons.com/gradchannel.

College of Engineering
Dr. Gary A. Gabriele, Dean
Programs in:
chemical engineering (MSChE)
civil engineering (MSCE)
communications systems (Certificate)
composite engineering (Certificate)
computer architecture (Certificate)
computer engineering (MSCE, Certificate)
electrical engineering (MSEE, Certificate)
electrical power systems (Certificate)
electro-mechanical systems (Certificate)
engineering (MSCE, MSChE, MSEE, MSME, MSTE, MSWREE, PhD, Certificate)
high frequency systems (Certificate)
intelligent systems (Certificate)
machinery dynamics (Certificate)
manufacturing (Certificate)

mechanical engineering (MSME)
thermofluid systems (Certificate)
transportation engineering (MSTE)
water resources and environmental engineering (MSWREE)
wireless and digital communications (Certificate)

College of Nursing

Dr. Marguerite K. Schlag, Assistant Dean and Director, Graduate Program
Programs in:
adult nurse practitioner (MSN, Post Master's Certificate)
clinical case management (MSN, Post Master's Certificate)
geriatric nurse practitioner (MSN, Post Master's Certificate)
health care administration (MSN)
nurse anesthetist (MSN, Post Master's Certificate)
nursing (PhD)
nursing education (MSN, Post Master's Certificate)
pediatric nurse practitioner (MSN, Post Master's Certificate)

Graduate School of Liberal Arts and Sciences

Dr. Gerald Long, Dean
Programs in:
applied statistics (MS)
biology (MA, MS)
chemistry (MS)
classics (MA)
communication (MA)
community counseling (MS)
computing sciences (MS)
counseling and human relations (MS)
criminal justice administration (MS)
educational leadership (MA)
elementary school counseling (MS)
elementary teacher education (MA)
English (MA)
Hispanic studies (MA)
history (MA)
human resource development (MS)
liberal arts and sciences (MA, MPA, MS, PhD)
liberal studies (MA)
mathematical sciences (MA)
philosophy (PhD)
political science (MA)
psychology (MS)
public administration (MPA)
secondary school counseling (MS)
secondary teacher education (MA)
theatre (MA)
theology (MA)

School of Law

Mark A. Sargent, Dean
Programs in:
law (JD, LL M)
tax (LL M)

Villanova School of Business

James M. Danko, Dean
Programs in:
accountancy (M Ac)
business (EMBA, M Ac, MBA, MS, MTM)
business administration (MBA)
executive business administration (EMBA)
finance (MS)
technology management (MTM)

■ WAYNESBURG COLLEGE

Waynesburg, PA 15370-1222
http://www.waynesburg.edu/

Independent-religious, coed, comprehensive institution. *Computer facilities:* 150 computers available on campus for general student use. A campuswide network can be accessed from student residence rooms and from off campus. Internet access and online class registration are available. *Library facilities:* Waynesburg College Library. *General application contact:* Director, 412-854-3600.

■ WEST CHESTER UNIVERSITY OF PENNSYLVANIA

West Chester, PA 19383
http://www.wcupa.edu/

State-supported, coed, comprehensive institution. CGS member. *Enrollment:* 12,882 graduate, professional, and undergraduate students; 547 full-time matriculated graduate/professional students (420 women), 1,514 part-time matriculated graduate/professional students (1,131 women). *Computer facilities:* 700 computers available on campus for general student use. A campuswide network can be accessed from student residence rooms and from off campus. Internet access and online class registration are available. *Library facilities:* Francis Harvey Green Library plus 1 other. *General application contact:* Information Contact, 610-436-2943.

Find University Details at www.petersons.com/gradchannel.

Graduate Studies

Dr. Janet Hickman, Interim Dean

College of Arts and Sciences

Dr. Gil Wiswall, Interim Dean
Programs in:
arts and sciences (M Ed, MA, MS, MSA, Certificate)
biology (MS)
chemistry (M Ed, MS)
clinical chemistry (MS)
clinical psychology (MA)
communication studies (MA)
computer science (MS, Certificate)
English (MA)
French (M Ed, MA)
general psychology (MA)
German (M Ed)
gerontology (Certificate)
history (M Ed, MA)
industrial organizational psychology (MA)
Latin (M Ed)
long term care (MSA)
mathematics (MA)
philosophy (MA)
physical science (MA)
Spanish (M Ed, MA)
teaching English as a second language (MA)

College of Visual and Performing Arts

Dr. Timothy Blair, Dean
Programs in:
music education (MM)
music history (MA)
performance (MM)
visual and performing arts (MA, MM)

School of Business and Public Affairs

Dr. Christopher Fiorentino, Dean
Programs in:
business and public affairs (MA, MBA, MS, MSA, MSW)
criminal justice (MS)
economics/finance (MBA)
executive business administration (MBA)
general business (MBA)
geography (MA)
health services (MSA)
human research management (MSA)
individualized (MSA)
leadership for women (MSA)
long-term care (MSA)
management (MBA)
public administration (MSA)
regional planning (MSA)
social work (MSW)
sport and athletic training (MSA)
technology and electronic commerce (MBA)
training and development (MSA)

School of Education

Dr. Joseph Malak, Dean
Programs in:
counseling and educational psychology (M Ed, MS)
early childhood and special education (M Ed)
educational research (MS)
elementary education (M Ed)
elementary school counseling (M Ed)
higher education counseling (MS)
literacy (M Ed)
professional and secondary education (M Ed, MS)
reading (M Ed)
secondary education (M Ed)
secondary school counseling (M Ed)
special education (M Ed)
teaching and learning with technology (Certificate)

School of Health Sciences

Dr. Donald E. Barr, Dean

West Chester University of Pennsylvania (continued)
Programs in:
- communicative disorders (MA)
- driver education (Certificate)
- emergency preparedness (Certificate)
- environmental health (MS)
- exercise and sport physiology (MS)
- gerontology (MS)
- health care administration (Certificate)
- health sciences (M Ed, MA, MPH, MS, MSA, MSN, Certificate)
- health services (MSA)
- integrative health (Certificate)
- nursing (MSN)
- nursing education (MSN)
- physical education (MS)
- public health (MPH, MS)
- school health (M Ed)
- sport and athletic administration (MSA)

■ WIDENER UNIVERSITY
Chester, PA 19013-5792
http://www.widener.edu/

Independent, coed, comprehensive institution. CGS member. *Computer facilities:* Computer purchase and lease plans are available. 345 computers available on campus for general student use. A campuswide network can be accessed from student residence rooms and from off campus. Internet access and online class registration, all library resources and special journals and services are available. *Library facilities:* Wolfgram Memorial Library. *General application contact:* Associate Provost for Graduate Studies, 610-499-4351.

Find University Details at www.petersons.com/gradchannel.

College of Arts and Sciences
Programs in:
- arts and sciences (MA, MPA)
- criminal justice (MA)
- liberal studies (MA)
- public administration (MPA)

Graduate Programs in Engineering
Programs in:
- chemical engineering (M Eng)
- civil engineering (M Eng)
- computer and software engineering (M Eng)
- engineering management (M Eng)
- management and technology (MSMT)
- mechanical engineering (M Eng)
- telecommunications engineering (M Eng)

School of Business Administration
Programs in:
- accounting information systems (MS)
- business administration (MBA, MHA, MHR, MS)
- health and medical services administration (MBA, MHA)
- human resource management (MHR, MS)
- taxation (MS)

School of Human Service Professions
Program in:
- human service professions (M Ed, MS, MSW, DPT, Ed D, Psy D)

Center for Education
Programs in:
- adult education (M Ed)
- counseling in higher education (M Ed)
- counselor education (M Ed)
- early childhood education (M Ed)
- educational foundations (M Ed)
- educational leadership (M Ed)
- educational psychology (M Ed)
- elementary education (M Ed)
- English and language arts (M Ed)
- health education (M Ed)
- higher education leadership (Ed D)
- home and school visitor (M Ed)
- human sexuality (M Ed)
- mathematics education (M Ed)
- middle school education (M Ed)
- principalship (M Ed)
- reading and language arts (Ed D)
- reading education (M Ed)
- school administration (Ed D)
- science education (M Ed)
- social studies education (M Ed)
- special education (M Ed)
- technology education (M Ed)

Center for Social Work Education
Program in:
- social work education (MSW)

Institute for Graduate Clinical Psychology
Program in:
- clinical psychology (Psy D)

Institute for Physical Therapy Education
Program in:
- physical therapy education (MS, DPT)

School of Law
Program in:
- law (JD)

School of Law at Wilmington
Programs in:
- corporate law and finance (LL M)
- health law (LL M, MJ, D Law)
- juridical science (SJD)
- law (JD)

School of Nursing
Program in:
- nursing (MSN, DN Sc, PMC)

■ WILKES UNIVERSITY
Wilkes-Barre, PA 18766-0002
http://www.wilkes.edu/

Independent, coed, comprehensive institution. *Enrollment:* 4,777 graduate, professional, and undergraduate students; 440 full-time matriculated graduate/professional students (265 women), 2,092 part-time matriculated graduate/professional students (1,439 women). *Computer facilities:* 700 computers available on campus for general student use. A campuswide network can be accessed from student residence rooms and from off campus. Internet access and online class registration are available. *Library facilities:* Eugene S. Farley Library. *General application contact:* Kathleen Houlihan, Director of Graduate Studies, 570-408-3235.

Graduate Studies and Continued Learning
Dr. Michael Speziale, Interim Dean

College of Arts, Humanities and Social Sciences
Dr. Darin Fields, Dean
Programs in:
- arts, humanities and social sciences (MA, MS Ed)
- classroom technology (MS Ed)
- creative writing (MA)
- educational computing (MS Ed)
- educational development and strategies (MS Ed)
- educational leadership (MS Ed)
- elementary education (MS Ed)
- instructional technology (MS Ed)
- school business leadership (MS Ed)
- secondary education (MS Ed)
- special education (MS Ed)

College of Science and Engineering
Dr. Dale Bruns, Dean
Programs in:
- electrical engineering (MSEE)
- engineering operations and strategy (MS)
- mathematics (MS, MS Ed)
- science and engineering (MS, MS Ed, MSEE)

Jay S. Sidhu School of Business and Leadership
Dr. Paul Browne, Dean
Programs in:
- accounting (MBA)
- entrepreneurship (MBA)
- finance (MBA)
- human resource management (MBA)
- international business (MBA)
- management (MBA)
- marketing (MBA)

Nesbitt College of Pharmacy and Nursing
Dr. Bernard Graham, Dean
Programs in:
- nursing (MSN)
- pharmacy (Pharm D)
- pharmacy and nursing (Pharm D, MSN)

Puerto Rico

■ BAYAMÓN CENTRAL UNIVERSITY

Bayamón, PR 00960-1725
http://www.ucb.edu.pr/

Independent-religious, coed, comprehensive institution. *Computer facilities:* 130 computers available on campus for general student use. A campuswide network can be accessed. Internet access is available. *Library facilities:* BCU Library plus 1 other. *General application contact:* Director of Admissions, 787-786-3030 Ext. 2100.

Graduate Programs

Programs in:
- accounting (MBA)
- administration and supervision (MA Ed)
- biblical studies (MA)
- commercial education (MA Ed)
- divinity (M Div)
- education of the autistic (MA Ed)
- elementary education (K–3) (MA Ed)
- elementary education (K–6) (MA Ed)
- elementary physical education (MA Ed)
- finance (MBA)
- general business (MBA)
- guidance and counseling (MA Ed)
- management (MBA)
- management of security and protection (MBA)
- marketing (MBA)
- pastoral theology (MA)
- pre-elementary teacher (MA Ed)
- psychology (MA)
- special education (MA Ed)
- theological studies (MA)
- theology (MA)

■ CARLOS ALBIZU UNIVERSITY

San Juan, PR 00901
http://www.albizu.edu/

Independent, coed, upper-level institution. *Enrollment:* 603 full-time matriculated graduate/professional students (515 women), 99 part-time matriculated graduate/professional students (77 women). *Graduate faculty:* 22 full-time (13 women), 61 part-time/adjunct (33 women). *General application contact:* Carlos Rodríguez, Director of Students Affairs, 787-725-6500 Ext. 21.

Graduate Programs in Psychology

Dr. Lourdes Garcia, Chancellor

Programs in:
- clinical psychology (MS, PhD, Psy D)
- general psychology (PhD)
- industrial/organizational psychology (MS, PhD)
- speech and language pathology (MS)

■ INTER AMERICAN UNIVERSITY OF PUERTO RICO, METROPOLITAN CAMPUS

San Juan, PR 00919-1293
http://metro.inter.edu/

Independent, coed, comprehensive institution. CGS member. *Computer facilities:* 400 computers available on campus for general student use. A campuswide network can be accessed from student residence rooms and from off campus. Internet access and online class registration are available. *Library facilities:* Centro de Acceso a la Informacion plus 1 other. *General application contact:* Information Contact, 787-765-1270.

Faculty of Economics and Administrative Sciences

Programs in:
- accounting (MBA)
- business and management development (PhD)
- business education (MA)
- finance (MBA)
- human resources (MBA)
- industrial management (MBA)
- labor relations (MA)
- marketing (MBA)

Faculty of Education

Programs in:
- administration and supervision (MA)
- education (Ed D)
- elementary education (MA)
- guidance and counseling (MA)
- health and physical education (MA)
- higher education (MA Ed)
- occupational education (MA)
- special education (MA Ed)
- teaching of science (MA Ed)
- vocational evaluation (MA)

Faculty of Liberal Arts

Programs in:
- humanistic studies (MA, PhD)
- Spanish (MA)
- teaching English as a second language (MA)
- theological studies (PhD)

Faculty of Science and Technology

Programs in:
- administration of laboratories (MS)
- educational computing (MA)
- medical technology (MS)
- micromolecular biology (MS)
- open information systems (MS)

School of Criminal Justice

Program in:
- criminal justice (MA)

School of Psychology

Program in:
- psychology (MA)

School of Social Work

Programs in:
- clinical services (MSW)
- social administration (MSW)

■ INTER AMERICAN UNIVERSITY OF PUERTO RICO, SAN GERMÁN CAMPUS

San Germán, PR 00683-5008
http://www.sg.inter.edu/

Independent, coed, university. *Enrollment:* 5,960 graduate, professional, and undergraduate students; 471 full-time matriculated graduate/professional students, 581 part-time matriculated graduate/professional students. *Graduate faculty:* 55 full-time, 48 part-time/adjunct. *Computer facilities:* 1,400 computers available on campus for general student use. A campuswide network can be accessed. Internet access and online class registration are available. *Library facilities:* Juan Cancio Ortiz Library. *Graduate expenses:* Tuition: part-time $175 per credit. Required fees: $238 per semester. Tuition and fees vary according to degree level. *General application contact:* Dr. Carlos E. Irizarry, Director of Graduate Studies Center, 787-264-1912 Ext. 7357.

Graduate Studies Center

Dr. Carlos E. Irizarry, Director of Graduate Studies Center

Programs in:
- accounting (MBA)
- administration and supervision (MA)
- applied mathematics (MA)
- art (MFA)
- business education (MA)
- ceramics (MFA)
- counseling psychology (MA, PhD)
- drawing (MFA)
- elementary education (MA)
- environmental sciences (MS)
- finance (MBA)
- guidance and counseling (MA)
- human resources (MBA, PhD)
- industrial relations (MBA)
- international business (PhD)
- interregional and international business (PhD)
- labor relations (PhD)
- library and information sciences (MLS)
- management information systems (MBA)
- marketing (MBA)
- music education (MA)
- painting (MFA)
- photography (MFA)
- physical education and scientific analysis of human body movement (MA)
- printmaking (MFA)
- quality organizational design (MBA)
- school psychology (MS, PhD)

Inter American University of Puerto Rico, San Germán Campus (continued)
- science education (MA)
- sculpture (MFA)
- special education (MA)
- teaching English as a second language (MA)

■ PONTIFICAL CATHOLIC UNIVERSITY OF PUERTO RICO

Ponce, PR 00717-0777

http://www.pucpr.edu/

Independent-religious, coed, university. *Computer facilities:* 419 computers available on campus for general student use. A campuswide network can be accessed from off campus. Internet access is available. *Library facilities:* Encarnacion Valdes Library plus 1 other. *General application contact:* Director of Admissions, 787-841-2000 Ext. 1000.

College of Arts and Humanities
Programs in:
- arts and humanities (MA)
- Hispanic studies (MA)
- history (MA)
- theology and philosophy (M Div)

College of Business Administration
Programs in:
- accounting (MBA)
- business administration (PhD)
- finance (MBA)
- general business (MBA)
- human resources (MBA)
- international business (MBA)
- management (MBA)
- management information systems (MBA)
- marketing (MBA)
- office administration (MBA)

College of Education
Programs in:
- commercial education (MRE)
- curriculum instruction (M Ed)
- education (PhD)
- education-general (MRE)
- English as a second language (MRE)
- religious education (MA Ed)
- scholar psychology (MRE)

College of Sciences
Programs in:
- chemistry (MS)
- environmental sciences (MS)
- medical technology (Certificate)
- medical-surgical nursing (MS)
- mental health and psychiatric nursing (MS)
- sciences (MS, Certificate)

Institute of Graduate Studies in Behavioral Science and Community Affairs
Programs in:
- clinical psychology (MA, MS)
- clinical social work (MSW)
- criminology (MA)
- industrial psychology (MS)
- psychology (PhD)
- public administration (MA)

School of Law
Program in:
- law (JD)

■ UNIVERSIDAD DEL TURABO

Gurabo, PR 00778-3030

http://www.suagm.edu/ut/

Independent, coed, comprehensive institution. *Computer facilities:* A campuswide network can be accessed from off campus. Internet access is available. *General application contact:* Director of Admissions and Financial Aid, 787-743-7979 Ext. 4352.

Graduate Programs
Programs in:
- bilingual education (MA)
- criminal justice studies (MPA)
- education administration and supervision (MA)
- environmental studies (MES)
- human services administration (MPA)
- school libraries administration (MA)
- special education (MA)
- teaching English as a second language (MA)

School in Business Administration
Programs in:
- accounting (MBA)
- logistics and materials management (MBA)
- management (MBA, DBA)
- management of information systems (DBA)
- marketing (MBA)

■ UNIVERSIDAD METROPOLITANA

San Juan, PR 00928-1150

http://www.suagm.edu/umet/

Independent, coed, comprehensive institution. *Computer facilities:* 50 computers available on campus for general student use. Internet access is available. *General application contact:* Director of Admissions and Financial Aid, 787-766-1717 Ext. 6587.

Graduate Programs in Education
Programs in:
- curriculum and teaching (MA)
- educational administration and supervision (MA)
- environmental education (MA)
- fitness management (MA)
- managing leisure services (MA)
- pre-school centers administration (MA)
- pre-school education (MA)
- special education (MA)
- teaching of physical education (MA)

School of Business Administration
Programs in:
- accounting (MBA)
- finance (MBA)
- human resources management (MBA)
- international business (MBA)
- management (MBA)
- marketing (MBA)
- public accounting (Certificate)

School of Environmental Affairs
Programs in:
- conservation and management of natural resources (MEM)
- environmental education (MA)
- environmental planning (MEM)
- environmental risk and assessment management (MEM)

■ UNIVERSITY OF PUERTO RICO, MAYAGÜEZ CAMPUS

Mayagüez, PR 00681-9000

http://www.uprm.edu

Commonwealth-supported, coed, university. *Enrollment:* 12,380 graduate, professional, and undergraduate students; 400 full-time matriculated graduate/professional students (178 women), 612 part-time matriculated graduate/professional students (330 women). *Graduate faculty:* 568 full-time (190 women). *Computer facilities:* 1,066 computers available on campus for general student use. A campuswide network can be accessed from off campus. Internet access and online class registration are available. *Library facilities:* General Library plus 1 other. *Graduate expenses:* Tuition, nonresident: full-time $4,655. Required fees: $210. One-time fee: $77 full-time. Part-time tuition and fees vary according to course load and reciprocity agreements. *General application contact:* Dra. Doris Ramírez, Director of Graduate Studies, 787-265-3809.

Graduate Studies
Dra. Doris Ramírez, Director of Graduate Studies

College of Agricultural Sciences
Dr. John Fernández-VanCleve, Dean
Programs in:
- agricultural economics (MS)
- agricultural education (MS)
- agricultural extension (MS)
- agricultural sciences (MS)
- agronomy (MS)
- animal industry (MS)
- crop protection (MS)

food science and technology (MS)
horticulture (MS)
soils (MS)

College of Arts and Sciences
Dr. Moisés Orengo-Avilés, Dean
Programs in:
applied chemistry (PhD)
applied mathematics (MS)
arts and sciences (MA, MS, PhD)
biology (MS)
chemistry (MS)
computational sciences (MS)
English education (MA)
geology (MS)
Hispanic studies (MA)
marine sciences (MS, PhD)
physics (MS)
pure mathematics (MS)
statistics (MS)

College of Business Administration
Prof. Eva Quinñones, Dean
Programs in:
business administration (MBA)
finance (MBA)
human resources (MBA)
industrial management (MBA)

College of Engineering
Dr. Ramón Vásquez, Dean
Programs in:
chemical engineering (ME, MS, PhD)
civil engineering (ME, MS, PhD)
computer engineering (ME, MS)
computing information science and engineering (PhD)
electrical engineering (ME, MS)
engineering (ME, MS, PhD)
industrial engineering (ME)
management systems (MS)
mechanical engineering (ME, MS)

■ UNIVERSITY OF PUERTO RICO, RÍO PIEDRAS
San Juan, PR 00931-3300
http://www.uprrp.edu/

Commonwealth-supported, coed, university. CGS member. *Enrollment:* 20,528 graduate, professional, and undergraduate students; 2,467 full-time matriculated graduate/professional students (1,660 women), 1,329 part-time matriculated graduate/professional students (916 women). *Computer facilities:* 170 computers available on campus for general student use. A campuswide network can be accessed from student residence rooms. Internet access is available. *Library facilities:* Jose M. Lazaro Library plus 10 others. *Graduate expenses:* Tuition, commonwealth resident: part-time $100 per credit. Tuition, nonresident: part-time $291 per credit. Required fees: $72 per semester. *General application contact:* Cruz B. Valentin-Arbelo, Admission Office Director, 787-764-0000 Ext. 5653.

College of Business Administration
Dr. Emilio Pontojas, Coordinator of Master Programs
Program in:
business administration (MBA, PhD)

College of Education
Dr. Angeles Molina Ilurrondo, Dean
Programs in:
biology education (M Ed)
chemistry education (M Ed)
child education (M Ed)
curriculum and teaching (Ed D)
education (M Ed, MS, Ed D)
educational research and evaluation (M Ed)
English education (M Ed)
exercise sciences (MS)
family ecology and nutrition (M Ed)
guidance and counseling (M Ed, Ed D)
history education (M Ed)
mathematics education (M Ed)
physics education (M Ed)
school administration and supervision (M Ed, Ed D)
secondary education (M Ed)
Spanish education (M Ed)
special education (M Ed)
teaching English as a second language (M Ed)

College of Humanities
Dr. Josè L. Romos Escobor, Dean
Programs in:
comparative literature (MA)
English (MA, PhD)
Hispanic studies (MA, PhD)
history (MA, PhD)
humanities (MA, PhD, Certificate)
linguistics (MA)
philosophy (MA)
translation (MA, Certificate)

College of Natural Sciences
Dr. Brad Weiner, Dean
Programs in:
biology (MS, PhD)
chemical physics (PhD)
chemistry (MS, PhD)
mathematics (MS, PhD)
natural sciences (MS, PhD)
physics (MS)

College of Social Sciences
Dr. Carlos Severino-Valdés, Acting Dean
Programs in:
economics (MA)
psychology (MA, PhD)
social sciences (MA, MPA, MRC, MSW, PhD)
sociology (MA)

Graduate School of Rehabilitation Counseling
Dr. Marilyn Mendoza-Lugo, Director
Program in:
rehabilitation counseling (MRC)

Graduate School of Social Work
Dr. Norma Rodriguez, Director
Program in:
social work (MSW, PhD)

School of Public Administration
Dr. Palmira González, Director
Program in:
public administration (MPA)

Graduate School of Information Sciences and Technologies
Dr. Nitza M. Hernández, Director
Programs in:
librarianship (Post-Graduate Certificate)
librarianship and information services (MLS)

Graduate School of Planning
Dr. Elías R. Gutierrez, Director
Program in:
planning (MP)

School of Architecture
Dr. Fernando Abruña, Dean
Program in:
architecture (M Arch)

School of Communication
Dr. Eliseo Colón, Director
Program in:
communication (MA)

School of Law
Dr. Efrén Rivera-Ramos, Dean
Program in:
law (JD, LL M)

Rhode Island

■ BROWN UNIVERSITY
Providence, RI 02912
http://www.brown.edu/

Independent, coed, university. CGS member. *Computer facilities:* Computer purchase and lease plans are available. 500 computers available on campus for general student use. A campuswide network can be accessed from student residence rooms and from off campus. Internet access and online class registration are available. *Library facilities:* John D. Rockefeller Library plus 5 others. *General application contact:* Admission Office, 401-863-2600.

Graduate School
Programs in:
American civilization (AM, PhD)
anthropology (AM, PhD)
art history (AM, PhD)
biochemistry (PhD)
chemistry (Sc M, PhD)
classics (AM, PhD)
cognitive science (Sc M, PhD)
comparative literature (AM, PhD)
comparative study of development (AM)
computer science (Sc M, PhD)

Brown University (continued)
economics (AM, PhD)
Egyptology (AM, PhD)
elementary education 1-6 (MAT)
English literature and language (AM, PhD)
French studies (AM, PhD)
geological sciences (MA, Sc M, PhD)
German (AM, PhD)
Hispanic studies (AM, PhD)
history (AM, PhD)
history of mathematics (AM, PhD)
Italian studies (AM, PhD)
Judaic studies (AM, PhD)
linguistics (AM, PhD)
mathematics (M Sc, MA, PhD)
music (AM, PhD)
neuroscience (PhD)
old world archaeology and art (AM, PhD)
philosophy (AM, PhD)
physics (Sc M, PhD)
political science (AM, PhD)
population studies (PhD)
psychology (AM, Sc M, PhD)
religious studies (AM, PhD)
Russian (AM, PhD)
secondary biology (MAT)
secondary English (MAT)
secondary social studies/history (MAT)
Slavic languages (AM, PhD)
sociology (AM, PhD)
theatre arts (AM)
writing (MFA)

A. Alfred Taubman Center for Public Policy and American Institutions
Program in:
public policy and American institutions (MPA, MPP)

Center for Environmental Studies
Osvaldo Sala, Director
Program in:
environmental studies (AM)

Center for Old World Archaeology and Art
Program in:
old world archaeology and art (AM, PhD)

Center for Portuguese and Brazilian Studies
Programs in:
Brazilian studies (AM)
Luso-Brazilian studies (PhD)
Portuguese studies and bilingual education (AM)

Division of Applied Mathematics
Program in:
applied mathematics (Sc M, PhD)

Division of Biology and Medicine
Programs in:
artificial organs, biomaterials, and cell technology (MA, Sc M, PhD)
biochemistry (M Med Sc, Sc M, PhD)
biology (MA, PhD)
biology and medicine (M Med Sc, MA, MPH, MS, Sc M, PhD)
biomedical engineering (MS, PhD)
biostatistics (MS, PhD)
cancer biology (PhD)
cell biology (M Med Sc, Sc M, PhD)
developmental biology (M Med Sc, Sc M, PhD)
ecology and evolutionary biology (PhD)
epidemiology (MS, PhD)
health services research (MS, PhD)
immunology (M Med Sc, Sc M, PhD)
immunology and infection (PhD)
medical science (PhD)
molecular microbiology (M Med Sc, Sc M, PhD)
molecular pharmacology and physiology (MA, Sc M, PhD)
neuroscience (PhD)
pathobiology (Sc M)
public health (MPH)
statistical science (MS, PhD)
toxicology and environmental pathology (PhD)

Division of Engineering
Programs in:
aerospace engineering (Sc M, PhD)
biomedical engineering (Sc M)
electrical sciences (Sc M, PhD)
fluid mechanics, thermodynamics, and chemical processes (Sc M, PhD)
materials science (Sc M, PhD)
mechanics of solids and structures (Sc M, PhD)

National Institutes of Health Sponsored Programs
Program in:
neuroscience (PhD)

Program in Medicine
Program in:
medicine (MD)

■ BRYANT UNIVERSITY
Smithfield, RI 02917-1284
http://www.bryant.edu/

Independent, coed, comprehensive institution. *Enrollment:* 3,651 graduate, professional, and undergraduate students; 420 part-time matriculated graduate/professional students (151 women). *Graduate faculty:* 49 full-time (13 women), 8 part-time/adjunct (1 woman). *Computer facilities:* Computer purchase and lease plans are available. 467 computers available on campus for general student use. A campuswide network can be accessed from student residence rooms and from off campus. Internet access and online class registration, e-mail, online library, wireless network, student Web hosts are available. *Library facilities:* Douglas and Judith Krupp Library. *Graduate expenses:* Tuition: part-time $1,998 per course. *General application contact:* Kristopher T. Sullivan, Assistant Dean of the Graduate School, 401-232-6230.

Graduate School
Kristopher T. Sullivan, Assistant Dean of the Graduate School

Graduate School of Business
Dr. Jack W. Trifts, Dean of the College of Business
Programs in:
accounting (MBA, CAGS)
business administration (MBA, CAGS)
computer information systems (MBA, CAGS)
e-strategy (MBA, CAGS)
finance (MBA, CAGS)
general business (MBA)
information systems (MSIS)
management (MBA, CAGS)
marketing (MBA, CAGS)
operations management (MBA)
professional accounting (MPAC)
taxation (MST, CAGS)

■ JOHNSON & WALES UNIVERSITY
Providence, RI 02903-3703
http://www.jwu.edu/

Independent, coed, comprehensive institution. *Enrollment:* 10,310 graduate, professional, and undergraduate students; 805 full-time matriculated graduate/professional students (417 women), 156 part-time matriculated graduate/professional students (91 women). *Graduate faculty:* 17 full-time (5 women), 14 part-time/adjunct (3 women). *Computer facilities:* 400 computers available on campus for general student use. A campuswide network can be accessed from student residence rooms and from off campus. Internet access and online class registration are available. *Library facilities:* Johnson & Wales University Library plus 1 other. *General application contact:* Dr. Allan G. Freedman, Director of Graduate Admissions, 401-598-1015.

Find University Details at www.petersons.com/gradchannel.

The Alan Shawn Feinstein Graduate School
Dr. Frank Pontarelli, Dean
Programs in:
accounting (MBA)
business education and secondary special education (MAT)
educational leadership (Ed D)
elementary education and special education (MAT)
event leadership (MBA)
financial management (MBA)
food service education and secondary special education (MAT)
international trade (MBA)
marketing (MBA)
organizational leadership (MBA)

■ PROVIDENCE COLLEGE
Providence, RI 02918
http://www.providence.edu/

Independent-religious, coed, comprehensive institution. *Enrollment:* 4,835 graduate, professional, and undergraduate students; 111 full-time matriculated graduate/professional students (72 women), 387 part-time matriculated graduate/professional students (246 women). *Graduate faculty:* 33 full-time (9 women), 55 part-time/adjunct (25 women). *Computer facilities:* 164 computers available on campus for general student use. A campuswide network can be accessed from student residence rooms and from off campus. Internet access and online class registration are available. *Library facilities:* Phillips Memorial Library. *Graduate expenses:* Tuition: full-time $6,573; part-time $939 per unit. *General application contact:* Dr. Thomas Flaherty, Dean of Graduate Studies, 401-865-2247.

Graduate Studies
Dr. Thomas Flaherty, Dean, Graduate Studies
Programs in:
administration (M Ed)
biblical studies (MA)
business administration (MBA)
education literacy (M Ed)
elementary administration (M Ed)
guidance and counseling (M Ed)
history (MA)
mathematics (MAT)
pastoral ministry (MA)
religious education (MA)
religious studies (MA)
secondary administration (M Ed)
special education (M Ed)

■ RHODE ISLAND COLLEGE
Providence, RI 02908-1991
http://www.ric.edu/

State-supported, coed, comprehensive institution. *Enrollment:* 8,939 graduate, professional, and undergraduate students; 230 full-time matriculated graduate/professional students (192 women), 410 part-time matriculated graduate/professional students (329 women). *Graduate faculty:* 135 full-time (62 women), 46 part-time/adjunct (27 women). *Computer facilities:* Computer purchase and lease plans are available. 350 computers available on campus for general student use. A campuswide network can be accessed from student residence rooms and from off campus. Internet access and online class registration are available. *Library facilities:* Adams Library. *Graduate expenses:* Tuition, state resident: part-time $244 per credit. Tuition, nonresident: part-time $512 per credit. Required fees: $12 per credit. $66 per term. Tuition and fees vary according to degree level, program and reciprocity agreements. *General application contact:* Dean of Graduate Studies, 401-456-8700.

School of Graduate Studies
Dean
Program in:
nursing (MSN)

Faculty of Arts and Sciences
Dr. Richard R. Weiner, Dean
Programs in:
art (MA)
art education (MAT)
arts and sciences (MA, MAT, MFA, MM Ed, MPA)
biology (MA)
creative writing (MA)
English (MA)
history (MA)
mathematics (MA)
media studies (MA)
music education (MAT, MM Ed)
psychology (MA)
public administration (MPA)
theatre (MFA)

Feinstein School of Education and Human Development
Dr. Julie Wollman, Interim Dean
Programs in:
bilingual/bicultural education (M Ed)
counseling (MA)
early childhood education (M Ed)
education (PhD)
education and human development (M Ed, MA, MAT, PhD, CAGS)
educational administration (CAGS)
educational leadership (M Ed)
elementary education (M Ed, MAT)
English (MAT)
French (MAT)
health education (M Ed)
history (MAT)
math (MAT)
reading (M Ed)
school administration (M Ed)
school counseling (CAGS)
secondary education (M Ed)
Spanish (MAT)
special education (M Ed, CAGS)
teaching English as a second language (M Ed, MAT)
technology education (M Ed)

School of Management
Dr. James Schweikart, Dean
Programs in:
accounting (MP Ac)
management (MP Ac)
personal financial planning (MP Ac)

School of Social Work
Dr. Carol Bennett-Speight, Dean
Program in:
social work (MSW)

■ ROGER WILLIAMS UNIVERSITY
Bristol, RI 02809
http://www.rwu.edu/

Independent, coed, comprehensive institution. *Enrollment:* 5,172 graduate, professional, and undergraduate students; 602 full-time matriculated graduate/professional students (298 women), 221 part-time matriculated graduate/professional students (132 women). *Graduate faculty:* 30 full-time (13 women), 7 part-time/adjunct (3 women). *Computer facilities:* Computer purchase and lease plans are available. 410 computers available on campus for general student use. A campuswide network can be accessed from student residence rooms and from off campus. Internet access and online class registration, telephone registration are available. *Library facilities:* Roger Williams University Library plus 2 others. *Graduate expenses:* Tuition: part-time $362 per credit. Tuition and fees vary according to program. *General application contact:* Suzanne Faubl, Director of Graduate Admissions, 401-254-3809.

Feinstein College of Arts and Sciences
Dr. Robert Cole, Interim Dean
Programs in:
arts and sciences (MA, MPA)
forensic psychology (MA)
public administration (MPA)

Ralph R. Papitto School of Law
David A. Logan, Dean
Program in:
law (JD)

School of Architecture, Art and Historic Preservation
Stephen White, Dean
Program in:
architecture (M Arch)

School of Education
Dr. Bruce Marlowe, Dean
Programs in:
education (MA, MAT)
elementary education (MAT)
literacy (MA)

School of Justice Studies
Stephanie Manzi, Dean
Program in:
criminal justice (MS)

■ SALVE REGINA UNIVERSITY
Newport, RI 02840-4192
http://www.salve.edu/

Independent-religious, coed, comprehensive institution. *Enrollment:* 2,589 graduate, professional, and undergraduate students; 76 full-time matriculated graduate/professional students (47 women), 333 part-time

Salve Regina University (continued)
matriculated graduate/professional students (183 women). *Graduate faculty:* 8 full-time (3 women), 32 part-time/adjunct (12 women). *Computer facilities:* 163 computers available on campus for general student use. A campuswide network can be accessed from student residence rooms and from off campus. Internet access is available. *Library facilities:* McKillop Library. *General application contact:* Karen E. Johnson, Graduate Admissions Counselor, 401-341-2153.

Find University Details at www.petersons.com/gradchannel.

Graduate Studies
Dr. Thomas M. Sabbagh, Dean
Programs in:
business administration (MBA)
business studies (Certificate)
expressive and creative arts (CAGS)
health services administration (MS, Certificate)
holistic counseling (MA)
homeland security (Certificate)
human resources management (Certificate)
humanities (MA, PhD)
international relations (MA, Certificate)
justice and homeland security (MS)
law enforcement leadership (MS, MSM)
management (Certificate)
mental health (CAGS)
mental health counseling (CAGS)
organizational development (Certificate)
rehabilitation counseling (MA)

■ UNIVERSITY OF RHODE ISLAND
Kingston, RI 02881
http://www.uri.edu

State-supported, coed, university. CGS member. *Enrollment:* 15,062 graduate, professional, and undergraduate students; 1,564 full-time matriculated graduate/professional students (958 women), 1,623 part-time matriculated graduate/professional students (1,067 women). *Graduate faculty:* 674 full-time, 32 part-time/adjunct. *Computer facilities:* 552 computers available on campus for general student use. A campuswide network can be accessed from off campus. *Library facilities:* University Library plus 1 other. *Graduate expenses:* Tuition, state resident: full-time $6,032; part-time $335 per credit. Tuition, nonresident: full-time $17,288; part-time $960 per credit. Required fees: $65 per credit. $30 per semester. One-time fee: $80 part-time. *General application contact:* Harold D. Bibb, Associate Dean of the Graduate School, 401-874-2262.

Graduate School
Karen Markin, Interim Vice Provost for Graduate Studies, Research and Outreach

College of Arts and Sciences
Winifed Brownell, Dean
Programs in:
applied mathematics (PhD)
arts and sciences (MA, MLIS, MM, MPA, MS, PhD, Certificate, Graduate Certificate)
behavioral science (PhD)
chemistry (MS, PhD)
clinical psychology (PhD)
computer science (MS, PhD)
digital forensics (Graduate Certificate)
English (MA, PhD)
history (MA)
library and information studies (MLIS)
mathematics (MS, PhD)
music (MM)
physics (MS, PhD)
political science (MA)
public policy and administration (MA, MPA, Certificate)
school psychology (MS, PhD)
Spanish (MA)
statistics (MS)

College of Business Administration
Mark Higgins, Dean
Programs in:
accounting (MS)
business administration (PhD)
finance (MBA, PhD)
international business (MBA)
international sports management (MBA)
management (MBA, PhD)
management science (MBA)
management sciences and information systems (PhD)
marketing (MBA, PhD)

College of Continuing Education
John McCray, Vice Provost for Urban Programs
Programs in:
clinical laboratory sciences (MS)
communication studies (MA)

College of Engineering
Bahram Nassersharif, Dean
Programs in:
chemical engineering (MS, PhD)
design/systems (MS, PhD)
electrical engineering (MS, PhD)
engineering (MS, MSCE, PhD)
environmental engineering (MSCE)
fluid mechanics (MS, PhD)
industrial and manufacturing engineering (PhD)
manufacturing systems engineering (MS)
ocean engineering (MS, PhD)
solid mechanics (MS, PhD)
structural engineering (MS, PhD)
thermal sciences (MS, PhD)
transportation engineering (MS, PhD)

College of Human Science and Services
W. Lynn McKinney, Dean
Programs in:
adult education (MA)
audiology (Au D)
college student personnel (MS)
elementary education (MA)
exercise science (MS)
human development and family studies (MS)
human science and services (MA, MM, MS, Au D, DPT)
marriage and family therapy (MS)
music education (MM)
physical education (MS)
physical therapy (DPT)
psychosocial aspects of physical activity and sport (MS)
reading education (MA)
secondary education (MA)
speech-language pathology (MS)
teaching and administration (MS)
textiles, fashion merchandising and design (MS)

College of Nursing
Dayle Joseph, Dean
Programs in:
administration (MS)
clinical specialist in gerontology (MS)
clinical specialist in psychiatric/mental health (MS)
family nurse practitioner (MS)
nurse midwifery (MS)
nursing (PhD)
nursing education (MS)

College of Pharmacy
Donald Letendre, Dean
Programs in:
biomedical and pharmaceutical sciences (MS, PhD)
medicinal chemistry and pharmacognosy (MS, PhD)
pharmaceutical sciences (MS, PhD)
pharmaceutics and pharmacokinetics (MS, PhD)
pharmacology and toxicology (MS, PhD)
pharmacy (Pharm D)
pharmacy practice (MS, PhD)

College of the Environment and Life Sciences
Jeffrey Seemann, Dean
Programs in:
animal health and disease (MS)
animal science (MS)
aquaculture (MS)
aquatic pathology (MS)
biochemistry (MS, PhD)
biological sciences (MS, PhD)
entomology (MS, PhD)
environment and life sciences (MA, MMA, MS, PhD)
environmental and natural resource economics (MS, PhD)
environmental sciences (PhD)
fisheries (MS)
food science (MS, PhD)
geosciences (MS)
marine affairs (MA, MMA, PhD)
microbiology (MS, PhD)
molecular genetics (MS, PhD)
nutrition (MS, PhD)
plant sciences (MS, PhD)

Graduate School of Oceanography
David Farmer, Dean
Program in:
oceanography (MO, MS, PhD)

Labor Research Center
Dr. Richard Scholl, Director
Programs in:
human resources (MS)
labor relations (MS)

South Carolina

■ BOB JONES UNIVERSITY
Greenville, SC 29614
http://www.bju.edu/

Independent-religious, coed, university. *Library facilities:* J.S. Mack plus 2 others.

■ CHARLESTON SOUTHERN UNIVERSITY
Charleston, SC 29423-8087
http://www.charlestonsouthern.edu/

Independent-religious, coed, comprehensive institution. *Computer facilities:* 190 computers available on campus for general student use. A campuswide network can be accessed from student residence rooms and from off campus. Internet access and online class registration, online course work are available. *Library facilities:* L. Mendel Rivers Library. *General application contact:* Vice President for Enrollment Management, 843-863-7050.

Program in Business
Programs in:
accounting (MBA)
finance (MBA)
health care administration (MBA)
information systems (MBA)
organizational development (MBA)

Program in Criminal Justice
Program in:
criminal justice (MSCJ)

Programs in Education
Programs in:
administration and supervision (M Ed)
elementary education (M Ed)
English (MAT)
science (MAT)
secondary education (M Ed)
social studies (MAT)

■ THE CITADEL, THE MILITARY COLLEGE OF SOUTH CAROLINA
Charleston, SC 29409
http://www.citadel.edu

State-supported, coed, comprehensive institution. *Enrollment:* 3,386 graduate, professional, and undergraduate students; 157 full-time matriculated graduate/professional students (108 women), 631 part-time matriculated graduate/professional students (346 women). *Graduate faculty:* 62 full-time (17 women), 19 part-time/adjunct (4 women). *Computer facilities:* 350 computers available on campus for general student use. A campuswide network can be accessed from student residence rooms and from off campus. Internet access and online class registration are available. *Library facilities:* Daniel Library. *Graduate expenses:* Tuition, state resident: part-time $259 per credit hour. Tuition, nonresident: part-time $482 per credit hour. *General application contact:* Dr. Raymond S. Jones, Associate Dean, College of Graduate and Professional Studies, 843-953-5089.

College of Graduate and Professional Studies
Brig. Gen. Harrison S. Carter, Provost/Dean of the College
Programs in:
biology (MA)
computer and information science (MS)
English (MA)
health, exercise, and sports science (MS)
history (MA)
physical education (MAT)
psychology (MA)
social science (MA)

School of Business Administration
Dr. Earl Walker, Head
Program in:
business administration (MBA)

School of Education
Dr. Tony Johnson, Head
Programs in:
education (M Ed, MA, MAT, Ed S)
educational administration (M Ed, Ed S)
guidance and counseling (M Ed)
reading (M Ed)
school psychology (MA, Ed S)
secondary education (MAT)

■ CLEMSON UNIVERSITY
Clemson, SC 29634
http://www.clemson.edu/

State-supported, coed, university. CGS member. *Enrollment:* 17,165 graduate, professional, and undergraduate students; 2,009 full-time matriculated graduate/professional students (849 women), 837 part-time matriculated graduate/professional students (452 women). *Graduate faculty:* 1,056 full-time (299 women), 90 part-time/adjunct (28 women). *Computer facilities:* Computer purchase and lease plans are available. 1,250 computers available on campus for general student use. A campuswide network can be accessed from student residence rooms and from off campus. Internet access and online class registration, wireless network are available. *Library facilities:* Robert Muldrow Cooper Library plus 1 other. *Graduate expenses:* Tuition, state resident: full-time $8,812; part-time $450 per hour. Tuition, nonresident: full-time $18,036; part-time $760 per hour. Required fees: $474; $5 per term. *General application contact:* Information Contact, 861-656-3195.

Find University Details at www.petersons.com/gradchannel.

Graduate School
Dr. J. Bruce Rafert, Dean
Programs in:
interdisciplinary studies (PhD, Certificate)
policy studies (PhD, Certificate)

College of Agriculture, Forestry and Life Sciences
Dr. Alan Sams, Dean
Programs in:
agricultural education (M Ag Ed)
agriculture, forestry and life sciences (M Ag Ed, MFR, MS, PhD)
animal and veterinary sciences (MS, PhD)
applied economics and statistics (MS)
biochemistry and molecular biology (MS, PhD)
biological sciences (MS, PhD)
biosystems engineering (MS, PhD)
environmental toxicology (MS, PhD)
food technology (PhD)
food, nutrition, and culinary science (MS)
forest resources (MFR, MS, PhD)
genetics (MS, PhD)
microbiology (MS, PhD)
packaging science (MS)
plant and environmental sciences (MS, PhD)
wildlife and fisheries biology (MS, PhD)
zoology (PhD)

College of Architecture, Arts, and Humanities
Dr. Janice Schach, Dean
Programs in:
architecture (M Arch, MS)
architecture, arts, and humanities (M Arch, MA, MCRP, MCSM, MFA, MLA, MRED, MS, PhD)
city and regional planning (MCRP)
construction science and management (MCSM)
developmental planning (MCRP)
digital production arts (MFA)
English (MA)
environmental design and planning (PhD)
historic preservation (MS)
history (MA)
landscape architecture (MLA)
professional communication (MA)
real estate development (MRED)
rhetorics, communication and information design (PhD)
visual arts (MFA)

College of Business and Behavioral Science
Dr. David Grigsby, Interim Dean

Clemson University (continued)
Programs in:
- accountancy and legal studies (MP Acc)
- applied economics (PhD)
- applied psychology (MS)
- applied sociology (MS)
- business administration (MBA)
- business and behavioral science (M E!Com, MA, MBA, MP Acc, MPA, MRED, MS, PhD)
- economics (MA)
- electronic commerce (M E!Com)
- graphic communications (MS)
- human factors psychology (PhD)
- industrial/organizational psychology (PhD)
- management (MS, PhD)
- marketing (MS)
- public administration (MPA)
- real estate development (MRED)

College of Engineering and Science
Dr. Esin Gulari, Dean
Programs in:
- applied and pure mathematics (MS, PhD)
- astronomy and astrophysics (MS, PhD)
- atmospheric physics (MS, PhD)
- automotive engineering (MS, PhD)
- bioengineering (MS, PhD)
- biophysics (MS, PhD)
- biosystems engineering (MS, PhD)
- chemical engineering (MS, PhD)
- chemistry (MS, PhD)
- civil engineering (MS, PhD)
- computational mathematics (MS, PhD)
- computer engineering (MS, PhD)
- computer science (MS, PhD)
- electrical engineering (M Engr, MS, PhD)
- engineering and science (M Engr, MS, PhD)
- environmental engineering and science (M Engr, MS, PhD)
- environmental health physics (MS)
- hydrogeology (MS)
- industrial engineering (MS, PhD)
- materials science and engineering (MS, PhD)
- mechanical engineering (MS, PhD)
- operations research (MS, PhD)
- physics (MS, PhD)
- polymer and fiber science (MS, PhD)
- statistics (MS, PhD)
- the environment (MS)

College of Health, Education, and Human Development
Dr. Larry Allen, Dean
Programs in:
- administration and supervision (M Ed, Ed S)
- community counseling (M Ed)
- counselor education (M Ed)
- curriculum and instruction (PhD)
- educational leadership (M Ed, PhD)
- elementary education (M Ed)
- English (M Ed)
- health, education, and human development (M Ed, MAT, MHRD, MPRTM, MS, PhD, Ed S)
- human resource development (MHRD)
- mathematics (M Ed)
- middle grades education (MAT)
- natural sciences (M Ed)
- nursing (MS)
- parks, recreation, and tourism management (MPRTM, MS, PhD)
- reading (M Ed)
- school counseling (M Ed)
- secondary education (M Ed)
- special education (M Ed)
- student affairs (M Ed)
- youth development (MS)

Institute on Family and Neighborhood Life
Dr. Sue Limber, Head
Programs in:
- family and neighborhood life (PhD)
- international and community studies (PhD)

■ COLLEGE OF CHARLESTON
Charleston, SC 29424-0001
http://www.cofc.edu/

State-supported, coed, comprehensive institution. *Computer facilities:* Computer purchase and lease plans are available. 578 computers available on campus for general student use. A campuswide network can be accessed from student residence rooms and from off campus. Internet access and online class registration are available. *Library facilities:* Marlene and Nathan Addlestone Library plus 1 other. *General application contact:* Assistant Director of Admissions, 843-953-5614.

Graduate School

School of Business and Economics
Programs in:
- accountancy (MS)
- business and economics (MS)

School of Education
Programs in:
- early childhood education (M Ed, MAT)
- education (M Ed, MAT, Certificate)
- elementary education (M Ed, MAT)
- English to speakers of other languages (Certificate)
- languages (M Ed)
- science and mathematics for teachers (M Ed)
- special education (M Ed)

School of Humanities and Social Sciences
Programs in:
- bilingual legal interpreting (MA, Certificate)
- English (MA)
- history (MA)
- humanities and social sciences (MA, MPA, Certificate)
- organizational and corporate communication (Certificate)
- public administration (MPA)

School of Sciences and Mathematics
Programs in:
- computer and information sciences (MS)
- environmental studies (MS)
- marine biology (MS)
- mathematics (MS, Certificate)
- sciences and mathematics (MS, Certificate)

■ COLUMBIA COLLEGE
Columbia, SC 29203-5998
http://www.columbiacollegesc.edu/

Independent-religious, Undergraduate: women only; graduate: coed, comprehensive institution. *Enrollment:* 1,446 graduate, professional, and undergraduate students; 234 full-time matriculated graduate/professional students (219 women), 69 part-time matriculated graduate/professional students (64 women). *Graduate faculty:* 5 full-time (3 women), 28 part-time/adjunct (17 women). *Computer facilities:* 150 computers available on campus for general student use. A campuswide network can be accessed. Internet access and online class registration, e-mail, data storage are available. *Library facilities:* J. Drake Edens Library plus 1 other. *Graduate expenses:* Tuition: part-time $300 per credit. *General application contact:* Carolyn Emeneker, Director of Graduate School and Evening College Admissions, 803-786-3766.

Graduate Programs
Dr. Laurie B. Hopkins, Provost and Vice President for Academic Affairs
Programs in:
- divergent learning (M Ed)
- human behavior and conflict management (MA)
- interpersonal relations/conflict management (Certificate)
- organizational behavior/conflict management (Certificate)

■ CONVERSE COLLEGE
Spartanburg, SC 29302-0006
http://www.converse.edu/

Independent, Undergraduate: women only; graduate: coed, comprehensive institution. *Enrollment:* 1,977 graduate, professional, and undergraduate students; 156 full-time matriculated graduate/professional students (136 women), 1,069 part-time matriculated graduate/professional students (847 women). *Graduate faculty:* 35 full-time (16 women), 17 part-time/adjunct (8 women). *Computer facilities:* 72 computers available on campus for general student use. A campuswide network can be accessed from student residence rooms and from off campus. Internet access and online class registration are available. *Library facilities:* Mickel Library. *Graduate expenses:* Tuition: part-time $305 per credit hour. Required fees: $20 per term. *General application contact:* Thomas M. Faulkenberry, Dr., 864-596-9082.

Carroll McDaniel Petrie School of Music

Dr. Scott M. Robbins, Sr., Interim Dean
Programs in:
- instrumental performance (M Mus)
- music education (M Mus)
- piano pedagogy (M Mus)
- vocal performance (M Mus)

School of Education and Graduate Studies

Thomas M. Faulkenberry, Dean of the School of Education and Graduate Studies
Programs in:
- administration and supervision (Ed S)
- art education (M Ed)
- biology (MAT)
- chemistry (MAT)
- curriculum and instruction (Ed S)
- early childhood education (MAT)
- education (Ed S)
- elementary education (M Ed, MAT)
- English (M Ed, MAT, MLA)
- gifted education (M Ed)
- history (MLA)
- leadership (M Ed)
- learning disabilities (MAT)
- liberal arts (MLA)
- marriage and family therapy (Ed S)
- mathematics (M Ed, MAT)
- mental disabilities (MAT)
- natural sciences (M Ed)
- political science (MLA)
- secondary education (M Ed, MAT)
- social sciences (M Ed, MAT)
- special education (M Ed, MAT)

■ FRANCIS MARION UNIVERSITY
Florence, SC 29501-0547
http://www.fmarion.edu/

State-supported, coed, comprehensive institution. *Enrollment:* 4,075 graduate, professional, and undergraduate students; 33 full-time matriculated graduate/professional students (27 women), 235 part-time matriculated graduate/professional students (192 women). *Graduate faculty:* 117 full-time (33 women), 8 part-time/adjunct (5 women). *Computer facilities:* 551 computers available on campus for general student use. A campuswide network can be accessed from student residence rooms and from off campus. Internet access and online class registration, Blackboard are available. *Library facilities:* James A. Rogers Library plus 1 other. *Graduate expenses:* Tuition, state resident: full-time $6,527; part-time $326 per credit hour. Tuition, nonresident: full-time $13,054; part-time $653 per credit hour. Required fees: $185; $5 per credit hour. $45 per term. *General application contact:* Rannie Gamble, Administrative Manager, 843-661-1286.

Graduate Programs

Provost's Office
Programs in:
- applied clinical psychology (MS)
- applied community psychology (MS)
- school psychology (MS)

School of Business

Dr. M. Barry O'Brien, Dean
Programs in:
- business (MBA)
- health management (MBA)

School of Education

Dr. James R. Faulkenberry, Dean
Programs in:
- early childhood education (M Ed)
- elementary education (M Ed)
- learning disabilities (M Ed, MAT)
- remedial education (M Ed)
- secondary education (M Ed)

■ FURMAN UNIVERSITY
Greenville, SC 29613
http://www.furman.edu/

Independent, coed, comprehensive institution. *Enrollment:* 3,010 graduate, professional, and undergraduate students; 115 full-time matriculated graduate/professional students (89 women), 76 part-time matriculated graduate/professional students (61 women). *Graduate faculty:* 26 full-time (15 women), 19 part-time/adjunct (15 women). *Computer facilities:* 340 computers available on campus for general student use. A campuswide network can be accessed from student residence rooms and from off campus. Internet access and online class registration are available. *Library facilities:* James Buchanan Duke Library plus 2 others. *Graduate expenses:* Tuition: part-time $347 per credit. *General application contact:* Troy M. Terry, Director of Graduate Studies, 864-294-2213.

Graduate Division

Troy M. Terry, Director of Graduate Studies
Programs in:
- chemistry (MS)
- early childhood education (MA)
- elementary education (MA)
- English as a second language (MA)
- middle school education (MA)
- reading (MA)
- school administration (MA)
- special education (MA)

■ SOUTH CAROLINA STATE UNIVERSITY
Orangeburg, SC 29117-0001
http://www.scsu.edu/

State-supported, coed, comprehensive institution. CGS member. *Enrollment:* 4,384 graduate, professional, and undergraduate students; 226 full-time matriculated graduate/professional students (167 women), 272 part-time matriculated graduate/professional students (201 women). *Graduate faculty:* 61 full-time (30 women), 13 part-time/adjunct (5 women). *Computer facilities:* 300 computers available on campus for general student use. A campuswide network can be accessed. Internet access is available. *Library facilities:* Miller F. Whittaker Library. *Graduate expenses:* Tuition, state resident: full-time $7,278. Tuition, nonresident: full-time $14,322. *General application contact:* Dr. Thomas Thompson, Dean of the School of Graduate Studies, 803-516-4734.

School of Graduate Studies

Dr. Thomas Thompson, Dean of the School of Graduate Studies
Programs in:
- agribusiness (MS)
- agribusiness and entrepreneurship (MBA)
- civil and mechanical engineering (MA, MS)
- early childhood and special education (M Ed)
- early childhood education (MAT)
- educational leadership (Ed D, Ed S)
- elementary counselor education (M Ed)
- elementary education (M Ed, MAT)
- engineering (MAT)
- general science (MAT)
- individual and family development (MS)
- mathematics (MAT)
- nutritional sciences (MS)
- rehabilitation counseling (MA)
- secondary counselor education (M Ed)
- secondary education (M Ed)
- special education (M Ed)
- speech/language pathology (MA)

■ SOUTHERN WESLEYAN UNIVERSITY
Central, SC 29630-1020
http://www.swu.edu/

Independent-religious, coed, comprehensive institution. *Computer facilities:* 92 computers available on campus for general student use. A campuswide network can be accessed from student residence rooms and from off campus. Internet access and online class registration are available. *Library facilities:* Rickman Library. *General application contact:* Regional Enrollment Manager, 800-345-4998.

Southern Wesleyan University (continued)

Program in Business Administration

Program in:
business administration (MBA)

Program in Christian Ministries

Program in:
Christian ministries (M Min)

Program in Education

Program in:
education (M Ed)

Program in Management

Program in:
management (MSM)

■ UNIVERSITY OF SOUTH CAROLINA

Columbia, SC 29208

http://www.sc.edu/

State-supported, coed, university. CGS member. *Computer facilities:* 2,432 computers available on campus for general student use. A campuswide network can be accessed from student residence rooms and from off campus. Internet access and online class registration are available. *Library facilities:* Thomas Cooper Library plus 7 others. *General application contact:* Director of Graduate Admissions, 803-777-4243.

Find University Details at www.petersons.com/gradchannel.

College of Pharmacy

Programs in:
pharmaceutical sciences (MS, PhD)
pharmacy (Pharm D, MS, PhD)

The Graduate School

Programs in:
biology (MS, PhD)
biology education (IMA, MAT)
ecology, evolution and organismal biology (MS, PhD)
gerontology (Certificate)
mathematics (MA, MS, PhD)
mathematics education (M Math, MAT)
molecular, cellular, and developmental biology (MS, PhD)

Arnold School of Public Health

Programs in:
alcohol and drug studies (Certificate)
biostatistics (MPH, MSPH, Dr PH, PhD)
communication sciences and disorders (MCD, MSP, PhD)
environmental health science (MS)
environmental quality (MPH, MSPH, PhD)
epidemiology (MPH, MSPH, Dr PH, PhD)
exercise science (MS, DPT, PhD)
general public health (MPH)
hazardous materials management (MPH, MSPH, PhD)
health education administration (Ed D)
health promotion and education (MAT, MPH, MS, MSPH, Dr PH, PhD)
health services policy and management (MHA, MPH, Dr PH, PhD)
industrial hygiene (MPH, MSPH, PhD)
physical activity and public health (MPH)
public health (MAT, MCD, MHA, MPH, MS, MSP, MSPH, DPT, Dr PH, Ed D, PhD, Certificate)
school health education (Certificate)

College of Arts and Sciences

Programs in:
anthropology (MA, PhD)
applied statistics (CAS)
archives (MA)
art education (IMA, MA, MAT)
art history (MA)
art studio (MA)
arts and sciences (IMA, MA, MAT, MFA, MIS, MMA, MPA, MS, PMS, PSM, PhD, CAS, Certificate)
chemistry and biochemistry (IMA, MAT, MS, PhD)
clinical/community psychology (MA, PhD)
comparative literature (MA, PhD)
creative writing (MFA)
criminology and criminal justice (MA)
English (MA, PhD)
English education (MAT)
environmental geoscience (PMS)
experimental psychology (MA, PhD)
foreign languages (MAT)
French (MA)
general psychology (MA)
geography (MA, MS, PhD)
geography education (IMA)
geological sciences (MS, PhD)
German (MA)
historic preservation (MA)
history (MA, PhD)
history education (IMA, MAT)
industrial statistics (MIS)
international studies (MA, PhD)
linguistics (MA, PhD)
marine science (MS, PhD)
media arts (MMA)
museum (MA)
museum management (Certificate)
philosophy (MA, PhD)
physics and astronomy (IMA, MAT, MS, PSM, PhD)
political science (MA, PhD)
public administration (MPA)
public history (MA, Certificate)
religious studies (MA)
school psychology (PhD)
sociology (MA, PhD)
Spanish (MA)
statistics (MS, PhD)
studio art (MFA)
teaching English to speakers of other languages (Certificate)
theater (IMA, MA, MAT, MFA)
women's studies (Certificate)

College of Education

Programs in:
art education (IMA, MAT)
business education (IMA, MAT)
community and adult education (M Ed)
counseling education (PhD, Ed S)
curriculum and instruction (Ed D)
early childhood education (M Ed, MAT, PhD)
education (IMA, M Ed, MA, MAT, MS, MT, Ed D, PhD, Certificate, Ed S)
educational administration (M Ed, MA, PhD, Ed S)
educational psychology, research (M Ed, PhD)
educational technology (M Ed)
elementary education (M Ed, MAT, PhD)
English (MAT)
foreign language (MAT)
foundations in education (PhD)
health education (MAT)
health education administration (Ed D)
higher education and student affairs (M Ed)
higher education leadership (Certificate)
language and literacy (M Ed, PhD)
mathematics (MAT)
physical education (IMA, MAT, MS, PhD)
science (IMA, MAT)
secondary education (IMA, M Ed, MA, MAT, MT, PhD)
social studies (IMA, MAT)
special education (M Ed, MAT, PhD)
teaching (Ed S)
theatre and speech (IMA, MAT)

College of Engineering and Information Technology

Programs in:
chemical engineering (ME, MS, PhD)
civil engineering (ME, MS, PhD)
computer science and engineering (ME, MS, PhD)
electrical engineering (ME, MS, PhD)
engineering and information technology (ME, MS, PhD)
mechanical engineering (ME, MS, PhD)
software engineering (MS)

College of Hospitality, Retail, and Sport Management

Programs in:
hospitality, retail, and sport management (MHRTM, MS)
hotel, restaurant and tourism management (MHRTM)
live sport and entertainment events (MS)
public assembly facilities management (MS)
retailing (MS)

College of Mass Communications and Information Studies

Programs in:
journalism and mass communications (MA, MMC, PhD)

library and information science (MLIS, Certificate, Specialist)
mass communication and information studies (MA, MLIS, MMC, PhD, Certificate, Specialist)

College of Nursing
Programs in:
acute care clinical specialist (MSN)
acute care nurse practitioner (MSN, Certificate)
adult nurse practitioner (MSN)
advanced practice clinical nursing (MSN, Certificate)
advanced practice nursing in primary care (MSN, Certificate)
advanced practice nursing in psychiatric mental health (MSN, Certificate)
clinical nursing (MSN)
community mental health and psychiatric health nursing (MSN)
community/public health clinical nurse specialist (MSN)
family nurse practitioner (MSN)
health nursing (MSN)
nursing administration (MSN)
nursing practice (DNP)
nursing science (PhD)
pediatric nurse practitioner (MSN)
psychiatric/mental health nurse practitioner (MSN)
psychiatric/mental health specialist (MSN)
women's health nurse practitioner (MSN)

College of Social Work
Program in:
social work (MSW, PhD)

The Darla Moore School of Business
Programs in:
accountancy (M Acc)
business administration (PMBA, PhD)
business measurement and assurance (M Acc)
economics (MA, PhD)
human resources (MHR)
international business administration (IMBA)

School of Music
Programs in:
composition (MM, DMA)
conducting (MM, DMA)
jazz studies (MM)
music education (MM Ed, PhD)
music history (MM)
music performance (Certificate)
music theory (MM)
opera theater (MM)
performance (MM, DMA)
piano pedagogy (MM, DMA)

School of the Environment
Programs in:
earth and environmental resources management (MEERM)
environment (MEERM)

School of Law
Program in:
law (JD)

School of Medicine
Programs in:
biomedical science (MBS, PhD)
genetic counseling (MS)
medicine (MD, MBS, MNA, MRC, MS, PhD, Certificate)
nurse anesthesia (MNA)
psychiatric rehabilitation (Certificate)
rehabilitation counseling (MRC, Certificate)

■ WINTHROP UNIVERSITY
Rock Hill, SC 29733
http://www.winthrop.edu/

State-supported, coed, comprehensive institution. *Enrollment:* 6,292 graduate, professional, and undergraduate students; 306 full-time matriculated graduate/professional students (189 women), 395 part-time matriculated graduate/professional students (279 women). *Graduate faculty:* 144 full-time (64 women), 79 part-time/adjunct (43 women). *Computer facilities:* 250 computers available on campus for general student use. A campuswide network can be accessed from student residence rooms and from off campus. Internet access is available. *Library facilities:* Dacus Library. *Graduate expenses:* Tuition, state resident: full-time $9,148; part-time $383 per hour. Tuition, nonresident: full-time $16,864; part-time $704 per hour. *General application contact:* Information Contact, 800-411-7041.

College of Arts and Sciences
Dr. Debra C. Boyd, Dean
Programs in:
arts and sciences (MA, MLA, MS, SSP)
biology (MS)
English (MA)
history (MA)
human nutrition (MS)
liberal arts (MLA)
psychology (MS, SSP)
social work (MA)
Spanish (MA)

College of Business Administration
Dr. Roger Weikle, Dean
Programs in:
business administration (MBA, MS, Certificate)
software development (MS)
software project management (Certificate)

College of Education
Dr. Patricia Graham, Dean
Programs in:
agency counseling (M Ed)
education (M Ed, MAT, MS)
educational leadership (M Ed)
middle level education (M Ed)
physical education (MS)
reading education (M Ed)
school counseling (M Ed)
secondary education (M Ed, MAT)
special education (M Ed)

College of Visual and Performing Arts
Dr. Elizabeth Patenaude, Dean
Programs in:
art (MFA)
art administration (MA)
art education (MA)
conducting (MM)
music education (MME)
performance (MM)
visual and performing arts (MA, MFA, MM, MME)

South Dakota

■ COLORADO TECHNICAL UNIVERSITY—SIOUX FALLS
Sioux Falls, SD 57108
http://www.ctu-siouxfalls.com/

Proprietary, coed, comprehensive institution. *Computer facilities:* Computer purchase and lease plans are available. 55 computers available on campus for general student use. A campuswide network can be accessed from off campus. Internet access is available. *Library facilities:* Resource Center. *General application contact:* Admissions Manager, 605-361-0200 Ext. 103.

Program in Computing
Programs in:
computer systems security (MSCS)
software engineering (MSCS)

Program in Criminal Justice
Program in:
criminal justice (MSM)

Programs in Business Administration and Management
Programs in:
business administration (MBA)
business management (MSM)
health science management (MSM)
human resources management (MSM)
information technology (MSM)
organizational leadership (MSM)
project management (MBA)
technology management (MBA)

■ MOUNT MARTY COLLEGE
Yankton, SD 57078-3724
http://www.mtmc.edu/

Independent-religious, coed, comprehensive institution. *Enrollment:* 1,220 graduate, professional, and undergraduate students; 70 full-time matriculated graduate/professional students (42 women). *Graduate faculty:* 4 full-time (3 women), 1 part-time/adjunct (0 women). *Computer facilities:* Computer purchase and lease plans are available. 21

Mount Marty College (continued)
computers available on campus for general student use. A campuswide network can be accessed from student residence rooms and from off campus. Internet access is available. *Library facilities:* Mount Marty College Library. *General application contact:* Brandi Tschumper, Vice President of Enrollment, 800-658-4552.

Graduate Studies Division
Brandi Tschumper, Vice President of Enrollment
Programs in:
business administration (MBA)
nurse anesthesia (MS)
pastoral ministries (MPM)

■ SOUTH DAKOTA STATE UNIVERSITY
Brookings, SD 57007
http://www.sdstate.edu/

State-supported, coed, university. CGS member. *Enrollment:* 11,303 graduate, professional, and undergraduate students; 317 full-time matriculated graduate/professional students (155 women), 964 part-time matriculated graduate/professional students (585 women). *Computer facilities:* 1,022 computers available on campus for general student use. A campuswide network can be accessed from student residence rooms and from off campus. Internet access and online class registration are available. *Library facilities:* H. M. Briggs Library. *General application contact:* Traci Johnson, Application Contact, 605-688-4181.

Graduate School
Dr. Kevin Kephart, Dean

College of Agriculture and Biological Sciences
Dr. Fred Cholick, Dean
Programs in:
agriculture and biological sciences (MS, PhD)
agronomy (PhD)
animal science (MS, PhD)
animal sciences (MS, PhD)
biological science (MS, PhD)
biological sciences (MS, PhD)
economics (MS)
plant science (MS)
rural sociology (MS)
sociology (PhD)
wildlife and fisheries sciences (MS, PhD)

College of Arts and Science
Dr. Herbert Cheever, Dean
Programs in:
arts and science (MA, MS, PhD)
chemistry (MS, PhD)
communication studies and journalism (MS)
English (MA)
geography (MS)
health, physical education and recreation (MS)

College of Education and Counseling
Dr. Dee Hopkins, Dean
Programs in:
counseling and human resource development (MS)
curriculum and instruction (M Ed)
education and counseling (M Ed, MS)
educational administration (M Ed)

College of Engineering
Dr. Duane Sander, Dean
Programs in:
biological sciences (MS, PhD)
computational science and statistics (PhD)
electrical engineering (PhD)
engineering (MS)
geospatial science and engineering (PhD)
industrial management (MS)
mathematics (MS)

College of Family and Consumer Sciences
Dr. Laurie Stenberg Nichols, Dean
Programs in:
apparel merchandising and interior design (MFCS)
family and consumer sciences (MFCS)
human development, consumer and family sciences (MFCS)
nutrition, food science and hospitality (MFCS)

College of Nursing
Dr. Sandra J. Bunkers, Department Head, Graduate Nursing
Program in:
nursing (MS, PhD)

College of Pharmacy
Dr. Danny Lattin, Dean
Programs in:
biological science (MS, PhD)
pharmacy (Pharm D, MS, PhD)

■ UNIVERSITY OF SIOUX FALLS
Sioux Falls, SD 57105-1699
http://www.usiouxfalls.edu/

Independent-religious, coed, comprehensive institution. *Enrollment:* 1,675 graduate, professional, and undergraduate students; 405 part-time matriculated graduate/professional students (245 women). *Graduate faculty:* 20 full-time (11 women), 20 part-time/adjunct (9 women). *Computer facilities:* 150 computers available on campus for general student use. A campuswide network can be accessed from student residence rooms and from off campus. Internet access is available. *Library facilities:* Norman B. Mears Library. *Graduate expenses:* Tuition: part-time $300 per semester hour. Required fees: $15 per term. Part-time tuition and fees vary according to program. *General application contact:* Student Contact, 605-331-5000.

Program in Business Administration
Rebecca T. Murdock, Director
Program in:
business administration (MBA)

Program in Education
Dawn Olson, Director of Graduate Education
Programs in:
leadership (M Ed)
reading (M Ed)
superintendent (Ed S)
teaching (M Ed)
technology (M Ed)

■ THE UNIVERSITY OF SOUTH DAKOTA
Vermillion, SD 57069-2390
http://www.usd.edu/

State-supported, coed, university. *Enrollment:* 8,746 graduate, professional, and undergraduate students; 2,233 matriculated graduate/professional students. *Graduate faculty:* 422 full-time, 41 part-time/adjunct. *Computer facilities:* 834 computers available on campus for general student use. A campuswide network can be accessed from student residence rooms and from off campus. Internet access and online class registration are available. *Library facilities:* I. D. Weeks Library plus 2 others. *Graduate expenses:* Tuition, state resident: part-time $120 per credit hour. Tuition, nonresident: part-time $355 per credit hour. Required fees: $90 per credit hour. *General application contact:* Jane M Olson, Registration Officer, 605-677-6287.

Find University Details at www.petersons.com/gradchannel.

Graduate School
Dr. Karen L Olmstead, Dean
Programs in:
administrative studies (MS)
interdisciplinary studies (MA)

College of Arts and Sciences
Dr. Matthew Moen, Dean
Programs in:
arts and sciences (MA, MNS, MPA, MS, Au D, PhD)
audiology (Au D)
biology (MA, MNS, MS, PhD)
chemistry (MA, MNS)
clinical psychology (MA, PhD)
communication studies (MA)
communications disorders (MA)
computational sciences and statistics (PhD)
computer science (MA)
English (MA, PhD)
history (MA)
human factors (MA, PhD)
mathematics (MA, MNS)
political science (MA)
public administration (MPA)
speech-language pathology (MA)

College of Fine Arts
Daniel Guyette, Dean
Programs in:
art (MFA)
fine arts (MA, MFA, MM)
music (MM)
theatre (MA, MFA)

School of Business
Dean Michael Keller, Dean
Programs in:
business (MBA, MP Acc)
business administration (MBA)
professional accountancy (MP Acc)

School of Education
Dr. Jeri Engelking, Campus Dean
Programs in:
counseling and psychology in education (MA, PhD, Ed S)
curriculum and instruction (Ed D, Ed S)
education (MA, MS, Ed D, PhD, Ed S)
educational administration (MA, Ed D, Ed S)
elementary education (MA)
health, physical education and recreation (MA)
secondary education (MA)
special education (MA)
technology for education and training (MS, Ed S)

School of Law
Barry R. Vickrey, Dean
Program in:
law (JD)

School of Medicine and Health Sciences
Dr. Rodney R. Parry, Dean
Programs in:
cardiovascular research (MS, PhD)
cellular and molecular biology (MS, PhD)
medicine (MD)
medicine and health science (MD, MS, DPT, PhD)
molecular microbiology and immunology (MS, PhD)
neuroscience (MS, PhD)
occupational therapy (MS)
physical therapy (MS, DPT)
physician assistant studies (MS)
physiology and pharmacology (MS, PhD)

Tennessee

■ AUSTIN PEAY STATE UNIVERSITY
Clarksville, TN 37044
http://www.apsu.edu/

State-supported, coed, comprehensive institution. CGS member. *Enrollment:* 9,207 graduate, professional, and undergraduate students; 228 full-time matriculated graduate/professional students (164 women), 488 part-time matriculated graduate/professional students (356 women). *Graduate faculty:* 109 full-time (46 women), 21 part-time/adjunct (10 women). *Computer facilities:* Computer purchase and lease plans are available. 650 computers available on campus for general student use. A campuswide network can be accessed from student residence rooms and from off campus. Internet access and online class registration are available. *Library facilities:* Felix G. Woodward Library. *Graduate expenses:* Tuition, state resident: full-time $5,138; part-time $272 per credit hour. Tuition, nonresident: full-time $14,832; part-time $693 per credit hour. Required fees: $1,009. *General application contact:* Dr. Charles Pinder, Dean, College of Graduate Studies, 931-221-7414.

College of Graduate Studies
Dr. Charles Pinder, Dean, College of Graduate Studies

College of Arts and Letters
James Diehr, Dean
Programs in:
arts and letters (M Mu, MA)
communication arts (MA)
English (MA)
military history (MA)
music education (M Mu)
performance (M Mu)

College of Professional Programs and Social Sciences
Dr. David Denton, Dean
Programs in:
curriculum and instruction (MA Ed)
education (M Ed, Ed S)
educational leadership studies (MA Ed)
guidance and counseling (MS)
health and physical education (MS)
management (MS)
nursing (MS)
psychology (MA)
reading (MA Ed)
social sciences (M Ed, MA, MA Ed, MS, Ed S)

College of Science and Mathematics
Dr. Susan Calovini, Interim Dean
Programs in:
biology (MS)
science and mathematics (MS)

■ BELMONT UNIVERSITY
Nashville, TN 37212-3757
http://www.belmont.edu/

Independent-religious, coed, comprehensive institution. *Enrollment:* 4,481 graduate, professional, and undergraduate students; 302 full-time matriculated graduate/professional students (236 women), 405 part-time matriculated graduate/professional students (221 women). *Graduate faculty:* 89 full-time (47 women), 52 part-time/adjunct (33 women). *Computer facilities:* 350 computers available on campus for general student use. A campuswide network can be accessed from student residence rooms and from off campus. Internet access and online class registration, individual student information via BANNER Web are available. *Library facilities:* Lila D. Bunch Library. *General application contact:* Dr. Kathryn Baugher, Dean of Enrollment Services, 615-460-6785.

College of Arts and Sciences
Dr. Larry M. Hall, Dean
Programs in:
arts and sciences (M Ed, MA, MAT, MSA)
literature (MA)
writing (MA)

School of Education
Dr. Trevor F. Hutchins, Associate Dean
Programs in:
education (MAT)
elementary education (M Ed)
English (M Ed)
history (M Ed)
mathematics (M Ed)
middle grade education (M Ed)
science (M Ed)
secondary education (M Ed)
sports administration (MSA)
technology (M Ed)

College of Health Sciences
Dr. Debra B. Wollaber, Dean
Program in:
health sciences (MSN, MSOT, DPT, OTD)

School of Nursing
Dr. Leslie J. Higgins, Director, Graduate Program
Program in:
nursing (MSN)

School of Occupational Therapy
Dr. Ruth Ford, Associate Dean
Program in:
occupational therapy (MSOT, OTD)

School of Physical Therapy
Dr. John S. Halle, Associate Dean
Program in:
physical therapy (DPT)

College of Visual and Performing Arts
Dr. Cynthia R. Curtis, Dean
Program in:
visual and performing arts (MM)

School of Music
Dr. Robert Gregg, Director
Programs in:
church music (MM)
composition (MM)
music education (MM)
pedagogy (MM)
performance (MM)

Jack C. Massey Graduate School of Business
Dr. Patrick Raines, Dean
Program in:
business (M Acc, MBA)

■ BETHEL COLLEGE
McKenzie, TN 38201
http://www.bethel-college.edu/

Independent-religious, coed, comprehensive institution. *Computer facilities:* Computer purchase and lease plans are available. 8 computers available on campus for general student use. A campuswide network can be accessed from student residence rooms. Internet access, each student receives a laptop computer are available. *Library facilities:* Burroughs Learning Center. *General application contact:* Chair, Division of Education and Health Sciences, 731-352-4025.

Program in Education
Programs in:
- administration and supervision (MA Ed)
- biology education K8-12 (MAT)
- elementary education (MAT)
- English education K8-12 (MAT)
- history education K8-12 (MAT)
- physical education K8-12 (MAT)
- special education K8-12 (MAT)

■ CARSON-NEWMAN COLLEGE
Jefferson City, TN 37760
http://www.cn.edu/

Independent-religious, coed, comprehensive institution. *Enrollment:* 1,949 graduate, professional, and undergraduate students; 98 full-time matriculated graduate/professional students (78 women), 52 part-time matriculated graduate/professional students (40 women). *Graduate faculty:* 7 full-time (4 women), 20 part-time/adjunct (12 women). *Computer facilities:* 200 computers available on campus for general student use. A campuswide network can be accessed from student residence rooms and from off campus. Internet access is available. *Library facilities:* Stephens-Burnett Library plus 1 other. *Graduate expenses:* Tuition: part-time $270 per credit hour. *General application contact:* Graduate Admissions and Services Adviser, 865-473-3468.

Department of Nursing
Dr. Patricia Kraft, Dean and Chair
Program in:
- family nurse practitioner (MSN)

Graduate Program in Education
Dr. Jean Love, Chair
Programs in:
- curriculum and instruction (M Ed)
- elementary education (MAT)
- school counseling (M Ed)
- secondary education (MAT)
- teaching English as a second language (MATESL)

■ CHRISTIAN BROTHERS UNIVERSITY
Memphis, TN 38104-5581
http://www.cbu.edu/

Independent-religious, coed, comprehensive institution. *Enrollment:* 1,776 graduate, professional, and undergraduate students; 60 full-time matriculated graduate/professional students (39 women), 261 part-time matriculated graduate/professional students (158 women). *Graduate faculty:* 19 full-time (8 women), 13 part-time/adjunct (6 women). *Computer facilities:* 300 computers available on campus for general student use. A campuswide network can be accessed from student residence rooms and from off campus. Internet access and online class registration, online class listings, e-mail, course assignments are available. *Library facilities:* Plough Memorial Library and Media Center. *General application contact:* Tonna R. Bruce, Dean, Graduate and Professional Studies Programs, 901-321-3296.

Graduate Programs

School of Arts
Dr. Marins Carriere, Dean
Programs in:
- Catholic studies (MACS)
- curriculum and instruction (M Ed)
- educational leadership (MSEL)
- teacher-leadership (M Ed)
- teaching (MAT)

School of Business
Dr. Mike R. Ryan, Dean
Programs in:
- business (MBA)
- executive leadership (MAEL)
- financial planning (Certificate)
- project management (Certificate)

School of Engineering
Dr. Eric B Welch, Dean
Program in:
- engineering (MEM, MSEM)

■ CUMBERLAND UNIVERSITY
Lebanon, TN 37087-3408
http://www.cumberland.edu/

Independent, coed, comprehensive institution. *Enrollment:* 1,345 graduate, professional, and undergraduate students; 33 full-time matriculated graduate/professional students (23 women), 275 part-time matriculated graduate/professional students (188 women). *Graduate faculty:* 11 full-time (4 women), 14 part-time/adjunct (5 women). *Computer facilities:* 150 computers available on campus for general student use. A campuswide network can be accessed from student residence rooms and from off campus. Internet access is available. *Library facilities:* Doris and Harry Vise Library. *Graduate expenses:* Tuition: full-time $10,890; part-time $605 per credit. *General application contact:* Eddie Pawlawski, Vice President for Enrollment Management, 615-444-2562 Ext. 1225.

Program in Business Administration
Dr. Paul Stumb, Dean of the Labry School of Business
Program in:
- business administration (MBA)

Program in Education
Dr. Kenneth C. Collier, Dean, School of Education
Program in:
- education (MAE)

Program in Organizational Leadership and Human Relations Management
Dr. William R. Cheatham, Associate Professor, Criminal Justice
Program in:
- organizational leadership and human relations management (MS)

Program in Public Service Administration
Dr. C. William McKee, Professor
Program in:
- public service administration (MS)

■ EAST TENNESSEE STATE UNIVERSITY
Johnson City, TN 37614
http://www.etsu.edu/

State-supported, coed, university. CGS member. *Computer facilities:* Computer purchase and lease plans are available. 550 computers available on campus for general student use. A campuswide network can be accessed. Internet access and online class registration are available. *Library facilities:* Sherrod Library plus 2 others. *General application contact:* Assistant Dean, 423-439-4221.

Find University Details at www.petersons.com/gradchannel.

James H. Quillen College of Medicine
Programs in:
- anatomy (MS, PhD)
- biochemistry (MS, PhD)
- biophysics (MS, PhD)
- medicine (MD, MS, PhD)
- microbiology (MS, PhD)
- pharmacology (MS, PhD)
- physiology (MS, PhD)

School of Graduate Studies

College of Arts and Sciences
Programs in:
- applied sociology (MA)
- art education (MA)
- art history (MA)

arts and sciences (MA, MFA, MS, MSW)
biology (MS)
chemistry (MS)
clinical psychology (MA)
communication (MA)
criminal justice and criminology (MA)
English (MA)
general psychology (MA)
general sociology (MA)
history (MA)
mathematics (MS)
microbiology (MS)
social work (MSW)
studio art (MA, MFA)

College of Business and Technology
Programs in:
accountancy (M Acc)
business administration (MBA, Certificate)
business and technology (M Acc, MBA, MCM, MPM, MS, Certificate)
city management (MCM)
clinical nutrition (MS)
community development (MPM)
computer science (MS)
digital media (MS)
engineering technology (MS)
general administration (MPM)
health care management (Certificate)
industrial arts/technology education (MS)
information systems science (MS)
municipal service management (MPM)
software engineering (MS)
urban and regional economic development (MPM)
urban and regional planning (MPM)

College of Education
Programs in:
7-12 (MAT)
administrative endorsement (M Ed, Ed D, Ed S)
advanced practitioner (M Ed)
classroom leadership (Ed D)
classroom technology (M Ed)
community agency counseling (M Ed, MA)
comprehensive concentration (M Ed)
counseling (M Ed, MA)
early childhood education (M Ed, MA)
early childhood general (M Ed)
early childhood special education (M Ed)
early childhood teaching (M Ed)
education (M Ed, MA, MAT, Ed D, Ed S)
educational communication (M Ed)
educational leadership (M Ed, Ed D, Ed S)
educational media/educational technology (M Ed)
elementary and secondary (school counseling) (M Ed, MA)
elementary education (M Ed, MAT)
exercise physiology (MA)
fitness leadership (MA)
K-12 (MAT)
marriage and family therapy (M Ed, MA)
modified concentration (M Ed)
physical education (M Ed, MA)
post secondary and private sector leadership (Ed D)
reading and storytelling (M Ed, MA)
reading education (M Ed, MA)
school leadership (Ed D)
school library media (M Ed)
school system leadership (Ed S)
secondary education (M Ed, MAT)
sports management (MA)
sports sciences (MA)
teacher leadership (Ed S)

College of Nursing
Programs in:
advanced nursing practice (Post Master's Certificate)
health care management (Certificate)
nursing (MSN, DSN)

College of Public and Allied Health
Programs in:
audiology (MS, Au D)
communicative disorders (MS)
community health (MPH)
environmental health (MSEH)
epidemiology (Certificate)
gerontology (Certificate)
health care management (Certificate)
physical therapy (DPT)
public and allied health (MPH, MS, MSEH, Au D, DPT, Certificate)
public health (MPH)
public health administration (MPH)
special education audiology pre-K-12 (MS)
special education speech pathology pre-K-12 (MS)
speech pathology (MS)

Division of Cross-Disciplinary Studies
Program in:
liberal studies (MALS)

■ FREED-HARDEMAN UNIVERSITY
Henderson, TN 38340-2399
http://www.fhu.edu/

Independent-religious, coed, comprehensive institution. *Enrollment:* 1,969 graduate, professional, and undergraduate students; 97 full-time matriculated graduate/professional students (59 women), 399 part-time matriculated graduate/professional students (274 women). *Graduate faculty:* 22 full-time (5 women), 10 part-time/adjunct (5 women). *Computer facilities:* Computer purchase and lease plans are available. 250 computers available on campus for general student use. A campuswide network can be accessed from student residence rooms and from off campus. Internet access and online class registration are available. *Library facilities:* Loden-Daniel Library. *Graduate expenses:* Tuition: part-time $334 per credit hour. Required fees: $10 per credit hour. *General application contact:* Dr. Samuel T. Jones, Vice President for Academics, 731-989-6004.

Program in Business Administration
Dr. Tom Deberry, Director of Graduate Studies, School of Business
Program in:
business administration (MBA)

Program in Counseling
Dr. Mike Cravens, Graduate Director
Program in:
counseling (MS)

Program in Education
Dr. Elizabeth Saunders, Graduate Director
Programs in:
curriculum and instruction (M Ed)
school counseling (M Ed)
school leadership (Ed S)

School of Biblical Studies
Dr. Earl Edwards, Director of Graduate Studies
Programs in:
biblical studies (M Div, M Min, MA)
divinity (M Div)
ministry (M Min)
New Testament (MA)

■ LEE UNIVERSITY
Cleveland, TN 37320-3450
http://www.leeuniversity.edu/

Independent-religious, coed, comprehensive institution. *Enrollment:* 4,012 graduate, professional, and undergraduate students; 153 full-time matriculated graduate/professional students (104 women), 135 part-time matriculated graduate/professional students (83 women). *Graduate faculty:* 72 full-time (18 women), 3 part-time/adjunct (0 women). *Computer facilities:* Computer purchase and lease plans are available. A campuswide network can be accessed from off campus. Internet access and online class registration are available. *Library facilities:* William G. Squires Library plus 3 others. *Graduate expenses:* Tuition: part-time $412 per credit. Required fees: $10 per semester. Tuition and fees vary according to course load. *General application contact:* Vicki Glasscock, Graduate Admissions Director, 423-614-8059.

Program in Behavioral Sciences
Dr. Doyle Goff, Director
Programs in:
mental health counseling (MS)
school counseling (MS)

Program in Education
Dr. Gary Riggins, Director

Lee University (continued)
Programs in:
- classroom teaching (M Ed)
- educational leadership (M Ed)
- elementary/secondary education (MAT)
- special education (elementary) (M Ed)
- special education (secondary) (M Ed, MAT)
- special education (severe disabilities) (M Ed)

Program in Music
Dr. Jim W. Burns, Director
Programs in:
- church music (MCM)
- music education (MME)
- performance (MMMP)

Program in Religion
Dr. Michael Fuller, Director
Programs in:
- biblical studies (MA)
- theological studies (MA)
- youth and family ministry (MA)

■ LINCOLN MEMORIAL UNIVERSITY
Harrogate, TN 37752-1901
http://www.lmunet.edu/

Independent, coed, comprehensive institution. *Enrollment:* 2,981 graduate, professional, and undergraduate students; 235 full-time matriculated graduate/professional students (177 women), 1,352 part-time matriculated graduate/professional students (1,013 women). *Graduate faculty:* 33 full-time (17 women), 11 part-time/adjunct (6 women). *Computer facilities:* 150 computers available on campus for general student use. A campuswide network can be accessed from student residence rooms. Internet access is available. *Library facilities:* Carnegie Library plus 1 other. *General application contact:* Barbara McCune, Senior Assistant, Graduate Office, 423-869-6374.

School of Business
Dr. Bill Hamby, Dean
Program in:
- business (MBA)

School of Education
Dr. Fred Bedelle, Dean, School of Graduate Studies
Programs in:
- administration and supervision (M Ed, Ed S)
- counseling and guidance (M Ed)
- curriculum and instruction (M Ed, Ed S)

School of Nursing and Allied Health
Dr. Mary Modorin, Dean
Program in:
- nursing (MSN)

■ LIPSCOMB UNIVERSITY
Nashville, TN 37204-3951
http://www.lipscomb.edu/

Independent-religious, coed, comprehensive institution. *Enrollment:* 2,563 graduate, professional, and undergraduate students; 128 full-time matriculated graduate/professional students (67 women), 146 part-time matriculated graduate/professional students (55 women). *Graduate faculty:* 21 full-time (4 women), 13 part-time/adjunct (6 women). *Computer facilities:* 245 computers available on campus for general student use. A campuswide network can be accessed from student residence rooms and from off campus. Internet access and online class registration are available. *Library facilities:* Beaman Library plus 1 other. *Graduate expenses:* Tuition: part-time $560 per semester hour. Tuition and fees vary according to program. *General application contact:* Dr. Randy Bouldin, Associate Provost for Graduate Studies, 615-966-5711.

Hazelip School of Theology
Dr. Mark Black, Director
Programs in:
- biblical studies (MA)
- Christian studies (MA)
- divinity (M Div)
- ministry (MA)
- New Testament (MA)
- Old Testament (MA)
- theological studies (MTS)
- theology (MA)

MBA Program
Dr. Steven K. Yoho, Associate Dean of Graduate Business Studies
Programs in:
- accounting (MBA)
- business administration (general) (MBA)
- conflict management (MBA)
- financial services (MBA)
- healthcare management (MBA)
- leadership (MBA)
- nonprofit management (MBA)

Program in Education
Dr. Junior High, Director
Programs in:
- instructional leadership (M Ed)
- learning and teaching (MALT)
- school administration and supervision (M Ed)
- special education instruction, K-12 (MASE)

■ MIDDLE TENNESSEE STATE UNIVERSITY
Murfreesboro, TN 37132
http://www.mtsu.edu/

State-supported, coed, university. CGS member. *Graduate faculty:* 352 full-time (140 women), 10 part-time/adjunct (6 women). *Computer facilities:* 2,300 computers available on campus for general student use. A campuswide network can be accessed from student residence rooms and from off campus. Internet access and online class registration are available. *Library facilities:* James E. Walker Library. *General application contact:* Dr. Donald L. Curry, Dean and Vice Provost for Research, 615-898-2840.

College of Graduate Studies
Dr. Abdul S. Rao, Vice Provost for Research/Dean

College of Basic and Applied Sciences
Dr. Thomas Cheatham, Dean
Programs in:
- aerospace education (M Ed)
- aviation administration (MS)
- basic and applied sciences (M Ed, MS, MSN, MST, MVTE, DA)
- biology (MS)
- chemistry (MS, DA)
- computer science (MS)
- engineering technology and industrial studies (MS, MVTE)
- mathematics (MS)
- mathematics education (MST)
- nursing (MSN)

College of Business
Dr. James E. Burton, Dean
Programs in:
- accounting (MS)
- business (MA, MBA, MBE, MS, PhD)
- business education (MBE)
- computer information systems (MS)
- economics and finance (MA, PhD)
- information systems (MS)
- management and marketing (MBA)

College of Education and Behavioral Science
Dr. Gloria Bonner, Dean
Programs in:
- administration and supervision (M Ed, Ed S)
- child development and family studies (MS)
- criminal justice administration (MCJ)
- curriculum and instruction (M Ed, Ed S)
- dyslexic studies (Graduate Certificate)
- early childhood education (M Ed)
- education and behavioral science (M Ed, MA, MCJ, MS, PhD, Ed S, Graduate Certificate)
- elementary education (M Ed, Ed S)
- English as a second language (M Ed)
- exercise science and health promotion (MS)
- health, physical education, recreation and safety (MS)
- human performance (PhD)
- industrial/organizational psychology (MA)
- middle school education (M Ed)
- nutrition and food science (MS)
- physical education (PhD)
- professional counseling (M Ed, Ed S)
- psychology (MA)
- reading (M Ed)
- school counseling (M Ed)
- school psychology (Ed S)
- special education (M Ed)

College of Liberal Arts
Dr. John McDaniel, Dean
Programs in:
- English (MA, PhD)
- foreign languages and literatures (MAT)
- geosciences (Graduate Certificate)
- gerontology (Graduate Certificate)
- health care management (Graduate Certificate)
- historic preservation (DA)
- history (MA, DA)
- liberal arts (MA, MAT, DA, PhD, Graduate Certificate)
- music (MA)
- public history (PhD)
- sociology (MA)

College of Mass Communication
Dr. Anantha Babbili, Dean
Programs in:
- journalism (MS)
- mass communication (MS)
- recording arts (MFA)

■ TENNESSEE STATE UNIVERSITY
Nashville, TN 37209-1561
http://www.tnstate.edu/

State-supported, coed, comprehensive institution. CGS member. *Enrollment:* 9,038 graduate, professional, and undergraduate students; 603 full-time matriculated graduate/professional students (431 women), 1,323 part-time matriculated graduate/professional students (937 women). *Graduate faculty:* 151 full-time (63 women), 20 part-time/adjunct (11 women). *Computer facilities:* 705 computers available on campus for general student use. A campuswide network can be accessed from student residence rooms and from off campus. Internet access and online class registration are available. *Library facilities:* Martha M. Brown/Lois H. Daniel Library plus 1 other. *General application contact:* Graduate School Contact, 615-963-5901.

The School of Graduate Studies and Research
Dr. Helen Barrett, Dean

College of Arts and Sciences
Dr. William Lawson, Dean
Programs in:
- arts and sciences (MA, MCJ, MS, PhD)
- biological sciences (MS, PhD)
- chemistry (MS)
- criminal justice (MCJ)
- English (MA)
- mathematical sciences (MS)
- music education (MS)

College of Business
Dr. Tilden J. Curry, Dean
Program in:
- business (MBA)

College of Education
Dr. Leslie Drummonds, Dean
Programs in:
- administration and supervision (M Ed, Ed D, Ed S)
- counseling and guidance (MS)
- counseling psychology (PhD)
- curriculum and instruction (M Ed, Ed D)
- education (M Ed, MA Ed, MS, Ed D, PhD, Ed S)
- elementary education (M Ed, MA Ed, Ed D)
- human performance and sports science (MA Ed)
- psychology (MS, PhD)
- school psychology (MS, PhD)
- special education (M Ed, MA Ed, Ed D)

College of Engineering, Technology, and Computer Science
Dr. Decatur B. Rogers, Dean
Programs in:
- computer and information systems engineering (MS)
- computer information systems engineering (PhD)
- engineering (ME)

College of Health Sciences
Dr. Kathleen McEnerney, Dean
Programs in:
- health sciences (MPT, MS, DPT)
- physical therapy (MPT, DPT)
- speech and hearing science (MS)

Institute of Government
Dr. Ann-Marie Rizzo, Director
Program in:
- public administration (MPA, PhD)

School of Agriculture and Consumer Sciences
Dr. Constantine Fenderson, Interim Dean
Program in:
- agricultural sciences (MS)

School of Nursing
Dr. Bernadeen Fleming, Interim Dean
Programs in:
- family nurse practitioner (MSN)
- holistic nursing (MSN)
- nursing administration (MSN)
- nursing education (MSN)
- nursing informatics (MSN)

■ TENNESSEE TECHNOLOGICAL UNIVERSITY
Cookeville, TN 38505
http://www.tntech.edu/

State-supported, coed, university. CGS member. *Enrollment:* 9,733 graduate, professional, and undergraduate students; 655 full-time matriculated graduate/professional students (396 women), 815 part-time matriculated graduate/professional students (535 women). *Graduate faculty:* 341 full-time (62 women). *Computer facilities:* 620 computers available on campus for general student use. A campuswide network can be accessed from student residence rooms and from off campus. Internet access and online class registration are available. *Library facilities:* Angelo and Jennette Volpe Library and Media Center. *Graduate expenses:* Tuition, state resident: full-time $8,748; part-time $319 per hour. Tuition, nonresident: full-time $23,524; part-time $740 per hour. *General application contact:* Dr. Francis O. Otuonye, Associate Vice President for Research and Graduate Studies, 931-372-3233.

Graduate School
Dr. Francis O. Otuonye, Associate Vice President for Research and Graduate Studies

College of Arts and Sciences
Dean
Programs in:
- arts and sciences (MA, MS, PhD)
- chemistry (MS)
- computer science (MS)
- English (MA)
- environmental biology (MS)
- environmental sciences (PhD)
- fish, game, and wildlife management (MS)
- mathematics (MS)

College of Business Administration
Dr. Bob G. Wood, Director
Program in:
- business administration (MBA)

College of Education
Dr. Larry Peach, Interim Dean
Programs in:
- curriculum (MA, Ed S)
- early childhood education (MA, Ed S)
- education (MA, PhD, Ed S)
- educational psychology (MA, Ed S)
- educational psychology and student personnel (MA, Ed S)
- elementary education (MA, Ed S)
- exceptional learning (PhD)
- exercise science, physical education and wellness (MA)
- instructional leadership (MA, Ed S)
- library science (MA)
- reading (MA, Ed S)
- secondary education (MA, Ed S)
- special education (MA, Ed S)

College of Engineering
Dr. Glen Johnson, Dean
Programs in:
- chemical engineering (MS, PhD)
- civil engineering (MS, PhD)
- electrical engineering (MS, PhD)
- engineering (MS, PhD)
- mechanical engineering (MS, PhD)

School of Nursing
Dr. Shelia Green, Interim Dean
Program in:
- nursing (MSN)

■ TREVECCA NAZARENE UNIVERSITY
Nashville, TN 37210-2877
http://www.trevecca.edu/

Independent-religious, coed, comprehensive institution. *Enrollment:* 2,217 graduate, professional, and undergraduate students; 798 full-time matriculated graduate/professional students (565 women), 172 part-time matriculated graduate/professional students (112 women). *Graduate faculty:* 48 full-time (28 women), 66 part-time/adjunct (30 women). *Computer facilities:* 200 computers available on campus for general student use. A campuswide network can be accessed from student residence rooms and from off campus. Internet access is available. *Library facilities:* Mackey Library. *Graduate expenses:* Tuition: full-time $6,390; part-time $355 per credit. Tuition and fees vary according to degree level and program. *General application contact:* Dr. Stephen M. Pusey, Provost and Chief Academic Officer, 615-248-1258.

Graduate Division
Dr. Stephen M. Pusey, Provost and Chief Academic Officer

Division of Natural and Applied Sciences
Dr. Mike Moredock, Chair
Programs in:
- natural and applied sciences (MS)
- physician assistant (MS)

Division of Social and Behavioral Sciences
Dr. Peter Wilson, Chair
Programs in:
- counseling (MA)
- counseling psychology (MA)
- marriage and family therapy (MMFT)

School of Business and Management
Dr. Jim Hiatt, Dean
Programs in:
- business administration (MBA)
- business and management (MBA, MSM)
- management (MSM)

School of Education
Dr. Esther Swink, Dean
Programs in:
- educational leadership (M Ed)
- English language learners (PreK-12) (M Ed)
- instructional effectiveness (M Ed)
- instructional technology (M Ed)
- leadership and professional practice (D Ed)
- library and information science (MLI Sc)
- reading PreK-12 (M Ed)
- teaching (MAT)
- teaching 7-12 (MAT)
- teaching K-6 (MAT)

School of Religion and Philosophy
Dr. Tim Green, Dean
Programs in:
- biblical studies (MA)
- preaching and practical theology (MA)
- systematic theology/historical theology (MA)

■ TUSCULUM COLLEGE
Greeneville, TN 37743-9997
http://www.tusculum.edu/

Independent-religious, coed, comprehensive institution. *Computer facilities:* 200 computers available on campus for general student use. A campuswide network can be accessed from student residence rooms and from off campus. Internet access is available. *Library facilities:* Albert Columbus Tate Library plus 2 others. *General application contact:* Information Contact, 423-693-1177 Ext. 330.

Graduate School
Programs in:
- adult education (MA Ed)
- K–12 (MA Ed)
- organizational management (MAOM)

■ UNION UNIVERSITY
Jackson, TN 38305-3697
http://www.uu.edu/

Independent-religious, coed, comprehensive institution. *Enrollment:* 2,934 graduate, professional, and undergraduate students; 580 full-time matriculated graduate/professional students (379 women), 207 part-time matriculated graduate/professional students (134 women). *Graduate faculty:* 69. *Computer facilities:* 236 computers available on campus for general student use. A campuswide network can be accessed from student residence rooms and from off campus. Internet access is available. *Library facilities:* Emma Waters Summar Library plus 1 other. *General application contact:* Robbie Graves, Director of Enrollment Services, 731-661-5008.

Institute for International and Intercultural Studies
Dr. Cynthia Powell Jayne, Director
Program in:
- international and intercultural studies (MAIS)

McAfee School of Business Administration
Program in:
- business administration (MBA)

School of Christian Studies
Dr. Gregory Thornburg, Dean
Program in:
- Christian studies (MCS)

School of Education
Dr. Tom R. Rosebrough, Dean
Programs in:
- education (M Ed, MA Ed)
- education administration generalist (Ed S)
- educational leadership (Ed D)
- educational supervision (Ed S)
- higher education (Ed D)

School of Nursing
Dr. Tim Smith, Dean
Programs in:
- nurse anesthetist (PMC)
- nursing education (MSN, PMC)

■ UNIVERSITY OF MEMPHIS
Memphis, TN 38152
http://www.memphis.edu/

State-supported, coed, university. CGS member. *Enrollment:* 20,562 graduate, professional, and undergraduate students; 2,076 full-time matriculated graduate/professional students (1,125 women), 2,559 part-time matriculated graduate/professional students (1,712 women). *Graduate faculty:* 516 full-time (156 women), 63 part-time/adjunct (28 women). *Computer facilities:* 2,000 computers available on campus for general student use. A campuswide network can be accessed from off campus. Internet access and online class registration are available. *Library facilities:* University of Memphis Libraries: McWherter Libraries plus 6 others. *General application contact:* Information Contact, 901-678-2531.

Find University Details at www.petersons.com/gradchannel.

Cecil C. Humphreys School of Law
James R. Smoot, Dean
Program in:
- law (JD)

Graduate School
Dr. Karen D. Weddle-West, Assistant Vice Provost for Graduate Studies
Programs in:
- accounting (MBA, MS, PhD)
- accounting systems (MS)
- automatic control systems (MS)
- biomedical engineering (MS, PhD)
- biomedical systems (MS)
- business and economics (MA, MBA, MS, PhD)
- civil engineering (PhD)
- communications and propagation systems (MS)
- computer engineering technology (MS)
- design and mechanical engineering (MS)
- economics (MBA, PhD)
- electrical engineering (PhD)
- electronics engineering technology (MS)
- energy systems (MS)
- engineering (MS, PhD)
- engineering computer systems (MS)
- environmental engineering (MS)
- executive business administration (MBA)
- finance (PhD)

finance, insurance, and real estate (MBA, MS)
foundation engineering (MS)
industrial engineering (MS)
international business administration (MBA)
management (MBA, MS, PhD)
management information systems (MBA, MS, PhD)
management science (MBA)
manufacturing engineering technology (MS)
marketing (MBA, MS)
marketing and supply chain management (PhD)
mechanical engineering (PhD)
mechanical systems (MS)
power systems (MS)
real estate development (MS)
structural engineering (MS)
taxation (MS)
transportation engineering (MS)
water resources engineering (MS)

College of Arts and Sciences
Programs in:
anthropology (MA)
applied mathematics (MS)
applied statistics (PhD)
arts and sciences (MA, MCRP, MFA, MHA, MPA, MS, PhD)
bioinformatics (MS)
biology (MS, PhD)
chemistry (MS, PhD)
city and regional planning (MCRP)
clinical psychology (PhD)
computer science (PhD)
computer sciences (MS)
creative writing (MFA)
criminology and criminal justice (MA)
earth sciences (MA, MS, PhD)
English (MA)
experimental psychology (PhD)
French (MA)
general psychology (MS)
health administration (MHA)
history (MA, PhD)
mathematics (MS, PhD)
nonprofit administration (MPA)
philosophy (MA, PhD)
physics (MS)
political science (MA)
public management and policy (MPA)
school psychology (MA, PhD)
sociology (MA)
Spanish (MA)
statistics (MS, PhD)
urban affairs and public policy (MA, MCRP, MHA, MPA)
urban management and planning (MPA)
writing and language studies (PhD)

College of Communication and Fine Arts
Programs in:
applied music (M Mu, DMA)
art history (MA)
ceramics (MFA)
communication (MA)
communication and fine arts (M Mu, MA, MFA, DMA, PhD)
communication arts (PhD)
composition (M Mu, DMA)
conducting (M Mu, DMA)
Egyptian art and archaeology (MA)
film and video production (MA)
general art history (MA)
general journalism (MA)
graphic design (MFA)
historical musicology (PhD)
interior design (MFA)
jazz and studio performance (M Mu)
journalism administration (MA)
music education (M Mu, DMA)
musicology (M Mu)
painting (MFA)
printmaking/photography (MFA)
sculpture (MFA)
theatre (MFA)

College of Education
Programs in:
adult education (Ed D)
clinical nutrition (MS)
community education (Ed D)
counseling (MS, Ed D)
counseling psychology (PhD)
early childhood education (MAT, MS, Ed D)
education (MAT, MS, Ed D, PhD)
educational leadership (Ed D)
educational psychology and research (MS, PhD)
elementary education (MAT)
exercise and sport science (MS)
health promotion (MS)
higher education (Ed D)
instruction and curriculum (MS, Ed D)
instruction design and technology (MS, Ed D)
leadership (MS)
middle grades education (MAT)
physical education teacher education (MS)
policy studies (Ed D)
reading (MS, Ed D)
school administration and supervision (MS)
secondary education (MAT)
special education (MAT, MS, Ed D)
sport and leisure commerce (MS)
student personnel (MS)

Fogelman College of Business and Economics
Rajiv Grover, Dean
Programs in:
accounting (MBA, MS, PhD)
accounting systems (MS)
business and economics (MA, MBA, MS, PhD)
economics (MBA, PhD)
executive business administration (MBA)
finance (PhD)
finance, insurance, and real estate (MBA, MS)
international business administration (MBA)
management (MBA, MS, PhD)
management information systems (MBA, MS, PhD)
management science (MBA)
marketing (MBA, MS)
marketing and supply chain management (PhD)
real estate development (MS)
taxation (MS)

Herff College of Engineering
Dr. Richard C. Warder, Dean
Programs in:
automatic control systems (MS)
biomedical engineering (MS, PhD)
biomedical systems (MS)
civil engineering (PhD)
communications and propagation systems (MS)
computer engineering technology (MS)
design and mechanical engineering (MS)
electrical engineering (PhD)
electronics engineering technology (MS)
energy systems (MS)
engineering (MS, PhD)
engineering computer systems (MS)
environmental engineering (MS)
foundation engineering (MS)
industrial engineering (MS)
manufacturing engineering technology (MS)
mechanical engineering (PhD)
mechanical systems (MS)
power systems (MS)
structural engineering (MS)
transportation engineering (MS)
water resources engineering (MS)

School of Audiology and Speech-Language Pathology
Dr. Maurice Mendel, Dean
Program in:
audiology and speech-language pathology (MA, Au D, PhD)

University College
Dr. Dan Lattimore, Dean
Programs in:
consumer science and education (MS)
family and consumer science (MS)
liberal studies (MALS)

■ THE UNIVERSITY OF TENNESSEE
Knoxville, TN 37996
http://www.tennessee.edu/

State-supported, coed, university. CGS member. *Enrollment:* 28,901 graduate, professional, and undergraduate students; 3,946 full-time matriculated graduate/professional students (2,223 women), 2,095 part-time matriculated graduate/professional students (1,120 women). *Graduate faculty:* 1,381 full-time (478 women), 31 part-time/adjunct (17 women). *Computer facilities:* Computer purchase and lease plans are available. 1,500 computers available on campus for general student use. A campuswide network can be accessed from student residence rooms and from off campus. Internet access and online class registration are available. *Library facilities:*

The University of Tennessee (continued)
John C. Hodges Library plus 6 others. *Graduate expenses:* Tuition, state resident: full-time $5,574. Tuition, nonresident: full-time $16,840. Required fees: $792. *General application contact:* Michael Ickowitz, Associate Director Graduate and International Admissions, 865-974-3251.

College of Law

Dr. Karen R. Britton, Director of Admissions, Financial Aid and Career Services
Program in:
law (JD)

Graduate School

Dr. Carolyn R. Hodges, Vice Provost and Dean, Graduate School
Programs in:
aviation systems (MS)
comparative and experimental medicine (MS, PhD)

College of Agricultural Sciences and Natural Resources

Dr. Caula Beyl, Dean
Programs in:
agricultural education (MS)
agricultural extension education (MS)
agricultural sciences and natural resources (MS, PhD)
animal anatomy (PhD)
biosystems engineering (MS, PhD)
biosystems engineering technology (MS)
breeding (MS, PhD)
entomology (MS, PhD)
floriculture (MS)
food science and technology (MS, PhD)
forestry (MS)
integrated pest management and bioactive natural products (PhD)
landscape design (MS)
management (MS, PhD)
nutrition (MS, PhD)
physiology (MS, PhD)
plant pathology (MS, PhD)
public horticulture (MS)
turfgrass (MS)
wildlife and fisheries science (MS)
woody ornamentals (MS)

College of Architecture and Design

Dr. John McRae, Interim Dean
Programs in:
architecture (professional) (M Arch)
architecture (research) (M Arch)
landscape architecture (MLA)
landscape architecture (research) (MA, MS)

College of Arts and Sciences

Dr. Bruce Bursten, Dean
Programs in:
accompanying (MM)
American history (PhD)
analytical chemistry (MS, PhD)
applied linguistics (PhD)
applied mathematics (MS)
archaeology (MA, PhD)
arts and sciences (M Math, MA, MFA, MM, MPA, MS, PhD)
audiology (MA, PhD)
behavior (MS, PhD)
biochemistry, cellular and molecular biology (MS, PhD)
biological anthropology (MA, PhD)
ceramics (MFA)
chemical physics (PhD)
choral conducting (MM)
clinical psychology (PhD)
composition (MM)
computer science (MS, PhD)
costume design (MFA)
criminology (MA, PhD)
cultural anthropology (MA, PhD)
drawing (MFA)
ecology (MS, PhD)
energy, environment, and resource policy (MA, PhD)
English (MA, PhD)
environmental chemistry (MS, PhD)
European history (PhD)
evolutionary biology (MS, PhD)
experimental psychology (MA, PhD)
French (MA, PhD)
genome science and technology (MS, PhD)
geography (MS, PhD)
geology (MS, PhD)
German (MA, PhD)
graphic design (MFA)
hearing science (PhD)
history (MA)
inorganic chemistry (MS, PhD)
instrumental conducting (MM)
inter-area studies (MFA)
Italian (PhD)
jazz (MM)
lighting design (MFA)
mathematical ecology (PhD)
mathematics (M Math, MS, PhD)
media arts (MFA)
medical ethics (MA, PhD)
microbiology (MS, PhD)
modern foreign languages (PhD)
music education (MM)
music theory (MM)
musicology (MM)
organic chemistry (MS, PhD)
painting (MFA)
performance (MFA, MM)
philosophy (MA, PhD)
physical chemistry (MS, PhD)
physics (MS, PhD)
piano pedagogy and literature (MM)
plant physiology and genetics (MS, PhD)
political economy (MA, PhD)
political science (MA, PhD)
polymer chemistry (MS, PhD)
Portuguese (PhD)
printmaking (MFA)
psychology (MA)
public administration (MPA)
religious studies (MA)
Russian (PhD)
scene design (MFA)
sculpture (MFA)
Spanish (MA, PhD)
speech and hearing science (PhD)
speech and language pathology (PhD)
speech and language science (PhD)
speech pathology (MA)
theatre technology (MFA)
theoretical chemistry (PhD)
watercolor (MFA)
zoo-archaeology (MA, PhD)

College of Business Administration

Dr. Jan Williams, Dean
Programs in:
accounting (M Acc, PhD)
business administration (M Acc, MA, MBA, MS, PhD)
economics (MA, PhD)
finance (MBA, PhD)
industrial and organizational psychology (PhD)
industrial statistics (MS)
logistics and transportation (MBA, PhD)
management (PhD)
management science (MS, PhD)
marketing (MBA, PhD)
operations management (MBA)
professional business administration (MBA)
statistics (MS, PhD)
systems (M Acc)
taxation (M Acc)
teacher licensure (MS)
training and development (MS)

College of Communication and Information

Dr. Michael Wirth, Dean
Programs in:
advertising (MS, PhD)
broadcasting (MS, PhD)
communications (MS, PhD)
information sciences (MS, PhD)
journalism (MS, PhD)
public relations (MS, PhD)
speech communication (MS, PhD)

College of Education, Health and Human Sciences

Dr. Robert Rider, Dean
Programs in:
adult education (MS)
applied educational psychology (MS)
art education (MS)
biomechanics/sports medicine (MS, PhD)
child and family studies (MS, PhD)
collaborative learning (Ed D)
college student personnel (MS)
community health (PhD)
community health education (MPH)
consumer services management (MS)
counseling education (PhD)
cultural studies in education (PhD)
curriculum (MS, Ed S)
curriculum, educational research and evaluation (Ed D, PhD)
early childhood education (MS, PhD)
early childhood special education (MS)
education of deaf and hard of hearing (MS)

education, health and human sciences (MPH, MS, Ed D, PhD, Ed S)
educational administration and policy studies (Ed D, PhD)
educational administration and supervision (MS, Ed S)
educational psychology (Ed D, PhD)
elementary education (MS, Ed S)
elementary teaching (MS)
English education (MS, Ed S)
exercise physiology (MS, PhD)
exercise science (MS, PhD)
foreign language/ESL education (MS, Ed S)
gerontology (MPH)
health planning/administration (MPH)
health promotion and health education (MS)
hospitality management (MS)
hotel, restaurant, and tourism management (MS)
instructional technology (MS, Ed D, PhD, Ed S)
literacy, language and ESL education (PhD)
literacy, language education, and ESL education (Ed D)
mathematics education (MS, Ed S)
mental health counseling (MS)
modified and comprehensive special education (MS)
nutrition (MS)
nutrition science (PhD)
reading education (MS, Ed S)
recreation and leisure studies (MS)
rehabilitation counseling (MS)
retail and consumer sciences (MS)
retailing and consumer sciences (PhD)
safety (MS)
school counseling (MS, Ed S)
school psychology (PhD, Ed S)
science education (MS, Ed S)
secondary teaching (MS)
social foundations (MS)
social science education (MS, Ed S)
socio-cultural foundations of sports and education (PhD)
special education (Ed S)
sport management (MS)
sport studies (MS, PhD)
teacher education (Ed D, PhD)
textile science (MS, PhD)
therapeutic recreation (MS)
tourism (MS)

College of Engineering
Dr. Way Kuo, Dean
Programs in:
aerospace engineering (MS, PhD)
applied artificial intelligence (MS)
biomedical engineering (MS, PhD)
chemical engineering (MS, PhD)
civil engineering (MS, PhD)
composite materials (MS, PhD)
computational mechanics (MS, PhD)
computer engineering (MS, PhD)
electrical engineering (MS, PhD)
engineering (MS, PhD)
engineering management (MS)
engineering science (MS, PhD)
environmental engineering (MS)
fluid mechanics (MS, PhD)
human factors engineering (MS)
industrial engineering (MS, PhD)
information engineering (MS)
manufacturing systems engineering (MS)
materials science and engineering (MS, PhD)
mechanical engineering (MS, PhD)
optical engineering (MS, PhD)
polymer engineering (MS, PhD)
radiological engineering (MS, PhD)
solid mechanics (MS, PhD)

College of Nursing
Dr. Joan L. Creasia, Dean
Program in:
nursing (MSN, PhD)

College of Social Work
Dr. Karen Sowers, Dean
Programs in:
clinical social work practice (MSSW)
social welfare management and community practice (MSSW)
social work (PhD)

College of Veterinary Medicine
Dr. Michael J. Blackwell, Dean
Program in:
veterinary medicine (DVM)

■ THE UNIVERSITY OF TENNESSEE AT CHATTANOOGA
Chattanooga, TN 37403-2598
http://www.utc.edu/

State-supported, coed, comprehensive institution. CGS member. *Enrollment:* 8,923 graduate, professional, and undergraduate students; 534 full-time matriculated graduate/professional students (352 women), 778 part-time matriculated graduate/professional students (452 women). *Graduate faculty:* 145 full-time (59 women), 22 part-time/adjunct (7 women). *Computer facilities:* 300 computers available on campus for general student use. A campuswide network can be accessed from student residence rooms and from off campus. Internet access and online class registration are available. *Library facilities:* Lupton Library. *Graduate expenses:* Tuition, state resident: full-time $5,434; part-time $339 per hour. Tuition, nonresident: full-time $14,830; part-time $861 per hour. Required fees: $940; $178 per hour. *General application contact:* Dr. Deborah E. Arfken, Dean of Graduate Studies, 423-425-4666.

Graduate School
Dr. Deborah E. Arfken, Dean of Graduate Studies

College of Arts and Sciences
Dr. Charles Nelson, Acting Dean
Programs in:
arts and sciences (MA, MM, MPA, MS, MSCJ)
criminal justice (MSCJ)
English (MA)
environmental sciences (MS)
industrial/organizational psychology (MS)
music (MM)
public administration (MPA)
research psychology (MS)

College of Business Administration
Dr. Richard P. Casavant, Dean
Programs in:
accountancy (M Acc)
business administration (M Acc, MBA)
general business administration (MBA)

College of Engineering and Computer Science
Dr. Ron Bailey, Dean
Programs in:
computational engineering (PhD)
computer science (MS, Graduate Certificate)
engineering (MS)
engineering and computer science (MS, PhD, Graduate Certificate)
engineering management (MS, Graduate Certificate)

College of Health, Education and Professional Studies
Dr. Mary Tanner, Dean
Programs in:
administration (MSN)
adult health (MSN)
counseling (M Ed)
education (MSN)
educational leadership (Ed D)
educational specialist (Ed S)
educational technology (Ed S)
elementary education (M Ed)
family nurse practitioner (MSN)
health and human performance (MS)
health, education and professional studies (M Ed, MS, MSN, DPT, Ed D, Ed S)
nurse anesthesia (MSN)
physical therapy (DPT)
school leadership (M Ed)
school psychology (Ed S)
secondary education (M Ed)
special education (M Ed)

■ THE UNIVERSITY OF TENNESSEE AT MARTIN
Martin, TN 38238-1000
http://www.utm.edu/

State-supported, coed, comprehensive institution. *Enrollment:* 6,893 graduate, professional, and undergraduate students; 501 matriculated graduate/professional students (347 women). *Graduate faculty:* 151. *Computer facilities:* 836 computers available on campus for general student use. A campuswide network can be accessed from student residence rooms and from off campus. Internet access and online class registration, online fee payments, grades, degree progress, financial aid data, housing applications, transcripts are available. *Library facilities:* Paul Meek Library. *Graduate*

The University of Tennessee at Martin (continued)

expenses: Tuition, state resident: part-time $303 per credit hour. Tuition, nonresident: part-time $829 per credit hour. *General application contact:* Linda S. Arant, Student Services Specialist, 731-881-7012.

Graduate Programs

Dr. Victoria S. Seng, Assistant Vice Chancellor and Dean of Graduate Studies

College of Agriculture and Applied Sciences

Dr. James Byford, Dean

Programs in:
- agricultural operations management (MSAOM)
- agriculture and applied sciences (MSAOM, MSFCS)
- dietetics (MSFCS)
- general family and consumer sciences (MSFCS)

College of Business and Public Affairs

Dr. Ernest Moser, Dean

Programs in:
- accountancy (M Ac)
- business (MBA)
- business and public affairs (M Ac, MBA)

College of Education and Behavioral Sciences

Dr. Mary Lee Hall, Dean

Programs in:
- advanced elementary (MS Ed)
- advanced secondary (MS Ed)
- education and behavioral sciences (MS Ed)
- educational administration and supervision (MS Ed)
- initial licensure comprehensive (MS Ed)
- initial licensure elementary (MS Ed)
- initial licensure secondary (MS Ed)
- mental health (MS Ed)
- school counseling (MS Ed)

■ VANDERBILT UNIVERSITY

Nashville, TN 37240-1001

http://www.vanderbilt.edu/

Independent, coed, university. CGS member. *Enrollment:* 11,607 graduate, professional, and undergraduate students; 4,565 full-time matriculated graduate/professional students (2,360 women), 623 part-time matriculated graduate/professional students (407 women). *Computer facilities:* 400 computers available on campus for general student use. A campuswide network can be accessed from student residence rooms and from off campus. Productivity and educational software available. *Library facilities:* Jean and Alexander Heard Library plus 7 others. *Graduate expenses:* Tuition: full-time $24,462. Required fees: $2,515. One-time fee: $30 full-time. Full-time tuition and fees vary according to course load, degree level and program. *General application contact:* Walter B. Bieschke, Program Coordinator for Admissions, 615-343-6321.

Divinity School

Dr. James Hudnut-Beumler, Dean

Program in:
- divinity (M Div, MTS)

Graduate School

Dennis G. Hall, Associate Provost for Research and Graduate Education

Programs in:
- analytical chemistry (MAT, MS, PhD)
- anthropology (MA, PhD)
- astronomy (MS)
- biochemistry (MS, PhD)
- biological sciences (MS, PhD)
- biomedical informatics (MS, PhD)
- cancer biology (MS, PhD)
- cell and developmental biology (MS, PhD)
- cellular and molecular pathology (PhD)
- classics (MA)
- community research and action (MS, PhD)
- creative writing (MFA)
- earth and environmental sciences (MS)
- economic development (MA)
- economics (MA, MAT, PhD)
- English (MA, MAT, PhD)
- French (MA, MAT, PhD)
- German (MA, MAT, PhD)
- history (MA, MAT, PhD)
- inorganic chemistry (MAT, MS, PhD)
- Latin (MAT)
- Latin American studies (MA)
- leadership and policy studies (PhD)
- learning, teaching and diversity (MS, PhD)
- liberal arts and science (MLAS)
- mathematics (MA, MAT, MS, PhD)
- microbiology and immunology (MS, PhD)
- molecular physiology and biophysics (MS, PhD)
- neuroscience (PhD)
- nursing science (PhD)
- organic chemistry (MAT, MS, PhD)
- pharmacology (PhD)
- philosophy (MA, PhD)
- physical chemistry (MAT, MS, PhD)
- physics (MA, MAT, MS, PhD)
- political science (MA, MAT, PhD)
- Portuguese (MA)
- psychological sciences (MA, PhD)
- religion (MA, PhD)
- sociology (MA, PhD)
- Spanish (MA, MAT, PhD)
- Spanish and Portuguese (PhD)
- special education (MS, PhD)
- theoretical chemistry (MAT, MS, PhD)

Law School

Edward L Rubin, Dean

Programs in:
- law (JD, LL M)
- law and economics (PhD)

Owen Graduate School of Management

Dr. James W. Bradford, Dean

Programs in:
- business administration (MBA)
- executive business administration (MBA)
- finance (PhD)
- management (MBA, MSF, PhD)
- marketing (PhD)
- operations management (PhD)
- organization studies (PhD)

Peabody College

Dr. Camilla P. Benbow, Dean

Programs in:
- child studies (M Ed)
- community development action (M Ed)
- curriculum and instructional leadership (M Ed)
- early childhood education (M Ed)
- early childhood leadership (Ed D)
- education (M Ed, MPP, Ed D)
- education policy (MPP)
- educational leadership and policy (Ed D)
- elementary education (M Ed)
- English education (M Ed)
- English language learners (M Ed)
- higher education (M Ed)
- higher education, leadership and policy (Ed D)
- human development counseling (M Ed)
- human resource development (M Ed)
- international education policy and management (M Ed)
- mathematics education (M Ed)
- organizational leadership (M Ed)
- reading education (M Ed)
- school administration (M Ed)
- science education (M Ed)
- secondary education (M Ed)
- special education (M Ed)

School of Engineering

Dr. Kenneth F. Galloway, Dean

Programs in:
- biomedical engineering (M Eng, MS, PhD)
- chemical engineering (M Eng, MS, PhD)
- civil engineering (M Eng, MS, PhD)
- computer science (M Eng, MS, PhD)
- electrical engineering (M Eng, MS, PhD)
- engineering (M Eng, MS, PhD)
- environmental engineering (M Eng, MS, PhD)
- environmental management (MS, PhD)
- materials science (M Eng, MS, PhD)
- mechanical engineering (M Eng, MS, PhD)

School of Medicine

Dr. Steven G. Gabbe, Dean

Programs in:
- audiology (Au D, PhD)
- biomedical and biological sciences (PhD)
- chemical and physical biology (PhD)
- clinical investigation (MS)
- education of the deaf (MED)
- hearing and speech sciences (MS)
- medical physics (MS)

medicine (MED, MPH, MS, Au D, PhD)
public health (MPH)
speech-language-pathology (MS)

School of Nursing
Dr. Colleen Conway-Welch, Dean
Programs in:
adult acute care nurse practitioner (MSN)
adult health nurse practitioner/forensic (MSN)
adult nurse practitioner/cardiovascular disease management and prevention (MSN)
adult nurse practitioner/palliative care (MSN)
clinical management (clinical nurse leader/specialist) (MSN)
family nurse practitioner (MSN)
gerontology nurse practitioner (MSN)
health systems management (MSN)
neonatal nurse practitioner (MSN)
nurse midwifery (MSN)
nursing informatics (MSN)
nursing science (PhD)
pediatric acute care nurse practitioner (MSN)
pediatric primary care nurse practitioner (MSN)
psychiatric-mental health nurse practitioner (MSN)
women's health nurse practitioner (MSN)

Texas

■ ABILENE CHRISTIAN UNIVERSITY
Abilene, TX 79699-9100
http://www.acu.edu/

Independent-religious, coed, comprehensive institution. CGS member. *Enrollment:* 4,777 graduate, professional, and undergraduate students; 299 full-time matriculated graduate/professional students (147 women), 317 part-time matriculated graduate/professional students (139 women). *Graduate faculty:* 14 full-time (2 women), 72 part-time/adjunct (27 women). *Computer facilities:* 700 computers available on campus for general student use. A campuswide network can be accessed from student residence rooms and from off campus. Internet access and online class registration are available. *Library facilities:* Brown Library. *Graduate expenses:* Tuition: full-time $12,504; part-time $521 per hour. Required fees: $700; $34 per hour. *General application contact:* William Horn, Graduate Admissions Counselor, 325-674-2656.

Graduate School
Dr. Carol G. Williams, Graduate Dean
Programs in:
communication sciences and disorders (MS)
education and human services (M Ed, MS, MSSW, Certificate)
educational diagnostician (M Ed)
higher education (M Ed)
leadership of learning (M Ed, Certificate)
liberal arts (MLA)
reading specialist (M Ed)
social work (MSSW)

College of Arts and Sciences
Dean
Programs in:
arts and sciences (MA, MS, Certificate)
clinical psychology (MS)
composition/rhetoric (MA)
conflict resolution and reconciliation (MA, Certificate)
counseling psychology (MS)
family studies (MS, Certificate)
general psychology (MS)
gerontology (MS, Certificate)
human communication (MA)
literature (MA)
organizational and human resource development (MS)
school psychology (MS)
writing (MA)

College of Biblical Studies
Dr. Jack Reese, Dean
Programs in:
biblical studies (M Div, MA, MACM, MMFT, D Min)
Christian ministry (MACM)
divinity (M Div)
history and theology (MA)
marriage and family therapy (MMFT)
ministry (D Min)
missions (MA)
New Testament (MA)
Old Testament (MA)

College of Business Administration
Bill Fowler, Department Chair
Program in:
business administration (M Acc)

School of Nursing
Dr. Jan Noles, Dean
Program in:
nursing (MSN)

■ AMBERTON UNIVERSITY
Garland, TX 75041-5595
http://www.amberton.edu/

Independent-religious, coed, upper-level institution. *Enrollment:* 1,648 graduate, professional, and undergraduate students; 289 full-time matriculated graduate/professional students (139 women), 700 part-time matriculated graduate/professional students (450 women). *Graduate faculty:* 16 full-time (7 women), 45 part-time/adjunct (20 women). *Computer facilities:* 30 computers available on campus for general student use. Internet access is available. *Library facilities:* Library Resource Center plus 1 other. *Graduate expenses:* Tuition: full-time $4,800; part-time $600 per course. *General application contact:* Adviser, 972-279-6511 Ext. 180.

Graduate School
Dr. Algia Allen, Academic Dean
Programs in:
counseling (MA)
general business (MBA)
human relations and business (MA, MS)
management (MBA)
professional development (MA)

■ ANGELO STATE UNIVERSITY
San Angelo, TX 76909
http://www.angelo.edu/

State-supported, coed, comprehensive institution. CGS member. *Enrollment:* 6,265 graduate, professional, and undergraduate students; 179 full-time matriculated graduate/professional students (114 women), 275 part-time matriculated graduate/professional students (168 women). *Graduate faculty:* 124 full-time (51 women). *Computer facilities:* 600 computers available on campus for general student use. A campuswide network can be accessed from student residence rooms and from off campus. Internet access and online class registration are available. *Library facilities:* Porter Henderson Library plus 1 other. *Graduate expenses:* Tuition, state resident: full-time $2,340; part-time $130 per hour. Tuition, nonresident: full-time $7,290; part-time $405 per hour. Required fees: $906; $56 per hour. *General application contact:* Brenda Stewart, Assistant to the Dean, College of Graduate Studies, 325-942-2169.

Find University Details at www.petersons.com/gradchannel.

College of Graduate Studies
Dr. Carol B. Diminnie, Dean of the College of Graduate Studies
Program in:
interdisciplinary studies (MA, MS)

College of Business and Professional Studies
Dr. Corbett Gaulden, Dean
Programs in:
accounting (MBA)
business (MBA, MPAC)
business administration (MBA)
professional accountancy (MPAC)

College of Education
Dr. John J. Miazga, Dean of the College of Education
Programs in:
curriculum and instruction (M Ed, MA)
education (M Ed, MA, MS)
educational diagnostics (M Ed)
guidance and counseling (M Ed)
kinesiology (MS)
reading specialist (M Ed)

Angelo State University (continued)
- school administration (M Ed)
- student development and leadership in higher education (M Ed)
- teacher education (M Ed, MA)

College of Liberal and Fine Arts
Dr. Kevin Lambert, Dean
Programs in:
- communication systems management (MA)
- English (MA)
- history (MA)
- liberal and fine arts (MA, MPA, MS)
- psychology (MS)
- public administration (MPA)

College of Sciences
Dr. Grady Blount, Dean
Programs in:
- adult nurse practitioner (MSN)
- animal science (MS)
- biology (MS)
- nurse educator (MSN)
- physical therapy (MPT)
- sciences (MPT, MS, MSN)

■ BAYLOR UNIVERSITY
Waco, TX 76798
http://www.baylor.edu/

Independent-religious, coed, university. CGS member. *Enrollment:* 14,040 graduate, professional, and undergraduate students; 1,867 full-time matriculated graduate/professional students (826 women), 330 part-time matriculated graduate/professional students (176 women). *Graduate faculty:* 350. *Computer facilities:* Computer purchase and lease plans are available. 1,500 computers available on campus for general student use. A campuswide network can be accessed from student residence rooms and from off campus. Internet access and online class registration are available. *Library facilities:* Moody Memorial Library plus 8 others. *General application contact:* Suzanne Keener, Administrative Assistant, 254-710-3588.

George W. Truett Seminary
Dr. Paul W. Powell, Dean
Program in:
- theology (M Div, MTS, D Min)

Graduate School
Dr. Larry Lyon, Dean

Academy of Health Sciences
Col. Darwin L. Fretwell, Dean
Programs in:
- health care administration (MHA)
- health sciences (MHA, MPT, DPT, Dr Sc PT)
- physical therapy (MPT, DPT, Dr Sc PT)

College of Arts and Sciences
Programs in:
- American studies (MA)
- applied sociology (PhD)
- arts and sciences (MA, MES, MFA, MIJ, MPPA, MS, MSCP, MSCSD, MSL, MSW, PhD, Psy D)
- biology (MA, MS, PhD)
- chemistry (MS, PhD)
- church-state studies (MA, PhD)
- clinical psychology (MSCP, Psy D)
- communication sciences and disorders (MA, MSCSD)
- communication studies (MA)
- directing (MFA)
- earth science (MA)
- English (MA, PhD)
- environmental biology (MS)
- environmental studies (MES, MS)
- geology (MS, PhD)
- history (MA)
- international journalism (MIJ)
- international studies (MA)
- journalism (MA)
- limnology (MSL)
- mathematics (MS, PhD)
- museum studies (MA)
- neuroscience (MA, PhD)
- philosophy (MA, PhD)
- physics (MA, MS, PhD)
- political science (MA, PhD)
- public policy and administration (MPPA)
- religion (MA, PhD)
- social work (MSW)
- sociology (MA)
- Spanish (MA)
- statistics (MA, PhD)

Hankamer School of Business
Dr. Gary Carini, Director of Graduate Programs
Programs in:
- accounting and business law (M Acc, MT)
- business (M Acc, MA, MBA, MBAIM, MIM, MS, MS Eco, MSIS, MT)
- business administration (MBA)
- economics (MS Eco)
- information systems (MSIS)
- information systems management (MBA)
- international economics (MA, MS)
- international management (MBA, MBAIM, MIM)

Institute of Biomedical Studies
Dr. Robert Kane, Interim Director
Program in:
- biomedical studies (MS, PhD)

Louise Herrington School of Nursing
Dr. Pauline Johnson, Graduate Program Director
Programs in:
- family nurse practitioner (MSN)
- neonatal nurse practitioner (MSN)
- nursing administration and management (MSN)

School of Education
Interim Dean
Programs in:
- curriculum and instruction (MA, MS Ed, Ed D, Ed S)
- education (MA, MS Ed, Ed D, PhD, Ed S)
- educational administration (MS Ed, Ed S)
- educational psychology (MA, MS Ed, PhD, Ed S)
- exercise, nutrition and preventive health (PhD)
- health, human performance and recreation (MS Ed)

School of Engineering and Computer Science
Dr. Greg Speegle, Graduate Program Director
Programs in:
- biomedical engineering (MSBE)
- computer science (MS)
- electrical and computer engineering (MSECE)
- engineering (ME, MSBE, MSECE, MSME)
- mechanical engineering (MSME)

School of Music
Dr. Harry Elzinga, Graduate Program Director
Programs in:
- church music (MM)
- composition (MM)
- conducting (MM)
- music education (MM)
- music history and literature (MM)
- music theory (MM)
- performance (MM)
- piano accompanying (MM)
- piano pedagogy and performance (MM)

School of Law
Dr. Bradley J. B. Toben, Dean
Program in:
- law (JD)

■ DALLAS BAPTIST UNIVERSITY
Dallas, TX 75211-9299
http://www.dbu.edu/

Independent-religious, coed, comprehensive institution. *Enrollment:* 5,153 graduate, professional, and undergraduate students; 474 full-time matriculated graduate/professional students (289 women), 1,069 part-time matriculated graduate/professional students (709 women). *Graduate faculty:* 49 full-time (21 women), 112 part-time/adjunct (46 women). *Computer facilities:* Computer purchase and lease plans are available. 182 computers available on campus for general student use. A campuswide network can be accessed from student residence rooms and from off campus. Internet access and online class registration are available. *Library facilities:* Vance Memorial Library. *Graduate expenses:* Tuition: full-time $8,370; part-time $465 per credit hour. Required fees: $465 per credit hour. *General application contact:* Kit P. Montgomery, Director of Graduate Programs, 214-333-5242.

College of Adult Education
Dr. Donovan Fredrickson, Acting Dean

Programs in:
- accounting (MA)
- adult education (MA, MLA)
- arts (MLA)
- business (MA)
- Christian ministry (MLA)
- church leadership (MA)
- corporate management (MA)
- counseling (MA)
- criminal justice (MA)
- English (MLA)
- English as a second language (MA, MLA)
- finance (MA)
- fine arts (MLA)
- higher education (MA)
- history (MLA)
- leadership studies (MA)
- management (MA)
- management information systems (MA)
- marketing (MA)
- missions (MA, MLA)
- political science (MLA)

College of Humanities and Social Sciences
Dr. Michael Williams, Dean
Programs in:
- counseling (MA)
- humanities and social sciences (MA)

Dorothy M. Bush College of Education
Dr. Charles Carona, Dean
Programs in:
- early childhood education (M Ed)
- education (M Ed, MAT)
- education in curriculum and instruction (M Ed)
- educational leadership (M Ed)
- elementary reading education (M Ed)
- general elementary education (M Ed)
- reading and ESL (M Ed)
- reading specialist (M Ed)
- school counseling (M Ed)
- teaching (MAT)

Graduate School of Business
Dr. Charlene Conner, Dean
Programs in:
- accounting (MBA)
- business (MA, MBA)
- business communication (MA, MBA)
- conflict resolution management (MA, MBA)
- e-business (MBA)
- entrepreneurship (MBA)
- finance (MBA)
- general management (MA)
- health care management (MA, MBA)
- human resource management (MA)
- international business (MBA)
- management (MBA)
- management information systems (MBA)
- marketing (MBA)
- project management (MBA)
- technology and engineering management (MBA)

School of Leadership and Christian Education
Dr. Rick Gregory, Dean
Programs in:
- adult ministry (MA)
- Baptist student ministry (MA)
- business ministry (MA)
- children's ministry (MA)
- Christian education: childhood ministry (MA)
- Christian education: student ministry (MA)
- collegiate ministry (MA)
- counseling ministry (MA)
- education ministry (MA)
- general ministry (MA)
- global leadership (MA)
- higher education (M Ed)
- leadership and Christian education (M Ed, MA)
- ministry with students (MA)
- missions ministry (MA)
- worship leadership (MA)
- worship ministry (MA)
- youth ministry (MA)

■ DEVRY UNIVERSITY
Irving, TX 75063-2439
http://www.devry.edu/

Proprietary, coed, comprehensive institution. *Computer facilities:* Computer purchase and lease plans are available. 442 computers available on campus for general student use. A campuswide network can be accessed from off campus. Internet access and online class registration are available. *Library facilities:* Learning Resource Center.

Keller Graduate School of Management
Program in:
- management (MAFM, MBA, MHRM, MISM, MNCM, MPA, MPM)

■ HARDIN-SIMMONS UNIVERSITY
Abilene, TX 79698-0001
http://www.hsutx.edu/

Independent-religious, coed, comprehensive institution. *Enrollment:* 2,372 graduate, professional, and undergraduate students; 204 full-time matriculated graduate/professional students (106 women), 187 part-time matriculated graduate/professional students (98 women). *Graduate faculty:* 74 full-time (28 women), 17 part-time/adjunct (5 women). *Computer facilities:* 224 computers available on campus for general student use. A campuswide network can be accessed from student residence rooms and from off campus. Internet access is available. *Library facilities:* Richardson Library plus 1 other. *Graduate expenses:* Tuition: full-time $9,090; part-time $505 per hour. Required fees: $490; $66 per semester. One-time fee: $50. Tuition and fees vary according to course load and degree level. *General application contact:* Dr. Gary Stanlake, Dean of Graduate Studies, 325-670-1298.

The Acton MBA in Entrepreneurship
Program in:
- entrepreneurship (MBA)

Graduate School
Dr. Gary Stanlake, Dean of Graduate Studies
Programs in:
- English (MA)
- family psychology (MA)
- history (MA)
- liberal arts (MA)
- religion (MA)
- theology (MA)

Holland School of Sciences and Mathematics
Dr. Christopher McNair, Dean
Programs in:
- environmental management (MS)
- physical therapy (DPT)
- sciences and mathematics (MS, DPT)

Irvin School of Education
Dr. Pam Williford, Dean
Programs in:
- advanced physical education (M Ed)
- counseling and human development (M Ed)
- education (M Ed)
- gifted education (M Ed)
- reading specialist (M Ed)
- sports and recreation management (M Ed)

Kelley College of Business
Dr. Charles Walts, Director
Program in:
- business (MBA)

School of Music
Dr. Leigh Anne Hunsaker, Director
Programs in:
- church music (MM)
- music education (MM)
- music performance (MM)
- theory-composition (MM)

School of Nursing
Dr. Janet Noles, Dean
Programs in:
- advanced healthcare delivery (MSN)
- family nurse practitioner (MSN)

■ HOUSTON BAPTIST UNIVERSITY
Houston, TX 77074-3298
http://www.hbu.edu/

Independent-religious, coed, comprehensive institution. *Computer facilities:* 95 computers available on campus for general student use. A campuswide network can be accessed from student residence rooms. Internet

Houston Baptist University (continued)
access is available. *Library facilities:* Moody Library. *General application contact:* Coordinator of Graduate Admissions, 281-649-3295.

College of Arts and Humanities
Programs in:
- arts and humanities (MATS, MLA)
- liberal arts (MLA)
- theological studies (MATS)

College of Business and Economics
Programs in:
- accounting (MACCT)
- business administration (MBA, MSM)
- business and economics (MACCT, MBA, MSHA, MSHRM, MSM)
- health administration (MSHA)
- human resources management (MSHRM)

College of Education and Behavioral Sciences
Programs in:
- bilingual education (M Ed)
- Christian counseling (MACC)
- counselor education (M Ed)
- curriculum and instruction (M Ed)
- education and behavioral sciences (M Ed, MACC, MAP)
- educational administration (M Ed)
- educational diagnostician (M Ed)
- psychology (MAP)
- reading education (M Ed)

■ LAMAR UNIVERSITY
Beaumont, TX 77710
http://www.lamar.edu/

State-supported, coed, university. CGS member. *Enrollment:* 609 full-time matriculated graduate/professional students (241 women), 378 part-time matriculated graduate/professional students (205 women). *Graduate faculty:* 178 full-time (64 women), 24 part-time/adjunct (11 women). *Computer facilities:* 120 computers available on campus for general student use. A campuswide network can be accessed from student residence rooms and from off campus. *Library facilities:* Mary and John Gray Library. *Graduate expenses:* Tuition, nonresident: part-time $33 per hour. Required fees: $43 per hour. $110 per semester. *General application contact:* Sandy Drane, Coordinator of Graduate Admissions, 409-880-8356.

Find University Details at www.petersons.com/gradchannel.

College of Graduate Studies
Dr. James W. Westgate, Assistant Dean

College of Arts and Sciences
Dr. Brenda S. Nichols, Dean
Programs in:
- applied criminology (MS)
- arts and sciences (MA, MPA, MS, MSN)
- biology (MS)
- chemistry (MS)
- community/clinical psychology (MS)
- computer science (MS)
- English (MA)
- history (MA)
- industrial/organizational psychology (MS)
- mathematics (MS)
- nursing administration online (MSN)
- nursing education online (MSN)
- public administration (MPA)

College of Business
Dr. Enrique R. Venta, Dean
Programs in:
- accounting (MBA)
- experiential business and Entrepreneurship (MBA)
- financial management (MBA)
- healthcare administration (MBA)
- information systems (MBA)
- management (MBA)

College of Education and Human Development
Dr. H. Lowery-Moore, Dean
Programs in:
- counseling and development (M Ed, Certificate)
- education (Ed D)
- education administration (M Ed)
- education and human development (M Ed, MS, DE, Ed D, Certificate)
- educational leadership (DE)
- family and consumer science (MS)
- kinesiology (MS)
- principal (Certificate)
- school superintendent (Certificate)
- supervision (M Ed)
- technology application (Certificate)
- vocational home economics (Certificate)

College of Engineering
Dr. Jack Hopper, Chair
Programs in:
- chemical engineering (ME, MES, DE, PhD)
- civil engineering (ME, MES, DE)
- electrical engineering (ME, MES, DE)
- engineering (ME, MEM, MES, MS, DE, PhD)
- engineering management (MEM)
- environmental engineering (MS)
- environmental studies (MS)
- industrial engineering (ME, MES, DE)
- mechanical engineering (ME, MES, DE)

College of Fine Arts and Communication
Dr. Russ A. Schultz, Dean
Programs in:
- art history (MA)
- audiology (MS, Au D)
- deaf studies/deaf education (MS, Ed D)
- fine arts and communication (MA, MM, MM Ed, MS, Au D, Ed D)
- music education (MM Ed)
- music performance (MM)
- photography (MA)
- speech language pathology (MS)
- studio art (MA)
- theatre (MS)
- visual design (MA)

■ LETOURNEAU UNIVERSITY
Longview, TX 75607-7001
http://www.letu.edu/

Independent-religious, coed, comprehensive institution. *Enrollment:* 3,975 graduate, professional, and undergraduate students; 217 full-time matriculated graduate/professional students (135 women), 123 part-time matriculated graduate/professional students (71 women). *Graduate faculty:* 7 full-time (0 women), 29 part-time/adjunct (7 women). *Computer facilities:* Computer purchase and lease plans are available. 191 computers available on campus for general student use. A campuswide network can be accessed from student residence rooms and from off campus. Internet access and online class registration are available. *Library facilities:* Margaret Estes Resource Center. *Graduate expenses:* Tuition: full-time $10,043; part-time $510 per credit hour. Required fees: $975; $50 per credit hour. One-time fee: $75 full-time. *General application contact:* Chris Fontaine, Assistant VP for Enrollment Management and Market Research, 903-233-3250.

Graduate and Professional Studies
Dr. Scott Ray, Associate Vice President for the school of Graduate and Professional Studies
Programs in:
- business administration (MBA)
- educational leadership (MBA)

■ LUBBOCK CHRISTIAN UNIVERSITY
Lubbock, TX 79407-2099
http://www.lcu.edu/

Independent-religious, coed, comprehensive institution. *Computer facilities:* 159 computers available on campus for general student use. A campuswide network can be accessed from student residence rooms and from off campus. Internet access and online class registration, e-mail are available. *Library facilities:* University Library. *General application contact:* Administrative Assistant, 806-720-7662.

Graduate Biblical Studies
Programs in:
- Bible and ministry (MS)
- biblical interpretation (MA)

■ MIDWESTERN STATE UNIVERSITY

Wichita Falls, TX 76308

http://www.mwsu.edu/

State-supported, coed, comprehensive institution. *Enrollment:* 6,042 graduate, professional, and undergraduate students; 107 full-time matriculated graduate/professional students (68 women), 427 part-time matriculated graduate/professional students (277 women). *Graduate faculty:* 78 full-time (29 women), 13 part-time/adjunct (8 women). *Computer facilities:* 402 computers available on campus for general student use. A campuswide network can be accessed from student residence rooms and from off campus. Internet access and online class registration are available. *Library facilities:* Moffett Library. *General application contact:* Barbara Ramos Merkle, Director of Admissions, 800-842-1922.

Graduate Studies
Dr. Emerson Capps, Dean and Associate Provost

College of Business Administration
Anthony Chelte, Dean
Programs in:
- business administration (MBA)
- health services administration (MBA)

College of Education
Dr. Grant Simpson, Dean
Programs in:
- curriculum and instruction (ME)
- education (M Ed, MA, ME)
- educational leadership and technology (ME)
- general counseling (MA)
- human resource development (MA)
- reading education (M Ed)
- school counseling (M Ed)
- special education (M Ed)
- training and development (MA)

College of Health Sciences and Human Services
Dr. Susan Sportsman, Dean
Programs in:
- family nurse practitioner (MSN)
- health sciences and human services (MHA, MPA, MSK, MSN, MSR)
- health services administration (MHA, MSN)
- kinesiology (MSK)
- nurse educator (MSN)
- public administration (MPA)
- public administration (administrative justice) (MPA)
- public administration (health services administration)
- with certificate (MPA)
- public administration (health services) (MPA)
- radiologic administration (MSR)
- radiologic education (MSR)
- radiologic sciences (MSR)
- radiologist assistant (MSR)

College of Humanities and Social Sciences
Dr. Samuel E. Watson, Dean
Programs in:
- English (MA)
- history (MA)
- humanities and social sciences (MA)
- political science (MA)
- psychology (MA)

College of Science and Mathematics
Dr. Betty Stewart, Dean
Programs in:
- biology (MS)
- computer science (MS)

■ OUR LADY OF THE LAKE UNIVERSITY OF SAN ANTONIO

San Antonio, TX 78207-4689

http://www.ollusa.edu/

Independent-religious, coed, comprehensive institution. *Computer facilities:* Computer purchase and lease plans are available. 230 computers available on campus for general student use. A campuswide network can be accessed from student residence rooms and from off campus. Internet access and online class registration are available. *Library facilities:* The Sueltenfuss Library plus 2 others. *General application contact:* Information Contact, 210-434-6711 Ext. 2314.

College of Arts and Sciences
Programs in:
- English (MA)
- English communication arts (MA)
- language and literature (MA)

School of Business
Programs in:
- general (MBA)
- health care management (MBA)

School of Education and Clinical Studies
Programs in:
- communication and learning disorders (MA)
- counseling psychology (MS, Psy D)
- curriculum and instruction (M Ed)
- human sciences (MA)
- leadership studies (PhD)
- learning resources (M Ed)
- marriage and family therapy (MS)
- principal (M Ed)
- school counseling (M Ed)
- school psychology (MS)
- sociology (MA)
- special education (MA)

Worden School of Social Service
Program in:
- social service (MSW)

■ PRAIRIE VIEW A&M UNIVERSITY

Prairie View, TX 77446-0519

http://www.pvamu.edu/

State-supported, coed, comprehensive institution. *Enrollment:* 7,912 graduate, professional, and undergraduate students; 737 full-time matriculated graduate/professional students (513 women), 1,473 part-time matriculated graduate/professional students (1,098 women). *Graduate faculty:* 79 full-time (19 women), 131 part-time/adjunct (49 women). *Computer facilities:* Computer purchase and lease plans are available. 500 computers available on campus for general student use. A campuswide network can be accessed from student residence rooms and from off campus. Internet access and online class registration, e-mail are available. *Library facilities:* John B. Coleman Library. *Graduate expenses:* Tuition, state resident: full-time $1,440; part-time $80 per credit. Tuition, nonresident: full-time $6,444; part-time $358 per credit. *General application contact:* Dr. Ben DeSpain, Head, 936-857-2312.

College of Agriculture and Human Sciences
Dr. Linda Willis, Dean
Programs in:
- agricultural economics (MS)
- animal sciences (MS)
- interdisciplinary human sciences (MS)
- soil science (MS)

College of Arts and Sciences
Dr. Danny Kelley, Dean
Programs in:
- arts and sciences (MA, MS)
- biology (MS)
- chemistry (MS)
- English (MA)
- mathematics (MS)
- sociology (MA)

Division of Social Work, Behavioral and Political Science
Dr. Walle Engedayehu, Division Head
Program in:
- sociology (MA)

College of Business
John W. Dyck, Dean
Programs in:
- accounting (MS)
- general business administration (MBA)

College of Education
Dr. M. Paul Mehta, Dean
Programs in:
- counseling (MA, MS Ed)
- curriculum and instruction (M Ed, MA Ed, MS Ed)
- education (M Ed, MA, MA Ed, MS, MS Ed, PhD)
- educational leadership (PhD)
- health education (M Ed, MS)

Prairie View A&M University (continued)
physical education (M Ed, MS)
school administration (M Ed, MS Ed)
school supervision (M Ed, MS Ed)
special education (M Ed, MS Ed)

College of Engineering
Dr. Milton R. Bryant, Dean
Programs in:
computer information systems (MSCIS)
computer science (MSCS)
electrical engineering (MSEE, PhDEE)
engineering (MS Engr)

College of Juvenile Justice and Psychology
Dr. Elaine Rodney, Dean
Programs in:
clinical adolescent psychology (PhD)
juvenile forensic psychology (MSJFP)
juvenile justice (MSJJ, PhD)

College of Nursing
Dr. Betty N. Adams, Dean
Programs in:
family nurse practitioner (MSN)
nursing administration (MSN)
nursing education (MSN)

School of Architecture
Dr. Ikhlas Sabouni, Dean
Programs in:
architecture (M Arch)
community development (MCD)

■ RICE UNIVERSITY
Houston, TX 77251-1892
http://www.rice.edu/

Independent, coed, university. CGS member. *Enrollment:* 5,119 graduate, professional, and undergraduate students; 1,916 full-time matriculated graduate/professional students (672 women), 89 part-time matriculated graduate/professional students (53 women). *Graduate faculty:* 597 full-time, 387 part-time/adjunct. *Computer facilities:* 523 computers available on campus for general student use. A campuswide network can be accessed from student residence rooms and from off campus. Internet access and online class registration are available. *Library facilities:* Fondren Library. *Graduate expenses:* Tuition: full-time $23,400; part-time $1,300 per hour. Required fees: $150; $75 per semester. Tuition and fees vary according to program. *General application contact:* Office of Graduate Studies, 713-348-4002.

Graduate Programs
Jordan Konisky, Vice Provost for Research and Graduate Studies
Program in:
education (MAT)

George R. Brown School of Engineering
Dr. Sallie Keller-McNulty, Dean of Engineering
Programs in:
bioengineering (MS, PhD)
biostatistics (PhD)
chemical and biomolecular engineering (MS, PhD)
chemical engineering (M Ch E)
circuits, controls, and communication systems (MS, PhD)
civil engineering (MCE, MS, PhD)
computational and applied mathematics (MA, MCAM, PhD)
computational finance (PhD)
computational science and engineering (MCSE, PhD)
computer science (MCS, MS, PhD)
computer science and engineering (MS, PhD)
computer science in bioinformatics (MCS)
electrical engineering (MEE)
engineering (M Ch E, M Stat, MA, MBE, MCAM, MCE, MCS, MCSE, MEE, MEE, MES, MME, MMS, MS, PhD)
environmental engineering (MEE, MES, MS, PhD)
environmental science (MEE, MES, MS, PhD)
lasers, microwaves, and solid-state electronics (MS, PhD)
materials science (MMS, MS, PhD)
mechanical engineering (MME, MS, PhD)
statistics (M Stat, MA, PhD)

Jesse H. Jones Graduate School of Management
Dr. William H. Glick, Dean
Program in:
business administration (EMBA, MBA, PMBA)

School of Architecture
Lars Lerup, Dean
Programs in:
architecture (M Arch, D Arch)
urban design (M Arch UD)

School of Humanities
Gary Wihl, Dean
Programs in:
English (MA, PhD)
French studies (MA, PhD)
history (MA, PhD)
humanities (MA, PhD)
linguistics (MA, PhD)
philosophy (MA, PhD)
religious studies (PhD)
Spanish (MA)

School of Social Sciences
Lyn Ragsdale, Dean
Programs in:
anthropology (MA, PhD)
cognitive sciences (MA, PhD)
economics (MA, PhD)
industrial-organizational/social psychology (MA, PhD)
political science (MA, PhD)
psychology (MA, PhD)
social sciences (MA, PhD)

Shepherd School of Music
Dr. Robert Yekovich, Dean
Programs in:
composition (MM, DMA)
conducting (MM)
history (MM)
performance (MM, DMA)
theory (MM)

Wiess School of Natural Sciences
Dr. Kathleen S. Matthews, Dean
Programs in:
biochemistry and cell biology (MA, PhD)
chemistry (MA)
earth science (MA, PhD)
ecology and evolutionary biology (MA, MS, PhD)
environmental analysis and decision making (MS)
geophysics (MS)
inorganic chemistry (PhD)
mathematics (MA, PhD)
nanoscale physics (MS)
natural sciences (MA, MS, MST, PhD)
organic chemistry (PhD)
physical chemistry (PhD)
physics (MA)
physics and astronomy (MS, MST, PhD)

Rice Quantum Institute
Dr. Peter Nordlander, Director
Program in:
quantum physics (MS, PhD)

■ ST. EDWARD'S UNIVERSITY
Austin, TX 78704
http://www.stedwards.edu/

Independent-religious, coed, comprehensive institution. *Enrollment:* 5,224 graduate, professional, and undergraduate students; 158 full-time matriculated graduate/professional students (115 women), 802 part-time matriculated graduate/professional students (450 women). *Graduate faculty:* 48 full-time (22 women), 52 part-time/adjunct (17 women). *Computer facilities:* 475 computers available on campus for general student use. A campuswide network can be accessed from student residence rooms and from off campus. Internet access and online class registration are available. *Library facilities:* Scarborough-Phillips Library. *Graduate expenses:* Tuition: full-time $11,682; part-time $649 per credit hour. Full-time tuition and fees vary according to course load and program. *General application contact:* Bridget Sowinski, Director, Center for Academic Progress, 512-428-1061.

New College
Dr. H. Ramsey Fowler, Dean
Programs in:
counseling (MA)
liberal arts (MLA, Certificate)

School of Education
Dr. Karen Jenlink, Dean
Program in:
education (MA)

School of Management and Business
Marsha Kelliher, Dean
Programs in:
- accounting (MBA)
- business management (MBA)
- computer information systems (MS)
- conflict resolution (Certificate)
- digital media management (MBA)
- entrepreneurship (MBA, Certificate)
- finance—general (MBA, Certificate)
- global business (MBA, Certificate)
- human resource management (MBA, Certificate)
- human services (MA)
- management and business (MA, MBA, MS, Certificate)
- management information systems (MBA, Certificate)
- marketing (MBA, Certificate)
- operations management (MBA, Certificate)
- organizational leadership and ethics (MS)
- personal financial planner (MBA, Certificate)
- project management (MS)
- sports management (MBA, Certificate)

■ ST. MARY'S UNIVERSITY OF SAN ANTONIO
San Antonio, TX 78228-8507
http://www.stmarytx.edu/

Independent-religious, coed, comprehensive institution. *Enrollment:* 3,904 graduate, professional, and undergraduate students; 964 full-time matriculated graduate/professional students (464 women), 540 part-time matriculated graduate/professional students (287 women). *Graduate faculty:* 44 full-time (14 women), 89 part-time/adjunct (30 women). *Computer facilities:* Computer purchase and lease plans are available. 100 computers available on campus for general student use. A campuswide network can be accessed from student residence rooms and from off campus. Internet access and online class registration, wireless campus; e-mail are available. *Library facilities:* Louis J. Blume Library plus 1 other. *Graduate expenses:* Tuition: full-time $10,890; part-time $605 per hour. Required fees: $500. Tuition and fees vary according to degree level. *General application contact:* Dr. Henry Flores, Dean of the Graduate School, 210-436-3101.

Graduate School
Dr. Henry Flores, Dean of the Graduate School
Programs in:
- Catholic principalship (Certificate)
- Catholic school administrators (Certificate)
- Catholic school leadership (MA, Certificate)
- Catholic school teachers (Certificate)
- clinical psychology (MA, MS)
- communication studies (MA)
- community counseling (MA)
- computer information systems (MS)
- computer science (MS)
- counseling (Sp C)
- counseling education and supervision (PhD)
- educational leadership (MA, Certificate)
- electrical engineering (MS)
- electrical/computer engineering (MS)
- engineering administration (MS)
- engineering computer applications (MS)
- engineering management (MS)
- engineering systems management (MS)
- English literature and language (MA)
- industrial engineering (MS)
- industrial/organizational psychology (MA, MS)
- inter-American administration (MPA)
- international relations (MA)
- marriage and family relations (Certificate)
- marriage and family therapy (MA, PhD)
- mental health (MA)
- mental health and substance abuse counseling (Certificate)
- operations research (MS)
- pastoral ministry (MA)
- political communications and applied science (MA)
- political science (MA)
- principalship (mid-management) (Certificate)
- public administration (MPA)
- public management (MPA)
- reading (MA)
- school psychology (MA)
- software engineering (MS)
- substance abuse (MA)
- theology (MA)

Bill Greehey School of Business
Dr. Keith A Russell, Dean
Programs in:
- accounting (M Acc)
- business administration (MBA)
- finance (MBA)
- international business (MBA)
- management (MBA)
- taxation (M Acc)

School of Law
Robert William Piatt, Dean
Program in:
- law (JD)

■ SAM HOUSTON STATE UNIVERSITY
Huntsville, TX 77341
http://www.shsu.edu/

State-supported, coed, university. *Enrollment:* 15,935 graduate, professional, and undergraduate students; 485 full-time matriculated graduate/professional students (297 women), 1,397 part-time matriculated graduate/professional students (999 women). *Graduate faculty:* 213 full-time (68 women), 1 part-time/adjunct (0 women). *Computer facilities:* 552 computers available on campus for general student use. A campuswide network can be accessed from student residence rooms and from off campus. Internet access and online class registration are available. *Library facilities:* Newton Gresham Library. *Graduate expenses:* Tuition, state resident: full-time $5,904; part-time $164 per semester hour. Tuition, nonresident: full-time $15,804; part-time $439 per semester hour. Required fees: $1,374; $462 per semester. *General application contact:* Dr. Mitchell Muehsam, Dean of Graduate Studies and Associate Vice President for Academic Affairs, 936-294-1971.

College of Arts and Sciences
Dr. Jaimie Hebert, Dean
Programs in:
- agriculture (MS)
- art (MA, MFA)
- arts and sciences (M Ed, MA, MFA, MM, MS)
- biology (MA, MS)
- chemistry (MS)
- computing and information science (MS)
- dance (MFA)
- industrial education (M Ed, MA)
- industrial technology (MA)
- mathematics (MA, MS)
- statistics (MS)
- vocational education (M Ed)

School of Music
Dr. James Bankhead, Chair
Programs in:
- conducting (MM)
- music (MM)
- music education (M Ed, MM)

College of Business Administration
Dr. R. Dean Lewis, Dean
Programs in:
- business administration (MBA)
- finance (MS)
- general business and finance (MS)

College of Criminal Justice
Dr. Vincent Webb, Dean
Programs in:
- criminal justice (MS, PhD)
- criminal justice and criminology (MA)
- criminal justice management (MS)
- forensic science (MS)

College of Education and Applied Science
Dr. Genevieve Brown, Dean
Programs in:
- administration (M Ed, MA)
- counseling (M Ed, MA)
- counselor education (MA, PhD)
- early childhood education (M Ed)
- education and applied science (M Ed, MA, MLS, Ed D, PhD)
- educational leadership (Ed D)
- elementary education (M Ed, MA)
- health and kinesiology (M Ed, MA)

Sam Houston State University (continued)
instructional leadership (M Ed, MA)
library science (MLS)
reading (M Ed, MA)
secondary education (M Ed, MA)
special education (M Ed, MA)

College of Humanities and Social Sciences
Dr. John deCastro, Dean
Programs in:
clinical psychology (MA, PhD)
English (MA)
family and consumer sciences (MA)
history (MA)
humanities and social sciences (MA, MPA, PhD)
political science (MA)
psychology (MA)
public administration (MPA)
school psychology (MA)
sociology (MA)

■ SOUTHERN METHODIST UNIVERSITY
Dallas, TX 75275
http://www.smu.edu/

Independent-religious, coed, university. CGS member. *Enrollment:* 10,941 graduate, professional, and undergraduate students; 2,199 full-time matriculated graduate/professional students (902 women), 2,028 part-time matriculated graduate/professional students (778 women). *Graduate faculty:* 613 full-time (205 women), 315 part-time/adjunct (111 women). *Computer facilities:* Computer purchase and lease plans are available. 758 computers available on campus for general student use. A campuswide network can be accessed from student residence rooms and from off campus. Internet access and online class registration, online billing/payment processing are available. *Library facilities:* Central University Library plus 7 others. *General application contact:* Dr. R. Hal Williams, Dean of Research and Graduate Studies, 214-768-4345.

Cox School of Business
Dr. Albert W. Niemi, Dean
Programs in:
accounting (MSA)
business (Exec MBA, MBA)
management (MSM)

Dedman College
Dr. R. Hal Williams, Interim
Programs in:
anthropology (PhD)
applied economics (MA)
applied geophysics (MS)
biological sciences (MA, MS, PhD)
chemistry (MS, PhD)
clinical and counseling psychology (MA)
clinical psychology (PhD)
computational and applied mathematics (MS, PhD)
economics (MA, PhD)
English (MA, PhD)
exploration geophysics (MS)
geology (MS, PhD)
geophysics (PhD)
history (MA, PhD)
medical anthropology (MA)
medieval studies (MA)
physics (MS, PhD)
religious studies (MA, PhD)
statistical science (MS, PhD)

Dedman School of Law
John B. Attanasio, Dean
Programs in:
comparative and international law (LL M)
law (JD, SJD)
law-general (LL M)
taxation (LL M)

Meadows School of the Arts
Jose Antonio Bowen, Dean
Programs in:
acting (MFA)
art history (MA)
arts (MA, MFA, MM, MSM, Certificate)
conducting (MM)
dance (MFA)
design (MFA)
joint business)
music composition (MM)
music education (MM)
music history (MM)
music theory (MM)
performance (MM, Certificate)
piano performance and pedagogy (MM)
sacred music (MSM)
studio art (MFA)

Division of Cinema—Television
Rick Worland, Chair
Program in:
cinema—television (MA)

Perkins School of Theology
Dr. William B. Lawrence, Dean
Program in:
theology (M Div, CMM, MSM, MTS, D Min)

School of Education and Human Development
Programs in:
education and human development (M Ed, MBE, MLS)
liberal arts (MLS)
literacy and language acquisition (MBE)
teacher education (M Ed)

School of Engineering
Dr. Geoffrey Orsak, Dean
Programs in:
applied science (MS, PhD)
civil engineering (MS, PhD)
computer engineering (MS Cp E, PhD)
computer science (MS, PhD)
electrical engineering (MSEE, PhD)
electronic and optical packaging (MS)
engineering (MS, MS Cp E, MSEE, MSEM, MSIEM, MSME, DE, PhD)
engineering management (MSEM, DE)
environmental engineering (MS)
environmental science (MS)
facilities management (MS)
information engineering and management (MSIEM)
manufacturing systems management (MS)
mechanical engineering (MSME, PhD)
operations research (MS, PhD)
security engineering (MS)
software engineering (MS)
systems engineering (MS)
telecommunications (MS)

■ STEPHEN F. AUSTIN STATE UNIVERSITY
Nacogdoches, TX 75962
http://www.sfasu.edu/

State-supported, coed, comprehensive institution. *Computer facilities:* 1,000 computers available on campus for general student use. A campuswide network can be accessed from student residence rooms and from off campus. Internet access and online class registration are available. *Library facilities:* Ralph W. Steen Library. *General application contact:* Associate Vice President for Graduate Studies and Research, 936-468-2807.

Graduate School

College of Applied Arts and Science
Programs in:
applied arts and science (MA, MIS, MSW)
communication (MA)
interdisciplinary studies (MIS)
mass communication (MA)
social work (MSW)

College of Business
Programs in:
business (MBA)
computer science (MS)
management and marketing (MBA)
professional accountancy (MPAC)

College of Education
Programs in:
athletic training (MS)
counseling (MA)
early childhood education (M Ed)
education (M Ed, MA, MS, Ed D)
educational leadership (Ed D)
elementary education (M Ed)
human sciences (MS)
kinesiology (M Ed)
school psychology (MA)
secondary education (M Ed)
special education (M Ed)
speech pathology (MS)

College of Fine Arts
Programs in:
art (MA)

design (MFA)
drawing (MFA)
fine arts (MA, MFA, MM)
music (MA, MM)
painting (MFA)
sculpture (MFA)

College of Forestry and Agriculture
Programs in:
agriculture (MS)
forestry (MF, MS, PhD)
forestry and agriculture (MF, MS, PhD)

College of Liberal Arts
Programs in:
English (MA)
history (MA)
liberal arts (MA, MPA)
psychology (MA)
public administration (MPA)

College of Sciences and Mathematics
Programs in:
biology (MS)
biotechnology (MS)
chemistry (MS)
environmental science (MS)
geology (MS, MSNS)
mathematics (MS)
mathematics education (MS)
physics (MS)
sciences and mathematics (MS, MSNS)
statistics (MS)

■ SUL ROSS STATE UNIVERSITY
Alpine, TX 79832
http://www.sulross.edu/

State-supported, coed, comprehensive institution. *Computer facilities:* 200 computers available on campus for general student use. A campuswide network can be accessed from student residence rooms and from off campus. Internet access is available. *Library facilities:* Bryan Wildenthal Memorial Library. *General application contact:* Dean of Admissions and Records, 915-837-8050.

Division of Agricultural and Natural Resource Science
Programs in:
agricultural and natural resource science (M Ag, MS)
animal science (M Ag, MS)
range and wildlife management (M Ag, MS)

Rio Grande College of Sul Ross State University
Programs in:
business administration (MBA)
teacher education (M Ed)

School of Arts and Sciences
Programs in:
art education (M Ed)
art history (M Ed)
arts and sciences (M Ed, MA, MS)
biology (MS)
English (MA)
geology and chemistry (MS)
history (MA)
political science (MA)
psychology (MA)
public administration (MA)
studio art (M Ed)

School of Professional Studies
Programs in:
bilingual education (M Ed)
counseling (M Ed)
criminal justice (MS)
educational diagnostics (M Ed)
elementary education (M Ed)
industrial arts (M Ed)
international trade (MBA)
management (MBA)
physical education (M Ed)
professional studies (M Ed, MBA, MS)
reading specialist (M Ed)
school administration (M Ed)
secondary education (M Ed)
supervision (M Ed)

■ TARLETON STATE UNIVERSITY
Stephenville, TX 76402
http://www.tarleton.edu/

State-supported, coed, comprehensive institution. *Enrollment:* 9,464 graduate, professional, and undergraduate students; 337 full-time matriculated graduate/professional students (203 women), 1,194 part-time matriculated graduate/professional students (821 women). *Graduate faculty:* 151 full-time (55 women), 115 part-time/adjunct (39 women). *Computer facilities:* 600 computers available on campus for general student use. A campuswide network can be accessed from student residence rooms and from off campus. Internet access and online class registration are available. *Library facilities:* Dick Smith Library plus 1 other. *General application contact:* Dr. Linda M. Jones, Dean, 254-968-9104.

College of Graduate Studies
Dr. Linda M. Jones, Dean

College of Agriculture and Human Sciences
Dr. Don Cawthon, Acting Dean
Programs in:
agriculture (MS)
agriculture and human sciences (MS)
agriculture education (MS)

College of Business Administration
Dr. Ruby Barker, Dean
Programs in:
business administration (MBA)
human resource management (MS)
information systems (MS)

College of Education
Dr. Jill Burk, Dean
Programs in:
counseling (M Ed)
counseling and psychology (M Ed)
counseling psychology (M Ed)
curriculum and instruction (M Ed)
education (M Ed, Ed D, Certificate)
educational administration (M Ed, Certificate)
educational leadership (Ed D)
educational psychology (M Ed)
physical education (M Ed)
secondary education (Certificate)
special education (Certificate)

College of Liberal and Fine Arts
Dr. Dean A. Minix, Dean
Programs in:
criminal justice (MCJ)
English (MA)
history (MA)
liberal and fine arts (MA, MCJ, MS)
liberal studies (MS)
political science (MA)

College of Science and Technology
Dr. Rueben Walter, Dean
Programs in:
biology (MS)
environmental science (MS)
mathematics (MS)
science and technology (MS)

■ TEXAS A&M INTERNATIONAL UNIVERSITY
Laredo, TX 78041-1900
http://www.tamiu.edu/

State-supported, coed, comprehensive institution. *Enrollment:* 4,917 graduate, professional, and undergraduate students; 151 full-time matriculated graduate/professional students, 800 part-time matriculated graduate/professional students. *Graduate faculty:* 70 full-time (20 women), 12 part-time/adjunct (1 woman). *Computer facilities:* 200 computers available on campus for general student use. A campuswide network can be accessed from off campus. *Library facilities:* Sue and Radcliff Killam Library. *Graduate expenses:* Tuition, state resident: full-time $1,580. Tuition, nonresident: full-time $5,432. Required fees: $3,808. *General application contact:* Dr. Jeff Brown, Director, office of Graduate Studies, 956-326-2596.

Office of Graduate Studies and Research
Dr. Jeff Brown, Director
Programs in:
educational administration (MS Ed)
generic special education (MS Ed)
school counseling (MS)

College of Arts and Sciences
Dr. Nasser Momayezi, Dean

Texas A&M International University (continued)
Programs in:
arts and sciences (MA, MACP, MAIS, MPA, MS, PhD)
biology (MS)
counseling psychology (MACP)
criminal justice (MS)
English (MA)
fine and performing arts)
Hispanic studies (PhD)
history (MA)
mathematical and physical science (MA, MAIS)
political science (MA)
psychology (MS)
public administration (MPA)
sociology (MA)
Spanish (MA)

College of Business Administration
Dr. Jacky So, Dean
Programs in:
accounting (MP Acc)
business administration (MBA, MP Acc, MSIS)
information systems (MSIS)
international banking (MBA)
international trade (MBA)

College of Education
Dr. Humberto Gonzalez, Dean
Programs in:
bilingual education (PhD)
curriculum and instruction (MS, PhD)
early childhood education (PhD)
education (MS, MS Ed, PhD)
reading (MS)

School of Nursing
Dr. Susan Walker, Director
Program in:
nursing (MSN)

■ TEXAS A&M UNIVERSITY
College Station, TX 77843
http://www.tamu.edu/

State-supported, coed, university. CGS member. *Enrollment:* 45,380 graduate, professional, and undergraduate students; 7,085 full-time matriculated graduate/professional students (2,889 women), 1,715 part-time matriculated graduate/professional students (860 women). *Graduate faculty:* 1,205 full-time (249 women), 160 part-time/adjunct (31 women). *Computer facilities:* 1,300 computers available on campus for general student use. A campuswide network can be accessed from student residence rooms and from off campus. Internet access and online class registration are available. *Library facilities:* Sterling C. Evans Library plus 4 others. *Graduate expenses:* Tuition, state resident: full-time $4,697. Tuition, nonresident: full-time $11,297. Required fees: $2,272. *General application contact:* Graduate Admissions, 979-845-1044.

College of Agriculture and Life Sciences
Dr. Elsa Murano, Vice Chancellor
Programs in:
agricultural economics (MAB, MS, PhD)
agricultural education (M Ed, MS, Ed D, PhD)
agriculture (M Agr)
agriculture and life sciences (M Agr, M Ed, M Eng, MAB, MS, DE, Ed D, PhD)
agronomy (M Agr, MS, PhD)
animal breeding (MS, PhD)
animal science (M Agr, MS, PhD)
biochemistry (MS, PhD)
biological and agricultural engineering (M Agr, M Eng, MS, DE, PhD)
biophysics (MS)
dairy science (M Agr, MS)
entomology (M Agr, MS, PhD)
forestry (MS, PhD)
genetics (PhD)
horticulture (PhD)
horticulture and floriculture (M Agr, MS)
molecular and environmental plant sciences (MS, PhD)
natural resources development (M Agr)
nutrition and food science (M Agr, MS, PhD)
physiology of reproduction (MS, PhD)
plant pathology (MS, PhD)
plant protection (M Agr)
poultry science (M Agr, MS, PhD)
rangeland ecology and management (M Agr, MS, PhD)
recreation resources development (M Agr)
recreation, park, and tourism sciences (MS, PhD)
soil science (MS, PhD)
wildlife and fisheries sciences (M Agr, MS, PhD)

College of Architecture
J. Thomas Regan, Dean
Programs in:
architecture (M Arch, MS Arch, PhD)
construction management (MS)
land development (MSLD)
landscape architecture (MLA)
urban and regional science (PhD)
urban planning (MUP)
visualization science (MS)

College of Education and Human Development
Doug Palmer, Interim Dean
Programs in:
counseling psychology (PhD)
curriculum and instruction (M Ed, MS, PhD)
education and human development (M Ed, MS, Ed D, PhD)
educational administration and human resource development (M Ed, MS, Ed D, PhD)
educational psychology (PhD)
educational technology (M Ed)
gifted and talented education (M Ed, MS)
health education (M Ed, MS, Ed D, PhD)
Hispanic bilingual education (M Ed, PhD)
human learning and development (MS)
intelligence, creativity, and giftedness (PhD)
kinesiology (M Ed, MS, Ed D, PhD)
learning, development, and instruction (PhD)
mathematics education (M Ed, MS, PhD)
multicultural/urban/ESL/international education (M Ed, MS, PhD)
reading/language arts (M Ed, MS, PhD)
research, measurement and statistics (MS)
research, measurement, and statistics (PhD)
school counseling (M Ed)
school psychology (PhD)
science education (M Ed, MS, PhD)
social studies education (M Ed, MS, PhD)
special education (M Ed, PhD)

College of Engineering
Dr. G. Kemble Bennett, Dean
Programs in:
aerospace engineering (M Eng, MS, PhD)
biomedical engineering (M Eng, MS, D Eng, PhD)
chemical engineering (M Eng, MS, PhD)
computer engineering (M En, M Eng, MS, PhD)
computer science (MCS, MS, PhD)
construction engineering and management (M Eng, MS, D Eng, PhD)
electrical engineering (MS, PhD)
engineering (M En, M Eng, MCS, MID, MS, D Eng, PhD)
engineering technology and industrial distribution (MID)
environmental engineering (M Eng, MS, D Eng, PhD)
geotechnical engineering (M Eng, MS, D Eng, PhD)
health physics (MS)
industrial and systems engineering (M Eng, MS)
industrial engineering (D Eng, PhD)
materials engineering (M Eng, MS, D Eng, PhD)
mechanical engineering (M Eng, MS, D Eng, PhD)
nuclear engineering (M Eng, MS, PhD)
ocean engineering (M Eng, MS, D Eng, PhD)
petroleum engineering (M Eng, MS, PhD)
structural engineering (M Eng, MS, D Eng, PhD)
transportation engineering (M Eng, MS, D Eng, PhD)
water resources engineering (M Eng, MS, D Eng, PhD)

College of Geosciences
Dr. Bjorn Kjerfve, Dean

Programs in:
- atmospheric sciences (MS, PhD)
- geography (MS, PhD)
- geology (MS, PhD)
- geophysics (MS, PhD)
- geosciences (MS, PhD)
- oceanography (MS, PhD)

College of Liberal Arts
Dr. Charles A. Johnson, Dean
Programs in:
- anthropology (MA, PhD)
- behavioral and cellular neuroscience (MS, PhD)
- clinical psychology (MS, PhD)
- cognitive psychology (MS, PhD)
- communication (MA, PhD)
- developmental psychology (MS, PhD)
- economics (MS, PhD)
- English (MA, PhD)
- Hispanic studies (MA, PhD)
- history (MA, PhD)
- industrial/organizational psychology (MS, PhD)
- liberal arts (MA, MS, PhD)
- philosophy (MA, PhD)
- political science (MA, PhD)
- science and technology journalism (MS)
- social psychology (MS, PhD)
- sociology (MS, PhD)

College of Science
H. Joseph Newton, Dean
Programs in:
- applied physics (PhD)
- biology (MS, PhD)
- botany (MS, PhD)
- chemistry (MS, PhD)
- mathematics (MS, PhD)
- microbiology (MS, PhD)
- molecular and cell biology (PhD)
- neuroscience (MS, PhD)
- physics (MS, PhD)
- science (MS, PhD)
- statistics (MS, PhD)
- zoology (MS, PhD)

College of Veterinary Medicine
Dr. H. Richard Adams, Dean
Program in:
- veterinary medicine (DVM, MS, PhD)

Graduate Programs in Veterinary Medicine
Dr. L. Garry Adams, Associate Dean, Research and Graduate Studies
Programs in:
- epidemiology (MS)
- food safety/toxicology (MS)
- genetics (MS, PhD)
- physiology and pharmacology (MS, PhD)
- toxicology (MS, PhD)
- veterinary anatomy (MS, PhD)
- veterinary integrative biosciences (MS, PhD)
- veterinary large animal clinical sciences (MS)
- veterinary medicine and surgery (MS)
- veterinary microbiology (MS, PhD)
- veterinary parasitology (MS)
- veterinary pathobiology (MS, PhD)
- veterinary pathology (MS, PhD)
- veterinary physiology and pharmacology (MS, PhD)
- veterinary public health (MS)
- veterinary small animal medicine and surgery (MS)

Faculty of Neuroscience
Program in:
- neuroscience (MS, PhD)

George Bush School of Government and Public Service
Richard A. Chilcoat, Dean
Programs in:
- international affairs (MPSA)
- public service and administration (MPSA)

Mays Business School
Dr. Jerry R. Strawser, Dean
Programs in:
- accounting (MS, PhD)
- business (EMBA, MBA, MLERE, MS, PhD)
- business administration (EMBA, MBA)
- finance (MS, PhD)
- human resource management (MS)
- management (PhD)
- management information systems (MS, PhD)
- management science (PhD)
- marketing (MS, PhD)
- production and operations management (PhD)
- real estate (MLERE)

■ TEXAS A&M UNIVERSITY–COMMERCE
Commerce, TX 75429-3011
http://www.tamu-commerce.edu/

State-supported, coed, university. CGS member. *Computer facilities:* 405 computers available on campus for general student use. A campuswide network can be accessed from student residence rooms and from off campus. Internet access and online class registration are available. *Library facilities:* Gee Library. *General application contact:* Graduate Admissions Adviser, 843-886-5167.

Graduate School

College of Arts and Sciences
Programs in:
- agricultural education (M Ed, MS)
- agricultural sciences (M Ed, MS)
- art (MA, MS)
- art history (MA)
- arts and sciences (M Ed, MA, MFA, MM, MS, MSW, PhD)
- biological and earth sciences (M Ed, MS)
- chemistry (M Ed, MS)
- college teaching of English (PhD)
- computer science (MS)
- English (MA, MS)
- fine arts (MFA)
- history (MA, MS)
- mathematics (MA, MS)
- music (MA, MS)
- music composition (MA, MM)
- music education (MA, MM, MS)
- music literature (MA)
- music performance (MA, MM)
- music theory (MA, MM)
- physics (M Ed, MS)
- social sciences (M Ed, MS)
- social work (MSW)
- sociology (MA, MS)
- Spanish (MA)
- studio art (MA)
- theatre (MA, MS)

College of Business and Technology
Programs in:
- business administration (MBA)
- business and technology (MA, MBA, MS)
- economics (MA, MS)
- industry and technology (MS)

College of Education and Human Services
Programs in:
- counseling (M Ed, MS, Ed D)
- early childhood education (M Ed, MA, MS)
- education (M Ed, MA, MS, Ed D, PhD)
- educational administration (M Ed, MS, Ed D)
- educational psychology (PhD)
- elementary education (M Ed, MS)
- health, kinesiology and sports studies (M Ed, MS, Ed D)
- higher education (MS)
- learning technology and information systems (M Ed, MS)
- psychology (MA, MS)
- reading (M Ed, MA, MS)
- secondary education (M Ed, MS)
- special education (M Ed, MA, MS)
- supervision of curriculum and instruction: elementary education (Ed D)
- supervision, curriculum, and instruction (Ed D)
- training and development (MS)

■ TEXAS A&M UNIVERSITY–CORPUS CHRISTI
Corpus Christi, TX 78412-5503
http://www.tamucc.edu/

State-supported, coed, comprehensive institution. CGS member. *Computer facilities:* 500 computers available on campus for general student use. A campuswide network can be accessed from student residence rooms and from off campus. Internet access and online class registration are available. *Library facilities:* Mary and Jeff Bell Library. *General application contact:* Records Evaluator, 361-825-5740.

Texas A&M University–Corpus Christi (continued)

Graduate Studies and Research

College of Business
Programs in:
- accounting (M Acc)
- health care administration (MBA)
- international business (MBA)

College of Education
Programs in:
- counseling (MS, PhD)
- counselor education (PhD)
- curriculum and instruction (MS, Ed D)
- early childhood education (MS)
- educational administration (MS)
- educational leadership (Ed D)
- educational technology (MS)
- elementary education (MS)
- kinesiology (MS)
- occupational training and development (MS)
- reading (MS)
- secondary education (MS)
- special education (MS)

College of Liberal Arts
Programs in:
- English (MA)
- history (MA)
- psychology (MA)
- public administration (MPA)
- studio arts (MA, MFA)

College of Nursing and Health Sciences
Programs in:
- clinical nurse specialist (MSN)
- family nurse practitioner (MSN)
- health care administration (MSN)
- leadership in nursing systems (MSN)

College of Science and Technology
Programs in:
- applied and computational mathematics (MS)
- biology (MS)
- coastal and marine system science (PhD)
- computer science (MS)
- curriculum content (MS)
- environmental science (MS)
- mariculture (MS)
- science and technology (MS, PhD)

■ TEXAS A&M UNIVERSITY–KINGSVILLE
Kingsville, TX 78363
http://www.tamuk.edu/

State-supported, coed, university. *Computer facilities:* 600 computers available on campus for general student use. A campuswide network can be accessed from student residence rooms and from off campus. *Library facilities:* James C. Jernigan Library. *General application contact:* Dean, College of Graduate Studies, 361-593-2808.

Find University Details at www.petersons.com/gradchannel.

College of Graduate Studies

College of Agriculture and Home Economics
Programs in:
- agribusiness (MS)
- agricultural education (MS)
- agriculture and home economics (MS, PhD)
- animal sciences (MS)
- human sciences (MS)
- plant and soil sciences (MS, PhD)
- range and wildlife management (MS)
- wildlife science (PhD)

College of Arts and Sciences
Programs in:
- applied geology (MS)
- art (MA, MS)
- arts and sciences (MA, MM, MS)
- biology (MS)
- chemistry (MS)
- communication (MS)
- English (MA, MS)
- gerontology (MS)
- history and political science (MA, MS)
- mathematics (MS)
- music education (MM)
- psychology (MA, MS)
- sociology (MA, MS)
- Spanish (MA)

College of Business Administration
Program in:
- business administration (MBA, MS)

College of Education
Programs in:
- adult education (M Ed)
- bilingual education (MA, MS, Ed D)
- early childhood education (M Ed)
- education (M Ed, MA, MS, Ed D, PhD)
- elementary education (MA, MS)
- English as a second language (M Ed)
- guidance and counseling (MA, MS)
- health and kinesiology (MA, MS)
- higher education administration leadership (PhD)
- reading (MS)
- school administration (MA, MS, Ed D)
- secondary education (MA, MS)
- special education (M Ed)
- supervision (MA, MS)

College of Engineering
Programs in:
- chemical engineering (ME, MS)
- civil engineering (ME, MS)
- computer science (MS)
- electrical engineering (ME, MS)
- engineering (ME, MS, PhD)
- environmental engineering (ME, MS, PhD)
- industrial engineering (ME, MS)
- mechanical engineering (ME, MS)
- natural gas engineering (ME, MS)

■ TEXAS A&M UNIVERSITY–TEXARKANA
Texarkana, TX 75505-5518
http://www.tamut.edu/

State-supported, coed, upper-level institution. *Enrollment:* 1,670 graduate, professional, and undergraduate students; 49 full-time matriculated graduate/professional students (36 women), 465 part-time matriculated graduate/professional students (332 women). *Computer facilities:* 133 computers available on campus for general student use. A campuswide network can be accessed from off campus. Internet access and online class registration are available. *Library facilities:* John F. Moss Library plus 1 other. *Graduate expenses:* Tuition, state resident: part-time $112 per credit hour. Tuition, nonresident: part-time $387 per credit hour. Required fees: $8 per credit hour. $8 per term. *General application contact:* Patricia E. Black, Director of Admissions and Registrar, 903-223-3068.

Graduate Studies and Research
Dr. David Allard, Dean

College of Arts and Sciences and Education
Dr. Rosannce Stripling, Dean
Programs in:
- adult education (MS)
- curriculum and instruction (MS)
- education (MS)
- educational administration (M Ed)
- English (MA)
- history (MS)
- instructional technology (MS)
- interdisciplinary studies (MA, MS)
- special education (M Ed, MS)

College of Business
Dr. Edward Bashaw, Dean
Programs in:
- accounting (MSA)
- business administration (MBA, MS)

College of Health and Behavioral Sciences
Dr. Jo Kahler, Dean
Program in:
- counseling psychology (MS)

■ TEXAS CHRISTIAN UNIVERSITY
Fort Worth, TX 76129-0002
http://www.tcu.edu/

Independent-religious, coed, university. CGS member. *Enrollment:* 8,865 graduate, professional, and undergraduate students; 610 full-time matriculated graduate/professional students, 988 part-time matriculated graduate/professional students. *Computer facilities:* Computer purchase and lease plans are available. A campuswide network can be accessed from student residence rooms and from off campus. Internet access and online class registration are available. *Library facilities:* Mary Couts Burnett Library. *Graduate expenses:* Tuition: part-time $800 per credit hour. *General application contact:* Admissions, TCU Graduate Studies Office, 817-257-7515.

AddRan College of Humanities and Social Sciences
Dr. Mary Volcansek, Dean
Programs in:
English (MA, PhD)
history (MA, PhD)
humanities and social sciences (MA, PhD)

Brite Divinity School
Dr. D. Newell Williams, President
Programs in:
Biblical interpretation (PhD)
Christian service (MACS)
divinity (M Div, D Min)
pastoral theology and pastoral counseling (PhD)
theological studies (MTS, CTS)
theology (Th M)

College of Communication
Dr. William T. Slater, Dean
Programs in:
advertising/public relations (MS)
communication (MS)
communication in human relations (MS)
news-editorial (MS)

College of Fine Arts
Dr. Scott Sullivan, Dean
Programs in:
art history (MA)
fine arts (M Mus, MA, MFA, MM Ed, Artist Diploma)
studio art (MFA)

School of Music
Dr. Richard Gipson, Director
Programs in:
conducting (M Mus)
music education (MM Ed)
musicology (M Mus)
organ performance (M Mus)
piano (Artist Diploma)
piano pedagogy (M Mus)
piano performance (M Mus)
string performance (M Mus)
theory/composition (M Mus)
vocal performance (M Mus)
voice pedagogy (M Mus)
wind and percussion performance (M Mus)

College of Science and Engineering
Dr. Michael McCracken, Dean
Programs in:
biology (MA, MS)
chemistry (MA, MS, PhD)
earth sciences (MS)
ecology (MS)
environmental sciences (MS)
geology (MS)
mathematics (MAT)
physics (MA, MS, PhD)
psychology (MA, MS, PhD)
science and engineering (MA, MAT, MS, PhD)

Graduate Studies and Research
Dr. Don Coerver, Director
Program in:
liberal arts (MLA)

Harris College of Nursing and Health Sciences
Dr. Paulette Burns, Dean
Programs in:
adult nursing (MSN)
kinesiology (MS)
nursing and health sciences (MS, MSN, MSNA)
speech-language pathology (MS)

School of Nurse Anesthesia
Dr. Kay K. Sanders, Director
Program in:
nurse anesthesia (MSNA)

M. J. Neeley School of Business
Dr. Daniel G. Short, Dean
Programs in:
accounting (M Ac)
business administration (MBA)
international management (MIM)

School of Education
Dr. Sam Deitz, Dean
Programs in:
counseling (M Ed)
education (M Ed, PhD, Certificate)
educational administration (M Ed)
educational foundations (M Ed)
educational studies: science education (PhD)
elementary education (M Ed, Certificate)
school counseling (Certificate)
science education (M Ed)
special education (M Ed)

■ TEXAS SOUTHERN UNIVERSITY
Houston, TX 77004-4584
http://www.tsu.edu/

State-supported, coed, university. CGS member. *Enrollment:* 11,224 graduate, professional, and undergraduate students; 1,434 full-time matriculated graduate/professional students (850 women), 683 part-time matriculated graduate/professional students (455 women). *Graduate faculty:* 118 full-time (48 women), 37 part-time/adjunct (11 women). *Computer facilities:* 500 computers available on campus for general student use. A campuswide network can be accessed. Internet access and online class registration, Blackboard Learning and Community Portal System (E-education) are available. *Library facilities:* Robert J. Terry Library plus 2 others. *General application contact:* Dr. Richard Pitre, Dean of the Graduate School, Acting, 713-313-7011 Ext. 7534.

College of Pharmacy and Health Sciences
Dr. Barbara Hayes, Dean
Program in:
pharmacy and health sciences (Pharm D, MHCA)

Graduate School
Dr. Richard Pitre, Dean of the Graduate School, Acting

College of Education
Dr. Jay Cummings, Dean
Programs in:
bilingual education (M Ed)
counseling (M Ed, Ed D)
counseling education (Ed D)
curriculum, instruction, and urban education (Ed D)
early childhood education (M Ed)
education (M Ed, MS, Ed D)
educational administration (M Ed, Ed D)
elementary education (M Ed)
health education (MS)
higher education administration (Ed D)
mid-management superintending (Ed D)
physical education (MS)
reading education (M Ed)
research education and certification (Ed D)
research education and education (Ed D)
secondary education (M Ed)
special education (M Ed)

College of Liberal Arts and Behavioral Sciences
Dr. Merline Pitre, Dean
Programs in:
English (MA, MS)
history (MA)
human services and consumer sciences (MS)
liberal arts and behavioral sciences (MA, MS)
music (MA)
psychology (MA)
sociology (MA)

Jesse H. Jones School of Business
Dr. Joseph Boyd, Dean
Programs in:
business (MBA)
business administration (MBA)

School of Public Affairs
Dr. Theophilus Herrington, Interim Dean
Programs in:
public administration (MPA)
public affairs (MCP, MPA)
urban planning and environmental policy (MCP)

School of Science and Technology
Dr. Victor Obot, Interim Dean
Programs in:
biology (MS)
chemistry (MS)
computer science (MS)
environmental toxicology (MS, PhD)
industrial technology (MS)
mathematics (MA, MS)
science and technology (MA, MS, PhD)
transportation (MS)

Texas Southern University (continued)

Tavis Smiley School of Communication
Dr. James Ward, Head
Programs in:
journalism (MA)
speech communications (MA)
telecommunications (MA)

Thurgood Marshall School of Law
McKen V. Carrington, Dean
Program in:
law (JD)

■ TEXAS STATE UNIVERSITY-SAN MARCOS
San Marcos, TX 78666
http://www.txstate.edu/

State-supported, coed, university. CGS member. *Enrollment:* 27,485 graduate, professional, and undergraduate students; 1,442 full-time matriculated graduate/professional students (905 women), 1,837 part-time matriculated graduate/professional students (1,177 women). *Graduate faculty:* 360 full-time (143 women), 58 part-time/adjunct (32 women). *Computer facilities:* Computer purchase and lease plans are available. 1,200 computers available on campus for general student use. A campuswide network can be accessed from student residence rooms and from off campus. Internet access and online class registration are available. *Library facilities:* Alkek Library. *General application contact:* Dr. J. Michael Willoughby, Dean of Graduate School, 512-245-2581.

Graduate School
Dr. J. Michael Willoughby, Dean
Programs in:
applied sociology (MAIS)
biology (MSIS)
criminal justice (MSIS)
educational administration and psychological services (MAIS)
elementary mathematics, science, and technology (MSIS)
health, physical education, and recreation (MAIS)
interdisciplinary studies in political science (MAIS)
international studies (MA)
modern languages (MAIS)
occupational education (MAIS, MSIS)
psychology (MAIS)

College of Applied Arts
Dr. Jaime Chahin, Dean
Programs in:
agriculture (M Ed)
applied arts (M Ed, MS, MSCJ)
criminal justice (MSCJ)
family and child studies (MS)
management of technical education (M Ed)

College of Education
Dr. Rosalinda Barrera, Dean
Programs in:
counseling and guidance (M Ed)
developmental and adult education (MA, PhD)
early childhood education (M Ed, MA)
education (M Ed, MA, MSRLS, PhD)
educational administration (M Ed, MA)
elementary education (M Ed, MA)
elementary education-bilingual/bicultural (M Ed, MA)
health and physical education (MA)
health education (M Ed)
physical education (M Ed)
professional counseling (MA)
reading education (M Ed)
recreation and leisure services (MSRLS)
school psychology (MA)
secondary education (M Ed, MA)
special education (M Ed)

College of Fine Arts and Communication
Dr. T. Richard Cheatham, Dean
Programs in:
communication studies (MA)
fine arts and communication (MA, MM)
journalism and mass communication (MA)
music education (MM)
music performance (MM)
theatre arts (MA)

College of Health Professions
Dr. Ruth Welborn, Dean
Programs in:
communication disorders (MA, MSCD)
health professions (MA, MHA, MS, MSCD, MSPT, MSW)
health services and research (MS)
health services research (MS)
healthcare administration (MHA)
healthcare human resources (MS)
physical therapy (MSPT)
social work (MSW)

College of Liberal Arts
Dr. Ann Marrie Ellis, Dean
Programs in:
anthropology (MA)
applied geography (MAG)
creative writing (MFA)
environmental geography (PhD)
environmental geography, geography education, and geography information science (PhD)
geographic information science (MAG)
geography (MAG, MS)
geography education (PhD)
health psychology (MA)
history (M Ed, MA)
information science (PhD)
land/area studies (MAG)
legal studies (MA)
liberal arts (M Ed, MA, MAG, MFA, MPA, MS, PhD)
literature (MA)
political science (MA)
public administration (MPA)
resource and environmental studies (MAG)
rhetoric and composition (MA)
sociology (MA, MS)
Spanish (MA)
technical communication (MA)

College of Science
Dr. Hector E. Flores, Dean
Programs in:
aquatic biology (MS)
biochemistry (MS)
biology (M Ed, MA, MS)
chemistry (MA, MS)
computer science (MA, MS)
industrial mathematics (MS)
industrial technology (MST)
mathematics (MS)
middle school mathematics teaching (M Ed)
physics (MS)
population and conservation biology (MS)
science (M Ed, MA, MS, MST)
software engineering (MS)
wildlife ecology (MS)

Emmett & Miriam McCoy College of Business Administration
Dr. Denise Smart, Dean
Programs in:
accounting (M Acy)
business administration (M Acy, MBA)

■ TEXAS TECH UNIVERSITY
Lubbock, TX 79409
http://www.ttu.edu/

State-supported, coed, university. CGS member. *Enrollment:* 27,996 graduate, professional, and undergraduate students; 3,570 full-time matriculated graduate/professional students (1,593 women), 1,575 part-time matriculated graduate/professional students (875 women). *Graduate faculty:* 768 full-time (225 women), 34 part-time/adjunct (5 women). *Computer facilities:* Computer purchase and lease plans are available. 3,000 computers available on campus for general student use. A campuswide network can be accessed from student residence rooms and from off campus. Internet access and online class registration, online degree plans, accounts, transcripts, schedules are available. *Library facilities:* Texas Tech Library plus 3 others. *Graduate expenses:* Tuition, state resident: full-time $4,440. Tuition, nonresident: full-time $11,040. Required fees: $2,136. *General application contact:* Dr. Duane Crawford, Assistant Dean of Graduate Admissions and Recruitment, 806-742-2781.

Find University Details at www.petersons.com/gradchannel.

Graduate School
Dr. John Borrelli, Dean
Programs in:
heritage management (MS)
interdisciplinary studies (MA, MS)
museum science (MA)

College of Agricultural Sciences and Natural Resources
Dr. Marvin J. Cepica, Dean
Programs in:
agribusiness (MAB)
agricultural and applied economics (MS, PhD)
agricultural education (MS, Ed D)
agricultural sciences and natural resources (M Agr, MAB, MLA, MS, Ed D, PhD)
agronomy (PhD)
animal science (MS, PhD)
crop science (MS)
entomology (MS)
fisheries science (MS, PhD)
food technology (MS)
horticulture (MS)
landscape architecture (MLA)
range science (MS, PhD)
soil science (MS)
wildlife science (MS, PhD)

College of Architecture
David Andrew Vernooy, Dean
Programs in:
architecture (M Arch, MS, PhD)
community design and development (MS)
historical preservation (MS)
land-use planning, management, and design (PhD)
visualization (MS)

College of Arts and Sciences
Dr. Jane L. Winer, Dean
Programs in:
anthropology (MA)
applied linguistics (MA)
applied physics (MS)
arts and sciences (MA, MPA, MS, PhD)
atmospheric sciences (MS)
biological informatics (MS)
biology (MS, PhD)
biotechnology (MS)
chemistry (MS, PhD)
classics (MA)
clinical psychology (PhD)
communication studies (MA)
counseling psychology (MA, PhD)
economics (MA, PhD)
English (MA, PhD)
environmental toxicology (MS, PhD)
exercise and sport sciences (MS)
experimental psychology (MA, PhD)
geoscience (MS, PhD)
German (MA)
history (MA, PhD)
mathematics (MA, MS, PhD)
microbiology (MS)
philosophy (MA)
physics (MS, PhD)
political science (MA, PhD)
psychology (MA, PhD)
public administration (MPA)
romance language (MA)
romance languages—Spanish (MA)
Romance languages-French (MA)
Romance languages-Spanish (PhD)
sociology (MA)
sports health (MS)
statistics (MS)
technical communication (MA)
technical communication and rhetoric (PhD)
zoology (MS, PhD)

College of Education
Dr. Sheryl Santos, Dean
Programs in:
bilingual education (M Ed)
counselor (Certificate)
counselor education (M Ed, PhD)
curriculum and instruction (M Ed, PhD)
education (M Ed, Ed D, PhD, Certificate)
education diagnostician (Certificate)
educational leadership (M Ed, Ed D)
educational psychology (M Ed, PhD)
elementary education (M Ed)
gifted and talented (Certificate)
higher education (M Ed, Ed D, PhD)
information processing technologist (Certificate)
instructional technology (M Ed, Ed D)
language and literacy education (M Ed)
principal (Certificate)
secondary education (M Ed)
special education (M Ed, Ed D)
special education counselor (Certificate)
superintendent (Certificate)
visually handicapped (Certificate)

College of Engineering
Dr. Pamela A. Eibeck, Dean
Programs in:
chemical engineering (MS Ch E, PhD)
civil engineering (MSCE, PhD)
computer science (MS, PhD)
electrical engineering (MSEE, PhD)
engineering (M Engr, MENVEGR, MS, MS Ch E, MSCE, MSEE, MSETM, MSIE, MSME, MSMSE, MSPE, MSSEM, PhD)
environmental engineering (MENVEGR)
environmental technology and management (MSETM)
industrial engineering (MSIE, PhD)
manufacturing systems and engineering (MSMSE)
mechanical engineering (MSME, PhD)
petroleum engineering (MSPE, PhD)
software engineering (MS)
systems and engineering management (MSSEM)

College of Human Sciences
Dr. Linda C. Hoover, Dean
Programs in:
consumer economics and environmental design (PhD)
environmental design (MS)
environmental design and consumer economics (PhD)
family and consumer sciences education (MS, PhD, Certificate)
gerontology (MS)
hospitality administration (PhD)
human development and family studies (MS, PhD)
human sciences (MS, PhD, Certificate)
marriage and family therapy (MS, PhD)
nutritional sciences (MS, PhD)
personal financial planning (MS)
restaurant, hotel and institutional management (MS)
restaurant, hotel, and institutional management (MS, PhD)

College of Mass Communications
Dr. Jerry C. Hudson, Dean
Program in:
mass communications (MA, PhD)

College of Visual and Performing Arts
Dr. Jonathan Marks, Interim Dean
Programs in:
art (MFA)
art education (MAE)
composition (MM, DMA)
conducting (DMA)
fine arts (PhD)
music performance (MM)
music theory (MM)
musicology (MM)
pedagogy (MM)
performance (DMA)
piano pedagogy (DMA)
theatre arts (MA, MFA)
visual and performing arts (MA, MAE, MFA, MM, MM Ed, DMA, PhD)

Jerry S. Rawls College of Business Administration
Dr. Allen T. McInnes, Dean
Programs in:
accounting (PhD)
agricultural business (MBA)
audit/financial reporting (MSA)
business administration (IMBA, MBA, MS, MSA, PhD, Certificate)
business statistics (MS, PhD)
entrepreneurship (MBA)
finance (MBA)
general business (MBA)
health organization management (MBA, MS)
international business (MBA)
management (PhD)
management and leadership skills (MBA)
management information systems (MBA, MS, PhD)
marketing (MBA, PhD)
production and operations management (MS, PhD)
statistics (MBA)

School of Law
Walter Burl Huffman, Dean
Program in:
law (JD)

■ TEXAS WESLEYAN UNIVERSITY
Fort Worth, TX 76105-1536
http://www.txwesleyan.edu/

Independent-religious, coed, comprehensive institution. *Enrollment:* 2,930 graduate, professional, and undergraduate students; 648 full-time matriculated graduate/

Texas Wesleyan University (continued)
professional students (336 women), 754 part-time matriculated graduate/professional students (429 women). *Graduate faculty:* 37 full-time (11 women), 40 part-time/adjunct (13 women). *Computer facilities:* 77 computers available on campus for general student use. A campuswide network can be accessed. Internet access is available. *Library facilities:* Eunice and James L. West Library plus 1 other. *Graduate expenses:* Tuition: full-time $4,230; part-time $470 per credit hour. Required fees: $53 per credit hour. Tuition and fees vary according to program. *General application contact:* Holly Kiser, Information Contact, 817-531-4458.

Graduate Programs
Dr. Allen Henderson, Provost
Programs in:
business administration (MBA)
education (M Ed, MAT, MS Ed)
geriatrics (MSHA)
health administration (MSHA)
nurse anesthesia (MHS, MSNA)
professional counseling (MA)
public health (MSHA)
school counseling (MS)

School of Law
Cynthia Fountaine, Interim Dean
Program in:
law (JD)

■ TEXAS WOMAN'S UNIVERSITY
Denton, TX 76201
http://www.twu.edu/

State-supported, coed, primarily women, university. CGS member. *Enrollment:* 11,832 graduate, professional, and undergraduate students; 1,812 full-time matriculated graduate/professional students (1,571 women), 2,800 part-time matriculated graduate/professional students (2,529 women). *Graduate faculty:* 354 full-time (272 women), 418 part-time/adjunct (300 women). *Computer facilities:* 700 computers available on campus for general student use. A campuswide network can be accessed from student residence rooms and from off campus. Internet access and online class registration are available. *Library facilities:* Blagg-Huey Library. *Graduate expenses:* Part-time $168 per unit. Tuition, state resident: full-time $4,369. Tuition, nonresident: full-time $9,373; part-time $443 per unit. Required fees: $20 per unit. $177 per term. *General application contact:* Samuel Wheeler, Coordinator of Graduate Admissions, 940-898-3188.

Graduate School
Dr. Jennifer L. Martin, Dean of the Graduate School

College of Arts and Sciences
Dr. Ann Staton, Dean
Programs in:
art (MA, MFA)
arts (MA, MFA, PhD)
arts and sciences (MA, MBA, MFA, MHSM, MS, PhD, SSP)
biology (MS)
biology teaching (MS)
chemistry (MS)
chemistry teaching (MS)
counseling psychology (MA, PhD)
dance (MA, MFA, PhD)
drama (MA)
English (MA)
government (MA)
history (MA)
management (MBA, MHSM)
mathematics (MA, MS)
mathematics teaching (MS)
molecular biology (PhD)
music (MA)
rhetoric (PhD)
school psychology (PhD)
science teaching (MS)
sociology (MA, PhD)
women's studies (MA)

College of Health Sciences
Dr. Jimmy Ishee, Dean
Programs in:
education of the deaf (MS)
exercise and sports nutrition (MS)
food science (MS)
health care administration (MHA)
health sciences (MA, MHA, MOT, MS, DPT, Ed D, PhD)
health studies (MS, Ed D, PhD)
institutional administration (MS)
kinesiology (MS, PhD)
nutrition (MS, PhD)
occupational therapy (MA, MOT, PhD)
physical therapy (MS, DPT, PhD)
speech-language pathology (MS)

College of Nursing
Dr. Marcia Hern, Dean
Programs in:
adult health nurse practitioner (MS)
health systems management (MS)
nursing (MS)
nursing education (MS)
nursing science (PhD)

College of Professional Education
Dr. Nan L. Restine, Interim Dean
Programs in:
child development (MS, PhD)
counseling and development (MS)
early childhood education (M Ed, MA, MS, Ed D)
education administration (M Ed, MA)
elementary education (M Ed, MA)
family studies (MS, PhD)
family therapy (MS, PhD)
library science (MA, MLS, PhD)
professional education (M Ed, MA, MAT, MLS, MS, Ed D, PhD)
reading education (M Ed, MA, MS, Ed D, PhD)
special education (M Ed, MA, PhD)
teaching (MAT)

■ TRINITY UNIVERSITY
San Antonio, TX 78212-7200
http://www.trinity.edu/

Independent-religious, coed, comprehensive institution. CGS member. *Enrollment:* 2,693 graduate, professional, and undergraduate students; 119 full-time matriculated graduate/professional students (78 women), 107 part-time matriculated graduate/professional students (66 women). *Graduate faculty:* 15 full-time (7 women), 21 part-time/adjunct (12 women). *Computer facilities:* 450 computers available on campus for general student use. A campuswide network can be accessed from student residence rooms and from off campus. Internet access and online class registration are available. *Library facilities:* Elizabeth Huth Coates Library. *General application contact:* Dr. Mary E. Stefl, Chair, 210-999-8424.

Department of Business Administration
Dr. Petrea K. Sandlin, Director of the Accounting Program
Program in:
accounting (MS)

Department of Education
Dr. Paul Kelleher, Chair
Programs in:
school administration (M Ed)
school psychology (MA)
teacher education (MAT)

Department of Health Care Administration
Dr. Mary E. Stefl, Chair
Program in:
health care administration (MS)

■ UNIVERSITY OF DALLAS
Irving, TX 75062-4736
http://www.udallas.edu/

Independent-religious, coed, university. *Enrollment:* 2,941 graduate, professional, and undergraduate students; 388 full-time matriculated graduate/professional students (151 women), 1,365 part-time matriculated graduate/professional students (559 women). *Graduate faculty:* 26 full-time (8 women), 66 part-time/adjunct (12 women). *Computer facilities:* Computer purchase and lease plans are available. 125 computers available on campus for general student use. A campuswide network can be accessed from student residence rooms and from off campus. Internet access is available. *Library facilities:* William A. Blakley Library. *General application contact:* Corey Ellis, Director of Admissions, 972-721-5356.

Braniff Graduate School of Liberal Arts
Dr. David Sweet, Dean
Programs in:
American studies (MAS)

art (MA, MFA)
English literature (MA, MEL)
humanities (M Hum, MA)
liberal arts (M Hum, M Pol, M Psych, M Th, MA, MAS, MCSL, MEL, MFA, MPM, MRE, MTS, PhD)
philosophy (MA)
politics (M Pol, MA)
psychology (M Psych, MA)
theology (M Th, MA)

Institute for Religious and Pastoral Studies
Dr. Brian Schmisek, Director
Program in:
religious and pastoral studies (MCSL, MPM, MRE, MTS)

Institute of Philosophic Studies
Programs in:
literature (PhD)
philosophy (PhD)
politics (PhD)

Graduate School of Management
Dr. J. Lee Whittington, Dean
Programs in:
accounting (MBA, MS)
business management (MBA)
corporate finance (MBA, MM)
engineering management (MBA, MM)
entrepreneurship (MBA, MM)
financial services (MBA, MM)
global business (MBA, MM)
health services management (MBA, MM)
human resource management (MBA, MM, MS)
information assurance (MBA, MM, MS)
information technology (MBA, MM, MS)
information technology service management (MBA)
IT service management (MS)
marketing (MM)
marketing management (MBA)
not-for-profit management (MBA)
organization development (MBA)
project management (MBA, MM)
sports and entertainment management (MBA, MM)
strategic leadership (MBA)
supply chain management (MBA)
supply chain management and market logistics (MM)
telecommunications management (MBA, MM)

■ UNIVERSITY OF HOUSTON
Houston, TX 77204
http://www.uh.edu/

State-supported, coed, university. CGS member. *Enrollment:* 34,334 graduate, professional, and undergraduate students; 4,486 full-time matriculated graduate/professional students (2,358 women), 2,448 part-time matriculated graduate/professional students (1,310 women). *Graduate faculty:* 655 full-time (174 women), 331 part-time/adjunct (119 women). *Computer facilities:* 825 computers available on campus for general student use. A campuswide network can be accessed from student residence rooms and from off campus. Internet access and online class registration are available. *Library facilities:* M.D. Anderson Library plus 6 others. *Graduate expenses:* Tuition, state resident: full-time $5,429; part-time $226 per credit. Tuition, nonresident: full-time $12,029; part-time $501 per credit. Required fees: $2,454. *General application contact:* Jeff Fuller, Executive Associate Director of Admission, 832-842-9047.

Bauer College of Business
Dr. Arthur Warga, Dean
Programs in:
accountancy (M Acy)
accounting (PhD)
business (M Acy, MBA, MS, PhD)
decision and information sciences (MBA, PhD)
finance (MS)
management (PhD)
marketing and entrepreneurship (PhD)

College of Architecture
Joseph Mashburn, Dean
Program in:
architecture (M Arch, MS)

College of Education
Robert K. Wimpelberg, Dean
Programs in:
allied health (M Ed, Ed D)
art education (M Ed)
bilingual education (M Ed)
counseling psychology (M Ed, PhD)
curriculum and instruction (Ed D)
early childhood education (M Ed)
education (M Ed, MS, Ed D, PhD)
education of the gifted (M Ed)
educational administration (M Ed, Ed D)
educational psychology (M Ed)
educational psychology and individual differences (PhD)
elementary education (M Ed)
exercise science (MS)
health education (M Ed)
higher education (M Ed)
historical, social, and cultural foundations of education (M Ed, Ed D)
kinesiology (PhD)
mathematics education (M Ed)
physical education (M Ed, Ed D)
reading and language arts education (M Ed)
science education (M Ed)
second language education (M Ed)
secondary education (M Ed)
social studies education (M Ed)
special education (M Ed, Ed D)
teaching (M Ed)

College of Liberal Arts and Social Sciences
Dr. John Antel, Dean
Programs in:
anthropology (MA)
applied English linguistics (MA)
clinical psychology (PhD)
economics (MA, PhD)
English and American literature (MA, PhD)
French (MA)
history (MA, PhD)
industrial/organizational psychology (PhD)
interior design (MA)
liberal arts and social sciences (MA, MFA, MM, DMA, PhD)
literature and creative writing (MA, MFA, PhD)
painting (MA)
philosophy (MA)
photography (MA)
political science (MA, PhD)
psychology (MA)
public history (MA)
sculpture (MA)
social psychology (PhD)
sociology (MA)
Spanish (MA, PhD)
speech language pathology (MA)

Moores School of Music
David Ashley White, Chairperson
Programs in:
accompanying (MM)
applied music (MM)
composition (MM, DMA)
conducting (DMA)
music education (MM, DMA)
music literature (MM)
music performance and pedagogy (MM)
music theory (MM)
performance (DMA)

School of Communication
Beth Olson, Chairperson
Programs in:
mass communication studies (MA)
public relations studies (MA)
speech communication (MA)

School of Theatre
Sidney Berger, Chairperson
Program in:
theatre (MA, MFA)

College of Natural Sciences and Mathematics
Dr. John L. Bear, Dean
Programs in:
biochemistry (MA, MS, PhD)
biology (MA, MS, PhD)
chemistry (MA, MS, PhD)
computer science (MA, MS, PhD)
geology (MA, MS, PhD)
geophysics (MA, MS, PhD)
mathematics (MA, MS, PhD)
natural sciences and mathematics (MA, MS, PhD)
physics (MA, MS, PhD)

College of Optometry
Earl Smith, Dean

University of Houston (continued)
Programs in:
optometry (OD)
physiological optics/vision science (MS Phys Op, PhD)

College of Pharmacy
Dr. Sunny Ohia, Dean
Programs in:
hospital pharmacy (MSPHR)
medical chemistry and pharmacology (MS)
pharmaceutics (MS, PhD)
pharmacology (MS, PhD)
pharmacy (Pharm D)
pharmacy administration (MSPHR)

College of Technology
William Fitzgibbon, Interim Dean
Programs in:
engineering technology (M Tech)
human development and consumer science (MS)
information and logistics technology (MS)
technology (M Tech, MS)

Conrad N. Hilton College of Hotel and Restaurant Management
John Bowen, Dean
Program in:
hotel and restaurant management (MHM, MS)

Cullen College of Engineering
Dr. Raymond W. Flumerfelt, Dean
Programs in:
aerospace engineering (MS, PhD)
biomedical engineering (MS)
chemical engineering (M Ch E, MS Ch E, PhD)
civil and environmental engineering (MCE, MS Env E, MSCE, PhD)
computer and systems engineering (MS, PhD)
electrical and computer engineering (MEE, MSEE, PhD)
engineering (M Ch E, MCE, MEE, MIE, MME, MS, MS Ch E, MS Env E, MSCE, MSEE, MSIE, MSME, PhD)
environmental engineering (MS, PhD)
industrial engineering (MIE, MSIE, PhD)
materials engineering (MS, PhD)
mechanical engineering (MME, MSME)
petroleum engineering (MS)

Graduate School of Social Work
Dr. Ira C. Colby, Dean
Program in:
social work (MSW, PhD)

Law Center
Raymond Nimmer, Interim Dean
Program in:
law (JD, LL M)

■ UNIVERSITY OF HOUSTON–CLEAR LAKE
Houston, TX 77058-1098
http://www.uhcl.edu/

State-supported, coed, upper-level institution. CGS member. *Enrollment:* 1,113 full-time matriculated graduate/professional students (676 women), 2,438 part-time matriculated graduate/professional students (1,559 women). *Graduate faculty:* 154 full-time (65 women), 120 part-time/adjunct (56 women). *Computer facilities:* 383 computers available on campus for general student use. A campuswide network can be accessed from off campus. Internet access and online class registration are available. *Library facilities:* Neumann Library. *General application contact:* Janis S. Bigelow, Assistant Director of Admissions, Recruitment and Communications, 281-283-2540.

School of Business
Dr. Wm. Theodore Cummings, Dean
Programs in:
accounting (MS)
business (MA, MBA, MHA, MS)
business administration (MBA)
environmental management (MS)
finance (MS)
healthcare administration (MHA)
human resource management (MA)
management information systems (MS)
professional accounting (MS)

School of Education
Dr. Dennis Spuck, Dean
Programs in:
counseling (MS)
curriculum and instruction (MS)
early childhood education (MS)
education (MS, Ed D)
educational leadership (Ed D)
educational management (MS)
instructional technology (MS)
multicultural studies (MS)
reading (MS)
school library and information science (MS)

School of Human Sciences and Humanities
Dr. Bruce Palmer, Dean
Programs in:
behavioral sciences (MA)
clinical psychology (MA)
criminology (MA)
cross-cultural studies (MA)
family therapy (MA)
fitness and human performance (MA)
history (MA)
human sciences and humanities (MA)
humanities (MA)
literature (MA)
school psychology (MA)

School of Science and Computer Engineering
Dr. Sadegh Davari, Interim Dean
Programs in:
biological sciences (MS)
biotechnology (MS)
chemistry (MS)
computer engineering (MS)
computer information systems (MS)
computer science (MS)
environmental science (MS)
mathematical sciences (MS)
physics (MS)
science and computer engineering (MS)
software engineering (MS)
statistics (MS)
system engineering (MS)

■ UNIVERSITY OF HOUSTON–VICTORIA
Victoria, TX 77901-4450
http://www.uhv.edu/

State-supported, coed, upper-level institution. *Enrollment:* 2,652 graduate, professional, and undergraduate students; 252 full-time matriculated graduate/professional students (153 women), 1,085 part-time matriculated graduate/professional students (692 women). *Graduate faculty:* 73 full-time (27 women). *Computer facilities:* 150 computers available on campus for general student use. A campuswide network can be accessed from off campus. Internet access and online class registration are available. *Library facilities:* VC/UHV Library plus 1 other. *Graduate expenses:* Tuition, state resident: full-time $3,168; part-time $176 per semester hour. Tuition, nonresident: full-time $7,218; part-time $401 per semester hour. Required fees: $756; $42 per semester hour. Tuition and fees vary according to course load. *General application contact:* Admissions and Records, 361-570-4114.

School of Arts and Sciences
Dr. Jeffrey Dileo, Interim Dean
Programs in:
arts and sciences (MA, MAIS, MS)
coputer science (MS)
interdisciplinary studies (MAIS)
psychology (MA)

School of Business Administration
Charles Bullock, Dean
Program in:
business administration (MBA)

School of Education and Human Development
Dr. John Stansell, Dean
Program in:
education (M Ed)

■ UNIVERSITY OF MARY HARDIN-BAYLOR
Belton, TX 76513
http://www.umhb.edu/

Independent-religious, coed, comprehensive institution. *Enrollment:* 2,738 graduate, professional, and undergraduate students; 52

full-time matriculated graduate/professional students (31 women), 86 part-time matriculated graduate/professional students (58 women). *Graduate faculty:* 25 full-time (11 women), 6 part-time/adjunct (2 women). *Computer facilities:* Computer purchase and lease plans are available. 262 computers available on campus for general student use. A campuswide network can be accessed from student residence rooms. Internet access is available. *Library facilities:* Townsend Memorial Library. *Graduate expenses:* Tuition: full-time $8,910; part-time $495 per hour. Required fees: $906; $47 per hour. $30 per term. Tuition and fees vary according to course load. *General application contact:* Robbin Steen, Director of Admissions and Recruiting, 254-295-4520.

College of Business

Programs in:
- accounting (MBA)
- business (MBA, MS)
- information systems (MS)
- management (MBA)
- sport management (MBA)

College of Education

Dr. Marlene Zipperlen, Dean
Programs in:
- educational administration (M Ed, Ed D)
- educational psychology (M Ed)
- exercise and sport science (M Ed)
- general studies (M Ed)
- reading education (M Ed)

College of Sciences and Humanities

Programs in:
- community counseling (MA)
- marriage and family Christian counseling (MA)
- psychology and counseling (MA)
- school counseling and psychology (MA)
- sciences and humanities (MA)

■ UNIVERSITY OF NORTH TEXAS

Denton, TX 76203
http://www.unt.edu/

State-supported, coed, university. CGS member. *Enrollment:* 33,443 graduate, professional, and undergraduate students; 2,519 full-time matriculated graduate/professional students (1,424 women), 4,326 part-time matriculated graduate/professional students (2,836 women). *Graduate faculty:* 924 full-time (335 women). *Computer facilities:* 2,006 computers available on campus for general student use. A campuswide network can be accessed from student residence rooms and from off campus. *Library facilities:* Willis Library plus 4 others. *Graduate expenses:* Tuition, state resident: full-time $3,573; part-time $198 per credit. Tuition, nonresident: full-time $8,577; part-time $476 per credit. Required fees: $1,258; $126 per credit. One-time fee: $150 full-time. Tuition and fees vary according to course load. *General application contact:* Dr. Sandra L. Terrell, Dean, 940-565-2383.

Find University Details at www.petersons.com/gradchannel.

Robert B. Toulouse School of Graduate Studies

Dr. Sandra L. Terrell, Dean

College of Arts and Sciences

Dr. Warren Burggren, Dean
Programs in:
- applied geography (MS)
- arts and sciences (MA, MFA, MJ, MS, Au D, PhD)
- audiology (Au D)
- biochemistry (MS, PhD)
- biology (MA, MS, PhD)
- chemistry (MS, PhD)
- clinical psychology (PhD)
- communication studies (MA, MS)
- counseling psychology (MA, MS, PhD)
- drama (MA, MS)
- economic research (MS)
- economics (MA)
- English (MA, PhD)
- environmental science (MS, PhD)
- experimental psychology (MA, MS, PhD)
- French (MA)
- health psychology and behavioral medicine (PhD)
- history (MA, MS, PhD)
- industrial psychology (MA, MS)
- journalism (MA, MJ)
- labor and industrial relations (MS)
- mathematics (MA, MS, PhD)
- molecular biology (MA, MS, PhD)
- philosophy (MA, PhD)
- physics (MA, MS, PhD)
- political science (MA, MS, PhD)
- psychology (MA, MS)
- radio, television and film (MA, MFA, MS)
- school psychology (MA, MS)
- Spanish (MA)
- speech-language pathology (MA, MS)

College of Business Administration

Dr. Kathleen Cooper, Dean
Programs in:
- accounting (MS, PhD)
- administrative management (MBA)
- banking (MBA, PhD)
- business administration (EMBA, MBA, MS, PhD)
- decision technologies (MS)
- finance (MBA, PhD)
- finance, insurance, real estate, and law (MS)
- information systems (PhD)
- information technology (MS)
- insurance (MBA)
- management (EMBA, MBA)
- management science (PhD)
- marketing and logistics (MBA, PhD)
- organization theory and policy (PhD)
- personnel and industrial relations (MBA, PhD)
- production/operations management (MBA, PhD)
- real estate (MBA)

College of Education

Dr. Jean Keller, Dean
Programs in:
- applied technology, training and development (M Ed, MS, Ed D, PhD)
- community health (MS)
- computer education and cognitive systems (MS, PhD)
- counseling (M Ed, MS, PhD)
- counseling and student services (M Ed, MS, PhD)
- counselor education (MS)
- curriculum and instruction (Ed D, PhD)
- development and family studies (MS)
- development, family studies, and early childhood education (MS, Ed D)
- early childhood education (MS, Ed D)
- education (M Ed, MS, Ed D, PhD, Certificate)
- educational administration (M Ed, Ed D, PhD)
- educational research (PhD)
- health promotion (MS)
- higher education (M Ed, MS, Ed D, PhD)
- kinesiology (MS)
- reading (M Ed, MS, Ed D, PhD)
- recreation and leisure studies (MS, Certificate)
- school health (MS)
- secondary education (M Ed, MS)
- special education (M Ed, MS, PhD)

College of Engineering

Dr. Oscar Garcia, Dean
Programs in:
- computer science (MS, PhD)
- electrical engineering (MS)
- engineering (MS, PhD)
- engineering technology (MS)
- materials science (MS, PhD)

College of Music

Dr. James C. Scott, Dean
Programs in:
- composition (MM, DMA, PhD)
- jazz studies (MM)
- music (MA)
- music education (MM, MME, PhD)
- music theory (MM, PhD)
- musicology (MM, PhD)
- performance (MM, DMA)

College of Public Affairs and Community Service

Dr. David W. Hartman, Dean
Programs in:
- aging (Certificate)
- applied anthropology (MA)
- applied economics (MS)
- applied gerontology (PhD)
- behavior analysis (MS)
- criminal justice (MS)
- general studies in aging (MA, MS)

University of North Texas (continued)
long term care, senior housing, and aging services (MA, MS)
public administration (MPA)
public affairs and community service (MA, MPA, MS, PhD, Certificate)
rehabilitation counseling (MS)
rehabilitation studies (MS)
sociology (MA, MS, PhD)
vocational evaluation (MS)
work adjustment services (MS)

Interdisciplinary Studies
Donna Hughes, Head
Program in:
interdisciplinary studies (MA, MS)

School of Library and Information Sciences
Dr. Herman Totten, Dean
Programs in:
information science (MS, PhD)
library science (MS)

School of Merchandising and Hospitality Management
Dr. Judith C. Forney, Dean
Programs in:
hotel/restaurant management (MS)
merchandising and fabric analytics (MS)

School of Visual Arts
Dr. Robert Milnes, Dean
Programs in:
art (PhD)
art education (MA, MFA, PhD)
art history (MA, MFA)
ceramics (MFA)
communication design (MFA)
fashion design (MFA)
fibers (MFA)
interior design (MFA)
metalsmithing and jewelry (MFA)
painting and drawing (MFA)
photography (MFA)
printmaking (MFA)
sculpture (MFA)

■ UNIVERSITY OF ST. THOMAS
Houston, TX 77006-4696
http://www.stthom.edu/

Independent-religious, coed, comprehensive institution. CGS member. *Enrollment:* 3,607 graduate, professional, and undergraduate students; 314 full-time matriculated graduate/professional students (136 women), 913 part-time matriculated graduate/professional students (578 women). *Graduate faculty:* 50 full-time (19 women), 29 part-time/adjunct (11 women). *Computer facilities:* 156 computers available on campus for general student use. A campuswide network can be accessed from student residence rooms and from off campus. Internet access is available. *Library facilities:* Doherty Library plus 1 other. *Graduate expenses:* Tuition: full-time $11,880; part-time $660 per credit. Required fees: $52; $21 per semester. *General application contact:* David Melton, Assistant Vice President of University Admissions, 713-525-3833.

Cameron School of Business
Dr. Bahman Mirshab, Dean
Program in:
business (MBA, MIB, MSA, MSIS)

Center for Thomistic Studies
Dr. Mary Catherine Sommers, Director
Program in:
philosophy (MA, PhD)

Program in Liberal Arts
Dr. Ravi Srinivas, Dean
Program in:
liberal arts (MLA)

School of Education
Dr. Ruth M. Strudler, Dean
Program in:
education (M Ed)

School of Theology
Dr. Sandra C. Magie, Dean
Program in:
theology (M Div, MAPS, MAT)

■ THE UNIVERSITY OF TEXAS AT ARLINGTON
Arlington, TX 76019
http://www.uta.edu/

State-supported, coed, university. CGS member. *Enrollment:* 24,825 graduate, professional, and undergraduate students; 2,364 full-time matriculated graduate/professional students (1,093 women), 3,230 part-time matriculated graduate/professional students (1,884 women). *Graduate faculty:* 336 full-time (90 women), 66 part-time/adjunct (25 women). *Computer facilities:* 1,000 computers available on campus for general student use. A campuswide network can be accessed from student residence rooms and from off campus. Internet access and online class registration are available. *Library facilities:* Central Library plus 2 others. *Graduate expenses:* Tuition, state resident: full-time $5,528. Tuition, nonresident: full-time $10,478. International tuition: $10,608 full-time. *General application contact:* Dr. Phil Cohen, Dean of Graduate Studies, 817-272-3186.

Graduate School
Dr. Phil Cohen, Dean of Graduate Studies
Program in:
interdisciplinary studies (MA, MS)

College of Business Administration
Dr. Daniel Himarios, Dean
Programs in:
accounting (MP Acc, MS, PhD)
business administration (PhD)
business statistics (PhD)
economics (MA)
finance (MBA)
health care administration (MS)
human resources (MSHRM)
information systems (MBA, MS, PhD)
management (MBA)
management sciences (MBA)
marketing (MBA, PhD)
marketing research (MS)
quantitative finance (MS)
real estate (MBA, MS)
taxation (MS)

College of Education
Dr. Jeanne M. Gerlach, Dean
Programs in:
curriculum and instruction (M Ed)
educational leadership and policy studies (M Ed)
physiology of exercise (MS)
teaching (M Ed T)

College of Engineering
Dr. Bill D. Carroll, Dean
Programs in:
aerospace engineering (M Engr, MS, PhD)
biomedical engineering (MS, PhD)
civil and environmental engineering (M Engr, MS, PhD)
computer science and engineering (M Engr, M Sw En, MCS, MS, PhD)
electrical engineering (M Engr, MS, PhD)
engineering (M Engr, M Sw En, MCS, MS, PhD)
engineering management (MS)
industrial and manufacturing systems engineering (M Engr, PhD)
logistics (MS)
materials science and engineering (M Engr, MS, PhD)
mechanical engineering (M Engr, MS, PhD)
systems engineering (MS)

College of Liberal Arts
Dr. Beth S. Wright, Dean
Programs in:
anthropology (MA)
communication (MA)
criminology and criminal justice (MA)
English (MA)
French (MA)
history (MA)
humanities (MA)
liberal arts (MA, MM, PhD)
linguistics (MA, PhD)
literature (PhD)
music (MM)
political science (MA)
rhetoric (PhD)
sociology (MA)
Spanish (MA)
teaching English to speakers of other languages (MA)
transatlantic history (PhD)

College of Science
Dr. Paul Paulus, Interim Dean
Programs in:
applied chemistry (PhD)
biology (MS)

chemistry (MS)
environmental and earth sciences (MS, PhD)
environmental science (MS, PhD)
experimental psychology (PhD)
geology (MS)
interdisciplinary science (MA)
math: geoscience (PhD)
mathematical sciences (PhD)
mathematics (MS)
physics (MS)
physics and applied physics (PhD)
psychology (MS)
quantitative biology (PhD)
science (MA, MS, PhD)

School of Architecture
Donald Gatzke, Director
Programs in:
architecture (M Arch, MLA)
landscape architecture (MLA)

School of Nursing
Dr. Elizabeth C. Poster, Dean
Programs in:
administration/supervision of nursing (MSN)
nurse practitioner (MSN)
nursing science (PhD)
teaching of nursing (MSN)

School of Social Work
Dr. Santos H. Hernandez, Dean
Program in:
social work (MSSW, PhD)

School of Urban and Public Affairs
Dr. Richard Cole, Dean
Programs in:
city and regional planning (MCRP)
public administration (MPA)
urban and public affairs (MA, MCRP, MPA, PhD)

■ THE UNIVERSITY OF TEXAS AT AUSTIN
Austin, TX 78712-1111
http://www.utexas.edu/

State-supported, coed, university. CGS member. *Computer facilities:* 4,000 computers available on campus for general student use. A campuswide network can be accessed from student residence rooms and from off campus. Internet access and online class registration, e-mail are available. *Library facilities:* Perry-Castañeda Library plus 17 others. *General application contact:* Director, Graduate and International Admissions Center, 512-475-7398.

College of Pharmacy
Program in:
pharmacy (Pharm D, MS Phr, PhD)

Graduate School
Programs in:
computational and applied mathematics (MA, PhD)
Russian, East European and Eurasian studies (MA)
science and technology commercialization (MS)
writing (MFA)

Cockrell School of Engineering
Programs in:
aerospace engineering (MSE, PhD)
architectural engineering (MSE)
biomedical engineering (MSE, PhD)
chemical engineering (MSE, PhD)
civil engineering (MSE, PhD)
electrical and computer engineering (MSE, PhD)
energy and mineral resources (MA, MS)
engineering (MA, MS, MSE, PhD)
engineering mechanics (MSE, PhD)
environmental and water resources engineering (MSE)
manufacturing systems engineering (MSE)
materials science and engineering (MSE, PhD)
mechanical engineering (MSE, PhD)
operations research and industrial engineering (MSE, PhD)
petroleum and geosystems engineering (MSE, PhD)

College of Communication
Programs in:
advertising (MA, PhD)
communication (MA, MFA, PhD)
communication sciences and disorders (MA, PhD)
communication studies (MA, PhD)
film/video production (MFA)
journalism (MA, PhD)
radio-television-film (MA, PhD)

College of Education
Programs in:
academic educational psychology (M Ed, MA)
counseling education (M Ed)
counseling psychology (PhD)
curriculum and instruction (M Ed, MA, Ed D, PhD)
education (M Ed, MA, MHRDL, Ed D, PhD)
educational administration (M Ed, Ed D, PhD)
foreign language education (MA, PhD)
health education (M Ed, MA, Ed D, PhD)
human development and education (PhD)
kinesiology (M Ed, MA, Ed D, PhD)
learning cognition and instruction (PhD)
mathematics education (M Ed, MA, PhD)
quantitative methods (PhD)
school psychology (PhD)
science education (M Ed, MA, PhD)
special education (M Ed, MA, Ed D, PhD)

College of Fine Arts
Programs in:
art education (MA)
art history (MA, PhD)
dance (MFA)
design (MFA)
fine arts (M Music, MA, MFA, DMA, PhD)
music (M Music, DMA, PhD)
studio art (MFA)
theatre (MA, MFA, PhD)

College of Liberal Arts
Programs in:
American studies (MA, PhD)
Arabic studies (MA, PhD)
archaeology (MA, PhD)
Asian cultures and languages (MA, PhD)
Asian studies (MA, PhD)
classics (MA, PhD)
comparative literature (MA, PhD)
economics (MA, MS Econ, PhD)
English (MA, PhD)
folklore and public culture (MA, PhD)
French (MA, PhD)
geography (MA, PhD)
Germanic studies (MA, PhD)
government (MA, PhD)
Hebrew studies (MA, PhD)
Hispanic literature (MA, PhD)
history (MA, PhD)
Ibero-Romance philology and linguistics (MA, PhD)
Latin American studies (MA, PhD)
liberal arts (MA, MS Econ, PhD)
linguistic anthropology (MA, PhD)
linguistics (MA, PhD)
Luso-Brazilian literature (MA, PhD)
Middle Eastern studies (MA, PhD)
Persian studies (MA, PhD)
philosophy (MA, PhD)
physical anthropology (MA, PhD)
psychology (PhD)
Romance linguistics (MA, PhD)
Slavic languages and literatures (MA, PhD)
social anthropology (MA, PhD)
sociology (MA, PhD)

College of Natural Sciences
Programs in:
analytical chemistry (MA, PhD)
astronomy (MA, PhD)
biochemistry (MA, PhD)
biological sciences (MA, PhD)
cell and molecular biology (PhD)
cellular and molecular biology (PhD)
child development and family relations (MA, PhD)
computer sciences (MA, MSCS, PhD)
ecology, evolution and behavior (PhD)
genetics and developmental biology (PhD)
geological sciences (MA, MS, PhD)
inorganic chemistry (MA, PhD)
marine science (MS, PhD)
mathematics (MA, PhD)
microbiology (MA, PhD)
microbiology and immunology (PhD)
natural sciences (MA, MS, MS Stat, MSCS, PhD)
nutrition (MA)
nutritional sciences (MA, PhD)

The University of Texas at Austin (continued)
- organic chemistry (MA, PhD)
- physical chemistry (MA, PhD)
- physics (MA, MS, PhD)
- plant biology (MA, PhD)
- statistics (MS Stat)

Graduate School of Library and Information Science
Program in:
- library and information science (MLIS, PhD)

The Institute for Neuroscience
Program in:
- neuroscience (MA, PhD)

Lyndon B. Johnson School of Public Affairs
Programs in:
- public affairs (MP Aff)
- public policy (PhD)

McCombs School of Business
Programs in:
- accounting (MPA, PhD)
- business (MBA)
- business administration (MBA, MHRDL, MPA, PhD)
- finance (PhD)
- human resource development leadership (MHRDL)
- management (PhD)
- management sciences and information systems (PhD)
- marketing administration (PhD)

School of Architecture
Programs in:
- architecture (M Arch, MLA, MS Arch St, MSCRP, PhD)
- community and regional planning (MSCRP, PhD)

School of Nursing
Program in:
- nursing (MSN, PhD)

School of Social Work
Program in:
- social work (MSSW, PhD)

School of Law
Lawrence Sager, Interim Dean
Program in:
- law (JD, LL M)

■ THE UNIVERSITY OF TEXAS AT BROWNSVILLE
Brownsville, TX 78520-4991
http://www.utb.edu/

State-supported, coed, upper-level institution. CGS member. *Computer facilities:* Computer purchase and lease plans are available. 650 computers available on campus for general student use. A campuswide network can be accessed from off campus. Internet access and online class registration are available. *Library facilities:* Arnulfo L. Oliveira Library. *General application contact:* Dean, Graduate Studies, 956-882-8812.

Graduate Studies

College of Liberal Arts
Programs in:
- behavioral sciences (MAIS)
- English (MA)
- government (MAIS)
- history (MAIS)
- interdisciplinary studies (MAIS)
- liberal arts (MA, MAIS, MPPM)
- public policy and management (MPPM)
- Spanish (MA)

College of Science, Mathematics and Technology
Programs in:
- biological sciences (MS, MSIS)
- mathematics (MS)
- physics (MS)

School of Business
Program in:
- business (MBA)

School of Education
Programs in:
- bilingual education (M Ed)
- counseling and guidance (M Ed)
- curriculum and instruction (M Ed)
- early childhood education (M Ed)
- educational administration (M Ed)
- educational technology (M Ed)
- English as a second language (M Ed)
- reading specialist (M Ed)
- special education/educational diagnostician (M Ed)

School of Health Sciences
Program in:
- health sciences (MSN)

■ THE UNIVERSITY OF TEXAS AT DALLAS
Richardson, TX 75083-0688
http://www.utdallas.edu/

State-supported, coed, university. CGS member. *Enrollment:* 14,523 graduate, professional, and undergraduate students; 2,169 full-time matriculated graduate/professional students (954 women), 2,268 part-time matriculated graduate/professional students (990 women). *Graduate faculty:* 369 full-time (79 women), 25 part-time/adjunct (5 women). *Computer facilities:* 630 computers available on campus for general student use. A campuswide network can be accessed from student residence rooms and from off campus. Internet access and online class registration, wireless network are available. *Library facilities:* Eugene McDermott Library plus 1 other. *General application contact:* Dr. Austin Cunningham, Dean for Graduate Studies, 972-883-2234.

Erik Jonsson School of Engineering and Computer Science
Dr. Robert Helms, Dean
Programs in:
- computer engineering (MS, PhD)
- computer science (MS, PhD)
- electrical engineering (MSEE, PhD)
- engineering and computer science (MS, MSEE, MSTE, PhD)
- materials science engineering (MS, PhD)
- microelectronics (MSEE, PhD)
- software engineering (MS, PhD)
- telecommunications (MSEE, MSTE, PhD)

School of Arts and Humanities
Dr. Dennis M. Kratz, Dean
Programs in:
- arts and technology (MFA)
- humanities (MA, MAT, PhD)

School of Behavioral and Brain Sciences
Dr. Bert Moore, Dean
Programs in:
- audiology (Au D)
- behavioral and brain sciences (MS, Au D, PhD)
- cognition and neuroscience (MS, PhD)
- communication disorders (MS)
- communication sciences (PhD)
- early childhood disorders (MS)
- psychological sciences (MS, PhD)

School of Economic, Political and Policy Sciences
Dr. Brian Berry, Dean
Programs in:
- applied economics (MS)
- economic, political and policy sciences (MPA, MPP, MS, PhD)
- economics (PhD)
- geospatial information sciences (MS, PhD)
- international political economy (MS)
- political science (PhD)
- public affairs (MPA, PhD)
- public policy (MPP)
- public policy and political economy (PhD)
- sociology (MS)

School of General Studies
Dr. George Fair, Dean
Program in:
- interdisciplinary studies (MA)

School of Management
Dr. Hasan Pirkul, Dean
Programs in:
- accounting and information management (MS)
- business administration (EMBA, MBA)
- information technology and management (MS)
- international management studies (MA, PhD)
- management (EMBA, MA, MBA, MS, PhD)
- management and administrative science (MS)
- management science (PhD)
- medical management (MS)

School of Natural Sciences and Mathematics
Dr. Myrm B. Salamon, Dean

Programs in:
- applied mathematics (MS, PhD)
- applied physics (MS)
- bioinformatics and computational biology (MS)
- biotechnology (MS)
- chemistry (MS, PhD)
- engineering mathematics (MS)
- geosciences (MS, PhD)
- mathematical science (MS)
- mathematics education (MAT)
- molecular and cell biology (MS, PhD)
- natural sciences and mathematics (MAT, MS, PhD)
- physics (PhD)
- science education (MAT)
- statistics (MS, PhD)

■ THE UNIVERSITY OF TEXAS AT EL PASO
El Paso, TX 79968-0001
http://www.utep.edu/

State-supported, coed, university. CGS member. *Computer facilities:* A campuswide network can be accessed from student residence rooms and from off campus. *Library facilities:* University Library. *General application contact:* Dean of the Graduate School, 915-747-5491 Ext. 7886.

Graduate School
Programs in:
- environmental science and engineering (PhD)
- materials science and engineering (PhD)

College of Business Administration
Programs in:
- accounting (MACY)
- business administration (MACY, MBA, MS)
- economics and finance (MS)

College of Education
Programs in:
- education (M Ed, MA, Ed D)
- educational administration (M Ed, MA, Ed D)
- educational curriculum and instruction (M Ed, MA)

College of Engineering
Programs in:
- civil engineering (MS, PhD)
- computer engineering (MS, PhD)
- computer science (MS)
- electrical engineering (MS)
- engineering (MEENE, MIT, MS, MSENE, PhD)
- environmental engineering (MEENE, MSENE)
- industrial engineering (MS)
- information technology (MIT)
- mechanical engineering (MS)
- metallurgical engineering (MS)

College of Health Sciences
Programs in:
- allied health (MPT, MS)
- community health (MSN)
- community health/family nurse practitioner (MSN)
- health and physical education (MS)
- health sciences (MPT, MS, MSN)
- kinesiology and sports studies (MS)
- nurse midwifery (MSN)
- nursing administration (MSN)
- nursing-clinical (MSN)
- physical therapy (MPT)
- post master's nursing (MSN)
- speech language pathology (MS)
- women's health care (MSN)

College of Liberal Arts
Programs in:
- art (MA)
- border history (MA)
- clinical psychology (MA)
- communication (MA)
- creative writing in English (MFA)
- creative writing in Spanish (MFA)
- English and American literature (MA)
- experimental psychology (MA)
- history (MA, PhD)
- liberal arts (MA, MAIS, MAT, MFA, MM, MPA, PhD)
- linguistics (MA)
- music education (MM)
- music performance (MM)
- political science (MA, MPA)
- professional writing and rhetoric (MA)
- psychology (PhD)
- sociology (MA)
- Spanish (MA)
- teaching English (MAT)
- theatre arts (MA)

College of Science
Programs in:
- bioinformatics (MS)
- biological science (MS, PhD)
- chemistry (MS)
- environmental science and engineering (PhD)
- geological sciences (MS, PhD)
- geophysics (MS)
- interdisciplinary studies (MSIS)
- mathematical sciences (MAT)
- mathematics (MS)
- physics (MS)
- science (MAT, MS, MSIS, PhD)
- statistics (MS)

■ THE UNIVERSITY OF TEXAS AT SAN ANTONIO
San Antonio, TX 78249-0617
http://www.utsa.edu/

State-supported, coed, university. CGS member. *Enrollment:* 28,380 graduate, professional, and undergraduate students; 1,283 full-time matriculated graduate/professional students (667 women), 2,565 part-time matriculated graduate/professional students (1,578 women). *Graduate faculty:* 435 full-time (161 women), 66 part-time/adjunct (16 women). *Computer facilities:* 800 computers available on campus for general student use. A campuswide network can be accessed from student residence rooms. Internet access and online class registration are available. *Library facilities:* UTSA Library plus 1 other. *Graduate expenses:* Tuition, state resident: full-time $1,730; part-time $192 per credit hour. Tuition, nonresident: full-time $6,680; part-time $742 per credit hour. Required fees: $733; $308,359 per credit hour. *General application contact:* Dr. Dorothy A. Flannagan, Dean of the Graduate School, 210-458-4330.

College of Business
Dr. Lynda Y. de la Viña, Dean
Programs in:
- accounting (MS, PhD)
- applied statistics (PhD)
- business (MA, MBA, MS, MSIT, MSMOT, MT, PhD)
- business economics (MBA)
- business finance (MBA)
- economics (MA)
- finance (MS, PhD)
- information systems (MBA, PhD)
- information technology (MSIT)
- international business (MBA)
- management (PhD)
- management accounting (MBA)
- management science (MBA)
- management technology (MSMOT)
- marketing management (MBA)
- statistics (MS)
- taxation (MBA, MT)

College of Education and Human Development
Dr. Betty M. Merchant, Dean
Programs in:
- bicultural studies (MA)
- bicultural-bilingual studies (MA)
- counseling (MA)
- counselor education (PhD)
- culture, literacy, and language (PhD)
- curriculum and instruction (MA)
- early childhood and elementary education (MA)
- education and human development (MA, Ed D, PhD)
- education-adult and higher education (MA)
- educational leadership (Ed D)
- educational leadership and policy studies (MA)
- educational psychology/special education (MA)
- instructional technology (MA)
- reading and literacy (MA)
- teaching English as a second language (MA)

College of Engineering
Dr. C. Mauli Agarwal, Dean
Programs in:
- biomedical engineering (PhD)
- civil engineering (MSCE)
- electrical engineering (MSEE, PhD)
- engineering (MSCE, MSEE, MSME, PhD)
- mechanical engineering (MSME)

College of Liberal and Fine Arts
Dr. Daniel J. Gelo, Dean

The University of Texas at San Antonio (continued)

Programs in:
- anthropology (MA, PhD)
- art history (MA)
- communication (MA)
- English (MA, PhD)
- Hispanic culture (MA)
- history (MA)
- liberal and fine arts (MA, MFA, MM, MS, PhD)
- music (MM)
- political science (MA)
- psychology (MS)
- sociology (MS)
- Spanish (MA)
- studio art (MFA)

College of Public Policy

Dr. Jesse T. Zapata, Vice Provost, Downtown

Programs in:
- applied demography (PhD)
- justice policy (MS)
- public administration (MPA)
- public policy (MPA, MS, MSW, PhD)
- social work (MSW)

College of Sciences

Dr. George Perry, Dean

Programs in:
- biology (MS, PhD)
- biotechnology (MS)
- chemistry (MS, PhD)
- computer science (MS, PhD)
- environmental science and engineering (PhD)
- environmental sciences (MS)
- geology (MS)
- mathematics education (MS)
- physics (MS, PhD)
- sciences (MS, PhD)

■ THE UNIVERSITY OF TEXAS AT TYLER

Tyler, TX 75799-0001

http://www.uttyler.edu/

State-supported, coed, comprehensive institution. *Enrollment:* 5,926 graduate, professional, and undergraduate students; 667 matriculated graduate/professional students. *Computer facilities:* 177 computers available on campus for general student use. A campuswide network can be accessed from student residence rooms and from off campus. Internet access and online class registration are available. *Library facilities:* Robert Muntz Library. *Graduate expenses:* Tuition, state resident: part-time $50 per credit hour. Tuition, nonresident: part-time $328 per credit hour. Required fees: $107 per credit hour. $426 per term. *General application contact:* Bonnie Purser, Office of Graduate Studies, 903-566-7142.

College of Arts and Sciences

Dr. Alisa White, Interim Dean

Programs in:
- art (MA, MAIS, MFA)
- arts and sciences (MA, MAIS, MAT, MFA, MPA, MS, MSIS)
- biology (MS)
- criminal justice (MS)
- English (MA)
- history (MA, MAT)
- interdisciplinary studies (MAIS, MSIS)
- mathematics (MS, MSIS)
- music (MAIS)
- political science (MA, MAT)
- public administration (MPA)
- sociology (MAT, MS)

College of Business and Technology

Programs in:
- business administration (MBA)
- general management (MBA)
- health care track (MBA)
- human resource development (MS)
- human resource development and technology (MS)
- industrial distribution (MS)
- industrial safety (MS)
- industrial technology (MS)
- instructional technology (MS)
- technology systems (MS)

College of Education and Psychology

Dr. William Geiger, Dean

Programs in:
- clinical psychology (MS)
- counseling psychology (MA)
- curriculum and instruction (M Ed)
- early childhood education (M Ed, MA)
- education and psychology (M Ed, MA, MAT, MS, MSIS)
- educational leadership (M Ed)
- interdisciplinary studies (MSIS)
- reading (M Ed, MA)
- school counseling (MA)
- secondary teaching (MAT)
- special education (M Ed, MA)

College of Engineering and Computer Science

Dr. Jim Nelson, Dean

Programs in:
- computer science (MS)
- engineering (M Engr)
- engineering and computer science (M Engr, MS, MSIS)
- interdisciplinary studies (MSIS)

College of Nursing and Health Sciences

Dr. Linda Klotz, Dean

Programs in:
- clinical exercise physiology (MS)
- health and kinesiology (M Ed)
- kinesiology (MS)
- nurse practitioner (MSN)
- nursing administration (MSN)
- nursing and health sciences (M Ed, MS, MSN)
- nursing education (MSN)

■ THE UNIVERSITY OF TEXAS OF THE PERMIAN BASIN

Odessa, TX 79762-0001

http://www.utpb.edu/

State-supported, coed, comprehensive institution. *Computer facilities:* Computer purchase and lease plans are available. 170 computers available on campus for general student use. A campuswide network can be accessed from student residence rooms and from off campus. Internet access and online class registration are available. *Library facilities:* J. Conrad Dunagan Library. *General application contact:* Director of Graduate Studies, 915-552-2530.

Office of Graduate Studies

College of Arts and Sciences

Programs in:
- applied behavioral analysis (MA)
- arts and sciences (MA, MS)
- biology (MS)
- clinical psychology (MA)
- criminal justice administration (MS)
- English (MA)
- geology (MS)
- history (MA)
- kinesiology (MS)
- psychology (MA)

School of Business

Programs in:
- accountancy (MPA)
- business (MBA, MPA)
- management (MBA)

School of Education

Programs in:
- bilingual/English as a second language education (MA)
- counseling (MA)
- early childhood education (MA)
- education (MA)
- educational leadership (MA)
- professional education (MA)
- reading (MA)
- special education (MA)

■ THE UNIVERSITY OF TEXAS–PAN AMERICAN

Edinburg, TX 78541-2999

http://www.utpa.edu/

State-supported, coed, comprehensive institution. CGS member. *Enrollment:* 17,337 graduate, professional, and undergraduate students; 608 full-time matriculated graduate/professional students (369 women), 1,653 part-time matriculated graduate/professional students (1,094 women). *Graduate faculty:* 232 full-time (78 women), 16 part-time/adjunct (9 women). *Computer facilities:* 500 computers available on campus for general student use. A campuswide network can be accessed from off campus. Internet access and online class registration are available. *Library facilities:* University Library. *Graduate expenses:*

Tuition, state resident: full-time $2,577; part-time $143 per credit hour. Tuition, nonresident: full-time $7,527; part-time $418 per credit hour. Required fees: $561. *General application contact:* Edel de la Garza, Administrative Clerk, 956-381-3661 Ext. 2207.

College of Arts and Humanities
Programs in:
art (MFA)
arts and humanities (M Mus, MA, MAIS, MFA, MSIS)
communication (MA)
English (MA, MAIS)
English as a second language (MA)
ethnomusicology (M Mus)
history (MA, MAIS)
interdisciplinary studies (MAIS)
music education (M Mus)
performance (M Mus)
Spanish (MA)
theatre (MA)

College of Business Administration
Programs in:
business administration (MBA, MS, PhD)
computer information systems (MS, PhD)

College of Education
Programs in:
bilingual education (M Ed)
counseling (M Ed)
early childhood education (M Ed)
education (M Ed, MA, MS, Ed D)
educational diagnostician (M Ed)
educational leadership (M Ed, Ed D)
elementary education (M Ed)
gifted education (M Ed)
kinesiology (MS)
reading (M Ed)
school psychology (MA)
secondary education (M Ed)
special education (M Ed)

College of Health Sciences and Human Services
Dr. Bruce Reed, Interim Dean
Programs in:
adult health nursing (MSN)
communication sciences and disorders (MS)
family nurse practitioner (MSN)
health sciences and human services (MS, MSN, MSSW)
occupational therapy (MS)
pediatric nurse practitioner (MSN)
rehabilitation counseling (MS)
social work (MSSW)

College of Science and Engineering
Programs in:
biology (MS)
computer science (MS)
mathematics (MS)
science and engineering (MS)

College of Social and Behavioral Sciences
Dr. Van A Reidhead, Dean
Programs in:
criminal justice (MS)
psychology (MA)
public administration (MPA)
social and behavioral sciences (MA, MPA, MS)
sociology (MS)

■ UNIVERSITY OF THE INCARNATE WORD
San Antonio, TX 78209-6397
http://www.uiw.edu/

Independent-religious, coed, comprehensive institution. *Enrollment:* 5,619 graduate, professional, and undergraduate students; 137 full-time matriculated graduate/professional students (97 women), 816 part-time matriculated graduate/professional students (529 women). *Graduate faculty:* 67 full-time (37 women), 42 part-time/adjunct (19 women). *Computer facilities:* Computer purchase and lease plans are available. 200 computers available on campus for general student use. A campuswide network can be accessed from student residence rooms and from off campus. Internet access and online class registration are available. *Library facilities:* J.E. and L.E. Mabee Library plus 1 other. *Graduate expenses:* Tuition: part-time $570 per credit hour. Required fees: $54 per credit hour. One-time fee: $195 part-time. Tuition and fees vary according to degree level. *General application contact:* Andrea Cyterski-Acosta, Dean of Enrollment, 210-829-6005.

Felk School of Pharmacy
Dr. Arcelia Johnson-Fannin, Founding Dean
Program in:
pharmacy (Pharm D)

School of Graduate Studies and Research
Dr. Kevin Vichcales, Dean

College of Humanities, Arts, and Social Sciences
Dr. Donna Aronson, Dean
Programs in:
English (MA)
humanities, arts, and social sciences (MA)
multidisciplinary studies (MA)
religious studies (MA)

Dreeben School of Education
Dr. Denise Staudt, Dean
Programs in:
adult education (M Ed, MA)
diversity education (M Ed, MA)
early childhood education (M Ed, MA)
education (M Ed, MA, MAT, PhD)
elementary teaching (MAT)
general education (M Ed, MA)
instructional technology (M Ed, MA)
international education and entrepreneurship (PhD)
kinesiology (M Ed, MA)
mathematics education (PhD)
organizational leadership (PhD)
organizational learning (M Ed, MA)
reading (M Ed, MA)
secondary teaching (MAT)
special education (M Ed, MA)

H-E-B School of Business and Administration
Dr. Robert Ryan, Dean
Programs in:
adult education (MAA)
applied administration (MAA)
business and administration (MAA, MBA, Certificate)
communication arts (MAA)
English (MAA)
instructional technology (MAA)
international business (MBA, Certificate)
multidisciplinary sciences (MAA)
nutrition (MAA)
organizational development (MAA, Certificate)
project management (Certificate)
sports management (MAA, MBA)
urban administration (MAA)

School of Interactive Media and Design
Dr. Cheryl Anderson, Dean
Programs in:
communication arts (MA)
interactive media and design (MA)

School of Mathematics, Sciences, and Engineering
Dr. Glen Edward James, Dean
Programs in:
biology (MA, MS)
mathematics (MS)
mathematics, sciences, and engineering (MA, MS)
multidisciplinary sciences (MA)
nutrition (MS)
teaching (MA)

School of Nursing and Health Professions
Dr. Kathleen Light, Dean
Programs in:
kinesiology (MS)
nursing (MSN)
nursing and health professions (MS, MSN)
sports management (MS)

■ WAYLAND BAPTIST UNIVERSITY
Plainview, TX 79072-6998
http://www.wbu.edu/

Independent-religious, coed, comprehensive institution. *Enrollment:* 1,072 graduate, professional, and undergraduate students; 7 full-time matriculated graduate/professional students (4 women), 95 part-time matriculated graduate/professional students (76 women). *Graduate faculty:* 16 full-time

Wayland Baptist University (continued)
(6 women), 1 (woman) part-time/adjunct. *Computer facilities:* 123 computers available on campus for general student use. A campuswide network can be accessed from student residence rooms and from off campus. Internet access is available. *Library facilities:* J.E. and L.E. Mabee Learning Resource Center. *Graduate expenses:* Tuition: full-time $6,120; part-time $340 per credit hour. Required fees: $50 per term. *General application contact:* Dr. Bobby Hall, Vice President of Academic Services, 806-291-3410.

Graduate Programs
Dr. Bobby Hall, Vice President of Academic Services
Programs in:
Christian ministry (MCM)
counseling (MA)
education (M Ed)
general business (MBA)
government administration (MPA)
health care administration (MBA)
human resource management (MBA)
international management (MBA)
justice administration (MPA)
management (MA, MBA)
management information systems (MBA)
multidisciplinary science (MS)
religion (MA)

■ WEST TEXAS A&M UNIVERSITY
Canyon, TX 79016-0001
http://www.wtamu.edu/

State-supported, coed, comprehensive institution. *Computer facilities:* 1,200 computers available on campus for general student use. A campuswide network can be accessed from student residence rooms and from off campus. Internet access and online class registration are available. *Library facilities:* Cornette Library. *General application contact:* Dean of the Graduate School, 806-651-2730.

College of Agriculture, Nursing, and Natural Sciences
Programs in:
agricultural business and economics (MS)
agriculture (PhD)
agriculture, nursing, and natural sciences (MS, MSN, PhD)
animal science (MS)
biology (MS)
chemistry (MS)
engineering technology (MS)
environmental science (MS)
mathematics (MS)
nursing (MSN)
plant science (MS)

College of Business
Programs in:
accounting (MP Acc)
accounting/business administration (MPA)
business (MBA, MP Acc, MPA, MS)
business administration (MBA)
finance and economics (MS)
professional accounting (MPA)

College of Education and Social Sciences
Programs in:
administration (M Ed)
counseling education (M Ed)
criminal justice (MA)
curriculum and instruction (M Ed)
education and social sciences (M Ed, MA, MS)
educational diagnostician (M Ed)
educational technology (M Ed)
history (MA)
political science (MA)
professional counseling (MA)
psychology (MA)
reading (M Ed)
special education (M Ed)
sports and exercise science (MS)

College of Fine Arts and Humanities
Programs in:
art (MA)
communication (MA)
communication disorders (MS)
English (MA)
fine arts and humanities (MA, MFA, MM, MS)
music (MA)
performance (MM)
studio art (MFA)

Program in Interdisciplinary Studies
Program in:
interdisciplinary studies (MA, MS)

Utah

■ BRIGHAM YOUNG UNIVERSITY
Provo, UT 84602-1001
http://www.byu.edu/

Independent-religious, coed, university. CGS member. *Enrollment:* 34,185 graduate, professional, and undergraduate students; 2,674 full-time matriculated graduate/professional students (995 women), 727 part-time matriculated graduate/professional students (248 women). *Graduate faculty:* 1,100 full-time (181 women), 149 part-time/adjunct (50 women). *Computer facilities:* Computer purchase and lease plans are available. 2,000 computers available on campus for general student use. A campuswide network can be accessed from student residence rooms and from off campus. Internet access and online class registration, intranet are available. *Library facilities:* Main library plus 2 others. *General application contact:* Adviser, 801-422-4541.

Graduate Studies
Bonnie Brinton, Dean

College of Family, Home, and Social Sciences
Dr. David B. Magleby, Dean
Programs in:
anthropology (MA)
clinical psychology (PhD)
family, home, and social sciences (MA, MS, MSW, PhD)
general psychology (MS)
history (MA)
marriage and family therapy (MS, PhD)
marriage, family and human development (MS, PhD)
psychology (PhD)
social work (MSW)
sociology (MS, PhD)

College of Fine Arts and Communications
Dr. Stephen M. Jones, Dean
Programs in:
art education (MA)
art history (MA)
composition (MM)
conducting (MM)
fine arts and communications (MA, MFA, MM)
mass communication (MA)
music education (MA, MM)
musicology (MA)
performance (MM)
production design (MFA)
studio art (MFA)
theatre and media arts (MA)

College of Health and Human Performance
Sara Lee Gibb, Dean
Programs in:
athletic training (MS)
exercise physiology (MS, PhD)
health and human performance (MPH, MS, PhD)
health promotion (MS, PhD)
health science (MPH)
physical medicine and rehabilitation (PhD)
sports pedagogy (MS)
youth and family recreation (MS)

College of Humanities
Dr. John R. Rosenberg, Dean
Programs in:
comparative literature (MA)
comparative studies (MA)
English (MA)
French studies (MA)
general linguistics (MA)
German studies (MA)
humanities (MA)
language acquisition and teaching (MA)
Portuguese linguistics (MA)

Portuguese literature (MA)
Spanish linguistics (MA)
Spanish teaching (MA)
Spanish/Latin American Literature (MA)
Spanish/Peninsular literature (MA)
teaching English as a second language (MA, Certificate)

College of Life Sciences
Dr. Rodney J. Brown, Dean
Programs in:
agronomy (MS)
biological science education (MS)
food science (MS)
genetics and biotechnology (MS)
integrative biology (MS, PhD)
life sciences (MS, PhD)
microbiology (MS, PhD)
molecular biology (MS, PhD)
neuroscience (MS, PhD)
nutrition (MS)
physiology and developmental biology (MS, PhD)
wildlife and wildlands conservation (MS, PhD)

College of Nursing
Dr. Mary Williams, Interim Dean
Program in:
family nurse practitioner (MS)

College of Physical and Mathematical Sciences
Earl M. Woolley, Dean
Programs in:
analytical chemistry (MS, PhD)
applied statistics (MS)
biochemistry (MS, PhD)
computer science (MS, PhD)
geology (MS)
inorganic chemistry (MS, PhD)
mathematics (MS, PhD)
mathematics education (MA)
organic chemistry (MS, PhD)
physical and mathematical sciences (MA, MS, PhD)
physical chemistry (MS, PhD)
physics (MS, PhD)
physics and astronomy (PhD)

College of Religious Education
Dr. Terry B. Ball, Dean
Program in:
religious education (MRE)

David O. McKay School of Education
Dr. K. Richard Young, Dean
Programs in:
counseling psychology (PhD)
education (M Ed, MA, MS, PhD, Ed S)
educational leadership and foundations (M Ed, PhD)
instructional psychology and technology (MS, PhD)
literacy education (M Ed, MA)
school psychology (Ed S)
special education (MS)
speech-language pathology (MS)
teacher education (M Ed, MA)

Ira A. Fulton College of Engineering and Technology
Dr. Alan R. Parkinson, Dean
Programs in:
chemical engineering (MS, PhD)
civil engineering (MS, PhD)
construction management (MS)
electrical and computer engineering (MS, PhD)
engineering and technology (MS, PhD)
information technology (MS)
manufacturing systems (MS)
mechanical engineering (MS, PhD)
technology teacher education (MS)

J. Reuben Clark Law School
Kevin J Worthen, Dean
Program in:
law (JD, LL M)

Marriott School of Management
Dr. Ned C. Hill, Dean
Programs in:
accountancy (M Acc)
business administration (MBA)
information systems (MISM)
management (EMPA, M Acc, MBA, MISM, MPA)
public management (EMPA, MPA)

■ SOUTHERN UTAH UNIVERSITY
Cedar City, UT 84720-2498
http://www.suu.edu/

State-supported, coed, comprehensive institution. *Enrollment:* 7,029 graduate, professional, and undergraduate students; 73 full-time matriculated graduate/professional students (31 women), 355 part-time matriculated graduate/professional students (224 women). *Graduate faculty:* 42 full-time (8 women), 12 part-time/adjunct (4 women). *Computer facilities:* 300 computers available on campus for general student use. A campuswide network can be accessed from student residence rooms and from off campus. *Library facilities:* Southern Utah University Library. *Graduate expenses:* Tuition, state resident: full-time $3,888. Tuition, nonresident: full-time $12,830. Required fees: $505. Tuition and fees vary according to program. *General application contact:* Abe Harraf, Provost, 435-586-7704.

College of Education
Dr. Prent Klag, Associate Professor of Teacher Education
Program in:
education (M Ed)

College of Humanities and Social Sciences
Dean Rodney D. Decker, Dean
Program in:
humanities and social sciences (MPC)

College of Performing and Visual Arts
Bill Byrnes, Dean
Program in:
arts administration (MFA)

School of Business
Dr. Carl Templin, Dean
Programs in:
accounting (M Acc)
business (M Acc, MBA)
business administration (MBA)

■ UNIVERSITY OF PHOENIX–UTAH CAMPUS
Salt Lake City, UT 84123-4617
http://www.phoenix.edu/

Proprietary, coed, comprehensive institution. *Enrollment:* 3,986 graduate, professional, and undergraduate students; 1,427 full-time matriculated graduate/professional students (671 women). *Graduate faculty:* 124 full-time (24 women), 404 part-time/adjunct (103 women). *Computer facilities:* A campuswide network can be accessed from off campus. Internet access is available. *Library facilities:* University Library. *Graduate expenses:* Tuition: full-time $9,104. Required fees: $760. *General application contact:* Campus Information Center, 801-263-1444.

The Artemis School
Dr. Adam Honea, Provost

College of Education
Dr. Marla LaRue, Dean/Executive Director
Programs in:
administration and supervision (MA Ed)
curriculum and instruction (MA Ed)
elementary education (MA Ed)
school counseling (MSC)
secondary education (MA Ed)

College of Health and Human Services
Dr. Gil Linne, Dean/Executive Director
Programs in:
business administration healthcare (MSN)
mental health counseling (MSC)
nursing (MSN)

John Sperling School of Business
Dr. William Pepicello, Provost and Senior Vice Presidnet of Academic Affairs
Program in:
business (MBA, MIS)

College of Graduate Business and Management
Dr. Brian Lindquist, Associate Vice President and Dean/Executive Director
Program in:
business administration (MBA)

College of Information Systems and Technology
Dr. Adam Honea, Provost/Dean, Vice President Academic Research and Development
Program in:
information systems and technology (MIS)

■ UNIVERSITY OF UTAH
Salt Lake City, UT 84112-1107
http://www.utah.edu/

State-supported, coed, university. CGS member. *Enrollment:* 28,619 graduate, professional, and undergraduate students; 4,844 full-time matriculated graduate/professional students (2,105 women), 1,620 part-time matriculated graduate/professional students (813 women). *Graduate faculty:* 862 full-time (296 women), 185 part-time/adjunct (79 women). *Computer facilities:* 8,000 computers available on campus for general student use. A campuswide network can be accessed from student residence rooms and from off campus. Internet access and online class registration, online classes are available. *Library facilities:* Marriott Library plus 3 others. *Graduate expenses:* Tuition, state resident: full-time $3,208. Tuition, nonresident: full-time $11,326. Required fees: $608. Tuition and fees vary according to class time and program. *General application contact:* Office of Admissions, 801-581-7281.

College of Pharmacy
Programs in:
- medicinal chemistry (MS, PhD)
- pharmaceutics and pharmaceutical chemistry (MS, PhD)
- pharmacology and toxicology (MS, PhD)
- pharmacy (Pharm D, MS, PhD)
- pharmacy practice (MS)

The Graduate School
Dr. David S. Chapman, Dean
Programs in:
- biological chemistry (PhD)
- biostatistics (MST)
- biotechnology (PSM)
- computational engineering and science (MS)
- computational science (PSM)
- econometrics (MST)
- economics (MST)
- environmental engineering (MS, PhD)
- environmental science (PSM)
- mathematics (MST)
- sciences instrumental (PSM)
- sociology (MST)
- statistics (M Stat, MST)

College of Architecture and Planning
Brenda Scheer, Dean
Programs in:
- architectural studies (M Arch, MS)
- urban planning (MUP)

College of Education
David J. Sperry, Dean
Programs in:
- counseling psychology (PhD)
- education (M Ed, M Phil, M Stat, MA, MAT, MS, Ed D, PhD)
- education, culture, and society (M Ed, MA, MS, PhD)
- educational leadership and policy (M Ed, M Phil, Ed D, PhD)
- educational psychology (MA)
- elementary education (MAT)
- professional counseling (MS)
- professional psychology (M Ed)
- school counseling (M Ed, MS)
- secondary education (MAT)
- special education (M Ed, M Phil, MS, PhD)
- statistics (M Stat)
- teaching and learning (M Ed, M Phil, MA, MS, PhD)

College of Engineering
Dr. Richard B. Brown, Dean
Programs in:
- bioengineering (ME, MS, PhD)
- chemical engineering (ME, MS, PhD)
- civil engineering (MS, PhD)
- computer science (M Phil, MS, PhD)
- computing (MS, PhD)
- electrical engineering (M Phil, ME, MS, PhD, EE)
- engineering (M Phil, ME, MS, PhD, EE)
- environmental engineering (ME, MS, PhD)
- materials science and engineering (ME, MS, PhD)
- mechanical engineering (ME, MS, PhD)
- nuclear engineering (ME, MS, PhD)

College of Fine Arts
Raymond Tymas Jones, Chair
Programs in:
- art history (MA)
- ballet (MFA)
- ceramics (MFA)
- community-based art education (MFA)
- drawing (MFA)
- film studies (MFA)
- fine arts (M Mus, MA, MFA, PhD)
- graphic design (MFA)
- illustration (MFA)
- modern dance (MA, MFA)
- music (M Mus, MA, PhD)
- painting (MFA)
- photography/digital imaging (MFA)
- printmaking (MFA)
- sculpture/intermedia (MFA)

College of Health
Dr. James E. Graves, Dean
Programs in:
- audiology (Au D)
- exercise and sport science (MS, PhD)
- health (M Phil, MA, MOT, MS, Au D, DPT, Ed D, PhD, PPDPT)
- health promotion and education (M Phil, MS, Ed D, PhD)
- nutrition (MS)
- occupational therapy (MOT)
- parks, recreation, and tourism (M Phil, MS, Ed D, PhD)
- physical therapy (DPT, PPDPT)
- speech-language pathology (MA, MS, PhD)

College of Humanities
Robert D. Newman, Dean and Associate Vice President of Interdisciplinary Studies
Programs in:
- American studies (MA, PhD)
- anthropology (MA)
- applied linguistics (MA, PhD)
- Arabic (MA, PhD)
- Arabic and linguistics (MA, PhD)
- British American literature (MA, PhD)
- communication (M Phil, MA, MS, PhD)
- comparative literature (MA, PhD)
- creative writing (MFA)
- English (PhD)
- French (MA, MALP)
- German (MA, MALP, PhD)
- Hebrew (MA)
- history (MA, PhD)
- humanities (M Phil, MA, MALP, MAT, MFA, MS, PhD)
- language pedagogy (MALP)
- linguistics (MA)
- literature and creative writing (PhD)
- Persian (MA, PhD)
- philosophy (MA, MS, PhD)
- political science (MA, PhD)
- rhetoric and composition (PhD)
- Spanish (MA, MALP, PhD)
- Turkish (MA)

College of Mines and Earth Sciences
Dr. Francis H. Brown, Dean
Programs in:
- environmental engineering (ME, MS, PhD)
- geological engineering (ME, MS, PhD)
- geology (MS, PhD)
- geophysics (MS, PhD)
- metallurgical engineering (ME, MS, PhD)
- meteorology (MS, PhD)
- mines and earth sciences (ME, MS, PhD)
- mining engineering (ME, MS, PhD)

College of Nursing
Maureen Keefe, Dean
Programs in:
- aging (MS, Certificate)
- nursing (MS, PhD, Certificate)

College of Science
Peter J. Stang, Dean
Programs in:
- biology (MS)
- chemical physics (PhD)
- chemistry (M Phil, MA, MS, PhD)
- ecology and evolutionary biology (MS, PhD)
- genetics (MS, PhD)
- mathematics (M Phil, M Stat, MA, MS, PhD)
- microbiology (PhD)
- molecular biology (PhD)
- physics (MA, MS, PhD)
- plant biology (PhD)
- science (M Phil, M Stat, MA, MS, PhD)
- science teacher education (MS)

College of Social and Behavioral Science
J. Steven Ott, Director
Programs in:
- anthropology (MA, MS, PhD)

economics (M Phil, M Stat, MA, MS, PhD)
family and consumer studies (MS)
geography (MA, MS, PhD)
political science (MA, MS, PhD)
psychology (M Stat, MA, MS, PhD)
public administration (MPA, Certificate)
social and behavioral science (M Phil, M Stat, MA, MPA, MS, PhD, Certificate)
sociology (M Stat, MA, MS, PhD)

College of Social Work
Jannah H. Mather, Dean
Program in:
social work (MSW, PhD)

David Eccles School of Business
Dr. Jack Brittain, Dean
Programs in:
accounting and information systems (M Pr A, PhD)
business (M Pr A, M Stat, MBA, MS, PhD)
business administration (M Stat, MBA, PhD)
finance (MS, PhD)
management (MBA, PhD)

School of Medicine
Dr. A. Lorris Betz, Executive Dean and Senior Vice President for Health Sciences
Programs in:
biochemistry (MS, PhD)
biostatistics (M Stat)
experimental pathology (PhD)
human genetics (MS, PhD)
laboratory medicine and biomedical science (MS)
medical informatics (MS, PhD)
medicine (MD, M Phil, M Stat, MPAS, MPH, MS, MSPH, PhD)
neurobiology and anatomy (PhD)
neuroscience (PhD)
oncological sciences (M Phil, MS, PhD)
physician assistant (MPAS)
physiology (PhD)
public health (MPH, MSPH, PhD)

S.J. Quinney College of Law
Hiram E. Chodosh, Dean
Program in:
law (JD, LL M)

■ UTAH STATE UNIVERSITY
Logan, UT 84322
http://www.usu.edu/

State-supported, coed, university. CGS member. *Enrollment:* 14,444 graduate, professional, and undergraduate students; 2,030 full-time matriculated graduate/professional students (800 women), 576 part-time matriculated graduate/professional students (276 women). *Graduate faculty:* 712 full-time (178 women), 163 part-time/adjunct (45 women). *Computer facilities:* Computer purchase and lease plans are available. 875 computers available on campus for general student use. A campuswide network can be accessed from student residence rooms and from off campus. Internet access and online class registration are available. *Library facilities:* Merrill Library plus 4 others. *General application contact:* Peter J. Morris, Admissions Officer, School of Graduate Studies, 435-797-1190.

School of Graduate Studies
Dr. Laurens H. Smith, Interim Dean

College of Agriculture
Noelle E. Cockett, Dean
Programs in:
agricultural systems technology (MS)
agriculture (MDA, MFMS, MS, PhD)
animal science (MS, PhD)
biometeorology (MS, PhD)
bioveterinary science (MS, PhD)
dairy science (MS)
dietetic administration (MDA)
ecology (MS, PhD)
family and consumer sciences education (MS)
food microbiology and safety (MFMS)
nutrition and food sciences (MS, PhD)
nutrition science (MS, PhD)
plant science (MS, PhD)
soil science (MS, PhD)
toxicology (MS, PhD)

College of Business
Caryn C. Beck-Dudley, Dean
Programs in:
accountancy (M Acc)
applied economics (MS)
business (M Acc, MA, MBA, MS, Ed D, PhD)
business administration (MBA)
business education (MS)
business information systems (MS)
business information systems and education (Ed D)
economics (MA, MS, PhD)
education (PhD)
human resource management (MS)

College of Education and Human Services
Dr. Carol Strong, Dean
Programs in:
audiology (Au D, Ed S)
business information systems (Ed D, PhD)
clinical/counseling/school psychology (PhD)
communication disorders and deaf education (M Ed)
communicative disorders and deaf education (MA, MS)
curriculum and instruction (Ed D, PhD)
disability disciplines (PhD)
education and human services (M Ed, MA, MFHD, MRC, MS, Au D, Ed D, PhD, Ed S)
elementary education (M Ed, MA, MS)
family and human development (MFHD)
family, consumer, and human development (MS, PhD)
health, physical education and recreation (M Ed, MS)
instructional technology (M Ed, MS, PhD, Ed S)
rehabilitation counselor education (MRC)
research and evaluation (PhD)
research and evaluation methodology (PhD)
school counseling (MS)
school psychology (MS)
secondary education (M Ed, MA, MS)
special education (M Ed, MS, Ed S)

College of Engineering
H. Scott Hinton, Dean
Programs in:
aerospace engineering (MS, PhD)
biological and agricultural engineering (MS, PhD)
civil and environmental engineering (ME, MS, PhD, CE)
electrical engineering (ME, MS, PhD)
engineering (ME, MS, PhD, CE)
industrial technology (MS)
irrigation engineering (MS, PhD)
mechanical engineering (ME, MS, PhD)

College of Humanities, Arts and Social Sciences
Dr. Gary H. Kiger, Dean
Programs in:
advanced technical practice (MFA)
American studies (MA, MS)
art (MA, MFA)
bioregional planning (MS)
design (MFA)
English (MA, MS)
folklore (MA, MS)
history (MA, MS)
humanities, arts and social sciences (MA, MFA, MLA, MS, MSLT, MSS, PhD)
interior design (MS)
journalism and communication (MA, MS)
landscape architecture (MLA)
political science (MA, MS)
second language teaching (MSLT)
sociology (MA, MS, MSS, PhD)
theatre arts (MA, MFA)
western American literature and culture (MA, MS)

College of Natural Resources
Dr. Nat Frazer, Dean
Programs in:
bioregional planning (MS)
ecology (MS, PhD)
fisheries biology (MS, PhD)
forestry (MS, PhD)
geography (MA, MS)
human dimensions of ecosystem science and management (MS, PhD)
natural resources (MA, MNR, MS, PhD)
range science (MS, PhD)
recreation resource management (MS, PhD)
watershed science (MS, PhD)
wildlife biology (MS, PhD)

College of Science
Don Fiesinger, Dean

Utah State University (continued)
Programs in:
biochemistry (MS, PhD)
biology (MS, PhD)
chemistry (MS, PhD)
computer science (MCS, MS, PhD)
ecology (MS, PhD)
geology (MS)
industrial mathematics (MS)
mathematical sciences (PhD)
mathematics (M Math, MS)
physics (MS, PhD)
science (M Math, MCS, MS, PhD)
statistics (MS)

■ WEBER STATE UNIVERSITY
Ogden, UT 84408-1001
http://weber.edu/

State-supported, coed, comprehensive institution. *Enrollment:* 18,303 graduate, professional, and undergraduate students; 147 full-time matriculated graduate/professional students (33 women), 350 part-time matriculated graduate/professional students (196 women). *Graduate faculty:* 44 full-time (14 women), 26 part-time/adjunct (10 women). *Computer facilities:* Computer purchase and lease plans are available. 558 computers available on campus for general student use. A campuswide network can be accessed from student residence rooms and from off campus. Internet access and online class registration, online grades are available. *Library facilities:* Stewart Library plus 1 other. *Graduate expenses:* Tuition, state resident: full-time $3,950; part-time $203 per semester. Tuition, nonresident: full-time $10,371; part-time $518 per semester. Required fees: $544; $24 per semester. Tuition and fees vary according to course load and program. *General application contact:* Christopher C. Rivera, Director of Admissions, 801-626-6046.

College of Social and Behavioral Sciences
Dr. Richard Sadler, Dean
Programs in:
criminal justice (MCJ)
social and behavioral sciences (MCJ)

Jerry and Vickie Moyes College of Education
Dr. Jack L. Rasmussen, Dean
Programs in:
curriculum and instruction (M Ed)
education (M Ed)

John B. Goddard School of Business and Economics
Dr. Lewis R Gale, Dean
Programs in:
accountancy (M Acc)
business administration (MBA)
business and economics (M Acc, MBA)

■ WESTMINSTER COLLEGE
Salt Lake City, UT 84105-3697
http://www.westminstercollege.edu/

Independent, coed, comprehensive institution. *Enrollment:* 2,479 graduate, professional, and undergraduate students; 223 full-time matriculated graduate/professional students (92 women), 297 part-time matriculated graduate/professional students (132 women). *Graduate faculty:* 43 full-time (23 women), 13 part-time/adjunct (9 women). *Computer facilities:* 400 computers available on campus for general student use. A campuswide network can be accessed from student residence rooms and from off campus. Internet access and online class registration are available. *Library facilities:* Giovale Library plus 1 other. *General application contact:* Joel Bauman, Vice President of Enrollment Services, 801-832-2200.

The Bill and Vieve Gore School of Business
James Clark, Dean
Programs in:
business administration (MBA, Certificate)
technology management (MBATM)

Program in Counseling Psychology
Janine Wanlass, Director
Program in:
counseling psychology (MSCP)

Program in Professional Communication
Dr. Helen Hodgson, Director
Program in:
professional communication (MPC)

School of Education
David Stokes, Interim
Program in:
education (M Ed, MAT)

School of Nursing and Health Sciences
Dr. Jean Dyer, Dean
Programs in:
family nurse practitioner (MSN)
nurse anesthesia (MSNA)
nursing (MSN)
nursing education (MSN)

Vermont

■ BENNINGTON COLLEGE
Bennington, VT 05201
http://www.bennington.edu/

Independent, coed, comprehensive institution. *Enrollment:* 657 graduate, professional, and undergraduate students; 120 full-time matriculated graduate/professional students (78 women), 14 part-time matriculated graduate/professional students (10 women). *Graduate faculty:* 39 full-time (18 women), 16 part-time/adjunct (8 women). *Computer facilities:* 61 computers available on campus for general student use. A campuswide network can be accessed from student residence rooms and from off campus. Internet access is available. *Library facilities:* Crossett Library plus 1 other. *Graduate expenses:* Tuition: full-time $20,000; part-time $2,800 per course. One-time fee: $75 full-time. Tuition and fees vary according to program. *General application contact:* Ken Himmelman, Dean of Admissions, 802-440-4312.

Graduate Programs
Dr. Wendy Hirsch, Associate Dean
Programs in:
allied and health sciences (Certificate)
art education (MAT)
creative writing (MFA)
dance (MFA)
drama (MFA)
early childhood (MAT)
education (MATSL)
elementary education (MAT)
English education (MAT)
foreign language education (MAT, MATSL)
French (MATSL)
mathematics education (MAT)
music (MFA)
music education (MAT)
science education (MAT)
secondary education (MAT)
social science education (MAT)
Spanish (MATSL)

■ CASTLETON STATE COLLEGE
Castleton, VT 05735
http://www.castleton.edu/

State-supported, coed, comprehensive institution. *Computer facilities:* Computer purchase and lease plans are available. 225 computers available on campus for general student use. A campuswide network can be accessed from student residence rooms. Internet access is available. *Library facilities:* Calvin Coolidge Library. *General application contact:* Director of Admissions, 802-468-1213.

Division of Graduate Studies
Programs in:
curriculum and instruction (MA Ed)
educational leadership (MA Ed, CAGS)
forensic psychology (MA)
language arts and reading (MA Ed, CAGS)
special education (MA Ed, CAGS)

■ COLLEGE OF ST. JOSEPH
Rutland, VT 05701-3899
http://www.csj.edu/

Independent-religious, coed, comprehensive institution. *Enrollment:* 509 graduate, professional, and undergraduate students; 54 full-time matriculated graduate/professional students (41 women), 169 part-time matriculated graduate/professional students (128 women). *Graduate faculty:* 13 full-time (4 women), 21 part-time/adjunct (11 women). *Computer facilities:* Computer purchase and lease plans are available. 30 computers available on campus for general student use. A campuswide network can be accessed from student residence rooms and from off campus. Internet access is available. *Library facilities:* Giorgetti Library. *Graduate expenses:* Tuition: full-time $10,990; part-time $300 per credit. Part-time tuition and fees vary according to program. *General application contact:* Tracy Gallipo, Director of Admissions, 802-773-5900 Ext. 3262.

Graduate Program
Dr. Gary M. Lawler, Vice President of Academic and Student Affairs

Division of Business
Robert Foley, Chair
Program in:
- business administration (MBA)

Division of Education
Dr. Kapi Reith, Chair
Programs in:
- elementary education (M Ed)
- English (M Ed)
- general education (M Ed)
- mathematics (M Ed)
- reading (M Ed)
- secondary education (M Ed)
- social studies (M Ed)
- special education (M Ed)

Division of Psychology and Human Services
Dr. Craig Knapp, Chair
Programs in:
- clinical mental health counseling (MS)
- clinical psychology (MS)
- community counseling (MS)
- school guidance counseling (MS)
- substance abuse counseling (MS)

■ GODDARD COLLEGE
Plainfield, VT 05667-9432
http://www.goddard.edu/

Independent, coed, comprehensive institution. *Enrollment:* 415 full-time matriculated graduate/professional students (306 women). *Graduate faculty:* 2 full-time (1 woman), 72 part-time/adjunct (53 women). *Computer facilities:* 27 computers available on campus for general student use. A campuswide network can be accessed from student residence rooms and from off campus. Internet access, library services are available. *Library facilities:* Eliot Pratt Center. *Graduate expenses:* Tuition: full-time $12,506; part-time $10,392 per year. Required fees: $998; $499 per term. *General application contact:* Brenda J. Hawkins, Director of Admissions, 800-906-8311 Ext. 240.

Graduate Program
Dr. Susan Fleming, Director
Programs in:
- consciousness studies (MA)
- environmental studies (MA)
- health arts and sciences (MA)
- interdisciplinary arts (MFA)
- organizational development (MA)
- psychology and counseling (MA)
- socially responsible business and sustainable communities (MA)
- teacher education (MA)
- transformative language arts (MA)
- writing (MFA)

■ JOHNSON STATE COLLEGE
Johnson, VT 05656-9405
http://www.johnsonstatecollege.edu/

State-supported, coed, comprehensive institution. *Enrollment:* 1,866 graduate, professional, and undergraduate students; 71 full-time matriculated graduate/professional students (51 women), 168 part-time matriculated graduate/professional students (112 women). *Graduate faculty:* 13 full-time (8 women), 12 part-time/adjunct (10 women). *Computer facilities:* 131 computers available on campus for general student use. A campuswide network can be accessed from student residence rooms and from off campus. Internet access is available. *Library facilities:* Library and Learning Center. *General application contact:* Catherine H. Higley, Administrative Assistant for Graduate Programs, 800-635-2356 Ext. 1244.

Graduate Program in Education
Programs in:
- applied behavior analysis (MA Ed)
- children's mental health (MA Ed)
- curriculum and instruction (MA Ed)
- developmental disabilities (MA Ed)
- education of the gifted (MA Ed)
- reading education (MA Ed)
- science education (MA Ed)
- secondary education (MA Ed, CAGS)
- special education (MA Ed)
- teaching all secondary students (MA Ed, CAGS)

Program in Counseling
Program in:
- counseling (MA)

Program in Fine Arts
Programs in:
- drawing (MFA)
- painting (MFA)
- sculpture (MFA)

■ NORWICH UNIVERSITY
Northfield, VT 05663
http://www.norwich.edu/

Independent, coed, comprehensive institution. *Enrollment:* 400 full-time matriculated graduate/professional students (150 women). *Graduate faculty:* 4 full-time (0 women), 152 part-time/adjunct (52 women). *Computer facilities:* 142 computers available on campus for general student use. A campuswide network can be accessed from student residence rooms and from off campus. Internet access is available. *Library facilities:* Kreitzberg Library. *General application contact:* Jane D. Joslin, Administrative Assistant, 802-485-2730.

School of Graduate Studies
Dr. William Clemments, Director
Programs in:
- business administration (MBA)
- civil engineering (MCE)
- education (M Ed)
- information assurance (MS)
- international (MA)
- justice administration (MJA)
- military history (MA)
- nursing administration (MSN)
- organizational leadership (MSOL)
- public administration (MPA)

■ SAINT MICHAEL'S COLLEGE
Colchester, VT 05439
http://www.smcvt.edu/

Independent-religious, coed, comprehensive institution. *Enrollment:* 2,437 graduate, professional, and undergraduate students; 86 full-time matriculated graduate/professional students (60 women), 220 part-time matriculated graduate/professional students (158 women). *Graduate faculty:* 25 full-time (11 women), 84 part-time/adjunct (49 women). *Computer facilities:* 233 computers available on campus for general student use. A campuswide network can be accessed from student residence rooms and from off campus. Internet access and online class registration are available. *Library facilities:* Durick Library. *General application contact:* Dee M. Goodrich, Director of Admissions and Marketing, Graduate Programs, 802-654-2251.

Graduate Programs
Dr. Jeffrey Trumbower, Dean
Programs in:
- administration (M Ed, CAGS)
- administration and management (MSA, CAMS)
- arts in education (CAGS)
- clinical psychology (MA)
- curriculum and instruction (M Ed, CAGS)
- information technology (CAGS)
- reading (M Ed)

Saint Michael's College (continued)
special education (M Ed, CAGS)
teaching English as a second language (MATESL, Certificate)
technology (M Ed)
theology (MA, CAS, Certificate)

■ SCHOOL FOR INTERNATIONAL TRAINING

Brattleboro, VT 05302-0676

http://www.sit.edu/

Independent, coed, graduate-only institution. *Graduate faculty:* 27 full-time (12 women), 19 part-time/adjunct (8 women). *Computer facilities:* 55 computers available on campus for general student use. A campuswide network can be accessed from student residence rooms and from off campus. Internet access is available. *Library facilities:* Donald B. Watt Library. *Graduate expenses:* Tuition: full-time $27,355; part-time $638 per credit hour. Required fees: $1,092. *General application contact:* Information Contact, 800-336-1616.

Find University Details at www.petersons.com/gradchannel.

Graduate Programs
Adam Weinberg, Provost/Executive Vice President
Programs in:
conflict transformation (MA)
English for speakers of other languages (MAT)
French (MAT)
intercultural service, leadership, and management (MA)
international education (MA)
management (MS)
social justice in intercultural relations (MA)
Spanish (MAT)
sustainable development (MA)

■ UNIVERSITY OF VERMONT

Burlington, VT 05405

http://www.uvm.edu/

State-supported, coed, university. CGS member. *Enrollment:* 11,870 graduate, professional, and undergraduate students; 1,772 matriculated graduate/professional students (1,068 women). *Graduate faculty:* 702 full-time, 604 part-time/adjunct. *Computer facilities:* Computer purchase and lease plans are available. 685 computers available on campus for general student use. A campuswide network can be accessed from student residence rooms and from off campus. Internet access and online class registration, e-mail, Web pages, on-line course support are available. *Library facilities:* Bailey-Howe Library plus 3 others. *Graduate expenses:* Tuition, state resident: part-time $434 per credit. Tuition, nonresident: part-time $1,096 per credit. *General application contact:* Patricia Stokowski, Assistant Dean, 802-656-3160.

College of Medicine
Dr. John Evans, Dean
Programs in:
anatomy and neurobiology (PhD)
biochemistry (MS, PhD)
medicine (MD, MS, PhD)
microbiology and molecular genetics (MS, PhD)
molecular physiology and biophysics (MS, PhD)
neuroscience (PhD)
pathology (MS)
pharmacology (MS, PhD)

Graduate College
Dr. Frances E. Carr, Vice President for Research and Dean of the Graduate College
Program in:
cell and molecular biology (MS, PhD)

College of Agriculture and Life Sciences
Dr. R. K. Johnson, Dean
Programs in:
agriculture and life sciences (MPA, MS, PhD)
animal sciences (MS, PhD)
animal, nutrition and food sciences (PhD)
botany (MS, PhD)
community development and applied economics (MPA, MS)
field naturalist (MS)
microbiology and molecular genetics (MS, PhD)
nutritional sciences (MS)
plant and soil science (MS, PhD)
public administration (MPA)

College of Arts and Sciences
Dr. Eleanor Miller, Dean
Programs in:
arts and sciences (MA, MAT, MS, MST, PhD)
biology (MS, PhD)
biology education (MST)
chemistry (MS, PhD)
clinical psychology (PhD)
communication sciences (MS)
English (MA)
French (MA)
geology (MS)
German (MA)
Greek (MA)
Greek and Latin (MAT)
historic preservation (MS)
history (MA)
Latin (MA)
physics (MS)
psychology (PhD)

College of Education and Social Services
Dr. Fayneese Miller, Dean
Programs in:
counseling (MS)
curriculum and instruction (M Ed)
education and social services (M Ed, MS, MSW, Ed D)
educational leadership (M Ed)
educational leadership and policy studies (Ed D)
educational studies (M Ed)
higher education and student affairs administration (M Ed)
interdisciplinary studies (M Ed)
reading and language arts (M Ed)
social work (MSW)
special education (M Ed)

College of Engineering and Mathematics
Dr. Domenico Grasso, Dean
Programs in:
biomedical engineering (MS)
biostatistics (MS)
civil and environmental engineering (MS, PhD)
computer science (MS, PhD)
electrical engineering (MS, PhD)
engineering and mathematics (MS, MST, PhD)
materials science (MS, PhD)
mathematics (MS, MST, PhD)
mathematics education (MST)
mechanical engineering (MS, PhD)
statistics (MS)

College of Nursing and Health Sciences
Dr. Betty Rambur, Dean
Programs in:
nursing (MS)
nursing and health sciences (MS, DPT)
physical therapy (DPT)

The Rubenstein School of Environment and Natural Resources
Dr. D. DeHayes, Dean
Programs in:
environment and natural resources (MS, PhD)
natural resources (MS, PhD)

School of Business Administration
Dr. R. DeWitt, Dean
Program in:
business administration (MBA)

Virginia

■ THE COLLEGE OF WILLIAM AND MARY

Williamsburg, VA 23187-8795

http://www.wm.edu/

State-supported, coed, university. CGS member. *Enrollment:* 7,709 graduate, professional, and undergraduate students; 1,494 full-time matriculated graduate/professional students (727 women), 383 part-time matriculated graduate/professional students (197 women). *Graduate faculty:* 594 full-time (212 women), 164 part-time/adjunct (83 women). *Computer facilities:* 225 computers available on campus for general student use. A campuswide network can be accessed from student residence rooms and from off campus. Internet access and online class registration are available. *Library facilities:* Swem Library plus 9 others. *Graduate expenses:* Tuition, state resident: full-time $6,100; part-time $260 per credit. Tuition, nonresident: full-time $18,790; part-time $725 per credit. Required fees: $3,314. Tuition and fees vary according to program. *General application contact:* Dr. Laurie Sanderson, Dean of Research and Graduate Studies, 757-221-2468.

Find University Details at www.petersons.com/gradchannel.

Faculty of Arts and Sciences
Dr. Laurie Sanderson, Dean of Research and Graduate Studies
Programs in:
- American studies (MA, PhD)
- anthropology (MA, PhD)
- applied science (MS, PhD)
- arts and sciences (MA, MPP, MS, PhD, Psy D)
- biology (MS)
- chemistry (MA, MS)
- clinical psychology (Psy D)
- computational operations research (MS)
- computer science (MS, PhD)
- general experimental psychology (MA)
- history (MA, PhD)
- physics (MS, PhD)
- public policy (MPP)

Mason School of Business
Dr. Lawrence Pulley, Dean
Programs in:
- accounting (M Acc)
- business administration (MBA)

School of Education
Dr. Virginia McLaughlin, Dean
Programs in:
- community and addictions counseling (M Ed)
- community counseling (M Ed)
- curriculum and educational technology (Ed D, PhD)
- curriculum leadership (Ed D, PhD)
- education (M Ed, MA Ed, Ed D, PhD, Ed S)
- educational counseling (Ed D, PhD)
- educational leadership (M Ed)
- educational policy, planning, and leadership (Ed D, PhD)
- elementary education (MA Ed)
- family counseling (M Ed)
- gifted education (MA Ed)
- gifted education administration (M Ed)
- reading education (MA Ed)
- school counseling (M Ed)
- school psychology (M Ed, Ed S)
- secondary education (MA Ed)
- special education (MA Ed)

School of Marine Science/ Virginia Institute of Marine Science
Dr. John T. Wells, Dean and Director
Program in:
- marine science (MS, PhD)

William & Mary Law School
W. Taylor Reveley, Dean
Program in:
- law (JD, LL M)

■ DEVRY UNIVERSITY
Arlington, VA 22202
http://www.devry.edu/

Proprietary, coed, comprehensive institution. *Computer facilities:* Computer purchase and lease plans are available. 380 computers available on campus for general student use. A campuswide network can be accessed from off campus. Internet access and online class registration are available. *Library facilities:* Learning Resource Center.

Keller Graduate School of Management
Program in:
- management (MAFM, MBA, MHRM, MISM, MNCM, MPA, MPM)

■ EASTERN MENNONITE UNIVERSITY
Harrisonburg, VA 22802-2462
http://www.emu.edu/

Independent-religious, coed, comprehensive institution. *Enrollment:* 1,324 graduate, professional, and undergraduate students; 111 full-time matriculated graduate/ professional students (49 women), 280 part-time matriculated graduate/professional students (213 women). *Graduate faculty:* 29 full-time (13 women), 43 part-time/adjunct (21 women). *Computer facilities:* 110 computers available on campus for general student use. A campuswide network can be accessed from student residence rooms and from off campus. Internet access is available. *Library facilities:* Sadie Hartzler Library. *General application contact:* Don A. Yoder, Director of Seminary and Graduate Admissions, 540-432-4257.

Eastern Mennonite Seminary
Dr. Ervin R. Stutzman, Seminary Dean
Programs in:
- church leadership (MA)
- divinity (M Div)
- ministry studies (Certificate)
- online theological studies (Certificate)
- religion (MA)
- theological studies (Certificate)

Program in Business Administration
Allon H. Lefever, Director MBA Program
Program in:
- business administration (MBA)

Program in Conflict Transformation
Dr. David Brubaker, Academic Director
Program in:
- conflict transformation (MA, Graduate Certificate)

Program in Counseling
Dr. P. David Glanzer, Professor of Counselor Education
Program in:
- counseling (MA)

Program in Education
Dr. Donovan D. Steiner, Director
Program in:
- education (MA)

■ GEORGE MASON UNIVERSITY
Fairfax, VA 22030
http://www.gmu.edu/

State-supported, coed, university. CGS member. *Enrollment:* 29,889 graduate, professional, and undergraduate students; 2,308 full-time matriculated graduate/ professional students (1,223 women), 7,015 part-time matriculated graduate/professional students (3,940 women). *Graduate faculty:* 1,108 full-time (431 women), 920 part-time/ adjunct (466 women). *Computer facilities:* 1,500 computers available on campus for general student use. A campuswide network can be accessed from student residence rooms and from off campus. Internet access, telephone registration are available. *Library facilities:* Fenwick Library plus 1 other. *Graduate expenses:* Tuition, state resident: full-time $5,724; part-time $238 per credit. Tuition, nonresident: full-time $16,896; part-time $704 per credit. Required fees: $1,656; $69 per credit. *General application contact:* Dan Robb, Director of Graduate Admissions, 703-993-4201.

College of Health and Human Services
Dr. Shirley S. Travis, Dean
Programs in:
- advanced clinical nursing (MSN)
- nurse practitioner (MSN)
- nursing (MSN, PhD)
- nursing administration (MSN)
- nursing education (Certificate)
- nursing educator (MSN)
- social work (MSW)

College of Humanities and Social Sciences
Jack Censer, Chair
Programs in:
- clinical psychology (PhD)
- communications (MA)
- creative writing (MFA)
- cultural studies (PhD)
- developmental psychology (PhD)
- economics (MA, PhD)
- English (MA)
- English literature (MA)
- experimental neuropsychology (MA)
- foreign languages (MA)

George Mason University (continued)
- history (MA, PhD)
- human factors engineering psychology (MA, PhD)
- humanities and social sciences (MA, MAIS, MFA, MPA, MS, MSW, DA Ed, PhD, Certificate)
- industrial/organizational psychology (MA, PhD)
- interdisciplinary studies (MAIS)
- liberal studies (MAIS)
- life-span development psychology (MA)
- linguistics (MA)
- professional writing and editing (MA)
- public administration (MPA)
- school psychology (MA)
- social work (MSW)
- sociology (MA)
- teaching writing and literature (MA)

The National Center for Community College Education
Nance Lucas, Interim Director
Program in:
- community college education (DA Ed, Certificate)

College of Science
Dr. Vikas E. Chandhoke, Director
Programs in:
- applied and engineering physics (MS)
- biodefense (MS, PhD)
- bioinformatics and computational biology (MS, PhD, Certificate)
- biology (MS, PhD)
- chemistry (MS)
- chemistry and biochemistry (MS)
- climate dynamics (PhD)
- computational and data sciences (MS, PhD, Certificate)
- computational social science (PhD)
- computational techniques and applications (Certificate)
- earth systems and geoinformation sciences (PhD, Certificate)
- earth systems geoinformation science (MS)
- environmental science and policy (MS, PhD)
- geographic and cartographic sciences (MS)
- geography (MS)
- mathematical sciences (MS, PhD)
- mathematics (MS, PhD)
- nanotechnology and nanoscience (Certificate)
- neuroscience (PhD)
- physical sciences (PhD)
- physics and astronomy (MS)
- remote sensing and earth image processing (Certificate)

College of Visual and Performing Arts
William Reeder, Dean
Programs in:
- dance (MFA)
- music (MA)
- music education (MA)
- visual and performing arts (MA, MFA)
- visual technologies (MA)

Graduate School of Education
Jeffrey Gorrell, Dean
Programs in:
- bilingual/multicultural/English as a second language education (M Ed)
- counseling and development (M Ed)
- early childhood education (M Ed)
- education (M Ed, MA, MS, PhD)
- education leadership (M Ed)
- exercise, fitness and health promotion (MS)
- initiatives in educational transformation (MA)
- instructional technology (M Ed)
- middle education (M Ed)
- reading (M Ed)
- secondary education (M Ed)
- special education (M Ed)

Institute for Conflict Analysis and Resolution
Dr. Sara Cobb, Director
Program in:
- conflict analysis and resolution (MS, PhD)

School of Law
Programs in:
- intellectual property (LL M)
- law (JD)
- law and economics (LL M)

School of Management
Richard Klimoski, Dean
Programs in:
- bio-science management (MS)
- business administration (EMBA, MBA)
- management (EMBA, MBA, MS)
- technology management (MS)

School of Public Policy
Dr. Kingsley Haynes, Dean
Programs in:
- international commerce and policy (MA)
- organization development and knowledge management (MNPS)
- peace operations (MNPS)
- public policy (MA, MNPS, MPP, PhD)
- transportation policy, operations and logistics (MA)

Volgenau School of Information Technology and Engineering
Lloyd Griffiths, Dean
Programs in:
- civil and infrastructure engineering (MS)
- computer science (MS, PhD)
- electrical and computer engineering (PhD)
- electrical engineering (MS)
- federal statistics (Certificate)
- information systems (MS)
- information technology (MS, PhD, Engr)
- information technology and engineering (MS, PhD, Certificate, Engr)
- operations research and management science (MS)
- software systems engineering (MS)
- statistical science (MS, PhD)
- systems engineering (MS)
- telecommunication (MS)

■ HAMPTON UNIVERSITY
Hampton, VA 23668
http://www.hamptonu.edu/

Independent, coed, university. CGS member. *Computer facilities:* Computer purchase and lease plans are available. 1,300 computers available on campus for general student use. A campuswide network can be accessed from student residence rooms and from off campus. Internet access and online class registration are available. *Library facilities:* William R. and Norma B. Harvey Library plus 3 others. *General application contact:* Vice President for Research and Dean of Graduate College, 757-727-5310.

Find University Details at www.petersons.com/gradchannel.

Graduate College
Programs in:
- applied mathematics (MS)
- biological sciences (MA, MS)
- business (MBA)
- chemistry (MS)
- college student development (MA)
- communicative sciences and disorders (MA)
- community agency counseling (MA)
- computer science (MS)
- counseling (MA)
- elementary education (MA)
- museum studies (MA)
- nursing (MS)
- physical therapy (DPT)
- physics (MS, PhD)
- special education (MA)
- teaching (MT)

■ HOLLINS UNIVERSITY
Roanoke, VA 24020-1603
http://www.hollins.edu/

Independent, Undergraduate: women only; graduate: coed, comprehensive institution. *Enrollment:* 1,061 graduate, professional, and undergraduate students; 179 full-time matriculated graduate/professional students (136 women), 148 part-time matriculated graduate/professional students (119 women). *Graduate faculty:* 23 full-time (9 women), 33 part-time/adjunct (17 women). *Computer facilities:* 100 computers available on campus for general student use. A campuswide network can be accessed from student residence rooms and from off campus. Internet access, applications software are available. *Library facilities:* Wyndham Robertson Library plus 1 other. *General application contact:* Cathy S. Koon, Manager of Graduate Services, 540-362-6326.

Find University Details at www.petersons.com/gradchannel.

Graduate Programs
Dr. Wayne Markert, Provost

Programs in:
- children's literature (MA, MFA)
- creative writing (MFA)
- dance (MFA)
- humanities (MALS)
- interdisciplinary studies (MALS)
- liberal studies (CAS)
- playwriting (MFA)
- screenwriting and film studies (MA, MFA)
- social science (MALS)
- teaching (MAT)
- visual and performing arts (MALS)

■ JAMES MADISON UNIVERSITY

Harrisonburg, VA 22807

http://www.jmu.edu/

State-supported, coed, comprehensive institution. CGS member. *Enrollment:* 17,393 graduate, professional, and undergraduate students; 762 full-time matriculated graduate/professional students (546 women), 376 part-time matriculated graduate/professional students (169 women). *Graduate faculty:* 228 full-time (100 women), 60 part-time/adjunct (31 women). *Computer facilities:* Computer purchase and lease plans are available. 600 computers available on campus for general student use. A campuswide network can be accessed from student residence rooms and from off campus. Internet access and online class registration are available. *Library facilities:* Carrier Library plus 2 others. *Graduate expenses:* Tuition, state resident: full-time $6,336; part-time $264 per credit hour. Tuition, nonresident: full-time $17,832; part-time $743 per credit hour. *General application contact:* Dr. Reid Linn, Dean, College of Graduate and Outreach Programs, 540-568-6131.

College of Graduate and Outreach Programs

Dr. Reid Linn, Dean, College of Graduate and Outreach Programs

College of Arts and Letters

Dr. David K. Jeffrey, Dean

Programs in:
- arts and letters (MA, MPA, MS)
- English (MA)
- history (MA)
- public administration (MPA)
- technical and scientific communication (MA, MS)

College of Business

Dr. Robert D. Reid, Dean

Programs in:
- accounting (MS)
- business (MBA, MS)
- business administration (MBA)

College of Education

Dr. Phillip M. Wishon, Dean

Programs in:
- adult education/human resource development (MS Ed)
- early childhood education (MAT)
- education (M Ed, MAT, MS Ed)
- educational leadership (M Ed)
- exceptional education (M Ed)
- middle education (MAT)
- reading education (M Ed)
- secondary education (MAT)

College of Integrated Science and Technology

Dr. A. Jerry Benson, Dean

Programs in:
- assessment and measurement (PhD)
- audiology (Au D, PhD)
- clinical audiology (PhD)
- college student personnel administration (M Ed)
- combined-integrated clinical and school psychology (Psy D)
- community counseling psychology (MA, Ed S)
- computer science (MS)
- health education (MS, MS Ed)
- integrated science and technology (M Ed, MA, MOT, MPAS, MS, MS Ed, MSN, Au D, PhD, Psy D, Ed S)
- kinesiology (MS)
- nursing (MSN)
- occupational therapy (MOT)
- physician assistant studies (MPAS)
- psychological sciences (MA)
- school counseling (M Ed, Ed S)
- school psychology (M Ed, MA, Ed S)
- speech-language pathology (MS, PhD)

College of Science and Mathematics

Dr. David F. Brakke, Dean

Programs in:
- biology (MS)
- mathematics and statistics (M Ed)
- science and mathematics (M Ed, MS)

College of Visual and Performing Arts

Dr. Marilou Johnson, Interim Dean

Programs in:
- art education (MA)
- art history (MA)
- ceramics (MFA)
- conducting (MM)
- drawing/painting (MFA)
- metal/jewelry (MFA)
- music education (MM)
- performance (MM)
- photography (MFA)
- printmaking (MFA)
- sculpture (MFA)
- studio art (MA)
- theory-composition (MM)
- visual and performing arts (MA, MFA, MM)
- weaving/fibers (MFA)

■ LIBERTY UNIVERSITY

Lynchburg, VA 24502

http://www.liberty.edu/

Independent-religious, coed, comprehensive institution. *Enrollment:* 17,606 graduate, professional, and undergraduate students; 1,137 full-time matriculated graduate/professional students (408 women), 2,935 part-time matriculated graduate/professional students (1,270 women). *Graduate faculty:* 56 full-time (9 women), 91 part-time/adjunct (20 women). *Computer facilities:* Computer purchase and lease plans are available. 406 computers available on campus for general student use. A campuswide network can be accessed from student residence rooms and from off campus. Internet access and online class registration are available. *Library facilities:* A. Pierre Guillermin Integrated Learning Resource Center plus 1 other. *General application contact:* Kyle A Falce, Director of Graduate Admissions, 800-424-9596.

College of Arts and Sciences

Dr. Ronald E. Hawkins, Dean

Programs in:
- counseling (MA)
- nursing (MSN)
- pastoral care and counseling (PhD)
- professional counseling (PhD)

Liberty Theological Seminary and Graduate School

Dr. Ergun Caner, Dean

Programs in:
- religious studies (M Div, MA, MAR, MRE, D Min)
- theology (Th M)

School of Business

Dr. Bruce K. Bell, Dean

Program in:
- business (MBA)

School of Communications

Dr. William G. Gribbin, Dean

Program in:
- communications (MA)

School of Education

Dr. Karen L. Parker, Dean

Programs in:
- administration and supervision (M Ed)
- curriculum and instruction (M Ed)
- early childhood education (M Ed)
- education specialist (Ed S)
- educational leadership (Ed D)
- elementary education (M Ed)
- gifted education (M Ed)
- reading specialist (M Ed)
- school counseling (M Ed)
- secondary education (M Ed)
- special education (M Ed)

School of Law

Mathew D. Staver, Dean

Program in:
- law (JD)

■ LONGWOOD UNIVERSITY
Farmville, VA 23909
http://www.longwood.edu/

State-supported, coed, comprehensive institution. CGS member. *Computer facilities:* Computer purchase and lease plans are available. 270 computers available on campus for general student use. A campuswide network can be accessed from student residence rooms and from off campus. Internet access and online class registration are available. *Library facilities:* The Janet D. Greenwood Library. *General application contact:* Assistant Dean of Graduate Studies, 434-395-2707.

Office of Graduate Studies
Programs in:
- 6-12 initial teaching/licensure (MA)
- creative writing (MA)
- criminal justice (MS)
- English education and writing (MA)
- literature (MA)

College of Business and Economics
Program in:
- retail management (MBA)

College of Education and Human Services
Programs in:
- communication sciences and disorders (MS)
- community and college counseling (MS)
- curriculum and instruction specialist-elementary (MS)
- curriculum and instruction specialist-secondary (MS)
- educational leadership (MS)
- guidance and counseling (MS)
- literacy and culture (MS)
- school library media (MS)

■ LYNCHBURG COLLEGE
Lynchburg, VA 24501-3199
http://www.lynchburg.edu/

Independent-religious, coed, comprehensive institution. *Enrollment:* 2,398 graduate, professional, and undergraduate students; 92 full-time matriculated graduate/professional students (73 women), 192 part-time matriculated graduate/professional students (142 women). *Graduate faculty:* 30 full-time (17 women), 9 part-time/adjunct (1 woman). *Computer facilities:* 217 computers available on campus for general student use. A campuswide network can be accessed from student residence rooms. Internet access is available. *Library facilities:* Knight-Capron Library. *Graduate expenses:* Tuition: full-time $6,300; part-time $350 per credit. Required fees: $100. *General application contact:* Dr. Edward Polloway, Vice President for Graduate and Community Advancement, 434-544-8655.

Graduate Studies
Dr. Edward Polloway, Vice President for Graduate and Community Advancement

School of Business and Economics
Dr. Dan Messerschmidt, Dean
Program in:
- business (MBA)

School of Education and Human Development
Dr. Jan Stenette, Dean
Programs in:
- community counseling (M Ed)
- counselor education (M Ed)
- early childhood special education (M Ed)
- educational leadership (M Ed)
- English education (M Ed)
- mental retardation (M Ed)
- school counseling (M Ed)
- science education (M Ed)
- severely/profoundly handicapped education (M Ed)
- special education (M Ed)
- teaching and learning (M Ed)
- teaching children with learning disabilities (M Ed)
- teaching the emotionally disturbed (M Ed)

■ MARY BALDWIN COLLEGE
Staunton, VA 24401-3610
http://www.mbc.edu/

Independent, coed, primarily women, comprehensive institution. *Enrollment:* 1,755 graduate, professional, and undergraduate students; 104 full-time matriculated graduate/professional students (76 women), 101 part-time matriculated graduate/professional students (85 women). *Graduate faculty:* 5 full-time (3 women), 38 part-time/adjunct (20 women). *Computer facilities:* 227 computers available on campus for general student use. A campuswide network can be accessed from student residence rooms and from off campus. Internet access and online class registration are available. *Library facilities:* Grafton Library. *General application contact:* Lisa Branson, Executive Director of Admissions and Financial Aid, 540-887-7260.

Graduate Studies
Programs in:
- acting (M Litt)
- directing (M Litt)
- elementary education (MAT)
- middle grades education (MAT)
- Shakespeare and Renaissance literature in performance (M Litt, MFA)
- teaching (M Litt, MAT)

■ MARYMOUNT UNIVERSITY
Arlington, VA 22207-4299
http://www.marymount.edu/

Independent-religious, coed, comprehensive institution. *Enrollment:* 3,604 graduate, professional, and undergraduate students; 437 full-time matriculated graduate/professional students (355 women), 861 part-time matriculated graduate/professional students (617 women). *Graduate faculty:* 69 full-time (48 women), 62 part-time/adjunct (33 women). *Computer facilities:* Computer purchase and lease plans are available. 177 computers available on campus for general student use. A campuswide network can be accessed from off campus. Internet access and online class registration are available. *Library facilities:* Emerson C. Reinsch Library plus 1 other. *Graduate expenses:* Tuition: full-time $11,160; part-time $620 per credit. Required fees: $113; $630 per credit. *General application contact:* Francesca Reed, Coordinator, Graduate Admissions, 703-284-5901.

Corporate Outreach Program
Dr. Stuart Werner, Director

School of Arts and Sciences
Dr. Teresa Reed, Dean
Programs in:
- arts and sciences (MA, MS, Certificate)
- computer science (MS, Certificate)
- computer security and information assurance (Certificate)
- forensic computing (Certificate)
- humanities (MA)
- humanities: teaching licensure in secondary English (MA)
- interior design (MA)
- literature and languages (MA)

School of Business Administration
James Ryerson, Dean
Programs in:
- advanced leadership (Certificate)
- business administration (MA, MBA, MS, Certificate)
- health care informatics (Certificate)
- health care management (MS)
- human resource management (MA, Certificate)
- information systems (MS, Certificate)
- information systems program management (Certificate)
- instructional design (Certificate)
- leading and managing change (Certificate)
- legal administration (MA)
- management (MS)
- management studies (Certificate)
- organization development (Certificate)
- paralegal studies (Certificate)
- project management (Certificate)

School of Education and Human Services
Dr. Wayne Lesko, Dean
Programs in:
- alternative teacher licensure (Certificate)
- Catholic school leadership (M Ed, Certificate)
- community counseling (MA, Certificate)
- community counseling and forensic psychology)

education and human services (M Ed, MA, Certificate)
elementary education (M Ed)
English as a second language (M Ed)
forensic psychology)
learning disabilities (M Ed)
pastoral and spiritual care (MA)
pastoral counseling (MA, Certificate)
professional studies (M Ed)
school counseling (MA)
secondary education (M Ed)

School of Health Professions
Dr. Tess Cappello, Dean
Programs in:
family nurse practitioner (MSN, Certificate)
health professions (MS, MSN, DPT, Certificate)
health promotion management (MS)
nursing administration (MSN, Certificate)
nursing education (MSN, Certificate)
physical therapy (DPT)
RN to MSN (MSN)

■ NORFOLK STATE UNIVERSITY
Norfolk, VA 23504
http://www.nsu.edu/

State-supported, coed, comprehensive institution. CGS member. *Computer facilities:* Computer purchase and lease plans are available. 512 computers available on campus for general student use. A campuswide network can be accessed. Internet access and online class registration are available. *Library facilities:* Lymon Beecher Brooks Library. *General application contact:* Director, Office of Graduate Studies, 757-823-8015.

School of Graduate Studies

School of Education
Programs in:
early childhood education (MAT)
education (MA, MAT)
pre-elementary education (MA)
principal preparation (MA)
secondary education (MAT)
severe disabilities (MA)
teaching (MA)
urban education/administration (MA)

School of Liberal Arts
Programs in:
applied sociology (MS)
community/clinical psychology (MA)
criminal justice (MA)
liberal arts (MA, MFA, MM, MS, Psy D)
media and communication (MA)
music (MM)
music education (MM)
performance (MM)
psychology (Psy D)
theory and composition (MM)
urban affairs (MA)
visual studies (MA, MFA)

School of Science and Technology
Programs in:
computer science (MS)
electronics engineering (MS)
materials science (MS)
optical engineering (MS)
science and technology (MS)

School of Social Work
Program in:
social work (MSW, PhD)

■ OLD DOMINION UNIVERSITY
Norfolk, VA 23529
http://www.odu.edu/

State-supported, coed, university. CGS member. *Enrollment:* 21,625 graduate, professional, and undergraduate students; 1,262 full-time matriculated graduate/professional students (802 women), 2,711 part-time matriculated graduate/professional students (1,486 women). *Graduate faculty:* 554 full-time (178 women), 105 part-time/adjunct (61 women). *Computer facilities:* 800 computers available on campus for general student use. A campuswide network can be accessed from student residence rooms and from off campus. Internet access and online class registration, online courses are available. *Library facilities:* Douglas and Patricia Perry Library plus 2 others. *Graduate expenses:* Part-time $285 per credit hour. Tuition, nonresident: part-time $715 per credit hour. Required fees: $94 per semester. *General application contact:* Alice McAdory, Director of Admissions, 757-683-3685.

Find University Details at www.petersons.com/gradchannel.

College of Arts and Letters
Dr. Chandra deSilva, Dean
Programs in:
applied linguistics (MA)
applied sociology (MA)
arts and letters (MA, MFA, MME, PhD)
creative writing (MFA)
criminology and criminal justice (PhD)
English (MA, PhD)
history (MA)
humanities (MA)
international studies (MA, PhD)
music education (MME)
visual studies (MA, MFA)

College of Business and Public Administration
Dr. Nancy Bagranoff, Dean
Programs in:
accounting (MS)
business administration (MBA, PhD)
business and public administration (MA, MBA, MPA, MS, MUS, PhD)
economics (MA)
finance (PhD)
management (PhD)
marketing (PhD)
policy analysis/program evaluation (MUS)
public administration (MPA)
public administration and urban policy (PhD)
public planning analysis (MUS)
urban administration (MUS)

College of Engineering and Technology
Dr. Oktay Baysal, Dean
Programs in:
aerospace engineering (ME, MS, PhD)
civil engineering (ME, MS, PhD)
computer engineering (ME, MS)
design and manufacturing (ME)
electrical and computer engineering (PhD)
electrical engineering (ME, MS)
engineering and technology (ME, MEM, MS, PhD)
engineering management (MEM, MS, PhD)
environmental engineering (ME, MS, PhD)
experimental methods (ME)
mechanical engineering (ME, MS, PhD)
modeling and simulation (ME, MS, PhD)
motorsports (ME)
systems engineering (ME)

College of Health Sciences
Dr. Andrew Balas, Dean
Programs in:
community health professions (MS)
dental hygiene (MS)
environmental health (MS)
health care administration (MS)
health sciences (MPH, MS, MSN, DPT, PhD)
health services research (PhD)
long-term care administration (MS)
nursing (MSN)
physical therapy (DPT)
public health (MPH)
wellness and promotion (MS)

College of Sciences
Dr. Chris Platsucas, Interim Dean
Programs in:
analytical chemistry (MS)
applied experimental psychology (PhD)
biochemistry (MS)
biology (MS)
biomedical sciences (PhD)
clinical chemistry (MS)
clinical psychology (Psy D)
computational and applied mathematics (MS, PhD)
computer science (MS, PhD)
ecological sciences (PhD)
environmental chemistry (MS)
human factors psychology (PhD)
industrial/organizational psychology (PhD)
ocean and earth sciences (MS)
oceanography (PhD)
organic chemistry (MS)
physical chemistry (MS)

Old Dominion University (continued)
physics (MS, PhD)
psychology (MS, PhD)
sciences (MS, PhD, Psy D)

Darden College of Education
Dr. William H. Graves, Dean
Programs in:
athletic training (MS Ed)
biology (MS Ed)
business and industry training (MS)
career and technical education (PhD)
chemistry (MS Ed)
community college leadership (PhD)
community college teaching (MS)
counseling (MS Ed, PhD, Ed S)
curriculum and instruction (MS Ed)
early childhood education (MS Ed, PhD)
education (MS, MS Ed, PhD, Ed S)
educational leadership (MS Ed, PhD, Ed S)
educational media (MS Ed)
educational training (MS Ed)
elementary education (MS Ed)
English (MS Ed)
exercise and wellness (MS Ed)
higher education (MS Ed, PhD, Ed S)
human movement science (PhD)
human resources training (PhD)
instructional design and technology (PhD)
instructional technology (MS Ed)
library science (MS Ed)
literacy leadership (PhD)
middle and secondary teaching (MS)
middle school education (MS Ed)
principal preparation (MS Ed)
reading education (MS Ed)
recreation and tourism studies (MS Ed)
secondary education (MS Ed)
special education (MS Ed, PhD)
speech-language pathology (MS Ed)
sport management (MS Ed)
technology education (PhD)

■ RADFORD UNIVERSITY
Radford, VA 24142
http://www.radford.edu/

State-supported, coed, comprehensive institution. CGS member. *Enrollment:* 9,220 graduate, professional, and undergraduate students; 501 full-time matriculated graduate/professional students (389 women), 585 part-time matriculated graduate/professional students (463 women). *Graduate faculty:* 111 full-time (54 women), 36 part-time/adjunct (24 women). *Computer facilities:* 500 computers available on campus for general student use. A campuswide network can be accessed from student residence rooms and from off campus. Internet access and online class registration, online financial aid status and student accounts payable are available. *Library facilities:* McConnell Library plus 1 other. *Graduate expenses:* Tuition, state resident: full-time $4,680; part-time $260 per credit hour. Tuition, nonresident: full-time $8,604; part-time $478 per credit hour. *General application contact:* Graduate Admissions Office, 540-831-5431.

Graduate College
Dr. Carole L. Seyfrit, Dean

College of Arts and Sciences
Dr. Judy Niehaus, Acting Dean
Programs in:
arts and sciences (MA, MS, Psy D, Ed S)
clinical psychology (MA, MS)
corporate and professional communication (MS)
counseling psychology (Psy D)
criminal justice (MA, MS)
English (MA, MS)
experimental psychology (MA)
industrial-organizational psychology (MA, MS)
school psychology (Ed S)

College of Business and Economics
Dr. William A. Dempsey, Dean
Programs in:
business administration (MBA)
business and economics (MBA)

College of Education and Human Development
Dr. Patricia Shoemaker, Acting Dean
Programs in:
content area studies (MS)
counseling and human development (MS)
curriculum and instruction (MS)
deaf and hard of hearing (MS)
early childhood education (MS)
early childhood special education (MS)
education (MS)
education and human development (MS)
educational leadership (MS)
educational technology (MS)
high incidence disability (MS)
library media (MS)
reading (MS)
severe disability (MS)
special education (MS)
teaching English as second language (MS)

College of Visual and Performing Arts
Dr. Joseph P. Scartelli, Dean
Programs in:
art (MFA)
music (MA)
music therapy (MS)
visual and performing arts (MA, MFA, MS)

Waldron College of Health and Human Services
Dr. Raymond Linville, Acting Dean
Programs in:
communication science and disorders (MA, MS)
health and human services (MA, MS, MSN, MSW)
nursing (MSN)
social work (MSW)

■ REGENT UNIVERSITY
Virginia Beach, VA 23464-9800
http://www.regent.edu/

Independent, coed, comprehensive institution. *Enrollment:* 4,266 graduate, professional, and undergraduate students; 1,408 full-time matriculated graduate/professional students (833 women), 1,812 part-time matriculated graduate/professional students (965 women). *Graduate faculty:* 144 full-time (42 women), 326 part-time/adjunct (138 women). *Library facilities:* Regent University Library plus 1 other. *General application contact:* Althea Bishard, Registrar and Executive Director of Enrollment and Academic Services, 800-373-5504.

Find University Details at www.petersons.com/gradchannel.

Graduate School
Dr. Randall Pannell, Vice President for Academic Affairs

Robertson School of Government
Dr. Charles W. Dunn, Dean
Programs in:
health care policy and administration (MA)
international politics (MA)
law and public policy (MA)
political leadership and management (MA)
political management (MA)
public administration (MA)
public policy (MA)
terrorism and homeland defense (MA)
world economies and political development (MA)

School of Communication and the Arts
Michael Patrick, Dean
Programs in:
acting and directing (MFA)
cinema arts (MA)
communication (MA, PhD)
fine arts (MFA)
journalism (MA)
script and screenwriting (MFA)
television arts (MA)
theatre arts (MA)

School of Divinity
Dr. Michael Palmer, Dean
Programs in:
biblical studies (MA)
leadership and renewal (D Min)
missiology (M Div, MA)
practical theology (M Div, MA)
renewal studies (PhD)

School of Education
Dr. Alan A. Arroyo, Dean
Programs in:
Christian school program (M Ed)
cross-categorical special education (M Ed)
education (M Ed, Ed D)
educational leadership (M Ed)

elementary education (M Ed)
individual degree plan (M Ed)
master teacher (M Ed)
special education leadership (Ed S)
TESOL (M Ed)

School of Global Leadership and Entrepreneurship
Dr. Bruce Winston, Dean
Programs in:
business administration (MBA)
management (MA)
organizational leadership (MA, PhD, Certificate)
strategic foresight (MA)
strategic leadership (DSL)

School of Law
Jeffrey Brauch, Dean
Program in:
law (JD)

School of Psychology and Counseling
Dr. Rosemarie Hughes, Dean
Programs in:
clinical psychology (Psy D)
counseling (MA)
counseling studies (CAGS)
counselor education and supervision (PhD)

■ SHENANDOAH UNIVERSITY
Winchester, VA 22601-5195
http://www.su.edu/

Independent-religious, coed, comprehensive institution. *Enrollment:* 3,105 graduate, professional, and undergraduate students; 663 full-time matriculated graduate/ professional students (458 women), 649 part-time matriculated graduate/professional students (442 women). *Graduate faculty:* 116 full-time (56 women), 37 part-time/ adjunct (17 women). *Computer facilities:* Computer purchase and lease plans are available. 175 computers available on campus for general student use. A campuswide network can be accessed from student residence rooms and from off campus. Internet access and online class registration, online grades and student account information are available. *Library facilities:* Alson H. Smith Jr. Library plus 1 other. *Graduate expenses:* Tuition: full-time $12,200; part-time $610 per credit. Required fees: $150. Full-time tuition and fees vary according to course load and program. *General application contact:* David Anthony, Dean of Admissions, 540-665-4581.

Byrd School of Business
Dr. Randy Boxx, Dean
Programs in:
business administration (MBA)
health care management (Certificate)
information systems and computer technology (Certificate)

College of Arts and Sciences
Dr. Calvin Allen, Dean
Programs in:
administrative leadership (D Ed)
advanced professional teaching English to speakers of other languages (Certificate)
education (MSE)
elementary education (Certificate)
middle school education (Certificate)
professional studies (Certificate)
professional teaching English to speakers of other languages (Certificate)
public management (Certificate)
secondary education (Certificate)
women's studies (Certificate)

School of Health Professions
Program in:
health professions (MS, MSN, DPT, Certificate)

Division of Athletic Training
Dr. Rose A. Schmieg, Director
Program in:
athletic training (MS)

Division of Nursing
Dr. Sheila Ralph, Director
Programs in:
family nurse practitioner (Certificate)
nurse-midwifery (Certificate)
nursing (MSN)
psychiatric mental health nurse practitioner (Certificate)

Division of Occupational Therapy
Dr. Deborah Maar, Director
Program in:
occupational therapy (MS)

Division of Physical Therapy
Dr. Rose A. Schmieg, Director
Program in:
physical therapy and non-traditional physical therapy (DPT)

Division of Physician Assistant Studies
Anthony A. Miller, Director
Program in:
physician assistant (MS)

School of Pharmacy
Dr. Alan McKay, Dean
Program in:
pharmacy and non-traditional pharmacy (Pharm D)

Shenandoah Conservatory
Dr. Laurence A. Kaptain, Dean
Programs in:
arts administration (MS)
church music (MM, Certificate)
composition (MM)
conducting (MM)
dance (MA, MFA, MS)
dance accompanying (MM)
music (MS)
music education (MME, DMA)
music therapy (MMT)
pedagogy (MM)
performance (MM, DMA, Artist Diploma)
piano accompanying (MM)

■ UNIVERSITY OF MARY WASHINGTON
Fredericksburg, VA 22401-5358
http://www.umw.edu/

State-supported, coed, comprehensive institution. *Enrollment:* 4,862 graduate, professional, and undergraduate students; 121 full-time matriculated graduate/ professional students (92 women), 507 part-time matriculated graduate/professional students (367 women). *Graduate faculty:* 25 full-time (17 women), 20 part-time/adjunct (10 women). *Computer facilities:* 244 computers available on campus for general student use. A campuswide network can be accessed from student residence rooms and from off campus. Internet access and online class registration are available. *Library facilities:* Simpson Library. *Graduate expenses:* Part-time $275 per credit hour. Tuition, state resident: part-time $626 per credit. Required fees: $25 per term. One-time fee: $45 part-time. *General application contact:* Matthew E. Mejia, Assistant Dean for Graduate and Professional Studies and Dean of the Faculty, 540-286-8017.

College of Graduate and Professional Studies
Dr. Meta R. Braymer, Vice President for Graduate and Professional Studies and Dean of the Faculty
Programs in:
business administration (MBA)
education (M Ed)
management information systems (MSMIS)

■ UNIVERSITY OF RICHMOND
Richmond, University of Richmond, VA 23173
http://www.richmond.edu/

Independent, coed, comprehensive institution. *Computer facilities:* Computer purchase and lease plans are available. 650 computers available on campus for general student use. A campuswide network can be accessed from student residence rooms and from off campus. Internet access and online class registration are available. *Library facilities:* Boatwright Memorial Library plus 2 others. *General application contact:* Director of the Graduate School, 804-289-8417.

Find University Details at www.petersons.com/gradchannel.

Graduate School of Arts and Sciences
Programs in:
arts and sciences (MA, MLA, MS)
biology (MS)
English (MA)
history (MA)
liberal arts (MLA)
psychology (MA)

University of Richmond (continued)

Robins School of Business
Dr. Jorge Haddock, Dean
Program in:
business (MBA)

School of Law
Program in:
law (JD)

■ UNIVERSITY OF VIRGINIA
Charlottesville, VA 22903
http://www.virginia.edu/

State-supported, coed, university. CGS member. *Enrollment:* 24,068 graduate, professional, and undergraduate students; 5,924 full-time matriculated graduate/professional students (2,637 women), 331 part-time matriculated graduate/professional students (206 women). *Graduate faculty:* 2,102 full-time (638 women), 202 part-time/adjunct (93 women). *Computer facilities:* Computer purchase and lease plans are available. 1,645 computers available on campus for general student use. A campuswide network can be accessed from student residence rooms and from off campus. Internet access and online class registration, online course management tool are available. *Library facilities:* Alderman Library plus 14 others. *General application contact:* Dean of Appropriate School, 434-924-0311.

College and Graduate School of Arts and Sciences
Edward L. Ayers, Dean
Programs in:
anthropology (MA, PhD)
arts and sciences (MA, MFA, MS, PhD)
astronomy (MS, PhD)
biology (MA, MS, PhD)
chemistry (MA, MS, PhD)
classical art and archaeology (MA, PhD)
classics (MA, PhD)
creative writing (MFA)
drama (MFA)
East Asian studies (MA)
economics (MA, PhD)
English (MA, PhD)
environmental sciences (MA, MS, PhD)
foreign affairs (MA, PhD)
French (MA, PhD)
German (MA, PhD)
government (MA, PhD)
history (MA, PhD)
history of art and architecture (MA, PhD)
immunology (PhD)
Italian (MA)
linguistics (MA)
mathematics (MA, MS, PhD)
music (MA, PhD)
philosophy (MA, PhD)
physics (MA, MS, PhD)
physics education (MA)
psychology (MA, PhD)
religious studies (MA, PhD)
Slavic languages and literatures (MA, PhD)
sociology (MA, PhD)
Spanish (MA, PhD)
statistics (MS, PhD)

Center for Biomedical Ethics
Jonathan Moreno, Director, Center for Biomedical Ethics
Program in:
bioethics (MA)

Curry School of Education
David W. Breneman, Dean
Programs in:
administration and supervision (M Ed, Ed D, Ed S)
clinical and school psychology (Ed D, PhD)
communication disorders (M Ed)
counselor education (M Ed, Ed D, Ed S)
curriculum and instruction (M Ed, Ed D, Ed S)
education (M Ed, MT, Ed D, PhD, Ed S)
educational policy and evaluation (M Ed, Ed D)
educational psychology (M Ed, Ed D, Ed S)
health and physical education (M Ed, Ed D)
higher education (Ed D, Ed S)
kinesiology (M Ed, Ed D)
special education (M Ed, Ed D, Ed S)

Darden Graduate School of Business Administration
Robert F. Bruner, Dean
Program in:
business administration (MBA, PhD)

McIntire School of Commerce
Carl P. Zeithaml, Dean
Programs in:
accounting (MS)
management of information technology (MS)

School of Architecture
Karen Van Lengen, Dean
Programs in:
architectural history (M Arch H, PhD)
architecture (M Arch)
landscape architecture (M Land Arch)
urban and environmental planning (MUEP)

School of Engineering and Applied Science
James H. Aylor, Dean
Programs in:
applied mechanics (MAM, MS)
biomedical engineering (ME, MS, PhD)
chemical engineering (ME, MS, PhD)
civil engineering (ME, MS, PhD)
computer engineering (ME, MS, PhD)
computer science (MCS, MS, PhD)
electrical engineering (ME, MS, PhD)
engineering and applied science (MAM, MCS, ME, MEP, MMSE, MS, PhD)
engineering physics (MEP, MS, PhD)
materials science (MMSE, MS, PhD)
mechanical and aerospace engineering (ME, MS, PhD)
systems and information engineering (ME, MS, PhD)

School of Law
John C. Jeffries, Dean
Program in:
law (JD, LL M, SJD)

School of Medicine
Arthur Garson, Jr., Vice President and Dean
Programs in:
biochemistry (PhD)
biological and physical sciences (MS)
biophysics (PhD)
cell biology (PhD)
clinical investigation and patient-oriented research (MS)
health evaluation sciences (MS)
informatics in medicine (MS)
medicine (MD, MPH, MS, PhD)
microbiology (PhD)
neuroscience (PhD)
pharmacology (PhD)
physiology (PhD)
public health (MPH)
surgery (MS)

School of Nursing
B. Jeanette Lancaster, Dean
Program in:
nursing (MSN, PhD)

■ VIRGINIA COMMONWEALTH UNIVERSITY
Richmond, VA 23284-9005
http://www.vcu.edu/

State-supported, coed, university. CGS member. *Enrollment:* 30,381 graduate, professional, and undergraduate students; 2,792 full-time matriculated graduate/professional students (1,819 women), 2,247 part-time matriculated graduate/professional students (1,471 women). *Graduate faculty:* 1,012 full-time. *Computer facilities:* 400 computers available on campus for general student use. A campuswide network can be accessed from student residence rooms and from off campus. Internet access and online class registration are available. *Library facilities:* Virginia Commonwealth University Libraries plus 6 others. *General application contact:* Dr. Mark J. Schaefermeyer, Director of Admissions and Recruitment, 804-828-4696.

Find University Details at www.petersons.com/gradchannel.

Center for the Study of Biological Complexity
Program in:
bioinformatics (MB, MS)

Graduate School
Dr. F. Douglas Boudinot, Dean, Graduate School
Programs in:
- integrative life sciences (PhD)
- interdisciplinary studies (MIS)

College of Humanities and Sciences
Dr. Robert D. Holsworth, Dean
Programs in:
- account management (MS)
- account planning (MS)
- analytical chemistry (MS, PhD)
- applied mathematics (MS)
- applied physics (MS)
- applied social research (CASR)
- art direction (MS)
- biology (MS)
- chemical physics (PhD)
- clinical psychology (PhD)
- community revitalization planning (MURP)
- copywriting (MS)
- counseling psychology (PhD)
- creative brand management (MS)
- creative media planning (MS)
- creative writing (MFA)
- criminal justice (MS, CCJA)
- environmental communication (MIS)
- environmental health (MIS)
- environmental planning (MURP)
- environmental policy (MIS)
- environmental sciences (MIS)
- forensic science (MS)
- gender violence intervention (Certificate)
- general psychology (PhD)
- geographic information systems (Certificate)
- historic preservation planning (Certificate)
- history (MA)
- homeland security and emergency preparedness (MA, Graduate Certificate)
- humanities and sciences (MA, MFA, MIS, MPA, MS, MURP, PhD, CASR, CCJA, CPM, CURP, Certificate)
- inorganic chemistry (MS, PhD)
- international development planning (MURP)
- literature (MA)
- mass communications (MS, PhD)
- mathematics (MS)
- media, art, and text (PhD)
- medical physics (MS, PhD)
- metropolitan planning (MURP)
- nonprofit management (Graduate Certificate)
- operations research (MS)
- organic chemistry (MS, PhD)
- physical chemistry (MS, PhD)
- physics (MS)
- planning information systems (Certificate)
- planning management (MURP)
- political science and public administration (MPA)
- public management (CPM)
- public policy and administration (PhD)
- scholastic journalism (MS)
- sociology (MS)
- statistical sciences and operations research (MS, Certificate)
- strategic public relations (MS)
- urban planning (MURP)
- urban revitalization (CURP)
- writing and rhetoric (MA)

School of Allied Health Professions
Dr. Cecil B. Drain, Dean
Programs in:
- advanced physical therapy (MS)
- aging studies (CAS)
- allied health professions (MHA, MS, MSHA, MSNA, MSOT, PhD, CAS, CPC)
- anatomy and neurobiology (PhD)
- clinical laboratory sciences (PhD)
- entry-level physical therapy (MS)
- gerontology (MS, PhD)
- health administration (MHA, MSHA, PhD)
- health related sciences (PhD)
- health services organization and research (PhD)
- nurse anesthesia (PhD)
- occupational therapy (PhD)
- patient counseling (MS, CPC)
- physical therapy (PhD)
- physiology (PhD)
- radiation sciences (PhD)
- rehabilitation counseling (MS, CPC)
- rehabilitation leadership (PhD)

School of Business
Dr. Michael L. Sesnowitz, Dean
Programs in:
- accountancy (M Acc, MBA, MS, PhD)
- accounting (M Acc, MBA, MS, PhD)
- business administration (MBA, PhD)
- decision sciences (MBA, MS)
- economics (MA, MBA, MS)
- finance, insurance, and real estate (MS)
- information systems (MS, PhD)
- management (Certificate)
- marketing and business law (Certificate)
- real estate and urban land development (MS, Certificate)
- tax (MS)
- taxation (M Tax)

School of Education
Dr. Beverly Warren, Chair
Programs in:
- adult literacy (M Ed)
- adults with disabilities (M Ed)
- athletic training (MS)
- counselor education (M Ed)
- curriculum and instruction (M Ed)
- early childhood (M Ed)
- early education (MT)
- education (M Ed, MS, MT, PhD, Certificate)
- educational leadership (PhD)
- emotionally disturbed (M Ed, MT)
- exercise science (MS)
- human resource development (M Ed)
- instructional leadership (PhD)
- learning disabilities (M Ed)
- mentally retarded (M Ed, MT)
- middle education (MT)
- reading (M Ed)
- recreation, parks and sports leadership (MS)
- rehabilitation and movement science (PhD)
- research and evaluation (PhD)
- secondary education (MT, Certificate)
- severely/profoundly handicapped (M Ed)
- special education (MT)
- teacher education (MS)
- urban services leadership (PhD)

School of Engineering
Dr. Russell Jamison, Dean
Programs in:
- biomedical engineering (MS, PhD)
- chemical and life science engineering (MS, PhD)
- computer science (MS, PhD, Certificate)
- electrical engineering (MS, PhD)
- engineering (PhD)
- mechanical engineering (MS, PhD)

School of Nursing
Dr. Nancy F. Langston, Dean
Programs in:
- adult health nursing (MS)
- child health nursing (MS)
- family health nursing (MS)
- health system (PhD)
- immunocompetence (PhD)
- nurse practitioner (MS, Certificate)
- nursing administration (MS)
- psychiatric-mental health nursing (MS)
- risk and resilience (PhD)
- women's health nursing (MS)

School of Social Work
Dr. Frank R. Baskind, Dean
Program in:
- social work (MSW, PhD)

School of the Arts
Dr. Richard E. Toscan, Dean
Programs in:
- acting (MFA)
- architectural history (MA)
- art education (MAE)
- art history (MA, PhD)
- arts (MA, MAE, MFA, MM, PhD)
- ceramics (MFA)
- costume design (MFA)
- design/visual communications (MFA)
- directing (MFA)
- education (MM)
- fibers (MFA)
- furniture design (MFA)
- glassworking (MFA)
- historical studies (MA)
- interior environment (MFA)
- jewelry/metalworking (MFA)
- kinetic imaging (MFA)
- museum studies (MA)
- painting (MFA)
- pedagogy (MFA)
- photography and film (MFA)
- printmaking (MFA)
- scene design/technical theater (MFA)
- sculpture (MFA)

Virginia Commonwealth University (continued)

Medical College of Virginia-Professional Programs
Dr. Sheldin M. Retchin, Vice President for Health Sciences
Program in:
medicine (DDS, MD, Pharm D, MPH, MS, PhD)

School of Dentistry
Dr. Ronald J. Hunt, Dean
Program in:
dentistry (DDS)

School of Medicine
Dr. Jerome F. Strauss, Dean
Programs in:
anatomy (MS, PhD)
anatomy and physical therapy (PhD)
biochemistry (MS, PhD)
biostatistics (MS, PhD)
epidemiology and community health (PhD)
genetic counseling (MS)
human genetics (PhD)
medicine (MD, MPH, MS, PhD)
microbiology and genetics (MS)
microbiology and immunology (MS, PhD)
molecular biology and genetics (MS, PhD)
neuroscience (MS, PhD)
pathology (MS, PhD)
pharmacology (PhD)
pharmacology and toxicology (MS)
physiology (MS, PhD)
public health (MPH)

School of Pharmacy
Dr. Victor A. Yanchick, Dean
Programs in:
pharmaceutics (Pharm D, MS, PhD)
pharmacy (Pharm D, MS, PhD)

■ VIRGINIA POLYTECHNIC INSTITUTE AND STATE UNIVERSITY
Blacksburg, VA 24061
http://www.vt.edu/

State-supported, coed, university. CGS member. *Enrollment:* 28,470 graduate, professional, and undergraduate students; 4,199 full-time matriculated graduate/professional students (1,818 women), 2,274 part-time matriculated graduate/professional students (1,037 women). *Graduate faculty:* 1,581 full-time (440 women), 18 part-time/adjunct (11 women). *Computer facilities:* Computer purchase and lease plans are available. 8,000 computers available on campus for general student use. A campuswide network can be accessed from student residence rooms and from off campus. Internet access and online class registration are available. *Library facilities:* Newman Library plus 4 others. *Graduate expenses:* Tuition, state resident: full-time $7,017; part-time $390 per credit hour. Tuition, nonresident: full-time $12,414; part-time $690 per credit hour. International tuition: $11,296 full-time. Required fees: $1,523; $256 per term. *General application contact:* Graduate School Receptionist, 540-231-9563.

Graduate School
Dr. Karen P. DePauw, Vice Provost for Graduate Studies and Dean of the Graduate School

College of Agriculture and Life Sciences
Dr. Sharron Quisenberry, Dean
Programs in:
agribusiness (MS)
agricultural economics (MS)
agriculture and life sciences (MS, PhD)
animal science (MS, PhD)
applied economics (MS)
crop and soil environmental sciences (MS, PhD)
developmental and international economics (PhD)
econometrics (PhD)
entomology (MS, PhD)
food science and technology (MS, PhD)
horticulture (MS, PhD)
human nutrition, foods and exercise (MS, PhD)
life sciences (MS, PhD)
macro and micro economics (PhD)
markets and industrial organizations (PhD)
plant pathology (MS, PhD)
plant physiology and weed science (MS, PhD)
plant protection (MS)
poultry science (MS, PhD)
public and regional/urban economics (PhD)
resource and environmental economics (PhD)

College of Architecture and Urban Studies
Dr. A.J. Davis, Dean
Programs in:
architecture and design (M Arch, MS)
architecture and urban studies (M Arch, MLA, MPA, MPIA, MS, MURP, PhD, CAGS)
building construction (MS)
environmental design and planning (PhD)
landscape architecture (MLA)
public administration and policy (MPA, PhD, CAGS)
public and international affairs (MPIA)
urban and regional planning (MURP)

College of Engineering
Dr. Richard C. Benson, Head
Programs in:
aerospace engineering (M Eng, MS, PhD)
biological systems engineering (M Eng, MS, PhD)
chemical engineering (M Eng, MS, PhD)
civil engineering (M Eng, MS, PhD)
computer engineering (M Eng, MS, PhD)
computer science (MS, PhD)
electrical engineering (M Eng, MS, PhD)
engineering (M Eng, MEA, MIS, MS, PhD)
engineering administration (MEA)
engineering mechanics (MS, PhD)
environmental engineering (M Eng, MS)
environmental sciences and engineering (MS)
industrial engineering (M Eng, MS, PhD)
information systems (MIS)
materials science and engineering (M Eng, MS, PhD)
mechanical engineering (M Eng, MS, PhD)
mining and minerals engineering (M Eng, MS, PhD)
ocean engineering (MS)
operations research (M Eng, MS, PhD)
systems engineering (M Eng, MS)

College of Liberal Arts and Human Sciences
Programs in:
administration and supervision of special education (Ed D, PhD, Ed S)
adult and continuing education (MA Ed, Ed D, PhD)
adult development and aging (MS, PhD)
adult learning and human resource development (MS, PhD)
apparel business and economics (MS, PhD)
apparel product design and analysis (MS, PhD)
apparel quality analysis (MS, PhD)
arts administration (MFA)
career and technical education (MS Ed, Ed D, PhD, Ed S)
child development (MS, PhD)
communication (MA)
consumer studies (MS, PhD)
costume design (MFA)
counselor education (MA Ed, Ed D, PhD, Ed S)
creative writing (MFA)
curriculum and instruction (MA Ed, Ed D, PhD, Ed S)
education (ITMA, MA Ed, MS Ed, Ed D, PhD, Ed S)
educational counseling (MA Ed, Ed D, PhD, Ed S)
educational leadership (MA Ed, Ed D, PhD)
educational research and evaluation (PhD)
English (MA)
family financial management (MS, PhD)
family studies (MS, PhD)
health and physical education (MS Ed)
history (MA)
household equipment (MS, PhD)
housing (MS, PhD)
instructional technology (ITMA)
interior design (MS, PhD)

liberal arts and human sciences (ITMA, MA, MA Ed, MFA, MS, MS Ed, Ed D, PhD, Ed S)
lighting design (MFA)
marriage and family therapy (MS, PhD)
philosophy (MA)
political science (MA)
property management (MFA)
resource management (MS, PhD)
rhetoric and writing (PhD)
scenic design (MFA)
science and technology studies (MS, PhD)
sociology (MS, PhD)
stage management (MFA)
technical theatre (MFA)

College of Natural Resources
Dr. J. Michael Kelly, Dean
Programs in:
fisheries and wildlife sciences (MS, PhD)
forest biology (MF, MS, PhD)
forest biometry (MF, MS, PhD)
forest management/economics (MF, MS, PhD)
forest products marketing (MF, MS, PhD)
geography (MS, PhD)
industrial forestry operations (MF, MS, PhD)
natural resources (MF, MNR, MS, PhD)
outdoor recreation (MF, MS, PhD)
wood science and engineering (MF, MS, PhD)

College of Science
Dr. Lay Nam Chang, Dean
Programs in:
applied mathematics (MS, PhD)
applied physics (MS, PhD)
bio-behavioral sciences (PhD)
botany (MS, PhD)
chemistry (MS, PhD)
clinical psychology (PhD)
developmental psychology (PhD)
ecology and evolutionary biology (MS, PhD)
economics (MA, PhD)
genetics and developmental biology (MS, PhD)
geological sciences (MS, PhD)
geophysics (MS, PhD)
industrial/organizational psychology (PhD)
mathematical physics (MS, PhD)
microbiology (MS, PhD)
physics (MS, PhD)
psychology (MS)
pure mathematics (MS, PhD)
science (MA, MS, PhD)
statistics (MS, PhD)
zoology (MS, PhD)

Intercollege
Programs in:
biomedical engineering (MS, PhD)
biomedical engineering and sciences (MS, PhD)
genetics, bioinformatics and computational biology (PhD)
information technology (MIT)
interdisciplinary studies (MIT, MS, PhD)
macromolecular science and engineering (MS, PhD)

Pamplin College of Business
Dr. Richard E. Sorensen, Dean
Programs in:
accounting and information systems (MACIS, PhD)
business (MACIS, MBA, MS, PhD)
business administration (PhD)
business administration/finance (MS, PhD)
business administration/management (MS, PhD)
business administration/marketing (MS, PhD)
business information technology (MS, PhD)
hospitality and tourism management (MS, PhD)

Virginia-Maryland Regional College of Veterinary Medicine
Dr. Gerhardt G Schurig, Dean
Programs in:
biomedical and veterinary sciences (MS, PhD)
veterinary medicine (DVM, MS, PhD)

■ VIRGINIA STATE UNIVERSITY

Petersburg, VA 23806-0001
http://www.vsu.edu/

State-supported, coed, comprehensive institution. *Computer facilities:* 750 computers available on campus for general student use. A campuswide network can be accessed from student residence rooms and from off campus. Internet access and online class registration are available. *Library facilities:* Johnston Memorial Library. *General application contact:* Dean, Graduate Studies, Research, and Outreach, 804-524-5985.

School of Graduate Studies, Research, and Outreach
Program in:
interdisciplinary studies (MIS)

School of Engineering, Science and Technology
Programs in:
biology (MS)
engineering, science and technology (M Ed, MS)
mathematics (MS)
mathematics education (M Ed)
physics (MS)
psychology (MS)

School of Liberal Arts and Education
Programs in:
economics (MA)
education (M Ed, MS)
educational administration and supervision (M Ed, MS)
English (MA)
guidance (M Ed, MS)
history (MA)
liberal arts and education (M Ed, MA, MS, CAGS)
vocational technical education (M Ed, MS, CAGS)

Washington

■ ANTIOCH UNIVERSITY SEATTLE

Seattle, WA 98121-1814
http://www.antiochsea.edu/

Independent, coed, upper-level institution. *Computer facilities:* 8 computers available on campus for general student use. A campuswide network can be accessed from off campus. Internet access is available. *Library facilities:* Antioch Seattle Library. *General application contact:* Dean of Student and Enrollment Services, 206-441-5352 Ext. 5200.

Graduate Programs
Programs in:
education (MA)
psychology (MA, Psy D)

Center for Creative Change
Programs in:
environment and community (MA)
management (MS)
organizational psychology (MA)
strategic communications (MA)
whole system design (MA)

■ CENTRAL WASHINGTON UNIVERSITY

Ellensburg, WA 98926
http://www.cwu.edu/

State-supported, coed, comprehensive institution. CGS member. *Enrollment:* 10,688 graduate, professional, and undergraduate students; 276 full-time matriculated graduate/professional students (149 women), 182 part-time matriculated graduate/professional students (110 women). *Graduate faculty:* 302 full-time (105 women). *Computer facilities:* 720 computers available on campus for general student use. A campuswide network can be accessed from student residence rooms and from off campus. Internet access is available. *Library facilities:* Central Washington University Library. *Graduate expenses:* Tuition, state resident: full-time $6,312. Tuition, nonresident: full-time $14,112. Tuition and fees vary according to course load and degree level. *General application contact:* Justine Eason, Admissions Program Coordinator, 509-963-3103.

Find University Details at www.petersons.com/gradchannel.

Central Washington University (continued)

Graduate Studies, Research and Continuing Education

Dr. Wayne S. Quirk, Associate Vice President for Graduate Studies, Research and Continuing Education
Program in:
individual studies (M Ed, MA, MS)

College of Arts and Humanities
Dr. Marji Morgan, Dean
Programs in:
art (MA, MFA)
arts and humanities (MA, MFA, MM)
English (MA)
history (MA)
music (MM)
teaching English as a second language (MA)
theatre production (MA)

College of Business
Dr. Roy Savoian, Dean
Programs in:
accounting (MPA)
business (MPA)

College of Education and Professional Studies
Dr. Rebecca Bowers, Dean
Programs in:
education and professional studies (M Ed, MS)
educational administration (M Ed)
engineering technology (MS)
family and consumer sciences education (MS)
family studies (MS)
health, physical education and nutrition (MS)
master teacher (M Ed)
nutrition (MS)
reading education (M Ed)
special education (M Ed)

College of the Sciences
Dr. Meghan Miller, Dean
Programs in:
biological sciences (MS)
chemistry (MS)
experimental psychology (MS)
geological sciences (MS)
mathematics (MAT)
mental health counseling (MS)
resource management (MS)
school counseling (M Ed)
school psychology (M Ed)
sciences (M Ed, MAT, MS)

■ CITY UNIVERSITY OF SEATTLE

Bellevue, WA 98005

http://www.cityu.edu/

Independent, coed, comprehensive institution. *Computer facilities:* 145 computers available on campus for general student use. A campuswide network can be accessed from off campus. Internet access is available. *Library facilities:* City University Library. *General application contact:* Information Contact, 800-426-5596.

Find University Details at www.petersons.com/gradchannel.

Graduate Division

Gordon Albright School of Education
Programs in:
curriculum and instruction (M Ed)
educational leadership (M Ed)
educational leadership: principal certification (M Ed, Certificate)
educational leadership: principal/ program administrator certification (Certificate)
educational leadership: program administrator certification (M Ed, Certificate)
guidance and counseling (M Ed, Certificate)
integrated arts and performance learning (M Ed)
professional certification-teachers (Certificate)
reading (Certificate)
reading and literacy (M Ed)
reading. literacy, and ESL/ELL (M Ed)
teacher certification (MIT)
technology, curriculum and instruction (M Ed)

School of Arts and Sciences
Program in:
counseling psychology (MA)

School of Management
Programs in:
accounting (MBA)
C++ programming (Certificate)
computer systems—C++ programming (MS)
computer systems—individualized study (MS)
computer systems—web programming in e-commerce (MS)
computer systems-web development (MS)
financial management (MBA, Certificate)
general management (MBA, MPA, Certificate)
general management-Europe (MBA)
human resource management (MPA)
individualized study (MBA)
information systems (MBA, Certificate)
management—general management (MA)
management—human resource management (MA)
management—individualized study (MA)
marketing (MBA, Certificate)
personal financial planning (MBA, Certificate)
project management (MBA, MS, Certificate)
technology management (MS, Certificate)
web development (Certificate)
web programming in e-commerce (Certificate)

■ EASTERN WASHINGTON UNIVERSITY

Cheney, WA 99004-2431

http://www.ewu.edu/

State-supported, coed, comprehensive institution. CGS member. *Computer facilities:* Computer purchase and lease plans are available. 200 computers available on campus for general student use. A campuswide network can be accessed from student residence rooms and from off campus. Internet access and online class registration, e-mail are available. *Library facilities:* John F. Kennedy Library plus 1 other. *General application contact:* Associate Dean for Graduate Studies, 509-359-6297.

Graduate Studies

Program in:
interdisciplinary studies (MA, MS)

College of Arts and Letters
Programs in:
arts and letters (M Ed, MA, MFA)
composition (MA)
creative writing (MFA)
English (MA)
French education (M Ed)
instrumental/vocal performance (MA)
music education (MA)
music history and literature (MA)

College of Business and Public Administration
Programs in:
business administration (MBA)
business and public administration (MBA, MPA, MURP)
public administration (MPA)
urban and regional planning (MURP)

College of Education and Human Development
Programs in:
adult education (M Ed)
college instruction (MA, MS)
college instruction in physical education (MS)
counseling psychology (MS)
curriculum and instruction (M Ed)
early childhood education (M Ed)
education and human development (M Ed, MA, MS)
educational leadership (M Ed)
elementary teaching (M Ed)
foundations of education (M Ed)
instructional media and technology (M Ed)
literacy specialist (M Ed)
physical education (MS)
school counseling (MS)
school library media administration (M Ed)
school psychology (MS)
science education (M Ed)
social science education (M Ed)
special education (M Ed)
supervising (clinic)
teaching (M Ed)

College of Science, Mathematics and Technology
Programs in:
biology (MS)
communication disorders (MS)
computer science (M Ed, MS)
mathematics (MS)
occupational therapy (MOT)
physical therapy (DPT)
science, mathematics and technology (M Ed, MOT, MS, DPT)

College of Social and Behavioral Sciences
Programs in:
communication studies (MS)
history (MA)
psychology (MS)
school psychology (MS)
social and behavioral sciences (MA, MS)

Intercollegiate College of Nursing
Program in:
nursing (MN)

School of Social Work and Human Services
Program in:
social work and human services (MSW)

■ THE EVERGREEN STATE COLLEGE
Olympia, WA 98505
http://www.evergreen.edu/

State-supported, coed, comprehensive institution. *Enrollment:* 4,416 graduate, professional, and undergraduate students; 128 full-time matriculated graduate/professional students (84 women), 164 part-time matriculated graduate/professional students (104 women). *Graduate faculty:* 18 full-time (10 women), 7 part-time/adjunct (2 women). *Computer facilities:* 300 computers available on campus for general student use. A campuswide network can be accessed from student residence rooms and from off campus. Internet access and online class registration are available. *Library facilities:* Daniel J. Evans Library. *Graduate expenses:* Tuition, state resident: full-time $6,546; part-time $218 per credit. Tuition, nonresident: full-time $19,982; part-time $666 per credit. Tuition and fees vary according to course load. *General application contact:* J. T. Austin, Graduate Studies Office, 360-867-6707.

Graduate Programs
Dr. Don Bantz, Vice President and Provost
Programs in:
environmental studies (MES)
public administration (MPA)
teaching (MIT)

■ GONZAGA UNIVERSITY
Spokane, WA 99258
http://www.gonzaga.edu/

Independent-religious, coed, comprehensive institution. *Enrollment:* 6,610 graduate, professional, and undergraduate students; 888 full-time matriculated graduate/professional students (431 women), 1,443 part-time matriculated graduate/professional students (842 women). *Graduate faculty:* 155 full-time (45 women), 45 part-time/adjunct (15 women). *Computer facilities:* Computer purchase and lease plans are available. 350 computers available on campus for general student use. A campuswide network can be accessed from student residence rooms and from off campus. Internet access and online class registration are available. *Library facilities:* Ralph E. and Helen Higgins Foley Center plus 1 other. *Graduate expenses:* Tuition: full-time $10,620; part-time $590 per credit. *General application contact:* Julie McCulloh, Dean of Admissions, 509-323-6592.

College of Arts and Sciences
Dr. Robert Prusch, Dean
Programs in:
arts and sciences (MA)
pastoral ministry (MA)
philosophy (MA)
religious studies (MA)
spirituality (MA)

Program in Teaching English as a Second Language
Dr. Mary Jeannot, Chairperson
Program in:
teaching English as a second language (MATESL)

School of Business Administration
Dr. Clarence H. Barnes, Dean
Program in:
business administration (M Acc, MBA)

School of Education
Dr. Shirley Williams, Dean
Programs in:
administration and curriculum (MAA)
anesthesiology education (M Anesth Ed)
counseling psychology (MAC, MAP)
education (M Anesth Ed, MA Ed Ad, MAA, MAC, MAP, MASPAA, MES, MIT, MTA)
educational administration (MA Ed Ad)
initial teaching (MIT)
special education (MES)
sports and athletic administration (MASPAA)
teaching at-risk students (MAT)

School of Law
Earl Martin, Dean
Program in:
law (JD)

School of Professional Studies
Dr. Mary McFarland, Dean
Programs in:
communication and leadership studies (MA)
leadership studies (PhD)
nursing (MSN)
organizational leadership (MOL)

■ HERITAGE UNIVERSITY
Toppenish, WA 98948-9599
http://www.heritage.edu/

Independent, coed, comprehensive institution. *Enrollment:* 328 full-time matriculated graduate/professional students (232 women), 146 part-time matriculated graduate/professional students (96 women). *Graduate faculty:* 21 full-time (13 women), 67 part-time/adjunct (35 women). *Computer facilities:* 158 computers available on campus for general student use. A campuswide network can be accessed from off campus. Internet access is available. *Library facilities:* Library and Resource Center. *General application contact:* Kathy Otto, Coordinator of Administrative Services, 509-865-8635.

Graduate Programs in Education
Jim Borst, Dean of the College of Education and Psychology
Programs in:
bilingual education/ESL (M Ed)
biology (M Ed)
counseling (M Ed)
educational administration (M Ed)
English and literature (M Ed)
professional studies (M Ed)
reading/literacy (M Ed)
special education (M Ed)
teaching (MIT)

■ PACIFIC LUTHERAN UNIVERSITY
Tacoma, WA 98447
http://www.plu.edu/

Independent-religious, coed, comprehensive institution. *Enrollment:* 3,640 graduate, professional, and undergraduate students; 186 full-time matriculated graduate/professional students (123 women), 105 part-time matriculated graduate/professional students (78 women). *Graduate faculty:* 16 full-time (3 women), 15 part-time/adjunct (9 women). *Computer facilities:* Computer purchase and lease plans are available. 200 computers available on campus for general student use. A campuswide network can be accessed from student residence rooms and from off campus. Internet access and online class registration are available. *Library facilities:* Mortvedt Library. *Graduate expenses:* Tuition: full-time $17,544. Part-time tuition and fees vary according to program. *General application contact:* Linda DuBay, Senior Office Assistant, 253-535-7151.

Find University Details at www.petersons.com/gradchannel.

Division of Graduate Studies
Dr. Patricia O'Connell Killen, Provost and Dean of Graduate Studies

Division of Humanities
Dr. Douglas E. Oakman, Dean
Program in:
creative writing (MFA)

Pacific Lutheran University (continued)

Division of Social Sciences
Dr. Norris Peterson, Dean
Programs in:
marriage and family therapy (MA)
social sciences (MA)

School of Business
Dr. Andrew Turner, Dean
Program in:
business administration (MBA)

School of Education
Dr. John Lee, Dean
Programs in:
education (MA)
educational leadership (MA)
teaching (MA)

School of Nursing
Dr. Terry Miller, Dean and Graduate Program Director
Programs in:
client systems management (MSN)
entry level nursing (MSN)
family nurse practitioner (MSN)
health care systems management (MSN)
nursing (MSN)

■ SAINT MARTIN'S UNIVERSITY
Lacey, WA 98503-1297
http://www.stmartin.edu/

Independent-religious, coed, comprehensive institution. *Computer facilities:* 153 computers available on campus for general student use. A campuswide network can be accessed from student residence rooms. Internet access is available. *Library facilities:* Saint Martin's College Library. *General application contact:* Information Contact, 360-438-4311.

Graduate Programs
Programs in:
administration (M Ed)
civil engineering (MCE)
counseling psychology (MAC)
engineering management (M Eng Mgt)
English as a second language (M Ed)
guidance and counseling (M Ed)
reading (M Ed)
special education (M Ed)
teaching (MIT)
technology in education (M Ed)

Division of Economics and Business Administration
Program in:
economics and business administration (MBA)

■ SEATTLE PACIFIC UNIVERSITY
Seattle, WA 98119-1997
http://www.spu.edu/

Independent-religious, coed, comprehensive institution. *Enrollment:* 3,830 graduate, professional, and undergraduate students; 217 full-time matriculated graduate/professional students (159 women), 523 part-time matriculated graduate/professional students (366 women). *Graduate faculty:* 52 full-time (23 women). *Computer facilities:* 150 computers available on campus for general student use. A campuswide network can be accessed from student residence rooms and from off campus. Internet access and online class registration are available. *Library facilities:* Seattle Pacific University Library. *General application contact:* John Glancy, Director, Graduate Admissions/Marketing, 206-281-2325.

Graduate School
Dr. Les L. Steele, Vice President for Academic Affairs

College of Arts and Sciences
Dr. Bruce Congdon, Dean
Programs in:
arts and sciences (MA)
fine arts (MA)
teaching English as a second language (MA)

School of Business and Economics
Gary Karns, Graduate Director
Programs in:
business administration (MBA)
business and economics (MBA, MS)
information systems management (MS)

School of Education
Dr. Rick Eigenbrood, Director of Graduate Programs
Programs in:
education (M Ed, MAT, Ed D)
educational leadership (M Ed, Ed D)
reading/language arts education (M Ed)
school counseling (M Ed)
secondary teaching (MAT)

School of Health Sciences
Dr. Lucille Kelley, Dean
Programs in:
health sciences (MSN, Certificate)
nurse practitioner (Certificate)
nursing leadership (MSN)

School of Psychology, Family and Community
Dr. Michèal Roe, Dean
Programs in:
clinical psychology (PhD)
marriage and family therapy (MS)
organizational psychology (MA, PhD)
psychology, family and community (MA, MS, PhD)

■ SEATTLE UNIVERSITY
Seattle, WA 98122-1090
http://www.seattleu.edu/

Independent-religious, coed, comprehensive institution. *Enrollment:* 7,226 graduate, professional, and undergraduate students; 1,415 full-time matriculated graduate/professional students (839 women), 1,547 part-time matriculated graduate/professional students (916 women). *Graduate faculty:* 167 full-time (94 women), 85 part-time/adjunct (47 women). *Computer facilities:* 401 computers available on campus for general student use. A campuswide network can be accessed from student residence rooms and from off campus. Internet access and online class registration are available. *Library facilities:* Lemieux Library plus 1 other. *General application contact:* Janet Shandley, Associate Dean of Graduate Admissions, 206-296-5900.

Albers School of Business and Economics
Dr. Joseph Phillips, Dean
Programs in:
business administration (MBA, MIB, Certificate)
business and economics (EMBA, MBA, MIB, MPAC, MSF, Certificate)
finance (MSF, Certificate)
leadership formation (EMBA, Certificate)
professional accounting (MPAC)

College of Arts and Sciences
Dr. Wallace Loh, Dean
Programs in:
arts and sciences (MA Psych, MACJ, MNPL, MPA, MSAL)
criminal justice (MACJ)
existential and phenomenological therapeutic psychology (MA Psych)
sport and exercise (MSAL)

The Center for Nonprofit and Social Enterprise Management
Dr. Michael Bisesi, Director
Program in:
nonprofit and social enterprise management (MNPL)

Institute of Public Service
Dr. Russell Lidman, Director
Program in:
public service (MPA)

College of Education
Dr. Sue Schmitt, Dean
Programs in:
adult education and training (M Ed, MA, Certificate)
counseling and school psychology (MA, Certificate, Ed S)
curriculum and instruction (M Ed, MA, Certificate)
education (M Ed, MA, MIT, Ed D, Certificate, Ed S, Post-Master's Certificate)
educational administration (M Ed, MA, Certificate, Ed S)
educational leadership (Ed D)
literacy (M Ed, Post-Master's Certificate)
special education (M Ed, MA, Certificate)
student development administration (M Ed, MA)
teacher education (MIT)
teaching English to speakers of other languages (M Ed, MA, Certificate)

College of Nursing
Dr. Mary Walker, Dean

Programs in:
advanced practice nursing immersion (MSN)
leadership in community nursing (MSN)
nursing (MSN)
primary care nurse practitioner (MSN)

College of Science and Engineering
Dr. Michael Quinn, Dean
Programs in:
science and engineering (MSE)
software engineering (MSE)

School of Law
Kellye Y. Testy, Dean
Program in:
law (JD)

School of Theology and Ministry
Dr. Mark Markuly, Dean
Programs in:
divinity (M Div)
pastoral counseling (MA)
pastoral studies (MAPS)
theology and ministry (M Div, MA, MAPS, MATS, Certificate)
transforming spirituality (MATS, Certificate)

■ UNIVERSITY OF PUGET SOUND
Tacoma, WA 98416
http://www.ups.edu/

Independent, coed, comprehensive institution. *Enrollment:* 2,819 graduate, professional, and undergraduate students; 198 full-time matriculated graduate/professional students (155 women), 57 part-time matriculated graduate/professional students (48 women). *Graduate faculty:* 23 full-time (16 women), 30 part-time/adjunct (25 women). *Computer facilities:* 314 computers available on campus for general student use. A campuswide network can be accessed from student residence rooms and from off campus. Internet access, financial aid, admission, student employment, library are available. *Library facilities:* Collins Memorial Library. *Graduate expenses:* Tuition: full-time $26,390. Tuition and fees vary according to course load. *General application contact:* Dr. George H. Mills, Vice President for Enrollment, 253-879-3211.

Graduate Studies
Dr. John M. Finney, Associate Dean

School of Education
Dr. Christine Kline, Dean
Programs in:
agency counseling (M Ed)
counselor education (M Ed)
education (M Ed, MAT)
elementary education (MAT)
middle school education (MAT)
pastoral counseling (M Ed)
secondary education (MAT)

School of Occupational Therapy and Physical Therapy
Head
Programs in:
occupational therapy (MOT, MSOT)
occupational therapy and physical therapy (MOT, MSOT, DPT)
physical therapy (DPT)

■ UNIVERSITY OF WASHINGTON
Seattle, WA 98195
http://www.washington.edu/

State-supported, coed, university. CGS member. *Computer facilities:* 285 computers available on campus for general student use. A campuswide network can be accessed from student residence rooms and from off campus. Internet access and online class registration are available. *Library facilities:* Suzzallo/Allen Library plus 21 others. *General application contact:* Information Contact, 206-543-2100.

Graduate School
Programs in:
biology for teachers (MS)
education (M Ed, Professional Certificate)
global trade, transportation, and logistics (Certificate)
K-8 education (Certificate)
museology (MA)
Near and Middle Eastern studies (PhD)
preservation planning and design (Certificate)
principalship (Certificate)
quantitative ecology and resource management (MS, PhD)
school administration (Certificate)
urban design (Certificate)

Business School
Programs in:
auditing and assurance (MP Acc)
business (PhD)
evening part-time (MBA)
executive (MBA)
full time (MBA)
global (MBA)
global executive (MBA)
taxation (MP Acc)
technology management (MBA)

College of Architecture and Urban Planning
Programs in:
architecture (M Arch)
architecture and urban planning (M Arch, MLA, MS, MSCM, MUP, PhD, Certificate)
computer design (Certificate)
construction management (MS, MSCM)
historic preservation (Certificate)
landscape architecture (MLA)
lighting (Certificate)
urban design (Certificate)
urban design and planning (PhD)
urban planning (MUP)

College of Arts and Sciences
Programs in:
acting (MFA)
anthropology (MA, PhD)
applied mathematics (MS, PhD)
art (MFA)
art and design (MFA)
art history (MA, PhD)
arts and sciences (M Mus, MA, MAIS, MAT, MC, MFA, MM, MS, DMA, PhD)
astronomy (MS, PhD)
atmospheric sciences (MS, PhD)
botany (MS, PhD)
Central Asian studies (MAIS)
chemistry (MS, PhD)
China studies (MAIS)
Chinese language and literature (MA, PhD)
classics (MA, PhD)
classics and philosophy (PhD)
communication (MA, MC, PhD)
comparative literature (MA, PhD)
comparative religion (MAIS)
costume design (MFA)
dance (MFA)
directing (MFA)
East European studies (MAIS)
economics (MA, PhD)
English (MA, MAT, MFA, PhD)
English as a second language (MAT)
French (MA, PhD)
French and Italian studies (MA, PhD)
geography (MA, PhD)
geology (MS, PhD)
geophysics (MS, PhD)
German language and literature (MA)
German literature and culture (PhD)
Hispanic literary and cultural studies (MA)
history (PhD)
international studies (MAIS)
Italian (MA)
Japan studies (MAIS)
Japanese language and literature (MA, PhD)
Korea studies (MAIS)
lighting design (MFA)
linguistics (MA, PhD)
mathematics (MA, MS, PhD)
Middle Eastern studies (MAIS)
music (M Mus, MA, MM, DMA, PhD)
music education (MA, PhD)
Near Eastern languages and civilization (MA)
philosophy (MA, PhD)
physics (MS, PhD)
political science (MA, PhD)
psychology (PhD)
Romance linguistics (MA, PhD)
Russian literature (MA, PhD)
Russian studies (MAIS)
Russian, East European and Central Asian studies (MAIS)
Scandinavian studies (MA, PhD)
scene design (MFA)
Slavic linguistics (MA, PhD)
sociology (MA, PhD)

University of Washington (continued)
South Asian language and literature (MA, PhD)
South Asian studies (MAIS)
Spanish and Portuguese (MA)
speech and hearing sciences (MS, PhD)
statistics (MS, PhD)
theory and criticism (PhD)
women studies (MA, PhD)
zoology (PhD)

College of Education
Programs in:
curriculum and instruction (M Ed, Ed D, PhD)
early childhood education (M Ed, Ed D, PhD)
educational leadership and policy studies (M Ed, Ed D, PhD)
educational psychology (M Ed, PhD)
elementary special education (M Ed, Ed D, PhD)
emotional and behavioral disabilities (M Ed)
general special education (M Ed, Ed D, PhD)
human development and cognition (M Ed, PhD)
measurement and research (M Ed, PhD)
school counseling (M Ed, PhD)
school psychology (M Ed, PhD)
severe disabilities (M Ed, Ed D, PhD)
special education (M Ed, Ed D, PhD)
teacher education (MIT)

College of Engineering
Dr. Matthew O'Donnell, Dean
Programs in:
aeronautics and astronautics (MAE, MSAA, PhD)
bioengineering (MME, MS, PhD)
chemical engineering (MS Ch E, MSE, PhD)
computer science (MS, PhD)
construction engineering (MSCE)
electrical engineering (MSEE, PhD)
engineering (MAE, MME, MS, MS Ch E, MSAA, MSCE, MSE, MSEE, MSIE, MSME, MSMSE, PhD)
environmental engineering (MS, MSCE, MSE, PhD)
hydrology, water resources, and environmental fluid mechanics (MS, MSCE, MSE, PhD)
industrial engineering (MSE, MSIE, PhD)
materials science and engineering (MSE, MSMSE, PhD)
materials science and engineering nanotechnology (PhD)
mechanical engineering (MSE, MSME, PhD)
structural and geotechnical engineering and mechanics (MS, MSCE, MSE, PhD)
technical communication (MS, PhD)
transportation and construction engineering (MS, MSE, PhD)
transportation engineering (MSCE)

College of Forest Resources
Programs in:
forest economics (MS, PhD)
forest ecosystem analysis (MS, PhD)
forest engineering/forest hydrology (MS, PhD)
forest products marketing (MS, PhD)
forest soils (MS, PhD)
paper science and engineering (MS, PhD)
quantitative resource management (MS, PhD)
silviculture (MFR)
silviculture and forest protection (MS, PhD)
social sciences (MS, PhD)
urban horticulture (MFR, MS, PhD)
wildlife science (MS, PhD)

College of Ocean and Fishery Sciences
Programs in:
aquatic and fishery sciences (MS, PhD)
biological oceanography (MS, PhD)
chemical oceanography (MS, PhD)
marine affairs (MMA)
marine geology and geophysics (MS, PhD)
ocean and fishery sciences (MMA, MS, PhD)
physical oceanography (MS, PhD)

Daniel J. Evans School of Public Affairs
Dr. Sandra Archibald, Dean
Program in:
public affairs (MPA, PhD)

The Information School
Harry Bruce, Professor and Dean
Programs in:
information management (MSIM)
information science (PhD)
library and information science (MLIS)

School of Nursing
Program in:
nursing (MN, MS, PhD)

School of Public Health and Community Medicine
Programs in:
biostatistics (MPH, MS, PhD)
environmental and occupational health (MPH)
environmental and occupational hygiene (PhD)
environmental health (MS)
epidemiology (MPH, MS, PhD)
genetic epidemiology (MS)
health services (MS, PhD)
health services administration (MHA)
health services administration and planning (EMHA)
industrial hygiene and safety (MS)
international health (MPH)
maternal/child health (MPH)
nutritional sciences (MPH, MS, PhD)
occupational medicine (MPH)
pathobiology (MS, PhD)
public health (MPH)
public health and community medicine (EMHA, MHA, MPH, MS, PhD)
public health genetics (MPH, MS, PhD)
safety and ergonomics (MS)
statistical genetics (PhD)
toxicology (MS, PhD)

School of Social Work
Program in:
social work (MSW, PhD)

School of Social Work, Tacoma Campus
Program in:
social work (MSW)

School of Dentistry
Program in:
dentistry (DDS, MS, MSD, PhD)

School of Law
Programs in:
Asian law (LL M, PhD)
intellectual property law and policy (LL M)
law (JD)
law of sustainable international development (LL M)
taxation (LL M)

School of Medicine
Programs in:
genome sciences (PhD)
medicine (MD, MOT, MS, MSE, DPT, PhD)

Graduate Programs in Medicine
Programs in:
biochemistry (PhD)
biological structure (PhD)
biomedical and health informatics (MS, PhD)
immunology (PhD)
laboratory medicine (MS)
medicine (MOT, MS, MSE, DPT, PhD)
microbiology (PhD)
molecular and cellular biology (PhD)
molecular basis of disease (PhD)
neurobiology (PhD)
neuroscience (PhD)
occupational therapy (MOT)
pathology (MS)
pharmacology (MS, PhD)
physical therapy (DPT)
physiology and biophysics (PhD)
rehabilitation science (PhD)
veterinary science (MS)

School of Pharmacy
Programs in:
medicinal chemistry (PhD)
pharmaceutics (MS, PhD)
pharmacy (Pharm D, MS, PhD)

■ UNIVERSITY OF WASHINGTON, BOTHELL
Bothell, WA 98011-8246
http://www.uwb.edu

State-supported, coed, upper-level institution. *Enrollment:* 1,683 graduate, professional, and undergraduate students; 119 full-time matriculated graduate/professional students (55 women), 116 part-time matriculated graduate/professional students (96 women). *Graduate faculty:* 30 full-time (17 women), 3 part-time/adjunct (2 women). *Library facilities:* UW Bothell Library plus 1 other. *General application contact:* Hung Dang, Registrar/Assistant Director of Student Affairs, 425-352-5305.

Program in Policy Studies
Prof. Jolynn Edwards, Director, Interdisciplinary Studies Program
Program in:
policy studies (MA)

■ UNIVERSITY OF WASHINGTON, TACOMA
Tacoma, WA 98402-3100
http://www.tacoma.washington.edu/

State-supported, coed, upper-level institution. *Library facilities:* University of Washington Tacoma Library.

■ WALLA WALLA COLLEGE
College Place, WA 99324-1198
http://www.wwc.edu/

Independent-religious, coed, comprehensive institution. *Enrollment:* 1,876 graduate, professional, and undergraduate students; 203 full-time matriculated graduate/professional students (156 women), 38 part-time matriculated graduate/professional students (23 women). *Graduate faculty:* 29 full-time (16 women), 22 part-time/adjunct (15 women). *Computer facilities:* 118 computers available on campus for general student use. A campuswide network can be accessed from student residence rooms and from off campus. Internet access and online class registration are available. *Library facilities:* Peterson Memorial Library plus 3 others. *Graduate expenses:* Tuition: full-time $20,124; part-time $516 per quarter hour. *General application contact:* Dr. Joe G. Galusha, Dean of Graduate Studies, 509-527-2421.

Graduate School
Dr. Joe G. Galusha, Dean
Program in:
biology (MS)

School of Education and Psychology
Dr. Julian Melgosa, Dean
Programs in:
counseling psychology (MA)
curriculum and instruction (M Ed, MA, MAT)
educational leadership (M Ed, MA, MAT)
literacy instruction (M Ed, MA, MAT)
students at risk (M Ed, MA, MAT)
teaching (MAT)

School of Social Work
Dr. Pamela Cress, Dean
Program in:
social work (MSW)

■ WASHINGTON STATE UNIVERSITY
Pullman, WA 99164
http://www.wsu.edu/

State-supported, coed, university. CGS member. *Enrollment:* 23,655 graduate, professional, and undergraduate students; 2,136 full-time matriculated graduate/professional students (1,074 women), 1,124 part-time matriculated graduate/professional students (613 women). *Graduate faculty:* 755 full-time (207 women), 34 part-time/adjunct (5 women). *Computer facilities:* 2,400 computers available on campus for general student use. A campuswide network can be accessed from student residence rooms and from off campus. Internet access and online class registration are available. *Library facilities:* Holland Library plus 5 others. *Graduate expenses:* Tuition, state resident: full-time $7,066. Tuition, nonresident: full-time $17,204. *General application contact:* Graduate School Admissions, 800-GRADWSU.

College of Veterinary Medicine
Dr. Warwick M. Bayly, Dean
Programs in:
neuroscience (MS, PhD)
veterinary and comparative anatomy, pharmacology, and physiology (MS, PhD)
veterinary clinical sciences (MS)
veterinary medicine (DVM, MS, PhD)
veterinary microbiology and pathology (MS, PhD)
veterinary science (MS, PhD)

Graduate School
Dr. Howard Grimes, Dean
Program in:
interdisciplinary studies (PhD)

College of Agricultural, Human, and Natural Resource Sciences
Dr. Daniel J. Bernardo, Dean
Programs in:
agribusiness (MA)
agricultural economics (MA, PhD)
agricultural, human, and natural resource sciences (MA, MS, MSLA, PhD, Certificate)
agriculture (MS)
animal sciences (MS, PhD)
apparel, merchandising, design and textiles (MA)
applied and theoretical options (MS)
applied economics (MA)
biological and agricultural engineering (MS, PhD)
crop sciences (MS, PhD)
economics (MA, PhD, Certificate)
entomology (MS, PhD)
environmental and natural resource sciences (PhD)
food science (MS, PhD)
horticulture (MS, PhD)
human development (MA)
human nutrition (MS)
interdisciplinary (PhD)
interior design (MA)
international business economics (Certificate)
landscape architecture (MSLA)
molecular plant sciences (MS, PhD)
natural resource sciences (MS)
nutrition (PhD)
plant pathology (MS, PhD)
soil sciences (MS, PhD)

College of Business
Dr. Eric Spangenberg, Dean
Programs in:
accounting and business law (M Acc)
accounting and information systems (M Acc)
accounting and taxation (M Acc)
business (M Acc, MBA, PhD, Certificate)
business administration (MBA, PhD)
finance, insurance and real estate (PhD)

College of Education
Dr. Judy Mitchell, Dean
Programs in:
counseling psychology (Ed M, MA, PhD)
curriculum and instruction (Ed D, PhD)
diverse languages (M Ed, MA)
education (Ed M, M Ed, MA, MIT, MS, Ed D, PhD)
educational leadership (M Ed, MA, Ed D, PhD)
educational psychology (Ed M, MA, PhD)
elementary education (M Ed, MA, MIT)
exercise science (MS)
higher education (Ed M, MA, Ed D, PhD)
higher education with sport management (Ed M)
literacy education (M Ed, MA, PhD)
math education (PhD)
secondary education (M Ed, MA)

College of Engineering and Architecture
Dr. Candis Claiborn, Dean
Programs in:
architecture (M Arch)
architecture design theory (MS)
chemical engineering (MS, PhD)
civil engineering (MS, PhD)
computer engineering (MS, PhD)
computer science (MS, PhD)
electrical engineering (MS, PhD)
engineering and architecture (M Arch, MS, Dr DES, PhD)
environmental engineering (MS)
material science engineering (MS)
mechanical engineering (MS, PhD)

College of Liberal Arts
Dr. Eric Lear, Dean
Programs in:
archaeology (MA, PhD)

Washington State University (continued)
- ceramics (MFA)
- clinical psychology (PhD)
- composition (MA)
- crime and deviance (MA, PhD)
- criminal justice (MA, PhD)
- cultural anthropology (MA, PhD)
- digital media (MFA)
- drawing (MFA)
- early and modern European history (MA, PhD)
- English (MA, PhD)
- environmental history (MA, PhD)
- environments, community and demographics (PhD)
- environments, community, and demographics (MA)
- ethnic studies (MA, PhD)
- evolutionary anthropology (MA, PhD)
- experimental psychology (PhD)
- feminist studies (MA, PhD)
- health communications (MA, PhD)
- history (MA, PhD)
- institutions and social organizations (MA, PhD)
- intercultural international communications (MA)
- intercultural/international communications (PhD)
- jazz (MA)
- Latin American history (MA, PhD)
- liberal arts (MA, MFA, MS, PhD)
- literature (MA, PhD)
- media and society (MA, PhD)
- media process and effects (MA, PhD)
- modern East Asia history (MA, PhD)
- music (MA)
- music education (MA)
- organizational communications (MA, PhD)
- painting (MFA)
- performance (MA)
- philosophy (MA)
- photography (MFA)
- political science (MA, PhD)
- political sociology (MA, PhD)
- print making (MFA)
- psychology (MS)
- public history (MA, PhD)
- sculpture (MFA)
- social inequality (MA, PhD)
- social psychology and life course (MA, PhD)
- Spanish (MA)
- teaching of English (MA)
- US history (MA, PhD)
- women's history (MA, PhD)
- world history (MA, PhD)

College of Pharmacy
Dr. James P. Kehrer, Dean
Programs in:
- health policy and administration (MHPA)
- pharmaceutical science (Pharm D)
- pharmacology and toxicology (MS, PhD)
- pharmacy (Pharm D, MHPA, MS, PhD)

College of Sciences
Dr. Michael Griswold, Dean
Programs in:
- applied mathematics (MS, PhD)
- biochemistry and biophysics (MS, PhD)
- biology (MS)
- botany (MS, PhD)
- chemistry (MS, PhD)
- environmental and natural resource sciences (MS, PhD)
- environmental science (MS, PhD)
- genetics and cell biology (MS, PhD)
- geology (MS, PhD)
- materials science (PhD)
- mathematics teaching (MS, PhD)
- microbiology (MS, PhD)
- molecular biosciences (MS, PhD)
- physics (MS, PhD)
- sciences (MS, PhD)
- zoology (MS, PhD)

■ WESTERN WASHINGTON UNIVERSITY
Bellingham, WA 98225-5996
http://www.wwu.edu/

State-supported, coed, comprehensive institution. CGS member. *Enrollment:* 14,035 graduate, professional, and undergraduate students; 773 matriculated graduate/professional students. *Graduate faculty:* 457 full-time, 160 part-time/adjunct. *Computer facilities:* 1,874 computers available on campus for general student use. A campuswide network can be accessed from student residence rooms and from off campus. Internet access and online class registration are available. *Library facilities:* Wilson Library plus 1 other. *Graduate expenses:* Tuition, state resident: full-time $6,609; part-time $199 per credit. Tuition, nonresident: full-time $16,845; part-time $540 per credit. *General application contact:* Graduate Office Admissions, 360-650-3170.

Graduate School
Dr. Moheb Ghali, Dean

College of Business and Economics
Dennis Murphy, Dean
Program in:
- business and economics (MBA)

College of Fine and Performing Arts
Dr. Carol D. Edwards, Dean
Programs in:
- fine and performing arts (M Mus, MA)
- music (M Mus)
- theatre arts (MA)

College of Humanities and Social Sciences
Dr. Ronald Kleinknecht, Dean
Programs in:
- anthropology (MA)
- communication sciences and disorders (MA)
- English (MA)
- exercise science (MS)
- experimental psychology (MS)
- history (MA)
- humanities and social sciences (M Ed, MA, MS)
- mental health counseling (MS)
- political science (MA)
- school counseling (M Ed)
- sport psychology (MS)

College of Sciences and Technology
Dr. Arlan Norman, Dean
Programs in:
- biology (MS)
- chemistry (MS)
- computer science (MS)
- geology (MS)
- mathematics (MS)
- sciences and technology (MS)

Huxley College of the Environment
Dr. Bradley F. Smith, Dean
Programs in:
- environment (M Ed, MS)
- environmental science (MS)
- geography (MS)
- marine and estuarine science (MS)
- natural science/science education (M Ed)

Woodring College of Education
Dr. Stephanie Salzman, Dean
Programs in:
- advanced classroom practice (M Ed)
- continuing and college education (M Ed)
- education (M Ed, MA, MIT)
- educational administration (M Ed)
- elementary education (M Ed)
- rehabilitation counseling (MA)
- secondary education (MIT)
- special education (M Ed)
- student affairs administration (M Ed)

■ WHITWORTH UNIVERSITY
Spokane, WA 99251-0001
http://www.whitworth.edu/

Independent-religious, coed, comprehensive institution. *Enrollment:* 2,504 graduate, professional, and undergraduate students; 58 full-time matriculated graduate/professional students (40 women), 190 part-time matriculated graduate/professional students (128 women). *Computer facilities:* Computer purchase and lease plans are available. 200 computers available on campus for general student use. A campuswide network can be accessed from student residence rooms and from off campus. Internet access and online class registration are available. *Library facilities:* Harriet Cheney Cowles Library plus 2 others. *General application contact:* Office of Admissions, 509-777-1000.

School of Education
Dr. Dennis Sterner, Dean
Program in:
- education (M Ed, MAT, MIT)

Graduate Studies in Education
Dr. Sharon Mowry, Director
Programs in:
- administration (M Ed)
- counseling (M Ed)
- elementary education (M Ed)

gifted and talented (MAT)
school counselors (M Ed)
secondary education (M Ed)
social agency/church setting (M Ed)
special education (MAT)
teaching (MIT)

School of Global Commerce and Management
Mary Alberts, Director, Graduate Studies in Business
Programs in:
business administration (MBA)
global commerce and management (MBA, MIM)
international management (MBA)

West Virginia

■ MARSHALL UNIVERSITY
Huntington, WV 25755
http://www.marshall.edu/

State-supported, coed, university. CGS member. *Enrollment:* 13,936 graduate, professional, and undergraduate students; 1,600 full-time matriculated graduate/professional students (993 women), 1,917 part-time matriculated graduate/professional students (1,416 women). *Graduate faculty:* 359 full-time (156 women), 147 part-time/adjunct (101 women). *Computer facilities:* 1,854 computers available on campus for general student use. A campuswide network can be accessed from student residence rooms and from off campus. Internet access and online class registration are available. *Library facilities:* John Deaver Drinko Library plus 2 others. *General application contact:* Information Contact, 304-746-1900.

Find University Details at www.petersons.com/gradchannel.

Academic Affairs Division
Dr. Sarah Denman, Provost and Senior Vice President for Academic Affairs
Program in:
forensic science (MS)

College of Education and Human Services
Dr. Rosalyn Anstine Templeton, Executive Dean
Programs in:
adult and technical education (MS)
counseling (MA, Ed S)
early childhood education (MA)
education (MAT)
education and human services (MA, MAT, MS, Ed D, Ed S)
education and professional development (MA, Ed D, Ed S)
elementary education (MA)
exercise science (MS)
exercise science, sports and recreation (MS)
family and consumer sciences (MA)
human development and allied technology (MA, MS)
leadership studies (MA, Ed D, Ed S)
reading education (MA, Ed S)
school psychology (Ed S)
secondary education (MA)
special education (MA)
sport administration (MS)

College of Fine Arts
Dr. Donald Van Horn, Dean
Programs in:
art (MA)
fine arts (MA)
music (MA)

College of Health Professions
Dr. Shortie McKinney, Dean
Programs in:
communication disorders (MA)
dietetics (MS)
health professions (MA, MS, MSN)
nursing (MSN)

College of Information, Technology and Engineering
Dr. Tony Szwilski, Interim Dean
Programs in:
engineering and computer science (MSE)
environmental science (MS)
environmental science and safety technology (MS)
information systems (MS)
information systems and technology management (MS)
information, technology and engineering (MS, MSE)
safety (MS)
technology management (MS)

College of Liberal Arts
Dr. Christina Murphy, Dean
Programs in:
clinical psychology (MA)
communication studies (MA)
criminal justice (MS)
English (MA)
general psychology (MA)
geography (MA, MS)
history (MA)
humanities (MA)
industrial and organizational psychology (MA)
liberal arts (MA, MS, Psy D)
political science (MA)
psychology (Psy D)
sociology and anthropology (MA)

College of Science
Dr. Andrew Rogerson, Dean
Programs in:
biological science (MA, MS)
chemistry (MS)
mathematics (MA, MS)
physical science (MS)
science (MA, MS)

Lewis College of Business
Dr. Paul Uselding, Dean
Programs in:
business (MBA, MS)
business administration (MBA)
health care administration (MS)
human resource management (MS)
management (MBA, MS)

School of Journalism and Mass Communications
Dr. Corley F. Dennison, Dean
Program in:
journalism and mass communications (MAJ)

Joan C. Edwards School of Medicine
Dr. Charles H. McKown, Dean and Vice President
Programs in:
biomedical sciences (MS, PhD)
medicine (MD, MS, PhD)

■ MOUNTAIN STATE UNIVERSITY
Beckley, WV 25802-9003
http://www.mountainstate.edu/

Independent, coed, comprehensive institution. *Enrollment:* 4,420 graduate, professional, and undergraduate students; 468 full-time matriculated graduate/professional students (259 women), 52 part-time matriculated graduate/professional students (32 women). *Graduate faculty:* 21 full-time (9 women), 67 part-time/adjunct (25 women). *Computer facilities:* 97 computers available on campus for general student use. A campuswide network can be accessed from student residence rooms and from off campus. Internet access is available. *Library facilities:* Mountain State University Library. *Graduate expenses:* Tuition: full-time $3,660; part-time $305 per credit. Tuition and fees vary according to course load and program. *General application contact:* Dinah Rock, Coordinator of Graduate Academic Services, 304-929-1588.

Graduate Studies
James G. Silosky, Executive Vice President and Chief Academic Officer
Programs in:
administration/education (MSN)
criminal justice administration (MCJA)
family nurse practitioner (MSN)
health science (MHS)
interdisciplinary studies (MA, MS)
nurse anesthesia (MSN)
physician assistant (MSPA)
registered nurse anesthetist (Certificate)
strategic leadership (MSSL)

■ WEST VIRGINIA UNIVERSITY
Morgantown, WV 26506
http://www.wvu.edu/

State-supported, coed, university. CGS member. *Enrollment:* 27,115 graduate, professional, and undergraduate students;

West Virginia University (continued)
4,370 full-time matriculated graduate/professional students (2,240 women), 2,155 part-time matriculated graduate/professional students (1,394 women). *Graduate faculty:* 1,422 full-time (463 women), 448 part-time/adjunct (235 women). *Computer facilities:* Computer purchase and lease plans are available. 2,500 computers available on campus for general student use. A campuswide network can be accessed from student residence rooms and from off campus. Internet access and online class registration are available. *Library facilities:* Downtown Library Complex plus 9 others. *Graduate expenses:* Tuition, state resident: full-time $4,926; part-time $276 per credit hour. Tuition, nonresident: full-time $14,278; part-time $796 per credit hour. Tuition and fees vary according to program. *General application contact:* Information Contact, 800-344-WVU1.

College of Business and Economics
Dr. R. Stephen Sears, Dean
Programs in:
- business administration (MBA)
- business and economics (MA, MBA, MPA, MSIR, PhD)
- industrial relations (MSIR)

Division of Accounting
Prof. Timothy Pearson, Director
Program in:
- accounting (MPA)

Division of Economics and Finance
Dr. William N. Trumbull, Director
Programs in:
- business analysis (MA)
- econometrics (PhD)
- industrial economics (PhD)
- international economics (PhD)
- labor economics (PhD)
- mathematical economics (MA, PhD)
- monetary economics (PhD)
- public finance (PhD)
- public policy (MA)
- regional and urban economics (PhD)
- statistics and economics (MA)

College of Creative Arts
Dr. Bernie Schultz, Dean
Programs in:
- acting (MFA)
- art education (MA)
- art history (MA)
- ceramics (MFA)
- creative arts (MA, MFA, MM, DMA, PhD)
- graphic design (MFA)
- music composition (MM, DMA)
- music education (MM, PhD)
- music history (MM)
- music performance (MM, DMA)
- music theory (MM)
- painting (MFA)
- printmaking (MFA)
- sculpture (MFA)
- studio art (MA)
- theatre design/technology (MFA)

College of Engineering and Mineral Resources
Dr. Eugene V. Cilento, Dean
Programs in:
- aerospace engineering (MSAE, PhD)
- chemical engineering (MS Ch E, PhD)
- civil engineering (MSCE, MSE, PhD)
- computer engineering (PhD)
- computer science (MSCS, PhD)
- electrical engineering (MSEE, PhD)
- engineering (MSE)
- engineering and mineral resources (MS, MS Ch E, MS Min E, MSAE, MSCE, MSCS, MSE, MSEE, MSIE, MSME, MSPNGE, MSSE, PhD)
- industrial engineering (MSE, MSIE, PhD)
- industrial hygiene (MS)
- mechanical engineering (MSME, PhD)
- mining engineering (MS Min E, PhD)
- occupational safety and health (PhD)
- petroleum and natural gas engineering (MSPNGE, PhD)
- safety management (MS)
- software engineering (MSSE)

College of Human Resources and Education
Dr. Anne H. Nardi, Dean
Programs in:
- audiology (Au D)
- autism spectrum disorder (5-adult) (Ed D)
- autism spectrum disorder (K-6) (Ed D)
- child development and family studies (MA)
- counseling (MA)
- counseling psychology (PhD)
- curriculum and instruction (Ed D)
- early intervention (preschool) (MA)
- early intervention/early childhood special education (MA)
- educational leadership (Ed D)
- educational psychology (MA)
- elementary education (MA)
- gifted education (1-12) (MA)
- higher education administration (MA)
- higher education curriculum and teaching (MA)
- human resources and education (MA, MS, Au D, Ed D, PhD)
- information and communication systems (MA)
- instructional design and technology (MA)
- multicategorical special education (5-adult) (Ed D)
- multicategorical special education (K-6) (Ed D)
- professional development (MA)
- public school administration (MA)
- reading (MA)
- rehabilitation counseling (MS)
- secondary education (MA)
- severe/multiple disabilities (K-adult) (MA)
- special education (Ed D)
- speech-language pathology (MS)
- technology and society (MA)
- technology education (MA)
- vision impairments (PreK-adult) (Ed D)

College of Law
John W. Fisher, Dean
Program in:
- law (JD)

Davis College of Agriculture, Forestry and Consumer Sciences
Dr. Cameron R. Hackney, Dean
Programs in:
- agricultural and extension education (MS)
- agricultural and resource economics (MS)
- agricultural extension education (MS)
- agricultural sciences (PhD)
- agriculture, forestry and consumer sciences (M Agr, MS, MSF, PhD)
- agronomy (MS)
- animal and food sciences (PhD)
- animal and nutritional sciences (MS)
- animal breeding (MS, PhD)
- biochemical and molecular genetics (MS, PhD)
- breeding (MS)
- cytogenetics (MS, PhD)
- descriptive embryology (MS, PhD)
- developmental genetics (MS)
- entomology (MS)
- environmental microbiology (MS)
- experimental morphogenesis/teratology (MS)
- food sciences (MS)
- forest resource science (PhD)
- forestry (MSF)
- horticulture (MS)
- human genetics (MS, PhD)
- immunogenetics (MS, PhD)
- life cycles of animals and plants (MS, PhD)
- molecular aspects of development (MS, PhD)
- mutagenesis (MS, PhD)
- nutrition (MS)
- oncology (MS, PhD)
- physiology (MS)
- plant and soil sciences (PhD)
- plant genetics (MS, PhD)
- plant pathology (MS)
- population and quantitative genetics (MS, PhD)
- production management (MS)
- recreation, parks and tourism resources (MS)
- regeneration (MS, PhD)
- reproduction (MS)
- reproductive physiology (MS, PhD)
- resource management and sustainable development (PhD)
- teaching vocational-agriculture (MS)
- teratology (PhD)
- toxicology (MS, PhD)
- wildlife and fisheries resources (MS)

Eberly College of Arts and Sciences
Dr. Mary Ellen Mazey, Dean
Programs in:
- African history (MA, PhD)
- African-American history (MA, PhD)

American history (MA, PhD)
American public policy and politics (MA)
analytical chemistry (MS, PhD)
Appalachian/regional history (MA, PhD)
applied mathematics (MS, PhD)
applied physics (MS, PhD)
arts and sciences (MA, MALS, MFA, MLS, MPA, MS, MSW, PhD)
astrophysics (MS, PhD)
behavior analysis (PhD)
cell and molecular biology (MS, PhD)
chemical physics (MS, PhD)
clinical psychology (MA, PhD)
communication in instruction (MA)
communication theory and research (MA)
comparative literature (MA)
condensed matter physics (MS, PhD)
corporate and organizational communication (MA)
creative writing (MFA)
development psychology (PhD)
discrete mathematics (PhD)
East Asian history (MA, PhD)
elementary particle physics (MS, PhD)
energy and environmental resources (MA)
English (MA, PhD)
environmental and evolutionary biology (MS, PhD)
European history (MA, PhD)
French (MA)
geographic information systems (PhD)
geography (MA, PhD)
geography-regional development (PhD)
geology (MS, PhD)
geomorphology (MS, PhD)
geophysics (MS, PhD)
German (MA)
GIS/cartographic analysis (MA)
history of science and technology (MA, PhD)
hydrogeology (MS)
hydrology (PhD)
inorganic chemistry (MS, PhD)
integrative organismal biology (PhD)
integrative organismal, biology (MS)
interdisciplinary mathematics (MS)
international and comparative public policy and politics (MA)
Latin American history (MA)
legal studies (MLS)
liberal studies (MALS)
linguistics (MA)
literary/cultural studies (MA, PhD)
materials physics (MS, PhD)
mathematics for secondary education (MS)
organic chemistry (MS, PhD)
paleontology (MS, PhD)
petrology (MS, PhD)
physical chemistry (MS, PhD)
plasma physics (MS, PhD)
political science (PhD)
psychology (MS)
public policy analysis (PhD)
pure mathematics (MS)
regional development (MA)
solid state physics (MS, PhD)
Spanish (MA)
statistical physics (MS, PhD)
statistics (MS)
stratigraphy (MS, PhD)
structure (MS, PhD)
teaching English to speakers of other languages (MA)
theoretical chemistry (MS, PhD)
theoretical physics (MS, PhD)
writing (MA)

School of Applied Social Science
Dr. Christopher L. Plein, Chair
Programs in:
aging and health care (MSW)
applied social research (MA)
applied social science (MA, MPA, MSW)
children and families (MSW)
community mental health (MSW)
public administration (MPA)

Perley Isaac Reed School of Journalism
Dr. Maryann Reed, Dean
Programs in:
integrated marketing communications (MS)
journalism (MSJ)

School of Dentistry
Dr. James J. Koelbl, Dean
Programs in:
dentistry (DDS, MS)
endodontics (MS)
orthodontics (MS)
prosthodontics (MS)

Division of Dental Hygiene
Amy D. Funk, Interim Director of Dental Hygiene
Program in:
dental hygiene (MS)

School of Medicine
Dr. John E. Prescott, Dean
Programs in:
community health/preventative medicine (MPH)
medicine (MD, MOT, MPH, MPT, MS, PhD)
occupational therapy (MOT)
physical therapy (MPT)
public health (MPH)
public health sciences (PhD)

Graduate Programs at the Health Sciences Center
Dr. Thomas Saba, Associate Vice President, Health Sciences Center Research and Graduate Education
Programs in:
biochemistry and molecular biology (MS, PhD)
cancer cell biology (PhD)
cellular and integrative physiology (MS, PhD)
exercise physiology (MS, PhD)
health sciences (MS, PhD)
immunology and microbial pathogenesis (MS, PhD)
neuroscience (PhD)
pharmaceutical and pharmacological sciences (MS, PhD)

School of Nursing
Dr. E. Jane Martin, Dean
Programs in:
nurse practitioner (Certificate)
nursing (MSN, PhD)

School of Pharmacy
Dr. Patricia A. Chase, Dean
Programs in:
administrative pharmacy (PhD)
behavioral pharmacy (MS, PhD)
biopharmaceutics/pharmacokinetics (MS, PhD)
clinical pharmacy (Pharm D)
industrial pharmacy (MS)
medicinal chemistry (MS, PhD)
pharmaceutical chemistry (MS, PhD)
pharmaceutics (MS, PhD)
pharmacology and toxicology (MS)
pharmacy (MS)
pharmacy administration (MS)

School of Physical Education
Programs in:
athletic coaching (MS)
athletic training (MS)
exercise physiology (Ed D)
physical education/teacher education (MS, Ed D)
sport management (MS)
sport psychology (MS, Ed D)

■ WHEELING JESUIT UNIVERSITY
Wheeling, WV 26003-6295
http://www.wju.edu/

Independent-religious, coed, comprehensive institution. *Enrollment:* 1,402 graduate, professional, and undergraduate students; 94 full-time matriculated graduate/professional students (53 women), 100 part-time matriculated graduate/professional students (81 women). *Graduate faculty:* 14 full-time (4 women), 9 part-time/adjunct (4 women). *Computer facilities:* 125 computers available on campus for general student use. A campuswide network can be accessed from student residence rooms and from off campus. Internet access is available. *Library facilities:* Bishop Hodges Library plus 1 other. *Graduate expenses:* Tuition: full-time $8,910; part-time $405 per credit hour. Required fees: $105 per semester. One-time fee: $380 full-time. Full-time tuition and fees vary according to course load, degree level and program. *General application contact:* Becky Forney, Associate Dean of Adult Education, 304-243-2250.

Department of Business
Dr. Edward W Younkins, Director
Programs in:
accounting (MS)
business administration (MBA)

Wheeling Jesuit University (continued)

Department of Nursing
Dr. Rose M. Kutlenios, Chair
Program in:
nursing (MSN)

Department of Physical Therapy
Dr. Luis G. Vargas, Director
Program in:
physical therapy (DPT)

Wisconsin

■ ALVERNO COLLEGE
Milwaukee, WI 53234-3922
http://www.alverno.edu/

Independent-religious, Undergraduate: women only; graduate: coed, comprehensive institution. *Enrollment:* 2,480 graduate, professional, and undergraduate students; 127 full-time matriculated graduate/professional students (109 women), 87 part-time matriculated graduate/professional students (73 women). *Graduate faculty:* 18 full-time (13 women), 19 part-time/adjunct (16 women). *Computer facilities:* 400 computers available on campus for general student use. A campuswide network can be accessed from student residence rooms and from off campus. Internet access, e-mail are available. *Library facilities:* Alverno College Library. *Graduate expenses:* Tuition: full-time $9,288; part-time $516 per credit. Required fees: $250; $125 per semester. Tuition and fees vary according to program. *General application contact:* Dianna K. Gaebler, Director, Graduate and Adult Admissions, 414-382-6133.

School of Business
William McEachern, MBA Program Director
Program in:
business (MBA)

School of Education
Dr. Mary Diez, Graduate Dean
Programs in:
adaptive education (MA)
administrative leadership (MA)
adult education and organizational development (MA)
adult educational and instructional design (MA)
adult educational and instructional technology (MA)
instructional leadership (MA)
instructional technology for K-12 settings (MA)
professional development (MA)
reading education (MA)
reading education with adaptive education (MA)
science education (MA)
teaching in alternative schools (MA)

School of Nursing
Julie Millenbruch, Program Director
Program in:
nursing (MSN)

■ CARDINAL STRITCH UNIVERSITY
Milwaukee, WI 53217-3985
http://www.stritch.edu/

Independent-religious, coed, comprehensive institution. *Computer facilities:* 236 computers available on campus for general student use. A campuswide network can be accessed from student residence rooms and from off campus. Internet access is available. *Library facilities:* Cardinal Stritch University Library. *General application contact:* Information Contact, 800-347-8822 Ext. 4042.

College of Arts and Sciences
Programs in:
arts and sciences (MA, MM)
clinical psychology (MA)
history (MA)
lay ministries (MA)
ministry (MA)
piano (MM)
religious studies (MA)
visual studies (MA)

College of Business and Management
Program in:
business and management (MBA, MSM)

College of Education
Programs in:
education (ME)
educational leadership (MS)
instructional technology (ME, MS)
leadership for the advancement of learning and service (Ed D, PhD)
literacy/English as a second language (MA)
reading/language arts (MA)
reading/learning disability (MA)
special education (MA)
teaching (MAT)
urban education (MA)

College of Nursing
Program in:
nursing (MSN)

■ CARROLL COLLEGE
Waukesha, WI 53186-5593
http://www.cc.edu/

Independent-religious, coed, comprehensive institution. *Enrollment:* 3,292 graduate, professional, and undergraduate students; 47 full-time matriculated graduate/professional students (39 women), 152 part-time matriculated graduate/professional students (114 women). *Graduate faculty:* 15 full-time (6 women), 12 part-time/adjunct (9 women). *Computer facilities:* 250 computers available on campus for general student use. A campuswide network can be accessed from student residence rooms and from off campus. Internet access and online class registration are available. *Library facilities:* Todd Wehr Memorial Library. *Graduate expenses:* Tuition: part-time $325 per credit. Part-time tuition and fees vary according to program. *General application contact:* Jennifer L. Wells-Sperry, Director of Graduate Admission, 262-524-7357.

Graduate Program in Education
Dr. Mary Ann Wisniewski, Director
Programs in:
education (M Ed)
learning and teaching (M Ed)

Program in Physical Therapy
Dr. Jane F. Hopp, Dean, Natural and Health Sciences
Program in:
physical therapy (MPT, DPT)

Program in Software Engineering
Dr. Chenglie Hu, Associate Professor of Computer Science and Program Director
Program in:
software engineering (MSE)

■ CONCORDIA UNIVERSITY WISCONSIN
Mequon, WI 53097-2402
http://www.cuw.edu/

Independent-religious, coed, comprehensive institution. *Enrollment:* 5,574 graduate, professional, and undergraduate students; 1,112 full-time matriculated graduate/professional students, 680 part-time matriculated graduate/professional students. *Graduate faculty:* 47 full-time, 81 part-time/adjunct. *Computer facilities:* 100 computers available on campus for general student use. A campuswide network can be accessed from student residence rooms and from off campus. Internet access is available. *Library facilities:* Rinker Memorial Library plus 1 other. *General application contact:* Mary Eberhardt, Graduate Admissions, 262-243-4551.

Graduate Programs
Dr. Marsha K. Konz, Dean of Graduate Studies
Programs in:
art education (MS Ed)
arts and sciences (MCM)
business and legal studies (MBA, MSSPA)
church music (MCM)
curriculum and instruction (MS Ed)
early childhood (MS Ed)
educational administration (MS Ed)
environmental education (MS Ed)
family nurse practitioner (MSN)
family studies (MS Ed)
finance (MBA)

geriatric nurse practitioner (MSN)
health and human services (MOT, MSN, MSPT, MSRS, DPT)
health care administration (MBA)
human resource management (MBA)
international business (MBA)
international business-English/Chinese (MBA)
management (MBA)
management information services (MBA)
managerial communications (MBA)
marketing (MBA)
nurse educator (MSN)
occupational therapy (MOT)
physical therapy (MSPT, DPT)
professional counseling (MPC)
public administration (MBA)
reading (MS Ed)
rehabilitation science (MSRS)
risk management (MBA)
school counseling (MS Ed)
special education (MS Ed)
student personnel administration (MSSPA)

■ EDGEWOOD COLLEGE
Madison, WI 53711-1997
http://www.edgewood.edu/

Independent-religious, coed, comprehensive institution. *Enrollment:* 2,565 graduate, professional, and undergraduate students; 68 full-time matriculated graduate/professional students (45 women), 493 part-time matriculated graduate/professional students (326 women). *Graduate faculty:* 121. *Computer facilities:* Computer purchase and lease plans are available. 140 computers available on campus for general student use. A campuswide network can be accessed from student residence rooms and from off campus. Internet access and online class registration are available. *Library facilities:* Oscar Rennebohm Library. *General application contact:* Paula O'Malley, Director for Admissions and Recruitment, 608-663-2217.

Program in Business
Dr. Gary Schroeder, Chair
Program in:
business (MBA)

Program in Education
Dr. Joseph Schmiedicke, Chair
Programs in:
director of instruction (Certificate)
director of special education and pupil services (Certificate)
education (MA Ed)
educational administration (MA)
educational leadership (Ed D)
emotional disturbances (MA, Certificate)
learning disabilities (MA, Certificate)
learning disabilities and emotional disturbances (MA, Certificate)
school business administration (Certificate)
school principalship K-12 (Certificate)

Program in Marriage and Family Therapy
Dr. Peter Fabian, Director
Program in:
marriage and family therapy (MS)

Program in Nursing
Dr. Margaret Noreuil, Chair
Program in:
nursing (MS)

Program in Religious Studies
Dr. John Leonard, Chairperson
Program in:
religious studies (MA)

■ LAKELAND COLLEGE
Sheboygan, WI 53082-0359
http://www.lakeland.edu/

Independent-religious, coed, comprehensive institution. *Computer facilities:* Computer purchase and lease plans are available. 100 computers available on campus for general student use. A campuswide network can be accessed from student residence rooms and from off campus. Internet access is available. *Library facilities:* Esch Memorial Library. *General application contact:* Graduate Program Coordinator, 920-565-1256.

Graduate Studies Division
Programs in:
business administration (MBA)
education (M Ed)
theology (MAT)

■ MARIAN COLLEGE OF FOND DU LAC
Fond du Lac, WI 54935-4699
http://www.mariancollege.edu/

Independent-religious, coed, comprehensive institution. *Enrollment:* 3,040 graduate, professional, and undergraduate students; 44 full-time matriculated graduate/professional students (29 women), 870 part-time matriculated graduate/professional students (582 women). *Graduate faculty:* 19 full-time (7 women), 40 part-time/adjunct (22 women). *Computer facilities:* 225 computers available on campus for general student use. A campuswide network can be accessed from student residence rooms. Internet access and online class registration are available. *Library facilities:* Cardinal Meyer Library. *Graduate expenses:* Tuition: part-time $310 per credit. Tuition and fees vary according to degree level and program. *General application contact:* Sheryl Ayala, Vice President for Academic Affairs, 920-923-7604.

Business Division
David McPhail, Dean of Lifelong Learning
Program in:
organizational leadership and quality (MS)

School of Education
Dr. Kathryn Polmanteer, Dean, School of Education
Programs in:
educational leadership (MA, PhD)
teacher development (MA)

School of Nursing
Dr. James C. McCann, Dean, School of Nursing
Programs in:
adult nurse practitioner (MSN)
nurse educator (MSN)

■ MARQUETTE UNIVERSITY
Milwaukee, WI 53201-1881
http://www.marquette.edu/

Independent-religious, coed, university. CGS member. *Enrollment:* 11,548 graduate, professional, and undergraduate students; 2,004 full-time matriculated graduate/professional students (1,017 women), 1,329 part-time matriculated graduate/professional students (666 women). *Graduate faculty:* 606 full-time (234 women), 438 part-time/adjunct (180 women). *Computer facilities:* Computer purchase and lease plans are available. 1,200 computers available on campus for general student use. A campuswide network can be accessed from student residence rooms and from off campus. Internet access is available. *Library facilities:* Raynor Memorial Libraries plus 1 other. *General application contact:* Erin Fox, Assistant Director for Recruitment, 414-288-5319.

Graduate School
Dr. William Wiener, Vice Provost for Research/Dean
Programs in:
interdisciplinary studies (PhD)
public service (MAPS)

College of Arts and Sciences
Dr. Michael A. McKinney, Dean
Programs in:
algebra (PhD)
American literature (PhD)
analytical chemistry (MS, PhD)
ancient philosophy (MA, PhD)
arts and sciences (MA, MAT, MS, PhD)
bio-mathematical modeling (PhD)
bioanalytical chemistry (MS, PhD)
bioinformatics (MS)
biophysical chemistry (MS, PhD)
British and American literature (MA)
British empiricism and analytic philosophy (MA, PhD)
British literature (PhD)
cell biology (MS, PhD)
chemical physics (MS, PhD)
Christian philosophy (MA, PhD)
clinical psychology (MS)
computers (MS)
computing (MS)
developmental biology (MS, PhD)

Marquette University (continued)

- early modern European philosophy (MA, PhD)
- ecology (MS, PhD)
- endocrinology (MS, PhD)
- ethics (MA, PhD)
- European history (MA, PhD)
- evolutionary biology (MS, PhD)
- genetics (MS, PhD)
- German philosophy (MA, PhD)
- historical theology (MA, PhD)
- inorganic chemistry (MS, PhD)
- international affairs (MA)
- mathematics (MS)
- mathematics education (MS)
- medieval history (MA)
- medieval philosophy (MA, PhD)
- microbiology (MS, PhD)
- molecular biology (MS, PhD)
- muscle and exercise physiology (MS, PhD)
- neurobiology (MS, PhD)
- organic chemistry (MS, PhD)
- phenomenology and existentialism (MA, PhD)
- philosophy of religion (MA, PhD)
- physical chemistry (MS, PhD)
- political science (MA)
- psychology (PhD)
- religious studies (PhD)
- Renaissance and Reformation (MA)
- reproductive physiology (MS, PhD)
- social and applied philosophy (MA)
- Spanish (MA, MAT)
- statistics (MS)
- systematic theology (MA, PhD)
- theology (MA)
- theology and society (PhD)
- United States (MA, PhD)

College of Business Administration
Dr. David Shrock, Dean
Programs in:

- accounting (MSA)
- business administration (MBA, MSA, MSAE, MSHR)
- business economics (MSAE)
- financial economics (MSAE)
- human resources (MSHR)
- international economics (MSAE)

College of Communication
Dr. Ana Garner, Dean
Programs in:

- advertising and public relations (MA)
- broadcasting and electronic communications (MA)
- communications studies (MA)
- journalism (MA)
- mass communications (MA)
- religious communications (MA)
- science, health and environmental communications (MA)

College of Engineering
Dr. Stan V. Jaskolski, Dean
Programs in:

- bioinstrumentation/computers (MS, PhD)
- biomechanics/biomaterials (MS, PhD)
- computing (MS)
- construction and public works management (MS, PhD)
- electrical engineering (MS, PhD)
- engineering (MS, PhD)
- engineering management (MS)
- environmental/water resources engineering (MS, PhD)
- functional imaging (PhD)
- healthcare technologies management (MS)
- mechanical engineering (MS, PhD)
- structural/geotechnical engineering (MS, PhD)
- systems physiology (MS, PhD)
- transportation planning and engineering (MS, PhD)

College of Health Sciences
Dr. Jack C. Brooks, Dean
Programs in:

- health sciences (MS, DPT)
- physical therapy (DPT)
- physician assistant studies (MS)
- speech-language pathology (MS)

College of Nursing
Dr. Lea Acord, Dean
Programs in:

- adult nurse practitioner (Certificate)
- advanced practice nursing (MSN)
- gerontological nurse practitioner (Certificate)
- neonatal nurse practitioner (Certificate)
- nurse-midwifery (Certificate)
- nursing (PhD)
- pediatric nurse practitioner (Certificate)

School of Education
Dr. Bill Henk, Dean
Program in:

- education (MA, Ed D, PhD, Spec)

Law School
Joseph D. Kearney, Dean
Program in:

- law (JD)

School of Dentistry
Programs in:

- advanced training in general dentistry (MS)
- dental biomaterials (MS)
- dentistry (DDS, MS)
- endodontics (MS)
- orthodontics (MS)
- prosthodontics (MS)

■ MOUNT MARY COLLEGE

Milwaukee, WI 53222-4597

http://www.mtmary.edu/

Independent-religious, Undergraduate: women only; graduate: coed, comprehensive institution. *Enrollment:* 1,732 graduate, professional, and undergraduate students; 97 full-time matriculated graduate/professional students (92 women), 153 part-time matriculated graduate/professional students (143 women). *Graduate faculty:* 12 full-time (11 women), 22 part-time/adjunct (19 women). *Computer facilities:* 170 computers available on campus for general student use. A campuswide network can be accessed from student residence rooms and from off campus. Internet access is available. *Library facilities:* Haggerty Library. *Graduate expenses:* Tuition: part-time $490 per credit. Required fees: $48 per term. Tuition and fees vary according to course load and program. *General application contact:* Dr. Douglas J. Mickelson, Associate Dean for Graduate and Continuing Education, 414-256-1252.

Graduate Programs
Dr. Douglas J. Mickelson, Associate Dean for Graduate and Continuing Education
Programs in:

- administrative dietetics (MS)
- art therapy (MS)
- business administration (MBA)
- clinical dietetics (MS)
- community counseling (MS)
- education (MA)
- English (MA)
- nutrition education (MS)
- occupational therapy (MS)
- professional development (MA)

■ SILVER LAKE COLLEGE

Manitowoc, WI 54220-9319

http://www.sl.edu/

Independent-religious, coed, comprehensive institution. *Enrollment:* 939 graduate, professional, and undergraduate students; 18 full-time matriculated graduate/professional students (16 women), 293 part-time matriculated graduate/professional students (230 women). *Graduate faculty:* 6 full-time (all women), 54 part-time/adjunct (33 women). *Computer facilities:* 50 computers available on campus for general student use. A campuswide network can be accessed from off campus. Internet access is available. *Library facilities:* The Erma M. and Theodore M. Zigmunt Library. *Graduate expenses:* Tuition: full-time $6,120; part-time $340 per credit. *General application contact:* Jamie Grant, Associate Director- Admissions, 800-236-4752 Ext. 186.

Division of Graduate Studies
Programs in:

- administrative leadership (MA)
- management and organizational behavior (MS)
- music education-Kodaly emphasis (MM)
- teacher leadership (MA)

■ UNIVERSITY OF WISCONSIN–EAU CLAIRE

Eau Claire, WI 54702-4004

http://www.uwec.edu/

State-supported, coed, comprehensive institution. CGS member. *Enrollment:* 10,505 graduate, professional, and undergraduate students; 111 full-time matriculated graduate/professional students (88 women), 312 part-time matriculated graduate/professional students (192 women). *Graduate faculty:* 345 full-time (128 women), 11 part-time/adjunct (6 women). *Computer facilities:* 1,150 computers available on campus for general student use. A campuswide network can be accessed from student residence rooms and from off campus. Internet access and online class registration are available. *Library facilities:* William D. McIntyre Library plus 1 other. *Graduate expenses:* Tuition, state resident: full-time $6,533; part-time $363 per credit. Tuition, nonresident: full-time $17,143; part-time $952 per credit. Tuition and fees vary according to program and reciprocity agreements. *General application contact:* Kristina Anderson, Director of Admissions, 715-836-5415.

College of Arts and Sciences
Dr. Donald Christian, Dean
Programs in:
- arts and sciences (MA, MS, MSE, Ed S)
- biology (MS)
- English (MA)
- history (MA)
- school psychology (MSE, Ed S)

College of Business
Dr. V. Thomas Dock, Dean
Programs in:
- business (MBA)
- business administration (MBA)

College of Education and Human Sciences
Dr. Katherine Rhoades, Dean
Programs in:
- biology (MAT, MST)
- communication sciences and disorders (MS)
- education and human sciences (MAT, MEPD, MS, MSE, MST)
- education and professional development (MEPD)
- elementary education (MST)
- English (MAT, MST)
- history (MAT, MST)
- mathematics (MAT, MST)
- reading (MST)
- special education (MSE)

College of Nursing and Health Sciences
Dr. Elaine Wendt, Dean
Programs in:
- environmental and public health (MS)
- nursing (MSN)
- nursing and health sciences (MS, MSN)

■ UNIVERSITY OF WISCONSIN–LA CROSSE
La Crosse, WI 54601-3742
http://www.uwlax.edu

State-supported, coed, comprehensive institution. CGS member. *Enrollment:* 9,818 graduate, professional, and undergraduate students; 411 full-time matriculated graduate/professional students (267 women), 1,164 part-time matriculated graduate/professional students (798 women). *Graduate faculty:* 121 full-time (44 women), 84 part-time/adjunct (55 women). *Computer facilities:* 600 computers available on campus for general student use. A campuswide network can be accessed from student residence rooms and from off campus. Internet access and online class registration are available. *Library facilities:* Murphy Library. *General application contact:* Kathryn Kiefer, Associate Director of Admissions, 608-785-8939.

Find University Details at www.petersons.com/gradchannel.

Office of University Graduate Studies
Dr. Vijendra Agarwal, Director

College of Business Administration
Dr. Bruce May, Dean
Program in:
- business administration (MBA)

College of Liberal Studies
Dr. John Mason, Dean
Programs in:
- college student development and administration (MS Ed)
- elementary education (MEPD)
- emotional disturbance (MS Ed)
- K–12 (MEPD)
- learning disabilities (MS Ed)
- liberal studies (MEPD, MS Ed, Ed S)
- professional development (MEPD)
- reading (MS Ed)
- school psychology (MS Ed, Ed S)
- secondary education (MEPD)
- special education (MS Ed)

College of Science and Health
Dr. Karen Palmer-McLean, Dean
Programs in:
- aquatic sciences (MS)
- athletic training (MS)
- biology (MS)
- cellular and molecular biology (MS)
- clinical exercise physiology (MS)
- clinical microbiology (MS)
- community health education (MPH, MS)
- human performance (MS)
- microbiology (MS)
- nurse anesthesia (MS)
- occupational therapy (MS)
- physical education teaching (MS)
- physical therapy (MSPT, DPT)
- physician assistant studies (MS)
- physiology (MS)
- recreation (MS)
- school health education (MS)
- science and health (MPH, MS, MSE, MSPT, DPT)
- software engineering (MSE)
- special/adapted physical education (MS)
- sport administration (MS)

■ UNIVERSITY OF WISCONSIN–MADISON
Madison, WI 53706-1380
http://www.wisc.edu/

State-supported, coed, university. CGS member. *Computer facilities:* Computer purchase and lease plans are available. A campuswide network can be accessed from student residence rooms and from off campus. Internet access and online class registration are available. *Library facilities:* Memorial Library plus 40 others. *General application contact:* Information Contact, 608-262-2433.

Development Studies Program
Ian Coxhead, Chairman
Program in:
- development studies (PhD)

Graduate School
Programs in:
- biophysics (PhD)
- cellular and molecular biology (PhD)
- engineering (PDD)
- neuroscience (MS, PhD)
- professional practice (ME)
- technical Japanese (ME)

College of Agricultural and Life Sciences
Programs in:
- agricultural and applied economics (MA, MS, PhD)
- agricultural and life sciences (MA, MS, PhD)
- agricultural journalism (MS)
- agroecology (MS)
- agronomy (MS, PhD)
- animal sciences (MS, PhD)
- bacteriology (MS)
- biochemistry (MS, PhD)
- biological systems engineering (MS, PhD)
- biometry (MS)
- dairy science (MS, PhD)
- entomology (MS, PhD)
- family and consumer journalism (MS)
- food science (MS, PhD)
- forest science (MS, PhD)
- forestry (PhD)
- genetics (PhD)
- horticulture (MS, PhD)
- landscape architecture (MA, MS)
- mass communication (PhD)
- medical genetics (MS)
- molecular and environmental toxicology (MS, PhD)
- natural resources (MA, MS, PhD)
- nutritional sciences (MS, PhD)
- plant breeding and plant genetics (MS, PhD)
- plant pathology (MS, PhD)
- recreation resources management (MS)
- soil science (MS, PhD)
- wildlife ecology (MS, PhD)

College of Engineering
Paul S. Peercy, Dean
Programs in:
- biomedical engineering (MS, PhD)
- chemical engineering (MS, PhD)
- civil and environmental engineering (MS, PhD)
- electrical engineering (MS, PhD)
- energy systems (ME)
- engineering (ME, MS, PhD, PDD)

University of Wisconsin–Madison (continued)

- engineering mechanics (MS, PhD)
- environmental chemistry and technology (MS, PhD)
- geological engineering (MS, PhD)
- industrial and systems engineering (MS, PhD)
- limnology and marine science (MS, PhD)
- manufacturing systems engineering (MS)
- materials engineering (MS, PhD)
- materials science (MS, PhD)
- mechanical engineering (MS, PhD)
- nuclear engineering and engineering physics (MS, PhD)
- polymers (ME)

College of Letters and Science
Programs in:

- African languages and literature (MA, PhD)
- Afro-American studies (MA)
- anthropology (MA, MS, PhD)
- applied English linguistics (MA)
- art history (MA, PhD)
- astronomy (PhD)
- atmospheric and oceanic sciences (MS, PhD)
- biology of brain and behavior (PhD)
- botany (MS, PhD)
- cartography and geographic information systems (MS)
- chemistry (MS, PhD)
- Chinese (MA, PhD)
- choral (MM, DMA)
- classics (MA, PhD)
- clinical psychology (PhD)
- cognitive neurosciences (PhD)
- communication arts (MA, PhD)
- communicative disorders (MS, PhD)
- comparative literature (MA, PhD)
- composition (MM, DMA)
- composition studies (PhD)
- computer sciences (MS, PhD)
- curriculum and instruction (PhD)
- developmental psychology (PhD)
- economics (PhD)
- English language and linguistics (PhD)
- ethnomusicology (MM, PhD)
- family and consumer journalism (PhD)
- French (MA, PhD)
- French studies (MFS, Certificate)
- geographic information systems (Certificate)
- geography (MS, PhD)
- geology (MS, PhD)
- geophysics (MS, PhD)
- German (MA, PhD)
- Greek (MA)
- Hebrew and Semitic studies (MA, PhD)
- history (MA, PhD)
- history of science (MA, PhD)
- industrial relations (MA, MS, PhD)
- instrumental (MM, DMA)
- international public affairs (MPIA)
- Italian (MA, PhD)
- Japanese (MA, PhD)
- journalism and mass communication (MA)
- languages and cultures of Asia (MA, PhD)
- Latin (MA)
- Latin American, Caribbean and Iberian studies (MA)
- letters and science (MA, MFA, MFS, MM, MPA, MPIA, MS, MSSW, DMA, PhD, Certificate)
- library and information studies (MA, PhD, Certificate)
- linguistics (MA, PhD)
- literature (MA, PhD)
- mass communication (PhD)
- mathematics (MA, PhD)
- music (MA, MM, DMA, PhD)
- music education (MM)
- musicology (MA, MM, PhD)
- perception (PhD)
- performance (MM, DMA)
- philosophy (MA, PhD)
- physics (MA, MS, PhD)
- political science (MA, PhD)
- Portuguese (MA, PhD)
- psychology (PhD)
- public affairs (MPA, MPIA)
- rural sociology (MS)
- Scandinavian studies (MA, PhD)
- Slavic languages and literature (MA, PhD)
- social and personality psychology (PhD)
- social welfare (PhD)
- social work (MSSW)
- sociology (MS, PhD)
- Southeast Asian studies (MA)
- Spanish (MA, PhD)
- statistics (MS, PhD)
- theatre and drama (MA, MFA, PhD)
- theory (MA, MM, PhD)
- urban and regional planning (MS, PhD)
- zoology (MA, MS, PhD)

Gaylord Nelson Institute for Environmental Studies
Peter J. Nowak, Chair
Programs in:

- conservation biology and sustainable development (MS)
- environmental monitoring (MS, PhD)
- environmental studies (MS, PhD)
- land resources (MS, PhD)
- water resources management (MS)

School of Business
Dr. Michael M. Knetter, Dean
Programs in:

- accounting and information systems (PhD)
- actuarial science (MS)
- applied corporate finance (MBA)
- applied security analysis (MBA)
- arts administration (MBA)
- brand and product management (MBA)
- business (MBA, MS, PhD)
- business administration (MBA)
- business statistics (PhD)
- entrepreneurial management (MBA)
- finance, investment, and banking (PhD)
- information systems (MBA)
- international business (PhD)
- management and human resources (PhD)
- marketing (PhD)
- marketing research (MBA)
- operations and technology management (MBA)
- quantitative financial management (MS)
- real estate (MBA)
- real estate and urban land economics (PhD)
- risk management and insurance (MBA)
- strategic human resource management (MBA)
- strategic management in the life and engineering sciences (MBA)
- supply chain management (MBA)

School of Education
Dr. Julie K. Underwood, Dean
Programs in:

- administration (Certificate)
- art (MA, MFA)
- art education (MA)
- counseling (MS)
- counseling psychology (PhD)
- curriculum and instruction (MS, PhD)
- education (MA, MFA, MS, PhD, Certificate)
- education and mathematics (MA)
- educational policy (MS, PhD)
- educational policy studies (MA, PhD)
- educational psychology (MS, PhD)
- French education (MA)
- German education (MA)
- kinesiology (MS, PhD)
- music education (MS)
- occupational therapy (MS, PhD)
- rehabilitation psychology (MA, MS, PhD)
- science education (MS)
- Spanish education (MA)
- special education (MA, MS, PhD)
- therapeutic science (MS)

School of Human Ecology
Robin A. Douthitt, Dean
Programs in:

- consumer behavior and family economics (MS, PhD)
- design studies (MFA, MS, PhD)
- human development and family studies (MS, PhD)

Law School
Kenneth B. Davis, Dean
Programs in:

- law (JD, LL M, MLI, SJD)
- legal institutions (MLI)

School of Medicine and Public Health
Dr. Robert N. Golden, Dean
Programs in:

- biomolecular chemistry (MS, PhD)
- cancer biology (PhD)
- endocrinology-reproductive physiology (MS, PhD)
- genetics and medical genetics (MS, PhD)
- health physics (MS)
- medical physics (MS, PhD)

medicine (MD, MPH, MS, PhD)
medicine and public health (MD, MPH, MS, PhD)
microbiology (PhD)
molecular and cellular pharmacology (PhD)
pathology and laboratory medicine (PhD)
physiology (PhD)
population health (MPH, MS, PhD)

School of Nursing
Dr. Katharyn A. May, Dean
Program in:
nursing (MS, PhD)

School of Pharmacy
Programs in:
pharmaceutical sciences (MS, PhD)
pharmacy (Pharm D, MS, PhD)
social and administrative sciences in pharmacy (MS, PhD)

School of Veterinary Medicine
Programs in:
anatomy (MS, PhD)
biochemistry (MS, PhD)
cellular and molecular biology (MS, PhD)
comparative biosciences (MS, PhD)
environmental toxicology (MS, PhD)
neurosciences (MS, PhD)
pharmacology (MS, PhD)
physiology (MS, PhD)
veterinary medicine (DVM, MS, PhD)

■ UNIVERSITY OF WISCONSIN–MILWAUKEE
Milwaukee, WI 53201-0413
http://www.uwm.edu/

State-supported, coed, university. CGS member. *Enrollment:* 28,309 graduate, professional, and undergraduate students; 2,102 full-time matriculated graduate/professional students (1,250 women), 2,137 part-time matriculated graduate/professional students (1,330 women). *Graduate faculty:* 787 full-time (285 women). *Computer facilities:* 310 computers available on campus for general student use. A campuswide network can be accessed from off campus. *Library facilities:* Golda Meir Library. *Graduate expenses:* Tuition, state resident: part-time $510 per credit. Tuition, nonresident: part-time $1,408 per credit. Tuition and fees vary according to program. *General application contact:* General Information Contact, 414-229-4982.

Graduate School
Dr. Abbas Ourmazd, Dean of Graduate School/Vice Chancellor for Research
Program in:
multidisciplinary studies (PhD)

College of Engineering and Applied Science
Dr. Al Ghorbanpoor, Interim Dean
Programs in:
computer science (MS, PhD)
engineering (MS, PhD, Certificate)
engineering and applied science (MS, PhD, Certificate)
medical informatics (PhD)

College of Health Sciences
Randall Lambrecht, Dean
Programs in:
clinical laboratory science (MS)
communication sciences and disorders (MS)
health sciences (MS, PhD)
healthcare informatics (MS)
kinesiology (MS)
occupational therapy (MS)

College of Letters and Sciences
G. Richard Meadows, Dean
Programs in:
anthropology (MS, PhD, Certificate)
art history (MA)
art museum studies (Certificate)
biological sciences (MS, PhD)
chemistry (MS, PhD)
classics and Hebrew studies (MAFLL)
clinical psychology (MS, PhD)
communication (MA, Certificate)
comparative literature (MAFLL)
economics (MA, PhD)
English (MA, PhD, Certificate)
French and Italian (MAFLL)
geography (MA, MS, PhD)
geological sciences (MS, PhD)
German (MAFLL)
history (MA, PhD)
human resources and labor relations (MHRLR, Certificate)
journalism and mass communication (MA)
letters and sciences (MA, MAFLL, MHRLR, MLS, MPA, MS, PhD, Certificate)
liberal studies (MLS)
mathematics (MS, PhD)
philosophy (MA)
physics (MS, PhD)
political science (MA, PhD)
psychology (MS, PhD)
public administration (MPA)
Slavic studies (MAFLL)
sociology (MA)
Spanish (MAFLL)
urban studies (MS, PhD)

College of Nursing
Karen Morin, Representative
Program in:
nursing (MS, PhD, Certificate)

Peck School of the Arts
William Robert Bucker, Dean
Programs in:
art (MA, MFA)
art education (MA, MFA, MS)
arts (MA, MFA, MM, MS, Certificate)
dance (MFA)
film (MFA)
music (MM, Certificate)
theatre (MFA)

School of Architecture and Urban Planning
Robert Greenstreet, Dean
Programs in:
architecture (M Arch, PhD, Certificate)
architecture and urban planning (M Arch, MUP, PhD, Certificate)
urban planning (MUP, Certificate)

School of Education
Alfonzo Thurman, Dean
Programs in:
administrative leadership (Certificate)
administrative leadership and supervision in education (MS)
cultural foundations of education (MS)
curriculum planning and instruction improvement (MS)
early childhood education (MS)
education (MS, PhD, Certificate, Ed S)
educational psychology (MS, Ed S)
elementary education (MS)
exceptional education (MS)
junior high/middle school education (MS)
reading education (MS)
school psychology (Ed S)
secondary education (MS)
teaching in an urban setting (MS)
urban education (PhD)

School of Information Studies
Johannes Britz, Dean
Program in:
information studies (MLIS, CAS)

School of Social Welfare
Stan Stojkovic, Dean
Programs in:
criminal justice (MS)
social welfare (MS, MSW, Certificate)
social work (MSW, Certificate)

Sheldon B. Lubar School of Business
Sarah Sandin, Representative
Program in:
business (MBA, MS, PhD, Certificate)

■ UNIVERSITY OF WISCONSIN–OSHKOSH
Oshkosh, WI 54901
http://www.uwosh.edu/

State-supported, coed, comprehensive institution. *Computer facilities:* 475 computers available on campus for general student use. A campuswide network can be accessed from student residence rooms and from off campus. Internet access and online class registration are available. *Library facilities:* Forrest R. Polk Library. *General application contact:* Director, Graduate Admissions and Records, 920-424-0007.

The School of Graduate Studies
Program in:
social work (MSW)

College of Business Administration
Programs in:
business administration (MBA, MS)
information systems (MS)

University of Wisconsin–Oshkosh (continued)

College of Education and Human Services
Programs in:
- counseling (MSE)
- cross-categorical (MSE)
- curriculum and instruction (MSE)
- early childhood: exceptional education needs (MSE)
- education and human services (MS, MSE)
- educational leadership (MS)
- non-licensure (MSE)
- reading education (MSE)

College of Letters and Science
Programs in:
- biology (MS)
- English (MA)
- experimental psychology (MS)
- general agency (MPA)
- health care (MPA)
- industrial/organizational psychology (MS)
- letters and science (MA, MPA, MS, MSW)
- mathematics education (MS)

College of Nursing
Programs in:
- adult health and illness (MSN)
- family nurse practitioner (MSN)

■ UNIVERSITY OF WISCONSIN–PLATTEVILLE
Platteville, WI 53818-3099
http://www.uwplatt.edu/

State-supported, coed, comprehensive institution. *Enrollment:* 6,732 graduate, professional, and undergraduate students; 110 full-time matriculated graduate/professional students (85 women), 401 part-time matriculated graduate/professional students (194 women). *Graduate faculty:* 5 full-time (2 women), 90 part-time/adjunct (16 women). *Computer facilities:* 1,000 computers available on campus for general student use. A campuswide network can be accessed from student residence rooms and from off campus. Internet access and online class registration are available. *Library facilities:* Karrmann Library. *Graduate expenses:* Tuition, state resident: part-time $365 per credit. Tuition, nonresident: part-time $955 per credit. *General application contact:* Kristal Prohaska, Admissions and Enrollment Management, 608-342-1125.

School of Graduate Studies
Dr. David P. Van Buren, Dean

College of Engineering, Mathematics and Science
Dr. Rich Shultz, Dean
Programs in:
- computer science (MS)
- engineering, mathematics and science (MS)

College of Liberal Arts and Education
Dr. Mittie Nimocks, Dean
Programs in:
- adult education (MSE)
- counselor education (MSE)
- elementary education (MSE)
- liberal arts and education (MSE)
- middle school education (MSE)
- secondary education (MSE)
- vocational and technical education (MSE)

Distance Learning Center
Dawn Drake, Executive Director
Programs in:
- criminal justice (MS)
- engineering (MS)
- project management (MS)

■ UNIVERSITY OF WISCONSIN–RIVER FALLS
River Falls, WI 54022-5001
http://www.uwrf.edu/

State-supported, coed, comprehensive institution. CGS member. *Computer facilities:* 387 computers available on campus for general student use. A campuswide network can be accessed from student residence rooms and from off campus. Internet access and online class registration are available. *Library facilities:* Chalmer Davee Library. *General application contact:* Program Assistant II, 715-425-3843.

Outreach and Graduate Studies
Program in:
- management (MM)

College of Agriculture, Food, and Environmental Sciences
Programs in:
- agricultural education (MS)
- agriculture, food, and environmental sciences (MS)

College of Arts and Science
Programs in:
- arts and science (MSE)
- mathematics education (MSE)
- science education (MSE)
- social science education (MSE)

College of Education and Professional Studies
Programs in:
- communicative disorders (MS)
- counseling (MSE)
- education (MS, MSE, Ed S)
- elementary education (MSE)
- reading (MSE)
- school psychology (MSE, Ed S)
- secondary education-communicative disorders (MSE)

■ UNIVERSITY OF WISCONSIN–STEVENS POINT
Stevens Point, WI 54481-3897
http://www.uwsp.edu/

State-supported, coed, comprehensive institution. *Enrollment:* 8,842 graduate, professional, and undergraduate students; 115 full-time matriculated graduate/professional students (86 women), 148 part-time matriculated graduate/professional students (109 women). *Graduate faculty:* 262 full-time (84 women), 24 part-time/adjunct (10 women). *Computer facilities:* 880 computers available on campus for general student use. A campuswide network can be accessed from student residence rooms and from off campus. Internet access and online class registration are available. *Library facilities:* Learning Resources Center. *Graduate expenses:* Tuition, state resident: full-time $5,910; part-time $328 per credit. Tuition, nonresident: full-time $16,520; part-time $918 per credit. Required fees: $756; $73 per credit. *General application contact:* Catherine Glennon, Director of Admissions, 715-346-2441.

College of Fine Arts and Communication
Jeff Morin, Dean
Programs in:
- fine arts and communication (MA, MM Ed)
- interpersonal communication (MA)
- mass communication (MA)
- music (MM Ed)
- organizational communication (MA)
- public relations (MA)

College of Letters and Science
Lance Grahn, Dean
Programs in:
- biology (MST)
- business and economics (MBA)
- English (MST)
- history (MST)
- letters and science (MBA, MST)

College of Natural Resources
Dr. Christine Thomas, Dean
Program in:
- natural resources (MS)

College of Professional Studies
Joan North, Dean

School of Communicative Disorders
Dr. Gary Cumley, Head
Program in:
- communicative disorders (MS, Au D)

School of Education
Dr. JoAnne Katzmarek, Associate Dean
Programs in:
- education—general/reading (MSE)
- education—general/special (MSE)
- educational administration (MSE)
- elementary education (MSE)
- guidance and counseling (MSE)

School of Health Promotion and Human Development
Marty Loy, Head
Programs in:
human and community resources (MS)
nutritional sciences (MS)

■ UNIVERSITY OF WISCONSIN–STOUT
Menomonie, WI 54751
http://www.uwstout.edu/

State-supported, coed, comprehensive institution. *Enrollment:* 8,327 graduate, professional, and undergraduate students; 294 full-time matriculated graduate/professional students (218 women), 337 part-time matriculated graduate/professional students (234 women). *Graduate faculty:* 196 full-time (81 women). *Computer facilities:* Computer purchase and lease plans are available. 590 computers available on campus for general student use. A campuswide network can be accessed from student residence rooms and from off campus. Internet access and online class registration, all undergraduates receive a laptop computer. are available. *Library facilities:* Library Learning Center. *Graduate expenses:* Tuition, state resident: part-time $317 per credit. Tuition, nonresident: part-time $543 per credit. Tuition and fees vary according to reciprocity agreements. *General application contact:* Anne E. Johnson, Graduate Student Evaluator, 715-232-1322.

Graduate School
Dr. Janice Coker, Associate Vice Chancellor

College of Human Development
Dr. John Wesolek, Dean
Programs in:
applied psychology (MS)
family studies and human development (MS)
food and nutritional sciences (MS)
human development (MS)
marriage and family therapy (MS)
mental health counseling (MS)
vocational rehabilitation (MS)

College of Technology, Engineering, and Management
Dr. Bob Meyer, Dean
Programs in:
information and communication technologies (MS)
manufacturing engineering (MS)
risk control (MS)
technology management (MS)
technology, engineering, and management (MS)
training and development (MS)

School of Education
Dr. Mary Hopkins-Best, Interim Dean
Programs in:
career and technical education (MS, Ed S)
education (MS, MS Ed, Ed S)
guidance and counseling (MS)
industrial/technology education (MS)
school psychology (MS Ed, Ed S)

■ UNIVERSITY OF WISCONSIN–SUPERIOR
Superior, WI 54880-4500
http://www.uwsuper.edu/

State-supported, coed, comprehensive institution. CGS member. *Computer facilities:* Computer purchase and lease plans are available. 161 computers available on campus for general student use. A campuswide network can be accessed from student residence rooms and from off campus. Internet access and online class registration are available. *Library facilities:* Jim Dan Hill Library. *General application contact:* Program Assistant/Status Examiner, 715-394-8295.

Graduate Division
Programs in:
art education (MA)
art history (MA)
art therapy (MA)
community counseling (MSE)
educational administration (MSE, Ed S)
elementary school counseling (MSE)
emotional/behavior disabilities (MSE)
human relations (MSE)
instruction (MSE)
learning disabilities (MSE)
mass communication (MA)
secondary school counseling (MSE)
special education (MSE)
speech communication (MA)
studio arts (MA)
teaching reading (MSE)
theater (MA)

■ UNIVERSITY OF WISCONSIN–WHITEWATER
Whitewater, WI 53190-1790
http://www.uww.edu/

State-supported, coed, comprehensive institution. *Enrollment:* 10,502 graduate, professional, and undergraduate students; 276 full-time matriculated graduate/professional students (164 women), 745 part-time matriculated graduate/professional students (447 women). *Graduate faculty:* 332. *Computer facilities:* 1,300 computers available on campus for general student use. A campuswide network can be accessed from student residence rooms and from off campus. Internet access and online class registration are available. *Library facilities:* Andersen Library. *Graduate expenses:* Tuition, state resident: full-time $3,311. Tuition, nonresident: full-time $8,616. Required fees: $368 per credit. *General application contact:* Sally A. Lange, School of Graduate Studies, 262-472-1006.

School of Graduate Studies
Dr. John Stone, Dean, School of Graduate Studies

College of Arts and Communications
Dr. John Heyer, Dean
Programs in:
arts and communications (MS)
corporate communication (MS)
mass communication (MS)

College of Business and Economics
Dr. Christine Clements, Dean
Programs in:
accounting (MPA)
business and economics (MBA, MPA, MS, MS Ed)
finance (MBA)
general business education (MS)
human resource management (MBA)
information technology management (MBA)
international business (MBA)
management (MBA)
marketing (MBA)
operations and supply chain management (MBA)
post-secondary business education (MS)
school business management (MS Ed)
secondary business education (MS)
technology and training (MBA)

College of Education
Dr. Jeffrey Barnett, Dean
Programs in:
communicative disorders (MS)
community counseling (MS Ed)
curriculum and instruction (MS)
education (MS, MS Ed)
higher education (MS Ed)
reading (MS Ed)
safety (MS)
school counseling (MS Ed)
special education (MS Ed)

College of Letters and Sciences
Dr. Mary Pinkerton, Interim Dean
Programs in:
letters and sciences (MS Ed, Ed S)
school psychology (MS Ed, Ed S)

■ VITERBO UNIVERSITY
La Crosse, WI 54601-4797
http://www.viterbo.edu/

Independent-religious, coed, comprehensive institution. *Computer facilities:* 278 computers available on campus for general student use. A campuswide network can be accessed from student residence rooms and from off campus. Internet access, e-mail; Blackboard courses; wireless classrooms are available. *Library facilities:* Todd Wehr Memorial Library. *General application contact:* Information Contact, 608-796-3000.

Graduate Program in Education
Program in:
education (MA)

Graduate Program in Nursing
Dr. Bonnie Nesbitt, Director

Viterbo University (continued)
Program in:
nursing (MSN)

Wyoming

■ UNIVERSITY OF WYOMING
Laramie, WY 82070
http://www.uwyo.edu/

State-supported, coed, university. CGS member. *Enrollment:* 13,203 graduate, professional, and undergraduate students; 1,060 full-time matriculated graduate/professional students (500 women), 917 part-time matriculated graduate/professional students (542 women). *Graduate faculty:* 578 full-time (152 women), 108 part-time/adjunct (48 women). *Computer facilities:* Computer purchase and lease plans are available. 950 computers available on campus for general student use. A campuswide network can be accessed from student residence rooms and from off campus. Internet access and online class registration are available. *Library facilities:* William Robertson Coe Library plus 8 others. *General application contact:* Michell Anderson, Credentials Analyst/Advising Assistant, 307-766-2287.

College of Law
Jerry Parkinson, Dean
Program in:
law (JD)

Graduate School
Dr. Don A. Roth, Dean

College of Agriculture
Dr. Frank D. Galey, Dean
Programs in:
agrecology (MS)
agricultural and applied economics (MS)
agriculture (MS, PhD)
agronomy (MS, PhD)
animal sciences (MS, PhD)
entomology (MS, PhD)
entomology/water resources (MS, PhD)
family and consumer sciences (MS)
food science and human nutrition (MS)
molecular biology (MS, PhD)
pathobiology (MS)
rangeland ecology and watershed management (MS, PhD)
rangeland ecology and watershed management/water resources (MS, PhD)
reproductive biology (MS, PhD)
soil science (MS)
soil science/water resources (PhD)

College of Arts and Sciences
B. Oliver Walter, Dean
Programs in:
American studies (MA)
anthropology (MA, PhD)
arts and sciences (MA, MAT, MFA, MM, MP, MPA, MS, MST, PhD)
botany (MS, PhD)
botany/water resources (MS)
chemistry (MS, PhD)
communication (MA)
community and regional planning and natural resources (MP)
creative writing (MFA)
English (MA)
French (MA)
geography (MA, MP, MST)
geography/water resources (MA)
geology (MS, PhD)
geophysics (MS, PhD)
German (MA)
history (MA, MAT)
international peace corps (MA)
international studies (MA)
mathematics (MA, MAT, MS, MST, PhD)
mathematics/computer science (PhD)
music education (MA)
performance (MM)
philosophy (MA)
political science (MA)
psychology (MA, MS, PhD)
public administration (MPA)
rural planning and natural resources (MP)
sociology (MA)
Spanish (MA)
statistics (MS, PhD)
zoology and physiology (MS, PhD)

College of Business
Dr. Brent A. Hathaway, Dean
Programs in:
accounting (MS)
business (MBA, MS, PhD)
business administration (MBA)
economics (MS, PhD)
economics and finance (MS)
finance (MS)

College of Education
Dr. Patricia McClurg, Dean
Programs in:
adult and post secondary education (Ed S)
adult and postsecondary education (MA, Ed D, PhD)
counselor education (MS, PhD)
curriculum and instruction (MA, Ed D, PhD)
distance education (Ed D, PhD)
education (MA, MS, MST, Ed D, PhD, Ed S)
educational leadership (MA, Ed D, PhD, Ed S)
instructional technology (MS, Ed D, PhD)
science and mathematics teaching (MS, MST)
special education (MA, Ed S)

College of Engineering
Dr. Ovid A. Plumb, Dean
Programs in:
atmospheric science (MS, PhD)
chemical engineering (MS, PhD)
civil engineering (MS, PhD)
computer science (MS, PhD)
electrical engineering (MS, PhD)
engineering (MS, PhD)
environmental engineering (MS)
mechanical engineering (MS, PhD)
petroleum engineering (MS, PhD)

College of Health Sciences
Dr. Robert O. Kelley, Dean
Programs in:
audiology (PhD)
health sciences (Pharm D, MS, MSW, PhD)
kinesiology and health (MS)
neuroscience (PhD)
nursing (MS)
pharmacy (Pharm D)
social work (MSW)
speech-language pathology (MS)

Index

Alphabetical Listing of Schools